Ray Rankins
Paul Bertucci
Chris Gallelli
Alex T. Silverstein

Microsoft® SQL Server 2008 R2 UNLEASHED

SAMS | 800 East 96th Street, Indianapolis, Indiana 46240 USA

Microsoft SQL Server 2008 R2 Unleashed

ISBN-13: 978-0-672-33056-8
ISBN-10: 0-672-33056-3

Library of Congress Cataloging-in-Publication Data is on file.

Printed in the United States of America

First Printing September 2010

Trademarks

Warning and Disclaimer

Bulk Sales

Pearson offers excellent discounts on this book when ordered in quantity for bulk purchases or special sales. For more information, please contact:

U.S. Corporate and Government Sales
1-800-382-3419
corpsales@pearsontechgroup.com

For sales outside of the U.S., please contact:

International Sales
+1-317-581-3793
international@pearsontechgroup.com

Publisher
Paul Boger

Editor In Chief
Karen Gettman

Acquisitions Editor
Neil Rowe

Development Editor
Mark Renfrow

Managing Editor
Sandra Schroeder

Project Editor
Seth Kerney

Copy Editor
Chuck Hutchinson

Indexer
Erika MIllen

Proofreader
Leslie Joseph
Debbie Williams

Technical Editor
Rebecca M. Riordan
J. Boyd Nolan

Publishing Coordinator
Romney French

Multimedia Developer
Dan Scherf

Designer
Gary Adair

Compositor
Mark Shirar

Contents at a Glance

Introduction 1

Part I Welcome to Microsoft SQL Server

1 SQL Server 2008 Overview 9

2 What's New in SQL Server 2008 35

3 Examples of SQL Server Implementations 51

Part II SQL Server Tools and Utilities

4 SQL Server Management Studio 63

5 SQL Server Command-Line Utilities 103

6 SQL Server Profiler 121

Part III SQL Server Administration

7 SQL Server System and Database Administration 165

8 Installing SQL Server 2008 185

9 Upgrading to SQL Server 2008 227

10 Client Installation and Configuration 263

11 Security and User Administration 291

12 Data Encryption 335

13 Security and Compliance 359

14 Database Backup and Restore 377

15 Database Mail 427

16 SQL Server Scheduling and Notification 449

17 Administering SQL Server 2008 with PowerShell 481

18 SQL Server High Availability 523

19 Replication 545

20 Database Mirroring 617

21 SQL Server Clustering 655

22 Administering Policy-Based Management 687

Part IV Database Administration

23 Creating and Managing Databases 709

24 Creating and Managing Tables 741

25 Creating and Managing Indexes 791

26 Implementing Data Integrity 811

27 Creating and Managing Views in SQL Server 837

28 Creating and Managing Stored Procedures 869

29 Creating and Managing User-Defined Functions....917
30 Creating and Managing Triggers....949
31 Transaction Management and the Transaction Log....995
32 Database Snapshots....1043
33 Database Maintenance....1069

Part V SQL Server Performance and Optimization

34 Data Structures, Indexes, and Performance....1091
35 Understanding Query Optimization....1209
36 Query Analysis....1301
37 Locking and Performance....1341
38 Database Design and Performance....1403
39 Monitoring SQL Server Performance....1427
40 Managing Workloads with the Resource Governor....1493
41 A Performance and Tuning Methodology....1519

Chapters on the CD

Part VI SQL Server Application Development

42 What's New for Transact-SQL in SQL Server 2008....1551
43 Transact-SQL Programming Guidelines, Tips, and Tricks....1637
44 Advanced Stored Procedure Programming and Optimization....1733
45 SQL Server and the .NET Framework....1787
46 SQLCLR: Developing SQL Server Objects in .NET....1825
47 Using XML in SQL Server 2008....1865
48 SQL Server Web Services....1927
49 SQL Server Service Broker....1959
50 SQL Server Full-Text Search....1997

Part VII SQL Server Business Intelligence Features

51 SQL Server 2008 Analysis Services....2029
52 SQL Server Integration Services....2099
53 SQL Server 2008 Reporting Services....2169

Part VIII Bonus Chapters

54 Managing Linked and Remote Servers....2243
55 Configuring, Tuning, and Optimizing SQL Server Options....2273
56 SQL Server Disaster Recovery Planning....2329

Index 2353

Table of Contents

Introduction 1

Part I Welcome to Microsoft SQL Server

1 SQL Server 2008 Overview 9

SQL Server Components and Features 9
- The SQL Server Database Engine....10
- SQL Server 2008 Administration and Management Tools 12
- Replication....15
- Database Mirroring....17
- Full-Text Search....17
- SQL Server Integration Services (SSIS)....18
- SQL Server Analysis Services (SSAS) 19
- SQL Server Reporting Services (SSRS)....20
- SQL Server Service Broker....22

SQL Server 2008 R2 Editions 23
- SQL Server 2008 Standard Edition 23
- SQL Server 2008 Enterprise Edition 24
- Differences Between the Enterprise and Standard Editions of SQL Server 25
- Other SQL Server 2008 Editions....26

SQL Server Licensing Models....30
- Web Edition 32
- Developer Edition Licensing 32
- Express Edition Licensing....32
- Compact Edition 3.5 Licensing....32
- Choosing a Licensing Model....32
- Mixing Licensing Models 33
- Passive Server/Failover Licensing 33
- Virtual Server Licensing....33
- Multiple Instances of SQL Server 34

Summary....34

2 What's New in SQL Server 2008 35

New SQL Server 2008 Features 35
- New Storage Features....36
- New Data Types 37
- New Transact-SQL Constructs 37
- New Performance Features 38
- New Security Features....39

New Database Administration Features 40
New SQL Server Management Studio Features 41
PowerShell Integration 42
New Premium SQL Server Editions 42
SQL Server Utility for Multiserver Management 43
PowerPivot for Excel and SharePoint 43
New Reporting Services Features 44
SQL Server 2008 Enhancements 45
SQL Server Management Studio 45
Dynamic Management Views 45
Database Mirroring 46
SQLCLR Enhancements 46
Replication Enhancements 46
SQL Server Integration Services Enhancements 47
Service Broker Enhancements 47
Analysis Services Enhancements 48
Installation Enhancements 49
Deprecated Features 49
Summary 50

3 Examples of SQL Server Implementations 51

Application Terms 52
OLTP Application Examples 53
OLTP ERP Example 53
OLTP Shopping Cart Example 56
DSS Application Examples 57
DSS Example One 57
DSS Example Two 58
DSS Example Three 59
Summary 61

Part II SQL Server Tools and Utilities

4 SQL Server Management Studio 63

What's New in SSMS 63
The Integrated Environment 64
Window Management 65
Integrated Help 68
Administration Tools 71
Registered Servers 71
Object Explorer 73
Activity Monitor 75

Log File Viewer 77
SQL Server Utility 79
Development Tools 85
The Query Editor 85
Managing Projects in SSMS 93
Integrating SSMS with Source Control....95
Using SSMS Templates....97
T-SQL Debugging 100
Multiserver Queries....101
Summary 102

5 SQL Server Command-Line Utilities 103

What's New in SQL Server Command-Line Utilities 104
The sqlcmd Command-Line Utility 105
Executing the sqlcmd Utility....106
Using Scripting Variables with sqlcmd 108
The dta Command-Line Utility....109
The tablediff Command-Line Utility....112
The bcp Command-Line Utility 115
The sqldiag Command-Line Utility....116
The sqlservr Command-Line Utility....118
Summary 119

6 SQL Server Profiler 121

What's New with SQL Server Profiler....121
SQL Server Profiler Architecture 122
Creating Traces....123
Events....125
Data Columns....127
Filters....130
Executing Traces and Working with Trace Output 132
Saving and Exporting Traces....132
Saving Trace Output to a File 133
Saving Trace Output to a Table 134
Saving the Profiler GUI Output....134
Importing Trace Files 135
Importing a Trace File into a Trace Table....135
Analyzing Trace Output with the Database Engine Tuning Advisor138
Replaying Trace Data 138
Defining Server-Side Traces....140
Monitoring Running Traces 153
Stopping Server-Side Traces 155

Profiler Usage Scenarios 157
Analyzing Slow Stored Procedures or Queries 157
Deadlocks 158
Identifying Ad Hoc Queries 159
Identifying Performance Bottlenecks 160
Monitoring Auto-Update Statistics 162
Monitoring Application Progress 162
Summary 164

Part III SQL Server Administration

7 SQL Server System and Database Administration 165

What's New in SQL Server System and Database Administration 165
System Administrator Responsibilities 166
System Databases 166
The master Database 167
The resource Database 168
The model Database 168
The msdb Database 168
The distribution Database 168
The tempdb Database 169
Maintaining System Databases 169
System Tables 170
System Views 171
Compatibility Views 172
Catalog Views 175
Information Schema Views 177
Dynamic Management Views 179
System Stored Procedures 181
Useful System Stored Procedures 182
Summary 183

8 Installing SQL Server 2008 185

What's New in Installing SQL Server 2008 185
Installation Requirements 186
Hardware Requirements 186
Software Requirements 188
Installation Walkthrough 192
Install Screens, Step by Step 192
Other Options Available in the SQL Server Installation Center 211
Installing SQL Server Using a Configuration File 212
Running an Automated or Manual Install 217

Installing Service Packs and Cumulative Updates 218
    Installing SP1 from the Command Line 220
Slipstream Installations...222
Summary 225

9 Upgrading to SQL Server 2008 227

What's New in Upgrading SQL Server..227
Using the SQL Server Upgrade Advisor (UA) 228
    Getting Started with the UA..229
    The Analysis Wizard 230
    The Report Viewer 235
Destination: SQL Server 2008 or SQL Server 2008 R2 236
    Side-by-Side Migration..236
    Upgrading In-Place 242
Upgrading Using a Configuration File 250
Slipstreaming Upgrades 251
    Upgrading from SQL Server 7 or SQL Server 6.5 252
Upgrading Other SQL Server Components 253
    Upgrading Analysis Services..253
    Upgrading Reporting Services 255
Summary 261

10 Client Installation and Configuration 263

What's New in Client Installation and Configuration 263
Client/Server Networking Considerations..264
    Server Network Protocols 264
    The Server Endpoint Layer..267
    The Role of SQL Browser 270
Client Installation...271
    Installation Requirements 271
    Installing the Client Tools...271
    Installing SNAC 272
Client Configuration 274
    Client Configuration Using SSCM 275
    Connection Encryption..278
Client Data Access Technologies 279
    Provider Choices...280
    Driver Choices 281
    Connecting Using the Various Providers and Drivers 281
    General Networking Considerations and Troubleshooting..............287
Summary 289

11 Security and User Administration 291

What's New in Security and User Administration 291
An Overview of SQL Server Security 292
Authentication Methods....294
  Windows Authentication Mode....294
  Mixed Authentication Mode....294
  Setting the Authentication Mode....295
Managing Principals 295
  Logins....296
  SQL Server Security: Users....298
  User/Schema Separation....301
  Roles....302
Managing Securables....309
Managing Permissions 311
Managing SQL Server Logins....313
  Using SSMS to Manage Logins 313
  Using T-SQL to Manage Logins 317
Managing SQL Server Users....318
  Using SSMS to Manage Users 318
  Using T-SQL to Manage Users 320
Managing Database Roles 321
  Using SSMS to Manage Database Roles....321
  Using T-SQL to Manage Database Roles....322
Managing SQL Server Permissions 322
  Using SSMS to Manage Permissions....323
  Using T-SQL to Manage Permissions....330
The Execution Context....331
  Explicit Context Switching 332
  Implicit Context Switching....333
Summary 334

12 Data Encryption 335

What's New in Data Encryption....336
An Overview of Data Security 336
An Overview of Data Encryption 338
SQL Server Key Management....339
  Extensible Key Management 341
Column-Level Encryption 343
  Encrypting Columns Using a Passphrase....344
  Encrypting Columns Using a Certificate 346

Transparent Data Encryption 350
Implementing Transparent Data Encryption 351
Managing TDE in SSMS 352
Backing Up TDE Certificates and Keys 353
Limitations of TDE 355
Column-Level Encryption Versus Transparent Data Encryption 356
Summary 357

13 Security and Compliance **359**

Exposure and Risk 360
Across the Life Cycle 361
The Security Big Picture 362
Identity Access Management Components 364
Compliance and SQL Server 366
SQL Server Auditing 368
Setting Up Auditing via T-SQL 372
SQL Injection Is Easy to Do 374
Summary 376

14 Database Backup and Restore **377**

What's New in Database Backup and Restore 377
Developing a Backup and Restore Plan 378
Types of Backups 379
Full Database Backups 380
Differential Database Backups 380
Partial Backups 381
Differential Partial Backups 381
File and Filegroup Backups 381
Copy-Only Backups 382
Transaction Log Backups 382
Recovery Models 382
Full Recovery 383
Bulk-Logged Recovery 384
Simple Recovery 385
Backup Devices 385
Disk Devices 386
Tape Devices 386
Network Shares 386
Media Sets and Families 387
Creating Backup Devices 387

Backing Up a Database 388
Creating Database Backups with SSMS 388
Creating Database Backups with T-SQL 390
Backing Up the Transaction Log 393
Creating Transaction Log Backups with SSMS...............................394
Creating Transaction Log Backups with T-SQL...............................394
Backup Scenarios..396
Full Database Backups Only 396
Full Database Backups with Transaction Log Backups 396
Differential Backups...397
Partial Backups...398
File/Filegroup Backups..400
Mirrored Backups..401
Copy-Only Backups 402
Compressed Backups 402
System Database Backups 403
Restoring Databases and Transaction Logs...403
Restores with T-SQL 404
Restoring by Using SSMS...409
Restore Information...411
Restore Scenarios..414
Restoring to a Different Database 414
Restoring a Snapshot 416
Restoring a Transaction Log 416
Restoring to the Point of Failure...417
Restoring to a Point in Time 419
Online Restores...421
Restoring the System Databases 421
Additional Backup Considerations..423
Frequency of Backups...423
Using a Standby Server...424
Snapshot Backups 425
Considerations for Very Large Databases..425
Maintenance Plans 426
Summary 426

15 Database Mail 427

What's New in Database Mail...427
Setting Up Database Mail 428
Creating Mail Profiles and Accounts...429
Using T-SQL to Update and Delete Mail Objects..............................432

Setting System-wide Mail Settings....433
Testing Your Setup....433
Sending and Receiving with Database Mail....434
The Service Broker Architecture....434
Sending Email....435
Receiving Email....441
Using SQL Server Agent Mail....441
Job Mail Notifications....442
Alert Mail Notifications....443
Related Views and Procedures....445
Viewing the Mail Configuration Objects....445
Viewing Mail Message Data....446
Summary....448

16 SQL Server Scheduling and Notification 449

What's New in Scheduling and Notification....450
Configuring the SQL Server Agent....450
Configuring SQL Server Agent Properties....450
Configuring the SQL Server Agent Startup Account....452
Configuring Email Notification....454
SQL Server Agent Proxy Account....455
Viewing the SQL Server Agent Error Log....456
SQL Server Agent Security....458
Managing Operators....458
Managing Jobs....461
Defining Job Properties....461
Defining Job Steps....462
Defining Multiple Jobs Steps....464
Defining Job Schedules....465
Defining Job Notifications....467
Viewing Job History....468
Managing Alerts....469
Defining Alert Properties....469
Defining Alert Responses....472
Scripting Jobs and Alerts....474
Multiserver Job Management....476
Creating a Master Server....476
Enlisting Target Servers....477
Creating Multiserver Jobs....477
Event Forwarding....477
Summary....479

17 Administering SQL Server 2008 with PowerShell 481

What's New with PowerShell....481

Overview of PowerShell....482

Start Using PowerShell Now....483

Common Terminology....483

Object-Based Functionality....484

SQL Server Management Objects....484

WMI....484

Installing PowerShell....485

PowerShell Console....485

Scriptable and Interactive....486

Default Security....486

Execution Policy....487

Profiles....487

Built-in Help Features....487

PowerShell Scripting Basics....490

A Few Basic Cmdlets....490

Creating a PowerShell Script....491

Adding Comments....491

Variables....491

Escaping Characters....492

Special Variable $_....493

Joining Variables and Strings....493

Passing Arguments....494

Using Param....494

Arrays....495

Operators....496

Conditional Statements....496

Functions....497

Looping Statements....498

Filtering Cmdlets....499

Formatting Cmdlets....500

Dealing with CSV Files....501

Dealing with Dates and Times....502

-WhatIf/-Confirm Parameters....503

PowerShell in SQL Server 2008....503

Adding PowerShell Support....503

Accessing PowerShell....505

SQL Server PowerShell....506

SQL Provider....507

SQL Cmdlets....508

SQL Server Agent Support....509

Step-By-Step Examples 509
General Tasks 509
Scheduling Scripts 510
Common OS-Related Tasks 512
SQL Server–Specific Tasks 514
Using the Provider 515
Creating a Database Table 515
Performing a Database Backup 516
Checking Server Settings 518
Checking the Database Usage 519
Getting Table Properties 520
Cmdlet Example: Invoke-SqlCmd 520
Cmdlet Example: Invoke-PolicyEvaluation 521
Joining Columns 521
Retrieving an Entry 522
Summary 522

18 SQL Server High Availability 523

What's New in High Availability 524
What Is High Availability? 525
The Fundamentals of HA 526
Hardware Factors 527
Backup Considerations 527
Operating System Upgrades 527
Vendor Agreements Followed 528
Training Kept Up to Date 528
Quality Assurance Done Well 528
Standards/Procedures Followed 528
Server Instance Isolation 528
Building Solutions with One or More HA Options 530
Microsoft Cluster Services (MSCS) 530
SQL Clustering 531
Data Replication 534
Log Shipping 535
Database Mirroring 537
Combining Failover with Scale-Out Options 538
Other HA Techniques That Yield Great Results 538
High Availability from the Windows Server Family Side 540
Microsoft Virtual Server 2005 541
Virtual Server 2005 and Disaster Recovery 542
Summary 542

19 Replication 545

What's New in Data Replication 546
What Is Replication? 547
The Publisher, Distributor, and Subscriber Magazine Metaphor 549
Publications and Articles 550
Filtering Articles 550
Replication Scenarios 555
The Central Publisher Replication Model 555
The Central Publisher with Remote Distributor Replication Model 557
The Publishing Subscriber Replication Model 558
The Central Subscriber Replication Model 559
The Multiple Publishers with Multiple Subscribers Replication Model 559
The Updating Subscribers Replication Model 560
The Peer-to-Peer Replication Model 561
Subscriptions 562
Anonymous Subscriptions (Pull Subscriptions) 563
The Distribution Database 564
Replication Agents 565
The Snapshot Agent 566
The Log Reader Agent 569
The Distribution Agent 569
The Merge Agent 570
Other Specialized Agents 571
Planning for SQL Server Data Replication 572
Autonomy, Timing, and Latency of Data 572
Methods of Data Distribution 573
SQL Server Replication Types 574
Snapshot Replication 574
Transactional Replication 574
Merge Replication 575
Basing the Replication Design on User Requirements 577
Data Characteristics 578
Setting Up Replication 579
Creating a Distributor and Enabling Publishing 580
Creating a Publication 584
Horizontal and Vertical Filtering 592
Creating Subscriptions 594
Scripting Replication 600
Monitoring Replication 603
Replication Monitoring SQL Statements 603
Monitoring Replication within SQL Server Management Studio 606

Troubleshooting Replication Failures 608
New and Improved Peer-to-Peer Replication 609
The Performance Monitor 610
Replication in Heterogeneous Environments 611
Backup and Recovery in a Replication Configuration 612
Some Thoughts on Performance 613
Log Shipping 614
Data Replication and Database Mirroring for Fault Tolerance and High Availability 614
Summary 615

20 Database Mirroring 617

What's New in Database Mirroring 617
What Is Database Mirroring? 618
Copy-on-Write Technology 620
When to Use Database Mirroring 621
Roles of the Database Mirroring Configuration 621
Playing Roles and Switching Roles 622
Database Mirroring Operating Modes 622
Setting Up and Configuring Database Mirroring 623
Getting Ready to Mirror a Database 624
Creating the Endpoints 627
Granting Permissions 629
Creating the Database on the Mirror Server 630
Identifying the Other Endpoints for Database Mirroring 632
Configuring Database Mirroring by Using the Wizard 633
Monitoring a Mirrored Database Environment 639
Removing Mirroring 643
Testing Failover from the Principal to the Mirror 645
Client Setup and Configuration for Database Mirroring 647
Migrate to Database Mirroring 2008 as Fast as You Can 649
Using Replication and Database Mirroring Together 651
Using Database Snapshots from a Mirror for Reporting 652
Summary 654

21 SQL Server Clustering 655

What's New in SQL Server Clustering 656
How Microsoft SQL Server Clustering Works 656
Understanding MSCS 658
Extending MSCS with NLB 662
How MSCS Sets the Stage for SQL Server Clustering 663

Installing SQL Server Clustering....665
Configuring SQL Server Database Disks....666
Installing Network Interfaces....668
Installing MSCS....668
Installing SQL Server....668
Failure of a Node....679
The Connection Test Program for a SQL Server Cluster....681
Potential Problems to Watch Out for with SQL Server Clustering....684
Summary....685

22 Administering Policy-Based Management **687**

Introduction to Policy-Based Management....687
Policy-Based Management Concepts....689
Facets....689
Conditions....693
Policies....693
Categories....693
Targets....693
Execution Modes....694
Central Management Servers....695
Implementing Policy-Based Management....697
Creating a Condition Based on a Facet....697
Creating a Policy....699
Creating a Category....701
Evaluating Policies....702
Importing and Exporting Policies....703
Sample Templates and Real-World Examples....704
Sample Policy Templates....704
Evaluating Recovery Models....705
Implementing Surface Area Configuration Checks....705
SQL Server Health Checks....705
Ensuring Object Naming Conventions....706
Checking Best Practices Compliance....706
Policy-Based Management Best Practices....706
Summary....707

Part IV Database Administration

23 Creating and Managing Databases **709**

What's New in Creating and Managing Databases....710
Data Storage in SQL Server....710

Database Files....711
Primary Files....712
Secondary Files....712
Using Filegroups....713
Using Partitions....716
Transaction Log Files....716
Creating Databases....717
Using SSMS to Create a Database....718
Using T-SQL to Create Databases....721
Setting Database Options....722
The Database Options....723
Using T-SQL to Set Database Options....725
Retrieving Option Information....726
Managing Databases....729
Managing File Growth....729
Expanding Databases....730
Shrinking Databases....731
Moving Databases....736
Restoring a Database Backup to a New Location....736
Using ALTER DATABASE....736
Detaching and Attaching Databases....737
Summary....740

24 Creating and Managing Tables 741

What's New in SQL Server 2008....741
Creating Tables....742
Using Object Explorer to Create Tables....742
Using Database Diagrams to Create Tables....743
Using T-SQL to Create Tables....744
Defining Columns....747
Data Types....747
Column Properties....755
Defining Table Location....761
Defining Table Constraints....763
Modifying Tables....765
Using T-SQL to Modify Tables....766
Using Object Explorer and the Table Designer to Modify Tables....769
Using Database Diagrams to Modify Tables....772
Dropping Tables....773
Using Partitioned Tables....774
Creating a Partition Function....776
Creating a Partition Scheme....778
Creating a Partitioned Table....779

Adding and Dropping Table Partitions 782
Switching Table Partitions 785
Creating Temporary Tables 789
Summary 790

25 Creating and Managing Indexes 791

What's New in Creating and Managing Indexes 791
Types of Indexes....792
Clustered Indexes 792
Nonclustered Indexes 793
Creating Indexes 795
Creating Indexes with T-SQL....795
Creating Indexes with SSMS....800
Managing Indexes....803
Managing Indexes with T-SQL 803
Managing Indexes with SSMS 806
Dropping Indexes 807
Online Indexing Operations....807
Indexes on Views 809
Summary 810

26 Implementing Data Integrity 811

What's New in Data Integrity....811
Types of Data Integrity 812
Domain Integrity....812
Entity Integrity 812
Referential Integrity....812
Enforcing Data Integrity....812
Implementing Declarative Data Integrity 812
Implementing Procedural Data Integrity....813
Using Constraints 813
The PRIMARY KEY Constraint 813
The UNIQUE Constraint 815
The FOREIGN KEY Referential Integrity Constraint....816
The CHECK Constraint 820
Creating Constraints 821
Managing Constraints 827
Rules 830
Defaults 831
Declarative Defaults....831
Bound Defaults 833
When a Default Is Applied....833
Restrictions on Defaults....835
Summary 836

27 **Creating and Managing Views in SQL Server** **837**

What's New in Creating and Managing Views 837
Definition of Views 837
Using Views 839
Simplifying Data Manipulation 839
Focusing on Specific Data 840
Abstracting Data 841
Controlling Access to Data 842
Creating Views 844
Creating Views Using T-SQL 845
Creating Views Using the View Designer 849
Managing Views 852
Altering Views 852
Dropping Views with T-SQL 853
Managing Views with SSMS 853
Data Modifications and Views 853
Partitioned Views 854
Modifying Data Through a Partitioned View 858
Distributed Partitioned Views 859
Indexed Views 860
Creating Indexed Views 861
Indexed Views and Performance 863
To Expand or Not to Expand 866
Summary 867

28 **Creating and Managing Stored Procedures** **869**

What's New in Creating and Managing Stored Procedures 869
Advantages of Stored Procedures 870
Creating Stored Procedures 871
Creating Procedures in SSMS 872
Temporary Stored Procedures 879
Executing Stored Procedures 880
Executing Procedures in SSMS 881
Execution Context and the EXECUTE AS Clause 882
Deferred Name Resolution 885
Identifying Objects Referenced in Stored Procedures 887
Viewing Stored Procedures 888
Modifying Stored Procedures 891
Viewing and Modifying Stored Procedures with SSMS 892
Using Input Parameters 893
Setting Default Values for Parameters 895
Passing Object Names as Parameters 898

Using Wildcards in Parameters 899
Using Table-Valued Parameters 901
Using Output Parameters...902
Returning Procedure Status 904
Debugging Stored Procedures Using SQL Server Management Studio......905
Using System Stored Procedures...908
Startup Procedures 911
Summary...915

29 Creating and Managing User-Defined Functions 917

What's New in SQL Server 2008...917
Why Use User-Defined Functions?...918
Types of User-Defined Functions...921
Scalar Functions...921
Table-Valued Functions 923
Creating and Managing User-Defined Functions...925
Creating User-Defined Functions...925
Viewing and Modifying User-Defined Functions 936
Managing User-Defined Function Permissions...941
Rewriting Stored Procedures as Functions...942
Creating and Using CLR Functions...944
Adding CLR Functions to a Database...944
Deciding Between Using T-SQL or CLR Functions 946
Summary...947

30 Creating and Managing Triggers 949

What's New in Creating and Managing Triggers 950
Using DML Triggers 950
Creating DML Triggers...951
Using AFTER Triggers...953
Using inserted and deleted Tables...957
Enforcing Referential Integrity by Using DML Triggers 961
Cascading Deletes 963
Cascading Updates...965
INSTEAD OF Triggers 967
Using DDL Triggers 976
Creating DDL Triggers 983
Managing DDL Triggers...986
Using CLR Triggers...988
Using Nested Triggers 991
Using Recursive Triggers 992
Summary...993

31 Transaction Management and the Transaction Log 995

What's New in Transaction Management 995
What Is a Transaction? 995
How SQL Server Manages Transactions....996
Defining Transactions....997
  AutoCommit Transactions 997
  Explicit User-Defined Transactions 998
  Implicit Transactions....1003
  Implicit Transactions Versus Explicit Transactions....1006
Transactions and Batches....1007
Transactions and Stored Procedures....1009
Transactions and Triggers 1014
  Triggers and Transaction Nesting....1015
  Triggers and Multistatement Transactions....1017
  Using Savepoints in Triggers 1019
Transactions and Locking....1021
  READ_COMMITTED_SNAPSHOT Isolation 1022
Coding Effective Transactions 1022
Transaction Logging and the Recovery Process 1023
  The Checkpoint Process 1024
  The Recovery Process....1028
  Managing the Transaction Log....1032
Long-Running Transactions....1037
Bound Connections....1039
Distributed Transactions....1040
Summary....1041

32 Database Snapshots 1043

What's New with Database Snapshots 1044
What Are Database Snapshots? 1044
Limitations and Restrictions of Database Snapshots 1048
Copy-on-Write Technology 1050
When to Use Database Snapshots....1051
  Reverting to a Snapshot for Recovery Purposes....1052
  Safeguarding a Database Prior to Making Mass Changes....1053
  Providing a Testing (or Quality Assurance) Starting Point (Baseline)....1054
  Providing a Point-in-Time Reporting Database 1054
  Providing a Highly Available and Offloaded Reporting Database from a Database Mirror 1055
Setup and Breakdown of a Database Snapshot....1056
  Creating a Database Snapshot....1057
  Breaking Down a Database Snapshot....1062

Reverting to a Database Snapshot for Recovery ... 1062
Reverting a Source Database from a Database Snapshot ... 1063
Using Database Snapshots with Testing and QA ... 1064
Setting Up Snapshots Against a Database Mirror ... 1064
Reciprocal Principal/Mirror Reporting Configuration ... 1065
Database Snapshots Maintenance and Security Considerations ... 1067
Security for Database Snapshots ... 1067
Snapshot Sparse File Size Management ... 1067
Number of Database Snapshots per Source Database ... 1067
Summary ... 1068

33 Database Maintenance 1069

What's New in Database Maintenance ... 1070
The Maintenance Plan Wizard ... 1070
Backing Up Databases ... 1072
Checking Database Integrity ... 1075
Shrinking Databases ... 1076
Maintaining Indexes and Statistics ... 1077
Scheduling a Maintenance Plan ... 1080
Managing Maintenance Plans Without the Wizard ... 1084
Executing a Maintenance Plan ... 1088
Maintenance Without a Maintenance Plan ... 1089
Database Maintenance Policies ... 1090
Summary ... 1090

Part V SQL Server Performance and Optimization

34 Data Structures, Indexes, and Performance 1091

What's New for Data Structures, Indexes, and Performance ... 1092
Understanding Data Structures ... 1093
Database Files and Filegroups ... 1093
Primary Data File ... 1095
Secondary Data Files ... 1095
The Log File ... 1096
File Management ... 1096
Using Filegroups ... 1097
FILESTREAM Filegroups ... 1100
Database Pages ... 1101
Page Types ... 1102
Data Pages ... 1103
Row-Overflow Pages ... 1109
LOB Data Pages ... 1110
Index Pages ... 1112

Space Allocation Structures....1113
- Extents....1113
- Global and Shared Global Allocation Map Pages....1114
- Page Free Space Pages....1115
- Index Allocation Map Pages....1115
- Differential Changed Map Pages....1116
- Bulk Changed Map Pages....1116

Data Compression....1117
- Row-Level Compression....1117
- Page-Level Compression....1119
- The CI Record....1122
- Implementing Page Compression....1122
- Evaluating Page Compression....1123
- Managing Data Compression with SSMS....1126

Understanding Table Structures....1127
- Heap Tables....1129
- Clustered Tables....1130

Understanding Index Structures....1132
- Clustered Indexes....1133
- Nonclustered Indexes....1136

Data Modification and Performance....1141
- Inserting Data....1141
- Deleting Rows....1144
- Updating Rows....1145

Index Utilization....1146

Index Selection....1149

Evaluating Index Usefulness....1150

Index Statistics....1153
- The Statistics Histogram....1155
- How the Statistics Histogram Is Used....1157
- Index Densities....1158
- Estimating Rows Using Index Statistics....1159
- Generating and Maintaining Index and Column Statistics....1161

SQL Server Index Maintenance....1169
- Setting the Fill Factor....1179
- Reapplying the Fill Factor....1181
- Disabling Indexes....1182
- Managing Indexes with SSMS....1183

Index Design Guidelines....1184
- Clustered Index Indications....1185
- Nonclustered Index Indications....1186
- Index Covering....1188

Included Columns 1190
Wide Indexes Versus Multiple Indexes 1191
Indexed Views 1192
Indexes on Computed Columns 1193
Filtered Indexes and Statistics 1195
Creating and Using Filtered Indexes 1196
Creating and Using Filtered Statistics 1198
Choosing Indexes: Query Versus Update Performance 1199
Identifying Missing Indexes 1201
The Database Engine Tuning Advisor 1201
Missing Index Dynamic Management Objects 1202
Missing Index Feature Versus Database Engine Tuning Advisor 1203
Identifying Unused Indexes 1205
Summary 1208

35 Understanding Query Optimization 1209

What's New in Query Optimization 1210
What Is the Query Optimizer? 1211
Query Compilation and Optimization 1212
Compiling DML Statements 1212
Optimization Steps 1213
Query Analysis 1213
Identifying Search Arguments 1214
Identifying OR Clauses 1214
Identifying Join Clauses 1215
Row Estimation and Index Selection 1216
Evaluating SARG and Join Selectivity 1216
Estimating Access Path Cost 1221
Using Multiple Indexes 1228
Optimizing with Indexed Views 1236
Optimizing with Filtered Indexes 1239
Join Selection 1241
Join Processing Strategies 1241
Determining the Optimal Join Order 1246
Subquery Processing 1248
Execution Plan Selection 1251
Query Plan Caching 1254
Query Plan Reuse 1254
Query Plan Aging 1256
Recompiling Query Plans 1257
Monitoring the Plan Cache 1258
Other Query Processing Strategies 1266
Predicate Transitivity 1266

Group by Optimization 1267
Queries with DISTINCT 1268
Queries with UNION 1268
Parallel Query Processing 1268
Parallel Query Configuration Options 1271
Identifying Parallel Queries 1272
Parallel Queries on Partitioned Objects 1273
Common Query Optimization Problems 1274
Out-of-Date or Insufficient Statistics 1274
Poor Index Design 1275
Search Argument Problems 1276
Large Complex Queries 1277
Triggers 1278
Managing the Optimizer 1278
Optimizer Hints 1280
Forced Parameterization 1285
Using the USE PLAN Query Hint 1287
Using Plan Guides 1290
Limiting Query Plan Execution with the Query Governor 1298
Summary 1300

36 Query Analysis 1301

What's New in Query Analysis 1302
Query Analysis in SSMS 1302
Execution Plan ToolTips 1304
Logical and Physical Operator Icons 1308
Analyzing Stored Procedures 1315
Saving and Viewing Graphical Execution Plans 1316
Displaying Execution Plan XML 1317
Missing Index Hints 1317
SSMS Client Statistics 1322
Using the SET SHOWPLAN Options 1324
SHOWPLAN_TEXT 1324
SHOWPLAN_ALL 1326
SHOWPLAN_XML 1327
Using sys.dm_exec_query_plan 1328
Query Statistics 1330
STATISTICS IO 1330
STATISTICS TIME 1333
Using datediff() to Measure Runtime 1336
STATISTICS PROFILE 1337
STATISTICS XML 1337

Query Analysis with SQL Server Profiler 1338
Summary 1340

37 **Locking and Performance** **1341**

What's New in Locking and Performance 1341
The Need for Locking 1342
Transaction Isolation Levels in SQL Server 1342
 Read Uncommitted Isolation 1344
 Read Committed Isolation 1344
 Read Committed Snapshot Isolation 1345
 Repeatable Read Isolation 1346
 Serializable Read Isolation 1346
 Snapshot Isolation 1347
The Lock Manager 1349
Monitoring Lock Activity in SQL Server 1350
 Querying the sys.dm_tran_locks View 1350
 Viewing Locking Activity with SQL Server Profiler 1355
 Monitoring Locks with Performance Monitor 1357
SQL Server Lock Types 1359
 Shared Locks 1360
 Update Locks 1360
 Exclusive Locks 1361
 Intent Locks 1362
 Schema Locks 1363
 Bulk Update Locks 1363
SQL Server Lock Granularity 1364
 Serialization and Key-Range Locking 1365
 Using Application Locks 1369
 Index Locking 1372
 Row-Level Versus Page-Level Locking 1373
 Lock Escalation 1374
Lock Compatibility 1376
Locking Contention and Deadlocks 1377
 Identifying Locking Contention 1378
 Setting the Lock Timeout Interval 1380
 Minimizing Locking Contention 1381
 Deadlocks 1382
Table Hints for Locking 1393
 Transaction Isolation–Level Hints 1393
 Lock Granularity Hints 1395
 Lock Type Hints 1395

Optimistic Locking 1396
Optimistic Locking Using the rowversion Data Type 1396
Optimistic Locking with Snapshot Isolation 1399
Summary 1401

38 Database Design and Performance 1403

What's New in Database Design and Performance 1403
Basic Tenets of Designing for Performance 1404
Logical Database Design Issues 1405
Normalization Conditions 1405
Normalization Forms 1406
Benefits of Normalization 1407
Drawbacks of Normalization 1407
Denormalizing a Database 1408
Denormalization Guidelines 1408
Essential Denormalization Techniques 1409
Database Filegroups and Performance 1415
RAID Technology 1417
RAID Level 0 1418
RAID Level 1 1419
RAID Level 10 1420
RAID Level 5 1421
SQL Server and SAN Technology 1422
What Is a SAN? 1423
SAN Considerations for SQL Server 1423
Summary 1425

39 Monitoring SQL Server Performance 1427

What's New in Monitoring SQL Server Performance 1428
Performance Monitoring Tools 1429
The Data Collector and the MDW 1429
SQL Server Utility 1451
SQL Server Extended Events 1455
Windows Performance Monitor 1465
A Performance Monitoring Approach 1477
Monitoring the Network Interface 1478
Monitoring the Processors 1480
Monitoring Memory 1485
Monitoring the Disk System 1488
Monitoring SQL Server's Disk Activity 1490
Monitoring Other SQL Server Performance Items 1492
Summary 1492

40 **Managing Workloads with the Resource Governor** 1493

Overview of Resource Governor....1494
Resource Governor Components....1495
    Classification....1495
    Workload Groups....1496
    Resource Pools....1496
Configuring Resource Governor....1498
    Enabling Resource Governor....1499
    Defining Resource Pools....1500
    Defining Workload Groups....1502
    Creating a Classification Function....1506
Monitoring Resource Usage....1509
Modifying Your Resource Governor Configuration....1513
    Deleting Workload Groups....1514
    Deleting Resource Pools....1515
    Modifying a Classification Function....1516
Summary....1517

41 **A Performance and Tuning Methodology** 1519

The Full Architectural Landscape....1520
Primary Performance and Tuning Handles....1521
A Performance and Tuning Methodology....1522
    Designing In Performance and Tuning from the Start....1523
    Performance and Tuning for an Existing Implementation....1528
Performance and Tuning Design Guidelines....1534
    Hardware and Operating System Guidelines....1534
    SQL Server Instance Guidelines....1536
    Database-Level Guidelines....1537
    Table Design Guidelines....1537
    Indexing Guidelines....1539
    View Design Guidelines....1541
    Transact-SQL Guidelines....1541
    Application Design Guidelines....1545
    Distributed Data Guidelines....1546
    High-Availability Guidelines....1546
Tools of the Performance and Tuning Trade....1547
    Microsoft Out-of-the-Box....1547
    Third-Party Performance and Tuning Tools....1548
Summary....1550

Chapters on the CD

Part VI SQL Server Application Development

42 What's New for Transact-SQL in SQL Server 2008 1551

MERGE Statement 1552
  MERGE Statement Best Practices and Guidelines 1558
Insert over DML 1559
GROUP BY Clause Enhancements 1561
  ROLLUP and CUBE Operator Syntax Changes 1561
  GROUPING SETS 1562
  The grouping_id() Function 1565
Variable Assignment in DECLARE Statement 1568
Compound Assignment Operators 1568
Row Constructors 1569
New date and time Data Types and Functions 1572
  Date and Time Conversions 1575
Table-Valued Parameters 1576
  Table-Valued Parameters Versus Temporary Tables 1580
Hierarchyid Data Type 1580
  Creating a Hierarchy 1580
  Populating the Hierarchy 1581
  Querying the Hierarchy 1583
  Modifying the Hierarchy 1587
Using FILESTREAM Storage 1592
  Enabling FILESTREAM Storage 1593
  Setting Up a Database for FILESTREAM Storage 1596
  Using FILESTREAM Storage for Data Columns 1597
Sparse Columns 1600
  Column Sets 1600
  Working with Sparse Columns 1601
  Sparse Columns: Good or Bad? 1604
Spatial Data Types 1605
  Representing Spatial Data 1606
  Working with Geometry Data 1607
  Working with Geography Data 1609
  Spatial Data Support in SSMS 1611
  Spatial Data Types: Where to Go from Here? 1614
Change Data Capture 1614
  The Change Data Capture Tables 1615
  Enabling CDC for a Database 1617
  Enabling CDC for a Table 1617

Querying the CDC Tables 1619
CDC and DDL Changes to Source Tables 1626
Change Tracking 1627
Implementing Change Tracking 1628
Identifying Tracked Changes 1630
Identifying Changed Columns 1633
Change Tracking Overhead 1634
Summary 1635

43 Transact-SQL Programming Guidelines, Tips, and Tricks 1637

General T-SQL Coding Recommendations 1638
Provide Explicit Column Lists 1638
Qualify Object Names with a Schema Name 1640
Avoid SQL Injection Attacks When Using Dynamic SQL 1643
Comment Your T-SQL Code 1652
General T-SQL Performance Recommendations 1653
UNION Versus UNION ALL Performance 1654
Use IF EXISTS Instead of SELECT COUNT(*) 1654
Avoid Unnecessary ORDER BY or DISTINCT Clauses 1654
Temp Tables Versus Table Variables Versus Common Table Expressions 1654
Avoid Unnecessary Function Executions 1656
Cursors and Performance 1656
Variable Assignment in UPDATE Statements 1659
T-SQL Tips and Tricks 1663
Date Calculations 1663
Sorting Results with the GROUPING Function 1669
Using CONTEXT_INFO 1671
Working with Outer Joins 1673
Generating T-SQL Statements with T-SQL 1682
Working with @@ERROR and @@ROWCOUNT 1683
De-Duping Data with Ranking Functions 1684
In Case You Missed It: New Transact-SQL Features in SQL Server 2005 1687
The xml Data Type 1687
The max Specifier 1688
TOP Enhancements 1689
The OUTPUT Clause 1693
Common Table Expressions 1698
Recursive Queries with CTEs 1700
Ranking Functions 1708
The ROW_NUMBER Function 1708
The RANK and DENSE_RANK Functions 1711

The NTILE Function 1712
Using Row Numbers for Paging Results 1714
PIVOT and UNPIVOT 1718
The APPLY Operator 1722
CROSS APPLY 1722
OUTER APPLY 1723
TRY...CATCH Logic for Error Handling 1724
The TABLESAMPLE Clause 1727
Summary 1731

44 Advanced Stored Procedure Programming and Optimization 1733

T-SQL Stored Procedure Coding Guidelines 1733
Calling Stored Procedures from Transactions 1735
Handling Errors in Stored Procedures 1738
Using Source Code Control with Stored Procedures 1741
Using Cursors in Stored Procedures 1743
Using CURSOR Variables in Stored Procedures 1748
Nested Stored Procedures 1753
Recursive Stored Procedures 1755
Using Temporary Tables in Stored Procedures 1759
Temporary Table Performance Tips 1760
Using the table Data Type 1762
Using Remote Stored Procedures 1764
Stored Procedure Performance 1764
Query Plan Caching 1765
The SQL Server Plan Cache 1766
Shared Query Plans 1766
Automatic Query Plan Recompilation 1767
Forcing Recompilation of Query Plans 1770
Using Dynamic SQL in Stored Procedures 1774
Using sp_executesql 1776
Installing and Using .NET CLR Stored Procedures 1779
Adding CLR Stored Procedures to a Database 1780
T-SQL or CLR Stored Procedures? 1781
Using Extended Stored Procedures 1782
Adding Extended Stored Procedures to SQL Server 1782
Obtaining Information on Extended Stored Procedures 1783
Extended Stored Procedures Provided with SQL Server 1783
Using xp_cmdshell 1784
Summary 1786

45 SQL Server and the .NET Framework 1787

What's New in SQL Server 2008 and the .NET Framework 1787
Getting Comfortable with ADO.NET 3.5 and SQL Server 2008 1788
    ADO.NET: Advanced Basics 1788
Developing with LINQ to SQL 1793
    Getting Started 1793
    Going Deeper 1796
    Uncovering LINQ to SQL with Linqpad 1798
Using ADO.NET Data Services 1803
    Getting Set Up 1803
    Essentials 1803
    Building Your Data Service 1806
    CRUD Operations 1811
Leveraging the Microsoft Sync Framework 1816
    Getting Started with MSF and Sync Services for ADO.NET 1817
    Building Our Example OCA 1818
Summary 1823

46 SQLCLR: Developing SQL Server Objects in .NET 1825

What's New for SQLCLR in SQL Server 2008 1825
Developing Custom Managed Database Objects 1825
    An Introduction to Custom Managed Database Objects 1826
    Managed Object Permissions 1827
    Developing Managed Objects with Visual Studio 2008 1829
    Developing Managed Stored Procedures 1830
    Developing Managed User-Defined Functions (UDFs) 1835
    Developing Managed User-Defined Types (UDTs) 1844
    Developing Managed User-Defined Aggregates (UDAs) 1853
    Developing Managed Triggers 1856
    Using Transactions 1861
    Using the Related System Catalogs 1863
Summary 1864

47 Using XML in SQL Server 2008 1865

What's New in Using XML in SQL Server 2008 1865
Understanding XML 1866
Relational Data As XML: The FOR XML Modes 1866
    RAW Mode 1867
    AUTO Mode 1873
    EXPLICIT Mode 1877
    PATH Mode 1881

FOR XML and the xml Data Type 1884
XML As Relational Data: Using OPENXML 1887
Using the xml Data Type 1890
Defining and Using xml Columns 1892
Using XML Schema Collections 1894
The Built-in xml Data Type Methods 1899
Indexing and Full-Text Indexing of xml Columns 1918
Indexing xml Columns 1918
Full-Text Indexing 1924
Summary 1925

48 SQL Server Web Services 1927

What's New in SQL Server Web Services 1927
Web Services Migration Path 1928
Web Services History and Overview 1928
The Web Services Pattern 1929
Building Web Services 1930
The AS HTTP Keyword Group 1934
The FOR SOAP Keyword Group 1938
Examples: A C# Client Application 1942
Example 1: Running a Web Method Bound to a Stored Procedure from C# 1942
Example 2: Running Ad Hoc T-SQL Batches from a SQL Server Web Service 1947
Example 3: Calling a Web Method–Bound Stored Procedure That Returns XML 1951
Using Catalog Views and System Stored Procedures 1954
Controlling Access Permissions 1955
Summary 1957

49 SQL Server Service Broker 1959

What's New in Service Broker 1959
Understanding Distributed Messaging 1960
The Basics of Service Broker 1960
Designing a Sample System 1964
Understanding Service Broker Constructs 1965
Defining Messages and Choosing a Message Type 1965
Setting Up Contracts for Communication 1970
Creating Queues for Message Storage 1970
Defining Services to Send and Receive Messages 1973
Planning Conversations Between Services 1974
Service Broker Routing and Security 1985

Using Certificates for Conversation Encryption 1985
A Final Note on the Sample System 1992
Troubleshooting SSB Applications with ssbdiagnose.exe 1993
Related System Catalogs 1994
Summary 1996

50 SQL Server Full-Text Search 1997

What's New in SQL Server 2008 Full-Text Search 1998
Upgrade Options in SQL Server 2008 1998
How SQL Server FTS Works 1999
Indexing 1999
Searching 2001
Implementing SQL Server 2008 Full-Text Catalogs 2002
Setting Up a Full-Text Index 2003
Using T-SQL Commands to Build Full-Text Indexes and Catalogs 2003
Using the Full-Text Indexing Wizard to Build Full-Text Indexes and Catalogs 2017
Full-Text Searches 2020
CONTAINS and CONTAINSTABLE 2020
FREETEXT and FREETEXTTABLE 2023
Full-Text Search Maintenance 2024
Full-Text Search Performance 2025
Full-Text Search Troubleshooting 2026
Summary 2028

Part VII SQL Server Business Intelligence Features

51 SQL Server 2008 Analysis Services 2029

What's New in SSAS 2029
Understanding SSAS and OLAP 2030
Understanding the SSAS Environment Wizards 2032
OLAP Versus OLTP 2036
An Analytics Design Methodology 2038
An Analytics Mini-Methodology 2038
An OLAP Requirements Example: CompSales International 2040
CompSales International Requirements 2040
OLAP Cube Creation 2042
Using SQL Server BIDS 2042
Creating an OLAP Database 2044
Generating a Relational Database 2081
Cube Perspectives 2082
KPIs 2082

Data Mining 2083
Security and Roles 2095
Summary 2097

52 SQL Server Integration Services 2099
What's New with SSIS 2100
SSIS Basics 2100
SSIS Architecture and Concepts 2105
SSIS Tools and Utilities 2110
A Data Transformation Requirement 2113
Running the SSIS Wizard 2115
The SSIS Designer 2126
The Package Execution Utility 2135
The dtexec Utility 2135
Running Packages 2137
Running Package Examples 2140
The dtutil Utility 2141
dtutil Examples 2144
Connection Projects in Visual Studio 2145
Change Data Capture Addition with R2 2147
Using bcp 2147
Fundamentals of Exporting and Importing Data 2151
File Data Types 2153
Format Files 2153
Using Views 2163
Logged and Nonlogged Operations 2163
Batches 2164
Parallel Loading 2164
Supplying Hints to bcp 2165
Summary 2167

53 SQL Server 2008 Reporting Services 2169
What's New in SSRS 2008 2169
Discontinued Functionality and Breaking Changes 2170
Enhancements 2172
Tool and Service Enhancements 2176
SharePoint Integration Improvements 2177
Service Changes and Improvements 2178
Programming Enhancements 2178
Reporting Services Architecture 2179
Installing and Configuring SSRS 2182
The Installation Sequence 2182

SSRS Configuration Using RSCM 2186
Developing Reports 2190
Tools of the Trade 2190
Report Basics 2191
Overview of the Report Development Process 2192
Data Planning and Preparation 2193
Using Shared Data Sources 2193
Using Datasets 2193
Using Shared Datasets 2194
Developing Reports Using BIDS 2196
Working with the Tablix 2199
Understanding Expressions 2200
Report Design Fundamentals 2202
Using the Data Visualization Controls: Sparkline, Indicator, and Data Bar 2204
Designing Reports Using Report Builder 2213
Report Builder and Report Model Security 2233
Enabling Report Builder 2233
Management and Security 2234
Securing Reports 2234
Subscriptions 2235
Report Execution Options 2237
Performance and Monitoring 2239
SSRS Trace Log 2239
Execution Log 2240
Windows Event Log 2240
Performance Counters 2240
Summary 2241

Part VIII Bonus Chapters

54 Managing Linked and Remote Servers 2243

What's New in Managing Linked and Remote Servers 2244
Managing Remote Servers 2244
Remote Server Setup 2246
Linked Servers 2251
Distributed Queries 2252
Distributed Transactions 2252
Adding, Dropping, and Configuring Linked Servers 2253
sp_addlinkedserver 2253
sp_linkedservers 2260
sp_dropserver 2261
sp_serveroption 2261

Mapping Local Logins to Logins on Linked Servers 2263
sp_addlinkedsrvlogin 2263
sp_droplinkedsrvlogin 2265
sp_helplinkedsrvlogin 2266
Obtaining General Information About Linked Servers 2267
Executing a Stored Procedure via a Linked Server 2268
Setting Up Linked Servers Using SQL Server Management Studio 2269
Summary 2272

55 Configuring, Tuning, and Optimizing SQL Server Options 2273

What's New in Configuring, Tuning, and Optimizing SQL Server Options 2274
SQL Server Instance Architecture 2274
Configuration Options 2275
Fixing an Incorrect Option Setting 2283
Setting Configuration Options with SSMS 2283
Obsolete Configuration Options 2283
Configuration Options and Performance 2284
access check cache bucket count 2284
access check cache quota 2285
ad hoc distributed queries 2285
affinity I/O mask 2286
affinity mask 2287
Agent XP 2289
awe enabled 2289
backup compression default 2291
blocked process threshold 2291
c2 audit mode 2291
clr enabled 2292
common criteria compliance enabled 2292
cost threshold for parallelism 2293
cross db ownership chaining 2293
cursor threshold 2294
default full-text language 2294
default language 2296
EKM provider enabled 2298
filestream_access_level 2299
fill factor 2299
index create memory 2300
in-doubt xact resolution 2300
lightweight pooling 2301
locks 2301

max degree of parallelism 2302
max server memory and min server memory 2302
max text repl size..........2304
max worker threads..........2305
min memory per query 2306
nested triggers..........2306
network packet size 2306
optimize for ad hoc workloads..........2307
PH_timeout..........2308
priority boost..........2308
query governor cost limit..........2309
query wait..........2310
recovery interval..........2310
remote admin connections 2311
remote login timeout 2311
remote proc trans 2312
remote query timeout..........2312
scan for startup procs 2313
show advanced options..........2313
user connections..........2313
user options 2315
XP-Related Configuration Options 2316
Database Engine Tuning Advisor..........2317
The Database Engine Tuning Advisor GUI 2317
The Database Engine Tuning Advisor Command Line 2321
Data Collection Sets..........2326
Summary..........2328

56 SQL Server Disaster Recovery Planning 2329

What's New in SQL Server Disaster Recovery Planning..........2330
How to Approach Disaster Recovery 2330
Disaster Recovery Patterns..........2332
Recovery Objectives..........2336
A Data-Centric Approach to Disaster Recovery 2337
Microsoft SQL Server Options for Disaster Recovery 2338
Data Replication 2338
Log Shipping..........2339
Database Mirroring and Snapshots 2341
The Overall Disaster Recovery Process 2342
The Focus of Disaster Recovery 2342
sqldiag.exe 2347
Planning and Executing a Disaster Recovery..........2349

Have You Detached a Database Recently? 2350
Third-Party Disaster Recovery Alternatives 2350
Summary 2351

Index 2353

About the Authors

Ray Rankins is owner and president of Gotham Consulting Services, Inc. (www.gotham-consulting.com), near Saratoga Springs, New York. Ray has been working with Sybase and Microsoft SQL Server for more than 23 years and has experience in database administration, database design, project management, application development, consulting, courseware development, and training. He has worked in a variety of industries, including financial, manufacturing, health care, retail, insurance, communications, public utilities, and state and federal government. His expertise is in database performance and tuning, query analysis, advanced SQL programming and stored procedure development, database design, data architecture, and database application design and development. Ray's presentations on these topics at user group conferences have been very well received. Ray is coauthor of *Microsoft SQL Server 2005 Unleashed, Microsoft SQL Server 2000 Unleashed* (first and second editions), *Microsoft SQL Server 6.5 Unleashed* (all editions), *Sybase SQL Server 11 Unleashed,* and *Sybase SQL Server 11 DBA Survival Guide,* Second Edition, all published by Sams Publishing. As an instructor, Ray brings his real-world experience into the classroom, teaching classes on SQL, advanced SQL programming and optimization, database design, database administration, and database performance and tuning. Ray can be reached at rrankins@gothamconsulting.com.

Paul Bertucci is the founder of Database Architechs (www.dbarchitechs.com), a global database consulting firm with offices in the United States and Paris, France. He has more than 30 years of experience with database design, data architecture, data replication, performance and tuning, master data management (MDM), data provenance/digital DNA, distributed data systems, data integration, high availability, and systems integration for numerous Fortune 500 companies, including Intel, 3COM, Coca-Cola, Apple, Toshiba, Lockheed, Wells Fargo, Safeway, Sony, Charles Schwab, Cisco, Sybase, Symantec, Veritas, and Honda, to name a few. He has authored numerous database articles, data standards, and high-profile database courses, such as Sybase's "Performance and Tuning" and "Physical Database Design" courses. Other Sams Publishing books that he has authored or coauthored include the highly popular *Microsoft SQL Server 2000 Unleashed, ADO.NET in 24 Hours, Microsoft SQL Server High Availability,* and *Microsoft SQL Server 2005 Unleashed.* Paul is a frequent speaker at industry conferences such as Informatica World, Oracle World, MDM Summits, and Microsoft-oriented conferences such as SQL Saturday's, PASS conferences, Tech Ed's, and SQL Server User Groups. He has deployed numerous systems with Microsoft SQL Server, Sybase, DB2, Postgres, MySQL, and Oracle database engines, and he has designed/architected several commercially available tools in the database, data modeling, performance and tuning, data integration, digital DNA, and multidimensional planning spaces. Formerly the Chief Data Architect at Symantec, Paul's current working arrangement is as Autodesk's Chief Enterprise Architect. Paul received his formal education in computer science and electrical engineering from the University of California, Berkeley (Go Bears!). He lives in the great Pacific northwest (Oregon) with his five children, Donny, Juliana, Nina, Marissa, and Paul Jr. Paul can be reached at pbertucci@dbarchitechs.com or bertucci@alum.calberkeley.org.

Chris Gallelli is the president of CGAL Consulting Services, Inc. His company focuses on consulting services in the areas of database administration, database tuning, and database programming using Microsoft Visual Studio. Chris has more than 15 years of experience with SQL Server and more than 25 years in the field of information technology. He has a bachelor's degree in electrical engineering and a master's degree in business administration from Union College. Chris currently lives near Albany, New York, with his lovely wife, Laura, and two daughters, Rachael and Kayla. Other Sams Publishing books that he has coauthored include *Microsoft SQL Server 2000 Unleashed* and *Microsoft SQL Server 2005 Unleashed*. Chris can be reached at cgallelli@gmail.com.

Alex T. Silverstein is owner and chief information officer of Unified Digital Group, LLC, a consulting and custom software development firm headquartered near Saratoga Springs, New York. He specializes in designing SQL Server and Microsoft .NET–powered solutions using the principles of agile development and the Rational Unified Process. Alex has more than a decade of experience providing application development, database administration, and training services worldwide to a variety of industries. He was also a coauthor for *Microsoft SQL Server 2005 Unleashed* and a contributing author for *Microsoft SQL Server 2000 Unleashed*, both published by Sams Publishing. You can reach Alex anytime via email at alex@unifieddigital.com.

About the Contributing Author

Hilary Cotter is a SQL Server MVP with more than 20 years of IT experience working for Fortune 500 clients. He is the author of a book on SQL Server Replication and coauthor of *Microsoft SQL Server 2008 Management and Administration* from Sams Publishing. Hilary has also written numerous white papers and articles on SQL Server and databases.

Dedication

I would like to dedicate this book in loving memory of my grandmother, Gertrude Holdridge, who recently passed away at the "young" age of 87. You will be dearly missed, "Gramma Gert."

—Ray Rankins

Dedicated to my children, for the countless times they heard me say "No, not now, I'm writing chapters!" Thanks, Paul Jr., Marissa, Nina, Juliana, and Donny; I love you all very much!

—Paul Bertucci

This book is dedicated to my Mom and Dad. My mother, Arlene Gallelli, is the perfect mom. Her love, kindness, and relentless support have helped me in all aspects of my life, including the creation of this book. My Dad, Joe Gallelli, is a great father and a great friend. He is an encyclopedia of knowledge, and I can always count on his wisdom and guidance. Thank you both.

—Chris Gallelli

My work on this book is dedicated to my father, Harry Silverstein, a fellow man of letters. For, while his stay with us on this planet was not nearly long enough, he left us with a feeling of kindness and a call to humanity and fellowship with all that has remained for a lifetime. Thank you, Harry, for having been you.

—Alex T. Silverstein

Acknowledgments

I would first like to thank my coauthors for their tireless efforts in helping to turn out a quality publication and their willingness to take on more work when needed to help keep things on track. I would also like to thank Neil Rowe at Sams Publishing for providing us the opportunity to write this book and for his seemingly infinite patience as we repeatedly missed our deadlines.

I would also like to acknowledge my colleague and friend David Solomon for developing the Word macro used to extract the code listings and examples presented in the chapters so we could make them available on the included CD. His efforts made that task significantly easier. I would also like to thank David for his help reviewing some of my chapters.

I would also like to acknowledge and thank Ross Mistry for providing content for the "Administering Policy Based Management" and "Automating SQL Server Tasks Using PowerShell" chapters.

Most of all, I wish to thank my loving wife, Elizabeth, for her patience and understanding during the long days, late nights, and lost weekends spent working on yet another book. I'll be getting to that "honey-do" list now, my dear.

—Ray Rankins

With any writing effort, there is always a huge sacrifice of time that must be made to properly research, demonstrate, and describe leading-edge subject matter. The brunt of the burden usually falls on those many people who are near and very dear to me. With this in mind, I desperately need to thank my family for allowing me to encroach on many months of what should have been my family's "quality time."

However, with sacrifice also comes reward in the form of technical excellence and high-quality business relationships. Many individuals were involved in this effort, both directly and indirectly, starting with the other authors (thanks RR, CG, and AS!), Steve Luk, Raymond Hardman, Jason Riedberger, John Martin, Gene Vilain, Yves Moison, Thierry Gerardin, Mark Ginnebaugh (of DesignMind), and Nathan Gustafson. Their expertise in and knowledge of database engines, SQL, performance and tuning, data replication, database mirroring, database snapshots, business intelligence, data integration, and high availability are unmatched.

—Paul Bertucci

Writing a book of this size and scope requires a tremendous amount of time and dedication. The time and dedication apply not only to the authors who are writing the book but also to their family members. My wife and daughters were very understanding while I was holed up working on this book, and that understanding helped make the book happen. My love and thanks to them.

I would also like to thank many of my clients who embraced SQL Server 2008 and gave me the opportunity to use it in the real world. In particular, I would like to thank Ray McQuade and his company, Spruce Computer Systems. Spruce has had tremendous success with SQL Server 2005 and SQL Server 2008.

—Chris Gallelli

I would like to acknowledge the following people for helping make my contribution to this book possible: Ray Rankins, Paul Bertucci, Chris Gallelli, Neil Rowe, Gregory Abbruzzese, Frank Esposito, Jonathan Rubenstein, Linda Motzkin, Lane McCarthy, Bob

Barter, Amatzia Segal, all the wonderful customers who keep Unified Digital in business, and, most importantly, El Shaddai. You all are the *sine qua non* of my world, and I thank you most heartily.

—Alex T. Silverstein

We Want to Hear from You!

As the reader of this book, *you* are our most important critic and commentator. We value your opinion and want to know what we're doing right, what we could do better, what areas you'd like to see us publish in, and any other words of wisdom you're willing to pass our way.

You can email or write me directly to let me know what you did or didn't like about this book—as well as what we can do to make our books stronger.

Please note that I cannot help you with technical problems related to the topic of this book, and that due to the high volume of mail I receive, I might not be able to reply to every message.

When you write, please be sure to include this book's title and author as well as your name and phone or email address. I will carefully review your comments and share them with the author and editors who worked on the book.

E-mail: neil.rowe@samspublishing.com

Mail: Neil Rowe
Executive Editor
Sams Publishing
800 East 96th Street
Indianapolis, IN 46240 USA

Reader Services

Visit our website and register this book at informit.com/register for convenient access to any updates, downloads, or errata that might be available for this book.

Introduction

Over the past decade, SQL Server has established itself as a robust and reliable database platform whose performance, scalability, and reliability meet the implementation needs of businesses and corporations from small desktop applications on up to multiterabyte enterprise-wide systems. The updates and enhancements in SQL Server 2008 and SQL Server 2008 R2 further solidify its position in the marketplace as a robust enterprise-wide database system that can compete on the same level as the other major enterprise-wide database products, providing a database engine foundation that can be highly available 7 days a week, 365 days a year.

NOTE

The position of SQL Server 2008 as a leader in the market of enterprise-wide database management systems (DBMS) was confirmed in a report released by Forrester Research on June 30, 2009 (The Forrester Wave: Enterprise Database Management Systems, Q2 2009). In this report, Forrester analyst Noel Yuhanna indicated that Microsoft along with Oracle and IBM DB2 were the leaders in the DBMS market. The report from Forrester Research indicated that Microsoft's strong commitment to its data platform starting with SQL Server 2005 and continuing with the latest iteration of the product, SQL Server 2008, had boosted Microsoft to the top of the DBMS market. Key findings in the report concluded that Microsoft received high scores in database programmability, security, availability, and application/data integration, and for delivering the best price performance for most business applications. The report also acknowledged that Microsoft "has shown increasing focus and commitment to going after the enterprise market," and that SQL Server 2008 has "enabled Microsoft to take market share in moderately sized to large enterprises, delivering good performance, scalability, security, and availability functionality." The report also indicated that "five years ago, hardly any enterprises ran multi-terabyte databases with SQL Server to support critical applications. Today, hundreds of enterprises are running 10-terabyte and larger transactional SQL Server databases."

One of the biggest challenges we face writing the *SQL Server Unleashed* series of books is how to provide comprehensive, in-depth, all-inclusive coverage of all the features of SQL Server within a single book. Over the past few releases, the number of SQL Server features and components has increased, and many of these features and components (for example, SQL Server Integration Services, Reporting Services, and .NET Framework integration) provide material enough to warrant their own separate titles. To cover each topic sufficiently would require more information than could reasonably fit in print in a single volume. Thus, we had to make some hard decisions as to what to include in print.

We decided that the printed portion of the book would provide detailed coverage of the core database server features and the day-to-day administrative and management aspects and tools of SQL Server 2008 and 2008 R2. We want to ensure that we provide enough of the necessary information, tips, and guidelines to get you started making effective use of these features. At the same time, there is a wealth of useful information we want to provide on additional SQL Server 2008 features and major components of SQL Server, such as SQL Server Integration Services, Reporting Services, Analysis Services, T-SQL programming, and SQL Server integration with the .NET Framework. Rather than leave this valuable information out entirely, we decided to include the chapters with this material on the CD provided with this book. Also, as in the past, the CD contains all our sample scripts, databases, and other code samples and material that support the book content.

Our other main goal when writing this book was for it to be more than just a syntax reference. SQL Server Books Online is a fine resource as a syntax reference. This book attempts to pick up where Books Online leaves off, by providing, in addition to syntax where necessary, valuable insight, tips, guidelines, and useful examples derived from our many years of experience working with SQL Server. Although we do provide the core, and sometimes advanced, syntax elements for the SQL commands discussed, SQL Server Books Online provides a much more extensive syntax reference than would make sense to try to duplicate here. As a matter of fact, at times, we may even direct you to Books Online for more detail on some of the more esoteric syntax options available for certain commands.

We hope that we have succeeded in meeting the goals we set out for this book and that it becomes an essential reference and source of expert information for you as you work with the either version of SQL Server 2008.

NOTE

Although this book includes coverage of SQL Server 2008 R2, most of the material presented applies to SQL Server 2008 as well. Actually, there are few significant differences in the core product between SQL Server 2008 and SQL Server 2008 R2. Most of the new features are related to enhancements to Reporting Services. You can be comfortable using this book as a reference for either version of SQL Server 2008. When the book discusses features available only in the R2 release, this fact is specifically spelled out in the chapter.

Who This Book Is For

This *Unleashed* book is intended for intermediate- to advanced-level users: for SQL Server administrators who want to understand SQL Server more completely to be able to effectively manage and administer their SQL Server environments, and for developers who want a more thorough understanding of SQL Server to help them write better Transact-SQL (T-SQL) code and develop more robust SQL Server applications. If you are responsible for analysis, design, implementation, support, administration, or troubleshooting of SQL Server 2008, this book provides an excellent source of experiential information for you. You can think of this as a book of applied technology. The emphasis is on the more complex aspects of the product, including using the new tools and features, administering SQL Server, analyzing and optimizing queries, implementing data warehouses, ensuring high availability, and tuning SQL Server performance.

This book is for both developers and SQL Server administrators who are new to SQL Server 2008 or SQL Server 2008 R2 as well as those who are already familiar with prior versions of SQL Server. At the beginning of each chapter is a brief summary of the major changes or new features or capabilities of SQL Server related to that topic. If you are already familiar with SQL Server, you can use this information to focus on the information in the chapters that covers the new features and capabilities in more detail.

This book is intended to provide a behind-the-scenes look into SQL Server, showing you what goes on behind the various wizards and GUI-based tools so you can learn what the underlying SQL commands are. Although the GUI tools can make your average day-to-day operations much simpler, every database administrator should learn the underlying commands to the tools and wizards to fully unlock the power and capabilities of SQL Server.

What This Book Covers

The book is divided into the following sections:

- **Part I, "Welcome to Microsoft SQL Server"**—This part introduces you to the Microsoft SQL Server 2008 environment, the various editions of SQL Server that are available, and the capabilities of each edition in the various Windows environments. In addition, it provides an overview of and introduction to the new features found in SQL Server 2008 and SQL Server 2008 R2, which are covered in more detail throughout the rest of the book.
- **Part II, "SQL Server Tools and Utilities"**—This part covers the tools and utility programs that SQL Server 2008 provides for you to administer and manage your SQL Server environments. You'll find information on the various management tools you use on a daily basis, such as SQL Server Management Studio and the new SQLCMD command-line query tool, along with information on SQL Server Profiler. If you are not familiar with these tools, you should read this part of the book early on because these tools are often used and referenced throughout many of the other chapters in the book.
- **Part III, "SQL Server Administration"**—This part discusses topics related to the administration of SQL Server at the database server level. It begins with an overview of what is involved in administering a SQL Server environment and then goes on to cover the tasks related to setting up and managing the overall SQL Server environment, including installing and upgrading to SQL Server 2008 and SQL Server 2008 R2 as well as installing SQL Server clients. This part also includes coverage of security and user administration, database backup and restore, replication, and using the Database Mail facility. Chapters on SQL Server clustering, database mirroring, and

SQL Server high availability provide some expert advice in these areas. Task scheduling and notification using SQL Server Agent and using the new Policy Based Management feature are also discussed in this part.

- **Part IV, "SQL Server Database Administration"**—This part delves into the administrative tasks associated with creating and managing a SQL Server 2008 database, including the creation and management of database objects, such as tables, indexes, views, stored procedures, functions, and triggers. It also provides coverage of the Database Snapshots and an overview of database maintenance tasks and responsibilities.
- **Part V, "SQL Server Performance and Optimization"**—This part provides information to help you get the best performance out of SQL Server. It begins with a discussion of data structures, indexes, and performance, key items to understand to help ensure good database performance. It then builds on that information with chapters on query optimization and analysis, locking, database design and performance, and ways to manage workloads using the new Resource Governor; then it finishes with a methodology for monitoring and optimizing SQL Server performance.
- **Part VI, "SQL Server Application Development"**—This part includes a comprehensive overview of what's new in T-SQL in SQL Server 2008 and SQL Server 2008 R, T-SQL programming guidelines, tips, and tricks, and advanced stored procedure programming and optimization. In addition, chapters in this Part provide an overview of .NET integration with SQL Server and creating .NET CLR objects information, working with XML in SQL Server, and working with additional SQL Server components that are not part of the core database engine such as Web Services, Service Broker, and Full-Text Search.
- **Part VII, "SQL Server Business Intelligence Features"**—This Part includes a comprehensive overview of SQL Server 2008 R2's built-in business intelligence features: Analysis Services, Integration Services, and Reporting Services, with a specific focus on the enhancements to Reporting Services introduced with the R2 release.
- **Bonus Chapters on the CD**—This Part provides a few chapters for which there just wasn't room enough to include elsewhere in the book. These chapters provide expert advice and information on managing remote and linked servers, configuring, tuning and optimizing SQL Server, and planning for SQL Server Disaster Recoverys.
- **Book Materials on the CD**—Also included on the CD are many of the code samples, scripts, databases, and other materials that supplement various chapters. This has always been one of the most valuable reasons to buy books in the *Unleashed* series. It is our goal not just to discuss a SQL technique or solution, but to also provide working samples and examples that actually do it. Learning by seeing is essential for understanding.

In addition to the included CD content, please visit the web page for this book at www.samspublishing.com periodically for any updated or additional bonus material as it becomes available.

Conventions Used in This Book

Names of commands and stored procedures are presented in a special `monospaced` computer typeface. We have tried to be consistent in our use of uppercase and lowercase for keywords and object names. However, because the default installation of SQL Server doesn't make a distinction between upper- and lowercase for SQL keywords or object names and data, you might find some of the examples presented in either upper- or lowercase.

Code and output examples are presented separately from regular paragraphs and are also in a `monospaced` computer typeface. The following is an example:

```
select object_id, name, type_desc
from sys.objects
where type = 'SQ'

object_id   name                            type_desc
----------- ------------------------------- ------------
1977058079  QueryNotificationErrorsQueue    SERVICE_QUEUE
2009058193  EventNotificationErrorsQueue    SERVICE_QUEUE
2041058307  ServiceBrokerQueue              SERVICE_QUEUE
```

When syntax is provided for a command, we have followed these conventions:

Syntax Element	Definition
`command`	These are command names, options, and other keywords.
`placeholder`	Monospaced italic indicates values you provide.
`{}`	You must choose at least one of the enclosed options.
`[]`	The enclosed value/keyword is optional.
`()`	Parentheses are part of the command.
`|`	You can select only one of the options listed.
`,`	You can select any of the options listed.
`[...]`	The previous option can be repeated.

Consider the following syntax example:

```
grant {all | permission_list} on object [(column_list)]
      to {public | user_or_group_name [, [...]]}
```

In this case, *object* is required, but *column_list* is optional. Note also that items shown in plain computer type, such as *grant*, public, and all, should be entered literally, as shown. Placeholders are presented in *italic*, such as *permission_list* and user_or_group_name. *A placeholder* is a generic term for which you must supply a specific value or values. The ellipsis *([...])* in the square brackets following *user_or_group_name* indicates that multiple user or group names can be specified, separated by commas. You can specify either the keyword public or one or more user or group names, but not both.

Some of the examples presented in this book make use of the AdventureWorks2008 and AdventureWorks2008R2 databases, which are not automatically installed with SQL Server 2008 or SQL Server 2008 R2. To install the AdventureWorks sample databases, you must first download the installer from the Microsoft SQL Server Samples and Community Projects website at http://www.codeplex.com/sqlserversamples.

NOTE

Most of the examples presented in this book that use the AdventureWorks database can be run in either AdventureWorks2008 or AdventureWorks2008R2. Structurally, these databases are identical. However, the following tables in AdventureWorks2008R2 have different data values for some of the columns:

- Person
- SalesPerson
- SalesOrderHeader
- SalesTerritory
- Shift
- TransactionHistory

If any of the examples use any of these tables, you may see different results depending on whether you run them in AdventureWorks2008 or AdventureWorks2008R2. When necessary, it will be stated in the chapter which version of the AdventureWorks database was used to generate the results displayed.

Although it is not necessary to install both versions of the AdventureWorks database, it is possible to install both versions in the same SQL Server instance if you wish.

For many of the examples presented in Part V, larger tables than what are available in the AdventureWorks database were needed to demonstrate many of the concepts with more meaningful examples. For many of the chapters in this part, as well as some other chapters throughout the book, the examples come from the bigpubs2008 database. A copy of the database, along with an Entity-Relationship (ER) diagram and table descriptions, is also on the CD.

To install the `bigpubs2008` database on your system so you can try the various examples, do the following:

1. Copy the `bigpubs2008.mdf` file into the SQL Server data folder where you want it to reside.
2. After copying the file to the destination folder, ensure that the `Read-Only` property of the bigpubs2008.mdf file is not enabled (this can happen when the file is copied from the CD). Right-click the file in Windows Explorer and select Properties to bring up the Properties dialog. Click the Read-Only check box to remove the check mark. Click OK to save the changes to the file attributes.
3. Attach the `bigpubs2008` database by using a command similar to the following:

   ```
   sp_attach_single_file_db 'bigpubs2008',
           N'D:\MSSQL\DATA\MSSQL.1\MSSQL\Data\bigpubs2008.mdf
   ```

   Note that you might need to edit the path to match the location where you copied the `bigpubs2008.mdf` file.

Alternatively, you can attach the database by using SQL Server Management Studio. To do this, right-click the `Databases` node in the Object Explorer and select Attach. When the Attach Databases dialog appears, click the Add button, locate the bigpubs2008.mdf file, and click OK. In the bottom window pane, click the transaction log file entry (it should say `Not Found` in the message column) and click the Remove button. Next, click the OK button to attach the database. A new transaction log file is automatically created in the same folder as the bigpubs2008.mdf file. For more information on attaching database files, see Chapters14, "Database Backup and Restore," and 23, "Creating and Managing Databases."

NOTE

In addition to the `bigpubs2008` database, the `.mdf` file for the database used for examples in Chapter 51, "SQL Server Analysis Services," is also provided. To install the `CompSales` database, do the following:

1. Copy the CompSales.mdf file into the SQL Server data folder where you want it to reside.
2. Ensure that the `Read-Only` property of the CompSales.mdf file is not enabled.
3. Attach the `CompSales` database by using a command similar to the following (edit the path to match the location of the CompSales.mdf file on your system):

   ```
   sp_attach_single_file_db 'CompSales',
   N'D:\MSSQL\DATA\MSSQL.1\MSSQL\Data\CompSales.mdf
   ```

Good Luck!

If you have purchased this book, you are on your way to getting the most from SQL Server 2008 or SQL Server 2008 R2. You have already chosen a fine platform for building database applications, one that can provide outstanding performance and rock-solid reliability and availability at a reasonable cost. With this book, you now have the information you need to make the best of it.

Many of us who worked on this book have been using SQL Server since it was first released. Writing about each new version challenges us to reassess our understanding of SQL Server and the way it works. It's an interesting and enjoyable process, and we learn a lot writing each of these books. We hope you get as much enjoyment and knowledge from reading this book as we have from writing it.

CHAPTER 1

SQL Server 2008 Overview

IN THIS CHAPTER

- SQL Server Components and Features
- SQL Server 2008 R2 Editions
- SQL Server Licensing Models

Exactly what is SQL Server 2008? When you first install the product, what are all the pieces you get, what do they do, and which of them do you need?

At its core, SQL Server 2008 is an enterprise-class database management system (DBMS) that is capable of running anything from a personal database only a few megabytes in size on a handheld Windows Mobile device up to a multiserver database system managing terabytes of information. However, SQL Server 2008 is much more than just a database engine.

The SQL Server product is made up of a number of different components. This chapter describes each of the pieces that make up the SQL Server product and what role each plays. Each of these topics is dealt with in more detail later in the book. In addition, this chapter looks at the environments that support SQL Server 2008 and SQL Server 2008 R2 and the features available in each of the various SQL Server editions.

SQL Server Components and Features

The main component of SQL Server 2008 is the Database Engine. Before you can use the other components and features of SQL Server 2008, which are discussed in the following sections, you need to have an instance of the Database Engine installed.

The SQL Server Database Engine

The Database Engine is the core application service in the SQL Server package for storing, processing, and securing data with SQL Server 2008. The SQL Server 2008 Database Engine is a Windows service that can be used to store and process data in a relational format, as XML documents, and new for 2008, as spatial data. The following are the main responsibilities of the Database Engine:

- Provide reliable storage for data
- Provide a means to rapidly retrieve this data
- Provide consistent access to the data
- Control access to the data through security
- Enforce data integrity rules to ensure that the data is reliable and consistent.

Each of these responsibilities is examined in greater detail in later chapters in this book. For now, this chapter provides just a brief overview on each of these points to show how Microsoft SQL Server fulfills these core responsibilities.

Reliable Storage

Reliable storage starts at the hardware level. This isn't the responsibility of the Database Engine, but it's a necessary part of a well-built database. Although you can put an entire SQL database on a single IDE or SATA drive (or even burn a read-only copy on a CD), it is preferable to maintain the data on RAID arrays. The most common RAID arrays can survive hardware failures at the disk level without loss of data.

NOTE

For more information on the reliability characteristics and performance implications of the various RAID configurations and guidelines for implementing RAID configurations with SQL Server, see Chapter 38, "Database Design and Performance."

Using whatever hardware you have decided to make available, the Database Engine manages all the data structures necessary to ensure reliable storage of your data. Rows of data are stored in *pages*, and each page is 8KB in size. Eight pages make up an *extent*, and the Database Engine keeps track of which extents are allocated to which tables and indexes.

NOTE

A *page* is an 8KB chunk of a data file, the smallest unit of storage available in the database. An *extent* is a collection of eight 8KB pages.

Another key feature the Database Engine provides to ensure reliable storage is the transaction log. The transaction log makes a record of every change that is made to the database.

For more information on the transaction log and how it's managed, see Chapter 31, "Transaction Management and the Transaction Log."

NOTE

It is not strictly true that the transaction log records *all* changes to the database; some exceptions exist. Operations on binary large objects—data of type `image` and `text`—can be excepted from logging, and bulk copy loads into tables can be minimally logged to get the fastest possible performance.

Rapid Data Access

SQL Server allows the creation of indexes, enabling fast access to data. See Chapter 34, "Data Structures, Indexes, and Performance," for an in-depth discussion of indexes.

Another way to provide rapid access to data is to keep frequently accessed data in memory. Excess memory for a SQL Server instance is used as a data cache. When pages are requested from the database, the SQL Server Database Engine checks to see if the requested pages are already in the cache. If they are not, it reads them off the disk and stores them in the data cache. If there is no space available in the data cache, the least recently accessed pages (that is, those that haven't been accessed in a while since they were read into memory) are flushed out of the data cache to make room for the newly requested pages. If the pages being flushed contain changes that haven't been written out yet, they are written to disk before being flushed from memory. Otherwise, they are simply discarded.

NOTE

With sufficient memory, an entire database can fit completely into memory, providing the best possible I/O performance for the database.

Consistent Data Access

Getting to your data quickly doesn't mean much if the information you receive is inaccurate. SQL Server follows a set of rules to ensure that the data you receive from queries is consistent.

The general idea with consistent data access is to allow only one client at a time to change the data and to prevent others from reading data from the database while it is undergoing changes. Data and transactional consistency are maintained in SQL Server by using transactional locking.

Transactional consistency has several levels of conformance, each of which provides a trade-off between accuracy of the data and concurrency. These levels of concurrency are examined in more detail in Chapter 37, "Locking and Performance."

Access Control

SQL Server controls access by providing security at multiple levels. Security is enforced at the server, database, schema, and object levels. Server-level access is enforced either by using a SQL Server username and password or through integrated network security, which uses the client's network login credentials to establish identity.

SQL Server security is examined in greater detail in Chapter 11, "Security and User Administration."

Data Integrity

Some databases have to serve the needs of more than a single application. A corporate database that contains valuable information might have a dozen different departments wanting to access portions of the database for different needs.

In this kind of environment, it is impractical to expect the developers of each application to agree on an identical set of standards for maintaining data integrity. For example, one department might allow phone numbers to have extensions, whereas another department may not need that capability. One department might find it critical to maintain a relationship between a customer record and a salesperson record, whereas another might care only about the customer information.

The best way to keep everybody sane in this environment—and to ensure that the data stays consistent and usable by everyone—is to enforce a set of data integrity rules within the database itself. This is accomplished through data integrity constraints and other data integrity mechanisms, such as triggers. See Chapter 26, "Implementing Data Integrity," for details.

SQL Server 2008 Administration and Management Tools

SQL Server 2008 and SQL Server 2008 R2 provide a suite of tools for managing and administering the SQL Server Database Engine and other components. The following sections provide an overview of the primary tools for day-to-day administration, management, and monitoring of your SQL Server environments.

SQL Server Management Studio (SSMS)

SSMS is the central console from which most database management tasks can be coordinated. SSMS provides a single interface from which all servers in a company can be managed. SSMS is examined in more detail in Chapter 4, "SQL Server Management Studio."

Figure 1.1 shows SSMS being used for some everyday administration tasks.

Figure 1.1 shows a list of registered servers in the upper-left pane. Below that is the Object Explorer, which lets you browse the contents of the databases within a SQL Server instance. The `bigpubs2008` database has been expanded, and the right pane shows the columns for the `authors` table.

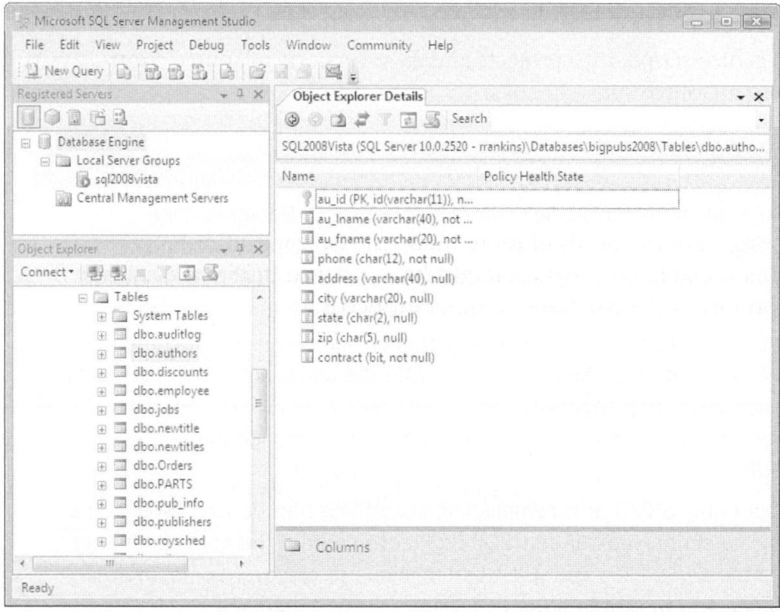

FIGURE 1.1 SSMS, showing a list of columns for the **authors** table in the **bigpubs2008** database.

Following are some of the tasks you can perform with SSMS. Most of these tasks are discussed in detail later in the book:

- Completely manage many servers in a convenient interface
- Set server options and configuration values, such as the amount of memory and number of processors to use, default language, and default location of the data and log files
- Manage logins, database users, and database roles
- Create, edit, and schedule automated jobs through the SQL Server Agent
- Back up and restore databases and define maintenance plans
- Create new databases
- Browse table contents
- Create and manage database objects, such as tables, indexes, and stored procedures
- Generate DDL scripts for databases and database objects
- Configure and manage replication
- Create, edit, execute, and debug Transact-SQL (T-SQL) scripts
- Define, implement, manage, and invoke SQL Server Policies

- Enable and disable features of SQL Server
- Manage and organize scripts into projects and save versions in source control systems such as Visual SourceSafe

NOTE

Much of SQL Server Managements Studio's interaction with SQL Server is done through standard T-SQL statements. For example, when you create a new database through the SSMS interface, behind the scenes, SSMS generates a `CREATE DATABASE` SQL statement to be executed in the target server. Essentially, whatever you can do through the SSMS GUI, you can do with T-SQL statements. As a matter of fact, nearly every dialog in SSMS provides the capability to generate the corresponding T-SQL script for the action(s) it performs. This capability can be very useful as a timesaver for tasks that you need to perform repeatedly, avoiding the need to step through the options presented in the GUI.

If you're curious about how SSMS is accomplishing something that doesn't provide the capability to generate a script, you can run SQL Profiler to capture the commands that SSMS is sending to the server. You can use this technique to discover some interesting internal information and insight into the SQL Server system catalogs.

SQL Server Configuration Manager

SQL Server Configuration Manager is a tool provided with SQL Server 2008 for managing the services associated with SQL Server and for configuring the network protocols used by SQL Server. Primarily, SQL Server Configuration Manager is used to start, pause, resume, and stop SQL Server services and to view or change service properties.

SQL Server Agent

SQL Server Agent is a scheduling tool integrated into SSMS that allows convenient definition and execution of scheduled scripts and maintenance jobs. SQL Server Agent also handles automated alerts—for example, if the database runs out of space.

SQL Server Agent is a Windows service that runs on the same machine as the SQL Server Database Engine. The SQL Server Agent service can be started and stopped through either SSMS, the SQL Server Configuration Manager, or the ordinary Windows Services Manager.

In enterprise situations in which many SQL Server machines need to be managed together, the SQL Server Agent can be configured to distribute common jobs to multiple servers through the use of Multiserver Administration. This capability is most helpful in a wide architecture scenario, in which many SQL Server instances are performing the same tasks with the databases. Jobs are managed from a single SQL Server machine, which is responsible for maintaining the jobs and distributing the job scripts to each target server. The results of each job are maintained on the target servers but can be observed through a single interface.

If you had 20 servers that all needed to run the same job, you could check the completion status of that job in moments instead of logging in to each machine and checking the status 20 times.

The SQL Server Agent also handles event forwarding. Any system events recorded in the Windows system event log can be forwarded to a single machine. This gives a busy administrator a single place to look for errors.

More information about how to accomplish these tasks, as well as other information on the SQL Server Agent, is available in Chapter 16, "SQL Server Scheduling and Notification."

SQL Server Profiler

The SQL Server Profiler is a GUI interface to the SQL Trace feature of SQL Server that captures the queries and results flowing to and from the database engine. It is analogous to a network sniffer, although it does not operate on quite that low a level. The Profiler can capture and save a complete record of all the T-SQL statements passed to the server and the occurrence of SQL Server events such as deadlocks, logins, and errors. You can use a series of filters to pare down the results when you want to drill down to a single connection or even a single query.

You can use the SQL Profiler to perform these helpful tasks:

- You can capture the exact SQL statements sent to the server from an application for which source code is not available (for example, third-party applications).
- You can capture all the queries sent to SQL Server for later playback on a test server. This capability is extremely useful for performance testing with live query traffic.
- If your server is encountering recurring access violations (AVs), you can use the Profiler to reconstruct what happened leading up to an AV.
- The Profiler shows basic performance data about each query. When your users start hammering your server with queries that cause hundreds of table scans, the Profiler can easily identify the culprits.
- For complex stored procedures, the Profiler can identify which portion of the procedure is causing the performance problem.
- You can audit server activity in real-time.

More information on SQL Server Profiler is available in Chapter 6, "SQL Server Profiler."

Replication

Replication is a server-based tool that you can use to synchronize data between two or more databases. Replication can send data from one SQL Server instance to another, or it can replicate data to Oracle, Access, or any other database that is accessible via ODBC or OLE DB.

SQL Server supports three kinds of replication:

- Snapshot replication
- Transactional replication
- Merge replication

The availability and functionality of replication might be restricted, depending on the edition of SQL Server 2008 you are running.

NOTE

Replication copies the changes to data from your tables and indexed views, but it does not normally re-create indexes or triggers at the target. It is common to have different indexes on replication targets than on the source to support different requirements.

Snapshot Replication

With snapshot replication, the server takes a picture, or snapshot, of the data in a table at a single point in time. Usually, if this operation is scheduled, the target data is simply replaced at each update. This form of replication is appropriate for small data sets, infrequent update periods (or for a one-time replication operation), or management simplicity.

Transactional Replication

Initially set up with a snapshot, the server maintains downstream replication targets by reading the transaction log at the source and applying each change at the targets. For every insert, update, and delete operation, the server sends a copy of the operation to every downstream database. This is appropriate if low-latency replicas are needed. Transactional replication can typically keep databases in sync within about five seconds of latency, depending on the underlying network infrastructure. Keep in mind that transactional replication does not guarantee identical databases at any given point in time. Rather, it guarantees that each change at the source will eventually be propagated to the targets. If you need to guarantee that two databases are transactionally identical, you should look into Distributed Transactions or database mirroring.

Transactional replication might be used for a website that supports a huge number of concurrent browsers but only a few updates, such as a large and popular messaging board. All updates would be done against the replication source database and would be replicated in near-real-time to all the downstream targets. Each downstream target could support several web servers, and each incoming web request would be balanced among the web farm. If the system needed to be scaled to support more read requests, you could simply add more web servers and databases and add the database to the replication scheme.

Merge Replication

With snapshot and transactional replication, a single source of data exists from which all the replication targets are replenished. In some situations, it might be necessary or desirable to allow the replication targets to accept changes to the replicated tables and merge these changes together at some later date.

Merge replication allows data to be modified by the subscribers and synchronized at a later time. This synchronization could be as soon as a few seconds, or it could be a day later.

Merge replication would be helpful for a sales database that is replicated from a central SQL Server database out to several dozen sales laptops. As the sales personnel make sales calls, they can add new data to the customer database or change errors in the existing data. When the salespeople return to the office, they can synchronize their laptops with the central database. Their changes are submitted, and the laptops get refreshed with whatever new data was entered since the last synchronization.

Immediate Updating

Immediate updating allows a replication target to immediately modify data at the source. This task is accomplished by using a trigger to run a distributed transaction. Immediate updating is performance intensive, but it allows for updates to be initiated from anywhere in the replication architecture.

More details on replication are available in Chapter 19, "Replication."

Database Mirroring

The database mirroring feature available in SQL Server 2008 provides a solution for increasing database availability. Essentially, database mirroring maintains two copies of a single database that reside on different instances of SQL Server, typically on server instances that reside on computers in different locations. In a typical database mirroring scenario, one server instance serves as the primary database to which the client applications connect, and the other server instance acts as a hot or warm standby server.

Database mirroring involves re-applying every modification operation that occurs on the primary database onto the mirror database as quickly as possible. This is accomplished by sending every active transaction log record generated on the primary server to the mirror server. The log records are applied to the mirror database, in sequence, as quickly as possible. Unlike replication, which works at the logical level, database mirroring works at the level of the physical log record. The mirror database is an exact copy of the primary database.

For more information on setting up and using database mirroring, see Chapter 20, "Database Mirroring."

Full-Text Search

SQL Server 2008 provides the capability to issue full-text queries against plain character-based data in your SQL Server tables. This capability is useful for searching large text fields, such as movie reviews, book descriptions, or case notes. Full-text queries can include words and phrases, or multiple forms of a word or phrase.

Full-Text Search capabilities in Microsoft SQL Server 2008 are provided by the Microsoft Full-Text Engine for SQL Server (MSFTESQL). The MSFTESQL service works together with the SQL Server Database Engine. You specify tables or entire databases that you want to index. The full-text indexes are built and maintained outside the SQL Server database files in special full-text indexes stored in the Windows file system. You can specify how often the full-text indexes are updated to balance performance issues with timeliness of the data.

The SQL Server Database Engine supports basic text searches against specific columns. For example, to find all the rows where a text column contained the word *guru*, you might write the following SQL statement:

```
select *
   from resume
   where description like '%guru%'
```

This statement finds all the rows in the resume table where the description contains the word *guru*. This method has a couple problems, however. First, the search is slow. Because the Database Engine can't index text columns, a full table scan has to be done to satisfy the query. Even if the data were stored in a varchar column instead of a text column, an index may not help because you're looking for *guru* anywhere in the column, not just at the beginning, so the index cannot be used to locate the matching rows. (Chapter 34 contains more information on avoiding such situations.)

What if you wanted to search for the word *guru* anywhere in the table, not just in the description column? What if you were looking for a particular set of skills, such as "SQL" and "ability to work independently"? Full-text indexing addresses these problems. To perform the same search as before with full-text indexing, you might use a query like this:

```
select *
   from resume
   where contains(description, 'guru')
```

To perform a search that looks for a set of skills, you might use a query like this:

```
select *
   from resume
   where contains(*, 'SQL and "ability to work independently"')
```

For more information on setting up and searching Full-Text Search indexes, see Chapter 50, "SQL Server Full-Text Search" (on the CD).

SQL Server Integration Services (SSIS)

SSIS is a platform for building high-performance data integration solutions and workflow solutions. You can build extract, transform, and load (ETL) packages to update data warehouses, interact with external processes, clean and mine data, process analytical objects, and perform administrative tasks. Following are some of the features of SSIS:

- Graphical tools and wizards for building, debugging, and deploying SSIS packages
- Workflow functions, such as File Transfer Protocol (FTP), SQL statement execution, and more
- SSIS Application Programming Interfaces (APIs)
- Complex data transformation for data cleansing, aggregation, merging, and copying

- An email messaging interface
- A service-based implementation
- Support for both native and managed code (C++ or any common language runtime [CLR]–compliant language, such as C# or J#)
- An SSIS object model

SSIS is a tool that helps address the needs of getting data—which is often stored in many different formats, contexts, file systems, and locations—from one place to another. In addition, the data often requires significant transformation and conversion processing as it is being moved around. Common uses of SSIS might include the following:

- Exporting data out of SQL Server tables to other applications and environments (for example, ODBC or OLE DB data sources, flat files)
- Importing data into SQL Server tables from other applications and environments (for example, ODBC or OLE DB data sources, flat files)
- Initializing data in some data replication situations, such as initial snapshots
- Aggregating data (that is, data transformation) for distribution to/from data marts or data warehouses
- Changing the data's context or format before importing or exporting it (that is, data conversion)

For more information on creating and using SSIS packages, see Chapter 52, "SQL Server Integration Services."

SQL Server Analysis Services (SSAS)

SSAS provides online analytical processing (OLAP) and data mining functionality for business intelligence (BI) solutions. SSAS provides a rich set of data mining algorithms to enable business users to mine data, looking for specific patterns and trends. These data mining algorithms can be used to analyze data through a Unified Dimensional Model (UDM) or directly from a physical data store.

SSAS uses both server and client components to supply OLAP and data mining functionality for BI applications. SSAS consists of the analysis server, processing services, integration services, and a number of data providers. It has both server-based and client-/local-based analysis services capabilities. This essentially provides a complete platform for SSAS. The basic components within SSAS are all focused on building and managing data cubes.

SSAS allows you to build dimensions and cubes from heterogeneous data sources. It can access relational OLTP databases, multidimensional data databases, text data, and any other source that has an OLE DB provider available. You don't have to move all your data into a SQL Server database first; you just connect to its source. In addition, SSAS allows a designer to implement OLAP cubes, using a variety of physical storage techniques directly tied to data aggregation requirements and other performance considerations.

You can easily access any OLAP cube built with SSAS via the Pivot Table Service, you can write custom client applications by using Multidimensional Expressions (MDX) with OLE DB for OLAP or ActiveX Data Objects Multidimensional (ADO MD), and you can use a number of third-party OLAP-compliant tools. MDX enables you to formulate complex multidimensional queries.

SSAS is commonly used to perform the following tasks:

- Perform trend analysis to predict the future. For example, based on how many widgets you sold last year, how many will you sell next year?
- Combine otherwise disconnected variables to gain insight into past performance. For example, was there any connection between widget sales and rainfall patterns? Searching for unusual connections between your data points is a typical data mining exercise.
- Perform offline summaries of commonly used data points for instant access via a web interface or custom interface. For example, a relational table might contain one row for every click on a website. OLAP can be used to summarize these clicks by hour, day, week, and month and then to further categorize them by business line.

Included for Analysis Services in SQL Server 2008 R2 is PowerPivot for Excel and PowerPivot for SharePoint. PowerPivot for Excel and SharePoint are client and server components that integrate Analysis Services with Excel and SharePoint. PowerPivot for Excel is an add-in that allows you to create PowerPivot workbooks that can assemble and relate large amounts of data from different sources. PowerPivot workbooks typically contain large, multidimensional datasets that you create in a separate client application and use with PivotTables and PivotCharts in a worksheet. The PowerPivot add-in removes the one million row limit for worksheets and provides rapid calculations for the large data that you assemble.

PowerPivot for SharePoint extends SharePoint 2010 and Excel Services to add server-side processing, collaboration, and document management support for the PowerPivot workbooks that you publish to SharePoint.

Together, the PowerPivot client add-in and server components provide an end-to-end solution that furthers business intelligence data analysis for Excel users on the workstation and on SharePoint sites.

SSAS is a complex topic. For more information on MDX, data cubes, and ways to use data warehousing analysis services, see Chapter 52, "SQL Server 2008 Analysis Services."

SQL Server Reporting Services (SSRS)

SQL Server Reporting Services is a server-based reporting platform that delivers enterprise, web-enabled reporting functionality so you can create reports that draw content from a variety of data sources, publish reports in various formats, and centrally manage security and subscriptions.

Reporting Services includes the following core components:

- A complete set of tools you can use to create, manage, and view reports
- A report server component that hosts and processes reports in a variety of formats, including HTML, PDF, TIFF, Excel, CSV, and more
- An API that allows developers to integrate or extend data and report processing into custom applications or to create custom tools to build and manage reports

There are two design tools for building reports: Report Designer, a powerful development tool integrated with Visual Studio, and Report Builder 3.0, which is a simpler point-and-click tool that you use to design ad hoc reports. Both report design tools provide a WYSIWYG experience.

Reports are described using the Report Definition Language (RDL). RDL contains the description of the report layout, formatting information, and instructions on how to fetch the data. After a report is defined, it can be deployed on the report server, where it can be managed, secured, and delivered to a variety of formats, including HTML, Excel, PDF, TIFF, and XML. Various delivery, caching, and execution options are also available, as are scheduling and historical archiving.

One major set of enhancements in SQL Server 2008 R2 includes the new and enhanced features in Reporting Services, which includes

- **New features for SharePoint integration with Reporting Services**—These features include support for multiple SharePoint Zones, support for the SharePoint Universal Logging service, and a query designer for SharePoint Lists as a data source.
- **Report parts**—These are reusable report items that are stored on a report server or on a SharePoint site integrated with a report server.
- **Shared datasets**—These datasets can be shared, stored, processed and cached externally from the report, thus providing a consistent set of data that can be shared by multiple reports.
- **Cache refresh plans**—These plans allow you to cache reports or shared dataset query results on first use or from a schedule.
- **Sparklines and data bars**—These simple charts convey a lot of information in a little space, often inline with text. Sparklines and data bars are often used in tables and matrices.
- **Indicators**—These minimal gauges convey the state of a single data value at a glance. Indicators can be used by themselves in dashboards or free-form reports, but they are most commonly used in tables or matrices to visualize data in rows or columns.
- **Calculating aggregates of aggregates**—You can now create expressions that calculate an aggregate of an aggregate.

- **Better report pagination**—Page breaks on tablix data regions (table, matrix, and list), groups, and rectangles give you better control of report pagination.
- **Map reports**—Report Designer now provides a Map Wizard and Map Layer Wizard to add maps and map layers to your report to help visualize data against a geographic background. A map layer displays map elements based on spatial data from a map in the Map Gallery, from a SQL Server query that returns SQL Server spatial data, or from an Environmental Systems Research Institute, Inc. (ESRI) shapefile.
- **Business Intelligence Development Studio Support for SQL Server 2008 Reports and Report Server projects**—Business Intelligence Development Studio now supports working with both SQL Server 2008 and SQL Server 2008 R2 reports, and with Report Server projects in the SQL Server 2008 R2 version of Business Intelligence Development Studio.
- **Improved Previewing of Report**—Report Builder 3.0 provides a better preview experience with the introduction of edit sessions that enable the reuse of cached datasets when previewing reports. Reports render more quickly when using the cached datasets.

Report Manager has also been updated in the SQL Server 2008 R2 release to provide an improved user experience and look and feel. This includes an updated color scheme and layout in an effort to provide easier navigation to manage report properties and Report Server items. You can now use a new drop-down menu on each report or Report Server item in a folder to access the various configuration options for the report or item you choose. Following are some of the key enhancements to Report Manager in SQL Server 2008 R2:

- Workflow has been improved for viewing and managing reports and report server items. You can use a new drop-down menu to access various configuration options for each report or report server item in a folder.
- The need to render a report before accessing and configuring report properties when in default view has been eliminated.
- The visible display area is now larger in the Report Viewer when rendering reports.
- An updated Report Viewer toolbar includes some updates to the toolbar controls, as well as the capability to export report data to an Atom service document and data feeds.

For more information on designing and deploying reports using Reporting Services and more information on the extensive R2 enhancements, see Chapter 53, "SQL Server 2008 Reporting Services."

SQL Server Service Broker

SQL Server Service Broker provides a native SQL Server infrastructure that supports asynchronous, distributed messaging between database-driven services. Service Broker handles all the hard work of managing coordination among the constructs required for distributed messaging, including transactional delivery and storage, message typing and validation, multithreaded activation and control, event notification, routing, and security.

Service Broker is designed around the basic functions of sending and receiving messages. An application sends messages to a *service*, which is a name for a set of related tasks. An application receives messages from a *queue*, which is a view of an internal table. Service Broker guarantees that an application receives each message exactly once, in the order in which the messages were sent.

Service Broker can be useful for any application that needs to perform processing asynchronously or that needs to distribute processing across a number of computers. An example would be a bicycle manufacturer and seller who must provide new and updated parts data to a company that implements a catalog management system. The manufacturer must keep the catalog information up-to-date with its product model data, or it could lose market share or end up receiving orders from distributors based on out-of-date catalog information. When the parts data is updated in the manufacturer's database, a trigger could be invoked to send a message to Service Broker with information about the updated data. Service Broker would then asynchronously deliver the message to the catalog service. The catalog service program would then perform the work in a separate transaction. When this work is performed in a separate transaction, the original transaction in the manufacturer's database can commit immediately. The application avoids system slowdowns that result from keeping the original transaction open while performing the update to the catalog database.

For more information on using Service Broker, see Chapter 49, "SQL Server Service Broker" (on the CD).

SQL Server 2008 R2 Editions

You can choose from several editions of SQL Server 2008 R2. The edition you choose depends on your database and data processing needs, as well as the Windows platform on which you want to install it.

For actual deployment of SQL Server in a production environment, you can choose from any edition of SQL Server 2008 except Developer Edition and Evaluation Edition. Which edition you choose to deploy depends on your system requirements and need for SQL Server components.

This following sections examine the different editions of SQL Server and discusses their features and capabilities. Using this information, you can better choose which edition provides the appropriate solution for you.

SQL Server 2008 Standard Edition

The Standard Edition of SQL Server 2008 is the version intended for the masses—those running small- to medium-sized systems who don't require the performance, scalability, and availability provided by Enterprise Edition. Standard Edition scalability is limited to up to four processors. There is no built-in memory limitation in SQL Server 2008 Standard Edition; it can utilize as much memory as provided by the operating system.

SQL Server 2008 Standard Edition includes the following features:

- CLR procedures, functions, and data types
- SQL Server Analysis Services
- Service Broker
- Reporting Services
- SQL Server Integration Services
- Full-Text Search
- Built-in XML support
- Spatial Indexes
- SQL Server Profiler and performance analysis tools
- SQL Server Management Studio
- Policy Based Management
- Replication
- Two-node failover clustering
- Database mirroring (safety full mode only)
- Log shipping
- Backup Compression (available in R2 only)

The Standard Edition can be installed on any of the Windows 2003 SP2 and Windows 2008 Server platforms, as well as Windows XP Professional, Windows Vista Ultimate, Enterprise, or Business Editions, and Windows 7 Ultimate, Enterprise, or Professional Editions.

The Standard Edition should meet the needs of most departmental and small- to mid-sized applications. However, if you need more scalability, availability, advanced security or performance features, or comprehensive analysis features, you should implement the Enterprise Edition of SQL Server 2008.

SQL Server 2008 Enterprise Edition

The Enterprise Edition of SQL Server 2008 is the most comprehensive and complete edition available. It provides the most scalability and availability of all editions and is intended for systems that require high performance and availability, such as large-volume websites, data warehouses, and high-throughput online transaction processing (OLTP) systems.

SQL Server 2008 Enterprise Edition supports as much memory and as many CPUs as supported by the operating system on which it is installed. It can be installed on any of the Windows 2003 SP2 and Windows 2008 Server platforms.

In addition, SQL Server 2008 Enterprise Edition provides performance enhancements, such as parallel queries, indexed views, and enhanced read-ahead scanning.

Which version is right for you? The next section explores the feature sets of Enterprise and Standard Editions so you can decide which one provides the features you need.

Differences Between the Enterprise and Standard Editions of SQL Server

For deploying SQL Server 2008 in a server environment, either the Standard Edition or Enterprise Edition of SQL Server is a logical choice. To help you decide between the two editions, Table 1.1 compares the major features that each edition supports.

TABLE 1.1 SQL Server 2008 Feature Comparison: Enterprise and Standard Editions

Feature	Enterprise Edition	Standard Edition
Max number of CPUs	8	4
64-bit support	Yes	Yes
CLR runtime integration	Yes	Yes
Full-Text Search	Yes	Yes
Native XML Support	Yes	Yes
FILESTREAM Support	Yes	Yes
Spatial Data Support	Yes	Yes
SQL Server Integration Services	Yes	Yes
Database Mail	Yes	Yes
Policy Based Management	Yes	Yes
SQL Profile	Yes	Yes
Integration Services with Basic Transforms	Yes	Yes
Integration Services with Advanced Data Mining and Cleansing Transforms	Yes	No
Star Join Query Optimization	Yes	No
Change Data Capture	Yes	No
Service Broker	Yes	Yes
Reporting Services	Yes	Yes
Replication	Yes	Yes
Log Shipping	Yes	Yes
Database mirroring	Yes	Yes (Single REDO thread with Safety FULL only)

TABLE 1.1 SQL Server 2008 Feature Comparison: Enterprise and Standard Editions

Feature	Enterprise Edition	Standard Edition
Database snapshots	Yes	No
Indexed views	Yes	Yes (Can be created, but automatic matching by Query Optimizer not supported)
Updatable distributed partitioned views	Yes	No
Table and index partitioning	Yes	No
Online index operations	Yes	No
Parallel index operations	Yes	No
Parallel DBCC	Yes	No
Online page and file restoration	Yes	No
Fast Recovery	Yes	No
Data Compression	Yes	No
Compressed Backups	Yes	Yes
Resource Governor	Yes	No
Fine Grained Encryption	Yes	No
Transparent Data Encryption	Yes	No
Failover clustering	Yes	Yes (2-node only)
Multiple-instance support	Yes (50 instances maximum)	Yes (16 instances maximum)
PowerPivot for SharePoint	Yes (R2 only)	No
Application and Multi-Server Management (R2 Only)	Yes	Yes (as a managed instance only)

Other SQL Server 2008 Editions

The Standard and Enterprise Editions of SQL Server 2008 are intended for server-based deployment of applications. In addition, the following editions are available for other specialized uses:

- Workgroup Edition
- Developer Edition
- Web Edition

- Express Edition
- Compact Edition

Workgroup Edition

SQL Server 2008 Workgroup Edition is intended for small organizations that need a database with no limits on database size or number of users but may not need the full capabilities of the Standard Edition. SQL Server 2008 Workgroup Edition can be used as a front-end web server or for departmental or branch office applications.

Workgroup Edition includes most of the core database features and capabilities of the SQL Server Standard Edition except for the following:

- It is limited to two CPUs and a maximum of 4GB of memory.
- It does not support failover clustering.
- Database mirroring support is limited to being a witness only.
- It does not include Analysis Services.
- It provides limited support for Integration Services and Reporting Services features.

Workgroup Edition can be installed in any of the following environments:

- Any Windows 2003 Server editions
- Any Windows 2008 Server editions
- Windows 7
- Windows Vista
- Windows XP

Developer Edition

The Developer Edition of SQL Server 2008 is a full-featured version intended for development and end-user testing only. It includes all the features and functionality of Enterprise Edition, at a much lower cost, but the licensing agreement prohibits production deployment of databases using Developer Edition.

To provide greater flexibility during development, Developer Edition can be installed in any of the following environments.

- Any Windows 2003 Server editions
- Any Windows 2008 Server editions
- Windows 7
- Windows Vista
- Windows XP

Web Edition

SQL Server 2008 Web Edition is a lower total-cost-of-ownership option, similar to the Workgroup Edition, but intended for small- to large-scale web hosts and websites.

Web Edition includes most of the core database features and capabilities of the SQL Server Standard Edition with the following key differences:

- It is limited to a maximum of 4 CPUs.
- Unlike the Workgroup Edition, memory in this edition is constrained only by the OS maximum memory limits.
- It does not support failover clustering.
- Database mirroring support is limited to being a witness only.
- It does not include Analysis Services.
- It includes only the basic version of SQL Server Management Studio (which lacks advanced features such as IntelliSense and version control support).
- It provides limited support for Integration Services and Reporting Services features.

Web Edition can be installed in any of the following environments.

- Any Windows 2003 Server editions
- Any Windows 2008 Server editions
- Windows 7
- Windows Vista
- Windows XP

Express Edition

SQL Server Express Edition is a free, lightweight, embeddable, and redistributable version of SQL Server 2008. It includes a stripped-down version of SQL Server Management Studio, called SQL Server Management Studio Express, for easily managing a SQL Server Express instance and its databases. The Express Edition of SQL Server 2008 is intended for users who are running applications that require a locally installed database, often on mobile systems, and who spend at least some time disconnected from the network. The core database engine of Express Edition is the same as the other SQL Server editions, so as your needs grow, your applications seamlessly work with the rest of the SQL Server product family.

The Express Edition can be installed in any of the following environments:

- Any Windows 2003 Server editions
- Any Windows 2008 Server editions
- Windows 7
- Windows Vista
- Windows XP

Express Edition supports most of the same features as the Workgroup Edition, with the following exceptions:

- It is limited to using a maximum of one CPU and 1GB of memory.
- It limits the maximum database size to 4GB.
- It does not include Full-Text Search, Reporting Services, or Analysis Services.
- It does not include SQL Server Integration Services.
- It supports Service Broker as a client only.
- It does not include SSMS.
- It can participate in replication only as a subscriber.

If you need a bit more than the Express Edition offers, but not as much as the Workgroup Edition, Microsoft also provides the Express Edition with Advanced Services. The Express Edition with Advanced Services includes support for Full-Text Search and limited support of Reporting Services for web reporting.

SQL Server Compact 3.5 Edition

SQL Server Compact 3.5 is a free, embedded version of SQL Server intended for building standalone and occasionally connected applications for mobile devices, desktops, and web clients on Windows platforms. The Compact 3.5 Edition provides general T-SQL compatibility and a cost-based Query Optimizer similar to that in SQL Server 2008. Developers who are familiar with SQL Server 2008 should feel comfortable developing for SQL Server Compact 3.5.

SQL Server Compact 3.5 Edition has a small footprint, requiring only about 2–3MB. It can connect directly with a SQL Server 2008 database through remote execution of T-SQL statements, and it also supports replication with SQL Server 2008 databases as a merge replication subscriber so that data can be accessed and manipulated offline and synchronized later with a server-based version of SQL Server 2008.

SQL Server 2008 R2 Premium Editions

SQL Server 2008 R2 introduces two new premium editions to meet the needs of large-scale datacenters and data warehouses:

- SQL Server 2008 R2 Datacenter
- SQL Server 2008 R2 Parallel Data Warehouse

SQL Server 2008 R2 Datacenter Edition is built on SQL Server 2008 R2 Enterprise and is designed to deliver a high-performing data platform that provides the highest levels of scalability for large application workloads, virtualization and consolidation, and management for an organization's database infrastructure. The Datacenter Edition provides the following key features:

- Application and Multi-Server Management for enrolling, gaining insights into, and managing over 25 instances
- Highest virtualization support for maximum ROI on consolidation and virtualization
- High-scale complex event processing with SQL Server StreamInsight

- Support for more than 8 processors and up to 256 logical processors for highest levels of scale
- Support for memory limits up to the OS maximum

SQL Server 2008 R2 Parallel Data Warehouse Edition is a highly scalable data warehouse appliance-based solution that delivers performance at low cost through a massively parallel processing (MPP) architecture and compatibility with hardware partners providing the ability to scale your data warehouse to tens and hundreds of terabytes. Following are some key features of the Parallel Data Warehouse Edition:

- Tens to hundreds of terabytes enabled by MPP architecture
- Advanced data warehousing capabilities such as Star Join Queries and Change Data Capture
- Integration with SSIS, SSRS, and SSAS
- Support for the industry standard data warehousing hub and spoke architecture and parallel database copy

SQL Server Licensing Models

In addition to feature sets, one of the determining factors in choosing a SQL Server edition is cost. With SQL Server 2008, Microsoft provides two types of licensing models: processor-based licensing and server-based licensing.

Processor-based licensing requires a single license for each physical CPU in the machine that is running a Microsoft Server product. This type of license includes unlimited client device access. Additional server licenses, seat licenses, and Internet connector licenses are not required. You must purchase a processor license for each installed processor on the server on which SQL Server 2008 will be installed, even if some processors will not be used for running SQL Server. The only exception is for systems with 16 or more processors that allow partitioning of the processors into groups so the SQL Server software can be delegated to a subset of the processors.

NOTE

For licensing purposes, Microsoft bases the number of CPUs in a machine on the number of CPU sockets on the motherboard, not the number of cores on the CPU chip itself. Thus, although a dual-core or quad-core processor chip may appear to the operating system as two or four CPUs, at the time of this writing, each of these types of chips is still considered a single CPU for licensing purposes if it occupies only a single CPU socket on the motherboard.

For those who prefer the more familiar server/client access license (CAL), or for environments in which the number of client devices connecting to SQL Server is small and known, two server/CAL-based licensing models are also available:

- **Device CALs**—A device CAL is required for a device (for example, PC, workstation, terminal, PDA, mobile phone) to access or use the services or functionality of Microsoft SQL Server. The server plus device CAL model is likely to be the more cost-effective choice if there are multiple users per device (for example, in a call center).
- **User CALs**—A SQL server user CAL is required for a user (for example, an employee, a customer, a partner) to access or use the services or functionality of Microsoft SQL Server. The server plus user CAL model is likely to be more cost effective if there are multiple devices per user (for example, a user who has a desktop PC, laptop, PDA, and so forth).

The server/CAL licensing model requires purchasing a license for the computer running SQL Server 2008 as well as a license for each client device or user that accesses any SQL Server 2008 installation. A fixed number of CALs are included with a server license and the server software. Additional CALs can be purchased as needed.

Server/per-seat CAL licensing is intended for environments in which the number of clients per server is relatively low, and access from outside the company firewall is not required. Be aware that using a middle-tier or transaction server that pools or multiplexes database connections does not reduce the number of CALs required. A CAL is still required for each distinct client workstation that connects through the middle tier. (Processor licensing might be preferable in these environments due to its simplicity and affordability when the number of clients is unknown and potentially large.)

The pricing listed in Table 1.2 is provided for illustrative purposes only and is based on pricing available at the time of publication. These estimated retail prices are subject to change and might vary from reseller pricing.

TABLE 1.2 SQL Server 2008 R2 Estimated Retail Pricing

Licensing Option	Enterprise Edition	Standard Edition	Workgroup Edition	Parallel Data Warehouse and Datacenter Editions
Processor Licensing	$28,749 per processor	$7,499 per processor	$3,899 per processor	$57,498 per processor
Server/per-seat CAL license with 5 workgroup CALs	N/A	N/A	$739	N/A
Server/per-seat CAL license with 5 CALs	N/A	$1,849	N/A	N/A
Server/per-seat CAL license with 25 CALs	$13,969	N/A	N/A	N/A

Web Edition Licensing

The Express Edition of SQL Server 2008 is available via free download from www.microsoft.com/sql. Developers can redistribute it with their applications at no cost by simply registering for redistribution rights with Microsoft. The Express Edition does not require a CAL when it is used on a standalone basis. If it connects to a SQL Server instance running Enterprise Edition, Standard Edition, or Workgroup Edition, a separate user or device CAL is required for the device running Express Edition unless the SQL Server instance it connects to is licensed using the per-processor model.

Developer Edition Licensing

The Developer Edition of SQL Server 2008 is available for a fixed price of $50. The Developer Edition is licensed per developer and must be used for designing, developing, and testing purposes only.

Express Edition Licensing

The Express Edition of SQL Server 2008 is available via free download from www.microsoft.com/sql. Developers can redistribute it with their applications at no cost by simply registering for redistribution rights with Microsoft. The Express Edition does not require a CAL when it is used on a standalone basis. If it connects to a SQL Server instance running Enterprise Edition, Standard Edition, or Workgroup Edition, a separate user or device CAL is required for the device running Express Edition unless the SQL Server instance it connects to is licensed using the per-processor model.

Compact Edition 3.5 Licensing

SQL Server 2008 Mobile Edition is available as a downloadable development product for mobile applications. You can deploy SQL Server Mobile to an unlimited number of mobile devices if they operate in standalone mode (that is, the device does not connect to or use the resources of any SQL Server system not present on the device). If the device connects to a SQL Server instance that is not on the device, a separate user or device CAL is required unless the SQL Server instance it connects to is licensed using the per-processor model.

Choosing a Licensing Model

Which licensing model should you choose? Per-processor licensing is generally required in instances in which the server will be accessed via the Web. This type of licensing includes servers used in Internet situations or servers that will be accessed from both inside and outside an organization's firewall. Per-processor licensing might also be appropriate and cost effective for internal environments in which there are a very large number of users in relation to the number of SQL Server machines. An additional advantage to the per-processor model is that it eliminates the need to count the number of devices connecting to SQL Server, which can be difficult to manage on an ongoing basis for a large organization.

Using the server/per-seat CAL model is usually the most cost-effective choice in internal environments in which client-to-server ratios are low.

Mixing Licensing Models

You can mix both per-processor and server/CAL licensing models in your organization. If the Internet servers for your organization are segregated from the servers used to support internal applications, you can choose to use processor licensing for the Internet servers and server/CAL licensing for internal SQL Server instances and user devices.

Keep in mind that you do not need to purchase CALs to allow internal users to access a server already licensed via a processor license: The processor licenses allow access to that server for all users.

Passive Server/Failover Licensing

In SQL Server 2008, two or more servers can be configured in a failover mode, with one server running as a passive server so that the passive server picks up the processing of the active server only in the event of a server failure. SQL Server 2008 offers three types of failover support:

- Database mirroring
- Failover clustering
- Log shipping

If your environment uses an active/passive configuration in which at least one server in the failover configuration does not regularly process information but simply waits to pick up the workload when an active server fails, no additional licenses are required for the passive server. The exception is if the failover cluster is licensed using the per-processor licensing model and the number of processors on the passive server exceeds the number of processors on the active server. In this case, additional processor licenses must be acquired for the number of additional processors on the passive computer.

In an active/active failover configuration, all servers in the failover configuration regularly process information independently unless a server fails, at which point one server or more takes on the additional workload of the failed server. In this environment, all servers must be fully licensed using either per-processor licensing or server/CAL licensing. Keep in mind that in some log shipping and database mirroring configurations, the standby (passive) server can be used as a read-only reporting server installation. Under this usage, the standby server is no longer "passive" and must be licensed accordingly.

Virtual Server Licensing

Virtualization is defined broadly as the running of software on a "virtual environment." A virtual environment exists when an operating system is somehow emulated (that is, does not run directly on the physical hardware). When you're running virtualization software on a system, one or several applications and their associated operating systems can run on one physical server inside their respective virtual environments.

Running SQL Server 2008 inside a virtual operating environment requires at least one license per virtual operating environment. Within each virtual operating environment, the license allows you to run one or more instances of SQL Server 2008. The license for a virtual operating environment can be a server/CAL license or a processor-based license. If using a processor-based license, you must purchase a processor license for each processor that the virtual machine accesses. The total number of physical and virtual processors used by the virtual operating system environments cannot exceed the number of software licenses assigned to that server. However, if you are running Enterprise Edition and all physical processors in the machine have been licensed, you may run an unlimited number of virtual operating environments on that same machine.

Multiple Instances of SQL Server

An option to virtualization is multi-instancing. With multi-instancing, multiple copies of SQL Server can be run concurrently in a single instance of an OS. Multi-instancing for SQL Server 2008 can take place both in a virtual environment or in a physical environment. Although multi-instancing offers a relatively high degree of isolation between copies of SQL Server 2008, this isolation takes place at the application level (instead of at the OS level).

In SQL Server 2008, the Workgroup and Standard Editions now allow you to run any number of instances of the server software in one physical or virtual operating system environment on the licensed server. Previously, only the Enterprise Edition of the server license allowed multi-instancing.

Summary

This chapter examined the various platforms that support SQL Server 2008 R2 and reviewed and compared the various editions of SQL Server 2008 that are available. Which platform and edition are appropriate to your needs depends on scalability, availability, performance, licensing costs, and limitations. The information provided in this chapter should help you make the appropriate choice.

Chapter 2, "What's New in SQL Server 2008," takes at closer look at the new features and capabilities provided with the various SQL Server 2008 editions.

CHAPTER 2

What's New in SQL Server 2008

IN THIS CHAPTER

- New SQL Server 2008 Features
- SQL Server 2008 Enhancements

SQL Server 2005 provided a number of significant new features and enhancements over what was available in SQL Server 2000. This is not too surprising considering there was a five-year gap between these major releases. Microsoft SQL Server 2008 is not as much of a quantum leap forward from SQL Server 2005, but it provides a number of new features and enhancements to further extend the performance, reliability, availability, programmability, and ease of use of SQL Server. This chapter explores the new features provided in SQL Server 2008 and SQL Server 2008 R2, as well as many of the enhancements to previously available features.

New SQL Server 2008 Features

So what does SQL Server 2008 have to offer over SQL Server 2005? Following is an overview of the new features provided in SQL Server 2008:

- **New storage features**—FILESTREAM storage, sparse columns and column sets, row-level and page-level data compression
- **New data types**—`Date`, `Time`, and `DATETIME2` data types; `Hierarchyid` data type; spatial data types; user-defined table type
- **New Transact-SQL (T-SQL) constructs**—Compound operators, `GROUPING SETS`, `MERGE` statement, row constructors, table-valued parameters, `INSERT` over DML, new date and time functions
- **New performance features**—Filtered indexes and statistics, `FORCESEEK` query hint, hash values for

finding similar queries in the plan cache, Plan Guide Successful and Plan Guide Unsuccessful event classes, Guided/Misguided Plan Executions/sec Performance Monitor counters, `LOCK ESCALATION` option for `ALTER TABLE`, hot-add CPUs

- **New security features**—Transparent data encryption, Extensible Key Management, SQL Server Audit
- **New database administration features**—Backup compression, Change Data Capture, Change Tracking, the Data Collector, Policy-Based Management, SQL Server Extended Events, Resource Governor
- **New SQL Server management features**—Transact-SQL Debugger, IntelliSense, error list window, multiserver queries, PowerShell integration

SQL Server 2008 R2 further enhances SQL Server 2008 with the following new features:

- Two new premium editions to meet the needs of large-scale datacenters and data warehouses:
    - SQL Server 2008 R2 Datacenter
    - SQL Server 2008 R2 Parallel Data Warehouse
- SQL Server Utility for Multi-Server Management
- PowerPivot for Excel and SharePoint
- A number of new Reporting Services features including Report Builder 3.0, report parts, shared datasets, Sparklines and data bars, indicators, calculating aggregates of aggregates, maps, lookup functions

The following sections take a closer look at each of these new features and, where appropriate, provide references to subsequent chapters where you can find more information and detail about the new features.

New Storage Features

SQL Server 2008 provides a set of new features to reduce storage requirements and improve performance.

One of the new features is FILESTREAM storage. *FILESTREAM storage* is a property that can be applied to `varchar(max)` columns; it enables SQL Server applications to store unstructured data, such as documents and images, directly in the NTFS file system while still maintaining the behavior of a database column. The advantages of FILESTREAM storage are improved performance and increased size of BLOB data, expanding from the 2GB limit of image columns to the available space in the file system. For more information on using FILESTREAM storage, see Chapter 42, "What's New for Transact-SQL in SQL Server 2008."

Other storage features introduced in SQL Server 2008 are sparse columns and column sets. *Sparse columns* are ordinary columns that have an optimized storage format for null values. If you use sparse columns, you can also define a column set on the table that will return all sparse columns in the table. A *column set* is an untyped XML representation that combines all the sparse columns of a table into a structured output. For more information on defining sparse columns and column sets, see Chapter 24, "Creating and Managing Tables."

Row-level and page-level data compression also are introduced in SQL Server 2008. *Data compression* helps to reduce both storage and memory requirements as the data is compressed both on disk and when brought into the SQL Server data cache. Row-level compression isn't true data compression but implements a more efficient storage format for fixed-length data. Page-level compression is true data compression, using both column prefix and dictionary-based compression. For more information on implementing data compression, see Chapter 24.

New Data Types

SQL Server 2008 introduces a handful of new data types. Two of the most welcome of these are the new `DATE` and `TIME` data types. These new data types allow you to store date-only and time-only values. In addition, SQL Server now supports the `DATETIME2` and `DATETIMEOFFSET` data types. `DATETIME2` is a variation of the `DATETIME` data type that supports datetime values from 0001-01-01 to 9999-12-31 23:59:59.999999. `DATETIMEOFFSET` supports UTC-based datetime values that are time zone aware.

The new `Hierarchyid` data type is a common language runtime (CLR) user-defined type (UDT) that provides a mechanism for representing and storing a tree structure in a table in an efficient manner. This data type is useful for storing data that represents a parent child, tree-like structure such as an organizational structure or a graph of links between web pages.

Spatial data types are introduced in SQL Server 2008 as well. There are two new spatial data types: `geometry` and `geography`. The `geometry` data type supports planar, or Euclidean (flat-earth), data. The `geography` data type stores ellipsoidal (round-earth) data, such as GPS latitude and longitude coordinates. These new data types support the storage and manipulation of spatial data objects such as linestrings, points, and polygons.

SQL Server 2008 also introduces a new user-defined table type that can be used as parameters in stored procedures and functions, as well as for defining table variables in a batch or the body of a stored procedure or function.

For more information and examples on using the new SQL Server 2008 data types, see Chapter 42.

New Transact-SQL Constructs

What would a new SQL Server release be without new T-SQL commands and constructs to further expand the power and capabilities of the T-SQL language? SQL Server 2008 is no exception (although SQL Server 2008 R2 is an exception because no new T-SQL constructs are introduced in R2). The new constructs provided in SQL Server 2008 include

- **Compound operators**—New operators that provide a shorthand method of performing an operation and assigning a value to a local variable (for example, `+=`, `*=`).

- **GROUPING SETS**—New operator added to the GROUP BY clause to perform multiple grouping operations in a single query.
- **MERGE** statement—New DML statement that can perform INSERT, UPDATE, or DELETE operations on a target table based on the results of a join with a source table.
- **Row constructors**—An enhancement to the VALUES clause that allows multiple row inserts within a single INSERT statement. Also provides the ability to use the VALUES clause to create a pseudo table of values in a subquery or common table expression.
- **Table-valued parameters**—New parameter type that can be assigned the new user-defined table types. Table-valued parameters enable you to pass a table variable containing multiple rows of data to a stored procedure or function without the need to create a temporary table.

To coincide with the new DATE and TIME data types, SQL Server 2008 also introduces a few new date and time functions:

- **SYSDATETIME()**—Returns the current system datetime as a DATETIME2(7) value
- **SYSDATETIMEOFFSET()**—Returns the current system datetime as a DATETIMEOFFSET(7) value
- **SYSUTCDATETIME**—Returns the current system datetime as a DATETIME2(7) value representing the current UTC time
- **SWITCHOFFSET (DATETIMEOFFSET, *time_zone*)**—Changes the DATETIMEOFFSET value from the stored time zone offset to the specified time zone
- **TODATETIMEOFFSET (*datetime, time_zone*)**—Converts a local datetime value for the specified time zone to a DATETIMEOFFSET UTC value

For more information and examples on using the new SQL Server 2008 T-SQL constructs, see Chapter 42.

New Performance Features

SQL Server 2008 also introduces some new features and enhancements for monitoring, managing, and improving query performance. Among these new features are filtered indexes and statistics. A *filtered index* is a nonclustered index defined on a subset of data using a filter predicate to index only a portion of rows in the table. *Filtered statistics* are statistics defined on a subset of data in the table using a filter predicate. A well-designed filtered index can improve query performance, reduce index maintenance costs, and reduce index storage costs compared with full-table indexes, especially when columns contain a large number of rows with null or a single value that isn't searched on but can skew the index and statistics. For more information on creating and using filtered indexes and statistics, see Chapter 34, "Data Structures, Indexes, and Performance."

SQL Server 2008 provides FORCESEEK as a new table and query hint for controlling how SQL Server optimizes a query; it forces the optimizer to use only an index seek operation to access the data in the referenced table or view. For more information on using the FORCESEEK hint, see Chapter 35, "Understanding Query Optimization."

Plan guides were a feature introduced in SQL Server 2005. *Plan guides* can be used to optimize the performance of queries when you cannot or do not want to change the text of the query directly (for example, when queries in a third-party database application are not performing as expected). SQL Server 2008 provides additional features related to plan guides to make implementing and managing them easier. Among these features are new event classes (Plan Guide Successful and Plan Guide Unsuccessful) that can be monitored via SQL Server Profiler to determine when plan guides are being applied. There are also two new Performance Monitor counters (Guided/Misguided Plan Executions/sec) that you can use to monitor via Performance Monitor how often plan guides are being used or not being used.

SQL Server 2008 also now generates hash values for query plans in the plan cache. The `sys.dm_exec_query_stats` and `sys.dm_exec_requests` dynamic management views (DMVs) now provide query hash and query plan hash values that you can use to help find similar queries in the plan cache. Locating similar queries can help you determine the aggregate resource usage for similar queries and similar query execution plans so that you can better focus your query tuning efforts and help identify which queries may get the most benefit from using plan guides. For more information on query plans and using plan guides, see Chapter 35.

To provide greater control of locking, SQL Server 2008 offers the new `LOCK ESCALATION` table option. This option specifies the allowed methods of lock escalation for a table. The default is `AUTO`, which allows the Database Engine to select the appropriate lock escalation level for the query if a table is partitioned. You can also specify `TABLE` to force full table-level locking whether or not a table is partitioned. A third option, `DISABLE`, prevents escalation to a table-level lock in most cases. For more details on locking and the `LOCK ESCALATION` option, see Chapter 37, "Locking and Performance."

One additional new feature in SQL Server 2008 Enterprise Edition is hot-add CPU. *Hot-add CPU* is the capability to dynamically add CPUs to a running system. Additional CPUs can be made available logically by online hardware partitioning, virtually through a virtualization layer, or even physically by adding new hardware on systems that support adding physical CPUs while the system is online. Hot-add CPU, which requires hardware support, is available only when you're running Windows Server 2008 Datacenter or Enterprise Edition.

New Security Features

SQL Server 2005 provided the capability to encrypt data at the column level. However, this encryption was not transparent to the end users or applications. Encrypting and decrypting the data required coding changes to use the built-in encryption and decryption functions. SQL Server 2008 introduces transparent data encryption (TDE), which allows for encrypting the entire database without affecting client applications. The purpose of TDE is to protect sensitive data in the event a database file or backup is stolen. Encryption is done in real-time at the page level as the data is written to disk and decrypted as the data is read from disk. The encryption is based on a database encryption key (DEK), which is a symmetric key secured by using a certificate stored in the `master` database of the server or an asymmetric key protected by an Extensible Key Management (EKM) module.

Extensible Key Management, which is also new with SQL Server 2008, enables you to store the keys used to encrypt data separately from the data it protects. SQL Server 2008 EKM enables the encryption keys that protect the database files to be stored in a removable device such as a smartcard, USB device, or a software-based Extensible Key Management (EKM)/Hardware Security Module (HSM) module. EKM facilitates separation of duties by taking key management out of the hands of the database administrators.

For more information on implementing and using transparent data encryption and extensible key management, see Chapter 12, "Data Encryption."

SQL Server already provides a number of existing audit methods (SQL Trace, C2 audit mode, DDL triggers). In addition to these, SQL Server 2008 adds an additional audit method: SQL Server Audit. SQL Server Audit, based on the new Extended Events feature, allows you to monitor server- or database-level events or groups of events. You can set up and monitor audit events at the server or database level and audit the audit actions themselves. For more information on SQL Server Audit, see Chapter 13, "Security and Compliance."

New Database Administration Features

SQL Server 2008 introduced backup compression for Enterprise Edition. With SQL Server 2008 R2, backup compression is supported in Standard and all higher editions (every edition of SQL Server 2008 and later can restore a compressed backup, however). In addition to the space savings provided by compressed backups, compressing a backup also typically increases backup speed because it requires less device I/O. However, the I/O cost savings comes at the expense of increased CPU usage caused by the compression process. For more information on compressing backups, see Chapter 14, "Database Backup and Restore."

Policy-Based Management is a new mechanism in SQL Server 2008 for managing one or more instances of SQL Server 2008. SQL Server Policy-Based Management can help to simplify management operations such as setting database options across multiple servers, checking SQL Server configurations, or enforcing naming conventions, helping to reduce the total cost of ownership (TCO) of administering multiple SQL Server instances. SQL Server Management Studio (SSMS) can be used to define and implement policies for managing SQL Server instances, databases, or other SQL Server objects as well as on-demand checking and enforcement of policies. Checking and enforcement of these policies can also be scheduled using SQL Server Agent. For more information on Policy-Based Management in SQL Server, see Chapter 22, "Administering Policy Based Management."

Currently, several options are available for troubleshooting or getting information about SQL Server–generated events: SQL Server Profiler, SQL Server Log, dynamic management views and functions, SQL Trace, trace flags, Windows Application and System logs, performance counters, and so on. SQL Server 2008 introduces a new event infrastructure, Extended Events. *Extended Events* is a general-purpose event-handling system for server systems. Currently, the Extended Events infrastructure supports the correlation of data from SQL Server and, under certain conditions, the correlation of data from the operating system and database applications. Extended Events has the potential to make other troubleshooting options obsolete in future releases and become the common denominator for troubleshooting purposes. As mentioned previously, the new SQL Server Audit feature is based on Extended Events. For more information on configuring and using Extended Events for monitoring SQL Server 2008, see Chapter 39, "Monitoring SQL Server Performance."

Resource Governor, another new technology in SQL Server 2008, enables you to manage and control the allocation of resources for SQL Server according to workload. Similarly sized queries or requests that can, and should be, treated the same are assigned to a workload group as the requests are received. Each workload group is associated to a pool of resources that represents the physical resources for SQL Server (currently, for SQL Server 2008, these resources are CPU and memory). Limits are specified on resource consumption for these incoming requests. In an environment where multiple distinct workloads are present on the same server, Resource Governor enables you to differentiate these workloads and allocate shared resources as they are requested, based on the limits you specify. For more information on implementing and configuring Resource Governor, see Chapter 40, "Managing Workloads with the Resource Governor."

Change Data Capture (CDC) and Change Tracking are new features in SQL Server 2008 with similar names but different purposes. *CDC* is an asynchronous mechanism that captures all changes of a data row from the transaction log and stores them in change tables. The information captured is available in relational format and can be accessed by client applications such as extract, transform, and load (ETL) processes. All intermediate values of a row are stored. Using Change Data Capture, you can avoid using expensive techniques such as triggers, time stamp columns, and join queries to identify and capture the changes made to data.

Change Tracking, on the other hand, is a lightweight synchronous mechanism that tracks data modifications but records only the fact that a row has changed. Applications can use Change Tracking to identify which rows have changed for a user table and refresh their data stores with the latest values from these rows by requerying the table.

For more information on using CDC and Change Tracking, see Chapter 42.

New SQL Server Management Studio Features

SQL Server Management Studio (SSMS) was first introduced in SQL Server 2005. SSMS is a full-featured, robust SQL Server administration and development tool. However, there was clearly room for improvement, and SQL Server 2008 provides some long-awaited enhancements.

One of the most anticipated (and missed) features in SSMS was a built-in T-SQL debugger. Prior to SQL Server 2005, SQL Server Enterprise Manager had a built-in T-SQL Debugger. A lot of users were disappointed a T-SQL debugger was not included with this version of SSMS. To debug T-SQL, you needed to install Visual Studio (VS). Fortunately, a built-in debugger returns to SSMS in SQL Server 2008.

Another long-awaited feature for SSMS is IntelliSense. IntelliSense is a useful feature in the Query Editor for looking up language elements and object names without having to leave the editor. IntelliSense can even automatically complete and insert language elements directly into your code.

In conjunction with IntelliSense, SSMS also provides the error list window The *error list window* displays all errors and warnings produced by IntelliSense as you develop your code in the Database Engine Query Editor. You can double-click the error message entry to jump to the error location. As you fix errors, they are automatically removed from the error list window.

One other new capability built in to SSMS in SQL Server 2008 is *multiserver queries*. This feature allows you to execute T-SQL statements against multiple servers defined in a server group at the same time. If you open a Query Editor from the server group in the Registered Servers window, the T-SQL statements in the current Query Editor are executed against all the servers in the group. The results from the query can be merged into a single results pane or can be returned in separate results panes for each server.

For more details on these new features in SSMS, see Chapter 4, "SQL Server Management Studio."

PowerShell Integration

SQL Server 2008 provides integrated support for Windows PowerShell, a powerful scripting shell that enables administrators and developers to automate server administration and application deployment. The Windows PowerShell language supports more complex logic than Transact-SQL scripts, enabling SQL Server administrators to build more robust and complex administration scripts.

SQL Server provides two snap-ins to Windows PowerShell for creating scripts to manage SQL Server:

- A SQL Server provider, which enables a simple navigation mechanism similar to file system paths where the drive is associated with a SQL Server management object model and the nodes are based on the object model classes. This allows you to use familiar commands such as `cd` and `dir` to navigate the paths similar to the way you navigate folders in a command prompt window.
- A set of cmdlets, which are commands used in Windows PowerShell scripts to specify a SQL Server action, such as running a SQLCMD script containing Transact-SQL or XQuery statements

For more information on managing SQL Server using PowerShell, see Chapter 17, "Administering SQL Server 2008 with PowerShell."

New Premium SQL Server Editions

SQL Server 2008 R2 introduces two new premium-level editions of SQL Server: Datacenter Edition and Parallel Data Warehouse.

Built on SQL Server 2008 R2 Enterprise, SQL Server 2008 R2 Datacenter is designed to deliver a high-performing data platform that provides the highest levels of scalability for large application workloads, virtualization and consolidation, and management for an organization's database infrastructure. Datacenter helps enable organizations to cost-effectively scale their mission-critical environment. Key features of Datacenter include

- Application and multiserver management for enrolling, gaining insights, and managing more than 25 instances
- Highest virtualization support for maximum return on investment (ROI) on consolidation and virtualization
- High-scale complex event processing with SQL Server StreamInsight
- Support for more than 8 processors and up to 256 logical processors

SQL Server 2008 R2 Parallel Data Warehouse is a highly scalable data warehouse appliance-based solution. Parallel Data Warehouse delivers performance at low cost through a massively parallel processing (MPP) architecture and compatibility with hardware partners, allowing you to scale your data warehouse to tens and even hundreds of terabytes. Key features provided by Parallel Data Warehouse include

- Advanced data warehousing capabilities such as Star Join Queries and Change Data Capture
- Integration with SSIS, SSRS, and SSAS
- Support for industry-standard data warehousing hub-and-spoke architecture and parallel database copy

SQL Server Utility for Multiserver Management

SQL Server 2008 R2 features new SSMS dashboards for observing information on more than one server from the same screen by utilizing the new SQL Server Utility. The SQL Server Utility models an organization's SQL Server–related entities in a unified view. Utility Explorer and SQL Server Utility viewpoints in SQL Server Management Studio provide administrators a holistic view of SQL Server resource health. Entities that can be viewed in the SQL Server Utility include

- Instances of SQL Server
- Data-tier applications
- Database files
- Volumes

SQL Server Utility is covered in more detail in Chapters 4 and 39.

PowerPivot for Excel and SharePoint

PowerPivot is a new tool that integrates SQL Server with Microsoft Excel and SharePoint to create a self-service business intelligence (BI) solution for the enterprise. PowerPivot for Excel and SharePoint are client and server components that integrate Analysis Services with Excel and SharePoint. PowerPivot for Excel is an add-in that allows you to create PowerPivot workbooks that can assemble and relate large amounts of data from different sources. PowerPivot for SharePoint extends SharePoint 2010 and Excel Services to add server-side processing, collaboration, and document management support for the PowerPivot workbooks that you publish to SharePoint. Together, the PowerPivot client add-in and server components provide an end-to-end solution that furthers business intelligence data analysis for Excel users on the workstation and on SharePoint sites.

For more information on PowerPivot, see Chapter 51, "Analysis Services."

New Reporting Services Features

SQL Server 2008 R2 introduces a number of new features for Reporting Services. The Reporting Services enhancements are probably the most significant aspect of the R2 release. One of the key changes in SQL Server 2008 R2 is an updated version of the Report Manager. The SQL Server 2008 R2 Report Manager provides an improved user experience via interface changes, including an updated color scheme and layout, in an effort to provide easier navigation for managing report properties and Report Server items. Following are some of the key enhancements to Report Manager in R2:

- An improved workflow for viewing and managing reports and Report Server items through the use of a new drop-down menu to access various configuration options for each report or Report Server item in a folder
- Elimination of the need to render a report before accessing and configuring report properties when in default view
- Increased screen space for the Report Viewer when rendering reports
- An updated Report Viewer toolbar, which includes some updates to the toolbar controls, as well as the capability to export report data to an Atom service document and data feeds

The set of new and enhanced features in SQL Server 2008 R2 for Reporting Services includes

- **Report parts**—You can store these reusable report items on a Report Server or on a SharePoint site that is integrated with a Report Server.
- **Sparklines and data bars**—These simple charts convey a lot of information in a little space, often inline with text.
- **Indicators**—These minimal gauges convey the state of a single data value at a glance. Indicators can be used by themselves in dashboards or free-form reports.
- **Calculation of aggregates of aggregates**—You can now create expressions that calculate an aggregate of an aggregate.
- **Improved report pagination**—Reporting Services provides more control over report pagination including dynamic updating of page names and numbers when a report is run, as well as disabling page breaks entirely.
- **Map reports**—Report Designer now provides a Map Wizard and Map Layer Wizard so that you can add maps and map layers to your report to help visualize data against a geographic background.

- **Shared datasets**—This Report Server feature can retrieve data from shared data sources that connect to external data sources, providing a way to share a query to help provide a consistent set of data for multiple reports.
- **Cache refresh plans**—These plans allow you to cache reports or shared dataset query results on first use or from a schedule.
- **Improved previewing of reports**—Report Builder 3.0 provides a better preview experience with the introduction of edit sessions that enable the reuse of cached datasets when you are previewing reports, which allows reports to render more quickly.

For more information on designing and deploying reports using Reporting Services and more information on the extensive set of new Reporting Services features in R2, see Chapter 53, "SQL Server 2008 Reporting Services."

SQL Server 2008 Enhancements

In addition to the brand new features in SQL Server 2008, there are a number of enhancements to existing features provided by SQL Server 2008 and SQL Server 2008 R2. The following sections provide an overview of the major enhancements.

SQL Server Management Studio

In addition to the new SSMS features discussed previously, SSMS has also received a number of enhancements in SQL Server 2008; you are now able to do the following:

- Customize the columns displayed by the Object Explorer Details window.
- Display the properties of a selected item from Object Explorer Details at the bottom of the window.
- View a color-coded status bar at the bottom of the window for Transact-SQL and MDX code editors which provide information about the editor connection. The status bar changes color when a code editor opens multiple connections.
- Customize the tab name for items in the title bar of the code editor windows.
- Configure the number of rows returned when you open tables via the Object Browser.
- Create and manage plan guides via the `Programmability` folder in Object Browser.

Dynamic Management Views

SQL Server 2008 adds five new dynamic management views to return memory-related information about SQL Server:

- **`sys.dm_os_memory_brokers`**—Returns information about memory brokers, the components that track memory allocations
- **`sys.dm_os_memory_nodes`**—Returns memory allocation information for memory allocated through SQL Server Memory Manager

- **sys.dm_os_nodes**—Returns information about SQL OS memory nodes, internal structures of SQL OS that abstract hardware processor locality
- **sys.dm_os_process_memory**—Returns complete information about memory allocated to SQL Server process space
- **sys.dm_os_sys_memory**—Describes the memory state for the operation system

In addition, the `cpu_ticks_in_ms` column in the `sys.dm_os_sys_info` dynamic management view has been discontinued, and two new columns, `sqlserver_start_time_ms_ticks` and `sqlserver_start_time`, have been added.

Database Mirroring

SQL Server 2008 provides a number of enhancements to database mirroring, mostly related to performance of database mirroring, including compression of the transaction log records being streamed to the mirror database, asynchronous write-ahead on the incoming log stream and read-ahead during the undo phase, and improved use of the log send buffers. For more information on database mirroring and the improvements, see Chapter 20, "Database Mirroring."

SQLCLR Enhancements

SQL Server 2008 extends the SQLCLR by extending the 8KB size limit for CLR user-defined types and CLR user-defined aggregates, supporting the definition of ordered table-valued functions, providing support for multiple input parameters for user-defined aggregates, and including the option to define static methods as user-defined functions.

For more information on the enhancements to SQL CLR, see Chapter 46, "Creating .NET CLR Objects in SQL Server 2008."

Replication Enhancements

SQL Server 2008 introduces a number of usability and manageability enhancements for peer-to-peer replication and the Replication Monitor.

Peer-to-peer replication includes the following significant usability and manageability improvements:

- A new option, enabled by default, that allows the Distribution Agent to detect conflicts during synchronization and to stop applying changes at the affected row.
- The capability to add nodes to a replication topology without quiescing the topology.
- The capability to configure a topology visually in the Configure Peer-to-Peer Topology Wizard. The Topology Viewer enables you to perform common configuration tasks, such as adding new nodes, deleting nodes, and adding new connections between existing nodes.

The Replication Monitor includes the following usability improvements:

- Most of the Replication Monitor grids allow you to specify which columns to view, sort by multiple columns, and filter rows in the grid based on column values.

- The Common Jobs tab for the Publisher node has been renamed to Agents.
- The single Warnings and Agents tab for the publication node has been split into separate Warnings and Agents tabs to emphasize the difference between administering performance warnings and monitoring replication agents.

For more information on configuring and using replication in SQL Server 2008, see Chapter 19, "Replication."

SQL Server Integration Services Enhancements

Integration Services in SQL Server 2008 received enhancements and improvements as well. Following are some of these enhancements:

- Improvements in the parallel execution of data flow pipeline paths on multiprocessor systems, going beyond the SQL Server 2005 limit of two engines.
- A new script environment. Visual Studio for Applications (VSA) has been replaced with Visual Studio Tools for Applications (VSTA). VSTA allows the development of scripts written on Visual C# and Visual Basic, providing support for the Script Task and Script Component. VSTA also supports debugging and adding managed assemblies to a script at design time.
- Increased performance and improved caching options for Lookup Transformations.
- Data profiling to improve data quality by identifying potential data quality problems.
- Support for the new Change Data Capture feature in SQL Server 2008, providing an effective method for performing incremental data loads from source tables to data marts and data warehouses.

For more information on using SQL Server Integration Services in SQL Server 2008, see Chapter 52, "SQL Server Integration Services."

Service Broker Enhancements

SQL Server 2008 provides the following enhancements to Service Broker:

- Support for conversation priorities. This support allows administrators and developers to specify that messages for important Service Broker conversations are sent and received before messages from less important conversations to ensure that low-priority work does not block higher-priority work.
- The new `ssbdiagnose` command-prompt utility to analyze and diagnose Service Broker configurations and conversations.
- A new performance object and counters that report how often Service Broker dialogs request transmission objects and how often inactive transmission objects are written to work tables in `tempdb`.
- Support for Service Broker in SQL Server Management Studio via new Service Broker Elements in Object Explorer.

For more information on the new features and capabilities of Service Broker, see Chapter 49.

Analysis Services Enhancements

SQL Server 2008 also introduces some new features and enhancements to Analysis Services. Following are some of the primary improvements:

- A new Aggregation Designer makes it easier to browse and modify aggregation designs.
- Aggregation design and usage-based optimization wizards have been simplified and enhanced.
- New AMO warning messages alert users when they depart from design best practices or make logical errors in database design.
- Simplified and enhanced cube and dimension wizards help you create better cubes and dimensions in fewer steps.
- A new Attribute Relationship designer makes it easier to browse and modify attribute relationships.
- A new Key Columns dialog box makes editing key columns easier.
- Key columns can now be edited in the Properties panel.
- An updated Dimension Structure tab helps make modifying attributes and hierarchies easier.
- A new storage structure is available and performance has been enhanced in all backup and restore scenarios.
- When creating a mining structure, you can now divide the data in the mining structure into training and testing sets.
- You can now attach filters to a mining model and apply the filter during both training and testing. Applying a filter to the model lets you control the data used to train the model and lets you more easily assess the performance of the model on subsets of the data.
- Cross-validation is now available in the Mining Accuracy Chart view of the Data Mining Designer.
- SQL Server 2008 supports the creation, management, and use of data mining models from Microsoft Excel when you use the SQL Server 2008 Data Mining add-ins for Office 2007.
- You are able to add aliases to columns in a mining model to make it easier to understand column content and reference the column in DMX statements.

For more information on the new features and capabilities of SQL Server Analysis Services (SSAS), see Chapter 51.

Installation Enhancements

Starting with SQL Server 2008 Service Pack 1, you can now perform slipstream installations of SQL Server 2008. *Slipstream* is the integration of the original installation media files with a service pack and/or a cumulative update so that they can be installed in a single step.

SQL Server 2008 also provides the capability to selectively uninstall cumulative updates and/or service packs via the Programs and Features control panel.

For more information on installing and upgrading SQL Server 2008, see Chapters 8, "Installing SQL Server 2008," and 9, "Upgrading to SQL Server 2008."

Deprecated Features

In addition to the new and enhanced features in SQL Server 2008, it's important to note the features for which support has been discontinued. Table 2.1 lists the unsupported/deprecated features along with their replacements, if any.

TABLE 2.1 Deprecated Features in SQL Server 2008

Deprecated Feature	Replacement
`sp_addalias`	None
`DUMP` and `LOAD` statements	`BACKUP` and `RESTORE`
`BACKUP LOG WITH NO_LOG` and `BACKUP LOG WITH TRUNCATE_ONLY`	None; however, changing the database to simple recovery clears the transaction log
`BACKUP TRANSACTION`	`BACKUP LOG`
`sp_helpdevice`	`sys.backupdevices` catalog view
60, 65, and 70 compatibility levels	Support is provided only for compatibility levels 80 and higher
User groups (`sp_addgroup`, `sp_changegroup`, `sp_dropgroup`, `sp_helpgroup`)	Roles
`Northwind` and `pubs` databases	`AdventureWorks` database

To help keep track of deprecated features so that you can identify potential future upgrade and compatibility problems, SQL Server 2008 provides the SQL Server: Deprecated Features performance counter and the Deprecation Announcement and Deprecation Final Support event classes, which you can monitor via SQL Server Profiler or SQL Trace.

Summary

SQL Server 2008 provides a number of new and long-awaited features and enhancements. This chapter provides an overview of the new features and enhancements that ship with SQL Server 2008 and SQL Server 2008 R2. To learn more, refer to the other chapters referenced here.

However, before we get into covering the features and capabilities of SQL Server 2008 and SQL Server 2008 R2, we'll first take a look at some real-world production implementations of SQL Server to give you an idea of what is possible with SQL Server in both the online transaction processing (OLTP) world and in the decision support systems (DSS)/business intelligence (BI) realms.

CHAPTER 3

Examples of SQL Server Implementations

IN THIS CHAPTER

- Application Terms
- OLTP Application Examples
- DSS Application Examples

As you will see in this chapter, companies use SQL Server for many types of applications and on most tiers now. Gone are the days when you would second guess yourself choosing to use SQL Server over a competing database engine (such as Oracle or DB2 on a UNIX platform) to ensure you got optimal transactional throughput, high availability, and the highest performance. In fact, SQL Server outnumbers both of these database vendors in installed sites globally. Microsoft SQL Server has arrived!

The *SQL Server Unleashed* team has gathered a few showcase SQL Server–based applications to give you an example of what is possible with SQL Server in both the online transaction processing (OLTP) world and in the decision support systems (DSS)/business intelligence (BI) realms. Each example in this chapter comes from real-life database applications running in production environments at major organizations around the world. In general, all the examples in this book come from our direct customer experiences. We often translate those real-life customer implementations into `AdventureWorks2008` or `bigpubs2008` database terms so that you can easily re-create them for your own use.

This chapter describes two OLTP applications: one is a traditional ERP system using SQL Server as the database layer, and the other is an online shopping system with shopping carts and both high-availability and high-performance requirements.

On the DSS/BI side, this chapter presents a traditional conformed-dimension star schema data warehouse implementation for a high-tech company and then shows you what this looks like implemented as an online analytical processing (OLAP) cube created by Analysis Services.

Under the DSS/BI examples, this chapter describes a hybrid distributed reporting example that uses multiple SQL Server technologies to get the most out of a complex application environment in the healthcare industry.

Application Terms

Online transaction processing, or OLTP, is a class of applications that facilitate and manage transaction-oriented processing, typically for data entry, complex business processes (such as order entry), and retrieval transactions. The term *transaction* in the context of computer or database transactions is a finite set of changes that are grouped together and can be undone together if any one piece does not complete (or fails). Often, however, we speak of transactions as a business "unit of work" that can span multiple database transactions as one logical business transaction. The term *OLTP* has also been used to refer to processing in which the system responds immediately to user requests. An automated teller machine (ATM) application for a bank is a classic example of this type of OLTP transaction.

In many applications, efficient OLTP applications may depend on sophisticated transaction management software and/or database optimization tactics to facilitate the processing of large numbers of concurrent users and updates to an OLTP-oriented database. In a geographic-distributed database system, OLTP brokering programs are used to distribute transaction processing among multiple computers on a network. These days, central OLTP is often underneath the covers and integrated into most service-oriented architectures (SOAs) and exposed as web services that can be easily orchestrated for different application functionality.

Decision support systems (DSS) have been around since the late 1960s, beginning with model-driven DSS and running the gamut of financial planning systems, spreadsheets, and massive multidimensional databases more recently. We speak of data warehouses, data marts, executive information systems, OLAP cubes, and business intelligence when referring to DSS. All enable complex decision support capabilities, multidimensional data analysis, online analytical processing, business intelligence, spatial DSS, and complex querying and reporting capabilities.

DSS system categories are

- Data analysis systems that support the manipulation, aggregation, and transformation of data for a specific task or purpose

- Pure analysis information systems that enable a series of decision-oriented databases and small models
- Complex accounting and financial models that calculate and forecast behavior based on business events and financial results
- Predictive models that estimate the consequences of actions on the basis of simulation models
- Optimization models that provide insight and possible actions a business can take by generating an optimal solution consistent with a series of constraints

Microsoft has the capability to fully address the first three types and is only now venturing into predictive and optimization modeling. The examples in this chapter illustrate a classic data warehouse (star schema/snowflake, multidimensional, measures/facts), a small distributed data mart, and an OLAP cube.

For each example in this chapter, we try to describe the overall purpose of the application, the major use cases, and the technology and architecture on which they were deployed. Where appropriate, we might showcase a data model diagram, a relational schema, or a distributed topology that gives you some insight into why the implementation was done a specific way. You are likely to recognize some use cases that may be the same in your environment and therefore possibly apply the same techniques or solutions to serve you as well.

OLTP Application Examples

The following sections describe what the major Enterprise Resource Planning (ERP) vendor SAP AG has implemented using SQL Server for its database layer.

OLTP ERP Example

SAP business solutions are composed of a comprehensive range of products that empower an enterprise with a flexible, end-to-end solution. A critical challenge in implementing an SAP solution is the selection of a data platform to deliver the advanced features and capabilities needed to support the most demanding workloads. The Microsoft SQL Server database software (either SQL Server 2008 or SQL Server 2005) is the relational database management system (RDBMS) of choice for deploying secure, reliable, highly available, high-performing, and scalable SAP installations. Plus, SQL Server high-availability features can minimize downtime for any SAP implementation.

The company's flagship applications are the NetWeaver-based SAP ERP/Business Suites and SAP R/3 industry solutions. Since 1993, SAP and Microsoft have been working together to provide a deeply integrated Microsoft platform with SAP solutions. Microsoft is currently the most selected platform for R/3 and SAP application deployments: more than 56,000 SAP application installations run on Windows, which is more than all other platforms combined. Of these, more than 23,000 SAP application installations worldwide are running with SQL Server as the RDBMS. In fact, this $11.5 billion company uses its own software for its internal ERP purposes completely deployed on the Microsoft SQL Server platform.

As you can see in Figure 3.1, SAP's ERP footprint is a three-tier architecture consisting of a variety of client types, a horizontally scalable application server tier, and a highly available, high-performance database tier.

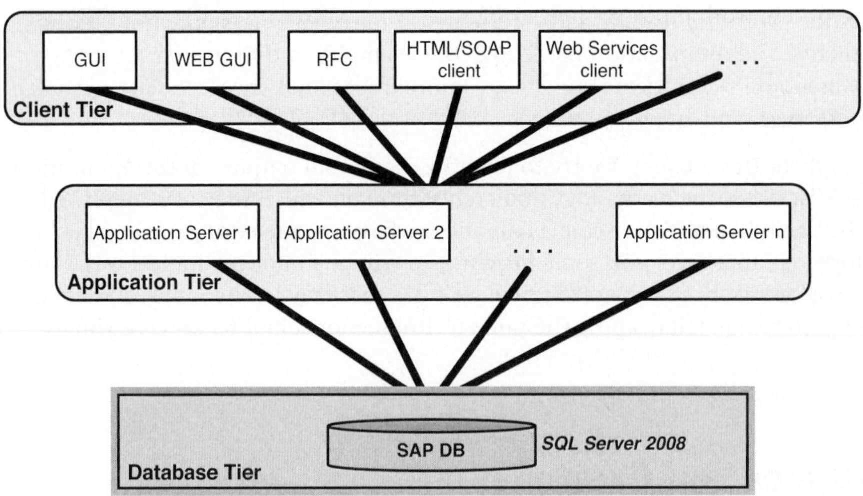

FIGURE 3.1 SAP multitier architecture with SQL Server as the database layer.

The SAP multitiered client/server architecture is composed of three levels:

- **Client/Presentation Tier**—This tier supports SAP graphic user interfaces (GUIs) such as SAP GUI, SAP WebGUI, and other products that connect to the SAP NetWeaver Application Server using one of the supported interfaces. The client tier also includes applications to access SAP using Web Services. For example, applications including smart clients and Microsoft Office applications can integrate SAP data, such as when the Microsoft Excel spreadsheet software is used with Web Services. Applications that use the SAP RFC interface are also part of the presentation tier. Especially in the Microsoft world, connecting to the application tier via RFC became common with the SAP .NET connector, which offers a bandwidth of .NET classes and methods that are mapped to SAP Business Application Programming Interfaces (BAPIs) that are accessible via RFC.

- **Application Tier**—This tier can contain multiple SAP NetWeaver Application Server instances. However, it needs to contain at least one application instance. If multiple instances are used in one system, each application instance is typically run on separate server hardware or virtual machines. The application tier and database tier can run on the same server hardware on small-scale systems and in some very large hardware configurations. The complete processing of the business transactions and workflow is handled on the application side. No business logic is pushed down for execution into the database layer. The database tier is used for data storage only. Technically, an SAP application instance is a collection of processes called *work processes* in SAP terminology. Based on a configuration profile for each individual instance, these work processes fulfill different tasks and requests. To share user contexts and user data, the work processes of one instance share larger areas of memory. The business logic itself was originally programmed in a 4GL language called ABAP; it has now been supplemented by the possibility to code business logic in Java as well.
- **Database Tier**—This tier supports the SAP database, including the SAP Business Suite or R/3 and other SAP applications hosted on SQL Server. The database tier typically runs one database schema for each SAP product using separate server hardware. The database servers can be connected to a storage area network (SAN), Network Attached Storage (NAS), or locally attached storage.

Each SAP application process establishes two connections to SQL Server (as shown in Figure 3.2). There is no sharing of connections between the different SAP processes of an instance. SAP does not use connection pooling. Every one of the processes establishes

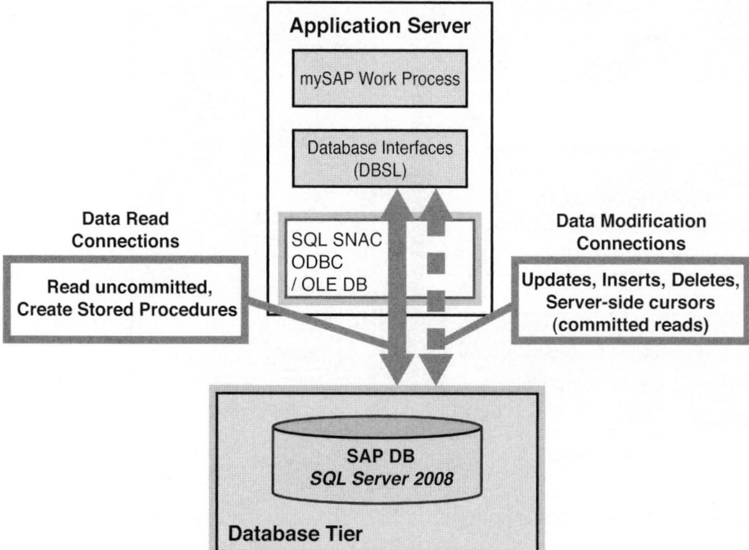

FIGURE 3.2 SAP multiple connections to SQL Server.

connections at startup and keeps them until the process is shut down or restarted. SAP uses Multiple Active Result Sets (MARS) and multiple open client-side cursors that can use the same connection. Each connection is used for different purposes. One performs uncommitted reads of the data or creates stored procedures as needed. The other connection is for data modifications such as updates, inserts, deletes, and server-side cursors. The application tier has been optimized around using these connections.

We featured this ERP application because SAP has proven to the world how rock solid SQL Server is and that the smallest company to companies as large as SAP itself can safely and confidently deploy on SQL Server without hesitation.

OLTP Shopping Cart Example

This shopping cart example features an Internet-based e-commerce implementation for a leading health and vitamin retailer. At the center of this high-availability application is the shopping cart and a global ordering and fulfillment capability. Approximately 5,000 to 10,000 users are online concurrently at any one time, and this application supports up to 50 million hits per day. A key to this application is that it is "stateless," and all database calls are extremely simple and shallow. This web-facing application is built on JRUN but features SQL Server at the database layer, as shown in Figure 3.3.

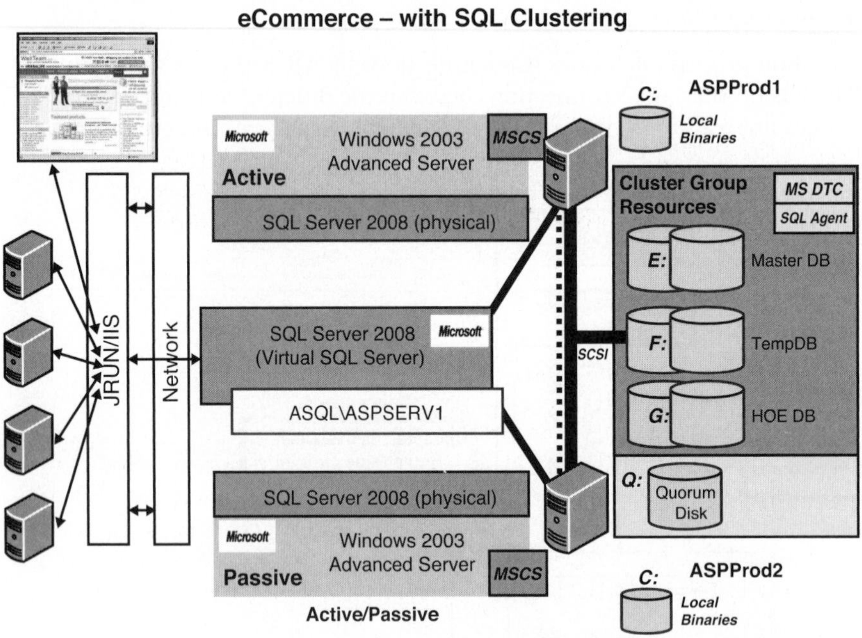

FIGURE 3.3 An e-commerce Internet application with a SQL Server database tier.

This e-commerce application is just a part of a much larger Application Service Provider (ASP) platform. This ASP company houses hundreds of other companies' applications in multiple data centers around the globe. To ensure high availability, this ecommerce application was built on a two-node Active/Passive SQL Clustering configuration. In the four years that this application has been running, the database tier has achieved a 99.99% uptime with rolling updates at both the operating system and SQL Server levels. The OLTP database on SQL Server is approximately 10TB and utilizes log shipping to create a reasonably current disaster recovery (DR) copy (that has never been utilized!). Ninety percent of the reporting is done off the DR copy (approximately one-hour old data on average). This is fully within the service-level requirements needed by the health and vitamin company.

It's important to note here is that if availability falls below 99.99 (four 9s), the ASP company must pay fairly large financial penalties as a part of its agreement with its customers. Each physical server in the cluster is a Dell 8 CPU server with 256GB RAM on SQL Server 2008 Enterprise editions on Windows 2003 Advanced Servers. This has been a rock-solid implementation from the very start.

DSS Application Examples

The DSS/BI examples start with a traditional star schema data warehouse deployment for a Silicon Valley high-tech company. The same data has also been deployed as an OLAP cube created by Analysis Services.

The last example, describes a hybrid distributed reporting system that, uses multiple SQL Server technologies such as data replication, database mirroring, and database snapshots to get the most out of a complex healthcare industry application environment.

DSS Example One

A Silicon Valley computer company implemented a traditional data warehouse using a star schema approach. A star schema provides multiple paths (dimensions) to the central data facts. As you can see in Figure 3.4, a decision support user can get to the Sales Units, Sales Price, and Sales Returns through Geographic, Time, and Product dimensions. This allows the user to ask questions such as "What were net sales for North America for a particular month for a specific computer product?" SQL Server Integration Services (SSIS) packages populate this data warehouse and conformed dimensions on a daily basis with deltas (new data changes only). The data warehouse is unavailable for about one hour each night as daily updates are rolled into this deployment.

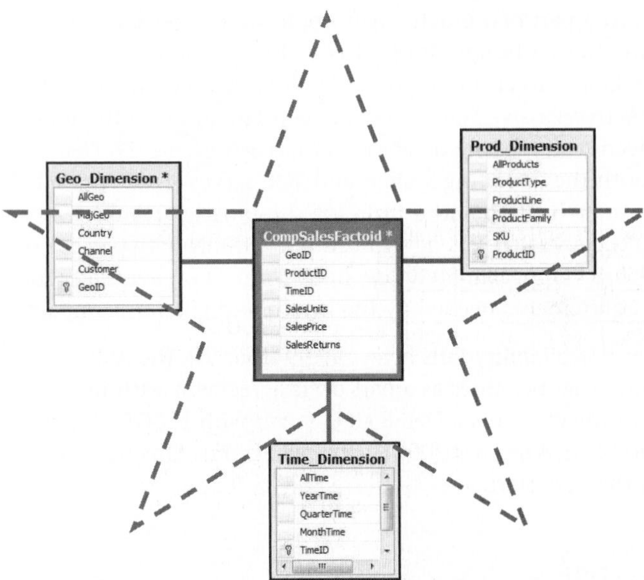

FIGURE 3.4 Star schema data warehouse for global computer sales.

This SQL Server instance is isolated from the OLTP application where the data is sourced. There are about 500–600 data warehouse users of this data globally. This data warehouse is approaching 5TB in size.

DSS Example Two

The same Silicon Valley computer company also implemented some of the same data in a more complex Analysis Services OLAP cube for data mining purposes. The company had many things it did not know about its sales data and wanted to do complex trending and forecasting to better understand the demand for products worldwide. Figure 3.5 shows the OLAP cube built in Analysis Services for this complex business intelligence purpose. Several demand forecasting and product sales trending models were developed to allow this company to predict sales by each of its products for each geographic region.

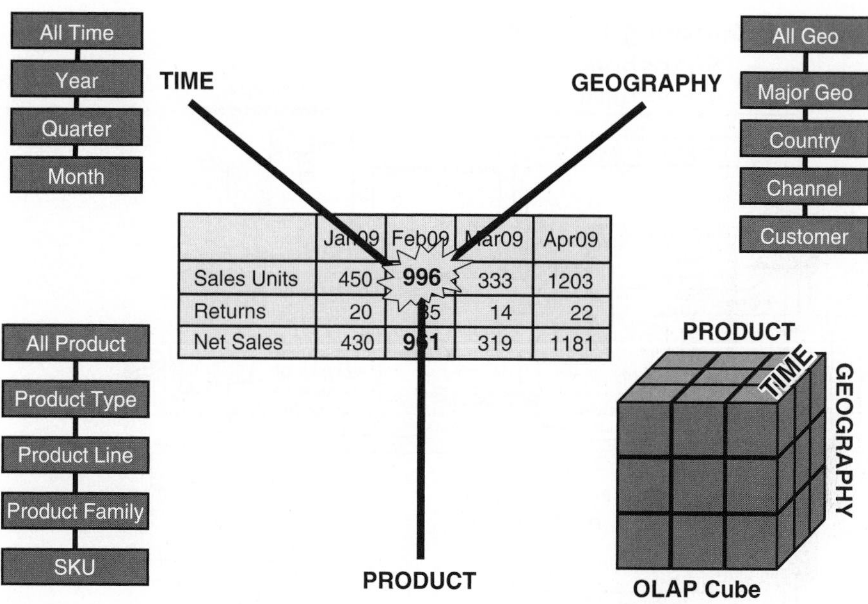

FIGURE 3.5 Multidimensional OLAP cube in Analysis Services.

DSS Example Three

This last example features a multitechnology hybrid data reporting solution that provides real-time reporting along with point-in-time reporting for a major healthcare organization in the Pacific Northwest. This solution starts with real-time data replication from its online transactional systems where all hospital transactions are taking place. This includes patient events, medications administered, surgeries done, hospital charges, and so on. By distributing this data to a highly available two-node SQL Cluster, the hospital is able to realize all its real-time reporting requirements that center around providing all known information for a particular patient in the hospital at any time. Figure 3.6 shows this OLTP-to-SQL cluster real-time, continuous data replication and the real-time reporting enabled by this data distribution.

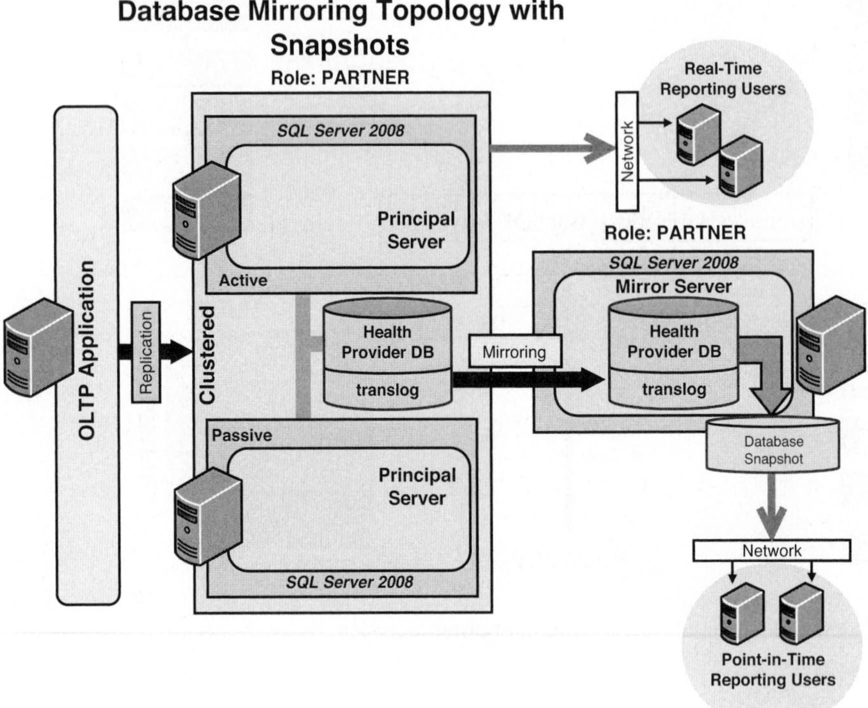

FIGURE 3.6 Hybrid SQL Server reporting configuration.

Another major reporting requirement for this health organization is not a real-time requirement, but rather a leisurely hourly snapshot, point-in-time reporting requirement. A much larger group of users must be served by this noncritical reporting need and cannot impact the real-time reporting environment in any way. To satisfy this point-in-time, noncritical reporting need, the health organization leveraged SQL Server database mirroring from the replicated SQL Server Health Provider DB. From the mirror, hourly database snapshots are created to satisfy all the point-in-time reporting needs of the organization. This configuration has been extremely stable since the SQL Server 2005 deployment.

Summary

This chapter described some truly interesting SQL Server–based implementations. These examples reflect how major software vendors such as SAP have utilized SQL Server as the core of their ERP data tier, how Internet-based companies rely on SQL Server to host their e-commerce applications, and how SQL Server can be used to fulfill various decision support and business intelligence needs of major corporations. We selected these examples because they are rock solid and reflect potentially similar scenarios that you may be faced with. It is this flexibility and reliability that will allow you to be successful as well.

The next chapter delves into the functionality of the SQL Server Management Studio environment.

CHAPTER 4
SQL Server Management Studio

IN THIS CHAPTER

- What's New in SSMS
- The Integrated Environment
- Administration Tools
- Development Tools

SQL Server Management Studio (SSMS) is an integrated application that provides access to most of the graphical tools you can use to perform administrative and development tasks on SQL Server 2008. SSMS was introduced with SQL Server 2005 and replaced the Enterprise Manager, Query Analyzer, and Analysis Manager that were available in SQL Server 2000. Microsoft consolidated all those tools into one, with a focus on providing a tool that suits the needs of both developers and database administrators (DBAs).

SSMS is a complicated tool that provides an entry point to almost all of SQL Server's functionality. The functionality that is accessible from SSMS is entirely too much to cover in one chapter. The aim of this chapter is to give a basic overview of SSMS while touching on the features that are new to SQL Server 2008. Others chapters in this book discuss the components of SSMS and provide more detailed coverage.

What's New in SSMS

SSMS is loaded with new features in SQL Server 2008. This tool was introduced in SQL Server 2005, and it brought quite a bit of change with it. There is also quite a bit of change with SQL Server 2008, but the basic look-and-feel of the application remains much the same as it was in SQL Server 2005.

The standout features in the SQL Server 2008 SSMS include four new features geared toward the administrator and three new features geared toward the developer. Of course, all these features could be used by both administrators and developers.

The new administrator features in SSMS include a beefed-up Activity Monitor, a new Object Search option, a customizable Object Explorer Details window, and a new management tool named SQL Server Utility that was added with SQL Server 2008 R2. The Activity Monitor now contains four separate graphs that look like graphs displayed in Task Manager, and they pull information similar to what you might see in System Monitor. The Object Search option allows you to search for database objects by name while changes to the Object Explorer Details window significantly expand the amount of available information and allow the user to change the information that is displayed. Finally, the new SQL Server Utility allows for the capture of resource information across multiple servers and provides one unified view for the display of this information.

Enhancements that are focused on the developer include IntelliSense in the Query Editor, an integrated Transact-SQL (T-SQL) Debugger, and a Multiserver Query execution option. IntelliSense helps with the completion of T-SQL code as you write it. This feature was much anticipated for SQL Server 2005, but it never made it to the released code. That anticipation continued with SQL Server 2008, and fortunately, Microsoft has delivered. This feature should not disappoint, and it will ultimately improve your productivity.

A debugging tool that is integrated into SSMS is another great new feature. Those who have developed stored procedures with thousands of lines of code will particularly appreciate this new feature. You can set breakpoints, evaluate variables, and step through the code line by line. This debugging capability applies to all T-SQL in the query editor window.

Multiserver queries is the last standout feature offered with SQL Server 2008. This feature allows you to run a single query against more than one server. The results returned from each server are displayed in a single result window. If you're managing many servers, this feature can be a real timesaver.

This chapter further explores the new features in SSMS. It first examines the features at the environmental level, focusing on how SSMS behaves and how to best utilize the environment. Next, it looks at the administrative tools and what changes have been made to help you better manage your SQL Server environment. Finally, this chapter looks at the development tools available with SSMS and changes made to improve your SQL Server development experience.

The Integrated Environment

If you have been working with SQL Server for a long time, you may remember the SQL Enterprise Manager that came with SQL Server 6.5. In some respects, with SSMS, Microsoft has moved back to the paradigm that existed then. Like the SQL Server 6.5 Enterprise Manager, SSMS provides an integrated environment where developers and DBAs alike can perform the database tasks they need. Say goodbye to Query Analyzer, Analysis Manager, and a number of other desparate tools used in SQL Server 2000 and say hello to SSMS, which provides "one-stop shopping" for most of your database needs.

Window Management

Figure 4.1 shows a sample configuration for the SSMS main display. The environment and windows displayed are completely customizable, with the exception of the document window area. Figure 4.1 shows the document window area displaying the Object Explorer Details page. The Object Explorer Details page is the default, but other pages, such as a query editor window, can take the focus in this tab-oriented section of the SSMS display.

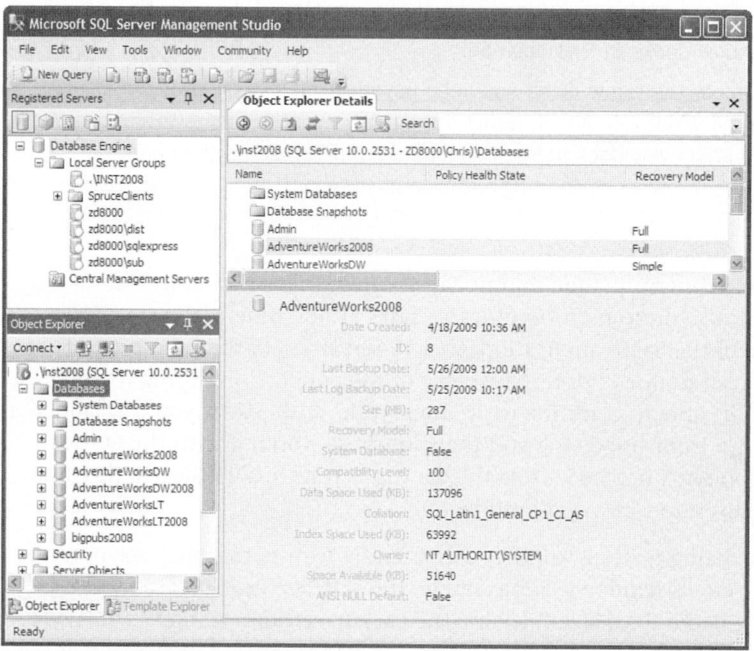

FIGURE 4.1 The SSMS main display.

The dialogs that form the rest of the SSMS display are referred to as *components* and include the Registered Servers and Object Explorer windows shown in Figure 4.1, as well as a number of other components that can be displayed via the View menu found at the top of the SSMS display. You can configure each of the component windows in a number of ways; for example, you can have them float, or you can hide, dock, autohide, or display them as tabbed documents in the document window area.

The configuration that you choose for your SSMS display depends on the type of work you do with SQL Server as well as the type of person you are. The Auto Hide feature causes the component window to shrink to a tab along the left or right side of the display. When you mouse over the tab, the window automatically expands and stays expanded as long as the mouse cursor remains in the component window area. Auto Hide helps maximize the working real estate available in the document window for query development and the like. Docking many windows can clutter the screen, but this feature allows you to view many different types of information all at once. This is a matter of personal preference, and SSMS has made it very easy to change.

TIP

You can reposition the component windows by dragging and dropping them to the desired locations. When you are in the middle of a drag and drop, rectangular icons with arrows are displayed at different locations on the SSMS window surface. If you mouse over one of these arrowed icons to select the window location, you see the window destination highlighted. If you release your mouse button while the destination is highlighted, the window docks in that position.

Some users at first ignore the arrow icons and keep hovering the window over the location where they want the window to go. Hovering the window over the desired location does not allow you to effectively dock it. You should save yourself some time and aggravation and use the arrow icons for drag-and-drop positioning.

The SSMS window environment include nonmodal windows that are sizable. The nonmodal windows allows you to perform multiple tasks at one time without needing to open another instance of the SSMS application. In SQL Server 2000, the Enterprise Manager users were forced to open another instance of the application during many administrative tasks to be able to continue with other work. With SSMS, you can launch a backup with the Back Up Database dialog and then continue working with the Object Explorer or other components in SSMS while the backup is running. This capability is a great timesaver and helps improve overall productivity.

Your ability to size the dialog boxes is another user-friendly feature that may seem minor but is quite handy on certain windows. For example, the SQL Server 2000 Enterprise Manager Restore dialog had a fixed size. Viewing the backup set information in this relatively small (nonsizable) dialog box was a challenge. The Restore dialog in SQL Server 2008's SSMS can contain a slew of information related to the backup sets available for restore. The capability to size the windows allows for much more information to be displayed.

The tabbed document window area provides some usability improvements as well. This area, as described earlier, is fixed and is always displayed in SSMS. Component windows can be displayed in this area, along with windows for the Query Editor, diagrams, and other design windows. If desired, you can change the environment from a tabbed display to multiple-document interface (MDI) mode. In this mode, each document is opened in its own window within the document window. The MDI mode manages windows like the SQL Server 2000 Query Analyzer and may be more user-friendly for some people. You can change to MDI mode by selecting Tools, Options and then selecting MDI Environment from the General page.

One particularly useful window that can be displayed in the document window is the Object Explorer Details page. This new window displays information relative to the node selected in the Object Explorer and includes options to produce detailed reports and graphs. The Object Explorer Details page is displayed in the document window by default when SSMS is launched, but you can also display it by pressing F7 or choosing Object Explorer Details from the View menu.

The Object Explorer Details page has been vastly improved in SQL Server 2008. If you're familiar with the previous version, you can see in Figure 4.1 that there is much more information displayed in SQL Server 2008 than there was in 2005. The nice part is that you can customize the information that is displayed and save those changes so that they are used the next time you open SSMS. For example, when you right-click on a column heading (such as Name), you see all the columns available for display. Only a handful are displayed by default, but more than 30 available columns relate to databases. The columns that are available depend on the type of object selected in the Object Explorer window.

TIP

You can copy some or all of the information shown in the Object Explorer Details window and paste it into another application such as Excel for a quick and easy report. For example, you can select the `Databases` node in Object Explorer, highlight the data shown in the Object Explorer Details page, press Ctrl+C to copy the data, and then paste it into Excel. All the columns related to database (including Headings) are captured and give you an easy way to review information about all your databases.

Another significant change in the Object Explorer Details page is the Object Search box. The Object Search box, located at the top of the Object Explorer Details page (next to the Search label), allows you to search for objects by name. You can use wildcards (for example, `Product%`), or you can type a specific name you are looking for. The results are displayed in the Object Explorer Details page. Keep in mind that the objects that are searched depend on what is selected in the Object Explorer window. For example, if you highlight the `Databases` node, you search all the databases on your SQL Server instance. If you select a specific database, only that database is searched.

TIP

In SQL Server 2000, you could select multiple objects for scripting by selecting the items from the Object Explorer tree in Enterprise Manager. You cannot use the Object Explorer tree to perform this operation with SQL Server 2008, and this has generated some confusion. The solution is the Object Explorer Details page, which provides a means for performing multiple selections of the objects it displays. You can hold down the Ctrl key and click only those items you want to script. After you select the items you want, you simply right-click one of the selected items and choose the preferred scripting method. This method also works with scheduled jobs displayed in the Object Explorer Details page. SQL Server 2000 did not offer this capability.

Integrated Help

SSMS offers an expanded set of help facilities as well as improved integration into the application environment. The Help sources have been expanded to include both local and online resources. Local help is similar to the Help resources available in past versions and references files installed on your machine during the installation process. Local help includes the local SQL Server Books Online resources. Local help files are static and are updated only if another documentation installation is run on the local machine.

Online help provides access to content that is not static and can be updated with the latest changes. Three default online resources are provided by default:

- **MSDN Online**—MSDN Online contains the latest version of the MSDN documentation, including the latest quarterly releases.
- **Codezone Community**—Codezone Community includes a set of third-party websites that have partnered with Microsoft and provide a wealth of information from sources outside Microsoft.
- **Questions**—The Questions option allows you to search the forum archives for answers to questions that others have already asked. It also allows you to post your own questions.

The help resources you use on your machine are configurable. You can choose to search online resources first, followed by local help, or you can choose an option that searches local help resources first, followed by online resources. You can also choose specific Codezone online resources to search, or you can eliminate the search of all online resources. Figure 4.2 shows the online help Options window, which allows you to configure your Help options. You access this dialog by selecting Tools, Options.

The Help resources you select are used when you search for content within the Help facility. When you use both local and online resources options, you see results from multiple locations in your search results. Figure 4.3 shows a sample Books Online Document Explorer window with results from a search on "Management Studio." Notice that the panel on the right side of the window lists entries under Local Help, MSDN Online, Codezone Community, and Questions. Each of these sections contains search results that

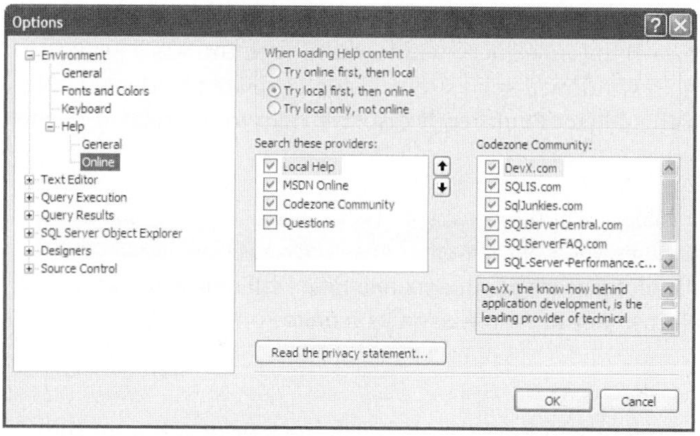

FIGURE 4.2 Setting Help options.

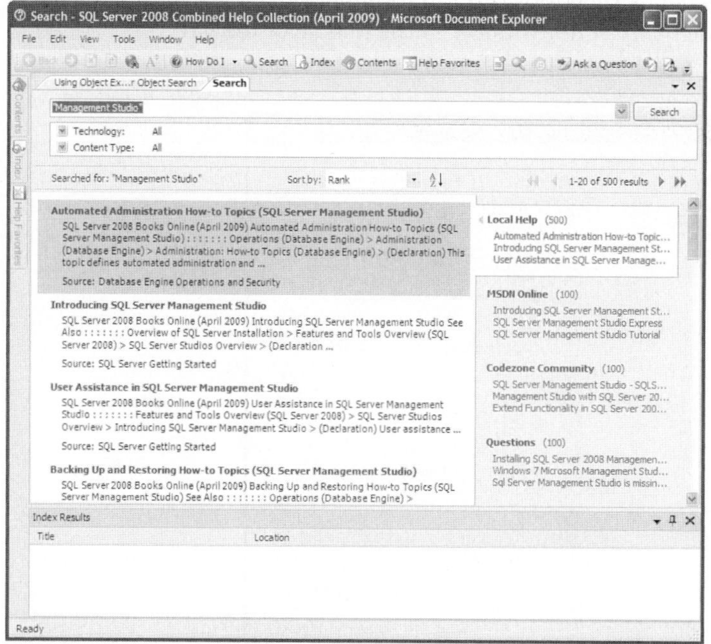

FIGURE 4.3 A Books Online search.

you can access by simply clicking on that area. The number of search results for each section is displayed in parentheses after the section name.

One other significant change to the help facilities in SSMS is the addition of Dynamic Help. Dynamic Help is a carryover from the Visual Studio environment. It is a help facility that automatically displays topics in a Help window that are related to what you are doing in SSMS. For example, if you are working in a query window and type the word SELECT to start your query, the Dynamic Help window displays several topics related to the SELECT statement. If you are working in the Object Explorer, it displays Help topics related to the Object Explorer.

NOTE

There is some processing overhead associated with Dynamic Help. You may find that your SSMS environment runs a bit slower when you use this feature.

Dynamic Help is one of the component windows that you can dock or position on the SSMS surface. To use Dynamic Help, you select Help, Dynamic Help. Figure 4.4 shows an example of the SSMS environment with the Dynamic Help window docked on the right side of the window. The Dynamic Help topics in this example are relative to the SELECT keyword that is typed in the query editor window in the middle of the screen.

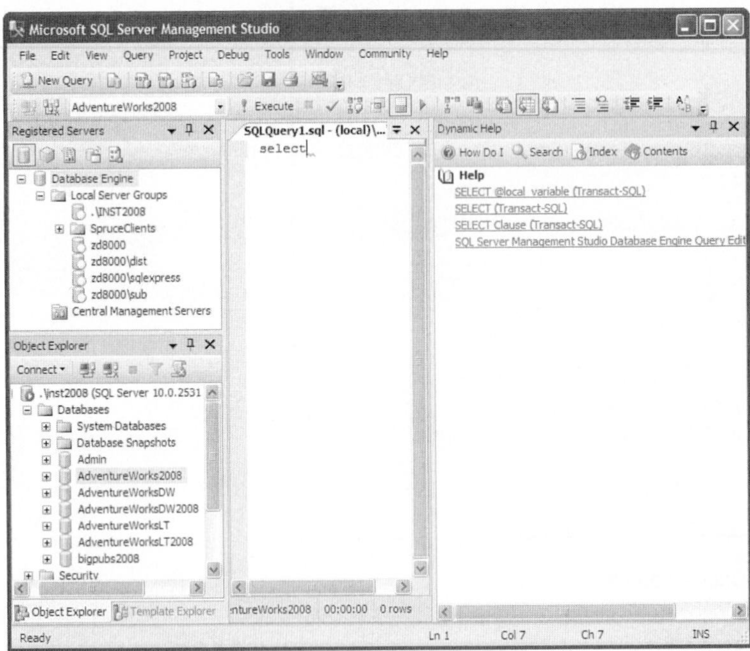

FIGURE 4.4 Dynamic Help.

Administration Tools

The tools available with SSMS can be broadly categorized into tools that are used for administering SQL Server and tools that are used for developing or authoring new SQL Server objects. As a matter of practice, developers use some of the administrative tools, and administrators use some of the development tools.

SSMS comes with an expanded set of tools to help with SQL Server administrative tasks. It builds on the functionality that was available in SQL Server 2005 and adds some new tools and functionality to help ease the administrative burden.

Registered Servers

Registered servers is a concept in SQL Server 2008 that represents a division between managing servers and registering servers. With the SQL Server 2000 Enterprise Manager, the Microsoft Management Console (MMC) tree was displayed on the left side of the Enterprise Manager screen, and it contained servers that had been registered via that tree. Any registered servers or groups were listed in the tree, along with any of the associated objects.

Registered servers are managed and displayed in the Registered Servers component window. Figure 4.5 shows an example of the Registered Servers window, with several server groups and their associated registered servers. You can add new groups or servers any time so that you have a handy way of organizing the servers you work with.

FIGURE 4.5 The Registered Servers window.

The servers listed in Figure 4.5 are all Database Engine servers. These server types are the conventional SQL Server instances, like those you could register in the SQL Server 2000 Enterprise Manager. You can also register several other types of servers. The icons across the top of the Registered Servers window indicate the types of servers that can be registered. In addition to Database Engine servers, you can also register servers for Analysis Services, Reporting Services, SQL Server Mobile, and Integration Services. The Registered Servers window gives you one consolidated location to register all the different types of servers available in SQL Server 2008. You simply click the icon associated with the appropriate server type, and the registered servers of that type are displayed in the Registered Servers tree.

NOTE

The SQL Server 2008 Registered Servers window enables you to register servers that are running SQL Server 2005, SQL Server 2000, and SQL Server 7.0. You can manage all the features of SQL Server 2005 and SQL Server 2000 with SQL Server 2008 tools. You can also have both sets of tools on one machine. The SQL Server 2000, SQL Server 2005, and SQL Server 2008 tools are compatible and function normally together.

Management tools from prior SQL Server versions cannot be used to manage SQL Server 2008 instances. For example, the SQL Server 2000 Enterprise Manager cannot be used to manage SQL Server 2008. You can connect the Query Analyzer to a SQL Server 2008 instance and run queries, but the Object Explorer and other tools are not compatible with SQL Server 2008.

When a server is registered, you have several options available for managing the server. You can right-click the server in the Registered Servers window to start or stop the related server, open a new Object Explorer window for the server, connect to a new query window, or export the registered servers to an XML file so that they can be imported on another machine.

TIP

The import/export feature can be a real timesaver, especially in environments where many SQL servers are managed. You can export all the servers and groups registered on one machine and save the time of registering them all on another machine. For example, you can right-click the `Database Engine` node, select Export, and then choose a location to store the XML output file. Then all you need to do to register all the servers and groups on another machine is move the file to that machine and import the file.

Object Explorer

The Object Explorer window that existed in the SQL Server 2000 Query Analyzer was integrated into SSMS in SQL Server 2005. SQL Server 2008 continues to use an integrated Object Explorer that behaves like SQL Server 2005.. The most significant feature for those folks managing a large number of database objects is the capability to populate the Object Explorer tree asynchronously. This may not hit home for folks who deal with smaller databases, but it can be a real time saver for those that are dealing with many databases on a single SQL Server instance or for those that work with databases that have a significant number of database objects. The Object Explorer tree in SSMS displays immediately and allows navigation in the tree and elsewhere in SSMS while the population of the tree is taking place.

The Object Explorer is adaptive to the type of server it is connected to. For a Database Engine server, the databases and objects such as tables, stored procedures, and so on are displayed in the tree. If you connect to an Integration Services server, the tree displays information about the packages defined on that type of server. Figure 4.6 shows an example of the Object Explorer with several different types of SQL Server servers displayed in the tree. Each server node has a unique icon that precedes the server name, and the type of server is also displayed in parentheses following the server name.

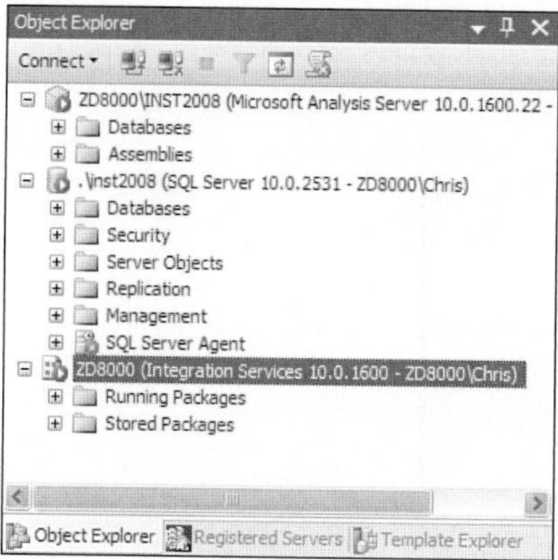

FIGURE 4.6 Multiple server types in Object Explorer.

The objects displayed in the Object Explorer tree can be filtered in SQL Server 2008. The number of filters is limited, but those that are available can be helpful. For example, you can filter the tables displayed in Object Explorer based on the name of the table, the schema that it belongs to, or the date on which it was created. Again, for those who deal with large databases and thousands of database objects, this feature is very helpful.

Administrators also find the enhanced scripting capabilities in the Object Explorer very useful. The scripting enhancements are centered mostly on the administrative dialog boxes. These dialogs now include a script button that allows you to see what SSMS is doing behind the scenes to effect your changes. In the past, the Profiler could be used to gather this information, but it was more time-consuming and less integrated than what is available now.

Figure 4.7 shows an example of an administrative dialog, with the scripting options selected at the top. You can script the commands to a new query window, a file, the Windows Clipboard, or a job that can be scheduled to run at a later time.

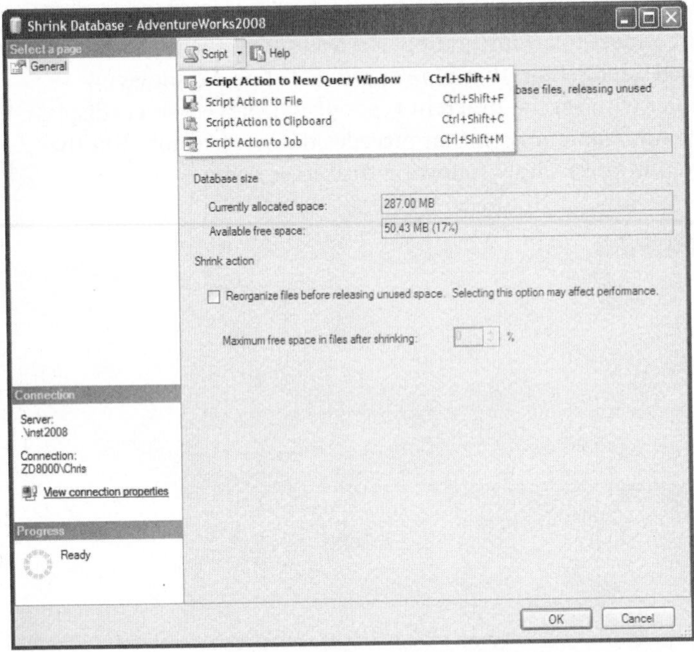

FIGURE 4.7 Scripting from administrative dialogs.

Aside from these features, many of the features and much of the functionality associated with the Object Explorer is similar to what was found in SQL Server 2000 and is almost identical to what was found in SQL Server 2005. Keep in mind that there are some additional nodes in the Object Explorer tree and that some of the objects are located in different places. For example, the `Management` node now contains nodes for `Policy Management`, `Data Collection`, and the `Resource Governor`, which are all new in SQL Server 2008.

One often-overlooked Object Explorer feature is the reports option that was added in SQL Server 2005 and still exists in SQL Server 2008. This option is available by right-clicking on a node in the Object Explorer. Reports are not available for every node in the Object Explorer tree, but many of them do have this option. Most reports are found in the top-level nodes in the tree. For example, if you right-click on a database in the Object Explorer tree and then select Reports and Standard Reports, you see more than a dozen available reports. These reports include Disk Usage, Backup and Restore Events, Top Transactions by Age, and a host of others. Graphs are included with some reports, and you can export or print all these reports. Figure 4.8 shows an example of the Disk Usage report for the `AdventureWorks2008` database.

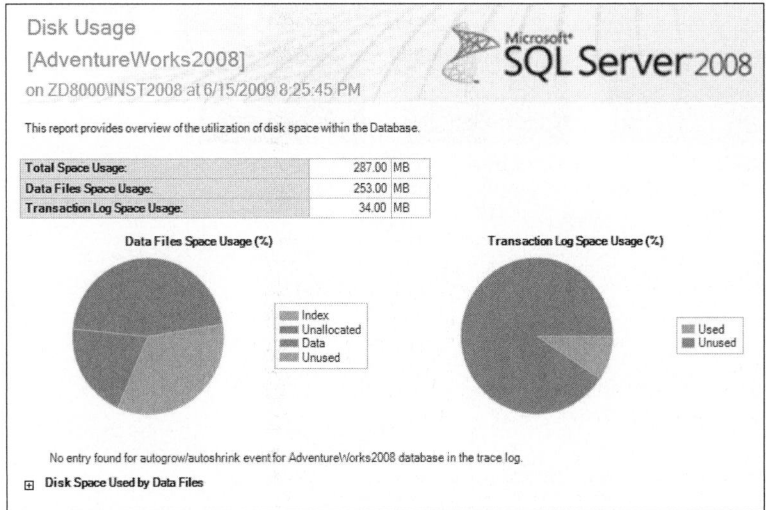

FIGURE 4.8 A Disk Usage Object Explorer Details report.

The graphs are easy to read, and some sections of the report can be expanded to provide more detail. Bullets at the bottom of a report are nodes that can be expanded. For example, the bullet Disk Space Used by Data Files at the bottom of Figure 4.8 can be expanded to display details about each of the data files.

Activity Monitor

The Activity Monitor has seen some dramatic changes in SQL Server 2008. These changes build on the foundation established in SQL Server 2005 and help provide much more information related to the performance of your SQL Server instance.

Before we get into the details of the Activity Monitor, let's make sure you know where to find it. It is no longer found in the `Management` node of the Object Explorer. Instead, you right-click on the name of the server instance in the Object Explorer, and you see a selection for Activity Monitor.

When the Activity Monitor launches, you see a new display with four different graphs, as shown in Figure 4.9. The graphs include % Processor Time (from SQL Server), Waiting Tasks, Database I/O and Batch Requests. These graphs give you a quick performance snapshot for your SQL Server in one spot without having to launch System Monitor or some other monitoring tool to view this kind of information.

You also find more detailed performance information below the graphs. This information is grouped into four categories: Processes, Resource Waits, Data File I/O and Recent Expensive Queries. Clicking on the expand button for one of these categories presents the details you are looking for. These details contain drop-down headings that allow you to filter the results and view only the information you need.

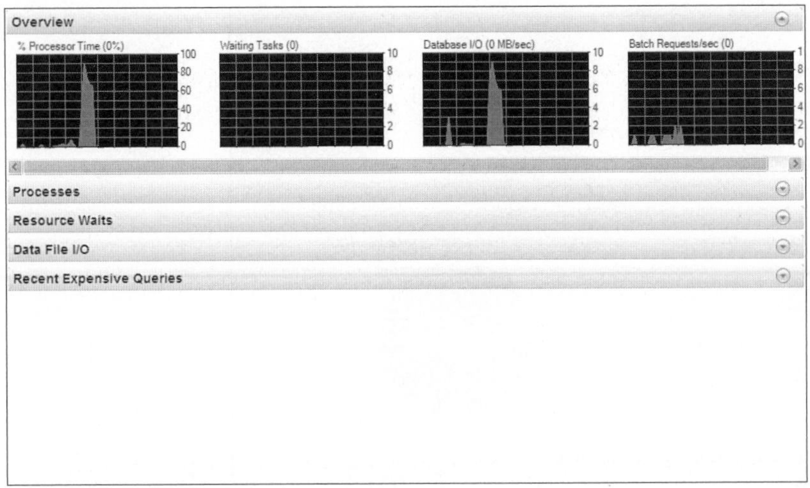

FIGURE 4.9 SQL Server 2008 Activity Monitor.

The Processes Details window contains information similar to what was displayed in the SQL Server 2005 Activity Monitor. These details include information similar to what is returned with the `sp_who` system stored procedure. The server process ID (SPID) is listed in a column named Session ID, and the related information for each SPID is displayed in the remaining columns. If you right-click on a particular process, you can see the details of that process. You can then kill that process or launch the SQL Server Profiler to trace the activity for the process. Figure 4.10 shows an example of the expanded Processes details window.

The Resource Waits window (that is displayed below the Process window) can help you identify bottlenecks on your server. It details the processes waiting for other resources on the server. The amount of time a process is waiting and the wait category (what the process is waiting for) are found in this display. If you click on the Cumulative Wait Time column, the rows are sorted by this column and you can find the wait category that has been waiting the longest. This sorting capability applies to all the columns in the display.

Se ID	U: Pr	Login	Datab	Task State	Comm	Applic	Wait Time (ms)	Wait Type	Wait Resou	Bl By	H Bl	Memo Use (KB)
51	1	ZD8000\...	master			Microsoft...	0					
52	1	ZD8000\...	tempdb	RUNNING	SELECT	Microsoft...	0					
53	1	ZD8000\...	master			Microsoft...	0					
54	1	ZD8000\...	master			Microsoft...	0					
55	1	ZD8000\...	master			Microsoft...	0					
56	1	ZD8000\...	master			Microsoft...	0					
57	1	NT AUT...	msdb			SQLAge...	0					

FIGURE 4.10 Processes Details window in the Activity Monitor.

The Data File I/O window lists each database and its related database files. The amount of disk I/O experienced by each of the files is detailed in the columns of this display. You can isolate the database and files that are most heavily hit with read or write activity as well as the databases that may be suffering from poor I/O response with this screen.

Finally, the Recent Expensive Queries window displays information similar to what you can obtain using catalog views. It provides statistics for all the databases on the instance and is a quick and easy way to find and tune expensive SQL statements. If you right-click on a row in the display and click Edit Query Text, you can see the entire SQL text associated with the query. You are able to click on one of the column headings such as CPU to sort the display according to the metric you feel defines cost. Best of all, you can right-click on a row and choose Show Execution Plan, and you have the Query Plan ready for analysis.

NOTE

When you mouse over the column headers in the detailed windows, ToolTips give you more information about the columns. This information includes the system view that the information is gathered from and where you can look in Books Online to obtain further information.

Log File Viewer

The Log File Viewer is another nonmodal window that is essential for administering your SQL Server. Like the Activity Monitor, it houses information that was previously displayed in the document window in the SQL Server 2000 Enterprise Manager. It can display log files that are generated from several different sources, including Database Mail, SQL Server Agent, SQL Server, and Windows NT.

The Log File Viewer can be launched from the related node in the SSMS Object Explorer. For example, you can select the `Management` node and expand `SQL Server Error Logs`. If you double-click one of the error logs listed, a new Log File Viewer window is launched, displaying the SQL Server log file entries for the log type selected (see Figure 4.11).

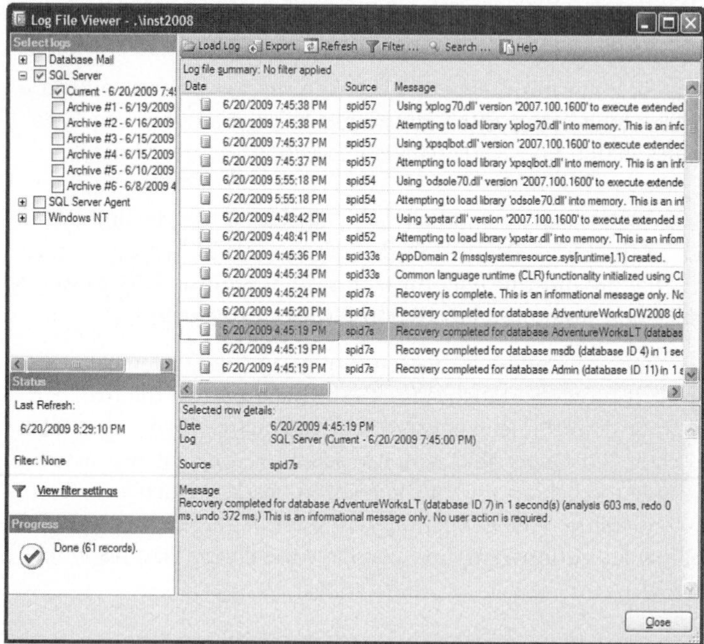

FIGURE 4.11 SQL Server logs displayed in the Log File Viewer.

NOTE

By default, entries are shown in the SQL Server Log File Viewer from newest to oldest. This is different from the default order in the SQL Server 2000 Enterprise Manager, which displayed the log file entries from oldest to newest.

One of the first things you notice when you launch the Log File Viewer is that a tree structure at the top-left corner of the screen shows the log files you are viewing. You can see that there are four different log types available: Database Mail, SQL Agent, SQL Server, and Windows NT. You can choose to display multiple log files within a given log type (for example, the current SQL Server log and Archive #1), or you can select logs from different sources. For example, you can display all the current log entries for SQL Server and the current log entry for the SQL Server Agent.

When multiple logs are selected, you can differentiate between the rows shown on the right side of the Log File Viewer by looking at the Log Source column and the Log Type column. The Log Source values match up with the names shown in the tree structure where the log was selected. The Log Type column shows the type of log, such as SQL Agent or SQL Server. Rows from the different log types are displayed together and sorted according to the date on which the row was created. The sort order cannot be changed.

TIP

You can rearrange the order of the columns shown in the Log File Viewer. You simply click the column header and drag the column to the desired location. When you are viewing rows for more than one log type or multiple logs, it is best to drag the Log Type and Log Source columns to a location that is easily viewed so that you can distinguish between the entries.

Other noteworthy features in the Log File Viewer include the capability to filter and load a log from an external source. You can filter on dates, users, computers, the message text, and the source of the message. You can import log files from other machines into the view by using the Load Log facility. This facility works hand-in-hand with the Export option, which allows you to export the log to a file. These files can be easily shared so that others can review the files in their own Log File Viewer.

SQL Server Utility

The SQL Server Utility was added in SQL Server 2008 R2 and is geared toward multiserver management. It provides several new hooks in the SSMS environment that improve visibility and control across multiple SQL Server environments. Access to these new hooks is provided through a new Utility Explorer that can be displayed within your SSMS environment. This Utility Explorer has a tree-like structure similar to the Object Explorer, and it provides rich content related to the health and integrity of the SQL Server environments you have selected to manage using the SQL Server Utility. Figure 4.12 shows an example of the type of information the Utility Explorer can display.

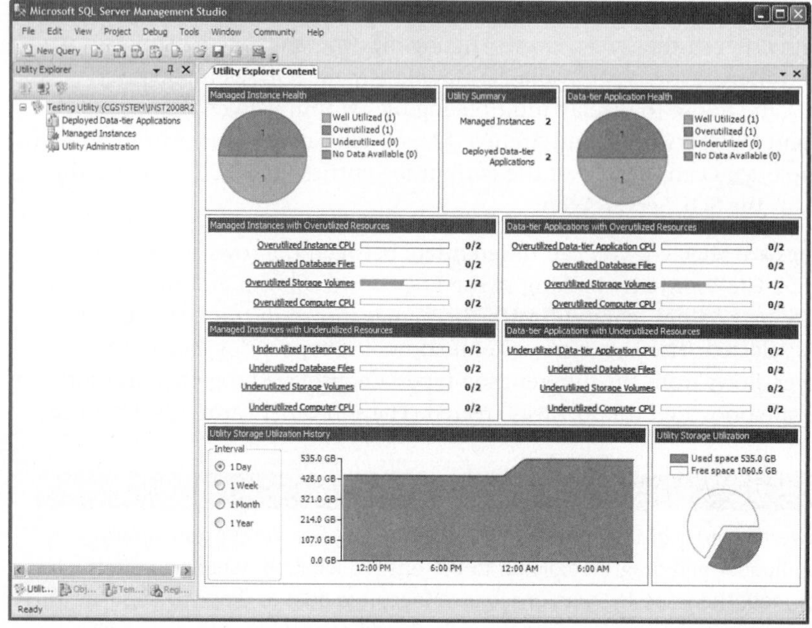

FIGURE 4.12 Utility Explorer content.

The SQL Server Utility must first be configured to facilitate the display of information in the Utility Explorer. The configuration is relatively straightforward, but you must meet several requirements before starting it. The following requirements apply to the utility control point (UCP), which is the SQL Server instance capturing the information and the SQL Server instances being managed by the UCP:

- SQL Server must be version 10.50 or higher.
- The SQL Server instance type must be Database Engine.
- The SQL Server Utility must operate within a single Windows domain or domains with two-way trust relationships.
- On Windows Server 2003, the SQL Server Agent service account must be a member of Performance Monitor User group.
- The SQL Server service accounts on the UCP and all managed instances of SQL Server must have read permission to Users in Active Directory.

In addition, the UCP must be running the Data Center, Developer, or Enterprise Edition of SQL Server.

When you have met these requirements, you are ready to start using the SQL Server Utility. The first steps are to establish a UCP and to enroll SQL Server instances for the UCP to manage. This is accomplished by selecting View on the SSMS menu bar and then selecting Utility Explorer. A content pane is displayed in SSMS that contains options for configuring the SQL Server Utility (see Figure 4.13). It also contains links to video that can guide you through each step.

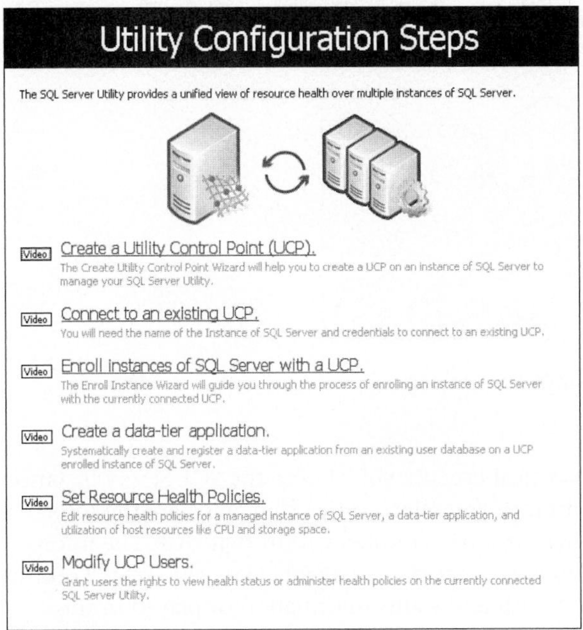

FIGURE 4.13 Utility Configuration Steps.

The first thing to do when configuring the SQL Server Utility is to click on the Create a Utility Control Point (UCP) link on the Getting Started tab. This initiates a wizard that will guide you through a five-step process that creates the UCP. The first wizard screen that outlines these steps is shown in Figure 4.14.

4

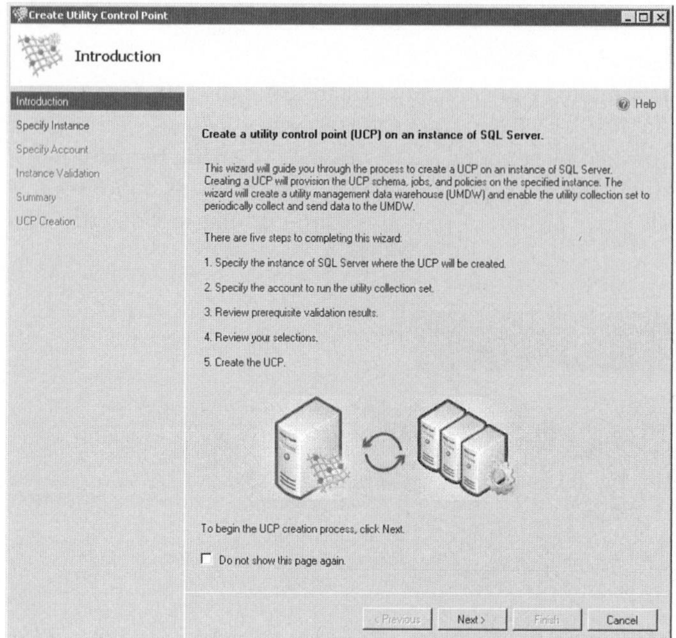

FIGURE 4.14 Create Utility Control Point Wizard screen.

The first step of the wizard is the most critical because you choose the SQL Server Instance that will be the UCP. The SQL Server instance you select in this step will store the information related to the UCP and any other instances enrolled within that UCP. The information collected by the UCP is stored in a database named `sysutility_mdw` created on the UCP instance. This database drives the health and status information displayed in the Utility Explorer.

After you complete the wizard steps to create a UCP, the UCP appears in the Utility Explorer Tree, and summary information about the UCP is displayed in the Utility Explorer Content tab. The UCP is the top-most node in the tree and contains other child nodes that contain the different types of information managed by the UCP. An example of the Utility Explorer tree is shown in Figure 4.15.

The first child node displayed in the Utility Explorer tree is named `Deployed Data-tier Applications`. A data-tier application, or DAC, is a single entity that contains all the database objects and related instance objects used by an application. This includes tables, stored procedures, SQL Server Logins, and so on. DACs can be created from a Visual Studio 2010 data-tier application project or by using the Extract Data-Tier Application Wizard in SSMS. The full scope of DAC capabilities is beyond the scope of this chapter, but it is important to see how they fit into the Utility Explorer Display.

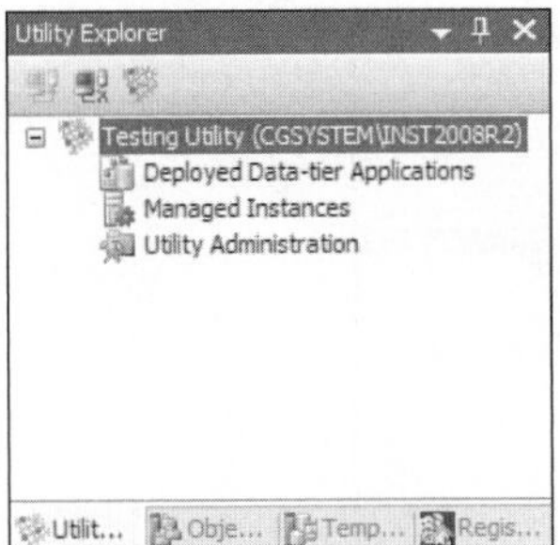

FIGURE 4.15 Utility Explorer tree.

NOTE

Two different SQL Server features use the same *DAC* acronym. The aforementioned *data-tier application* is one of them, but a *dedicated administrator connection* is also referred to as a DAC.

After creating a DAC deployment package, you can deploy it to another SQL Server instance. This deployment creates the related database, the database objects along with the related server objects. If the server to which the DAC is deployed is managed by the UCP, you can show the deployed DAC information by clicking on the `Deployed Data-tier Applications` node of the Utility Explorer.

The next node in the Utility Explorer tree, named `Managed Instances`, contains information about SQL Server instances enrolled in the UCP. Enrolling an instance essentially means you want to manage the instance through the UCP and gather information about it. You can easily enroll this instance by right-clicking on the `Managed Instances` node and selecting Enroll Instance.

Each instance enrolled in the UCP is listed at the top of the Utility Explorer Content tab. When a managed instance is selected from this list, a set of resource and policy information is made available in the lower half of the window. The available tabs in this window which define the type of information that is captured include CPU Utilization, Storage Utilization, Policy Details and Property Details. Figure 4.16 shows two managed instances and the related CPU Utilization graphs for the top-most SQL Server instance.

The last node, `Utility Administration`, can be used to manage policy, security, and data warehouse settings for a SQL Server Utility. These settings drive the SQL Server Utility summary screen and set thresholds across the entities defined in the utility. Figure 4.17 shows an example of the Policy information that can be managed with Utility Administration.

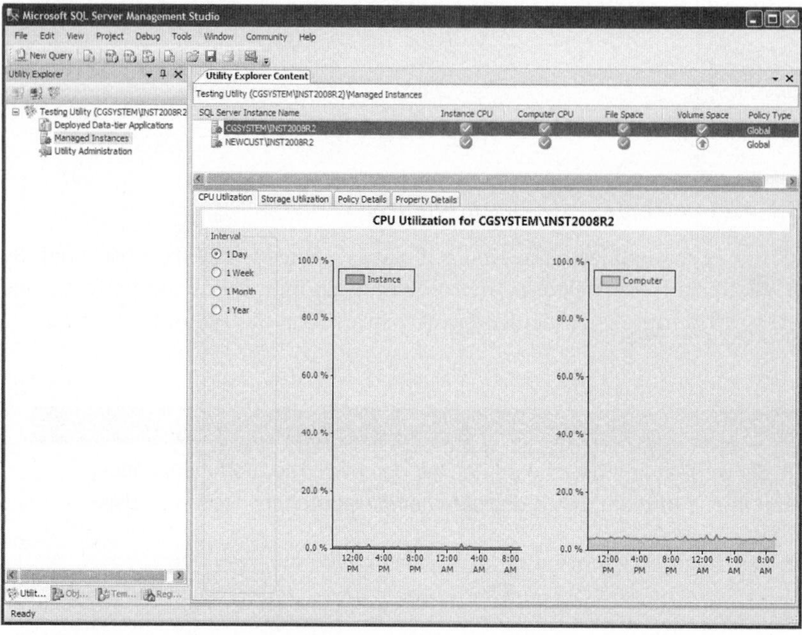

FIGURE 4.16 Managed Instances.

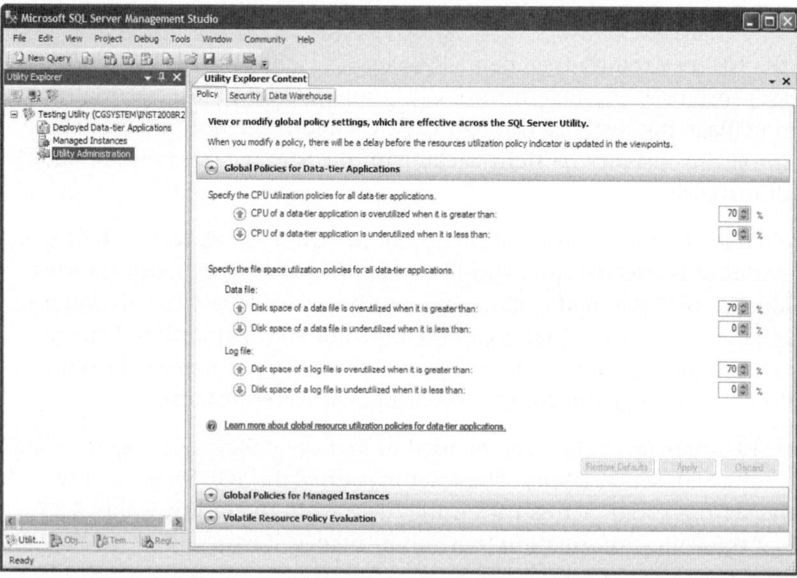

FIGURE 4.17 Utility Administration.

The Policy tab is one of three tabs available on the Utility Administration window. You can see in Figure 4.17 that there are also Security and Data Warehouse tabs. The Security tab allows you to manage permissions for logins that can administer or read from the UCP. Logins can be assigned to the Utility Reader role on this screen, which allows them to connect to the SQL Server Utility and read information from the Utility Explorer in SSMS. The Data Warehouse tab allows you to adjust the amount of time data will be retained in the UCP data warehouse. The default time period is one year.

Over time, the amount of data collected in the UCP data warehouse can be substantial. By default, each managed instance enrolled in the UCP sends configuration and performance data to the UCP every 15 minutes. Consequently, the space used by the utility management data warehouse (UMDW) needs to be monitored. The UMDW database, named `sysutility_mdw`, is listed as a user database in the Object Explorer.

Development Tools

SSMS delivers an equally impressive number of features for database developers. Many of the features were available with SQL Server 2005, but SQL Server 2008 has added some new ones as well. T-SQL Debugging, IntelliSense in the Query Editor, and multiserver queries are a few of those new tools for developers found in SQL Server 2008. These new tools and the other essential developer tools from SSMS are discussed in the following sections.

The Query Editor

The Query Editor sits at the top of the list for development tools in SSMS. The Query Editor, as its name indicates, is the editing tool for writing queries in SSMS. It contains much of the functionality that was contained in SQL Server 2000's Query Analyzer. The capability to write T-SQL queries, execute them, return results, generate execution plans, and use many of the other features you may be familiar with in Query Analyzer are also available with the Query Editor.

One main difference with the Query Editor is that is has been integrated into the SSMS environment. In SQL Server 2000, the Query Analyzer was a separate application with its own independent interface. In SQL Server 2008, SSMS houses the query-editing capabilities along with all the administrative capabilities.

NOTE

The biggest upside to the integration of the query-editing tool into the SSMS environment is that you can find almost anything you need to administer or develop on your SQL Server database in one spot. There is no need to jump back and forth between applications. One possible downside, however, is that SSMS may be much more than some database developers need.

Clicking the New Query button, opening a file, and selecting the Script to File option from a list of database objects in the Object Explorer are just a few of the ways to launch the Query Editor. Figure 4.18 shows the query editor window with a sample `SELECT` statement from the `AdventureWorks2008` database. The query editor window is displayed on the right side of the screen and the Object Explorer on the left side.

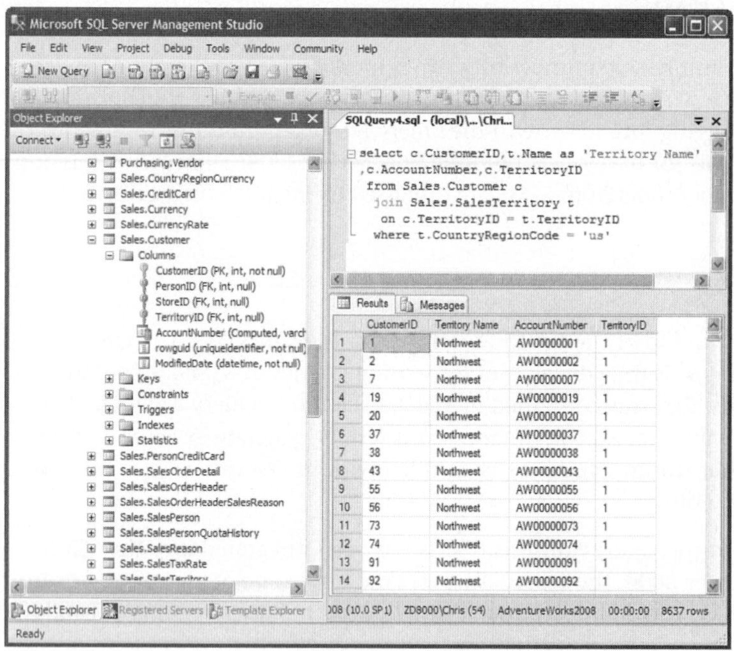

FIGURE 4.18 The query editor window in SSMS.

The basic editing environment within the Query Editor is similar to Query Analyzer. The top portion of the query editor window contains the query. The bottom portion contains the results of an executed query. The results can be displayed as text, displayed in a grid format, or output as XML. However, in the Query Editor, windows are by default managed differently than with Query Analyzer. Multiple query editor windows are displayed in a tabbed format; in comparison, Query Analyzer displayed a separate window for each query.

TIP

The tabbed document display has some advantages, but you can set an option in SSMS that causes the Query Editor to behave much like the Query Analyzer. To do this, you select Tools, Options to launch the Options dialog. The default page has a section named Environmental Layout. If you choose the MDI Environment option, you set SSMS in MDI mode instead of the tabbed layout.

IntelliSense

IntelliSense has finally made it to the SQL Server Query Editor. This much-anticipated tool was slated for SQL Server 2005, but it was pulled before making it to the marketplace. Fortunately, it made it to SQL Server 2008, and it was worth the wait. This is especially true for those developers who have been working with Visual Studio or other Microsoft development tools that have this feature.

IntelliSense is a handy tool that helps you complete queries as you are typing them in the query editor window. Start typing and you will see. For example, type `SELECT * FROM A` in the query editor window, and a drop-down appears in the query editor window after you start typing the first letter after the `FROM` clause. The drop-down, in this case, contains the databases and tables from which you can select data. If you type in a stored procedure name to execute, a drop-down shows you the parameters that the stored procedure accepts. Type `SYS.` in the query editor window, and you see a drop-down of all the objects available in the *SYS* schema. This includes catalog views and the related columns that these views contain. If you type in a query that is incorrect, IntelliSense places a red squiggly line under the part of the query that is syntactically incorrect.

The value of this tool will become more apparent as you use it. It can be confusing at times, but it will ultimately speed up your development time. It can also reduce the number of times you need to go to Books Online or some other help source and will make your development life easier.

NOTE

IntelliSense works only with SQL Server 2008 databases. If you start typing a query against a database from a prior version, the handy IntelliSense drop-downs do not appear.

Query Editor Types

The Query Editor in SQL Server 2008 enables you to develop different types of queries. You are not limited to database queries based on SQL. You can use the Query Editor to develop all types of SQL Server Scripts, including those for SQL Server Analysis Services (SSAS) and SQL Server Mobile Edition. The SSAS queries come in three different flavors: multidimensional expressions (MDX), data mining expressions (DMX), and XML for analysis (XMLA). Only one selection exists for creating SQL Server Mobile Edition scripts.

You see these new query options when you create a new query. When you select New from the SSMS menu, you can choose what type of query to create. You use the Database Engine Query choice to create a T-SQL query against the Database Engine. The other new query options correspond to SSAS and SQL Server Mobile Edition. The SSMS toolbar has icons that correspond to each type of query that can be created.

Each query type has a code pane that works much the same way across all the different types of queries. The code pane, which is the topmost window, color-codes the syntax that is entered, and it has sophisticated search capabilities and other advanced editing features that make it easy to use.

Disconnected Editing

SQL Server 2008 is able to use the code editor without a database connection. When creating a new query, you can choose to connect to a database or select Cancel to leave the code pane disconnected. To connect to the database later, you can right-click in the code pane window and select the Connect option. You can also disconnect the Query Editor at any time or choose the Change Connection option to disconnect and connect to another database all at once.

Along with disconnected editing are some changes to the Windows behavior that are worth noting. The biggest changes relate to the behavior of query windows currently open at the time a file is opened for editing. With SQL Server 2000 Query Analyzer, the currently selected window would be populated with the contents of the file you were opening. Prior to this replacement, a prompt would be displayed asking whether you wanted to save your results. If the query window was empty, the contents would be replaced without the prompt for saving.

With SQL Server 2008, a new query window is opened every time a new file is opened. The new window approach is faster but can lead to many more open windows in the document window. You need to be careful about the number of windows/connections you have open. Also, you need to be aware that the tabbed display shows only a limited number of windows. Additional connections can exist even if their tabs are not in the active portion of the document window.

Editing `sqlcmd` Scripts in SSMS

`sqlcmd` is a command-line utility introduced in SQL Server 2008. You can use it for ad hoc interactive execution of T-SQL statements and scripts. It is basically a replacement for the `ISQL` and `OSQL` commands used in versions prior to SQL Server 2005. (`OSQL` still works with SQL Server 2008, but `ISQL` has been discontinued.)

You can write, edit, and execute `sqlcmd` scripts within the Query Editor environment. The Query Editor in SSMS treats `sqlcmd` scripts in much the same way as other scripts. The script is color-coded and can be parsed or executed. This is possible only if you place the Query Editor in SQLCMD mode, which you do by selecting Query, SQLCMD Mode or selecting the SQLCMD mode icon from the SSMS toolbar.

Figure 4.19 shows a sample `sqlcmd` script in SSMS that can be used to back up a database. This example illustrates the power and diversity of a `sqlcmd` script that utilizes both T-SQL and `sqlcmd` statements. It uses environment variables set within the script. The script variables `DBNAME` and `BACKUPPATH` are defined at the top of the script with the `SETVAR` command. The `BACKUP` statement at the bottom of the script references these variables, using the convention `$(`*`variablename`*`)`, which substitutes the value in the command.

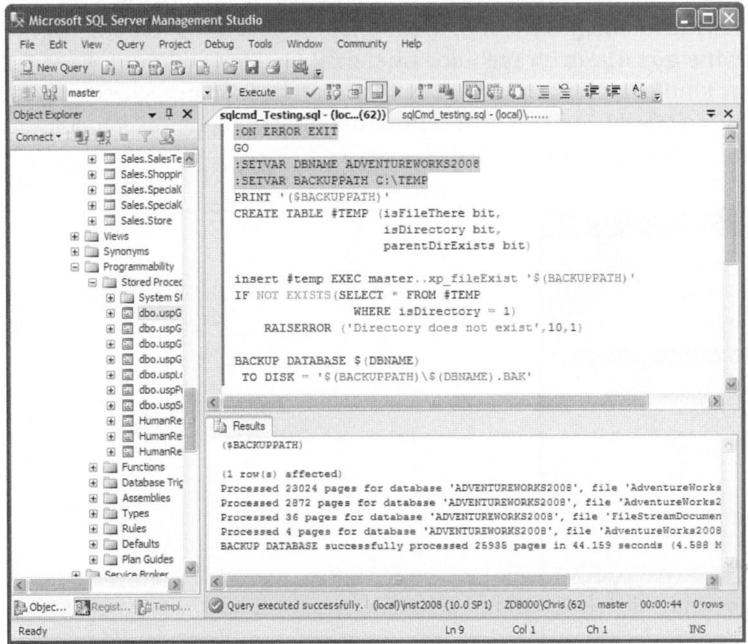

FIGURE 4.19 Editing a **`sqlcmd`** script in SSMS.

`sqlcmd` scripts that are edited in SSMS can also be executed within SSMS. The results are displayed in the results window of the query editor window, just like any other script. After you test a script, you can execute it by using the `sqlcmd` command-line utility. The `sqlcmd` command-line utility is a powerful tool that can help automate script execution. For more information on using `sqlcmd` in SSMS, refer to the Books Online topic "Editing SQLCMD Scripts with Query Editor." The `sqlcmd` command-line utility is discussed in more detail in Chapter 5, "SQL Server Command-Line Utilities."

Regular Expressions and Wildcards in SSMS

SSMS has a robust search facility that includes the use of regular expressions. Regular expressions provide a flexible notation for finding and replacing text, based on patterns within the text. Regular expressions are found in other programming languages and applications, including the Microsoft .NET Framework. The regular expressions in SSMS work in much the same way as these other languages, but there are some differences in the notation.

The option to use regular expressions is available whenever you are doing a find or replace within an SSMS script. You can use the find and replace option in the code pane or results window. You can use the Find and Replace option from the Edit menu or press either the Ctrl+F or Ctrl+H shortcut keys to launch the Find and Replace dialog box. Figure 4.20 shows an example of the Find and Replace dialog that utilizes a regular expression. This example is searching for the text *Customer*, preceded by the @ character and not followed by the *Id* characters. This kind of search could be useful for searching a large stored procedure where you want to find the customer references but don't want to see the variables that contain *customer* in the first part of the variable name.

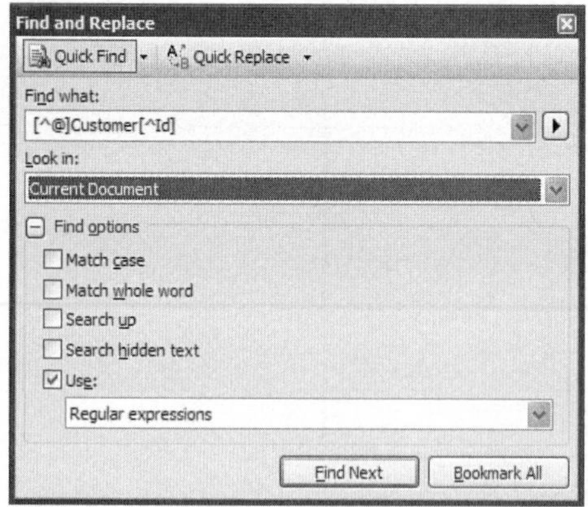

FIGURE 4.20 A find and replace with regular expressions.

You use regular expressions only when the Use check box in the Find and Replace dialog is selected. When this option is selected, you can choose either Regular Expressions or Wildcards. Wildcard searches work much the same way in SSMS as they do in file searches. For example, if you want to find any references to the word *zip*, you could enter `*zip*` in the Find What text box. The wildcard options are limited but very effective for simple searches.

Regular expressions have a much more extensive number of available search options. When you choose the option to use regular expressions, the arrow button is enabled to the right of the text box where you enter your search text. If you click this button, you are given an abbreviated list of regular expression characters that you can use in your searches. A brief description of what each character represents in the search is listed next to the character. For a complete list of characters, you can choose the Complete Character List option at the bottom of the list. This option brings you to the Books

Online topic "How to: Search with Regular Expressions," which gives a comprehensive review of all the characters.

Enhanced Performance Output

The Query Editor in SSMS has an extensive set of options available for capturing and distributing performance-related data. It contains many of the familiar performance features that you may have grown accustomed to in SQL Server 2000 Query Analyzer—plus more. If you're familiar with the SQL Server 2005 performance output, you will find that that the SQL Server 2008 performance output has changed very little. The Execution Plan tab that is displayed in the results window and the Results and Messages tab are still there in SQL Server 2008. The Execution Plan tab can be populated with two different types of plans: estimated plans and actual plans. The actual execution plan shows the plan that was used in generating the actual query results. The actual plan is generated along with the results when the Include Actual Execution Plan option is selected. This option can be selected from the SSMS toolbar or from the Query menu. Figure 4.21 shows an example of an actual execution plan generated for a query against the `AdventureWorks2008` database.

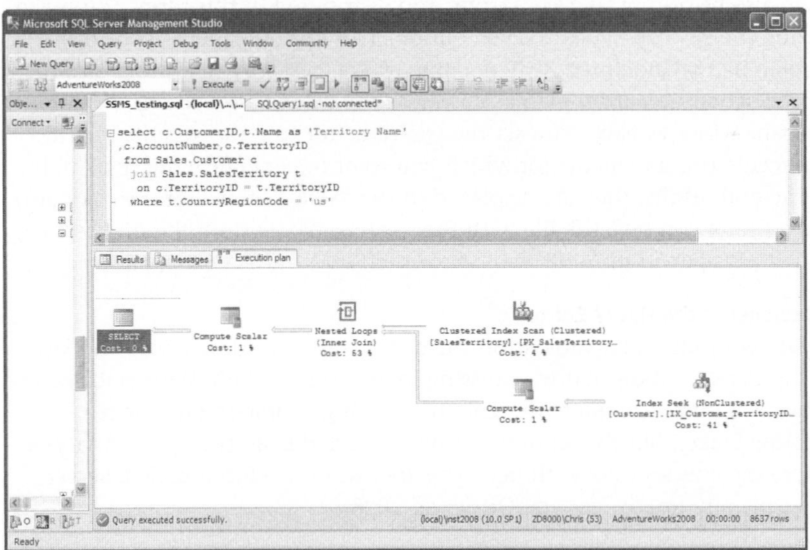

FIGURE 4.21 Displaying an actual execution plan in Query Editor.

The familiar treelike structure that was also present in SQL Server 2000 is still used in SQL Server 2005 and SQL Server 2008. The ToolTips displayed when you mouse over a node in the execution plan include additional information; you can see that information in a more static form in the Properties window if you right-click the node and select Properties. The display is generally easy to read and should be read from right to left.

NOTE

The Manage Indexes and Manage Statistics options available in the SQL Server 2000 Query Analyzer are not present in the Query Editor in SQL Server 2008. Those options in Query Analyzer were accessible by right-clicking a node in the query plan. You can use the Database Engine Tuning Advisor (DTA) in SQL Server 2008 to analyze the Query Editor statements or open the Table Designer to manage the indexes on a specific table.

Query plans generated in the Query Editor are easy to distribute in SQL Server 2008. You have several options for capturing query plan output so that you can save it or send it to someone else for analysis. If you right-click an empty section of the Execution Plan window, you can select the Save Execution Plan As option, which allows you to save the execution plan to a file. By default, the file has the extension `.sqlplan`. This file can be opened using SSMS on another machine to display the graphical output.

The query plan can also be output in XML format and distributed in this form. You make this happen by using the `SET SHOWPLAN_XML ON` option. This option generates the estimated execution plan in a well-defined XML document. The best way to do this is to turn off the display of the actual execution plan and execute the `SET SHOWPLAN_XML ON` statement in the code pane window. Next, you set the Query Editor to return results in grid format and then execute the statements for which you want to generate a query plan. If you double-click the grid results, they are displayed in the SSMS XML editor. You can also save the results to a file. If you save the file with the `.sqlplan` extension, the file displays the graphical plan when opened in SSMS.

Using the Query Designer in the Query Editor

A graphical query design tool is accessible from the query editor window where you write your queries. This is a great option that was missing in SQL Server 2000. With SQL Server 2000, you could access a graphical query designer by opening a table in Enterprise Manager and selecting Query, but this option was disconnected from the Query Analyzer environment, where the queries were authored. This tool was introduced in SQL Server 2005 and remains generally unchanged in SQL Server 2008.

With SQL Server 2008, you can right-click in the query editor window and choose Design Query in Editor. A dialog box appears, allowing you to add tables to the graphical query designer surface. The selected tables are shown in a window that allows you to select the columns you want to retrieve. Selected columns appear in a `SELECT` statement displayed at the bottom of the Query Designer window. Figure 4.22 shows an example of the Query Designer window that contains two tables from the `AdventureWorks2008` database. The two tables selected in this figure are related, as indicated by the line between them.

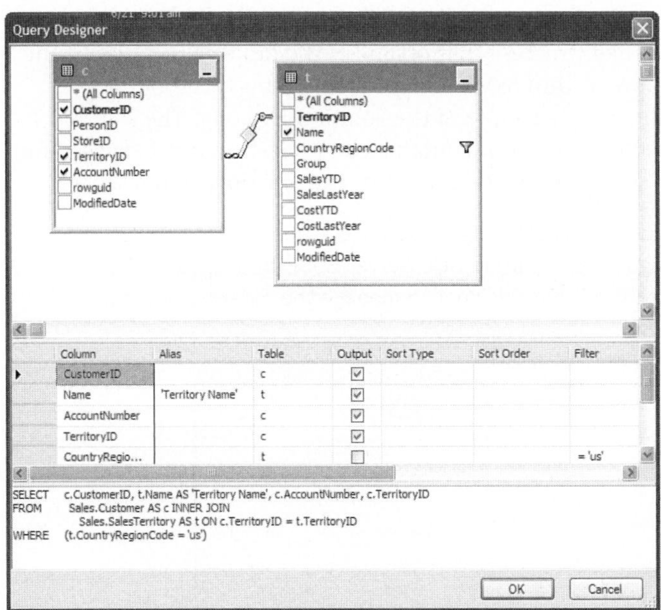

FIGURE 4.22 Designing queries in the Query Editor.

The T-SQL statements are generated automatically as you select various options on the Query Designer screen. If you select Sort Type, an `ORDER BY` clause is added. If you choose an alias for a column, it is reflected in the T-SQL. If tables are related, the appropriate joins are generated.

When you click OK on the Query Designer window, the related T-SQL is automatically placed in the query editor window. You can edit the T-SQL as needed or use it as is. You can imagine the time savings you can achieve by using this tool.

TIP

The Query Designer has a very impressive feature that allows you to view a T-SQL query visually. If you copy a valid T-SQL statement, open the Query Designer, and paste the T-SQL into the SQL pane at the bottom of the Query Designer, it tries to resolve the T-SQL into a graphical display. The tables in the `FROM` clause are shown in the designer panel, and information related to the selected columns is listed as well. The Query Designer cannot resolve all T-SQL statements and may fail to generate a visual display for some complex T-SQL.

Managing Projects in SSMS

Project management capabilities like those available in Visual Studio are available in SSMS. Queries, connections, and other files that are related can be grouped into projects. A project or set of projects is further organized or grouped as a solution. This type of organization is the same as in the Visual Studio environment.

Projects and solutions are maintained and displayed with the Solution Explorer. The Solution Explorer contains a tree-like structure that organizes the projects and files in the solution. It is a component window within SSMS that you launch by selecting View, Solution Explorer. Figure 4.23 shows an example of the Solution Explorer. The solution in this example is named `EmployeeUpgrade`, and it contains two projects, named `Phase1` and `Phase2`. Each project contains a set of connections, a set of T-SQL scripts, and a set of miscellaneous files.

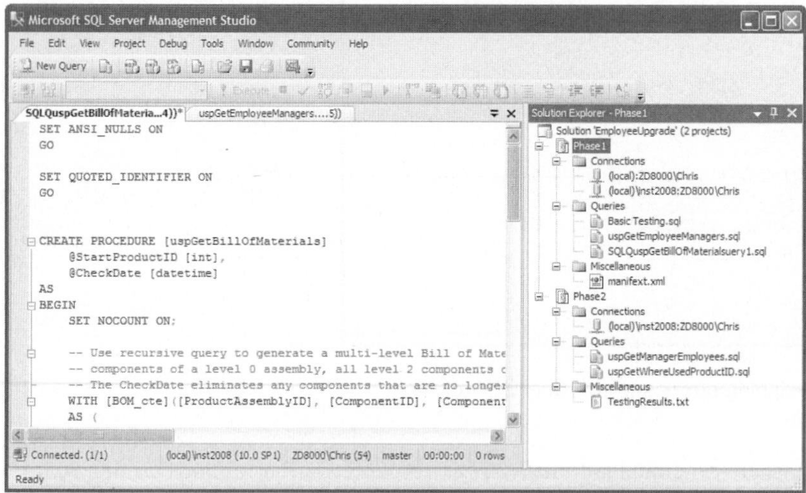

FIGURE 4.23 Solutions and projects listed in the Solution Explorer.

The first thing to do when using the project management capabilities in SSMS is to add a project. To do this, you select File, New, and when the New dialog appears, you select Project to add a new project. When adding the new project, you are given a choice of the type of project, and you must select either SQL Server Scripts, Analysis Services Scripts, or SQL Mobile Scripts. Each one of these project types is geared toward the respective SQL Server technology.

The solution that is related to the project is created at the same time that the project is created. The Solution Name is entered at the bottom of the New Project window and an option to create a separate directory for the solution is provided. There is no option to create the solution separately.

After the project is added, you can add the related connections and files. To add a new connection, you simply right-click the `Connections` node. The `Connections` entries allow you to store SQL Server connection information that relates to the project you are working on. For example, you could have a connection to your test environment and another connection to the production environment that relates to the project. When a connection is included in the project, you can double-click it, and a new query window for that connection is established.

SQL script files are added to a project in a similar fashion to connections: You right-click the `Queries` node and select the New Query option. A new query editor window appears, allowing you to enter the T-SQL commands. Any T-SQL script is viable for this category, including those that relate to database objects such as stored procedures, triggers, and tables.

You can also add existing files to a project. To do this, you right-click the project node, select Add, and then select Existing Item. The file types listed in the drop-down at the bottom of the Add Existing Item dialog include SQL Server files (`*.sql`), SQL deadlock files (`*.xdl`), XML files (`*.xml`), and execution plan files (`*.sqlplan`). SQL Server files are added, by default, to the `Queries` node. All the other file types are added to the `Miscellaneous` node. The connection entries are not stored in a separate file but are contained in the project file itself.

Integrating SSMS with Source Control

SSMS has the capability to integrate database project files into a source control solution. Source control provides a means for protecting and managing files. Source control applications typically contain features that allow you to track changes to files, control and track who uses the files, and provide a means for tagging the files with a version stamp so that the files can be retrieved at a later time, by version.

SSMS can integrate with a number of different source control applications. Visual SourceSafe is Microsoft's basic source control solution, but other source control applications can be used instead. The source control client application must be installed on the machine on which SSMS is running. When the installation is complete, you can set the source control application that SSMS will use within SSMS. To do this, you select Tools, Options and navigate to the `Source Control` node. The available source control clients are listed in the Current Source Control Plug-in drop-down.

The link between SSMS and the source control application is the database solution. After a solution is created, it can be added to the source control. To add a solution to a source control application, you open the Solution Explorer and right-click the solution or any of the projects in the solution. You then see the Add Solution to Source Control option. You must then log in to the source control application and select a source control project to add the solution to.

When the solution is added to a source control application, all the related projects and project files are added as well. The projects and files in the source control application have additional options available in the Solution Explorer. Figure 4.24 shows a sample solution added to a source control application. A subset of the source control options available when you right-click project files are shown in this figure as well.

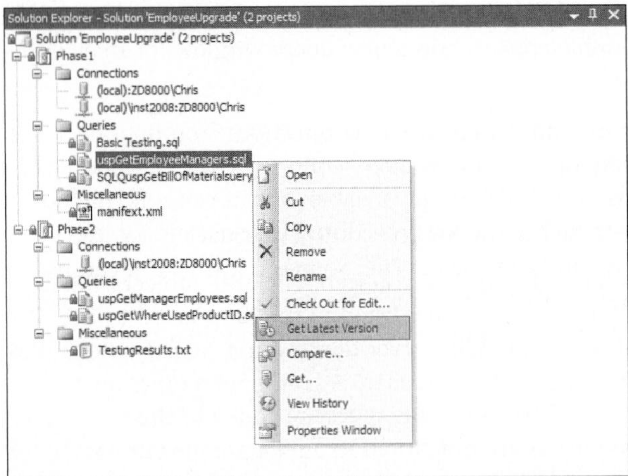

FIGURE 4.24 Source control options in the Solution Explorer.

The options related to source control are listed toward the bottom of the options list. The options that are available depend on the status of the selected file. For example, if a file has been checked out, additional options are displayed that relate to checking the file back in. Following are some of the common source control options:

- **Check Out for Edit**—This option allows you to get a copy of the file from the source control application so that you can modify the file. When you check out the file, the source control provider can keep track of the user who has checked out the file, and it can also prevent other users from checking out the file.
- **Check In**—This option copies the locally modified file into the source control solution. The file must first be checked out for editing before you can use the Check In option. A new version for the file is established, and any prior versions of the file are retained as well.
- **Get Latest Version**—This option gets a read-only copy of the latest version of the project file from the source control application. The file is not checked out with this option.
- **Compare**—This option enables you to compare versions of source control files. The default comparison that is shown is between the file in the source control application and the local file on your machine.
- **Get**—This option is similar to the Get Latest Version option, but it retrieves a read-only copy of the file. With this option, a dialog box appears, allowing you to select the file(s) that you want to retrieve.
- **View History**—This option lists all versions of the files checked into the source control application. The History dialog box has many options that you can use with the different versions of the file. You can view differences between versions of the

files, view the contents of a specific version, generate reports, or get an older version of the file.

- **Undo Checkout**—This option changes the checkout status in the source control application and releases the file to other source control users. Any changes made to the local copy of the file are not added to the source control version.

Other source control options are available via the Source Control menu in SSMS. You select an item in the Solution Explorer and then select File, Source Control. You can use this menu to check the status of a file by using the SourceSafe Properties option, set source control properties, launch the source control application, and perform other source control operations.

Using SSMS Templates

Templates provide a framework for the creation of database objects in SSMS. They are essentially boilerplate files that help generate scripts for common database objects. They can speed up the development of these scripts and help enforce consistency in the generation of the underlying database objects.

The Template Explorer is a component window available in SSMS and replaces the Template tab available in the SQL Server 2000 Query Analyzer. Figure 4.25 shows the Template Explorer and the available SQL Server template folders. Separate templates also exist for Analysis Services and SQL Server Mobile Edition. You can view them by selecting the related icon at the top of the Template Explorer.

You access the available templates by expanding the template folder in the Template Explorer tree. For example, if you expand the `Index` folder, you see six different types of index templates. If you double-click one of the templates, a new query editor window appears, populated with the template script. Figure 4.26 shows the template script displayed when you open the Create Index Basic template.

The template script contains template parameters that have the following format within the script:

```
<parameter_name, data_type, value>
```

You can manually replace these parameters in the script, or you can use the Specify Values for Template Parameters option from the Query menu to globally replace the parameters in the script with the desired values. Selecting Query, Specify Values for Template Parameters launches the Specify Values for Template Parameters dialog box, which enables you to enter the parameter values (see Figure 4.27).

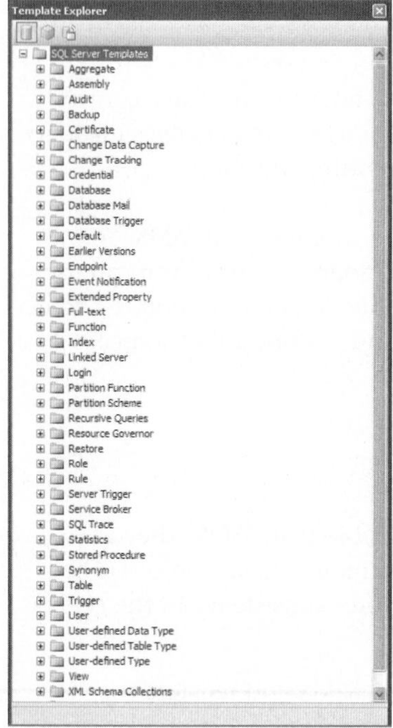

FIGURE 4.25 The SSMS Template Explorer.

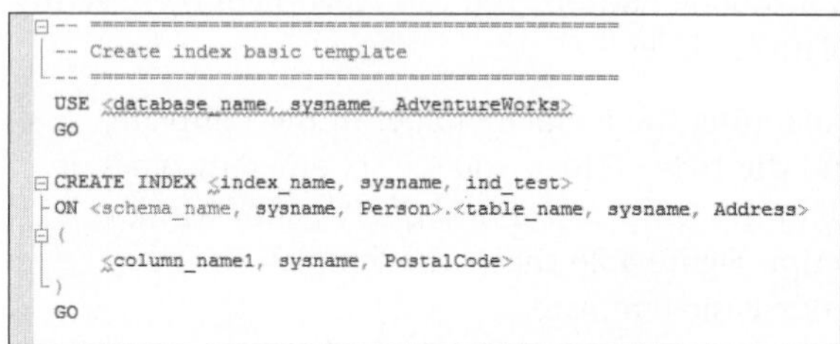

FIGURE 4.26 The template script for creating a basic index.

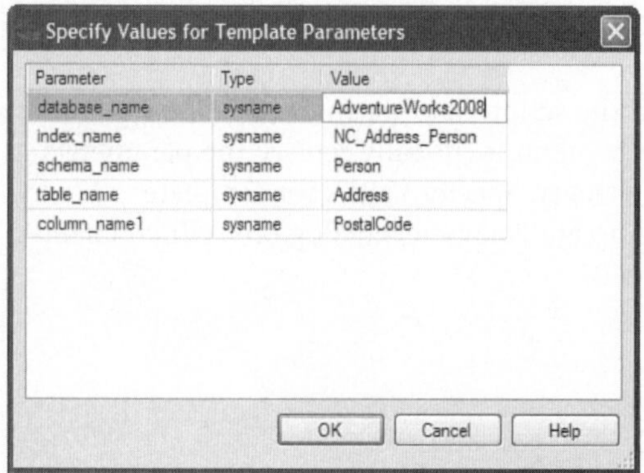

FIGURE 4.27 The Specify Values for Template Parameters dialog box.

TIP

When you use the Specify Values for Template Parameters option, some parameters may be missed if the parameter text has been altered. For example, if you add a carriage return after *parameter_name*, the Parameters dialog box does not list that parameter. It is best to leave the template script unchanged before you specify values for the parameters. You should make changes to the script after the values have been specified.

After you enter the parameter values and click OK, the values are reflected in the script. For example, the values shown in Figure 4.27 for the basic index template result in the following script:


```
-- =============================================
-- Create index basic template
-- =============================================
USE AdventureWorks2008
GO
CREATE INDEX NC_Address_Person
ON Person.Address
(
    PostalCode
)
GO
```

You also have the option of creating your own custom templates. These templates can contain parameters just like those available with the default templates. You can also create your own template folder that will be displayed in the Template Explorer tree. To create a new template folder, you right-click the `SQL Server Templates` node in the Template Explorer tree and select New, Folder. A new folder appears in the tree, and you can specify a new folder name. Figure 4.28 shows the Template Explorer with a set of custom templates found under the `_mytemplates` folder. The code pane in this figure shows the contents of a new custom template named `sys.objectSelectWithParameters`. This custom template contains two parameter declarations: `object_type` and `modify_date`. When you select the Specify Values for Template Parameters options for this custom template, you have the opportunity to change the values, just as you can with the default templates.

NOTE

When you double-click a template in the Template Explorer tree, you create a script based on the template. Changes made to the script do not affect the template; they affect only the script generated from the template. To change the actual template, you need to right-click the template and select Edit. After you complete your changes, you need to make sure to save the template.

Also, you should keep in mind that there is no requirement to have parameters in your templates. Templates are handy tools for accessing any code snippet you might use. After the code snippet is added as a template, you can open a new query editor window based on the template or simply drag and drop the template from the Template Explorer to an existing query editor window, and the code for the template is pasted into the window.

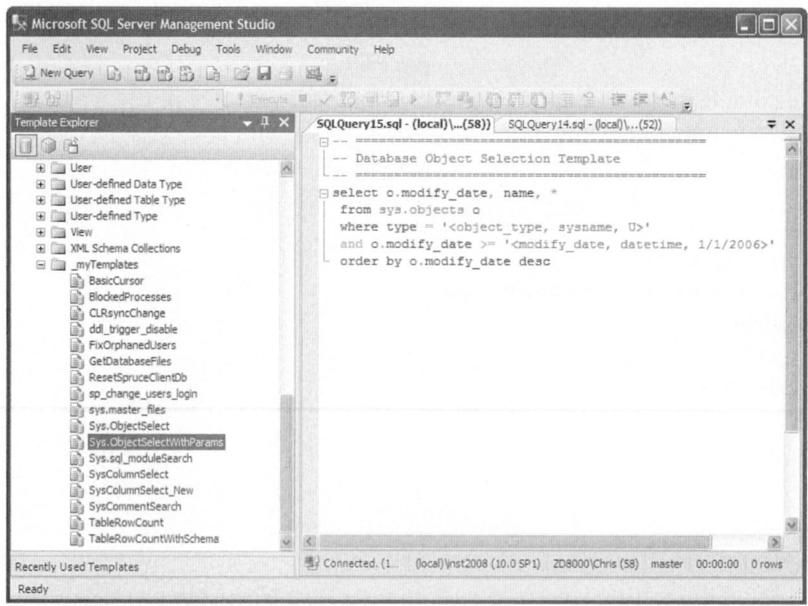

FIGURE 4.28 A custom template example.

T-SQL Debugging

Finally, you are able to debug T-SQL from within the SQL Server development environment. Yes, you could do this kind of thing using Visual Studio, but database developers should be able to debug in the environment where they generally develop their SQL statements—within SSMS. SQL Server 2008 provides this capability, and it works well.

The trickiest part of debugging may be starting the debugger. It is not all that difficult but may be less than obvious for some. For example, let's say you want to debug a stored procedure. To do this, you right-click on the stored procedure in the Object Explorer and select Script Stored Procedure As, Execute To, New Query Editor Window, and a script for executing the procedure is generated. If the stored procedure has parameters, you add the SQL to assign a value to those parameters to the script. Now you are ready to debug this script and the related stored procedure.

To initiate debugging, you click on the green arrow on the SQL Server menu bar. When you start debugging, several new debugging windows are added to the SSMS display, and the query editor window shows a yellow arrow in the left margin next to the line in the script that is about to be run. You can now use the debug toolbar at the top of the SSMS screen to step through your code. If you click the Step Into button, the current statement executes, and the script progresses to the next available statement. Figure 4.29 shows an example of the T-SQL Debugging Environment while debugging is in progress. The debugging environment enables you to view values assigned to variables, review the call stack, set breakpoints, and perform debugging much like you would do in development environments such as Visual Studio.

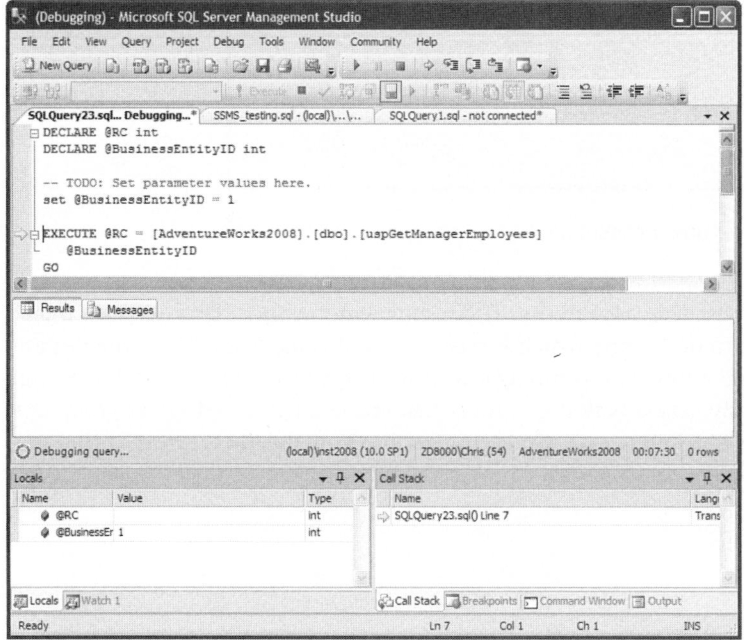

FIGURE 4.29 The T-SQL Debugging Environment.

Multiserver Queries

Another slick new option available with SQL Server 2008 is the capability to execute a script on multiple servers at once. Multiserver queries allow the contents of a single query editor window to be run against all the servers defined in a given registered server group. After the group is created and servers are registered in the group, you can right-click on the group and select the New Query option to create a query window that can be run against all the servers in the group. Click on the Execute button, and the query is run against all the servers. Figure 4.30 shows a server group named `MyTestGroup` containing three servers registered in that group, a sample query to run against these servers, and a single result window that shows the results of the query for all servers in the group.

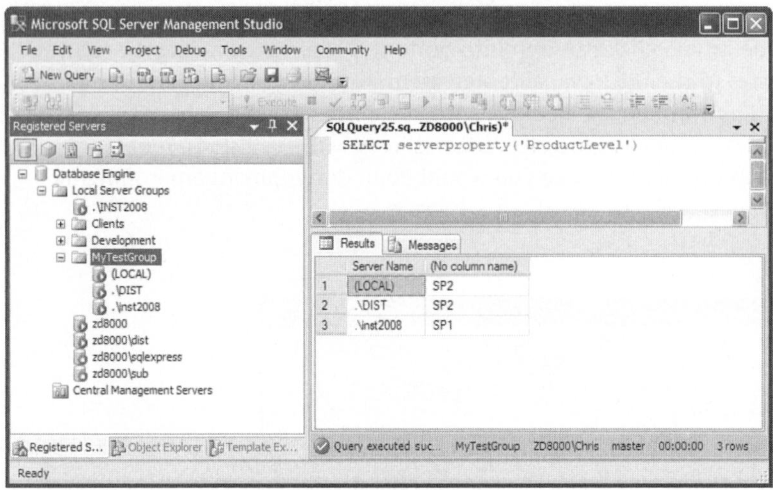

FIGURE 4.30 Multiserver query execution.

Multiserver queries are relatively easy to use. The results window includes a Server Name column that allows you to determine which server the result came from. These queries are backward compatible and allow you to run against prior versions of SQL Server, including SQL Server 2005. The only caveat is that you must first create a registered server group and the related registered servers before you run the query, but you already know that this task is also relatively easy.

Summary

The number of tools and features available in SSMS is extensive and can be daunting when you first enter the environment. Remember that you can customize this environment and hide many of the windows that are displayed. You can start with a fairly simple SSMS configuration that includes the Object Explorer and a query editor window. This configuration may allow you to accomplish a majority of your SQL Server tasks. As you become more familiar with the environment, you can introduce new tools and features to help improve your overall productivity.

The discussion of SSMS does not end with this chapter. Further details related to SSMS are covered throughout this book. You can use the new features described in this chapter as a starting point and look to other chapters for more detailed discussion of database features accessible through SSMS.

Chapter 5 looks at the SQL Server utilities that can be run from the command prompt. These tools allow you to perform some of the same tasks available in SSMS. The capability to launch these utilities from the command line can be useful when you're automating tasks or accessing SQL Server when a GUI tool such as SSMS is not available.

CHAPTER 5

SQL Server Command-Line Utilities

IN THIS CHAPTER

- What's New in SQL Server Command-Line Utilities
- The **sqlcmd** Command-Line Utility
- The **dta** Command-Line Utility
- The **tablediff** Command-Line Utility
- The **bcp** Command-Line Utility
- The **sqldiag** Command-Line Utility
- The **sqlservr** Command-Line Utility

This chapter explores various command-line utilities that ship with SQL Server. These utilities give administrators a different way to access the database engine and its related components. In some cases, they provide functionality that is also available with SQL Server's graphical user interface (GUI). Other command-line utilities provide functionality that is available only from the command prompt. For each utility, this chapter provides the command syntax along with the most commonly used options. For the full syntax and options available for the utility, see SQL Server Books Online.

NOTE

This chapter focuses on command-line utilities that are core to SQL Server and the SQL Server database engine. Several other command-line utilities that are used less frequently or geared toward other SQL Server services are not covered in this chapter. These utilities include `dtexec` and `dtutil`, which can be used with SQL Server Integration Services (SSIS). Reporting Services has the `rs`, `rsconfig`, and `rskeymgmt` command-line utilities. Lastly, there are several executable files documented as utilities in Books Online (such as `ssms`, which opens the SQL Server Management Studio) that have limited parameters and are basically used to launch their related applications.

Table 5.1 lists the command-line utilities discussed in this chapter. This table lists the physical location of each utility's executable. The location is needed to execute the utility in most cases, unless the associated path has been added to the `Path` environmental variable.

TABLE 5.1 Command-Line Utility Installation Locations

Utility	Install Location
sqlcmd	x:\Program Files\Microsoft SQL Server\100\Tools\Binn
dta	x:\Program Files\Microsoft SQL Server\100\Tools\Binn
tablediff	x:\Program Files\Microsoft SQL Server\100\COM
bcp	x:\Program Files\Microsoft SQL Server\100\Tools\Binn
sqldiag	x:\Program Files\Microsoft SQL Server\100\Tools\Binn
sqlservr	x:\Program Files\Microsoft SQL Server\MSSQL10.MSSQLSERVER\MSSQL\Binn

NOTE

The `tablediff` utility is installed when SQL Server replication is installed. If you can't find the tablediff.exe in the location specified in Table 5.1, check to see whether the replication was installed.

When you are testing many of these utilities, it is often easiest to set up a batch file (`.BAT`) that contains a command to change the directory to the location shown in Table 5.1. After you make this directory change, you can enter the command-line utility with the relevant parameters. Finally, you should enter a `PAUSE` command so that you can view the output of the utility in the command prompt window. Following is an example you can use to test the `sqlcmd` utility (which is discussed in more detail later in this chapter):

```
CD "C:\Program Files\Microsoft SQL Server\100\Tools\Binn"
SQLCMD -S(local) -E -Q "select @@servername"
pause
```

After you save the commands in a file with a `.BAT` extension, you can simply double-click the file to execute it. This approach is much easier than retyping the commands many times during the testing process.

What's New in SQL Server Command-Line Utilities

The SQL Server command-line utilities available in SQL Server 2008 are basically the same as those offered with SQL Server 2005. This has some key benefits for those who are familiar with the 2005 utilities. Very little has changed in the syntax, and batch files or scripts you have used with these utilities in the past should continue to work unchanged.

A few command-line utilities have been added in SQL Server 2008, however, and some have been removed. The sqlps utility is new to SQL Server 2008. This utility can be used to run PowerShell commands and scripts. The sqlps utility and the PowerShell Windows–based command-line management tool are discussed in detail in Chapter 17, "Administering SQL Server 2008 with PowerShell."

Utilities removed from SQL Server 2008 include sac. The sac utility can be used in SQL Server 2005 to import or export settings available in the graphical Surface Area Configuration (SAC) tool. Both the sac command-line utility and SAC graphical tool have been removed. Similar functionality is now available via policy-based management and the Configuration Manager tool.

The sqlcmd Command-Line Utility

The sqlcmd command-line utility is the next generation of the isql and osql utilities that you may have used in prior versions of SQL Server. It provides the same type of functionality as isql and osql, including the capability to connect to SQL Server from the command prompt and execute T-SQL commands. The T-SQL commands can be stored in a script file, entered interactively, or specified as command-line arguments to sqlcmd.

5

NOTE

The isql and osql command-line utilities are not covered in this chapter. The isql utility was discontinued in SQL Server 2005 and is not supported in SQL Server 2008. The osql utility is still supported but will be removed in a future version of SQL Server. Make sure to use sqlcmd in place of osql to avoid unnecessary reworking in the future.

The syntax for sqlcmd follows:

```
sqlcmd
[{ { -U login_id [ -P password ] } ¦ -E trusted connection }]
[ -z new password ] [ -Z new password and exit]
[ -S server_name [ \ instance_name ] ] [ -H wksta_name ] [ -d db_name ]
[ -l login time_out ] [ -A dedicated admin connection ]
[ -i input_file ] [ -o output_file ]
[ -f < codepage > | i: < codepage > [ < , o: < codepage > ] ]
[ -u unicode output ] [ -r [ 0 | 1 ] msgs to stderr ]
[ -R use client regional settings ]
[ -q "cmdline query" ] [ -Q "cmdline query" and exit ]
[ -e echo input ] [ -t query time_out ]
[ -I enable Quoted Identifiers ]
[ -v var = "value"...] [ -x disable variable substitution ]
[ -h headers ][ -s col_separator ] [ -w column_width ]
[ -W remove trailing spaces ]
```

```
[ -k [ 1 | 2 ] remove[replace] control characters ]
[ -y display_width ] [-Y display_width ]
[ -b on error batch abort ] [ -V severitylevel ] [ -m error_level ]
[ -a packet_size ][ -c cmd_end ]
[ -L [ c ] list servers[clean output] ]
[ -p [ 1 ] print statistics[colon format]]
[ -X [ 1 ] ] disable commands, startup script, environment variables [and exit]
[ -? show syntax summary ]
```

The number of options available for `sqlcmd` is extensive, but many of the options are not necessary for basic operations. To demonstrate the usefulness of this tool, we look at several different examples of the `sqlcmd` utility, from fairly simple (using few options) to more extensive.

Executing the `sqlcmd` Utility

Before we get into the examples, it is important to remember that `sqlcmd` can be run in several different ways. It can be run interactively from the command prompt, from a batch file, or from a Query Editor window in SSMS. When run interactively, the `sqlcmd` program name is entered at the command prompt with the required options to connect to the database server. When the connection is established, a numbered row is made available to enter the T-SQL commands. Multiple rows of T-SQL can be entered in a batch; they are executed only after the `GO` command has been entered. Figure 5.1 shows an example with two simple `SELECT` statements that were executed interactively with `sqlcmd`. The connection in this example was established by typing `sqlcmd` at the command prompt to establish a trusted connection to the default instance of SQL Server running on the machine on which the command prompt window is opened.

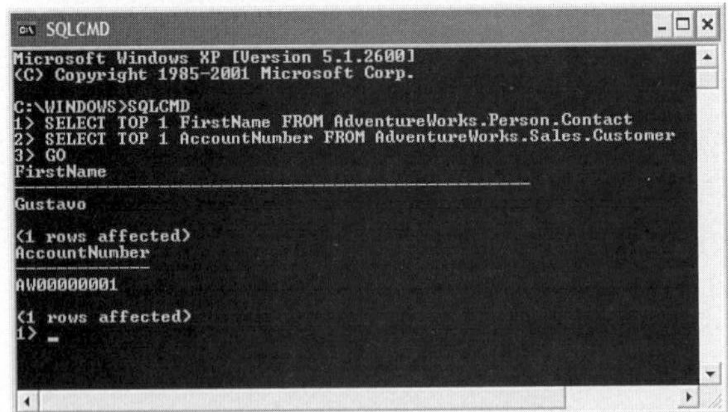

FIGURE 5.1 Executing **sqlcmd** interactively.

The capability to edit and execute `sqlcmd` scripts was added to SSMS with SQL Server 2005. A `sqlcmd` script can be opened or created in a Query Editor window within SSMS. To edit these scripts, you must place the editor in SQLCMD Mode. You do so by selecting Query, SQLCMD Mode or by clicking the related toolbar button. When the editor is put in SQLCMD Mode, it provides color coding and the capability to parse and execute the commands within the script. Figure 5.2 shows a sample `sqlcmd` script opened in SSMS in a Query Editor window set to SQLCMD Mode. The shaded lines are `sqlcmd` commands.

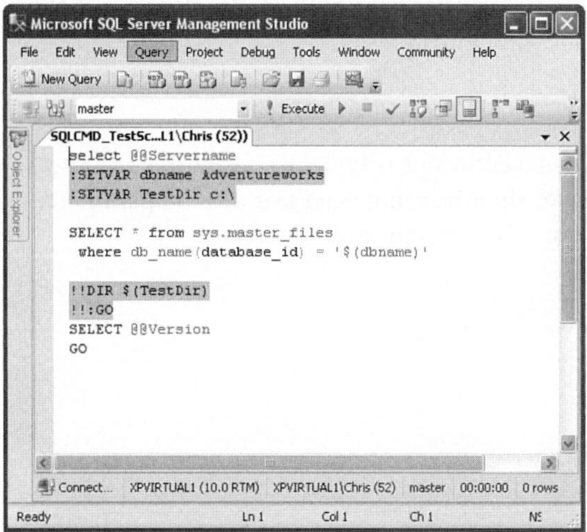

FIGURE 5.2 Executing and editing **sqlcmd** scripts in SSMS.

The most common means for executing `sqlcmd` utility is via a batch file. This method can provide a great deal of automation because it allows you to execute a script or many scripts by launching a single file. The examples shown in this section are geared toward the execution of `sqlcmd` in this manner. The following simple example illustrates the execution of `sqlcmd`, using a trusted connection to connect to the local database, and the execution of a simple query that is set using the `-Q` option:

```
sqlcmd -S (local) -E -Q"select getdate()"
```

You can expand this example by adding an output file to store the results of the query and add the `-e` option, which echoes the query that was run in the output results:

```
sqlcmd -S (local) -E -Q"select getdate()" -o c:\TestOutput.txt -e
```

The contents of the `c:\TestOutput.txt` file should look similar to this:

```
select getdate()
-----------
2008-09-10 20:29:05.645
 (1 rows affected)
```

Using a trusted connection is not the only way to use `sqlcmd` to connect to a SQL Server instance. You can use the `-U` and `-P` command-line options to specify the SQL Server user and password. `sqlcmd` also provides an option to specify the password in an environmental variable named `sqlcmdPASSWORD`, which can be assigned prior to the `sqlcmd` execution and eliminates the need to hard-code the password in a batch file.

sqlcmd also provides a means for establishing a dedicated administrator connection (DAC) to the server. The DAC is typically used for troubleshooting on a server that is having problems. It allows an administrator to get onto the server when others may not be able to. If the DAC is enabled on the server, a connection can be established with the -A option and a query can be run, as shown in the following example:

```
sqlcmd -S (local) -A -Q"select getdate()"
```

If you need to manage more complex T-SQL execution, it is typically easier to store the T-SQL in a separate input file. The input file can then be referenced as a sqlcmd parameter. For example, say that you have the following T-SQL stored in a file named C:\TestsqlcmdInput.sql:

```
BACKUP DATABASE Master
 TO DISK = 'c:\master.bak'

BACKUP DATABASE Model
 TO DISK = 'c:\model.bak'

BACKUP DATABASE MSDB
 TO DISK = 'c:\msdb.bak'
```

The sqlcmd execution, which accepts the C:\TestsqlcmdInput.sql file as input and executes the commands within the file, looks like this:

```
sqlcmd -S (local) -E -i"C:\TestsqlcmdInput.sql" -o c:\TestOutput.txt –e
```

The execution of the preceding example backs up three of the system databases and writes the results to the output file specified.

Using Scripting Variables with sqlcmd

sqlcmd provides a means for utilizing variables within sqlcmd input files or scripts. These scripting variables can be assigned as sqlcmd parameters or set within the sqlcmd script. To illustrate the use of scripting variables, let's change our previous backup example so that the database that will be backed up is a variable. A new input file named c:\BackupDatabase.sql should be created, and it should contain the following command:

```
BACKUP DATABASE $(DatabaseToBackup)
 TO DISK = 'c:\$(DatabaseToBackup).bak'
```

The variable in the preceding example is named DatabaseToBackup. Scripting variables are referenced using the $( ) designators. These variables are resolved at the time of execution, and a simple replacement is performed. This allows variables to be specified within quotation marks, if necessary. The -v option is used to assign a value to a variable at the command prompt, as shown in the following example, which backs up the model database:

```
sqlcmd -S (local) -E -i"C:\BackupDatabase.sql" -v DatabaseToBackup = model
```

If multiple variables exist in the script, they can all be assigned after the -v parameter. These variables should not be separated by a delimiter, such as a comma or semicolon. Scripting variables can also be assigned within the script, using the :SETVAR command. The input file from the previous backup would be modified as follows to assign the DatabaseToBackup variable within the script:

```
:SETVAR DatabaseToBackup Model
BACKUP DATABASE $(DatabaseToBackup)
 TO DISK = 'c:\$(DatabaseToBackup).bak'
```

Scripts that utilize variables, sqlcmd commands, and the many available options can be very sophisticated and can make your administrative life easier. The examples in this section illustrate some of the basic features of sqlcmd, including some of the features that go beyond what is available with osql.

The dta Command-Line Utility

dta is the command-line version of the graphical Database Engine Tuning Advisor. Both the command-line utility and graphical tool provide performance recommendations based on the workload provided to them. The syntax for dta is as follows:

```
       Dta [ -? ] |
[
     [ -S server_name[ \instance ] ]
     {
         { -U login_id [-P password ] }
         | -E              }
         { -D database_name [ ,...n ] }
             [-d database_name ]
             [ -Tl table_list | -Tf table_list_file ]
         { -if workload_file | -it workload_trace_table_name }
         { -s session_name | -ID session_ID }
             [ -F ]
                     [ -of output_script_file_name ]
                     [ -or output_xml_report_file_name ]
                     [ -ox output_XML_file_name ]
                     [ -rl analysis_report_list [ ,...n ] ]
                     [ -ix input_XML_file_name ]
                     [ -A time_for_tuning_in_minutes ]
                     [ -n number_of_events ]
             [ -m minimum_improvement ]
                     [ -fa physical_design_structures_to_add ]
                     [ -fp partitioning_strategy ]
                     [ -fk keep_existing_option ]
```

```
                [ -fx drop_only_mode ]
        [ -B storage_size ]
        [ -c max_key_columns_in_index ]
        [ -C max_columns_in_index ]
                [ -e | -e tuning_log_name ]
                [ -N online_option]
                [ -q ]
                [ -u ]
            [ -x ]
            [ -a ]
]
```

An extensive number of options is available with this utility, but many of them are not required to do basic analysis. At a minimum, you need to use options that provide connection information to the database, a workload to tune, a tuning session identifier, and the location to store the tuning recommendations. The connection options include `-S` for the server name, `-D` for the database, and either `-E` for a trusted connection or `-U` and `-P`, which can be used to specify the user and password.

The workload to tune is either a workload file or workload table. The `-if` option is used to specify the workload file location, and the `-it` option is used to specify a workload table. The workload file must be a Profiler trace file (`.trc`), SQL script (`.sql`) that contains T-SQL commands, or SQL Server trace file (`.log`). The workload table is a table that contains output from a workload trace. The table is specified in the form *`database_name.owner_name.table_name`*.

The tuning session must be identified with either a session name or session ID. The session name is character based and is specified with the `-s` option. If the session name is not provided, a session ID must be provided instead. The session ID is numeric and is set using the `-ID` option. If the session name is specified instead of the session ID, the `dta` generates an ID anyway.

The last options required for a basic `dta` execution identify the destination to store the `dta` performance recommendations, which can be stored in a script file or in XML. The `-of` option is used to specify the output script filename. XML output is generated when the `-or` or `-ox` option is used. The `-or` option generates a filename if one is not specified, and the `-ox` option requires a filename. The `-F` option can be used with any of the output options to force an overwrite of a file with the same name, if one exists.

To illustrate the use of `dta` with basic options, let's look at an example of tuning a simple `SELECT` statement against the `AdventureWorks2008R2` database. To begin, you use the following T-SQL, which is stored in a workload file named `c:\myScript.sql`:

```
USE AdventureWorks2008R2 ;
GO
select *
 from Production.transactionHistory
 where TransactionDate = '9/1/04'
```

The following example shows the basic dta execution options that can be used to acquire performance recommendations:

```
dta -S xpvirtual1 -E -D AdventureWorks2008R2 -if c:\MyScript.sql
-s MySessionX -of C:\MySessionOutputScript.sql -F
```

NOTE

dta and other utilities executed at the command prompt are executed with all the options on a single line. The preceding example and any others in this chapter that are displayed on more than one line should actually be executed at the command prompt or in a batch file on a single line. They are broken here because the printed page can accommodate only a fixed number of characters.

The preceding example utilizes a trusted connection against the AdventureWorks2008R2 database, a workload file named c:\MyScript.sql, and a session named MySessionX, and it outputs the performance recommendations to a text file named c:\MySessionOutputScript.sql. The -F option is used to force a replacement of the output file if it already exists. The output file contains the following performance recommendations:

```
se [AdventureWorks2008R2]
go

CREATE NONCLUSTERED INDEX [_dta_index_TransactionHistory_5]
 ON [Production].[TransactionHistory]
(
    [TransactionDate] ASC
)
INCLUDE ( [TransactionID],
[ProductID],
[ReferenceOrderID],
[ReferenceOrderLineID],
[TransactionType],
[Quantity],
[ActualCost],
[ModifiedDate])
 WITH (SORT_IN_TEMPDB = OFF, IGNORE_DUP_KEY = OFF,
  DROP_EXISTING = OFF, ONLINE = OFF) ON [PRIMARY]
go
```

In short, the dta output recommends that a new index be created on the TransactionDate column in the TransactionHistory table. This is a viable recommendation, considering that there was no index on the TransactionHistory.TransactionDate column, and it was used as a search argument in the workload file.

Many other options (that go beyond basic execution) can be used to manipulate the way dta makes recommendations. For example, a list can be provided to limit which tables the dta looks at during the tuning process. Options can be set to limit the amount of time that the dta tunes or the number of events. These options go beyond the scope of this chapter, but you can gain further insight into them by looking at the graphical DTA, which contains many of the same types of options. You can refine your tuning options in the DTA, export the options to an XML file, and use the -ix option with the dta utility to import the XML options and run the analysis.

The tablediff Command-Line Utility

The tablediff utility enables you to compare the contents of two tables. It was originally developed for replication scenarios to help troubleshoot nonconvergence, but it is also very useful in other scenarios. When data in two tables should be the same or similar, this tool can help determine whether they are the same, and if they are different, it can identify what data in the tables is different.

The syntax for tablediff is as follows:

```
tablediff
[ -? ] |
{
        -sourceserver source_server_name[\instance_name]
        -sourcedatabase source_database
        -sourcetable source_table_name
    [ -sourceschema source_schema_name ]
    [ -sourcepassword source_password ]
    [ -sourceuser source_login ]
    [ -sourcelocked ]
        -destinationserver destination_server_name[\instance_name]
        -destinationdatabase subscription_database
        -destinationtable destination_table
    [ -destinationschema destination_schema_name ]
    [ -destinationpassword destination_password ]
    [ -destinationuser destination_login ]
    [ -destinationlocked ]
    [ -b large_object_bytes ]
    [ -bf number_of_statements ]
    [ -c ]
    [ -dt ]
    [ -et table_name ]
    [ -f [ file_name ] ]
    [ -o output_file_name ]
    [ -q ]
    [ -rc number_of_retries ]
    [ -ri retry_interval ]
```

```
    [ -strict ]
    [ -t connection_timeouts ]
}
```

The `tablediff` syntax requires source and destination connection information to perform a comparison. This information includes the servers, databases, and tables that will be compared. Connection information must be provided for SQL Server authentication but can be left out if Windows authentication can be used. The source and destination parameters can be for two different servers or the same server, and the `tablediff` utility can be run on a machine that is neither the source nor the destination.

To illustrate the usefulness of this tool, let's look at a sample comparison in the `AdventureWorks2008R2` database. The simplest way to create some data for comparison is to select the contents of one table into another and then update some of the rows in one of the tables. The following `SELECT` statement makes a copy of the `AddressType` table in the `AdventureWorks2008R2` database to the `AddressTypeCopy` table:

```
select *
 into Person.AddressTypeCopy
 from Person.AddressType
```

In addition, the following statement updates two rows in the `AddressTypeCopy` table so that you can use the `tablediff` utility to identify the changes:

```
UPDATE Person.AddressTypeCopy
 SET Name = 'Billing New'
 WHERE AddressTypeId = 1

UPDATE Person.AddressTypeCopy
 SET Name = 'Shipping New',
  ModifiedDate = '20090918'
 WHERE AddressTypeId = 5
```

The `tablediff` utility can be executed with the following parameters to identify the differences in the `AddressType` and `AddressTypeCopy` tables:

```
tablediff -sourceserver "(local)" -sourcedatabase "AdventureWorks2008R2"
-sourceschema "Person"-sourcetable "AddressType"
-destinationserver "(local)" -destinationdatabase "AdventureWorks2008R2"
-destinationschema "Person" -destinationtable "AddressTypeCopy"
-f c:\TableDiff_Output.txt
```

The destination and source parameters are the same as in the previous example, except for the table parameters, which have the source `AddressType` and the destination `AddressTypeCopy`. The execution of the utility with these parameters results in the following output to the command prompt window:

```
User-specified agent parameter values:
-sourceserver (local)
-sourcedatabase AdventureWorks2008R2
-sourceschema Person
-sourcetable AddressType
-destinationserver (local)
-destinationdatabase AdventureWorks2008R2
-destinationschema Person
-destinationtable AddressTypeCopy
-f c:\TableDiff_Output

Table [AdventureWorks2008R2].[Person].[AddressType] on (local)
and Table [AdventureWorks2008R2].[Person].[AddressTypeCopy] on (local)
have 2 differences.
Fix SQL written to c:\TableDiff_Output.sql.
Err      AddressTypeID   Col
Mismatch        1        Name
Mismatch        5        ModifiedDate Name
The requested operation took 0.296875 seconds.
```

The output first displays a summary of the parameters used and then shows the comparison results. In this example, it found the two differences that are due to updates performed on AddressTypeCopy. In addition, the -f parameter used in the example caused the tablediff utility to output a SQL file that can be used to fix the differences in the destination table. The output file from this example looks as follows:

```
— Host: (local)
— Database: [AdventureWorks2008R2]
— Table: [Person].[AddressTypeCopy]
SET IDENTITY_INSERT [Person].[AddressTypeCopy] ON
UPDATE [Person].[AddressTypeCopy]
 SET [Name]='Billing'
 WHERE [AddressTypeID] = 1
UPDATE [Person].[AddressTypeCopy]
 SET [ModifiedDate]='2002-06-01 00:00:00.000',
 [Name]='Shipping' WHERE [AddressTypeID] = 5
SET IDENTITY_INSERT [Person].[AddressTypeCopy] OFF
```

NOTE

The tablediff utility requires the source table to have at least one primary key, identity, or ROWGUID column. This gives the utility a key that it can use to try to match a corresponding row in the destination table. If the -strict option is used, the destination table must also have a primary key, identity, or ROWGUID column.

Keep in mind that several different types of comparisons can be done with the tablediff utility. The -q option causes a quick comparison that compares only record counts and looks for differences in the schema. The -strict option forces the schemas of each table to be the same when the comparison is run. If this option is not used, the utility allows some columns to be of different data types, as long as they meet the mapping requirements for the data type (for example, INT can be compared to BIGINT).

The tablediff utility can be used for many different types of comparisons. How you use this tool depends on several factors, including the amount and type of data you are comparing.

The bcp Command-Line Utility

You use the bcp (bulk copy program) tool to address the bulk movement of data. This utility is bidirectional, allowing for the movement of data into and out of a SQL Server database.

bcp uses the following syntax:

```
bcp {[[database_name.][owner].]{table_name | view_name} | "query"}
    {in | out | queryout | format} data_file
    [-mmax_errors] [-fformat_file] [-x] [-eerr_file]
    [-Ffirst_row] [-Llast_row] [-bbatch_size]
    [-n] [-c] [-N] [-w] [-V (60 | 65 | 70 | 80)] [-6]
    [-q] [-C { ACP | OEM | RAW | code_page } ] [-tfield_term]
    [-rrow_term] [-iinput_file] [-ooutput_file] [-apacket_size]
    [-Sserver_name[\instance_name]] [-Ulogin_id] [-Ppassword]
    [-T] [-v] [-R] [-k] [-E] [-h"hint [,...n]"]
```

Some of the commonly used options—other than the ones used to specify the database, such as user ID, password, and so on—are the -F and -L options. These options allow you to specify the first and last row of data to be loaded from a file, which is especially helpful in large batches. The -t option allows you to specify the field terminator that separates data elements in an ASCII file. The -E option allows you to import data into SQL Server fields that are defined with identity properties.

TIP

The BULK INSERT T-SQL statement and SSIS are good alternatives to bcp. The BULK INSERT statement is limited to loading data into SQL Server, but it is an extremely fast tool for loading data. SSIS is a sophisticated GUI that allows for both data import and data export, and it has capabilities that go well beyond those that were available in SQL Server 2000's Data Transformation Services (DTS).

This section barely scratches the surface when it comes to the capabilities of bcp. For a more detailed look at bcp, refer to the section, "Using bcp" in Chapter 52, "SQL Server Integration Services."

The sqldiag Command-Line Utility

sqldiag is a diagnostic tool that you can use to gather diagnostic information about various SQL Server services. It is intended for use by Microsoft support engineers, but you might also find the information it gathers useful in troubleshooting a problem. sqldiag collects the information into files that are written, by default, to a folder named SQLDIAG, which is created where the file sqldiag.exe is located (for example, C:\Program Files\Microsoft SQL Server\100\Tools\binn\SQLDIAG\). The folder holds files that contain information about the machine on which SQL Server is running in addition to the following types of diagnostic information:

- SQL Server configuration information
- SQL Server blocking output
- SQL Server Profiler traces
- Windows performance logs
- Windows event logs

The syntax for sqldiag changed quite a bit in SQL Server 2005, but very little has changed in SQL Server 2008. Some of the options that were used in versions prior to SQL Server 2005 are not compatible with the current version. The full syntax for sqldiag is as follows:

```
sqldiag
     { [/?] }
     |
     { [/I configuration_file]
       [/O output_folder_path]
       [/P support_folder_path]
       [/N output_folder_management_option]
       [/C file_compression_type]
       [/B [+]start_time]
       [/E [+]stop_time]
       [/A SQLdiag_application_name]
       [/T { tcp [ ,port ] | np | lpc | via } ]
       [/Q] [/G] [/R] [/U] [/L] [/X] }
     |
     { [START | STOP | STOP_ABORT] }
     |
     { [START | STOP | STOP_ABORT] /A SQLdiag_application_name }
```

NOTE

Keep in mind that many of the options for `sqldiag` identify how and when the `sqldiag` utility will be run. The utility can be run as a service, scheduled to start and stop at a specific time of day, and it can be configured to change the way the output is generated. The details about these options are beyond the scope of this chapter but are covered in detail in SQL Server Books Online. This section is intended to give you a taste of the useful information that this utility can capture.

By default, the `sqldiag` utility must be run by a member of the Windows Administrators group, and this user must also be a member of the sysadmin fixed SQL Server role. To get a flavor for the type of information that `sqldiag` outputs, open a command prompt window, change the directory to the location of the `sqldiag.exe` file, and type the following command:

```
sqldiag
```


No parameters are needed to generate the output. The command prompt window scrolls status information across the screen as it collects the diagnostic information. You see the message "SQLDIAG Initialization starting..." followed by messages that indicate what information is being collected. The data collection includes a myriad of system information from `MSINFO32`, default traces, and SQLDumper log files. When you are ready to stop the collection, you can press Ctrl+C.

If you navigate to the `sqldiag` output folder, you find the files created during the collection process. In this output folder, you should find a file with `MSINFO32` in its name. This file contains the same type of information that you see when you launch the System Information application from Accessories or when you run `MSINFO32.EXE`. This is key information about the machine on which SQL Server is running. This information includes the number of processors, the amount of memory, the amount of disk space, and a slew of other hardware and software data.

You also find a file named *`xxx_sp_sqldiag_Shutdown.out`*, where *`xxx`* is the name of the SQL Server machine. This file contains SQL Server–specific information, including the SQL Server error logs, output from several key system stored procedures, including *`sp_helpdb`* and `sp_configure`, and much more information related to the current state of SQL Server.

You find other files in the `sqldiag` output directory as well. Default trace files, log files related to the latest `sqldiag` execution, and a copy of the XML file containing configuration information are among them. Microsoft documentation on these files is limited, and you may find that the best way to determine what they contain is simply to open the files and review the wealth of information therein.

The `sqlservr` Command-Line Utility

The `sqlservr` executable is the program that runs when SQL Server is started. You can use the `sqlservr` executable to start SQL Server from a command prompt. When you do that, all the startup messages are displayed at the command prompt, and the command prompt session becomes dedicated to the execution of SQL Server.

CAUTION

If you start SQL Server from a command prompt, you cannot stop or pause it by using SSMS, Configuration Manager, or the Services applet in the Control Panel. You should stop the application only from the command prompt window in which SQL Server is running. If you press Ctrl+C, you are asked whether you want to shut down SQL Server. If you close the command prompt window in which SQL Server is running, SQL Server is automatically shut down.

The syntax for the `sqlserver` utility is as follows:

```
sqlservr [-sinstance_name] [-c] [-dmaster_path] [-f]
     [-eerror_log_path] [-lmaster_log_path] [-m]
     [-n] [-Ttrace#] [-v] [-x] [-gnumber] [-h]
```

Most commonly, you start SQL Server from the command prompt if you need to troubleshoot a configuration problem. The `-f` option starts SQL Server in minimal configuration mode. This allows you to recover from a change to a configuration setting that prevents SQL Server from starting. You can also use the `-m` option when you need to start SQL Server in single-user mode, such as when you need to rebuild one of the system databases.

SQL Server functions when started from the command prompt in much the same way as it does when it is started as a service. Users can connect to the server, and you can connect to the server by using SSMS. What is different is that the SQL Server instance running in the command prompt appears as if it is not running in some of the tools. SSMS and SQL Server Service Manager show SQL Server as being stopped because they are polling the SQL Server service, which is stopped when running in the command prompt mode.

TIP

If you simply want to start the SQL Server service from the command prompt, you can use the `NET START` and `NET STOP` commands. These commands are not SQL Server specific but are handy when you want to start or stop SQL Server, especially in a batch file. The SQL Server service name must be referenced after these commands. For example, `NET START MSSQLSERVER` starts the default SQL Server instance.

Summary

SQL Server provides a set of command-line utilities that allow you to execute some of the available SQL Server programs from the command prompt. Much of the functionality housed in these utilities is also available in graphical tools, such as SSMS. However, the capability to initiate these programs from the command prompt is invaluable in certain scenarios.

Chapter 6, "SQL Server Profiler," covers a tool that is critical for performance tuning in SQL Server 2008. SQL Server Profiler provides insight by monitoring and capturing the activity occurring on a SQL Server instance. It is a "go-to" tool for many DBAs and developers because of the wide variety of information that it can capture.

CHAPTER 6

SQL Server Profiler

IN THIS CHAPTER

- What's New with SQL Server Profiler
- SQL Server Profiler Architecture
- Creating Traces
- Executing Traces and Working with Trace Output
- Saving and Exporting Traces
- Replaying Trace Data
- Defining Server-Side Traces
- Profiler Usage Scenarios

This chapter explores the SQL Server Profiler, one of SQL Server's most powerful auditing and analysis tools. The SQL Server Profiler gives you a basic understanding of database access and helps you answer questions such as these:

- Which queries are causing table scans on my invoice history table?
- Am I experiencing deadlocks, and, if so, why?
- What SQL queries is each application submitting?
- Which were the 10 worst-performing queries last week?
- If I implement this alternative indexing scheme, how will it affect my batch operations?

SQL Server Profiler records activity that occurs on a SQL Server instance. The tool has a great deal of flexibility and can be customized for your needs. You can direct SQL Server Profiler to record output to a window, file, or table. You can specify which events to trace, the information to include in the trace, how you want that information grouped, and what filters you want to apply.

What's New with SQL Server Profiler

The SQL Server 2008 Profiler is essentially the same as the SQL Server 2005 profiler. This is not surprising because many new features that were added with SQL Server 2005 addressed gaps identified in previous versions. The changes made in SQL Server 2008 are generally minor and include several new trace events, one new trace column, and several other minor changes to the profiler GUI screens.

SQL Server Profiler Architecture

SQL Server 2008 has both a server and a client-side component for tracing activity on a server. The SQL trace facility is the server-side component that manages queues of events initiated by event producers on the server. Extended stored procedures can be used to define the server-side events that are to be captured. These procedures, which define a SQL trace, are discussed later in this chapter, in the section, "Defining Server-Side Traces."

The SQL Profiler is the client-side tracing facility. It comes with a fully functional GUI that allows for real-time auditing of SQL Server events. When it is used to trace server activity, events that are part of a trace definition are gathered at the server. Any filters defined as part of the trace definition are applied, and the event data is queued for its final destination. The SQL Profiler application is the final destination when client-side tracing is used. The basic elements involved in this process are shown in Figure 6.1.

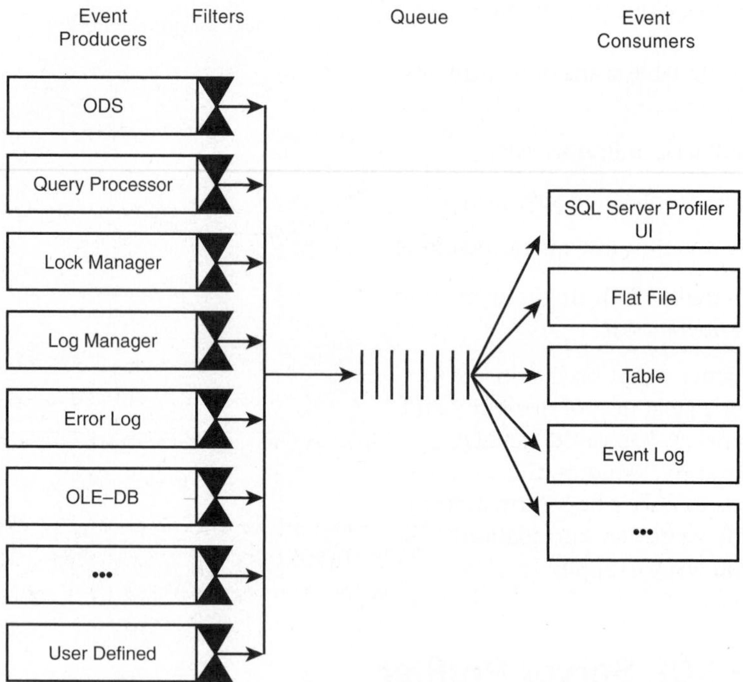

FIGURE 6.1 SQL Server Profiler's architecture.

This figure illustrates the following four steps in the process when tracing from the SQL Server Profiler:

1. Event producers, such as the Query Processor, Lock Manager, ODS, and so on, raise events for the SQL Server Profiler.
2. The filters define the information to submit to SQL Server Profiler. A producer will not send events if the event is not included in the filter.

3. SQL Server Profiler queues all the events.
4. SQL Server Profiler writes the events to each defined consumer, such as a flat file, a table, the Profiler client window, and so on.

In addition to obtaining its trace data from the event producers listed in step 1, you can also configure SQL Profiler so that it obtains its data from a previously saved location. This includes trace data saved in a file or table. The "Saving and Exporting Traces" section, later in this chapter, covers using trace files and trace tables in more detail.

Creating Traces

Because SQL Server Profiler can trace numerous events, it is easy to get lost when reading the trace output. You need to roughly determine the information you require and how you want the information grouped. For example, if you want to see the SQL statements that each user is submitting through an application, you could trace incoming SQL statements and group them by user and by application.

When you have an idea about what you want to trace, you should launch the SQL Server Profiler by selecting Start, then SQL Server 2008, then Performance Tools, and finally SQL Server Profiler. You also can launch it from within SSMS from the Tools menu. When you launch the Profiler, you are presented with an application window that is basically empty. To start a new trace, you select the File menu and choose New Trace. In the connection dialog that is displayed, you can enter the connectivity information for the server you want to trace. After the connection is established, the General tab of the Trace Properties window (see Figure 6.2) is displayed.

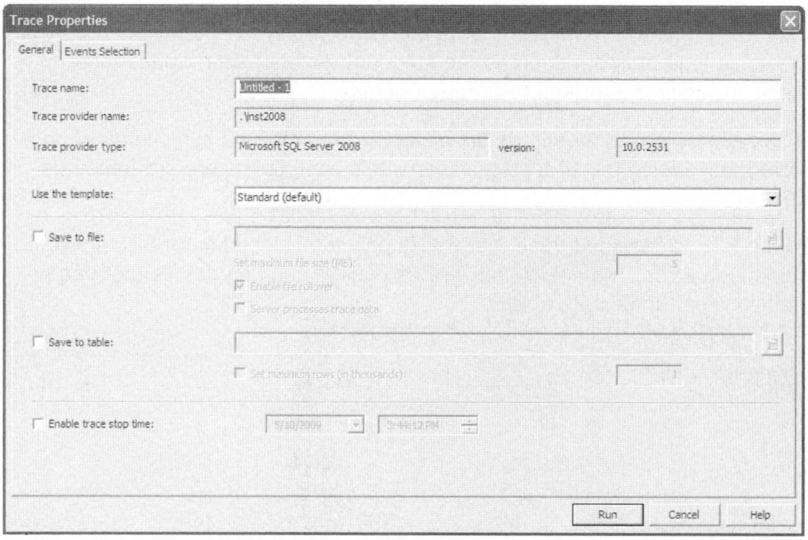

FIGURE 6.2 General trace properties.

The first place you should look when creating a new trace is at the trace templates. These templates contain predefined trace settings that address some common auditing needs. They have preset events, data columns, and filters targeted at specific profiling scenarios. The available trace templates, found in the template drop-down on the General tab of the Trace Properties window, are listed in Table 6.1.

TABLE 6.1 SQL Profiler Templates

Template	Description
`SP_Counts`	Tracks all the stored procedures as they start. No event except for the stored procedure starting is traced.
`Standard`	Traces the completion of SQL statements and Remote Procedure Calls (RPCs) as well as key connection information.
`TSQL`	Traces the start of SQL statements and RPCs. This template is useful for debugging client applications where some of the statements are not completing successfully.
`TSQL_Duration`	Traces the total execution time for each completed SQL statement or RPC.
`TSQL_Grouped`	Traces the start of SQL statements and RPCs, grouped by `Application`, `NTUser`, `LoginName`, and `ClientProcessId`.
`TSQL_Locks`	Traces the completion of SQL statements along with the key lock information that can be used to troubleshoot lock timeouts, deadlocks, and lock escalation issues.
`TSQL_Replay`	Captures profiling information that is useful for replay. This template contains the same type of information as the standard template, but it adds more detail, including cursor and RPC output details.
`TSQL_SPs`	Traces stored procedures in detail, including the start and completion of each stored procedure. The SQL statements within each procedure are traced as well.
`Tuning`	Performs a streamlined trace that tracks only the completion of SQL statements and RPCs. The completion events provide duration details that can be useful for performance tuning.

Keep in mind that the templates that come with SQL Server 2008 are not actual traces. They simply provide a foundation for you in creating your own traces. After you select a template, you can modify the trace setting and customize it for your own needs. You can then save the modified template as its own template file that will appear in the template drop-down list for future trace creation.

`Trace Name` is another property you can modify on the General tab. `Trace Name` is a relatively unimportant trace property for future traces. When you create a new trace, you can specify a name for the trace; however, this trace name will not be used again. For instance, if you have a trace definition you like, you can save the trace definition as a template file. If you want to run the trace again in the future, you can create a new trace and select the template file that you saved. You will not be selecting the trace to run based on the trace name you entered originally. `Trace Name` is useful only if you are running multiple traces simultaneously and need to distinguish between them more easily.

TIP

Do yourself a favor and save your favorite trace definitions in your own template. The default set of templates that come with SQL Server are good, but you will most likely want to change the position of a column or add an event that you find yourself using all the time. It is not hard to adjust one of the default templates to your needs each time, but if you save your own template with exactly what you need, it makes the task all the more easy. After you save your own template, you can set it as the default template, and it will be used by default every time you start the Profiler.

The Save to File and Save to Table options on the General tab of the Trace Properties page allow you to define where the trace output is stored. You can save the output to a flat file or SQL Server table. These options are discussed in more detail later in the chapter, in the section "Saving and Exporting Traces."

The last option on the General tab of the Trace Properties window is the Enable Trace Stop Time option. This scheduling-oriented feature allows you to specify a date and time at which you want to stop tracing. This capability is handy if you want to start a trace in the evening before you go home. You can set the stop time so that the trace will run for a few hours but won't affect any nightly processing that might occur later in the evening.

Events

The events and data columns that will be captured by your Profiler trace are defined on the Events Selection tab. An example of the Events Selection tab is shown in Figure 6.3.

The Events Selection tab consolidates the selection of events, data columns, and filters on one screen. One of the biggest advantages of the SQL Server 2008 Events Selection tab is that you can easily determine which data columns will be populated for each event by looking at the columns that have check boxes available for the event. For example, the Audit Login event has check boxes for `Text Data`, `ApplicationName`, and others but does not have a check box available for `CPU`, `Reads`, `Writes`, and other data columns that are not relevant to the event. For those data columns that have check boxes, you have the

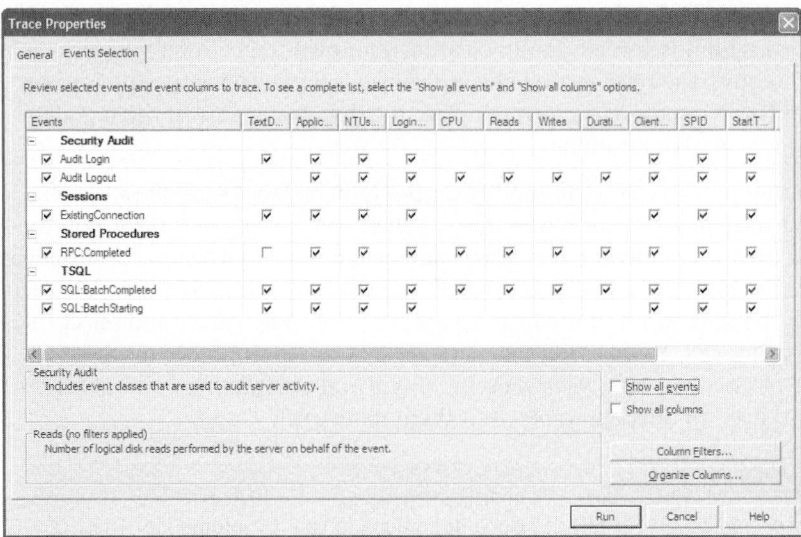

FIGURE 6.3 The Events Selection tab.

option of unchecking the box so that the data column will not be populated for the event when the trace is run.

You may find that adding events in SQL Server 2008 is a bit confusing. When you select a template, the event categories, selected events in those categories, and selected columns are displayed in the Events Selection tab. Now, if you want to add additional events, how do you do it? The answer to this question lies in the Show All Events check box in the lower-right corner of the Events Selection tab. When you click this check box, all the available event categories are listed on the screen. The events and columns that you had previously selected may or may not be visible on the screen. They are not lost, but you may need to scroll down the Events Selection tab to find the event categories that contain the events you had selected prior to selecting the Show All Events check box.

You will also notice that all the events in the categories in which you had events selected are displayed. In other words, if you had only 2 events selected in the Security Audit category and then selected the Show All Events check box, you see all 42 events listed. The only 2 events selected are the ones you had selected previously, but you need to wade through many events to see them. One upside to this kind of display is that you can easily view all the events for a category and the columns that relate to the events. One possible downside is that the Events Selection tab can be very busy, and it may take a little extra time to find what you are looking for.

TIP

If you capture too many events in one trace, the trace becomes difficult to review. Instead, you can create several traces, one for each type of information that you want to examine, and run them simultaneously. You can also choose to add or remove events after the trace has started. Keep in mind that you can pause a running trace, change the selected events, and restart the trace without losing the output that was there prior to pausing the trace.

Your ability to select and view events is made easier by using the tree control available on each event. The tree control allows you to expand or compress an event category. When you click the + icon next to a category, all the events are displayed. When you click the – icon, the event category is collapsed to a single row on the display. When an event has been selected for use within a category, the category name is shown in bold. If you want to add all the events in a category to your trace, you can simply right-click the category name and choose the Select Event Category option. You can also remove all events in a category by right-clicking the category name and choosing the Deselect Event Category option.

Understanding what each of the events captures can be a challenging task. You can refer to "SQL Server Event Class Reference" in Books Online for a detailed description, or you can use the simple Help facility available on the Events Selection tab. The Events Selection tab has a Help facility that describes each of the events and categories. The Help text is displayed on the Events Selection tab below the list of available events. When you mouse over a particular event or event category, a description of that item is shown. This puts the information you need at your fingertips.

NOTE

If you are going to use SQL Server Profiler, you should spend some time getting to know the events first and the type of output that Profiler generates. You should do this first in a development environment or standalone environment where the Profiler's effect on performance does not matter. It's a good idea to start a trace with a few events at a time and execute some relevant statements to see what is displayed for each event. You will soon realize the strength of the SQL Server Profiler and the type of valuable information it can return.

Data Columns

The columns of information captured in a Profiler trace are determined by the Data Columns selected. The Events Selection tab has the functionality you need to add columns, organize the columns, and apply filters on the data returned in these columns. As mentioned earlier, you can select and deselect the available columns for a particular event by using the check boxes displayed for the listed events. To understand what kind of information a column is going to return, you can simply mouse over the column, and Help for that item is displayed in the second Help box below the event list. Figure 6.4 shows an example of the Help output. In this particular case, the mouse pointer is over the `ApplicationName` column returned for the `SQL:BatchCompleted` event. The first Help box displays information about the `SQL:BatchCompleted` event, and the second Help box shows information about the data column.

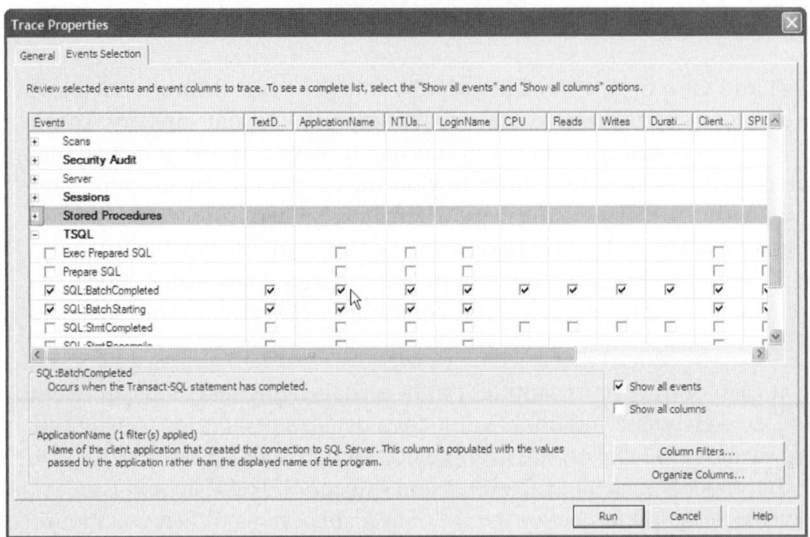

FIGURE 6.4 Help for data columns on the Events Selection tab.

Keep in mind that there is a default set of columns displayed for each event. You can view additional columns by selecting the Show All Columns check box. When you choose this option, an additional set of columns is displayed in the Events Selection tab. The additional columns are shown with a dark gray background, and you may need to scroll to the right on the Events Selection tab to be able to see them. Figure 6.5 shows an example of the additional columns displayed for the `Performance` event when the Show All Columns option is used. Some of the additional columns available for selection in this example are `BigintData1` and `BigintData2`.

To organize the columns you have selected, you can choose the Organize Columns selection on the Events Selection tab. This Organize Columns window allows you to change the order of the columns in the trace output as well as group the data by selected columns. Figure 6.6 shows an example of the Organize Columns window with the groups and columns selected by default when you use the `TSQL_Grouped` template.

To change the order of a column, you simply select the column in the list and use the Up or Down buttons to move it. The same movement can be done with columns selected for grouping. You add columns to groups by selecting the column in the data list and clicking the Up button until the column is moved out of the Columns list and into the Groups

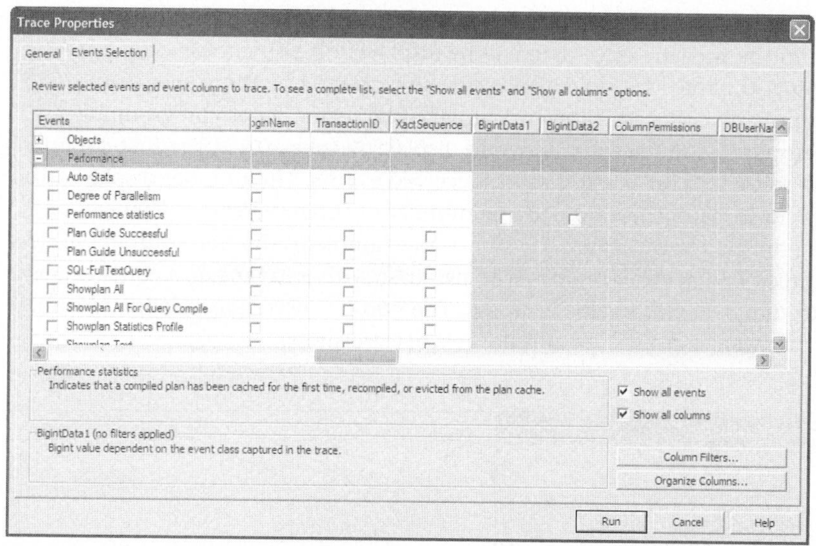

FIGURE 6.5 Additional columns displayed with the Show All Columns option.

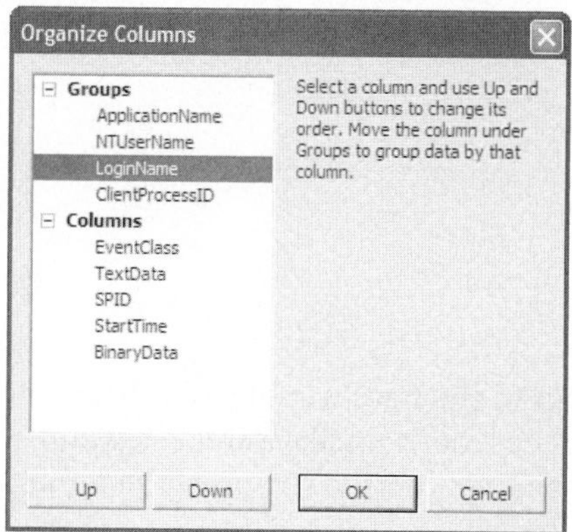

FIGURE 6.6 Organizing columns in the Events Selection tab.

list. For example, in Figure 6.6, you can group the `SPID` column by selecting it and clicking the Up button until it moves into the Groups tree structure instead of the Columns tree structure.

TIP

You can select a particular column for all events by right-clicking the column header in the Events Selection tab and choosing the Select Column option. This causes all the check boxes on the grid to be selected. To remove a column from all events, you right-click the column header and choose Deselect Column.

The number of columns selected for grouping and the order of the columns are both important factors in the way the trace data will be displayed. If you choose only one column for grouping, the trace window displays events grouped by the values in the grouped data column and collapses all events under it. For example, if you group by `DatabaseId`, the output in the trace window grid displays `DatabaseId` as the first column, with a + sign next to each `DatabaseId` that has received events. The number displayed to the right of the event in parentheses shows the number of collapsed events that can be viewed by clicking on the + sign. Figure 6.7 shows an example of the trace output window that has been grouped by `DatabaseId` only. The database with a `DatabaseId` equal to `6` is shown at the bottom of the grid in this example. The grid has been expanded, and some of the 20 events that were captured for this `DatabaseId` are shown.

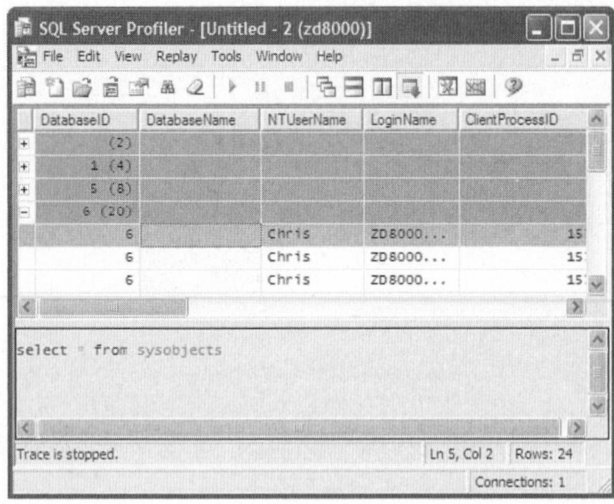

FIGURE 6.7 Grouping on a single column.

If you select multiple columns for grouping, the output in the trace window is ordered based on the columns in the grouping. The events are not rolled up like a single column, but the trace output grid automatically places the incoming events in the proper order in the output display.

TIP

The organization of columns in a trace can happen after a trace has been defined and executed. If you save the trace to a file or table, you can open it later and specify whatever ordering or grouping you want to reorganize the output. This flexibility gives you almost endless possibilities for analyzing the trace data.

Filters

Filters restrict the event data returned in your trace output. You can filter the events captured by the SQL Profiler via the Column Filters button on the Events Selection tab. An example of the Edit Filter window is shown in Figure 6.8. All the available columns for the trace are shown on the left side of the Edit Filter window. Those columns that have filters on them have a filter icon displayed next to the column in the column list.

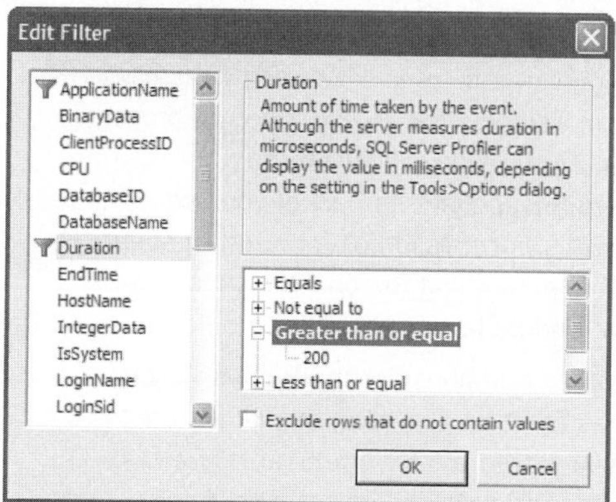

FIGURE 6.8 Editing filter properties.

The filtering options in SQL Server 2008 are similar to those available in SQL Server 2005. Which options are available depends on the type of column you are filtering on. The different filtering options are as follows:

- **Like/Not Like**—This option enables you to include or exclude events based on a wildcard. You should use the % character as your wildcard character. When you have completed a filter definition you can press Enter to create an entry space for another filter definition. For example, with the `ApplicationName` filter, you can specify `Like Microsoft%`, and you get only those events related to applications that match the wildcard, such as Microsoft SQL Server Management Studio. This filtering option is available for text data columns and data columns that contain name information, such as `NTUserName` and `ApplicationName`.
- **Equals/Not Equal To/Greater Than or Equal/Less Than or Equal**—Filters with this option have all four of these conditions available. For the Equals and Not Equal To conditions, you can specify a single value or a series of values. For a series of values, you hit enter after each value is entered and a new entry space is created for you to enter the next value. For the other conditional types, a single value is supplied. For example, you can filter on `DataBaseID` and input numeric values under the `Equals To` node of the filtering tree. This filtering option is available for numeric data columns such as `Duration`, `IndexId`, and `ObjectId`.
- **Greater Than/Less Than**—This type of filtering option is available only on time-based data columns. This includes `StartTime` and `EndTime` filters. These filters expect date formats of the form YYYY-MM-DD or YYYY-MM-DD HH:MM:SS.

Each data column can use one of these three filtering options. When you click the data column available for filtering, you see the filtering options for that column displayed in the right pane of the Edit Filter window. You enter the values on which you want to filter in the data entry area on the filter tree. This input area is shown when you select a specific filtering option. For multiple filter values, you press the Enter key after you enter each value. This causes a new data entry area to appear below the value you were on.

CAUTION

Filters applied to columns that are not available or selected for an event do not prevent the event data from being returned. For example, if you place a filter on the `ObjectName` column and choose the `SQL:StmtStarting` event as part of your trace, the event data is not filtered because `ObjectName` is not a valid column for that event. This behavior may seem relatively intuitive, but it is something to consider when you are receiving output from a trace that you believe should have been filtered out.

Also, be careful when specifying multiple filter values and consider the Boolean logic applied to them. When you specify multiple values for the `Like` filter, the values are evaluated with an `OR` condition. For example, if you create a filter on `ObjectName` and have a `Like` filter with values of `A%`, `B%`, and `C%`, the filter returns object names that start with A or B or C. When you use the `Not Like` filter, the `AND` condition is used on multiple values. For example, `Not Like` filter values for `ObjectName` of `A%` and `C%` result in objects with names that do not start with A and object names that do not start with C.

Executing Traces and Working with Trace Output

After you define the events and columns you want to capture in a trace, you can execute the Profiler trace. To do so, you click the Run button on the Trace Properties window, and the Profiler GUI starts capturing the events you have selected. The GUI contains a grid that is centrally located on the Profiler window, and newly captured events are scrolled on the screen as they are received. Figure 6.9 shows a simple example of the Profiler screen with output from an actively running trace.

The Profiler GUI provides many different options for dealing with an actively running trace. You can turn off scrolling on the trace, pause the trace, stop the trace, and view the properties of an actively running trace. You can find strings within the trace output, and you can even move the columns around in the display so that they are displayed in a different order. These options provide a great deal of flexibility and allow you to focus on the output that is most important to you.

Saving and Exporting Traces

In many cases, you want to save or export the trace output generated by a Profiler trace. The output can be analyzed, replayed, imported, or manipulated at a later time after it has been saved. Trace output can be saved as the trace is running or saved after it has been generated to the Profiler GUI. The Trace Properties window provides options for saving trace output while the trace is running. The options are defined using the Save to File and Save to Table options on the General tab of the Trace Properties window. You can save to a file, a table, or both a table and a file. Figure 6.10 shows an example of a trace that will save to both a file and table while it is executing.

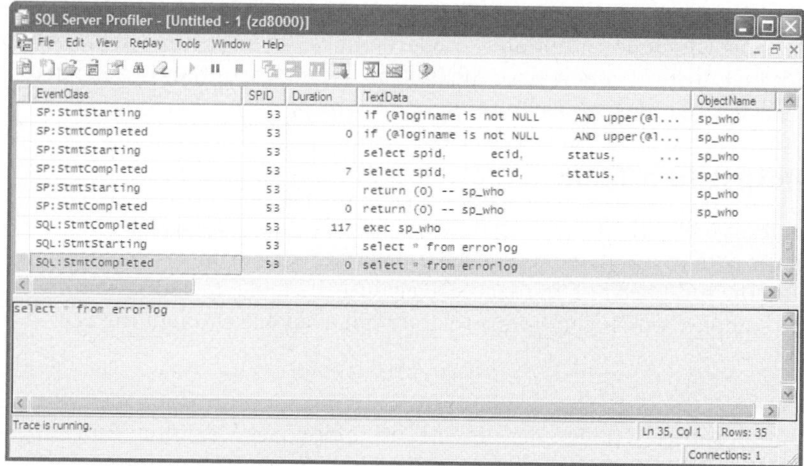

FIGURE 6.9 The Profiler GUI with an active trace.

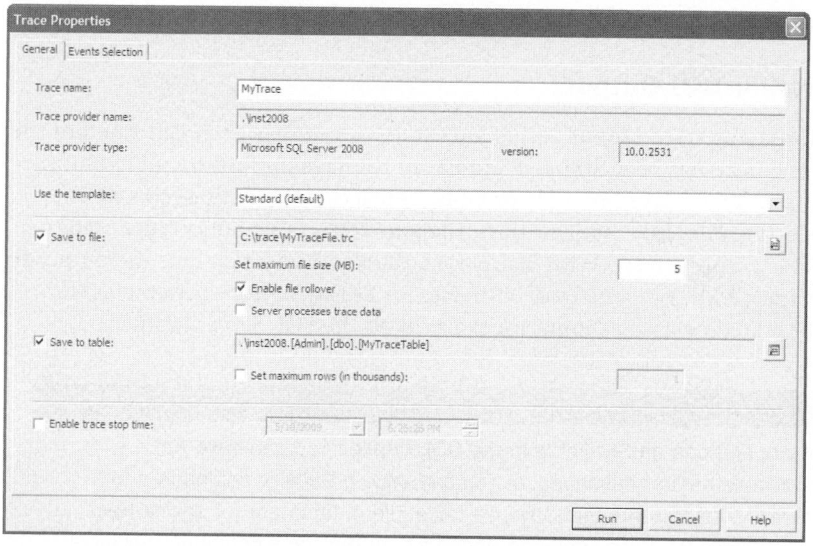

Trace Properties
General | Events Selection
Trace name: MyTrace
Trace provider name: .\inst2008
Trace provider type: Microsoft SQL Server 2008 version: 10.0.2531
Use the template: Standard (default)
Save to file: C:\trace\MyTraceFile.trc
Set maximum file size (MB): 5
Enable file rollover
Server processes trace data
Save to table: .\inst2008.[Admin].[dbo].[MyTraceTable]
Set maximum rows (in thousands):
Enable trace stop time:
Run Cancel Help

FIGURE 6.10 Saving trace output while a trace is running.

Saving Trace Output to a File

When you save a running trace to a file, you have several options for controlling the output. One option you should always consider is the Set Maximum File Size (MB) option. This option prevents a trace output file from exceeding the specified size. Controlling the size helps make the file more manageable and, more importantly, it can save you from having a trace file gobble up all the disk space on the drive you are writing to. Remember that the amount of trace data written to a file on a busy production system can be extensive. You can also use this file size option in conjunction with the Enable File Rollover option. When the Enable File Rollover option is used, the trace does not stop when the file size maximum is met. Instead, a new trace file is created, and the output is generated to that file until it reaches the file size maximum.

Saving Trace Output to a Table

The Save to Table option writes the trace output directly to a SQL Server table as the trace is running. Having the data in a SQL table provides a great deal of flexibility for analyzing the data. You can use the full power of Transact-SQL against the table, including sorting, grouping, and more complex search conditions that are not available through the SQL Profiler filters.

You need to consider both the disk space requirements and impact on performance when the Save to Table option is used. The Profiler provides an option, Set Maximum Rows (in Thousands), to limit the amount of output generated from the trace. The performance impact depends on the volume of data being written to the table. Generally, you should avoid writing the trace output to a table when using high-volume SQL servers. The best option for high-volume servers is to first write the trace output to a file and then import the file to a trace table at a later time.

Saving the Profiler GUI Output

Another option for saving trace output occurs after trace output has been generated to the Profiler GUI and the trace has been stopped. Similar to the save options for an executing trace, the GUI output can be saved to a file or table. You access the options to save the GUI output by selecting File, Save As. The Trace File and Trace Table options are used to save to a file or table consecutively. With SQL Server 2008, you can also save the output to an XML file. The Trace XML File and Trace XML File for Replay options generate XML output that can be edited or used as input for replay with the SQL Server Profiler.

NOTE

Two distinct save operations are available in the SQL Profiler. You can save trace events to a file or table as just described, or you can save a trace definition in a template file. The Save As Trace Table and Save As Trace File options are for saving trace events to a file. The Save As Trace Template option saves the trace definition. Saving a trace template saves you the trouble of having to go through all the properties each time to set up the events, data columns, and filters for your favorite traces.

An alternative to saving all the event data associated with a particular trace is to select specific event rows from the SQL Profiler windows. You can capture all the trace information associated with a trace row by selecting a row in the trace output window of Profiler and choosing Edit, Copy. Or, you can just copy the event text (typically a SQL statement) by selecting the row, highlighting the text in the lower pane, and using the Copy option. You can then paste this data into SSMS or the tool of your choice for further execution and more detailed analysis. This capability can be particularly useful during performance tuning. After you identify the long-running statement or procedure, you can copy the SQL, paste it into SSMS, and display the query plan to determine why the query was running so long.

Importing Trace Files

A trace saved to a file or table can be read back into SQL Profiler at a later time for more detailed analysis or to replay the trace on the same SQL Server or another SQL Server instance. You can import data from a trace file or trace table by choosing File, Open and then selecting either a trace file or trace table. If you choose to open a trace file, you are presented with a dialog to locate the trace file on the local machine. If you choose to import a trace table, you are first presented with a connection dialog to specify the SQL Server name, the login ID, and the password to connect to it. When you are successfully connected, you are presented with a dialog to specify the database and name of the trace table you want to import from. After you specify the trace file or trace table to import into Profiler, the entire contents of the file or table are read in and displayed in a Profiler window.

You may find that large trace files or trace tables are difficult to analyze, and you may just want to analyze events associated with a specific application or table, or specific types of queries. To limit the amount of information displayed in the Profiler window, you can filter out the data displayed via the Properties dialog. You can choose which events and data columns you want to display and also specify conditions in the Filters tab to limit the rows displayed from the trace file or trace table. These options do not affect the information stored in the trace file or trace table—only what information is displayed in the Profiler window.

Importing a Trace File into a Trace Table

Although you can load a trace file directly into Profiler for analysis, very large files can be difficult to analyze. Profiler loads an entire file. For large files, this process can take quite awhile, and the responsiveness of Profiler might not be the best. Multiple trace output files for a given trace can also be cumbersome and difficult to manage when those files are large.

You can use the trace filters to limit which rows are displayed but not which rows are imported into Profiler. You often end up with a bunch of rows displayed with no data in the columns you want to analyze. In addition, while the filters allow you to limit which rows are displayed, they don't really provide a means of running more complex reports on the data, such as generating counts of events or displaying the average query duration.

Fortunately, SQL Server 2008 provides a way for you to selectively import a trace file into a trace table. When importing a trace file into a trace table, you can filter the data before it goes into the table as well as combine multiple files into a single trace table. When the data is in a trace table, you can load the trace table into Profiler or write your own queries and reports against the trace table for more detailed analysis than is possible in Profiler.

Microsoft SQL Server also includes some built-in user-defined functions for working with Profiler traces. The `fn_trace_gettable` function is used to import trace file data into a trace table. Following is the syntax for this function:

```
fn_trace_gettable( [ @filename = ] filename , [ @numfiles = ] number_files )
```

This function returns the contents of the specified file as a table result set. You can use the result set from this function just as you would any table. By default, the function returns all possible Profiler columns, even if no data was captured for the column in the trace. To limit the columns returned, you specify the list of columns in the query. If you want to limit the rows retrieved from the trace file, you specify your search conditions in the `WHERE` clause. If your Profiler trace used rollover files to split the trace across multiple files, you can specify the number of files you want it to read in. If the default value of `default` is used, all rollover files for the trace are loaded. Listing 6.1 provides an example of creating and populating a trace table from a trace file, using `SELECT INTO`, and then adding rows by using an `INSERT` statement. Note that this example limits the columns and rows returned by specifying a column list and search conditions in the `WHERE` clause.

LISTING 6.1 Creating and Inserting Trace Data into a Trace Table from a Trace File

```
/*******************************************************************
** NOTE - you will need to edit the path/filename on your system if
**        you use this code to load your own trace files
*******************************************************************/

select EventClass,
       EventSubClass,
       TextData = convert(varchar(8000), TextData),
       BinaryData,
       ApplicationName,
       Duration,
       StartTime,
       EndTime,
       Reads,
       Writes,
       CPU,
       ObjectID,
       IndexID,
       NestLevel
    into TraceTable
    FROM ::fn_trace_gettable('c:\temp\sampletrace_ 20090510_0622.trc', default)
    where TextData is not null
      or EventClass in (16, — Attention
                        25, — Lock:Deadlock
```

```
                                        27, — Lock:Timeout
                                        33, — Exception
                                        58, — Auto Update Stats
                                        59, — Lock:Deadlock Chain
                                        79, — Missing Column Statistics
                                        80, — Missing Join Predicate
                                        92, — Data File Auto Grow
                                        93, — Log File Auto Grow
                                        94, — Data File Auto Shrink
                                        95) — Log File Auto Shrink

Insert into TraceTable (EventClass, EventSubClass,
            TextData, BinaryData,
            ApplicationName, Duration, StartTime, EndTime, Reads, Writes,
            CPU, ObjectID, IndexID, nestlevel)
     select EventClass, EventSubClass,
            TextData = convert(varchar(7900), TextData), BinaryData,
            ApplicationName, Duration, StartTime, EndTime, Reads, Writes,
            CPU, ObjectID, IndexID, nestlevel
        FROM ::fn_trace_gettable('c:\temp\sampletrace_ 20090510_0205.trc', -1)
        where TextData is not null
           or EventClass in (16, —  Attention
                             25, — Lock:Deadlock
                             27, — Lock:Timeout
                             33, — Exception
                             58, — Auto Update Stats
                             59, — Lock:Deadlock Chain
                             79, — Missing Column Statistics
                             80, — Missing Join Predicate
                             92, — Data File Auto Grow
                             93, — Log File Auto Grow
                             94, — Data File Auto Shrink
                             95) — Log File Auto Shrink
go
```

After the trace file is imported into a trace table, you can open the trace table in Profiler or run your own queries against the trace table from a query editor window in SSMS. For example, the following query returns the number of lock timeouts encountered for each table during the period the trace was running:

```
select object_name(ObjectId), count(*)
    from TraceTable
    where EventClass = 27 — Lock:Timout Event
    group by object_name(ObjectId)
go
```

Analyzing Trace Output with the Database Engine Tuning Advisor

In addition to being able to manually analyze traces in Profiler, you can also use the Database Engine Tuning Advisor to analyze the queries captured in a trace and recommend changes to your indexing scheme. The Database Engine Tuning Advisor is a replacement for the Index Tuning Wizard that was available in SQL Server 2000. You can invoke it from the Tools menu in SQL Profiler. The Database Engine Tuning Advisor can read in a trace that was previously saved to a table or a file. This feature allows you to capture a workload, tune the indexing scheme, and re-run the trace to determine whether the index changes improved performance as expected.

Because the Database Engine Tuning Advisor analyzes SQL statements, you need to make sure that the trace includes one or more of the following events:

```
SP:StmtCompleted
SP:StmtStarting
SQL:BatchCompleted
SQL:BatchStarting
SQL:StmtCompleted
SQL:StmtStarting
```

One of each class (one `SP:` and one `SQL:`) is sufficient to capture dynamic SQL statements and statements embedded in stored procedures. You should also make sure that the trace includes the text data column, which contains the actual queries.

The Database Engine Tuning Advisor analyzes the trace and gives you recommendations, along with an estimated improvement-in-execution time. You can choose to create indexes now or at a later time, or you can save the `CREATE INDEX` commands to a script file.

Replaying Trace Data

To replay a trace, you must have a trace saved to a file or a table. The trace must be captured with certain trace events to enable playback. The required events are captured by default if you use the Profiler template `TSQL_Replay`. You can define a trace to be saved when you create or modify the trace definition. You can also save the current contents of the trace window to a file or table by using the Save As Trace File or Save As Trace Table options in the File menu.

To replay a saved trace, you choose File and then Open to open a trace file or trace table. After you select the type of trace to replay, a grid with the trace columns selected in the original trace is displayed. At this point, you can either start the replay of the trace step-by-step or complete execution of the entire trace. The options for replaying the trace are found under the Replay menu. When you start the replay of the trace, the Connect to

Server dialog is displayed, enabling you to choose the server that you want to replay the traces against. When you are connected to a server, a Replay Configuration dialog like the one shown in Figure 6.11 is displayed.

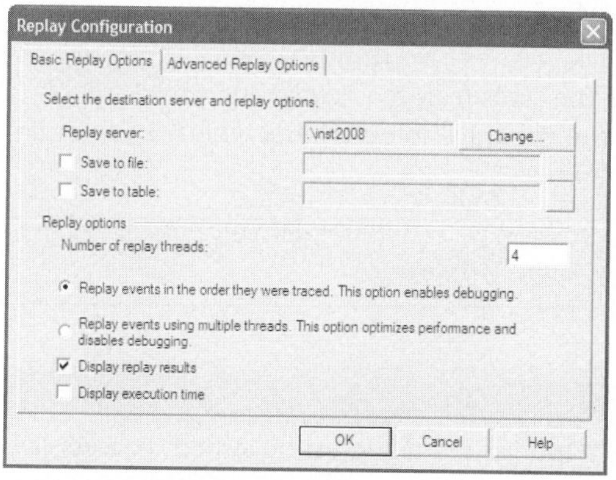

FIGURE 6.11 Basic replay options.

The first replay option, which is enabled by default, replays the trace in the same order in which it was captured and allows for debugging. The second option takes advantage of multiple threads; it optimizes performance but disables debugging. A third option involves specifying whether to display the replay results. You would normally want to see the results, but for large trace executions, you might want to forgo displaying the results and send them to an output file instead.

If you choose the option that allows for debugging, you can execute the trace in a manner similar to many programming tools. You can set breakpoints, step through statements one at a time, or position the cursor on a statement within the trace and execute the statements from the beginning of the trace to the cursor position.

NOTE

Automating testing scripts is another important use of the SQL Profiler Save and Replay options. For instance, a trace of a heavy production load can be saved and rerun against a new release of the database to ensure that the new release has similar or improved performance characteristics and returns the same data results. The saved traces can help make regression testing much easier.

You also have the option of specifying advanced replay options in SQL Server 2008. These options are found on the Advanced Replay Options tab of the Replay Configuration dialog (see Figure 6.12).

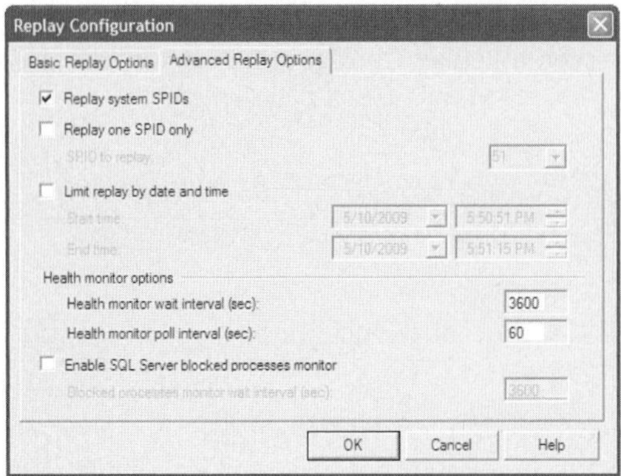

FIGURE 6.12 Advanced replay options.

The first two options on the Advanced Replay Options tab relate to the system process IDs (SPIDs) targeted for replay. If the Replay System SPIDs option is selected, the trace events for every SPID in the trace file will be replayed. If you want to target activity for a specific SPID, you should choose the Replay One SPID Only option and select the SPID from the drop-down menu. You can also limit the events that will be replayed based on the timing of the events. If you want to replay a specific time-based section of the trace, you can use the Limit Replay by Date and Time option. Only those trace events that fall between the data range you specify will be replayed.

The last set of advanced options is geared toward maintaining the health of the server on which you are replaying the trace. The Health Monitor Wait Interval (sec) option determines the amount of time a thread can run during replay before being terminated. This helps avoid an excessive drain on the server's resources. The Health Monitor Poll Interval (sec) option determines how often the health monitor will poll for threads that should be terminated. The last advanced option on the screen relates to blocked processes. When it is enabled, the monitor polls for blocked processes according to the interval specified.

Defining Server-Side Traces

Much of the SQL Server Profiler functionality can also be initiated through a set of system stored procedures. Through these procedures, you can define a server-side trace that can be run automatically or on a scheduled basis, such as via a scheduled job, instead of through the Profiler GUI. Server-side traces are also useful if you are tracing information over an extended period of time or are planning on capturing a large amount of trace information. The overhead of running a server-side trace is less than that of running a client-side trace with Profiler.

To start a server-side trace, you need to define the trace by using the trace-related system procedures. These procedures can be called from within a SQL Server stored procedure or batch. You define a server-side trace by using the following four procedures:

- **sp_trace_create**—This procedure is used to create the trace definition. It sets up the trace and defines the file to store the captured events. sp trace create returns a trace ID number that you need to reference from the other three procedures to further define and manage the trace.
- **sp_trace_setevent**—You need to call this procedure once for each data column of every event that you want to capture.
- **sp_trace_setfilter**—You call this procedure once for each filter you want to define on an event data column.
- **sp_trace_setstatus**—After the trace is defined, you call this procedure to start, stop, or remove the trace. You must stop and remove a trace definition before you can open and view the trace file.

You will find that manually creating procedure scripts for tracing can be rather tedious. Much of the tedium is due to the fact that many numeric parameters drive the trace execution. For example, the sp_trace_setevent procedure accepts an eventid and a columnid that determine what event data will be captured. Fortunately, SQL Server 2008 provides a set of catalog views that contain these numeric values and what they represent. The sys.trace_categories catalog view contains the event categories. The sys.trace_events catalog view contains the trace events, and sys.trace_columns contains the trace columns. The following SELECT statement utilizes two of these system views to return the available events and their related categories:

```
select e.trace_event_id, e.name 'Event Name', c.name 'Category Name'
 from sys.trace_events e
  join sys.trace_categories c on e.category_id = c.category_id
 order by e.trace_event_id
```

The results of this SELECT statement are shown in Table 6.2.

TABLE 6.2 Trace Events and Their Related Categories

trace_event_id	Event Name	Category Name
10	RPC:Completed	Stored Procedures
11	RPC:Starting	Stored Procedures
12	SQL:BatchCompleted	T-SQL
13	SQL:BatchStarting	T-SQL

6

TABLE 6.2 Trace Events and Their Related Categories

trace_event_id	Event Name	Category Name
14	Audit Login	Security Audit
15	Audit Logout	Security Audit
16	Attention	Errors and Warnings
17	ExistingConnection	Sessions
18	Audit Server Starts And Stops	Security Audit
19	DTCTransaction	Transactions
20	Audit Login Failed	Security Audit
21	EventLog	Errors and Warnings
22	ErrorLog	Errors and Warnings
23	Lock:Released	Locks
24	Lock:Acquired	Locks
25	Lock:Deadlock	Locks
26	Lock:Cancel	Locks
27	Lock:Timeout	Locks
28	Degree of Parallelism	Performance
33	Exception	Errors and Warnings
34	SP:CacheMiss	Stored Procedures
35	SP:CacheInsert	Stored Procedures
36	SP:CacheRemove	Stored Procedures
37	SP:Recompile	Stored Procedures
38	SP:CacheHit	Stored Procedures
40	SQL:StmtStarting	T-SQL
41	SQL:StmtCompleted	T-SQL
42	SP:Starting	Stored Procedures
43	SP:Completed	Stored Procedures
44	SP:StmtStarting	Stored Procedures
45	SP:StmtCompleted	Stored Procedures

TABLE 6.2 Trace Events and Their Related Categories

trace_event_id	Event Name	Category Name
46	Object:Created	Objects
47	Object:Deleted	Objects
50	SQLTransaction	Transactions
51	Scan:Started	Scans
52	Scan:Stopped	Scans
53	CursorOpen	Cursors
54	TransactionLog	Transactions
55	Hash Warning	Errors and Warnings
58	Auto Stats	Performance
59	Lock:Deadlock Chain	Locks
60	Lock:Escalation	Locks
61	OLEDB Errors	OLEDB
67	Execution Warnings	Errors and Warnings
68	Showplan Text (Unencoded)	Performance
69	Sort Warnings	Errors and Warnings
70	CursorPrepare	Cursors
71	Prepare SQL	T-SQL
72	Exec Prepared SQL	T-SQL
73	Unprepare SQL	T-SQL
74	CursorExecute	Cursors
75	CursorRecompile	Cursors
76	CursorImplicitConversion	Cursors
77	CursorUnprepare	Cursors
78	CursorClose	Cursors
79	Missing Column Statistics	Errors and Warnings
80	Missing Join Predicate	Errors and Warnings
81	Server Memory Change	Server

TABLE 6.2 Trace Events and Their Related Categories

trace_event_id	Event Name	Category Name
82	UserConfigurable:0	User configurable
83	UserConfigurable:1	User configurable
84	UserConfigurable:2	User configurable
85	UserConfigurable:3	User configurable
86	UserConfigurable:4	User configurable
87	UserConfigurable:5	User configurable
88	UserConfigurable:6	User configurable
89	UserConfigurable:7	User configurable
90	UserConfigurable:8	User configurable
91	UserConfigurable:9	User configurable
92	Data File Auto Grow	Database
93	Log File Auto Grow	Database
94	Data File Auto Shrink	Database
95	Log File Auto Shrink	Database
96	Showplan Text	Performance
97	Showplan All	Performance
98	Showplan Statistics Profile	Performance
100	RPC Output Parameter	Stored Procedures
102	Audit Database Scope GDR Event	Security Audit
103	Audit Schema Object GDR Event	Security Audit
104	Audit Addlogin Event	Security Audit
105	Audit Login GDR Event	Security Audit
106	Audit Login Change Property Event	Security Audit
107	Audit Login Change Password Event	Security Audit
108	Audit Add Login to Server Role Event	Security Audit

TABLE 6.2 Trace Events and Their Related Categories

trace_event_id	Event Name	Category Name
109	Audit Add DB User Event	Security Audit
110	Audit Add Member to DB Role Event	Security Audit
111	Audit Add Role Event	Security Audit
112	Audit App Role Change Password Event	Security Audit
113	Audit Statement Permission Event	Security Audit
114	Audit Schema Object Access Event	Security Audit
115	Audit Backup/Restore Event	Security Audit
116	Audit DBCC Event	Security Audit
117	Audit Change Audit Event	Security Audit
118	Audit Object Derived Permission Event	Security Audit
119	OLEDB Call Event	OLEDB
120	OLEDB QueryInterface Event	OLEDB
121	OLEDB DataRead Event	OLEDB
122	Showplan XML	Performance
123	SQL:FullTextQuery	Performance
124	Broker:Conversation	Broker
125	Deprecation Announcement	Deprecation
126	Deprecation Final Support	Deprecation
127	Exchange Spill Event	Errors and Warnings
128	Audit Database Management Event	Security Audit
129	Audit Database Object Management Event	Security Audit
130	Audit Database Principal Management Event	Security Audit
131	Audit Schema Object Management Event	Security Audit
132	Audit Server Principal Impersonation Event	Security Audit

TABLE 6.2 Trace Events and Their Related Categories

trace_event_id	Event Name	Category Name
133	Audit Database Principal Impersonation Event	Security Audit
134	Audit Server Object Take Ownership Event	Security Audit
135	Audit Database Object Take Ownership Event	Security Audit
136	Broker:Conversation Group	Broker
137	Blocked process report	Errors and Warnings
138	Broker:Connection	Broker
139	Broker:Forwarded Message Sent	Broker
140	Broker:Forwarded Message Dropped	Broker
141	Broker:Message Classify	Broker
142	Broker:Transmission	Broker
143	Broker:Queue Disabled	Broker
144	Broker:Mirrored Route State Changed	Broker
146	Showplan XML Statistics Profile	Performance
148	Deadlock graph	Locks
149	Broker:Remote Message Acknowledgement	Broker
150	Trace File Close	Server
151	Database Mirroring Connection	Database
152	Audit Change Database Owner	Security Audit
153	Audit Schema Object Take Ownership Event	Security Audit
154	Audit Database Mirroring Login	Security Audit
155	FT:Crawl Started	Full text
156	FT:Crawl Stopped	Full text
157	FT:Crawl Aborted	Full text
158	Audit Broker Conversation	Security Audit

TABLE 6.2 Trace Events and Their Related Categories

trace_event_id	Event Name	Category Name
186	TM: Commit Tran completed	Transactions
187	TM: Rollback Tran starting	Transactions
188	TM: Rollback Tran completed	Transactions
189	Lock:Timeout (timeout > 0)	Locks
190	Progress Report: Online Index Operation	Progress Report
191	TM: Save Tran starting	Transactions
192	TM: Save Tran completed	Transactions
193	Background Job Error	Errors and Warnings
194	OLEDB Provider Information	OLEDB
195	Mount Tape	Server
196	Assembly Load	CLR
198	XQuery Static Type	T-SQL
199	QN: Subscription	Query Notifications
200	QN: Parameter table	Query Notifications
201	QN: Template	Query Notifications
202	QN: Dynamics	Query Notifications
212	Bitmap Warning	Errors and Warnings
213	Database Suspect Data Page	Errors and Warnings
214	CPU threshold exceeded	Errors and Warnings
215	PreConnect:Starting	Sessions
216	PreConnect:Completed	Sessions
217	Plan Guide Successful	Performance
218	Plan Guide Unsuccessful	Performance
235	Audit Fulltext	Security Audit

The numeric IDs for the trace columns can be obtained from the sys.trace_columns catalog view, as shown in the following example:

```
select trace_column_id, name 'Column Name', type_name 'Data Type'
 from sys.trace_columns
 order by trace_column_id
```

Table 6.3 shows the results of this SELECT statement and lists all the available trace columns.

TABLE 6.3 Trace Columns Available for a Server-Side Trace

trace_column_id	Column Name	Data Type
1	TextData	text
2	BinaryData	image
3	DatabaseID	int
4	TransactionID	bigint
5	LineNumber	int
6	NTUserName	nvarchar
7	NTDomainName	nvarchar
8	HostName	nvarchar
9	ClientProcessID	int
10	ApplicationName	nvarchar
11	LoginName	nvarchar
12	SPID	int
13	Duration	bigint
14	StartTime	datetime
15	EndTime	datetime
16	Reads	bigint
17	Writes	bigint
18	CPU	int
19	Permissions	bigint
20	Severity	int
21	EventSubClass	int
22	ObjectID	int
23	Success	int

TABLE 6.3 Trace Columns Available for a Server-Side Trace

trace_column_id	Column Name	Data Type
24	IndexID	int
25	IntegerData	int
26	ServerName	nvarchar
27	EventClass	int
28	ObjectType	int
29	NestLevel	int
30	State	int
31	Error	int
32	Mode	int
33	Handle	int
34	ObjectName	nvarchar
35	DatabaseName	nvarchar
36	FileName	nvarchar
37	OwnerName	nvarchar
38	RoleName	nvarchar
39	TargetUserName	nvarchar
40	DBUserName	nvarchar
41	LoginSid	image
42	TargetLoginName	nvarchar
43	TargetLoginSid	image
44	ColumnPermissions	int
45	LinkedServerName	nvarchar
46	ProviderName	nvarchar
47	MethodName	nvarchar
48	RowCounts	bigint
49	RequestID	int
50	XactSequence	bigint
51	EventSequence	bigint

TABLE 6.3 Trace Columns Available for a Server-Side Trace

trace_column_id	Column Name	Data Type
52	BigintData1	bigint
53	BigintData2	bigint
54	GUID	uniqueidentifier
55	IntegerData2	int
56	ObjectID2	bigint
57	Type	int
58	OwnerID	int
59	ParentName	nvarchar
60	IsSystem	int
61	Offset	int
62	SourceDatabaseID	int
63	SqlHandle	image
64	SessionLoginName	nvarchar
65	PlanHandle	image
66	GroupID	int

You have to call the sp_trace_setevent procedure once for each data column you want captured for each event in the trace. Based on the number of events and number of columns, you can see that this can result in a lot of executions of the sp_trace_setevent procedure for a larger trace definition.

To set up filters, you must pass the column ID, the filter value, and numeric values for the logical operator and column operator to the sp_trace_setfilter procedure. The logical operator can be either 0 or 1. A value of 0 indicates that the specified filter on the column should be ANDed with any other filters on the column, whereas a value of 1 indicates that the OR operator should be applied. Table 6.4 describes the values allowed for the column operators.

TABLE 6.4 Column Operator Values for **sp_trace_setfilter**

Value	Comparison Operator
0	= (equal)
1	<> (not equal)
2	> (greater than)
3	< (less than)
4	>= (greater than or equal)
5	<= (less than or equal)
6	`LIKE`
7	`NOT LIKE`

Fortunately, there is an easier way of generating a trace definition script. You can set up your traces by using the SQL Profiler GUI and script the trace definition to a file. After you define the trace and specify the events, data columns, and filters you want to use, you select File, Export, Script Trace Definition. The SQL commands (including calls to the aforementioned system stored procedures) to define the trace, start the trace, and write the trace to a file are generated into one script file. You have the option to generate a script that works with SQL Server 2000, 2005 or 2008. Listing 6.2 shows an example of a trace definition exported from the Profiler. It contains the trace definitions for the `TSQL` trace template. You must replace the text `InsertFileNameHere` with an appropriate filename, prefixed with its pathname, before running this script.

LISTING 6.2 A SQL Script for Creating and Starting a Server-Side Trace

```
/****************************************************/
/* Created by: SQL Server 2008 Profiler          */
/* Date: 05/10/2009  07:20:54 PM         */
/****************************************************/


-- Create a Queue
declare @rc int
declare @TraceID int
declare @maxfilesize bigint
```

```
set @maxfilesize = 5

— Please replace the text InsertFileNameHere, with an appropriate
— filename prefixed by a path, e.g., c:\MyFolder\MyTrace. The .trc extension
— will be appended to the filename automatically. If you are writing from
— remote server to local drive, please use UNC path and make sure server has
— write access to your network share

exec @rc = sp_trace_create @TraceID output, 0, N'InsertFileNameHere', @maxfilesize,
NULL
if (@rc != 0) goto error

— Client side File and Table cannot be scripted

— Set the events
declare @on bit
set @on = 1
exec sp_trace_setevent @TraceID, 10, 2, @on
exec sp_trace_setevent @TraceID, 10, 12, @on
exec sp_trace_setevent @TraceID, 10, 13, @on
exec sp_trace_setevent @TraceID, 12, 1, @on
exec sp_trace_setevent @TraceID, 12, 12, @on
exec sp_trace_setevent @TraceID, 12, 13, @on


— Set the Filters
declare @intfilter int
declare @bigintfilter bigint

— Set the trace status to start
exec sp_trace_setstatus @TraceID, 1

— display trace id for future references
select TraceID=@TraceID
goto finish

error:
select ErrorCode=@rc
finish:


go
```

TIP

If you want to always capture certain trace events when SQL Server is running, such as auditing events, you can create a stored procedure that uses the `sp_trace` stored procedures to create a trace and specify the events to be captured. You can use the code in Listing 6.2 as a basis to create the stored procedure. Then you can mark the procedure as a startup procedure by using the `sp_procoption` procedure to set the `autostart` option. The trace automatically starts when SQL Server is started, and it continues running in the background.

Just be aware that although using server-side traces is less intrusive than using the SQL Profiler client, some overhead is necessary to run a trace. You should try to limit the number of events and number of columns captured to minimize the overhead as much as possible.

Monitoring Running Traces

SQL Server 2008 provides some additional built-in user-defined functions to get information about currently running traces. Like the `fn_trace_gettable` function discussed previously, these functions return the information as a tabular result. The available functions are as follows:

- **`fn_trace_getinfo(`*`trace_id`*`)`**—This function is passed a `traceid`, and it returns information about the specified trace. If passed the value of `default`, it returns information about all existing traces. An example of the output from this function is shown in Listing 6.3.
- **`fn_trace_geteventinfo(`*`trace_id`*`)`**—This function returns a list of the events and data columns being captured for the specified trace. Only the event and column ID values are returned. You can use the information provided in Tables 6.2 and 6.3 to map the IDs to the more meaningful event names and column names.
- **`fn_trace_getfilterinfo(`*`trace_id`*`)`**—This function returns information about the filters being applied to the specified trace. Again, the column ID and logical and comparison operator values are returned as integer IDs that you need to decipher. See Table 6.4 for a listing of the column operator values.

LISTING 6.3 An Example of Using the Built-in User-Defined Functions for Monitoring Traces

```
SELECT * FROM ::fn_trace_getinfo(default)


traceid      property     value
------------ ------------ -------------------------
1            1            2
1            2            C:\Program Files\Microsoft SQL Server\MSSQL.1\
                           MSSQL\LOG\log_376.trc
```

```
1          3          20
1          4          NULL
1          5          1
2          1          0
2          2          c:\trace\mytrace.trc.trc
2          3          5
2          4          NULL
2          5          1


select * from ::fn_Trace_getfilterinfo(2)

columnid    logical_operator comparison_operator value
------ ---------- ----------- ------
3           0                0                   6
10          0                7                   Profiler
10          0                7                   SQLAgent
```

NOTE

You may be wondering why there is always a `traceid` with a value of 1 running when you run the `fn_trace_getinfo` procedure. This is the default trace that SQL Server automatically initiates when it starts. The default trace is enabled by default. You can identify which trace is the default by selecting from the `sys.traces` catalog view and examining the `is_default` column. The default trace captures a number of different types of events, including object creates and drops, errors, memory and disk changes, security changes, and more. You can disable this default trace, but it is generally lightweight and should be left enabled.

The output from the functions that return trace information is relatively cryptic because many of the values returned are numeric. For example, the property values returned by `fn_trace_getinfo` are specified as integer IDs. Table 6.5 describes of each of these property IDs.

TABLE 6.5 Description of Trace Property ID Values

Property ID	Description
1	Trace options specified in `sp_trace_create`
2	Trace filename
3	Maximum size of trace file, in MB
4	Date and time the trace will be stopped
5	Current trace status

Stopping Server-Side Traces

It is important to keep track of the traces you have running and to ensure that "heavy" traces are stopped. Heavy traces are typically traces that capture a lot of events and are run on a busy SQL Server. These traces can affect the overall performance of your SQL Server machine and write a large amount of information to the trace output file. If you specified a stop time when you started the trace, it automatically stops and closes when the stop time is reached. For example, in the SQL script in Listing 6.2, if you wanted the trace to run for 15 minutes instead of indefinitely, you would set the value for the stoptime variable at the beginning of the script, using a command similar to the following:

```
set @stoptime = dateadd(minute, 15, getdate())
```

To otherwise stop a running server-side trace, you use the sp_trace_setstatus stored procedure and pass it the trace ID and a status of 0. Stopping a trace only stops gathering trace information and does not delete the trace definition from SQL Server. Essentially, it pauses the trace. You can restart the trace by passing sp_trace_setstatus a status value of 1.

After you stop a trace, you can close the trace and delete its definition from SQL Server by passing sp_trace_setstatus the ID of the trace you want to stop and a status value of 2. After you close the trace, you must redefine it before you can restart it.

If you don't know the ID of the trace you want to stop, you can use the fn_trace_getinfo function or the sys.traces catalog view to return a list of all running traces and select the appropriate trace ID. The following example shows how to stop and close a trace with a trace ID of 2:

```
-- Set the trace status to stop
exec sp_trace_setstatus 2, 0
go

-- Close and Delete the trace
exec sp_trace_setstatus 2, 2
go
```

If you want to stop and close multiple traces, you must call sp_trace_setstatus twice for each trace. Listing 6.4 provides an example of a system stored procedure that you can create in SQL Server to stop a specific trace or automatically stop all currently running traces.

LISTING 6.4 A Sample System Stored Procedure to Stop Profiler Traces

```
use master
go
if object_id ('sp_stop_profiler_trace') is not null
    drop proc sp_stop_profiler_trace
go

create proc sp_stop_profiler_trace @TraceID int = null
as

if @TraceID is not null
begin
    -- Set the trace status to stop
    exec sp_trace_setstatus @TraceID, 0

    -- Delete the trace
    exec sp_trace_setstatus @TraceID, 2
end
else
begin
-- the following cursor does not include the default trace
    declare c1 cursor for
    SELECT distinct traceid FROM :: fn_trace_getinfo (DEFAULT)
        WHERE traceId not in (select ID from sys.traces where is_default = 1)
    open c1
    fetch c1 into @TraceID
    while @@fetch_status = 0
    begin
        -- Set the trace status to stop
        exec sp_trace_setstatus @TraceID, 0

        -- Delete the trace
        exec sp_trace_setstatus @TraceID, 2
        fetch c1 into @TraceID
    end
    close c1
    deallocate c1
end
```

Profiler Usage Scenarios

This chapter has already covered many of the technical aspects of SQL Profiler, but what about some practical applications? Beyond the obvious uses of identifying what SQL statements an application is submitting, the following sections look at a few scenarios in which the SQL Profiler can be useful. These scenarios are presented to give you some ideas about how SQL Profiler can be used. You'll see that the monitoring and analysis capabilities of SQL Profiler are limited only by your creativity and ingenuity.

Analyzing Slow Stored Procedures or Queries

After you identify that a particular stored procedure is running slowly, what should you do? You might want to look at the estimated execution plan for the stored procedure, looking for table scans and sections of the plan that have a high cost percentage. But what if the execution plan has no obvious problems? This is the time you should consider using the SQL Profiler.

You can set up a trace on the stored procedure that captures the execution of each statement within it, along with its duration, in milliseconds. Here's how:

1. Create a new trace, using the `TSQL_Duration` template.
2. Add the `SP:StmtCompleted` event from the stored procedure event class to the trace.
3. Add a filter on the `Duration` column with the duration not equal to `0`. You can also set the filter to a larger number to exclude more of the short-running statements.

If you plan to run the procedure from SSMS, you might want to add a filter on the `SPID` column as well. Set it equal to the process ID for your session; the SPID is displayed at the bottom of the SSMS window next to your username, in parentheses. This traces only those commands that are executed from your SSMS query editor window.

When you run the trace and execute the stored procedure, you see only those statements in the procedure that have nonzero duration. The statements are listed in ascending duration order. You need to look to the bottom of the Profiler output window to find your longer-running statements. You can isolate these statements, copy them to SSMS, and perform a separate analysis on them to determine your problem.

You can also add showplan events to your Profiler trace to capture the execution plan as the trace is running. SQL Server now has showplan events that capture the showplan results in XML format. Traces with this type of XML output can have a significant impact on server performance while they are running but make the identification of poorly performing statements much easier. When you are tracing stored procedure executions, it is a good idea to add a filter on the specific stored procedure you are targeting to help minimize the impact on performance.

After you run a trace with an XML showplan event, you can choose to extract the showplan events to a separate file. To do so, in the SQL Server Profiler you select File, Export,

Extract SQL Server Events, Extract Showplan Events. At this point, you can save the showplan events in a single file or to a separate file for each event. The file(s) is saved with a `SQLPlan` file extension. This file can then be opened in SSMS, and the graphical query execution plan is displayed.

Deadlocks

Deadlocks are a common occurrence in database management systems (DMBSs). In simple terms, deadlocks occur when a process (for example, SPID 10) has a lock on a resource that another process (for example, SPID 20) wants. In addition, the second process (SPID 20) wants the resource that the first process has locked. This cyclic dependency causes the DBMS to kill one of the processes to resolve the deadlock situation.

Resolving deadlocks and identifying the deadlock participants can be difficult. In SQL Server 2008 and past versions, trace flag 1204 can be set to capture the processes involved in the deadlock. The output is text based but provides valuable information about the types of locks and the statements that were executing at the time of the deadlock. In addition to this approach, SQL Server 2008 offers the capability to capture detailed deadlock information via the SQL Server Profiler. This type of tracing can be accomplished as follows:

1. Create a new trace, using a `Blank` template; this leaves the selection of all the events, data columns, and filters to you.
2. Add the `Locks:Deadlock graph` event to the trace from the `Locks` category. An additional tab named Event Extraction Settings appears on the Trace Properties window.
3. Click the Save Deadlock XML Events Separately check box. This causes the deadlock information to be written to a separate file. You could also export the results after the trace has been run by using the File, Export option.

When you run this trace, it captures any deadlock event that occurs and writes it to the XML file specified. To test this, you can open two query editor windows and execute the following statements, in the order listed, and in the query window specified:

```
-- In Query Window # 1
--Step1
USE ADVENTUREWORKS2008
GO
BEGIN TRAN
   UPDATE HumanResources.Employee SET ModifiedDate = GETDATE()

-- In Query Window # 2
--Step2
USE ADVENTUREWORKS2008
GO
BEGIN TRAN
   UPDATE HumanResources.Department SET ModifiedDate = GETDATE()
   SELECT * FROM  HumanResources.Employee

-- In Query Window # 1
```

```
--Step3
  SELECT * FROM  HumanResources.Department
```

When the deadlock occurs, the results pane for one of the query windows contains a message similar to the following:

```
Msg 1205, Level 13, State 51, Line 3
Transaction (Process ID 55) was deadlocked on lock resources with another
process and has been chosen as the deadlock victim. Rerun the transaction.
```

When the row with the `Deadlock graph` event is selected in the Profiler output grid, a graph like the one shown in Figure 6.13 is displayed.

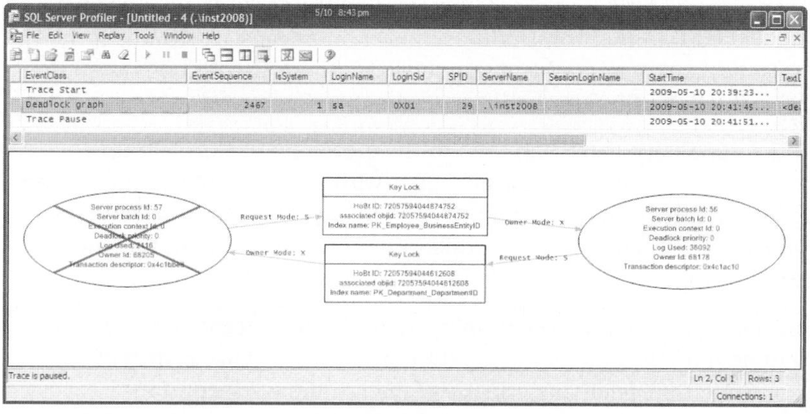

FIGURE 6.13 Output from the **Deadlock graph** event.

The `Deadlock graph` event contains a wealth of information about the deadlock occurrence. The oval nodes represent the processes involved in the deadlock. The oval with an X mark across it is the deadlock victim that had its process killed. The other oval represents the process that was allowed to complete when the deadlock was resolved. The boxes in the middle of the graph display lock information about the specific objects involved in the deadlock.

The graph is interactive and displays relevant information about the processes that were running when the deadlock occurred. For example, when you mouse over the oval nodes, pop-up text appears, displaying the SQL statement that was executing at the time of the deadlock. This is the same type of information that is displayed when the aforementioned trace flag is used, but the graph tends to be easier to decipher.

Identifying Ad Hoc Queries

One problem that can plague a production system is the execution of ad hoc queries against the production database. If you want to identify ad hoc queries, the application, and the users who are running them, SQL Profiler is your tool. You can create a trace as follows:

1. Create a new trace, using the `SQLProfilerStandard` template.
2. Add a new `ApplicationName` filter with `Like Microsoft%`.

When this trace is run, you can identify database access that is happening via SSMS or Microsoft Access. The user, the duration, and the actual SQL statement are captured. An alternative would be to change the `ApplicationName` filter to trace application access for all application names that are not like the name of your production applications, such as `Not Like MyOrderEntryApp%`.

Identifying Performance Bottlenecks

Another common problem with database applications is identifying performance bottlenecks. For example, say that an application is running slow, but you're not sure why. You tested all the SQL statements and stored procedures used by the application, and they were relatively fast. Yet you find that some of the application screens are slow. Is it the database server? Is it the client machine? Is it the network? These are all good questions, but what is the answer? SQL Profiler can help you find out.

You can start with the same trace definition used in the preceding section. For this scenario, you need to specify an `ApplicationName` filter with the name of the application you want to trace. You might also want to apply a filter to a specific `NTUserName` to further refine your trace and avoid gathering trace information for users other than the one that you have isolated.

After you start your trace, you use the slow-running application's screens. You need to look at the trace output and take note of the duration of the statements as they execute on the database server. Are they relatively fast? How much time was spent on the execution of the SQL statements and stored procedures relative to the response time of the application screen? If the total database duration is 1,000 milliseconds (1 second), and the screen takes 10 seconds to refresh, you need to examine other factors, such as the network or the application code.

With SQL Server 2008, you also combine Windows System Monitor (Perfmon) output with trace output to identify performance bottlenecks. This feature helps unite system-level metrics (for example, CPU utilization, memory usage) with SQL Server performance metrics. The result is a very impressive display that is synchronized based on time so that a correlation can be made between system-level spikes and the related SQL Server statements.

To try out this powerful new feature, you open the Perfmon application and add a new performance counter log. For simplicity, you can just add one counter, such as `% Processor Time`. Then you choose the option to manually start the log and click OK. Now, you want to apply some kind of load to the SQL Server system. The following script does index maintenance on two tables in the `AdventureWorks2008` database and can be used to apply a sample load:

```
USE [AdventureWorks2008]
GO
ALTER INDEX [PK_SalesOrderDetail_SalesOrderID_SalesOrderDetailID]
 ON [Sales].[SalesOrderDetail]
```

```
 REORGANIZE WITH ( LOB_COMPACTION = ON )
GO
PRINT 'FIRST INDEX IS REBUILT'
WAITFOR DELAY '00:00:05'
USE [AdventureWorks2008]
GO
ALTER INDEX [PK_Person_BusinessEntityID]
 ON [Person].[Person] REBUILD WITH
 ( PAD_INDEX  = OFF, STATISTICS_NORECOMPUTE  = OFF,
   ALLOW_ROW_LOCKS  = ON, ALLOW_PAGE_LOCKS  = ON,
   SORT_IN_TEMPDB = OFF )
GO
PRINT 'SECOND INDEX IS REORGANIZED'
```

Next, you open the script in SSMS, but you don't run it yet. You open SQL Profiler and create a trace by using the `Standard Profiler` template. This template captures basic SQL Server activity and also includes the `StartTime` and `EndTime` columns that are necessary to correlate with the Perfmon counters. Now you are ready to start the performance log and the SQL Server Profiler trace. When they are running, you can run the sample load script. When the script has completed, you stop the performance log and Profiler trace. You save the Profiler trace to a file and then open the file in the Profiler application.

The correlation of the Perfmon log to the trace output file is accomplished from within the Profiler application. To do this, you select File, Import Performance Data. Then you select the performance log file that was just created; these files are located by default in the `c:\perflogs` folder. After you import the performance data, a new performance graph and associated grid with the performance counters is displayed in the Profiler, as shown in Figure 6.14

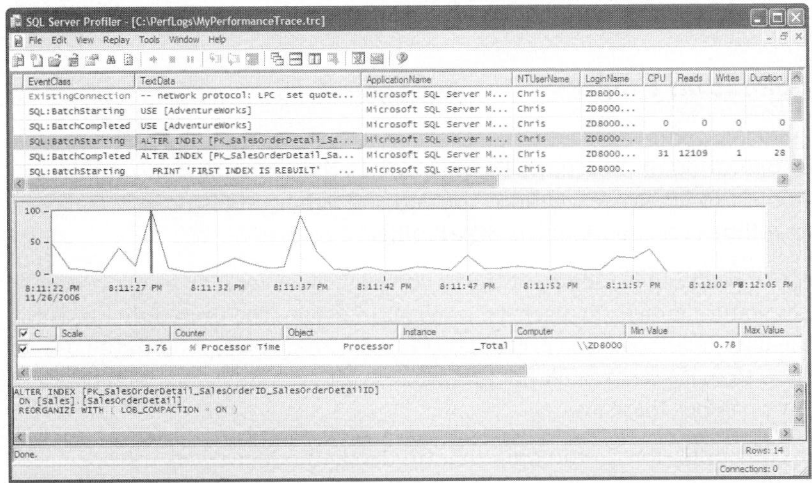

FIGURE 6.14 System Monitor counters correlated within a Profiler trace.

Now the fun begins! If you click one of the statements captured in the Profiler grid, a vertical red line appears in the Perfmon graph that reflects the time at which the statement was run. Conversely, if you click a location in the graph, the corresponding SQL statement that was run at that time is highlighted in the grid. If you see a spike in CPU in the Perfmon graph, you can click the spike in the graph and find the statement that may have caused the spike. This can help you quickly and efficiently identify bottlenecks and the processes contributing to it.

Monitoring Auto-Update Statistics

As discussed in Chapter 35, "Understanding Query Optimization," SQL Server updates index statistics automatically as data is changed in a table. In some environments, excessive auto-updating of statistics can affect system performance while the statistics are being updated. SQL Profiler can be used to monitor auto-updating of statistics as well as automatic statistics creation.

To monitor auto-updating of statistics, you create a trace and include the `AutoStats` event from the `Performance` event category. Then you select the `TextData`, `Integer Data`, `Success`, and `Object ID` columns. When the `AutoStats` event is captured, the `Integer Data` column contains the number of statistics updated for a given table, the `Object ID` is the ID of the table, and the `TextData` column contains names of the columns together with either an `Updated:` or `Created:` prefix. The `Success` column contains potential failure indication.

If you see an excessive number of `AutoStats` events on a table or index, and the duration is high, it could be affecting system performance. You might want to consider disabling auto-update for statistics on that table and schedule statistics to be updated periodically during nonpeak periods. You may also want to utilize the `AUTO_UPDATE_STATISTICS_ASYNC` database setting, which allows queries that utilize affected statistics to compile without having to wait for the update of statistics to complete.

Monitoring Application Progress

The 10 user-configurable events can be used in a variety of ways, including for tracking the progress of an application or procedure. For instance, perhaps you have a complex procedure that is subject to lengthy execution. You can add debugging logic in this procedure to allow for real-time benchmarking via SQL Profiler.

The key to this type of profiling is the use of the `sp_trace_generateevent` stored procedure, which enables you to launch the `User configurable` event. The procedure needs to reference one of the `User configurable` event IDs (`82` to `91`) that correspond to the `User configurable` event `0` to `9`. If you execute the procedure with `eventid = 82`, then `User configurable` event `0` catches these events.

Listing 6.5 contains a sample stored procedure that (in debug mode) triggers the trace events that SQL Profiler can capture.

LISTING 6.5 A Stored Procedure That Raises **User configurable** Events for SQL Profiler

```
CREATE PROCEDURE SampleApplicationProc (@debug bit = 0)
as
declare @userinfoParm nvarchar(128)
select @userinfoParm = getdate()

--if in debug mode, then launch event for Profiler
--    indicating Start of Application Proc
if @debug =1
begin
       SET @userinfoParm = 'Proc Start: ' + convert(varchar(30),getdate(),120)
       EXEC sp_trace_generateevent @eventid = 83, @userinfo = @userinfoparm
end

--Real world would have complex proc code executing here
--The WAITFOR statement was added to simulate processing time
WAITFOR DELAY '00:00:05'

---if debug mode, then launch event indicating next significant stage
if @debug =1
begin
       SET @userinfoParm = 'Proc Stage One Complete: '
                              + convert(varchar(20),getdate(),120)
       EXEC sp_trace_generateevent @eventid = 83, @userinfo = @userinfoparm
end

--Real world would have more complex proc code executing here
--The WAITFOR statement was added to simulate processing time
WAITFOR DELAY '00:00:05' —5 second delay

---if debug mode, then launch event indicating next significant stage
if @debug =1
begin
       SET @userinfoParm = 'Proc Stage Two Complete: '
                              + convert(varchar(30),getdate(),120)
       EXEC sp_trace_generateevent @eventid = 83, @userinfo = @userinfoparm
end

--You get the idea

GO
```

Now you need to set up a new trace that includes the `UserConfigurable:1` event. To do so, you choose the `TextData` data column to capture the `User configurable` output and any other data columns that make sense for your specific trace. After this task is complete, you can launch the sample stored procedure from Listing 6.5 and get progress information via SQL Profiler as the procedure executes. You can accumulate execution statistics over time with this kind of trace and summarize the results. The execution command for the procedure follows:

```
EXEC  SampleApplicationProc @debug = 1
```

The resulting SQL Profiler results are shown in Figure 6.15.

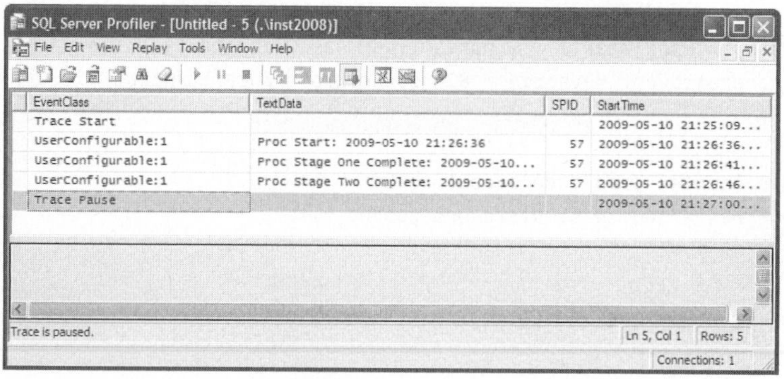

EventClass	TextData	SPID	StartTime
Trace Start			2009-05-10 21:25:09...
UserConfigurable:1	Proc Start: 2009-05-10 21:26:36	57	2009-05-10 21:26:36...
UserConfigurable:1	Proc Stage One Complete: 2009-05-10...	57	2009-05-10 21:26:41...
UserConfigurable:1	Proc Stage Two Complete: 2009-05-10...	57	2009-05-10 21:26:46...
Trace Pause			2009-05-10 21:27:00...

FIGURE 6.15 **`User configurable`** trace results.

There are many other applications for `User configurable` events. How you use them depends on your specific need. As is the case with many Profiler scenarios, there are seemingly endless possibilities.

Summary

Whether you are a developer or database administrator, you should not ignore the power of the SQL Profiler. It is often one of the most underused applications in the SQL Server toolkit, yet it is one of the most versatile. Its auditing capabilities and ability to unravel complex server processes define its value.

This chapter wraps up the introduction to the tools and utilities available with SQL Server. Now you should be equipped to start administering and working with SQL Server.

The chapters in the next section focus on the overall administration of SQL, using some of the tools that you have been exposed to thus far. Chapter 7, "SQL Server System and Database Administration," gives you some insight into the inner workings of SQL Server and what it takes to effectively administer a SQL Server instance.

CHAPTER 7

SQL Server System and Database Administration

IN THIS CHAPTER

- What's New in SQL Server System and Database Administration
- System Administrator Responsibilities
- System Databases
- System Tables
- System Views
- System Stored Procedures

This chapter outlines the role of a SQL Server system administrator and explores some of the methods that an administrator can use to query important system data. As with any other job, understanding the roles and responsibilities of the job is critical to doing the job well. The responsibilities of an administrator vary depending on the job, but there are some core responsibilities covered in this chapter.

You also need the right tools and right information to do the job well and do it efficiently. The system data covered in this chapter provides some of the key information. The methods discussed to access this information are among the tools you will need. System data discloses information that can be invaluable when assessing your SQL Server environment and is an essential part of administering a SQL Server database.

What's New in SQL Server System and Database Administration

The means for accessing system information has changed very little from SQL Server 2005 to SQL Server 2008. The new systems views that were introduced in SQL Server 2005 are still the preferred means for getting at that all-important system information. These views, which include catalog, compatibility, and dynamic views, are discussed in detail later in this chapter.

What is new in SQL Server 2008 is an expanded set of system views. These new views are geared toward some of the new functionality offered with SQL Server 2008. For example, new catalog and dynamic management views that return information about Change Tracking and the Resource Governor have been added to cover these new features.

System Administrator Responsibilities

A system administrator is responsible for the integrity and availability of the data in a database. This is a simple concept, but it is a huge responsibility. Some large corporations place a valuation on their data as high as $1 million per 100MB. The investment in dollars is not the only issue; many companies that lose mission-critical data simply never recover.

Job descriptions for system administrators vary widely. In small shops, the administrator might lay out the physical design, install SQL Server, implement the logical design, tune the installation, and then manage ongoing tasks, such as backups. At larger sites, tasks might be broken out into separate job functions. Managing users and backing up data are common examples. However, a lead administrator should still be in place to define policy and coordinate efforts.

Whether performed by an individual or as a team, the core administration tasks are as follows:

- Install and configure SQL Server.
- Plan and create databases.
- Manage data storage.
- Control security.
- Tune the database.
- Perform backup and recovery.

Another task sometimes handled by administrators is managing stored procedures. Because stored procedures for user applications often contain complex Transact-SQL (T-SQL) code, they tend to fall into the realm of the application developer. However, because stored procedures are stored as objects in the database, they are also the responsibility of the administrator. If an application calls custom stored procedures, the system administrator must be aware of this and coordinate with the application developers.

The system administration job can be stressful, frustrating, and demanding, but it is a highly rewarding, interesting, and respected position. As a system administrator, you are expected to know all, see all, and predict all, but you should be well compensated for your efforts.

System Databases

SQL Server uses system databases to support different parts of the database management system (DBMS). Each database plays a specific role and stores information that SQL Server needs to do its job. The system databases are much like the user databases created in SQL Server. They store data in tables and contain the views, stored procedures, and other database objects that you also see in user databases. They also have associated database files (that is, `.mdf` and `.ldf` files) that are physically located on the SQL Server machine. Table 7.1 lists system databases and their related database filenames.

TABLE 7.1 System Databases and Their Associated Database Files

Database	.mdf Filename	.ldf Filename
master	master.mdf	mastlog.ldf
resource	mssqlsystemresource.mdf	mssqlsystemresource.ldf
model	model.mdf	modellog.ldf
msdb	msdbdata.mdf	msdblog.ldf
distribution	distmdl.ldf	distmdl.mdf
tempdb	tempdb.mdf	templog.ldf

TIP

You can use the `sys.master_files` catalog view to list the physical locations of the system database files as well as the user database files. This catalog view contains a myriad of information, including the logical name, current state, and size of each database file.

The folder where each of these database files is located depends on the SQL Server installation. By default, the installation process places these files in a folder named *`<drive>:\Program Files\Microsoft SQL Server\MSSQL.1\MSSQL\Data\`*. You can move these files after the installation by using special procedures that are documented in the SQL Server Books Online topic "Moving System Databases."

The following sections describe the function of each system database.

The `master` Database

The `master` database contains server-wide information about the SQL Server system. This server-wide information includes logins, linked server information, configuration information for the server, and information about user databases created in the SQL Server instance. The actual locations of the database files and key properties that relate to each user database are stored in the `master` database.

SQL Server cannot start without a `master` database. This is not surprising, given the type of information that it contains. Without the `master` database, SQL Server does not know the location of the databases that it services and does not know how the server is configured to run.

The resource Database

The resource database contains all the system objects deployed with SQL Server 2008. These system objects include the system stored procedures and system views that logically appear in each database but are physically stored in the resource database. Microsoft moved all the system objects to the resource database to simplify the upgrade process. When a new release of the software is made available, upgrading the system objects is accomplished by simply copying the single resource database file to the local server. Similarly, rolling back an upgrade only requires overwriting the current version of the resource database with the older version.

You do not see the resource database in the list of system databases shown in SQL Server Management Studio (SSMS). You also cannot add user objects to the resource database. For the most part, you should not be aware of the existence of the resource database. It has database files named mssqlsystemresources.mdf and mssqlsystemresources.ldf that are located in the Binn folder, but you cannot access the database directly. In addition, you do not see the database listed when selecting databases using system views or with system procedures, such as sp_helpdb.

The model Database

The model database is a template on which all user-created databases are based. All databases must contain a base set of objects known as the *database catalog*. When a new database is created, the model is copied to create the requisite objects. Conveniently, objects can be added to the model database. For example, if you want a certain table created in all your databases, you can create the table in the model database, and it is then propagated to all subsequently created databases.

The msdb Database

The msdb database is used to store information for the SQL Server Agent, the Service Broker, Database Mail, log shipping, and more. When you create and schedule a SQL Server Agent job, the job's parameters and execution history are stored in msdb. Backups and maintenance plan information are stored in msdb as well. If log shipping is implemented, critical information about the servers and tables involved in this process is stored in msdb.

The distribution Database

The distribution database, utilized during replication, stores metadata and history information for all types of replication. It is also used to store transactions when transactional replication is utilized. By default, replication is not set up, and you do not see the distribution database listed in SSMS. However, the actual data files for the distribution database are installed by default.

Refer to Chapter 19, "Replication," for a more detailed discussion of the intricacies of replication.

The tempdb Database

The tempdb database stores temporary data and data objects. The temporary data objects include temporary tables, temporary stored procedures, and any other objects you want to create temporarily. The longevity of data objects in the temporary database depends on the type of object created. Ultimately, all temporary database objects are removed when the SQL Server service is restarted. The tempdb database is re-created, and all objects and data added since the last restart of SQL Server are lost.

tempdb can also be used for some of SQL Server's internal operations. Large sort operations are performed in tempdb before the result set is returned to the client. Certain index operations can be performed in tempdb to offload some of the space requirements or to spread I/O. SQL Server also uses tempdb to store row versions that are generated from database modifications in databases that use row versioning or snapshot isolation transactions. Refer to Chapter 37 "Locking and Performance," for a more detailed discussion of transaction isolation levels and row versioning.

Maintaining System Databases

You should give system databases the same attention that you give your user databases. These databases should be backed up on a regular basis and secured in the event that one of them needs to be restored. All the system databases, with the exception of tempdb and resource, can be backed up. These same databases can also be restored to bring them back to a previous state.

7

NOTE

Although you cannot back up the resource database using SQL Server's BACKUP and RESTORE commands, you can make a backup copy of it by performing a file-based or disk-based backup of the mssqlsystemresource.mdf file (SQL Server must not be running at the time). Likewise, you can manually restore a backup copy of the mssqlsystemresource.mdf file only when SQL Server is not running. You must be careful not to overwrite the current resource database with a version for a different release level of SQL Server.

It's important that you monitor the size of your system databases. The amount of data that accumulates in these databases can be significant. This is particularly true for the tempdb, msdb, and distribution databases. Large sort or index operations can increase the size of your tempdb database in a short period of time. The msdb and distribution databases contain a great deal of historical information. Consider, for example, a server with hundreds of databases that have log backups occurring every 15 minutes. The information captured for each individual backup is not significant, but the total number of databases and frequency of the backups cause many rows to be stored in the msdb database. Cleanup tasks and similar activities that remove older historical data can help keep the database size manageable.

System Tables

System tables contain data about objects in the SQL Server databases (that is, metadata) as well as information that SQL Server components use to do their job. Many of the system tables are now hidden (in the resource database) and are no longer available for direct access by end users. In SQL Server 2008, compatibility views, which are discussed later in this chapter, have the same names as the system tables available in SQL Server 2000. For example, if you had a query in SQL Server 2000 that selected from syscolumns, this query continues to work in SQL Server 2008, but the results come from a view instead of a system table.

The system tables that you can view are now found in some of the system databases, such as msdb or master. You can use the Object Explorer in SSMS to view the system tables in these databases. Figure 7.1 shows the system tables listed for the master database in the Object Explorer.

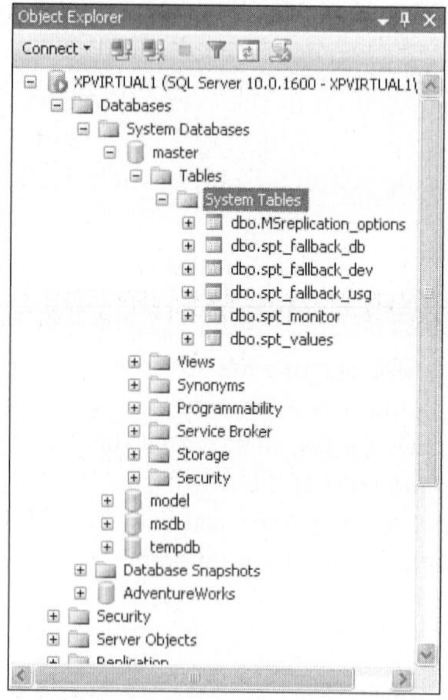

FIGURE 7.1 System tables listed in Object Explorer.

The most significant number of viewable system tables is found in the msdb system database. The system tables there support backup and restore, log shipping, maintenance plans, Notification Services, the SQL Server Agent, and more. You can retrieve a tremendous amount of information from these system tables if you know what you are looking for. The following query selects from the system tables in `msdb` to report on recent restores for the `AdventureWorks2008R2` database:

```
select destination_database_name 'database', h.restore_date, restore_type,
   cast((backup_size/1024)/1024 as numeric(8,0)) 'backup_size MB',
   f.physical_device_name
 from msdb..restorehistory h (NOLOCK)
    LEFT JOIN msdb..backupset b (NOLOCK)
        ON h.backup_set_id = b.backup_set_id
    LEFT JOIN msdb..backupmediafamily f (NOLOCK)
        ON b.media_set_id = f.media_set_id
 where h.restore_date > getdate() - 5
    and UPPER(h.destination_database_name) = 'AdventureWorks2008R2'
 order by UPPER(h.destination_database_name), h.restore_date desc
```

One of the challenges with using system tables is determining the relationships between them. Some vendors offer diagrams of these tables, and you can also determine the relationships by reviewing the foreign keys on these tables and by referring to SQL Server 2008 Books Online, which describes the use for each column in the system table.

CAUTION

Microsoft does not recommend querying system tables directly. It does not guarantee the consistency of system tables across versions and warns that queries that may have worked against system tables in past versions may no longer work. Catalog views or information schema views should be used instead, especially in production code.

Queries against system tables are best used for ad hoc queries. The values in system tables should never be updated, and an object's structure should not be altered, either. Making changes to the data or structure could cause problems and cause SQL Server or one of its components to fail.

System Views

System views are virtual tables that expose metadata that relates to many different aspects of SQL Server. Several different types of views target different data needs. SQL Server 2008 offers an extended number of system views and view types that should meet most, if not all, your metadata needs.

The available system views can be shown in the Object Explorer in SSMS. Figure 7.2 shows the Object Explorer with the `System Views` node highlighted. There are far too many views to cover in detail in this chapter, but we cover each type of view and provide an example of each to give you some insight into their value. Each system view is covered in detail in SQL Server Books Online, which includes descriptions of each column in the view.

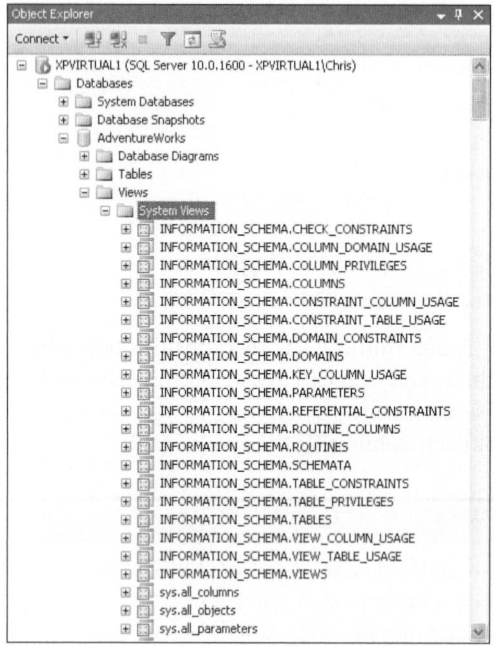

FIGURE 7.2 System views listed in Object Explorer.

Compatibility Views

Compatibility views were retained in SQL Server 2008 for backward compatibility. Many of the system tables available in SQL Server 2000 and prior versions of SQL Server are now implemented as compatibility views. These views have the same name as the system tables from prior versions and return the same metadata available in SQL Server 2000. They do not contain information that was added after SQL Server 2000.

You can find most of the compatibility views in the Object Explorer by looking for system views that have names starting with `sys.sys`. For example, `sys.syscolumns`, `sys.syscomments`, and `sys.sysobjects` are all compatibility views. The first part of the name indicates the schema that the object belongs to (in this case, `sys`). All system objects are part of this `sys` schema or the `INFORMATION_SCHEMA` schema. The second part of the name is the view name, which corresponds to the name of a system table in SQL Server 2000.

TIP

To see a list of compatibility views, use the index lookup in SQL Server 2008 Books Online and look for `sys.sys`. The index is placed at the beginning of a list of compatibility views, starting with `sys.sysaltfiles`. Objects in the list that are compatibility views have the text `compatibility view` following the object name, so you can easily identify them and get help.

You also can use the new IntelliSense feature available with SQL Server 2008 to obtain information about the compatibility views and other system views. Simply open a query window in SSMS and start typing a `SELECT` statement. When you start typing the name of the view that you want to select from (for example, `sys.`) the IntelliSense drop-down appears listing the views that start with the letters `sys`. You can also determine the columns available from the view by referencing the view or alias for the view in the column selection list. When you enter the period following the view or alias, the IntelliSense drop-down shows you the available columns.

You should transition from the use of compatibility views to the use of other system views, such as catalog views. The scripts that were created in SQL Server 2000 and reference SQL Server 2000 system tables should continue to function in SQL Server 2008, but this capability is strictly for backward compatibility. Table 7.2 provides a list of SQL Server 2000 system tables and alternative SQL Server 2008 system views you can use instead.

TABLE 7.2 SQL Server 2008 Alternatives for SQL Server 2000 System Tables

SQL Server 2000 System Table	SQL Server 2008 System View	View Type
`sysaltfiles`	`sys.master_files`	Catalog view
`syscacheobjects`	`sys.dm_exec_cached_plans`	DMV
	`sys.dm_exec_plan_attributes`	DMV
	`sys.dm_exec_sql_text`	DMV
`syscharsets`	`sys.syscharsets`	Compatibility view
`syscolumns`	`sys.columns`	Catalog view
`syscomments`	`sys.sql_modules`	Catalog view
`sysconfigures`	`sys.configurations`	Catalog view
`sysconstraints`	`sys.check_constraints`	Catalog view
	`sys.default_constraints`	Catalog view
	`sys.key_constraints`	Catalog view

TABLE 7.2 SQL Server 2008 Alternatives for SQL Server 2000 System Tables

SQL Server 2000 System Table	SQL Server 2008 System View	View Type
	sys.foreign_keys	Catalog view
syscurconfigs	sys.configurations	Catalog view
sysdatabases	sys.databases	Catalog view
sysdepends	sys.sql_dependencies	Catalog view
sysdevices	sys.backup_devices	Catalog view
sysfilegroups	sys.filegroups	Catalog view
sysfiles	sys.database_files	Catalog view
sysforeignkeys	sys.foreign_keys	Catalog view
sysfulltextcatalogs	sys.fulltext_catalogs	Catalog view
sysindexes	sys.indexes	Catalog view
	sys.partitions	Catalog view
	sys.allocation_units	Catalog view
	sys.dm_db_partition_stats	DMV
sysindexkeys	sys.index_columns	Catalog view
syslanguages	sys.syslanguages	Compatibility view
syslockinfo	sys.dm_tran_locks	DMV
syslocks	sys.dm_tran_locks	DMV
syslogins	sys.sql_logins (transact-sql)	Catalog view
sysmembers	sys.database_role_members	Catalog view
sysmessages	sys.messages	Catalog view
sysobjects	sys.objects	Catalog view
sysoledbusers	sys.linked_logins	Catalog view
sysopentapes	sys.dm_io_backup_tapes	DMV
sysperfinfo	sys.dm_os_performance_counters	DMV
syspermissions	sys.database_permissions	Catalog view
	sys.server_permissions	Catalog view
sysprocesses	sys.dm_exec_connections	DMV

TABLE 7.2 SQL Server 2008 Alternatives for SQL Server 2000 System Tables

SQL Server 2000 System Table	SQL Server 2008 System View	View Type
	sys.dm_exec_sessions	DMV
	sys.dm_exec_requests	DMV
sysprotects	sys.database_permissions	Catalog view
	sys.server_permissions	Catalog view
sysreferences	sys.foreign_keys	Catalog view
sysremotelogins	sys.remote_logins	Catalog view
sysservers	sys.servers	Catalog view
systypes	sys.types	Catalog view
sysusers	sys.database_principals	Catalog view

Catalog Views

Using catalog views is the preferred method for returning information used by the Microsoft SQL Server database engine. There is a catalog view to return information about almost every aspect of SQL Server. The number of catalog views is far too large to list here, but you can gain some insight into the range of information available by looking at the following list, which shows the categories of information covered by catalog views:

- Change Tracking
- Common language runtime (CLR) assembly
- Data spaces and full text
- Database mirroring
- Data spaces
- Endpoint
- Extended properties
- Linked servers
- Messages (for errors)
- Objects
- Partition function
- Resource Governor
- Scalar types
- Schemas

- Security
- Server-wide configuration
- Service Broker
- SQL Server Extended Events
- XML schemas (XML type system)

Some of the catalog views return information that is new to SQL Server 2008. Examples include the Change Tracking and Resource Governor catalog views. Other catalog views provide information that may have been available in prior versions through system tables, system procedures, and so on, but the new catalog views expand on the information returned and include elements that are new to SQL Server 2008.

To demonstrate the use of a catalog view, let's compare a simple SQL Server 2000 `SELECT` statement that returns object information to a `SELECT` statement in SQL Server 2008 that returns similar information. The following example shows a `SELECT` statement written in SQL Server 2000 to return any stored procedure created after a given date:

```
select o.crdate, o.name
 from sysobjects o
 where type = 'p'
  and crdate > '1/1/08'
 order by crdate, name
```

Now, compare this `SELECT` statement to one that uses a SQL Server 2008 catalog view. The `sys.objects` catalog view is a new alternative to the SQL Server 2000 `sysobjects` system table. The following `SELECT` uses the `sys.objects` catalog view to return the same type of information as the preceding example:

```
select o.create_date, o.modify_date, name
 from sys.objects o
 where type = 'p'
 and (create_date > '1/1/08'
   or o.modify_date >= '1/1/08')
 order by  1, 2, 3
```

As you can see, the `modify_date` column has been added to the `SELECT` statement. This column did not exist with the `sysobjects` system table. The addition of this column allows you to identify objects that were created as well as objects that were modified or altered.

Let's look at an example of using a catalog view to return the same kind of information returned in SQL Server 2000 with a system procedure. The handy `sp_helpfile` system procedure returns information about database files associated with a given database. This SQL Server 2000 procedure is still available in SQL Server 2008. An alternative to this procedure is the new `sys.master_files` catalog view. This view returns all the information that `sp_helpfile` returns and more. The following example shows a `SELECT` statement using the sys.master_files catalog view to return the database files for the AdventureWorks2008R2 database:

```
select *
 from sys.master_files
 where db_name(database_id) = 'AdventureWorks2008R2'
```

You have the distinct advantage of being able to select the database files for all the databases on your server by using this catalog view. You can also tailor your SELECT statement to isolate database files based on the size of the database or the location of the physical database files. For example, to return all database files that are found somewhere on your C drive, you could use the following SELECT:

```
select db_name(database_id), physical_name
 from sys.master_files
 where physical_name like 'c:\%'
```

There are plenty of catalog views that provide information about SQL Server. When you are looking to return information about SQL Server components, you should look to the catalog views first. These views provide a great deal of flexibility and allow you to isolate the specific information you need.

Information Schema Views

Information schema views provide another system table–independent option for accessing SQL Server metadata. This type of view was available in prior versions of SQL Server. Using information schema views is a viable alternative for accessing SQL Server metadata from a production application. The information schema views enable an application that uses them to function properly even though the underlying system tables may have changed. Changes to the underlying system tables are most prevalent when a new version of SQL Server is released (such as SQL Server 2008), but changes can also occur as part of service packs to an existing version.

The information schema views also have the advantage of being SQL-92 compatible. Compliance with the SQL-92 standard means that SQL statements written against these views work with other DBMSs that also adhere to the SQL-92 standard. The SQL-92 standard supports a three-part naming convention, which SQL Server has implemented as *database.schema.object.*

In SQL Server 2008, all the information schema views are in the same schema, named INFORMATION_SCHEMA. The following information schema views or objects are available:

- CHECK_CONSTRAINTS
- COLUMN_DOMAIN_USAGE
- COLUMN_PRIVILEGES
- COLUMNS
- CONSTRAINT_COLUMN_USAGE

- CONSTRAINT_TABLE_USAGE
- DOMAIN_CONSTRAINTS
- DOMAINS
- KEY_COLUMN_USAGE
- PARAMETERS
- REFERENTIAL_CONSTRAINTS
- ROUTINES
- ROUTINE_COLUMNS
- SCHEMATA
- TABLE_CONSTRAINTS
- TABLE_PRIVILEGES
- TABLES
- VIEW_COLUMN_USAGE
- VIEW_TABLE_USAGE
- VIEWS

When you refer to information schema views in a SQL statement, you must use a qualified name that includes the schema name. For example, the following statement returns all the tables and columns in a given database, using the `tables` and `columns` information schema views:

```
select t.TABLE_NAME, c.COLUMN_NAME
 from INFORMATION_SCHEMA.TABLES t
  join INFORMATION_SCHEMA.COLUMNS c on t.TABLE_NAME = c.TABLE_NAME
 order by t.TABLE_NAME, ORDINAL_POSITION
```

TIP

You can expand the `Views` node in a given database in the Object Explorer and open the `System Views` node to see a list of the available information schema views. The information schema views are listed at the top of the `System Views` node. If you expand the `Column` node under each information schema view, you see the available columns to select from the view. You can then drag the column into a query window for use in a `SELECT` statement. You can also use IntelliSense in a query window determine the columns.

Fortunately, the names of the information schema views are fairly intuitive and reflect the kind of information they contain. The relationships between the information schema views can be derived from the column names shared between the tables.

Dynamic Management Views

Dynamic management views (DMVs), which were introduced in SQL Server 2005, provide a simple means for assessing the state of a server. These views provide a lightweight means for gathering diagnostic information without the heavy burden associated with the tools available in SQL Server 2000. The SQL Server 2000 diagnostic tools, such as heavy Profiler traces, PerfMon, `dbcc` executions, and `pssdiag`, are still available, but oftentimes, the information returned from the DMVs is enough to determine what may be ailing a SQL Server machine.

An extensive number of DMVs are available in SQL Server 2008. Some DMVs are scoped at the server level, and others are scoped at the database level. They are all found in the `sys` schema and have names that start with `dm_`. Table 7.3 lists the different types of DMVs. The DMVs in this table are categorized based on function as well as the starting characters in the DMV names. The naming convention gives you an easy means for identifying the type of each DMV.

TABLE 7.3 Types of DMVs

Category	Name Prefix	Information Captured
Auditing	`dm_audit`	New Auditing information
Service Broker	`dm_broker`	Server Broker statistics, including activated tasks and connections
Change Data	`dm_cdc`	New Change Data Capture information
CLR	`dm_clr`	CLR information, including the CLR loaded assemblies
Cryptographic	`dm_cryp`	Security related data
TDE	`dm_database`	Transparent Data Encryption
Database	`dm_db`	Databases and database objects
Execution	`dm_exec`	Execution of user code
Full-Text	`dm_fts`	Full-Text Search information
I/O	`dm_io`	Input and output on network disks
Operating system	`dm_os`	Low-level operating system information, including memory and locking information
Provider	`dm_provider`	Extensible Key Management (EKM)
Query Notification	`dm_qn`	Active Query Notification subscriptions
Replication	`dm_repl`	Replication information, including the articles, publications, and transaction involved in replication

7

TABLE 7.3 Types of DMVs

Category	Name Prefix	Information Captured
Server	dm_server	Server Audit status
Transaction	dm_tran	Transactions and isolation-level information
Object	dm_sql	Object References
Extended Events	dm_xe	New event handling infrastructure

TIP

You can expand the `Views` node in a given database in the Object Explorer and open the `System Views` node to see a list of the available DMVs. The DMVs are all listed together and start with `dm_`. If you expand the `Column` node under each DMV, you see the available columns to select from the view. You can then drag the column into a query window to be included in a `SELECT` statement.

To illustrate the value of the DMVs, let's look at a performance scenario and compare the SQL Server 2000 approach to a SQL Server 2008 approach using DMVs. A common performance-related question is "What stored procedures are executing most frequently on my server?" With SQL Server 2000, the most likely way to find out is to run a Profiler trace. You must have a Profiler trace that has already been running to capture the stored procedure executions, or you must create a new trace and run it for a period of time to answer the performance question. The trace takes time to create and can affect server performance while it is running.

With SQL Server 2008, you can use one of the DMVs in the execution category to answer the same performance question. The following example uses the `sys.dm_exec_query_stats` DMV along with a dynamic management function named `dm_exec_sql_text`. It returns the object IDs of the five most frequently executed stored procedures, along with the actual text associated with the procedure:

```
select top 5 q.execution_count, q.total_worker_time,
 s.dbid, s.objectid, s.text
 from sys.dm_exec_query_stats q
 CROSS APPLY sys.dm_exec_sql_text (q.sql_handle) s
 ORDER BY q.execution_count desc
```

The advantage of using a DMV is that it can return past information without having to explicitly create a trace or implement some other performance tool. SQL Server automatically caches the information so that you can query it at any time. The collection of the data starts when the SQL Server instance is started, so you can get a good cross-section of information. Keep in mind that your results can change as the server continues to collect information over time.

Many of the performance scenarios such as those that relate to memory, CPU utilization, blocking, and recompilation can be investigated using DMVs. You should consider using

DMVs to address performance problems before using other methods in SQL Server 2008. In many cases, you may be able to avoid costly traces and glean enough information from the DMV to solve your problem.

NOTE

Dynamic management functions return the same type of information as DMVs. The dynamic management functions also have names that start with dm_ and reside in the sys schema. You can find the dynamic management functions listed in the Object Explorer within the master database. If you select Function, System Functions, Table-Valued Functions, you see the dynamic management functions listed at the top.

DMVs are also a great source of information that does not relate directly to performance. For example, you can use the dm_os_sys_info DMV to gather important server information, such as the number of CPUs, the amount of memory, and so on. The following example demonstrates the use of the dm_os_sys_info DMV to return CPU and memory information:

```
select cpu_count, hyperthread_ratio, physical_memory_in_bytes
 from sys.dm_os_sys_info

/* Results from prior select

cpu_count   hyperthread_ratio physical_memory_in_bytes
----------- ----------------- ------------------------
2           2                 2146357248
*/
```

The cpu_count column returns the number of logical CPUs, hyperthread_ratio returns the ratio between physical CPUs and logical CPUs, and the last column selected returns the physical memory on the SQL Server machine.

System Stored Procedures

System stored procedures have been a favorite of SQL Server DBAs since the inception of SQL Server. They provide a rich set of information that covers many different aspects of SQL Server. They can return some of the same types of information as system views, but they generally return a fixed set of information that cannot be modified as you can when using a SELECT statement against the system views. That is not to say that they are not valuable; they are valuable, and they are particularly useful for people who have been using SQL Server for a long time. System stored procedures such as sp_who, sp_lock, and sp_help are tools for a database professional that are as basic as a hammer is to a carpenter.

System stored procedures have names that start with sp_, and they are found in the sys schema. They are global in scope, which allows you to execute them from any database, without qualifying the stored procedure name. They also run in the context of the database where you are working. In other words, if you execute `sp_helpfile` in the `AdventureWorks2008R2` database, the database files for the `AdventureWorks2008R2` database are returned. This same type of behavior exists for any stored procedure that is created in the `master` database with a name that starts with `sp_`. For example, if you create a procedure named `sp_helpme` in the `master` database and execute that procedure in the `AdventureWorks2008R2` database, SQL Server ultimately looks for and finds the procedure in the `master` database.

NOTE

It is often useful to create your own system stored procedures to make it easier to execute complex queries against the system views (or to provide information not provided by the built-in system procedures). For more information and tips on creating your own system stored procedures, refer to Chapter 28, "Creating and Managing Stored Procedures."

System stored procedures are listed in the Object Explorer, in the `Programmability` node within `Stored Procedures` and then `System Stored Procedures`. There are far too many system stored procedures to list or discuss them all here. A quick check of the `master` database lists more than 1,000 procedures. SQL Server Books Online provides detailed help on these procedures, which it groups into 18 different categories.

Useful System Stored Procedures

You are likely to use only a handful of system stored procedures on a regular basis. What procedures you use depends on the type of work you do with SQL Server and your capacity to remember their names. Table 7.4 contains a sample set of system stored procedures that you may find useful.

TABLE 7.4 Useful System Stored Procedures

System Stored Procedure	Description
`sp_configure`	Displays or changes server-wide configuration settings.
`sp_createstats`	Creates statistics that are used by the Query Optimizer for all tables in a database.
`sp_help`	Provides details about the object that is passed to it. If a table name is passed to this procedure, it returns information on the columns, constraints, indexes, and more.
`sp_helpdb`	If no parameters are supplied, returns relevant database information (including the space used) for all the databases on an instance of SQL Server.

TABLE 7.4 Useful System Stored Procedures

System Stored Procedure	Description
sp_helpfile	Lists the database files associated with the database you are connected to.
sp_lock	Displays current locking information for the entire SQL Server instance.
sp_spaceused	Provides the number of rows and disk space used by the table, indexed view, or queue passed to it.
sp_who	Lists current processes that are connected to an instance of SQL Server.

Many of the administrative functions performed by SSMS can also be accomplished with system stored procedures. Examples include procedures that start with `sp_add` and `sp_delete`, which can be used to add and delete database objects. In addition, more than 90 system stored procedures start with `sp_help`, which return help information on database objects.

TIP

You can use the `sys.all_objects` catalog view to search for available system stored procedures. This catalog view lists objects that are schema scoped as well as system objects. For example, the query `SELECT * FROM sys.all_objects WHERE name LIKE 'sp_help%'` returns all the system stored procedures that start with `sp_help`. You can turn to Books Online for detailed help on any of the system stored procedures. Just enter `sp_` in the index search, and you see a list of them all.

Becoming familiar with some of the system stored procedures is well worth your while. Using them is a very fast and effective means for gathering information from SQL Server. They do not require the formation of a `SELECT` statement, and using them is often the easiest way to get information via a query window.

Summary

Administering SQL Server can be a complex and time-consuming job. Understanding the SQL Server internals and some of the easy ways to obtain information about a SQL Server instance can make this job a lot easier. Taking the time to learn what makes SQL Server tick expands your knowledge of this comprehensive DBMS and helps you make better decisions when working with it.

Now that you know a bit about managing SQL Server, you may need to install an instance of SQL Server to administer. Take a look at Chapter 8, "Installing SQL Server 2008," which guides you through the installation process.

CHAPTER 8

Installing SQL Server 2008

IN THIS CHAPTER

- What's New in Installing SQL Server 2008
- Installation Requirements
- Installation Walkthrough
- Installing SQL Server Using a Configuration File
- Installing Service Packs and Cumulative Updates
- Slipstream Installations

Installing SQL Server is the first and one of the easiest tasks you'll accomplish as an administrator. And even though it may take as little as 15 minutes to get SQL Server 2008 up and running by clicking through the install screens and accepting the defaults (Next, Next, Next...), it is crucial to first understand the meaning of each install option and its ramifications for your environment.

What's New in Installing SQL Server 2008

The installation process has been completely revamped for SQL Server 2008, introducing enhancements to simplify the installation compared to SQL Server 2005. The new installation features for SQL Server 2008 include the following:

- A new SQL Server 2008 Installation Center landing page, which includes a number of options for planning, installing, and maintaining a SQL Server implementation, as well as links to SQL Server documentation for planning and reviewing before starting the install.
- New maintenance tasks available in the installation process, allowing DBAs to either repair a corrupt SQL Server 2008 installation or conduct a feature upgrade. The Feature Upgrade Wizard allows DBAs to upgrade or change their installed edition of SQL Server 2008 (for example, upgrading from Standard Edition to Enterprise Edition without having to perform a complete reinstall).

- A discovery report that provides details on all SQL Server components, features, and settings associated with an installation.
- The potential to automate SQL Server installations by using an existing configuration file.
- An Advanced Cluster Preparation tool, which streamlines and prepares a SQL Server 2008 failover cluster installation.

With the release of Service Pack 1, SQL Server 2008 also now supports Slipstream installation. Slipstreaming is a method of integrating a SQL Server 2008 update (such as a service pack or cumulative update) with the original installation media so that the original media and update are installed at the same time. This capability can be a huge timesaver over having to manually apply service packs or cumulative updates after performing a full installation.

Installation Requirements

Before you install SQL Server 2008 on your server, it's a good idea (even if you own the latest-and-greatest system) to review the hardware and software requirements. The next two sections gather all the fine print into a few conveniently organized tables.

NOTE

The SQL Server 2008 installer helps determine whether your system meets the minimum requirements by running the new System Configuration Checker (SCC) early in the install. SCC conveniently provides a savable (via a button click) textual report on its results (and displays them onscreen). SCC is covered in detail later in this chapter.

Hardware Requirements

To install SQL Server 2008, you must ensure your system possesses a few basic components:

- A pointing device
- A display device with resolution of at least 1024×768 (required by SQL Server Management Studio [SMSS])
- A DVD-ROM or CD-ROM drive (for installation from disc)

Table 8.1 lists server environment hardware requirements, by SQL Server edition, with reference to processor type and/or word length. This table lists the base minimum hardware requirements. In most installations, you want to have at least 2GB of memory and a 2GHz or faster processor. In addition, installation using a redundant array of disks (RAID) on production systems is highly recommended.

Of course, faster editions of processors, increased RAM, and more disk space don't negatively impact any installation either. One final (and perhaps obvious) note: The more SQL Server components you install, the more disk space you need. Analysis Services, for example, requires an additional 90MB of disk space for the install.

The hard disk space requirements for SQL Server are dependent on which SQL Server components are installed. Table 8.2 breaks down the disk space requirements by feature.

TABLE 8.1 SQL Server 2008 Minimum Hardware Requirements, by Edition

SQL Server Editions	Memory (RAM)	Processors (CPU)
Enterprise, Datacenter, Standard, Workgroup, Web, and Developer (32-bit)	1GB	1GHz Pentium III
Enterprise, Datacenter, Standard, Workgroup, Web, and Developer (64-bit)	1GB	1.4GHz AMD Opteron, AMD Athlon 64, Intel Xeon with Intel EM64T support, or Intel Pentium IV with EM64T support
Enterprise, Standard, and Developer (Itanium)	1GB	1GHz Itanium
Express (64-bit)	256MB	1.4GHz AMD Opteron, AMD Athlon 64, Intel Xeon with Intel EM64T support, or Intel Pentium IV with EM64T support
Express (32-bit)	256MB	1GHz Pentium III
Express with Tools and Express with Advanced Services (32-bit)	512MB	1GHz Pentium III

NOTE

Licensing for multicore processors is the same as for single-core processors: only a single license is required for each multicore processor. Another way of saying this is licensing is per CPU socket, not per processor core.

TABLE 8.2 SQL Server 2008 Disk Space Requirements, by Feature

SQL Server Feature	Disk Space Requirement
Database Engine and data files, Replication, and Full-Text Search	280MB
Analysis Services and data files	90MB
Reporting Services and Report Manager	120MB
Integration Services	120MB
Client Components	850MB
SQL Server Books Online	240MB

Software Requirements

The following software prerequisites must be installed on any server running any SQL Server edition:

- Microsoft Internet Explorer 6.0 Service Pack 1 (SP1) or later (required because it is a dependency of SMSS, Books Online, Business Intelligence Development Studio [for Analysis Services], and the Report Designer)
- Windows Installer 4.5 or later (sometimes distributed by Microsoft Windows Update services; also will be installed by the SQL Server Installation Center)
- .NET Framework 3.5 SP1, SQL Server Native Client and SQL Server Setup support files (if not installed already, these are also installed by SQL Server Installation Center)

Table 8.3 lists the software and operating system requirements for SQL Server 2008, by edition.

TABLE 8.3 SQL Server 2008 R2 Software Requirements, by Edition

SQL Server Editionµs	Supported Operating Systems
Enterprise and Datacenter (32-bit)	Windows Server 2003 Standard, Enterprise, and Datacenter Editions with SP2 or later Windows Server 2008 Web, Standard, Enterprise, and Datacenter Editions with SP2 or later Windows Server 2008 R2 Web, Standard, Enterprise, and Datacenter Editions
Enterprise and Datacenter (64-bit)	Windows Server 2003 Standard, Enterprise, and Datacenter x64 Editions with SP2 or later Windows Server 2008 Standard, Web, Enterprise, and Datacenter x64 Editions with SP2 or later Windows Server 2008 R2 Standard, Web, Enterprise, and Datacenter x64 Editions
Enterprise (Itanium)	Windows Server 2003 Enterprise and Datacenter 64-bit Itanium Editions SP2 or later Windows Server 2008 64-bit Itanium with SP2 or later Windows Server 2008 R2 64-bit Itanium

TABLE 8.3 SQL Server 2008 R2 Software Requirements, by Edition

SQL Server Editionµs	Supported Operating Systems
Standard and Developer (32-bit)	Windows XP SP3 or later Windows Vista SP2 Ultimate, Enterprise, Business, and Home Basic/Premium Editions Windows 7 Ultimate, Enterprise, Professional, and Home Basic/Premium x64 Editions Windows Server 2003 Enterprise, Standard, and Datacenter Editions with SP2 or later Windows Server 2008 R2 Web Standard, Enterprise, and Datacenter Editions Windows Server 2008 Web, Standard, Enterprise, and Datacenter Editions
Standard and Developer (64-bit)	Windows Server 2003 Standard, Enterprise, and Datacenter x64 Editions with SP2 or later Windows XP Professional x64 Edition Windows Vista Ultimate, Enterprise, Business, and Home Basic/Premium x64 Editions Windows 7 Ultimate, Enterprise, Professional, and Home Basic/Premium x64 Editions Windows Server 2008 Web, Standard, Datacenter, and Enterprise x64 Editions Windows Server 2008 R2 Web, Standard, Datacenter, and Enterprise x64 Editions
Developer (Itanium)	Windows Server 2003 Enterprise and Datacenter Editions for Itanium-based systems with SP2 or later Windows Server 2008 64-bit Itanium Enterprise and Datacenter Edition SP2 or later Windows Server 2008 R2 64-bit Itanium Enterprise Edition
Workgroup (32-bit)	Windows XP SP3 and later Windows Server 2003 Standard, Enterprise, and Datacenter Editions with SP2 or later Windows Vista SP2 Ultimate, Enterprise, Business, and Home Basic/Premium Editions Windows 7 Ultimate, Enterprise, Professional, and Home Basic/Premium Editions Windows Server 2008 SP2 Web, Standard, Enterprise, and Datacenter Editions Windows Server 2008 R2 Web, Standard, Enterprise, and Datacenter Editions

TABLE 8.3 SQL Server 2008 R2 Software Requirements, by Edition

SQL Server Editionµs	Supported Operating Systems
Workgroup (64-bit)	Windows XP x64 Professional
	Windows Server 2003 Standard, Enterprise, and Datacenter x64 Editions with SP2 or later
	Windows Vista Ultimate, Home Premium, Home Basic, Enterprise, and Business x64 Editions
	Windows 7 Ultimate, Enterprise, Professional, and Home Basic/Premium x64 Editions
	Windows Server 2008 SP2 Web, Standard, Enterprise, and Datacenter x64 Editions
	Windows Server 2008 R2 Web, Standard, Enterprise, and Datacenter x64 Editions
Web (32-bit)	Windows Server 2003 Standard, Enterprise, and Datacenter Editions with SP2 or later
	Windows Server 2008 SP2 Web, Standard, Enterprise, and Datacenter Editions
	Windows Server 2008 R2 Web, Standard, Enterprise, and Datacenter Editions
Web (64-bit)	Windows Server 2003 Standard, Enterprise, and Datacenter x64 Editions with SP2 or later
	Windows Server 2008 SP2 Web, Standard, Enterprise, and Datacenter x64 Editions
	Windows Server 2008 R2 Web, Standard, Enterprise, and Datacenter x64 Editions
Express (32-bit)	Windows XP (Home, Tablet, Professional, and Media Editions) SP2 or later
	Windows Server 2003 (Web, Standard, Enterprise, and Datacenter Editions with SP2 or later)
	Windows Vista SP2 Ultimate, Home Premium, Home Basic, Enterprise, and Business Editions
	Windows 7 Ultimate, Enterprise, Professional, and Home Basic/Premium Editions
	Windows Server 2008 SP2 Web, Standard, Enterprise, and Datacenter Editions
	Windows Server 2008 R2 Web, Standard, Enterprise, and Datacenter Editions

TABLE 8.3 SQL Server 2008 R2 Software Requirements, by Edition

SQL Server Editionµs	Supported Operating Systems
Express (64-bit)	Windows Server 2003 Standard, Enterprise, and Datacenter x64 Editions with SP2 or later
	Windows Vista Ultimate, Home Premium, Home Basic, Enterprise, and Business x64 Editions
	Windows 7 Ultimate, Enterprise, Professional, and Home Basic/Premium x64 Editions
	Windows Server 2008 SP2 Web, Standard, Enterprise, and Datacenter x64 Editions
	Windows Server 2008 R2 Web, Standard, Enterprise, and Datacenter x64 Editions

Network Protocol Support

The following network protocols are supported for all editions (where applicable):

- Shared memory (but not for failover clusters)
- Named pipes
- TCP/IP (required for SQL Server endpoint communications)
- Virtual Interface Adapter (VIA)

Running Multiple Simultaneous Editions

You can install multiple editions of SQL Server 2008 on the same machine and run them simultaneously. This capability comes in handy when you need to test code or other feature functionality on one edition versus another, such as when your development and deployment environments differ. In fact, you can even install and run SQL Server 2008 Enterprise Evaluation Edition on XP SP2 (not supported for the non–Evaluation Enterprise Edition) if you need to test an Enterprise Edition feature on a non–Windows Server system.

NOTE

You can quickly ascertain the SQL Server edition you're running by executing this T-SQL query:

```
select serverproperty('edition')
```

Installation Walkthrough

The following sections walk you through a typical installation scenario step by step. We bring up important points of information along the way, providing a real-world perspective on the process. No past experience with SQL Server is required to understand these sections.

NOTE

SQL Server 2008 is actually version 10 of the product, just as SQL Server 2005 is version 9, and SQL Server 2000 was version 8, which succeeded SQL Server 7. SQL Server 2008 R2 is considered version 10.5. Although versioning by year *seems* straightforward, it may obfuscate the reasoning behind the naming convention used for many installed items, such as shared folder names (for example, `Microsoft SQL Server\100`), SQL Server instance folder names (for example, \MSSQL10_50.MSSQLSERVER), and so on. In addition, SQL Server 2000 servers appear as version 8 when registered in SSMS (and elsewhere). You can still administer many aspects of SQL Server 2000 instances via the 2008 and 2008 R2 management tools.

Install Screens, Step by Step

The first step in installing SQL Server 2008 or 2008 R2 is, of course, to launch the SQL Server Installation Center. You do this by inserting the install DVD in the drive and double-clicking `setup.exe` in the root folder (if AutoPlay is enabled, setup runs automatically). If you're installing from a decompressed `.iso` file or network share, locate the root folder and double-click the `setup.exe` file in the root folder.

If Windows Installer 4.5 or Microsoft .NET Framework 3.5 Service Pack 1 are not installed, the SQL Server Setup program first needs to install them before you can continue. If this is the case, you see a dialog like the one shown in Figure 8.1

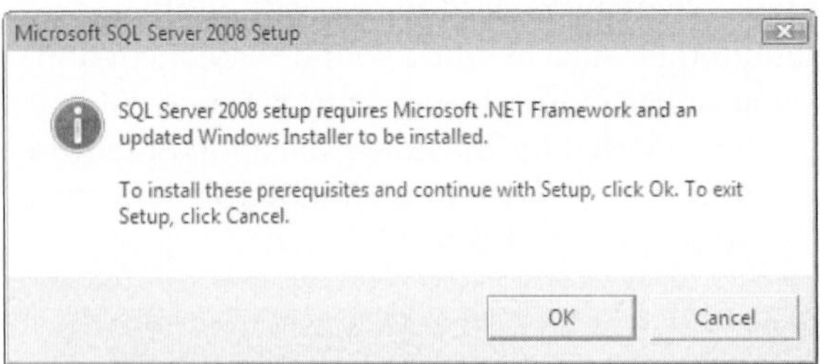

FIGURE 8.1 SQL Server 2008 prerequisites warning dialog.

NOTE

If the prerequisites for the Installer need to be installed, you likely need to restart the computer for the updates to take effect. After restarting, rerun `setup.exe` to continue the installation.

When the prerequisites are installed, the Installation Wizard runs the SQL Server Installation Center, as shown in Figure 8.2.

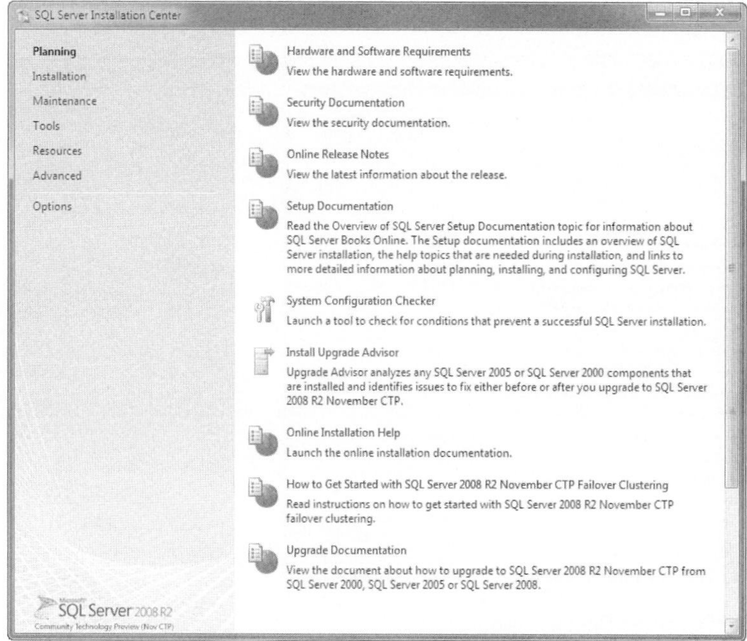

FIGURE 8.2 SQL Server 2008 Installation Center window.

NOTE

The same installation program is used whether you want to perform a full SQL Server installation or to install just the client tools. You have the option to choose which components to install on the Feature Selection screen, which is displayed after you install the Setup Support Files.

The first thing you'll notice is that there is a great deal of content immediately available from the SQL Server Installation Center Planning window, including documentation on hardware and software requirements, release notes, security and upgrade documentation, and the System Configuration Checker. You typically first want to run the System Configuration Checker to confirm that your system meets the minimum hardware and software requirements for installing SQL Server 2008. Click on the link for the System Configuration Checker to bring up the screen shown in Figure 8.3. This is essentially the Setup Support Rules screen that also runs during the actual installation. It's better to find out now if there will be any issues with the installation before you get into the actual installation.

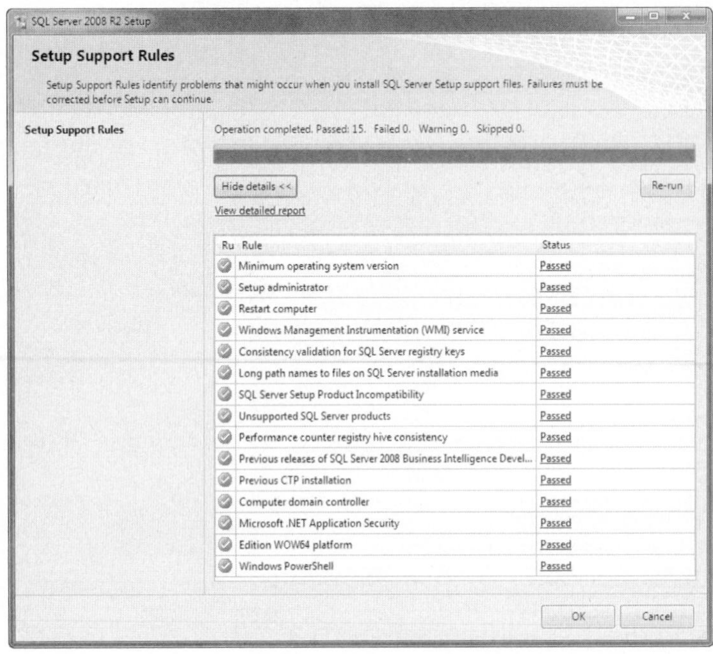

FIGURE 8.3 System Configuration Checker window

When the SCC scan is complete, overall status of the check is detailed at the top of the main window. You can click the Show Details button to view a detailed report of the checks performed. This report notes any issues found. If any checks fail, or a warning is raised, click the hyperlink in the Status column for more detailed report with specifics and suggestions for resolution. Click the View Detailed Report link to see the SCC results in an HTML report format, which is also saved to a file (see Figure 8.4).

After you verify that the system configuration is sufficient to support the SQL Server 2008 installation, click OK to go back to the SQL Server Installation Center. Then click on the Installation option in the menu on the left of the SQL Server Installation Center. This brings up the installation options. To install a new instance of SQL Server, select the New Installation or Add Features to an Existing Installation option, as shown in Figure 8.5.

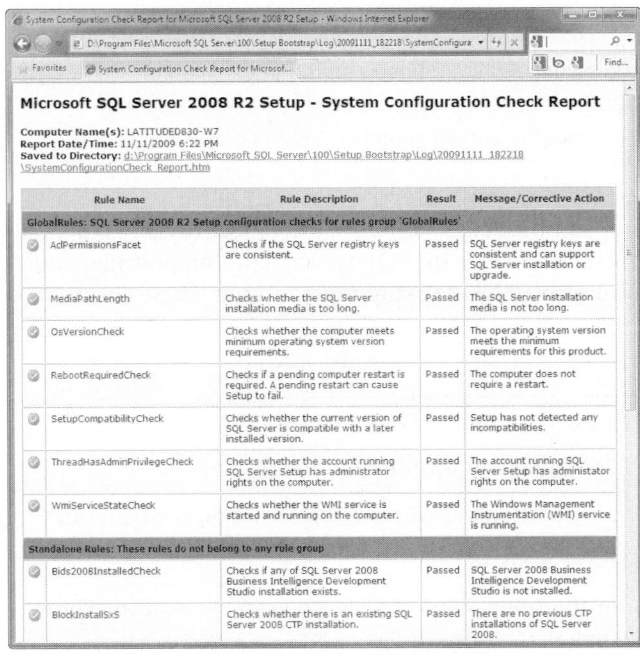

FIGURE 8.4 System Configuration Checker HTML report.

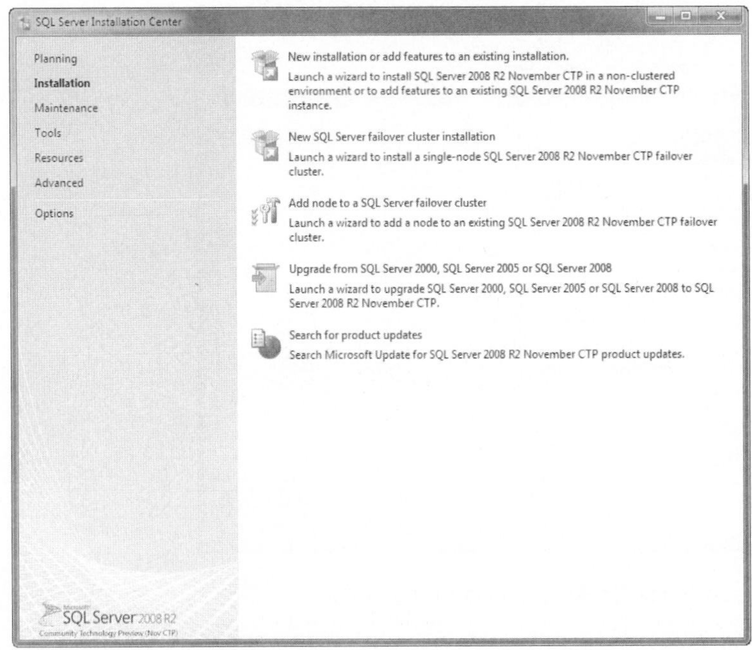

FIGURE 8.5 SQL Server Installation menu.

NOTE

The following installation steps and screenshots are based on the installation of SQL Server 2008 R2. For SQL Server 2008 installations, the order of the install screens and options may be slightly different, but the screen contents and options are similar.

The first step of the installation is to run the Setup Support Rules to identify any potential issues that might occur when the installer installs the SQL Server Setup support files and lists any items that may need to be corrected before Setup can continue. These checks include the following:

- Operating system version
- Whether there are any reboots pending from other installers
- Whether the logged-in user is a system administrator (a must)
- Whether there is support for long pathnames where the installation media resides
- The consistency of any SQL Server Registry keys

After the Setup Support Rules run for the Setup Support Files, you can click on the Show Details button to display a window like that shown in Figure 8.6.

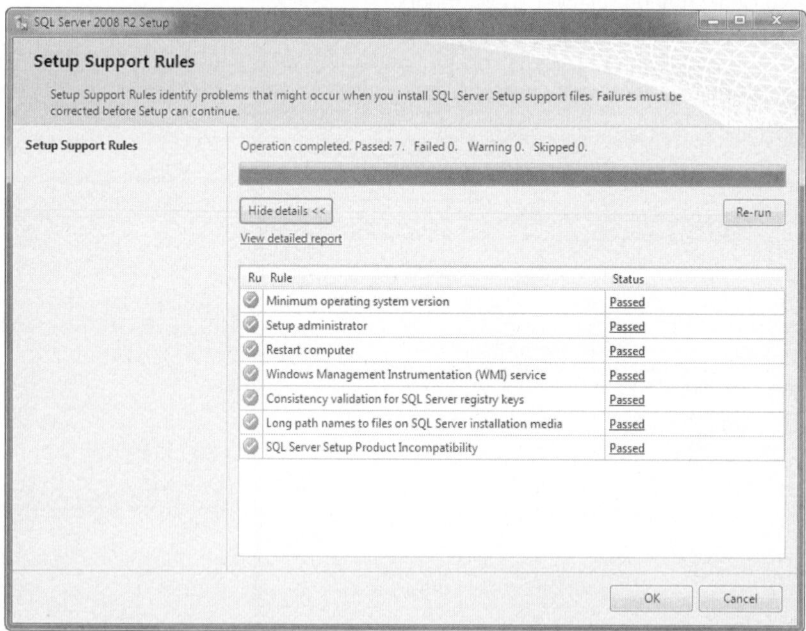

FIGURE 8.6 Setup Support Rules for Setup Support Files Detail.

If any tests fail, you can click on the View Detailed Report link to see a more detailed report file. You can also click on the hyperlink in the Status column of the failed rule to view specifics on the failed rule. If there are no failed Setup Support Rules to hinder installation, click OK to continue to the installation of the Setup Support Files (see Figure 8.7). The Setup Support Files are components that need to be installed so that the actual SQL Server product installation can proceed. Click Install to initiate the installation of the Setup Support Files.

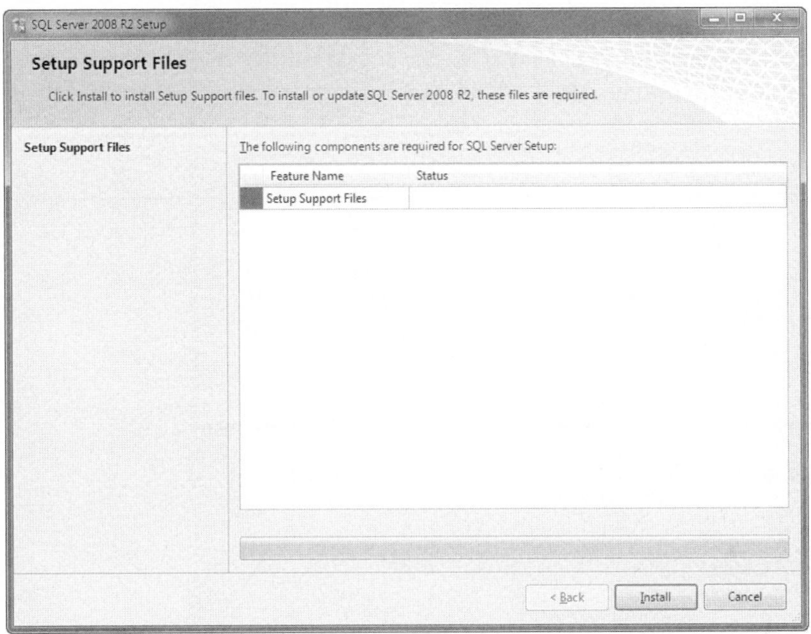

FIGURE 8.7 Setup Support Files installation screen.

After the installation of the Setup Support Files has completed successfully, the Installer reruns the Setup Support Rules, this time running additional checks to verify that the system will support the installation of SQL Server and its features. Again, if any of the tests fail or a warning is generated, you typically need to address this situation before continuing to ensure a successful SQL Server installation. For example, Figure 8.8 shows a warning regarding Windows Firewall. Clicking on the Warning hyperlink in the Status column brings up a dialog with more information about the warning. In this case, the warning indicates that if Windows Firewall is enabled, the network ports for SQL Server need to be opened to allow remote clients to access SQL Server on this machine.

If no tests have failed and all warnings have been reviewed or resolved, click Next to bring up the Product Key page to enter any necessary product keys if you are installing a version of SQL Server 2008 that is not free (see Figure 8.9).

After entering the product key (if needed), click Next to review the License Terms for SQL Server 2008 R2 (see Figure 8.10). Note that you need to accept the license agreement that follows; otherwise, you can't proceed. Click the check box indicating your acceptance of the license terms and click Next to bring up the Setup Role page, as shown in Figure 8.11.

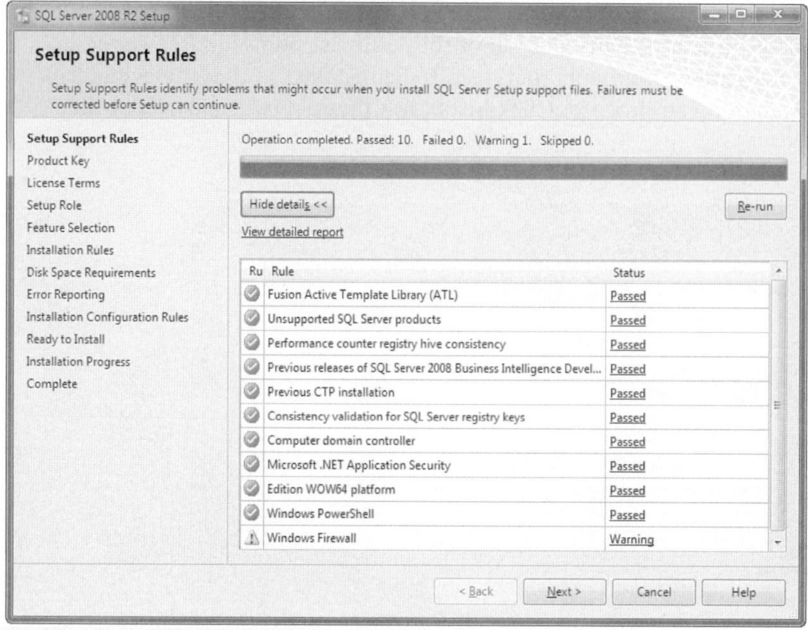

FIGURE 8.8 Setup Support Rules for SQL Server installation detail.

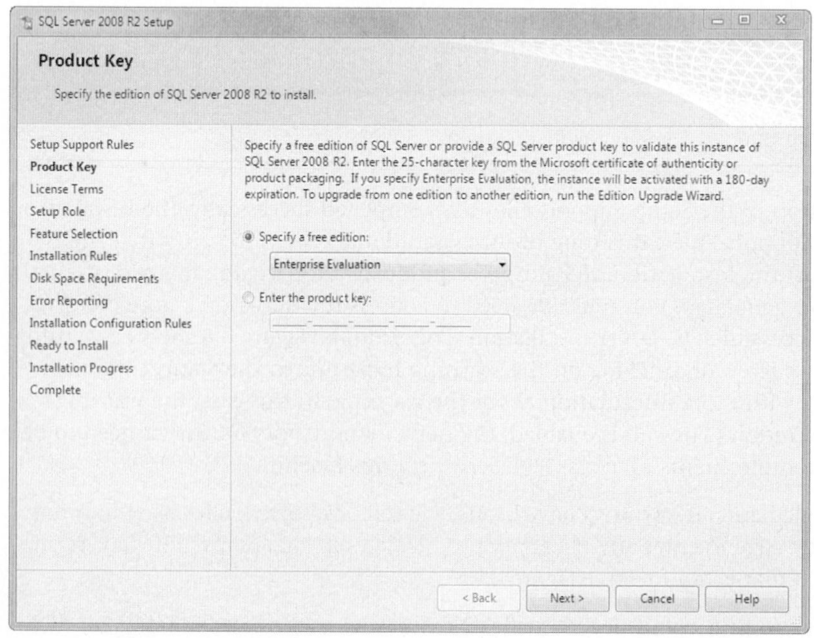

FIGURE 8.9 Product Key entry page.

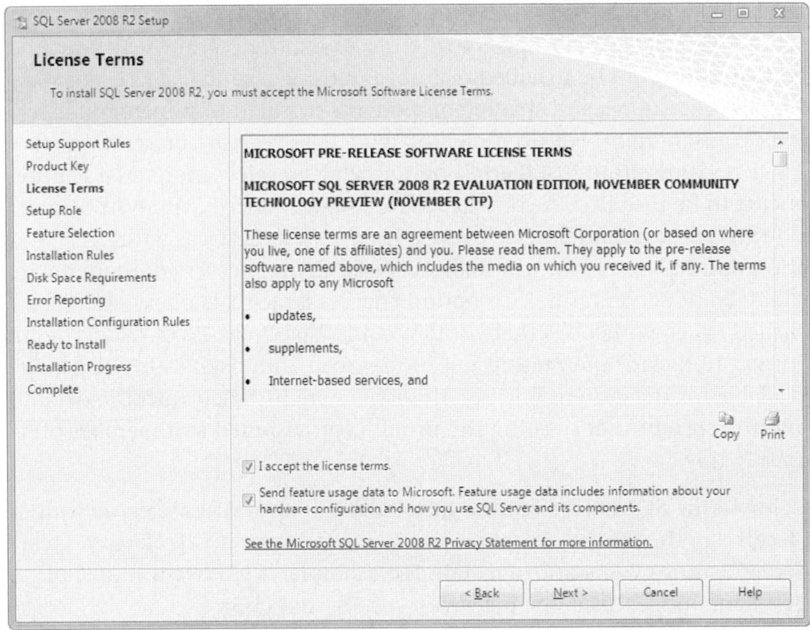

FIGURE 8.10 License Terms page.

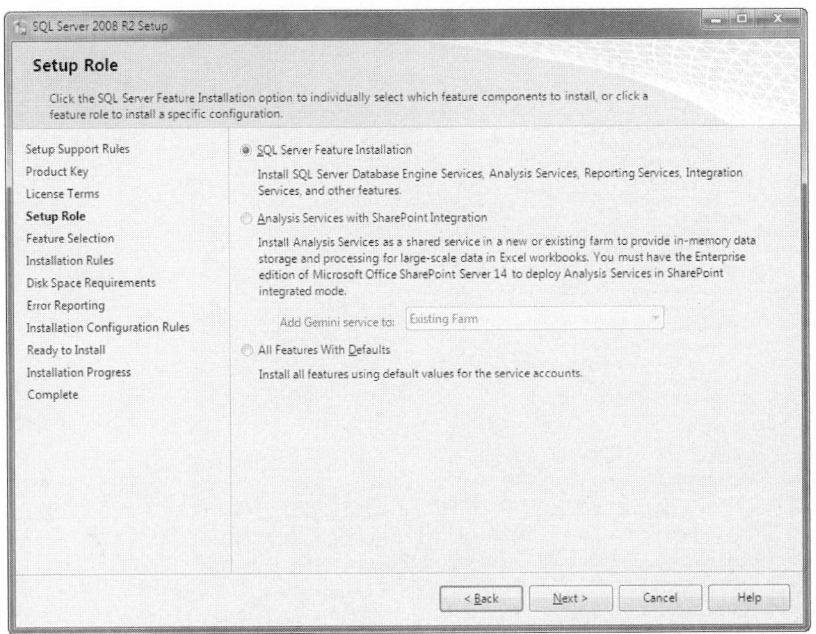

FIGURE 8.11 Setup Role page.

The Setup Role page is new with SQL Server 2008 R2. This page was not available in SQL Server 2008. The Setup Role page lets you specify whether to use the Feature Selection page to select individual features to be installed or to install using a setup role. A *setup role* is a fixed selection of all the features and shared components required to implement a predefined SQL Server configuration. For example, in Figure 8.11, you are presented with three options. The SQL Server Feature Installation option lets you select individual features and shared components to be installed, such as Database Engine Services, Analysis Services (native mode), Reporting Services, and Service Broker. The Analysis Services with SharePoint Integration option allows you to install Analysis Services server components in a Microsoft Office SharePoint Server farm. This option enables large-scale query and data processing for published Excel workbooks that contain embedded PowerPivot data. The All Features with Defaults option skips the Feature Selection screen and installs all SQL Server 2008 R2 features available for the current release. All services are installed with the default system accounts, and the current user running the install is provisioned as a member of the SQL Server `sysadmin` role.

In most cases, you choose the SQL Server Feature Installation option. After selecting this option, click Next to display the Feature Selection window (see Figure 8.12). Here, you can select which SQL Server features you want to install. For example, if you want to install only the SQL Server Client Tools, this is the place you specify that choice.

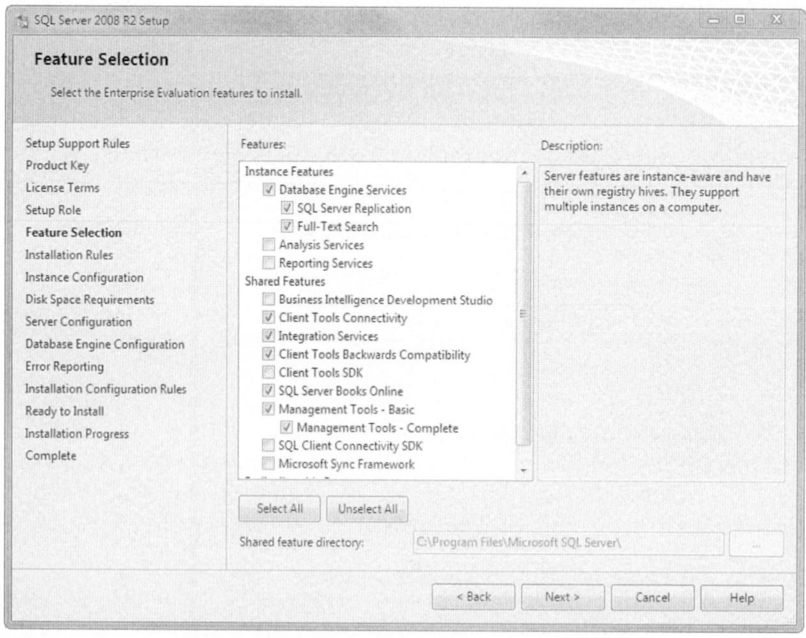

FIGURE 8.12 The Feature Selection page.

Following are the most commonly available features (detailed in subsequent chapters of this book):

- **Database Engine Services**—Includes the core Database Engine services, optional replication (see Chapter 19, "Replication"), and Full-Text Search (see Chapter 50, "SQL Server Full-Text Search") services.
- **Analysis Services**—Includes the engine used to create business intelligence solutions that rely on OLAP and data mining (see Chapter 51, "SQL Server 2008 Analysis Services").
- **Reporting Services**—Includes the engine and tools used to generate and deploy data-centric reports (see Chapter 53, "SQL Server 2008 Reporting Services").
- **Shared Features**—Includes optional features shared among multiple SQL Server instances on the same system, such as Business Intelligence Development Studio, Client Tools Connectivity components, Integration Services, SQL Server Books Online, SQL Server Management Tools, and the Microsoft Sync Framework.

If you are uncertain about the need for a specific feature, when you click on it in this window, a description of the feature and what will be installed is displayed in the Description pane on the right.

The Feature Selection page is also the place where you can change the installation location for the shared features (if this is the first time any of the shared features are being installed on the system). The default location is `C:\Program Files\Microsoft SQL Server`. In most production installations, you'll most likely want the shared features to remain in the `Program Files` folder.

After you finish making your selections, click Next to move on to the Installation Rules page (see Figure 8.13).

NOTE

In versions of SQL Server 2008 prior to R2, the installation rules were not run until later in the installation process.

The Installation Rules page runs a check to determine whether there are any issues that will block the installation of the selected features. From this page, you can address any issues and rerun the rules until they all pass or only warning messages are displayed. Like the Setup Support Rules page, this page enables you to get detailed information on the rule checks performed by clicking on the Show Details button. You can get more information on a specific rule by clicking the hyperlink in the Status column. A detailed HTML report can be generated as well by clicking on the View Detailed Report hyperlink.

When no errors are displayed on the Installation Rules page, click Next to proceed to the Instance Configuration page.

You can choose to install SQL Server as the default instance (if a default instance has not already been installed) or as a named instance. SQL Server supports multiple instances of SQL Server on a single server or workstation, but only one instance can be the default instance. The default instance can be an installation of SQL Server 2000, SQL Server 2005, or SQL Server 2008. All other instances must be named instances. The named instances

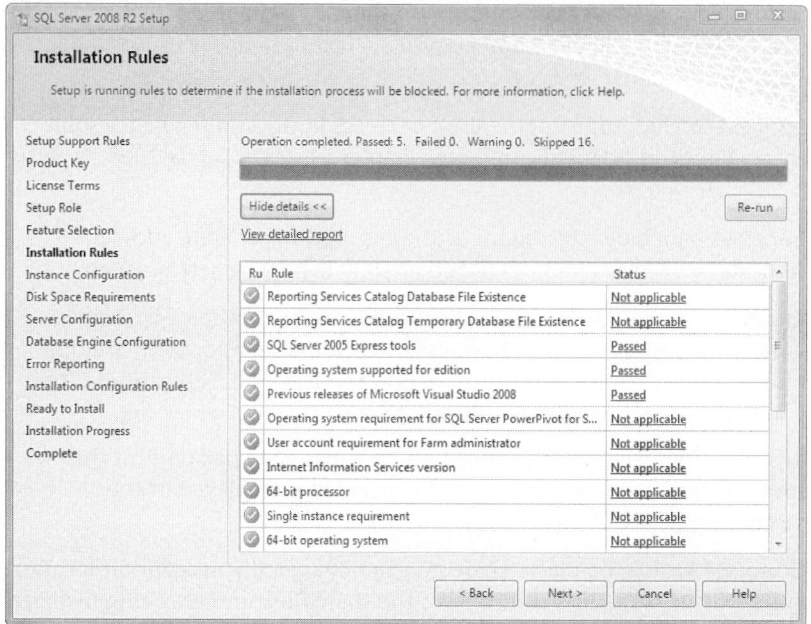

FIGURE 8.13 The Installation Rules page.

can be different versions and/or editions of SQL Server. You can run multiple instances of SQL Server concurrently on the same machine with each instance running independently of other instances. You can also install SQL Server as a named instance without installing a default instance first. If any instances are already installed, they are listed in the Installed Instances list. (For example, Figure 8.14 shows that an instance of the Shared Components from SQL Server 2005 is already installed.)

Another option you can specify on this screen is the Instance Root Directory. This determines where the data files for the system databases for the SQL Server instance will be installed. The installation path for SQL Server 2008 defaults to the system drive of the machine to which you are installing, followed by the root default folder: `[system drive letter]:Program Files\Microsoft SQL Server`. From here, two main subfolders branch out:

- **`100`**—This is the version-specific parent folder (SQL Server 2008 is version 10.0, hence 100) for shared features such as Integration Services (under `DTS`), client tools (under `Tools`), shared tools (under `Shared`), and COM components (under `COM`).
- **`MSSQL10_50.InstanceName`**—This is the parent folder for Database Engine components (under `MSSQL/Binn`) and data files (under `MSSQL/Data`). *`InstanceName`* is determined by the value specified during the installation process.
- **`MSAS10_50.InstanceName`**—This is the parent folder for Analysis Services components.

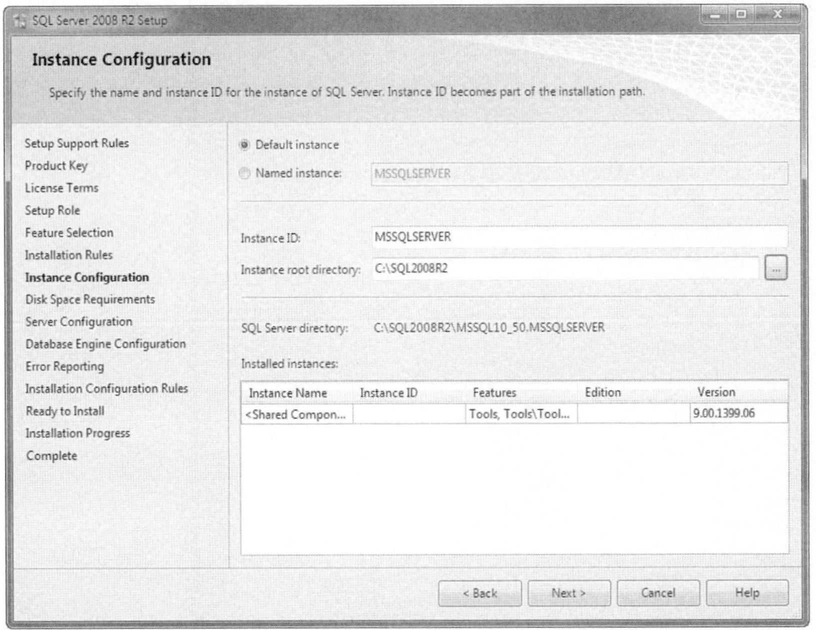

FIGURE 8.14 Instance Configuration page.

- **`MSRS10_50.`*`InstanceName`***—This is the parent folder for Reporting Services components.

After you finish configuring the instance, click Next to bring up the Disk Space Requirements page. This information screen shows only the disk space requirements for the features you've chosen to install and the available space in the drives you selected to install to. If you want to change the install locations, click on the Back button to return to the screen where the installation directory you want to change is specified. When you are satisfied with your selections, click Next to move onto the Server Configuration page (see Figure 8.15).

On the Server Configuration page, you can specify the specific user accounts and passwords to use for the selected SQL Server services you chose to install. To simplify matters, you can click the Use the Same Account for All SQL Server Services button to specify a single local or domain account dedicated for SQL Server 2008 R2 use and assign it to all services. However, for improved security, it is recommended that you create multiple accounts, one for each service. This helps reinforce the least-privileged user account approach, which states that a user should have only the privileges required to get the job done—and no more. Having multiple accounts also makes it clearer for network administrators to determine which SQL Server services (as opposed to the multitude of other running services) are requesting access to a resource. If you don't specify a user account, the services are set up to run under the Local System account, which is an account with local admin privileges that does not have access to any network resources. The Installer provides warnings if you specify an account with insufficient privileges or credentials.

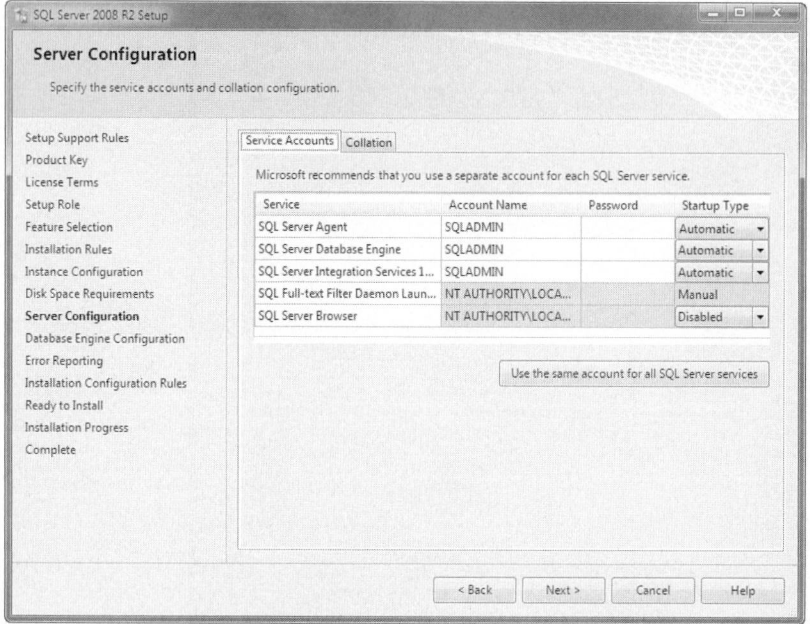

FIGURE 8.15 Server Configuration page.

Also on the Service Accounts tab, you can select the server startup options for the SQL Server services being installed by selecting the startup type in the drop-down selection list to the right of the service. It is highly recommended to autostart the SQL Server service so it's available when the system is started. (If necessary, you can change the startup options for the SQL Server services later, using the SQL Server Configuration Manager.)

NOTE

The SQL Server Browser service is installed only once, no matter how many instances you install.

NOTE

If you are not sure what accounts to set up for the various services, don't worry too much at this point. You can always change the service accounts later using the SQL Server Configuration Manager.

The Server Configuration page also allows you to override the default SQL Server collation settings. You do so by first clicking on the Collation tab (see Figure 8.16). Collations are important because they are used to determine case sensitivity of textual data for comparisons, sort order in indexes, and so on.

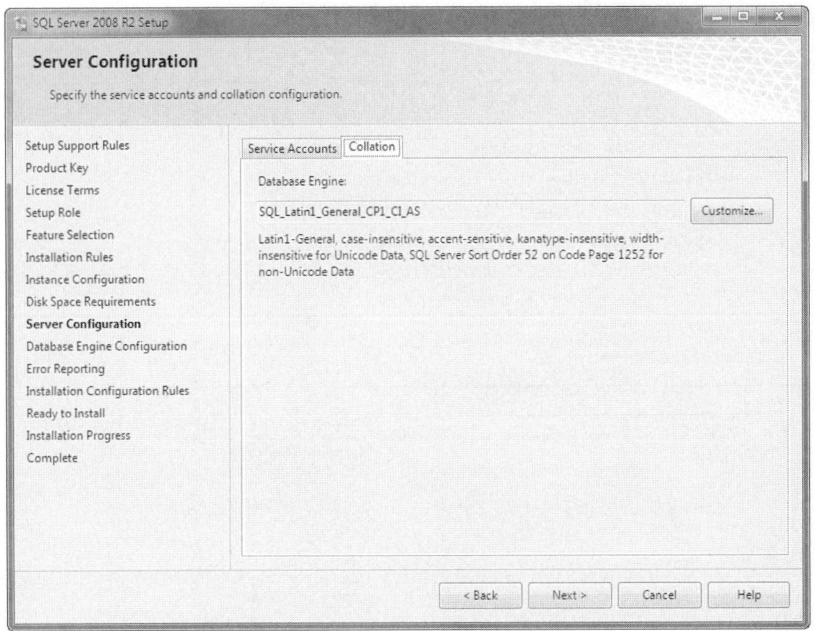

FIGURE 8.16 Server Configuration Collation setting.

If you're running Windows in the United States, the collation selection defaults to `SQL_Latin1_General_CP1_CI_AS` for the Database Engine. The default settings should be changed only if the collation setting for this installation of SQL Server needs to match the collation settings used by another instance of SQL Server, or if it needs to match the Windows system locale of another computer. If you need to change the collation settings, click on the Customize button. This brings up the Database Engine Collation Customization dialog, where you can select from standardized SQL Collations or customize your own by specifying a Windows collation setting and the desired sort options.

After making your selections on the Server Configuration page, click Next to move onto the Database Engine Configuration page. On this page, you can specify the authentication mode to use for SQL Server. This is done on the Account Provisioning tab (see Figure 8.17). The default setting is for Windows Authentication only. However, Mixed Mode authentication is required if you plan to have any clients authenticating to SQL Server 2008 R2 but will not be authenticating to a Windows domain. If you do select Mixed Mode authentication, you also have to enter a password to use for the built-in in SQL Server administration account (`sa`). A strong `sa` password is recommended. The Account Provisioning page also provides the opportunity to specify local or domain accounts to be mapped to the `sysadmin` role in SQL Server (you must provide at least one). These accounts have unrestricted access to SQL Server for performing SQL Server administration and maintenance tasks. For more information on user accounts, passwords, and server roles, see Chapter 11, "Security and User Administration."

8

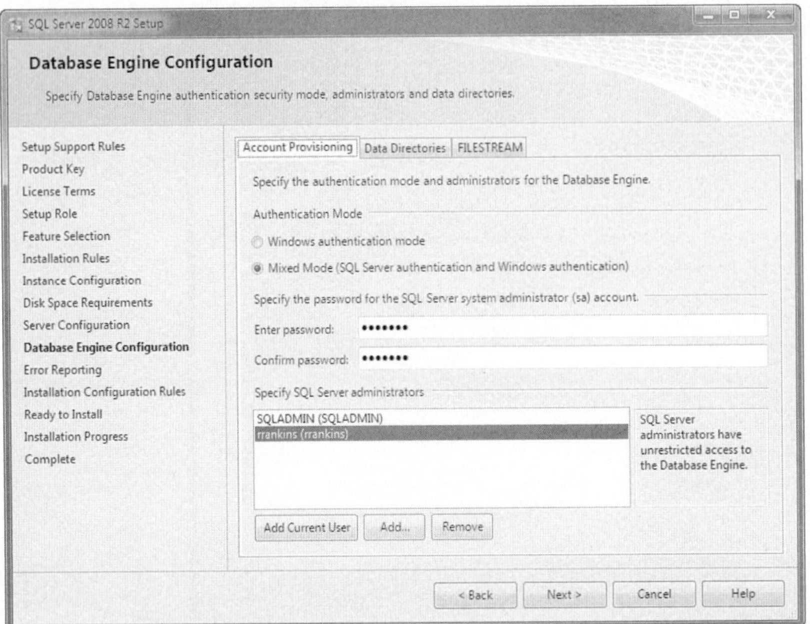

FIGURE 8.17 The Account Provisioning tab.

On the Data Directories tab (see Figure 8.18), you can configure the data root directory and default directories where the `user` and `tempdb` data and log files will be created, as well as the default location for the Backup directory. Note that the System Database Directory cannot be changed here; you need to return to the Instance Configuration page and modify the Instance Root directory. In a production installation, for performance reasons, you should set up multiple drives or drive arrays to store the data and log files. Typically, you do not want the system data files stored on the `C:` drive, especially buried in the `Program Files` folder. You likely want to locate the data files on a high-performance drive setup specifically for database files and away from the system swap file and other applications. For recoverability purposes, you also should keep your backup files on a separate drive from your data files. (For more information on database devices and performance, see Chapter 38, "Database Design and Performance.") As a general rule, you also should place the log files on separate disks from the data files, and placing `tempdb` on its own disk further helps improve performance

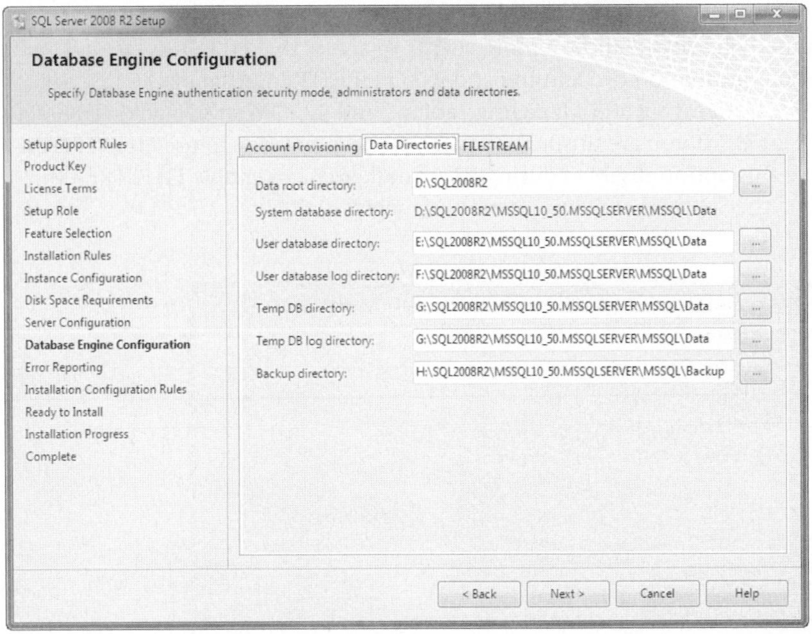

FIGURE 8.18 The Data Directories tab.

NOTE

If you are planning on installing multiple SQL Server instances on the same server, consider using separate subdirectories for each instance's data and log files. This way, you avoid potential conflicts between data and log filenames for databases with the same names created in more than on SQL Server instance. As you notice, by default, the SQL Server Installer creates subdirectories under the specified root directory name using the SQL Server version number and instance name (for example, `MSSQL10_50.MSSQLSERVER`) and then an additional subdirectory for the services type (`MSSQL` for SQL Server, `MSAS` for Analysis Services, and `MSRS` for Reporting Services).

The final tab on the Database Engine Configuration tab is FILESTREAM (see Figure 8.19). The FILESTREAM data type is a column property available in SQL Server 2008. FILESTREAM storage is implemented as a `varbinary(max)` column, but the actual data is stored as BLOBs in the file system. Because of security considerations, FILESTREAM, by default, is disabled. If you want to use the FILESTREAM option, click the Enable FILESTREAM for Transact-SQL Access check box to enable FILESTREAM capabilities. This control must be checked before the other control options will be available. The Enable FILESTREAM for File I/O Streaming Access check box enables Win32 streaming access for FILESTREAM. If this option is selected, you can specify the name of the Windows share in which the FILESTREAM data will be stored. The Allow Remote Clients to Have Streaming Access to FILESTREAM Data check box determines whether to allow remote clients to access this FILESTREAM data on this server. For more information on defining and using FILESTREAM data in SQL Server 2008, see Chapters 24, "Creating and Managing Tables," and 42, "What's New for Transact-SQL in SQL Server 2008." If you are unsure whether you need or want to use FILESTREAM data, you can leave this option disabled during the install. You can enable FILESTREAM data at any time via the SQL Server Configuration Manager.

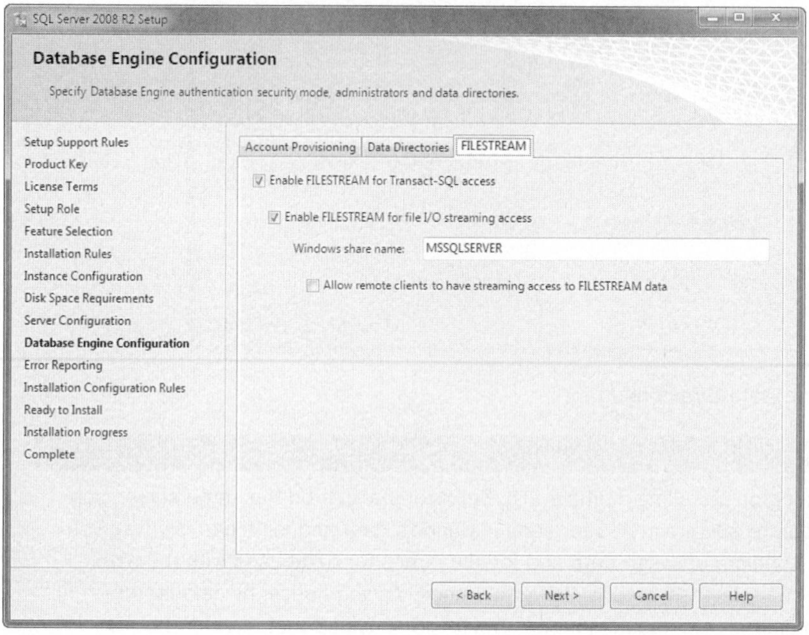

FIGURE 8.19 The FILESTREAM tab.

Some of the remaining configuration screens depend on which features you selected in the Feature Selection page. For example, if you chose to install Analysis Services or Reporting Services, you have configuration pages to specify the installation options for these features. For more information on configuring Analysis Services and Reporting Services, see Chapters 51, "SQL Server 2008 Analysis Services," and 53, "SQL Server 2008 Reporting Services." As with the FILESTREAM option, you do not have to install Analysis Services or Reporting Services during the initial install. You can always run the SQL Server Installation Center later to add these features to an existing SQL Server instance.

After you finish making your selections, click Next to move on to the Error Reporting page. On the Error Reporting page, you have the option to indicate whether you want to have error reports sent to Microsoft automatically for any of the SQL Server services that run without user interaction. This option, if enabled, helps Microsoft improve future releases of SQL Server features by sending error reports to Microsoft automatically. This process is colloquially known as "phoning home," and you may be inclined to keep this option unchecked. Note that doing so reduces Microsoft's capability to gather important information that can helpful for identifying possible bugs and developing fixes in future service pack releases. Specify whether you want to participate and click Next to continue to the Installation Configuration Rules page, as shown in Figure 8.20.

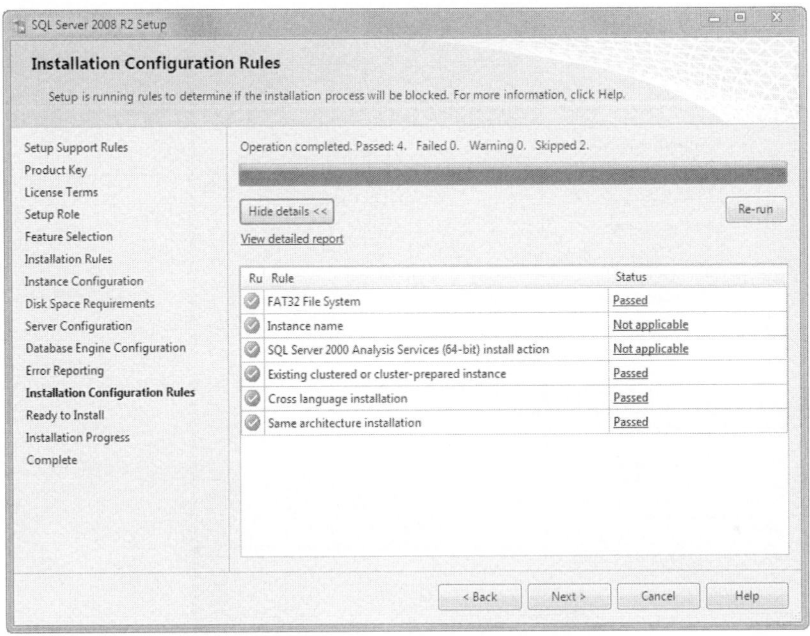

FIGURE 8.20 The Installation Configuration Rules page.

NOTE

In SQL Server 2008, the Error Reporting page was referred to as the Error and Usage Reporting page. In addition to the option to have error reports sent to Microsoft automatically, it also provided the option to participate in the Customer Experience Improvement program.

The Installation Configuration Rules page runs a final set of checks to determine if there are any issues that will prevent a successful installation of SQL Server 2008. If no errors are reported, click Next to continue to the Ready to Install page (see Figure 8.21). This page displays a summary of the installation options chosen as well as the file locations specified. Review this information to ensure the features and file locations match what you specified during the previous screens. This page also displays the location of the Configuration file path where you can find the `ConfigurationFile.ini` file generated by the installer. This `.ini` file can be used for unattended installations, which are discussed later in this chapter. The `ConfigurationFile.ini` file is located in the same place where you can find the installation log files, which you can review if any problems occur during the installation.

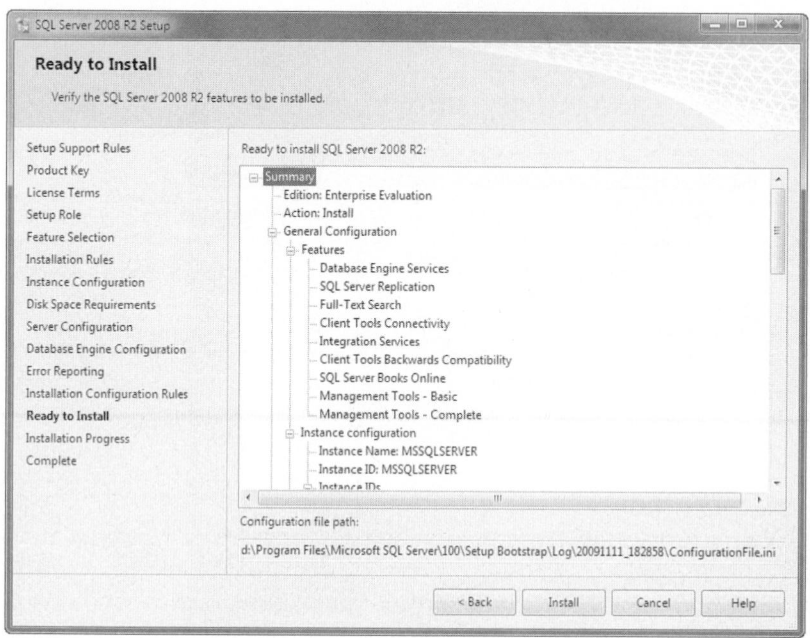

FIGURE 8.21 The Ready to Install Page.

If everything looks satisfactory on the Ready to Install Page, click the Install button to proceed with the SQL Server installation. This displays the Installation Progress screen, which shows a progress bar and messages to allow you to track the progress of the installation. When the setup process is complete, the Installer displays the Complete page, which contains a hyperlink to the Installer log file and supplemental information about the installation.

One of the notes that may be displayed in the Supplemental Information section of the Complete page refers to the installation of the SQL Server sample databases. If you've worked with previous versions of SQL Server, you may remember that there was an option to install the sample databases during the SQL Server installation. With SQL Server 2008, the sample databases are not part of the SQL Server Installation Center, nor are they available on the install media. To install the sample databases and sample code for non-Express editions of SQL Server 2008, you need to go to the Microsoft CodePlex website to download the installer for the sample databases. There is a link to the SQL Server samples on the CodePlex website on the Resources page of the SQL Server Installation Center.

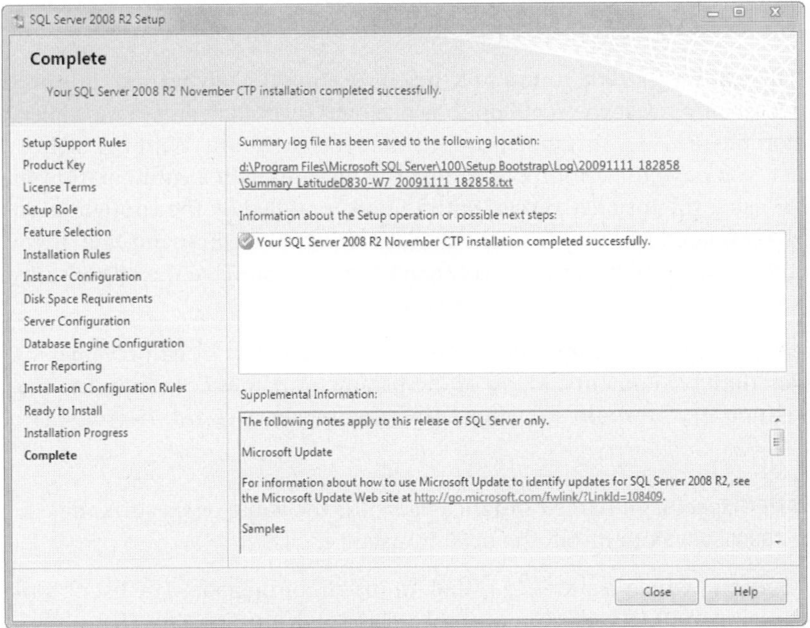

FIGURE 8.22 The Complete page.

The Supplemental Information section also provides a link to the latest `readme` file for the release of SQL Server installed and a note regarding how SQL Server updates are now available via Microsoft Update. Before leaving the Installation Center, you might want to click the Search for Product Update link on the Installation page to see whether there are any critical hotfixes or service packs already available for your SQL Server installation.

Other Options Available in the SQL Server Installation Center

Before leaving the SQL Server Installation Center, let's explore a few other utilities available from the main menu. The Maintenance menu provides tools to upgrade an installed SQL Server 2008 Edition (for example, from Standard Edition to Enterprise Edition), repair a corrupt installation, or remove a node from a SQL Server 2008 cluster. The Tools menu provides links to the System Configuration Checker, the Installed features discovery report that generates information regarding all SQL Server products and features installed on the local machine, and a utility to upgrade existing SQL Server 2005 Integration Services packages to the SQL Server 2008 Integration Services package format.

Finally, on the Advanced menu, there are options to prepare and complete a SQL Server failover cluster and to install in instance of SQL Server 2008 from an existing configuration file. Installing using an existing configuration file allows you to repeat an installation without having to go through all the individual steps and enter/select all the options you normally have to go through with the installation wizard.

Installing SQL Server Using a Configuration File

If you need to install SQL Server 2008 to multiple machines, you'll likely want to do so without having to manually select the same options over and over. Running the installer using a configuration file provides this much-needed timesaving feature. With the SQL Server 2008 installer, you have the option of running the installer with a configuration file in a couple of ways: using the Installer Wizard with options prefilled by the configuration file or using a fully automated and unattended installation from the command line. If you use the GUI with the options prefilled by the configuration file, you have the opportunity to review and change options along the way as necessary.

The `ConfigurationFile.ini` file is a text file composed of parameters in name/value pairs along with descriptive comments. Many of the parameter names correspond to the screens and screen options you would see when using the Installer Wizard. Here are some examples:

- **INSTANCENAME**—Specifies a named instance name for the value or specifies the special value `MSSQLSERVER` to install the default instance.
- **FEATURES**—Specifies which features to install, uninstall, or upgrade. The list of top-level features include SQL, AS, RS, IS, and Tools. The SQL feature installs the Database Engine, Replication, and Full-Text. The Tools feature installs Management Tools, Books Online, Business Intelligence Development Studio, and other shared components.
- **INSTALLSHAREDIR**—Specifies the root installation directory for native shared components.
- **INSTANCEDIR**—Specifies the installation directory for instance-specific components.
- **INSTALLSQLDATADIR**—Specifies the Database Engine root data directory.
- **SQLBACKUPDIR**—Specifies the default directory for the Database Engine backup files.
- **SQLUSERDBDIR**—Specifies the default directory for the Database Engine user databases.
- **SQLUSERDBLOGDIR**—Specifies the default directory for the Database Engine user database logs.
- **SQLTEMPDBDIR**—Specifies the directory for Database Engine `tempdb` files.
- **SQLCOLLATION** or **ASCOLLATION**—Specifies values to set the collation for SQL Server or Analysis Services.
- **SQLSVCACCOUNT**—Specifies the user account for the SQL Server service: domain\user or system account.
- **TCPENABLED**—Specifies whether the TCP/IP protocol is enabled (`1`) or disabled (`0`).
- **NPENABLED**—Specifies whether the Named Pipes protocol is enabled (`1`) or disabled (`0`).

- **SECURITYMODE**—Specifies authentication mode for SQL Server. You can use the special value "`SQL`" here to override the default of Windows-only authentication.

The following example shows the contents of a configuration file for SQL Server 2008 R2:

```
;SQLSERVER2008 Configuration File
[SQLSERVER2008]

; Specify the Instance ID for the SQL Server features you have specified. SQL
 Server directory structure, registry structure, and service names will reflect
 the instance ID of the SQL Server instance.
INSTANCEID="MSSQLSERVER"

; Specifies a Setup work flow, like INSTALL, UNINSTALL, or UPGRADE. This is a
 required parameter.
ACTION="Install"

; Specifies features to install, uninstall, or upgrade. The list of top-level
 features include SQL, AS, RS, IS, and Tools. The SQL feature will install the
 database engine, replication, and full-text. The Tools feature will install
 Management Tools, Books online, Business Intelligence Development Studio, and
 other shared components.
FEATURES=SQLENGINE,REPLICATION,FULLTEXT,CONN,IS,BC,BOL,SSMS,ADV_SSMS

; Displays the command line parameters usage
HELP="False"

; Specifies that the detailed Setup log should be piped to the console.
INDICATEPROGRESS="False"

; Setup will not display any user interface.
QUIET="False"

; Setup will display progress only without any user interaction.
QUIETSIMPLE="False"

; Specifies that Setup should install into WOW64. This command line argument is
not supported on an IA64 or a 32-bit system.
X86="False"

; Detailed help for command line argument ENU has not been defined yet.
ENU="True"

; Parameter that controls the user interface behavior. Valid values are Normal for
 the full UI, and AutoAdvance for a simplied UI.
UIMODE="Normal"
```

8

```
; Specify if errors can be reported to Microsoft to improve future SQL Server
 releases. Specify 1 or True to enable and 0 or False to disable this feature.
ERRORREPORTING="True"

; Specify the root installation directory for native shared components.
INSTALLSHAREDDIR="C:\Program Files\Microsoft SQL Server"

; Specify the installation directory.
INSTANCEDIR="C:\SQL2008R2"

; Specify that SQL Server feature usage data can be collected and sent to
 Microsoft. Specify 1 or True to enable and 0 or False to disable this feature.
SQMREPORTING="True"

; Specify a default or named instance. MSSQLSERVER is the default instance for
 non-Express editions and SQLExpress for Express editions. This parameter is
 required when installing the SQL Server Database Engine (SQL), Analysis Services
 (AS), or Reporting Services (RS).
INSTANCENAME="MSSQLSERVER"

; Agent account name
AGTSVCACCOUNT="SQLADMIN"

; Auto-start service after installation.
AGTSVCSTARTUPTYPE="Automatic"

; Startup type for Integration Services.
ISSVCSTARTUPTYPE="Automatic"

; Account for Integration Services: Domain\User or system account.
ISSVCACCOUNT="SQLADMIN"

; Startup type for the SQL Server service.
SQLSVCSTARTUPTYPE="Automatic"

; Level to enable FILESTREAM feature at (0, 1, 2 or 3).
FILESTREAMLEVEL="1"

; Specifies a Windows collation or an SQL collation to use for the Database Engine.
SQLCOLLATION="SQL_Latin1_General_CP1_CI_AS"

; Account for SQL Server service: Domain\User or system account.
SQLSVCACCOUNT="SQLADMIN"
```

```
; Windows account(s) to provision as SQL Server system administrators.
SQLSYSADMINACCOUNTS="SQLADMIN"

; The default is Windows Authentication. Use "SQL" for Mixed Mode Authentication.
SECURITYMODE="SQL"

; The Database Engine root data directory.
INSTALLSQLDATADIR="C:\SQL2008R2"

; Default directory for the Database Engine backup files.
SQLBACKUPDIR="C:\SQL2008R2\MSSQL10_50.MSSQLSERVER\MSSQL\Backup"

; Default directory for the Database Engine user databases.
SQLUSERDBDIR="C:\SQL2008R2\MSSQL10_50.MSSQLSERVER\MSSQL\Data"

; Default directory for the Database Engine user database logs.
SQLUSERDBLOGDIR="C:\SQL2008R2\MSSQL10_50.MSSQLSERVER\MSSQL\Data"

; Directory for Database Engine TempDB files.
SQLTEMPDBDIR="C:\SQL2008R2\MSSQL10_50.MSSQLSERVER\MSSQL\Data"

; Provision current user as a Database Engine system administrator for
 SQL Server 2008 R2 Express.
ADDCURRENTUSERASSQLADMIN="False"

; Specify 0 to disable or 1 to enable the TCP/IP protocol.
TCPENABLED="0"

; Specify 0 to disable or 1 to enable the Named Pipes protocol.
NPENABLED="0"

; Startup type for Browser Service.
BROWSERSVCSTARTUPTYPE="Disabled"

; Add description of input argument FTSVCACCOUNT
FTSVCACCOUNT="NT AUTHORITY\LOCAL SERVICE"
```

Depending on which options you chose during an install, other options may be listed in the `Configuration.ini` file, some of which are designed solely for clustered installs, Analysis Services, Reporting Services, Integration Services, or Tools.

To create a configuration file (sorry, no configuration file template is available on the installation media), run the installation program and follow the wizard all the way through to the Ready to Install page where the location of the `Configuration.ini` file generated is specified (see Figure 8.21). If you do not want to continue with an actual

8

installation at this point, simply click the Cancel button to cancel the setup. At this point, you can copy the `Configuration.ini` file to another location so you can make edits to it.

NOTE

The Installer writes out all the appropriate parameters for the options and values specified, with the exception of sensitive information such as passwords. For an unattended install, these values can be provided at the command prompt when you run `setup.exe`. In addition, the new SQL Server 2008 R2 `/IAcceptSQLServerLicenseTerms` parameter is also not written out to the configuration file and requires either you modify the configuration file or supply a value at the command prompt.

The `setup.exe` command-line program can be found at the root level of the installation media. To use a configuration file to install a standalone SQL Server instance, run the installation through the command-line `setup.exe` program and supply the `ConfigurationFile.ini` using the `ConfigurationFile` parameter, as in the following example:

```
Setup.exe /ConfigurationFile=CustomConfigurationFile.INI
```

If you want to override any of the values in the configuration file or provide values not specified in the configuration file, you can provide additional command-line parameters to `setup.exe`. For example, to avoid having to enter the service account passwords during the installation, you can enter them on the command line using the password parameters to `config.exe`:

```
Setup.exe /SQLSVCPASSWORD="mypassword" /AGTSVCPASSWORD="mypassword"
 /ASSVCPASSWORD="mypassword" /ISSVCPASSWORD="mypassword"
 /RSSVCPASSWORD="mypassword" /ConfigurationFile=CustomConfigurationFile.INI
```

NOTE

The password parameters are required to run a fully unattended installation. Also, if the `SECURITYMODE` setting is set to SQL in the configuration file or via the command-line parameter, you need to provide the `/SAPWD` parameter to provide a password for the `sa` account.

Most of the other available `setup.exe` command-line parameters are the same as the parameter names used in the configuration file as listed previously. For full details of the available `setup.exe` parameters, refer to SQL Server Books Online.

Running an Automated or Manual Install

When installing SQL Server from the command prompt, you can also specify what level of the installer interface you want to run, either silent, basic, or full interaction. SQL Server supports full quiet mode by using the `/Q` parameter or Quiet Simple mode by using the `/QS` parameter. The `/Q` switch is intended for running unattended installations. With this switch provided, Setup runs in quiet mode without any user interface. The `/QS` switch only shows progress via the GUI; it does not accept any input and displays no error messages if encountered.

Regardless of the installation method chosen, you are required to confirm acceptance of the software license terms as an individual or on behalf of an entity, unless your use of the software is governed by a separate agreement such as a Microsoft volume licensing agreement or a third-party agreement with an ISV or OEM. For full unattended installations (using the `/Q` or `/QS` parameters) with SQL Server 2008 R2, you must include the `/IACCEPTSQLSERVERLICENSETERMS` parameter to avoid the display of the License Terms page. Following is a sample command line for running an unattended installation of SQL Server 2008:

```
C:\Documents and Settings\rrankins\My Documents\Downloads\SQL2008\R2
 Nov CTP>setup.exe /configurationfile=customconfigurationfile.ini
 /Q /IACCEPTSQLSERVERLICENSETERMS  /SQLSVCPASSWORD="riddler"
 /AGTSVCPASSWORD="riddler"  /SAPWD="riddler"
```

SQL Server 2008 R2 introduces a new option to the `setup.exe` that allows you to run a somewhat more attended mode of the installation that gives you a bit more control over the install than the `/Q` and `/QS` parameters, while streamlining the install somewhat. You can now specify the `/UIMODE` parameter instead of the `/Q` or `/QS` switches. The `/UIMODE` parameter specifies whether to present the full set of Installer Wizard pages for review and confirmation while running the setup or to present a minimum number of pages during setup. `/UIMODE=Normal`, the default option, presents all setup dialog boxes for the selected features, allowing you to review the values or manually enter values not provided in the configuration file (such as service account passwords). You can specify the `/UIMODE=AutoAdvance` option to skip nonessential dialogs and auto advances through a number of pages, including the Ready to Install page.

8

NOTE

Although SQL Server 2008 `Configuration.ini` files are compatible with the SQL Server 2008 R2 `setup.exe` program, some of the options generated in a SQL Server 2008 R2 `Configuration.ini` file are not compatible with the pre-R2 installer, such as the `ENU`, `UIMODE`, `FARMADMINPORT`, and `IACCEPTSQLSERVERLICENSETERMS` parameters.

Installing Service Packs and Cumulative Updates

If you are installing SQL Server 2008 instead of SQL Server 2008 R2, it is recommended that you install SQL Server 2008 Service Pack 1. SQL Server 2008 SP1 doesn't provide any significant new features for SQL Server 2008 but does provide a number of fixes to the GA release version of SQL Server 2008 (Microsoft Knowledge Base article `968369` lists all the fixes).

Service Pack 1 does provide a few new features primarily to ease the deployment of service packs and cumulative updates. The first of these is Slipstream installations. *Slipstreaming* is an installation method that integrates the base installation files for SQL Server with its service packs and cumulative updates and enables you to install them in a single step. You can slipstream SQL Server 2008 SP1 and subsequent cumulative updates with the original installation media so that original media and the updates are installed at the same time. The next section in this chapter describes how to set up a Slipstream installation.

SQL Server 2008 SP1 also provides the capability to uninstall SQL Server 2008 cumulative updates or service packs via the Programs and Features Control Panel (or the Add/Remove Programs Control Panel in Windows XP or Windows Server 2003).

Before installing SP1, you should make sure to back up all user-created databases, as well as the system databases `master`, `model`, `msdb`, and any replicated databases. If you have installed Analysis Services, back up the entire `OLAP` directory (as discussed earlier in this chapter, in the "Installation Paths" section) and all its subdirectories.

You also should make sure to close all open connections to the instance to which you are applying SP1 (including any connections via the management tools; setup should prompt you to close them) and make sure the various SQL Server services are started in the Services Control Panel. Also, be sure `master` and `msdb` each have 500KB free (or that they are autogrow enabled).

When you're ready, log on to the machine as an admin and start the downloaded SP1 executable. After extracting the contents to a temporary folder on the `C:` drive, the SP1 setup launches, displaying the Welcome screen shown in Figure 8.23. As you can see from this window, the SP1 Welcome screen runs the SP1 setup support rules to verify that the SP1 install can be run.

Click Next to display the License Agreement screen. Click the check box to select the license agreement and then click Next again to advance to the Select Features screen to display and select the installed features to be updated (see Figure 8.24). The ensuing Feature Selection window lists (again) the features to be updated, organized in tree fashion, by SQL Server instance name. You can uncheck the features or instances you do not want to upgrade to SP1, except for shared features, which are required to be updated.

Click Next to move onto the Check Files in Use screen (see Figure 8.25). This screen identifies any open or running files that the SP1 setup program needs access to during the install. If any files are listed, you have the option to shut down the services or applications associated with the files and run the check again to see whether the all items are cleared from the list. Note that it is not critical for the Files in Use list to be empty, but if

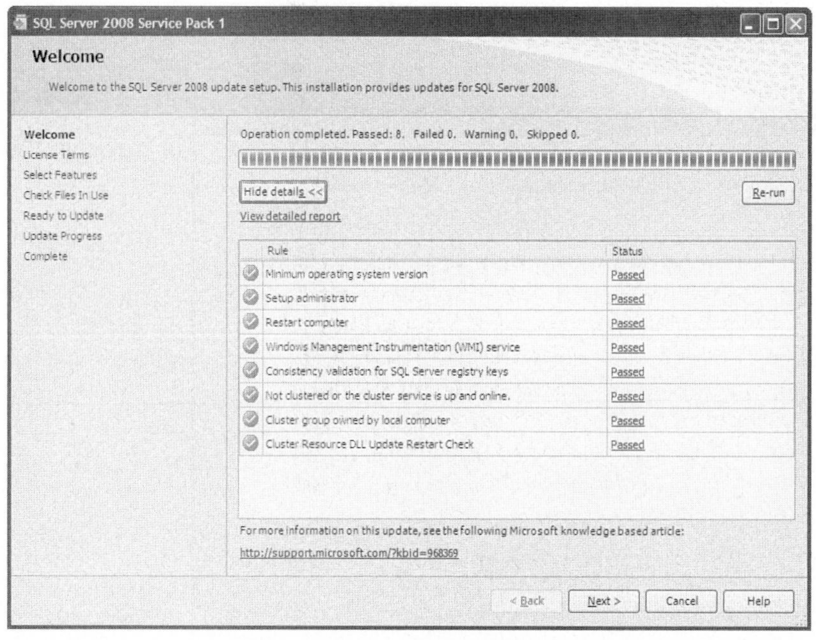

FIGURE 8.23 SQL Server 2008 SP1 Welcome screen.

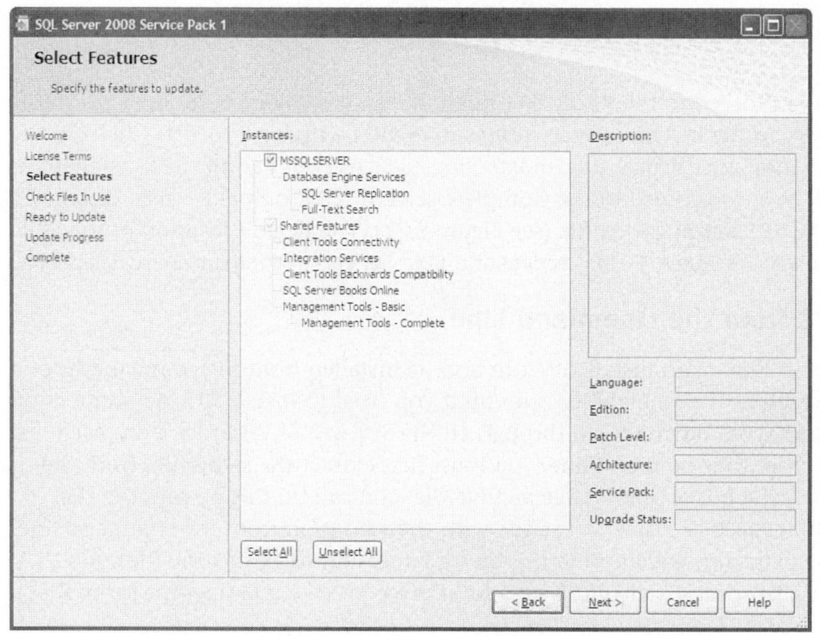

FIGURE 8.24 SQL Server 2008 SP1 Feature Selection screen.

any files are listed, you need to reboot the system after running the SP1 setup to complete the installation.

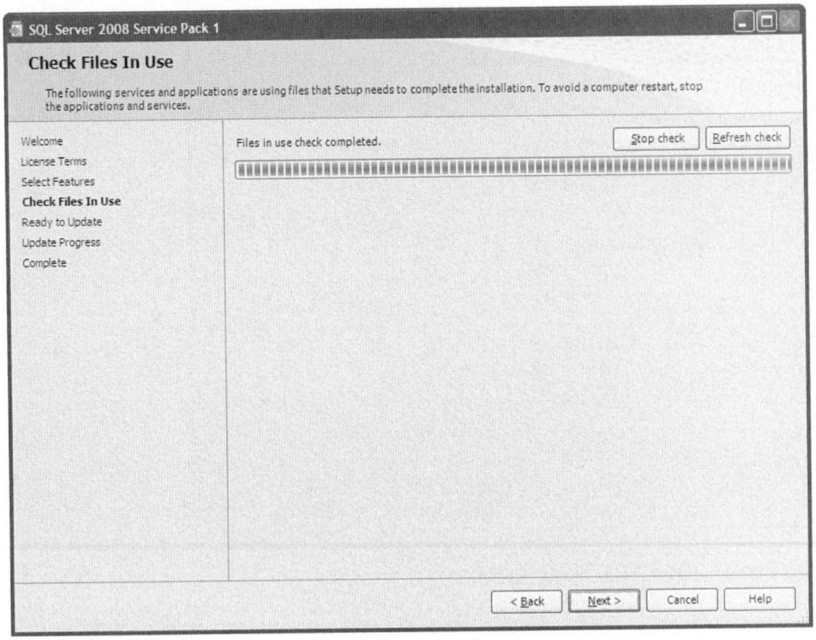

FIGURE 8.25 SQL Server 2008 SP1 Check Files in Use screen.

Click Next again to proceed to the Ready to Update screen (see Figure 8.26), which displays a summary of the instances and features that will be updated to SP1. Click Update to start the installation and display the Update Progress screen. When the SP1 installation is complete, click Next to proceed to the Complete screen. The Complete screen displays the location of the SP1 summary log file (see Figure 8.27). The default location of the SP1 summary log file is `C:\Program Files\Microsoft SQL Server\100\Setup Bootstrap\LOG`.

Installing SP1 from the Command Line

Like the SQL Server 2008 main install, SP1 can also be installed from the command line with no user interaction. This capability is useful if you need to install SP1 to a number of servers and want to avoid having to go through all the SP1 Install Wizard screens each time. To run SP1 from the command line, you must first extract the setup files from the SP1 download file, which is an executable archive file. You can do this by running the `SQLServer2008SP1-KB968369-x64-ENU.exe` file with the `/x` option from the command line. This launches the extractor, which prompts you for a location to extract the files to. Alternatively, you can specify a directory on a local drive to have it extract the setup files to automatically:

```
SQLServer2008SP1-KB968369-x64-ENU.exe /x:C:\SP1
```

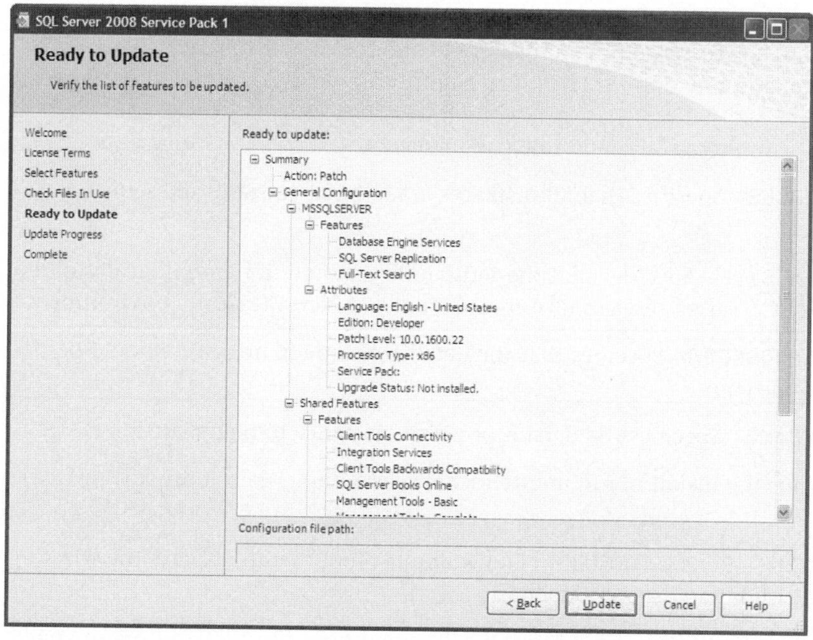

FIGURE 8.26 SQL Server 2008 SP1 Ready to Update screen.

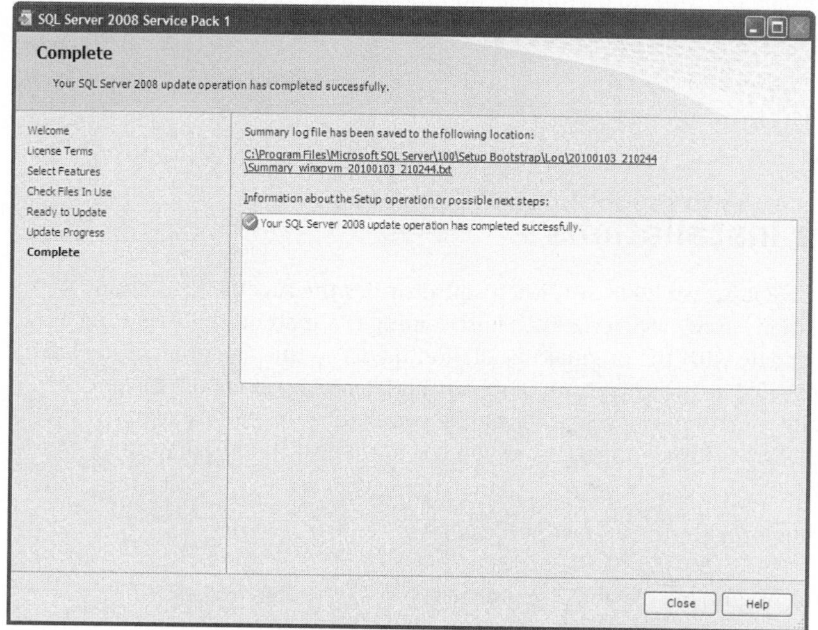

FIGURE 8.27 SQL Server 2008 SP1 Installation Complete screen.

8

After extracting the SP1 setup files to a folder, you can run the `setup.exe` program from the command line. The SP1 setup program supports options similar to the SQL Server 2008 installer command-line options (although significantly fewer options are available):

- **/HELP**—Displays these command-line parameters.
- **/ALLINSTANCES**—Specifies that all instances are to be included in the setup operation.
- **/CLUSTERPASSIVE**—Specifies that the setup utility should not automatically start and stop the SQL Server services if running in a non-Microsoft cluster environment.
- **/INDICATEPROGRESS**—Specifies that the detailed Setup log messages should be displayed to the console.
- **/INSTANCENAME**—Specifies the default or named instance to be updated
- **/QUIET**—Runs the install in full unattended mode. Setup does not display any user interface.
- **/QUIETSIMPLE**—Runs the install in Quiet Simple mode. Setup displays the wizard screens but without any user interaction.
- **/X86**—Specifies that Setup should install a 32-bit edition into WOW64 on an x64-based system.

For example, to install SP1 with no user interaction for all instances on a server, you would run the following command:

```
setup.exe /quiet /allinstances
```

Slipstream Installations

With the release of SQL Server 2008 SP1, Microsoft provides the capability to create Slipstream installations of SQL Server 2008. Slipstreaming is a method of integrating a SQL Server 2008 update with the original installation media so that the original media and update are installed at the same time. This capability can be a huge timesaver over having to manually run a service pack and possible cumulative update installations after running a full SQL Server install, especially if you have to repeat the installation in multiple environments.

Slipstreaming is supported in the following scenarios:

- Installing the original media and a service pack
- Installing the original media, a service pack, and a cumulative update to the service pack

NOTE

Slipstreaming a cumulative update for SQL Server 2008 with the original media but without a service pack is not supported because slipstreaming wasn't supported until SQL Server 2008 SP1 was released. Also, a Slipstream installation cannot be performed to update a SQL Server 2008 instance to SQL Server 2008 R2.

If you are doing a single install of SQL Server 2008 and at the same time want to apply SP1 and possibly a cumulative update as well, you can run the Slipstream installation by performing the following steps:

1. If they are not installed already on the target machine, install the required prerequisites for the SQL Server 2008 Installer (.NET Framework 3.5 SP1 and Windows Installer 4.5). You can install them manually from the SQL Server install disk (the installers are located in the `Drive_Letter:\platform\redist\Windows Installer` folder). Alternatively, after you extract the service pack files, run the `sqlsupport.msi` file from within the folder where the service pack files have been extracted. For example, if you extracted the Service pack to the `C:\sql2k8xp1` folder on an X86 platform, this file would be found in the `C:\SQL2K8SP1\x86\setup\1033` folder.

NOTE

To confirm whether the setup support files are installed, search for the Microsoft SQL Server 2008 Setup Support Files entry in the Programs and Features Control Panel (or the Add or Remove Programs Control Panel in operating systems prior to Windows Vista or Windows Server 2008).

NOTE

On the IA-64 platform, the .NET Framework 3.5 is not supported. The .NET Framework 2.0 SP2 is required instead. The .NET Framework 2.0 SP2 is located in the `Drive_Letter:\ia64\redist\2.0\NetFx20SP2_ia64.exe` folder on the source media.

---

2. If not done already, download the Service Pack (PCU) package that matches your system architecture and, if desired, the cumulative update (CU) package you want to install.
3. For each package you want to include in the Slipstream installation, extract the contents to a folder on the local drive by running a command similar to the following at the command prompt from within the folder where you downloaded the package(s):

```
Name_of_the_PCU_or_CU_package.exe /x:Root_of_path_to_extract_to\<PCU | CU>
```

4. Now things get a bit tricky. Because Slipstream support is introduced with SP1, the `setup.exe` program that shipped with the original SQL Server 2008 installation media doesn't support the `/PCUSource` or `/CUSource` options that allow you to specify the locations of the service pack and cumulative updates to be slipstreamed. Instead, you need to run the SQL Server 2008 Setup program for Service Pack 1 and specify the action as `INSTALL`, and the file paths for the original media, as well as service pack and cumulative update files. These are specified using the `/ACTION`, `/MEDIASource`, `/PCUSource`, and `/CUSource` parameters. The following example shows how to run a slipstream install of SQL Server 2008 from the install CD in the `D:` drive with SP1 extracted to the `C:\SQLServer2008SP1` folder:

   ```
   C:\SQLServer2008SP1>setup.exe /PCUSource=C:\SQLServer2008SP1 /ACTION=INSTALL
    /MEDIASOURCE=D:\
   ```

   This command runs the SQL Server installation in the normal GUI mode, requiring you to specify and confirm all settings. If you want, you can also choose to run the install in a limited interface or automated mode, as described previously in this chapter in the section describing how to use a configuration file. However, the first time you run a Slipstream installation, you should at least use an interface that allows you to view the Ready to Install page before running the installation so that you can verify whether the desired Slipstream installation is being performed. If the setup utility is running a Slipstream installation, it is indicated in the Action field, as shown in Figure 8.28.

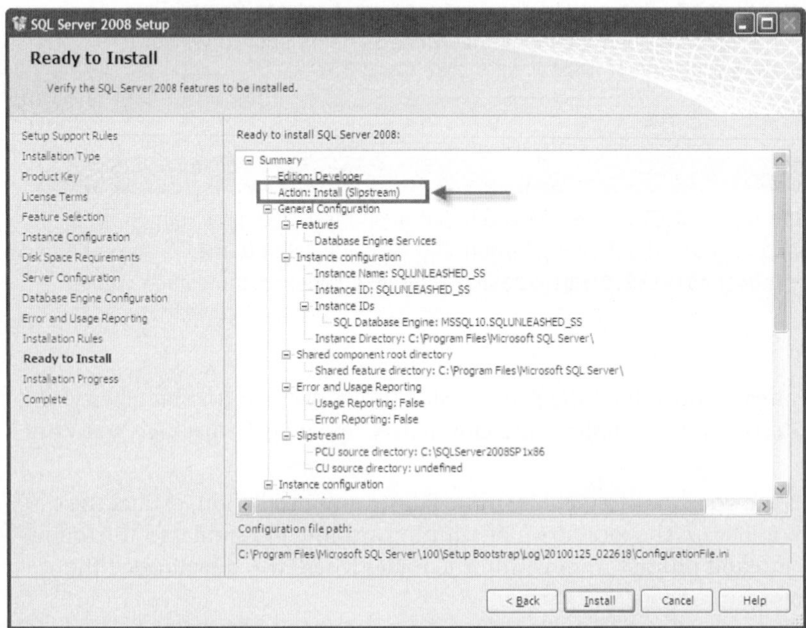

FIGURE 8.28 Verifying a Slipstream installation on the Ready to Install page.

Summary

This chapter provides a fairly detailed overview of the SQL Server 2008 install process from start to finish. The chapter shows how the new Installer Wizard makes it easy to install as many instances as you like, with whatever feature sets and in whatever configuration you choose.

The chapter also shows how the installer reports progress, failure, and success on an individual task basis rather than with one seemingly endless progress bar, making it a lot easier to rectify problems without calling Microsoft or scouring the newsgroups to figure out what went wrong.

Chapter 9, "Upgrading to SQL Server 2008," takes a similar approach to examining the process of upgrading from SQL Server 2000 or SQL Server 2005 to SQL Server 2008 or SQL Server 2008 R2.

CHAPTER 9

Upgrading to SQL Server 2008

IN THIS CHAPTER

- What's New in Upgrading SQL Server
- Using the SQL Server Upgrade Advisor (UA)
- Destination: SQL Server 2008 or SQL Server 2008 R2
- Upgrading Using a Configuration File
- Slipstreaming Upgrades74
- Upgrading Other SQL Server Components

SQL Server 2008 offers a number of new features and improvements that make upgrading desirable. You can upgrade instances of SQL Server 2000 and SQL Server 2005 to SQL Server 2008 or SQL Server 2008 R2, as well as upgrade SQL Server 2008 to SQL Server 2008 R2. Whether you're a gung-ho developer or the most conservative of administrators, there's an upgrade path to suit your comfort level. This chapter provides best practices and recommendations for upgrading to SQL Server 2008 with minimal issues.

What's New in Upgrading SQL Server

SQL Server 2008 provides a new installer program for performing installations and upgrades. The new features of the SQL Server 2008 Installer include

- A new SQL Server 2008 Installation Center landing page, which includes a number of options for planning, installing, and maintaining a SQL Server implementation; links to SQL Server documentation for planning and reviewing before starting the upgrade; and a link to install the Upgrade Advisor.
- The Feature Upgrade Wizard, which allows DBAs to upgrade or change the installed edition of SQL Server 2008 or SQL Server 2008 R2 (for example, upgrading from Standard Edition to Enterprise Edition without having to perform a complete reinstall).

- A discovery report that provides a detailed information regarding all SQL Server components, features, and settings associated with an install or upgrade.
- The potential to automate SQL Server upgrades by using a configuration file.
- A tool that allows for a smooth transition of SQL Server Integration Services (SSIS) packages by automatically upgrading them from SQL Server 2005 to the SQL Server 2008 Integration Services format.

Also new in SQL Server 2008 is a refined Upgrade Advisor. The Upgrade Advisor tool allows a DBA to fully analyze existing SQL Server 2005 and SQL Server 2000 installations for issues that may surface when upgrading to SQL Server 2008 or SQL Server 2008 R2. Addressing these issues before conducting the upgrade should lead to a smoother experience when transitioning to SQL Server 2008.

With the release of Service Pack 1, SQL Server 2008 also now supports Slipstream installations. Slipstreaming is a method of integrating a SQL Server 2008 update (such as a service pack or cumulative update) with the original installation media so that the original media and update are installed at the same time. This can be a huge timesaver over having to manually apply service packs or cumulative updates after performing a full installation or upgrade.

NOTE

The focus of this chapter is on upgrade options and best practices rather than a screen-by-screen walkthrough of the upgrade process. An upgrade installation is not much different from a new installation. See Chapter 8, "Installing SQL Server 2008," for a detailed walkthrough and description of the installer screens and options.

Using the SQL Server Upgrade Advisor (UA)

It would be a daunting task indeed to try to test every stored procedure and function, every table and view, every online analytical processing (OLAP) cube, every Data Transformation Services (DTS) or SQL Server Integration Services (SSIS) package, and so on that your team has built to make sure they still work after you migrate them to SQL Server 2008.

With the availability of the SQL Server Upgrade Advisor (UA), you can relax a bit and let the combined experience and testing of early adopters and the SQL Server development team go to work for you.

NOTE

Even though the UA is a great tool, if you have the resources to do so, it is a good idea to set up an additional test environment just for SQL Server 2008. Also, you should thoroughly test your upgraded objects and code *after the upgrade* on a dry run, just to be sure you don't miss anything. Remember to make full backups!

The UA advises on which aspects of your current setup should or need to be changed to become compatible with SQL Server 2008. Let's look at how it works.

Getting Started with the UA

Before running the Upgrade Advisor, you must first install it. The easiest way to install the Upgrade Advisor is to start the SQL Server 2008 Installer. On the Installer Landing page is an option to install the Upgrade Advisor (see Figure 9.1). Alternatively, the Upgrade Advisor is available in the `Servers\redist\Upgrade Advisor` folder of the SQL Server installation media, or from the Microsoft Download Center. The Upgrade Advisor has the following system requirements:

- Windows XP Service Pack 2 (SP2) or later, Windows Vista, Windows Server 2003 SP2 or later, or Windows Server 2008 SP2, Windows 7, and Windows Server 2008 R2.
- Windows Installer beginning with version 4.5 (required by the .NET Framework; you can install Windows Installer from the Windows Installer website)
- The .NET Framework

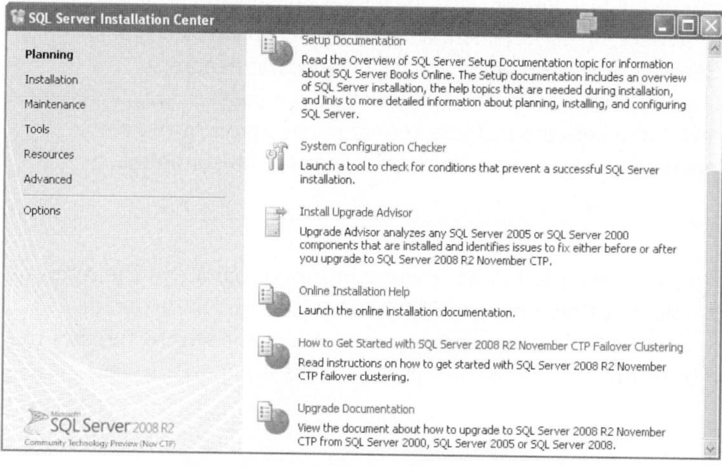

FIGURE 9.1 Installing the Upgrade Advisor from the SQL Server 2008 Installer.

NOTE

If not installed already, the .NET Framework 2.0 is available on the SQL Server 2008 product media, and from the SDK, redistributable, and service pack download website. To install the .NET Framework 2.0 from the SQL Server 2008 media, locate the root of the disk drive. Then double-click the `\redist` folder, double-click the `\2.0` folder, and run `Dotnetfx.exe` (for 32-bit) or `Dotnetfx64.exe` (for 64-bit), depending on your operating system.

If you run the SQL Server Installer, it installs the Windows Installer and .NET Framework requirements automatically if they are not detected.

If upgrading from SQL Server 2000 Analysis Services, you need to install the SQL Server 2000 Decision Support Objects (DSOs) on the system where UA will be run to scan upgrade issues in Analysis Services. To install DSOs, run the SQL Server 2000 Setup program and click Install SQL Server 2000 Components. Click Analysis Services to start the Analysis Services Setup program. In Select Components, make sure that the Decision Support Objects component is selected.

Additionally, if you are upgrading SQL Server 2000 DTS packages, the SQL Server 2000 client components are required to scan SQL Server 2000 DTS packages. The SQL Server 2000 client components can be installed from the SQL Server 2000 installation disk.

If you are upgrading from SQL Server 2005 DTS packages that were migrated from SQL Server 2000, you need to install the SQL Server 2005 backward-compatibility components to scan SQL Server 2005 DTS. Use the SQL Server 2005 installation disk to install backward-compatibility components.

NOTE

The location where you can install SQL Server Upgrade Advisor depends on what you will be analyzing. Upgrade Advisor supports remote analysis of all supported components except Reporting Services. If you are not scanning instances of Reporting Services, you can install Upgrade Advisor on any computer that can connect to your instance of SQL Server and that meets the Upgrade Advisor prerequisites. If you are scanning instances of Reporting Services, you must install Upgrade Advisor on the Report Server.

As described in the following sections, the UA has two main functional areas: the Analysis Wizard and Report Viewer. The first time you use Upgrade Advisor, run the Upgrade Advisor Analysis Wizard to analyze SQL Server components. When the wizard finishes the analysis, you can view the resulting reports in the Upgrade Advisor Report Viewer.

The Analysis Wizard

You'll be glad to know that the analysis process does not modify any code or data; that is left for you to do (or not do) at a later time. As an example, let's run the UA's Analysis Wizard against all the SQL Server components of a locally installed SQL Server 2005 instance. The Analysis Wizard examines objects that can be accessed, such as scripts, stored procedures, triggers, and trace files. Upgrade Advisor cannot analyze desktop applications or encrypted stored procedures.

To start the process, click the Launch Upgrade Advisor Analysis Wizard hyperlink at the bottom of the Welcome page (see Figure 9.2). When the Analysis Wizard's Welcome page appears, click Next. When you reach the SQL Server Components screen, choose all the components to be analyzed by checking their corresponding check boxes (see Figure 9.3).

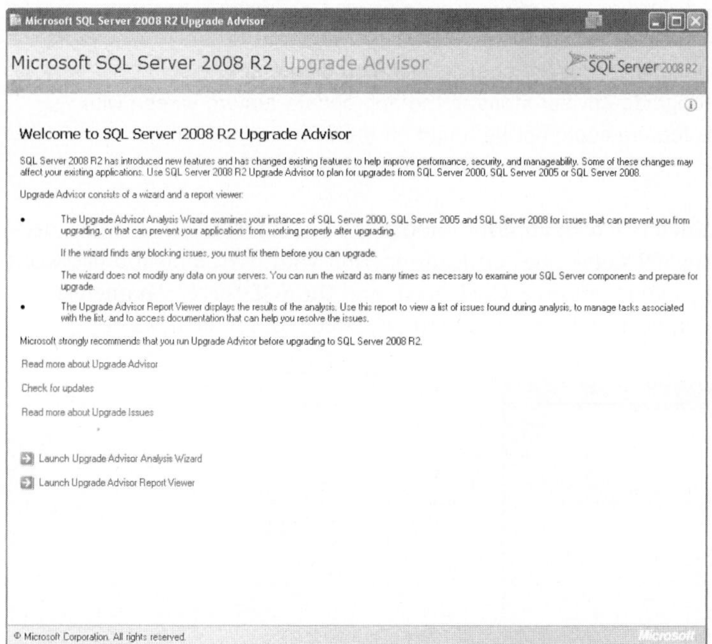

FIGURE 9.2 The Upgrade Advisor Welcome page.

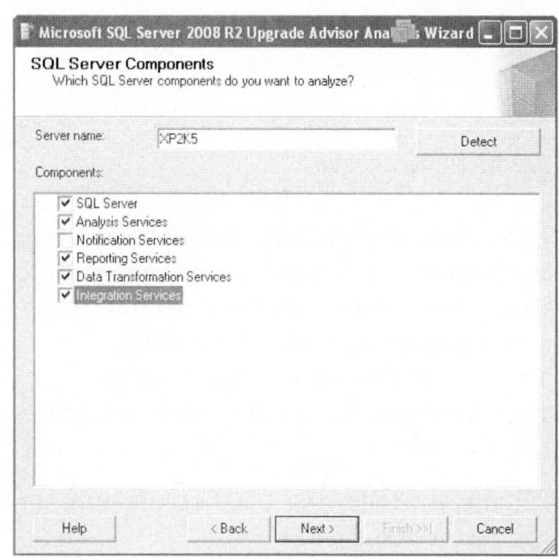

FIGURE 9.3 Choosing the components to be analyzed by the UA's Analysis Wizard.

NOTE

Be sure to select only components that are actually installed on the server being upgraded; otherwise, the Upgrade Advisor stalls at the appropriate feature screen with an error message that the feature could not be found on the specified server.

When the Connection Parameters screen appears, choose the target server, select an authentication method, and if using SQL Server authentication, enter your username and password so that the UA can connect to your instance. Click Next, and the SQL Server Parameters screen, shown in Figure 9.4, appears. Choose which (if any) databases to analyze.

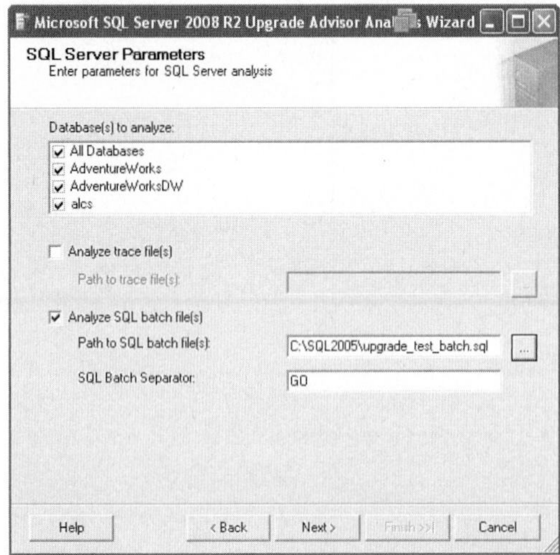

FIGURE 9.4 Choosing the databases and files for the UA to analyze.

You can also use this screen to ask the UA to analyze one or more SQL Profiler trace (`.trc`) files. This feature is useful for analyzing the T-SQL statements submitted from one or more applications for deprecated or discontinued features. You would want to set up and run a trace in SQL Profiler ahead of time to capture a representative sample of the T-SQL executed against the server. You can also scan T-SQL batch files (maintenance scripts, procedures, functions, triggers, and so on) to check for deprecated or discontinued features used in the SQL scripts.

For this example, create a SQL batch file that contains the following T-SQL commands, most of which are deprecated in SQL Server 2008, just to test the UA:

```
use bigpubs2008
go

EXEC sp_configure 'set working set size'
```

```
SELECT * FROM master..syslockinfo

DECLARE @ptr varbinary(16)

SELECT @ptr = TEXTPTR(pr_info)
FROM pub_info
WHERE pub_id = '6380'

SELECT *
FROM Stores s, Stores s2
WHERE s.Stor_Id *= s2.Stor_Id
AND s.Stor_name <> s2.Stor_name

READTEXT pub_info.pr_info @ptr 0 25
```

When you're ready, click Next, and the Upgrade Advisor presents screens for each of the SQL Server components you selected previously (refer to Figure 9.3) asking for login information or to select packages to analyze. Note that if you selected a component, but that component isn't installed on the server you are upgrading, the Upgrade Advisor reports that no instances of that component could be found on the server and you cannot proceed until you go back and deselect the component.

If you selected to analyze DTS or SSIS packages, the DTS and SSIS Parameters screens (shown in Figure 9.5) give you the option to analyze all the packages stored in the target instance or to specify one or more package files to be analyzed.

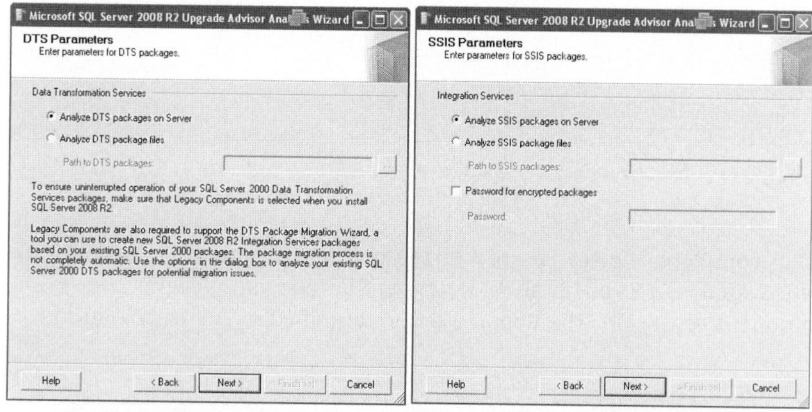

FIGURE 9.5 Choosing the DTS and SSIS packages to analyze.

Note that the DTS Parameters screen advises that you must install the Legacy Components feature when installing SQL Server 2008; otherwise, SQL Server 2008 will not be able to run your DTS packages (unless they are upgraded to the new SSIS format). To upgrade your DTS packages, you need to use the DTS Migration Wizard, which is installed with SSIS and discussed later in this chapter, in the section "Migrating DTS Packages."

When you're all set with your DTS and SSIS selections, click Next to reach the Confirm Upgrade Advisor Settings screen. Make sure that all the SQL Server services you are analyzing are running and (if you're happy with your selections) click the Run button to begin the analysis.

As you can see from the Upgrade Advisor Progress screen that appears (see Figure 9.6), the wizard performs a task-based study of each component, providing per-step reporting, similar to the installer and the System Configuration Checker (both discussed in Chapter 8).

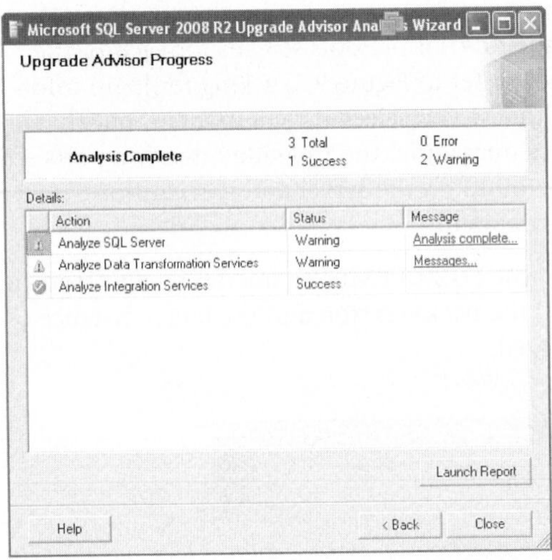

FIGURE 9.6 The Upgrade Advisor Progress screen.

When the analysis is complete, the UA Progress screen presents a Launch Report button. The output of the UA Analysis Wizard is an XML report that you can view via the second major component of the UA, the Report Viewer, described in the next section.

NOTE

You can view your last-generated report by using the Report Viewer; you can find the link to launch it on the main screen. If you run the UA more than once against the same SQL Server instance, however, you must save your previously generated reports to a directory other than the default output directory; otherwise, the previously generated report will be overwritten.

UA reports are saved by default to the folder `My Documents\SQL Server 2008 R2 Upgrade Advisor Reports\`*`Servername`*, and then they are broken down into separate XML files by component (for example, `AS.xml` for Analysis Services, `DE.xml` for the Database Engine).

You can launch the Report Viewer to figure out what to do about the issues the UA may have uncovered. Click the Launch Report button to proceed.

The Report Viewer

The Report Viewer is one of the most important tools in the upgrade process because it provides per-issue messaging, resolution tracking, and (in many cases) hyperlinks to the compiled help documentation distributed with the UA.

Issues are organized in the Report Viewer on a per-server and then per-component basis. They can be filtered by type (that is, all issues, all upgrade issues, pre-upgrade issues, all migration issues, and resolved issues), and you can track your resolution progress by checking the This Issue Has Been Resolved check boxes. Figure 9.7 shows the main user interface of the Report Viewer.

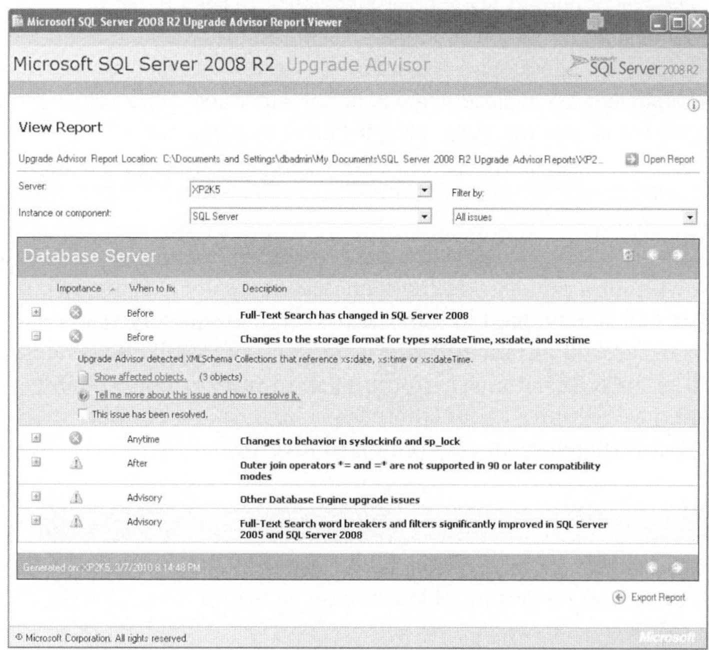

FIGURE 9.7 SQL Server UA's Report Viewer.

Destination: SQL Server 2008 or SQL Server 2008 R2

Now that you have become familiar with how to use the helpful Upgrade Advisor, you're ready to begin your extensive pre-upgrade testing phase. After you resolve all the issues you can, it's time to take the next step: install SQL Server 2008 (in your test and development environments first, of course).

Two different paths lead from SQL Server 2000 or 2005 to SQL Server 2008:

- You can upgrade your existing SQL Server 2000 SP4 or later and SQL Server 2005 SP2 or later instances in-place, using the SQL Server Installer.
- You can install SQL Server 2008 side by side with your current SQL Server instances and then migrate your data and other content to SQL Server 2008.

The same upgrade paths exist for upgrading from SQL Server 2008 to SQL Server 2008 R2.

The path you choose depends primarily on two factors: your comfort level with the new platform and the scope of feature use in your current environment. When you have become familiar with what it takes to travel either path, you'll find it much easier to make your decision. The first approach we explore in this chapter is the more conservative side-by-side migration path.

NOTE

If the server environment where your current SQL Server installation resides is not a supported platform for performing an in-place upgrade, a side-by-side migration may be your only option. For example, if you are upgrading from SQL Server 7 or running in a Windows 2000 server environment, an in-place upgrade is not supported. For a list of supported in-place upgrade paths, see the "Upgrading In-Place" section, later in this chapter.

Side-by-Side Migration

SQL Server 2008 can coexist without a problem on the same servers as any existing SQL Server 2000 or 2005 instances. SQL Server 2008 R2 can coexist on the same servers as any existing SQL Server 2000, 2005, or 2008 instances. This means you can install one or more instances of SQL Server 2008 or 2008 R2 without performing an in-place upgrade of any pre-2008 instances. You don't have to worry about whether you're breaking existing functionality. Side-by-side migration is therefore an easy option to investigate.

NOTE

If you are doing a side-by-side installation, be sure your server has sufficient resources (CPU, memory, disk space) to support running multiple instances of SQL Server.

Many administrators favor the side-by-side approach to upgrading because it gives everyone on the development team (including eager software folks) a chance to get comfortable with the new features in the new SQL Server release *before* committing to it in production environments.

In addition, it is far easier to roll back to your previous-version SQL Server components because installing side by side leaves them intact (unlike upgrading in-place, which replaces them). When you are reasonably comfortable with the new SQL Server release, you can go forward confidently in migrating all your objects (presuming that, if you're leaving previous versions intact, you're also ready to perform necessary tasks, such as changing connection strings, server aliases, and so on).

Avoiding an Unintentional In-Place Upgrade During Setup

If you do intend to go ahead with a side-by-side installation, there's a small gotcha you need to watch out for when installing a new instance of SQL Server 2008. When you run the Setup program, the Instance Name screen is somewhat lengthy in its header's verbiage, and if you don't take the time to read it closely, you might unintentionally upgrade all your components. This is the lowdown:

- If you choose the Default Instance radio button and you already have a SQL Server default instance, that default instance is upgraded.
- If you the choose the Named Instance radio button, you need to make sure to enter a name that you know is not in use as an instance name; otherwise, the existing named instance is upgraded.

Figure 9.8 shows an example of how to make the right choice and use an instance name, `SQL2008R2`, that makes it abundantly clear you are installing a new instance.

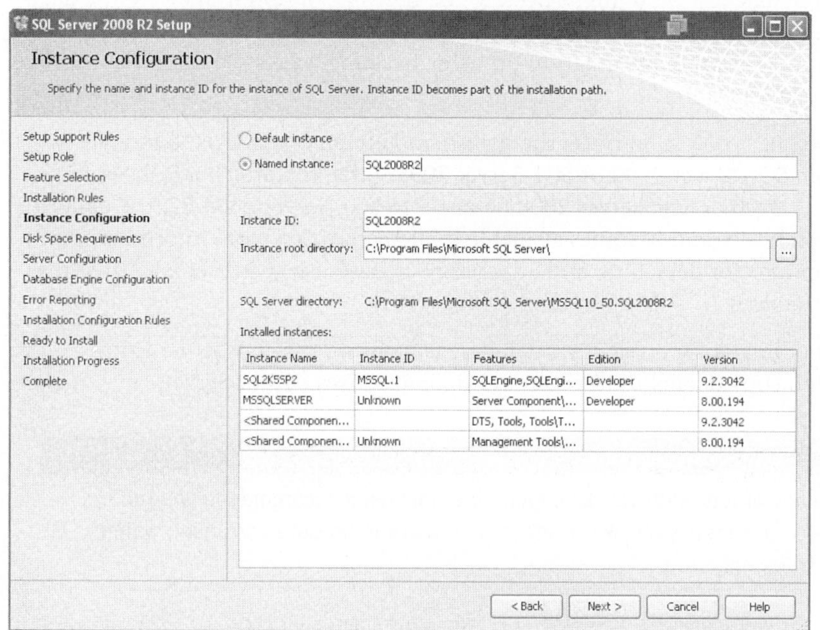

FIGURE 9.8 Installing a new named SQL Server 2008 R2 instance.

Migrating Databases

Now it's time for the most important task: migrating your databases to SQL Server 2008. One method of migrating to SQL Server 2008 or 2008 R2 is by backing up your SQL Server 2000 and 2005 databases and restoring them to SQL Server 2008. Another method is to attach or restore a database from a prior version of SQL Server to SQL Server 2008. When you migrate using either of these methods, the database is upgraded automatically during the attach/restore process.

NOTE

Database backups created by using SQL Server 7.0 or earlier are in an incompatible format and cannot be restored in SQL Server 2008 or 2008 R2. For information on how to migrate a database from SQL Server 6.5 or 7.0 to SQL Server 2008, see the section "Upgrading from SQL Server 7 or SQL Server 6.5," later in this chapter.

When you use backup and restore to copy a database to another instance of SQL Server, the source and destination computers can be any platform on which SQL Server runs. The general steps to upgrade using backup and restore are as follows:

1. Back up the source database that resides on an instance of SQL Server 2000, SQL Server 2005, SQL Server 2008, or SQL Server 2008 R2.
2. Restore the backup of the source database on the destination SQL Server. Restoring the database automatically creates all the database files and upgrades the database.

When restoring the database, you might need to use the `MOVE` option to relocate the database files because SQL Server 2008 and SQL Server 2008 R2 use a different default path than earlier versions. For more information on using backup and restore, see Chapter 14, "Database Backup and Restore."

In SQL Server 2008 R2, you can also use the detach and attach operations to migrate a user database from SQL Server 2000 or SQL Server 2005. After you attach a SQL Server 2005 or SQL Server 2000 or SQL Server 2008 database to SQL Server 2008 R2, the database is upgraded automatically and becomes available immediately. For more information on the syntax and options for detaching and attaching databases, see Chapter 23, "Creating and Managing Databases."

Another method of migrating an existing database is by using the SQL Server Copy Database Wizard to copy databases between multiple instances of SQL Server.

TIP

Before you use any of the methods described here, Microsoft recommends you run the appropriate `DBCC` consistency checks to make sure there is no data corruption within the databases to be migrated.

Using the Copy Database Wizard Using the Copy Database Wizard is probably the easiest approach to use to migrate your databases to SQL Server 2008 or 2008 R2. To run the

Copy Database Wizard, using SQL Server Management Studio (SSMS), connect the Object Explorer to your previous SQL Server version's instance. Expand `Databases` and then select and right-click the database you want to copy (or move) into SQL Server 2008. Then select Tasks, Copy Database.

When the wizard's initial Welcome page is displayed, click Next and then select your source server (the 2000 or 2005 instance). Click Next again and select your destination server (your newly installed SQL Server 2008 or SQL Server 2008 R2 instance). Click Next again to bring up the Select the Transfer Method screen. This screen provides two options for copying or moving your databases to SQL Server 2008:

- **Detach and Attach**—This option is the same as the detach/attach method described previously. It's fast, but it takes the database offline during the migration process.
- **Use the SQL Server Management Objects (SMO) to Import the Database**—This option is slower, but it keeps the source database online during the process.

NOTE

When you use the detach and attach method, SSIS uses the service account of SQL Server Agent that is running on the 2008 (destination) instance. This account must be able to access the file systems of both servers; otherwise, the wizard will fail.

Select the option that works best for you and then click Next. The Select Databases screen appears, and, as Figure 9.9 shows, you should check the Copy (not Move) check boxes for the databases you want to migrate.

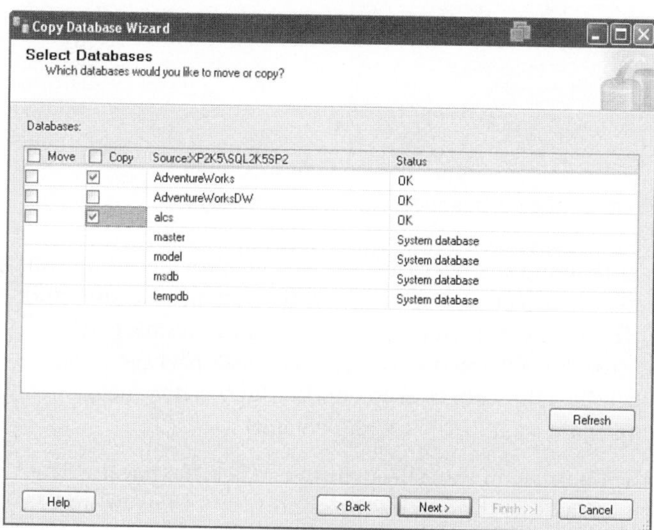

FIGURE 9.9 Selecting the databases to copy to SQL Server 2009.

CAUTION

After a pre-2008 database is upgraded (in case you choose the Move Database option or you perform an attach or restore and delete the original), it cannot be downgraded back to its former version—not even if you attempt to detach/attach or restore it to SQL 2000 or 2005. Thus, it is especially important to create full backup copies of all your databases before you upgrade. It's also a good idea to back up the entire `Program Files/Microsoft SQL Server` directory tree.

After you make your database selections, click Next, and the Configure Destination Database screen appears for each database you selected in the previous step. This screen allows you to rename the database on the destination server if you so desire (see Figure 9.10). It also provides options to overwrite any existing databases or MDF (data) and LDF (log) files on the destination server or to create new ones in the folders of your choice. Make your selections and click Next.

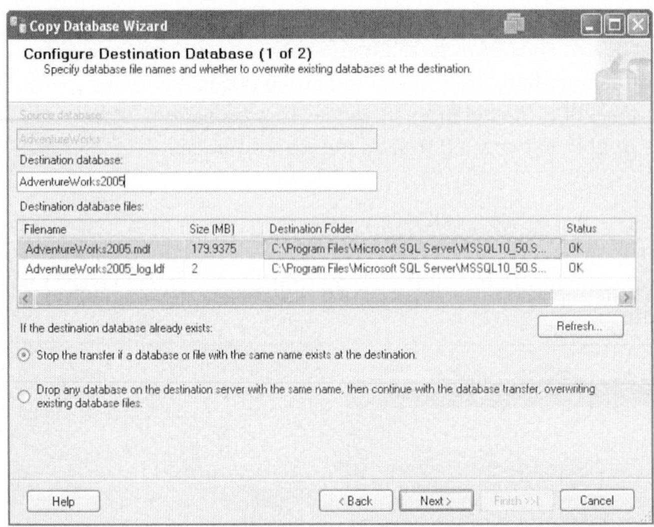

FIGURE 9.10 Copy Database Wizard Configure Destination Database screen.

The Select Database Objects screen that appears next (see Figure 9.11) provides some real power because it allows the server-wide objects (those stored in the system databases and source database) to be imported. These objects include stored procedures residing in `master`, SQL Server Agent jobs, custom user-defined error messages, SSIS packages, and SQL Server logins. You need to click the ellipsis button to choose the specific ones you want to import (rather than choosing them all, which is the default).

When you're finished selecting the objects you want brought over, click Next again. The Configure the Package screen that appears next provides the opportunity to name and save the SSIS package created for migrating the database, and to specify how you want to log the messages generated during the transfer. Click Next to present the Schedule the

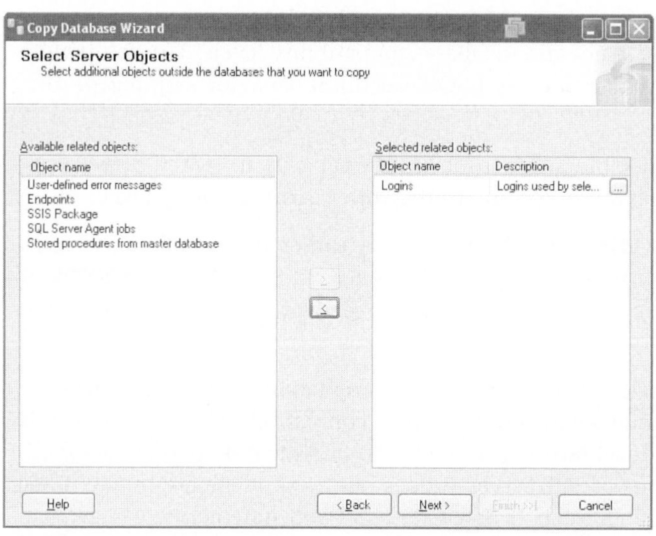

FIGURE 9.11 Importing server-wide objects, using the Copy Database Wizard.

Package screen, which allows you to run the transfer immediately or schedule it to run at a specific time. You are also given an opportunity to specify an SSIS proxy account to use to run the transfer (you should make sure it's an account that has appropriate permissions on both the source and destination servers to ensure a successful transfer).

After you make your scheduling choices, click Next to display the Complete the Wizard screen (see Figure 9.12). Here, you have an opportunity to review the choices you've made on the prior screens. If everything looks okay, click Finish to complete the wizard and start or schedule the Copy Database package.

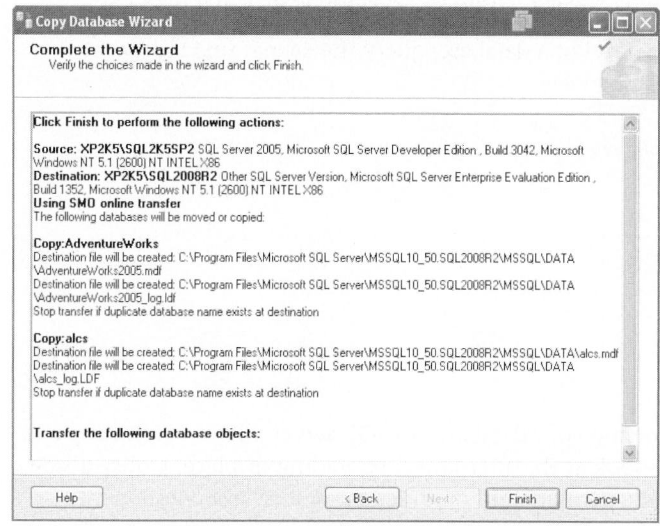

FIGURE 9.12 The Copy Database Complete the Wizard screen.

Database Compatibility Level Migrating pre-2008 databases into SQL Server 2008 brings up the question of compatibility issues and database compatibility levels. The compatibility level is a per-database setting that controls T-SQL execution behavior with regard to SQL Server's versioning system.

The T-SQL execution engine is flexible insofar as it has the capacity to switch between varying, version-dependent behaviors according to the current compatibility-level setting.

When a database is upgraded to SQL Server 2008 from any earlier version of SQL Server, the database retains its existing compatibility level if it is at least 80 (SQL Server 2000). Upgrading a database with a compatibility level below 80 sets the database to compatibility level 80.

Compatibility level affects behaviors only for the specified database, not for the entire server. An important point to understand about database compatibility levels, however, is that the database compatibility-level setting is intended to provide only partial backward compatibility with earlier versions of SQL Server. It does not prevent the use of new T-SQL features available in SQL Server 2008 such as new data types and statements.

The compatibility-level setting is provided primarily as an interim migration aid to work around version differences in the behaviors that are controlled by the relevant compatibility-level setting. Essentially, it allows T-SQL code that may be using deprecated features or expects pre-100 level behaviors for certain commands to continue operating as it did in the prior version of SQL Server. Using the compatibility-level setting should not be viewed as a permanent solution. It should be used only until the T-SQL code affected by behavioral differences in SQL Server 2008 can be converted to work properly in SQL Server 2008. Then you can use `ALTER DATABASE` to change the compatibility level to 100.

You can find a full list of the behavioral differences between the compatibility-level settings in the Books Online article associated with the "ALTER DATABASE Compatibility Level" topic. This option can be used to set the compatibility level for a particular database.

To view the current compatibility level of a database, query the `compatibility_level` column in the `sys.databases` catalog view:

```
select compatibility_level from sys.databases where name = db_name()
go

compatibility_level
-------------------
90
```

Upgrading In-Place

Now that you've seen how to migrate your databases to SQL Server 2008 by following the side-by-side migration path, let's look at the alternative: upgrading in-place. Unlike a side-by-side install, an in-place upgrade permanently modifies the SQL Server components, data, and metadata objects, and there is no going back. You will likely be more comfortable taking the side-by-side migration path than doing an in-place upgrade, unless a side-by-side migration is not possible because of disk space limitations, you have very few SQL Server features in use, or you are fairly confident about the potential success of the upgrade process because you've done extensive issue resolution with the assistance of the Upgrade Assistant.

If you are performing an in-place upgrade of the Database Engine, it is strongly recommended that you first do the following:

- Create full, verified backups of your existing SQL Server databases.
- Run the appropriate `DBCC` consistency checks (for example, `DBCC CHECKDB` and `DBCC CHECKFILEGROUP`).
- Make sure the system databases on your pre-2008 instances (for example, `master`, `msdb`, `tempdb`, and `model`) are all set to auto-grow.
- Disable any startup stored procedures that get kicked off when the SQL Server service starts.
- Disable database replication and empty the replication log.

After you perform all these actions, you are ready to begin the upgrade process.

Upgrading the Database Engine

You perform an in-place upgrade by running the SQL Server Installation Center. On the Installation page, you can invoke the Upgrade Wizard to upgrade from SQL Server 2000, 2005, or 2008 (see Figure 9.13). After first running the Setup Rules check and installing the Setup Support Files, the Upgrade Wizard essentially runs the installation process. (The installation process and all its screens are described in Chapter 8 under the heading, "Install Screens, Step by Step.") The key differences between running a new install versus an upgrade is that during the upgrade process, you choose an existing default or named instance on the Select Instance screen (see Figure 9.14).

After selecting the instance to upgrade, you see the Feature Selection page. The features to be upgraded are preselected. You cannot change the features to be upgraded, and you cannot add features during an upgrade operation. To add features, you need to run the Installation Center again after the upgrade operation is complete.

After making choices on the Features Selection page, step through the Instance Configuration, Disk Space Requirements, and Server Configuration screens, making changes as necessary. For example, authentication and login information are carried forward from the previous instance of SQL Server. You can assign the same login account to all SQL Server services, or you can configure each service account individually. You can also specify whether services start automatically, are started manually, or are disabled.

Next, you are presented with options for upgrading your full-text catalogs. In SQL Server 2005 and earlier versions, each full-text index resided in a full-text catalog that belonged to its own filegroup and was treated as a database file. In SQL Server 2008, a full-text catalog is a logical concept that refers to a group of full-text indexes and is no longer treated as a separate database file with a physical path. However, during upgrade of any

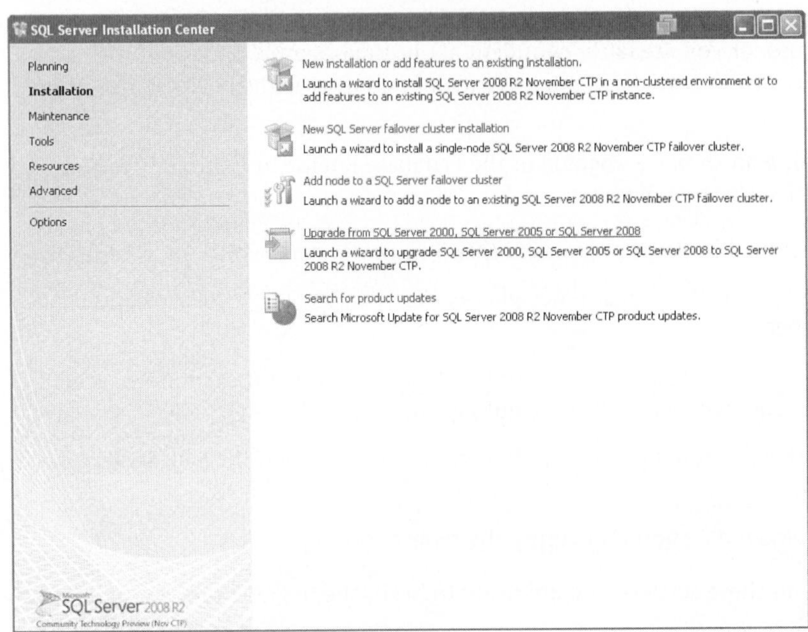

FIGURE 9.13 Running the Upgrade Wizard from the Installation Center.

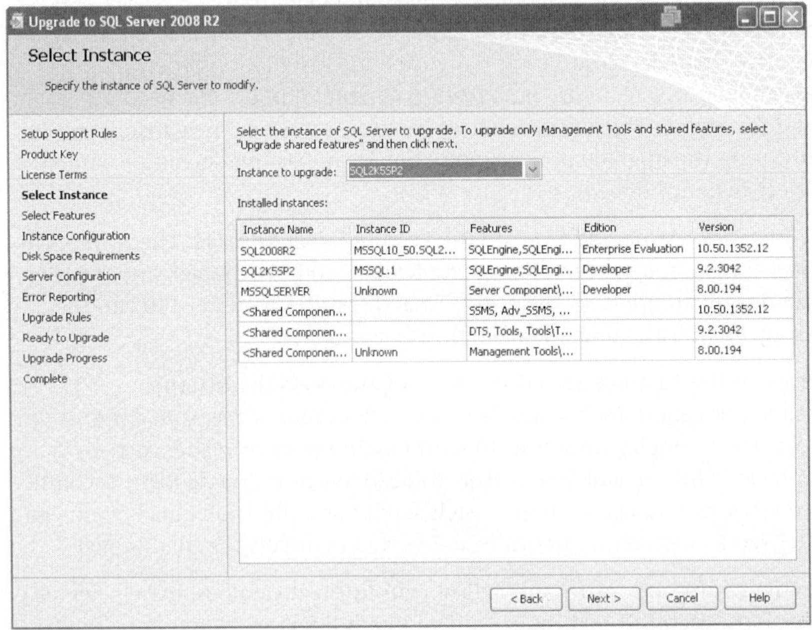

FIGURE 9.14 The Select Instance screen in the SQL Server Installation Center.

full-text catalog, a new filegroup is still created on the same disk to maintain the pre-upgrade disk I/O behavior. If the old full-text catalog path is invalid, though, the upgrade places the full-text index in the same filegroup as the base table or in the primary filegroup if the table is partitioned.

Three options are available for upgrading your existing full-text catalogs:

- **Import**—Typically, import is the fastest method of upgrading, but an imported full-text catalog does not use the new and enhanced word breakers introduced in SQL Server 2008, so you might want to rebuild your full-text catalogs eventually if not during the upgrade.
- **Rebuild**—This method uses the new SQL Server 2008 word breakers, but rebuilding indexes can take awhile.
- **Reset**—When you use this method, SQL Server 2005 full-text catalog files are removed, but the metadata for full-text catalogs and full-text indexes is retained. The catalog remains empty until you manually issue a full population after the upgrade completes.

After choosing your full-text upgrade option, you next choose your Error Reporting options, and then the Upgrade Rules check is run to validate your system configuration with the options and features chosen during the upgrade process. If all the rules pass, you can review the upgrade operation on the Ready to Upgrade page, which also displays the path to the upgrade configuration file (this is useful for setting up and performing unattended upgrades from the command line, as discussed later in this chapter). If everything looks okay, click Upgrade to begin the upgrade process. The upgrade process automatically upgrades all objects that are common to all databases, including the following:

- Tables, views, indexes, and constraints
- Stored procedures, functions, and triggers
- User-defined types, rules, and defaults
- Logins, users, and permissions
- Database diagrams

You can monitor the upgrade progress on the Upgrade Progress screen. Depending on your hardware configuration and the features to be upgraded, the upgrade operation can take from approximately 30 minutes to several hours. The databases on the instance being upgraded remain unavailable until the upgrade is complete.

When the upgrade finishes, it displays the upgrade status of each component and also provides the location of the upgrade log. A system restart may be required in some cases if any upgraded components were in use during the upgrade process.

When your upgrade of the Database Engine is complete, it is recommended that you perform the following on all databases (also recommended for side-by-side migration):

- Repopulate your full-text catalogs if you chose not to rebuild them during the upgrade.
- Run the `sp_updatestats` system stored procedure to update statistics.
- Reregister your server in SSMS.

The SQL Server 2008 Upgrade Matrix

No software upgrade section would be complete without an illustrative table showing the versions and editions of SQL Server for which the upgrade methods described thus far are supported. They are presented in Table 9.1.

TABLE 9.1 Supported Upgrade Paths to SQL Server 2008 and 2008 R2

Previous SQL Server Edition	Supported Upgraded Edition
SQL Server 2000 Enterprise Edition SP4	SQL Server 2008 Enterprise Edition SQL Server 2008 R2 Enterprise Edition SQL Server 2008 R2 Datacenter Edition
SQL Server 2000 IA64 Enterprise Edition SP4	SQL Server 2008 IA64 Enterprise Edition SQL Server 2008 R2 IA64 Enterprise Edition SQL Server 2008 R2 IA64 Datacenter Edition
SQL Server 2000 Developer Edition SP4	SQL Server 2008 Developer Edition SQL Server 2008 R2 Developer Edition
SQL Server 2000 IA64 Developer Edition SP4	SQL Server 2008 IA64 Developer Edition SQL Server 2008 IA64 R2 Developer Edition
SQL Server 2000 Standard Edition SP4	SQL Server 2008 Standard Edition SQL Server 2008 Enterprise Edition SQL Server 2008 R2 Standard Edition SQL Server 2008 R2 Enterprise Edition
SQL Server 2000 Workgroup Edition SP4	SQL Server 2008 Workgroup Edition SQL Server 2008 Standard Edition SQL Server 2008 Enterprise Edition SQL Server 2008 R2 Workgroup Edition SQL Server 2008 R2 Standard Edition SQL Server 2008 R2 Enterprise Edition
SQL Server 2000 Personal Edition SP4	Not supported
SQL Server 2000 Evaluation Edition	Not supported

TABLE 9.1 Supported Upgrade Paths to SQL Server 2008 and 2008 R2

Previous SQL Server Edition	Supported Upgraded Edition
SQL Server 2000 MSDE 2000 SP4	SQL Server 2008 Express SQL Server 2008 Express with Tools SQL Server 2008 Express with Advanced Services SQL Server 2008 Workgroup SQL Server 2008 R2 Express SQL Server 2008 R2 Express with Tools SQL Server 2008 R2 Express with Advanced Services SQL Server 2008 R2 Workgroup
SQL Server 2005 Enterprise Edition SP2	SQL Server 2008 Enterprise Edition SQL Server 2008 R2 Enterprise Edition SQL Server 2008 R2 Datacenter Edition
SQL Server 2005 IA64 Enterprise Edition SP2	SQL Server 2008 IA64 Enterprise Edition SQL Server 2008 R2 IA64 Enterprise Edition SQL Server 2008 R2 IA64 Datacenter Edition
SQL Server 2005 X64 Enterprise Edition SP2	SQL Server 2008 X64 Enterprise Edition SQL Server 2008 R2 X64 Enterprise Edition SQL Server 2008 R2 X64 Datacenter Edition
SQL Server 2005 Developer Edition SP2	SQL Server 2008 Developer Edition SQL Server 2008 R2 Developer Edition
SQL Server 2005 IA64 Developer Edition SP2	SQL Server 2008 IA64 Developer Edition SQL Server 2008 IA64 R2 Developer Edition
SQL Server 2005 X64 Developer Edition SP2	SQL Server 2008 X64 Developer Edition SQL Server 2008 X64 R2 Developer Edition
SQL Server 2005 Standard Edition SP2	SQL Server 2008 Standard Edition SQL Server 2008 Enterprise Edition SQL Server 2008 R2 Standard Edition SQL Server 2008 R2 Enterprise Edition
SQL Server 2005 IA64 Standard Edition SP2	SQL Server 2008 IA64 Enterprise Edition SQL Server 2008 R2 IA64 Enterprise Edition
SQL Server 2005 X64 Standard Edition SP2	SQL Server 2008 X64 Standard Edition SQL Server 2008 R2 X64Standard Edition SQL Server 2008 X64 Enterprise Edition SQL Server 2008 R2 X64 Enterprise Edition

TABLE 9.1 Supported Upgrade Paths to SQL Server 2008 and 2008 R2

Previous SQL Server Edition	Supported Upgraded Edition
SQL Server 2005 Workgroup Edition SP2	SQL Server 2008 Workgroup Edition SQL Server 2008 Standard Edition SQL Server 2008 Enterprise Edition SQL Server 2008 R2 Workgroup Edition SQL Server 2008 R2 Standard Edition SQL Server 2008 R2 Enterprise Edition
SQL Server 2005 Personal Edition SP2	Not supported
SQL Server 2005 Evaluation Edition	Not supported
SQL Server 2005 Express SP2	SQL Server 2008 Express SQL Server 2008 Express with Tools SQL Server 2008 Express with Advanced Services SQL Server 2008 Workgroup SQL Server 2008 Standard Edition SQL Server 2008 Enterprise Edition SQL Server 2008 R2 Express SQL Server 2008 R2 Express with Tools SQL Server 2008 R2 Express with Advanced Services SQL Server 2008 R2 Workgroup SQL Server 2008 R2 Standard Edition SQL Server 2008 R2 Enterprise Edition
SQL Server 2005 Express SP2 Advanced	SQL Server 2008 Express with Advanced Services SQL Server 2008 Workgroup SQL Server 2008 Standard Edition SQL Server 2008 Enterprise Edition SQL Server 2008 R2 Express with Advanced Services SQL Server 2008 R2 Workgroup SQL Server 2008 R2 Standard Edition SQL Server 2008 R2 Enterprise Edition
SQL Server 2008 Enterprise Edition	SQL Server 2008 R2 Enterprise Edition SQL Server 2008 R2 Datacenter Edition
SQL Server 2008 IA64 Enterprise Edition	SQL Server 2008 R2 IA64 Enterprise Edition SQL Server 2008 R2 IA64 Datacenter Edition
SQL Server 2008 X64 Enterprise Edition	SQL Server 2008 R2 X64 Enterprise Edition SQL Server 2008 R2 X64 Datacenter Edition

TABLE 9.1 Supported Upgrade Paths to SQL Server 2008 and 2008 R2

Previous SQL Server Edition	Supported Upgraded Edition
SQL Server 2008 Developer Edition	SQL Server 2008 R2 Developer Edition SQL Server 2008 R2 Datacenter Edition
SQL Server 2008 IA64 Developer Edition	SQL Server 2008 R2 IA64 Developer Edition SQL Server 2008 R2 IA64 Datacenter Edition
SQL Server 2008 X64 Developer Edition	SQL Server 2008 R2 X64 Developer Edition SQL Server 2008 R2 X64 Datacenter Edition
SQL Server 2008 Standard Edition	SQL Server 2008 R2 Standard Edition SQL Server 2008 R2 Enterprise Edition SQL Server 2008 R2 Datacenter Edition
SQL Server 2008 X64 Standard Edition	SQL Server 2008 R2 X64Standard Edition SQL Server 2008 R2 X64 Enterprise Edition SQL Server 2008 R2 X64 Datacenter Edition
SQL Server 2008 Workgroup Edition	SQL Server 2008 R2 Workgroup Edition SQL Server 2008 R2 Standard Edition SQL Server 2008 R2 Enterprise Edition SQL Server 2008 R2 Datacenter Edition
SQL Server 2008 X64 Workgroup Edition	SQL Server 2008 R2 X64 Workgroup Edition SQL Server 2008 R2 X64 Standard Edition SQL Server 2008 R2 X64 Enterprise Edition SQL Server 2008 R2 X64 Datacenter Edition
SQL Server 2008 Web Edition	SQL Server 2008 R2 Web Edition SQL Server 2008 R2 Standard Edition SQL Server 2008 R2 Enterprise Edition
SQL Server 2008 X64 Web Edition	SQL Server 2008 R2 X64 Web Edition SQL Server 2008 R2 X64 Standard Edition SQL Server 2008 R2 X64 Enterprise Edition
SQL Server 2008 Express	SQL Server 2008 R2 Express SQL Server 2008 R2 Express with Tools SQL Server 2008 R2 Express with Advanced Services SQL Server 2008 R2 Workgroup SQL Server 2008 R2 Standard Edition SQL Server 2008 R2 Enterprise Edition SQL Server 2008 R2 Datacenter Edition

TABLE 9.1 Supported Upgrade Paths to SQL Server 2008 and 2008 R2

Previous SQL Server Edition	Supported Upgraded Edition
SQL Server 2008 Express Advanced	SQL Server 2008 R2 Express with Advanced Services SQL Server 2008 R2 Workgroup SQL Server 2008 R2 Standard Edition SQL Server 2008 R2 Enterprise Edition SQL Server 2008 R2 Datacenter Edition
SQL Server 2008 Evaluation Edition	Not supported

NOTE

As you see in Table 9.1, direct upgrades from versions prior to SQL Server 2000 SP4 or SQL Server 2005 versions prior to SP2 are not supported. Options for migrating databases from these versions of SQL Server are presented later in this chapter.

Upgrading Using a Configuration File

If you need to upgrade multiple SQL Server 2008 instances, you'll likely want to do so without having to run the Installation Center utility each time and manually select the same options over and over. Fortunately, you can run an upgrade via the Installation Center using a configuration file. Using a configuration file, you have a couple options for how you run the upgrade: using the Upgrade Wizard with options prefilled by the configuration file or as a fully automated and unattended installation from the command line. If you run using the GUI with the options prefilled by the configuration file, you have the opportunity to review and change options along the way as necessary.

NOTE

If you've never run a SQL Server installation using the setup feature of SQL Server, you should refer to the "Installing SQL Server Using a Configuration File" section in Chapter 8 for a detailed description of the process and options available.

Following are a few of the parameters relevant to running an upgrade using a configuration file:

- **/ACTION=UPGRADE**—Specifies that you are running an upgrade.
- **/INSTANCENAME**—Specifies the SQL Server instance to be upgraded. For the default instance, you use the special value MSSQLSERVER.
- **/CONFIGURATIONFILE**—Specifies the configuration file to use for the upgrade.
- **/INSTANCEDIR**—Specifies a nondefault installation directory for shared components to be upgraded.
- **/UIMODE**—Specifies whether to present only the minimum number of dialog boxes during setup. Normal presents all setup dialogs; AutoAdvance skips nonessential dialog boxes.
- **/FTUPGRADEOPTION**—Specifies the full-text catalog upgrade option. Valid values are REBUILD, RESET, and IMPORT.

To create an upgrade configuration file, run the Upgrade Wizard as described previously and follow it all the way through to the Ready to Install page where the location of the generated Configuration.ini file is specified. At this point, you can click the Cancel button if you don't want to actually perform the upgrade. Then copy the Configuration.ini file to another location so you can make any necessary edits to it.

To run an upgrade using a configuration file, you need to run the setup.exe program, which can be found at the root level of the installation media. If you want to override any of the values in the configuration file or provide values not specified in the configuration file, you can provide additional command-line parameters. For example, to avoid having to enter the service account passwords during the installation, you can enter them on the command line using the password parameters to config.exe. Following is a sample execution to upgrade the default instance and specify the account and password for Reporting Services and the service account for Integration Services:

```
Setup.exe /q /ACTION=upgrade /INSTANCENAME=MSSQLSERVER
 /RSUPGRADEDATABASEACCOUNT="myRSaccount" /RSUPGRADEPASSWORD="myRSpassword"
 /ISSVCAccount="NT Authority\Network Service" /IACCEPTSQLSERVERLICENSETERMS
```

Note also that the preceding example specifies the /q parameter, which runs the upgrade in Full Quiet mode, which is intended for running unattended installations. With this switch provided, Setup runs without any user interface. Another option is to run with the /QS switch, which shows progress via the GUI but does not accept any input and displays no error messages if encountered.

Slipstreaming Upgrades

If you are upgrading to SQL Server 2008, you'll likely want to install Service Pack 1 as well and possibly the latest cumulative update. In the past, this meant running the upgrade and then running the Service Pack 1 (SP1) install and cumulative update separately. This process can be tedious and time consuming. Fortunately with the release of SP1, SQL Server 2008 supports Slipstream installations and upgrades. As mentioned previously, slip-streaming is a method of integrating a SQL Server 2008 update with the original installation media so that the original media and the update are installed at the same time.

Because slipstreaming was introduced with SQL Server 2008 SP1 and not with the initial release, a slipstream upgrade must be run from the `setup.exe` program provided with SQL Server 2008 SP1. If you run from the SP1 media folder, you need to specify the location of the SQL Server 2008 installation media using the `MEDIASOURCE` parameter, as shown in the following example:

```
setup.exe /PCUSource=C:\SQLServer2008SP1 /ACTION=UPGRADE  /MEDIASOURCE=D:\
 /INSTANCENAME=MSSQLSERVER
```

The `/PCUSource` parameter is used to specify the location of the SP1 package. You use the `/CUSource` parameter to specify the location of a Cumulative Update package you want to apply as well, if any.

NOTE

A slipstream install cannot be used to update a SQL Server 2008 instance to SQL Server 2008 R2.

For a full description and more detailed examples on how to set up and run a Slipstream installation, refer to Chapter 8.

Upgrading from SQL Server 7 or SQL Server 6.5

SQL Server supports upgrading from SQL Server 2000 SP4 and later and SQL Server 2005 SP2 and later. Unfortunately, upgrading directly from SQL Server 7.0 or earlier versions is not supported. The supported migration path is to first migrate your SQL Server 7.0 (or earlier) databases to SQL Server 2000 SP4 or 2005 SP2 (upgrades that are supported) and then upgrade from one of these versions to SQL Server 2008 or 2008 R2.

If you have a SQL Server 2000 SP2 or SQL Server 2005 SP4 instance available, the easiest way to upgrade your SQL Server 7.0 or earlier databases is to detach them from the source server and then attach the databases to an instance running either SQL Server 2000 SP2 or SQL Server 2005 SP4. When the database is attached, it is upgraded to that version, and then you can upgrade the database to SQL Server 2008 R2. Generally, this is the preferred method.

Another option is to use the SQL Server Import and Export Wizard to copy data from a 7.0 or earlier instance of SQL Server. The main disadvantage of this approach is that it brings over only tables and data. You have to manually script your stored procedures, functions, triggers, views, and other database objects and re-create them on the upgraded target database.

Upgrading Other SQL Server Components

Now that you've seen how to migrate databases, jobs, logins, custom error messages, and full-text catalogs, let's discuss how you can migrate the rest of your SQL Server objects. First, let's look at Analysis Services.

Upgrading Analysis Services

The following sections highlight some important considerations you should be aware of when upgrading Analysis Services.

Upgrading from SQL Server 2005 Analysis Services

You can upgrade an existing instance of SQL Server 2005 Analysis Services to SQL Server 2008 Analysis Services using the Upgrade Wizard. The wizard automatically migrates existing databases from the old instance to the new instance. The metadata and binary data is compatible between the SQL Server 2005 and SQL Server 2008, so the data is retained after you upgrade. You do not have to manually migrate the data. To upgrade an existing instance of SQL Server 2005 Analysis Services, run the Upgrade Wizard and specify the name of the existing AS instance as the name of the new AS instance. The AS databases are upgraded automatically.

NOTE

Users running in a 64-bit environment must upgrade Analysis Services *before* upgrading the SQL Server Database Engine. You can, of course, run setup more than once, so in this situation it is recommended that you upgrade Analysis Services first (separately) and then upgrade your other components on subsequent runs.

Upgrading from SQL Server 2000 Analysis Services

Because of changes to the underlying architecture of Analysis Services between SQL Server 2000 and SQL Server 2008, you cannot perform an in-place upgrade. You have to migrate your SQL Server 2000 AS databases to SQL Server 2008.

The first task is to install a new named instance of SQL Server 2008 Analysis Services (SSAS) by using the SQL Server 2008 Installation Center program. When this process is complete, you can use the Analysis Services Migration Wizard to import your SQL Server 2000 Analysis Services content into the SQL Server 2008 AS format. This wizard re-creates your existing OLAP structures on the new instance, without altering the original source material.

If you remove the prior instance of SQL Server 2000 Analysis Services after you have migrated its databases, you can use the Analysis Services Instance Rename tool to make the named instance of SQL Server 2008 Analysis Services the default instance on the server.

To launch the Analysis Services Migration Wizard, open the Object Browser and connect to Analysis Services. Then navigate to the top-level `Analysis Services` node to find the wizard. You can also simply select Start, Run and then enter the command `MigrationWizard.exe`. You need to make sure that `MSSQLServerOLAPService` is running before you begin; you can verify this by using the SQL Server Service Manager.

Click Next on the Welcome page, and the Specify Source and Destination screen appears (see Figure 9.15). You need to enter the name of your SQL Server 2000 Analysis Services server as the source. Then you have two options:

- **Server**—You can choose this radio button and enter the name of your new SSAS instance to immediately migrate your OLAP databases.
- **Script File**—If you select this radio button and enter a filename, the wizard can generate an XML for Analysis (XMLA) script, which you can later run to perform the same migration.

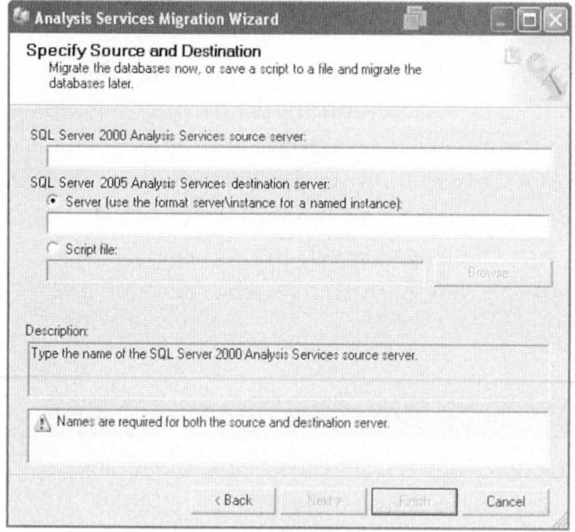

FIGURE 9.15 The Analysis Services Migration Wizard's Specify Source and Destination screen.

Click Next, and the Select Databases to Migrate screen appears; this screen is fairly self-explanatory. Make your selections and then click Next. The Validating Databases screen appears. At this point, the wizard performs the migration and reports on its progress, noting any issues along the way.

When the wizard is done, click Next, and the Completing the Wizard screen appears, showing a summary report.

NOTE

According to Microsoft, the Analysis Services Migration Wizard is unable to migrate three OLAP constructs: linked cubes, drill-through options, and remote partitions. You need to manually re-create these constructs.

When your migration is complete, you need to remember to reprocess your cubes; otherwise, you are unable to query the new database. In addition, the migrated database doesn't yet exploit the features of SSAS's Unified Dimensional Model (UDM) in your existing cubes. To fully explore that topic and learn more about other new features and functionality in Analysis Services, check out Chapter 51, "SQL Server 2008 Analysis Services."

Upgrading Reporting Services

SQL Server 2008 supports upgrading from the following earlier editions of Reporting Services:

- SQL Server 2000 Reporting Services with Service Pack 2 (SP2)
- SQL Server 2005 Reporting Services

You can choose to perform an in-place upgrade or migrate a Reporting Services Installation to SQL Server 2008. You can run the Upgrade Advisor tool on the Report Server computer to determine any issues that might prevent a successful upgrade. Known upgrade issues currently include the following:

- There is no upgrade support for a Report Server that uses a remote SQL Server 2000 Database Engine instance to host the Report Server database.
- There is no support for the SQL Server 2000 Report Server Web service in SQL Server 2008 because this endpoint is discontinued, and any custom features that point to the ReportServer2000 endpoint no longer run.
- There is no support for earlier versions of the Reporting Services WMI provider because the Reporting Services WMI provider is not backward compatible with previous versions. You cannot use the SQL Server 2008 Reporting Services WMI provider with earlier versions of Reporting Services.

Performing an In-Place Upgrade of Reporting Services

If you've run the Upgrade Advisor and it doesn't report any issues that would prevent a successful upgrade (or you've addressed any issues it raises), you can perform an in-place upgrade of any instance of SQL Server 2000 Reporting Services SP2 or SQL Server 2005 Reporting Services.

Before upgrading Reporting Services, you should first back up the following:

- The symmetric key (by using the `RSKEYMGMT` tool)
- Your Report Server databases
- Configuration files: `Rsreportserver.config`, `Rswebapplication.config`, `Rssvrpolicy.config`, `Rsmgrpolicy.config`, `Reportingservicesservice.exe.config`, `Web.config` (for both the Report Server and Report Manager ASP.NET applications), and `Machine.config` (for ASP.NET if you modified it for Report Server operations)
- Any customizations to existing Reporting Services virtual directories in IIS
- Your reports

Before running the upgrade, you first need to stop IIS and the Report Services Windows service on each machine on which you will be running the in-place upgrade. (For a Web farm [now known as a *scale-out* implementation] the upgrade must be run on every node.)

Then run the Installation Center and select your existing instance for upgrade at the appropriate screen. The Installation Center upgrades the instance in-place, including all its components and any published reports and snapshots.

Upgrading Reporting Services also requires updates to your Report Server databases. Because the Report Server database schema can change with each new release of Reporting Services, it is required that the database version match the version of the Report Server instance you are using. In most cases, a Report Server database can be upgraded automatically with no specific action on your part. The following list identifies all the conditions under which a Report Server database is upgraded:

- After a Reporting Services instance is upgraded, the database schema is automatically upgraded after service startup and the Report Server determines that the database schema version does not match the server version.
- At service startup, the Report Server checks the database schema version to verify that it matches the server version. If the database schema version is an older version, it is automatically upgraded to the schema version that is required by the Report Server. Automatic upgrade is especially useful if you restored or attached an older Report Server database. A message is entered in the Report Server trace log file indicating that the database schema version was upgraded.
- The Reporting Services Configuration tool upgrades a local or remote Report Server database when you select an older version to use with a newer Report Server instance. In this case, you must confirm the upgrade action before it happens.

NOTE

The Reporting Services Configuration tool no longer provides a separate Upgrade button or upgrade script. Those features are obsolete in SQL Server 2008 due to the automatic upgrade feature of the Report Server service.

After the database schema is updated, you cannot roll back the upgrade to an earlier version. Always back up the Report Server database in case you need to re-create a previous installation.

SQL Server 2008 introduces changes to the Report Definition Language (RDL), the report object model, and the rendering object model that affect reports created in earlier versions of the software. When you upgrade a Reporting Services installation from a prior version to a SQL Server 2008 Reporting Services installation, existing reports and snapshots that have been uploaded to a Report Server are automatically upgraded to the new schema the first time they are processed. If a report cannot be automatically upgraded, the report is processed using the backward-compatibility mode. Also, if you open an `.rdl` file in Report Designer that was created for the SQL Server 2000 or SQL Server 2005 namespace, Report Designer automatically upgrades the report to the current namespace. After you save the report, you cannot open it in earlier versions of Report Designer.

If you are unable to perform an in-place upgrade of your existing installation for any reason, your other option is to install a new instance of SQL Server 2008 Reporting Services and then migrate your Report Server database and configuration files to the new instance.

Migrating to Reporting Services 2008

The migration process for Reporting Services includes a combination of manual and automated steps. The following tasks are required to perform a Reporting Services migration:

- Back up your Report Server databases, applications, and configuration files.
- Back up the encryption key.
- If it is not installed already, install a new instance of SQL Server 2008 or 2008 R2.
- Move your Report Server database(s) from your SQL Server 2000 or 2005 installation to your new installation using the detach/attach or backup/restore method.
- Move any custom report items, assemblies, or extensions to the new installation.
- Configure the Report Server.
- Edit the `RSReportServer.config` file to include any custom settings from your previous installation.
- Optionally, configure custom Access Control Lists (ACLs) for the new Reporting Services Windows service group.
- Remove unused applications and tools after you have confirmed that the new instance is fully operational.

When you are backing up the Report Server configuration files, the files to back up include

- `Rsreportserver.config`
- `Rswebapplication.config`
- `Rssvrpolicy.config`
- `Rsmgrpolicy.config`
- `Reportingservicesservice.exe.config`
- `Web.config` for both the Report Server and Report Manager ASP.NET applications
- `Machine.config` for ASP.NET if you modified it for Report Server operations

During the install of your new instance of Reporting Services, when you reach the Reporting Services screen, you need to be sure to select the Install but Do Not Configure option. After moving your Report Server databases, launch the new Reporting Services Configuration tool and select the Report Server database that you've moved from the previous installation to automatically upgrade it. Then restore your backed-up encryption key.

Just as with an in-place upgrade, to upgrade the reports themselves, all you need to do is open them in the Report Designer, which automatically converts them to the new Report Definition Language format.

After you successfully migrate your Report Server to a SQL Server 2008 Reporting Services instance, you might want to perform the following steps to remove programs and files that are no longer necessary:

- Uninstall the previous version of Reporting Services if it's no longer needed.
- Remove IIS if you no longer need it on the computer (it's no longer needed by Reporting Services 2008).
- Delete `RSActivate.exe` (if you migrated from SQL Server 2000 installations only).

Upgrading SSIS Packages

When you upgrade an instance of SQL Server 2005 to SQL Server 2008, your existing SQL Server 2005 Integration Services packages are not automatically upgraded to the package format that SQL Server 2008 Integration Services uses. You have to manually upgrade your SQL Server 2005 packages.

There are multiple methods to upgrade SQL Server 2005 packages. Some of the methods are only temporary. For others, the upgrade is permanent. Table 9.2 lists each of the upgrade methods and whether the upgrade is temporary or permanent.

TABLE 9.2 SSIS Upgrade Methods

Upgrade Method	Type of Upgrade
Using the `dtexec` utility installed with SQL Server 2008	The package upgrade and script migration are temporary. The changes are not saved.
Adding a SQL Server 2005 package to an existing project or opening a SQL Server 2005 package in SQL Server 2008 Integration Services	The package upgrade is permanent if you save the package. The script migration is permanent if you add the package to an existing project or if you open the package and save the conversion changes.
Using the SSIS Package Upgrade Wizard	The package upgrade and script migration are permanent.
Using the Upgrade method to upgrade one or more Integration Services packages.	The package upgrade and script migration are permanent.

The SSIS Package Upgrade Wizard is the recommended approach for upgrading your SQL Server 2005 SSIS packages. Because you can configure the wizard to back up your original packages, you can continue to use the original packages if you experience upgrade difficulties. You can run the SSIS Package Upgrade Wizard from SQL Server Management Studio, from SQL Server Installation Center, or at the command prompt.

To run the wizard from SQL Server Management Studio, connect to Integration Services, expand the `Stored Packages` node, right-click the `File System` or `MSDB` node, and then click Upgrade Packages. To run the wizard from SQL Server Installation Center, click

Tools and then click Upgrade Integration Services packages. At the command prompt, run the `SSISUpgrade.exe` file from the `C:\Program Files\Microsoft SQL Server\100\DTS\Binn` folder.

Migrating DTS Packages

SSIS is a complete rewrite of the DTS runtime, and this is why your DTS packages are not automatically migrated to SQL Server 2008 when running an in-place upgrade. You essentially have two options for how to handle your existing DTS packages:

- Install runtime support for DTS packages so you can continue to run your existing DTS packages.
- Migrate your DTS packages to SSIS using the DTS Package Migration Wizard.

Full DTS support in SQL Server 2008 consists of multiple components. The first component is the Client Tools Backward Compatibility option. During an installation or upgrade, on the Feature Selection page, select Integration Services and choose to install the Client Tools Backward Compatibility option. This option installs the Execute DTS 2000 Package task for SSIS.

The next component you need to install is DTS runtime support. To install runtime support for Data Transformation Services packages, go to the Microsoft Download Center and locate the Microsoft SQL Server 2008 Feature Pack page. From there, download the Microsoft SQL Server 2005 Backward Compatibility Components (this component has not been updated for SQL Server 2008). If you also want to use the SQL Server 2008 tools to open and view DTS packages, you have to download and install the design-time support as well. This support can also be found in the Microsoft Download Center on the Feature Pack for Microsoft SQL Server 2005 page.

After you install the DTS runtime support, your DTS packages can run as before. You can run your DTS packages one of the following ways:

- From the command prompt using the `dtsrun.exe` utility
- Via SQL Server Agent Jobs by setting the job step to Operating system (`CmdExec`) and use the `dtsrun` utility (`dtsrun.exe`) to run the package
- Via Integration Services Packages using the Execute DTS 2000 Package task

9

If you also installed the design-time support, you are able to continue to edit and manage your DTS packages. You can manage your DTS packages from SQL Server Management Studio under the `Data Transformation Services` node, which is available in the `Management/Legacy` folder. Here, you can open existing DTS packages stored on the file system or in the `msdb` database, or add additional packages to the server by clicking the Import button. Although DTS packages can be modified and renamed, you cannot create new DTS packages within SSMS.

The DTS runtime support is intended to be used only on a temporary basis until you have the opportunity to migrate your DTS packages to SSIS. To migrate your DTS packages to SSIS, you can use the DTS Package Migration Wizard.

To run the DTS Package Migration Wizard, you first need to make sure that the SSIS service is in the running state. In SSMS, open the Object Explorer and navigate to the `Legacy` node, under `Management`. Then right-click the `Data Transformation Services` (DTS) node and select the Package Migration Wizard option to migrate one or more packages (those stored on a server or as files) to SSIS.

NOTE

The Package Migration Wizard is available only in the Developer, Standard, and Enterprise Editions of SQL Server 2008.

When you run the Package Migration Wizard, you first need to select the source and destination servers (the source must be a SQL Server 7 or 2000 instance, and the destination must be a 2008 instance with SSIS running) on the Choose Source Location and Choose Destination Location screens.

Then click Next to reach the List Packages screen (see Figure 9.16), where you check the check boxes for the packages you want to bring over. The name for each imported package is listed in the Destination Package column, and you can click there to edit it.

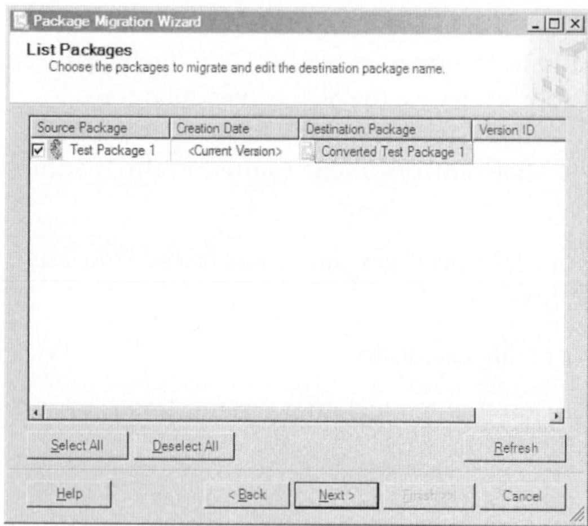

FIGURE 9.16 The Package Migration Wizard's List Packages screen.

At the next screen, you can specify a log file for the process. You click Next again and then click Finish to complete the migration.

As with all the other wizards provided with SQL Server 2008, the Package Migration Wizard reports progress and any issues on a per-package basis, offering an exportable report at the end.

After migration is complete, the original DTS package is still available on the SQL Server 7 or 2000 instance, in unmodified form. You can import packages into SQL Server in SSMS by connecting to SSIS in the Object Explorer and then navigating to the `Stored Packages` node and then the `MSDB` node. If you selected a file system folder as the destination, right-click the `File System` node and then select Import Package to display the migrated packages.

Summary

Now that you've taken in a great deal of information to help your organization transition to SQL Server 2008, it's time to put that knowledge to work by actively taking the plunge.

If you need even more documentation, you can look to the many other chapters in this book and even more resources on the Web that can assist you. Of course, there's an abundance of content on Microsoft's website (after all, it's in Microsoft's interests that customers upgrade to SQL Server 2008), including webcasts, TechNet, and online learning courses available to MSDN subscribers.

When your new environment is ready to go, you can move on to Chapter 10, "Client Installation and Configuration," to learn how to get your clients up and running with your new installation of SQL Server 2008.

CHAPTER 10

Client Installation and Configuration

IN THIS CHAPTER

- What's New in Client Installation and Configuration
- Client/Server Networking Considerations
- Client Installation
- Client Configuration
- Client Data Access Technologies

SQL Server 2008 offers a robust client/server architecture that provides speed and security, simple configuration and maintenance, and enhanced management capabilities.

This chapter contains the latest information on how to install, configure, and connect to SQL Server 2008 from the client side, and it offers key server-side insights that will help provide a complete understanding of what you need to do establish a database connection.

What's New in Client Installation and Configuration

Client installation and configuration in SQL Server 2008 is similar to SQL Server 2005 but does have its share of changes. First and foremost is the introduction of a new net-library named SQL Native Client 10.0 (SNAC10). SNAC10 gives applications access to the new features and data types available with SQL Server 2008. It builds on the data access component distribution strategy introduced in SQL Server 2005 that was simply called SQL Native Client (SNAC or SNAC9).

The good news is that your applications can continue to access SQL Server 2008 with the older SNAC components. Both SNAC9 and SNAC10 can be used on the same client system. SNAC9 is not able to reference new features in SQL Server 2008, however, so you have to upgrade to SNAC10 to gain access to them.

Another big change in SQL Server 2008 is the removal of the Surface Area Configuration (SAC) tool. The SAC tool was introduced in SQL Server 2005 and was a key part of client configuration. The functionality made available in this tool has now been replaced with Policy-Based Management features and changes in the SQL Server Configuration Manager (SSCM) tool. For example, the option to allow Remote Connections that was available in SAC is no longer there. You should look to the SSCM tool and enable or disable the protocols for which you want to allow connections. The details of this change are discussed later in this chapter, and a full discussion of Policy-Based Management is provided in Chapter 22, "Administering Policy Based Management."

One last change in SQL Server 2008 Client Installation and Configuration that may rear its head relates to the `BUILTIN\Administrator` windows group. By default, this group is no longer included in the SQL Server `sysadmin` fixed server role on new SQL Server 2008 installations. So, by default, network administrators and administrators of the machine where SQL Server is running are not able to log in to SQL Server and administer it. In past versions of SQL Server, the `BUILTIN\Administrator` windows group was added to the `sysadmin` role. To grant administrators permission to SQL Server, you can manually add the `BUILTIN\Administrator` group to the `sysadmin` SQL Server role, or you can add each individual network administrator that needs to access SQL Server to that role.

The change to the `BUILTIN\Administrator` windows group is in line with Microsoft's strategy to "secure by design, secure by default, and secure in deployment." This strategy relates to many aspects of SQL Server, including installation, security, and client installation and configuration. The strategy is a good one but can cause you, as the administrator, some extra grief if you are not aware of the impact that these changes can have on you and your users.

Client/Server Networking Considerations

Before we delve into the features on the client side in SQL Server, it's important to make note of a few server-side features. This information will help you gain an understanding of which networking features are initially configured on the server (after an installation or upgrade) as well as how incoming connections are dealt with. Such knowledge can be invaluable in diagnosing connectivity issues.

If you've been following along chapter by chapter, you've learned how to install or upgrade an instance of SQL Server 2008. To get your clients up and running fast, you must be sure the Database Engine is listening for them.

The following sections describe how to set up the server's basic network configuration, including configuring it to accept remote connections, learning which protocols it supports, and understanding how it listens for and responds to client requests.

Server Network Protocols

The first and most basic step after a SQL Server installation or upgrade is to make sure the appropriate network protocols are configured on the server.

NOTE

Note that the term *server* is used here to refer to an instance of the SQL Server 2008 Database Engine. The term *client* is used generally to mean any program that needs to communicate with a server. The server and client may reside on the same physical machine (especially when using SQL Server Mobile and Express Editions).

First, you should ensure that the protocols your clients once used to connect to SQL Server 7, 2000 or 2005 (or that your clients would like to use) are still supported by SQL Server 2008 and configured.

You might be surprised to learn that the following protocols that were supported in SQL Server 2000 are not supported by SQL Server 2005 or SQL Server 2008:

- AppleTalk
- Banyan VINES
- Multiprotocol
- NW Link IPX/SPX

If you were using these protocols and you've upgraded from SQL Server 2000, your clients are no longer able to connect. Following are the only protocols that SQL Server 2008 supports:

- Named pipes
- Shared memory
- TCP/IP
- Virtual Interface Adapter (VIA)

If you were using any of these protocols and you just upgraded, Setup copies your pre-upgrade settings over to SQL Server 2008, including the enabled state, IP addresses, TCP ports, pipe names, and so on. Clients can simply test their connections to be sure the upgrade was successful, and in most cases, no changes need to be made.

NOTE

The Shared memory protocol works only for connections both to and from the same machine hosting the Database Engine. Shared memory is used by client tools such as SQL Server Management Studio (SSMS) and SQLCMD, and it's also a good choice for use by locally running custom applications because it is secure by design. (It is the default protocol used by local applications that do not specify otherwise.)

All remote connections to SQL Server are thus disabled by default. Following is an extremely common client-side error message illustrating connection failure due to disabled remote connectivity:

```
A network-related or instance-specific error occurred while
establishing a connection to SQL Server. The server was not found
or was not accessible. Verify that the instance name is correct and
that SQL Server is configured to allow remote connections.
```

The exact wording of this message varies slightly, depending on the particular client or connection method used. The same error also occurs when the Database Engine service is stopped.

In SQL Server 2008, remote connections must be enabled for each network protocol on which you want the server to communicate. This is easily accomplished using the SQL Server Configuration Manager (SSCM). You launch SSCM from the SQL Server 2008 `Configuration Tools` menu group. In SSCM, you expand `SQL Server Network Configuration` and then select the `Protocols` entry for the SQL Server instance that you want to configure. In the Details pane, right-click on one of the available protocols (for example, Named Pipes) and select Enable to allow connections for this protocol (see Figure 10.1). SSCM serves many purposes and is discussed in detail later in this chapter.

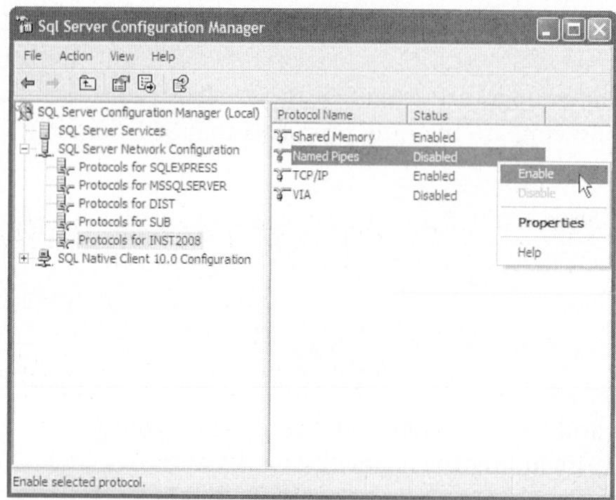

FIGURE 10.1 Enabling remote connections over named pipes using SSCM.

When the protocol is enabled, SQL Server is configured to listen for connections from clients using the same protocol. You must restart the SQL Server instance for the changes to take effect and for SQL Server to actually start listening for connections. You can verify that SQL Server is listening on the protocol that you have enabled by looking at the SQL Server error log. Each time the SQL Server instance is restarted, messages are written to the log indicating which protocols it is listening on. The following sample error log messages show what SQL Server is listening for:

```
Server is listening on [ 'any' <ipv4> 1719].
Server named pipe provider is ready to accept connection on
[ \\.\pipe\MSSQL$INST2008\sql\query ].
```

SQL Server listens on all configured protocols simultaneously, giving no preference or priority to any. This is in contrast to the explicitly prioritized manner in which clients attempt to connect via all configured protocols. The client configuration is discussed in detail later in this chapter.

NOTE

In SQL Server 2005, the Surface Area Configuration (SAC) tool also could be used to allow remote connections and to configure the protocols on which they communicate. The SAC tool has been removed in SQL Server 2008, so you need to look to the SSCM to configure your protocols.

The Server Endpoint Layer

A networking feature in SQL Server 2008 adds an additional layer to the client/server network structure: Tabular Data Stream (TDS) endpoints. When you install (or upgrade to) SQL Server 2008, a default system endpoint is created on the server for each available protocol on the server. These endpoints cannot be dropped, and they are created regardless of whether the protocol is disabled or otherwise unavailable.

NOTE

The term *endpoint* in this context refers to the combination of a protocol selection, one or more IP addresses (or pipe names), and any associated port numbers.

These are the default system endpoints:

- `TSQL Local Machine` (for shared memory)
- `TSQL Named Pipes`
- `TSQL Default TCP`
- `TSQL Default VIA`
- `Dedicated Admin Connection` (also known as the DAC)

You can view these endpoints and check their status by executing the following T-SQL statement:

```
Use Master
GO
SELECT * FROM sys.endpoints WHERE principal_id = 1
```

By default, all users are granted access to these endpoints (except the DAC, which is only for members of the `sysadmin` role). Administrators can create new endpoints on the server to increase connection security by stopping (or disabling) the default system endpoints and then creating new user-defined endpoints that only specific clients can access.

(Creating a new system endpoint automatically revokes permission on the default endpoint of the same protocol to the `public` group.)

NOTE

Only one named pipe and one shared memory endpoint can exist per instance, but multiple VIA or TCP endpoints (with different port and address settings) can coexist.

Each endpoint communicates with clients via TDS packets, which are formatted on the server side by SNAC and on the client side by SNAC or another of the net-libraries.

Administrators have the option of stopping and starting endpoints while sessions are still active, preventing new connections from being made while still supporting existing ones.

An administrator can grant or revoke endpoint access to specific users or groups (for example, preventing backdoor access through client tools). It is therefore important for clients to know that this structure exists and to learn how they receive permission to connect to endpoints through a server-side process known as *provisioning*.

Client Access Provisioning

There are three fairly straightforward rules of access provisioning. If any one of these rules is met by an incoming client, that client may access the endpoint. If none are met, the client is denied access. These are the rules:

- If the client specifies an IP address and a TCP port that match those of a specific endpoint, the client may connect to it, if the client has permission to do so.
- If only the TCP port specified by the client matches that of a specific endpoint, and the endpoint is configured to listen on all IP addresses, the client may connect to it, if the client has permission to do so.
- If neither the TCP port nor IP address is specified, but the default endpoint for the protocol is enabled, the client may attempt to connect to the endpoint.

NOTE

If the endpoint to which access is successfully provisioned is currently stopped, or if the user does not have permission to connect to it, no further endpoints are tried and the client cannot continue.

For example, let's say a server has three TCP/IP endpoints defined:

- The default (`TSQL Default TCP`), which listens on all IP addresses and Port 1433 (a default SQL Server 2008 instance)
- A user-created endpoint called `TCP_UserCreated 101_91`, configured to listen on IP address 192.168.1.101 and Port 91

- A second user-created endpoint, called `TCP_UserCreated Any_91`, which is configured to listen on all IP addresses and Port 91

A client attempts to connect specifically to 192.168.1.101:91. Because this is an exact address and port match, the client can try to connect to `TCP_UserCreated 101_91`. Having an exact address and port match meets the first provisioning rule.

A second client attempts to connect to any IP address on Port 91. Because there is no exact address match, the client cannot attempt to connect to `TCP_UserCreated 101_91`. However, the client can attempt to connect to `TCP_UserCreated Any_91` because it is configured to listen on all IP addresses. This meets the second provisioning rule.

A third client attempts to connect on any port and any address. If `TSQL Default TCP` is started, the client is granted permission to attempt to connect. This meets the third provisioning rule.

NOTE

Settings such as IP addresses and TCP ports are used to implicitly connect to specific endpoints. These values are specified by clients in connection strings, data source names (DSNs), and server aliases, all of which are discussed later in this chapter in the "Client Configuration" section.

TIP

If, at any time, you want to discover which protocol and endpoint a connected client is currently using, you can run the following T-SQL to list the current connections and related protocols. The `session_id` identifies the server process ID (SPID), and an additional `WHERE` clause can be added to the `SELECT` statement that selects only the SPID you are interested in:

```
SELECT name, net_transport, session_id, e.endpoint_id
FROM sys.dm_exec_connections d
JOIN sys.endpoints e
ON e.endpoint_id = d.endpoint_id
go
name                    net_transport     session_id    endpoint_id
TSQL Local Machine    Shared memory    53            2
```


Following is an example of the client-side error message that results if the `TSQL Default TCP` endpoint is stopped and you try to connect to it:

```
A connection was successfully established with the server, but then an error
occurred during the login process
```

Now that you know a bit about endpoints, let's go a bit deeper and explore how client connections are facilitated on the server.

The Role of SQL Browser

You might be surprised to learn that when clients try to connect to SQL Server 2008, their first network access is made over UDP Port 1434 to the SQL Browser service.

NOTE

Regardless of the encryption status of the connection itself, login credentials are always encrypted when passed to SQL Server 2008 (to foil any malicious packet sniffing). If a certificate signed by an external authority (such as VeriSign) is not installed on the server, SQL Server automatically generates a self-signed certificate for use in encrypting login credentials.

SQL Browser is the upgrade to the SQL Server Resolution Protocol (SSRP) and its job is to hand out instance names, version numbers, and connection information for each (nonhidden) instance of the Database Engine (and Analysis Services) residing on a server—not only for SQL Server 2008 instances, but for SQL Server 2000 and 2005 instances as well.

When clients connect by name, SQL Browser searches for that name in its list and then hands out the connection data for that instance. It can also provide a list of available servers and help make connections to the correct server instance or to make a connection on the dedicated administrator connection (DAC).

Ports, Pipes, and Instances

Default instances of SQL Server 2008 are automatically configured (just as in previous editions) to listen on all IP addresses and TCP Port 1433.

Named instances, on the other hand, are automatically configured to listen on all IP addresses, using dynamic TCP port numbers that change when the Database Engine is restarted. (Most often, these change only when the port number last used by the service is in use by a different application.)

If the SQL Browser service is not running, the client might need to provide additional connection information to be able to connect to SQL Server. The additional connection information includes the specific port or pipe that the SQL Server instance may be listening on. The only exception to this is if the server is listening on the default port of 1433. Otherwise, the client must specify the port when connecting with TCP/IP. When dynamic ports are used, the port number can change at any given time and cause your clients to have to change their port to match the new server port.

SQL Browser, therefore, is configured to autostart on servers that contain one or more named instances so that clients can connect by simply providing the server name. The complexity associated with providing additional port or pipe information is avoided when the SQL Browser service is running. SQL Browser is also required for enumerating the server lists used to connect with client tools such as SMSS.

NOTE

If named instances have fixed port numbers known to clients, or if a pipe name is well known, SQL Browser is not required to connect.

NOTE

For named pipes, the default instance's pipe name is `\sql\query`; for named instances, the pipe name is `MSSQL$instancename\sql\query`.

When a link is made, endpoint provisioning kicks in to finalize (or reject) the connection.

Client Installation

Now that you have acquired some knowledge about the most important server-side networking considerations, it's time to learn how to install and configure the client-side half of the equation.

Installation Requirements

All SQL Server 2008 installations (including client-tools-only or SNAC-only installations) require Windows Installer 4.5, which is freely downloadable from Microsoft. It can also be installed as part of the SQL Server Installation Wizard or manually installed from the SQL Server media. The location of the installer media varies depending on the media you are using but an example of the location is as follows:

```
D:\English\SQL2008\Enterprise\X86\redist\Windows Installer\x86
```

The same operating system requirements for server installations apply to client tools and SNAC installations, with one exception: When you install SNAC by itself on top of Windows XP, only SP1 is required, and when you install SNAC on top of Windows Server 2003, SP1 is not required. You can review the complete list of requirements in Chapter 8, "Installing SQL Server 2008," in the section "Installation Requirements."

Note that SNAC and the client tools both depend on the presence of the .NET Framework 3.5 SP1, and the client tools in turn depend on SNAC. Setup automatically installs both Framework 3.5 SP1 and SNAC, when required, on the target machine. If incompatible or beta versions exist that must be uninstalled first, Setup lets you know to use Installer 4.5.

Installing the Client Tools

To install the SQL Server 2008 client tools, you start Setup normally and follow the prompts as described in Chapter 8. When the Feature Selection screen appears, you check only the Client Tools Connectivity check box, as shown in Figure 10.2.

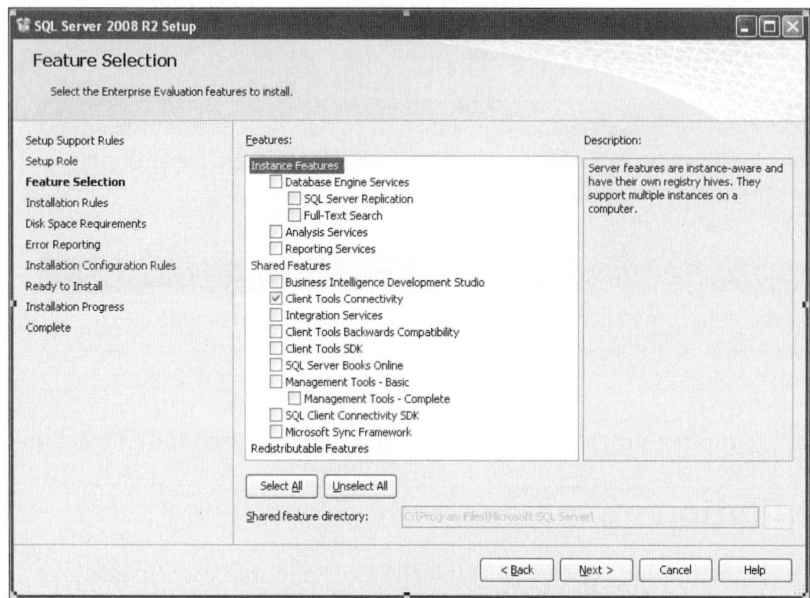

FIGURE 10.2 Performing a client-tools-only installation.

The same kind of install can be done quietly from the command line (Setup doubles as a command-line application), using the following:

```
driveletter:\Servers\Setup> Setup.exe /q /ACTION=Install /FEATURES=CONN
 /INSTANCENAME=INST2008
```

That's all there is to it!

You will be happy to learn that the SQL Server 2008 client tools can safely be installed side by side with your SQL Server 2000 or 2005 client tools. You can even access databases and other objects created in either edition (with a few notable exceptions, such as database diagrams) by using either toolset.

The sections that follow describe how to install and use a few of the client tools for client configuration and testing.

Installing SNAC

This section shows how easy it is to install SNAC, the key net-library for SQL Server 2008 and beyond.

As mentioned earlier, both the SQL Server 2008 Database Engine and the client tools depend on SNAC. SNAC is installed when you install the SQL Server connectivity tools, or you can simply launch it on its own from the SQL Server installation medium by running `driveletter:\Servers\Setup\sqlncli.msi`.

Table 10.1 describes the files that the Microsoft Installer (MSI) package installs.

TABLE 10.1 Files Installed by the SNAC MSI Package

Filename	Purpose	Installed To
Sqlncli.h	C++ header file (replaces sqloledb.h)	*Program Files*\Microsoft SQL Server\100\SDK
sqlncli10.lib	C++ library file for calling BCP functions (replaces odbcbcp.lib)	*Program Files*\Microsoft SQL Server\100\SDK
sqlncli10.dll	Main library, containing both the ODBC driver and OLE DB provider (houses all functionality)	*WINDIR*\system32
sqlnclir10.rll	Resource file	*WINDIR*\system32
s10ch_sqlncli.chm	Compiled help file for creating data sources using SNAC	*WINDIR*\system32

TIP

For detailed information on how to write C++ code by using the header and library files included in the SNAC software development kit (SDK), see the Books Online topic "Using the SQL Native Client Header and Library Files."

The SNAC installer has two primary options (shown in Figure 10.3):

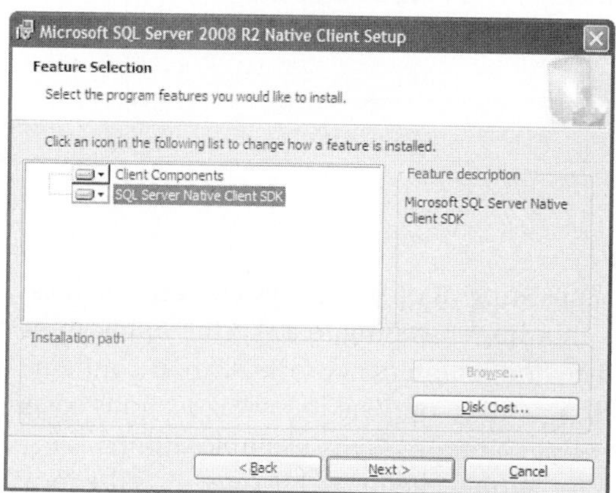

FIGURE 10.3 SNAC's installation options.

- Install SNAC by itself
- Install the SNAC SDK files along with it

NOTE

By default, all network protocols except for VIA are enabled on the client during installation.

That's all there is to installing SNAC!

Redistributing SNAC with Custom Client Applications

If you build an application that relies on SNAC, you need to be aware that it can be redistributed in two ways:

- As part of any SQL Server 2008 installation or upgrade
- As a custom application installation dependency

When you are building MSI files for an application, it is important that you register `sqlncli.msi` as a package dependency (and, of course, to install it as well, if it is not present on the destination machine). This helps ensure that SNAC will not be accidentally uninstalled from the destination machine without first flashing a warning to users, indicating that any application that relies on it will break. To do this, you execute the following command early in your application's installation process:

```
msiexec /i sqlncli.msi APPGUID={unique identifier for your product}
```

NOTE

The program name for SNAC found in the Add or Remove Programs Control Panel applet is Microsoft SQL Server 2008 Native Client, not SQL Native Client, as it is commonly known.

Client Configuration

Client configuration is a many-leveled beast, consisting of operating system tasks such as installing protocols, application tasks such as choosing or coding to a specific Application Programming Interface (API), provider, or driver, and maintenance tasks such as configuring network settings, building connection strings, and so on. The following sections cover a broad range of these tasks, focusing on the most common. Many examples utilize TCP/IP both because it is the default protocol for remote clients and because it is the most widely used.

No chapter can cover all the possible ways of connecting, but this one is designed to give you the tools you need to get set up right from the start and to navigate your way in case specific issues arise.

The first client configuration tool we look at is SSCM.

Client Configuration Using SSCM

The Client Network Utility available prior to SQL Server 2005 has been decommissioned, and all its functionality is now built into SSCM. This includes the capability to create server aliases, to enable and prioritize network protocols, to control the various SQL Server services, and more.

NOTE

One thing Microsoft is keen on including in Books Online is that neither Setup nor `sqlncli.msi` installs the actual network protocols themselves, nor do they enable them at the operating system level. This means that if you do not have TCP/IP installed and you need to start using it, you have to first set it up by using the Network Connections Control Panel applet (if you're using Windows, that is).

You can launch SSCM directly from its Start menu icon, or you can access it in the `Services and Applications` node of the Computer Management console. When you have SSCM up and running, to access its client-side functionality, you expand its top-level node (`SQL Server Configuration Manager` *`(servername)`*`)` and then you click the `SQL Native Client 10.0 Configuration` node. Below it, you click the `Client Protocols` node to reveal the enabled state and priority order of each protocol, in grid format, in the right pane (see Figure 10.4).

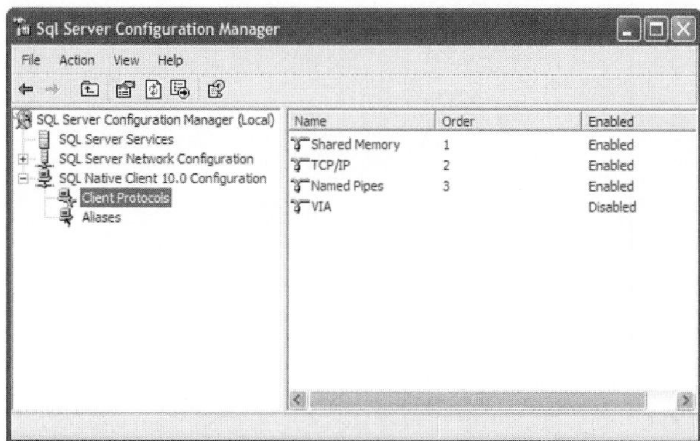

FIGURE 10.4 SSCM's Client Protocols screen.

From this screen, you can right-click any of the protocols to change their enabled state, view Properties pages, or change the default connection order (except that of shared memory, which is always tried first and whose order cannot be changed). The following is the default connection order for clients connecting without the benefit of a server alias, connection string, or other means:

- Shared memory
- TCP/IP
- Named pipes

(As the grid shows, VIA is disabled by default.) When you are connecting remotely, TCP/IP is the first protocol attempted because shared memory is local only.

NOTE

When a client does not specify a connection protocol, SNAC automatically tries each protocol in the list in sequence, according to the Order column. The first protocol to connect successfully wins.

If the winning connection is subsequently rejected by the server for any reason, no other protocols are tried.

Note also that local clients using MDAC 2.8 or lower cannot connect using shared memory, and they are automatically switched to named pipes if they attempt to do so.

Let's examine one of the protocols. To start, you need to double-click TCP/IP under the Name column to open the TCP/IP Properties screen (see Figure 10.5).

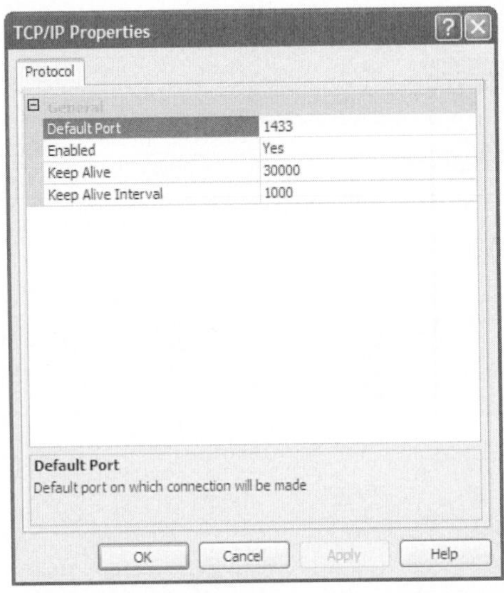

FIGURE 10.5 The TCP/IP Properties screen.

The values stored here are used by TCP/IP clients as default connection values, and they are applied only when a specific server alias or other configuration mechanism is not in use. They are also used by the SQL Server 2008 client tools when shared memory is not available.

As you can see, the default port, 1433, is set up to connect to the more commonly configured default instances of SQL Server. By editing the values on this page, you can change the default port number, enabled state, keep-alive values, and other settings (when editing other protocols). You should edit and enable the protocols according to your specific needs.

Server Aliases

A *server alias* is a name that is used like a server name that represents a group of server settings for use by connecting clients. Server aliases are very handy because of the way they simplify connection parameters: clients need only specify the alias name, and SNAC pulls the rest of the information (such as the IP address, TCP port number, and pipe name) from SSCM at connection time.

To create a server alias, you right-click the `Aliases` node under `SQL Native Client Configuration` and choose New Alias. On the Alias - New screen that appears (see Figure 10.6), you specify the alias name, protocol (except shared memory, for which you cannot create an alias), and server name. (*`local`*, ., and *`localhost`* also work for local connections over TCP/IP or named pipes.)

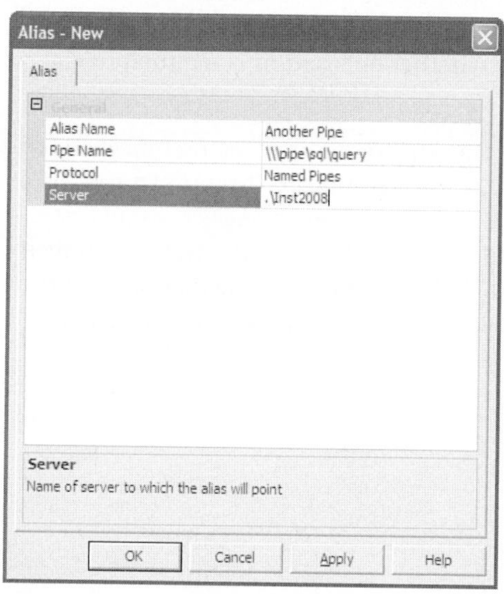

FIGURE 10.6 Alias properties for a new named pipe server alias.

When you make your protocol selection, the grid rows change to dynamically reveal the settings particular to that protocol. When you are finished, you click OK, and your alias is ready for use.

Connection Encryption

With SQL Server 2008, it is easy to set up Secure Sockets Layer (SSL) encrypted client/server communication over all protocols. The SNAC net-library handles the tasks of encryption and decryption on both the server and client ends. (Note that this process does cause a slight decrease in performance.) Setting it up requires both server-side and client-side configuration changes; this section covers only the client-side changes in detail.

SQL Server 2008 enables encryption using two types of certificates:

- Certificates generated by and obtained from an external certification authority such as VeriSign
- Certificates generated by SQL Server 2008 (known as *self-signed certificates*)

The bit strength of the encryption (40-bit or 128-bit) depends on the bit strength of the operating systems of the computers involved in the connection.

To set up the server for encryption, your administrator registers a certificate on the server operating system (using the Certificates Management console) and then installs it in the Database Engine.

If an externally signed certificate is not installed on the server, SQL Server uses its built-in self-signed certificate. (A server administrator may also create and save a self-signed certificate by using SQL Server 2008 via the new `CREATE CERTIFICATE` and `BACKUP CERTIFICATE` T-SQL syntax.) It is also up to the server to decide whether encryption is required or optional for connecting clients.

The client's half of the job is to have installed what is known as a *root-level certificate* that is issued by the same certification authority as the server's certificate. To install a root-level certificate, you right-click the certificate itself (a `.cer` or `.crt` file) and select Install Certificate to launch the Certificate Import Wizard. You click Next on the welcome screen to reach the Certificate Store screen (see Figure 10.7). Then you select the first radio button (Automatically Select the Certificate Store) and then click Next. Finally, you click Finish.

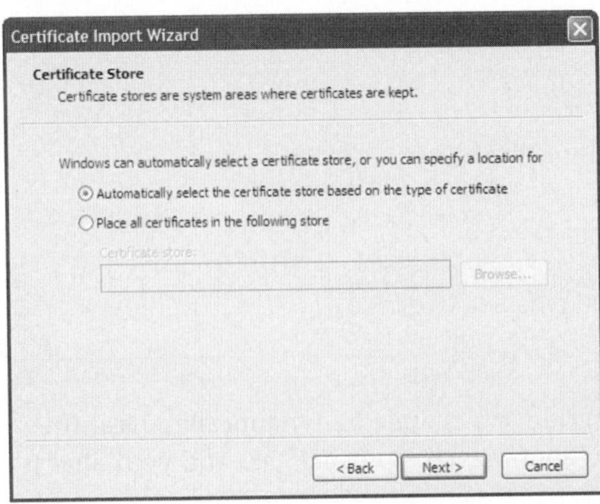

FIGURE 10.7 Importing a certificate on the client computer using the Certificate Import Wizard.

Next, you launch SSCM, right-click the `SQL Native Client 10.0 Configuration` node, and then select Properties. The Flags tab appears (see Figure 10.8) in the Properties window.

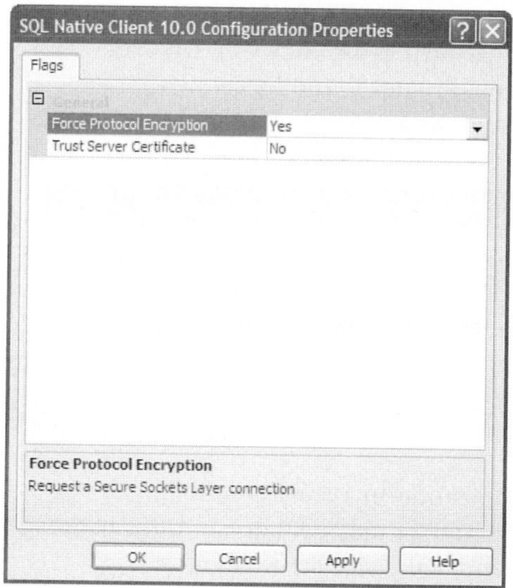

FIGURE 10.8 Forcing clients to request an encrypted connection using SSCM.

You set the `Force Protocol Encryption` property value to `Yes`. This causes clients to request an SSL-encrypted connection when communicating with the Database Engine. If the server does not respond in kind, the connection is killed.

The `Trust Server Certificate` property gives clients a choice in how they deal with server certificates:

- To use a self-signed certificate, you set the property value to `Yes`. This option prevents SNAC from validating the server's certificate.
- To use an externally signed certificate, you set the property value to `No`, which causes SNAC to validate the server's certificate.

SSMS can also connect over an encrypted connection. When connecting using the Connect to Server dialog, you click the Options button and then click the Connection Properties tab. Then you choose your database and protocol and, at the bottom left, check the Encrypt Connection check box.

Client Data Access Technologies

The question of which data access technology to use with SQL Server 2008 is a common one, with a seemingly easy answer: you use SNAC because it has all the latest and greatest functionality, all rolled into one. (You learn how to use SNAC in the sections that follow.)

A more correct answer is that your choice depends on which software technologies your clients currently use and what their specific needs are.

Your data access options consist of providers and drivers, whose functionality is often encapsulated inside code libraries known as *net-libraries* (such as SNAC's `sqlncli10.dll`). In addition to these net-libraries, supporting services such as MDAC's OLE DB Core Services are also available, providing useful functionality not found in the net-libraries, such as connection pooling. (ADO.NET also functions as a service, to a certain degree.)

NOTE

The Microsoft Data Access Components (MDAC) has a new name that started with the Vista operating system. The data access components are now called Windows Data Access Components or Windows DAC or WDAC. References to MDAC in this chapter also apply to the Windows DAC.

Provider Choices

A *provider* is software used for accessing various data stores in a consistent manner conforming to a specification, such as OLE DB. A provider may contain an API. Clients that use providers are known as *consumers*. SMSS and SQLCMD, for example, are consumers of the SNAC OLE DB provider.

You can choose from the following providers:

- **SQL Native Client OLE DB provider**—This is the latest OLE DB provider, and it is built into SNAC; it is also known as SQLNCLI. COM applications might want to switch to this provider to access the latest functionality; doing so also provides access to SQL Server 7 and 2000 databases.
- **.NET Framework data provider for SQL Server**—This data provider is built in to the `System.Data.SqlClient` namespace in the .NET Framework. Managed code applications should use it to access the latest SQL Server 2008 functionality from .NET 3.5 applications. .NET 1.0, 1.1, and 2.0 applications do not have access to all the latest SQL Server 2008 functionality through this provider.
- **Microsoft OLE DB provider for SQL Server**—This OLE DB provider, known as `SQLOLEDB`, is specialized for accessing SQL Server data and is distributed with MDAC. COM applications may continue to use it to access SQL Server 2008, or they can switch to SQLNCLI for the latest functionality.
- **Microsoft OLE DB provider for ODBC**—This deprecated OLE DB provider, known as `MSDASQL`, is distributed with MDAC. ADO applications can continue to use it to access SQL Server 2008, but SQL Server does not support the latest SNAC-specific OLE DB functionality.

Microsoft has also made available a few implementation-specific OLE DB providers, such as the OLE DB provider for DB2, a COM component for integrating IBM DB2 and SQL Server 2008 data.

Driver Choices

A *driver* in this context can be defined as software that conforms to a standard such as Open Database Connectivity (ODBC) and provides an API for accessing a specific type of data store. `osql.exe` is a good example of an application that uses an ODBC driver (the SNAC driver).

These are the available drivers:

- **SQL Native Client ODBC driver**—This is the latest ODBC driver, and it is built into SNAC. COM applications might want to switch to this driver to access the latest functionality.
- **Microsoft ODBC driver for SQL Server**—This is the ODBC driver distributed with MDAC for accessing SQL Server databases. COM applications can continue to use it to access SQL Server 2008, or they can switch to the SNAC ODBC driver for the latest functionality. This driver also provides access to SQL Server 7, 2000, and 2005 databases.
- **Java Database Connectivity (JDBC) driver**—The JDBC driver was built specifically for accessing SQL Server data from Java code.

CAUTION

Although it is still possible to connect to SQL Server 2008 by using DB-library and Embedded SQL, Microsoft has deprecated them both, and they will not be supported in future editions.

Connecting Using the Various Providers and Drivers

Now that you know what your options are in terms of providers and drivers, the following sections detail them one by one, with a special focus on putting the features in SQL Server 2008 to work.

Using SNAC

SNAC is a net-library that contains both the latest OLE DB provider and ODBC driver for using the rich features in SQL Server 2008 databases. It is compatible for accessing SQL Server 7, 2000, and 2005 databases as well.

The code for SNAC is contained in the single dynamic link library `sqlncli10.dll`, and it serves as provider, driver, and API for applications that call its underlying COM functions from unmanaged code (that is, from C or C++).

The bottom line with SNAC is that if you're building applications that need to exploit the latest features of SQL Server 2008, you need to use its APIs. If you don't, your application will continue to work without SNAC, but those new features will not be available.

NOTE

A large number of connection keywords are available for use with SNAC connections. A few of them are illustrated in the examples that follow, but for a complete reference, see the Books Online topic "Using Connection String Keywords with SQL Native Client."

Using OLE DB with SNAC Applications that call the COM APIs for OLE DB need to have the connection provider value changed from `SQLOLEDB` to `SQLNCLI10`. You also need to use the SNAC header file, as in the following example:

```
include "sqlncli.h";
```

`sqlncli.h` contains the latest function prototypes and other definitions for use with SNAC. This file is named the same as it was in SQL Server 2005, but it is installed in a different location.

NOTE

The SNAC OLE DB provider is OLE DB version 2.0 compliant.

Using ODBC with SNAC To connect to SQL Server 2008 using ODBC, you use a connection string or a DSN that is accessible to the client application at runtime. The ODBC driver used with SQL Server 2000 (simply called SQL Server) can still be used but is not the best option for SQL Server 2005 or 2008. To get the latest SNAC functionality, you must use the driver called SQL Native Client 10.0 (for example, `DRIVER={SQL Native Client 10.0}`).

To create a SNAC ODBC DSN, you run the Data Sources (ODBC) applet found in your operating system's administrative tools. You create a system, file, or user DSN, and you need to be sure to select the SQL Server Native Client 10.0 driver on the Create New Data Source screen that appears. On this screen, you click the Advanced button to enter any SNAC-specific connection string keyword-value pairs, as shown in Figure 10.9.

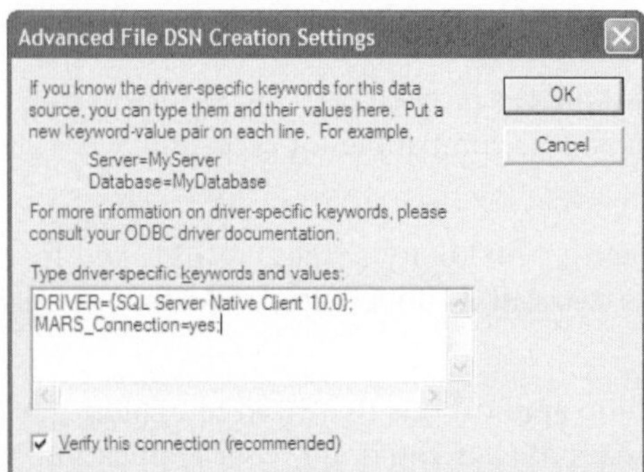

FIGURE 10.9 Using the Data Sources (ODBC) tool to configure MARS with a SNAC ODBC DSN.

You finish the wizard by entering the configuration data as you normally would, and you can use you new DSN just as you would any other. For more information on building COM applications that utilize SNAC, see the Books Online topic "Creating a SQL Native Client ODBC Driver Application."

Using ADO with SNAC Of course, the first recommendation is that if you're still using ADO, you should switch to ADO.NET if you can. If that isn't feasible, you can still access SQL Server 2008 from your ADO applications. But you should do so only if you need the new features; in this case, you need to start using the SNAC OLE DB provider in your code. To do so, you first install SNAC, and then you update your connection strings (or DSNs) to use the new `SQLNCLI` value for the `Provider` connection string keyword. Then you set the `DataTypeCompatibility` keyword to `80`. Here's an example (in Visual Basic 6 code):

```
Dim MyConnection As New ADODB.Connection
Dim MyFirstOpenRecordset As New ADODB.Recordset
Dim MySecondOpenRecordset As New ADODB.Recordset
Dim ConnString As String
Dim SelectResultsCount As Integer

Connstring =
    "Provider=SQLNCLI; DataTypeCompatibility=80; Database=MyAppsDB;" & _
    "Server=.\SQLEXPRESS; AttachDBFileName=c:\MyDBs\MyAppsDB.mdf;" & _
    "MARS Connection=true; Integrated Security=SSPI;"
MyConnection.ConnectionString = ConnString
MyConnection.Open
' Using 2 open recordsets on one connection puts MARS to work:
Set MyFirstOpenRecordset =
    MyConnection.Execute(
        "SELECT TOP 10 * FROM MyTable",
        SelectResultsCount,
        adCmdText
    )
Set MySecondOpenRecordset =
    MyConnection.Execute("SELECT TOP 10 * FROM MySecondTable", _
        SelectResultsCount, adCmdText)

' and so on...
```

Note the use of the `AttachDBFileName` connection string keyword, which instructs SQL Server 2008 to attach the specified Microsoft data file (`MyAppsDB.mdf`).

10

Using the .NET Framework Data Provider for SQL Server

.NET applications that use the `System.Data.SqlClient` namespace rely on the .NET Framework data provider and ADO.NET. To use this provider, you simply add the following statement to your C# code file:

```
using System.Data.SqlClient;
```

For VB .NET, you use this:

```
Imports System.Data.SqlClient
```

And for JScript .NET, you use this:

```
import System.Data.SqlClient;
```

Note that the .NET provider supports a variety of connection string styles, including ODBC, OLE DB, and OLE DB/SNAC, and you can mix and match some of their respective connection string keywords. For example, `Database` and `Initial Catalog` mean the same thing to ADO.NET, and so do `Server` and `Data Source`. But don't let this fool you: Under the covers, only the .NET provider is always in use. (This is probably why changing the value passed to the `Provider` keyword seems to have no noticeable effect.)

Applications built on .NET Framework 1.0 and 1.1 can access SQL Server 2008 databases without issue. The only caveat is that those earlier versions of ADO.NET can't make use of certain SQL Server 2008 features, such as asynchronous command execution, cache synchronization, bulk copy, and the new data types. (However, implicit conversions such as from `varchar` to `xml` and from UDTs to `varbinary` allow their use as T-SQL input from .NET Framework 1.1 applications.) ADO.NET 2.0 applications, however, have access to the full gamut of new functionality in SQL Server 2008.

The following is an example of two connection strings (in different styles) that both turn on the MARS feature for ADO.NET 2.0 applications:

The following is in ODBC style:

```
Driver={SQL Native Client 10.0}; Database=AdventureWorks2008;
Server=MyServer/SQL08;
Encrypt=yes; Trusted_Connection=yes; MARS_Connection=yes
```

The following is in OLE DB style:

```
Provider=SQLNCLI10; Database=AdventureWorks2008; Server=MyServer/SQL08;
Encrypt=yes; Trusted_Connection=yes; MultipleActiveResultSets=true
```

Notice the use of the keywords `MARS_Connection` (`MultipleActiveResultSets` also works) and `Encrypt` (which requests connection encryption from the server).

The SQLCLR Context Connection When you need to connect to SQL Server 2008 from within a managed stored procedure, function, or trigger (known as *SQLCLR code*), which is possible only with .NET 2.0 or greater, you use a special type of connection, known as a *context connection*. This feature prevents you from having to open a new connection because the code itself is already running within the context of an open connection.

The connection string for context connections is extremely easy to use (`"context connection=true"`), as the C# example in Listing 10.1 illustrates.

LISTING 10.1 Using the Context Connection from a Managed Stored Procedure

```
using System;
using System.Data;
using System.Data.SqlClient;
using System.Data.SqlTypes;
using Microsoft.SqlServer.Server;

public partial class StoredProcedures
{
    [Microsoft.SqlServer.Server.SqlProcedure]
    public static void ContextConnectionTest()
    {
        using (SqlConnection Context =
            new SqlConnection("context connection=true"))
        {
            using (SqlCommand TestCommand =
                new SqlCommand("SELECT TOP 10 * FROM Person.Person", Context))
            {
                using (SqlDataAdapter Adapter =
                    new SqlDataAdapter(TestCommand))
                {
                    using (DataSet MyData = new DataSet())
                    {
                        Adapter.Fill(MyData);
                    }
                }
            }
        }
    }
}
```

For more information on building SQLCLR client libraries, see Chapter 43, "SQLCLR: Developing SQL Server Objects in .NET"

Using MDAC

MDAC contains the OLE DB provider for SQL Server (`SQLOLEDB`) and the ODBC driver for SQL Server. MDAC is officially part of the operating system, and, as mentioned earlier, MDAC and SNAC are distributed and developed on separate tracks: MDAC with the operating system and SNAC with SQL Server. They do interrelate, however, in that applications that use SNAC can make use of the core services provided by MDAC, including support for connection pooling, client-side cursors, ADO support, and memory management. As mentioned earlier, to make use of the latest SQL Server 2008 functionality, you need to use SNAC.

TIP

If, at any time, you want to discover which version of MDAC is installed on a machine, you can simply check the value of the following Registry key (using `regedit.exe` or from code):

```
HKEY_LOCAL_MACHINE\SOFTWARE\Microsoft\DataAccess\Version
```

Note also that the planned MDAC version 10.0 release has been killed and superseded by SNAC.

If you choose to upgrade from MDAC to SNAC, it's important to note some key differences between the two that could affect your applications:

- Return values from SQL Server 2008 to MDAC applications are implicitly type converted, as shown in Table 10.2.

TABLE 10.2 Implicit Type Conversions for SQL Server 2008 Data Types

SQL Server 2008 Data Type	Converted to Data Type
`varbinary(MAX)`	`Image`
`xml`	`ntext`
`nvarchar(MAX)`	`ntext`
`varchar(MAX)`	`text`
UDTs	`varbinary`

- Warning and error messages and message handling differ between MDAC and SNAC.
- SNAC requires that T-SQL parameters begin with the `@` character; MDAC does not.
- SNAC, unlike MDAC, is not compatible with Visual Studio Analyzer or PerfMon.

For further details, see the Books Online topic "Updating an Application to SQL Native Client from MDAC."

Using ODBC with MDAC You can configure an ODBC connection by using a connection string or DSN that specifies the Microsoft ODBC driver for SQL Server.

For connection strings, you use the keyword-value pair `Provider={SQL Server}`.

To use a DSN, you run the Data Sources (ODBC) applet, as mentioned earlier. When choosing a driver, you select the one simply named SQL Server.

Using OLE DB with MDAC You can access SQL Server 2008 databases by using the Microsoft OLE DB provider for SQL Server (`SQLOLEDB`). In connection strings or property values, you use the `Provider` keyword and the value `SQLOLEDB`.

NOTE

Unlike with SNAC's OLE DB provider, with SQLOLEDB you can access both SQL Server data and data from non–SQL Server data sources. Also, SNAC is not dependent on any particular version of MDAC because it expects that a compatible MDAC version will be present on the operating system, as enforced by its own installation requirements.

Using JDBC

Microsoft released a freely downloadable, JDBC 4.0-compliant, Type 4 driver for use with SQL Server 2008. It can be used from all types of Java programs and servers via the J2EE connection API.

The following is the basic syntax for a JDBC connection string:

```
jdbc:sqlserver://ServerName\InstanceName:port;property=value[;property=value]
```

For complete details on using JDBC, check out Microsoft's JDBC product documentation at http://msdn.microsoft.com/en-us/library/ee229547(v=SQL.10).aspx. You might also find the newsgroup microsoft.public.sqlserver.jdbcdriver helpful.

General Networking Considerations and Troubleshooting

This section provides guidelines for solving some common connectivity issues. You can perform the following steps as a first line of defense when your connections fail:

1. Check whether the server is configured (via SSCM, as detailed earlier in this chapter, in the section "Server Network Protocols") to accept remote connections.
2. Ensure that the SQL Browser service is started.
3. Determine whether clients are specifying the correct port (for using fixed ports with named instances) in the server alias or connection string.
4. Check whether the client's network protocols are enabled and configured to correctly handshake with those of the server. They should use SSCM on both sides, as explained earlier in this chapter, in the section "Client Configuration Using SSCM."
5. Be sure you have permission to connect on the server's endpoints.
6. When using encryption, be sure the server and client certificates match (that is, check their *Common Name* (CN) and any other relevant attributes) and are installed and configured correctly on both sides. (See the section "Connection Encryption," earlier in this chapter.)
7. Make certain that your firewalls are configured to permit the required network traffic. (See the following section, "Firewall Considerations.")
8. Check to see whether your users have permission to log in to the server and access the specified database.
9. Make sure that your clients' choices of providers support the SQL Server 2008 features they are trying to use.
10. Make sure the provider, driver, DSN, server alias, or other connection mechanism is still valid and hasn't been altered or removed from the system.

11. Network administrators are no longer added to the SQL Server `sysadmin` role by default. If the user trying to connect is a network administrator, he or she must be granted explicit permission with SQL Server 2008. See the topic named "Database Engine Configuration - Account Provisioning" in Books Online for more information.

Firewall Considerations

For clients to successfully connect through a firewall, it must be configured to allow the following:

- **Bidirectional traffic on UDP Port 1434**—This is required only for communications to and from the SQL Browser service; when SQL Browser is not in use, you can close this port.
- **Bidirectional traffic on any TCP port used by SQL Server**—Be sure to open port 1433 for default instances and also open any fixed ports assigned to your named or default instances. (TCP high port numbers must be opened only when dynamic ports are used by named instances. Using dynamic port numbers for named instances is not recommended.) You can determine the ports currently in use via SSCM.

When using Windows Firewall, you can easily open these ports. To do this, you run Windows Firewall from the Control Panel, and on the main screen that appears, you click the Exceptions tab. Then you click the Add Port button and enter the required names (either `SQL Server` or `SQL Browser`, for example) and port numbers, one at a time, on the Add a Port screen that appears (see Figure 10.10).

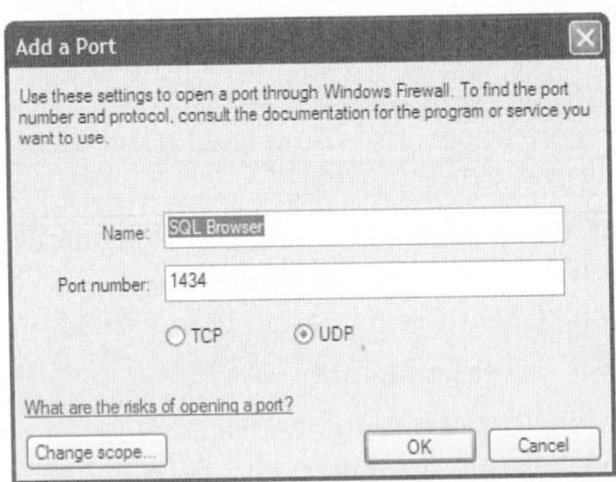

FIGURE 10.10 Creating port exceptions for SQL Server 2008, using Windows Firewall.

Tools for Testing Connections

It's always helpful to have a few tools on your belt for testing client connectivity.

SSCM is a tool that is usually easily accessible, and you can use its Connect to Server dialog to select a protocol to test (as described earlier in this chapter, in the section "Client Data Access Technologies"). You can also use `SQLCMD` with the `-S` parameter to connect to a particular server. This is the syntax:

```
SQLCMD -Sprotocol_prefix:ServerName,PortNumber -E
```

In this syntax, *protocol_prefix* takes one of the following values:

- np (for named pipes)
- tcp (for TCP/IP)
- lpc (for shared memory)
- via (for VIA)

In the following example, -E indicates the use of a trusted connection:

```
SQLCMD -Stcp:.\SQL08,1435 -E
```

When all else fails, you can use telnet to test the openness of a port on the firewall. Here's an example:

```
telnet IP_Address Port_Number
```

Summary

This chapter covers a lot of ground regarding client-side (and even a bit of server-side) communication with SQL Server 2008. Some of the sections are admittedly dense enough to bear rereading, and you probably have questions about your specific setup. You can always refer to the sections presented in this chapter to pick up tips on how to best configure and troubleshoot the varying environments you may encounter. And you can (and should) use the extremely helpful Usenet groups that are devoted to the subject (for example, microsoft.public.sqlserver.clients or microsoft.public.sqlserver.programming).

Now that your client configuration is complete, you can move on to Chapter 11, "Security and User Administration," to learn how to securely administer the Database Engine.

CHAPTER 11

Security and User Administration

IN THIS CHAPTER

- What's New in Security and User Administration
- An Overview of SQL Server Security
- Authentication Methods
- Managing Principals
- Managing Securables
- Managing Permissions
- Managing SQL Server Logins
- Managing SQL Server Users
- Managing Database Roles
- Managing SQL Server Permissions
- The Execution Context

Securing your database environment and providing the right type of access to your users are critical administrative tasks. This chapter examines the security features in SQL Server 2008 that relate to user administration and the objects that users can access.

What's New in Security and User Administration

Several new security enhancements have been added to SQL Server 2008 to help make it more secure than any prior version. These enhancements build upon the myriad of security-related changes made in SQL Server 2005 and follow the policy of "least privileges" that Microsoft has been pushing. Several of these new changes follow:

- **`BUILTIN\Administrators`**—This local Windows group is no longer included in the SQL Server `sysadmin` fixed server role. In prior versions, the BUILTIN\Administrators account was part of this role, which meant that network administrators could access the SQL Server instance even though they were not given explicit permission. You still have the option of manually adding this group to the `sysadmin` role, but it is not installed this way by default.
- **Surface Area Configuration** (SAC)—This GUI tool, which was introduced in SQL Server 2005, has been removed in SQL Server 2008. It was used to enable or disable SQL Server features and options, but it has been replaced in part by the new Policy-Based

Management feature and in part by an enhanced SQL Server Configuration Manager. Right-click on the server instance in Object Explorer and choose Facets. You get a quick look at the number of settings available via facets that are part of Policy-Based Management. If you select Server Configuration from the drop-down, you see features such as CLR Integration (that is, `CLRIntegrationEnabled`) that you could have set in the past with the Surface Area Configuration tool.

- **Local Groups Removed from `sysadmin`**—Several local network groups that were added to the `sysadmin` server role in past versions are no longer added to this role. These accounts include `SQLServerMSSQLUser$ COMPUTERNAME $ INSTANCENAME` and `SQLServerSQLAgentUser$ COMPUTERNAME $ INSTANCENAME`. Only the SQL Server Service and SQL Server Agent Service accounts are added to the `sysadmin` role.

An Overview of SQL Server Security

The SQL Server 2008 security model is the best place to start to understand SQL Server security. The model is based on three categories that separate the basic elements of security:

- **Principals**—Principals are the entities that request security to SQL Server resources. They include Windows users, SQL Server users, and database users.
- **Securables**—Securables are the SQL Server resources to which permissions can be granted.
- **Permissions**—Permissions link principals with securables.

Table 11.1 shows the security components contained in each tier of the SQL Server 2008 security model. The columns are ordered from left to right, based on the way security is established.

TABLE 11.1 SQL Server 2008 Security Components

Principals	Permissions	Securables
Windows:	GRANT/REVOKE/DENY	Server Scope
Groups	CREATE	Login
Domain Login	ALTER	Endpoint
Local Login	DROP	Database
SQL Server:	CONTROL	Database Scope
SQL Login	CONNECT	User
Server Role	SELECT	Role

TABLE 11.1 SQL Server 2008 Security Components

Principals	Permissions	Securables
Database:	EXECUTE	Application role
User	UPDATE	Assembly
Database Role	DELETE	Message Type
Application Role	INSERT	Route
	REFERENCES	Service
	RECEIVE	Remote Service
		Binding
	VIEW DEFINITION	Fulltext Catalog
	TAKE OWNERSHIP	Certificate
	CONTROL	Asymmetric Key
	VIEW CHANGE TRACKING	Symmetric Key
		Contract
		Schema
		Schema Scope
		Table
		View
		Function
		Procedure
		Queue
		Type
		Synonym
		Aggregate
		XML Schema
		Collection

The implementation of the security model is relatively straightforward: you choose the principal from Column 1, the desired permission from Column 2, and the securable to assign the permission from Column 3. For example, a `SQL LOGIN` (the principal) needs to `CREATE` (the permission) databases (the securable). Together, these three elements represent a complete security assignment.

Some complexity has been introduced, based on the hierarchical nature of some of the security components. Security can be established on these hierarchical components, which in turn cascades the security to the underlying components. In addition, not all the permission components apply to every securable. Many of the securables have a select number of permissions that apply to them; conversely, many permissions apply only to a select number of securables. For example, `SELECT` permission is applicable to securables such as tables and views but would not be appropriate for stored procedures.

The following sections discuss the tiers of the security model and their underlying components.

Authentication Methods

The first level of security encountered when accessing SQL Server is known as *authentication*. The authentication process performs the validation needed to allow a user or client machine to connect to SQL Server. This connection can be granted via a Windows login or SQL Server login.

Windows Authentication Mode

Windows Authentication mode validates the account name and password, using information stored in the Windows operating system. A Windows account or group must be established first, and then security can be established for that account in SQL Server. This mode has the advantage of providing a single login account and the capability to leverage domain security features, such as password length and expiration, account locking, encryption, and auditing. Microsoft recommends this approach.

Mixed Authentication Mode

Mixed authentication allows for both Windows authentication and SQL Server authentication. SQL Server authentication is based on a login that is created in SQL Server and lives in SQL Server only. No Windows account is involved with SQL Server authentication. The account and password are established and maintained in SQL Server. SQL Server logins can be created with stronger password enforcement that help better protect the login. This topic is discussed in more detail in the section "Managing SQL Server Logins," later in this chapter.

SQL Server authentication is useful in environments in which a Windows domain controller does not control network access. It can also be useful for Web applications or legacy applications, where it may be cumbersome to establish a Windows user account for every connection to the database server.

Setting the Authentication Mode

You can select the authentication mode when you install SQL Server, and you can change it after the installation. To change the authentication mode after installation, you right-click the server node in the Object Explorer and choose the Properties option. When the Server Properties dialog appears, you select the Security page (see Figure 11.1). The Security page allows you to specify Windows Authentication mode or SQL Server and Windows Authentication mode (that is, mixed authentication). Any changes to the authentication mode require a restart of SQL Server to make the change effective.

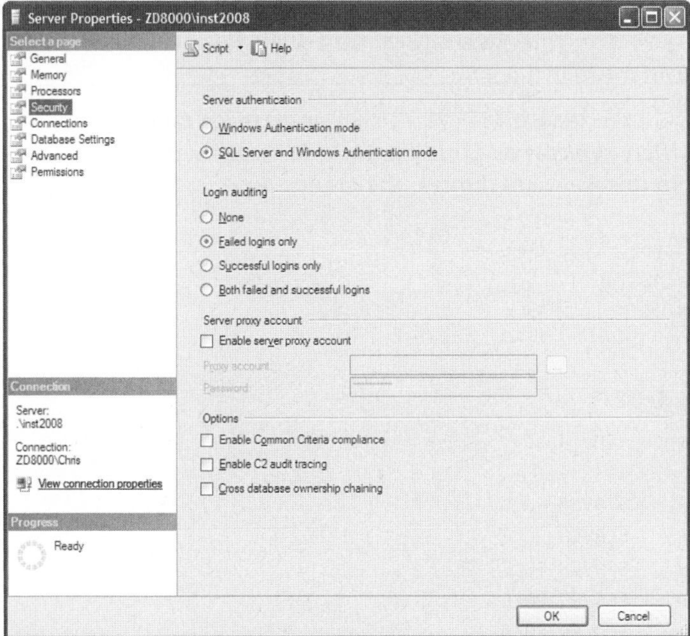

FIGURE 11.1 Changing the authentication mode.

Managing Principals

Principals are the entities that can request permission to SQL Server resources. They are made up of groups, individuals, or processes. Each principal has its own unique identifier on the server and is scoped at the Windows, server, or database level. The principals at the Windows level are Windows users or groups. The principals at the SQL Server level include SQL Server logins and server roles. The principals scoped at the database level include database users, data roles, and application roles.

Logins

Every principal granted security to SQL Server must have an associated login. The login provides access to SQL Server and can be associated with principals scoped at the Windows and server levels. These logins can be associated with Windows accounts, Windows groups, or SQL Server logins.

Logins are stored in the master database and can be granted permission to resources scoped at the server level. Logins provide the initial permission needed to access a SQL Server instance and allow you to grant access to the related databases. Permissions to specific database resources must be granted via a database user. The important point to remember is that logins and users are directly related to each other but are different entities. It is possible to create a new login without creating an associated database user, but a new database user must have an associated login.

To better understand logins, you can look at the `sys.server_principals` catalog view. This view contains a row for every server-level principal, including each server login. The following example selects from this view and displays the results:

```
select left(name,25) name, type, type_desc
 from sys.server_principals AS log
WHERE (log.type in ('U', 'G', 'S', 'R'))
 order by 3,1

/*Results from previous query
name                      type type_desc
------------------------- ---- ------------
bulkadmin                 R    SERVER_ROLE
dbcreator                 R    SERVER_ROLE
diskadmin                 R    SERVER_ROLE
processadmin              R    SERVER_ROLE
public                    R    SERVER_ROLE
securityadmin             R    SERVER_ROLE
serveradmin               R    SERVER_ROLE
setupadmin                R    SERVER_ROLE
sysadmin                  R    SERVER_ROLE
sa                        S    SQL_LOGIN
DBSVRXP\LocalUser1        U    WINDOWS_LOGIN
HOME\Administrator        U    WINDOWS_LOGIN
NT AUTHORITY\SYSTEM       U    WINDOWS_LOGIN
*/
```

The results from the `sys.server_principals` selection include the name of the server principal as well as the type of principal. The rows that have a `type_desc` value of `SQL_LOGIN`, `WINDOWS_GROUP`, or `WINDOWS_LOGIN` are all logins established on the SQL Server instance. A login with a `type_desc` of `SQL_LOGIN` represents a login created with SQL Server authentication. Logins with a `type_desc` of `WINDOWS_GROUP` or `WINDOWS_LOGIN` are

Windows groups or individual Windows users granted logins to SQL Server. The other entries with type_desc of SERVER_ROLE are fixed server roles discussed later in this chapter.

The logins established for Windows logins or groups can be part of the local domain of the SQL Server machine, or they can be part of another domain. In the previous example, DBSVRXP\LocalUser1 is a login established for a local user on a database server named DBSVRXP. The HOME\Administrator login is also a Windows login, but it is part of a network domain named HOME. Both logins are preceded by the domain that they are part of and are displayed this way in SQL Server.

NOTE

In SQL Server 2000, logins were stored in the syslogins system table in the master database. The syslogins table is still available for selection as a view, but it is available only for backward compatibility. The catalog views (including sys.server_principals) are recommended for use instead.

You might have noticed in the earlier sys.server_principals output that two other logins are listed that we have not discussed yet. These logins (SA and NT AUTHORITY\SYSTEM) are system accounts installed by default at installation time. Each of these accounts serves a special purpose in SQL Server.

The SA account is a SQL_LOGIN assigned to the sysadmin fixed server role. The SA account and members of the sysadmin fixed server role have permission to perform any activity within SQL Server. The SA account cannot be removed, and it can always be used to gain access to SQL Server. The SA account should always have a strong password to prevent malicious attacks, and it should be used only by database administrators. Users or logins requiring full administrative privileges can be assigned a separate SQL Server login that is assigned to the sysadmin fixed server role. This improves the audit trail and limits the amount of use on the SA account.

The NT AUTHORITY\SYSTEM login is an account related to the local system account under which SQL Server services can run. It is also added as a member of the sysadmin fixed server role and has full administrative privileges in SQL Server. This account can also be removed if the SQL Server services are not running with the local system account. This should be done with caution, however, because it can affect applications such as Reporting Services.

One other special account was not listed, but it would have been in SQL Server 2005. The BUILTIN\Administrators login is a Windows group that corresponds to the local administrators group for the machine that SQL Server is running on. The BUILTIN\Administrators group is no longer added by default as a SQL Server login during installation. In SQL Server 2005, it was also added as a member of the sysadmin fixed server role, but this is no longer the case. This change improves the security of SQL Server out of the box by limiting the number of people that have access (by default) to the SQL Server instance.

NOTE

The BUILTIN\Administrators group can be manually added in SQL Server 2008 if desired. This allows domain administrators and anyone else who has been added to the local administrators group to have sysadmin privileges. Adding this group is not recommended but can be done if you want to set network privileges that are similar to past versions of SQL Server.

SQL Server Security: Users

Database users are principals scoped at the database level. Database users establish a link between logins (which are stored at the server level) and users (which are stored at the database level). Database users are required to use the database and are also required to access any object stored in the database.

Generally, the login name and database username are the same, but this is not a requirement. If desired, you could add a login named Chris and assign it to a user named Kayla. This type of naming convention would obviously cause some confusion and is not recommended, but SQL Server has the flexibility to allow you to do it. In addition, a user can be associated with a single person or a group of people. This capability is tied to the fact that a login can be related to a single account or group. For example, a login named training could be created and tied to a Windows group (that is, *domain\training*) that contains all the training personnel. This login could then be tied to a single database user. That single database user would control database access for all the users in the Windows group.

TIP

The relationship between logins and users can be broken when databases are moved or copied between servers. The reason is that a database user contains a reference to the associated login. Logins are referenced based on a unique identifier called a security identifier (SID). When a database is copied from one server to another, the users in that database contain references to logins that may not exist on the destination server or that may have different SIDs.

You can use the sp_change_users_login system stored procedure to identify and fix these situations. You can run the following command against a newly restored or attached database to check for orphaned users:

```
EXEC sp_change_users_login 'Report'
```

If orphaned users are shown in the results, you can rerun the procedure and fix the problems. For example, if the results indicate that a user named Chris is orphaned, you can run the following command to add a new login named Chris and tie the orphaned database user to this newly created login:

```
EXEC sp_change_users_login 'Auto_Fix', 'Chris', NULL, 'pw'
```

Refer to SQL Server Books Online for full documentation on the sp_change_users_login system stored procedure.

You can use the sys.database_principals catalog view to list all the users in a given database. The following example shows a SELECT statement using this view and the results from the SELECT:

```
SELECT
left(u.name,25) AS [Name],
type,
left(type_desc,15) as type_desc
FROM
sys.database_principals AS u
WHERE
(u.type in ('U', 'S', 'G'))
ORDER BY 1

/*Results from previous query
Name                      type type_desc
------------------------- ---- ---------------
dbo                       S    SQL_USER
DBSVRXP\LocalUser1        U    WINDOWS_USER
guest                     S    SQL_USER
INFORMATION_SCHEMA        S    SQL_USER
sys                       S    SQL_USER
*/
```

The SELECT statement in this example returns five rows (that is, five users). This SELECT was run against the AdventureWorks2008 database, and the only user explicitly added to the database was the Windows user DBSVRXP\LocalUser1. The other users are special users who are added by default to each database. These users do not have corresponding server logins named the same. These users are discussed in the following sections.

The dbo User

The dbo user is the database owner and cannot be deleted from the database. Members of the sysadmin server role are mapped to the dbo user in each database, which allows them to administer all databases. Objects owned by dbo that are part of the dbo schema can be referenced by the object name alone. When an object is referenced without a schema name, SQL Server first looks for the object in the default schema for the user that is connected. If the object is not in the user's default schema, the object is retrieved from the dbo schema. Users can have a default schema that is set to dbo.

Schemas and their relationship to users are discussed in more detail in the section "User/Schema Separation," later in this chapter.

The guest User

The guest user is created by default in each database when the database is created. This account allows users that do not have a user account in the database to access the database. By default, the guest user does not have permission to connect to the database. To allow logins without a specific user account to connect to the database, you need to grant

CONNECT permission to the guest account. You can run the following command in the target database to grant the CONNECT permission:

```
GRANT CONNECT TO GUEST
```

When the guest account is granted CONNECT permission, any login can use the database. This opens a possible security hole. The default permissions for the guest account are limited by design. You can change the permissions for the guest account, and all logins that use it will be granted those permissions. Generally, you should create new database users and grant permissions to these users instead of using the guest account.

If you want to lock down the guest account, you can. You cannot drop the guest user, but you can disable it by revoking its CONNECT permission. The following example demonstrates how to revoke the CONNECT permission for the guest user:

```
REVOKE CONNECT FROM guest
```

If you decide to grant additional access to the guest account, you should do so with caution. The guest account can be used as a means for attacking your database.

The INFORMATION_SCHEMA User

The INFORMATION_SCHEMA user owns all the information schema views installed in each database. These views provide an internal view of the SQL Server metadata that is independent of the underlying system tables. Some examples of these views include INFORMATION_SCHEMA.COLUMNS and INFORMATION_SCHEMA.CHECK_CONSTRAINTS. The INFORMATION_SCHEMA user cannot be dropped from the database.

The sys User

The sys account gives users access to system objects such as system tables, system views, extended stored procedures, and other objects that are part of the system catalog. The sys user owns these objects. Like the INFORMATION_SCHEMA user, it cannot be dropped from the database.

TIP

If you are interested in viewing the specific objects owned by any of the special users discussed in these sections, you can use a SELECT statement like the following:

```
--Find all objects owned by a given user
SELECT name, object_id, schema_id, type_desc
FROM sys.all_objects
WHERE OBJECTPROPERTYEX(object_id, N'OwnerId') = USER_ID(N'sys')
ORDER BY 1
```

The SELECT in this example shows all the objects owned by the sys user. To change the user, you simply change the parameter of the USER_ID function in the SELECT statement from 'sys' to whatever user you want.

User/Schema Separation

The changes to schema security introduced in SQL Server 2005 have been carried forward to SQL Server 2008. Versions of SQL Server before SQL Server 2005 had schemas, but they did not conform to the American National Standards Institute (ANSI) definition of schemas. ANSI defines a schema as a collection of database objects that one user owns and that forms a single namespace. A single namespace is one in which each object name is unique and there are no duplicates. So, for example, if you have two tables named `customer`, they cannot exist in the same namespace.

To fully understand the user/schema changes in SQL Server 2008, you need to understand how schemas were used in prior versions of SQL Server. In SQL Server 7.0 and 2000, a default schema was created for each user, and it had the same name as the user. For example, if you created a new user named `Rachael`, a corresponding schema named `Rachael` would be created as well. There was no option in those releases to change the default schema for a user, and each user was forever bound to a schema with the same name. When the user created new objects, the objects were created by default in that user's schema, which is always the name of the user. So, if `Rachael` created an object named `customer`, it was placed in the `Rachael` schema, and the object was owned by `Rachael`. When `Rachael` wanted to reference the object, she could use a three-part name with the format *`database.owner.object`*. If a linked server was used, according to the SQL Server 2000 documentation, the object in the linked server could be referenced with the four-part name `linked_server.catalog.schema.object`. (for example `myserver.AdventureWorks2008.Rachael.Customer)`. You can see that the schema name is used prior to the object name when the object is outside the local server. The bottom line is that the schema and owner were basically the same thing in SQL Server 7.0 and 2000.

With SQL Server 2005 and SQL Server 2008, the owner and schema have been separated. This is made possible in part by allowing a database user to have a default schema different from the name of the user. For example, our sample user `Rachael` could be assigned the default schema `Sales`. When `Rachael` creates objects in the database, her objects are created, by default, in the `Sales` schema. If `Rachael` wants to reference an object that she created, she can reference the table in a number of different ways. She can use the full four-part name (*`server.database.schema.object`*) *that includes the* `Sales` schema name to reference the object via a linked server. She can simply refer to the object with the object name alone, and the `Sales` schema will be searched first for the object. She can also use a three-part name or a two part name. If the object name is not found in the `Sales` schema, the dbo schema will be searched. This concept is illustrated in the following sample SELECT statements that all retrieve the same rows from the Region table that was created by Rachael in the Adventureworks2008 database.

```
select * from region
select * from sales.region
select * from AdventureWorks2008.Sales.Region
```

The important point to remember is that owners and schemas are different from one another in SQL Server 2008. For example, you can have a customer table created in the Sales schema, and that table can be owned by a user named Chris. The object should be referenced with the schema name qualifier, such as Sales.Customer, not Chris.Customer. This has the distinct advantage of allowing object ownership to change without affecting the code that references the object. The reason is that database code that references an object uses the schema name instead of the object owner.

The schema enhancements in SQL Server 2008 go well beyond the user/schema separation. Schemas are an integral part of all the database objects that exist in SQL Server. As we delve into more details about SQL Server security and the assignment of permissions, you will see that schemas play a very important part.

Roles

Roles provide a consistent yet flexible model for security administration. Roles are similar to the groups used in administering networks. Permissions are applied to a role, and then members are added to the role. Any member of the role has all the permissions that the role has.

The use of roles simplifies the administrative work related to security. Roles can be created based on job function, application, or any other logical group of users. With roles, you do not have to apply security to each individual user. Any required changes to permissions for the role can be made to the role security, and the members of the role receive those changes.

SQL Server has the following three types of roles:

- **Fixed server and fixed database roles**—These roles are installed by default and have a predefined set of permissions.
- **User-defined roles**—These roles are created in each database, with a custom set of permissions for each set of users assigned to it.
- **Application roles**—These special roles can be used to manage database access for an application.

These roles are discussed in the following sections.

Fixed Server Roles

Fixed server roles are scoped at the server level, which means that the permissions for these roles are oriented toward server-level securables. These roles contain a variety of fixed permissions geared toward common administrative tasks. Logins (not users) are assigned to these roles.

The same fixed server roles available in SQL Server 2000 and SQL Server 2005 are also available in SQL Server 2008. There is, however, one new role named `public` that has been added. Server principals, by default, are granted the permissions that have been granted to the `public` role. There are a limited number of permissions that are initially granted to the `public` role, but you can change the permissions if you like. A complete list of all the fixed server roles and their related permissions is shown in Table 11.2.

TABLE 11.2 Fixed Server Roles

Role	Permission
`bulkadmin`	Allowed to run the `BULK INSERT` statement.
`dbcreator`	Allowed to use `CREATE`, `ALTER`, `DROP`, and `RESTORE` on any database.
`diskadmin`	Allowed to manage disk files that are used by SQL Server.
`processadmin`	Allowed to terminate SQL Server processes.
`public`	Assigned to all logins. Permissions granted to this role are assigned to every login by default.
`securityadmin`	Allowed to use `GRANT`, `DENY`, and `REVOKE` permissions for logins at the server and database levels. Members of this role can reset passwords for SQL Server logins.
`serveradmin`	Allowed to change server-wide configuration properties and shut down the server, if needed.
`setupadmin`	Allowed to add and remove linked servers and execute some system stored procedures.
`sysadmin`	Allowed to perform any activity in the server.

A single login can be assigned to one or more of these fixed server roles. When multiple roles are assigned, the combination of all the permissions is allocated to the login.

NOTE

Keep in mind that when a login is assigned to certain fixed server roles, they have implied permissions that cascade to the database level. For example, if a login is assigned to the `sysadmin` role, that login can perform any activity on the server, and it can also perform any action on any database on that server. Similarly, if a login is added to the `securityadmin` role, the login can change permissions at the database level as well as the server level.

All the fixed server roles are listed in the SQL Server Management Studio (SSMS) Object Explorer. Figure 11.2 shows the Object Explorer with the `Server Roles` node expanded. You can right-click any of the roles and select Properties to display the logins that are currently members of the role.

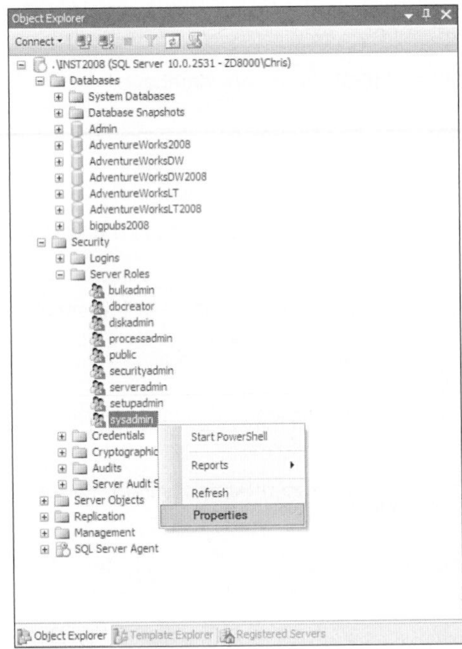

FIGURE 11.2 Fixed server roles in Object Explorer.

Fixed Database Roles

SQL Server provides fixed roles that define a common set of permissions at the database level. These fixed database roles are assigned to database users. The permissions defined for the fixed database roles cannot be changed. Table 11.3 shows the fixed database roles and their permissions.

TABLE 11.3 Fixed Database Roles

Role	Permission
db_accessadmin	Allowed to add or remove database access for logins.
db_backupoperator	Allowed to back up the database.
db_datareader	Allowed to read all user table data.
db_datawriter	Allowed to change the data in all user tables.
db_ddladmin	Allowed to run any Data Definition Language (DDL) command against the database. This includes commands to create, alter, and drop database objects.
db_denydatareader	Denied the right to read all user table data.
db_denydatawriter	Denied the right to change the data in any of the user tables.
db_owner	Allowed to perform any action on the database. Members of the sysadmin fixed server role are mapped to this database role.
db_securityadmin	Allowed to manage permissions for database users, including membership in roles.
dbm_monitor	Allowed to view the most recent status in the Database Mirroring Monitor.

NOTE

You can find a more granular breakdown of permissions associated with fixed database roles in the SQL Server Books Online documentation. Look for the subject "Permissions of Fixed Database Roles." The extensive table in this documentation defines the specific permissions for each role. For example, the table shows that the db_backupoperator role is granted the BACKUP DATABASE, BACKUP LOG, and CHECKPOINT permissions. This gives you more insight into what the members of this role can do. Some fixed database roles have a large number of permission defined for them, such as db_ddladmin, which has more than 30 individual permissions. The types of permissions and improved granularity available with SQL Server 2008 are discussed in the "Managing Permissions" section, later in this chapter.

You can also find a list of fixed database roles in the Object Explorer. Figure 11.3 shows the fixed database roles for the AdventureWorks2008 database. The roles are found under the Security node within each database. You can right-click a fixed database role and select Properties to view the member users.

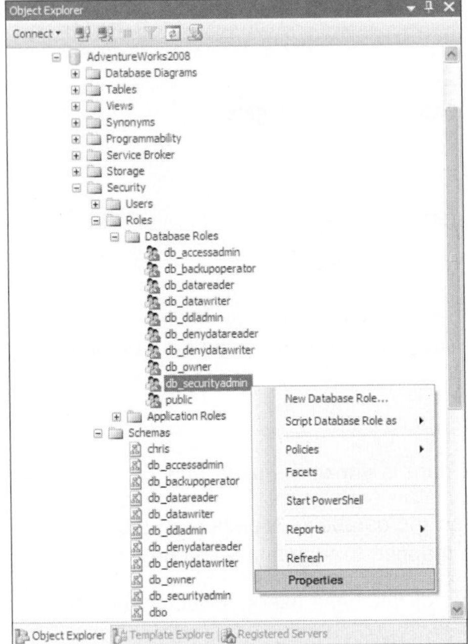

FIGURE 11.3 The fixed database roles in Object Explorer.

Fixed database roles and schemas are related. Figure 11.3 shows the expanded `Schemas` node for the `AdventureWorks2008` database. You can see that there is a corresponding schema for each of the fixed database roles. These schemas are automatically created, and each is owned by the related database role.

The `public` Role

The `public` role is a special database role that is like a fixed database role except that its permissions are not fixed. The permissions for this role can be altered. Every user in a database is automatically made a member of the `public` role and in turn receives any permissions that have been granted to the `public` role. Database users cannot be removed from the `public` role.

The `public` role is similar in function to the `guest` user that is installed by default in each database. The difference is that the permissions granted to the `guest` user are used by any login that does not have a user account in the database. In this case, the login is allowed to enter the database via the `guest` account. In the case of the `public` role, the login has been added as a user of the database and in turn picks up any permissions that have been granted to the `public` role.

To view the permissions associated with the `public` role, you can use a `SELECT` statement like the following:

```
SELECT top 5 g.name,
    object_name(major_id) as 'Object',
```

```
   permission_name
 from sys.database_permissions p
 join sys.database_principals g
  on p.grantee_principal_id = g.principal_id
   and g.name = 'public'
order by 1,2

/*Results from the previous select
name    Object          permission_name
------  --------------  ---------------
public  all_columns     SELECT
public  all_objects     SELECT
public  all_parameters  SELECT
public  all_sql_modules SELECT
public  all_views       SELECT
*/
```

This `SELECT` utilizes two catalog views that contain security information. The `SELECT` returns only the first five permissions for the `public` role, but the `TOP` clause can be removed to return all the permissions.

User-Defined Roles

SQL Server enables you to create your own custom database roles. Like the fixed roles, user-defined roles can be used to provide a common set of permissions to a group of users. The key benefit behind using user-defined roles is that you can define your own set of custom permissions that fit your needs. User-defined roles can have a broad range of permissions, including the more granular set of permissions made available with SQL Server 2008.

To demonstrate the power of a user-defined database role, let's look at a simple example. Let's say that you have a group of users who need to read all the tables in a database but should be granted access to update only one table. If you look to the fixed database roles, you have the `db_datareader` and `db_datawriter` roles, which give you a partial solution. You can use the `db_datareader` role to allow the read capability you need, but the `db_datawriter` role gives write permission to all the tables—not just one.

One possible solution would be to give every user in the group membership to the `db_datareader` group and assign the specific `UPDATE` permission to each user as well. If the group contains hundreds of users, you can see that this would be rather tedious. Another solution might be to create a Windows group that contains every user who needs the permissions. You can then assign a login and database user to this group and grant the appropriate permissions. The Windows group is a viable solution but can sometimes be difficult to implement in a complex Windows domain.

Another approach to this challenge is to use a user-defined database role. You can create the role in the database that contains the tables in question. After you create the role, you can include it in the `db_datareader` role, and you can establish the `UPDATE` permission to the single table. Finally, you can assign the individual users or group of users to the role. Any future permission changes for this set of users can be administered through the user-defined database role. The script in Listing 11.1 steps through a process that demonstrates and tests the addition of a database role. This is similar to the example we just walked through. Parts of the script need to be run by an administrator, and other parts should be run in a query editor window that is connected to the database with the newly created `testuser`.

LISTING 11.1 An Example of User-Defined Database Roles

```
--The following statements must be run by an administrator to add
--a login and database user with no explicit permissions granted
CREATE LOGIN [TestUser] WITH PASSWORD=N'pw',
DEFAULT_DATABASE=[master], CHECK_EXPIRATION=OFF, CHECK_POLICY=OFF
GO

GO
USE [AdventureWorks2008]
GO
CREATE USER [TestUser] FOR LOGIN [TestUser]
go
--the following statement fails when executed by the TestUser
--which has no explicit permissions defined in the AdventureWorks2008 database
select top 5 * from person.person
UPDATE person.person SET suffix = 'Jr.'
 WHERE FirstName = 'Ken'
--The following statement is run by an administrator to:
--1)add a new TestDbRole with permission to UPDATE
--2)grant UPDATE permission on the Person.person table
--3)add the TestUser to the TestDbRole database role
USE [AdventureWorks2008]
GO
--1)
CREATE ROLE [TestDbRole] AUTHORIZATION [dbo]
--2)
GRANT UPDATE ON [Person].[Person] TO [TestDbRole]
GRANT SELECT ON [Person].[Person] TO [TestDbRole]
--3)
EXEC sp_addrolemember N'TestDbRole', N'TestUser'

--the following statements now succeed when executed
--by the TestUser because the role that it
--was added to has SELECT and UPDATE permission
--on that table
select top 5 * from person.person
UPDATE person.person SET suffix = 'Jr.'
 WHERE ContactID = 1
```

```
--the following select fails because 'testdbrole'
--does not permit SELECT on any table but person.person
select * from person.ContactType
--The following statement is run by an administrator
--to add the TestDbRole database role to the db_datareader
--fixed-database role
EXEC sp_addrolemember N'db_datareader', N'TestDbRole'
GO
--Finally, the testuser can update the Person.person table
-- and select from any other table in the database
select * from person.ContactType
```

Database roles and permissions are discussed in more detail later in this chapter, in the sections "Managing Database Roles" and "Managing Permissions."

Application Roles

Unlike other roles, application roles contain no database users. When an application role is created (see the section "Managing Database Roles," later in this chapter), rather than add a list of users who belong to the role, you specify a password. To obtain the permissions associated with the role, the connection must set the role and supply the password. This is done using the stored procedure `sp_setapprole`. You set the role to the `sales` application role (with the password `PassW0rd`) as follows:

```
EXEC sp_setapprole 'sales', 'PassW0rd'
```

You can also encrypt the password:

```
EXEC sp_setapprole 'sales', {ENCRYPT N ' PassW0rd'}, 'odbc'
```

When an application role is set, all permissions from that role apply, and all permissions inherited from roles other than `public` are suspended until the session is ended.

So why is it called an application role? The answer is in how it is used. An application role is used to provide permissions on objects through an application, *and only through the application*. Remember that you must use `sp_setapprole` and provide a password to activate the role; this statement and password are not given to the users; rather, they are embedded in the application's `CONNECT` string. This means that the user can get the permissions associated with the role only when running the application. The application can have checks and balances written into it to ensure that the permissions are being used for the forces of good and not evil.

Managing Securables

Securables are the entities in SQL Server on which permissions can be granted. In other words, principals (for example, users or logins) obtain permission to securables. This chapter describes many examples of securables, including tables, databases, and many entities that have been part of the SQL Server security model in past versions. SQL Server 2008's security model contains a granular set of securables for applying permissions.

Securables are hierarchical in nature and are broken down into nested hierarchies of named scopes. Three scopes are defined: at the server, database, and schema levels. Table 11.4 list the securables for each scope.

TABLE 11.4 SQL Server 2008 Securables

Server	Database	Schema
Logins	User	Table
Endpoints	Role	View
Databases	Application role	Function
	Assembly	Procedure
	Message Type	Queue
	Route	Type
	Service	Synonym
	Remote Service Binding	Aggregate
	Fulltext Catalog	XML Schema Collection
		Certificate
	Asymmetric Key	
	Symmetric Key	
	Contract	
	Schema	

As mentioned earlier, a hierarchy exists within each scope; in addition, relationships cross scope boundaries. Servers contain databases, databases contain schemas, and schemas contain a myriad of objects that are also hierarchical. When certain permissions are granted on a securable at the server level the permissions cascade; meaning permission is granted at the database and schema levels. For example, if a login is granted `control` permission at the server level, `control` is implicitly granted at the database and schema levels. The relationships between securables and permissions can be complicated. The next section details the different types of permissions and sheds some light on how these permissions affect securables.

Managing Permissions

Database security is mainly about managing permissions. Permissions are the security mechanisms that tie principals (for example, logins) to securables (for example, tables). With SQL Server 2008, permissions can be applied at a granular level that provides a great deal of flexibility and control.

Permissions in SQL Server 2008 revolve around three commands: `GRANT`, `REVOKE`, and `DENY`. These three commands were also used in SQL Server 2005 and SQL Server 2000. When permission is granted, the user or role is given permission to perform an action, such as creating a table. The `DENY` statement denies permission on an object and prevents the principal from gaining `GRANT` permission based on membership in a group or role. The `REVOKE` statement removes a permission that was previously granted or denied.

When specifying permissions, you need to carefully consider the hierarchy that exists between `GRANT`, `REVOKE`, and `DENY`. This is particularly important when the principal (for example, user or login) is part of a group or role and permissions have been granted on securables at different scopes of the security model. Following are some examples of the precedence that exists between these statements:

- A `GRANT` of a permission removes any `REVOKE` or `DENY` on a securable. For example, if a table has `SELECT` permission denied on it and then the `SELECT` permission is granted, the `DENY` permission is then removed on that table.
- `DENY` and `REVOKE` remove any `GRANT` permission on a securable.
- `REVOKE` removes any `GRANT` or `DENY` permission on a securable.
- Permissions denied at a higher scope in the security model override grants on that permission at a lower scope. Keep in mind that the security model has the server scope at the highest level, followed by database and schema. So, if `INSERT` permission is denied on tables at the database level, and `INSERT` on a specific table in that database is granted at the schema level, the result is that `INSERT` is denied on all tables. In this example, a database-level `DENY` overrides any `GRANT` at the lower schema level.
- Permissions granted at a higher scope in the security model are overridden by a `DENY` permission at a lower level. For example, if `INSERT` permission is granted on all tables at the database scope, and `INSERT` is denied on a specific table in the database (schema scope), `INSERT` is then denied on that specific table.

The assignment of a permission includes the `GRANT`, `DENY`, or `REVOKE` statements plus the permission that these statements affect. The number of available permissions increased in SQL Server 2005 and has been carried forward to SQL Server 2008. Familiar permissions such as `EXECUTE`, `INSERT`, and `SELECT` that were available in SQL Server 2000 are still around, plus the new permissions that were added in SQL Server 2005. Following are some of the new types that were added in SQL Server 2005:

- **CONTROL**—This type confers all defined permissions on the securable. This ownership-like capability also cascades to any lower-level objects in the security hierarchy.
- **ALTER**—This type confers the capability to change the securable's properties but does not include the capability to make ownership changes. If ALTER is applied on a scope such as a database or a schema, the capability to use ALTER, CREATE, or DROP on any object in the scope is allocated as well.
- **IMPERSONATE**—This type allows the principal to impersonate another user or login.
- **VIEW DEFINITION**—This type allows access to SQL Server metadata. This type of data is not granted by default in SQL Server 2008; therefore, the VIEW DEFINITION permission was added to manage access.

The combination of available permissions and the securables that they can be applied to is extensive. The permissions that are applicable depend on the particular securable. SQL Server Books Online lists the permissions for specific securables. You can use the index feature at Books Online to look for "permissions [SQL Server]." There, you will find a section named "Permissions Applicable to Specific Securables" as well as a section named "SQL Server Permissions" that lists each securable and its related permissions.

You can also view the available permissions by using system functions and catalog views. The following example uses the sys.fn_builtin_permissions function to retrieve a partial listing of all the available permissions:

```
SELECT top 5 class_desc, permission_name, parent_class_desc
 FROM sys.fn_builtin_permissions(default)
order by 1,2
/* Results from previous query
class_desc              permission_name parent_class_desc
----------------        --------------- -----------------
APPLICATION ROLE        ALTER           DATABASE
APPLICATION ROLE        CONTROL         DATABASE
APPLICATION ROLE        VIEW DEFINITION DATABASE
ASSEMBLY                ALTER           DATABASE
ASSEMBLY                CONTROL         DATABASE
*/
```

The granularity with which permissions can be applied with SQL Server 2008 is impressive and, to some degree, challenging. When you look at all the available permissions, you will see that some planning is needed to manage them. In the past, fixed database roles were simple to use but in many cases provided permissions that went beyond what the user needed. Microsoft has supplied the tools to facilitate the concept of "least privileges," which means providing only the privileges that are needed and nothing more. The tools to help you manage permissions are discussed later in this chapter, in the section "Managing SQL Server Permissions."

Managing SQL Server Logins

You can create and administer logins easily using SSMS. You can use T-SQL as well, but the GUI screens are often the best choice. The GUI screens present the configurable properties for a login, including the available options, databases, and securables that can be assigned to a login. The number of configurable options is extensive and can be difficult to manage with T-SQL.

Using SSMS to Manage Logins

The visual tools for managing logins in SSMS are accessible via the Object Explorer. You need to expand the `Security` node in Object Explorer and right-click the `Logins` node. Then you select the New Login option, and the new login screen, shown in Figure 11.4, appears.

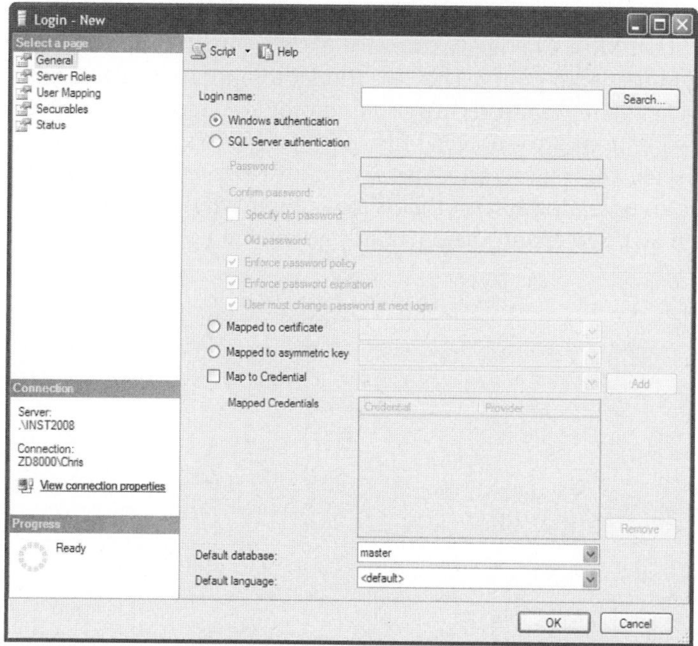

FIGURE 11.4 Creating a login in SSMS with Windows Authentication.

The default authentication mode for a new login is Windows Authentication. If you want to add a login with Windows Authentication, you need to type the name of your Windows user or group in the Login Name text box. You can also click the Search button to search for Windows logins. In either case, the login entered for Windows Authentication should be in the form *`<DOMAIN>\<UserName>`* (*for example,* `mydomain\Chris`) or in the form *`user@company.com`*.

With Windows Authentication, you have an option to restrict access to the server for the new login when it is created. If you select Deny Server Access, a command to deny access to SQL Server is issued immediately after the login is created (for example, `DENY CONNECT SQL TO [DBSVRXP\Chris]`). This option can be useful for staging new logins and waiting until all the appropriate security has been applied prior to allowing the login to access your SQL Server instance. After you completing the security setup for the login, you can select the login properties and choose the `GRANT SERVER ACCESS` option.

You can use the same new login screen shown in Figure 11.4 to add a login with SQL Server Authentication. Again, you need to provide a login name, but with the standard SQL Server login, there is no domain associated with the user. The login is independent of any Windows login and can be named as desired. The login and password for SQL Server Authentication are stored and maintained in SQL Server.

When SQL Server Authentication is selected, several options related to passwords are enabled. These options, as shown in Figure 11.5, include Enforce Password Expiration, Enforce Password Policy, and User Must Change Password at Next Login. These options are all associated with a more rigid password policy. They are similar to options available with Windows accounts and provide a more robust security solution for SQL Server logins. The catch is that the new password options are enforced only on the Windows 2003 Server operating system and versions above. You can select these options when running SQL Server on a machine that has an operating system that is lower than Windows 2003 Server, but the hooks between SQL Server and the operating system are not in place to enforce the password policy.

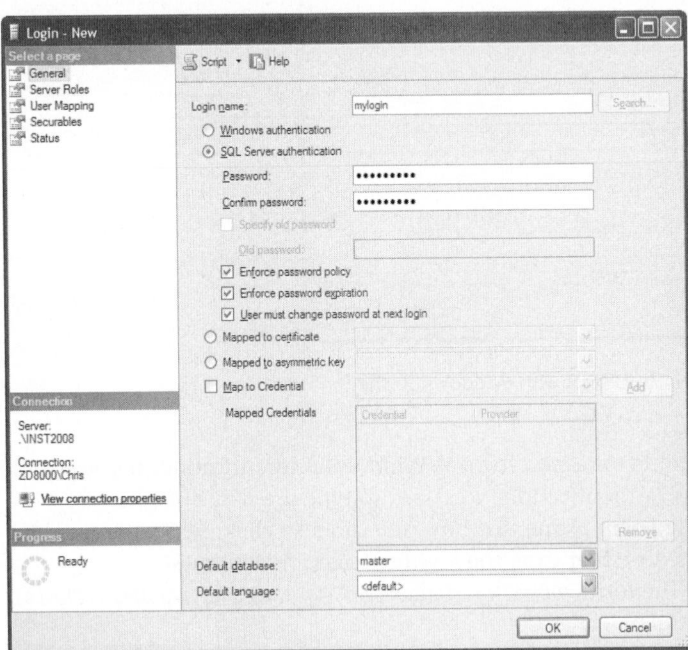

FIGURE 11.5 Creating a login in SSMS with SQL Server Authentication.

The next set of options on the General page of the new login allows you to map the login to a certificate, asymmetric key, or credential. The certificate and asymmetric key selections allow you to create a certificate-mapped login or an asymmetric key-mapped login. A certificate-mapped login and an asymmetric key-mapped login are used only for code signing and cannot be used to connect to SQL Server. If these options are used, the certificate or asymmetric key must exist on the server before you map the logins to them. The capability to map the login to a credential on the General page is new to SQL Server 2008. This option simply links the login to an existing credential, but its capabilities may be expanded.

The default database and default language are the final options located on the General page of the new login screen. These options are available regardless of the authentication method selected. The default database is the database that the login will connect to by default. The `master` database is selected, but it is generally not the best database to select for your default. You should choose the default database that your login will use most often and avoid using any of the system databases as your default. This helps prevent database users from executing statements against the wrong database, and it also removes the step of having to change the database every time the user connects. You should make sure that the login is given access to whatever database you select as the default. (The Database Access page is discussed later in this chapter.)

The default language determines the default language used by the login. If no default language is specified and the `<default>` entry is left in the Language drop-down, the server's default language is used. The default language for the server can be retrieved or set by using the `sp_configure` system stored procedure. The language selection affects many things, including date formats, month names, and names of days. To see a list of languages available on the server and the related options, you use the `sys.syslanguages` catalog view.

The new login screen has four other pages available for selection when creating your new login: Server Roles, User Mapping, Securables, and Status. The Server Roles page allows you to select one or more fixed server roles for the login to participate in. Figure 11.6 shows the new login screen with the Server Roles page selected. For a more detailed review of the permissions related to each server role, refer to the section "Fixed Server Roles," earlier in this chapter.

The User Mapping page allows you to select the databases that the login will have access to. When the Map check box is selected for a database, the Default Schema and User cells are enabled. The default schema is the schema that will contain the database objects created by the login. The login can create objects in schemas other than the default if the login has permission to use the other schemas. If no schema is specified, the default schema is used. The default schema also comes into play when you're retrieving database objects. If no schema is specified on database retrievals, the default schema is searched first for the database object. If no Default Schema is specified on the Database Access screen, the default schema is set to `dbo`. The User data entry area allows you to enter a database username that is different from the login name. By default, the database username is the same as the login name, but you can change it.

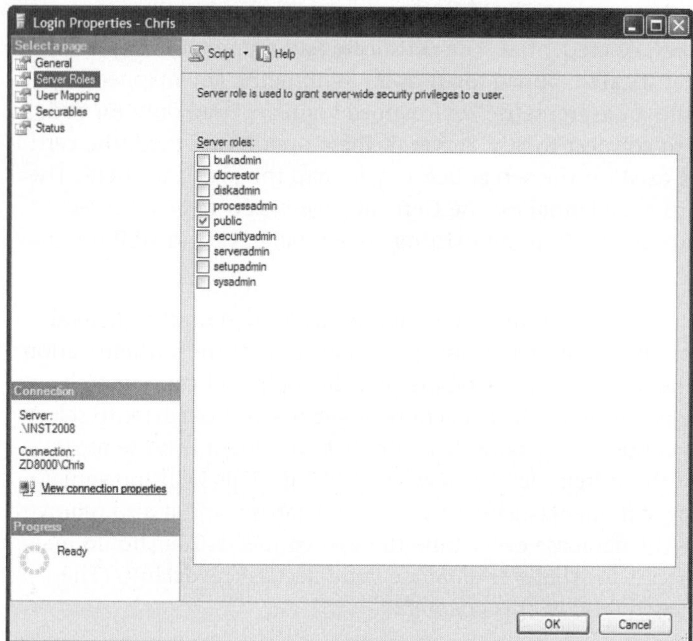

FIGURE 11.6 Choosing a server role.

The other thing that happens when you select the Map check box on the database is that the list of database roles is enabled in the bottom portion of the screen. You can select one or more database roles for the login. Both fixed and user-defined database roles are available for selection. The `public` database role is selected by default and cannot be deselected.

The Securables page allows you to select server objects for login permissions. The server objects are limited to object types scoped at the server level. They include `Servers`, `Endpoints`, `Logins`, and `Server Roles` object types. The management of all permissions, including those for `Logins`, is discussed in detail in the "Managing Permissions" section, earlier in the chapter.

The last page listed for selection is the Status page, which allows you to configure some authorization and authentication options. You can grant or deny access to the database engine on this page, and you can enable or disable the login. You also might need to visit this page if the login gets locked out. If this happens, you have an option on this page to reenable the login so that it is not longer locked out.

To modify a login, you right-click the login in the `Security` node and select Properties. The same set of property pages available when you create a new login are displayed. You cannot change the authentication mode after the login has been created, but you can change all the other settings, if desired.

To delete a login, you right-click the login and select Delete. The Delete Object screen appears, and you can click OK to delete the login. A warning message appears, stating "Deleting server logins does not delete the database users associated with the logins." If the login has associated database users, and the login deletion is performed, database users are orphaned, and you have to manually delete the users associated with the login in each database.

Using T-SQL to Manage Logins

You can manage logins by using T-SQL statements. This approach is generally not as easy as using the user-friendly GUI screens that come with SSMS, but sometimes using T-SQL is better. For example, with installations and upgrades that involve changes to logins, you can use T-SQL to script the changes and produce a repeatable process.

SQL Server 2008 includes system stored procedures and an `ALTER LOGIN` statement that you can use to manage logins. The same system stored procedures available in prior versions are still available in SQL Server 2008, but they have been deprecated and will not be available in a future version. Table 11.5 lists the available system stored procedures and the basic function and current state of each one. The state indicates whether the procedure has been deprecated and whether an alternative exists in SQL Server 2008.

TABLE 11.5 System Stored Procedures for Managing Logins

Store Procedure	Function	Status
`sp_addlogin`	Add a SQL Server login.	Deprecated; use `CREATE LOGIN`
`sp_defaultdb`	Change the default database.	Deprecated; use `ALTER LOGIN` instead.
`sp_defaultlanguage`	Change the default language.	Deprecated; use `ALTER LOGIN` instead.
`sp_denylogin`	Deny server access to a Windows login.	Deprecated.
`sp_droplogin`	Drop a SQL Server login.	Deprecated; use `DROP LOGIN` instead.
`sp_grantlogin`	Add a Windows login.	Deprecated.
`sp_password`	Change a login's password.	Deprecated; use `ALTER LOGIN` instead.
`sp_revokelogin`	Drop a Windows login.	Deprecated; use `DROP LOGIN` instead.

The system stored procedures have a variety of parameters, which are documented in Books Online. Because they have been deprecated, they are not the focus of this section. Instead, this section focuses on a number of examples that utilize the CREATE, ALTER, and DROP statements. The following example creates a SQL Server login with a password that must be changed the first time the login connects:

```
CREATE LOGIN Laura WITH PASSWORD=N'mypassw0rd$'
   MUST_CHANGE, CHECK_EXPIRATION=ON
```

You can then use the following ALTER LOGIN statement to change the default database, language, and password for the new Laura login:

```
ALTER LOGIN [Laura] WITH
 DEFAULT_DATABASE=[AdventureWorks2008],
 DEFAULT_LANGUAGE=[British],
 PASSWORD=N'myStr0ngPW'
```

Finally, you can drop the Laura login by using the following:

```
DROP LOGIN [Laura]
```

As you can see, the T-SQL statements for Logins are relatively easy to use. To simplify matters, you can generate T-SQL statements from SSMS. To do so, you click the Script button available on the screen that appears after you specify a login action. For example, if you right-click a login and select Delete, the Delete Object screen appears. At the top of this screen is a Script button. When you click this button, SSMS scripts the related T-SQL statements into a query editor window for you to review and execute.

Managing SQL Server Users

The SSMS has a set of friendly user interfaces to manage SQL Server users as well. The screens are similar to the screens for logins and are also launched from the Object Explorer. You can also use a set of T-SQL statements to manage users.

Using SSMS to Manage Users

To manage users via SSMS, you open the Object Explorer and expand the Security node followed by the Users node. The Users node contains a list of the current database users. To add a new database user, you can right-click the Users node and select New User. Figure 11.7 shows the Object Explorer window with the option to create a new user selected for the AdventureWorks2008 database.

Figure 11.8 shows the new database user screen displayed after you select the New User option. In this figure, a login named Chris is used, and the database user name is Chris as well. These two names do not need to match but are often the same for consistency. The login must exist before you can create the user. You can click the ellipsis button next to the login name to view a list of available logins. After you click the ellipsis, you can click the Browse button to see the logins that have already been added to SQL Server.

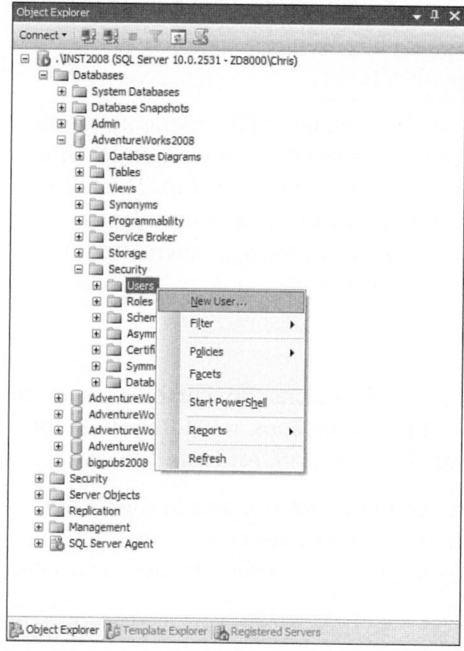

FIGURE 11.7 The New User option in Object Explorer.

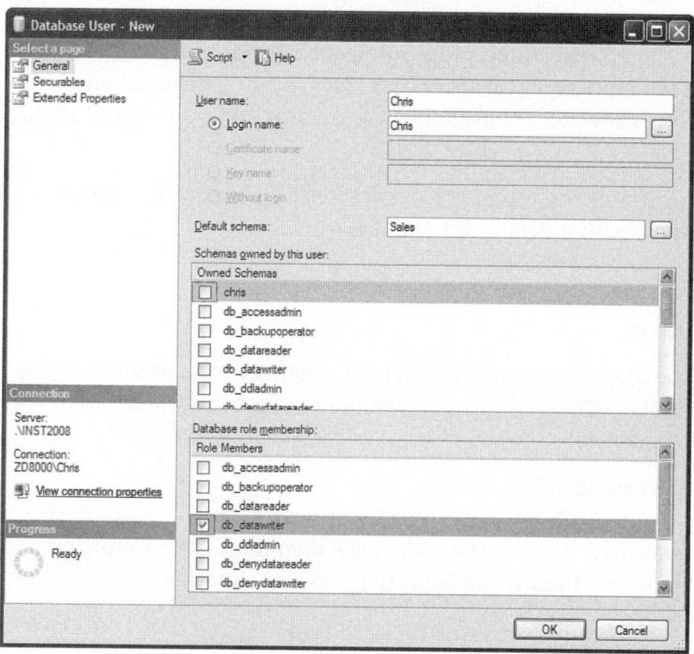

FIGURE 11.8 Using SSMS to create a new user.

The default schema must be a valid schema created in the database. If the default schema is left blank, it defaults to dbo. After the default schema has been set, it is used as the default location for storing and retrieving database objects.

You can select one or more schemas to be owned by the user, but a given schema can be owned by only one user in the database. When a schema is selected for ownership for a user, the previous owner loses ownership, and the new user gains ownership. The following example shows the type of T-SQL statement that you can run to accomplish the ownership change. This example changes the ownership on the Person schema to the user Laura:

```
ALTER AUTHORIZATION ON SCHEMA::[Person] TO [Laura]
```

When you select the Permissions page, you can assign permissions to securables scoped at the database and schema levels. The management of all permissions, including those for users, is discussed in detail in the "Managing Permissions" section, earlier in the chapter.

To modify or delete an existing database user, you can right-click the user in the Object Explorer and choose the related option. To modify the user, you select Properties, and a screen similar to the one you use to add the user is displayed. To delete the user, you select the Delete option.

Using T-SQL to Manage Users

CREATE USER, ALTER USER, and DROP USER are the T-SQL commands you use most often to manage database users. These commands are replacements for the system stored procedures used in prior versions. The system stored procedures, such as sp_adduser, sp_dropuser, sp_grantdbaccess, and sp_revokedbaccess, have been deprecated and will be removed in a future version. They are still available for use now, but you should avoid them when possible.

The following example demonstrates the use of the CREATE USER statement to create a new database user named Laura, with a default schema Sales:

```
CREATE USER Laura FOR LOGIN Laura
    WITH DEFAULT_SCHEMA = Sales
```

You can use the ALTER USE statement to change the default schema or the username. The following example uses the ALTER USER statement to change the name of the database user currently named Laura to LauraG:

```
ALTER USER Laura WITH NAME = LauraG
```

If you want to delete a database user, you use the DROP USER command. The following example demonstrates how to delete the LauraG from the previous example:

```
DROP USER [LauraG]
```

When dropping database users, you must keep in mind that you cannot drop them if they are the owners of database objects. An object's ownership must be transferred to another database user before that object can be deleted. This applies to schemas that can be owned by the user as well.

Managing Database Roles

Database roles are custom roles that you can define to group your users and simplify the administration of permissions. Generally, custom database roles (non-fixed) are created if the fixed database roles do not meet the security needs of the administrator. (The assignment of logins and users to fixed server and fixed database roles is covered earlier in this chapter.)

Using SSMS to Manage Database Roles

You can find database roles in the Object Explorer for each database, under the `Security` node, which contains a `Roles` node. The `Roles` node contains a `Database Roles` node, which lists both fixed and nonfixed database roles. To add a new custom database role (nonfixed), you right-click the `Database Roles` node and select New Database Role. A new database role dialog box appears, as shown in Figure 11.9.

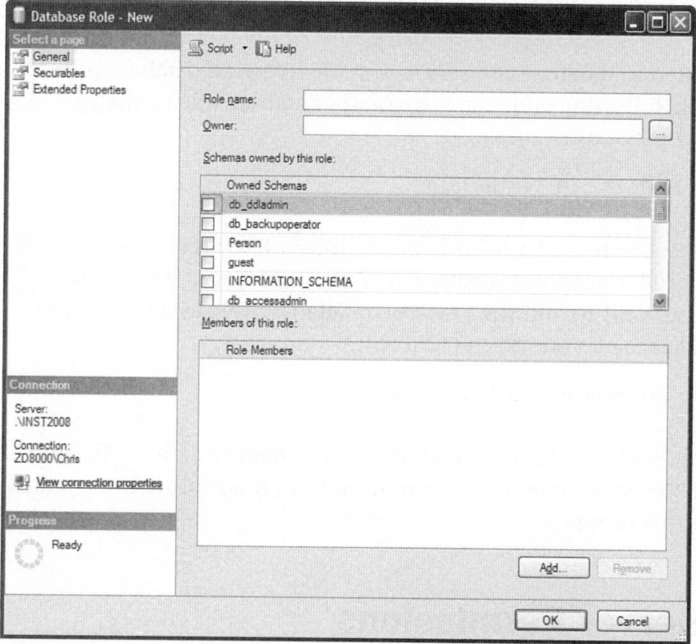

FIGURE 11.9 The new database role dialog box.

You need to enter a name for the role and name for the owner of the role. Like a database user, a database role can also own schemas. If you click the Add button, you can add database users from the current database to the role.

If you select the Permissions page, you can define the permission for the database role. This definition includes the selection of database objects scoped at the database and schema levels. These permissions are discussed in detail in the "Managing Permissions" section, earlier in this chapter.

Using T-SQL to Manage Database Roles

Some of the T-SQL system stored procedures used in prior versions to manage roles have been deprecated, including `sp_addrole` and `sp_droprole`. The `sp_addrolemember` and `sp_droprolemember` procedures have not been deprecated and are still good choices for adding members to a role.

The `CREATE ROLE` and `DROP ROLE` statements are the new replacements for `sp_addrole` and `sp_droprole`. The following example uses the `CREATE ROLE` statement to create a new database role named `DevDbRole`:

```
CREATE ROLE [DevDbRole]
```

To assign a user named `Chris` to the new `DevDbRole` role, you can use the following:

```
EXEC sp_addrolemember N'DevDbRole', N'chris'
```

Role membership is not limited to database users. It is possible to assign database roles as members of another role. The following adds the `TestDbRole` database role to the `DevDbRole` role created in the previous example:

```
EXEC sp_addrolemember N'DevDbRole', N'TestDbRole'
```

You cannot use `sp_addrolemember` to add a fixed database role, a fixed server role, or `dbo` to a role. You can, however, add a nonfixed database role as a member of a fixed database role. If, for example, you want to add the `DevDbRole` database role as a member of the fixed database role `db_dataread`, you use the following command:

```
EXEC sp_addrolemember N'db_datareader', N'DevDbRole'
```

The `ALTER ROLE` statement exists but is limited to changing the name of a role. To drop a database role, you use the `DROP ROLE` statement. Keep in mind that all role members must be dropped before a role can be dropped.

Managing SQL Server Permissions

You can use T-SQL or the visual tools available in SSMS to manage permissions. Based on the number of available permissions and their complexity, it is recommended that you use the SSMS tools. The following sections cover these tools from several different angles and look at the management of permissions at different levels of the security model. You learn how to use T-SQL to manage the permissions as well.

Using SSMS to Manage Permissions

The Object Explorer in SSMS enables you to manage permissions at many different levels of the permission hierarchy. You can manage permissions at a high level, such as the entire server, or you can manage permissions at the very lowest level, including a specific object, such as a table or stored procedure. The degree of granularity you use for permissions depends on your security needs. To demonstrate the scope of permissions, let's look at managing permissions at several different levels, starting at a high level and working down to the object level.

NOTE

There are many different ways to achieve a security goal in SSMS. For example, you can manage permissions for a database user from the database or from the user. You can apply permissions on schema objects for the entire schema or to individual objects. You should always try to choose the permission solution that allows you to achieve your security goals with the least amount of administrative overhead.

Using SSMS to Manage Permissions at the Server Level

Logins can be granted explicit permissions at the server level. Earlier we looked at fixed server roles as one means for assigning permissions, but you can manage individual server-level securables as well. Figure 11.10 shows the Login Properties window for a login named `Chris`. You launch this window by right-clicking the login and selecting Properties. Figure 11.10 shows the Securables page, which allows you to add specific securables to the grid.

NOTE

You can open a Permissions page like the one shown in Figure 11.10 from many different places in the Object Explorer. The title of the dialog box and the content of the grid vary, depending on the object selected, but the screen is generally the same, no matter where it is launched. This provides consistency and simplifies the overall management of permissions.

You can click the Search button shown toward the top of Figure 11.10 to add objects to the securables grid. When you click this button, the Add Objects window shown in Figure 11.11 is displayed. This window allows you to choose the types of objects you want to add. If you select Specific Objects, you are taken directly to the Select Objects window. If you choose All Objects of the Types, you are taken to an intermediate screen that allows you to select the type of objects you want to assign permissions to.

Again, the Add button and the means for adding objects are fairly consistent for all permissions. What varies is the object types available for selection. For example, at the server level, the types of objects available to assign permissions are scoped at the server level. Figure 11.12 shows the Select Object Types window displayed when you choose the

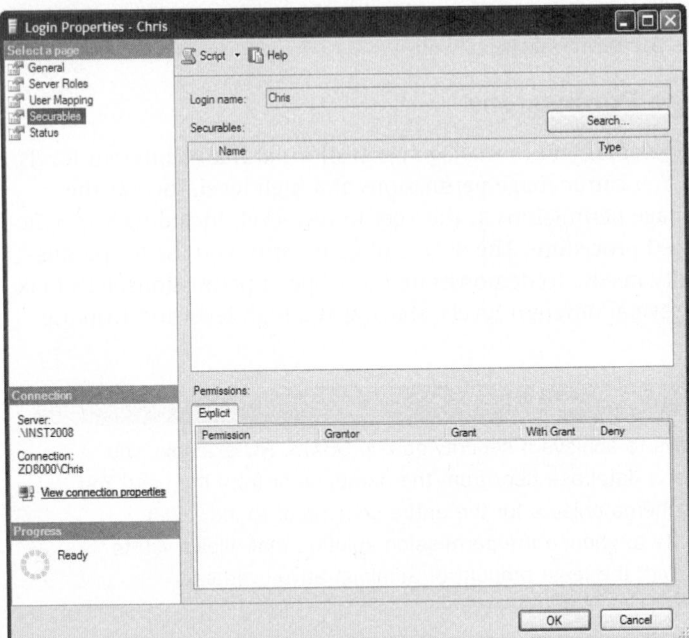

FIGURE 11.10 Server-level permissions.

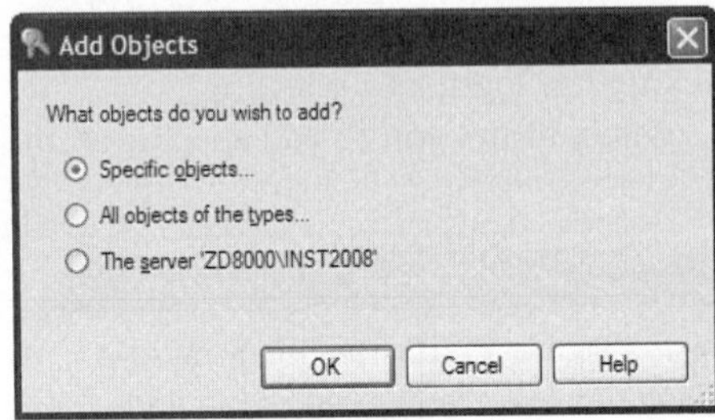

FIGURE 11.11 The Add Objects window.

All Objects of the Types option at the server level. You can see that the available objects are all scoped at the server level.

If the `endpoints` objects are selected, the securables grid is populated with all the available endpoints that have permissions to manage. Figure 11.13 shows the Login Properties window with the `endpoints` securables populated. The `TSQL Named Pipes` securable is selected, which allows you to specify the explicit permissions for the securable in the bottom grid. In this example, the Grant and With Grant check boxes have been selected for the control permission. This gives the login named `Chris` the right to control the `Named Pipes` endpoint and also allows him to grant this control right (because With Grant is selected) to other logins.

The examples we just walked through are related to the assignment of explicit permission on a specific instance of a securable. You can also apply server permissions at a higher

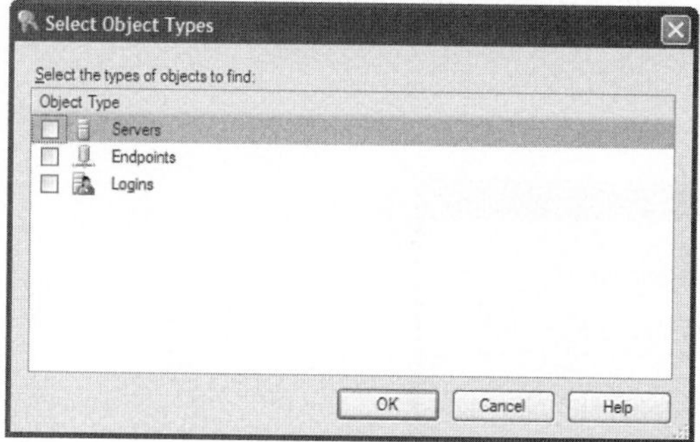

FIGURE 11.12 Server-level object types.

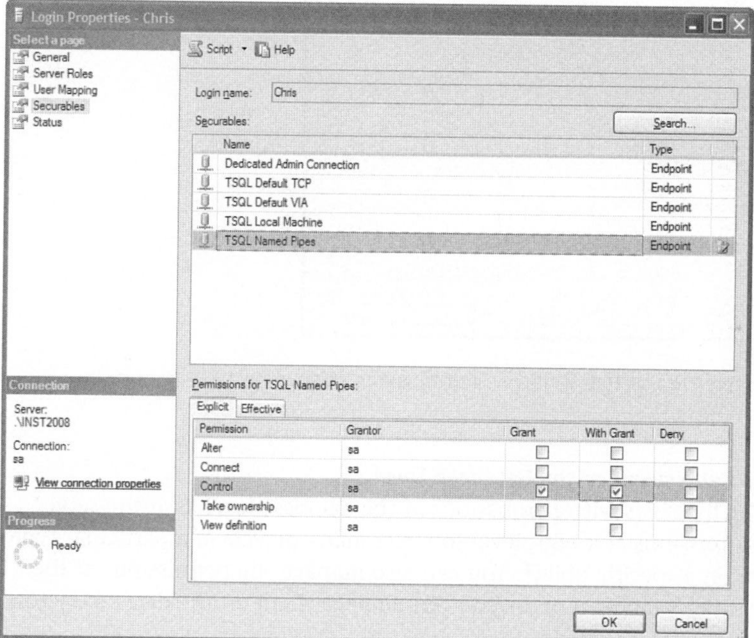

FIGURE 11.13 Server-level securables.

level. For example, you might want to specify permissions for a login to allow that login to control all server endpoints instead of specific endpoints. You can accomplish this in several ways. One way to do it is to select the `Server` object from the list of object types when adding permissions for a specific login. Another way is to right-click the server name in the Object Explorer and select Properties. The Server Properties window that appears has a Permissions page that lists all the logins for the server, along with the macro-level permissions scoped for the server. Figure 11.14 shows the Server Properties window with the login `Chris` selected. The explicit permissions listed in this case are at a higher level and are not just for one instance. The example shown in Figure 11.14 allows the login `Chris` to alter any database or any endpoint on the server. This is based on the Grant check boxes selected.

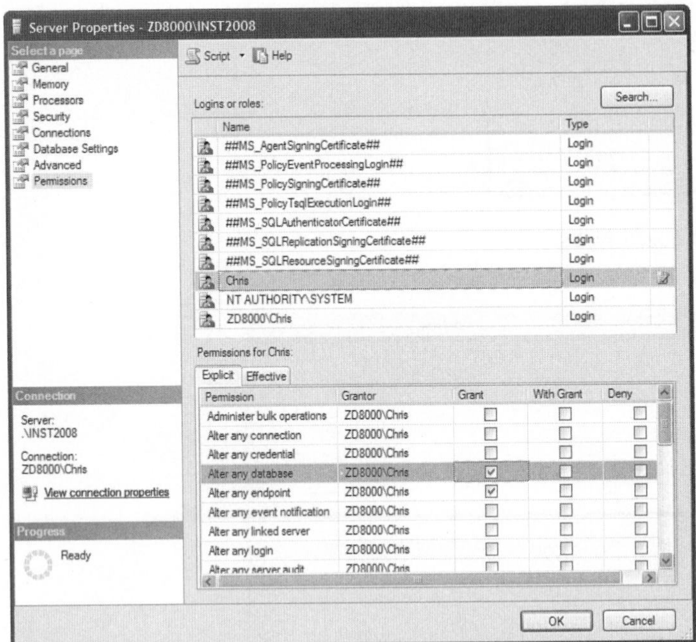

FIGURE 11.14 The Server Properties window's Permissions page.

Using SSMS to Manage Permissions at the Database Level

The same type of hierarchy exists with permissions at the database level as at the server level. You can apply permissions at a high level to affect many objects of a particular type, or you can apply them on a specific object. You can also manage the permissions at the database level on a specific database user, or you can manage them on the database across many users.

To demonstrate the differences between object types available at the database level, let's first look at managing permissions for a specific database user. As with logins, you can right-click a database user and select Properties. On the Properties window that appears, you select the Securables page, and you get a screen to assign permissions that is very similar to the login permissions screen. The difference at the database level is in the object types available for selection. Figure 11.15 shows the object types available when you choose the All Objects of Types choice during the addition of securables for a database user.

When a low-level object type such as a table or stored procedure is selected, you are able to apply explicit permissions to a specific object instance. Figure 11.16 shows an example of low-level securables available when the `Table` object type is selected.

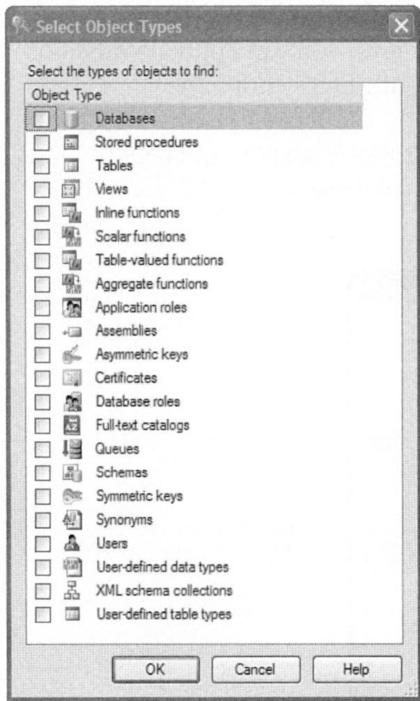

FIGURE 11.15 Database-level object types.

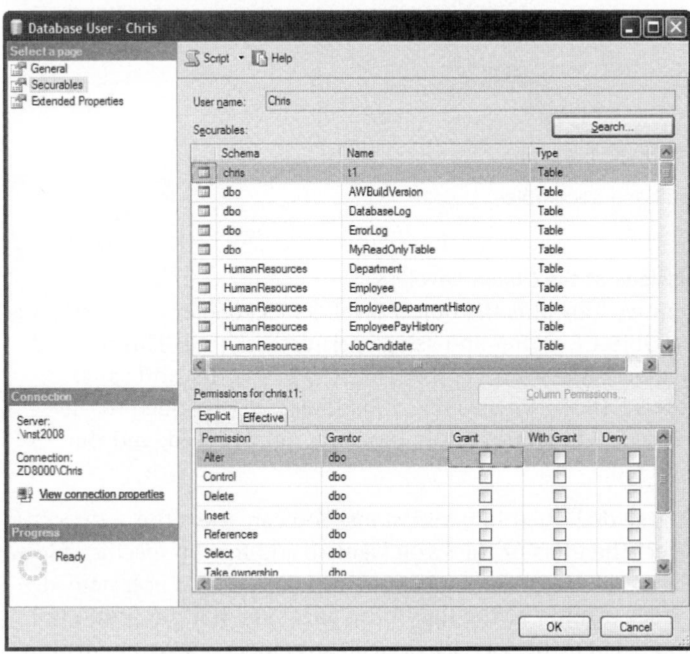

FIGURE 11.16 Low-level database securables.

To apply permissions at a higher level in the database, you choose the object type `Databases`. With this securable added to the permissions grid, you can apply permissions to a group of objects by selecting a single permission. Figure 11.17 shows the `AdventureWorks2008` database selected as the securable and the related permissions available. In this example, the login `Chris` has been granted `INSERT`, `SELECT`, and `UPDATE` permissions to all the tables in the `AdventureWorks2008` database.

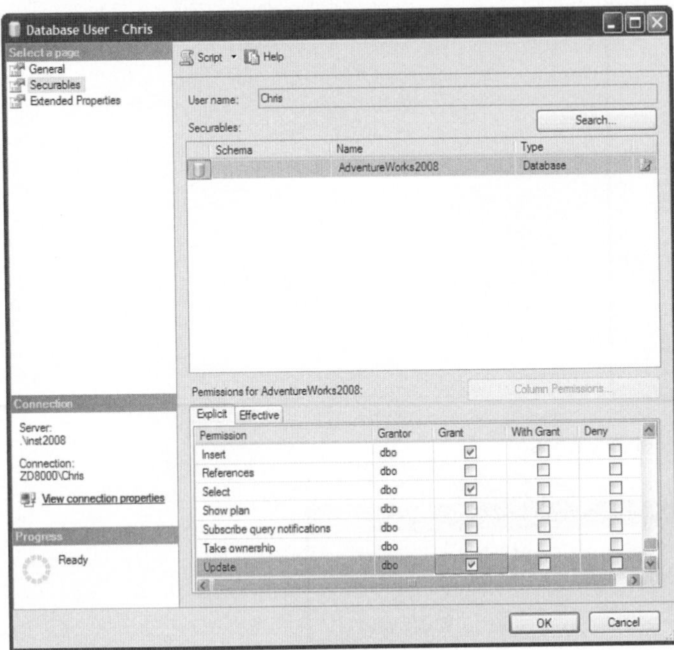

FIGURE 11.17 High-level database securables.

Using SSMS to Manage Permissions at the Object Level

The last permission assignment we look at is the object level. SSMS enables you to select a specific object instance in the Object Explorer and assign permissions to it. This method allows you to navigate to the object you want via the Object Explorer tree and assign permissions accordingly. Figure 11.18 shows the Object Explorer tree expanded to the `Stored Procedures` node. A specific stored procedure has been right-clicked, and the Properties option has been selected.

The Properties window has a page dedicated to permissions. You can select the Permissions page and then select the users or roles you want to add for the specific object, such as a stored procedure. Figure 11.19 shows the Permissions page with a user named `Chris` added to the Users or Roles window at the top of the page. The bottom portion of the page shows explicit permissions for the user `Chris`, which includes a `DENY` permission on the stored procedure selected.

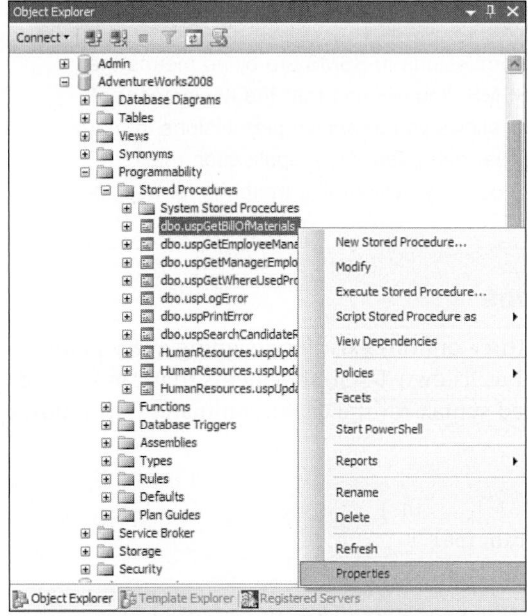

FIGURE 11.18 Object-level permissions selected via Object Explorer.

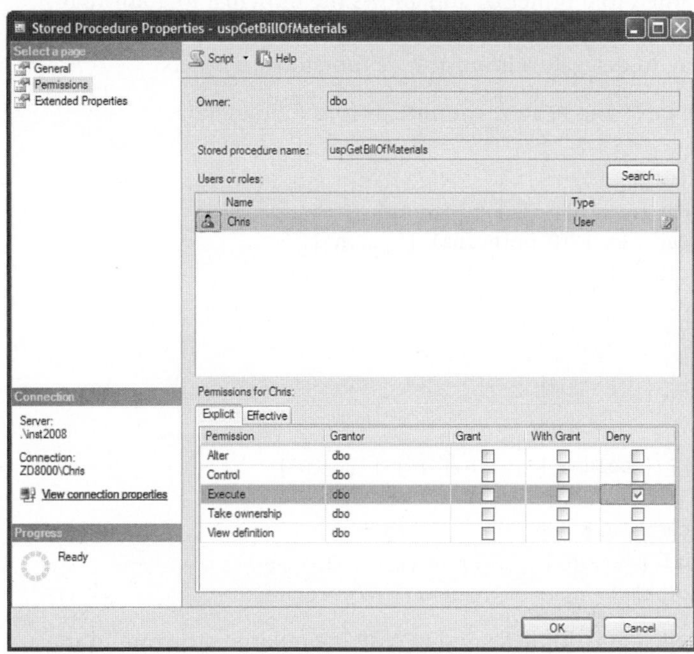

FIGURE 11.19 Object-level permissions.

NOTE

The methods described here for managing permissions in SSMS are by no means the only ways you can manage permissions in SSMS. You will find that the assignment of permissions pervades SSMS and that SSMS allows you to assign permissions in many different ways. The point to keep in mind is that database roles, application roles, schemas, and other objects in the security model all have similar methods for assigning permissions.

Using T-SQL to Manage Permissions

As you saw in the SSMS Permissions pages, three options exist for assigning every permission: GRANT, DENY, and REVOKE. Each option has its own T-SQL statements that can be used to manage permissions as well. The simplified syntax for the GRANT command is as follows:

```
GRANT { ALL [ PRIVILEGES ] }
      | permission [ ( column [ ,...n ] ) ] [ ,...n ]
      [ ON [ class :: ] securable ] TO principal [ ,...n ]
      [ WITH GRANT OPTION ] [ AS principal ]
```

This basic GRANT syntax is similar to that in SQL Server 2000, but the addition of many permissions and securables in SQL Server 2005 and SQL Server 2008 has expanded the scope of the command. SQL Server 2005 also introduced the WITH GRANT option which allows a permission to be granted to a principal and allows the principal to grant that permission to another principal. The WITH GRANT option has been carried forward to SQL Server 2008 and is a good way to delegate administrative functions to others.

The simplified syntax for the DENY and REVOKE commands is as follows:

```
DENY { ALL [ PRIVILEGES ] }
      | permission [ ( column [ ,...n ] ) ] [ ,...n ]
      [ ON [ class :: ] securable ] TO principal [ ,...n ]
      [ CASCADE] [ AS principal ]

REVOKE [ GRANT OPTION FOR ]
      {
        [ ALL [ PRIVILEGES ] ]
        |
                permission [ ( column [ ,...n ] ) ] [ ,...n ]
      }
      [ ON [ class :: ] securable ]
      { TO | FROM } principal [ ,...n ]
      [ CASCADE] [ AS principal ]
```

You can see that the simplified syntax for DENY and REVOKE is similar in structure to the GRANT statement. All the statements must identify the permission, securable, and principal that will receive the permission.

The ALL clause has been deprecated in SQL Server 2008. If ALL is specified, it does not affect all permissions on the object; it affects only a subset of the permissions related to the securable. The subset of permissions is dependent on the securable.

The following examples demonstrate several different types of permissions you can manage by using T-SQL commands:

```
--Grant permissions to create a table
-- to a user named Chris
GRANT CREATE TABLE TO Chris

--Grant ALL permissions on a stored procedure
-- to a database role named TestDBRole
GRANT ALL ON dbo.uspGetBillOfMaterials TO TestDBRole

--DENY UPDATE permission on the Customer table
-- to user named Laura
DENY UPDATE ON OBJECT::sales.customer TO Laura

--REVOKE UPDATE permissions on the Customer table
-- to user named Laura.
REVOKE UPDATE ON OBJECT::sales.customer TO Laura
```

There are many different flavors of the GRANT, DENY, and REVOKE statements, depending on the securable they are affecting. Books Online outlines the syntax for each securable and the permissions that can be applied.

Remember that you can use the Script option to generate the T-SQL from SSMS. The Script button is available when you're managing permissions, and using it is a great way to familiarize yourself with the T-SQL that is used to effect changes. You can select the permissions you want to apply via the GUI screen and then click the Script button to generate the T-SQL.

The Execution Context

The execution context determines what permissions are checked when statements are executed or actions are performed on the database server. By default, the execution context is set to the principal connected to the server or database. If a user named Chris connects to the AdventureWorks2008 database, the permissions assigned to Chris are checked.

In SQL Server 2008, you can change the execution context so that permissions are checked for a principal other than that to which you are connected. You can make this change in execution context (called *context switching*) explicitly or implicitly.

Explicit Context Switching

With explicit context switching, you can use the EXECUTE AS statement to change the user or login used to check permissions. This is similar to the SET USER statement available in SQL Server 2000 and SQL Server 2005. It is extremely useful for administrators who are testing the permissions they have set for users or logins. The following example demonstrates the use of the explicit EXECUTE AS statement:

```
--Assume that you are connected as an administrator (DBO)
--and want to prevent members of the Public role from
--selecting from the Sales.Customer table
DENY SELECT ON sales.customer TO Public

--We can check that user Laura cannot select from the
-- Sales.Customer table using the EXECUTE AS statement
EXECUTE AS USER = 'laura'
SELECT TOP 1 * FROM sales.customer

-- Revert to the previous execution context.
REVERT
```

You can also do explicit context switching at the login level. You can use the EXECUTE AS statement to switch the execution context to another login instead of a user.

Context switching is linked to the IMPERSONATE permission. As an administrator, you can grant IMPERSONATE to a login or user to enable that user to execute as that user. For example, an administrator can temporarily enable another login to run in the same execution context by using the IMPERSONATE permission and EXECUTE AS statement. The following example demonstrates the assignment of the IMPERSONATE permission to a login named Laura:

```
--Chris grants the right to Laura to impersonate him
GRANT IMPERSONATE ON LOGIN::[chris] TO [laura]
GO

--Laura can then connect with her login and use
-- the EXECUTE AS command to run commands that
-- normally only Chris has permission to run
EXECUTE AS Login = 'Chris'
DBCC CHECKDB (AdventureWorks2008)
SELECT USER_NAME()
--Revert back to Laura's execution context
REVERT
SELECT USER_NAME()
```

Laura can now use EXECUTE as Chris, who is an administrator. This capability can be particularly useful when a user or login has many custom permissions that would take a lot of time to establish for another user or login.

Implicit Context Switching

With implicit context switching, the execution context is set within a module such as a stored procedure, trigger, or user-defined function. The EXECUTE AS clause is placed in the module and is set to the user that the module will be run as. The context switch is implicit because the user who runs the module does not have to explicitly specify the context before running the module. The context is set within the module.

The EXECUTE AS clause has several different options to establish the execution context. All modules are able to set the context to a specific user or login. Functions, stored procedures, and Data Manipulation Language (DML) triggers can also execute as CALLER, SELF, or OWNER. DDL triggers can run as CALLER or SELF. Queues can run as SELF or OWNER. The CALLER option is the default, and it runs the module in the context of the user who called the module. The SELF option causes the module to run in the context of the user or login that created the procedure. The OWNER option causes the module to run in the context of the current owner of the module.

The following example demonstrates the creation and execution of a stored procedure with the EXECUTE AS clause on a specific user named Chris:

```
CREATE PROCEDURE dbo.usp_TestExecutionContext
WITH EXECUTE AS 'chris'
AS SELECT USER_NAME() as 'User'

--Set the user to someone other than chris to test the
-- implicit EXECUTE AS
SETUSER 'DBO'
EXEC usp_TestExecutionContext

/*Results of the prior execution
User
------
chris
*/
```

This example shows that the USER_NAME retrieved in the stored procedure is Chris, regardless of who executed the procedure.

Implicit execution context can be particularly useful in situations in which permissions cannot be granted to a user directly. For example, TRUNCATE TABLE permissions cannot be granted explicitly to a user, but a database owner can run this command. Instead of granting dbo rights to a user needing TRUNCATE permissions, you can create a stored procedure that does the truncation. You can create the stored procedure with the execution context of dbo, and you can grant the user rights to execute the stored procedure that does the truncation. When you use this method, the user can perform the truncation but does not have any of the other permissions related to a database owner.

Summary

SQL Server 2008 continues the trend of providing more security and more flexible security to the SQL Server database environment. Several new enhancements have been added to SQL Server 2008 that add to the slew of security changes added to SQL Server 2005. The granularity of the permissions and the other security-related features covered in this chapter allow you to keep your SQL Server environment safe.

Chapter 12, "Data Encryption," looks at another aspect of SQL Server that helps secure your database environment. It covers encryption methods that can be implemented to further protect your data from unauthorized access.

CHAPTER 12
Data Encryption

IN THIS CHAPTER

- What's New in Data Encryption
- An Overview of Data Security
- An Overview of Data Encryption
- SQL Server Key Management
- Column-Level Encryption
- Transparent Data Encryption
- Column-Level Encryption Versus Transparent Data Encryption

With all the concern about identity theft these days, there has been increasingly more attention paid to how all the Personally Identifiable Information (PII) and other sensitive information stored in databases is being protected. It is necessary to secure and protect this data to avoid any potential liability should the PII or sensitive data fall into the wrong hands, and in some cases, doing so may even be required by law (for example, Health Insurance Portability and Accountability Act, or HIPAA, requirements).

Chapter 11, "Security and User Administration," discusses methods to secure and control the access to your SQL Server data via login and user security. This type of security is usually sufficient to prevent access to the data by anyone other than properly authorized users. But what if you need to prevent authorized users, such as your database or server administrators, from viewing sensitive data? How can you protect sensitive data from hackers or in the event that a database backup is stolen?

One method is to encrypt the data. This chapter looks at two methods provided in SQL Server 2008 for encrypting data: column-level encryption and transparent data encryption (TDE). In addition to describing how to implement both methods, the chapter presents the features and limitations of each of these methods to help you decide which data encryption method may help you meet your data security needs.

What's New in Data Encryption

In SQL Server 2000 and earlier, if you wanted to encrypt data in your databases, you usually needed to implement some form of client-side encryption. SQL Server itself did not provide any means of encrypting data at the database level, so all the encryption and decryption occurred in the application itself. This required custom-written applications to encrypt and decrypt the data, and only those applications would be able to view the encrypted data.

SQL Server 2005 introduced the capability to perform column-level (sometimes called *cell-level*) encryption. This provided the capability to encrypt data within the database itself at the column level. However, this method is still not transparent to the applications and requires changes to the database schema as well as changes to your applications and T-SQL code to include the proper function calls to encrypt and decrypt the data as it is stored and retrieved.

SQL Server 2008 introduces a new form of database encryption: transparent data encryption. TDE allows you to encrypt an entire database without affecting client applications. The purpose of TDE is to prevent scenarios in which the physical media (such as database files or backups) containing sensitive data are stolen and then read by attaching the database files or restoring the backups.

NOTE

Both column-level and transparent data encryption are available only in the Enterprise and Developer Editions of SQL Server 2008 and SQL Server 2008 R2.

Another new feature in SQL Server 2008 is Extensible Key Management (EKM). EKM enables parts of the cryptographic key hierarchy to be managed by an external source such as Hardware Security Module (HSM), referred to as a *cryptographic provider*. Encryption and decryption operations using these keys are handled by the cryptographic provider. This allows for flexibility and choice in cryptographic providers as well as common key management.

An Overview of Data Security

Security is important for every product and every business. By following some simple security best practices, you can avoid many security vulnerabilities. This section discusses some security recommendations that you should consider for your SQL Server implementations. Securing SQL Server can be viewed as a series of steps, involving four areas: the platform, authentication, objects (including data), and applications that access the system.

The platform for SQL Server includes the physical hardware and networking systems connecting clients to the database servers. The first step in securing your SQL Server environment is to provide sufficient physical security by limiting access to the physical server and hardware components. To enhance the physical security of the SQL Server installation, you should consider placing the server in a room accessible only by authorized personnel, ideally a locked computer room with monitored flood detection and fire detection or suppression systems. In addition, you should physically secure your backup media by storing it at a secure offsite location.

Next, you need to ensure your system provides sufficient physical network security by keeping unauthorized users off the network by limiting access to the network to authorized users only. Make sure your database servers are installed in a secure zone of your company's intranet behind a firewall. Do not connect your SQL Servers directly to the Internet. Always make sure there is a firewall between your servers and the Internet and set it up to block all traffic except for that which is required.

Next, you need to ensure that you have secured your operating system and files. SQL Server uses operating system files for operation and data storage. Be sure to restrict access to these files to system administrators only. Use the NTFS file system because it is more stable and recoverable than FAT file systems. NTFS also enables security options such as file and directory Access Control Lists (ACLs) and Encrypting File System (EFS) file encryption.

For your installed SQL Server instances, you can enhance the security of the SQL Server installation by running your SQL Server services under service accounts granted the minimal permissions necessary for operation (do not run under the Windows Administrator account!). These accounts should be low-privileged Windows local user or domain user accounts.

Surface area reduction is also an important security measure. Surface area reduction helps improve security by providing fewer avenues for potential attacks on a system. In addition to running services under "least privilege" accounts, this measure also involves stopping or disabling unused components.

You should also enhance the security of the SQL Server instances through limiting the individuals, groups, and processes granted access to SQL Server and appropriately limiting access to the databases and objects the database contains. One way is to require Windows authentication for connections to SQL Server. If you are using SQL Server authentication as well, you should be sure to enforce password policies that require strong passwords and password expiration for all SQL Server logins. For more information on setting up SQL Server logins and managing database users and object permissions, see Chapter 11.

Even if you follow the recommendations presented here for securing your environment, you still can be vulnerable to access control problems. Encryption provides another way to enhance security by limiting data loss even in the rare occurrence that access controls are bypassed. For example, if a malicious user hacks into the database host computer and obtains sensitive data, such as credit card numbers, that stolen information might be useless if it is encrypted.

An Overview of Data Encryption

Encryption is the process of obfuscating data by the use of a key or password. This can make the data useless without the corresponding decryption key or password. Encryption does not solve access control problems. However, it enhances security by limiting data loss even if access controls are bypassed.

Encryption is actually the conversion of readable plaintext into ciphertext, which cannot be easily understood by unauthorized people. The concrete procedure of carrying out the encryption is called an *algorithm*. Decryption is the process of converting ciphertext back into its original form so it can be understood. Both encryption and decryption require a key, which must be kept secret because it enables the holder to carry out the decryption.

There are two primary methods of encryption: symmetric key encryption and asymmetric key encryption. Symmetric key encryption uses the same key for both encryption and decryption. Asymmetric key encryption, also called public-key encryption, uses two different keys for encryption and decryption, which together form a key pair. The key used for encryption is called a *public key*. The key used for decryption is referred to as a *private key*.

Symmetric key encryption is inherently less secure because it uses the same key for both encryption and decryption operations, and the exchange of data requires transfer of the key, which introduces a potential for its compromise. This can be avoided with an asymmetric key because individuals encrypting and decrypting data have their own, separate keys. However, asymmetric encryption is based on algorithms that are more complex, and its impact on performance is more significant, making it often unsuitable in scenarios involving larger amounts of data. However, it is possible to take advantage of the strengths of both methods by encrypting data with a symmetric key and then protecting the symmetric key with asymmetric encryption.

One solution to the dilemma of key distribution is to use digital certificates. A certificate is a digitally signed piece of software that associates a public key with the identity of the private key owner, assuring its authenticity. There is an inherent problem with this approach—namely, how to assure the identity of the certificate issuer. To resolve this issue, Microsoft provides a number of trusted certificate authorities (known as Trusted Root Certification Authorities) with the operating system. These certificate authorities are responsible for verifying that organizations requesting certificates are really what they claim to be.

Typically, the algorithms used for encryption are industry standard, such as the Advanced Encryption Standard (AES). The fact that the algorithms are published doesn't make them weaker, but rather helps ensure they are strong and robust. Because these algorithms have been reviewed by thousands of experts around the globe, they have stood the test of time. SQL Server 2008 allows administrators and developers to choose from among several algorithms, including DES, Triple DES, TRIPLE_DES_3KEY, RC2, RC4, 128-bit RC4, DESX, 128-bit AES, 192-bit AES, and 256-bit AES. No one algorithm is ideal for all situations, and a discussion on the merits of each is beyond the scope of this chapter. However, the following general principles apply:

- Strong encryption generally consumes more CPU resources than weak encryption.
- Long keys generally yield stronger encryption than short keys.
- Asymmetric encryption is stronger than symmetric encryption using the same key length, but it is slower.
- Long, complex passwords are stronger than short passwords.
- If you are encrypting lots of data, you should encrypt the data using a symmetric key and encrypt the symmetric key with an asymmetric key.

However, what really protects your data from third parties is not so much the algorithm but the encryption key, which you must keep secure. Keys must be stored securely and made available only on a need-to-know basis. Ideally, authorized people or systems should be able to use but not necessarily have a copy of the key. It's also a security best practice to implement key rotation, changing keys periodically in case a key has been compromised. For greater key security, you can also make use of Extensible Key Management, allowing keys to be managed by an external source such as Hardware Security Module.

SQL Server 2008 provides support for not only encryption of data, but also encryption of user network connections and stored procedures. The remainder of this chapter discusses the two methods of data encryption, column-level encryption and transparent data encryption. Client network encryption is covered in Chapter 10, "Client Installation and Configuration." Encryption of stored procedure code is discussed in Chapter 28, "Creating and Managing Stored Procedures."

NOTE

Although encryption is a valuable tool to help ensure security, it does incur overhead and can affect performance, and any use of encryption requires a maintenance strategy for your passwords, keys, and certificates.

Therefore, encryption should not be automatically considered for all data or connections. When you are deciding whether to implement encryption, consider how users access the data. If access is over a public network, data encryption may be required to increase data security. However, if all access is via a secure intranet configuration, encryption may not be required.

This chapter describes the encryption methods available in SQL Server 2008 and SQL Server 2008 R2 along with the pros and cons of implementing these encryption methods. This information should help you to determine whether using encryption is appropriate for implementing your data security solutions.

SQL Server Key Management

SQL Server 2008 provides rich support for various types of data encryption using symmetric and asymmetric keys and digital certificates. As an administrator, you probably need to manage at least the upper level of keys in the hierarchy shown in Figure 12.1. Each key protects its child keys, which in turn protect their child keys, down through the tree. The one exception is when a password is used to protect a symmetric key or certificate. This is how SQL Server lets users manage their own keys and take responsibility for keeping the key secret.

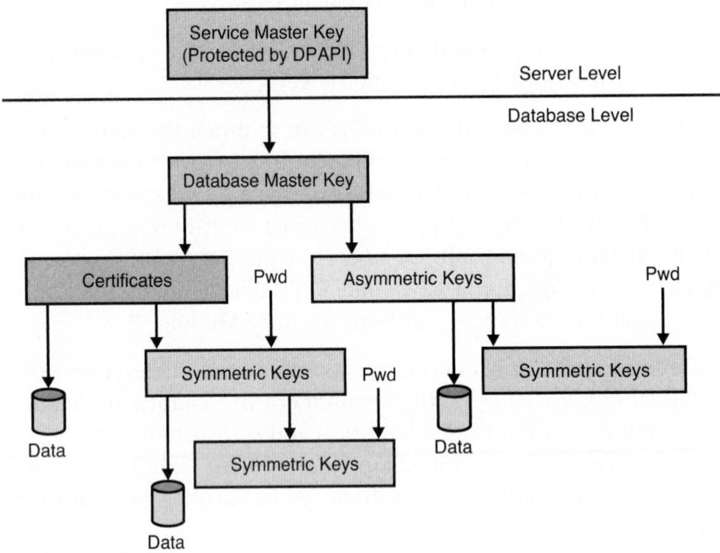

FIGURE 12.1 Key hierarchy in SQL Server 2008.

Each SQL Server instance has its *service master key*. The service master key is the one key that rules them all. It is a symmetric key created automatically during SQL Server installation and is encrypted and protected by the Data Protection API (DPAPI), which is provided by the underlying Windows OS, using the credentials of the SQL Server service account. Protection of this key is critical because if it is compromised, an attacker can eventually decipher every key in the server managed by SQL Server. SQL Server manages the service master key for you, although you can perform maintenance tasks on it to dump it to a file, regenerate it, and restore it from a file. However, most of the time you will not need or want to make any of these changes to the key, although administrators are advised to back up their service master keys in the event of key corruption.

The main purpose of the server master key is to secure system data, such as passwords used in instance-level settings such as linked servers or connection strings. The service master key is also used to secure each of the *database master keys*. Within each database, the database master key serves as the basis for creating certificates or asymmetric keys, which subsequently can be applied to protect data directly or to further extend the encryption hierarchy (for example, by creating symmetric keys). Creation, storage, and other certificate and key management tasks can be handled internally, without resorting to features of the operating system or third-party products.

Each database can have a single master key. You must create a database master key before using it by using the CREATE MASTER KEY Transact-SQL statement with a user-supplied password:

```
CREATE MASTER KEY ENCRYPTION BY PASSWORD = 'R@nD0m!T3%t'
```


SQL Server encrypts the database master key using a triple DES key derived from the password as well as the service master key. The first copy is stored in the database, and the second is stored in the master database. Having the database master key protected by the server master key makes it possible for SQL Server to decrypt the database master key automatically when required. The application or user does not need to open the master key explicitly using the password. This is a major benefit of having the keys protected in the hierarchy.

NOTE

Detaching a database with an existing master key and moving it to another server can be an issue. The problem is that the new server's database master key is different from that of the old server. As a result, the server cannot automatically decrypt the database master key. This situation can be circumvented by opening the database master key with the password with which it is encrypted and using the ALTER MASTER KEY statement to encrypt it with the new database master key.

When the database master key exists, developers can use it to create any of three types of keys, depending on the type of encryption required:

- Asymmetric keys
- Symmetric keys
- Certificates

TIP

Microsoft recommends against using certificates or asymmetric keys for encrypting data directly. Asymmetric key encryption is many times slower, and the amount of data that you can protect using this mechanism is limited, depending on the key modulus. It is recommended that you protect certificates and asymmetric keys using a password instead of by the database master key.

Extensible Key Management

Another new feature in SQL Server 2008 that provides greater key security is Extensible Key Management. EKM enables you to manage your encryption keys via an external provider. This allows for flexibility and choice in encryption providers as well as common key management across your enterprise.

With the growing demand for regulatory compliance and concern for data privacy, organizations are taking advantage of encryption as a way to provide a "defense in depth" solution. As organizations increasingly use encryption and keys to secure their data, key management becomes more complex. Some high security databases use thousands of keys, and you must employ a system to store, retire, and regenerate these keys. This approach is often impractical using only database encryption management tools. As a solution, various hardware vendors provide products to store encryption keys on hardware or software modules. These products also provide a more secure key management solution because the encryption keys do not reside with encryption data. They also move the key management workload from SQL Server to a dedicated key management system.

Extensible key management in SQL Server 2008 also supports the use of Hardware Security Module, which enables the encryption keys used to protect your data to be stored in an off-box device such as a smartcard, USB device, or EKM/HSM module, providing a physical separation of keys from data. SQL Server 2008 Extensible Key Management enables third-party EKM/HSM vendors to register their modules in SQL Server. When registered, SQL Server users can use the encryption keys stored on EKM modules. This enables SQL Server to access the advanced encryption features these modules support such as bulk encryption and decryption, and key management functions such as key aging and key rotation.

SQL Server 2008 Extensible Key Management also provides data protection from database administrators. Data can be encrypted by using encryption keys that only the database user has access to on the external EKM/HSM module.

To summarize, SQL Server 2008 Extensible Key Management provides the following benefits:

- An additional authorization check that enables separation of duties between database administration and key management
- Improved performance through hardware-based encryption/decryption rather than software-based encryption/decryption
- External encryption key generation
- Physical separation of data and keys
- Encryption key retrieval
- External encryption key retention and encryption key rotation
- Easier encryption key recovery
- Manageable encryption key distribution
- Secure encryption key disposal

When possible, it is highly recommended that you use EKM with both database- and column-level encryption for more comprehensive key management and hardware-based cryptography.

Column-Level Encryption

Column-level encryption (sometimes referred to as cell-level encryption) was introduced in Microsoft SQL Server 2005 and is still fully supported in SQL Server 2008 R2. Column-level encryption offers a more granular level of encryption than TDE, allowing you to encrypt specific data columns in the context of specific users.

Column-level encryption is implemented as a series of built-in functions and a key management hierarchy. Implementing column-level encryption is a manual process that requires a re-architecture of the application to call the encryption and decryption functions explicitly when storing or retrieving data. In addition, the tables must be modified to store the encrypted data as `varbinary`. The data is then recast back to the appropriate data type when it is read.

Column-level encryption and decryption are provided by pairs of functions that complement each other:

- **`EncryptByCert()` and `DecryptByCert()`**—Encrypts and decrypts data using the public key of a certificate to generate a private asymmetric key
- **`EncryptByAsymKey()` and `DecryptByAsymKey()`**—Encrypts and decrypts data using an asymmetric key
- **`EncryptByKey()` and `DecryptByKey()`**—Encrypts and decrypts data by using a symmetric key
- **`EncryptByPassphrase()` and `DecryptByPassphrase()`**—Encrypts and decrypts data by using a passphrase to generate a symmetric key

Before you can begin generating keys to encrypt columns, you must first make sure a database master key has been created:

```
USE AdventureWorks2008R2;
GO

--If there is no master key, create one now.
IF NOT EXISTS
    (SELECT * FROM sys.symmetric_keys
            WHERE symmetric_key_id = 101)
    CREATE MASTER KEY ENCRYPTION
       BY PASSWORD = 'Th15i$aS7riN&ofR@nD0m!T3%t'
GO
```

NOTE

The examples in this chapter make use of the `AdventureWorks2008R2` database but can be run in the `AdventureWorks2008` database as well; however, there may be differences in the data values returned. For more information on downloading and installing the `AdventureWorks` databases, see the Introduction.

Encrypting Columns Using a Passphrase

As our first example, let's keep things simple and look at how to encrypt a column using a passphrase. To do so, let's look at the `Sales.CreditCard` table, which currently stores card numbers in cleartext:

```
select top 5 * from Sales.CreditCard
go

CreditCardID CardType       CardNumber     ExpMonth ExpYear ModifiedDate
------------ -------------- -------------- -------- ------- -----------
1            SuperiorCard   33332664695310 11       2006    2007-08-30
2            Distinguish    55552127249722 8        2005    2008-01-06
3            ColonialVoice  77778344838353 7        2005    2008-02-15
4            ColonialVoice  77774915718248 7        2006    2007-06-21
5            Vista          11114404600042 4        2005    2007-03-05
```

Credit card numbers really should not be stored in their cleartext form in the database, so to fix this, first create a copy of the `Sales.CreditCard` table and define the `CardNumber_encrypt` column as a `varbinary(256)` so you can store the encrypted credit card numbers in the column (encrypted columns in SQL Server 2008 can be stored only as `varbinary` values):

```
USE AdventureWorks2008R2;
GO

select CreditCardID,
       CardType,
       CardNumber_encrypt = CONVERT(varbinary(256), CardNumber),
       ExpMonth,
       ExpYear,
       ModifiedDate
into Sales.CreditCard_encrypt
from Sales.CreditCard
where 1 = 2
```

Now, you can populate the `CreditCard_encrypt` table with rows from the original `CreditCard` table using the `EncryptByPassPhrase` function to encrypt the credit card numbers as the rows are copied over:

```
declare @passphrase varchar(128)
set @passphrase = 'unencrypted credit card numbers are bad, um-kay'
insert Sales.CreditCard_encrypt (
       CardType,
       CardNumber_encrypt,
       ExpMonth,
       ExpYear,
```

```
        ModifiedDate
)
select top 5
        CardType,
        CardNumber_encrypt = EncryptByPassPhrase(@passphrase, CardNumber),
        ExpMonth,
        ExpYear,
        ModifiedDate
from Sales.CreditCard
```

Now, try a query against the `CreditCard_encrypt` table without decrypting the data and see what it returns (note, for display purposes, the values in the `CardNumber_encrypt` column have been truncated):

```
select * from Sales.CreditCard_encrypt
go

CreditCardID CardType      CardNumber_encrypt    ExpMonth ExpYear ModifiedDate
------------ ------------- --------------------- -------- ------- -----------
1            SuperiorCard  0x010000007C65089E... 11       2006    2007-08-30
2            Distinguish   0x010000000C624987... 8        2005    2008-01-06
3            ColonialVoice 0x01000000AA8761A0... 7        2005    2008-02-15
4            ColonialVoice 0x010000002C2857CC... 7        2006    2007-06-21
5            Vista         0x0100000095F6730D... 4        2005    2007-03-05
```

In the preceding results, you can see that the credit card numbers have been encrypted as a `varbinary` value, and no meaningful information can be obtained from this. To view the data in its unencrypted form, you need to use the `DecryptByPassPhrase` function and convert the value back to an `nvarchar(25)`:

```
declare @passphrase varchar(128)
set @passphrase = 'unencrypted credit card numbers are bad, um-kay'
select CreditCardID,
        CardType,
        CardNumber = convert(nvarchar(25), DecryptByPassPhrase(@passphrase,
  CardNumber_encrypt)),
        ExpMonth,
        ExpYear,
        ModifiedDate
from Sales.CreditCard_encrypt
GO
```

```
CreditCardID CardType        CardNumber     ExpMonth ExpYear ModifiedDate
------------ -------------- -------------- -------- -------------------
1            SuperiorCard   33332664695310 11       2006     2007-08-30
2            Distinguish    55552127249722 8        2005     2008-01-06
3            ColonialVoice  77778344838353 7        2005     2008-02-15
4            ColonialVoice  77774915718248 7        2006     2007-06-21
5            Vista          11114404600042 4        2005     2007-03-05
```

So that's a simple example showing how to encrypt a column. You may be thinking, however, using a passphrase like this probably isn't very secure. The passphrase used to encrypt the column would have to be shared with all users and applications that need to store or retrieve data in the CreditCard_encrypt table. A shared passphrase like this can be easily compromised, and then the data is visible to anyone who can gain access to the database. It is usually more secure to encrypt data using a symmetric key or certificate.

Encrypting Columns Using a Certificate

One solution to the problem of encrypting using a shared passphrase is to encrypt the data using a certificate. A primary benefit of certificates is that they relieve hosts of the need to maintain a set of passwords for individual subjects. Instead, the host merely establishes trust in a certificate issuer, which may then sign an unlimited number of certificates.

Certificates can be created within SQL Server 2008 using the CREATE CERTIFICATE command. The certificate created is a database-level securable that follows the X.509 standard and supports X.509 V1 fields. The CREATE CERTIFICATE command can load a certificate from a file or assembly, or it can also generate a key pair and create a self-signed certificate. The ENCRYPTION BY PASSWORD option is not required; the private key of the certificate is encrypted using the database master key. When the private key is encrypted using the database master key, you do not have to specify a decryption password when retrieving the data using the certificate.

The first step is to create the certificate with the CREATE CERTIFICATE command:

```
USE AdventureWorks2008R2;
CREATE CERTIFICATE BillingDept01
   WITH SUBJECT = 'Credit Card Billing'
GO
```

After you create the certificate, the next step is to create a symmetric key that will be encrypted by the certificate. You can use many different algorithms for encrypting keys. The supported encryption algorithms for the symmetric key are DES, TRIPLE_DES, RC2, RC4, RC4_128, DESX, AES_128, AES_192, and AES_256. The following code creates a symmetric key using the AES_256 encryption algorithm and encrypts it using the BillingDept01 certificate:

```
USE AdventureWorks2008R2;
CREATE SYMMETRIC KEY BillingKey2010 WITH ALGORITHM = AES_256
    ENCRYPTION BY CERTIFICATE BillingDept01;
GO
```

Now you empty out the rows inserted previously in the `CreditCard_encrypt` table using the `PassPhrase` encryption method by truncating it:

```
USE AdventureWorks2008R2;
Truncate table Sales.CreditCard_encrypt
```


Next reinsert rows from the `CreditCard` table, this time using the symmetric key associated with the certificate to encrypt the data using the `EncryptByKey` function. The `EncryptByKey` function requires the GUID of the symmetric key as the first parameter. You can look up this identifier by running a query against the `sys.symmetric_keys` table or simply use the `KEY_GUID()` function, as in this example:

```
USE AdventureWorks2008R2;
-- First, decrypt the key using the BillingDept01 certificate
OPEN SYMMETRIC KEY BillingKey2010
     DECRYPTION BY CERTIFICATE BillingDept01
-- Now, insert the rows using the symmetric key
-- encrypted by the certificate
insert Sales.CreditCard_encrypt (
       CardType,
       CardNumber_encrypt,
       ExpMonth,
       ExpYear,
       ModifiedDate
)
select top 5
       CardType,
       CardNumber_encrypt = EncryptByKey(KEY_GUID('BillingKey2010'),
                                         CardNumber),
       ExpMonth,
       ExpYear,
       ModifiedDate
from Sales.CreditCard
```

If you examine the contents of the `CreditCard_encrypt` table, you can see that they have been encrypted:

```
select * from Sales.CreditCard_encrypt
go

CreditCardID CardType     CardNumber_encrypt     ExpMonth ExpYear ModifiedDate
------------ ------------ -------------------- -------- ------- -----------
1            SuperiorCard 0x0046C380E7A27749... 11       2006    2007-08-30
2            Distinguish  0x0046C380E7A27749... 8        2005    2008-01-06
```

```
3           ColonialVoice 0x0046C380E7A27749... 7          2005     2008-02-15
4           ColonialVoice 0x0046C380E7A27749... 7          2006     2007-06-21
5           Vista         0x0046C380E7A27749... 4          2005     2007-03-05
```

Now, an authorized user that specifies the appropriate certificate can retrieve the data by using `DecryptByKey` function:

```
USE AdventureWorks2008R2;
OPEN SYMMETRIC KEY BillingKey2010
     DECRYPTION BY CERTIFICATE BillingDept01
select CardType,
       CardNumber = convert(nvarchar(25), DecryptByKey(CardNumber_encrypt)),
       ExpMonth,
       ExpYear,
       ModifiedDate
from Sales.CreditCard_encrypt
go

CreditCardID CardType      CardNumber     ExpMonth ExpYear ModifiedDate
------------ ------------- -------------- -------- ------- ----------
1            SuperiorCard  33332664695310 11       2006    2007-08-30
2            Distinguish   55552127249722 8        2005    2008-01-06
3            ColonialVoice 77778344838353 7        2005    2008-02-15
4            ColonialVoice 77774915718248 7        2006    2007-06-21
5            Vista         11114404600042 4        2005    2007-03-05
```

When you are done using a key, it is good practice to close the key using the `CLOSE SYMMETRIC KEY` statement:

```
CLOSE SYMMETRIC KEY BillingKey2010
```

The keys defined in a database can be viewed through the system catalog table, `sys.symmetric_keys`:

```
select name,
       pvt_key_encryption_type,
       issuer_name,
       subject,
       expiry_date = CAST(expiry_date as DATE),
       start_date = CAST(start_date as DATE)
  from sys.certificates
go

name         pvt_key_encryption_type issuer_name
subject              expiry_date start_date
------------ -------------------- ------------------
------------------ ----------- ----------
```

```
BillingDept01 MK                    Credit Card Billing
Credit Card Billing 2011-05-01  2010-05-01
```

The certificates defined in a database can be viewed through the system catalog tables, `sys.certificates`:

```
select name,
       key_length,
       key_algorithm,
       algorithm_desc,
       create_date = CAST(create_date as DATE),
       modify_date = CAST(create_date as DATE),
       key_guid
    from sys.symmetric_keys
go

name                     key_length  key_algorithm algorithm_desc
create_date modify_date key_guid
------------------------ ----------- ------------- -------------
----------- ----------- ------------------------------------
##MS_DatabaseMasterKey## 128         D3            TRIPLE_DES
2010-04-30  2010-04-30  A3550B00-6BAE-41E2-A1BC-D784DC35779E
BillingKey2010           256         A3            AES_256
2010-04-30  2010-04-30  10C5C800-0B4C-44C2-9F71-5415007C2E81
```

If the usage of the key and certificate are no longer needed, they should be dropped from the database:

```
DROP SYMMETRIC KEY BillingKey2010
DROP CERTIFICATE BillingDept01
```

NOTE

There is a lot more information about column-level encryption and key management that could be discussed at this point, but such discussion would be beyond the scope of this chapter; our intent here is to merely introduce the concepts of data encryption. For more information on column-level encryption, refer to SQL Server 2008 Books Online.

Transparent Data Encryption

As mentioned previously, transparent data encryption (TDE) is a new feature introduced in SQL Server 2008 that allows an entire database to be encrypted. Unlike column-level encryption, in TDE the encryption and decryption of data is performed automatically by the Database Engine, and this is fully transparent to the end user and applications. No changes to the database or applications are needed. Consequently, TDE is the simpler choice when bulk encryption of data is required to meet regulatory compliance or corporate data security standards.

The encryption of a database using TDE helps prevent the unauthorized access of data in the scenario in which physical media or backups have been lost or stolen. Transparent data encryption uses a database encryption key (DEK) for encrypting the database. The DEK is stored in the database boot record and is secured by a certificate stored in the master database. The database master key is protected by the service master key, which is in turn protected by the Data Protection API. When TDE is enabled on a database, attaching data files to another SQL Server instance or the restoring of a backup to another SQL Server instance is not permitted until the certificate that was used to secure the DEK is available.

NOTE

Optionally, the DEK can be secured by an asymmetric key that resides in a Hardware Security Module with the support of Extensible Key Management. The private key of the certificate is encrypted with the database master key that is a symmetric key, which is usually protected with a strong password.

For example, if a hard drive that contains database files is stolen, without TDE, those database files can be attached in another SQL Server instance, thus allowing access to the nonencrypted data in those files. With TDE, the data and log files are automatically encrypted, and the data within these files cannot be accessed without an encryption key. Additionally, backups of databases that have TDE enabled are also encrypted automatically. We're all familiar with stories about how backup tapes containing sensitive information have been lost or stolen. With TDE, the data in the backup files is completely useless without also having access to the key used to encrypt that data.

The encryption and decryption of data with TDE are performed at the page level as data moves between the buffer pool and disk. Data residing in the buffer pools is not encrypted. TDE's specific purpose is to protect data at rest by encrypting the physical files of the database, rather than the data itself. These physical files include the database file (`.mdf`), transaction log file (`.ldf`), and backup files (`.bak`). Data pages are encrypted as they are written from the buffer pool to the database files on disk. Conversely, the data is decrypted at the page level when the data is read in from the files on disk into the buffer pool. The encryption and decryption are done using a background process transparent to the database user. Although additional CPU resources are required to implement TDE, overall, this approach offers much better performance than column-level encryption. According to Microsoft, the performance hit averages only about 3–5%.

TDE supports several different encryption options, such as AES with 128-bit, 192-bit, or 256-bit keys or 3 Key Triple DES. You make your choice when implementing TDE.

Implementing Transparent Data Encryption

Like many encryption scenarios, TDE is dependent on an encryption key. The TDE database encryption key is a symmetric key that secures the encrypted database. The DEK is protected using a certificate stored in the `master` database of the SQL Server instance where the encrypted database is installed.

Implementing TDE for a specific database is accomplished by following these steps:

- Create a master key.
- Create or obtain a certificate protected by the master key.
- Create a database encryption key and protect it by the certificate.
- Configure the database to use encryption.

Listing 12.1 demonstrates the commands needed to encrypt the `AdventureWorks2008R2` database, including the creation of a master key, certificate, and DEK protected by the certificate.

LISTING 12.1 Encrypting the **AdventureWorks2008R2** Database

```
USE master;
GO

--Create the master key which is stored in the master database
CREATE MASTER KEY ENCRYPTION BY PASSWORD = 'mystrongpassword$$';
GO

-- Create a certificate that is also stored in the master
-- database. This certificate will be used to encrypt a user database
CREATE CERTIFICATE MyCertificate
 with SUBJECT = 'Certificate stored in Master Db'
GO

-- Create a Database Encryption Key (DEK) that is based
-- on the previously created certificate
-- The DEK is stored in the user database
USE AdventureWorks2008R2
GO
CREATE DATABASE ENCRYPTION KEY
WITH ALGORITHM = AES_256
ENCRYPTION BY SERVER CERTIFICATE MyCertificate
GO
```

```
-- Turn the encryption on for the AdventureWorks2008R2
ALTER DATABASE AdventureWorks2008R2
SET ENCRYPTION ON
 GO
```

After you enable TDE, you might want to monitor the progress of the encryption. This can be done by running the following query:

```
SELECT DBName = DB_NAME(database_id), encryption_state
FROM sys.dm_database_encryption_keys ;
GO

DBName               encryption_state
-------------------- ----------------
tempdb               3
AdventureWorks2008R2 3
```

This query returns the database encryption state. A database encryption state of 2 means that encryption has begun, and an encryption state of 3 indicates that encryption has completed. When the `tempdb` database and `user` database you are encrypting reach a state of 3, the entire `user` database and `tempdb` database are encrypted.

When TDE is enabled for a given database, encryption is applied to a variety of files related to the database, including the following:

- **Database Data Files**—All data files that contain the database data are encrypted. These files typically have the extension `.mdf` or `.ndf`.
- **Database Log Files**—The transaction log files are encrypted so that no clear text is visible in the files. These files typically have the extension `.ldf`.
- **Database Backups**—All database backups, including full, differential, and log, are encrypted.
- **`Tempdb`**—If any databases on a server are encrypted with TDE, the `tempdb` database is also encrypted.

In addition to these files, you can also manually enable TDE on the distribution and subscriber database involved in replication. This encrypts a portion of data involved in replication, but there are still some unencrypted files. Snapshots from snapshot replication as well as the initial distribution of data for transactional and merge replication are not encrypted.

Managing TDE in SSMS

You can also view and manage transparent data encryption in SQL Server Management Studio. To do so, right-click on the database in the Object Explorer for which you want to configure TDE and select Tasks; then select Manage Database Encryption. If you are setting up the initial configuration for TDE in a database, you see a dialog like that shown in Figure 12.2.

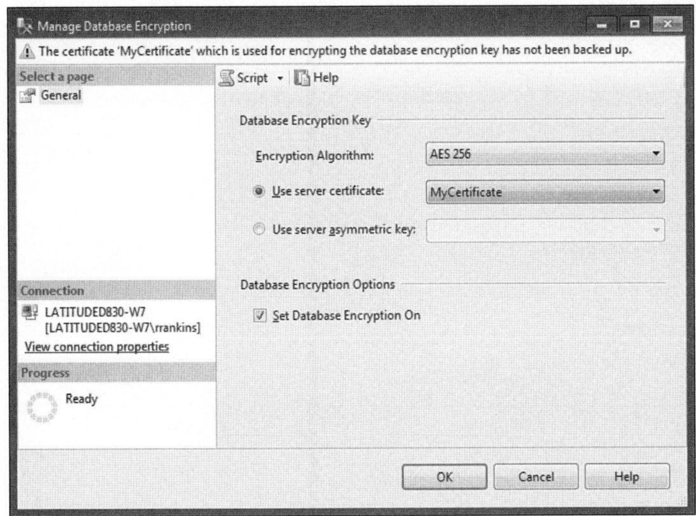

FIGURE 12.2 Enabling TDE in SSMS.

The options available in this dialog correspond to commands shown in Listing 12.1. You specify the encryption algorithm to be used and the server certificate used to protect the database encryption key. When you are ready to enable TDE for the database, put a check mark in the Set Database Encryption On check box.

If TDE is already enabled for a database, the dialog changes to provide you with options to re-encrypt the database encryption key and to regenerate the DEK using a different encryption algorithm. You can also enable/disable database encryption (see Figure 12.3). A second page displays the current TDE properties and encryption state of the database (see Figure 12.4).

Backing Up TDE Certificates and Keys

The most important issue to consider when using TDE is that you must back up and retain the certificate and private key associated with the encryption. If these things are lost or unavailable, you are not able to restore or attach the encrypted database files on another server. The following warning message displayed after creating a certificate drives home this point:

```
Warning: The certificate used for encrypting the database
encryption key has not been backed up. You should immediately
back up the certificate and the private key associated with the
certificate. If the certificate ever becomes unavailable or if you
must restore or attach the database on another server, you must have
backups of both the certificate and the private key or you will not
be able to open the database.
Backup up the certificate and private key
```

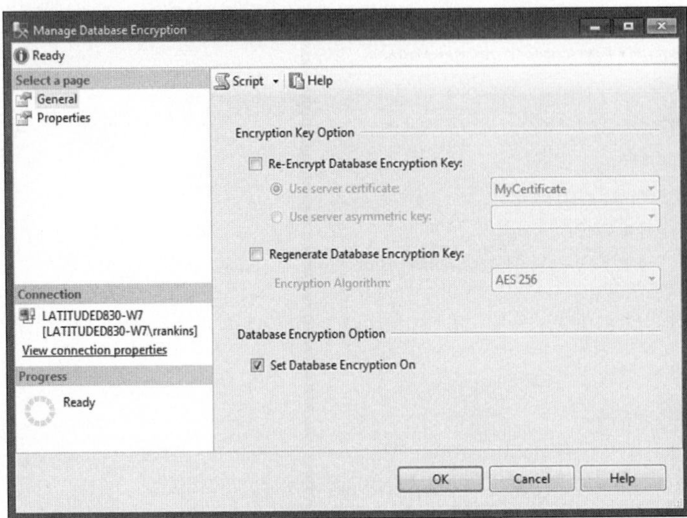

FIGURE 12.3 Modifying TDE properties in SSMS.

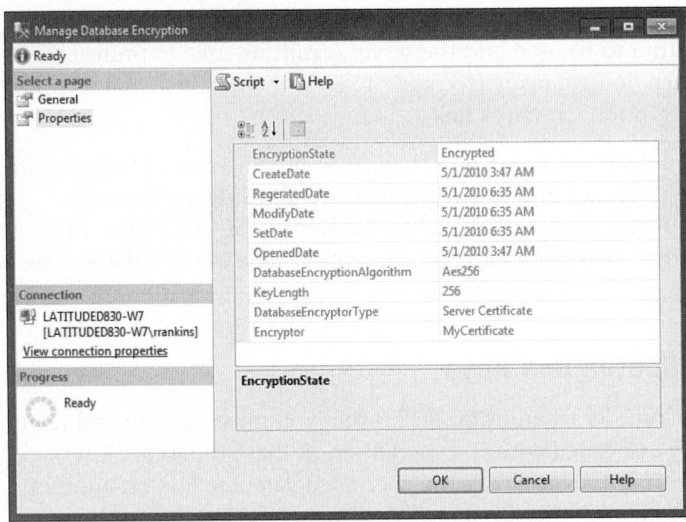

FIGURE 12.4 Viewing TDE properties in SSMS.

Backing up the certificate, private key, and master key for the server is relatively straightforward. An example of backing up the master key is shown in the following SQL statement:

```
BACKUP MASTER KEY TO FILE = 'c:\mssql2008\backup\masterkey'
    ENCRYPTION BY PASSWORD = 'somekeybackuppassword$$'
```

Backing up the certificate and associated private key also uses the BACKUP command. The following example backs up the certificate created in Listing 12.1:

```
BACKUP CERTIFICATE MyCertificate TO FILE = 'c:\mssql2008\backup\MyCertificate'
    WITH PRIVATE KEY ( FILE = 'c:\mssql2008\backup\MyCertificatePrivateKey' ,
    ENCRYPTION BY PASSWORD = 'somecertbackuppassword$$' )
```


If you want to restore a database backup on another server instance, a master key for the server must exist. If one does not exist, you can create one by using the CREATE MASTER KEY ENCRYPTION syntax. After creating the master key, you are able to create the TDE certificate from a backup of the certificate from the original SQL Server instance, as shown in the following example:

```
CREATE CERTIFICATE MyCertificate
     FROM FILE = 'c:\mssql2008\backup\MyCertificate'
     WITH PRIVATE KEY (FILE = 'c:\mssql2008\backup\MyCertificatePrivateKey',
     DECRYPTION BY PASSWORD = 'somecertbackuppassword$$')
```

After the certificate is restored on the other server instance, you can restore the encrypted database backup. At this point, the restore can be performed just as you would restore any unencrypted database backup. The restored database is also encrypted and behaves like the original TDE database.

TDE is a relatively simple and effective way to encrypt and protect your data. Other encryption methods that exist with SQL Server can protect different elements of your database. Encryption can be applied to columns of data, an entire table, as well as the communication that occurs between databases and the clients that access them. The level of encryption and need to use it depend on the type of data you are securing.

Limitations of TDE

Although TDE offers many benefits over column-level encryption, it has some of its own limitations, which are important to consider. They include

- TDE is not granular like column-level encryption. The entire database is encrypted, but only on disk. Sensitive data such as Social Security numbers or credit card numbers can be seen by anyone who has permission to access those columns. TDE also does not prevent DBAs from viewing any data in the database.
- TDE does not protect communications between client applications and SQL Server. Network encryption methods should be used to protect sensitive data flowing over the network.
- FILESTREAM data is not encrypted.
- When any one database on a SQL Server instance has TDE enabled, the tempdb database is also automatically encrypted. This can affect performance for both encrypted and nonencrypted databases running on the same instance.

- Databases encrypted with TDE can't take advantage of SQL Server 2008's new backup compression. If you want to take advantage of both backup compression and encryption, you have to use a third-party application, such as Idera's SQL Safe Backup or Redgate's SQL Backup, which both have the capability to both compress and encrypt backups.

Column-Level Encryption Versus Transparent Data Encryption

So is column-level encryption or transparent data encryption the right solution for your systems? Both column-level encryption and transparent data encryption provide a means of obfuscating sensitive data to protect it from unauthorized access. However, they do so in different ways.

TDE prevents the unauthorized access of the contents of the database files and backups, but does not protect sensitive data within the database from being viewed by authorized users or database administrators. Column-level encryption provides more granular control over the data being encrypted but is not transparent to your applications.

Table 12.1 lists the similarities and differences between column-level encryption and TDE.

TABLE 12.1 Comparison of Column-Level Encryption and Transparent Data Encryption

Features/Limitations	Column-Level Encryption	Transparent Data Encryption
Data is encrypted on disk and backups	Yes	Yes
Supports HSMs	Yes	Yes
Data level of encryption	Granular, at the column level	Encrypts the entire database only
User level of encryption	Encrypted data can be restricted at the user level on a need-to-know basis	Any user with sufficient database permissions can view encrypted data
Impact on applications	Database applications need to be modified	Completely transparent to applications and end users
Indexing of encrypted data	Encrypted columns cannot be indexed	No restrictions on indexes
Performance impact	May be significant depending on the type of encryption key used	Small impact on performance (3–5%)

For some organizations, you might want to consider implementing both column-level encryption along with TDE for a database. Although this combination is more complex to set up and administer, it offers greater security and encryption granularity than does either method used alone. TDE protects the database files and backups from unauthorized access, whereas column-level encryption protects sensitive data within the database from being accessed by authorized users, including DBAs. Implementing TDE in conjunction with cell-level encryption provides a layered approach to data security, which enhances its effectiveness.

The main disadvantage to implementing column-level encryption is that it isn't transparent to the end-user applications. In addition to requiring changes to the database schema, it also requires changes in the applications to include the proper function calls to encrypt and decrypt the data as it is stored and retrieved. Another issue with column-level encryption is that you cannot index encrypted columns, nor can you generate statistics on the encrypted columns. This can affect query performance because search arguments that reference encrypted columns cannot be optimized. For this reason, typically only the most sensitive columns of a table that do not need to be indexed are encrypted.

Summary

Chapter 11, "Security and User Administration," discusses methods to secure and control the access to your SQL Server data via login and user security to prevent unauthorized users from accessing your SQL Server instances and databases. Column-level encryption, as discussed here, takes these protections a step further by preventing authorized users, such as your database or server administrators, from viewing sensitive data within a database. Transparent data encryption protects all your data from being accessed by unauthorized users in the event that your database files or backups are lost or stolen.

Chapter 13, "Security and Compliance," discusses security methods available in SQL Server and how they can be implemented to meet your security compliance requirements. It also covers the new data auditing methods you can use to track changes to your data and database objects.

CHAPTER 13

Security and Compliance

IN THIS CHAPTER

- Exposure and Risk
- Across the Life Cycle
- The Security Big Picture
- Identity Access Management Components
- Compliance and SQL Server
- SQL Server Auditing
- Setting Up Auditing via T-SQL
- SQL Injection Is Easy to Do

As you complete what you think is your best database design and application on the planet, you stop yourself dead in your tracks and say, with hesitation, "What about the security and compliance implications?" Now is not the time to start thinking about these aspects. In fact, as we show you in this chapter, you should start considering these issues from the beginning of the development life cycle.

With the growth of software and database development in the world, there is a rise in the demand for security best practices to achieve the goals of creating secure software. Best practices must start from the glass and reach through the application, to the database layer, and even to the operating system and the physical file levels. Best practices are also meant to be scrutinized for overall results on the basis of the level of security, efficiency, and complexity they provide. How much and which best practice to use can also be considered on the basis of confidentiality, integrity, and availability (which is known as *CIA*). Software security must be considered at many layers and is additive in nature—each layer providing the necessary security and compliance of one part of the bigger puzzle. To get it right, you must "design in" security from the beginning.

In this chapter we discuss security aspects in conjunction with a traditional development life cycle; this includes aspects such as vulnerability assessments, threat modeling, and identity management. You can take many steps to prevent *SQL injection*, for example, and other vulnerabilities. We also talk about compliance aspects in regards to global and regional regulations such as the Health Insurance Portability and Accountability Act (also known as HIPAA), the Payment Card Industry (PCI) standards, and data privacy regulations such as Personally Identifiable Information (PII).

We also provide a simple example of using the SQL Server Auditing feature that can be extremely useful in identifying and monitoring compliance of access and usage at the SQL Server database or object levels. And lastly, we show you how to do some malicious damage with SQL injection. We show you how to do this so that you can learn how to prevent it. But first, let's try to better understand what exposure and risk are all about.

Exposure and Risk

You must understand that security is really "risk management" or "risk mitigation." It can be very difficult to completely secure an application or environment. However, you are able to control or limit damage by following certain practices. Your data and applications have different levels of security requirements depending on the exposure endpoints (an *exposure endpoint* is defined by who is using the application and data). Figure 13.1 shows a simple matrix of data and application sensitivity versus the exposure endpoints of that application. By definition, the more external facing your application is (such as to the Internet) and the higher the sensitivity of the data involved, the higher risk precautions you have to take.

Exposure End Points

Data/Application	Limited Exposure (Internal/Intranet Only)	Exposable (External Internet)
Low Sensitivity (Public)	Low Risk	Medium Risk
Medium Sensitivity (Confidential)	Medium Risk	High Risk
High Sensitivity (Highly Confidential)	High Risk	High Risk

FIGURE 13.1 The exposure endpoints "risk" by category of data/application sensitivity.

Let's say you have an internal company SQL Server–based application that has only very low sensitivity data (public-facing data such as benefits data). You freely share this type of data with whoever wants to see it. The types of controls or rigor are likely very small for this type of application—perhaps as simple as an integrated Active Directory with your SQL Server and read-only access for all user roles.

On the other side of the spectrum, you may have applications generating financial transactions with credit card data that must have zero vulnerabilities, encrypt data across the network, encrypt data at rest within SQL Server, and use the new SQL auditing feature for database-level monitoring of all data accesses.

A big part of the risk management aspect is understanding what the impact of this risk would be if your system is compromised. It is always best to identify this aspect up front in some type of risk "cost" or "impact." Many financially strong companies have gone out of business as a result of security breaches they had not anticipated or considered. It is better to plan for such risk from the beginning.

Another aspect to consider is staying compliant with data you use in nonproduction environments. Often, companies needlessly put their entire livelihood at risk by using live data values in nonproduction environments. If PII or other company-sensitive data is available in your nonproduction environments (such as in Development, Test, and Quality Assurance platforms), you are violating laws and regulations around the globe and putting your company and your customers at risk. You can easily employ data subsetting and masking to your nonproduction data. Putting this practice in place is a great idea.

Across the Life Cycle

We introduce formal development life-cycle concepts in other chapters. In those chapters, such as Chapter 41, "A Performance and Tuning Methodology," the emphasis is on designing in performance from the beginning. A part of good design is how you have complied with laws and regulations, how you have protected the data you access or store, how you have secured your application and data, and how you have verified all this. For these reasons, we provide some details and describe what must be done across the development life cycle to properly address security and compliance. We term this process the "risk mitigation" of what you build.

Figure 13.2 shows a formal waterfall development life cycle with key security and compliance items identified at each relevant phase. Getting into the risk mitigation business starts by giving security and compliance the full commitment and recognition they deserve.

This step starts with a clear statement of security and compliance objectives as you are sizing up your application in the assessment phase. These objectives often take the form of stating how you will address the rules, laws, data sensitivities, access considerations, and eventual end users (and the countries they reside in).

Next, you focus on the clear identification and specification of all security and scope of compliance. You look at the details of exactly where the compliance or security lines need to be, determine how you must fully address them, and clearly identify which must be adhered to for your application. Often, organizations have security information analysts and data privacy groups that contribute to this part of your development efforts. They, in turn, bring others to the table, such as legal, auditing, and even corporate communications folks.

As you go into the design phase, you must complete the full analysis and design of every security and compliance element for your application. As part of this analysis and design phase, you should start enumeration test plans that must be completely verified before your application can be delivered to its users.

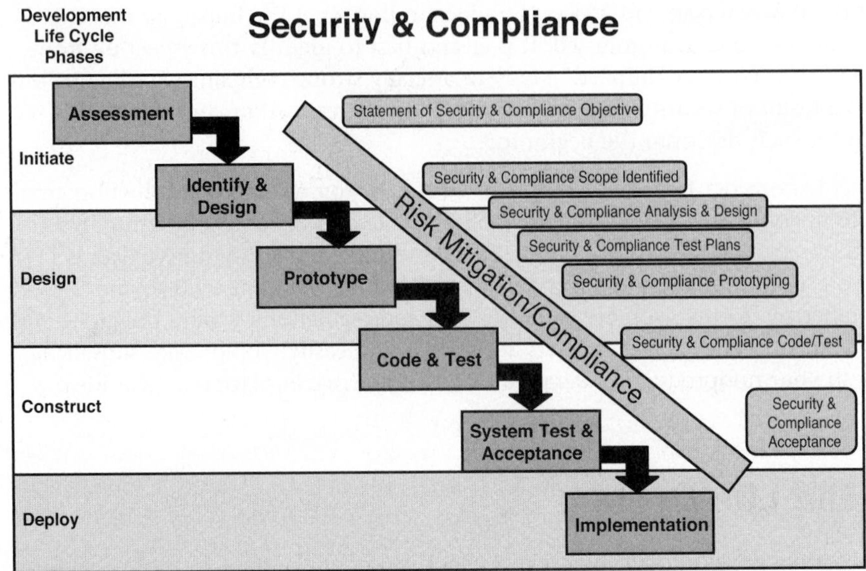

FIGURE 13.2 Security and compliance across the development life cycle.

In the prototyping phase, you have a chance to start demonstrating how security, access, privacy, and compliance will be addressed. This phase is very important because of all the complications, rules, laws, and issues that are at stake and must be verified. We have not run a development effort without extensive prototyping of as many security and compliance tests as are humanly possible. It is this risk that must be fully addressed early and never as an afterthought!

As you fully code and test your database and application, you must never skip the security testing and validation. It is best to put these tests *first* in your overall test plans. As your application completely takes shape, a complete application scan for vulnerabilities can be performed. Popular tools such as AppScan are essential tools of the trade for performing this task.

Finally, as you near deployment, you should make sure all the security and compliance acceptance tests are met. You need to capture these results fully because the successful completion of this part of acceptance testing can be shown in SOX compliance auditing.

The Security Big Picture

Now, let's turn to the bigger security and compliance picture that shows many of the layers involved in a broader security enforcement approach. Figure 13.3 shows many of these layers, starting at the top with solid guidelines, policies, and compliance-reporting capabilities. You must start with these components to guarantee that you are aware of what must be done and have a way to show you are doing what the policies outline.

Next, you must define and create other aspects of security and compliance, such as security event management, alerting and monitoring, complete threat models, and vulnerability

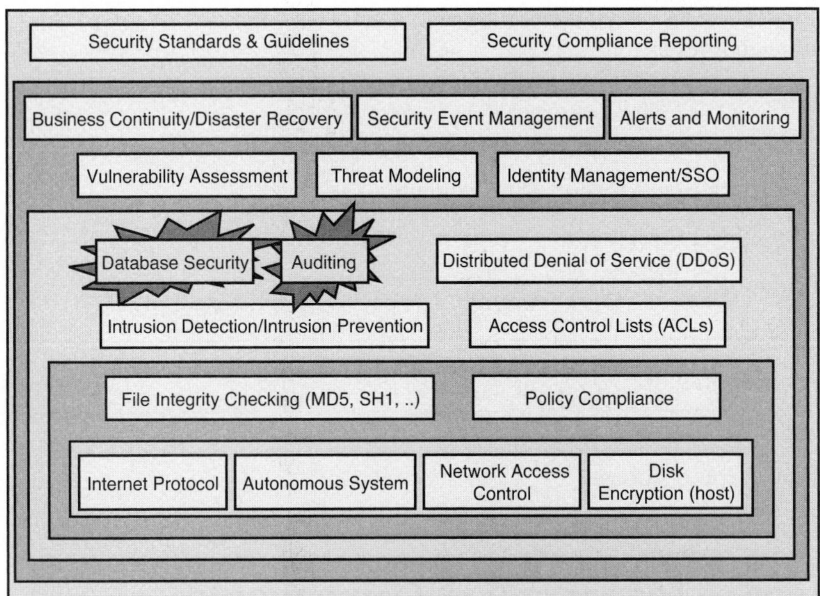

FIGURE 13.3 Security enforcement layers and components.

assessment objectives. These types of components must also reach into and be enforceable across major events such as disaster recovery (to ensure business continuity) and continue to support what you have deployed around identity management and single sign-on.

The next inner layer is where your database security is defined, along with any database-level or database instance–level auditing you put into place. It is also this layer where messy things such as SQL injection can occur and Denial of Service often surfaces. Getting some type of intrusion detection and prevention scheme into place is essential. Clear access controls are also essential. Later in this chapter, we describe some basic SQL Server–based auditing at the database level. Chapters 11, "Security and User Administration," and 12, "Data Security," also describe much of what you must do around overall security administration and database-level security. Figure 13.3 highlights these two critical areas.

Moving further down the layers of security, you find file integrity checking, secure Internet protocols, disk-level encryption, and other security-enhancing items. They all work together to bring you what should be a more secure (and compliant) place to deploy your applications within.

With SQL Server 2008 R2, you are essentially out-of-the-box ready to do absolutely *nothing*. In other words, Microsoft has taken the policy to "allow nothing," and any access, execution, or other action must be explicitly granted. Believe it or not, this is the right thing to do. This approach ensures that all objects and accesses are explicitly declared and, by definition, are fulfilling security and many compliance regulations.

The Open Web Application Security Project (OWASP; www.owasp.org) lists its recent top 10 application vulnerabilities as follows:

- SQL Injection
- Cross-Site Scripting
- Broken Authentication and Session Management
- Insecure Direct Object References
- Cross-Site Request Forgery
- Security Misconfiguration
- Failure to Restrict URLs
- Unvalidated Redirects and Forwards
- Insecure Cryptographic Storage
- Insufficient Transport Layer Protection

Identity Access Management Components

One of the key areas identified in the security big picture (as you can see looking back at Figure 13.3) is identity management. It is key in the sense that well-managed identities are essential to well-managed security. There is a quite a bit to consider when talking about identities. Figure 13.4 shows a common "identity universe" for a company that has both internal- and external-facing applications. In other words, identities are both customers that interact with the business and internal identities such as employees and other workforce identities (contractors, temps, partners, and so on). Both sets of identities must be managed well, and often there are overlapping identities that require accesses (and identity management) in both areas (internal and external).

Often, companies use one internal-facing LDAP directory such as Microsoft's Active Directory for managing their internal identities and then another LDAP directory such as Sun One LDAP for managing all external-facing identities (for forums, eStore, and so on). Then they create triggers or synchronization jobs that do a "search before create" type of processing when new identities are created within either LDAP directory. Because overlap is rare, not much extra "create" overhead occurs, but when they do overlap, only one identity (such as a partner identity that might be in that company's internal and external LDAP directories) gets created. This is effectively "mastering" the user identities. It is recommended that you consider both sources of identities at all times. You should also establish strict access roles for all identities with the least rights going to anonymous identities.

More and more companies are also now moving to concepts such as Open ID, where a company can utilize the authentication and identification established by third-party Open ID providers and grant trust to these identities with very high confidence. The industry is moving this way fast. Figure 13.5 shows the logical components of identity access management.

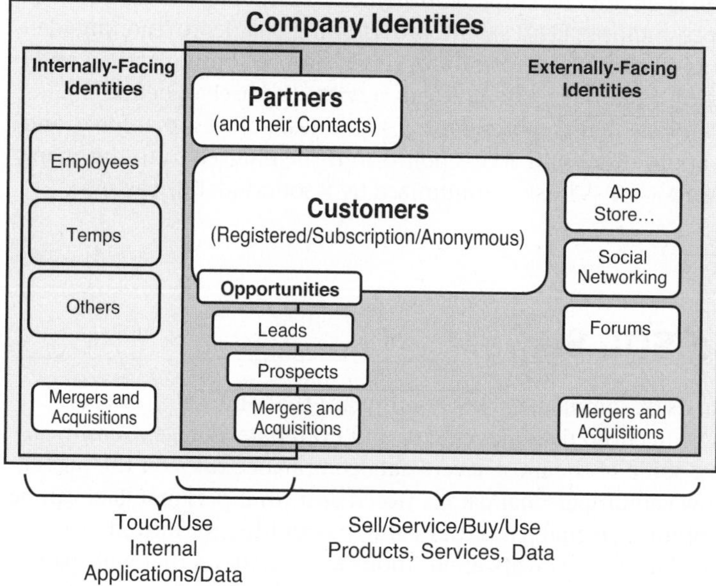

FIGURE 13.4 Identity universes (internal and external-facing applications).

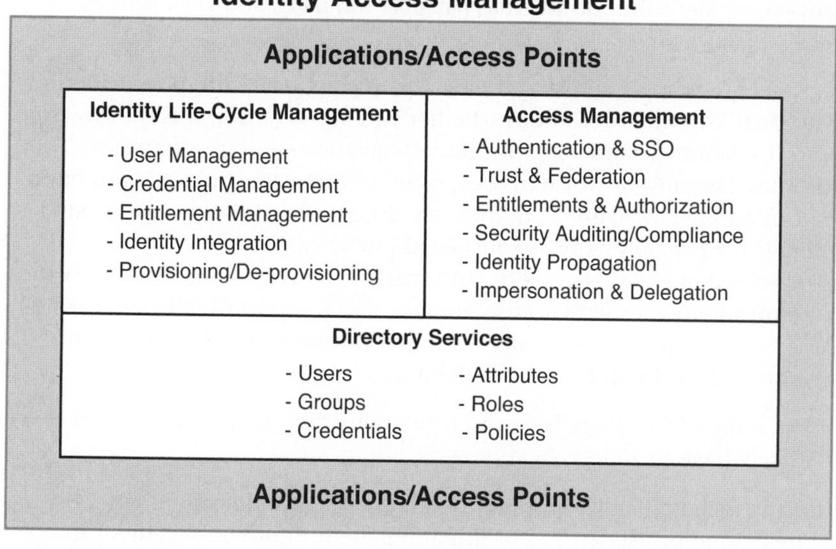

FIGURE 13.5 Logical components of identity access management.

13

This figure shows that you must carefully address full identity life-cycle management, which includes user ID management, credential management, entitlement management, identity integration (between multiple LDAPs), and provisioning *and* deprovisioning identities. Access management is all about authentication, single sign-on, authorization, and impersonation and delegation rules. And, the directory services themselves define the users, groups, all attributes (or elements) of a user or group, roles, policies to enforce, and credentials to be used. All applications and access points must be plugged in to this identity access management framework. All risk is minimized by a sound identity access management foundation.

Compliance and SQL Server

On the global level, hundreds of compliance laws are in place that affect almost every aspect of data access, data protection, data movement, and even data storage. Countries such as Germany now have some of the most severe data compliance rules on the planet, such as strict control of how certain personal data is stored and what personal data can be stored; these rules even prohibit personal data from being transmitted (or moved) across German borders. If you are planning to create applications and databases that will span countries or contain sensitive or private data, you must "design in" the rules and enforcements from the beginning (as we have been stressing throughout this chapter).

Let's address the most common "sensitive" data: Personal Identifiable Information (or PII for short). PII data is at the center of most global data privacy laws and regulations. As you can see from a subset of the PII data model in Figure 13.6, PII data is any personal information that identifies an individual, such as name; address; driver's license number; other government-issued identification (such as passport number); and even gender, ethnicity, and age.

If you have any databases or applications that have this type of data in it, you are bound by local and/or regional laws and regulations whether you like it or not. It is the law. You must then protect this data in accordance with those regulations and laws; otherwise, you become liable for fines, lawsuits, or worse (risk exposure of that data could put you out of business). As you can also see in Figure 13.6, there are different sensitivity levels around PII data. Something like a person's name is considered low sensitivity, whereas an employee ID is considered medium sensitivity. And marital status, gender, Social Security number, bank account number, driver's license number, and passport number are considered high sensitivity and often must be treated with special care and feeding with capabilities such as encryption in transit and at rest (while stored in a table).

Following is a list of some of the many laws and regulations that have been put into effect and that you will likely have to address in your application:

- The Health Insurance Portability and Accountability Act (also known as HIPAA) was introduced in 1996 to protect critical health and patient information. HIPAA forces companies to strictly control data identified under its jurisdiction.

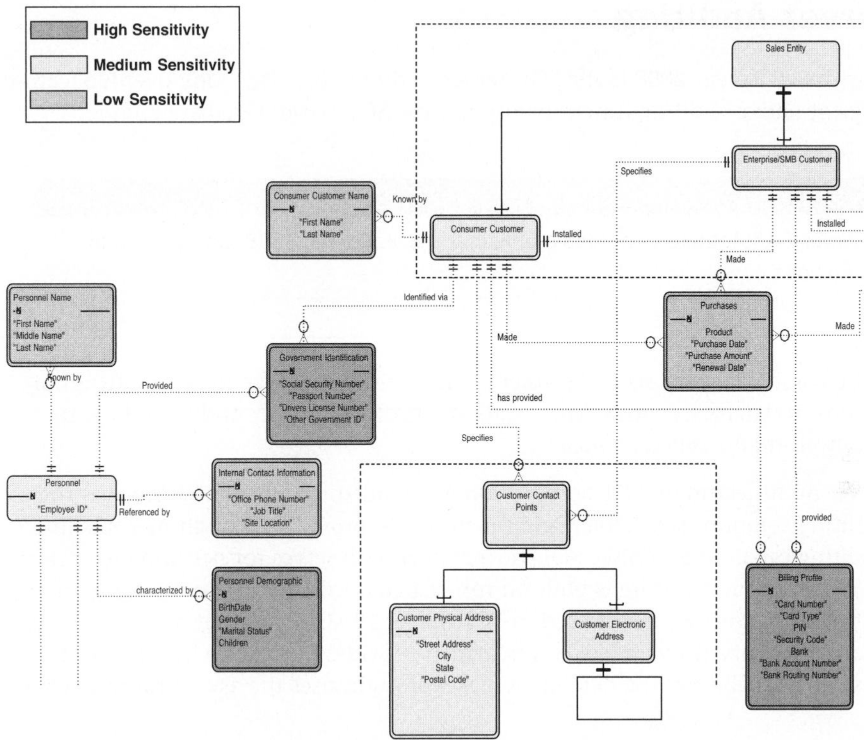

FIGURE 13.6 Personally Identifiable Information (PII).

- The Sarbanes-Oxley Act (known as SOX), put into place in 2002, requires auditors to assess and report on the effectiveness of a company's internal controls on information and extend into the authorization of access and updates to data.
- The Gramm-Leach-Bliley Act (GLBA) of 1999 further defines steps that must be taken by financial institutions to protect, secure, and prevent access of core financial data.
- California's Information Practices Act of 2005 details strict controls around PII data, what needs to be encrypted, and laws surrounding breaches of controlled data.
- The Children's Online Privacy Protection Act, passed in 1998, focuses on the procedures to protect the confidentiality, security, and integrity of personal information collected from children.

Other industry-oriented laws and regulations have emerged, such as the Payment Card Industry data security standard (PCI standard). It is focused on what must be done to ensure credit card information is secure from the moment a customer makes a purchase until the merchant disposes of the credit card transactions.

Two great books on security and compliance are *Cryptography in the Database* by Kevin Kenan (2006, Addison-Wesley) and *The Executive Guide to Information Security* by Mark Egan (2005, Addison-Wesley). These books will make great focused additions to your technology library.

SQL Server Auditing

Introduced with SQL Server 2008 is the SQL Server Audit feature. This long-overdue feature now adds a great native auditing functionality into the SQL Server Database Engine.

NOTE

The SQL Server Audit feature is available only in the SQL Server 2008 Enterprise and Developer Editions.

An *audit* is the combination of several elements into a single package for a specific group of server actions or database actions. The components of SQL Server Audit combine to produce an output that is called an *audit*.

The SQL Server Audit feature in SQL Server 2008 is intended to replace SQL Trace as the preferred auditing solution. SQL Server Audit is meant to provide full auditing capabilities, and only auditing capabilities, unlike SQL Trace, which also serves for performance debugging. The SQL Server Audit feature is built on top of Extended Events, a new high-performance eventing infrastructure introduced in SQL Server 2008. SQL Server Audit leverages the performance benefits of Extended Events, which provides both asynchronous and synchronous write capabilities (by default, SQL Server Audit uses the asynchronous eventing model).

NOTE

By default, the audit events are written to the audit target in an asynchronous fashion for performance reasons. When tighter guarantees of audit records being written to the audit log are required, you can select synchronous write, with the understanding that some amount of performance degradation should be expected. The choice of asynchronous or synchronous is controlled by the `QUEUE_DELAY` option of the `CREATE AUDIT DDL`.

SQL Server Audit is also tightly integrated with the Windows operating systems and can push (write) its audits to the Windows Application or Security Event Log. With SQL Server Auditing, you can set up auditing of just about any event or execution within SQL Server, and it can be as granular as you need (right down to a table and operation level). This capability is important because not only can you track all these events, but you can use this auditing capability to fulfill application and database audit compliance and look for patterns of misuse, or even specific "hot" objects that contain the most sensitive data in your database.

As you can see in Figure 13.7, a branch under each database called `Security` contains several of the common security-related nodes that you've seen before (`Users`, `Roles`, `Schemas`, and so on). But now, there is a `Database Audit Specifications` branch from which you can set up and view the database audit specifications you have defined. You can have as many specifications as you want, and again, they can be at varying levels of granularity.

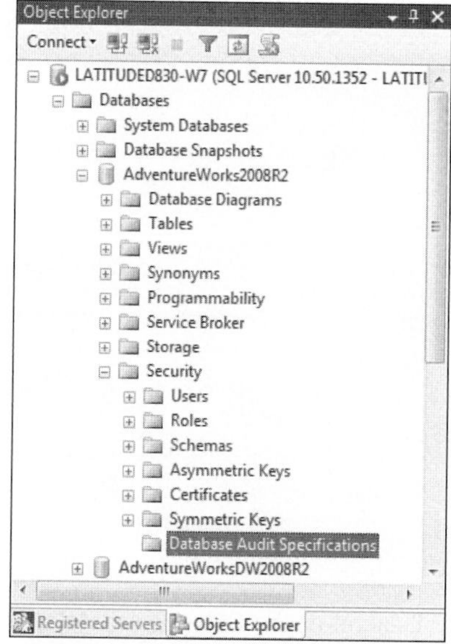

FIGURE 13.7 The new `Database Audit Specifications` item in the SQL Server Management Studio (SSMS) Object Explorer.

Before you can set up a Database Audit Specification, however, you must first set up a SQL Server Audit object. To do this, you must use a couple of new entries in the Object Explorer under the `Security` folder at the SQL Server instance level: Audits and Server Audit Specifications.

Essentially, three main objects describe audits in SQL Server 2008:

- **The Server Audit object**—Used to describe the target for audit data, plus some top-level configuration settings. This destination can be a file, the Windows Application log, or the Windows Security log. The Server Audit object contains no information about what is being audited—just *where* the audit data is going. Multiple Server Audit objects can be defined with each object independent from one another (that is, they can each specify a different destination).

- **The Server Audit Specification object**—Used to describe what to audit at a server instance-wide level. A server audit specification must be associated with a Server Audit object to define where the audit data is written. There is a one-to-one relationship between the Server Audit Specification object and the Server Audit object.

- **The Database Audit Specification**—Used to describe *what* to audit at a specific database level. Where the audit data is written is determined by the Server Audit object it is associated with. Each database audit specification can be associated with only one server audit. A server audit can be associated with audit specifications for multiple databases, but only one database audit specification per database.

To create a new Server Audit object, right-click on the `Audits` item in Object Explorer and select New Audit (see Figure 13.8).

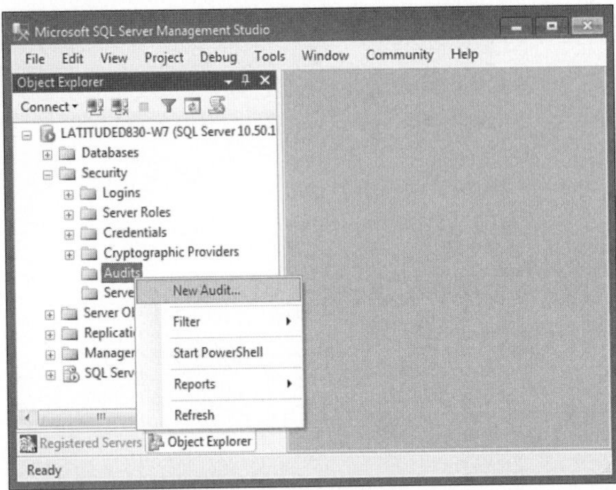

FIGURE 13.8 Creating a new Server Audit object in Object Explorer at the Server instance level.

When you set up a Server Audit object, you specify where the audit information will be written to. In Figure 13.9, you can see that we are creating a server audit named `NEW_SQL_Server_Audit` and are defining it to use the Application log at the Windows operating system level as the audit destination. You can also choose to write to the Windows Security log or to a text file. Events written to the Application or Security Event log can be accessed with Event Viewer or with specialized Event log management software, such as Microsoft Systems Center Operations Manager.

NOTE

Depending on the volume of audit targets being monitored, better performance may be achieved by using a file as the audit target rather than the Windows Event log. Also, when written to a file, the audit data is accessible through a built-in table-valued function (`fn_get_audit_file`), which allows the use of regular `SELECT` syntax to query the audit trail.

NOTE

You can also configure the Audit object to shut down the SQL Server instance if, for whatever reason, SQL Server Audit is unable to write its audit events to the audit target. Although shutting down the server instance may seem drastic, doing so may be necessary for certain scenarios, to ensure that the server cannot operate without its activity being audited.

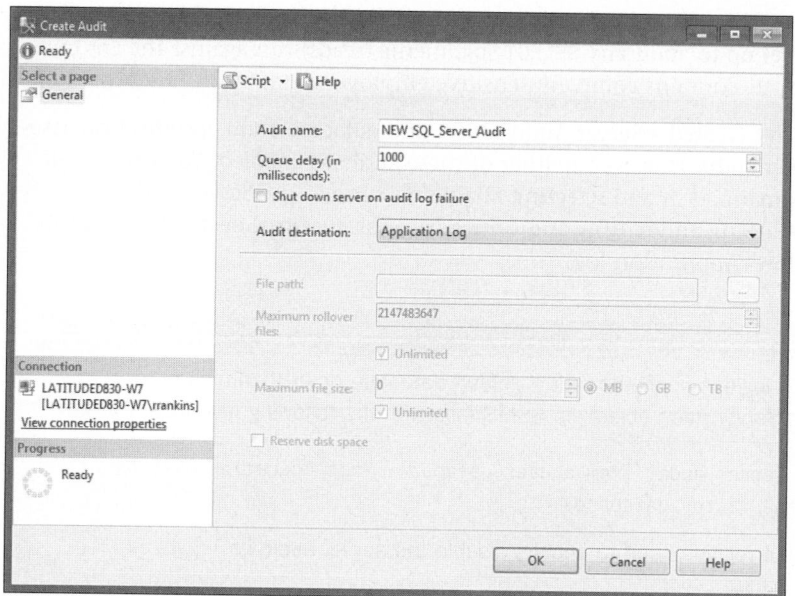

FIGURE 13.9 The Create Audit dialog.

After you set up the Server Audit object, the next step is to go to the `Database Audit Specifications` folder, as shown in Figure 13.7, in the database for which you want to set up auditing. Right-click this folder and select New Database Audit Specification to bring up the dialog shown in Figure 13.10. This is where you define your database-level audits.

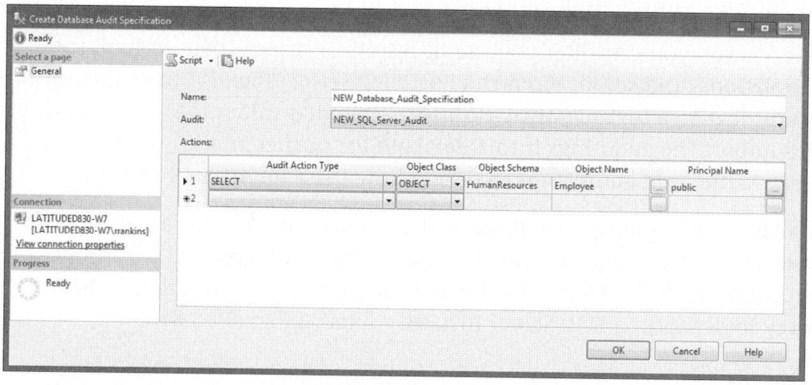

FIGURE 13.10 The Create Database Audit Specification dialog.

In the Create Database Audit Specification dialog, you specify the name of the Database Audit object and the Server Audit object it will be running under. In this example, the Database Audit name is `NEW_Database_Audit_Specification`, and it will be running under the NEW_SQL_Server_Audit Audit object defined in Figure 13.9. In this example, the database audit is being set up to audit any SELECT statements (reads) run against the Employee table (which, of course, contains company-sensitive employee data) by any user (public).

At this point you have created a Server Audit object and database audit specification associated with the server audit. However, neither of these audits is enabled. You can enable them by right-clicking on each and selecting Enable. As soon as the Server Audit object is enabled, it begins auditing and writing audit records to the specified destination (in this example, the Windows Application log).

NOTE

If your SQL Server login is configured for a default database other than master, enabling the SQL Server Audit object via SSMS fails with the following message:

```
Cannot alter a server audit from a user database. This operation must be
 performed in the master database.
```

If you receive this error, you need to enable/disable the server audit via T-SQL, as shown in Listing 13.1.

You can review the details by right-clicking on the Server Audit and selecting View Audit Logs or, if you are auditing to the Windows Application or Security Event Log, by opening the Windows Event Viewer directly. One of the advantages of opening the Audit log from within SSMS is that it automatically filters the log to show only SQL Server Audit events. In Figure 13.11, you can see that we've opened the Log File Viewer and selected to view the Application log (where we directed our SQL Server Audit to go). A few SELECT statements were run against the Employee table and, sure enough, the audit information of the SELECT statements shows up in the Application log.

Within the Log File Viewer, you can filter your audit results or search them to look for patterns, specific violations, and so on. From the Log File Viewer, you also have the option of exporting the audit logs to a text file or to a comma-separated values (CSV) file. With a CSV file, you could import the audit logs into a database for further analysis and correlation. It's up to your security and audit team to decide how these audits are to be used.

In addition to database-level auditing of actions at the database level, you can also set up auditing of server-level events, such as management changes and logon and logoff operations. These are set up in the SSMS Object Explorer through the Server Audit Specifications item in the Security folder for the SQL Server instance (refer to Figure 13.8).

Setting Up Auditing via T-SQL

Alternatively, you can set up auditing with T-SQL statements and also switch the audit off and on using the ALTER SERVER AUDIT command by using WITH (STATE=ON) or WITH (STATE=OFF), as shown in Listing 13.1.

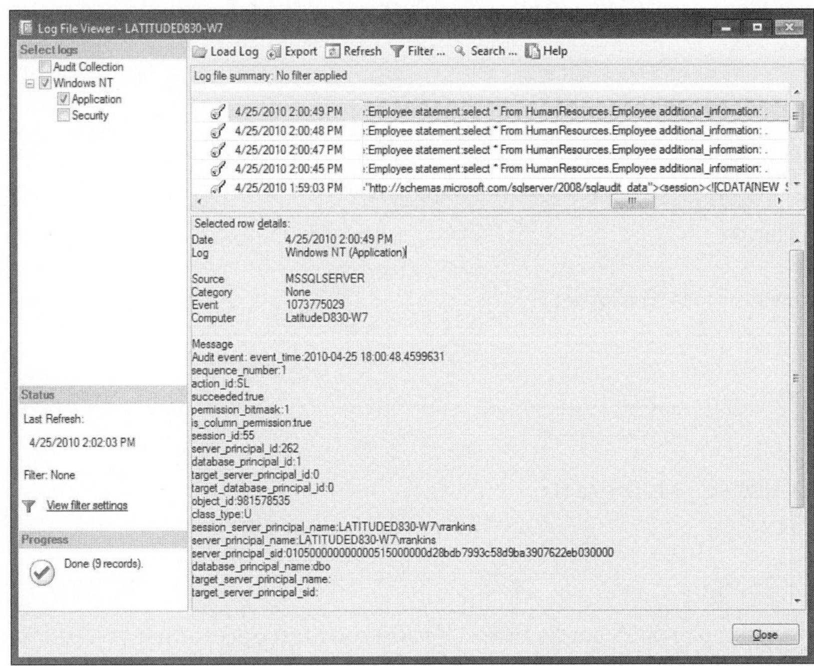

FIGURE 13.11 Log File Viewer showing the audit events of a SQL Server Audit object.

LISTING 13.1 Setting Up Auditing with T-SQL

```
/* Create the SQL Server Audit object, and send the results to the
  Windows Application event log. */
USE master;
go
CREATE SERVER AUDIT NEW_SQL_Server_Audit
    TO APPLICATION_LOG
    WITH ( QUEUE_DELAY = 1000,  ON_FAILURE = CONTINUE);
GO

/* Create the Database Audit Specification object using an Audit event */
USE AdventureWorks2008R2;
GO
CREATE DATABASE AUDIT SPECIFICATION NEW_Database_Audit_Specification
FOR SERVER AUDIT NEW_SQL_Server_Audit
    ADD (SELECT
           ON OBJECT::[HumanResources].[Employee]
           BY [public])
    WITH (STATE = ON);
GO
```

```
/* Enable the audit. */
USE master;
go
ALTER SERVER AUDIT NEW_SQL_Server_Audit
WITH (STATE = ON);

/* Test the audit is working */
USE AdventureWorks2008R2;
GO
SELECT * from HumanResources.Employee;
GO

/* Disable the audit. */
USE master;
GO
ALTER SERVER AUDIT NEW_SQL_Server_Audit
WITH (STATE = OFF);
 GO
```

It is recommended that you create your audit specifications with scripts so that you can easily manage them and not have to re-create them via SSMS dialogs.

SQL Injection Is Easy to Do

As we previously stated, SQL injection is the number-one security vulnerability globally as reported and tracked by the Open Web Application Security Project (OWASP; www.owasp.org). Because of this continued vulnerability, we decided to show you how to do SQL injection. However, keep in mind that we are showing you how to do it so that you can prevent this situation from happening to you. You need to make sure you include the vulnerability checks as a part of your coding and design reviews. Then this will never happen to you.

If you have a typical .NET forms application that prompts users to provide filter criteria to locate information, this is often a perfect place for hackers to add their own malicious code to do damage. Even your own employees might be hackers or want to cause harm. We call these folks "Evil SQL'ers."

The most common way SQL injection occurs is with the direct insertion of code into a variable that is part of a SQL statement. In other words, a user-defined variable is concatenated with a partially defined SQL statement and then subsequently executed as part of the application. The hacker adds a terminating character to the first part of the input and then follows it up with his or her own destructive SQL statement.

Let's consider the following simple Contact Name search application as an example. A .NET forms application might define a variable called `ContactFirstName` and then prompt the end user for a value to search for any contact's first name that begins with a set of characters such as "Don." Such an operation might result in finding "Don," "Donald," and "Donny" matching rows. The code might look like this:

```
var ContactFirstName;
ContactFirstName = Request.form ("ContactFirstName");
var sql = "SELECT * FROM [AdventureWorks].[Person].[Contact]
           WHERE [FirstName] like '" + ContactFirstName + "%'";
```

The subsequent SQL code that would be submitted to SQL Server for execution would be as follows:


```
SELECT * FROM  [AdventureWorks].[Person].[Contact]
WHERE [FirstName] Like 'Don%';
```

This code works perfectly.

To test this code as if you are an "Evil SQL'er," create a table named `XtraContactsTable` that you can pretend is your primary contacts table where all your company's contacts are stored. Go ahead and create this empty table for this evil test. The simple `CREATE` statement could be

```
CREATE TABLE [dbo].[XtraContactsTable]
([ContactFirstName] [nchar](10) NULL) ON [PRIMARY];
```

To be really evil, attempt to drop this table and cause severe damage to this company using the SQL injection method. Now, at the applications prompt for a contact first name, you, acting as the evil SQL'er, can instead type the following:

```
Don'; drop table [dbo].[XtraContactsTable] --
```

The subsequent SQL code that is sent to SQL Server for execution is

```
SELECT * FROM  [AdventureWorks].[Person].[Contact]
WHERE [FirstName] Like 'Don%';
drop table [dbo].[XtraContactsTable] --
```

The first part of the query is executed, followed by the `DROP TABLE` statement. Try this with the table you just created. After you execute the entire "valid" SQL statement, you see rows returned from the first part of the query, and the drop of the `XtraContactsTable` is also executed. If the evil code had simply used the `Employee` table name or the `Contact` table name, all your company's most sacred data would be gone in a flash.

That is SQL injection! It is easier to do than you think. And now you know how to do it, which means you must also prevent this and other SQL injection vulnerabilities from the beginning. In this case, you should write code to reject quotation marks, specific delimiters (such as `;`), and comment characters such as `- -` and `/*...*/`. We have included this SQL code example on the CD with this book as well.

Another popular method by Evil SQL'ers is to put a nasty piece of code into text or char data that will be stored as data in a table. When (or if) the data is ever used as part of a

SQL statement (and concatenated to SQL code as just demonstrated), the code in the data is executed. Pretty tricky! Sort of like a time bomb waiting to explode.

FIGURE 13.12 Reprinted with permission from xkcd.com.

NOTE

For additional examples of SQL injection and SQL coding tips to help prevent SQL injection attacks, see Chapter 43, "Transact-SQL Programming Guidelines, Tips, and Tricks."

Summary

As stated earlier, best practices for security and compliance must start from the glass and reach through the application, to the database layer, and even to the operating system and the physical file levels. This chapter describes an orderly process to follow as you develop applications that include security and compliance reviews and add testing all along the way. You should never wait until your application is done to start checking for security vulnerabilities; verify adherence to compliance rules or regulations; or determine what data needs to be protected, encrypted, or perhaps not even stored.

Taking advantage of the new SQL Server Auditing feature can be extremely useful in identifying and monitoring compliance of access and usage at the SQL Server database or object levels. Now you know how to do a little damage via SQL injection. You should also know how to prevent this type of damage. Remember, software security is really risk management. It is this risk that must be analyzed thoroughly. After you analyze it, responding in a known situation is always easier. Risks can appear due to architectural problems or with holes in applications (such as with SQL injection). The main aim of software security is to just fall safely and carefully and to limit the damage. We don't want to read about your failing in the newspaper or on Twitter.

In the next chapter, you learn about database backup and restores. To fix damage caused by security issues like those described in this chapter, you may have to restore your database to its state before the attack occurred. We hope that this never happens to you.

CHAPTER 14

Database Backup and Restore

IN THIS CHAPTER

- What's New in Database Backup and Restore
- Developing a Backup and Restore Plan
- Types of Backups
- Recovery Models
- Backup Devices
- Backing Up a Database
- Backing Up the Transaction Log
- Backup Scenarios
- Restoring Databases and Transaction Logs
- Restore Scenarios
- Additional Backup Considerations

You need to perform database backups to protect your investment in data. Making backups may seem mundane, but consider Murphy's Law ("If anything can go wrong, it will") when you are considering your backup plan. For example, if you forget to add a new database to your backup plan, that database will crash. If you neglect to run a test restore of your backups, those backups will not restore properly. This type of thinking may seem a bit defeatist, but it can help you create a robust backup solution that allows you to sleep comfortably knowing you have a good plan.

Fortunately, SQL Server comes with many different backup and restore options you can use to develop a robust backup plan and avoid those worst-case scenarios. This chapter covers the key considerations in developing a backup and restore plan and then covers the options available with SQL Server to implement that plan.

What's New in Database Backup and Restore

The majority of the backup and restore features that existed in SQL Server 2005 still exist in SQL Server 2008. A few options, however, have been eliminated or deprecated. For example, the backup options used to truncate the transaction log in prior versions are no longer supported. Specifically, the `NO_LOG` and `TRUNCATE_ONLY` options have been eliminated. The alternative for performing this kind of operation is to set the database recovery model to simple.

Several other deprecated features are still available in SQL Server 2008 but will be removed in a future version of SQL

Server. The Tape backup option is one example. The option to set a password on a backup or media-set will be removed in the next version of SQL Server. The protection provided by these passwords is weak, which is the reason they are being removed.

The biggest enhancement in backup and restore is the ability to create a compressed backup. Compressed backups use less space and can be created in less time than conventional backups. The creation of compressed backups can be established server-wide or can be enabled on a single backup using the `COMPRESSION` option. This feature is available only in SQL Server 2008 Enterprise and Developer Editions.

Developing a Backup and Restore Plan

Developing a solid backup and restore plan for SQL Server is one of the most critical tasks an administrator performs. Simply put, if you are a database administrator (DBA) and have a significant loss of data in a database you are responsible for, your job may be on the line. You need to carefully examine the backup needs of your organization, document those needs, and deliver a plan that defines how your backup and restore plan will meet those needs.

The best place to start in identifying the backup requirements is to ask the right questions. The following questions can help drive out the answers you need:

- How much data loss is acceptable? For example, if you choose to do only full database backups each night, would it be acceptable to lose all the data added to the database during the next day? This could happen if you had a failure and had to restore to the last full backup.
- What is the nature of the database? For example, is the database used for a data warehouse, or is it used for a high-volume transaction processing system?
- How often does the data in the database change? Some databases may change very little or not at all during the day but sustain heavy batch updates during the evening.
- What is the acceptable recovery time in the event a database must be restored from previous backups? This question is directly related to the amount of downtime acceptable for the applications using the database.
- Is there a maintenance window for the application/database? The maintenance window is typically a period of time when the database or server can be taken offline. What are the exact times of the maintenance windows?
- What is the size of the database(s) you need to back up?
- What media is available for backup, and where is the media located?
- What is the budget for database backup and recovery? If no budget has been established, the answers to some of the preceding questions drive the cost of the solution.

Some of the questions that need to be asked to come up with a good backup and restore plan may raise some eyebrows. For example, you may find that the answer you get for the question "How much data loss is acceptable?" is "None!" Don't panic. There are sensible responses for these types of answers. The reality is that you can deliver a solution that virtually eliminates the possibility of data loss—but that comes at a cost. The cost may come in the form of real dollars as well as other costs, such as performance or disk space. As with many other technical solutions, you need to consider trade-offs to come up with the right plan.

NOTE

Many of the questions that relate to database backup and restore are related to system backups as well. System-wide backups, which happen independently of SQL Server backups, capture all or most of the files on a server and write them to appropriate media. These server backups are often performed by DBAs, system administrators, and the like. You should consider having the person or persons responsible for the system backups present when asking the database backup and restore questions. This will help with the coordination and timing of the backups.

When you have the answers to these questions, you need to document them, along with your recommended solution. You should identify any assumptions and make sure to outline any portion of the plan that has not met the requirements.

The good news is that the implementation of the plan is often less difficult than coming up with the plan itself. Microsoft provides a myriad of tools to create database backups that can meet the needs of your organization. The remainder of this chapter focuses on the details required to finalize a solid backup and recovery plan.

Types of Backups

SQL Server offers several different types of backups you can use to restore a database to a former state. Each of these backups uses a file or set of files to capture the database state. The files are found outside the SQL Server database and can be stored on media such as tape or hard disk.

As described in the following sections, these backup types are available with SQL Server 2008:

- Full database backups
- Differential database backups
- Partial backups
- Differential partial backups
- File and filegroup backups
- Copy-only backups
- Transaction log backups

Full Database Backups

A full database backup is an all-inclusive backup that captures an entire database in one operation. This full backup can be used to restore a database to the state it was in when the database backup completed. The backup is transactionally consistent, contains the entire database structure, and contains the related data stored in these structures.

As with many other backups, SQL Server allows for updates to the database while a full backup is running. It keeps track of the changes occurring during the backup by capturing a portion of the transaction log in the database backup. The backup also records the log sequence number (LSN) when the database backup is started, as well as the LSN when the database backup completes. The LSN is a unique sequential number you can use to determine the order in which updates occur in the database. The LSNs recorded in the backup are used in the restore process to recover the database to a point in time that has transactional consistency.

A full database backup is often used in conjunction with other backup types; it establishes a base for these other types if a restore operation is needed. The other backup types are discussed in the following sections, but it is important not to forget about the full backup that must be restored first in order to utilize other backup types. For example, let's say you are making hourly transaction log backups. If the database is to be recovered using those transaction log backups, the last full database backup must be restored first, and then the subsequent log backups can be applied.

Differential Database Backups

Differential database backups capture changes to any data extent that happened since the last full database backup. The last full database backup is referred to as the *differential base* and is required to make the differential backup useful. Each data extent that is monitored consists of eight physically contiguous data pages. As changes are made to the pages in an extent, a flag is set to indicate that a change has been made to the extent. When the differential database backup is executed, only those extents that have had pages modified are written to the backup.

Differential database backups can save backup space and improve the overall speed of recovery. The savings in space and time are directly related to the amount of change that occurs in the database. The amount of change in the database depends on the amount of time between differential backups. When the number of database changes since the last backup is relatively small, you achieve the best results. If, however, a significant number of changes occur to the data between differential backups, the value of this type of backup is diminished.

Ultimately the number of data pages that are affected by the changes determine the number of pages that must be included in the differencial backup. The number of pages is affected by the indexing structure as well as the nature of the updates. If for example, there are many rows that are changed but those rows are all clustered on a limited number of data pages then the differencial backup will not be that large.

Partial Backups

Partial backups provide a means for eliminating read-only data from a backup. In some implementations, a portion of the data in a database may not change and is strictly used for inquiry. If this data is placed on a read-only filegroup, you can use partial backups to back up everything except the read-only data. This technique reduces the size of your backup and reduces the time it takes to complete the backup. The read-only filegroups should still be backed up, but this needs to occur only after the read-only data is loaded.

Differential Partial Backups

Differential partial backups work like differential database backups but are focused on the same type of data as partial backups. The extents that have changed in filegroups that are not read-only are captured in this type of backup. This includes the primary filegroup and any read/write filegroups defined at the time of the backup. Like differential database backups, these backups also require a differential base, but it must be a single differential base. In other words, multiple base backups that have been taken at different times for different database files will not work. You must use a single base backup that encompasses all of the database files.

File and Filegroup Backups

File and filegroup backups are targeted at databases that contain more than one filegroup. In these situations, the filegroup or files in the filegroups can be backed up independently. If a filegroup is backed up, all the files defined in the filegroup are backed up.

File and filegroup backups are often used for larger databases where the creation time for a full database backup takes too long or the resulting backup is too large. In these situations, you can stagger the backups of the files or filegroups and write them to different locations.

The main disadvantage of this type of backup is the increase in administrative overhead. Each of the files in the database must be backed up, and a complete set of these files must be retained to restore the database. For a full recovery model, the transaction log backups must also be retained.

NOTE

SQL Server 2008 supports file and filegroup backups for all recovery models, including simple recovery. The catch with simple recovery is that the files and filegroups are limited to read-only secondary filegroups. SQL Server 2000 did not allow these types of backups with simple recovery.

Copy-Only Backups

Copy-only backups allow a backup of any type to be taken without affecting any other backups. Normally, a database backup is recorded in the database itself and is identified as part of a chain that can be used for restore. For example, if a full database backup is taken, any subsequent differential database backups use this full database backup as their base. A restore process utilizing the differential database backups would have a reference to the full database backup, and that backup would have to be available.

Copy-only backups do not affect the restore chain. They are useful in situations in which you simply want to get a copy of the database for testing purposes or things of this nature. Microsoft has made it easier to make this kind of backup by adding the Copy Only Backup check box when performing a backup using SQL Server Management Studio (SSMS). In SQL Server 2005, the Copy Only Backup had to be performed via the Transact-SQL (T-SQL) `BACKUP` command. An example of the copy-only backup is provided later in this chapter, in the section "Backing Up a Database."

Transaction Log Backups

Transaction log backups capture records written to the transaction log file(s) defined for a database. The full and bulk-logged recovery models are the only models that support transaction log backups. These models cause transaction events to be retained in the transaction log so that they can be backed up. Simple recovery mode causes the transaction log to be truncated periodically and thus invalidates the usefulness of the transaction log backups.

The transaction log backups and their strong ties to the recovery model are discussed in more detail in the next section.

Recovery Models

Each database has a recovery model that determines how transactions will be written to the transaction log. The recovery model you choose has a direct impact on your ability to recover from a media failure. These following three recovery models are available with SQL Server 2008:

- Full recovery
- Bulk-logged
- Simple

You set the recovery model via T-SQL or the Database Properties window in SSMS. The following example shows the T-SQL command you can use to change the `AdventureWorks2008` database to the bulk-logged model:

```
ALTER DATABASE [AdventureWorks2008] SET RECOVERY BULK_LOGGED WITH NO_WAIT
```

Figure 14.1 shows the Options page on the Database Properties window, which also allows you to select a recovery model.

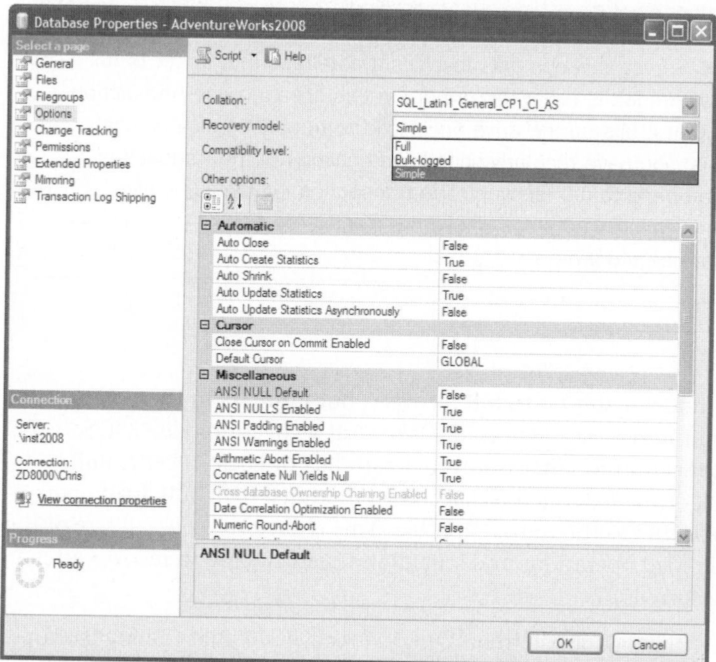

FIGURE 14.1 Setting the recovery model in SSMS.

Full Recovery

The full recovery model gives you the most protection against data loss. A database set to full recovery will have all database operations written to the transactions log. These operations include insertions, updates, and deletions, as well as any other statements that change the database. In addition, the full recovery model captures any database inserts that are the result of a `BCP` command or `BULK INSERT` statement.

In the event of a media failure, a database that is in full recovery can be restored to the point in time at which the failure occurred. Your ability to restore to a point in time is dependent on your database backup plan. If a full database backup is available, along with the transaction log backups that occurred after the full database backup, you can recover to the point of the last transaction log backup. In addition, if your current transaction log is available, you can restore up to the point of the last committed transaction in the transaction log.

This recovery model is the most comprehensive, but in some respects, it is the most expensive. It is expensive in terms of the transaction log space needed to capture all the database operations. The space can be significant with databases that have a lot of update activity or with databases that have large bulk load operations. It is also expensive in terms of server overhead because every transaction is captured and retained in the transaction log so that they can be recovered in the event of a failure.

TIP

A common problem in SQL Server environments involves a database that is set to full recovery but whose transaction log is never backed up. In this scenario, the transaction log can grow to the point that it fills up the drive on which the transaction log is located. You need to ensure that you have regularly scheduled backups of the transaction log if you have set your database to full recovery. The transaction log backups allow you to recover from a media failure and also remove the inactive portion of the transaction log so that it does not need to grow.

Bulk-Logged Recovery

The bulk-logged recovery model is similar to full recovery, but it differs in the way that bulk operations are captured in the transaction log. With full recovery mode, SQL Server writes every row to the transaction log that is inserted with `BCP` or `BULK INSERT`. Bulk-logged recovery keeps track of the extents that have been modified by a bulk load operation but does not write each row to the transaction log. This reduces the overall size of the transaction log during bulk load operations and still allows the database to recover after a bulk load operation has occurred.

The biggest downside to setting a database to bulk-logged recovery is that the log backups for the databases can be large. The log backups are large because SQL Server copies all the data extents that have been affected by bulk load operations since the last backup of the transaction log. Remember that data extents consist of eight data pages each, and each page is 8KB in size. This may not seem like much by today's standards, but it can be significant when you're bulk loading a large table. For example, consider a table occupying 1GB of space that is truncated each week and reloaded with a bulk insert. The bulk insert operation goes relatively fast because the rows are not being written to the transaction log, but the backup of the transaction log is much larger.

NOTE

In testing we did on a table with approximately 2.4 million rows (that occupied 500MB of space), the log file grew over 2GB during a bulk insert operation that reloaded all rows in a full recovery mode database. In contrast, the same bulk insert operation on the database with bulk-logged recovery grew the log by only 9MB. However, the backup of the 9MB transaction log was approximately 500MB. This is much larger than the actual log itself because the bulk operation caused all the modified extents from the bulk insert operation to be stored in the log backup as well.

The other downside to bulk-logged recovery is that with it, you may sacrifice the ability to restore to the most recent point in time. This situation occurs if a bulk insert operation has occurred since the last database backup and a media failure occurs. In this case, the restores can occur for any backups that were taken that do not contain a bulk insert operation, but any outstanding changes that were retained in the transaction log cannot be applied. The reason is that bulk operations are not written to the log directly in this model and cannot be recovered. Only bulk operations captured in a backup can be restored.

If transactions have occurred in a database since the last backup, and no bulk insert operations have occurred, you can recover those pending transactions as long as the media containing the transaction log is still available. The tail of the transaction log can be backed up and applied during a restore operation. The tail of the log and other restore scenarios are discussed in the "Restore Scenarios" section, later in this chapter.

Simple Recovery

The simple recovery model is the easiest to administer, but it is the option that has the greatest possibility for data loss. In this mode, your transactions log is truncated automatically based on a checkpoint in the database. These checkpoints happen often, and they cause the data in the transaction log to be truncated frequently.

NOTE

Prior to SQL Server 2000, the `trunc. log on checkpoint` database option was used to truncate the log on a checkpoint and produce the same type of behavior as simple recovery. This database option and the equivalent backup options `NO_LOG` and `TRUNCATE_ONLY` are no longer supported. The only supported method for truncating the transaction log in SQL Server 2008 is to switch the database to use the simple recovery model.

The most important point to remember about the simple recovery model is that with it, you cannot back up the transaction log that captures changes to your database. If a media failure occurs, you are not able to recover the database activity that has occurred since the last database backup. This is a major exposure, so simple recovery is not recommended for production databases. However, it can be a good option for development databases where the loss of some transactions is acceptable. In these types of environments, simple recovery can equate to saved disk space because the transaction log is constantly truncated. The administration in these environments is reduced as well because the transaction log backups are not an option and thus do not need to be managed.

For a more detailed discussion of the transaction log, see Chapter 31, "Transaction Management and the Transaction Log."

Backup Devices

A backup device is used to provide a storage destination for the database backups created with SQL Server. Backups can be written to logical or physical devices. A logical device is essentially an alias to the physical device and makes it easier to refer to the device when performing database backups. The physical backup devices that SQL Server can write to include files on local disks, tape, and network shares.

Disk Devices

A disk device is generally stored in a folder on a local hard drive. This should not be the same hard drive where your data is stored! Disk devices have several advantages, including speed and reliability. If you have ever had a backup fail because you forgot to load a tape, you can appreciate the advantage of disk backups. On the other hand, if backups are stored on a local disk and the server is destroyed, you lose your backups as well.

NOTE

Disks have become increasingly popular media as the prices have fallen. Storage area networks (SANs) and other large-scale disk solutions have entered mainstream usage and offer a large amount of storage at a relatively inexpensive price. They also offer redundancy and provide fault tolerance to mitigate the chance of losing data on a disk. Finally, increased network bandwidth across LANs and WANs has allowed for the movement of backups created on disk to alternate locations. This is a simple way to achieve additional fault tolerance.

Tape Devices

Tape devices are used to back up to tape. Tape devices must be directly connected to the server, and parallel backups to multiple drives are supported to increase throughput. Tape backups have the advantage of being scalable, portable, and secure. Scalability is important as a database grows; available disk space often precludes the use of disk backups for large databases. Because tapes are removable media, they can easily be transported offsite, where they can be secured against theft and damage.

SQL Server supports the Microsoft Tape Format (MTF) for backup devices, which means that SQL Server backups and operating system backups can share the same tape. This capability is convenient for small sites with shared use servers and only one tape drive. You can schedule your SQL Server backups and file backups without having to be onsite to change the tape.

Network Shares

SQL Server 2008 allows the use of both mapped network drives and Universal Naming Convention (UNC) paths in the backup device filename. A mapped network drive must be mapped as a network drive in the session in which SQL Server is running. This is prone to error and generally not recommended. UNC paths are much simpler to administer. With UNC backup devices, the SQL Server service account must be able to see the UNC path on the network. This is accomplished by granting the service account full control permission on the share or by making the service account a member of the `Administrators` group on the remote computer.

Keep in mind that backups performed on a network share should be done on a dedicated or high-speed network connection, and the backup should be verified to avoid potential corruption introduced by network error. The time it takes a backup to complete over the network depends on network traffic, so you need to take this factor into consideration when planning your backups.

Media Sets and Families

When you're backing up to multiple devices, the terms *media set* and *media family* are used to describe the components of the backup. A *media set* is the target destination of the database backup and comprises several individual media. All media in a media set must be of the same type (for example, all tape or all disk). A *media family* is the collection of media associated with an individual backup device. For example, a media family could be a collection of five tapes contained in a single tape device.

The first tape in the media family is referred to as the *initial* media, and the subsequent tapes are referred to as *continuation* media. All the media families combined are referred to as the *media set*. If, for example, a backup is written to 3 backup devices (each with 4 tapes), the media set would contain 3 media families and consist of a total of 12 tapes. It is recommended to use the `MEDIANAME` parameter of the `BACKUP` command to specify a name for the media set. This parameter associates the multiple devices as members of the media set. The `MEDIANAME` parameter can then be referenced in future backup operations.

Creating Backup Devices

You can create logical backup devices by using T-SQL or SSMS. The T-SQL command for creating these logical backup devices is `sp_addumpdevice`, which has the following syntax:

```
sp_addumpdevice [ @devtype = ] 'device_type'
        , [ @logicalname = ] 'logical_name'
        , [ @physicalname = ] 'physical_name'
      [ , { [ @cntrltype = ] controller_type |
            [ @devstatus = ] 'device_status' }
      ]
```

The following sample script demonstrates the creation of the different types of backup devices:

```
-- Local Disk
EXEC sp_addumpdevice 'disk', 'diskdev1',
    'c:\mssql2008\backup\AdventureWorks2008.bak'
-- Network Disk
EXEC sp_addumpdevice 'disk', 'networkdev1',
    '\\myserver\myshare\AdventureWorks2008.bak'
-- Tape
EXEC sp_addumpdevice 'tape', 'tapedev1', '\\.\tape0'
```

To create backup devices with SSMS, you navigate to the `Server Objects` node in the Object Explorer and right-click `Backup Devices` and then `New Backup Device`; the Backup

Device screen appears. This screen includes a text box for the device name, along with a section to select the destination for the device. This is the physical location, and you can select either Tape or File.

Backing Up a Database

Now that you know the types of backups, the recovery models they relate to, and the devices you can write to, you are ready to back up your database. You can create backups with SQL Server 2008 by using either the SSMS or T-SQL. Some backups are supported only through T-SQL, but the vast majority can be accomplished with either tool.

Creating Database Backups with SSMS

The backup options in SSMS are accessible through the Object Explorer. For example, you can right-click the `AdventureWorks2008` database in the SSMS Object Explorer, select Tasks and Backup, and a backup window like the one shown in Figure 14.2 appears.

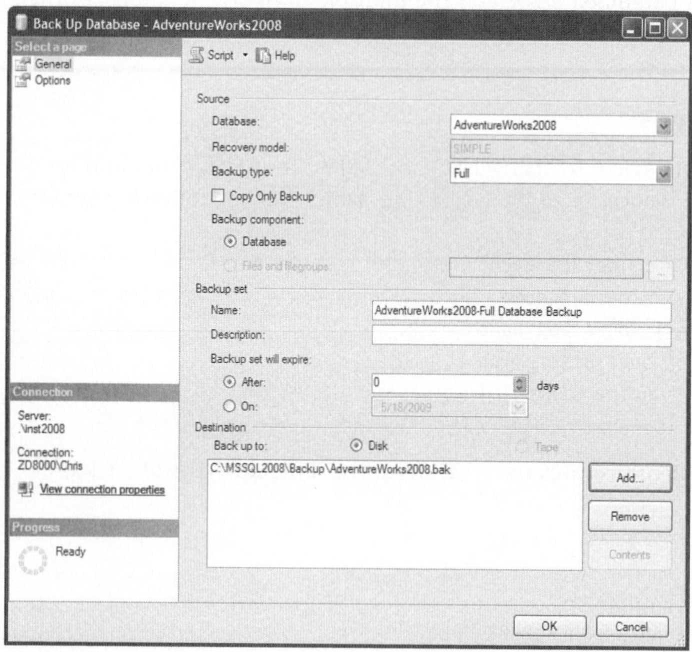

FIGURE 14.2 The Back Up Database window in SSMS.

The Source section on the Back Up Database window contains information relative to the database that will be backed up. The target database is displayed in the first drop-down, along with the recovery model set for the database. The backup types available in the drop-down are dependent on the recovery model. For simple recovery, only full and differential backup types are available. For full recovery and bulk-logged recovery models, all backup types are available in the drop-down.

The Backup Set section allows you to give the backup a meaningful name and specify when the backup set will expire. When the backup set expires, the backup can be overwritten and is no longer retained. If the backup is set to expire after 0 days, it will never expire.

The Destination section identifies the disk or tape media that will contain the backup. You can specify multiple destinations in this section by clicking the Add button. For disk media, you can specify a maximum of 64 disk devices. The same limit applies to tape media. If multiple devices are specified, the backup information is spread across those devices. All the devices must be present for you to be able to restore the database. If no tape devices are attached to the database server, the Tape option is disabled.

You can select several different types of options for a database backup. Figure 14.3 shows the options page available when you back up a database by using SSMS.

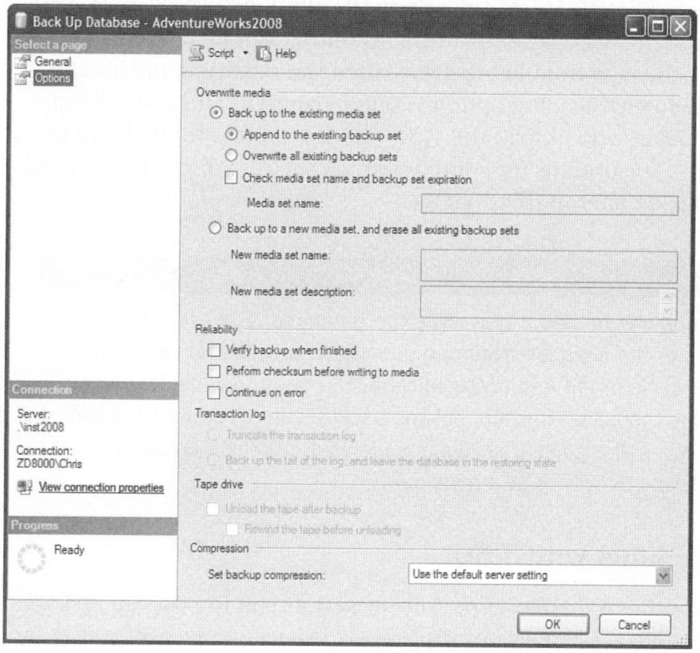

FIGURE 14.3 The Back Up Database Options page in SSMS.

The Overwrite Media section allows you to specify options relative to the destination media for the backup. Keep in mind that a given media set can contain more than one backup. This can occur if the Append to the Existing Backup Set options is selected. With this option, any prior backups contained on the media set are preserved, and the new backup is added to it. With the Overwrite All Existing Backup Sets option, the media set contains only the latest backup, and no prior backups are retained.

You can use the options in the Reliability section to ensure that the backup that has been created can be used reliably in a restore situation. Verifying the backup when finished is highly recommended, but doing so causes the backup time to be extended during the verification. Similarly, the Perform Checksum Before Writing to Media option helps ensure that you have a sound backup, but again, it causes the database backup to run longer.

The options in the Transaction Log section are available for databases in the full recovery or bulk-logged model. These options are disabled in the simple recovery model. The Truncate the Transaction Log option causes any inactive portion of the transaction log to be removed after the database backup is complete. The inactive portion of the log and other detail of the transaction log are discussed in more detail in Chapter 30 "Transaction Management and the transaction log". This option, the default, helps keep the size of the transaction log manageable. The Back Up the Tail of the Log option is related to point-in-time restores and is discussed in more detail in the "Restore Scenarios" section later in this chapter.

The set of options in the Tape Drive section are enabled only when tape has been selected for the destination media. Selecting the Unload the Tape After Backup option causes the media tape to be ejected when the backup completes. This option can help identify the end of a backup and prevent the tape from being overwritten the next time the backup runs. The Rewind the Tape Before Unloading option is self-explanatory; it causes the tape to be released and rewound before you unload the tape. The last set of options relate to compressed database backups. The options for compressed backups are discussed in detail in the Compressed Backup secion later in this chapter.

NOTE

Keep in mind that all backups can be performed while the database is in use. SQL Server is able to keep track of the changes occurring during the backup and can maintain transactional consistency as of the end of the backup. You need to consider some performance overhead during the actual backup, but the backup can occur during active database hours. However, it is still a good idea to schedule your database backups during off-hours, when database activity is at a minimum.

Creating Database Backups with T-SQL

The T-SQL `BACKUP` command offers a myriad of options to perform all the backup operations available in SSMS. However, SSMS does not support some backup operations that can be performed only with T-SQL.

The `BACKUP` command comes in three different flavors. The first flavor involves the backup of a database. The command syntax starts with `BACKUP DATABASE`, followed by the relevant parameters and options. The second flavor involves the backup of a file or filegroup that is part of the database. The command syntax for this type of backup also utilizes the `BACKUP`

DATABASE command, but a file or filegroup is specified after the database name to identify which parts of the database should be backed up. The last flavor involves the backup of the database's transaction log. The syntax for backing up the transaction log starts with BACKUP LOG. Each flavor shares many of the same options. The basic syntax for backing up a database follows:

```
BACKUP DATABASE { database_name | @database_name_var }
TO < backup_device > [ ,...n ]
[ [ MIRROR TO < backup_device > [ ,...n ] ] [ ...next-mirror ] ]
[ WITH
    [ BLOCKSIZE = { blocksize | @blocksize_variable } ]
    [ [ , ] { CHECKSUM | NO_CHECKSUM } ]
    [ [ , ] COMPRESSION | NO_COMPRESSION]
    [ [ , ] COPY_ONLY ]
    [ [ , ] { STOP_ON_ERROR | CONTINUE_AFTER_ERROR } ]
    [ [ , ] DESCRIPTION = { 'text' | @text_variable } ]
    [ [ , ] DIFFERENTIAL ]
    [ [ , ] EXPIREDATE = { date | @date_var }
    | RETAINDAYS = { days | @days_var } ]
    [ [ , ] PASSWORD = { password | @password_variable } ]
    [ [ , ] { FORMAT | NOFORMAT } ]
    [ [ , ] { INIT | NOINIT } ]
    [ [ , ] { NOSKIP | SKIP } ]
    [ [ , ] MEDIADESCRIPTION = { 'text' | @text_variable } ]
    [ [ , ] MEDIANAME = { media_name | @media_name_variable } ]
    [ [ , ] MEDIAPASSWORD = { mediapassword | @mediapassword_variable } ]
    [ [ , ] NAME = { backup_set_name | @backup_set_name_var } ]
    [ [ , ] { NOREWIND | REWIND } ]
    [ [ , ] { NOUNLOAD | UNLOAD } ]
    [ [ , ] RESTART ]
    [ [ , ] STATS [ = percentage
 ] ]
]
```

The number of options is extensive, but many of them are optional. A BACKUP DATABASE command can be as simple as the following example:

```
BACKUP DATABASE [AdventureWorks2008]
 TO  DISK = N'C:\mssql2008\backup\AdventureWorks2008_COPY.bak'
```

The first part of the BACKUP command is related to the database you want to back up (*database_name*), followed by the location to which you want to write the backup (backup_device). The remainder of the syntax relates to the options that can be specified following the WITH clause. These options determine how your backup will be created and the properties of the resulting backup. Table 14.1 outlines these options.

14

TABLE 14.1 **BACKUP DATABASE** Options

Option	Description
BLOCKSIZE	The physical block size that will be used to create the backup. The default is 64KB.
CHECKSUM | NO_CHECKSUM	When CHECKSUM is specified, a checksum is calculated before the backup is written to validate that the backup is not corrupt. The default is NO_CHECKSUM.
COMPRESSION | NO_COMPRESSION	This new option in SQL Server 2008, available only with the Enterprise or Developer Edition, causes the backup file to be compressed. The default is NO_COMPRESSION.
STOP_ON_ERROR | CONTINUE_AFTER_ERROR	This option is used in conjunction with the CHECKSUM option. The STOP_ON_ERROR option, which is the default, causes the backup to fail if the checksum cannot be validated.
DESCRIPTION	This is a 255-character description of the backup set.
DIFFERENTIAL	This option causes a differential backup to occur, which captures changes only since the last backup.
EXPIREDATE	This option specifies the date on which the backup set will expire and be overwritten.
RETAINDAYS	This option specifies the number of elapsed days before the backup set can be overwritten.
PASSWORD	This is a password that must be specified when restoring the backup set.
FORMAT | NOFORMAT	FORMAT causes the existing media header and backup set to be overwritten. The default is NOFORMAT.
INIT | NOINIT	The INIT option causes a backup set to be overwritten. The backup set is not overwritten if the backup set has not expired or if it does not match the media name specified with the NAME option. NOINIT, which is the default, causes the backup set to be appended to the existing media.
NOSKIP | SKIP	NOSKIP, which is the default, allows backup sets to be overwritten if they have expired. The SKIP option skips expiration and media name checks and is used to prevent the overwriting of backup sets.
MEDIADESCRIPTION	This is a 255-character description for the entire backup media containing the backup sets.

TABLE 14.1 **BACKUP DATABASE** Options

Option	Description
MEDIANAME	This is a 128-character name for the backup media. If it is specified, the target media must match this name.
MEDIAPASSWORD	This is a password for the media set. When media is created with this password, the password must be supplied to be able to create a backup set on that media or to restore from that media.
NAME	This is a 128-character name for the backup set.
NOREWIND | REWIND	This option is used for tape operations. REWIND, which is the default, causes the tape to be released and rewound after it fills.
NOUNLOAD | UNLOAD	This option is used for tape operations. NOUNLOAD, which is the default, causes the tape to remain in the tape drive after a backup completes. UNLOAD causes the tape to be rewound and unloaded when the backup completes.
RESTART	This option has no effect and is in place only for backward compatibility.
STATS	This option causes completion statistics to be displayed at the specified interval to assess progress.
COPY_ONLY	This option allows a backup to be made without affecting the normal sequence of backups.

The "Backup Scenarios" section, later in this chapter, provides some examples of how to use these options.

Backing Up the Transaction Log

As discussed, the full and bulk-logged recovery models cause transactions to be written to the database's transaction log. These transactions should be backed up periodically for two main reasons. First, the transaction log backups can be used in case of a media failure to restore work completed in the database. These backups limit your exposure to data loss and enable you to reapply changes that have occurred.

The second reason for backing up the transaction log is to keep the size of the log manageable. Keep in mind that SQL Server is a write-ahead database management system (DBMS) and thus writes most changes to the transaction log first, before it updates the actual data files. This type of DBMS is great for recovery purposes, but it can be a real headache if you do not periodically clear those transactions from the log. Without a backup or manual truncation, the log can fill to a point where it will use up all the space on your disk.

Creating Transaction Log Backups with SSMS

The same backup screen utilized for database backups in SSMS can also be used for transaction log backups. Figure 14.4 shows the Back Up Database window with Transaction Log selected as the backup type. A device must be selected to write the backup to, and some additional options on the Options page that relate to the transaction log are enabled.

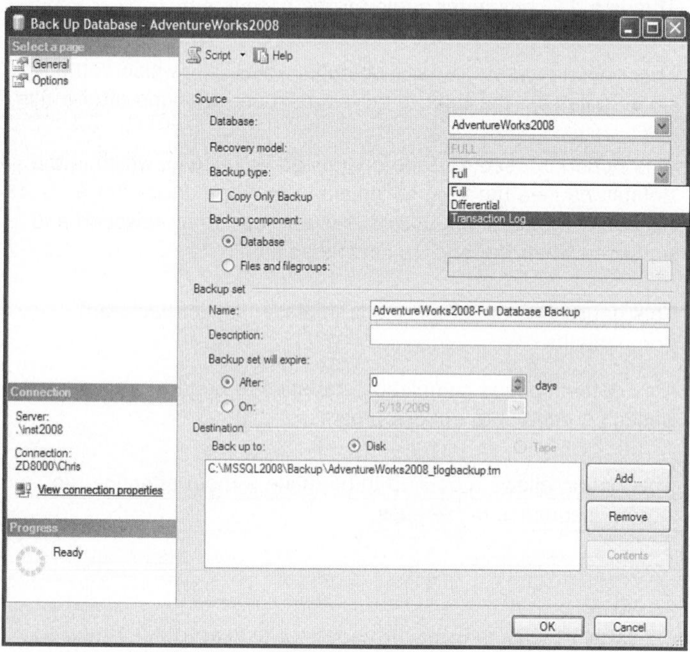

FIGURE 14.4 Backing up the transaction log in SSMS.

Creating Transaction Log Backups with T-SQL

When you back up a transaction log by using T-SQL, you use the `BACKUP LOG` command, which includes all the previously listed options except the `DIFFERENTIAL` option. (Differential backups do not apply to transaction logs.) Several additional options are available for transaction log backups. The following abbreviated syntax for the `BACKUP LOG` command shows the options used exclusively for backing up transaction logs:

```
BACKUP LOG { database_name | @database_name_var }
TO < backup_device > [ ,...n ]
[ [ MIRROR TO < backup_device > [ ,...n ] ] [ ...next-mirror ] ]
[ WITH
```

```
......
    [ [ , ] NO_TRUNCATE ]
    [ [ , ] { NORECOVERY | STANDBY = undo_file_name } ]
```

The options specific to BACKUP LOG are discussed in detail in the following sections.

The NO_TRUNCATE Option

You use the NO_TRUNCATE option when the log is available, but the database is not. This option prevents the truncation of the transaction log after a backup occurs. Under normal circumstances, the BACKUP LOG command not only writes to the transaction log, but also signals a checkpoint for the database to flush any dirty buffers from memory to the database files. This behavior becomes a problem when the media containing the database is unavailable and you must capture the current contents of a log to a backup file for recovery. If you last did a log backup four hours ago, this would mean the loss of all the input since then. If your log is on a separate disk that is not damaged, you have those four hours of transactions available to you, but BACKUP LOG fails because it can't run a checkpoint on the data files. You run BACKUP LOG with the NO_TRUNCATE option, and the log is backed up, but the checkpoint is not run because the log is not actually cleared. You now have this new log backup to restore as well, enabling recovery to the time of failure. The only transactions lost are those that were not yet committed.

The NORECOVERY | STANDBY= *undo_file_name* Options

The NORECOVERY option causes the tail of the log to be backed up and leaves the database in a RESTORING state, which allows additional transaction logs to be applied, if necessary. The tail of the log is the active portion of the log that contains transactions not yet backed up. This "tail" is critical in restore situations in which all committed transactions are reapplied. Typically, the NORECOVERY option is used with the NO_TRUNCATE option to retain the contents of the log.

The STANDBY option also backs up the tail of the log, but it leaves the database in a read-only/standby state. The read-only state allows inquiry on the database and allows additional transaction logs to be applied to the database as well. *undo_file_name* must be supplied with the STANDBY command so that transactions not committed and rolled back at the time of the backup can be reapplied if additional transaction logs are applied to the database. This STANDBY option produces the same results as executing BACKUP LOG WITH NORECOVERY followed by a RESTORE WITH STANDBY command.

NOTE

As mentioned earlier, Microsoft has removed the NO_LOG and TRUNCATE_ONLY options available with earlier versions of SQL Server, including SQL Server 2005. Setting a database to use the simple recovery model is the alternative to these options.

Backup Scenarios

Typically, several different types of backups are used in a comprehensive backup plan. These backups are often combined to produce maximum recoverability while balancing the load on the system and amount of time to recover the database. The following backup scenarios outline some of the ways SQL Server backups are used.

NOTE

Many of the examples that follow utilize a backup directory named `c:\mssql2008\backup`. If you are interested in running some of these examples on your own system, you need to create this directory on the database server first before running the scripts that reference this directory. You can use backup and data directories different from the default directory to simplify the directory structure for the SQL Server files. Typically, these directories should not be on the `C:` drive, but the `C:` drive is used here for simplicity.

Full Database Backups Only

A full database backup, without the use of other database backups, is often found in nonproduction environments where the loss of transactional data is relatively unimportant. Some development environments are good examples of this. In these environments, a nightly full backup is sufficient to ensure that recent Data Definition Language (DDL) changes and the related development data for the day are captured. If a catastrophic failure occurs during the day and causes a restore to occur, the database can be restored from the prior night's backup. The following example shows a full backup of the `AdventureWorks2008` database:

```
--Full Database Backup to a single disk device
BACKUP DATABASE [AdventureWorks2008]
 TO  DISK = N'C:\mssql2008\backup\AdventureWorks2008.bak'
 WITH NOFORMAT, INIT,  NAME = N'AdventureWorks2008-Full Database Backup',
 SKIP, NOREWIND, NOUNLOAD,  STATS = 10
```

The sole use of daily full database backups needs to be carefully considered. The benefits of limited administration and limited backup space requirements have to be weighed against the costs of losing an entire day's transactions.

Full Database Backups with Transaction Log Backups

Compared to making a full database backup only, a more comprehensive approach to database backups includes the use of transaction log backups to augment the recoverability of full database backups. Transaction log backups that are taken periodically capture incremental database activity that can be applied to a full database backup during database restore.

You need to measure the frequency of the transaction log backup against the tolerance for data loss. For example, if the requirement is to prevent no more than one hour's worth of work, the transaction log backups should be taken hourly. If the media on which the backup is stored is accessible, you should lose no more than one hour's worth of data.

As mentioned earlier, the database must be placed in full or bulk-logged recovery mode to capture transaction log backups. Listing 14.1 shows the commands necessary to place the AdventureWorks2008 database in full recovery mode, the required backup to establish a base, followed by the command to perform the actual transaction log backup.

LISTING 14.1 Full Backups with Transaction Logs

```
--First need to change the recovery model from simple to full
--so that the tlogs are available for backup
ALTER DATABASE [AdventureWorks2008] SET RECOVERY FULL WITH NO_WAIT

--*** A Full database backup must be taken after the
--*** recovery mode has been changed
--*** in order to set a base for future tlog backups.
--*** If the full backup is not taken
--*** then tlog backups will fail.
--The Following full backup utilizes two devices on the same drive.
--Often times multiple devices are backed up to different drives.
--Backing up to different drives
-- can speed up the overall backup
time and help when you are running low on space on a drive
-- where your backups are written.

BACKUP DATABASE [AdventureWorks2008]
 TO  DISK = N'C:\mssql2008\backup\AdventureWorks2008_Full_Dev1.bak',
     DISK = N'C:\mssql2008\backup\AdventureWorks2008_Full_Dev2.bak'
 WITH NOFORMAT, NOINIT, SKIP, NOREWIND, NOUNLOAD,  STATS = 10

--Transaction log backups can be taken now that a base has been established
--The following tlog backup is written to a single file
BACKUP LOG [AdventureWorks2008]
 TO  DISK = N'C:\mssql2008\backup\log\AdventureWorks2008_FirstAfterFull.trn'
 WITH NOFORMAT, INIT,  NAME = N'AdventureWorks2008-Transaction Log  Backup',
 SKIP, NOREWIND, NOUNLOAD,  STATS = 10, CHECKSUM
```

Differential Backups

Differential backups can be used to reduce the amount of time required to restore a database and can be particularly useful in environments where the amount of data that changes is limited. Differential backups capture only the database extents that have changed since the last database backup—typically, a full database backup.

The addition of differential backups to a plan that includes full database backups and transaction log backups can significantly improve the overall recovery time. The differential database backup eliminates the need to apply any transaction log backups that have occurred from the time of the last full backup up until the completion of the differential backup. Figure 14.5 depicts a backup plan that includes full database backups, transaction log backups, and differential backups. The differential backups are executed on a daily basis between the full backups.

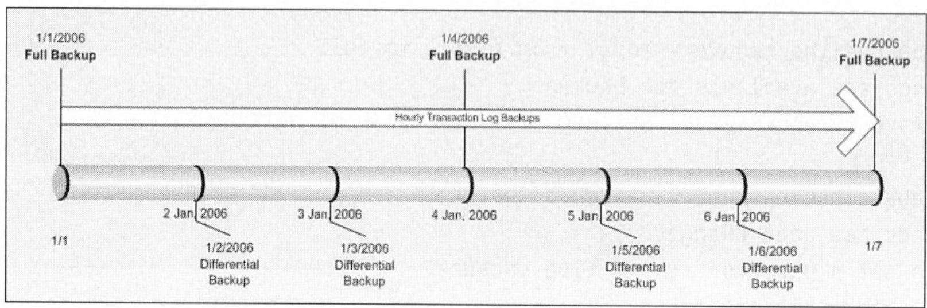

FIGURE 14.5 A backup plan that includes differential backup.

It is important to remember that differential backups are cumulative and contain all changes since the last differential base. There is no need to apply previous differential backups if the new differential base has not been established. For example, in the backup plan shown in Figure 14.5, if a media failure occurred in the middle of the day on January 3, the differential backup that would be used is the one taken at the beginning of the day on January 3; the differential backup that occurred on January 2 would not be needed. The full backup from January 1, the differential from January 3, and any transaction log backups that had occurred since the differential on January 3 would be used to restore the database.

You can create differential backups by using SSMS or T-SQL. The following example demonstrates the creation of a differential backup for the `AdventureWorks2008` database using T-SQL:

```
BACKUP DATABASE [AdventureWorks2008]
 TO  DISK = N'C:\mssql2008\backup\AdventureWorks2008_Diff2.bak'
 WITH  DIFFERENTIAL , NOFORMAT, INIT,
 NAME = N'AdventureWorks2008-Differential Database Backup',
 SKIP, NOREWIND, NOUNLOAD,  STATS = 10
```

Partial Backups

Partial backups are useful when read-only files or filegroups are part of a database. Listing 14.2 contains the commands necessary to add a read-only filegroup to the `AdventureWorks2008` database. The commands in Listing 14.2 do not perform a partial backup, but they do modify a sample database so that a partial database would make sense.

LISTING 14.2 Adding a Read-Only Filegroup to a Database

```
--Need to add a read only filegroup first to demonstrate
ALTER DATABASE AdventureWorks2008
ADD FILEGROUP ReadOnlyFG1
GO
-- Add a file to the Filegroup
ALTER DATABASE AdventureWorks2008
ADD FILE
(    NAME = AdventureWorks2008_ReadOnlyData,
    FILENAME = 'C:\mssql2008\data\AdventureWorks2008_ReadOnlyData.ndf',
    SIZE = 5MB,
    MAXSIZE = 100MB,
    FILEGROWTH = 5MB) TO FILEGROUP ReadOnlyFG1
go
--Create a table on the ReadOnly filegroup
CREATE TABLE AdventureWorks2008.dbo.MyReadOnlyTable
  ( FirstName varchar(50),
    LastName varchar(50),
    EMailAddress char(1000) )
ON ReadOnlyFG1

--Insert some data into the new read only Filegroup
insert AdventureWorks2008.dbo.MyReadOnlyTable
 select LastName, FirstName, 'xxx'
 from AdventureWorks2008.person. person

--Make the filegroup readonly
 ALTER DATABASE [AdventureWorks2008] MODIFY FILEGROUP [ReadOnlyFG1] READONLY
```

When you have a filegroup that contains read-only data, a partial backup can be valuable. The partial backup by default excludes any read-only filegroups and backs up only the read/write data that could have changed.

Listing 14.3 contains three separate backup commands that relate to the partial backup. The first backup command is not a partial backup but instead backs up the read-only filegroup. If the read-only filegroup is not backed up prior to the partial backup, the read-only filegroup is backed up, as is part of the partial backup. The second backup command creates the actual partial backup. The key parameter in this backup is `READ_WRITE_FILEGROUPS`, which causes the backup to skip the read-only data. The third backup command in Listing 14.3 shows that it is possible to perform a partial backup that includes the read-only data as well. This command includes a specific reference to the read-only filegroup, which causes it to be backed up as well.

LISTING 14.3 Making a Partial Backup

```
--Need to backup the readonly filegroup that was created
-- or it will be included in the partial backup
BACKUP DATABASE [AdventureWorks2008]
 FILEGROUP = N'ReadOnlyFG1'
 TO  DISK = N'C:\mssql2008\backup\AdventureWorks2008_ReadOnlyFG.bak'
 WITH NOFORMAT, NOINIT,  NAME = N'AdventureWorks2008-Full Filegroup Backup',
 SKIP, NOREWIND, NOUNLOAD,  STATS = 10

--Create the Partial Database Backup
--It will not contain the data from readonly filegroup
--The partial database backup can be restored without affecting
-- the data in the readonly filegroup
BACKUP DATABASE [AdventureWorks2008] READ_WRITE_FILEGROUPS
 TO  DISK = N'C:\mssql2008\backup\AdventureWorks2008_Partial.bak'
 WITH NOFORMAT, INIT,  NAME = N'AdventureWorks2008-Partial Database Backup',
 SKIP, NOREWIND, NOUNLOAD,  STATS = 10

--It is possible to backup the readonly filegroup(s) as well
--by listing the readonly filegroups in the backup command as shown in the
--following backup command
BACKUP DATABASE [AdventureWorks2008] FILEGROUP = 'ReadOnlyFG1',
 READ_WRITE_FILEGROUPS
 TO  DISK = N'C:\mssql2008\backup\AdventureWorks2008_Partial_WithReadOnly.bak'
 WITH NOFORMAT, INIT,  NAME = N'AdventureWorks2008-Partial Database Backup',
  SKIP, NOREWIND, NOUNLOAD,  STATS = 10
```

File/Filegroup Backups

Much of our discussion thus far has focused on backing up an entire database, but it is possible to back up only particular files or a group of files in a filegroup. A SQL Server database, by default, has only two files: the data file (with the file extension `.mdf`) and the log file (with the extension `.ldf`). You can add additional files and filegroups that contain these files to extend the database beyond the original two files. These additional files are often data files added to larger databases that require additional space. With very large databases, performing a full backup that contains all the database files can take too much time. In such a case, the individual files or filegroups can be backed up separately, enabling you to spread out the backup.

Listing 14.4 shows the T-SQL command that can be used to back up the read-only file you added to the `AdventureWorks2008` database in Listing 14.3.

LISTING 14.4 Creating a File Backup

```
BACKUP DATABASE [AdventureWorks2008] FILE = 'AdventureWorks2008_ReadOnlyData'
 TO  DISK = N'C:\mssql2008\backup\AdventureWorks2008_ReadOnlyData.bak'
 WITH NOFORMAT, INIT,  NAME = N'AdventureWorks2008-Readonly File Backup',
  SKIP, NOREWIND, NOUNLOAD,  STATS = 10
```

There is some additional administrative overhead associated with file and filegroup backups. Unlike a full database backup that produces one file that contains the entire database, the file backups do not stand by themselves and require other backups to be able to create the entire database. You need to keep the following points in mind when performing file and filegroup backups:

- A file or filegroup backup does not back up any portion of the transaction log. To restore a file or filegroup backup, you must have the transaction log backups since the last file or filegroup backup, including the tail of the log, for the database system to ensure transactional consistency. This also implies that the database must be in full or bulk-logged recovery because these are the only models that support transaction log backups.
- Individual file or filegroup backups can be restored from a full database backup.
- Point-in-time recovery is not permitted with file or filegroup backups.
- Differential backups can be combined with file or filegroup backups. These differential backups capture only those extents that have changed since the file or filegroup backup was made.

File and filegroup backups can be very powerful options for very large databases, but you need to ensure that the relevant backups can be accounted for. In all backup situations, the key to a successful plan is testing your backup strategy; this is particularly true with file and filegroup backups.

Mirrored Backups

The use of mirrored backups can help diminish the possibility of losing a database backup. Database backups can be your lifeline to recovery, and you do not want to lose them. Mirrored backups simultaneously write the backup information to more than one media set. You can mirror the backup to two, three, or four different media sets. Listing 14.5 gives an example of a mirrored backup that writes two different media sets.

LISTING 14.5 Creating a Mirrored Backup

```
BACKUP DATABASE AdventureWorks2008
TO disk = 'C:\mssql2008\backup\AdventureWorks2008_Mirror1a.bak',
```

```
   disk = 'C:\mssql2008\backup\AdventureWorks2008_Mirror1b.bak'
MIRROR TO disk = 'c:\mssql2008\backup\AdventureWorks2008_Mirror2a.bak',
   disk = 'C:\mssql2008\backup\AdventureWorks2008_Mirror2b.bak'
WITH FORMAT,
    MEDIANAME = 'AdventureWorks2008MirrorSet'
```

The example in Listing 14.5 is simplistic and demonstrates only the backup's capability to write to two different locations. At the end of the backup example, four files will exist. Each pair of files can be used to restore the database. In the real world, a backup like that in Listing 14.5 would write to two different disk or tape drives. Storing the media on the same drive is very risky and does not give you all the advantages a mirror can afford.

Copy-Only Backups

If you want a backup that will not affect future or past backups, copy-only backups are for you. The copy-only backup allows you to make a database or log backup without identifying the backup as one that should be included in a restore sequence.

Contrast this with a full database backup: If a full database backup is taken, the information related to this backup is captured in the system tables. This backup can form the base for other backups, such as transaction log backups or differential backups, and must be retained to be able to restore the backups that depend on the base.

The following example shows a copy-only backup; the `COPY_ONLY` parameter is the key to creating this kind of backup:

```
BACKUP DATABASE [AdventureWorks2008]
 TO  DISK = N'C:\mssql2008\backup\AdventureWorks2008_COPY.bak'
 WITH COPY_ONLY
```

Compressed Backups

How would you like to create a backup file that is smaller and takes less time to create? Sign me up. This has got to be an option that the average database user would love to use. Compressed backups are smaller in size than uncompressed backups. The reduced size of a compressed backup typically requires less device I/O and can therefore reduce backup times significantly.

You must be aware that there are some trade-offs, however. First, this feature is available only with Enterprise Edition or Developer Edition. Second, the creation of a compressed backup can impact on the performance of concurrent operations on your database server while the backup is being created. Specifically, CPU usage increases during the backup. This may or may not be an issue for you. Consider that many full database backups are taken during off-hours, so there are more CPU cycles available during this time. Either way, you should monitor the CPU usage using compression versus not using compression to evaluate the impact. Another option is to create low-priority compressed backups in a session whose CPU usage is limited by the Resource Governor. (For more information on using the Resource Governor, see Chapter 40, "Managing Workloads with the Resource Governor.")

When you get past these hurdles, the creation of a compressed backup is straightforward. One option is to set a server option so that all backups are created as compressed files by default. You can use the sp_configure stored procedure to set the backup compression default. If this is set to true, future backups will be created in a compressed format unless the backup is specifically created with the NO_COMPRESS option.

You also have the option of creating a compressed backup regardless of the server option. This is done using the new COMPRESSION option available with the T-SQL BACKUP command. The following example shows how to create an AdventureWorks2008 backup in the compressed format:


```
BACKUP DATABASE [AdventureWorks2008]
TO  DISK = N'C:\MSSQL2008\Backup\AdventureWorks2008_compressed.bak'
WITH NOFORMAT, NOINIT,
 NAME = N'AdventureWorks2008-Full Database Backup',
SKIP, NOREWIND, NOUNLOAD, COMPRESSION,  STATS = 10
```

The compression is quite impressive. In some simple tests performed on the AdventureWorks2008 database, the compressed backup was one fourth the size of a noncompressed backup. The compression ratio varies depending on the type of data in the database that you are backing up but can be as good as or better than 4:1.

System Database Backups

The system databases are the master, model, msdb, resource, tempdb, and distribution databases. SQL Server uses these databases as part of its internal workings. All these databases should be part of your backup plan, except for resource and tempdb. You can find detailed descriptions of these databases in Chapter 7, "SQL Server System and Database Administration." The important point to remember about all these databases is that they contain key information about your SQL Server environment. The msdb database contains information about backups and scheduled jobs. The master database contains information about all the user databases stored on the server. This information can change over time.

To ensure that you do not lose the information the system databases contain, you should back up these databases as well. Typically, nightly full database backups of these databases suffice. You can use the same backup T-SQL syntax or SSMS screens that you use for a user databases to accomplish this task.

Restoring Databases and Transaction Logs

A database restore allows a database or part of a database to be recovered to a state that it was in previously. This state includes the physical structure of the database, configuration options, and data contained in the database. The options you have for recovery are heavily dependent on the backup plan you have in place and way you have configured your database. Databases that are set to simple recovery mode have limited options for database restore. Databases that are in full recovery mode and have frequent backups have many more restore options. Following are the basic options for restore:

- Restore an entire database.
- Perform a partial restore.
- Restore a file or page from a backup.
- Restore a transaction log.
- Restore a database to a point in time by using a database snapshot.

The following sections delve further into the restore options listed here. They focus on the means for accomplishing these restores and some of the common restore scenarios you might encounter.

Restores with T-SQL

The command to restore a database in SQL Server is aptly named `RESTORE`. The `RESTORE` command is similar to the `BACKUP` command in that it can be used to restore a database, part of a database, or a transaction log. You restore an entire database or part of a database by using the `RESTORE DATABASE` syntax. You do transaction log restores by using the `RESTORE TRANSACTION` syntax.

Database Restores with T-SQL

Listing 14.6 shows the full syntax for `RESTORE DATABASE`.

LISTING 14.6 **RESTORE DATABASE** Syntax

```
--To Restore an Entire Database from a Full database backup (a Complete Restore):
RESTORE DATABASE { database_name | @database_name_var }
[ FROM <backup_device> [ ,...n ] ]
[ WITH
   [ { CHECKSUM | NO_CHECKSUM } ]
   [ [ , ] { CONTINUE_AFTER_ERROR | STOP_ON_ERROR } ]
   [ [ , ] ENABLE_BROKER ]
   [ [ , ] ERROR_BROKER_CONVERSATIONS ]
   [ [ , ] FILE = { file_number | @file_number } ]
   [ [ , ] KEEP_REPLICATION ]
   [ [ , ] MEDIANAME = { media_name | @media_name_variable } ]
   [ [ , ] MEDIAPASSWORD = { mediapassword |
                   @mediapassword_variable } ]
   [ [ , ] MOVE 'logical_file_name' TO 'operating_system_file_name' ]
               [ ,...n ]
   [ [ , ] NEW_BROKER ]
   [ [ , ] PARTIAL ]
   [ [ , ] PASSWORD = { password | @password_variable } ]
   [ [ , ] { RECOVERY | NORECOVERY | STANDBY =
```

```
        {standby_file_name | @standby_file_name_var }
   } ]
   [ [ , ] REPLACE ]
   [ [ , ] RESTART ]
   [ [ , ] RESTRICTED_USER ]
   [ [ , ] { REWIND | NOREWIND } ]
   [ [ , ] STATS [ = percentage ] ]
   [ [ , ] { STOPAT = { date_time | @date_time_var }
    | STOPATMARK = { 'mark_name' | 'lsn:lsn_number' }
            [ AFTER datetime ]
    | STOPBEFOREMARK = { 'mark_name' | 'lsn:lsn_number' }
            [ AFTER datetime ]
   } ]
   [ [ , ] { UNLOAD | NOUNLOAD } ]
]
```


Once again, there are many available options for restoring a database, but a simple restore is fairly straightforward. The following example demonstrates a full restore of the `AdventureWorks2008` database:

```
RESTORE DATABASE [AdventureWorks2008]
FROM  DISK = N'C:\mssql2008\backup\AdventureWorks2008_FullRecovery.bak'
WITH  FILE = 1,  NOUNLOAD,  REPLACE,  STATS = 10
```

For more sophisticated restores, you can specify options following the `WITH` clause. Table 14.2 briefly describes these options. Many of the options are the same as for the `BACKUP` command and provide similar functionality.

TABLE 14.2 **RESTORE DATABASE** Options

Option	Description
CHECKSUM | NO_CHECKSUM	When CHECKSUM is specified, a checksum is calculated before the backup is restored. If the checksum validation fails, the restore fails as well. The default is NO_CHECKSUM.
STOP_ON_ERROR | CONTINUE_AFTER_ERROR	The STOP_ON_ERROR option, which is the default, causes the backup to fail if an error is encountered. CONTINUE_AFTER_ERROR allows the restore to continue if an error is encountered.
ENABLE_BROKER	This option starts the Service Broker so that messages can be received.

TABLE 14.2 **RESTORE DATABASE** Options

Option	Description
ERROR_BROKER_CONVERSATIONS	Service Broker conversations with the database being restored are ended, with an error stating that the database is attached or restored.
FILE = { *file_number* | *@file_number* }	This option identifies the backup set number to be restored from the backup media. The default is 1, which indicates the latest backup set.
KEEP_REPLICATION	This option prevents replication settings from being removed during a restore operation. This is important when setting up replication to work with log shipping.
MEDIANAME	This is a 128-character name for the backup media. If it is specified, the target media must match this name.
MEDIAPASSWORD	This is a password for the media set. If the media was created with a password, the password must be supplied to restore from that media.
MOVE	This option causes the specified *logical_file_name* to be moved from its original file location to another location.
NEW_BROKER	This option creates a new *service_broker_guid.*
PARTIAL	This option causes a partial restore to occur that includes the primary filegroup and any specified secondary filegroup(s).
PASSWORD	This password is specific to the backup set. If a password was used when creating the backup set, a password must be used to restore from the media set.
RECOVERY | NORECOVERY | STANDBY	The RECOVERY option, which is the default, restores the database so that it is ready for use. NORECOVERY renders the database inaccessible but able to restore additional transaction logs. The STANDBY option allows additional transaction logs to be applied but the database to be read. These options are discussed in more detail later in this section.

TABLE 14.2 **RESTORE DATABASE** Options

Option	Description
REPLACE	This option causes the database to be created with the restore, even if the database already exists.
RESTART	This option allows a previously interrupted restore to restart where it was stopped.
RESTRICTED_USER	This option restricts access to the database after it has been restored. Only members of the db_owner, dbcreator, or sysadmin role can access it.
REWIND | NOREWIND	This option is used for tape operations. REWIND, which is the default, causes the tape to be released and rewound.
STATS	This option causes completion statistics to be displayed at the specified interval to assess progress.
STOPAT | STOPATMARK | STOPBEFOREMARK	This option causes a restore to recover to a specified date/time or to recover to a point defined by a specific transaction. The STOPAT option restores the database to the state it was in at the date and time. The STOPATMARK and STOPBEFOREMARK options restore based on the specified marked transaction or LSN.
UNLOAD | NOUNLOAD	This option is used for tape operations. NOUNLOAD cause the tape to remain in the tape drive after a restore completes. UNLOAD, which is the default, causes the tape to be rewound and unloaded when the restore completes.

14

Various options are utilized in the "Restore Scenarios" section, later in this chapter. Those restore scenarios provide a frame of reference for the options and further meaning about what they can accomplish.

Transaction Log Restores with T-SQL

The syntax details and options for restoring a transaction log backup are similar to those for RESTORE BACKUP. The options not available with RESTORE LOG include ENABLE_BROKER, ERROR_BROKER_CONVERSATIONS, NEW_BROKER, and PARTIAL.

The RECOVERY | NORECOVERY | STANDBY options are particularly important when performing transaction log restores and also when restoring a database that will have transaction logs applied. If these options are used incorrectly, you can render your database inaccessible or unable to restore subsequent transaction log backups. With the RECOVERY option, any uncommitted transactions are rolled back, and the database is made available for use. When a restore (of either a database or transaction log) is run with this option, no further transaction logs can be applied. The NORECOVERY and STANDBY options do allow subsequent transaction logs to be applied. When the NORECOVERY option is specified, the database is completely unavailable after the restore and is left in a restoring state. In this state, you cannot read the database, update the database, or obtain information about the database, but you can restore transaction logs.

With the STANDBY option, the database is left in a read-only state that allows some database access. *standby_file_name* must be specified with the *STANDBY* option. The standby file contains uncommitted transactions rolled back to place the database in a consistent state for read operations. If subsequent transaction log backups are applied to the *STANDBY* database, the uncommitted transactions in the standby file are reapplied to the database.

CAUTION

Take note of the *standby_file_name* name used when restoring with the STANDBY option and make sure the file is secure. If another restore operation is performed and the same *standby_file_name* is used, the previous standby file is overwritten. The database cannot be fully recovered without the standby file, so you have to perform all the restore operations again.

We speak from personal experience on this one. During a data recovery drill, for a large database (approximately 1TB), we spent hours restoring the transaction logs on a set of log-shipped databases. We manually restored the last log to be applied to place the database in STANDBY mode. Another database also in the data recovery drill was also placed in STANDBY, and unfortunately, the same standby file was used on this database. This caused more than one person a very long night. Be careful!

Some of the other options of the RESTORE DATABASE command are covered in the "Restore Scenarios" section, later in this chapter. Once again, many of these options are not required for most types of restores. For example, the following command uses basic options to restore a transaction log backup to the AdventureWorks2008 database:

```
RESTORE LOG [AdventureWorks2008] FROM
DISK =
N'C:\mssql2008\backup\AdventureWorks2008\AdventureWorks2008_backup_200906091215.trn'
WITH  FILE = 1,  NOUNLOAD,  STATS = 10, NORECOVERY
```

Typically, the individual restore commands you will use are along the lines of the preceding example. The restores become more complicated when many restores of different types are involved in a recovery option. Fortunately, SSMS can help ease this pain.

Restoring by Using SSMS

The restore capabilities in SSMS are comprehensive and can reduce the amount of time needed to perform a restore and limit the number of errors. This is partly due to the fact that SSMS keeps track of the backups that have occurred on a server. When a restore operation is requested for a database, SQL Server reads from its own system tables and presents a list of backups that it knows about that can be restored. In situations in which many files need to be restored, SSMS can be an invaluable tool.

You access the restore functions in SSMS by right-clicking the database in the Object Explorer and selecting Tasks and then Restore. The options available for restore include Database, File and Filegroups, and Transaction Log. Which restore options are enabled depends on the state of the database being restored. The Transaction Log option is disabled for databases that were restored with the `RECOVERY` option or are set to simple recovery mode. Figure 14.6 shows an example of the restore screen that is displayed when you select a database restore for the `AdventureWorks2008` database.

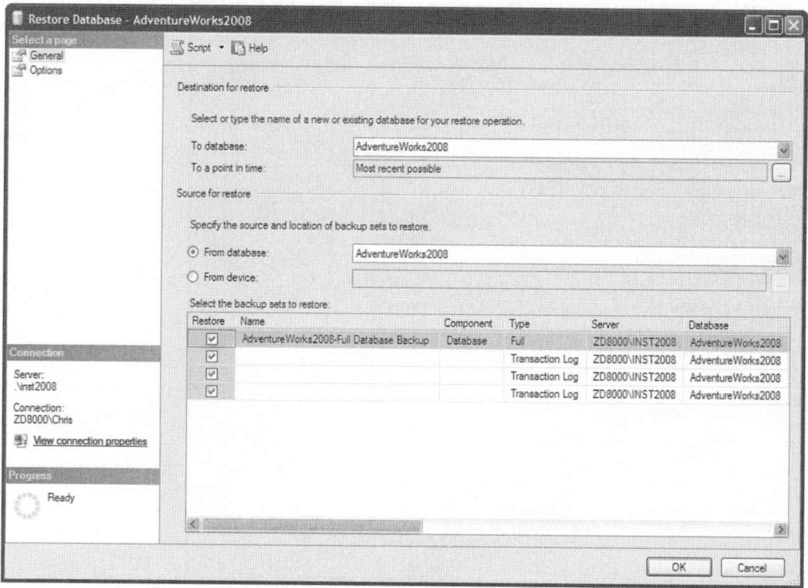

FIGURE 14.6 A database restore with SSMS.

The Restore Database window can show more than one type of backup, depending on what is available. The first backup shown in Figure 14.6 is a full backup, followed by a series of transaction log backups. The beauty of this screen is that the backups are shown in the order in which they should be applied. This order is very important with restores because they must be applied in the order in which they occurred. You can choose to apply all the backups or selectively choose the backups you want to apply. If you uncheck the first full database backup, all subsequent log backups are unchecked as well. If you recheck the full database backup and click one of the transaction log backups toward the bottom of the list, all the required backups that happened prior to the selected backups are also selected.

Figure 14.7 shows an example or the Options page of the Restore Database window for the `AdventureWorks2008` database. The Options page allows you to specify many of the T-SQL `RESTORE` options reviewed previously. The Overwrite the Existing Database option is equivalent to the `REPLACE` parameter and forces a replacement of the restored database if it exists already. The Preserve the Replication Settings option is equivalent to `KEEP_REPLICATION`. The Restrict Access to the Restored Database option is the same as using the `RESTRICTED_USER` option with the T-SQL `RESTORE` command. The Prompt Before Restoring Each Backup option does not have a T-SQL equivalent; it displays a prompt before restoring each backup set to ask whether you want to restore it.

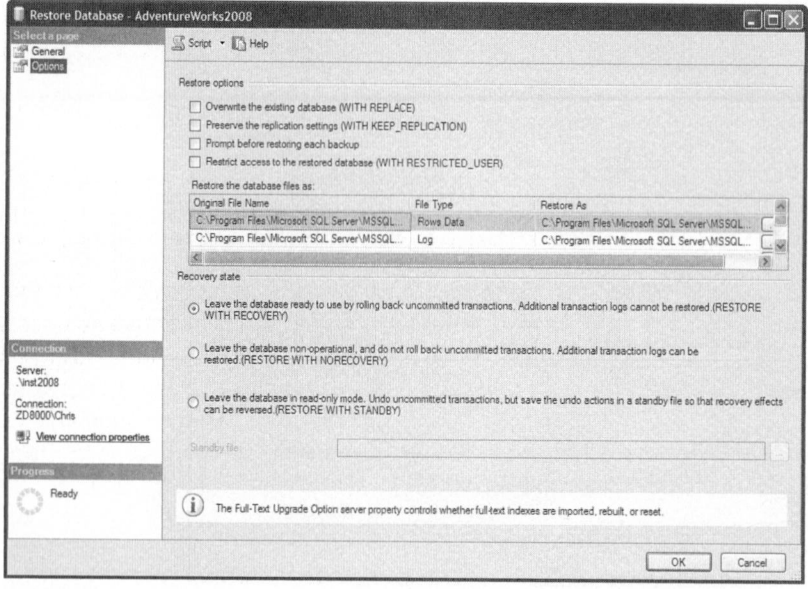

FIGURE 14.7 Restore options with SSMS.

The last three options on the Options page relate the recovery state of the last backup set restored. The first option is synonymous with the `RECOVERY` option, the second option is the same as `NORECOVERY`, and the last option is equivalent to the `STANDBY` option. The standby filename must be supplied with the `STANDBY` option and defaults to the default backup directory for the server. By default, the name of the file contains the name of the database being restored.

TIP

You should click the Script button available on the Restore Database window if you want to see what is going on under the hood of the SSMS restores or want to run a restore later. You can learn a lot about the T-SQL options and how they work by scripting out the commands.

Restore Information

Backup files and system tables contain a wealth of information about what can be restored or already has been restored. You can retrieve information from the backup files by using variations of the RESTORE command. These variations do not actually perform the restore operation but provide information about the backups that can be restored. The RESTORE commands and some useful system tables are detailed in the following sections.

The RESTORE FILELISTONLY Command

The RESTORE FILELISTONLY command returns a result set that contains a list of the database and log files contained in the backup. An example of this command follows:

```
RESTORE FILELISTONLY
FROM DISK = 'C:\mssql2008\backup\AdventureWorks2008_Partial.bak'
```

The results from this type of restore include the logical and physical filenames, the type of each file, and the size of each file.

The RESTORE HEADERONLY Command

The RESTORE HEADERONLY command returns a result set that contains the backup header data for all backup sets on the specified backup device. This command is useful when multiple backup sets are written to the same device. An example of this command follows:

```
RESTORE HEADERONLY
FROM DISK = 'C:\mssql2008\backup\AdventureWorks2008_Partial.bak'
```

More than 50 columns are returned in the result set. Some particularly useful pieces of information include the start and finish time for the backup, recovery mode when the backup was taken, type of backup, and name of the computer from which the backup was performed.

The RESTORE VERIFYONLY Command

The RESTORE VERIFYONLY command verifies that a backup set is complete and readable. The restore does not attempt to verify the structure of the data in the backups, but it has been enhanced to run additional checks on the data. The checks are designed to increase the probability of detecting errors. An example of this command follows:

```
RESTORE VERIFYONLY
FROM DISK = 'C:\mssql2008\backup\AdventureWorks2008_Partial.bak'

/*Result from the prior RESTORE VERIFYONLY command
The backup set on file 1 is valid.
*/
```

The results from the prior example show that the `RESTORE VERIFYONLY` command does not contain much output, but the value of this command is in helping ensure that the backups are sound.

Backup and Restore System Tables

The system tables for backups and restores are found in the `msdb` system database. These system tables are used to keep historical information about the backups and restores that have occurred on the server. These system tables are listed in Table 14.3.

TABLE 14.3 Backing Up and Restoring System Tables

`msdb` **System Table**	**Description**
`backupfile`	Contains one row for each data or log file of a database.
`backupfilegroup`	Contains one row for each filegroup in a database at the time of backup.
`backupmediafamily`	Contains a row for each media family.
`backupmediaset`	Contains one row for each backup media set.
`backupset`	Contains a row for each backup set.
`logmarkhistory`	Contains one row for each marked transaction that has been committed.
`restorefile`	Contains one row for each restored file. These include files restored indirectly, by filegroup name.
`restorefilegroup`	Contains one row for each restored filegroup.
`restorehistory`	Contains one row for each restore operation.
`suspect_pages`	Contains one row per page that failed with an 824 error (with a limit of 1,000 rows).
`sysopentapes`	Contains one row for each currently open tape device.

Refer to "Backup and Restore Tables" in the "System Tables" section of SQL Server Books Online for a detailed description of each table, including each column that can be retrieved.

You are able to query these tables to obtain a variety of information related to backups and restores. You can tailor these queries to look at a specific database or a specific time frame. The following example retrieves restore information for the AdventureWorks2008 database:

```
select destination_database_name 'database', h.restore_date, restore_type,
 cast((backup_size/1024)/1024 as numeric(8,0)) 'backup_size MB',
  f.physical_device_name
 from msdb..restorehistory h (NOLOCK)
   LEFT JOIN msdb..backupset b (NOLOCK)
   ON h.backup_set_id = b.backup_set_id
   LEFT JOIN msdb..backupmediafamily f (NOLOCK)
   ON b.media_set_id = f.media_set_id
 where h.restore_date > getdate() - 5
    and UPPER(h.destination_database_name) = 'AdventureWorks2008'
 order by UPPER(h.destination_database_name), h.restore_date desc
```

This example displays information related to restores that have been executed in the past five days for the AdventureWorks2008 database. The restore date, type of restore, size of the backup, and physical location of the file used for the restore are displayed when you run this query.

CAUTION

Queries against system tables are acceptable and can provide a wealth of information, but you need to exercise caution whenever you are dealing with a system table. SQL Server uses these tables, and problems can occur if the values in them are changed or their physical structure is altered.

Backup and Restore Report

A set of standard reports that come with SQL Server 2008 provide a variety of information about your databases, including recent restores and backups. You can access these reports by right-clicking on a database in the SSMS Object Explorer, then Reports, and then Standard Reports. You see over a dozen reports ready for you to run.

A report particularly useful for obtaining restore and backup information is named Backup and Restore Events. This report details the latest backup and restore events that have occurred on a particular database. An example of this report is shown in Figure 14.8.

The interactive report allows you to drill down into each backup or restore event to obtain more information. For example, the restore information shown in Figure 14.8 was obtained by clicking on the plus button next to the Successful Restore Operations label. You can then drill down into an individual restore to obtain more information, including the physical files involved in the operation.

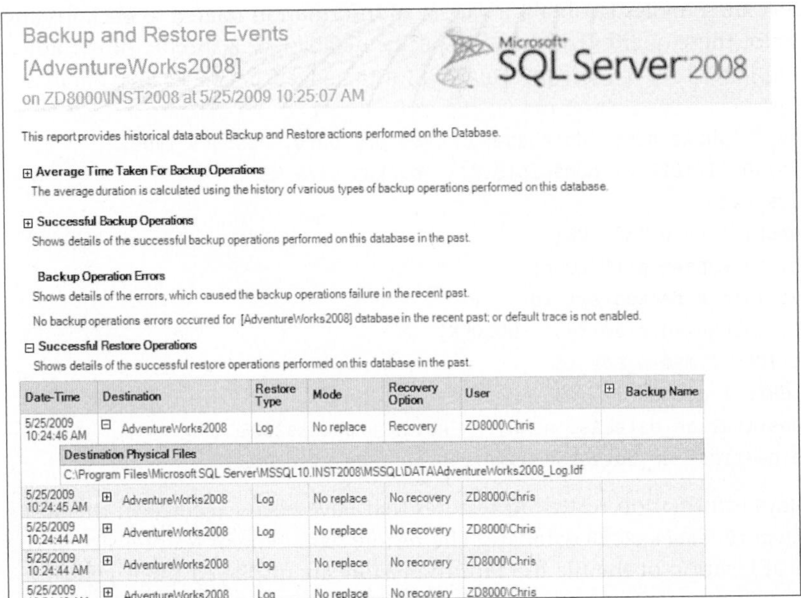

FIGURE 14.8 Backup and Restore Events report.

Restore Scenarios

Restore scenarios are as varied as the backup scenarios that drive them. The number of scenarios is directly related to the types of backups taken and frequency of those backups. If a database is in simple recovery mode and full database backups are taken each night, your restore options are limited. Conversely, full recovery databases that have multiple filegroups and take a variety of different types of backups have a greater number of options that can be used to restore the database.

The following sections describe a number of restore scenarios to give you a taste of the types of restores you may encounter. The scenarios include some restores performed with T-SQL and others performed with SSMS.

Restoring to a Different Database

You can restore a database backup to a different database. The database you're restoring to can be on the same server or a different server, and the database can be restored to a different name, if needed. These types of restores are common in development environments where a production backup is recovered on a development server or multiple copies of the same development database are restored to different database names for use by different groups.

Listing 14.7 shows the T-SQL `RESTORE` command you can use to create a new database named `AdventureWorks2008_COPY` from the backup of the `AdventureWorks2008` database. Take note of the `MOVE` options that specify where the database files for the new

AdventureWorks2008_COPY database will exist. Each MOVE option must refer to the logical name for the file and include a physical file location that is a valid location on the server. In addition, the referenced file cannot be used by another database. The only exception is when you are restoring to the database that is using the files and the REPLACE option is used.

LISTING 14.7 Restore to a Different Database

```
RESTORE DATABASE [AdventureWorks2008_COPY]
 FROM  DISK = N'C:\mssql2008\backup\AdventureWorks2008.bak'
 WITH  FILE = 1,
 MOVE N'AdventureWorks2008_Data' TO
N'C:\mssql2008\data\AdventureWorks2008_Copy.mdf',
 MOVE N'AdventureWorks2008_Log' TO
N'C:\mssql2008\data\AdventureWorks2008_Copy_log.ldf',
  NOUNLOAD,  STATS = 10
```


TIP

A restore of a database backup taken from another server can cause problems after the restore completes. The problems are caused by broken relationships between the database users captured in the backup file and the associated logins on the server to which the backup is restored. The relationships are broken because each login receives a unique ID assigned to it when it is added. These unique IDs can and will be different across servers, even though the logins may have the same name. The unique ID from the login is stored with each database user in order to identify the login that the user is associated with. When the unique ID for the login is different or not found, you get spurious errors when trying to connect to the database with these users or when trying to administer these users in SSMS.

The sp_change_users_login system stored procedure is designed to correct these broken relationships. You can run this procedure with the "report" option in the database in question to help identify any problems (that is, sp_change_users_login "report"). The stored procedure also has options to fix the broken relationships. For example, sp_change_users_login "autofix", "myuser" fixes the relationship for the "myuser" database user. You should check SQL Server Books Online for further options and details on this stored procedure.

Another quick-and-dirty means for fixing orphaned database users is to delete the users from the database and then re-create them. Of course, the login must exist on the server, and all the permissions associated with the database user must be reestablished. Permissions can be overlooked or missed with this method, so it is safer to stick with the sp_change_users_login procedure.

Restoring a Snapshot

Database snapshots, which were introduced in SQL Server 2005, provide a fast method for capturing a transactionally consistent view of a database. The snapshot is created as another read-only database linked to the original database from which the snapshot was taken. As changes are made to the original database, the database engine uses a copy-on-write method to keep the snapshot consistent.

After a snapshot is taken, you can revert back to the snapshot at a later time and restore the original database to the state it was in when the snapshot was taken. You do not create the snapshot by backing up a database, but you can restore it using methods similar to restoring a backup. The following examples shows the syntax to revert a database back to a database snapshot:

```
RESTORE DATABASE { database_name | @database_name_var }
FROM DATABASE_SNAPSHOT database_snapshot_name
```

Database snapshots are available only with the Enterprise or Development Editions of SQL Server. They are discussed in more detail in Chapter 32, "Database Snapshots."

Restoring a Transaction Log

Transaction log restores deserve special attention because of their dependency on other backup types. Typical transaction log restores occur after a full or differential database restore has occurred. After this base is established, the transaction log restores must be done in the same sequential order as the backups that were taken.

Fortunately, SSMS does a good job of presenting the available backups in the order in which they must be applied. You can do the entire restore sequence with SSMS, including a full restore followed by a restore of any other backups, including transaction log backups. To restore transaction log backups (independent of other backups), you can select the Transaction Log option. Figure 14.9 shows a sample screen for restoring transaction logs in the `AdventureWorks2008` database.

The transaction logs shown in Figure 14.9 are listed in the order in which they were taken and the order in which they need to be applied. You can uncheck some of the available backups, but you are not allowed to select backups that are not in the correct sequence. In other words, you can uncheck backups from the bottom of the list, but if you uncheck backups toward the top of the list, all backups found below that item are unchecked as well.

It is important to remember that you can restore transaction log backups only to a database that is in the `NORECOVERY` or `STANDBY` state. Make sure that every restore prior to the last one uses one of these options. When you restore the last transaction log, you should use the `RECOVERY` option so that the database is available for use.

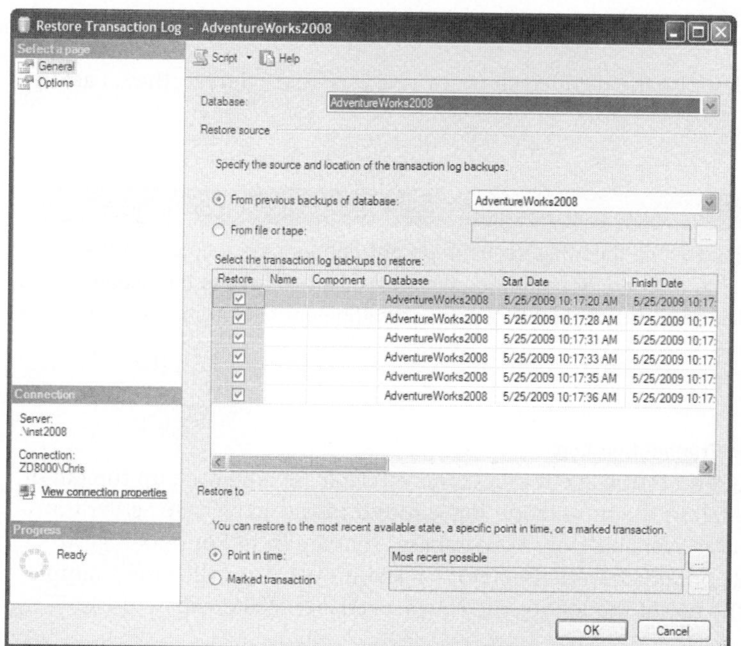

FIGURE 14.9 Transaction Log Restore.

Restoring to the Point of Failure

A disk failure on a drive that houses database files is a reality that some database administrators must deal with. This situation can give pause to the most seasoned administrators, but it is a situation that can be addressed with little or no data loss. Don't panic! You need to first identify the available backups.

NOTE

It is hoped the disk that experienced a failure is not the same disk that houses your backups. Database backups should always be stored on separate media. One of the best approaches is to write the backups to a drive that does not contain any other SQL Server files and write the contents of that drive to tape. This minimizes the possibility of losing one of those all-important backups.

The backup components that you need to restore to the point of failure include the following:

- A backup of the tail of the transaction log
- A full database backup or file/filegroup backup to establish a base

- The full sequence of transaction log backups created since the full database backup

The following sections describe the detailed steps for recovery that relate to these backup components.

NOTE

The restore steps outlined in the following sections do not address the recovery of the actual disk that failed. The recovery of hardware, such as a disk, is beyond the scope of this book, but it needs to be addressed to get your environment back to the state it was in prior to the failure.

Backing Up the Tail of the Transaction Log

The first thing you should do in the event of a damaged database is to back up the tail of the transaction log. The tail of the transaction log is found in the active SQL Server transaction log file(s). This tail is available only for databases that are in full or bulk-logged recovery mode. This tail contains transactions not backed up yet. The following example shows how to back up the tail of the log for the AdventureWorks2008 database using T-SQL:

```
BACKUP LOG [AdventureWorks2008]
 TO  DISK = N'C:\mssql2008\backup\log\AdventureWorks2008_Tail.trn'
 WITH  NO_TRUNCATE
```

NO_TRUNCATE prevents the transactions in the log from being removed and allows the transaction log to be backed up, even if the database is inaccessible. This type of backup is possible only if the transaction log file is accessible and was not on the disk that had the failure.

Recovering the Full Database Recovery

After you back up the tail of the transaction log, you are ready to perform a full database restore. This restore, which is based on a full database backup or a file/filegroup backup, overwrites the existing database. It is imperative that the full database restore be done with the NORECOVERY option so that the transaction log backups and tail of the log can be applied to the database as well. The following example restores a full backup of the AdventureWorks2008 database, using the T-SQL RESTORE command:

```
RESTORE DATABASE [AdventureWorks2008]
 FROM  DISK = N'C:\mssql2008\backup\AdventureWorks2008.bak'
 WITH  FILE = 1,  NORECOVERY,  NOUNLOAD,  REPLACE,  STATS = 10
```

Upon completion of this type of restore, the database appears in the SSMS Object Explorer with "(Restoring...)" appended to the end of the database name. The database is now ready for transaction log backups to be applied.

Restoring the Transaction Log Backup

The final step in recovery is to apply the transaction log backups. These backups include all the transaction log backups since the last full backup plus the tail of the log you backed up after the media failure. If differential backups were taken since the last full backup, you can apply the last differential backup and apply only those transaction log backups that have occurred since the last differential backup.

You can restore transaction log backups by using T-SQL or SSMS. To restore with SSMS, you can right-click the database in the restoring state and select the Transaction Log Restore option. The Restore Transaction Log screen lists the available transaction log backups, including the backup of the transaction log tail. You need to select all the transaction logs, including the tail. You should make sure to go to the Options tab and select the Recovery option so that your database is available after the restore completes.

Alternatively, you can use T-SQL to perform the transaction log backup restores. The following example shows a series of transaction log restores. The first two restores are done with the `NORECOVERY` option. The last command restores the tail of the log and uses the `RECOVERY` option to make the database available for use:


```
RESTORE LOG [AdventureWorks2008]
 FROM  DISK =
N'C:\mssql2008\backup\AdventureWorks2008_backup_200906180922.trn'
 WITH  FILE = 1,  NORECOVERY,  NOUNLOAD,  STATS = 10
GO
RESTORE LOG [AdventureWorks2008]
 FROM  DISK =
  N'C:\mssql2008\backup\AdventureWorks2008_backup_200906180923.trn'
 WITH  FILE = 1,  NORECOVERY,  NOUNLOAD,  STATS = 10
GO
RESTORE LOG [AdventureWorks2008]
 FROM  DISK =
  N'C:\mssql2008\backup\log\AdventureWorks2008_Tail.trn'
 WITH  FILE = 3,  NOUNLOAD,  STATS = 10
GO
```

When many transaction log backups are involved, using T-SQL to perform the restores can be challenging. The restores must occur in the proper order and refer to the proper location of the backup file(s). Restores done with SSMS are typically less prone to error.

Restoring to a Point in Time

Databases in the full or bulk-logged recovery models can be restored to a point in time. This type of restore is similar to the point-of-failure scenario covered previously, but it allows for a more precise restore operation. These restores allow the database to be recovered to a time prior to a particular event. Malicious attacks or erroneous updates are some examples of events that would justify a point-in-time restore.

> **NOTE**
>
> There are some limitations on point-in-time restores of databases set to the bulk-logged recovery model. Point-in-time restores are not possible on transaction log backups that contain bulk load operations. Point-in-time restores can occur using transaction log backups that occurred prior to the bulk load operation, as long as a bulk load did not occur during the time of these backups.

A point-in-time restore can be done using one of the following:

- A specific date/time within the transaction log backup
- A specific transaction name inserted in the log
- An LSN

Point-in-time restores can be done with T-SQL or SSMS. Figure 14.10 shows the General page that allows you to specify the Point in Time option. The default is to restore to the most recent time possible, but you can click on the ellipsis to display the Point in Time Restore dialog box, which is shown in the middle of Figure 14.10. You can select the date to restore to by using the date drop-down and enter the time to restore to as well.

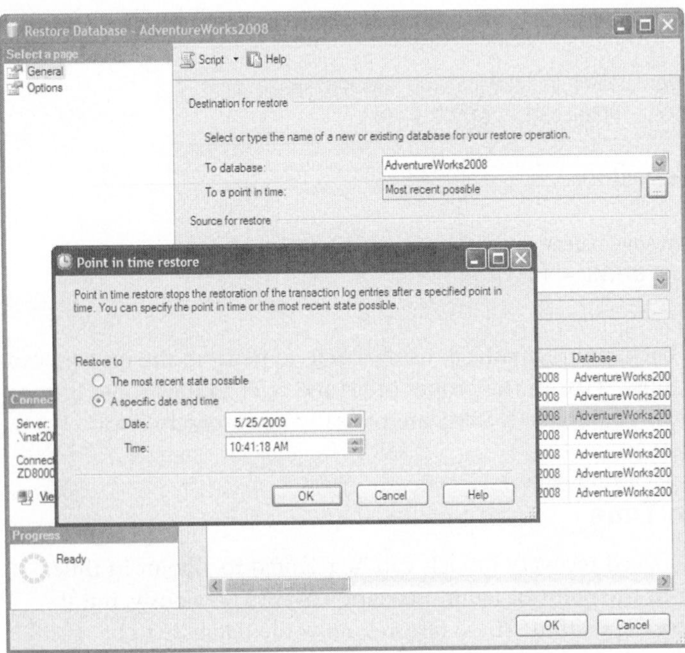

FIGURE 14.10 A point-in-time restore.

Online Restores

Online restores were new to SQL Server 2005 and continue to be supported in SQL Server 2008. They allow a filegroup, file, or specific page within a file to be restored while the rest of the database is online. The file or filegroup that is being restored to must be offline during the duration of the online restore.

TIP

You should take a full backup of a database immediately before taking a read-only file offline. This simplifies the online restore process and eliminates the need to apply a bunch of transaction log backups prior to the online restore. This applies only to databases in full or bulk-logged recovery.

The following example demonstrates how to take a read-only file offline:

```
ALTER DATABASE AdventureWorks2008
MODIFY FILE (NAME = 'AdventureWorks2008_ReadOnlyData', OFFLINE)
```

When the file is offline, you can perform a restore to that file without affecting the rest of the database. The following example shows an example of an online restore of a read-only file to the `AdventureWorks2008` database:

```
RESTORE DATABASE [AdventureWorks2008]
 FILE = N'AdventureWorks2008_ReadOnlyData'
 FROM  DISK = N'C:\mssql2008\backup\AdventureWorks2008_ReadOnlyData.bak'
 WITH  FILE = 1,  NOUNLOAD,  STATS = 10, RECOVERY
```

Restoring the System Databases

The SQL Server 2008 system databases that can be restored are the `master`, `msdb`, `model`, and `distribution` databases. Each of these databases performs an essential role in the operation of SQL Server. If these databases are damaged or lost, they can be restored from database backup files in a similar fashion to user databases.

The `master` database, which contains information about other databases and is required to start SQL Server, has some special restore considerations. It must be operational before restores of other system databases can be considered. When you are restoring the `master` database, there are two basic scenarios. The first scenario involves a restore of the `master` database when the `master` database currently used by SQL Server is operational. In the second scenario, the `master` database is unavailable, and SQL Server is unable to start.

The first `master` database restore scenario is less involved and typically less stressful than the second. In the first scenario, your SQL Server can be up and running until the time you want to do the restore. When you are ready to do the restore, the SQL Server instance must be running in single-user mode. The server can be started in single-user mode via a command prompt window. You stop the currently running SQL Server service, open a command prompt window, navigate to the directory where the `sqlservr.exe` file exists (typically `C:\Program Files\Microsoft SQL Server\MSSQL.1\MSSQL\Binn\`), and run the following command:

```
sqlservr.exe -m
```

When this command is executed, the SQL Server instance is running in the command prompt window. This window must be kept open for the SQL Server instance to keep running. The service for SQL Server appears as stopped, but the database engine is truly running.

The `-m` parameter places the server in single-user mode and allows a single administrator connection to the server. You can use that one connection to connect to the server to use the Object Explorer, a database query window in SSMS, SQLCMD, or any other tool that allows you to establish a connection and run commands against the database server. If you use the SSMS Object Explorer connection, you can right-click on the `master` database and select the Restore option. You need to enter `master` for the database to restore and select the overwrite option. You can instead run a T-SQL `RESTORE` command to achieve the same result.

When the restore of the `master` database is complete, SQL Server is automatically shut down. If you performed the restore using Object Explorer, you can expect to get an error message at the end of the restore process because SQL Server was shut down. You can simply close the command prompt window you used earlier and establish a new connection to the database server. All the databases, logins, and so on that were present prior to the backup are reestablished.

In the second scenario, the `master` database is damaged or unavailable, and SQL Server cannot start. If SQL Server is unable to start, you must reestablish a base environment like that which existed when SQL Server was initially installed. Using the `REBUILDDATABASE` option in `setup.exe` is one way to re-create all the system databases and reestablish this base environment. The `REBUILDDATABASE` parameter is part of a SQL Server installation that is done from the command prompt. You need the installation media for the edition of SQL Server installed on the machine. After you insert the disk and when you have access to the installation files, you can use the following syntax to launch the Setup program from a command prompt window:

```
start /wait <CD or DVD Drive>\setup.exe /qn
INSTANCENAME=<InstanceName> REINSTALL=SQL_Engine
REBUILDDATABASE=1 SAPWD=<NewStrongPassword>
```

`InstanceName` should be set to `MSSQLSERVER` for a default instance of SQL Server or the name of the instance, if it is not the default. In addition, a new `SA` password needs to be supplied for the `SAPWD` parameter. The `/qn` parameter suppresses all the setup dialog boxes and error messages and causes the installation to run silently. If you want to receive more information during the installation, you can specify the `/qb` parameter.

NOTE

If you get a message about a missing Windows Installer, you can find that software on the SQL Server media in the `Redist` folder. You may also find that the `setup.exe` file is not found on the root of your installation media. If this is the case, you need to change the directory in the command prompt window to the location of the `setup.exe` file on the installation media prior to executing the command to launch the setup program. Finally, remember to reinstall any service packs or patches you may have installed. The execution of the command prompt setup reverts the server back to the original software release.

At the end of the installation, all the system database files are installed to their original locations. This includes the original `master.mdf`, `mastlog.ldf`, `msdbdata.mdf`, and `msdblog.ldf` files, as well as the related database files for the other system databases. Any of the user databases you may have added to the server are no longer known by the `master` database and in turn are not available in the Object Explorer or other database tools.

If you have a backup of the `master` database, you can restore it after the command prompt installation is complete. You follow the procedures outlined in the first scenario, earlier in this section, to restore the `master` database from a backup. At the completion of the restore, any user databases present at the time of the `master` database backup are now available. You can also run restores for other system databases at this time, including the `msdb` database, which contains all your scheduled jobs and history.

If you do not have a backup of the `master` database, this is not the end of the world. You still have the option of manually attaching your user databases or restoring them from backup files. Attaching the database is typically much faster than restores from backup files and is the preferred method. You must also reestablish logins, backup devices, server triggers, and any other server-level objects stored in the `master` database. Depending on your environment, this can be a lengthy operation, but you can easily avoid it by making those all-important system database backups.

Additional Backup Considerations

A sound backup plan goes beyond the commands and tools described thus far in this chapter. There are several other considerations, detailed in the following sections, that should be considered as well.

Frequency of Backups

How often you back up your databases depends on many factors, including the following:

- The size of your databases and your backup window (that is, the time allocated to complete the task of backing up the database)

- The frequency of changes to the data and method by which it is changed
- The acceptable amount of data loss in the event of a failure
- The acceptable recovery time in the event of a failure

First, you must establish what your backup window will be. Because SQL Server allows dynamic backups, users can still access the database during backups; however, this affects performance. This means you should still schedule backups for low-activity periods and have them complete in the shortest possible time.

After you establish your backup window, you can determine your backup method and schedule. For example, if it takes 4 hours for a full backup to complete, and the database is quiescent between midnight and 6:00 a.m., you have time to perform a full backup each night. On the other hand, if a full backup takes 10 hours, and you have a 2-hour window, you should consider monthly or weekly backups, perhaps in conjunction with filegroup, differential, and transaction log backups. In many decision-support databases populated with periodic data loads, it might suffice to back up once after each data load.

Backup frequency is also directly tied to acceptable data loss. In the event of catastrophic failure, such as a fire in the server room, you can recover data only up to the point of the last backup moved offsite. If it is acceptable to lose a day's worth of data entry, nightly backups might suffice. If your acceptable loss is an hour's worth of data, hourly transaction log backups would have to be added to the schedule.

Your backup frequency affects your recovery time. In some environments, a weekly full backup plus transaction log backups taken every 10 minutes provide an acceptable data loss factor. A failure a few days after backup would require a full database restore and the application of hundreds of transaction logs. Adding a daily differential backup in this case would vastly improve restore time. The full and differential backups would be restored, and then six logs would be applied for each hour between the differential backup and the time of failure.

Using a Standby Server

If the ability to quickly recover from failure is crucial to your operation, you might consider implementing a standby server. Implementing a standby server involves backing up the production server and then restoring it to the standby server, leaving it in recovery mode. As transaction logs are backed up on the production server, they are applied to the standby server. If a failure occurs on the production server, the standby server can be recovered and used in place of the production server. If the production server is still running, you should not forget to back up the current log with the `NO_TRUNCATE` option and restore it to the standby server as well before bringing it online.

NOTE

Another advantage of restoring backups to a standby server is that it immediately validates your backups so you can be assured of whether they are valid. There is nothing worse than finding out during a recovery process that one of the backup files is damaged or missing.

The STANDBY =*undo_file_name* option plays a key role in the application of transaction logs to the standby server. When the database and subsequent log backups are restored to the standby server with this option, the database is left in recovery mode but is available as a read-only database. Now that the standby database is available for queries, it can actually reduce load on the production database by acting as a decision support system (DSS). Database Consistency Checks (DBCC) can be run on it as well, further reducing the load on the production system.

For the database to be available for reads, the data must be in a consistent state. This means that all uncommitted transactions must be rolled back. This rollback is usually handled by the RECOVERY option during a restore. In the case of a standby server, this would cause a problem because you would intend to apply more logs, which could, in fact, commit those transactions. This situation is handled by the *undo_file_name* clause of the STANDBY option. The file specified here holds a copy of all uncommitted transactions rolled back to bring the standby server to a consistent, read-only state. If those transactions subsequently commit a log restore, this undo information can be used to complete the transaction.

The application of hundreds or thousands of transaction logs to the standby server can be challenging. Fortunately, SQL Server 2008 includes log shipping, which automates the transfer of logs to the standby server. Log shipping, which can be configured in SSMS, uses SQL Server Agent jobs on the primary server to back up the transaction log and copy it to a folder on the standby server. SQL Server Agent on the standby server then executes a load job to restore the log. Automating your standby server with log shipping reduces administration and helps to ensure that the standby database is up-to-date. For further details on log shipping, see Chapter 19, "Replication." Log shipping isn't a form of replication but is covered in Chapter 19 as an alternative to replication.

Snapshot Backups

Snapshot backups are developed in conjunction with independent hardware and software vendors. These backups are not related to SQL Server database snapshots and are not accessible from any of the SQL Server tools. They utilize backup and restore technology and can provide relatively fast backup and restore operations. Snapshot backups are typically utilized on very large databases that are unable to perform database backups and restores in a timely fashion using SQL Server's conventional backup and restore resources.

Considerations for Very Large Databases

When it comes to backup and recovery, special consideration must be given to very large databases, which are known as VLDBs. A VLDB has the following special requirements:

- **Storage**—Size might dictate the use of tape backups over the network or a disk.
- **Time**—As your time to backup increases, the frequency of backups might have to be adjusted.
- **Method**—How you back up your database is affected by its size. Differential or file and filegroup backups might have to be implemented.

- **Recovery**—Partial database recovery, such as restoring a file or filegroup, might be required due to the prohibitive time required to restore the entire database.

When designing a VLDB, you must integrate your backup plan with storage, performance, and availability requirements. Larger databases take longer to back up because the backup sizes are larger, and restores on this type of database can take much longer to complete than with a smaller database.

Maintenance Plans

SQL Server includes maintenance plans that provide database maintenance tasks, including optimization, integrity checks, and backups. The backup options available in the maintenance plans are comprehensive and include the capability to regularly schedule full, differential, and transaction log backups. This type of automation is essential to ensure that your backups are taken with a reliable tool at regular intervals.

You can create maintenance plans from within SSMS. If you open the `Management` node in the Object Explorer, you see a node named `Maintenance Plans`. If you right-click this node, you can select New Maintenance Plan to create a plan from scratch, or you can select Maintenance Plan Wizard to have a wizard guide you through the creation of a new maintenance plan. The following options that relate to backups are available as part of a maintenance plan:

- Back Up Database (Full)
- Back Up Database (Differential)
- Back Up Database (Transaction Log)

Using these tasks in a maintenance plan is a great start to a solid backup and recovery plan. Refer to Chapter 33, "Database Maintenance," for further details about creating a maintenance plan.

Summary

Having a database environment without a solid backup and recovery plan is like owning a home without an insurance policy to protect it. If you develop a plan to minimize the possibility of losing a database, you have essentially bought an insurance policy for your data. In the event of a problem, you can call on the backups that you have invested in and recover the loss with a minimal amount of cost.

Chapter 15, "Database Mail," explores a comprehensive mail feature offered with SQL Server 2008. Database Mail allows you to send email notifications from SQL Server. These notifications can be tied to scheduled jobs and alerts within SQL Server, including jobs that can execute those all-important database backups.

CHAPTER 15

Database Mail

IN THIS CHAPTER

- What's New in Database Mail
- Setting Up Database Mail
- Sending and Receiving with Database Mail
- Using SQL Server Agent Mail
- Related Views and Procedures

Database Mail is SQL Server 2008's emailing component, built as the replacement for SQL Mail. Although SQL Mail can still be enabled in SQL Server 2008 (for backward compatibility, although it is deprecated), it's a simple task to convert all your existing SQL Mail code and SQL Agent Mail notifications to Database Mail. And you'll surely want to.

What's New in Database Mail

Database Mail is an enterprise-class implementation designed with all the features you'd expect from this next-generation database server, most of which are not available in SQL Mail. These features include support for multiple email profiles and accounts, asynchronous (queued) message delivery via a dedicated process in conjunction with Service Broker, cluster-awareness, 64-bit compatibility, greater security options (such as governing of mail attachment size and prohibition of file extensions), and simplified mail auditing. Database Mail also utilizes the industry-standard Simple Mail Transfer Protocol (SMTP), signaling the end of reliance on Extended Messaging Application Programming Interface (Extended MAPI).

Database Mail has more capabilities and is more scalable and reliable than SQL Mail, especially when stressed with the heavier usage scenarios common today. And, thankfully, it's a good deal easier to successfully configure than its predecessor.

Setting Up Database Mail

Unlike with SQL Mail, setting up profiles and accounts for use with Database Mail is easy to accomplish, thanks mainly to the Database Mail Configuration Wizard, found in the SQL Server Management Studio (SSMS) Object Browser. You can use this wizard both to set up and manage Database Mail. Before using it, you need to switch on the Database Mail feature, which is off by default, in keeping with Microsoft's secure-by-default approach. Follow these steps to do so.

Configure the `Database Mail XPs` configuration option by running the following T-SQL code in a new query window (while logged in as `sysadmin`, of course):

```
use Master
GO
sp_configure 'show advanced options', 1;
GO
RECONFIGURE;
GO
sp_configure 'Database Mail XPs', 1;
GO
RECONFIGURE
GO
Configuration option 'show advanced options' changed from 0 to 1. Run the
RECONFIGURE statement to install.
Configuration option 'Database Mail XPs' changed from 0 to 1. Run the
RECONFIGURE statement to install.
```

If you ever want to disable Database Mail, you can run this:

```
sp_configure 'Database Mail XPs', 0;
```

This statement prevents Database Mail from starting in response to a call to `sysmail_start_sp` (discussed later in this chapter). If Database Mail is running when you make this call, it sends unsent queued mail until the mail sending process (`DatabaseMail.exe`) has been idle for the duration of the `DatabaseMailExeMinimumLifeTime` configuration setting (discussed later in this chapter); then it stops.

You also need to enable Service Broker in `msdb` (if not done already) because Database Mail relies on it as part of its implementation. To do this, you stop the SQL Server Agent service and then execute the following script:

```
USE master
GO
ALTER DATABASE msdb SET ENABLE_BROKER
```

You can check the status of Service Broker on msdb by using the following code:

```
Use Master
GO
SELECT is_broker_enabled
FROM sys.databases
WHERE name = 'msdb'
GO
is_broker_enabled
---------.
1
(1 row(s) affected)
```

To receive message send requests from outside the SQL Server instance, you need to create an endpoint (preferably a certificate-secured one) associated with Service Broker. To accomplish this, refer to the "Service Broker Routing and Security" section in Chapter 49, "SQL Server Service Broker" (on the CD), or consult the "Create Endpoint" topic in Books Online.

To complete this configuration, you need to return to SSMS and establish a connection to the same SQL Server instance for which you just enabled Database Mail. You connect the Object Browser to that instance and expand the Management folder to reveal the `Database Mail` node. Then you right-click the `Database Mail` node and select the Configure Database Mail menu option to launch the Database Mail Configuration Wizard.

Creating Mail Profiles and Accounts

After you pass the Database Mail Configuration Wizard's welcome screen, you are presented with the opportunity to set up Database Mail ("for the first time"). You can achieve this by creating the required profiles, profile security settings, SMTP accounts, and system-wide mail settings. You should leave the first radio button (Set Up Database Mail by Performing the Following Tasks) selected and then click Next.

NOTE

In Database Mail, you use mail profiles. A *mail profile* is simply a securable container for a group of SMTP accounts that is used when sending mail. In contrast to SQL Mail, with Database Mail, you can set up multiple profiles containing multiple accounts, allowing for finer-grained administrative control. You can create one profile for admintrators and another for regular users, for example, or create distinct profiles dedicated to various software applications.

Note also that to use Database Mail, you no longer need to run the SQL Server or SQL Server Agent Windows services under user accounts (rather than using the default, `LocalSystem`), nor do you need to install Microsoft Outlook (or any other Extended MAPI client) on the machine hosting SQL Server 2008.

In the New Database Mail Account screen that appears (see Figure 15.1), you name (using a valid `sysname`) and describe your first profile in the provided text boxes, and then you click Add to add your first SMTP account. This process is much like the process of setting up the SMTP (or sending) portion of your email accounts with your regular email client software. To create the SMTP account, you specify a name, an optional description, a user display name, an email address, an optional reply address, a server name, a port, and an authentication mode, which is used to authenticate to the specified SMTP server (as required by your SMTP provider). For many non-Windows SMTP providers, anonymous (no authentication) or basic (simple user name/password) authentication is usually required. If your provider requires Windows Authentication, the credentials under which the SQL Server Windows service runs are supplied to the SMTP server at runtime.

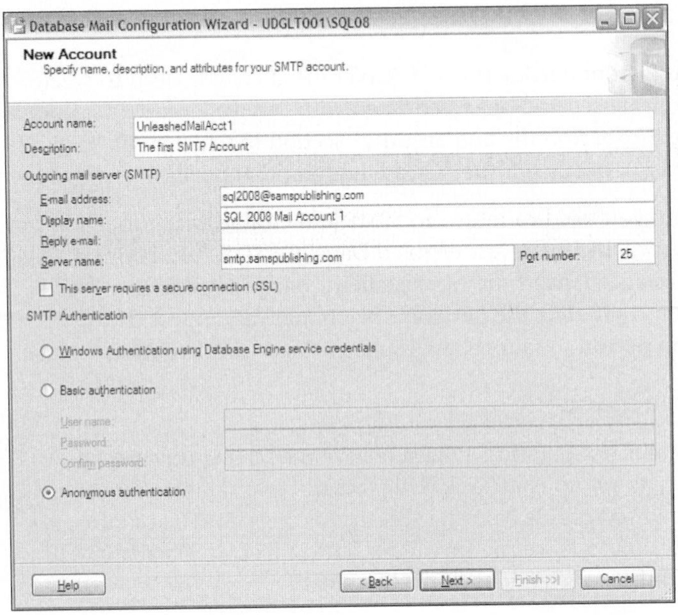

FIGURE 15.1 Using the Database Mail Configuration Wizard to set up SMTP accounts.

Instead of using the wizard, you can add a new profile via T-SQL. For example, the following three examples introduce the Database Mail stored procedures `sysmail_add_profile_sp`, `sysmail_add_account_sp`, and `sysmail_add_profileaccount_sp`.

The first script creates the new profile:

```
EXEC msdb.dbo.sysmail_add_profile_sp
    @profile_name = 'Default SQL 2008 Profile',
    @description = 'Used for general-purpose emailing.'
```

The second script creates the new SMTP account:

```
EXEC msdb.dbo.sysmail_add_account_sp
    @account_name = 'UnleashedMailAcct1',
```

```
    @description = 'The first SMTP Account.',
    @email_address = 'sql2008@samspublishing.com',
    @display_name = 'SQL 2008 Mail Account 1',
    @mailserver_name = 'smtp.samspublishing.com' ;
```

The third script associates this new account with the new profile:

```
EXEC msdb.dbo.sysmail_add_profileaccount_sp
    @profile_name = 'Default SQL 2008 Profile',
    @account_name = 'UnleashedMailAcct1',
    @sequence_number =1;
```

The great thing you'll find when adding SMTP accounts is that Database Mail allows you to provide more than one SMTP account for the same profile. You can order the SMTP accounts by priority (using the Move Up/Move Down buttons) so that if a mail send via the top-level (or first) account fails, the second account will be used to retry sending, and so on. This is called *SMTP failover priority*, and there are two mail settings that control how it works. These settings, found on the Configure System Parameters screen of the wizard, are AccountRetryAttempts and AccountRetryDelay. AccountRetryAttempts specifies how many mail send retries Database Mail will make before failing over to the SMTP account of next-highest priority. AccountRetryDelay specifies (in seconds) how long to wait between mail send retries. These features represent a big improvement in reliability over SQL Mail, which had no such retry capabilities.

After adding the new account to the profile, click Next to set up the profile security settings on the Manage Profile Security screen. Database Mail profiles have two levels of security (with two corresponding tabs on the wizard screen):

- **Public**—The profile can be used by all msdb users.
- **Private**—The profile can be used only by specific users or members of a specific role. (Note that to send mail, users must have DatabaseMailUserRole membership in msdb. Use sp_addrolemember to accomplish this.) Specify these users on the Private Profiles tab of the Manage Profile Security screen.

In this case, check the check box under the Public column of the data grid on the Public tab; then click the word No under the Default Profile column. A drop-down list appears, allowing you to make the profile the default (by changing the selection to Yes). The default profile on the server is used when you invoke sp_send_dbmail (the successor to xp_sendmail) without specifying any profile name for the @profile_name parameter. It's a good idea to have a default profile set up for general mailing purposes, especially when testing.

To set profile security using T-SQL, run the following call to the stored procedure sysmail_add_principalprofile_sp:

```
exec msdb.dbo.sysmail_add_principalprofile_sp
    @profile_name = 'Default SQL 2008 Profile',
    @principal_name = 'public',
    @is_default = 1 ;
```

A third way to configure all the previously mentioned mail objects (in the form of a T-SQL script) is to use an SMSS Database Mail query template. To do this, you open the Template Explorer via the View menu (or by pressing Ctrl+Alt+T), and then you expand to the `Database Mail` folder and double-click Simple Mail Database Configuration. Then you connect to your SQL Server instance and, from the Query menu, select the Specify Values for Template Parameters option (or press Ctrl+Shift+M) to fill in the desired parameter values, which correspond to the parameters of the stored procedures mentioned previously.

Using T-SQL to Update and Delete Mail Objects

To delete or update profiles, accounts, profile-account associations, and profile security settings (note: do so in reverse order), you use the stored procedures shown in Table 15.1.

TABLE 15.1 T-SQL Stored Procedures

Stored Procedure Name	Purpose
`sysmail_delete_profile_sp`	Delete a profile
`sysmail_delete_account_sp`	Delete an account
`sysmail_delete_principalprofile_sp`	Delete the association between a profile and a user or role (revokes permission for the principal on use of the profile)
`sysmail_delete_profileaccount_sp`	Delete the association between a profile and an account
`sysmail_update_profile_sp`	Update a profile
`sysmail_update_account_sp`	Update an account
`sysmail_update_principalprofile_sp`	Update the association between a profile and a user or role
`sysmail_update_profileaccount_sp`	Update the association between a profile and an account

For example, to delete a profile, you execute this:

```
exec msdb.dbo.sysmail_delete_profile_sp @profile_name='Undesireable Profile Name'
```

To update a profile's security, changing it from the default to the nondefault profile, you execute the following:

```
exec msdb.dbo.sysmail_update_principalprofile_sp
    @profile_name = 'Default SQL 2008 Profile',
```

```
@principal_name = 'public',
@is_default = 0;
```

Alternatively, you can simply return to the wizard and select one of the Manage options to alter or drop any of the settings or objects. (Of course, under the covers, the wizard probably uses all these stored procedures.)

Setting System-wide Mail Settings

You use the Configure System Parameters screen in the Database Mail Configuration Wizard to configure the system-wide Database Mail settings. (Click Next on the Select Configuration Task screen to reach this screen, if you haven't already.) You've seen the first two settings that appear in the grid (`AccountRetryAttempts` and `AccountRetryDelay`) in an earlier section ("Creating Mail Profiles and Accounts") as they relate to SMTP failover priority. These are the other four:

- **Maximum File Size (Bytes)**—This setting specifies the maximum size of any one email attachment.
- **Prohibited Attachment File Extensions**—This setting specifies which potentially dangerous or undesirable attachment types to ban from exchanged emails.
- **Database Mail Executable Minimum Lifetime (seconds)**—This setting specifies how long (minimally) the database mail process (that is, `DatabaseMail.exe`, which is activated by Service Broker) should run idly before closing after it finishes emptying the mail send queue.
- **Logging Level**—This setting specifies the quality of email auditing to use, and it can be set to Normal (errors only), Extended (errors, warnings, and informational messages; this is the default), or Verbose (the same as Extended, plus success messages and other messages that are useful when you debug problems with `DatabaseMail.exe`). To view Database Mail's primary log, right-click the `Database Mail` folder in the Object Browser and then click the View Database Mail Log menu option. Examine and maintain the log by using the Log File Viewer that is launched. You can also use the built-in stored procedure `sysmail_delete_log_sp` to clear the log, or query the `msdb` `sysmail_event_log` view to see its contents in tabular format.

To change any of these configuration settings via T-SQL script, use the `sysmail_configure_sp` stored procedure. `sysmail_configure_sp` takes two parameters: the name of the setting (minus any spaces) and its new value. The following example uses the `sysmail_configure_sp` procedure to change `AccountRetryDelay` to two minutes:

```
exec msdb.dbo.sysmail_configure_sp 'AccountRetryDelay', 1200
```

Testing Your Setup

The final step in setting up Database Mail is to ask SQL Server to send a test email. To do this, right-click the `Database Mail` folder in the Object Browser and then click the Send Test E-mail menu option.

If the test fails, click Troubleshoot, and SMSS opens the "Troubleshooting Database Mail" Books Online topic, which provides a solid set of troubleshooting steps to get you started.

If the mail is sent by SQL Server and successfully received in your client software's inbox, you can proceed to the next section to learn how to use the `sp_send_dbmail` stored procedure to send email from T-SQL. Otherwise, look for more troubleshooting help in the "Related Views and Procedures" section of this chapter.

Sending and Receiving with Database Mail

If you're building client applications that rely heavily on Database Mail, it's crucial to gain an in-depth understanding of its underlying architecture. The following sections provide detailed information on its inner workings.

The Service Broker Architecture

As noted earlier, SQL Server relies on Service Broker (SSB) to activate the Database Mail process (`DatabaseMail.exe`) used to send mail. `DatabaseMail.exe` uses ADO.NET to connect to SQL Server and to read from and write to SSB queues (found in `msdb`) that hold send requests and send statuses in the form of typed SSB messages. You can view these queues (`InternalMailQueue` and `ExternalMailQueue`) in the Object Browser by selecting `Service Broker` and then the `Queues` folder. If you look a bit further in the Object Browser, you see how the mail transmission architecture is implemented (in part) as an SSB application, as you find the corresponding internal and external Database Mail SSB services (`InternalMailService` and `ExternalMailService`), SSB message types (`SendMail` and `SendMailStatus`), and a single SSB contract (`SendMail/v1.0`).

SSB's involvement with Database Mail works like this:

1. `sp_send_dbmail` (as the SSB *initiator*) is invoked and returns immediately. Under the covers, this adds an SSB message of type `SendMail` to the SSB mail queue, activating the undocumented internal stored procedure `sp_ExternalMailQueueListener`. Note that the mail message itself is saved to one or more of the `msdb` tables (such as `sysmail_unsentitems` and `sysmail_attachments`) if there are any attachments.
2. SSB launches `DatabaseMail.exe` (running under the credentials of the SQL Server service), which, in turn, connects back to SQL Server, using Windows Authentication.
3. `DatabaseMail.exe` reads the queued SSB send message, retrieves the mail message data, sends the email, and, finally (acting as the SSB *target*), places a message of type `SendMailStatus` in the mail status queue, reporting on the mail sending success or failure.
4. When there's nothing left to be sent in the outbound queue, and the maximum process idle time has been reached, `DatabaseMail.exe` exits.

By using SSB, Database Mail inherits the reliability of the SSB message transmission architecture. If you want to learn more about Service Broker and how its constructs work, consult Chapter 49 (on the CD) for full details.

Sending Email

The SSB queues that Database Mail uses must first be enabled before you can send mail from a session. You do this by executing the msdb stored procedure sysmail_start_sp. This procedure is similar to its predecessor, xp_startmail (as it must be called before sending), except that it has no parameters and, of course, has nothing to do with MAPI. It returns 0 or 1, indicating success or failure. If you don't call this procedure, you receive this error message:

```
Mail not queued. Database Mail is stopped. Use sysmail_start_sp to
start Database Mail.
```

To temporarily disable SSB's activation of the mail process, you execute sysmail_stop_sp (also with no parameters), which returns 0 or 1. If you send mail from code after this disabling this process, these messages will be queued. The external process is not started until sysmail_start_sp is called again. To check on the status of Database Mail, you can execute sysmail_help_status_sp (with no parameters). To check on the status of the queues, you execute sysmail_help_queues_sp.

After you execute sysmail_start_sp, you're ready to begin sending mail using the sp_send_dbmail stored procedure. It has 21 parameters, most of which are optional. As the query engine will tell you if you try to execute it with no or too few parameters, at least one of the following parameters must be specified: @body, @query, @file_attachments, or @subject. You also must specify one of the following: @recipients, @copy_recipients, or @blind_copy_recipients.

NOTE

For the following T-SQL examples to work, you must first configure a default profile using either the Database Mail Configuration Wizard or Database Mail stored procedures, as detailed earlier.

A minimally parameterized test call might look like the following:

```
exec msdb.dbo.sp_send_dbmail @body='Testing...', @subject='A Test',
@recipients='test@samspublishing.com'
go
Mail Queued.
```

Table 15.2 describes the parameters, their types, and the xp_sendmail parameters to which they may correspond, to help you along in converting your existing T-SQL code.

TABLE 15.2 Parameters for Database Mail Stored Procedure sp_send_dbmail

Parameter	Description	xp_sendmail **Parameter to Which It Corresponds**
@profile_name	The sysname of the profile whose SMTP accounts will be used to send.	Not available in xp_sendmail.
@recipients	A varchar(max) semicolon-delimited list of the recipients' email addresses.	Same as xp_sendmail.
@copy_recipients	A varchar(max) semicolon-delimited list of the carbon copy recipients' email addresses.	Same as xp_sendmail.
@blind_copy_recipients	A varchar(max) semicolon-delimited list of the blind carbon copy recipients' email addresses.	Same as xp_sendmail.
@subject	The nvarchar(255) email subject.	Same as xp_sendmail.
@body	The nvarchar(max) email body.	Was @message in xp_sendmail.
@body_format	One of the two varchar (20) email format type strings, either 'HTML' or 'TEXT' (the default).	Not available in xp_sendmail.
@importance	One of the three varchar (6) email importance strings, either 'Low', 'Normal' (the default), or 'High'.	Not available in xp_sendmail.
@sensitivity	One of the four varchar (12) email sensitivity strings, either 'Normal' (the default), 'Personal', 'Private', or 'Confidential'.	Not available in xp_sendmail.
@file_attachments	An nvarchar(max) semicolon-delimited list of absolute paths to files to attach.	Was @attachments in xp_sendmail.

TABLE 15.2 Parameters for Database Mail Stored Procedure sp_send_dbmail

Parameter	Description	xp_sendmail **Parameter to Which It Corresponds**
@query	An nvarchar(max) T-SQL code string to be executed when the message is sent. The code is executed in a different session than the calling session, so variable scope is a consideration.	Same as xp_sendmail.
@execute_query_database	The sysname of the database in which the T-SQL in query is to be executed.	Was @dbuse in xp_sendmail.
@attach_query_result_as_file	A bit value indicating whether the results of the T-SQL in query should be an attachment (1) or appended to the body (0; the default).	Was @attach_results in xp_sendmail.
@query_attachment_filename	The nvarchar(255) filename for the attached query results (as per @query and @attach_query_result_as_file). If not specified, the generated filename is arbitrary (usually QueryResults [some number].txt)	In xp_sendmail, the first filename in @attachments was used.
@query_result_header	A bit value indicating whether the query result (1; the default) should include the column headers.	Was @no_header in xp_sendmail.
@query_result_width	An int value (defaulting to 256; you specify a number between 10 and 32767) indicating how wide a line in the query results should be before line wrapping occurs.	Was @width in xp_sendmail.
@query_result_separator	A char(1) value (defaulting to a space) that indicates the query results column separator.	Was @separator in xp_sendmail.

15

TABLE 15.2 Parameters for Database Mail Stored Procedure sp_send_dbmail

Parameter	Description	xp_sendmail **Parameter to Which It Corresponds**
@exclude_query_output	A bit value that indicates whether to suppress the query output (such as rowcounts, print statements, and so forth) from being printed on the query console. 0 (do not suppress) is the default.	Was @no_output in xp_sendmail.
@append_query_error	A bit value that indicates whether to send the email if the query to be executed raises an error. If set to 1, the error message is appended to the query output, and the query window for the session also displays the error ("A severe error occurred on the current command. The results, if any, should be discarded."). If set to 0 (the default), the message is not sent, and sp_send_dbmail returns 1.	Not available in xp_sendmail, but similar to @echo_error.
@query_no_truncate	A bit value that indicates whether to truncate query results having long values (such as varchar(max), text, xml, and so on) greater than 256. It defaults to 0 (off). Microsoft warns that using this can slow things down, but it is the only way to properly send these types.	Not available in xp_sendmail.
@mailitem_id	An output parameter, an int value indicating the unique mailitem_id of the message. You see this as a column in the views discussed in the section "Related Views and Procedures," later in this chapter.	Not available in xp_sendmail.

Note that the @type and @set_user parameters for xp_sendmail are not available. @type, of course, is obsolete because it is MAPI specific. @set_user is also obsolete because the content of the T-SQL to be executed may contain an EXECUTE AS statement.

Now that you're familiar with the flurry of mail sending options, let's look at a few examples and then examine how to track your sent messages by using the system views. Both of the following examples rely on sending via the default profile of the current user context. If the user has a default private profile assigned, it is used. If not, the default public profile is used (as in these examples). If there is no default public profile, an error is raised.

The example shown in Listing 15.1 sends an email containing an `xml` result to a recipient as an attached Extensible Application Markup Language (XAML) document, retrieved from the `AdventureWorks2008.Production.Illustration` column.

LISTING 15.1 Sending XML as an Attachment with Database Mail

```
USE AdventureWorks2008
GO
DECLARE
    @subject nvarchar(255),
    @body varchar(max),
    @query nvarchar(max),
    @IllustrationId int,
    @query_attachment_filename nvarchar(255),
    @mailitem_id int

SELECT
    @IllustrationId = pi.IllustrationId,
    @subject = 'XAML for "' + pm.Name + '" attached. '
FROM Production.Illustration pi
JOIN Production.ProductModelIllustration pmi
ON pmi.IllustrationId = pi.IllustrationId
JOIN Production.ProductModel pm
ON pm.ProductModelID = pmi.ProductModelID

SELECT
    @body =
        N'Attached, please find the XAML diagram for illustration #' +
        CAST(@IllustrationId as nvarchar(10)) +
        '. A XAML browser plug-in is required to view this file.'

SELECT @query =
    N'SELECT Diagram FROM Production.Illustration
    WHERE IllustrationId = ' + CAST(@IllustrationId as nvarchar(10))

SELECT @query_attachment_filename = N'PM_' +
    CAST(@IllustrationId as nvarchar(10)) + '.xaml'
```

15

```
exec msdb.dbo.sp_send_dbmail
    @subject=@subject,
    @body=@body,
    @recipients='test@samspublishing.com',
    @query=@query,
    @execute_query_database='AdventureWorks2008',
    @attach_query_result_as_file=1,
    @query_attachment_filename=@query_attachment_filename,
    @query_no_truncate=1,
    @exclude_query_output=1,
    @query_result_width=32767,
    @mailitem_id=@mailitem_id OUTPUT

SELECT sent_status, sent_date
FROM msdb.dbo.sysmail_allitems
WHERE mailitem_id = @mailitem_id
GO
sent_status sent_date
-----. ----.
unsent      NULL
 (1 row(s) affected)
```

Note that you must set `@query_no_truncate` to 1 and `@query_result_width` to the maximum (to be safe) value for the attached query results to contain consistently well-formed XML. In addition, you should not include any carriage returns or line feeds in the body of the message, or the SMTP servers may not be able to send it.

The example in Listing 15.2 sends some query results as a comma-separated value (CSV) file that can be imported into programs such as Microsoft Excel. (You need to use the Get External Data command to accomplish this with Excel 9.)

LISTING 15.2 Sending CSV Data as an Attachment with Database Mail

```
USE AdventureWorks2008
GO
DECLARE @mailitem_id int, @tab char(1)
SET @tab = char(13)

exec msdb.dbo.sp_send_dbmail
    @subject='D. Margheim, Contact Info',
    @body='Attached is Diane Margheim''s contact info, in CSV format.',
    @recipients='test@samspublishing.com',
    @query=N'SELECT BusinessEntityID, Title, FirstName, MiddleName, LastName
        FROM Person.Person
        WHERE BusinessEntityId = 8',
    @execute_query_database='AdventureWorks2008',
```

```
    @attach_query_result_as_file=1,
    @query_attachment_filename='DMargheim.csv',
    @exclude_query_output=1,
    @query_result_separator=',',
    @mailitem_id=@mailitem_id OUTPUT

SELECT sent_status, sent_date
FROM msdb.dbo.sysmail_allitems
WHERE mailitem_id = @mailitem_id
GO
sent_status sent_date
------ -----
unsent      NULL
 (1 row(s) affected)
```

Notice that in both of these code listings, the values selected from the `sent_status` and `sent_date` columns of `sysmail_allitems` indicate that the mail has not yet been sent. The reason is that mail sending (like all other SSB messaging) is asynchronous: The message is immediately queued, and the Mail process later picks it up and sends it. To find out more about system views such as `sysmail_allitems`, see the section "Related Views and Procedures," later in this chapter.

15

Receiving Email

The only way for SQL Server 2008 to receive email is by using the legacy stored procedures, such as `sp_processmail`, with SQL Mail. Database Mail does not support receiving incoming messages because there is no IMAP or POP3 support. This may have something to do with the fact that receiving email can represent a major security risk. Imagine what a denial-of-service attack on a database cluster could do to an organization. Or consider the danger of an incoming email request resulting in the execution of a query such as `DROP DATABASE X`. Most SQL Server data is too precious to jeopardize in this manner. Microsoft has also made it clear that SQL Mail will be phased out in the next release of SQL Server. Plus, there are many better alternatives to using this methodology, such as using native Web services (as discussed in Chapter 48, "SQL Server Web Services"), using .NET CLR-integrated assembly code (as discussed in Chapter 45, "SQL Server and the .NET Framework"), or building a dedicated Service Broker application (as discussed in Chapter 49).

Using SQL Server Agent Mail

As with SQL Server 2000, SQL Server 2008's Agent has the capability to send email notifications. They may be triggered by alerts or scheduled task completions, such as jobs. SQL Server 2008 provides the option of using either SQL Mail or Database Mail to do the sending, but SQL Mail will soon be phased out, and Database Mail is by far the more robust choice. As with Database Mail, SQL Server Agent Mail is turned off by default, and you must configure it via SMSS or T-SQL, as described in the following sections.

Job Mail Notifications

The following sections show an example in which you create a SQL Server Agent Mail operator that SQL Server Agent will notify when a job completes.

Creating an Operator

First, you need to create an operator. To do so, using the Object Browser, you expand the `SQL Server Agent` node and then right-click the `Operators` folder and select New Operator. Then you should name this new operator `Test Database Mail Operator` and provide an email address for testing purposes in the Email Name text box. You can use any valid email address you can access with your email client software. You click OK to save the new operator.

Enabling SQL Agent Mail

Next, you need to enable SQL Server Agent to use Database Mail. You right-click the `SQL Server Agent` node and then select Properties. On the left side of the Properties dialog that appears (see Figure 15.2), you click the Alert System link. Under the Mail Session group, you check the Enable Mail Profile check box. In the Mail System drop-down list, you select Database Mail (this is also the place where you can choose SQL Mail, if you desire). In the Mail Profile drop-down list, you select the default SQL 2008 profile you created earlier and then click OK. By doing this, you are telling SQL Server Agent to use the SMTP servers in your default profile to send email. You need to restart SQL Server Agent by using the right-click menu.

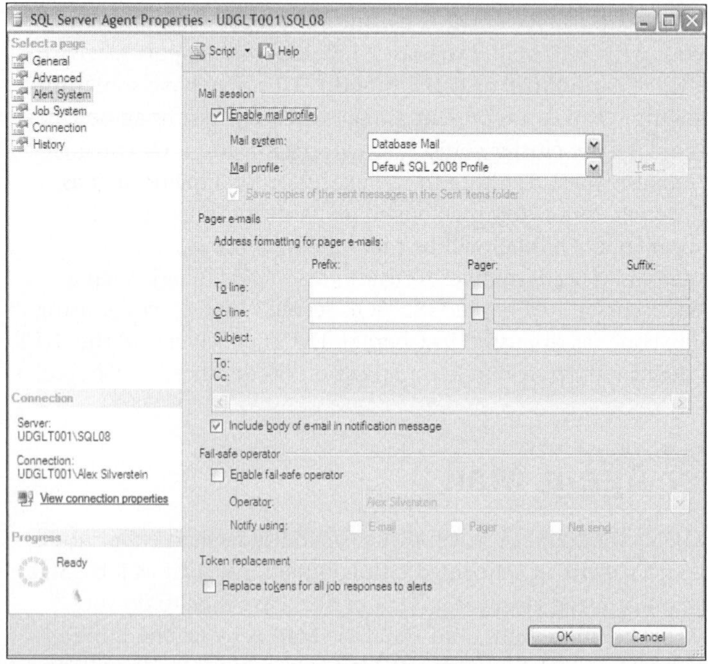

FIGURE 15.2 Using the SQL Server Agent Properties dialog to configure Database Mail.

Creating the Job

Next, you need to create the job. You begin by right-clicking the `Jobs` folder and then selecting New Job. You should name the job `Database Mail Test Job` and select an owner. Then you should check the Enabled check box near the bottom of the dialog and click the Steps link on the left side of the dialog. Next, you click the New button and add a step named `Test Mail Step 1`. You should leave the type as Transact-SQL and then change the database selection to AdventureWorks2008. In the Command text box, you enter the following code:

```
RAISERROR('This is simply a test job.', 10, 1)
```

Next, you click the Advanced link on the left side of the dialog, and in the On Success Action drop-down list, you select Quit the Job Reporting Success. Then you click the Notifications link on the left side of the dialog. Next, under Actions to Perform When the Job Completes, you check the Email check box and select the operator you just created. From the drop-down to the right, you select When the Job Completes and then click OK to save the job.

Testing the Job-Completion Notification

To test the email configuration and notification you just set up, you right-click the job name under the `Jobs` folder and then select Start Job. If everything is set up properly, an email message appears in your inbox, indicating the job's successful completion. Its body text might look something like this:

```
JOB RUN:     'Database Mail Test Job' was run on 5/7/2009 at 8:37:22 PM
DURATION:     0 hours, 0 minutes, 0 seconds
STATUS:     Succeeded
MESSAGES:     The job succeeded.  The Job was invoked by User [TestUser].
    The last step to run was step 1 (Test Mail Step 1).
```

Alert Mail Notifications

As another example, in the following sections, you'll create a simple user-defined alert that you can trigger directly from T-SQL script.

Creating an Alert

You start by creating an alert. To do this, you use the Object Browser to expand the `SQL Server Agent` node; then you right-click the `Alerts` node and select New Alert. In the Alert Properties dialog that appears (see Figure 15.3), you name the new alert `Database Mail Test Alert` and make sure the Enabled check box is checked. For the Event type, you leave the selection on SQL Server Event Alert. Under Event Alert Definition, select AdventureWorks2008 from the Database Name drop-down list, and then click the Severity option button and choose 010 - Information. Next, check the Raise Alert When Message Contains check box and type the phrase `This is a Test` in the Message Text text box.

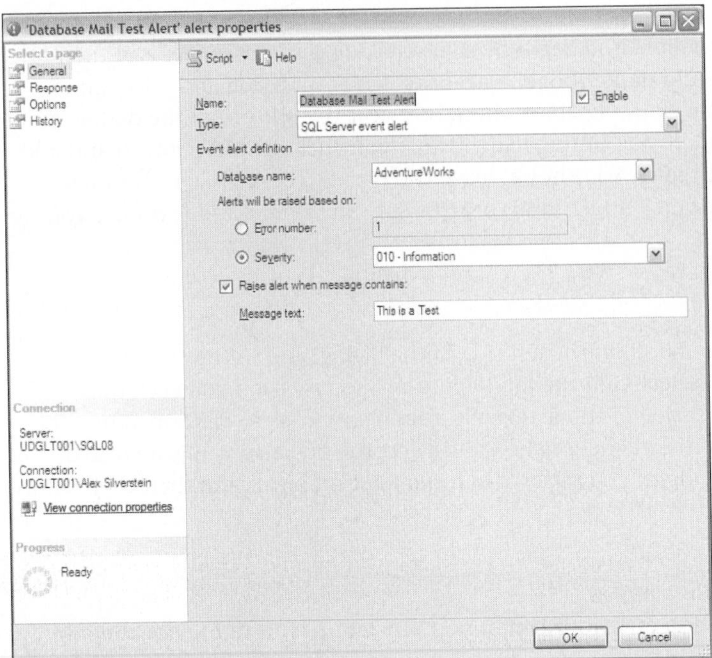

FIGURE 15.3 Creating a SQL Server event alert with a Database Mail notification.

On the left side of the alert properties dialog, you click the Response link. Then you check the Notify Operators check box and, in the Operator list, check the Email check box to the right of the Test Database Mail Operator grid row. Finally, you click OK to close and save the new custom alert.

Testing the Alert Notification

To test your new alert notification, you open a new query window in SMSS and enter the following code:

```
USE AdventureWorks2008
go
RAISERROR('This is an alert mail test', 10, 1) WITH LOG
go
'This is an alert mail test'
```

Because you specified `WITH LOG`, this simple statement writes an event to the Windows Event log, which in turn triggers the alert because the database context, message text, and severity all match the conditions of the alert. An email message should have appeared in your inbox, indicating the alert's successful triggering. This message should contain body text such as this:

```
DATE/TIME:     5/7/2009 9:00:45 PM
DESCRIPTION:     Error: 50000 Severity:  10 State: 1 This is an alert
```

```
    mail test
COMMENT:     (None)
JOB RUN:     (None)
```

Related Views and Procedures

To report on the status of all your Database Mail objects without relying on wizards and properties pages, you need some tabular views and stored procedures. msdb contains many system tables, views, and corresponding stored procedures that make this task easy. The following section lists the tables (or views) and their columns, noting the stored procedure (if any) that you can use to read from them.

Viewing the Mail Configuration Objects

The first set of msdb objects we'll review are those related to system objects such as profiles, profile security, and accounts:

- **sysmail_profile**—Contains basic profile data, including the unique profile_id, name, description, last_mod_datetime, and last_mod_user name. You execute sysmail_help_profile_sp to retrieve this data by @profile_name or @profile_id.
- **sysmail_principalprofile**—Contains profile security settings, including the profile_id, associated principal (or user) (principal_SID), profile default status (is_default: 1 for yes or 0 for no), last_mod_datetime, and last_mod_user name. You execute sysmail_help_principalprofile_sp to retrieve this data by @profile_name, @profile_id, @principal_name, or @principal_id (not principal SID). Here's an example:

  ```
  exec msdb.dbo.sysmail_help_principalprofile_sp
      @profile_name='Default SQL 2008 Profile'
  ```

- **sysmail_account**—Contains basic account data, including the unique account_id, name, description, email_address, display_name, replyto_address, last_mod_datetime, and last_mod_user name. You execute sysmail_help_account_sp to retrieve this data by @account_id or @account_name.
- **sysmail_server**—Contains account SMTP server data, including the unique related account_id and servertype, servername, port, server username, server authentication data (credential_id), SSL status (enable_SSL), last_mod_datetime, and last_mod_user name. (sysmail_help_account_sp returns data from this table as well.)
- **sysmail_servertype**—Contains servertype data for accounts' servers. (SMTP is the only currently supported type, although it seems this system was built for extensibility, as the columns is_incoming and is_outgoing may leave the door open for adding POP or IMAP servers sometime in the future.) Also includes last_mod_datetime and last_mod_user name. (sysmail_help_account_sp returns data from this table as well.)

To join sysmail_account, sysmail_server, and sysmail_servertype (as sysmail_help_account_sp seems to do), you can try a query such as the following:

```
SELECT *
FROM msdb.dbo.sysmail_account a
JOIN msdb.dbo.sysmail_server s
ON a.account_id = s.account_id
JOIN msdb.dbo.sysmail_servertype st
ON st.servertype = s.servertype
```

- **sysmail_profileaccount**—Maintains the profile-account relationship, including the profile_id, account_id, account priority sequence_number, last_mod_datetime, and last_mod_user name. You execute sysmail_help_profileaccount_sp to retrieve this data by @account_id, @account_name, @profile_id, or @profile_name.
- **sysmail_configuration**—Contains the system-wide mail configuration settings (paramname, paramvalue, description), and when and by whom each was last modified (last_mod_datetime and last_mod_user name). You execute sysmail_help_configure_sp to query this data by @parameter_name. Here's an example:

```
exec msdb.dbo.sysmail_help_configure_sp
    @parameter_name='accountretrydelay'
```

Viewing Mail Message Data

The second set of msdb objects (and perhaps the more important ones) we'll review are those used to discover the status of mail messages.

The first thing you need to do is to check on the status of the mail messages you've attempted to send, without relying on inboxes to tell you if they've been received. Several views in msdb enable this, most of which may be filtered by mail account, sending user, send date, status, and more. To begin this process, you query the view sysmail_allitems, which contains all the data about your messages (subjects, recipients, importance, and so on) as well as send_request_date, sent_date, and sent_status. Here's an example:

```
SELECT mailitem_id, subject, sent_status
FROM msdb.dbo.sysmail_allitems
go
mailitem_id    subject                                            sent_status
-----------------------------------------------------------------------------


1              Database Mail Test                                 sent
2              C. Adams, Contact Info                             sent
3              XAML for HL Touring Seat/Saddle attached.          sent
4              SQL Server Job System: 'Database Mail Test Job'    sent

(4 row(s) affected)
```

Because all these messages have a sent_status of sent, the contents of this recordset are analogous to what you'd find if you queried the view sysmail_sentitems. But suppose your sent_status column read failed. In that case, you'd start by querying the sysmail_faileditems view (a subset of sysmail_allmailitems) in conjunction with sysmail_event_log (which contains the detailed textual reasons why failures have occurred). Here's an example:

```
SELECT f.subject, f.mailitem_id, l.description
FROM msdb.dbo.sysmail_event_log l
JOIN msdb.dbo.sysmail_faileditems f
ON f.mailitem_id = l.mailitem_id
WHERE event_type = 'error'
ORDER BY log_date
go
subject              mailitem_id    description
----------------------------------------------------------------------------
Database Mail Test   3              The mail could not be sent because[...]the
string is not in the form required for an e-mail address

(1 row(s) affected)
```


Note that the quality of the contents of sysmail_event_log depends on the Log Level system-wide mail configuration setting (discussed earlier in the section "Setting System-wide Mail Settings"). The Log File Viewer also uses this table's contents. To permanently delete its contents, you use the stored procedure sysmail_delete_log_sp.

To query how many messages are queued (waiting to be sent) and for how long, you use the sysmail_unsentitems view. Here's an example:

```
SELECT
    mailitem_id,
    subject,
    DATEDIFF(hh, send_request_date, GETDATE()) HoursSinceSendRequest
FROM msdb.dbo.sysmail_unsentitems
```

If you're unsure why messages aren't being sent, you can try the following:

- Execute sysmail_help_queue_sp, whose resulting state column tells the state of the mail transmission queues: INACTIVE (off) or RECEIVES_OCCURRING (on). To see the status for only the mail (outbound) or status (send status) queues, you use the @queue_type parameter.
- Execute sysmail_help_status_sp, whose resulting Status column tells you the state of Database Mail itself: STOPPED or STARTED.

Summary

This chapter showed how Database Mail has elevated the status of emailing with SQL Server from somewhat difficult to use to enterprise class. Microsoft has achieved this goal by relying on cross-platform industry standards, by making configuration easy, by providing a comprehensive set of system objects for storage and tracking, by adding failover capability, and by utilizing the Service Broker infrastructure.

Chapter 16, "SQL Server Scheduling and Notification," digs much deeper into configuring SQL Server Agent jobs and alerts, as well as using Database Mail for job and alert notifications.

CHAPTER 16

SQL Server Scheduling and Notification

IN THIS CHAPTER

- What's New in Scheduling and Notification
- Configuring the SQL Server Agent
- Viewing the SQL Server Agent Error Log
- SQL Server Agent Security
- Managing Operators
- Managing Jobs
- Managing Alerts
- Scripting Jobs and Alerts
- Multiserver Job Management
- Event Forwarding

Automation is the key to efficiency, and the SQL Server Agent is your automation tool in SQL Server 2008. This chapter delves into the administrative capabilities of the SQL Server Agent and its capability to schedule server activity and respond to server events.

The SQL Server Agent, which runs as a Windows service, is responsible for running scheduled tasks, notifying operators of events, and responding with predefined actions to errors and performance conditions. The SQL Server Agent can perform these actions without user intervention, utilizing the following:

- **Alerts**—*Alerts* respond to SQL Server or user-defined errors, and they can also respond to performance conditions. An alert can be configured to run a job as well as notify an operator.
- **Jobs**—A *job* is a predefined operation or set of operations, such as transferring data or backing up a transaction log. A job can be scheduled to run on a regular basis or called to run when an alert is fired.
- **Operators**—An *operator* is a user who should be notified when an alert fires or a job requests notification. The operator can be notified by email, by pager, or via the `NET SEND` command.

NOTE

The SQL Server Agent is not supported with the SQL Server Express Edition or SQL Server Express Advanced Edition. It is supported in all the other editions of SQL Server 2008, however. You can use the Windows Task Scheduler as an alternative for scheduling when using the SQL Server Express Editions. The Task Scheduler has basic scheduling capabilities but does not compare to the robust features found in the SQL Server Agent.

What's New in Scheduling and Notification

A new feature added to SQL Server 2008 Scheduling and Notification is the capability to execute PowerShell scripts. PowerShell is a command-line scripting language that allows administrators to achieve greater control and productivity. SQL Server 2008 comes with several PowerShell snap-ins that give you access to a variety of SQL Server objects. Scripts that are written to access these objects can be run from SQL Server jobs using the new PowerShell job type. You can find a more detailed discussion of PowerShell's capabilities in the next chapter, "Administering SQL Server 2008 with PowerShell."

Policy-Based Management is another new feature in SQL Server 2008. This feature does not fall directly under Scheduling and Notification, but it provides related management features. For example, some of the multiserver concepts discussed later in this chapter can be replaced or augmented through the use of Policy-Based Management. This feature is covered in Chapter 22, "Administering Policy Based Management."

Configuring the SQL Server Agent

The primary configuration settings for the SQL Server Agent are located within the Object Explorer and SQL Server Configuration Manager. Most of the settings that define how the SQL Server Agent will execute are defined via the SQL Server Agent Properties accessible from the Object Explorer. The SQL Server Configuration Manager contains settings related to the SQL Server Agent's service. The service settings are limited but contain important properties such as the Startup Account for the SQL Server Agent.

Configuring SQL Server Agent Properties

Figure 16.1 shows the SQL Server Agent Properties dialog that appears when you right-click and select Properties on the `SQL Server Agent` node located on the root of the Object Explorer tree.

You can set several different types of properties in the SQL Server Agent Properties dialog. The General options are displayed by default, and they include the capability to set the

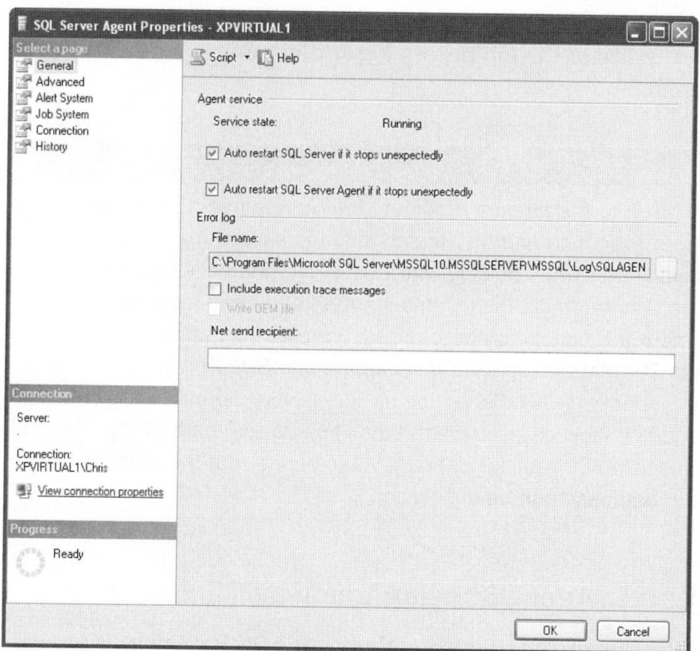

FIGURE 16.1 SQL Server Agent properties.

auto restart options and define an error log for the SQL Server Agent. Selecting the option Auto Restart SQL Server Agent If It Stops Unexpectedly is best for most installations. There is usually a heavy dependency on the Agent performing its actions, and you probably want the service to be restarted if it has been inadvertently stopped.

The Advanced page contains options for event forwarding and idle CPU conditions. The event forwarding options are discussed in detail in the section "Event Forwarding," later in this chapter. The idle CPU options define conditions related to the execution of jobs that have been set up to run when the CPU is idle. You can define idle CPU conditions such as the average CPU percentage that the CPU must be below to be considered idle.

The Alert System page is related to configuring email notification and is discussed in the "Configuring Email Notification" section, later in this chapter.

The Job System page has an option to set the shutdown time-out interval. This option determines the amount of time the SQL Server Agent waits for jobs to complete before finalizing the shutdown process. There is also an option related to proxy accounts discussed in the "SQL Server Agent Proxy Account" section, later in this chapter.

The Connection page includes an option to set an alias for the local host server. This option is useful if you cannot use the default connection properties for the local host and need to define an alias instead.

The History page options are related to the amount of job history that will be retained. You have the option to limit the size of the job history log and/or remove job history that is older than a set period of time.

TIP

Careful attention should be given to the amount of history that is retained. Every time a job is run, the history of that execution and the related detail is saved. The need for careful monitoring is particularly true when dealing with SQL Server instances that have a large number of databases. The msdb database contains the job history records and can become sizable over time if the history is not removed. For example, we have seen environments where close to 700 databases were installed on one SQL Server instance. The company was performing SQL Server log backups every 15 minutes on each of these databases and full backups each night. When you do the math (4 log backups/hour * 700 databases = 2800 backups/hour), you can see that the amount of history written to the msdb database can be significant.

Configuring the SQL Server Agent Startup Account

The startup account defines the Microsoft Windows account the SQL Server Agent service uses. The selection of this account is critical in defining the level of security that the SQL Server Agent will have. Access to resources on the server on which SQL Server is running and access to network resources are determined by the startup account. This selection is particularly important in cases in which the SQL Server Agent needs to access resources on other machines. Examples of network access that the SQL Server Agent might need include jobs that write backups to a drive on another machine and jobs that look for files found on other servers on the network.

The startup account for the SQL Server Agent is set initially during the installation of SQL Server, but you can change it by using several different tools such as the Windows Service Control Manager and SQL Server Configuration Manager. The Windows Service Control Manager is a good tool for viewing all the services on your server, but changes to the SQL Server services are better made through the SQL Server Configuration Manager. The Configuration Manager is more comprehensive and makes additional configuration settings, such as Registry permissions, that ensure proper operation.

The SQL Server Configuration Manager is a consolidated tool that allows you to manage network options and services related to SQL Server. To launch this tool, you select Start, Microsoft SQL Server 2008, Configuration Tools. Figure 16.2 shows an example of the Configuration Manager with the SQL Server 2008 services selected for viewing. To change the startup account for the SQL Server Agent, you can right-click on its service and select Properties.

The startup account used by the SQL Server Agent is initially determined during the installation of SQL Server. You have the option of choosing one of several built-in accounts, or you can select a domain account. The built-in accounts are available by default and do not

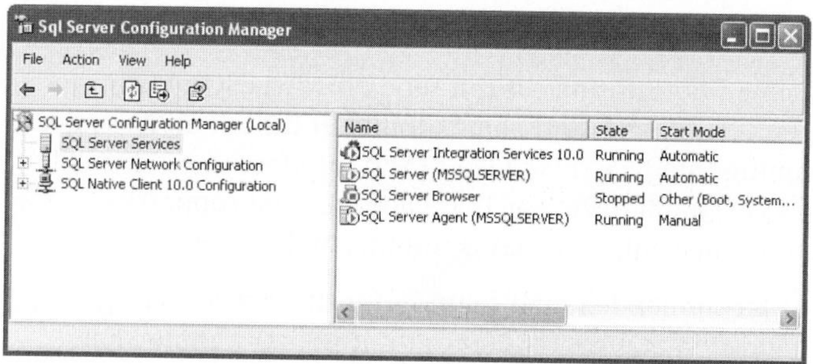

FIGURE 16.2 SQL Server Agent service properties.

require any network administration to use them. These accounts, however, should be used with caution because they can provide network access to the SQL Server Agent that may not be desired. Generally, you want to provide the minimum amount of security necessary for the SQL Server Agent to perform its tasks.

The recommended startup account for the SQL Server Agent is a Windows account. You specify a Windows startup account for SQL Server Agent by using the This Account option on the Service Properties window. The Windows account can be a local user account or domain user account. It must be a member of the SQL Server `sysadmin` fixed server role on the local SQL Server instance. The use of this type of startup account provides the most flexibility and allows you to tailor the network and local resources that the SQL Server Agent has permission to access.

16

The Windows account does not have to be a member of the Windows `administrators` group. In fact, exclusion from the `administrators` group is recommended in most cases. This approach adheres to the principle of least privileges, which says that you should limit the amount of security provided to only that which is needed. In many cases, inclusion in the `administrators` group is not needed and only increases exposure to security threats.

The Windows account you choose with the This Account option must have certain security rights to be able to function as the startup account for SQL Server. The account must have permission to log on as a service. You can set this permission and others by using the Local Security Policy application, which can be found under Administrative Tools. You can select the `Local Policies` node and then select `User Rights Assignment` to display a list of all the security settings, including Log On as a Service Policy. You should make sure the account you chose or the group that it is in is included in this policy.

TIP

The Local Security Policy editor can be hard to find. In most operating systems, you can click `Start` `Run` then enter **`secpol.msc`** to launch the Local Security Policy editor.

Configuring Email Notification

The SQL Server Agent can send email notifications; it can send email via SQL Mail or Database Mail. SQL Mail was retained for backward compatibility. It utilizes an Extended Messaging Application Programming Interface (Extended MAPI) interface to send email and requires that you install an email application (such as Outlook) that supports Extended MAPI communication on the computer that is running SQL Server.

Database Mail, which is now the recommended mail solution for the SQL Server Agent, is the focus of this section. It was added in SQL Server 2005, and it utilizes Simple Mail Transfer Protocol (SMTP) instead of Extended MAPI to send mail. This simplifies email setup and has many benefits over SQL Mail, including the following:

- There is no requirement that an email client be installed on the SQL Server machine.
- Email is queued for later delivery if the mail server stops or fails.
- Multiple SMTP servers can be specified so that mail continues to be delivered in the event that one of the SMTP servers stops.
- Database Mail is cluster aware.

Database Mail is disabled by default in SQL Server 2008 but can be enabled using the Database Mail Configuration Wizard. This wizard provides a comprehensive means for configuring Database Mail. The Database Mail Configuration Wizard is not launched from the `SQL Server Agent` node. Instead, you can launch it by expanding the `Management` node, right-clicking Database Mail, and selecting Configure Database Mail. This wizard guides you through the configuration of mail profiles, SMTP accounts, and other options relevant to Database Mail. The Configuration Wizard and many other details related to Database Mail are discussed in detail in Chapter 15, "Database Mail."

After you set up Database Mail and confirm that it is working properly, you can select it as your mail system for the SQL Server Agent to send mail. You do this by right-clicking the `SQL Server Agent` node in the Object Explorer and selecting Properties. Then you select the Alert System page in the SQL Server Agent Properties dialog, and the screen shown in Figure 16.3 appears. In this figure, Database Mail is selected as the mail system, along with a mail profile for Database Mail created with the Database Mail Configuration Wizard. The mail profile you select can have multiple SMTP accounts assigned to it. This allows for redundancy in the event that the mail cannot be sent to one of the SMTP accounts.

To ensure proper functioning of the alert system, you should restart the SQL Server Agent service after the alert system has been configured. If you experience problems sending notifications via the SQL Server Agent, you should check the service account that SQL Server is running under. If the SQL Server Agent is running with the local system account, resources outside the SQL Server machine will be unavailable; this includes mail servers that are on other machines. You should change the service account for the SQL Server Agent to a domain account to resolve this issue. Chapter 15 provides more information on using Database Mail in SQL Server 2008.

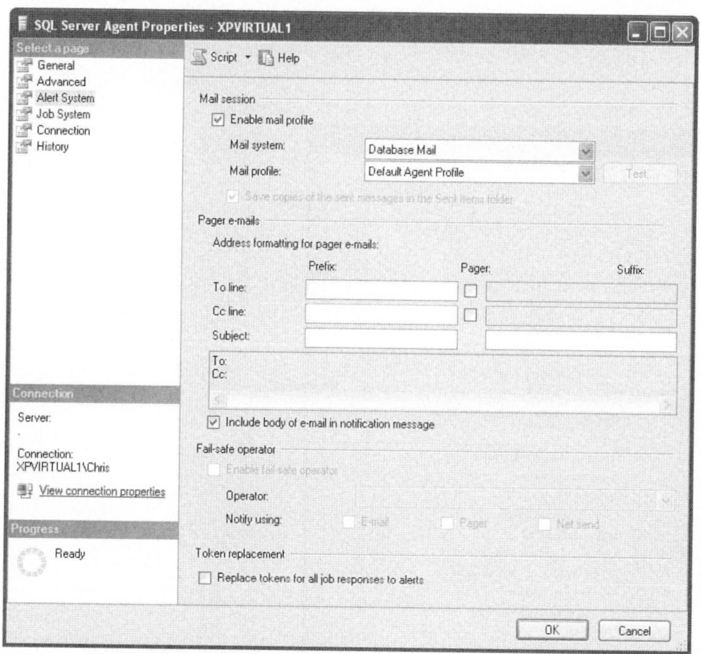

FIGURE 16.3 The Alert System page of the SQL Server Agent Properties dialog.

SQL Server Agent Proxy Account

Proxy accounts allow non–Transact-SQL (non–T-SQL) job steps to execute under a specific security context. By default, only users in the `sysadmin` role can execute these job steps. Non-`sysadmin` users can be assigned to a proxy account to allow them to run the special job steps. In SQL Server 2000, a single proxy account was provided for this function. With SQL Server 2008, multiple proxy accounts can be established, each of which can be assigned to a different SQL Server Agent subsystem.

To establish a proxy account for the SQL Server Agent, you must first create a credential. A *credential* contains the authentication information necessary to connect to a resource outside SQL Server. The credential is typically linked to a Windows account that has the appropriate rights on the server. To create a credential, you open the `Security` node in the Object Explorer, right-click the `Credentials` node, and select New Credential. You give the credential a name, enter an identity value that corresponds to a valid Windows account, and provide a password for the account.

After creating a credential, you can create a new proxy account and link it to the credential. To create a new proxy account, you expand the `SQL Server Agent` node in the Object Explorer tree, right-click `Proxies`, and select New Proxy Account. Figure 16.4 shows an example of the New Proxy Account dialog. In this example, the proxy name and credential name are the same, but they do not need to be. The only subsystem selected for the sample proxy account in Figure 16.4 is the operating system, but a proxy account can be linked to multiple subsystems.

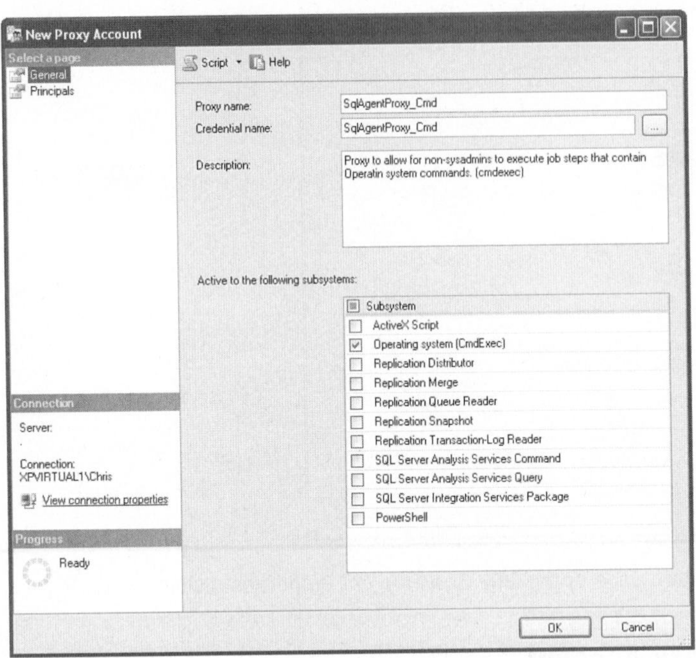

FIGURE 16.4 Creating a new proxy account.

After a proxy account is created, a `sysadmin` can assign one or more SQL logins, `msdb` roles, or server roles to the proxy. You do this by using the Principals page of the New Proxy Account dialog. A proxy account can have zero or many principals assigned to it. Conversely, a principal can be assigned to many different proxies. Linking non-admin principals to the proxy allows the principal to create job steps for subsystems that have been assigned to the proxy.

Proxy accounts are referenced within a SQL Server Agent job step. The General page of the Job Step Properties dialog contains a Run As drop-down that lists valid accounts or proxies that can be used to run the particular job step. After you add a proxy account, you see it in this drop-down list. Keep in mind that the account is not visible for a T-SQL job step that does not utilize a proxy account. Steps that utilize the T-SQL subsystem execute under the job owner's context and they do not utilize a proxy account.

Viewing the SQL Server Agent Error Log

The SQL Server Agent maintains an error log that records information, warnings, and error messages concerning its operation. A node named `Error Logs` is located in the `SQL Server Agent` tree in the Object Explorer. The `Error Logs` node contains multiple versions of the

SQL Server Agent error log. By default, a maximum of 10 versions of the error log are displayed under the `Error Logs` node. The versions displayed include the current error log and the last 9 versions. Each time the SQL Server Agent is restarted, a new error log is generated, with a name that includes a time stamp. The first part of the current version's name is `Current`. Names of older logs start with `Archive #`, followed by a number; the newer logs have lower numbers. The SQL Server error log works in much the same way as the SQL Server Agent's error log.

TIP

You can cycle the error log at any time without stopping and starting the SQL Server Agent. To do so, you right-click the `Error Logs` node in the Object Explorer and select Recycle; a new error log is then generated. You can also use the `msdb.dbo.sp_cycle_agent_errorlog` stored procedure to cycle the error log. You need to remember to also select the Refresh option to show the latest available error logs.

To view the contents of any of the logs, you need to double-click the particular log. Double-clicking a particular log file launches the Log File Viewer. The Log File Viewer contains the SQL Server Agent error logs in addition to logs that are associated with other SQL Server components, including Database Mail, SQL Server, and Windows NT. Figure 16.5 shows a sample Log File Viewer screen with the current SQL Server Agent error log selected for display. The Log File Viewer provides filtering capabilities that allow you to focus on a particular type of error message, along with other viewing capabilities that are common to all the logs available for viewing.

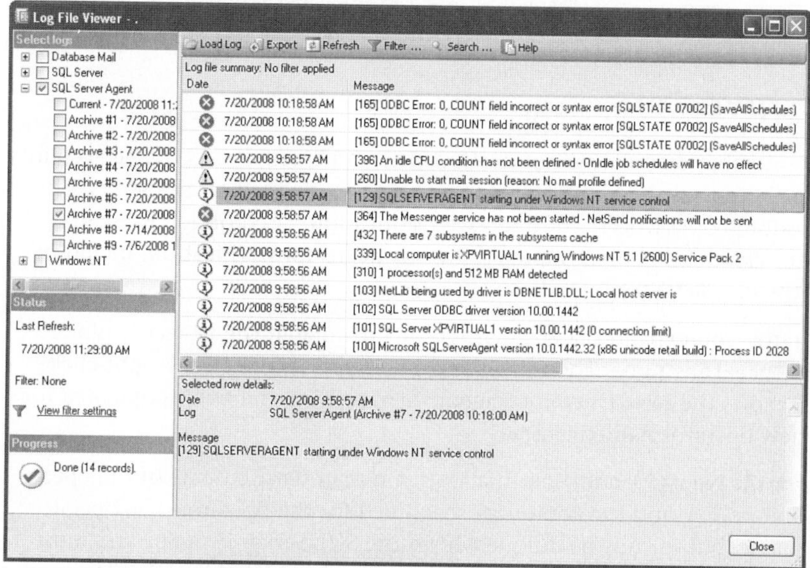

FIGURE 16.5 The SQL Server Agent error log.

SQL Server Agent Security

Many changes were made to the security model related to the SQL Server Agent in SQL Server 2005. In the past, everyone could view the SQL Server Agent. Starting in SQL Server 2005, logins must be a part of the `sysadmin` server role or assigned to one of three `msdb` database roles to be able to view and modify the SQL Server Agent. The `SQL Server Agent` node does not appear in the Object Explorer tree if the login does not have the appropriate permissions. Following are the `msdb` database roles and their basic permissions:

- **`SQLAgentUserRole`**—Users with this permission can create and manage local jobs and job schedules that they own. They cannot create multiserver jobs or manage jobs that they do not own.
- **`SQLAgentReaderRole`**—Users with this permission can view jobs that belong to other users in addition to all the permissions associated with `SQLAgentUserRole`.
- **`SQLAgentOperatorRole`**—Users with this permission can view operators and alerts and control jobs owned by other users. The job control on jobs owned by other users is limited to stopping or starting and enabling or disabling those jobs. `SQLAgentOperatorRole` also has all the permissions available to `SQLAgentUserRole` and `SQLAgentReaderRole`.

`SQLAgentUserRole` has the fewest privileges, and each subsequent role has increasing levels of security. In addition, each subsequent role inherits the permissions of the roles with fewer permissions. For example, `SQLAgentReaderRole` can do everything that `SQLAgentUserRole` can do and more. Refer to the topic "Implementing SQL Server Agent Security" in SQL Server Books Online for a detailed list of all the permissions related to the new database roles.

Managing Operators

Operators are accounts that can receive notification when an event occurs. These accounts are not linked directly to the user and login accounts that are defined on the server. They are basically aliases for people who need to receive notification based on job execution or alerts. Each operator can define one or more electronic means for notification, including email, pager, and the `NET SEND` command.

To add a new operator, you expand the `SQL Server Agent` node in the Object Explorer and right-click the `Operators` node. Then you select New Operator from the right-click menu. Figure 16.6 shows the New Operator screen, with many of the fields populated for the creation of a new operator named `LauraG`.

The General page of the New Operator screen allows you to enter the name of the operator, the notification options, and the "on duty" scheduled for the operator. The operator name can be any name, but it must be unique within the SQL Server instance and must be no more than 128 characters. The operator name can be the same as another login or user on the server, but this is not required.

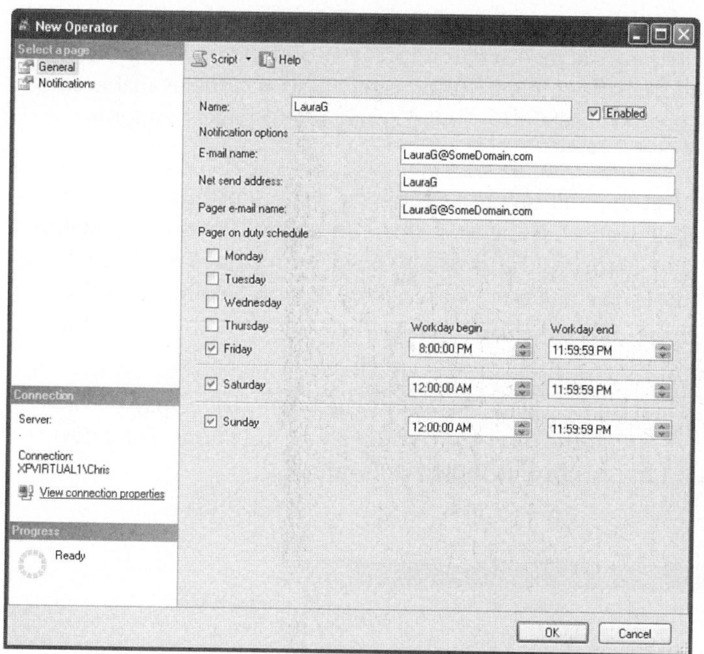

FIGURE 16.6 Creating a new operator.

The notifications options are the key to operators. You create operators so that you can then define notification options and have messages sent from SQL Server.

If you use the email notification option, the email address you specify must be a valid address that can be reached via Database Mail or SQL Mail. One of the two mail options must be configured before the email functionality will work. If Database Mail is configured, the email is sent via an SMTP server. To send email with SQL Mail, SQL Server must be able to access a Microsoft Exchange server, and you must have the Extended MAPI client installed on the SQL Server machine.

The `NET SEND` notification option causes a pop-up window to appear on the recipient's computer; this window contains the notification text. In the Net Send Address text box, you specify the name of the computer or user that is visible on the network to the SQL Server machine. For `NET SEND` to work, the Messenger service on SQL Server must be started. This Messenger service must also be started on the machine that is receiving the `NET SEND` message. You can test the basic `NET SEND` capabilities by executing `NET SEND` at the command prompt. The basic syntax for `NET SEND` follows:

```
NET SEND {name | * | /domain[:name] | /users} message
```

The following example uses the `NET SEND` command to send the message "Test net send message" to the operator `LauraG`:

```
NET SEND LauraG "Test net send message"
```

The final notification option is through a pager email address. Pager email requires that third-party software be installed on the mail server to process inbound email and convert it to a pager message. The methods for implementing pager email and the available software are dependent on the pager provider. You should contact your pager vendor for implementation details.

If you implement pager notification, you can also define the pager schedule for the operator. The Pager on Duty Schedule section of the New Operator dialog allows you to define the days and times when the operator will be available to receive a page. The General page includes a check box for each day the operator can receive a page. It also includes the Workday Begin and Workday End settings, which you can use to define the valid time periods to receive a page.

The other page available when defining a new operator is the Notifications page, which displays the alerts and jobs for which the operator will receive notifications. For a new operator, the Alert List or Job List is empty, as shown in Figure 16.7.

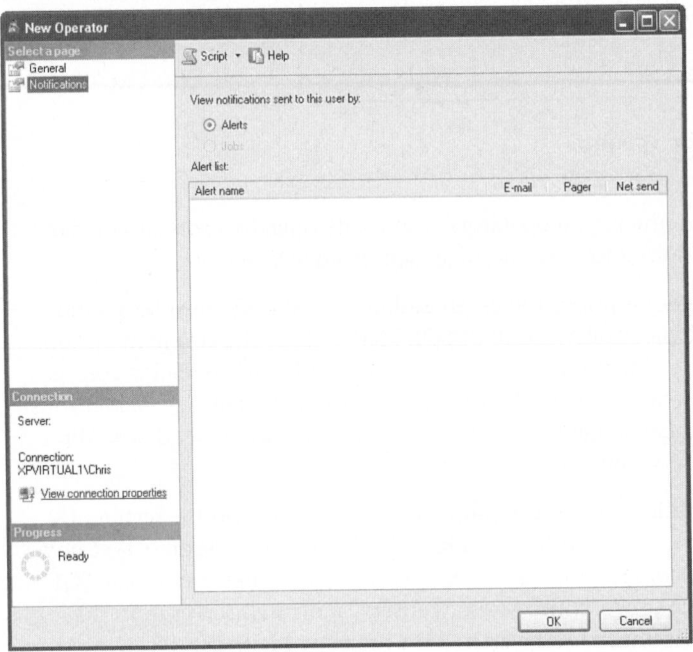

FIGURE 16.7 The Notifications page of the New Operator dialog.

You'll have a better understanding of the usefulness of operators after you read the following discussions of jobs and alerts. Jobs and alerts can have operators linked to them for notification purposes.

Managing Jobs

A *job* is a container for operations that can be executed by the SQL Server Agent. Jobs can be run once or scheduled to run on a regular basis. Jobs provide the basis for SQL Server automation and allow for the execution of many different types of operations, including T-SQL, SQL Server Integration Services (SSIS) packages, and operating system commands.

Defining Job Properties

The `Jobs` node is located under `SQL Server Agent` in the Object Explorer. You right-click the `Jobs` node and select New Job to create a new SQL Server Agent job. A New Job dialog like the one shown in Figure 16.8 appears.

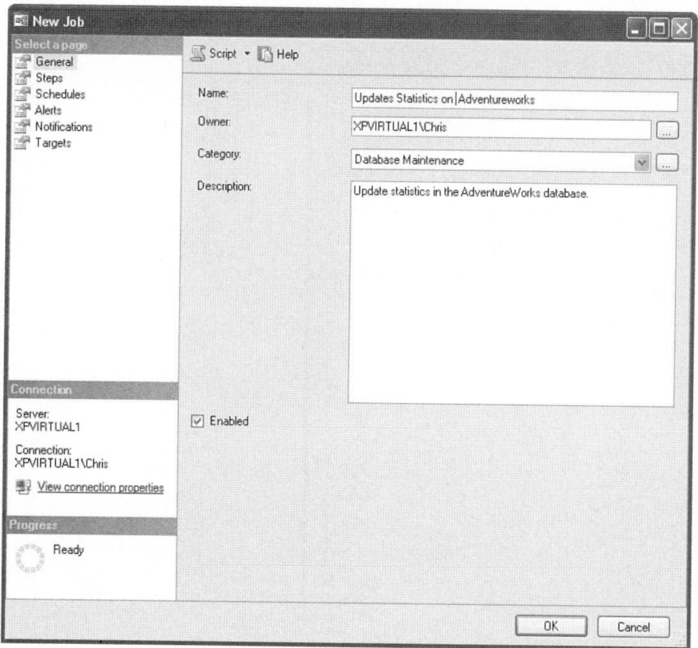

FIGURE 16.8 The New Job dialog.

> **NOTE**
>
> Only logins that are part of one of the `msdb` fixed database roles or are members of the `sysadmin` fixed server role are able to create or modify jobs.

The General properties page shown in Figure 16.8 contains the basic information about the job, including the name and description. The owner of the job defaults to the login for the person creating the job; however, if the login of the person creating the job is part of the sysadmin fixed server role, the default can be changed. You use the Category selection to group or organize jobs. There are several predefined categories for selection, including Database Maintenance and Log Shipping. The default category is set to [Uncategorized(local)].

Defining Job Steps

After you add the general information for a new job, you are ready to add the job steps that actually perform the work. To do this, you select the Steps page on the left side of the New Job dialog, and the job steps for this job are listed. To create a new job step, you click the New button, and a New Job Step dialog like the one shown in Figure 16.9 appears.

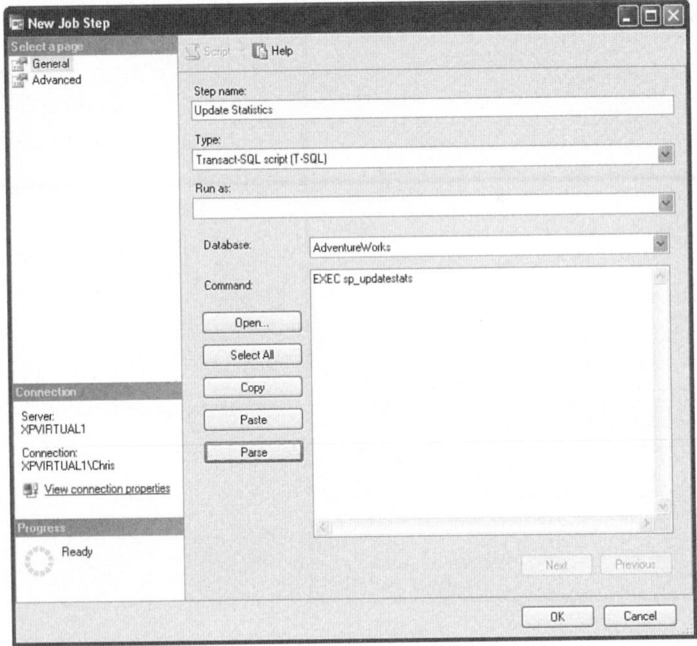

FIGURE 16.9 The New Job Step dialog.

A step name is the first piece of information you need to provide for the job step. It can be up to 128 characters long and must be unique within the job. Then you need to select a job step type. The SQL Server Agent can run a variety of types of job steps, including the following:

- ActiveX script (Visual Basic, Java, Perl script)
- Operating System (CmdExec)
- PowerShell

- `Replication Distributor`
- `Replication Merge`
- `Replication Queue Reader`
- `Replication Snapshot`
- `Replication Transaction Log Reader`
- `SQL Server Analysis Services Command`
- `SQL Server Analysis Services Query`
- `SQL Server Integration Services Package`
- `Transact-SQL script (T-SQL)`

`SQL Server Analysis Services Command`, `Server Analysis Services Query`, and `SQL Server Integration Services Package` are types that were added in SQL Server 2005. They provide integration with SQL Server Analysis Services (SSAS) and SSIS. Chapters 45, "SQL Server and the .NET Framework," and 46, "SQLCLR: Developing SQL Server Objects in .NET," provide detailed discussions of these technologies. The PowerShell job type was added in SQL Server 2008; further information on PowerShell is provided in Chapter 17, "Administering SQL Server 2008 with PowerShell."

The Step properties page displays different information, depending on the type of step selected. When the `Transact-SQL script (T-SQL)` type is selected, you see a window similar to the one shown in Figure 16.9. If you choose the `SQL Server Integration Services Package` type, the Step properties page changes to allow you to enter all the relevant information needed to execute an SSIS package.

In many cases (including T-SQL), a command window is available to input the step commands. With a T-SQL command, you can enter the same type of commands you would enter in a query window. You click the Parse button to validate the SQL and ensure proper syntax. The `Operating system (CmdExec)` type allows you to enter the same types of commands that you can enter in a command prompt window. Each step type has its own command syntax that you can test in the native environment to ensure proper operation.

You can select the Advanced page to configure job flow information and other information related to the job step. On Success Action allows you to specify the action to perform when the current job step completes. Actions include the execution of the next job step (if one exists) and the ability to set job status based on the step completion. The same selection options also exist for On Failure Action.

The Retry options define the options that relate to retrying the job step in the event that the job step fails. Retry Attempts defines the number of times the job step will be re-executed if it fails. Retry Intervals (Minutes) defines the amount of time (in minutes) between retry attempts.

TIP

The Retry options are useful for polling scenarios. For example, you might have a job step that tests for the existence of a file during a given period of the day. The job can be scheduled to start at a time of day when the file is expected. If the file is not there and the step fails, Retry Attempts can be set to poll again for the file. Retry Interval determines how often it retries, and the combination of Retry Attempts and Retry Interval determines the total polling window. For example, if you want to check for the file for 2 hours, you can set Retry Attempts to 24 with a Retry Interval of 5 minutes. If the job step fails more than the number of retries, the step completes in failure.

The last set of options on the Advanced page relate to the output from the job step. Job step output can be saved to an output file that can be overwritten each time the job step is run, or the output can be appended each time. The Log to Table option writes the job step output to the `sysjobstepslogs` table in the `msdb` database. The table contains one row for each job step with the Log to Table option enabled. If Append Output to Existing Entry in Table is enabled, the `sysjobstepslogs` data row for the step can contain output for more than one execution. If this option is not selected, the table contains only execution history for the last execution of the step.

CAUTION

If you choose the Append Output to Existing Entry in Table option, the size of the `sysjobstepslogs` table will grow over time. You should consider using the `sp_delete_jobsteplog` stored procedure to remove data from the `sysjobstepslogs` table. This stored procedure has several different parameters that allow you to filter the data that will be removed. You can use these parameters to remove log data by job, job step, date, or size of the log for the job step.

Defining Multiple Jobs Steps

You can define multiple jobs steps in a single job. This allows you to execute multiple dependent job actions. The job steps run one at a time (serially), and you can specify the order of the job steps. The job order and the related dependencies are called *control of flow*.

Figure 16.10 shows an example of a job that has multiple dependent job steps. Take note of the On Success and On Failure columns, which define the control of flow. For example, if step 1 succeeds, the next step occurs. If step 1 fails, no further steps are executed, and the job quits, reporting a job failure. The control of flow is slightly different for the second step, whereby the control of flow passes to the next step on success but flows to the fourth step if a failure occurs.

The control of flow is defined on each job step. As discussed earlier in this chapter, the Advanced tab of the New Job Step dialog provides drop-down lists that allow you to specify the actions to take on success and on failure. In addition, the Steps page that lists all of a job's steps allows you to specify the start step for the job. The drop-down box at

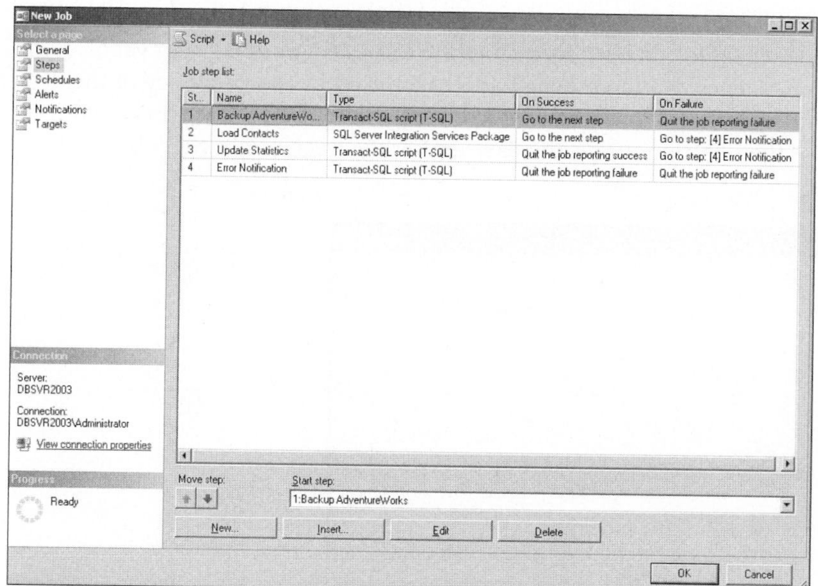

FIGURE 16.10 Multiple job steps.

the bottom of the Steps page provides this function. You can also use the Move Step arrows to change the start step. Manipulating the start step is useful when you're restarting a job manually, as in the case of a job failure; in this situation, you might want to set the job to start on a step other than the first step.

NOTE

SSIS provides the same type of flow control capabilities as the SQL Server Agent. In fact, maintenance plans that contain multiple related actions (such as optimization, backup, and reporting) utilize SSIS packages. A scheduled job starts an SSIS package, which executes the package in a single step, but the actual maintenance steps are defined within the package. The SSIS Designer utilizes a graphical tool that depicts the flow of control and allows you to modify the individual steps.

Defining Job Schedules

The SQL Server Agent contains a comprehensive scheduling mechanism you can use to automate the execution of your jobs. A job can have zero, one, or more schedules assigned to it. You can view the schedules associated with a job by selecting the Schedules page of the Job Properties screen. To create a new schedule for a job, you can click the New button at the bottom of the Schedules page. Figure 16.11 shows the New Job Schedule Properties page, with a sample schedule and options defined. The options on this screen vary, depending on the frequency of the job schedule. For example, if the frequency of the schedule shown in Figure 16.11 were changed from daily to weekly, the screen would change to allow for the selection of specific days during the week to run the job.

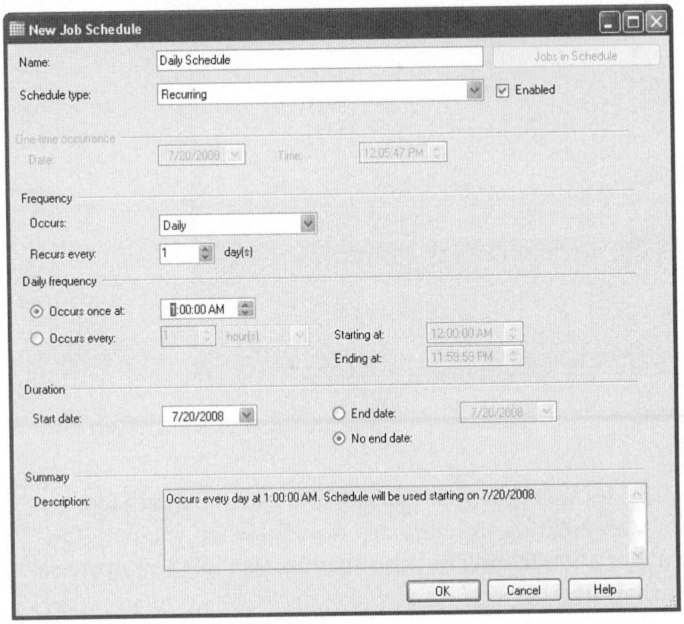

FIGURE 16.11 The New Job Schedule Properties page.

You have the ability to share job schedules so that one job schedule can be utilized by more than one job. When you select the Schedule page, a Pick button is available at the bottom of the page. If you click the Pick button, a screen appears showing all the defined schedules. If you highlight one of the schedules in the list and click OK, the schedule is linked to the related job. You can also view all the jobs associated with a particular schedule by editing the schedule and clicking the Jobs in Schedule button in the top-right portion of the Job Schedule Properties screen.

Tracking multiple job schedules and schedule execution can be challenging in an environment that has many jobs and schedules. The `sp_help_jobs_in_schedule`, and `sp_help_jobactivity` stored procedures are helpful system stored procedures that are found in the `msdb` database. The `sp_help_jobs_in_schedule` stored procedure provides information about the relationship between jobs and schedules. The `sp_help_jobactivity` stored procedure provides point-in-time information about the runtime state of SQL

Server jobs. This stored procedure returns a lot of information, including recent job executions, the status of those executions, and the next scheduled run date.

Defining Job Notifications

The Notifications page of the Job Properties dialog, as shown in Figure 16.12, allows you to define the notification actions to perform when a job completes.

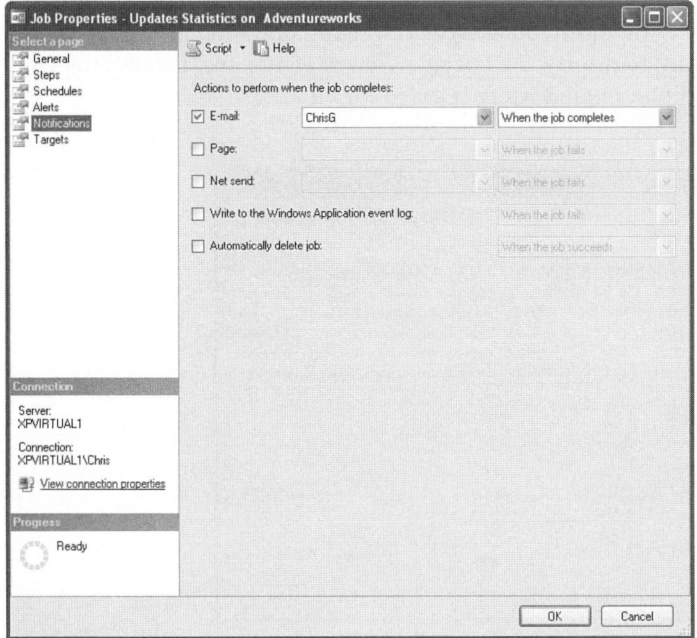

FIGURE 16.12 The Notifications page of the Job Properties dialog.

As discussed earlier in this chapter, notifications can be sent via email, pager, or `NET SEND` command. The notifications for a Schedule Job can be sent based on the following events:

- When the job succeeds
- When the job fails
- When the job completes

Each of these events can have a different notification action defined for it. For example, a notification might send an email if the job succeeds but page someone if it fails.

You also have the option of writing notification information into the Windows Application event log or automatically deleting the job when it completes. These two options are also available on the Notifications page. Writing events to the Application log is a useful tracking mechanism. Monitoring software is often triggered by events in the application log. The automatic job deletion options are useful for jobs that will be run only once. As with the other notification options, you can set up the delete job action such that it is deleted only when a specific job event occurs. For example, you might want to delete the job only if the job succeeds.

Viewing Job History

You view job history via the Log File Viewer, which is a comprehensive application that allows for many different types of logs to be viewed. You right-click a job in the SQL Server Agent and select History to display the Log File Viewer. Figure 16.13 shows the Log File Viewer with several examples of job history selected for viewing.

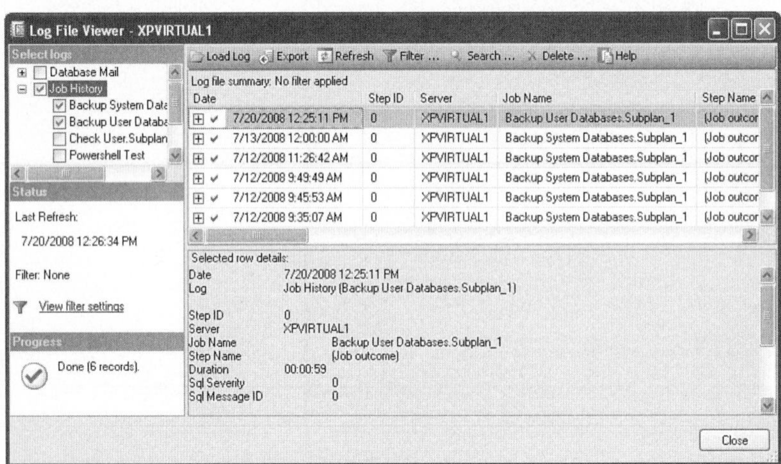

FIGURE 16.13 Job history shown in the Log File Viewer.

Compared to viewing job history in SQL Server versions prior to SQL Server 2005, the current form of the Log File Viewer has some distinct advantages for viewing job history. In the Log File Viewer, you can select multiple jobs for viewing at one time. To view job step details, you expand the job entries and select a job step. You can use the row details shown below the log file summary to troubleshoot job errors and isolate problems. The Log File Viewer also has filtering capabilities that allow you to isolate the jobs to view. Click on the `Filter` button and the Filter Settings dialog appears. You can filter jobs by using a number of different settings, including User, Start Date, and Message Text. You must click the Apply Filter button for the selected filtering option to take effect.

The amount of history that is kept is based on the history settings defined for the SQL Server Agent. You access the history settings by right-clicking the `SQL Server Agent` node, selecting Properties, and then selecting the History page on the left part of the screen. The settings available on the History page are shown in Figure 16.14. By default, the job history log is limited to 1,000 rows, with a maximum of 100 rows per job. You can also select the Automatically Remove Agent History option and select a period of time to retain history. This setting causes the SQL Server Agent to periodically remove job history from the log. This is a good approach for keeping the size of the log manageable.

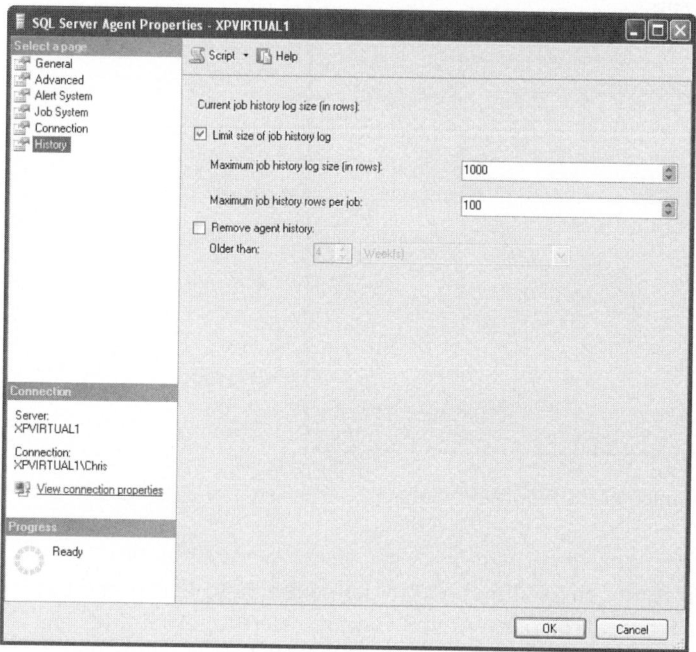

FIGURE 16.14 Job history settings.

Managing Alerts

The SQL Server Agent can monitor events that occur on the database server and automatically respond to these events with alerts. Alerts can be fired based on SQL Server events, performance conditions, and Windows Management Instrumentation (WMI) events. After an alert is fired, the SQL Server Agent can respond by notifying an operator or executing a job. This provides a proactive means for identifying and reacting to critical conditions on a database server.

Defining Alert Properties

To define alerts, you select the `SQL Server Agent` node in the Object Explorer tree and then right-click on the `Alerts` node and select New Alert. Figure 16.15 shows an example of the New Alert dialog that appears.

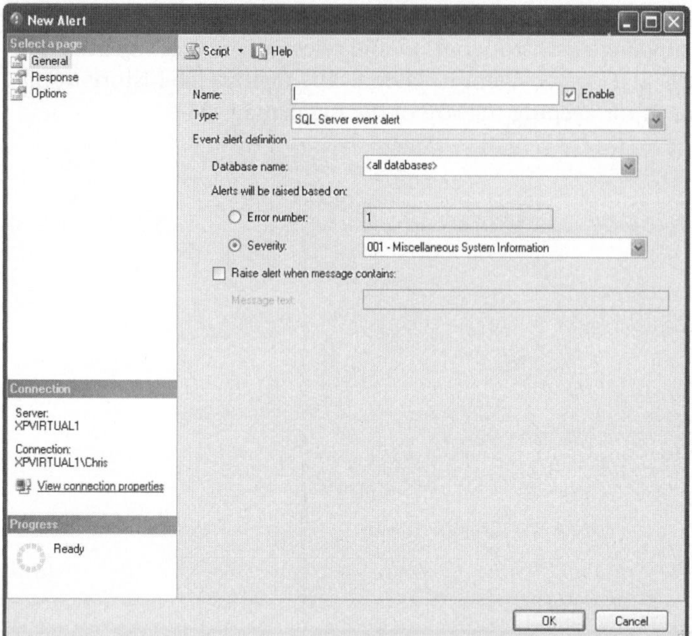

FIGURE 16.15 The General page of the New Alert dialog.

The General page selected in Figure 16.15 allows you to define the basic alert properties, including the name of the alert and type of event you want the alert to respond to. The default type of alert, the SQL Server event alert, is triggered by SQL Server events that write to the Windows Application event log. SQL Server writes to the Application event log when the following events occur:

- When `sysmessages` errors with a severity of 19 or higher are generated. You can use the `sys.sysmessages` catalog view to view all the `sysmessages` that are stored in the server. You can create new user-defined messages by using the `sp_addmessage` stored procedure; they must have a `msg_id` (or error number) that is greater than 50,000. The error message must be created before you can reference the error number in an alert.
- When `sysmessages` errors are generated by the database engine. These messages have error numbers lower than 50,000 and are installed by default.
- When any `RAISERROR` statement is invoked with the `WITH LOG` option. The `WITH LOG` statement forces the event to be written to the Application event log. Messages generated with `RAISERROR` that have a severity level greater than 18 are required to write to the Application event log.

- When sysmessages have been altered with the sp_altermessage statement to write to the application log. The sp_altermessage command has a write_to_log parameter that you can use to modify error numbers found in sys.messages. When the write_to_log parameter is set to WITH_LOG, these message automatically write to the Application event log, regardless of whether the WITH_LOG option is used when the error is raised.
- When application calls are made to xp_logevent to log an event to the application log.

The bottom portion of the General page of the New Alert dialog allows you to define which events in the Application event log the alert should respond to. You can have the event respond to a specific error number, the error severity level, or specific text that is contained in the error message. The sys.sysmessages catalog view contains a complete list of all the error message details for all the supported languages. You can use the following SELECT statement to list the error messages for the English language:

```
SELECT * FROM SYS.SYSMESSAGES
where msglangid = 1033
order by msglangid, error
```

You can define an alert for hundreds of messages. For example, you can define an alert that responds to changes to database options. You do this by selecting error number 5084, which is triggered whenever a change is made to the database options. You can also narrow the scope of the alert to look at a specific database by using the Database Name drop-down. This limits the alert to errors that occur in the specific database you choose. The default option is to look at all databases.

The two other types of alerts you can define are SQL Server performance condition alerts and WMI event alerts. A SQL Server performance condition alert reacts to performance conditions on the server. Figure 16.16 shows an example of this type of alert.

When you select a SQL Server performance condition alert, you need to select the performance object and counter for that object to monitor. The SQL Server performance objects and counters available on the General page of the New Alert dialog are a subset of those available in the Windows Performance Monitor application. These performance metrics encompass key indicators, such as memory, CPU, and disk space.

After selecting the object and counter, you need to define the performance threshold for the alert at the bottom of the General page, below the Alert if Counter label. In the example shown in Figure 16.16, the alert is monitoring the transaction log file for the AdventureWorks database. The threshold has been set such that the alert will fire if the transaction log for this database rises above 2KB.

The WMI event alerts use WMI to monitor events in an instance of SQL Server. The SQL Server Agent can access SQL Server events by using the WMI provider for server events by issuing WMI Query Language (WQL) statements. WQL is a scaled-down version of SQL that contains some WMI-specific extensions. When a WMI query is run, it essentially creates an event notification in the target database so that a related event will fire. The

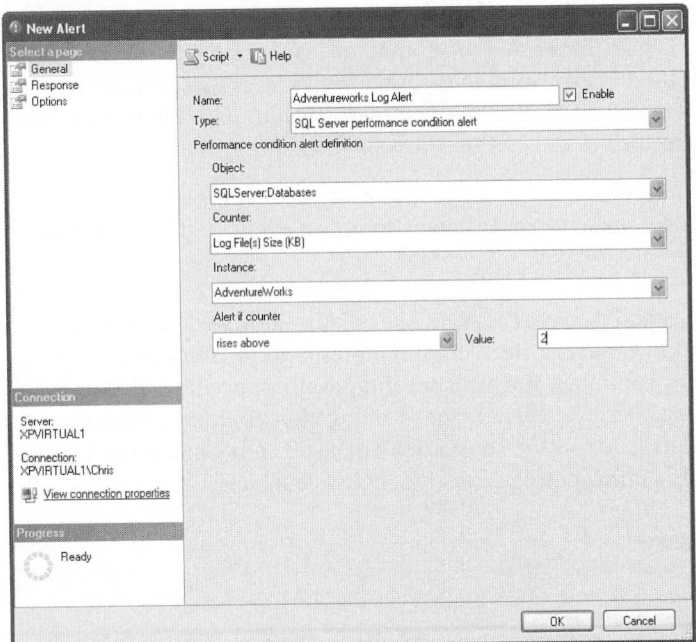

FIGURE 16.16 A SQL Server performance condition alert on the General page.

number of WMI events is extensive. Refer to the "WMI Provider for Server Events Classes and Properties" topic in SQL Server Books Online for a complete list.

Figure 16.17 shows an example of a WMI event alert. This example uses a WQL query that detects any Data Definition Language (DDL) changes to any of the databases on the server. After the alert is created, you can test it by running a DDL statement against the database (for example, `alter table Person.address add newcol int null`).

Defining Alert Responses

The definition of an alert has two primary components. As discussed earlier in this chapter, the first component involves the identification of the event or performance condition that will trigger the alert. The second part of an alert definition involves the desired response when the alert condition is met. You can define an alert response by using the Response page on the alert's Properties screen. Figure 16.18 shows a sample response that has been configured to use `NET SEND` on a message to the operator named `ChrisG`.

Operator notification and job execution are the two responses to an alert. Operator notification allows for one or more operators to be notified via email, pager, or the `NET SEND` command. Job execution allows for the execution of a job that has been defined in the SQL Server Agent. For example, you could execute a job that does a database backup for an alert that is triggered based on database size. You can define both job execution and operator notification in a single alert; they are not mutually exclusive.

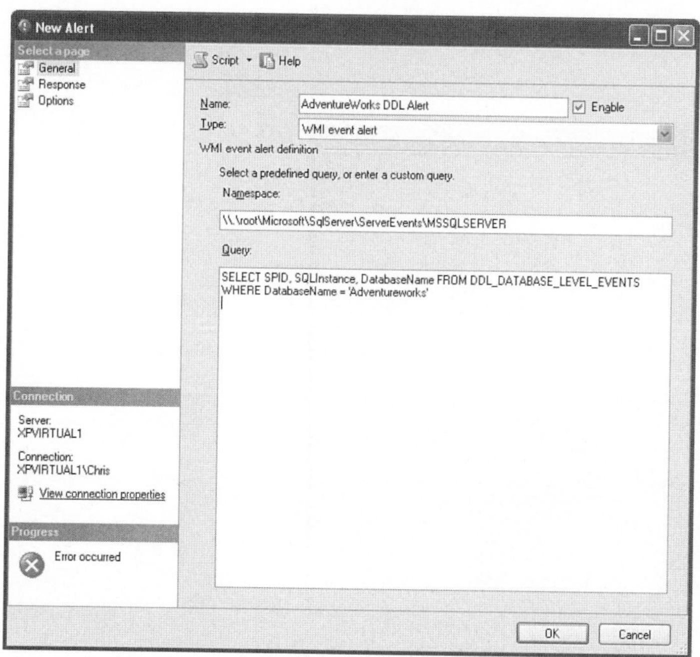

FIGURE 16.17 The General page showing a WMI event alert.

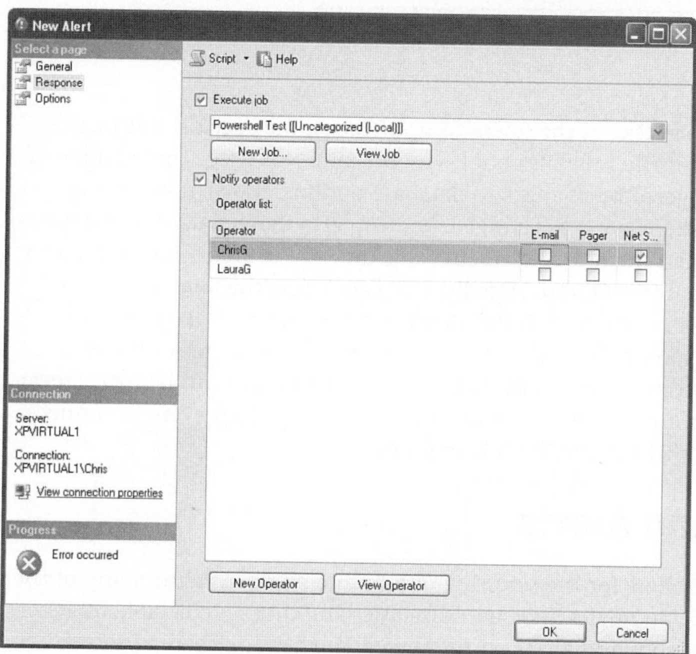

FIGURE 16.18 Configuring an alert response.

You can further define an alert response by using the Options page of an alert's Properties window (see Figure 16.19).

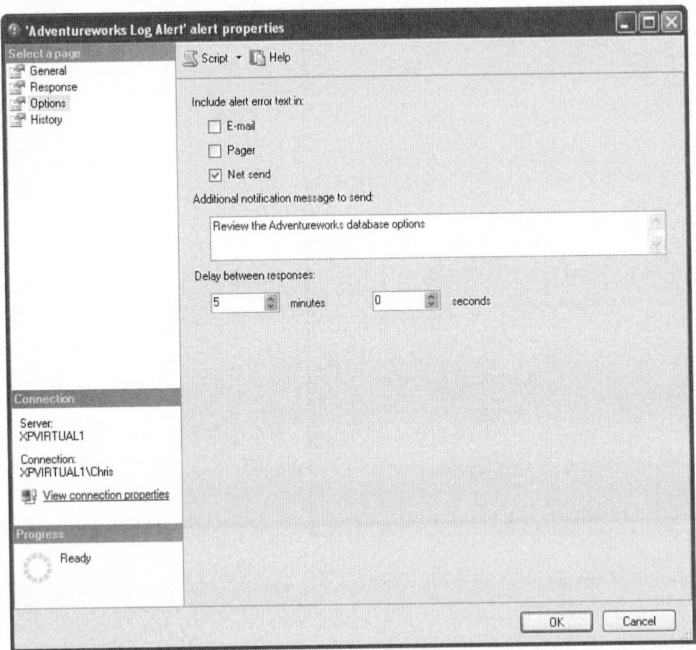

FIGURE 16.19 Alert options.

You can include an alert's error text in the operator notification message on this page. This alert error text provides further details about why the alert was fired. For example, if you have an alert that is triggered by changes to database options, the alert error text would include the actual option that was changed. You can also define additional notification text that is included when the message is sent. This message could include directives for the operators or additional instructions. Finally, you can define the amount of time that the alert will wait before responding to the alert condition again. You do this by using the Delay Between Responses drop-downs (Minutes and Seconds) to set the wait time. This capability is useful in situations in which an alert condition can happen repeatedly within a short period of time. You can define a response delay to prevent an unnecessarily large number of alert notifications from being sent.

Scripting Jobs and Alerts

SQL Server has options that allow for the scripting of jobs and alerts. As with many of the other objects in SQL Server, you might find that it is easier and more predictable to generate a script that contains the jobs and alerts on the server. You can use these scripts to reinstall the jobs and alerts or deploy them to another server. You can right-click the job or alert you want to script and choose a scripting option to generate the T-SQL for the individual object. You can also select the `Job` or `Alerts` node to view the Object Explorer Details that lists all the objects. You can also display the Object Explorer Details through the View menu or by selecting it as the active tab. When Object Explorer Details is selected, you have the option of selecting one or more jobs to script. You can select multiple jobs by holding down the Ctrl key and clicking the jobs you want to script.

Figure 16.20 shows a sample Object Explorer Details for jobs, with several of the jobs selected for scripting. To generate the script, you simply right-click one of the selected jobs and select the Script Job As menu option to generate the desired type of script.

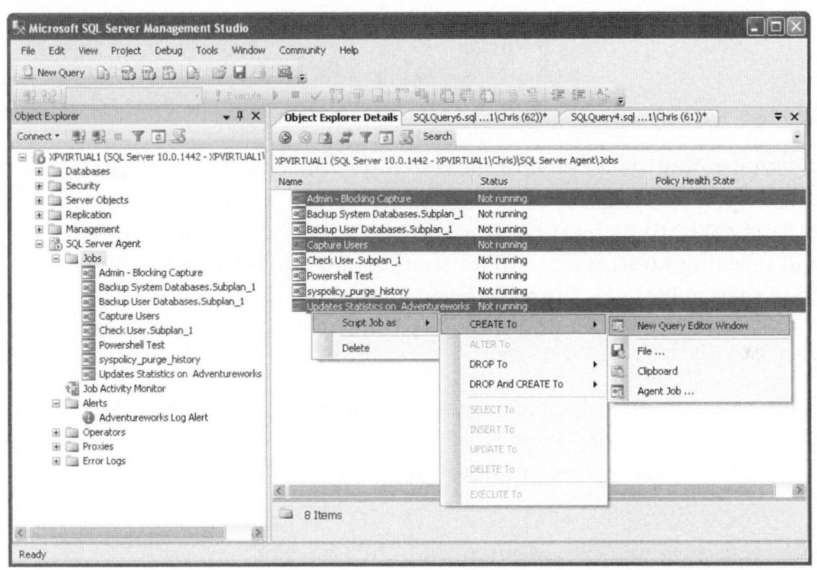

FIGURE 16.20 Script generation for jobs.

NOTE

With SQL Server 2008, you can also filter the jobs you want to script by using the filtering capabilities that are available on the Object Explorer Details. For example, you can filter on jobs whose names contain specific text. After you filter the jobs, you can script the jobs that are displayed. The filtering options and the capability to selectively script jobs are particularly useful in environments in which many jobs and alerts exist.

16

Multiserver Job Management

Multiserver job management allows you to centralize the administration of multiple *target* servers on a single *master* server. The master server is a SQL Server instance that contains the job definitions and status information for all the enlisted target servers. The target servers are SQL Server instances that obtain job information from the master server and continually update the master server with job statistics.

Multiserver job management is beneficial in SQL Server environments in which there are many instances to manage. You can establish jobs, operators, and execution schedules one time on the master server and then deploy them to all the target servers. This promotes consistency across the enterprise and can ease the overall administrative burden. Without multiserver job management, administrative jobs must be established and maintained on each server.

Creating a Master Server

The first step in creating a multiserver environment involves the creation of a master server. SQL Server 2008 provides the Master Server Wizard, which simplifies this task. You launch the Master Server Wizard by right-clicking the `SQL Server Agent` node in the Object Explorer and selecting Multi Server Administration and Make This a Master. The Master Server Wizard then guides you through the creation of an operator to receive multiserver job notifications and allows you to specify the target servers for SQL Server Agent jobs.

Figure 16.21 shows the Master Server Wizard screen that allows you to add information related to the master server's operator. The operator created on the master server, named `MSXOperator`, is the only one that can receive notifications for multiserver jobs.

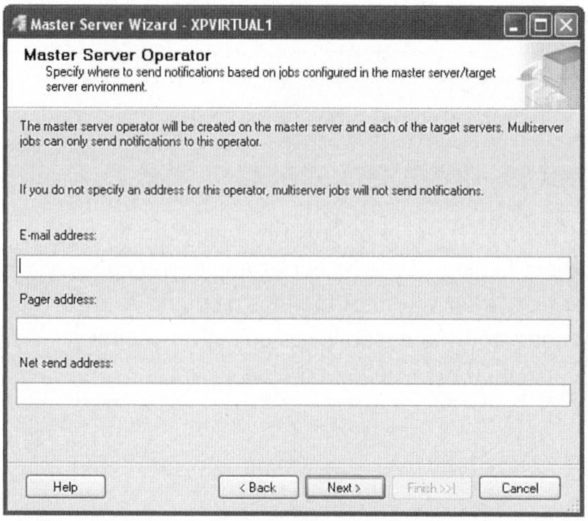

FIGURE 16.21 The Master Server Wizard.

The Master Server Wizard also validates the service accounts that the SQL Server Agent uses on the target servers. These accounts are typically Windows domain accounts that are in the same domain as the master server. The service accounts are important because the target servers utilize Windows security to connect to the master server and download jobs for the SQL Server Agent. The validation process and security considerations are simplified if the master server and target servers are run with the same domain account.

Enlisting Target Servers

The Master Server Wizard allows you to enlist one or more target servers. Enlisting a target server identifies it to the master server and allows the master server to manage the administration of its jobs. You can also enlist additional target servers after the wizard completes. You do this by right-clicking the `SQL Server Agent` node of the target server and then selecting Multi Server Administration and then Make This a Target. Doing so launches the Target Server Wizard, which guides you through the addition of another target server. The Target Server Wizard performs some of the same actions as the Master Server Wizard, including the following:

- It ensures that the SQL Server versions on the two servers are compatible.
- It ensures that the SQL Server Agent on the master server is running.
- It ensures that the Agent Startup account has rights to log in as a target server.
- It enlists the target server.

Creating Multiserver Jobs

After setting up the master and target servers, you can create jobs on the master server and specify which target servers they should run on. Periodically, the target servers poll the master server. If any jobs defined for them have been scheduled to run since the last polling interval, the target server downloads the jobs and runs them. When a job completes, the target server uploads the job outcome status to the master server.

Event Forwarding

Event forwarding is another multiserver feature that allows a single SQL Server instance to process events for other servers in your SQL Server environment. This involves the designation of an alerts management server to which other servers can forward their events. You enable the alerts management server by right-clicking the `SQL Server Agent` node and selecting Properties. When the Properties pages appears, you click the Advanced page (see Figure 16.22).

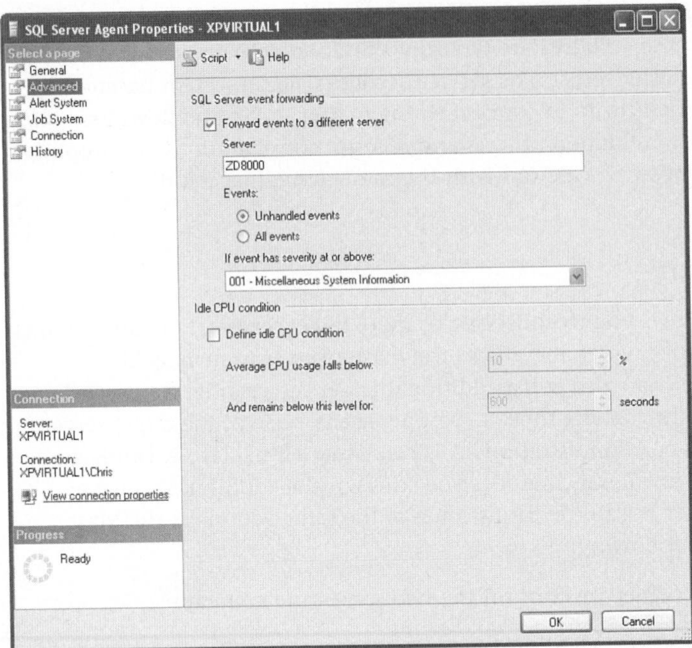

FIGURE 16.22 Configuring event forwarding.

To configure event forwarding, you select the Forward Events to a Different Server option on the Advanced page. You can then select the SQL Server instance you want as the alerts management server by using the Server drop-down. The servers shown in the drop-down are those that have been registered in SSMS. If the server you want does not appear in the drop-down, you need to choose Registered Servers from the View menu and ensure that the server is registered.

You can choose to forward unhandled events, all events, or only a subset of the events. The default is to send all unhandled events, but you can customize this for your needs. You can further limit the messages that are forwarded by specifying the severity level that the message must have in order to be forwarded. For example, you can configure the servers to forward only fatal error messages that have a severity greater than or equal to Level 19. In this scenario, you could define alerts on the alerts management server that respond to these fatal errors and notify operators that specialize in their resolution.

You need to consider a number of trade-offs when using event forwarding. You need to weigh the benefits of central administration and a lack of redundancy against the disadvantages of having a single point of failure and increased network traffic. The available network bandwidth, number of servers involved in event forwarding, and stability of the alerts management server are some of the key factors you need to think about in making your decision.

Summary

The SQL Server Agent in SQL Server 2008 delivers a powerful set of tools to make your administrative life easier. It provides automation in the form of jobs, operators, and alerts that help you deliver a consistent and healthy database environment. After you have set up the appropriate automation with the SQL Server Agent, you can rest assured that you have been proactive in managing your database environment.

PowerShell is another tool to help with your automation needs. This new tool, that was integrated into SQL Server 2008, provides a powful command-line facility you can use to access SQL Server objects. This tool is discussed in Chapter 17.

CHAPTER 17

Administering SQL Server 2008 with PowerShell

- Overview of PowerShell
- PowerShell Scripting Basics
- PowerShell in SQL Server 2008
- Step-By-Step Examples

Windows PowerShell is Microsoft's next-generation scripting language. More and more server-based products are being released with various levels of support for this scripting language.

This chapter provides an overview of what Windows PowerShell is and describes some of the basic features of Windows PowerShell that SQL Server 2008 users should find useful. It also presents examples that demonstrate the use of these features with SQL Server 2008.

SQL Server 2008 includes additional features to support PowerShell. The chapter also presents step-by-step examples showing how to use Windows PowerShell for various OS and database tasks.

What's New with PowerShell

The integration of Windows PowerShell into the SQL Server environment is new to SQL Server 2008. The PowerShell scripting language has been around for some time, but it was not installed with prior versions of SQL Server or integrated into the SQL Server environment. With SQL Server 2008, it is installed, and there are now means for easily accessing SQL Server objects via this powerful scripting shell.

The `SQLPS` utility is at the crux of the new PowerShell integration in SQL Server 2008. `SQLPS` is a command-line shell that loads and registers SQL Server snap-ins that provide access to SQL Server via PowerShell. There is no need to manually reference or load the SQL Server libraries, which is necessary if you launch the PowerShell environment independently using the native PowerShell (`powershell.exe`) utility.

In SQL Server 2008, the new `SQLPS` utility has also been integrated into the SQL Server Management Studio (SSMS) environment. You can launch a `SQLPS` session by right-clicking on an object in the Object Explorer tree and selecting Start PowerShell. A `SQLPS` command window is launched with the path for that object already referenced. You can now work with the properties of that object in a command-line environment that provides options that go beyond the traditional GUI environment.

The integration of `SQLPS` is also visible in the SQL Server Agent. You can now add PowerShell job steps to SQL Server jobs. The PowerShell commands that you can enter for the job step are the same as you would enter interactively in a PowerShell session. This new kind of job step allows you to schedule PowerShell commands and integrate PowerShell actions with other SQL Server Agent job steps.

Overview of PowerShell

Windows PowerShell is Microsoft's next-generation automation and scripting language. It is built on the Microsoft .NET 2.0 Framework.

Windows PowerShell was first released to the public in November 2006 as version 1.0. It was released as a separate install for Windows XP and Windows 2003, and shortly after, an install for Windows Vista was made available. Since its release, Windows PowerShell has been downloaded over two million times.

NOTE

From this point on, we refer to Windows PowerShell simply as *PowerShell*.

When Windows Server 2008 was released, PowerShell was provided with the operating system. To have access to PowerShell, you simply had to add the Windows PowerShell feature through the new Server Manager.

NOTE

Currently, PowerShell is not available on Windows Server 2008 Core because of the .NET Framework requirement. Server 2008 Core officially doesn't support the .NET Framework.

In 2008, Microsoft announced that PowerShell is now part of its Common Engineering Criteria for 2009 and beyond. This announcement basically means that all of Microsoft's server products should have some level of PowerShell support. Microsoft Exchange 2007 was the earliest server-class product to come out with full PowerShell support. In fact, all of Exchange's administrative tasks are based on PowerShell. The PowerShell functionality in Exchange is actually named Exchange Management Shell.

NOTE

PowerShell 1.0 is installed by default when SQL Server 2008 client software or Database Services are installed. Keep in mind that PowerShell 1.0 is not the latest version available. The next version, PowerShell version 2, is available for download and is installed by default with newer operating systems such as Windows Server 2008 R2. V2 introduces a number of new features that are not covered in this chapter.

NOTE

The intent of this chapter is to introduce the basic concepts and functionality of PowerShell and how it integrates with SQL Server 2008. Use of more advanced features is beyond the scope of what can be covered in a single chapter.

For more information on PowerShell, be sure to check out the main PowerShell address at http://www.microsoft.com/powershell and also the PowerShell team blog at http://blogs.msdn.com/powershell.

A number of script examples and resources are also available in the Microsoft Technet PowerShell Script Center: http://technet.microsoft.com/en-us/scriptcenter/powershell.aspx

If you want to get into some of the more advanced features and capabilities of PowerShell, you may also want to check out a PowerShell-specific book such as *Windows PowerShell Unleashed* from Sams Publishing.

Start Using PowerShell Now

PowerShell supports all the regular DOS commands and can run scripts written in any other language (the script engine specific to that scripting language still needs to be used). If any kind of scripting is currently being done, there is no reason why users can't start using PowerShell now, even if they are not using its vast functionality.

Common Terminology

Here are some of the common terms used when working with PowerShell:

- **Cmdlet**—This is the name given to the built-in commands in PowerShell. Cmdlets are the most basic component within PowerShell and are used when doing anything in PowerShell. They are always of the form "verb-noun." Cmdlets also have arguments called *parameters*, and values can be passed to these parameters.
- **Script**—With automation comes the requirement for scripts. Using scripts is as simple as putting a single cmdlet in a file and then executing the file. In PowerShell, scripts have the extension `.ps1` and can be executed or invoked by simply calling it as `./my_script.ps1`.
- **Pipeline**—This PowerShell functionality allows a series of cmdlets to be combined together using the pipe character (|). The output from one cmdlet is then piped to the following cmdlet for further processing.

- **Provider**—Using this PowerShell functionality, a data store is presented to the user in a format similar to a file system. Some of the "core" cmdlets are typically used to do various tasks such as creating items like files and/or folders.
- **Snap-in**—PowerShell functionality can be extended with the use of snap-ins. They are basically DLL files written in a .NET programming language such as C# or VB.NET. DBAs can load these snap-ins in their PowerShell session to add additional functionality such as additional cmdlets and/or providers.
- **Tab completion**—This PowerShell functionality allows the user to press the Tab key to autocomplete supported commands and parameters.
- **Aliases**—Theseare shorter names that can be used for cmdlets. For example, some typical UNIX and DOS commands have had aliases for them created in PowerShell. These aliases map to the actual PowerShell cmdlet.

Object-Based Functionality

As mentioned earlier, PowerShell is built on the .NET Framework. This implies that everything within PowerShell is object based. This is a familiar concept for anyone who is already familiar with the .NET Framework or .NET programming languages such as C# or VB.NET.

This object-based functionality is an important concept to remember if you want to dive deeper into PowerShell. PowerShell provides many features, and it can also use additional features provided by other .NET assemblies.

SQL Server Management Objects

SQL Server Management Objects (SMO) are a very useful tool to advanced users and developers when dealing with the automation of SQL Server 2005 and 2008. A lot of the features within SQL Server (core engine, agent, mail, and so on) are packaged into easy-to-access .NET libraries that can be accessed from PowerShell.

Most of the functionality provided by the new PowerShell support in SQL 2008 is based on SMO.

As for SQL Server 2005, PowerShell can still be used to administer this version via SMO. The only difference is that the relevant assemblies must be loaded manually.

WMI

Windows Management Instrumentation (WMI) is a Windows service that provides remote control and management. PowerShell provides some built-in support for retrieving information via WMI.

Although the main goal of WMI may be to provide remote access, it can also be used locally and can provide a wealth of information about a system. For example, WMI can be used to easily query disk space and installed patches. Examples of using WMI are shown later in this chapter.

Installing PowerShell

As of Windows Server 2008, adding the PowerShell feature is easy using the new Server Manager application. With previous versions of Windows, PowerShell was a separate install, which required downloading and installing an external package.

To install PowerShell on Server 2008, start Server Manager, go to the `Features` node, then click Add Features, and simply check the box for Windows PowerShell, as shown in Figure 17.1.

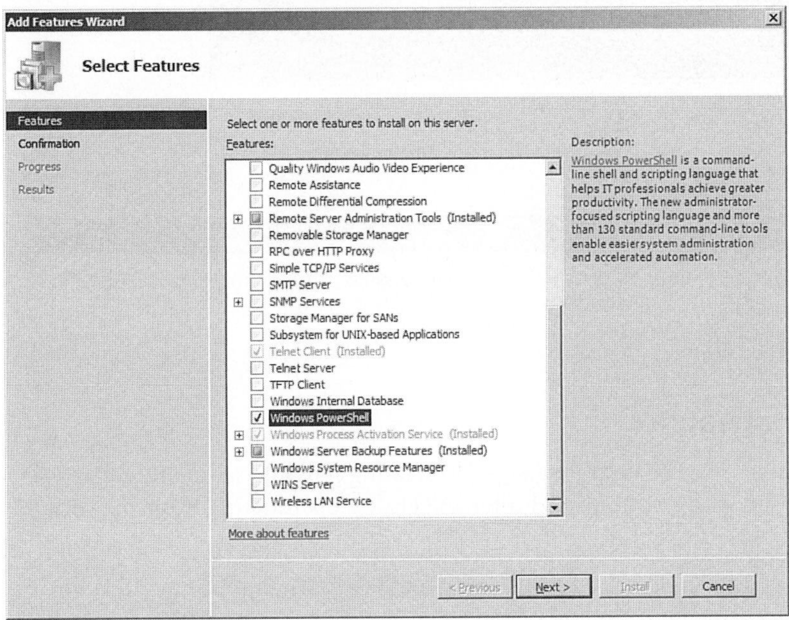

FIGURE 17.1 Selecting the Windows PowerShell feature.

PowerShell Console

You can accessing PowerShell directly from the Start menu, by opening All Programs, and choosing Windows PowerShell 1.0, then finally Windows PowerShell (alternatively, on some systems, such as Windows 7, you can find the Windows PowerShell folder under the Accessories folder in the Start menu). The Windows PowerShell console opens, as shown in Figure 17.2.

FIGURE 17.2 Opening the PowerShell console.

NOTE

The prompt displayed in examples of the PowerShell console in this chapter has been changed from the default.

Scriptable and Interactive

PowerShell can be used as a scripting language, by creating reusable scripts that can automate various tasks, and it can also be used interactively, by opening up a console window and entering commands line by line.

In interactive mode, PowerShell is intelligent enough to know when a command is not complete and actually displays >> on a new line when it believes a complete command has not been entered.

Default Security

After PowerShell has been installed, it is very secure out of the box. Here are two of the default security features:

- PowerShell cannot run any scripts. If you attempt to double-click on any `.ps1` script, it simply opens the contents in Notepad.
- PowerShell cannot be accessed remotely.

Execution Policy

By default, PowerShell can only be used interactively from the console. This is part of the default security. To be able to actually run scripts, you must set the execution policy. The easiest way to set this policy is to use the `Set-ExecutionPolicy` cmdlet, as follows:

```
PS>Set-ExecutionPolicy RemoteSigned
```

Basically, when you use the value `RemoteSigned`, PowerShell is set to be able to run scripts that have been created locally, but if a script is downloaded from the Internet, for example, it must be signed.

NOTE

The details of the different execution policy settings available or the advantages and disadvantages of different possibilities are not covered in this chapter. Using `RemoteSigned` is one of the better trade-offs between functionality and security for most users.

Profiles

As users become more and more familiar with PowerShell, they typically develop customizations that they may want to save for the next time PowerShell is opened. PowerShell has several profiles that can be used to configure user and system-wide settings. The system-wide profile is easy to access using the following:

```
PS>notepad $profile
```

NOTE

On a new install, this file typically doesn't exist, so don't be surprised if a window pops up asking you to create the file. Adding commands to the profile is usually as easy as adding the exact same commands that you would execute in the shell directly into the profile.

Built-in Help Features

As mentioned earlier, cmdlets are the most basic component of PowerShell. Three of these cmdlets are essential in attempting to learn PowerShell. Even advanced users may still use these cmdlets on a daily basis:

- **`Get-Command`**—This cmdlet is essential in discovering what commands can be used and what might be available on the system to help with a certain task.
- **`Get-Help`**—When you are looking for additional details, specifically on other cmdlets, this is the main cmdlet to use.

- **Get-Member**—Absolute beginners don't typically start using this cmdlet when first initiated into PowerShell, but for advanced users, and easier discovery, this cmdlet is very useful.

Let's look at each of these cmdlets in more detail.

Get-Command

The `Get-Command` cmdlet can be used to get a listing of an entire list of cmdlets on the system, but it can also be used to get cmdlets that can be used for a specific task or purpose. For example, `Get-Command` alone in the console prints the entire list of available cmdlets available in the current console:

```
PS>Get-Command
```

If this is the first time you have ever opened a PowerShell console, how do you write to the console? How about displaying something as simple as "Welcome to SQL 2008"? You can pass something basic to `Get-Command`, such as the string `"*write*"`:

```
PS>Get-Command *write*
```

What results is a listing of all the cmdlets that have the string `"write"` in any part of their name.

In addition, the preceding command also displays any applications and aliases (aliases are discussed later in this chapter) found in the current user's path.

PowerShell can be pretty smart. The preceding sample is actually a shortcut for something longer like this:

```
PS>Get-Command -Name *write*
```

Based on how the cmdlet is programmed, cmdlets can automatically assign a particular value to a parameter even when the parameter isn't explicitly typed out.

Originally, we were looking for a cmdlet to display something on the console and found the cmdlet `Write-Host`. Let's try it:

```
PS>Write-Host "Welcome to SQL 2008"
```

Get-Help

The learning curve with PowerShell can be relatively steep. Sometimes you can find a particular command for a particular task, such as the `Write-Host` cmdlet in the preceding section, but you might not always be sure how to actually use it. `Write-Host` is simple, but what if `Write-Host` had other useful features, or help was required for some other cmdlet?

`Get-Help` is a very useful cmdlet. Just using `Get-Help` alone provides some default help information:

```
PS>Get-Help
```

To get help on a particular cmdlet, you can use `Get-Help` and pass the other cmdlet as an argument:

```
PS>Get-Help Write-Host
```

That approach might not provide a lot of useful information; perhaps the `-Full` and `-Examples` parameters are more useful:

```
PS>Get-Help Write-Host -Full
```

Passing the `-Full` parameter gives a detailed description of the cmdlet and all its parameters (including what types of values they accept). If you are a more experienced user, the `-Examples` parameter is very useful, because it just gives some examples of using the cmdlet, which is an easy way to remember the syntax of a particular command:

```
PS>Get-Help Write-Host -Examples
```

NOTE

`Get-Help` works on other cmdlets, but it can also be used when you are looking for additional details on other concepts in PowerShell. To get a listing of the built-in help for various concepts in PowerShell, you can run the command `Get-Help about_*`.

Get-Member

Because everything in PowerShell is object based, some of the features that can be accessed are always visible. To find out more about a particular object, you can use the `Get-Member` cmdlet to look at all its members (the more interesting members of a .NET object are usually its properties and methods).

Using something simple like `"AdventureWorks2008R2"`, you can easily look at PowerShell's members (possibly without having to consult any .NET developer-focused documentation). `"AdventureWorks2008R2"` is a string—in other words, a combination of alphanumeric characters (that can include spaces). The following example is another way to display a string in the PowerShell console:

```
PS>"AdventureWorks2008R2"
```

PowerShell automatically recognizes this is a simple string and displays it.

A string can be easily displayed to the console, but what else can you do with a string object? In the .NET Framework, a string is really a `System.String` object. The .NET Framework provides a lot of functionality that can be used to deal with strings. Now let's consider another example:

```
PS>" AdventureWorks2008R2"|Get-Member
```

From the preceding command, more information is displayed now, including `TypeName:System.String`, which confirms that this is a `System.String` object. One particular feature that `Get-Member` indicates is that there is a `ToLower` method supported by this particular object:

```
PS>"AdventureWorks2008R2".ToLower()
```

In this example, the `ToLower` method of the `System.String` object is used to change the string into all lowercase letters.

PowerShell Scripting Basics

The following sections cover some of the basics of scripting with PowerShell. We hope this information will help you understand how you can use PowerShell in various situations to automate various tasks.

A Few Basic Cmdlets

Following is a list of a few basic cmdlets and how they can be used, with a brief example:

- **`Get-ChildItem`** (aka `dir`, `gci`)—Cmdlet used to list child items in a provider. Mostly used to list things such as files and directories in a file system. Example: `Get-ChildItem *.ps1`
- **`Select-Object`**—Cmdlet used to retrieve only specific properties. See `Get-Help Select-Object -Examples` for examples.
- **`Group-Object`**—Cmdlet used to group objects based on their properties. See `Get-Help Group-Object -Examples` for examples.
- **`Sort-Object`**—Cmdlet used to sort objects based on their properties. See `Get-Help Sort-Object -Examples` for examples.
- **`Read-Host`**—Cmdlet used to read input from the screen, usually from a user, before continuing. Example: `Read-Host "Enter a database name"`.
- **`Measure-Command`**—Cmdlet used to measure how much time a particular scriptblock took to run. Example: `Measure-Command {Get-Command}`.
- **`Write-Host`**—Cmdlet used to basically display output to the console. This cmdlet was covered earlier.
- **`New-Object`**—Cmdlet used to create an instance of a .NET (or COM) object. Examples are provided later.
- **`Get-Alias`**—Cmdlet used to get a listing of the aliases on the system. `Get-Alias`, with no arguments, lists all the aliases configured on the local system.
- **`Get-Content`**—Cmdlet used to read the contents of a file. Typically, only text-based files are supported. Example: `Get-Content my_script.ps1`.

- **`Add-Content`**—Cmdlet used to add or append content to a file. Example: `Add-Content my_file.txt "testing"`.
- **`Set-Content`**—Cmdlet used to set the contents of a file (it overwrites any existing content). Example: `Set-Content my_file.txt "testing 123"`.
- **`Start-Transcript`**—Cmdlet used also with `Stop-Transcript` to record everything in the console to a specific text file. Example: `Start-Transcript`.

Creating a PowerShell Script

Creating a PowerShell script is as simple as placing a few commands into a `.ps1` script and then invoking that script. Here's a simple example of putting the `Write-Host` cmdlet into a script and then running it.

```
PS> add-content c:\temp\test.ps1 "Write-Host `testing`"
PS>c:\temp\test.ps1
testing
PS>
```

In the preceding example, a `Write-Host` cmdlet was placed in a file named `test.ps1`, and then the file was invoked. The output resulted in the string `"testing"` being output to the script. Notepad or any other simple text editor could also be used to create more complicated scripts.

Sample PowerShell scripts that directly apply to SQL Server administration are provided later in this chapter. Refer to the "The Step-By-Step Examples" section.

Adding Comments

Adding comments to a PowerShell script is as simple as adding the # character at the beginning of the line. To comment out entire blocks of code, you must use a # on each line.

NOTE

Another way to comment out blocks of code is to use something called a *here string*. This technique is not covered in this book.

Variables

Strings and objects were discussed earlier in this chapter. A very useful feature of PowerShell, and thus of SQL-PowerShell, is the ability to place objects into a variable. This allows you to run any kind of command and place any objects produced into a variable for later use.

Examples of using variables are presented later in this chapter. For now, a string can be easily saved as a variable:

```
PS>$var="AdventureWorks2008R2"
```

```
PS>$var
AdventureWorks2008R2
```

In the preceding example, the string is saved as the variable `$var` and then output to the script when the variable is simply invoked:

```
PS>$database=read-host "Enter a database name"
Enter a database name:AdventureWorks2008R2
PS>$database
AdventureWorks2008R2
```

The `Read-Host` cmdlet was introduced briefly already. In this example, the `Read-Host` cmdlet is used to read input from the console, and the information input is passed to the `$database` variable.

NOTE

When you perform certain actions in a script, a function, and even from the command line, the scope assigned to the variable or function determines how this variable will be seen by other scripts, functions, and so on. The details of scoping are not discussed any further, but it is still an important concept to remember as you use PowerShell more and more.

NOTE

You can issue the `Get-Help about_shell_variable` and `Get-Help about_scope` commands in Powershell for more information and examples about shell variables.

An example provided later in this chapter demonstrates that objects much more complicated than simple strings can be saved to a variable for later use.

Escaping Characters

Often a special character may be used—for example, in DOS commands—but PowerShell tries to interpret it differently. Let's consider the dollar sign character (`$`). PowerShell normally tries to interpret it as a variable:

```
PS C:\> $var="$5 discount"
PS C:\> $var
 discount
PS C:\> $var="`$5 discount"
PS C:\> $var
$5 discount
PS C:\>
```

The preceding example shows how the escape character, which is the backtick (`), is used to escape the dollar sign, so that PowerShell doesn't try to interpret the character literally as the beginning of a variable.

NOTE

You can execute the `Get-Help about_escape_character` command in PowerShell for more information and examples.

Special Variable $_

In PowerShell, $_ is a special variable that represents the current object in the pipeline. When several cmdlets are piped together, this special variable may be used often. Several examples of using this special variable are shown later in this chapter.

NOTE

A special variable named `$input` also represents objects passed along the pipeline, but we do not look at this variable in any further detail in this chapter.

NOTE

See `Get-Help about_automatic_variables` for more information and examples.

Joining Variables and Strings

The concept of objects was already introduced briefly. When you are dealing with simple strings, you can easily concatenate them together using the plus (+) sign to create a new string:

```
PS>$last_name="Doe"
PS>$first_name="John"
PS>$full_name=$last_name+", "+$first_name
PS>$full_name
Doe, John
PS>
```

In this example, two variables containing simple strings are defined, and they are simply concatenated together to create a third variable, which is then displayed to the console.

NOTE

This kind of concatenation works when both variables are strings. An error may be returned if the variable is of another data type.

An example is provided later with the `AdventureWorks2008R2` database where string variables from two different columns in the same table will be joined together using this feature.

Passing Arguments

PowerShell has a special reserved variable named `$args`. It can be used with scripts and functions, and represents any arguments passed to the script or function when it is invoked, as shown here:

```
PS>add-content c:\temp\parameter.ps1 "`$args.count"
PS>add-content c:\temp\parameter.ps1 "`$args[0]"
PS>c:\temp\parameter.ps1 1 2 3
3
1
PS>
```

In the preceding example, a two-line script is created, and then it is invoked while passing some arguments to it. `$args.count` displays the number of arguments passed to the script, whereas `$args[0]` displays the value of the first argument only.

Later, an example of a PowerShell script that can do a database backup is provided. The example is extended to show how a script could be used to accept an argument that would be the name of the database the script will back up.

Using `Param`

A special construct, `param`, can be used to force the way arguments are passed to a script or function:

```
PS>function test_param {
>> param([string]$arg1)
>> write-host "Argument 1 is $arg1"
>> }
>>PS>test_param "testing"
Argument 1 is testing
PS>test_param -arg1 "testing"
Argument 1 is testing
PS>
```

In this example, `param` is used to specify that a parameter passed to this script will be a string object and will be contained in the variable `$arg1` for later use in the script.

NOTE

The biggest difference between using `param` or `$args` with arguments occurs when the number of arguments is known versus unknown. The `param` keyword should not be used when the number of arguments passed is not known.

NOTE

`[string]` is a shortcut in PowerShell where you specify that the argument, as in the preceding example, will be a string, and not something else such as a number or integer. A dozen or so of these shortcuts are available in PowerShell, and they are typically known as *type accelerators*.

Arrays

To PowerShell, *arrays* are simply a listing of data. They can be used for various tasks and can be created easily, as you can see here:

```
PS>$var="foo","bar"
PS>$var
foo
bar
PS>
```

In this example, an array is created with two values, and then it is simply invoked, which simply results in outputting each element of the array, one per line. When an array is created, a reference can be made to a particular element of the array using a special "[]" syntax, like this:

```
PS>$var[0]
foo
PS>
```

NOTE

The first element of an array is the element zero; therefore, the first record in an array is retrieved by referencing the element `id [0]`.

The `count` property is also useful as a property of array objects (remember that everything n PowerShell is a .NET object:

```
PS>$var.count
2
PS>
```

The `count` property is used to iterate through each element of an array.

NOTE

Arrays can also be defined in at least two other ways: with a type accelerator (`[array]$var` is an example) or using a notation like this:

```
$var=@("foo","bar").
```

Several other type accelerators are used in PowerShell, but they are not described in this chapter.

NOTE

You can execute the `Get-Help about_array` command for more information and examples on using arrays in PowerShell.

In a later example, this feature of retrieving a particular element of an array is used with the `AdventureWorks2008R2` database.

Operators

A task commonly performed both from the console and also in scripts is to compare two strings against each other. The most common operators are as follows:

- **Arithmetic**—When comparing numbers or integers, for example:

  ```
  5 -gt 4
  ```

- **Comparison**—When comparing strings, for example:

  ```
  "user" -eq "user"
  ```

  In both of these cases, a Boolean value is returned (`True` or `False`).

NOTE

Execute the `Get-Help about_operator` command for more information and examples.

Conditional Statements

Often in scripting, some kind of decision must be made by comparing values before a script or set of commands continues.

Operators can provide a simple example of how conditional statements work, as shown here:

```
PS>if("userA" -eq "userA")
>> {
>>   Write-Host "Equal"
```

```
>> }
>> else
>> {
>>   Write-Host "Not equal"
>> }
>>Equal
PS>$user="userB"
PS>if("userA" -eq "$user")
>> {
>>   Write-Host "Equal"
>> }
>> else
>> {
>>   Write-Host "Not equal"
>> }
>>Not equal
PS>
```

The preceding code provides a simple example and shows how interactive the PowerShell console can be. The >> character is simply PowerShell informing the user that the commands entered are basically not complete, and more input is required.

A later example using the AdventureWorks2008R2 database uses a conditional statement to make a particular decision based on the results from evaluating a particular expression.

Functions

Quite often, as the usage of SQL-PowerShell increases, some efficiencies are gained by using functions. Functions are especially useful when you are creating things that are done on a regular basis either directly in the console or in a script.

For example, a long script may have been developed that contains several checks for the existence of a file, such as a long database filename, as in the following:

```
PS>Function test {
>> param($user1,$user2)
>> if("$user1" -eq "$user2")
>> {
>>   Write-Host "Equals"
>> }
>> else
>> {
>>   Write-Host "Not equal"
>> }
>> }
>>PS>test "userA" "userB"
Not equal
PS>test "userA" "userA"
```

```
Equals
PS>
```

Using the earlier example of comparing two strings, this example writes a function named `test`, so if future comparisons are required, the typing requirements will be greatly reduced.

> **NOTE**
>
> Execute the `Get-Help about_function` command in PowerShell for more information and examples.

In a later example, a function is used to create a quick reference for sending out an email via PowerShell.

Looping Statements

Often a script needs to loop through items and act on each. PowerShell supports several looping constructs. Examples of the `for` and `foreach` constructs are demonstrated here. Others, such as `while`, also exist but are not covered in this chapter.

```
PS>for($i=0;$i -lt 5;$i+=2){
>> $i
>> }
>>0
2
4
PS>
```

The preceding example shows a `for` loop. The method to jump or way to use a step is shown. A jump or step is indicated by the last part of the preceding `for` loop, where `$i+=2` is used. If this example had used `$i++` instead, the output would be each number from 0 to 5.

Here's an example of using `foreach`:

```
PS C:\book>dir
    Directory: Microsoft.PowerShell.Core\FileSystem::C:\book
Mode                LastWriteTime     Length Name
----                -------------     ------ ----
d----          8/4/2008  11:29 PM            directory
-a---          8/5/2008  12:01 AM         53 database.csv
-a---          8/4/2008  11:27 PM          0 file.ps1
-a---          8/4/2008  11:27 PM          0 file.txt
-a---          8/4/2008  11:47 PM       1813 list.csv
PS C:\book>$contents=dir
PS C:\book>$contents
```

```
    Directory: Microsoft.PowerShell.Core\FileSystem::C:\book
Mode                LastWriteTime     Length Name
----                -------------     ------ ----
d----         8/4/2008  11:29 PM            directory
-a---         8/5/2008  12:01 AM         53 database.csv
-a---         8/4/2008  11:27 PM          0 file.ps1
-a---         8/4/2008  11:27 PM          0 file.txt
-a---         8/4/2008  11:47 PM       1813 list.csv
PS C:\book>foreach($each in $contents){
>> $each.name
>> }
>>directory
database.csv
file.ps1
file.txt
list.csv
PS C:\book>
```

In this example, within the `foreach` scriptblock, any number of commands could have been added, and they would have acted on each object.

NOTE

Use the `Get-Help about_for`, `Get-Help about_foreach`, and `Get-Help about_while` commands for more information and examples.

NOTE

Another feature that can also be useful in scripting is keywords, such as `break`, `continue`, and `return`. They can be used in various circumstances to basically end the execution of conditional statements and also looping statements. See `Get-Help about_break` and `Get-Help about_continue` for more information and examples.

Filtering Cmdlets

PowerShell also has a few useful filtering cmdlets:

- **`Where-Object`** (alias **`where`** and ?)—Participates in a pipeline by helping to narrow down the objects passed along the pipeline based on some specific criteria.
- **`ForEach-Object`** (alias **`foreach`** and %)—Participates in a pipeline by applying a scriptblock to every object passed along the pipeline.

By looking at a few files and a directory contained within a test directly, we can easily demonstrate the use of both cmdlets:

```
PS C:\book> dir
```

17

```
    Directory: Microsoft.PowerShell.Core\FileSystem::C:\book

Mode                LastWriteTime     Length Name
----                -------------     ------ ----
d----          8/4/2008  11:29 PM            directory
-a---          8/4/2008  11:27 PM          0 file.ps1
-a---          8/4/2008  11:27 PM          0 file.txt

PS C:\book> dir|ForEach-Object{$_.Name.ToUpper()}
DIRECTORY
FILE.PS1
FILE.TXT
PS C:\book> dir|Where-Object{$_.PsIsContainer}

    Directory: Microsoft.PowerShell.Core\FileSystem::C:\book

Mode                LastWriteTime     Length Name
----                -------------     ------ ----
d----          8/4/2008  11:29 PM            directory

PS C:\book>
```

In this example, first the `ForEach-Object` cmdlet is demonstrated, where each object passed along from the `dir` command is acted on, and the name of the object (filename or directory name) is changed to uppercase.

Next, the `Where-Object` cmdlet is demonstrated, where each object passed along is evaluated this time to determine whether it is a file or directory. If it is a directory (the scriptblock `{$_.PsIsContainer}` returns as True), the object continues along the pipeline, but in this case, the pipeline has ended.

NOTE

There is a `ForEach-Object` cmdlet and a `foreach` keyword, and they are not the same. Something useful to remember is that `ForEach-Object` would be used as part of a pipeline.

Formatting Cmdlets

Several formatting cmdlets are very useful:

- **`Format-Table`** (alias ft)—Cmdlet that prints out properties in a table-based format.
- **`Format-List`** (alias fl)—Cmdlet that prints out properties in a list-style format.

Some simple examples of `Format-Table` can be easily demonstrated, as you can see here:

```
PS C:\book\test> Get-Process powershell
Handles  NPM(K)    PM(K)      WS(K) VM(M)   CPU(s)
```

```
Id ProcessName
------- ------    -----      ----- -----    ------
-- -----------
    548      13    54316      13192   164     25.55
2600 powershell

PS C:\book\test> Get-Process powershell| `
>> Format-Table -autosize handles,id
>>
Handles   Id
-------   --
    561 2600

PS C:\book\test>
```

In this example, you use the `Get-Process` cmdlet to list the properties of the `powershell.exe` process. By default, the PowerShell formatting subsystem determines what properties to display. Using `Format-Table`, you modify the properties displayed. The `-autosize` parameter is used to shorten and align all the columns neatly.

NOTE

There are also `Format-Custom` and `Format-Wide` cmdlets. See the built-in help for each cmdlet for more information and examples.

Dealing with CSV Files

PowerShell provides two cmdlets that help greatly when you are dealing with files in the comma-separated value (CSV) format:

- **`Import-Csv`**—This cmdlet reads in a CSV file and creates objects from its contents.
- **`Export-Csv`**—This cmdlet takes an object (or objects) as input and create sa CSV file, as shown here:

```
PS>dir | Export-Csv c:\temp\file.csv
```

This simple example shows how to output the contents of the current directory to a CSV-formatted file. Looking at the contents of this file displays information about the objects, though, instead of just plain strings such as filenames.

The following example creates a simple CSV-formatted file and then is read in using the `Import-Csv` cmdlet. The `Select-Object` cmdlet is used to display only the database column:

```
PS C:\> cd c:\temp
PS C:\temp> Add-Content database.csv "server,database"
PS C:\temp> Add-Content database.csv "server1,database1"
PS C:\temp> Add-Content database.csv "server2,database2"
PS C:\temp> Get-Content database.csv
```

17

```
server,database
server1,database1
server2,database2
PS C:\temp> Import-Csv database.csv|Format-Table -AutoSize
server database
------ --------
server1 database1
server2 database2

PS C:\temp> Import-Csv database.csv|Select-Object database
database
--------
database1
database2

PS C:\temp>
```

NOTE

The `Format-Table` cmdlet is used in the preceding example simply to format the data in a more appropriate format for this book.

Dealing with Dates and Times

Being able to do date/time calculations is very useful. Fortunately PowerShell provides all kinds of quick date/time calculations. Some of the more common tricks are shown in the following example:

```
PS>[DateTime]::Now
Tuesday, August 05, 2008 2:01:22 PM

PS>([DateTime]::Now).AddDays(-1)
Monday, August 04, 2008 2:01:44 PM

PS>
```

Here, a .NET method is used to get a new value from the original object. This is done in a "single step," in contrast to saving the object to a variable and then using the method on the variable. The use of a minus sign indicates that a value is being requested from the past.

Other common date/time methods include

- **AddHours**—Add/subtract based on a number of hours.
- **AddMilliseconds**—Add/subtract based on a number of milliseconds.
- **AddMinutes**—Add/subtract based on a number of minutes.

- **AddMonths**—Add/subtract based on a number of months.
- **AddSeconds**—Add/subtract based on a number of seconds.
- **AddYears**—Add/subtract based on a number of years.

-WhatIf/-Confirm Parameters

Several of the core PowerShell cmdlets support -whatif and/or -confirm parameters. The cmdlets that support these parameters could actually make system changes that cannot be reserved, such as deleting a file.

Consider the following example using these parameters:

```
PS>New-Item -Type File -Path file.tmp


    Directory: Microsoft.PowerShell.Core\FileSystem::C:\book

Mode                LastWriteTime     Length Name
----                -------------     ------ ----
-a---          8/4/2008  10:33 PM          0 file.tmp

PS>Remove-Item -Path file.tmp -WhatIf
What if: Performing operation "Remove File" on Target
"C:\book\file.tmp".
PS>
```

Two new cmdlets are demonstrated in the preceding example: New-Item, used to create things such as files, and Remove-Item, used to delete or remove things such as files.

PowerShell in SQL Server 2008

This section covers what has been specifically added to SQL Server 2008 to provide support for PowerShell.

Adding PowerShell Support

NOTE

This discussion is based on SQL Server 2008 Enterprise Edition. SQL Server 2008 Express doesn't provide all the same features. For example, the Express version doesn't provide the SQL Server Agent functionality briefly discussed later.

Either during the initial installation of SQL 2008 or afterward while changing the installed features, you are able to add the SQL Server–specific PowerShell features by using the setup utility. The Management Tools-Basic feature must be added, as shown in Figure 17.3.

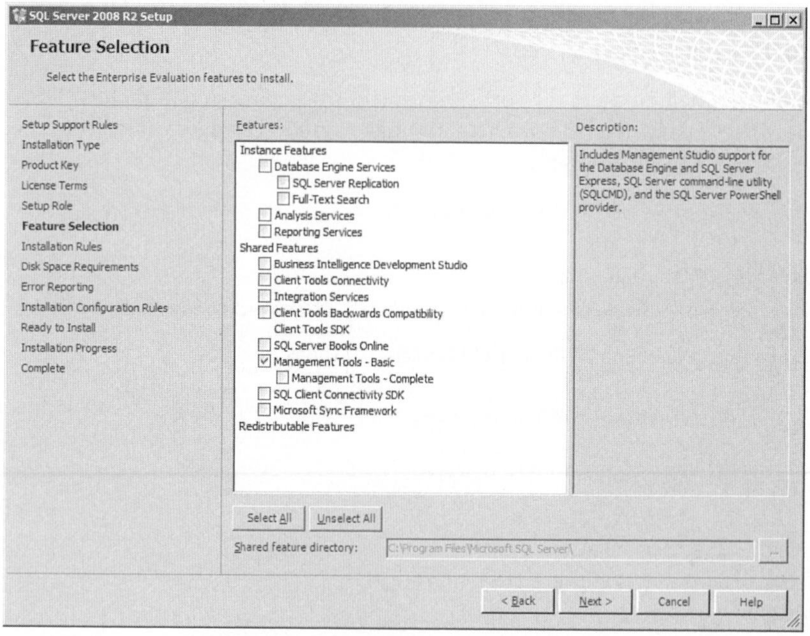

FIGURE 17.3 Installing the PowerShell features.

The Management Studio add-on is also required to get the PowerShell-specific features installed. This specific feature adds the following:

- **Management Studio**—The graphical user interface for managing SQL Server 2008
- **SQLCMD**—The utility that SQL scripters should already be familiar with
- **SQL Server PowerShell provider**—The PowerShell-specific extra functionality

NOTE

An added bonus is that you can install Management Studio by itself on either the server or another remote system, and be able to administer your SQL Server database remotely. Consideration should be given to whether the SQL Server is set up for remote connections, and the appropriate firewall changes have been made to the network and on the database server, if applicable.

Accessing PowerShell

Now that you have added the SQL Server–specific PowerShell features, you can access a SQL Server PowerShell session.

NOTE

From this point on, we make the distinction between PowerShell and SQL Server PowerShell. The details are discussed shortly, but for now *PowerShell* is the basic or default PowerShell console, and *SQL Server PowerShell* is a more restricted version of PowerShell that has all the SQL Server–specific PowerShell features packaged within it.

SQL Server PowerShell can be accessed in either of two ways:

- You can open SQL Server PowerShell via the SQL Server Management Studio by right-clicking on a particular object in the Object Explorer and selecting Start PowerShell, as shown in Figure 17.4. This way is handy because it provides a prompt in the SQL provider (which is discussed shortly) in the location of the object that was right-clicked.

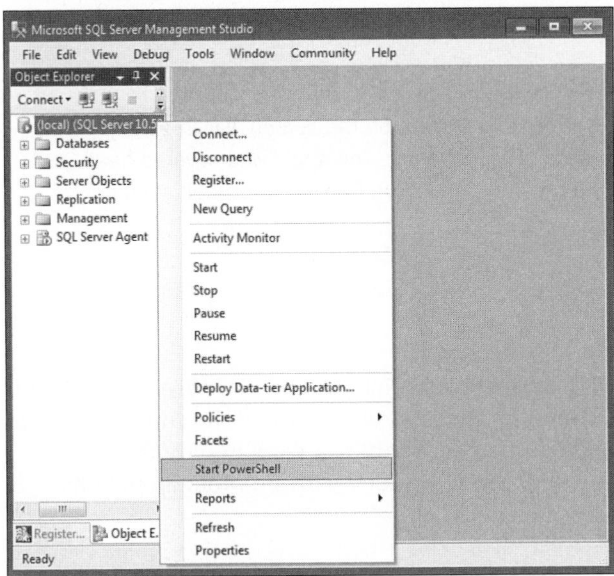

FIGURE 17.4 Accessing PowerShell via SSMS.

- You also can open SQL Server PowerShell directly from regular DOS or a regular PowerShell console by simply navigating to the appropriate location, as shown in Figure 17.5.

17

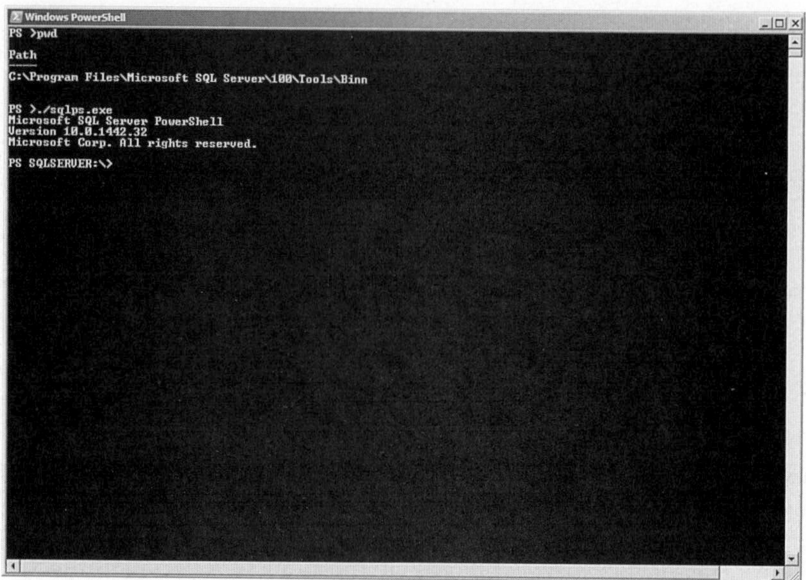

FIGURE 17.5 Accessing PowerShell using **sqlps.exe**.

NOTE

When you first open the shell, some errors may appear on the screen, which simply indicates that PowerShell execution policy should be set. This topic was covered near the beginning of the chapter. The execution policy for SQL Server PowerShell should also be `RemoteSigned`, at least.

SQL Server PowerShell

When you first get into SQL Server PowerShell, you might notice that this is a restricted version of the default PowerShell console. In other words, several of the core cmdlets are not available in SQL Server PowerShell, and others might not work exactly the same way. For example, invoking the `Get-Command` cmdlet alone with no other arguments does not list all the available commands.

NOTE

Running `Get-Command` in SQL Server PowerShell without any parameters might generate the following message:

```
Get-Command : Object reference not set to an instance of an object.
```

However, other invocations of this command work fine (such as the other examples of `Get-Command` in this section). Microsoft has identified this issue but as of this writing has not released a fix for it. Because the error occurs only within the SQL provider, the current workaround is to switch from the SQL Server provider to a different drive (such as `C:\`) before running `Get-Command`:

```
PS SQLSERVER:\> cd c:\
PS C:\> Get-Command
  <output deleted>
PS C:\> cd SQLSERVER:
PS SQLSERVER:\>
```

NOTE

Profiles were discussed earlier in this chapter. The SQL Server PowerShell minishell also has its own profile, and you can manage it by simply typing `notepad $profile` in SQL Server PowerShell. A prompt may come up that the file cannot be found and asking whether it should be created.

SQL Provider

Earlier in this chapter, the term *provider* was briefly introduced. The SQL team decided to implement a SQL Server provider. What this provides is a layout of the SQL object structure, which resembles that of a regular file system.

You use the SQL provider when accessing SQL Server PowerShell via SQL Server Management Studio: depending on what object you right-click to access SQL Server PowerShell, a prompt opens in the context of that particular object. Basically, the way certain commands work is also affected by the current location within the SQL Server provider. Here are two different examples of being placed in different locations within the SQL Server provider. In the first example, the `AdventureWorks2008R2` database was right-clicked within SSMS, as shown in Figure 17.6. In the second example, a specific table (`Person.Address`) within the `AdventureWorks2008R2` database was right-clicked, as shown in Figure 17.7.

When you start the SQL Server PowerShell minishell by simply invoking `sqlps.exe` as seen earlier, a prompt opens at the root of the SQL Server provider.

NOTE

Some of the core cmdlets like `Get-Item`, `Remove-Item`, and `New-Item` are typically used within providers to retrieve, remove, and create items, respectively. Within the SQL Server provider, creating items using the `New-Item` cmdlet is currently not supported. Other methods are required to actually create items.

17

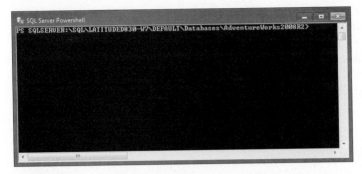

FIGURE 17.6 SQL Server provider at the database level.

FIGURE 17.7 SQL Server provider at the table level.

NOTE

Four SQL-based providers are actually available in SQL Server 2008 and six in SQL Server 2008 R2. We look only at the SQL provider that provides functionality for the database engine itself in any detail in this chapter. Refer to the SQL Server Books Online documentation for more information on the other providers (SQLPolicy, SQLRegistration, DataCollection, Utility, and DAC). The Utility and DAC providers are available only in SQL Server 2008 R2.

SQL Cmdlets

A number of cmdlets available in SQL Server PowerShell are part of the basic PowerShell functionality. However, within SQL Server PowerShell, five additional cmdlets are available only after the minishell is started (or if the snap-in is loaded manually, which is not covered in any detail here):

- **`Invoke-PolicyEvaluation`**—A cmdlet that evaluates a SQL Server Policy-Based Management policy (or policies) against a target server.
- **`Invoke-SqlCmd`**—A cmdlet that runs any regular T-SQL command and any languages and commands supported by the `sqlcmd` utility, which may be more familiar to most users.

- **Encode-SqlName**—A cmdlet that helps to encode SQL Server identifiers into a format that PowerShell can use.
- **Decode-SqlName**—A cmdlet that helps to return the original SQL Server identifiers from a value previously given by the `Encode-SqlName` cmdlet.
- **Convert-UrnToPath**—A cmdlet that converts the SMO Uniform Resource Name to a SQL Server provider path.

Later, examples of using the core cmdlets are provided, as well as the first two cmdlets introduced in the preceding list.

NOTE

For more details on the three other cmdlets not discussed here, see the built-in help for more information and examples.

NOTE

The intent is to ship more cmdlets as part of SQL-PowerShell in the future after more database users become more familiar with SQL Server PowerShell.

SQL Server Agent Support

PowerShell has been integrated into the SQL Server Agent subsystem. In other words, you can create jobs that call PowerShell-specific commands to run.

Consult SQL Server Books Online for more details on incorporating PowerShell into your SQL Server Agent job steps.

Step-By-Step Examples

The following sections provide examples of using PowerShell both for general tasks and for SQL Server 2008–specific tasks. We expand on some of the basic concepts introduced earlier with SQL Server 2008–specific examples.

General Tasks

Often you might be required to send out emails containing particular reports and/or output from commands run.

To do so, you use features from the .NET Framework via PowerShell to send out emails, as shown in here:

```
Function Send-Mail {
param([string]$To,[string]$From,[string]$Subject, `
```

```
  [string]$Body,[string]$File,[string]$SmtpServer)
  If($SmtpServer -eq ""){
    $SmtpServer = "FQDN of your SMTP server here"
  }
  $Smtp = New-Object System.Net.Mail.SMTPclient($SmtpServer)
  $Message = New-Object
  System.Net.Mail.MailMessage($From,$To,$Subject,$Body)
  If ($File -ne "") {
    $Attach = New-Object System.Net.Mail.Attachment $File
    $Message.Attachments.Add($Attach)
  }
  $smtp.Send($message)
}
```

You can enter the preceding code into a script or directly to the console. If you type the code in the console, you must press the Enter key twice (once to close the function and another time on an empty line) before the PowerShell prompt returns.

In the preceding code listing, functionality from the .NET Framework is used to get SMTP functionality. A function is used so that this code could be easily copied as required into new scripts, and so on. Calling the function is then easy, and passing the command-line arguments is shown here (the PowerShell prompt can vary depending on whether the default PowerShell is used or the new SQL minishell):

```
PS>Send-Mail  -To "end_user@user.com " -From "user@user.com" -Subject
"Automated Email" -Body "Testing" -File "C:\reports\report.txt"
```

NOTE

You might need to configure some antivirus programs to allow the `PowerShell.exe` process (or `sqlps.exe`) to “talk” over the SMTP protocol port (TCP 25).

Scheduling Scripts

From time to time, it may be useful to have a method to schedule PowerShell scripts to run automatically based on a particular schedule (when the SQL Server Agent isn't available locally, for example).

You can easily view the method to call PowerShell scripts by simply typing `powershell.exe /?` from a PowerShell session, as shown here:

```
PS>powershell.exe /?
...
PowerShell -Command "& {Get-EventLog -LogName security}"
...
```

Only a very small section of the text displayed is shown in this example. The `powershell.exe` can be used for scheduling regular PowerShell scripts. `sqlps.exe` works similarly, and you can also access its help by passing a slash and question mark (`/?`) to the command:

```
PS SQLSERVER:\> sqlps.exe /?


sqlps [ [ [-NoLogo] [-NoExit] [-NoProfile]
          [-OutputFormat {Text | XML}] [-InputFormat {Text | XML}]
        ]
        [-Command { -
                  | <string> [ <command_parameters> ]
                  | <script_block> [ -args <argument_array> ]
                  }
        ]
      ]
      [ -Help | -?]

-NoLogo
    Do not display the copyright banner on startup.
-NoExit
    Keep running after completing all startup commands.
-NoProfile
    Do not load a user profile.
-OutputFormat
    Format the output of all objects as either text strings (Text) or in a
    serialized CLIXML format (XML).
-InputFormat
    The input from stdin is formatted as either text strings (Text) or in a
    serialized CLIXML format (XML).
-Command
    sqlps runs the commands specified and then exits, unless -NoExit is also
    specified. Do not specify other characters after the -Command switch,
    they will be read as command arguments.
      -
          Read input commands from the keyboard by using stdin.
      <string> [ <command_parameters> ]
          Specifies a string containing the PowerShell commands to be run. Use
          the format "&{<command>}". The quotation marks identify a string and
          the invocation operator (&) causes sqlps to run the command.
      <script_block> [ -args <argument_array> ]
          Specifies a block of PowerShell commands to be run. Use the format
          {<script_block>}.
-Help | -?
    Show the syntax summary help.
```

17

NOTE

How do you know whether to use `powershell.exe` or `sqlps.exe` when scheduling jobs? If you're using anything relating to SMO and/or the SQL cmdlets in the script, `sqlps.exe` would seem to be easier to use because all the prerequisites to using SMO and the SQL cmdlets are already loaded, which can save several lines in a script. As a reminder, the SQL minishell is limited in its functionality, so `powershell.exe` may be required in particular if you need to load some PowerShell functionality from another application, such as Exchange.

As discussed briefly earlier, SQL Server Agent can also be used to run scheduled PowerShell commands.

Common OS-Related Tasks

Now let's look at some more OS-related tasks, while keeping our focus on SQL Server–related tasks.

Let's check the status of the SQL Server service using the `Get-Service` cmdlet in the regular PowerShell console:

```
PS>Get-Service "mssqlserver"
Status   Name               DisplayName
------   ----               -----------
Stopped  MSSQLSERVER   SQL Server (MSSQLSERVER)
PS>
```

NOTE

When multiple instances are in use, the service name is something like `MSSQL$INSTANCE01`. To start such an instance from PowerShell or even the SQL minishell, you would have to use the following syntax for the service name: `` MSSQL`$INSTANCE01 ``. The dollar sign ($) character is escaped so that PowerShell doesn't try to interpret this as the beginning of a variable when the string is parsed.

The service is stopped. When you use the pipeline feature of PowerShell, the service is started:

```
PS>Get-Service "mssqlserver"|Start-Service
WARNING: Waiting for service 'SQL Server (SQLSERVER)
```

```
  (MSSQLSERVER)' to finish starting...
WARNING: Waiting for service 'SQL Server (SQLSERVER)
  (MSSQLSERVER)' to finish starting...
PS>
```

This example demonstrates using the pipeline to chain commands together. Alternatively, you could use `Start-Service` directly:

```
PS>Start-Service "mssqlserver"
```

The difference between the two methods demonstrates some of the power in PowerShell. When you use `Get-Service`, a service object is retrieved. When you use the pipeline, this object is passed to `Start-Service`. `Start-Service` is built to basically accept input from the pipeline and autofills its parameters based on what was input; thus, it knows to start the SQL Server service.

NOTE

You could use SQL Server PowerShell, but because SQL Server wasn't started, Management Studio would not have been able to connect, and you could not open SQL Server PowerShell by right-clicking. You could use PowerShell to start `sqlps.exe`, though, and then you could use the `Get-Service` and `Start-Service` cmdlets to start SQL Server. If you use SQL Server PowerShell by calling `sqlps.exe` directly from within a default PowerShell console, the SQL Server could still be started, but a connection wouldn't be automatically made to the default instance of the database.

Most administrators have probably already used the Windows Task Manager to look at the SQL Server processes. Perhaps it was to determine whether SQL seemed to be using too much memory or some other issue. PowerShell provides the `Get-Process` cmdlet, shown here, to look at running processes:

```
PS>Get-Process sqlservr
Handles  NPM(K)    PM(K)      WS(K) VM(M)   CPU(s)
  Id ProcessName
-------  ------    -----      ----- -----   ------
  -- -----------
    318      45    64156      44288  1554     2.03
  572 sqlservr
PS>
```

Another common OS-related task is to look for events in the Windows application event log:

```
PS>Get-EventLog Application -New 10
PS>Get-EventLog Application -New 10| `
```

```
  Where {$_.EntryType -eq "Error"}
PS>Get-EventLog Application -New 10| `
  Where {$_.EntryType -eq "Error"}|Select-Object TimeWritten
```

The preceding example demonstrates another useful feature of the PowerShell pipeline where you can join several commands together to get specific results. First, only the 10 newest entries are retrieved; then a pipe is used to get only the entries classified as an error, and finally, only the `TimeWritten` property is displayed.

We mentioned WMI earlier in this chapter as a method for remote control and administration of servers. WMI is packed full of features that are useful for system administration. A few examples of using PowerShell's built-in WMI features are shown here.

- Getting a listing of all the fixed local logical drives:

  ```
  PS>Get-WmiObject -query "select * from Win32_LogicalDisk   where
  DriveType='3'"
  ```

- Getting a listing of all the fixed remote logical drives:

  ```
  PS>Get-WmiObject -computerName server -query
    "select * from Win32_LogicalDisk where DriveType='3'"
  ```

- Getting a listing of all the local patches/hotfixes installed (the `-computerName` parameter could be used with a value to retrieve this information from a remote system):

  ```
  PS>Get-WmiObject Win32_QuickFixEngineering
  ```

NOTE

Remote WMI connections may require that appropriate firewall rules be open in the network and also with a client firewall on the remote system. In addition, remote WMI queries must also be authenticated. By default, WMI queries use the current user's authentication credentials. In some scenarios WMI authentication can be more complicated.

The preceding examples show only the beginning of all the things WMI can provide quick access to. Another common task is trying to find files or folders. You can use the `Get-ChildItem` cmdlet to recursively search through a directory structure. The following example shows how to search for the location of the `powershell.exe` executable:

```
PS>Get-ChildItem c:\ -recurse powershell.exe
```

SQL Server–Specific Tasks

Before jumping into more hardcore SQL Server PowerShell features, let's briefly look at the SQL Server event log. Fortunately, the log simply contains text-based files, which PowerShell can read. You could use the `Get-Content` cmdlet to view the entire log, but instead you can use the `Select-String` cmdlet to look for a specific string or pattern in the error log file. First, you change the current location to the SQL Server log directory:

```
PS>Set-Location "C:\Program Files\Microsoft SQL Server"
PS>Set-Location (join-path $pwd "MSSQL10_50.MSSQLSERVER\MSSQL\Log")
PS>Select-String "error" ERRORLOG
```

The PowerShell prompt in the preceding example is simply a generic one because the preceding commands would work both in the default PowerShell console and in the SQL Server PowerShell minishell.

An example of taking this further would be to retrieve all the errors in the `ERRORLOG` file. When you use `Get-Member` and `Format-List` to look at the object output by `Select-String`, the date is hidden inside a string in the `Line` property:

```
PS >
Select-String "error" ERRORLOG|foreach{$_.line}|where{$_ -match "^20*"}|
foreach{$date,$time=$_.split()[0],$_.split()[1];[datetime]$($date+" "+$time) }
PS >
```

The preceding example demonstrates how to look for the string `"error"` in the current SQL Server `ERRORLOG` file. For all the lines that match, the `Line` property is passed along the pipeline. Next, based on some testing, it appears that you want to search only lines that start with `"20*-"`. From that object, two values are retrieved: `$_.split()[0]` and `$_.split[1]`. These values are placed in the `$date` and `$time` variables, respectively. From there, they are recombined, and a type accelerator is used to indicate that this is a date/time object, so any calculations against this value will be simplified. What is finally output is the time stamp showing when the error occurred.

17

Using the Provider

Using the SQL Server provider can be very handy in navigating the system. Starting PowerShell from SSMS, DBAs can easily find their way through different objects as if working with files and directories.

When the SSMS is used to start PowerShell at the server level, the databases are down one level, and from there tables and users, for example, can also be easily accessed.

In the session shown in Figure 17.8, we navigated to a particular database and entered a `dir Tables` command. The output from the last command would scroll beyond the current screen, so only the first part of the output is displayed.

Creating a Database Table

Creating a database and a table are common tasks that a DBA may undertake. You can use T-SQL with the `Invoke-SqlCmd` cmdlet to do this, but a demonstration on how to do this with the SQL Server PowerShell minishell using SMO is presented here to help you better understand the new functionality that is available:

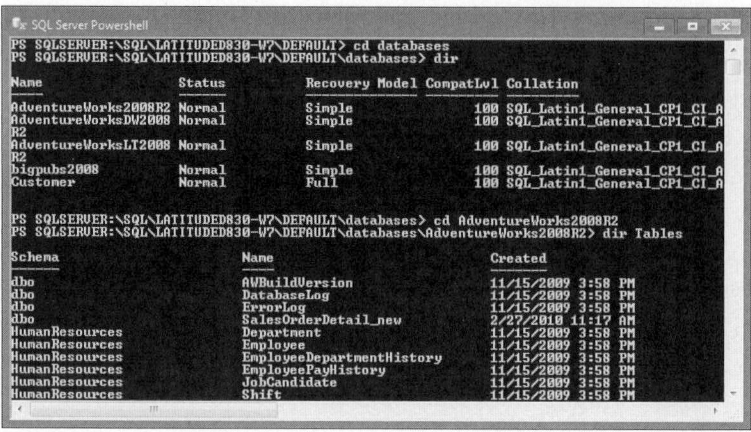

FIGURE 17.8 Navigating the SQL Server provider.

```
cd databases
$my_db=New-Object Microsoft.SqlServer.Management.Smo.Database
$my_db.Name="my_database"
$my_db.Parent=(Get-Item ..)
$my_db.Create()
cd my_database
cd tables
$my_tbl=New-Object Microsoft.SqlServer.Management.Smo.Table
$my_tbl.Name="my_table"
$my_tbl.Parent=(Get-Item ..)
$my_col=New-Object Microsoft.SqlServer.Management.Smo.Column
$my_col.Name="my_column"
$my_col.Parent=$my_tbl
$my_col.DataType= ([Microsoft.SqlServer.Management.Smo.DataType]::Int)
$my_tbl.Columns.Add($my_col)
$my_tbl.Create()
```

In the preceding example, some new objects are created, some of their properties are set, and some methods are called. You can search for the particular SMO classes used in this example to gain further information.

In the future, there may be something like `New-Database` and `New-Table` cmdlets that help to create a database and table, which would likely reduce the preceding code to fewer than five lines.

Performing a Database Backup

Another example that may be useful is performing a database backup using SMO. Using the `AdventureWorks2008R2` database, you can back up the database using just a few lines:

```
$server=New-Object Microsoft.SqlServer.Management.Smo.Server
```

```
$backup=new-object Microsoft.SqlServer.Management.Smo.Backup
$file=new-object Microsoft.SqlServer.Management.Smo.BackupDeviceItem
$file.Name="C:\backup\AW_DB.bak"
$backup.Devices.Add($file)
$backup.Database="AdventureWorks2008R2"
$backup.SqlBackup($server)
```

The preceding code could be copied into a `.ps1` file (for this example, assume it's copied to `c:\temp\backup.ps1`), and it could be changed to accept two arguments. The preceding code could be modified to the following code snippet so that it accepts parameters from the command line:

```
param([string]$device=$(throw Write-Host "Device required"), [string]
$database=$(throw Write-Host "Database required"))
Write-Host "backup of $database to $device starting..."
$server=New-Object Microsoft.SqlServer.Management.Smo.Server
$backup=new-object Microsoft.SqlServer.Management.Smo.Backup
$file=new-object Microsoft.SqlServer.Management.Smo.BackupDeviceItem
$file.Name=$device
$backup.Devices.Add($file)
$backup.Database=$database
$backup.SqlBackup($server)
Write-Host "backup complete"
Get-Item $device
```

The changes in the preceding example introduce a new keyword, `throw`. Without it, error messages would be thrown to the console, but this might not help the end user to understand why it failed. For the purpose of printing feedback to the console, the `Write-Host` and `Get-Item` cmdlets were also added to provide a limited amount of feedback and to finally provide the details of the final backup file.

Then to invoke the script, as shown in the following example, you simply need to pass two parameters to the script: the names of the file to back up to and the database to actually back up.

```
PS>$backup_to="C:\backup\AdventureWorks2008R2.bak"
PS>$db="AdventureWorks2008R2"
PS> c:\temp\backup.ps1 $backup_to $db
```

As an example of using a conditional statement in the preceding script, perhaps a check could be done to see whether a backup has already been completed within the past seven days. To accomplish this, you would add this particular section of code just before the line `Write-Host "backup of $database to $device starting..."`:

```
If((Test-Path $device) -and (Get-Item $device).LastWriteTime `
  -gt (Get-Date).AddDays(-7)){
  "Backup has been performed in last 7 days"  Break
}
```

17

In the preceding code, a conditional statement is added to accomplish the check. The `AddDays()` method is passed a negative number which subtracts days from the current date..

NOTE

When you use the `param` keyword, this section of code must be on the first noncommented line in all scripts. Otherwise, the PowerShell parser returns an error.

Again, using SMO isn't necessarily for beginners, but the good thing is that scripts can easily be created and passed around. The preceding example shows the bare minimum required to do a database backup; several other options are available, and the preceding code would actually overwrite the backup each time it is run. There also isn't any error checking of any sort, which isn't the best way to develop scripts.

Along with the `New-Database` and `New-Table` cmdlets that may come in the future, maybe a `Start-DbBackup` will be another good cmdlet to have available.

Checking Server Settings

From the SSMS, by right-clicking on the `SQL Server` node and then starting a SQL Server PowerShell session, you can open a console directly in the root of the default SQL Server in the example.

From here, you can easily obtain information on the SQL Server. First, the location is set to the instance that is to be queried, and then an object representing the SQL Server is saved to a variable (this demonstrates the advanced features mentioned earlier where objects can be saved to variables). The properties of that variable can then be accessed as follows:

```
PS>Set-Location SQLSERVER:\SQL\<servername>\<instance_name>
PS>$sql_server=get-item .
PS>$sql_server.Information.VersionString
```

Using the `Get-Member` cmdlet discussed earlier, you can easily discover other members of the object contained in `$sql_server`, but this is left as an exercise for you to perform on your own.

NOTE

This example demonstrates an important feature of the SQL Server provider: context sensitivity. In the preceding example, the current location was in the root of the SQL Server provider or database, and the command `Get-Item.` was used. The dot in this command basically indicates that you want an object that represents the current location in the provider. If the dot were moved to a different location, this command would no longer work the same way.

Checking the Database Usage

Using the object retrieved in the $sql_server variable, you can create a quick report of database usage using the databases property of that object, as shown here:

```
PS SQLSERVER:\SQL\<servername>\<instancename>>
$sql_server.databases| Format-Table -autosize Name,@{
    Label= "% Used"
    Expression={[math]::round((($_.spaceavailable/1kb)/$_.size),2)}
  }Name                      % Used
----                      ------
AdventureWorks2008R2        0.02
AdventureWorksDW2008R2         0
AdventureWorksLT2008R2      0.02
bigpubs2008                 0.18
Customer                    0.74
master                      0.24
model                       0.39
msdb                        0.02
my_database                 0.38
tempdb                       0.8
```

Using the Format-Table cmdlet, you can easily and quickly create all kinds of reports. Some capabilities we haven't discussed yet were used to create this report:

- **Calculated properties**—The values displayed by Format-Table can be calculated using scriptblocks. That allows the logic to be highly customized. These scriptblocks are laid out as follows:

  ```
  @{Label="some text value"
    Expression={the scriptblock to evaluate here}
  }
  ```

- **Direct access to the .NET Framework**—The following line is directly from the .NET Framework:

  ```
  "[math]::round(value,decimal)"
  ```

  .NET functionality is being used to round out the numbers to the second decimal point.

  PowerShell has special meaning for 1kb, 1mb, 1gb and 1tb, which all present the value of the counterpart in number of bytes—for example, 1kb=1024. The values can also be uppercase.

Getting Table Properties

Another common task is to get a row count of the tables in a particular database:

```
PS SQLSERVER:\SQL\<servername>\<instancename>\Databases\
AdventureWorks2008R2\Tables> Get-ChildItem .| Sort-Object -descending|Select-
Object -First 10| Format-Table -autosize Name,RowCountNote
```

NOTE

An easy-to-remember alias for `Get-ChildItem` is basically `dir`.

In the preceding example using the `AdventureWorks2008R2` database, the top 10 tables with the highest row count value are returned.

NOTE

The preceding example shows how many features are packaged within PowerShell, which applies not only to SQL tables, but also to all .NET objects. Simply using `Get-Item` on a particular table returns only the default properties of `Schema`, `Name`, and `Created`. Piping something like `Get-Item [table_name]` to either `Format-Table *` or `Get-Member` exposes all the properties available for a particular object.

Cmdlet Example: `Invoke-SqlCmd`

The `Invoke-SqlCmd` cmdlet was mentioned earlier. It will likely be the most commonly used cmdlet currently provided. Here is a simple example using this cmdlet:

```
Invoke-sqlcmd -query "exec sp_help"
```

Using `Invoke-SqlCmd`, you can simply pass any T-SQL–based query as a value to the cmdlet. The preceding basic example is provided by running a basic built-in stored procedure: `sp_help`.

This example demonstrates several important issues, especially how powerful the provider can be. Based on the location in the SQL provider, some of the values passed to the cmdlet are automatically provided to the cmdlet by the provider itself: the server and database to query aren't required in the command line.

Let's consider this example a bit further and do a few extra things with it.

First, this cmdlet can accept input from the pipeline:

```
"exec sp_help"|ForEach-Object{Invoke-SqlCmd $_}
```

The preceding line demonstrates a few more issues that have already been discussed: the `ForEach-Object` cmdlet, the special variable $_, and also the way parameters can automatically match values to parameters even when the parameter name isn't explicitly added to the command entered.

The sp_help stored procedure provides a lot of information. What if only the extended stored procedures were required?

When Get-Member is used, the members from this particular query are inspected, and it is determined that the Object_type property is the value that indicates what kind of stored procedure is being dealt with.

The query to get only extended stored procedures is now the following:

```
"exec sp_help"|ForEach-Object{Invoke-SqlCmd $_}| `
  Where{$_.Object_type -eq "extended stored proc"}|Select Name
```

Finally, the output consists only of extended stored procedures.

Cmdlet Example: Invoke-PolicyEvaluation

Another one of the provided cmdlets is Invoke-PolicyEvaluation. This cmdlet is used to specify a SQL Server Policy-Based Management policy (or policies) that will be evaluated against the target server. You can easily cycle through all the available policies and evaluate each one, or simply provide a list of policies to evaluate separated by a comma. Consider this example:

```
sl "C:\Program Files\Microsoft SQL Server\100\Tools\Policies\DatabaseEngine\1033"
Invoke-PolicyEvaluation -Policy "Database Auto Shrink.xml" -TargetServerName
"MSSQLSERVER"
```

The preceding command returns the output to the console of the result of the policy evaluation. By default, the particular policy passed to the cmdlet is only checked. In other words, by default, properties are actually changed so that they are now compliant with the policy.

Joining Columns

Quite often, databases provide a table for users. Frequently, these users have their last name and first name in separate columns. Because these are typically simple strings, a feature, already discussed, allows two strings to be easily joined together.

The following code snippet shows how two columns from the AdventureWorks2008R2 database are easily joined together from within the SQL minishell:

```
PS SQLSERVER:\SQL\D830\DEFAULT\databases\adventureworks2008r2> Invoke-SqlCmd
 "Select * from Person.Person"| `
>>   Select-Object -First 10|ForEach-Object{$_.LastName + ", " + $_.FirstName}
Sánchez, Ken
Duffy, Terri
Tamburello, Roberto
Walters, Rob
```

```
Erickson, Gail
Goldberg, Jossef
Miller, Dylan
Margheim, Diane
Matthew, Gigi
Raheem, Michael
```

Here, the first 10 records are selected, and then the `LastName` and `FirstName` values are combined together.

Retrieving an Entry

On occasion, you might need to get a particular entry from a table. When the following code snippet is run, an array is automatically returned:

```
PS SQLSERVER:\SQL\D830\DEFAULT\databases\adventureworks2008r2>  Invoke-SqlCmd
 "Select * from Person.Person"
```

PowerShell provides a simple way to look at particular elements within an array. In the following example, entry 100 is returned and then entries 95 to 105:

```
PS SQLSERVER:\SQL\D830\DEFAULT\databases\adventureworks2008r2>  (Invoke-SqlCmd
 "Select * from Person.Person")[100]
PS SQLSERVER:\SQL\D830\DEFAULT\databases\adventureworks2008r2>  (Invoke-SqlCmd
 "Select * from Person.Person")[95..105]
```

NOTE

The first element of an array is the element zero; therefore, the first record in an array is retrieved by referencing the element id `[0]`.

Summary

This chapter provides an overview of PowerShell and how it has been specifically implemented in SQL Server 2008. Microsoft is putting a lot of effort into integrating PowerShell into all its server-based products, including SQL Server. Support for PowerShell in SQL Server 2008 still has a way to go before it could ever be considered the main scripting language, but the functionality available now is worth looking at.

The next chapter delves into high availability and the options available in SQL Server 2008.

CHAPTER 18

SQL Server High Availability

IN THIS CHAPTER

- What's New in High Availability144
- What Is High Availability?145
- The Fundamentals of HA147
- Building Solutions with One or More HA Options150
- Other HA Techniques That Yield Great Results159
- High Availability from the Windows Server Family Side162

With SQL Server 2008, Microsoft continues to push the high availability (HA) bar higher and higher. Extensive high-availability options, coupled with a variety of Windows server family enhancements, provide almost everyone with a chance at achieving the mythical "five-nines" (that is, 99.999% uptime).

Understanding your high-availability requirements is only the first step in implementing a successful high-availability application. Knowing what technical options exist is equally as important. Then, by following a few basic design guidelines, you can match your requirements to the best high-availability technical solution.

This chapter introduces a variety of fundamental HA options—such as redundant hardware configurations, RAID, and MSCS clustering—as well as more high-level options—such as SQL clustering, data replication, and database mirroring—that should lead you to a solid high-availability foundation. Microsoft has slowly been moving in the direction of trying to make SQL Server (and the Windows operating systems) as continuously available as possible for as many of its options as possible. Remember that Microsoft is competing with the UNIX/Linux-based worlds that have offered (and achieved) much higher uptime levels for years. The SQL Server RDBMS engine itself and the surrounding services, such as Analysis Services, Integration Services, Notification Services, and Reporting Services, have all taken big steps toward higher availability.

What's New in High Availability

In general, a couple of Microsoft SQL Server 2008 configuration options offer a very strong database engine foundation that can be highly available (7 days a week, 365 days a year). Microsoft's sights are set on being able to achieve five-nines reliability with almost everything it builds. An internal breakthrough introduced with SQL Server 2005 called "copy-on-write" technology, has enabled Microsoft to greatly enhance several of its database high availability options.

Here are a few of the most significant enhancements and new features that have direct or indirect effects on increasing high availability for a SQL Server 2008–based implementation:

- **Increased number of nodes in a SQL cluster**—You can create a SQL cluster of up to 64 nodes on Windows Server Data Center 2008.
- **Enhancements to do unattended cluster setup**—Instead of having to use wizards to set up SQL clustering, you can use the Unattended Cluster Setup mode. This is very useful for fast re-creation or remote creation of SQL clustering configurations.
- **All SQL Server 2008 services as cluster managed resources**—All SQL Server 2008 services are now cluster aware.
- **SQL Server 2008 database mirroring**—Database mirroring creates an automatic failover capability to a "hot" standby server. (Chapter 20, "Database Mirroring," covers this topic in detail.)
- **SQL Server 2008 peer-to-peer replication**—This option of data replication uses a publisher-to-publisher model (hence peer-to-peer).
- **SQL Server 2008 automatic corruption recovery from mirror**—This enhancement in database mirroring recognizes and corrects corrupt pages during mirroring.
- **SQL Server 2008 mirroring transaction record compression**—This feature allows for compression of the transaction log records used in database mirroring to increase the speed of transmission to the mirror.
- **SQL Server 2008 fast recovery**—Administrators can reconnect to a recovering database after the transaction log has been rolled forward (and before the rollback processing has finished).
- **Online restore**—Database administrators can perform a restore operation while the database is still online.
- **Online indexing**—The online index option allows concurrent modifications (updates, deletes, and inserts) to the underlying table or clustered index data and any associated indexes during index creation time.
- **Database snapshot**—SQL Server 2008 allows for the generation and use of a read-only, stable view of a database. The database snapshot is created without the overhead of creating a complete copy of the database or having completely redundant storage.

- **Hot additions**—This feature allows for hot additions to memory and CPU.
- **Addition of a snapshot isolation level**—A new snapshot isolation (SI) level is being provided at the database level. With SI, users can access the last committed row, using a transactionally consistent view of the database.
- **Dedicated administrator connection**—SQL Server 2008 supports a dedicated administrator connection that administrators can use to access a running server even if the server is locked or otherwise unavailable. This capability enables administrators to troubleshoot problems on a server by executing diagnostic functions or Transact-SQL statements without having to take down the server.

At the operating system (OS) level, Virtual Server 2005 has firmly established virtualization for both development and production environments and allows entire application and database stacks to run on a completely virtual operating system footprint that will never bring down the physical server.

NOTE

Microsoft has announced that log shipping will be deprecated soon. Although it has been functionally replaced with database mirroring, log shipping remains available in SQL Server 2008. However, you should plan to move off log shipping as soon as you can.

Keep in mind that Microsoft already has an extensive capability in support of high availability. The new HA features add significant gains to the already feature-rich offering.

What Is High Availability?

The availability continuum depicted in Figure 18.1 shows a general classification of availability based on the amount of downtime an application can tolerate without impacting the business. You would write your service-level agreements (SLAs) to support and try to achieve one of these continuum categories.

Topping the chart is the category extreme availability, so named to indicate that this is the least tolerant category and is essentially a zero (or near zero) downtime requirement (that is, sustained 99.5% to 100% availability). The mythical five-nines falls at the high end of this category. Next is the high availability category, which has a minimal tolerance for downtime (that is, sustained 95% to 99.4% availability). Most "critical" applications would fit into this category of availability need. Then comes the standard availability category, with a more normal type of operation (that is, sustained 83% to 94% availability). The acceptable availability category is for applications that are deemed noncritical to a company's business, such as online employee benefit package self-service applications. These applications can tolerate much lower availability ranges (sustained 70% to 82% availability) than the more critical services. Finally, the marginal availability category is for nonproduction custom applications, such as marketing mailing label applications that can tolerate significant downtime (that is, sustained 0% to 69% availability). Again, remember that availability is measured by the planned operation times of the application.

Availability Continuum

	Characteristic	Availability Range
Extreme Availability	Near zero downtime!	(99.5%-100%) 1.8 days/yr–5.26 min/yr
High Availability	Minimal downtime	(95%-99.4%) 18 days/yr–2.0 days/yr
Standard Availability	With some downtime tolerance	(83%-94%)
Acceptable Availability	Non-critical Applications	(70%-82%)
Marginal Availability	Non-production Applications	(up to 69%)

Availability Range describes the percentage of time relative to the "planned" hours of operations

8,760 hours/year I 168 hours/week I 24 hours/day
525,600 minutes/year I 7,200 minutes/week I 1,440 minutes/day

FIGURE 18.1 Availability continuum.

NOTE

Another featured book from Sams Publishing, called *Microsoft SQL Server High Availability*, can take you to the depths of high availability from every angle. This landmark offering provides a complete guide to high availability, beginning with ways to gather and understand your HA requirements, assess your HA needs, and completely build out high-availability implementations for the most common business scenarios in the industry. Pick up this book if you are serious about achieving five-nines of reliability.

Achieving the mythical five-nines (that is, a sustained 99.999% availability) falls into the extreme availability category (which tolerates between 5.26 minutes and 1.8 days of down time per year). In general, the computer industry calls this high availability, but we push this type of near-zero downtime requirement into its own extreme category, all by itself. Most applications can only dream about this level of availability because of the costs involved, the high level of operational support required, the specialized hardware that must be in place, and many other extreme factors.

The Fundamentals of HA

Every minute of downtime you have today translates into losses that you cannot well afford. You must fully understand how the hardware and software components work together and how, if one component fails, the others will be affected. High availability of an application is a function of all the components together, not just one by itself. Therefore, the best approach for moving into supporting high availability is to work on shoring up the basic foundation components of hardware, backup/recovery, operating system upgrading, ample vendor agreements, sufficient training, extensive quality assurance/testing, rigorous standards and procedures, and some overall risk-mitigating strategies, such as spreading out critical applications over multiple servers. By addressing these first, you add a significant amount of stability and high-availability capability across your hardware/system stack. In other words, you are moving up to a necessary level before you completely jump into a particular high-availability solution. If you do nothing further from this point, you have already achieved a portion of your high-availability goals.

Hardware Factors

You need to start by addressing your basic hardware issues for high availability and fault tolerance. This includes redundant power supplies, UPS systems, redundant network connections, and ECC memory (error correcting). Also available are "hot-swappable" components, such as disks, CPUs, and memory. In addition, most servers are now using multiple CPUs, fault-tolerant disk systems such as RAID, mirrored disks, storage area networks (SANs), Network Attached Storage (NAS), redundant fans, and so on.

Cost may drive the full extent of what you choose to build out. However, you should start with the following:

- Redundant power supplies (and UPSs)
- Redundant fan systems
- Fault-tolerant disks, such as RAID (1 through 10), preferably "hot swappable"
- ECC memory
- Redundant Ethernet connections

Backup Considerations

After you consider hardware, you need to look at the basic techniques and frequency of your disk backups and database backups. For many companies, the backup plan isn't what it needs to be to guarantee recoverability and even the basic level of high availability. At many sites, database backups are not being run, are corrupted, or aren't even considered necessary. You would be shocked by the list of Fortune 1000 companies where this occurs.

Operating System Upgrades

You need to make sure that all upgrades to your OS are applied and also that the configuration of all options is correct. This includes making sure you have antivirus software installed (if applicable), along with the appropriate firewalls for external-facing systems.

Vendor Agreements Followed

Vendor agreements come in the form of software licenses, software support agreements, hardware service agreements, and both hardware and software service-level agreements. Essentially, you are trying to make sure you can get all software upgrades and patches for your OS and for your application software at any time, as well as get software support, hardware support agreements, and both software and hardware SLAs in place to guarantee a level of service within a defined period of time.

Training Kept Up to Date

Training is multifaceted in that it can be for software developers to guarantee that the code they write is optimal, for system administrators who need to administer applications, and even for end users themselves to make sure they use the system correctly. All these types of training play into the ultimate goal of achieving high availability.

Quality Assurance Done Well

Testing as much as possible—and doing it in a very formal way—is a great way to guarantee a system's availability. Dozens of studies over the years have clearly shown that the more thoroughly you test (and the more formal your QA procedures), the fewer software problems you will have. Many companies foolishly skimp on testing, which has a huge impact on system reliability and availability.

Standards/Procedures Followed

Standards and procedures are interlaced tightly with training and QA. Coding standards, code walkthroughs, naming standards, formal system development life cycles, protection of tables from being dropped, use of governors, and so on all contribute to more stable and potentially more highly available systems.

Server Instance Isolation

By design, you may want to isolate applications (such as SQL Server's applications and their databases) away from each other to mitigate the risk of such an application causing another to fail.

Plain and simple, you should never put applications in each other's way if you don't have to. The only things that might force you to load up a single server with all your applications would be expensive licensing costs for each server's software and perhaps hardware scarcity (strict limitations to the number of servers available for all applications). A classic example occurs when a company loads up a single SQL Server instance with between two and eight applications and their associated databases. The problem is that the applications are sharing memory, CPUs, and internal work areas, such as `tempdb`. Figure18.2 shows an overloaded SQL Server instance that is being asked to service seven major applications (Appl 1 DB through Appl 7 DB).

The single SQL Server instance in Figure 18.2 is sharing memory (cache) and critical internal working areas, such as `tempdb`, with all seven major applications. Everything runs fine

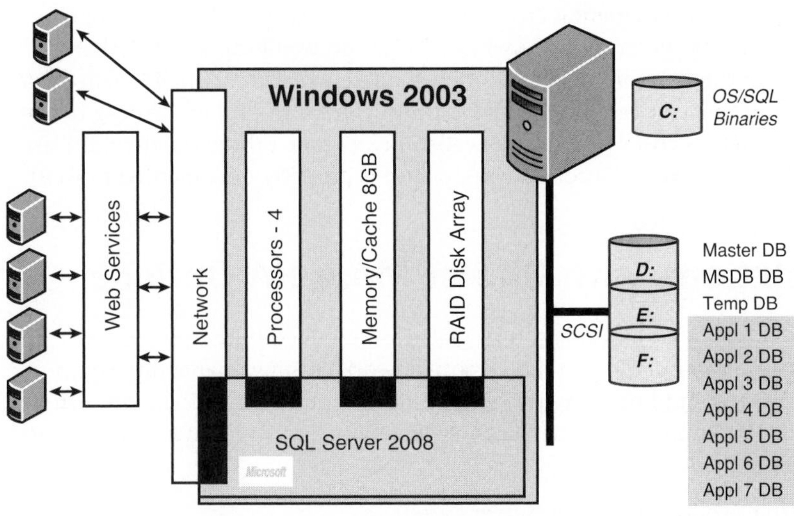

FIGURE 18.2 High risk: Many applications sharing a single SQL Server 2008 instance.

until one of these applications submits a runaway query, and all other applications being serviced by that SQL Server instance come to a grinding halt. Most of this built-in risk could be avoided by simply putting each application (or perhaps two applications) onto their own SQL Server instance, as shown in Figure 18.3. This fundamental design approach greatly reduces the risk of one application affecting another.

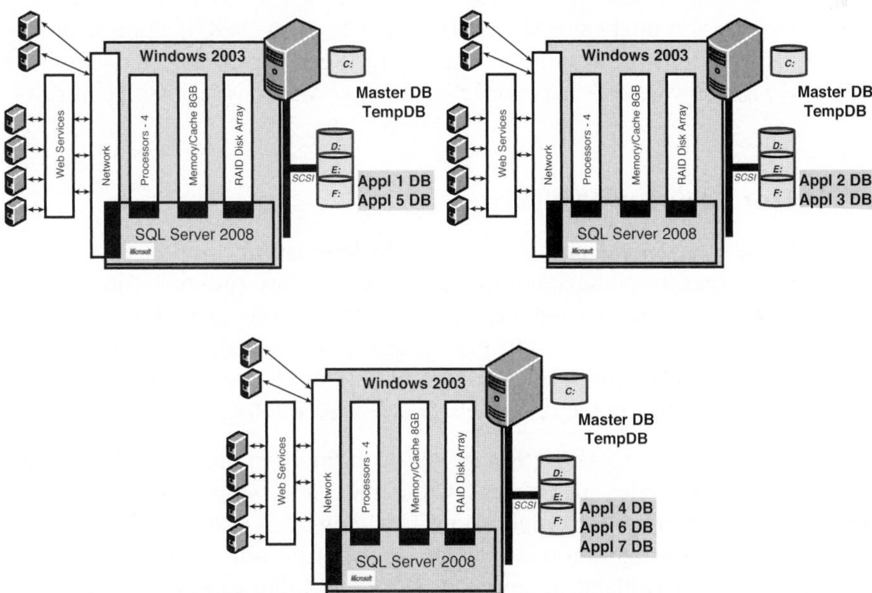

FIGURE 18.3 Mitigated risk: Isolating critical applications away from each other.

18

Many companies make this fundamental error. The trouble is that they keep adding new applications to their existing server instance without a full understanding of the shared resources that underpin the environment. It is often too late when they finally realize that they are hurting themselves "by design." You have now been given proper warning of the risks. If other factors, such as cost or hardware availability, dictate otherwise, then at least it is a calculated risk that is entered into knowingly (and is properly documented as well).

Building Solutions with One or More HA Options

When you have the fundamental foundation in place, as described in the preceding section, you can move on to building a tailored software-driven high-availability solution. Which HA option(s) you should be using really depends on your HA requirements. The following high-availability options are used both individually and, very often, together to achieve different levels of HA:

- Microsoft Cluster Services (non–SQL Server based)
- SQL clustering
- Data replication (including peer-to-peer configurations)
- Log shipping
- Database mirroring

All these options are readily available "out of the box" from Microsoft, from the Windows Server family of products and from Microsoft SQL Server 2008.

It is important to understand that some of these options can be used together, but not all go together. For example, you might use Microsoft Cluster Services (MSCS) along with Microsoft SQL Server 2008's SQL Clustering to implement the SQL clustering database configuration, whereas, you wouldn't necessarily need to use MSCS with database mirroring.

Microsoft Cluster Services (MSCS)

MSCS could actually be considered a part of the basic HA foundation components described earlier, except that it's possible to build a high-availability system without it (for example, a system that uses numerous redundant hardware components and disk mirroring or RAID for its disk subsystem). Microsoft has made MSCS the cornerstone of its clustering capabilities, and MSCS is utilized by applications that are cluster enabled. A prime example of a cluster-enabled technology is Microsoft SQL Server 2008.

MSCS is the advanced Windows operating system configuration that defines and manages between 2 and 16 servers as "nodes" in a cluster. These nodes are aware of each other and can be set up to take over cluster-aware applications from any node that fails (for example, a failed server). This cluster configuration also shares and controls one or more disk subsystems as part of its high-availability capability. Figure 18.4 illustrates a basic two-node MSCS configuration.

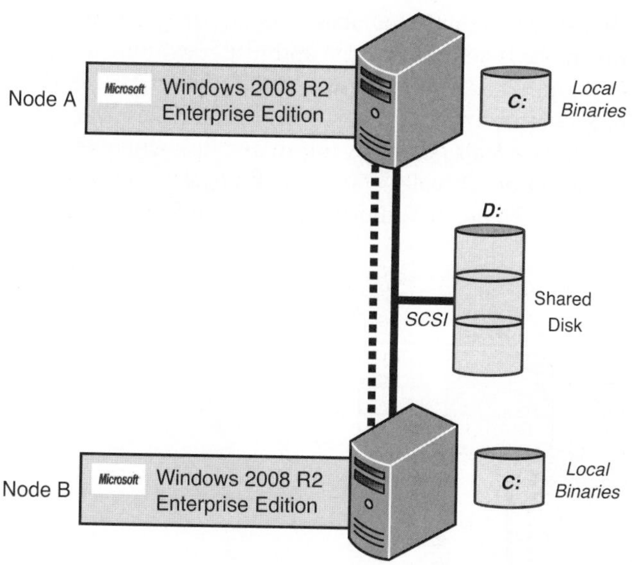

FIGURE 18.4 Basic two-node MSCS configuration.

MSCS is available only with Microsoft Windows Enterprise Edition and Data Center operating system products. Don't be alarmed, though. If you are looking at a high-availability system to begin with, there is a great probability that your applications are already running with these enterprise-level OS versions.

MSCS can be set up in an active/passive or active/active mode. Essentially, in an active/passive mode, one server sits idle (that is, is passive) while the other is doing the work (that is, is active). If the active server fails, the passive one takes over the shared disk and the cluster-aware applications instantaneously.

SQL Clustering

If you want a SQL Server instance to be clustered for high availability, you are essentially asking that this SQL Server instance (and the database) be completely resilient to a server failure and completely available to the application without the end user ever even noticing that there was a failure (or at least with minimal interruption). Microsoft provides this capability through the SQL Clustering option. SQL Clustering is built on top of MSCS for its underlying detection of a failed server and for its availability of the databases on the shared disk (which is controlled by MSCS). SQL Server is said to be a "cluster-aware/enabled" technology.

A SQL Server instance that is clustered can be created by actually creating a virtual SQL Server instance that is known to the application (the constant in the equation) and then two physical SQL Server instances that share one set of databases. In an active/passive configuration, only one SQL Server instance is active at a time and just goes along and does its work. If that active server fails (and with it, the physical SQL Server instance), the passive server (and the physical SQL Server instance on that server) simply takes over instantaneously. This is possible because MSCS also controls the shared disk where the databases are. The end user and application never really know which physical SQL Server instance they are on or whether one failed. Figure 18.5 illustrates a typical SQL Clustering configuration built on top of MSCS.

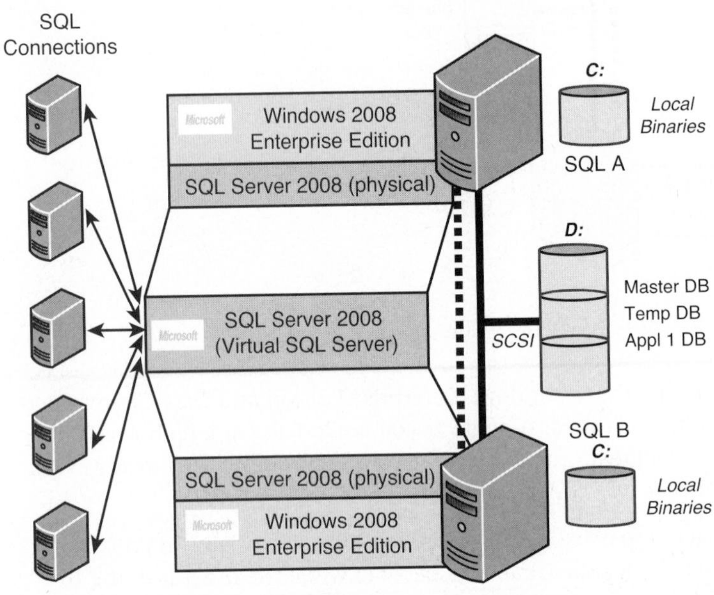

FIGURE 18.5 Basic SQL Clustering two-node configuration (active/passive).

Setup and management of this type of configuration are much easier than you might think. More and more often, SQL Clustering is the method chosen for most high-availability solutions. Later in this chapter, you see that other methods may also be viable for achieving high availability (based on the application's HA requirements). Chapter 21, "SQL Server Clustering," covers this topic in more detail.

Extending the clustering model to include Network Load Balancing (NLB) pushes this particular solution even further into higher availability—from client traffic high availability to back-end SQL Server high availability. Figure 18.6 shows a four-host NLB cluster architecture acting as a virtual server to handle the network traffic coupled with a two-node SQL cluster on the back end. This setup is resilient from top to bottom.

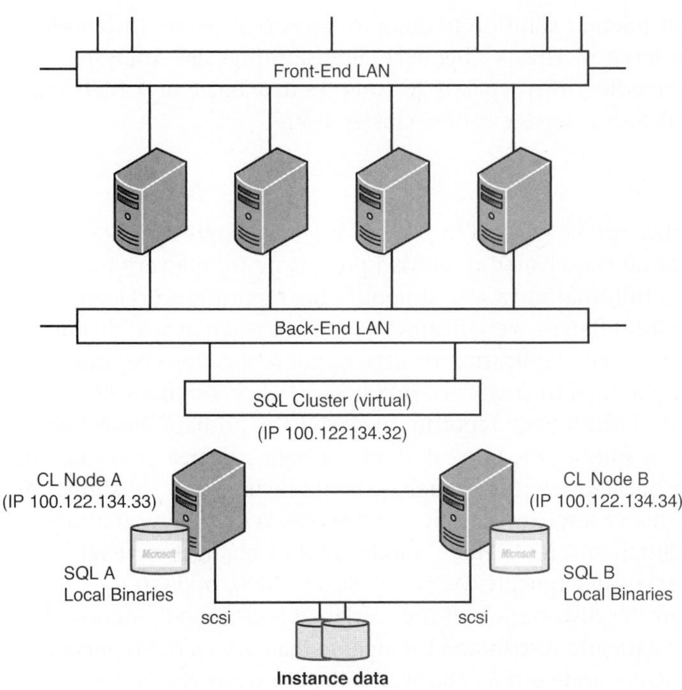

FIGURE 18.6 An NLB host cluster with a two-node server cluster.

The four NLB hosts work together, distributing the work efficiently. NLB automatically detects the failure of a server and repartitions client traffic among the remaining servers.

The following apply to SQL Clustering in SQL Server 2008:

- **Full SQL Server 2008 Services as cluster-managed resources**—All SQL Server 2008 services, including the following, are cluster aware:
    - SQL Server DBMS engine
    - SQL Server Agent
    - SQL Server Full-Text Search
    - Analysis Services
    - Integration Services
    - Notification Services
    - Reporting Services
    - Service Broker

Now, you can extend this fault-tolerant solution to embrace more SQL Server instances and *all* of SQL Server's related services. This is a big deal because things like Analysis Services previously had to be handled with separate techniques to achieve near high availability. Not anymore; each SQL Server service is now cluster aware.

Data Replication

The next technology option that can be utilized to achieve high availability is data replication. Originally, data replication was created to offload processing from a very busy server (such as an OLTP application that must also support a big reporting workload) or to geographically distribute data for different, very distinct user bases (such as worldwide product ordering applications). As data replication (transactional replication) became more stable and reliable, it started to be used to create "warm" (almost "hot") standby SQL Servers that could also be used to fulfill basic reporting needs. If the primary server ever failed, the reporting users would still be able to work (hence a higher degree of availability achieved for them), and the replicated reporting database could be used as a substitute for the primary server, if needed (hence a warm-standby SQL Server). When doing transactional replication in the "instantaneous replication" mode, all data changes were replicated to the replicate servers extremely quickly. With SQL Server 2000, updating subscribers allowed for even greater distribution of the workload and, overall, increased the availability of the primary data and distributed the update load across the replication topology. There are plenty of issues and complications involved in using the updating subscribers approach (for example, conflict handlers, queues).

With SQL Server 2005, Microsoft introduced peer-to-peer replication, which is not a publisher/subscription model, but a publisher-to-publisher model (hence peer-to-peer). It is a lot easier to configure and manage than other replication topologies, but it still has its nuances to deal with. This peer-to-peer model allows excellent availability for this data and great distribution of workload along geographic (or other) lines. This may fit some companies' availability requirements and also fulfill their distributed reporting requirements as well.

The top of Figure 18.7 shows a typical SQL data replication configuration of a central publisher/subscriber using continuous transactional replication. This can serve as a basis for high availability and also fulfills a reporting server requirement at the same time. The bottom of Figure 18.7 shows a typical peer-to-peer continuous transactional replication model that is also viable.

The downside of peer-to-peer replication comes into play if ever the subscriber (or the other peer) needs to become the primary server (that is, take over the work from the original server). This takes a bit of administration that is *not* transparent to the end user. Connection strings have to be changed, ODBC data sources need to be updated, and so on. But this process may take minutes as opposed to hours of database recovery time, and it may well be tolerable to end users. Peer-to-peer configurations handle recovery a bit better in that much of the workload is already distributed to either of the nodes. So, at most, only part of the user base will be affected if one node goes down. Those users can easily be redirected to the other node (peer), with the same type of connection changes described earlier.

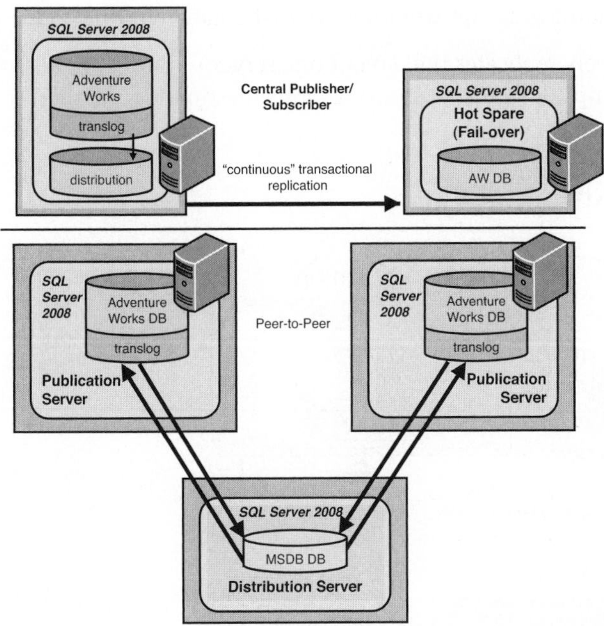

FIGURE 18.7 Basic data replication configurations for HA.

With either the publisher/subscriber or peer-to-peer replication approach, there is a risk of not having all the transactions from the publishing server. However, often, a company is willing to live with this small risk in favor of availability. Remember that a replicated database is an approximate image of the primary database (up to the point of the last update that was successfully distributed), which makes it very attractive as a warm standby. For publishing databases that are primarily read-only, using a warm standby is a great way to distribute the load and mitigate the risk of any one server failing. Chapter 19, "Replication," covers data replication and all the various implementation scenarios that you might ever need to use.

Log Shipping

Another, more direct, method of creating a completely redundant database image is to utilize log shipping. Microsoft "certifies" log shipping as a method of creating an "almost hot" spare. Some folks even use log shipping as an alternative to data replication (it has been referred to as "the poor man's data replication"). There's just one problem: Microsoft has formally announced that log shipping (as we know and love it) will be deprecated in the near future. The reasons are many, but the primary one is that it is being replaced by database mirroring (referred to as *real-time log shipping*, when it was first being conceived). If you still want to use log shipping, it is perfectly viable—for now.

Log shipping does three primary things:

- Makes an exact image copy of a database on one server from a database dump
- Creates a copy of that database on one or more other servers from that dump

- Continuously applies transaction log dumps from the original database to the copy

In other words, log shipping effectively replicates the data of one server to one or more other servers via transaction log dumps. Figure 18.8 shows a source/destination SQL Server pair that has been configured for log shipping.

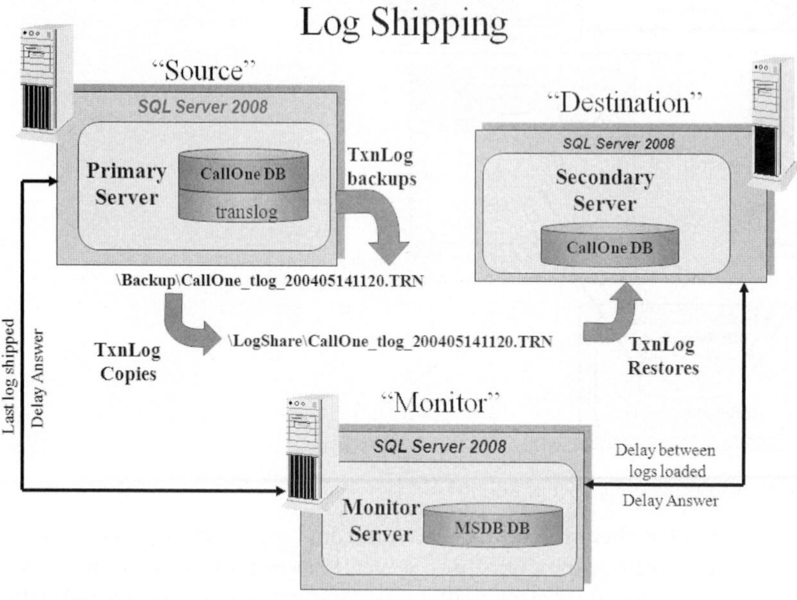

FIGURE 18.8 Log shipping in support of high availability.

Log shipping is a great solution when you have to create one or more failover servers. It turns out that, to some degree, log shipping fits the requirement of creating a read-only subscriber as well. The following are the gating factors for using log shipping as a method of creating and maintaining a redundant database image:

- Data latency lag is the time that exists between the transaction log dumps on the source database and when these dumps are applied to the destination databases.
- Sources and destinations must be the same SQL Server version.
- Data is read-only on the destination SQL Server until the log shipping pairing is broken (as it should be to guarantee that the transaction logs can be applied to the destination SQL Server).

The data latency restriction might quickly disqualify log shipping as an instantaneous high-availability solution (if you need rapid availability of the failover server). However, log shipping might be adequate for certain situations. If a failure ever occurs on the primary SQL Server, a destination SQL Server that was created and maintained via log shipping can be swapped into use fairly quickly. The destination SQL Server would contain exactly what was on the source SQL Server (right down to every user ID, table, index, and file allocation map, except for any changes to the source database that occurred after the last log dump was applied). This directly achieves a level of high availability. It is still not completely transparent, though, because the SQL Server instance names are different, and the end user may be required to log in again to the new server instance.

NOTE

Log shipping is not covered further in this book because of its limited life going forward. The *SQL Server 2000 Unleashed* version of this book covers log shipping in extensive detail. Remember that log shipping is not data replication and uses a completely different technology than data replication.

Database Mirroring

Another failover option with SQL Server is database mirroring. Database mirroring essentially extends the old log shipping feature of SQL Server and creates an automatic failover capability to a "hot" standby server. Database mirroring is being billed as creating a fault-tolerant database that is an "instant" standby (ready for use in less than three seconds).

At the heart of database mirroring is the "copy-on-write" technology. Copy-on-write means that transactional changes are shipped to another server as the logs are written. All logged changes to the database instance become immediately available for copying to another location. As you can see in Figure 18.9, database mirroring utilizes a witness server as well as client components to insulate the client applications from any knowledge of a server failure.

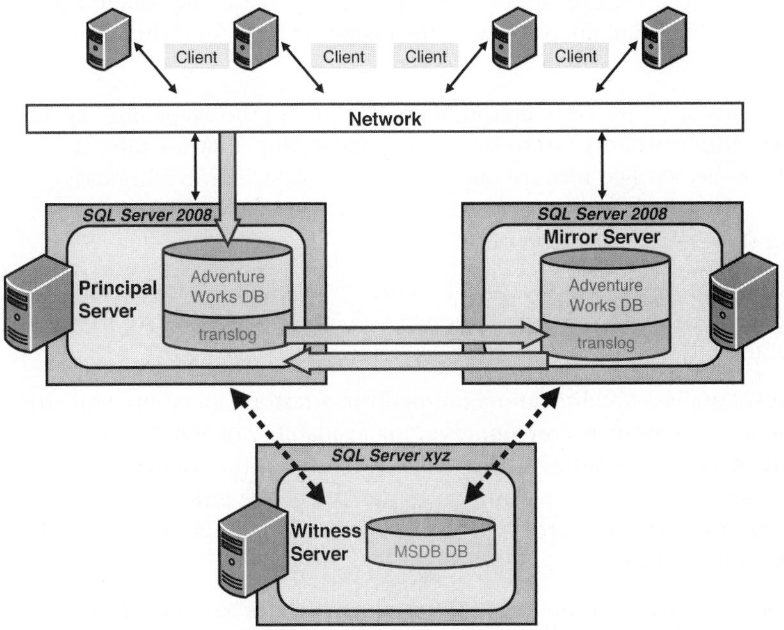

FIGURE 18.9 SQL Server 2008 database mirroring high-availability configuration.

Chapter 20 dives much more deeply into database mirroring setup, configuration, and architecture. It is sufficient to say here that with database mirroring, an application can possibly be failed over to the mirrored database in 3 seconds or less, with nearly complete client transparency. You can also leverage this mirrored database for offloading reporting by creating a snapshot from it. Again, this topic is covered in Chapter 20.

Combining Failover with Scale-Out Options

SQL Server 2008 pushes combinations of options to achieve higher availability levels. A prime example would be combining data replication with database mirroring to provide maximum availability of data, scalability to users, and fault tolerance via failover, potentially at each node in the replication topology. By starting with the publisher and perhaps the distributor, you make them both database mirror failover configurations.

Building up a combination of both options together is essentially the best of both worlds: the super-low latency of database mirroring for fault tolerance and high availability (and scalability) of data through replication. Check out Chapter 20 for more details on this creative configuration.

Other HA Techniques That Yield Great Results

Microsoft has been revisiting (and architecting) several operations that previously required a table or whole database to be offline. For several critical database operations (such as recovery operations, restores, indexing, and others), Microsoft has either made the data in the database available earlier in the execution of the operation or made the data in the database completely available simultaneously with the operation. The following primary areas are now addressed:

- **Fast recovery**—This faster recovery option directly improves the availability of SQL Server databases. Administrators can reconnect to a recovering database after the transaction log has been rolled forward (and before the rollback processing has finished). Figure 18.10 illustrates how Microsoft makes a SQL Server 2008 database available earlier than would SQL Server 2000.

  In particular, a database in SQL Server 2008 becomes available when committed transaction log entries are rolled forward (termed *redo*) and no longer have to wait for the "in flight" transactions to be rolled back (termed *undo*).

- **Online restore**—Database administrators can perform a restore operation while the database is still online. Online restore improves the availability of SQL Server because only the data being restored is unavailable; the rest of the database remains online and available to users. In addition, the granularity of the restore has changed to be at the filegroup level and even at the page level, if needed. The remainder of the database remains available.

- **Online indexing**—Concurrent modifications (updates, deletes, and inserts) to the underlying table or clustered index data and any associated indexes can now be done during index creation time. For example, while a clustered index is being

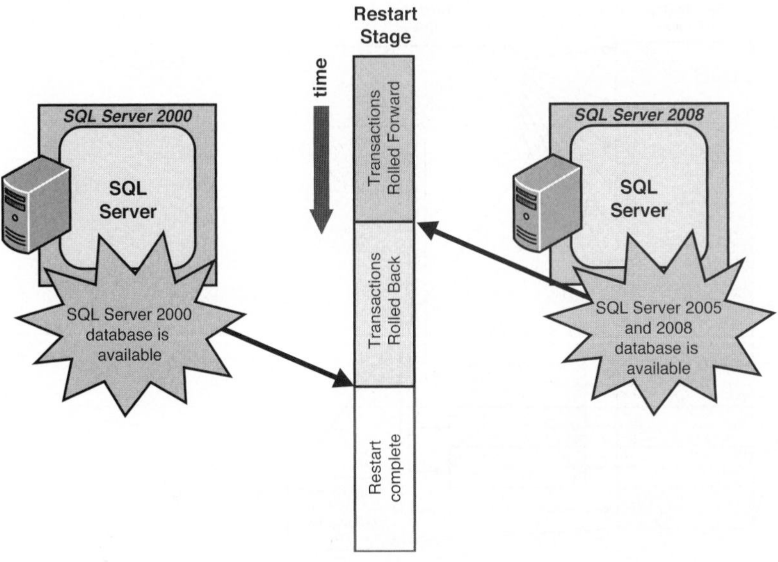

FIGURE 18.10 SQL Server 2008 databases become available earlier than databases with SQL Server 2000 database recovery (fast recovery).

rebuilt, you can continue to make updates to the underlying data and perform queries against the data.

- **Database snapshots**—You can now create a read-only, stable view of a database. A database snapshot is created without the overhead of creating a complete copy of the database or having completely redundant storage. A database snapshot is simply a reference point of the pages used in the database (that is defined in the system catalog). When pages are updated, a new page chain is started that contains the data pages changed since the database snapshot was taken, as illustrated in Figure 18.11.

  As the original database diverges from the snapshot, the snapshot gets its own copy of original pages when they are modified. The snapshot can even be used to recover an accidental change to a database by simply reapplying the pages from the snapshot back to the original database.

  The copy-on-write technology used for database mirroring also enables database snapshots. When a database snapshot is created on a database, all writes check the system catalog of "changed pages" first; if not there, the original page is copied (using the copy-on-write technique) and is put in a place for reference by the database snapshot (because this snapshot must be kept intact). In this way, the database snapshot and the original database share the data pages that have not changed.

- **Data partitioning improvements**—Data partitioning has been enhanced with native table and index partitioning. It essentially allows you to manage large tables and indexes at a lower level of granularity. In other words, a table can be defined to identify distinct partitions (such as by date or by a range of key values). This approach effectively defines a group of data rows that are unique to a partition.

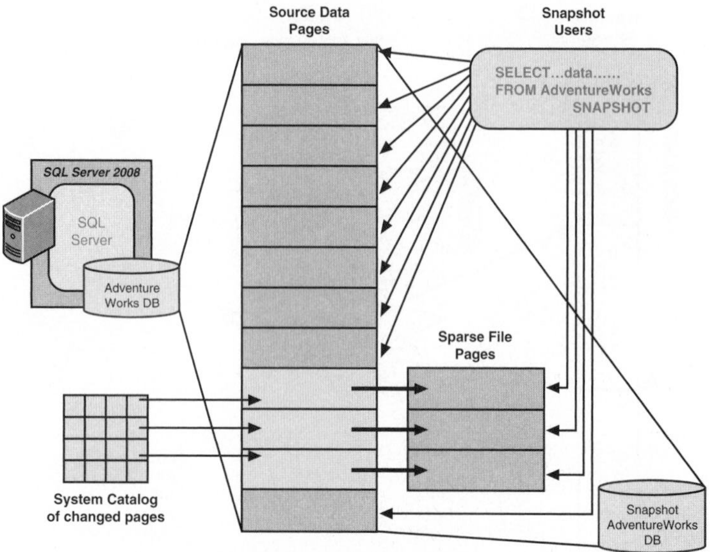

FIGURE 18.11 Database snapshots and the original database share pages and are managed within the system catalog of SQL Server 2008.

These partitions can be taken offline, restored, or loaded independently while the rest of the table is available.

- **Addition of a snapshot isolation level**—This snapshot isolation (SI) level is a database-level capability that allows users to access the last committed row, using a transactionally consistent view of the database. This capability provides improved scalability and availability by not blocking data access of this previously unavailable data state. This new isolation level essentially allows data reading requests to see the last committed version of data rows, even if they are currently being updated as part of a transaction (for example, they see the rows as they were at the start of the transaction without being blocked by the writers, and the writers are not blocked by readers because the readers do not lock the data). This isolation level is probably best used for databases that are read-mostly (with few writes/updates) due to the potential overhead in maintaining this isolation level.
- **Dedicated administrator connection**—This feature introduces a dedicated administrator connection that administrators can use to access a running server even if the server is locked or otherwise unavailable. This capability enables administrators to troubleshoot problems on a server by executing diagnostic functions or Transact-SQL statements without having to take down the server.

High Availability from the Windows Server Family Side

To enhance system uptimes, numerous system architecture enhancements that directly reduce unplanned downtime, such as improved memory management and driver verification, were made in Windows 2000, 2003, and 2008 R2. New file protection capabilities prevent new software installations from replacing essential system files and causing failures. In addition, device driver signatures identify drivers that may destabilize a system. And, perhaps another major step toward stabilization is the use of virtual servers.

Microsoft Virtual Server 2005

Virtual Server 2005 is a much more cost-effective virtual machine solution designed on top of Windows Server 2008 to increase operational efficiency in software testing and development, application migration, and server consolidation scenarios. Virtual Server 2005 is designed to increase hardware efficiency and help boost administrator productivity, and it is a key Microsoft deliverable toward the Dynamic Systems Initiative (eliminating reboots of servers, which directly affects downtime!). As shown in Figure 18.12, the host operating system—Windows Server 2008 in this case—manages the host system (at the bottom of the stack).

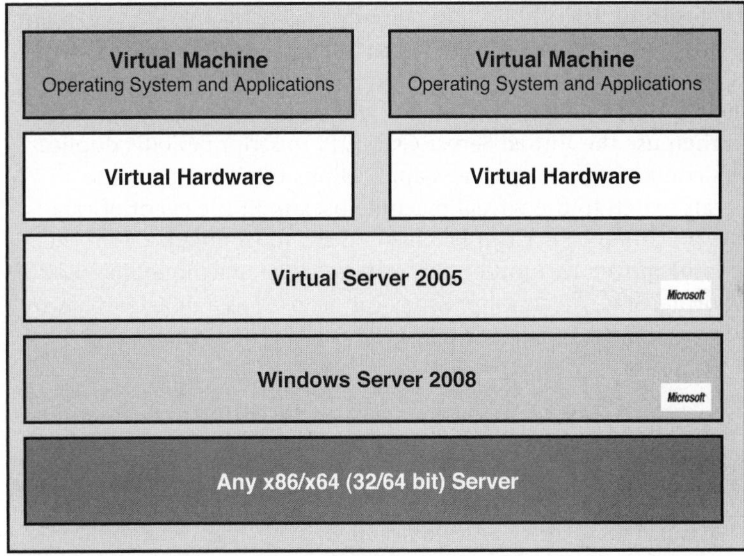

FIGURE 18.12 Microsoft Virtual Server 2005 server architecture.

Virtual Server 2005 provides a Virtual Machine Monitor (VMM) virtualization layer that manages virtual machines and provides the software infrastructure for hardware emulation. As you move up the stack, each virtual machine consists of a set of virtualized devices, the virtual hardware for each virtual machine.

A guest operating system and applications run in the virtual machine—unaware, for example, that the network adapter they interact with through Virtual Server is only a software simulation of a physical Ethernet device. When a guest operating system is running, the special-purpose VMM kernel takes mediated control over the CPU and hardware during virtual machine operations, creating an isolated environment in which the guest operating system and applications run close to the hardware at the highest possible performance.

Virtual Server 2005 is a multithreaded application that runs as a system service, with each virtual machine running in its own thread of execution; I/O occurs in child threads. Virtual Server derives two core functions from the host operating system: the underlying host operating system kernel schedules CPU resources, and the device drivers of the host operating system provide access to system devices. The Virtual Server VMM provides the software infrastructure to create virtual machines, manage instances, and interact with guest operating systems. An often-discussed example of leveraging Virtual Server 2005 capabilities would be to use it in conjunction with a disaster recovery implementation.

Virtual Server 2005 and Disaster Recovery

Virtual Server 2005 enables a form of server consolidation for disaster recovery. Rather than maintaining redundancy with costly physical servers, customers can use Virtual Server 2005 to back up their mission-critical functionality in a cost-effective way by means of virtual machines. The Virtual Machine Monitor (VMM) and Virtual Hard Disk (VHD) technologies in Virtual Server 2005, coupled with the comprehensive COM API, can be used to create similar failover functionality as standard, hardware-driven disaster recovery solutions. Customers can then use the Virtual Server COM API to script periodic duplication of physical hard disks containing vital business applications to virtual machine VHDs. Additional scripts can switch to the virtual machine backup in the event of catastrophic failure. In this way, a failing device can be taken offline to troubleshoot, or the application or database can be moved to another physical or virtual machine. Moreover, because VHDs are a core Virtual Server technology, they can be used as a disaster recovery agent, wherein business functionality and data can be easily archived, duplicated, or moved to other physical machines.

Summary

As you come to completely understand and assess your application's high-availability requirements, you can create a matching high-availability solution that will serve you well for years to come. The crux of high availability is laying a fundamentally sound foundation that you can count on when failures occur and then, when failures do occur, determining how much data loss you can tolerate, how much downtime is possible, and what the downtime is costing you.

The overall future seems to be improving greatly in all the basic areas of your Microsoft platform footprint, including

- Cheaper and more reliable hardware components that are highly swappable
- The advent of virtual server capabilities (with Windows Virtual Server 2005) to insulate software failures from affecting hardware
- Enhancements that Microsoft is making to SQL Server 2008 that address availability

The critical enhancements to the cornerstone availability capabilities of SQL Clustering will help this fault-tolerant architecture grow more reliable for years to come. The big bonuses come with the features of database mirroring as another fault-tolerant solution at the database level and the database snapshots feature to make data more available to more users more quickly than the older method of log shipping.

To top it all off, Microsoft is making great strides in the areas of online maintenance operations (online restores, online index creates, and so on) and leaping into the realm of one or more virtual server machines (with Virtual Server 2005) that will not bring down a physical server that houses them (which is very UNIX-like).

Chapter 19 delves into the complexities of the major data replication options available with SQL Server 2008.

CHAPTER 19
Replication

IN THIS CHAPTER

- What's New in Data Replication
- What Is Replication?
- The Publisher, Distributor, and Subscriber "Magazine" Metaphor
- Replication Scenarios
- Subscriptions
- Replication Agents
- Planning for SQL Server Data Replication
- SQL Server Replication Types
- Basing the Replication Design on User Requirements
- Setting Up Replication
- Scripting Replication
- Monitoring Replication

There is no such thing as a typical configuration or application anymore. Companies now have to support numerous hardware and software configurations in multitiered, distributed environments. These diverse configurations and applications (and users of the applications) come in all sizes and shapes. And, of course, you need a way to deal with varied data access requirements for these different physical locations; these remote or mobile users over a local area network, wide area network, wireless connections, and dial-up connections; and any needs over the Internet. Microsoft's data replication facility allows for a great breadth of capability to deal with many of these demands. However, to build a proper data replication implementation that meets many of these user requirements, you must have a thorough understanding of the business requirements and technical capabilities of data replication. Data replication is a set of technologies for storing and forwarding data and database objects from one database to another and then synchronizing this data between databases to maintain consistency. With SQL Server 2008, the data replication feature set offers numerous improvements in manageability, availability, programmability, mobility, scalability, and performance.

This chapter does the following:

- Helps you understand what data replication is
- Shows you how to understand and analyze user requirements of data
- Allows you to choose which replication configuration best meets these requirements (if any)

- Demonstrates how to implement a replication configuration
- Describes how to administer and monitor a data replication implementation

What's New in Data Replication

Much of what's new for Microsoft SQL Server data replication revolves around simplifying setup, administration, and monitoring of a data replication topology. This is the result of years of practical experience and thousands of production replication implementations around the globe. The overall data replication approach that Microsoft has developed (since replication's inception back in SQL Server 6.5 days) has been so solid that competitors, such as Oracle (with its Oracle Streams technology), have tried to mimic this architectural approach.

Among many others, the following are some of the new replications features and enhancements that make SQL Server 2008 data replication one of the best data distributions tools on the market:

- **Highly available replication node additions**—SQL Server 2008 offers the capability to add nodes to a replication topology without quiescing the topology.
- **Topology Viewer**—Enhancements have been made to the Peer-to-Peer Topology Wizard so that you can now visually see what the peer-to-peer topology looks like with the Topology Viewer.
- **Capability to centrally monitor all agents and jobs at the Publisher**—You are able to view information about all the agents and jobs associated with publications at the selected Publisher.
- **Minor Replication Monitor enhancements**—Replication Monitor has undergone slight tweaks to make it easier to monitor your full replication topologies. It allows you to monitor the overall health of a replication topology and provides detailed information about the status and performance of publications and subscriptions.
- **Capability to replicate switch partition ALTER**—Enhanced Transactional Replication Support for Partitioned Tables is now available, including the capability to replicate the switch partition `ALTER` for Tables.
- **Scripting integrated into wizards**—You can almost completely script your replication setup or breakdown during or after wizard executions.
- **Conflict Viewer**—This feature helps you view and resolve any conflicts that occurred during the synchronization of a merge subscription or queued updating subscription.
- **Peer-to-peer transactional replication**—Further enhancements have been introduced to the peer-to-peer replication model. They allow replication between identical participants in the topology (a master/master or symmetric publisher concept).
- **Peer-to-peer conflict detection**—The capability to detect conflicts during synchronization in a peer-to-peer replication topology has been added.

- **More replication mobility**—Merge replication provides the capability to replicate data over HTTPS with the web synchronization option, which is useful for synchronizing data from mobile users over the Internet or synchronizing data between Microsoft SQL Server databases across a corporate firewall.
- **Microsoft Sync Framework**—This comprehensive synchronization platform enables collaboration and offline access for applications, services, and devices. It features technologies and tools that enable roaming, sharing, and taking data offline. By using Sync Framework, developers can build sync ecosystems that integrate any application with any data from any store that uses any protocol over any network. We mention it here because of its replication-like behavior for "occasionally connected" applications.

Many of these terms and references might be new or foreign to you now, but they are all explained in this chapter. At the end of this chapter, when you review these new features, you'll be able to appreciate much more readily their significance.

What Is Replication?

Long before you ever start setting up and using SQL Server data replication, you need to have a solid grasp of what data replication is and how it can be used to meet your company's needs. In its classic definition, data replication is based on the "store-and-forward" data distribution model, as shown in Figure 19.1. In other words, data that is inserted, updated, or deleted in one location (stored) is automatically distributed (forwarded) to one or more locations.

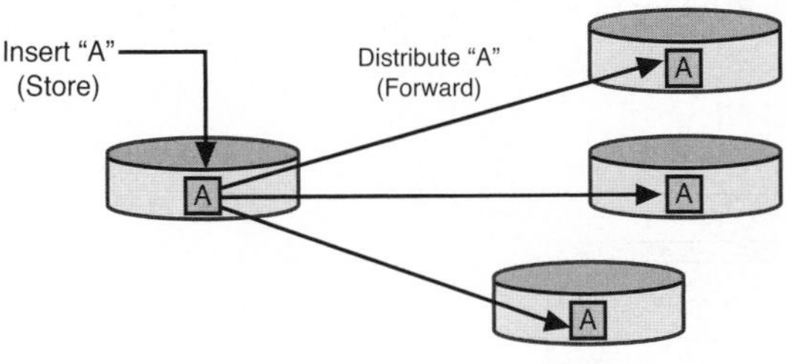

FIGURE 19.1 The store-and-forward data distribution model.

Of course, the data distribution model addresses all the other complexities of updates, deletes, data latency, autonomy, and so on. It is this data distribution model that Microsoft's data replication facility serves to implement. It has come a long way since the early days of Microsoft SQL Server replication (earlier than 6.5) and is now easily categorized as "production worthy." Numerous worldwide data replication scenarios have been implemented for some of the biggest companies in the world without a hitch. These scenarios fall into five major types:

- **Offloading**—You might need to deliver data to different locations to eliminate network traffic and unnecessary load on a single server (for example, when you need to isolate reporting activity away from your online transaction processing). The industry trend is to create an operational data store (ODS) data architecture that replicates core transactional data to a separate platform in real-time and delivers the data to the reporting systems, web services, and other data consumers without impacting the transactional systems in any way.
- **Enabling**—You might need to enable a group of users with a copy of data or a subset of data (vertically or horizontally) for their private use.
- **Partitioning**—You might need to move data off a single server onto several other servers to provide for high availability and decentralization of data (or partitioning of data). This might be the basis of serving customer call centers around the globe that must service "active" support calls (partitioned on active versus closed service requests).
- **Regionalization**—You might have regional ownership of data (for example, regional customers and their orders). In this case, it is possible to set up data replication to replicate data bidirectionally from two or more publishers of the same data.
- **Failover**—You could be replicating all data on a server to another server (that is, a failover server) so that if the primary server crashes, users can switch to the failover server quickly and continue to work with little downtime or data loss.

Figure 19.2 illustrates the topology of some of these replication variations.

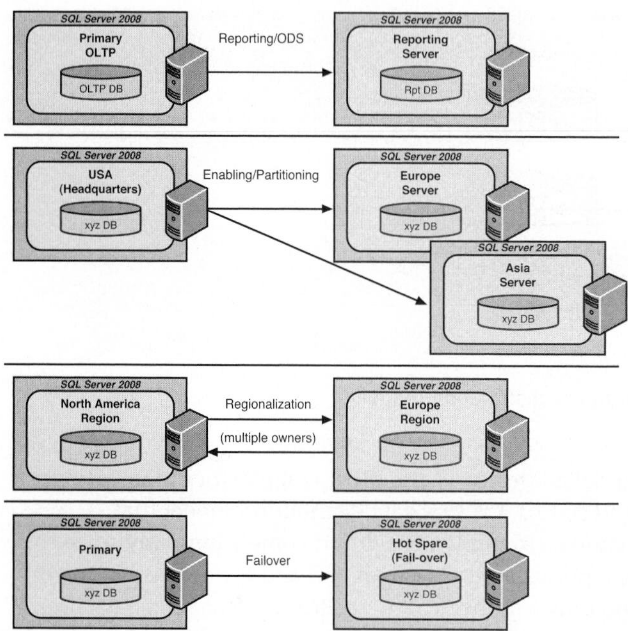

FIGURE 19.2 Data replication scenarios.

As you may notice, you can use data replication for many reasons. Many of these reasons are discussed later in this chapter. First, however, you need to understand some of the common terms and metaphors Microsoft uses in relationship to data replication. They started with the "magazine" concept as the basis of the metaphor. A magazine is created by a publisher, distributed via the mail, and delivered to only those who have a subscription to the magazine. The frequency of the magazine publication can vary, as can the frequency of the subscription (depending on how often the subscriber wants to receive a new magazine). The publication (magazine) consists of one or more articles. One or more articles can be subscribed to.

The Publisher, Distributor, and Subscriber Magazine Metaphor

Any SQL Server can play up to three distinct roles in a data replication environment:

- **Publication server**—The publication server (or publisher) contains the database or databases that will be published (the magazine!). This is the source of the data that is to be replicated to other servers. In Figure 19.3, the `Customer` table (an article in the magazine) in the `AdventureWorks2008` database is the data to be published. To publish data, the database that contains the data that will be published must first be enabled for publishing. Full publishing configuration requirements are discussed later in this chapter, in the section "Setting Up Replication."

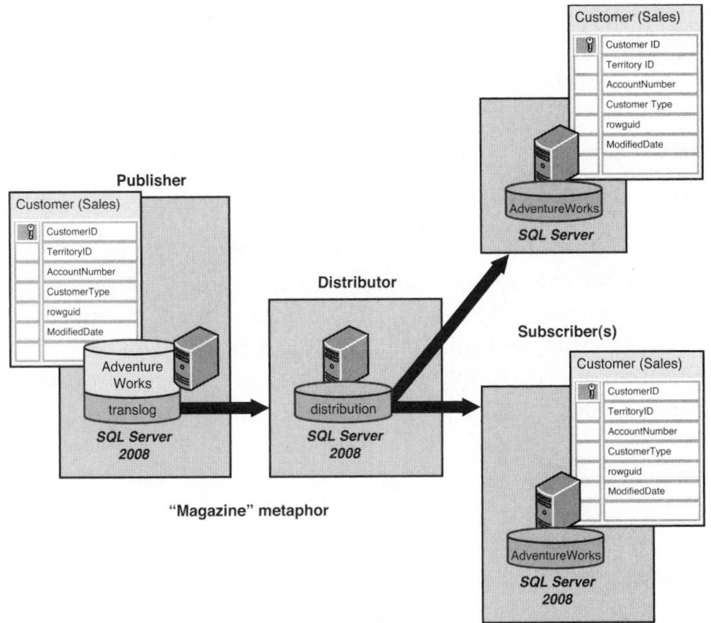

FIGURE 19.3 The publisher, distributor, and one or more subscribers.

19

- **Distribution server**—The distribution server (or distributor) can either be on the same server as the publication server or on a different server (in which case it is a remote distribution server). This server contains the distribution database. This database, also called the store-and-forward database, holds all the data changes that are to be forwarded from the published database to any subscription servers that subscribe to the data. A single distribution server can support several publication servers. The distribution server is truly the workhorse of data replication; it is essentially the mail system that picks up the magazine and delivers it to the subscription holder.
- **Subscription server**—The subscription server (or subscriber) contains a copy of the database or portions of the database being published (for example, the `Customer` table in the `AdventureWorks2008` database). The distribution server sends any changes made to this table (in the published database) to the subscription server's copy of the `Customer` table. This is known as *store-and-forward*. Some data replication configurations send the data to the subscription server, and then the data is read-only. It is also possible for subscribers (known as updating subscribers) to make updates, which are sent back to the publisher. More on this in the Updating Subscribers Replication Model section.

There are now new variations of this update subscriber option called *peer-to-peer replication*. Peer-to-peer allows for more than one publisher of the same data (table) at the same time! Essentially, each publisher is also a subscriber at the same time (hence, peer-to-peer). This chapter provides more information on updating subscribers and peer-to-peer configurations in the "The Updating Subscribers Replication Model" section, later.

Along with enabling distinct server roles (publisher, distributor, and subscriber), Microsoft utilizes a few more magazine metaphors, including publications and articles. A *publication* is a group of one or more *articles* and is the basic unit of data replication. An *article* is simply a pointer to a single table, or a subset of rows or columns out of a table, that will be made available for replication.

Publications and Articles

A single database can contain more than one publication. You can publish data from tables, from database objects, from the execution of stored procedures, and even from schema objects, such as referential integrity constraints, clustered indexes, nonclustered indexes, user triggers, extended properties, and collation. Regardless of what you plan to replicate, all articles in a publication are synchronized at the same time. Figure 19.4 shows an example of a publication (named `Cust_Orders` publication) with three articles (three tables from the `AdventureWorks2008` database). You can also choose to replicate whole tables or just parts of tables via filtering.

Filtering Articles

You can create articles within a publication in several different ways. The basic way to create an article is to publish all the columns and rows contained in a table. Although this is the easiest way to create articles, your business needs might require that you publish only specific columns or certain rows of a table. This is referred to as *filtering vertically* or

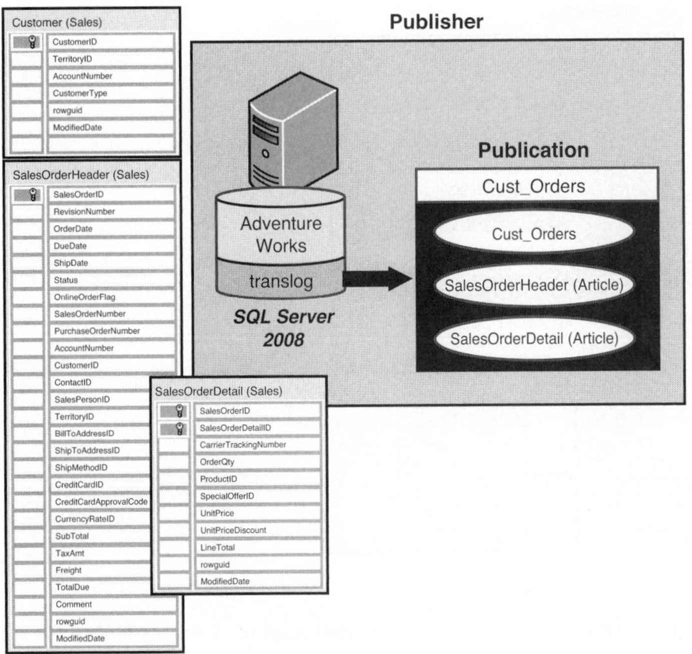

FIGURE 19.4 The **Cust_Orders** publication (in the **AdventureWorks2008** database).

horizontally. When you filter vertically, you filter only specific columns, whereas with horizontal filtering, you filter only specific rows. In addition, SQL Server 2008 provides the added functionality of join filters and dynamic filters.

As Figure 19.5 shows, you might need to replicate only a customer's `CustomerID`, `TerritoryID`, and `CustomerType` to various subscribing servers around your company. In your company, the other data, such as `AccountNumber`, may be restricted information that should not be replicated for general use. For that reason, you simply create an article for data replication that contains a subset of the `Customer` table that will be replicated to these other locations and excludes `AccountNumber` (and `rowguid` and `ModifiedDate` as well).

As another example, you might need to publish only the `Customer` table data for a specific customer type, such as "individual" customers ((`CustomerType = 'I'`) or customers that are "stores" (`CustomerType = 'S'`). This process, as shown in Figure 19.6, is known as horizontal filtering.

It is possible to combine horizontal and vertical filtering, as shown in Figure 19.7. This way, you can weed out unneeded columns *and* rows that aren't required for replication (that is, are not needed by the subscribers). For example, you might need only the customers that are stores and need only `CustomerID`, `TerritoryID`, and `CustomerType` data to be published.

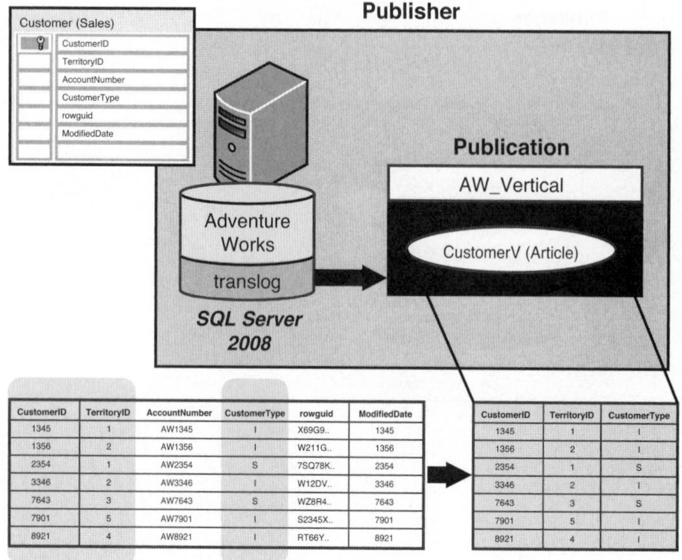

FIGURE 19.5 Vertical filtering creates a subset of columns from a table to be replicated to subscribers.

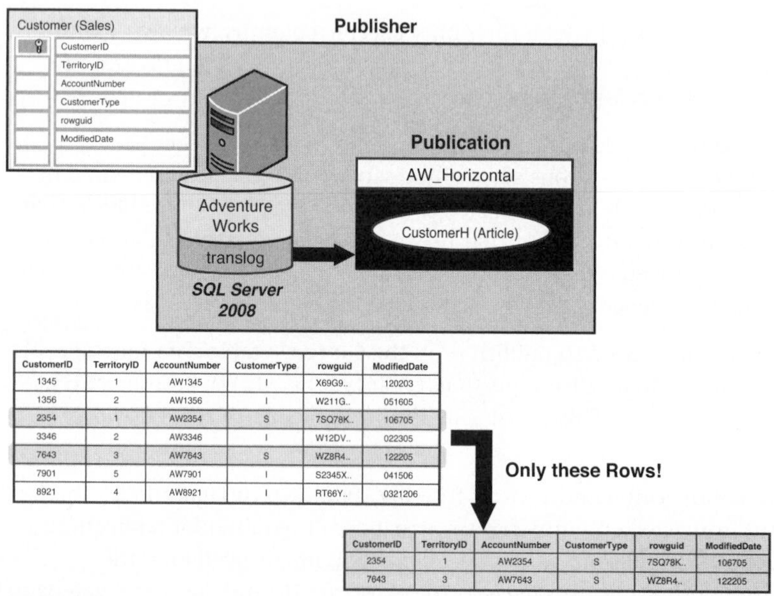

FIGURE 19.6 Horizontal filtering creates a subset of rows from a table to be replicated to subscribers.

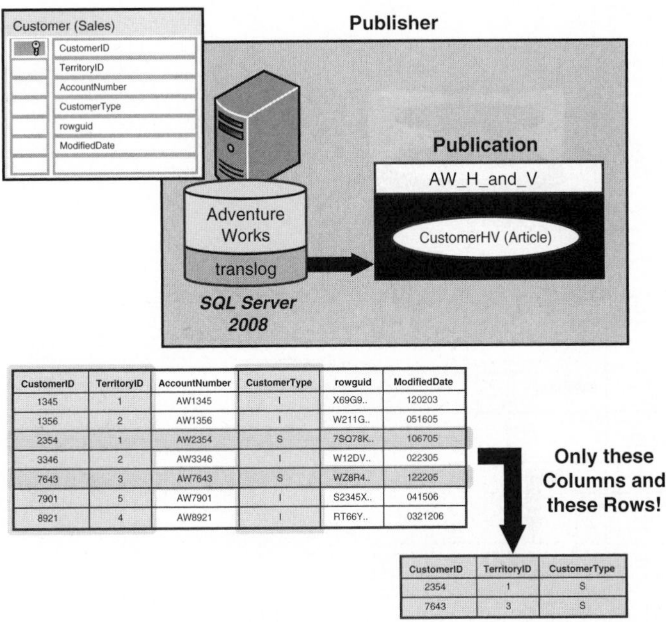

FIGURE 19.7 Combining horizontal and vertical filtering allows you to pare down the information in an article to only the important information needed by the subscribers.

As mentioned earlier, it is now possible to use join filters. Join filters enable you to use the values of one article (that is, values from a table) to determine what gets replicated from another article (that is, what values can be associated with another table) via a join. In other words, if you are publishing the `Customer` table data based on the customers that are stores, you can extend filtering (that is, a join filter) to replicate only those orders for these types of customers (as shown in Figure 19.8). This way, you replicate only orders for customers that are stores to a subscriber that needs to see only this filtered data. This type of replication can be efficient if it is done well.

You also can publish stored procedure executions, along with their parameters, as articles. This can be either a standard procedure execution article or a serializable procedure execution article. The difference is that the latter is executed as a serializable transaction; the serializable option is recommended because it replicates the procedure execution only if the procedure is executed within the context of a serializable transaction. If that same stored procedure is executed from outside a serializable transaction, changes to data in published tables are replicated as a series of DML statements. In general, replicating stored procedure executions gives you a major reduction in the number of SQL statements being replicated across the network versus standard DML statements.

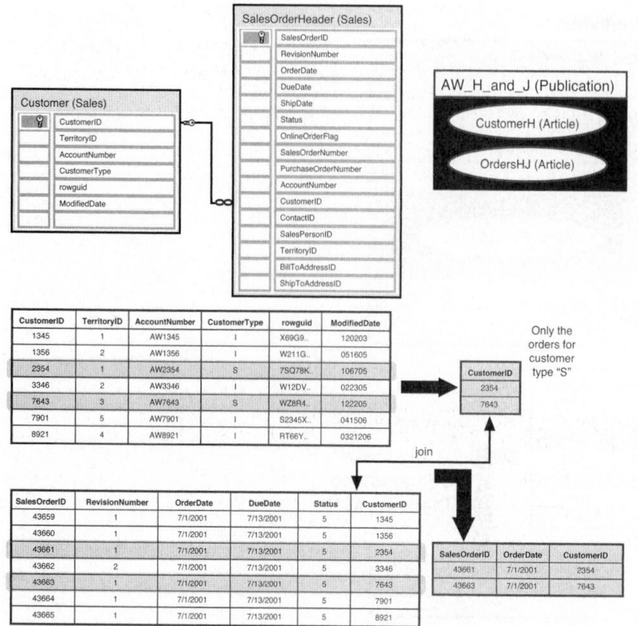

CustomerID	TerritoryID	AccountNumber	CustomerType	rowguid	ModifiedDate
1345	1	AW1345	I	X69G9..	120203
1356	2	AW1356	I	W211G..	051605
2354	1	AW2354	S	7SQ78K..	106705
3346	2	AW3346	I	W12DV..	022305
7643	3	AW7643	S	WZ8R4..	122205
7901	5	AW7901	I	S2345X..	041506
8921	4	AW8921	I	RT66Y..	0321206

CustomerID
2354
7643

SalesOrderID	RevisionNumber	OrderDate	DueDate	Status	CustomerID
43659	1	7/1/2001	7/13/2001	5	1345
43660	1	7/1/2001	7/13/2001	5	1356
43661	1	7/1/2001	7/13/2001	5	2354
43662	2	7/1/2001	7/13/2001	5	3346
43663	1	7/1/2001	7/13/2001	5	7643
43664	1	7/1/2001	7/13/2001	5	7901
43665	1	7/1/2001	7/13/2001	5	8921

SalesOrderID	OrderDate	CustomerID
43661	7/1/2001	2354
43663	7/1/2001	7643

FIGURE 19.8 Horizontal and Join publication: Joining customers that are stores (type "S") to corresponding **SalesOrderHeader** rows.

For instance, if you wanted to update the `Customer` table for every customer via an `UPDATE` SQL statement, the resulting `Customer` table updates would be replicated as a large multistep transaction involving at least 5,000 separate `UPDATE` statements at a minimum. This number of statements would significantly bog down your network. However, with stored procedure execution articles, only the execution of the stored procedure is replicated to the subscription server, and the stored procedure—not the numerous update statements—is executed on that subscription server. Figure 19.9 illustrates the difference in execution described earlier. Some subtleties when utilizing this type of data replication processing can't be overlooked, such as making sure the published stored procedure behaves the same on the subscribing server side.

Many more data replication terms are presented in this chapter, but it is essential that you first learn about the different types of replication scenarios that can be built and the reasons any of them would be desired over the others. It is also worth noting that Microsoft SQL Server 2008 supports replication to and from many different "heterogeneous" data sources. In other words, OLE DB and ODBC data sources can subscribe to SQL Server publications, and they can receive data replicated from a number of data sources, including Microsoft Exchange, Microsoft Access, Oracle, and DB2.

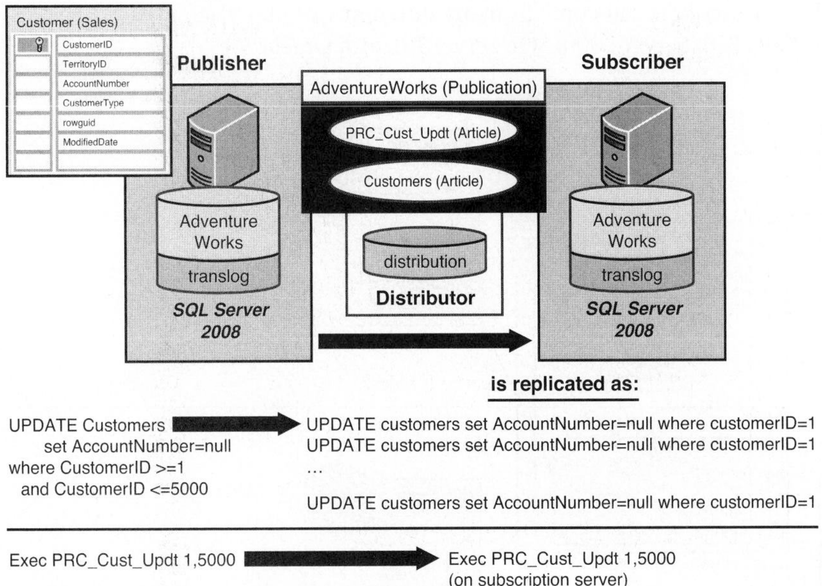
Customer (Sales)
CustomerID
TerritoryID
AccountNumber
CustomerType
rowguid
ModifiedDate
Publisher
Subscriber
AdventureWorks (Publication)
PRC_Cust_Updt (Article)
Customers (Article)
Adventure Works
translog
SQL Server 2008
distribution
Distributor
Adventure Works
translog
SQL Server 2008
is replicated as:
UPDATE Customers
set AccountNumber=null
where CustomerID >=1
and CustomerID <=5000
UPDATE customers set AccountNumber=null where customerID=1
UPDATE customers set AccountNumber=null where customerID=1
...
UPDATE customers set AccountNumber=null where customerID=1
Exec PRC_Cust_Updt 1,5000
Exec PRC_Cust_Updt 1,5000
(on subscription server)

FIGURE 19.9 Comparison of stored procedure execution and standard SQL statement replication.

Replication Scenarios

In general, depending on your business requirements and hardware or network constraints, one of several different data replication models can be implemented, including the following:

- Central publisher
- Central publisher with a remote distributor
- Publishing subscriber
- Central subscriber
- Multiple publishers with multiple subscribers
- Updating subscribers
- Peer-to-peer

19

The Central Publisher Replication Model

The central publisher replication model, shown in Figure 19.10, is Microsoft's default scenario and a common model used if your primary server has plenty of spare CPU cycles and you want a simple replication model. In this scenario, one SQL Server performs the function of both publisher and distributor. The publisher/distributor can have any number of subscribers. These subscribers can come in many different varieties, such as SQL Server 2008, SQL Server 2005, SQL Server 2000, SQL Server 7.0, and Oracle.

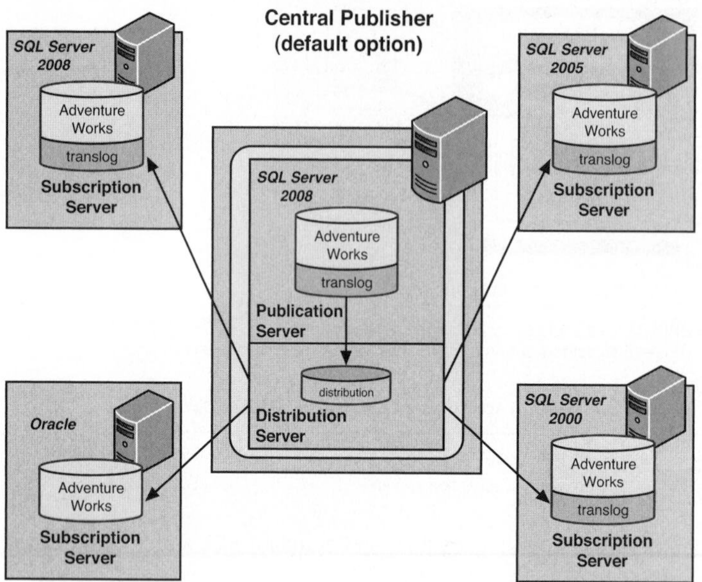

FIGURE 19.10 The central publisher scenario is fairly simple and is a replication model used often.

The central publisher scenario can be used in the following situations:

- Creation of a copy of a database for ad hoc queries and report generation (classic use)
- Publication of master lists to remote locations, such as master customer lists or master price lists
- Maintenance of a remote copy of an online transaction processing (OLTP) database that could be used by the remote sites during communication outages
- Maintenance of a spare copy of an OLTP database that could be used as a "hot spare" in case of server failure

However, it's important to consider the following for this replication model:

- If your OLTP server's activity is substantial and affects greater than 10% of your total data per day, this scenario is not for you. Other scenarios or configurations will better fit your needs.
- If your OLTP server is maximized on CPU, memory, and disk utilization, you should also consider another data replication scenario because this one is not for you either.

The Central Publisher with Remote Distributor Replication Model

The central publisher with remote distributor scenario, as shown in Figure 19.11, is similar to the central publisher scenario and would be used in the same general situations. The major difference between the two is that in the central publisher with remote distributor scenario, a second server is used to perform the role of distributor. This is highly desirable when you need to free the publishing server from having to perform the distribution task from a CPU, disk, and memory point of view. This is also the best scenario from which to expand the number of publishers and subscribers. Remember that a single distribution server can distribute changes for several publishers. The publisher and distributor must be connected to each other via a reliable, high-speed data link. This remote distributor scenario is proving to be one of the best data replication configurations due to its minimal impact on the publication server and maximum distribution capability to any number of subscribers.

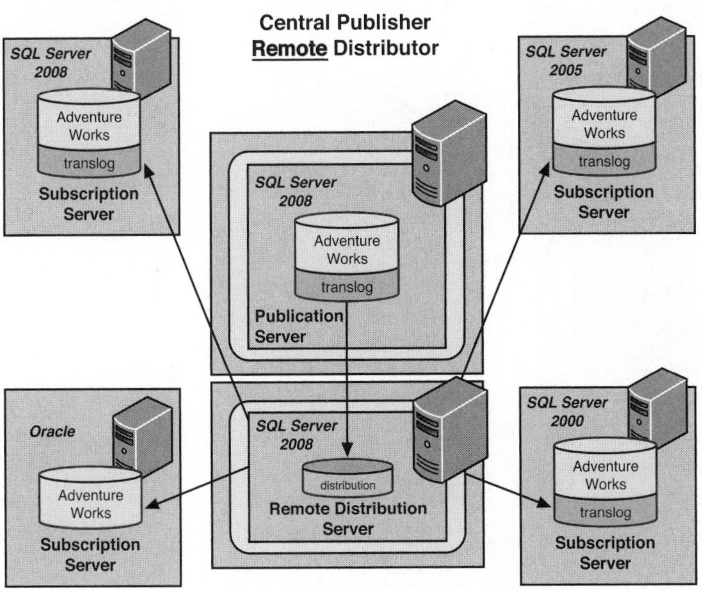

FIGURE 19.11 You use the central publisher with remote distributor scenario when you need to offload the distribution work to another server (to minimize the impact to the publishing server).

As mentioned previously, the central publisher/remote distributor approach can be used for all the same purposes as the central publisher scenario, and it also provides the added benefit of having minimal resource impact on the publication servers. If your OLTP server's activity affects more than 10% of your total data per day, this scenario can usually handle it without much issue. If your OLTP server has overburdened CPU, memory, and disk utilization, implementing this model easily solves these issues as well. The central publisher/remote distribution model is useful for the vast majority of all the data replication configurations due to its optimal characteristics. Nine out of ten replication scenarios that this author has implemented used the remote distributor replication model.

The Publishing Subscriber Replication Model

In the publishing subscriber scenario, as shown in Figure 19.12, the publication server also has to act as a distribution server to one subscriber. This subscriber, in turn, immediately publishes the data to any number of other subscribers. The configuration depicted here does not use a remote distribution configuration option but serves the same distribution model purpose. This scenario is best used when a slow or expensive network link exists between the original publishing server and all the other potential subscribers. This allows the initial (critical) publication of the data to be distributed from the original publishing server to that single subscriber across the slow, unpredictable, or expensive network line. Then, each of the many other subscribers can subscribe to the data, using faster, more predictable, "local" network lines than they would have with the publishing subscriber server.

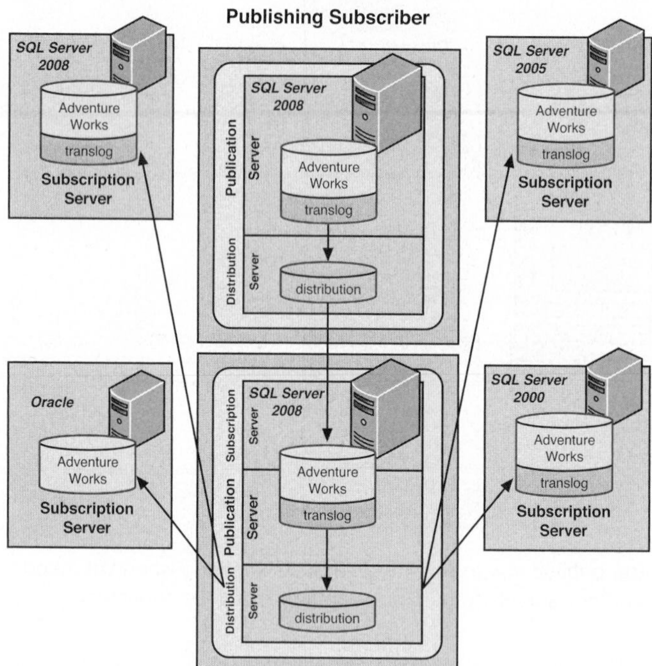

FIGURE 19.12 The publishing subscriber scenario works well when you have to deal with slow, unpredictable, or expensive network links in diverse geographic situations.

A classic example of this model is a company whose main office is in San Francisco and has several branch offices in Europe. Instead of replicating changes to all the branch offices in Europe, it replicates the updates to a single publishing subscriber server in Paris. This publishing subscriber server in Paris then replicates the updates to all other subscriber servers around Europe.

The Central Subscriber Replication Model

In the central subscriber scenario, as shown in Figure 19.13, several publishers replicate data to a single, central subscriber. Basically, this supports the concept of consolidating data at a central site. An example of this might be consolidating all new orders from regional sales offices to company headquarters. In such a situation, you now have several publishers of the `Orders` table, and you need to take some form of precaution, such as filtering by region. This would guarantee that no one publisher could update another region's orders.

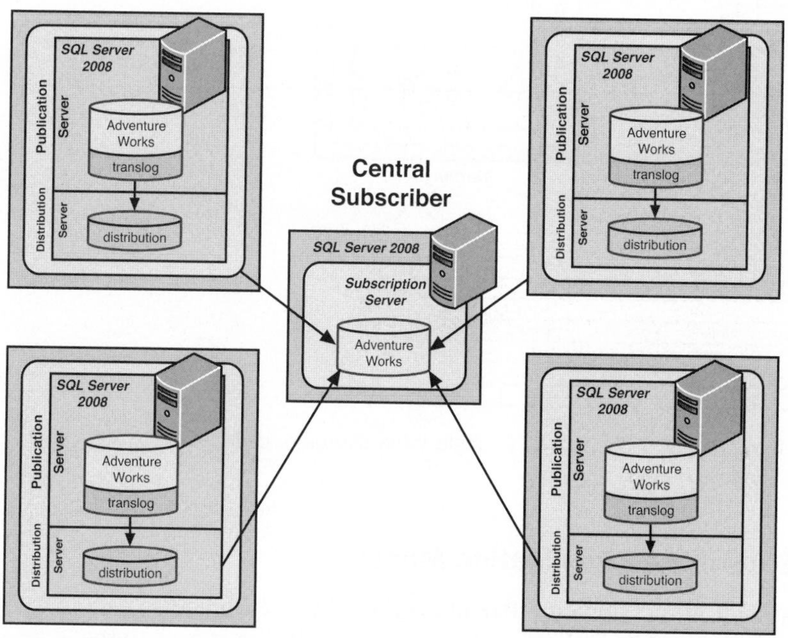

FIGURE 19.13 With the central subscriber scenario, several publishers send data to a single, central subscriber.

The Multiple Publishers with Multiple Subscribers Replication Model

In the multiple publishers with multiple subscribers scenario, as shown in Figure 19.14, a common table (such as the `Customer` table) is maintained on every server participating in the scenario. Each server publishes a particular set of rows (for example, the customer rows in a customer's own territory) that pertain to it—usually via filtering on something that identifies that site to the data rows it owns—and subscribes to the rows that all the other servers are publishing. The result is that each server has all the data at all times and can make changes to its data only. You must be careful when implementing this scenario to ensure that all sites remain synchronized. The most frequently used applications of this system are regional order processing systems and reservation tracking systems. When setting up this type of system, you need to make sure that only local users update local data. This check can be implemented through the use of stored procedures, restrictive views, or a check constraint.

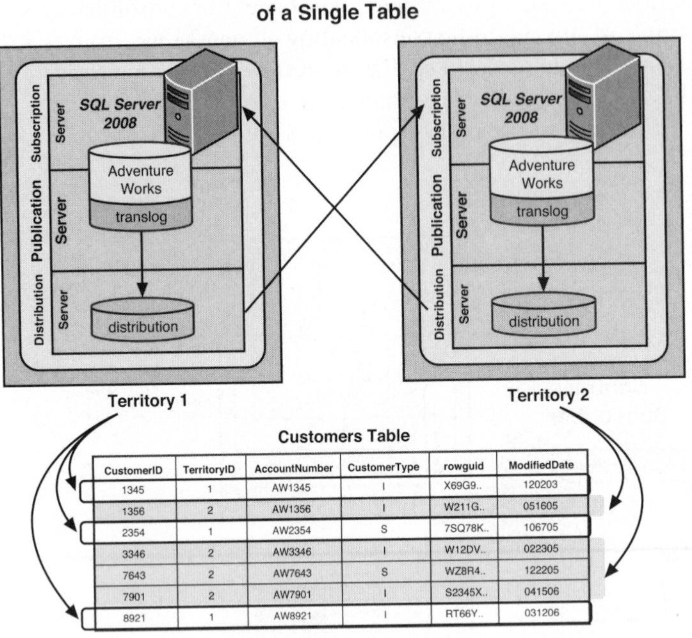

CustomerID	TerritoryID	AccountNumber	CustomerType	rowguid	ModifiedDate
1345	1	AW1345	I	X69G9..	120203
1356	2	AW1356	I	W211G..	051605
2354	1	AW2354	S	7SQ78K..	106705
3346	2	AW3346	I	W12DV..	022305
7643	2	AW7643	S	WZ8R4..	122205
7901	2	AW7901	I	S2345X..	041506
8921	1	AW8921	I	RT66Y..	031206

FIGURE 19.14 In the multiple publishers of a single table scenario, every server in the scenario maintains a common table.

The Updating Subscribers Replication Model

SQL Server 2008 has built-in functionality that allows the subscriber to update data in a table to which it subscribes and have those updates automatically made back to the publisher through either immediate or queued updates. This model, called the updating subscribers model, utilizes a two-phase commit process to update the publishing server as the changes are made on the subscribing server. These updates are then replicated to any other subscribers, but not to the subscriber that made the update.

Immediate updating allows subscribers to update data only if the publisher will accept these updates immediately. If the changes are accepted at the publisher, they are propagated to the other subscribers. The subscribers must be continuously and reliably connected to the publisher to make changes at the subscriber.

Queued updating allows subscribers to update data and then store those updates in a queue while disconnected from the publisher. When the subscriber reconnects to the publisher, the updates are propagated to the publisher. This functionality utilizes SQL Server 2008 queues and the queue reader agent or Microsoft Message Queuing (MSMQ).

A combination of immediate updating with queued updating allows the subscriber to use immediate updating but switch to queued updating if a connection cannot be maintained between the publisher and subscribers. After switching to queued updating, reconnecting to the publisher, and emptying the queue, the subscriber can switch back to immediate updating mode. An updating subscriber is shown in Figure 19.15.

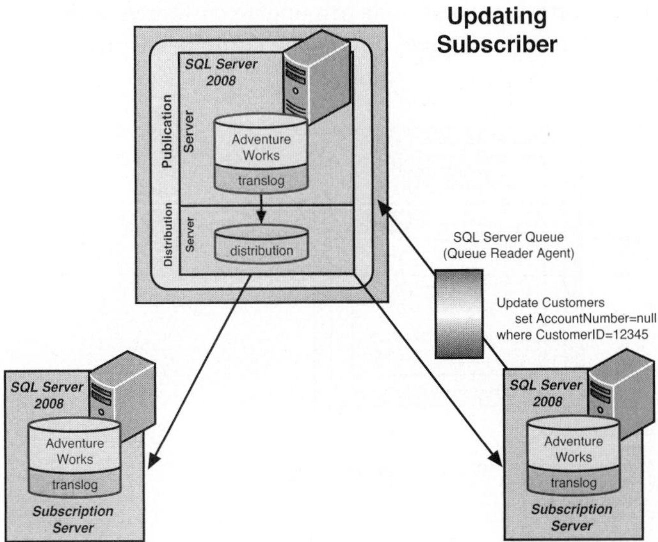

FIGURE 19.15 An updating subscriber updating its copy of a customer table and queuing the changes back to the publisher.

The Peer-to-Peer Replication Model

In SQL Server 2008, the peer-to-peer replication model can provide a simpler way for all nodes to have the same data and also gives them the capability to update this data independently. Peer-to-peer replication is different from subscriber updating in that there is no publisher/subscriber hierarchical relationship. Each peer is equal in level. They establish peer originator IDs so that each can keep track of where updates are coming from and can be utilized if conflicts arise. Peers do not subscribe to each other's data; they share each other's data. There are several limitations with peer-to-peer replication, most of which are to protect this peer-to-peer relationship from being corrupted or from having major data conflicts arise. There are no queues or immediate updating mechanisms involved, thus making this approach very useful when you need to have the same data in more than one place and need to update your local data to your heart's content. If your peers typically do not update the same rows (as in regional data peer-to-peers), this replication model can be very reliable with minimal issues. This type of replication model also allows for any number of peers and provides a separate, very graphic wizard to configure each node in the topology.

NOTE

New peer nodes can also be added to the topology without having to quiesce the topology, thus increasing the availability of the entire replication model.

Figure 19.16 illustrates a typical peer-to-peer configuration with each peer using a remote distribution server. Also note that with peer-to-peer replication, you might decide to prohibit updates to the other nodes' data by putting into place some type of stored procedure or view restrictions that allow the local node to update only its own local data. The example in Figure 19.16 shows that North American users can update customers with customer IDs between `1` and `3000`, whereas Asian users can update customers with customer IDs between `3001` and `9000`.

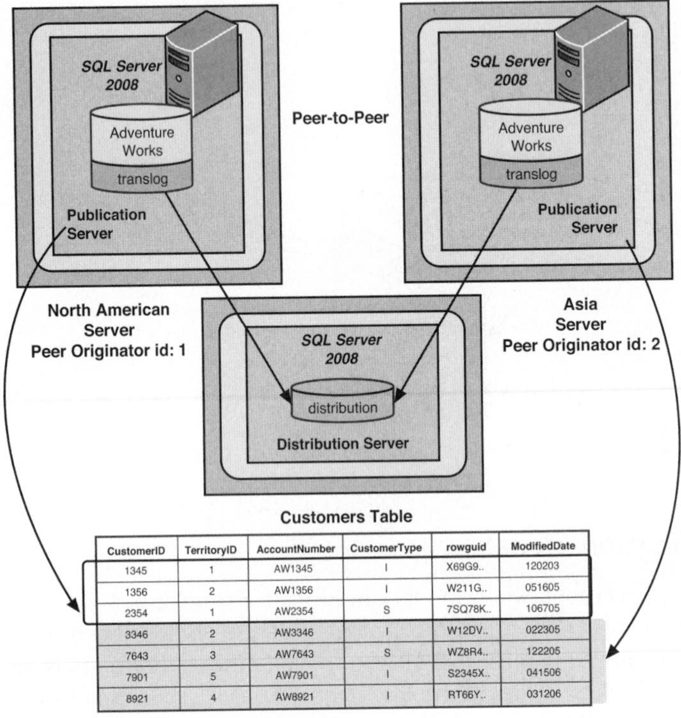

FIGURE 19.16 Peer-to-peer replication.

Subscriptions

A *subscription* is essentially a formal request and registration of that request for data that is being published. By definition, you subscribe to all articles of a publication.

When a subscription is being set up, you have the option of either having the data "pushed" to the subscriber server or "pulling" the data to the subscription server when it is needed. This is referred to as either a *push subscription* or *pull subscription*.

As shown in Figure 19.17, a pull subscription is set up and managed by the subscription server. The biggest advantage here is that pull subscriptions allow the system administrators of the subscription servers to choose what publications they will receive and when they receive them. With pull subscriptions, publishing and subscribing are separate acts and are not necessarily performed by the same user. In general, pull subscriptions are best when the publication does not require high security or if subscribing is done intermittently when the subscriber's data needs to be periodically brought up to date.

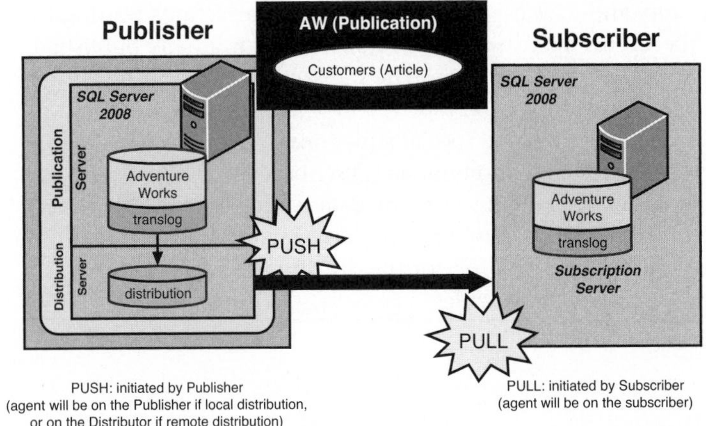

FIGURE 19.17 Push or pull subscriptions.

As you can also see in Figure 19.17, a push subscription is created and managed by the publication and distribution server. In effect, the distribution server and all the agents that do the work are pushing the publication to the subscription server. The advantage of using push subscriptions is that all the administration takes place in a central location (on the publication/distribution server side). In addition, publishing and subscribing happen at the same time, and many subscribers can be set up at once. This type of subscription is also recommended when dealing with heterogeneous subscribers because of the lack of pull capability on the subscription server side.

Anonymous Subscriptions (Pull Subscriptions)

It is possible to have "anonymous" subscriptions. An anonymous subscription is a special type of pull subscription that can be used in the following circumstances:

- When you are publishing data to the Internet
- When you have a huge number of subscribers
- When you don't want the overhead of maintaining extra information at the publisher or distributor
- When all the rules of your pull subscriptions apply to all your anonymous subscribers

Normally, information about all the subscribers, including performance data, is stored on the distribution server. Therefore, if you have a large number of subscribers or you do not want to track detailed information about the subscribers, you might want to allow anonymous subscriptions to a publication. Then little is kept at the distribution server, but it then becomes the responsibility of the subscriber to initiate the subscription and to keep synchronized.

The Distribution Database

The distribution database is a special type of database installed on the distribution server. This database, which is as a store-and-forward database, holds all transactions waiting to be distributed to any subscribers. This database receives transactions from any published databases that have designated it as their distributor. The transactions are held here until they are sent to the subscribers successfully. After a period of time, these transactions are purged from the distribution database. In some special situations, the transactions might not be purged for a longer period, enabling anonymous subscribers ample time to synchronize. The distribution database is the heart of the data replication facility. As you can see in Figure 19.18, the distribution database has several `MS` tables, such as `MSarticles`. These tables contain all the necessary information for the distribution server to fulfill the distribution role. Following are some of these tables:

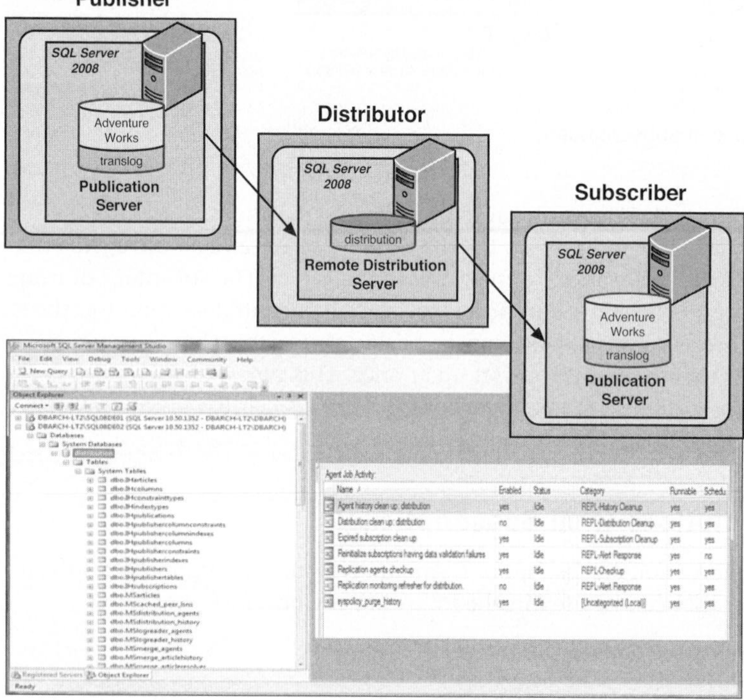

FIGURE 19.18 Tables of the distribution database and the distribution agents.

- **All the different publishers who will use this distribution server**—Stored in the `MSpublisher_databases` and `MSpublication_access` tables.
- **The publications and articles that will be distributed**—Stored in the `MSpublications` and `MSarticles` tables.
- **The complete information for all the distribution agents to perform their tasks**—Stored in the `MSdistribution_agents` table.
- **The complete information of the executions of these agents**—Stored in the `MSdistribution_history` table.

- **The subscribers**—Stored in `MSsubscriber_info`, `MSsubscriptions`, and other related tables.
- **Any errors that occur during replication and synchronization states**—Stored in `MSrepl_errors`, `MSsync_state`, and related tables.
- **The actual commands and transactions that are to be replicated**—Stored in the `MSrepl_commands` and `MSrepl_transactions` tables.
- **Heterogeneous (non-SQL Server) publishers' or subscribers' information**—Kept in the tables whose names begin with `IH`, such as `IHpublishers`, that will contain one row for each non-SQL Server publisher for which this distribution server distributes information.

Replication Agents

SQL Server utilizes replication agents to do different tasks during the replication process. These agents are constantly waking up at some frequency and fulfilling specific jobs. As you can see in Figure 19.19, several replication agent categories are listed under the Job Activity Monitor when you expand the SQL Server Agents branch (SQL Server Agent, Jobs, Job Activity Monitor branch).

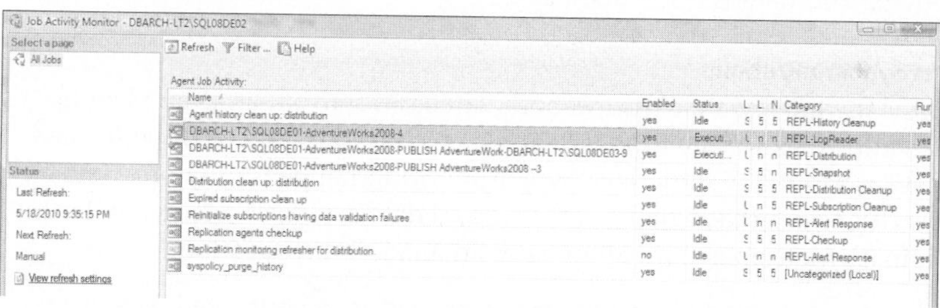

FIGURE 19.19 Replication agent jobs. Replication job category entries are prefixed with **REPL-**.

Here are the main replication agent categories:

- Snapshot Agent
- Log Reader Agent
- Distribution Agent
- Merge Agent (for updating subscribers)
- History Cleanup Agent
- Distribution Cleanup Agent
- Expired Subscription Cleanup Agent

- Reinitialize Subscriptions Having Data Validation Failures Agent
- Replication Monitoring Refresher for Distribution Agent
- Replication Agent Cleanup Agent

The Snapshot Agent

The snapshot agent is responsible for preparing the schema and initial data files of published tables and stored procedures, storing the snapshot on the distribution server, and recording information about the synchronization status in the distribution database. Each publication has its own snapshot agent that runs on the distribution server. It takes on the name of the publication within the publishing database within the machine on which it executes (that is, *[Machine]*`[Publishing database][Publication Name]`).

Figure 19.19 shows what this snapshot agent looks like under the SQL Server Agent, Job Activity Monitor branch in SQL Server Management Studio (SSMS). The snapshot agent (REPL-Snapshot category name) is named `DBARCH-LT2\SQL08DE01-AdventureWorks2008-PUBLISH AdventureWorks2008 - Tra-1`. In addition, these agents can be referenced from the Replication Monitor option (when you launch the Replication Monitor by right-clicking from the Replication branch in SQL Server Management Studio). Most often you are likely to use the SQL Server Agent path to these agents though.

It's worth noting that the snapshot agent might not even be used if the initialization of the subscriber's schema and data is done manually.

The Snapshot Agent Synchronization

The snapshot agent is the process that ensures both databases start on an even playing field. This process is known as *synchronization*. The synchronization process is performed whenever a publication has a new subscriber. Synchronization happens only one time for each new subscriber. It ensures that database schema and data are exact replicas on both servers. After the initial synchronization, all updates are made via replication.

When a new server subscribes to a publication, synchronization is performed. When synchronization begins, a copy of the table schema is copied to a file with the `.sch` extension. This file contains all the information necessary to create the table and any indexes on the tables, if they are requested. Next, a copy is made of the data in the table to be synchronized and written to a file (or several files) with the `.bcp` extension. The data file is a BCP, or bulk copy file. Both files are stored in the temporary working directory on the distribution server.

After the synchronization process has started and the data files have been created, any inserts, updates, and deletes are stored in the distribution database. These changes are not replicated to the subscription database until the synchronization process is complete.

When the synchronization process starts, only new subscribers are affected. Any subscriber that has been synchronized already and has been receiving modifications is unaffected. The synchronization set is applied to all servers waiting for initial synchronization. After the schema and data have been re-created, all transactions that have been stored in the distribution server are sent to the subscriber.

When you set up a subscription, it is possible to manually load the initial snapshot onto the server. This is known as *manual synchronization*. For extremely large databases, it is frequently easier to dump the database and then reload the database on the subscription server. If you load the snapshot this way, SQL Server assumes that the databases are already synchronized and automatically begins sending data modifications.

Snapshot Agent Processing

Figure 19.20 shows the details of the snapshot agent execution for a typical push subscription. You can see the execution history by simply right-clicking the snapshot job and choosing View History.

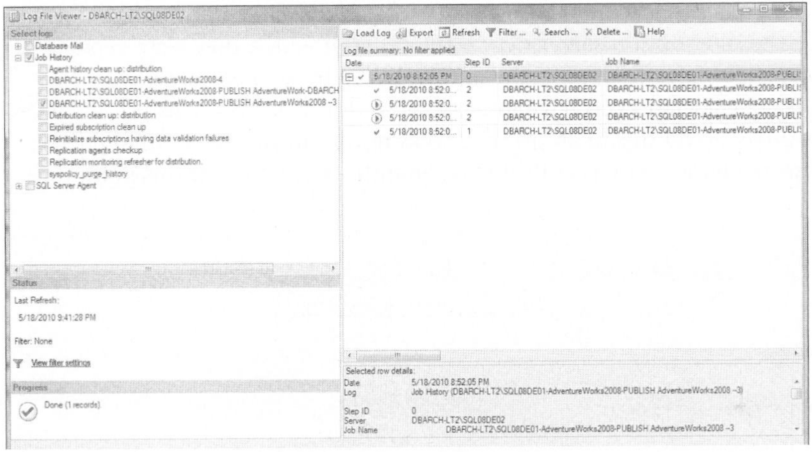

FIGURE 19.20 Snapshot agent execution job history.

The following sequence of tasks occurs with the snapshot agent:

1. The snapshot agent is initialized. This initialization can be immediate or at a designated time in the company's nightly processing window.
2. The agent connects to the publisher.
3. The agent generates schema files with the `.sch` file extension for each article in the publication. These schema files are written to a temporary working directory on the distribution server. These are the create table statements and such that will be used to create all objects needed on the subscription server side. They exist only for the duration of the snapshot processing.
4. All the tables in the publication are locked (held). The lock is required to ensure that no data modifications are made during the snapshot process.
5. The agent extracts a copy of the data in the publication and writes it to the temporary working directory on the distribution server. If all the subscribers are SQL Server machines, the data is written using a SQL Server native format, with the `.bcp` file extension. If you are replicating to databases other than SQL Server, the data is stored in standard text files with the `.txt` file extension. The `.sch` file and `.txt`

files/`.bmp` files are known as a *synchronization set*. Every table or article has a synchronization set.

CAUTION

It's important to make sure you have enough disk space on the drive that contains the temporary working directory. The snapshot data files will potentially be huge, and this size is the most common reason for snapshot failure.

6. As you can see in Figure 19.21, the agent executes the object creations and bulk copy processing at the subscription server side in the order in which they were generated (or it skips the object creation part if the objects have already been created on the subscription server side and you have indicated this during setup). This process takes awhile, so it is best to do this in an off time so as not to impact the normal processing day. Network connectivity is critical here. Snapshots often fail at this point.

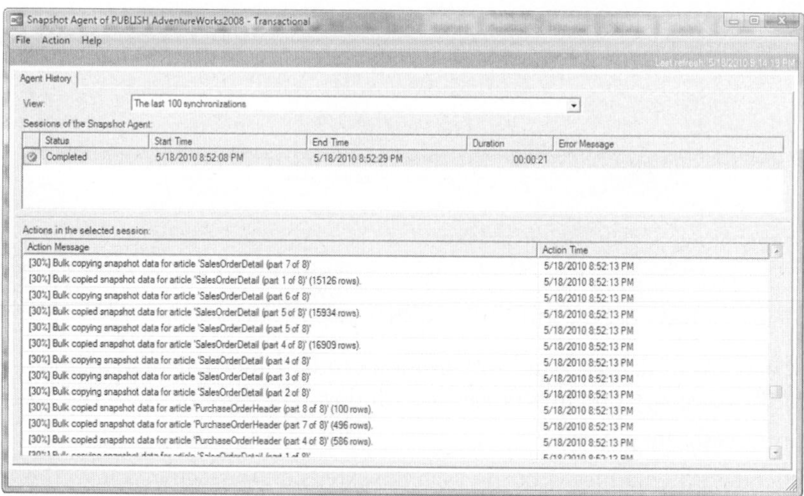

FIGURE 19.21 Snapshot agent delivering the snapshot to the subscriber (most recent operation on the top).

7. The snapshot agent posts the fact that a snapshot has occurred and what articles/publications were part of the snapshot to the distribution database. This is the only information sent to the distribution database.
8. When all the synchronization sets are finished being executed, the agent releases the locks on all the tables of this publication. The snapshot is now considered finished.

The Log Reader Agent

The log reader agent is responsible for moving transactions marked for replication from the transaction log of the published database to the distribution database. Each database published using transactional replication has its own log reader agent that runs on the distribution server. It is easy to find because it takes on the name of the publishing database whose transaction log it is reading (*[Machine name][Publishing DB name]*) and the REPL-LogReader category. Figure 19.19 shows the log reader agent (REPL-LogReader category name) for the AdventureWorks2008 database. It is named DBARCH-LT2\SQL08DE01-AdventureWorks2008-4.

After initial synchronization has taken place, the log reader agent begins to move transactions from the publication server to the distribution server. All actions that modify data in a database are logged to the transaction log in that database. This log is used not only in the automatic recovery process, but also in the replication process. When an article is created for publication and the subscription is activated, all entries about that article are marked in the transaction log. For each publication in a database, a log reader agent reads the transaction log and looks for any marked transactions. When the log reader agent finds a change in the log, it reads the changes and converts them to SQL statements that correspond to the action taken in the article. The SQL statements are then stored in a table on the distribution server, waiting to be distributed to subscribers.

Because replication is based on the transaction log, several changes are made in the way the transaction log works. During normal processing, any transaction that has either been successfully completed or rolled back is marked inactive. When you are performing replication, completed transactions are not marked inactive until the log reader process has read them and sent them to the distribution server.

Truncating and fast bulk-copying into a table are nonlogged processes. In tables marked for publication, you cannot perform nonlogged operations unless you temporarily turn off replication.

NOTE

One of the major changes in the transaction log comes when you have the Truncate Log on Checkpoint option turned on. When this option is on, SQL Server truncates the transaction log every time a checkpoint is performed, which can be as often as every several seconds. With replication, the inactive portion of the log is not truncated until the log reader process has read the transaction.

The Distribution Agent

A distribution agent moves transactions and snapshot jobs held in the distribution database out to the subscribers. This agent isn't created until a push subscription is defined for a subscriber. The distribution agent takes on the name of the publication database along with the subscriber information (*[Machine name][Publication DB name][Subscriber machine name]*). If you look back at Figure 19.19, you see a distribution agent (the *REPL-Distribution category* name) for the AdventureWorks2008 database to a subscriber. It is named `DBARCH-LT2\SQL08DE01--AdventureWorks2008 - PUBLISH AdventureWork - DBARCH-LT2\SQL08DE03-9`, where `SQL08DE01` is the publisher and `SQL08DE03` is the subscriber.

Those not set up for immediate synchronization share a distribution agent that runs on the distribution server. Pull subscriptions, to either snapshot or transactional publications, have a distribution agent that runs on the subscriber. Merge publications do not have a distribution agent at all. Rather, they rely on the merge agent, discussed next.

In transactional replication, the transactions have been moved into the distribution database, and the distribution agent either pushes out the changes to the subscribers or pulls them from the distributor, depending on how the servers are set up. All actions that change data on the publishing server are applied to the subscribing servers in the same order they were incurred. Figure 19.22 shows the latest history of the distribution agent and the total duration of the current subscription (11:20:56:4830000 hours, minutes, seconds, milliseconds in this example).

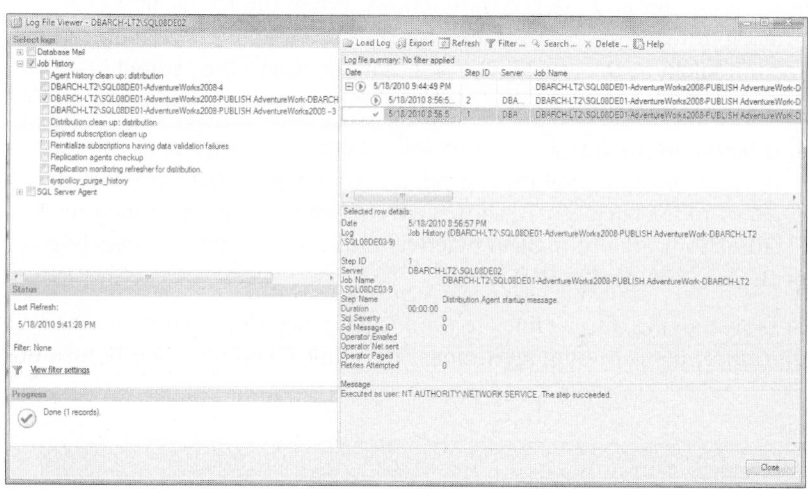

FIGURE 19.22 Distribution agent job history.

The Merge Agent

When you are dealing with merge publications, the merge agent moves and reconciles incremental data changes that occur after the initial snapshot was created. Each merge publication has a merge agent that connects to the publishing server and the subscribing server and updates both as changes are made. In a full merge scenario, the agent first uploads all changes from the subscriber where the generation is `0` or greater than the last generation sent to the publisher. The agent gathers the rows in which changes were made, and the rows without conflicts are applied to the publishing database.

A conflict can arise when changes are made at both the publishing server and subscription server to a particular row(s) of data. A conflict resolver handles these conflicts. Conflict resolvers are associated with an article in the publication definition. These conflict resolvers are sets of rules or custom scripts that can handle any complex conflict situation that might occur. The agent then reverses the process by downloading any changes from the publisher to the subscriber. Push subscriptions have merge agents that run on the publication server, whereas pull subscriptions have merge agents that run on the subscription server. Snapshot and transactional publications do not use merge agents.

Other Specialized Agents

In Figure 19.19, you can see that several other agents have been set up to do house cleaning around the replication configuration:

- **Agent history clean up: Distribution**—This agent clears out agent history from the distribution database every 10 minutes (by default). Depending on the size of the distribution, you might want to vary the frequency of this agent.
- **Distribution clean up: Distribution**—This agent clears out replicated transactions from the distribution database every 72 hours by default. This agent is used for snapshot and transactional publications only. If the volume of transactions is high, the frequency of this agent should be adjusted downward so you don't have too large of a distribution database. However, the frequency of synchronization with subscribers drives this frequency adjustment.
- **Expired subscription clean up**—This agent detects and removes expired subscriptions from the published databases. As part of the subscription setup, an expiration date is set. This agent usually runs once per day by default. You don't need to change this frequency.
- **Reinitialize subscriptions having data validation failures**—This agent is manually invoked. It is not on a schedule, but it could be. It automatically detects the subscriptions that failed data validation and marks them for re-initialization. This can then potentially lead to a new snapshot being applied to a subscriber that had data validation failures.
- **Replication monitoring refresher for distribution**—Microsoft SQL Server Replication Monitor is designed to efficiently monitor a large number of computers. The queries that Replication Monitor uses to perform calculations and gather data are cached and refreshed on a periodic basis. Caching reduces the number of queries and calculations required as you view different pages in Replication Monitor and allows monitoring to scale well for multiple users. Cache refresh is handled by the Replication monitoring refresher for distribution agent. This job runs continuously,

but the cache refresh schedule is based on waiting a certain amount of time after the previous refresh:

If there were agent history changes since the cache was last created, the wait time is a minimum of 4 seconds or the amount of time taken to create the previous cache.

If there were no agent history changes since the cache was last created, the wait time is a maximum of 30 seconds or the amount of time taken to create the previous cache. You don't need to change this frequency.

- **Replication agents checkup**—This agent detects replication agents that are not actively logging history. This checkup is critical because debugging replication errors is often dependent on an agent's history that has been logged.

Planning for SQL Server Data Replication

You must consider many factors when choosing a method to distribute data. Your business requirements determine which is the right method for you. In general, you need to understand the timing and latency of your data, its independence at each site, and your specific need to filter or partition the data.

Autonomy, Timing, and Latency of Data

Distributed data implementations can be accomplished using a few different facilities in Microsoft: Integration Services (IS), Distributed Transaction Coordinator (DTC), and Data Replication. The trick is to match the right facility to the type of data distribution you need to get done.

In some applications, such as online transaction processing and inventory control systems, data must be synchronized at all times. This requirement, called *immediate transactional consistency*, was known as tight consistency in previous versions of SQL Server.

SQL Server implements immediate transactional consistency data distribution in the form of two-phase commit processing. A *two-phase commit*, sometimes known as *2PC*, ensures that transactions are committed on all servers, or the transaction is rolled back on all servers. This ensures that all data on all servers is 100% in sync at all times. One of the main drawbacks of immediate transactional consistency is that it requires a high-speed LAN to work. This type of solution might not be feasible for large environments with many servers because occasional network outages can occur. These types of implementations can be built with DTC and IS.

In other applications, such as decision support and report generation systems, 100% data synchronization all the time is not terribly important. This requirement, called *latent transactional consistency*, was known as loose consistency in previous versions of SQL Server.

Latent transactional consistency is implemented in SQL Server via data replication. Replication allows data to be updated on all servers, but the process is not a simultaneous one. The result is "real-enough-time" data. This is known as latent transactional consistency because a lag exists between the data updated on the main server and the replicated data. In this scenario, if you could stop all data modifications from occurring on all servers, all the servers would eventually have the same data. Unlike the two-phase consistency model, replication works over both LANs and WANs, as well as slow or fast links.

When planning a distributed application, you must consider the effect of one site's operation on another. This is known as *site autonomy*. A site with complete autonomy can continue to function without being connected to any other site. A site with no autonomy cannot function without being connected to all other sites. For example, applications that utilize two-phase commits rely on all other sites being able to immediately accept changes sent to them. In the event that any one site is unavailable, no transactions on any server can be committed. In contrast, sites using merge replication can be completely disconnected from all other sites and continue to work effectively, not guaranteeing data consistency. Luckily, some solutions combine both high data consistency and site autonomy.

Methods of Data Distribution

After you have determined the amount of transactional latency and site autonomy needed, based on your business requirements, you need to select the data distribution method that corresponds. Each different type of data distribution has a different amount of site autonomy and latency. With these distributed data systems, you can choose from several methods:

- **Distributed transactions**—Distributed transactions ensure that all sites have the same data at all times. You pay a certain amount of overhead cost to maintain this consistency. (We do not discuss this nondata replication method here.)
- **Transactional replication with updating subscribers**—Users can change data at the local location, and those changes are applied to the source database at the same time. The changes are then eventually replicated to other sites. This type of data distribution combines replication and distributed transactions because data is changed at both the local site and source database.
- **Peer-to-peer replication**—A variation on the Transactional replication with updating subscribers theme is peer-to-peer replication, which is essentially full transactional replication between two (or more) sites, but is publisher-to-publisher (not update subscriber). There is no hierarchy—publisher (parent) and subscriber (child).
- **Transactional replication**—With transactional replication, data is changed only at the source location and is sent out to the subscribers. Because data is changed at only a single location, conflicts cannot occur.
- **Snapshot replication with updating subscribers**—This method is much like transactional replication with updating subscribers; users can change data at the local location, and those changes are applied to the source database at the same time. The entire changed publication is then replicated to all subscribers. This type of replication provides higher autonomy than transactional replication.

- **Snapshot replication**—A complete copy of the publication is sent out to all subscribers. This includes both changed and unchanged data.
- **Merge replication**—All sites make changes to local data independently and then update the publisher. It is possible for conflicts to occur, but they can be resolved.

SQL Server Replication Types

Microsoft has narrowed the field to three major types of data replication approaches within SQL Server: snapshot, transactional, and merge. Each replication type applies to only a single publication. However, it is possible to have multiple replication types per database.

Snapshot Replication

Snapshot replication makes an image of all the tables in a publication at a single moment in time and then moves that entire image to the subscribers. Little overhead on the server is incurred because snapshot replication does not track data modifications as the other forms of replication do. It is possible, however, for snapshot replication to require large amounts of network bandwidth, especially if the articles being replicated are large. Snapshot replication is the easiest form of replication to set up and is used primarily with smaller tables for which subscribers do not have to perform updates. An example of this might be a phone list that is to be replicated to many subscribers. This phone list is not considered to be critical data, and the frequency of it being refreshed is more than enough to satisfy all its users.

The primary agents used for snapshot replication are the snapshot agent and distribution agent.

- The snapshot agent creates files that contain the schema of the publication and the data. The files are temporarily stored in the snapshot folder of the distribution server, and then the distribution jobs are recorded in the distribution database.
- The distribution agent is responsible for moving the schema and data from the distributor to the subscribers.

A few other agents are also used; they deal with other needed tasks for replication, such as cleanup of files and history. In snapshot replication, after the snapshot has been delivered to all the subscribers, these agents delete the associated `.bcp` and `.sch` files from the distributor's working directory.

Transactional Replication

Transactional replication is the process of capturing transactions from the transaction log of the published database and applying them to the subscription databases. With SQL Server transactional replication, you can publish all or part of a table, views, or one or more stored procedures as an article. All data updates are then stored in the distribution database and sent and applied to any number of subscribing servers. Obtaining these updates from the publishing database's transaction log is extremely efficient. No direct reading of tables is required except during initial snapshot, and only the minimal amount of traffic is generated over the network. This has made transactional replication the most often used method.

As data changes are made, they are propagated to the other sites at nearly real-time; you determine the frequency of this propagation. Because changes are usually made only at the publishing server, data conflicts are avoided for the most part. As an example, push subscribers usually receive updates from the publisher in a minute or less, depending on the speed and availability of the network. Subscribers also can be set up for pull subscriptions. This capability is useful for disconnected users who are not connected to the network at all times.

The primary agents used for transactional replication are the snapshot agent, log agent, and distribution agent:

- The snapshot agent creates files that contain the schema of the publication and the data. The files are stored in the snapshot folder of the distribution server, and the distribution jobs are recorded in the distribution database.
- The log reader agent monitors the transaction log of the database that it is set up to service. Each database published has its own log reader agent set up for replication, and it will copy the transactions from the transaction log of that published database into the distribution database.
- The distribution agent is responsible for moving the schema and data from the distributor to the subscribers for the initial synchronization and then moving all the subsequent transactions from the published database to each subscriber as they come in. These transactions are stored in the distribution database for a certain length of time and are eventually purged.

A few other agents deal with the other housekeeping issues surrounding data replication, such as schema files cleanup, history cleanup, and transaction cleanup.

Merge Replication

Merge replication involves getting the publisher and all subscribers initialized and then allowing data to be changed at all sites involved in the merge replication at the publisher and at all subscribers. All these changes to the data are subsequently merged at certain intervals so that, again, all copies of the database have identical data.

Occasionally, data conflicts have to be resolved. The publisher does not always win in a conflict resolution. Instead, the winner is determined by whatever criteria you establish.

The primary agents used for merge replication are the snapshot agent and merge agent:

- The snapshot agent creates files that contain the schema of the publication and the data. The files are stored in the snapshot folder of the distribution server, and the distribution jobs are recorded in the distribution database. This is essentially the same behavior as with all other types of replication methods.

- The merge agent takes the initial snapshot and applies it to all the subscribers. It then reconciles all changes made on all the servers, based on the rules you configure.

Preparing for Merge Replication

When you set up a table for merge replication, SQL Server performs three schema changes to the database. First, it must either identify or create a unique column for each row that will be replicated. This column is used to identify the different rows across all the different copies of the table. If the table already contains a column with the `ROWGUIDCOL` property, SQL Server automatically uses that column for the row identifier. If not, SQL Server adds a column called `rowguid` to the table. SQL Server also places an index on this `rowguid` column.

Next, SQL Server adds triggers to the table to track changes that occur to the data in the table and record them in the merge system tables. The triggers can track changes at either the row or column level, depending on how you set it up. SQL Server supports multiple triggers of the same type on a table, so merge triggers do not interfere with user-defined triggers on the table.

Finally, SQL Server adds new system tables to the database that contains the replicated tables. The `MSMerge_contents` and `MSMerge_tombstone` tables track the updates, inserts, and deletes. These tables rely on `rowguid` to track which rows have actually been changed.

The merge agent is responsible for moving changed data from the site where it was changed to all other sites in the replication scenario. When a row is updated, the triggers added by SQL Server fire off and update the new system tables, setting the generation column equal to `0` for the corresponding `rowguid`. When the merge agent runs, it collects the data from the rows where the generation column is `0` and then resets the generation values to values higher than the previous generation numbers. This allows the merge agent to look for data that has already been shared with other sites without having to look through all the data. The merge agent then sends the changed data to the other sites.

When the data reaches the other sites, the data is merged with existing data according to rules you have defined. These rules are flexible and highly extensible. The merge agent evaluates existing and new data and resolves conflicts based on priorities or which data was changed first. Another available option is that you can create custom resolution strategies using the Component Object Model (COM) and custom stored procedures. After conflicts have been handled, synchronization occurs to ensure that all sites have the same data.

The merge agent identifies conflicts using the `MSMerge_contents` table. In this table, a column called `lineage` is used to track the history of changes to a row. The agent updates the `lineage` value whenever a user makes changes to the data in a row. The entry into this column is a combination of a site identifier and the last version of the row created at the site. As the merge agent is merging all the changes that have occurred, it examines each site's information to see whether a conflict has occurred. If a conflict has occurred, the agent initiates conflict resolution based on the criteria mentioned earlier.

Basing the Replication Design on User Requirements

As mentioned earlier, business requirements drive your replication configuration and method. In addition, nailing down all the details of the business requirements is the hardest part of a data replication design process. After you have completed the requirements gathering, the replication design usually just falls into place from it easily. The requirements gathering is highly recommended to get a prototype up and running as quickly as possible to measure the effectiveness of one approach over the other. You must understand several key aspects to make the right design decisions, including the following:

- What is the number of sites, and what is the site autonomy in the scope (location)?
- Which sites have the master data (data ownership)?
- What is the data latency requirement (by site)?
- What types of data accesses are being made (by site)?
    - Reads
    - Writes
    - Updates
    - Deletes

  This information needs to include exactly what data and data subsets that drive filtering are needed for the data accesses (by site).
- What is the volume of activity/transactions, including the number of users (by site)?
- How many machines do you have to work with (by site)?
- What are the available processing power (CPU and memory) and disk space on each of these machines (by site)?
- What are the stability, speed, and saturation level of the network connections between machines (by site)?
- What is the dial-in, Internet, or other access mechanism requirement for the data?
- What potential subscriber or publisher database engines are involved?

Figure 19.23 shows the factors that contribute to replication designs and the possible data replication configuration that would best be used. It is only a partial table because of the numerous factors and many replication configuration options available. However, it gives a good idea of the general design approach described here. Perhaps 95% of user requirements can be classified fairly easily. The other 5% might take some imagination in determining the best overall solution. Depending on the requirements that need to be supported, you might even end up with a solution using something like database mirroring or other distribution techniques.

Data Access	Latency	Autonomy	Sites (locations)	Frequency	Network	Machines	Owner	Other	REPLICATION
Read Only Reporting	short	high	many	high	fast/ stable	1 server/site	1 OLTP site	Each site only needs regional data	**Central Publisher Transactional repl filter by region**
Read Only Reporting	long	high	many	low	fast/ stable	1 server/site	1 OLTP site	Each site only needs regional data	**Central Publisher Snapshot repl filter by region**
Read Mostly A few updates	short	high	< 10	medium	fast/ stable	1 server/site	1 OLTP site	Regional updates on one table	**Central Publisher Transactional repl Updating Subs**
Read Mostly A few updates	medium	high	< 10	medium	slow/ unreliab	1 server/site	All update	Regional update all tables	**Central Publisher Merge repl**
Read equal Equal updates	short	high	< 10	medium	fast/ stable	n server/site	All update	Regional update all tables	**Peer-to-Peer Transactional repl**
Inserts (new orders)	short	high	many	high	fast/ stable	1 server/site	n update sites	Each site only needs regional data	**Central Subscriber Transactional repl**
Hot/Warm Spare	Very short	high	< 2	high	fast/ stable	1 server/site	1 OLTP site	Fail-over	**Central Publisher Remote Distributor Transactional repl**

FIGURE 19.23 Replication design factors.

Data Characteristics

You need to analyze the underlying data types and characteristics thoroughly. Issues such as collation or character set and data sorting come into play. You must be aware of what they are set to on all nodes of your replication configuration. SQL Server 2008 does not convert the replicated data and might even mistranslate the data as it is replicated because it is impossible to map all characters between character sets. It is best to look up the character set "mapping chart" for SQL Server replication to all other data target environments. Most are covered well, but problems arise with certain data types, such as `image`, `timestamp`, and `identity`. Sometimes, using the Unicode data types at all sites is best for consistency. Following is a general list of issues to watch out for in this regard:

- Collation consistency across all nodes of replication.
- Time stamp column data in replication. It might not be what you think.
- `identity`, `uniqueidentifier`, and `guid` column behavior with data replication.
- `text` or `image` data types to heterogeneous subscribers.
- Missing or unsupported data types because of prior versions of SQL Server or heterogeneous subscribers as part of the replication configuration.

- Maximum row size limitations between merge replication and transactional replication.

Figure 19.24 lists further SQL Server 2008 replication object limitations.

Microsoft SQL Server 2008 Replication object	Maximum sizes/numbers (32-bit)	Maximum sizes/numbers (64-bit)
Articles (merge publication)	256	256
Articles (snapshot or transactional publication)	32,767	32,767
Columns in a table (merge publication)	246	246
Columns in a table (SQL Server snapshot or transactional publication)	1000	1000
Columns in a table (Oracle snapshot or transactional publication)	995	995
Bytes for a column used in a row filter (merge publication)	1024	1024
Bytes for a column used in a row filter (snapshot or transactional publication)	8000	8000

FIGURE 19.24 SQL Server 2008 replication object limitations.

NOTE

If you have triggers on your tables and you want them to be replicated along with your table, you might want to add the line of code `NOT FOR REPLICATION` so that the trigger code isn't executed redundantly on the subscriber side.

Setting Up Replication

In general, SQL Server 2008 data replication is exceptionally easy to set up via SQL Server Management Studio wizards. However, if you use the wizards, you need to be sure to generate SQL scripts for every phase of replication configuration. In a production environment, you are likely to rely heavily on scripts and not have the luxury of having much time to set up and break down production replication configurations via wizards. Generating SQL scripts also eases the setup/breakdown process in development, test, and user acceptance environments.

You always have to define any data replication configuration in the following order:

1. Create or enable a distributor to enable publishing.
2. Enable publishing. (A distributor must be designated for a publisher.)
3. Create a publication and define articles within the publication.
4. Define subscribers and subscribe to a publication.

Figure 19.25 shows SQL Server Management Studio Object Explorer with three separate server connections. These three servers represent a possible replication topology.

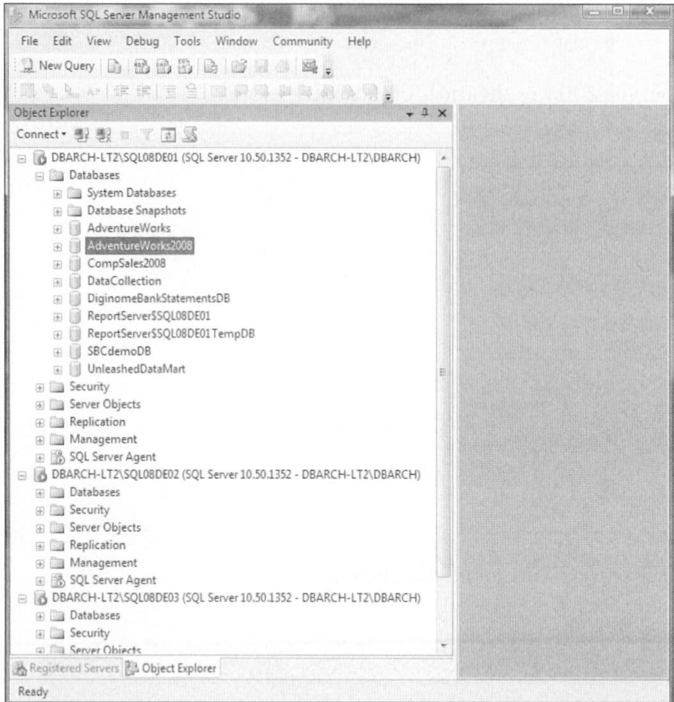

FIGURE 19.25 Three servers to be used in the replication topology (central publisher, remote distributor, and subscriber).

The following section takes you through the process of building up a typical central publisher/remote distribution data replication configuration. The following SQL Server named instances are used for different purposes (as shown in Figure 19.25):

- **Publisher**—A `SQL08DE01` named instance
- **Distributor**—A `SQL08DE02` named instance (REMOTE distributor)
- **Subscriber**—A `SQL08DE03` named instance

The following section highlights the different areas in SQL Server Management Studio that are needed to create this replication configuration.

Creating a Distributor and Enabling Publishing

Before setting up a publisher, you have to designate a distribution server to be used by that publisher. As discussed earlier, you can either configure the local server as the distribution server or choose a remote server as the distributor (not on the same machine as the publication server). You can configure the server as a distributor and publisher at the same time, or you can configure the server as a dedicated distributor on the remote server separately. In the sample topology described here, you start by creating a remote distributor separately so you can orient yourself to what is happening on each server in the topology as it is being built up. You are also able to enable a specific SQL Server instance as the publisher that will use this distributor (all in one wizard sequence). This method is very efficient.

Before you can configure replication, you must be a member of the `sysadmin` server role, so you should ensure that now. Then you use the following steps to configure a server as a distributor (remote distributor):

1. In SQL Server Management Studio, locate the `Replication` node under the server that will be the distributor (under the `SQL08DE02` named instance node). Right-click the `Replication` node and choose Configure Distribution. This starts you through the wizard, which provides three options:
    - Configure this server to be a distributor.
    - Configure this server to be both a publisher and distributor.
    - Configure this server to be a publisher that uses another server as its distributor.
2. When the wizard starts, click past the initial Configure Distribution Wizard splash page. Then choose the first radio button, which should say 'DBARCH-LT2\SQL08DE02' Will Act as Its Own Distributor (as shown in Figure 19.26). This designates this server as a distributor for one or more publishers. The distribution database and log are created here as well (and not on the publication server).

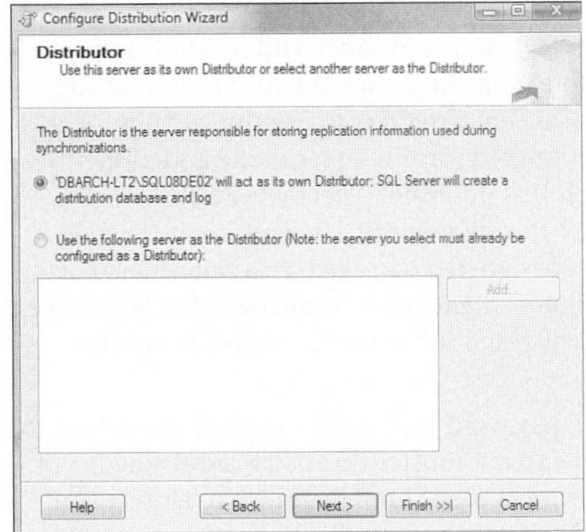

FIGURE 19.26 Configuring a separate distributor (REMOTE) wizard.

19

3. You are then asked how you want the replication agents to be started. Select the agents to be started automatically (the Yes option).
4. Next comes the location for the snapshot folder. Give it the proper network full pathname. Remember that potentially a large amount of data will be coming here, and it should be on a drive that can support the snapshot concept without filling up the drive.
5. When you are asked to configure the distribution database, select the default settings. Figure 19.27 shows all the distribution database name and location information.

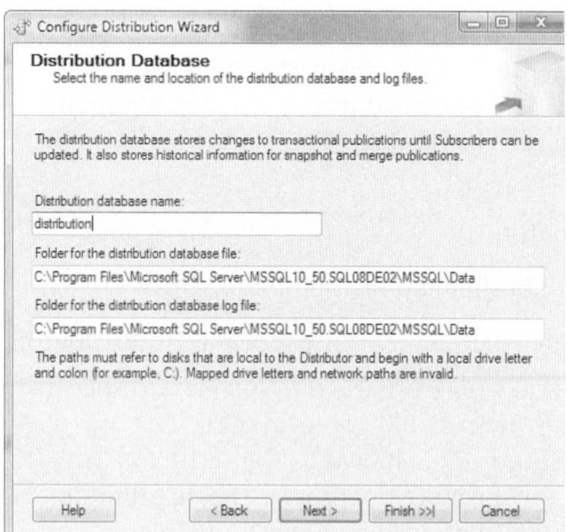

FIGURE 19.27 Specification of the distribution database name and location.

6. Identify the publisher if you know which SQL Server instance will be publishing the data that this distributor will distribute for. To do this, click the Add button at the bottom-left corner of the Publishers page to enable servers to use this distributor when they become publishers. You are prompted for the server name and authentication method for the distributor to reach this publisher. Specify `DBARCH-LT2\SQL08DE01` as a publisher that will use this distributor. The end result, as shown in Figure 19.28, is `DBARCH-LT2\SQL08DE01` designated (checked) as a publisher that will use this distribution database (distributor). Remember to uncheck the SQL Server named instance of the distribution server if you don't want to publish from that server (the `SQL08DE02` named instance).
7. Specify a distributor password. This is the password that will be used by publishers to connect to the distributor. You will be able to administer this password through SQL Server Management Studio directly. The wizard then summarizes what actions you want to take place, such as configure the distribution server or generate a script file with steps to configure distribution. Choose both. It's always good to have the scripts created now so you can start script-based configurations immediately. A

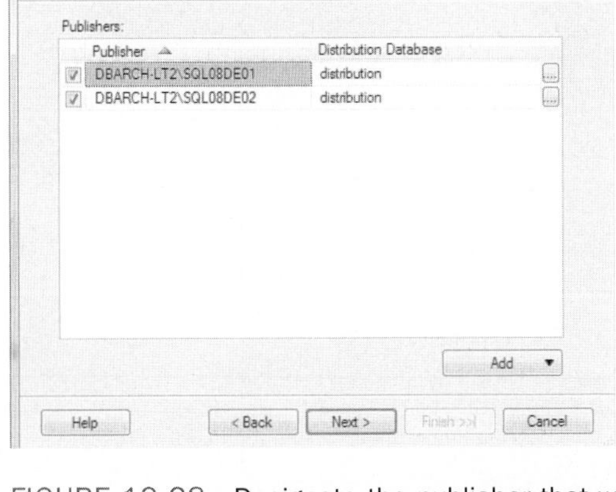

FIGURE 19.28 Designate the publisher that will use this remote distributor.

Complete the Wizard page is displayed, describing all the tasks that are about to happen, along with their configuration specifications. Figure19.29 show this summary.

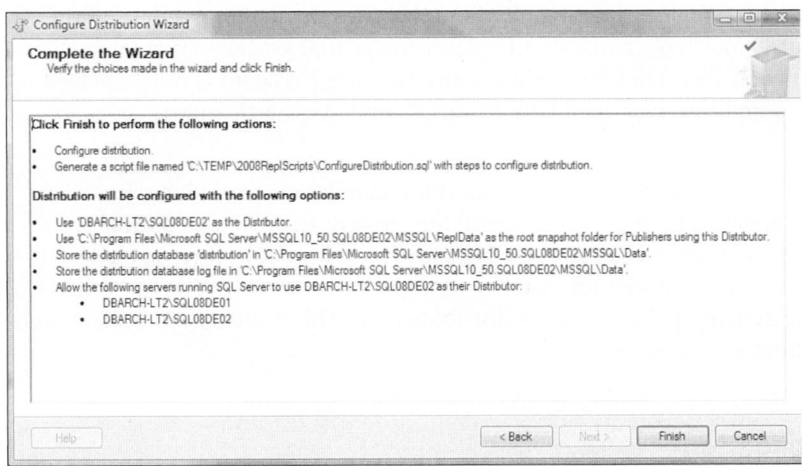

FIGURE 19.29 Completing the configuration of the distributor and enabling the publisher.

When you click Finish, several things begin to occur. First, a configuring dialog page comes up and spins its wheels through each step you have requested (as shown in Figure 19.30). A summary of steps, errors, and warnings is displayed on this page. When it completes, you can explore any issues (errors or warnings) by drilling down in the Report option (lower-right side of this dialog). Make sure you see Success after each step of this configuration.

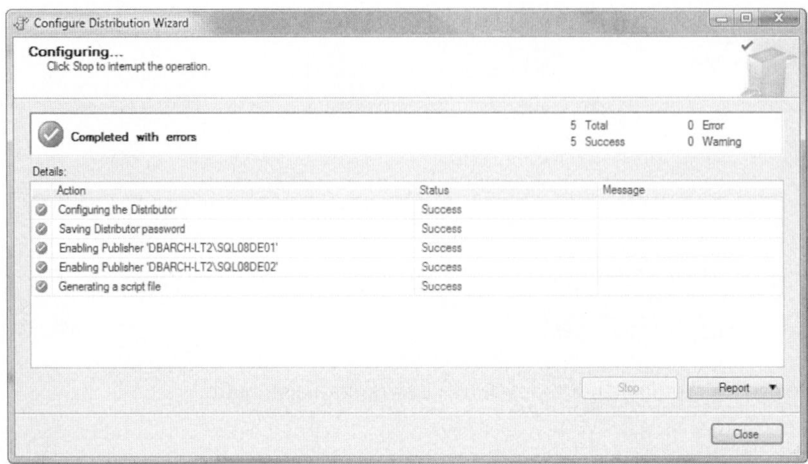

FIGURE 19.30 Configuring the distributor and enabling a publisher in progress.

Now is probably a good time to locate that distributor setup and enabling publication script and drop it into your replication administrator folder that you keep in a safe place. Figure 19.31 shows what this script looks like. Notice that the password is not displayed. The details of these scripts are described later in this chapter, in the "Scripting Replication" section.

When the distributor is configured and the distribution database is created, a series of replication agents (managed by SQL Server Agent) are created, with various duties, as described earlier in this chapter. Figure 19.32 shows the initial set of agents created on the distribution server (as seen from the Job Activity Monitor under the SQL Server Agent). No agents exist yet that actually publish data or distribute data. Those agents are created later, as you start publishing and subscribing.

Creating a Publication

When the distribution database has been created and publishing has been enabled on the server, you can create and configure a publication. In SQL Server Management Studio, you start by locating the `Replication` node under the publication server from which you want to publish data (the `DBARCH-LT2\SQL08DE01` named instance in this example). Figure 19.33 shows the program item option when you right-click the `Replication` node under what will be the publication server. As you can see, there are three options; one to create a new publication, one to create a new Oracle publication, and one to create a new subscription.

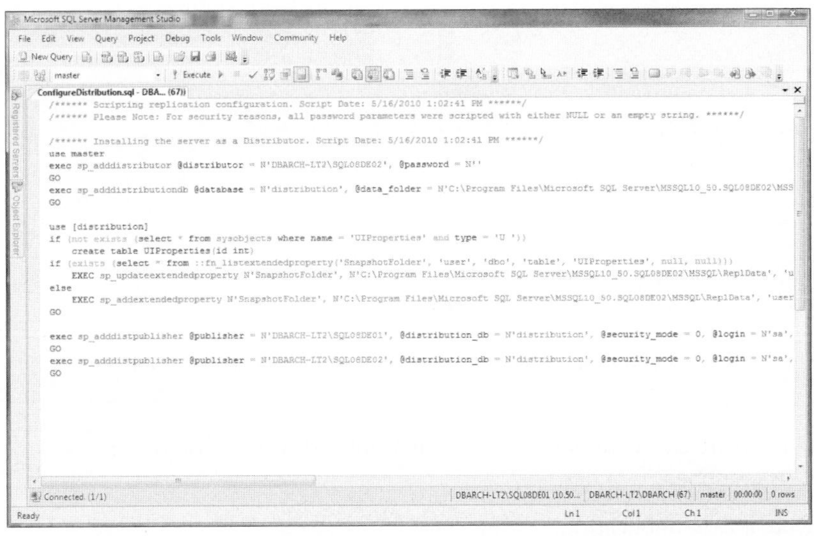

FIGURE 19.31 The script generated for creating the distributor and enabling a publisher.

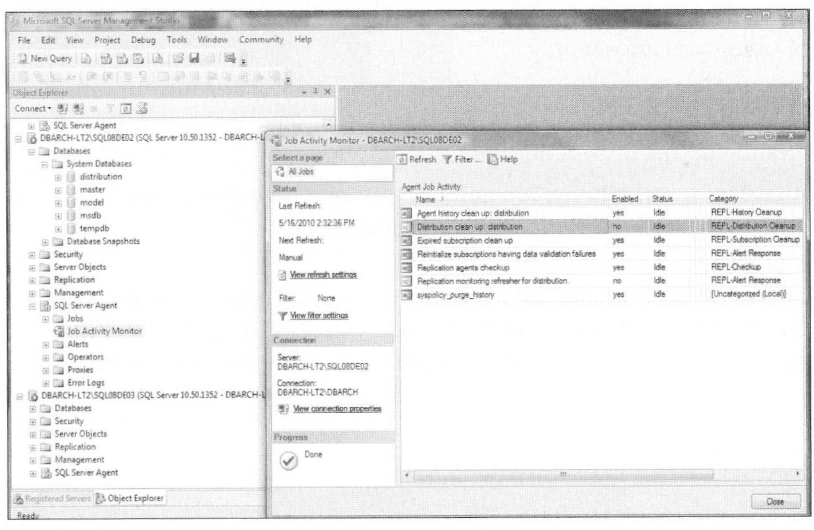

FIGURE 19.32 Initial replication agents on the distributor.

19

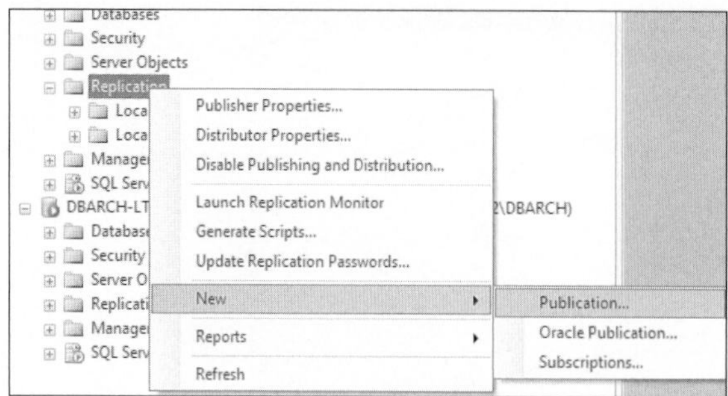

FIGURE 19.33 The New Publication item option on the server that will be the publisher.

You should choose to create a new publication (the first option). When you do, the New Publication Wizard is launched.

Here's how you create a new publication:

1. The first New Publication Wizard page outlines the two things that can be done with this wizard. The options are "Select the data and database objects you want to replicate" and "Filter the published data so that subscribers receive only the data they need." After this splash page, you need to specify how you want to distribute the data for this new publication. As you can see in Figure 19.34, you should use a remote distributor (the `DBARCH-LT2\SQL08DE02` named instance) to distribute data for this new publication you are defining.
2. When you are asked to provide a password that will be used to establish the administrative link to the distributor, supply it. It should be the same one you specified earlier when setting up the distribution server.
3. Identify the database on which you are going to set up a publication (see Figure 19.35). For this example, choose to create a publication on the `AdventureWorks2008` database.
4. Choose the type of replication method for this publication: Snapshot Publication, Transactional Publication, Transactional Publication with Updateable Subscriptions, or Merge Publication Method of Replication. For this example, select Transactional Publication.

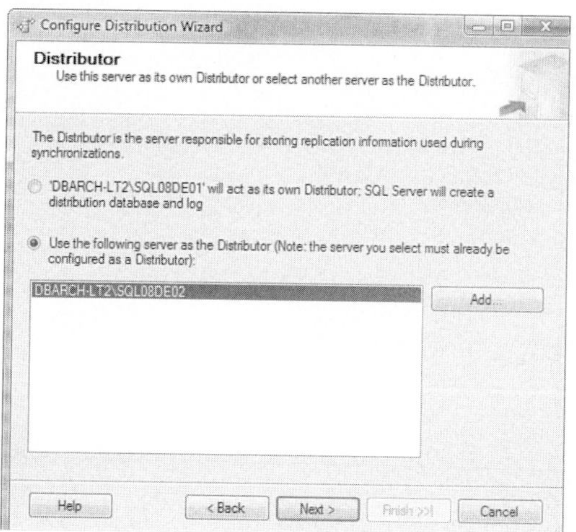

FIGURE 19.34 Specifying the remote distribution server for the new publication.

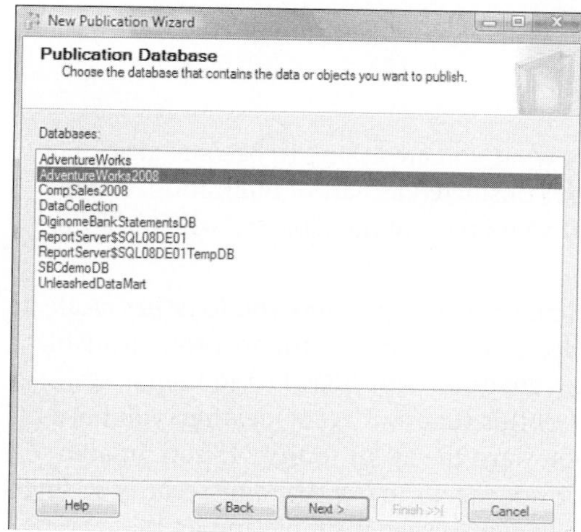

FIGURE 19.35 Choosing the database that contains the data or objects you want to publish.

5. Next, you are presented with the place where you specify what tables and other objects to publish. These will become your articles. You can specify filtering of any selected articles, where appropriate. To keep this simple, just choose the primary stored procedures, views, indexed views, user-defined functions, and tables of the `AdventureWorks2008` database for this publication. (You do not select any filtering at this time.) Figure 19.36 shows the Articles specification page. Also in Figure 19.36, you can view the article properties that dictate how all article objects should be handled by replication (via the Article Properties button in the upper-right corner of this wizard screen). An example of this is specifying the delete delivery format behavior for this publication (for all tables) to be Do Not Replication Delete Statements or Use Stored Procedures to Do the Deletes and not individual delete statements.

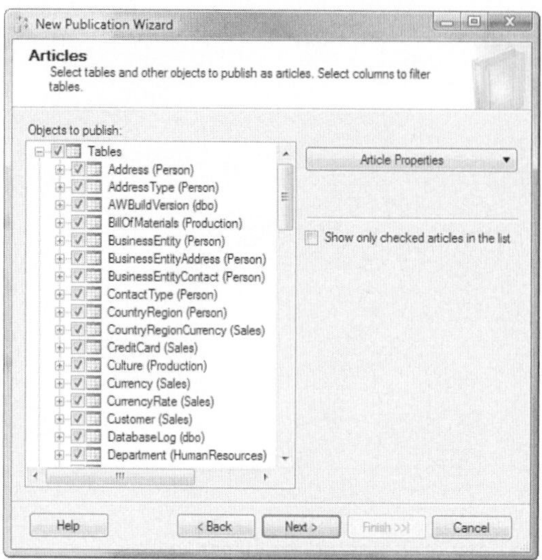

FIGURE 19.36 Choosing the tables and other objects that determine the articles to publish.

The next wizard screen carefully analyzes what you are asking to become articles and highlights any dependencies that must be considered as part of replication. A good example of an article issueis that indexed views require the tables to which they are bound to be part of the replication.

6. When the Snapshot Agent wizard configuration screen prompts you to either create a snapshot immediately or at some scheduled time and to keep the snapshot available to initialize subscriptions, select to create a snapshot immediately and keep it available to initialize the subscription. As part of this snapshot agent creation, you have to specify under what security credentials you want the agent security to run. In addition, you can specify if you want the log reader agent to use the same security settings as the snapshot agent. The rule of thumb here is to keep it simple and let these agents use the same security settings (as shown in Figure 19.37).
7. The wizard now has enough information to create the publication. When the wizard actions are summarized for you, choose to create the publication and generate a script file with all the steps to create the publication in it. Again, this script generation part is highly recommended. You certainly don't want to have to go through this wizard over and over. Once is enough.
8. When the summary of all choices made in the creation of a new publication is listed in the Complete the Wizard screen, name the publication appropriately. Your publication names should contain the type of publication method being used (for example, `Snapshot`, `Transactional`, `Merge`) and any other identifying qualifier that seems appropriate (usually reflecting the scope of the publication). Figure 19.38 shows this summary of actions and the publication name `PUBLISH AdventureWorks2008 - Transactional`.

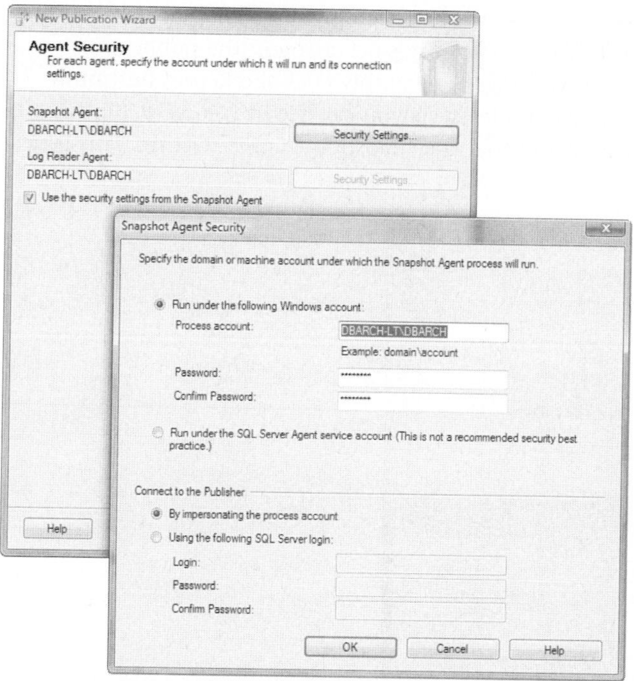

FIGURE 19.37 Agent security for snapshot agent and log reader agent.

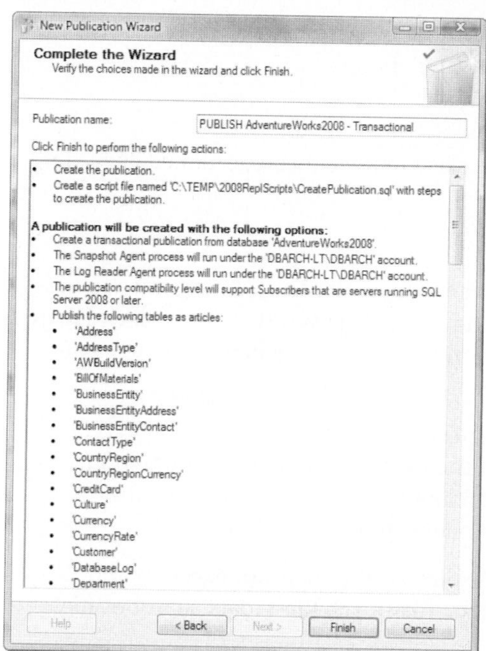

FIGURE 19.38 Publication action summary and naming the publication before it is created.

The actual creation of the publication is next. An action progress screen appears, showing each step (action) and indicating any errors or warnings occurring in the publication creation process. To view any errors or warnings, you simply click the Report button in the lower-right side after the processing completes. As you can see in Figure 19.39, this report lists, by name, all articles created and that the snapshot agent is starting. This is where all the initial action takes place.

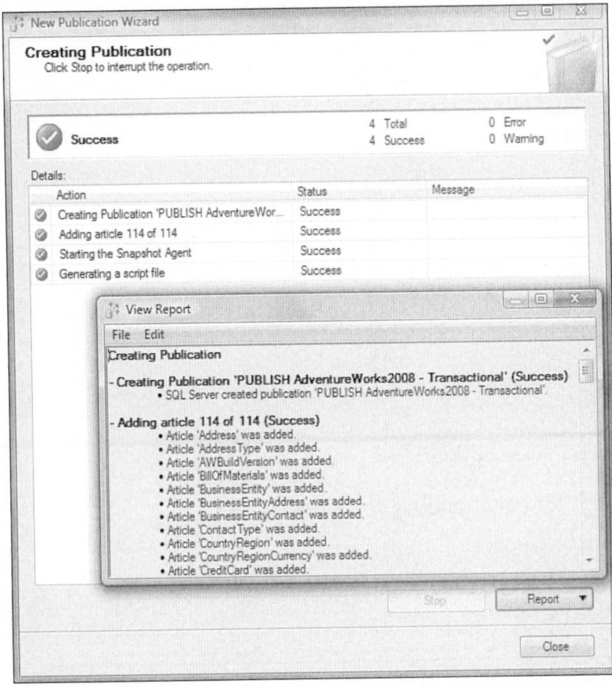

FIGURE 19.39 The publication steps and status, along with the report generated during this process.

As part of this process, several new agents (jobs) are added; they implement this publication using the designated distributor. There are no subscribers yet; they come later. Figure 19.40 shows the new jobs (agents) and publication entries. You are now ready to create subscriptions against this publication.

As you can see in Figure 19.41, if you launch Replication Monitor (from the `Replication` node under the publication server), you can see the newly created publication and its status, and you have access to any servers subscribing to it (none yet), along with the common replication jobs that are servicing this publication.

Because you chose to execute the snapshot immediately, the snapshot executes and utilizes the snapshot folder to generate the schema files (`.sch` files), data snapshot files

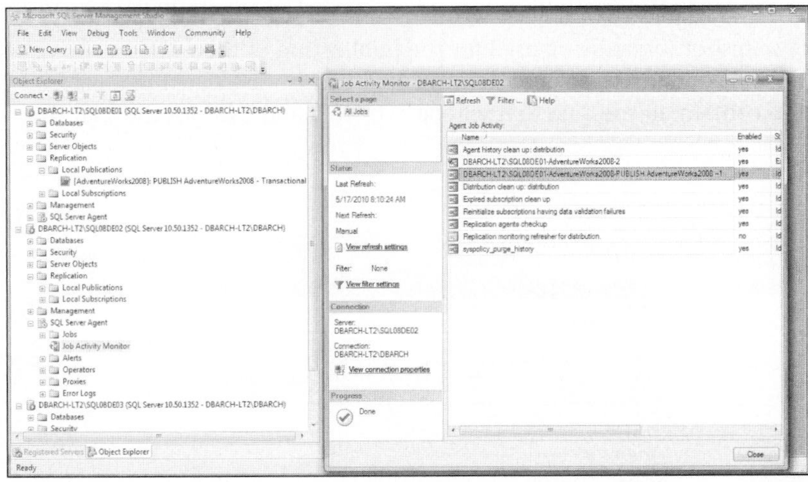

FIGURE 19.40 SQL Server Management Studio and the new publication agents (snapshot agent, distribution agent, and so on) and the new local publication.

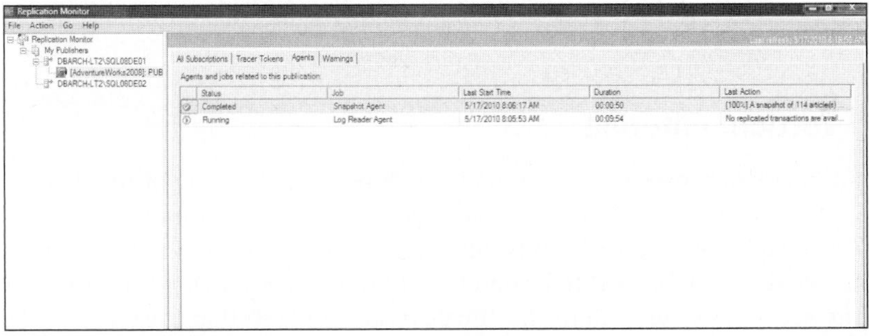

FIGURE 19.41 Replication Monitor, viewing the status of the newly created publication (from the publisher).

(`.bcp`), and so on to fully enable a subscription when one is created. Figure 19.42 shows the contents of the snapshot folder being used for the publication of the `AdventureWorks2008` publication. Remember that this folder must be located in a place that is big enough to contain all the data that will be extracted and used for the snapshot; plan ahead.

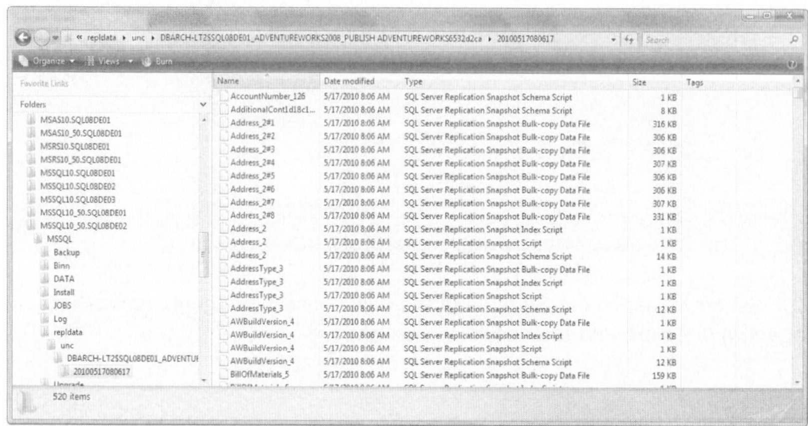

FIGURE 19.42 Contents of the snapshot folder produced for the publication.

Horizontal and Vertical Filtering

During the publication creation process, you could have done some filtering of the data, either horizontally or vertically (or both at the same time). The concept of filtering was covered earlier in this chapter. Figure 19.43 illustrates all you need to do to vertically filter (in terms of limiting what gets published to a subset of columns of a table). As you can see, you uncheck the `AccountNumber` column for the `Customer` table so that it isn't included in the article for that object in this publication. This might be done because account number information needs to be more tightly controlled within your company and shouldn't be part of what is viewed by any subscribing systems.

In addition, you can specify horizontal filters by using the Filter Rows option on a publication (publication properties). This allows you to specify horizontal filtering on any table you publish. Figure 19.44 shows a typical row filter on the `Customer` table that results in publishing North East Territory customers only (that is, those with `TerritoryID` values of `1` or `2`).

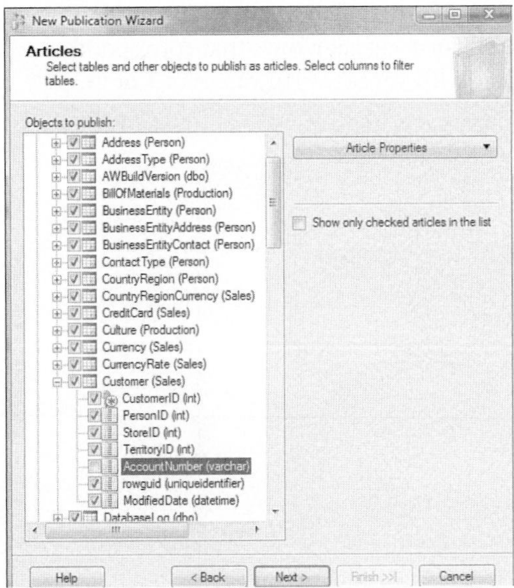

FIGURE 19.43 Specifying a vertical filter on the Customer table (limiting the columns to be published).

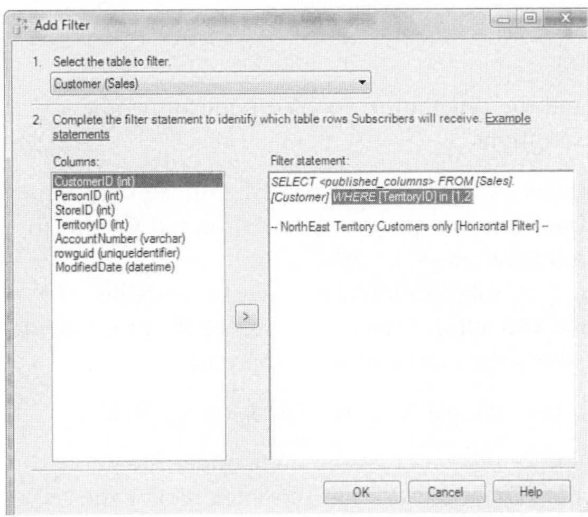

FIGURE 19.44 Specifying a horizontal filter on the **Customer** table (limiting the rows to be published).

Join filtering allows you to limit the rows you will publish, via join criteria, to another table. Figure 19.45 shows a complex join that filters `SalesOrderHeader` rows that correspond to North East Territory customers only (that is, those with `TerritoryID` values of `1` or `2`).

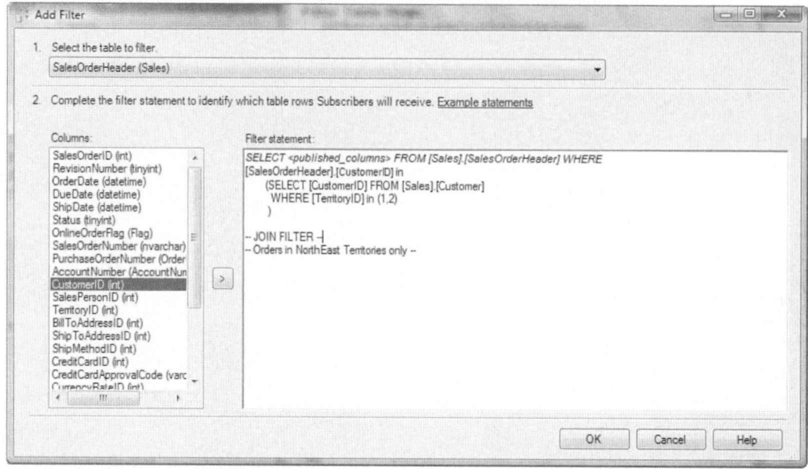

FIGURE 19.45 Specifying a join filter on the **SalesOrderHeader** table (limiting the sales rows that will be published by joining for the North East customers only).

Creating Subscriptions

Now that you have installed and configured the distributor, enabled publishing, and created a publication, you can create subscriptions.

Remember that two types of subscriptions can be created: push or pull. Pull subscriptions allow remote sites to subscribe to any publication that they are allowed to, but for this to work, you must be confident that the administrators at the other sites have properly configured the subscriptions at their sites. Push subscriptions are easier to create because all the subscription processes are performed and administered from the publication/distributor point of view. This also makes using them the most common approach.

For this example, we use the New Subscription Wizard to create a *push* subscription:

1. In SQL Server Management Studio, locate the `Replication` node under the publication server (the `DBARCH-LT2\SQL08DE01` named instance in this example) or the `Replication` node under the subscription server (the `DBARCH-LT2\SQL08DE03` named instance in this example). You can create a push subscription from either (but we use the subscription server here). Open the `Replication` node, navigate to the Local Subscription branch, right-click, and choose the New Subscriptions option. As you can see in Figure 19.46, choosing this option launches the New Subscription Wizard, where you can create one or more subscriptions to a publication and specify where and when to run the agents that synchronize the subscription.

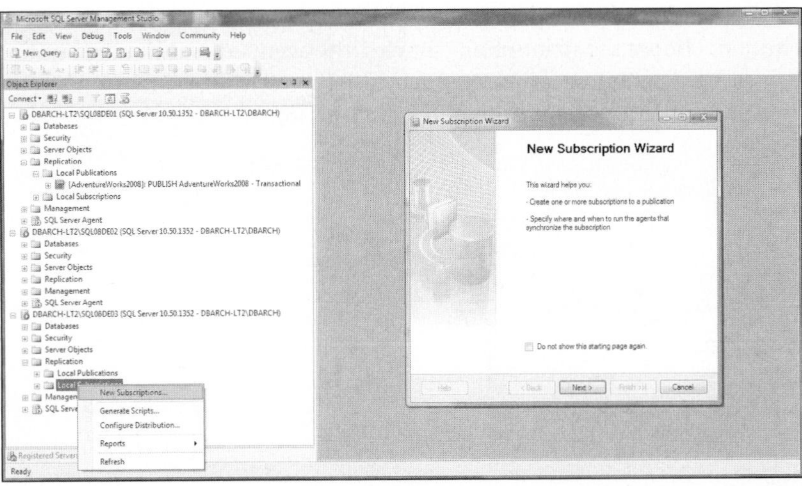

FIGURE 19.46 Launching the New Subscription Wizard from SQL Server Management Studio.

2. You first need to identify the publisher and publication from which you want to create one or more subscriptions. As you can see in Figure 19.47, we have specified the publisher (`DBARCH-LT2\SQL08DE01`) and the publication that has been created for the `AdventureWorks2008` database.

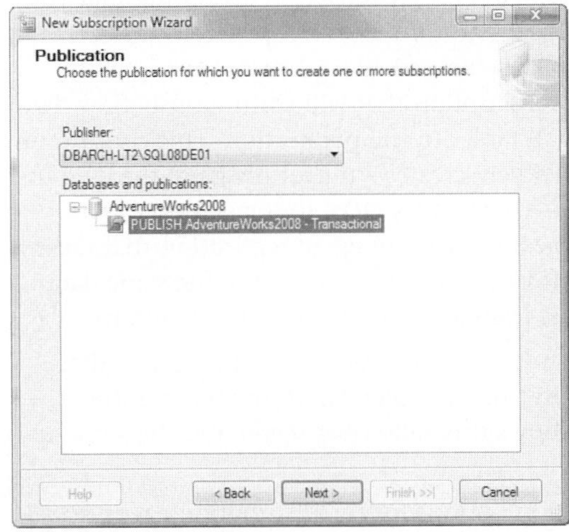

FIGURE 19.47 Identifying the publication from which to subscribe.

3. When you are presented with the option of where the replication agents will be run for the subscription, choose the first option—having the agents run at the distributor. This makes it a push subscription, which is much easier to control and manage centrally than a pull subscription (as shown in Figure 19.48).

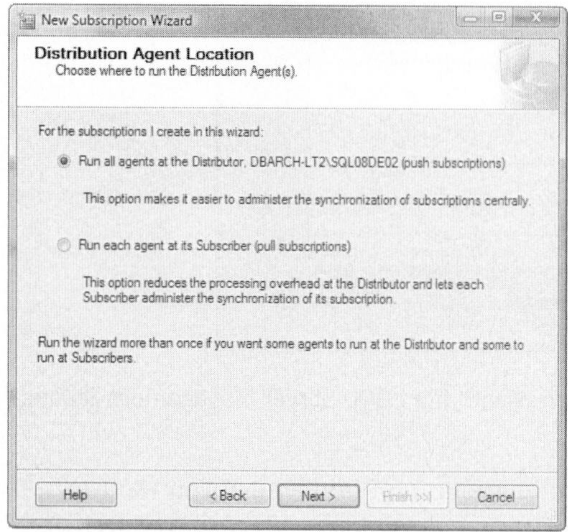

FIGURE 19.48 Run all agents at the Distributor (push subscriptions).

4. Next, the New Database dialog appears, asking you to identify the database target for the subscription and the physical database files for its allocation (assuming that you want to create this from scratch using this wizard process). Figure 19.49 shows this New Database dialog, with the target database named `AdventureWorks2008ODS`. Essentially, we have decided to create a subscription that will continuously flow data from the publisher to the subscriber for all tables in the publication. This continuous replication at the transactional level effectively creates a mirror image of the data for operational usage. That's why we have used the suffix ODS, for Operational Data Store, for the new database. This is a typical industry usage of replication that takes all read-only access to OLTP data and offloads it to the ODS copy of the same data (which is as close to up-to-date as the last transaction that was replicated to it).
5. In the Subscribers screen, with the new entry for the target subscriber server (the `DBARCH-LT2\SQL08DE03` named instance in this example), check the box for the target subscription server. Figure 19.50 shows this subscriber server and the subscription database target.
6. Specify the process account and connection options for the distribution agent (to connect to the subscription server). Typically, you choose the option to use a domain account or choose to impersonate the process account (shown in Figure 19.51).
7. Specify the synchronization schedule for each agent. You want the distribution agent to run continuously, but you also have the options to run on a schedule and on demand (as shown in Figure 19.51).

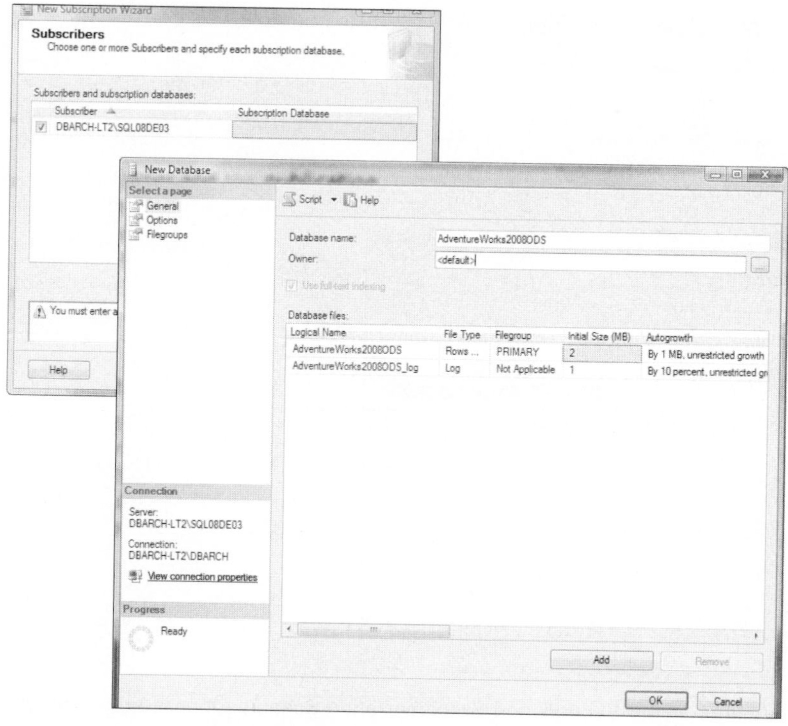

FIGURE 19.49 The New Database dialog specifying the target database (AdventureWorks2008ODS).

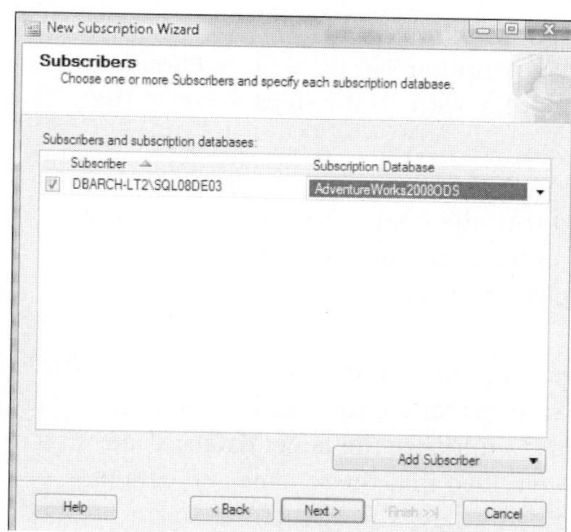

FIGURE 19.50 Specifying the subscription server target database.

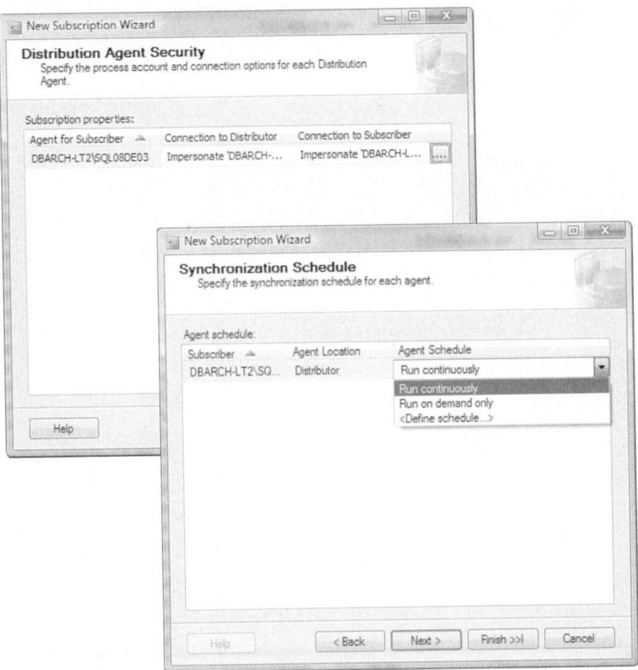

FIGURE 19.51 Distribution Agent Security and Synchronization Schedule for the subscription (Run Continuously).

8. Specify the initialization of the subscription. You want the subscription to be initialized immediately, but, depending on the size of the database, this might be accomplished manually with a database backup of the publication database.
9. On the next screen, which lists the New Subscription Wizard actions, choose to create the subscription and generate a script file with all the steps to create the subscription for use later.
10. On the next wizard dialog, identify the location of the script to be generated. As shown in Figure 19.52, you are presented with the final wizard summary screen. Click Finish to create your subscription, initialize the subscription database, and enjoy a full transactional replication implementation.

    After you click Finish, the create subscription process starts and goes through each step. Remember to check for errors or warnings if any errors occur. When this process completes, you wait for the agents to initialize the target database and start replication to the subscriber. If you have specified that the schema and data be created immediately, things start happening quickly. The distribution agent finishes the job. As you can see in Figure 19.53, the distribution agent applies the schemas to the subscriber (as viewed from the Replication Monitor's Distributor to Subscriber History tab). The bulk copying of the data into the tables on the subscriber side follows accordingly. After this bulk copying is done, the initialization step is completed, and active replication begins.

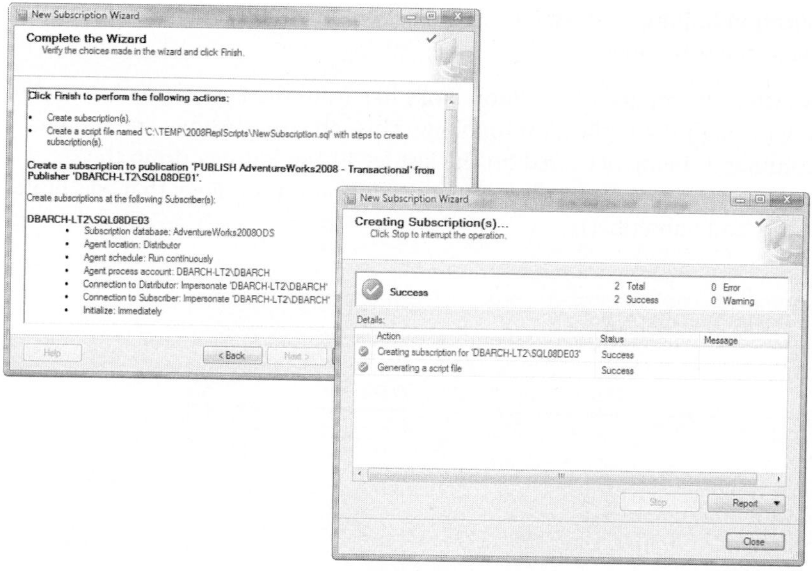

FIGURE 19.52 The New Subscription Wizard summary.

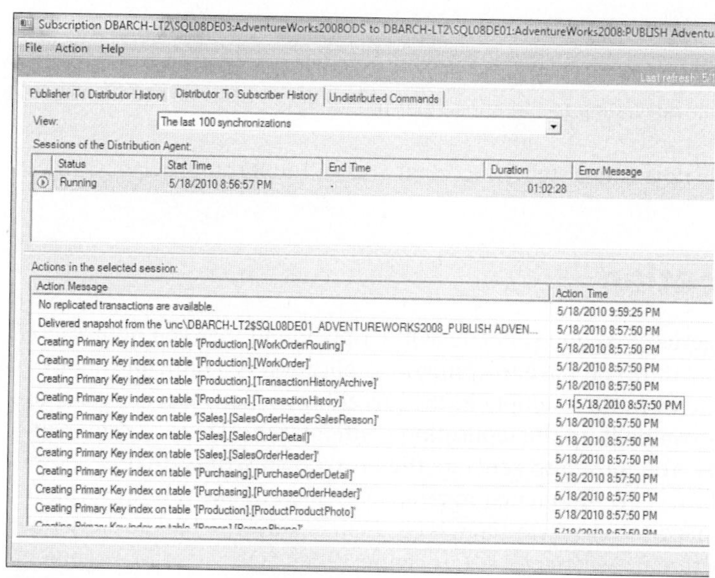

FIGURE 19.53 Delivering schemas and data to the subscriber.

The complete replication buildup is finished, and you should be fully functional for replicating transactions to the subscriber.

Figure 19.54 shows what the replication buildup looks like from the Replication Monitor as transactions flow through the replication topology. This screenshot shows the transaction counts and commands being delivered on the last leg in the journey (from the distributor to a subscriber). Figure 19.55 shows the full replication topology that was built (Publisher, Distributor and Subscriber).

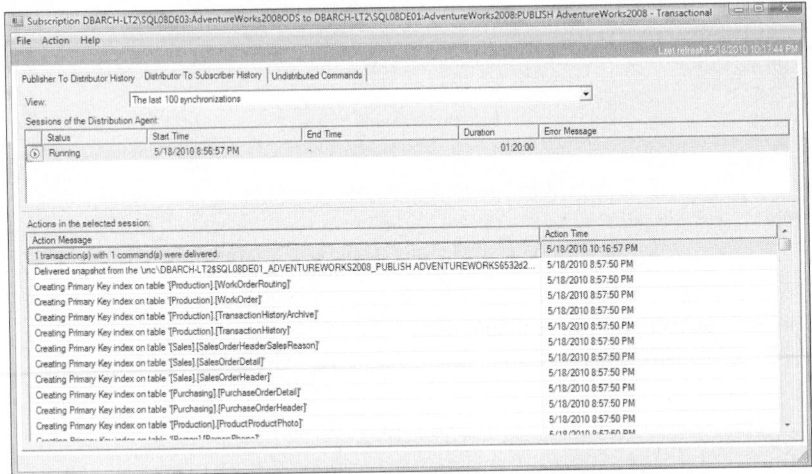

FIGURE 19.54 Transactions replicating to the subscriber (pushed).

Your replication topology is now completely functional and will replicate flawlessly for as long as you require.

Scripting Replication

Earlier, it was strongly suggested that you generate SQL scripts for all that you do because going through wizards every time you have to configure replication is a difficult way to run a production environment. In the example in the preceding section, you always chose to generate these scripts as you built up the replication configuration. This was only half the scripts needed, however. You must also generate the breakdown scripts (that is, those that drop and remove replication components) to remove each component of the replication topology in case you need to start from scratch or, as an example, rebuild a subscriber that is completely nonfunctional. As you can see in Figure 19.56, SQL Server Management Studio has a great feature that allows the complete generation of all aspects of replication topology (including disabling and removing replication).

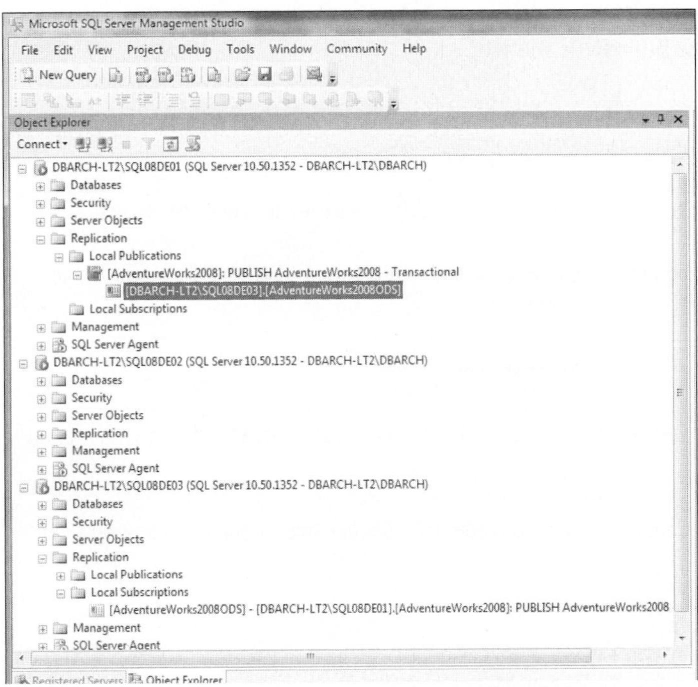

FIGURE 19.55 Full replication topology that was built (Publisher, Distributor, Subscriber).

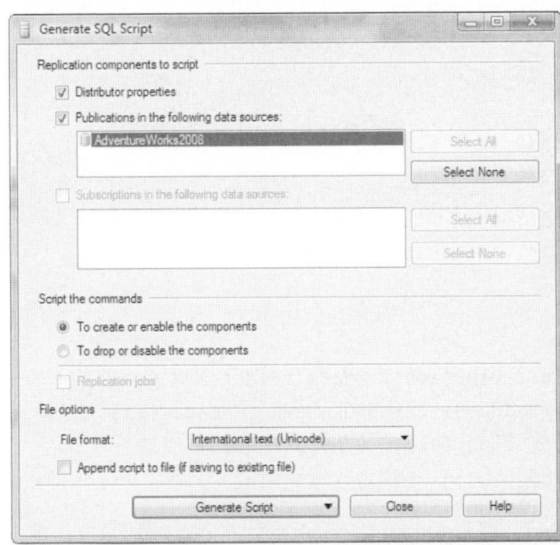

FIGURE 19.56 A script-generation feature for all replication topology components.

NOTE

Remember that working from scripts minimizes the errors you make while supporting your data replication environments (especially at 3:00 a.m.).

The following example shows the SQL scripts needed to generate the part of the data replication configuration you just built with the wizard:

```
------------------------------
-- From distribution Server --
------------------------------
/****** Scripting replication configuration. Script Date: 6/30/2009 10:49:03 AM
******/
/****** Please Note: For security reasons, all password parameters were scripted
with either NULL or an empty string. ******/

/****** Begin: Script to be run at Distributor ******/

/****** Installing the server as a Distributor. Script Date: 6/30/2009 10:49:03 AM
******/
use master
exec sp_adddistributor @distributor = N'DBARCH-LT2\SQL08DE02', @password = N''
GO

-- Adding the agent profiles
-- Updating the agent profile defaults
exec sp_MSupdate_agenttype_default @profile_id = 1
GO
exec sp_MSupdate_agenttype_default @profile_id = 2
GO
exec sp_MSupdate_agenttype_default @profile_id = 4
GO
exec sp_MSupdate_agenttype_default @profile_id = 6
GO
exec sp_MSupdate_agenttype_default @profile_id = 11
GO

-- Adding the distribution databases
use master
exec sp_adddistributiondb @database = N'distribution', @data_folder = N'C:\
Program Files\Microsoft SQL Server\MSSQL10.SQL08DE02\MSSQL\Data', @data_file =
 N'distribution.MDF', @data_file_size = 6, @log_folder = N'C:\Program Files\
Microsoft SQL Server\MSSQL10.SQL08DE02\MSSQL\Data', @log_file =
 N'distribution.LDF', @log_file_size = 3, @min_distretention = 0,
 @max_distretention = 72, @history_retention = 48, @security_mode = 1
GO

-- Adding the distribution publishers
exec sp_adddistpublisher @publisher = N'DBARCH-LT2\SQL08DE01', @distribution_db =
 N'distribution', @security_mode = 1, @working_directory = N'C:\Program
 Files\Microsoft SQL Server\MSSQL10.SQL08DE02\MSSQL\ReplData', @trusted = N'false',
```

```
 @thirdparty_flag = 0, @publisher_type = N'MSSQLSERVER'
GO

/****** End: Script to be run at Distributor ******/
use master
GO
```

The complete set of buildup and breakdown scripts for the example used here are available on this book's CD. They are labeled `CreatingXXX.sql` for the buildup scripts and `RemoveXXX.sql` for the breakdown scripts.

Monitoring Replication

After replication is up and running, it is important for you to monitor it and see how things are running. You can do this in several ways, including using SQL statements, SQL Server Management Studio, and Windows Performance Monitor. You are interested in the agent's successes and failures, the speed at which replication is done, and the synchronization state of tables involved in replication. Other issues to watch for are the sizes of the distribution database, growth of the subscriber databases, and available space on the distribution server's snapshot working directory.

Replication Monitoring SQL Statements

One way to look at the replication configuration and validate row counts, for example, is to use various replication stored procedures, including the following:

- **`sp_helppublication`**—Information on the publication server
- **`sp_helparticle`**—Article definition information
- **`sp_helpdistributor`**—Distributor information
- **`sp_helpsubscriberinfo`**—Subscriber server information
- **`sp_helpsubscription`**—Subscription information

These stored procedures are all extremely useful for verifying exactly how the replication configuration is really configured. If you execute these stored procedures (from the publication database), you get a great documentation of your complete replication topology that can be included in run books or other system documentation. Here's what you might do to see how the current replication configuration has been built out:

19

```
use AdventureWorks2008
go
exec sp_helppublication
exec sp_helparticle @publication='PUBLISH AdventureWorks2008 - Transactional'
exec sp_helpdistributor
exec sp_helpsubscriberinfo
exec sp_helpsubscription
go
```

It yields this result:

```
1 PUBLISH AdventureWorks2008 - Transactional       0     1     1     0
-----------------------------------------------------------------------
1  Address              [Person].[Address]                Address
2  AddressType          [Person].[AddressType]            AddressType
3  AWBuildVersion       [dbo].[AWBuildVersion]            AWBuildVersion
4  BillOfMaterials      [Production].[BillOfMaterials]    BillOfMaterials
5  Contact              [Person].[Contact]                Contact
6  ContactCreditCard    [Sales].[ContactCreditCard]       ContactCreditCard
7  ContactType          [Person].[ContactType]            ContactType
...
```

In addition, `sp_replcounters` shows the activity of this replication session. You can see the volume of traffic and the throughput here:

```
exec sp_replcounters
go
```

It yields this result:

```
database repl_trans rate trans/sec latency (sec) etc.
AdventureWorks2008    0       1562.5    1.243
```

For actual row count validation, you can use `sp_publication_validation`, which goes through and checks the row counts of the publication and subscribers:

```
exec sp_publication_validation @publication
    = 'PUBLISH AdventureWorks2008 - Transactional'
go
```

It yields this result:

```
Generated expected rowcount value of 19614 for Address.
Generated expected rowcount value of 6 for AddressType.
Generated expected rowcount value of 1 for AWBuildVersion.
Generated expected rowcount value of 2679 for BillOfMaterials.
Generated expected rowcount value of 19972 for Contact.
Generated expected rowcount value of 19118 for ContactCreditCard.
Generated expected rowcount value of 20 for ContactType.
Generated expected rowcount value of 238 for CountryRegion.
Generated expected rowcount value of 109 for CountryRegionCurrency.
Generated expected rowcount value of 19118 for CreditCard.
Generated expected rowcount value of 8 for Culture.
```

Another way to monitor replication is to look at the actual data being replicated. To do this, you first run the `SELECT count (*) FROM tblname` statement against the table where data is being replicated. Then you verify directly whether the most current data available is in the database. If you make a change to the data in the published table, do the changes show up in the replicated tables? If not, you might need to investigate how replication was configured on the server.

If you are allowing updatable subscriptions, the replication queue comes into play. You need to learn all about the `queueread` command prompt utility. This utility configures and begins the queue reader agent, which reads messages stored in the SQL Server queue or a Microsoft message queue and applies those messages to the publisher.

To help you visualize how replication works, and to help you monitor replication, the following sample stored procedure, called `REPL_ROWS_GENERATOR`, takes one parameter (the number of rows [new customers in the `Customer` table] you want to have inserted at a time) and generates new rows in the `Customer` table that can reflect different data activity that will be published (this stored procedure has been included on the CDROM for this book. Pull it off the CDROM and create it quickly within the AdventureWorks2008 Database.):

```
Use AdventureWorks2008
Go
-------------------------------------------------------
-- generate 500 new customers for replication testing --
-------------------------------------------------------
exec REPL_ROWS_GENERATOR 500
go
```

This example shows how to execute this stored procedure to insert 500 new customers. If you don't supply any parameter, the default is 100 new customers. Try it out.

The following messages appear after you execute the `REPL_ROWS_GENERATOR` stored procedure:

```
INSERTING ROW: 1
INSERTING ROW: 2
INSERTING ROW: 3
INSERTING ROW: 4
INSERTING ROW: 5
INSERTING ROW: 6
INSERTING ROW: 7
INSERTING ROW: 8
INSERTING ROW: 9
INSERTING ROW: 10
...
INSERTING ROW: 500
```

Figure 19.57 shows this stored procedure, which is included on the CD for this book.

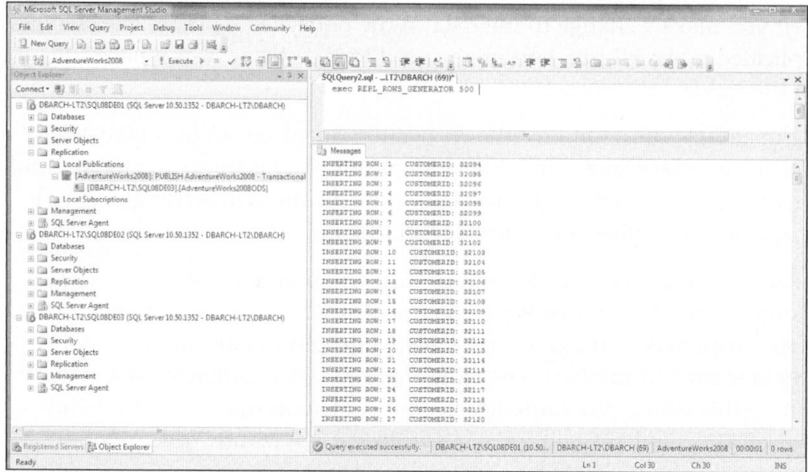

FIGURE 19.57 The executing **REPL_ROWS_GENERATOR** stored procedure for testing data replication.

Monitoring Replication within SQL Server Management Studio

As you can imagine, SQL Server Management Studio provides considerable information about the status of replication. Most of this information is available via Replication Monitor. In Replication Monitor, you can see the activity for publishers, distributors, and subscribers; you can see all agent details; and you can configure alerts.

Through Replication Monitor, you also can invoke validation subscriptions processing to see if replication is in sync. You just navigate to the publication whose subscription you want to validate, right-click, and choose Validate Subscription option. This allows you to verify that the subscriber has the same number of rows of replicated data as the publisher. You can validate all subscriptions or just a particular one. Validation options are extensive and include using fast row count methods, actual row count methods, and even checksum comparisons of row data. This is a huge feature for SQL Server 2008. Figure 19.58 shows the results of running a complete subscription validation.

Another great feature to help monitor replication is tracer tokens. Essentially, you create a marker (called a token) that flows through the full replication topology (from publisher to distributor to subscriber). It does not affect data tables! This flow is monitored and measured, down to the millisecond, and is for a specific publisher-to-subscriber path. Figure 19.59 shows the Tracer Tokens tab of the Replication Monitor and the Insert Tracer

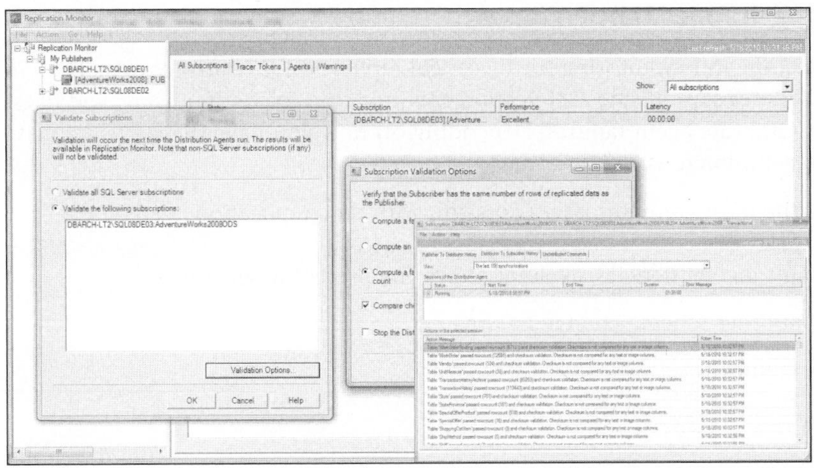

FIGURE 19.58 Validation of subscriptions via Replication Monitor.

button that you can click to fire off the token through the topology. You can click this button to quickly see where bottlenecks exist (for example, from publisher to distributor, from distributor to subscriber) and the latency of the data flow along the way. In this example, it took the tracer token 2 seconds in total to traverse from the publisher to the distributor and to the subscriber.

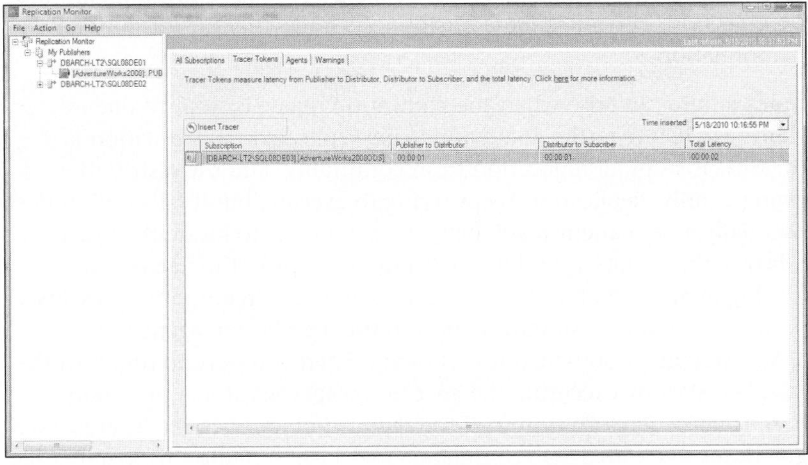

FIGURE 19.59 Tracer tokens for monitoring data replication throughput.

Troubleshooting Replication Failures

Configuring replication and monitoring for successful replication is relatively easy. The fun begins when failures start arising. Replication Monitor pays for itself quickly. Red flags begin appearing to indicate agent failures. Depending on how you have the alerts defined, you probably also get numerous emails or pages.

The following are the most common issues you find with data replication:

- Data row count inconsistencies, as discussed in the preceding section
- Subscriber/publisher schema change failures
- Connection failures
- Agent failures

For the conventional replication situations, if the problem is with the validation of subscriptions processing, it is usually best to resynchronize the subscription by dropping it and resubscribing or by reinitializing the subscription.

Another common issue is that the SQL Server Agent service doesn't start. Manually attempting to restart this service usually shakes things loose. Sometimes an object on the subscriber becomes messed up. The solution is usually to create that object again and reload its data via BCP or IS. Then you can resynchronize the subscription. In such a case, the subscription included this object originally, but it has become invalid in some way. With a heterogeneous subscriber, you often see connection errors due to invalid login IDs used in the ODBC connection. The quick fix is usually to just redefine the ODBC data source connection information.

A much more complex failure can arise when the replication queue is stopped due to some type of SQL language failure in the command being replicated. This situation is extremely serious because it stops all replication from continuing, and the distribution database starts growing rapidly. Replication keeps trying to execute, but it fails each time. This situation is essentially a permanent roadblock. The solution is to locate the exact transaction in the distribution database and delete it physically from the transaction queue. This action is highly unusual, but it is necessary when the circumstance presents itself. First, by looking at the error detail information in the distribution agent history, you can isolate the SQL statement on which it is choking. Then you have to find it in the distribution database. You start by executing the `sp_browsereplcmds` stored procedure from the distribution database. This gives you all the replication transactions (that is, each `xact_seqno`) along with the associated SQL command. You have to pump this to a text file for searching. You then search this data for the matching SQL command. When you locate it, you look for its associated transaction number (`xact_seqno`). You use this `xact_seqno` value to delete it from the `Msrepl_commands` table in the distribution database. This frees up the roadblock. You see this type of issue only about once every six months, if at all (it is hoped).

New and Improved Peer-to-Peer Replication

For data distribution requirements that must have updates in multiple nodes, peer-to-peer replication is ideal. You must worry about conflicts, but typically they are rare and very easily handled by a simple conflict handler. Peer-to-peer replication is transactional replication based, and can have any number of peers. A separate wizard is used to set up peer-to-peer replication because of its unique characteristics. Remember, there are essentially no subscribers, just publishers. All peers are handled by one or more distributors and are assigned a unique peer originator ID value to help in transactional consistency and conflict resolution. If you have been doing replication since the SQL Server 6.5 days, the peer-to-peer configuration topology viewer is much like that old user interface. Figure 19.60 shows the special invocation of peer-to-peer creation from SQL Server Management Studio.

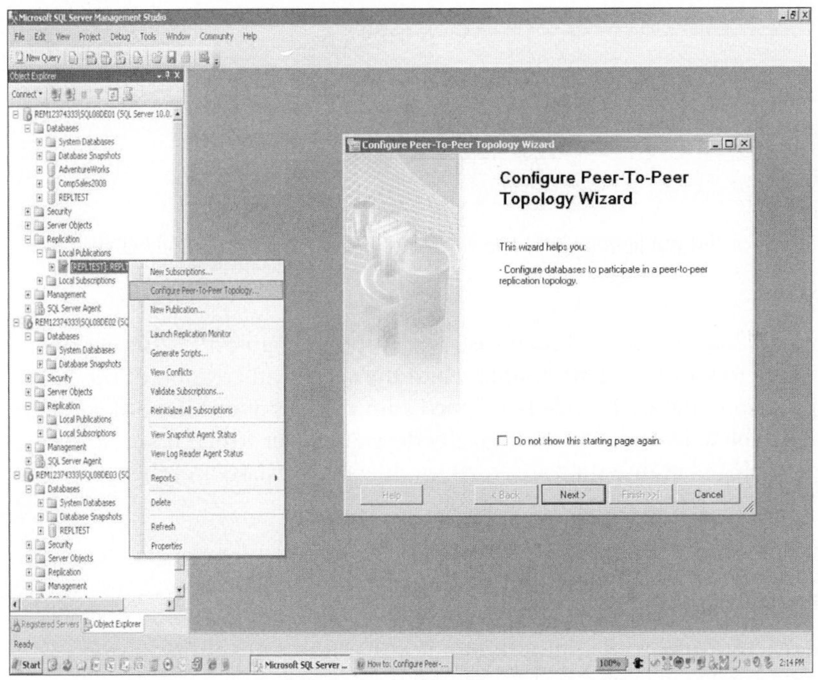

FIGURE 19.60 Peer-to-peer wizard launch.

You basically create publications that become shared in the peer-to-peer topology. You add "nodes" on an equal hierarchical level that participate in the publication equally. You can add any number of peers (nodes), and new in SQL Server 2008, this can be done without interrupting the existing replication topology. Figure 19.61 shows the setup of a publication for a database named REPLTEST_PEER2PEER and the addition of two nodes to the topology.

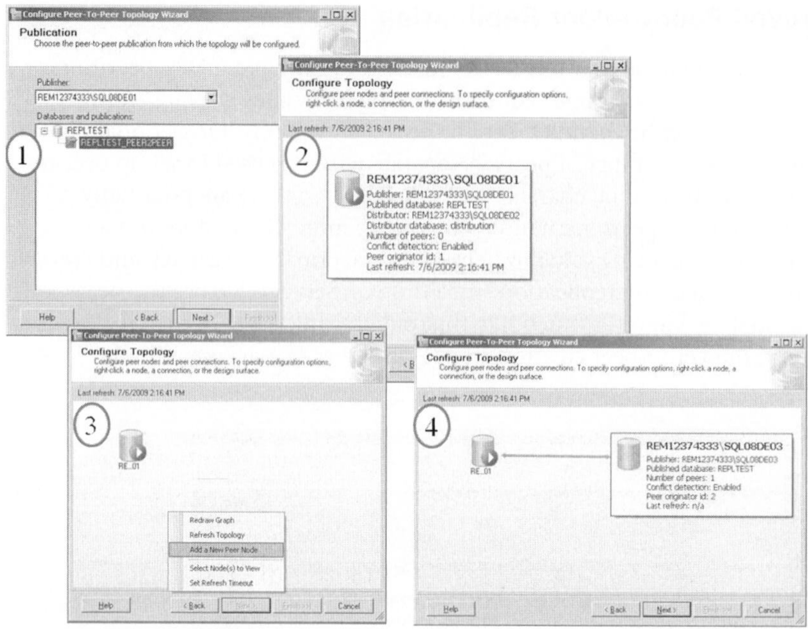

FIGURE 19.61 Setup of the publication and two nodes in a peer-to-peer topology (1 thru 4).

Peers are typically initialized manually for consistency purposes. Figure 19.62 shows the Configure Peer-to-Peer Topology Wizard summary and the successful creation of the full (two-node) topology. Note that each node is assigned a unique originator ID, and conflict detection has been enabled. Notice also that it really doesn't matter which node is listed first in the wizard topology because they are equal (no hierarchy exists) and the arrow is bidirectional.

The Performance Monitor

You can use Windows Performance Monitor to monitor the health of your replication scenario. When you install SQL Server, you get several new objects and counters in Performance Monitor:

- **`SQLServer:Replication Agents`**—This object contains counters used to monitor the status of all replication agents, including the total number running.
- **`SQLServer:Replication Dist`**—This object contains counters used to monitor the status of the distribution agents, including the latency and number of transactions transferred per second.
- **`SQLServer:Replication Logreader`**—This object contains counters used to monitor the status of the log reader agent, including the latency and number of transactions transferred per second.

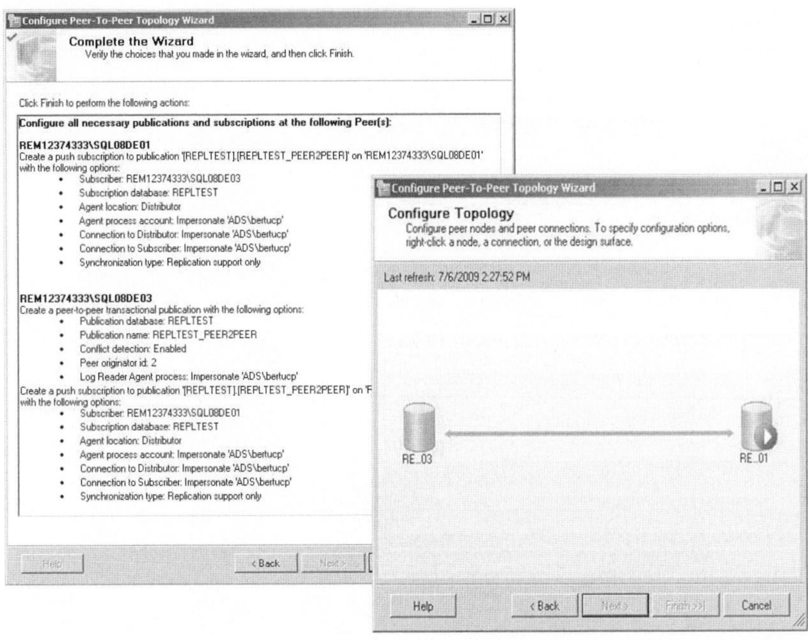

FIGURE 19.62 Configure Peer-to-Peer Topology Wizard summary and complete topology.

- **`SQLServer:Replication Merge`**—This object contains counters used to monitor the status of the merge agents, including the number of transactions and number of conflicts per second.
- **`SQLServer:Replication Snapshot`**—This object contains counters used to monitor the status of the snapshot agents, including the number of transactions per second.

As you can see in Figure 19.63, we chose to monitor the typical things critical for replication: the LogReader counters, the distribution server counters, some default processor times, and disk queue lengths to keep an eye on load at the publisher. Figure 19.63 shows some spikes during log reader activity as big transactions hit the publisher. However, they drop off quickly, easily handling the large transaction volumes.

Replication in Heterogeneous Environments

SQL Server 2008 allows for transactional and snapshot replication of data into and out of environments other than SQL Server. This is termed *heterogeneous* replication. The easiest way to set up this replication is to use ODBC or OLE DB and create a push subscription to the subscriber. This is much easier to make work than you might imagine. SQL Server can publish to the following database types:

- Microsoft Access
- Oracle
- Sybase

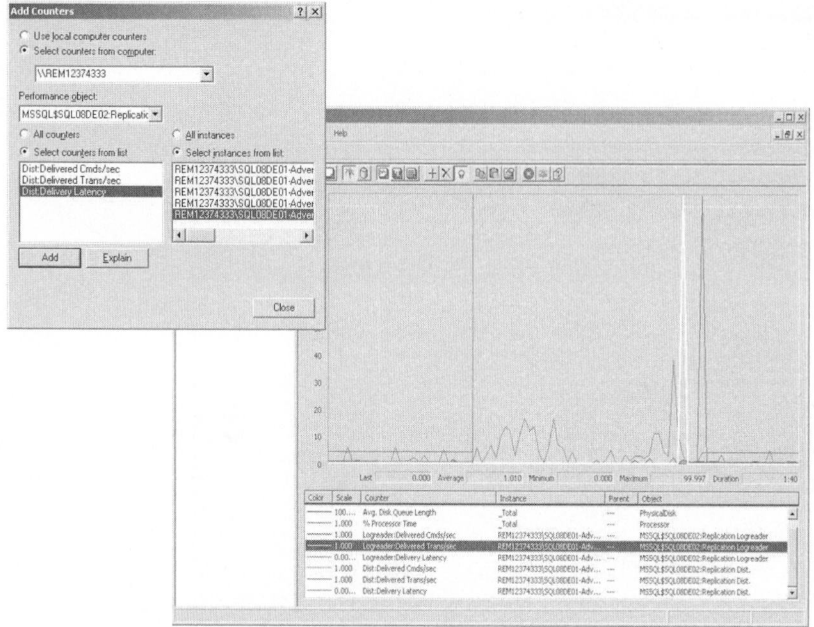

FIGURE 19.63 Performance Monitor counters for replication monitoring.

- IBM DB2/AS400
- IBM DB2/MVS

SQL Server can replicate data to any other type of database, provided that the following are true:

- The driver must be ODBC Level 1 compliant.
- The driver must be 32-bit, thread safe, and designed for the processor architecture on which the distribution process runs.
- The driver must support transactions.
- The driver and underlying database must support Data Definition Language (DDL).
- The underlying database cannot be read-only.

Backup and Recovery in a Replication Configuration

A replication-oriented backup strategy will reap major benefits for you after you have implemented a data replication configuration. You must realize that the scope of data and what you must back up together have changed. In addition, you must be aware of the recovery time frame and plan your backup/recovery strategy accordingly. You might not have multiple hours available to you to recover an entire replication topology. You now have databases that are conceptually joined, and you might need to back them up together in one synchronized backup. Figure 19.64 shows overall backup strategies for the most common recovery needs.

Recovery Need	Backup Strategy
100% data, All sites, Small Recovery Window	Coordinated DB backups at all sites involved in the replication configuration (publisher, distributor and all subscribers). Somewhat complex to do.
100% data, All sites, Medium Recovery Window	Backup Publication DB and Distribution DB together. Replication can be recovered from this point very easily without reconfiguring anything. Just have to re-initialize the subscribers. This is the most common approach being used.
100% data, All sites Big Recovery Window	Backup of Publication DB only. Can then reconfigure replication via scrips and reinitialize distribution, and all subscribers fairly easily.

FIGURE 19.64 Common backup strategies for different recovery needs.

When backing up environments, you need to back up the following at each site:

- Publisher (published database, `msdb`, and `master`)
- Distributor (distribution database, `msdb`, and `master`)
- Subscribers (subscriber database, optionally `msdb`, and `master` when pull subscriptions are being done)

You should always make copies of your replication scripts and keep them handy. At a minimum, you need to keep copies at the publisher and distributor and one more location, such as at one of your subscribers. You will use them for recovery someday.

You shouldn't forget to back up `master` and `msdb` when any new replication object is created, updated, or deleted.

If you have allowed updating of subscribers using queued updates, you need to expand your backup capability to include these queues.

In general, you will find that even when you walk up and pull the plug on your distribution server, publication server, or any subscribers, automatic recovery works well to get you back online and replicating quickly, without human intervention.

Some Thoughts on Performance

From a performance point of view, the replication configuration defaults err on the side of optimal throughput. That's the good news. The bad news is that everybody is different in some way, so you have to consider a bit of tuning of your replication configuration. In general, you can get your replication configuration working well by doing the following:

- Keeping the amount of data to be replicated at any one point small by running agents continuously, instead of at long, scheduled intervals.

- Setting a minimum amount of memory allocated to SQL Server by using the Min Server Memory option to guarantee ample memory across the board.
- Using good disk drive physical separation rules, such as keeping the transaction log on a separate disk drive from the data portion. Your transaction log is much more heavily used when you opt for transactional replication.
- Putting your snapshot working directory on a separate disk drive to minimize disk drive arm contention. You should use a separate snapshot folder for each publication.
- Publishing only what you need. By selectively publishing only the minimum amount of data required, you implement a much more efficient replication configuration, which is faster overall.
- Trying to run snapshots in nonpeak times so your network and production environments aren't bogged down.
- Minimizing transformation of data involved with replication.

Log Shipping

If you have a small need to create a read-only (ad hoc query/reporting) database environment that can tolerate a high degree of data latency, you might be a candidate for using log shipping. Log shipping is still a feature for SQL Server 2008, but it will be deprecated by the next release. In other words, it might be easy to use and easy to manage, but it is being phased out as a feature of SQL Server. For this reason, we do not describe it in this book (it is described in detail in *SQL Server 2000 Unleashed*, though). For those who have current log shipping configurations, it is time to move to database mirroring. This transition will be easy because the two capabilities are so much alike. (Actually, many aspects of database mirroring came from log shipping.)

Data Replication and Database Mirroring for Fault Tolerance and High Availability

SQL Server 2008 allows you to use combinations of options to achieve higher availability levels. A prime example is combining data replication with database mirroring to provide maximum availability of data, scalability to users, and fault tolerance via failover at potentially each node in the replication topology. You can start with the publisher and distributor, making them both database mirror failover configurations. Building up a combination of both options together is the best of both worlds: the super low latency of database mirroring for fault tolerance and the high availability (and scalability) of data through replication. (For more information, see Chapter 20, "Database Mirroring.")

Summary

Replication is a powerful feature of SQL Server that can be used in many business situations. Companies can use replication for anything from roll-up reporting to relieving the main server from ad hoc queries and reporting. It is critical to let your company's requirements drive the type of replication technique to use. Determining the replication option and configuration to use is difficult, but actually setting it up is reasonably easy. Microsoft has come a long way in this regard. Peer-to-peer replication seems to have the most promise of delivering master-master symmetric replication in a production environment. Microsoft's overall architectural approach and implementation is the model for the industry. You should not be afraid to use this facility. It is more than production-worthy, and the flexibility it offers and the overall performance are just short of incredible, incredible, incredible (replication humor for you).

In Chapter 20 we delve into the capability to make an image of a database (a mirror) for failover purposes using the database mirroring mechanism available within SQL Server 2008. This is a landmark addition for SQL Server.

CHAPTER 20

Database Mirroring

IN THIS CHAPTER

- What's New in Database Mirroring
- What Is Database Mirroring?
- Roles of the Database Mirroring Configuration
- Setting Up and Configuring Database Mirroring
- Testing Failover from the Principal to the Mirror
- Client Setup and Configuration for Database Mirroring
- Migrate to Database Mirroring 2008 as Fast as You Can
- Using Replication and Database Mirroring Together
- Using Database Snapshots from a Mirror for Reporting

Database mirroring is such a huge technology jump in capabilities that even the smallest company can now provide near-real-time database failover without the fancy, expensive hardware required with more complex configurations, such as with SQL Server Clustering (that is built on Microsoft Cluster Services [MSCS]). MSCS requires shared resources, separate network connections for internal heartbeat communication, and so on. In addition, multiple layers of software are involved (MSCS plus SQL Server). With database mirroring, you can set up a near-real-time database failover environment using all conventional, low-cost machines, without any complex hardware compatibility requirements, and database mirroring can fail over in as little as 3 seconds!

Database mirroring effectively allows anyone to immediately step up to nearly 99.9% (at least three nines) availability at the database layer at a very low cost, and it is easily configured and managed.

What's New in Database Mirroring

Performance, performance, and more performance! This is the key improvement for database mirroring in SQL Server 2008. This performance improvement was brought about by Microsoft's efforts to isolate and resolve the bottleneck in database mirroring that existed with SQL Server 2005. That bottleneck centered around the bulky transmission of full-size log records from one SQL Server to another. Improvements in SQL Server 2008 are centered around the data compression used on the log records sent from one server to the other. Later in this chapter we show you some results of a benchmark involving SQL Server 2005 and SQL Server 2008 that show the major impact of this enhancement. In addition, as records are being written to the mirror, automatic page repair can occur if SQL Server finds any page that is not intact, adding more reliability and stability to the overall SQL Server platform. A few more interesting performance counters and new dynamic management views that provide visibility into the health of your mirroring implementation round out the new features.

Microsoft SQL Server 2008 is shifting very strongly to a goal of providing a Database Engine foundation that can be highly available 7 days a week, 365 days a year. With database mirroring, Microsoft is providing the masses with the opportunity to achieve that dream much more quickly. Database mirroring was first introduced in SQL Server 2005. It was earlier known as Real-time Log Shipping (RTLS) and then had another name for a while, and it finally ended up being called *database mirroring*—which is what it really is.

The key breakthrough that allowed Microsoft to offer database mirroring was something called "copy-on-write" technology. We describe it in more detail in a bit. Suffice it to say that with copy-on-write technology, a transaction can be distributed (that is, written) to another completely separate SQL Server database immediately, and that other database can, in turn, be used as a failover (that is, it can be used to fail over to in less than 3 seconds).

NOTE

The examples in this chapter are based on the SQL Server 2005 version of the AdventureWorks database rather than the newer AdventureWorks2008 or AdventureWorks2008R2 sample databases used for many of the examples in the other chapters in this book. The reason for this is because Database Mirroring cannot be implemented on a database that is also configured for FILESTREAM storage. The 2008 and 2008R2 versions of the AdventureWorks database make use of FILESTREAM storage.

Fortunately, the 2005 version of the AdventureWorks database can be installed using the same installer that installs the AdventureWorks2008 or AdventureWorks2008R2 database. If you didn't install AdventureWorks when you installed either of these sample databases, simply relaunch the installer and choose to install the AdventureWorks OLTP database.

For more information on downloading and installing the AdventureWorks sample databases, see the Introduction chapter.

What Is Database Mirroring?

When you mirror a database, you are essentially asking for a complete copy of a database to be created and maintained, with as much up-to-the-second completeness as possible; you are asking for a mirror image. Database mirroring is a database-level feature. This means that there is no support for filtering, subsetting, or any form of partitioning. You mirror a complete database or nothing at all. This limitation actually keeps database mirroring simple and clean to implement. It also certainly provides some drawbacks, such as burning up twice the amount of disk storage, but what you get in return is well worth the cost in storage.

Database mirroring works through the transaction log of the principal database (of the database that is to be mirrored). You can mirror only a database that uses the full database recovery model. Otherwise, it would not be possible to forward transaction log entries to another server. Through the use of copy-on-write technology, a change to data in a primary server's database (as reflected in active transaction log entries) is first "copied" to the target server, and then it is "written" (that is, applied or restored) to the target database server (that is, to the mirror server) transaction log. That is why it's called *copy-on-write*.

Database mirroring is very different from data replication. With replication, database changes are at the logical level (insert, update, delete statements; stored procedure executions; and so on), whereas database mirroring uses the actual physical log entries on both the primary database server side and the mirror database server side. Effectively, the physical "active" log records from the transaction log of the principal database are copied and written directly to the transaction log of the mirror database. These physical log record-level transactions can be applied extremely quickly. As these physical log records are being applied to the mirror database, even the data cache reflects the forward application of the log records. This makes the entire database and data cache ready for the principal to take over extremely quickly. And, now with SQL Server 2008, the log records are compressed on the principal side before transmission, which allows more records per transmission to be sent to the mirror server, thus speeding up the whole topology quite a bit.

Figure 20.1 shows a typical database mirroring configuration that has three components:

- **Principal database server**—This is the source of the mirroring. You can mirror one or more databases on a single SQL Server instance to another SQL Server instance. You cannot mirror a database on one SQL Server instance to itself (that is, the same SQL Server instance). Remember, you mirror a database, not a subset of the database or a single table. It's all or nothing.
- **Mirror database server**—The mirror server is the recipient of the mirroring from the principal database server. This mirrored database is kept in hot standby mode and cannot be used directly in any way. In fact, after you configure database mirroring, this database shows its status as being in continuous "restore" mode. The reason is that the physical transaction records are continuously applied to this mirror database. This database is essentially a hot standby database and is not available for direct database usage of any kind. The reason is that it is used in case the principal fails and must not be tainted in any way (it must be the exact mirror image of the principal. The one exception to this nonusage scenario is creating database snapshots from the mirror database (creating database snapshots with a database mirror is described in more detail later in this chapter and in Chapter 32 "Database Snapshots").

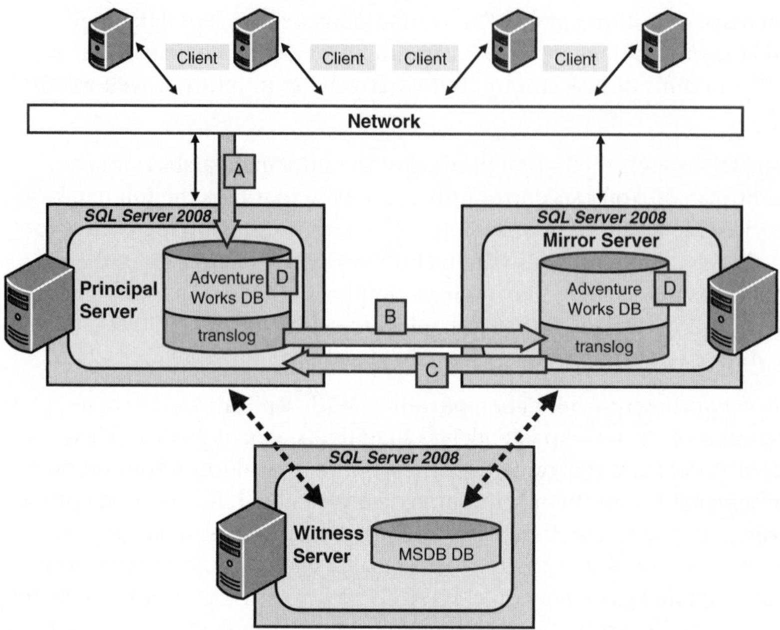

FIGURE 20.1 A basic database mirroring configuration with principal, mirror, and witness servers.

- **Witness database server**—You use the witness database server, which is optional, when you want to be continually checking to see if any failures have occurred to the primary database server and to help make the decision to fail over to the mirror database server. Using a witness server is a sound way to configure database mirroring. If you do not identify a witness server, the principal and mirror are left on their own to decide whether to fail over. With the witness server, a quorum is formed (that is, two out of three servers), and it takes the quorum to make a failover decision. A typical scenario is that the principal server fails for some reason, the witness sees this failure, the mirror also sees the failure, and together they agree that the principal is lost and that the mirror must take over the principal role. If the witness still sees that the principal is alive and well, but the communication between the mirror and principal has been broken, the witness does not agree to fail over to the mirror (even though the mirror thinks it must do this because it lost connection to the principal). Witness servers are usually put on separate physical servers.

Copy-on-Write Technology

The copy-on-write technology is at the core of the database mirroring capability. Look back at Figure 20.1, and notice what happens in a High Safety with Automatic Failover mode (synchronous mode):

1. A transaction from a client connection to the principal server (A) is written to the `AdventureWorks` database (D).
2. When the transaction is written to the principal server's transaction log, it is immediately copied (B) and written to the mirror server (D).
3. When this physical log record is written to the mirror server, it sends back an acknowledgment (C) to the principal of its write success.

This is the copy-on-write technology. The end result is that the mirror server is in exactly the same state as the principal server (if the physical log record has been successfully written on the mirror side). If failure occurs now, the mirror server can pick up all processing from the clients extremely quickly and without data loss.

NOTE

Database mirroring cannot be used for any of SQL Server's internal databases—`tempdb`, `masterdb`, `msdb`, or `modeldb`. Database mirroring is fully supported in SQL Server Standard Edition, Developer Edition, and Enterprise Edition, but it is *not* supported in SQL Server Workgroup Edition or Express Edition. However, machines running these server editions could be used as witness servers.

When to Use Database Mirroring

As mentioned earlier in this chapter, database mirroring elevates the availability level of a SQL Server–based application to a very high level without any special hardware and extra administration staff skills. However, when you should use database mirroring varies depending on your true needs.

Basically, if you need to increase the availability of the database layer, have automatic data protection (that is, redundant storage of data), or decrease the downtime that would normally be required to do upgrades, you should use database mirroring. An ever more popular scenario for database mirroring is when you need to offload reporting that is easily satisfied with periodic database snapshots. This usage provides great relief from heavily burdened transactional servers also used for reporting. Finally, if you need data distribution, high availability, and high data resiliency, using data replication with database mirroring is also a good idea. We discuss these latter two ideas later in this chapter.

Roles of the Database Mirroring Configuration

As you have seen, a typical database mirroring configuration has a principal server, mirror server, and witness server. Each of these servers plays a role at some point. The principal and mirror switch roles, so it is important to understand what these roles are and when a server is playing a particular role.

Playing Roles and Switching Roles

A *role* corresponds to what a server is doing at a particular point in time. There are three possible roles:

- **Witness role**—If a server is playing a witness role, it is essentially standing alongside both partners of a database mirror configuration and is used to settle all arguments. It is getting together with any one of the other servers and forming a quorum to come up with decisions. The decision that it will participate in is whether to fail over. That is it. As mentioned before, the witness server can be any edition of a SQL Server (even SQL Server Express, the free version).
- **Principal role**—If a server is playing a principal role, it is the server that the application will be connected to and that is generating the transactions. One of the partners in the database mirror must start out as the principal. After a failure, the mirror server takes over the principal role, and the roles reverse.
- **Mirror role**—If a server is playing a mirror role, it is the server that is having transactions written to it. It is in a constant recovery state (that is, the database state needed to be able to accept physical log records). One of the partners in the database mirroring configuration must start out in the mirror role. Then, if a failure occurs, the mirror server changes to the principal role.

Database Mirroring Operating Modes

With database mirroring, you have the option of deploying in one of three modes: high safety *with* automatic failover mode (high availability with a witness server), high safety *without* automatic failover mode (high protection without a witness server), and high-performance mode. Each mode has different failure and protection characteristics and uses the database mirroring configurations slightly differently. As you might expect, the high-performance mode offers the least amount of protection; you must sacrifice levels of protection for performance.

Database mirroring runs with either asynchronous or synchronous operations:

- **Synchronous operations**—With synchronous operations, a committed transaction is committed (that is, written) on both partners of the database mirroring pair. This obviously adds some latency cost to a complete transaction because it is across two servers. High-safety modes use synchronous operations.
- **Asynchronous operations**—With asynchronous operations, transactions commit without waiting for the mirror server to write the log to disk. This can speed up performance significantly. High-performance mode uses asynchronous operations.

Whether the operations are asynchronous or synchronous depends on the transaction safety setting. You control this setting through the `SAFETY` option when configuring with Transact-SQL (T-SQL) commands. The default for `SAFETY` is `FULL` (which provides synchronous operations). You set it to `OFF` for asynchronous operations. If you are using the mirroring wizard, this option is set for you automatically.

Of the three modes, only the high safety with automatic failover mode (high-availability mode) requires the witness server. The others can operate fine without this third server in their configuration. Remember that the witness server is looking at both the principal and mirror server and will be utilized (in a quorum) for automatic failover.

Role switching is the act of transferring the principal role to the mirror server. It is the mirror server that acts as the failover partner for the principal server. When a failure occurs, the principal role is switched to the mirror server, and its database is brought online as the principal database.

Failover variations are

- **Automatic failover**—Automatic failover is enabled with a three-server configuration involving a principal, mirror, and witness server. Synchronous operations are required, and the mirror database must already be synchronized (that is, in sync with the transactions as they are being written to the principal). Role switching is done automatically. This is for high-availability mode.
- **Manual failover**—Manual failover is needed when there is no witness server and you are using synchronous operations. The principal and mirror are connected to each other, and the mirror database is synchronized. Role switching is done manually. This is for high safety without automatic failover mode (high-protection mode). You are making the decision to start using the mirror server as the principal (no data loss).
- **Forced service**—In the case of a mirror server being available but possibly not synchronized, the mirror server can be forced to take over when the principal server has failed. This possibly means data loss because the transactions were not synchronized. This is for either high safety without automatic failover mode (high-protection mode) or high-performance mode.

Setting Up and Configuring Database Mirroring

Microsoft uses a few other concepts and technologies in database mirroring. You have already learned about the copy-on-write technology. Microsoft also uses *endpoints*, which are assigned to each server in a database mirroring configuration. In addition, establishing connections to each server is much more tightly controlled and requires service accounts or integrated (domain-level) authentication. Within SQL Server, grants must also be given to the accounts that will be executing database mirroring.

You can completely set up database mirroring by using T-SQL scripts, or you can use the Database Mirroring Wizard within SQL Server Management Studio (SSMS). We always advise that you use something that is repeatable, such as SQL scripts, and you can easily generate SQL scripts by using the new wizard. It's not fun to have to re-create or manage a database mirroring configuration in the middle of the night. Having this whole process in a script reduces almost all errors.

Getting Ready to Mirror a Database

Before you start setting up and configuring a database mirroring environment, it is always best to run through a simple checklist of basic requirements:

1. Verify that all server instances are at the same service pack level. In addition, the SQL Server edition you have must support database mirroring.
2. Verify that you have as much or more disk space available on the mirror server as on the principal server. You also need the same room for growth on both.
3. Verify that you have connectivity to each server from the others. You can most easily do this by trying to register each SQL Server instance in SSMS. If you can register the server, the server can be used for database mirroring. Do this for the principal, mirror, and witness servers.
4. Verify that the principal server database that is to be mirrored is using the full database recovery model. Right-click on the database you intend to mirror, choose Tasks, and then Mirroring. This brings you to the database mirroring properties dialog where you can configure mirroring. If you try to start configuring database mirroring and the database recovery model is not full for the principal database, you get a nasty message to that effect (see Figure 20.2). Because database mirroring is transaction log based, it makes sense to be using the full database recovery model: all transactions are written to the transaction log and are not truncated, as with other database recovery models.

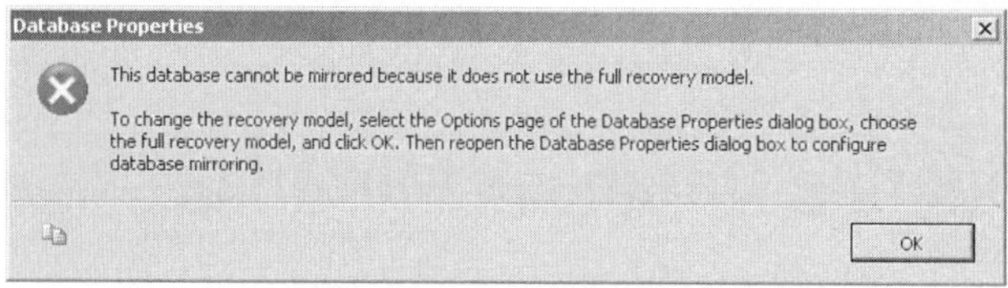

FIGURE 20.2 Trying to mirror a database that is not using the full database recovery model.

Before you go any further, you must establish the endpoints for each of the servers that will be a part of the database mirroring configuration. You can use the Configure Security option of the wizard to do this, but getting into the practice of using SQL scripts is really the best approach. Using SQL scripts is very easy, as you will soon see.

Endpoints utilize TCP/IP addressing and listening ports for all communication between the servers. Within a server, the endpoint is given a specific name (that is, an endpoint name) for easy reference and to establish the partner roles that this server (endpoint) will possibly play. In addition, a connection `GRANT` is needed for access to be allowed from each server to the other, and a service account should be used for this. This service account is usually a particular login that is known to the domain and is to be used for all connections in the database mirroring topology. Figure 20.3 shows the mirroring database properties of the `AdventureWorks` database on a SQL Server instance named `SQL08DE01`. As you can see, no server network addresses are set up for database mirroring of any kind, and the mirroring status says "This Database Has Not Been Configured for Mirroring."

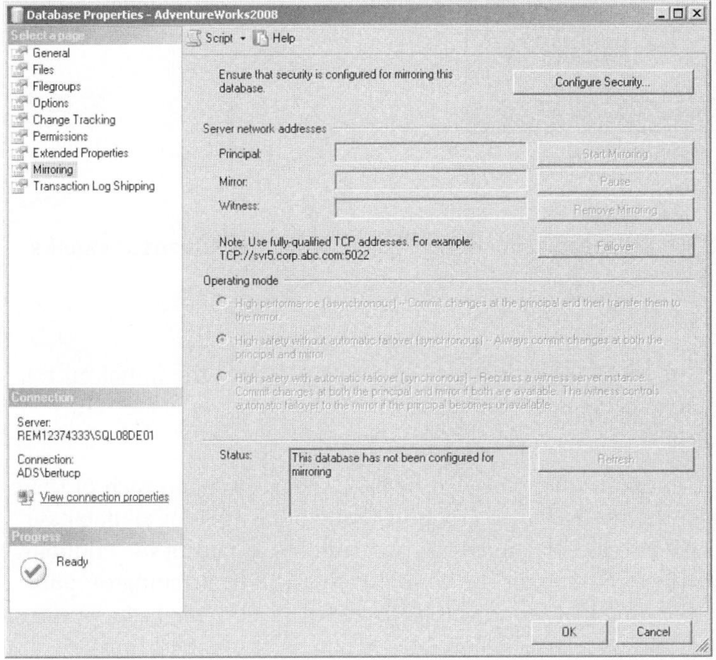

FIGURE 20.3 The Database Properties Mirroring page: mirroring network addressing and mirroring status.

Next, we look at how to set up high safety with automatic failover mode (high-availability mode) database mirroring with principal, mirror, and witness servers. For this, you can mirror the old reliable `AdventureWorks` database that Microsoft provides with SQL Server 2008.

Figure 20.4 illustrates the database mirroring configuration to set up.

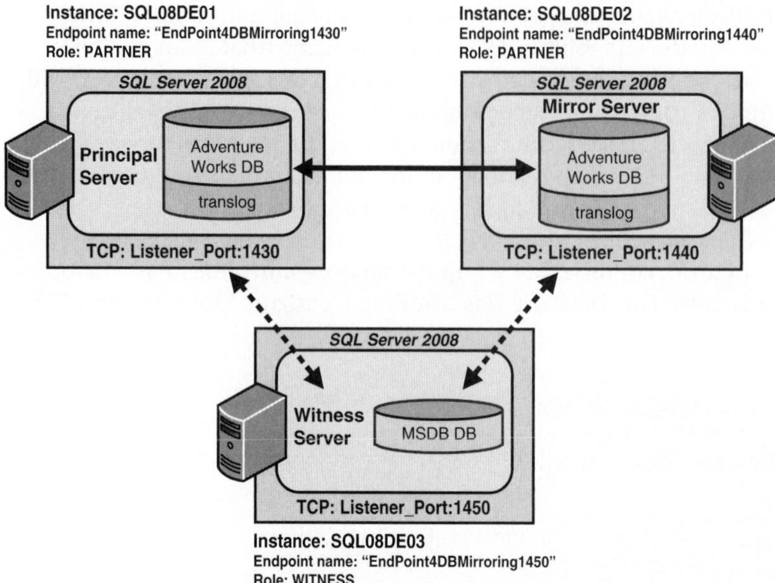

FIGURE 20.4 A high-availability database mirroring configuration with the **AdventureWorks** database.

The initial principal server is the SQL Server instance named `SQL08DE01`, the initial mirror server is the SQL Server instance named `SQL08DE02`, and the witness server is the SQL Server instance named `SQL08DE03`.

You need to establish a local endpoint named `EndPoint4DBMirroring9`*`xxx`* on each of these SQL Server instances and identify the TCP listening port that will be used for all database mirroring communication. We also like to embed the port number as part of the endpoint name, such as `EndPoint4DBMirroring1430` for the endpoint that will be listening on port 1430. In our configuration, the principal server will be listening on Port 1430, the mirror server on Port 1440, and the witness server on Port 1450. These port numbers must be unique within a single server machine, and the machine name and port combination must be unique within the network. An example of the fully qualified network address name of this server and the listing port is `TCP://REM1237433.ads.autodesk.com:1430`, where `REM1237433.ads.autodesk.com` is the machine name within the domain, and `1430` is the listening port created with the endpoint. In addition, each server's initial role needs to be specified. The `SQL08DE01` instance can play any partner role (that is, a mirror and/or principal), the `SQL08DE02` instance can play any partner role as well, and the `SQL08DE03` instance should play the witness role only.

We have included three SQL script templates with this book (in the Chapter 20 code directory on the CD) that have working examples of creating the endpoints, granting connection permissions to a login for the endpoints, verifying that the endpoints were created, altering the endpoints, backing up and restoring databases, and backing up and restoring transaction logs.

The first ones to look at are `2008 Create EndPoint Partner1.SQL`, `2008 Create EndPoint Partner2.SQL`, and `2008 Create EndPoint Witness.SQL`. You can leverage these templates to start the setup process if you are not using the Configure Security Wizard.

Now that we've verified all aspects of our planned mirroring topology, let's configure full database mirroring!

Creating the Endpoints

Each server instance in the database mirroring configuration must have an endpoint defined so that the other servers can communicate with it. This is sort of like a private phone line to your friends. Let's use the scripts provided as opposed to using the Configure Security Wizard. The first endpoint script is in the file `2008 Create EndPoint Partner1.SQL`.

From SSMS, you need to open a new query connection to your principal database by selecting File, New and in the New Query dialog, selecting Query with Current Connection. Open the SQL file for the first endpoint.

The following `CREATE ENDPOINT` T-SQL creates the endpoint named `EndPoint4DBMirroring1430`, with the `listener_port` value of `1430`, and the database mirroring role `Partner`:

```
-- create endpoint for principal server --
CREATE ENDPOINT [EndPoint4DBMirroring1430]
    STATE=STARTED
    AS TCP (LISTENER_PORT = 1430, LISTENER_IP = ALL)
    FOR DATA_MIRRORING (ROLE = PARTNER, AUTHENTICATION = WINDOWS NEGOTIATE
, ENCRYPTION = REQUIRED ALGORITHM RC4)
```

After this T-SQL runs, you should quickly run the following `SELECT` statements to verify that the endpoint has been correctly created:

```
select name,type_desc,port,ip_address from sys.tcp_endpoints;


SELECT db.name, m.mirroring_role_desc
FROM sys.database_mirroring m
JOIN sys.databases db
ON db.database_id = m.database_id
WHERE db.name = N'AdventureWorks';

select name,role_desc,state_desc from sys.database_mirroring_endpoints;
```

Figure 20.5 shows the desired result set from these queries.

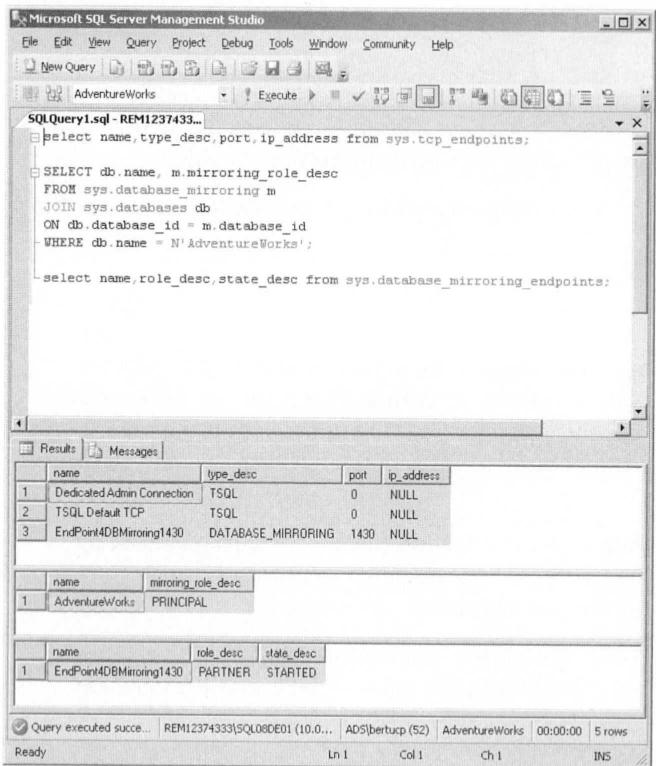

FIGURE 20.5 Verifying that an endpoint is created for database mirroring.

If you also look at the database properties for the AdventureWorks database on the principal server (SQL08DE01, in this example), you see the server network address for the principal server automatically appear now when you look at the Database Properties Mirroring page (see Figure 20.6).

Starting with the sample SQL scripts `2008 Create EndPoint Partner2.SQL` and `2008 Create EndPoint Witness.SQL`, you need to repeat the endpoint creation process for the mirror server (using a listener_port value of 1440) and the witness server (using a listener_port value of 1450) by opening a query connection to each one of these servers and running the following `CREATE ENDPOINT` commands:

```
-- create endpoint for mirror server --
CREATE ENDPOINT [EndPoint4DBMirroring1440]
    STATE=STARTED
    AS TCP (LISTENER_PORT = 1440, LISTENER_IP = ALL)
    FOR DATA_MIRRORING (ROLE = PARTNER, AUTHENTICATION = WINDOWS NEGOTIATE
, ENCRYPTION = REQUIRED ALGORITHM RC4)
```

For the witness server (notice that the role is now Witness), you run the following:

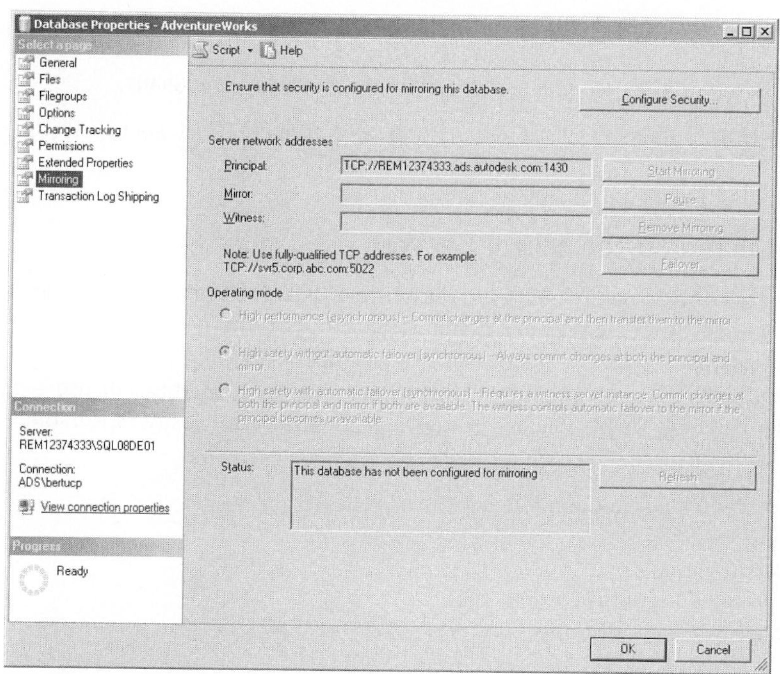

FIGURE 20.6 The Mirroring page of the **AdventureWorks** database on the principal server.

```
-- create endpoint for witness server --
CREATE ENDPOINT [EndPoint4DBMirroring1450]
    STATE=STARTED
    AS TCP (LISTENER_PORT = 1450, LISTENER_IP = ALL)
    FOR DATA_MIRRORING (ROLE = WITNESS, AUTHENTICATION = WINDOWS NEGOTIATE
, ENCRYPTION = REQUIRED ALGORITHM RC4)
```

Granting Permissions

It is possible to have an `AUTHORIZATION [login]` statement in the `CREATE ENDPOINT` command that establishes the permissions for a login account to the endpoint being defined. However, separating this out into a `GRANT` greatly stresses the point of allowing this connection permission. From each SQL query connection, you run a `GRANT` to allow a specific login account to connect on the `ENDPOINT` for database mirroring. If you don't have a specific login account to use, default it to `[NT AUTHORITY\SYSTEM]`.

First, from the principal server instance (`SQL08DE01`), you run the following `GRANT` (substituting `[DBARCHLT\Paul Bertucci]` with your specific login account to be used by database mirroring):

```
GRANT CONNECT ON ENDPOINT::EndPoint4DBMirroring1430 TO [DBARCHLT\Paul Bertucci];
```

Then, from the mirror server instance (`SQL08DE02`), you run the following `GRANT`:

20

```
GRANT CONNECT ON ENDPOINT:: EndPoint4DBMirroring1440 TO [DBARCHLT\Paul Bertucci];
```

Then, from the witness server instance (SQL08DE03), you run the following GRANT:

```
GRANT CONNECT ON ENDPOINT:: EndPoint4DBMirroring1450 TO [DBARCHLT\Paul Bertucci];
```

Creating the Database on the Mirror Server

When the endpoints are configured and roles are established, you can create the database on the mirror server and get it to the point of being able to mirror. You must first make a backup copy of the principal database (AdventureWorks, in this example). This backup will be used to create the database on the mirror server. You can use SSMS tasks or use SQL scripts to do this. The SQL scripts (DBBackupAW2008.sql), which are easily repeatable, are used here.

On the principal server, you make a complete backup as follows:

```
BACKUP DATABASE [AdventureWorks]
    TO DISK = N'C:\Program Files\Microsoft SQL
Server\MSSQL.2\MSSQL\Backup\AdventureWorks4Mirror.bak'
    WITH FORMAT
GO
```

Next, you copy this backup file to a place where the mirror server can reach it on the network. When that is complete, you can issue the following database RESTORE command to create the AdventureWorks database on the mirror server (using the WITH NORECOVERY option):

```
-- use this restore database(with NoRecovery option)
to create the mirrored version of this DB --
RESTORE FILELISTONLY
   FROM DISK = 'C:\Program Files\Microsoft SQL
Server\MSSQL.2\MSSQL\Backup\AdventureWorks4Mirror.bak'
go
RESTORE DATABASE AdventureWorks
   FROM DISK = 'C:\Program Files\Microsoft SQL
               Server\MSSQL.2\MSSQL\Backup\AdventureWorks4Mirror.bak'
  WITH NORECOVERY,
        MOVE 'AdventureWorks_Data' TO 'C:\Program Files\Microsoft SQL
               Server\MSSQL.4\MSSQL\Data\AdventureWorks_Data.mdf',
        MOVE 'AdventureWorks_Log'  TO 'C:\Program Files\Microsoft SQL
               Server\MSSQL.4\MSSQL\Data\AdventureWorks_Log.ldf'
GO
```

Because you don't necessarily have the same directory structure on the mirror server, you use the MOVE option as part of this restore to place the database files in the location you desire.

The restore process should yield something that looks like the following result set when restoring the AdventureWorks database that is shipped with SQL Server 2008:

```
-- Processed 21200 pages for database 'AdventureWorks',
                  file 'AdventureWorks_Data' on file 1.
-- Processed 2 pages for database 'AdventureWorks',
                  file 'AdventureWorks_Log' on file 1.
-- RESTORE DATABASE successfully processed 21202 pages
                  in 14.677 seconds (11.833 MB/sec).
```

Basically, this result set says you are not ready to get into the mirroring business yet. You must now apply at least one transaction log dump to the mirror database. This brings the mirror database to a point of synchronization with the principal and leaves the mirror database in the Restoring state. At this database recovery point, you can run through the mirroring wizard and start mirroring for high availability.

From the principal server, you dump (that is, back up) a transaction log as follows:

```
BACKUP LOG [AdventureWorks] TO
DISK = N'C:\Program Files\Microsoft SQL
Server\MSSQL.2\MSSQL\Backup\AdventureWorksLog.bak'
Go
Processed 8 pages for database 'AdventureWorks', file 'AdventureWorks_Log' on file 2.
```

Then you move this backup to a place where it can be reached by the mirror server. When that is done, you restore the log to the mirror database. From the mirror server, you restore the transaction log as follows. Note the following `WITH FILE =` statement; the file number must match the value in the backup log results (see the `on file 2` reference in the previous code):

```
RESTORE LOG [AdventureWorks]
   FROM  DISK = N'C:\Program Files\Microsoft SQL
         Server\MSSQL.4\MSSQL\Backup\AdventureWorksLog.bak'
   WITH  FILE = 2, NORECOVERY
GO
```

The restore log process should yield something that looks like the following result set:

```
RESTORE LOG successfully processed 8 pages
        in 0.034 seconds (9.396 MB/sec).
```

NOTE

You might need to update the `FILE = x` *entry in the RESTORE LOG* command to correspond to the "on file" value given during the log backup.

You are now ready to mirror the database in high-availability mode.

Identifying the Other Endpoints for Database Mirroring

To get each node in the topology to see each other, you have to identify the endpoints and listener port values to the databases involved in the database mirroring configuration (the principal and mirror). This also activates database mirroring. This process requires altering the database by using either the `SET PARTNER` or `SET WITNESS` statements within the `ALTER DATABASE` command. The Database Mirroring Wizard can also do this step for you, but doing it manually is easy.

We identify the unique endpoint listening port values for each endpoint that are unique within the server. They are port values 1430, 1440, and 1450 in our example.

Remember, you will be doing this *after* you create the `AdventureWorks` database on the mirror server side. After creating that database, you can run the following `ALTER DATABASE` command on the mirror server to identify the principal for the mirror to partner with:

```
-- From the Mirror Server Database: identify the principal server endpoint --
ALTER DATABASE AdventureWorks
    SET PARTNER = ' TCP://REM1237433.ads.autodesk.com:1430'
GO
```

Now, you are ready for the final step. From the principal server, you identify the mirror and witness. After you complete these step, the database mirroring topology tries to synchronize itself and begin database mirroring. The following statements identify the mirror server endpoint and witness server endpoint to the principal server's database:

```
-- From the Principal Server Database: identify the mirror server endpoint --
ALTER DATABASE AdventureWorks
    SET PARTNER = 'TCP://REM1237433.ads.autodesk.com:1440'
GO
-- From the Principal Server Database: identify the witness server endpoint --
ALTER DATABASE AdventureWorks
  SET WITNESS = 'TCP://REM1237433.ads.autodesk.com:1450'
GO
```

You do not have to alter any database from the witness server.

When this process completes successfully, you are mirroring! Yes, in fact, with this configuration, you are in automatic failover mode.

If you have issues or just want to start over, you can drop an endpoint or alter an endpoint quite easily. To drop and existing endpoint, you use the `DROP ENDPOINT` command. In this example, the following command would drop the endpoint you just created:

```
-- To DROP an existing endpoint --
DROP ENDPOINT EndPoint4DBMirroring1430;
```

Altering an endpoint (for example, to change the `listener_port` value) is just as easy as dropping one. The following example shows how to alter the currently defined endpoint to a new `listener_port` value of `1435` because of a conflict at the network level. (However, because we use the port in the endpoint name, it might have been best to just drop and create a new endpoint to fit the naming convention. Either way, you can easily manipulate these endpoints to fit your networking needs.)

```
-- To ALTER an existing endpoint --
ALTER ENDPOINT EndPoint4DBMirroring1430
   STATE = STARTED
   AS TCP( LISTENER_PORT = 1435 )
   FOR DATABASE_MIRRORING (ROLE = PARTNER)
```

Configuring Database Mirroring by Using the Wizard

After you have the endpoints created, the roles established, the connections to the endpoints granted, and the mirror database restored on the mirror server, you could easily run through the final short steps in the Database Mirroring Wizard to enable and start mirroring. Figure 20.7 shows the Mirror option from the `AdventureWorks` database (reached by right-clicking the database name) from what will be the principal server. Because this database is not enabled for mirroring yet, you must run through the Configure Security option on the top portion of the Mirroring page (refer to Figure 20.6). At this point, you can probably see only the network server address of the principal server. Don't worry; the rest (mirror and witness network server addresses) will be established and identified during the Configure Database Mirroring Security Wizard steps.

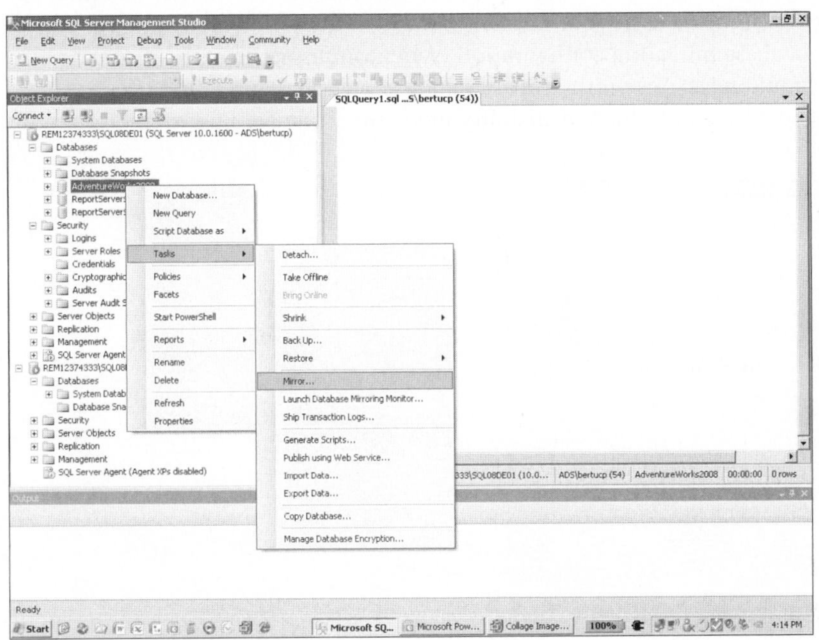

FIGURE 20.7 The Mirror option for the principal database server (`AdventureWorks`).

You need to click the Configure Security button on the Mirroring page. This immediately launches the Configure Database Mirroring Security Wizard for the database you have selected (`AdventureWorks`, in this example). Figure 20.8 shows this initial wizard splash page.

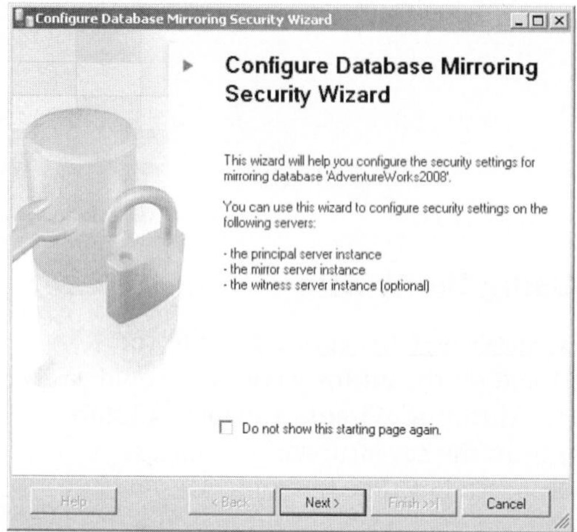

FIGURE 20.8 The Configure Database Mirroring Security Wizard for the **`AdventureWorks`** database.

You must configure all three server instances (principal, mirror, and witness servers) for the high-availability mode. The first option that must be indicated is whether you plan to include a witness server instance in your mirroring configuration. You are configuring a high-availability database mirroring configuration (synchronous mode with automatic failover), so you should select Yes on the wizard dialog shown in Figure 20.9; you do so because you want to create a full high-availability mode for automated failover.

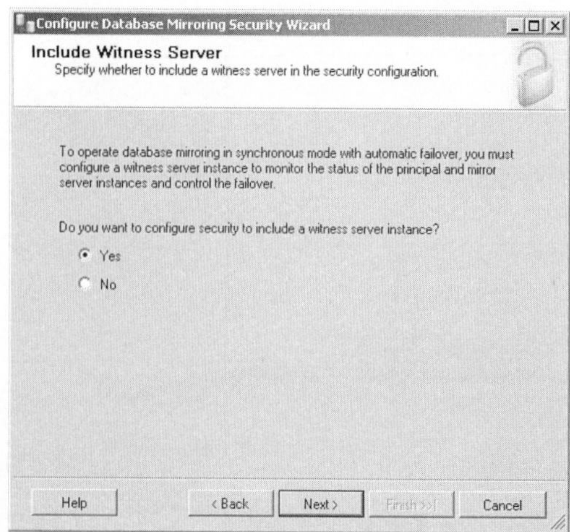

FIGURE 20.9 Including the witness server instance in the mirroring configuration.

The next page in the wizard prompts you to decide where to save the security configurations for database mirroring. You have no choice for the principal and mirror server instances; their security configuration information must be stored with them. You must also choose the default location for the witness server instance. The wizard then takes you through each server instance in the database mirroring configuration to establish all needed connection information to implement database mirroring. As you can see in Figure 20.10, this starts with the principal server instance. The wizard should find the endpoint and `listener_port` values you set up earlier (`listener_port` value 1430 and endpoint name `EndPoint4DBMirroring1430`, in this example).

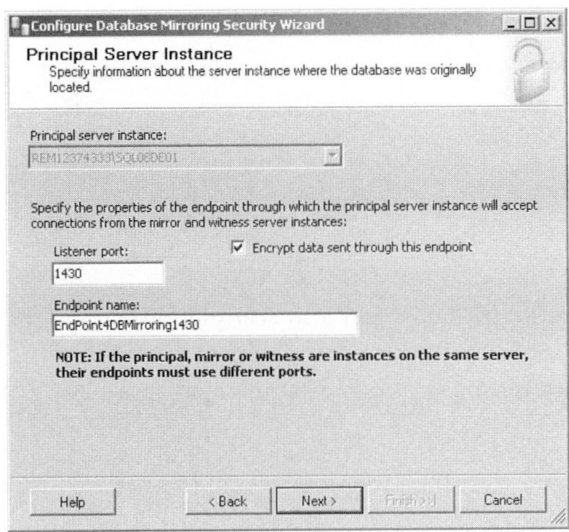

FIGURE 20.10 The Principal Server Instance screen of the Configure Database Mirroring Security Wizard.

Next comes the specification of the listener and endpoint entry for the mirror server instance (where the mirror copy of the database will be located). Initially, this page lists all server instances available on your network (that is, possible mirror server instances) and does not have a listener port or endpoint name specified yet. You need to identify which server you want to use as the mirror server instance (`REM12374333\SQL08DE02`, in this example) and click the Connect button to establish a valid (authorized) connection to the mirror server instance. Because you already set up the endpoint on this server (and granted connection permission, using a specific login ID), when you complete the connection dialog, the endpoint (`EndPoint4DBMirroring1440`, in this example) and `listener_port` value (1440, in this example) should be enabled, as shown in Figure 20.11.

Finally, you need to specify the witness server instance. Again, this dialog page lists all server instances available on the network (that is, possible witness server instances) and does not have a listener port or an endpoint name specified yet. You need to identify which server you want to use as the witness server instance (`REM12374333\SQL08DE03`, in this example) and click the Connect button to establish a valid (authorized) connection to the witness server instance. Because you already set up the endpoint on this server (and

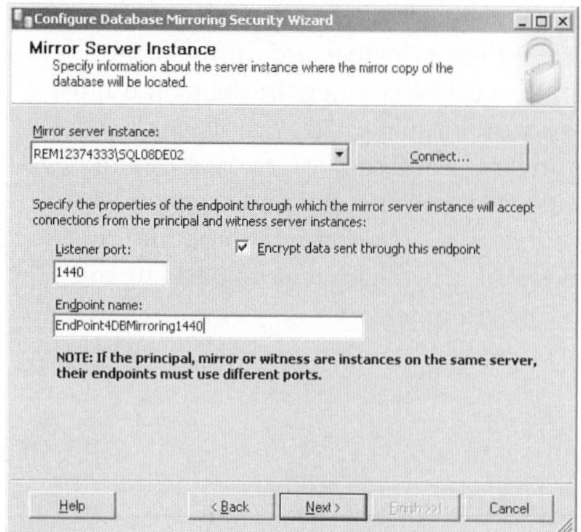

FIGURE 20.11 The Mirror Server Instance screen of the Configure Database Mirroring Security Wizard.

granted connection permission, using a specific login ID), when you complete the connection dialog, the endpoint (`EndPoint4DBMirroring1450`, in our example) and `listener_port` value (1450, in this example) should be enabled, as shown in Figure 20.12.

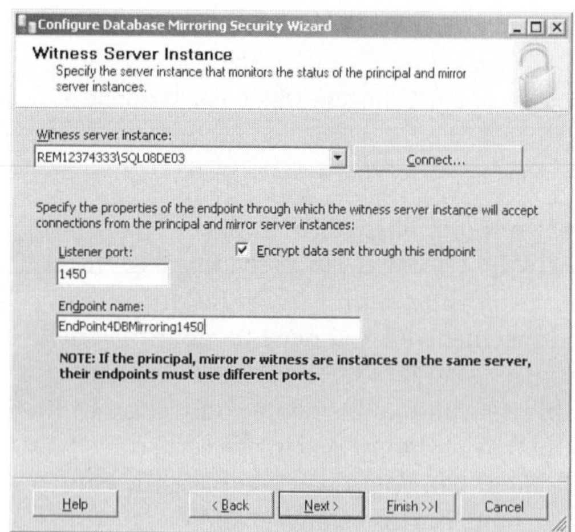

FIGURE 20.12 The Witness Server Instance screen of the Configure Database Mirroring Security Wizard.

The last step in the Configure Database Mirroring Security Wizard is to identify any service accounts that you want to use for the server instances in this database mirroring configuration. You are already using a single domain login ID for this purpose and explicitly granted connect permissions on each endpoint. Therefore, nothing more needs to be done here. If the server instances use different accounts in the same or a trusted domain as their service accounts for SQL Server, you can enter these accounts here. It is best to do this via scripts (as you saw earlier, when you created the endpoints on each server instance).

As you can see in Figure 20.13, the Configure Database Mirroring Security Wizard now presents a summary list of all the actions on each server instance that it will perform. You click Finish to execute them.

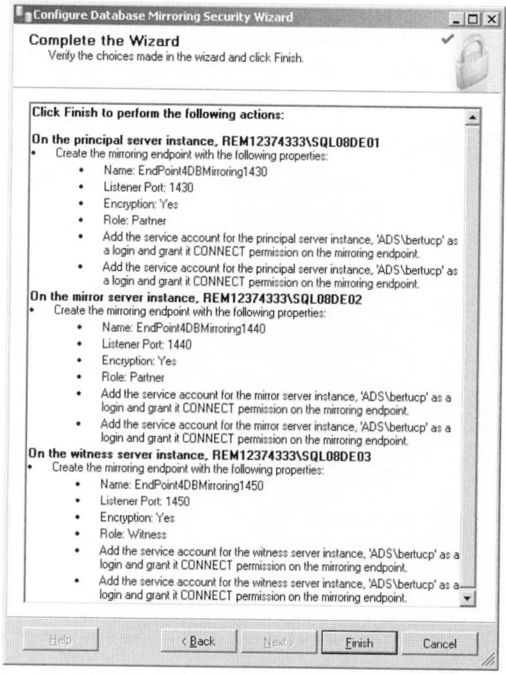

FIGURE 20.13 Summary of actions to be performed for the database mirroring configuration.

A report is generated, telling the total number of actions taken (three, in this case) and the status of each action. If any errors or warnings result, you can drill down into the Report button option in the bottom-right corner of this summary of actions page to determine what has occurred. If each status shows success, a Database Properties dialog, as shown in Figure 20.14, appears when you close this report page. This dialog gives you the option to start mirroring immediately or not start mirroring (because you will start mirroring at some other time). For this example, you want to start mirroring right away, so click the Start Mirroring button.

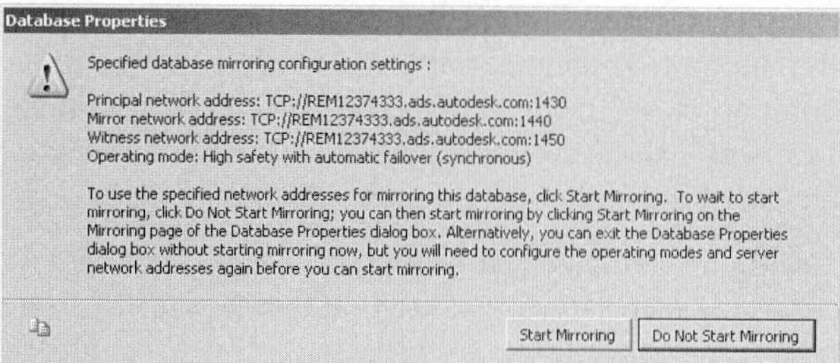

FIGURE 20.14 Specifying to start database mirroring for high safety with automatic failover.

Figure 20.15 shows the full Database Properties screen for the `AdventureWorks` database, all server network addresses, and the operating mode for mirroring.

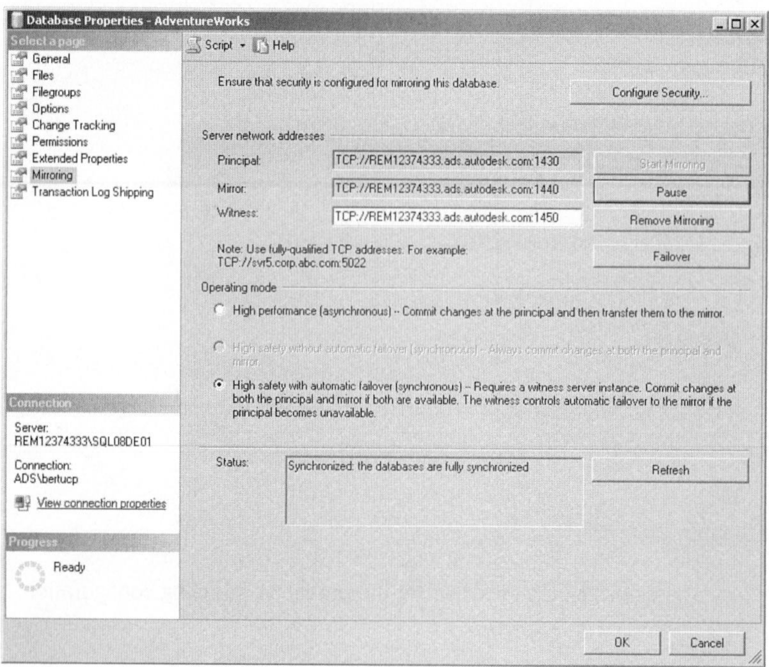

FIGURE 20.15 Fully configured properties and active mirroring for database mirroring.

If you look at the SQL Server log file (that is, the current log), you can see log entries indicating that database mirroring is active:

```
2/21/2009 22:33:33,spid21s,Unknown,Database mirroring is
          active with database 'AdventureWorks' as the
          principal copy. This is an informational message
          only. No user action is required.
2/21/2009 22:33:09,spid17s,Unknown,Starting up database 'AdventureWorks'.
```

```
2/21/2009 22:33:07,Server,Unknown,SQL Server is now
          ready for client connections. This is an
          informational message; no user action is required.
2/21/2009 22:33:00,spid12s,Unknown,The Database
           Mirroring protocol transport is now listening for connections.
2/21/2009 22:33:00,spid12s,Unknown,Server is
        listening on [ 'any' <ipv4> 1430].
```

Congratulations. You are now mirroring a database!

Monitoring a Mirrored Database Environment

After active mirroring has started, you can monitor the complete mirrored topology in a few ways. You can start by registering the database being mirrored to a new facility within SSMS called Database Mirroring Monitor. Database Mirroring Monitor allows you to monitor roles of the mirroring partnership (that is, principal, mirror, and witness), see the history of transactions flowing to the mirror server, see the status and speed of this transaction flow, and set thresholds to alert you if failures or other issues occur. In addition, you can administer the logins/service accounts being used in the mirrored database topology.

Figure 20.16 shows how you launch the Database Mirroring Monitor from SSMS: you right-click the principal database being mirrored, choose Tasks, and then choose Launch Database Mirroring Monitor.

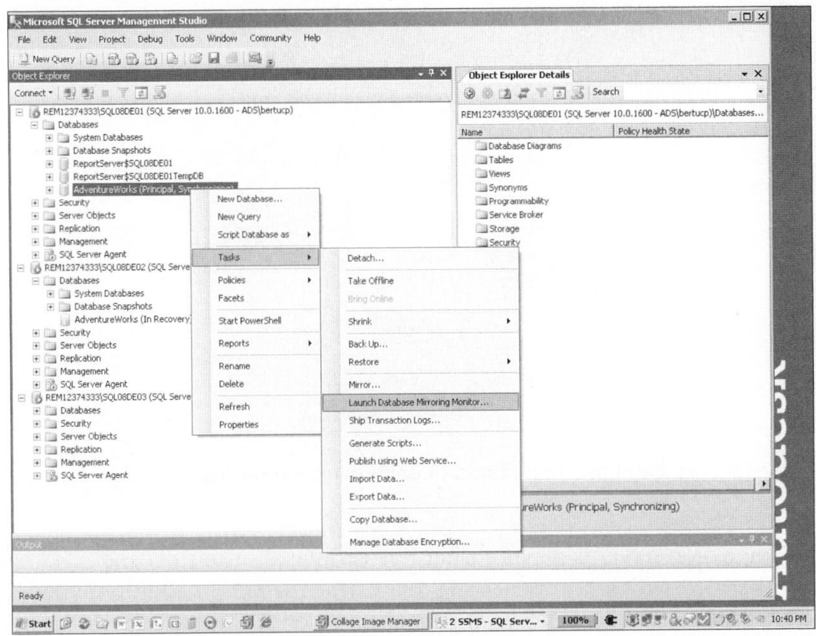

FIGURE 20.16 Launching Database Mirroring Monitor from SSMS.

You must register the database being mirrored. To do so, you select the principal or mirror server instance and set the Register check box for the database. Database Mirroring Monitor registers the database and both partner server instances, as shown in Figure 20.17.

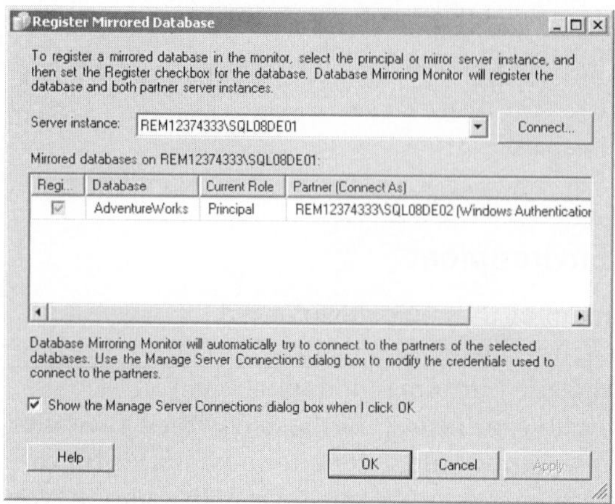

FIGURE 20.17 Registering the mirrored database within the Database Mirroring Monitor.

After the database is registered, all partners and the witness server instances show up in the Database Mirroring Monitor, as shown in Figure 20.18.

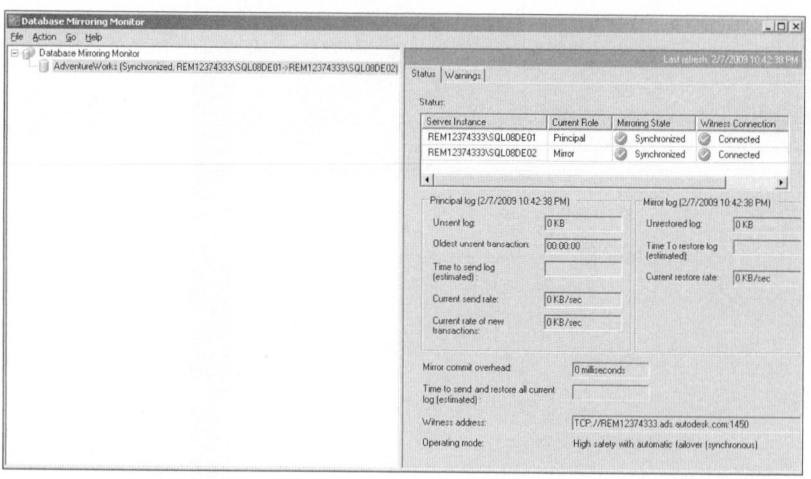

FIGURE 20.18 The registered database and status of each mirroring partner.

At a glance, you can see which server is playing what role (principal or mirror) and whether each partner has defined and is connecting to a witness server. In addition, you can see the unsent log (in size), the un-restored log (in size), when the oldest unsent transaction occurred, the amount of time it took to send the transaction to the mirror server instance, the send rate (KB/second), the current rate at which the transactions get restored

(KB/second), the mirror commit overhead (in milliseconds), the listener port of the witness server instance, and the operating mode of the mirroring (in this case, high safety with automatic failover—synchronous).

Figure 20.19 shows the detailed transaction history for a particular part of the mirroring flow (either the send out of the principal part or the restore to the mirror part). You can click the appropriate partner to see all transaction history details of the mirrored copy and restore process.

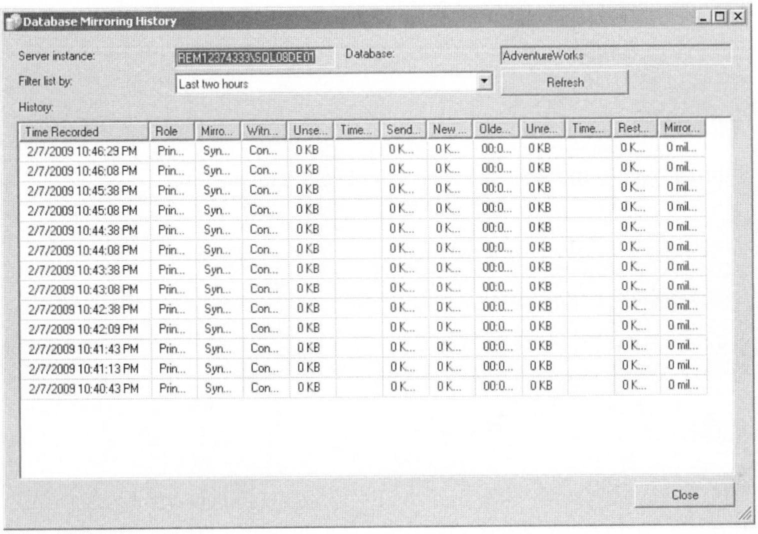

Database Mirroring History

Server instance: REM12374333\SQL08DE01 Database: AdventureWorks

Filter list by: Last two hours Refresh

History:

Time Recorded	Role	Mirro...	Witn...	Unse...	Time...	Send...	New ...	Olde...	Unre...	Time...	Rest...	Mirror...
2/7/2009 10:46:29 PM	Prin...	Syn...	Con...	0 KB		0 K...	0 K...	00:0...	0 KB		0 K...	0 mil...
2/7/2009 10:46:08 PM	Prin...	Syn...	Con...	0 KB		0 K...	0 K...	00:0...	0 KB		0 K...	0 mil...
2/7/2009 10:45:38 PM	Prin...	Syn...	Con...	0 KB		0 K...	0 K...	00:0...	0 KB		0 K...	0 mil...
2/7/2009 10:45:08 PM	Prin...	Syn...	Con...	0 KB		0 K...	0 K...	00:0...	0 KB		0 K...	0 mil...
2/7/2009 10:44:38 PM	Prin...	Syn...	Con...	0 KB		0 K...	0 K...	00:0...	0 KB		0 K...	0 mil...
2/7/2009 10:44:08 PM	Prin...	Syn...	Con...	0 KB		0 K...	0 K...	00:0...	0 KB		0 K...	0 mil...
2/7/2009 10:43:38 PM	Prin...	Syn...	Con...	0 KB		0 K...	0 K...	00:0...	0 KB		0 K...	0 mil...
2/7/2009 10:43:08 PM	Prin...	Syn...	Con...	0 KB		0 K...	0 K...	00:0...	0 KB		0 K...	0 mil...
2/7/2009 10:42:38 PM	Prin...	Syn...	Con...	0 KB		0 K...	0 K...	00:0...	0 KB		0 K...	0 mil...
2/7/2009 10:42:09 PM	Prin...	Syn...	Con...	0 KB		0 K...	0 K...	00:0...	0 KB		0 K...	0 mil...
2/7/2009 10:41:43 PM	Prin...	Syn...	Con...	0 KB		0 K...	0 K...	00:0...	0 KB		0 K...	0 mil...
2/7/2009 10:41:13 PM	Prin...	Syn...	Con...	0 KB		0 K...	0 K...	00:0...	0 KB		0 K...	0 mil...
2/7/2009 10:40:43 PM	Prin...	Syn...	Con...	0 KB		0 K...	0 K...	00:0...	0 KB		0 K...	0 mil...

Close

FIGURE 20.19 Transaction history of mirroring partners.

If you click the Warnings tab of the Database Mirroring Monitor, you can set various thresholds within the monitor to alert you when they have been reached (see Figure 20.20). Basically, you want to set thresholds that monitor the effectiveness of the mirroring operation.

If these key thresholds are ever exceeded, you want to be notified that something is very wrong and that failover may be in jeopardy. When a threshold is exceeded, an event is logged to the Application event log. You can configure an alert on this event by using SSMS or Microsoft Management Operations Manager (MOM). The threshold levels depend on your own failover tolerance. Our advice is to monitor the transaction and transfer rates for a peak period and then set the thresholds to be 100% higher than that. For example, if you see a peak mirror commit overhead value of 750 milliseconds, you should set the threshold to 1,500 milliseconds. This should be within the tolerance for commit overhead in your organization.

Figure 20.21 shows how easy it is to administer the service accounts/login IDs being used for database mirroring. You simply click an Edit button to change or set the login account you want to use for database mirroring at each instance in the mirroring topology.

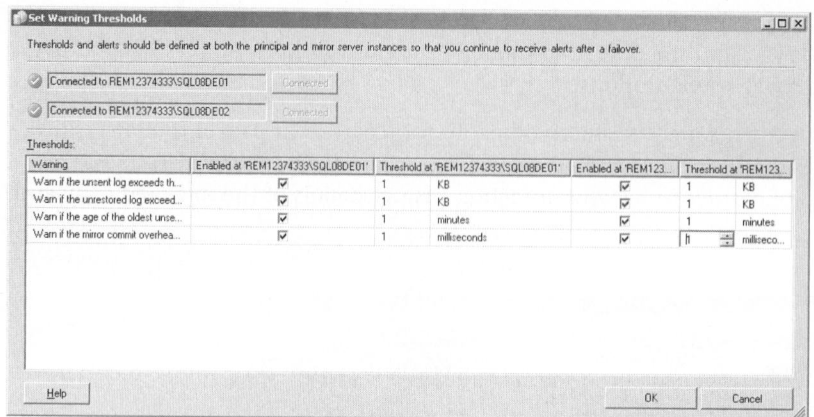

FIGURE 20.20 Setting thresholds to monitor mirroring effectiveness.

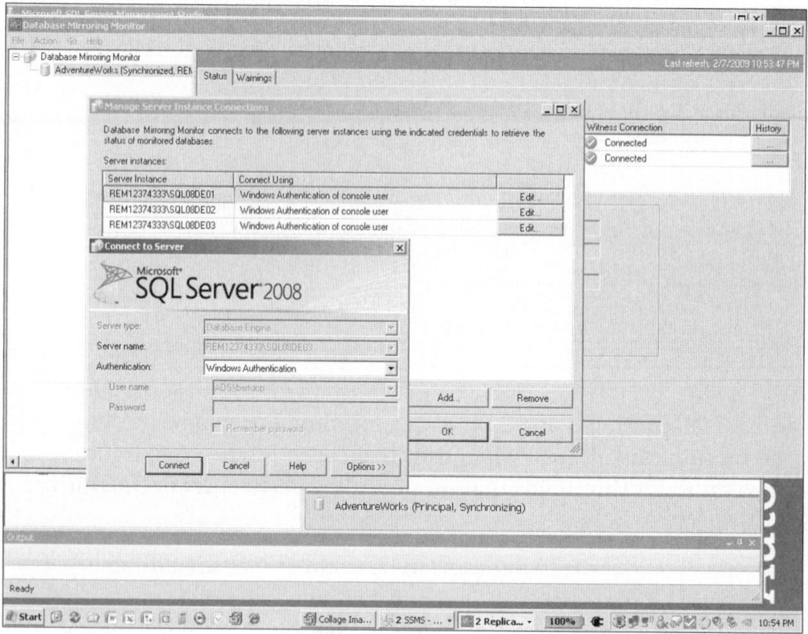

FIGURE 20.21 Setting service accounts/login IDs within the mirroring topology.

From the Database Properties Mirroring page, you can easily pause (and resume) database mirroring if you suspect that there are issues related to the mirroring operation. In addition, you can easily see what role each server instance is playing.

Removing Mirroring

Very likely, you will have to remove all traces of database mirroring from each server instance of a database mirroring configuration at some point. Doing so is actually pretty easy. Basically, you have to disable mirroring of the principal, drop the mirror server's database, and remove all endpoints from each server instance. You can simply start from the Database Properties page and the Mirroring option and do the whole thing. Alternatively, you can do this through SQL scripts. Let's first use the Mirroring options. Looking at the options on Figure 20.22, you simply choose to remove mirroring (from the principal server instance). This is just a bit too easy to do—almost dangerous!

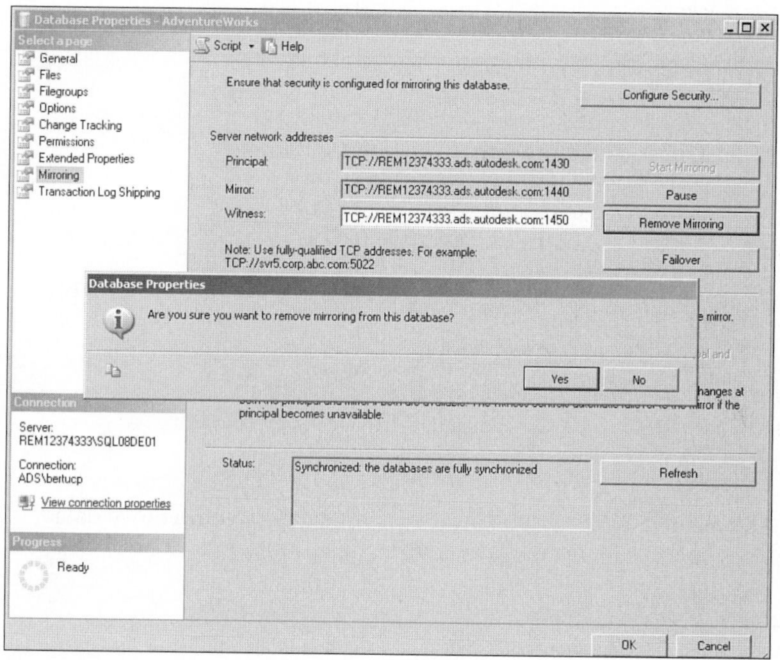

FIGURE 20.22 Removing database mirroring.

The mirroring process is immediately disabled. When mirroring is disabled, you can drop the database on the mirror server instance, remove the endpoints on each server instance (that is, principal, mirror, and witness instances), and be done—all through SSMS. This approach is straightforward.

If you're removing mirroring with SQL scripts, however, you need to break the mirroring from the principal, remove the principal's endpoint, drop the mirror database and remove the mirror's endpoint, and then drop the witness server's endpoint. At this point, all mirroring is removed. Follow along as we remove the database mirroring configuration we just set up.

The ALTER DATABASE and DROP ENDPOINT SQL commands break mirroring on the principal and remove the endpoint:

```
ALTER DATABASE AdventureWorks set partner off
go
DROP ENDPOINT EndPoint4DBMirroring1430
go
```

From the mirror server instance (not the principal!), you run the DROP DATABASE and DROP ENDPOINT SQL commands, as follows:

```
DROP DATABASE AdventureWorks
go
DROP ENDPOINT EndPoint4DBMirroring1440
go
```

From the witness server instance, you remove the endpoint as follows:

```
DROP ENDPOINT EndPoint4DBMirroring1450
go
```

To verify that you have removed these endpoints from each server instance, you simply run the following SELECT statements:

```
select name,type_desc,port,ip_address from sys.tcp_endpoints
select name,role_desc,state_desc from sys.database_mirroring_endpoints
```

All references to the endpoints and roles are removed.

You can also take a peek at the SQL Server log entries being made as you remove database mirroring:

```
02/05/2009 13:06:42,spid55,Unknown,The Database
           Mirroring protocol transport is disabled or not configured.
02/05/2009 13:06:40,spid55,Unknown,The Database Mirroring
           protocol transport has stopped listening for connections.
02/05/2009 12:52:55,spid19s,Unknown,Database mirroring
           connection error 4 'An error occurred while receiving
           data: '64(The specified network name is no longer
           available.)'.' for 'TCP:// REM1233..:1440'.
02/05/2009 12:52:55,spid19s,Unknown,Error: 1474
           <c/> Severity: 16<c/> State: 1.
02/05/2009 12:52:55,spid19s,Unknown,Database mirroring
           connection error 4 'An error occurred while
           receiving data: '64(The specified network name is
           no longer available.)'.' for 'TCP://REM1233..:1450'.
02/05/2009 12:52:55,spid19s,Unknown,Error: 1474
```

```
          <c/> Severity: 16<c/> State: 1.
02/05/2009 12:51:14,spid21s,Unknown,Database mirroring
          has been terminated for database 'AdventureWorks'.
```

These are all informational messages only. No user action is required. As you can see from these messages, you are now in a state of no database mirroring. You have to completely build up database mirroring again if you want to mirror the database again.

Testing Failover from the Principal to the Mirror

From the SSMS, you can easily fail over from the principal to the mirror server instance (and back again) by using the Failover button on the Database Properties Mirroring page, as shown in Figure 20.23.

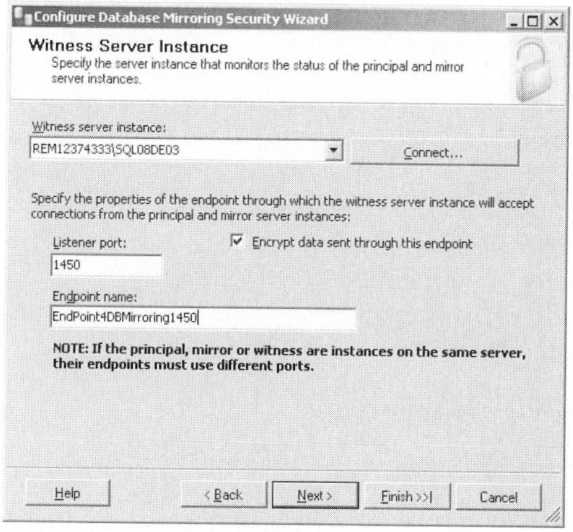

FIGURE 20.23 Testing failover of a mirrored database.

You must test this failover at some point to guarantee that it works. When you click the Failover button for this database mirroring configuration, you are prompted to continue with the failover by clicking Yes or No, as in the dialog shown in Figure 20.24.

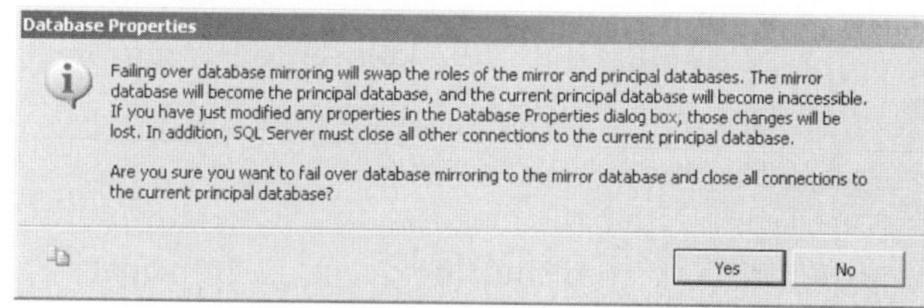

FIGURE 20.24 The failover message for database mirroring.

Remember that clicking Yes closes all connections to the principal server instance that are currently connected to this database. Later, we show you how to make your clients aware of both the principal and mirror server instances so that they can just pick up and run against either server instance, by design.

Now, if you look at the Database Properties Mirroring page (see Figure 20.25), you see that the principal and mirror listener port values have switched: the principal instance is now port value 1440, and the mirror instance is port value 1430. The server instances have completely switched their roles. You must now go to the server instance playing the principal role to fail over back to the original operating mode. If you try to open the current mirror server instance database, you get an error stating that you cannot access this database because it is in restore mode.

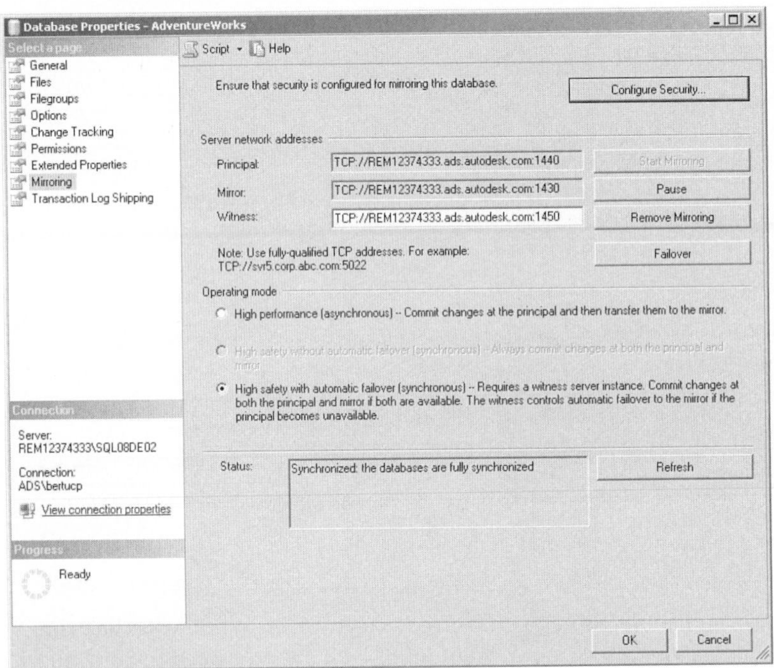

FIGURE 20.25 Server instances switch roles following a failover.

You can also manually run an `ALTER DATABASE` command to force failover to the mirrored server as follows:

```
ALTER DATABASE AdventureWorks set partner FAILOVER;
```

This command has the same effect as using SSMS or even shutting down the principal SQL Server instance service.

One last note with mirroring a database is that you cannot bring the principal offline as you would be able to do in an unmirrored configuration.

Client Setup and Configuration for Database Mirroring

Microsoft has enhanced the client connection capabilities to become mirroring aware. In other words, a client application is now able to connect to either partner in a mirrored configuration. The client would, of course, be connecting only to the server instance that is the current principal. With the help of an extension to the client connection configuration file, all .NET applications can easily add both partners to their connection string information, and when a principal fails, they can automatically establish a connection to the new principal (in a mirrored configuration). Figure 20.26 shows the added connection string information that you provide in the configuration file (`app.config`) for your application. This enhancement uses the `Failover Partner=` addition that identifies the proper failover server instance for this mirrored configuration.

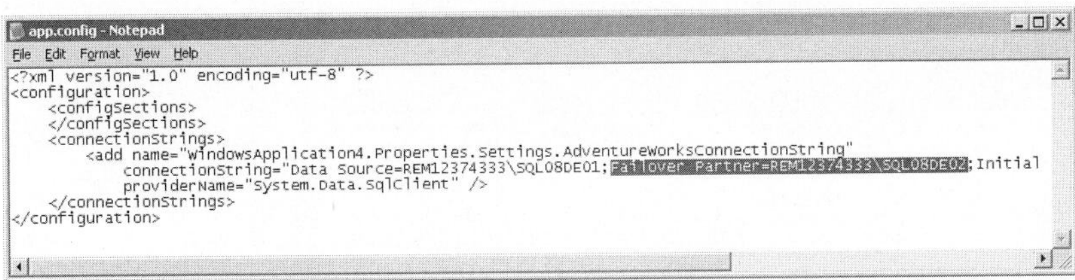

FIGURE 20.26 A client connection string configuration identifying the failover partner.

As a bonus, we have provided a small .NET C# client application that you can easily use to test client connections in a database mirroring configuration. This C# solution file, `SQL Client DB Mirroring Test.zip`, is included in the Chapter 20 code samples on the CD supplied with this book. When you expand this file, it builds a complete .NET solution directory with all code needed for this test application. With Visual Studio, you just open the `WindowsApplication4.sln` file (solution file), and the entire application comes up in Visual Studio. Figure 20.27 shows this simple application in Visual Studio.

This simple test program displays data from the `Product` table in the `AdventureWorks` database (which you are mirroring), along with the exact date and time of the data retrieval, the name of the server instance the data came from, and the SQL process ID (SPID) of the current server instance. This way, you can easily see which physical server the data is coming from. If you are trying to use this program, all you have to do is update the `app.config` file connection string entry with your two partner server instance names (`REM12374333\SQL08DE01` and `REM12374333\SQL08DE02`, in this example):

```
ConnectionString=
"Server= REM12374333\SQL08DE01;
 Failover Partner= REM12374333\SQL08DE02;
 Database=AdventureWorks;...."
```

Then you execute the test application. This application automatically connects to the current principal database (`AdventureWorks` on the `REM12374333\SQL08DE01` server instance, in this example), as you can see in Figure 20.28.

20

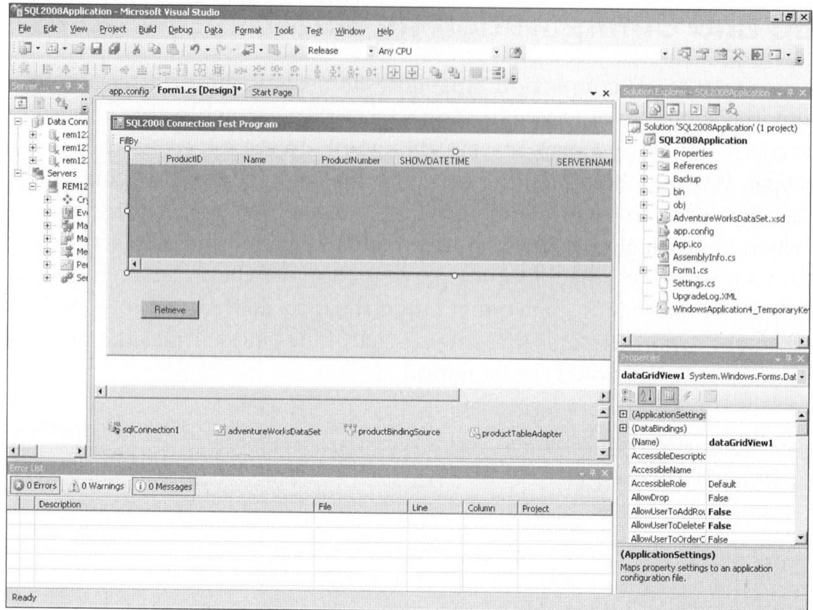

FIGURE 20.27 A SQL client test program for database mirroring in Visual Studio.

SQL2008 Connection Test Program

FillBy

ProductID	Name	ProductNumber	SHOWDATETIME	SERVERNAME	SPID
320	Chainring Bolts	CB-2903	Feb 8 2009 12:15:19:750AM	REM12374333\SQL08DE01	59
321	Chainring Nut	CN-6137	Feb 8 2009 12:15:19:750AM	REM12374333\SQL08DE01	59
322	Chainring	CR-7833	Feb 8 2009 12:15:19:750AM	REM12374333\SQL08DE01	59
323	Crown Race	CR-9981	Feb 8 2009 12:15:19:750AM	REM12374333\SQL08DE01	59
324	Chain Stays	CS-2812	Feb 8 2009 12:15:19:750AM	REM12374333\SQL08DE01	59

Retrieve

FIGURE 20.28 A SQL client test against the current principal server instance.

Next, you can fail over the principal to the mirror server, using the Database Properties Mirroring page's Failover button (refer to Figure 20.22). After you have failed this server over to its mirror (that is, switched roles), you simply click the Retrieve button at the bottom of the client test program to access the data in the `AdventureWorks` database again. Figure 20.29 shows this subsequent data retrieval. The test application shows the same data rows, along with the date and time of this data retrieval and the name of the server instance from which it got its data.

In this case, the data came from the other partner server instance (`AdventureWorks` on the `REM12374333\SQL08DE02` server instance, in this example). The test application simply uses the added connection information to reestablish its connection to the failed-over server instance (that is, the mirror server), completely transparently to the application.

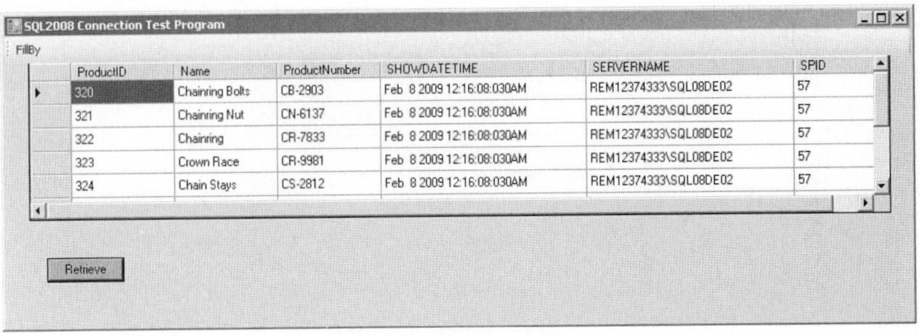

SQL2008 Connection Test Program

FillBy

ProductID	Name	ProductNumber	SHOWDATETIME	SERVERNAME	SPID
320	Chainring Bolts	CB-2903	Feb 8 2009 12:16:08:030AM	REM12374333\SQL08DE02	57
321	Chainring Nut	CN-6137	Feb 8 2009 12:16:08:030AM	REM12374333\SQL08DE02	57
322	Chainring	CR-7833	Feb 8 2009 12:16:08:030AM	REM12374333\SQL08DE02	57
323	Crown Race	CR-9981	Feb 8 2009 12:16:08:030AM	REM12374333\SQL08DE02	57
324	Chain Stays	CS-2812	Feb 8 2009 12:16:08:030AM	REM12374333\SQL08DE02	57

Retrieve

FIGURE 20.29 A SQL client test against the current principal server instance (formerly the mirror server) after failover.

Migrate to Database Mirroring 2008 as Fast as You Can

During our ramp-up on SQL Server 2008, we decided to conduct a benchmark that pitted SQL Server 2005 database mirroring against the exact same configuration with SQL Server 2008 database mirroring. Microsoft had described some performance improvements and other added features that sounded like viable reasons to upgrade to SQL Server 2008. At the heart of our benchmark we would be seeing how much performance improvement was possible with the changes that Microsoft has made to compression of the transaction log records on the principal side, their transmission to the mirror, and the restore to the mirror. Using identical servers, we conducted a fully loaded test with heavy transaction rates—first on SQL Server 2005 and then the exact same database mirroring configuration and transaction load on SQL Server 2008 database mirroring. The results may astound you! First, we ran a transaction sequence of 100,000 iterations of complex update and insert processing against the SQL Server 2005 database mirroring configuration that we built up in this chapter. Figure 20.30 shows the overall load and elapsed time that execution took on SQL Server 2005.

As you can see from Figure 20.30, the load was heavy, and it took 6 hours and 5 minutes to complete the 100,000 transactions on the SQL Server 2005 database mirroring configuration. We then upgraded the exact same machines to SQL Server 2008 and ran the same transaction load. No other changes of any kind were made. Figure 20.31 shows the overall load and elapsed time of that identical transaction load (100,000 transactions) on SQL Server 2008.

As you can see, the exact same transaction load took 3 hours and 34 minutes to complete. This result is nearly 50% faster and is completely transparent from the database and transaction point of view. Truly remarkable. This translates into being roughly 50% faster in high availability and failover. We think this example provides more than enough justification to upgrade to SQL Server 2008 as fast as you can.

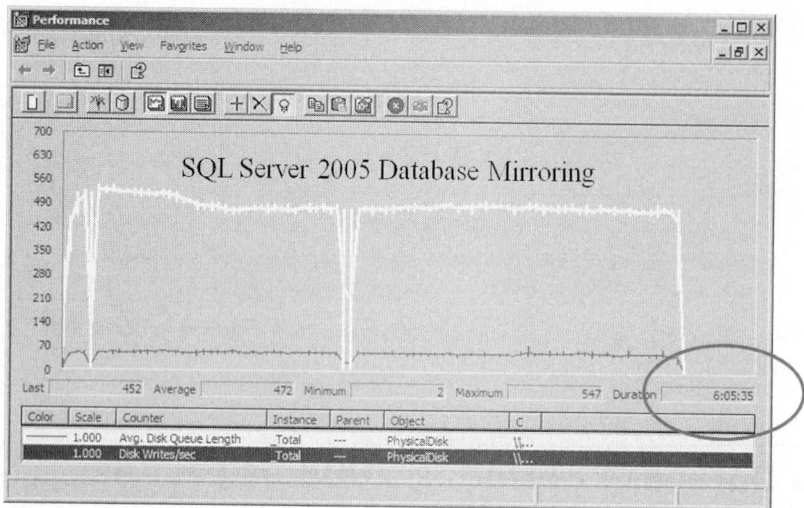

FIGURE 20.30 Transaction benchmark against SQL Server 2005 database mirroring.

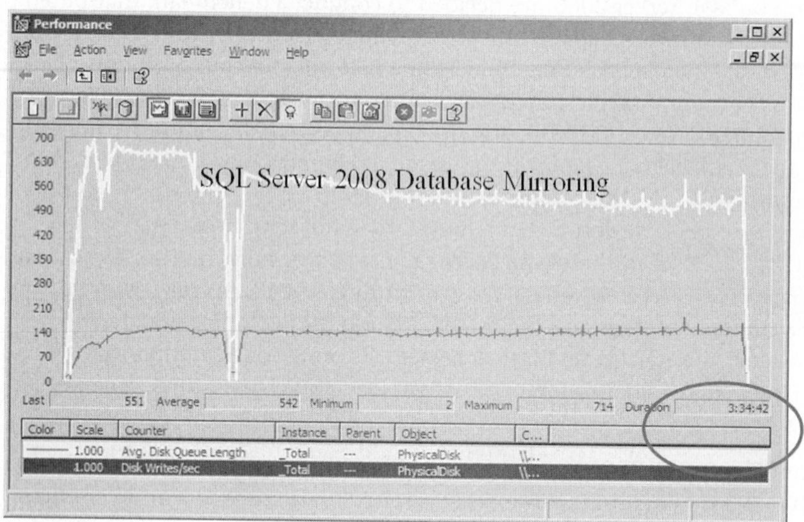

FIGURE 20.31 Transaction benchmark against SQL Server 2008 database mirroring.

Summarizing, the benchmark results are as follows:

- Overall send rate 41% faster (2008 versus 2005)
- Overall restore rate 52% faster (2008 versus 2005)
- Overall availability topology inherits the restore rate yielding ~50% more availability.

We would like to thank the Peace Health database team of John Martin and Jason Riedberger for flawless benchmarking on both of these topologies.

Using Replication and Database Mirroring Together

SQL Server 2008 allows you to use combinations of options to achieve higher availability levels. A prime example would be to combine data replication with database mirroring to provide maximum availability of data, scalability to users, and fault tolerance via failover, potentially at each node in a replication topology. By starting with the publisher and perhaps the distributor, you make them both database mirror failover configurations. Figure 20.32 shows a possible data replication and database mirroring configuration (database mirroring of the publisher and database mirroring of the distributor). For further explanation of a transactional replication topology, see Chapter 19, "Replication."

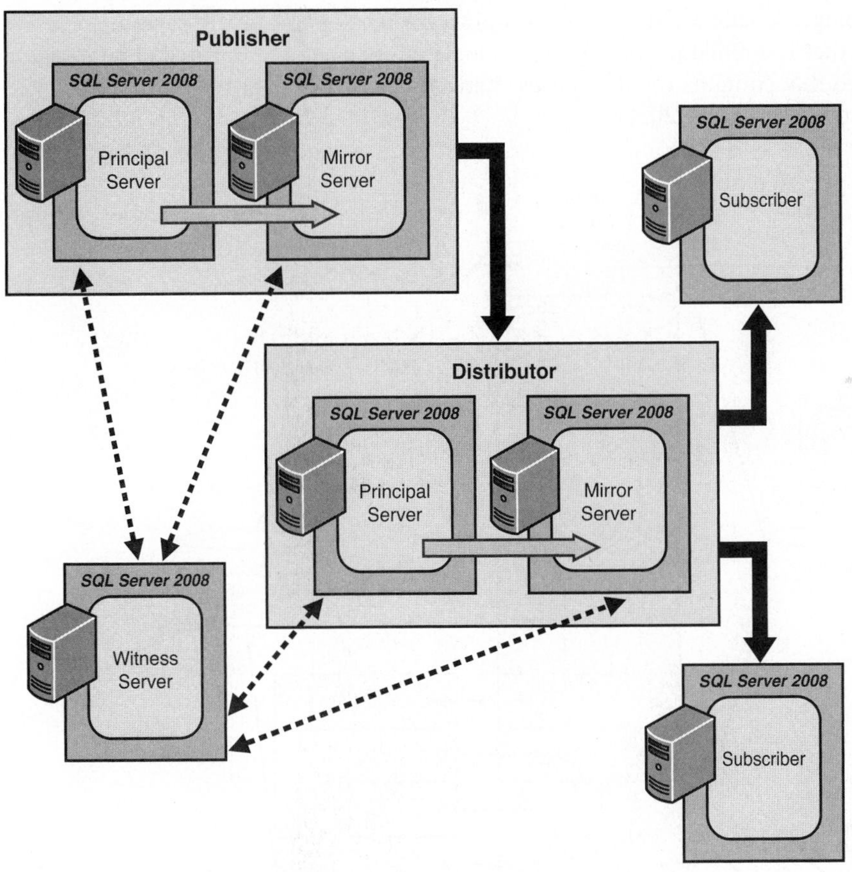

FIGURE 20.32 Rolling out database mirroring failover within data replication for scalability, availability, and fault tolerance.

Using database mirroring and replication together is essentially the best of both worlds: you get the super-low latency of database mirroring for fault tolerance, and you get high availability (and scalability) of data through replication. The downside of this type of combined capability is that it requires additional servers (for mirroring of the databases). The upside is the increased scalability and resilience of your applications.

Using Database Snapshots from a Mirror for Reporting

A powerful configuration to help offload reporting workload is to use database snapshots with database mirroring. A database snapshot is a highly efficient feature of SQL Server 2008 that allows for the generation and use of a read-only, stable view of a database at a moment in time (hence, it's called a snapshot). The database snapshot is also created without the overhead of creating a complete copy of the database or having completely redundant storage. A database snapshot is simply a reference point of the pages used in the database (that is defined in the system catalog). When pages are updated, a new page chain is started that contains the data pages changed since the database snapshot was taken, as illustrated in Figure 20.33.

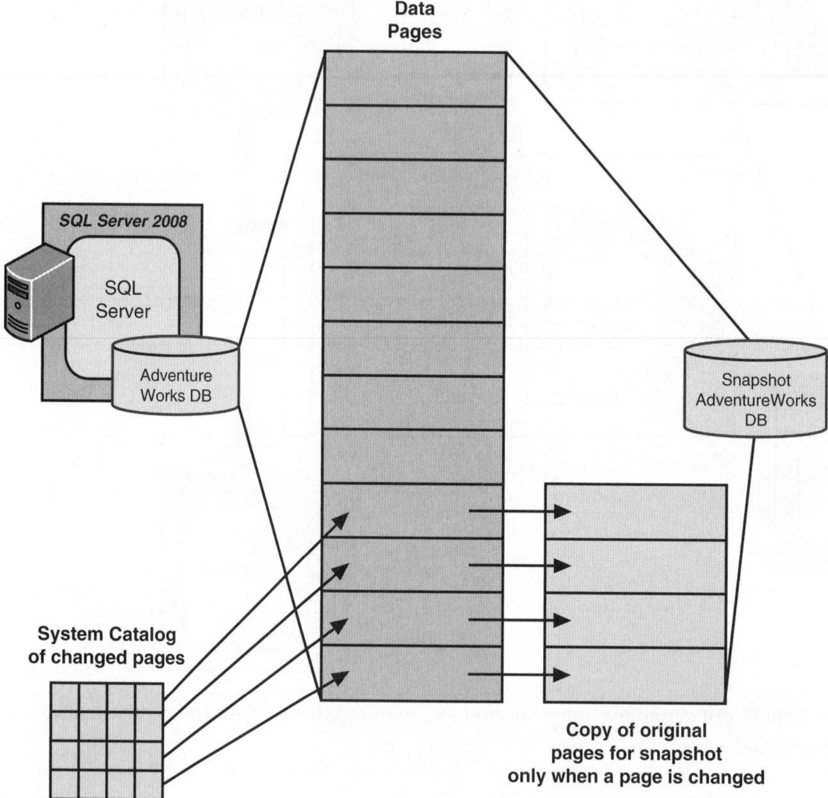

FIGURE 20.33 Database snapshots and the original database share pages and are managed within the system catalog of SQL Server 2008.

As the original database diverges from a snapshot, the snapshot gets its own copy of original pages when they are modified. The copy-on-write technology used for database mirroring also enables a database snapshot. When a database snapshot is created on a database (a mirror database, in this case), all writes check the system catalog of changed pages first; if the snapshot is not there, the original page is copied (using copy-on-write) and is put in a place for reference by the database snapshot (because the snapshot must be kept intact). In this way, a database snapshot and the original database share the data pages that have not changed.

Unlike a mirror database, a database snapshot can be accessed by a reporting client in read-only mode, as shown in Figure 20.34. As long as the mirror server is communicating to the principal, reporting clients can access the snapshot database.

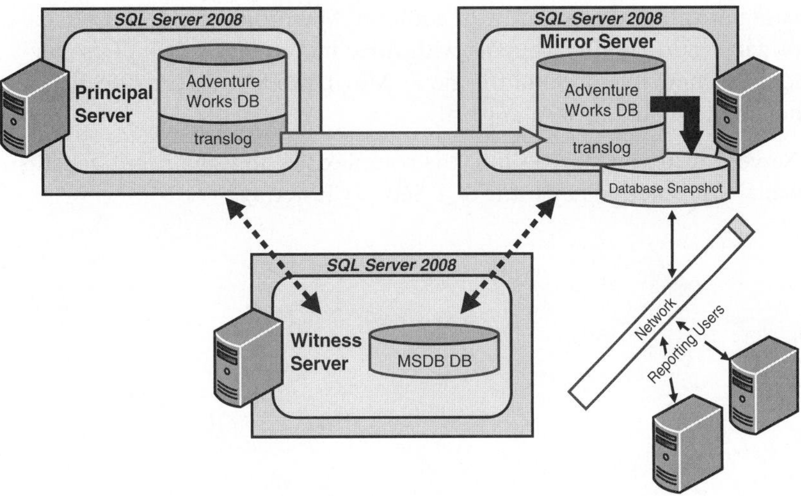

FIGURE 20.34 A database snapshot defined from a mirror server for reporting use.

If the principal fails over to the mirror server, the connections to the snapshot database are disconnected during the database restart process (which makes the mirror server the new principal server). It is possible to reconnect the reporting clients to the database snapshot after a failover is completed, but you must remember that now both the transactional clients and reporting clients are connected to a single SQL Server instance. This may not be acceptable from a performance point of view. Also, it is always a good idea to keep the number of snapshots to a minimum when creating them against a database mirror.

Chapter 32, "Database Snapshots," covers how to create database snapshots.

Summary

Database mirroring is one of the most significant SQL Server features to come along in a long time. This feature has provided a way for users to get to a minimum level of high availability for their databases and applications without having to use complex hardware and software configurations (as are needed with MSCS and SQL Server Clustering configurations).

To mirror a database, you essentially ask for a complete copy of a database to be created and maintained up to the last committed transaction. The ease and simplicity of creating and monitoring database mirroring will quickly make it a configuration that many people use. Adding variations to this configuration, such as enhancing data replication or offloading reporting users, adds even more availability, resilience, and scalability possible than ever existed before. And, as you have seen, it is very easy to have your applications take advantage of database mirroring transparently. In addition, Microsoft has now improved on its overall performance and stability, coupled with three more years' worth of production implementations by companies around the globe. Moving to SQL Server 2008 database mirroring is now more than a rock solid path.

Chapter 21, "SQL Server Clustering," delves into the complexities and significant benefits of building high-availability solutions by using SQL Server Clustering.

CHAPTER 21

SQL Server Clustering

IN THIS CHAPTER

- What's New in SQL Server Clustering
- How Microsoft SQL Server Clustering Works
- Installing SQL Server Clustering

Enterprise computing requires that the entire set of technologies you use to develop, deploy, and manage mission-critical business applications be highly reliable, scalable, and resilient. These technologies include the network, entire technology stack, operating systems on the servers, applications you deploy, database management systems, and everything in between.

An enterprise must now be able to provide a complete solution in regards to the following:

- **Scalability**—As organizations grow, so does the need for more computing power. The systems in place must enable an organization to leverage existing hardware and to quickly and easily add computing power as needs demand.
- **Availability**—As organizations rely more on information, it is critical that the information be available at all times and under all circumstances. Downtime is not acceptable. Moving to five-nines reliability (which means 99.999% uptime) is a must, not a dream.
- **Interoperability**—As organizations grow and evolve, so do their information systems. It is impractical to think that an organization will not have many heterogeneous sources of information. It is becoming increasingly important for applications to get to all the information, regardless of its location.
- **Reliability**—An organization is only as good as its data and information. It is critical that the systems providing that information be bulletproof.

It is assumed that you will provide a certain level of foundational capabilities in regard to network, hardware, and operating system resilience. The good news is that you can achieve many of your enterprise's demands easily and inexpensively by using Microsoft Cluster Services (MSCS), Network Load Balancing (NLB), and SQL Server Clustering (or combinations of them).

What's New in SQL Server Clustering

Much of what's new for MSCS and SQL Server Clustering has to do with the expanded number of nodes that can be managed together and several ease-of-use enhancements in MSCS, including the following:

- **Setup changes for SQL Server failover clustering**—One option forces you to run the Setup program on each node of the failover cluster. To add a node to an existing SQL Server failover cluster, you must run SQL Server Setup on the node that is to be added to the SQL Server failover cluster instance. Another option creates an enterprise push to nodes from the active node.
- **Cluster nodes residing on different subnets**—With Windows 2008, cluster nodes can now reside on different network subnets across network routers. You no longer have to stretch virtual local area networks to connect geographically separated cluster nodes. This opens the door to clustered disaster recovery options.
- **Instances per cluster**—SQL Server 2008 Enterprise Edition supports up to 25 SQL Server instances per cluster (up to 50 for a nonclustered server).
- **More cluster-aware applications**—Many of the MS SQL Server 2008 products are cluster aware, such as Analysis Services, Full Text Search, Integration Services, Reporting Services, FILESTREAM, and others, making these applications more highly available and resilient.
- **Isolation of the quorum disk in MSCS**—A shared disk partition that is *not* on the same physical drive/LUN as the quorum drive must be available in an attempt to reduce failure dependencies.
- **Number of nodes in a cluster**—With Windows 2003 Enterprise Edition (or Datacenter), you can now create up to 8 nodes in a single cluster, and with Windows 2008 Enterprise Edition (or Datacenter), you can create up to 16 nodes.

These new features and enhancements combine to make setting up SQL Server Clustering an easy high-availability proposition. They take much of the implementation risk out of the equation and make this type of installation available to a broader installation base.

How Microsoft SQL Server Clustering Works

Put simply, SQL Server 2008 allows failover and failback to or from another node in a cluster. This is an immensely powerful tool for achieving higher availability virtually transparently. There are two approaches to implementing SQL Server Clustering: active/passive or active/active modes.

In an active/passive configuration, an instance of SQL Server actively services database requests from one of the nodes in a SQL Server cluster (that is, the active node). Another node is idle until, for whatever reason, a failover occurs (to the passive node). With a failover situation, the secondary node (the passive node) takes over all SQL Server resources (for example, databases and the Microsoft Distributed Transaction Coordinator [MSDTC]) without the end user ever knowing that a failover has occurred. The end user might experience a brief transactional interruption because SQL Server Failover Clustering cannot take over in-flight transactions. However, the end user still just looks at a single (virtual) SQL Server and truly doesn't care which node is fulfilling requests.

Figure 21.1 shows a typical two-node SQL Server Clustering configuration using active/passive mode, in which Node 2 is idle (that is, passive).

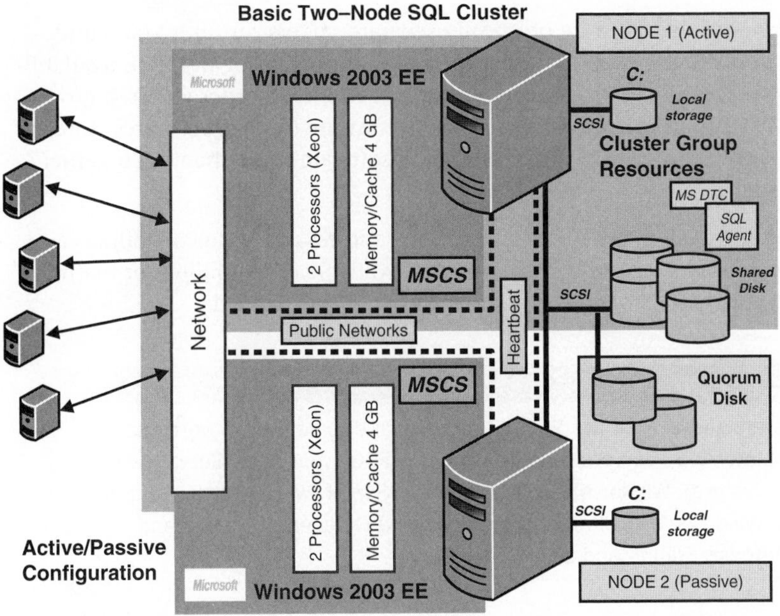

FIGURE 21.1 A typical two-node active/passive SQL Server Clustering configuration.

In an active/active configuration, SQL Server runs multiple servers simultaneously with different databases. This gives organizations with more constrained hardware requirements a chance to use a clustering configuration that can fail over to or from any node, without having to set aside idle hardware.

As previously mentioned, SQL Server Clustering is actually created within (on top of) MSCS. MSCS, not SQL Server, is capable of detecting hardware or software failures and automatically shifting control of the managed resources to a healthy node. SQL Server 2008 implements failover clustering based on the clustering features of the Microsoft Clustering Service. In other words, SQL Server is a fully cluster-aware application and becomes a set of resources managed by MSCS. The failover cluster shares a common set of cluster resources (or cluster groups), such as clustered (that is, shared) disk drives.

NOTE

You can install SQL Server on as many servers as you want; the number is limited only by the operating system license and SQL Server edition you have purchased. However, MSCS (for Windows 2008) can manage only up to 16 instances of Microsoft SQL Server Standard Edition at a time and up to 25 instances of Microsoft SQL Server Enterprise Edition at a time.

Understanding MSCS

A *server cluster* is a group of two or more physically separate servers running MSCS and working collectively as a single system. The server cluster, in turn, provides high availability, scalability, and manageability for resources and applications. In other words, a group of servers is physically connected via communication hardware (network), shares storage (via SCSI or Fibre Channel connectors), and uses MSCS software to tie them all together into managed resources.

Server clusters can preserve client access to applications and resources during failures and planned outages. If one of the servers in a cluster is unavailable due to failure or maintenance, resources and applications move to another available cluster node.

NOTE

You cannot do clustering with Windows 2000 Professional or older server versions. Clustering is available only on servers running Windows 2000 Advanced Server (which supports two-node clusters), Windows 2000 Datacenter Server (which supports up to four-node clusters), Windows 2003 Enterprise Edition and Datacenter Server, and Windows 2008 Enterprise Edition and Datacenter Server.

Clusters use an algorithm to detect a failure, and they use failover policies to determine how to handle the work from a failed server. These policies also specify how a server is to be restored to the cluster when it becomes available again.

Although clustering doesn't guarantee continuous operation, it does provide availability sufficient for most mission-critical applications and is the building block of numerous high-availability solutions. MSCS can monitor applications and resources, automatically recognizing and recovering from many failure conditions. This capability provides great flexibility in managing the workload within a cluster, and it improves the overall availability of the system. Technologies that are "cluster aware"—such as SQL Server, Microsoft Message Queuing (MSMQ), Microsoft Distributed Transaction Coordinator (MSDTC), and file shares—have already been programmed to work within (under the control of) MSCS.

TIP

In previous versions of MSCS, the `COMCLUST.EXE` utility had to be run on each node to cluster the MSDTC. It is now possible to configure MSDTC as a resource type, assign it to a resource group, and then have it automatically configured on all cluster nodes.

MSCS is relatively sensitive to the hardware and network equipment you put in place. For this reason, it is imperative that you verify your own hardware's compatibility *before* you go any further in deploying MSCS (check the hardware compatibility list at http://msdn.microsoft.com/en-us/library/ms189910.aspx). In addition, SQL Server failover cluster instances are not supported where the cluster nodes are also domain controllers.

Let's look a little closer at a two-node active/passive cluster configuration. As you can see in Figure 21.2, the *heartbeat* (named `ClusterInternal` in this figure) is a private network set up between the nodes of the cluster that checks whether a server is up and running ("is alive"). This occurs at regular intervals, known as *time slices*. If the heartbeat is not functioning, a failover is initiated, and another node in the cluster takes over for the failed node. In addition to the heartbeat private network, at least one public network (named `ClusterPublic` in this figure) must be enabled so that external connections can be made to the cluster. Each physical server (node) uses separate network adapters for each type of communication (public and internal heartbeat).

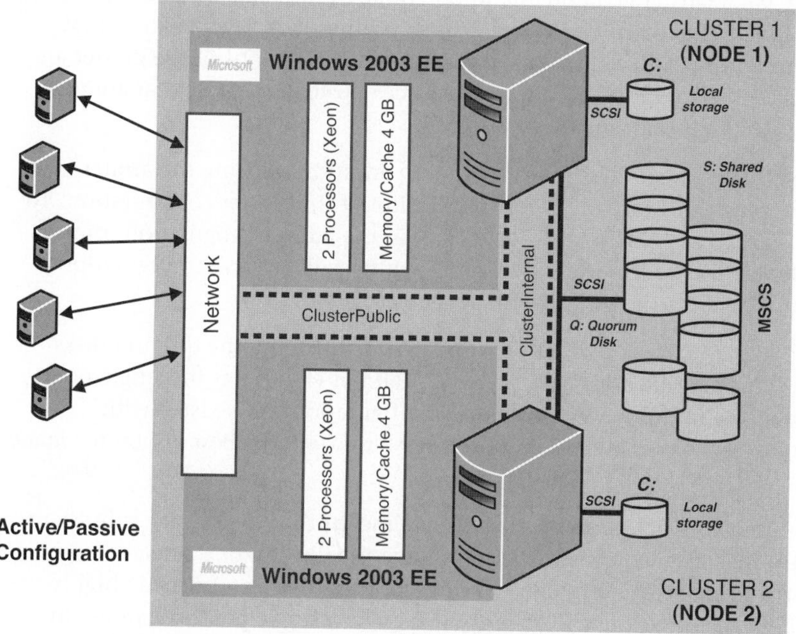

FIGURE 21.2 A two-node active/passive MSCS cluster configuration.

The *shared disk* array is a collection of physical disks (SCSI RAID or Fibre Channel–connected disks) that the cluster accesses and controls as resources. MSCS supports *shared nothing* disk arrays, in which only one node can own a given resource at any given moment. All other nodes are denied access until they own the resource. This protects the data from being overwritten when two computers have access to the same drives concurrently.

The *quorum drive* is a logical drive designated on the shared disk array for MSCS. This continuously updated drive contains information about the state of the cluster. If this drive becomes corrupt or damaged, the cluster installation also becomes corrupt or damaged.

NOTE

In general (and as part of a high-availability disk configuration), the quorum drive should be isolated to a drive all by itself and be mirrored to guarantee that it is available to the cluster at all times. Without it, the cluster doesn't come up at all, and you cannot access your SQL databases.

The MSCS architecture requires there to be a single quorum resource in the cluster that is used as the tie-breaker to avoid split-brain scenarios. A *split-brain scenario* happens when all the network communication links between two or more cluster nodes fail. In these cases, the cluster may be split into two or more partitions that cannot communicate with each other. MSCS guarantees that even in these cases, a resource is brought online on only one node. If the different partitions of the cluster each brought a given resource online, this would violate what a cluster guarantees and potentially cause data corruption. When the cluster is partitioned, the quorum resource is used as an arbiter. The partition that owns the quorum resource is allowed to continue. The other partitions of the cluster are said to have "lost quorum," and MSCS and any resources hosted on nodes that are not part of the partition that has quorum are terminated.

The quorum resource is a storage-class resource and, in addition to being the arbiter in a split-brain scenario, is used to store the definitive version of the cluster configuration. To ensure that the cluster always has an up-to-date copy of the latest configuration information, you should deploy the quorum resource on a highly available disk configuration (using mirroring, triple-mirroring, or RAID 10, at the very least).

Starting with Windows 2003, a more durable approach of managing the quorum disks with clustering was created, called *majority node set*. It all but eliminates the single-point-of-failure weakness in the traditional quorum disk configuration that existed with Windows 2000 servers. However, even this approach isn't always the best option for many clustered scenarios.

The notion of quorum as a single shared disk resource means that the storage subsystem has to interact with the cluster infrastructure to provide the illusion of a single storage device with very strict semantics. Although the quorum disk itself can be made highly available via RAID or mirroring, the controller port may be a single point of failure. In addition, if an application inadvertently corrupts the quorum disk or an operator takes down the quorum disk, the cluster becomes unavailable.

This situation can be resolved by using a majority node set option as a single quorum resource from an MSCS perspective. In this set, the cluster log and configuration information are stored on multiple disks across the cluster. A new majority node set resource ensures that the cluster configuration data stored on the majority node set is kept consistent across the different disks.

The disks that make up the majority node set could, in principle, be local disks physically attached to the nodes themselves or disks on a shared storage fabric (that is, a collection of centralized shared storage area network [SAN] devices connected over a switched-fabric or Fibre Channel–arbitrated loop SAN). In the majority node set implementation that is provided as part of MSCS in Windows Server 2003 and 2008, every node in the cluster uses a directory on its own local system disk to store the quorum data, as shown in Figure 21.3.

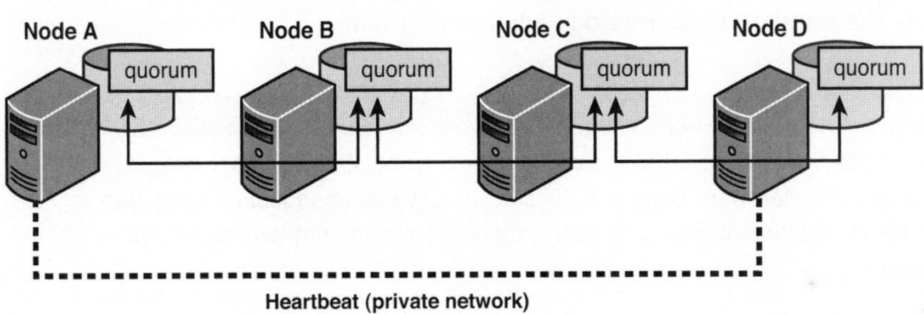

FIGURE 21.3 A majority node set.

If the configuration of the cluster changes, that change is reflected across the different disks. The change is considered to have been committed (that is, made persistent) only if that change is made to a majority of the nodes (that is, [Number of nodes configured in the cluster]/2) + 1). In this way, a majority of the nodes have an up-to-date copy of the data. MSCS itself starts up only if a majority of the nodes currently configured as part of the cluster are up and running as part of MSCS.

If there are fewer nodes, the cluster is said *not* to have quorum, and therefore MSCS waits (trying to restart) until more nodes try to join. Only when a majority (or quorum) of nodes are available does MSCS start up and bring the resources online. This way, because the up-to-date configuration is written to a majority of the nodes, regardless of node failures, the cluster always guarantees that it starts up with the most up-to-date configuration.

With Windows 2008, a few more quorum drive configurations are possible that address various voting strategies and also support geographically separated cluster nodes.

In Windows Server 2008 failover clustering, you have four choices on how to implement the quorum:

- One option is to use Node majority; a vote is given to each node of the cluster, and the cluster continues to run as long as a majority of nodes are up and running.
- A second option is to use both the nodes and the standard quorum disk, a common option for two-node clusters. Each node gets a vote, and the quorum, now called a *witness disk*, also gets a vote. As long as two of the three are running, the cluster continues. The cluster can actually lose the witness disk and still run.
- A third option is to use the classic/legacy model and assign a vote to the witness disk only. This type of quorum equates to the well-known, tried-and-true model that has been used for years.
- A fourth option is, of course, to use the majority node set (MNS) model with a file share witness.

We describe only the standard majority node set approach here.

TIP

A quick check to see whether your hardware (server, controllers, and storage devices) is listed on Microsoft's Hardware Compatibility List will save you headaches later. See the hardware pre-installation checklist at http://msdn.microsoft.com/en-us/library/ms189910.aspx.

Extending MSCS with NLB

You can also use a critical technology called Network Load Balancing (NLB) to ensure that a server is always available to handle requests. NLB works by spreading incoming client requests among a number of servers linked together to support a particular application. A typical example is to use NLB to process incoming visitors to your website. As more visitors come to your site, you can incrementally increase capacity by adding servers. This type of expansion is often referred to as *software scaling,* or *scaling out.* Figure 21.4 illustrates this extended clustering architecture with NLB.

By using both MSCS and NLB clustering technologies together, you can create an *n*-tier infrastructure. For instance, you can create an *n*-tiered e-commerce application by deploying NLB across a front-end web server farm and use MSCS clustering on the back end for your line-of-business applications, such as clustering your SQL Server databases. This approach gives you the benefits of near-linear scalability without server- or application-based single points of failure. This, combined with industry-standard best practices for designing high-availability networking infrastructures, can ensure that your Windows-based, Internet-enabled business will be online all the time and can quickly scale to meet

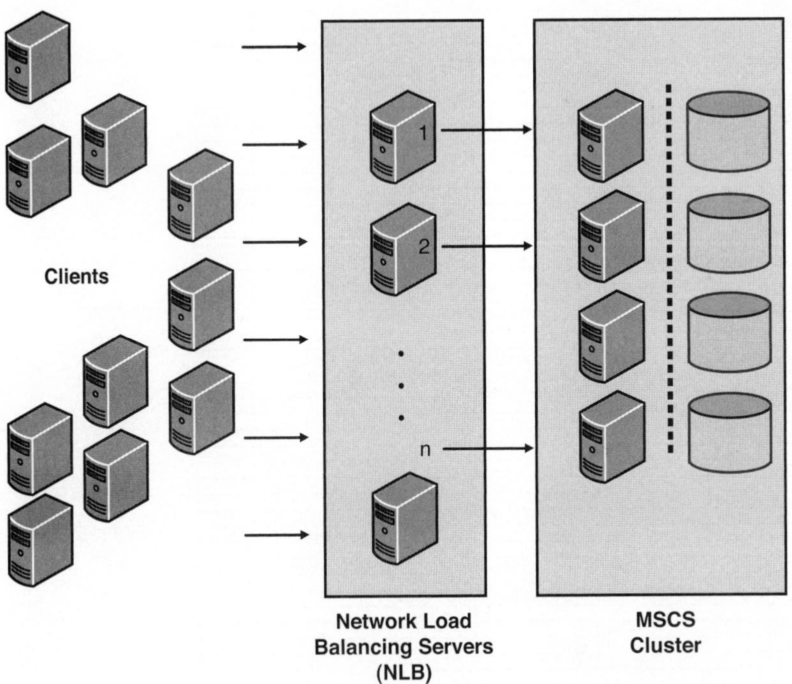

FIGURE 21.4 An NLB configuration.

demand. Other tiers could be added to the topology, such as an application-center tier that uses component load balancing. This further extends the clustering and scalability reach for candidate applications that can benefit from this type of architecture.

How MSCS Sets the Stage for SQL Server Clustering

Figure 21.5 shows an Excel spreadsheet that documents all the needed Internet Protocol (IP) addresses, network names, domain definitions, and SQL Server references to set up a two-node SQL Server Clustering configuration (configured in an active/passive mode). `CLUSTER1` is the first node, `CLUSTER2` is the second node, and the cluster group name is `CLUSTER >GROUP` (simple naming is used here to better illustrate the point). The public network name is `ClusterPublic`, and the internal heartbeat network name is `ClusterInternal`. This spreadsheet has also been included in the download files on the CD for this book. It's a good idea to fill out this spreadsheet *before* you start installing and configuring your servers.

Microsoft Excel non-commercial use - MSCSClustering2008 [Compatibility Mode]

	A	B	C	D	E
1	SS2K8CLUST	Node A	Node B	Cluster	
2	Name (netbios)	CLUSTER1	CLUSTER2	CLUSTER GROUP	
3	ClusterPublic	192.168.3.101	192.168.3.102	192.168.3.100	
4	> Mask	255.255.255.0	255.255.255.0	255.255.255.0	
5	> Default Gateway	192.168.3.1	192.168.3.1		
6	> Name Resolution	DNS/WINS	DNS/WINS		
7	> DNS	192.168.3.20	192.168.3.20		
8	> WINS	192.168.3.20	192.168.3.20		
9					
10	ClusterInternal	172.20.22.1	172.20.22.2		
11	> Mask	255.255.255.0	255.255.255.0		
12	> Default Gateway	none	none		
13	> Name Resolution	hosts file	hosts file		
14	> DNS	none	none		
15	> WINS	none	none		
16					
17	Domain (full)	GOTHAM.LOCAL	GOTHAM.LOCAL	GOTHAM.LOCAL	
18	(netbios)	GOTHAM	GOTHAM	GOTHAM	
19					
20	Domain\GroupName	For each clustered service being installed			
21	SQL Server	GOTHAM\Domain Admins			
22	SQL Server Agent	GOTHAM\Domain Admins			
23	Full-Text Search	GOTHAM\Domain Admins			
24					
25	UserID/Password				
26	Remote Account	\\CLUSTER1\Administrator:pswd	\\CLUSTER2\Administrator:pswd	\\GOTHAM\Administrator:pswd	
27	or	\\GOTHAM\Administrator:pswd	\\GOTHAM\Administrator:pswd	\\GOTHAM\Clusteradmin:pswd	
28	Service Account	\\GOTHAM\Clusteradmin:pswd	\\GOTHAM\Clusteradmin:pswd		
29					
30	Windows 2003 EE disk	C: (local)	C: (local)		
31	Shared Disk (s)	S:	S:		
32	Quorum Disk	Q:	Q:		
33	SCSI Controller	NETRAID 3si	NETRAID 3si		
34					
35	SQL Server 2008				
36	> Virtual Server Name			VSQLSERVER2008	
37	> SQL Instance Name			use default (no named instance)	
38	> SQL IP Address			192.168.3.110	
39	> SQL Server binaries	C:\Program Files\Microsoft SQL Ser	C:\Program Files\Microsoft SQL Server\MSSQL10_50.MSSQLSERVER\MSSQL\Binn		
40	> SQL Data Location	S:\MSSQL10_50.MSSQLSERVER\M	S:\MSSQL10_50.MSSQLSERVER\MSSQL\DATA		
41	> SQL Log Location	S:\MSSQL10_50.MSSQLSERVER\M	S:\MSSQL10_50.MSSQLSERVER\MSSQL\DATA		
42					
43	MSDTC	192.168.3.100	192.168.3.100		
44	SQL Agent	192.168.3.100	192.168.3.100	VSQLSERVER2008	
45	SQL Full Text	192.168.3.100	192.168.3.100	VSQLSERVER2008	
46					

FIGURE 21.5 An Excel spreadsheet for a two-node active/passive SQL Cluster configuration.

The cluster controls the following resources:

- Physical disks (`Q:` is for the quorum disk, `S:` is for the shared disks, and so on.)
- The cluster IP address
- The cluster name (network name)
- The Distributed Transaction Coordinator (MSDTC)
- The SQL Server virtual IP address
- The SQL Server virtual name (network name)
- SQL Server
- SQL Server Agent
- The SQL Server Full-Text Search service instance (if installed)

After you successfully install, configure, and test your cluster (MSCS), you are ready to add the SQL Server components as resources to be managed by MSCS. This is where the magic happens. Figure 21.6 shows how the Cluster Administrator should look after you install/configure MSCS. It doesn't have SQL Server 2008 installed yet.

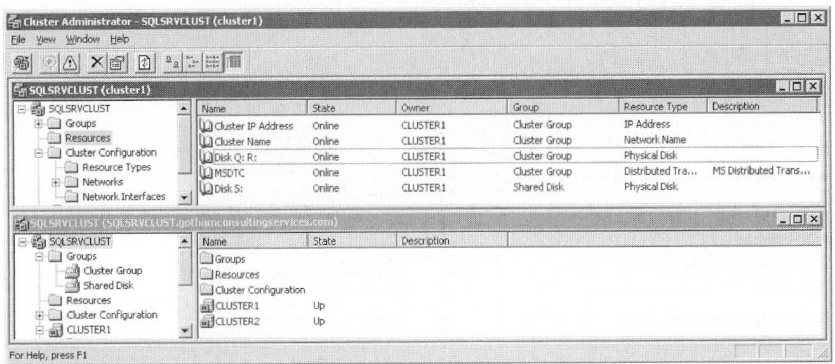

FIGURE 21.6 Windows 2003 Cluster Administrator, showing managed resources prior to installing SQL Server.

Installing SQL Server Clustering

When you install SQL Server in a clustered server configuration, you create it as a virtual SQL Server. A virtual SQL Server is not tied to a specific physical server; it is associated with a virtualized SQL Server name that is assigned a separate IP address (not the IP address or name of the physical servers on which it runs). Handling matters this way allows for your applications to be completely abstracted away from the physical server level.

Failover clustering has a new workflow for all Setup scenarios in SQL Server 2008. The two options for installation are

- **Integrated installation**—This option creates and configures a single-node SQL Server failover cluster instance. Additional nodes are added by using the Add Node functionality in Setup. For example, for Integrated installation, you run Setup to create a single-node failover cluster. Then you run Setup again for each node you want to add to the cluster.
- **Advanced/Enterprise installation**—This option consists of two steps; the prepare step prepares all nodes of the failover cluster to be operational. Nodes are defined and prepared during this initial step. After you prepare the nodes, the Complete step is run on the active node—the node that owns the shared disk—to complete the failover cluster instance and make it operational.

Figure 21.7 shows the same two-node cluster configuration as Figure 21.1, with all the SQL Server components identified. This virtual SQL Server is the only thing the end user will ever see. As you can also see in Figure 21.7, the virtual server name is `VSQLSERVER2008`, and the SQL Server instance name defaults to `blank` (you can, of course, give your instance a name). Figure 21.7 also shows the other cluster group resources that will be part of the SQL Server Clustering configuration: MSDTC, SQL Agent, SQL Server Full-Text Search, and the shared disk where the databases will live.

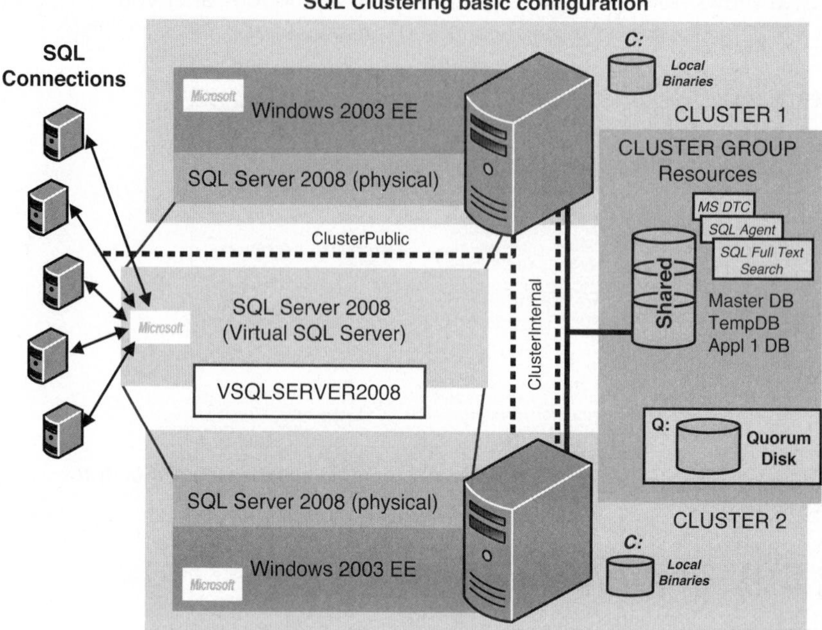

FIGURE 21.7 A basic SQL Server Clustering configuration.

SQL Server Agent will be installed as part of the SQL Server installation process, and it is associated with the SQL Server instance it is installed for. The same is true for SQL Server Full-Text Search; it is associated with the particular SQL Server instance that it is installed to work with. The SQL Server installation process completely installs all software on all nodes you designate.

Configuring SQL Server Database Disks

Before we go too much further, we need to talk about how you should lay out a SQL Server implementation on the shared disks managed by the cluster. The overall usage intent of a particular SQL Server instance dictates how you might choose to configure your shared disk and how it might be best configured for scalability and availability.

In general, RAID 0 is great for storage that doesn't need fault tolerance; RAID 1 or RAID 10 is great for storage that needs fault tolerance but doesn't have to sacrifice too much performance (as with most online transaction processing [OLTP] systems); and RAID 5 is great for storage that needs fault tolerance but whose data doesn't change that much (that is, low data volatility, as in many decision support systems [DSSs]/read-only systems).

All this means that there is a time and place to use each of the different fault-tolerant disk configurations. Table 21.1 provides a good rule of thumb to follow for deciding which SQL Server database file types should be placed on which RAID level disk configuration. (This would be true regardless of whether or not the RAID disk array was a part of a SQL Server cluster.)

TABLE 21.1 SQL Server Clustering Disk Fault-Tolerance Recommendations

Device	Description	Fault Tolerance
Quorum drive	The quorum drive used with MSCS should be isolated to a drive by itself (often mirrored as well, for maximum availability).	RAID 1 or RAID 10
OLTP SQL Server database files	For OLTP systems, the database data/index files should be placed on a RAID 10 disk system.	RAID 10
DSS SQL Server database files	For DSSs that are primarily read-only, the database data/index files should be placed on a RAID 5 disk system.	RAID 5
tempdb	This is a highly volatile form of disk I/O (when not able to do all its work in the cache).	RAID 10
SQL Server transaction log files	The SQL Server transaction log files should be on their own mirrored volume for both performance and database protection. (For DSSs, this could be RAID 5 also.)	RAID 10 or RAID 1

TIP

A good practice is to balance database files across disk arrays (that is, controllers). In other words, if you have two (or more) separate shared disk arrays (both RAID 10) available within a cluster group's resources, you should put the data file of Database 1 on the first cluster group disk resource (for example, `DiskRAID10-A`) and its transaction log on the second cluster group disk resource (for example, `DiskRaid10-B`). Then you should put the data file of Database 2 on the second cluster group disk resource of `DiskRAID10-B` and its transaction log on the first cluster group disk resource of `DiskRAID10-A`. In this way, you can stagger these allocations and in general balance the overall RAID controller usage, minimizing any potential bottlenecks that might occur on one disk controller. In addition, FILESTREAM filegroups must be put on a shared disk, and FILESTREAM must be enabled on each node in the cluster that will host the FILESTREAM instance. You can also use geographically dispersed cluster nodes, but additional items such as network latency and shared disk support must be verified before you get started. Check the Geographic Cluster hardware Compatibility List (http://msdn.microsoft.com/en-us/library/ms189910.aspx). On Windows 2008, most hardware and ISCSI supported hardware can be used, without the need to use "certified hardware." When you are creating a cluster on Windows 2008, you can use the cluster validation tool to validate the Windows cluster; it also blocks SQL Server Setup when problems are detected with the Windows 2008 cluster.

Installing Network Interfaces

You might want to take a final glance at Cluster Administrator so that you can verify that both `CLUSTER1` and `CLUSTER2` nodes and their private and public network interfaces are completely specified and their state (status) is up. If you like, you should also double-check the IP addresses and network names against the Excel spreadsheet created for this cluster specification.

Installing MSCS

As you can see in Figure 21.8, the MSCS "service" is running and has been started by the `ClusterAdmin` login account for the `GOTHAM` domain.

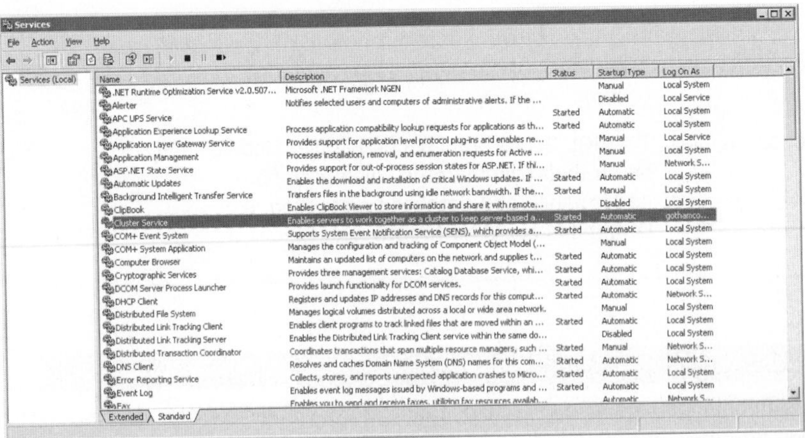

FIGURE 21.8 You need to make sure MSCS is running and started by the cluster account for the domain.

> **NOTE**
>
> If MSCS is not started and won't start, you cannot install SQL Server Clustering. You have to remove and then reinstall MSCS from scratch. You should browse the Event Viewer to familiarize yourself with the types of warnings and errors that can appear with MSCS.

Installing SQL Server

For SQL Clustering, you must install a new SQL Server instance within a minimum two-node cluster. You should not move a SQL Server instance from a nonclustered configuration to a clustered configuration. If you already have SQL Server installed in a nonclustered environment, you need to make all the necessary backups (or detach databases) first, and then you need to uninstall the nonclustered SQL Server instance. Some upgrade paths and migration paths are possible from prior versions of SQL Server and Windows server. You are also limited to a maximum of 25 instances of SQL Server per failover cluster. There is no uninstall SQL Server failover cluster option; you must run Setup from the node that is to be removed. You must specify the same product key on all the nodes that you are preparing for the same failover cluster. You also should make sure you use the same SQL Server instance ID for all the nodes that are prepared for the failover cluster.

With all MSCS resources running and in the online state, you run the SQL Server Setup program from the node that is online (for example, `CLUSTER1`). You are asked to install all software components required prior to installing SQL Server (.NET Framework 3.0 or 3.5, Microsoft SQL Native Client, and the Microsoft SQL Server 2008 Setup support files).

SQL Server integrated failover cluster installation consists of the following steps:

1. Create and configure a single-node SQL Server failover cluster instance. When you configure the node successfully, you have a fully functional failover cluster instance. At this point, it does not have high availability because there is only one node in the failover cluster.
2. On each node to be added to the SQL Server failover cluster, run Setup with Add Node functionality to add that node.

Alternatively, you can use the following SQL Server Advanced/Enterprise failover cluster installation:

1. On each node that will be an owner of the new SQL Server failover cluster, follow the Prepare Failover Cluster setup steps listed in the Prepare section. After you run the Prepare Failover Cluster on one node, Setup creates the `Configuration.ini` file, which lists all the settings you specified. On the additional nodes to be prepared, instead of following these steps, you can supply the `Configuration.ini` file from first node as an input to the Setup command line. This step prepares the nodes ready to be clustered, but there is no operational instance of SQL Server at the end of this step.
2. After the nodes are prepared for clustering, run Setup on one of the prepared nodes, preferably on the node that owns the shared disk that has the Complete Failover Cluster functionality. This step configures and finishes the failover cluster instance. After completing this step, you have an operational SQL Server failover cluster instance. and all the nodes prepared previously for that instance are the possible owners of the newly created SQL Server failover cluster.

After you take these steps, the standard Welcome to SQL Server Installation Center Wizard begins. It starts with a System Configuration check of the node in the cluster (`CLUSTER1`). Figure 21.9 shows the SQL Server Installation Center launch dialog and the results of a successful system check for `CLUSTER1`.

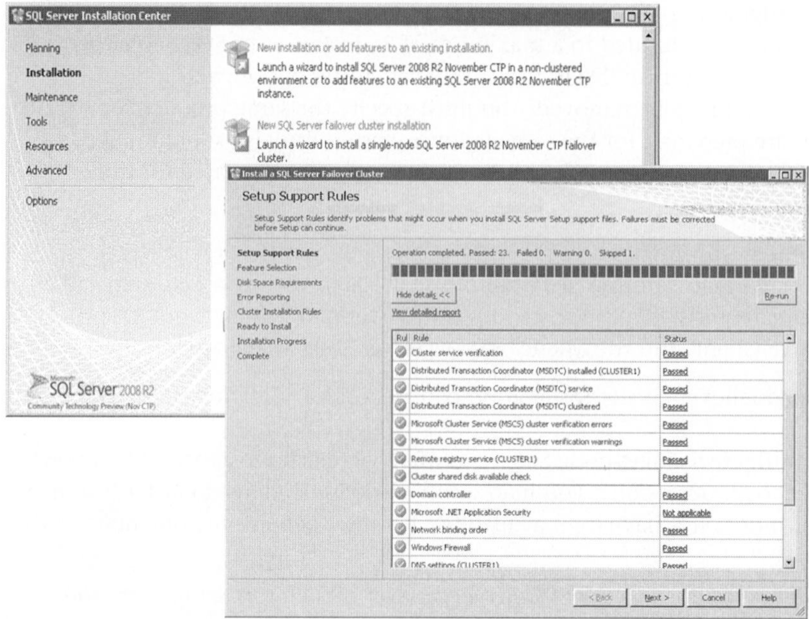

FIGURE 21.9 A Microsoft SQL Server Setup Support Rules check.

NOTE

SQL Server Clustering is available with SQL Server 2008 Standard Edition, Enterprise Edition, and Developer Edition. However, Standard Edition supports only a two-node cluster. If you want to configure a cluster with more than two nodes, you need to upgrade to SQL Server 2008 Enterprise Edition.

If this check fails (warnings are acceptable), you must resolve them before you continue. If the check is successful, you are then prompted for the checklist of features you want to install. Figure 21.10 shows the Feature Selection to install dialog.

You then see the Instance Configuration dialog, as shown in Figure 21.11, where you specify the network name for the new SQL Server failover cluster (the Virtual Server name, `VSQLSERVER2008` in this example) and then either can use the default SQL Server instance name (no name) or specify a unique SQL Server instance name (we chose to use the default instance name of `MSSQLSERVER`).

This virtual SQL Server name is the name the client applications will see (and to which they will connect). When an application attempts to connect to an instance of SQL Server 2008 that is running on a failover cluster, the application must specify both the virtual server name and instance name (if an instance name was used), such as `VSQLSERVER2008\VSQLSRV1` (virtual server name\SQL Server instance name) or `VSQLSERVER2008` (just the virtual server name without the default SQL Server instance

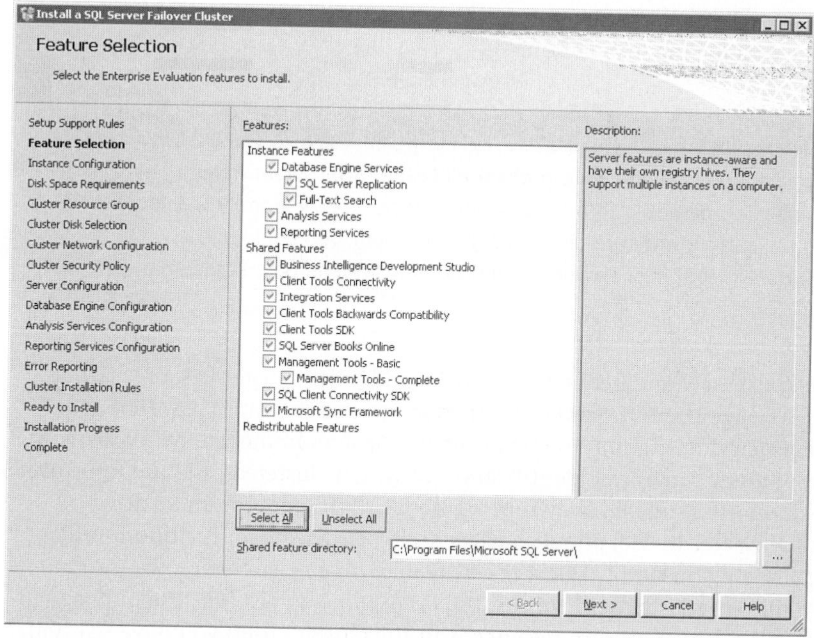

FIGURE 21.10 The SQL Server Setup Feature Selection dialog for a SQL Server Failover Cluster.

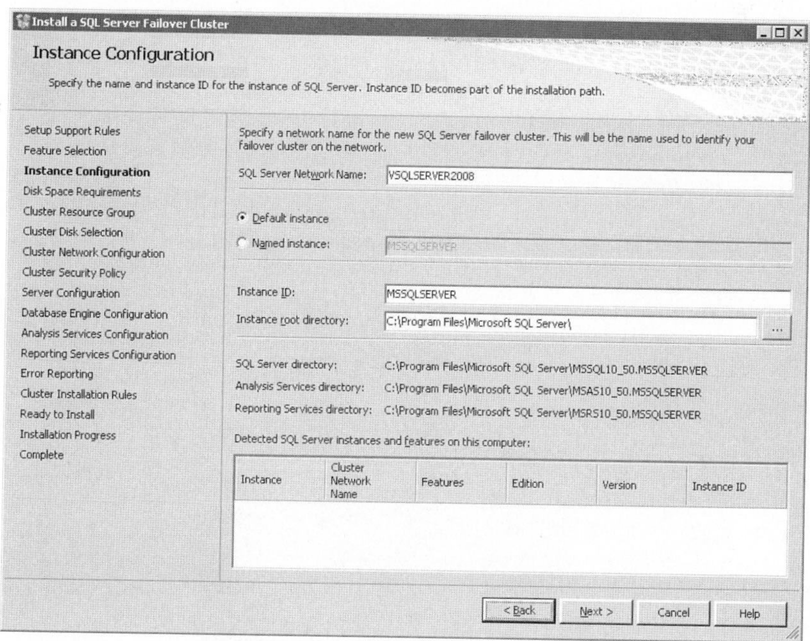

FIGURE 21.11 Specifying the virtual server name (VSQLSERVER2008) and default instance.

name). The virtual server name must be unique on the network. You also specify the local directory locations (root) for the installation.

NOTE

A good naming convention to follow is to preface all virtual SQL Server names and virtual SQL Server instance names with a *V*. This way, you can easily identify which SQL Server machines on your network are clustered. For example, you could use `VSQLSERVER2008` as a virtual SQL Server name and `VSQLSRV1` as an instance name.

Next comes the disk space requirements dialog, followed by the Cluster Resource Group specification. This is where the SQL Server resources are placed within MSCS. Here, you use the existing resource cluster group (named `Cluster Group`). Immediately following the resource group assignment comes the identification of which clustered disks are to be used via the Cluster Disk Selection dialog, shown in Figure 21.12. It contains an `S:` drive (which you want SQL Server to use) and `Q:` and `R:` drive being used for the quorum files (do not select this drive!). You simply select the available drive(s) where you want to put your SQL database files (the `S:` drive in this example). As you can also see, the only "qualified" disk is the `S:` drive. If the quorum resource is in the cluster group you have selected, a warning message is issued, informing you of this fact. A general rule of thumb is to isolate the quorum resource to a separate cluster group.

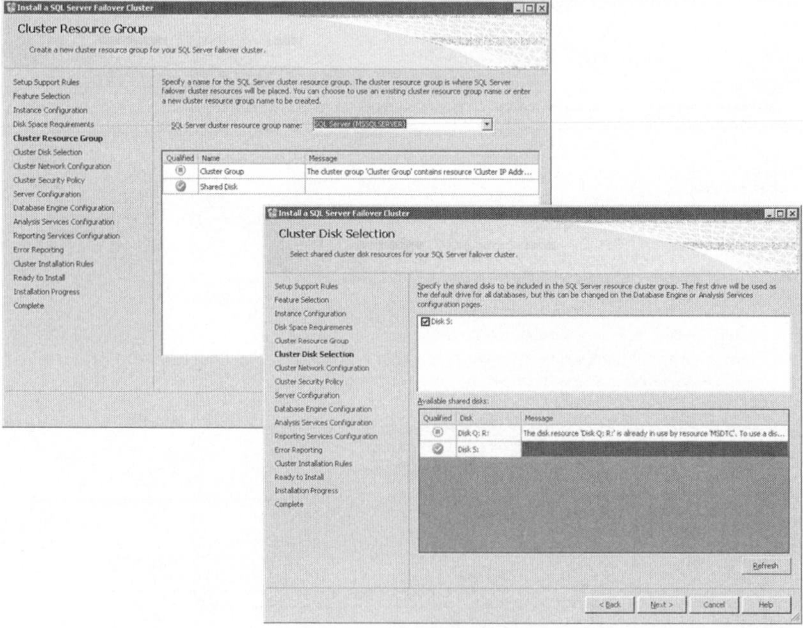

FIGURE 21.12 Cluster resource group specification and Cluster Disk Selection.

The next thing you need to do for this new virtual server specification is to identify an IP address and which network it should use. As you can see in the Cluster Network Configuration dialog, shown in Figure 21.13, you simply type in the IP address (for example, 192.168.3.110) that is to be the IP address for this virtual SQL Server for the available networks known to this cluster configuration (in this example, it is for the `ClusterPublic` network). If the IP address being specified is already in use, an error occurs.

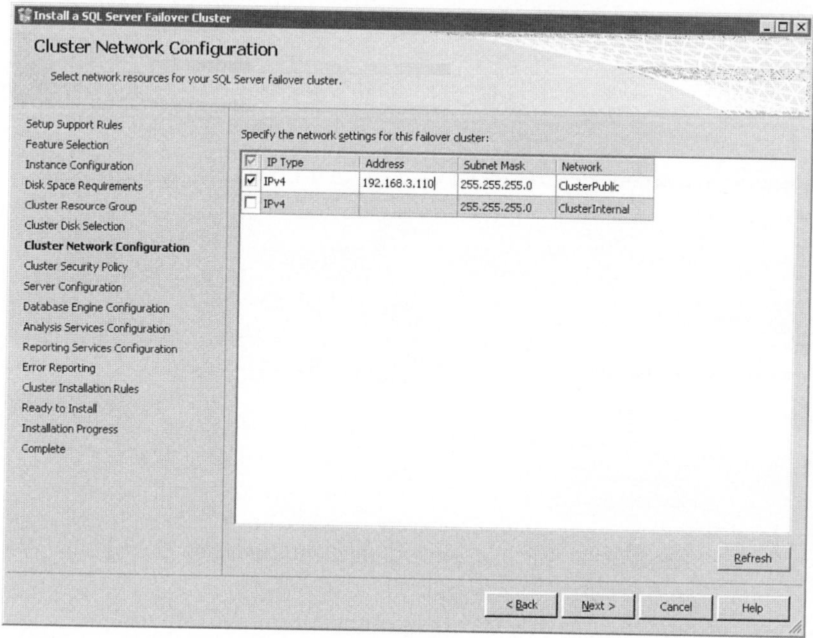

FIGURE 21.13 Specifying the virtual SQL Server IP address and which network to use.

NOTE

Keep in mind that you are using a separate IP address for the virtual SQL Server that is completely different from the cluster IP addresses. In a nonclustered installation of SQL Server, the server can be referenced using the machine's IP address. In a clustered configuration, you do not use the IP addresses of the servers themselves; instead, you use this separately assigned IP address for the "virtual" SQL Server.

Figure 21.14 shows the next step in identifying the Cluster Security Policy for each SQL Server component (Database Engine, SQL Server Agent, and Analysis Services). Here, you use the domain Admin group. Figure 21.14 also shows the Server Configuration "service accounts" to use for all the services within this SQL Server install. You use a ClusterAdmin account set up for this purpose. Remember, this account must have `administrator` rights within the domain and on each server (that is, it must be a member of the Administrators local group on any node in the cluster). This is followed by the Database Engine Configuration dialog, where you set what type of authentication mode to use, the data directories for the root and subfolders, and the FILESTREAM options. Needless to say, the Data root directory is on the `S:` drive.

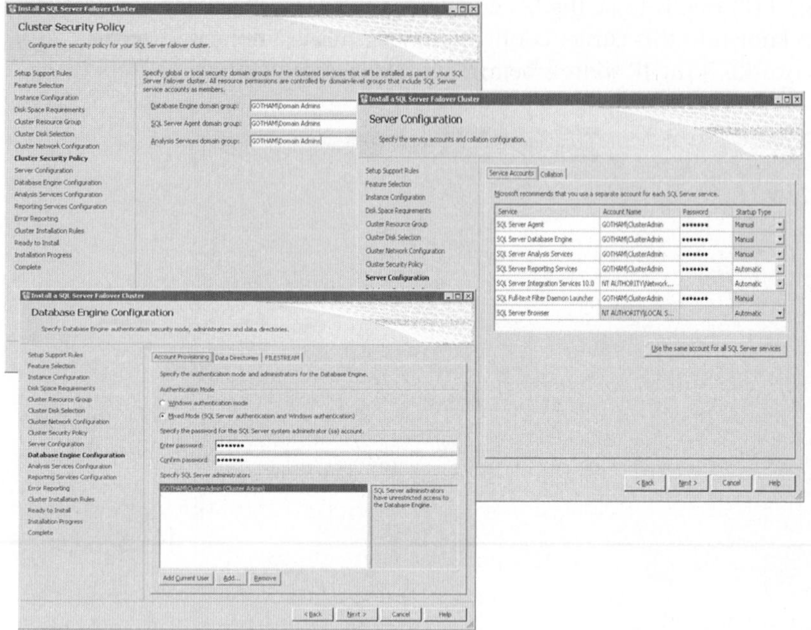

FIGURE 21.14 Specifying Cluster Security Policy, Server Config and Database Engine Config.

You then are prompted through the Analysis Services Configuration and Reporting Services Configuration dialogs. Your Analysis Services Data directories are within a subfolder of `S:\OLAP\`.

At this point, you have worked your way down to the Cluster Installation Rules check to determine if everything specified to this point is correct. Figure 21.15 shows this rules check "passing" status, a summary of what is about to be done, and the location of the configuration file (and path) that can be used later if you are doing command-line installs of new nodes in the cluster. A box appears around this configuration file path location at the bottom right of the Ready to Install dialog to show you where it is being created (if needed).

The next step is to click on the Install button.

The setup process installs SQL Server binaries locally on each node in the cluster (that is, in `C:\Program Files\Microsoft SQL Server`). The database files for the `master`, `model`, `tempdb`, and `msdb` databases are placed on the `S:` drive in this example. This is the shared disk location that must be available to all nodes in the SQL Server cluster.

When the process is complete, you can pop over into the Cluster Administrator and see all the resources just installed within the failover cluster. This is not highly available yet because you have completed only one node of the two-node failover cluster. But, as you

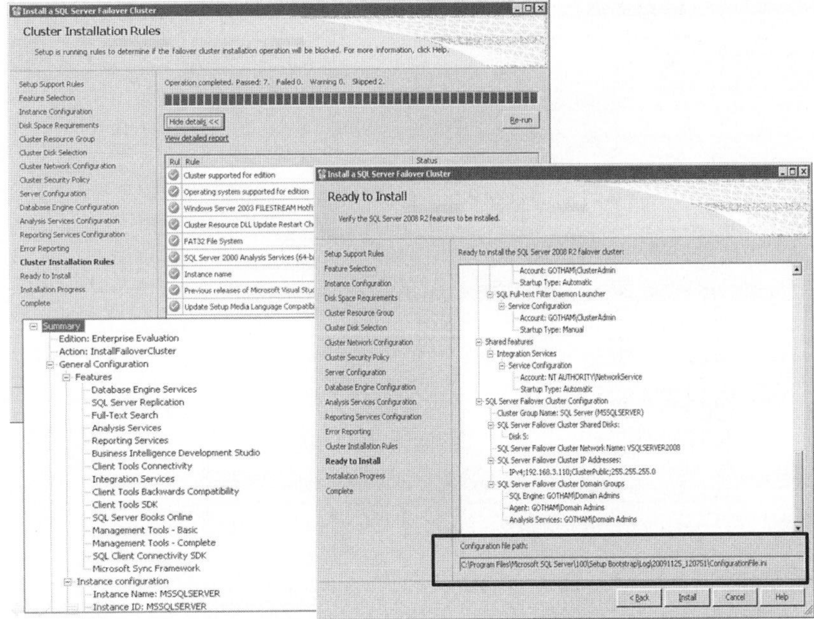

FIGURE 21.15 Cluster Installation Rules check and Ready to Install dialog.

can see in Figure 21.16, the SQL Server components have been successfully installed and are usable within the cluster.

Adding the next node (and any more subsequent nodes) to the cluster will make this configuration highly available because you will have other nodes to fail over to. To install the second node, you must now start back over that the Setup process (using SQL Server Installation Center). But this time, you can choose the Add Node to a SQL Server Failover Cluster option, as shown in Figure 21.17. Just as before, the Setup Support Rules check occurs for the next cluster node (`CLUSTER2`, in this example). As you can also see, adding a node is much simpler (many fewer steps) than creating a completely new SQL Server failover cluster installation.

If all items have passed on the new node, you come to the Cluster Node Configuration dialog, as shown in Figure 21.18. Here, you can see that the name of this node (`CLUSTER2`) is being associated with(added to) the original cluster node (`CLUSTER1`). This is truly where the magic occurs. You are then prompted to specify the service accounts and collation configuration of this second node. Again, you should specify the domain account that was specified in the first cluster configuration setup (`ClusterAdmin` in this example).

Now you are ready to verify that the rules for adding this node are being followed. If any check doesn't pass, you must correct it before the node can be added. Figure 21.19 shows this Add Node Rules check along with the summary of all the features to be installed as part of the add node operation.

Again, click the Install button to install the SQL Server features and add this node to the cluster.

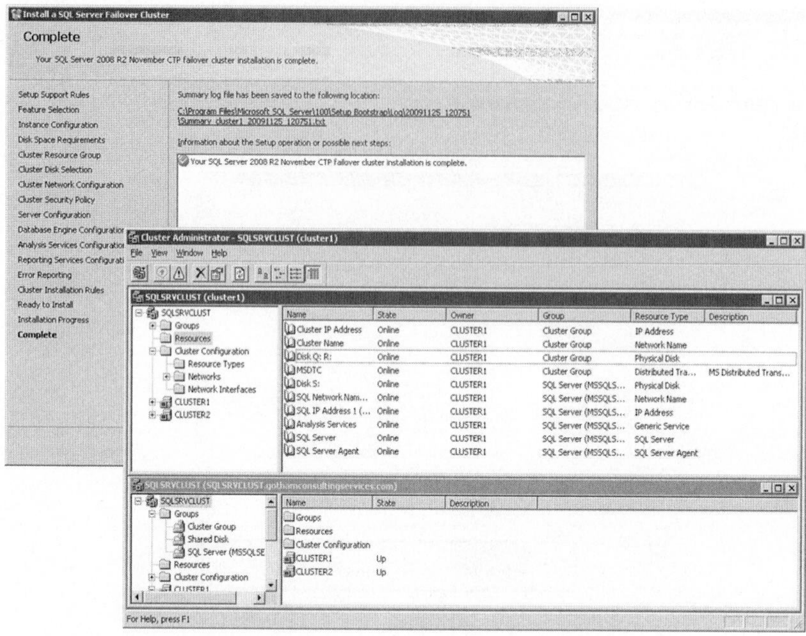

FIGURE 21.16 SQL Server Failover Cluster Node 1 install complete and within the Cluster Administrator.

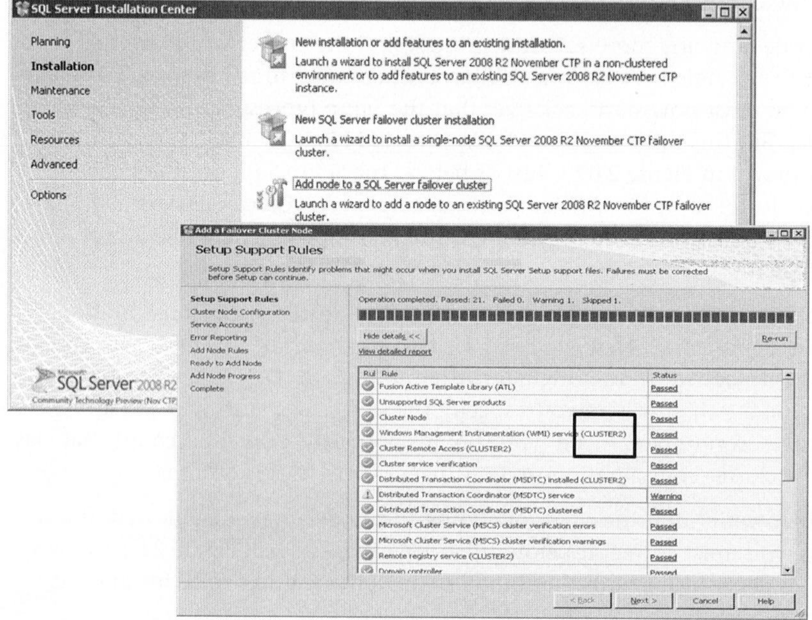

FIGURE 21.17 Adding a node to a SQL Server failover cluster and doing a Setup Support Rules check for the new cluster node.

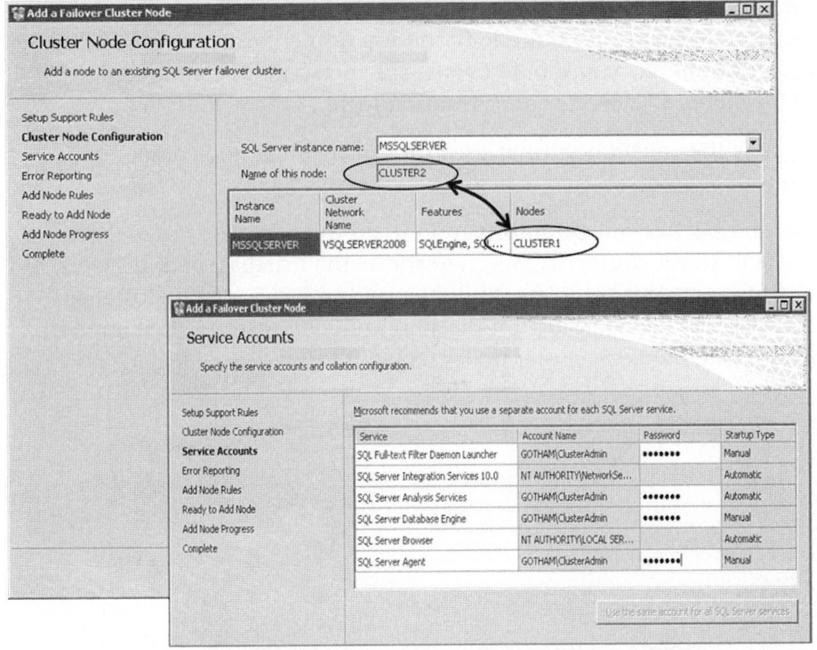

FIGURE 21.18 Specifying the cluster node configuration and the service accounts for the second node.

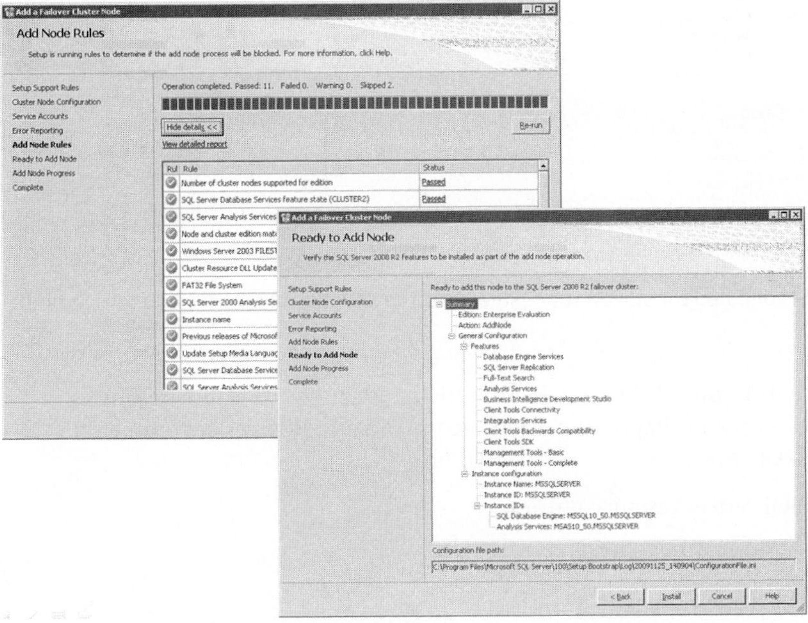

FIGURE 21.19 Cluster Installation Rules check and Ready to Install second node.

You must specify what type of authentication mode you want for SQL Server access: Windows Authentication (only) or mixed mode (Windows Authentication and SQL Server Authentication). For this example, you should choose the mixed mode option and provide a password for the sa SQL Server administration login.

Finally, you must specify the collation settings used for sorting order and compatibility with previous versions of SQL Server.

The SQL Setup program now has enough information to do the complete installation of the new node in the SQL Server cluster. Figure 21.20 shows the installation of the new SQL Server Failover Cluster node is complete. In particular, binaries are being installed locally, additional services are being created on the second node for SQL Server, and SQL resources are being associated to both cluster nodes.

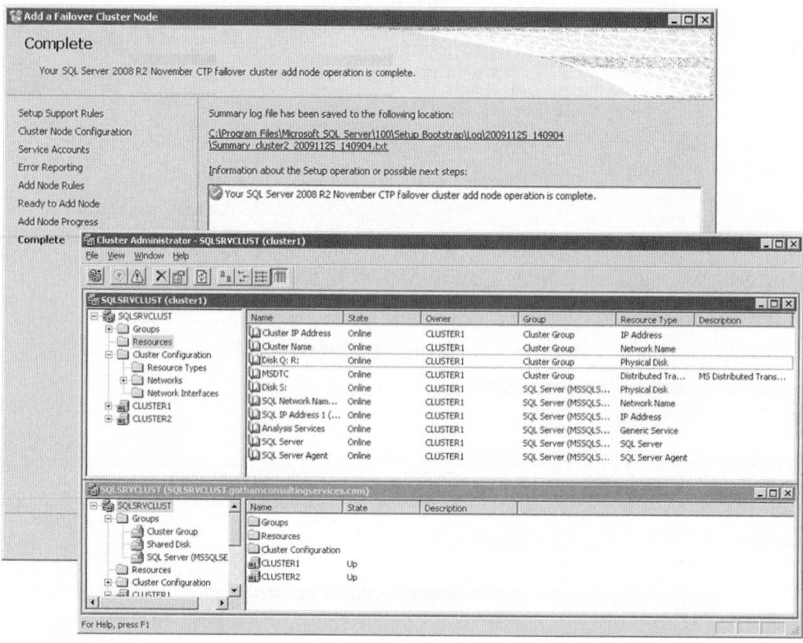

FIGURE 21.20 Second node installed (Complete) and the Cluster Administrator showing both nodes up.

As you can also see in Figure 21.20, Cluster Administrator shows the online resources within the cluster group and that both clusters are up and all resources are online (but controlled by `CLUSTER1` now).

Following are the SQL Server resource entries:

- The SQL Server virtual IP address
- The SQL Server network name
- SQL Server (`MSSQLSERVER`)

- SQL Server Agent (for the instance)
- Analysis Services
- Disk `S:` (physical disks where the DBs reside)
- MSDTC

Each resource entry should say `Online` in the State column and be owned by the same node (`CLUSTER1` in this example).

In the Cluster Administrator, you can easily view the properties of each of the new SQL Server resources by right-clicking a resource and selecting Properties. Figure 21.21 shows the properties of the Networks and Network Interface IP Address resources.

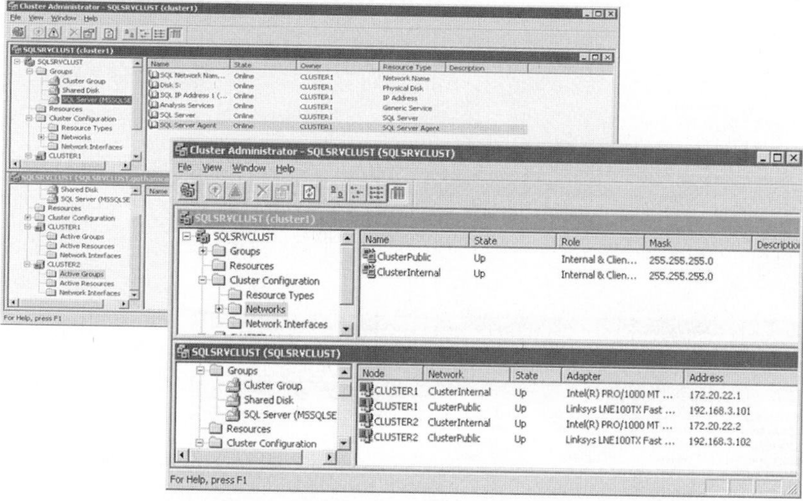

FIGURE 21.21 Properties of the Networks and Network Interfaces.

When you right-click a resource entry in the Cluster Administrator, you have an option to take the resource offline or to initiate a failure. You sometimes need to do this when you're trying to fix or test a SQL Server Clustering configuration. However, when you're initiating full SQL Server failover to another node (for example, from `CLUSTER1` to `CLUSTER2`), you typically use the Move Group cluster group technique because you want all the resources for the cluster group to fail over—not just one specific resource. Figure 21.22 shows that you simply right-click the Cluster Group item entry and select Move Group. All resources then fail over to `CLUSTER2`.

Failure of a Node

As you can see in Figure 21.23, one of the nodes in the SQL Server cluster (`CLUSTER1`) has failed, and MSCS is in the middle of failing over to the other node in the cluster (`CLUSTER2`). As you can also see, the `CLUSTER2` node item group has an hourglass on it, indicating that an MSCS operation is under way. The states of the resources on `CLUSTER2` are mostly Online Pending. In other words, these resources are in the middle of failing over to this node. As they come up successfully, Online Pending turns to Online.

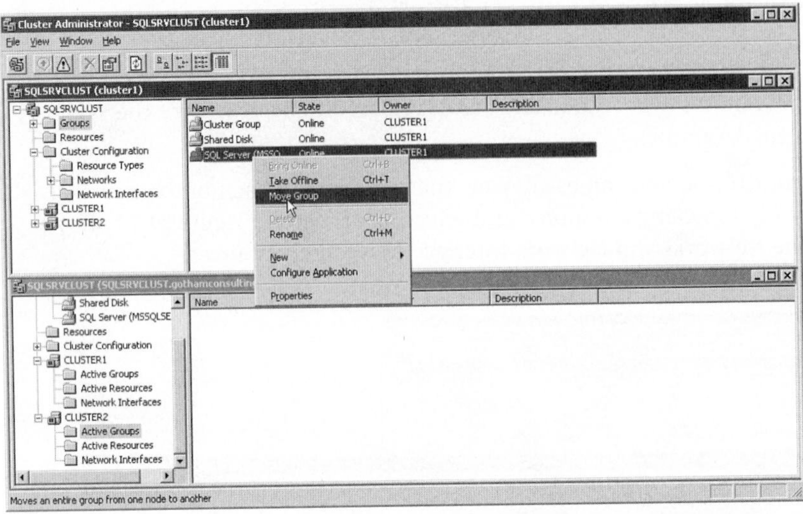

FIGURE 21.22 Using Move Group to fail over to another node in a cluster.

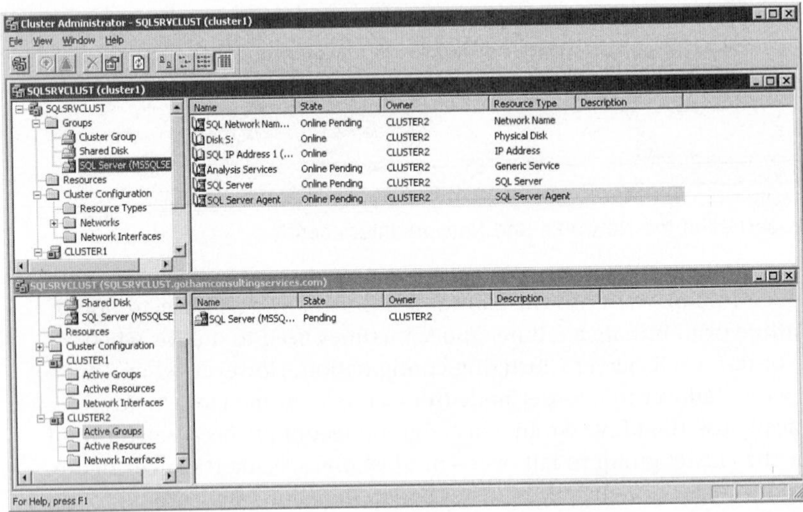

FIGURE 21.23 Failing over from **CLUSTER1** to **CLUSTER2**, Online Pending state.

In addition, the failure of a node (for any reason) is also written to the System event log.

This example showed an intentional failure of the SQL Server instance via the Cluster Administrator. SQL Server Failover Clustering does the right thing by failing over to the other node. This serves to verify that SQL Server Clustering is working properly. The next section illustrates what this effect has on a typical client application point of view, using a custom client test program called Connection Test Program.

Congratulations! You are now up and running, with your SQL Server Failover Cluster intact and should now be able to start achieving significantly higher availability for your end users. You ca easily register this new virtual SQL Server (`VSQLSERVER2008`) within SQL Server Management Studio (SSMS) and completely manage it as you would any other SQL Server instance.

The Connection Test Program for a SQL Server Cluster

To help in visualizing exactly what effect a SQL Server failure and subsequent failover may have on an end-user application, we have created a small test program using Visual Studio 2008. This small C# test program accesses the `AdventureWorks2008` database available for SQL Server 2008 (see the Introduction chapter for information on how to download and install the AdventureWorks2008 sample database), and it was created in about 10 minutes. It displays a few columns of data, along with a couple system variables that show connection information, including the following:

- **`ProductID`**, **`Name`**, and **`ProductNumber`**—This is a simple three-column display of data from the `Product` table in the `AdventureWorks2008` database.
- **`SHOWDATETIME`**—This shows the date and time (to the millisecond) of the data access being executed.
- **`SERVERNAME`**—This is the SQL Server name that the client is connected to.
- **`SPID`**—This is the SQL Server process ID (SPID) that reflects the connection ID to SQL Server itself by the client application.

This type of small program is useful because it always connects to the virtual SQL Server. This enables you to see what effect a failover would have with your client applications.

To populate this display grid, you execute the following SQL statement:

```
SELECT ProductID, Name, ProductNumber,
CONVERT (varchar(32), GETDATE(), 9) AS SHOWDATETIME,
@@SERVERNAME AS SERVERNAME,
@@SPID AS SPID
FROM Production.Product WHERE (ProductID LIKE '32%')
```

You use Visual Studio 2008 to set up a simple Windows form like the one shown in Figure 21.24. You build a simple button that will retrieve the data from the SQL Server database on the virtual server and also show the date, time, server name, and SPID information for each access invocation.

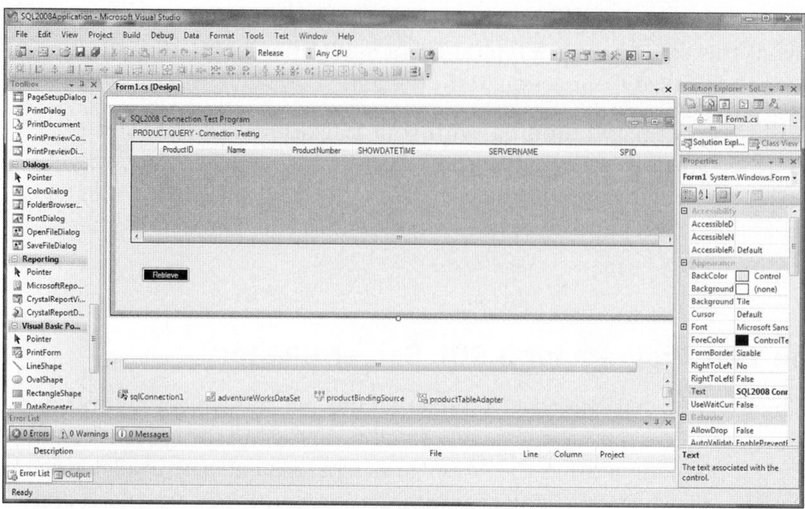

FIGURE 21.24 Visual Studio 2008 Windows form and data adapters needed for the test client C# program.

The Visual Studio 2008 project files for the Connection Test Program are available on the CD included with this book. The program, called `WindowsApplication4.sln SQLClientTest4` Visual Studio 2008 project, is zipped up in a file named `SQL Client SQL Clustering test program .zip`. If you want to install this program, you just unzip the `SQLClientTest.zip` file and locate the `WindowsApplication4.sln` solution file. You open this from your Visual Studio 2008 start page. Then you rebuild and deploy it after you have modified the connection string of the dataset adapter.

After deploying this simple test program, you simply execute it from anywhere on your network. As you can see in the `App.config` XML file for this application, shown here, the connection string references the `VSQLSERVER2008` virtual server name only:

```
<?xml version="1.0" encoding="utf-8" ?>
<configuration>
    <configSections>
    </configSections>
    <connectionStrings>
        <add name="WindowsApplication4.Properties.Settings.
       AdventureWorksConnectionString"
       connectionString="Data Source=VSQLSERVER2008;Initial
Catalog=AdventureWorks2008;
Integrated Security=True"
            providerName="System.Data.SqlClient" />
    </connectionStrings>
</configuration>
```

Figure 21.25 shows the first execution of the Connection Test Program. If you click the Retrieve button, the program updates the data grid with a new data access to the virtual SQL Server machine, shows the name of the server that the client program is connecting to (SERVERNAME), shows the date and time information of the data access (in the SHOWDATETIME column), and displays the SQL SPID that it is using for the data access (in the SPID column). You are now executing a typical C# program against the virtual SQL Server. Note that the SPID value is 55; this represents the SQL connection to the virtual SQL Server machine servicing the data request.

SQL2008 Connection Test Program

FillBy

ProductID	Name	ProductNumber	SHOWDATETIME	SERVERNAME	SPID
320	Chainring Bolts	CB-2903	Nov 25 2009 5:44:10:203PM	VSQLSERVER2008	55
321	Chainring Nut	CN-6137	Nov 25 2009 5:44:10:203PM	VSQLSERVER2008	55
322	Chainring	CR-7833	Nov 25 2009 5:44:10:203PM	VSQLSERVER2008	55
323	Crown Race	CR-9981	Nov 25 2009 5:44:10:203PM	VSQLSERVER2008	55
324	Chain Stays	CS-2812	Nov 25 2009 5:44:10:203PM	VSQLSERVER2008	55

Retrieve

FIGURE 21.25 Executing the Connection Test Program with current connection information.

Now let's look at how this high-availability approach works from the client application point of view. To simulate the failure of the active node, you simply turn off the machine (CLUSTER1 in this case). This is the best (and most severe) test case of all. Or, if you like, you can use the Cluster Administrator Move group approach shown earlier.

After you simulate this failure, you click the Retrieve button in the Connection Test Program again, and an unhandled exception occurs (see Figure 21.26). You can view the details of the error message, choose to quit the application, or choose to continue. You should click Continue for now.

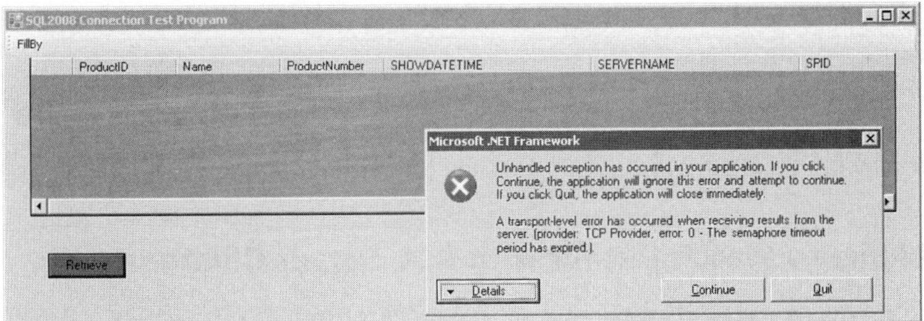

FIGURE 21.26 An unhandled exception has occurred; it is a transport-level error (that is, a TCP provider error).

What has happened is that the application can no longer connect to the failed SQL Server (because you turned off CLUSTER1), and it is still in the middle of failing over to CLUSTER2 in the two-node cluster.

A failover occurs in a short amount of time; the actual amount of time varies, depending on the power and speed of the servers implemented and the number of in-flight transactions that need to be rolled back or forward at the time of the failure. (A complete SQL failover often occurs in about 15 to 45 seconds. This is very minor and well within most service-level agreements and high-availability goals.) You then simply click the Retrieve button again in the Connection Test Program, and you are talking to SQL Server again, but now to CLUSTER2.

As you can see in Figure 21.27, the data connection has returned the customer data, SHOWDATETIME has been updated, and SERVERNAME still shows the same virtual SQL Server name that the application needs to connect to, but the SPID has changed from 55 to 52. This is due to the new connection of the Connection Test Program to the newly owned (failed-over) SQL Server machine. The Connection Test Program has simply connected to the newly started SQL Server instance on CLUSTER2. The unhandled exception (error) goes away, and the end user never knows a complete failover occurred; the user simply keeps processing as usual.

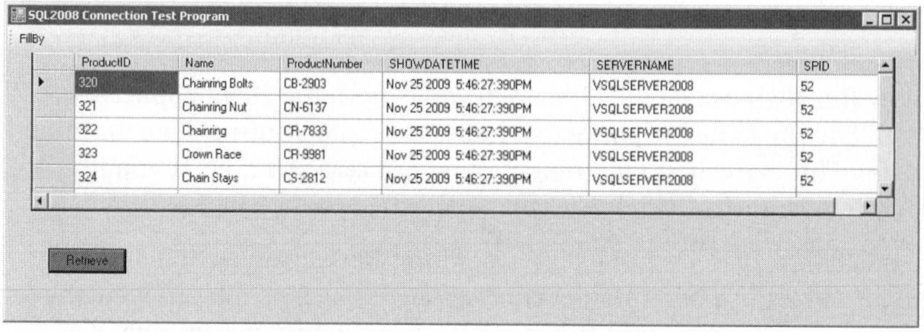

SQL2008 Connection Test Program

FillBy

ProductID	Name	ProductNumber	SHOWDATETIME	SERVERNAME	SPID
320	Chainring Bolts	CB-2903	Nov 25 2009 5:46:27:390PM	VSQLSERVER2008	52
321	Chainring Nut	CN-6137	Nov 25 2009 5:46:27:390PM	VSQLSERVER2008	52
322	Chainring	CR-7833	Nov 25 2009 5:46:27:390PM	VSQLSERVER2008	52
323	Crown Race	CR-9981	Nov 25 2009 5:46:27:390PM	VSQLSERVER2008	52
324	Chain Stays	CS-2812	Nov 25 2009 5:46:27:390PM	VSQLSERVER2008	52

Retrieve

FIGURE 21.27 Executing the Connection Test Program again against the failed-over cluster node.

NOTE

You could program better error handling that would not show the "unhandled exception" error. You might want to display a simple error message, such as "database momentarily unavailable—please try again," which would be much more user friendly.

Potential Problems to Watch Out for with SQL Server Clustering

Many potential problems can arise during setup and configuration of SQL Server Clustering. Following are some items you should watch out for:

- SQL Server service accounts and passwords should be kept the same on all nodes, or a node will not be able to restart a SQL Server service. You can use administrator or a designated account (for example, `Cluster` or `ClusterAdmin`) that has administrator rights within the domain and on each server.

- Drive letters for the cluster disks must be the same on all nodes (servers). Otherwise, you might not be able to access a clustered disk.
- You might have to create an alternative method to connect to SQL Server if the network name is offline and you cannot connect using TCP/IP. You can use named pipes, specified as `\\.\pipe\$$\SQLA\sql\query`.
- It is likely that you will run into trouble getting MSCS to install due to hardware incompatibility. Be sure to check Microsoft's Hardware Compatibility List before you venture into this installation.

Summary

Building out your company's infrastructure with clustering technology at the heart is a huge step toward achieving five-nines reliability. If you do this, every application, system component, or database you deploy on this architecture has that added element of resilience. And, in many cases, the application or system component changes needed to take advantage of these clustering technologies are completely transparent. Utilizing a combination of NLB and MSCS allows you not only to fail over applications but to scale for increasing network capacity.

The two-node, active/passive node is one of the most common SQL Server Clustering configurations used. As you become more familiar with SQL Server Clustering and your high-availability requirements get closer to five-nines), you might need to put in place other, more advanced configurations, such as four-node SQL Server clusters and/or datacenter-class clusters (of up to eight-node SQL Server clusters and active/active variations). If you follow the basic guidelines of disk configurations and database allocations across these disk configurations, as described in this chapter, you can guarantee a certain level of stability, performance, and scalability. SQL Server Clustering is one of the best, most cost-effective solutions, and it is literally "out of the box" with SQL Server and the Windows family of servers.

Remember that SQL Server 2008 supports other concepts related to high availability, such as data replication, log shipping (soon to be deprecated), and database mirroring. You might use these solutions rather than SQL Server Clustering, depending on your requirements.

Clustering is a very complex subject. The information contained in this chapter is sufficient to start you in this area, but for a much more complete and thorough understanding of how to assess your high-availability needs, to evaluate what you should build for high availability, and to implement a high-availability platform that uses MSCS and SQL Server Clustering, you should find a copy of *Microsoft SQL Server High Availability* by Paul Bertucci (Sams Publishing). This book is loaded with full explanations, a formal approach to achieving five-nines reliability, and numerous live examples.

Chapter 22, "Administering Policy-Based Management," explains how to affectively administer servers using the Declarative Management Framework.

Summary

CHAPTER 22

Administering Policy-Based Management

IN THIS CHAPTER

- Introduction to Policy-Based Management
- Policy-Based Management Concepts
- Implementing Policy-Based Management
- Sample Templates and Real-World Examples
- Policy-Based Management Best Practices

Policy-Based Management is one of the new management features introduced in SQL Server 2008. Policy-Based Management enables an organization to define policies to manage one or more SQL Server instances, databases, or objects within the enterprise. In addition, policies can be evaluated against target systems to ensure that the standard configuration settings are not out of compliance. Policy-Based Management was developed in response to the following industry trends:

- Increasing amounts of data being stored
- Data center consolidation and virtualization
- Growing product capabilities
- Proliferation of SQL Server systems within the enterprise
- Need for a way to manage SQL Server settings from a holistic perspective
- Regulatory compliance demanding secure and standardized settings

Introduction to Policy-Based Management

A data explosion has been occurring over the past several years. In a 2006 study, International Data Corporation (IDC; http://www.idc.com) reported that 5 exabytes of digital media (5 billion gigabytes) were stored in 2003, and in 2006 this had ballooned to 161 exabytes. Not only is more data being stored, but users are accessing more data than before. Part of this data growth is a result of the need for business intelligence (BI) systems to deliver actionable insights becoming more critical in the enterprise. Obtaining these insights requires large data volumes for trending and forecasting. As a result, data warehouses are becoming more critical in every enterprise.

This data explosion frequently results in a proliferation of SQL Servers.

Essentially, DBAs are being required to do more, frequently with less. In addition, the increasing complexities of the SQL Server product set are forcing DBAs to focus on efficient, scalable management and standardization. Due to the large numbers of SQL Servers involved, management by automation becomes critical as well to lessen the administrative burden. Monitoring also becomes more important to provide proactive support.

A well-managed SQL Server enterprise that follows best practices offers the following advantages:

- **Standardization**—Every SQL Server will have a common disk layout and settings, as well as consistent naming standards. As a result, DBAs moving from one SQL Server to another will not be surprised by different disk layouts or unusual settings that could account for a performance problem.
- **Best practices**—Microsoft internal studies have shown that 80% of the support calls to their Customer Service and Support (CSS) could have been avoided if the customer had been following best practices. Best practices not only offer performance advantages but also lead to fewer failure events caused by poorly configured SQL Servers, and security breaches due to SQL Servers that have not been hardened (security holes not locked down).
- **Ease of deployment**—A well-managed data center will have automated procedures for building SQL Servers (that is, unattended installations using configuration files) that require less time to build and minimal administrative interaction, resulting in fewer mistakes in a build and a reduction in administrative tasks.
- **Regulatory compliance**—By maintaining controlled and standardized settings, organizations can easily adhere to the demanding requirements of regulations such as Sarbanes-Oxley, the Health Insurance Portability and Accountability Act (HIPAA), and Payment Card Industry (PCI) standards.

The intent of Policy-Based Management is to provide a management framework that allows DBAs to automate management in their enterprise according to their own set of predefined standards. By implementing Policy-Based Management within a SQL Server infrastructure, organizations can reap the following benefits: total cost of ownership associated with managing SQL Server systems will be reduced, configuration changes to the SQL Server system can be monitored, unwanted system configuration changes can be prevented, and policies will ensure compliance.

The stated goals of Policy-Based Management fall into three categories:

- **Management by intent**—Allows DBAs to enforce standards and best practices from the start rather than in response to a performance problem or failure event

- **Intelligent monitoring**—Allows DBAs to detect changes that have been made to their SQL Server environments that deviate from the desired configuration
- **Virtualized management**—Provides a scalable framework that allows for management across the enterprise

Microsoft SQL Server 2008 and SQL Server 2008 R2 also ship with several predefined policies. These policies are not automatically imported into a default installation of SQL Server 2008. However, you can manually import them into SQL Server and use them as is or as a foundation for defining your own similar policies. These sample policies can be found in `C:\Program Files\Microsoft SQL Server\100\Tools\Policies\DatabaseEngine\1033`. Note that there are also policies for Reporting Services and Analysis Services, which can be found in the `ReportingServices` and `AnalysisServices` subdirectories of the `Policies` directory. Also note that Policy-Based Management can be used to manage SQL 2005 and 2000 servers.

NOTE

Microsoft has a blog focusing on Policy-Based Management (http://blogs.msdn.com/sqlpbm/) where it publishes scripts that can be used to enforce Microsoft best practices for SQL Server, as well as tips, tricks, and tutorials for using Policy-Based Management.

Policy-Based Management Concepts

Before we start learning about enforcing Policy-Based Management, there are a few key concepts DBAs must understand. These concepts include

- Facets
- Conditions
- Policies
- Categories
- Targets
- Execution mode
- Central Management Servers

Facets

A *facet* is a logical grouping of predefined SQL Server 2008 configuration settings. When a facet is coupled with a condition, a policy is formed and can be applied to one or more SQL Server instances and systems. Common facets include Surface Area Configuration, Server Audit, Database File, and Databases. Table 22.1 illustrates the complete list of predefined facets that can be selected, along with an indication of how each facet can be automated. Check On Schedule uses a SQL Server Agent job to evaluate a policy. Check On

Change uses event notification to evaluate based on when changes occur. Facets are included with SQL Server 2008 and cannot be modified.

TABLE 22.1 Facets for Policy-Based Management

Facet Name	Check on Change: Prevent	Check on Change: Log	Check on Schedule
Application Role	X	X	X
Asymmetric Key	X	X	X
Audit			X
Backup Device			X
Broker Priority			X
Broker Service			X
Certificate			X
Credential			X
Cryptographic Provider			X
Data File			X
Database			X
Database Audit Specification			X
Database DDL Trigger			X
Database Maintenance			X
Database Option		X	X
Database Performance			X
Database Role	X	X	X
Database Security			X
Default			X
Endpoint	X	X	X
File Group			X
Full Text Catalog			X
Full Text Index			X
Full Text Stop List			X
Index			X

TABLE 22.1 Facets for Policy-Based Management

Facet Name	Check on Change: Prevent	Check on Change: Log	Check on Schedule
Linked Server			X
Log File			X
Login			X
Login Options	X	X	X
Message Type			X
Multipart Name	X	X	X
Name			X
Partition Function			X
Partition Scheme			X
Plan Guide			X
Remote Service Binding			X
Resource Governor			X
Resource Pool	X	X	X
Rule			X
Schema	X	X	X
Server			X
Server Audit			X
Server Audit Specification			X
Server Configuration		X	X
Server DDL Trigger			X
Server Information			X
Server Performance			X
Server Security			X
Server Settings			X
Server Setup			X
Service Contract			X
Service Queue			X

TABLE 22.1 Facets for Policy-Based Management

Facet Name	Check on Change: Prevent	Check on Change: Log	Check on Schedule
Service Route			X
Statistic			X
Stored Procedure	X	X	X
Surface Area		X	X
Surface Area for AS			
Surface Area for RS			
Symmetric Key			X
Synonym			X
Table			X
Table Options	X	X	X
Trigger			X
User			X
User Defined Aggregate			X
User Defined Data Type			X
User Defined Function	X	X	X
User Defined Table Type			X
User Defined Type			X
User Options	X	X	X
View			X
View Options	X	X	X
Workload Group	X	X	X
Xml Schema Collection			X

The complete list of facets can be viewed in SQL Server 2008 Management Studio by expanding the `Management` folder, the `Policy-Based Management` node, and then the `Facets` folder. Alternatively, to view facets applied to a specific database, you can right-click the database and select Facets.

NOTE

Currently, there are 74 facets available for use. Going forward, Microsoft will undoubtedly create more facets, which will be included with upcoming service packs.

Conditions

A *condition* is a Boolean expression that dictates an outcome or desired state of a specific management condition, also known as a facet. Condition settings are based on properties, comparative operators, and values such as `String`, `equal`, `not equal`, `LIKE`, `NOT LIKE`, `IN`, or `NOT IN`. For example, a check condition could verify that data and log files reside on separate drives, that the state of the database recovery model is set to Full Recovery, that database file sizes are not larger than a predefined value, and that database mail is disabled.

Policies

A *policy* is a standard for a single setting of an object. It ultimately acts as a verification mechanism of one or more conditions of the required state of SQL Server targets. Typical scenarios for creating policies include imposing Surface Area Configuration settings, enforcing naming conventions on database objects, enforcing database and transaction log placement, and controlling recovery models. As mentioned earlier, a tremendous number of policies can be created against SQL Server 2008 systems. Surface Area Configurations are a very common policy, especially because the SQL Server 2005 Surface Area Configuration tool has been deprecated in SQL Server 2008.

NOTE

A policy can contain only one condition and can be either enabled or disabled.

Categories

Microsoft recognized that although you may want to implement a set of rigid standards for your internal SQL Server development or deployments, your enterprise may have to host third-party software that does not follow your standards. Although your internally developed user databases will subscribe to your own policies, the third-party user applications will subscribe to their own categories. To provide flexibility, you can select which policies you want a table, database, or server to subscribe to and group them into groups called *categories*, and then have a database subscribe to a category and unsubscribe from a group of other policies if necessary. A policy can belong to only one policy category.

Targets

A *target* is one or more SQL Server instances, databases, or database objects that you want to apply your categories or policies to. Targets can be only SQL Server 2008 R2, 2008, 2005, or 2000 systems. All targets in a server instance form a target hierarchy. A target set is the set of targets that results from applying a set of target filters to the target hierarchy—for example, all the tables in a database contained in a specific schema.

Execution Modes

When you are implementing policies, there are three types of execution modes. The On Change mode has two variations:

- **On Demand**—The On Demand policy ensures that a target or targets are in compliance. This task is invoked manually by right-clicking on the policy in the `Management` folder, `Policy Management` folder, `Policy` folder, and selecting Evaluate. The policy is not enforced and is only verified against all targets that have been subscribed to that policy. You can evaluate a policy also by right-clicking on the database and selecting Policies and Evaluate.
- **On Schedule**—Policies can be evaluated on a schedule. For example, a policy can be scheduled to check all SQL Server 2008 systems once a day. If any anomalies arise, these out-of-compliance policies are logged to a file. This file should be reviewed on a periodic basis. In addition, whenever a policy fails, the complete tree in SQL Server Management Studio displays a downward-pointing arrow next to the policy, as shown in Figure 22.1.

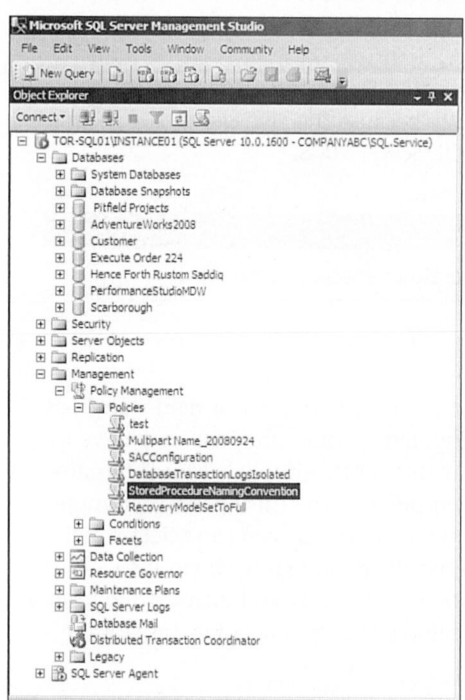

FIGURE 22.1 SQL Server management tree illustrating failed policies for table name.

- **On Change Prevent**—The On Change Prevent execution mode prevents changes to server, server object, database, or database objects that would make them out of compliance. For example, if you select a policy that restricts table names to only those that begin with the prefix `tbl`, and you attempt to create a table called `MyTable`, you get the following error message, and your table is not be created:

```
Policy 'table name' has been violated by
'/Server/(local)/Database/iFTS/Table/dbo.mytable'.
This transaction will be rolled back.
Policy description: ''
Additional help: '' : ''.
Msg 3609, Level 16, State 1, Procedure sp_syspolicy_
dispatch_event, Line 50
The transaction ended in the trigger.
The batch has been aborted.
```

- **On Change Log Only**—If you select On Change Log Only, a policy condition that is evaluated as failed is logged in the SQL Server Error log. The change does not prevent out-of-compliance changes.

Central Management Servers

In large enterprises, organizations most likely have more than one SQL Server system they want to effectively manage from a Policy-Based Management perspective. Therefore, if DBAs want to implement policies to multiple servers, they have two options. The first option includes exporting the policy and then importing it into different SQL Server systems. After the policy is imported, it must be configured to be evaluated on demand, on schedule, or on change.

The second option includes creating one or more Central Management Servers in SQL Server 2008. Basically, by registering one or more SQL Servers with a Central Management Server, a DBA can deploy multiserver policies and administration from a central system.

For example, you could create two Central Management Servers, one called OLAP and another called OLTP, and then register servers into each Central Management Server, import the different policies into each Central Management Server, and then evaluate the polices on each different Central Management Server. So, on your OLTP Central Management Server, the servers OLTP1, OLTP2, OLTP3, which are registered in the OLTP Central Management Server, would have the OLTP policies evaluated on them.

Creating a Central Management Server

Follow these steps to register a Central Management Server:

1. In SQL Server Management Studio, open the View menu and click Registered Servers.
2. In Registered Servers, expand the Database Engine node, right-click Central Management Servers, and then select Register Central Management Server.

3. In the New Server Registration dialog, specify the name of the desired Central Management Server.
4. If necessary, specify additional connection properties on the Connection Properties tab or click Save.

Registering SQL Server Instances in a Central Management Server

The next task registers SQL Server instances to be associated with a Central Management Server. The following steps outline this task:

1. Right-click on the Central Management Server with which you want to associate your SQL Server instance.
2. Select New Server Registration.
3. In the New Server Registration dialog, specify the name of the SQL Server Instance and the proper connection information and click Save
4. Repeat steps 1-3 for all SQL Server instances that you want to register with this Central Management Server.

Figure 22.2 illustrates a Central Management Server with one Server Group and two SQL Server instances registered.

FIGURE 22.2 Central Management Server with Registered SQL Server instances.

Importing and Evaluating Polices to the Central Management Server

After the Central Management Server is established, the Server Group is created, and the desired SQL Server instances are registered, it is time to import and evaluate policies. You can import policies for multiple instances by right-clicking the Central Management Server or Server Group and selecting Import Policies. After the policies are imported, the next step is to evaluate the policies by right-clicking the Central Management Server or Server

Group and selecting Evaluate. The output indicates the status of policies associated with all the SQL Server instances associated with the Central Management Server or Server Group.

NOTE

Importing, exporting, and evaluating policies are covered throughout the rest of the chapter.

Implementing Policy-Based Management

Now that you understand the basic purpose and concepts behind Policy Based Management, let's look at how to administer Policy-Based Management, then how to apply it to a server, and then a group of servers.

There are essentially six steps to implementing and administering Policy-Based Management:

- Creating a condition based on a facet
- Creating a policy based on that condition
- Creating a category
- Creating a Central Management Server
- Subscribing to a category
- Exporting or importing a policy

Let's look at each of these steps in turn. The upcoming sections explain each step in its entirety.

Creating a Condition Based on a Facet

When you are creating conditions, the general principle includes three elements: selecting a property, an operator, and then a value. The following example walks through the steps to create a condition based on a facet which will enforce a naming standard on a table:

1. To create a condition, connect to a SQL Server 2008 instance on which you want to create a policy.
2. Launch SQL Server Management Studio (SSMS). In Object Explorer, expand the `Management` folder, expand the `Policy Management` folder, and then expand the `Facets` folder.
3. Within the `Facets` folder, browse to the desired facet on which you want to create the policy (in this case, the Table facet).

4. To invoke the Create New Condition window, right-click the facet and select New Condition.
5. In the Create New Condition dialog, type a name for the condition (for example, `Table Name Convention`) and ensure that the facet selected is correct.
6. In the Expression section, perform the following tasks:
    a. Select the property on which you want to create your condition. For this example, use the `@Name` property.
    b. In the Operator drop-down box, select the `NOT LIKE` operator.
    c. In the value text box, enter `'tbl%'`.
7. Repeat step 6 for any additional expressions. For this example, the following expressions were entered, as displayed in Figure 22.3.

AndOr	Field	Operator	Value
	`@Name`	`NOT LIKE`	`'tbl%'`
AND	`Len(@Name)`	`<=`	`50`
AND	`@Name`	`NOT LIKE`	`'%s'`

8. Click OK to finalize the creation of the condition. You may have to click on the Field text box again for the OK button to be enabled.

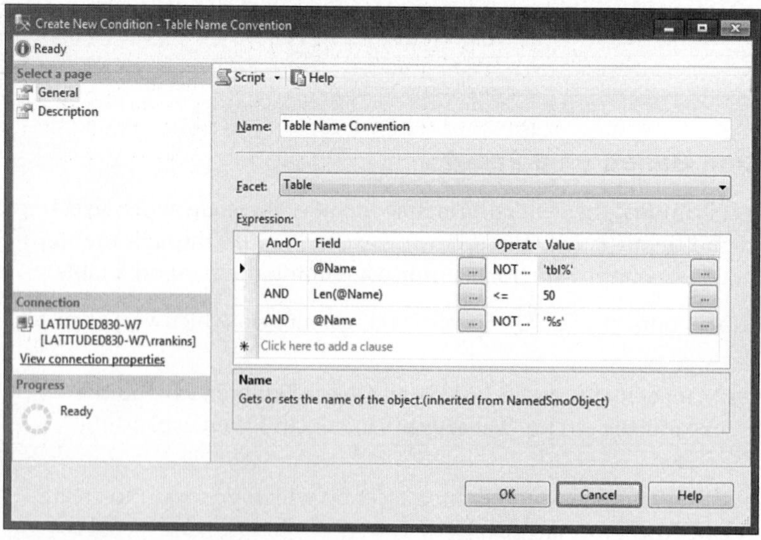

FIGURE 22.3 Creating a condition based on a facet.

NOTE

You can create conditions that query Windows Management Instrumentation (WMI) (using the `ExecuteWSQL` function) or SQL Server (using the `ExecuteSQL` function). For example, you can create conditions to check on available disk space or number of processors on the server. WMI allows you to issue SQL-like queries against management objects, which can return information on the physical machine hosting SQL Server and configuration and performance information, which is not accessible from within SQL Server itself.

Creating a Policy

After creating the condition or conditions, you need to create the policy. The *policy* is a standard that can be enforced on one or more SQL Server instances, systems, server objects, databases, or database objects. Follow these steps to create a policy with SQL Server Management Studio:

1. In Object Explorer, expand the `Management` folder, expand the `Policy Management` folder, and then click on `Policies`.
2. Right-click on the `Policies` folder and select New Policy.
3. On the General tab of the Create New Policy dialog, enter a name for the new policy, such as `Check Table Naming Conventions`.
4. In the Check Condition drop-down box, select a condition, such as the one created in the previous example, or select New to generate a new condition from scratch.
5. The Against Targets section indicates which objects the policy should be evaluated against. For example, you could create a new condition that applies to a specific database, all databases, a specific table, all tables, or to databases created after a specific date. In the Action Targets section, indicate which targets this condition should apply to.
6. Specify the Evaluation Mode by selecting one of the options in the drop-down menu. The options include On Demand, On Schedule, On Change Log Only, and On Change Prevent.

NOTE

If On Schedule is selected for the Evaluation Mode, specify a schedule from the predefined list or enter a new schedule.

7. The final drop-down box is Server Restriction. You can restrict which servers you do not want the policy to be evaluated against or enforced on by creating a server condition. Create a server restriction or leave the default setting None. An example of the policy settings for checking table name conventions is displayed in Figure 22.4.

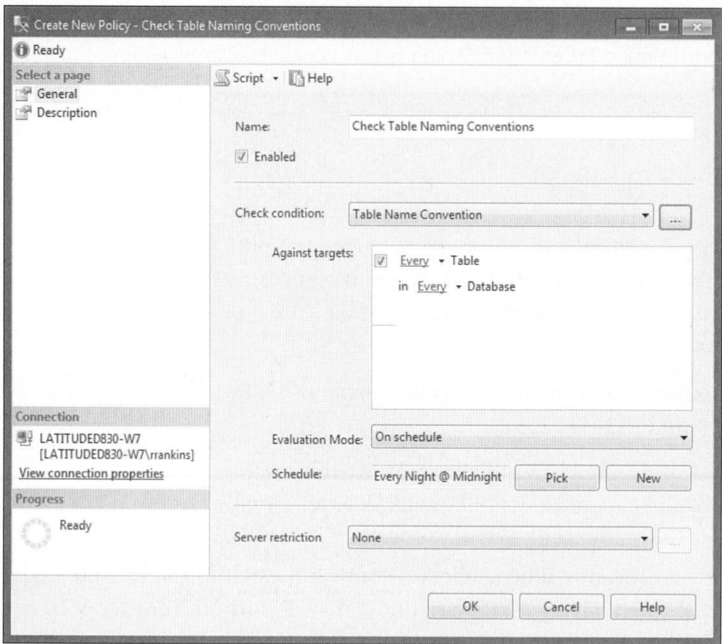

FIGURE 22.4 The Create New Policy dialog.

8. Before you close the Create New Policy dialog, ensure that the policy is enabled (the Enabled check box is selected) and then click on the Description page. The Description page allows you to categorize your policy, but it also allows you to display a custom text message when a policy is violated and a hyperlink where the DBA/developer can go for more information about the policy.
9. Click OK to finalize the creation of the new policy.

An Alternative to Creating Policies

As you can imagine, for complex policies you might need to create many conditions. In some cases it may be easier to create a table, database, or server configured to conform to the policy you want to create and then right-click on the specific object and select Facets. This brings up the View Facets page. Click on the Export Current State as Policy button. This exports a policy and a single condition to which the existing object will conform.

Figure 22.5 illustrates the dialog that prompts you for a name for your policy and condition as well as where you want to store the policy. You can store it in the file system and then import it to a Central Management Server or other servers where you want the policy to be evaluated, or you can import it directly to a server. Note that this policy will contain conditions specific to the object you use as a template; for example, if you use the `AdventureWorks2008` database, the policy will test for the condition where the database name is equal to `AdventureWorks2008`. For this feature to be useful, you likely need to edit the conditions to ensure that they are generic and evaluate exceptions correctly.

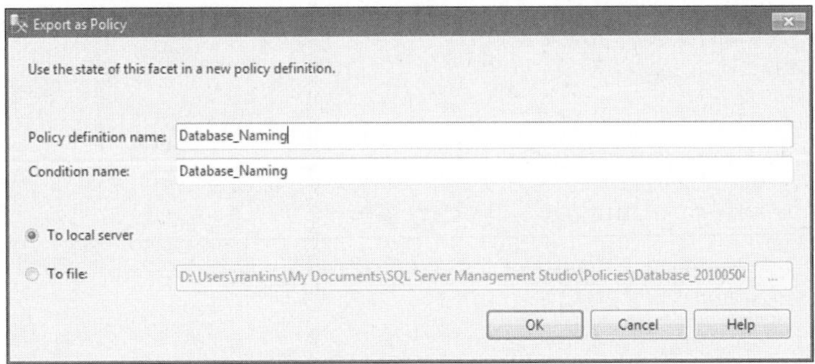

FIGURE 22.5 Exporting a policy based on an existing object.

Creating a Category

After you create a policy, it should be categorized. Categorization allows you to group policies into administrative or logical units and then allow database objects to subscribe to specific categories. It is worth mentioning that server objects can't subscribe to policies.

To create a category, click on the Description page in the Create New Policy dialog. Policies can be placed in the default category or a specific category, or you can create a new category. Specifying a category is illustrated in Figure 22.6.

You can also create categories by right-clicking on `Policy Management` and selecting Manage Categories.

If you choose to create a new category, click on the New button. This presents a dialog that allows you to name the category. By default, this policy is parked in the new category.

You can also select which category you want policies to belong to by selecting a specific category in the drop-down box. After you categorize your policies, you can select which categories you want your database to subscribe to. Right-click on the `Policy Management` folder and select Manage Categories. The Manage Policy Categories dialog (illustrated in Figure 22.7) appears. Check the categories to which you want all databases on your server to subscribe and deselect the ones that you do not want your server database to be subscribed to by default.

Other than the default category, DBAs can select which category (and policies belonging to that category) they want their databases to subscribe to. For example, if you have third-party software that does not follow your naming standards, you should ensure that the policies that enforce your naming standards are not in the default category. Then selectively have each of your user databases on your server subscribe to these databases.

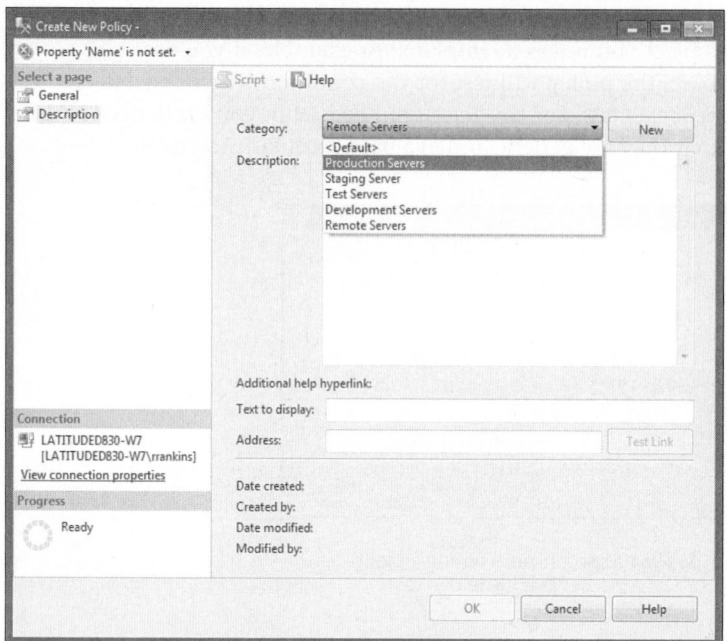

FIGURE 22.6 The category selection dialog.

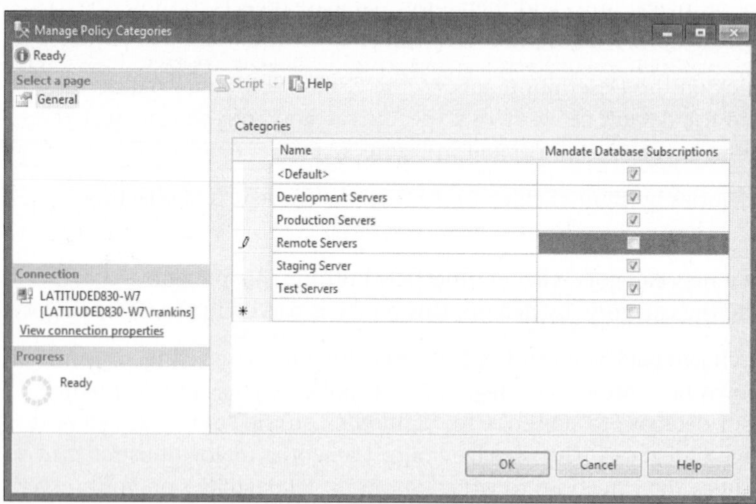

FIGURE 22.7 The Manage Policy Categories dialog.

Evaluating Policies

After you create an organization's policies and categories, you need to evaluate them to determine which of your servers and databases are out of compliance. There are three management points that can be leveraged to evaluate policies:

- For the first alternative, right-click on a server, server object, database, or database object in SQL Server Management Studio 2008 and select Policies and then Evaluate.
- For the second alternative, expand the `Management` folder, expand `Policy Management`, right-click on Policies, and select Evaluate. In the Evaluate Policies page displayed, check the policy or policies you want to evaluate and click the Evaluate button. It is also possible to select an individual policy. To do so, in the `Policy` folder, right-click on it and select Evaluate.
- Finally, the preferred way to evaluate all your servers, or a group of your servers, is to connect to display the Registered Servers list in SSMS. Expand the Central Management Servers node and right-click on the name of a Central Management Server and select Evaluate Policies. The policies you select to evaluate are evaluated on all SQL Servers defined on that Central Management Server—for example, all member servers in all Server Groups. If you select a Server Group, all member servers in that Server Group are evaluated. To evaluate the policies, you need to right-click on the Central Management Server, Server Group, or even Member Server and select Evaluate Policies.

When you right-click on the Central Management Server or Server Group and select Evaluate Polices, you are presented with a dialog that prompts you for a source, with a Choose Source prompt. For Select Source, enter the server name into which you have imported your policies or browse to a file share. Then highlight all the policies you want to import and click on the Close button to close the dialog.

After the policies are imported, you can select the individual policies you want to run and click Evaluate. The policies are then evaluated on the member servers, and the results are displayed in the Evaluation Results pane, as illustrated in Figure 22.8.

The Evaluation Results pane displays servers where a policy has failed. In the Target Details section, there is a View hyperlink, which allows you to browse to get more details on why the individual target server and policy target failed compliance to the policy you evaluated.

Importing and Exporting Policies

In some situations a DBA might want to export one or many policies with their conditions from one or many SQL Server systems and import them to another SQL Server instance or system. Fortunately, you can perform this task easily with an export and import wizard that generates or reads the policy definitions as XML files.

Follow these steps to export a policy with SQL Server Management Studio:

1. In Object Explorer, expand the `Management` folder, expand the `Policy Management` node, and then expand the `Policies` folder.
2. Within the `Policies` folder, right-click a desired policy to export and then select Export Policy.
3. In the Export Policy dialog, specify a name and path for the policy and click Save.

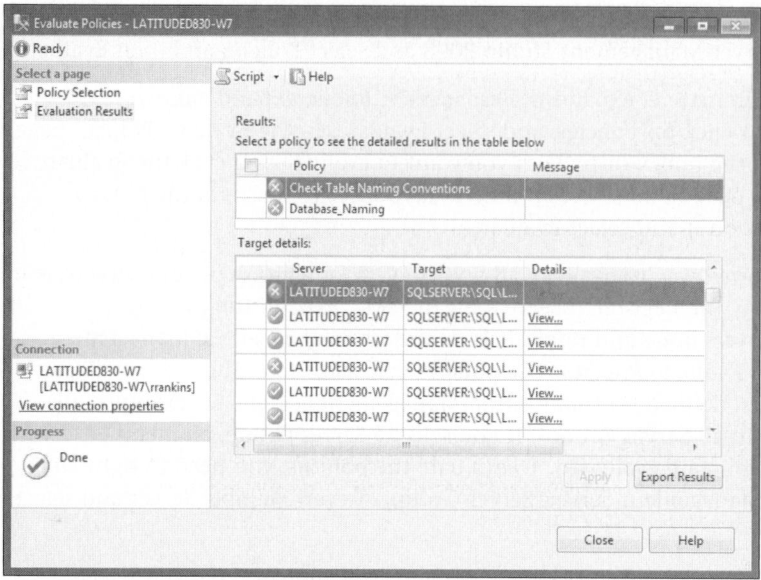

FIGURE 22.8 The Evaluation Results pane.

Importing a policy from an XML file is just as simple. Follow these steps to import a policy with SQL Server Management Studio:

1. In Object Explorer, expand the `Management` folder, expand the `Policy Management` node, and then select `Policies`.
2. Right-click on the `Policies` folder and select Import.
3. The import screen has three options you need to be aware of:

    a. First, provide the path of the file to import.

    b. Second, enable the option Replace Duplicate Items When Imported.

    c. Finally, in the Policy State drop-down box, specify the state of the policy being imported. The options include Preserve Policy State on Import, Enable All Policies on Import, and Disable All Policies on Import.

Sample Templates and Real-World Examples

The following sections illustrate the sample policy templates included with SQL Server 2008 and real-world examples for using Policy-Based Management.

Sample Policy Templates

SQL Server 2008 includes a plethora of predefined sample policies, which can be leveraged by importing them into a SQL Server 2008 system. The policies available for import are located in the default installation drive at `C:\Program Files\Microsoft SQL`

Server\100\Tools\Policies. As mentioned earlier, you can import the desired policies by right-clicking the Policies node and selecting Import. The sample templates are categorized by SQL Server feature such as Database Engine, Reporting Services, and Analysis Services.

Evaluating Recovery Models

Recovery models determine how SQL Server uses the transaction log. On OLTP systems, the most appropriate recovery model is generally the Full Recovery model. For OLAP systems, the most appropriate recovery model is generally the simple recovery model. For most development environments, the most appropriate recovery model is also the simple recovery model.

For mission-critical databases, or databases where point-in-time recovery is important, having a transaction log backed up every five minutes may be required. Policy-Based Management can be used to determine whether the appropriate recovery model is in place for each user database for each server type. Central Management Servers could be created for each server type and a policy can be created to ensure that the appropriate recovery model is in place across all servers managed within a management server.

Implementing Surface Area Configuration Checks

SQL Server 2005 shipped with the SQL Server Surface Area Configuration (SAC) tool. This tool allowed you to enable or disable various components and services on individual SQL 2005 Servers. This feature was deprecated in SQL Server 2008 because the Microsoft team felt that the better way to handle these configuration tasks was through Policy-Based Management.

If you want to implement the Surface Area Configuration feature in SQL Server 2008 to configure components and services, import the following policies:

- Surface Area Configuration for Database Engine 2005 and 2000 Features.xml
- Surface Area Configuration for Database Engine 2008 Features.xml
- Surface Area Configuration for Service Broker Endpoints.xml
- Surface Area Configuration for SOAP Endpoints.xml

SQL Server Health Checks

One of the SQL Server Support Engineers has posted blog entries on how to perform server health checks using Policy-Based Management. You can access his blog using this URL: http://blogs.msdn.com/bartd/archive/2008/09/11/defining-complex-server-health-policies-in-sql-2008.aspx.

The main part of the SQL Server health check revolves around ensuring the disk response times are less than 100ms. The Policy uses ExecuteSQL to query the dynamic management view sys.dm_io_virtual_file_stats to ensure that the disk response time is within this limit. You can extend this policy to query other DMVs for other health checks—for example, the use of excessive parallelism or checking to ensure that cumulative wait stats have not exceeded desired boundaries.

Ensuring Object Naming Conventions

Your company may have standards for naming objects. For example, stored procedures must start with the prefix `usp`, tables must start with the prefix `tbl`, and functions must start with the prefix `ufn`. Policy-Based Management can be used to ensure that all objects are compliant with this policy. This policy can be implemented to execute as On Change Prevent, which prevents the creation of such noncompliant objects.

Checking Best Practices Compliance

You can implement policies that check for SQL Server best practices. For example, databases can be configured with the autoclose and autoshrink options. Although these options have their place on some systems, they are not recommended to be enabled in production environments because the autoclose option causes a time delay while the database is opened by a connection trying to access it. This can lead to timeouts. The autoshrink option can lead to fragmentation and is in general not recommended. A policy can check for these settings and other settings to ensure that all your databases are following best practices.

Policy-Based Management Best Practices

Following are some best practices to consider when implementing Policy-Based Management in SQL Server 2008:

- When deploying Policy-Based Management in your environment, you should be very careful about using On Change Prevent. For example, a policy that prevents stored procedure creation with the `sp_` prefix prevents the enabling of replication on a SQL Server.
- When you create a policy that you want enforced on all user databases, you should place this policy in the default category so that it is subscribed to all databases. Otherwise, you need to manually subscribe all databases to the categories that contain the policies you want enforced.
- You should make use of multiple Configuration Servers or Server Groups to group your SQL Servers according to logical groupings on which you want to group your policies.
- Importing policies into centralized SQL Server 2008 servers makes it easier to deploy groups of policies against groups of servers using Central Management Servers—for example, to store data warehouse policies on Server A. You should use this server as a source when selecting policies to evaluate against your data warehouse servers registered in the Data Warehousing Central Management Server.
- You might find that your environment contains third-party user applications/databases that are not in compliance with the policies you have created for your enterprise. Policy-Based Management uses the opt-in metaphor such that all policies are enforced by default. For databases on which you do not want the policy to be enforced, you need to tag the database, perhaps with an extended property or a

specially named table that the server exception category or target will detect and exempt that server or database from the policy.

- You should use the ExecuteWSQL task to issue WMI queries to extend conditions and policies beyond the SQL Server environment—for example, to check what other services may be running on a server hosting SQL Server.

Summary

Policy-Based Management is a new component in SQL Server 2008 that allows you to manage your SQL 2000, 2005, and 2008 servers by creating policies that can be used to enforce compliance to best practices or to report on out-of-compliance servers. It provides a highly granular, flexible, and extensible toolset that allows you to manage all aspects of your SQL Server. Properly used, it is a great tool to enforce standardization in your environment and to ease the management burden.

The next part of this book, Part IV, "Database Administration," explores the tasks involved in creating and managing databases and database objects, just the sorts of things you want to apply many of your best practices and policies against.

CHAPTER 23

Creating and Managing Databases

IN THIS CHAPTER

- What's New in Creating and Managing Databases
- Data Storage in SQL Server
- Database Files
- Creating Databases
- Setting Database Options
- Managing Databases

A *database* is a collection of tables and related objects that help protect and organize data. It must exist before you can create all database objects, including tables, indexes, and stored procedures. This chapter focuses on how to create a sound database that can house database objects and how to manage the database after the objects are created. The creation and management of the various database objects is discussed in the remaining chapters in Part IV, "Database Administration."

NOTE

It is important to remember that SQL Server actually uses its own set of databases that are installed by default when SQL Server is installed. These databases are referred to as *system databases*. The databases that users create are aptly named *user databases*. The system databases include `master`, `model`, `msdb`, `tempdb`, and `resource`. Each of these databases performs a key function in the operation of SQL Server. For example, the `master` database contains an entry for every user database created and contains server-wide information critical to the operation of SQL Server. The `model` database is basically a template database for any newly created databases. Each system database is based on a structure similar to user databases and contain database objects like those contained in user databases. The system databases are discussed in detail in Chapter 7, "SQL Server System and Database Administration."

What's New in Creating and Managing Databases

SQL Server 2008 offers several new features that provide improved security and manageability. The primary security enhancement is the capability to encrypt an entire database using Transparent Data Encryption (TDE). This transparent data encryption applies to the data files and log files that make up a database. It allows for an entire database to be secure via encryption without the need to change existing applications or the individual database objects. Transparent Data Encription is covered in Chapter 12, "Data Encryption."

The manageability improvements in SQL Server 2008 are centered around data compression and enhanced database mirroring. The data compression improvements help reduce the amount of space that your database files occupy. The enhancements in database mirroring include automatic page repair, improved performance, and enhanced supportability via additional performance counters and new dynamic management views. Database mirroring is discussed in more detail in Chapter 20, "Database Mirroring."

Data Storage in SQL Server

A database is a storage structure for database objects. It is made up of at least two files. One file, referred to as a *data file*, stores the database objects, such as tables and indexes. The second file, referred to as the *transaction log file*, records changes to the data. A data file or log file can belong to only one database.

SQL Server stores data on the data file in 8KB blocks, known as pages. A *page* is the smallest unit of input/output (I/O) that SQL Server uses to transfer data to and from disk. An 8KB page is equal to 1024 bytes × 8, or 8192 bytes. There is some overhead associated with each data page, so the maximum number of bytes of data that can be stored on a page is 8060 bytes. The overhead on a data page includes a 96-byte page header that contains system information about the page. This system information includes the page number, page type, and amount of free space on the page.

Generally, a row of data in a SQL Server database is limited to the 8060-byte maximum. With SQL Server 2008, there are some exceptions to this 8060-byte limit if the table contains columns that have the data types `text/image`, `varchar`, `nvarchar`, `varbinary`, or `sql variant`. With these data types, SQL Server can store the data in a separate data structure when the size of the row exceeds the 8060-byte limit. When the 8060-byte limit is exceeded, SQL Server stores a pointer to the separate data structure so that the information in these columns can be accessed.

In an effort to reduce internal operations and increase I/O efficiency, SQL Server, when allocating space to a table or an index, allocates space in extents. An *extent* is eight contiguous pages, or 64KB of storage. There are actually two types of extents. Every table or index is initially allocated space in a *mixed extent*. As the name implies, mixed extents store pages from more than one object. When an index or a table is first created, it is assigned an index allocation map (IAM), which is used to track space usage for the object, and at least one data page. The IAM and data page are assigned to a mixed extent in an effort to save space because dedicating an extent to a table with a few small rows would be wasteful. Up to eight initial pages are assigned this way. When an object requires more than eight pages of storage, all further space is allocated from uniform extents. A *uniform extent* stores pages for only a single index or table. This allows SQL Server to optimize read and write operations and reduce fragmentation because the data is stored in units of 64KB (that is, eight pages) as opposed to individual 8KB pages being scattered throughout the data file.

For more detailed information on the internal storage structures and how to manage them in SQL Server databases, see Chapter 38, "Database Design and Performance."

Database Files

SQL Server maps a database over a set of operating system files visible to the SQL Server machine. Microsoft recommends that the files be located on a storage area network (SAN), on an iSCSI-based network, or on a locally attached disk. These three storage options provide the best performance and reliability for a SQL Server database. You have an option of storing database files on a network, but this option is turned off by default. You can use the trace flag 1807 to enable network-based database files, but it is generally not recommended that you do so.

Each database can contain a maximum of 32,767 files. Each database file serves a different purpose for the database engine. These files have a standard layout that allows SQL Server to organize and read the data within the files. SQL Server needs to keep track of the allocated space in each data file; it does so by allocating special pages in the first extent of each file. Because the data stored on these pages is dense and the files are accessed often, they are usually found in memory; therefore, they can be retrieved quickly.

The first page (page 0) in every file is the file header page. This page contains information about the file, such as the database to which the file belongs, the filegroup it is in, the minimum size, and its growth increment.

The second page (page 1) in each file is the page free space (PFS) page. The PFS page keeps track of the other pages in the database file. The PFS uses 1 byte for each page. This byte keeps track of whether the page is allocated, whether it is empty, and, if it is not empty, how full the page is. A single PFS page can keep track of 8,000 contiguous pages. Additional PFS pages are created as needed.

The third page (page 2) in each file is the global allocation map (GAM) page. This page tracks allocated extents. Each GAM page tracks 64,000 extents, and additional GAM pages are allocated as needed. The GAM page contains 1 bit for each extent, which is set to `0` if the extent is allocated to an object and to `1` if it is free.

The fourth page (page 3) is the secondary GAM (SGAM) page. The SGAM page tracks allocated mixed extents. Each SGAM page tracks 64,000 mixed extents, and additional SGAM pages are allocated as needed. A bit set to `1` for an extent indicates a mixed extent with pages available.

Primary Files

The *primary data file* is the data file that keeps track of all the other data files used by the database. It is an operating system file that typically has the file extension `.mdf`. SQL Server does not require that it have this `.mdf` extension, but it is recommended for consistency. The primary data file is the first file created for a database. Each database must have only one primary file. This file stores data for any database objects mapped to it, and it contains references to any other database files created.

In many cases, the primary data file is the only data file. There is no requirement to have more than one data file, and often, a database contains only one primary data file (for example, `C:\mssql\mydb.mdf`) and only one log file (for example, `C:\mssql\mydb_log.ldf`).

Secondary Files

You can create zero or more secondary data files in a database. These files, by default, are identified with the `.ndf` extension, but the extension can be different. Secondary data files provide an opportunity to spread the data that SQL Server stores over more than one physical file. This capability can be particularly useful for larger databases and can help with performance and management of database files. Consider, for example, a situation in which a database server has four physical drives available for the data file(s). Each drive is 1GB in size, but the database you are creating is 2GB. In this example, the database will not fit on one drive. A solution to this problem is to create a primary data file on one of the drives and a secondary data file on each of the three remaining drives. SQL Server automatically spreads the 2GB database across the four data files located on four separate drives.

Secondary files also provide some added flexibility for backing up or copying databases. This is most apparent with large databases. For example, let's say you have a 100GB database, and it contains only a primary data file. If you want to move this database to another environment, you must have a drive that is at least 100GB to store the primary data file. If you want to copy the database to a server that has 10 50GB drives, you cannot do it. You have the space across all 10 drives, but you do not have a single drive that can hold the primary data file. If, however, you create the database with several secondary files, you have the option of placing each of the secondary files on a separate drive.

TIP

You can use the `sys.master_files` catalog view to list the database files for all the databases. For example, `SELECT db_name(database_id),* from sys.master_files order by 1` returns all the database files, ordered by the name of the database they belong to. You can change the sort order for the `SELECT` statement and order it by `physical_name` to quickly locate a database file and find which database is using that file.

Using Filegroups

Filegroups allow you to align certain database objects with specific data files. Tables, indexes, and large object (LOB) data can be assigned to a filegroup. A filegroup can be associated with one or more data files. The alignment of data and indexes to filegroups can provide performance benefits and improve manageability. Each database has at least one filegroup, called the *primary filegroup*. This filegroup, by default, contains the primary data file and any other secondary data files that have not been specifically aligned with another filegroup. Any database object that you create without specifying a filegroup is created in the primary filegroup.

Additional filegroups can be created and aligned with secondary data files. There is no requirement to have more than one filegroup, but additional filegroups give you added flexibility. Filegroups can be aligned with data files that can be stored on separate disk drives to improve data access. This improvement is facilitated by concurrent disk access across the disk drives assigned to the filegroups.

TIP

If too many outstanding I/Os are causing bottlenecks in the disk I/O subsystem, you might want to consider spreading the files across more disk drives. Performance Monitor can identify I/O bottlenecks by monitoring the `PhysicalDisk` object and `Disk Queue Length` counter. You should consider spreading the files across multiple disk drives if the `Disk Queue Length` counter is greater than two times the number of spindles on the disk. For more information on monitoring SQL Server performance, see Chapter 39, "Monitoring SQL Server Performance."

For example, you could create a filegroup called `UserData_FG`, consisting of three files spread over three physical drives. You could create another filegroup named `Index_FG`, with a single file, on a fourth drive. Then, when you create the tables, you can create them on the `UserData_FG` filegroup. You can create indexes on the `Index_FG` filegroup. This reduces contention between tables because the data is spread over three disks and can be accessed independently of the indexes. If more storage is required in the future, you can easily add additional files to the index or data filegroup, as appropriate.

You can create filegroups at the time the database is created, or you can add them after the database is created. When you create filegroups along with the database, the definition for the filegroup is contained in the `CREATE DATABASE` statement. Following is an example of a `CREATE DATABASE` statement with filegroup definitions:

```
CREATE DATABASE [mydb] ON  PRIMARY
( NAME = N'mydb',
     FILENAME = N'C:\mssql2008\data\mydb.mdf' ,
     SIZE = 2048KB , FILEGROWTH = 1024KB ),
 FILEGROUP [Index_FG]
```

```
( NAME = N'mydb_index1',
    FILENAME = N'I:\mssql2008\data\mydb_index1.ndf' ,
    SIZE = 2048KB , FILEGROWTH = 1024KB ),
 FILEGROUP [UserData_FG]
( NAME = N'mydb_userdata1',
    FILENAME = N'D:\mssql2008\data\mydb_userdata1.ndf' ,
    SIZE = 2048KB , FILEGROWTH = 1024KB ),
( NAME = N'mydb_userdata2',
    FILENAME = N'E:\mssql2008\data\mydb_userdata2.ndf' ,
    SIZE = 2048KB , FILEGROWTH = 1024KB ),
( NAME = N'mydb_userdata3',
    FILENAME = N'F:\mssql2008\data\mydb_userdata3.ndf' ,
    SIZE = 2048KB , FILEGROWTH = 1024KB )
 LOG ON
( NAME = N'mydb_log',
    FILENAME = N'L:\mssql2008\log\mydb_log.ldf' ,
    SIZE = 1024KB , FILEGROWTH = 10%)
```

This example creates a database named `mydb` that has three filegroups. The first filegroup, `PRIMARY`, contains the `.mdf` file. `Index_FG` contains one file: `I:\mssql2008\data\mydb_index1.ndf`. The third filegroup, `UserData_FG`, contains three data files located on the `D:`, `E:`, and `F:` drives. This example demonstrates the relationship between databases, filegroups, and the underlying operating system files. (The T-SQL for creating a database is discussed in detail later in this chapter.)

After you create a database with multiple filegroups, you can then create a database object on a specific filegroup. In the preceding example, you could use the filegroup named `UserData_FG` to hold user-defined tables, and you could use the filegroup named `Index_FG` for the database indexes. You assign database objects at the time you create the object. The following example demonstrates the creation of a user-defined table on the `UserData_FG` filegroup and the creation of an index for that table on the `Index_FG` filegroup:

```
CREATE TABLE dbo.Table1
   (TableId int NULL,
   TableDesc varchar(50) NULL)
  ON [UserData_FG]

CREATE CLUSTERED INDEX [CI_Table1_TableID] ON [dbo].[Table1]
( [TableId] ASC)
  ON [Index_FG]
```

Any objects not explicitly created on a filegroup are created on the default filegroup. The `PRIMARY` filegroup is the default filegroup when a database is created. You can change the default filegroup, if necessary. If you want to change the default group to another group, you can use the `ALTER DATABASE` command. For example, the following command changes the default filegroup for the `mydb` database:

```
ALTER DATABASE [mydb] MODIFY FILEGROUP [UserData_FG] DEFAULT
```

You can also change the default filegroup by right-clicking the database in the Object Explorer, choosing Properties, and selecting the Filegroups page. Then you select the check box labeled Default to make the given filegroup the default. Figure 23.1 shows the filegroups for the `AdventureWorks2008` database, with the primary filegroup selected as the default.

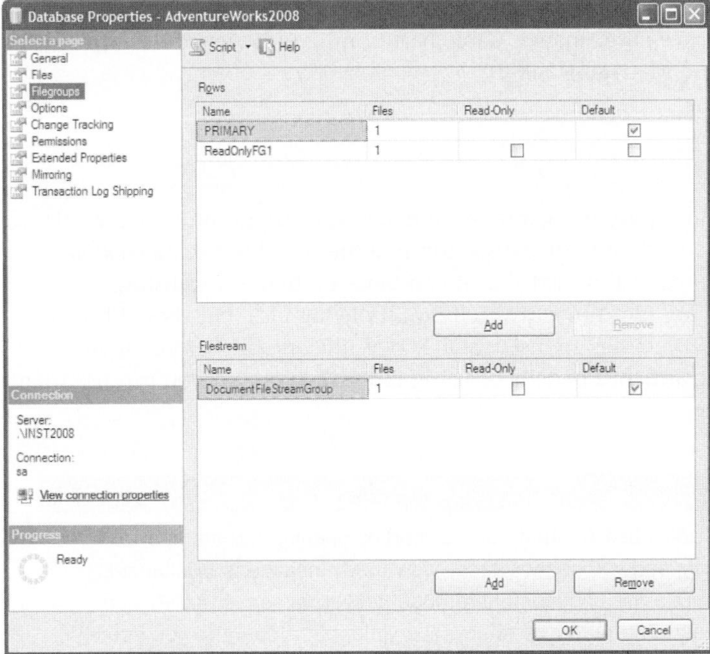

FIGURE 23.1 Setting the default filegroup in SQL Server Management Studio (SSMS).

When creating filegroups, you should keep in mind the following restrictions:

- You can't move a data file to another filegroup after it has been added to the database.
- Filegroups apply only to data files and not to log files.
- A data file can be part of only one filegroup and cannot be spread across multiple filegroups.
- You can have a maximum of 32,767 filegroups for each database.

NOTE

Using SANs and RAID arrays for the database disk subsystem diminishes the need for filegroups. SAN and RAID systems typically have many disks mapped to a single data drive. This inherently allows for concurrent disk access without requiring the creation of a filegroup with multiple data files.

Using Partitions

Partitioning in SQL Server 2008 allows for a single table or index to be aligned to more than one filegroup. This capability was introduced in SQL Server 2005. Prior to SQL Server 2005, you could use filegroups to isolate a table or an index to a single filegroup, but the table or index could not be spread across multiple filegroups or data files. The ability to spread a table or an index across multiple filegroups is particularly useful for large tables. You can partition a table across multiple filegroups and have data files live on separate disk drives to improve performance. Table partitioning is discussed in more detail in Chapter 24, "Creating and Managing Tables."

Transaction Log Files

A *transaction* is a mechanism for grouping a series of database changes into one logical operation. SQL Server keeps track of each transaction in a file called the *transaction log*. This log file usually has the extension `.ldf`, but it can have a different extension. Typically, there is only one log file. You can specify multiple log files, but these files are accessed sequentially. If multiple files are used, SQL Server fills one file before moving to the next. You realize no performance benefit by using multiple files, but you can use them to extend the size of the log.

NOTE

The transaction log file is not a text file that can be read by opening the file in a text editor. The file is proprietary, and you cannot easily view the transactions or changes within it. However, you can use the undocumented `DBCC LOG` *`(database name)`* command to list the log contents. The output is relatively cryptic, but it can give you some idea of the type of information that is stored in the log file.

Because the transaction log file keeps track of all changes applied to a database, it is very important for database recovery. The transaction log is your friend: it can prevent significant data loss and provide recovery that is not possible without it. Consider, for example, a case in which a database is put in simple recovery mode. In short, this causes transaction detail to be automatically removed from the transaction log. This option is often selected because the transaction log is seen as taking too much disk space. The problem with simple mode is that it limits your ability to recover transactions. If a catastrophic failure occurs, you can restore your last database backup, but that may be it. If that backup was taken the night before, all the database work done that day is lost.

If your database is not in simple mode (Full or Bulk-Logged), and the transaction log is intact, you have much better recovery options. For example, if you back up your transaction log periodically (for example, every hour) and a catastrophic error occurs, your data loss is limited. You still need to restore your last database backup, but you have the option of applying all the database changes stored in your transaction log. With hourly backups, you should lose no more than an hour's worth of work. This topic is covered in detail in Chapter 14, "Database Backup and Restore."

How the Transaction Log Works

SQL Server utilizes a write-ahead log. As changes are made to data through transactions, those changes are written immediately to the transaction log when the transaction is complete. The write-ahead log guarantees that all data modifications are written to the log prior to being written to disk. By writing each change to the transaction log before it is written to the database, SQL Server can increase I/O efficiency to the data files and ensure data integrity in case of system failure.

To fully understand the write-ahead log, you must first understand the role of SQL Server's cache or memory as it relates to database updates. SQL Server does not write updates directly to the data page on disk. Instead, SQL Server writes a change to a copy of the data page that has been placed in memory. Pages changed in memory and not yet written to disk are called *dirty pages*. The same basic approach is used for transaction log updates. The update to the log is performed in the log cache first, and it is written to disk at a later time. The time when the updates are actually written from cache to disk is called a *checkpoint*. The checkpoint occurs periodically, and SQL Server ensures that dirty pages are not written to disk before the corresponding log entry is written to disk.

The write-ahead log was designed for performance reasons, and it is critical for the recovery process after a system failure. If the system fails, an automatic recovery process is initiated when SQL Server restarts. This recovery process can use the checkpoint marker in the log file as a starting point for recovery. SQL Server examines all transactions after the checkpoint. If they are committed transactions, they are rolled forward; if they are incomplete transactions, they are rolled back, or undone.

NOTE

Changes were made in SQL Server 2005 that improve the availability of the database during the recovery process. These changes have been carried forward to SQL Server 2008. In versions prior to SQL Server 2005, the database was not available until it was completely recovered and the roll-forward and roll-back processes were complete. In versions following SQL Server 2005, the database is made available right after the roll-forward process. The roll-back or undo process can occur while users are in the database. This feature, known as Fast Recovery, is available only with the Enterprise Edition of SQL Server 2008.

For more detailed information on this topic, see Chapter 31, "Transaction Management and the Transaction Log."

Creating Databases

Database creation is a relatively straightforward operation that you can perform by using T-SQL statements or SSMS. Because the data and log files are created at the time the database is created, the time it takes for the database to be created depends on the size and number of files you specify when you create the database. If there is not enough disk space to create any of the files specified, SQL Server returns an error, and none of the files are created.

NOTE

Enhancements that were added in SQL Server 2005 and still exist in SQL Server 2008 have reduced the amount of time it takes to create a database. The reduction in creation time is attributed to a change in the way the database files are initialized. The initialization of the file with binary zeros is now deferred until the file is accessed via SQL queries. This results in much faster database creation and expansion. For example, we created a database with a 1GB data file on a machine running SQL Server 2008. The database was created in approximately 1 second. The same database was then created in SQL Server 2000, running on the same machine. The creation of the database on SQL Server 2000 took approximately 36 seconds. This new feature will make a lot of folks who create and support large databases very happy.

Using SSMS to Create a Database

The Object Explorer in SSMS makes creating a database simple. You right-click the `Databases` node and select New Database. The New Database dialog appears, as shown in Figure 23.2. The General page is selected by default. It allows you to select the essential information needed to create a database, including the database name, database owner, and location of the database files.

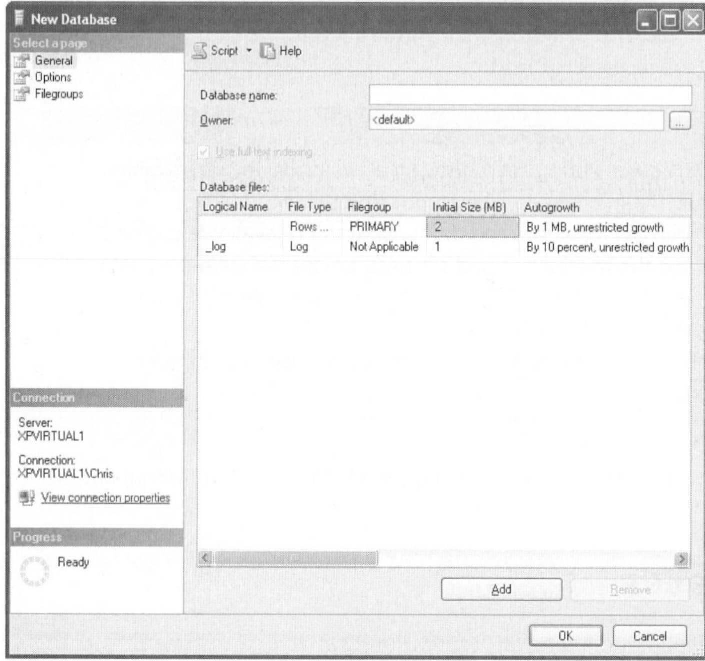

FIGURE 23.2 Creating a database by using SSMS.

Some related information is populated when you enter the database name. For example, the logical name of the database files is populated using the database name. The data file (which is identified with the file type `Data`) is named the same as the database. The log file (file type `Log`) has a database name with the suffix `_log`. The logical filename can be changed, but it must be unique within the database.

The location of the database files is an important decision. The location for each file is entered in the Path column in the Database Files grid. This column, located on the right side of the Database Files grid, includes an ellipsis that can help you navigate the directory structure on your server. When you select the location of these files, you should keep in mind the following:

- **Disk space**—Databases, by nature, grow over time. You need to make sure the location where you place your database files has sufficient space for growth.
- **Performance**—The location of your database files can affect performance. Generally, the data and log files should be placed on separate disk drives (with separate controllers) to maximize performance.
- **Organization**—Choosing a common location or directory for your database files can help keep things organized. For example, you could choose to place your data files in directories named `\mssql\data\` and `\mssql\log` instead of using the long pathname that SQL Server uses by default.

There are several restrictions related to the database files specified. Each filename must be unique and cannot be used by another database. The files specified for a database must be located on a local drive of the machine where SQL Server is installed, a SAN drive, or an iSCSI-based network drive. Finally, you need to make sure the path specified exists on the drive prior to creating the database.

NOTE

The default path for the database files is populated based on database settings values specified in the Server Properties dialog. To open this dialog, you right-click the server in the Object Explorer and choose Properties. When the Server Properties dialog appears, you choose the Database Settings page, where you see the database default locations. If the database default locations for the log and data files are not specified, the paths to the `master` database files are used. You can determine the paths to the `master` database files by looking at the startup parameters for the SQL Server instance. You can view these startup parameters within the SQL Server Configuration Manager. After you open this application, you right-click the SQL Server service and select Properties. On the Advanced tab of the Properties dialog that appears, you find the setting named Startup Parameters. The `-d` parameter identifies the location of the data file for the `master` database. The `-l` parameter identifies the location of the log file for the `master` database.

The remaining pages in the New Database dialog allow you to set database options, utilize filegroups, and set extended properties. The Options page contains many settings discussed in the "Setting Database Options" section later in this chapter. Three settings at the top of the Options page deserve special attention: Collation, Recovery Model, and Compatibility Level. Figure 23.3 shows the Options page.

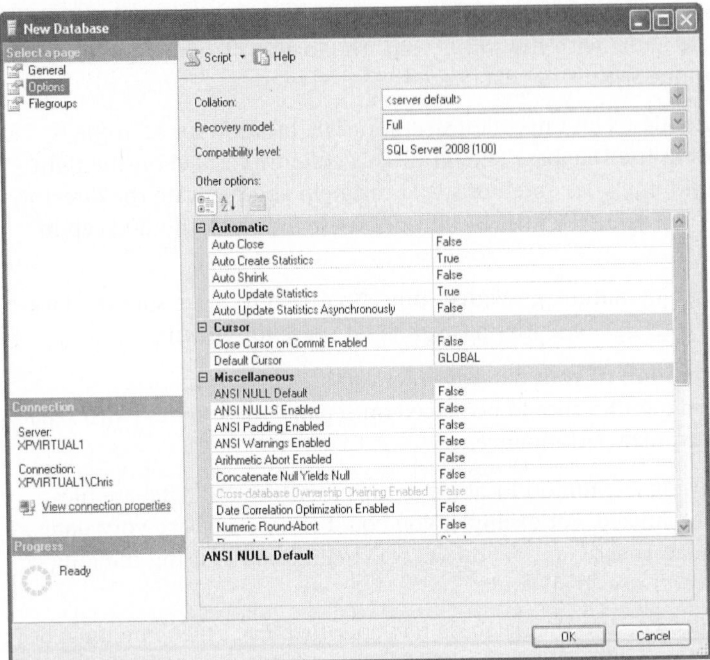

FIGURE 23.3 The Options page for creating a database.

Collation specifies how strings are sorted and compared. The selection of collation is language dependent and addresses differences in the way characters are ordered. The default collation for a database is based on the server default, which is set during the installation of SQL Server. The server default for many U.S.-based installations is `SQL_Latin1_General_CP1_CI_AS`. The collation name provides some insight into how the collation will work. For example, `CI` is an acronym for Case Insensitive, and `AS` indicates that the collation will be Accent Sensitive. The following `SELECT` statement can be used to list all the available collations and relates details about how the collation behaves:

```
SELECT * from ::fn_helpcollations()
```

The Recovery Model setting is critical in determining how much data can be recovered in the event of a media failure. The default is Full, which provides the greatest level of recovery. With Full recovery, all changes to the database (inserts, updates, and deletions) are written to the transaction log, and so are any changes that may have occurred using `BCP` or `BULK INSERT`. If a failure occurs on one of the database files, you can restore the database by using the last full backup. All the changes captured in the transaction log since the last full backup can be reapplied to the database as well.

The Bulk-Logged recovery setting is similar to Full recovery but has some differences in the way that operations (`BCP` or `BULK INSERT`) are logged. With Bulk-Logged recovery, you can still restore all the transaction log backups to recover your database to a point in time.

NOTE

When either Full recovery or Bulk-Logged settings is selected, it is important to set up a job or maintenance plan that performs periodic backups of the transaction log. A backup of the transaction log removes data from the log and keeps the size of the transaction log manageable. If regular backups of the transaction log are not made, the transaction log will continue to grow as every change in the database is written to it.

Simple recovery mode offers the simplest backup/recovery model but the greatest possibility of losing changes to the database. This is based on the fact that changes recorded in the transaction log are automatically truncated when the database is placed in Simple recovery mode. Recovery with Simple mode is limited to using full or differential database backups that have been taken. Simple recovery mode is a good option for read-only databases and for development databases that can afford the loss of changes since the last database backup. All the recovery models are discussed in detail in Chapter 14.

The last setting on the Options page that deserves special attention is Compatibility Level. The Compatibility Level determines the level of backward compatibility the database engine uses. For many newly created databases in SQL Server 2008, the default of SQL Server 2008 (100) will suffice. With this setting, all the new features available with SQL Server 2008 are utilized. In some situations, however, you might want a SQL Server 2008 database to behave as though it were a SQL Server 2005 database or SQL Server 2000 database. You can accomplish this by setting Compatibility Level to SQL Server 2005 (90) or SQL Server 2000 (80). Generally, you select older compatibility levels to allow code that was developed for prior versions of SQL Server to work as it did with those versions.

NOTE

The Compatibility Level setting is intended to allow a database to behave as if it were running in a previous version of SQL Server by providing similar query behavior or by allowing deprecated features to still work as they did in the previous version. However, setting the Compatibility Level to a prior version does not prevent new SQL Server 2008 features from being implemented in the database. The intent of this functionality is to provide a means for moving a database and application developed for a previous release of SQL Server to SQL Server 2008 and allow it to work as it did while enabling you to start taking advantage of new features and capabilities as you migrate the system to SQL Server 2008.

Using T-SQL to Create Databases

Instead of using SSMS, you can use T-SQL to create a database. The T-SQL command to do this is `CREATE DATABASE`. The `CREATE DATABASE` syntax is extensive and is best illustrated with an example. Listing 23.1 shows a sample script to create a database called `mydb`. This script was generated using the Script option available on the New Database screen.

LISTING 23.1 Using T-SQL to Create a Database

```
CREATE DATABASE [mydb] ON  PRIMARY
( NAME = N'mydb', FILENAME = N'C:\mssql2008\data\mydb.mdf' ,
    SIZE = 2048KB , FILEGROWTH = 1024KB )
 LOG ON
( NAME = N'mydb_log', FILENAME = N'C:\mssql2008\log\mydb_log.ldf',
    SIZE = 1024KB , FILEGROWTH = 10%)
GO
```

The database created in Listing 23.1 is relatively simple. It is named `mydb` and contains one data file and one log file. The data file is created on the `PRIMARY` filegroup; it is named `mydb.mdf` and is created in the `C:\mssql2008\data` folder. The `mydb.mdf` file is initially created with a size of 2048KB, or 2MB. If the database utilizes the entire 2MB, the file can be expanded by the amount specified in the `FILEGROWTH` parameter. In this case, the file can grow in 1MB increments. (Managing file growth is discussed in the section "Managing Databases," later in this chapter.)

The log file is defined using the `LOG ON` clause in the `CREATE DATABASE` command. The `mydb` database created in Listing 23.1 has a log file named `mydb_log.ldf` that is also created in the `C:\mssql2008\data` folder. The initial size of the file is 1MB, and it can expand by 10% of the current log file size. You need to use caution with large databases when using a percentage to define `FILEGROWTH`. For example, you may have problems if you have a large database that has a 30GB log file and a `FILEGROWTH` of 10%. If the database file is set to autogrow, and the 30GB log file is full, it attempts to expand the log file by 3GB. An expansion of this size could be detrimental to performance, and the disk drive where the log file is located might not have that much disk space remaining.

You can specify many of the other options that define a database after the database is created by using the `ALTER DATABASE` statement. The T-SQL scripting option available on the `CREATE DATABASE` screen generates the basic `CREATE DATABASE` syntax shown in Listing 23.1, and then it generates a series of `ALTER DATABASE` commands that further define the database. These options are discussed in the next section.

Setting Database Options

You can use an abundance of database options to refine the behavior of a database. These options fall into the following categories, which are part of the option specification:

- Auto Options
- Cursor Options
- Database Availability Options
- Date Correlation Optimization Options
- External Access Options
- Parameterization Options

Recovery Options

Service Broker Options

Snapshot Isolation Options

SQL Options

For each category, you can set one or more options. You can find a full list of options for each category in the section "Setting Database Options" in SQL Server Books Online. Some of the options are discussed in further detail in the chapters of this book that relate to the database options. For example, the recovery options are discussed in detail in Chapter 14, the Service Broker options are discussed in Chapter 49, "SQL Server Service Broker" (on the CD), and database mirroring options are discussed in Chapter 20, "Database Mirroring."

The following section focuses on the database options displayed on the Options page in SSMS.

The Database Options

You can access many of the most common database options via the Options page of the Database Properties dialog. To get to this dialog, you right-click a database in the SSMS Object Explorer and select Properties. When the dialog appears, you select the Options page from the list on the left side of the Database Properties dialog. Figure 23.4 shows the Options page for the `AdventureWorks2008` database. The options listed under Other Options can be listed alphabetically or by category. The default display mode is by category.

The default settings for these options suffice for most installations. However, some options deserve special attention. The options listed under the Automatic category are among these options. The Auto Close option could cause problems in prior versions of SQL Server. This option is intended for desktop implementations in which the database does not need to be online all the time. When users are not accessing the database and this option is selected, the database files are closed. When the first user accesses the database, the database is brought back online. The problem in prior versions was that the synchronous operation of opening and closing the database files caused performance problems. This issue has been addressed in SQL Server 2008 because the operations are now performed asynchronously. The Auto Close option defaults to `true` only for SQL Server 2008 Express Edition and should generally be left set to `false` for all other versions.

The Auto Create Statistics and Auto Update Statistics options also deserve special attention in situations in which the creation or updating of statistics is affecting performance. Generally, the creation or updating of statistics improves performance. These statistics enable the Query Optimizer to make the best decisions when determining the access path to the data. In some rare circumstances, there may be performance problems at the time statistics are created or updated automatically. When these situations arise, you can turn off the Auto Statistics options and schedule the statistics operations to occur during off-hours.

Enabling the Auto Shrink option is a good idea for keeping a nonproduction database as small as possible. This option automatically performs a database shrink operation against the database files when more than 25% of a file contains unused space. The default setting

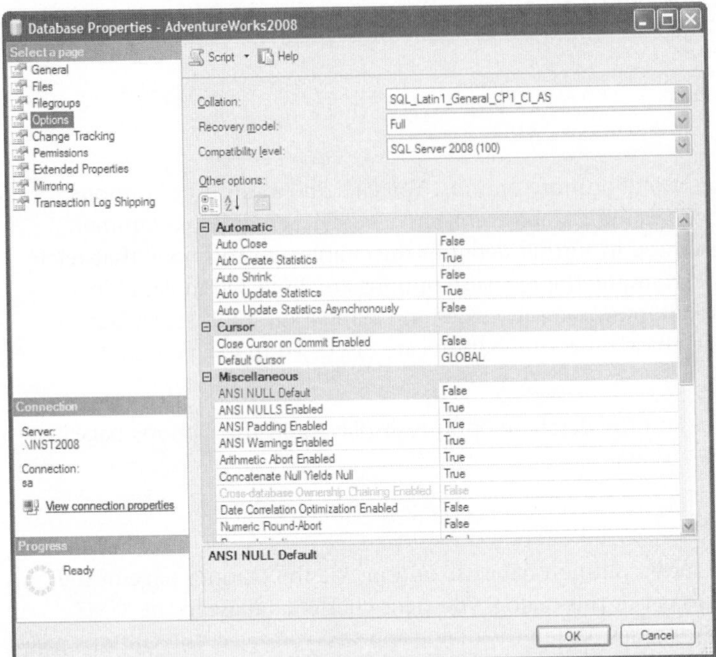

FIGURE 23.4 Database options in SSMS.

is `false` because this option can cause performance problems (related to the timing of the shrink operation) in a production database. Because the operation is automatic, it can run at any time, including times when there may be heavy production load.

The Page Verify option in the Recovery category was enhanced in SQL Server 2005. That enhancement came in the form of a new `CHECKSUM` option. This `CHECKSUM` option is the default; it causes a checksum calculation to occur across the entire database page. Prior to the availability of the `CHECKSUM` option, page verification was done with `TORN_PAGE_DETECTION`. Both of these options help detect damaged database pages, but `CHECKSUM` is the method that Microsoft recommends. The `CHECKSUM` calculation can be complicated but it basically tells SQL Server to calculate a number based on the contents of each data / index page. The `CHECKSUM` value is stored in the page header when it is written to disk. When the page is read from the disk, the checksum is computed again and compared to the value in page header to help ensure that the contents of each page are valid.

Database Read-Only and Restrict Access are two other commonly used options in the State category. You can set Database Read-Only to `true` to prevent updates from occurring in the database. Databases used for reference and not updated are perfect candidates for this option. The Restrict Access options are handy when you're executing system maintenance or mass updates in which you want to restrict users from accessing the database. Single User allows only one user to access the database. The Restricted option allows only members of `db_owner`, `dbcreator`, and `sysadmin` to access the database. With the

Restricted option, there is no limit on the number of users in these groups that can access the database.

You can easily set up the options reviewed in this section as well as the other options mentioned by using the Database Properties dialog. The current value for each option is shown in the right-hand column. To set an option to another value, you click the current value, and a drop-down arrow appears. When you click the drop-down arrow, you can select from the list of valid values for the option. After making all your option changes, you can click OK for the changes to take effect immediately, or you can click the Script button to generate the T-SQL code to change the options. The T-SQL code used to change the options is discussed in the next section.

Using T-SQL to Set Database Options

If you prefer to use T-SQL, or if the option you need to set doesn't appear in the Database Properties dialog, you can use the ALTER DATABASE command to set options. For example, the following command sets AUTO_UPDATE STATISTICS to OFF in the AdventureWorks2008 database:

```
ALTER DATABASE [AdventureWorks2008] SET AUTO_UPDATE_STATISTICS OFF WITH NO_WAIT
```

You can also change some of the options by using the system stored procedure sp_dboption. This feature is scheduled to be removed in a future release of SQL Server but is still available in this release. You might still be using this procedure based on prior releases, and old habits are hard to break. Following is an example of one of the sp_dboption commands many people have been using for years:

```
EXEC sp_dboption 'AdventureWorks2008', 'single user', 'TRUE'
```

This command sets the AdventureWorks2008 database to single-user mode. Setting a database to single-user mode is useful when you're performing certain database operations. For example, you might use sp_dboption to set a database to single-user mode prior to renaming the database with the sp_renamedb system procedure. It is important to break old habits and move on to using the ALTER DATABASE command. The single-user option and database name change have both been integrated into the ALTER DATABASE syntax. The following example shows how to set the single-user mode option and change the database name by using ALTER DATABASE:

```
ALTER DATABASE [AdventureWorks2008] SET  SINGLE_USER WITH NO_WAIT
GO
ALTER DATABASE [AdventureWorks2008] MODIFY NAME = [AdventureWorks2008_New]
GO
```

As you can see, using ALTER DATABASE is fairly straightforward and offers a consistent approach for modifying a database and its options.

TIP

Databases can be brought offline in SQL Server 2008 using SSMS or the T-SQL ALTER DATABASE command. When databases are offline no one can access them and the related database files can be moved. For example, you use the following T-SQL command to take the AdventureWorks2008 database offline:

```
ALTER DATABASE [AdventureWorks2008] SET OFFLINE WITH NO_WAIT
```

You can also specify an option with the ALTER DATABASE command that sets the database into an emergency state. This state marks the database as read-only, logging is disabled, and access to the database is limited to members of the sysadmin fixed server role. This option quickly prevents normal users from getting at the database but leaves the database available for inquiry for administrators. This is particularly useful when a database had been marked as suspect and is inaccessible. An example of setting a database to the emergency state follows:

```
ALTER DATABASE [AdventureWorks2008] SET emergency WITH NO_WAIT.
```

The offline option and emergency options can be invaluable when you want to quickly prevent or limit access to you database.

Retrieving Option Information

You can retrieve database settings by using several different methods. You can use the Database Properties dialog in SSMS (as described in the preceding section) to display commonly accessed options. You can also use the DATABASEPROPERTYEX function or the sp_dboption system stored procedure to display individual database options. As mentioned previously, sp_dboption is slated for removal in a future release, so the DATABASEPROPERTYEX function is preferred. This function accepts input values for the database name and the option for which you want to retrieve the value. The following is an example of a SELECT statement you can use to retrieve the Auto Shrink option for the AdventureWorks2008 database:

```
SELECT DATABASEPROPERTYEX ('AdventureWorks2008', 'IsAutoShrink')
```

This function returns a value of 1 or 0 for Boolean values—with 1 being "on" or "true"—and returns the actual value for non-Booleans. Table 23.1 lists the valid properties for the DATABASEPROPERTYEX function.

TABLE 23.1 **DATABASEPROPERTYEX** Properties

Property	Explanation
Collation	This is the default collation name for the database.
ComparisonStyle	This is the Windows comparison style of the collation.

TABLE 23.1 **DATABASEPROPERTYEX** Properties

Property	Explanation
`IsAnsiNullDefault`	The database follows SQL-92 rules for allowing null values.
`IsAnsiNullsEnabled`	All comparisons to a null evaluate to unknown.
`IsAnsiPaddingEnabled`	Strings are padded to the same length before comparison or insertion.
`IsAnsiWarningsEnabled`	Error or warning messages are issued when standard error conditions occur.
`IsArithmeticAbortEnabled`	Queries are ended when an overflow or divide-by-zero error occurs during query execution.
`IsAutoClose`	The database shuts down cleanly and frees resources after the last user exits.
`IsAutoCreateStatistics`	Existing statistics are automatically updated when the statistics become out-of-date because the data in the tables has changed.
`IsAutoShrink`	Database files are candidates for automatic periodic shrinking.
`IsAutoUpdateStatistics`	The `AUTO_UPDATE_STATISTICS` database option is enabled.
`IsCloseCursorsOnCommitEnabled`	Cursors that are open when a transaction is committed are closed.
`IsFulltextEnabled`	The database is full-text enabled.
`IsInStandBy`	The database is online as read-only, with the restore log allowed.
`IsLocalCursorsDefault`	Cursor declarations default to `LOCAL`.
`IsMergePublished`	The tables in a database can be published for merge replication, if replication is installed.
`IsNullConcat`	The null concatenation operand yields `NULL`.
`IsNumericRoundAbortEnabled`	Errors are generated when loss of precision occurs in expressions.
`IsParameterizationForced`	The `PARAMETERIZATION` database `SET` option is `FORCED`.

23

TABLE 23.1 **DATABASEPROPERTYEX** Properties

Property	Explanation
`IsPublished`	The tables of the database can be published for snapshot or transactional replication, if replication is installed.
`IsQuotedIdentifiersEnabled`	Double quotation marks can be used on identifiers.
`IsRecursiveTriggersEnabled`	Recursive firing of triggers is enabled.
`IsSubscribed`	The database is subscribed to a publication.
`IsSyncWithBackup`	The database is either a published database or a distribution database and can be restored without disrupting transactional replication.
`IsTornPageDetectionEnabled`	The SQL Server database engine detects incomplete I/O operations caused by power failures or other system outages.
`LCID`	This is the Windows locale ID (LCID) for the collation.
`Recovery`	This is the recovery model for the database.
`SQLSortOrder`	This indicates the SQL Server sort order ID supported in earlier versions of SQL Server.
`Status`	This is the database status.
`Updateability`	This indicates whether data can be modified.
`UserAccess`	This indicates which users can access the database.
`Version`	This is the internal version number of the SQL Server code with which the database was created. It is for internal use only by SQL Server tools and in upgrade processing.

If you would like to retrieve all the options set for a database, you have a couple of choices. The option that has been around for a while is `sp_helpdb`. You can pass to this system stored procedure the database name, and it returns several pieces of information about the database, including the options set. The database options are returned in the first result set from `sp_helpdb` in a column named Status. The database options are displayed in a comma-delimited format in the Status column. All Boolean options that are set to `ON` are returned in the Status column, and all non-Boolean values are returned with the value to which they are set.

The syntax for sp_helpdb is as follows:

```
sp_helpdb database_name
```

The sys.databases catalog view is another good resource for displaying all the database options. This catalog view has a separate column for each of the database options and is much easier to read than the sp_helpdb output. The view also has the added flexibility of allowing you to choose a set of options to return. The following example shows a SELECT statement that uses the sys.databases catalog view to return a common set of options:

```
select name, is_auto_close_on, is_auto_shrink_on,
    is_auto_create_stats_on, is_auto_update_stats_on
from sys.databases
where name = 'AdventureWorks2008'
```

The results from this SELECT statement return Boolean values in each column, indicating whether the option is set to on or off. The number of columns available for selection is extensive and similar to those options available with the DATABASEPROPERTYEX function.

TIP

Selecting the column you want from the sys.databases catalog view is easier when you use the Object Explorer. To set it, you go to the master database and expand the Views node, followed by the System Views node. When you see the sys.databases view listed under System Views, you expand the columns for the sys.databases view to see a list of all the available columns. You can then drag the options you want to view into a database query window for use in a SELECT statement.

You can also use the new IntelliSense feature available in the SQL Server 2008 query window. When creating a SELECT statement that retrieves from the sys.databases catalog view (or any other catalog view), you are given a drop-down list of available columns when you reference the view in the select list. See chapter 4 for a more in-depth discussion of the object explorer and IntelliSense.

Managing Databases

After you create a database, you have the ongoing task of managing it. At the database level, this task generally involves manipulating the file structure and setting options appropriate for the usage of the database.

Managing File Growth

As discussed earlier in this chapter, SQL Server manages file growth by automatically growing files by preset intervals when a need for additional space arises. However, this is a very loose definition of the word *manages*. What actually happens is that when the database runs out of space, it suspends all update activity, checks whether it is allowed additional space, and if space is available, it increases the file size by the value defined by FILEGROWTH. When the database fills up again, the whole process starts over.

When all the files in a filegroup are full and are configured to autogrow, SQL Server automatically expands one file at a time in a round-robin fashion to accommodate more data. For example, if a filegroup consists of multiple files, and no free space is available in any file in the filegroup, the first file is expanded by the specified file-growth setting. When the first file is full again, and there is no more free space elsewhere in the filegroup, the second file is expanded. When the second file is full, and there is no more free space elsewhere in the filegroup, the third file is expanded, and so on.

Because `FILEGROWTH` can be defined as small as 64KB, automatically increasing the file size can be detrimental to performance if it happens too frequently. When you think of managing file growth, you can think of the database administrator proactively monitoring the size of files and increasing the size before SQL Server runs out of space when allocating new extents. That's not to say automatic file growth is a bad thing; it is, in fact, a great "safety valve" to accommodate unpredictable data growth or a lack of attention on the part of the administrator.

Expanding Databases

As previously discussed, databases can be expanded automatically, or you can intervene and expand them manually. The manual expansion can be accomplished by adding more files to the database or by increasing the size of the existing files. The database expansions can be accomplished with either SSMS or T-SQL.

To expand the size of the data files using SSMS, you right-click the database in the Object Explorer and select Properties. When the Database Properties dialog appears, you select the Files page to list all the files associated with the database. The Initial Size (MB) column displays the current disk allocation for each file. You can enter the new size directly into the column or use the up arrow to increase the size. After establishing the new size, you can simply click OK to expand the database file, or you can script the change by using the Script button at the top of the Database Properties window.

You can also use the Files page of the Database Properties dialog in SSMS to add files to a database. You do this by clicking the Add button, which adds a new file entry row into the Database Files grid. You must supply a logical name for the new file, which typically contains the database name. In addition, you must supply the other data values in the row, including the file type, filegroup, initial size, autogrowth parameters, and path to the file.

The T-SQL `ALTER DATABASE` command is another option you can use for expanding a database. Listing 23.2 shows an `ALTER DATABASE` example that increases the size of a data file in the `AdventureWorks2008` database to 200MB.

LISTING 23.2 Using T-SQL to Increase the Size of a Database File

```
ALTER DATABASE [AdventureWorks2008]
 MODIFY FILE ( NAME = N'AdventureWorks2008_Data', SIZE = 200MB )
GO
```

You can also use the ALTER DATABASE command to add a new file to a database. Listing 23.3 shows an example that adds a new data file to the AdventureWorks2008 database.

LISTING 23.3 Using T-SQL to Add a New Database File

```
ALTER DATABASE [AdventureWorks2008]
 ADD FILE ( NAME = N'AdventureWorks2008_Data2',
 FILENAME = N'C:\Program Files\Microsoft SQL
Server\MSSQL.1\MSSQL\DATA\AdventureWorks2008_Data2.ndf',
  SIZE = 2048KB , FILEGROWTH = 1024KB ) TO FILEGROUP [PRIMARY]
GO
```


Shrinking Databases

Shrinking database files is a bit more involved than expanding them. Generally, you do database shrink operations manually, using DBCC commands. SQL Server does have the AUTOSHRINK database option, but it is usually reserved for development databases and should not be used in production. The reason it is not recommended for production is that the AUTOSHRINK operation can run at peak usage time and affect performance. AUTOSHRINK is executed when more than 25% of a file contains unused space. This event can occur, for example, after a large deletion.

If you want to shrink a database manually, you can do so by using DBCC SHRINKDATABASE, DBCC SHRINKDATAFILE, or SSMS. The following sections describe these three methods.

NOTE

Generally, you should avoid shrinking database files if you believe that the files are going to grow to the same larger size again. The continual expansion of a database can affect performance while the expansion is occurring. Also, if a database file is repeatedly shrunk and expanded, the database file itself can become fragmented within the file system, which can degrade I/O performance for the file.

Using DBCC SHRINKDATABASE to Shrink Databases

The DBCC SHRINKDATABASE statement attempts to shrink all the files in a database and leave a specified target percentage of free space. The following is an example of the DBCC SHRINKDATABASE syntax and running the command against the AdventureWorks2008 database:

```
DBCC SHRINKDATABASE
( 'database_name' | database_id | 0
     [ ,target_percent ]
     [ , { NOTRUNCATE | TRUNCATEONLY } ]
)
[ WITH NO_INFOMSGS ]
--Shrink Example
DBCC SHRINKDATABASE (AdventureWorks2008, 25)
```

The first parameter of the DBCC SHRINKDATABASE command is the *database_name* or *database_id*, and the second parameter is the desired percentage that will be left free. In the preceding example, an attempt will be made to shrink the database file and leave 25% free space in the files. This operation is done one data file at a time, and the log files are treated as one unit and shrunk together.

There are quite a few things to consider when you use the DBCC SHRINKDATABASE command. The following are some of the most important considerations:

- DBCC SHRINKDATABASE does not shrink a file smaller than its minimal size. The minimal size is the size of the file when it was initially created or the size of the file after it was explicitly resized. Explicit resizing can be accomplished with the DBCC SHRINKFILE command.
- The TRUNCATEONLY option frees any unused space at the end of a file but does not attempt any page movement within the file. The target percentage is ignored when this option is specified.
- The NOTRUNCATE option attempts to move pages in the files to push all free space to the end of the file. This option does not actually return the space to the operating system, and the physical file does not end up smaller when this option is used.
- If neither the NOTRUNCATE nor TRUNCATEONLY options are specified, this is equivalent to running DBCC SHRINKDATABASE WITH NOTRUNCATE followed by DBCC SHRINKDATABASE WITH TRUNCATEONLY. The first part attempts to push all the free space to the end of the file; then the free space is released to the operating system, and the file ends up smaller.
- The database files can never be shrunk to a size smaller than the data contained within them.

For smaller databases, the DBCC SHRINKFILE command is often considered to be a good choice because it is all inclusive and applies to all the database files. For larger databases or situations in which you need more control, you should consider using the DBCC SHRINKFILE command, which is discussed in the next section.

Using DBCC SHRINKFILE to Shrink Databases

The DBCC SHRINKFILE command operates on individual database files. For databases that contain many database files, you must execute multiple commands to shrink the entire database. This task requires some extra work, but the increased control is often worth the effort. This, combined with the fact that you can shrink a file below its minimum specified size, makes it a very good option.

The following example shows the syntax for the DBCC SHRINKFILE command and a simple example for the AdventureWorks2008 database:

```
DBCC SHRINKFILE
(
    { ' file_name ' | file_id }
```

```
    { [ , EMPTYFILE]
    | [ [ , target_size ] [ , { NOTRUNCATE | TRUNCATEONLY } ] ]
    }
)
[ WITH NO_INFOMSGS ]
-- sample shrink command
USE [AdventureWorks2008]
GO
DBCC SHRINKFILE (N'AdventureWorks2008_Data' , 180)
GO
DBCC SHRINKFILE (N'AdventureWorks2008_Log' , 10)
GO
```


Note that with this option, a filename or an ID is supplied, rather than the database name. `DBCC SHRINKFILE` must be run in the database that the file belongs to. You specify `TARGET_SIZE` in megabytes; this is the desired size for the file after the shrink completes. If `TARGET_SIZE` is not specified or the target size is too small, the command tries to shrink the file as much as possible. The `EMPTYFILE` option migrates all data in the file to other files in the same filegroup. No further data can be placed on the file. The file can subsequently be dropped from the database. This capability can be useful when you want to migrate a data file to a new disk. The `NOTRUNCATE` and `TRUNCATEONLY` options for `DBCC SHRINKDATAFILE` work the same way as with `DBCC SHRINKDATABASE`. Refer to the previous section for details.

TIP

If you would like to shrink every database file by using the `DBCC SHRINKFILE` command, you can generate the commands by using a `SELECT` statement. The following `SELECT` is an example of this:

```
SELECT 'PRINT ''LOGICAL NAME: ' + rtrim(name) +
    ' FILENAME: ' + rtrim(filename) + '''' + char(10) +
    'go' + char(10) +
    ' DBCC SHRINKFILE (' + convert(varchar(8),fileid) + ',1)' +
char(10) + 'go' + char(10)
from sysfiles  order by fileid
```

The results from this `SELECT` produce the `DBCC SHRINKFILE` commands for all the files in the database that it is run against. You can then paste the results into another query window and execute them. This particular example uses a fixed target size of 1MB, but you can adjust this size in the `SELECT` statement. You could also modify this `SELECT` statement so that it uses the `sys.master_files` catalog view instead of using `sysfiles`.

Shrinking the Log File

The data file most likely to grow beyond a normal size and require periodic shrinking is the transaction log file. If a user process issues a large update transaction, the log file grows to the size needed to hold the records generated by the transaction. This could be significantly larger than the normal growth of the transaction log.

As with data files, shrinking of the log file in SQL Server 2008 can take place only from the end of the log file. However, you must first back up or truncate the log to remove the inactive log records and reduce the size of the logical log. You can then run the `DBCC SHRINKFILE` or `DBCC SHRINKDATABASE` command to release the unused space in the log file.

Transaction log files are divided logically into segments, called virtual log files. The Database Engine chooses the size of the virtual log files dynamically while it is creating or extending log files. Transaction log files can only be shrunk to a virtual log file boundary. It is therefore not possible to shrink a log file to a size smaller than the size of a virtual log file, even if the space is not being used. The size of the virtual log files in a transaction log increase as the size of the log file increases. For example, a database defined with a log file of 1GB may have virtual log files 128MB in size. Therefore, the log can be shrunk to only about 128MB.

Because of the overhead incurred when the autoshrink process attempts to shrink database files, it is not recommended that you enable this option for the transaction log because it could be triggered numerous times during the course of a business day. It is better to schedule the shrinking of the log file to be performed during normal daily maintenance, when production system activity is at a minimum.

Using SSMS to Shrink Databases

In addition to shrinking a database by using T-SQL, you can do so through SSMS. In the Object Explorer, you right-click the database you want to shrink, and then you choose Tasks, followed by Shrink. You can then select either Database or Files. Selecting the Database option displays the Shrink Database dialog (see Figure 23.5). The currently allocated size and free space for the database are shown. You have the option of selecting the Shrink Action and checking the Reorganize Files Before Releasing Unused Space check box.

You can click the Script button to generate the T-SQL that will be used to perform the database shrink operation. When you do, a `DBCC SHRINKDATABASE` command is generated.

If you want to shrink database files, you choose the Files option instead of Database. Figure 23.6 shows the Shrink File dialog displayed when you select Files. You can shrink one database file at a time using this window. If you choose the shrink option Release Unused Space, SMSS uses the `DBCC SHRINKFILE` command with the `TRUNCATEONLY` option. If you choose the Reorganize Pages Before Releasing Unused Space option, SMSS uses the `DBCC SHRINKFILE` command without the `TRUNCATEONLY` or `NOTRUNCATE` option. As mentioned earlier, this causes page movement to free as much space as possible. A `TRUNCATE` operation then releases the free space back to the operating system.

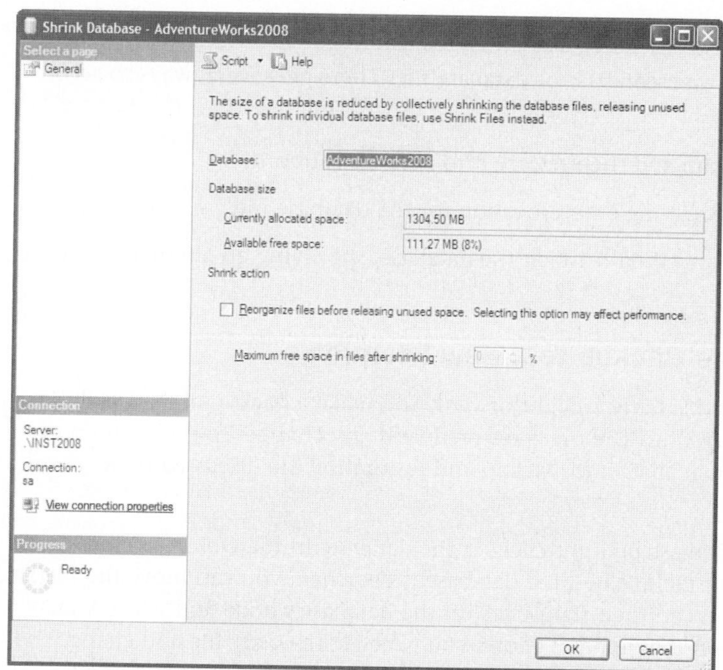

FIGURE 23.5 Shrinking an entire database using SSMS.

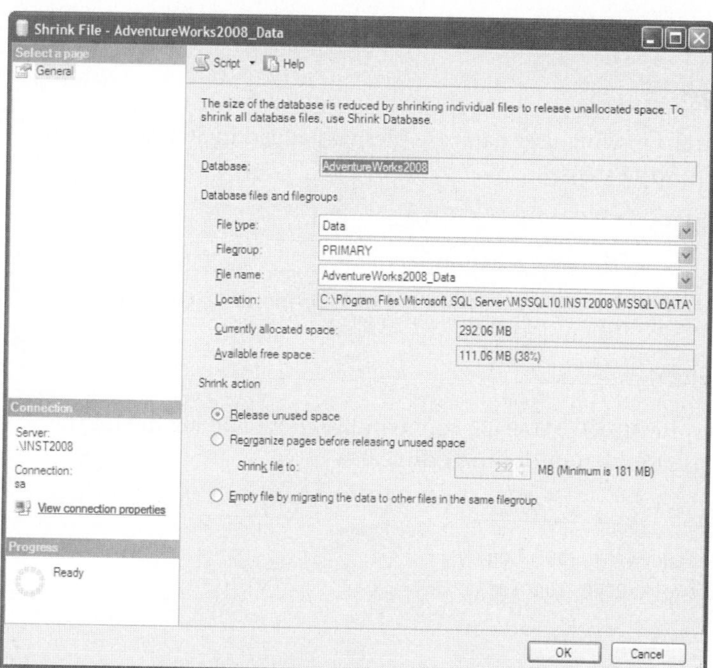

FIGURE 23.6 Shrinking database files in SSMS.

Moving Databases

Sometimes you need to move a database or database file. There are several ways to accomplish this task:

- Make a database backup and then restore it to a new location.
- Alter the database, specifying a new location for the database file.
- Detach the database and then reattach the database, specifying an alternate location.

Restoring a Database Backup to a New Location

The database backup option is fairly straightforward. You make a backup of the database and then write it to a file or files. The file is restored, and any changes to the location of the database files are made at that time. Backup and restoration are discussed in detail in Chapter 14.

You can easily detach a database by right-clicking the database in the Object Explorer and choosing Tasks and then Detach. When the database is detached, you can move the file(s) to the desired location. You can then right-click on the database's node and select Attach. The Attach Databases screen that appears allows you to select the `.mdf` file and change the file location for any of the related database files. The steps involved in detaching and attaching a database are discussed in detail in the later section "Detaching and Attaching Databases."

Using ALTER DATABASE

The `ALTER DATABASE` option for moving user database files was added in SQL Server 2005. This option involves the following steps:

1. Take the database offline.
2. Manually move the file(s) to the new location.
3. Run the `ALTER DATABASE` command to set the `FILENAME` property to the new file location.
4. Bring the database online.

The following example uses the `ALTER DATABASE` command to move the log file for the `AdventureWorks2008` database to the root of the `C:` drive.

```
ALTER DATABASE AdventureWorks2008
 MODIFY FILE (NAME = AdventureWorks2008_Log,
  FILENAME = 'C:\AdventureWorks2008_log.ldf')
```

CAUTION

Use caution when specifying the `FILENAME` parameter to move a database log file. If the `FILENAME` setting specified in the `ALTER DATABASE` command is incorrect and the file does not exist, the command still completes successfully. When the database is brought back online, a message stating that the file can't be found appears, and a new log file is created for you. This invalidates the old log file.

Detaching and Attaching Databases

A convenient way to move or copy database files is to detach and attach databases. Detaching database files removes the database from an instance of SQL Server but leaves the database files intact. After the database is detached, the files associated with the database (that is, `.mdf`, `.ndf`, and `.ldf` files) can be copied or moved to an alternate location. You can then reattach the relocated files by using the `CREATE DATABASE` command with the `FOR ATTACH` option.

TIP

The process of detaching and attaching a database is extremely fast. It is therefore a good alternative to `BACKUP` and `RESTORE` when you're copying a database to another location. The catch with detaching a database is that all users must be disconnected from the database, and the database is unavailable during the detach and copy of the database files.

To detach a database, you right-click the database in Object Explorer and select Tasks and then Detach. Figure 23.7 shows an example of the Detach Database dialog box for detaching the `AdventureWorks2008` database. You can specify several options, including a handy option (called Drop Connections) to kill any user processes (SPIDs) that may still be connected to the database when the detach operation is running. If you do not select the Drop Connections option, and users are still connected to the database, the detach operation fails.

Other options available during the detach operation are also useful. The Update Statistics option updates out-of-date statistics for all the database tables before you detach the database. The statistics update can take some time on larger databases, so this slows down the overall detach operation. The other option, Keep Full Text Catalogs, is new to SQL Server 2008. It allows you to detach any full-text catalogs associated with the database. These detached full-text catalogs are then reattached along with the database when the files are attached. See chapter 56 for a more in-depth discussion of full-text catalogs.

The attach operation is simple to execute through SMSS. In Object Explorer, you simply right-click the database's node and select the Attach option. The Attach Databases dialog box appears, allowing you to specify the database file(s) you want to attach. You need to click the Add button to be able to select a database file for restoration. When you select the main `.mdf` file associated with the database, the associated file information for the other related database files is populated as well.

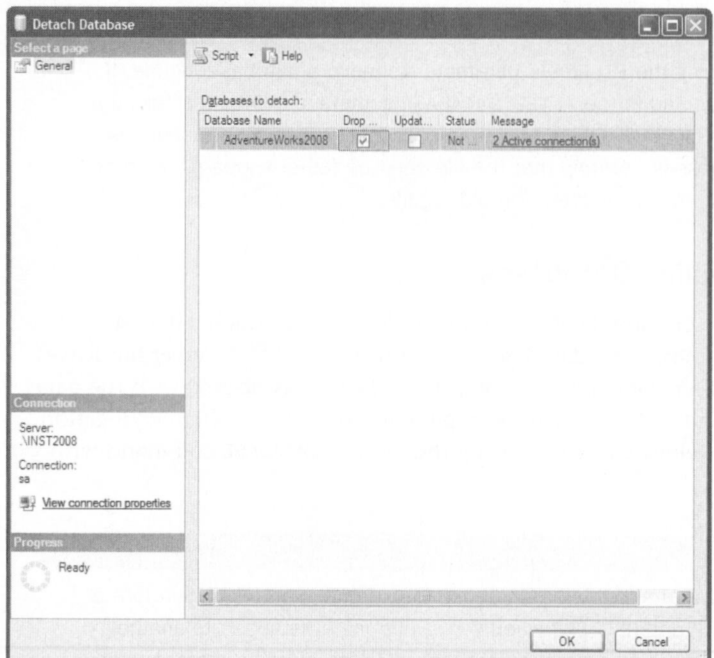

FIGURE 23.7 Detaching a database by using SSMS.

23.8 shows the Attach Databases dialog box for the AdventureWorks2008 database. The top portion of the dialog box lists the main (.mdf) database file selected for the AdventureWorks2008 database. The bottom portion lists the related files. You have an option to attach the database with a different name by changing the Attach As name located at the top of the screen. You can also edit the database details at the bottom of the screen and enter the location of the database files that will be attached. The Current File Path column displays the original file locations determined from the .mdf file. If the files were moved to a new location, this is the place to change the current file path to the new location.

You can also accomplish the detach and attach operations by using T-SQL. You perform the detach operation with the sp_detach_db system stored procedure. You perform the attach operation with the CREATE DATABASE command, using the FOR ATTACH option. The following is an example of T-SQL commands for detaching and attaching the AdventureWorks2008 database:

```
--Detach the database
EXEC master.dbo.sp_detach_db
 @dbname = N'AdventureWorks2008', @keepfulltextindexfile=N'false'
GO
--Attach the database
CREATE DATABASE [AdventureWorks2008] ON
( FILENAME = 'C:\Program Files\Microsoft SQL
```

```
Server\MSSQL.1\MSSQL\Data\AdventureWorks2008_Data.mdf' ),
( FILENAME = 'C:\Program Files\Microsoft SQL
Server\MSSQL.1\MSSQL\Data\AdventureWorks2008_log.LDF' )
 FOR ATTACH
```

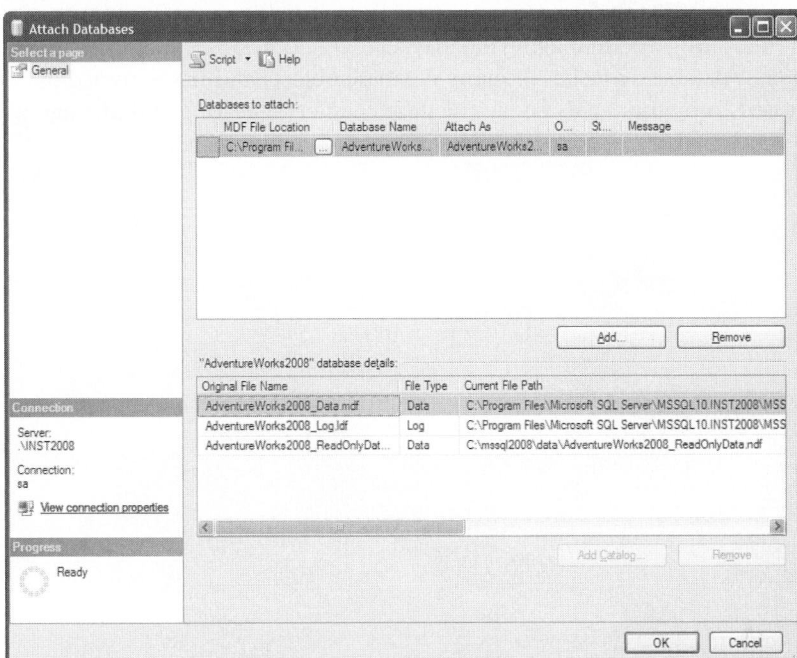

FIGURE 23.8 Attaching a database by using SSMS.

NOTE

You can use the `sp_attach_db` procedure to attach a database, but Microsoft recommends that you use the `CREATE DATABASE ... FOR ATTACH` command instead. The `sp_attach_db` procedure has been deprecated and is slated for removal in a future release of SQL Server.

SQL Server 2008 has the capability to attach a database without all the log files. You do this by using the `ATTACH_REBUILD_LOG` clause when creating the database. When you use this clause, SQL Server rebuilds the log files for you. This capability is useful on large databases that may have large logs that are not needed in the environment where the database files are attached. For example, a `READ_ONLY` database would not need the log files that may be associated with its production counterpart. The following example uses the `ATTACH_REBUILD_LOG` clause to create a copy of the `AdventureWorks2008` database:

```
CREATE DATABASE [AdventureWorks2008Temp] ON
( FILENAME = 'C:\Temp\AdventureWorks2008_Data.mdf' )
```

```
FOR ATTACH_REBUILD_LOG
```

Summary

The steps involved in creating and managing databases are by no means limited to the topics in this chapter. A database consists of many database objects and has a myriad of other features discussed throughout this book. The next chapter, "Creating and Managing Tables," delves into one of the most basic elements of a database: the table.

CHAPTER 24

Creating and Managing Tables

IN THIS CHAPTER

- What's New in SQL Server 2008
- Creating Tables
- Defining Columns
- Defining Table Location
- Defining Table Constraints
- Modifying Tables
- Dropping Tables
- Using Partitioned Tables
- Creating Temporary Tables

Tables are logical constructs used for the storage and manipulation of data in databases. Tables contain *columns*, which describe data, and *rows*, which are instances of table data. Basic relational database design determines the table and column names as well as the distribution of columns within tables.

This chapter gives you the administrative knowledge you need to create tables and manage them within your enterprise. It focuses on the basic constructs for tables and the table-level features that can make your tables robust and efficient objects to house your data.

What's New in SQL Server 2008

Most of the new table-oriented features available with SQL Server 2008 are related to the columns that define a table. Columns can now be defined with several new data types that further expand the type of data that SQL Server can store and manage. Some of these new types, such as the `FILESTREAM` storage and the `geometry` and `geography` data types take SQL Server beyond the typical relational model. `FILESTREAM` storage provides a reference point to a flat file in the operating system where the data actually resides, and the `geometry` and `geography` data types bring you into the world of spatial data storage.

The `hierarchyid` data type is system-provided. You use `hierarchyid` as a data type to create tables with a hierarchical structure or to reference the hierarchical structure of data in another location. You use `hierarchyid` functions to query and perform work with hierarchical data by using Transact-SQL (T-SQL).

There have also been additions to more traditional relational data types. For example, SQL Server 2008 now offers separate data types for date and time. The new `date` data type contains only the date, whereas the new `time` data type contains only the time portion. In the past, the `datetime` or `smalldatetime` data types combined the date and time components into a single data type. Other `date` and `time` data type enhancements are discussed later in the chapter.

SQL Server 2008 also introduces new ways to organize or access columns. Sparse columns and column sets are example of this. A *sparse column* is a column where the majority of the column's values contain null values. A sparse column is an ordinary column but is given the `SPARSE` keyword when it is added to a table so that the SQL Server Database Engine can optimize the storage of these types of columns. The related *column set* is another type of column that is XML-typed and identifies all the sparse columns added to a table. These data types and all the new data types are discussed later in this chapter.

The good news is that the management of tables and their related columns has remained relatively unchanged in SQL Server 2008. You will find that the facilities available in the SQL Server Management Studio are as familiar and as easy to use as they were in SQL Server 2005.

NOTE

This chapter uses examples from Bigpubs2008 database and the Adventureworks2008 database. Instructions for installing the BigPubs2008 database are located in the Introduction chapter at the beginning of this book.

Creating Tables

SQL Server 2008 supports the creation of tables using T-SQL, the SQL Server Management Studio (SSMS) Object Explorer and the SSMS Database Diagram Editor. Regardless of the tool you choose, creating a table involves naming the table, defining the columns, and assigning properties to the columns. The visual tools (such as Object Explorer and database diagrams) are usually the best starting point for creating tables. These tools offer drop-down boxes that allow you to choose the data types for your columns and check boxes that allow you to define their nullability.

This chapter first looks at the visual tools and then delves into the specific parameters related to the underlying T-SQL statements that ultimately create a table.

Using Object Explorer to Create Tables

The Object Explorer in SSMS has a `Tables` node under each database listed. You can add tables via the Object Explorer by right-clicking this `Tables` node. Figure 24.1 shows the New Table option displayed after you right-click the `Tables` node in Object Explorer. The top-right side of the screen shown in Figure 24.1 is the table creation screen that allows you to enter the column name and data type and to set the Allow Nulls option.

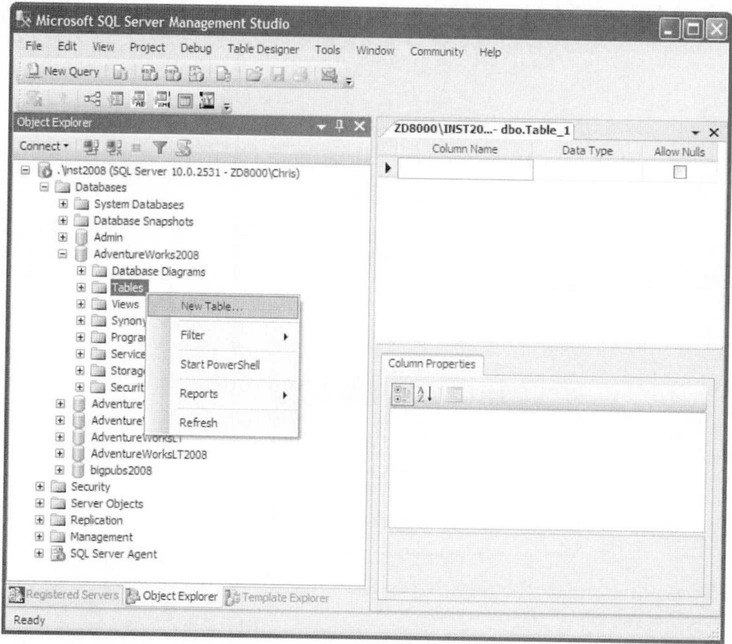

FIGURE 24.1 Using Object Explorer to create a table.

The data entry area under Column Name is a free-form area where you can define a column name. You can select the data type from the Data Type drop-down, which displays the data types available with SQL Server. The Allow Nulls option is Boolean in nature and is either checked or not checked. For each column selected, a Column Properties section is displayed in SSMS, providing a myriad of additional properties that you can assign to each column. These properties are discussed in more detail in the "Defining Columns" section, later in this chapter.

Using Database Diagrams to Create Tables

You can use the database diagrams for a more robust visual representation of your tables. You view them from within SSMS, and they give you the distinct advantage of being able to display multiple tables and the relationships between these tables. The Database Diagram Editor behaves similarly to other data modeling tools that allow you to move related tables around in the diagram and group them accordingly.

Figure 24.2 shows several screens related to database diagrams. The left side of Figure 24.2 shows the Object Explorer and the resulting New Database Diagram option that is displayed if you right-click the `Database Diagrams` node. The right side of the screen shows the diagram design window. In this example, the existing `Department` table from the AdventureWorks2008 database was added to the diagram, and a new Printer table was added as well. The printer table was added by right-clicking in the diagram design window and selecting the New Table option.

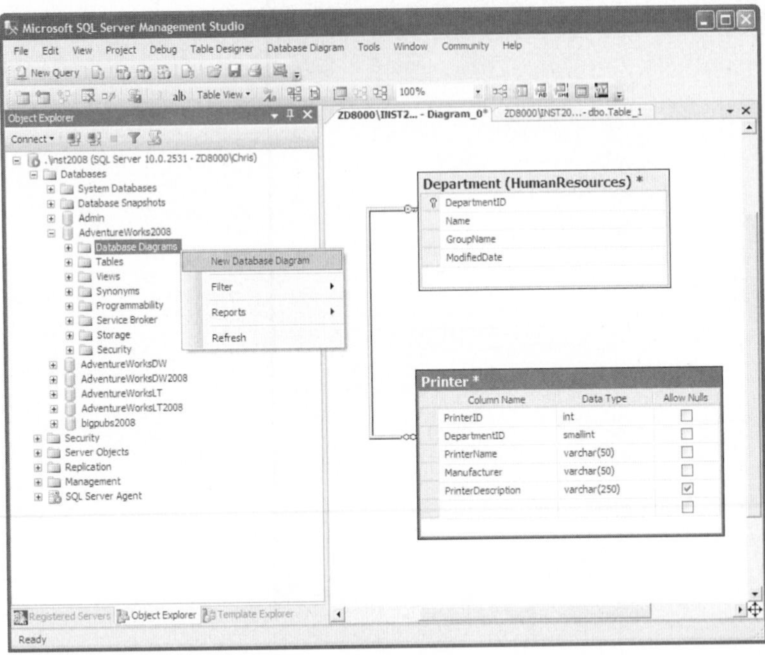

FIGURE 24.2 Using database diagrams to create a table.

The column names and related attributes for the new Printer table in Figure 24.2 were added using the table entry fields. The data entry screen for the table is similar to the one provided with the Object Explorer. You enter column names, along with their associated data types and nullability option.

The advantage of database diagrams is that you can define relationships and show them with a visual representation. This visual view provides a much easier way to view the table structures in a database. In the example shown in Figure 24.2, the line drawn between the Department and Printer tables represents a relationship between these two tables. You define such a foreign key relationship in the database diagram by dragging the related column from one table to the other related table. Table relationships and constraints are discussed later in this chapter, in the section "Defining Table Constraints."

Using T-SQL to Create Tables

Ultimately, all the tables created with the visual tools can also be created by using T-SQL. As with many of the SSMS tools, database objects can be resolved or scripted into T-SQL statements. Let's examine the T-SQL syntax to better understand some of the table creation options; then we can discuss the definition of the columns in each table.

The full T-SQL `CREATE TABLE` syntax is extensive. It includes options to define table constraints, indexes, and index options. SQL Server Books Online shows the full syntax and describes each of these options in detail. Listing 24.1 shows the basic T-SQL syntax; the first part of the syntax is listed in Books Online. This syntax is enough to enable you to create a table with its associated column definitions.

LISTING 24.1 Basic T-SQL **CREATE TABLE** Syntax

```
CREATE TABLE
    [ database_name . [ schema_name ] . | schema_name . ] table_name
        ( { <column_definition> | <computed_column_definition> }
        [ <table_constraint> ] [ ,...n ] )
    [ ON { partition_scheme_name ( partition_column_name ) | filegroup
        | "default" } ]
    [ { TEXTIMAGE_ON { filegroup | "default" } ]
[ ; ]

<column_definition> ::=
column_name <data_type>
    [ COLLATE collation_name ]
    [ NULL | NOT NULL ]
    [
        [ CONSTRAINT constraint_name ] DEFAULT constant_expression ]
      | [ IDENTITY [ ( seed ,increment ) ] [ NOT FOR REPLICATION ]
    ]
    [ ROWGUIDCOL ] [ <column_constraint> [ ...n ] ]

<data type> ::=
[ type_schema_name . ] type_name
    [ ( precision [ , scale ] | max |
        [ { CONTENT | DOCUMENT } ] xml_schema_collection ) ]
```

The number of options in this basic syntax can be daunting, but the reality is that you can exclude many of the options and execute a relatively simple statement. Listing 24.2 is an example of a simple statement you can use to create a table. This listing shows a `CREATE TABLE` statement that you can use to create the `Printers` table that was shown in Figure 24.2.

LISTING 24.2 A Basic T-SQL **CREATE TABLE** Example

```
CREATE TABLE Printer
    (
    PrinterID int NOT NULL,
    DepartmentID smallint NOT NULL,
    PrinterName varchar(50) NOT NULL,
```

```
Manufacturer varchar(50) NOT NULL,
PrinterDescription varchar(250) NULL
)
```

The `CREATE TABLE` statement in Listing 24.2 specifies the table to create, followed by an ordered list of columns to add to the table. The following section describes the specifics related to defining the columns.

TIP

SSMS provides several methods for generating the T-SQL code to create tables. Therefore, you rarely need to type the `CREATE TABLE` statements from scratch. Instead, you can use the friendly graphical user interface (GUI) screens that enable you to define the table, and then you can generate the T-SQL script. For example, you can right-click a new table in the database diagram and select Generate Change Script to generate the associated T-SQL for the table.

One of the important considerations during table creation is schema assignment. *Schemas* allow you to logically group objects (including tables) and define ownership, independent of the individual users in the database. Schema enhancements introduced in SQL Server 2005 are still available in SQL Server 2008 and can play a significant role in the definition of tables in a database. Consider, for example, the `AdventureWorks2008` database that ships with SQL Server 2008. The tables in this database have been assigned to schemas that group the tables according to their functional areas. The schemas in the `AdventureWorks2008` database include `Sales`, `Purchasing`, `Person`, `Production`, `HumanResources`, and `dbo`. Some sample tables in the `Person` schema include the `Person` and `Address` tables. The `Purchasing` schema includes tables that relate to purchasing, including the `PurchaseOrderHeader` and `Vendor` tables.

The designation of a schema in the `CREATE TABLE` statement is relatively simple. Listing 24.3 includes a three-part table name for the creation of a `Printer` table in the `HumanResources` schema. The database name (`AdventureWorks2008`) is the first part of the name, followed by a schema name (`HumanResources`). The last part of Listing 24.3 shows a sample `SELECT` statement against the `Printer` table that is owned by the `HumanResources` schema. The schema name must precede the table, when referenced. The only exception to this rule is tables that belong to the default schema assigned to the user executing the query.

LISTING 24.3 Using T-SQL **CREATE TABLE** in a Schema

```
CREATE TABLE AdventureWorks2008.HumanResources.Printer
    (
    PrinterID int NOT NULL,
    DepartmentID smallint NOT NULL,
    PrinterName varchar(50) NOT NULL,
```

```
    Manufacturer varchar(50) NOT NULL,
    PrinterDescription varchar(250) NULL
    )
go
 select * from HumanResources.Printer
```

The creation of schemas and assignment of tables to schemas requires some forethought. This task, which is permission oriented, is discussed in more detail in Chapter 11, "Security and User Administration."

Defining Columns

A *table* is defined as a collection of columns. Each column represents an attribute of the database table and has characteristics that define its scope and the type of data it can contain. In defining a column, you must assign a name and a data type. For consistency and readability, the column names should adhere to a naming convention that you define for your environment. Naming conventions often use a set of standard suffixes that indicate the type of data the column will contain. For example, you can add the `Date` suffix to a column name (for example, `OrderDate`) to identify it as a column that contains date/time data, or you can add the suffix `ID` (for example, `PrinterID`) to indicate that the column contains a unique identifier.

When creating and naming columns, you need to keep the following restrictions in mind:

- You can define up to 1,024 columns (nonsparse + computed) for each table. This number is increased to 30,000 columns if the table has a defined column set using sparse columns.
- Column names must be unique within a table.
- A row can hold a maximum of 8,060 bytes. Some data types can be stored off the 8KB data page to allow a row to exceed this limit.
- A data type must be assigned to each column.

These restrictions provide a framework for a column definition. The next consideration in defining a column is the data type. The following section discusses the various data types.

Data Types

SQL Server 2008 has an extensive list of data types to choose from, including some that are new to SQL Server 2008. New data types include `date`, `time`, `datetime2`, `datetimeoffset`, `filestream`, and `geometry`. Each data type is geared toward a specific type of data that will be stored in the column. Table 24.1 provides a complete list of the data types available in SQL Server 2008.

TABLE 24.1 Table Data Types

Data Type	Range/Description	Storage
`bigint`	-2^{63} (–9,223,372,036,854,775,808) to $2^{63\text{-}1}$ (9,223,372,036,854,775,807)	8 bytes
`binary (n)`		Binary data with a length of n bytes The number of bytes defined by n, up to 8,000
`bit`	An integer data type that can take a value of `1`, `0`, or `NULL`	1 byte for every eight columns that are defined as bits on the table
`char`	Up to 8,000 characters	1 byte per character
`date`	0001-01-01 through 9999-12-31	3 bytes
`datetime` through	8 bytes; accurate to December 31, 9999	January 1, 1753, 3.33 milliseconds
`datetime2` through	8 bytes; accurate to December 31, 9999	January 1, 0001, 100 nanoseconds
`datetimeoffset` through	10 bytes December 31, a time zone offset	January 1, 0001, 9999; includes
`decimal`	Based on the precision	-10^{38+1} to $10^{38\text{-}1}$
`float`	–1.79E + 38 to –2.23E – 38, 0 and 2.23E – 38 to 1.79E + 38	4 or 8 bytes, depending on the allocation mantissa
`geography` representing	round-earth data such as GPS latitude and longitude coordinates	.NET CLR data type
`geometry` CLR data type representing	data in a Euclidean (flat) coordinate system	.NET
`hierarchyid` levels	Up to 892 bytes	User defined nodes and
`image`	Variable-length binary data	Up to $2^{31\text{-}1}$ (2,147,483,647) bytes
`int`	-2^{31} (–2,147,483,648) to $2^{31\text{-}1}$ (2,147,483,647)	4 bytes

TABLE 24.1 Table Data Types

Data Type	Range/Description	Storage
money	–922,337,203,685,477.5808 to 922,337,203,685,477.5807	8 bytes
nchar	Up to 4,000 Unicode characters	Two times the number of characters entered
ntext	Up to 2^{30-1} (1,073,741,823) characters	Two times the number of characters entered
numeric (p,s) 10^{38-1}	Based on the precision	-10^{38+1} through
nvarchar(n)		Up to 4,000 Unicode characters Two times the number of characters entered
nvarchar(max)	Unicode characters up to the maximum storage capacity of	Two times the number plus 2 bytes, up to 2^{30-1}
real	–1.18E – 38, 0 and 1.18E – 38 to 3.40E + 38	4 bytes
smalldatetime		January 1, 1900, through June 6, 2079 4 bytes; accurate to 1 minute
smallint to 2^{15-1} (32,767)	2 bytes	-2^{15} (–32,768)
smallmoney 214,748.3647	4 bytes	–214,748.3648 to
sql_variant values of	Up to 8,016 bytes various SQL Server 2008–supported data types, except text, ntext, image, timestamp, and sql_variant	A data type that stores
text	Up to 231-1	2,147,483,647) characters Up to 2,147,483,647 bytes
time	00:00:00.0000000 to 23:59:59.9999999	5 bytes
timestamp/rowversion generated, unique binary	numbers within a database; generally used for version stamping rows	Automatically 8 bytes

24

TABLE 24.1 Table Data Types

Data Type	Range/Description	Storage
`tinyint`	0 to 255	1 byte
`uniqueidentifier` unique identifier	16 bytes (GUID)	A 16-byte globally
`varbinary(n)`		Binary data with a length of n bytes The number of bytes defined by *n*, up to 8,000
`varbinary(max)`	Binary data up to the maximum storage capacity	Two times the number of characters entered plus 2 bytes, up to 2^{30-1}
`varchar (n)`	1 byte per character	Up to 8,000 characters
`varchar (max)`	Non-Unicode characters up to the maximum storage capacity	1 byte per character; maximum 2^{31-1} bytes
`xml`	XML instances or a variable of XML type	2GB

The data type you select is important because it provides scope for the column. For example, if you define a column as type `int`, you can be assured that only integer data will be stored in the column and that character data will not be allowed. The advantages of data typing are fairly obvious but sometimes overlooked.

You should avoid defining most of your columns with a single data type, such as `varchar`. As mentioned earlier in this chapter, the visual tools provide a great way for you to select a data type: you simply select a data type from a drop-down selection box that lists the available data types.

TIP

The Object Explorer has a categorized list of all the system data types. To get to it, you open the `Programmability` node under your database and then expand the `Types` node. You then see a node named `System Data Types` that lists all the data type categories, including `Exact Numbers`, `Approximate Numbers`, and `Date and Time`. The data types for each category are listed under each category node. If you mouse over the particular data type, you see a brief description, including the valid range of values.

Several data types in SQL Server 2008 deserve special attention. Some of these data types are new to SQL Server 2008 and some of them were introduced in SQL Server 2005. The following sections discuss these data types.

New Date/Time Data Types

Several new date/time data types were added in SQL Server 2008. These data types were added to enhance SQL Server's date/time capabilities. The `date` and `time` data types were added to separate these two date/time components. The `date` data type contains only the month, day, and year components, whereas the `time` data type contains only the time components. The separation of `date` and `time` was planned for SQL Server 2005 but never made it to the final release.

The precision and scale of date/time data types has been expanded in SQL Server 2008 as well. The `datetime2` data type is similar to the `datetime` data type, but it has a larger range of dates (January 1, 0001, through December 31, 9999), and the time portion of this data type contains fractional seconds with seven digits of precision. The `datetime` data type is accurate only to within 3 milliseconds, whereas the new `datetime2` data type is accurate to 100 nanoseconds.

Finally, SQL Server introduces time zone support in a new data type named `datetimeoffset`. This data type has precision in fractional seconds (like `datetime2`), but it also contains an extra date/time component that defines the time zone offset for the date. The time zone offset is two digits that represent the offset hours and two digits that represent the offset minutes. The offset is used against the UTC date. The following example shows how this new data type can be used:

```
select CAST('2009-07-08 11:33:22.1234567-04:00' AS datetimeoffset(7))
```

The `xml` Data Type

The `xml` data type (introduced in SQL Server 2005) enables you to store XML documents and XML fragments in a SQL Server database. (An XML fragment is an XML instance that is missing a single top-level element.) Use of the `xml` data type is discussed in more detail in Chapter 47, "Using XML in SQL Server 2008."

The `hierarchyid` Data Type

The `hierarchyid` data type is new in SQL Server 2008. The `hierarchyid` data type is a variable-length system data type used to represent a position in a tree hierarchy. A column of type `hierarchyid` does not automatically represent a tree. It is up to the application to generate and assign `hierarchyid` values in such a way that the desired relationship between rows is reflected in the values. For more information and examples for using the `hierarchyid` data type, see Chapter 42, "What's New for Transact-SQL in SQL Server 2008."

Spatial Data Types

SQL Server 2008 introduces support for storing geographical data with the inclusion of new spatial data types. Spatial data types provide a comprehensive, high-performance, and extensible data storage solution for spatial data, enabling organizations of any scale to integrate geospatial features into their applications and services.

Spatial data types can be used to store and manipulate location-based information and come in the form of two new data types: `geography` and `geometry`. The `geography` data type is a .NET CLR data type that provides a storage structure for geodetic data, sometimes referred to as round earth data because it assumes a roughly spherical model of the world. It provides a storage structure for spatial data that is defined by latitude and longitude coordinates using an industry standard ellipsoid such as WGS84, the projection method used by Global Positioning System (GPS) applications. The `geometry` data type is a .NET CLR data type that supports the planar model/data, which assumes a flat projection and is therefore sometimes called flat earth. `geometry` data is represented as points, lines, and polygons on a flat surface, such as maps and interior floor plans where the curvature of the earth does not need to be taken into account.

For more information on and examples using spatial data types, see Chapter 42.

Large-Value Data Types

Three large-value data types added in SQL Server 2005 allow you to store a significant amount of data in a single column. They allow you to store up to 2^{31} bytes of non-Unicode data and 2^{30} bytes of Unicode data. All these data types have the `(max)` designator: `varchar(max)`, `nvarchar(max)`, and `varbinary(max)`. The `varchar`, `nvarchar`, and `varbinary` data types were available prior to SQL Server 2005, but the `max` parameter gave these types additional scope.

The great thing about these data types is that they are much easier to work with than large object (LOB) data types. LOB data types (which include `text`, `ntext`, and `image`) require special programming when retrieving and storing data. The large-value data types do not have these restrictions. They can be used much like their smaller counterparts `varchar(n)`, `nvarchar(n)`, and `varbinary(n)` that are defined without the `max` keyword. So if you want to select data from a `varchar(max)` column, you can simply execute a `SELECT` statement against it, regardless of the amount of data stored in it. Consider, for example, the following `SELECT` statement, executed against a `varchar(max)` column named `DocumentSummary` in the `AdventureWorks2008.Production.Document` table:

```
select Title, substring(DocumentSummary,1,30) 'DocumentSummary'
from production.document
where LEFT(DocumentSummary,30) like 'Reflector%'

/* results from previous select statement
Title                                             DocumentSummary
------------------------------------------------- ------------------------------
Front Reflector Bracket Installation              Reflectors are vital safety co
*/
```

This works fine with the `varchar(max)` column, but the `LEFT` function used in the `WHERE` clause would cause an error if the column were a `text` column instead.

The large-value data types can be stored in the data row or in a separate data page, based on the setting of the `sp_tableoption 'large value types out of row'` option. If the option is set to `OFF`, up to 8,000 characters can be stored in this column in the actual data row. If the option is set to `ON`, data for this column is stored in a separate data page if its length would result in the data row exceeding 8,060 bytes. The actual location of the column data is transparent to any user accessing the table.

Large Row Support

In SQL Server 2000, there was a strict limit of 8,060 bytes that could be stored in a single row. If the total amount of data exceeded this limit, the update or insert would fail. Enhancements were made in SQL Server 2005 to dynamically manage rows that exceed the 8,060-byte limit. This dynamic behavior is designed for columns that are defined as varchar, nvarchar, varbinary, or sql_variant. If the values in these columns cause the total size of the row to go beyond the 8,060-byte limit, SQL Server moves one or more of the variable-length columns to pages in the ROW_OVERFLOW_DATA allocation unit. A pointer to this separate storage location, rather than the actual data, is kept in the data row. If the data row shrinks below the 8,060-byte limit at a later time, SQL Server dynamically moves the data from the ROW_OVERFLOW_DATA allocation unit back into the data page.

The following example creates a table that has columns that could exceed the 8,060-byte limit, with a total of 9,000 characters:


```
CREATE TABLE t1
(col1 varchar(4000), col2 varchar(5000))

insert t1
select replicate('x', 4000),replicate('x', 5000)
```

If you execute the CREATE TABLE statement, you do not get any warning message related to the 8,060-byte limit. After the table is created, you can execute an insert into the table that exceeds the 8,060-byte limit. The insert succeeds, and the dynamic allocation previously described is handled automatically.

User-Defined Data Types

User-defined data types allow you to create custom data types that are based on the existing system data types. These data types are also called *alias data types* in SQL Server 2008. You create a user-defined data type and give it a unique name that you can then use in the definitions of tables. For example, you can create a user-defined data type named ShortDescription, defined as varchar(20), and assign it to any column. This promotes data type consistency across your tables.

You can create user-defined data types by using T-SQL in a couple of different ways. Using the sp_addtype system stored procedure and using the new CREATE TYPE command are two possibilities. The sp_addtype system stored procedure is slated to be removed in a future version of SQL Server, so using the CREATE TYPE command is preferred. The following example shows how to create the ShortDescription user-defined data type:

```
CREATE TYPE [dbo].[ShortDescription] FROM [varchar](20) NOT NULL
```

After a user-defined data type is created, you can use it in the definition of tables. The following is an example of a table created with the new ShortDescription user-defined data type:

```
CREATE TABLE [dbo].CodeTable
 (TableId int identity,
  TableDesc ShortDescription)
```

When you look at the definition of the `CodeTable` table in Object Explorer, you see the `TableDesc` column displayed with the `ShortDescription` data type as well as the underlying data type `varchar(20)`.

You can use the Object Explorer to create user-defined data types as well. To do so, you right-click the `User-Defined Data Types` node, then select `Programmability`, and then select `Types`. Then you choose the New User-Defined Data Type option, and you can create a new user-defined data type through a friendly GUI screen. If you create a user-defined data type in the model database, this user-defined data type is created in any newly created database.

CLR User-Defined Types

SQL Server 2008 continues support for user-defined types (UDTs) implemented with the Microsoft .NET Framework common language runtime (CLR). CLR UDTs enable you to extend the type system of the database and also enable you to define complex structured types.

A UDT may be simple or structured and of any degree of complexity. A UDT can encapsulate complex, user-defined behaviors. You can use CLR UDTs in all contexts where you can use a system type in SQL Server, including in columns in tables, in variables in batches, in functions or stored procedures, as arguments of functions or stored procedures, or as return values from functions.

A UDT must first be implemented as a managed class or structure in any one of the CLR languages and compiled into a .NET Framework assembly. You can then register it with SQL Server by using the `CREATE ASSEMBLY` command, as in the following example:

```
CREATE ASSEMBLY latlong FROM 'c:\samplepath\latlong.dll'
```

After registering the assembly, you can create the CLR UDTs by using a variation of the `CREATE TYPE` command shown previously:

```
CREATE TYPE latitude EXTERNAL NAME latlong.latitude
CREATE TYPE longitude EXTERNAL NAME latlong.longitude
```

When a CLR UDT is created, you can use it in the definition of tables. The following example shows a table created with the new `latitude` and `longitude` UDTs:

```
CREATE TABLE [dbo].StoreLocation
 (StoreID int NOT NULL,
  StoreLatitude latitude,
  StoreLongitude longitude)
```

For more details on programming and defining CLR UDTs, see Chapter 45, "SQL Server and the .NET Framework."

Column Properties

Name and data type are the most basic properties of a column, but many other properties can be defined for a column. You do not have to specify these properties to be able to create the columns, but you can use them to further refine the type of data that can be stored within a column. Note that many of the available column properties relate to indexes and constraints that are beyond the scope of this section. The following sections describe some of the column properties you are most likely to encounter.

The NULL and NOT NULL Keywords

When you are defining tables, it is always good idea to explicitly state whether a column should or should not contain nulls. You do this by specifying the `NULL` or `NOT NULL` keywords after the column data type. If the nullability option is not specified, the SQL Server default is to allow nulls unless the `ANSI_NULL_DFLT_OFF` option is enabled for the session or no setting is specified for the session, and the `ANSI_NULL_DEFAULT` option for the database is set to `OFF`. Because of this uncertainty, it is best to always explicitly specify the desired nullability option for each column. Listing 24.4 creates a new table named `PrinterCartridge` that has the `NULL` or `NOT NULL` property specified for each column.

LISTING 24.4 Defining Column **NULL** Properties by Using **CREATE TABLE**

```
CREATE TABLE dbo.PrinterCartridge
    (
    CartridgeId int NOT NULL,
    PrinterID int NOT NULL,
    CartridgeName varchar(50) NOT NULL,
    CartridgeColor varchar(50) NOT NULL,
    CartrideDescription varchar(255) NULL,
    InstallDate datetime NOT NULL
    )
GO
```

NOTE

It is beyond the scope of this section to debate whether columns should ever allow nulls. In some organizations, nulls are heavily used, and in others they are not allowed. There is no right answer, but it is important for a development team to be aware of the existence of nulls so that it can create appropriate code to handle them.

Identity Columns

A property commonly specified when creating tables is `IDENTITY`. This property automatically generates a unique sequential value when it is assigned to a column. It can be assigned only to columns that are of the following types:

- decimal
- int
- numeric
- smallint
- bigint
- tinyint

Only one identity column can exist for each table, and that column cannot allow nulls.

When implementing the IDENTITY property, you supply a seed and an increment. The *seed* is the starting value for the numeric count, and the *increment* is the amount by which it grows. A seed of 10 and an increment of 10 would produce values of 10, 20, 30, 40, and so on. If not specified, the default seed value is 1, and the increment is 1. Listing 24.5 adds an IDENTITY value to the PrinterCartridge table used in the previous example.

LISTING 24.5 Defining an Identity Column by Using **CREATE TABLE**

```
IF  EXISTS (SELECT * FROM dbo.sysobjects
WHERE id = OBJECT_ID(N'dbo.PrinterCartridge')
AND OBJECTPROPERTY(id, N'IsUserTable') = 1)
DROP TABLE dbo.PrinterCartridge

CREATE TABLE dbo.PrinterCartridge
    (
    CartridgeId int IDENTITY (1000, 1) NOT NULL,
    PrinterID int NOT NULL,
    CartridgeName varchar(50) NOT NULL,
    CartridgeColor varchar(50) NOT NULL,
    CartrideDescription varchar(255) NULL,
    InstallDate datetime NOT NULL
    )
GO

insert PrinterCartridge
 (PrinterID, CartridgeName, CartridgeColor, CartrideDescription, InstallDate)
values (1, 'inkjet', 'black','laser printer cartridge', '8/1/09')

select CartridgeId, PrinterID, CartridgeName
 from PrinterCartridge

/* results from previous SELECT statement
CartridgeId PrinterID   CartridgeName
----------- ----------- --------------------------------------------------
1000        1           inkjet
*/
```

In this listing, the seed value has been set to `1000`, and the increment has been set to `1`. An insert into the `PrinterCartridge` table and a subsequent `SELECT` from that table follows the `CREATE TABLE` statement in the listing. Notice that the results of the `SELECT` show a value of `1000` for the identity column `CartridgeID`. This is the seed or starting point that is defined.

ROWGUIDCOL Columns

An alternative to an identity column is a column defined with the `ROWGUIDCOL` property. Like the `IDENTITY` property, the `ROWGUIDCOL` property is autogenerating and unique. The difference is that the `ROWGUIDCOL` option generates column values that will be unique on any networked database anywhere in the world. The identity column generates values that are unique only within the table that contains the column.

You can have only one `ROWGUIDCOL` column per table. You must create this `ROWGUIDCOL` column with the `uniqueidentifier` data type, and you must assign a default of `NEWID()` to the column to generate the unique value. Keep in mind that users can manually insert values directly into columns defined as `ROWGUIDCOL`. These manual inserts could cause duplicates in the column, so a `UNIQUE` constraint should be added to the column as well to ensure uniqueness.

Listing 24.6 shows the creation of a table with a `ROWGUIDCOL` column. Several rows are inserted into the newly created table, and those rows are selected at the end of the listing.

LISTING 24.6 Defining a **ROWGUIDCOL** Column

```
CREATE TABLE SomeUniqueTable
   (UniqueID   UNIQUEIDENTIFIER      DEFAULT NEWID(),
   EffectiveDate datetime )
GO
INSERT INTO SomeUniqueTable (EffectiveDate) VALUES ('7/1/09')
INSERT INTO SomeUniqueTable (EffectiveDate) VALUES ('8/1/09')
GO
select * from SomeUniqueTable
/* Results from previous select statement
UniqueID                             EffectiveDate
------------------------------------ -----------------------
614181BC-D7B9-4108-B2BD-C2F39E999424 2009-07-01 00:00:00.000
62368A2D-3557-4727-9DD3-FBCA38705B1B 2009-08-01 00:00:00.000
*/
```

You can see that the `ROWGUIDCOL` values are fairly large. They are 16-byte `binary` values that are significantly larger than most of the data types used for identity columns. For example, an identity column defined as data type `int` occupies only 4 bytes. You need to consider the storage requirements for `ROWGUIDCOL` when you select this data type.

24

Computed Columns

A *computed column* is a column whose value is calculated based on other columns. Generally speaking, the column is a virtual column because it is calculated on the fly, and no value is stored in the database table. With SQL Server 2008, you have an option of actually storing the calculated value in the database. You do so by marking the column as persisted. If the computed column is persisted, you can create an index on this column as well.

Listing 24.7 includes several statements that relate to the creation of a computed column. It starts with an ALTER TABLE statement that adds a new computed column named SetRate to the Sales.CurrencyRate table in the AdventureWorks2008 database. The new rate column is based on an average of two other rate columns in the table. A SELECT statement is executed after that; it returns several columns, including the new SetRate computed column. The results are shown after the SELECT. Finally, an ALTER TABLE statement is used to change the newly added column so that its values are stored in the database. This is accomplished with the ADD PERSISTED option.

LISTING 24.7 Defining a Computed Column

```
--Add a computed column to the Sales.CurrencyRate Table named SetRate
ALTER TABLE Sales.CurrencyRate
 ADD SetRate AS ( (AverageRate + EndOfDayRate) / 2)
go
--Select several columns including the new computed column
select top 5 AverageRate, EndOfDayRate , SetRate
 from sales.currencyrate

/*Results from previous SELECT statement
AverageRate           EndOfDayRate          SetRate
--------------------- --------------------- ---------------------
1.00                  1.0002                1.0001
1.5491                1.55                  1.5495
1.9379                1.9419                1.9399
1.4641                1.4683                1.4662
8.2781                8.2784                8.2782
*/

--Alter the computed SetRate column to be PERSISTED
ALTER TABLE Sales.CurrencyRate
 alter column SetRate ADD PERSISTED
```

NOTE

You can use the `sp_spaceused` stored procedure to check the space allocated to the `Sales.CurrencyRate` table. You need to check the size before the column is persisted, and then you need to check the space allocated to the table after the column is persisted. As you would expect, the space allocated to the table is increased only after the column is persisted.

FILESTREAM Storage

SQL Server 2008 introduces `FILESTREAM` storage for storing unstructured data, such as documents, images, and videos. In previous versions of SQL Server, there were two ways of storing unstructured data. One method was to store it in the database as a binary large object (BLOB) in an image or `varbinary(max)` column. The other method was to store the data outside the database, separate from the structured relational data, storing a reference or pathname to the unstructured data in a `varchar` column in a table. Neither of these methods is ideal for unstructured data.

`FILESTREAM` storage helps to solve the issues with using unstructured data by integrating the SQL Server Database Engine with the NTFS file system for storing the unstructured data, such as documents and images, on the file system with the database storing a pointer to the data. Although the actual data resides outside the database in the NTFS file system, you can still use T-SQL statements to insert, update, query, and back up `FILESTREAM` data, while maintaining transactional consistency between the unstructured data and corresponding structured data with same level of security.

To specify that a column should store data on the file system when creating or altering a table, you specify the `FILESTREAM` attribute on a `varbinary(max)` column. This causes the Database Engine to store all data for that column on the file system, but not in the database file. After you complete these tasks, you can use Transact-SQL and Win32 to manage the `FILESTREAM` data.

NOTE

To use `FILESTREAM` storage, you must first enable `FILESTREAM` storage at the Windows level as well as at the SQL Server Instance level. You can enable `FILESTREAM` at the Windows level during installation of SQL Server 2008 or at any time using SQL Server Configuration Manager. After you enable `FILESTREAM` at the Windows level, you next need to enable `FILESTREAM` for the SQL Server Instance. You can do this either through SQL Server Management Studio or via T-SQL. For more information on enabling and using `FILESTREAM` storage, see Chapter 42.

Sparse Columns and Column Sets

SQL Server 2008 provides a new space-saving storage option referred to as *sparse columns*. Sparse columns are ordinary columns that provide optimized storage for null values. If the value of a column defined as a sparse column is `NULL`, it doesn't consume any space at all.

You can define a column as a sparse column by specifying the SPARSE keyword after the data type in the CREATE TABLE or ALTER TABLE statement, as shown in Listing 24.8.

LISTING 24.8 Specifying a Sparse Column in a Create Table Statement

```
CREATE TABLE DBO.SPARSE_TABLE
(ID INT IDENTITY(1,1),
 FIRST_NAME VARCHAR (50),
 MIDDLE_NAME VARCHAR (50) SPARSE NULL,
 LASTNAME VARCHAR (50)
)
```

The space savings of sparse columns come with a trade-off, however, requiring extra space for storing non-null values in the sparse column. Fixed-length and precision data types require 4 extra bytes, and variable-length data types require 2 extra bytes. For this reason, you should consider using sparse columns only when the space saved is at least 20% to 40%.

SQL Server stores sparse columns in a single XML column that appears to external applications and end users as a normal column. Storing the sparse columns in a single XML column allows up to 30,000 sparse columns in a single table, exceeding the limitation of 1,024 columns if sparse columns are not used. In addition, because sparse columns have many null-valued rows, they are good candidates for filtered indexes. A filtered index on a sparse column can index only the rows that have non-null values stored in the column. This creates smaller and more efficient indexes. (For more information on filtered indexes, see Chapters 25, "Creating and Managing Indexes," and 34, "Data Structures, Indexes, and Performance.")

Sparse columns can be of any SQL Server data type and behave like any other column with the following restrictions:

- A sparse column must be nullable and cannot have the ROWGUIDCOL or IDENTITY properties. A sparse column cannot be of the following data types—text, ntext, image, timestamp, user-defined data type, geometry, or geography—or have the FILESTREAM attribute.
- A sparse column cannot have a default value.
- A sparse column cannot be bound to a rule.
- A computed column cannot be marked as sparse.
- A sparse column cannot be part of a clustered index or a unique primary key index.

When the number of sparse columns in a table is large, and operating on them individually is cumbersome, you may want to define a column set. A column set is an untyped XML representation that combines all the sparse columns of a table into a structured set. A column set is like a calculated column in that the column set is not physically stored in the table, but the column set is directly updatable. Applications may see some performance improvement when they select and insert data by using column sets on tables that have lots of columns.

To define a column set, use the `<column_set_name> FOR ALL_SPARSE_COLUMNS` keywords in the `CREATE TABLE` or `ALTER TABLE` statements, as shown in Listing 24.9.

LISTING 24.9 Defining a Column Set

```
CREATE TABLE emp_info
(ID INT IDENTITY(1,1),
 FIRST_NAME VARCHAR (50),
 MIDDLE_NAME VARCHAR (50) SPARSE NULL ,
 LASTNAME VARCHAR (50),
 HOMEPHONE VARCHAR(10) SPARSE NULL,
 BUSPHONE VARCHAR(10) SPARSE NULL,
 CELLPHONE VARCHAR(10) SPARSE NULL,
 FAX VARCHAR(10) SPARSE NULL,
 EMAIL VARCHAR(30) SPARSE NULL,
 WEBSITE VARCHAR(30) SPARSE NULL,
 CSet XML COLUMN_SET FOR ALL_SPARSE_COLUMNS
)
```

A column set is created as an untyped XML column and is treated as any other XML column with a maximum XML data size limit of 2GB. Only one column set per table is allowed. You cannot add a column set to a table if the table already contains sparse columns.

To specify a column as a sparse column using SQL Server Management Studio (SSMS), set the `Is Sparse` property to Yes in the column properties for the selected column (see Figure 24.3). Similarly, if a column needs to be declared as column set, set the `Is Columnset` property to Yes in the column properties.

For more information on using and working with sparse columns and column sets, see Chapter 42.

Defining Table Location

As databases scale in size, the physical location of database objects, particularly tables and indexes, becomes crucial. Consider two tables, `Authors` and `Titles`, that are always queried together. If they are located on the same physical disk, contention for hardware resources may slow performance. SQL Server addresses this issue by enabling you to specify where a table (or an index) is stored.

The mechanism for specifying the physical table location is the filegroup. Filegroups are aligned to physical data files. By default, each database has a primary filegroup and a data file that matches the name of the database. You can create additional filegroups and align them to other data files. When these filegroups are created, SQL Server enables you to create your database tables on a specific filegroup.

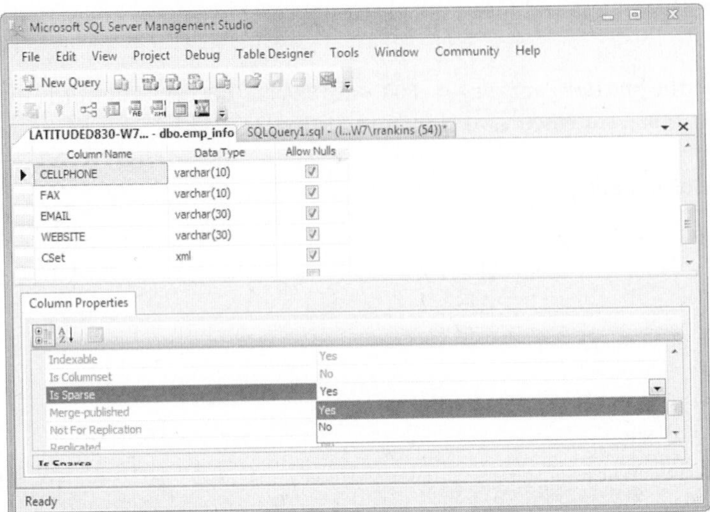

FIGURE 24.3 Setting a column as a sparse column.

NOTE

Using partitioned tables is a way to specify table location. This SQL Server 2008 feature allows you to divide a table into partitions and align those partitions with filegroups. This concept is discussed in detail in the "Using Partitioned Tables" section, later in this chapter.

The placement of tables on separate filegroups has some distinct advantages, including performance benefits. You can achieve performance improvements by storing filegroups on different disks. You can also achieve some manageability improvements by using filegroups because you can back up and manipulate filegroups separately. This capability is particularly important for large tables.

You specify the location of a table by using the `ON` clause during table creation. Listing 24.10 shows an example of creating two filegroups in the `BigPubs2008` database, followed by the creation of two new tables on those filegroups. Note that the filegroups must exist before the tables are created. For more information on filegroups, see Chapter 23, "Creating and Managing Databases."

LISTING 24.10 An Example of Creating Tables on Specific Filegroups

```
--Add the filegroups
ALTER DATABASE BigPubs2008 ADD FILEGROUP FG1
ALTER DATABASE BigPubs2008 ADD FILEGROUP FG2
GO
--Add files to the filegroups
ALTER DATABASE BigPubs2008 ADD FILE
```

```
(   NAME = FG1_File,
    FILENAME = 'c:\BigPubs2008FG1.ndf',
    SIZE = 2MB) TO FILEGROUP FG1
go

ALTER DATABASE BigPubs2008 ADD FILE
(   NAME = FG2_File,
    FILENAME = 'c:\BigPubs2008FG2.ndf',
    SIZE = 2MB) TO FILEGROUP FG2
go

CREATE TABLE [dbo].[authors_NEW](
    [au_id] [dbo].[id] NOT NULL,
    [au_lname] [varchar](40) ,
    [au_fname] [varchar](20) ,
    [phone] [char](12),
    [address] [varchar](40)  NULL,
    [city] [varchar](20)  NULL,
    [state] [char](2)  NULL,
    [zip] [char](5)  NULL,
    [contract] [bit] NOT NULL,
) ON FG1
go

CREATE TABLE [dbo].[titles_NEW](
    [title_id] [dbo].[tid] NOT NULL,
    [title] [varchar](80)  NOT NULL,
    [type] [char](12)  NOT NULL,
    [pub_id] [char](4)  NULL,
    [price] [money] NULL,
    [advance] [money] NULL,
    [royalty] [int] NULL,
    [ytd_sales] [int] NULL,
    [notes] [varchar](400)  NULL,
    [pubdate] [datetime] NOT NULL,
) ON FG2
```


Defining Table Constraints

Constraints provide a means to enforce data integrity. In addition to NULL/NOT NULL, discussed earlier in this chapter, SQL Server provides five constraint types: PRIMARY KEY, FOREIGN KEY, UNIQUE, CHECK, and DEFAULT. These constraints help further define the type of data you can store in tables.

Constraints are covered in detail in Chapter 26, "Implementing Data Integrity." This chapter introduces the basic means for adding constraints to a table. You can add constraints at the time of table creation, or you can add them after a table has been created, by using the ALTER TABLE statement.

Listing 24.11 shows a CREATE TABLE statement that has an example of each one of the five constraint types listed. The PRIMARY KEY constraint is created at the bottom of the script and is named PK_TitleHistory. The FOREIGN KEY constraint is created on the title_id column and is named FK_titles_titleHistory. The UNIQUE constraint is part of the primary key and can be identified with the UNIQUE keyword. The CHECK constraint is created on the price column; it checks to make sure the price is greater than zero. Finally, a DEFAULT constraint is created on the modify_user column; it sets the user to the value of system if no explicit value is specified.

LISTING 24.11 Example of Creating Constraints with **CREATE TABLE**

```
CREATE TABLE dbo.TitleHistory(
   title_id dbo.tid
      CONSTRAINT FK_titles_titleHistory
      REFERENCES titles (title_id)NOT NULL ,
   change_date datetime NOT NULL,
   title varchar(80) NOT NULL,
   type char(12)  NOT NULL,
   price money NULL
      CONSTRAINT CK_TitleHistory_Price CHECK  (Price>0),
   modify_user nchar(10) NOT NULL
      CONSTRAINT DF_TitleHistory_modify_user  DEFAULT (N'system'),
 CONSTRAINT PK_TitleHistory UNIQUE CLUSTERED
(  title_id ASC,
   change_date ASC ) )
```

You can create the same constraints as in Listing 24.11 by using the ALTER TABLE statement. This means you can first create the table (without the constraints) and then add the constraints afterward. Listing 24.12 shows the creation of the same titleHistory table, with the constraints added later via the ALTER TABLE statement.

LISTING 24.12 Example of Creating Constraints with **ALTER TABLE**

```
IF  EXISTS (SELECT * FROM dbo.sysobjects
WHERE id = OBJECT_ID(N'[dbo].[TitleHistory]')
AND OBJECTPROPERTY(id, N'IsUserTable') = 1)
DROP TABLE [dbo].[TitleHistory]

CREATE TABLE dbo.TitleHistory(
   title_id dbo.tid NOT NULL,
```

```
    change_date datetime NOT NULL,
    title varchar(80) NOT NULL,
    type char(12) NOT NULL,
    price money NULL,
    modify_user nchar(10) NOT NULL )
GO

--PRIMARY KEY/UNIQUE CONSTRAINT
ALTER TABLE dbo.TitleHistory
    ADD  CONSTRAINT PK_TitleHistory UNIQUE CLUSTERED
     (
        title_id ASC,
        change_date ASC
     )WITH (SORT_IN_TEMPDB = OFF, ONLINE = OFF)
go
--FOREIGN KEY CONSTRAINT
ALTER TABLE dbo.TitleHistory  WITH CHECK
    ADD  CONSTRAINT FK_titles_titleHistory FOREIGN KEY(   title_id)
     REFERENCES dbo.titles (title_id)
GO
--CHECK CONSTRAINT
ALTER TABLE dbo.TitleHistory  WITH CHECK
    ADD  CONSTRAINT CK_TitleHistory_Price CHECK  ((Price>(0)))
GO
--DEFAULT CONSTRAINT
ALTER TABLE dbo.TitleHistory
    ADD  CONSTRAINT DF_TitleHistory_modify_user
      DEFAULT (N'system') FOR modify_user
```

24

Modifying Tables

You often need to modify database tables after you create them. Fortunately, you can use several tools to accomplish this task. These tools are the same set of tools you can use to add, modify, and delete tables: the SSMS Object Explorer, Table Designer, Database Diagram Editor, and T-SQL. The following sections touch on each of these tools but focus most heavily on the use of T-SQL.

Regardless of the method you use, you must always exercise caution when modifying tables, particularly in a production environment. Table relationships and the impact to data that may already exist in a table are key considerations in modifying a table. A visual tool such as a database diagram can assist you in determining the impact to related tables and can be used to generate the T-SQL script. The following section looks at the underlying T-SQL that can be used to modify a table, and then we delve into the visual tools that can simplify your life and generate some of the T-SQL for you.

Using T-SQL to Modify Tables

You can modify tables in many different ways, including making changes to the columns, constraints, and indexes associated with a table. Some of the changes have a bigger impact on the database than others. Some modifications require that the modified table be dropped and re-created to effect the change. Fortunately, you can use the T-SQL `ALTER TABLE` statement to mitigate the database impact and help streamline many of the most common modifications. You can make the following types of changes by using the `ALTER TABLE` statement:

- Change a column property, such as a data type or `NULL` property.
- Add new columns or drop existing columns.
- Add or drop constraints.
- Enable or disable `CHECK` and `FOREIGN KEY` constraints.
- Enable or disable triggers.
- Reassign partitions.
- Alter an index associated with a constraint.

The following sections discuss a few examples of these types of changes to familiarize you with the `ALTER TABLE` command. The full syntax for the `ALTER TABLE` command is extensive, and you can find it in SQL Server Books Online.

Changing a Column Property

You can use the `ALTER COLUMN` clause of the `ALTER TABLE` command to modify column properties, including the `NULL` property or the data type of a column. Listing 24.13 shows an example of changing the data type of a column.

LISTING 24.13 Changing the Data Type of a Column by Using **ALTER TABLE**

```
alter table titles
  alter column notes varchar(400) null
```

You must be aware of several restrictions when you modify the data type of a column. The following rules apply when altering columns:

- You cannot modify a `text`, `image`, `ntext`, or `timestamp` column.
- The column cannot be the `ROWGUIDCOL` for the table.
- The column cannot be a computed column or be referenced by a computed column.

- The column cannot be a replicated column.
- If the column is used in an index, the column length can only be increased in size. In addition, it must be of varchar, nvarchar, or varbinary data type, and the data type cannot change.
- If statistics have been generated using CREATE STATISTICS, the statistics must first be dropped before the column can be altered.
- The column cannot have a PRIMARY KEY or FOREIGN KEY constraint or be used in a CHECK or UNIQUE constraint. The exception is that a column with a CHECK or UNIQUE constraint, if defined as variable length, can have the length altered.
- A column with a default defined for it can have only the length, nullability, or precision and scale altered.
- If a column has a schema-bound view defined on it, the same rules that apply to columns with indexes apply.

TIP

Changing some data types can result in changing the data. For example, changing from nchar to char could result in any extended characters being converted. Similarly, changing precision and scale could result in data truncation. Other modifications, such as changing from char to int, might fail if the data doesn't match the restrictions of the new data type. Before you change data types, you should always validate that the data conforms to the desired new data type.

Adding and Dropping Columns

You add columns to a table by using the ADD COLUMN clause. Listing 24.14 illustrates the addition of a new column named ISBN to the titles table.

LISTING 24.14 Adding a Column by Using **ALTER TABLE**

```
ALTER TABLE titles
  add ISBN int null
```

When you use the ALTER TABLE statement to add a column, the new column is added at the end of the table. In most cases, this location is acceptable. The location of the column in the table generally has no bearing on the use of the table. There are, however, situations in which it is desired to have the new column added in the middle of the table. The ALTER TABLE statement does not work for this situation. To add a column in the middle of the table, you need to create a new version of the table with a different name and the columns in the desired order, copy the data from the old table, drop the old table, and rename the new table with the old table name. Alternatively, you can also accomplish this by using SSMS, as described in the following section.

There are also some issues you need to consider with regard to the null option specified for a new column. In the case of a column that allows nulls, there is no real issue: SQL Server adds the column and allows a `NULL` value for all rows. If `NOT NULL` is specified, however, the column must be an identity column or have a default specified. Note that even if a default is specified, if the column allows nulls, the column is not populated with the default if no value is provided for the column. You use the `WITH VALUES` clause as part of the default specification to override this and populate the column with the default.

With some restrictions, columns can also be dropped from a table. Listing 24.15 shows the syntax for dropping a column. You can specify to drop multiple columns, separated by commas.

LISTING 24.15 Dropping a Column by Using **ALTER TABLE**

```
alter table titles
  drop column ISBN
```

The following columns cannot be dropped:

- A column in a schema-bound view
- An indexed column
- A replicated column
- A column used in a `CHECK`, `FOREIGN KEY`, `UNIQUE`, or `PRIMARY KEY` constraints
- A column associated with a default or bound to a default object
- A column bound to a rule

NOTE

Be careful when using `ALTER TABLE` to modify columns that hold existing data. When you add, drop, or modify columns, SQL Server places a schema lock on the table, preventing any other access until the operation completes. Changes to columns in tables that have many rows can take a long time to complete and generate a large amount of log activity.

As mentioned earlier, the `ALTER TABLE` statement is not the only T-SQL statement you can use to modify tables. You accomplish some table changes by using T-SQL that drops and re-creates the tables that are being modified. The following sections look at some examples of these types of changes.

Using Object Explorer and the Table Designer to Modify Tables

The Object Explorer in SSMS is your window into the various tables available for modification in a database. You expand the `Tables` node in the Object Explorer tree and right-click the table you would like to modify. Then you select the Design option, and a Table Designer window appears, showing all the table columns. In addition, a Table Designer menu option appears at the top of the SSMS window. The Table Designer menu includes many options, including Insert Columns, Delete Columns, and Remove Primary Key. The full list of available options is shown in Figure 24.4. A Table Designer window for the `BigPubs2008.Authors` table is shown as the active tab on the right side of Figure 24.4.

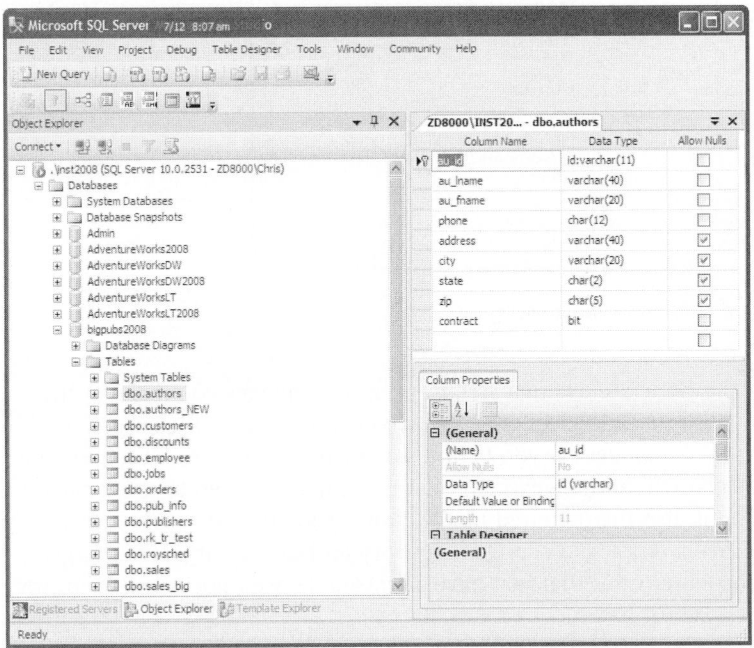

FIGURE 24.4 The Table Designer.

To illustrate the power of the Table Designer, let's add a new column to the `authors` table. You can add the column to the middle of the table, just prior to the `address` column. You do this by highlighting the entire `address` row in the Table Designer grid and then selecting Table Designer, Insert Column. A new data entry row is added to the Table Designer grid, where you can specify the name of the new column, the data type, and a null option. For this example, you can name the new column `Gender`, with a data type of `char(1)` and the setting `ALLOW NULLS`. Figure 24.5 shows the Table Designer grid with the newly added `Gender` column highlighted. In addition, the figure shows the Table Designer menu options with the newly enabled Generate Change Script option selected.

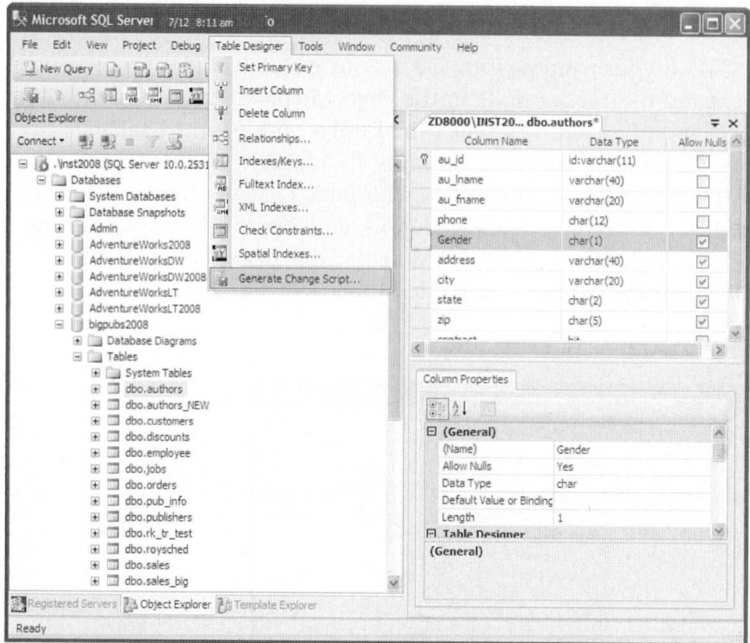

FIGURE 24.5 Inserting a column in Table Designer.

You do not need to use the Generate Change Script option for changes you make in the Table Designer. You can close the Table Designer tab where you made your changes, and the Table Designer makes the changes for you behind the scenes. Sometimes, though, you might want to script the changes and see exactly what is going to happen to the database. Clicking the Script button is also the preferred method for deploying changes to other environments. You can save a script in a change repository and execute it in your target environments. This approach ensures that you have a repeatable, well-documented means for making table changes.

Listing 24.16 shows the contents of a script that would be generated based on the new `Gender` column you added to the `authors` table. For the sake of space, some of the initial script options and the triggers associated with the `authors` table have been removed from the script. The important point to note is how extensive this script is. A new temporary `authors` table is created, and it includes the new column; the data from the `authors` table is copied into the temporary table; and then the table is renamed. In addition, the script must manage the constraints, indexes, and other objects associated with the `authors` table. The good news is that Table Designer does most of the work for you.

LISTING 24.16 Changing Script Generated from the Table Designer

```
ALTER TABLE dbo.authors
   DROP CONSTRAINT DF__authors__phone__04C4C0F4
GO
```

```
CREATE TABLE dbo.Tmp_authors
   (
   au_id dbo.id NOT NULL,
   au_lname varchar(40) NOT NULL,
   au_fname varchar(20) NOT NULL,
   phone char(12) NOT NULL,
   Gender char(1) NULL,
   address varchar(40) NULL,
   city varchar(20) NULL,
   state char(2) NULL,
   zip char(5) NULL,
   contract bit NOT NULL
   )  ON [PRIMARY]
GO
ALTER TABLE dbo.Tmp_authors ADD CONSTRAINT
   DF__authors__phone__04C4C0F4 DEFAULT ('UNKNOWN') FOR phone
GO
IF EXISTS(SELECT * FROM dbo.authors)
    EXEC('INSERT INTO dbo.Tmp_authors (au_id, au_lname,
      au_fname, phone, address, city, state, zip, contract)
      SELECT au_id, au_lname, au_fname, phone, address,
         city, state, zip, contract
      FROM dbo.authors WITH (HOLDLOCK TABLOCKX)')
GO
ALTER TABLE dbo.titleauthor
   DROP CONSTRAINT FK__titleauth__au_id__14070484
GO
DROP TABLE dbo.authors
GO
EXECUTE sp_rename N'dbo.Tmp_authors', N'authors', 'OBJECT'
GO
ALTER TABLE dbo.authors ADD CONSTRAINT
   UPKCL_auidind PRIMARY KEY CLUSTERED
   (
   au_id
   ) WITH( STATISTICS_NORECOMPUTE = OFF, IGNORE_DUP_KEY = OFF,
      ALLOW_ROW_LOCKS = ON, ALLOW_PAGE_LOCKS = ON) ON [PRIMARY]
GO
CREATE NONCLUSTERED INDEX aunmind ON dbo.authors
   (
   au_lname,
   au_fname
   ) WITH( STATISTICS_NORECOMPUTE = OFF, IGNORE_DUP_KEY = OFF,
      ALLOW_ROW_LOCKS = ON, ALLOW_PAGE_LOCKS = OFF) ON [PRIMARY]
GO
ALTER TABLE dbo.authors WITH NOCHECK ADD CONSTRAINT
```

```
   CK__authors__au_id__03D09CBB
      CHECK (([au_id] like
      '[0-9][0-9][0-9]-[0-9][0-9]-[0-9][0-9][0-9][0-9]'))
GO
ALTER TABLE dbo.authors WITH NOCHECK ADD CONSTRAINT
   CK__authors__zip__05B8E52D
      CHECK (([zip] like '[0-9][0-9][0-9][0-9][0-9]'))
GO
```

You will find that you can make most of the changes you want to make by using the Table Designer. To make other changes, you can use the same approach you just used to add a column. This approach involves making the changes via the Table Designer menu options and then using the option to script the change. This is a great way to evaluate the impact of your changes and to save those changes for later execution.

Using Database Diagrams to Modify Tables

Database diagrams offer an excellent visual view of your database tables that you can also use to modify tables. You do this by adding the table you want to modify to a new or existing database diagram. Oftentimes, it is best to also add all the related tables to the diagram as well. You can easily do this by right-clicking the table and choosing the Add Related Tables option.

With a database diagram, you have the same options that you have with the Table Designer, plus you have diagramming options. Both the Table Designer and Database Diagrams menus are shown when a database diagram is in focus. These menus disappear if you change the tabbed window to a Database Engine query window, so remember that you must select the diagram window to be able to display the menu options.

Figure 24.6 shows a database diagram for the `HumanResouces.Department` table, along with its related table. The Table Designer menu is selected to show that it is available when you work with a database diagram. You must have one of the tables selected to enable all the menu options. In Figure 24.6, the `Department` table has been highlighted, and a new `ModifiedUser` column has been added to the end of the table. Figure 24.6 also shows that the Database Diagram menu is available for selection. This menu includes options to add tables to the diagram and manipulate the tables within the diagram.

The same scripting options are available with a database diagram as are available in the Table Designer. You can make your changes from within the diagram and then choose the Generate Change Script menu option. Listing 24.17 shows the change script generated based on the addition of the `ModifiedUser` column to the end of the `Department` table. As expected, this change is accomplished with an `ALTER TABLE` statement.

LISTING 24.17 The Change Script Generated from a Database Diagram

```
ALTER TABLE HumanResources.Department ADD
    ModifiedUser varchar(20) NULL
GO
```

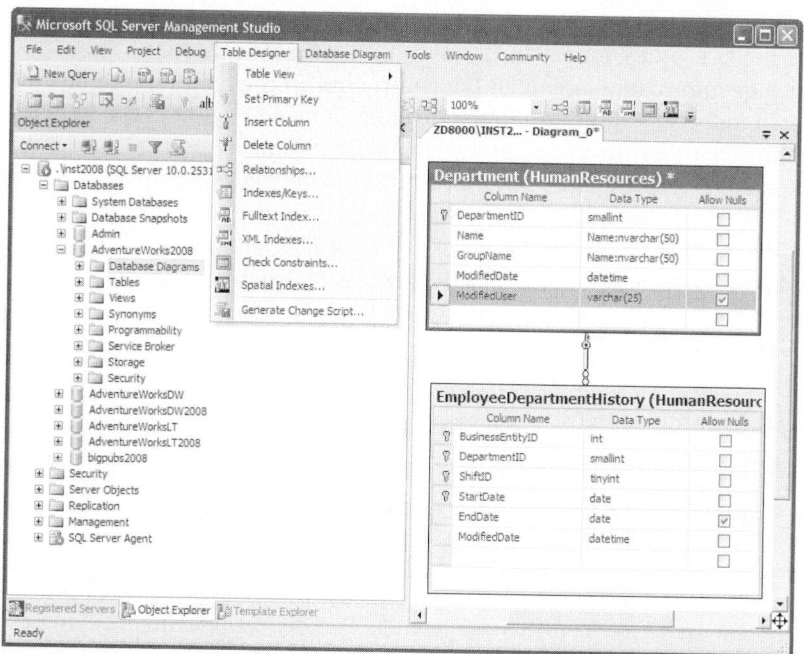

FIGURE 24.6 Modifying tables by using a database diagram.

The use of the ALTER TABLE statement in this listing brings us full circle, back to our initial method for making table modifications. Using all the tools discussed in this section together will usually give you the best results.

Dropping Tables

There are several different methods for dropping (or deleting) a table. You can right-click the table in the SSMS Object Explorer and select Delete, you can right-click a table in a database diagram and choose Delete Tables from Database, or you can use the old-fashioned method of utilizing T-SQL. Here's an example of the T-SQL DROP TABLE statement:

```
DROP TABLE [HumanResources].[Department]
```

You can reference multiple tables in a single DROP TABLE command by separating the table names with commas. Any triggers and constraints associated with the table are also dropped when the table is dropped.

A big consideration when dropping a table is the table's relationship to other tables. If a foreign key references the table that you want to drop, the referencing table or foreign key constraint must be dropped first. In a database that has many related tables, dropping elements can get complicated. Fortunately, a few tools can help you through this. The system stored procedure sp_helpconstraint is one of these tools. This procedure lists all the foreign key constraints that reference a table. Listing 24.18 shows an execution of this stored procedure for the `Sales.Store` table in the `AdventureWorks2008` database. The procedure results include information about all the constraints on the table. The results to focus on are those that follow the heading Table Is Referenced by Foreign Key. The partial results shown in Listing 24.18 for the `Sales.Store` table indicate that `FK_StoreContact_Store_CustomerID` must be dropped first before you can drop the `Sales.Store` table.

LISTING 24.18 Using **sp_helpconstraint** to Find Foreign Key References

```
sp_helpconstraint [Sales.Store]


/*partial results of sp_helpconstraint execution
Table is referenced by foreign key
----------------------------------------------------------------
AdventureWorks2008.Sales.StoreContact: FK_StoreContact_Store_CustomerID
 */
```

Two other approaches are useful for identifying foreign key references prior to dropping a table. The first is using a database diagram. You can create a new database diagram and add the table that you are considering for deletion. After the table is added, you right-click the table in Object Explorer and select Add Related Tables. The related tables, including those that have foreign key references, are then added. You can then right-click the relationship line connecting two tables and select Delete Relationships from Database. When you have deleted all the foreign key relationships from the diagram, you can right-click the table you want to delete and select Generate Change Script to create a script that can be used to remove the foreign key relationship(s).

The other approach is to right-click the table in Object Explorer and choose View Dependencies. The dialog that appears gives you the option of viewing the objects that depend on the table or viewing the objects on which the table depends. If you choose the option to view the objects that depend on the table, all the dependent objects are displayed, but you can focus on the objects that are tables.

Using Partitioned Tables

In SQL Server 2008, tables are stored in one or more partitions. *Partitions* are organizational units that allow you to divide data into logical groups. By default, a table has only a single partition that contains all the data. The power of partitions comes into play when you define multiple partitions for a table that is segmented based on a key column. This column allows the data rows to be horizontally split. For example, a date/time column can be used to divide each month's data into a separate partition. These partitions can also be aligned to different filegroups for added flexibility, ease of maintenance, and improved performance.

The important point to remember is that you access tables with multiple partitions (which are called *partitioned tables*) the same way you access tables with a single partition. Data Manipulation Language (DML) operations such as `INSERT` and `SELECT` statements reference the table the same way, regardless of partitioning. The difference between these types of tables has to do with the back-end storage and the organization of the data.

Generally, partitioning is most useful for large tables. *Large* is a relative term, but these tables typically contain millions of rows and take up gigabytes of space. Often, the tables targeted for partitioning are large tables experiencing performance problems because of their size. Partitioning has several different applications, including the following:

- **Archival**—Table partitions can be moved from a production table to another archive table that has the same structure. When done properly, this partition movement is very fast and allows you to keep a limited amount of recent data in the production table while keeping the bulk of the older data in the archive table.
- **Maintenance**—Table partitions that have been assigned to different filegroups can be backed up and maintained independently of each other. With very large tables, maintenance activities on the entire table (such as backups) can take a prohibitively long time. With partitioned tables, these maintenance activities can be performed at the partition level. Consider, for example, a table that is partitioned by month: all the new activity (updates and insertions) occurs in the partition that contains the current month's data. In this scenario, the current month's partition would be the focus of the maintenance, thus limiting the amount of data you need to process.
- **Query performance**—Partitioned tables joined on partitioned columns can experience improved performance because the Query Optimizer can join to the table based on the partitioned column. The caveat is that joins across partitioned tables not joining on the partitioned column may actually experience some performance degradation. Queries can also be parallelized along the partitions.

Now that we have discussed some of the reasons to use partitioned tables, let's look at how to set up partitions. There are three basic steps:

1. Create a partition function that maps the rows in the table to partitions based on the value of a specified column.
2. Create a partition scheme that outlines the placement of the partitions in the partition function to filegroups.
3. Create a table that utilizes the partition scheme.

These steps are predicated on a good partitioning design, based on an evaluation of the data within the table and the selection of a column that will effectively split the data. If multiple filegroups are used, those filegroups must also exist before you execute the three steps in partitioning. The following sections look at the syntax related to each step, using simple examples. These examples utilize the `BigPubs2008` database.

Creating a Partition Function

A partition function identifies values within a table that will be compared to the column on which you partition the table. As mentioned previously, it is important that you know the distribution of the data and the specific range of values in the partitioning column before you create the partition function. The following query provides an example of determining the distribution of data values in the sales_big table by year:

```
--Select the distinct yearly values
SELECT year(ord_date) as 'year', count(*) 'rows'
 FROM sales_big
 GROUP BY year(ord_date)
 ORDER BY 1
go

year        rows
----------- -----------
       2005          30
       2006      613560
       2007      616450
       2008      457210
```

You can see from the results of the SELECT statement that there are four years' worth of data in the sales_big table. Because the values specified in the CREATE PARTITION FUNCTION statement are used to establish data ranges, at a minimum, you would need to specify at least three data values when defining the partition function, as shown in the following example:

```
--Create partition function with the yearly values to partition the data
CREATE PARTITION FUNCTION SalesBigPF1 (datetime)
   AS RANGE RIGHT FOR VALUES
   ('01/01/2006', '01/01/2007',
      '01/01/2008')
GO
```

In this example, four ranges, or partitions, would be established by the three RANGE RIGHT values specified in the statement:

- **values < 01/01/2006**—This partition includes any rows prior to 2006.
- **values >= 01/01/2006 AND values < 01/01/2007**—This partition includes all rows for 2006.
- **values >= 01/01/2007 AND values < 01/01/2008**—This partition includes all rows for 2007.
- **values > 01/01/2008**—This includes any rows for 2008 or later.

This method of partitioning would be more than adequate for a static table that is not going to be receiving any additional data rows for different years than already exist in the table. However, if the table is going to be populated with additional data rows after it has been partitioned, it is good practice to add additional range values at the beginning and end of the ranges to allow for the insertion of data values less than or greater than the existing range values in the table. To create these additional upper and lower ranges, you would want to specify five values in the VALUES clause of the CREATE PARTITION FUNCTION, as shown in Listing 24.19. The advantages of having these additional partitions are demonstrated later in this section.

LISTING 24.19 Creating a Partition Function

```
if exists (select 1 from sys.partition_functions where name = 'SalesBigPF1')
   drop partition function SalesBigPF1
go
--Create partition function with the yearly values to partition the data
Create PARTITION FUNCTION SalesBigPF1 (datetime)
   AS RANGE RIGHT FOR VALUES
   ('01/01/2005', '01/01/2006', '01/01/2007',
      '01/01/2008',  '01/01/2009')
GO
```


In this example, six ranges, or partitions, are established by the five range values specified in the statement:

- **values < 01/01/2005**—This partition includes any rows prior to 2005.
- **values >= 01/01/2005 AND values < 01/01/2006**—This partition includes all rows for 2005.
- **values >= 01/01/2006 AND values < 01/01/2007**—This partition includes all rows for 2006.
- **values >= 01/01/2007 AND values < 01/01/2008**—This partition includes all rows for 2007.
- **values >= 01/01/2008 AND values < 01/01/2009**—This partition includes all rows for 2008.
- **values >= 01/01/2009**—This partition includes any rows for 2009 or later.

An alternative to the RIGHT clause in the CREATE PARTITION FUNCTION statement is the LEFT clause. The LEFT clause is similar to RIGHT, but it changes the ranges such that the < operands are changed to <=, and the >= operands are changed to >.

TIP

Using RANGE RIGHT partitions for datetime values is usually best because this approach makes it easier to specify the limits of the ranges. The datetime data type can store values only with accuracy to 3.33 milliseconds. The largest value it can store is 0.997 milliseconds. A value of 0.998 milliseconds rounds down to 0.997, and a value of 0.999 milliseconds rounds up to the next second.

If you used a RANGE LEFT partition, the maximum time value you could include with the year to get all values for that year would be 23:59:59.997. For example, if you specified 12/31/2006 23:59:59.999 as the boundary for a RANGE LEFT partition, it would be rounded up so that it would also include rows with datetime values less than or equal to 01/01/2007 00:00:00.000, which is probably not what you would want. You would redefine the example shown in Listing 24.19 as a RANGE LEFT partition function as follows:

```
CREATE PARTITION FUNCTION SalesBigPF1 (datetime)
   AS RANGE LEFT FOR VALUES
   ('12/31/2004 23:59:59.997', '12/31/2005 23:59:59.997',
    '12/31/2006 23:59: 59.997', '12/31/2007 23:59:59.997',
    '12/31/2008 23:59:59.997')
```

As you can see, it's a bit more straightforward and probably less confusing to use RANGE RIGHT partition functions when dealing with datetime values or any other continuous-value data types, such as float or numeric.

Creating a Partition Scheme

After you create a partition function, the next step is to associate a partition scheme with the partition function. A partition scheme can be associated with only one partition function, but a partition function can be shared across multiple partition schemes.

The core function of a partition scheme is to map the values defined in the partition function to filegroups. When creating the statement for a partition scheme, you need to keep in mind the following:

- A single filegroup can be used for all partitions, or a separate filegroup can be used for each individual partition.
- Any filegroup referenced in the partition scheme must exist before the partition scheme is created.
- There must be enough filegroups referenced in the partition scheme to accommodate all the partitions. The number of partitions is one more than the number of values specified in the partition function.
- The number of partitions is limited to 1,000.
- The filegroups listed in the partition scheme are assigned to the partitions defined in the function based on the order in which the filegroups are listed.

Listing 24.20 creates a partition schema that references the partition function created in Listing 24.19. This example assumes that the referenced filegroups have been created for each of the partitions. (For more information on creating filegroups and secondary files, see Chapter 23.)

NOTE

If you would like to create the same filegroups and files used by the examples in this section, check out the script file called `Create_Filegroups_and_Files_for_Partitioning.sql` on the included CD in the code listings directory for this chapter. If you run this script, it creates all the necessary file groups and files referenced in the examples. Note that you need to edit the script to change the `FILENAME` value if you need the files to be created in a directory other than `C:\MSSQL2008\DATA`.

LISTING 24.20 Creating a Partition Scheme

```
--Create a partition scheme that is aligned with the partition function
CREATE PARTITION SCHEME SalesBigPS1
    AS PARTITION SalesBigPF1
    TO ([Older_data], [2005_data], [2006_data],
        [2007_data], [2008_data], [2009_data])
GO
```


Alternatively, if all partitions are going to be on the same filegroup, such as the PRIMARY filegroup, you could use the following:

```
Create PARTITION SCHEME SalesBigPS1
    as PARTITION SalesBigPF1
    ALL to ([PRIMARY])
go
```

Notice that `SalesBigPF1` is referenced as the partition function in Listing 24.20. This ties together the partition scheme and partition function. Figure 24.7 shows how the partitions defined in the function would be mapped to the filegroup(s). At this point, you have made no changes to any table, and you have not even specified the column in the table that you will partition. The next section discusses those details.

Creating a Partitioned Table

Tables are partitioned only when they are created. This is an important point to keep in mind when you are considering adding partitions to a table that already exists. Sometimes, performance issues or other factors may lead you to determine that a table you have already created and populated may benefit from being partitioned.

The re-creation of large tables in a production environment requires some forethought and planning. The data in the table must be retained in another location for you to re-create the table. Bulk copying the data to a flat file and renaming the table are two possible solutions for retaining the data. After you determine the data retention method, you can re-create the table, with the new partition scheme. For simplicity's sake, the example in Listing 24.21 creates a new table named `sales_big_Partitioned` instead of using the

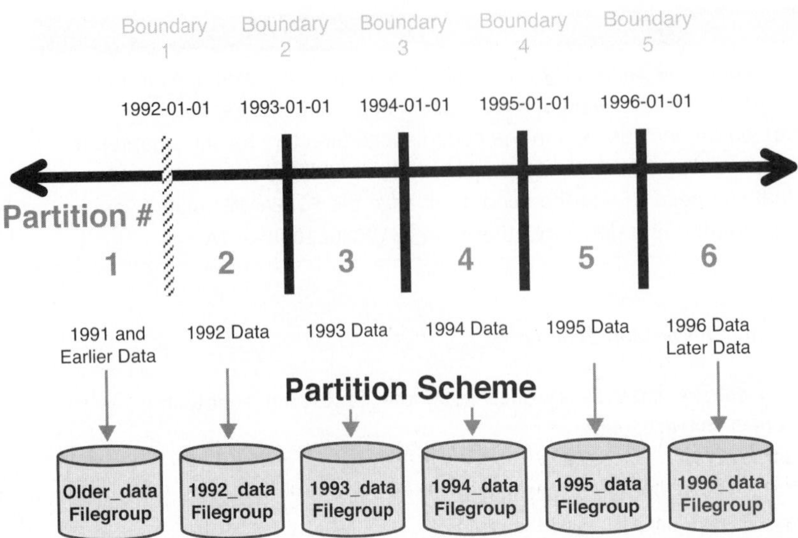

FIGURE 24.7 Mapping of partitions to filegroups, using a **RANGE RIGHT** partition function.

original sales_big table. The second part of Listing 24.21 copies the data from the sales_big table into the sales_big_Partitioned table.

LISTING 24.21 Creating a Partitioned Table

```
CREATE TABLE dbo.sales_big_Partitioned(
        sales_id int IDENTITY(1,1) NOT NULL,
        stor_id char(4) NOT NULL,
        ord_num varchar(20) NOT NULL,
        ord_date datetime NOT NULL,
        qty smallint NOT NULL,
        payterms varchar(12) NOT NULL,
        title_id dbo.tid NOT NULL
) ON SalesBigPS1 (ord_date)  --this statement is key to Partitioning the table
GO

GO

--Insert data from the sales_big table into the new sales_big_partitioned table
SET IDENTITY_INSERT sales_big_Partitioned ON
GO
INSERT sales_big_Partitioned with (TABLOCKX)
 (sales_id, stor_id, ord_num, ord_date, qty, payterms, title_id)
 SELECT sales_id, stor_id, ord_num, ord_date, qty, payterms, title_id
  FROM sales_big
```

```
go
SET IDENTITY_INSERT sales_big_Partitioned OFF
GO
```

The key clause to take note of in this listing is `ON SalesBigPS1 (ord_date)`. This clause identifies the partition scheme on which to create the table (`SalesBigPS1`) and the column within the table to use for partitioning (`ord_date`).

After you create the table, you might wonder whether the table was partitioned correctly. Fortunately, there are some catalog views related to partitions that you can query for this kind of information. Listing 24.22 shows a sample `SELECT` statement that utilizes the `sys.partitions` view. The results of the statement execution are shown immediately after the `SELECT` statement. Notice that there are six numbered partitions and that the estimated number of rows for each partition corresponds to the number of rows you saw when you selected the data from the unpartitioned `SalesBig` table.

LISTING 24.22 Viewing Partitioned Table Information

```
select convert(varchar(16), ps.name) as partition_scheme,
       p.partition_number,
       convert(varchar(10), ds2.name) as filegroup,
       convert(varchar(19), isnull(v.value, ''), 120) as range_boundary,
       str(p.rows, 9) as rows
   from sys.indexes i
   join sys.partition_schemes ps on i.data_space_id = ps.data_space_id
   join sys.destination_data_spaces dds
        on ps.data_space_id = dds.partition_scheme_id
   join sys.data_spaces ds2 on dds.data_space_id = ds2.data_space_id
   join sys.partitions p on dds.destination_id = p.partition_number
                      and p.object_id = i.object_id and p.index_id = i.index_id
   join sys.partition_functions pf on ps.function_id = pf.function_id
   LEFT JOIN sys.Partition_Range_values v on pf.function_id = v.function_id
           and v.boundary_id = p.partition_number - pf.boundary_value_on_right
   WHERE i.object_id = object_id('sales_big_partitioned')
     and i.index_id in (0, 1)
   order by p.partition_number

/* Results from the previous SELECT statement
partition_scheme partition_number filegroup  range_boundary      rows
---------------- ---------------- ---------- ------------------- ---------
SalesBigPS1                     1 Older_Data                             0
SalesBigPS1                     2 2005_Data  2005-01-01 00:00:00        30
SalesBigPS1                     3 2006_Data  2006-01-01 00:00:00    613560
SalesBigPS1                     4 2007_Data  2007-01-01 00:00:00    616450
SalesBigPS1                     5 2008_Data  2008-01-01 00:00:00    457210
SalesBigPS1                     6 2009_Data  2009-01-01 00:00:00         0
*/
```

Adding and Dropping Table Partitions

One of the most useful features of partitioned tables is that you can add and drop entire partitions of table data in bulk. If the table partitions are set up properly, these commands can take place in seconds, without the expensive input/output (I/O) costs of physically copying or moving the data. You can add and drop table partitions by using the SPLIT RANGE and MERGE RANGE options of the ALTER PARTITION FUNCTION command:

```
ALTER PARTITION FUNCTION partition_function_name()
{ SPLIT RANGE ( boundary_value ) | MERGE RANGE ( boundary_value ) }
```

Adding a Table Partition

The SPLIT RANGE option adds a new boundary point to an existing partition function and affects all objects that use this partition function. When this command is run, one of the function partitions is split in two. The new partition is the one that contains the new boundary point. The new partition is created to the right of the boundary value if the partition is defined as a RANGE RIGHT partition function or to the left of the boundary if it is a RANGE LEFT partition function. If the partition is empty, the split is instantaneous.

If the partition being split contains data, any data on the new side of the boundary is physically deleted from the old partition and inserted into the new partition. In addition to being I/O intensive, a split is also log intensive, generating log records that are four times the size of the data being moved. In addition, an exclusive table lock is held for the duration of the split. If you want to avoid this costly overhead when adding a new partition to the end of the partition range, it is recommended that you always keep an empty partition available at the end and split it before it is populated with data. If the partition is empty, SQL Server does not need to scan the partition to see whether there is any data to be moved.

NOTE

Avoiding the overhead associated with splitting a partition is the reason the code in Listing 24.19 defined the SalesBigPF1 partition function with a partition for 2009, even though there is no 2009 data in the sales_big_partitioned table. As long as you split the partition before any 2009 data is inserted into the table and the 2009 partition is empty, no data needs to be moved, so the split is instantaneous.

Before you split a partition, a filegroup must be marked to be the NEXT USED partition by the partition scheme that uses the partition function. You initially allocate filegroups to partitions by using a CREATE PARTITION SCHEME statement. If a CREATE PARTITION SCHEME statement allocates more filegroups than there are partitions defined in the CREATE PARTITION FUNCTION statement, one of the unassigned filegroups is automatically marked as NEXT USED by the partition scheme, and it will hold the new partition.

If there are no filegroups currently marked `NEXT USED` by the partition scheme, you must use `ALTER PARTITION SCHEME` to either add a filegroup or designate an existing filegroup to hold the new partition. This can be a filegroup that already holds existing partitions. Also, if a partition function is used by more than one partition scheme, all the partition schemes that use the partition function to which you are adding partitions must have a `NEXT USED` filegroup. If one or more do not have a `NEXT USED` filegroup assigned, the `ALTER PARTITION FUNCTION` statement fails, and the error message displays the partition scheme or schemes that lack a `NEXT USED` filegroup.

The following SQL statement adds a `NEXT USED` filegroup to the `SalesBigPS1` partition scheme. Note that in this example, the filegroup specified is a new filegroup, `2010_DATA`:

```
ALTER PARTITION SCHEME SalesBigPS1 NEXT USED '2010_Data'
```

Now that you have specified a `NEXT USED` filegroup for the partition scheme, you can go ahead and add the new range for 2010 and later data rows to the partition function, as in the following example:

```
--Alter partition function with the yearly values to partition the data
ALTER PARTITION FUNCTION SalesBigPF1 () SPLIT RANGE ('01/01/2010')
GO
```

Figure 24.8 shows the effects of splitting the 2009 table partition.

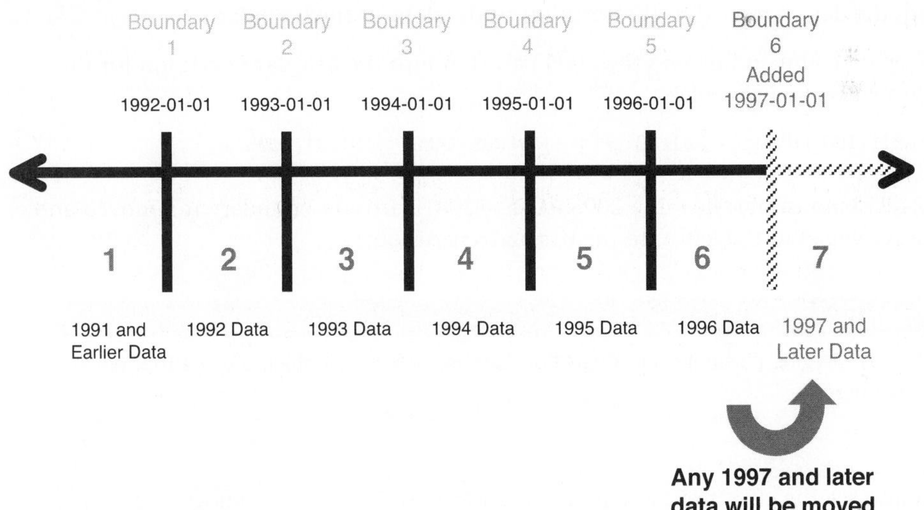

FIGURE 24.8 The effects of splitting a **RANGE RIGHT** table partition.

You can also see the effects of splitting the partition on the system catalogs by running the same query as shown earlier, in Listing 24.22:

```
/* New results from the SELECT statement in Listing 24.22
partition_scheme partition_number filegroup  range_boundary      rows
---------------- ---------------- ---------- ------------------- ---------
SalesBigPS1                     1 Older_Data                             0
SalesBigPS1                     2 2005_Data  2005-01-01 00:00:00        30
SalesBigPS1                     3 2006_Data  2006-01-01 00:00:00    613560
SalesBigPS1                     4 2007_Data  2007-01-01 00:00:00    616450
SalesBigPS1                     5 2008_Data  2008-01-01 00:00:00    457210
SalesBigPS1                     6 2009_Data  2009-01-01 00:00:00         0
SalesBigPS1                     7 2010_Data  2010-01-01 00:00:00         0
*/
```

Dropping a Table Partition

You can drop a table partition by using the `ALTER PARTITION FUNCTION ... MERGE RANGE` command. This command essentially removes a boundary point from a partition function as the partitions on each side of the boundary are merged into one. The partition that held the boundary value is removed. The filegroup that originally held the boundary value is removed from the partition scheme unless it is used by a remaining partition or is marked with the `NEXT USED` property.

Any data that was in the removed partition is moved to the remaining neighboring partition. If a `RANGE RIGHT` partition boundary was removed, the data that was in that boundary's partition is moved to the partition to the left of boundary. If it was a `RANGE LEFT` partition, the data is moved to the partition to the right of the boundary.

The following command merges the 2005 partition into the `Old_Data` partition for the `sales_big_partitioned` table:

```
ALTER PARTITION FUNCTION SalesBigPF1 () MERGE RANGE ('01/01/2005')
```

Figure 24.9 demonstrates how the 2005 `RANGE RIGHT` partition boundary is removed and the data is merged to the left, into the `Old_Data` partition.

CAUTION

Splitting or merging partitions for a partition function affects all objects using that partition function.

You can also see the effects of merging the partition on the system catalogs by running the same query as shown in Listing 24.22:

```
/* New results from the SELECT statement in Listing 24.20
partition_scheme partition_number filegroup  range_boundary      rows
---------------- ---------------- ---------- ------------------- ---------
SalesBigPS1                     1 Older_Data                            30
SalesBigPS1                     3 2006_Data  2006-01-01 00:00:00    613560
```

```
SalesBigPS1                    4 2007_Data  2007-01-01 00:00:00    616450
SalesBigPS1                    5 2008_Data  2008-01-01 00:00:00    457210
SalesBigPS1                    6 2009_Data  2009-01-01 00:00:00         0
SalesBigPS1                    7 2010_Data  2010-01-01 00:00:00         0
*/
```

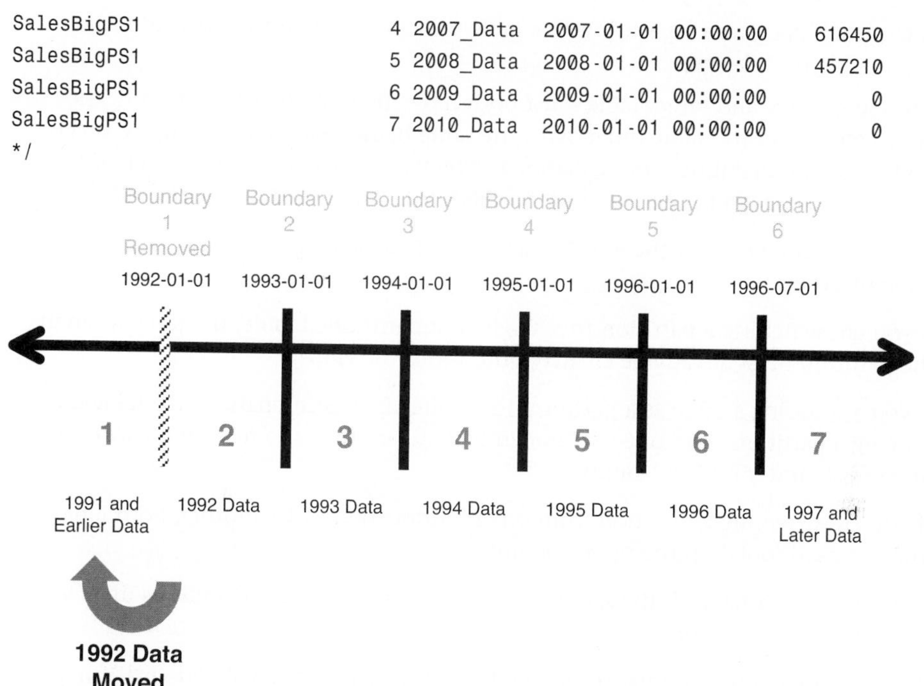

FIGURE 24.9 The effects of merging a **RANGE RIGHT** table partition.

Like the split operation, the merge operation occurs instantaneously if the partition being merged is empty. The process can be very I/O intensive if the partition has a large amount of data in it. Any rows in the removed partition are physically moved into the remaining partition. This operation is also very log intensive, requiring log space approximately four times the size of data being moved. An exclusive table lock is held for the duration of the merge.

If you no longer want to keep the data in the table for a partition you are merging, you can move the data in the partition to another empty table or empty table partition by using the `SWITCH PARTITION` option of the `ALTER TABLE` command. This option is discussed in more detail in the following section.

Switching Table Partitions

One of the great features of table partitions is that they enable you to instantly swap the contents of one partition to an empty table, the contents from a partition on one table to a partition in another table, or an entire table's contents into another table's empty partition. This operation performs changes only to metadata in the system catalogs for the affected tables/partitions, with no actual physical movement of data.

For you to switch data from a partition to a table or from a table into a partition, the following criteria must be met:

- The source table and target table must both have the same structure (that is, the same columns in the same order, with the same names, data types, lengths, precisions, scales, nullabilities, and collations). The tables must also have the same primary key constraints and settings for `ANSI_NULLS` and `QUOTED_IDENTIFIER`.
- The source and target of the `ALTER TABLE...SWITCH` statement must reside in the same filegroup.
- If you are switching a partition to a single, nonpartitioned table, the table receiving the partition must already be created, and it must be empty.
- If you are adding a table as a partition to an already existing partitioned table or moving a partition from one partitioned table to another, the receiving partition must exist, and it must be empty.
- If you are switching a partition from one partitioned table to another, both tables must be partitioned on the same column.
- The source must have all the same indexes as the target, and the indexes must also be in the same filegroup.
- If you are switching a nonpartitioned table to a partition of an already existing partitioned table, the nonpartitioned table must have a constraint defined on the column corresponding to the partition key of the target table to ensure that the range of values fits within the boundary values of the target partition.
- If the target table has any `FOREIGN KEY` constraints, the source table must have the same foreign keys defined on the corresponding columns, and those foreign keys must reference the same primary keys that the target table references.

If you are switching a partition of a partitioned table to another partitioned table, the boundary values of the source partition must fit within those of the target partition. If the boundary values do not fit, a constraint must be defined on the partition key of the source table to make sure all the data in the table fits into the boundary values of the target partition.

CAUTION

If the tables have `IDENTITY` columns, partition switching can result in the introduction of duplicate values in `IDENTITY` columns of the target table and gaps in the values of `IDENTITY` columns in the source table. You can use `DBCC_CHECKIDENT` to check the identity values of tables and correct them if necessary.

When you switch a partition, data is not physically moved. Only the metadata information in the system catalogs indicating where the data is stored is changed. In addition, all associated indexes are automatically switched, along with the table or partition.

To switch table partitions, you use the ALTER TABLE command:

```
ALTER TABLE table_name SWITCH [ PARTITION source_partition_number_expression ]
   TO target_table [ PARTITION target_partition_number_expression ]
```

You can use the ALTER TABLE...SWITCH command to switch an unpartitioned table into a table partition, switch a table partition into an empty unpartitioned table, or switch a table partition into another table's empty table partition. The code shown in Listing 24.23 creates a table to hold the data from the 2006 partition and then switches the 2006 partition from the sales_big_partitioned table to the new table.

LISTING 24.23 Switching a Partition to an Empty Table

```
CREATE TABLE dbo.sales_big_2006(
        sales_id int IDENTITY(1,1) NOT NULL,
        stor_id char(4) NOT NULL,
        ord_num varchar(20) NOT NULL,
        ord_date datetime NOT NULL,
        qty smallint NOT NULL,
        payterms varchar(12) NOT NULL,
        title_id dbo.tid NOT NULL
) ON '2006_data'  -- required in order to switch the partition to this table
go
alter table sales_big_partitioned
    switch partition $PARTITION.SalesBigPF1 ('1/1/2006')
    to sales_big_2006
go
```


Note that Listing 24.23 uses the $PARTITION function. You can use this function with any partition function name to return the partition number that corresponds with the specified partitioning column value. This prevents you from having to query the system catalogs to determine the specific partition number for the specified partition value.

You can run the query from Listing 24.22 to show that the 2006 partition is now empty:

```
partition_scheme partition_number filegroup  range_boundary      rows
---------------- ---------------- ---------- ------------------- ---------
SalesBigPS1                     1 Older_Data                            30
SalesBigPS1                     2 2006_Data  2006-01-01 00:00:00         0
SalesBigPS1                     3 2007_Data  2007-01-01 00:00:00    616450
SalesBigPS1                     4 2008_Data  2008-01-01 00:00:00    457210
SalesBigPS1                     5 2009_Data  2009-01-01 00:00:00         0
SalesBigPS1                     6 2010_Data  2010-01-01 00:00:00         0
```

Now that the 2006 data partition is empty, you can merge the partition without incurring the I/O cost of moving the data to the Older_data partition:

```
ALTER PARTITION FUNCTION SalesBigPF1 () merge RANGE ('1/1/2006')
```

Rerunning the query in Listing 24.22 now returns the following result set:

```
partition_scheme partition_number filegroup  range_boundary      rows
---------------- ---------------- ---------  ------------------- ---------
SalesBigPS1                     1 Older_Data                            30
SalesBigPS1                     2 2007_Data  2007-01-01 00:00:00    616450
SalesBigPS1                     3 2008_Data  2008-01-01 00:00:00    457210
SalesBigPS1                     4 2009_Data  2009-01-01 00:00:00         0
SalesBigPS1                     5 2010_Data  2010-01-01 00:00:00         0
```

To demonstrate switching a table into a partition, you can update the date for all the rows in the sales_big_2006 table to 2009 and switch it into the 2009 partition of the sales_big_partitioned table. Note that before you can do this, you need to copy the data to a table in the 2009_data filegroup and also put a check constraint on the ord_date column to make sure all rows in the table are limited to values that are valid for the 2009_data partition. Listing 24.24 shows the commands you use to create the new table and switch it into the 2009 partition of the sales_big_partitioned table.

LISTING 24.24 Switching a Table to an Empty Partition

```
CREATE TABLE dbo.sales_big_2009(
        sales_id int IDENTITY(1,1) NOT NULL,
        stor_id char(4)  NOT NULL,
        ord_num varchar(20)  NOT NULL,
        ord_date datetime NOT NULL
         constraint CK_sales_big_2009_ord_date
            check (ord_date >= '1/1/2009' and ord_date < '1/1/2010'),
        qty smallint NOT NULL,
        payterms varchar(12)  NOT NULL,
        title_id dbo.tid NOT NULL
) ON '2009_data'  -- required to switch the table to the 2009 partition
go
set identity_insert sales_big_2009 on
go
insert sales_big_2009 (sales_id, stor_id, ord_num,
                       ord_date, qty, payterms, title_id)
   select sales_id, stor_id, ord_num,
          dateadd(yy, 3, ord_date),
          qty, payterms, title_id
      from sales_big_2006
go
set identity_insert sales_big_2009 off
```

```
go
alter table sales_big_2009
  switch to sales_big_partitioned
  partition $PARTITION.SalesBigPF1 ('1/1/2009')
go
```

Rerunning the query from Listing 24.22 now returns the following result:

```
partition_scheme partition_number filegroup  range_boundary      rows
---------------- ---------------- ---------  ------------------- ---------
SalesBigPS1                     1 Older_Data                            30
SalesBigPS1                     2 2007_Data  2007-01-01 00:00:00    616450
SalesBigPS1                     3 2008_Data  2008-01-01 00:00:00    457210
SalesBigPS1                     4 2009_Data  2009-01-01 00:00:00    613560
SalesBigPS1                     5 2010_Data  2010-01-01 00:00:00         0
```


TIP

Switching data into or out of partitions provides a very efficient mechanism for archiving old data from a production table, importing new data into a production table, or migrating data to an archive table. You can use `SWITCH` to empty or fill partitions very quickly. As you've seen in this section, split and merge operations occur instantaneously if the partitions being split or merged are empty first. If you must split or merge partitions that contain a lot of data, you should empty them first by using `SWITCH` before you perform the split or merge.

Creating Temporary Tables

A *temporary table* is a special type of table that is automatically deleted when it is no longer used. Temporary tables have many of the same characteristics as permanent tables and are typically used as work tables that contain intermediate results.

You designate a table as temporary in SQL Server by prefacing the table name with a single pound sign (#) or two pound signs (##). Temporary tables are created in `tempdb`; if a temporary table is not explicitly dropped, it is dropped when the session that created it ends or the stored procedure it was created in finishes execution.

If a table name is prefaced with a single pound sign (for example, `#table1`), it is a *private* temporary table, available only to the session that created it.

A table name prefixed with a double pound sign (for example, `##table2`) indicates that it is a *global* temporary table, which means it is accessible by all database connections. A global temporary table exists until the session that created it terminates. If the creating session terminates while other sessions are accessing the table, the temporary table is available to those sessions until the last session's query ends, at which time the table is dropped.

A common way of creating a temporary table is to use the SELECT INTO method as shown in the following example:

```
SELECT* INTO #Employee2 FROM Employee
```

This method creates a temporary table with a structure like the table that is being selected from. It also copies the data from the original table and inserts it into this new temporary table. All of this is done with this one simple command.

NOTE

Table variables are a good alternative to temporary tables. These variables are also temporary in nature and have some advantages over temporary tables. Table variables are easy to create, are automatically deleted, cause fewer recompilations, and use fewer locking and logging resources. Generally speaking, you should consider using table variables instead of temporary tables when the temporary results are relatively small. Parallel query plans are not generated with table variables, and this can impede overall performance when you are accessing a table variable that has a large number of rows.

For more information on using temporary tables and table variables, see Chapter 43, "Transact-SQL Programming Guidelines, Tips, and Tricks," that is found on the bonus CD.

Tables created without the # prefix but explicitly created in tempdb are also considered temporary, but they are a more permanent form of a temporary table. They are not dropped automatically until SQL Server is restarted and tempdb is reinitialized.

Summary

Tables are the key to a relational database system. When you create tables, you need to pay careful attention to choosing the proper data types to ensure efficient storage of data, adding appropriate constraints to maintain data integrity, and scripting the creation and modification of tables to ensure that they can be re-created, if necessary.

Good table design includes the creation of indexes on a table. Tables without indexes are generally inefficient and cause excessive use of resources on your database server. Chapter 25, "Creating and Managing Indexes," covers indexes and their critical role in effective table design.

CHAPTER 25

Creating and Managing Indexes

IN THIS CHAPTER

- What's New in Creating and Managing Indexes
- Types of Indexes
- Creating Indexes
- Managing Indexes
- Dropping Indexes
- Online Indexing Operations
- Indexes on Views

Just like the index in this book, an index on a table or view allows you to efficiently find the information you are looking for in a database. SQL Server does not require indexes to be able to retrieve data from tables because it can perform a full table scan to retrieve a result set. However, doing a table scan is analogous to scanning every page in this book to find a word or reference you are looking for.

This chapter introduces the different types of indexes available in SQL Server 2008 to keep your database access efficient. It focuses on creating and managing indexes by using the tools Microsoft SQL Server 2008 provides. For a more in-depth discussion of the internal structures of indexes and designing and managing indexes for optimal performance, see Chapter 34, "Data Structures, Indexes, and Performance."

What's New in Creating and Managing Indexes

The creation and management of indexes are among the most important performance activities in SQL Server. You will find that indexes and the tools to manage them in SQL Server 2008 are very similar to those in SQL Server 2005. New to SQL Server 2008 is the capability to compress indexes and tables to reduce the amount of storage needed for these objects. This new data compression feature is discussed in detail in Chapter 34.

Also new to SQL Server 2008 are filtered indexes. Filtered indexes utilize a `WHERE` clause that filters or limits the number of rows included in the index. The smaller filtered index allows queries that are run against rows in the index to run faster. These can also save on the disk space used by the index.

Spatial indexes also are new to SQL Server 2008. These indexes are used against spatial data defined by coordinates of latitude and longitude. The spatial data is essential for efficient global navigation. The Spatial indexes are grid based and help optimize the performance of searches against the Spatial data. Spatial indexes are also discussed in more detail in Chapter 34.

Types of Indexes

SQL Server has two main types of indexes: clustered and nonclustered. They both help the query engine get at data faster, but they have different effects on the storage of the underlying data. The following sections describe these two main types of indexes and provide some insight into when to use each type.

Clustered Indexes

Clustered indexes sort and store the data rows for a table, based on the columns defined in the index. For example, if you were to create a clustered index on the `LastName` and `FirstName` columns in a table, the data rows for that table would be organized or sorted according to these two columns. This has some obvious advantages for data retrieval. Queries that search for data based on the clustered index keys have a sequential path to the underlying data, which helps reduce I/O.

A clustered index is analogous to a filing cabinet where each drawer contains a set of file folders stored in alphabetical order, and each file folder stores the files in alphabetical order. Each file drawer contains a label that indicates which folders it contains (for example, folders A–D). To locate a specific file, you first locate the drawer containing the appropriate file folders, then locate the appropriate file folder within the drawer, and then scan the files in that folder in sequence until you find the one you need.

A clustered index is structured as a balanced tree (B-tree). Figure 25.1 shows a simplified diagram of a clustered index defined on a last name column.

The top, or root, node is a single page where searches via the clustered index are started. The bottom level of the index is the leaf nodes. With a clustered index, the leaf nodes of the index are also the data pages of the table. Any levels of the index between the root and leaf nodes are referred to as *intermediate nodes*. All index key values are stored in the clustered index levels in sorted order. To locate a data row via a clustered index, SQL Server starts at the root node and navigates through the appropriate index pages in the intermediate levels of the index until it reaches the data page that should contain the desired data row(s). It then scans the rows on the data page until it locates the desired value.

There can be only one clustered index per table. This restriction is driven by the fact that the underlying data rows can be sorted and stored in only one way. With very few exceptions, every table in a database should have a clustered index. The selection of columns

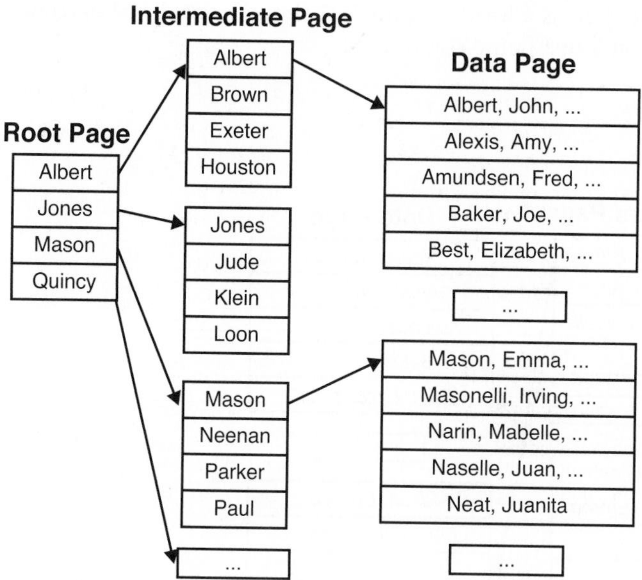

FIGURE 25.1 A simplified diagram of a clustered index.

for a clustered index is very important and should be driven by the way the data is most commonly accessed in the table. You should consider using the following types of columns in a clustered index:

- Those that are often accessed sequentially
- Those that contain a large number of distinct values
- Those that are used in range queries that use operators such as `BETWEEN`, >, >=, <, or <= in the `WHERE` clause
- Those that are frequently used by queries to join or group the result set

When you are using these criteria, it is important to focus on the most critical data access: the queries that are run most often or that must have the best performance. This approach can be challenging but ultimately reduces the number of data pages and related I/O for the queries that matter.

Nonclustered Indexes

A nonclustered index is a separate index structure, independent of the physical sort order of the data rows in the table. You are therefore not restricted to creating only 1 nonclustered index per table; in fact, in SQL Server 2008 you can create up to 999 nonclustered indexes per table. This is an increase from SQL Server 2005, which was limited to 249.

A nonclustered index is analogous to an index in the back of a book. To find the pages on which a specific subject is discussed, you look up the subject in the index and then go to the pages referenced in the index. With nonclustered indexes, you may have to jump around to many different nonsequential pages to find all the references.

A nonclustered index is also structured as a B-tree. Figure 25.2 shows a simplified diagram of a nonclustered index defined on a first name column.

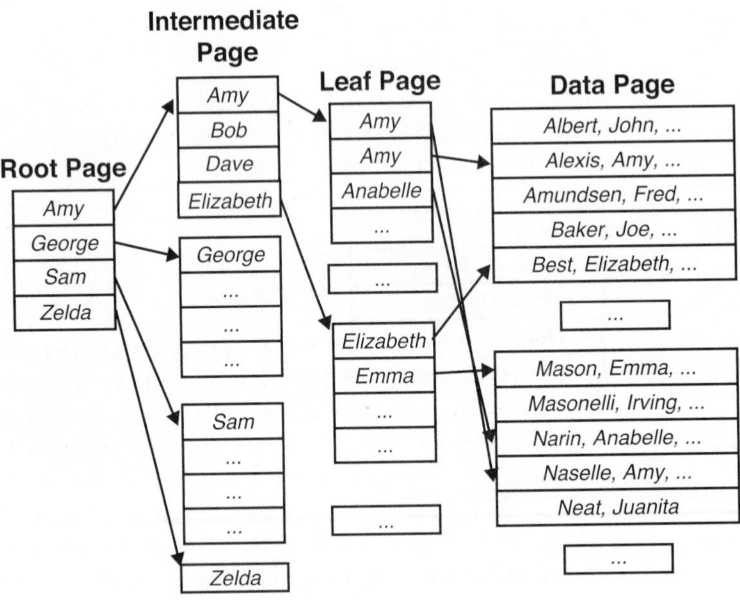

FIGURE 25.2 A simplified diagram of a nonclustered index.

As with a clustered index, in a nonclustered index, all index key values are stored in the nonclustered index levels in sorted order, based on the index key(s). This sort order is typically different from the sort order of the table itself. The main difference between a nonclustered index and clustered index is that the leaf row of a nonclustered index is independent of the data rows in the table. The leaf level of a nonclustered index contains a row for every data row in the table, along with a pointer to locate the data row. This pointer is either the clustered index key for the data row, if the table has a clustered index on it, or the data page ID and row ID of the data row if the table is stored as a heap structure (that is, if the table has no clustered index defined on it).

To locate a data row via a nonclustered index, SQL Server starts at the root node and navigates through the appropriate index pages in the intermediate levels of the index until it reaches the leaf page, which should contain the index key for the desired data row. It then scans the keys on the leaf page until it locates the desired index key value. SQL Server then uses the pointer to the data row stored with the index key to retrieve the corresponding data row.

NOTE

For a more detailed discussion of clustered tables versus heap tables (that is, tables with no clustered indexes) and more detailed descriptions of clustered and nonclustered index key structures and index key rows, as well as how SQL Server internally maintains indexes, see Chapter 34.

The efficiency of the index lookup and the types of lookups should drive the selection of nonclustered indexes. In the book index example, a single page reference is a very simple lookup for the book reader and requires little work. If, however, many pages are referenced in the index, and those pages are spread throughout the book, the lookup is no longer simple, and much more work is required to get all the information.

You should choose your nonclustered indexes with the book index example in mind. You should consider using nonclustered indexes for the following:

- Queries that do not return large result sets
- Columns that are frequently used in the WHERE clause that return exact matches
- Columns that have many distinct values (that is, high cardinality)
- All columns referenced in a critical query (a special nonclustered index called a *covering index* that eliminates the need to go to the underlying data pages)

Having a good understanding of your data access is essential to creating nonclustered indexes. Fortunately, SQL Server comes with tools such as the SQL Server Profiler and Database Engine Tuning Advisor that can help you evaluate your data access paths and determine which columns are the best candidates. SQL Profiler is discussed in more detail in Chapter 6, "SQL Server Profiler." In addition, Chapter 34 discusses the use of the SQL Server Profiler and Database Engine Tuning Advisor to assist in developing an optimal indexing strategy.

Creating Indexes

The following sections examine the most common means for creating indexes in SQL Server. Microsoft provides several different methods for creating indexes, each of which has advantages. The method used is often a matter of personal preference, but there are situations in which a given method has distinct advantages.

Creating Indexes with T-SQL

Transact-SQL (T-SQL) is the most fundamental means for creating an index. This method was available in all previous versions of SQL Server. It is a very powerful option for creating indexes because the T-SQL statements that create indexes can be stored in a file and run as part of a database installation or upgrade. In addition, T-SQL scripts that were used in prior SQL Server versions to create indexes can be reused with very little change.

You can create indexes by using the T-SQL `CREATE INDEX` command. Listing 25.1 shows the basic `CREATE INDEX` syntax. Refer to SQL Server 2008 Books Online for the full syntax.

LISTING 25.1 **CREATE INDEX** Syntax

```
CREATE [ UNIQUE ] [ CLUSTERED | NONCLUSTERED ] INDEX index_name
    ON <object> ( column [ ASC | DESC ] [ ,...n ] )
    [ INCLUDE ( column_name [ ,...n ] ) ]
    [ WHERE <filter_predicate> ]
    [ WITH ( <relational_index_option> [ ,...n ] ) ]
```

Table 25.1 lists the `CREATE INDEX` arguments.

TABLE 25.1 Arguments for **CREATE INDEX**

Argument	Explanation
`UNIQUE`	Indicates that no two rows in the index can have the same index key values. Inserts into a table with a `UNIQUE` index will fail if a row with the same value already exists in the table.
`CLUSTERED | NON-CLUSTERED`	Defines the index as clustered or nonclustered. `NON-CLUSTERED` is the default. Only one clustered index is allowed per table.
index_name	Specifies the name of the index to be created.
object	Specifies the name of the table or view to be indexed.
column_name	Specifies the column or columns that are to be indexed.
`ASC | DESC`	Specifies the sort direction for the particular index column. `ASC` creates an ascending sort order and is the default. The `DESC` option causes the index to be created in descending order.
`INCLUDE (`*column [,... n]* `)`	Allows a column to be added to the leaf level of an index without being part of the index key. This is a new argument.

TABLE 25.1 Arguments for **CREATE INDEX**

Argument	Explanation
WHERE <filter_predicate>	This argument, new to SQL Server 2008, is used to create a filtered index. The filter_predicate contains a WHERE clause that limits the number of rows in the table that are included in the index.
relational_index_option	Specifies the index option to use when creating the index.

Following is a simple example using the basic syntax of the CREATE INDEX command:

```
CREATE NONCLUSTERED INDEX [NC_Person_LastName]
ON [Person].[Person]
(
[LastName] ASC
)
```

This example creates a nonclustered index on the person.person table, based on the LastName column. The NONCLUSTERED and ASC keywords are not necessary because they are the defaults. Because the UNIQUE keyword is not specified, duplicates are allowed in the index (that is, multiple rows in the table can have the same LastName).

Unique indexes are more involved because they serve two roles: they provide fast access to the data via the index's columns, but they also serve as a constraint by allowing only one row to exist on a table for the combination of column values in the index. They can be clustered or nonclustered. Unique indexes are also defined on a table whenever you define a unique or primary key constraint on a table. The following example shows the creation of a nonclustered unique index:

```
CREATE UNIQUE NONCLUSTERED INDEX [AK_CreditCard_CardNumber]


ON [Sales].[CreditCard]
(
        [CardNumber] ASC
)
```

This example creates a nonclustered index named AK_CreditCard_CardNumber on the Sales.CreditCard table. This index is based on a single column in the table. When it is created, this index prevents credit card rows with the same credit card number from being inserted into the CreditCard table.

25

The relational index options listed in Table 25.2 allow you to define more sophisticated indexes or specify how an index is to be created.

TABLE 25.2 Relational Index Options for **CREATE INDEX**

Argument	Explanation
`PAD_INDEX = {ON | OFF}`	Determines whether free space is allocated to the non-leaf-level pages of an index. The percentage of free space is determined by `FILLFACTOR`.
`FILLFACTOR =` *`fillfactor`*	Determines the amount of free space left in the leaf level of each index page. The *`fillfactor`* *values represent a percentage, from* `0` to `100`. The default value is `0`. If *`fillfactor`* *is* `0` or `100`, the index leaf-level pages are filled to capacity, leaving only enough space for at least one more row to be inserted.
`SORT_IN_TEMPDB = {ON | OFF}`	Specifies whether intermediate sort results that are used to create the index are stored in `tempdb`. Using them can speed up the creation of the index (if `tempdb` is on a separate disk), but it requires more disk space.
`IGNORE_DUP_KEY = {ON | OFF}`	Determines whether multirow inserts will fail when duplicate rows in the insert violate a unique index. When this option is set to `ON`, duplicate key values are ignored, and the rest of the multirow insert succeeds. When it is `OFF` (the default), the entire multirow insertfails if a duplicate is encountered.
`STATISTICS_NO_RECOMPUTE = {ON | OFF}`	Determines whether distribution statistics used by the Query Optimizer are recomputed. When `ON`, the statistics are not automatically recomputed.
`DROP_EXISTING = {ON | OFF}`	Determines whether an index with the same name is dropped prior to re-creation. This can provide some performance benefits over dropping the existing index first and then creating. Clustered indexes see the most benefit.
`ONLINE = {ON | OFF}`	Determines whether the index is built such that the underlying table is still available for queries and data modification during the index creation. This new feature is discussed in more detail in the "Online Indexing Operations" section, later in this chapter.

TABLE 25.2 Relational Index Options for **CREATE INDEX**

Argument	Explanation
ALLOW_ROW_LOCKS = {ON | OFF}	Determines whether row locks are allowed when accessing the index. The default for this new feature is ON.
ALLOW_PAGE_LOCKS = {ON | OFF}	Determines whether page locks are allowed when accessing the index. The default for this new feature is ON.
MAXDOP = *number of processors*	Determines the number of processors that can be used during index operations. The default for this new feature is 0, which causes an index operation to use the actual number of processors or fewer, depending on the workload on the system. This can be a useful option for index operations on large tables that may impact performance during the operation. For example, if you have four processors, you can specify MAXDOP = 2 to limit the index operation to use only two of the four processors.
DATA_COMPRESSION = { NONE | ROW | PAGE} [ON PARTITIONS ({ <partition_number_expression> | <range> } [, ...n])	Determines whether data compression is used on the specified index. The compression can be done on the row or page level and specific index partitions can be compressed if the index uses partitioning.

The following example creates a more complex index that utilizes several of the index options described in Table 25.2:

```
CREATE NONCLUSTERED INDEX [
IX_Person_LastName_FirstName_MiddleName] ON [Person].[Person]
(
   [LastName] ASC,
   [FirstName] ASC,
   [MiddleName] ASC
  )WITH (SORT_IN_TEMPDB = OFF, IGNORE_DUP_KEY = OFF, DROP_EXISTING = OFF, FILLFAC-
TOR=80)
```

This example creates a nonclustered composite index on the person's last name (LastName), first name (FirstName), and middle name (MiddleName). It utilizes some of the commonly used options and demonstrates how multiple options can be used in a single CREATE statement.

TIP

SQL Server Management Studio (SSMS) has several methods for generating the T-SQL code that creates indexes. You therefore rarely need to type index `CREATE` statements from scratch. Instead, you can use the friendly GUI screens that enable you to specify the common index options, and then you can generate the T-SQL script that can be executed to create the index.

Additional syntax options (not listed here) relate to backward compatibility and the creation of indexes on XML columns. Refer to Chapter 47, "Using XML in SQL Server 2008," and the SQL Server Books Online documentation for further details.

Creating Indexes with SSMS

SQL Server 2008 has many options for creating indexes within SSMS. You can create indexes within SSMS via the Database Engine Tuning Advisor, database diagrams, the Table Designer, and several places within the Object Explorer. The means available from the Object Explorer are the simplest to use and are the focus of this section. The other options are discussed in more detail in related chapters of this book.

Index creation in the Object Explorer is facilitated by the New Index screen. You can launch this screen from SMSS by expanding the database tree in the Object Explorer and navigating to the `Indexes` node of the table that you want to add the index to. Then you right-click the `Indexes` node and select New Index. A screen like the one shown in Figure 25.3 is displayed.

The name and options that are populated in Figure 25.3 are based on the person index created in the previous T-SQL section. The `LastName`, `FirstName`, and `MiddleName` columns were selected and added as part of this new index by clicking the Add button, which displays a screen with all the columns in the table that are available for the index. You simply select the column(s) you want to include on the index. This populates the Index Key Columns grid on the default General page.

You can select other options for an index by changing the Select a Page options available on the top-left side of the New Index screen. The Options, Included Columns, Storage, Spatial, and Filter pages each provide a series of options that relate to the corresponding category and are utilized when creating the index.

Of particular interest is the Included Columns page. This page allows you to select columns that you want to include in the leaf-level pages of the index but don't need as part of the index key. For example, you could consider using included columns if you have a critical query that often selects last name, first name, and address from a table but uses only the last name and first name as search arguments in the `WHERE` clause. This may be a situation in which you would want to consider the use of a covering index that places all the referenced columns from the query into a nonclustered index. In the case of our critical query, the address column can be added to the index as an included column. It is not included in the index key, but it is available in the leaf-level pages of the index so that the additional overhead of going to the data pages to retrieve the address is not needed.

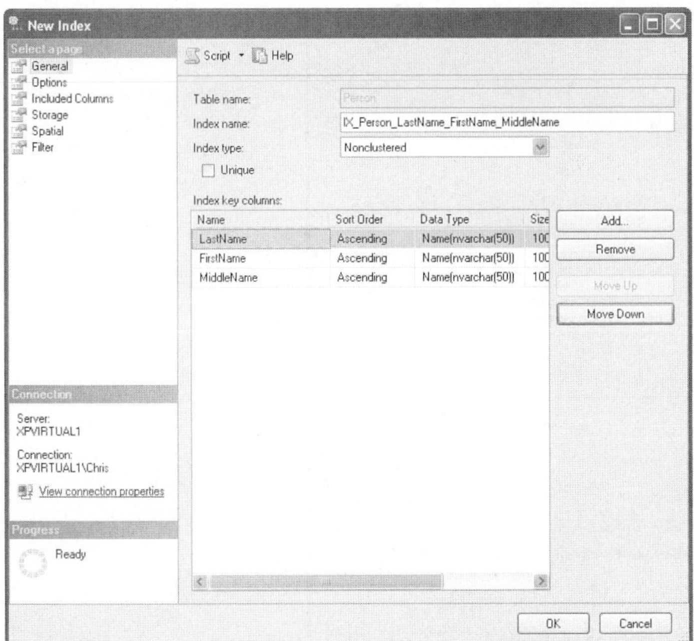

FIGURE 25.3 Using Object Explorer to create indexes.

The Spatial and Filter option pages are new to SQL Server 2008. The Spatial page can be used to create spatial indexes on a column that is defined as a spatial data type; that is either type `geometry` or `geography`. If your table contains a column of this data type, you can use the Index Type drop-down to change the index type to Spatial. After this is done, you can add a column that is defined as a spatial data type to the index. Finally, you can select the Spatial option page, as shown in Figure 25.4, that allows you to fully define a spatial index. The meaning of the parameters on this page are beyond the scope of this chapter and are discussed in more detail in Chapter 34.

The Filter option page allows you to define a filtering criterion to limit the rows that are included in the index. The page, shown in Figure 25.5, is relatively simple with a single input area that contains your filtering criterion. This criterion is basically the contents of a `WHERE` clause that is similar to what you would use in a query window to filter the rows in your result. The filter expression shown in Figure 25.5 was defined for an index on the `PersonType` column, which is found in the `Person.Person` table of the `AdventureWorks2008` sample database. Many of the rows in this table have a `PersonType` value equal to `'IN'` so a filtered index that does not include rows with this value will dramatically reduce the size of the index and make searches on values other than `'IN'` relatively fast.

After selecting all the options you want for your index via the New Index screen, you have several options for actually creating the index. You can script the index, schedule the index creation for a later time, or simply click OK to allow the New Index screen to add the index immediately. As mentioned earlier, it is a good idea to use this New Index

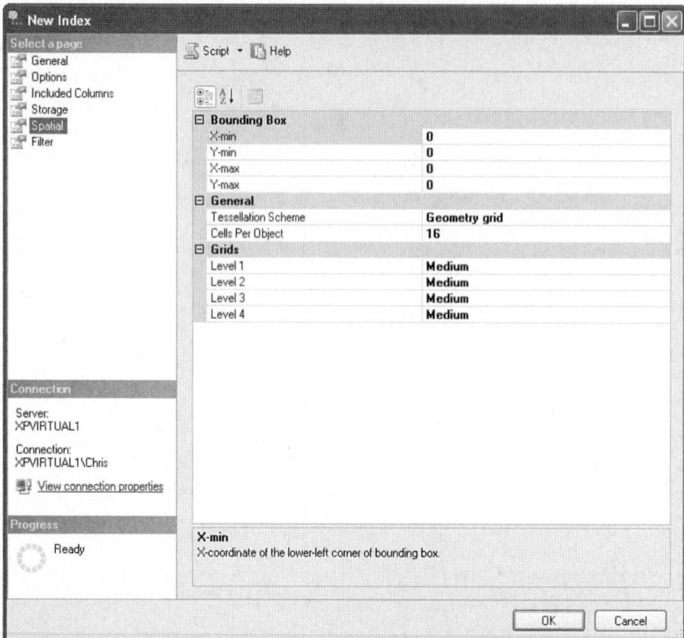

FIGURE 25.4 Spatial Index options page.

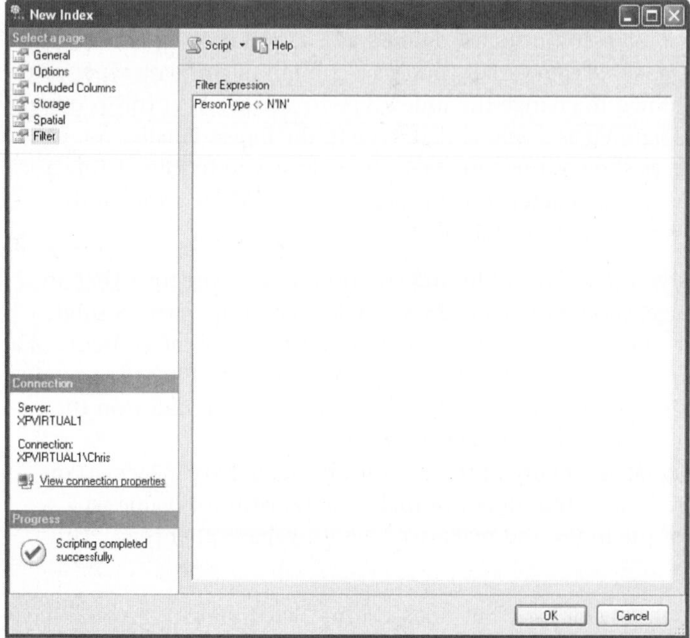

FIGURE 25.5 Filter Index options page.

screen to specify the index options, and then you can click the Script button to generate all the T-SQL statements needed to create the index. You can then save this script to a file to be used for generating a database build script or for maintaining a record of the indexes defined in a database.

Managing Indexes

There are two different aspects to index management. The first aspect is the management of indexes by the SQL Server database engine. Fortunately, the engine does a good job of managing the indexes internally so that limited manual intervention is required. This is predicated on a well-designed database system and the use of SQL Server features, such as automatic updates to distribution statistics.

The other aspect of index management typically comes into play when performance issues arise. Index adjustments and maintenance of these indexes make up the bulk of this effort.

Managing Indexes with T-SQL

One of the T-SQL features available with SQL Server 2008 is the ALTER INDEX statement. This statement simplifies many of the tasks associated with managing indexes. Index operations such as index rebuilds and changes to fill factor that were previously handled with DBCC commands are now available via the ALTER INDEX statement. The basic syntax for ALTER INDEX is as follows:

```
ALTER INDEX {index_name | ALL}
   ON [{database_name.[schema_name]. | schema_name.}]
     {table_or_view_name}
   { REBUILD [WITH(<rebuild_index_option>[,...n])]
   | REORGANIZE [ WITH( LOB_COMPACTION = {ON | OFF})]
   | DISABLE
   | SET (<set_index_option>[,...n]) }
```

Let's look at a few examples that demonstrate the power of the ALTER INDEX statement. The first example simply rebuilds the primary key index on the Production.Product table:

```
ALTER INDEX [PK_Product_ProductID] ON [Production].[Product] REBUILD
```

This offline operation is equivalent to the DBCC DBREINDEX command. The specified index is dropped and re-created, removing all fragmentation from the index pages. This is done dynamically, without the need to drop and re-create constraints that reference any of the affected indexes. If it is run on a clustered index, the data pages of the table are defragmented as well. If you specify the ALL option for the ALTER INDEX command, all indexes as well as the data pages of the table (if the table has a clustered index) are defragmented.

NOTE

If the REBUILD option is run on a heap table (that is, a table with no clustered index), the rebuild operation does not affect the underlying table. Only the specified nonclustered indexes are rebuilt.

For added flexibility, you can also specify index options as part of the REBUILD operation. The options available with the REBUILD command are the same options available when you are creating indexes. The only exception is that the DROP EXISTING option is not available with the REBUILD operation. (Table 25.2, earlier in this chapter, provides detailed descriptions of the options.) The following example rebuilds the clustered index on the Production.Product table and specifies several of the available REBUILD options:

```
ALTER INDEX [PK_Product_ProductID]
 ON [
Production].[Product] REBUILD WITH ( PAD_INDEX  = OFF,
  STATISTICS_NORECOMPUTE = OFF,
ALLOW_ROW_LOCKS = ON,
  ALLOW_PAGE_LOCKS = ON, ONLINE = OFF, SORT_IN_TEMPDB = OFF,
  DATA_COMPRESSION = NONE )
```

An alternative to the REBUILD operation is the REORGANIZE operation. The REORGANIZE operation is equivalent to the DBCC INDEX DEFRAG command. During the REORGANIZE operation, the leaf-level pages of the index are physically reordered to match the logical order of the index keys. The indexes are not dropped. The REORGANIZE operation is always an online operation and does not require long-term table locks to complete.

TIP

The REORGANIZE operation can generate a large number of transactions during its execution. You need to be sure to carefully evaluate the amount of space available in the transaction log and monitor the free space during this operation. If the transaction log is set to AUTOGROW, you need to make sure you have adequate free space on the drive where your transaction log lives. This is especially true for very large tables. Several options are available for mitigating the growth of the log during these operations, such as setting the recovery model on the database to BULK-LOGGED.

The REORGANIZE operation has just one option: LOB_COMPACTION. When the LOB_COMPACTION option is set to ON, the data for columns with large object (LOB) data types is compacted. This consolidates the data and frees disk space. LOB data types include image, text, ntext, varchar(max), nvarchar(max), varbinary(max), and xml. The following example performs a REORGANIZE operation on the clustered index of the Production.Product table with the LOB_COMPACTION option set to OFF:

```
ALTER INDEX [PK_Product_ProductID] ON [Production].[Product]
```

```
REORGANIZE WITH ( LOB_COMPACTION = ON )
```

Disabling an index is another capability introduced with SQL Server 2005 that can be accomplished with the ALTER INDEX statement. When the DISABLE option is used on an index, the index is no longer available for retrieving data from a table. If a clustered index is disabled, the entire table is made unavailable. The data remains in the table, but no Data Manipulation Language (DML) operations can be performed on the table until the index is dropped or rebuilt. Unlike dropping an index, when an index is disabled, SQL Server retains the index definition in metadata so it can easily be re-enabled; index statistics are still maintained for nonclustered indexes that have been disabled.

After an index is disabled, you can re-enable it only by re-creating the index. You can accomplish this using the ALTER INDEX REBUILD command or CREATE INDEX WITH DROP_EXISTING command.

Disabling indexes can be particularly useful for testing purposes. Let's say you have a nonclustered index on a table that you believe is used very little. You can disable the index initially before removing it to evaluate the change. The definition of the index is still contained in the database. If you ultimately determine that the index is still needed, you can rebuild the index to make it available again.

TIP

Another reason for disabling a nonclustered index is to reduce the space requirements when rebuilding the index. If an index to be rebuilt is not disabled, SQL Server requires enough temporary disk space in the database to store both the old and new versions of the index. However, if the index is disabled first, SQL Server can reuse the space required for the disabled index to rebuild it. No additional disk space is necessary except for temporary space required for sorting, which is only about 20% of the index size.

The following example disables a nonclustered index on the Production.Product table:

```
ALTER INDEX [AK_Product_Name] ON [Production].[Product] DISABLE
```

One point to keep in mind when an index is disabled is that it is not readily apparent in SSMS that the index has been disabled. The index still appears in the Object Explorer tree under the Indexes node, and there are no indicators on the index display to alert you to the fact that it has been disabled. You can, however, use other methods to determine if the index has been disabled. The sys.indexes catalog view is one of these methods. Refer to the is_disabled column returned with this view. A value of 1 in the is_disabled column indicates that it has been disabled, and a value of 0 indicates that it is enabled. The following SELECT statement shows an example of how to use the sys.indexes catalog view:

```
select  is_disabled,* from sys.indexes
 where object_name(object_id) = 'Product'
```

You can also easily change options on an index with the `ALTER INDEX` statement. The following example sets several of the available options for a nonclustered index on the `authors` table:

```
ALTER INDEX [AK_Product_ProductNumber] ON [Production].[Product]
 SET (
    ALLOW_PAGE_LOCKS = ON,
    ALLOW_ROW_LOCKS = OFF,
    IGNORE_DUP_KEY = ON,
    STATISTICS_NORECOMPUTE = ON
    )
```

Other options exist for managing indexes with T-SQL, but the `ALTER INDEX` statement provides the bulk of what you need. Many of the other T-SQL options that you may have used for managing indexes in SQL Server 2000 and earlier, such as `DBCC DBREINDEX`, are still available in SQL Server 2008 for backward compatibility.

For more information and guidelines on managing indexes for performance, such as why and when to rebuild an index, see Chapter 34.

Managing Indexes with SSMS

Several tools are available in SSMS for managing indexes. You can use tools such as the Database Engine Tuning Advisor, database diagrams, and the Table Designer to view indexes and make modifications. These tools have many features that are geared toward specific tasks, but again, in most cases the Object Explorer provides the simplest means for managing indexes.

Figure 25.6 shows the index options available by right-clicking an index in the Object Explorer. Many of these options are geared toward index management, including the options Rebuild, Reorganize, and Disable.

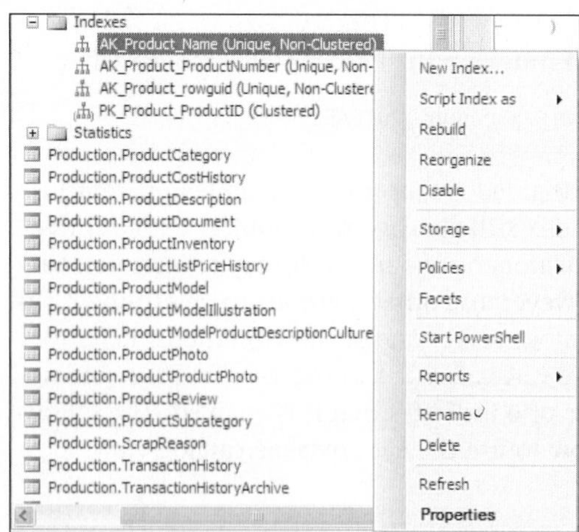

FIGURE 25.6 Using Object Explorer to manage indexes.

Similar options are also available from the `Indexes` node of the Object Explorer that enable you to rebuild, reorganize, or disable all the indexes for the table.

TIP

You can right-click an index in the Object Explorer and choose Properties to display the index columns and other relevant information. This option was not available with the SQL Server 2000 Object Explorer. You can also run the `SP_HELPINDEX` command on any table in a database to list all the indexes on the table and their related columns. This command must be run in a database engine query window. For example, `sp_helpindex [Production.Product]` returns all the indexes for the `Product` table in the `AdventureWorks` database. Make sure to enclose the table name with brackets when including the schema name.

Dropping Indexes

You can drop indexes by using T-SQL or via tools in the SSMS. To drop indexes with T-SQL, you use the `DROP INDEX` command, a simple example of which follows:

```
DROP INDEX [IX_WorkOrder_ScrapReasonID] ON [Production].[WorkOrder]
```

This command drops the index named `IX_WorkOrder_ScrapReasonID` on the `Production.WorkOrder` table.

Using the Object Explorer in SSMS is the simplest alternative for dropping indexes. In the Object Explorer, you simply right-click the index you want to drop and then select Delete. The same execution options available for adding and modifying indexes are also available after you select Delete. This includes the option to script the T-SQL statements like that shown in the preceding `DROP INDEX` example.

NOTE

If you drop a clustered index on a table, SQL Server needs to rebuild all the remaining nonclustered indexes on the table. The reason is that when a clustered index exists on a table, the nonclustered indexes include the clustered index key in the nonclustered index rows as a pointer to the corresponding data rows. When the clustered index is dropped, the clustered index key needs to be replaced with page and row pointers. If a large number of nonclustered indexes exist on the table, the operation to rebuild the nonclustered indexes can be very time consuming and I/O intensive. For more information on the internal structures of clustered and nonclustered indexes, see Chapter 34.

Online Indexing Operations

One of the great features available with SQL Server 2008 is online indexing. This feature, available only with the Enterprise or Developer Edition, allows you to create, rebuild, or drop indexes without having exclusive access to the index or table. This means that users can have concurrent access to the underlying tables and indexes while the index operation is in progress. This bodes well for high-availability applications and databases that have limited downtime available for offline operations.

Following is an example of the T-SQL syntax for an online index operation:

```
ALTER INDEX [PK_Product_ProductID] ON [Production].[Product]
REBUILD WITH ( ONLINE = ON)
```

The `ONLINE = ON` parameter is the key to making the index operation an online operation.

To accomplish online indexing, SQL Server must maintain the old and new versions of the affected indexes during the operation. The old version (referred to as the *source*) includes any table or indexes that are affected by the index operation. For example, if a clustered index is part of the online operation, the clustered index and all the nonclustered indexes that reference the clustered index are maintained as part of the source. The new version (referred to as the *target*) is the new index or indexes that are being created or rebuilt. In the case of a table without a clustered index, a structure known as a heap is used as the source and target.

During online index operations, the following three phases occur:

- **Preparation**—Concurrent activity is temporarily suspended while a snapshot of the source index structure is taken and written as an empty structure to the target.
- **Building**—The source index structures are scanned, sorted, merged, and inserted into the target. User `SELECT` statements are satisfied via the source. Insertions, updates, and deletions to the affected table are written to both the source and target.
- **Final**—Concurrent activity is temporarily suspended while the source is replaced by the newly created structures (target).

When the final phase is complete, all the query and update plans that were using the old structures are invalidated. Future queries utilize the newly created index structures after this point.

When considering online indexing, you need to account for the following:

- **Disk space**—Generally, the disk space requirements for online operations are the same as those for offline operations. The exception to this is online index operations on clustered indexes. These operations use a temporary mapping index that requires additional disk space. The temporary mapping index contains one row for each record in the table.
- **Performance**—Online index operations are generally slower and take more system resources than offline operations. Primarily, the reason is that the old and new index structures are maintained during the index operation. Heavy updates to the tables involved in the index operation can cause an overall decrease in performance and a spike in CPU utilization and I/O as the two index structures are maintained.
- **Transaction log**—Online index operations are fully logged. You may therefore encounter a heavy burden on your transaction log during online index operations

for large tables. This can cause your transaction log to fill quickly. The transaction log can be backed up, but it cannot be truncated during online index operations. You need to make sure you have enough space for your log to grow; otherwise, the online index operation could fail.

Indexes on Views

SQL Server 2008 supports the creation of indexes on views. Like indexes on tables, indexes on views can dramatically improve the performance of the queries that reference the views. By nature, a view is a virtual table and does not have a separate data structure as does a table, even though it can be referenced like a table. After an index is created on a view, the result set of the view is stored in the database, just as it would be for a table. The indexed view is no longer virtual because it requires maintenance as rows are added to, deleted from, or modified in the tables referenced by the view. Refer to Chapter 27, "Creating and Managing Views in SQL Server," for a more detailed discussion of views.

The first index created on a view must be a unique clustered index. After that is created, other nonclustered indexes can be built on the view for additional performance gains.

The most difficult part of the index creation process is identifying a view that is valid for index creation. Many requirements must be met for a view to qualify. Refer to the SQL Server Books Online documentation for a complete list of all the restrictions. The following is a partial list of the most common requirements:

- All the tables in the view must be in the same database as the view and have the same owner as the view.
- The view must not reference any other views.
- The view must be created with `SCHEMABINDING`, and any function referenced in the view must also be created with `SCHEMABINDING`.
- A two-part name with the schema prefix must be used for every table or user-defined function referenced in the view.
- Many `SET` options, including `ANSI_NULLS`, `ANSI_PADDING`, `ANSI_WARNINGS`, `CONCAT_NULL_YIELDS_NULL`, and `QUOTED_IDENTIFIER` must be set to `ON`.
- Any functions referenced in the view must be deterministic. (See Chapter 29, "Creating and Managing User-Defined Functions," for more information on deterministic functions.)
- Views with aggregate functions must also include `COUNT_BIG(*)`.

The following example shows the creation of a view that can have an index created on it:

```
CREATE VIEW titleview
 WITH SCHEMABINDING AS
      select title, au_ord, au_lname, price, ytd_sales, pub_id
        from dbo.authors, dbo.titles, dbo.titleauthor
```

```
    where authors.au_id = titleauthor.au_id
      AND titles.title_id = titleauthor.title_id
```

The SCHEMABINDING clause and database schema qualifier (dbo) for each table are necessary in the view definition to be able to make the view valid for index creation. The following example creates an index on the titleview view:

```
CREATE UNIQUE CLUSTERED INDEX [AK_vw_Employee] ON [dbo].[vw_Employee]
( [JobTitle] ASC, [LoginID] ASC)
```

After the index is created, you can manage it in much the same way that you manage the indexes on tables. You can use both T-SQL and SSMS to manage these indexes.

For more information and guidelines on creating and using indexed views, see Chapter 27.

Summary

Index creation is an important part of managing a database. Creating useful indexes can vastly improve query performance and should not be overlooked. Fortunately, SQL Server 2008 makes the creation and management of indexes quite easy.

In Chapter 26, "Implementing Data Integrity," you see how you can use indexes and other methods to enforce data integrity. Subsequent chapters cover the internal working of indexes and give you more insight into their role in performance.

CHAPTER 26

Implementing Data Integrity

IN THIS CHAPTER

- What's New in Data Integrity
- Types of Data Integrity
- Enforcing Data Integrity
- Using Constraints
- Rules
- Defaults

The value of your data is determined by its integrity. You may have heard the phrase "garbage in, garbage out." In the database world, "garbage in" refers to data that has been loaded into a database without validation or without data integrity. This "garbage" data can then be retrieved ("garbage out"), and erroneous decisions can result because of it.

Implementing good data integrity measures is your best defense against the "garbage in, garbage out" scenario. This involves identifying valid values for tables and columns and deciding how to enforce the integrity of those values. This chapter covers the different types of data integrity and the methods for enforcing them.

What's New in Data Integrity

Much of the functionality related to data integrity has remained the same in SQL Server 2008. Several features that were added in SQL Server 2005, such as cascading integrity constraints, are still supported in SQL Server 2008. The lack of change in this area is generally a blessing. The tools available to enforce data integrity were comprehensive in 2005 and remain so in 2008.

Keep in mind that bound defaults, which were deprecated in SQL Server 2005, are still available in SQL Server 2008. For now, you can still use this statement to create a default that is bound to one or more columns. Microsoft recommends using the `DEFAULT` keyword with `ALTER TABLE` or `CREATE TABLE` instead.

Types of Data Integrity

How integrity is enforced depends on the type of integrity being enforced. As described in the following sections, the types of data integrity are domain, entity, and referential integrity.

Domain Integrity

Domain integrity controls the validation of values for a column. You can use domain integrity to enforce the type, format, and possible values of data stored in a column. SQL Server provides several mechanisms to enforce domain integrity:

- You can control the type of data stored in a column by assigning a data type to the column.
- You can use `CHECK` constraints and rules to control the format of the data.
- You can control the range of values stored in a column by using `FOREIGN KEY` constraints, `CHECK` constraints, default definitions, nullability, and rules.

Entity Integrity

Entity integrity requires that all rows in a table be unique. You can enforce entity integrity in SQL Server by using `PRIMARY KEY` constraints, `UNIQUE` constraints, and `IDENTITY` properties.

Referential Integrity

Referential integrity preserves the defined relationships between tables. You can define such a relationship in SQL Server by relating foreign key columns on one table to the primary key or unique key of another table. When it is defined, referential integrity ensures that values inserted in the foreign key columns have corresponding values in the primary table. It also controls changes to the primary key table and ensures that related foreign key rows are not left orphaned.

Enforcing Data Integrity

You can enforce data integrity by using declarative or procedural methods. Implementing declarative data integrity requires little or no coding. Implementing procedural data integrity is more flexible but requires more custom coding.

Implementing Declarative Data Integrity

Declarative integrity is enforced within the database, using constraints, rules, and defaults. This is the preferred method of enforcing integrity because it has low overhead and requires little or no custom programming. It can be centrally managed in the database, and it provides a consistent approach for ensuring the integrity of data.

Implementing Procedural Data Integrity

Procedural integrity can be implemented with stored procedures, triggers, and application code. It requires custom programming that defines and enforces the integrity of the data. The biggest benefits of implementing procedural data integrity are flexibility and control. You can implement the custom code in many different ways to enforce the integrity of your data. The custom code can also be a detriment; the lack of consistency and potential inefficiencies in the way the data integrity is performed can be a real problem.

In general, declarative data integrity should be used as the primary means for control. Procedural data integrity can be used to augment declarative data integrity, if needed.

Using Constraints

Constraints—including PRIMARY KEY, FOREIGN KEY, UNIQUE, CHECK, and DEFAULT—are the primary method used to enforce data integrity. You can implement defaults as constraints or as objects in a database; for more information, see the "Defaults" section, later in this chapter.

The PRIMARY KEY Constraint

The PRIMARY KEY constraint is one of the key methods for ensuring entity integrity. When this constraint is defined on a table, it ensures that every row can be uniquely identified with the primary key value(s). The primary key can have one or more columns as part of its definition. None of the columns in the primary key definition can allow nulls. When multiple columns are used in the definition of the primary key, the combination of the values in all the primary key columns must be unique. Duplication can exist in a single column that is part of a multicolumn primary key.

There can be only one primary key defined for each table. When a primary key is defined on a table, a unique index is automatically created as well. This index contains all the columns in the primary key and ensures that the rows in this index are unique. Generally, every table in a database should have a primary key. The primary key and its associated unique index provide fast access to a database table.

Figure 26.1 shows the Adventureworks2008 database Employee table, which is an example of a table that has a primary key defined. The primary key in this table is EmployeeID, and it is denoted in the dialog shown in Figure 26.1 with a key symbol in the leftmost column.

The existing primary key on the Employee table in the Adventureworks2008 database was generated as a T-SQL script, as shown in the following example:

```
ALTER TABLE [HumanResources].[Employee]
  ADD  CONSTRAINT [PK_Employee_BusinessEntityID] PRIMARY KEY CLUSTERED
(BusinessEntityID ASC)
```

In general, you try to choose a primary key that is relatively short. BusinessEntityID, for example, is a good choice because it is an integer column and takes only 4 bytes of

XPVIRTUAL1.A...rces.Employee

Column Name	Data Type	Allow Nulls
EmployeeID	int	☐
NationalIDNumber	nvarchar(15)	☐
ContactID	int	☐
LoginID	nvarchar(256)	☐
ManagerID	int	☑
Title	nvarchar(50)	☐
BirthDate	datetime	☐
MaritalStatus	nchar(1)	☐
Gender	nchar(1)	☐
HireDate	datetime	☐
SalariedFlag	Flag:bit	☐
VacationHours	smallint	☐
SickLeaveHours	smallint	☐
CurrentFlag	Flag:bit	☐
rowguid	uniqueidentifier	☐
ModifiedDate	datetime	☐
		☐

FIGURE 26.1 A primary key example.

storage. This is particularly important when the primary key is `CLUSTERED`, as in the case of `PK_Employee_BusinessEntityID`. The key values from the clustered index are used by all nonclustered indexes as lookup keys. If the clustered key is large, this consumes more space and affects performance.

Surrogate keys are often good choices for primary keys. The `BusinessEnityID` column in the `Person.BusinessEntity` table is an example of a surrogate key. Surrogate keys consist of a single column that automatically increments and is inherently unique, as in the case of an identity column. Surrogate keys are good candidates for primary keys because they are implicitly unique and relatively short in length. You should avoid using large, multi-column indexes as primary keys. They can impede performance because fewer index rows can be stored on each index page. The performance implications related to primary key indexes and other indexes are discussed in more detail in Chapter 34, "Data Structures, Indexes, and Performance."

NOTE

Over the years, there has been much debate over the use of surrogate keys for primary keys. One school of thought is to avoid surrogate keys because insertions always occur at the end of the primary key index and are not distributed. This can lead to "hot spots" in the index because the insert activity is always on the last page of the index. In addition, surrogate keys have no real meaning and are less intuitive than primary keys that have meaning, such as `lastname` and `firstname`.

The other school of thought, in favor of using surrogate keys for primary keys, emphasizes the importance of defining primary keys that are not based on meaningful columns. If meaningful columns are used and the definitions of those columns change, this can have a significant impact on the table that contains the primary key and any tables related to it. Those in favor of using surrogate keys as primary keys also focus on the relatively small key size, which is good for performance and reduces pages splits because the values are always inserted into the index sequentially.

The UNIQUE Constraint

The UNIQUE constraint is functionally similar to PRIMARY KEY. It also uses a unique index to enforce uniqueness, but unlike PRIMARY KEY, it allows nulls in the columns that participate in the UNIQUE constraint. The definition of a UNIQUE constraint with columns that are nulls is generally impractical. The value of NULL is considered a unique value, so you are limited to the number of rows that can be inserted with NULL values. For example, only one row with a NULL value in the constraint column can be inserted if the UNIQUE constraint is based on a single column. UNIQUE constraints with multiple nullable columns can have more than one row with null values in the constraint keys, but the number of rows is limited to the combination of unique values across all the columns.

An alternate unique key on the SalesTaxRate table is a good example of a unique constraint in the AdventureWorks2008 database. The AK_SalesTaxRate_StateProvinceID_TaxType index contain the StateProvinceId and TaxType columns. Each of these columns is defined as NOT NULL. In simple terms this means that TaxTypes must be unique within each state or province. If, however, the StateProvinceID was nullable then you could have one row for a given TaxType that is null then all other rows for that tax type must have the StateProvinceID to make the combination of StateProvinceId and Tax Type unique.

26

You generally use a UNIQUE constraint when a column other than the primary key must be guaranteed to be unique. For example, consider the Employee table example used in the previous section. The primary key on the identity column EmployeeID ensures that a unique value will be assigned to each employee row, but it does not prevent duplication in any of the other columns. For example, every row in the Employee table could have the same LoginID setting if no other UNIQUE constraints were found on this table. Generally, each employee should have his or her own unique LoginID. You can enforce this policy by adding a UNIQUE constraint on the LoginID column. The following example demonstrates the creation of a UNIQUE constraint on the EmployeeID column:

```
ALTER TABLE [HumanResources].[Employee]
 ADD CONSTRAINT AK_Employee_LoginID
  UNIQUE NONCLUSTERED (LoginID ASC)
```

As with PRIMARY KEY constraints, a unique index is created whenever a UNIQUE constraint is created. If you drop the UNIQUE constraint, you drop the unique index as well.

Conversely, if you drop the unique index, you indirectly drop the UNIQUE constraint, too. You can implement a UNIQUE constraint as a constraint or an index. To illustrate this, the following example shows the creation of the same UNIQUE constraint on Employee_LoginID as before, this time using an index:

```
CREATE UNIQUE NONCLUSTERED INDEX [AK_Employee_LoginID]
 ON [HumanResources].[Employee]
(LoginID ASC)
```

NOTE

Although UNIQUE constraints and unique indexes achieve the same goal, they must be managed based on how they were created. In other words, if you create a UNIQUE constraint on a table, you cannot directly drop the associated unique index. If you try to drop the unique index directly, you get a message stating that an explicit DROP INDEX is not allowed and that it is being used for unique key constraint enforcement. To drop the UNIQUE constraint, you must use the DROP CONSTRAINT syntax associated with the ALTER TABLE statement. Similarly, if you create a unique index, you cannot drop that index by using a DROP CONSTRAINT statement; you must use DROP INDEX instead.

You can have more than one unique constraint per table. When creating unique constraints, you have all the standard index-creation options available. These options include how the underlying index is clustered, the fill factor, and a myriad of other index options.

The FOREIGN KEY Referential Integrity Constraint

The basic premise of a relational database is that tables are related. These relationships are maintained and enforced via referential integrity. FOREIGN KEY constraints are the declarative means for enforcing referential integrity in SQL Server. You implement FOREIGN KEY constraints by relating one or more columns in a table to the columns in a primary key or unique index. The columns in the referencing table can be referred to as *foreign key columns*. The table with the primary key or unique index can be referred to as the *primary table*. Figure 26.2 shows a relationship between the BusinessEntityAddress table and BusinessEntityAddress table. The foreign key in this example is AddressTypeID on the BusinessEntityAddress table. AddressTypeID on this table is related to the primary key on the AddressTypeID table. The foreign key relationship in this diagram is denoted by the line between these two tables.

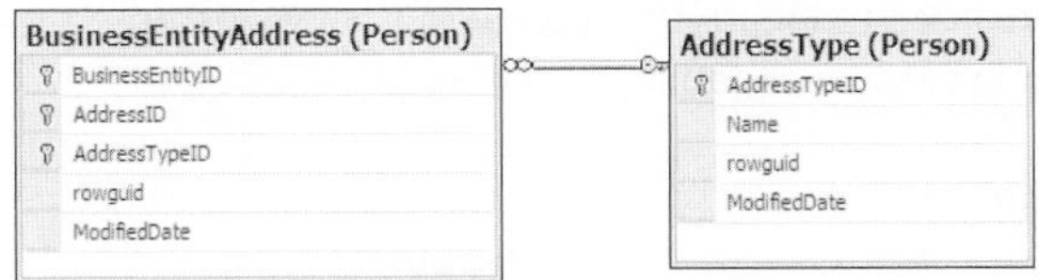

FIGURE 26.2 A foreign key constraint on the **BusinessEntityAddress** table.

Once defined, a foreign key, by default, enforces the relationship between the tables in the following ways:

- Values in the foreign key columns must have a corresponding value in the primary table. If the new values in the foreign key columns do not exist in the primary table, the insert or update operation fails.
- Values in the primary key or unique index that are referenced by the foreign key table cannot be deleted. If an attempt is made to delete a referenced value in the primary table, the delete fails.
- Values in the primary key or unique index that are referenced by the foreign key table cannot be modified. If an attempt is made to change a referenced value in the primary table, the update fails.

In the case of the `AddressType/BusinessEntityAddress` relationship shown in Figure 26.2, any `AddressTypeID` used in the `BusinessEntityAddress` table must have a corresponding value in the `AddressType` table. Listing 26.1 shows an `INSERT` statement in the `BusinessEntityAddress` table that does not have a valid `AddressTypeID` entry in the `AddressType` table. The statement fails, and the resulting message is shown after the `INSERT` statement. A similar error message is displayed if an attempt is made to delete or update values in the primary key or unique index that does not satisfy the foreign key contraint.

LISTING 26.1 A Foreign Key Conflict with **INSERT**

```
INSERT Person.BusinessEntityAddress
 (BusinessEntityID,AddressID, AddressTypeID, rowguid, ModifiedDate)
 VALUES (1,249, 9, NEWID(), GETDATE())
/* RESULTS OF INSERT FOLLOW
Msg 547, Level 16, State 0, Line 1
The INSERT statement conflicted with the FOREIGN KEY
constraint "FK_BusinessEntityAddress_AddressType_AddressTypeID".
The conflict occurred in database "AdventureWorks2008",
table "Person.AddressType", column 'AddressTypeID'.
The statement has been terminated.*/
```

The following example shows the T-SQL needed to create the foreign key relationship between the AddressType and BusinessEntityAddress tables:

```
ALTER TABLE [Person].[BusinessEntityAddress]
ADD  CONSTRAINT [FK_BusinessEntityAddress_AddressType_AddressTypeID]
  FOREIGN KEY([AddressTypeID])
REFERENCES [Person].[AddressType]
([AddressTypeID])
```

When you create a FOREIGN KEY constraint, the related primary key or unique index must exist first. In the case of the AddressType/BusinessEntityAddress relationship, the AddressType table and primary key on AddressTypeID must exist before you can create the FK_BusinessEntityAddress_AddressType_AddressTypeID foreign key. In addition, the data types of the related columns must be the same. The related columns in the two tables can actually have different names, but in practice the columns are usually named the same. Naming the columns the same makes your database much more intuitive.

NOTE

In addition to relating two different tables with a foreign key, you can also relate a table to itself. These self-referencing relationships are often found in organization tables or employee tables. For example, you could have an Employee table with a primary key of EmployeeID . This table could also have a ManagerID column. In this case, ManagerID on the Employee table has a relationship to the primary key index on EmployeeID. The manager is an employee, so it makes sense that they should have a valid EmployeeID. A foreign key on the Employee table will enforce this relationship and ensure that any ManagerID points to a different row in the table with a valid EmployeeID.

Cascading Referential Integrity

Cascading referential integrity has been around for some time and was introduced with SQL Server 2000. This type of integrity allows for updates and deletions on the primary table to be cascaded to the referencing foreign key tables. By default, a FOREIGN KEY constraint prevents updates and deletions to any primary key or unique index values referenced by a foreign key. With cascading referential integrity, you can bypass this restriction and are able to define the type of action you want to occur when the updates and deletions happen.

You define the cascading actions on the FOREIGN KEY constraint, using the ON DELETE and ON UPDATE clauses. The ON DELETE clause defines the cascading action for deletions to the primary table, and the ON UPDATE clause defines the actions for updates. These clauses are used with the CREATE TABLE or ALTER TABLE statements and are part of the REFERENCES clause of these statements.

You can specify the same cascading actions for updates and deletions:

- **NO ACTION**—This action, the default, causes deletions and updates to the primary table to fail if the rows are referenced by a foreign key.

- **CASCADE**—This option causes updates and deletions to cascade to any foreign key records that refer to the affected rows in the primary table. If the CASCADE option is used with the ON DELETE clause, any records in the foreign key table that refer to the deleted rows in the primary table are also deleted. When CASCADE is used with the ON UPDATE clause, any updates to the primary table records are also made in the related rows of the foreign key table.

- **SET NULL**—This option was new in SQL Server 2005. It is similar to the CASCADE option except that the affected rows in the foreign key table are set to NULL when deletions or updates are performed on the related primary table. The value of NULL is assigned to every column that is defined as part of the foreign key and requires that each column in the foreign key allow null values.

- **SET DEFAULT**—This option also was new in SQL Server 2005. It is similar to the CASCADE option except that the affected rows in the foreign key table are set to the default values defined on the columns when deletions or updates are performed on the related primary table. If you want to set this option, each column in the foreign key must have a default definition assigned to it, or it must be defined as nullable. If no default definition is assigned to the column, NULL is used as the default value. It is imperative that the primary table have related records for the default or null entries that can result from the cascading action. For example, if you have a two-column foreign key, and each column has a default of 1, a corresponding record with the key values of 1 and 1 needs to exist in the primary table, or the cascade action fails. The integrity of the relationship must be maintained.

To illustrate the power of cascading actions, consider the AddressType/BusinessEntityAddress relationship used in previous examples. Let's say you want to remove the associated BusinessEntityAddress records when an AddressType record is deleted. The addition of the ON DELETE CASCADE clause at the bottom of the following foreign key definition achieves this result:

```
ALTER TABLE [Person].[BusinessEntityAddress]
ADD  CONSTRAINT [FK_BusinessEntityAddress_AddressType_AddressTypeID]
  FOREIGN KEY([AddressTypeID])
REFERENCES [Person].[AddressType]
([AddressTypeID])
ON DELETE CASCADE
```

Keep in mind that other factors affect the successful execution of a cascading deletion. If other foreign keys exist on the table, and they do not have ON DELETE CASCADE specified, the cascading actions do not succeed if a foreign key violation occurs on these tables. In addition, you need to consider the existence of triggers that may prevent deletions from occurring. Also, you need to consider that a series of cascading actions can be initiated by a single DELETE statement. This happens when you have many related tables, each of which has cascading actions defined. This approach works fine as long as there are no circular references that cause one of the tables in the cascading tree to be affected by a table lower in the tree.

If you want to specify the cascading action for updates, you can add an additional ON UPDATE clause, along with the ON DELETE clause. For example, you can change the foreign key in the previous example so that BusinessEntityAddress records are set to NULL when an update is made to the related key on the primary table. This can be accomplished with the following foreign key definition:

```
ALTER TABLE [Person].[BusinessEntityAddress]
ADD  CONSTRAINT [FK_BusinessEntityAddress_AddressType_AddressTypeID]
  FOREIGN KEY([AddressTypeID])
REFERENCES [Person].[AddressType]
([AddressTypeID])
ON DELETE CASCADE
 ON UPDATE SET NULL
```

You can see that cascading referential integrity is a powerful tool. However, it must be used with caution. Consider the fact that foreign keys without cascading actions may prevent erroneous actions. For example, if a DELETE statement is mistakenly executed against the entire AddressType table, the deletion would fail before the records could be deleted because foreign key tables are referencing the AddressType table. This failure would be a good thing. If, however, the ON DELETE CASCADE clause were used in the foreign key definitions, the erroneous deletion would succeed, and all the foreign key records would be deleted as well.

The CHECK Constraint

You can use the CHECK constraint to enforce domain integrity and to provide a means for restricting the values that can be entered in a column. A CHECK constraint is implemented as a Boolean expression, and it must not be FALSE if the insertion or update is to proceed. The Boolean expression can reference other columns in the same table, but it cannot reference other tables. Foreign keys and triggers can be used to reference columns in other tables, if needed. The expression can also include functions that do not return results. A CHECK constraint that is defined on a specific column can reference only the values in the column.

CHECK constraints are good for ensuring the format of data inserted in a column and for defining a list of acceptable values. Columns with phone numbers or Social Security numbers are good candidates for CHECK constraints that enforce formatting restrictions. Columns that have the data types money or integer can use CHECK constraints to ensure that the values are always greater than or equal to zero. A column that has a small fixed number of valid values is also a good candidate for a CHECK constraint. A fixed number of values can be defined in the CHECK constraint, and no additional table lookup or coding is necessary to ensure that the valid values are inserted. The following example shows a CHECK constraint on the Employee table that checks the values for the Gender column:

```
ALTER TABLE [HumanResources].[Employee]  WITH CHECK
 ADD  CONSTRAINT [CK_Employee_Gender]
 CHECK  ((upper([Gender])='F' OR upper([Gender])='M'))
```

The CHECK constraint in this example ensures that only F or M is inserted in this column. These types of CHECK constraints are relatively fast and are preferred over FOREIGN KEY constraints when the values are fixed.

NOTE

Be careful with CHECK constraint expressions that can evaluate to NULL. CHECK constraints allow insertions and updates to the table to proceed when the CHECK constraint expression does not evaluate to FALSE. A NULL value is considered to be unknown and does not evaluate to FALSE, so the insertion or update succeeds. For example, if you have a nullable column that has a constraint specifying that the value must be greater than or equal to zero, this constraint does not prevent a NULL value from being inserted into the column.

Keep in mind that the creation of a CHECK constraint on a table that already has data in it may fail. This is due to a validation performed when the constraint is created. If existing data violates the constraint, the constraint is not created. The only exception is to create the constraint by using the NOCHECK option. When this option is used, the existing data is not checked, but any future updates or insertions are. The following example shows the creation of a CHECK constraint on the Employee table:

```
ALTER TABLE [HumanResources].[Employee]  WITH NOCHECK
ADD  CONSTRAINT [CK_Employee_Gender_F]
CHECK  ((upper([Gender])='F'))
```


The constraint is on the Gender column that already has a check constraint on it, which ensures that the data values are only F or M. The new constraint on the Gender column specifies that the value must be F. The existing data has values of F and M, but the NOCHECK option allows you to add the constraint anyway.

Any new rows added to the Employee table after the new CK_Employee_Gender_F CHECK constraint has been added are then checked. With multiple CHECK constraints defined on a column, the constraints are evaluated in the order in which they were added to the table. In the preceding example, the CK_Employee_Gender constraint is evaluated first, and then the new CK_Employee_Gender_F constraint is evaluated. If a Gender value of F is entered, both constraints evaluate to TRUE, and the change is accepted. If a value of M is inserted in the Gender column, the CK_Employee_Gender constraint succeeds, but the CK_Employee_Gender_F constraint fails, and the change is rejected.

Creating Constraints

You can define constraints on a single column or on multiple columns. Single-column constraints are referred to as *column-level* constraints. You can define this type of constraint when you create the column on the table. Constraints that reference multiple columns must be defined on the table and are considered *table-level* constraints. Table-level constraints must be defined after all the referenced columns in the table are created.

Using T-SQL to Create Constraints

You can create constraints with T-SQL by using the CREATE TABLE or ALTER TABLE statement. When you create a column-level constraint by using the CREATE TABLE statement, the CONSTRAINT keyword and constraint definition are included immediately after the column definition. Table-level constraints defined with the CREATE TABLE statement are specified after the column list in the table definition.

The Customer table in the Adventureworks2008 database is a good example of a table that has several different types of constraints. Listing 26.2 shows the CREATE TABLE command, along with the constraint definitions for a table named Customer2 that is modeled after the Customer table. All the constraints in this example have been included in the CREATE TABLE statement. The constraints on this table include PRIMARY KEY, FOREIGN KEY, and CHECK constraints. You can find all the constraints in the CREATE TABLE statement by looking for the CONSTRAINT keyword.

LISTING 26.2 Creating Constraints by Using a **CREATE TABLE** Statement

```
CREATE TABLE [Sales].[Customer2](
   [CustomerID] [int] IDENTITY(1,1) NOT FOR REPLICATION NOT NULL,
   [TerritoryID] [int] NULL,
   [AccountNumber]  AS
      (isnull('AW'+[dbo].[ufnLeadingZeros]([CustomerID]),'')),
   [CustomerType] [nchar](1) NOT NULL
      CONSTRAINT CK_Customer_CustomerType2 CHECK
       ((upper([CustomerType])='I' OR upper([CustomerType])='S')),
   [rowguid] [uniqueidentifier] ROWGUIDCOL  NOT NULL
      CONSTRAINT [DF_Customer_rowguid2]  DEFAULT (newid()),
   [ModifiedDate] [datetime] NOT NULL
      CONSTRAINT [DF_Customer_ModifiedDate2]  DEFAULT (getdate()),
 CONSTRAINT [PK_Customer_CustomerID2] PRIMARY KEY CLUSTERED
   ([CustomerID] ASC),
 CONSTRAINT FK_Customer_SalesTerritory_TerritoryID2 FOREIGN KEY
   ([TerritoryID])
   REFERENCES [Sales].[SalesTerritory] ([TerritoryID])
)
GO
```

Generally, it is easier to manage constraints by using the ALTER TABLE statement than by integrating them into the CREATE TABLE statement. One of the biggest reasons is that the scripting capability in SQL Server Management Studio (SSMS) generates ALTER TABLE statements for many of the constraints. You can easily script a table and its constraints by using SSMS, and you will find that SSMS uses the ALTER TABLE statement extensively. Listing 26.3 includes a statement to remove the Customer2 table and a subsequent set of statements that re-creates the Customer2 table and utilizes the ALTER TABLE statement to create several of the constraints. The statements to re-create the Customer2 table were generated using the Object Explorer in SSMS. Some of the constraints are created within the initial CREATE TABLE statement, and some are created with the ALTER TABLE statement.

LISTING 26.3 Creating Constraints by Using **ALTER TABLE**

```
IF  EXISTS (SELECT * FROM dbo.sysobjects WHERE id
   = OBJECT_ID(N'[Sales].[Customer2]') AND OBJECTPROPERTY(id, N'IsUserTable') = 1)
 DROP TABLE [Sales].[Customer2]
go

CREATE TABLE [Sales].[Customer2](
   [CustomerID] [int] IDENTITY(1,1) NOT FOR REPLICATION NOT NULL,
   [TerritoryID] [int] NULL,
   [AccountNumber]  AS (isnull('AW'+[dbo].[ufnLeadingZeros]([CustomerID]),'')),
   [CustomerType] [nchar](1) COLLATE SQL_Latin1_General_CP1_CI_AS NOT NULL,
   [rowguid] [uniqueidentifier] ROWGUIDCOL  NOT NULL
    CONSTRAINT [DF_Customer_rowguid2]  DEFAULT (newid()),
   [ModifiedDate] [datetime] NOT NULL
    CONSTRAINT [DF_Customer_ModifiedDate2]  DEFAULT (getdate()),
 CONSTRAINT [PK_Customer_CustomerID2] PRIMARY KEY CLUSTERED
(
   [CustomerID] ASC
) ON [PRIMARY]
) ON [PRIMARY]

GO
ALTER TABLE [Sales].[Customer2]  WITH CHECK
 ADD  CONSTRAINT [FK_Customer_SalesTerritory_TerritoryID2]
  FOREIGN KEY(   [TerritoryID])
   REFERENCES [Sales].[SalesTerritory] (   [TerritoryID])
GO
ALTER TABLE [Sales].[Customer2]  WITH CHECK
 ADD  CONSTRAINT [CK_Customer_CustomerType2]
  CHECK  ((upper([CustomerType])='I' OR upper([CustomerType])='S'))
```

Using SSMS to Create Constraints

Most of the examples used so far in this chapter use T-SQL to demonstrate constraints. SSMS simplifies the administration of constraints by providing a user-friendly interface that allows you to view and manage constraints. The visual tools available for managing constraints in SSMS include the Object Explorer, Database Diagram Editor, and Table Designer.

Figure 26.3 shows the Object Explorer with the Constraints node expanded for the Employee table and the New Constraint option selected. The Constraints node contains the CHECK and DEFAULT constraints for the table. Notice in the Object Explorer that some of the constraints (`PRIMARY KEY`, `UNIQUE`, and `FOREIGN KEY`) are actually contained under the `Keys` node.

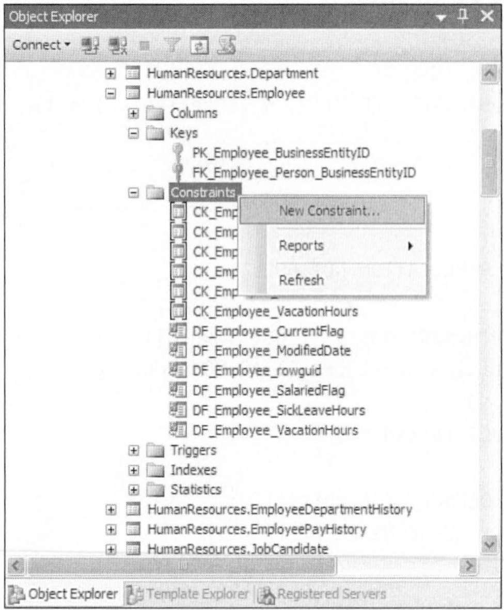

FIGURE 26.3 Constraints in Object Explorer.

When you select the New Constraint option from the Object Explorer, the Check Constraints dialog, shown in Figure 26.4, appears. This dialog gives you the option to define a new `CHECK` constraint on the table selected. You simply fill in a valid expression for the constraint, give it a unique name, and select the options you want.

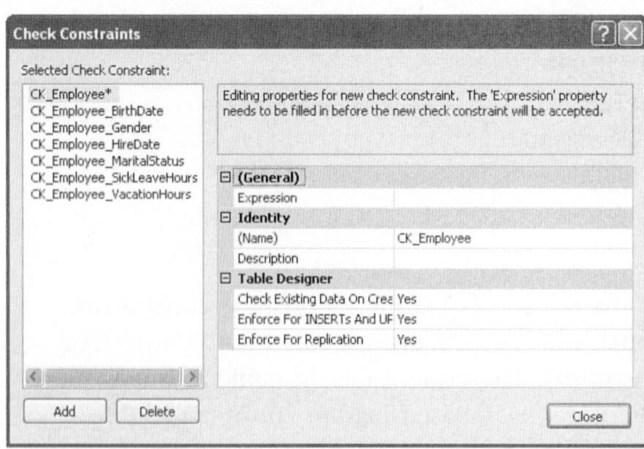

FIGURE 26.4 A new **CHECK** constraint in Object Explorer.

Similarly, you can right-click the `Keys` node and select New Foreign Key to add a new `FOREIGN KEY` constraint. Figure 26.5 shows the Foreign Key Relationships dialog displayed after you select New Foreign Key. You click the ellipsis to the right of Tables and Columns Specification, and you can select the primary key table you want the foreign key to relate to. Finally, you select the desired options, and you are ready to add your new `FOREIGN KEY` constraint.

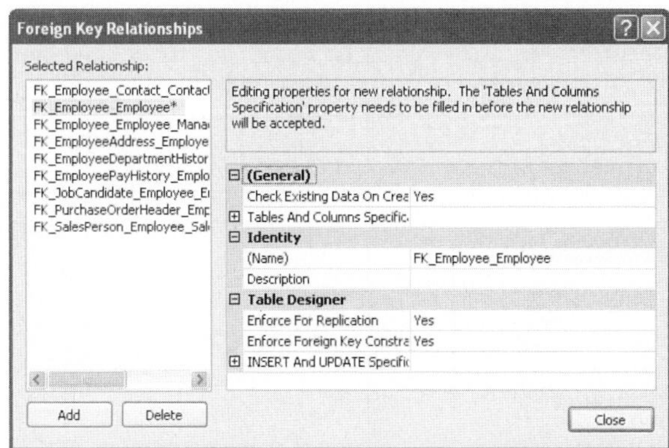

FIGURE 26.5 A new **FOREIGN KEY** constraint in Object Explorer.

> **TIP**
>
> When you use the Object Explorer to add or modify constraints, two windows are important to this process. The first window is the Constraint window, which allows you to input the constraint information. The Table Designer window that displays the column properties for the table is the other window that is important to the change process. It is launched in the background, and you can view it on the tabbed display of SSMS. When you make changes using the Constraint window, those changes are not applied via SSMS until the Table Designer window is closed. This may cause some confusion because even though you close your Constraint window with your changes, those changes may not be reflected in the database. You must close the Table Designer window to be able to actually make the changes to the table. When you close the Table Designer window, a prompt appears, asking whether you want to save the changes to the table. If you click Yes, your constraint changes are applied to the database. If you click No, none of the constraint changes you have made are applied. You can also use the Table Designer menu to script out the related changes and apply them manually via a database engine query window.

The Database Diagram Editor is another great visual tool for adding constraints. This tool is particularly useful for viewing and adding foreign key relationships to tables. Consider, for example, the database diagram shown in Figure 26.6. This diagram shows the `AddressType` and `BusinessEntityAddress` tables and the relationships that exist between them. To add a new relationship, you right-click the table you want to add the foreign key to and select the Relationships option. After you fill in the appropriate information for the relationship, you can generate a change script by using the Table Designer menu, or you can simply close the database diagram window and respond to the prompt to save changes. You can also see options to add other constraints, such as CHECK constraints, by right-clicking the table in the database diagram and selecting the desired option.

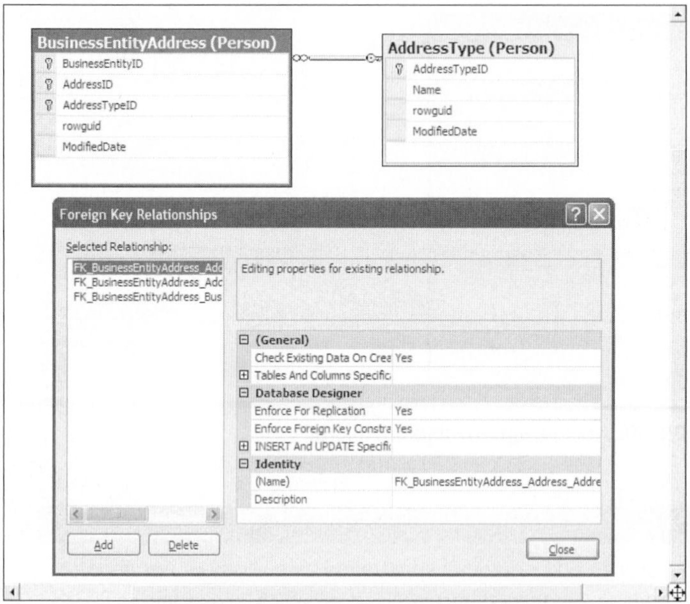

FIGURE 26.6 Adding constraints by using a database diagram.

You can also launch windows for adding constraints from the Table Designer menu. To enable the Table Designer menu, you right-click the table in Object Explorer that you want to add constraints to and select the Design option. The table and column properties are displayed, and the Table Designer menu is enabled. The Table Designer menu includes options to manage relationships, indexes/keys, and CHECK constraints.

TIP

It is a good idea to generate a script to implement changes made using SSMS visual tools. You can review the script for accuracy, run it at a later time, and save it in a file to keep track of the changes. You can also apply the saved script to other environments, if needed.

Managing Constraints

Managing constraints consists of gathering information about constraints, disabling and re-enabling constraints, and dropping constraints. These actions are discussed in the following sections.

Gathering Constraint Information

You can obtain information about constraints by using the visual tools, system stored procedures, and `information_schema` views. The visual tools (including the Object Explorer, Table Designer, and database diagrams) were introduced in the previous section. These tools offer a simple, user-friendly means for obtaining information related to constraints. These tools allow you to view a table's constraints and display the relative information.

The `sp_help` and `sp_helpconstraint` system stored procedures are another good source of information about constraints. Like the visual tools, these procedures allow you to gather constraint information about a specific table. The `sp_helpconstraint` procedure provides the most concise information related to constraints. Figure 26.7 shows the `sp_helpconstraint` output for the `Sales.Customer` table. You need to make sure to enclose the table name in brackets, as shown here, when the schema name is included. The output from `sp_helpconstraint` includes all the constraints for the table, and it supplies a list of tables that have foreign key references to the table.

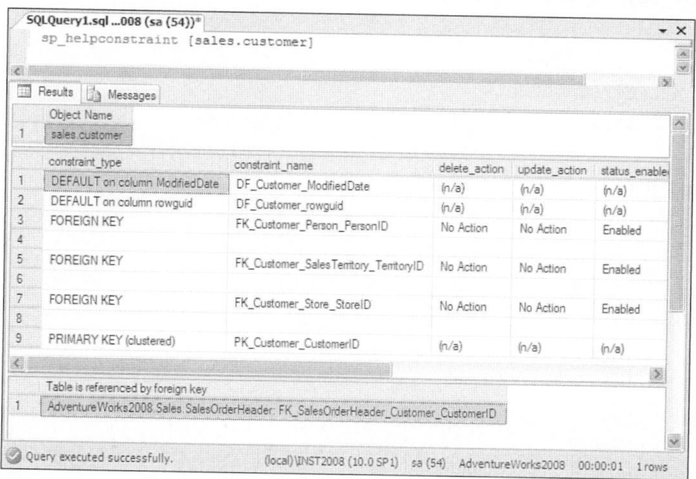

FIGURE 26.7 Executing **`sp_helpconstraint`** on the **`Customer`** table.

Catalog views offer a flexible alternative for returning information about constraints. SQL Server Books Online recommends using the `sys.key_constraints`, `sys.check_constraints`, and `sys.default_constraints` catalog views. These catalog views allow you to obtain constraint information for more than one table at a time. They are very flexible and allow you to customize the type of data you want to return simply by adjusting the selection criterion.

Listing 26.4 shows a sample `SELECT` statement for each of the catalog views related to constraints and the resulting output. The `SELECT` statements in this example have a `WHERE` clause in them that limits the results to the `SalesTax` table, but you can remove this clause to retrieve constraints for all the tables.

LISTING 26.4 Using Catalog Views to Display Constraint Information

```
select LEFT(name,30) NAME, type from sys.key_constraints
    where object_name(parent_object_id) = 'SalesTaxRate'
    order by 1

select LEFT(name,30) NAME, type from sys.check_constraints
    where object_name(parent_object_id) = 'SalesTaxRate'
    order by 1

select LEFT(name,30) NAME, type from sys.default_constraints
    where object_name(parent_object_id) = 'SalesTaxRate'
    order by 1

/* Results of the previous SELECT statements
NAME                           type
------------------------------ ----
PK_SalesTaxRate_SalesTaxRateID PK

(1 row(s) affected)

NAME                           type
------------------------------ ----
CK_SalesTaxRate_TaxType        C

(1 row(s) affected)

NAME                           type
------------------------------ ----
DF_SalesTaxRate_ModifiedDate   D
DF_SalesTaxRate_rowguid        D
DF_SalesTaxRate_TaxRate        D
```

```
(3 row(s) affected)
*/
```

Dropping Constraints

You can drop constraints by using the visual tools or by using T-SQL. You can right-click a constraint in the Object Explorer and select the Delete option to drop that constraint. The Object Explorer also offers a script option that generates the T-SQL statements used to drop the constraint. The `ALTER TABLE` command is the T-SQL command you use to make the change. For example, to drop the `CK_Employee_Gender` constraint on the `Employee` table, you can use the following command:

```
ALTER TABLE [HumanResources].[Employee]
DROP CONSTRAINT [CK_Employee_Gender]
```

You should use caution when dropping constraints because some constraints affect other tables. For example, if you drop the `PRIMARY KEY` constraint on a table and that table is referenced by foreign keys, the drop statement fails.

Disabling Constraints

You can disable `CHECK` and `FOREIGN KEY` constraints by using the `NOCHECK` clause. This capability allows you to stop the constraints from being checked without removing the constraints from your database. The following `ALTER TABLE` command allows you to disable the `FK_Customer_SalesTerritory_TerritoryID` foreign key constraint on the `Customer` table:

```
ALTER TABLE Sales.Customer
    NOCHECK CONSTRAINT FK_Customer_SalesTerritory_TerritoryID
```

When the constraint is disabled, it no longer performs validation. You should disable constraints with caution because the integrity of your data can be compromised. In the previous example, disabling the `FOREIGN KEY` constraint would allow an invalid `TerritoryID` to be inserted in the `Customer` table.

Why would you disable constraints? One possible reason would be to disable the constraints during large data loads. The execution of constraints can slow the load process. To facilitate the fastest load speed, you can disable constraints and then re-enable them when the data load is complete. To re-enable a constraint, you use the `CHECK` keyword in the `ALTER TABLE` statement. The following example re-enables the `FOREIGN KEY` constraint for the `Customer` table:

```
ALTER TABLE Sales.Customer
    CHECK CONSTRAINT FK_Customer_SalesTerritory_TerritoryID
```

Keep in mind that enabling a constraint does not necessarily mean the underlying data is being validated against the constraint. In fact, the default behavior when enabling a constraint in SQL Server 2008 is not to check the data against the constraint when a constraint in enabled. The default behavior when a constraint is added is to validate the data. You can force the data in the table to be validated using the WITH CHECK option. The following WITH CHECK option could be used to force the validation of the underlying data when a constraint is enabled:

```
ALTER TABLE Sales.Customer
    WITH CHECK CHECK CONSTRAINT FK_Customer_SalesTerritory_TerritoryID
```

Rules

You can use rules as another method to enforce domain integrity. Rules are similar to CHECK constraints but have some limitations. The biggest advantage when using a rule is that one rule can be bound to multiple columns or user-defined data types. This capability can be useful for columns that contain the same type of data and are found in multiple tables in a database. The syntax for creating a rule is as follows:

```
CREATE RULE [ schema_name . ] rule_name
AS condition_expression
[ ; ]
```

condition_expression can include any statement that can be placed in a WHERE clause. It includes one variable that is preceded with the @ symbol. This variable contains the value of the bound column that is supplied with the INSERT or UPDATE statement. The name of the variable is not important, but the conditions and formatting within the expression are. Only one variable can be referenced per rule. The following example illustrates the creation of a rule that could be used to enforce the format of data inserted in phone number columns:

```
CREATE RULE phone_rule AS
@phone LIKE '([0-9][0-9][0-9]) [0-9][0-9][0-9]-[0-9][0-9][0-9][0-9]'
```

The variable in the condition expression is @phone, and it contains the inserted or updated value for any column that the rule is bound to. The following example binds the phone_rule rule to the PhoneNumber column in the person.PersonPhone table:

```
sp_bindrule phone_rule, 'Person.PersonPhone.PhoneNumber'
```

When a rule is bound to a column, any future insertions or updates to data in the bound column are constrained by the rule. Existing data is not affected at the time the rule is bound to the column. For example, many different phone number formats in the person.PersonPhone table do not conform to phone_rule, but phone_rule can be bound to this table successfully. To illustrate this point, the following UPDATE statement can be run against the person.PersonPhone table after the phone_rule rule is bound to the PhoneNumber column:

```
update person.contact
 set phone = phone
```

The preceding update sets the PhoneNumber value to itself, but this causes phone_rule to execute. The following error message is displayed after the update is run because the existing data in the person.contact table violates the phone_rule rule:

```
Msg 513, Level 16, State 0, Line 2
A column insert or update conflicts with a rule imposed
by a previous CREATE RULE statement.
The statement was terminated.
The conflict occurred in database 'Adventureworks2008',
table 'PersonPhone', column 'PhoneNumber'.
The statement has been terminated.
```

Although rules are powerful objects, Microsoft has slated them for removal in a future version of SQL Server. Microsoft recommends using CHECK constraints on each column instead of rules. CHECK constraints provide more flexibility and a consistent approach, and multiple CHECK constraints can be applied to a single column.

Defaults

A default provides a value for a column when a value is not supplied. Defaults can be anything that evaluates to a constant, such as a constant, built-in function, or mathematical expression. Defaults are of two types: declarative and bound. The two types are functionally the same; the difference is in how they are implemented.

Declarative Defaults

A *declarative default* is a constraint defined as part of the table definition. Using declarative defaults is the preferred method for assigning default values to columns. You can use the CREATE TABLE or ALTER TABLE statement to create a default and assign it to a column. Declarative defaults are assigned to a single column and cannot be reused for other columns in the database. The following example shows the creation of a new column namedCustomerType in the SalesCustomer table followed by the creation of a new default on that column:

```
ALTER TABLE Sales.Customer
 ADD CustomerType CHAR(1)
ALTER TABLE Sales.Customer ADD CONSTRAINT
```

```
    DF_Customer_CustomerType DEFAULT 'I' FOR CustomerType
```

It is important to remember that a default constraint stores the default value only when a value is not provided during the insertion of a row into the table. The creation of a default constraint does not affect the existing data in the table. UPDATE statements do not utilize the values specified in the default constraint, either, unless the DEFAULT keyword is explicitly referenced; this issue is discussed later in this chapter, in the section "When a Default Is Applied." Generally, the only time a default comes into play is when the row is initially inserted. The following example shows an INSERT statement that causes the default value defined in the DF_Customer_CustomerType constraint to be used:

```
INSERT Sales.Customer
 (TerritoryID)
 SELECT TOP 1 TerritoryID from Sales.SalesTerritory

select CustomerID, CustomerType from Sales.Customer
 where CustomerID = @@identity

/*Results from previous select statement
CustomerID  CustomerType
----------- ------------
30119       I
*/
```

The Sales.Customer table in the Adventureworks2008 database is an interesting table because most of the columns have defaults defined, are identity columns, or are nullable. This table has eight columns, but only one value is supplied in the previous example. The rest of the columns, including the CustomerType column, have default definitions that automatically populate the values upon insertion or default to null.

One common misconception with defaults is that a default value is stored when a NULL value is supplied for a column on insertion. However, NULL is considered a value, so the default value is not used in this situation. This is demonstrated in the following example, where the CustomerType column is altered to accept NULL values and then a NULL value is specified for the CustomerType column in the INSERT statement:

```
ALTER TABLE Sales.Customer
 ALTER COLUMN CustomerType nchar(1) null

INSERT Sales.Customer
 (TerritoryID, CustomerType)
 SELECT TOP 1 TerritoryID, null
  from Sales.SalesTerritory
```

The insertion in this example succeeds, and the Null value is stored in the CustomerType column that has a default defined on it.

To remove a declarative default constraint, you use ALTER TABLE with the DROP CONSTRAINT clause. The following example removes the DF_Customer_CustomerType constraint from the Sales.Customer table:

```
ALTER TABLE Sales.Customer DROP CONSTRAINT DF_Customer_CustomerType
```

Bound Defaults

Bound defaults are similar to rules in that you first create a bound default and then bind it to a column or set of columns. Bound defaults are also similar to rules in that they are slated for removal in a future version of SQL Server. This section covers the basics of bound defaults, but you should keep in mind that Microsoft recommends you avoid using them for new development work.

You use the CREATE DEFAULT command to establish a default that can be bound to a column at a later time. The CREATE DEFAULT syntax is as follows:

```
CREATE DEFAULT [ schema_name . ] default_name
AS constant_expression [ ; ]
```

constant_expression can include any constant, built-in function, or mathematical expression. It cannot include user-defined functions. Character and data values that are part of the expression should be enclosed in single quotation marks. Monetary, integer, and floating-point constants do not require the single quotation marks.

The following example creates a default named password_df that can be used to supply a default password for any password-oriented columns:

```
CREATE DEFAULT password_df AS 'defaultpw'
```

After you create a default, you can bind it to a column. The following example binds the password_df default to the passwordSalt column on the person.password table:

```
sp_bindefault password_df, 'person.password.PasswordSalt'
```

As you can see, a bound default appears to require an extra step, but after it is created, it offers an advantage: you can bind it to other columns. This capability provides some consistency across all the columns that the default is bound to and reduces the overall number of database objects.

When a Default Is Applied

Defaults are applied only when no value is specified for a column during an insertion. They can also be applied during insertions and updates when the DEFAULT keyword is used. To demonstrate the application of defaults, consider the following examples:

```
CREATE TABLE test_default
(id int IDENTITY NOT NULL,
```

```
tmstmp timestamp NOT NULL,
password char(13) NOT NULL DEFAULT 'defaultpw',
Shortdesc VARCHAR(50) NULL)
```

The table in this example has a unique characteristic: each column has some sort of default value associated with it. One column has a default of NULL because it is nullable. The IDENTITY and TIMESTAMP columns automatically generate values because of their data type, and the password column has an explicit default definition. In this scenario, you can supply the keywords DEFAULT VALUES in the INSERT statement to insert a row of data, as shown in the following example:

```
INSERT test_default DEFAULT VALUES
select * from test_default
/* results from previous select statement
id          tmstmp              password      Shortdesc
------ ---------- ------- -------------
1           0x00000000000007D1 defaultpw     NULL
*/
```

You can see from the results of the SELECT statement in this example that a row was inserted in the new table, and this row includes default values for all the columns. If you want to supply values for some of the columns and allow the defaults to be used for other columns, you can simply exclude the columns with defaults from the column listing in the INSERT statement. The following example demonstrates how to do this:

```
INSERT test_default (ShortDesc)
 VALUES('test default insertion')
SELECT * FROM test_default
 where ShortDesc = 'test default insertion'

/* results from previous select statement
id  tmstmp              password  Shortdesc
-- ---------- ----- ------------
2   0x00000000000007D2 defaultpw  test default insertion
*/
```

The DEFAULT keyword can also be listed explicitly in the VALUE listing of the INSERT statement, as shown in the following example:

```
INSERT test_default (tmstmp, password, ShortDesc)
 VALUES(DEFAULT, DEFAULT, DEFAULT)
SELECT * FROM test_default where id = @@identity
/*
(1 row(s) affected)
id  tmstmp              password     Shortdesc
-- ---------- ------- -----
3   0x00000000000007D5 defaultpw     NULL
*/
```

All the examples so far have dealt with INSERT statements, but there is one scenario in which a default value can be applied with an UPDATE statement. This scenario is similar to the preceding example and requires the use of the DEFAULT keyword. The following example demonstrates the use of the DEFAULT keyword in an UPDATE statement:

```
UPDATE top (1) test_default
 SET PASSWORD = DEFAULT
GO
SELECT top 1 * from test_default
/*
id          tmstmp             password     Shortdesc
------.  ----------  -------.  ------.
1           0x00000000000007DE defaultpw    NULL
*/
```

Keep in mind that default values are *not* used for updates unless the DEFAULT keyword is explicitly referenced in the SET clause of the UPDATE statement.

Restrictions on Defaults

When creating defaults, you need to keep in mind the following restrictions:

- A default cannot be created on columns that have been defined with TIMESTAMP, IDENTITY, or ROWGUIDCOL properties.
- Only one default can be assigned to a given column. This restriction applies to both declarative and bound defaults.
- Only one default can exist per column.
- The default value must be compatible with the data type of the column.
- A default that is bound cannot be dropped if the default is currently bound to a column. The default must be unbound from the column first.
- The expression in a default cannot include the names of any columns or other database objects.

There are also some considerations related to the interaction of rules, defaults, and constraints:

- If a column has both a rule and default, the default is not inserted if it violates the rules.
- If a default value violates a CHECK constraint, the default is not inserted. Ultimately, all the rules, defaults, and constraints that are active are validated. If the change to the data violates any of them, it is rejected.

Summary

This chapter covers the basic tools you can use to ensure the integrity of the data in a database. The integrity of data is directly related to its value; remember the concept of "garbage in, garbage out." If you take the time to implement the constraints and other methods discussed in this chapter, you provide a solid foundation for the storage of data and avoid the headaches related to dealing with "garbage" data.

Chapter 27, "Creating and Managing Views in SQL Server," discusses a means for virtually accessing the data in tables. Virtual tables, or views, allow you to selectively choose the data elements on one or more tables that you want to present as a single window into your data.

CHAPTER 27

Creating and Managing Views in SQL Server

IN THIS CHAPTER

- What's New in Creating and Managing Views
- Definition of Views
- Using Views
- Creating Views
- Managing Views
- Data Modifications and Views
- Partitioned Views
- Indexed Views

Views offer a window into your data that does not require physical storage. They are essentially virtual tables that are defined by a SELECT statement. This chapter describes the benefits and advantages of these powerful database objects.

What's New in Creating and Managing Views

Much of the core functionality associated with standard views has remained unchanged in SQL Server 2008. However, some storage enhancements have been added to SQL Server 2008 that can be used with views. These storage enhancements include disk storage compression in both row and page format. It is available on indexed views and can be used on tables and indexes as well. This data compression is not covered in this chapter but is covered in detail in Chapter 34, "Data Structures, Indexes, and Performance."

Definition of Views

Views are a logical way of viewing data in the underlying physical tables. They are tied to a SELECT statement that retrieves data from one or more tables or views in the same database or a different database. In most cases, there is no physical storage of data associated with the view, and the SELECT that is associated with the view is run dynamically whenever the view is referenced.

The following T-SQL statement can be used to create a simple view in the Adventureworks2008 database:

```
CREATE VIEW [dbo].[vw_CustomerAddress]
AS
SELECT     Sales.Customer.CustomerID, Sales.Customer.AccountNumber,
 Person.Address.AddressLine1,
 Person.Address.StateProvinceID, Person.Address.City,
 Person.Address.PostalCode
FROM Sales.Customer
 INNER JOIN Person.Person
  ON Sales.Customer.PersonID = Person.Person.BusinessEntityID
 INNER JOIN Person.BusinessEntityAddress
  ON Person.Person.BusinessEntityID = Person.BusinessEntityAddress.BusinessEntityID
  INNER JOIN Person.Address   ON Person.BusinessEntityAddress.AddressID =
Person.Address.AddressID
```

The vw_CustomerAddress view in this example selects from four different tables in the Adventureworks2008 database: Sales.Customer, Person.Person, Person.Business EntityAddress, and Person.Address. After the view is created, it can be used in the FROM clause of another SELECT statement. The following data retrieval example uses the newly created view:

```
select c.AccountNumber, s.OrderDate, c.city , c.StateProvinceId
  from vw_CustomerAddress c
   INNER JOIN Sales.SalesOrderHeader s
    ON c.CustomerID = s.CustomerID
 WHERE StateProvinceId = 14
  AND s.OrderDate = '9/21/01'
 ORDER BY c.city


AccountNumber OrderDate               city                 StateProvinceId
AW00020060    2001-09-21 00:00:00.000 Runcorn              14
AW00011333    2001-09-21 00:00:00.000 Newcastle upon Tyne  14
```

You can see from the sample SELECT that the view is treated much like a table that is referenced in a SELECT statement. The view can be joined to other tables, individual columns from the view can be selected, and those columns can be included in the ORDER BY clause. All the retrieval is done dynamically when the view is referenced, and the underlying tables that are part of the view definition are implicitly accessed, without the need to know the underlying structure of the view.

Using Views

Views are useful in many scenarios. Some of the most common scenarios include the following:

- Simplifying data manipulation
- Focusing on specific data
- Abstracting data
- Controlling access to data

Simplifying Data Manipulation

Views can be used to simplify data access. Common queries that utilize complex joins, UNION queries, and more involved SQL can be defined as views. This minimizes the amount of complex code that must be written or rewritten and provides a simple way of organizing your common data access.

SQL Server 2008 comes with a set of system views that demonstrate the views' capability to mask complex queries and simplify data manipulation. These system views include catalog views, information schema views, and compatibility views. In many cases, the definition of these views is hidden, but some of them can be analyzed using the sp_helptext system procedure. For example, sys.triggers, a catalog view defined in SQL Server 2008, has the following definition associated with it:

```
CREATE VIEW sys.triggers AS
   SELECT o.name,
    object_id = o.id,
    parent_class = o.pclass,
    parent_class_desc = pc.name,
    parent_id = o.pid,
    type = o.type,
    type_desc = n.name,
    create_date = o.created,
    modify_date = o.modified,
    is_ms_shipped = sysconv(bit, o.status & 1),        — OBJALL_MSSHIPPED
    is_disabled = sysconv(bit, o.status & 256),        — OBJTRG_DISABLED
    is_not_for_replication = sysconv(bit, o.status & 512),     — OBJTRG_NOTFORREPL
    is_instead_of_trigger = sysconv(bit, o.status & 1024)     — OBJTRG_INSTEADOF
   FROM sys.sysschobjs o
   LEFT JOIN sys.syspalnames n ON n.class = 'OBTY' AND n.value = o.type
   LEFT JOIN sys.syspalvalues pc ON pc.class = 'UNCL' AND pc.value = o.pclass
   WHERE o.type IN ('TA','TR') AND o.pclass <> 100
      AND has_access('TR', o.id, o.pid, o.nsclass) = 1
```

To select the relevant data from the sys.triggers view, you need only reference the columns in the view that are of interest, and the complexity of the view is hidden. The following query demonstrates the simplicity of a SELECT statement against the sys.triggers view:

```
select name, type, create_date
 from sys.triggers
 where name like 'i%'
```

You can see from the sys.triggers example why the folks at Microsoft are big proponents of views. Complex queries such as the sys.triggers view can be written and tested once, and subsequent data retrieval can be accomplished by selecting from the view.

Focusing on Specific Data

Views allow users or developers to focus on the specific data elements they need to work with. Tables that contain hundreds of columns or columns that have limited value for the end user can be filtered with a view such that only the relevant data elements are returned.

The HumanResources.vEmployee view in the Adventureworks2008 database is a good example of a view that focuses on specific data and simplifies data access. The view definition follows:

```
ALTER VIEW [vEmployee]
AS
SELECT
    e.[BusinessEntityID]
    ,p.[Title]
    ,p.[FirstName]
    ,p.[MiddleName]
    ,p.[LastName]
    ,p.[Suffix]
    ,e.[JobTitle]
    ,pp.[PhoneNumber]
    ,pnt.[Name] AS [PhoneNumberType]
    ,ea.[EmailAddress]
    ,p.[EmailPromotion]
    ,a.[AddressLine1]
    ,a.[AddressLine2]
    ,a.[City]
    ,sp.[Name] AS [StateProvinceName]
    ,a.[PostalCode]
    ,cr.[Name] AS [CountryRegionName]
    ,p.[AdditionalContactInfo]
FROM [HumanResources].[Employee] e
        INNER JOIN [Person].[Person] p
        ON p.[BusinessEntityID] = e.[BusinessEntityID]
    INNER JOIN [Person].[BusinessEntityAddress] bea
```

```
    ON bea.[BusinessEntityID] = e.[BusinessEntityID]
    INNER JOIN [Person].[Address] a
    ON a.[AddressID] = bea.[AddressID]
    INNER JOIN [Person].[StateProvince] sp
    ON sp.[StateProvinceID] = a.[StateProvinceID]
    INNER JOIN [Person].[CountryRegion] cr
    ON cr.[CountryRegionCode] = sp.[CountryRegionCode]
    LEFT OUTER JOIN [Person].[PersonPhone] pp
    ON pp.BusinessEntityID = p.[BusinessEntityID]
    LEFT OUTER JOIN [Person].[PhoneNumberType] pnt
    ON pp.[PhoneNumberTypeID] = pnt.[PhoneNumberTypeID]
    LEFT OUTER JOIN [Person].[EmailAddress] ea   ON p.[BusinessEntityID] =
ea.[BusinessEntityID]
```

The HumanResources.vEmployee view filters out much of the data that is sensitive or superfluous when gathering the basic information about an employee.

Abstracting Data

Data abstraction, in its simplest form, isolates the client code from changes to the underlying structure. A view can be used to implement data abstraction within your database schema. If, for example, you have client code that will retrieve data from a database table that is likely to change, you can implement a view that retrieves data from the underlying table. The client code will then reference the view and never access the underlying table directly. If the underlying tables change or the source of the data for the view changes, these changes can be isolated from the referencing client code.

To demonstrate this scenario, let's look at the following SELECT statement, which retrieves data directly from the Sales.SalesOrderHeader table:

```
select TerritoryID, sum(TotalDue)
 from Sales.SalesOrderHeader
  group by TerritoryID
order by TerritoryID
```

The client code could certainly utilize this kind of query to retrieve the territory data. You may find, however, that the data retrieval would be better placed within a view if the summarized territory data were slated to be rolled up into an aggregate table at a later time. In this scenario, a view like the following could be created initially:

```
CREATE VIEW vw_TerritoryOrders AS
select TerritoryID, sum(TotalDue) 'TotalSales'
 from Sales.SalesOrderHeader
  group by TerritoryID
```

The client code that needs the territory data would then reference the vw_TerritoryOrders view. If the source of the territory data changes and it is rolled up in an aggregate table, the view can be changed to reflect the new source for the data, but the client code remains unchanged. The following example alters the vw_TerritoryOrders view such that the source of the data is changed:

```
ALTER VIEW vw_TerritoryOrders AS
select TerritoryID, SalesYTD 'TotalSales'
 from Sales.SalesTerritory
```

Changing a single view in these types of scenarios can be much easier than changing the client code that has direct references to the table. This type of abstraction also applies to partitioned views, which are discussed later in this chapter.

Controlling Access to Data

Views can be used as a security mechanism to limit a user's access to specific data. This type of view security can be used to limit the columns that a user has access to or the rows that the user has access to. A view that limits the accessible columns can be referred to as *vertical security*, or *column-level security*. A view that restricts the rows that are returned is referred to as *horizontal security*, or *row-level security*.

With vertical security, a view is created that contains only the data elements or columns that you want to make visible. Columns that are sensitive in nature (for example, payroll data) can be excluded from a view so that they are not seen when the user selects from the view.

After the view is created, security can be granted on the view. If the owner of the objects referenced in the view is the same as the owner of the view itself, the user who is granted permission to the view does not need to have permission granted to the underlying objects. Listing 27.1 gives an example of this scenario.

LISTING 27.1 Security with Views

```
USE adventureworks2008
go
CREATE LOGIN OwnerLogin WITH PASSWORD = 'pw'
CREATE USER OwnerLogin FOR LOGIN OwnerLogin
EXEC sp_addrolemember N'db_owner', N'OwnerLogin'

CREATE LOGIN NonOwnerLogin WITH PASSWORD = 'pw'
CREATE USER NonOwnerLogin FOR LOGIN NonOwnerLogin

—Connect as the OwnerLogin at this point
Go

CREATE VIEW OwnerView as
 select LoginID, JobTitle, BirthDate, Gender, HireDate, SalariedFlag
  from HumanResources.Employee go

GRANT SELECT ON [dbo].[OwnerView] TO [NonOwnerLogin]
```

```
—Connect as the NonOwnerLogin at this point

—The following select succeeds because the owner of the
—view that was granted permission is the same as the underlying
—table in the view
select * from OwnerView

—The following SELECT against the underlying table fails
—because the NonOwnerLogin does not have permission to
—select from the table.  He can only select through the view
select * from HumanResources.Employee
```

Listing 27.1 outlines a scenario where one login creates a view that selects specific columns from the `HumanResources.Employee` table. The `Employee` table is part of the `HumanResources` schema, and it is owned by `DBO`. The view that is created is also owned by `DBO` because the login (`OwnerLogin`) that created the view is a member of the `db_owner` role. Ultimately, `NonOwnerLogin` is granted permission to the view. When the `NonOwnerLogin` user connects to the database, that user can select rows from the view and will see only the columns in the `Employee` table that have been selected in the view. If that user tries to select rows directly from the underlying `HumanResources.Employee` table, a permission-related error fires. Ownership chaining is the key to making this scenario work.

With ownership chaining, SQL Server automatically authorizes a user to access the underlying tables, views, or functions referenced in the view. This happens only if the view has the same owner as the underlying objects and the user has been granted permission to the view. If, however, you have various owners of the underlying objects that a view references, permissions must be checked at each level. If access is denied at any level, access to the view is denied. Ownership chaining was available in prior versions and is still available in SQL Server 2008 for backward compatibility.

27

Horizontal security can also be implemented with a view. With horizontal security, a `WHERE` clause is included in the view's `SELECT` statement to restrict the rows that are returned. The following example demonstrates a simple view that utilizes horizontal security:

```
CREATE VIEW EmpViewHorizontal
  as
 select EmployeeID, BirthDate, Gender, HireDate, SalariedFlag
  from HumanResources.Employee
 where HireDate >  '3/1/03'

—Sample SELECT results from the view:

LoginID                  BirthDate   Gender   HireDate    SalariedFlag
adventure-works\syed0    1965-02-11  M        2003-04-15  1
adventure-works\lynn0    1961-04-18  F        2003-07-01  1
```

```
adventure-works\rachel0 1965-08-09  F         2003-07-01  1
```

Only the rows in the Employee table with a HireDate value greater than March 1, 2003, are returned when you select everything from the view. Separate views can be created based on geography, demographics, or any other data element that requires a different set of security.

Keep in mind that additional conditions can be applied when selecting from a view. You can utilize another WHERE clause in the SELECT statement that uses a view. This is demonstrated in the following example:

```
select * from EmpViewHorizontal
 where HireDate >= '7/1/03'
  and BirthDate > '1/1/65'

LoginID                 BirthDate  Gender  HireDate   SalariedFlag
adventure-works\rachel0 1965-08-09 F       2003-07-01 1
```

As you can see, a view with horizontal security restricts your initial result set but does not prevent you from applying additional conditions to obtain the desired result.

Creating Views

You can create several different types of views in SQL Server 2008, including standard views, indexed views, and partitioned views. Standard views are like those that have been discussed thus far in this chapter; they let you achieve most of the benefits associated with views. An indexed view has a unique clustered index defined on it that causes the view to be materialized. In other words, the creation of the index causes physical storage of the data related to the view's index. Partitioned views join horizontally partitioned data from a set of distinct tables. They can be locally partitioned, meaning that the tables are on the same server; or they can be distributed, meaning that some of the tables exist on other servers. Partitioned views and indexed views are discussed in detail later in this chapter.

All types of views share a common set of restrictions:

- Every column (including derived columns) must have a name.
- The SELECT statement used in the view cannot include the COMPUTE BY clause or the INTO keyword.
- The SELECT statement used in the view cannot include the ORDER BY clause.
- The SELECT statement used in the view cannot contain temporary tables.
- You cannot associate AFTER triggers with views, but you can associate INSTEAD OF triggers.
- You cannot associate rules or default definitions with a view.
- You cannot define a full-text index on a view.

A view can have a maximum of 1,024 columns. You can select all the columns for a view by using a `SELECT *` statement, but you need to use some caution when doing so. In particular, you must keep in mind that the view will not display columns that have been added to the view's underlying tables after the view has been created. The fact that the new columns are not displayed can be a good thing but is sometimes overlooked. You can prevent changes to the underlying objects (for example, tables) by creating the view with `SCHEMABINDING`. `SCHEMABINDING` is discussed in the next section.

If you want the changes to the underlying objects to be reflected in the views, you can use the `sp_refreshview` stored procedure. This stored procedure updates the metadata for the specified non-schema-bound view.

TIP

SQL Server Books Online lists a handy script that can be used to update any view that has a dependency on an object. The script is shown in the `sp_refreshview` examples. The script, listed here, is coded such that it will generate output that can be run to generate the `sp_refreshview` statements for the `Person.Person` table in the `Adventureworks2008` database:

```
SELECT DISTINCT 'EXEC sp_refreshview ''' + name + ''''
FROM sys.objects so INNER JOIN sys.sql_dependencies sd
ON so.object_id = sd.object_id
WHERE type = 'V'
AND sd.referenced_major_id = object_id('Person.Person')
```

To generate the executions for another object, you simply change the name of the object (that is, `Person.Person`) found at the end of the script to the name of the object you want to investigate.

With these guidelines in mind, you are now ready to create your view. Views can be created in SQL Server 2008 using T-SQL or SQL Server Management Studio (SSMS).

Creating Views Using T-SQL

The `CREATE VIEW` statement is used to create views with T-SQL. The syntax for the `CREATE VIEW` statement follows:

```
CREATE VIEW [ schema_name . ] view_name [ (column [ ,...n ] ) ]
[ WITH <view_attribute> [ ,...n ] ]
AS select_statement [ ; ]
[ WITH CHECK OPTION ]
```

```
<view_attribute> ::=
{
    [ ENCRYPTION ]
    [ SCHEMABINDING ]
    [ VIEW_METADATA ]     }
```

This statement and the related options are essentially the same in SQL Server 2008 as they were in SQL Server 2005 and SQL Server 2000. We first look at a simple example for creating a view with T-SQL and then delve into several other examples that utilize the view attributes. Listing 27.2 shows a sample T-SQL statement for creating a simple view.

LISTING 27.2 Creating a Simple View with T-SQL

```
CREATE VIEW Sales.vw_OrderSummary as
select datepart(yy, orderdate) as 'OrderYear',
    datepart(mm, orderdate) as 'OrderMonth',
    sum(TotalDue) as 'OrderTotal'
 from Sales.SalesOrderHeader
 group by datepart(yy, orderdate), datepart(mm, orderdate)
```

There are several important aspects to notice in the example in Listing 27.2. First, all the columns in the `SELECT` statement are derived columns and do not simply reference a column in a table. You do not need to have a derived column in your view, but if you do, the derived column(s) must have a name or an alias assigned to it to be able to create the view. The column name allows you to reference the derived column when selecting from the view. If the derived columns in the `SELECT` statement are not named, the `CREATE VIEW` statement will fail.

Another notable characteristic of the simple view example is that an aggregate is used in the `SELECT` statement. Aggregates are allowed in views and are common implementations of views. Views with aggregates can be used instead of summary tables that denormalize data and use additional disk space. Keep in mind that the results of any view (including those with aggregates) are not returned in any particular order. Views cannot be created with the `ORDER BY` clause, but the `ORDER BY` clause can be utilized in a `SELECT` statement that references the view. The following example shows the first five rows of the `vw_OrderSummary` view created in Listing 27.2:

```
select top 5 * from Sales.vw_OrderSummary

OrderYear   OrderMonth  OrderTotal
------      ------      -----------
2003        5           4449886.2315
2001        11          3690018.6652
```

```
2003        8            6775857.0745
2002        7            3781879.0708
2003        11           5961182.6761
```

You can see from the results of the SELECT that the summarized order information is not returned in any particular order. If you want to sort the results, you can treat the view like a table in a SELECT statement and use the ORDER BY clause to produce the desired results. The following example shows a SELECT statement from the vw_OrderSummary view and the ordered results:

```
select top 5 *
 from Sales.vw_OrderSummary
 where OrderYear >= 2004
 order by OrderYear, OrderMonth

OrderYear   OrderMonth  OrderTotal
----------- ----------- ---------------------
2004        1           3691013.2227
2004        2           5207182.5122
2004        3           5272786.8106
2004        4           4722890.7352
2004        5           6518825.2262
```

TIP

In many cases, it is best to create views that include the primary key columns from the underlying tables. This allows the views to be joined to other tables. Consider, for example, a view created on the Employee table in the Adventureworks2008 database. If you want to join that view to another table (such as EmployeeAddress), you need the primary key of the table (that is, Employee.EmployeeID) in the view.

Views can also be created with the following special view attributes: ENCRYPTION, SCHEMABINDING, and VIEW_METADATA. Each of these attributes and some other specialized views are discussed in the following sections.

ENCRYPTION

The ENCRYPTION attribute causes the view definition to be stored as encrypted text in sys.syscomments. This feature is also available for stored procedures and other database code that you may want to protect. One issue to consider when you create a view using the ENCRYPTION option is that this option prevents the view from being published as part of SQL Server replication.

The following example shows the creation of one of the prior views with the ENCRYPTION attribute:

```
IF  EXISTS (SELECT * FROM sys.views WHERE
object_id = OBJECT_ID(N'[Sales].[vw_OrderSummary]'))
DROP VIEW [Sales].[vw_OrderSummary]
GO

CREATE VIEW Sales.vw_OrderSummary
    WITH ENCRYPTION AS
select datepart(yy, orderdate) as 'OrderYear',
    datepart(mm, orderdate) as 'OrderMonth',
    sum(TotalDue) as 'OrderTotal'
 from Sales.SalesOrderHeader
 group by datepart(yy, orderdate), datepart(mm, orderdate)
go
```

The following SELECT statement from sys.syscomments retrieves the text related to the encrypted view and shows that the view definition is not visible in the Text column:

```
SELECT id, OBJECT_NAME(ID) 'ViewName', text
FROM SYS.sysCOMMENTS
 WHERE OBJECT_NAME(ID) LIKE '%vw_OrderSummary%'

id          ViewName             text
----------  -------------------- --------------------
919674324   vw_OrderSummary      NULL
```

SCHEMABINDING

The SCHEMABINDING attribute binds a view to the schema of the underlying table(s) referenced in the view's SELECT statement. This binding action prevents any changes to the underlying tables that would affect the view definition. For example, if you have a view that includes the Employee.Title column, this column cannot be altered or dropped in the Employee table. If schema changes are attempted on the underlying tables, an error message is returned, and the change is not allowed. The only way to make the change is to drop the view or alter the view to remove the SCHEMABINDING attribute.

TIP

Views created with SCHEMABINDING have been used in the past to simply prevent changes to the underlying schema. Any table for which you wanted to prevent schema changes was included in a view, and this essentially locked the definition of the table. This approach is no longer needed because you can accomplish the same thing using DDL triggers, which can react to schema changes and prevent them if desired.

VIEW_METADATA

When the VIEW_METADATA option is specified, SQL Server returns information about the view, as opposed to the base tables. This happens when browse-mode metadata is requested for a query that references the view via a database API. Browse-mode metadata is additional information returned by SQL Server to client-side DBLIB, ODBC, and OLE DB APIs, which allows them to implement client-side updatable cursors.

WITH CHECK OPTION

WITH CHECK OPTION forces all data modifications made through a view to adhere to the conditions in the view. The example shown in Listing 27.3 shows a view created using WITH CHECK OPTION.

LISTING 27.3 View using a **WITH CHECK OPTION**

```
CREATE VIEW HumanResources.vw_MaleEmployees
 AS
SELECT LoginID, Gender
 FROM HumanResources.Employee
 WHERE Gender = 'M'
 WITH CHECK OPTION
```

The following UPDATE statement fails when executed against the view created in Listing 27.3 because the Gender change would cause it to no longer be seen by the view:

```
UPDATE HumanResources.vw_MaleEmployees
 SET Gender = 'F'
 WHERE LoginId = 'adventure-works\taylor0'
```


Updates and other modifications made though a view are discussed further in the "Data Modifications and Views" section, later in this chapter.

Creating Views Using the View Designer

SQL Server 2008 provides a graphical tool, called the View Designer, you can use to create views. This tool can be an invaluable aid when you are creating or modifying a view. The View Designer is equipped with four panes that provide the information relative to the view. Figure 27.1 shows the View Designer display for the Person.vStateProvinceCountryRegion view installed in the Adventureworks2008 database. To view an existing view in the View Designer, right-click on the view listed in the Object Explorer and select Design. To create a new view via the View Designer, right-click the Views node in the Object Explorer and select New View. An empty View Designer is displayed.

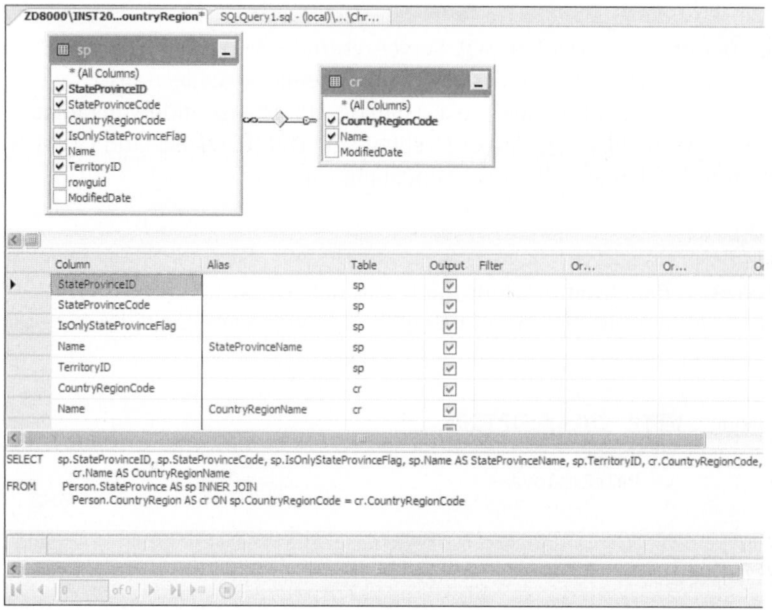

FIGURE 27.1 The View Designer window.

The View Designer has these four panes:

- **Diagram pane**—Gives a graphical view of the tables that are part of the view. This includes the columns in the tables and relationships between the tables contained in the view.
- **Criteria pane**—Displays all the columns selected in the view and allows for sorting, filtering, and other related column-oriented criteria.
- **SQL pane**—Renders the T-SQL associated with the view.
- **Results pane**—Shows the results of that view's `SELECT` statement.

The panes in the View Designer are dependent on each other. If you add a `WHERE` clause in the SQL pane, the corresponding `Filter` value is added in the Criteria pane. Similarly, if you right-click in the Diagram pane and add a table to the view, the Criteria and SQL panes are updated to reflect this change.

TIP

One of the most amazing features of the View Designer is the capability to render a SQL statement into its graphical form. You can copy T-SQL into the SQL pane, and the View Designer reverse-engineers the tables into the Diagram pane, giving you a graphical display of the query. Some complex SQL statements cannot be rendered, but many of them can. Give it a try; you will be impressed.

You can control the View Designer via the Query Designer menu option as well. Adding a new table, verifying the T-SQL, and changing the panes displayed are just some of the options available on this menu.

NOTE

The View Designer does not allow you to set every attribute of a view. It is a great starting point for creating a view, but you need to set some attributes using T-SQL after creating the view. For example, you cannot specify `WITH CHECK OPTION` in the View Designer, but you can set it by altering the view after it has been created.

There is also no option to script a view from the View Designer. You must close the View Designer first, and then you are asked whether you want to save the view. If you click Yes, a prompt allows you to specify a name.

The Properties window displays information about the view and also allows you to enter additional view properties. If this window is not visible, you can select the Properties window from the View menu or simply press F4. The properties you can set on the view include (but are not limited to) a description, the schema that owns the view, and whether to bind the view to the schema. Figure 27.2 shows the Properties window for the `Person.vStateProvinceCountryRegion` view that we looked at earlier.

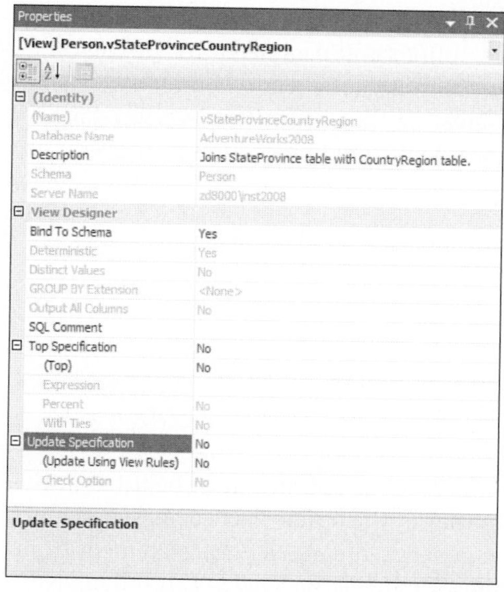

FIGURE 27.2 The view's Properties window.

After defining a view using the panes in the View Designer and setting its properties, you can choose to save the view. You are prompted to give it a name. After you save the view, it appears in the Object Explorer tree.

Managing Views

After creating your view, you can manage the view via T-SQL or the View Designer. The T-SQL commands for managing views are the `ALTER VIEW` and `DROP VIEW` statements. The `ALTER VIEW` statement is used to modify the properties or definition of the view, and the `DROP VIEW` statement is used to remove the view from the database.

Altering Views with T-SQL

The `ALTER VIEW` syntax follows:

```
ALTER VIEW [ schema_name . ] view_name [ ( column [ ,...n ] ) ]
[ WITH <view_attribute> [ ,...n ] ]
AS select_statement [ ; ]
[ WITH CHECK OPTION ]

<view_attribute> ::=
{
    [ ENCRYPTION ]
    [ SCHEMABINDING ]
    [ VIEW_METADATA ]
}
```

The `ALTER VIEW` statement utilizes the same set of options and parameters as the `CREATE VIEW` statement. You should consider using the `ALTER VIEW` statement when making changes to your view instead of dropping and re-creating the view. Altered views retain their associated permissions and do not affect dependent stored procedures or triggers.

An example of the `ALTER VIEW` statement follows:

```
 ALTER VIEW [dbo].[vw_employee]
 with SCHEMABINDING
 AS
SELECT TITLE, GENDER
   FROM HumanResources.Employee
 WITH CHECK OPTION
```

The entire definition of the view, including any attributes or options, must be listed in the `ALTER VIEW` statement. This behavior is similar to that of the `ALTER PROCEDURE` statement and some of the other `ALTER` statements. You can generate the `ALTER VIEW` statement from the Object Explorer by right-clicking the view and selecting Script View As and then choosing Alter To. This allows you to script the `ALTER` statement to a new query editor window, a file, or the Clipboard.

Dropping Views with T-SQL

You can drop views from a database by using the DROP VIEW statement. The syntax for DROP VIEW follows:

```
DROP VIEW [ schema_name . ] view_name [ ...,n ] [ ; ]
```

You can drop more than one view by using one DROP VIEW statement and listing all the targeted views, separated by commas. You should consider running the sp_depends stored procedure against the targeted views before dropping them. This procedure lists the objects dependent on the view you are dropping.

TIP

You can also drop more than one view via SSMS. Simply select the Views node in Object Explorer and then activate the Object Explorer Details window. The Object Explorer Details window displays all the views and allows you to select multiple views that are displayed. After selecting the views you want to delete, you can right-click a selection and choose Delete to remove all the views selected.

Managing Views with SSMS

You can use the Object Explorer in SQL Server Management Studio to alter or drop views as well. To do so, you right-click a view in the Object Explorer and choose Design to launch the View Designer. The View Designer allows you to modify a view in an easy-to-use graphical interface. Refer to the "Creating Views Using the View Designer" section, earlier in this chapter, for a detailed review of the View Designer.

To drop a view, you right-click the view in the Object Explorer and choose Delete. You can drop the view by clicking OK on the Delete Object screen, or you can script the drop statement for later execution.

Data Modifications and Views

Data modifications are allowed through a view under certain circumstances. Views that meet these criteria are sometimes called *updatable views*. Updatable views can be referenced in an INSERT, UPDATE, or DELETE statement, and these statements ultimately affect the underlying table(s) in the view.

The following example contains a SQL statement to create an updatable view, followed by an UPDATE statement that performs a data modification using the view:

```
CREATE VIEW vw_CreditCard
AS
SELECT     CreditCardID, CardType, CardNumber, ExpMonth, ExpYear
```

```
FROM        Sales.CreditCard

UPDATE vw_CreditCard
 SET ExpYear = ExpYear + 1
 WHERE ExpYear < 2006
```

In general, updatable views are similar to the previous example. The following specific conditions allow a view to be updatable:

- Any data modification via a view must reference columns from a single base table. This does not restrict a view to only one table, but the columns referenced in the data modification can be for only one of the tables defined in the view.
- The columns affected by the data modification must directly reference the underlying tables. They cannot be derived through an aggregate function (for example, `AVG`, `COUNT`, `SUM`) and cannot contain computations from an expression that utilizes columns from another table.
- The `TOP` clause cannot be part of the `SELECT` statement that defines the view when the `WITH CHECK OPTION` clause is used.
- The columns affected by the data modification cannot be affected by `GROUP BY`, `HAVING`, or `DISTINCT` clauses in the view definition.

You can overcome these restrictions by using `INSTEAD OF` triggers to perform the data modifications. You can create `INSTEAD OF` triggers on a view, and the logic within the triggers performs the actual database updates. `INSTEAD OF` triggers are discussed in detail in Chapter 30, "Creating and Managing Triggers."

Partitioned views are another means for performing data modifications via a view. Partitioned views can be updatable and are not subject to all the restrictions listed for conventional views. However, some additional restrictions apply to partitioned views. These additional restrictions and other details about partitioned views are discussed in the next section.

Partitioned Views

Partitioned views are used to access data that has been horizontally split, or partitioned, across multiple tables. These tables can be in the same or different databases—or even spread across multiple servers. Partitioning of tables is done to spread the I/O and processing load of large tables across multiple disks or servers.

You combine the tables in a partitioned view by using a `UNION ALL` statement that causes the data from the separate tables to appear as if they were one table. These separate tables are referred to as *member tables* or *base tables*. The member tables in a `SELECT` statement of the view must all be structured in the same way, and the view must adhere to the following restrictions:

- All the columns from the member tables should be included in the view definition.

- Columns with the same ordinal position in the SELECT list should have the same data type.
- The same column cannot be used multiple times in the SELECT list.
- A partitioning column that segments the data must be identified and needs to have the same ordinal position across all the member table SELECT statements.
- The partitioning column cannot be a computed column, an identity, a default, or a time stamp.
- The data values in the partitioning column cannot overlap in the underlying tables.
- The partitioning column must be part of the primary key of the member table.
- The member tables in the partitioned view need a CHECK constraint on the partitioning column.
- A table can appear only once as part of the UNION ALL statement.
- The member tables cannot have indexes created on computed columns in the table.
- The number of columns in the member table primary key constraints should be the same.
- All member tables should have the same ANSI PADDING setting when created.

The list of restrictions for creating partitioned views is extensive, but the creation of a partitioned view is relatively straightforward and intuitive. Consider, for example, the Sales.SalesOrderHeader table in the Adventureworks2008 database. This table is relatively small, but it is the type of table that could have a large number of rows and experience heavy utilization. To balance the workload against this table, you could use a partitioned view that utilizes base tables that each contain a separate year's data. Listing 27.4 shows the CREATE TABLE statements to create the base tables for each year. The yearly tables are intended to hold summarized daily numbers, and each contains only a subset of the columns in the Sales.SalesOrderHeader table.

LISTING 27.4 Creating the Base Tables for a Partitioned View

```
CREATE TABLE Sales.Sales_2001
(
    OrderDay datetime NOT NULL
        CHECK (OrderDay BETWEEN '20010101' AND '20011231'),
    SubTotal money NOT NULL ,
    TaxAmt money not null,
    Freight money not null,
 CONSTRAINT PK_Sales_2001_OrderDay PRIMARY KEY CLUSTERED (OrderDay ASC)
)

CREATE TABLE Sales.Sales_2002
(
```

```
    OrderDay datetime NOT NULL,
        CHECK (OrderDay BETWEEN '20020101' AND '20021231'),
    SubTotal money NOT NULL ,
    TaxAmt money not null,
    Freight money not null,
 CONSTRAINT PK_Sales_2002_OrderDay PRIMARY KEY CLUSTERED (OrderDay ASC)
)

CREATE TABLE Sales.Sales_2003
(
    OrderDay datetime NOT NULL
        CHECK (OrderDay BETWEEN '20030101' AND '20031231'),
    SubTotal money NOT NULL ,
    TaxAmt money not null,
    Freight money not null,
 CONSTRAINT PK_Sales_2003_OrderDay PRIMARY KEY CLUSTERED (OrderDay ASC)
)

CREATE TABLE Sales.Sales_2004
(
    OrderDay datetime NOT NULL
        CHECK (OrderDay BETWEEN '20040101' AND '20041231'),
    SubTotal money NOT NULL ,
    TaxAmt money not null,
    Freight money not null,
 CONSTRAINT PK_Sales_2004_OrderDay PRIMARY KEY CLUSTERED (OrderDay ASC)
)
```

Notice that each table has a primary key on `OrderDay`, the partitioning column. Also notice that a `CHECK` constraint is defined for each table; it ensures that only orders for the given year can be stored in the table.

To demonstrate the power of a partitioned view, it is best to populate the base tables that will be used by the view. Listing 27.5 contains a series of `INSERT` statements that select from the `Sales.SalesOrderHeader` table and populate the base tables. The `SELECT` statements summarize several key columns by day and contain a `WHERE` clause that limits the result to orders for the respective years.

LISTING 27.5 Populating the Base Tables for a Partitioned View

```
INSERT Sales.Sales_2001
   SELECT CONVERT(VARCHAR(8),OrderDate,112),
      SUM(SubTotal), SUM(TaxAmt), SUM(Freight)
    FROM Sales.SalesOrderHeader
    WHERE OrderDate between '20010101' AND '20011231'
    GROUP BY CONVERT(VARCHAR(8),OrderDate,112)
```

```
INSERT Sales.Sales_2002
   SELECT CONVERT(VARCHAR(8),OrderDate,112),
      SUM(SubTotal), SUM(TaxAmt), SUM(Freight)
    FROM Sales.SalesOrderHeader
    WHERE OrderDate between '20020102' AND '20021231'
    GROUP BY CONVERT(VARCHAR(8),OrderDate,112)

INSERT Sales.Sales_2003
   SELECT CONVERT(VARCHAR(8),OrderDate,112),
      SUM(SubTotal), SUM(TaxAmt), SUM(Freight)
    FROM Sales.SalesOrderHeader
    WHERE OrderDate between '20030101' AND '20031231'
    GROUP BY CONVERT(VARCHAR(8),OrderDate,112)

INSERT Sales.Sales_2004
   SELECT CONVERT(VARCHAR(8),OrderDate,112),
      SUM(SubTotal), SUM(TaxAmt), SUM(Freight)
    FROM Sales.SalesOrderHeader
    WHERE OrderDate between '20040102' AND '20041231'
    GROUP BY CONVERT(VARCHAR(8),OrderDate,112)
```

Now that you have the populated base table, you can create a partitioned view and ensure that the view is selecting only from the base tables that it needs.

Two types of partitioned views are discussed in this chapter: local and distributed. A local partitioned view utilizes base tables found on the same server. A distributed partitioned view contains at least one base table that resides on a different (remote) server. The focus in the section is on local partitioned views; distributed partitioned views are discussed later in this chapter. The T-SQL for creating a local partitioned view named `Sales.vw_Sales_Daily` is shown in Listing 27.6.

27

LISTING 27.6 Creating a Local Partitioned View

```
Create View Sales.vw_Sales_Daily
 as
      SELECT * FROM Sales.Sales_2001
       UNION ALL
      SELECT * FROM Sales.Sales_2002
       UNION ALL
      SELECT * FROM Sales.Sales_2003
       UNION ALL
      SELECT * FROM Sales.Sales_2004
```

The best way to validate that a partitioned view is working properly is to run a conditional SELECT against the view and display the execution plan. If the partitioned view is functioning properly, it should be accessing only the base tables it needs to satisfy the SELECT and should not access all the tables in the view unless it needs to. The following example shows a sample SELECT against the new partitioned view:

```
SELECT * FROM Sales.vw_Sales_Daily
 WHERE OrderDay > '20040701'
   and SubTotal > 2000
```

If you execute this statement and review the actual execution plan, you see that an index seek is performed against the Sales.Sales_2004 table. This is the correct result, given that the SELECT statement is targeting order data from 2004.

NOTE

SQL Server Books Online states that the recommended method for partitioning data on a local server in SQL Server 2008 is through the use of partitioned tables and indexes. Partitioned tables and indexes are discussed in Chapter 24, "Creating and Managing Tables."

Modifying Data Through a Partitioned View

You can modify data via a partitioned view if the SQL statement performing the modification meets certain conditions, as described here:

- All columns in the partitioned view must be specified in the INSERT statement. Columns that include a DEFAULT constraint or allow nulls are also subject to this requirement.
- The DEFAULT keyword cannot be used on inserts to partitioned views or on updates to partitioned views.
- UPDATE statements cannot modify PRIMARY KEY columns if the member tables have text, ntext, or image columns.
- Inserts and updates to a partitioned view are not allowed if the view contains a time stamp.
- Identity columns in a partitioned view cannot be modified by an INSERT or UPDATE statement.
- INSERT, UPDATE, and DELETE statements are not allowed against a partitioned view if there is a self-join with the same view or with any of the member tables in the statement.

NOTE

Data can be modified through partitioned views only in the Enterprise and Developer Editions of SQL Server 2008.

In addition to the conditions shown in this list, you must also satisfy any restrictions that apply to the member tables. Check constraints, foreign key constraints, and any other table-level restrictions must be accounted for in the modification statement. The user executing the modification against the partitioned view must have the appropriate `INSERT`, `UPDATE`, or `DELETE` permissions on the member tables for the update to succeed.

Distributed Partitioned Views

Microsoft provides distributed partitioned views (DPVs) as a primary means to scale out a database server. Scalability allows an application or a database to utilize additional resources, which allows it to perform more work. There are two kinds of scalability: scaleup and scaleout. A scaleup solution focuses on a single server scaled to provide more processing power than its predecessor. An example of scaleup would be migrating from a server with a single dual-core processor to a machine with 4-quad-core processor. Scaleout solutions include the addition of servers to augment the overall processing power.

DPVs are similar to local partitioned views, but they utilize one or more tables located on a remote server. The placement of partitioned data on remote servers allows the processing power of more than one server to be utilized. The partitioning is intended to be transparent to the application and allow for additional partitions and servers as the application's needs scale.

The following list outlines the basic requirements for creating a DPV:

- A linked server definition is added to each member server that will contain the partitioned data. The linked server contains the connection information required to run distributed queries on another member server.
- The `lazy schema validation` option is set to `true` on each of the member servers, using `sp_serveroption`. This option is set for performance reasons and allows the query processor to skip schema checking of remote tables if the query can be satisfied on a single member server.
- A DPV is created on each member server. This DPV references the local tables in addition to the tables found on the other member servers.

27

Listing 27.7 shows SQL commands that can be used to satisfy the requirements in the preceding list. The DPV created in the last portion of the script is similar to the local partitioned view created in the previous section. The key difference in this DPV example is the inclusion of a distributed query that retrieves records for `Sales.Sales_2002` from a remote server. The remote server in this example is named `DbSvrXP`.

LISTING 27.7 Creating a Distributed Partitioned View

```
Exec sp_addlinkedserver @server='dbsvrxp',
      @srvproduct='',
      @provider='MSDASQL',
      @provstr='DRIVER={SQL Server};
SERVER=dbsvrxp;UID=linklogin;PWD=pw;Initial Catalog=Adventureworks2008'
```

```
—Set the server option for improved DPV performance
exec sp_serveroption dbsvrxp, 'lazy schema validation', true

Create View Sales.vw_Sales_Daily
 as
      SELECT * FROM Sales.Sales_2001
       UNION ALL
      SELECT * FROM dbsvrxp.Adventureworks2008.Sales.Sales_2002
       UNION ALL
      SELECT * FROM Sales.Sales_2003
       UNION ALL
      SELECT * FROM Sales.Sales_2004
```

The DPV created in Listing 27.7 contains only one remote table. The example could be further expanded to have each table in the UNION clause on a different remote server. Keep in mind that the DPV CREATE statement needs to be adjusted when run on the remote server(s). The tables that are local on one server are now remote on the other server, and those that are remote can now be local.

If the DPVs are properly defined, SQL Server 2008 attempts to optimize their performance by minimizing the amount of data transferred between member servers. The query processor retrieves the CHECK constraint definitions from each member table. This allows the query processor to map the specified search arguments to the appropriate table(s). The query execution plan then accesses only the necessary tables and retrieves only the remote rows needed to complete the SQL statement.

Data can be modified through a DPV as well. Updatable DPVs, which were introduced in SQL Server 2000, are still available in SQL Server 2008. Data modifications are performed against a view, allowing true transparency. The view is accessed as if it were a base table, and the user or application is unaware of the actual location of the data. If it is configured properly, SQL Server determines via the WHERE clause specified in the update query which partition defined in the view must be updated rather than updating all tables in the join.

NOTE

Data can be modified through distributed partitioned views only in the Enterprise and Developer Editions of SQL Server 2008.

Indexed Views

You establish indexed views by creating a unique clustered index on the view itself, independent of the member tables that it references. The creation of this unique index transforms a view from an object that is virtual in nature to one that has physical storage associated with it. Like all other indexes, the index on a view takes up physical storage, requires maintenance, and, most importantly, can provide performance benefits that justify its creation.

Creating Indexed Views

Indexed views were first available for creation in SQL Server 2000 and continue to be a viable means for improving query performance in SQL Server 2008. An index can be created on a view in all versions of SQL Server 2008, but there are limitations on some of the versions. The Developer and Enterprise Editions of SQL Server 2008 are the only editions that support the use of indexed views for queries that don't specifically reference the views. Other editions of SQL Server must reference the view by name in the SQL statements and must also use the `NOEXPAND` keyword in the query. The details of `NOEXPAND` are discussed in the section "To Expand or Not to Expand," later in this chapter.

Regardless of the edition of SQL Server you are running, some basic requirements must be satisfied for you to create an indexed view. These requirements, which follow, are detailed in SQL Server 2008 Books Online:

- The `ANSI_NULLS` and `QUOTED_IDENTIFIER` options must be set to `ON` when the `CREATE VIEW` statement is executed.
- The `ANSI_NULLS` option must be set to `ON` for the execution of all `CREATE TABLE` statements that create tables referenced by the view.
- The view must not reference any other views, only base tables.
- All base tables referenced by the view must be in the same database as the view and have the same owner as the view.
- The view must be created with the `SCHEMABINDING` option. Schema binding binds the view to the schema of the underlying base tables.
- User-defined functions referenced in the view must be created with the `SCHEMABINDING` option.
- Tables and user-defined functions must be referenced via two-part names in the view. One-part, three-part, and four-part names are not allowed.
- All functions referenced by expressions in the view must be deterministic.
- If the view definition uses an aggregate function, the `SELECT` list must also include `COUNT_BIG (*)`.
- The `DATA ACCESS` property of a user-defined function must be `NO SQL`, and the `EXTERNAL ACCESS` property must be `NO`.
- CLR functions can appear only in the `SELECT` list of the view and can reference only fields that are not part of the clustered index key. They cannot appear in the `WHERE` clause of the view or the `ON` clause of a `JOIN` operation in the view.
- CLR functions and methods of CLR user-defined types used in the view definition must have the properties set as `DETERMINISTIC = TRUE`, `PRECISE = TRUE`, `DATA ACCESS = NO SQL`, and `EXTERNAL ACCESS = NO`.

- If GROUP BY is specified, the view SELECT list must contain a COUNT_BIG(*) expression, and the view definition cannot specify HAVING, CUBE, or ROLLUP.
- The view cannot contain any of the T-SQL elements shown in the following list:

* or tablename.*	An expression on a column found in the GROUP BY clause	A derived table
A common table expression (CTE)	A rowset function	The UNION, EXCEPT, or INTERSECT operators
Subqueries	Outer joins or self-joins	The TOP clause
The ORDER BY clause	The DISTINCT keyword	COUNT (COUNT_BIG is allowed)
AVG, MAX, MIN, STDEV, STDEVP, VAR, or VARP	A SUM function that references a nullable expression	A CLR user-defined aggregate function
The full text predicate	COMPUTE or COMPUTE BY CONTAINS or FREETEXT	CROSS APPLY or OUTER APPLY operators
Table hints	Join hints	

You can see from this list that the number of requirements is extensive. It can therefore be difficult to determine whether all the requirements have been met for a particular view. To simplify this determination, you can query the IsIndexable property, using the OBJECTPROPERTY function. The following example demonstrates the use of the IsIndexable property against the sys.views catalog view:

```
SELECT name AS ViewName
  ,SCHEMA_NAME(schema_id) AS SchemaName
  ,OBJECTPROPERTYEX(object_id,'IsIndexed') AS IsIndexed
  ,OBJECTPROPERTYEX(object_id,'IsIndexable') AS IsIndexable
  ,create_date
  ,modify_date
FROM sys.views;
```

The IsIndexable property returns a 1 (or TRUE) if an index can be created on the view and a 0 if it is not indexable. Most of the views in the Adventureworks2008 database are not indexable, but the database does contain a couple of examples of views that have been indexed. The following example shows the CREATE statement for an index on the vProductAndDescription view. The SET options required when creating the index are included in the example as well:

```
SET ARITHABORT ON  — for 80 compatibility or earlier
GO
SET CONCAT_NULL_YIELDS_NULL ON
GO
```

```
SET QUOTED_IDENTIFIER ON
GO
SET ANSI_NULLS ON
GO
SET ANSI_PADDING ON
GO
SET ANSI_WARNINGS ON
GO
SET NUMERIC_ROUNDABORT OFF
GO

CREATE UNIQUE CLUSTERED INDEX [IX_vProductAndDescription]
 ON [Production].[vProductAndDescription]
(
      [CultureID] ASC,
      [ProductID] ASC
)
```

The following example shows the `Production.vProductAndDescript` view that the index was created on:

```
CREATE VIEW [Production].[vProductAndDescription]
WITH SCHEMABINDING
AS
View (indexed or standard) to display products
—and product descriptions by language.
SELECT
    p.[ProductID]
    ,p.[Name]
    ,pm.[Name] AS [ProductModel]
    ,pmx.[CultureID]
    ,pd.[Description]
FROM [Production].[Product] p
    INNER JOIN [Production].[ProductModel] pm
    ON p.[ProductModelID] = pm.[ProductModelID]
    INNER JOIN [Production].[ProductModelProductDescriptionCulture] pmx
    ON pm.[ProductModelID] = pmx.[ProductModelID]
    INNER JOIN [Production].[ProductDescription] pd
    ON pmx.[ProductDescriptionID] = pd.[ProductDescriptionID];
```

Indexed Views and Performance

Adding indexes to tables is a generally accepted means for improving database performance. Indexes provide a keyed lookup to rows of data that can improve database access and avoid the performance nightmare of a table scan where the entire contents of a table are searched. The same basic principles apply to indexes on views, but indexed views are best utilized to increase performance in the following scenarios:

- Aggregations such as SUM or AVG can be precomputed and stored in the index to minimize the potentially expensive computations during query execution.
- Large table joins can be persisted to eliminate the need to write a join when retrieving the data.
- A combination of aggregations and large table joins can be stored.

The performance improvements from the aforementioned scenarios can be significant and can justify the use of an index. The Query Optimizer can use the precomputed results stored in the view's index and avoid the cost of aggregating or joining the underlying tables. Keep in mind that the Query Optimizer may still use the indexes found on the member tables of the view instead of the index on the view. The Query Optimizer uses the following conditions in determining whether the index on the view can be utilized:

- The tables in the query FROM clause must be a superset of the tables in the indexed view's FROM clause. In other words, the query must contain all the tables in the view. The query can contain additional tables not contained in the view.
- The join conditions in the query must be a superset of the view's join conditions.
- The aggregate columns in the query must be derivable from a subset of the aggregate columns in the view.
- All expressions in the query SELECT list must be derivable from the view SELECT list or from the tables not included in the view definition.
- All columns in the query search condition predicates that belong to tables in the view definition must appear in the GROUP BY list, the SELECT list if there is no GROUP BY, or the same or equivalent predicate in the view definition.

NOTE

Predicting the Query Optimizer's use of an indexed view can be complicated and depends on the complexity of the view that is indexed and the complexity of the query that may utilize the view. A detailed discussion of these scenarios is beyond the scope of this chapter, but the Microsoft TechNet article "Improving Performance with SQL Server 2005 Indexed Views" provides that detail. This article includes more than 20 examples that illustrate the use of indexed views and the conditions the Query Optimizer uses in selecting an indexed view. As you can see from the title, this article was written for SQL Server 2005, but the content is still relative for SQL Server 2008.

The flip side of performance with indexes (including those on views) is that there is a cost in maintaining an index. This cost can adversely affect the performance of data modifications against objects that have these indexes. Generally speaking, indexes should *not* be placed on views that have underlying data sets that are frequently updated. Caution must be exercised when placing indexes on views that support online transaction processing (OLTP) applications. A balance must be struck between improving the performance of database modification and improving the performance of database inquiry. Indexed views improve database inquiry. Databases used for data warehousing and decision support are usually the best candidates for indexed views.

The impact of data modifications on indexed views is exacerbated by the fact that the complete result set of a view is stored in the database. When the clustered index is created on a view, you specify the clustered index key(s) in the `CREATE UNIQUE CLUSTERED INDEX` statement, but more than the columns in the key are stored in the database. As in a clustered index on a base table, the B-tree structure of the clustered index contains only the key columns, but the data rows contain all the columns in the view's result set.

The increased space utilized by the index view is demonstrated in the following examples. This first example creates a view and an associated index view similar to the `Adventureworks2008 Production.vProductAndDescription` view used in a prior example:

```
result setCREATE VIEW [Production].[vProductAndDescription_2]
WITH SCHEMABINDING
AS
View (indexed or standard) to display products and
— product descriptions by language.
SELECT
    p.[ProductID]
    ,pmx.[CultureID]
FROM [Production].[Product] p
    INNER JOIN [Production].[ProductModel] pm
    ON p.[ProductModelID] = pm.[ProductModelID]
    INNER JOIN [Production].[ProductModelProductDescriptionCulture] pmx
    ON pm.[ProductModelID] = pmx.[ProductModelID]
    INNER JOIN [Production].[ProductDescription] pd
    ON pmx.[ProductDescriptionID] = pd.[ProductDescriptionID];
go
CREATE UNIQUE CLUSTERED INDEX [IX_vProductAndDescription_2]
  ON [Production].[vProductAndDescription_2]
(
      [CultureID] ASC,
      [ProductID] ASC
)
```

The difference with this new view is that the result set returns only the two columns in the clustered index; there are no additional columns in the result set.

When the new view and associated index are created, you can compare the amount of physical storage occupied by each. The following example shows the `sp_spaceused` commands for each view and the associated results:

```
exec sp_spaceused 'Production.vProductAndDescription'
```

27

```
/* results
name                        rows      reserved    data      index_size  unused
------------                --        ----        ---       ------      ---
vProductAndDescription      1764      592 KB      560 KB    16 KB       16 KB
*/
exec sp_spaceused 'Production.vProductAndDescription_2'
/* results
name                        rows      reserved    data      index_size  unused
------------                --        ----        ---       ------      ---
vProductAndDescription_2    1764      64 KB       48 KB     16 KB       0 KB
*/
```

Take note of the reserved space and data results for each view. The view that was created with only two result columns takes much less space than the view that has an index with five result columns. You need to consider the overhead of storing these additional result columns along with the index when creating the view and related index. Changes made to any of the columns in the base tables that are part of the view results must also be maintained for the index view as well.

Nonclustered indexes can be created on a view, and they can also provide added query performance benefits when used properly. Typically, columns that are not part of the clustered index on a view are added to the nonclustered index. Like nonclustered indexes on tables, the nonclustered indexes on the view provide additional options for the Query Optimizer when it is choosing the best query path. Common search arguments and foreign key columns that may be joined in the view are common targets for nonclustered indexes.

To Expand or Not to Expand

The expansion of a view to its base tables is a key consideration when evaluating the use of indexes on views. The SQL Server Query Optimizer can expand a view to its base tables or decide to utilize indexes that are found on the view itself. The selection of an index on a view is directly related to the edition of SQL Server 2008 you are running and the expansion options selected for a related query.

As mentioned earlier, the Enterprise and Developer Editions are the only editions that allow the Query Optimizer to use an indexed view to solve queries that structurally match the view, even if they don't refer to the view by name. For other editions of SQL Server 2008, the view must be referenced in the query, and the NOEXPAND hint must be used as well for the Query Optimizer to consider the index on the view. The following example demonstrates the use of the NOEXPAND hint:

```
SELECT *
FROM Production.vProductAndDescription (NOEXPAND)
 WHERE cultureid = 'he'
```

When this example is run against the Adventureworks2008 database, the execution plan indicates that a clustered index seek will be performed, using the index on the view. If the NOEXPAND hint is removed from the query, the execution plan will ignore the index on the view and return the results from the base table(s). The only exception to this is when the Enterprise or Developer Edition is used. These editions can always consider indexed views but may or may not choose to use them.

SQL Server also has options to force the Query Optimizer to use the expanded base tables and ignore indexed views. The (EXPAND VIEWS) query hint ensures that SQL Server will process a query by accessing data directly from the base tables. This option might seem counterproductive, but it can be useful in situations in which contention exists on an indexed view. It is also handy for testing indexed views and determining overall performance with and without the use of indexed views.

The following example, which utilizes the same view as the previous example, demonstrates the use of the (EXPAND VIEWS) query hint:

```
SELECT *
FROM Production.vProductAndDescription
 WHERE cultureid = 'he'
 OPTION (EXPAND VIEWS)
```

The query plan in this example shows the use of the base tables, and the index on the view is ignored. For more information on query optimization and indexes, see Chapter 34.

Summary

Views provide a broad spectrum of functionality, ranging from simple organization to improved overall query performance. They can simplify life for developers and users by filtering the complexity of a database. They can help organize data access and provide a security mechanism that helps keep a database safe. Finally, they can provide performance improvements via the use of partitioned views and indexed views that help keep your database fast.

Some of the same benefits, including performance and security benefits, can also be achieved through the use of stored procedures. Chapter 28, "Creating and Managing Stored Procedures," delves into these useful and powerful database objects.

CHAPTER 28

Creating and Managing Stored Procedures

IN THIS CHAPTER

- What's New in Creating and Managing Stored Procedures
- Advantages of Stored Procedures
- Creating Stored Procedures
- Executing Stored Procedures
- Deferred Name Resolution
- Viewing Stored Procedures
- Modifying Stored Procedures
- Using Input Parameters
- Using Output Parameters
- Returning Procedure Status
- Debugging Stored Procedures Using SQL Server Management Studio
- Using System Stored Procedures
- Startup Procedures

A *stored procedure* is one or more SQL commands stored in a database as an executable object. Stored procedures can be called interactively, from within client application code, from within other stored procedures, and from within triggers. Parameters can be passed to and returned from stored procedures to increase their usefulness and flexibility. A stored procedure can also return a number of result sets and a status code.

What's New in Creating and Managing Stored Procedures

Unlike SQL Server 2005 with its addition of .NET CLR stored procedures, SQL Server 2008 doesn't introduce any significant changes to the creation and functionality of stored procedures. However, one of the most welcome enhancements is the return of the Transact-SQL (T-SQL) debugger to SQL Server Management Studio (SSMS). System administrators can now debug stored procedures without having to install Visual Studio (VS). An introduction to debugging stored procedures is provided later in this chapter in the section "Debugging Stored Procedures Using SQL Server Management Studio."

One small enhancement to the functionality of stored procedures in SQL Server 2008 is the capability to use table-valued parameters. Table-valued parameters allow you to pass table variables as input parameters to stored procedures so that the contents may be accessed from within the stored procedure. In previous versions of SQL Server, it was not possible to access the contents of table variables outside the scope in which they were declared. The "Using Table-Valued Parameters" section in this chapter provides a description and examples on how to make use of this new feature.

One other enhancement in SQL Server 2008 is that there is no longer a maximum size for your stored procedure source code.

Advantages of Stored Procedures

Using stored procedures provides many advantages over executing large and complex SQL batches from client applications. Following are some of them:

- **Modular programming**—Subroutines and functions are often used in ordinary 3GL and 4GL languages (such as C, C++, and Microsoft Visual Basic) to break code into smaller, more manageable pieces. The same advantages are achieved when using stored procedures, with the difference that the stored procedure is stored in SQL Server and can be called by any client application.
- **Restricted, function-based access to tables**—A user can have permission to execute a stored procedure without having permissions to operate directly on the underlying tables.
- **Reduced network traffic**—Stored procedures can consist of many individual SQL statements but can be executed with a single statement. This allows you to reduce the number and size of calls from the client to the server.
- **Faster execution**—Stored procedures' query plans are kept in memory after the first execution. The code doesn't have to be reparsed and reoptimized on subsequent executions.
- **Enforced consistency**—If users modify data only through stored procedures, problems that often result from ad hoc modifications (such as omitting a crucial `WHERE` clause) are eliminated.
- **Reduced operator and programmer errors**—Because less information is being passed, complex tasks can be executed more easily, with less likelihood of SQL errors.
- **Automating complex or sensitive transactions**—If all modifications of certain tables take place in stored procedures, you can guarantee the data integrity on those tables.

Some of the disadvantages of using stored procedures (depending on the environment) are as follows:

- **Increase in server processing requirements**—Using stored procedures can increase the amount of processing that takes place on the server. In a large user environment with considerable activity in the server, it may be more desirable to offload some of the processing to the client workstation.
- **Less cross-DBMS portability**—Although the ANSI-99 SQL standard provides a standard for stored procedures in database management systems (DBMSs), the format and structure are different from those of SQL Server stored procedures. These

procedures would all have to be rewritten to be compatible with another DBMS environment.

Should you use stored procedures? The answer is (as it often is), it depends.

If you are working in a two-tier environment, using stored procedures is often advantageous. The trend is shifting to three- (or more) tier environments. In such environments, business logic is often handled in some middle tier (possibly ActiveX objects managed by Microsoft Transaction Server). If you operate in that type of environment, you might want to restrict the stored procedures to performing basic data-related tasks, such as retrievals, insertions, updates, and deletions.

NOTE

You can use stored procedures to make a database sort of a "black box" as far as the developers and the application code are concerned. If all database access is managed through stored procedures, the applications are shielded from possible changes to the underlying database structures.

For example, one organization found the need to split one table across multiple databases. By simply modifying the existing stored procedures to handle the multiple tables and by using distributed partitioned views, the company was able to make this change without requiring any changes to the front-end application code.

Creating Stored Procedures

To create a stored procedure, you need to give the procedure a unique name within the schema and then write the sequence of SQL statements to be executed within the procedure. Following is the basic syntax for creating stored procedures:

```
CREATE { PROC | PROCEDURE } [schema_name.]procedure_name [ ; number ]
    [ { @parameter [ schema_name.]data_type }
        [ VARYING ] [ = default ] [ OUT | OUTPUT ] [READONLY]
    ] [ ,...n ]
[ WITH  {  [ ENCRYPTION ]
          , [ RECOMPILE ]
          , [ EXECUTE_AS_Clause ]
          [ ,...n] ]
[ FOR REPLICATION ]
AS
[BEGIN]
    SQL_Statements
[   RETURN scalar_expression ]
[END]
```

It is good programming practice to always end a procedure with the `RETURN` statement and to specify a return status other than `0` when an error condition occurs. Listing 28.1 shows a simple stored procedure that returns book titles and the names of the authors who wrote them.

LISTING 28.1 A Sample Stored Procedure

```
use bigpubs2008
go
IF EXISTS ( SELECT * FROM sys.procedures
            WHERE schema_id = schema_id('dbo')
              AND name = N'title_authors')
   DROP PROCEDURE dbo.title_authors
GO
CREATE PROCEDURE title_authors
AS
BEGIN
   SELECT a.au_lname, a.au_fname, t.title
      FROM titles t INNER JOIN
           titleauthor ta ON t.title_id = ta.title_id RIGHT OUTER JOIN
           authors a ON ta.au_id = a.au_id
   RETURN 0
END
```

NOTE

Unless stated otherwise, all examples in this chapter run in the context of the bigpubs2008 database.

Creating Procedures in SSMS

To create a stored procedure in SSMS, open the object tree for the database in which you want to create the procedure, open the Programmability folder, right-click the Stored Procedures folder, and from the context menu, choose New Stored Procedure. SSMS opens a new query window, populated with code that is based on a default template for stored procedures. Listing 28.2 shows an example of the default template code for a stored procedure that would be opened into a new query window.

LISTING 28.2 An Example of a New Stored Procedure Creation Script Generated by SSMS

```
-- ================================================
-- Template generated from Template Explorer using:
-- Create Procedure (New Menu).SQL
--
-- Use the Specify Values for Template Parameters
-- command (Ctrl-Shift-M) to fill in the parameter
-- values below.
```

```
--
-- This block of comments will not be included in
-- the definition of the procedure.
-- ================================================
SET ANSI_NULLS ON
GO
SET QUOTED_IDENTIFIER ON
GO
-- =============================================
-- Author:          <Author,,Name>
-- Create date: <Create Date,,>
-- Description:     <Description,,>
-- =============================================
CREATE PROCEDURE <Procedure_Name, sysname, ProcedureName>
     - Add the parameters for the stored procedure here
     <@Param1, sysname, @p1> <Datatype_For_Param1, , int> =
 <Default_Value_For_Param1, , 0>,
     <@Param2, sysname, @p2> <Datatype_For_Param2, , int> =
 <Default_Value_For_Param2, , 0>
AS
BEGIN
     - SET NOCOUNT ON added to prevent extra result sets from
     - interfering with SELECT statements.
     SET NOCOUNT ON;

    -- Insert statements for procedure here
     SELECT <@Param1, sysname, @p1>, <@Param2, sysname, @p2>
END
GO
```


You can modify the template code as necessary to set the procedure name and to specify the parameters, return value, and procedure body. When you are finished, you can execute the contents of the query window to create the procedure. After you have created the procedure successfully, it is recommended that you save the source code to a file by choosing the Save or Save As option from the File menu. This way, you can re-create the stored procedure from the file if it is accidentally dropped from the database.

TIP

When you create a new stored procedure in SSMS, the procedure does not show up in the `Stored Procedures` folder in the Object Browser unless you right-click the `Stored Procedures` folder and choose the Refresh option.

One thing you might notice about the stored procedure template is that it contains template parameters for parameter names, procedure name, author name, create date, and so on. These template parameters are in the format `<parameter, type, value>`:

- `parameter_name` is the name of the template parameter in the script.
- `data_type` is the optional data type of the template parameter.
- `value` is the default value to be used to replace every occurrence of the template parameter in the script

You can auto substitute values for template parameters by selecting Query, Specify Values for Template Parameters or by pressing Ctrl+Shift+M. This brings up the dialog shown in Figure 28.1.

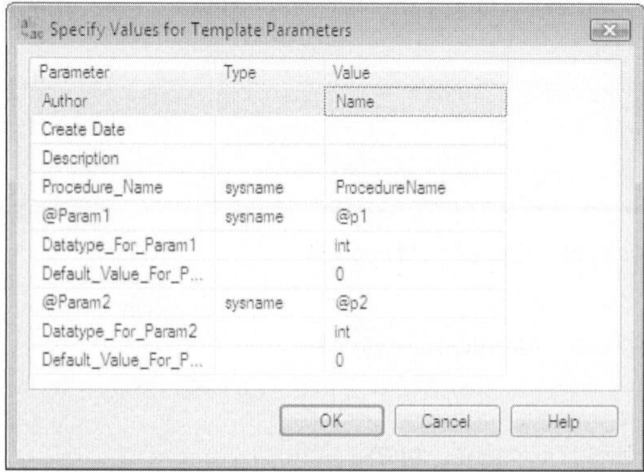

FIGURE 28.1 Using the Specify Values for Template Parameters dialog in SSMS.

You enter the values for the template parameters in the Value column and then click OK. SSMS then substitutes any values you specified wherever the template parameter is used within the template.

An alternative way to create a stored procedure from a template is to use the Template Explorer in SSMS. You can open the Template Explorer by selecting View, Template Explorer in SSMS or by pressing Ctrl+Alt+T. The Template Explorer window appears in SSMS, as shown in Figure 28.2.

You can double-click the name of the stored procedure template you want to use or right-click the desired template and then select Open. SSMS opens a new query window, populated with the template code.

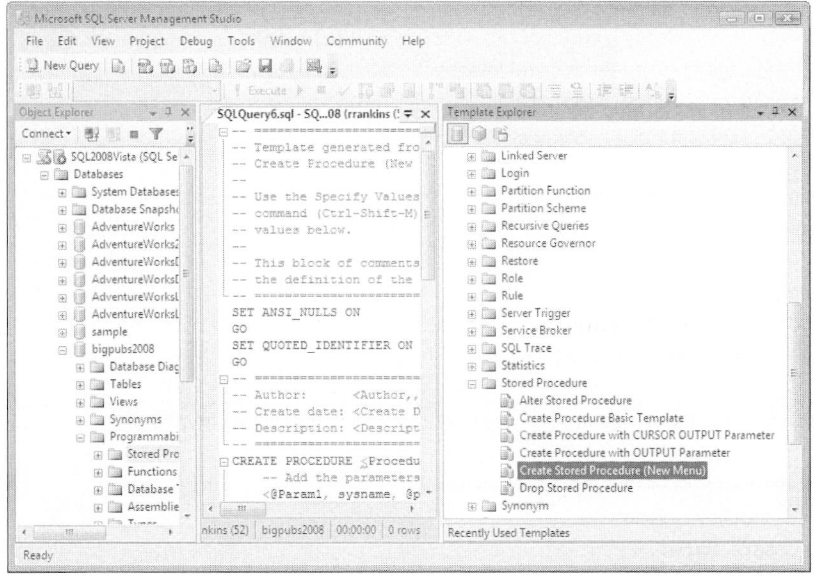

FIGURE 28.2 Using the Template Explorer for creating stored procedures in SSMS.

NOTE

It is also possible to edit the provided stored procedure templates available in the Template Explorer by right-clicking them and selecting the Edit option. You can then customize the templates to include code fragments, comments, or structure that is more to your preference and save the changes to the template file. However, it is generally recommended that you not modify the provided templates and instead create your own custom templates.

Creating Custom Stored Procedure Templates

To create a custom stored procedure template, right-click the `Stored Procedure` folder in the Template Explorer and select New. SSMS then creates an entry in the Template Explorer, and you can specify the name for the template.

To begin adding code to the template, right-click the template and select Edit. This opens a query window in which you can start entering the new template code. Probably the best way to get started is to copy the template code from one of the templates provided with SQL Server 2008 and then modify it as you desire. You then select File, Save to save the template code to the file.

Listing 28.3 shows an example of a new stored procedure template.

LISTING 28.3 An Example of Custom Stored Procedure Template

```
-- ================================================
-- Create basic stored procedure template
-- ================================================

-- Drop stored procedure if it already exists
IF EXISTS (
  SELECT *
    FROM sys.procedures
   WHERE schema_id = schema_id('dbo')
     AND name = N'<Proc_Name, sysname, myproc>'
)
   DROP PROCEDURE <Schema_Name, sysname, dbo>.<Proc_Name, sysname, myproc>
GO
-- ================================================
-- Author:        <Author,,Name>
-- Create date: <Create Date,,>
-- Description:    <Description,,>
-- ================================================
CREATE PROCEDURE <Schema_Name, sysname, dbo>.<Proc_Name, sysname, myproc>
    — Add the parameters for the stored procedure here
    <@param1, sysname, @p1> <param1_type, , int> = <param1_default, , 0>,
    <@param2, sysname, @p2> <param2_type, , int> = <param2_default, , 0>,
    <@param3, sysname, @p3> <param3_type, , int>  OUTPUT
AS
BEGIN
    -- SET NOCOUNT ON added to prevent extra result sets from
    -- interfering with SELECT statements.
    SET NOCOUNT ON;

    DECLARE @trancnt int
    SELECT @trancnt = @@TRANCOUNT

    if @trancnt = 0
        BEGIN TRAN <Proc_Name, sysname, myproc>
    else
        SAVE TRAN <Proc_Name, sysname, myproc>

    /* Insert processing code here */

    if (@@error != 0) -- check for error condition
    begin
        -- rollback to savepoint, or begin tran
        rollback tran <Proc_Name, sysname, myproc>
        -- return error code indicating rollback
```

```
        return -101
    end

    /* Insert more processing here if required */


    -- set value of output parameter
    set <@param3,sysname, @p3> = <@param1,sysname, @p1> + <@param2,sysname, @p2>

    if @trancnt = 0     -- this proc issued begin tran
      -- commit tran, decrement @@trancount to 0
      commit tran <Proc_Name, sysname, myproc>
    -- commit not required with save tran

    return 0 /* successful return */

END
GO


— =============================================
— Example to execute the stored procedure
— =============================================
DECLARE <@output_variable, sysname, @p3_output> <output_datatype, , int>

EXECUTE <Schema_name, sysname, dbo>.<Proc_name, sysname, myproc>
        <@param1, sysname, @p1> = <param1_value, , 1>,
        <@param2, sysname, @p2> = <param2_value, , 1>,
        <@param3, sysname, @p3> = <@output_variable, sysname, @p3_output> OUTPUT

SELECT <@output_variable, sysname, @p3_output>
GO
```


After you define a custom stored procedure template, you can use it as you would use the built-in templates. You can double-click it or right-click and select Open, and SSMS opens a new query window with a new stored procedure creation script based on the custom template. If you use the default values for the template parameters, after the parameter substitution, the `CREATE PROCEDURE` script looks like the one in Listing 28.4.

LISTING 28.4 An Example of a **CREATE PROCEDURE** Script Generated from the Custom Stored Procedure Template

```
-- =============================================
-- Create basic stored procedure template
-- =============================================
```

```
-- Drop stored procedure if it already exists
IF EXISTS (
  SELECT *
    FROM sys.procedures
   WHERE schema_id = schema_id('dbo')
     AND name = N'myproc'
)
   DROP PROCEDURE dbo.myproc
GO

-- ===============================================
-- Author:          Name
-- Create date:
-- Description:
-- ===============================================
CREATE PROCEDURE dbo.myproc
    — Add the parameters for the stored procedure here
    @p1 int = 0,
    @p2 int = 0,
    @p3 int  OUTPUT
AS
BEGIN
    -- SET NOCOUNT ON added to prevent extra result sets from
    -- interfering with SELECT statements.
    SET NOCOUNT ON;

    DECLARE @trancnt int
    SELECT @trancnt = @@TRANCOUNT

    if @trancnt = 0
        BEGIN TRAN myproc
    else
        SAVE TRAN myproc

    /* Insert processing code here */

    if (@@error != 0) -- check for error condition
    begin
        -- rollback to savepoint, or begin tran
        rollback tran myproc
        -- return error code indicating rollback
        return -101
    end

    /* Insert more processing here if required */
```

```
    -- set value of output parameter
    set @p3 = @p1 + @p2

    if @trancnt = 0      -- this proc issued begin tran
      -- commit tran, decrement @@trancount to 0
      commit tran myproc
    -- commit not required with save tran

    return 0 /* successful return */

END
GO

-- =============================================
-- Example to execute the stored procedure
-- =============================================
DECLARE @p3_output int

EXECUTE dbo.myproc
        @p1 = 1,
        @p2 = 1,
        @p3 = @p3_output OUTPUT

SELECT @p3_output
GO
```


Temporary Stored Procedures

SQL Server enables you to create private and global temporary stored procedures. Temporary stored procedures are analogous to temporary tables in that they can be created with the # and ## prefixes added to the procedure name. The # prefix denotes a local temporary stored procedure; ## denotes a global temporary stored procedure. A local temporary stored procedure can be executed only by the connection that created it, and the procedure is automatically deleted when the connection is closed. A global temporary stored procedure can be accessed by multiple connections and exists until the connection used by the user who created the procedure is closed and any currently executing versions of the procedure by any other connections are completed.

If a stored procedure not prefixed with # or ## is created directly in the `tempdb` database, the stored procedure exists until SQL Server is shut down. Procedures created directly in `tempdb` continue to exist even after the creating connection is terminated.

Temporary stored procedures are provided for backward compatibility with earlier versions of SQL Server that did not support the reuse of execution plans for T-SQL statements or batches. Applications connecting to SQL Server 2000 and higher should use the `sp_executesql` system stored procedure to execute dynamic SQL statements instead of creating temporary stored procedures.

TIP

It is strongly recommended that `sp_executesql` be used instead of temporary stored procedures. Excessive use of temporary stored procedures can lead to locking contention on the system tables in `tempdb`, which can adversely affect overall system performance. For more information on using sp_executesql, see Chapter 44, "Advanced Stored Procedure Programming and Optimization."

Executing Stored Procedures

To execute a stored procedure, you simply invoke it by using its name (the same way you probably have already executed system stored procedures, such as `sp_help`). If the execution of the stored procedure isn't the first statement in a batch, you need to precede the procedure name with the `EXEC` keyword. Following is the basic syntax for executing stored procedures:

```
[EXEC[UTE]] [@status =] [schema].procedure_name[; number]
  [[@param_name =] expression [output][, ... ]]
[WITH RECOMPILE]
```

NOTE

The reason you need the `EXEC` keyword when invoking a stored procedure in a batch or other stored procedure is quite simple. SQL Server parses the commands sent to it in a batch by searching for keywords. Stored procedure names aren't keywords. If SQL Server finds a procedure name among the SQL statements, chances are that SQL Server will return an error message because it tries to treat it as part of the preceding command. Sometimes the execution is successful, but SQL Server doesn't execute what you want. Consider this example:

```
SELECT * FROM titles
sp_help
```

The `SELECT` statement runs fine, but the procedure is not executed. The reason is that `sp_help` ends up being used as a table alias for the `titles` table in the `SELECT` statement.

However, if you precede the procedure name with `EXEC`, like this, you get the expected behavior:

```
SELECT * FROM titles
```

```
EXEC sp_help
```

Why don't you have to put EXEC in front of the procedure name if the procedure is the first statement in a batch? If SQL Server doesn't recognize the first string in a batch, it simply assumes that it is a name of a stored procedure. For example, execute the following string and notice the error message:

```
Dsfdskgkghk
go


Msg 2812, Level 16, State 62, Line 1
Could not find stored procedure 'Dsfdskgkghk'.
```

As good programming practice, it is best to always precede stored procedures with the EXEC keyword. This way, it will always work as expected, whether or not it's the first statement in a batch.

Executing Procedures in SSMS

To execute a stored procedure in SSMS, open the object tree for the database, open the `Programmability` folder, and open the `Stored Procedures` folder. Then right-click the stored procedure, and from the context menu, choose Execute Stored Procedure. SSMS then presents you with the Execute Procedure dialog, as shown in Figure 28.3. In this window, you can enter values for any parameters contained in the stored procedure. If you want to pass a `NULL` value to a parameter, you need to be sure to place a check mark in the Pass Null Value check box for that parameter.

After you specify values for all the parameters, SSMS opens a new query window with the generated execute statement and automatically executes it. It displays any results in the Results window. If the stored procedure contains output parameters, SSMS generates local variables for the output parameters and uses a `SELECT` statement to display the values returned to the output parameters. Listing 28.5 shows an example of the execute script and its results for the procedure invoked in Figure 28.3 (this procedure is the one generated from the custom procedure template, as shown in Listing 28.4).

LISTING 28.5 A Procedure Execution Script Generated by SSMS

```
USE [bigpubs2008]
GO

DECLARE     @return_value int,
        @p3 int

EXEC @return_value = [dbo].[myproc]
        @p1 = 100,
        @p2 = 200,
        @p3 = @p3 OUTPUT
```

```
SELECT @p3 as N'@p3'

SELECT 'Return Value' = @return_value

GO


@p3
-----------
300

Return Value
------------
0
```

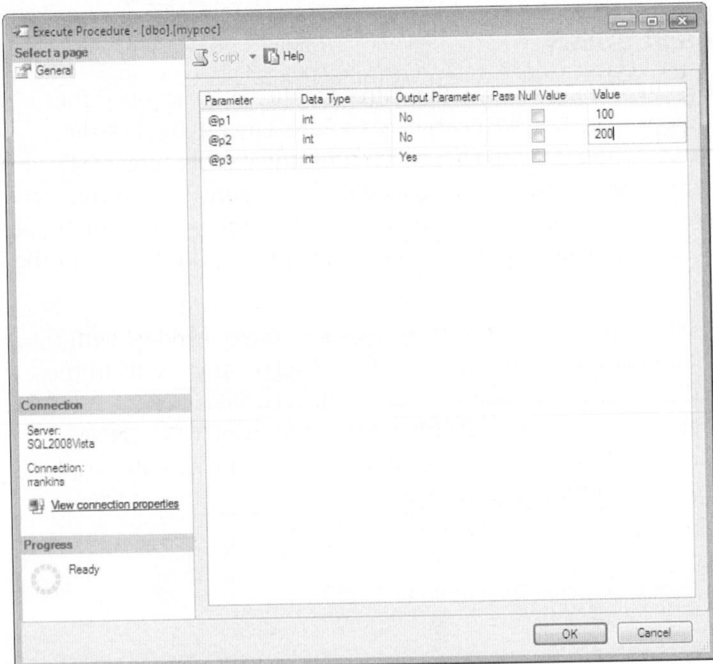

FIGURE 28.3 Using the Execute Procedure dialog in SSMS.

Execution Context and the EXECUTE AS Clause

Normally, stored procedures execute within the security context of the current user. The user must have execute permission on the procedure and if the objects referenced within the stored procedure are not owned by the user who created the stored procedure, the current user must also have the necessary permissions granted on the referenced objects. The current user does not inherit the permissions of the procedure creator. The only exception to this occurs when the objects referenced by a stored procedure *are* owned by the same user who created the stored procedure. In this case, permissions on the referenced objects in the stored procedure are dependent on the ownership chain that exists between the calling procedure and referenced objects. For example, if the creator of a stored procedure also owns the table that it references, the user executing the stored procedure inherits the rights on the referenced table from the owner within the context of the stored procedure, without having to be granted explicit rights on the table by the table owner.

However, there are limitations to using ownership chaining alone for inheriting access permissions:

- The rights inherited by ownership chaining apply only to DML statements: `SELECT`, `INSERT`, `UPDATE`, and `DELETE`.
- The owners of the calling and called objects must be the same.
- The rights inherited by ownership chaining do not apply to dynamic queries inside the stored procedure.

In SQL Server 2008, you can implicitly define the execution context of functions (except inline table-valued functions), stored procedures, and triggers by specifying the `EXECUTE AS` clause. The `EXECUTE AS` clause allows you to go beyond ownership chaining to specify the security context under which a stored procedure will execute and what access rights the user will have on the referenced objects. The `EXECUTE AS` clause allows you to specify explicitly the security context under which the stored procedure will execute. In other words, it allows you to specify which user account SQL Server should use to validate permissions on the database objects referenced by the stored procedure. The user executing the stored procedure, in effect, impersonates the user specified in the `EXECUTE AS` clause within the context of the execution of the stored procedure.

The `EXECUTE AS` clause can be specified when the stored procedure is created to set the default security context for all users when executing the stored procedure. Alternatively, the `EXECUTE AS` clause can be specified explicitly within the stored procedure code or within each individual user session. When specified in a user session, the security context switches to that specified until the connection is closed, a `REVERT` statement is run, or another `EXECUTE AS` statement is run.

28

The syntax of the `EXECUTE AS` clause for stored procedures is as follows:

```
{ EXEC | EXECUTE } AS { CALLER | SELF | OWNER | 'user_name' }
```

You can specify the following security context options when using the `EXECUTE AS` clause:

- **CALLER**—This option specifies that the statements inside the stored procedure are executed in the context of the caller of the module (that is, the current user). The user executing the stored procedure must have execute permission on the stored procedure and also permissions on any database objects that are referenced by the stored procedure that are not owned by the procedure creator. **CALLER** is the default behavior for all stored procedures, and it is the same as SQL Server 2000 behavior.

- **SELF**—This option is equivalent to **EXECUTE AS** *user_name*, where the specified user is the person creating or modifying the stored procedure.
- **OWNER**—This option specifies that the statements inside the stored procedure execute in the context of the current owner of the stored procedure. If the procedure does not have a specified owner, the owner of the schema in which the procedure was created is used. **OWNER** must map to a single user account and cannot be a role or group.
- '*user_name*'—This option specifies that the statements inside the stored procedure execute in the context of the **user_name** specified. Permissions for any objects within the stored procedure are verified against this user. The user specified must exist in the current database and cannot be a group, role, certificate, key, or built-in account.

To determine the execution context of a stored procedure, you can query the *execute_as_principal_id* column in either the sys.sql_modules or sys.assembly_modules catalog view.

Specifying an execution context for a stored procedure can be very useful when you want to define custom permission sets. For example, some actions, such as TRUNCATE TABLE, cannot be explicitly granted to other users. However, if you use the EXECUTE AS clause to set the execution context of a stored procedure to a user who does have truncate table permissions (for example, a user who has permissions to alter the table), you can then incorporate the TRUNCATE TABLE statement within the procedure. Any user to whom you then grant EXECUTE permission on the stored procedure is able to run it to execute the TRUNCATE TABLE command contained in it.

TIP

When using the EXECUTE AS clause to customize the permission set for a stored procedure, it is good security policy to specify a login or user that has the least privileges required to perform the operations defined in the stored procedure. Do not specify an account such as a database owner account unless those permissions are required.

To specify the EXECUTE AS clause when you create or modify a stored procedure and specify a user account other than your own, you must have impersonate permissions on the specified user account in addition to having permissions to create or alter the stored procedure. When no execution context is specified or EXECUTE AS CALLER is specified, impersonate permissions are not required.

The following example demonstrates how the user context changes when you use the EXECUTE AS clause in the creation of a stored procedure:

```
use bigpubs2008
go
sp_addlogin fred, fred2008
go
```

```
sp_grantdbaccess fred
go

create proc test_execute_as
with EXECUTE AS 'fred'
as
select user_name() as 'User context within proc'
go

select user_name() as 'User context before EXEC'
exec test_execute_as


User context before EXEC
------------------------------
dbo

User context within proc
------------------------------
fred
```

Deferred Name Resolution

In SQL Server 2008, the object names that a stored procedure references do not have to exist at the time the procedure is created. SQL Server 2008 checks for the existence of database objects at the time the stored procedure is executed and returns an error message at runtime if the referenced object doesn't exist. The only exception is when a stored procedure references another stored procedure that doesn't exist. In that case, a warning message is issued, but the stored procedure is still created (see Listing 28.6).

28

LISTING 28.6 Procedure Name Resolution During Stored Procedure Creation

```
create proc p2
as
exec p3
go

The module 'p2' depends on the missing object 'p3'. The module will still be
  created; however, it cannot run successfully until the object exists.
```

When a table or view *does* exist at procedure creation time, the column names in the referenced table are validated. If a column name is mistyped or doesn't exist, the procedure is not created (see Listing 28.7).

LISTING 28.7 Column Name Validation in Stored Procedures

```
IF EXISTS ( SELECT * FROM sys.procedures
               WHERE schema_id = schema_id('dbo')
                 AND name = N'get_authors_and_titles')
   DROP PROCEDURE dbo.get_authors_and_titles
GO
create proc get_authors_and_titles
as

select a.au_lname, au_fname, title, isbn_number
   from authors a join titleauthor ta on a.au_id = ta.au_id
   join titles t on t.title_id = ta.title_id
return
go

Server: Msg 207, Level 16, State 1, Procedure get_authors_and_titles, Line 4
Invalid column name 'isbn_number'.
```

One advantage of delayed (or deferred) name resolution is the increased flexibility when creating stored procedures; the order of creating procedures and the tables they reference does not need to be exact. Delayed name resolution is an especially useful feature when a stored procedure references a temporary table that isn't created within that stored procedure. However, at other times, it can be frustrating to have a stored procedure create successfully only to have it fail when it runs due to a missing table, as shown in Listing 28.8.

LISTING 28.8 Runtime Failure of a Stored Procedure with an Invalid Object Reference

```
create proc get_authors_and_titles
as

select a.au_lname, au_fname, title, pub_date
   from authors a join titleauthor ta on a.au_id = ta.au_id
   join books t on t.title_id = ta.title_id

go

EXEC get_authors_and_titles
go

Server: Msg 208, Level 16, State 1, Procedure get_authors_and_titles, Line 4
 Invalid object name 'books'.
```

Another issue to be careful of with deferred name resolution is that you can't rename objects referenced by stored procedures and have the stored procedure continue to work. In versions of SQL Server prior to 7.0, after the stored procedure was created, object references within the stored procedure were made via the object ID rather than the object name. This allowed stored procedures to continue to function properly if a referenced object was renamed. However, now that object names are resolved at execution time, the procedure fails at the statement referencing the renamed object. For the stored procedure to execute successfully, it needs to be altered to specify the new object name.

Identifying Objects Referenced in Stored Procedures

Because changing the name of a table can cause stored procedures to no longer work, you might want to identify which stored procedures reference a specific table so you know which stored procedures will be affected by changes to the table name or columns. You can view the dependencies between database objects by querying the `sys.sql_dependencies` object catalog view. Unfortunately, all you really see if you query the `sys.sql_dependencies` view is a bunch of numbers—just the IDs of the objects and columns that have a dependency relationship, along with some additional status information.

The better way to display a list of stored procedures that reference a specific table or view, or to display a list of objects referenced by a stored procedure, is to use the `sys.dm_sql_referencing_entities` and `sys.dm_sql_referenced_entities` dynamic management functions.

```
sys.dm_sql_referencing_entities ( ' schema_name.table_or_view_name ' , ' OBJECT ' )
sys.dm_sql_referenced_entities ( ' schema_name.proc_name ' , ' OBJECT ' )
```

For example, to display the stored procedures, triggers, functions, and views that reference the `titles` table, you would execute the following:

```
select referencing_schema_name, referencing_entity_name
 From sys.dm_sql_referencing_entities ( 'dbo.titles' , 'OBJECT' )
go
```

In the `bigpubs2008` database, the `titles` table is referenced by the following:

```
referencing_schema_name   referencing_entity_name
-----------------------------------------------
dbo                       AverageBookPrice
dbo                       AverageBookPrice2
dbo                       AveragePricebyType
dbo                       AveragePricebyType2
dbo                       reptq1
dbo                       reptq2
dbo                       reptq3
dbo                       title_authors
```

```
dbo                      titleview
dbo                      valid_book_types
```

To display the objects referenced by the `title_authors` stored procedure, you could execute the following:

```
select distinct
    referenced_entity_name as table_name,
    referenced_minor_name as column_name
 From sys.dm_sql_referenced_entities ('dbo.title_authors' , 'OBJECT' )
go
```

In the current database, the specified object references the following:

```
table_name      column_name
----------------------------
authors         NULL
authors         au_fname
authors         au_id
authors         au_lname
titleauthor     NULL
titleauthor     au_id
titleauthor     title_id
titles          NULL
titles          title
titles          title_id
```

You can also see dependency information in SSMS by right-clicking an object and choosing View Dependencies. This brings up the Object Dependencies window, as shown in Figure 28.4. You can view either the objects that depend on the selected object or objects on which the selected object depends. You can also expand the dependency tree for the objects listed in the Dependencies pane.

Viewing Stored Procedures

You can view the source code for stored procedures in SQL Server 2008 by querying the `definition` column of the object catalog view `sys.sql_modules` or by using the system procedure `sp_helptext` (see Listing 28.9).

LISTING 28.9 Viewing Code for a Stored Procedure by Using **sp_helptext**

```
exec sp_helptext title_authors
go

Text
------------------------------------------------------------
CREATE PROCEDURE title_authors
```

```
AS
BEGIN
   SELECT a.au_lname, a.au_fname, t.title
      FROM titles t INNER JOIN
           titleauthor ta ON t.title_id = ta.title_id RIGHT OUTER JOIN
           authors a ON ta.au_id = a.au_id
   RETURN
END
```

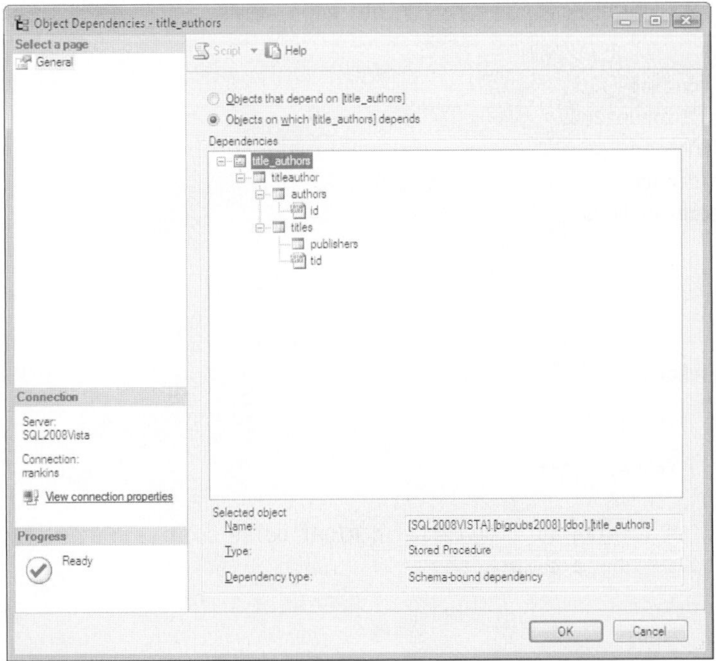

FIGURE 28.4 Viewing object dependencies in SSMS.

By default, all users have permission to execute `sp_helptext` to view the SQL code for the stored procedures in a database. If you want to protect the source code of stored procedures and keep its contents from prying eyes, you can create a procedure by using the `WITH ENCRYPTION` option. When this option is specified, the source code stored in the database is encrypted.

NOTE

If you use encryption when creating stored procedures, be aware that although SQL Server can internally decrypt the source code, no mechanisms exist for the user or for any of the end-user tools to decrypt the stored procedure text for display or editing. With this in mind, make sure that you store a copy of the source code for those procedures in a file in case you need to edit or re-create them. Also, procedures created by using the `WITH ENCRYPTION` option cannot be published as part of SQL Server replication.

You can, however, attach a debugger to the server process and retrieve a decrypted procedure from memory at runtime.

You can also view the text of a stored procedure by using the ANSI INFORMATION_SCHEMA view routines. The routines view is an ANSI standard view that provides the source code for the stored procedure in the routine_description column. The following example uses the INFORMATION_SCHEMA.routines view to display the source code for the title_authors stored procedure:

```
select routine_definition
from INFORMATION_SCHEMA.routines
where specific_catalog = 'bigpubs2008'
  and specific_schema = 'dbo'
  and routine_type = 'Procedure'
  and routine_name = 'title_authors'
go

routine_definition
-------------------------------------------------------------------------
CREATE PROCEDURE title_authors
AS
BEGIN
   SELECT a.au_lname, a.au_fname, t.title
      FROM titles t INNER JOIN
           titleauthor ta ON t.title_id = ta.title_id RIGHT OUTER JOIN
           authors a ON ta.au_id = a.au_id
   RETURN
END
```

However, the routine_description column is limited to only the first 4,000 characters of the stored procedure code. A better way to view the code with a query is to use the sys.sql_modules object catalog view:

```
select definition
    from sys.sql_modules
    where object_id = object_id('title_authors')
go

CREATE PROCEDURE title_authors
AS
BEGIN
   SELECT a.au_lname, a.au_fname, t.title
      FROM titles t INNER JOIN
           titleauthor ta ON t.title_id = ta.title_id RIGHT OUTER JOIN
           authors a ON ta.au_id = a.au_id
```

```
    RETURN
END
```

Finally, one other method of displaying the source code for a stored procedure is to use the new `object_definition()` function. This function takes the object ID as a parameter. If you, like most other people, do not know the object ID of the procedure in question, you can use the `object_id()` function. The following is an example of using the `object_definition()` function:

```
select object_definition(object_id('dbo.title_authors'))
go

---------------------------------------------------------------------------------
CREATE PROCEDURE title_authors @state char(2) = '%'
AS
BEGIN
    SELECT a.au_lname, a.au_fname, t.title
        FROM titles t INNER JOIN
             titleauthor ta ON t.title_id = ta.title_id RIGHT OUTER JOIN
             authors a ON ta.au_id = a.au_id
    RETURN
END
```

TIP

If you are running these queries to display the procedure code in a query window in SSMS, you probably need to modify the query results options to have the procedures display correctly. From the Query menu, select Query Options. Expand the Results item and select Text. Enter a value up to 8192 for the Maximum Number of Characters Displayed in Each Column setting and click OK.

You probably also want to have the results displayed as text rather than in the grid. To make this change, under the Query menu, select the Results To submenu and then select Results to Text. As a shortcut, you can press Ctrl+T to switch to Results to Text. You can press Ctrl+D to switch back to Results to Grid.

Modifying Stored Procedures

You can modify the text of a stored procedure by using the `ALTER PROCEDURE` statement. The syntax for `ALTER PROCEDURE` is similar to the syntax for `CREATE PROCEDURE` (see Listing 28.10). Using `ALTER PROCEDURE` has a couple advantages over dropping and re-creating a procedure to modify it. The main advantage is that you don't have to drop the procedure first to make the change, so it remains available, even if the `ALTER PROCEDURE` command fails due to a syntax or object reference error. The second advantage is that because you don't have to drop the procedure, you don't have to worry about reassigning permissions to it after modifying it.

LISTING 28.10 Modifying a Stored Procedure by Using **ALTER PROCEDURE**

```
ALTER PROCEDURE title_authors @state char(2) = '%'
AS
BEGIN
    SELECT a.au_lname, a.au_fname, t.title, t.pubdate
       FROM titles t
       INNER JOIN titleauthor ta ON t.title_id = ta.title_id
       RIGHT OUTER JOIN authors a ON ta.au_id = a.au_id
       where state like @state
    RETURN
END
```

Viewing and Modifying Stored Procedures with SSMS

You can also use SSMS to create, view, and modify stored procedures.

To edit a stored procedure in SSMS, expand the `Programmability` folder and then the `Stored Procedures` folder, right-click the name of the procedure you want to modify, and select Modify (see Figure 28.5).

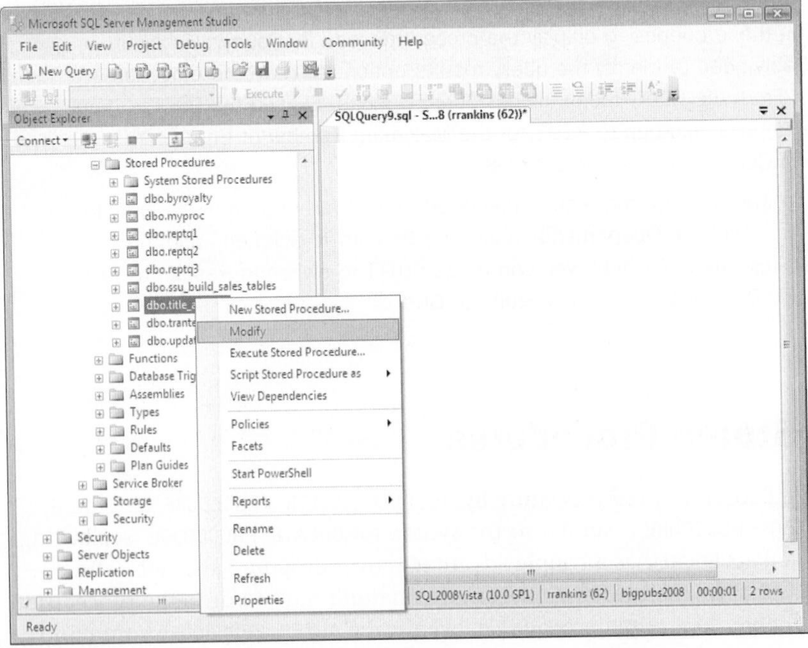

FIGURE 28.5 Modifying stored procedures in SSMS.

SSMS then extracts the `ALTER PROCEDURE` statement for the selected procedure into a new query window. Here, you can edit the procedure code as needed and then execute the contents of the query window to modify the procedure. In addition, the Object Browser in SSMS provides other options for extracting the stored procedure source code. It can generate code to create, alter, or drop the selected stored procedure. You can script the stored procedure source code to a new window, to a file, or to the Windows Clipboard by right-clicking the stored procedure name in the Object Browser and choosing the appropriate option (see Figure 28.6).

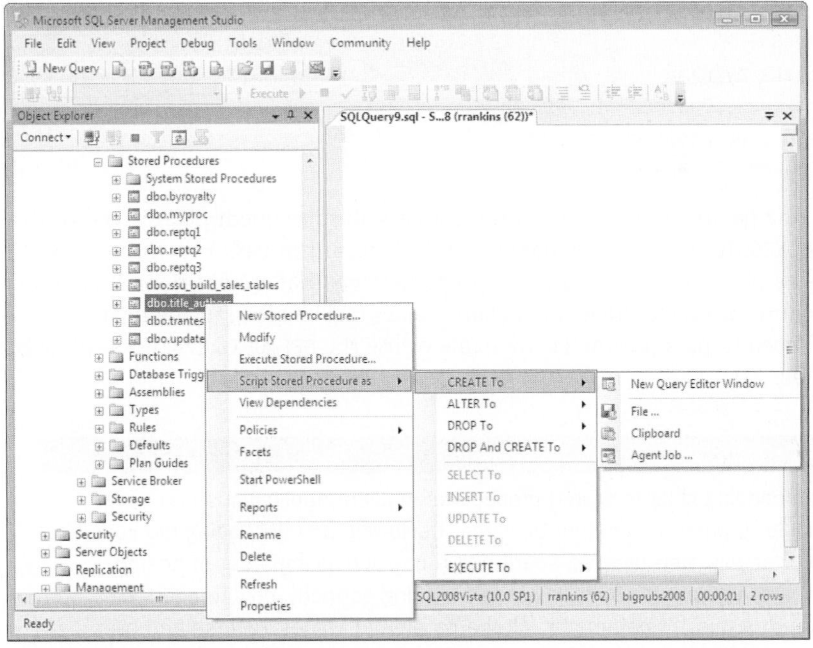

FIGURE 28.6 Extracting stored procedure source code to a new query window.

Using Input Parameters

To increase the flexibility of stored procedures and perform more complex processing, you can pass parameters to procedures. The parameters can be used anywhere that local variables can be used within the procedure code.

The following example is a stored procedure that requires three parameters:

```
CREATE PROC myproc
 @parm1 int, @parm2 int, @parm3 int
AS
```

```
-- Processing goes here
RETURN
```

If you want to help identify the data values for which the parameters are defined, it is recommended that you give your parameters meaningful names. Parameter names, like local variables, can be up to 128 characters in length, including the @ sign, and they must follow SQL Server rules for identifiers. Up to 2,100 parameters can be defined for a stored procedure.

When you execute a procedure, you can pass the parameters by position or by name:

```
--Passing parameters by position
EXEC myproc 1, 2, 3
--Passing parameters by name
EXEC myproc @parm2 = 2, @parm2 = 1, @parm3 =3
--Passing parameters by position and name
EXEC myproc 1, @parm3 =3, @parm2 = 2
```

After you specify one parameter by name, you must pass all subsequent parameters for the procedure in that EXECUTE statement by name as well. You cannot pass any of the subsequent parameters by position. If you want to skip parameters that are not the last parameter(s) in the procedure and have them take default values (as described in the next section), you also need to pass parameters by name or use the DEFAULT keyword in place of the parameter value.

TIP

When you are embedding calls to stored procedures in client applications and script files, it is advisable to pass parameters by name. Reviewing and debugging the code becomes easier that way. One time we spent half a day debugging a set of nested stored procedures to figure out why they weren't working correctly, only to find the problem was due to a missed parameter; all the parameter values were shifted over one place and the wrong values ended up being passed to the wrong parameters. This resulted in the queries not finding any matching values. Had the parameters been passed by name, this issue would not have occurred. This was a lesson learned the hard way!

Input parameter values passed in can be only explicit constant values, local variables, parameters, or, new for SQL Server 2008, table-valued parameters. However, you cannot specify a function or another expression as an input parameter value. You would have to store a return value from the function or expression value in a local variable and pass the local variable as the input parameter. Likewise, you cannot use a function or another expression as a default value for a parameter.

Setting Default Values for Parameters

You can assign a default value to a parameter by specifying a value in the definition of the parameter, as shown in Listing 28.11.

LISTING 28.11 Assigning a Default Value for a Parameter in a Stored Procedure

```
ALTER PROCEDURE title_authors @state char(2) = '%'
AS
SELECT a.au_lname, a.au_fname, t.title
   FROM titles t
   INNER JOIN titleauthor ta ON t.title_id = ta.title_id
   RIGHT OUTER JOIN authors a ON ta.au_id = a.au_id
    WHERE a.state like @state
RETURN
 GO
```

You can have SQL Server apply the default value for a parameter during execution by not specifying a value or by specifying the DEFAULT keyword in the position of the parameter, as shown in Listing 28.12.

LISTING 28.12 Applying a Default Value for a Parameter When Executing a Stored Procedure

```
EXEC title_authors
EXEC title_authors DEFAULT
EXEC title_authors @state = DEFAULT
```

TIP

If you are involved in creating stored procedures that other people will use, you probably want to make the stored procedures as easy to use as possible.

If you leave out a parameter that is required, SQL Server presents an error message. The myproc procedure, shown earlier in this section, requires three parameters: @parm1, @parm2, and @parm3:

```
EXEC myproc

Server: Msg 201, Level 16, State 4, Procedure myproc, Line 0
Procedure 'myproc' expects parameter '@parm1', which was not
 supplied.
```

Note that SQL Server complains only about the first missing parameter. The programmer passes the first parameter, only to find out that more parameters are required. This is a good way to annoy a programmer or an end user.

When you execute a command-line program, you probably expect that you can use /? to obtain a list of the parameters the program expects. You can program stored procedures in a similar manner by assigning NULL (or some other special value) as a default value to the parameters and checking for that value inside the procedure. The following is an outline of a stored procedure that presents the user with information about the parameters expected if the user doesn't pass parameters:

```
CREATE PROC MyProc2
 @parm1 int = NULL, @parm2 int = 32, @parm3 int = NULL
AS
IF (@parm1 IS NULL or @parm1 NOT BETWEEN 1 and 10) OR
   @parm3 IS NULL
PRINT 'Usage:
 EXEC MyProc2
 @parm1 int,   (Required: Can be between 1 and 10)
 @parm2 = 32,  (Optional: Default value of 32)
 @parm3 int,   (Required: Any number within range)'
-- Processing goes here
RETURN
GO

EXEC MyProc2
GO

Usage:
 EXEC MyProc2
 @parm1 int,   (Required: Can be between 1 and 10)
 @parm2 = 32,  (Optional: Default value of 32)
 @parm3 int,   (Required: Any number within range)
```

You can develop your own standards for the way the message is presented to the user, but what is important is that the information is presented at all.

To display the parameters defined for a stored procedure, you can view them in the SSMS Object Explorer (see Figure 28.7) or by executing the sp_help stored procedure, as shown in Listing 28.13. (Note that the output has been edited to fit the page.)

LISTING 28.13 Displaying Stored Procedure Parameters by Using **sp_help**

```
exec sp_help title_authors
Name                Owner      Type                Created_datetime
```

```
------------- ----- ------ ---- ------- ----------- -----------------------
title_authors    dbo        stored procedure  2008-09-15 21:15:06.540


Parameter_name Type  Length Prec Scale Param_order Collation
-------------- ----- ------ ---- ------- ----------- ------------------------
@state          char  2      2    NULL            1 SQL_Latin1_General_CP1_CI_AS
```

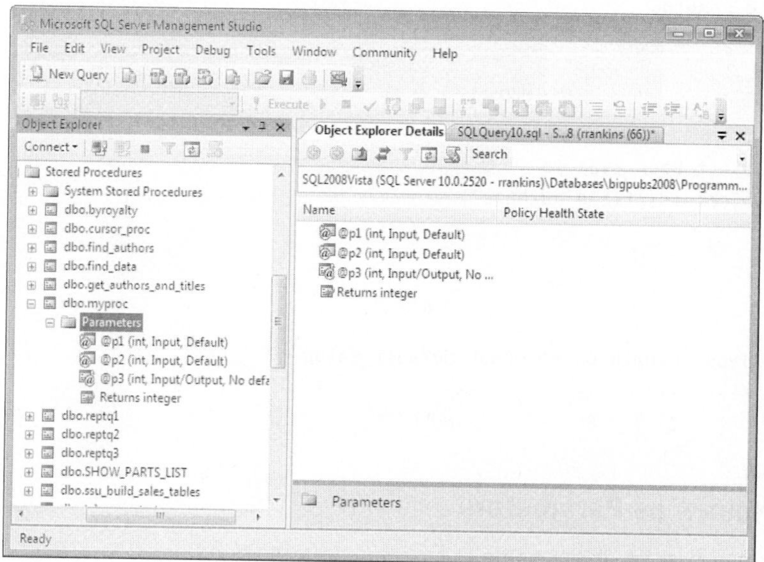

FIGURE 28.7 Displaying stored procedure parameters in SSMS.

You can also display the stored procedure parameters by running a query against the `INFORMATION_SCHEMA` view `parameters`:

```
select substring(Parameter_NAME,1, 30) as Parameter_name,
       substring (DATA_TYPE, 1, 20) as Data_Type,
       CHARACTER_MAXIMUM_LENGTH as Length,
       ordinal_position as param_order,
       Collation_name
from INFORMATION_SCHEMA.parameters
where specific_name = 'title_authors'
  and specific_schema = 'dbo'
order by ordinal_position

go
```

```
Parameter_name   Data_Type     Length  param_order Collation_name
---------------- ------------- ------- ----------- ----------------------------
@state           char                2           1 SQL_Latin1_General_CP1_CI_AS
```

You can view parameter information for a stored procedure as well using the `sys.parameters` catalog view:

```
select substring(p.name,1, 30) as Parameter_name,
       substring (t.name, 1, 20) as Data_Type,
       p.max_length as Length,
       parameter_id as param_order,
       default_value
from sys.parameters p
inner join sys.types t
     on p.user_type_id = t.user_type_id
where p.object_id = object_id('title_authors')
order by parameter_id

go

Parameter_name  Data_Type  Length param_order default_value
--------------- ---------- ------ ----------- -------------
@state          char       2      1           NULL
```

Passing Object Names as Parameters

In SQL Server 2008, if you pass an object name as a parameter to a stored procedure, SQL Server attempts to treat it as a table-valued parameter unless the object name is used either as an argument in a `WHERE` clause or in a dynamic SQL query. For example, the code in Listing 28.14 generates an error message when you try to create the stored procedure.

LISTING 28.14 Attempting to Create a Stored Procedure by Using a Parameter to Pass in a Table Name

```
CREATE  proc find_data @table varchar(128)
as

select * from @table

GO

Msg 1087, Level 16, State 1, Procedure find_data, Line 4
 Must declare the table variable "@table".
```

As you can see, when the parameter is used in the `FROM` clause, SQL Server expects it to be defined as a `table` variable. To use the value in the parameter as a table name, you can build a dynamic SQL query similar to the example shown in Listing 28.15.

LISTING 28.15 Passing a Table as a Parameter to a Stored Procedure for Dynamic SQL Execution

```
CREATE  proc find_data @table varchar(128)
as

exec ('select * from ' + @table)
return
go

exec find_data @table = 'publishers'
go

pub_id pub_name                       city             state country
------ ------------------------------ ---------------- ----- ----------
0736   New Moon Books                 Boston           MA    USA
0877   Binnet & Hardley               Washington       DC    USA
1389   Algodata Infosystems           Berkeley         CA    USA
1622   Five Lakes Publishing          Chicago          IL    USA
1756   Ramona Publishers              Dallas           TX    USA
...
9952   Scootney Books                 New   York       NY    USA
9999   Lucerne Publishing             Paris            NULL  France
```

Using Wildcards in Parameters

Wildcards can be included in varchar-based input parameters and used in a LIKE clause in a query to perform pattern matching. However, you should not use the char data type for parameters that will contain wildcard characters because SQL Server pads spaces onto the value passed in to the parameter to expand it to the specified size of the char data type. For example, if you declared an @lastname parameter as char(40) and passed in 'S%', SQL Server would search not for a string starting with 'S' but for a string starting with 'S', any characters, and ending with up to 38 spaces. This would likely not match any actual data values.

Also, to increase the flexibility of a stored procedure that searches for character strings, you can default the parameter to '%', as in the following example:

```
IF EXISTS ( SELECT * FROM sys.procedures
               WHERE schema_id = schema_id('dbo')
                 AND name = N'find_authors')
   DROP PROCEDURE dbo.find_authors
GO
 create proc find_authors @lastname varchar(40) = '%'
as
    select au_id, au_lname, au_fname
```

```
        from authors
        where au_lname like @lastname
        order by au_lname, au_fname
```

This procedure, if passed no parameter, returns data for all authors in the authors table. If passed a string containing wildcard characters, this procedure returns data for all authors matching the search pattern specified. If a string containing no wildcards is passed, the query performs a search for exact matches against the string value.

Unfortunately, wildcard searches can be performed only against character strings. If you want to have similar flexibility searching against a numeric value, such as an integer, you can default the value to NULL and when the parameter is NULL, compare the column with itself, as shown in the following example:

```
IF EXISTS ( SELECT * FROM sys.procedures
               WHERE schema_id = schema_id('dbo')
                 AND name = N'find_titles_by_sales')
   DROP PROCEDURE dbo.find_titles_by_sales
GO
create proc find_titles_by_sales @ytd_sales int = null
as
    select title_id, title, ytd_sales
        from titles
        where ytd_sales = isnull(@ytd_sales, ytd_sales)
```

However, the problem with this approach is that the procedure returns all rows from the titles table except those in which ytd_sales contains a NULL value. The reason is that NULL is never considered equal to NULL; you cannot compare an unknown value with another unknown value. To return all rows, including those in which ytd_sales is NULL, you need to implement a dual-query solution, as in the following example:

```
IF EXISTS ( SELECT * FROM sys.procedures
               WHERE schema_id = schema_id('dbo')
                 AND name = N'find_titles_by_sales')
   DROP PROCEDURE dbo.find_titles_by_sales
GO
create proc find_titles_by_sales @ytd_sales int = null
as
if @ytd_sales is null
    select title_id, title, ytd_sales
        from titles
else
    select title_id, title, ytd_sales
        from titles
        where ytd_sales= @ytd_sales
```

Using Table-Valued Parameters

In previous versions of SQL Server, it was not possible to share the contents of table variables between stored procedures. SQL Server 2008 changes that with the introduction of table-valued parameters, which allow you to pass table variables to stored procedures. Table-valued parameters provide more flexibility and, in many cases, better performance than temporary tables as a means to pass result sets between stored procedures.

NOTE

For more information on using temporary tables and the `table` data type in stored procedures, see Chapter 44.

Table-valued parameters provide many of the same performance advantages as table data types. Table-valued parameters also share some of the same restrictions as table variables, such as SQL Server not maintaining statistics on table-valued parameters and table-valued parameters not permitted as the target of a `SELECT INTO` or `INSERT EXEC` statement. In addition, table-valued parameters can be passed only as `READONLY` input parameters to stored procedures. DML operations, such as `UPDATE`, `INSERT`, and `DELETE`, cannot be performed on table-valued parameters within the body of a stored procedure.

To create and use table-valued parameters, you must first create a user-defined table type and define the table structure. You do so using the `CREATE TYPE` command, as in the following example:

```
if exists (select * from sys.systypes t where t.name = 'ytdsales_tabletype'
                and t.uid = USER_ID('dbo'))
     drop type ytdsales_tabletype
go
CREATE TYPE ytdsales_tabletype AS TABLE
(title_id char(6),
 title varchar(50),
 pubdate date,
 ytd_sales int)
go
```

After the table data type is created, you can use it for declaring local table variables and for stored procedure parameters. To use the table-valued parameter in a procedure, you create a procedure to receive and access data through a table-valued parameter:

```
/* Create a procedure to receive data for the table-valued parameter. */
if OBJECT_ID('tab_parm_test') is not null
    drop proc tab_parm_test
go
create proc tab_parm_test
```

```
        @pubdate datetime = null,
        @sales_minimum int = 0,
        @ytd_sales_tab ytdsales_tabletype READONLY
as
set nocount on

if @pubdate is null
    -- if no date is specified, set date to last year
    set @pubdate = dateadd(month, -12, getdate())

select * from @ytd_sales_tab
where pubdate > @pubdate
and ytd_sales >= @sales_minimum
return
go
```

Then, when calling that stored procedure, you declare a local table variable using the table data type defined previously, populate the table variable with data, and then pass the table variable to the stored procedure:

```
/* Declare a variable that references the type. */
declare @ytd_sales_tab ytdsales_tabletype

/* Add data to the table variable. */
insert @ytd_sales_tab
    select title_id, convert(varchar(50), title), pubdate, ytd_sales
      from titles

/* Pass the table variable populated with data to a stored procedure. */
exec tab_parm_test '6/1/2001', 10000, @ytd_sales_tab
go

title_id title                                              ytd_sales
-------- -------------------------------------------------- -----------
BU2075   You Can Combat Computer Stress!                    18722
MC3021   The Gourmet Microwave                              22246
TC4203   Fifty Years in Buckingham Palace Kitchens          15096
```

Using Output Parameters

If a calling batch passes a variable as a parameter to a stored procedure and that parameter is modified inside the procedure, the modifications are not passed to the calling batch unless you specify the OUTPUT keyword for the parameter when executing the stored procedure.

If you want a procedure to be able to pass parameter values out from the procedure, you need to use the keyword OUTPUT when creating the procedure. The following example shows a stored procedure that accepts two parameters, one of which is used as an output parameter:

```
IF EXISTS ( SELECT * FROM sys.procedures
               WHERE schema_id = schema_id('dbo')
                 AND name = N'ytd_sales')
   DROP PROCEDURE dbo.ytd_sales
GO
CREATE PROC ytd_sales
@title varchar(80), @ytd_sales int OUTPUT
AS
SELECT @ytd_sales = ytd_sales
   FROM titles
   WHERE title = @title
RETURN
```

The calling batch (or stored procedure) needs to declare a variable to store the returned value. The execute statement must include the OUTPUT keyword as well, or the modifications won't be reflected in the calling batch's variable:

```
DECLARE @sales_up_to_today  int
EXEC ytd_sales 'Life Without Fear', @sales_up_to_today OUTPUT
PRINT 'Sales this year until today''s date: ' +
      CONVERT(VARCHAR(10), @sales_up_to_today) + '.'

Sales this year until today's date: 111.
```

You can also pass the output parameter by name:

```
DECLARE @sales_up_to_today  int
EXEC ytd_sales 'Life Without Fear',
      @ytd_sales = @sales_up_to_today OUTPUT
PRINT 'Sales this year until today''s date: ' +
      CONVERT(VARCHAR(10), @sales_up_to_today) + '.'
```

Note that when you pass an output parameter by name, the parameter name (@ytd_sales, in this example) is listed on the left side of the expression, and the local variable (@sales_up_to_today), which is set equal to the value of the output parameter, is on the right side of the expression. An output parameter can also serve as an input parameter.

Output parameters can also be passed back and captured in a client application by using ADO, ODBC, OLE DB, and so on.

Returning Procedure Status

Most programming languages are able to pass a status code to the caller of a function or subroutine. A value of 0 generally indicates that the execution was successful. SQL Server stored procedures are no exception.

SQL Server automatically generates an integer status value of 0 after successful completion of a stored procedure. If SQL Server detects a system error, a status value between -1 and -99 is returned. You can use the RETURN statement to explicitly pass a status value less than -99 or greater than 0. The calling batch or procedure can set up a local variable to retrieve and check the return status.

In Listing 28.16, the stored procedure returns the year-to-date sales for a given title as a result set. If the title does not exist, to avoid returning an empty result set, the procedure returns the status value -101. In the calling batch or stored procedure, you need to create a variable to hold the return value. The variable name is passed the EXECUTE keyword and the procedure name as shown in Listing 28.16.

LISTING 28.16 Returning a Status Code from a Stored Procedure

```
IF EXISTS ( SELECT * FROM sys.procedures
               WHERE schema_id = schema_id('dbo')
                 AND name = N'ytd_sales2')
   DROP PROCEDURE dbo.ytd_sales2
GO
--Create the procedure
CREATE PROC ytd_sales2 @title varchar(80)
AS
IF NOT EXISTS (SELECT * FROM titles WHERE title = @title)
    RETURN -101
SELECT ytd_sales
   FROM titles
   WHERE title = @title
RETURN
GO

-- Execute the procedure
DECLARE @status int
EXEC @status = ytd_sales2 'Life without Fear'
IF @status = -101
    PRINT 'No title with that name found.'
go

ytd_sales
---------
111
```

```
-- Execute the procedure
DECLARE @status int
EXEC @status = ytd_sales2 'Life without Beer'
IF @status = -101
    PRINT 'No title with that name found.'
go

 No title with that name found.
```

Return values can also be passed back and captured by client applications developed in ADO, ODBC, OLE DB, and so on.

Debugging Stored Procedures Using SQL Server Management Studio

One of the great tools available in the SQL Server 2000 Query Analyzer, the built-in SQL Debugger, was left out of SQL Server Management Studio (SSMS) in SQL Server 2005. Fortunately, SQL Server 2008 brings the T-SQL debugger back to SSMS.

The Transact-SQL debugger in SQL Server Management Studio enables you to step through Transact-SQL scripts, stored procedures, triggers, and functions as they are running. The Transact-SQL debugger allows you to do the following:

- Step through the Transact-SQL statements in the Query Editor line by line or set breakpoints to stop at specific lines.
- Step into or over Transact-SQL stored procedures, functions, or triggers run by the code in the query editor window.
- Watch the values assigned to variables and observe system objects such as the call stack and threads.

If you want to run the T-SQL Debugger, the query editor window must be connected to SQL Server as a member of the `sysadmin` server role.

NOTE

Debugging of T-SQL code should be done only on a test or development server, not on a production server. Debugging sessions can often run for long periods of time while you are investigating the operations of your Transact-SQL statements. If the code being debugged involves a multistatement transaction, locks acquired by the session could be held for extended periods while the code is paused in the debugger until the debugging session is ended or the transaction committed or rolled back. This could lead to extensive locking contention or blocking for other applications accessing production data.

You start the debugger in a query editor window by either clicking the Debug button on the Query toolbar or by clicking Start Debugging on the Debug menu, as shown in Figure 28.8.

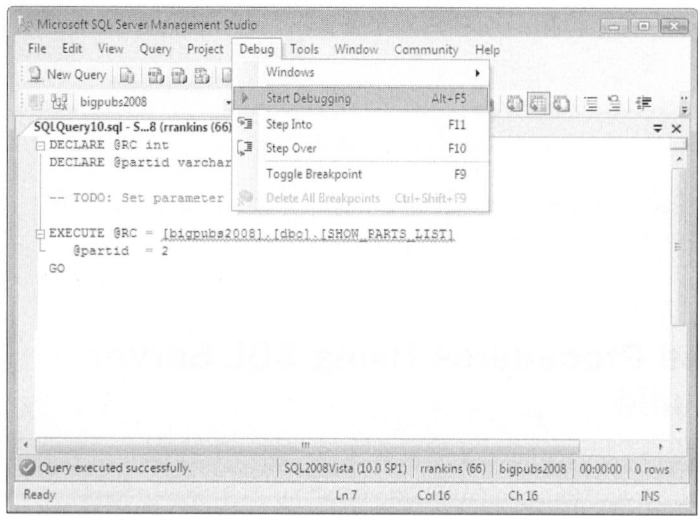

FIGURE 28.8 Invoking the T-SQL debugger in SSMS.

When the query editor window enters debug mode, the debugger initially stops on the first line of code in the stored procedure, as shown in Figure 28.9. You can then set any breakpoints and run to the breakpoints or step through the procedure code one line at a time. You can press F10 to step through the code one line at a time. If the SQL code invokes a stored procedure or function, or a DML statement invokes a trigger, you can press F11 to step into the called routine. If you step into a routine in the T-SQL Debugger, SQL Server Management Studio opens a new query editor window populated with the source code for the routine, places the window into debug mode, and then pauses execution on the first statement in the routine. You can then step through or set breakpoints in the code for that routine.

Located near the bottom of the debugger window are some useful information windows. The first group of windows is the Locals/Watch window, which displays the contents of local variables or any watch expressions you have defined. The Locals window displays the current values in all the local variables within the current scope. You can also modify the values of the variables in the Locals window to test various scenarios or to adjust data values so the code executes differently. To modify the value of a variable, right-click the row and select Edit Value.

In the four Watch windows, you can add variables or expressions whose values you want to watch, such as the global variables `@@NESTLEVEL`, `@@FETCH_STATUS`, or `@@ROWCOUNT`. To add an expression to a Watch window, you can either select Add Watch in the QuickWatch dialog box or enter the name of the expression in the Name column of an empty row in a Watch window. The Watch windows, like the other tabbed windows in the debugger, can be set as docked or floating windows, allowing you to view multiple windows simultaneously (Figure 28.9 shows an example of the Watch1 window set as a floating window).

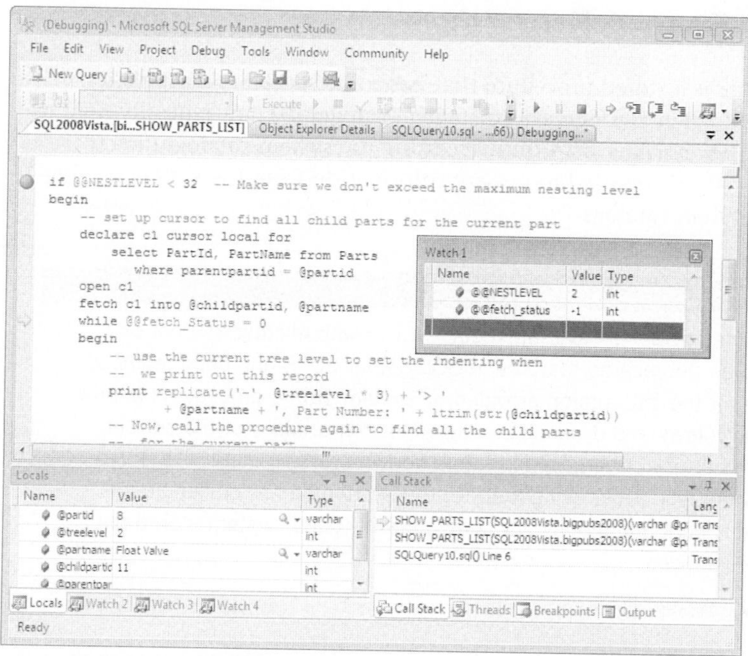

FIGURE 28.9 Debugging a T-SQL stored procedure in SSMS.

The second group of windows is the Call Stack, Breakpoints, Output, and Results and Messages windows. The Call Stack window displays the current execution location and also displays information about how execution passed from the original query editor window to the current execution location through any other functions, procedures, or triggers. The Breakpoints window lets you view information about the breakpoints you have set. From this window, you can also jump to the source code where the breakpoint is set or disable or delete the breakpoint. The Output window displays various messages and program data, including system messages from the debugger. The Results and Messages tabs on the query editor window display the results of previously executed Transact-SQL statements within the debugging session. The query editor window stays in debug mode until either the last statement in the query editor window is executed or you manually stop debugging. You can stop debugging, along with any further statement execution, using any one of the following methods:

- On the Debug menu, click Stop Debugging.
- On the Debug toolbar, click the Stop Debugging button.
- On the Query menu, click Cancel Executing Query.

- On the Query toolbar, click the Cancel Executing Query button.

If you want to stop debugging but allow the remaining Transact-SQL statements to run to completion, click Detach All on the Debug menu.

Using System Stored Procedures

A system stored procedure is a stored procedure that has some special characteristics. These procedures, created when SQL Server is installed or upgraded, are generally used to administer SQL Server. They shield a DBA from accessing the system catalogs directly. Some system stored procedures are used to present information from the system catalog, and others modify the system catalogs.

NOTE

System stored procedures seem to have fallen out of favor with Microsoft. Most of them have been listed as deprecated features in SQL Server 2008 and been replaced with T-SQL commands, or the information provided by system stored procedures is now available via the catalog views and dynamic management views. Many of the current system stored procedures may be removed in future versions of Microsoft SQL Server, so it is recommended that you avoid using many of the system stored procedures in any of your development work and modify any code currently using system stored procedures to use the alternatives.

Although many of the system stored procedures have been deprecated and are not as critical to administering SQL Server as they once were, it is still a good idea to be familiar with the basic system stored procedures. There are currently around 400 documented system stored procedures in SQL Server 2008, so it would be a tough job to learn the names and syntax for all of them. The total number of system stored procedures is more than 1,400. Some of the undocumented stored procedures are called by other procedures, and others are called from SSMS or other SQL Server tools and utility programs.

The following attributes characterize a system stored procedure:

- The stored procedure name begins with `sp_`.
- The stored procedure resides in the `Resource` database.
- The procedure is defined in the `sys` schema.

These attributes make the procedure *global*, which means you can execute the procedure from any database without qualifying the database name. The procedure executes within the current database context.

Although system stored procedures reside in the `Resource` database, they also run in any database context when fully qualified with a database name, regardless of the current database context. For instance, `sp_helpfile` shows information about the files configured for the current database. In the following example, when not qualified, `sp_helpfile` returns file information for the master database, and when qualified with bigpubs2008.., it returns file information for the bigpubs2008 database:

```
exec sp_helpfile
go

name     fileid filename                                                    filegroup
size     maxsize  growth usage
-------- ------ ----------------------------------------------------------- ---------
-------- -------- ------ ----------
master   1      C:\MSSQL2008\MSSQL10.SQL2008UNLEASHED\MSSQL\DATA\master.mdf  PRIMARY
4096 KB  Unlimited 10%    data only
mastlog  2      C:\MSSQL2008\MSSQL10.SQL2008UNLEASHED\MSSQL\DATA\mastlog.ldf NULL
512 KB   Unlimited 10%    log only


exec bigpubs2008..sp_helpfile
go

name             fileid filename                               filegroup size
 maxsize   growth usage
---------------------------------------------------------------------------------------
------------------------
bigpubs2008      1      E:\MSSQL2008\DATA\bigpubs2008.mdf      PRIMARY   214912 KB
 Unlimited 10%    data only
bigpubs2008_log  2      E:\MSSQL2008\DATA\bigpubs2008_log.LDF  NULL      504 KB
 Unlimited 10%    log only
```

Table 28.1 describes the categories of system stored procedures.

TABLE 28.1 System Stored Procedure Categories

Category	Description
Catalog stored procedures	Used to implement ODBC data dictionary functions and isolate ODBC applications from changes to underlying system tables.
Cursor stored procedures	Used to implement cursor variable functionality.
Database engine stored procedures	Used for general maintenance of the SQL Server Database Engine.
Database mail stored procedures	Used to perform email operations from within an instance of SQL Server.
Database maintenance plan procedures	Used to set up core database maintenance tasks.
Distributed queries stored procedures	Used to link remote servers and manage distributed queries.

TABLE 28.1 System Stored Procedure Categories

Category	Description
Full-text search stored procedures	Used to implement and query full-text indexes.
Log shipping stored procedures	Used to configure, modify, and monitor log shipping configurations.
Automation stored procedures	Allow OLE automation objects to be used within a T-SQL batch.
Notification services stored procedures	Used to manage SQL Server 2008 Notification Services.
Replication stored procedures	Used to manage replication.
Security stored procedures	Used to manage security, such as login IDs, usernames, and so on.
SQL Server Profiler stored procedures	Used by SQL Server Profiler to monitor performance and activity.
SQL Server Agent stored procedures	Used by SQL Server Agent to manage scheduled and event-driven activities.
Web task stored procedures	Used for creating web pages.
XML stored procedures	Used for XML text management.
General extended stored procedures	Provide an interface from an instance of SQL Server to external programs for various maintenance activities (for example, `xp_sqlmaint`)

Some of the more useful system stored procedures are listed in Table 28.2.

TABLE 28.2 Useful System Stored Procedures

Procedure Name	Description
`sp_who` and `sp_who2`	Return information about current connections to SQL Server.
`sp_help [`*`object_name`*`]`	Lists the objects in a database or returns information about a specified object.
`sp_helpdb`	Returns a list of databases or information about a specified database.
`sp_configure`	Lists or changes configuration settings.

Startup Procedures

A SQL Server administrator can create stored procedures that are marked for execution automatically whenever SQL Server starts. They are often referred to as *startup procedures*. Startup procedures are useful for performing housekeeping-type tasks or starting up a background process when SQL Server starts. Some possible uses for startup procedures include the following:

- Automatically perform system or maintenance tasks in `tempdb`, such as creating a global temporary table.
- Enable custom SQL Server Profiler traces automatically whenever SQL Server is running. (For more information on SQL Server Profiler traces, see Chapter 6.)
- Automatically start other external processes on the SQL Server machine, using `xp_cmdshell`. (Using `xp_cmdshell` is discussed in the section "Using Extended Stored Procedures," in Chapter 44.)
- Prime the data cache with the contents of your critical, frequently used tables.
- Prime the plan cache by executing procedures or functions you want to have compiled and cached before applications start using them.

To create a startup procedure, you log in as a system administrator and create the procedure in the `master` database. Then you set the procedure startup option to `true` by using `sp_procoption`:

```
sp_procoption procedure_name, startup, true
```

If you no longer want the procedure to run at startup, remove the `startup` option by executing the same procedure and changing the value to `false`.

By default, a startup procedure runs in the context of the system administrator, but it can use `SETUSER` to impersonate another account, if necessary. If you need to reference objects in other databases from within a startup procedure, you need to fully qualify the object with the appropriate database and owner names.

Startup procedures are launched asynchronously; that is, SQL Server doesn't wait for them to complete before continuing with additional startup tasks. This allows a startup procedure to execute in a loop for the duration of the SQL Server process, or it allows several startup procedures to be launched simultaneously. While a startup procedure is running, it runs as a separate worker thread.

TIP

If you need to execute a series of stored procedures in sequence during startup, you can nest the stored procedure calls within a single startup procedure. This approach consumes only a single worker thread.

Any error messages or print statements generated by a startup procedure are written to the SQL Server error log. For example, consider the following whimsical but utterly useless startup procedure:

```
use master
go
create procedure good_morning
as
print 'Good morning, Dave'
return
go
sp_procoption good_morning, startup, true
go
```

When SQL Server is restarted, the following entries would be displayed in the error log:

```
2009-06-12 13:21:00.04 spid5s      Recovery is complete. This is an
 informational message only. No user action is required.
2009-06-12 13:21:00.15 spid5s      Launched startup procedure 'good_morning'.
2009-06-12 13:21:00.15 spid51s     Good morning, Dave
```

Any result sets generated by a startup procedure vanish into the infamous bit bucket. If you need to return result sets from a startup procedure, the procedure should be written to insert the results into a table. The table needs to be a permanent table and not a temporary table because a temporary table would be automatically dropped when the startup procedure finished executing.

The following example is a startup procedure that could preload all tables within the `Sales` and `Purchasing` schemas in the `AdventureWorks` database into data cache memory on SQL Server startup:

```
use master
go
create procedure prime_cache
as
declare @tablename varchar(128),
        @schemaname varchar(128)
```

```
declare c1 cursor for
select s.name, o.name
     from AdventureWorks.sys.objects o
     join AdventureWorks.sys.schemas s
         on o.schema_id = s.schema_id
     where type = 'U'
     and s.name in ('Sales', 'Purchasing')

open c1
fetch c1 into @schemaname, @tablename
while @@fetch_status = 0
begin
    print 'Loading ''' + @schemaname + '.' + @tablename + ''' into data cache'
    exec ('select * from AdventureWorks.' + @schemaname + '.' + @tablename)
    fetch c1 into @schemaname, @tablename
end
close c1
deallocate c1
return
go

sp_procoption prime_cache, startup, true
go
```

The error log output from this startup procedure would be similar to the following:

```
2009-06-15 19:39:18.970 spid7s      Launched startup procedure 'prime_cache'.
2009-06-15 19:39:20.550 spid30s     Loading 'Sales.Store' into data cache
2009-06-15 19:39:20.870 spid30s     Loading 'Sales.StoreContact' into data cache
2009-06-15 19:39:20.870 spid30s     Loading 'Purchasing.ProductVendor' into data
 cache
2009-06-15 19:39:20.950 spid30s     Loading 'Purchasing.Vendor' into data cache
2009-06-15 19:39:21.010 spid30s     Loading 'Purchasing.PurchaseOrderDetail' into
 data cache
2009-06-15 19:39:21.140 spid30s     Loading 'Purchasing.VendorAddress' into data
 cache
2009-06-15 19:39:21.150 spid30s     Loading 'Purchasing.VendorContact' into data
 cache
2009-06-15 19:39:21.160 spid30s     Loading 'Purchasing.PurchaseOrderHeader' into
 data cache
2009-06-15 19:39:21.220 spid30s     Loading 'Sales.ContactCreditCard' into data
 cache
2009-06-15 19:39:21.310 spid30s     Loading 'Sales.CountryRegionCurrency' into
 data cache
2009-06-15 19:39:21.420 spid30s     Loading 'Sales.CreditCard' into data cache
2009-06-15 19:39:21.540 spid30s     Loading 'Sales.Currency' into data cache
```

```
2009-06-15 19:39:21.570 spid30s      Loading 'Sales.SalesOrderDetail' into data
 cache
2009-06-15 19:39:22.040 spid30s      Loading 'Sales.CurrencyRate' into data cache
2009-06-15 19:39:22.120 spid30s      Loading 'Sales.Customer' into data cache
2009-06-15 19:39:22.420 spid30s     Loading 'Sales.SalesOrderHeader' into data cache
2009-06-15 19:39:23.170 spid30s      Loading 'Sales.CustomerAddress' into data
 cache
2009-06-15 19:39:23.290 spid30s      Loading 'Sales.SalesOrderHeaderSalesReason'
 into data cache
2009-06-15 19:39:23.340 spid30s      Loading 'Sales.SalesPerson' into data cache
2009-06-15 19:39:23.360 spid30s      Loading 'Sales.SalesPersonQuotaHistory' into
 data cache
2009-06-15 19:39:23.380 spid30s      Loading 'Sales.SalesReason' into data cache
2009-06-15 19:39:23.380 spid30s      Loading 'Sales.Individual' into data cache
2009-06-15 19:39:23.950 spid30s      Loading 'Sales.SalesTaxRate' into data cache
2009-06-15 19:39:23.970 spid30s      Loading 'Sales.SalesTerritory' into data cache
2009-06-15 19:39:24.000 spid30s      Loading 'Sales.SalesTerritoryHistory' into
 data cache
2009-06-15 19:39:24.060 spid30s      Loading 'Purchasing.ShipMethod' into data
 cache
2009-06-15 19:39:24.090 spid30s      Loading 'Sales.ShoppingCartItem' into data
 cache
2009-06-15 19:39:24.100 spid30s      Loading 'Sales.SpecialOffer' into data cache
2009-06-15 19:39:24.110 spid30s      Loading 'Sales.SpecialOfferProduct' into data
 cache
```

If you want to disable the automatic execution of all startup procedures, you can use `sp_configure` to disable the `scan for startup procs` configuration option. Setting this option to `0` disables the running of startup procedures on subsequent SQL Server restarts.

If SQL Server is not currently running and you want to skip running the startup procedures, you can specify Trace Flag 4022 as a startup parameter. You can set the trace flag for a SQL Server instance by using the SQL Server Configuration Manager. In SQL Server Configuration Manager, perform the following steps:

1. Click on SQL Server 2008 Services.
2. In the right pane, right-click the SQL Server instance you want to set the trace flag for and select Properties.
3. Go to the Advanced tab and select the Startup Parameters box.
4. Click the expand arrow to the right of the input field to expand the entire field.
5. Place your cursor at the end of the value and type a semicolon (**;**).
6. Type **-T4022** (see Figure 28.10).
7. Click OK.

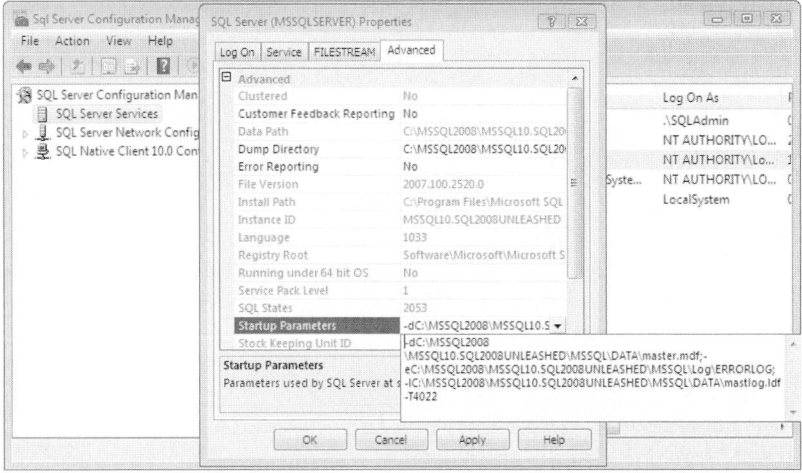

FIGURE 28.10 Setting Trace Flag 4022 to prevent startup procedures from executing.

Also, if you start SQL Server with minimal configuration (by using the `-f` flag), the startup stored procedures are not executed.

Summary

Stored procedures are among the premier features of Microsoft SQL Server. They provide a number of benefits over using ad hoc SQL, including faster performance; restricted, function-based access to tables; protection of application code from database changes; and the ability to simplify complex tasks into a simple stored procedure call.

In the next chapter, you learn how to expand the capabilities of your T-SQL code by creating and using user-defined functions developed in T-SQL.

CHAPTER 29

Creating and Managing User-Defined Functions

IN THIS CHAPTER

- What's New in SQL Server 2008
- Why Use User-Defined Functions?
- Types of User-Defined Functions
- Creating and Managing User-Defined Functions
- Rewriting Stored Procedures as Functions
- Creating and Using CLR Functions

SQL Server provides a number of predefined functions that are built in to the T-SQL language. The supplied functions help extend the capabilities of T-SQL, providing the ability to perform string manipulation, mathematic calculations, data type conversions, and so on within T-SQL code. Although SQL Server provides a reasonably extensive set of functions, you might sometimes wish you had available a function that is not provided. You could create a stored procedure to perform custom processing, but you can't use the result of a stored procedure in a `WHERE` clause or as a column in a `SELECT` list. For this type of situation, SQL Server 2008 provides user-defined functions.

A user-defined function can return a single scalar value, like the majority of the built-in functions, or it can return a result set as a table result, similarly to a table variable.

This chapter takes a look at how to create and manage user-defined functions as well as when it may be better to rewrite stored procedures as functions.

What's New in SQL Server 2008

Not much has really changed with user-defined functions in SQL Server 2008 from SQL Server 2005. No real new functionality or features have been added beyond the ability to specify up to 2,100 parameters instead of 1,024. User-defined functions can still be created in T-SQL or using the .NET common language runtime (CLR). Being able to define functions in the CLR significantly extends what you can do in user-defined functions by opening up the power and capabilities of the .NET Framework languages. This means you can develop functions in SQL Server that are either impossible or very difficult to achieve using T-SQL alone. Later in this chapter, in the section "Creating and Using CLR Functions," you learn about CLR functions and some general guidelines on when to use CLR functions versus T-SQL functions.

NOTE

This chapter focuses primarily on creating T-SQL functions. For more information and examples related to creating and coding examples of CLR functions, see Chapter 46, "SQLCLR: Developing SQL Server Objects.."

Why Use User-Defined Functions?

The main benefit of user-defined functions is that they mean you are not limited to just the functions SQL Server provides. You can develop your own functions to meet your specific needs or to simplify complex SQL code. For example, the `getdate()` function returns the current system date and time. It always includes both a date component and time component, with accuracy down to the milliseconds. What if you wanted to return a `datetime` value with just the date and have the time always set to midnight? To do this, you would have to pass the result from `getdate()` through some other functions to zero out the time component. The following is one possible solution:

```
select convert(datetime, convert(date, getdate()))
```

Each time you wanted just the date, with the time always set to midnight, you would have to perform this same conversion operation on the result of the `getdate()` function. As an alternative, you could create a user-defined function that performs the operations on `getdate()` automatically and always returns the current date, with a time value of midnight, as in this example:

```
USE bigpubs2008
go

CREATE FUNCTION getonlydate ()
RETURNS datetime
AS
BEGIN   RETURN (select convert(datetime, convert(date, getdate())))
END
GO
```

You could then use the user-defined function in your SQL code in place of the more complex conversion operation on the `getdate()` function each time. Like the built-in system functions, user-defined functions can be used in `SELECT` lists, `SET` clauses of `UPDATE` statements, `VALUES` clauses of `INSERT` statements, as default values, and so on. For example, the following query uses the user-defined function `getonlydate()` to return the current date, with a time of midnight:

```
select dbo.getonlydate()
```

The following examples show how you could use the `getonlydate()` user-defined function in other statements:

```
USE bigpubs2008
go
CREATE TABLE Orders (
       OrderID int IDENTITY (1, 1) NOT NULL Primary Key,
       CustomerID nchar (5) COLLATE SQL_Latin1_General_CP1_CI_AS NULL ,
       EmployeeID int NULL ,
       OrderDate datetime NULL default dbo.getonlydate(),
       RequiredDate datetime NULL ,
       ShippedDate datetime NULL
)
go

insert Orders (CustomerID, EmployeeID, RequiredDate)
    values ('BERGS', 3, dbo.getonlydate() + 7)
go

update Orders
     set ShippedDate = dbo.getonlydate()
     where OrderID = 1
go

select OrderDate,
       RequiredDate,
       ShippedDate
    from Orders
  where OrderDate = dbo.getonlydate()
go

OrderDate               RequiredDate            ShippedDate
----------------------- ----------------------- -----------------------
2008-06-03 00:00:00.000 2008-06-10 00:00:00.000 2008-06-03 00:00:00.000
```

If you use the `getonlydate()` function consistently when you want to store only dates with a time value of midnight, searching against `datetime` columns is easier because you don't have to concern yourself with the time component. For example, if you use `getdate()` instead of `getonlydate()`, you have to account for the time component in your queries against `OrderDate` to ensure that you find all records for a particular day:

29

```
SELECT OrderDate,
       RequiredDate,
       ShippedDate
    from Orders
  where OrderDate >= convert(varchar(10), getdate(), 110)
    and OrderDate < convert(varchar(10), getdate() + 1, 110)
```

From this example, you can see how much using the `getonlydate()` user-defined function can simplify your queries.

TIP

Another way to avoid the issues related to storing a time component in your date-valued columns in SQL Server 2008 is to use the new `DATE` data type instead of `DATETIME`. This new data type is discussed in more detail in Chapter 42, "What's New for Transact-SQL in SQL Server 2008."

In addition to functions that return scalar values, you can also define functions that return table results. You can use functions that return table results anywhere in queries that a table or view can be used, including joins, subqueries, and so on. The following examples show how to use a user-defined table-valued function that returns a list of valid book types:

```
use bigpubs2008
go
create function valid_book_types()
returns TABLE
as
return (SELECT distinct type from titles)
go

select * from dbo.valid_book_types()
go
insert titles
select * from newtitles
where type in (select * from dbo.valid_book_types())
```

Essentially, this example reduces a query to a simple function that you can now use anywhere a table can be referenced.

With a few restrictions—which are covered later in this chapter, in the "Creating and Managing User-Defined Functions" section—you can write all types of functions in SQL Server to perform various calculations or routines. For example, you could create a T-SQL function that returns a valid list of code values, a function to determine the number of days items are backordered, a function to return the average price of all books, and so on. Plus, with the capability to create CLR-based functions, you can create significantly more powerful functions than what can be accomplished using T-SQL alone. Examples of CLR-based functions include a more robust `soundex()` function, a function to return the factorial of a number, and an address comparison function. The possibilities are nearly endless. As you have can see, user-defined functions significantly increase the capabilities and flexibility of T-SQL.

Types of User-Defined Functions

SQL Server supports three types of user-defined functions:

- Scalar functions
- Inline table-valued functions
- Multistatement table-valued functions

The next few sections take an in-depth look at the differences between the function types and how and where you can use them.

Scalar Functions

A scalar function is like the standard built-in functions provided with SQL Server. It returns a single scalar value that can be used anywhere a constant expression can be used in a query. (You saw an example of this in the earlier description of the `getonlydate()`function.)

A scalar function typically takes one or more arguments and returns a value of a specified data type. Every T-SQL function must return a result using the `RETURN` statement. The value to be returned can be contained in a local variable defined within the function, or the value can be computed in the `RETURN` statement. The following two functions are variations of a function that returns the average price for a specified type of book from the `titles` table:

```
use bigpubs2008
go
CREATE FUNCTION AverageBookPrice(@booktype varchar(12) = '%')
RETURNS money
AS
BEGIN
    DECLARE @avg money
    SELECT @avg = avg(price)
    FROM titles
    WHERE type like @booktype

    RETURN @avg
END
go
```

```
CREATE FUNCTION AverageBookPrice2(@booktype varchar(12) = '%')
RETURNS money
AS
BEGIN
    RETURN ( SELECT avg(price)
             FROM titles
             WHERE type like @booktype)
END
```

As mentioned earlier in this chapter, a scalar function can be used anywhere a constant expression can be used. For example, SQL Server doesn't allow aggregate functions in a `WHERE` clause unless they are contained in a subquery. The `AvgBookPrice()` function lets you compare against the average price without having to use a subquery:

```
select title_id, type, price from titles
where price > dbo.AverageBookPrice('popular_comp')
go

title_id type         price
-------- ------------ ---------------------
PC1035   popular_comp 17.1675
PS2091   psychology   17.0884
```

When invoking a user-defined scalar function, you must include the schema name. If you omit the schema name, you get the following error, even if the function is created in your default schema or exists only in the `dbo` schema in the database:

```
select AverageBookPrice('popular_comp')
go

Server: Msg 195, Level 15, State 10, Line 1
'AverageBookPrice' is not a recognized function name.
```

You can return the value from a user-defined scalar function into a local variable in two ways. You can assign the result to a local variable by using the `SET` statement or an assignment select, or you can use the `EXEC` statement. The following commands are functionally equivalent:

```
declare @avg1 money,
        @avg2 money,
        @avg3 money
select @avg1 = dbo.AverageBookPrice('popular_comp')
set @avg2 = dbo.AverageBookPrice('popular_comp')
exec @avg3 = dbo.AverageBookPrice 'popular_comp'
select @avg1 as avg1, @avg2 as avg2, @avg3 as avg3
go
```

```
Warning: Null value is eliminated by an aggregate or other SET operation.
avg1                 avg2                 avg3
-------------------- -------------------- --------------------
16.0643              16.0643              16.0643
```

Notice, however, that when you use a function in an EXEC statement, you invoke it similarly to the way you invoke a stored procedure, and you do not use parentheses around the function parameters. Also, when you invoke a function in the EXEC statement, the function generates the following warning message: "Warning: Null value is eliminated by an aggregate or other SET operation." This warning isn't generated when the function is invoked in the SET or SELECT statement. To avoid confusion, you should stick to using the EXEC statement for stored procedures and invoke scalar functions as you would normally invoke a SQL Server built-in function.

Table-Valued Functions

A table-valued user-defined function returns a rowset instead of a single scalar value. You can invoke a table-valued function in the FROM clause of a SELECT statement, just as you would a table or view. In some situations, a table-valued function can almost be thought of as a view that accepts parameters, so the result set is determined dynamically. A table-valued function specifies the keyword TABLE in its RETURNS clause.

Table-valued functions are of two types: inline and multistatement. The two types of table-valued functions return the same thing, and they are also invoked the same way. The only real difference between them is the way the function is written to return the rowset. The next couple sections look at each of these types of table-valued functions.

Inline Table-Valued Functions

An inline table-valued function specifies only the TABLE keyword in the RETURNS clause, without table definition information. The code inside the function is a single RETURN statement that invokes a SELECT statement. For example, you could create an inline table-valued function that returns a rowset of all book types and the average price for each type, where the average price exceeds the value passed into the function:

```
use bigpubs2008
go
CREATE FUNCTION AveragePricebyType (@price money = 0.0)
RETURNS table
AS

   RETURN ( SELECT type, avg(isnull(price, 0)) as avg_price
            FROM titles
            group by type
            having avg(isnull(price, 0)) > @price)
```

29

You can invoke the function by referencing it in a FROM clause as you would a table or view:

```
select * from AveragePricebyType (15.00)
go

type         avg_price
------------ ---------------------
business     15.0988
mod_cook     15.4236
```

Notice that when you invoke a table-valued function, you do not have to specify the schema name as you do with a user-defined scalar function.

Multistatement Table-Valued Functions

Multistatement table-valued functions differ from inline functions in two major ways:

- The RETURNS clause specifies a table variable and its definition.
- The body of the function contains multiple statements, at least one of which populates the table variable with data values.

You define a table variable in the RETURNS clause by using the TABLE data type. The syntax to define the table variable is similar to the CREATE TABLE syntax. Note that the name of the table variable comes before the TABLE keyword:

```
RETURNS @variable TABLE ( column definition | table_constraint [, ...] )
```

The scope of the table variable is limited to the function in which it is defined. Although the contents of the table variable are returned as the function result, the table variable itself cannot be accessed or referenced outside the function.

Within the function in which a table variable is defined, that table variable can be treated like a regular table. You can perform any SELECT, INSERT, UPDATE, or DELETE statement on the rows in a table variable, except for SELECT INTO. Here's an example:

```
INSERT INTO @table SELECT au_lname, au_fname from authors
```

The following example defines the inline table-valued function AveragePricebyType() as a multistatement table-valued function called AveragePricebyType2():

```
use bigpubs2008
go
CREATE FUNCTION AveragePricebyType2 (@price money = 0.0)
RETURNS @table table (type varchar(12) null, avg_price money null)
AS
begin
    insert @table
       SELECT type, avg(isnull(price,0)) as avg_price
             FROM titles
             group by type
```

```
            having avg(isnull(price, 0)) > @price
    return
end
```

Notice the main differences between this version and the inline version: in the multistatement version, you have to define the structure of the table rowset you are returning and also have to include the BEGIN and END statements as wrappers around the multiple statements that the function can contain. Other than that, both functions are invoked the same way and return the same rowset:

```
select * from AveragePricebyType2 (15.00)
go

type         avg_price
------------ --------------------
business     15.0988
mod_cook     15.4236
```

Why use multistatement table-valued functions instead of inline table-valued functions? Generally, you use multistatement table-valued functions when you need to perform further operations (for example, inserts, updates, or deletes) on the contents of the table variable before returning a result set. You would also use them if you need to perform more complex logic or additional processing on the input parameters of the function before invoking the query to populate the table variable.

Creating and Managing User-Defined Functions

In the preceding sections of this chapter, you saw some examples of creating functions. The following sections discuss in more detail the CREATE FUNCTION syntax and the types of operations allowed in functions. These sections also show how to create and manage T-SQL functions by using SQL Server Management Studio (SSMS).

Creating User-Defined Functions

You create T-SQL functions by using T-SQL statements. You can enter the T-SQL code in sqlcmd, SSMS, or any other third-party query tool that allows you to enter ad hoc T-SQL code. The following sections first show the basic syntax for creating functions and then show how you can create functions by using the features of SSMS.

Creating T-SQL Functions

User-defined functions can accept 0–2,100 input parameters but can return only a single result: either a single scalar value or table result set.

The T-SQL syntax for the CREATE FUNCTION command for scalar functions is as follows:

```
CREATE FUNCTION [ schema_name. ] function_name
    ( [ { @parameter_name [AS] [ schema_name.]scalar_datatype [ = default ] }
```

```
    [ ,...n ] ] )
RETURNS scalar_datatype
[ WITH { [ ENCRYPTION ]
         [ , SCHEMABINDING ]
         [ , RETURNS NULL ON NULL INPUT | CALLED ON NULL INPUT ]
         [ , EXECUTE_AS_Clause ]
       } ]
 [ AS ]
BEGIN
    SQL_Statements
    RETURN scalar_expression
END
```

The syntax for the CREATE FUNCTION command for inline table-valued functions is as follows:

```
CREATE FUNCTION [ schema_name. ] function_name
    ( [ { @parameter_name [AS] [ schema_name.]scalar_datatype [ = default ] }
      [ ,...n ] ] )
RETURNS TABLE
[ WITH { [ ENCRYPTION ]
         [ , SCHEMABINDING ]
         [ , RETURNS NULL ON NULL INPUT | CALLED ON NULL INPUT ]
         [ , EXECUTE_AS_Clause ]
       } ]
[ AS ]
RETURN [ ( ] select-stmt [ ) ]
```

The syntax for the CREATE FUNCTION command for multistatement table-valued functions is as follows:

```
CREATE FUNCTION [ schema_name. ] function_name
    ( [ { @parameter_name [AS] [ schema_name.]scalar_datatype [ = default ] }
      [ ,...n ] ] )
RETURNS @table_variable TABLE ( { column_definition | table_constraint }
                                  [ ,...n ] )
[ WITH { [ ENCRYPTION ]
         [ , SCHEMABINDING ]
         [ , RETURNS NULL ON NULL INPUT | CALLED ON NULL INPUT ]
         [ , EXECUTE_AS_Clause ]
       } ]
 [ AS ]
BEGIN
    SQL_Statements
    RETURN
END
```

The types of SQL statements allowed in a function include the following:

- `DECLARE` statements to define variables and cursors that are local to the function.
- Assignments of values to variables that are local to the function, using the `SET` command or an assignment select.
- Cursor operations on local cursors that are declared, opened, closed, and de-allocated within the function. `FETCH` statements must assign values to local variables by using the `INTO` clause.
- Control-of-flow statements such as `IF`, `ELSE`, `WHILE`, `GOTO`, and so on, excluding the `TRY...CATCH` statements.
- `UPDATE`, `INSERT`, and `DELETE` statements that modify table variables defined within the function.
- `EXECUTE` statements that call an extended stored procedure. (Any results returned by the extended stored procedure are discarded.)
- Other user-defined functions, up to a maximum nesting level of 32.

If you specify the `ENCRYPTION` option, the SQL statements used to define the function are stored encrypted in the `syscomments` table. This prevents anyone from viewing the function source code in the database.

NOTE

If you choose to encrypt the function code, you should be sure to save a copy of the script used to create the function to a file outside the database, in case you ever need to modify the function or re-create it. After the source code for the function is encrypted, you cannot extract the original unencrypted source code from the database.

If a function is created with the `SCHEMABINDING` option, the database objects that the function references cannot be altered or dropped unless the function is dropped first or the schema binding of the function is removed, using the `ALTER FUNCTION` command and without specifying the `SCHEMABINDING` option. A `CREATE FUNCTION` statement with the `SCHEMABINDING` option specified fails unless all the following conditions are met:

- Any user-defined functions and views referenced within the function are also schema bound.
- Any objects referenced by the function are referenced using a two-part name (*`schema.object_name`*).
- The function and the objects it references belong to the same database.
- The user executing the `CREATE FUNCTION` statement has `REFERENCES` permission on all database objects that the function references.

You can specify the SCHEMABINDING option only for T-SQL functions. The following example modifies the AveragePricebyType2 function by specifying the SCHEMABINDING option:

```
ALTER FUNCTION AveragePricebyType2 (@price money = 0.0)
RETURNS @table table (type varchar(12) null, avg_price money null)
with schemabinding
AS
begin
    insert @table
       SELECT type, avg(price) as avg_price
             FROM dbo.titles
             group by type
             having avg(price) > @price
    return
end
```

The following example shows what happens if you try to modify a column in the titles table referenced by the function:

```
alter table titles alter column price smallmoney null
go

Msg 5074, Level 16, State 1, Line 1
The object 'AveragePricebyType2' is dependent on column 'price'.
Msg 5074, Level 16, State 1, Line 1
The statistics 'price' is dependent on column 'price'.
Msg 4922, Level 16, State 9, Line 1
ALTER TABLE ALTER COLUMN price failed because one or more objects access this
column.
```

If the RETURNS NULL ON NULL INPUT option is specified, the function automatically returns NULL as a result, without invoking the function body. If this option is not specified, the default option of CALLED ON NULL INPUT is applied. The following example shows the difference between these two options:

```
CREATE FUNCTION striptime (@datetimeval datetime)
RETURNS datetime
AS
BEGIN
    DECLARE @dateval datetime
    SELECT @dateval = convert(date, isnull(@datetimeval, getdate()))
    RETURN @dateval
END
GO
```

```
CREATE FUNCTION striptime2(@datetimeval datetime)
RETURNS datetime
WITH RETURNS NULL ON NULL INPUT
AS
BEGIN
    DECLARE @dateval datetime
    SELECT @dateval = convert(date, isnull(@datetimeval, getdate()))
    RETURN @dateval

END
GO

select dbo.striptime(NULL), dbo.striptime2(NULL)

----------------------- -----------------------
2006-06-05 00:00:00.000 NULL
```

The `EXECUTE AS` clause allows you to specify the security context under which the user-defined function will execute. This way, you can control which user account SQL Server uses to validate permissions on any database objects referenced by the function. This option cannot be specified for inline table-valued functions.

Another key restriction on user-defined functions is that SQL statements within a function cannot generate side effects; that is, a user-defined function cannot generate permanent changes to any resource whose scope extends beyond the function. For example, a function cannot modify data in a table, operate on cursors not local to the function, create or drop database objects, issue transaction control statements, or generate a result set other than the defined function result via a `SELECT` statement or an extended stored procedure that would be returned to the user. The only changes that can be made by the SQL statements in a function are to the objects local to the function, such as local cursors or variables.

A new feature in SQL Server 2008 is that you can now include most built-in system functions within a user-defined function, even ones that are nondeterministic (that is, functions that can return different data values on each call). For example, the `getdate()` function is considered nondeterministic because even though it is always invoked with the same argument, it returns a different value each time it is executed. However, the following nondeterministic built-in functions are still not allowed in user-defined functions:

- `newid()`
- `newsequentialid()`
- `rand()`
- `textptr()`

User-defined functions can also call other user-defined functions, with a limit of 32 levels of nesting. Nesting of functions can help improve the modularity and reusability of function code. For example, the following version of the getonlydate() function uses the striptime() function example shown earlier in this chapter:

```
CREATE FUNCTION dbo.getonlydate()
RETURNS datetime
as
BEGIN
DECLARE @date datetime
SET @date = dbo.striptime( getdate())
RETURN @date
end
```

Using SSMS to Create Functions

To create a function by using SSMS, open the Object Explorer to the database in which you want to create the function. Then select the Programmability node, right-click the Functions node, select New, and then choose one of the three available options as shown in Figure 29.1:

- Inline Table-Valued Function
- Multistatement Table-Valued Function
- Scalar-Valued Function

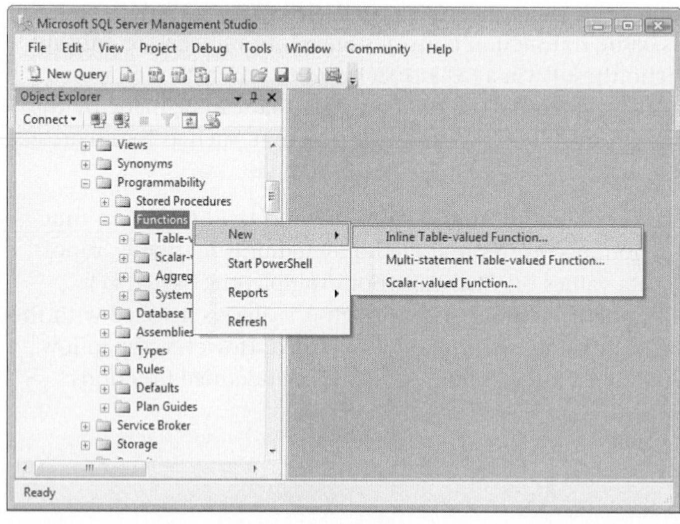

FIGURE 29.1 Creating a new function from the Object Browser in SSMS.

SSMS opens a new query window populated with a template for that type of function. Listing 29.1 shows an example of the default template code for an inline table-valued function that would be opened into a new query window.

LISTING 29.1 An Example of a New Function Creation Script Generated by SSMS

```
-- ================================================
-- Template generated from Template Explorer using:
-- Create Inline Function (New Menu).SQL
--
-- Use the Specify Values for Template Parameters
-- command (Ctrl-Shift-M) to fill in the parameter
-- values below.
--
-- This block of comments will not be included in
-- the definition of the function.
-- ================================================
SET ANSI_NULLS ON
GO
SET QUOTED_IDENTIFIER ON
GO
-- =============================================
-- Author:          <Author,,Name>
-- Create date: <Create Date,,>
-- Description:     <Description,,>
-- =============================================
CREATE FUNCTION <Inline_Function_Name, sysname, FunctionName>
(
     -- Add the parameters for the function here
     <@param1, sysname, @p1> <Data_Type_For_Param1, , int>,
     <@param2, sysname, @p2> <Data_Type_For_Param2, , char>
)
RETURNS TABLE
AS
RETURN
(
     -- Add the SELECT statement with parameter references here
     SELECT 0
)


GO
```

You can modify the template code as necessary to name the function and to specify the parameters, return value, and function body. When you are finished, you execute the contents of the query window to create the function. After you create a function successfully, you should save the source code to a file by choosing File, Save or File, Save As. This way, you can re-create the function from the file if it is accidentally dropped from the database.

One thing you might notice about the function templates is that they contain template parameters for parameter names and function names, for example. These template parameters are in the format `<parameter_name, data_type, value>`:

- `parameter_name` is the name of the template parameter in the script.
- `data_type` is the optional data type of the template parameter.
- `value` is the default value to be used to replace every occurrence of the template parameter in the script.

You can automatically substitute values for template parameters by selecting Query, Specify Values for Template Parameters or by pressing Ctrl+Shift+M. The Specify Values for Template Parameters dialog, shown in Figure 29.2, appears.

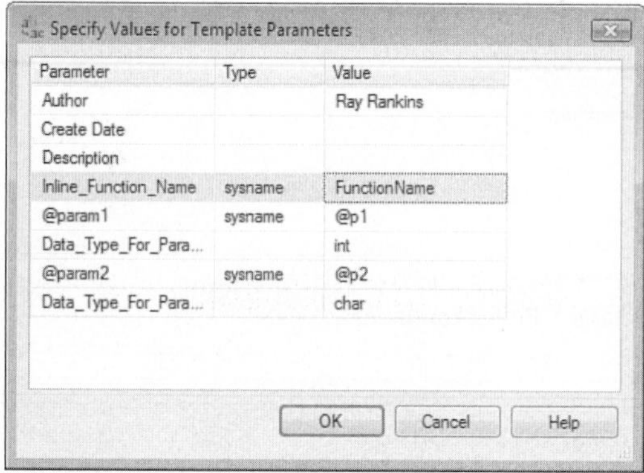

FIGURE 29.2 Using the Specify Values for Template Parameters dialog with functions in SSMS.

Enter the values for the template parameters in the Value column and then click OK. SSMS then substitutes any values you specified wherever the template parameter is defined within the template.

An alternative way to create a function from a template is to use the Template Explorer in SSMS. You can open the Template Explorer by selecting View, Template Explorer in SSMS (see Figure 29.3) or by pressing Ctrl+Alt+T. The Template Explorer window appears in SSMS (which is also shown in Figure 29.3).

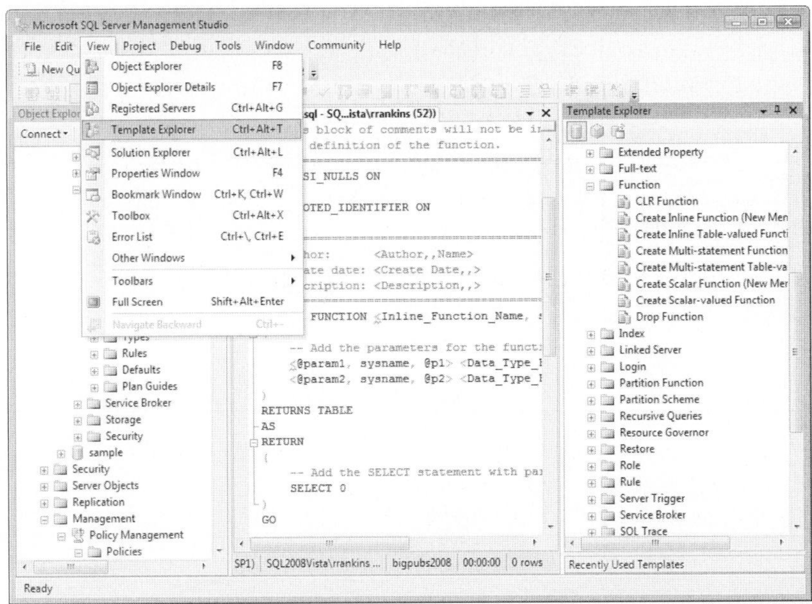

FIGURE 29.3 Opening the Template Explorer to create functions in SSMS.

You can double-click the template for the type of function you want to create or right-click the desired template and then select Open. SSMS opens a new query window populated with the template code.

NOTE

You are also able to edit the provided function templates available in the Template Explorer by right-clicking them and selecting Edit. You can then customize the templates to include code fragments, comments, or a structure that is more to your preferences and save the changes to the template file. However, it is generally recommended that you not modify the provided templates alone and instead create your own custom templates.

Creating Custom Function Templates

To create a custom function template, right-click the `Function` folder in the Template Explorer and select New. SSMS then creates an entry in the Template Explorer, and you can specify the name for the template, as shown in Figure 29.4.

To begin adding code to the template, you double-click it or right-click and select Open. A blank query window appears, and you can use it to enter the new template code. Probably the best way to get started is to copy the template code from one of the templates provided with SQL Server 2008.

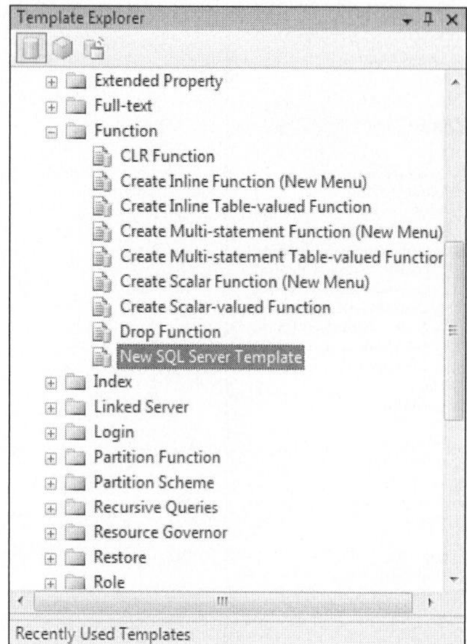

FIGURE 29.4 Creating a new function template in SSMS.

Listing 29.2 shows an example of a new function template.

LISTING 29.2 An Example of Custom Function Template

```
--==========================================
-- SQL Server 2008 Unleashed Sample
--  Create scalar-valued function template
--==========================================

USE <database_name, sysname, bigpubs2008>
GO

IF OBJECT_ID (N'<schema_nm, sysname, dbo>.<func_nm, sysname, fn_myfunc>')
      IS NOT NULL
   DROP FUNCTION <schema_nm, sysname, dbo>.<func_nm, sysname, fn_myfunc>
GO

CREATE FUNCTION <schema_nm, sysname, dbo>.<func_nm, sysname, fn_myfunc>
    (<parameter1, sysname, @param1> <parameter1_datatype,, int>,
     <parameter2, sysname, @param2> <parameter2_datatype,, int>,
     <parameter3, sysname, @param3> <parameter3_datatype,, int>)
RETURNS <return_value_datatype,,int>
WITH EXECUTE AS CALLER
AS
-- place the body of the function here
```

```
BEGIN
    DECLARE <variable1, sysname, @var1> <variable1_datatype,, int>,
            <variable2, sysname, @var2> <variable2_datatype,, int>

    select <variable1, sysname, @var1> = isnull(<parameter1, sysname, @param1> )
    <T-SQL_Body,,>

    RETURN <variable1, sysname, @var1>
END
 GO
```

After you define a custom function template, you can use it as you do the built-in templates. You can double-click it or right-click and select Open, and SSMS opens a new query window with a new function creation script based on the custom template. If you use the default values for the template parameters, after the parameter substitution, your CREATE FUNCTION script should look like the one in Listing 29.3.

LISTING 29.3 An Example of a **CREATE FUNCTION** Script Generated from a Custom Function Template

```
--==========================================
-- SQL Server 2008 Unleashed Sample
--  Create scalar-valued function template
--==========================================

USE bigpubs2008
GO

IF OBJECT_ID (N'dbo.fn_myfunction') IS NOT NULL
   DROP FUNCTION dbo.fn_myfunction
GO

CREATE FUNCTION dbo.fn_myfunction
    (@param1 int,
     @param2 int,
     @param3 int)
RETURNS int
WITH EXECUTE AS CALLER
AS
-- place the body of the function here
BEGIN
    DECLARE @var1 int,
            @var2 int
```

```
    select @var1 = isnull(@param1 )


    RETURN @var1
END
 GO
```

Viewing and Modifying User-Defined Functions

Besides using T-SQL commands to create functions, you can also use them to view and modify functions. You can get information by using the provided system procedures and queries against the `INFORMATION_SCHEMA.routines` view. The following sections describe these methods.

Using T-SQL to View Functions

To view the source code for a user-defined function, you can use the `sp_helptext` procedure:

```
use bigpubs2008
go
exec sp_helptext getonlydate
go

Text
------------------------------------------------------------------------------

CREATE FUNCTION getonlydate ()
RETURNS datetime
AS
BEGIN   RETURN (select convert(datetime, convert(date, getdate())))
END
```

NOTE

To display the source code for the functions clearly, configure the SSMS query window to display results as text rather than in the grid by pressing Ctrl+T.

In addition to `sp_helptext`, you can write queries against the `INFORMATION_SCHEMA.routines` view to display the source code for a function:

```
SELECT routine_definition
from INFORMATION_SCHEMA.routines
where routine_name = 'getonlydate'
and specific_schema = 'dbo'
```

```
and specific_catalog = 'bigpubs2008'

routine_definition
------------------------------------------------------------------------------
CREATE FUNCTION getonlydate ()
RETURNS datetime
AS
BEGIN   RETURN (select convert(datetime, convert(date, getdate())))
END
```

If you want to display information about the input parameters for a function, you use the `INFORMATION_SCHEMA.parameters` view. For scalar functions, the view also displays information for the return parameter, which has an ordinal position of `0` and no parameter name:

```
select substring(parameter_name,1,20) as parameter_name,
       substring(data_type, 1, 20) as data_type,
       Parameter_mode,
       ordinal_position
from INFORMATION_SCHEMA.parameters
where specific_name = 'striptime'
and specific_schema = 'dbo'
and specific_catalog = 'bigpubs2008'
order by ordinal_position
go

parameter_name       data_type            Parameter_mode ordinal_position
-------------------- -------------------- -------------- ----------------
                     datetime             OUT            0
@datetimeval         datetime             IN             1
```

If you want to display information about the result columns returned by a table-valued function, use the `INFORMATION_SCHEMA.routine_columns` view:

```
select substring(column_name, 1, 20) as column_name,
       substring (data_type, 1, 12)
             + case when character_maximum_length is not null
                 then '(' + cast(character_maximum_length as varchar(4)) + ')'
                      else ''
                      end
              as datatype,
       numeric_precision as 'precision',
       numeric_scale as scale,
       ordinal_position
from INFORMATION_SCHEMA.routine_columns
where table_name = 'AveragePricebyType'
order by ordinal_position
go
```

```
column_name          datatype           precision scale       ordinal_position
-------------------- ------------------ --------- ----------- ----------------
type                 char(12)           NULL      NULL        1
avg_price            money              19        4           2
```

In addition, SQL Server provides the OBJECTPROPERTY function, which you can use to get information about functions. One of the things you can find out is whether a function is a multistatement table function, an inline function, or a scalar function. The OBJECTPROPERTY function accepts an object ID and an object property parameter, and it returns the value 1 if the property is true, 0 if it is false, or NULL if an invalid function ID or property parameter is specified. The following property parameters are appropriate for functions:

- **IsTableFunction**—Returns 1 if the function is a table-valued function but not an inline function.
- **IsInlineFunction**—Returns 1 if the function is an inline table-valued function.
- **IsScalarFunction**—Returns 1 if the function is a scalar function.
- **IsSchemaBound**—Returns 1 if the function was created with the SCHEMABINDING option.
- **IsDeterministic**—Returns 1 if the function is deterministic (that is, it always returns the same result each time it is called with a specific set of input values).

The following example demonstrates a possible use of the OBJECTPROPERTY function with the INFORMATION_SCHEMA.routines view:

```
select convert(varchar(10), specific_Schema) as 'schema',
  convert(varchar(20), specific_name) as 'function',
  case objectproperty(object_id(specific_name), 'IsScalarFunction')
      when 1 then 'Yes' else 'No' end as IsScalar,
  case objectproperty(object_id(specific_name), 'IsTableFunction')
      when 1 then 'Yes' else 'No' end as IsTable,
  case objectproperty(object_id(specific_name), 'IsInlineFunction')
      when 1 then 'Yes' else 'No' end as IsInline,
  case objectproperty(object_id(specific_name), 'IsSchemaBound')
      when 1 then 'Yes' else 'No' end as IsSchemaBnd,
  case objectproperty(object_id(specific_name), 'IsDeterministic')
      when 1 then 'Yes' else 'No' end as IsDtrmnstc
from information_Schema.routines
where routine_type = 'FUNCTION'
order by specific_name
go

schema     function             IsScalar IsTable IsInline IsSchemaBnd IsDtrmnstc
---------- -------------------- -------- ------- -------- ----------- ----------
dbo        AverageBookPrice     Yes      No      No       No          No
```

```
dbo        AverageBookPrice2    Yes      No       No       No         No
dbo        AveragePricebyType   No       Yes      Yes      No         No
dbo        AveragePricebyType2  No       Yes      No       Yes        Yes
dbo        getdateonly          Yes      No       No       No         No
dbo        getonlydate          Yes      No       No       No         No
dbo        striptime            Yes      No       No       No         No
dbo        striptime2           Yes      No       No       No         No
```

Using T-SQL to Modify Functions

You can use the ALTER FUNCTION command to change a function's definition without having to drop and re-create it. The syntax for the ALTER FUNCTION command is identical to the syntax for CREATE FUNCTION, except that you replace the CREATE keyword with the ALTER keyword. The following example modifies the AveragePricebyType2 function:

```
ALTER FUNCTION AveragePricebyType2 (@price money = 0.0)
RETURNS @table table (type varchar(12) null, avg_price money null)
with schemabinding
AS
begin
    insert @table
       SELECT type, avg(price) as avg_price
             FROM dbo.titles
             group by type
             having avg(price) > @price
        order by avg(price) desc
    return
end
```

Using the ALTER FUNCTION command has a couple advantages over dropping and re-creating a function to modify it. The main advantage, as mentioned earlier, is that you don't have to drop the function first to make the change. The second advantage is that, because you don't have to drop the function, you don't have to worry about reassigning permissions to the function. To determine whether a function has been altered since it was created, you can query the LAST_ALTERED column in the INFORMATION_SCHEMA.routines view for that function.

One limitation of the ALTER FUNCTION command is that you cannot use this command to change a table-valued function to a scalar function or to change an inline function to a multistatement function. You have to drop and re-create the function.

Using SSMS to View and Modify Functions

To view or edit a function within SSMS, open the Object Explorer to the database in which you want to create the function. Then select the Programmability node, right-click the Functions node, and then select either the Table-Valued Functions folder or the Scalar-Valued Functions folder. SSMS then displays a list of the functions of that type defined in that database within the Object Explorer as well as in the Summary window.

NOTE

If the function you want to view or edit is not shown in the list, it was probably created after the list of functions in the Object Explorer was populated. You might need to refresh the function list in Object Explorer. To do this, you right-click the `Functions` folder and choose Refresh.

When you right-click a function name in either the Object Explorer or the Summary window, you are presented with a number of options for viewing or modifying the function, as shown in Figure 29.5.

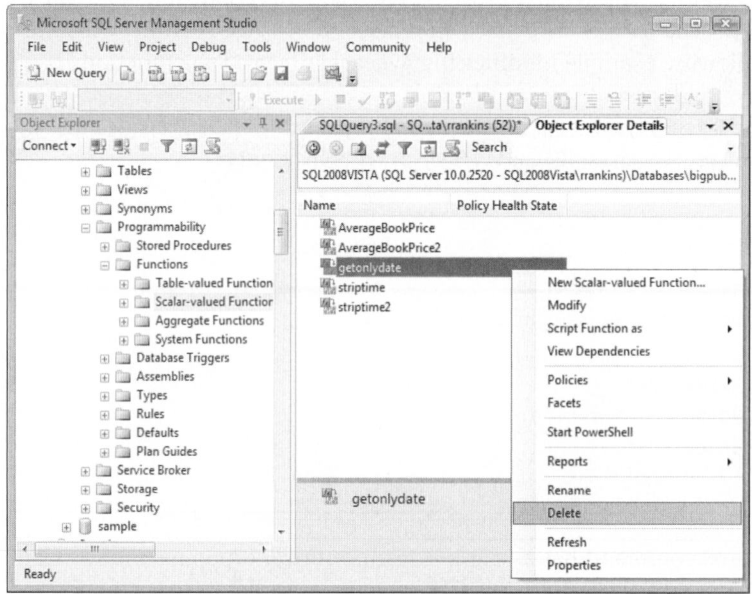

FIGURE 29.5 The Options menu for viewing and editing functions in SSMS.

You can view or edit the function properties, view the function dependencies, delete the function, rename it, modify it, or script the function definition. If you choose to edit the function by clicking Modify, SSMS opens a new query window with the source code of the function extracted from the database as an `ALTER FUNCTION` command. You can edit the function as needed and execute the code in the query window to modify the function.

There are also options for scripting a function as a `CREATE`, `ALTER`, `DROP`, or `SELECT` command to either a new query window, a file, or the Clipboard, as shown in Figure 29.6.

You can also view the function properties by selecting the Properties option from the context menu. The Properties dialog appears, as shown in Figure 29.7. Unfortunately, except for the function permissions and extended properties, the properties shown are read-only.

For more information on the features and options for SSMS and for scripting objects, see Chapter 4, "SQL Server Management Studio."

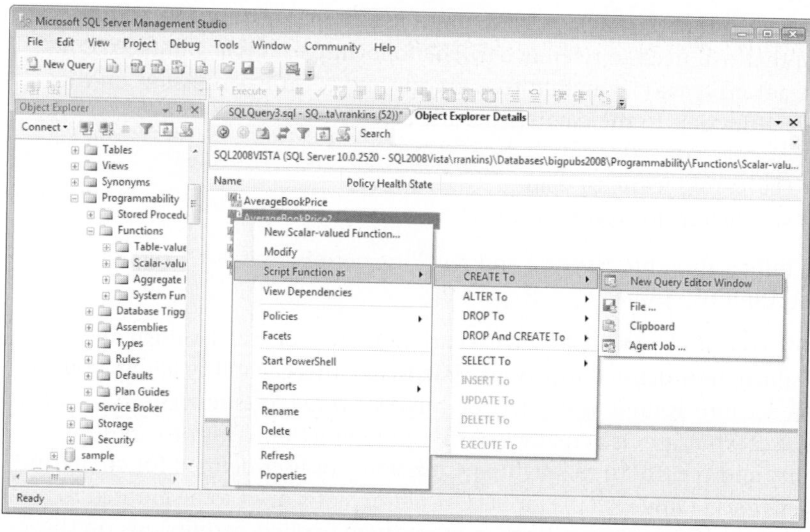

FIGURE 29.6 Options for scripting functions in SSMS.

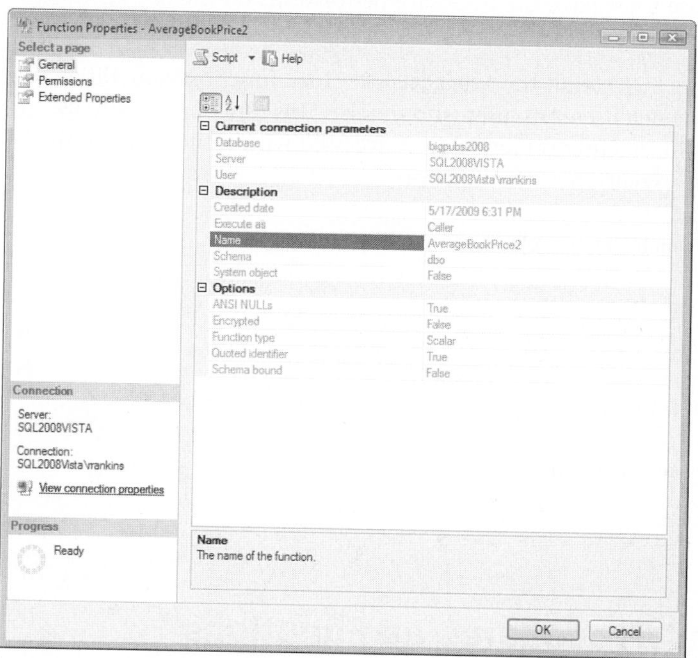

FIGURE 29.7 The Function Properties dialog in SSMS.

Managing User-Defined Function Permissions

When a function is initially created, the only user who has permission to execute the function is the user who created it. To allow other users to execute a scalar function, you need to grant EXECUTE permission on the function to the appropriate user(s), group(s), or role(s). For a table-valued function, you need to grant SELECT permission to the user(s), group(s), or role(s) that will need to reference it. The following example grants EXECUTE permission on the getonlydate() function to everyone and SELECT permission on the AveragePriceByType function to the database user fred:

```
GRANT EXECUTE on dbo.getonlydate to public
GRANT SELECT on AveragePricebyType to fred
```

For more detailed information on granting and revoking permissions, see Chapter 11, "Security and User Administration."

In SQL Server 2008, you can also specify the execution context of scalar-valued and multi-statement, table-valued, user-defined functions. Essentially, this capability allows you to control which user account is used to validate permissions on objects referenced by the function, regardless of what user is actually executing the function. This provides additional flexibility and control in managing permissions for user-defined functions and the objects they reference. Only EXECUTE or SELECT permissions need to be granted to users on the function itself; you do not have to grant them explicit permissions on the referenced objects. Only the user account defined as the execution context for the function by the EXECUTE AS clause must have the necessary permissions on the objects the function accesses.

For example, in the following SQL script, the AverageBookPrice2 function is modified to run within the context of the dbo user. Any user who invokes this function essentially inherits the permissions of the dbo user on any objects accessed within the scope of the function temporarily for the execution of the function:

```
ALTER FUNCTION [dbo].[AverageBookPrice2](@booktype varchar(12) = '%')
RETURNS money
WITH EXECUTE AS 'dbo'
AS
BEGIN
    RETURN ( SELECT avg(price)
             FROM titles
             WHERE type like @booktype)
END
GO
```

Rewriting Stored Procedures as Functions

In releases of SQL Server prior to SQL Server 2000, if you wanted to do custom processing within SQL code, your only real option was to create stored procedures to do things that often would have worked much better as functions. For example, you couldn't use the result set of a stored procedure in a WHERE clause or to return a value as a column in a select list. Using a stored procedure to perform calculations on columns in a result set often required using a cursor to step through each row in a result set and pass the column values fetched, one at a time, to the stored procedure as parameters. This procedure then typically returned the computed value via an output parameter, which had to be mapped to another local variable. Another alternative was to retrieve the initial result set into a temporary table and then perform additional queries or updates against the temporary table to modify the column values, which often required multiple passes. Neither of these methods was an efficient means of processing the data, but prior to SQL Server 2000, few alternatives existed. If you needed to join against the result set of a stored procedure, you had to insert the result set into a temporary table first and then join against the temporary table, as shown in the following code fragment:

```
...
insert #results exec result_proc
select * from other_Table
   join #results on other_table.pkey = #results.keyfield
...
```

Now that SQL Server supports user-defined functions, you might want to consider rewriting some of your old stored procedures as functions to take advantage of the capabilities of functions and improve the efficiency of your SQL code. You mainly want to do this in situations in which you would like to be able to invoke a stored procedure directly from within a query. If the stored procedure returns a result set, it is a candidate for being written as a table-valued function. If it returns a scalar value, usually via an output parameter, it is a candidate for being written as a scalar function. However, the following criteria also are indications that a procedure is a good candidate for being rewritten as a function:

- The procedure logic is expressible in a single `SELECT` statement; however, it is written as a stored procedure, rather than a view, because of the need for it to be parameter driven.
- The stored procedure does not perform update operations on tables, except against table variables.
- There are no dynamic SQL statements executed via the `EXECUTE` statement or `sp_executesql`.
- The stored procedure returns no more than a single result set.
- If the stored procedure returns a result set, its primary purpose is to build an intermediate result that is typically loaded into a temporary table, which is then queried in a `SELECT` statement.

29

The `result_proc` stored procedure, used earlier in this section, could possibly be rewritten as a table-valued function called `fn_result()`. The preceding code fragment could then be rewritten as follows:

```
SELECT *
    FROM fn_results() fn
    join other_table o.pkey = fn.keyfield
```

Creating and Using CLR Functions

Prior to SQL Server 2005, the only way to extend the functionality of SQL Server beyond what was available using the T-SQL language was to create extended stored procedures or Component Object Model (COM) components. The main problem with these types of extensions was that if not written very carefully, they could have an adverse impact on the reliability and security of SQL Server. For example, extended stored procedures are implemented as DLLs that run in the same memory space as SQL Server. An access violation raised in a poorly written extended stored procedure could crash SQL Server itself.

In addition, neither extended stored procedures nor COM components allow you to create custom user-defined functions that can be written in any programming language other than T-SQL, which has a limited command set for operations such as complex string comparison and manipulation and complex numeric computations.

In SQL Server 2008, you can write custom user-defined functions in any Microsoft .NET Framework programming language, such as Microsoft Visual Basic .NET or Microsoft Visual C#. SQL Server supports both scalar and table-valued CLR functions, as well as CLR user-defined aggregate functions. These extensions written in the CLR are much more secure and reliable than extended stored procedures or COM components.

For information on the methods and tools to actually create and compile CLR user-defined functions, see Chapter 46. This chapter focuses only on how to install and use CLR functions in a SQL Server database.

NOTE

The CLR function examples presented in the following sections are provided as illustrations only. The sample code will not execute successfully because the underlying CLR assemblies have not been provided.

Adding CLR Functions to a Database

If you've already created and compiled a CLR function, your next task is to install that CLR function in the database. The first step in this process is to copy the .NET assembly to a location that SQL Server can access, and then you need to load it into SQL Server by creating an assembly. The syntax for the `CREATE ASSEMBLY` command is as follows:

```
CREATE ASSEMBLY AssemblyName [AUTHORIZATION Owner_name]
FROM  { <client_assembly_specifier> | <assembly_bits> [ ,...n ] }
[WITH PERMISSION_SET = (SAFE | EXTERNAL_ACCESS | UNSAFE) ]
```

AssemblyName is the name of the assembly. *client_assembly_specifier* specifies the local path or network location where the assembly being uploaded is located, and also the manifest filename that corresponds to the assembly. It can be expressed as a fixed string or an expression evaluating to a fixed string, with variables. The path can be a local path, but often the path is a network share. *assembly_bits* is the list of binary values that make up the assembly and its dependent assemblies.

The WITH clause is optional, and it defaults to SAFE. Marking an assembly with the SAFE permission set indicates that no external resources (for example, the Registry, Web services, file I/O) are going to be accessed.

The CREATE ASSEMBLY command fails if it is marked as SAFE and assemblies like System.IO are referenced. Also, if anything causes a permission demand for executing similar operations, an exception is thrown at runtime.

Marking an assembly with the EXTERNAL_ACCESS permission set tells SQL Server that it will use resources such as networking, files, and so forth. Assemblies such as System.Web.Services (but not System.Web) can be referenced with this set. To create an EXTERNAL_ACCESS assembly, the creator must have EXTERN ACCESS_permission.

Marking an assembly with the UNSAFE permission set tells SQL Server that not only might external resources be used, but unmanaged code may be invoked from managed code. An UNSAFE assembly can potentially undermine the security of either SQL Server or the CLR. Only members of the sysadmin role can create UNSAFE assemblies.

After the assembly is created, the next step is to associate the method within the assembly with a user-defined function. You do this with the CREATE FUNCTION command, using the following syntax:

```
CREATE FUNCTION [ schema_name. ] function_name
    ( [ { @parameter_name [AS] [ schema_name.]scalar_datatype [ = default ] }
      [ ,...n ] ] )
RETURNS { return_data_type | TABLE ( { column_name data_type } [ ,...n ] ) }
[ WITH { [ , RETURNS NULL ON NULL INPUT | CALLED ON NULL INPUT ]
         [ , EXECUTE_AS_Clause ] } ]
[ AS ] EXTERNAL NAME assembly_name.class_name.method_name
```

After creating the CLR function successfully, you can use it just as you would a T-SQL function. The following example shows how to manually deploy a table-valued CLR function:

```
CREATE ASSEMBLY fn_EventLog
FROM 'F:\assemblies\fn_EventLog\fn_eventlog.dll'
WITH PERMISSION_SET = SAFE
GO
CREATE FUNCTION ShowEventLog(@logname nvarchar(100))
RETURNS TABLE (logTime datetime,
               Message nvarchar(4000),
               Category nvarchar(4000),
               InstanceId bigint)
AS
EXTERNAL NAME fn_EventLog.TabularEventLog.InitMethod
GO
SELECT * FROM dbo.ReadEventLog(N'System') as T
go
```

NOTE

The preceding examples show the steps involved in manually registering an assembly and creating a CLR function. If you use Visual Studio's `Deploy` feature, the `CREATE/ALTER ASSEMBLY` and `CREATE FUNCTION` commands are issued automatically by Visual Studio. For more details on using Visual Studio to create and deploy user-defined CLR functions, see Chapter 46.

Deciding Between Using T-SQL or CLR Functions

One question that often comes up regarding user-defined functions is whether it's better to develop functions in T-SQL or in the CLR. The answer really depends on the situation and what the function will be doing.

The general rule of thumb is that if the function will be performing data access or large set-oriented operations with little or no complex procedural logic, it's better to create that function in T-SQL to get the best performance. The reason is that T-SQL works more closely with the data and doesn't require multiple transitions between the CLR and SQL Server engine.

On the other hand, most benchmarks have shown that the CLR performs better than T-SQL for functions that require a high level of computation or text manipulation. The CLR offers much richer APIs that provide capabilities not available in T-SQL for operations such as text manipulation, cryptography, I/O operations, data formatting, and invoking of web services. For example, T-SQL provides only rudimentary string manipulation capabilities, whereas the .NET Framework supports capabilities such as regular expressions, which are much more powerful for pattern matching and replacement than the T-SQL `replace()` function.

Another good candidate for CLR functions is user-defined aggregate functions. User-defined aggregate functions cannot be defined in T-SQL. To compute an aggregate value over a group in T-SQL, you would have to retrieve the values as a result set and then enumerate over the result set, using a cursor to generate the aggregate. This results in slow and complicated code. With CLR user-defined aggregate functions, you need to implement the code only for the accumulation logic. The query processor manages the iteration, and any user-defined aggregates referenced by the query are automatically accumulated and returned with the query result set. This approach can be orders of magnitude faster than using cursors, and it is comparable to using SQL Server built-in aggregate functions. For example, the following shows how you might use a user-defined aggregate function that aggregates all the authors for a specific `BookId` into a comma-separated list:

```
use bigpubs2008
go
SELECT t.Title_ID, count(*), dbo.CommaList(a.au_lname) as AuthorNames
   FROM Authors a
   JOIN titleauthor ta on a.au_id = ta.au_id
```

```
   JOIN Titles t on ta.title_id = t.title_id
GROUP BY t.title_id
having count(*) > 2
go

Title_ID AuthorNames
-------- ------------------------------------------------------------------
TC7777   O'Leary, Gringlesby, Yokomoto
```

NOTE

The preceding example will not execute successfully because we have not created the `CommaList()` CLR function. It is provided merely as an example showing how such a function could be used if it was created.

In a nutshell, performance tests have generally shown that T-SQL generally performs better for standard CRUD (create, read, update, delete) operations, whereas CLR code performs better for complex math, string manipulation, and other tasks that go beyond data access.

Summary

User-defined functions in SQL Server 2008 allow you to create reusable routines that can help make your SQL code more straightforward and efficient.

In this chapter, you saw how to create and modify scalar functions and inline and multi-statement table-valued functions and how to invoke and use them in queries. Scalar functions can be used to perform more complex operations than those provided by the built-in scalar functions. Table-valued functions provide a way to create what are essentially parameterized views, and you can include them inline in your queries, just as you would in a table or view.

With the introduction of CLR-based functions, SQL Server 2008 greatly increases the power and capabilities of user-defined functions, and CLR functions can also provide performance improvements over T-SQL functions that need to perform complex computations or string manipulations.

In the next chapter, you learn how to create and manage triggers in SQL Server 2008.

CHAPTER 30

Creating and Managing Triggers

IN THIS CHAPTER

- What's New in Creating and Managing Triggers
- Using DML Triggers
- Using DDL Triggers
- Using CLR Triggers
- Using Nested Triggers
- Using Recursive Triggers

A *trigger* is a special type of stored procedure executed automatically based on the occurrence of a database event. Prior to SQL Server 2005, the database events that fired triggers were based only on data manipulations, such as insertions, updates, or deletions. Triggers in SQL Server 2005 and SQL Server 2008 can also fire on events related to the definition of database objects. The two types of triggering events are referred to as Data Manipulation Language (DML) and Data Definition Language (DDL) events.

Most of the benefits derived from triggers are based on their event-driven nature. Once created, triggers automatically fire (without user intervention) based on an event in the database. This differs from other database code, which must be called explicitly in order to execute.

Say, for example, that you would like to keep track of historical changes to the data in several key tables in a database. Whenever a change is made to the data in the tables, you would like to put a copy of the data in a historical table before the change is made. You could accomplish this via the application code that is making the change to the data. The application code could copy the data to the history table before the change occurs and then execute the actual change. You could also manage this in other ways, such as by using stored procedures that are called by the application and subsequently insert records into the history tables.

These solutions work, but a trigger-based solution has some distinct advantages over them. With a trigger-based solution, a trigger can act on any modifications to the key tables. In the case of the history table example, triggers would automatically insert records into the history table whenever a modification was made to the data. This would all happen within the scope of the original transaction and would write history records for any changes made to these tables, including ad hoc changes that may have been made directly to the tables outside the application.

This is just one example of the benefits and uses of triggers. This chapter discusses the different types of triggers and further benefits they can provide.

What's New in Creating and Managing Triggers

The features and methods available for creating and managing triggers are essentially the same in SQL Server 2008 as they were in SQL Server 2005. The upside to this is that you can take the knowledge and skills that you have with SQL Server 2005 and apply them directly to SQL Server 2008.

One area that has had some minor changes in SQL Server 2008 relates to events captured by DDL triggers. In SQL Server 2008 more system stored procedures that perform DDL-like operations fire DDL triggers and event notification. In SQL Server 2005 certain system stored procedures would fire DDL triggers, but there are many more included in SQL Server 2008. For example, the execution of the `sp_rename` stored procedure would not fire a DDL trigger in SQL Server 2005, but it does in SQL Server 2008. Refer to the "Using DDL Triggers" section later in this chapter for a complete list of DDL statements and system stored procedures that DDL triggers respond to.

Using DML Triggers

DML triggers are invoked when a DML event occurs in the database. DML events manipulate or modify the data in a table or view. These events include insertions, updates, and deletions.

DML triggers are powerful objects for maintaining database integrity and consistency. They are able to evaluate data before it has been committed to the database. During this evaluation period, these triggers can perform a myriad of actions, including the following:

- Compare before and after versions of data.
- Roll back invalid modifications.
- Read from other tables, including those in other databases.
- Modify other tables, including those in other databases.
- Execute local and remote stored procedures.

Based on the nature of these actions, triggers were originally used in many cases to enforce referential integrity. Triggers were used when foreign key columns in one table had to be validated against primary keys or unique index values in another table. The triggers could fire when data was modified, and validations could be performed to ensure that referential integrity was maintained.

The advent of declarative referential integrity (DRI) diminished the need for referential integrity triggers. DRI is now generally implemented with database objects such as foreign key constraints that perform the referential integrity validation internally. Because of this, triggers generally handle more complex integrity concepts and enforce restrictions that cannot be handled through data types, constraints, defaults, or rules. Following are some examples of trigger uses:

- **Maintenance of duplicate and derived data**—A denormalized database generally introduces data duplications (that is, redundancy). Instead of exposing this redundancy to end users and programmers, you can keep the data in sync by using triggers. If the derived data is allowed to be out of sync, you might want to consider handling refreshes through batch processing or some other method instead.
- **Complex column constraints**—If a column constraint depends on other rows within the same table or rows in other tables, using a trigger is the best method for that column constraint.
- **Complex defaults**—You can use a trigger to generate default values based on data in other columns, rows, or tables.
- **Inter-database referential integrity**—When related tables are found in two different databases, you can use triggers to ensure referential integrity across the databases.

You can use stored procedures for all these tasks, but the advantage of using triggers is that they fire on all data modifications. Stored procedure code or SQL in application code is executed only when it makes the data modifications. With triggers, all data modifications are subject to the trigger code, except for bulk copy and a few other nonlogged actions. Even if a user utilizes an ad hoc tool, such as SQL Server Management Studio (SSMS) to make changes to the database, the integrity rules cannot be bypassed after the trigger is in place.

NOTE

Triggers and stored procedures are not mutually exclusive. You can have both triggers and stored procedures that perform modifications and validation on that same table. If desired, you can perform some tasks via triggers and other tasks via stored procedures.

Creating DML Triggers

You can create and manage triggers in SQL Server Management Studio or directly via Transact-SQL (T-SQL) statements. The Object Explorer in SSMS provides a simple means of creating triggers that you can use to generate the underlying T-SQL code. You expand the Object Explorer tree to the user table level and then right-click the `Triggers` node. When you select the New Trigger option, as shown in Figure 30.1, the trigger template shown in the right pane of Figure 30.1 appears.

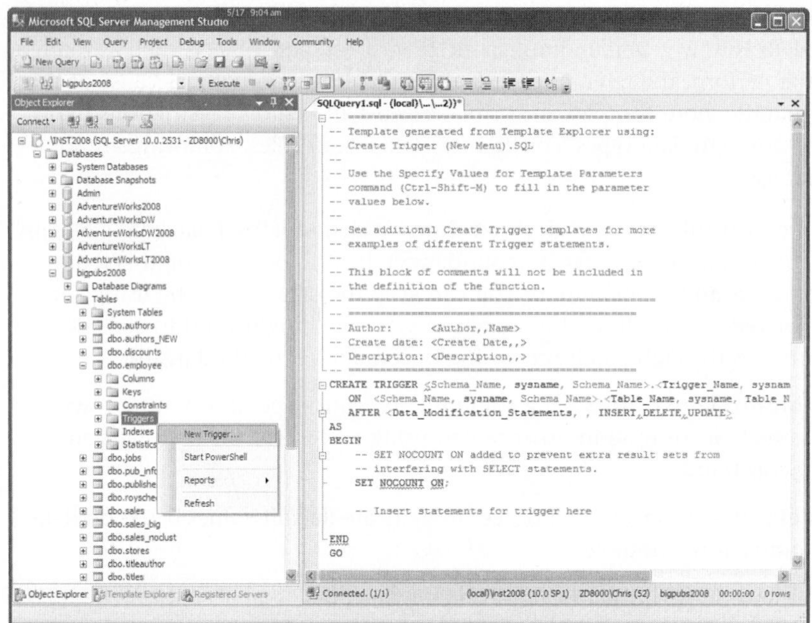

FIGURE 30.1 Using SSMS to create triggers.

You can populate the trigger template by manually editing it, or you can select the Query menu option Specify Values for Template Parameters. When you select Specify Values for Template Parameters, a screen appears, allowing you to fill in the basic values for the trigger, including the table that the trigger will be on and the events to respond to.

You can launch the New Trigger template and other templates related to triggers via the Template Explorer, which you open by selecting View, Template Explorer in SSMS. Figure 30.2 shows a partial list of the available templates, including those related to triggers.

All the trigger templates provide a basic framework for you to create a trigger, but the core logic is up to you. Existing triggers or sample triggers are often good alternatives to the templates because they offer more of the core logic. You can right-click a trigger in the Object Explorer and select the Script Trigger As option. This option contains several different methods to script the trigger. After you script a trigger, you can modify it as necessary to meet your needs.

TIP

Using the `sys.triggers` catalog view is a good way to list all the triggers in a database. To use it, you simply open a new query editor window in SSMS and select all the rows from the view as shown in the following example:

```
SELECT * FROM sys.triggers
```

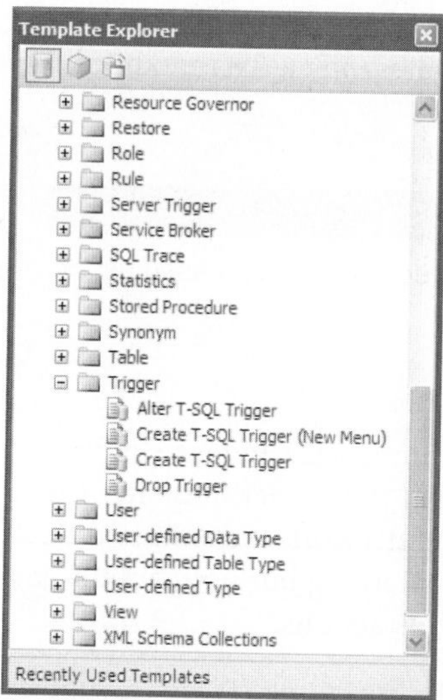

FIGURE 30.2 The Template Explorer.

After you have a basic trigger template, you can code the trigger, with limited restrictions. Almost every T-SQL statement you would use in a SQL batch or stored procedure is also available for use in the trigger code. However, you cannot use the following commands in a DML trigger:

- `ALTER DATABASE`
- `CREATE DATABASE`
- `DISK RESIZE`
- `DROP DATABASE`
- `LOAD DATABASE` and `LOAD LOG`
- `RECONFIGURE`
- `RESTORE DATABASE` and `RESTORE LOG`

The following sections describe the different types of DML triggers that can be coded and some of their common uses.

Using AFTER Triggers

An `AFTER` trigger is the original mechanism that SQL Server created to provide an automated response to data modifications. Prior to the release of SQL Server 2000, the `AFTER` trigger was the only type of trigger, and the word `AFTER` was rarely used in its name. Any trigger written for prior versions of SQL Server or documentation referring to these triggers is for `AFTER` triggers.

30

SQL Server 2000 introduced a new type of trigger called an `INSTEAD OF` trigger. This trigger is discussed later in the section titled "`INSTEAD OF` Triggers." The introduction of that new trigger and inclusion of the word AFTER in the name of the old trigger have helped accentuate the behavior of the AFTER trigger: the AFTER trigger executes *after* a data modification has taken place.

NOTE

Throughout the rest of this chapter, if the trigger type is not specified, you can assume that it is an AFTER trigger.

The fact that an AFTER trigger fires *after* a data modification might seem to be a simple concept, but it is critical to understanding how it works. The AFTER trigger fires after the data modification statement completes but before the statement's work is committed to the databases. The statement's work is captured in the transaction log but not committed to the database until the trigger has executed and performed its actions.

The trigger has the capability to roll back its actions as well as the actions of the modification statement that invoked it. This is possible because an implicit transaction exists that includes both the modification statement and trigger it fires. If the trigger does not issue a rollback, an implicit COMMIT of all the work is issued when the trigger completes.

The basic syntax for creating an AFTER trigger is as follows:

```
CREATE TRIGGER trigger_name
ON table_name
AFTER { INSERT | UPDATE | DELETE }
AS
SQL statements
```

The AFTER trigger is the default type of DML trigger, so the AFTER keyword is optional.

Listing 30.1 shows the code you use to create a trigger in the BigPubs2008 database. (You can find instructions for creating the BigPubs2008 database in the introduction chapter at the beginning of this book.) This new trigger prints a message, stating the number of rows updated by an UPDATE statement. You then execute a couple of UPDATE statements to see whether the trigger works.

LISTING 30.1 An Example of a Simple **AFTER** Trigger

```
CREATE TRIGGER tr_au_upd ON authors
AFTER UPDATE
AS
PRINT 'TRIGGER OUTPUT: ' +CONVERT(VARCHAR(5), @@ROWCOUNT)
+ ' rows were updated.'
GO

UPDATE authors
SET au_fname = au_fname
```

```
WHERE state = 'UT'
GO
--TRIGGER OUTPUT: 1 rows were updated.

UPDATE authors
SET au_fname = au_fname
WHERE state = 'CA'
GO
--TRIGGER OUTPUT: 37 rows were updated.
```

Even though you do not actually change the contents of the `au_fname` column (because you set it to itself), the trigger fires anyway. Listing 30.1 does not show the typical use of a trigger, but it gives you some insight into how and when a trigger fires. The fact that the trigger fires, regardless of what is updated, causes many developers to test the `@@rowcount` value at the beginning of the trigger code. If `@@rowcount` is equal to zero, the trigger can return without executing the remainder of the trigger code. This is a good tactic for optimizing the performance of triggers.

NOTE

Triggers are meant to guarantee the integrity of data. Although you can return result sets and messages in triggers, doing so is not recommended. The programmers who write applications that perform modifications on a table are probably not prepared to get unexpected result sets or messages when they submit data modification statements.

The exception is returning an error with the `RAISERROR` command. If a trigger performs `ROLLBACK TRAN`, it should also execute `RAISERROR` to communicate the failure to the application.

Executing AFTER Triggers

You know that the `AFTER` trigger fires when a data modification (such as an insertion, an update, or a deletion) takes place. What about the trigger's execution in relationship to other events, including the execution of constraints? The following events take place before an `AFTER` trigger executes:

- **Constraint processing**—This includes `CHECK` constraints, `UNIQUE` constraints, and `PRIMARY KEY` constraints.
- **Declarative referential actions**—These actions are defined by `FOREIGN KEY` constraints that ensure the proper relationships between tables. This includes cascading `FOREIGN KEY` constraints.
- **Triggering action**—This data modification caused the trigger to fire. The action occurs before the trigger fires, but the results are not committed to the database until the trigger completes.

You need to consider this execution carefully when you design triggers. For example, if you have a constraint and trigger defined on the same column, any violations to the constraint abort the statement, and the trigger execution does not occur. For example, if you have a foreign key constraint on a table that ensures referencial integrity and a trigger that that does some validation on that same foreign key column then the trigger validation will only execute if the foreign key validation is successful.

Specifying Trigger Firing Order

You can create more than one trigger on a table for each data modification action. In other words, you can have multiple triggers responding to an `INSERT`, an `UPDATE`, or a `DELETE` command. This can be useful in certain situations, but it can generate confusion because you might not know the order in which the triggers fire for the particular action.

Some of the confusion has been alleviated by the fact that SQL Server 2008 allows you to specify the first and last trigger that fire for a particular action. If you have four triggers responding to updates on a given table, you can set the order for two of the triggers (first and last), but the order of the remaining two triggers remains unknown.

The `sp_settriggerorder` procedure is the tool you use to set the trigger order. This procedure takes the trigger name, order value (`FIRST`, `LAST`, or `NONE`), and action (`INSERT`, `UPDATE`, or `DELETE`) as parameters. For example, you could use the following to set the firing order on the trigger used in this chapter's simple example:

```
sp_settriggerorder tr_au_upd, FIRST, 'UPDATE'
```

The execution of this command sets the `tr_au_upd` trigger as the first trigger to fire when an update happens to the table on which this trigger has been placed. If an `ALTER` statement is executed against the trigger after the trigger order has been defined, the firing order is lost. The `sp_settriggerorder` procedure must be run again to reestablish the firing order.

NOTE

It is recommended that you avoid defining multiple triggers for the same event on the same table when possible. Often, it is possible to include all the logic in one trigger defined for an action. This can simplify your database and avoid the uncertainty of the firing order.

Special Considerations with AFTER Triggers

Following are a few other considerations for `AFTER` triggers:

- `AFTER` triggers can be used on tables that also have cascading referential integrity constraints. The cascading feature, which was new to SQL Server 2000, allows you to define cascading actions when a user updates or deletes a primary key to which a foreign key points. This new feature is discussed in more detail in Chapter 24, "Creating and Managing Tables."
- `WRITETEXT` and `TRUNCATE TABLE` do not fire triggers. `BCP`, by default, does not fire triggers either, but the `FIRE_TRIGGERS` bulk copy hint can be specified to cause both `AFTER` and `INSTEAD OF` triggers to execute.

- Triggers are objects, so they must have unique names within the database. If you try to add a trigger with a name that already exists, you get an error message. You can, however, use ALTER on an existing trigger.

The following restrictions apply to AFTER triggers:

- AFTER triggers can be placed only on tables, not on views.
- A single AFTER trigger cannot be placed on more than one table.
- The text, ntext, and image columns cannot be referenced in the AFTER trigger logic.

Using inserted and deleted Tables

In most trigger situations, you need to know what changes were made as part of the data modification. You can find this information in the inserted and deleted tables. For the AFTER trigger, these temporary memory-resident tables contain the rows modified by the statement. With the INSTEAD OF trigger, the inserted and deleted tables are actually temporary tables created on-the-fly.

The inserted and deleted tables have identical column structures and names as the tables that were modified. Consider running the following statement against the BigPubs2008 database:

```
UPDATE titles
 SET price = $15.05
 WHERE type LIKE '%cook%'
```

When this statement is executed, a copy of the rows to be modified is recorded, along with a copy of the rows after the modification. These copies are available to the trigger in the deleted and inserted tables.

If you want to be able to see the contents of the deleted and inserted tables for testing purposes, you can create a copy of the table and then create a trigger on that copy (see Listing 30.2). You can perform data modification statements and view the contents of these tables without the modification actually taking place.

LISTING 30.2 Viewing the Contents of the **inserted** and **deleted** Tables

```
--Create a copy of the titles table in the BigPubs2008 database
SELECT *
 INTO titles_copy
 FROM titles
GO
--add an AFTER trigger to this table for testing purposes
CREATE TRIGGER tc_tr ON titles_copy
 FOR INSERT, UPDATE, DELETE
 AS
 PRINT 'Inserted:'
 SELECT title_id, type, price FROM inserted
```

```
PRINT 'Deleted:'
SELECT title_id, type, price FROM deleted
 ROLLBACK TRANSACTION
```

The inserted and deleted tables are available within the trigger after INSERT, UPDATE, and DELETE. Listing 30.3 shows the contents of inserted and deleted, as reported by the trigger when executing the preceding UPDATE statement.

LISTING 30.3 Viewing the Contents of the **inserted** and **deleted** Tables When Updating the **titles_copy** Table

```
UPDATE titles_copy
 SET price = $15.05
 WHERE type LIKE '%cook%'

Inserted:
title_id type         price
-------- ------------ --------------------
TC7777   trad_cook    15.05
TC4203   trad_cook    15.05
TC3218   trad_cook    15.05
MC3021   mod_cook     15.05
MC2222   mod_cook     15.05

Deleted:
title_id type         price
-------- ------------ --------------------
TC7777   trad_cook    14.3279
TC4203   trad_cook    14.595
TC3218   trad_cook    0.0017
MC3021   mod_cook     15.894
MC2222   mod_cook     14.9532
```

NOTE

In SQL Server 2008, an error message is displayed after a rollback is initiated in a trigger. The error message indicates that the transaction ended in the trigger and that the batch has been aborted. Prior to SQL Server 2005, an error message was not displayed when a rollback was encountered in the trigger.

The nature of the inserted and deleted tables enables you to determine the action that fired the trigger. For example, when an INSERT occurs, the deleted table is empty because there were no previous values prior to the insertion. Table 30.1 shows the DML triggering events and the corresponding contents in the deleted and inserted tables.

TABLE 30.1 Determining the Action That Fired a Trigger

Statement	Contents of `inserted`	Contents of `deleted`
`INSERT`	Rows added	Empty
`UPDATE`	New rows	Old rows
`DELETE`	Empty	Rows deleted

NOTE

Triggers do not fire on a row-by-row basis. One common mistake in coding triggers is to assume that only one row is modified. However, triggers are set-based. If a single statement affects multiple rows in the table, the trigger needs to handle the processing of all the rows that were affected, not just one row at a time.

One common approach to dealing with the multiple rows in a trigger is to place the rows in a cursor and then process each row that was affected, one at a time. This approach works, but it can have an adverse effect on the performance of the trigger. To keep your trigger execution fast, you should try to use rowset-based logic instead of cursors in triggers when possible.

Rowset-based logic will typically join to the inserted or deleted table that are available to a trigger. You can join these tables to other tables that are being manipulated by the trigger. For example, a trigger on a Job table can update a related employee table with rowset-based logic such as :

```
UPDATE employee
   SET employee.job_lvl = i.min_lvl
  FROM inserted i
 WHERE employee.emp_id = i.emp_id
```

This kind of logic will allow the trigger update to work correctly if one job record is changed or many job rows are changed at once. This is much more efficient than loading all of the rows from the inserted table into a cursor which updates the employee records one at a time within the cursor loop.

Checking for Column Updates

The `UPDATE()` function is available inside `INSERT` and `UPDATE` triggers. `UPDATE()` allows a trigger to determine whether a column was affected by the `INSERT` or `UPDATE` statement that fired the trigger. By testing whether a column was actually updated, you can avoid performing unnecessary work.

For example, suppose a rule mandates that you cannot change the city for an author (a silly rule, but it demonstrates a few key concepts). Listing 30.4 creates a trigger for both `INSERT` and `UPDATE` that enforces this rule on the `authors` table in the `BigPubs2008` database.

LISTING 30.4 Using the **UPDATE()** Function in a Trigger

```
CREATE TRIGGER tr_au_ins_upd ON authors
FOR INSERT, UPDATE
AS
IF UPDATE(city)
 BEGIN
 RAISERROR ('You cannot change the city.', 15, 1)
 ROLLBACK TRAN
 END
GO
UPDATE authors
SET city = city
WHERE au_id = '172-32-1176'

Server: Msg 50000, Level 15, State 1, Procedure
 tr_au_ins_upd, Line 5
 You cannot change the city.
```

Listing 30.4 shows how you generally write triggers that verify the integrity of data. If the modification violates an integrity rule, an error message is returned to the client application, and the modification is rolled back.

The `UPDATE()` function evaluates to `TRUE` if you update the column in the `UPDATE` statement. As shown in the preceding example, you do not have to change the value in the column for the `UPDATE()` function to evaluate to `TRUE`, but the column must be referenced in the `UPDATE` statement. For example, with the `author` update, the `city` column was set it to itself (the value does not change), but the `UPDATE()` function still evaluates to `TRUE`.

NOTE

If you created the `tr_au_upd` trigger on the `authors` table as part of the `AFTER` trigger example earlier in this chapter, you might have also seen the `TRIGGER OUTPUT: 1 rows were updated` message. This trigger was set to be the first trigger to fire, and it executes in addition to the new `ins_upd` trigger added in the example from this section.

Now you can add a couple of `INSERT` statements on the `authors` table:

```
INSERT authors (au_id, au_lname, au_fname, city, contract)
VALUES('111-11-1111', 'White', 'Johnson','Menlo Park', 1)

--Results from the previous insert
Server: Msg 50000, Level 15, State 1
You cannot change the city.
```

The UPDATE() function evaluates to TRUE and displays the error message. This outcome is expected because the trigger was created for INSERT as well, and the IF UPDATE condition is evaluated for both insertions and updates.

Now you can see what happens if you change the INSERT statement so that it does not include the city column in the INSERT:

```
INSERT authors (au_id, au_lname, au_fname, contract)
VALUES('111-11-2222', 'White', 'Johnson', 1)

Server: Msg 50000, Level 15, State 1
You cannot change the city.
```

The error message is still displayed, even though the insertion was performed without the city column. This process might seem counterintuitive, but the IF UPDATE condition always returns a TRUE value for INSERT actions. The reason is that the columns have either explicit default values or implicit (NULL) values inserted, even if they are not specified. The IF UPDATE conditions see this as a change and evaluate to TRUE.

If you change the tr_au_ins_upd trigger to be for UPDATE only (not INSERT and UPDATE), the insertions can take place without error.

Enforcing Referential Integrity by Using DML Triggers

Several options, including foreign key constraints and stored procedures, are available to enforce referential integrity, but using a trigger is still a viable alternative. A trigger provides a great deal of flexibility and allows you to customize your referential integrity solution to fit your needs. Some of the other alternatives, such as foreign keys, do not provide the same degree of customization.

TIP

In a database environment in which multiple databases are used with related data, a trigger can be invaluable for enforcing referential integrity. The trigger can span databases, and it can ensure that data rows inserted into a table in one database are valid based on rows in another database.

Listing 30.5 shows how to re-create and populate the customers and orders tables in the sample BigPubs2008 database.

LISTING 30.5 Creating and Populating the **customers** and **orders** Tables

```
if exists (select * from sysobjects
   where id = object_id('orders') and sysstat & 0xf = 3)
       drop table orders
GO
if exists (select * from sysobjects
```

```
  where id = object_id('customers') and sysstat & 0xf = 3)
      drop table customers
GO

CREATE TABLE customers
(customer_id INT PRIMARY KEY NOT NULL,
customer_name NVARCHAR(25) NOT NULL,
customer_comments NVARCHAR(22) NULL)
CREATE TABLE orders
(order_id INT  PRIMARY KEY NOT NULL,
customer_id INT,
order_date DATETIME,
CONSTRAINT FK_orders_customers
       FOREIGN KEY (customer_id) REFERENCES customers (customer_id))

INSERT customers (customer_id, customer_name, customer_comments)
VALUES(1, 'Hardware Suppliers AB','Stephanie is contact.')
INSERT customers (customer_id, customer_name, customer_comments)
VALUES(2, 'Software Suppliers AB','Elisabeth is contact.')
INSERT customers (customer_id, customer_name, customer_comments)
VALUES(3, 'Firmware Suppliers AB','Mike is contact.')

INSERT orders (order_id, customer_id, order_date)
VALUES(100, 1, GETDATE())
INSERT orders (order_id, customer_id, order_date)
VALUES(101, 1, GETDATE())
INSERT orders (order_id, customer_id, order_date)
VALUES(102, 1, GETDATE())
```

```
SELECT * FROM customers
SELECT * FROM orders
customer_id customer_name             customer_comments
----------- ------------------------- ----------------------
1           Hardware Suppliers AB     Stephanie is contact.
2           Software Suppliers AB     Elisabeth is contact.
3           Firmware Suppliers AB     Mike is contact.

order_id    customer_id order_date
----------- ----------- -----------------------
100         1           2009-06-17 05:16:49.233
101         1           2009-06-17 05:16:49.233
102         1           2009-06-17 05:16:49.233
```

When foreign key constraints are used to enforce referencial integrity, they prohibit several different types of changes to the data in the related tables. These restrictions ensure the that the integrity of the relationships is maintained. For example, the FOREIGN KEY constraint FK_orders_customers on the orders table prohibits the following:

- Inserting rows into the orders table for customer numbers that don't exist in the customers table
- Updating the orders table by changing the customer number to values that don't exist in the customers table
- Deleting rows in the customers table for which orders exist
- Updating the customers table by changing the customer number for which orders exist

You might want a cascading action instead of prohibiting the deletion or update of rows on the customers table. This would include automatically cascading the DELETE or UPDATE statement executed on the customers table to the related orders table. You can do this by using triggers.

Cascading Deletes

A cascading delete is relatively simple to create. Listing 30.6 shows a cascading delete trigger for the customers table.

TIP

SQL Server 2000 added a feature that allows you to define cascading actions on a FOREIGN KEY constraint. When defining the constraints on a table, you can use the ON UPDATE CASCADE or ON DELETE CASCADE clause, which causes changes to the primary key of a table to cascade to the related foreign key tables. Refer to Chapter 26, "Implementing Data Integrity," for further information on this option.

LISTING 30.6 A Cascading Delete for the **customers** Table

```
CREATE TRIGGER cust_del_orders ON customers
FOR DELETE
AS
IF @@ROWCOUNT = 0
 RETURN
DELETE orders
 FROM orders o , deleted d
 WHERE o.customer_id = d.customer_id
IF @@ERROR <> 0
 BEGIN
  RAISERROR ('ERROR encountered in cascading trigger.', 16, 1)
```

```
ROLLBACK TRAN
RETURN
END
```

The following DELETE statement deletes the row for Customer 1, so all three rows for that customer in the orders table should be deleted by the trigger:

```
DELETE customers WHERE customer_id = 1


Server: Msg 547, Level 16, State 1
The DELETE statement conflicted with COLUMN REFERENCE
constraint 'FK_orders_customers'.
The conflict occurred in database 'BigPubs2008',
table 'orders', column 'customer_id'.
The statement has been terminated.
```

This result might not be what you expected. The FOREIGN KEY constraint here restricts the DELETE statement, so the trigger never fires. The trigger in this example is an AFTER trigger. Therefore, the trigger does not fire, and the cascading action never takes place. You have several options to get around this situation:

- Remove the FOREIGN KEY constraint from orders to customers.
- Disable the FOREIGN KEY constraint from orders to customers.
- Keep the FOREIGN KEY constraint and perform all cascading actions in stored procedures.
- Keep the FOREIGN KEY constraint and perform all cascading actions in the application.
- Use an INSTEAD OF trigger in place of the AFTER trigger.
- Use the new cascading referential integrity constraints.

Listing 30.7 shows how you can disable the FOREIGN KEY constraint so that a cascading delete can occur.

LISTING 30.7 Disabling the **FOREIGN KEY** Constraint to the **customers** Table So That a Cascading Delete Can Occur

```
ALTER TABLE orders
 NOCHECK CONSTRAINT FK_orders_customers
GO

GO
DELETE customers WHERE customer_id = 1
SELECT * FROM customers
SELECT * FROM orders
customer_id customer_name              customer_comments
```

```
----------- ------------------------- ---------------------
2           Software Suppliers AB     Elisabeth is contact.
3           Firmware Suppliers AB     Mike is contact.

order_id    customer_id order_date
----------- ----------- --------------------------
```

In Listing 30.7, the cascading deletes occur via the trigger because the FOREIGN KEY constraint is disabled. Compared to a trigger for cascading deletes, a trigger for cascading updates is more complex and not as common. This issue is discussed in more detail in the next section.

If you disable the FOREIGN KEY constraint, you have a potential integrity problem. If rows are inserted or updated in the orders table, there are no constraints to ensure that the customer number exists in the customer table. You can take care of this situation by using an INSERT and UPDATE trigger on the orders table (see Listing 30.8). The trigger in Listing 30.8 tests for the existence of a customer before the order is inserted or updated.

LISTING 30.8 Handling a Restriction by Using a Trigger on the **orders** Table

```
if exists (select * from sysobjects where id = object_id('dbo.ord_ins_upd_cust')
        and sysstat & 0xf = 8)
        drop trigger dbo.ord_ins_upd_cust
GO

CREATE TRIGGER ord_ins_upd_cust ON orders
FOR INSERT, UPDATE
AS
IF EXISTS (SELECT * FROM inserted
           WHERE customer_id NOT IN
          (SELECT customer_id FROM customers))
 BEGIN
  RAISERROR('No customer with such customer number', 16, 1)
  ROLLBACK TRAN
  RETURN
  END
```

Cascading Updates

A cascading update with a trigger is a bit tricky to achieve. Modifying a primary key, per definition, really involves deleting a row and inserting a new row. The problem is that you lose the connection between the old row and new row in the customers table. How do you know which changes to cascade to which rows?

This situation is simpler if you can restrict the changes to one row (see Listing 30.9) because you have only one row in the `deleted` and `inserted` tables. You know the customer number before and after the modification.

LISTING 30.9 A Cascading Update in a Trigger

```
if exists (select * from sysobjects where id = object_id('dbo.cust_upd_orders')
        and sysstat & 0xf = 8)
        drop trigger dbo.cust_upd_orders
GO

CREATE TRIGGER cust_upd_orders ON customers
FOR UPDATE
AS
DECLARE @rows_affected int, @c_id_before int, @c_id_after int
SELECT @rows_affected = @@ROWCOUNT
IF @rows_affected = 0
 RETURN -- No rows changed, exit trigger
IF UPDATE(customer_id)
BEGIN
 IF @rows_affected = 1
 BEGIN
   SELECT @c_id_before = customer_id FROM deleted
   SELECT @c_id_after = customer_id FROM inserted
   UPDATE orders
    SET customer_id = @c_id_after
    WHERE customer_id = @c_id_before
 END
ELSE
  BEGIN
     RAISERROR ('Cannot update more than 1 row.', 16, 1)
     ROLLBACK TRAN
     RETURN
 END
END
```

If several rows are updated, it's not easy to know which order belongs to which customer. You can easily modify the trigger shown in Listing 30.9 to handle a situation in which several rows change to the same value; however, this is not allowed because of the primary key on the `customers` table. Instances in which several rows are modified and the primary key value is changed are rare, and you are not likely to encounter such situations.

NOTE

The cascading FOREIGN KEY constraints are an excellent alternative to triggers, and they are efficient. If you choose not to use the cascading feature, you might still want to enjoy the simplicity of constraints. Then you need to handle cascading actions only in stored procedures or in client applications.

Stored procedures are often a good choice because they essentially give application developers a function-based interface for modifications. If the implementation details (for example, the table structure or rules) change, client applications can be isolated from the changes, as long as the interfaces to the stored procedures stay the same. The question of how to handle a cascade is a matter of personal preference, however.

Handling cascading updates in a client application or stored procedure is a chicken-and-egg situation: you cannot change the primary key table first because other tables reference it. You also cannot change the referencing table because no row exists in the primary key table with a corresponding value. The solution is to insert in the referenced table a new row that contains the new primary key value, change the referencing rows, and then delete the old row from the referenced table.

INSTEAD OF Triggers

SQL Server 2000 introduced a type of trigger called an INSTEAD OF trigger. This type of trigger extends SQL Server's trigger capabilities and provides an alternative to the AFTER trigger that was heavily utilized in prior versions of SQL Server.

The name of the trigger gives you some insight into how this trigger operates: this trigger performs its actions *instead of* the action that fired it. This is much different from the AFTER trigger, which performs its actions *after* the statement that caused it to fire has completed. This means you can have an INSTEAD OF update trigger on a table that successfully completes but does not include the actual update to the table.

The basic syntax for creating an INSTEAD OF trigger is as follows:

```
CREATE TRIGGER trigger_name
ON table_name
INSTEAD OF { INSERT | UPDATE | DELETE }
AS
SQL statements
```

Listing 30.10 shows how to create a trigger that prints a message stating the number of rows updated by an UPDATE statement. It then executes an UPDATE against the table that has the trigger on it. Finally, it selects the rows from the table for review.

LISTING 30.10 A Simple **INSTEAD OF** Trigger

```
if exists (select * from sysobjects where id = object_id('dbo.cust_upd_orders')
        and sysstat & 0xf = 8)
        drop trigger dbo.cust_upd_orders
GO
CREATE TRIGGER trI_au_upd ON authors
INSTEAD OF UPDATE
AS
PRINT 'TRIGGER OUTPUT: '
+CONVERT(VARCHAR(5), @@ROWCOUNT) + ' rows were updated.'
GO

UPDATE authors
SET au_fname = 'Rachael'
WHERE state = 'UT'
GO
TRIGGER OUTPUT: 1 rows were updated.

SELECT au_fname, au_lname FROM authors
WHERE state = 'UT'
GO
au_fname             au_lname
-------------------- ----------------------------------------
Johann Wolfgang      von Goethe
```

As you can see from the results of the `SELECT` statement, the first name (`au_fname`) column is not updated to `'Rachael'`. The `UPDATE` statement is correct, but the `INSTEAD OF` trigger logic does not apply the update from the statement as part of its `INSTEAD OF` action. The only action the trigger carries out is to print its message.

The important point to realize is that after you define an `INSTEAD OF` trigger on a table, you need to include all the logic in the trigger to perform the actual modification as well as any other actions that the trigger might need to carry out.

Executing INSTEAD OF Triggers

To gain a complete understanding of the `INSTEAD OF` trigger, you must understand its execution in relationship to the other events that are occurring. The following key events are important when the `INSTEAD OF` trigger fires:

- **Triggering action**—The `INSTEAD OF` trigger fires *instead of* the triggering action. As shown earlier, the actions of the `INSTEAD OF` trigger replace the actions of the original data modification that fired the trigger.

- **Constraint processing**—Constraint processing—including `CHECK` constraints, `UNIQUE` constraints, and `PRIMARY KEY` constraints—happens *after* the `INSTEAD OF` trigger fires.

Listing 30.11 demonstrates the trigger execution order.

LISTING 30.11 **INSTEAD OF** Trigger Execution

```
CREATE TRIGGER employee_insInstead
ON employee
INSTEAD OF insert
AS

DECLARE @job_id smallint

--Insert the jobs record for the employee if it does not already exist
IF NOT EXISTS
(SELECT 1
   FROM jobs j, inserted i
  WHERE i.job_id = j.job_id)
BEGIN
   INSERT jobs
       (job_desc, min_lvl, max_lvl)
      SELECT 'Automatic Job Add', i.job_lvl, i.job_lvl
       FROM inserted i

--Capture the identify value for the job just inserted
--This will be used for the employee insert later
   SELECT @job_id = @@identity

   PRINT 'NEW job_id ADDED FOR NEW EMPLOYEE:' + convert(char(3),@job_id)

END

--Execute the original insert action with the newly added job_id
INSERT employee
       (emp_id, fname, minit, lname, job_id, job_lvl, pub_id, hire_date)
   SELECT emp_id, fname, minit, lname, @job_id, job_lvl, pub_id, hire_date
     FROM Inserted

GO
```


The trigger in Listing 30.11 can be created in `BigPubs2008`. The key feature of this `INSTEAD OF` trigger is that it can satisfy a referential integrity constraint that was not satisfied before the `INSERT` was executed. Note the `FOREIGN KEY` constraint on the `employee` table that references `job_id` on the `jobs` table. The trigger first checks whether the `jobs` record associated with the `job_id` of the employee being inserted exists. If the `jobs` record does not exist for the inserted employee's `job_id`, the trigger inserts a new `jobs` record and uses it for the insertion of the employee record.

If you execute the following `INSERT` statement, which has a `job_id` that does not exist, it succeeds:

```
INSERT EMPLOYEE
       (emp_id, fname, minit, lname, job_id, job_lvl, pub_id, hire_date)
 VALUES ('KNN33333F', 'Kayla', 'N', 'Nicole', 20, 100, 9952, getdate())
Go
```

This statement succeeds because the constraint processing happens after the `INSTEAD OF` trigger completes its actions. Conversely, if you were to create the same trigger as an `AFTER` trigger, the `FOREIGN KEY` constraint would execute before the `AFTER` trigger, and the following error message would be displayed:

```
INSERT statement conflicted with COLUMN FOREIGN KEY constraint
'FK__employee__job_id__1BFD2C07'. The
conflict occurred in database 'BigPubs2008', table 'jobs', column 'job_id'.
-->The statement has been terminated.
```

Notice with the previous `INSTEAD OF` trigger example that the last action the trigger performs is the actual insertion of the employee record. The trigger was created to fire when an employee was inserted, so the trigger must perform the actual insertion. This insertion occurs in addition to any other actions that justify the trigger's creation.

Using AFTER Versus INSTEAD OF Triggers

Now that you have seen some of the key differences between `AFTER` and `INSTEAD OF` triggers, you need to decide which trigger to use. In the previous example (Listing 30.11), the `INSTEAD OF` trigger is the only trigger option for this kind of functionality. However, you can often use either trigger type to attain the same result.

Something you should consider when choosing one of these triggers is the efficiency of the overall modification. For example, if you have a modification that will cause a trigger to fire and often reject the modification, you might want to consider using the `INSTEAD OF` trigger. The rationale is that the `INSTEAD OF` trigger does not perform the actual modification until after the trigger completes, so you do not need to undo the modification. If you were to use an `AFTER` trigger in the same scenario, any modifications that were rejected would need to be rolled back because they have already been written to the transaction log by the time the `AFTER` trigger fires.

Conversely, if you have a situation in which the vast majority of the updates are not rejected, the `AFTER` trigger might be your best choice.

The particular situation dictates the preferred trigger, but you should keep in mind that `INSTEAD OF` triggers tend to be more involved than `AFTER` triggers because an `INSTEAD OF` trigger must perform the actual data modification that fired it.

Using AFTER and INSTEAD OF Triggers Together

An important consideration when coding an INSTEAD OF trigger is that it can exist on the same table as an AFTER trigger. INSTEAD OF triggers can also execute based on the same data modifications as AFTER triggers.

Consider, for example, the INSTEAD OF trigger from Listing 30.11 that you placed on the employee table in the BigPubs2008 database. An AFTER trigger already existed on the employee table. Listing 30.12 shows the code for the existing AFTER trigger on the employee table.

LISTING 30.12 An **AFTER** Trigger Placed on the Same Table as an **INSTEAD OF** Trigger

```
if exists (select * from sysobjects where id = object_id('dbo.employee_insupd')
        and sysstat & 0xf = 8)
        drop trigger dbo.employee_insupd
GO

CREATE TRIGGER employee_insupd
ON employee
FOR INSERT, UPDATE
AS
--Get the range of level for this job type from the jobs table.
declare @min_lvl tinyint,
   @max_lvl tinyint,
   @emp_lvl tinyint,
   @job_id smallint
select @min_lvl = min_lvl,
   @max_lvl = max_lvl,
   @emp_lvl = i.job_lvl,
   @job_id = i.job_id
from employee e, jobs j, inserted i
where e.emp_id = i.emp_id AND i.job_id = j.job_id
IF (@job_id = 1) and (@emp_lvl <> 10)
begin
   raiserror ('Job id 1 expects the default level of 10.',16,1)
   ROLLBACK TRANSACTION
end
ELSE
IF NOT (@emp_lvl BETWEEN @min_lvl AND @max_lvl)
begin
   raiserror ('The level for job_id:%d should be between %d and %d.',
      16, 1, @job_id, @min_lvl, @max_lvl)
   ROLLBACK TRANSACTION
End
go
```

This AFTER trigger checks whether the job level assigned to the employee falls within a valid range for the job_id assigned to the employee. It is fired for both insertions and updates, and it can exist on the same table as the employee_insInstead INSTEAD OF trigger described earlier. The combined effect on an employee insertion with both the triggers on the employee table is to have the following actions happen:

1. The INSERT data modification is executed.
2. The INSTEAD OF trigger fires, completes its validation, and ultimately does the employee insertion that is written to the transaction log.
3. Constraint processing completes.
4. The AFTER trigger fires, performing its actions on the employee record inserted by the INSTEAD OF trigger.
5. The AFTER trigger completes and commits the transaction to the database.

One of the key points in this example is that the AFTER trigger performs its actions on the row inserted by the INSTEAD OF trigger. It does not use the record from the original INSERT that started the trigger execution. Therefore, in this chapter's example, where the INSTEAD OF trigger generates a new job_id, the new job_id value—not the job_id that was originally inserted—is used in the AFTER trigger.

You need to consider rollback and recovery in this scenario as well, but they are beyond the scope of this discussion. This example simply shows that INSTEAD OF and AFTER triggers can be combined and that you need to consider the order of execution when designing a trigger solution.

Using Views with INSTEAD OF Triggers

One of the most powerful applications of an INSTEAD OF trigger is to a view. The INSTEAD OF trigger, unlike the AFTER trigger, can be applied to a view and triggered based on modifications to the view. For more information on views, see Chapter 27, "Creating and Managing Views."

The creation of INSTEAD OF triggers on views is important because data modifications against views have many restrictions. The list is extensive, but following are a few examples:

- You cannot use data modification statements that apply to more than one table in the view in a single statement.
- All columns defined as NOT NULL in the underlying tables that are being inserted must have the column values specified in the INSERT statement.
- If the view was defined with the WITH CHECK OPTION clause, rows cannot be modified in a way that will cause them to disappear from the view.

You can use the INSTEAD OF trigger to overcome some of these restrictions. In particular, the first restriction (related to making a single table modification) can be addressed with the INSTEAD OF trigger. The INSTEAD OF trigger fires before the actual modification takes place, so it can resolve the modifications to the underlying tables associated with the view. It can then execute the modification directly against those base tables. The following example demonstrates this capability:

```
Use BigPubs2008
go
CREATE VIEW employeeJobs
AS
select j.min_lvl, j.max_lvl, j.job_id, j.job_desc, e.job_lvl, e.emp_id
 from employee e, jobs j
where e.job_id = j.job_id
GO
```

This example creates a view in the `BigPubs2008` database that joins data from the `employee` and `jobs` tables. It retrieves the job types and the associated levels, the employees assigned to the job types, and each employee's current job level. Following is a sample set of rows from the view:

```
min_lvl max_lvl job_id job_desc                                    job_lvl emp_id
------- ------- ------ ------------------------------------------- ------- ---------
25      100     14     Designer                                    35      ENL44273F
25      100     14     Designer                                    89      PSA89086M
25      100     14     Designer                                    100     KFJ64308F
25      100     12     Editor                                      32      Y-L77953M
25      100     12     Editor                                      35      H-B39728F
25      100     12     Editor                                      100     HAS54740M
```

Let's say you want to change the minimum job level (`min_lvl`) for the `Designer` job to `40` and at the same time set the job level (`job_lvl`) for any employees who have this job to `40`. If you execute the following update—without an `INSTEAD OF` trigger—against the view, you get the message shown:

```
UPDATE employeeJobs
   SET min_lvl = 40,
       job_lvl = 40
 WHERE job_id = 12
GO
View or function 'employeeJobs' is not updateable
because the modification affects multiple base tables.
```

To get around this problem, you can use an `INSTEAD OF` trigger. The trigger can decipher the update to the view and apply the updates to the base table without causing the error. This functionality is demonstrated in the `INSTEAD OF` trigger shown in Listing 30.13.

30

LISTING 30.13 A Basic View with an **INSTEAD OF** Trigger

```
CREATE TRIGGER employeeJobs_updInstead
ON employeeJobs
INSTEAD OF UPDATE
AS
IF @@ROWCOUNT = 0 RETURN
```

```
--update the data related to the jobs table
UPDATE jobs
   SET jobs.min_lvl = i.min_lvl,
       jobs.max_lvl = i.max_lvl,
       jobs.job_desc = i.job_desc
  FROM inserted i
 WHERE jobs.job_id = i.job_id
   AND (jobs.min_lvl <> i.min_lvl
       OR jobs.max_lvl <> i.max_lvl
       OR jobs.job_desc <> i.job_desc)

--update the data related to the employee table
UPDATE employee
   SET employee.job_lvl = i.min_lvl
  FROM inserted i
 WHERE employee.emp_id = i.emp_id
GO
```

A section in Listing 30.13 checks the fields related to the `jobs` table and updates the base table if any of the values have changed. Another section updates the `employee` table for the employee fields that have been changed in the view.

NOTE

You could enhance the trigger in Listing 30.13 to include logic to check for specific updates or to update only those employees who are assigned to the job and have a job level below the new minimum. These enhancements are not included in the listing to keep the example simple.

If you now execute the same `UPDATE` statement, you don't get an error message:

```
UPDATE employeeJobs
   SET min_lvl = 40,
       job_lvl = 40
 WHERE job_id = 12
GO
```

The following results show values selected from the `employeeJobs` view after the update is executed successfully:

```
min_lvl max_lvl job_id job_desc                                    job_lvl emp_id
------- ------- ------ ------------------------------------------- ------- ---------
25      100     14     Designer                                    35      ENL44273F
25      100     14     Designer                                    89      PSA89086M
```

```
25    100   14   Designer                                   100   KFJ64308F
25    100   13   Sales Representative                       35    PMA42628M
25    100   13   Sales Representative                       64    CGS88322F
25    100   13   Sales Representative                       100   TPO55093M
40    100   12   Editor                                     40    Y-L77953M
40    100   12   Editor                                     40    H-B39728F
40    100   12   Editor                                     40    HAS54740M
```

Notice that the `Editor` job now has a minimum level (`min_lvl`) equal to `40` and that all the employees who have that job level (`job_lvl`) are also set to `40`.

You can see the added flexibility that you get by using the `INSTEAD OF` trigger on a basic view. This flexibility is also applicable to a more sophisticated view called a *distributed partitioned view*. With this type of view, data for the view can be partitioned across different servers. Partitioning this way enables you to scale a database solution and still have a single view of the data that appears as one table.

You can make data modifications via a distributed partitioned view, but some restrictions exist. If you do not meet the requirements for updating the view, you can use the `INSTEAD OF` trigger to bypass these restrictions; this is similar to adding an `INSTEAD OF` trigger on a nonpartitioned view.

INSTEAD OF Trigger Restrictions

`INSTEAD OF` triggers have many capabilities, but they also have limitations. Following are some of them:

- `INSTEAD OF` triggers do not support recursion. This means they cannot call themselves, regardless of the setting of the `Recursive Triggers` database option. For example, if an `INSERT` is executed on a table that has an `INSTEAD OF` trigger, and the `INSTEAD OF` trigger performs an `INSERT` on this same table, the `INSTEAD OF` trigger for this `INSERT` does not fire a second time. Any `AFTER` triggers defined on the same table for `INSERT` fire based on the `INSTEAD OF` trigger `INSERT`.
- You can define only one `INSTEAD OF` trigger for each action on a given table. Therefore, you can have a maximum of three `INSTEAD OF` triggers for each table: one for `INSERT`, one for `UPDATE`, and one for `DELETE`.
- A table cannot have an `INSTEAD OF` trigger and a `FOREIGN KEY` constraint with `CASCADE` defined for the same action. For example, you cannot have an `INSTEAD OF` trigger defined for `DELETE` on a given table as well as a foreign key with a `CASCADE DELETE` definition. You get an error if you attempt to do this. In this situation, you could have `INSTEAD OF` triggers defined on `INSERT` and `UPDATE` without receiving errors.

Using DDL Triggers

DDL triggers were introduced in SQL Server 2005. These triggers focus on changes to the definition of database objects as opposed to changes to the actual data. The definition of database objects is dictated by the DDL events that these triggers respond to.

The DDL events that these triggers fire on can be broken down into two main categories. The first category includes DDL events that are scoped at the database level and affect the definition of objects such as tables, indexes, and users. The second category of DDL triggers is scoped at the server level. These triggers apply to server objects, such as logins.

The number of DDL events at the database level far exceeds the number at the server level. Table 30.2 lists the DDL statements and system stored procedures that DDL triggers can fire on.

TABLE 30.2 DDL Statements and System Stored Procedures*

Create/Grant/Bind/Add	Alter/Update/Deny	Drop/Revoke/Unbind
Statements and System Stored Procedures with Database-Level Scope		
CREATE_APPLICATION_ROLE	ALTER_APPLICATION_ROLE	DROP_APPLICATION_ROLE
(sp_addapprole)	(sp_approlepassword)	(sp_dropapprole)
CREATE_ASSEMBLY	ALTER_ASSEMBLY	DROP_ASSEMBLY
	ALTER_AUTHORIZATION_ DATABASE (sp_changedbowner)	
CREATE_CERTIFICATE	ALTER_CERTIFICATE	DROP_CERTIFICATE
CREATE_CONTRACT		DROP_CONTRACT
CREATE_DATABASE	ALTER_DATABASE	DROP_DATABASE
CREATE_DEFAULT		DROP_DEFAULT
BIND_DEFAULT		UNBIND_DEFAULT
GRANT_DATABASE	DENY_DATABASE	REVOKE_DATABASE
CREATE_EVENT_NOTIFICATION		DROP_EVENT_NOTIFICATION
CREATE_EXTENDED_PROPERTY	ALTER_EXTENDED_PROPERTY	DROP_EXTENDED_PROPERTY
(sp_addextendedproperty)	(sp_updateextendedproperty)	(sp_dropextended property)
CREATE_FULLTEXT_INDEX	ALTER_FULLTEXT_INDEX DROP_FULLTEXT_INDEX	
(sp_fulltexttable)	(sp_fulltextcatalog)	(sp_fulltexttable)

TABLE 30.2 DDL Statements and System Stored Procedures*

Create/Grant/Bind/Add	Alter/Update/Deny	Drop/Revoke/Unbind
	(sp_fulltext_column)	
CREATE_FUNCTION	ALTER_FUNCTION	DROP_FUNCTION
CREATE_INDEX	ALTER_INDEX	DROP_INDEX
	(sp_indexoption)	
CREATE_MASTER_KEY	ALTER_MASTER_KEY	DROP_MASTER_KEY
CREATE_MESSAGE_TYPE	ALTER_MESSAGE_TYPE	DROP_MESSAGE_TYPE
CREATE_PARTITION_FUNCTION	ALTER_PARTITION_FUNCTION	DROP_PARTITION_FUNCTION
CREATE_PARTITION_SCHEME	ALTER_PARTITION_SCHEME	DROP_PARTITION_SCHEME
CREATE_PLAN_GUIDE	ALTER_PLAN_GUIDE	DROP_PLAN_GUIDE
(sp_create_plan_guide)	(sp_control_plan_guide)	(sp_control_plan_guide)
CREATE_PROCEDURE	ALTER_PROCEDURE	DROP_PROCEDURE
CREATE_QUEUE	ALTER_QUEUE	DROP_QUEUE
CREATE_REMOTE_SERVICE_	ALTER_REMOTE_SERVICE_	DROP_REMOTE_SERVICE_
BINDING	BINDING	BINDING
RENAME		
(sp_rename)		
CREATE_ROLE	ALTER_ROLE	DROP_ROLE
(sp_addrole and sp_addgroup)		(sp_droprole and sp_dropgroup)
ADD_ROLE_MEMBER	ALTER_ROUTEDROP_ROLE_MEMBER	
CREATE_ROUTE	ALTER_ROUTE	DROP_ROUTE
CREATE_RULE		DROP_RULE
BIND_RULE		UNBIND_RULE
(sp_bindrule)		(sp_unbindrule)
CREATE_SCHEMA	ALTER_SCHEMA	DROP_SCHEMA
(sp_addrole and sp_adduser)	(sp_changeobjectowner)	
(sp_addgroup and sp_grantdbaccess)		

TABLE 30.2 DDL Statements and System Stored Procedures*

Create/Grant/Bind/Add	Alter/Update/Deny	Drop/Revoke/Unbind
CREATE_SERVICE	ALTER_SERVICE	DROP_SERVICE
ADD_SIGNATURE		DROP_SIGNATURE
CREATE_SPATIAL_INDEX	ALTER_INDEX	DROP_INDEX
CREATE_STATISTICS	UPDATE_STATISTICS	DROP_STATISTICS
CREATE_SYMMETRIC_KEY	ALTER_SYMMETRIC_KEY	DROP_SYMMETRIC_KEY
CREATE_SYNONYM		DROP_SYNONYM
CREATE_TABLE	ALTER_TABLE	DROP_TABLE
	(sp_tableoption)	
CREATE_TRIGGER	ALTER_TRIGGER	DROP_TRIGGER
	(sp_settriggerorder)	
CREATE_TYPE		DROP_TYPE
(sp_addtype)		(sp_droptype)
CREATE_USER	ALTER_USER	DROP_USER
(sp_adduser and sp_grantdbaccess)	(sp_change_users_login)	(sp_dropuser and sp_revokedbaccess)
CREATE_VIEW	ALTER_VIEW	DROP_VIEW
CREATE_XML_INDEX	ALTER_INDEX	DROP_INDEX
CREATE_XML_SCHEMA_	ALTER_XML_SCHEMA_	DROP_XML_SCHEMA_
COLLECTION	COLLECTION	COLLECTION
Statements and System Stored Procedures with Server-Level Scope		
ALTER_AUTHORIZATION_SERVER		
CREATE_DATABASE	ALTER_DATABASE	DROP_DATABASE
	(sp_fulltext_database)	
CREATE_ENDPOINT	ALTER_ENDPOINTDROP_ENDPOINT	
CREATE_EXTENDED_PROCEDURE		DROP_EXTENDED_PROCEDURE
(sp_addextendedproc)		(sp_dropextendedproc)
ALTER_INSTANCE		

TABLE 30.2 DDL Statements and System Stored Procedures*

Create/Grant/Bind/Add	Alter/Update/Deny	Drop/Revoke/Unbind
(sp_configure and sp_addserver)		
CREATE_LINKED_SERVER	ALTER_LINKED_SERVER	DROP_LINKED_SERVER
(sp_addlinkedserver)	(sp_serveroption)	(sp_dropserver)
CREATE_LINKED_SERVER_LOGIN		DROP_LINKED_SERVER_LOGIN
(sp_addlinkedsrvlogin)		(sp_droplinkedsrvlogin)
CREATE_LOGIN	ALTER_LOGIN	DROP_LOGIN
(sp_addlogin and sp_grantlogin)	(sp_defaultdb and sp_defaultlanguage)	(sp_droplogin and sp_revokelogin
(xp_grantlogin and sp_denylogin)	(sp_password, sp_change_users_login)	(xp_revokelogin)
CREATE_MESSAGE	ALTER_MESSAGE	DROP_MESSAGE
(sp_addmessage)	(sp_altermessage)	(sp_dropmessage)
CREATE_REMOTE_SERVER	ALTER_REMOTE_SERVER	DROP_REMOTE_SERVER
(sp_addserver)	(sp_setnetname)	(sp_dropserver)
GRANT_SERVER	DENY_SERVER	REVOKE_SERVER
ADD_SERVER_ROLE_MEMBER		DROP_SERVER_ROLE_MEMBER
Statements and System Stored Procedures with Database-Level Scope		
Create/Grant/Bind/Add	**Alter/Update/Deny**	**Drop/Revoke/Unbind**
CREATE_APPLICATION_ROLE	ALTER_APPLICATION_ROLE	DROP_APPLICATION_ROLE
(sp_addapprole)	(sp_approlepassword)	(sp_dropapprole)
CREATE_ASSEMBLY	ALTER_ASSEMBLY	DROP_ASSEMBLY
	ALTER_AUTHORIZATION_DATABASE(sp_changedbowner)	
CREATE_CERTIFICATE	ALTER_CERTIFICATE	DROP_CERTIFICATE
CREATE_CONTRACT		DROP_CONTRACT
CREATE_DATABASE	ALTER_DATABASE	DROP_DATABASE
CREATE_DEFAULT		DROP_DEFAULT
BIND_DEFAULT		UNBIND_DEFAULT

TABLE 30.2 DDL Statements and System Stored Procedures*

Create/Grant/Bind/Add	Alter/Update/Deny	Drop/Revoke/Unbind
GRANT_DATABASE	DENY_DATABASE	REVOKE_DATABASE
CREATE_EVENT_ NOTIFICATION		DROP_EVENT_ NOTIFICATION
CREATE_EXTENDED_ PROPERTY (sp_addextendedproperty)	ALTER_EXTENDED_PROPERTY (sp_updateextendedproperty)	DROP_EXTENDED_PROPERTY (sp_dropextendedproperty)
CREATE_FULLTEXT_INDEX (sp_fulltexttable)	ALTER_FULLTEXT_INDEX (sp_fulltextcatalog) (sp_fulltext_column)	DROP_FULLTEXT_INDEX (sp_fulltexttable)
CREATE_FUNCTION	ALTER_FUNCTION	DROP_FUNCTION
CREATE_INDEX	ALTER_INDEX (sp_indexoption)	DROP_INDEX
CREATE_MASTER_KEY	ALTER_MASTER_KEY	DROP_MASTER_KEY
CREATE_MESSAGE_TYPE	ALTER_MESSAGE_TYPE	DROP_MESSAGE_TYPE
CREATE_PARTITION_FUNCTION	ALTER_PARTITION_FUNCTION	DROP_PARTITION_ FUNCTION
CREATE_PARTITION_SCHEME	ALTER_PARTITION_SCHEME	DROP_PARTITION_SCHEME
CREATE_PLAN_GUIDE (sp_create_plan_guide)	ALTER_PLAN_GUIDE (sp_control_plan_guide)	DROP_PLAN_GUIDE (sp_control_plan_guide)
CREATE_PROCEDURE	ALTER_PROCEDURE	DROP_PROCEDURE
CREATE_QUEUE	ALTER_QUEUE	DROP_QUEUE
CREATE_REMOTE_SERVICE_BIN DING	ALTER_REMOTE_SERVICE_BINDIN G	DROP_REMOTE_SERVICE_BIN DING
RENAME (sp_rename)		
CREATE_ROLE (sp_addrole and sp_addgroup)	ALTER_ROLE	DROP_ROLE (sp_droprole and sp_dropgroup)
ADD_ROLE_MEMBER	ALTER_ROUTE	DROP_ROLE_MEMBER

TABLE 30.2 DDL Statements and System Stored Procedures*

Create/Grant/Bind/Add	Alter/Update/Deny	Drop/Revoke/Unbind
CREATE_ROUTE	ALTER_ROUTE	DROP_ROUTE
CREATE_RULE		DROP_RULE
BIND_RULE		UNBIND_RULE
(sp_bindrule)		(sp_unbindrule)
CREATE_SCHEMA	ALTER_SCHEMA	DROP_SCHEMA
(sp_addrole and sp_adduser)	(sp_changeobjectowner)	
(sp_addgroup and sp_grantdbaccess)		
CREATE_SERVICE	ALTER_SERVICE	DROP_SERVICE
ADD_SIGNATURE		DROP_SIGNATURE
CREATE_SPATIAL_INDEX	ALTER_INDEX	DROP_INDEX
CREATE_STATISTICS	UPDATE_STATISTICS	DROP_STATISTICS
CREATE_SYMMETRIC_KEY	ALTER_SYMMETRIC_KEY	DROP_SYMMETRIC_KEY
CREATE_SYNONYM		DROP_SYNONYM
CREATE_TABLE	ALTER_TABLE	DROP_TABLE
	(sp_tableoption)	
CREATE_TRIGGER	ALTER_TRIGGER	DROP_TRIGGER
	(sp_settriggerorder)	
CREATE_TYPE		DROP_TYPE
(sp_addtype)		(sp_droptype)
CREATE_USER	ALTER_USER	DROP_USER
(sp_adduser and sp_grantdbaccess)	(sp_change_users_login)	(sp_dropuser and sp_revokedbaccess)
CREATE_VIEW	ALTER_VIEW	DROP_VIEW
CREATE_XML_INDEX	ALTER_INDEX	DROP_INDEX
CREATE_XML_SCHEMA_COLLECTION	ALTER_XML_SCHEMA_COLLECTION	DROP_XML_SCHEMA_COLLECTION
Statements and System Stored Procedures with Server-Level Scope		
ALTER_AUTHORIZATION_SERVER		

TABLE 30.2 DDL Statements and System Stored Procedures*

Create/Grant/Bind/Add	Alter/Update/Deny	Drop/Revoke/Unbind
CREATE_DATABASE	ALTER_DATABASE	DROP_DATABASE
	(sp_fulltext_database)	
CREATE_ENDPOINT	ALTER_ENDPOINT	DROP_ENDPOINT
CREATE_EXTENDED_PROCEDURE		DROP_EXTENDED_PROCEDURE
(sp_addextendedproc)		(sp_dropextendedproc)
ALTER_INSTANCE		
(sp_configure and sp_addserver)		
CREATE_LINKED_SERVER	ALTER_LINKED_SERVER	DROP_LINKED_SERVER
(sp_addlinkedserver)	(sp_serveroption)	(sp_dropserver)
CREATE_LINKED_SERVER_ LOGIN		DROP_LINKED_SERVER_ LOGIN
(sp_addlinkedsrvlogin)		(sp_droplinkedsrvlogin)
CREATE_LOGIN	ALTER_LOGIN	DROP_LOGIN
(sp_addlogin and sp_grantlogin)	(sp_defaultdb and sp_defaultlanguage)	(sp_droplogin and sp_revokelogin
(xp_grantlogin and sp_denylogin)	(sp_password, sp_change_users_login)	(xp_revokelogin)
CREATE_MESSAGE	ALTER_MESSAGE	DROP_MESSAGE
(sp_addmessage)	(sp_altermessage)	(sp_dropmessage)
CREATE_REMOTE_SERVER	ALTER_REMOTE_SERVER	DROP_REMOTE_SERVER
(sp_addserver)	(sp_setnetname)	(sp_dropserver)
GRANT_SERVER	DENY_SERVER	REVOKE_SERVER
ADD_SERVER_ROLE_MEMBER		DROP_SERVER_ROLE_MEMBER

System stored procedures are enclosed in parentheses.

Triggers created on the DDL events are particularly important for auditing purposes. In the past, it was very difficult to isolate changes to the definition of a database or to secure them from change. With DDL triggers, you have the tools necessary to manage these changes.

Creating DDL Triggers

The basic syntax for creating a DDL trigger follows:

```
CREATE TRIGGER trigger_name
ON { ALL SERVER | DATABASE }
[ WITH <ddl_trigger_option> [ ,...n ] ]
{ FOR | AFTER } { event_type | event_group } [ ,...n ]
AS { sql_statement  [ ; ] [ ...n ] | EXTERNAL NAME < method specifier >  [ ; ] }
```

The best way to illustrate the use of the DDL trigger syntax and power of these triggers is to look at a few examples. The example shown in Listing 30.14 illustrates the creation of a DDL trigger that is scoped at the database level and prevents table-level changes.

LISTING 30.14 A Database-Scoped DDL Trigger for Tables

```
CREATE TRIGGER tr_TableAudit
ON DATABASE
FOR CREATE_TABLE, ALTER_TABLE, DROP_TABLE
AS
   PRINT 'You must disable the TableAudit trigger in order
      to change any table in this database'
   ROLLBACK
GO
```

This trigger is fired whenever the `CREATE`, `ALTER`, or `DROP TABLE` statements are executed. Consider, for example, the following statements that can be run against the `BigPubs2008` database:

```
ALTER table titles
 add new_col int null
alter table titles
 drop column new_col

You must disable the TableAudit trigger in order to change any table in this
database
Msg 3609, Level 16, State 2, Line 1
The transaction ended in the trigger. The batch has been aborted.
```

These `ALTER` statements add a column to the `titles` table and then remove the column. With the `tr_TableAudit` trigger in place on the `BigPubs2008` database, the error message is displayed after the first `ALTER` statement is executed.

30

This type of trigger is useful for controlling development and production database environments. It goes beyond the normal security measures and helps manage unwanted change. For development environments, this type of trigger enables the database administrator to lock down an environment and focus all changes through that person.

The previous examples include events scoped at the database level. Let's look at an example that applies to server-level events. The script in Listing 30.15 creates a trigger scoped at the server level. It prevents changes to the server logins. When this trigger is installed, it displays a message and rolls back any login changes that are attempted.

LISTING 30.15 A Server-Scoped DDL Trigger for Logins

```
CREATE TRIGGER tr_LoginAudit
ON ALL SERVER
FOR CREATE_LOGIN, ALTER_LOGIN, DROP_LOGIN
AS
   PRINT 'You must disable the tr_LoginAudit trigger before making login changes'
   ROLLBACK
```

The DDL trigger examples we have looked at thus far have targeted specific events listed in Table 30.2. These individual events can also be referenced via an event group. Event groups are hierarchical in nature and can be referenced in DDL triggers instead of the individual events. For example, the table-level trigger from Listing 30.14 can be changed as shown in Listing 30.16 to accomplish the same result. In Listing 30.16, the `DDL_TABLE_EVENTS` group reference replaces the individual event references to `CREATE_TABLE`, `ALTER_TABLE`, and `DROP_TABLE`.

LISTING 30.16 An Example of a DDL Trigger Referencing an Event Group

```
USE [BigPubs2008]
IF  EXISTS (SELECT * FROM sys.triggers
   WHERE name = N'tr_TableAudit' AND parent_class=0)
DROP TRIGGER [tr_TableAudit] ON DATABASE
go

CREATE TRIGGER tr_TableAudit
ON DATABASE
FOR DDL_TABLE_EVENTS
AS
   PRINT 'You must disable the TableAudit trigger in
      order to change any table in this database'
   ROLLBACK
GO
```

SQL Server Books Online has an excellent diagram listing all the event groups that can be used to fire DDL triggers. Refer to the "DDL Event Groups" topic in Books Online, which shows the event groups and related DDL events they contain. Event groups simplify administration and allow for auditing at a high level.

The DDL trigger examples we have looked at thus far have executed simple print statements. To further extend the functionality of DDL triggers, you can code them to capture event information related to the DDL trigger execution. You do this by using the `EVENTDATA` function. The `EVENTDATA` function returns an XML string that includes the time of the event, server process ID (SPID), and type of event that fired the trigger. For some events, additional information, such as the object name or T-SQL statement, is included in the XML string as well.

The `EVENTDATA` function is essentially the replacement for the `inserted` and `deleted` tables available with DML triggers but not available with DDL triggers. It gives you information you can use to implement an auditing solution that captures changes to a data definition. This function is particularly useful in situations in which you do not want to prevent changes to your definition, but you want a record of the changes that occur.

Listing 30.17 shows an auditing solution with a DDL trigger that utilizes the `EVENTDATA` function to capture any changes to indexes in the `BigPubs2008` database. Several event data elements are selected from the `EVENTDATA` XML string and displayed whenever a change is made to an index.

LISTING 30.17 An Example of a DDL Trigger That References an Event Group

```
CREATE TRIGGER tr_ddl_IndexAudit
ON DATABASE
FOR CREATE_INDEX, ALTER_INDEX, DROP_INDEX
AS
  DECLARE @EventData XML
-- Capture event data from the EVENTDATA function
  SET @EventData = EVENTDATA()
-- Select the auditing info from the XML stream
  SELECT   @EventData.query (''data(/EVENT_INSTANCE/PostTime)'')
              AS [Event Time],
           @EventData.query (''data(/EVENT_INSTANCE/EventType)'')
              AS [Event Type],
           @EventData.query (''data(/EVENT_INSTANCE/ServerName)'')
              AS [Server Name],
           @EventData.query (''data(/EVENT_INSTANCE/TSQLCommand/CommandText)'')
              AS [Command Text]
GO
```

To test the DDL trigger in Listing 30.17, you can run the following statement to create an index on the `titles` table in the `BigPubs2008` database:

```
CREATE NONCLUSTERED INDEX [nc_titles_type] ON [dbo].[titles] ( [type] ASC )
```

The `INDEX CREATE` statement completes successfully, and the event-specific information appears in the Results pane.

You can further extend the auditing capabilities of this type of DDL trigger by writing the results to an audit table. This would give you a quick way of tracking changes to database objects. This type of approach dramatically improves change control and reporting on database changes.

NOTE

DDL triggers can also execute managed code based on the CLR. This topic is discussed in the section "Using CLR Triggers," later in this chapter.

Managing DDL Triggers

The administration of DDL triggers is similar to the administration of DML triggers, but DDL triggers are located in a different part of the Object Explorer tree. The reason is that DDL triggers are scoped at the server or database level, not at the table level. Figure 30.3 shows the Object Explorer tree and the nodes related to DDL triggers at both the server and database levels. The `tr_TableAudit` trigger you created earlier in this chapter is shown under the `Database Triggers` node. Figure 30.3 shows the options available when you right-click a database trigger in the Object Explorer tree.

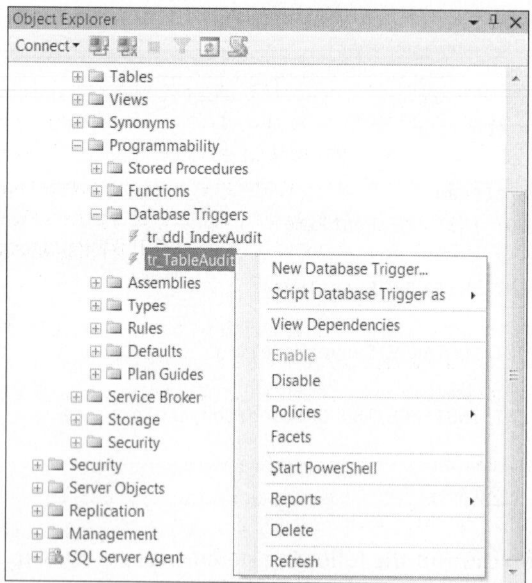

FIGURE 30.3 Using SSMS to manage DDL triggers.

The DDL triggers scoped at the server level are found in the `Triggers` node under the `Server Objects` node of the Object Explorer tree. (The `Server Objects` node is near the bottom of Figure 30.3.)

You can obtain information about DDL triggers by using catalog views. These views provide a convenient and flexible means for querying database objects, including DDL triggers. Table 30.3 lists the catalog views that relate to triggers. The table includes the scope of the trigger that the view reports on and a brief description of what it returns.

TABLE 30.3 Catalog Views for DDL Triggers

Catalog View	Description
Statements with Database-Level Scope	
`sys.triggers`	All triggers, including DDL database-scoped triggers
`sys.trigger_events`	All trigger events, including those that fire DDL database-scoped triggers
`sys.sql_modules`	All SQL-defined modules, including trigger definitions
`sys.assembly_modules`	All CLR-defined modules, including database-scoped triggers
Statements with Server-Level Scope	
`sys.server_triggers`	Server-scoped DDL triggers
`sys.server_trigger_events`	Events that fire server-scoped triggers
`sys.sql_modules`	DDL trigger definitions for server-scoped triggers
`sys.server_assembly_modules`	CLR trigger definitions for server-scoped triggers

Listing 30.18 shows sample `SELECT` statements that utilize the catalog views. These statements use the `sys.triggers` and `sys.server_triggers` views. The `SELECT` against the `sys.triggers` table uses a `WHERE` clause condition that checks the `parent_class` column to retrieve only DDL triggers. The `SELECT` from `sys.server_triggers` does not need a `WHERE` clause because it inherently returns only DDL triggers. The results of each statement are shown below each `SELECT` in the listing.

LISTING 30.18 Viewing DDL Triggers with Catalog Views

```
--DATABASE SCOPED DDL TRIGGERS
select left(name,20) 'Name', create_date, modify_date, is_disabled
 from sys.triggers
 where parent_class = 0
```

```
--Name                 create_date             modify_date             is_disabled
---------------------- ----------------------- ----------------------- -----------
--tr_TableAudit        2009-06-18 12:48:43.140 2009-06-18 12:48:43.140 0
--tr_ddl_IndexAudit    2009-06-22 06:35:10.233 2009-06-22 06:35:10.233 0

--SERVER SCOPED DDL TRIGGERS
select left(name,20) 'Name', create_date, modify_date, is_disabled
 from sys.server_triggers

--Name                 create_date             modify_date             is_disabled
---------------------- ----------------------- ----------------------- -----------
--tr_LoginAudit        2009-06-18 12:13:46.077 2005-06-18 12:13:46.077 0
```

Using CLR Triggers

CLR triggers are triggers based on the CLR. CLR integration, which was added with SQL Server 2008, allows for database objects (such as triggers) to be coded in one of the supported .NET languages, including Visual Basic .NET and C#.

The decision to code triggers and other database objects by using the CLR depends on the type of operations in the trigger. Typically, objects that have heavy computations or require references to objects outside SQL are coded in the CLR. Triggers strictly geared toward database access should continue to be coded in T-SQL.

You can code both DDL and DML triggers by using a supported CLR language. Generally speaking, it is much easier to code a CLR trigger in the Visual Studio .NET Integrated Development Environment (IDE), but you can create them outside the IDE as well. Visual Studio .NET provides a development environment that offers IntelliSense, debugging facilities, and other user-friendly capabilities that come with a robust IDE. The .NET Framework and development environment are discussed in more detail in Chapter 4, "SQL Server and the .NET Framework."

The following basic steps are required to create a CLR trigger:

1. Create the CLR class. You code the CLR class module with references to the namespaces required to compile CLR database objects.
2. Compile the CLR class into an assembly or a DDL file, using the appropriate language compiler.
3. Load the CLR assembly into SQL Server so that it can be referenced.
4. Create the CLR trigger that references the loaded assembly.

The following listings provide examples of each of these steps.

NOTE

The CLR must be enabled on your server before you can add CLR components. The CLR option is disabled by default. To enable the CLR, you use the `sp_configure 'clr enabled', 1` T-SQL command followed by the `RECONFIGURE` command. You can also enable CLR integration by using SQL Server 2008 Surface Area Configuration and then choosing the Surface Area Configuration for Features and selecting the Enable CLR Integration option.

Listing 30.19 contains C# code that can be used for the first step: creating the CLR class. This simple example selects rows from the `inserted` table.

LISTING 30.19 A CLR Trigger Class Created with C#

```
using System;
using System.Data;
using System.Data.Sql;
using Microsoft.SqlServer.Server;
using System.Data.SqlClient;
using System.Data.SqlTypes;
using System.Xml;
using System.Text.RegularExpressions;

public class clrtriggertest
{
    public static void showinserted()
    {
        SqlTriggerContext triggContext = SqlContext.TriggerContext;
        SqlConnection conn = new SqlConnection ("context connection = true");
        conn.Open();
        SqlCommand sqlComm = conn.CreateCommand();
        SqlPipe sqlP = SqlContext.Pipe;
        SqlDataReader dr;
                sqlComm.CommandText = "SELECT pub_id, pub_name from inserted";
                dr = sqlComm.ExecuteReader();
                while (dr.Read())
                        sqlP.Send((string)dr[0] + ", " + (string)dr[1]);

    }
}
```

The CLR class in Listing 30.19 needs to be compiled so that SQL Server can use it. The compiler for C# is located in the .NET Framework path, which is

C:\WINDOWS\Microsoft.NET\Framework*version* by default. The last part of the path, version, is the number of the latest version installed on your machine. For simplicity's sake, you can add the full .NET Framework path to your path variable in the Advanced tab of your System Properties dialog. If you add the .NET Framework path to your path variable, you can run the executable for the compiler without navigating to that location.

You can save the code from Listing 30.19 in a text file named clrtriggertesting.cs. Then you can open a command prompt window and navigate to the folder where you saved the clrtriggertesting.cs file. The command shown in Listing 30.20 compiles the clrtriggertesting.cs file into clrtriggertesting.dll. This command can be run from any directory if you have added the .NET Framework path (for example, C:\WINDOWS\Microsoft.NET\Framework\v3.5) to your path variable. Without the additional path entry, you need to navigate to the .NET Framework path prior to executing the command.

LISTING 30.20 A CLR Trigger Class Compilation

```
csc /target:library clrtriggertesting.cs
```

After compiling clrtriggertesting.dll, you need to load the assembly into SQL Server. Listing 30.21 shows the T-SQL command you can execute to create the assembly for clrtriggertesting.dll.

LISTING 30.21 Using **CREATE ASSEMBLY** in SQL Server

```
CREATE ASSEMBLY triggertesting
 from 'c:\clrtrigger\clrtriggertesting.dll'
 WITH PERMISSION_SET = SAFE
```

The final step is to create the trigger that references the assembly. Listing 30.22 shows the T-SQL commands to add a trigger on the publishers table in the BigPubs2008 database.

LISTING 30.22 Creating a CLR Trigger

```
CREATE TRIGGER tri_publishers_clr
ON publishers
FOR INSERT
AS
 EXTERNAL NAME triggertesting.clrtriggertest.showinserted
```

Listing 30.23 contains an INSERT statement to the publishers table that fires the newly created CLR trigger.

LISTING 30.23 Using an `INSERT` Statement to Fire a CLR Trigger

```
INSERT publishers
 (pub_id, pub_name)
 values ('9922','Sams Publishing')
```

The trigger simply echoes the contents of the `inserted` table. The output from the trigger based on the insertion in Listing 30.23 is as follows:

```
9922, Sams Publishing
```

The `tri_publishers` trigger demonstrates the basic steps for creating a CLR trigger. The true power of CLR triggers lies in performing more complex calculations, string manipulations and things of this nature that the can be done much more efficiently with CLR programming languages than they can in T-SQL.

NOTE

For more detailed information and examples of CLR triggers, see Chapter 45.

Using Nested Triggers

Triggers can be nested up to 32 levels. If a trigger changes a table on which another trigger exists, the second trigger is fired and can then fire a third trigger, and so on. If the nesting level is exceeded, the trigger is canceled, and the transaction is rolled back.

The following error message is returned if the nesting level is exceeded:

```
Server: Msg 217, Level 16, State 1, Procedure ttt2, Line 2
Maximum stored procedure nesting level exceeded (limit 32).
```

You can disable nested triggers by setting the `nested triggers` option of `sp_configure` to `0` (off):

```
EXEC sp_configure 'nested triggers', 0
GO
RECONFIGURE WITH OVERRIDE
GO
```

After the `nested triggers` option is turned off, the only triggers to fire are those that are part of the original data modification: the top-level triggers. If updates to other tables are made via the top-level triggers, those updates are completed, but the triggers on those tables do not fire. For example, say you have an `UPDATE` trigger on the `jobs` table in the `BigPubs2008` database and an `UPDATE` trigger on the `employee` table as well. The trigger on the `jobs` table updates the `employee` table. If an update is made to the `jobs` table, the `jobs` trigger fires and completes the updates on the `employee` table. However, the trigger on the `employee` table does not fire.

The default configuration is to allow nested triggers, but there are reasons for turning off the `nested triggers` option. For example, you might want triggers to fire on direct data modifications but not on modifications that are made by another trigger. Say you have a trigger on every table that updates the audit time. You might want the audit time for a table to be updated by a trigger when that table is being updated directly, but you might not want the audit date updated on any of the other tables that are part of the nested trigger executions. This can be accomplished by turning off the `nested triggers` option.

Using Recursive Triggers

Recursive triggers were introduced in SQL Server 7.0. If a trigger modifies the same table where the trigger was created, the trigger does not fire again unless the `recursive triggers` option is turned on. `recursive triggers` is a database option turned off by default.

The first command in the following example checks the setting of `recursive triggers` for the `BigPubs2008` database, and the second sets `recursive triggers` to `TRUE`:

```
EXEC sp_dboption BigPubs2008, 'recursive triggers'

EXEC sp_dboption BigPubs2008, 'recursive triggers', TRUE
```

If you turn off nested triggers, recursive triggers are automatically disabled, regardless of how the database option is set. The maximum nesting level for recursive triggers is the same as for nested triggers: 32 levels.

You should use recursive triggers with care. It is easy to create an endless loop, as shown in Listing 30.24, which creates a recursive trigger on a new test table in the `BigPubs2008` database.

LISTING 30.24 The Error Message Returned for an Endless Loop with Recursive Triggers

```
--The first statement is used to disable the previously created
--DDL trigger which would prevent any changes.
DISABLE TRIGGER ALL ON DATABASE
EXEC sp_configure 'nested triggers', 1
RECONFIGURE WITH OVERRIDE
EXEC sp_dboption BigPubs2008, 'recursive triggers', TRUE
CREATE TABLE rk_tr_test (id int IDENTITY)
GO
CREATE TRIGGER rk_tr ON rk_tr_test FOR INSERT
AS INSERT rk_tr_test DEFAULT VALUES
GO
INSERT rk_tr_test DEFAULT VALUES

Server: Msg 217, Level 16, State 1, Procedure rk_tr, Line 2
Maximum stored procedure nesting level exceeded (limit 32).
```

The recursion described thus far is known as *direct recursion*. Another type of recursion exists as well: indirect recursion. With *indirect recursion*, a table that has a trigger fires an update to another table, and that table, in turn, causes an update to happen to the original table on which the trigger fired. This action causes the trigger on the original table to fire again.

With indirect recursion, setting the `recursive triggers` database setting to `FALSE` does not prevent the recursion from happening. The only way to prevent this type of recursion is to set the `nested triggers` setting to `FALSE`, which, in turn, prevents all recursion.

Summary

Triggers are among the most powerful tools for ensuring the quality of data in a database. The range of commands that can be executed from within triggers and their capability to automatically fire give them a distinct role in defining sound database solutions.

Chapter 31, "Transaction Management and the Transaction Log," looks at the methods for defining and managing transactions within SQL Server 2008.

CHAPTER 31

Transaction Management and the Transaction Log

IN THIS CHAPTER

- What's New in Transaction Management
- What Is a Transaction?
- How SQL Server Manages Transactions
- Defining Transactions
- Transactions and Batches
- Transactions and Stored Procedures
- Transactions and Triggers
- Transactions and Locking
- Coding Effective Transactions
- Transaction Logging and the Recovery Process
- Long-Running Transactions
- Bound Connections
- Distributed Transactions

Transaction management is an important area in database programming. The transactions you construct and issue can have a huge impact on the performance of SQL Server and the consistency of your databases. This chapter looks at the methods for defining and managing transactions in SQL Server 2008.

What's New in Transaction Management

Not much has really changed in SQL Server 2008 related to transactions, transaction logging, and transaction management. About the only real change is the removal of the `WITH TRUNCATE_ONLY` and `WITH NO_LOG` options from the `BACKUP LOG` command. These options are no longer available in SQL Server 2008 to prune the transaction log. The alternative is to switch the database to simple recovery model.

What Is a Transaction?

A *transaction* is one or more SQL statements that must be completed as a whole or, in other words, as a single logical unit of work. Transactions provide a way of collecting and associating multiple actions into a single all-or-nothing multiple-operation action. All operations within the transaction must be fully completed or not performed at all.

Consider a bank transaction in which you move $1,000 from your checking account to your savings account. This transaction is, in fact, *two* operations: a decrement of your checking account and an increment of your savings account. Consider the impact on your finances if the bank's server went down after it completed the first step and never got to the second! When the two operations are combined, as a transaction, they either both succeed or both fail as a single, complete unit of work.

A transaction is a logical unit of work that has four special characteristics, known as the ACID properties:

- **Atomicity**—Associated modifications are an all-or-nothing proposition; either all are done or none are done.
- **Consistency**—After a transaction finishes, all data is in the state it should be in, all internal structures are correct, and everything accurately reflects the transaction that has occurred.
- **Isolation**—One transaction cannot interfere with the processes of another transaction.
- **Durability**—After the transaction has finished, all changes made are permanent.

The responsibility for enforcing the ACID properties of a transaction is split between T-SQL developers and SQL Server. The developers are responsible for ensuring that the modifications are correctly collected together and that the data is going to be left in a consistent state that corresponds with the actions being taken. SQL Server ensures that the transaction is isolated and durable, undertakes the atomicity requested, and ensures the consistency of the final data structures. The transaction log of each database provides the durability for the transaction. As you see in this chapter, you have some control over how SQL Server handles some of these properties.

How SQL Server Manages Transactions

SQL Server uses the database's transaction log to record the modifications that occur within the database. Each log record is labeled with a unique log sequence number (LSN), and all log entries that are part of the same transaction are linked together so that they can be easily located if the transaction needs to be undone or redone. The primary responsibility of logging is to ensure transaction durability—either ensuring that the completed changes make it to the physical database files or ensuring that any unfinished transactions are rolled back in the event of an error or a server failure.

What is logged? Obviously, the start and end of a transaction are logged, but SQL Server also logs the actual data modification, page allocations and de-allocations, and changes to indexes. SQL Server keeps track of a number of pieces of information, all with the aim of ensuring the ACID properties of the transaction.

After a transaction has been committed, it cannot be rolled back. The only way to undo a committed transaction is to write another transaction to reverse the changes made. A transaction can be rolled back before it is committed, however.

SQL Server provides transaction management for all users, using the following components:

- Transaction-control statements to define the logical units of work
- A write-ahead transaction log
- An automatic recovery process
- Data-locking mechanisms to ensure consistency and transaction isolation

Defining Transactions

You can carry out transaction processing with Microsoft SQL Server in three ways:

- **AutoCommit**—Every T-SQL statement is its own transaction and automatically commits when it finishes. This is the default mode in which SQL Server operates.
- **Explicit**—This approach provides programmatic control of the transaction, using the `BEGIN TRAN` and `COMMIT/ROLLBACK TRAN/WORK` commands.
- **Implicit**—In this mode, when you issue certain SQL commands, SQL Server automatically starts a transaction. You must finish the transaction by explicitly issuing the `COMMIT/ROLLBACK TRAN/WORK` commands.

Each of these methods is discussed in the following sections.

NOTE

The terms for explicit and implicit transactions can be somewhat confusing. The way to keep them straight is to think of how a multistatement transaction is initiated, not how it is completed. AutoCommit transactions are in a separate category because they are both implicitly started and committed.

Implicit and explicit transactions have to be explicitly ended, but explicit transactions must also be explicitly started with the `BEGIN TRAN` statement, whereas no `BEGIN TRAN` is necessary to start a multistatement transaction when in implicit transaction mode.

AutoCommit Transactions

AutoCommit is the default transaction mode for SQL Server. Each individual T-SQL command automatically commits or rolls back its work at the end of its execution. Each SQL statement is considered to be its own transaction, with begin and end control points implied. Following is an example:

```
[implied begin transaction]
UPDATE account
   SET balance = balance + 1000
   WHERE account_no = "123456789"
[implied commit or rollback transaction]
```

If an error is present in the execution of the statement, the action is undone (that is, rolled back); if no errors occur, the action is completed, and the changes are saved.

Now let's consider the banking transaction mentioned at the beginning of this chapter that involved moving money from a savings account to a checking account. Assume that it is written as follows in T-SQL:

```
declare @checking_account char(10),
        @savings_account char(10)
select @checking_account = '0003456321',
       @savings_account = '0003456322'
update account
   set balance = balance - $1000
   where account_number = @checking_account
update savings_account
   set balance = balance + $1000
   where account_number = @savings_account
```

What would happen if an error occurred in updating the savings account? With AutoCommit, each statement is implicitly committed after it completes successfully, so the update for the checking account has already been committed. You would have no way of rolling it back except to write another separate update to add the $1,000 back to the account. If the system crashed during the updates, how would you know which updates, if any, completed, and whether you need to undo any of the changes because the subsequent commands were not executed? You would need some way to group the two commands together as a single logical unit of work so they can complete or fail as a whole. SQL Server provides transaction control statements that allow you to explicitly create multistatement user-defined transactions.

Explicit User-Defined Transactions

To have complete control of a transaction and define logical units of work that consist of multiple data modifications, you need to write explicit user-defined transactions. Any SQL Server user can make use of the transaction control statements; no special privileges are required.

To start a multistatement transaction, use the `BEGIN TRAN` command, which optionally takes a transaction name:

```
BEGIN TRAN[SACTION] [transaction_name [WITH MARK ['description']]]
```

The transaction name is essentially meaningless as far as transaction management is concerned, and if transactions are nested (which is discussed later in this chapter), the name is useful only for the outermost `BEGIN TRAN` statement. Rolling back to any other name, besides a savepoint name (savepoints are covered in the next section), generates an error message similar to the following error message and does not roll back the transaction:

```
Msg 6401, Level 16, State 1, Line 5
Cannot roll back t2. No transaction or savepoint of that name was found.
```

Naming transactions is really useful only when you use the `WITH MARK` option. If the `WITH MARK` option is specified, a transaction name must be specified. `WITH MARK` allows for restoring a transaction log backup to a named mark in the transaction log. (For more information on restoring database and log backups, see Chapter 14, "Database Backup and Restore.") This option allows you to restore a database to a known state or to recover a set of related databases to a consistent state. However, you need to be aware that `BEGIN TRAN` records are written to the log only if an actual data modification occurs within the transaction.

You complete an explicit transaction by issuing either a `COMMIT TRAN` or `COMMIT [WORK]` statement, and you can undo an explicit transaction by using either `ROLLBACK TRAN` or `ROLLBACK [WORK]`. The syntax of these commands is as follows:

```
COMMIT [TRAN[SACTION] [transaction_name]] | [WORK]

ROLLBACK [TRAN[SACTION] [transaction_name | savepointname]] | [WORK]
```

The `COMMIT` statement marks the successful conclusion of a transaction. This statement can be coded as `COMMIT`, `COMMIT WORK`, or `COMMIT TRAN`. The only difference is that the first two versions are SQL-92 ANSI compliant.

The `ROLLBACK` statement unconditionally undoes all work done within the transaction. This statement can also be coded as `ROLLBACK`, `ROLLBACK WORK`, or `ROLLBACK TRAN`. The first two commands are ANSI-92 SQL compliant and do not accept user-defined transaction names. `ROLLBACK TRAN` is required if you want to roll back to a savepoint within a transaction.

The following example shows how you could code the previously mentioned banking example as a single transaction in SQL Server:

```
declare @checking_account char(10),
        @savings_account char(10)
select @checking_account = '0003456321',
       @savings_account = '0003456322'
begin tran
update account
   set balance = balance - $1000
   where account_number = @checking_account
if @@error != 0
begin
    rollback tran
    return
end
update savings_account
   set balance = balance + $1000
   where account_number = @savings_account
if @@error != 0
```

```
begin
    rollback tran
    return
end
commit tran
```

Certain commands cannot be specified within a user-defined transaction, primarily because they cannot be effectively rolled back in the event of a failure. In most cases, because of their long-running nature, you would not want them to be specified within a transaction anyway. Following are the commands you cannot specify in a user-defined transaction:

```
ALTER DATABASE
ALTER FULLTEXT CATALOG
ALTER FULLTEXT INDEX
BACKUP DATABASE
BACKUP LOG
CREATE DATABASE
CREATE FULLTEXT CATALOG
CREATE FULLTEXT INDEX
DROP DATABASE
DROP FULLTEXT CATALOG
DROP FULLTEXT INDEX
RESTORE DATABASE
RECONFIGURE
RESTORE LOG
UPDATE STATISTICS
```

Savepoints

A savepoint allows you to set a marker in a transaction that you can roll back to undo a portion of the transaction but commit the remainder of the transaction. The syntax is as follows:

```
SAVE TRAN[SACTION] savepointname
```

Savepoints are not ANSI-SQL 92 compliant, so you must use the SQL Server–specific transaction management commands that allow you to specify a named point within the transaction and then recover back to it.

The following code illustrates the differences between the two types of syntax when using the `SAVE TRAN` command:

SQL-92 Syntax	SQL Server–Specific Syntax
`BEGIN TRAN mywork`	`BEGIN TRAN mywork`
`UPDATE table1...`	`UPDATE table1...`
`SAVE TRAN savepoint1`	`SAVE TRAN savepoint1`
`INSERT INTO table2...`	`INSERT INTO table2...`
`DELETE table3...`	`DELETE table3...`
`IF @@error = -1`	`IF @@error = -1`
`ROLLBACK WORK`	`ROLLBACK TRAN savepoint1`
`COMMIT WORK`	`COMMIT TRAN`

Note the difference between the SQL-92 syntax on the left and the SQL Server–specific syntax on the right. In the SQL-92 syntax, when you reach the `ROLLBACK WORK` command, the *entire* transaction is undone rather than undoing only to the point marked by the savepoint. You have to use the SQL Server–specific `ROLLBACK TRAN` command and specify the savepoint name to roll back the work to the savepoint and still be able to subsequently roll back or commit the rest of the transaction.

Nested Transactions

As a rule, you can't have more than one active transaction per user session within SQL Server. However, suppose you have a SQL batch that issues a `BEGIN TRAN` statement and then subsequently invokes a stored procedure, which also issues a `BEGIN TRAN` statement. Because you can have only one transaction active, what does the `BEGIN TRAN` inside the stored procedure accomplish? In SQL Server, this leads to an interesting anomaly referred to as *nested transactions*.

To determine whether transactions are open and how deep they are nested within a connection, you can use the global function `@@trancount`. If no transaction is active, the transaction nesting level is `0`. As a transaction is initiated, the transaction nesting level is incremented; as a transaction completes, the transaction nesting is decremented. The overall transaction remains open and can be entirely rolled back until the transaction nesting level returns to `0`.

You can use the `@@trancount` function to monitor the current status of a transaction. For example, what would SQL Server do when encountering the following transaction (which produces an error because of the reference constraint on the `titles` table)?

```
use BIGPUBS2008
go
BEGIN TRAN
   DELETE FROM publishers
   WHERE pub_id = '0736'
go

Msg 547, Level 16, State 0, Line 2
The DELETE statement conflicted with the REFERENCE constraint
 "FK__pub_info__pub_id__2BDE8E15". The conflict occurred in database
 "bigpubs2008", table "dbo.pub_info", column 'pub_id'.
The statement has been terminated.
```

Is the transaction still active? You can find out by using the @@trancount function:

```
select @@trancount
go

------
          1
```

In this case, @@trancount returns a value of 1, which indicates that the transaction is still open and in progress. This means that you can still issue commands within the transaction and commit the changes, or you can roll back the transaction. Also, if you were to log out of the user session from SQL Server before the transaction nesting level reached 0, SQL Server would automatically roll back the transaction.

Although nothing prevents you from coding a BEGIN TRAN within another BEGIN TRAN, doing so has no real benefit, even though such cases might occur. However, if you nest transactions in this manner, you must execute a COMMIT statement for each BEGIN TRAN statement issued. The reason is that SQL Server modifies the @@trancount with each transaction statement and considers the transaction finished only when the transaction nesting level returns to 0. Table 31.1 shows the effects that transaction control statements have on @@trancount.

TABLE 31.1 Transaction Statements' Effects on **@@trancount**

Statement	Effect on @@trancount
BEGIN TRAN	+1
COMMIT	–1
ROLLBACK	Sets to 0
SAVE TRAN *savepoint*	No effect
ROLLBACK TRAN *savepoint*	No effect

Following is a summary of how transactional control relates to the values reported by:

- When you log in to SQL Server, the value of @@trancount for your session is initially 0.
- Each time you execute begin transaction, SQL Server increments @@trancount.
- Each time you execute commit transaction, SQL Server decrements @@trancount.
- Actual work is committed only when @@trancount reaches 0 again.
- When you execute ROLLBACK TRANSACTION, the transaction is canceled and @@trancount returns to 0. Notice that ROLLBACK TRANSACTION cuts straight through

any number of nested transactions, canceling the overall main transaction. This means that you need to be careful how you write code that contains a ROLLBACK statement. You need to be sure to check for the return status up through all levels and exit accordingly so you don't continue executing data modifications that were meant to be part of the larger overall transaction.

- Setting savepoints and rolling back to a savepoint do not affect @@trancount or transaction nesting in any way.
- If a user connection is lost for any reason when @@trancount is greater than 0, any pending work for that connection is automatically rolled back. SQL Server requires that multistatement transactions be explicitly committed.
- Because the BEGIN TRAN statement increments @@trancount, each BEGIN TRAN statement must be paired with a COMMIT for the transaction to complete successfully.

Let's look at some sample code to see the values of @@trancount as the transaction progresses. This first example is a simple explicit transaction with a nested BEGIN TRAN:

SQL Statement	@@trancount Value
SELECT "Starting....."	0
BEGIN TRAN	1
DELETE FROM table1	1
BEGIN TRAN	2
INSERT INTO table2	2
COMMIT	1
UPDATE table3	1
COMMIT	0

Transactions are nested *syntactically only*. The only commit tran statement that has an impact on real data is the last one, the statement that returns @@trancount to 0. That statement fully commits the work done by the initial and nested transactions. Until that final COMMIT TRAN is encountered, all the work can be rolled back with a ROLLBACK statement.

As a general rule of thumb, if a transaction is already active, you shouldn't issue another BEGIN TRAN statement. You should check the value of @@trancount to determine whether a transaction is already active. If you want to be able to roll back the work performed within a nested transaction without rolling back the entire transaction, you can set a savepoint instead of issuing a BEGIN TRAN statement. Later in this chapter, you see an example showing how to check @@trancount within a stored procedure to determine whether the stored procedure is being invoked within a transaction and then issue a BEGIN TRAN or SAVE TRAN, as appropriate.

Implicit Transactions

AutoCommit transactions and explicit user-defined transactions, which are the default transaction mode in SQL Server 2008, are not ANSI-92 SQL compliant. The ANSI-92 SQL standard states that any data retrieval or modification statement issued should implicitly begin a multistatement transaction that remains in effect until an explicit ROLLBACK or COMMIT statement is issued. Microsoft refers to this transation mode as IMPLICIT_TRANSACTIONS.

To enable implicit transactions for a connection in SQL Server 2008, you need to enable the IMPLICIT_TRANSACTIONS session setting using the following command:

```
SET IMPLICIT_TRANSACTIONS ON
```

After this option is turned on, transactions are implicitly started, if they are not already in progress, whenever any of the following commands are executed:

- ALTER TABLE
- CREATE
- DELETE
- DROP
- FETCH
- GRANT
- INSERT
- OPEN
- REVOKE
- SELECT
- TRUNCATE TABLE
- UPDATE

Note that neither the ALTER VIEW nor ALTER PROCEDURE statement starts an implicit transaction.

You must explicitly complete implicit transactions by issuing a COMMIT or ROLLBACK; a new transaction is started again on the execution of any of the preceding commands. If you plan to use implicit transactions, the main issue to be aware of is that locks are held until you explicitly commit the transaction. This can cause problems with concurrency and the system's capability to truncate the transaction log.

Even when using implicit transactions, you can still issue the BEGIN TRAN statement and create transaction nesting. In the following example, IMPLICIT_TRANSACTIONS ON is turned on to see the effect this has on the value of @@trancount.

SQL Statements	@@trancount Value
SET IMPLICIT_TRANSACTIONS ON	0
go	0
INSERT INTO table1	1
UPDATE table2	1
COMMIT	0

```
go
SELECT * FROM table1              1
BEGIN TRAN                        2
DELETE FROM table1                2
COMMIT                            1
go
DROP TABLE table1                 1
COMMIT                            0
```

As you can see in this example, if a `BEGIN TRAN` is issued while a transaction is still active, transaction nesting occurs, and a second `COMMIT` is required to finish the transaction. The main difference between this example and the preceding one is that here, a `BEGIN TRAN` is *not* required to start the transaction. The first `INSERT` statement initiates the transaction. When you are running in implicit transaction mode, you don't need to issue a `BEGIN TRAN` statement; in fact, you should avoid doing so to prevent transaction nesting and the need for multiple commits.

The following example shows the previous banking transaction using implicit transactions:

```
set implicit_transactions on
go

declare @checking_account char(10),
        @savings_account char(10)
select @checking_account = '0003456321',
       @savings_account = '0003456322'
update account
   set balance = balance - $1000
   where account_number = @checking_account
if @@error != 0
begin
    rollback
    return
end
update savings_account
   set balance = balance + $1000
   where account_number = @savings_account
if @@error != 0
begin
    rollback
```

```
    return
end
commit
```

This example is nearly identical to the explicit transaction example except for the lack of a BEGIN TRAN statement. In addition, when in implicit transaction mode, you cannot roll back to a named transaction because no name is assigned when the transaction is invoked implicitly. You can, however, still set savepoints and roll back to savepoints to partially roll back work within an implicit transaction.

TIP

If you need to know within your SQL code whether implicit transactions are enabled so you can avoid issuing explicit BEGIN TRAN statements, you can check the @@options function. @@options returns a bitmap that indicates which session-level options are enabled for the current session. If bit 2 is on, implicit transactions are enabled. The following code snippet can be used in stored procedures or SQL batches to check this value and decide whether to issue a BEGIN TRAN statement:

```
if @@options & 2 != 2 — if bit 2 is not turned on
  BEGIN TRAN —a begin tran can be issued since implicit transactions
are off
...
```

Implicit Transactions Versus Explicit Transactions

When would you want to use implicit transactions versus explicit transactions? If you are porting an application from another database environment, such as DB2 or Oracle, that uses implicit transactions, that application converts over to SQL Server more easily and with fewer code changes if you run in implicit transaction mode. Also, if the application you are developing needs to be ANSI compliant and run across multiple database platforms with minimal code changes, you might want to use implicit transactions.

If you use implicit transactions in your applications, you need to be sure to issue COMMIT statements as frequently as possible to prevent leaving transactions open and holding locks for an extended period of time, which can have an adverse impact on concurrency and overall system performance.

If an application is going to be hosted only on SQL Server, it is recommended that you use AutoCommit and explicit transactions so that changes are committed as quickly as possible and so that only those logical units of work that are explicitly defined contain multiple commands within a transaction.

Transactions and Batches

There is no inherent transactional quality to batches. As you have seen already, unless you provide the syntax to define a single transaction made up of several statements, each individual statement in a batch is its own separate transaction, and each statement is carried to completion or fails individually.

The failure of a transaction within a batch does not cause the batch to stop processing. In other words, transaction flow does not affect process flow. After a `ROLLBACK TRAN` statement, processing continues with the next statement in the batch or stored procedure. For this reason, you should be sure to check for error conditions after each data modification within a transaction and exit the batch or stored procedure, as appropriate.

Consider the banking transaction again, this time removing the `RETURN` statements:

```
declare @checking_account char(10),
        @savings_account char(10)
select @checking_account = '0003456321',
       @savings_account = '0003456322'
begin tran
update account
   set balance = balance - $1000
   where account_number = @checking_account
if @@error != 0
    rollback tran
update savings_account
   set balance = balance + $1000
   where account_number = @savings_account
if @@error != 0
    rollback tran
commit tran
```

Assume that a check constraint on the account prevents the balance from being set to a value less than 0. If the checking account has less than $1,000 in it, the first update fails, and the T-SQL code catches the error condition and rolls back the transaction. At this point, the transaction is no longer active, but the batch still contains additional statements to execute. Without a return after the rollback, SQL Server continues with the next statement in the batch, which in this case is the update to the savings account. However, this now executes as its own separate transaction, and it automatically commits if it completes successfully. This is not the result you want because now that second update is its own separate unit of work, so you have no way to roll it back.

The key concept to keep in mind here is that transaction flow does not affect program flow. In the event of an error within a transaction, you need to make sure you have the proper error checking and a means to exit the transaction in the event of an error. This prevents the batch from continuing with any remaining modifications that were meant to be a part of the original transaction. As a general rule, a RETURN statement should almost always follow a rollback.

In addition to being able to define multiple transactions within a batch, you can also have transactions that span multiple batches. For example, you could write an application that begins a transaction in one batch and then asks for user verification during a second batch. The SQL might look like this:

First batch:

```
use bigpubs2008
go
begin transaction
insert publishers (pub_id, pub_name, city, state)
    values ('1111', 'Joe and Marys Books', 'Northern Plains', 'IA')
if @@error = 0
    print 'publishers insert was successful. Please go on.'
else
    print 'publisher insert failed. Please roll back'
```

Second batch:

```
update titles
    set pub_id = '1111'
    where pub_id = '1234'
delete authors
    where state = 'CA'
commit transaction
```

Writing transactions that span multiple batches is almost always a bad idea. The locking and concurrency problems can become complicated, with awful performance implications. What if the application prompted for user input between batches, and the user went out to lunch? Locks would be held until the user got back and continued the transaction. In general, you want to enclose each transaction in a single batch, using conditional programming constructs to handle situations like the preceding example. Following is a better way to write that code:

```
begin transaction
insert publishers (pub_id, pub_name, city, state)
    values ('1111', 'Joe and Marys Books', 'Northern Plains', 'IA')
if @@error = 0
begin
    print 'publishers insert was successful. Continuing.'
    update titles
        set pub_id = '1111'
        where pub_id = '1234'
    delete authors
```

```
        where state = 'CA'
    commit transaction
end
else
begin
    print 'publisher insert failed. rolling back transaction'
    rollback transaction
end
```

The important point in this example is that the transaction now takes place within a single batch for better performance and consistency. As you see in the next section, it is usually best to encode transactions in stored procedures for even better performance and to avoid the possibility of unfinished transactions.

Transactions and Stored Procedures

Because SQL code in stored procedures runs locally on the server, it is recommended that entire transactions be completely encapsulated within stored procedures to speed transaction processing. This way, the entire transaction executes within a single stored procedure call from the client application, rather than being executed across multiple requests. The less network traffic that occurs between the client application and SQL Server during transactions, the faster they can finish.

Another advantage of using stored procedures for transactions is that doing so helps you avoid the occurrence of partial transactions—that is, transactions that are started but not fully committed. Using stored procedures this way also avoids the possibility of user interaction within a transaction. The stored procedure keeps the transaction processing completely contained because it starts the transaction, carries out the data modifications, completes the transaction, and returns the status or data to the client.

Stored procedures also provide the additional benefit that if you need to fix, fine-tune, or expand the duties of the transaction, you can do all this at one time, in one central location. Your applications can share the same stored procedure, providing consistency for the logical unit of work across your applications.

Although stored procedures provide a useful solution to managing transactions, you need to know how transactions work within stored procedures and code for them appropriately. Consider what happens when one stored procedure calls another, and they both do their own transaction management. Obviously, they now need to work in concert with each other. If the called stored procedure has to roll back its work, how can it do so correctly without causing data integrity problems?

The issues you need to deal with go back to the earlier topics of transaction nesting and transaction flow versus program flow. Unlike a rollback in a trigger (see the next section), a rollback in a stored procedure does not abort the rest of the batch or the calling procedure.

For each BEGIN TRAN encountered in a nested procedure, the transaction nesting level is incremented by 1. For each COMMIT encountered, the transaction nesting level is decremented by 1. However, if a rollback other than to a named savepoint occurs in a nested procedure, it rolls back all statements to the outermost BEGIN TRAN, including any work performed inside the nested stored procedures that has not been fully committed. It then continues processing the remaining commands in the current procedure as well as the calling procedure(s).

To explore the issues involved, you can work with the sample stored procedure shown in Listing 31.1. The procedure takes a single integer argument, which it then attempts to insert into a table (test_table). All data entry attempts—whether successful or not—are logged to a second table (auditlog). Listing 31.1 contains the code for the stored procedure and the tables it uses.

LISTING 31.1 Sample Stored Procedure and Tables for Transaction Testing

```
CREATE TABLE test_table (col1 int)
go
CREATE TABLE auditlog (who varchar(128), valuentered int null)
go
CREATE PROCEDURE trantest @arg INT
AS
BEGIN TRAN
   IF EXISTS( SELECT * FROM test_table WHERE col1 = @arg )
   BEGIN
      RAISERROR ('Value %d already exists!', 16, -1, @arg)
      ROLLBACK TRANSACTION
   END
   ELSE
   BEGIN
      INSERT INTO test_table (col1) VALUES (@arg)
      COMMIT TRAN
   END
INSERT INTO auditlog (who, valuentered) VALUES (USER_NAME(), @arg)
return
```

Now explore what happens if you call this stored procedure in the following way and check the values of the two tables:

```
set nocount on
EXEC trantest 1
EXEC trantest 2
SELECT * FROM test_table
SELECT valuentered FROM auditlog
go
```

The execution of this code gives the following results:

```
col1
-----.
1
2

valuentered
-----.
1
2
```

These would be the results you would expect because no errors would occur, and nothing would be rolled back.

Now, if you were to run the same code a second time, `test_table` would still have only two rows because the procedure would roll back the attempted insert of the duplicate rows. However, because the procedure and batch are not aborted, the code would continue processing, and the rows would still be added to the `auditlog` table. The result would be as follows:

```
set nocount on
EXEC trantest 1
EXEC trantest 2
SELECT * FROM test_table
SELECT valuentered FROM auditlog
go

Msg 50000, Level 16, State 1, Procedure trantest, Line 6
Value 1 already exists!

Msg 50000, Level 16, State 1, Procedure trantest, Line 6
Value 2 already exists!

col1
-----.
1
2


valuentered
-----.
1
2
1
2
```

Now explore what happens when you execute the stored procedure from within a transaction:

```
set nocount on
BEGIN TRAN
EXEC trantest 3
EXEC trantest 1
EXEC trantest 4
COMMIT TRAN
SELECT * FROM test_table
SELECT valuentered FROM auditlog
go
```

The execution of this code gives the following results:

```
Msg 50000, Level 16, State 1, Procedure trantest, Line 6
Value 1 already exists!

Msg 266, Level 16, State 2, Procedure trantest, Line 0
Transaction count after EXECUTE indicates that a COMMIT or ROLLBACK TRANSACTION
 statement is missing. Previous count = 1, current count = 0.

Msg 3902, Level 16, State 1, Line 6
The COMMIT TRANSACTION request has no corresponding BEGIN TRANSACTION.

col1
------
1
2
4

valuentered
------
1
2
1
2
1
4
```

A number of problems are occurring now. For starters, you get a message telling you that the transaction nesting level was messed up. More seriously, the results show that the value 4 made it into the `test_table` table anyway and that the `auditlog` table picked up the inserts of 1 and the 4 but lost the fact that you tried to insert a value of 3. What happened?

Let's examine this example one step at a time. First, you start the transaction and insert the value 3 into trantest. The stored procedure starts its own transaction, adds the value to test_table, commits that, and then adds a row to auditlog. Next, you execute the procedure with the value 1. This value already exists in the table, so the procedure raises an error and rolls back the transaction. Remember that a ROLLBACK undoes work to the outermost BEGIN TRAN—which means the start of this batch. This rolls back everything, including the insert of 3 into trantest and auditlog. The auditlog entry for the value 1 *is* inserted and not rolled back because it occurred after the transaction was rolled back and is a standalone, automatically committed statement now.

You then receive an error regarding the change in the transaction nesting level because a transaction should leave the state of a governing procedure in the same way it was entered; it should make no net change to the transaction nesting level. In other words, the value of @@trancount should be the same when the procedure exits as when it was entered. If it is not, the transaction control statements are not properly balanced.

Also, because the batch is not aborted, the value 4 is inserted into trantest, an operation that completes successfully and is automatically committed. Finally, when you try to commit the transaction, you receive the last error regarding a mismatch between BEGIN TRAN and COMMIT TRAN because no transaction is currently in operation.

The solution to this problem is to write the stored procedures so that transaction nesting doesn't occur and so the stored procedure rolls back only its own work. When a rollback occurs, it should return an error status so that the calling batch or procedure is aware of the error condition and can choose to continue or abort the work at that level. You can manage this by checking the current value of @@trancount and determining what needs to be done. If a transaction is already active, the stored procedure should not issue a BEGIN TRAN and nest the transaction; rather, it should set a savepoint. This allows the procedure to perform a partial rollback of its work. If no transaction is active, the procedure can safely begin a new transaction. The following SQL code fragment is an example of using this approach:

```
DECLARE @trancount INT
/* Capture the value of the transaction nesting level at the start */
SELECT @trancount = @@trancount
IF (@trancount = 0)   — no transaction is currently active, start one
   BEGIN TRAN mytran
ELSE                  — a transaction is active, set a savepoint only
   SAVE TRAN mytran
.
.
/* This is how to trap an error. Roll back either to your
   own BEGIN TRAN or roll back to the savepoint. Return an
   error code to the caller to indicate an internal failure.
   How the caller handles the transaction is up to the caller.*/
```

```
IF (@@error <> 0)
BEGIN
   ROLLBACK TRAN mytran
   RETURN -1969
END
.
.
/* Once you reach the end of the code, you need to pair the BEGIN TRAN,
   if you issued it, with a COMMIT TRAN. If you executed the SAVE TRAN
   instead, you have nothing else to do...end of game! */
IF (@trancount = 0)
  COMMIT TRAN

RETURN 0
```

If you apply these concepts to all stored procedures that need to incorporate transaction processing as well as the code that calls the stored procedures, you should be able to avoid problems with transaction nesting and inconsistency in your transaction processing. You just need to be sure to check the return value of the stored procedure and determine whether the whole batch should be failed or whether that one call is of little importance to the overall outcome and the transaction can continue.

For additional examples of and discussion about coding guidelines for stored procedures in transactions, see Chapter 44, "Advanced Stored Procedure Programming and Optimization."

Transactions and Triggers

SQL Server 2008 provides two types of Data Manipulation Language (DML) triggers: `AFTER` and `INSTEAD OF`. `INSTEAD OF` triggers perform their actions before any modifications are made to the actual table the trigger is defined on.

Whenever a trigger is invoked, it is *always* invoked within another transaction, whether it's a single-statement AutoCommit transaction or a user-defined multistatement transaction. This is true for both `AFTER` triggers and `INSTEAD OF` triggers. Even though an `INSTEAD OF` trigger fires before, or "instead of," the data modification statement itself, if a transaction is not already active, an AutoCommit transaction is still automatically initiated as the data modification statement is invoked and prior to the invocation of the `INSTEAD OF` trigger. (For more information on `AFTER` and `INSTEAD OF` triggers, see Chapter 30, "Creating and Managing Triggers.")

NOTE

Although the information presented in this section applies to both `AFTER` and `INSTEAD OF` triggers, the examples presented pertain primarily to `AFTER` triggers.

Because the trigger is already operating within the context of a transaction, the only transaction control statements you should ever consider using in a trigger are `ROLLBACK` and

SAVE TRAN. You don't need to issue a BEGIN TRAN because a transaction is already active; a BEGIN TRAN would only serve to increase the transaction nesting level, and that would complicate things further.

Triggers and Transaction Nesting

To demonstrate the relationship between a trigger and the transaction nesting level, you can use the following SQL code to create a trigger on the employee table:

```
use bigpubs2008
go
CREATE TRIGGER tD_employee ON employee
FOR DELETE
AS
   DECLARE @msg VARCHAR(255)

   SELECT @msg = 'Trancount in trigger = ' + CONVERT(VARCHAR(2), @@trancount)

   PRINT @msg

   RETURN
go
```

The purpose of this trigger is simply to show the state of the @@trancount within the trigger as the deletion is taking place.

If you now execute code for implied and explicit transactions, you can see the values of @@trancount and behavior of the batch. First, here's the implied transaction:

```
set nocount on
print 'Trancount before delete = ' + CONVERT(VARCHAR(2), @@trancount)
DELETE FROM employee WHERE emp_id = 'PMA42628M'
print 'Trancount after delete = ' + CONVERT( VARCHAR(2), @@trancount)
go
```

The results of this are as follows:

```
Trancount before delete = 0
Trancount in trigger = 1
Trancount after delete = 0
```

Because no transaction starts until the DELETE statement executes, the first value of @@trancount indicates this with a value of 0. Within the trigger, the transaction count has a value of 1; you are now inside the implied transaction caused by the DELETE. After the trigger returns, the DELETE is automatically committed, the transaction is finished, and @@trancount returns to 0 to indicate that no transaction is currently active.

Now explore what happens within an explicit transaction:

```
begin tran
print 'Trancount before delete = ' + CONVERT(VARCHAR(2), @@trancount)
DELETE FROM employee WHERE emp_id = 'PMA42628M'
print 'Trancount after delete = ' + CONVERT( VARCHAR(2), @@trancount)
commit tran
print 'Trancount after commit = ' + CONVERT( VARCHAR(2), @@trancount)
go
```

This code gives the following results:

```
Trancount before delete = 1
Trancount in trigger = 1
Trancount after delete = 1
Trancount after commit = 0
```

In this example, a transaction is already active when the `DELETE` is executed. The `BEGIN TRAN` statement initiates the transaction, and `@@trancount` is 1 before the `DELETE` is executed. The trigger becomes a part of that transaction, which is not committed until the `COMMIT TRAN` statement is executed.

What would happen, however, if the trigger performed a rollback? You can find out by modifying the trigger to perform a rollback as follows:

```
ALTER TRIGGER tD_employee ON employee
FOR DELETE
AS
print 'Trancount in trigger = ' + CONVERT(VARCHAR(2), @@trancount)

ROLLBACK TRAN

return
```

Now rerun the previous batch. The outcome this time is as follows:

```
Trancount before delete = 1
Trancount in trigger = 1
Msg 3609, Level 16, State 1, Line 3
The transaction ended in the trigger. The batch has been aborted.
```

Notice in this example that the batch did not complete, as evidenced by the missing output from the last two `print` statements. When a rollback occurs within a trigger, SQL Server aborts the current transaction, continues processing the commands in the trigger, and after the trigger returns, aborts the rest of the batch and returns error message 3609 to indicate that the batch has been aborted because the transaction ended within the trigger. A `ROLLBACK TRAN` statement in a trigger rolls back all work to the first `BEGIN TRAN` statement. It is not possible to roll back to a specific named transaction, although you can roll back to a named savepoint, as discussed later in this section.

Again, the batch and transaction are aborted when the trigger rolls back; any subsequent statements in the batch are not executed. The key concept to remember is that the trigger becomes an integral part of the statement that fired it and of the transaction in which that statement occurs.

It is important to note, however, that although the batch is aborted immediately after the trigger that performed a rollback returns, any statements within the trigger that follow the ROLLBACK TRAN statement but before it returns are executed. For example, you can modify the previous trigger further to include a print statement after the ROLLBACK TRAN statement:

```
ALTER TRIGGER tD_employee ON employee
FOR DELETE
AS
print 'Trancount in trigger = ' + CONVERT(VARCHAR(2), @@trancount)

ROLLBACK TRAN

print 'Trancount in trigger after rollback = ' + CONVERT(VARCHAR(2), @@trancount)

return
```

Now, if you rerun the previous batch, you can see the print statement after the ROLLBACK TRAN but before the RETURN statement is executed:

```
Trancount before delete = 1
Trancount in trigger = 1
Trancount in trigger after rollback = 0
Msg 3609, Level 16, State 1, Line 3
The transaction ended in the trigger. The batch has been aborted.
```

Notice that the Trancount after the ROLLBACK TRAN in the trigger is now 0. If the trigger subsequently performed any data modifications following the ROLLBACK TRAN, they would now be running as AutoCommit transactions. For this reason, you must be sure to issue a RETURN statement to exit the trigger after a ROLLBACK TRAN is issued to avoid the trigger performing any operations that would then be automatically committing, leaving no opportunity to roll them back.

Triggers and Multistatement Transactions

Now let's look at another example. First, you need to create a trigger to enforce referential integrity between the titles table and publishers table:

```
--The first statement is used to disable any previously created
--DDL triggers in the database which would prevent creating a new trigger.
```

```
DISABLE TRIGGER ALL ON titles
go
create trigger tr_titles_i on titles for insert as
declare @rows int  — create variable to hold @@rowcount
select @rows = @@rowcount
if @rows = 0 return
if update(pub_id) and (select count(*)
        from inserted i, publishers p
        where p.pub_id = i.pub_id ) != @rows
  begin
        rollback transaction
        raiserror ('Invalid pub_id inserted', 16, 1)
  end
return
go
```

Next, for the trigger to take care of the referential integrity, you might first need to disable the foreign key constraint on the titles table with a command similar to the following:

```
alter table titles nocheck constraint FK__titles__pub_id__0F424F67
```

NOTE

The system-generated name for the foreign key constraint may possibly be different on your database. You can use sp_helpconstraint titles to verify the name of the foreign key constraint on the pub_id column of the titles table and use it in place of the constraint name specified in this example.

Now, run a multistatement transaction with an invalid pub_id in the second insert statement:

```
/* transaction inserts rows into a table */
begin tran add_titles
insert titles (title_id, pub_id, title)
       values ('XX1234', '0736', 'Tuning SQL Server')
insert titles (title_id, pub_id, title)
       values ('XX1235', 'abcd', 'Tuning SQL Server')
insert titles (title_id, pub_id, title)
       values ('XX1236', '0877', 'Tuning SQL Server')
commit tran
go

Msg 50000, Level 16, State 1, Procedure tr_titles_i, Line 10
Invalid pub_id inserted
Msg 3609, Level 16, State 1, Line 4
The transaction ended in the trigger. The batch has been aborted.
```

How many rows are inserted if 'abcd' is an invalid pub_id? In this example, no rows are inserted because the ROLLBACK TRAN in the trigger rolls back all modifications made by the trigger, including the insert with the bad pub_id and all statements preceding it within the transaction. After the RETURN statement is encountered in the trigger, the rest of the batch is aborted.

CAUTION

You should never issue a BEGIN TRAN statement in a trigger because a transaction is already active at the time the trigger is executed. Rolling back to a named transaction in a trigger is illegal and generates a runtime error, rolling back the transaction and immediately terminating processing of the trigger and batch. The only transaction control statements you should ever consider including in a trigger are ROLLBACK TRAN and SAVE TRAN.

Using Savepoints in Triggers

Although BEGIN TRAN statements are not recommended within a trigger, you can set a savepoint in a trigger and roll back to the savepoint. This technique rolls back only the operations within the trigger subsequent to the savepoint. The trigger and transaction it is a part of are still active until the transaction is subsequently committed or rolled back. The batch continues processing.

Savepoints can be used to avoid a trigger's arbitrarily rolling back an entire transaction. You can roll back to the named savepoint in the trigger and then issue a raiserror and return immediately to pass the error code back to the calling process. The calling process can then check the error status of the data modification statement and take appropriate action, either rolling back the transaction, rolling back to a savepoint in the transaction, or ignoring the error and committing the data modification.

The following example shows a trigger that uses a savepoint:

```
alter trigger tr_titles_i on titles for insert as
declare @rows int  — create variable to hold @@rowcount
select @rows = @@rowcount
if @rows = 0 return
save tran titlestrig
if update(pub_id) and (select count(*)
        from inserted i, publishers p
        where p.pub_id = i.pub_id ) != @rows
  begin
       rollback transaction titlestrig
       raiserror ('Invalid pub_id inserted', 16, 1)
  end
return
```

This trigger rolls back all work since the savepoint and returns an error number of 50000. In the transaction, you can check for the error number and make the decision about whether to continue the transaction, roll back the transaction, or, if savepoints were set in the transaction, roll back to a savepoint and let the transaction continue. The following example rolls back the entire transaction if either of the first two inserts fail, but it rolls back to the named savepoint only if the third insert fails, allowing the first two to be committed:

```
begin tran add_titles
insert titles (title_id, pub_id, title)
       values ('XX1234', '0736', 'Tuning SQL Server')
if @@error = 50000 — roll back entire transaction and abort batch
   begin
   rollback tran add_titles
   return
   end
insert titles (title_id, pub_id, title)
       values ('XX1236', '0877', 'Tuning SQL Server')
 if @@error = 50000 — roll back entire transaction and abort batch
   begin
   rollback tran add_titles
   return
   end
save tran keep_first_two  — set savepoint for partial rollback
insert titles (title_id, pub_id, title)
       values ('XX1235', 'abcd', 'Tuning SQL Server')
 if @@error = 50000  — roll back to save point, continue batch
   begin
   rollback tran keep_first_two
   end
commit tran
```

TIP

When you use a savepoint inside a trigger, the trigger does not roll back the transaction. Therefore, the batch is not automatically aborted. You must explicitly return from the batch after rolling back the transaction to prevent subsequent statements from executing.

NOTE

Don't forget to reenable the constraint on the titles table when you are finished testing:

```
alter table titles check constraint FK__titles__pub_id__0F424F67
```

Transactions and Locking

SQL Server issues and holds on to locks for the duration of a transaction to ensure the isolation and consistency of the modifications. Data modifications that occur within a transaction acquire exclusive locks, which are then held until the completion of the transaction. Shared locks, or read locks, are held for only as long as the statement needs them; usually, a shared lock is released as soon as data has been read from the resource (for example, row, page, table). You can modify the length of time a shared lock is held by using keywords such as `HOLDLOCK` in a query or setting the `REPEATABLE_READ` or `SERIALIZABLE` lock isolation levels. If one of these options is specified, shared locks are held until the completion of the transaction.

What this means for you as a database application developer is that you should try to hold on to as few locks or as small a lock as possible for as short a time as possible to avoid locking contention between applications and to improve concurrency and application performance. The simple rule when working with transactions is to keep them short and keep them simple. In other words, you should do what you need to do in the most concise manner, in the shortest possible time. You should keep any extraneous commands that do not need to be part of the logical unit of work—such as `SELECT` statements, commands for dropping temporary tables, commands for setting up local variables, and so on—outside the transaction.

To modify the manner in which a transaction and its locks can be handled by a `SELECT` statement, you can issue the `SET TRANSACTION ISOLATION LEVEL` statement. This statement allows the query to choose how much it is protected against other transactions modifying the data being used. The `SET TRANSACTION ISOLATION LEVEL` statement has the following mutually exclusive options:

- **`READ COMMITTED`**—This setting is the default for SQL Server. Modifications made within a transaction are locked exclusively, and the changes cannot be viewed by other user processes until the transaction completes. Commands that read data only hold shared locks on the data for as long as they are reading it. Because other transactions are not blocked from modifying the data after you have read it within your transaction, subsequent reads of the data within the transaction might encounter *nonrepeatable reads* or *phantom data*.
- **`READ UNCOMMITTED`**—With this level of isolation, one transaction can read the modifications made by other transactions prior to being committed. This is, therefore, the least restrictive isolation level, but it is one that allows the reading of dirty and uncommitted data. This option has the same effect as issuing `NOLOCK` within `SELECT` statements, but it has to be set only once for your connection. This option should never be used in an application in which accuracy of the query results is required.
- **`REPEATABLE READ`**—When this option is set, as data is read, locks are placed and held on the data for the duration of the transaction. These locks prevent other transactions from modifying the data you have read so that you can carry out multiple passes across the same information and get the same results each time. This isolation

level is obviously more restrictive than READ COMMITTED and READ UNCOMMITTED, and it can block other transactions. However, although it prevents nonrepeatable reads, it does not prevent the addition of new rows or *phantom rows* because only *existing* data is locked.

- **SERIALIZABLE**—This option is the most restrictive isolation level because it places a range lock on the data. This prevents any modifications to the data being read from until the end of the transaction. It also avoids phantom reads by preventing rows from being added or removed from the data range set.
- **SNAPSHOT**—Snapshot isolation specifies that data read by any statement will see only data modifications that were committed before the start of the transaction. The effect is as if the statements in a transaction see a snapshot of the committed data as it existed at the start of the transaction. The ALLOW_SNAPSHOT_ISOLATION database option must be set to ON for a transaction to specify the SNAPSHOT isolation level.

READ_COMMITTED_SNAPSHOT Isolation

In addition to the SNAPSHOT isolation level, SQL Server also supports a special form of read-committed isolation, referred to as READ_COMMITTED_SNAPSHOT. This form of isolation is similar to snapshot isolation, but unlike snapshot isolation, which sees the version of the data at the start of the transaction, read committed snapshot queries see the version of the data at the start of the statement.

To enable the READ_COMMITTED_SNAPSHOT isolation level for queries, you need to enable the READ_COMMITTED_SNAPSHOT database option. Any queries that normally would run at the standard READ_COMMITTED isolation level automatically run at the READ_COMMITTED_SNAPSHOT isolation level, without requiring any code changes.

For more information on transaction isolation levels and their effect on lock types, locking behavior, and performance, see Chapter 37, "Locking and Performance."

Coding Effective Transactions

Poorly written or inefficient transactions can have a detrimental effect on concurrency of access to data and overall application performance. SQL Server can hold locks on a number of resources while the transaction is open; modified rows acquire exclusive locks, and other locks might also be held, depending on the isolation level used. To reduce locking contention for resources, transactions should be kept as short and efficient as possible. During development, you might not even notice that a problem exists; the problem might become noticeable only after the system load is increased and multiple users are executing transactions simultaneously. Following are some guidelines to consider when coding transactions to minimize locking contention and improve application performance:

- Do not return result sets within a transaction. Doing so prolongs the transaction unnecessarily. Perform all data retrieval and analysis outside the transaction.

- *Never* prompt for user input during a transaction. If you do, you lose all control over the duration of the transaction. (Even the best programmers miss this one on occasion.) On the failure of a transaction, be sure to issue the rollback before putting up a message box telling the user that a problem occurred.
- Keep the start and end of a transaction together in the same batch or, better yet, use a stored procedure for the operation.
- Keep the transaction short. Start the transaction at the point where you need to do the modifications. Do any preliminary work beforehand.
- Make careful use of different locking schemes and transaction isolation levels.
- If user input is unavoidable between data retrieval and modification and you need to handle the possibility of another user modifying the data values read, use optimistic locking strategies or snapshot isolation rather than acquiring and holding locks by using `HOLDLOCK` or other locking options. Chapter 37 covers optimistic locking methods and snapshot isolation in more detail.
- Collect multiple transactions into one transaction, or batch transactions together, if appropriate. This advice might seem to go against some of the other suggestions, but it reduces the amount of overhead SQL Server will encounter to start, finish, and log the transactions.

Transaction Logging and the Recovery Process

Every SQL Server database has its own transaction log that keeps a record of all data modifications in a database (for example, `insert`, `update`, `delete`) in the order in which they occur. This information is stored in one or more log files associated with the database. The information stored in these log files cannot be modified or viewed effectively by any user process.

SQL Server uses a write-ahead log. The buffer manager guarantees that changes are written to the transaction log before the changes are written to the database. The buffer manager also ensures that the log pages are written out in sequence so that transactions can be recovered properly in the event of a system crash.

The following is an overview of the sequence of events that occurs when a transaction modifies data:

1. Writes a `BEGIN TRAN` record to the transaction log in buffer memory.
2. Writes data modification information to transaction log pages in buffer memory.
3. Writes data modifications to the database in buffer memory.
4. Writes a `COMMIT TRAN` record to the transaction log in buffer memory.
5. Writes transaction log records to the transaction log file(s) on disk.
6. Sends a `COMMIT` acknowledgment to the client process.

The end of a typical transaction is indicated by a `COMMIT` record in the transaction log. The presence of the `COMMIT` record indicates that the transaction must be reflected in the database or be redone, if necessary. A transaction aborted during processing by an explicit rollback or a system error has its changes automatically undone.

Notice that the data records are not written to disk when a `COMMIT` occurs. This is done to minimize disk I/O. All log writes are done synchronously to ensure that the log records are physically written to disk and in the proper sequence. Because all modifications to the data can be recovered from the transaction log, it is not critical that data changes be written to disk right away. Even in the event of a system crash or power failure, the data can be recovered from the log if it hasn't been written to the database.

SQL Server ensures that the log records are written before the affected data pages by recording the log sequence number (LSN) for the log record making the change on the modified data page(s). Modified, or "dirty," data pages can be written to disk only when the LSN recorded on the data page is less than the LSN of the last log page written to the transaction log.

When and how are the data changes written to disk? Obviously, they must be written out at some time; otherwise, it could take an exceedingly long time for SQL Server to start up if it had to redo all the transactions contained in the transaction log. Also, how does SQL Server know during recovery which transactions to reapply, or roll forward, and which transactions to undo or roll back? The following section looks at the mechanisms involved in the recovery process.

The Checkpoint Process

During recovery, SQL Server examines the transaction log for each database and verifies whether the changes reflected in the log are also reflected in the database. In addition, it examines the log to determine whether any data changes that were written to the data were caused by a transaction that didn't complete before the system failure.

As discussed earlier, a `COMMIT` writes the log records for a transaction to the transaction log (see Figure 31.1). Dirty data pages are written out either by the Lazy Writer or checkpoint process. The Lazy Writer process runs periodically to check whether the number of free buffers has fallen below a certain threshold, reclaims any unused pages, and writes out any dirty pages that haven't been referenced recently.

The checkpoint process also scans the buffer cache periodically and writes all dirty log pages and dirty data pages to disk (see Figure 31.2). The purpose of the checkpoint is to sync up the data stored on disk with the changes recorded in the transaction log. Typically, the checkpoint process finds little work to do because most dirty pages have been written out previously by the worker threads or Lazy Writer process.

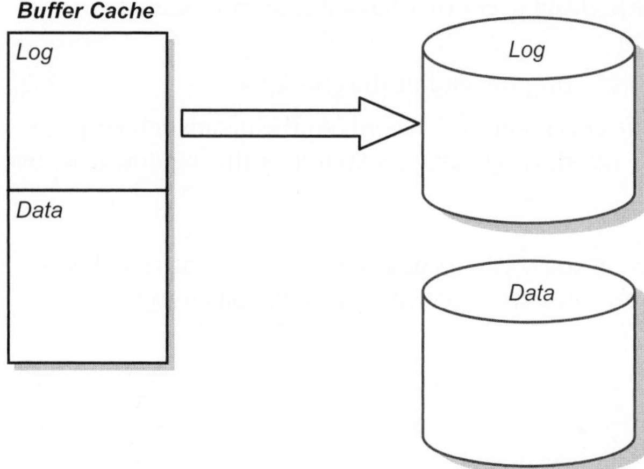

FIGURE 31.1 A commit writes all "dirty" log pages from cache to disk.

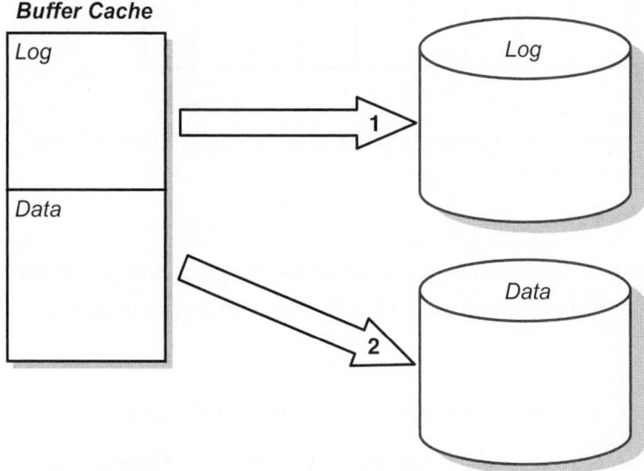

FIGURE 31.2 A checkpoint writes log pages from cache to disk and then writes all "dirty" data pages.

SQL Server performs the following steps during a checkpoint:

1. Writes a record to the log file to record the start of the checkpoint.
2. Stores information recorded for the checkpoint in a chain of checkpoint log records.
3. Records the minimum recovery LSN (MinLSN), which is the first log image that must be present for a successful database-wide rollback. The MinLSN is either the LSN of the start of the checkpoint, LSN of the oldest active transaction, or LSN of the oldest transaction marked for replication that hasn't yet been replicated to all subscribers.
4. Writes a list of all outstanding, active transactions to the checkpoint records.
5. Writes all modified log pages to the transaction log on disk.

6. Writes all dirty data pages to disk. (Data pages that have not been modified are not written back to disk to save I/O.)
7. Writes a record to the log file, indicating the end of the checkpoint.
8. Writes the LSN of the start of the checkpoint log records to the database boot page. (This is done so that SQL Server can find the last checkpoint in the log during recovery.)

Figure 31.3 shows a simplified version of the contents of a transaction log after a checkpoint. (For simplicity, the checkpoint records are reflected as a single log entry.)

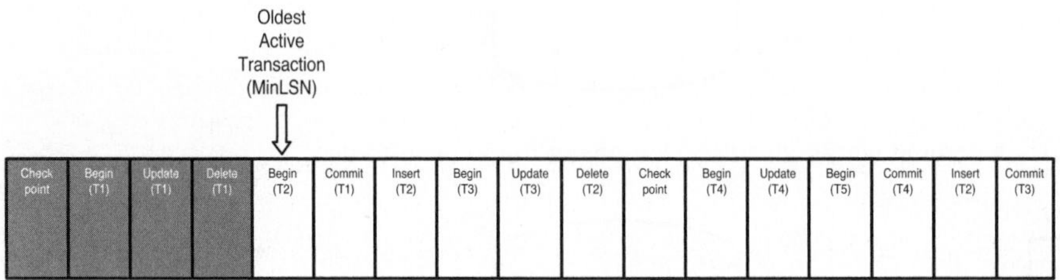

FIGURE 31.3 A simplified view of the end of the transaction log with various completed and active transactions, as well as the last checkpoint.

The primary purpose of a checkpoint is to reduce the amount of work the server needs to do at recovery time to redo or undo database changes. A checkpoint can occur under the following circumstances:

- When a checkpoint statement is executed explicitly for the current database.
- When `ALTER DATABASE` is used to change a database option. `ALTER DATABASE` automatically checkpoints the database when database options are changed.
- When an instance of SQL Server is shut down gracefully either due to the execution of the `SHUTDOWN` statement or because the SQL Server service was stopped.

NOTE

The `SHUTDOWN WITH NOWAIT` statement does not perform what is considered a graceful shutdown of SQL Server. This statement forces a shutdown of SQL Server without waiting for current transactions to complete and *without* executing a checkpoint of each database. This type of shutdown may cause the subsequent restart of SQL Server to take a longer time to recover the databases on the server.

- When SQL Server periodically generates automatic checkpoints in each database to reduce the amount of time the instance would take to recover the database.

Automatic Checkpoints

The frequency of automatic checkpoints is determined by the setting of the recovery interval for SQL Server. However, the determination of when to perform a checkpoint is based on the number of records in the log, not a specific period of time. The time interval between the occurrences of automatic checkpoints can be highly variable. If few modifications are made to the database, the time interval between automatic checkpoints could be quite long. Conversely, automatic checkpoints can occur quite frequently if the update activity on a database is high.

The recovery interval does not state how often automatic checkpoints should occur. The recovery interval is actually related to an estimate of the amount of time it would take SQL Server to recover the database by applying the number of transactions recorded since the last checkpoint. By default, the recovery interval is set to `0`, which means SQL Server determines the appropriate recovery interval for each database. It is recommended that you keep this setting at the default value unless you notice that checkpoints are occurring too frequently and are impairing performance. You should try increasing the value in small increments until you find one that works well. You need to be aware that if you set the recovery interval higher, fewer checkpoints will occur, and the database will likely take longer to recover following a system crash.

If the database is using either the full or bulk-logged recovery model, an automatic checkpoint occurs whenever the number of log records reaches the number that SQL Server estimates it can process within the time specified by the `recovery interval` option.

If the database is using the simple recovery model, an automatic checkpoint occurs whenever the number of log records reaches the number that SQL Server estimates it can process during the time specified by the recovery interval option or the log becomes 70% full and the database is in log truncate mode. A database is considered to be in log truncate mode when the database is using the simple recovery model and one of the following events has occurred since the last full backup of the database:

- A minimally logged operation is performed in the database, such as a minimally logged bulk copy operation or a minimally logged `WRITETEXT` statement.
- An `ALTER DATABASE` statement is executed that adds or deletes a file in the database.
- A `BACKUP LOG` statement referencing the database is executed with either the `NO_LOG` or `TRUNCATE_ONLY` option.

When a database is configured to use the simple recovery model, the automatic checkpoint also truncates the unused portion of the transaction log prior to the oldest active transaction.

Manual Checkpoints

In addition to automatic checkpoints, a checkpoint can be explicitly initiated by members of the `sysadmin` fixed server role or the `db_owner` or `db_backupoperator` fixed database roles. The syntax for the `CHECKPOINT` command is as follows:

```
CHECKPOINT [ checkpoint_duration ]
```

To minimize the performance impact on other applications, SQL Server 2008 by default adjusts the frequency of the writes that a checkpoint operation performs. SQL Server uses this strategy for automatic checkpoints and for any `CHECKPOINT` statement that does not specify the *`checkpoint_duration`* value.

You can use the *`checkpoint_duration`* option to request the amount of time, in seconds, for the checkpoint to complete. When *`checkpoint_duration`* is specified, SQL Server attempts to perform the checkpoint within the requested duration. The performance impact of using *`checkpoint_duration`* depends on the number of dirty pages, the activity on the system, and the actual duration specified. For example, if the checkpoint would normally complete in 120 seconds, specifying a *`checkpoint_duration`* of 60 seconds causes SQL Server to devote more resources to the checkpoint than would be assigned by default to be able to complete the checkpoint in half the time. In contrast, specifying a *`checkpoint_duration`* of 240 seconds causes SQL Server to assign fewer resources than would be assigned by default. In other words, a short *`checkpoint_duration`* increases the resources devoted to the checkpoint, and a longer *`checkpoint_duration`* reduces the resources devoted to the checkpoint.

Regardless of the checkpoint duration specified, SQL Server always attempts to complete a checkpoint when possible. In some cases, a checkpoint may complete sooner than the specified duration, and at times it may run longer than the specified duration.

The Recovery Process

When SQL Server is started, it verifies that completed transactions recorded in the log are reflected in the data and that incomplete transactions whose changes are reflected in the data are rolled back out of the database. This is the recovery process. Recovery is an automatic process performed on each database during SQL Server startup. Recovery must be completed before the database is made available for use.

The recovery process guarantees that all completed transactions recorded in the transaction log are reflected in the data and all incomplete transactions reflected in the data are rolled back. During recovery, SQL Server looks for the last checkpoint record in the log.

Only the changes that occurred or were still open since the last checkpoint need to be examined to determine the need for any transactions to be redone (that is, rolled forward) or undone (that is, rolled back). After all the changes are rolled forward or rolled back, as necessary, the database is checkpointed, and recovery is complete.

The recovery algorithm has three phases centered around the last checkpoint record in the transaction log, as shown in Figure 31.4.

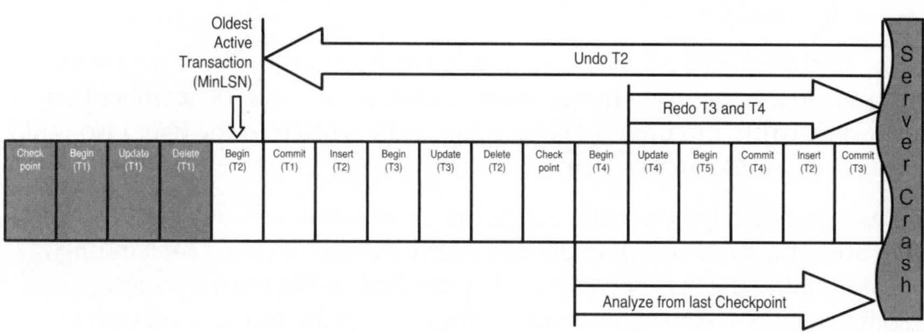

FIGURE 31.4 The phases of the recovery process.

These phases are as follows:

1. **Analysis phase**—SQL Server reads forward from the last checkpoint record in the transaction log. This pass identifies a list of pages (the dirty page table [DPT]) that might have been dirty at the time of the system crash or when SQL Server was shut down, as well as a list of the uncommitted transactions at the time of the crash.
2. **Redo (roll-forward) phase**—During this phase, SQL Server rolls forward all the committed transactions recorded in the log since the last checkpoint. This phase returns the database to the state it was in at the time of the crash. The starting point for the redo pass is the LSN of the oldest committed transaction within the DPT, so that only changes not previously checkpointed (only the committed dirty pages) are reapplied.
3. **Undo (rollback) phase**—This phase moves backward from the end of the log to the oldest active transaction at the time of the system crash or shutdown. All transactions that were not committed at the time of the crash but had pages written to the database are undone so that none of their changes are actually reflected in the database.

Now let's examine the transactions in the log in Figure 31.4 and determine how they will be handled during the recovery process:

- Transaction T1 is started and committed prior to the last checkpoint. No recovery is necessary.

- Transaction T2 started before the last checkpoint but had not completed at the time of the system crash. The changes written out by the checkpoint process for this transaction have to be rolled back.
- Transaction T3 started before the last checkpoint was issued and committed after that checkpoint but prior to the system crash. The changes made to the data after the checkpoint need to be rolled forward.
- Transaction T4 started and committed after the last checkpoint. This entire transaction needs to be rolled forward.
- Transaction T5 started after the last checkpoint, but no changes to the data were recorded in the log, so no data changes were written to the data. (Remember that changes must be written to the log before they can be written to the data.) No undo action is required for this transaction.

In a nutshell, this type of analysis is pretty much the same analysis the recovery process would do. To identify the number of transactions rolled forward or rolled back during recovery, you can examine the SQL Server error log and look at the recovery startup messages for each database. Following is a sample fragment of the recovery messages you might see in the SQL Server error log:

```
2009-05-22 10:37:04.440 spid15s      Starting up database 'tempdb'.
2009-05-22 10:37:04.630 spid18s      Starting up database 'msdb'.
2009-05-22 10:37:04.640 spid19s      Starting up database 'sample'.
2009-05-22 10:37:04.660 spid20s      Starting up database 'AdventureWorks'.
2009-05-22 10:37:04.670 spid21s      Starting up database 'bigpubs2008'.
2009-05-22 10:37:05.140 spid20s      1 transactions rolled forward in database
 'AdventureWorks' (6). This is an informational message only. No user action is
 required.
2009-05-22 10:37:05.150 spid19s      1 transactions rolled forward in database
 'sample' (5). This is an informational message only. No user action is required.
2009-05-22 10:37:05.240 spid19s      0 transactions rolled back in database
 'AdventureWorks' (6). This is an informational message only. No user action is
 required.
2009-05-22 10:37:05.260 spid20s      0 transactions rolled back in database
 'sample' (5). This is an informational message only. No user action is required.
2009-05-22 10:37:05.260 spid19s      Recovery is writing a checkpoint in database
 'AdventureWorks' (6). This is an informational message only. No user action is
 required.
2009-05-22 10:37:05.300 spid20s      Recovery is writing a checkpoint in database
 'sample' (5). This is an informational message only. No user action is required.
2009-05-22 10:37:05.340 spid18s      50 transactions rolled forward in database
 'msdb' (4). This is an informational message only. No user action is required.
2009-05-22 10:37:05.350 spid19s      Starting up database 'AdventureWorksDW'.
2009-05-22 10:37:05.460 spid20s      0 transactions rolled back in database 'msdb'
 (4). This is an informational message only. No user action is required.
```

```
2009-05-22 10:37:05.470 spid20s      Recovery is writing a checkpoint in database
 'msdb' (4). This is an informational message only. No user action is required.
2009-05-22 10:37:05.480 spid20s      Starting up database 'AdventureWorksLT'.
2009-05-22 10:37:05.520 spid21s      1 transactions rolled forward in database
 'bigpubs2008' (7). This is an informational message only. No user action is
 required.
2009-05-22 10:37:05.610 spid7s       1 transactions rolled back in database
 'bigpubs2008' (7). This is an informational message only. No user action is
 required.
2009-05-22 10:37:05.610 spid7s       Recovery is writing a checkpoint in database
 'bigpubs2008' (7). This is an informational message only. No user action is
 required.
2009-05-22 10:37:05.630 spid19s      1 transactions rolled forward in database
 'AdventureWorksDW' (8). This is an informational message only. No user action is
 required.
2009-05-22 10:37:05.680 spid18s      0 transactions rolled back in database
 'AdventureWorksDW' (8). This is an informational message only. No user action is
 required.
2009-05-22 10:37:05.700 spid18s      Recovery is writing a checkpoint in database
 'AdventureWorksDW' (8). This is an informational message only. No user action is
 required.
2009-05-22 10:37:05.740 spid20s      1 transactions rolled forward in database
 'AdventureWorksLT' (9). This is an informational message only. No user action is
 required.
2009-05-22 10:37:05.760 spid20s      0 transactions rolled back in database
 'AdventureWorksLT' (9). This is an informational message only. No user action is
 required.
2009-05-22 10:37:05.770 spid20s      Recovery is writing a checkpoint in database
 'AdventureWorksLT' (9). This is an informational message only. No user action is
 required.
2009-05-22 10:37:05.770 spid18s      Starting up database 'AdventureWorks2008'.
2009-05-22 10:37:05.780 spid19s      Starting up database 'AdventureWorksDW2008'.
2009-05-22 10:37:05.790 spid21s      Starting up database 'AdventureWorksLT2008'.
2009-05-22 10:37:05.900 spid19s      1 transactions rolled forward in database
 'AdventureWorksDW2008' (11). This is an informational message only. No user action
 is required.
2009-05-22 10:37:05.910 spid21s      1 transactions rolled forward in database
 'AdventureWorksLT2008' (12). This is an informational message only. No user action
 is required.
2009-05-22 10:37:05.940 spid18s      9 transactions rolled forward in database
 'AdventureWorks2008' (10). This is an informational message only. No user action
 is required.
2009-05-22 10:37:05.950 spid7s       0 transactions rolled back in database
 'AdventureWorksDW2008' (11). This is an informational message only. No user action
```

```
 is required.
2009-05-22 10:37:05.950 spid19s      0 transactions rolled back in database
 'AdventureWorksLT2008' (12). This is an informational message only. No user action
 is required.
2009-05-22 10:37:05.960 spid7s       Recovery is writing a checkpoint in database
 'AdventureWorksDW2008' (11). This is an informational message only. No user action
 is required.
2009-05-22 10:37:05.970 spid19s      Recovery is writing a checkpoint in database
 'AdventureWorksLT2008' (12). This is an informational message only. No user action
 is required.
2009-05-22 10:37:06.530 spid19s      0 transactions rolled back in database
 'AdventureWorks2008' (10). This is an informational message only. No user action
 is required.
2009-05-22 10:37:06.630 spid19s      Recovery is writing a checkpoint in database
 'AdventureWorks2008' (10). This is an informational message only. No user action
 is required.
2009-05-22 10:37:08.220 spid19s      Recovery completed for database
AdventureWorks2008 (database ID 10) in 1 second(s) (analysis 73 ms, redo 1 ms, undo
 572 ms.) This is an informational message only. No user action is required.
2009-05-22 10:37:08.250 spid7s       Recovery is complete. This is an informational
message only. No user action is required.
```

Managing the Transaction Log

Each database in SQL Server has at least one transaction log file. The transaction log file contains the transaction log records for all changes made in that database. By default, transaction log files have the file extension `.ldf`.

A database can have several log files, and each log file can have a maximum size of 32TB. A log file cannot be part of a filegroup. No information other than transaction log records can be written to a log file.

Regardless of how many physical files have been defined for the transaction log, SQL Server treats it as one contiguous file. The transaction log for a database is actually managed as a set of virtual log files (VLFs). VLFs have no fixed size, and there is no fixed number of VLFs for a physical log file. The size and number of VLFs is not configurable. SQL Server determines the size of the VLFs dynamically, based on the total size of all the log files and the growth increment specified for the log. Figure 31.5 shows an example of a physical log file divided into multiple virtual log files.

The transaction log is essentially a wrap-around file. Initially, the logical log file begins at the start of the physical log file. As transactions are committed, new log records are added to the end of the logical log, and the logical log expands toward the end of the physical log. When the logical log reaches the end of the physical log file, SQL Server attempts to wrap around and start writing log records back at the beginning of the physical log file, as shown in Figure 31.6.

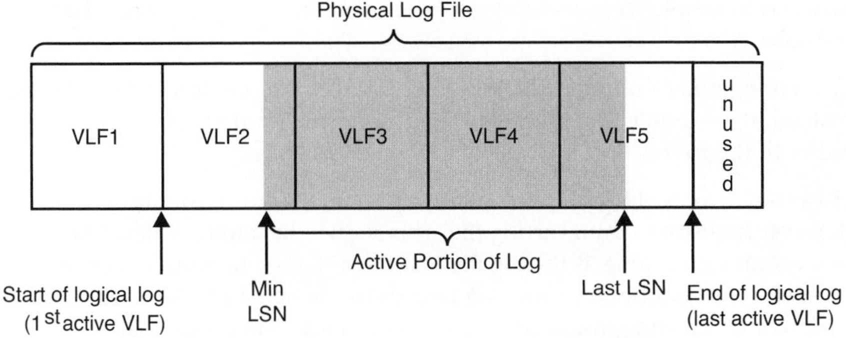

FIGURE 31.5 The structure of a physical log file showing VLFs.

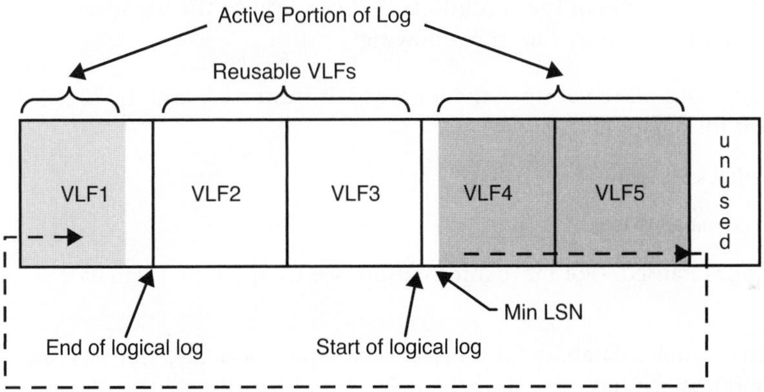

FIGURE 31.6 An example of the active portion of a log cycling around to reusable VLF at the beginning of a log file.

SQL Server, however, can reuse only the first VLF if it is no longer part of the logical log; that is, the VLF does not contain any active log records, and the contents of the inactive VLFs have been truncated. Log truncation frees any virtual logs whose records all appear before the MinLSN. The MinLSN is the log sequence number of the oldest log record required for a successful database recovery.

In environments where the log is not being maintained, SQL Server automatically truncates and reuses the space in the VLFs at the beginning of the log file as soon as it reaches the end of the log file. This can occur as long as the VLFs at the beginning of the log file do not contain the MinLSN. SQL Server assumes that the log is not being maintained when the database is in simple recovery mode, or when you have never performed a full backup of the database.

If the database is configured to use the bulk-logged or full recovery models so that the log is being maintained, the reusable portion of the log prior to the MinLSN cannot be truncated or purged until the transaction log has actually been backed up.

If the first VLF cannot be reused because it contains the MinLSN or it hasn't been truncated yet, SQL Server needs to expand the log file. This is done by adding a new VLF to the end of the physical log (as long as the log file is still configured to grow automatically). SQL Server can then continue writing log records to the new VLF. However, if the log file is not configured to auto-grow, a 9002 error is generated, indicating that the log file is out of space.

Certain conditions can cause log records to remain active, preventing the MinLSN from moving out of the first VLF, which in turn prevents the VLFs at the beginning of the physical log file from being reused. Some of the conditions that can lead to the log space not being reused include, but are not limited to, the following:

- No checkpoint has taken place yet since the log was last truncated, and the log records are needed for database recovery.
- A database or log backup is in progress.
- A long-running transaction is still active.
- Database mirroring is paused. (For more information, see Chapter 20, "Database Mirroring.")
- The database is the primary database for transactional replication, and transactions relevant to the publications have not yet been delivered to the distribution database. (For more information on replication, see Chapter 19, "Replication.")
- A database snapshot is being created (for more information, see Chapter 32, "Database Snapshots").

If something is preventing the log from being truncated, SQL Server 2008 provides information in the system catalogs to determine what is preventing log truncation. This information is available in the `log_reuse_wait_desc` column of the `sys.databases` catalog view, which you can display by using a query similar to the following:

```
select name, log_reuse_wait_desc
  from sys.databases
  where name = db_name()
```

When a log file is configured to auto-grow and there is significant update activity against the database and the inactive portion of the transaction log is not being truncated frequently enough (or at all) to allow for the reuse of VLFs, the log file size can become excessive. This can lead to insufficient disk space in the file system that contains the log file. This can subsequently also lead to a 9002 out-of-space error if the log file needs to grow and not enough disk space is available. At times, you might need to shrink the log file to reduce its size.

Shrinking the Log File

After the log has been backed up and the active portion of the log has wrapped around to the beginning of the log file, the VLFs at the end of the physical log can be deleted from the log file, and the log file can be reduced in size.

When you shrink a log file, the space freed can only come from the end of the log file. The unit of size reduction is the size of the virtual log file. For example, if you have a 1GB log file that has been divided into five 200MB virtual log files, the log file can only be shrunk in 200MB increments. The file size can be reduced to sizes such as 800MB or 400MB, but the file cannot be reduced to sizes such as 333MB or 750MB.

SQL Server 2008 provides the `DBCC SHRINKFILE` command for shrinking the transaction log file. Its syntax is as follows:

```
DBCC SHRINKFILE ( { 'file_name' } { [,EMPTYFILE] | [,target_size ] } )
   [ WITH NO_INFOMSGS ]
```

If no target size is specified for the `DBCC SHRINKFILE` command, SQL Server removes as many of the inactive virtual log files from the end of the physical log file as possible to restore the transaction log file to its default size. The default size of the transaction log file is the size specified when the log file was created or the last size set by using the `ALTER DATABASE` command.

If a target size is specified for `DBCC SHRINKFILE`, SQL Server attempts to remove as many VLFs from the end of the log file as possible to reduce the log file to as close to the target size as possible without making the log smaller than the specified target size. After shrinking, the log file is typically somewhat larger than the target size, especially if the target size is not a multiple of the VLF size.

If no VLFs beyond the *`target_size`* mark contain an active portion of the log, all the VLFs that come after the `target_size` mark are freed, and the `DBCC SHRINKFILE` statement completes successfully, with no messages. However, if any VLF beyond the *`target_size`* mark does contain an active portion of the log, SQL Server frees from the end of the physical log file as many of the VLFs as possible that do not contain active portions of the log. When this occurs, the `DBCC SHRINKFILE` command returns an informational message indicating that not all the requested space was freed. When the active portion of the log moves off the VLF(s) at the end of the physical log file, you can reissue the `DBCC SHRINKFILE` statement again to free the remaining space.

You can also use SQL Server Management Studio (SSMS) to shrink the transaction log file. In the Object Browser, expand the `Databases` folder and right-click the target database. Then select Tasks, Shrink, and Files. The Shrink File dialog appears, as shown in Figure 31.7.

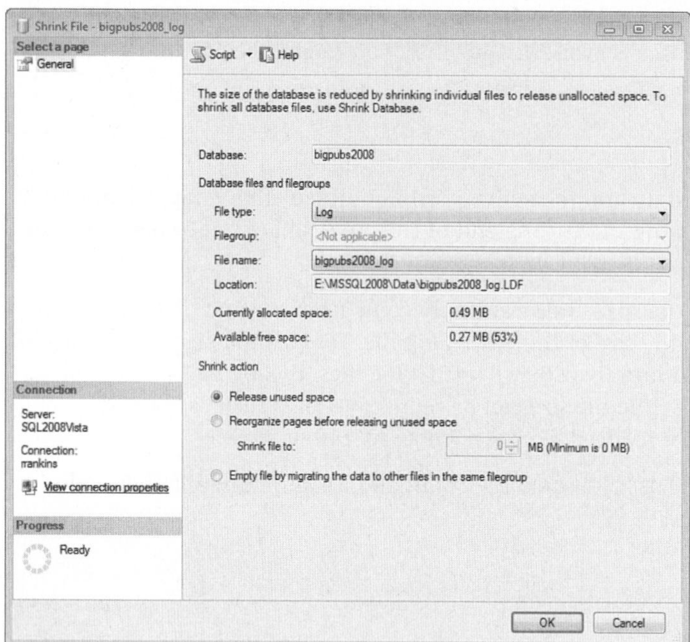

FIGURE 31.7 The SSMS Shrink File dialog.

In the File Type drop-down list, select Log. To shrink the log file to its default size, click the radio button next to Release Unused Space in the Shrink Action area of the dialog box. To shrink the log file to a desired size, click the radio button next to Reorganize Pages Before Releasing Unused Space and specify the desired target size. After you choose the desired shrink option, click OK.

In addition to manually shrinking the transaction log, SQL Server also provides a database option, AUTO_SHRINK, that can be enabled to shrink the log and database files automatically when space is available at the end of the file. If you are regularly backing up or truncating the log, the AUTO_SHRINK option keeps the size of the log file in check. The auto-shrink process runs periodically and determines whether the log file can be shrunk. The Log Manager keeps track of how much log space has been used since the auto-shrink process last ran. The auto-shrink process then shrinks the log either to 125% of the maximum log space used since auto-shrink last ran or the default size of the transaction log file, whichever is larger.

TIP

Repeated growing and shrinking of the log file can lead to excessive file fragmentation, which can have an adverse impact on the file I/O performance. It is recommended that instead of using `AUTO_SHRINK`, you set the transaction log to the size it is expected to grow to during normal processing and enable the auto-grow option so that it doesn't run out of space if something prevents the log from being truncated. By doing so, you help avoid the need for the log file to be constantly expanded during normal processing and also avoid excessive fragmentation of the log file. If something causes the log file to auto-grow and exceed the normal log file size, you can always manually shrink the file back to its normal size.

Long-Running Transactions

As you have already seen, transaction information is recorded in each database's transaction log. However, long-running transactions can be a cause of consternation to a system administrator who is attempting to back up and prune the transaction log. Only the inactive portion of the log can be truncated during this operation. The inactive portion of the log is the pages that contain log records for all completed transactions prior to the first log record of the oldest still-active transaction (see Figure 31.8). Even if completed transactions follow the first record of the oldest active transaction, they cannot be removed from the log until the oldest active transaction completes. The reason is that the log is pruned by clearing out entire pages of information prior to the oldest active transaction. Pages after that point cannot be cleared because they might contain records for the active transaction that would be needed in the event of a rollback or database recovery.

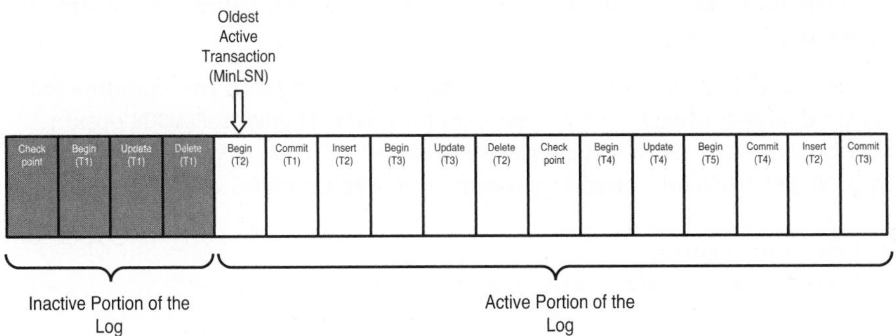

FIGURE 31.8 The inactive portion of the log is the pages in the log prior to the oldest active transaction.

In addition to preventing the log from being pruned, long-running transactions can degrade concurrency by holding locks for an extended period of time, preventing other users from accessing the locked data.

To get information about the oldest active transaction in a database, you can use the DBCC OPENTRAN command, whose syntax is as follows:

```
DBCC OPENTRAN [('DatabaseName' | DatabaseId)]
[WITH TABLERESULTS [, NO_INFOMSGS]]
```

The following example displays a sample of the oldest active transaction for the bigpubs2008 database:

```
DBCC OPENTRAN (bigpubs2008)
go

Transaction information for database 'bigpubs2008'.

Oldest active transaction:
    SPID (server process ID): 56
    UID (user ID) : -1
    Name          : add_titles
    LSN           : (1926:170:6)
    Start time    : May 26 2009 12:17:09:220AM
    SID           : 0xe6810e075514c744bc8d03b34c27b004
DBCC execution completed. If DBCC printed error messages, contact your system
administrator.
```

DBCC OPENTRAN returns the server process ID (SPID) of the process that initiated the transaction, user ID, name of the transaction (naming transactions are helpful here because the names might help you identify the SQL code that initiated the transaction), LSN of the page containing the initial BEGIN TRAN statement for the transaction, and, finally, time the transaction was started.

If you specify the TABLERESULTS option, this information is returned in two columns that you can load into a table for logging or comparison purposes. The NO_INFOMSGS option suppresses the display of the 'DBCC execution completed...' message. The following example runs DBCC OPENTRAN and inserts the results into a temp table:

```
CREATE TABLE #opentran_results
( result_label VARCHAR(30), result_value VARCHAR(46))

insert #opentran_results
    exec ('dbcc opentran (bigpubs2008) WITH TABLERESULTS,  no_infomsgs')

select * from #opentran_results
go
```

```
result_label                    result_value
------------------------------- ----------------------------
OLDACT_SPID                     57
OLDACT_UID                      -1
OLDACT_NAME                     add_titles
OLDACT_LSN                      (1926:203:1)
OLDACT_STARTTIME                May 26 2009 12:20:10:407AM
OLDACT_SID                      0xe6810e075514c744bc8d03b34c27b004
```

If no open transactions exist for the database, you receive the following message from `DBCC OPENTRAN`:

```
No active open transactions.
DBCC execution completed. If DBCC printed error messages, contact your
 system administrator.
```

`DBCC OPENTRAN` provides a means for you to identify which transactions are potential problems, based on their longevity. If you capture the process information at the same time, using `sp_who`, you can identify who or what application is causing the longest-running transaction(s). Using this information, you can terminate the process, if necessary, or you can just have a quiet word with the user if the query is ad hoc or with the application developers if it is SQL code generated by a custom application.

Bound Connections

During the course of a transaction, the process that initiated the transaction acquires exclusive locks on the data that is modified. These locks prevent other user processes or connections from seeing any of these changes until they are committed. However, it is common for some SQL Server applications to have multiple connections to SQL Server. Even though each connection might be for the same user, SQL Server treats each connection as an entirely separate SQL Server process, and by default, one connection cannot see the uncommitted changes of another nor modify records locked by the other connection.

Bound connections provide a means of linking multiple connections together to share the same lock space and participate in the same transaction. This capability can be useful, especially if an application makes use of extended stored procedures. Extended stored procedures, although invoked from within a user session, run externally in a separate session. An extended stored procedure might need to call back into the database to access data. Without bound connections between the original process and extended stored procedure, the extended stored procedure would be blocked by the locks held on the data by the originating process.

NOTE

In earlier versions of SQL Server, bound sessions were primarily used in developing extended stored procedures that needed to execute T-SQL statements on behalf of the process calling them. In SQL Server 2008, it is recommended that extended stored procedures be replaced with stored procedures written using the common language runtime (CLR). CLR-stored procedures are more secure, scalable, and stable than extended stored procedures. In addition, CLR-stored procedures use the `SqlContext` object to join the context of the calling session rather than bound connections.

Bound connections are of two types: local and distributed. Local bound connections are two or more connections within a single server that are bound into a single transaction space. Distributed bound connections make use of the Microsoft Distributed Transaction Coordinator (MS DTC; described in more detail in the following section, "Distributed Transactions") to share a transaction space across connections from more than one server.

Distributed Transactions

Typically, transaction management controls only the data modifications made within a single SQL Server instance. However, the increasing interest and implementation of distributed systems brings up the need to access and modify data distributed across multiple SQL Server instances within a single unit of work.

What if in the banking example, the checking accounts reside on one SQL Server instance and the savings accounts on another? Moving money from one account to another would require updates to two separate SQL Server instances. How do you modify data on two different instances and still treat it as a single unit of work? You need some way to ensure that the distributed transaction retains the same ACID properties as a local transaction. To provide this capability, SQL Server ships with the MS DTC service, which provides the capability to control and manage the integrity of multiserver transactions. MS DTC uses the industry-standard two-phase commit protocol to ensure the consistency of all parts of any distributed transaction passing through SQL Server and any referenced linked servers.

Chapter 54, "Managing Linked and Remote Servers" (on the CD), covers the process of configuring servers and writing SQL code to support distributed transactions.

Summary

A transaction is a logical unit of work as well as a unit of recovery. The successful control of transactions is of the utmost importance to the correct modification of related information. In this chapter, you learned how to define and control transactions, examined different transaction-management schemes, learned how the recovery process works, and discovered how to correctly code transactions within triggers and stored procedures. You also learned methods for optimizing transactions to improve application performance, and you got an overview of locking and distributed transactions. Locking is covered in more detail in Chapter 37, and distributed transactions are covered in more detail in Chapter 54. In addition, this chapter discussed the snapshot isolation options available in SQL Server 2008. Snapshot isolation provides the capability to keep versions of row data that existed prior to the start of a transaction.

Chapter 32 discusses the concept of database snapshots, which provide a way to keep a read-only, static view of a database.

CHAPTER 32

Database Snapshots

IN THIS CHAPTER

- What's New with Database Snapshots
- What Are Database Snapshots?
- Limitations and Restrictions of Database Snapshots
- Copy-on-Write Technology
- When to Use Database Snapshots
- Setup and Breakdown of a Database Snapshot
- Reverting to a Database Snapshot for Recovery
- Setting Up Snapshots Against a Database Mirror
- Database Snapshots Maintenance and Security Considerations

Database snapshots have been a feature of competing database products (Oracle and DB2) for years. Database snapshots are great for fulfilling point-in-time reporting requirements, reverting a database back to a point in time (recoverability and availability), and for potentially reducing the processing impact of querying against your primary transactional databases (via database mirroring and database snapshots).

Keep in mind that database snapshots are point in time and read-only. Database snapshots are not materialized views. Materialized views become part of the data object (table) that they are touching (that is, that are bound to them); when data changes in the base tables, materialized views change (that is, are updated). Database snapshots are point-in-time reflections of an entire database and are not bound to the underlying database objects from which they pull their data. They provide a full, read-only copy of the database at a specific point in time. Because of this point-in-time aspect, data latency must be well understood for all users of this feature: snapshot data is only as current as at the time the snapshot was made.

Database snapshots make huge use of Microsoft's copy-on-write technology. In fact, the copy-on-write technology is the primary enabling mechanism for snapshots. If you recall from Chapter 20, "Database Mirroring," the copy-on-write technology is what enables database mirroring. Database snapshots can also be used in conjunction with database mirroring to provide a highly available transactional system and a reporting platform that is created from the database mirror and offloads the reporting away from the primary transactional database, without any data loss impact whatsoever. This is a very powerful reporting and availability configuration.

What's New with Database Snapshots

With SQL Server 2005, everything about database snapshots was new because this was a completely new feature for SQL Server. With SQL Server 2008, there is little new to this feature other than under-the-cover improvements to the copy-on-write mechanisms and three more years of production implementations under their belt. One hundred percent of the SQL code you have set up for creating and managing snapshots will work perfectly with SQL Server 2008. No upgrade pain here.

Database snapshots have solved many companies' reporting, data safeguarding, and performance issues and directly contributed to higher availability across the board. Be aware, though, there are plenty of restrictions with doing database snapshots. In fact, these restrictions may prohibit you from using snapshots at all. We talk about these restrictions and when you can safely do database snapshots in a bit.

NOTE

The examples in this chapter are based on the SQL Server 2005 version of the AdventureWorks database rather than the newer AdventureWorks2008 or AdventureWorks2008R2 sample databases used for many of the examples in the other chapters in this book. The reason for this is because of the examples presented that create a snapshot from a Database Mirror. Database Mirroring cannot be implemented on a database that is also configured for FILESTREAM storage. The 2008 and 2008R2 versions of the AdventureWorks database make use of FILESTREAM storage.

Fortunately, the 2005 version of the AdventureWorks database can be installed using the same installer that installs the AdventureWorks2008 or AdventureWorks2008R2 database. If you didn't install AdventureWorks when you installed either of these sample databases, simply relaunch the installer and choose to install the AdventureWorks OLTP database.

For more information on downloading and installing the AdventureWorks sample databases, see the Introduction chapter.

What Are Database Snapshots?

Microsoft has kept up its commitment of providing a database engine foundation that can be highly available 7 days a week, 365 days a year. Database snapshots contribute to this goal in several ways:

- They decrease recovery time of a database because you can restore a troubled database with a database snapshot—referred to as *reverting*.
- They create a security blanket (safeguard) prior to running mass updates on a critical database. If something goes wrong with the update, the database can be reverted in a very short amount of time.

- They provide a read-only, point-in-time reporting database for ad hoc or canned reporting needs quickly (thus, increasing reporting environment availability).
- They create a read-only, point-in-time reporting and off-loaded database for ad hoc or canned reporting needs quickly from a database mirror (again, increasing reporting environment availability and also offloading reporting impact away from your production server/principal database server).
- As a bonus, database snapshots can be used to create testing or QA synchronization points to enhance and improve all aspects of critical testing (thus decreasing bad code from going into production that directly affects the stability and availability of that production implementation).

A database snapshot is simply a point-in-time full database view. It's not a copy—at least not a full copy when it is originally created. We talk about this more in a moment. Figure 32.1 shows conceptually how a database snapshot can be created from a source database on a single SQL Server instance.

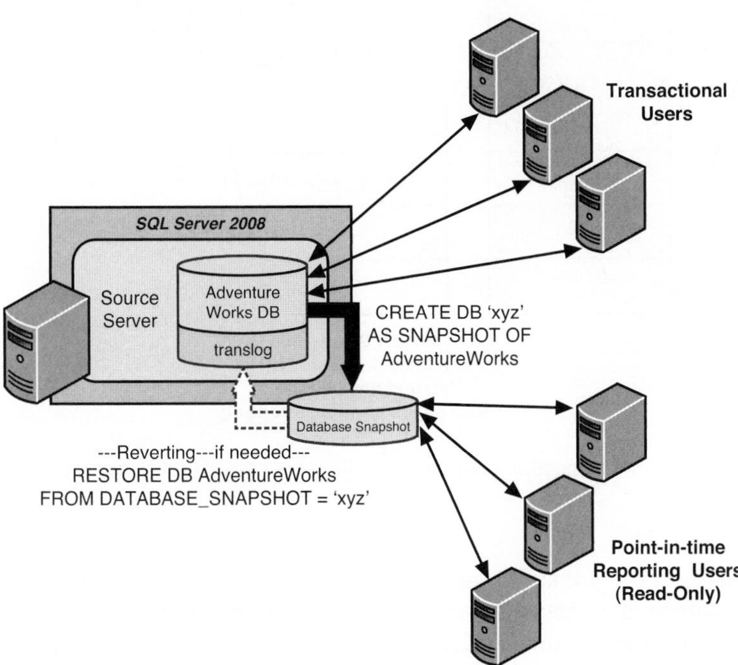

FIGURE 32.1 Basic database snapshot concept: a source database and its database snapshot, all on a single SQL Server instance.

This point-in-time view of a database's data never changes, even though the data (data pages) in the primary database (the source of the database snapshot) may change. It is truly a snapshot at a point in time. For a snapshot, it always simply points to data pages that were present at the time the snapshot was created. If a data page is updated in the source database, a copy of the original source data page is moved to a new page chain termed the *sparse file*. This utilizes copy-on-write technology. Figure 32.2 shows the sparse file that is created, alongside the source database itself.

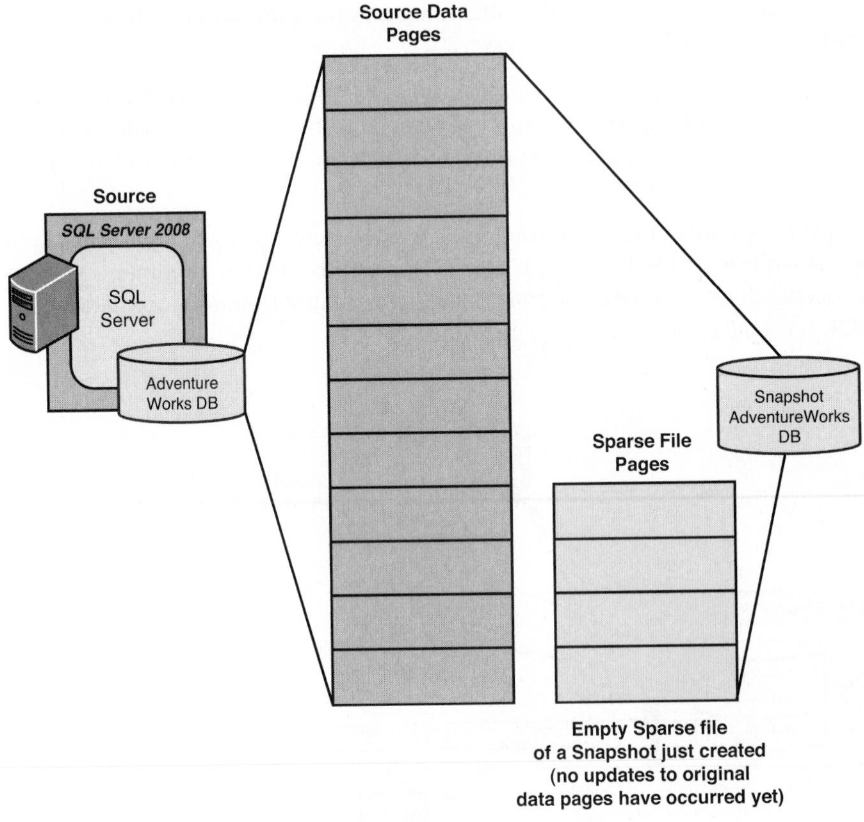

FIGURE 32.2 Source database data pages and the sparse file data pages that comprise the database snapshot.

A database snapshot really uses the primary database's data pages up until the point that one of these data pages is updated (changed in any way). As already mentioned, if a data page is updated in the source database, the original copy of the data page (which is referenced by the database snapshot) is written to the sparse file page chain as part of an update operation, using the copy-on-write technology. It is this new data page in the sparse file that still provides the correct point-in-time data to the database snapshot that it serves. Figure 32.3 illustrates that as more data changes (updates) occur in the source database, the sparse file gets larger and larger with the old original data pages.

Eventually a sparse file could contain the entire original database if all data pages in the primary database were changed. As you can also see in Figure 32.3, which data pages the database snapshot uses from the original (source) database and which data pages are used

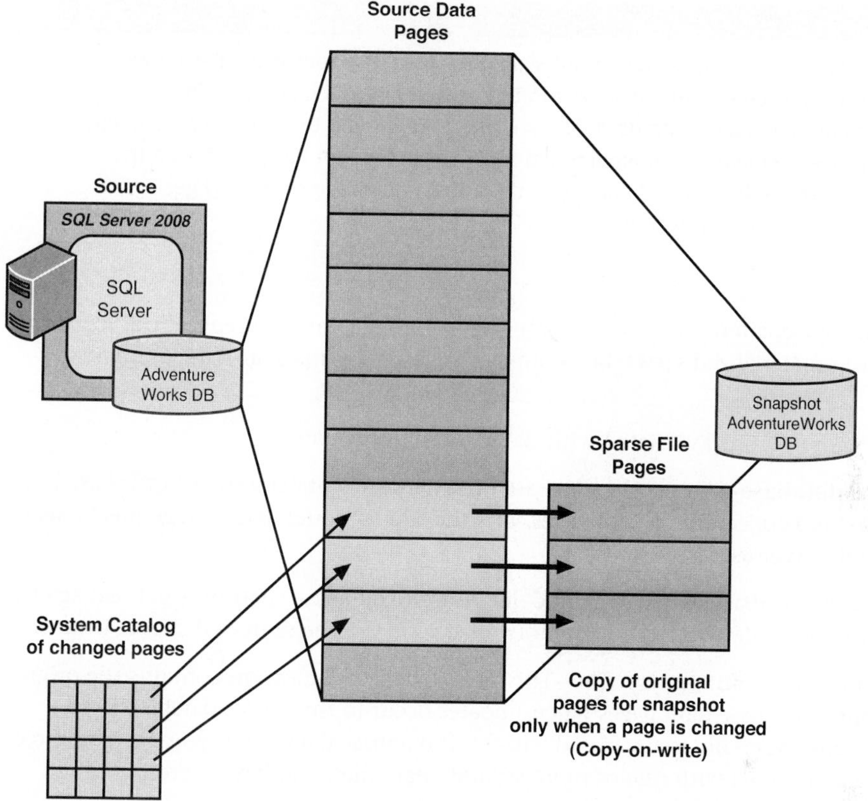

FIGURE 32.3 Data pages being copied to the sparse file for a database snapshot as pages are being updated in the source database.

from the sparse file are all managed by references in the system catalog for the database snapshot. This setup is incredibly efficient and represents a major breakthrough of providing data to others. Because SQL Server is using the copy-on-write technology, a certain amount of overhead is used during write operations. This is one of the critical factors you must sort through if you plan on using database snapshots. Nothing is free. The overhead includes the copying of the original data page, the writing of this copied data page to the sparse file, and then the subsequent metadata updating to the system catalog that manages the database snapshot data page list. Because of this sharing of data pages, it should also be clear why database snapshots must be within the same instance of a SQL Server: both the source database and snapshot start out as the same data pages and then diverge as source data pages are updated. In addition, when a database snapshot is created, SQL Server rolls back any uncommitted transactions for that database snapshot; only the committed transactions are part of a newly created database snapshot. And, as you might expect of something that shares data pages, database snapshots become unavailable if the source database becomes unavailable (for example, if it is damaged or goes offline).

NOTE

You might plan to do a new snapshot after about 30% of the source database has changed to keep overhead and file sizes in the sparse file at a minimum. The most frequent problem that occurs with database snapshots is related to sparse file sizes and available space. Remember, the sparse file has the potential of being as big as the source database itself (if all data pages in the source database eventually get updated). Plan ahead for this situation!

There are, of course, alternatives to database snapshots, such as data replication, log shipping, and even materialized views, but none are as easy to manage and use as database snapshots.

The most common terms associated with database snapshots are

- **Source database**—This is the database on which the database snapshot is based. A database is a collection of data pages. It is the fundamental data storage mechanism that SQL Server uses.
- **Snapshot databases**—There can be one or more database snapshots defined against any one source database. All snapshots must reside in the same SQL Server instance.
- **Database snapshot sparse file**—This new data page allocation contains the original source database data pages when updates occur to the source database data pages. One sparse file is associated with each database data file. If you have a source database allocated with one or more separate data files, you have corresponding sparse files of each of them.
- **Reverting to a database snapshot**—If you restore a source database based on a particular database snapshot that was done at a point in time, you are reverting. You are actually doing a database `RESTORE` operation with a `FROM DATABASE_SNAPSHOT` statement.
- **Copy-on-write technology**—As part of an update transaction in the source database, a copy of the source database data page is written to a sparse file so that the database snapshot can be served correctly (that is, still see the data page as of the snapshot point in time).

As Figure 32.4 illustrates, any data query using the database snapshot looks at both the source database data pages and the sparse file data pages at the same time. And these data pages always reflect the unchanged data pages at the point in time the snapshot was created.

Limitations and Restrictions of Database Snapshots

Many restrictions or limitations are involved with using database snapshots in SQL Server. Some of them are pretty restrictive and may determine whether you can consider using snapshots. With the current release of SQL Server Management Studio, you cannot even

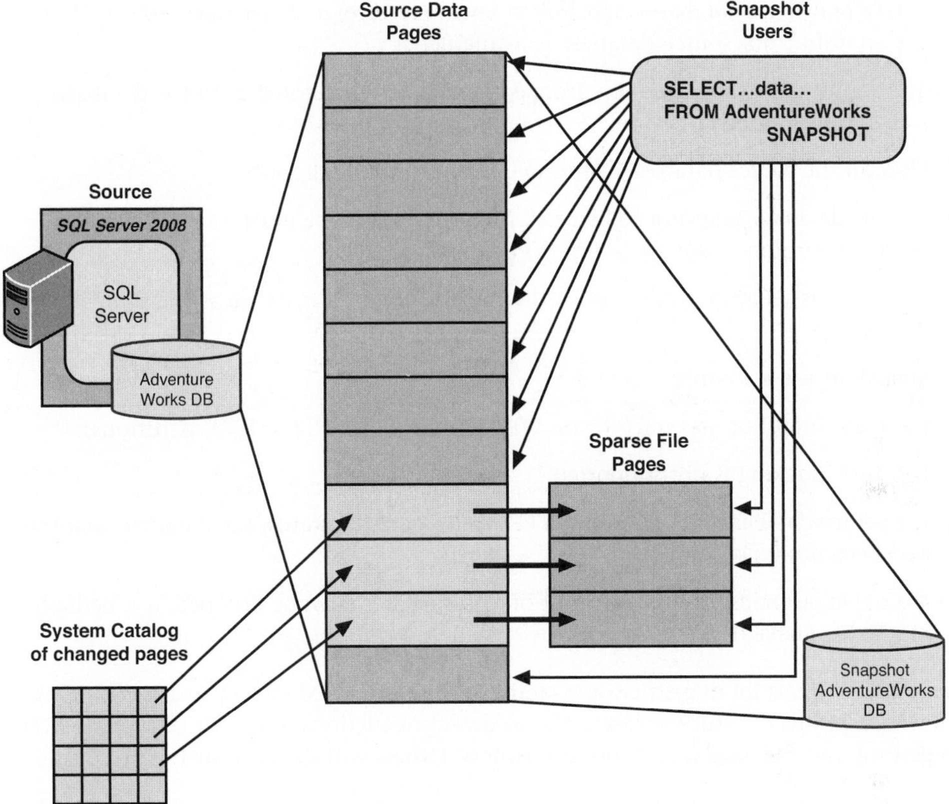

FIGURE 32.4 A query using the database snapshot touches both source database data pages and sparse file data pages to satisfy a query.

set up database snapshots with this GUI or a wizard; it must all be done using T-SQL statements (which is not that bad a deal). The following are some of the other restrictions:

- You must drop all other database snapshots when using a database snapshot to revert a source database.
- You lose visibility to the source database's uncommitted transactions in the database snapshot when it is created.
- The more updates to pages in the source database, the bigger your database snapshot sparse files become.
- A database snapshot can be done only for an entire database, not for a subset of the database.
- No additional changes can be made to a database snapshot. It is read-only and can't even have additional indexes created for it to make reporting queries run faster.
- Additional overhead is incurred on update operations on the source database due to the copy-on-write technique (not with SELECT statements).

- If you're using a database snapshot to revert (restore) a source database, neither the snapshot nor source database is available.
- The source database cannot be dropped, detached, or restored until the database snapshot is dropped first.
- Files on the source database or the snapshot cannot be dropped.
- For the database snapshot to be used, the source database must also be online (unless the source database is a mirrored database).
- The database snapshot must be on the same SQL Server instance as the source database.
- Snapshots are read-only.
- Database snapshot files must be on NTFS only (not FAT 32 or RAW partitions).
- Full-text indexing is not supported.
- If a source database ever goes into a `RECOVERY_PENDING` status, the database snapshot also becomes unavailable.
- If a database snapshot ever runs out of disk space, it must be dropped; it is actually marked as `SUSPECT`.

This may seem like a lot of restrictions—and it is. But look to Microsoft to address many of these restrictions in future releases. These current restrictions may disqualify many folks from getting into the database snapshot business. Others will thrive in its use out of the box.

Copy-on-Write Technology

The copy-on-write technology that Microsoft first introduced with SQL Server 2005 is at the core of both database mirroring and database snapshot capabilities. How it is used in database mirroring is explained in Chapter 20. In this section, we walk through a typical transactional user's update of data in a source database.

As you can see in Figure 32.5, an update transaction is initiated against the `AdventureWorks` database (labeled A). As the data is being updated in the source database's data page and the change is written to the transaction log (labeled B), the copy-on-write technology also copies the original source database data page in its unchanged state to the sparse data file (also labeled B) and updates the metadata page references in the system catalog (also labeled B) with this movement.

The original source data page is still available to the database snapshot. This adds extra overhead to any transaction that updates, inserts, or deletes data from the source database. After the copy-on-write technology finishes its write on the sparse file, the original update transaction is properly committed, and acknowledgment is sent back to the user (labeled C).

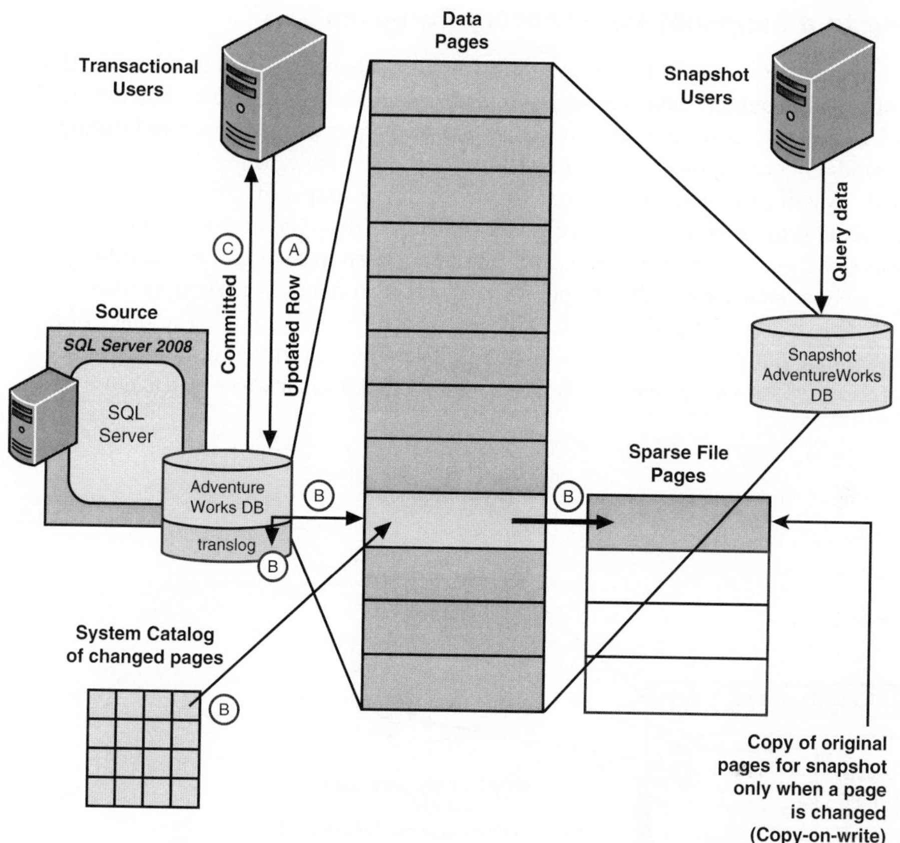

FIGURE 32.5 Using the copy-on-write technology with database snapshots.

NOTE

Database snapshots cannot be used for any of SQL Server's internal databases—`tempdb`, `master`, `msdb`, or `model`. Also, database snapshots are supported only in the Enterprise Edition of SQL Server 2008.

When to Use Database Snapshots

As mentioned previously, there are a few basic ways you can use database snapshots effectively. Each use is for a particular purpose, and each has its own benefits. After you have factored in the limitations and restrictions mentioned earlier, you can consider these uses. Let's look at each of them separately.

Reverting to a Snapshot for Recovery Purposes

Probably the most basic usage of database snapshots is decreasing recovery time of a database by restoring a troubled database with a database snapshot—referred to as *reverting*. As Figure 32.6 shows, one or more regularly scheduled snapshots can be generated during a 24-hour period, effectively providing you with data recovery milestones that can be rapidly used. As you can see in this example, four database snapshots are six hours apart (6:00 a.m., 12:00 p.m., 6:00 p.m., and 12:00 a.m.). Each is dropped and re-created once per day, using the same snapshot name. Any one of these snapshots can be used to recover the source database rapidly in the event of a logical data error (such as rows deleted or a table being dropped). This technique is not supposed to take the place of a good maintenance plan that includes full database backups and incremental transaction log dumps. However, it can be extremely fast to get a database back to a particular milestone.

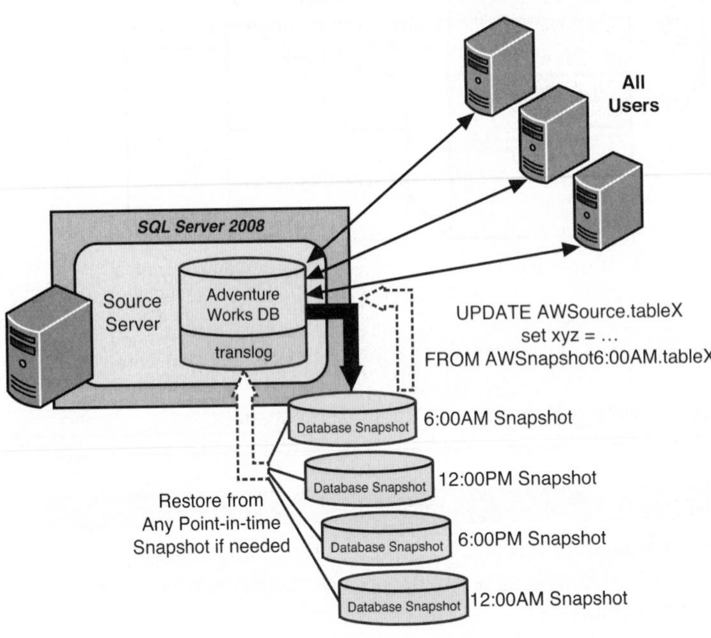

FIGURE 32.6 Basic database snapshot configuration: a source database and one or more database snapshots at different time intervals.

To revert to a particular snapshot interval, you simply use the `RESTORE DATABASE` command with the `FROM DATABASE_SNAPSHOT` statement. This is a complete database restore; you cannot limit it to just a single database object. In addition, you must drop all other database snapshots before you can use one of them to restore a database.

As you can also see in Figure 32.6, a targeted SQL statement variation from a complete database restore from a snapshot could be used instead if you knew exactly what you wanted to restore at the table and row level. You could simply use SQL statements (such as an UPDATE SQL statement or an INSERT SQL statement) from one of the snapshots to selectively apply only the fixes you are sure need to be recovered (reverted). In other words, you don't restore the whole database from the snapshot, you only use some of the snapshots' data with SQL statements and bring the messed-up data row values back in line with the original values in the snapshot. This is at the row and column level and usually requires quite a bit of detailed analysis before it can be applied to a production database.

It is also possible to use a snapshot to recover a table that someone accidentally dropped. There is a little data loss since the last snapshot, but it is a simple INSERT INTO statement from the latest snapshot before the table drop. So be careful here, but consider the value as well.

Safeguarding a Database Prior to Making Mass Changes

Often, you plan regular events against your database tables that result in some type of mass update being applied to big portions of the database. If you do a quick database snapshot *before* any of these types of changes, you are essentially creating a nice safety net for rapid recovery in the event you are not satisfied with the mass update results. Figure 32.7 illustrates this type of safeguarding technique.

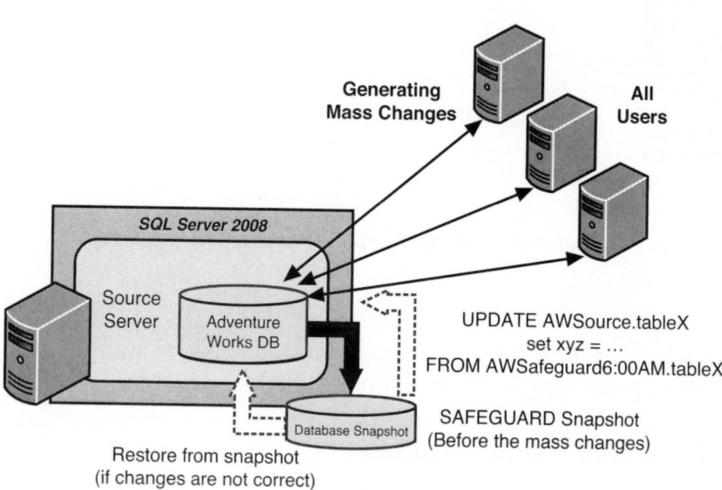

FIGURE 32.7 Creating a before database snapshot prior to scheduled mass updates to a database.

If you are not satisfied with the entire update operation, you can use RESTORE DATABASE from the snapshot and revert it to this point. Or, if you are happy with some updates but not others, you can use the SQL statement UPDATE to selectively update (restore) particular values back to their original values using the snapshot.

Providing a Testing (or Quality Assurance) Starting Point (Baseline)

In testing and the QA phases of your development life cycle, you often need to conduct tests over and over. These are either logic tests or even performance tests. To aid testing and QA, database snapshots can be made of a test database prior to full testing (create a testing baseline database snapshot) and then the test database can be reverted back to its original state at a moment's notice, using that baseline snapshot. This procedure can be done any number of times. Figure 32.8 shows how easy it is to simply create a testing reference point (or synchronization point) with a database snapshot.

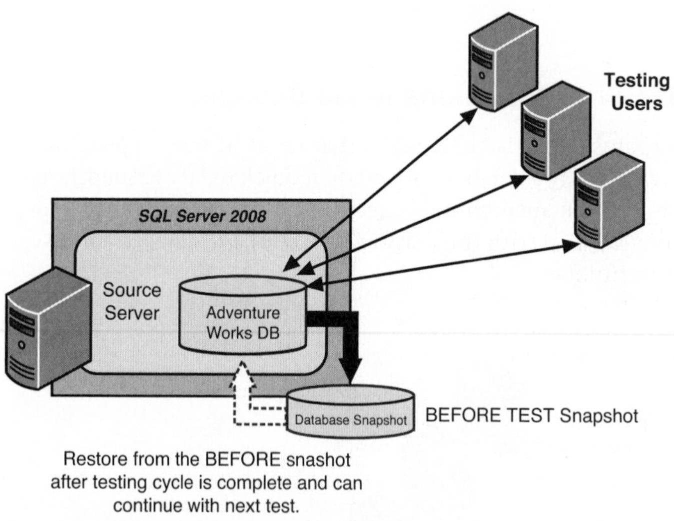

FIGURE 32.8 Establishing a baseline testing database snapshot before running tests and then reverting when finished.

You then just run your test scripts or do any manual testing—as much as you want—and then revert back to this starting point rapidly. Then you run more tests again.

Providing a Point-in-Time Reporting Database

If what you really need is a true point-in-time reporting database from which you can run ad hoc or canned reports, often a database snapshot can serve this purpose much better than resorting to log shipping or data replication. Key to determining when you can use this database snapshot technique is whether the reporting load on this database server instance can easily support the reporting workload and whether the update transactions against this database are adversely affected by the database snapshot overhead of each transaction. Figure 32.9 shows the typical database snapshot configuration for one or more database snapshots that are to be used for reporting.

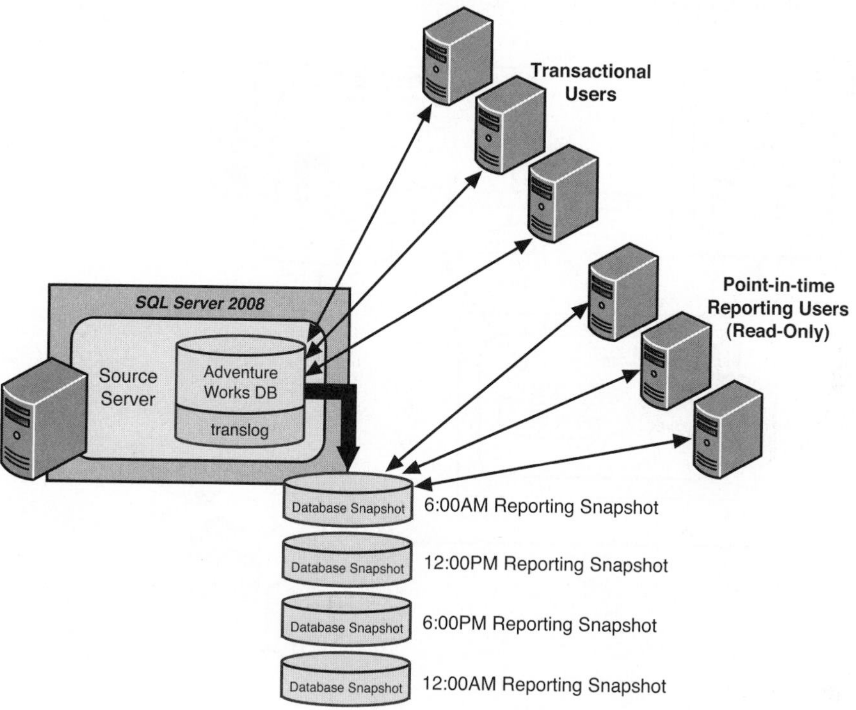

FIGURE 32.9 A point-in-time reporting database via a database snapshot.

Remember, this is a point-in-time snapshot of the source database. How frequently you need to create a new snapshot is dictated by your reporting requirements for data latency (how old the data can be in these reports).

Providing a Highly Available and Offloaded Reporting Database from a Database Mirror

If you are using database mirroring to improve your availability, you can also create a database snapshot against this mirrored database and expose the snapshot to your reporting users. Even though the mirrored database cannot be used for any access whatsoever (it is in constant restore mode), SQL Server allows a snapshot to be created against it (as shown in Figure 32.10). This is a very powerful configuration in that a database snapshot against a mirror does not impact the load of the principal server—guaranteeing high performance against the principal server. Also, when the database snapshot is isolated over to the mirror server, the performance of the reporting users is also more predictable because they are not competing with the transactional users for resources on the principal server. The only real issues arise when the principal server fails over to the mirror database. You now have both transactional and reporting users using the same database server instance, and the performance of them all is affected.

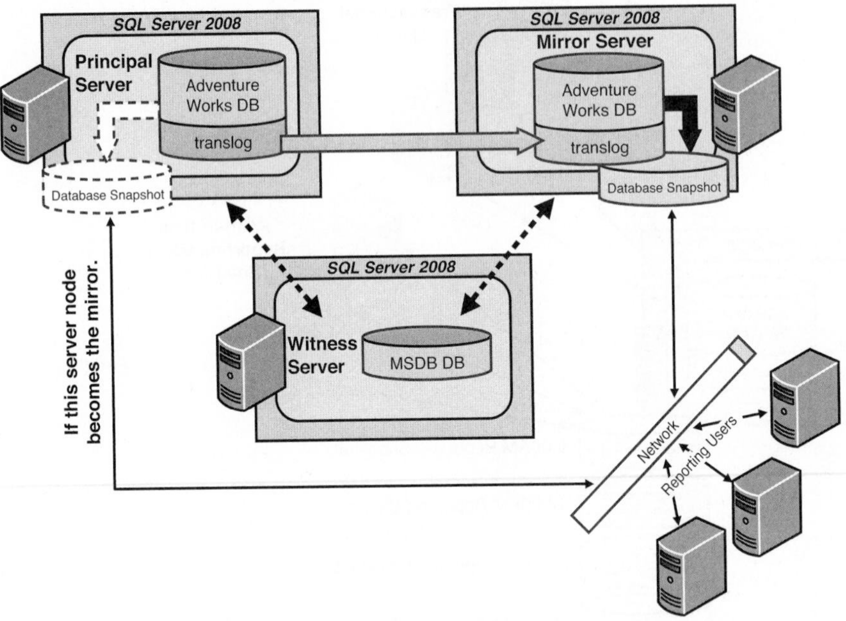

FIGURE 32.10 Creating a database snapshot for reporting against a mirrored database to offload the reporting impact on the principal server.

A possible solution to this situation would be to automatically (or manually) drop the database snapshot on the mirror server if it becomes the principal and create a new snapshot on the old principal server if it is available (it is now the mirror). You then just point all your reporting users to this new database snapshot. This task can be handled fairly easily in an application server layer. This solution is basically a reciprocal principal/mirror reporting configuration approach that always tries to get the database snapshot that is used for reporting to be on the server that is the mirror server. You would never really want to have active database snapshots on both the principal server and mirror server at the same time. This is way too much overhead for both servers. You want just the database snapshots to be on the mirror server. For a full explanation of all the capabilities of a database mirroring configuration, refer to Chapter 20.

Setup and Breakdown of a Database Snapshot

You might actually be surprised to find out how easily you can set up a database snapshot. This simplicity is partly due to the level at which database snapshots are created: at the database level and not at the table level. Setting up a database snapshot only entails running a CREATE DATABASE with the AS SNAPSHOT OF statement. You cannot create database snapshots from SQL Server Management Studio or from any other GUI or wizard for that matter. All must be done using SQL scripts. All SQL scripts for this chapter are available to you as a download from the Sams Publishing website for this book title (www.samspublishing.com) and on this book's CD. The script file, named DBSnapshotSQL2008.sql, also contains a variety of other useful SQL statements to help you better manage a database snapshot environment.

Creating a Database Snapshot

One of the first things you must figure out before you create a database snapshot is whether your source database data portion has more than one physical file in its allocation. All these file references must be accounted for in the snapshot. You execute the system stored procedure sp_helpdb with the source database name as the parameter, as shown here:

```
EXEC SP_HELPDB AdventureWorks
Go
```

The detailed file allocations of this database are as follows:

```
Name                          FileID        File Name
AdventureWorks_Data   1       C:\Server\
MSSQL10.SQL08DE01\MSSQL\DATA\AdventureWorks_Data.mdf
AdventureWorks_Log    2       C:\Server\
MSSQL10.SQL08DE01\MSSQL\DATA\AdventureWorks_Log.ldf
```

You need to worry about only the data portion of the database for the snapshot:

```
CREATE DATABASE SNAP_AdventureWorks_6AM
ON
 ( NAME = AdventureWorks_Data,
   FILENAME= 'C:\Server\ MSSQL10.SQL08DE01\MSSQL\DATA\SNAP_AW_data_6AM.snap'
AS SNAPSHOT OF AdventureWorks
go
```

Creating the database snapshot is really that easy. Now let's walk through a simple example showing how to create a series of four database snapshots against the AdventureWorks source database that represent snapshots six hours apart (refer to Figure 32.6). Here is the next snapshot to be run at 12:00 p.m.:

```
CREATE DATABASE SNAP_AdventureWorks_12PM
ON
 ( NAME = AdventureWorks_Data,
   FILENAME= 'C:\Server\ MSSQL10.SQL08DE01\MSSQL\DATA\SNAP_AW_data_12PM.snap')
AS SNAPSHOT OF AdventureWorks
go
```

These represent snapshots at equal time intervals and can be used for reporting or reverting.

NOTE

We use a simple naming convention for the database names for snapshots and for the snapshot files themselves. The database snapshot name is the word SNAP, followed by the source database name, followed by a qualifying description of what this snapshot represents, all separated with underscores. For example, a database snapshot that represents a 6:00 a.m. snapshot of the AdventureWorks database would have this name:

```
"SNAP_AdventureWorks_6AM"
```

The snapshot file-naming convention is similar. The name would start with the word SNAP, followed by the database name that the snapshot is for (AdventureWorks, in our example), followed by the data portion indication (for example, data, data1), a short identification of what this snapshot represents (for example, 6AM), and then the filename extension .snap to distinguish it from .mdf and .ldf files. For example, the snapshot filename for the preceding database snapshot would look like this:

```
"SNAP_AdventureWorks_data_6AM.snap"
```

We use the AdventureWorks database for this example. AdventureWorks currently uses only a single data file allocation for its data portion. Here's how you create the first snapshot, to reflect a 6:00 a.m. snapshot:

1. Create the snapshot on the source database AdventureWorks:

```
Use [master]
go
CREATE DATABASE SNAP_AdventureWorks_6AM
ON ( NAME = AdventureWorks_Data, FILENAME= 'C:\Program Files\
    Microsoft SQL Server\ MSSQL10.SQL08DE01\MSSQL\DATA\
    SNAP_AdventureWorks_data_6AM.snap')
AS SNAPSHOT OF AdventureWorks
   Go
```

2. Look at this newly created snapshot from the SQL Server instance point of view, using a SQL query against the sys.databases system catalog, as follows:

```
Use [master]
go
SELECT name,
       database_id,
       source_database_id, — source DB of the snapshot
       create_date,
       snapshot_isolation_state_desc
FROM sys.databases
   Go
```

This shows the existing source database and the newly created database snapshot:

```
name                 database_id source_database_id  create_date  snapshot_
                                                            isolation_state_desc
-------------------------------------------------------------------------------
AdventureWorks               7          NULL          2009-02-17 23:37:02.763
                                                                   OFF
SNAP_AdventureWorks_6AM   9           7          2009-12-05 06:18:36.597
                                                                      ON
```

Note that `source_database_id` for the newly created database snapshot contains the database ID of the source database. Of course, you can also look at the database snapshot properties by using SQL Server Management Studio, as shown in Figure 32.11.

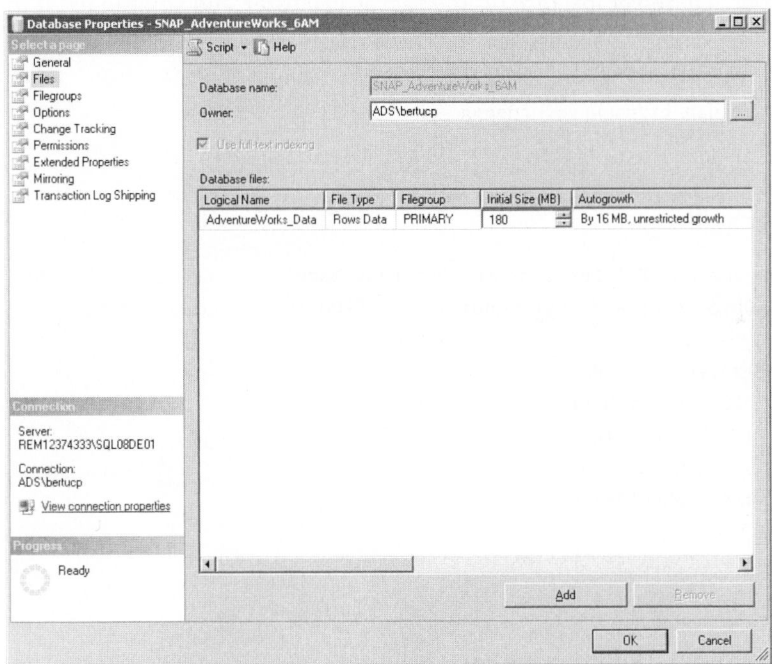

FIGURE 32.11 Using SQL Server Management Studio to view the database snapshot properties.

3. Look at the newly created physical file for the sparse file (for the database snapshot) by querying the `sys.master_files` system catalog:

```
SELECT database_id, file_id, name, physical_name
FROM sys.master_files
WHERE Name = 'AdventureWorks_data'
```

```
and is_sparse = 1
  go
```

Note that we are focusing on only the sparse files for the newly created database snapshot (that is, the `is_sparse = 1` qualification). This query results in the following:

```
database_id file_id     name                     physical_name
----------- ----------- -----------------------------------------------------
9           1          AdventureWorks_Data  C:\Prog...\DATA\
                                          SNAP_AdventureWorks_data_6AM.snap
```

4. To see the number of bytes that a snapshot sparse file is burning up, you can issue a series of SQL statements against system catalog views/tables by using `fn_virtualfilestats` and `sys.master_files`. However, the following is a quick-and-dirty stored procedure that should make this task much easier. Just create this stored procedure on your SQL Server instance (in the `master` database), and you can use it to see the sizes of any database snapshot sparse file on your server (also available in the downloadable SQL script file for this chapter):

```
CREATE PROCEDURE SNAP_SIZE_UNLEASHED2008
       @DBDATA varchar(255) = NULL
AS
if @DBDATA is not null
   BEGIN
      SELECT B.name as 'Sparse files for Database Name',
             A.DbId, A.FileId, BytesOnDisk      FROM fn_virtualfilestats
 (NULL, NULL) A,
           sys.master_files B
      WHERE A.DbID = B.database_id
        and A.FileID = B.file_id
        and B.is_sparse = 1
        and B.name = @DBDATA
   END
ELSE
   BEGIN
      SELECT B.name as 'Sparse files for Database Name',
             A.DbId, A.FileId, BytesOnDisk
      FROM fn_virtualfilestats (NULL, NULL) A,
           sys.master_files B
      WHERE A.DbID = B.database_id
        and A.FileID = B.file_id
        and B.is_sparse = 1
   END
  Go
```

When the `SNAP_SIZE_UNLEASHED2008` stored procedure is created, you run it with or without the name of the data portion of the database for which you have created a snapshot. If you do not supply the data portion name, you see all sparse files and their sizes on the SQL Server instance. The following example shows how to execute this stored procedure to see the sparse file current size for the AdventureWorks_data portion:

```
EXEC SNAP_SIZE_UNLEASHED2008 'AdventureWorks_Data'
  Go
```

This results in the detail bytes that the sparse file is using on disk:

```
Sparse files for Database Name  DbId   FileId   BytesOnDisk
------------------------------------------------------------------------------
  AdventureWorks_Data                 9      1       196608
```

Currently, the sparse file is very small (196KB) because it was recently created. Little to no source data pages have changed, so it is basically empty right now. It will start growing as data is updated in the source database and data pages are copied to the sparse file (by the copy-on-write mechanism). You can use the SNAP_SIZE_UNLEASHED2008 stored procedure to keep an eye on the sparse file size.

5. Believe it or not, the database snapshot is ready for you to use. The following SQL statement selects rows from this newly created database snapshot for a typical point-in-time–based query against the CreditCard table:

```
Use [SNAP_AdventureWorks_6AM]
go
SELECT [CreditCardID]
      ,[CardType]
      ,[CardNumber]
      ,[ExpMonth]
      ,[ExpYear]
      ,[ModifiedDate]
  FROM [SNAP_AdventureWorks_6AM].[Sales].[CreditCard]
WHERE CreditCardID = 1
  go
```

This statement delivers the correct, point-in-time result rows from the database snapshot:

```
CreditCardID CardType       CardNumber        ExpMonth ExpYear
                                                         ModifiedDate
______ ___________________________
                                                         ----------------
1            SuperiorCard   33332664695310    1        2010
                                                       2009-12-03 00:00:39.560
```

You can take a look at how this all looks from SQL Server Management Studio. Figure 32.12 shows the database snapshot database SNAP_AdventureWorks_6AM along with the source database AdventureWorks. It also shows the results of the system queries on these database object properties.

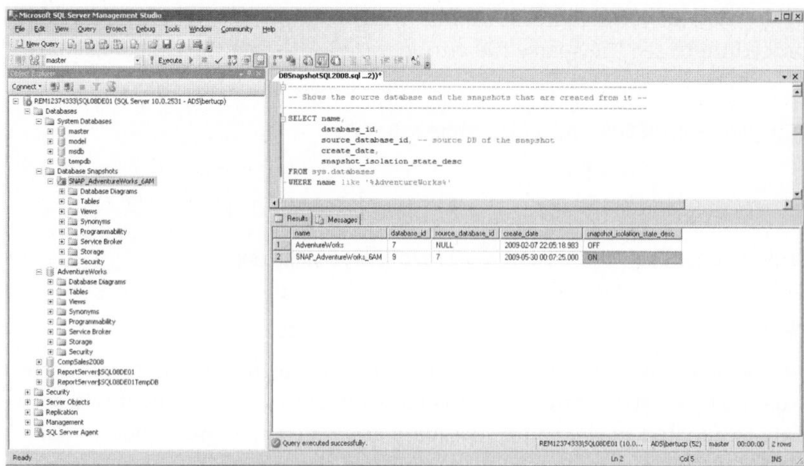

FIGURE 32.12 SSMS snapshot properties, system query results, and snapshot isolation state.

You are now in the database snapshot business!

Breaking Down a Database Snapshot

If you want to get rid of a snapshot or overlay a current snapshot with a more up-to-date snapshot, you simply use the `DROP DATABASE` command and then create it again. The `DROP DATABASE` command immediately removes the database snapshot entry and all sparse file allocations associated with the snapshot. It's very simple indeed. The following example drops the database snapshot just created:

```
Use [master]
go
DROP DATABASE SNAP_AdventureWorks_6AM
go
```

If you'd like, you can also drop (delete) a database snapshot from SQL Server Management Studio by right-clicking the database snapshot entry and choosing the Delete option. However, it's best to do everything with scripts so that you can accurately reproduce the same action over and over.

Reverting to a Database Snapshot for Recovery

If you have a database snapshot defined for a source database, you can use that snapshot to revert the source database to that snapshot's point-in-time milestone. In other words, you consciously overlay a source database with the point-in-time representation of that database (which you got when you created a snapshot). You must remember that you will lose all data changes that occurred from that point-in-time moment and the current state of the source database. However, this may be exactly what you intend.

Reverting a Source Database from a Database Snapshot

Reverting is just a logical term for using the DATABASE RESTORE command with the FROM DATABASE_SNAPSHOT statement. It effectively causes the point-in-time database snapshot to become the source database. Under the covers, much of this is managed from the system catalog metadata level. However, the results are that the source database will be in exactly the same state as the database snapshot. When you use a database snapshot as the basis of a database restore, all other database snapshots that have the same source database must first be dropped. Again, to see what database snapshots may be defined for a particular database, you can execute the following query:

```
Use [master]
go
SELECT name,
       database_id,
       source_database_id, — source DB of the snapshot
       create_date,
       snapshot_isolation_state_desc
FROM sys.databases
Go
```

This query shows the existing source database and the newly created database snapshot, as follows:

```
name                database_id source_database_id  create_date  snapshot_isolation_
                                                                     state_desc
------------------------------------------------------------------------------------

                                                                     ------------
AdventureWorks              7        NULL          2009-02-17 23:37:02.763
                                                                     OFF
SNAP_AdventureWorks_6AM    9          7          2009-12-05 06:01:36.597
                                                                     ON
SNAP_AdventureWorks_12PM  10          7           2009-12-05 12:00:36.227
                                                                     ON
```

In this example, there are two snapshots against the AdventureWorks database. The one you don't want to use when reverting must be dropped first. Then you can proceed to restore the source database with the remaining snapshot that you want. These are the steps:

1. Drop the unwanted snapshot(s):

```
Use [master]
go
DROP DATABASE SNAP_AdventureWorks_12PM
   go
```

2. Issue the RESTORE DATABASE command with the remaining snapshot:

```
USE [master]
```

```
go
RESTORE DATABASE AdventureWorks FROM DATABASE_SNAPSHOT =
'SNAP_AdventureWorks_6AM'
   go
```

When this process is complete, the source database and snapshot are essentially the same point-in-time database. But the source database quickly diverges, as updates begin to flow in again.

Using Database Snapshots with Testing and QA

Reverting to a "golden" copy of a database via a database snapshot is going to be popular going forward because of the simplicity that creating and reverting provides. Testing and QA groups will thrive on this feature, and this will directly affect the velocity of testing in your organization. With the increase in the frequency and stability of your testing and QA environments, a direct improvement in the quality of your application should be attainable. Essentially, these are the steps:

1. Create the golden database snapshot *before* you run your testing:

```
Use [master]
go
CREATE DATABASE SNAP_AdventureWorks_GOLDEN
ON ( NAME = AdventureWorks_Data, FILENAME= 'C:\Program Files\
    Microsoft SQL Server\ MSSQL10.SQL08DE01\MSSQL\DATA\
              SNAP_AdventureWorks_data_GOLDEN.snap')
AS SNAPSHOT OF AdventureWorks
   Go
```

2. Run tests or QA to your heart's content.
3. Revert to the golden copy when the testing is completed so that the process can be repeated again, regression testing can be run, stress testing can be done, performance testing can be started, or further application testing can be done:

```
USE [master]
go
RESTORE DATABASE AdventureWorks
FROM DATABASE_SNAPSHOT = 'SNAP_AdventureWorks_GOLDEN'
   go
```

Setting Up Snapshots Against a Database Mirror

If you are using database mirroring to improve your availability, you can also create a database snapshot against this mirrored database and expose the snapshot to your reporting users. Doing so further enhances the overall database availability to all end users (transactional and reporting users). In addition, it serves to isolate the reporting users from the transactional users. The reporting users are connected to the mirror server's version of the database (via a database snapshot of the mirrored database), and their reporting queries do not impact the principal server in any way. Remember that the mirrored database is not usable for any access whatsoever (it is in constant restore mode). SQL Server allows a snapshot to be created against it (refer to Figure 32.10). As mentioned previously, the only real issues arise when the principal server fails over to the mirror database. When the mirror server takes over for the principal, the database snapshot terminates its reporting user connections. The reporting users only need to reconnect to pick up where they left off. However, you now have both transactional and reporting users using the same database server instance, and performance of all is affected.

A possible solution to this situation would be to automatically (or manually) drop the database snapshot on the mirror server if it becomes the principal and create a new snapshot on the old principal server if it is available (it is now the mirror). You then just point all your reporting users to this new database snapshot. This process can be handled fairly easily in an application server layer. This is basically a reciprocal principal/mirror reporting configuration approach that always tries to get the database snapshot that is used for reporting to be on the server that is the mirror server. You would never really want to have active database snapshots on both the principal server and mirror server at the same time.

Reciprocal Principal/Mirror Reporting Configuration

The following steps outline the method to create the snapshot on the mirror, drop it when the mirror becomes the principal, and create a new snapshot against the old principal (now the mirror):

1. Create the database snapshot on a mirrored database server for reporting on the mirror server (`REM12374333\SQL08DE02`):

```
Use [master]
go
CREATE DATABASE SNAP_AdventureWorks_REPORTING
ON ( NAME = AdventureWorks_Data, FILENAME= 'C:\Program Files\
    Microsoft SQL Server\MSSQL10.SQL08DE02\MSSQL\DATA\
       SNAP_AdventureWorks_data_REPORTING.snap')
AS SNAPSHOT OF AdventureWorks
  Go
```

   As you can see in Figure 32.13, this would be the live configuration of the principal server (`REM12374333\SQL08DE01`), the mirror server (`REM12374333\SQL08DE02`), and the reporting database snapshot (`SNAP_AdventureWorks_REPORTING`), as shown from SQL Server Management Studio.

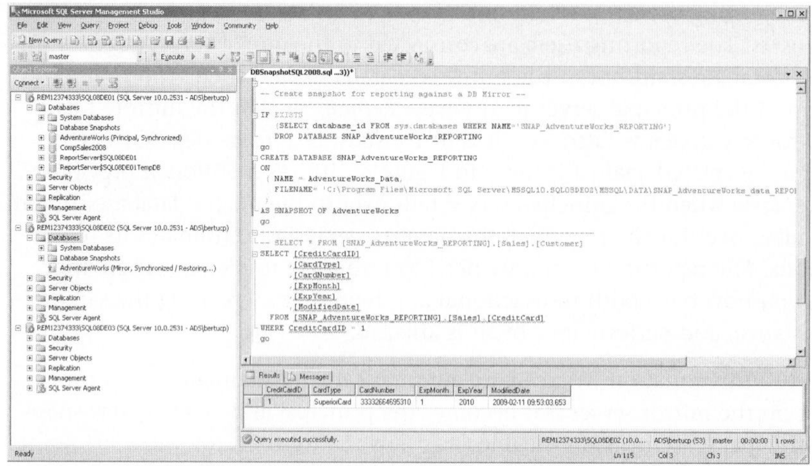

FIGURE 32.13 SQL Server Management Studio, showing database mirroring with a database snapshot for reporting configuration.

If the principal fails over to the mirror, you would drop the database snapshot that is currently created off that database and create a new one on the old principal (now the mirror), as shown in the following steps.

2. Drop the reporting database snapshot on the new principal server (the principal is now REM12374333\SQL08DE02):

```
Use [master]
go
DROP DATABASE SNAP_AdventureWorks_REPORTING
  go
```

3. Create the new reporting database snapshot on the new mirrored database server (the mirror is now REM12374333\SQL08DE01):

```
Use [master]
go
CREATE DATABASE SNAP_AdventureWorks_REPORTING
ON ( NAME = AdventureWorks_Data, FILENAME= 'C:\Program Files\
    Microsoft SQL Server\ MSSQL10.SQL08DE01\MSSQL\DATA\
        SNAP_AdventureWorks_data_REPORTING.snap')
AS SNAPSHOT OF AdventureWorks
  Go
```

That's it. You now have your reporting users completely isolated away from your principal server (and the transactional users) again. Life can return to normal very quickly.

Database Snapshots Maintenance and Security Considerations

With regard to database snapshots, several things need to be highly managed: snapshot sparse file size management, data latency management that corresponds to your users' needs, the location of the sparse files within your physical deployment, the sheer number of database snapshots you are willing to support against a single database instance, and the security and access needs of users of database snapshots.

Security for Database Snapshots

By default, you get the security roles and definitions that you have created in the source database available to you within the database snapshot *except* for roles or individual permissions that you have in the source database used for updating data or objects. This is referred to as "inherited from the source database." These updating rights are not available to you in a database snapshot. A database snapshot is a read-only database! If you have specialized roles or restrictions you want to be present in the database snapshot, you need to define them in the source database, and you get them instantly. You manage from a single place, and everyone is happy.

Snapshot Sparse File Size Management

Sparse file size is probably the most critical aspect to deal with when managing database snapshots. It is imperative that you keep a close watch on the growing size of any (and all) database snapshot sparse files you create. If your snapshot runs out of space because you didn't manage file size well, it becomes suspect and is not available to use. The only path out of this scenario is to drop the snapshot and re-create it. Following are some issues to consider for sparse files:

- Monitor sparse files regularly. Make use of stored procedures such as the `SNAP_SIZE_UNLEASHED2008` stored procedure to help with this situation.
- Pay close attention to the volatility of the source database. This rate of change directly translates to the size of the sparse file and how fast it grows. The rule of thumb is to match your drop and re-create of a database snapshot frequency to when the sparse file is at around 30% of the size of the source database. Your data latency user requirements may demand a faster rate of drop/re-create.
- Isolate sparse files away from the source database data files. You do not want to compete with disk arm movement in any way. Always work to get disk I/O as parallel as possible.

Number of Database Snapshots per Source Database

In general, you shouldn't have too many database snapshots defined on a database because of the copy-on-write overhead each snapshot requires. However, this all depends on the volatility of the source database and a server's capacity. If there is low volatility and the server is not using much CPU, memory, and disk capacity, this database could more readily support many separate database snapshots at once. If the volatility is high and CPU, memory, and perhaps disk capacity are saturated, you should minimize drastically the number of database snapshots.

Summary

Database snapshots can be thought of as an enabling capability with many purposes. They are great for fulfilling point-in-time reporting requirements easily, reverting a database to a point in time (recoverability and availability), insulating a database from issues that may arise during mass updates, and potentially reducing the processing impact of querying against the primary transactional databases (via database mirroring and database snapshots). You must remember that database snapshots are point in time and read-only. The only way to update a snapshot is to drop it and re-create it. Data latency of this point-in-time snapshot capability must always be made very clear to any of its users.

Database snapshots are snapshots of the entire database, not a subset. This clearly makes data snapshots very different from alternative data access capabilities such as data replication and materialized views. This feature has been made possible via a major breakthrough from Microsoft called copy-on-write technology. This is certainly an exciting extension to SQL Server but is not to be used as a substitute for good old database backups and restores. This is one capability that we recommend you consider using as soon as possible.

Chapter 33, "Database Maintenance," provides a detailed explanation of the best practices surrounding maintaining a database.

CHAPTER 33

Database Maintenance

IN THIS CHAPTER

- What's New in Database Maintenance
- The Maintenance Plan Wizard
- Managing Maintenance Plans Without the Wizard
- Executing a Maintenance Plan
- Maintenance Without a Maintenance Plan
- Database Maintenance Policies

Database maintenance is an essential part of database administration needed to keep databases healthy. It includes tasks performed after your database is created to ensure the integrity of the data in the database, provide performance improvements, and help keep your database safe.

This chapter examines some of the key tasks that should be included in your database maintenance plan. It discusses the means for creating these plans, including tools such as the Maintenance Plan Wizard that is part of SQL Server 2008. These tools make the creation of a solid database maintenance plan easier and provide a framework that allows you to create the plan once and let automation do the rest of the work.

What Needs to Be Maintained

The core tasks related to the maintenance of a SQL Server database are backing up the database and log, rebuilding indexes, updating statistics, and running integrity checks against the database. These ongoing, repetitive tasks are best run on a scheduled basis and are the backbone of the maintenance plan. Other tasks related to maintenance involve managing access by the users, maintaining data files, and monitoring performance. These tasks are more apt to be performed on an ad hoc basis when the need arises.

What's New in Database Maintenance

The required database maintenance tasks in SQL Server 2008 have remained the same as in earlier versions, and the tools to perform that maintenance are generally the same as they were in SQL Server 2005. Maintenance plans are still the core tool for performing database maintenance. These plans and the tools to create the plans (such as the Maintenance Plan Wizard) look and behave much like they did in SQL Server 2005. Enhancements to the maintenance plans that were introduced in SQL Server 2005 service packs have been carried on to SQL Server 2008.

One new feature related to database maintenance in SQL Server 2008 is the introduction of Database Maintenance Policies (a subset of the Policy-Based Management feature introduced in SQL Server 2008). Policy-Based Management is discussed in detail in Chapter 22, "Administering Policy-Based Management." In this chapter, we briefly cover the basics of using policies for performing database maintenance.

The Maintenance Plan Wizard

The Maintenance Plan Wizard is a tool that is available in SSMS. It provides an automated means for creating the basic tasks needed to maintain a database. It does not include all the tasks available for use in a maintenance plan but is a great starting point that allows you to quickly generate the basic elements of a good plan.

You launch the Maintenance Plan Wizard by expanding the `Management` node in SSMS and then right-clicking Maintenance Plans and selecting Maintenance Plan Wizard. The Maintenance Plan Wizard is like most other Microsoft wizards in that it presents sequential dialog boxes that allow you to incrementally provide the information needed to create the wizard's objective.

The Maintenance Plan Wizard first displays an introductory dialog box. When you click Next, it displays a dialog box (like the one shown in Figure 33.1) that allows you to specify the name and a description for your maintenance plan. You should choose a naming convention that will allow you to easily identify a maintenance plan and the type of maintenance it is performing. The name is displayed in the Object Explorer tree, and a good naming convention will make it easier to locate the plan you want.

The Select Plan Properties screen also allows you to specify the schedule for the maintenance plan. This schedule will be tied to the corresponding scheduled job that is created when the Maintenance Plan Wizard completes. You will find that the scheduling dialog that appears when you click on the Change button is very flexible and consistent with other places in SQL Server where a schedule can be defined.

After you name the maintenance plan and specify the schedule, you can click Next. The dialog box that appears next allows you to select the maintenance tasks you would like to perform on the server. Figure 33.2 shows the Select Maintenance Tasks dialog, with the tasks that are available from the wizard. You can select more than one task for a given plan. As mentioned earlier, the tasks listed in the wizard are not all the tasks available in a maintenance plan.

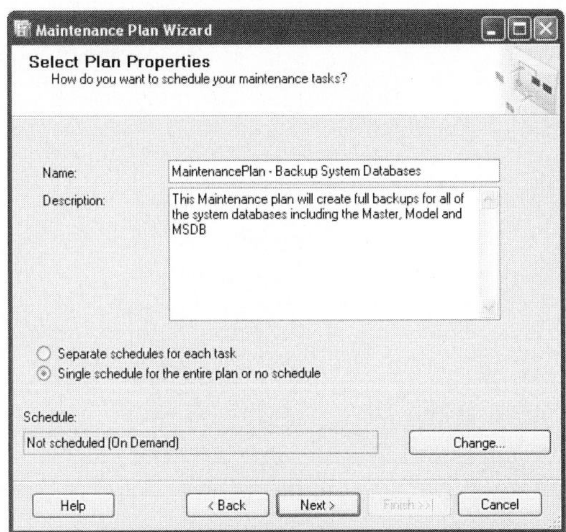

FIGURE 33.1 Setting the Maintenance Plan Properties using the Maintenance Plan Wizard.

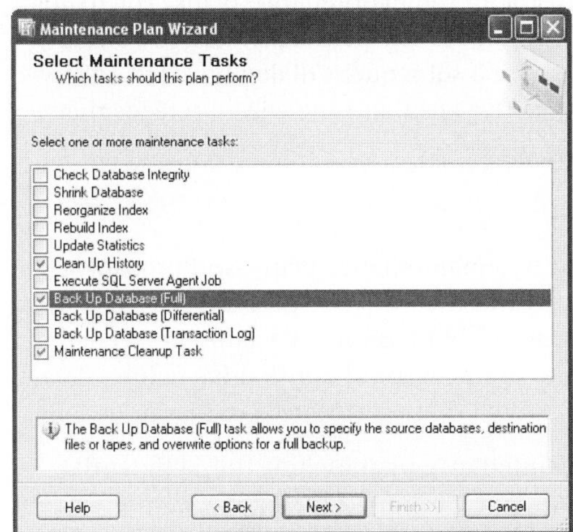

FIGURE 33.2 Selecting maintenance tasks in the Maintenance Plan Wizard.

The dialog box that appears next, as shown in Figure 33.3, allows you to specify the order in which the tasks are executed. Obviously, the order of the tasks can be a critical factor and is dependent on the type of tasks you are running. You can click the Move Up and Move Down buttons to change the order of the tasks.

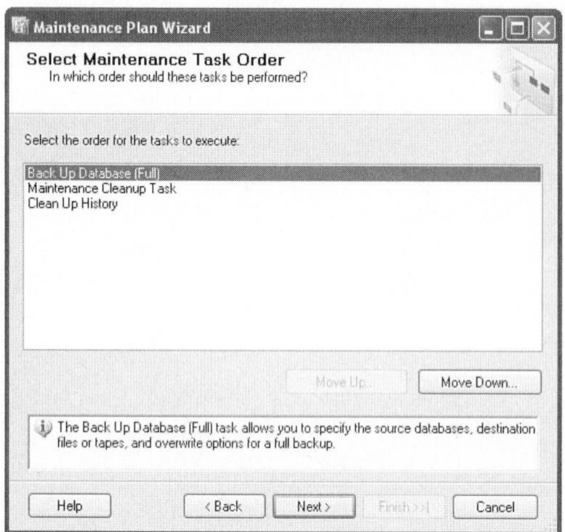

FIGURE 33.3 Selecting the order of the maintenance tasks in the Maintenance Plan Wizard.

The dialog boxes discussed so far are consistent for all the maintenance plans. The dialog boxes that follow are dependent on the tasks selected for the plan. Each task has a relevant set of properties that are displayed for entry in a subsequent dialog box. The following sections cover some of the common maintenance tasks and the wizard screens that relate to them.

Backing Up Databases

Backing up databases is the most basic element of a maintenance plan—and probably the most important part. The importance of backups and the role they play are discussed in detail in Chapter 14, "Database Backup and Restore," but basically, backups are needed to help limit the amount of data loss. For example, in the event of a disk drive failure, database backups can be used to restore the database data that was located on that drive.

The database backup options available via a maintenance plan include full, differential, and transaction log backups. The type of backup you select for a plan is heavily dependent on the type of environment you are maintaining and the type of database you are backing up. Databases that have very few changes may only need a nightly full backup and do not require transaction log or differential backups.

In most cases, it is a good idea to take a full backup of your system and user databases each night. Figure 33.4 shows the backup options the wizard displays for a full backup.

To set the properties for a full backup, you need to first define the databases you want to back up. You select the databases by using the Databases drop-down at the top of the screen. This drop-down is unique in that it gives you a variety of radio button options

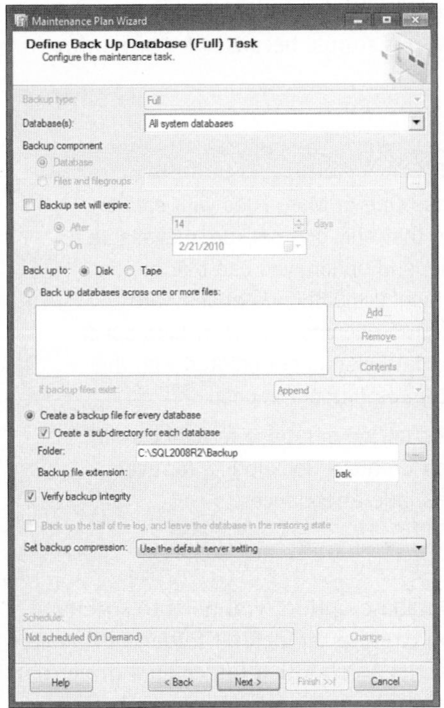

FIGURE 33.4 Full backup options in the Maintenance Plan Wizard.

rather than just a simple list. You can choose to back up all databases, all system databases, or all user databases, or you can select specific databases.

After you select the database(s) you want to back up, you must select a destination for the backup files. The destination includes the type of media (that is, tape or disk) and the file or files on that medium. The option Back Up Databases Across One or More Files allows you to specify one or more fixed files that the database backup will always be written to. With this option, you can choose to append each backup to the file(s) or overwrite the contents of the file(s) each time the backup is performed. If you choose to overwrite the backup each time, you have only the latest backup available for restoration. If you choose to append to the file, older backups are retained on this file, and the file continues to grow with each subsequent backup.

The preferred option for creating full backups with the wizard is the option Create a Backup File for Every Database. This option creates a separate file for each database in the maintenance plan. The backup file that is created has the database name as the first part of the filename, followed by `_backup_` and then a time stamp that indicates when the backup was created. For example, a backup named `AdventureWorks2008_backup_200608231402.bak` would be a backup file created using this option for the `AdventureWorks2008` database. Multiple versions of backups can be retained with this option, and the identification of the backup is simple because of the naming convention.

CAUTION

You should use the option Back Up Databases Across One or More Files with caution. The pitfall with overwriting the file with this option is that only one backup is available for restoration. When this option is used with the Append option, you can eat up all your disk space if the file is not cleaned up. In addition, if multiple databases are backed up with the plan, all these backups will be spread across the file or files specified for the destination. A separate backup for each database is not created with this option. This can lead to confusion and complicate the restoration process.

Generally speaking, you should steer clear of backing up the database to a single file or set of files. Instead, you should choose the option Create a Backup File for Every Database. This option has fewer pitfalls and requires little attendance.

When you use the Create a Backup File for Every Database option, you need to specify a folder for the database backups to be written to. You can use the default folder, or you can change it to a folder of your choice. It is a good practice to choose a folder on a drive that is different from the drive where your database files reside. Having backups on the same drive as your data could be a big problem if that drive fails and your only backups are on that drive. If you select the option Create a Sub-directory for Each Database, each database has a separate subfolder under the folder specified for the backup.

CAUTION

The main pitfall associated with the option Create a Backup File for Every Database is that many backup files can be created and are not automatically deleted by default. This point has been mentioned already, but it is a critical consideration. The good news is that you can now add the deletion of the older backups to the maintenance plan using the Maintenance Plan Wizard. To accomplish this, you need to select the Maintenance Cleanup task and provide the desired retention information that determines when the older backups are removed.

Another useful option on the Define Back Up Database screen is Verify Backup Integrity. If you select this option, SQL Server checks the integrity of the backup files that were written as part of the backup operation. Selecting this option extends the execution time for the backup plan but is generally a good idea to ensure that you have a viable backup for recovery. It is particularly useful when backups have been written across multiple files. Unfortunately, the backup task does not allow you to utilize the checksum options available with the SQL Server 2008 `BACKUP` command, but the basic `VERIFY` option suffices in most instances.

New to SQL Server 2008 is an option to define the compression for the database backup file. The Set Backup Compression drop-down at the bottom of the screen determines whether compression will be used. If the default for the server is set to compress backup or the specific option Compress Backup is selected, the backup file is created in a compressed format that will reduce the size of the backup file and save disk space. The trade-off when using compressed backups is that the creation of these backups takes additional CPU resources during their creation. However, the additional CPU processing time is typically offset by the faster I/O as a result of the reduced size of the backup file.

NOTE

In SQL Server 2008, compressed backups can only be performed in the Enterprise Edition. Beginning in SQL Server 2008 R2, compressed backups can be created in the Standard and all higher editions of SQL Server 2008 R2. Every edition of SQL Server 2008 and later can restore compressed backups, however.

Checking Database Integrity

The Define Database Check Integrity Task screen of the Maintenance Plan Wizard, shown in Figure 33.5, allows you to schedule the database consistency command `DBCC CHECKDB`, which checks the data pages for inconsistencies and is a good tool for ensuring that a database is healthy. The integrity checks can be made before each backup or on an independent schedule.

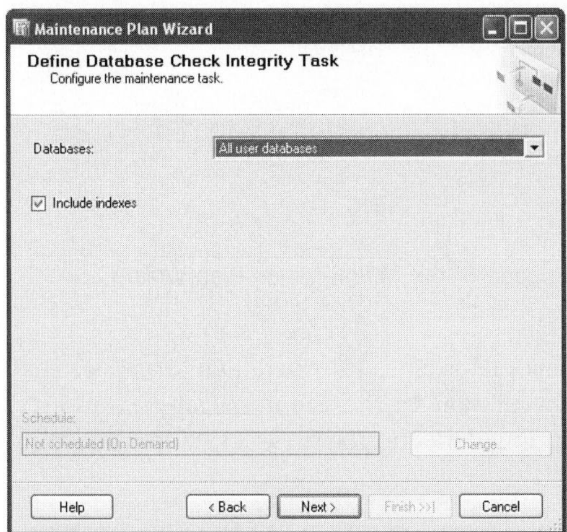

FIGURE 33.5 The Define Database Check Integrity Task screen of the Maintenance Plan Wizard.

The options available for checking database integrity via the wizard are limited.

Checking the Include Indexes check box causes integrity checks to be performed on the index pages as well. Checking the index pages for each table extends the amount of time the task runs, but it is the most thorough way to perform an integrity check. If problems are found, you can run the DBCC CHECKDB command manually with additional options to repair the problems. For more information on resolving DBCC errors, see Chapter 56, "SQL Server Disaster Recovery Planning" (on the CD). In some cases, the problems cannot be fixed without the possibility of data loss. You should consider contacting Microsoft support if you receive consistency errors in a critical database.

Shrinking Databases

The Define Shrink Database Task page of the Maintenance Plan Wizard, shown in Figure 33.6, can be useful for keeping the size of your databases manageable. As its name implies, this task is used to reduce the overall size of a database. This task's execution is essentially the equivalent to running the DBCC SHRINKDATABASE command, and it contains task options that mirror the options available with the DBCC command.

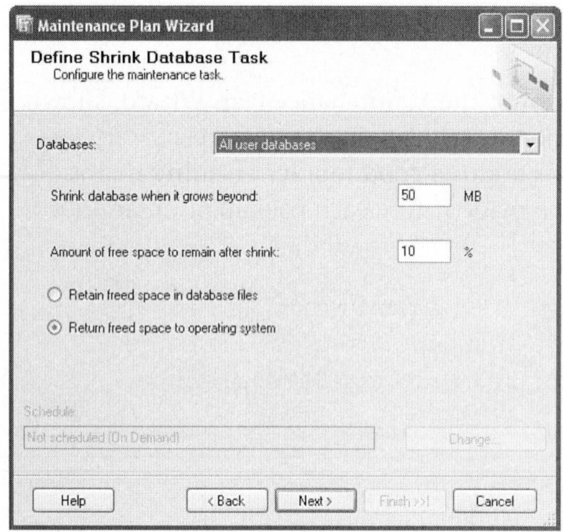

FIGURE 33.6 The Define Shrink Database Task page of the Maintenance Plan Wizard.

The setting Shrink Database When It Grows Beyond specifies the overall database size that must be exceeded for the shrink operation to occur. You set the size in megabytes, and it must be a whole number. If the database, including data and log files, is smaller than this size, the shrink operation does not occur.

The remaining options determine how the shrink operation runs when the shrink threshold is exceeded. The Amount of Free Space to Remain After Shrink option determines how much space is left in the database files after the shrink operation is finished. This is a target percentage and may not be feasible if the amount of disk space is limited. SQL Server does its best to achieve the target percentage, but it is not guaranteed. Generally, in environments where you have abundant disk space, it is best to leave at least 10% free after the operation so that the database can grow without the need for expanding the size of the database files.

The last settings on the screen determine how free space beyond the target percentage is handled. For example, let's assume that a large number of rows were deleted from a database and the target free space percentage is set to 10%. The shrink operation is run and is able to shrink the database such that 40% is now free. You can choose to retain in the database files the 30% beyond the target that is free by selecting the Retain Freed Space in Database Files option. Choosing this option is the same as running the `DBCC SHRINK DATABASE` command with the `NOTRUNCATE` option. With this option, you do not see any changes to the size of the database files, and the free space on the disk remains unchanged.

The other option, Return Freed Space to Operating System, can reduce the size of the database files and return that space to the operating system. This option utilizes the `TRUNCATEONLY` option that comes with the `DBCC SHRINK DATABASE` command and is the option needed to free up disk space on a server.

TIP

Running the Shrink Database task for every database is not necessarily a good idea. With the Shrink Database task, the database is condensed so that the data is located on contiguous pages in the database data file(s). This involves the movement of pages from one part of the file to another. This movement can cause fragmentation in tables and indexes. The fragmentation can, in turn, cause performance problems and undo work that may have been done with other tasks, such as rebuilding the indexes.

The other problem with shrinking the database relates to the cost of expanding the database at a later time. For example, let's say you have a database that has grown to 1GB. You shrink the database so that it is now only 800MB, but normal use of the database causes it to expand again. The expansion of the database files can be expensive and cause performance problems during the actual expansion, especially on high-volume production systems. The best solution is to purchase the appropriate amount of disk space and size the database so that database files do not need to expand frequently and the shrink operation is not needed. This is easier said than done, but it is the right answer nonetheless.

Maintaining Indexes and Statistics

Maintaining indexes and statistics is essential in most database environments, including those that have frequent changes to the data. These changes can cause tables and their indexes to become fragmented and inefficient. These types of environments can also lead to outdated statistics on indexes. Outdated statistics can cause the query engine to make less-than-optimal choices when determining the best access path to the data.

The maintenance of indexes and statistics is facilitated through the use of three different tasks in the Maintenance Plan Wizard: Reorganize Index, Rebuild Index, and Update Statistics. Using the Reorganize Index task is equivalent to running the `ALTER INDEX REORGANIZE` command. This task defragments and compacts clustered and nonclustered indexes on tables and views. This helps improve index-scanning performance and should improve overall response time. The operation is always done online and is also equivalent to running the `DBCC INDEXDEFRAG` command.

Figure 33.7 shows the screen you use to define the Reorganize Index task. This screen allows you select tables, views, or tables and views. You can also select specific tables or views that you want to reorganize. The Compact Large Objects option is equivalent to `ALTER INDEX LOB_COMPACTION = ON`. It causes data in large object (LOB) data types, such as `image` or `text` objects, to be compacted.

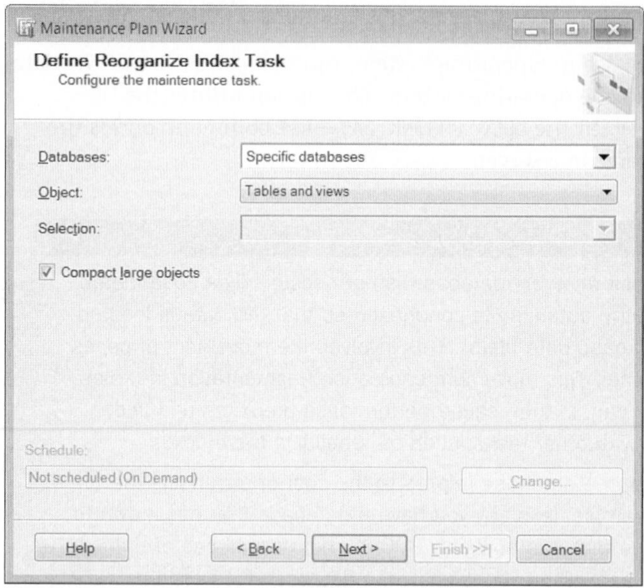

FIGURE 33.7 The Reorganize Index task options in the Maintenance Plan Wizard.

The Reorganize Index task moves the leaf-level pages so that they match the logical ordering of the index. This behavior improves performance, but it is not as extensive as the Rebuild Index task, which is equivalent to the `ALTER INDEX REBUILD` command. It is also equivalent to the `DBCC DBREINDEX` command. When the Rebuild Index task is executed, it rebuilds the indexes from scratch. This rebuilding can achieve the best performance results, but it also has the most impact on users of the database.

Figure 33.8 shows the options available for rebuilding an index with the Maintenance Plan Wizard.

The options for rebuilding are separated into two sections: Free Space Options and Advanced Options. The Free Space Options section pertains to the amount of free space left in the index pages after the rebuild operation completes. This free space is defined by the fill factor for the index. When the Reorganize Pages with the Default Amount of Free Space option is used, the fill factor is reset to the value used when the index was created. The other option, Change Free Space per Page Percentage To, allows you to choose a new fill factor value to be used for all indexes that have been selected for the rebuild operation.

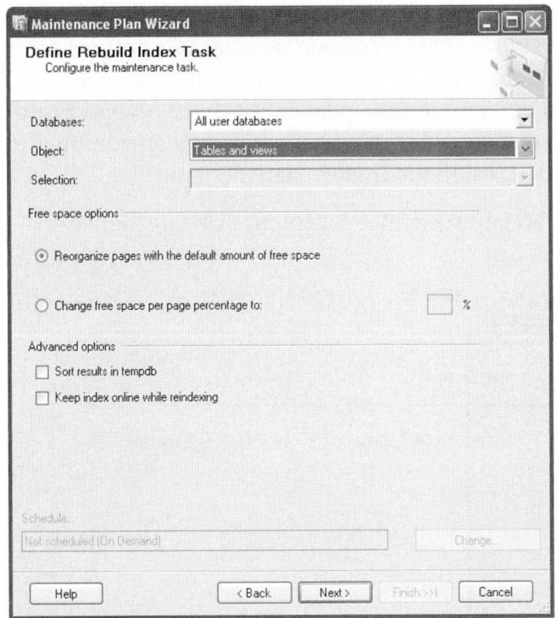

FIGURE 33.8 The Rebuild Index task options in the Maintenance Plan Wizard.

The following advanced Rebuild Index task options are available:

- **Sort Results in `tempdb`**—This option is equivalent to the `SORT_IN_TEMPDB` option for the index. It causes `tempdb` to be used to store intermediate results while rebuilding the index. If this option is not used, these intermediate results are stored in the database in which the index resides. Storing the results in `tempdb` can help prevent unnecessary growth of the user database in which the index is being rebuilt.
- **Keep Index Online While Reindexing**—This option is equivalent to the `ONLINE` option for the index. It allows users to access the underlying table and associated indexes during the index rebuild operation. If this option is not used, the index rebuild is on offline operation, and a table lock is held on the table that is having its indexes rebuilt.

These index options and further information regarding indexes are discussed in Chapter 25, "Creating and Managing Indexes." Refer to Chapter 34, "Data Structures, Indexes, and Performance," for details on the performance impact of some of the index options discussed.

The maintenance of statistics can be just as important as the maintenance of indexes on a table. Statistics contain information about the distribution of data in tables and indexes and provide valuable information to the SQL Server query engine. When the statistics are outdated, the query engine may not make the best decisions for getting the data.

Fortunately, there are database options that cause statistics to be automatically updated. The AUTO UPDATE STATISTICS and AUTO UPDATE STATISTICS ASYNCHRONOUSLY options cause index statistics to be created automatically. However, in some situations the automatic update of statistics does not happen often enough, or the update happens at inopportune times and can cause performance issues. You can address these situations by scheduling the updating of statistics via a maintenance plan, using the Update Statistics task.

Figure 33.9 shows the Maintenance Plan Wizard screen for setting the Update Statistics task options.

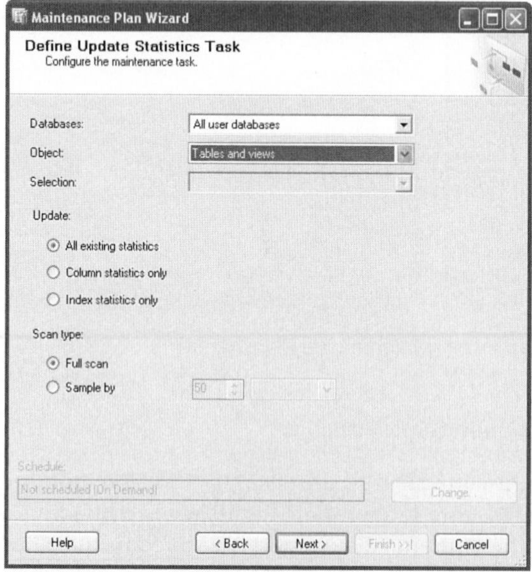

FIGURE 33.9 The Update Statistics task options in the Maintenance Plan Wizard.

The top portion of the Define Update Statistics Task screen is much like the option screens for maintaining indexes. You can choose the type of objects (tables or views) on which you want to update statistics, or you can focus on specific tables or views. The Update options at the bottom of the screen identify the types of statistics to be updated. If the All Existing Statistics option is selected, statistics for both indexes and columns are updated. Statistics on columns exist if the AUTO CREATE STATISTICS option has been set to ON or the statistics were manually created. The other two update options on the screen allow you to focus the update of statistics on columns only or indexes only.

Scheduling a Maintenance Plan

One of the greatest features of a maintenance plan is that you can schedule it. Scheduling takes manual work off your plate and provides consistency that might be missed if the plan had to be run manually. History is kept for each of the scheduled executions, which provides an audit trail, and notifications can be tied to the scheduled plans to allow a user to respond to failures or other results from the plan.

A schedule can be created for an entire maintenance plan or individual schedules can be created for each task in the plan. The scheduling selection is available on the Select Plan Properties screen, which is one of the first screens displayed while using the Maintenance Plan Wizard (refer to Figure 33.1). Choose the Separate Schedules for Each Task option to create a schedule for each task. The default option is Single Schedule for the Entire Plan or No Schedule. If you choose the option for separate schedules, the Schedule Change button is enabled on the task definition screen and this schedule is tied to that specific task.

Both scheduling options utilize the same scheduling screen. The screen to set scheduling options, the Job Schedule Properties dialog box shown in Figure 33.10, appears when you click on the Schedule Change button. This screen contains the same flexible scheduling features available in the SQL Server Agent.

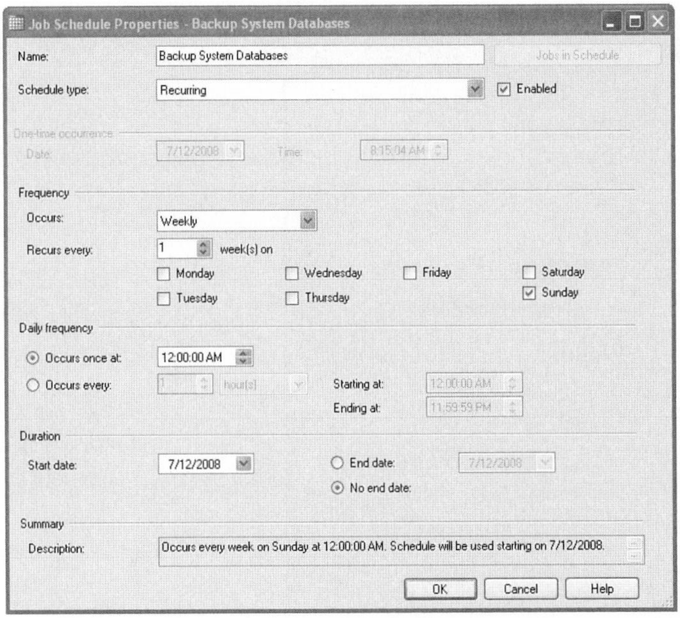

FIGURE 33.10 Scheduling options in the Maintenance Plan Wizard.

When a maintenance plan is saved, a scheduled job with the same name as the maintenance plan is created. The job schedule defined for the maintenance plan is applied to the scheduled job, and the SQL Server Agent manages the execution of the job, based on the schedule. Scheduling changes made to the maintenance plan are automatically reflected in the scheduled job. In addition, if the name of the maintenance plan is changed, the name of the scheduled job is changed as well. If an attempt is made to delete the scheduled job related to the maintenance plan, an error is returned, disallowing the deletion.

TIP

Scheduling in the Maintenance Plan Wizard is limited to one schedule per plan or task depending on which option you choose. You can surpass this limitation by adding additional schedules to the scheduled job associated with the maintenance plan. To do so, you simply open the associated scheduled job located in the `SQL Server Agent` node in SSMS and create the additional schedules. This capability is handy when you want a varied execution, such as a weekly schedule combined with daily executions of the same plan.

The scheduled job associated with a maintenance plan executes an SSIS package. Figure 33.11 shows an example of the scheduled job step for a SQL Server 2008 maintenance plan.

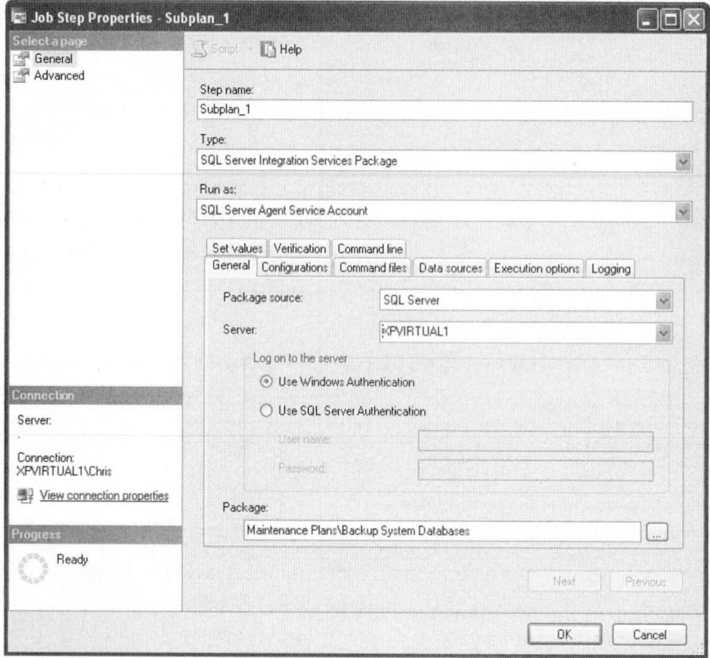

FIGURE 33.11 Scheduling jobs for a maintenance plan.

The utilization of SSIS in the execution of maintenance plans was a significant change in SQL Server 2005. SSIS provides added workflow capabilities and extends the feature set for maintenance plans. The scheduled job step that executes an SSIS package for the maintenance plan shows some of the options and flexibility of SSIS, but the real power is in the maintenance plan editor and the Business Intelligence Design Studio (BIDS) used to manage all SSIS packages. Chapter 52, "SQL Server Integration Services," provides further details on SSIS. The maintenance plan editor is discussed in the following section.

An integral part of a scheduled maintenance plan is the notification and reporting capabilities. The Select Report Options screen is displayed at the end of the Maintenance Plan Wizard (see Figure 33.12).

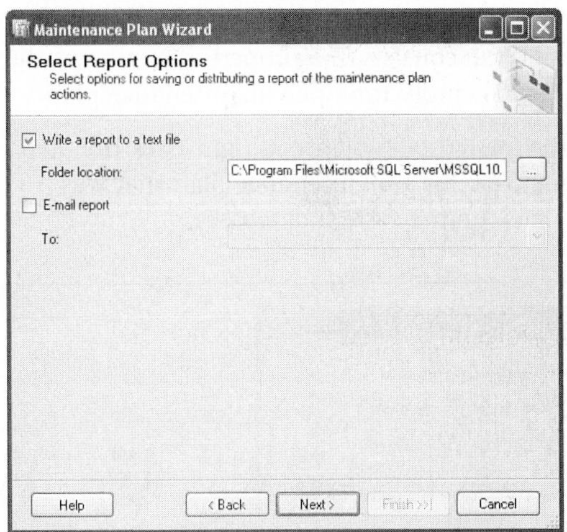

FIGURE 33.12 Reporting options in the Maintenance Plan Wizard.

The option Write a Report to a Text File provides details about the execution of each maintenance plan. This option should be selected for most plans, and it provides excellent information for researching past executions and diagnosing any maintenance plan failures.

The E-mail Report option provides a means for notifying a SQL Server operator when a task fails. You must have Database Mail enabled to be able to use this option, and the operator selected must have a valid email address to receive the notification. You can also edit the job associated with the maintenance plan after it has been created and set up notification there. The notification options on the scheduled job are more extensive than those in the Maintenance Plan Wizard.

CAUTION

If you have a maintenance plan generate a report, you need to make sure you have a means for cleaning up the files. The wizard does not create a plan that deletes the older report files. You can address this situation by modifying the plan after the wizard has created it and adding a Maintenance Cleanup task. This same task can be used to delete old database backup files. The modification of a maintenance plan and addition of the Maintenance Cleanup task are discussed in the following section.

Managing Maintenance Plans Without the Wizard

You can create or modify maintenance plans in SQL Server 2008 without using the Maintenance Plan Wizard. To create a new maintenance plan without the wizard, you right-click the `Maintenance Plan` node in the Object Explorer and select New Maintenance Plan. You are prompted for a maintenance plan name and then taken to the Design tab for the maintenance plan. The Design tab consists of a properties section at the top of the screen and a plan designer surface that is empty for a new maintenance plan.

Existing maintenance plans are displayed in the Design tab when you right-click the plan and select Modify. Figure 33.13 shows the Design tab for a maintenance plan that was created with the Maintenance Plan Wizard to back up the system databases.

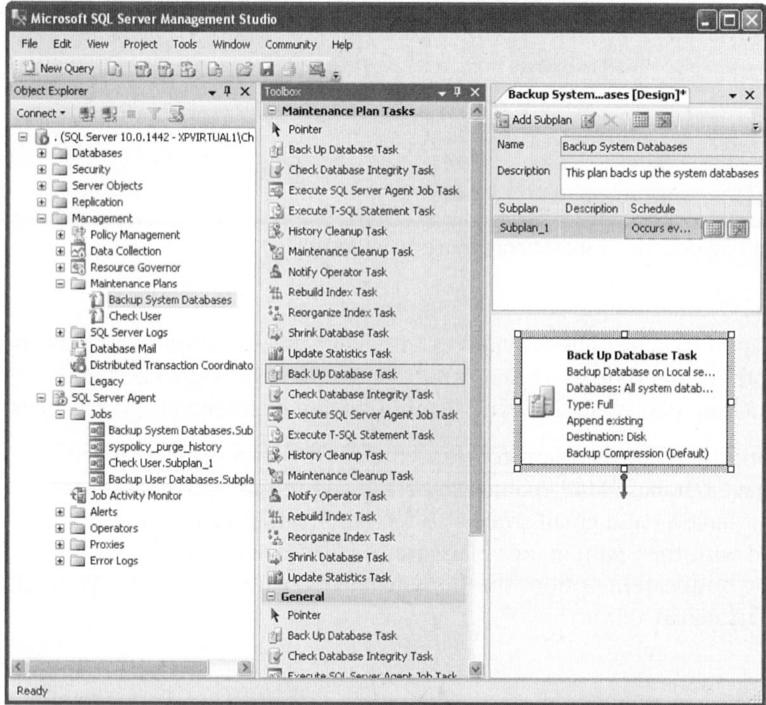

FIGURE 33.13 The maintenance plan Design tab.

The Design tab represents a significant difference from the way maintenance plans were managed in SQL Server 2000. The plan designer surface on the Design tab has drag-and-drop capabilities that allow you to add maintenance tasks to your plan. The available tasks are located in the Toolbox component. The Toolbox and the related tasks are shown in Figure 33.13 in the middle portion of the screen. To add a tool from the Toolbox, you drag the item from the Toolbox to the plan designer surface. Alternatively, you can double-click the task, and the task appears on the plan designer surface.

On the plan designer surface, you can move each of the tasks around, link them to other tasks, and edit them by double-clicking them. You can also right-click a task to edit it, group it with other tasks, autosize it, and gain access to other task options. You can right-click an empty section of the plan designer surface to add annotations or comments that provide additional information about the task or the overall plan.

NOTE

The dialog boxes displayed when you edit a task are unique for each task. The available maintenance plan tasks display an options screen like the one displayed during the execution of the Maintenance Plan Wizard. This provides consistency that is in place regardless of where the task is defined.

Adding a task to an existing maintenance plan is a good starting point to become familiar with the workings of the Design tab. Consider, for example, the maintenance plan shown in Figure 33.13. This plan, which was initially created with the Maintenance Plan Wizard, is used to create full database backups of all the system databases. One critical aspect that is missing from this plan is a task to remove older database backups. The task that can help you with this is the Maintenance Cleanup task. If you double-click that task in the Toolbox, the task is added to the plan designer surface, as shown in Figure 33.14.

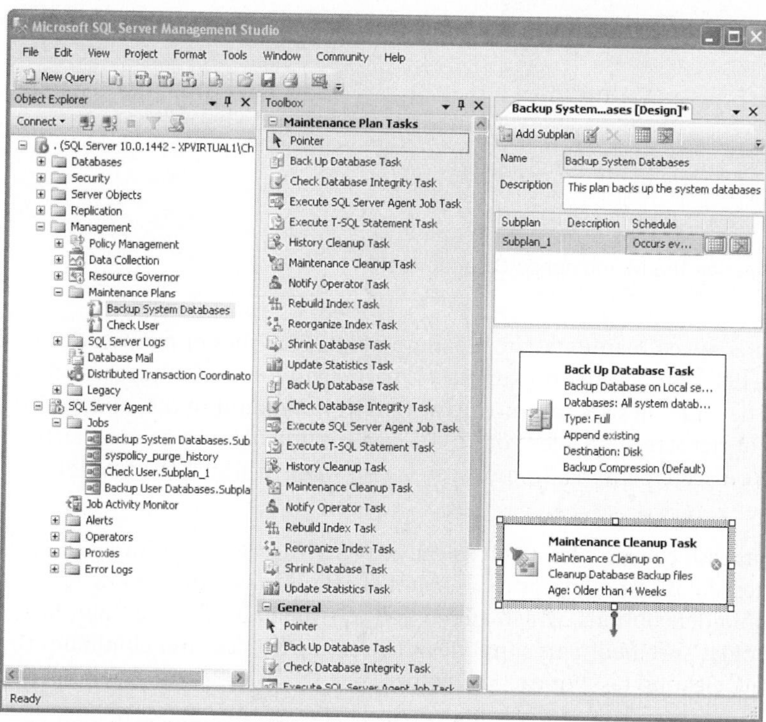

FIGURE 33.14 Adding a task to the plan designer surface.

After you add a task to the plan designer surface, you need to configure it. Note that a small red X icon appears on the right side of the task if the task has not yet been configured. To configure the Maintenance Cleanup task, you double-click it on the plan designer surface. Figure 33.15 shows the screen that appears so you can configure the Maintenance Cleanup task.

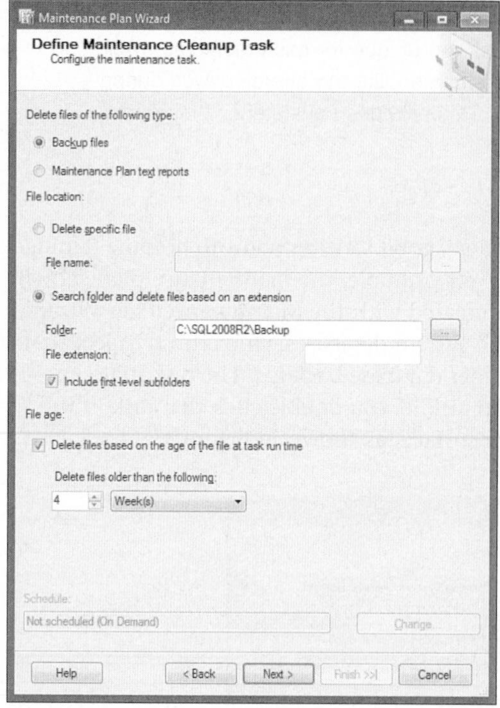

FIGURE 33.15 Configuring the Maintenance Cleanup task.

You can use the Maintenance Cleanup task to clean up old backup files or maintenance plan text reports. The deletion of older backup files is particularly important because database backups tend to be large files and can use up a significant amount of disk space. The File Location section of the screen enables you to delete a specific file, or you can delete files in a folder based on search criteria. In most cases, you want to search the folder to delete older files.

When cleaning up database backup files, you typically specify the file extension `.bak`. If you chose to write each database's backups to a separate folder, you should choose the Include First-Level Subfolders options, which allows you to search all first-level subfolders that exist under the folder specified. This simplifies the cleanup process and eliminates the need to have a separate cleanup task for each subfolder.

In the last section of the configuration screen for the Maintenance Cleanup task, you specify how old a file must be in order to be deleted. The default is four weeks, but you can adjust this setting to the desired time frame by using the related drop-downs. If you uncheck Delete Files Based on the Age of the File at Task Run Time, all files in the folder or subfolders are deleted, regardless of age.

NOTE

The deletion of database backup files is not based on the file dates or the name of the backup file. The Maintenance Cleanup task uses a procedure named `xp_delete_file` that examines the database backup and time the backup was created. Renaming the database backup file does not affect its inclusion in the deletion process.

After configuring the options for the Maintenance Cleanup task, you can click the View T-SQL button at the bottom of the screen. This feature reveals what is going on behind the scenes when the plan executes. Prior to SQL Server 2005, you had to obtain this kind of information by using the Profiler.

When you click OK, the task is ready to use in the maintenance plan. The task runs in parallel with the other tasks defined in the plan unless a precedence or link is established between the tasks. To establish a link between the tasks, you select the first task that you want to execute. When the task is selected, a green arrow is shown at the bottom of the task's box in the plan designer surface. You click the green arrow and drag it to the task that you want to run next. The green arrow is then connected to the other task. If you double-click the green arrow (or right-click and choose Edit), the Precedence Constraint Editor appears, as shown in Figure 33.16.

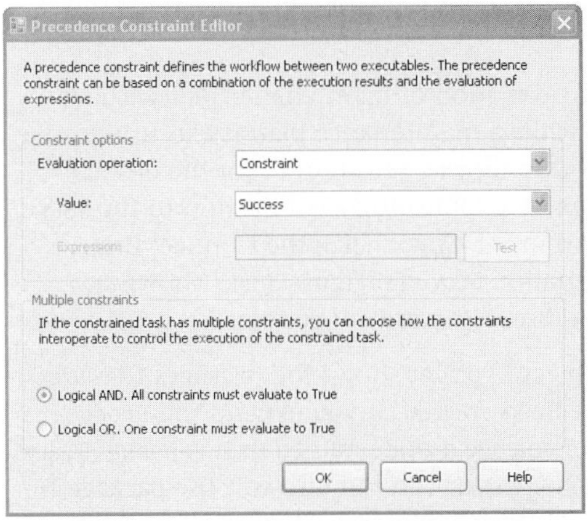

FIGURE 33.16 The Precedence Constraint Editor.

The paragraph at the top of the Precedence Constraint Editor gives a good description of what a precedence constraint is. In short, it can link tasks together based on the results of their execution. For example, if a backup database task succeeds, a Maintenance Cleanup task can be defined to run next. You can also set the constraint value so that the next task will run only if the first task fails, or you can have the next task run based on the prior task's completion, regardless of whether if succeeds or fails. In addition, you can link multiple tasks together with precedence. You define the logical relationship between tasks in the Multiple Constraints section of the Precedence Constraint Editor.

The workflow and relationships that can be defined between tasks for a maintenance plan are extensive and beyond the scope of this chapter. Many of the workflow concepts are similar to those of the DTS designer in SQL Server 2000 and the SSIS designer in SQL Server 2008.

Executing a Maintenance Plan

Maintenance plans that have been scheduled run automatically according to the schedule defined. You can also run maintenance plans manually by right-clicking a maintenance plan and selecting Execute or by selecting the SQL Server Agent job associated with the maintenance plan and starting the job. The execution behavior is different, depending on the means you use. If you choose to run the maintenance plan from the `Management` node, the SSIS package is launched, and the Execute Maintenance Plan window displays the current status of the plan execution.

If you run the SQL Server Agent job to execute the maintenance plan, a dialog box indicating the execution status of the job appears. The dialog does not indicate success for the maintenance plan until the entire maintenance plan has completed. The dialog box for the job can be closed, and the job will still continue to run. The Execute Maintenance Plan window, on the other hand, does not have an option to close it, and it must stay open until the plan completes.

There are two other means for monitoring the execution of maintenance plans. The Job Activity Monitor shows a status of executing while a maintenance plan is executing. You can set the refresh settings on the Job Activity Monitor to auto-refresh for the desired increment. You can also monitor the execution by establishing a connection to the SSIS server in SSMS. To establish an SSIS connection in SSMS, you click the Connect drop-down in the Object Explorer and choose Integration Services. Figure 33.17 shows an example of the Object Explorer with an Integration Services connection.

The Integration Services connection in the Object Explorer shows the packages that are running in addition to the packages that have been created. If you expand the `Stored Packages` node and navigate to the `MSDB` node, you see a node named `Maintenance Plans` that shows all the SSIS packages that have been created. You can also edit the package with BIDS, but that topic is beyond the scope of this chapter. See Chapter 52 for more information.

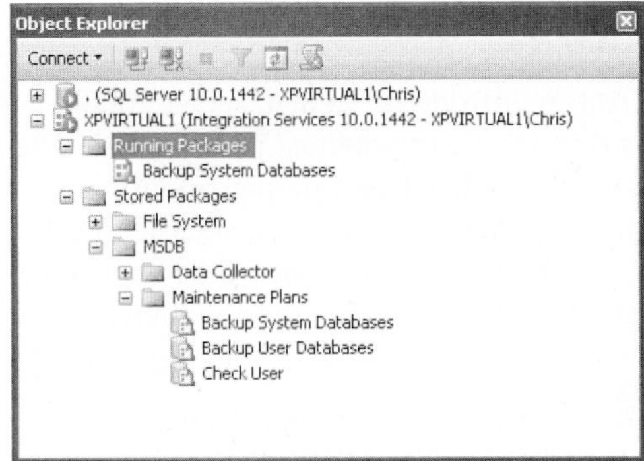

FIGURE 33.17 The Object Explorer with an Integration Services connection.

NOTE

SSIS does not need to be installed on the SQL Server machine to be able to create and execute maintenance plans. In the initial release of SQL Server 2005, this was a requirement but was changed with SQL Server 2005 SP2. This change carried over to SQL Server 2008, and maintenance plans are now fully functional with the SQL Server Database Services installation.

Maintenance Without a Maintenance Plan

You can perform database maintenance without the use of the built-in maintenance plans that come with SQL Server. The additional complexity in SQL Server 2008 may steer some people away from the use of these plans. In addition, these plans cannot be scripted, so deployment to multiple environments is not straightforward.

Database maintenance that is performed without a maintenance plan is often performed using custom scripts or stored procedures that execute the T-SQL commands to perform the maintenance. Other methods include manually executing the `SQLMAINT` utility to perform various maintenance tasks such as database backups and consistency checks. Often these maintenance commands or custom scripts are then scheduled to run on a regular basis by manually setting up jobs within the SQL Server Agent job scheduler in SQL Server Management Studio. (For more information on setting up and scheduling jobs in SQL Server Agent, see Chapter 16, "SQL Server Scheduling and Notification.")

Setting up maintenance tasks manually is a viable option, especially for the more experienced DBA because it requires additional development work and familiarity with the maintenance commands and options. However, even the experienced DBA should consider using maintenance plans because maintenance tasks set up manually may lack the integration with other SQL Server components that is offered with the SQL Server 2008 maintenance plans.

Database Maintenance Policies

Policy-Based Management, a new management feature introduced in SQL Server 2008, allows you to manage your SQL Server instances through clearly defined policies, reducing the potential for administrative errors or oversight. The policy-based framework implements the policies you defined via a Policy Engine, SQL Server Agent jobs, SQLCLR, DDL triggers, and Service Broker. You can choose to have the policies you defined be applied or evaluated against a single server or a group of servers, thus improving the scalability of monitoring and administration.

Policy-Based Management allows you to prescribe the way you want your databases maintained, and the system will help ensure things stay that way. Essentially, Policy-Based Management allows you to define rules for one or more SQL Servers and evaluate them. The goal of this feature is to make it easier for you to manage one or more servers by notifying you when servers are out of compliance with the database maintenance policies you have defined.

For example, you could define a policy to ensure that transaction log backups are being performed on the appropriate intervals on your OLTP databases. Policy-Based Management allows you to determine when one of your databases is not in compliance with your log backup policy. You can set up this policy to be evaluated on demand or via a schedule.

For more information on defining and using policies, see Chapter 22.

Summary

Establishing a database maintenance plan is important. Just like your car or your home, a database needs maintenance to keep working properly. The powerful features available with the SQL Server 2008 maintenance plans and Maintenance Plan Wizard make the creation of a robust maintenance plan relatively easy. If you establish your maintenance plans early in the life of your databases, you will save yourself time and aggravation in the long run.

Chapter 34 delves further into the importance of indexes and their relationship to performance. It expands on the optimization of indexes mentioned in this chapter and describes the role that indexes play in keeping databases running fast.

CHAPTER 34

Data Structures, Indexes, and Performance

IN THIS CHAPTER

- What's New for Data Structures, Indexes, and Performance
- Understanding Data Structures
- Database Files and Filegroups
- Database Pages
- Understanding Table Structures
- Understanding Index Structures
- Data Modification and Performance
- Index Utilization
- Index Selection
- Evaluating Index Usefulness
- Index Statistics
- SQL Server Index Maintenance
- Index Design Guidelines
- Indexed Views
- Indexes on Computed Columns
- Filtered Indexes and Statistics
- Choosing Indexes: Query Versus Update Performance
- Identifying Missing Indexes
- Identifying Unused Indexes

A number of factors affect SQL Server performance. One of the key factors is your table and index design; poor table and index design can result in excessive I/O and poor performance. To aid in developing a good table and index design in an effort to improve SQL Server performance by minimizing I/O, you need to have a good understanding of SQL Server data structures and indexes.

Proper table and index design is a key issue in achieving optimum SQL Server application performance. For example, you can often realize substantial performance gains in your SQL Server applications by creating the proper indexes to support the queries and operations being performed. At the same time, it's important to keep in mind that although many indexes on a table can help improve response time for queries and reports, too many indexes can hurt the performance of inserts, updates, and deletes due to the overhead required to maintain the index and data rows. Additionally, other index design decisions, such as which column(s) to create a clustered index on, might be influenced as much by how the data is inserted and modified and what the possible locking implications might be as they are by the query response time alone.

In this chapter, you learn about the underlying structures of databases, tables, rows, and indexes and how SQL Server maintains index and data structures because this information provides a basis for understanding the performance of your tables and indexes. This chapter discusses the storage structures in SQL Server and how these storage structures are maintained and managed. The chapter also discusses how SQL Server evaluates and uses indexes to improve query response time. Using this information, you should have a better understanding of the issues and factors that influence good table and index design.

What's New for Data Structures, Indexes, and Performance

SQL Server 2008 provides a number of new features related to data structures, indexes, and performance.

Among these new features are *filtered indexes* and *statistics*. Filtered indexes utilize a `WHERE` clause that filters or limits the number of rows included in the index. The smaller filtered index allows queries run against rows containing data values in the index to run faster. These filtered indexes can also save on the disk space used by the index. A well-designed filtered index can improve query performance, reduce index maintenance costs, and reduce index storage costs compared with full-table indexes.

Also new to SQL Server 2008 is the capability to compress data in indexes and tables to reduce the amount of storage space required and, in turn, reduce the I/O needed for these objects. *Page-level data compression* helps to reduce both storage and memory requirements as the data is compressed both on disk and when brought into the SQL Server data cache. *Row-level compression* isn't true data compression but implements a more efficient storage format for fixed-length data.

Other storage features introduced in SQL Server 2008 to reduce storage space requirements are *sparse columns* and *column sets*. Sparse columns are ordinary columns that use an optimized storage format for `NULL` values.

FILESTREAM storage was also introduced in SQL Server 2008 as a new storage mechanism for binary large object (BLOB) data. FILESTREAM storage is a property that can be applied to `varbinary(max)` columns and enables SQL Server applications to store unstructured data, such as documents and images, directly in the NTFS file system while still maintaining the behavior of a database column. The advantages of FILESTREAM storage are improved performance and increased size of BLOB data, expanding from the 2GB limit of image columns to the available space in the file system.

Spatial indexes are new to SQL Server 2008 as well. These indexes are used against spatial data defined by coordinates of latitude and longitude. The spatial data is essential for efficient global navigation. The spatial indexes are grid-based and help optimize the performance of searches against the spatial data.

NOTE

This chapter assumes that you already have an understanding of the different types of indexes and how to define them. For more information on index types and how to create indexes, see Chapter 25, "Creating and Managing Indexes."

Understanding Data Structures

SQL Server DBAs and users do not see data and storage the same way SQL Server does. A DBA or end user sees a database more logically as the following:

- Databases, physically stored in files
- Tables and indexes, placed in filegroups within databases
- Rows, stored in tables

SQL Server internally sees these storage structures at a lower, physical level as

- Databases, physically stored in data and log files
- Pages within these files, allocated to tables and indexes
- Data and index rows, stored in slots on pages

Database Files and Filegroups

Databases in SQL Server 2008 span at least two, and optionally several, database files. There must always be at least one file for data and one file for the transaction log. These database files are normal operating system files created in a directory within the operating system. These files are created when the database is created or when a database is expanded.

Each database file has the following set of properties:

- **A logical filename**—This name is used for internal reference to the file.
- **A physical filename**—This name is the actual physical pathname of the file.
- **An initial size**—If no size is specified for primary data file, its initial size, by default, is the minimum size required to hold the contents of the model database.
- **An optional maximum size**—A maximum file size limit can be specified.
- **A file growth increment**—This amount is specified in megabytes or as a percentage.

The information and properties about each file for a database are stored in the database visible via the system catalog view called `sys.database_files`. This view exists in every database and contains information about each of the database files. The `master` database contains a similar view, `sys.master_files`, that contains file information for all databases within the SQL Server instance. Table 34.1 lists the most useful columns in the `sys.database_files` view.

TABLE 34.1 The **sysfiles** Table

Column Name	Description
file_id	A file identification number that is unique within each database
file_guid	GUID for the file
type	File type (0=rows [that is, data files], 1=log, 2=FILESTREAM, 4=Full-text catalogs prior to SQL Server 2008
type_desc	Description of the file type (ROWS, LOG, FILESTREAM, FULLTEXT)
data_space_id	0 represents a log file; values > 0 represent the ID of the filegroup the data file belongs to
name	The logical name of the file
filename	The physical name of the file, including path
state	File state (0 = OFFLINE, 1 = RESTORING, 2 = RECOVERING, 3 = RECOVERY_PENDING, 4 = SUSPECT, 6 = OFFLINE, 7=DEFUNCT)
state_desc	Description of the file state (OFFLINE, RESTORING, RECOVERING, RECOVERY_PENDING, SUSPECT, OFFLINE, DEFUNCT)
size	Current size of the file in 8KB pages
max_size	Maximum file size in 8KB pages
growth	File growth setting (0=fixed, >0=autogrow in units of 8KB pages or by percentage if is_percent_growth is set to 1)
is_media_read_only	1=file is on read-only media
is_read_only	1= file is marked read-only
is_sparse	1=file is a sparse file
is_percent_growth	1=growth of file value is percentage

SQL Server uses the file location information visible in the sys.master_files catalog view most of the time. However, the Database Engine uses the file location information stored in the primary file to initialize the file location entries in the master database when attaching a database using the CREATE DATABASE statement with either the FOR ATTACH or FOR ATTACH_REBUILD_LOG options.

Every database can have three types of files:

- Primary data file
- Secondary data files
- Log files

In addition, in SQL Server 2008, databases can also have FILESTREAM data files and full-text data files.

Primary Data File

Every database has only one primary database file. The location of the primary database file is stored in the `master` database (visible via the `filename` column in the `sys.master_files` view). When SQL Server opens a database, it looks for this file and then reads from the file information on the other files defined for the database.

The file extension for the primary database file defaults to `.mdf`. The primary database file always belongs to the default filegroup. It is often sufficient to have only one database file for storing your tables and indexes (the primary database file). The file can, of course, be created on a RAID partition to help spread I/O. However, if you need finer control over placement of your tables across disks or disk arrays, or if you want to be able to back up only a portion of your database via filegroups, you can create additional, secondary data files for a database.

Secondary Data Files

A database can have any number of secondary files (in reality, the maximum number of files per database is 32,767, but that should be sufficient for most implementations). You can put a secondary file in the default filegroup or in another filegroup defined for the database. Secondary data files have the file extension `.ndf` by default.

Following are some situations in which the use of secondary database files might be beneficial:

- You want to perform a partial backup. A backup can be performed for the entire database or a subset of the database. The subset is specified as a set of files or filegroups. The partial backup feature is useful for large databases, where it is impractical to back up the entire database. When recovering with partial backups, a transaction log backup must also be available. For more information about backups, see Chapter 14, "Database Backup and Restore."
- You want more control over placement of database objects. When you create a table or index, you can specify the filegroup in which the object is created. This could help you spread I/O by placing your most active tables or indexes on separate filegroups defined on separate disks or disk arrays.
- Creating multiple files on a single disk provides no real performance benefit but could help in recovery. If you have a 90GB database in a single file and have to restore it, you need to have enough disk space available to create a new 90GB file. If you don't have 90GB of space available on a single disk, you cannot restore the database. On the other hand, if the database was created with three files each 30GB in size, you more likely will be able to find three 30GB chunks of space available on your server.

The Log File

Each database must have at least one log file. The log file contains the transaction log records of all changes made in a database (for more information on what is contained in the transaction log, see Chapter 31, "Transaction Management and the Transaction Log"). By default, log files have the file extension `.ldf`.

A database can have several log files, and each log file can have a maximum size of 32TB. A log file cannot be part of a filegroup. No information other than transaction log records can be written to a log file.

For more information on the log file and log file management, see Chapter 31.

File Management

In SQL Server 2008, you can specify that a database file should grow automatically as space is needed. SQL Server can also shrink the size of the database if the space is not needed. You can control whether to use this feature along with the increment by which the file is to be expanded. The increment can be specified as a fixed number of megabytes or as a percentage of the current size of the file. You can also set a limit on the maximum size of the file or allow it to grow until no more space is available on the disk.

Listing 34.1 provides an example of a database being created with a 10MB growth increment for the first database file, 20MB for the second, and 20% growth increment for the log file.

LISTING 34.1 Creating a Database with Autogrowth

```
CREATE DATABASE Customer
ON ( NAME='Customer_Data',
    FILENAME='D:\SQL_data\Customer_Data1.mdf',
    SIZE=50,
    MAXSIZE=100,
    FILEGROWTH=10),
   ( NAME='Customer_Data2',
    FILENAME='E:\SQL_data\Customer_Data2.ndf',
    SIZE=100,
    FILEGROWTH=20)
LOG ON ( NAME='Customer_Log',
    FILENAME='F:\SQL_data\Customer_Log.ldf',
    SIZE=50,
    FILEGROWTH=20%)
GO
```

The `Customer_Data` file has an initial size of 50MB, a maximum size of 100MB, and a file increment of 10MB.

The `Customer_Data2` file has an initial size of 100MB, has a file growth increment of 20MB, and can grow until the `E:` disk partition is full.

The transaction log has an initial size of 50MB; the file increases by 20% with each file growth. The increment is based on the *current* file size, not the size originally specified.

When creating or expanding data files in SQL Server 2008, SQL Server uses fast file initialization. This allows for the fast execution of the file creation and growth. With fast file initialization, the space is added to the data file immediately, but without initializing the logical pages in the data file with zeros. The existing disk content in the data file is not overwritten until new data is written to the files. This provides a huge performance advantage when a data file autogrows while an application is attempting to write data to the database. The application does not need to wait until the space is initialized; it can begin writing to the database immediately.

SQL Server also provides an option to autoshrink databases as well as manually shrink databases. However, shrinking a database is a resource-intensive process and should be done only if it is absolutely imperative to reclaim disk space. Also, if a data file is constantly shrinking and growing, it can lead to excessive file fragmentation at the file system level as well as excessive logical fragmentation within the file, both of which can lead to poor I/O performance.

Using Filegroups

All databases have a primary filegroup that contains the primary data file. There can be only one primary filegroup. If you don't create any other filegroups or change the default filegroup to a filegroup other than the primary filegroup, all files will be in the primary file group unless specifically placed in another filegroup.

In addition to the primary filegroup, you can add one or more filegroups to the database, and a filegroup can contain one or more files. The main purpose of using filegroups is to provide more control over the placement of files and data on your server. When you create a table or index, you can map it to a specific filegroup, thus controlling the placement of data. A typical SQL Server database installation generally uses a single RAID array to spread I/O across disks and create all files in the primary filegroup; more advanced installations or installations with very large databases spread across multiple array sets can benefit from the finer level of control of file and data placement afforded by additional filegroups.

For example, for a simple database such as `AdventureWorks`, you can create just one primary file that contains all data and objects and a log file that contains the transaction log information. For a larger and more complex database, such as a securities trading system where large data volumes and strict performance criteria are the norm, you might create the database with one primary file and four additional secondary files. You can then set up filegroups so you can place the data and objects within the database across all five files. If you have a table that itself needs to be spread across multiple disk arrays for performance reasons, you can place multiple files in a filegroup, each of which resides on a different disk, and create the table on that filegroup. For example, you can create three files (`Data1.ndf`, `Data2.ndf`, and `Data3.ndf`) on three disk arrays, respectively, and then assign them to the filegroup called spread_group. Your table can then be created specifically on the filegroup spread_group. Queries for data from the table are spread across the three disk arrays, thereby improving I/O performance.

If a filegroup contains more than one file, when space is allocated to objects stored in that filegroup, the data is stored proportionally across the files. In other words, if you have one file in a filegroup with twice as much free space as another, the first file has two extents allocated from it for each extent allocated from the second file (extents and space allocation are discussed in more detail later in this chapter).

Listing 34.2 provides an example of using filegroups in a database to control the file placement of the customer_info table.

LISTING 34.2 Using a Filegroup to Control Placement for a Table

```
CREATE DATABASE Customer
ON ( NAME='Customer_Data',
    FILENAME='C:\SQLData\Customer_Data1.mdf',
    SIZE=50,
    MAXSIZE=100,
    FILEGROWTH=10)
LOG ON ( NAME='Customer_Log',
    FILENAME='C:\SQLData\Customer_Log.ldf',
    SIZE=50,
    FILEGROWTH=20%)
GO

ALTER DATABASE Customer
 ADD FILEGROUP Cust_table
GO

ALTER DATABASE Customer
 ADD FILE
   ( NAME='Customer_Data2',
    FILENAME='G:\SQLData\Customer_Data2.ndf',
    SIZE=100,
    FILEGROWTH=20)
 TO FILEGROUP Cust_Table
GO

USE Customer
CREATE TABLE customer_info
(cust_no INT, cust_address NCHAR(200), info NVARCHAR(3000))
 ON Cust_Table
GO
```

The CREATE DATABASE statement in Listing 34.2 creates a database with a primary database file and log file. The first ALTER DATABASE statement adds a filegroup. A secondary database file is added with the second ALTER DATABASE command. This file is added to the Cust_Table filegroup. The CREATE TABLE statement creates a table; the ON Cust_Table clause places the table in the Cust_Table filegroup (the Customer_Data2 file on the G: disk partition).

The sys.filegroups system catalog view contains information about the database filegroups defined within a database, as shown in Table 34.2.

TABLE 34.2 The **sys.filegroups** System Catalog View

Column Name	Description
name	Name of the data space, unique within the database.
data_space_id	Data space ID number, unique within the database.
type	FG = Filegroup.
type_desc	Description of data space type: ROWS_FILEGROUP.
is_default	1 = This is the default data space. The default data space is used when a filegroup or partition scheme is not specified in a CREATE TABLE or CREATE INDEX statement. 0 = This is not the default data space.
filegroup_guid	GUID for the filegroup. NULL = PRIMARY filegroup.
log_filegroup_id	Not used; value is NULL.
is_read_only	1 = Filegroup is read-only. 0 = Filegroup is read/write.

The following statement returns the filename, size in megabytes (not including autogrow), and the name of the filegroup to which each file belongs:

```
SELECT
    convert(varchar(30), sf.name) as filename,
    size/128 as size_in_MB,
    convert(varchar(30), sfg.name) as filegroupname
 FROM sys.database_files sf
 INNER JOIN sys.filegroups sfg
 ON sf.data_space_id = sfg.data_space_id
```

```
go

filename                      size_in_MB  filegroupname
----------------------------- ----------- ------------------------
Customer_Data                 50          PRIMARY
Customer_Data2                100         Cust_table
```

FILESTREAM Filegroups

FILESTREAM storage is a new feature in SQL Server 2008 for storing unstructured data, such as documents, images, and videos. FILESTREAM storage helps to solve the issues with using unstructured data by integrating the SQL Server Database Engine with the NTFS file system for storing the unstructured data, such as documents and images, on the file system with the database storing a pointer to the data. Although the actual data resides outside the database in the NTFS file system, you can still use Transact-SQL (T-SQL) statements to insert, update, query, and back up FILESTREAM data, while maintaining transactional consistency between the unstructured data and corresponding structured data with same level of security.

NOTE

To use FILESTREAM storage, you must first enable FILESTREAM storage at the Windows level as well as at the SQL Server instance level. You can enable FILESTREAM at the Windows level during installation of SQL Server 2008 or at any time using SQL Server Configuration Manager. After you enable FILESTREAM at the Windows level, you next need to enable FILESTREAM for the SQL Server instance. You can do this either through SQL Server Management Studio (SSMS) or via T-SQL.

After you enabled FILESTREAM for the SQL Server instance, you can enable it for a database by creating a FILESTREAM filegroup. You can do this when the database is created (or to an existing database) by adding a filegroup and including the `CONTAINS FILESTREAM` clause. Unlike regular filegroups, a FILESTREAM filegroup can contain only a single file reference, which is actually a file system folder rather than an actual file. The actual folder must not exist (although the path up to the folder must exist); SQL Server creates the `filestream` folder. For example, in Listing 34.3, the code adds a FILESTREAM filegroup called `CustFSGroup` and adds the folder `G:\SQLData\custinfo_FS` into the file group. This `custinfo_FS` folder is created by SQL Server in the `G:\SQLData` folder.

LISTING 34.3 Using a Filegroup to Control Placement for a Table

```
ALTER DATABASE Customer
 ADD FILEGROUP Cust_FSGroup CONTAINS FILESTREAM

ALTER DATABASE Customer
```

```
    ADD FILE
      ( NAME=custinfo_FS,
        FILENAME = 'G:\SQLData\custinfo_FS')
        to FILEGROUP Cust_FSGroup
GO
```

If you look in the `G:\SQLData\custinfo_FS` folder, you should see a `Filestream.hdr` file and an `$FSLOG` folder. The `Filestream.hdr` file is a FILESTREAM container header file that should not be moved or modified.

As you can see in the example in Listing 34.3, for FILESTREAM files or file groups, unlike regular files, you do not specify size or growth information. No space is preallocated. The file and filegroup grow as data is added to tables that have been created with FILESTREAM columns.

As you create tables with FILESTREAM columns, a subfolder is created in the filegroup folder for each table. The filenames are GUIDs. Each FILESTREAM column created in the table results in another subfolder created under the table subfolder. The column subfolder name is also a GUID. At this point, there still are no actual files created. That happens after you start adding rows to the table. A file is created in the column subfolder for each row inserted into the table with a non-`NULL` value for the FILESTREAM column.

For more information on creating and using tables with FILESTREAM columns, see Chapter 42, "What's New for Transact-SQL in SQL Server 2008."

Database Pages

All information in SQL Server is stored at the page level. The *page* is the smallest level of I/O in SQL Server and is the fundamental storage unit. Pages contain the data itself or information about the physical layout of the data. The page size is the same for all page types: 8KB, or 8,192 bytes. The pages are arranged in two basic types of storage structures: linked data pages and index trees.

Databases are divided into logical 8KB pages. Within each file allocated to a database, the pages are numbered contiguously from 0 to *n*. The actual number of pages in the database file depends on the size of the file. Pages in a database are uniquely referenced by specifying the database ID, the file ID for the file the page resides in, and the page number within the file. When you expand a database with `ALTER DATABASE`, the new space is added at the end of the file, and the page numbers continue incrementing from the previous last page in the file. If you add a completely new file, its first page number is 0. When you shrink a database, pages are removed from the end of the file only, starting at the highest page in the database and moving toward lower-numbered pages until the database reaches the specified size or a used page that cannot be removed. This ensures that page numbers within a file are always contiguous.

Page Types

There are eight page types in SQL Server, as listed in Table 34.3.

TABLE 34.3 Page Types

Page Type	Stores
Data	Data rows for all data except `text`, `ntext`, `image`, `nvarchar(max)`, `varchar(max)`, `varbinary(max)`, and `xml` data
Row Overflow	Data columns that cause a data row to exceed the 8,060 bytes per page limit
LOB	Large object types (`text`, `ntext`, `image`, `nvarchar(max)`, `varchar(max)`, `varbinary(max)`, `xml` data, and `varchar`, `nvarchar`, `varbinary`, and `sqlvariant` when data row size exceeds 8KB)
Index	Index entries and pointers
Global Allocation Map	Information about allocated (used) extents
Page Free Space	Information about page allocation and free space on pages
Index Allocation Map	Information about extents used by a table or an index
Differential Changed Map	Information about which extents have been modified since the last full database backup
Bulk Changed Map	Information about which extents have been used in a minimally logged or bulk-logged operation since the last `BACKUP LOG` statement

All pages, regardless of type, have a similar layout. They all have a page header, which is 96 bytes, and a body, which consequently is 8,096 bytes. The page layout is shown in Figure 34.1.

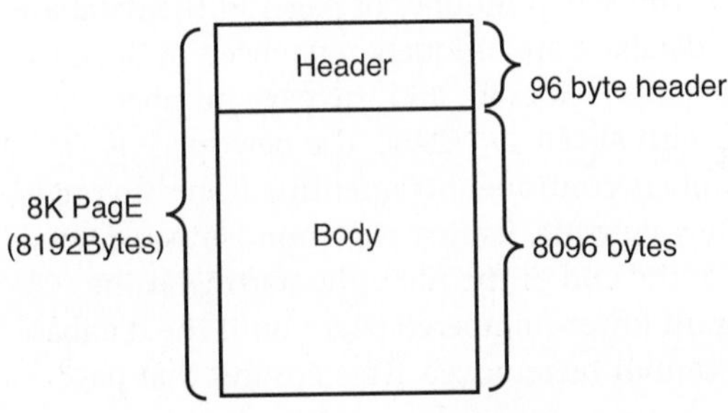

FIGURE 34.1 SQL Server page layout.

Data Pages

The actual data rows in tables are stored on data pages. Figure 34.2 shows the basic structure of a data page.

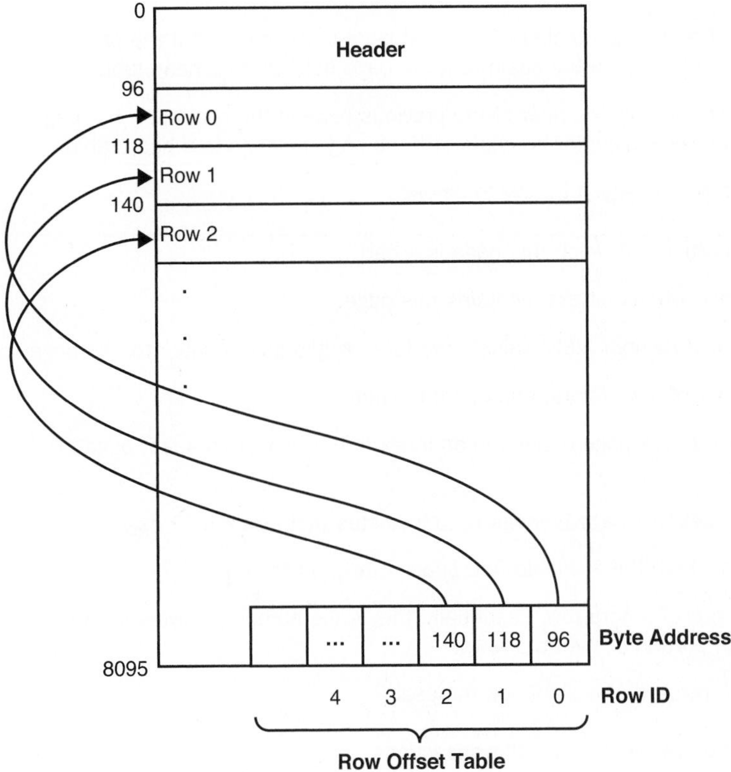

FIGURE 34.2 The structure of a SQL Server data page.

The following sections discuss and examine the contents of the data page.

The Page Header

The *page header* contains control information for the page. Some fields assist when SQL Server checks for consistency among its storage structures, and some fields are used when navigating among the pages that constitute a table. Table 34.4 describes the more useful fields contained in the page header.

TABLE 34.4 Information Contained in the Page Header

Page Header Fields	Description
`PageID`	Unique identifier for the page. It consists of two parts: the file ID number and page number.
`NextPage`	File number and page number of the next page in the chain (`0` if the page is the last or only page in the chain or if the page belongs to a heap table).
`PrevPage`	File number and page number of the previous page in the chain (`0` if the page is the first or only page in the chain or if the page belongs to a heap table).
`ObjectID`	ID of the object to which this page belongs.
`PartitionID`	ID of the partition of which this page is a part.
`AllocUnitID`	ID of the allocation unit that contains this page.
`LSN`	Log sequence number (LSN) value used for changes and updates to this page.
`SlotCnt`	Total number of rows (slots) used on the page.
`Level`	Level at which this page resides in an index tree (`0` indicates a leaf page or data page).
`IndexID`	ID of the index this page belongs to (`0` indicates that it is a data page).
`freedata`	Byte offset where the available free space starts on the page.
`Pminlen`	Minimum size of a data row. Essentially, this is the number of bytes in the fixed-length portion of the data rows.
FreeCnt	Number of free bytes available on the page.
reservedCnt	Number of bytes reserved by all transactions.
Xactreserved	Number of bytes reserved by the most recently started transaction.
tornBits	Bit string containing 1 bit per sector for detecting torn page writes (or checksum information if `torn_page_detection` is not on).
`flagBits`	Two-byte bitmap that contains additional information about the page.

The Data Rows

Following the page header, starting at byte 96 on the page, are the actual data rows. Each data row has a unique row number within the page. Data rows in SQL Server cannot cross page boundaries. The maximum available space in a SQL Server page is 8,060 bytes of in-row data. When a data row is logged in the transaction log (for an insert, for example), additional logging information is stored on the log page along with the data row. Because log pages are 8,192 bytes in size and also have a 96-byte header, a log page has only 8,096 bytes of available space. If you want to store the data row and logging information on a single log page, the in-row data cannot be more than 8,060 bytes in size. This, in effect, limits the maximum in-row data row size for a table in SQL Server 2008 to 8,060 bytes as well.

> **NOTE**
>
> Although 8,060 bytes is the maximum size of in-row data, 8,060 bytes is not the maximum row size limit in SQL Server 2008. Data rows can also have row-overflow and large object (LOB) data stored on separate pages, as you see later in this chapter.

The number of rows stored on a page depends on the size of each row. For a table that has all fixed-length, non-nullable columns, the size of the row and the number of rows that can be stored on a page are always the same. If the table has any variable or nullable fields, the number of rows stored on the page depends on the size of each row. SQL Server attempts to fit as many rows as possible in a page. Smaller row sizes allow SQL Server to fit more rows on a page, which reduces page I/O and allows more data pages to fit in memory. This helps improve system performance by reducing the number of times SQL Server has to read data in from disk.

Because each data row also incurs some overhead bytes in addition to the actual data, the maximum amount of actual *data* that can be stored in a single row on a page is slightly less than 8,060 bytes. The actual amount of overhead required per row depends on whether the table contains any variable-length columns. If you attempt to create a table with a minimum row size including data and row overhead that exceeds 8,060 bytes, you receive an error message as shown in the following example (remember that a multibyte character set data type such as `nchar` or `nvarchar` requires 2 bytes per character, so an `nchar(4000)` column requires 8,000 bytes):

```
CREATE TABLE customer_info2
(cust_no INT, cust_address NCHAR(25), info NCHAR(4000))
go

Msg 1701, Level 16, State 1, Line 1
Creating or altering table 'customer_info2' failed because the
 minimum row size would be 8061, including 7 bytes of internal
overhead. This exceeds the maximum allowable table row size of 8060
bytes.
```

If the table contains variable-length or nullable columns, you can create a table for which the minimum row size is less than 8,060 bytes, but the data rows could conceivably exceed 8,060 bytes. SQL Server allows the table to be created. If you then try to insert a row that exceeds 8,060 bytes of data and overhead, the data that exceeds the 8,060-byte limit for in-row data is stored in a row-overflow page.

The Structure of Data Rows The data for all fixed-length data fields in a table is stored at the beginning of the row. All variable-length data columns are stored after the fixed-length data. Figure 34.3 shows the structure of the data row in SQL Server.

Status Byte A (1 byte)	Status Byte B (1 byte) *not used*	Length of Fixed Length Data (2 bytes)	Fixed Length Data Columns (n bytes)	Number of Columns (2 bytes)	Null Bitmap (1 bit for each column)	Number of Variable Length Columns (2 bytes)	Column Offset Array (2 x number of variable columns)	Variable Length Data Columns (*n* bytes)

FIGURE 34.3 The structure of a SQL Server data row.

The total size of each data row is a factor of the sum of the size of the columns plus the row overhead. Seven bytes of overhead is the minimum for any data row:

- 1 byte for status byte A.
- 1 byte for status byte B (in SQL Server 2008, only 1 bit is used indicating that the record is a ghost-forwarded row).
- 2 bytes to store the length of the fixed-length columns.
- 2 bytes to store the number of columns in the row.
- 1 byte for every multiple of 8 columns (`ceiling(numcols / 8)` in the table for the `NULL` bitmap. A 1 in the bitmap indicates that the column allows `NULL`s.

The values stored in status byte A are as follows:

- **Bit 0**—This bit provides version information. In SQL Server 2008, it's always `0`.
- **Bits 1 through 3**—This 3-bit value indicates the nature of the row. `0` indicates that the row is a primary record, `1` indicates that the row has been forwarded, `2` indicates a forwarded stub, `3` indicates an index record, `4` indicates a blob fragment, `5` indicates a ghost index record, `6` indicates a ghost data record, and 7 indicates a ghost version record. (Many of these topics, such as forwarded and ghost records, are discussed in further detail later in this chapter.)
- **Bit 4**—This bit indicates that a `NULL` bitmap exists. This is somewhat unnecessary in SQL Server 2008 because a `NULL` bitmap is always present, even if no `NULL`s are allowed in the table.
- **Bit 5**—This bit indicates that one or more variable-length columns exists in the row.
- **Bit 6**—This bit indicates the row contains versioning information.
- **Bit 7**—This bit is not currently used in SQL Server 2008.

If the table contains any variable-length columns, the following additional overhead bytes are included in each data row:

- 2 bytes to store the number of variable-length columns in the row.
- 2 bytes times the number of variable-length columns for the offset array. This is essentially a table in the row identifying where each variable-length column can be found within the variable-length column block.

Within each block of fixed-length or variable-length data, the data columns are stored in the column order in which they were defined when the table was created. In other words, all fixed-length fields are stored in column ID order in the fixed-length block, and all nullable or variable-length fields are stored in column ID order in the variable-length block.

Storage of the `sql_variant` Data Type The `sql_variant` data type can contain a value of any column data type in SQL Server except for `text`, `ntext`, `image`, variable-length columns with the `MAX` qualifier, and `timestamp`. For example, a `sql_variant` in one row could contain character data; in another row, an `integer` value; and in yet another row, a `float` value. Because they can contain any type of value, `sql_variant` columns are always considered variable length. The format of a `sql_variant` column is as follows:

- Byte 1 indicates the actual data type being stored in the `sql_variant`.
- Byte 2 indicates the `sql_variant` version, which is always `1` in SQL Server 2008.
- The remainder of the `sql_variant` column contains the data value and, for some data types, information about the data value.

The data type value in byte 1 corresponds to the values in the `xtype` column in the `systypes` database system table. For example, if the first byte contains a hex 38, that corresponds to the `xtype` value of 56, which is the `int` data type.

Some data types stored in a `sql_variant` column require additional information bytes stored at the beginning of the data value (after the `sql_variant` version byte). The data types requiring additional information bytes and the values in these information bytes are as follows:

- Numeric and decimal data types require 1 byte for the precision and 1 byte for the scale.
- Character strings require 2 bytes to store the maximum length and 4 bytes for the collation ID.
- Binary and varbinary data values require 2 bytes to store the maximum length.

Storage of Sparse Columns A new storage feature introduced in SQL Server 2008 is sparse columns. Sparse columns are ordinary columns that use an optimized storage format for `NULL` values. Sparse columns reduce the space requirements for `NULL` values at the cost of more overhead to retrieve non-`NULL` values. A rule of thumb is to consider using sparse columns when you expect at least 90% of the rows to contain `NULL` values. Prime candidates are tables that have many columns where most of the attributes are `NULL` for most rows—for example, when different attributes apply to different subsets of rows and, for each row, only a subset of columns are populated with values.

The sparse columns feature significantly increases the number of possible columns in a table from 1,024 to 30,000. However, not all 30,000 can contain values. The number of actual populated columns you can have depends on the number of bytes of data in the rows. With sparse columns, storage of `NULL` values is optimized, requiring no space at all for storing `NULL` values. This is unlike nonsparse columns, which, as you saw earlier, do need space even for `NULL` values (a fixed-length `NULL` value requires the full column width, and a variable-length `NULL` requires at least 2 bytes of storage in the column offset array).

Although sparse columns themselves require no space for NULL values, there is some fixed overhead space required to allow rows to contain sparse columns. This space is needed to add the sparse vector to the end of the data row. A sparse vector is added to the end of a data row only if at least one sparse column is defined on the table.

The sparse vector is used to keep track of the physical storage of sparse columns in the row. It is stored as the last variable-length column in the row. No bit is stored in the NULL bitmap for the sparse vector column but it is included in the count of the variable columns (refer to Figure 34.3 for the general structure of a data row). The bytes stored in the sparse vector are shown in Table 34.5.

TABLE 34.5 Bytes Stored in the Sparse Vector

Name	Number of Bytes	Description
Complex column header	2	A value of 05 indicates the column is a sparse vector
Sparse column count	2	Number of sparse columns
Column ID set	2 × # of sparse columns	The column IDs of each column with a value stored in the sparse vector
Column offset table	2 × # of sparse columns	The offset of the ending position of each sparse column
Sparse data	Depends on actual values	The actual data values for each sparse column stored in column ID order

With the required overhead space for the sparse vector, the maximum size of all fixed-length non-NULL sparse columns is reduced to 8,019 bytes per row.

As you can see, the contents of a sparse vector are like a data row structure within a data row. If you refer to Figure 34.3, you can see that the structure of the sparse vector is similar to the shaded structure of a data row. One of the main differences is that the sparse vector stores no information for any sparse columns that contain NULL values. Also, fixed-length and variable-length columns are stored the same within the sparse vector. However, if you have any variable-length columns in the sparse vector that are too large to fit in the 8,019-byte limit of the data row, they are stored on row-overflow pages.

The Row Offset Table

The location of a row within a page is identified by the *row offset table*, which is located at the end of the page. To find a specific row within a page, SQL Server looks up the starting byte address for a given row ID in the row offset table, which contains the offset of the row from the beginning of the page (refer to Figure 34.2). Each entry in the row offset table is 2 bytes in size, so for each row in a table, an additional 2 bytes of space is added in from the end of the page for the row offset entry.

The row offset table keeps track of the logical order of rows on a data page. If a table has a clustered index defined on it, the data rows are stored in clustered index order. However, they may not be physically stored in clustered key order on the page itself. Instead, the row offset array indicates the logical clustered key order of the data rows. For example, row offset slot 0 refers to the first row in the clustered index key order, slot 1 refers to the second row, slot 2 refers to the third row, and so on. The physical location of the rows on the page may be in any order, depending on when rows on the page were inserted or deleted.

Row-Overflow Pages

While the maximum in-row size is 8,060 bytes per row, SQL Server 2008 allows actual rows to exceed this size for tables that contain `varchar`, `nvarchar`, `varbinary`, `sql_variant`, or common language runtime (CLR) user-defined type columns. Although the length of each one of these columns must still fall within the limit of 8,000 bytes, the combined width of the row can exceed the 8,060-byte limit.

When a combination of `varchar`, `nvarchar`, `varbinary`, `sql_variant`, or CLR user-defined type columns exceeds the 8,060-byte limit, SQL Server moves the record column with the largest width to another page in the `ROW_OVERFLOW_DATA` allocation unit, while maintaining a 24-byte pointer to the row-overflow page on the original page. Moving large records to another page occurs dynamically as records are lengthened based on update operations. Update operations that shorten records may cause records to be moved back to the original page in the `IN_ROW_DATA` allocation unit.

Row-overflow pages are used only under certain circumstances. For one, the row itself has to exceed 8,060 bytes; it does not matter how full the data page itself is. If a row is less than 8,060 bytes and there's not enough space in the data page, normal page splitting occurs to store the row. Also, each column in a table must be completely on the row or completely off it. A variable-length column cannot have some of its data on the regular data page and some of its data on the row-overflow page. One row can span multiple row-overflow pages depending on how many large variable-length columns there are.

Be aware that having data rows that require a row-overflow page increases the I/O cost of retrieving the data row. Querying and performing other select operations, such as sorts or joins on large records that contain row-overflow data, also slow processing time because these records are processed synchronously instead of asynchronously.

Therefore, when you design a table with multiple `varchar`, `nvarchar`, `varbinary`, `sql_variant`, or CLR user-defined type columns, you might want to consider the percentage of rows that are likely to require row overflow and the frequency with which this overflow data is likely to be queried. If there are likely to be frequent queries on many rows of row-overflow data, you should consider normalizing the table so that some columns are moved to another table, reducing the overall row size so that the rows fit within 8,060 bytes. The data can then be recombined in a query using an asynchronous `JOIN` operation.

TIP

Because of the performance implications, row-overflow pages are intended to be a solution for situations in which most of your data rows fit completely on your data pages and you only occasionally have rows that require a row-overflow page. Row-overflow pages allow SQL Server to handle the large data rows effectively without requiring a redesign of your table. However, if you find more than a few of your rows exceed the in-row size, you probably should look into using the LOB data types or redesigning your table.

LOB Data Pages

If you want to store large amounts of text or binary data, you can use the `text`, `ntext`, and `image` data types, as well as the `varchar(max)`, `nvarchar(max)`, and `varbinary(max)` data types. (For information about how to use these data types, see Chapter 24, "Creating and Managing Tables," and Chapter 38, "Database Design and Performance.") Each column for a row of these data types can store up to 2GB (minus 2 bytes) of data. By default, the LOB values are not stored as part of the data row, but as a collection of pages on their own. For each LOB column, the data page contains a 16-byte pointer, which points to the location of the initial page of the LOB data. A row with several LOB columns has one pointer for each column.

The pages that hold LOB data are 8KB in size, just like any other page in SQL Server. An individual LOB page can hold LOB data for multiple columns and also from multiple rows. A LOB data page can even contain a mix of LOB data. This helps reduce the storage requirements for the LOB data, especially when smaller amounts of data are stored in these columns. For example, if SQL Server could store data for only a single column for a single row on a single LOB data page and the data value consisted of only a single character, it would still use an entire 8KB data page to store that data! Definitely not an efficient use of space.

A LOB data page can hold LOB data for only a single table, however. A table with a LOB column has a single set of pages to hold all its LOB data.

LOB information is presented externally (to the user) as a long string of bytes. Internally, however, the information is stored within a set of pages. The pages are not necessarily organized sequentially but are logically organized as a B-tree structure. (B-tree structures are covered in more detail later in this chapter.) If an operation addresses some information in the middle of the data, SQL Server can navigate through the B-tree to find the data. In previous versions, SQL Server had to follow the entire page chain from the beginning to find the desired information.

If the amount of the data in the LOB field is less than 32KB, the 16-byte pointer in the data row points to an 84-byte root structure in the LOB B-tree. This root structure points to the pages and location where the actual LOB data is stored (see Figure 34.4). The data itself can be placed anywhere within the LOB pages for the table. The root structure keeps track of the location of the information in a logical manner. If the data is less than 64 bytes, it is stored in the root structure itself.

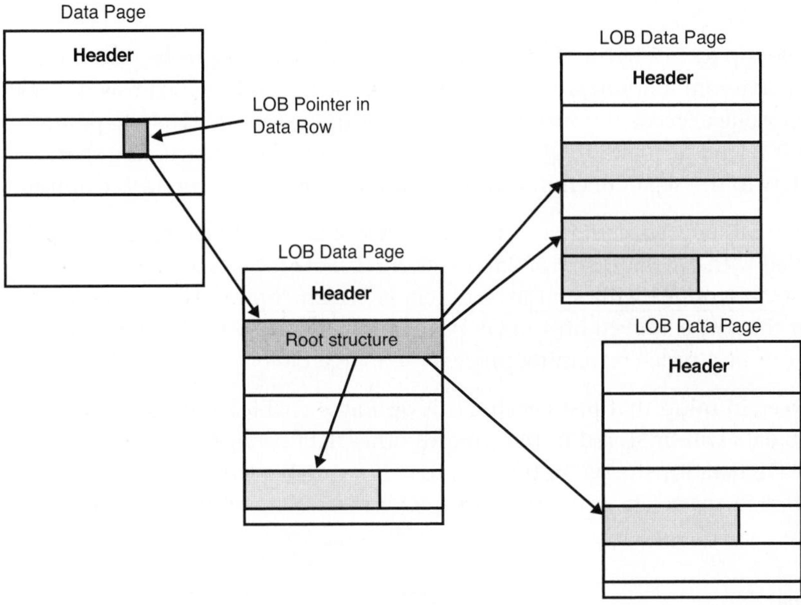

FIGURE 34.4 LOB data root structure pointing at the location of LOB data in the LOB B-tree.

If the amount of LOB data exceeds 32KB, SQL Server allocates intermediate B-tree index nodes that point to the LOB pages. In this situation, the intermediate node pages are stored on pages not shared between different occurrences of LOB columns; the intermediate node pages store nodes for only one LOB column in a single data row.

Storing LOB Data in the Data Row

To further conserve space and help minimize I/O, SQL Server 2008 supports storing LOB data in the actual data row. When the LOB data is stored outside the data row pages, at a minimum, SQL Server needs to perform one additional page read per row to get the LOB data.

Why would you want to store LOB data in the row? Why not just store the data in a `varchar(8000)`? Well, primarily because there is an upper limit of 8KB if the data is stored within the data row (not counting the other columns). Using a LOB data type, you can store more than 2 *billion* bytes of text. If you know most of your records will be small, but on occasion, some very large values will be stored, the `text in row` option provides optimum performance and better space efficiency for the majority of your LOB values, while providing the flexibility you need for the occasional large values. This option also provides the benefit of keeping the data all in a single column instead of having to split it across multiple columns or rows when the data exceeds the size limit of a single row.

If you want to enable the `text in row` option for a table with a LOB column, use the `sp_tableoption` stored procedure:

```
exec sp_tableoption pub_info, 'text in row', 512
```

This example enables up to 512 bytes of LOB data in the `pub_info` table to be stored in the data row. The maximum amount of LOB data that can be stored in a data row is 7,000 bytes. When a LOB value exceeds the specified size, rather than store the 16-byte pointer in the data row as it would normally, SQL Server stores the 24-byte root structure that contains the pointers to the separate chunks of LOB data for the row in the LOB column.

The second parameter to `sp_tableoption` can be just the option `ON`. If no size is specified, the option is enabled with a default size of 256 bytes. To disable the `text in row` option, you can set its value to `0` or `OFF` with `sp_tableoption`. When the option is turned off, all LOB data stored in the row is moved off to LOB pages and replaced with the standard 16-byte pointer. This can be a time-consuming process for a large table.

Also, you should keep in mind that just because this option is enabled it doesn't always mean that the LOB data will be stored in the row. All other data columns that are not LOB take priority over LOB data for storage in the data row. If a variable-length column grows and there is not enough space left in the row or page for the LOB data, the LOB data is moved off the page.

Storage of MAX Data

An alternative to the text and image data types in SQL Server 2008 is the option of defining variable-length data using the `MAX` specifier. When you use the `MAX` specifier with `varchar`, `nvarchar`, and `varbinary` columns, SQL Server determines automatically whether to store the data as a regular `varchar`, `nvarchar`, or `varbinary` value or as a LOB. Essentially, if the actual length is less than 8,000 bytes, SQL Server treats it as if it were one of the regular variable-length data types, including using row-overflow pages if necessary. If the `MAX` column exceeds 8,000 bytes, it is stored like LOB data.

Index Pages

Index information is stored on index pages. An *index page* has the same layout as a data page. The difference is the type of information stored on the page. Generally, a row in an index page contains the index key and a pointer to the page or row at the next (lower) level.

The actual information stored in an index page depends on the index type and whether it is a leaf-level page. A leaf-level clustered index page is the data page itself; you've already seen its structure. The information stored on other index pages is as follows:

- **Clustered indexes, nonleaf pages**—Each index row contains the index key and a pointer (the `fileId` and a page address) to a page in the index tree at the next lower level.
- **Nonclustered index, nonleaf pages**—Each index row contains the index key and a page-down pointer (the file ID and a page address) to a page in the index tree at

the next lower level. For nonunique indexes, the nonleaf row also contains the row locator information for the corresponding data row.

- **Nonclustered index, leaf pages**—Rows on this level contain an index key and a reference to a data row. For heap tables, this is the Row ID; for clustered tables, this is the clustered key for the corresponding data row.

The actual structure and content of index rows, as well as the structure of the index tree, are discussed in more detail later in this chapter.

Space Allocation Structures

When a table or index needs more space in a database, SQL Server needs a way to determine where space is available in the database to be allocated. If the table or index is still fewer than eight pages in size, SQL Server must find a mixed extent with one or more pages available that can be allocated. If the table or index is eight pages or larger in size, SQL Server must find a free uniform extent that can be allocated to the table or index.

Extents

If SQL Server allocated space one page at a time as pages were needed for a table (or an index), SQL Server would be spending a good portion of its time just allocating pages, and the data would likely be scattered noncontiguously throughout the database. Scanning such a table would not be very efficient. For these reasons, pages for each object are grouped together and allocated in *extents*; an extent consists of eight logically contiguous pages.

When a table or index is created, it is initially allocated a page on a mixed extent. If no mixed extents are available in the database, a new mixed extent is allocated. A mixed extent can be shared by up to eight objects (each page in the extent can be assigned to a different table or index).

As the table grows to at least eight pages in size, all future allocations to the table are done as *uniform extents*.

Figure 34.5 shows the use of mixed and uniform extents.

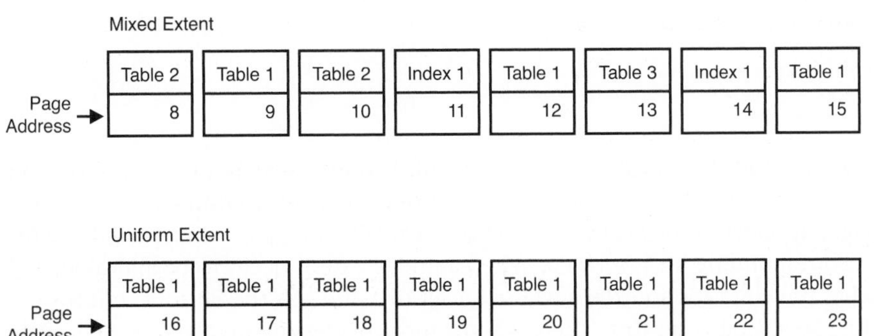

FIGURE 34.5 Mixed and uniform extents.

If SQL Server had to search throughout an entire database file to find free extents, it wouldn't be efficient. Instead, SQL Server uses two special types of pages to record which extents have been allocated to tables or indexes and whether it is a mixed or uniform extent:

- Global allocation map pages (GAMs)
- Shared global allocation map pages (SGAMs)

Global and Shared Global Allocation Map Pages

The allocation map pages track whether extents have been allocated to objects and indexes and whether the allocation is for mixed extents or uniform extents. As mentioned in the preceding section, there are two types of GAMs:

- **Global allocation map (GAM)**—The GAM keeps track of all allocated extents in a database, regardless of what it's allocated to. The structure of the GAM is straightforward: each bit in the page outside the page header represents one extent in the file, where `1` means that the extent is not allocated, and `0` means that the extent is allocated. Nearly 8,000 bytes (64,000 bits) are available in a GAM page after the header and other overhead bytes are taken into account. Therefore, a single GAM covers approximately 64,000 extents, or 4GB (64,000 * 64KB) of data.
- **Shared global allocation map (SGAM)**—The SGAM keeps track of mixed extents that have free space available. An SGAM has a structure similar to a GAM, with each bit representing an extent. A value of `1` means that the extent is a mixed extent and there is free space (at least one unused page) available on the extent. A value of `0` means that the extent is not currently allocated, that the extent is a uniform extent, or that the extent is a mixed extent with no free pages.

Table 34.6 summarizes the meaning of the bit in GAMs and SGAMs.

TABLE 34.6 Meaning of the GAM and SGAM Bits

Extent Usage	GAM Bit	SGAM Bit
Free, not used	1	0
Uniform or mixed with no free pages	0	0
Mixed, with free pages available	0	1

When SQL Server needs to allocate a uniform extent, it simply searches the GAM for a bit with a value of `1` and sets it to `0` to indicate it has been allocated. To find a mixed extent with free pages, it searches the SGAM for a bit set to `1`. When all pages in a mixed extent are used, its corresponding bit is set to `0`. When a mixed extent needs to be allocated, SQL Server searches the GAM for an extent whose bit set to `1` and sets the bit to `0`, and the corresponding SGAM bit is set to `1`. There is some more processing involved as well, such as spreading the data evenly across database files, but the allocation algorithms are still relatively simple.

SQL Server is able to easily locate GAM pages in a database because the first GAM page is located at the third page in the file (page number 2). There is another GAM every 511,230 pages after the first GAM. The fourth page (page number 3) in each database file is the SGAM page, and there is another SGAM each 511,230 pages after the first SGAM.

Page Free Space Pages

A *page free space (PFS)* page records whether each page is allocated and the amount of free space available on the page. Each PFS covers 8,088 contiguous pages in the file. For each of the 8,088 pages, the PFS has a 1-byte record that contains a bitmap for each page indicating whether the page is empty, 1 to 50% full, 51 to 80% full, 81 to 95% full, or more than 95% full. The first PFS page in a file is located at page number 1, the second PFS page is located at page 8088, and each additional PFS page is located every 8,088 pages after that. SQL Server uses PFS pages to find free pages on extents and to find pages with space available on extents when a new row needs to be added to a table or index.

Figure 34.6 shows the layout of GAM, SGAM, and PFS pages in a database file. Note that every file has a single file header located at page 0.

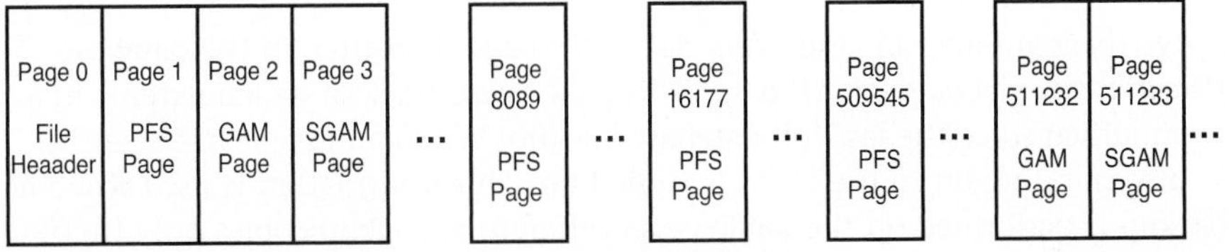

FIGURE 34.6 The layout of GAM, SGAM, and PFS pages in a database file.

Index Allocation Map Pages

Index allocation map (IAM) pages keep track of the extents used by a heap or index. Each heap table and index has at least one IAM page for each file where it has extents. An IAM cannot reference pages in other database files; if the heap or index spreads to a new database file, a new IAM for the heap or index is created in that file. IAM pages are allocated as needed and are spread randomly throughout the database files.

An IAM page contains a small header that has the address of the first extent in the range of pages being mapped by the IAM. It also contains eight page pointers that keep track of index or heap pages that are in mixed extents. These pointers might or might not contain any information, depending on whether any data has been deleted from the tables and the page(s) released. Remember, an index or heap will have no more than eight pages in mixed extents (after eight pages, it begins using uniform extents), so only the first IAM page stores this information. The remainder of the IAM page is for the allocation bitmap. The IAM bitmap works similarly to the GAM, indicating which extents over the range of extents covered by the IAM are used by the heap or index the IAM belongs to. If a bit is on, the corresponding extent is allocated to the table.

Each IAM covers a possible range of 63,903 extents (511,224 pages), covering a 4GB section of a file. Each bit represents an extent within that range, whether or not the extent is allocated to the object that the IAM belongs to. If the bit is set to `1`, the relative extent in the range is allocated to the index or heap. If the bit is set to `0`, the extent is either not allocated or might be allocated to another heap or index.

For example, assume that an IAM page resides at page 649 in the file. If the bit pattern in the first byte of the IAM is `1010 0100`, the first, third, and sixth extents within the range of the IAM are allocated to the heap or index. The second, fourth, fifth, seventh, and eighth extents are not.

NOTE

For a heap table, the data pages and rows within them are not stored in any specific order. Unlike versions of SQL Server prior to 7.0, the pages in a heap structure are not linked together in a page chain. The only logical connection between data pages is the information recorded in the IAM pages, which are linked together. The structure of heap tables is examined in more detail later in this chapter.

Differential Changed Map Pages

The seventh page (page number 6), and every 511,232nd page thereafter, in the database file is the *differential changed map (DCM)* page. This page keeps track of which extents in a file have been modified since the last full database backup. When an extent has been modified, its corresponding bit in the DCM is turned on. This information is used when a differential backup is performed on the database. A differential backup copies only the extents changed since the last full backup was made. Using the DCM, SQL Server can quickly tell which extents need to be backed up by examining the bits on the DCM pages for each data file in the database. When a full backup is performed for the database, all the bits are set back to `0`.

Bulk Changed Map Pages

The eighth page (page number 7), and every 511,232nd page thereafter, in the database file is the *bulk changed map (BCM)*. When you perform a minimally or bulk-logged operation in SQL Server 2008 in `BULK_LOGGED` recovery mode, SQL Server logs only the fact that the operation occurred and doesn't log the actual data changes. The operation is still fully recoverable because SQL Server keeps track of what extents were actually modified by the bulk operation in the BCM page. Similar to the DCM page, each bit on a BCM page represents an extent within its range, and if the bit is set to `1`, that indicates that the corresponding extent has been changed by a minimally logged bulk operation since the last full database backup. All the bits on the BCM page are reset to `0` whenever a full database backup or log backup occurs.

When you initiate a log backup for a database using the `BULK_LOGGED` recovery model, SQL Server scans the BCM pages and backs up all the modified extents along with the contents of the transaction log itself. You should be aware that the log file itself might be small, but the backup of the log can be many times larger if a large bulk operation has been performed since the last log backup.

Data Compression

SQL Server 2008 introduced a new data compression feature that is available in Enterprise and Datacenter Editions. Data compression helps to reduce both storage and memory requirements as the data is compressed both on disk and when brought into the SQL Server data cache.

When compression is enabled and data is written to disk, it is compressed and stored in the designated compressed format. When the data is read from disk into the buffer cache, it remains in its compressed format. This helps reduce both storage requirements and memory requirements. It also reduces I/O because more data can be stored on a data page when it's compressed. When the data is passed to another component of SQL Server, however, the Database Engine then has to uncompress the data on the fly. In other words, every time data has to be passed to or from the buffered cache, it has to be compressed or uncompressed. This requires extra CPU overhead to accomplish. However, in most cases, the amount of I/O and buffer cache saved by compression more than makes up for the CPU costs, boosting the overall performance of SQL Server.

Data compression can be applied on the following database objects:

- Tables (clustered or heap)
- Nonclustered indexes
- Indexed views

As the DBA, you need to evaluate which of the preceding objects in your database could benefit from compression and then decide whether you want to compress it using either row-level or page-level compression. Compression is enabled or disabled at the object level There is no single option you can enable that turns compression on or off for all objects in the database. Fortunately, other than turning compression on or off for the preceding objects, you don't have to do anything else to use data compression. SQL Server handles data compression transparently without your having to re-architect your database or your applications.

Row-Level Compression

Row-level compression isn't true data compression. Instead, space savings are achieved by using a more efficient storage format for fixed-length data to use the minimum amount of space required. For example, the `int` data type uses 4 bytes of storage regardless of the value stored, even `NULL`. However, only a single byte is required to store a value of `100`. Row-level compression allows fixed-length values to use only the amount of storage space required.

Row-level compression saves space and reduces I/O by

- Reducing the amount of metadata required to store data rows
- Storing fixed-length numeric data types as if they were variable-length data types, using only as many bytes as necessary to store the actual value
- Storing `CHAR` data types as variable-length data types
- Not storing `NULL` or `0` values

Row-level data compression provides less compression than page-level data compression, but it also incurs less overhead, reducing the amount of CPU resources required to implement it.

Row-level compression can be enabled when creating a table or index or using the `ALTER TABLE` or `ALTER INDEX` commands by specifying the `WITH (DATA_COMPRESSION = ROW)` option. The following example enables row compression on the `titles` table in the `bigpubs2008` database:

```
ALTER TABLE titles REBUILD WITH (DATA_COMPRESSION=ROW)
```

Additionally, if a table or index is partitioned, you can apply compression at the partition level.

When row-level compression is applied to a table, a new row format is used that is unlike the `standard data row` format discussed previouslywhich has a fixed-length data section separate from a variable-length data section (see Figure 34.3). This new row format is referred to as column descriptor, or CD, format. The name of this row format refers to the fact the every column has description information contained in the row itself. Figure 34.7 illustrates a representative view of the CD format (a definitive view is difficult because, except for the header, the number of bytes in each region is completely dependent on the values in the data row).

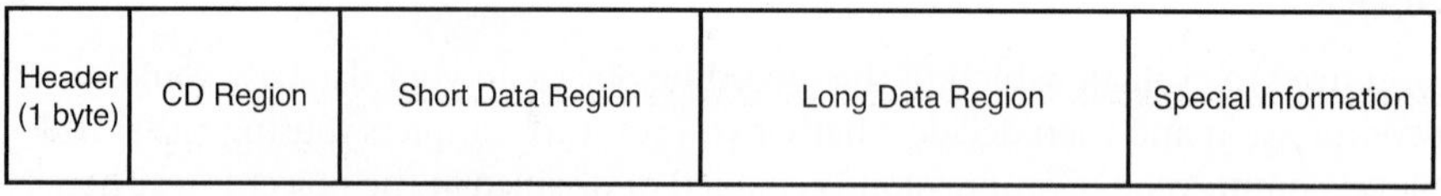

Header (1 byte)	CD Region	Short Data Region	Long Data Region	Special Information

FIGURE 34.7 A representative structure of a CD format row.

The row header is always 1 byte in length and contains information similar to Status Bits A in a normal data row:

- **Bit 0**—This bit indicates the type of record (*1* = CD record format).
- **Bit 1**—This bit indicates whether the row contains versioning information.
- **Bits 2–4**—This three-bit value indicates what kind of information is stored in the row (such as primary record, ghost record, forwarding record, index record).
- **Bit 5**—This bit indicates whether the row contains a Long data region (with values greater than 8 bytes in length).
- **Bits 6 and 7**—These bits are not used.

The CD region consists of two parts. The first is either a 1- or 2-byte value indicating the number of short columns (8 bytes or less). If the most significant bit of the first byte is set to `0`, it's a 1-byte field representing up to 127 columns; if it's `1`, it's a 2-byte field representing up to 32,767 columns. Following the first 1 or 2 bytes is the CD array. The CD array uses 4 bits for each column in the table to represent information about the length of the column. A bit representation of `0` indicates the column is `NULL`. A bit representation of the values `1` to `9` indicates the column is 0 to 8 bytes in length, respectively. A bit representation of `10` (`0xa`) indicates that the corresponding column value is a long data value and uses no space in the short data region. A bit representation of `11` (`0xb`) represents a bit column with a value of `1`, and a bit representation of `12` (`0xc`) indicates that the corresponding value is a 1-byte symbol representing a value in the page compression dictionary (the page compression dictionary is discussed next in the page-level compression section).

The short data region contains each of the short data values. However, because accessing the last columns can be expensive if there are hundreds of columns in the table, columns are grouped into clusters of 30 columns. At the beginning of the short data region, there is an area called the *short data cluster array*. Each entry in the array is a single byte, which indicates the sum of the sizes of all the data in the previous cluster in the short data region; the value is essentially a pointer to the first column of the cluster (no row offset is needed for the first cluster because it starts immediately after the CD region).

Any data value in the row longer than 8 bytes is stored in the long data region. This can include LOB and row-overflow pointers. Long data needs an actual offset value to allow SQL Server to locate each value. This offset array looks similar to the offset array used in the `standard data` row structure. The long data region consists of three parts: an offset array, a long data cluster array, and the long data. The long data cluster array is similar to the short data cluster array; it has one entry for each 30-column cluster (except for the last one) and serves to limit the cost of locating columns near the end of a long list of columns.

The special information section at the end of the row contains three optional pieces of information. The existence of any or all of this information is indicated by bits in the first 1-byte header at the beginning of the row. The three special pieces of information are

- **Forwarding pointer**—This pointer is used in a heap when a row is forwarded due to an update (forward pointers are discussed later in this chapter).
- **Back pointer**—If the row is a forwarded row, it contains a pointer back to the original row location.
- **Versioning information**—If snapshot isolation is being used, 14 bytes of versioning information are appended to the row.

Page-Level Compression

Page-level compression is an implementation of true data compression, using both column prefix and dictionary-based compression. Data is compressed be storing repeating values or common prefixes only once and then referencing those values from other columns and rows. When you implement page compression for a table, row compression is applied as well. Page-level compression offers increased data compression over row-level compression alone but at the expense of greater CPU utilization. It works using these techniques:

- First, row-level data compression is applied to fit as many rows as it can on a single page.

- Next, column prefix compression is run. Essentially, repeating patterns of data at the beginning of the values of a given column are removed and substituted with an abbreviated reference, which is stored in the compression information (CI) structure stored after the page header.
- Finally, dictionary compression is applied on the page. Dictionary compression searches for repeated values anywhere on a page and stores them in the CI.

Page compression is applied only after a page is full and if SQL Server determines that compressing a page will save a meaningful amount of space.

The amount of compression provided by page-level data compression is highly dependent on the data stored in a table or index. If a lot of the data repeats itself, compression is more efficient. If the data is more randomly discrete values, fewer benefits are gained from using page-level compression.

Column prefix compression looks at the column values on a single page and chooses a common prefix that can be used to reduce the storage space required for values in that column. The longest value in the column that contains the prefix is chosen as the anchor value. A row that represents the prefix values for each column is created and stored in the CI structure that immediately follows the page header. Each column is then stored as a delta from the anchor value, where repeated prefix values in the column are replaced by a reference to the corresponding prefix. If the value in a row does not exactly match the selected prefix value, a partial match can still be indicated.

For example, consider a page that contains the following data rows before prefix compression as shown in Figure 34.8.

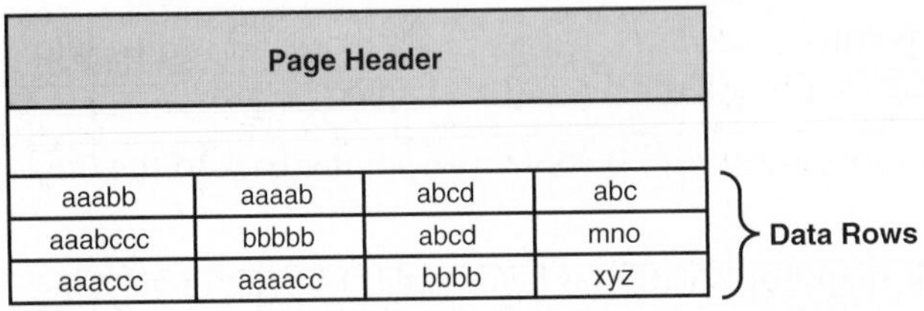

Page Header

aaabb	aaaab	abcd	abc
aaabccc	bbbbb	abcd	mno
aaaccc	aaaacc	bbbb	xyz

Data Rows

FIGURE 34.8 Sample page of a table before prefix compression.

After you apply column prefix compression on the page, the CI structure is stored after the page header holding the prefix values for each column. The columns then are stored as the difference between the prefix and column value, as shown in Figure 34.9.

In the first column in the first data row, the value `4b` represents that the first four characters of the prefix (`aaab`) are present at the beginning of the column for that row and also the character `b`. If you append the character `b` to the first four values of the prefix, it rebuilds the original value of `aaabb`. For any columns values that are [empty], the column matches the prefix value exactly. Any column value that starts with `0` means that none of the first characters of the column match the prefix. For the fourth column, there is no common prefix value in the columns, so no prefix value is stored in the CI structure.

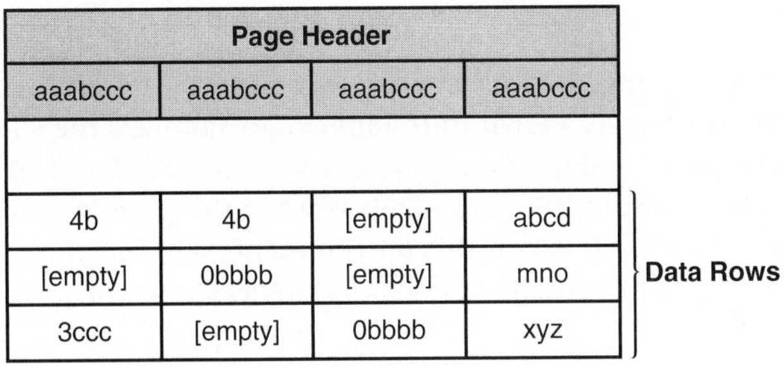

Page Header			
aaabccc	aaabccc	aaabccc	aaabccc
4b	4b	[empty]	abcd
[empty]	0bbbb	[empty]	mno
3ccc	[empty]	0bbbb	xyz

Data Rows

FIGURE 34.9 Sample page of a table after prefix compression.

After column prefix compression is applied to every column individually on the page, SQL Server then looks to apply dictionary compression. Dictionary compression looks for repeated values anywhere on the page and also stores them in the CI structure after the column prefix values. Dictionary compression values replace repeated values anywhere on a page. The following illustrates the same page shown previously after dictionary compression has been applied:

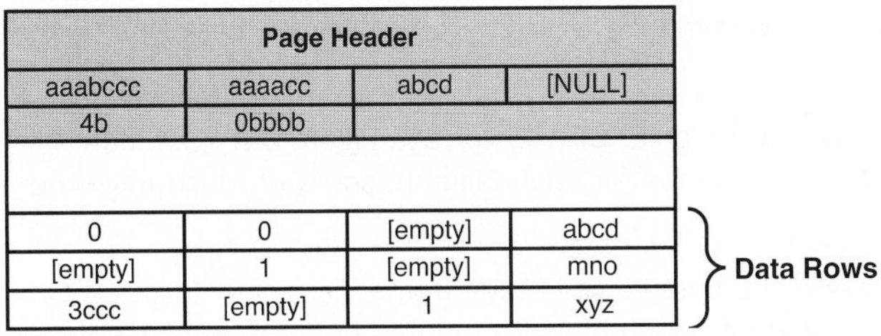

Page Header			
aaabccc	aaaacc	abcd	[NULL]
4b	0bbbb		
0	0	[empty]	abcd
[empty]	1	[empty]	mno
3ccc	[empty]	1	xyz

Data Rows

FIGURE 34.10 Sample page of a table after dictionary compression.

The dictionary is stored as a set of these duplicate values and a symbol to represent these values in the columns on the page. As you can see in this example, `4b` is repeated in multiple columns in multiple rows, and the value is replaced by the symbol `0` throughout the page. The value `0bbbb` is replaced by the symbol `1`. SQL Server recognizes that the value stored in the column is a symbol and not a data value by examining the coding in the CD array, as discussed earlier.

Not all pages contain both the prefix record and a dictionary. Having them both depends on whether the data has enough repeating values or patterns to warrant either a prefix record or a dictionary.

The CI Record

The CI record is the only main structural change to a page when it is page compressed versus a page that uses row compression only. As shown in the previous examples, the CI record is located immediately after the page header. There is no entry for the CI record in the row offset table because its location is always the same. A bit is set in the page header to indicate whether the page is page compressed. When this bit is present, SQL Server knows to look for the CI record. The CI record contains the data elements shown in Table 34.7.

TABLE 34.7 Data Elements Within the CI Record

Name	Description
Header	This structure contains 1 byte to keep track of information about the CI. Bit 0 is the version (currently always `0`), Bit 1 indicates the presence of a column prefix anchor record, and Bit 2 indicates the presence of a compression dictionary.
`PageModCount`	This value keeps track of the number of changes to the page to determine whether the compression on the page should be reevaluated and the CI record rebuilt.
Offsets	This element contains values to help SQL Server find the dictionary. It contains the offset of the end of the Column prefix anchor record and offset of the end of the CI record itself.
Anchor Record	This record looks exactly like a regular CD record (see Figure 34.7). Values stored are the common prefix values for each column, some of which might be `NULL`.
Dictionary	The first 2 bytes represent the number of entries in the dictionary, followed by an offset array of 2-byte entries, which indicate the end offset of each dictionary entry, and then the actual dictionary values.

Implementing Page Compression

Page compression can be implemented for a table at the time it is created or by using the `ALTER TABLE` command, as in the following example:

```
ALTER TABLE sales_big REBUILD WITH (DATA_COMPRESSION=PAGE)
```

Unlike row compression, which is applied immediately on the rows, page compression isn't applied until the page is full. The rows cannot be compressed until SQL Server can determine what encodings for prefix and dictionary substitution are going to be used to replace the actual data. When you enable page compression for a table or a partition, SQL Server examines every full page to determine the possible space savings. Any pages that are not full are not considered for compression. During the compression analysis, the prefix and dictionary values are created, and the column values are modified to reflect the prefix and dictionary values. Then row compression is applied. If the new compressed page can hold at least five additional rows, or 25% more rows than the page currently holds, the page is compressed. If neither one of these criteria is met, the compressed version of the page is discarded.

New rows inserted into a compressed page are compressed as they are inserted. However, new entries are not added to the prefix list or dictionary based on a single new row. The prefix values and dictionary symbols are rebuilt only on an all-or-nothing basis. After the page is changed a sufficient number of times, SQL Server evaluates whether to rebuild the CI record. The `PageModCount` field in the CI record is used to keep track of the number of changes to the page since the CI record was last built or rebuilt. This value is updated every time a row is updated, deleted, or inserted. If SQL Server encounters a full page during a data modification and the `PageModCount` is greater than 25 or the `PageModCount` divided by the number of rows on the page is greater than 25%, SQL Server reapplies the compression analysis on the page. Again, only if recompressing the page creates room for five additional rows, or 25% more rows than the page currently holds, the new compressed page replaces the existing page.

In B-tree structures (nonclustered indexes or a clustered table), only the leaf-level and data pages are considered for compression. When you insert a new row into a leaf or data page, if the compressed row fits, it is inserted and nothing more is done. If it doesn't fit, SQL Server attempts to recompress the page and then recompress the row based on the new CI record. If the row fits after recompression, it is inserted and nothing more is done. If the row still doesn't fit, the page needs to be split. When a compressed page is split, the CI record is copied to the new page exactly as it was, along with the rows moved to the new page. However, the `PageModCount` value is set to 25, so that when the new page gets full, it will be immediately analyzed for recompression. Leaf and data pages are also checked for recompression whenever you run an index rebuild or shrink operation.

If you enable compression on a heap table, pages are evaluated for compression only during rebuild and shrink operations. Also, if you drop a clustered index on a table, turning it into a heap, SQL Server runs compression analysis on any full pages. Compression is avoided during normal data modification operations on a heap to avoid changes to the Row IDs, which are used as the row locators for any indexes on the heap. (See the "Understanding Index Structures" section later in this chapter for a discussion of row locators.) Although the `RowModCounter` is still maintained, SQL Server essentially ignores it and never tries to recompress a page based on the `RowModCounter` value.

Evaluating Page Compression

Before choosing to implement page compression, you should determine if the overhead of page compression will provide sufficient benefit in space savings. To determine how changing the compression state will affect a table or an index, you can use the SQL Server 2008 `sp_estimate_data_compression_savings` stored procedure, which is available only in the editions of SQL Server that support data compression. This stored procedure evaluates the effects of compression by sampling up to 5,000 pages in the table and creating a copy of these 5,000 pages of the table in `tempdb`, performing the compression, and then using the sample to estimate the overall size for the table after compression. The syntax for `sp_estimate_data_compression_savings` is as follows:

```
sp_estimate_data_compression_savings
      [ @schema_name = ] 'schema_name'
     , [ @object_name = ] 'object_name'
    , [@index_id = ] index_id
     , [@partition_number = ] partition_number
    , [@data_compression = ] 'data_compression'
```

You can estimate the data compression savings for a table for either row or page compression by specifying either `'ROW'` or `'PAGE'` as the value for the `@data_compression` parameter. You can also estimate the average size of the compressed table if compression is disabled by specifying `NONE` as the value for `@data_compression`. You can also use the `sp_estimate_data_compression_savings` procedure to estimate the space savings for compression on a specific index or partition. The following example estimates the space savings if page compression were applied to the `big_sales` table in the `bigpubs2008` table versus row compression:

```
use bigpubs2008
go
exec sp_estimate_data_compression_savings 'dbo', 'sales_big', null, null, 'PAGE'
go

object_name  schema_name  index_id  partition_number
size_with_current_compression_setting(KB)
size_with_requested_compression_setting(KB)
sample_size_with_current_compression_setting(KB)
sample_size_with_requested_compression_setting(KB)
----------- ----------- -------- ----------------
-----------------------------------------
------------------------------------------
-------------------------------------------------
-------------------------------------------------
sales_big    dbo          1         1
116512
39128
40016
13440
sales_big    dbo          2         1
36648
22128
10904
6584


exec sp_estimate_data_compression_savings 'dbo', 'sales_big', null, null, 'ROW'
go
```

```
object_name  schema_name  index_id  partition_number
size_with_current_compression_setting(KB)
size_with_requested_compression_setting(KB)
sample_size_with_current_compression_setting(KB)
sample_size_with_requested_compression_setting(KB)

----------- ----------- -------- --------------
-----------------------------------------
-----------------------------------------
------------------------------------------------
------------------------------------------------
sales_big    dbo          1         1
116512
97936
40344
33912
sales_big    dbo          2         1
36648
27176
10992
8152
```

You can see in this example that the space savings from page compression would be significant, with an estimated reduction in the size of the table itself (`index_id = 1`) from 113MB (116,512 KB) to 38MB (39,128 KB), a savings of more than 66%. Row compression would not provide nearly as significant a savings, with an estimated reduction in size from 113MB to only 95MB (97,936 KB) , only a 16% savings.

If you compress the table, you can compare the estimated space savings to the actual size. For example, let's look at the initial size of the `sales_big` table:

```
use bigpubs2008
go

select sum(page_count) as pages, sum(compressed_page_count) as compressed_pages
from sys.dm_db_index_physical_stats (DB_ID(),
OBJECT_ID('sales_big'), 1, null, 'DETAILED')
where index_level = 0

SELECT SUM(used_page_count/ 128.0) AS size_in_MB
FROM sys.dm_db_partition_stats
WHERE object_id=OBJECT_ID('dbo.sales_big') AND index_id=1
GO

pages                compressed_pages
------------------------------------------
14519                0
```

```
size_in_MB
---------------------------------------
113.742187
```

Now, implement page compression on the `sales_big` table:

```
ALTER TABLE sales_big REBUILD WITH (DATA_COMPRESSION=PAGE)
```

Now, re-examine the size of the sales_big table:

```
select sum(page_count) as pages, sum(compressed_page_count) as compressed_pages
from sys.dm_db_index_physical_stats (DB_ID(),
OBJECT_ID('sales_big'), 1, null, 'DETAILED')
where index_level = 0

SELECT SUM(used_page_count/ 128.0) AS size_in_MB
FROM sys.dm_db_partition_stats
WHERE object_id=OBJECT_ID('dbo.sales_big') AND index_id=1
GO

pages                    compressed_pages
---------------------------------------
4452                     4451

size_in_MB
---------------------------------------
34.906250
```

In this example, you can see that the table was reduced in size significantly, from 14,519 pages to 4,452 pages (113.7MB to 34.9MB), pretty much right in line with the estimated space savings. You can also see that compression was reasonably effective, compressing 4,451 of 4,452 pages.

Be aware that you may not always receive the space savings predicted due to the effects of fill factor and the actual size of the rows. For example, if you have a row that is 8,000 bytes long and compression reduces its size by 40%, only one row can still be fit on the data page, so there is no space savings for that page. If the results of running `sp_estimate_data_compression_savings` indicate that the table will grow, this indicates that many of the rows in the table are using nearly the full precision of the data types, and the addition of the small overhead needed for the compressed format is more than the savings from compression. In this, it is obvious that there is no advantage to enabling compression.

Managing Data Compression with SSMS

The preceding examples show the T-SQL commands you can use to evaluate and manage row and page compression in SQL Server 2008. SSMS provides a Data Compression Wizard for evaluating and performing data compression activities. To invoke the Data

Compression Wizard, right-click on the table in the Object Explorer and select Storage and then select Manage Compression. Click Next to move past the Welcome page to bring up the Select Compression Type page, as shown in Figure 34.11.

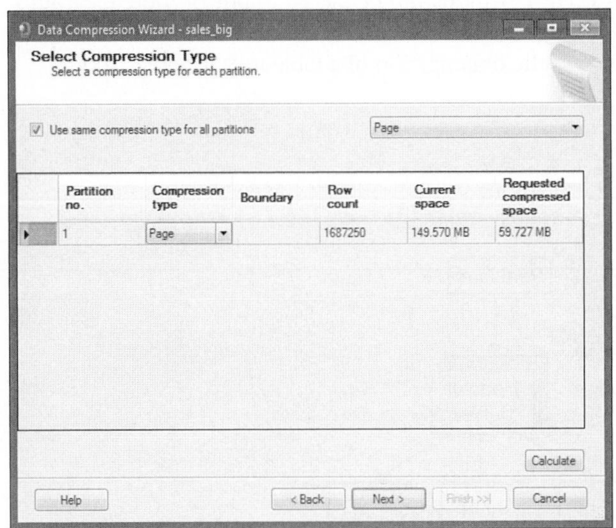

FIGURE 34.11 The Data Compression Wizard's Select Compression Type page.

On the Compression Type Page, you can choose the compression type to use at the partition level or to use the same compression type for all partitions. You can also see the estimated savings for selected compression type by clicking on the Calculate button. After you click on Calculate, the wizard displays the current partition size and requested compression size in the corresponding columns (note that it might take a few moments to do the calculation).

After making your selections, click on Next to display the Select and Output Option page. Here, you have the opportunity to have the wizard generate a script of commands you can run manually to implement the selected compression type. If you choose to generate a script, you have the option to save the script to a file, the Clipboard, or to a new query window in SSMS. You also have the option to run the compression changes immediately or schedule a SQL Agent job to run the changes at a specified time.

Understanding Table Structures

A table is logically defined as a set of columns with certain properties, such as the data type, nullability, constraints, and so on. Information about data types, column properties, constraints, and other information related to defining and creating tables can be found in Chapters 24, "Creating and Managing Tables," and 27, "Creating and Managing Views."

Internally, a table is contained in one or more partitions. A *partition* is a user-defined unit of data organization. By default, a table has at least one partition that contains all the table pages. This partition resides in a single filegroup, as described earlier. When a table has multiple partitions, the data is partitioned horizontally so that groups of rows are mapped into individual partitions, based on a specified column. The partitions can be placed in one or more filegroups in the database. The table is treated as a single logical entity when queries or updates are performed on the data. Figure 34.12 shows the organization of a table in SQL Server 2008.

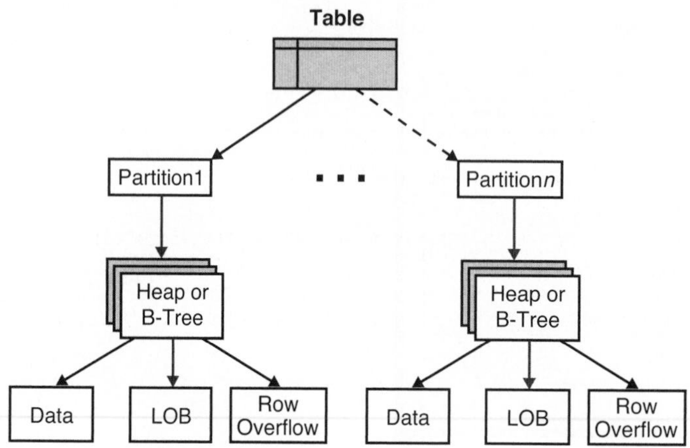

FIGURE 34.12 Table organization in SQL Server 2008.

Each table has one row in the `sys.objects` catalog view, and each table and index in a database is represented by a single row in the `sys.indexes` catalog view. Each partition of a table or index is represented by one or more rows in the `sys.partitions` catalog view. Each partition can have three types of data, each stored on its own set of pages: in-row data pages, row-overflow pages, and LOB data pages. Each of these types of pages has an allocation unit, which is contained in the `sys.allocation_units` view. There is always at least one allocation unit for the in-row data. The following sample query shows how to view the partition and allocation information for the `databaselog` and `currency` tables in the `AdventureWorks2008R2` database:

```
use AdventureWorks2008R2
go
SELECT convert(varchar(15), o.name) AS table_name,
     p.index_id as indid,
     convert(varchar(30), i.name) AS index_name ,
      convert(varchar(18), au.type_desc) AS allocation_type,
      au.data_pages as d_pgs,
      partition_number as ptn
FROM sys.allocation_units AS au
    JOIN sys.partitions AS p ON au.container_id = p.partition_id
    JOIN sys.objects AS o ON p.object_id = o.object_id
    JOIN sys.indexes AS i ON p.index_id = i.index_id AND i.object_id = p.object_id
```

```
WHERE o.name = N'databaselog' OR o.name = N'currency'
ORDER BY o.name, p.index_id;

table_name  indid index_name                   allocation_type   d_pgs ptn
----------- ----- ---------------------------- ----------------- ----- ---
Currency    1     PK_Currency_CurrencyCode     IN_ROW_DATA       1     1
Currency    2     AK_Currency_Name             IN_ROW_DATA       1     1
DatabaseLog 0     NULL                         IN_ROW_DATA       753   1
DatabaseLog 0     NULL                         LOB_DATA          0     1
DatabaseLog 0     NULL                         ROW_OVERFLOW_DATA 0     1
DatabaseLog 2     PK_DatabaseLog_DatabaseLogID IN_ROW_DATA       3     1
```

In this example, you can see that the DatabaseLog table (which is a heap table) has three allocation units associated with the table—LOB, row-overflow, and in-row data—and one allocation unit for the nonclustered index PK_DatabaseLog_DatabaseLogID. The currency table (which is a clustered table) has a single in-row allocation unit for both the table (index_id = 1) and the nonclustered index (AK_Currency_Name).

In SQL Server 2008, there are two types of tables: heap tables and clustered tables. Let's look at how they are stored.

Heap Tables

A table without a clustered index is a *heap table*. There is no imposed ordering of the data rows for a heap table. Additionally, there is no direct linkage between the pages in a heap table.

By default, a heap has a single partition. Heaps have one row in sys.partitions, with an index ID of 0 for each partition used by the heap. When a heap has multiple partitions, each partition has a heap structure that contains the data for that specific partition. For example, if a heap has four partitions, there are four heap structures (one in each partition) and four rows in sys.partitions.

Depending on the data types in the heap, each heap structure has one or more allocation units to store and manage the data for each partition. At a minimum, each heap has one IN_ROW_DATA allocation unit per partition. The heap also has one LOB_DATA allocation unit per partition, if it contains large object columns. It also has one ROW_OVERFLOW_DATA allocation unit per partition if it contains variable-length columns that exceed the 8,060-byte row size limit.

To access the contents of a heap, SQL Server uses the IAM pages. In SQL Server 2008, each heap table has at least one IAM page. The address of the first IAM page is available in the undocumented sys.sytem_internals_allocation_units system view. The column first_iam_page points to the first IAM page in the chain of IAM pages that manage the space allocated to the heap in a specific partition. The following query returns the first IAM pages for each of the allocation units for the heap table DatabaseLog in AdventureWorks2008R2:

```
use AdventureWorks2008R2
go
select p.partition_number as ptn,
     type_desc,
     filegroup_id,
     first_iam_page
from sys.system_internals_allocation_units i
inner join
sys.partitions p
on p.hobt_id = i.container_id
where p.object_id = OBJECT_ID('DatabaseLog')
and index_id = 0
go

ptn         type_desc            filegroup_id first_iam_page
----------- -------------------- ------------ --------------
1           IN_ROW_DATA          1            0xAA0000000100
1           LOB_DATA             1            0xB90000000100
1           ROW_OVERFLOW_DATA    1            0x000000000000
```

Note that the value `0x000000000000` for the `first_iam_page` for `ROW_OVERFLOW_DATA` indicates that no extents have yet been allocated for storing row-overflow data.

NOTE

The `sys.system_internals_allocation_units` system view is reserved for Microsoft SQL Server internal use only. Future compatibility and availability of this view is not guaranteed.

The data pages and rows in the heap are not sorted in any specific order and are not linked. The IAM page registers which extents are used by the table. SQL Server can then simply scan the allocated extents referenced by the IAM page, in physical order. This essentially avoids the problem of page chain fragmentation during reads because SQL Server always reads full extents in sequential order. Using the IAM pages to set the scan sequence also means that rows from the heap often are not returned in the order in which they were inserted.

As discussed earlier, each IAM can map a maximum of 63,903 extents for a table. As a table uses extents beyond the range of those 63,903 extents, more IAM pages are created for the heap table as needed. A heap table also has at least one IAM page for each file on which the heap table has extents allocated. Figure 34.13 illustrates the structure of a heap and how its contents are traversed using the IAM pages.

Clustered Tables

A *clustered table* is a table that has a clustered index defined on it. When you create a clustered index, the data rows in the table are physically sorted in the order of the columns in the index key. The data pages are chained together in a doubly linked list (each page points

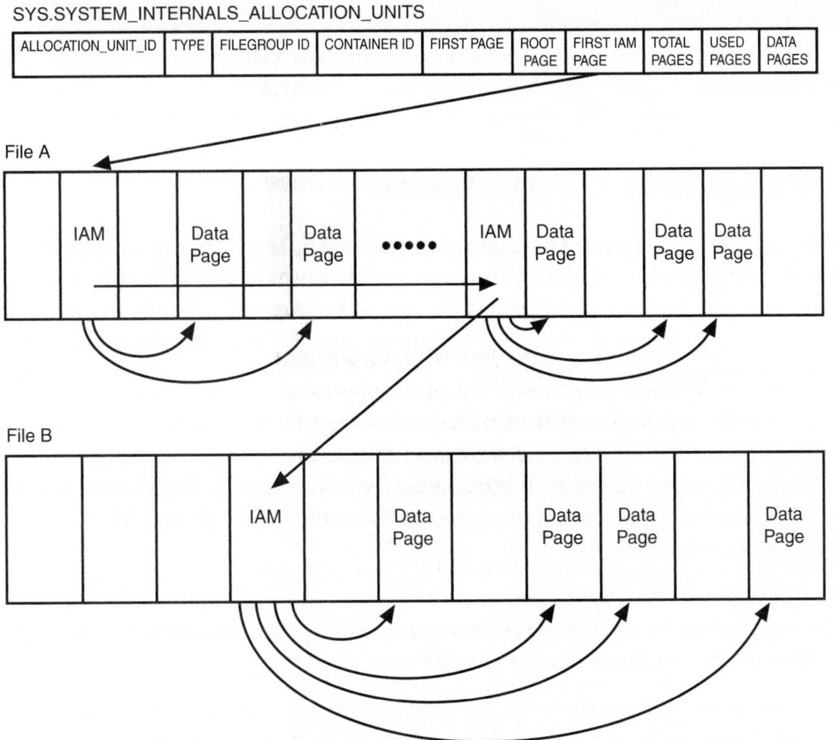

FIGURE 34.13 The structure of a heap table.

to the next page and to the previous page). Normally, data pages are not linked. Only index pages within a level are linked in this manner to allow for ordered scans of the data in an index level. Because the data pages of a clustered table constitute the leaf level of the clustered index, they are chained as well. This allows for an ordered table scan. The page pointers are stored in the page header. Figure 34.14 shows a simplified example of the data pages of a clustered table. (Note that the figure shows only the data pages.)

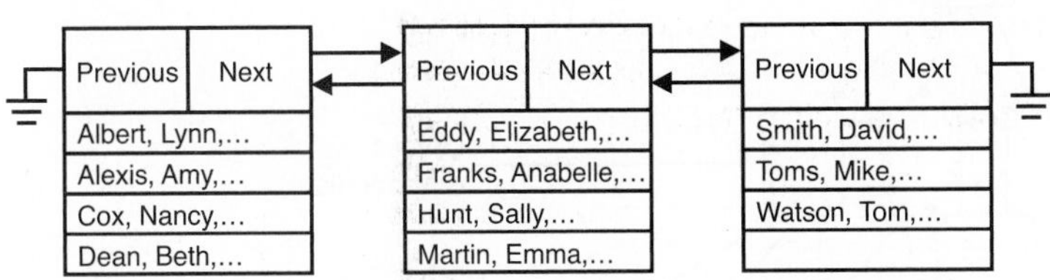

FIGURE 34.14 The data page structure of a clustered table.

TIP

More details on the structure and maintenance of clustered tables are provided in the remainder of this chapter.

Understanding Index Structures

When you run a query against a table that has no indexes, SQL Server has to read every page of the table, looking at every row on each page to find out whether each row satisfies the search arguments. SQL Server has to scan all the pages because there's no way of knowing whether any rows found are the only rows that satisfy the search arguments. This search method is referred to as a *table scan*.

A table scan is *not* an efficient way to retrieve data unless you really need to retrieve all rows. The Query Optimizer in SQL Server always calculates the cost of performing a table scan and uses that as a baseline when evaluating other access methods. The various access methods and query plan cost analysis are discussed in more detail in Chapter 35, "Understanding Query Optimization."

Suppose that a table is stored on 10,000 pages; even if only one row is to be returned or modified, all the pages must be searched, resulting in a scan of approximately 80MB of data (that is, 10,000 pages × 8KB per page = 80,000KB).

Indexes are structures stored separately from the actual data pages; they contain pointers to data pages or data rows. Indexes are used to speed up access to the data; they are also the mechanism used to enforce the uniqueness of key values.

Indexes in SQL Server are balanced trees (B-trees; see Figure 34.12). There is a single root page at the top of the tree, which branches out into *N* pages at each intermediate level until it reaches the bottom (leaf level) of the index. The leaf level has one row stored for each row in the table. The index tree is traversed by following pointers from the upper-

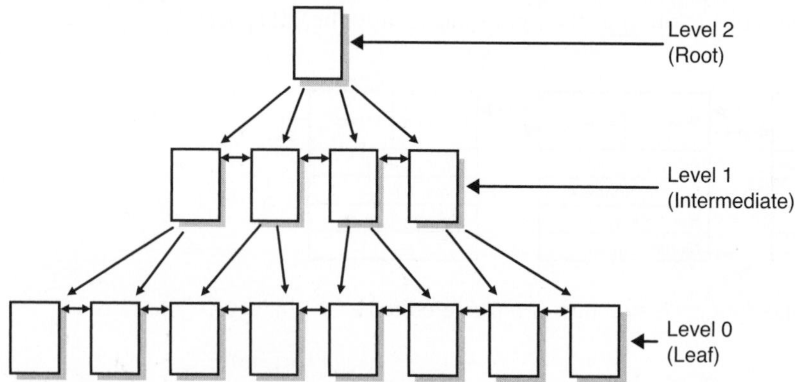

FIGURE 34.15 The basic structure of a B-tree index.

level pages down through the lower-level pages. Each level of the index is linked as a doubly linked list.

An index can have many intermediate levels, depending on the number of rows in the table, index type, and index key width. The maximum number of columns in an index is 16; the maximum width of an index row is 900 bytes.

To provide a more efficient mechanism to identify and locate specific rows within a table quickly and easily, SQL Server supports two types of indexes: clustered and nonclustered.

Clustered Indexes

When you create a clustered index, all rows in the table are sorted and stored in the clustered index key order. Because the rows are physically sorted by the index key, you can have only one clustered index per table. You can think of the structure of a clustered index as being similar to a filing cabinet: the data pages are like folders in a file drawer in alphabetical order, and the data rows are like the records in the file folder, also in sorted order.

You can think of the intermediate levels of the index tree as the file drawers, also in alphabetical order, that assist you in finding the appropriate file folder. Figure 34.16 shows an example of a clustered index tree structure.

In Figure 34.16, note that the data page chain is in clustered index order. However, the rows on each page might not be physically sorted in clustered index order, depending on when rows were inserted or deleted in the page. SQL Server still keeps the proper sort order of the rows via the row IDs and the row offset table. A clustered index is useful for range-retrieval queries or searches against columns with duplicate values because the rows within the range are physically located in the same page or on adjacent pages.

The data pages of the table are also the leaf level of a clustered index. To find all clustered index key values, SQL Server must eventually scan all the data pages.

SQL Server performs the following steps when searching for a value using a clustered index:

1. Queries the system catalogs for the page address for the root page of the index. (For a clustered index, the `root_page` column in `sys.system_internals_allocation_units` points to the top of the clustered index for a specific partition.)
2. Compares the search value against the key values stored on the root page.
3. Finds the highest key value on the page where the key value is less than or equal to the search value.
4. Follows the page pointer stored with the key to the appropriate page at the next level down in the index.
5. Continues following page pointers (that is, repeats steps 3 and 4) until the data page is reached.
6. Searches the rows on the data page to locate any matches for the search value. If no matching row is found on that data page, the table contains no matching values.

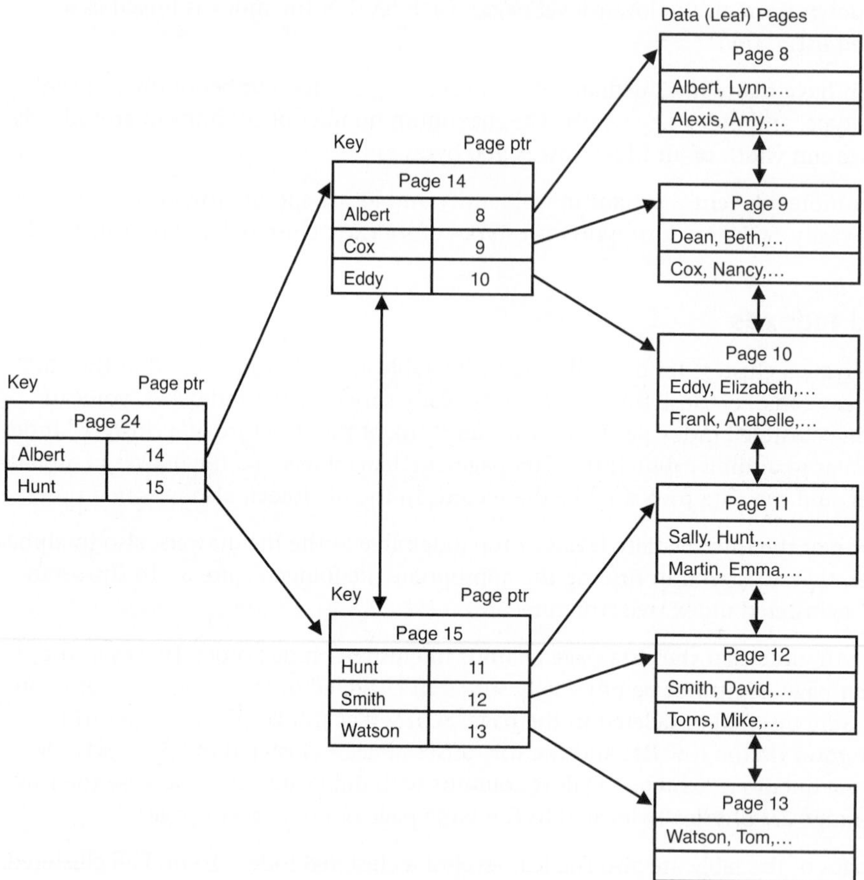

FIGURE 34.16 The structure of a clustered index.

By default, a clustered index has a single partition and thus has at least one row in `sys.partitions` with `index_id = 1`. When a clustered index has multiple partitions, a separate B-tree structure contains the data for that specific partition.

Depending on the data types in the clustered index, each clustered index structure has one or more allocation units in which to store and manage the data for a specific partition. At a minimum, each clustered index has one `IN_ROW_DATA` allocation unit per partition. If the table contains any LOB data, the clustered index also has one `LOB_DATA` allocation unit per partition and one `ROW_OVERFLOW_DATA` allocation unit per partition if the table contains any variable-length columns that exceed the 8,060-byte row size limit.

Clustered Index Row Structure

The structure of a clustered index row is similar to the structure of a data row except that it contains only key columns; this structure is detailed in Figure 34.17.

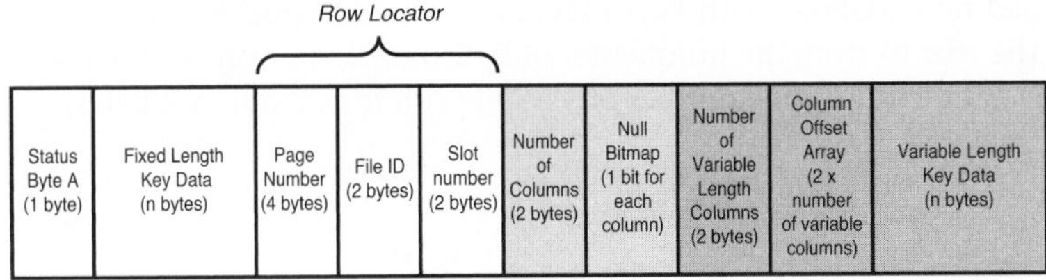

FIGURE 34.17 Clustered index row structure.

Notice that unlike a data row, index rows do not contain the status byte B or the 2 bytes to hold the length of fixed-length data fields. Instead of storing the length of the fixed-length data, which also indicates where the fixed-length portion of a row ends and the variable-length portion begins, the page header `pminlen` value is used to help describe an index row. The `pminlen` value is the minimum length of the index row, which is essentially the sum of the size of all fixed-width fields and overhead. Therefore, if no variable-length or nullable fields are in the index key, `pminlen` also indicates the width of each index row.

The null bitmap field and field for the number of columns in the index row are present only when an index key contains nullable columns. The number of columns value is only needed to determine how many bits are needed in the null bitmap and therefore how many bytes are required to store the null bitmap (1 byte per eight columns). The data contents of a clustered index row include the key values along with a 6-byte down-page pointer (the first 2 bytes are the file ID, and the last 4 bytes are the page number). The down-page pointer is the last value in the fixed-data portion of the row.

Nonunique Clustered Indexes

When a clustered index is defined on a table, the clustered index keys are used as row locators to identify the data rows being referenced by nonclustered indexes (more on this topic in the following section on nonclustered indexes). Because the clustered keys are used as unique row pointers, there needs to be a way to uniquely refer to each row in the table. If the clustered index is defined as a unique index, the key itself uniquely identifies every row. If the clustered index was not created as a unique index, SQL Server adds a 4-byte integer field, called a *uniqueifier*, to the data row to make each key unique when necessary. When is the uniqueifier necessary? SQL Server adds the uniqueifier to a row when the row is added to a table and that new row contains a key that is a duplicate of the key for an already-existing row.

The uniqueifier is added to the variable-length data area of the data row, which also results in the addition of the variable-length overhead bytes. Therefore, each duplicate row in a clustered index has a minimum of 4 bytes of overhead added for the additional uniqueifier. If the row had no variable-length keys previously, an additional 8 bytes of overhead are added to the row to store the uniqueifier (4 bytes) plus the overhead bytes required for the variable data (storing the number of variable columns requires 2 bytes, and the column offset array requires 2 bytes).

Nonclustered Indexes

A nonclustered index is a separate index structure, independent of the physical sort order of the data rows in the table. You can have up to 999 nonclustered indexes per table.

A nonclustered index is similar to the index in the back of a book. To find the pages on which a specific subject is discussed, you look up the subject in the index and then go to the pages referenced in the index. This method is efficient as long as the subject is discussed on only a few pages. If the subject is discussed on many pages, or if you want to read about many subjects, it can be more efficient to read the entire book.

A nonclustered index works similarly to the book index. From the index's perspective, the data rows are randomly spread throughout the table. The nonclustered index tree contains the index key values, in sorted order. There is a row at the leaf level of the index for each

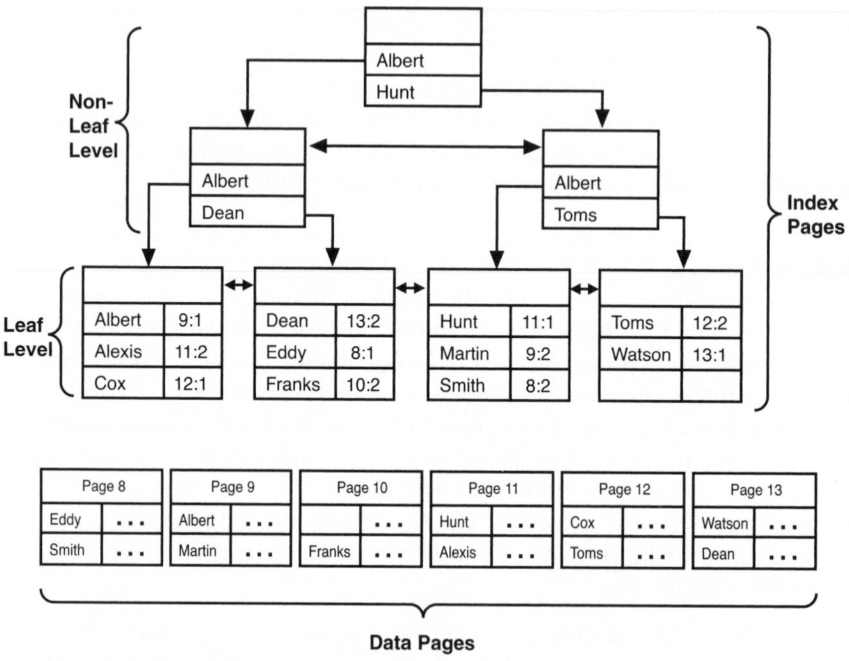

FIGURE 34.18 A nonclustered index on a heap table.

data row in the table. Each leaf-level row contains a data row locator to locate the actual data row in the table.

If no clustered index is created for the table, the data row locator for the leaf level of the index is an actual pointer to the data page and the row number within the page where the row is located (see Figure 34.18).

Nonclustered indexes on clustered tables use the associated clustered index key value for the record as the data row locator. When SQL Server reaches the leaf level of a nonclus-

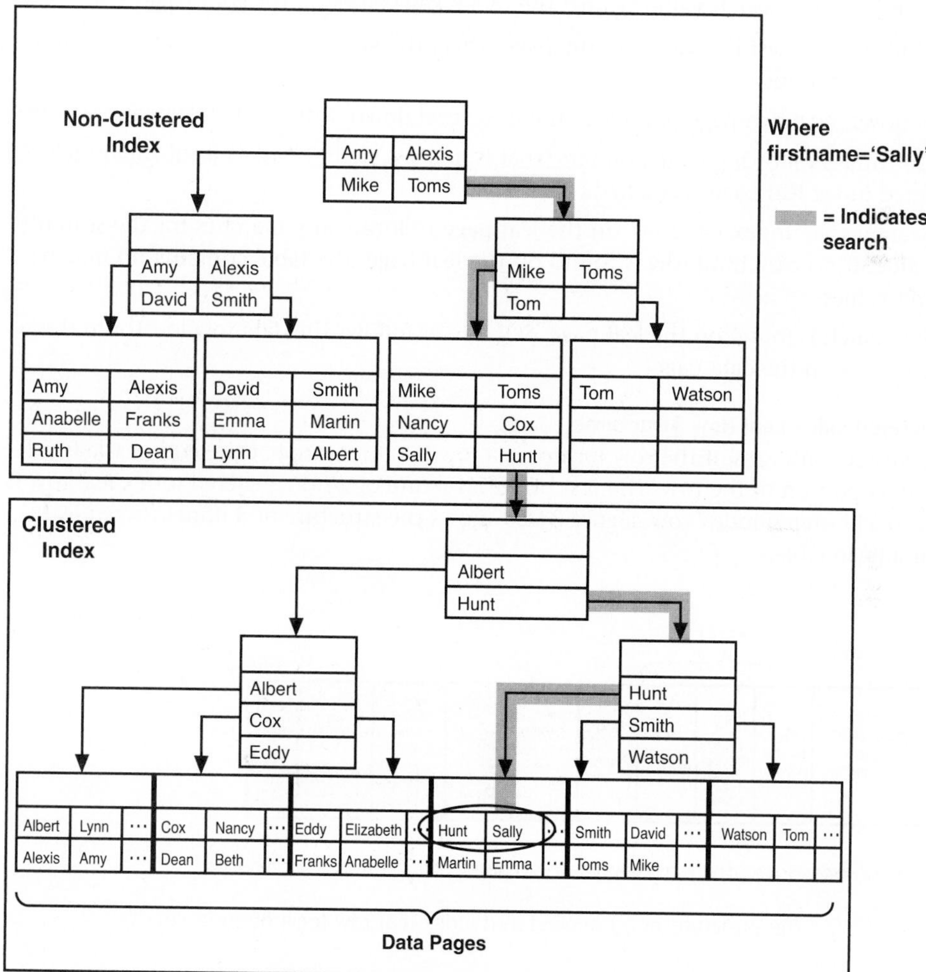

FIGURE 34.19 A nonclustered index on a clustered table.

tered index, it uses the clustered index key to start searching through the clustered index to find the actual data row (see Figure 34.19). This adds some I/O to the search itself, but the benefit is that if a page split occurs in a clustered table, or if a data row is moved (for example, as a result of an update), the nonclustered index row locator stays the same. As long as the clustered index key value itself is not modified, no data row locators in the nonclustered index have to be updated.

SQL Server performs the following steps when searching for a value by using a nonclustered index:

1. Queries the system catalog to determine the page address for the root page of the index.
2. Compares the search value against the index key values on the root page.
3. Finds the highest key value on the page where the key value is less than or equal to the search value.
4. Follows the down-page pointer to the next level down in the nonclustered index tree.
5. Continues following page pointers (that is, repeats steps 3 and 4) until the nonclustered index leaf page is reached.
6. Searches the index key rows on the leaf page to locate any matches for the search value. If no matching row is found on the leaf page, the table contains no matching values.
7. If a match is found on the leaf page, SQL Server follows the data row locator to the data row on the data page.

Nonclustered Index Leaf Row Structures

In nonclustered indexes, if the row locator is a row ID, it is stored at the end of the fixed-length data portion of the row. The rest of the structure of a nonclustered index leaf row is similar to a clustered index row. Figure 34.20 shows the structure of a nonclustered leaf row for a heap table.

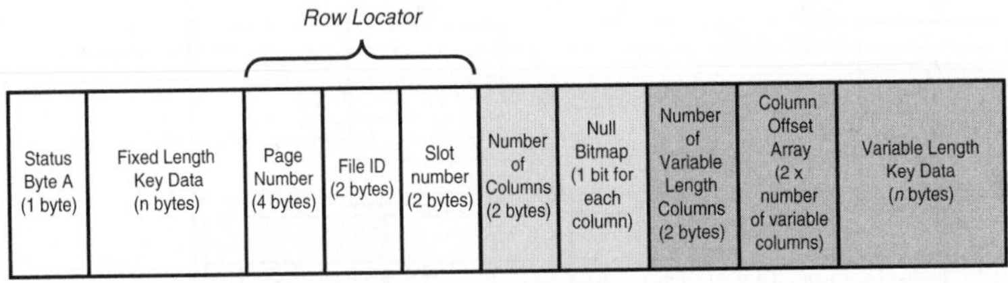

FIGURE 34.20 The structure of a nonclustered index leaf row for a heap table.

If the row locator is a clustered index key value, the row locator resides in either the fixed or variable portion of the row, depending on whether the clustered key columns were defined as fixed or variable length. Figure 34.21 shows the structure of a nonclustered leaf row for a clustered table.

When the row locator is a clustered key value and the clustered and nonclustered indexes share columns, the data value for the key is stored only once in the nonclustered index row. For example, if your clustered index key is on `lastname` and you have a nonclustered

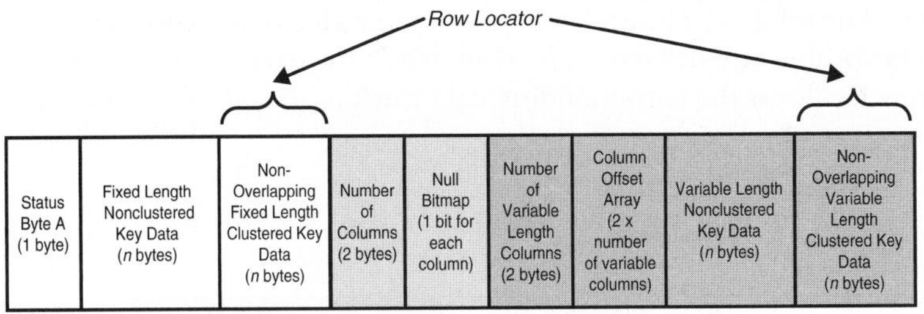

FIGURE 34.21 The structure of a nonclustered index leaf row for a clustered table.

index defined on both `firstname` and `lastname`, the index rows do not store the value of `lastname` twice, but only once for both keys.

Nonclustered Index Nonleaf Row Structures

The nonclustered index nonleaf rows are similar in structure to clustered index nonleaf rows in that they contain a page-down pointer to a page at the next level down in the index tree. The nonleaf rows don't need to point to data rows; they only need to provide the path to traverse the index tree to a leaf row. If the nonclustered index is defined as unique, the nonleaf index key row contains only the index key value and page-down pointer. Figure 34.22 shows the structure of a nonleaf index row for a unique nonclustered index.

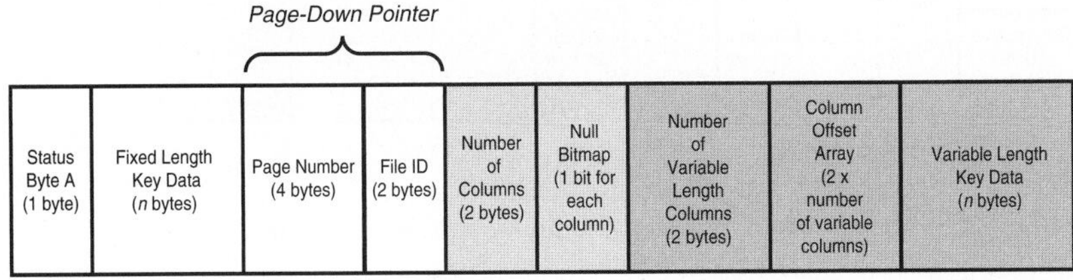

FIGURE 34.22 The structure of a nonclustered nonleaf index row for a unique index.

If the nonclustered index is not defined as a unique index, the nonleaf rows also contain the row locator information for the corresponding data row. Storing the row locator in the nonleaf index row ensures each index key row is unique (because the row locator, by its nature, must be unique). Ensuring each index key row is unique allows any corresponding nonleaf index rows to be located and deleted more easily when the data row is deleted. For a heap table, the row locator is the corresponding data row's page and row pointer, as shown in Figure 34.23.

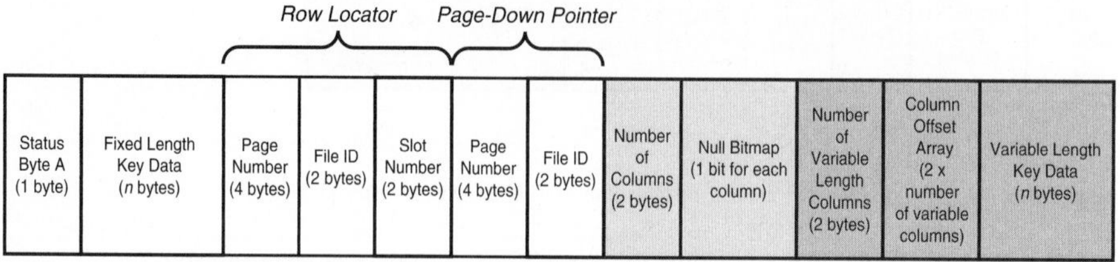

FIGURE 34.23 The structure of a nonclustered nonleaf index row for a nonunique index on a heap table.

If the table is clustered, the clustered key values are stored in the nonleaf index rows of the nonunique nonclustered index just as they are in the leaf rows, as shown in Figure 34.24.

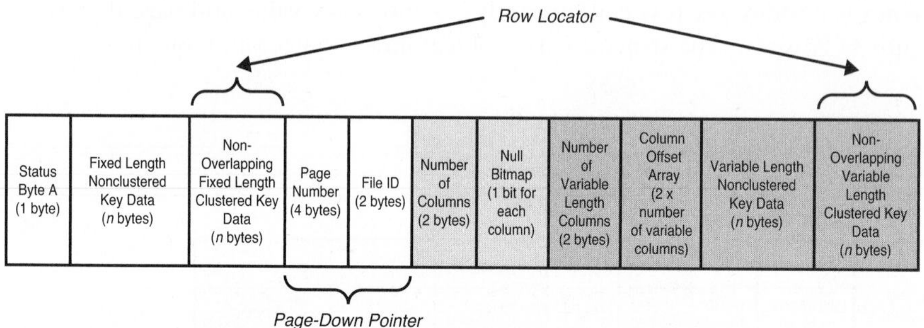

FIGURE 34.24 The structure of a nonclustered nonleafindex row for a nonunique index on a clustered table.

As you can see, it's possible for the index pointers and row overhead to exceed the size of the index key itself. This is why, for I/O and storage reasons, it is always recommended that you keep your index keys as small as possible.

Data Modification and Performance

Now that you have a better understanding of the storage structures in SQL Server, it's time to look at how SQL Server maintains and manages those structures when data modifications are taking place in the database.

Inserting Data

When you add a data row to a heap table, SQL Server adds the row to the heap wherever space is available. SQL Server uses the IAM and PFS pages to identify whether any pages with free space are available in the extents already allocated to the table. If no free pages are found, SQL Server uses the information from the GAM and SGAM pages to locate a free extent and allocate it to the table.

For clustered tables, the new data row is inserted to the appropriate location on the appropriate data page relative to the clustered index key order. If no more room is available on the destination page, SQL Server needs to link a new page in the page chain to make room available and add the row. This is called a *page split*.

In addition to modifying the affected data pages when adding rows, SQL Server needs to update all nonclustered indexes to add a pointer to the new record. If a page split occurs, this incurs even more overhead because the clustered index needs to be updated to store the pointer for the new page added to the table. Fortunately, because the clustered key is used as the row locator in nonclustered indexes when a table is clustered, even though the page and row IDs have changed, the nonclustered index row locators for rows moved by a page split do not have to be updated as long as the clustered key column values remain the same.

Page Splits

When a page split occurs, SQL Server looks for an available page to link into the page chain. It first tries to find an available page in the same extent as the pages it will be linked to. If no free pages exist in the same extent, it looks at the IAM to determine whether there are any free pages in any other extents already allocated to the table or index. If no free pages are found, a new extent is allocated to the table.

When a new page is found or allocated to the table and linked into the page chain, the original page is "split." Approximately half the rows are moved to the new page, and the rest remain on the original page (see Figure 34.25). Whether the new page goes before or after the original page when the split is made depends on the amount of data to be moved. In an effort to minimize logging, SQL Server moves the smaller rows to the new page. If the smaller rows are at the beginning of the page, SQL Server places the new page before the original page and moves the smaller rows to it. If the larger rows are at the beginning of the page, SQL Server keeps them on the original page and moves the smaller rows to the new page after the original page.

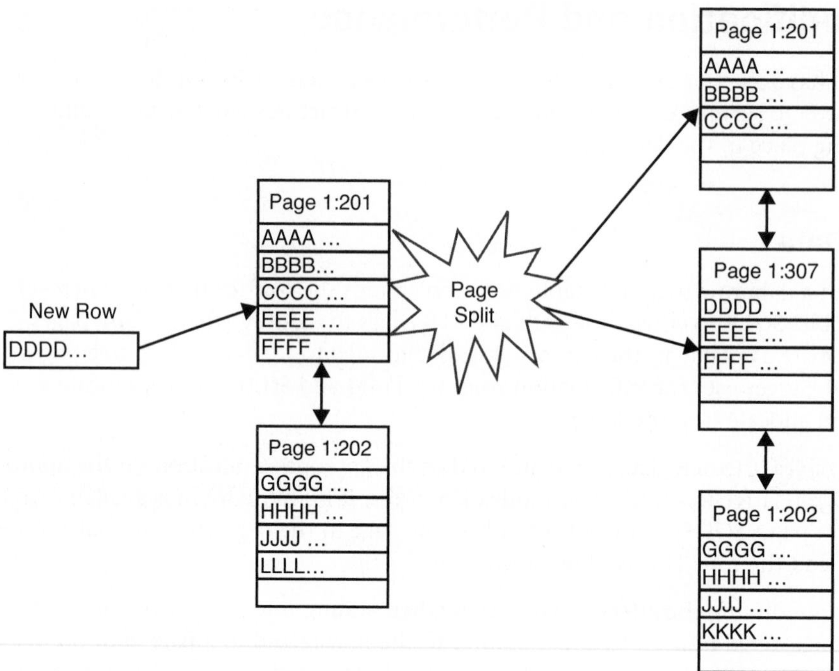

FIGURE 34.25 Page splitting due to inserts.

After determining where the new row goes between the existing rows and whether the new page is to be added before or after the original page, SQL Server has to move rows to the new page. The simplified algorithm for determining the split point is as follows:

1. Place first row (with the lowest clustered key value) at the beginning of first page.
2. Place the last row (with the highest clustered key value) on the second page.
3. Place the row with the next lowest clustered key value on the first page after the existing row(s).
4. Place the next-to-last row (with the second highest clustered key value) on the second page.
5. Continue alternating back and forth until the space between the two pages is balanced or one of the pages is full.

In some situations a double split can occur. If the new row has to go between two existing rows on a page, but the new row is too large to fit on either page with any of the existing rows, a new page is added after the original. The new row is added to the new page, a second new page is added after that, and the remaining original rows are inserted into the second new page. An example of a double split is shown in Figure 34.26.

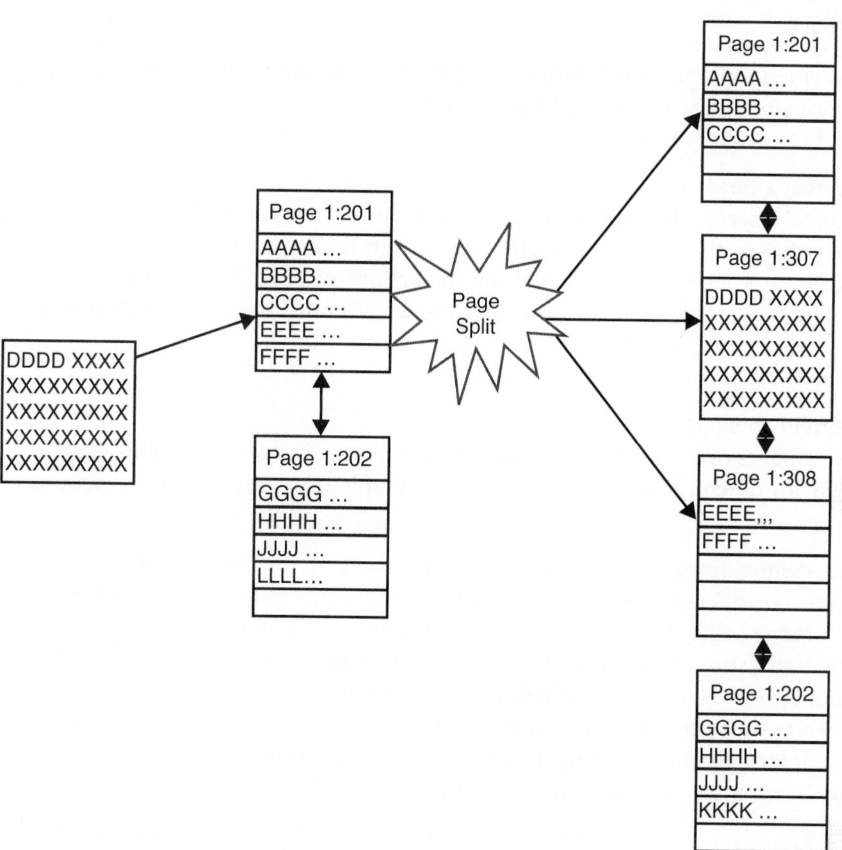

FIGURE 34.26 Double page split due to large row insert.

NOTE

Although page splits are expensive when they occur, they do generate free space in the split pages for future inserts into those pages. Page splits also help keep the index tree balanced as rows are added to the table. However, if you monitor the system with Performance Monitor and are seeing hundreds of page splits per second, you might want to consider rebuilding the clustered index on the table and applying a lower fill factor to provide more free space in the existing pages. This can help improve system performance until eventually the pages fill up and start splitting again. For this reason, some shops supporting high-volume online transaction processing (OLTP) environments with a lot of insert activity rebuild the indexes with a lower fill factor on a daily basis.

Deleting Rows

What happens when rows are deleted from a table? How, and when, does SQL Server reclaim the space when data is removed from a table?

Deleting Rows from a Heap

In a heap table, SQL Server does not automatically compress the space on a page when a row is removed; that is, the rows are not all moved up to the beginning of the page to keep all free space at the end, as SQL Server did in versions prior to 7.0. To optimize performance, SQL Server holds off on compacting the rows until the page needs contiguous space for storing a new row.

Deleting Rows from an Index

Because the data pages of a clustered table are actually the leaf pages of the clustered index, the behavior of data row deletes on a clustered table is the same as row deletions from an index page.

When rows are deleted from the leaf level of an index, they are not actually deleted but are marked as ghost records. Keeping the row as a ghost record makes it easier for SQL Server to perform key-range locking (key-range locking is discussed in Chapter 37, "Locking and Performance"). If ghost records were not used, SQL Server would have to lock the entire range surrounding the deleted record. With the ghost record still present and visible internally to SQL Server (it is not visible in query result sets), SQL Server can use the ghost record as an endpoint for the key-range lock to prevent "phantom" records with the same key value from being inserted, while allowing inserts of other values to proceed.

Ghost records do not stay around forever, though. SQL Server has a special internal housekeeping process that periodically examines the leaf level of B-trees for ghost records and removes them. This is the same thread that performs the autoshrink process for databases.

Whenever you delete a row, all nonclustered indexes need to be updated to remove the pointers to the deleted row. Nonleaf index rows are not ghosted when deleted. As with heap tables, however, the space is not compressed on the nonleaf index page until space is needed for a new row.

Reclaiming Space

Only when the last row is deleted from a data page is the page deallocated from the table. The only exception is if it is the last page remaining; all tables must have at least one page allocated, even if it's empty. When a deletion of an index row leaves only one row remaining on the page, the remaining row is moved to a neighboring page, and the now-empty index page is deallocated.

If the page to be deallocated is the last remaining used page in a uniform extent allocated to the table, the extent is deallocated from the table as well.

Updating Rows

SQL Server 2008 performs row updates by evaluating the number of rows affected, whether the rows are being accessed via a scan or index retrieval and whether any index keys are being modified, and automatically chooses the appropriate and most efficient update strategy for the rows affected. SQL Server can perform two types of update strategies:

- In-place updates
- Not-in-place updates

In-Place Updates

In SQL Server 2008, in-place updates are performed as often as possible to minimize the overhead of an update. An *in-place update* means that the row is modified where it is on the page, and only the affected bytes are changed.

When an in-place update is performed, in addition to the reduced overhead in the table itself, only a single modify record is written to the log. However, if the table has a trigger on it or is marked for replication, the update is still done in place but is recorded in the log as a delete followed by an insert (this provides the before-and-after image for the trigger that is referenced in the `inserted` and `deleted` tables).

In-place updates are performed whenever a heap is being updated and the row still fits on the same page, or when a clustered table is updated and the clustered key itself is not changed. You can get an in-place update if the clustered key changes but the row does not have to move; that is, the sorting of the rows wouldn't change.

Not-In-Place Updates

If the change to a clustered key prevents an in-place update from being performed, or if the modification to a row increases its size such that it can no longer fit on its current page, the update is performed as a delete followed by an insert; this is referred to as a *not-in-place update*.

When performing an update that affects multiple index keys, SQL Server keeps a list of the rows that need to be updated in memory, if it's small enough; otherwise, it is stored in `tempdb`. SQL Server then sorts the list by index key and type of operation (delete or insert). This list of operations, called the *input stream*, consists of both the old and new values for every column in the affected rows as well as the unique row identifier for each row.

SQL Server then examines the input stream to determine whether any of the updates conflict or would generate duplicate key values while processing (if they were to generate a duplicate key after processing, the update cannot proceed). It then rearranges the operations in the input stream in a manner to prevent any intermediate violations of the unique key.

For example, consider the following update to a table with a unique key on a sequential primary key:

```
update table1 set pkey = pkey + 1
```

Even though all values would still be unique when the update finished, if the update were performed internally one row at a time in sequential order, it would generate duplicates during the intermediate processing as the pkey value was incremented and matched the next pkey value. SQL Server would rearrange and rework the updates in the input stream to process them in a manner that would avoid the duplicates and then process them a row at a time. If possible, deletes and inserts on the same key value in the input stream are collapsed into a single update. In some cases, you might still get some rows that can be updated in place.

Forward Pointers

As mentioned earlier, when page splits on a clustered table occur, the nonclustered indexes do not need to be updated to reflect the new location of the rows because the row locator for the row is the clustered index key rather than the page and row ID. When an update operation on a heap table causes rows to move, the row locators in the nonclustered index would need to be updated to reflect the new location or the rows. This could be expensive if there were a larger number of nonclustered indexes on the heap.

SQL Server 2008 addresses this performance issue through the use of forward pointers. When a row in a heap moves, it leaves a forward pointer in the original location of the row. The forward pointer avoids having to update the nonclustered index row locator. When SQL Server is searching for the row via the nonclustered index, the index pointer directs it to the original location, where the forward pointer redirects it to the new row location.

A row never has more than one forward pointer. If the row moves again from its forwarded location, the forward pointer stored at the original row location is updated to the row's new location. There is never a forward pointer that points to another forward pointer. If the row ever shrinks enough to fit back into its original location, the forward pointer is removed, and the row is put back where it originated.

When a forward pointer is created, it remains unless the row moves back to its original location. The only other circumstance that results in forward pointers being deleted occurs when the entire database is shrunk. When a database file is shrunk and the data reorganized, all row locators are reassigned because the rows are moved to new pages.

Index Utilization

Now that you have an understanding of table and index structures and the overhead required to maintain your data and indexes, you might want to put things into practice to actually come up with an index design for your database, defining the appropriate indexes to support your queries. To effectively determine the appropriate indexes that should be created, you need to determine whether they'll actually be used by the SQL Server Query Optimizer. If an index is not being used effectively, it's just wasting space and creating unnecessary overhead during updates.

The main criterion to remember is that SQL Server does not use an index for the more efficient row locator lookup if at least the first column of the index is not included in a valid search argument (SARG) or join clause. You should keep this point in mind when choosing the column order for composite indexes. For example, consider the following index on the `stores` table in the `bigpubs2008` database:

```
create index nc1_stores on stores (city, state, zip)
```

NOTE

Unless stated otherwise, all sample queries from this point on in this chapter are run in the `bigpubs2008` database, which is available on the included CD or via download from this book's website at www.samspublishing.com. Instructions on installing this database is provided in the Introduction.

Each of the following queries could use the index because they include the first column, `city`, of the index as part of the SARG:

```
select stor_name from stores
   where city = 'Frederick'
     and state = 'MD'
     and zip = '21702'

select stor_name from stores
   where city = 'Frederick'
     and state = 'MD'

select stor_name from stores
   where city = 'Frederick'
     and zip = '21702'
```

However, the following queries do not use the index for a row locator lookup because they don't specify the `city` column as a SARG:

```
select stor_name from stores
   where state = 'MD'
     and zip = '21702'

select stor_name from stores
   where zip = '21702'
```

For the index `nc1_stores` to be used for a row locator lookup in the last query, you would have to reorder the columns so that `zip` is first—but then the index wouldn't be useful for any queries specifying only `city` and/or `state`. Satisfying all the preceding queries in this case would require additional indexes on the `stores` table.

NOTE

For the two preceding queries, if you were to display the execution plan information (as described in Chapter 36, "Query Analysis"), you might see that the queries actually use the `nc1_stores` index to retrieve the result set. However, if you look closely, you can see the queries are not using the index in the most efficient manner; the index is being used to perform an index scan rather than an index seek. An index seek is what we are really after. (Alternative query access methods are discussed in more detail in Chapter 35). In an index *seek*, SQL Server searches for the specific SARG by walking the index tree from the root level down to the specific row(s) with matching index key values and then uses the row locator value stored in the index key to directly retrieve the matching row(s) from the data page(s); the row locator is either a specific row identifier or the clustered key value for the row.

For an index *scan*, SQL Server searches all the rows in the leaf level of the index, looking for possible matches. If any are found, it then uses the row locator to retrieve the data row.

Although both seeks and scans use an index, the index scan is still more expensive in terms of I/O than an index seek but slightly less expensive than a table scan, which is why it is used. However, in this chapter you learn to design indexes that result in index seeks, and when this chapter talks about queries using an index, index seeks are what it refers to (except for the section on index covering, but that's a horse of a slightly different color).

You might think that the easy solution to get row locator lookups on all possible columns is to index all the columns on a table so that any type of search criteria specified for a query can be helped by an index. This strategy might be somewhat appropriate in a read-only decision support system (DSS) environment that supports ad hoc queries, but it is not likely because many of the indexes probably still wouldn't even be used. As you see in the section "Index Selection," later in this chapter, just because an index is defined on a column doesn't mean that the Query Optimizer is necessarily always going to use it if the search criteria are not selective enough. Also, creating that many indexes on a large table could take up a significant amount of space in the database, increasing the time required to back up and run `DBCC` checks on the database. As mentioned earlier, too many indexes on a table in an OLTP environment can generate a significant amount of overhead during inserts, updates, and deletes and have a detrimental impact on performance.

TIP

A common design mistake often made is too many indexes defined on tables in OLTP environments. In many cases, some of the indexes are redundant or are never even considered by the SQL Server Query Optimizer to process the queries used by the applications. These indexes end up simply wasting space and adding unnecessary overhead to data updates.

A case in point was one client who had eight indexes defined on a table, four of which had the same column, which was a unique key, as the first column in the index. That column was included in the `WHERE` clauses for all queries and updates performed on the table. Only one of those four indexes was ever used.

It is hoped that, by the end of this chapter, you understand why all these indexes were unnecessary and are able to recognize and determine which columns benefit from having indexes defined on them and which indexes to avoid.

Index Selection

To determine which indexes to define on a table, you need to perform a detailed query analysis. This process involves examining the search clauses to see what columns are referenced, knowing the bias of the data to determine the usefulness of the index, and ranking the queries in order of importance and frequency of execution. You have to be careful not to examine individual queries and develop indexes to support one query, without considering the other queries that are executed on the table as well. You need to come up with a set of indexes that work for the best cross-section of your queries.

TIP

A useful tool to help you identify your frequently executed and critical queries is SQL Server Profiler. I've found SQL Server Profiler to be invaluable when going into a new client site and having to identify the problem queries that need tuning. SQL Server Profiler allows you to trace the procedures and queries being executed in SQL Server and capture the runtime, reads and writes, execution plans, and other processing information. This information can help you identify which queries are providing substandard performance, which ones are being executed most often, which indexes are being used by the queries, and so on.

You can analyze this information yourself manually or save a trace to analyze with the Database Engine Tuning Advisor. The features of SQL Server Profiler are covered in more detail in Chapter 6, "SQL Server Profiler." The Database Engine Tuning Advisor is discussed in more detail in Chapter 55, "Configuring, Tuning, and Optimizing SQL Server Options."

Because it's usually not possible to index for everything, you should index first for the queries most critical to your applications or those run frequently by many users. If you have a query that's run only once a month, is it worth creating an index to support only that query and having to maintain it throughout the rest of the month? The sum of the additional processing time throughout the month could conceivably exceed the time required to perform a table scan to satisfy that one query.

TIP

If, due to query response time requirements, you must have an index in place when a query is run, consider creating the index only when you run the query and then dropping the index for the remainder of the month. This approach is feasible as long as the time it takes to create the index and run the query that uses the index doesn't exceed the time it takes to simply run the query without the index in place.

Evaluating Index Usefulness

SQL Server provides indexes for two primary reasons: as a method to enforce the uniqueness of the data in the database tables and to provide faster access to data in the tables. Creating the appropriate indexes for a database is one of the most important aspects of physical database design. Because you can't have an unlimited number of indexes on a table, and it wouldn't be feasible anyway, you should create indexes on columns that have high selectivity so that your queries will use the indexes. The selectivity of an index can be defined as follows:

Selectivity ratio = Number of unique index values / Number of rows in table

If the selectivity ratio is high—that is, if a large number of rows can be uniquely identified by the key—the index is highly selective and useful to the Query Optimizer. The optimum selectivity would be 1, meaning that there is a unique value for each row. A low selectivity means that there are many duplicate values and the index would be less useful. The SQL Server Query Optimizer decides whether to use any indexes for a query based on the selectivity of the index. The higher the selectivity, the faster and more efficiently SQL Server can retrieve the result set.

For example, say that you are evaluating useful indexes on the `authors` table in the `bigpubs2008` database. Assume that most of the queries access the table either by author's last name or by state. Because a large number of concurrent users modify data in this table, you are allowed to choose only one index—author's last name or state. Which one should you choose? Let's perform some analysis to see which one is a more useful, or selective, index.

First, you need to determine the selectivity based on the author's last name with a query on the `authors` table in the `bigpubs2008` database:

```
select count(distinct au_lname) as '# unique',
   count(*) as '# rows',
   str(count(distinct au_lname) / cast (count(*) as real),4,2) as 'selectivity'
from authors
go

# unique    # rows      selectivity
----------- ----------- -----------
160         172         0.93
```

The selectivity ratio calculated for the au_lname column on the authors table, 0.93, indicates that an index on au_lname would be highly selective and a good candidate for an index. All but 12 rows in the table contain a unique value for last name.

Now, look at the selectivity of the state column:

```
select count(distinct state) as '# unique',
    count(*) '# rows',
    str(count(distinct state) / cast (count(*) as real),4,2) as 'selectivity'
from authors
go

# unique    # rows      selectivity
----------- ----------- -----------
38          172         0.22
```


As you can see, an index on the state column would be much less selective (0.22) than an index on the au_lname column and possibly not as useful.

One of the questions to ask at this point is whether a few values in the state column that have a high number of duplicates are skewing the selectivity or whether there are just a few unique values in the table. You can determine this with a query similar to the following:

```
select state,
       count(*) as numrows,
       count(*)/b.totalrows * 100 as percentage
from authors a,
     (select convert(numeric(6,2), count(*)) as totalrows from  authors) as b
group by state, b.totalrows
having count(*) > 1
order by 2 desc
go

state numrows     percentage
----- ----------- -----------------------------------
CA    37          21.5116200
NY    18          10.4651100
TX    15          8.7209300
OH    9           5.2325500
FL    8           4.6511600
IL    7           4.0697600
NJ    7           4.0697600
WA    6           3.4883700
PA    6           3.4883700
CO    5           2.9069700
LA    5           2.9069700
MI    5           2.9069700
```

```
MN    3    1.7441800
MO    3    1.7441800
OK    3    1.7441800
AZ    3    1.7441800
AK    2    1.1627900
IN    2    1.1627900
GA    2    1.1627900
MA    2    1.1627900
NC    2    1.1627900
NE    2    1.1627900
SD    2    1.1627900
VA    2    1.1627900
WI    2    1.1627900
WV    2    1.1627900
```

As you can see, most of the `state` values are relatively unique, except for one value, `'CA'`, which accounts for more than 20% of the values in the table. Therefore, `state` is probably not a good candidate for an indexed column, especially if most of the time you are searching for authors from the state of California. SQL Server would generally find it more efficient to scan the whole table rather than search via the index.

NOTE

When a single value skews the selectivity of an index, as in this example with the `state` column, this type of column might be a candidate for a filtered index, a new feature in SQL Server 2008. See the section "Filtered Indexes and Statistics," later in this chapter.

As a general rule of thumb, if the selectivity ratio for a nonclustered index key is less than 0.85 (in other words, if the Query Optimizer cannot discard at least 85% of the rows based on the key value), the Query Optimizer generally chooses a table scan to process the query rather than a nonclustered index. In such cases, performing a table scan to find all the qualifying rows is more efficient than seeking through the B-tree to locate a large number of data rows.

NOTE

You can relate the concept of selectivity to a hypothetical example. Say that you need to find every instance of the word *SQL* in this book. Would it be easier to do it by using the index and going back and forth from the index to all the pages that contain the word, or would it be easier just to scan each page from beginning to end to locate every occurrence? What if you had to find all references to the word *squonk*, if any? *Squonk* would definitely be easier to find via the index (actually, the index would help you determine that it doesn't even exist). Therefore, the selectivity for *Squonk* would be high, and the selectivity for *SQL* would be much lower.

How does SQL Server determine whether an index is selective and which index, if it has more than one to choose from, would be the most efficient to use? For example, how would SQL Server know how many rows the following query might return?

```
select * from table
    where key between 1000000 and 2000000
```

If the table contains 10,000,000 rows with values ranging between 0 and 20,000,000, how does the Query Optimizer know whether to use an index or a table scan? There could be 10 rows in the range, or 900,000. How does SQL Server estimate how many rows are between 1,000,000 and 2,000,000? The Query Optimizer gets this information from the index statistics, as described in the next section.

Index Statistics

As mentioned earlier, the selectivity of a key is an important factor that determines whether an index will be used to retrieve the data rows that satisfy a query. SQL Server stores the selectivity and a histogram of sample values of the key; based on the statistics stored for the key columns for the index and the SARGs specified for the query, the Query Optimizer decides which index to use.

To see the statistical information stored for an index, use the `DBCC SHOW_STATISTICS` command, which returns the following pieces of information:

- A histogram that contains an even sampling of the values for the first column in the index key. SQL Server stores up to 200 sample values in the histogram.
- Index densities for the combination of columns in the index. Index density indicates the uniqueness of the index key(s) and is discussed later in this section.
- The number of rows in the table at the time the statistics were computed.
- The number of rows sampled to generate the statistics.
- The number of sample values (steps) stored in the histogram.
- The average key length.
- Whether the index is defined on a string column.
- The date and time the statistics were generated.

The syntax for `DBCC SHOW_STATISTICS` is as follows:

```
DBCC SHOW_STATISTICS (tablename, index)
```

Listing 34.4 displays the abbreviated output from `DBCC SHOW_STATISTICS`, showing the statistical information for the `aunmind` nonclustered index on the `au_lname` and `au_fname` columns of the `authors` table.

LISTING 34.4 **DBCC SHOW_STATISTICS** Output for the **aunmind** Index on the **authors** Table

```
dbcc show_statistics (authors, aunmind )
go

Name      Updated              Rows Rows Sampled  Steps  Density
Average key length String Index Filter Expression   Unfiltered Rows
--------- ------------------- ---- -------------- ------ -------
---------------------------------------------------- ---------------
aunmind   Mar 14 2010 10:20PM  172  172            148    1
24.06977          YES          NULL                  172

(1 row(s) affected)

All density   Average Length Columns
------------ ------------- -------------------------
0.00625       6.406977      au_lname
0.005813953   13.06977      au_lname, au_fname
0.005813953   24.06977      au_lname, au_fname, au_id

(3 row(s) affected)

RANGE_HI_KEY   RANGE_ROWS EQ_ROWS DISTINCT_RANGE_ROWS  AVG_RANGE_ROWS
-----------------------------------------------------------------------
Ahlberg        0          2       0                    1
Alexander      0          1       0                    1
Amis           0          1       0                    1
Arendt         0          1       0                    1
Arnosky        0          1       0                    1
Bate           0          1       0                    1
Bauer          0          1       0                    1
Benchley       0          1       0                    1
Bennet         0          1       0                    1
Blotchet-Halls 0          1       0                    1
...
del Castillo   0          1       0                    1
Dillard        0          1       0                    1
Doctorow       0          1       0                    1
Doyle          0          1       0                    1
Durrenmatt     2          1       2                    1
Eastman        0          1       0                    1
...
Gringlesby     0          1       0                    1
Grisham        0          1       0                    1
Gunning        0          1       0                    1
```

```
Hill          0       1     0             1
Hutchins      3       2     3             1
Ionesco       0       1     0             1
Ishiguro      0       1     0             1
...
Tyler         0       1     0             1
Van Allsburg  0       1     0             1
Van der       0       1     0             1
Van der Meer  0       1     0             1
von Goethe    0       1     0             1
Walker        0       1     0             1
Warner        0       1     0             1
White         0       2     0             1
Wilder        0       1     0             1
Williams      0       2     0             1
Wilson        0       1     0             1
Yates         0       1     0             1
Yokomoto      0       1     0             1
Young         0       1     0             1
```

Looking at the output, you can determine that the statistics were last updated on March 14, 2010. At the time the statistics were generated, the table had 172 rows, and all 172 rows were sampled to generate the statistics (no filtering was applied). The average key length is 24.06977 bytes. From the `All density` information, you can see that this index is highly selective. (A low density means high selectivity; index densities are covered shortly.)

After the general information and the index densities, the index histogram is displayed.

The Statistics Histogram

Up to 200 sample values can be stored in the statistics histogram. Each sample value is called a *step*. The sample value stored in each step is the endpoint of a range of values. Three values are stored for each step:

- **RANGE_ROWS**—This indicates how many other rows are inside the range between the current step and the step prior, not including the step values themselves.
- **EQ_ROWS**—This is the number of rows that have the same value as the sample value. In other words, it is the number of duplicate values for the step.
- **Range density**—This indicates the number of distinct values within the range. The range density information is actually displayed in two separate columns, `DISTINCT_RANGE_ROWS` and `AVG_RANGE_ROWS`:
  - `DISTINCT_RANGE_ROWS` is the number of distinct values between the current step and the step prior, not including the step values itself.
  - `AVG_RANGE_ROWS` is the average number of rows per distinct value within the range of the step.

34

In the output in Listing 34.4, distinct key values in the first column of the index are stored as the sample values in the histogram. Because most of the values for `au_lname` are unique, most of the range values are `0`. You can see that there is a duplicate in the index key for the last name of `Hutchins` (`EQ_ROWS` is `2`). For comparison purposes, Listing 34.5 shows a snippet of the `DBCC SHOW_STATISTICS` output for the `titleidind` index on the `sales` table in `bigpubs2008`.

LISTING 34.5 DBCC **SHOW_STATISTICS** Output for the **titleidind** Index on the **sales** Table in the **bigpubs2008** Database

```
dbcc show_statistics (sales, 'titleidind')
go

Name        Updated             Rows    Rows Sampled Steps  Density
Average key length String Index Filter Expression Unfiltered Rows
----------- ------------------ ------- ------------ ------ ------------
----------------- ----------- ---------------- --------------
titleidind  Mar 14 2010 10:39PM  168725  152432       188    0.003537365
26.40519            YES          NULL             168725

All density   Average Length Columns
------------- -------------- ------------------------------------------------
0.001858736   6              title_id
5.99844E-06   10             title_id, stor_id
5.926804E-06  26.4007        title_id, stor_id, ord_num

RANGE_HI_KEY RANGE_ROWS EQ_ROWS  DISTINCT_RANGE_ROWS  AVG_RANGE_ROWS
------------ ---------- -------- -------------------- --------------
BI0194       0          274.8199 0                    1
BI2184       639.6047   312.9337 2                    277.1448
BI2915       893.1208   271.811  3                    261.8779
BI3976       637.2789   260.778  2                    276.137
BI8448       1685.068   281.8409 6                    300.0652
BU1111       616.3464   276.8259 2                    267.0668
BU7832       357.0157   299.8948 1                    296.2236
CH0249       1067.558   279.8349 3                    313.0259
CH0639       1019.879   284.8499 3                    299.0454
CH0671       316.3136   259.7751 1                    262.4521
CH0847       1333.867   266.796  5                    295.557
CH1260       1069.884   287.8589 3                    313.7079
CH1380       612.8576   311.9307 2                    265.5551
CH1568       645.4193   286.8559 2                    279.6643
CH1692       974.525    275.8229 3                    285.7469
CH2080       329.1057   285.8529 1                    273.066
CH2240       715.1943   273.817  2                    309.8983
CH2256       352.364    310.9277 1                    292.364
```

```
CH2360     630.3014   293.8768 2          273.1136
CH2480     626.8126   311.9307 2          271.6019
CH2574     679.1439   279.8349 2          294.2774
CH2610     334.9203   280.8379 1          277.8905
CH2706     343.0607   300.8978 1          284.6448
CH2856     326.7799   287.8589 1          271.1362
...
FI9853     623.3239   295.8828 2          270.0902
FI9965     625.6497   323.9666 2          271.098
LC1680     629.1384   286.8559 2          272.6097
LC5292     647.7451   265.793  2          280.6721
MC3021     610.5318   244.7302 2          264.5473
NF2924     652.3968   266.796  2          282.6877
NF8918     669.8406   310.9277 2          290.2462
PC9999     665.1889   275.8229 2          288.2306
PS2106     709.3798   259.7751 2          307.3788
TC3218     617.5093   291.8708 2          267.5707
TC4203     29.23513   293.8768 0          284.9097
TC7777     29.23513   269.805  0          284.9097
```

As you can see in this example, there are a greater number of rows per range and a greater number of duplicates for each step value. Also, 188 steps in the histogram are used, and the sample values for the 168,725 rows in the table are distributed across those 188 step values. Also, in this example, 152,432 rows, rather than the whole table, were sampled to generate the statistics.

How the Statistics Histogram Is Used

The histogram steps are used for SARGs only when a constant expression is compared against an indexed column and the value of the constant expression is known at query compile time. The following SARG examples show where histogram steps can be used:

- `where col_a = getdate()`
- `where cust_id = 12345`
- `where monthly_sales < 10000 / 12`
- `where l_name like "Smith" + "%"`

Some constant expressions cannot be evaluated until query runtime. They include search arguments that contain local variables or subqueries and also join clauses, such as the following:

- `where price = @avg_price`
- `where total_sales > (select sum(qty) from sales)`
- `where titles.pub_id = publishers.pub_id`

For these types of statements, you need some other way of estimating the number of matching rows. In addition, because histogram steps are kept only on the first column of the index, SQL Server must use a different method for determining the number of matching rows for SARGs that specify multiple column values for a composite index, such as the following:

```
select * from sales
   where title_id = 'BI3976'
     and stor_id = 'P648'
```

When the histogram is not used or cannot be used, SQL Server uses the index density values to estimate the number of matching rows.

Index Densities

SQL Server stores the density values of each column in the index for use in queries where the SARG value is not known until runtime or when the SARG is on multiple columns of the index. For composite keys, SQL Server stores the density for the first column of the composite key; for the first and second columns; for the first, second, and third columns; and so on. This information is shown in the `All density` section of the `DBCC SHOW_STATISTICS` output in Listings 34.4 and 34.5.

Index density essentially represents the inverse of all unique key values of the key. The density of each key is calculated by using the following formula:

Key density = 1.00 / Count of distinct key values in the table

Therefore, the density for the `au_lname` column in the `authors` table in the `bigpubs2008` database is calculated as follows:

```
Select Density = 1.00/ (select count(distinct au_lname) from authors)
go
Density
---------------------------------------
0.0062500000000
```

The density for the combination of the columns `au_lname` and `au_fname` is as follows:

```
Select Density = 1.00/ (select count(distinct au_lname + au_fname) from authors)
go
Density
----------------
0.0058139534883
```

Notice that, unlike with the selectivity ratio, a *smaller* index density indicates a more selective index. As the density value approaches 1, the index becomes less selective and essentially useless. When the index selectivity is poor, the Query Optimizer might choose to do a table scan or a leaf-level index scan rather than perform an index seek because it is more cost-effective.

TIP

Watch out for database indexes that have poor selectivity. Such indexes are often more of a detriment to the performance of the system than they are a help. Not only are they usually not used for data retrieval, but they also slow down your data modification statements because of the additional index overhead. You should identify such indexes and consider dropping them.

Typically, the density value should become smaller (that is, more selective) as you add more columns to the key. For example, in Listing 34.5, the densities get progressively smaller (and thus, more selective) as additional columns are factored in, as shown in Table 34.8.

TABLE 34.8 Index Densities for the **titleidind** Index on the **sales** Table

Key Column	Index Density
`title_id`	0.001858736
`title_id, stor_id`	5.99844E-06 (.00000599844)
`title_id, stor_id, ord_num`	5.926804E-06 (.000005926804)

Estimating Rows Using Index Statistics

How does the Query Optimizer use the index statistics to estimate the number of rows that match the SARGs in a query?

SQL Server uses the histogram information when searching for a known value being compared to the leading column of the index key column, especially when the search spans a range or when there are duplicate values in the key. Consider this query on the `sales` table in the `bigpubs2008` database:

```
select * from sales
    where title_id = 'BI3976'
```

Because there are duplicates of `title_id` in the table, SQL Server uses the histogram on `title_id` (refer to Listing 34.5) to estimate the number of matching rows. For the value of `BI3976`, it would look at the `EQ_ROWS` value, which is `260.778`. This indicates that there are approximately 261 rows in the table that have a `title_id` value of `BI3976`.

When an exact match for the search argument is not found as a step in the histogram, SQL Server uses the `AVG_RANGE_ROWS` value for the next step greater than the search value. For example, SQL Server would estimate that for a search value of `'BI4184'`, on average, it would >match approximately 300.0652 rows because that is the `AVG_RANGE_ROWS` value for the step value of `'BI8448'`, which is the next step greater than `'BI3976'`.

When the query is a range retrieval that spans multiple steps, SQL Server sums the RANGE_ROWS and EQ_ROWS values between the endpoints of the range retrieval. For example, when we use the histogram in Listing 34.5, if the search argument were where title_id <= 'BI3976', the row estimate would be 274.8199+639.6047+312.9337+893.1208+271.811+637.2789+260.778, or 3290.3470 rows.

As mentioned previously, when the histogram cannot be used, SQL Server uses just the index density to estimate the number of matching rows. The formula is straightforward for an equality search; it looks like this:

Row Estimate = Number of Rows in Table × Index Density

For example, to estimate the number of matching rows for any given title_id in the sales table, multiply the number of rows in the sales table by the index density for the title_id key (0.001862197), as follows:

```
select count(*) * 0.001862197 as 'Row Estimate'
from sales
go

Row Estimate
-------------------
314.199188825
```

If a query specifies both the title_id and stor_id as SARGs, and if the SARG for title_id is a constant expression that can be evaluated at optimization time, SQL Server uses both the index density on title_id and stor_id as well as the histogram on title_id to estimate the number of matching rows. For some data values, the estimated number of matching rows for title_id and stor_id calculated using the index density could be greater than the estimated number of rows that match the specific title_id, as determined by the histogram. SQL Server uses whichever is the smaller of the two to calculate the row estimate.

Multiplying the number of rows in the sales table by the index density for title_id, stor_id (5.997505E-06), you can see that it is nearly unique, essentially matching only a single row:

```
select count(*) * 5.997505E-06 as 'Row Estimate'
from sales

Row Estimate
--------------
1.011929031125
```

In this example, SQL Server would use the index density on title_id and stor_id to estimate the number of matching rows. In this case, it is estimated that the query will return, on average, one matching row.

Generating and Maintaining Index and Column Statistics

At this point, you might ask, "How do the index statistics get created?" and "How are they maintained?" The index statistics are first created when you create the index on a table that already contains data rows or when you run the `UPDATE STATISTICS` command. Index statistics can also be automatically updated by SQL Server. SQL Server can be configured to constantly monitor the update activity on the indexed key values in a database and update the statistics through an internal process, when appropriate.

Auto-Update Statistics

To automatically update statistics, an internal SQL Server process monitors the updates to a table's columns to determine when statistics should be updated. SQL Server internally keeps track of the number of modifications made to a column via column modification counters (`colmodctrs`). SQL Server uses information about the table and the `colmodctrs` to determine whether statistics are out of date and need to be updated. Statistics are considered out of date in the following situations:

- When the table size has gone from 0 to >0 rows
- When the number of rows in the table at the time the statistics were gathered was 500 or fewer and the `colmodctr` of the leading column of the statistics object has changed by more than 500
- When the table had more than 500 rows at the time the statistics were gathered and the `colmodctr` of the leading column of the statistics object has changed by more than 500 + 20% of the number of rows in the table

If the statistics are defined on a temporary table, there is an additional threshold for updating statistics every six column modifications if the table contains fewer than 500 rows.

The `colmodctrs` are incremented in the following situations:

- When a row is inserted into the table
- When a row is deleted from the table
- When an indexed column is updated

Whenever the index statistics have been updated for a column, the `colmodctr` for that column is reset to `0`.

When SQL Server generates an update of the column statistics, it generates the new statistics based on a sampling of the data values in the table. Sampling helps minimize the overhead of the AutoStats process. The sampling is random across the data pages, and the values are taken from the table or the smallest nonclustered index on the columns needed to generate the statistics. After a data page containing a sampled row has been read from disk, all the rows on the data page are used to update the statistical information.

CAUTION

Having up-to-date statistics on tables helps ensure that optimum execution plans are being generated for queries at all times. In most cases, you would want SQL Server to automatically keep the statistics updated. However, it is possible that Auto-Update Statistics can cause an update of the index statistics to run at inappropriate times in a production environment or in a high-volume environment to run too often. If this problem is occurring, you might want to turn off the AutoStats feature and set up a scheduled job to update statistics during off-peak periods. Do not forget to update statistics periodically; otherwise, the resulting performance problems might end up being much worse than the momentary ones caused by the AutoStats process.

To determine how often the AutoStats process is being run, you can use SQL Server Profiler to determine when an automatic update of index statistics is occurring by monitoring the `Auto Stats` event in the `Performance` event class. (For more information on using SQL Server Profiler, see Chapter 6.)

If necessary, it is possible to turn off the AutoStats behavior by using the `sp_autostats` system stored procedure. This stored procedure allows you to turn the automatic updating of statistics on or off for a specific index or all the indexes of a table. The following command turns off the automatic update of statistics for an index named `aunmind` on the `authors` table:

```
Exec sp_autostats 'authors', 'OFF', 'aunmind'
```

When you run `sp_autostats` and simply supply the table name, it displays the current setting for the table as well as the database. Following are the settings for the `authors` table:

```
Exec sp_autostats 'authors'
go

Global statistics settings for [bigpubs2008]:
  Automatic update statistics: ON
  Automatic create statistics: ON

settings for table [authors]

Index Name                        AUTOSTATS Last Updated
------------------------ --------- -----------------------
[UPKCL_auidind]          ON        2009-10-19 01:23:47.263
[aunmind]                OFF       2010-03-14 22:20:52.177
[_WA_Sys_state_4AB81AF0] ON        2009-10-19 01:23:47.263
[au_fname]               ON        2009-10-19 01:23:47.280
[phone]                  ON        2009-10-19 01:23:47.293
[address]                ON        2009-10-19 01:23:47.310
[city]                   ON        2009-10-19 01:23:47.310
[zip]                    ON        2009-10-19 01:23:47.310
```

There are three other ways to disable auto-updating of statistics for an index:

- Specify the STATISTICS_NORECOMPUTE clause when creating the index.
- Specify the NORECOMPUTE option when running the UPDATE STATISTICS command.
- Specify the NORECOMPUTE option when creating statistics with the CREATE STATISTICS command. (You learn more about this command in the "Creating Statistics" section, later in the chapter.)

You can also turn AutoStats on or off for the entire database by setting the database option in SQL Server Management Studio; to do this, right-click the database in Object Explorer to bring up the Database Properties dialog, select the Options page, and set the Auto Update Statistics option to False. You can also disable or enable the AutoStats option for a database by using the ALTER DATABASE command:

```
ALTER DATABASE dbname SET AUTO_UPDATE_STATISTICS { ON | OFF }
```


NOTE

What actually happens when you execute sp_autostats or use the NORECOMPUTE option in the UPDATE STATISTICS command to turn off auto-update statistics for a specific index or table? SQL Server internally sets a flag in the system catalog to inform the internal SQL Server process not to update the index statistics for the table or index that has had the option turned off using any of these commands. To re-enable Auto Update Statistics, you either run UPDATE STATISTICS without the NORECOMPUTE option or execute the sp_autostats system stored procedure and specify the value 'ON' for the second parameter.

Asynchronous Statistics Updating

In versions prior to SQL Server 2005, when SQL Server determined that the statistics being examined to optimize a query were out of date, the query would wait for the statistics update to complete before compilation of the query plan would continue. This is still the default behavior in SQL Server 2008. However, the database option, AUTO_UPDATE_STATISTICS_ASYNC, can be enabled to support asynchronous statistics updating.

When the AUTO_UPDATE_STATISTICS_ASYNC option is enabled, queries do not have to wait for the statistics to be updated before compiling. Instead, SQL Server puts the out-of-date statistics on a queue to be updated by a worker thread, which runs as a background process. The query and any other concurrent queries compile immediately by using the existing out-of-date statistics. Because there is no delay for updated statistics, query response times are more predictable, even if the out-of-date statistics may cause the Query Optimizer to choose a less-efficient query plan. Queries that start after the updated statistics are ready use the updated statistics.

Manually Updating Statistics

Whether or not you've disabled AutoStats, you can still manually update index statistics by using the `UPDATE STATISTICS` T-SQL command, whose syntax is as follows:

```
UPDATE STATISTICS table | view
    [ { { index | statistics_name }
          | ( { index |statistics_name } [ ,...n ] ) } ]
   [ WITH [ [ FULLSCAN ]
            | SAMPLE number { PERCENT | ROWS } ]
            | RESAMPLE
        [ [ , ] [ ALL | COLUMNS | INDEX ]
        [ [ , ] NORECOMPUTE ] ]
```

If neither the `FULLSCAN` nor `SAMPLE` option is specified, the default behavior is to perform a sample scan to calculate the statistics, and SQL Server automatically computes the appropriate sample size.

The `FULLSCAN` option forces SQL Server to perform a full scan of the data in the table or index to calculate the statistics. This generates more accurate statistics than using sampling but is also the most time-consuming and I/O-intensive method. When you use the `SAMPLE` option, you can specify a fixed number of rows or a percentage of rows to sample to build or update the index statistics. If the sampling ratio specified ever results in too few rows being sampled, SQL Server automatically corrects the sampling, based on the number of existing rows in the table or view. At a minimum, approximately 1,000 data pages are sampled.

The `RESAMPLE` option specifies that the statistics be generated using the previously defined sampling ratio. This `RESAMPLE` option is useful for indexes or column statistics created with different sampling values. For example, if the index statistics were created using `FULLSCAN`, and the column statistics were created using a 50% sample, specifying the `RESAMPLE` option would update the statistics using `FULLSCAN` on the indexes and using the 50% sample for the others.

Specifying `ALL`, `COLUMNS`, or `INDEX` specifies whether the `UPDATE STATISTICS` command affects all existing statistics or only column or index statistics. By default, if no option is specified, the `UPDATE STATISTICS` statement affects all statistics.

As previously discussed, SQL Server automatically updates the index statistics by default. If you specify the `NORECOMPUTE` option with `UPDATE STATISTICS`, it disables AutoStats for the table or index.

When the `automatic update statistics` option is turned off, you should run the `UPDATE STATISTICS` command periodically, when appropriate. To determine the last time statistics were updated, you run the following command:

```
select STATS_DATE(tableid, indexid)
```

Following is an example:

```
select STATS_DATE(object_id('authors'), 1)
go

-----------------------
2010-03-15 00:04:51.407
```

TIP

You can get the index ID from sys.indexes for each index on a table by using the following query:

```
select name, index_id from sys.indexes
   Where object_id = object_id('table_name') and index_id > 0
```


Column-Level Statistics

In addition to statistics on indexes, SQL Server can also store statistics on individual columns that are not part of any indexes. Knowing the likelihood of a particular value being found in a nonindexed column can help the Query Optimizer better estimate the number of matching rows for SARGs on the nonindexed columns. This helps it determine the optimal execution plan, whether or not SQL Server is using an index to actually locate the rows.

For example, consider the following query:

```
select stor_name
   from stores st
   join sales s on (st.stor_id = s.stor_id)
   where s.qty <= 100
```

SQL Server knows the density of the `stor_id` column in both the `sales` and `stores` tables because of indexes on the column in those tables. There is no index on `qty`. However, if the Query Optimizer were to know how many rows in the `sales` table had a `qty` less than 100, it would be better able to choose the most efficient query plan for joining between `sales` and `stores`. For example, assume that, on average, there are approximately 500 sales per store. However, there are only approximately 5 sales per store where the `qty` is less than 100. With the statistics on `qty`, SQL Server has the opportunity to determine this, and knowing there might be only 5 matching rows per store in `sales` versus 500, it might choose a different, more efficient, join strategy between the two tables.

Being able to keep statistics on the `qty` column without having to add it to an existing index with `stor_id` or create a separate index on `qty` provides SQL Server with the selectivity information it needs for optimization. By not having to create an index on `qty` to generate statistics on the column, you avoid incurring the overhead of having to maintain the index key rows for each insert, update, and delete that occurs on the table. Only the index statistics on `qty` need to be maintained, which is required only after many modifications to the data have occurred.

By default, SQL Server generates column statistics automatically when queries are optimized and the column is specified in a SARG or join clause. If no column statistics exist and the Query Optimizer needs to estimate the approximate density or distribution of column values, SQL Server automatically generates statistics for that column. This rule has two exceptions:

- Statistics are not automatically created for columns when the cost of creating the statistics exceeds the cost of the query plan itself.
- Statistics are not automatically created when SQL Server is too busy (that is, when there are too many outstanding query compilations in progress).

If you want to disable or re-enable the database option to autocreate statistics in the database, you use the `ALTER DATABASE` command:

```
ALTER DATABASE dbname SET AUTO_CREATE_STATISTICS { ON | OFF }
```

You can also turn the Auto Create Statistics option on or off for the entire database by setting the database option in SSMS. In Object Explorer, right-click the database to bring up the Database Properties dialog, select the Options page, and set the Auto Create Statistics option to True or False.

Column statistics are stored in the system catalogs. General information about them can be viewed in the `sys.stats` catalog view. Autogenerated statistics have a name in the format `_WA_Sys_colname_systemgeneratednumber`. You can retrieve a list of autogenerated column statistics with a query similar to the following:

```
SELECT cast(object_name(object_id) as varchar(30)) as 'table',
       cast (name as varchar(30)) as autostats
   FROM sys.stats
   WHERE auto_created = 1
     AND objectproperty (object_id, 'IsUserTable') = 1
go
table                          autostats
------------------------------ ------------------------------
table                          autostats
------------------------------ ------------------------------
authors                        _WA_Sys_state_4AB81AF0
sales                          _WA_Sys_ord_num_628FA481
sales                          _WA_Sys_qty_628FA481
stores                         _WA_Sys_state_6477ECF3
stores                         _WA_Sys_zip_6477ECF3
titles                         _WA_Sys_type_6A30C649
```

Creating Statistics

If you want finer control over how the column statistics are generated, you can use the CREATE STATISTICS command. Its syntax is similar to that of UPDATE STATISTICS, with the exception that you specify a column or list of columns instead of an index on which to create statistics:

```
CREATE STATISTICS statistics_name ON table (column [,...n])
    [     WITH  [ [ FULLSCAN | SAMPLE number { PERCENT | ROWS } ] [,] ]
        [ NORECOMPUTE]      ]
```

Any column that can be specified as an index key can also be specified for statistics, except for XML columns or when the maximum allowable size of the combined column values exceeds the 900-byte limit on an index key. Statistics can also be created on computed columns if the ARITHABORT and QUOTED_IDENTIFIER database options are set to ON. In addition, statistics can be created on CLR user-defined type columns if the CLR type supports binary ordering.

If you want to create single-column statistics on all eligible columns in a database, you can use the sp_createstats system procedure:

```
sp_createstats [[@indexonly =] 'indexonly']
        [,[@fullscan =] 'fullscan']
        [,[@norecompute =] 'norecompute']
```

The created statistics have the same name as the column on which they are created. Statistics are not created on columns that already have statistics on them (for example, the first column of an index or a column that already has explicitly created statistics).

To display a list of all column statistics, whether autogenerated or manually created, you use a query similar to the previous one, but you include user-created statistics as well:

```
SELECT cast(object_name(object_id) as varchar(30)) as 'table',
       cast (name as varchar(30)) as name,
       stats_id
   FROM sys.stats
   WHERE objectproperty (object_id, 'IsUserTable') = 1
     and (auto_created = 1 or user_created = 1)
order by 1, 3
go

table                          name                           stats_id
------------------------------ ------------------------------ -----------
authors                        _WA_Sys_state_4AB81AF0         3
authors                        au_fname                       4
authors                        phone                          5
authors                        address                        6
authors                        city                           7
authors                        zip                            8
```

```
discounts                   discounttype                2
discounts                   stor_id                     3
discounts                   lowqty                      4
discounts                   highqty                     5
discounts                   discount                    6
employee                    fname                       3
employee                    minit                       4
employee                    job_id                      5
employee                    job_lvl                     6
employee                    pub_id                      7
employee                    hire_date                   8
jobs                        job_desc                    2
jobs                        min_lvl                     3
jobs                        max_lvl                     4
publishers                  pub_name                    2
publishers                  city                        3
publishers                  state                       4
publishers                  country                     5
roysched                    lorange                     3
roysched                    hirange                     4
roysched                    royalty                     5
sales                       _WA_Sys_ord_num_628FA481    3
sales                       ord_date                    4
sales                       _WA_Sys_qty_628FA481        5
sales                       payterms                    6
stores                      _WA_Sys_state_6477ECF3      3
stores                      _WA_Sys_zip_6477ECF3        4
stores                      stor_name                   5
stores                      stor_address                6
titleauthor                 au_ord                      4
titleauthor                 royaltyper                  5
titles                      _WA_Sys_type_6A30C649       3
titles                      pub_id                      4
titles                      price                       5
titles                      advance                     6
titles                      royalty                     7
titles                      ytd_sales                   8
titles                      notes                       9
titles                      pubdate                     10
```

To remove a collection of statistics on one or more columns for a table in the current database, you use the `DROP STATISTICS` command, which has the following syntax:

```
DROP STATISTICS {table | view}.statistics_name
```

Be aware that dropping the column statistics could affect how your queries are optimized, and less efficient query plans might be chosen. Also, if the Auto Create Statistics option is enabled for the database, SQL Server is likely to automatically create statistics on the columns the next time they are referenced in a SARG or join clause for a query.

String Summary Statistics

SQL Server 2008 supports string summary statistics for estimating the selectivity of `LIKE` conditions. String summary statistics are statistical summaries of substring frequency distribution for character columns. String summary statistics can be created on columns of type `text`, `ntext`, `char`, `varchar`, and `nvarchar`. String summary statistics allow SQL Server to estimate the selectivity of `LIKE` conditions, where the search string may have any number of wildcards in any combination, including `LIKE` conditions where the first character is a wildcard. In previous versions of SQL Server, row estimates could not be accurately obtained when the leading character of a search string was a wildcard character. String summary statistics allow SQL Server to estimate the selectivity of any of the following predicates:

- `Column LIKE 'string%'`
- `Column LIKE '%string'`
- `Column LIKE '%string%'`
- `Column LIKE 'str[abc]ing'`
- `Column LIKE '%abc%xy'`

String summary statistics include additional information beyond what is displayed by `DBCC SHOW_STATISTICS` for the histogram. You can determine whether string summary statistics have been created for a column or an index by examining the `String Index` column returned by `DBCC SHOW_STATISTICS`. If the value is `YES`, the statistics for that column or index also include a string summary. However, `DBCC SHOW_STATISTICS` does not display the actual contents of the string summary.

SQL Server Index Maintenance

SQL Server indexes are self-maintaining, which means that any time a data modification (such as an update, a delete, or an insert) takes place on a table, the index B-tree is automatically updated to reflect the correct data values and current rows. Generally, you do not have to do any maintenance of the indexes, but indexes and tables can become fragmented over time. There are two types of fragmentation: external fragmentation and internal fragmentation.

External fragmentation occurs when the logical order of pages does not match the physical order or the extents allocated to the table are not contiguous. These situations occur typically with clustered tables as a result of page splits and pages being allocated and linked into the page chain from other extents. External fragmentation is usually not much of an issue for most queries performing small result set retrievals via an index. It's more of a performance issue for ordered scans of all or part of a table or index. If the table is heavily fragmented and the pages are not contiguous, scanning the page chain is more expensive.

Internal fragmentation occurs when an index is not using up all the space within the pages in the table or index. Fragmentation within an index page can happen for the following reasons:

- As more records are added to a table, space is used on the data page and on the index page. As a result, the page eventually becomes completely full. If another insert takes place on that page and there is no more room for the new row, SQL Server splits the page into two, each page now being about 50% full. If the clustered key values being inserted are not evenly distributed throughout the table (as often happens with clustered indexes on sequential keys), this extra free space might not be used.
- Frequent `update` statements can cause fragmentation in the database at the data and index page level because the updates cause rows to move to other pages. Again, if future clustered key values inserted into the table are not evenly distributed throughout the table, the empty slots left behind might not be used.
- As rows are deleted, space becomes freed up on data and index pages. If no new rows within the range of deleted values on the page are inserted, the page remains sparse.

NOTE

Internal fragmentation is not always a bad thing. Although pages that are not completely full use up more space and require more I/O during retrieval, free space within a page allows for rows to be added without having to perform an expensive page split. For some environments where the activity is more insert intensive than query intensive, you might want more free space in pages. This can be accomplished by applying the fill factor when creating the index on the table. Applying the fill factor is described in more detail in the next section.

Usually, in a system, all these factors contribute to the fragmentation of data within the data pages and index pages. In an environment subject to a lot of data modification, you might see a lot of fragmentation on the data and index pages over a period of time. These sparse and fragmented pages remain allocated to the table or index even if they have only a single row or two, and the extent containing the page remains allocated to the table or index.

Data fragmentation can adversely affect performance for table or index scanning operations because the data is spread across more pages than necessary. More I/Os are required to retrieve the data. SQL Server provides a dynamic management view, `sys.dm_db_index_physical_stats`, which is a multistatement table-valued function that returns size and fragmentation information for the data and indexes of a specified table or view. The results from the function are returned by a normal `SELECT` statement and thus can be saved to a table for reporting purposes and historical analysis. The syntax of `dm_db_index_physical_stats` is as follows:

```
sys.dm_db_index_physical_stats (
    { database_id | NULL | 0 | DEFAULT }
```

```
, { object_id | NULL | 0 | DEFAULT }
, { index_id | NULL | 0 | -1 | DEFAULT }
, { partition_number | NULL | 0 | DEFAULT }
, { mode | NULL | DEFAULT } )
```

The parameters for dm_db_index_physical_stats are summarized in Table 34.9.

TABLE 34.9 **dm_db_index_physical_stats** Parameters

Parameter	Description
database_id	The ID of the database. The default is 0, which returns information for all databases. NULL, 0, and DEFAULT are equivalent values in this context. If you specify NULL or 0, for *database_id*, you must specify NULL for *object_id*, *index_id*, and *partition_number*.
object_id	The object ID of the table or view the index is on. Valid inputs are the ID number of a table or view, NULL, 0, or DEFAULT. The default is 0, which returns information for all tables and views in the specified database. NULL, 0, and DEFAULT are equivalent values in this context.
index_id	The ID of the index. Valid inputs are the ID number of an index, 0 if *object_id* is a heap, NULL, -1, or DEFAULT. The default is -1, which returns information for all indexes for a table or view. NULL, -1, and DEFAULT are equivalent values in this context. If you specify NULL for *index_id*, you must also specify NULL for *partition_number*.
partition_number	The partition number in the object. Valid inputs are the *partition_number* of an index or a heap, NULL, 0, or DEFAULT. The default is 0, which returns information for all partitions of the object. NULL, 0, and DEFAULT are equivalent values in this context. Use a *partition_number* of 1 for a nonpartitioned index or heap.
mode	The scan level used to obtain physical index statistics. Valid inputs are DEFAULT, NULL, LIMITED, SAMPLED, or DETAILED. The default mode is LIMITED. NULL and DEFAULT are equivalent values in this context.

The sys.dm_db_index_physical_stats function requires only an Intent-Shared table lock, regardless of the mode in which it runs. This provides for the capability to run the sys.dm_db_index_physical_stats function online without blocking update activity on a table.

The scan-level mode determines the level of scanning performed by the function to obtain the physical statistics for the index. The LIMITED mode is the fastest and scans the smallest number of pages. It scans all data pages for a heap but scans only leaf-level pages for an index. It also returns only a subset of the data columns, as shown in Table 34.10. The SAMPLED mode returns statistics based on a 1% sample of all the pages in the index or heap. If the index or heap has fewer than 10,000 pages, DETAILED mode is used instead of SAMPLED. The SAMPLED scan mode displays information for only data pages of a heap and leaf-level pages of an index. The DETAILED mode scans all pages and returns all statistics for all data and index levels.

TIP

The scan modes get progressively slower from LIMITED to DETAILED because more work is performed in each mode. To quickly gauge the size or fragmentation level of a table or an index, first use the LIMITED mode. It is the fastest and does not return a row for each nonleaf level in the IN_ROW_DATA allocation unit of the index.

Table 34.10 describes the result columns returned by the dm_db_index_physical_stats table-valued function.

TABLE 34.10 **dm_db_index_physical_stats** Result Columns

Column Name	Data Type	Description	Displayed in LIMITED Scan Mode
database_id	Smallint	A database ID database containing the table or view.	Yes
object_id	int	The object ID of the table or view where the index is located.	Yes
index_id	int	The index ID of the index. 0 indicates a heap.	Yes
partition_number	int	A partition number within the owning table, view, or index.	Yes
index_type_desc	nvarchar (60)	The index type. Values are HEAP, CLUSTERED INDEX, NONCLUSTERED INDEX, PRIMARY XML INDEX, and XML INDEX.	Yes
alloc_unit_type_desc	nvarchar (60)	A description of the allocation unit type. Values are IN_ROW_DATA, LOB_DATA, and ROW_OVERFLOW_DATA.	Yes
index_depth	tinyint	The number of index levels.	Yes
index_level	tinyint	The current level of the index. 0 indicates index leaf levels, heaps, and LOB_DATA or ROW_OVERFLOW_DATA allocation units.	Yes
avg_fragmentation_in_percent	float	The percentage of logical fragmentation (out-of-order pages in the index).	Yes

TABLE 34.10 **dm_db_index_physical_stats** Result Columns

Column Name	Data Type	Description	Displayed in LIMITED Scan Mode
fragment_count	bigint	The number of fragments (physically consecutive leaf pages) in the index.	Yes
avg_fragment_size_in_pages	float	The average number of pages in one fragment in an index.	Yes
page_count	bigint	The total number of index or data pages at the current level.	Yes
avg_page_space_used_in_percent	Float	The average percentage of available data storage space used in all pages.	No
record_count	Bigint	The total number of records at the current level.	No
ghost_record_count	Bigint	The number of ghost records ready for removal by the ghost cleanup task.	No
version_ghost_record_count	Bigint	The number of ghost records retained by an outstanding snapshot isolation transaction in an allocation unit.	No
min_record_size_in_bytes	Int	The minimum record size, in bytes.	No
max_record_size_in_bytes	Int	The maximum record size, in bytes.	No
avg_record_size_in_bytes	Float	The average record size, in bytes.	No
forwarded_record_count	Bigint	The number of forwarded records in a heap.	No
*compressed_page_count_*	Bigint	The number of compressed pages in a heap.	No

Listing 34.6 shows examples of running `sys.dm_db_index_physical_stats` on the `sales_big` table, using both `LIMITED` and `DETAILED` scan modes.

LISTING 34.6 **`sys.dm_db_index_physical_stats`** Examples

```
use bigpubs2008
go
select str(index_id,3,0) as indid,
      left(index_type_desc, 20) as index_type_desc,
      index_depth as idx_depth,
      index_level as idx_level,
      str(avg_fragmentation_in_percent, 5,2) as avg_frgmnt_pct,
      str(page_count, 10,0) as pg_cnt
  FROM sys.dm_db_index_physical_stats
      (db_id(), object_id('sales_big'),null, 0, 'LIMITED')

select str(index_id,3,0) as indid,
      left(index_type_desc, 20) as index_type_desc,
      index_depth as idx_depth,
      index_level as idx_level,
      str(avg_fragmentation_in_percent, 5,2) as avg_frgmnt_pct,
      str(page_count, 10,0) as pg_cnt
  FROM sys.dm_db_index_physical_stats
    (db_id(), object_id('sales_big'),null, 0, 'DETAILED')
go

indid index_type_desc      idx_depth idx_level avg_frgmnt_pct pg_cnt
----- -------------------- --------- --------- -------------- ----------
  1   CLUSTERED INDEX      3         0         63.42               14519
  2   NONCLUSTERED INDEX   3         0         14.90                4571

indid index_type_desc      idx_depth idx_level avg_frgmnt_pct pg_cnt
----- -------------------- --------- --------- -------------- ----------
  1   CLUSTERED INDEX      3         0         63.42               14519
  1   CLUSTERED INDEX      3         1         92.11                  38
  1   CLUSTERED INDEX      3         2          0.00                   1
  2   NONCLUSTERED INDEX   3         0         14.90                4571
  2   NONCLUSTERED INDEX   3         1         87.50                   8
  2   NONCLUSTERED INDEX   3         2          0.00                   1
```

Again, you can see from the output in Listing 34.6 that the logical fragmentation (`avg_frgmnt_pct`) is 63.42% for the leaf level of the clustered index (`idx_level = 0`). This indicates that nearly two thirds of the data pages are out of sequence in relation to ordering of the clustered key values. If you want to improve the performance of table scans or clustered index scans for the `sales_big` table, you need to decide whether to rebuild the index or simply defragment the index.

The degree of fragmentation helps you decide which defragmentation method to use. A rough guideline to use to help decide is to examine the `avg_fragmentation_in_percent` value returned by the `sys.dm_db_index_physical_stats` function. If the `avg_fragmentation_in_percent` value is greater than 5% but less than 30%, you should reorganize the index. If the `avg_fragmentation_in_percent` value is greater than 30%, you should consider rebuilding the index. If you also have a dedicated maintenance window large enough to perform a rebuild instead of simply reorganizing the index, you may as well run a rebuild because it performs a more thorough defragmentation than reorganizing the index.

Another factor in determining whether an index needs to be defragmented is how the data is accessed. If your applications are performing primarily single-row lookups, randomly accessing individual rows of data, the internal or external fragmentation is not a factor when it comes to query performance. Accessing one row from a fragmented table is just as easy as from an unfragmented table. However, if your applications are performing ordered range scan operations and reading all or large numbers of the pages in a table, excessive fragmentation can greatly slow down the scan. The more contiguous and full the pages, the better the performance will be of the scanning operations.

TIP

If you have very low levels of fragmentation (less than 5%), it is recommended that you not bother with either a reorganization or a rebuild because the benefit of removing such a small amount of fragmentation is not enough to justify the cost of reorganizing or rebuilding the index.

In SQL Server 2008, the `ALTER INDEX` command provides options for defragmenting an index. Following is the syntax for the `ALTER INDEX` command:

```
ALTER INDEX { index_name | ALL }
    ON  [ database_name. [ schema_name ] . | schema_name. ]
        table_or_view_name
    { REBUILD
        [ [PARTITION = ALL]
                    [ WITH ( <rebuild_index_option> [ ,...n ] ) ]
          | [ PARTITION = partition_number
                [ WITH ( <single_partition_rebuild_index_option>
                        [ ,...n ] )
                ]
            ]
        ]
    | DISABLE
```

```
    | REORGANIZE
        [ PARTITION = partition_number ]
        [ WITH ( LOB_COMPACTION = { ON | OFF } ) ]
  | SET ( <set_index_option> [ ,...n ] )
    }
[ ; ]

<rebuild_index_option > ::=
{
    PAD_INDEX = { ON | OFF }
  | FILLFACTOR = fillfactor
  | SORT_IN_TEMPDB = { ON | OFF }
  | IGNORE_DUP_KEY = { ON | OFF }
  | STATISTICS_NORECOMPUTE = { ON | OFF }
  | ONLINE = { ON | OFF }
  | ALLOW_ROW_LOCKS = { ON | OFF }
  | ALLOW_PAGE_LOCKS = { ON | OFF }
  | MAXDOP = max_degree_of_parallelism
  | DATA_COMPRESSION = { NONE | ROW | PAGE }
      [ ON PARTITIONS ( { <partition_number_expression> | <range> }
      [ , ...n ] ) ]
}
<range> ::=
<partition_number_expression> TO <partition_number_expression>
}

<single_partition_rebuild_index_option> ::=
{
    SORT_IN_TEMPDB = { ON | OFF }
  | MAXDOP = max_degree_of_parallelism
  | DATA_COMPRESSION = { NONE | ROW | PAGE } }
}

<set_index_option>::=
{
    ALLOW_ROW_LOCKS = { ON | OFF }
  | ALLOW_PAGE_LOCKS = { ON | OFF }
  | IGNORE_DUP_KEY = { ON | OFF }
  | STATISTICS_NORECOMPUTE = { ON | OFF }
}
```

The `REORGANIZE` option is always performed online, regardless of which edition of SQL Server 2008 you are running, allowing for other users to continue to update and query the underlying data in the table while the `REORGANIZE` process is running. The `REBUILD` option can be executed online only if you are running SQL Server 2008 Enterprise or Developer Editions. In all other editions of SQL Server 2008, the `REBUILD` option is executed offline. When it is executed offline, SQL Server acquires exclusive locks on the underlying data and associated indexes so any data modifications to the table are blocked until the rebuild completes.

Reorganizing an index uses minimal system resources to defragment only the leaf level of clustered and nonclustered indexes of tables and views. The first phase of the reorganization process compacts the rows on the leaf pages, reapplying the current fill factor value to reduce the internal fragmentation. To view the current fill factor setting, you can run a query such as the following against the sys.indexes system catalog view:

```
select cast(name as varchar(30)) as name, index_id, fill_factor
   from sys.indexes
   where object_id = object_id('sales_big')
go
name                           index_id    fill_factor
------------------------------ ----------- -----------
ci_sales_big                   1           0
idx1                           2           0
```


For more information on fill factor and how to set it, see the "Setting the Fill Factor" section, later in this chapter.

The second phase of the reorganization process involves the rearranging of the leaf-level pages so that the logical and physical order of the pages match, thereby reducing the external fragmentation of the leaf level of the index. SQL Server 2008 runs a REORGANIZATION of an index online because the second phase processes only two pages at a time, in an operation similar to a bubble sort. When defragmenting the index, SQL Server 2008 determines the first physical page belonging to the leaf level and the first logical page in the leaf level, and it swaps the data on those two pages. It then identifies the next logical and physical page and swaps them, and so on, until no more swaps need to be made. At this point, the logical page ordering matches the physical page ordering. While swapping the logical and physical pages, SQL Server uses an additional new page as a temporary storage area. After each page swap, SQL Server releases all locks and latches and saves the key of the last moved page.

The following example uses ALTER TABLE to reorganize the clustered index on the sales_big table:

```
ALTER INDEX ci_sales_big on sales_big REORGANIZE
```

After running this command, you can run a query similar to the query in Listing 34.6 to display the fragmentation of the ci_sales_big index on the sales_big table:

```
select str(s.index_id,3,0) as indid,
       left(i.name, 20) as index_name,
       left(index_type_desc, 20) as index_type_desc,
       index_depth as idx_depth,
       index_level as level,
       str(avg_fragmentation_in_percent, 5,2) as avg_frgmnt_pct,
```

```
       str(page_count, 10,0) as pg_cnt
   FROM sys.dm_db_index_physical_stats
       (db_id('bigpubs2008'), object_id('sales_big'),1, 0, 'DETAILED') s
     join sys.indexes i on s.object_id = i.object_id and s.index_id = i.index_id
go

indid index_name   index_type_desc idx_depth level avg_frgmnt_pct pg_cnt
----- ----------- ------------ --------- ----- ------------- ------
  1   ci_sales_big CLUSTERED INDEX 3          0       0.32           14519
  1   ci_sales_big CLUSTERED INDEX 3          1      92.11              38
  1   ci_sales_big CLUSTERED INDEX 3          2       0.00               1
```

As you can see, the average fragmentation percentage is down to .32% from 63.42%, indicating that the index is now mostly defragmented. However, the average fragmentation percentage of the intermediate level of the index (`level = 1`) is still 92.11%, indicating that it is heavily fragmented. To defragment the nonleaf levels of the index, you need to rebuild the index. The following example shows how to rebuild the index using the `ALTER INDEX` command:

```
ALTER INDEX ci_sales_big on sales_big REBUILD
```

After running this command, you can again run a query similar to the query in Listing 34.6 to display the fragmentation of the `ci_sales_big` index on the `sales_big` table:

```
select str(s.index_id,3,0) as indid,
       left(i.name, 20) as index_name,
       left(index_type_desc, 20) as index_type_desc,
       index_depth as idx_depth,
       index_level as level,
       str(avg_fragmentation_in_percent, 5,2) as avg_frgmnt_pct,
       str(page_count, 10,0) as pg_cnt
   FROM sys.dm_db_index_physical_stats
       (db_id('bigpubs2008'), object_id('sales_big'),1, 0, 'DETAILED') s
     join sys.indexes i on s.object_id = i.object_id and s.index_id = i.index_id
go

indid index_name   index_type_desc idx_depth level avg_frgmnt_pct pg_cnt
----- ----------- ------------ --------- ----- ------------- --------
  1   ci_sales_big CLUSTERED INDEX 3          0       0.01           14520
  1   ci_sales_big CLUSTERED INDEX 3          1       5.26              38
  1   ci_sales_big CLUSTERED INDEX 3          2       0.00               1
```

You can see from these results that the `REBUILD` option performs a more thorough defragmentation of the `ci_sales_big` index than `REORGANIZE`. The average fragmentation percentage of both the leaf and intermediate levels is significantly less.

NOTE

When you rebuild a nonclustered index, the rebuild operation requires enough temporary disk space to store both the old and new indexes. However, if the index is disabled before being rebuilt, the disk space made available by disabling the index can be reused by the subsequent rebuild or any other operation. No additional space is required except for temporary disk space for sorting, which is typically only about 20% of the index size.

Therefore, if disk space is limited, it may be helpful to disable a nonclustered index before rebuilding it. For more information on disabling indexes, see the "Disabling Indexes" section, later in this chapter.

One of the other options to the `CREATE INDEX` and `ALTER INDEX` commands is the `FILLFACTOR` option. The fill factor allows you to specify, as a percentage, the fullness of the pages at the data and leaf index page levels, essentially deciding how much free space to create in the index and data pages to make room for new rows and avoid page splits.

Setting the Fill Factor

Fill factor is a setting you can use when creating an index to specify, as a percentage, how full you want your data pages or leaf-level index pages to be when the index is created. A lower fill factor has the effect of spreading the data and leaf index rows across a greater number of pages by leaving more free space in the pages. This reduces page splitting and dynamic reorganization of index and data pages, which can improve performance in environments where there are a lot of inserts and updates to the data, while at the same time reducing performance for queries because an increased number of pages need to be read to retrieve multiple rows. A higher fill factor has the effect of packing more data and index rows per page by leaving less free space in the pages. Using a higher fill factor is useful in environments where the data is relatively static because it reduces the number of pages required for storing the data and its indexes, and it helps improve performance for queries by reducing the number of pages that need to be accessed.

By default, when you create an index on a table, if you don't specify a value for `FILLFACTOR`, the default value is `0`. With a `FILLFACTOR` setting of `0`, or `100`, the data pages for a clustered index and the leaf pages for a nonclustered index are created completely full. However, space is left within the nonleaf nodes of the index for one or two more rows. The default fill factor to be used when creating indexes is a server-level configuration option. If you want to change the server-wide default for the fill factor, you use the `sp_configure` command:

```
sp_configure 'fill factor',N
```

It is generally recommended that you leave the server-wide default for fill factor as `0` and specify your `FILLFACTOR` settings on an index-by-index basis. You can specify a specific fill factor value for an index by including the FILLFACTOR option for the CREATE INDEX statement:

```
CREATE [UNIQUE] [CLUSTERED | NONCLUSTERED] INDEX index_name
   ON [ [database_name.][schema_name.]] table_or_view_name
    [ WITH ( <relational_index_option> [ ,...n ] ) ]
<relational_index_option> ::=
{ PAD_INDEX  = { ON | OFF }
  | FILLFACTOR = fillfactor
  | SORT_IN_TEMPDB = { ON | OFF }
  | IGNORE_DUP_KEY = { ON | OFF }
  | STATISTICS_NORECOMPUTE = { ON | OFF }
  | DROP_EXISTING = { ON | OFF }
  | ONLINE = { ON | OFF }
  | ALLOW_ROW_LOCKS = { ON | OFF }
  | ALLOW_PAGE_LOCKS = { ON | OFF }
  | MAXDOP = max_degree_of_parallelism }
```

The FILLFACTOR option for the CREATE INDEX command allows you to specify, as a percentage, how full the data or leaf-level index pages should be when you create an index on a table. The specified percentage can be from 1 to 100. Specifying a value of 80 would mean that each data or leaf page would be filled approximately 80% full at the time you create the index. It is important to note that as more data gets modified or added to a table, the fill factor is not maintained at the level specified during the CREATE INDEX command. Over a period of time, you will find that each page has a different percentage of fullness as rows are added and deleted.

TIP

A fill factor setting specified when creating a nonclustered index affects only the nonclustered index pages and doesn't affect the data pages. To apply a fill factor to the data pages in a table, you must provide a fill factor setting when creating a clustered index on the table. Also, it is important to remember that the fill factor is applied only at index creation time and is *not* maintained by SQL Server. When you begin updating and inserting data, the fill factor is eventually lost. Therefore, specifying a fill factor when creating your indexes is useful only if the table already contains data or if you simply want to set a default fill factor for the index other than 0 that will be used when indexes are rebuilt or reorganized by ALTER INDEX.

If you specify only the FILLFACTOR option, only the data or leaf-level index pages are affected by the fill factor. To specify the level of fullness for nonleaf pages, use the PAD_INDEX option together with FILLFACTOR. This option allows you to specify how much space to leave open on each node of the index, which can help to reduce page splits within the nonleaf levels of the index. You don't specify a value for PAD_INDEX; it uses the same percentage value specified with the FILLFACTOR option. For example, to apply a 50% fill factor to the leaf and nonleaf pages in a nonclustered index on title_id in the titles table, you would execute the following:

```
CREATE INDEX title_id_index on titles (title_id)
        with (FILLFACTOR = 50, PAD_INDEX = ON)
```

TIP

When you use PAD_INDEX, the value specified by FILLFACTOR cannot be such that the number of rows on each index node falls below two. If you do specify such a value, SQL Server internally overrides it so that the number of rows on an intermediate index page is never less than two.

Reapplying the Fill Factor

When might you need to reestablish the fill factor for your indexes or data? As data gets modified in a table, the value of FILLFACTOR is not maintained at the level specified in the CREATE INDEX statement. As a result, each page can reach a different level of fullness. Over a period of time, this can lead to heavy fragmentation in the database if insert/delete activity is not evenly spread throughout the table, and it could affect performance. In addition, if a table becomes very large and then very small, rows could become isolated within data pages. This space will likely not be recovered until the last row on the page is deleted and the page is marked as unused. To either spread out rows or to reclaim space by repacking more rows per page, you need to reapply the fill factor to your clustered and nonclustered indexes.

In environments where insert activity is heavy, reapplying a low fill factor might help performance by spreading out the data and leaving free space on the pages, which helps to minimize page splits and possible page-locking contention during heavy OLTP activity. You can use Performance Monitor to monitor your system and determine whether excessive page splits are occurring. (See Chapter 39, "Monitoring SQL Server Performance" for more information on using Performance Monitor.)

A DBA must manually reapply the fill factor to improve the performance of the system. This can be done by using the ALTER INDEX command discussed earlier or by dropping and re-creating the index. ALTER INDEX is preferred because, by default, it applies the original fill factor specified when the index was created, or you can provide a new fill factor to override the default. The original fill factor for an index is stored in sys.indexes in the fill_factor column. In addition, if you use the ALTER INDEX command to reorganize or rebuild your table or index, it attempts to reapply the index's original fill factor when it reorganizes the pages.

Disabling Indexes

Another feature available in SQL Server 2008 is the capability to set an index as disabled. When an index is disabled, the definition of the index is maintained in the system catalogs, but the index itself contains no index key rows. Disabling an index prevents user access to the index. Disabling a clustered index also prevents access to the underlying table data.

You can manually disable an index at any time by using the `ALTER INDEX DISABLE` statement:

```
ALTER INDEX titleidind ON sales DISABLE
```

The reasons you might want to disable an index include the following:

- Correcting a disk I/O or allocation error on an index page and then rebuilding the index later
- Temporarily removing the index for troubleshooting purposes
- Saving temporary disk space while rebuilding nonclustered indexes

When you disable an index, the index is not maintained while it is disabled, and the Query Optimizer does not consider the index when creating query execution plans. However, statistics on a disabled nonclustered index remain in place and are updated automatically if the AutoStats option is in effect.

If you disable a clustered index, all nonclustered indexes on the table are automatically disabled as well. The nonclustered index cannot be re-enabled until the clustered index is either enabled or dropped. After you enable the clustered index, the nonclustered indexes must be explicitly enabled unless the clustered index was enabled by using the `ALTER INDEX ALL REBUILD` statement. Because the data rows of the table cannot be accessed while the clustered index is disabled, the following operations cannot be performed on the table:

- `SELECT`, `UPDATE`, `DELETE`, and `INSERT`
- `CREATE INDEX`
- `CREATE STATISTICS`
- `UPDATE STATISTICS`
- `ALTER TABLE` statements that modify table columns or constraints

After an index is disabled, it remains in a disabled state until it is rebuilt or dropped. You can enable a disabled index by rebuilding it by using one of the following methods:

- `ALTER INDEX` statement with the `REBUILD` clause
- `CREATE INDEX` with the `DROP_EXISTING` clause
- `DBCC DBREINDEX`

To determine whether an index is currently disabled, you can use the `INDEXPROPERTY` function (a value of 1 indicates the index is disabled):

```
select indexproperty(object_id('sales'), 'titleidind', 'IsDisabled')

-----------
1
```

Managing Indexes with SSMS

So far, you've seen the commands necessary for index management. In addition to these commands, SSMS provides tools for managing indexes.

To reorganize or rebuild an index using SSMS, in the Object Explorer, connect to an instance of the SQL Server 2008 Database Engine and then expand that instance. Then expand Databases, expand the database that contains the table with the specified index, and expand Tables. Next, expand the table in which the index belongs and then expand Indexes. Finally, right-click the index to rebuild and then click Rebuild or Reorganize. To rebuild or reorganize all indexes on a table, right-click Indexes and select Rebuild All or Reorganize All.

You can also disable indexes in SSMS. In the Object Explorer, right-click the index you want to disable and then select the Disable option. To disable all indexes on a table, right-click on Indexes and select Disable All.

You can also use SSMS to modify indexes. In the Object Explorer, right-click the index you want to modify and then click Properties. In the Properties dialog that appears (see Figure 34.27), you can add or remove columns from the index, change the uniqueness setting, set the index option, set the fill factor, rebuild the index, view the index fragmentation, reorganize the index, and so on.

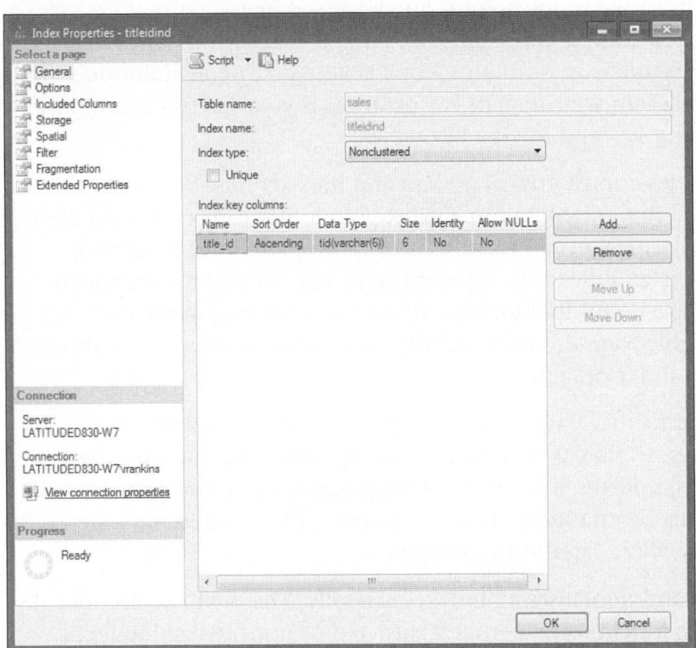

FIGURE 34.27 Setting and viewing index properties in SSMS.

Index Design Guidelines

SQL Server indexes are mostly transparent to end users and T-SQL developers. Indexes are typically not specified in queries unless you use table hints to force the Query Optimizer to use a particular index. (Although forcing indexes is generally not advised, using Query Optimizer table hints is covered in more detail in Chapter 35.) Normally, based on the index key histogram or density values, the SQL Server cost-based Query Optimizer automatically chooses the index that is least expensive from an I/O standpoint.

Chapter 35 goes into greater detail on how the Query Optimizer estimates I/O and determines the most efficient query plan. In the meantime, the following are some of the main guidelines to follow in creating useful indexes that the Query Optimizer can use effectively:

- For composite indexes, try to keep the more selective columns leftmost in the index. The first element in the index should be the most unique (if possible), and index column order in general should be from most to least unique. However, remember that selectivity doesn't help if the first ordered index column is not specified in your SARGs or join clauses. To ensure that the index is used for the largest number of queries, be sure the first ordered column is the column used most often in your queries.

- Be sure to index columns used in joins. Joins are processed inefficiently if no index on the column(s) is specified in a join. Remember that a `PRIMARY KEY` constraint automatically creates an index on a column, but a `FOREIGN KEY` constraint does not. You should create indexes on your foreign key columns if your queries commonly join between the primary key and foreign key tables.

- Tailor your indexes for your most critical queries and transactions. You cannot index for every possible query that might be run against your tables. However, your applications will perform better if you can identify your critical and most frequently executed queries and design indexes to support them. SQL Server Profiler, which is covered in Chapter 6, is a useful tool for identifying the most frequently executed queries. SQL Server Profiler can also help identify slow-running queries that might benefit from improved index design.

- Avoid indexes on columns that have poor selectivity. The Query Optimizer is not likely to use the indexes, so they would simply take up space and add unnecessary overhead during inserts, updates, and deletes. One possible exception occurs when the index can be used to cover a query. Index covering is discussed in more detail in the "Index Covering" section, later in this chapter.

- Choose your clustered and nonclustered indexes carefully. The next two sections discuss tips and guidelines for choosing between clustered or nonclustered indexes, based on the data contained in the columns and the types of queries executed against the columns.

Clustered Index Indications

Searching for rows via a clustered index is almost always faster than searching for rows via a nonclustered index—for two reasons. One reason is that a clustered index contains only pointers to pages rather than pointers to individual data rows; therefore, a clustered index is more compact than a nonclustered index. Because a clustered index is smaller and doesn't require an additional lookup via the row locator to find the matching rows, the rows can be found with fewer page reads than with a similarly defined nonclustered index. The second reason is that because the data in a table with a clustered index is physically sorted on the clustered key, searching for duplicate values or for a range of clustered key values is faster; the rows are adjacent to each other, and SQL Server can simply locate the first qualifying row and then search the rows in sequence until the last qualifying row is found. However, because you are allowed to create only one clustered index per table, you must judiciously choose the column or columns on which to define the clustered index.

If you require only a single index on a table, it's typically advantageous to make it a clustered index; the resulting overhead of maintaining clustered indexes during updates, inserts, and deletes can be considerably less than the overhead incurred by nonclustered indexes.

By default, the primary key on a table is defined as a clustered unique index. In most applications, the primary key column on a table is almost always retrieved in single-row lookups. For single-row lookups, a nonclustered index usually costs you only a few more I/Os than a similar clustered index. Are you or the users really going to notice a difference between three page reads to retrieve a single data row versus four- to six-page reads to retrieve a single data row? Not at all. However, if you have to perform a range retrieval, such as a lookup on last name, will you notice a difference between scanning 10% of the table versus having to find the rows using a full table scan? Most definitely. With this in mind, you might want to consider creating your primary key as a unique nonclustered index and choosing another candidate for your clustered index.

Following are guidelines to consider for other potential candidates for clustered indexes:

- **Columns with a number of duplicate values searched frequently (for example, `WHERE last_name = 'Smith'`)**—Because the data is physically sorted, all the duplicate values are kept together. Any query that tries to fetch records against such keys finds all the values, using a minimum of I/O. SQL Server locates the first row that matches the SARG and then scans the data rows in order until it finds the last row matching the SARG.

- **Columns often specified in the `ORDER BY`** clause—Because the data is already sorted, SQL Server can avoid having to re-sort the data if the `ORDER BY` is on the clustered index key and the data is retrieved in clustered key order. Remember that even for a table scan, the data is retrieved in clustered key order because the data in the table is in clustered key order. The only exception is if a parallel query operation is used to retrieve the data rows; in that case, the results needs to be re-sorted when the result sets from each parallel thread are merged. (For more information on parallel query strategies, see Chapter 35.)

- **Columns often searched for within a range of values (for example, `WHERE price between $10 and $20`)**—A clustered index can be used to locate the first qualifying row in the range of values. Because the rows in the table are in sorted order, SQL Server can simply scan the data pages in order until it finds the last qualifying row within the range. When the result set within the range of values is large, a clustered index scan is significantly more efficient in terms of total logical I/O performed than repeated row locator lookups via a nonclustered index.
- **Columns, other than the primary key, frequently used in join clauses**—Clustered indexes tend to be smaller than nonclustered indexes; the amount of page I/O required per lookup is generally less for a clustered index than for a nonclustered index. It can be a significant difference when joining many records. An extra page read or two might not seem like much for a single-row retrieval, but add those additional page reads to 100,000 join iterations, and you're looking at a total of 100,000 to 200,000 additional page reads.

When you consider columns for a clustered index, you might want to try to keep your clustered indexes on relatively static columns to minimize the re-sorting of data rows when an indexed column is updated. Any time a clustered index key value changes, the entire data row has to be moved to keep the clustered data values in physical sort order. In addition, all nonclustered indexes using the clustered key as the row locator to that row also need to be updated.

You should also avoid creating clustered indexes on wide keys that are made up of several columns, especially several large-size columns. The reason is that the clustered key values are incorporated in all nonclustered indexes as the row locater. Because the nonclustered index entries contain the clustering key in addition to the key columns defined for that nonclustered index, the nonclustered indexes end up being significantly larger and less efficient in terms of I/O.

Because you can physically sort the data in a table in only one way, you can have only one clustered index per table. Any other columns you want to index have to be defined with nonclustered indexes.

Nonclustered Index Indications

SQL Server allows you to create a maximum of 999 nonclustered indexes on a table. Until tables become extremely large, the actual space taken by a nonclustered index is a minor expense compared to the increased access performance. You need to keep in mind, however, that as you add more indexes to the system, database modification statements get slower due to the index maintenance overhead.

Also, when defining nonclustered indexes, you typically want to define indexes on columns that are more selective (that is, columns with low density values) so that they can be used effectively by the Query Optimizer. A high number of duplicate values in a nonclustered index can often make it more expensive (in terms of I/O) to process the query using the nonclustered index than a table scan. Let's look at a hypothetical example:

```
select title from titles
   where price between $5. and $10.
```

Assume that you have 1 million rows within the range; those 1 million rows could be randomly scattered throughout the table. Although the index leaf level has all the index rows in sorted order, reading all data rows one at a time would require a separate lookup via the row locator for each row in the worst-case scenario.

Thus, the worst-case I/O estimate for range retrievals using a nonclustered index is as follows:

Number of levels in the nonclustered index

+ Number of index pages scanned to find all matching rows

+ (Number of matching rows × Number of pages per lookup via the row locator)

If you have no clustered index on the table, the row locator is simply a page and row pointer and requires one data page read to find the matching data row. If 1 million rows are in the range, the worst-case cost estimate to search via the nonclustered index with no clustered index on the table would be as follows:

Number of index page reads to find all the row locators

+ (1 million matching rows × 1 data page read)

= 1 million + I/O

If you have a clustered index on the table, the row locator is a clustered index key for the data row. Using the row locator to find the matching row requires searching the clustered index tree to locate the data row. Assuming that the clustered index has two nonleaf levels, it would cost three pages to find each qualifying row on a data page. If the range has 1 million rows, the worst-case cost estimate to search via the nonclustered index with a clustered index on the table would be as follows:

Number of index page reads to find all the row locators

+ (1 million matching rows × 3 pages per lookup via the row locator)

= 3 million + I/O

Contrast each of these scenarios with the cost of a table scan. If the entire table takes up 50,000 pages, a full table scan would cost only 50,000 in terms of I/O. Therefore, in this example, doing a table scan would actually be more efficient than using the nonclustered index.

The following guidelines help you identify potential candidates for nonclustered indexes for your environment:

- Columns referenced in SARGs or join clauses that have a relatively high selectivity (the density value is low).

- Columns referenced in both the WHERE clause and the ORDER BY clause. When the data rows are retrieved using a nonclustered index, they are retrieved in nonclustered index key order. If the result set is to be ordered by the nonclustered index key(s) as well, SQL Server can avoid having to re-sort the result set, resulting in a more efficient query. In the following sample query, SQL Server can avoid the extra step of sorting the result set if a nonclustered index is on state and the index is used to retrieve the matching rows:

  ```
  select * from authors
     where state like 'C%'
     order by state
  ```

In general, nonclustered indexes are useful for single-row lookups, joins, queries on columns that are highly selective, or queries with small range retrievals. Also, when considering your nonclustered index design, you should not overlook the benefits of index covering, as described in the following section.

Index Covering

Index covering is a situation in which all the information required by the query in the SELECT and WHERE clauses can be found entirely within the nonclustered index itself. Because the nonclustered index contains a leaf row corresponding to every data row in the table, SQL Server can satisfy the query from the leaf rows of the nonclustered index. This results in faster retrieval of data because all the information can come directly from the index page, and SQL Server avoids lookups of the data pages.

Because the leaf pages in a nonclustered index are linked together, the leaf level of the index can be scanned just like the data pages in a table. Because the leaf index rows are typically much smaller than the data rows, a nonclustered index that covers a query will be faster than a clustered index on the same columns because fewer pages would need to be read.

In the following example, a nonclustered index on the au_lname and au_fname columns of the authors table would cover the query because the result columns and the SARGs can all be derived from the index itself:

```
Select au_lname, au_fname
   From authors
   Where au_lname like 'M%'
Go
```

Many other queries that use an aggregate function (such as MIN, MAX, AVG, SUM, and COUNT) or simply check for existence of criteria also benefit from index covering. The following aggregate query samples can take advantage of index covering:

```
select count(au_lname) from authors where au_lname like 'M%'


select count(*) from authors where au_lname like 'M%'


select count(*) from authors
```

You might wonder how the last query, which doesn't even specify a SARG, can use an index. SQL Server knows that by its nature, a nonclustered index contains a row for every data row in the table; it can simply count all the rows in any of the nonclustered indexes instead of scanning the whole table. For the last query, SQL Server chooses the smallest nonclustered index—that is, the one with the smallest number of leaf pages.

Index covering can sometimes occur when you are not expecting it. As discussed previously in this chapter, when you have a clustered index defined on a table, the clustered key is carried into all the nonclustered indexes to be used as the row locator to locate the actual data row. Having the additional clustered key column values in the nonclustered index provides more data values that can be used in index covering.

For example, assume that the `authors` table has a clustered index on `au_lname` and `au_fname` and a nonclustered primary key defined on `au_id`. Each row in the nonclustered index on `au_id` would contain the clustered key values for `au_lname` and `au_fname` for its corresponding data row. Because of this, the following query would actually be covered by the nonclustered index on `au_id`:


```
select au_lname, au_fname
   from authors
   where au_id like '123%'
```

Explicitly adding additional columns to nonclustered indexes to promote the occurrence of index covering has historically been a common method of improving query response time. Consider the following query:

```
select royalty from titles
   where price between $10 and $20
```

If you create an index on only the `price` column, SQL Server can find the rows in the index where `price` is between $10 and $20, but it has to access the data rows to retrieve `royalty`. With 100 rows in the range, the worst-case I/O cost to retrieve the data rows would be as follows:

Number of index levels

+ Number of index pages to find the 100 matching rows

+ (100 × Number of pages per lookup via the row locator)

If the `royalty` column were added to the index on the `price` column, SQL Server could scan the index to retrieve the results instead of having to perform the lookups via the row locator against the table, resulting in faster query response. The I/O cost using index covering would be lower, as follows:

Number of index levels

+ Number of index pages to scan to find the 100 matching rows

If you are considering padding your indexes to take advantage of index covering, beware of making an index too wide. As index row width approaches data row width, the benefits of covering are lost as the number of pages in the leaf level increases. As the number of leaf-level index pages approaches the number of pages in the table, the number of index levels also increases, increasing the I/O cost of using the index to locate data.

You should also avoid adding to the index columns that are frequently updated. Remember that any changes to the columns in the data rows cascade into the indexes as well. This increases the index maintenance overhead, which can adversely affect update performance.

As an alternative to adding columns to the nonclustered index key to encourage index covering, you might want to consider taking advantage of the included columns feature in SQL Server 2008.

Included Columns

A feature available for nonclustered indexes in SQL Server 2008 is included columns. Included columns allow you to add nonkey columns to the leaf level of a nonclustered index for the purpose of index covering.

One advantage of included columns is that because the nonkey columns are stored only in the leaf level of the index, the nonleaf rows of the index are smaller, which helps reduce the overall size of the index, thereby helping reduce the I/O cost of using the index. Another advantage is that this feature allows you to exceed the SQL Server maximum limits of 16 index key columns and 900-byte index key size. The included nonkey columns are not factored in when calculating the number of index key columns or index key size. All data types are allowed as included columns except for the `text`, `ntext`, and `image` data types. To add included columns to an index, specify the `INCLUDE` clause to the `CREATE INDEX` statement:

```
CREATE INDEX NC_titles_price on titles (price) INCLUDE (royalty)
```

An additional advantage of included columns is that you can add columns to a unique index for index covering purposes without affecting the uniqueness of the actual index key(s) and without having to create a second index on the unique key column(s) and the additional covering columns. For example, consider that you have a large number of queries that search titles by `title_id` to retrieve the price value. Creating a covering index on `title_id` and `price` could improve performance of these queries. However, creating a unique index on `title_id` and `price` would not enforce uniqueness on `title_id` alone (it would allow the insertion of multiple rows with the same `title_id` as long as they had different prices). Without using included columns, you would have to create a unique index on `title_id` and an additional nonunique index on `title_id` and `price` to enforce uniqueness on `title_id` and also have a covering index on `title_id` and `price`. However, with the included column feature, you can create just a single unique index on `title_id` with `price` as an included column:

```
CREATE INDEX UQ_titleid_price on titles (title_id) INCLUDE (price)
```

TIP

If you have existing nonclustered indexes with a large index key size, you might want to consider redesigning them so that only columns used for searching and lookups are key columns. You should make all other columns that were added for index covering into included columns. This way, you still have all columns needed to cover your queries, but the index key itself is smaller and more efficient.

You still should be careful to avoid adding unnecessary columns as included columns of an index. Adding too many index columns, key or nonkey, can adversely affect performance for the following reasons:

- Fewer index leaf rows fit on a page, which can increase I/O costs to search the leaf level of the index and also reduce data cache efficiency.
- Because of the increased leaf row size, more disk space is required to store the index, especially if you are adding `varchar(max)`, `nvarchar(max)`, `varbinary(max)`, or `xml` data types as nonkey index columns. Because the column values are also copied into the index leaf level, you are essentially storing the data values twice.
- Changes to the included columns in the data rows cascade into the leaf rows of the index as well. This increases the index maintenance overhead, which can adversely affect performance of data modifications.

Wide Indexes Versus Multiple Indexes

As an index key gets wider, the selectivity of the key generally becomes higher as well. It might seem that creating wide indexes would result in better performance. This is not necessarily true. The reason is that the wider the key, the fewer rows SQL Server stores on the index pages, requiring more pages at each level; this results in a higher number of levels in the index B-tree. To get to specific rows, SQL Server must perform more I/O.

To get better performance from queries, instead of creating a few wide indexes, you should consider creating multiple narrower indexes. The advantage here is that with smaller keys, the Query Optimizer can quickly scan through multiple indexes to determine the most efficient access plan. SQL Server has the option of performing multiple index lookups within a single query and merging the result sets together to generate an intersection of the indexes. Also, with more indexes, the Query Optimizer can choose from a wider variety of query plan alternatives.

If you are considering creating a wide key, you should individually check the distribution of values for each member of the composite key. If the selectivity on the individual columns is high, you might want to break up the index into multiple indexes. If the selectivity of individual columns is low but is high for combined columns, it makes sense to have wider keys on the table. To get to the right combination, you can populate your table with real-world data, experiment with creating multiple indexes, and check the distribution of values for each column. Based on the histogram steps and index density, you can make the decisions for an index design that works best for your environment.

Indexed Views

As discussed in Chapter 27, "Creating and Managing Views," SQL Server 2008 allows you to create indexed views. An *indexed view* is any view that has a clustered index defined on it. When a `CREATE INDEX` statement is executed on a view, the result set for the view is materialized and stored in the database with the same structure as a table with a clustered index. Changes made to the data in the underlying tables of the view are automatically reflected in the view the same way any changes to a table are reflected in its indexes. In addition to a clustered index, you can create additional nonclustered indexes on indexed views to provide additional query performance. Additional indexes on views might provide more options for the Query Optimizer to choose from during the optimization process.

In the Developer and Enterprise Editions of SQL Server 2008, when an indexed view exists on a table and you access the view directly within a query, the Query Optimizer automatically considers using the index on the view to improve query performance, just as an index on a table is used to improve performance. The Query Optimizer also considers using the indexed view, even for queries that do not directly name the view in the `FROM` clause. In other words, when a query might benefit from using the indexed view, the Query Optimizer can use the indexed view to satisfy the query in place of an existing index on the table itself. (For more information on how indexed views are used in query plans, see Chapter 35.)

It is important to note that although indexed views can be created in all editions of SQL Server 2008, only the Developer and Enterprise Editions automatically use indexed views to optimize queries. In the other editions, indexed views are not used to improve query performance unless the view is explicitly specified in the query and the `NOEXPAND` hint is specified as well. Without the `NOEXPAND` hint, SQL Server expands the view to its underlying base tables and optimizes based on the table indexes. The following example shows the use of the `NOEXPAND` option to force SQL Server to use the indexed view specified in the query:

```
select * from sales_Qty_Rollup WITH (NOEXPAND)
   where stor_id between 'B914' and 'B999'SET ARITHABORT ON
```

Indexed views add overhead and can be more complex for SQL Server to maintain over time than normal indexes. Each time an underlying table of a view is modified, SQL Server has to update the view result set and potentially the index on that view. The scope of a view's index can be larger than that of any single table's index, especially if the view is defined on several large tables. The overhead associated with maintaining a view and its index during updates can negate any benefit that queries gain from the indexed view. Because of this additional maintenance overhead, you should create indexes only on views where the advantage provided by the improved speed in retrieving the results outweighs the increased maintenance overhead.

Following are some guidelines to consider when you design indexed views:

- Create indexes on views where the underlying table data is relatively static.
- Create indexed views that will be used by several queries.
- Keep the indexes small. As with table indexes, a smaller index allows SQL Server to access the data more efficiently.
- Create indexed views that will be significantly smaller than the underlying table(s). An indexed view might not provide significant performance gains if its size is similar to the size of the original table.
- You need to specify the `NOEXPAND` hint in editions of SQL Server other than the Developer and Enterprise Editions of SQL Server; otherwise, the indexed view is not used to optimize the query.

Indexes on Computed Columns

SQL Server 2008 allows you to build indexes on computed columns in your tables. Computed columns can participate at any position of an index, along with your other table columns, including in a `PRIMARY KEY` or `UNIQUE` constraint. To create an index on computed columns, you must set the following `session options` as shown:

- `SET CONCAT_NULL_YIELDS_NULL ON`
- `SET QUOTED_IDENTIFIER ON`
- `SET ANSI_NULLS ON`
- `SET ANSI_PADDING ON`
- `SET ANSI_WARNINGS ON`
- `SET NUMERIC_ROUNDABORT OFF`

If any of these six `SET` options were not in effect when you created the table, you get the following message when you try to create an index on the computed column:

```
Server: Msg 1934, Level 16, State 1, Line 2
CREATE INDEX failed because the following SET options
 have incorrect settings: '<OPTION NAME>'.
```

In addition, the functions in the computed column must be deterministic. A *deterministic* function is one that returns the same result every time it is called with the same set of input parameters.

When you create a clustered index on a computed column, it is no longer a virtual column in the table. The computed value for the column is stored in the data rows of the table. If you create a nonclustered index on a computed column, the computed value is stored in the nonclustered index rows but not in the data rows, unless you also have a clustered index on the computed column.

Be aware of the overhead involved with indexes on computed columns. Updates to the columns that the computed columns are based on result in updates to the index on the computed column as well.

Indexes on computed columns can be useful when you need an index on large character fields. As discussed earlier, the smaller an index, the more efficient it is. You could create a computed column on the large character field by using the `CHECKSUM()` function. `CHECKSUM()` generates a 4-byte integer that is relatively unique for character strings but not absolutely unique. (Different character strings can generate the same checksum, so when searching against the checksum, you need to include the character string as an additional search argument to ensure that you are matching the right row.) The benefit is that you can create an index on the 4-byte integer generated by the `CHECKSUM()` that can be used to search against the character string instead of having to create an index on the large character column itself. Listing 34.7 shows an example of applying this solution.

LISTING 34.7 Using an Index on a Computed Checksum Column

```
--The first statement is used to disable any previously created
--DDL triggers in the database which would prevent creating a new constraint.
DISABLE TRIGGER ALL ON DATABASE
go
-- First add the computed column to the table
alter table titles add title_checksum as CHECKSUM(title)
go

-- Next, create an index on the computed column
create index NC_titles_titlechecksum on titles(title_checksum)
go

-- In your queries, include both the checksum column and the title column in
--   your search argument
select title_id, ytd_sales
   from titles
   where title_checksum = checksum('Fifty Years in Buckingham Palace Kitchens')
     and title = 'Fifty Years in Buckingham Palace Kitchens'
```

SQL Server 2008 also supports persisted computed columns. With persisted computed columns, SQL Server stores the computed values in the table without requiring an index on the computed column. Like indexed computed columns, persisted computed columns are updated when any other columns on which the computed column depends are updated.

Persisted computed columns allow you to create an index on a computed column that is defined with a deterministic, but imprecise, expression. This option enables you to create an index on a computed column when SQL Server cannot determine with certainty whether a function that returns a computed column expression—for example, a CLR function that is created in the Microsoft .NET Framework—is both deterministic and precise.

Filtered Indexes and Statistics

As discussed earlier in this chapter, a nonclustered index contains a row for every row in the table, even rows with a large number of duplicate key values where the nonclustered index will not be an effective method for finding those rows. For these situations, SQL Server 2008 introduces filtered indexes. Filtered indexes are an optimized form of nonclustered indexes, created by specifying a search predicate when defining the index. This search predicate acts as a filter to create the index on only the data rows that match the search predicate. This reduces the size of the index and essentially creates an index that covers your queries, which return only a small percentage of rows from a well-defined subset of data within your table.

Filtered indexes can provide the following advantages over full-table indexes:

- **Improved query performance and plan quality**—A well-designed filtered index improves query performance and execution plan quality because it is smaller than a full-table nonclustered index and has filtered statistics. Filtered statistics are more accurate than full-table statistics because they cover only the rows contained in the filtered index.
- **Reduced index maintenance costs**—Filtered indexes are maintained only when data modifications affect the data values contained in the index. Also, because a filtered index contains only the frequently accessed data, the smaller size of the index reduces the cost of updating the statistics.
- **Reduced index storage costs**—Filtered indexes can reduce disk storage for nonclustered indexes when a full-table index is not necessary. You can replace a full-table nonclustered index with multiple filtered indexes without significantly increasing the storage requirements.

Following are some of the situations in which filtered indexes can be useful:

- When a column contains mostly `NULL` values, but your queries search only for rows where data values are `NOT NULL`.
- When a column contains a large number of duplicate values, but your queries typically ignore those values and search only for the more unique values.

- When you want to enforce uniqueness on a subset of values—for example, a column on which you want to allow NULL values. A unique constraint allows only one NULL value; however, a filtered index can be defined as unique over only the rows that are NOT NULL.
- When queries retrieve only a particular range of data values and you want to index these values but not the entire table. For example, you have a table that contains a large number of historical values, but you want to search only values for the current year or quarter. You can create a filtered index on the desired range of values and possibly even use the INCLUDE option to add columns so your index fully covers your queries.

Now, you may be asking, "Can't some of the preceding solutions be accomplished using indexed views?" Yes, they can, but filtered indexes provided a better alternative. The most significant advantage is that filtered indexes can be used in any edition of SQL Server 2008, whereas indexed views are chosen by the optimizer only in the Developer, Enterprise, and Datacenter Editions unless you use the NOEXPAND hint in other editions. In addition, filtered indexes have reduced index maintenance costs (the query processor uses fewer CPU resources to update a filtered index than an indexed view); the Query Optimizer considers using a filtered index in more situations than the equivalent indexed view; you can perform online rebuilds of filtered indexes (online index rebuilds are not supported for indexed views); and filtered indexes can be nonunique, whereas indexed views must be unique.

Based on these advantages, it is recommended that you use filtered indexes instead of indexed views when possible. Consider replacing indexed views with filtered indexes when the view references only one table, the view query doesn't return computed columns, and the view predicate uses simple comparison logic and doesn't contain a view.

Creating and Using Filtered Indexes

To define filtered indexes, you use the normal CREATE INDEX command but include a WHERE condition as a search predicate to specify which data rows the filtered index should include. In the current implementation, you can specify only simple search predicates such as IN; the comparison operators IS NULL, IS NOT NULL, =, <>, !=, >, >=, !>, <, <=, !<; and the logical operator AND. In addition, filtered indexes cannot be created on computed columns, user-defined data types, Hierarchyid, or spatial types.

For example, assume you need to search only the sales table in the bigpubs2008 database for sales since 9/1/2008. The majority of the rows in the sales table have order dates prior to 9/1/2008. To create a filtered index on the ord_date column, you would execute a command like the following:

```
create index ord_date_filt on sales (ord_date)
    WHERE ord_date >= '2008-09-01 00:00:00.000'
```

Now, let's look at a couple queries that may or may not use the new filtered index. First, let's consider the following query looking for any sales for 9/15/2008:

```
select * from sales
where ord_date = '9/15/2008'
```

If you look at the execution plan in Figure 34.28, you can see that the filtered index, `ord_date_filt`, is used to locate the qualifying row values. The clustered index, `UPKCL_sales`, is used as the row locator to retrieve the data rows (as described earlier in the "Nonclustered Indexes" section).

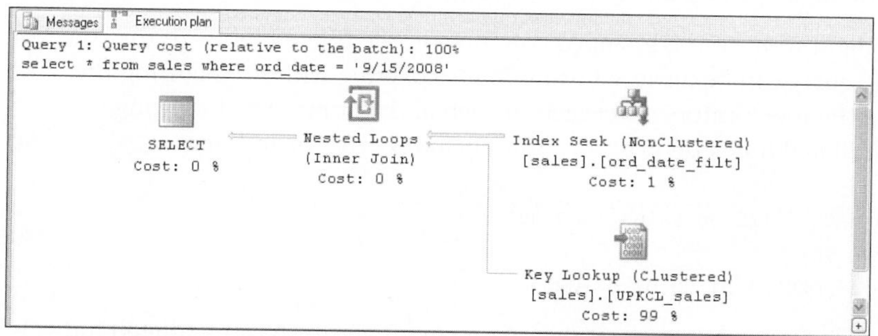

FIGURE 34.28 Query plan for a query that uses a filtered index.

NOTE

For more information on understanding and analyzing query plans, see Chapter 36.

If you run the following query using a data values that's outside the range of values stored in the filtered index, you see that the filtered index is not used (see Figure 34.29):

```
select * from sales
where ord_date = '9/15/2008'
```

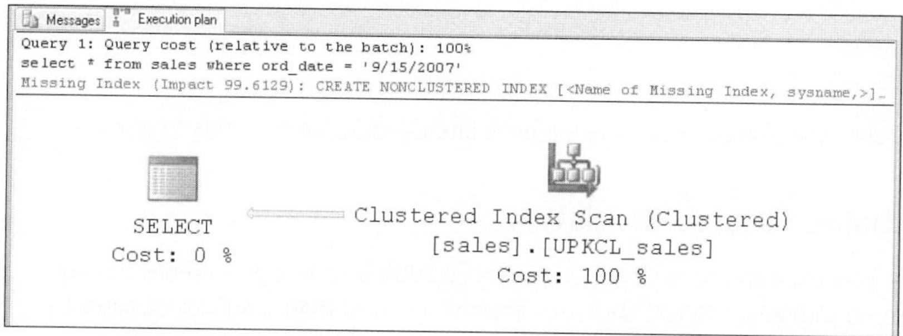

FIGURE 34.29 Query plan for a query using a value not in the filtered index.

Now let's consider a query that you might expect would use the filtered index but does not:

```
select stor_id, qty from sales
where ord_date > '9/15/2008'
```

Now, you might expect that this query would use the filtered index because the data values are within the range of values for the filtered index, but due to the number of rows that match, SQL Server determines that the I/O cost of using the filtered nonclustered index to locate the matching rows and then retrieve the data rows using the clustered index row locators requires more I/Os than simply performing a clustered index scan of the entire table (the same query plan as shown in Figure 34.29).

In this case, you might want to use included columns on the filtered index so that the data values for the query can be retrieved using index covering without incurring the extra cost of using the row locators to retrieve the actual data rows. The following example creates a filtered index on `ord_date` that includes `stor_id` and `qty`:

```
create index ord_date_filt2 on sales (ord_date)
INCLUDE (qty, stor_id)
WHERE ord_date >= '2008-09-01 00:00:00.000'
```

If you rerun the same query and examine the query plan, you see that the filtered index is used this time, and SQL Server uses index covering (see Figure 34.30). You can tell that it's using index covering with the `ord_dat_filt2` index because there is no use of the clustered index to retrieve the data rows. Using the row locators is unnecessary because all the information requested by the query can be retrieved from the index leaf rows that contain the values of the included columns as well.

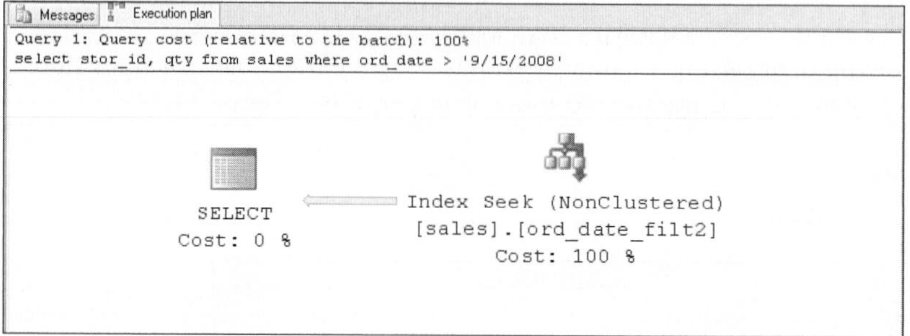

FIGURE 34.30 Query plan using index covering on a filtered index with included columns.

Creating and Using Filtered Statistics

Similar to the way you use filtered indexes, SQL Server 2008 also lets you create filtered statistics. Like filtered indexes, filtered statistics are also created over a subset of rows in the table based on a specified filter predicate. Creating a filtered index on a column autocreates the corresponding filtered statistics. In addition, filtered statistics can be created explicitly by including the `WHERE` clause with the `CREATE STATISTICS` statement.

Filtered statistics can be used to avoid a common issue with statistics where the cardinality estimation is skewed due to a large number of NULL or duplicate values, or due to a data correlation between columns. For example, let's consider the titles table in the bigpubs2008 database. All the cooking books (type = 'trad_cook' or 'mod_cook') are published by a single publisher (pub_id = '0877'). However, SQL Server stores column-level statistics on each of these columns independent of each other. Based on the statistics, SQL Server estimates there are six rows in the titles table where pub_id = '0877', and five rows where the type is either 'trad_cook' or 'mod_cook'.

However, let's assume you were to execute the following query:

```
select * from titles where pub_id = '0877'
and type in ('trad_cook', 'mod_cook')
```

When the Query Optimizer estimates the selectivity of this query where each search predicate is part of an AND condition, it assumes the conditions are independent of one another and estimates the number of matching rows by taking the intersection of the two conditions. Essentially, it multiplies the selectivity of each of the two conditions together to determine the total selectivity. The selectivity of each is 0.011 (6/537) and 0.009 (5/537), which, when multiplied together, comes out to approximately 0.0001, so the optimizer estimates at most only a single row will match. However, because all five cooking books are published by pub_id '0877', in actuality a total of five rows match.

Now, in this example, the difference between one row and five rows is likely not significant enough to make a big difference in query performance, but a similar estimation error could be quite large with other data sets, leading the optimizer to possibly choose an inappropriate, and considerably more expensive, query plan.

Filtered statistics can help solve this problem by letting you capture these types of data correlations in your column statistics. For example, to capture the fact that all cooking books are also published by the same publisher, you could create the filtered statistics using the following statement:

```
create statistics pub_id_type on titles (pub_id, type)
where pub_id = '0877' and type in ('trad_cook', 'mod_cook')
```

When these filtered statistics are defined and the same query is run, SQL Server uses the filtered statistics to determine that the query will match five rows instead of only one.

Although using this solution could require having to define a number of filtered statistics, it can be effective to help fix your most critical queries where cardinality estimates due to data correlation or data skew issues are causing the Query Optimizer to choose poorly performing query plans.

Choosing Indexes: Query Versus Update Performance

I/O is the primary factor in determining query performance. The challenge for a database designer is to build a physical data model that provides efficient data access. Creating indexes on database tables allows SQL Server to access data with fewer I/Os. Defining useful indexes during the logical and physical data modeling step is crucial. The SQL Server Query Optimizer relies heavily on index key distribution and index density to determine which indexes to use for a query. The Query Optimizer in SQL Server can use multiple indexes in a query (through index intersection) to reduce the I/O required to retrieve information. In the absence of indexes, the Query Optimizer performs a table scan, which can be costly from an I/O standpoint.

Although indexes provide a means for faster access to data, they slow down data modification statements due to the extra overhead of having to maintain the index during inserts, updates, and deletes.

In a DSS environment, defining many indexes can help your queries and does not create much of a performance issue because the data is relatively static and doesn't get updated frequently. You typically load the data, create the indexes, and forget about it until the next data load. As long as you have the necessary indexes to support the user queries and they're getting decent response time, the penalties of having too many indexes in a DSS environment are the space wasted for indexes that possibly won't be used, the additional time required to create the excessive indexes, and the additional time required to back up and run `DBCC` checks on the data.

In an OLTP environment, on the other hand, too many indexes can lead to significant performance degradation, especially if the number of indexes on a table exceeds four or five. Think about it for a second. Every single-row insert is at least one data page write and one or more index page writes (depending on whether a page split occurs) for every index on the table. With eight nonclustered indexes, that would be a minimum of nine writes to the database for a single-row insert. Therefore, for an OLTP environment, you want as few indexes as possible—typically only the indexes required to support the update and delete operations and your critical queries, and to enforce your uniqueness constraints.

The natural solution, in a perfect world, would be to create a lot of indexes for a DSS environment and as few indexes as possible in an OLTP environment. Unfortunately, in the real world, you typically have an environment that must support both DSS and OLTP applications. How do you resolve the competing indexing requirements of the two environments? Meeting the indexing needs of DSS and OLTP applications requires a bit of a balancing act, with no easy solution. It often involves making hard decisions as to which DSS queries might have to live with table scans and which updates have to contend with additional overhead.

One solution is to have two separate databases: one for DSS applications and another for OLTP applications. Obviously, this method requires some method of keeping the databases in sync. The method chosen depends on how up-to-date the DSS database has to be. If you can afford some lag time, you could consider using a dump-and-load mechanism, such as Log Shipping or periodic full database restores. If the DSS system requires up-to-the-minute concurrency, you might want to consider using replication or database mirroring.

Another possible alternative is to have only the required indexes in place during normal processing periods to support the OLTP requirements. At the end of the business day, you can create the indexes necessary to support the DSS queries and reports, and they can run as batch jobs after normal processing hours. When the DSS reports are complete, you can drop the additional indexes, and you're ready for the next day's processing. Note that this solution assumes that the time required to create the additional indexes is offset by the time saved by the faster running of the DSS queries. If the additional indexes do not result in substantial time savings, they are probably not necessary and need not be created in the first place. The queries need to be more closely examined to select the appropriate indexes to best support your queries.

As you can see, it is important to choose indexes carefully to provide a good balance between data search and data modification performance. The application environment usually governs the choice of indexes. For example, if the application is mainly OLTP with transactions requiring fast response time, creating too many indexes might have an adverse impact on performance. On the other hand, the application might be a DSS with few transactions doing data modifications. In that case, it makes sense to create a number of indexes on the columns frequently used in queries.

Identifying Missing Indexes

When developing an index design for your database and applications, you should make sure you create appropriate indexes for the various queries that will be executed against your tables. However, it can be quite a chore to identify all the queries you may need to create indexes for. Fortunately, SQL Server 2008 provides a couple of tools to help you identify any indexes you may need in your database: The Database Engine Tuning Advisor and the missing index dynamic management objects.

The Database Engine Tuning Advisor

The Database Engine Tuning Advisor is a tool that can analyze a SQL Script file or a set of queries captured in a SQL Profiler trace and recommend changes to your indexing scheme. After performing its analysis, the Database Engine Tuning Advisor provides recommendations for new or more effective indexes, indexed views, and partitioning schemes, along with the estimated improvement in execution time should the recommendation be implemented. You can choose to implement the recommendations immediately or later, or you can save the SQL statements to a script file. For detailed information on using the Database Engine Tuning Advisor, see Chapter55.

Although the Database Engine Tuning Advisor is a useful tool, and improvements have been made since it was introduced in SQL Server 2005 to improve its recommendations, it does still have some limitations. For one, because the Database Engine Tuning Advisor gathers statistics by sampling the data, repeatedly running the tool on the same workload may produce different results as different samples are used. In addition, if you impose constraints, such as specifying maximum disk space for tuning recommendations, the Database Engine Tuning Advisor may be forced to drop certain existing indexes, and the resulting recommendation may produce a negative expected improvement. The Database Engine Tuning Advisor may also not make recommendations under the following circumstances:

- The table being tuned contains fewer than 10 data pages.

- The recommended indexes would not offer enough improvement in query performance over the current physical database design.
- The user who runs the Database Engine Tuning Advisor is not a member of the `db_owner` database role or the `sysadmin` fixed server role.

Missing Index Dynamic Management Objects

In addition to the Database Engine Tuning Advisor, SQL Server 2008 introduces the missing index dynamic management objects to help identify potentially missing indexes in your database. The *missing index dynamic management objects* are a set of new dynamic management objects introduced in SQL Server 2008:

- **`sys.dm_db_missing_index_group_stats`**—Returns summary information about missing index groups, such as the performance improvements that could be gained by implementing a specific group of missing indexes.
- **`sys.dm_db_missing_index_groups`**—Returns information about a specific group of missing indexes, such as the group identifier and identifiers of all missing indexes contained in that group.
- **`sys.dm_db_missing_index_columns`**—Returns detailed information about a missing index; for example, it returns the name and identifier of the table where the index is missing, and the columns and column types that should make up the missing index.
- **`sys.dm_db_missing_index_details`**—Returns information about the database table columns missing an index.

After running a typical workload on SQL Server, you can query the dynamic management functions to retrieve information about possible missing indexes. Listing 34.8 provides a sample query that displays the missing index information for a query on the sales table that was run between 10:30 and 10:40 p.m. on 2/21/2010.

LISTING 34.8 Querying the Missing Index Dynamic Management Objects

```
SELECT
     mig.index_group_handle as handle,
     convert(varchar(30), statement) AS table_name,
         convert(varchar(12), column_name) AS Column_name,
         convert(varchar(10), column_usage) as ColumnUsage,
         avg_user_impact as avg_impact
FROM sys.dm_db_missing_index_details AS mid
CROSS APPLY sys.dm_db_missing_index_columns (mid.index_handle)
INNER JOIN sys.dm_db_missing_index_groups AS mig
ON mig.index_handle = mid.index_handle
inner join sys.dm_db_missing_index_group_stats AS migs
ON migs.group_handle = mig.index_group_handle
where mid.object_id = object_id('sales')
and last_user_seek between '2010-02-21 22:30' and '2010-02-21 22:40'
```

```
ORDER BY mig.index_group_handle, mig.index_handle, column_id;
GO

handle      table_name                      Column_name  ColumnUsage  avg_impact
----------- ------------------------------- ------------ ------------ ----------
2           [bigpubs2008].[dbo].[sales]     stor_id      INCLUDE      87.46
2           [bigpubs2008].[dbo].[sales]     qty          INEQUALITY   87.46
```

In this example, the optimizer recommends an index on the `qty` column to support an inequality operator. It is also recommended that the `stor_id` column be specified as an included column in the index. This index is estimated to improve performance by 87.46%.

Although the missing index feature provides some helpful information for identifying potentially missing indexes in your database, it too has a few limitations:

- It is not intended to fine-tune the existing indexes, only to recommend additional indexes when no useful index is found that can be used to satisfy a search or join condition.
- It reports only included columns for some queries. You need to determine whether the included columns should be specified as additional index key columns instead.
- It may return different costs for the same missing index group for different executions.
- It does not suggest filtered indexes.
- It is unable to provide recommendations for clustered indexes, indexed views, or table partitioning (you should use the Database Engine Tuning Advisor instead for these recommendations).

Probably the key limitation is that although the missing index feature is helpful for identifying indexes that may be useful for you to define, it's not a substitute for a well-thought-out index design.

Missing Index Feature Versus Database Engine Tuning Advisor

The missing indexes dynamic management objects are a lightweight, server-side, always-on feature for identifying and correcting potential indexing oversights. The Database Engine Tuning Advisor, on the other hand, is a comprehensive client-side tool that can be used to assess the physical database design and recommend new physical design structures for improving performance, including not only indexes, but also indexed views or partitioning schemes.

The Database Engine Tuning Advisor and missing indexes feature can possibly return different recommendations, even for a single-query workload. The reason is that the missing indexes dynamic management objects' index key column recommendations are not order sensitive. On the other hand, the Database Engine Tuning Advisor recommendations include ordering of the key columns for indexes to optimize query performance.

Table 34.11 details some other differences between the missing indexes feature and Database Engine Tuning Advisor in greater detail.

TABLE 34.11 Differences Between Missing Index Features and Database Engine Tuning Advisor

Comparison Point	Missing Indexes Feature	Database Engine Tuning Advisor
Execution method	Server side, always on	Client-side, standalone application
Scope of analysis	Quick, ad hoc analysis, providing limited information about missing indexes only	Thorough workload analysis, providing full recommendation report about the best physical database design configuration in the context of a submitted workload
Statements analyzed	`SELECT` statements only	`SELECT`, `UPDATE`, `INSERT`, and `DELETE`
Available disk storage space	Not factored into analysis	Factored into analysis; recommendations are not provided if they would exceed available storage space
Columns ordering	Recommended index column order not provided	Optimal index column order determined based on query execution cost
Index type	Nonclustered only	Both clustered and nonclustered index recommendations provided
Indexed views recommendations	Not provided	Recommended in supported editions
Partitioning recommendations	Not provided	Recommended in supported editions
Impact analysis	An approximate impact of adding a missing index is reported via the `sys.dm_db_missing_index_group_stats` dynamic management view (DMV)	Up to 15 different analysis reports generated to provide information about the impact of implementing recommendations

Identifying Unused Indexes

As mentioned previously in this chapter, each index on a table adds additional overhead for data modifications because the indexes also need to be maintained as changes are made to index key columns. In an OLTP environment, excessive indexes on your tables can be almost as much of a performance issue as missing indexes. To improve OLTP performance, you should limit the number of indexes on your tables to only those absolutely needed; you definitely should eliminate any unnecessary and unused indexes that may be defined on your tables to eliminate the overhead they introduce.

Fortunately, SQL Server provides a DMV that you can use to identify which indexes in your database are not being used: `sys.dm_db_index_usage_stats`. The columns in the `sys.dm_db_index_usage_stats` are shown in Table 34.12.

TABLE 34.12 Columns in the **`sys.dm_db_index_usage_stats`** DMV

Column Name	Description
database_id	ID of the database on which the table or view is defined
object_id	ID of the table or view on which the index is defined
index_id	ID of the index
user_seeks	Number of seeks by user queries
user_scans	Number of scans by user queries
user_lookups	Number of bookmark lookups by user queries
user_updates	Number of updates by user queries
last_user_seek	Time of last user seek
last_user_scan	Time of last user scan
last_user_lookup	Time of last user lookup
last_user_update	Time of last user update
system_seeks	Number of seeks by system queries
system_scans	Number of scans by system queries
system_lookups	Number of lookups by system queries
system_updates	Number of updates by system queries
last_system_seek	Time of last system seek
last_system_scan	Time of last system scan
last_system_lookup	Time of last system lookup
last_system_update	Time of last system update

Every individual seek, scan, lookup, or update on an index by a query execution is counted as a use of that index, and the corresponding counter in the view is incremented. Thus, you can run a query against this DMV to see whether there are any indexes that your queries are not using, that is, indexes that either have no rows in the DMV or have `0` values in the `user_seeks`, `user_scans`, or `user_lookups` columns (or the time values of the `last_user_*` columns are significantly in the past). You especially need to focus on any indexes that don't show any user query activity but do have a high value in the `last_user_update` column. This indicates an index that's adding significant update overhead but not being used by any queries for locating data rows.

For example, the query shown in Listing 34.9 returns all indexes in the current database that have never been accessed; that is, they would have no records at all in the `sys.dm_db_index_usage_stats` table.

LISTING 34.9 A Query for Unused Indexes

```
SELECT  convert(varchar(12), OBJECT_SCHEMA_NAME(I.OBJECT_ID)) AS SchemaName,
        convert(varchar(20), OBJECT_NAME(I.OBJECT_ID)) AS ObjectName,
        convert(varchar(30), I.NAME) AS IndexName
FROM    sys.indexes I
WHERE   -- only get indexes for user created tables
        OBJECTPROPERTY(I.OBJECT_ID, 'IsUserTable') = 1
        -- ignore heaps
        and I.index_id > 0
        -- find all indexes that exist but are NOT used
        AND NOT EXISTS (
                    SELECT  index_id
                    FROM    sys.dm_db_index_usage_stats
                    WHERE   OBJECT_ID = I.OBJECT_ID
                            AND I.index_id = index_id
                            AND database_id = DB_ID())
ORDER BY SchemaName, ObjectName, IndexName
```

Also, you should be aware that that the information is reported in the DMV both for operations caused by user-submitted queries and for operations caused by internally generated queries, such as scans for gathering statistics. If you run `UPDATE STATISTICS` on a table, the `sys.dm_db_index_usage_stats` table will have a row for each index for the system scan performed by the `UPDATE STATISTICS` command. However, the index may still be unused by any queries in your applications. Consequently, you might want to modify the previous query to look for indexes with `0` values in the `last_user_*` columns instead of indexes with no row at all in the DMV. Listing 34.10 provides an alternative query.

LISTING 34.10 A Query for Indexes Unused by Appliation Queries

```
SELECT  convert(varchar(12), OBJECT_SCHEMA_NAME(I.OBJECT_ID)) AS SchemaName,
        convert(varchar(20), OBJECT_NAME(I.OBJECT_ID)) AS ObjectName,
        convert(varchar(30), I.NAME) AS IndexName
FROM    sys.indexes I
          LEFT OUTER JOIN
          sys.dm_db_index_usage_stats u
          on I.index_id = u.index_id
          and u.database_id = DB_ID()
WHERE   -- only get indexes for user created tables
        OBJECTPROPERTY(I.OBJECT_ID, 'IsUserTable') = 1
        -- ignore heaps
        and I.index_id > 0
        -- find all indexes that exist but are NOT used
          and isnull(u.last_user_seek, 0) = 0
          and isnull(u.last_user_scan, 0) = 0
          and isnull(u.last_user_lookup, 0) = 0
ORDER BY SchemaName, ObjectName, IndexName
```

Note that the information returned by sys.dm_db_index_usage_stats is useful only if your server has been running long enough and has processed a sufficient amount of your standard and peak workflow. Also, you should be aware that the data in the DMV is cleared each time SQL Server is restarted, or if a database is detached and reattached. To prevent losing useful information, you might want to create a scheduled job that periodically queries the DMVs and saves the information to your own tables so you can track the information over time for more thorough and complete analysis.

Summary

One of the most important aspects of improving SQL Server performance is proper table and index design. Choosing the appropriate indexes for SQL Server to use to process queries involves thoroughly understanding the queries and transactions being run against the database, understanding the bias of the data, understanding how SQL Server uses indexes, and staying aware of the performance implications of overindexing tables in an OLTP environment. In general, you should consider using clustered indexes to support range retrievals or when data needs to be sorted in clustered index order; you should use nonclustered indexes for single- or discrete-row retrievals or when you can take advantage of index covering.

To really make good index design choices, you should have an understanding of the SQL Server Query Optimizer to know how it uses indexes and index statistics to develop query plans. This would be a good time to continue on and read Chapter 35.

CHAPTER 35

Understanding Query Optimization

IN THIS CHAPTER

- What's New in Query Optimization
- What Is the Query Optimizer?
- Query Compilation and Optimization
- Query Analysis
- Row Estimation and Index Selection
- Join Selection
- Execution Plan Selection
- Query Plan Caching
- Other Query Processing Strategies
- Parallel Query Processing
- Common Query Optimization Problems
- Managing the Optimizer

Query optimization is the process SQL Server goes through to analyze individual queries and determine the best way to process them. To achieve this end, SQL Server uses a cost-based Query Optimizer. As a cost-based Query Optimizer, the Query Optimizer's purpose is to determine the query plan that will access the data with the least amount of processing time in terms of CPU and logical and physical I/O. The Query Optimizer examines the parsed SQL queries and, based on information about the objects involved (for example, number of pages in the table, types of indexes defined, index statistics), generates a query plan. The query plan is the set of steps to be carried out to execute the query.

To allow the Query Optimizer to do its job properly, you need to have a good understanding of how the Query Optimizer determines query plans for queries. This knowledge will help you to understand what types of queries can be optimized effectively and to learn techniques to help the Query Optimizer choose the best query plan. This knowledge will help you write better queries, choose better indexes, and detect potential performance problems.

NOTE

To better understand the concepts presented in this chapter, you should have a reasonable understanding of how data structures and indexes affect performance. If you haven't already read Chapter 34, "Data Structures, Indexes, and Performance," it is recommended that you review it now.

NOTE

Occasionally throughout this chapter, graphical execution plans are used to illustrate some of the principles discussed. Chapter 36, "Query Analysis," provides a more detailed discussion of the graphical execution plan output and describes the information contained in the execution plans and how to interpret it. In this chapter, the execution plans are provided primarily to give you an idea of what you can expect to see for the different types of queries presented when you are doing your own query analysis.

What's New in Query Optimization

SQL Server 2008 introduces a few new features and capabilities related to query optimization and query performance in an attempt to deliver on the theme of "predictable performance." The primary new features and enhancements are as follows:

- An enhancement has been added to the `OPTIMIZE FOR` query hint option to include a new `UNKNOWN` option, which specifies that the Database Engine use statistical data to determine the values for one or more local variables during query optimization, instead of the initial values.
- Table hints can now be specified as query hints in the context of plan guides to provide advanced query performance tuning options
- A new `FORCESEEK` table hint has been added. This hint specifies that the query optimizer should use only an index seek operation as the access path to the data referenced in the query.
- Hash values are available for finding and tuning similar queries. The `sys.dm_exec_query_stats` and `sys.dm_exec_requests` catalog views provide query hash and query plan hash values that you can use to help determine the aggregate resource usage for similar queries and similar query execution plans. This can help you find and tune similar queries that individually consume minimal system resources but collectively consume significant system resources.
- The new filtered indexes feature in SQL Server 2008 is considered for estimating index usefulness.
- Parallel query processing on partitioned objects has been improved.

One of the key improvements in SQL Server 2008 is the simplification of the creation and use of plan guides:

- The `sp_create_plan_guide` stored procedure now accepts XML execution plan output directly via the `@hints` parameter instead of having to embed the output in the `USE PLAN` hint.
- A new stored procedure, `sp_create_plan_guide_from_handle`, allows you to create one or more plan guides from an existing query plan in the plan cache.
- You can create multiple `OBJECT` or SQL plan guides for the same query and batch or module although only one of these plan guides can be enabled at any given time.

- A new system function, `sys.fn_validate_plan_guide`, enables you to validate a plan guide.
- New SQL Profiler event classes, Plan Guide Successful and Plan Guide Unsuccessful, enable you to verify whether plan guides are being used by the Query Optimizer.
- New Performance Monitor counters in the SQL Server, SQL Statistics Object—Guided Plan Executions/sec and Misguided Plan Executions/sec—can be used to monitor the number of plan executions in which the query plan has been successfully or unsuccessfully generated by using a plan guide.
- Built-in support is now available for creating, deleting, enabling, disabling, or scripting plan guides in SQL Server Management Studio (SSMS). Plan guides now are located in the `Programmability` folder in Object Explorer.

NOTE

Many of the internals of the Query Optimizer and its costing algorithms are considered proprietary and have not been made public. Much of the information provided here is based on analysis and observation of query plans generated for various queries and search values.

The intent of this chapter is therefore not so much to describe the specific steps, algorithms, and calculations implemented by the Query Optimizer, but rather to provide a general overview of the query optimization process in SQL Server 2008 and what goes into estimating and determining an efficient query plan. Also, there are a number of possible ways SQL Server can optimize and process queries. The examples presented in this chapter focus on some of the more common optimization strategies.

What Is the Query Optimizer?

For any given SQL statement, the source tables can be accessed in many ways to return the desired result set. The Query Optimizer analyzes all the possible ways the result set can be generated and chooses the most appropriate method, called the *query plan* or *execution plan*. SQL Server uses a cost-based Query Optimizer. The Query Optimizer assigns a cost to every possible execution plan in terms of CPU resource usage and page I/O. The Query Optimizer then chooses the execution plan with the lowest associated cost.

Thus, the primary goal of the Query Optimizer is to find the least expensive execution plan that minimizes the total time required to process a query. Because I/O is the most significant factor in query processing time, the Query Optimizer analyzes the query and primarily searches for access paths and techniques to minimize the number of logical and physical page accesses as much as possible. The lower the number of logical and physical I/Os performed, the faster the query should run.

The process of query optimization in SQL Server is extremely complicated and is based on sophisticated costing models and data access algorithms. It is beyond the scope of a single chapter to explain in detail all the various costing algorithms that the Query Optimizer currently employs. This chapter is intended to help you better understand some of the concepts related to how the Query Optimizer chooses an execution strategy and provide an overview of the query optimization strategies employed to improve query processing performance.

Query Compilation and Optimization

Query compilation is the complete process from the submission of a query to its actual execution. There are many steps involved in query compilation—one of which is optimization. All T-SQL statements are compiled, but not all are optimized. Primarily, only the standard SQL Data Manipulation Language (DML) statements—`SELECT`, `INSERT`, `UPDATE`, and `DELETE`—require optimization. The other procedural constructs in T-SQL (`IF`, `WHILE`, local variables, and so on) are compiled as procedural logic but do not require optimization. DML statements are set-oriented requests that the Query Optimizer must translate into procedural code that can be executed efficiently to return the desired results.

NOTE

SQL Server also optimizes some Data Definition Language (DDL) statements, such as `CREATE INDEX` or `ALTER TABLE`, against the data tables. For example, a displayed query plan for the creation of an index shows optimization steps for accessing the table, sorting data, and inserting into the index tree. However, the focus in this chapter is on optimization of DML statements.

Compiling DML Statements

When SQL Server compiles an execution plan for a DML statement, it performs the following basic steps:

1. The query is parsed and checked for proper syntax, and the T-SQL statements are parsed into keywords, expressions, operators, and identifiers to generate a query tree. The query tree (sometimes referred to as the *sequence tree*) is an internal format of the query that SQL Server can operate on. It is essentially the logical steps needed to transform the query into the desired result.
2. The query tree is then normalized and simplified. During normalization, the tables and columns are verified, and the metadata (data types, null properties, index statistics, and so on) about them is retrieved. In addition, any views are resolved to their underlying tables, and implicit conversions are performed (for example, an integer compared with a float value). Also during this phase, any redundant operations (for example, unnecessary or redundant joins) are removed, and the query tree is simplified.
3. The Query Optimizer analyzes the different ways the source tables can be accessed and selects the series of steps that return the results fastest while typically using the fewest resources. The query tree is updated with the optimized series of steps, and an execution plan (also referred to as query plan) is generated from the final, optimized version of the sequence tree.

4. After the optimized execution plan is generated, SQL Server stores the optimized plan in the procedure cache.
5. SQL Server reads the execution plan from the procedure cache and executes the query plan, returning the result set (if any) to the client.

The optimized execution plan is then left in the procedure cache. If the same query or stored procedure is executed again and the plan is still available in the procedure cache, the steps to optimize and generate the execution plan are skipped, and the stored query execution plan is reused to execute the query or stored procedure.

Optimization Steps

When the query tree is passed to the Query Optimizer, the Query Optimizer performs a series of steps to break down the query into its component pieces for analysis to generate an optimal execution plan:

1. **Query analysis**—The query is analyzed to determine search arguments and join clauses. A search argument is defined as a `WHERE` clause that compares a column to a constant. A join clause is a `WHERE` clause that compares a column from one table to a column from another table.
2. **Row estimation and index selection**—Indexes are selected based on search arguments and join clauses (if any exist). Indexes are evaluated based on their distribution statistics and are assigned a cost.
3. **Join selection**—The join order is evaluated to determine the most appropriate order in which to access tables. In addition, the Query Optimizer evaluates the most appropriate join algorithm to match the data.
4. **Execution plan selection**—Execution costs are evaluated, and a query execution plan is created that represents the most efficient solution found by the optimizer.

The next four sections of this chapter examine each of these steps in more detail.

NOTE

Unless stated otherwise, the examples presented in this chapter operate on the tables in the `bigpubs2008` database. A copy of the `bigpubs2008` database is available on the CD included with this book. Instructions on how to install the database are presented in the Introduction.

Query Analysis

The first step in query optimization is to analyze each table in the query to identify all search arguments (SARGs), `OR` clauses, and join clauses. The SARGs, `OR` clauses, and join clauses are used in the second step, index selection, to select useful indexes to satisfy a query.

Identifying Search Arguments

A SARG is defined as a `WHERE` clause that compares a column to a constant. The format of a SARG is as follows:

```
Column operator constant_expression [and...]
```

SARGs provide a way for the Query Optimizer to limit the rows searched to satisfy a query. The general goal is to match a SARG with an index to avoid a table scan. Valid operators for a SARG are =, >, <, >=, and <=, `BETWEEN`, and `LIKE`. Multiple SARGs can be combined with the `AND` clause. (A single index might match some or all of the SARGs `AND`ed together.) Following are examples of SARGs:

- `flag = 7`
- `salary > 100000`
- `city = 'Saratoga' and state = 'NY'`
- `price between $10 and $20` (the same as `price > = $10 and price <= $20`)
- `100 between lo_val and hi_val` (the same as `lo_val <= 100 and hi_val >= 100`)
- `au_lname like 'Sm%'` (the same as `au_lname >= 'Sm' and au_lname < 'Sn'`)

In some cases, the column in a SARG might be compared with a constant expression rather than a single constant value. The constant expression can be an arithmetic operation, a built-in function, a string concatenation, a local variable, or a subquery result. As long as the left side of the SARG contains a column, it's considered an optimizable SARG.

Identifying OR Clauses

The next statements the Query Optimizer looks for in the query are `OR` clauses. `OR` clauses are SARGable expressions combined with an `OR` condition rather than an `AND` condition and are treated differently than standard SARGs. The format of an `OR` clause is

```
SARG or SARG [or ...]
```

with all columns involved in the `OR` belonging to the same table.

This `IN` statement

```
column in ( constant1, constant2, ...)
```

is also treated as an `OR` clause, becoming this:

```
column = constant1 or column = constant2 or ...
```

Some examples of `OR` clauses are as follows:

```
where au_lname = 'Smith'  or au_fname = 'Fred'
where (type = 'business' and price > $25) or pub_id = "1234"
where au_lname in ('Smith', 'Jones', 'N/A')
```

An OR clause is a disjunction; all rows matching either of the two criteria appear in the result set. Any row matching both criteria should appear only once.

The main issue is that an OR clause cannot be satisfied by a single index search. Consider the first example just presented:

```
where au_lname = 'Smith'  or au_fname = 'Fred'
```

An index on au_lname and au_fname helps SQL Server find all the rows where au_lname = 'Smith' AND au_fname = 'Fred', but searching the index tree does not help SQL Server efficiently find all the rows where au_fname = 'Fred' and the last name is any value. Unless an index on au_fname exists as well, the only way to find all rows with au_fname = 'Fred' is to search every row in the table or scan every row in a nonclustered index that contains au_fname as a nonleading index key.

An OR clause can typically be resolved by either a table scan or by using the OR strategy. Using a table scan, SQL Server reads every row in the table and applies each OR criteria to each row. Any row that matches any one of the OR criteria is put into the result set.

A table scan is an expensive way to process a query, so the Query Optimizer looks for an alternative for resolving an OR. If an index can be matched against all SARGs involved in the OR clause, SQL Server evaluates the possibility of applying the index union strategy described later in this chapter, in the section "Using Multiple Indexes."

Identifying Join Clauses

The next type of clause the Query Optimizer looks for during the query analysis phase is the join clause. A join condition is specified in the FROM clause using the JOIN keyword, as follows:

```
FROM table1 JOIN table2  on table1.column = table2.column
```

Alternatively, join conditions can be specified in the WHERE clause using the old-style join syntax, as shown in the following example:

```
Table1.Column Operator Table2.Column
```

A join clause always involves two tables, except in the case of a self-join, but even in a self-join, you must specify the table twice in the query. Here's an example:

```
select employee = e.LastName + ', ' + e.FirstName,
       manager = m.LastName + ', ' + m.FirstName
    from Northwind..Employees e left outer join Northwind..Employees m
    on e.ReportsTo = m.EmployeeID
   order by 2, 1
```

SQL Server treats a self-join just like a normal join between two different tables.

In addition to join clauses, the Query Optimizer also looks for subqueries, derived tables, and common table expressions and makes the determination whether they need to be flattened into joins or processed using a different strategy. Subquery optimization is discussed later in this chapter.

Row Estimation and Index Selection

When the query analysis phase of optimization is complete and all SARGs, `OR` clauses, and join clauses have been identified, the next step is to determine the selectivity of the expressions (that is, the estimated number of matching rows) and to determine the cost of finding the rows. The costs are measured primarily in terms of logical and physical I/O, with the goal of generating a query plan that results in the lowest estimated I/O and processing cost. Primarily, the Query Optimizer attempts to identify whether an index exists that can be used to locate the matching rows. If multiple indexes or search strategies can be considered, their costs are compared with each other and also against the cost of a table or clustered index scan to determine the least expensive access method.

An index is typically considered useful for an expression if the first column in the index is used in the expression and the search argument in the expression provides a means to effectively limit the search. If no useful indexes are found for an expression, typically a table or clustered index scan is performed on the table. A table or clustered index scan is the fallback tactic for the Query Optimizer to use if no lower-cost method exists for returning the matching rows from a table.

Evaluating SARG and Join Selectivity

To determine selectivity of a SARG, which helps in determining the most efficient query plan, the Query Optimizer uses the statistical information stored for the index or column, if any. If no statistics are available for a column or index, SQL Server automatically creates statistics on nonindexed columns specified in a SARG if the `AUTO_CREATE_STATISTICS` option is enabled for the database. SQL Server also automatically generates and updates the statistics for any indexed columns referenced in a SARG if the `AUTO_UPDATE_STATISTICS` option is enabled. In addition, you can explicitly create statistics for a column or set of columns in a table or an indexed view by using the `CREATE STATISTICS` command. Both index statistics and column statistics (whether created automatically or manually with the `CREATE STATISTICS` command) are maintained and kept up-to-date, as needed, if the `AUTO_UPDATE_STATISTICS` option is enabled or if the `UPDATE STATISTICS` command is explicitly run for a table, index, or column statistics. Available and up-to-date statistics allow the Query Optimizer to more accurately assess the cost of different query plans and choose a high-quality plan.

If no statistics are available for a column or an index and the `AUTO CREATE STATISTICS` and `AUTO UPDATE STATISTICS` options have been disabled for the database or table, SQL Server cannot make an informed estimate of the number of matching rows for a SARG and resorts to using some built-in percentages for the number of matching rows for various types of expressions. These percentages currently are as follows:

Operator	Row Estimate
=	(# of rows in table)$^{.75}$
between, > and <	9% (closed-range search)
>, <, >=, <=	30% (open-range search)

Using these default percentages almost certainly results in inappropriate query execution plans being chosen. You should always try to ensure that you have up-to-date statistics available for any columns referenced in your SARGs and join clauses.

When the value of a SARG can be determined at the time of query optimization, the Query Optimizer uses the statistics histogram to estimate the number of matching rows for the SARG. The histogram contains a sampling of the data values in the column and stores information on the number of matching rows for the sampled values, as well as for values that fall between the sampled values. If the statistics are up-to-date, this is the most accurate estimate of the number of matching rows for a SARG. (For a more detailed discussion of index and column statistics and the information contained in them, see Chapter 34.)

If the SARG contains an expression that cannot be evaluated until runtime (for example, a local variable or scalar function) but is an equality expression (=), the Query Optimizer uses the density information from the statistics to estimate the number of matching rows. The density value reflects the overall uniqueness of the data values in the column or index. Density information does not estimate the number of matching rows as accurately as the histogram because its value is determined across the entire range of values in a column or an index key and can be skewed higher by one or more values that have a high number of duplicates. Expressions that cannot be evaluated until runtime include comparisons against local variables or function expressions that cannot be evaluated until query execution.

If an expression cannot be evaluated at the time of optimization and the SARG is not an equality search but a closed- or open-range search, the density information cannot be used. The same percentages are used for the row estimates as when no statistics are available (9% for a closed-range search and 30% for an open-range search).

As a special case, if a SARG contains the equality (=) operator and a unique index exists that matches the SARG, based on the nature of a unique index, the Query Optimizer knows, without having to analyze the index statistics, that one and only one row can match the SARG.

If the query contains a join clause, SQL Server determines whether any usable indexes or column statistics exist that match the column(s) in the join clause. Because the Query Optimizer has no way of determining what value(s) will join between rows in the table at optimization time, it can't use the statistics histogram on the join column to estimate the number of matching rows. Instead, it uses the density information, as it does for SARGs that are unknown during optimization.

A lower density value indicates a more selective index. As the density approaches 1, the join condition becomes less selective. For example, if a nonclustered index has a high density value, it will likely be more expensive in terms of I/O to retrieve the matching rows using the nonclustered index than to perform a table scan or clustered index scan and the index likely will not be used.

NOTE

For a more thorough and detailed discussion of indexes and index and column statistics, see Chapter 34.

SARGs and Inequality Operators

In previous versions of SQL Server, when a SARG contained an inequality operator (!= or <>), the selectivity of the SARG could not be determined effectively for the simple reason that index or column statistics can help you estimate only the number of matching rows for a specific value, not the number of nonmatching rows. However, for some SARGs with inequality operators, if index or column statistics are available, SQL Server 2008 is able to estimate the number of matching rows. For example, consider the following SARG:

```
WHERE qty <> 1000
```

Without any available index or column statistics on the `qty` column, SQL Server would treat the inequality SARG as a SARG with no available statistics. Potentially every row in the table could satisfy the search criteria, so it would estimate the number of matching rows as all rows in the table.

However, if index or column statistics were available for the `qty` column, the Query Optimizer would look up the search value (`1000`) in the statistics and estimate the number of matching rows for the search value and then determine the number of matching rows for the query as the total number of rows in the table minus the estimated number of matching rows for the search value. For example, if there are 150,000 rows in the table and the statistics indicate that 1,570 rows match, where `qty = 1000`, the number of matching rows would be calculated as follows:

150,000	rows
– 1,570	rows (where `qty = 1000`)
= 148,430	rows (where `qty <> 1000`)

In this example, with the large number of estimated rows where `qty <> 1000`, SQL Server would likely end up performing a table scan to resolve the query. However, if the Query Optimizer estimates that there is a very small number of rows where `qty <> 1000`, the Query Optimizer might determine that it would be more efficient to use an index to find the nonmatching rows. You may be wondering how SQL Server efficiently searches the index for the rows where `qty <> 1000` without having to look at every row. In this case, internally, it converts the inequality SARG into two range retrievals by using an `OR` condition:

```
WHERE qty < 1000 OR qty > 1000
```

NOTE

Even if an inequality SARG is optimizable, that doesn't necessarily mean an index will be used. It simply allows the Query Optimizer to make a more accurate estimate of the number of rows that will match a given SARG. More often than not, an inequality SARG will result in a table or clustered index scan. You should try to avoid using inequality SARGs whenever possible.

SARGs and `LIKE` Clauses

In SQL Server versions prior to SQL Server 2005, the Query Optimizer would estimate the selectivity of a `LIKE` clause only if the first character in the string was a constant. Every row would have to be examined to determine if it was a match. SQL Server 2008 uses string summary statistics, which were introduced in SQL Server 2005, for estimating the selectivity of `LIKE` conditions.

String summary statistics provide a statistical summary of substring frequency distribution for character columns. String summary statistics can be created on columns of type `text`, `ntext`, `char`, `varchar`, and `nvarchar`. String summary statistics allow SQL Server to estimate the selectivity of `LIKE` conditions where the search string may have any number of wildcards in any combination, including when the first character is a wildcard. In versions of SQL Server prior to 2005, row estimates could not be accurately obtained when the leading character of a search string was a wildcard character. SQL Server 2008 can estimate the selectivity of `LIKE` predicates similar to the following:

- `au_lname LIKE 'Smith%'`
- `stor_name LIKE '%Books'`
- `title LIKE '%Cook%'`
- `title_id LIKE 'BU[1234567]001'`
- `title LIKE '%Cook%Chicken'`

The string summary statistics result in fairly accurate row estimates. However, if there is a user-specified escape character in a `LIKE` pattern (for example, `stor_name LIKE '%abc#_%' ESCAPE '#'`), SQL Server 2008 has to guess at the selectivity of the SARG.

The values generated for string summary statistics are not visible via `DBCC SHOW_STATISTICS`. However, `DBCC SHOW_STATISTICS` does indicate if string summary statistics have been calculated; if the value `YES` is specified in the `String Index` field in the first rowset returned by `DBCC SHOW_STATISTICS`, the statistics also include a string summary. Also, if the strings are more than 80 characters in length, only the first and last 40 characters are used for creating the string summary statistics. Accurate frequency estimates cannot be determined for substrings that do not appear in the first and last 40 characters of a string.

SARGS on Computed Columns

In versions of SQL Server prior to 2005, for a SARG to be optimizable, there had to be no computations on the column itself in the SARG. In SQL Server 2008, expressions involving computations on a column might be treated as SARGs during optimization if SQL Server can simplify the expression into a SARG. For example, the SARG

```
ytd_sales/12 = 1000
```

can be simplified to this:

```
ytd_sales = 12000
```

The simplified expression is used only during optimization to determine an estimate of the number of matching rows and the usefulness of the index. During actual execution, the conversion is not done while traversing the index tree because it won't be able to do the repeated division by 12 for each row while searching through the tree. However, doing the conversion during optimization and getting a row estimate from the statistics helps the Query Optimizer decide on other strategies to consider, such as index scanning versus table scanning, or it might help to determine an optimal join order if it's a multi-table query.

SQL Server 2008 supports the creation, update, and use of statistics on computed columns. The Query Optimizer can make use of the computed column statistics even when a query doesn't reference the computed column by name but rather contains an expression that matches the computed column expression. This feature avoids the need to rewrite the SARGs in queries with expressions that match a computed column expression to SARGs that explicitly contain the computed column itself.

When the SARG has a more complex operation performed on it, such as a function, it can potentially prevent effective optimization of the SARG. If you cannot avoid using a function or complex expression on a column in the search expression, you should consider creating a computed column on the table and creating an index on the computed column. This materializes the function result into an additional column on the table that can be indexed for faster searching, and the index statistics can be used to better estimate the number of matching rows for the SARG expression that references the function.

An example of using this approach would be for a query that has to find the number of orders placed in a certain month, regardless of the year. The following is a possible solution:

```
select distinct stor_id
   from sales
   where datepart(month, ord_date) = 6
```

This query gets the correct result set but ends up having to do so with a full table or index scan because the function on the `ord_date` column prevents the Query Optimizer from using an index seek against any index that might exist on the `ord_date` column.

If this query is used frequently in the system and quick response time is critical, you could create a computed column on the function and index it as follows:

```
alter table sales add ord_month as datepart(month, ord_date)
create index nc_sales_ordmonth on sales(ord_month)
```

Now, when you run the query on the table again, if you specify the computed column in the `WHERE` clause, the Query Optimizer can use the index on the computed column to accurately estimate the number of matching rows and possibly use the nonclustered index to find the matching rows and avoid a table scan, as it does for the following query:

```
select distinct stor_id
   from sales
   where ord_month = 6
```

Even if the query still ends up using a table scan, it at least has statistics available to know how many rows it can expect to match where the month matches the value specified. In addition, if a computed column exists that exactly matches the SARG expression, SQL Server 2008 can still use the statistics and index on the computed column to optimize the query, even if the computed column is not specified in the query itself. For example, with the `ord_month` column defined on the `sales` table and an index created on it, the following query can also use the statistics and index to optimize the query:

```
select distinct stor_id
   from sales
   where datepart(month, ord_date) = 6
```

TIP

The automatic matching of computed columns in SQL Server 2008 enables you to create and exploit computed columns without having to change the queries in your application. Be aware, though, that computed column matching is based on identical comparison. For example, a computed column of the form A + B + C does not match an expression of the form A + C + B.

Estimating Access Path Cost

After the selectivity of each of the SARGs, `OR` clauses, and join clauses is determined, the next phase of optimization is estimating the access path cost of the query. The Query Optimizer attempts to identify the total cost of various access paths to the data and determine which path results in the lowest cost to return the matching rows for an expression.

The primary cost of an access path, especially for single-table queries, is the number of logical I/Os required to retrieve the data. Using the available statistics and the information stored in SQL Server regarding the average number of rows per page and the number of pages in the table, the Query Optimizer estimates the number of logical page reads necessary to retrieve the estimated number of rows using a table scan or any of the candidate indexes. It then ranks the candidate indexes to determine which access path would retrieve the matching data rows with the lowest cost, typically the access path that requires the fewest number of logical and physical I/Os.

NOTE

A logical I/O occurs every time a page is accessed. If the page is not in cache, a physical I/O is first performed to bring the page into cache memory, and then a logical I/O is performed against the page. The Query Optimizer has no way of knowing whether a page will be in memory when the query actually is executed, so it always assumes a cold cache, that the first read of a page will be from disk. In a very few cases (for example, small OLTP queries), this assumption may result in a slightly slower plan being chosen that optimizes for the number of initial I/Os required to process the query. However, the cold cache assumption is a minor factor in the query plan costing, and it's actually the total number of logical I/Os that is the primary factor in determining the cost of the access path.

TIP

The following sections assume a general understanding of SQL Server index structures. If you haven't done so already, now is a good time to read through Chapter 34.

Clustered Index Cost

Clustered indexes are efficient for lookups because the rows that match the SARGs are clustered on the same page or over a range of adjacent pages. SQL Server needs only to find its way to the first page and then read the rows from that page and any subsequent pages in the page chain until no more matching rows are found.

Therefore, the I/O cost estimate for a clustered index is calculated as follows:

  Number of index levels in the clustered index

\+ Number of pages to scan within the range of values

The number of pages to scan is based on the estimated number of matching rows divided by the number of rows per page. For example, if SQL Server can store 250 rows per page for a table, and 600 rows are within the range of values being searched, SQL Server would estimate that it requires at least three page reads to find the qualifying rows. If the index is three levels deep, the logical I/O cost would be as follows:

  3 (index levels to find the first row)

\+ 3 (data pages: 600 rows divided by 250 rows per page)

= 6 logical page I/Os

For a unique clustered index and an equality operator, the logical I/O cost estimate is one data page plus the number of index levels that need to be traversed to access the data page.

When a clustered index is used to retrieve the data rows, you see a query plan similar to the one shown in Figure 35.1.

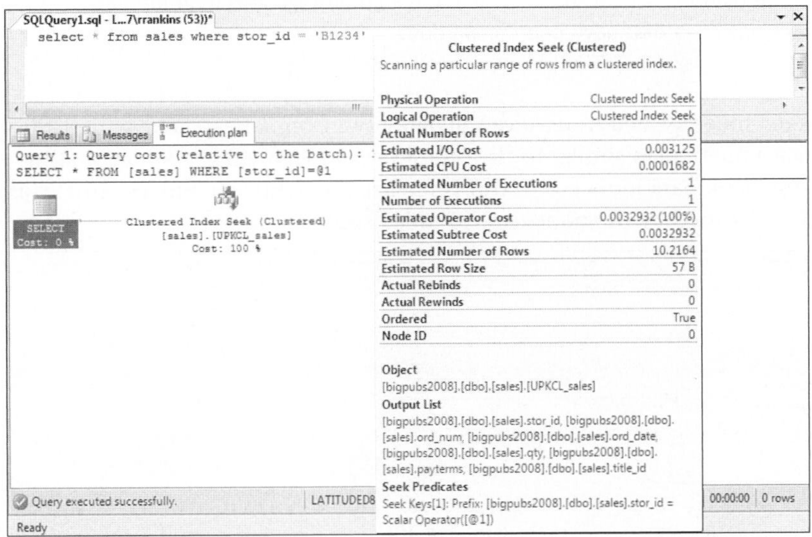

FIGURE 35.1 An execution plan for a clustered index seek.

Nonclustered Index Cost

When searching for values using a nonclustered index, SQL Server reads the index key values at the leaf level of the index and uses the bookmark to locate and read the data row. SQL Server has no way of knowing if matching search values will be on the same data page until it has read the bookmark. It is possible that while retrieving the rows, SQL Server might find all data rows on different data pages, or it might revisit the same data page multiple times. Either way, a separate logical I/O is required each time it visits the data page.

The I/O cost is therefore based on the depth of the index tree, the number of index leaf rows that need to be scanned to find the matching key values, and the number of matching rows. The cost of retrieving each matching row depends on whether the table is clustered or is a heap table (that is, a table with no clustered index defined on it). For a heap table, the nonclustered row bookmark is the page and row pointer (the row ID [RID]) to the actual data row. A single I/O is required to retrieve the data row. Therefore, the worst-case logical I/O cost for a heap table can be estimated as follows:

  Number of nonclustered index levels
+ Number of leaf pages to be scanned
+ Number of qualifying rows (each row represents a separate data page read)

NOTE

This estimate assumes that the data rows have not been forwarded. In a heap table, when a row has been forwarded, the original row location contains a pointer to the new location of the data row; therefore, an additional page read is required to retrieve the actual data row. The actual I/O cost would be one page greater per row than the estimated I/O cost for any rows that have been forwarded.

When a nonclustered index is used to retrieve the data rows from a heap table with a clustered index, you see a query plan similar to the one shown in Figure 35.2. Notice that in SQL Server 2008, the bookmark lookup operator is replaced by a RID lookup, essentially as a join with the RIDs returned by the nonclustered index seek.

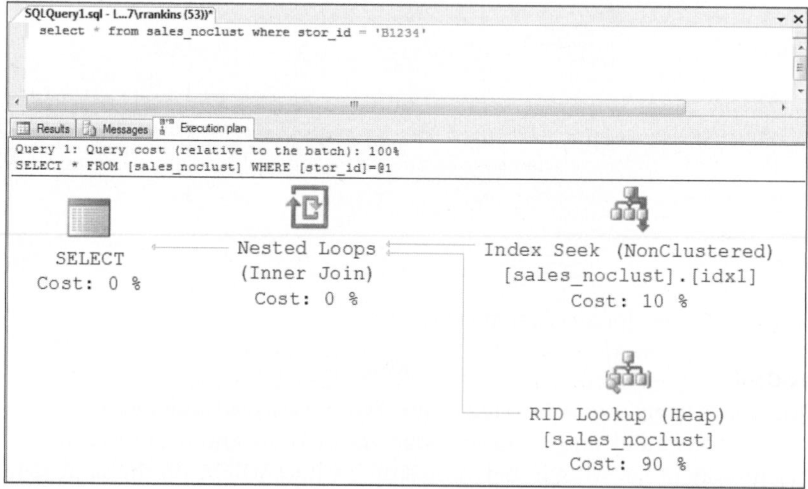

FIGURE 35.2 An execution plan for a nonclustered index seek against a heap table.

If the table is clustered, the row bookmark is the clustered key for the data row. The number of I/Os to retrieve the data row depends on the depth of the clustered index tree because SQL Server has to use the clustered index to find each row. The logical I/O cost of finding a row using the nonclustered index on a clustered table is therefore as follows:

Number of nonclustered index levels

\+ Number of leaf pages to be scanned

\+ Number of qualifying rows × Number of page reads to find a single row via the clustered index

For example, consider a heap table with a nonclustered index on last name. Assume that the index holds 800 rows per page (they're really big last names!), and 1,700 names are within the range you are looking for. If the index is three levels deep, the estimated logical I/O cost for the nonclustered index would be as follows:

3	(index levels)
+ 3	(leaf pages: 1,700 leaf rows/800 rows per page)
+ 1,700	(data page reads)
= 1,706	total logical I/Os

Now, assume that the table has a clustered index on it, and the size of the nonclustered index is the same. If the clustered index is three levels deep, including the data page, the estimated logical I/O cost of using the nonclustered index would be as follows:

3	(nonclustered index levels)
+ 3	(leaf pages: 1,700 leaf rows/800 rows per page)
+ 5,100	(1,700 rows × 3 clustered page reads per row)
= 5,106	(total logical I/Os)

NOTE

Although the I/O cost is greater for bookmark lookups in a nonclustered index when a clustered index exists on the table, the cost savings during row inserts, updates, and deletes using the clustered index as the bookmark are substantial, whereas the couple extra logical I/Os per row during retrieval do not substantially impact query performance.

For a unique nonclustered index using an equality operator, the I/O cost is estimated as the number of index levels traversed to access the bookmark plus the number of I/Os required to access the data page via the bookmark.

When a nonclustered index is used to retrieve the data rows on a table with a clustered index, you see a query plan similar to the one shown in Figure 35.3. Notice that in SQL Server 2008, the bookmark lookup operator is replaced by a clustered index seek, essentially as a join between the clustered index and the clustered index keys returned by the nonclustered index seek.

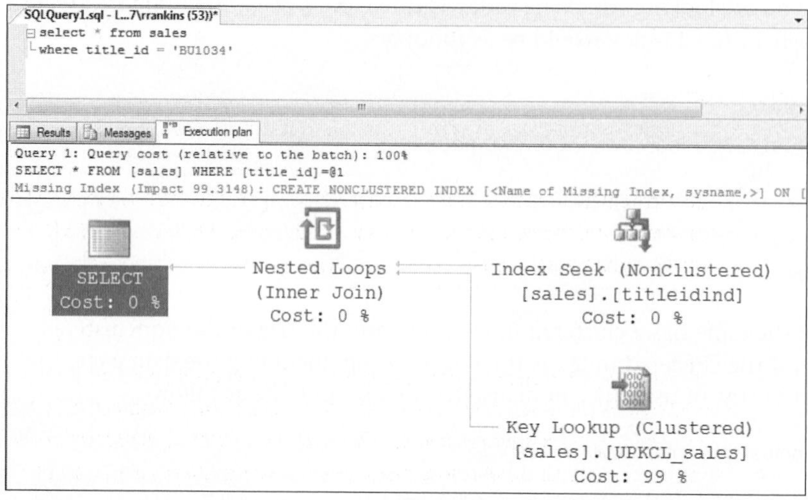

FIGURE 35.3 An execution plan for a nonclustered index seek against a table with a clustered index.

Covering Nonclustered Index Cost

When analyzing a query, the Query Optimizer considers any possibility to take advantage of index covering. *Index covering* is a method of using the leaf level of a nonclustered index to resolve a query when all the columns referenced in the query (in both the column list and WHERE clause, as well as any GROUP BY columns) are included in the index leaf row as either index key columns or included columns.

Index covering can save a significant amount of I/O because the query doesn't have to access the data page to return the requested information. In most cases, a nonclustered index that covers a query is faster than a similarly defined clustered index on the table because of the greater number of rows per page in the index leaf level compared to the number of rows per page in the table itself. (As the nonclustered leaf row size approaches the data row size, the I/O cost savings are minimal, if any.)

If index covering can take place in a query, the Query Optimizer considers it and estimates the I/O cost of using the nonclustered index to cover the query. The estimated I/O cost of index covering is as follows:

	Number of index levels
+	Number of leaf level index pages to scan

The number of leaf-level pages to scan is based on the estimated number of matching rows divided by the number of leaf index rows per page. For example, if index covering could be used on the nonclustered index on `title_id` for the query in the previous example, the I/O cost would be the following:

3	(nonclustered index levels)
+ 3	(leaf pages: 1,700 leaf rows/800 rows per page)
= 6	total logical I/Os

NOTE

For more information on index covering and when it can take place, as well as the included columns feature introduced in SQL Server 2008, see Chapter 34.

When index covering is used to retrieve the data rows, you might see a query plan similar to the one shown in Figure 35.4. If the entire leaf level of the index is searched, it displays as an index scan, as shown in this example.

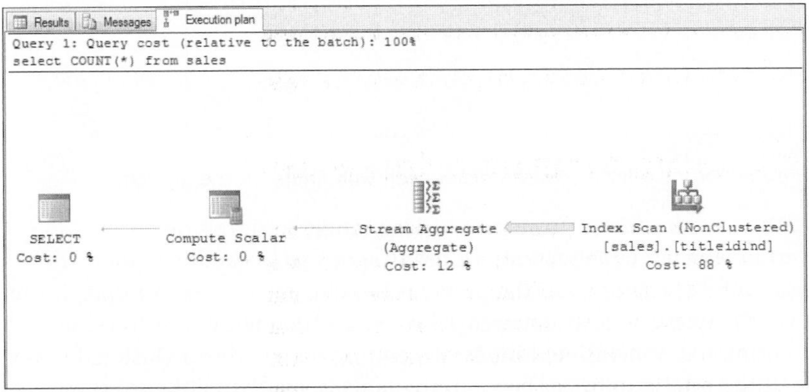

FIGURE 35.4 An execution plan for a covered index scan without limits on the search.

Other times, if the index keys can be searched to limit the range, you might see an index seek used, as shown in Figure 35.5. Note that the difference here from a normal index lookup is the lack of the RID or clustered index lookup because SQL Server does not need to go to the data row to find the needed information.

Table Scan Cost

If no usable index exists that can be matched with a SARG or a join clause, the Query Optimizer's only option is to perform a table scan. The estimate of the total I/O cost is simply the number of pages in the table, which is stored in the system catalogs and can be viewed by querying the `used_page_count` column of the `sys.dm_db_partition_stats` dynamic management view (DMV):

```
select used_page_count
   from sys.dm_db_partition_stats
   where object_id = object_id('sales_noclust')
     and (index_id = 0      -- data pages for heap table
          or index_id = 1) -- data pages for clustered table
go

used_page_count
--------------------
1244
```

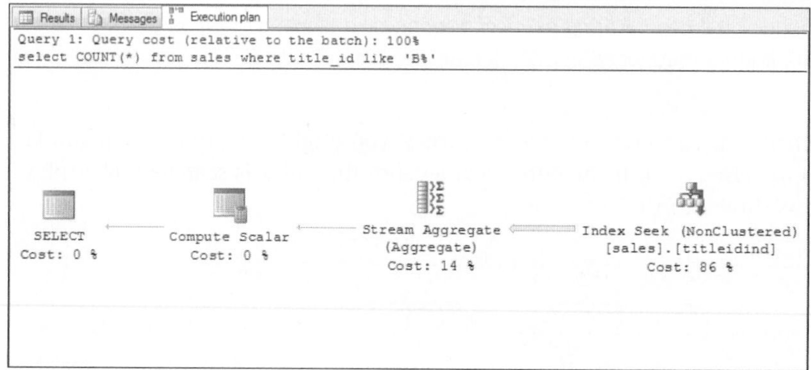

FIGURE 35.5 An execution plan for a covered index seek with limits on the search.

Keep in mind that there are instances (for example, large range retrievals on a nonclustered index column) in which a table scan might be cheaper than a candidate index in terms of total logical I/O. For example, in the previous nonclustered index example, if the index does not cover the query, it costs between 1,706 and 5,106 logical I/Os to retrieve the matching rows using the nonclustered index, depending on whether a clustered index exists on the table. If the total number of pages in the table is less than either of these values, a table scan would be more efficient in terms of total logical I/Os than using a nonclustered index.

When a table scan is used to retrieve the data rows from a heap table, you see a query plan similar to the one shown in Figure 35.6.

When a table scan is used to retrieve the data rows from a clustered table, you see a query plan similar to the one shown in Figure 35.7. Notice that it displays as a clustered index scan because the table is the leaf level of the clustered index.

Using Multiple Indexes

SQL Server allows the creation of multiple indexes on a table. If a query has multiple SARGs that can each be efficiently searched using an available index, the Query Optimizer in SQL Server can make use of multiple indexes by intersecting the indexes or using the index union strategy.

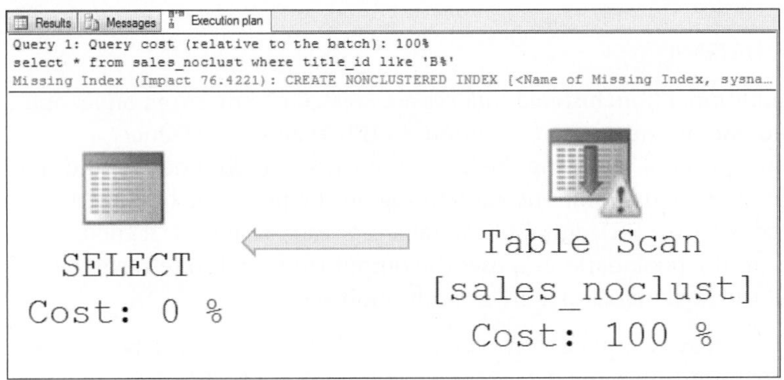

FIGURE 35.6 A table scan on a heap table.

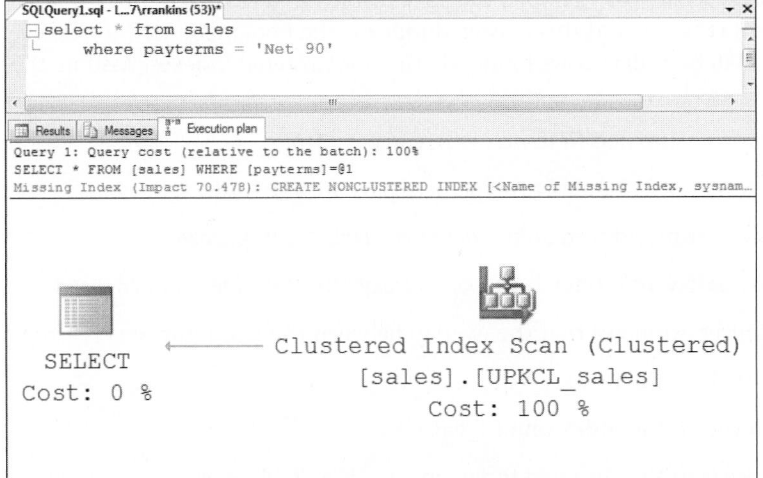

FIGURE 35.7 A table scan on a clustered table.

Index Intersection

Index intersection is a mechanism that allows SQL Server to use multiple indexes on a table when you have two or more SARGs in a query and each can be efficiently satisfied using an index as the access path. Consider the following example:

```
--First, create 2 additional indexes on sales to support the query
create index ord_date_idx on sales(ord_date)
create index qty_idx on sales(qty)
go
select * from sales
```

```
where qty = 816
  and ord_date = '1/2/2008'
```

In this example, two additional nonclustered indexes are created on the sales table: one on the qty column and one on the ord_date column. In this example, the Query Optimizer considers the option of searching the index leaf rows of each index to find the rows that meet each of the search conditions and joining on the matching bookmarks (either the clustered index key or RIDs if it's a heap table) for each result set. It then performs a merge join on the bookmarks and uses the output from that to retrieve the actual data rows for all the bookmarks that are in both result sets.

The index intersection strategy is applied only when the cost of retrieving the bookmarks for both indexes and then retrieving the data rows is less than that of retrieving the qualifying data rows using only one of the indexes or using a table scan.

You can go through the same analysis as the Query Optimizer to determine whether an index intersection makes sense. For example, the sales table has a clustered index on stor_id, ord_num, and title_id, and this clustered index is the bookmark used to retrieve the data rows for the matching data rows found via the nonclustered indexes. Assume the following statistics:

- There are 1,200 rows estimated to match where qty = 816.
- There are approximately 215 index rows per leaf page for the index on qty.
- There are 212 rows estimated to match where ord_date = '1/2/2008'.
- There are approximately 185 index rows per leaf page for the index on ord_date.
- The Query Optimizer estimates that the overlap between the two result sets is 1 row.
- The number of levels in the index on qty is 3.
- The number of levels in the index on ord_date is 3.
- The number of levels in the clustered index on the sales table is 3.
- The sales table is 1,252 pages in size.

Using this information, you can calculate the I/O cost for the different strategies the Query Optimizer can consider.

A table scan would cost 1,252 pages.

A standard data row retrieval via the nonclustered index on qty would have the following approximate cost:

2	index page reads (root and intermediate pages to locate first leaf page)
+ 6	leaf page reads (1200 rows / 215 rows per page)
+ 3600	(1,200 rows × 3 pages per bookmark lookup via the clustered index)
= 3,608	pages

A standard data row retrieval via the nonclustered index on `ord_date` would have the following approximate cost:

2	nonclustered index page reads (root and intermediate pages)
+ 2	nonclustered leaf page reads (212 rows / 185 rows per page)
+ 636	(212 rows × 3 pages per bookmark lookup via clustered index)
= 640	pages

The index intersection is estimated to have the following cost:

8	pages (1 root page + 1 intermediate page + the 6 leaf pages to find all the bookmarks for the 1,200 matching index rows on `qty`)
+ 4	pages (1 root page + 1 intermediate page + 2 leaf pages to find all the bookmarks for the 212 matching index rows on `ord_date`)
+ 3	page reads to find the 1 estimated overlapping row between the two indexes using the clustered index
= 15	pages

As you can see from these examples, the index intersection strategy is definitely the cheapest approach. If at any point the estimated intersection cost reaches 640 pages, SQL Server just uses the single index on `ord_date` and checks both search criteria against the 212 matching rows for `ord_date`. If the estimated cost of using an index in any way ever exceeds 1,252 pages, a table scan is likely to be performed, with the criteria checked against all rows.

When an index intersection is used to retrieve the data rows from a table with a clustered index, you see a query plan similar to the one shown in Figure 35.8.

If the table does not have a clustered index (that is, a heap table like the sales_noclust table in the bigpubs2008 database) and has supporting nonclustered indexes for an index intersection, you see a query plan similar to the one shown in Figure 35.9.

Notice that in the example shown in Figure 35.9, the Query Optimizer performs a hash join rather than a merge join on the RIDs returned by each nonclustered index seek and uses the results from the hash join to perform an RID lookup to retrieve the matching data rows.

NOTE

To duplicate the query plan shown in Figure 35.9, you need to create the following two additional indexes on the `sales_noclust` table:

```
create index ord_date_idx on sales_noclust(ord_date)
create index qty_idx on sales_noclust(qty)
```

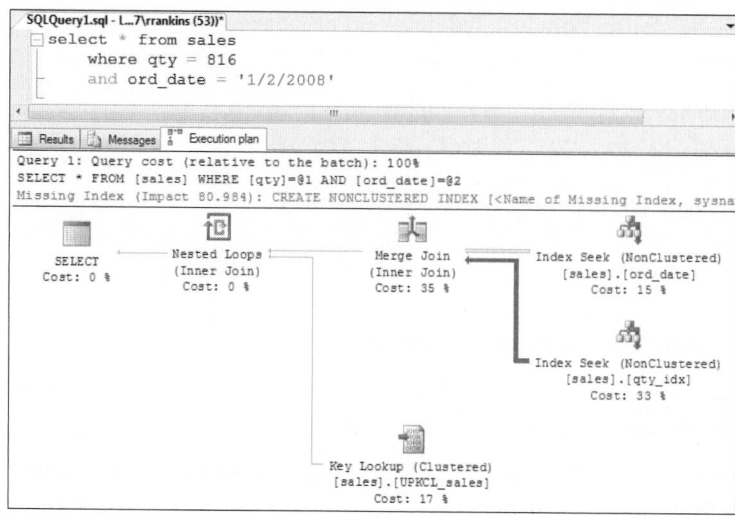

FIGURE 35.8 An execution plan for an index intersection on a clustered table.

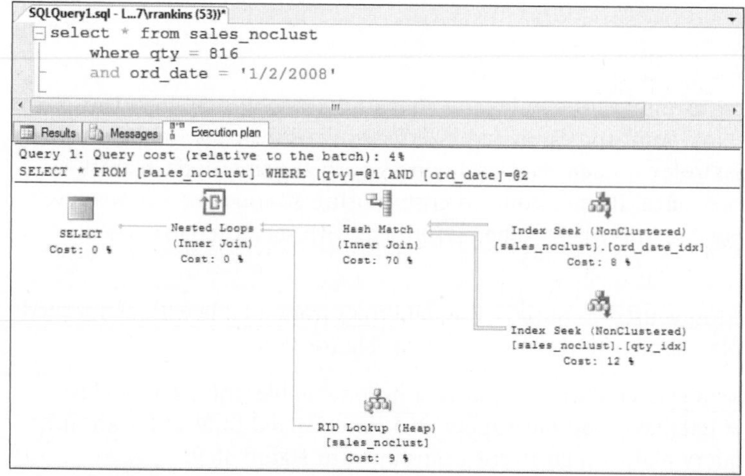

FIGURE 35.9 An execution plan for an index intersection on a heap table.

The Index Union Strategy

You see a strategy similar to an index intersection applied when you have an `OR` condition between your SARGs, as in the following query:

```
select * from sales
   where title_id = 'DR8514'
      or ord_date = '2006-01-01 00:00:00.000'
```

The index union strategy (often referred to as the `OR` strategy) is similar to an index intersection, with one slight difference. With the index union strategy, SQL Server executes each part separately, using the index that matches the SARG, but after combining the results with a merge join, it removes any duplicate bookmarks for rows that match both search arguments. It then uses the unique bookmarks to retrieve the result rows from the base table.

When the index union strategy is used on a table with a clustered index, you see a query plan similar to the one shown in Figure 35.10. Notice the addition of the stream aggregation step, which differentiates it from the index intersection query plan. The stream aggregation step performs a grouping on the bookmarks returned by the merge join to eliminate the duplicate bookmarks.

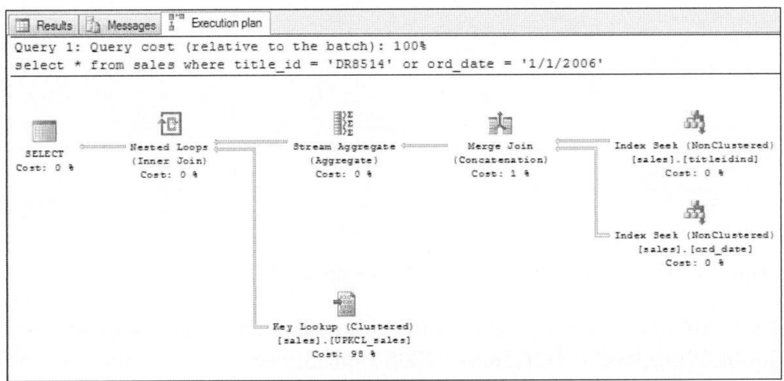

FIGURE 35.10 An execution plan for an index union strategy on a clustered table.

The following steps describe how SQL Server determines whether to use the index union strategy:

1. Estimate the cost of a table scan and the cost of using the index union strategy. If the cost of the index union strategy exceeds the cost of a table scan, stop here and simply perform a table scan. Otherwise, continue with the succeeding steps to perform the index union strategy.
2. Break the query into multiple parts, as in this example:

```
select * from sales where title_id = 'DR8514'
  select * from sales where ord_date = '2006-01-01 00:00:00.000'
```

3. Match each part with an available index.
4. Execute each piece and perform a join on the row bookmarks.
5. Remove any duplicate bookmarks.
6. Use the resulting list of unique bookmarks to retrieve all qualifying rows from the base table.

If any one of the `OR` clauses needs to be resolved via a table scan for any reason, SQL Server simply uses a table scan to resolve the whole query rather than applying the index union strategy.

When the index union strategy is used on a heap table (such as the sales_noclust table), you see a query plan similar to the one shown in Figure 35.11. Notice that the merge join is replaced with a concatenation operation, and the stream aggregate is replaced with distinct sort operation. Although the steps are slightly different from the index intersection strategy, the result is similar: a list of unique RIDs is returned, and they are used to retrieve the matching data rows in the table itself.

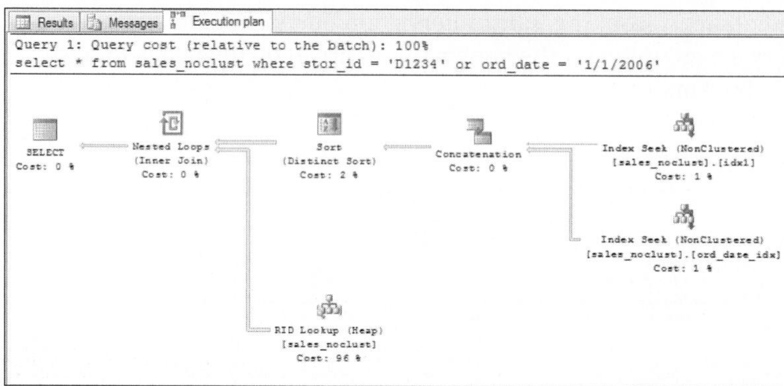

FIGURE 35.11 An execution plan for an index union strategy on a heap table.

When the OR in the query involves only a single column and a nonclustered index exists on the column, the Query Optimizer in SQL Server 2008 typically resolves the query with an index seek against the nonclustered index and then a bookmark lookup to retrieve the data rows. Consider the following query:

```
select * from sales
   where ord_date in ('6/15/2005', '9/28/2008', '6/25/2008')
```

This query is the same as the following:

```
select * from sales
   where ord_date = '6/15/2005'
     or ord_date =  '9/28/2008'
     or ord_date =  '6/25/2008'
```

To process this query, SQL Server performs a single index seek that looks for each of the search values and then joins the list of bookmarks returned with either the clustered index or the RIDs of the target table. No removal of duplicates is necessary because each OR condition matches a distinct set of rows. Figure 35.12 shows an example of the query plan for multiple OR conditions against a single column.

Index Joins

Besides using the index intersection and index union strategies, another way of using multiple indexes on a single table is to join two or more indexes to create a covering index. This is similar to an index intersection, except that the final bookmark lookup is not required because the merged index rows contain all the necessary information. Consider the following example:

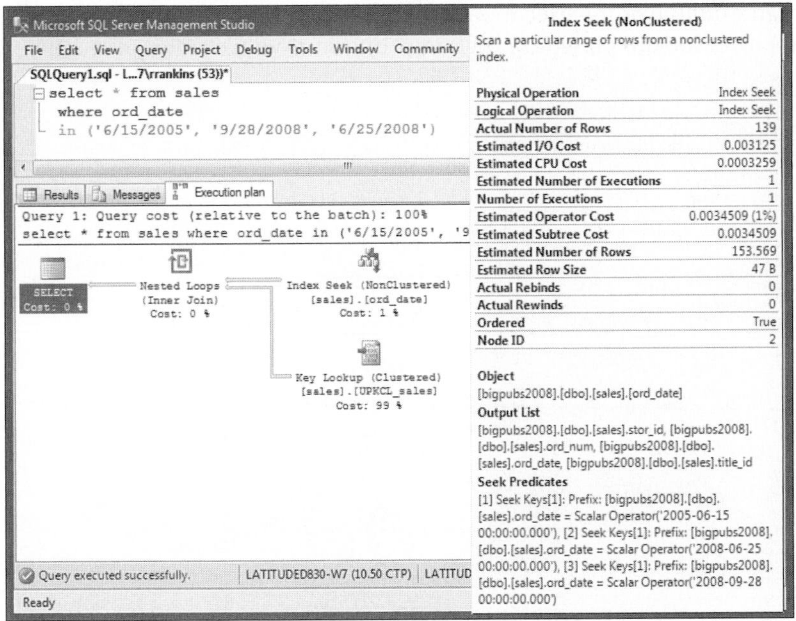

FIGURE 35.12 An execution plan using index seek to retrieve rows for an **OR** condition on a single column.


```
select stor_id from sales
   where qty = 816
     and ord_date = '1/2/2008'
```

Again, the `sales` table contains indexes on both the `qty` and `ord_date` columns. Each of these indexes contains the clustered index as a bookmark, and the clustered index contains the `stor_id` column. In this instance, when the Query Optimizer merges the two indexes using a merge join, joining them on the matching clustered indexes, the index rows in the merge set have all the information needed to resolve the query because `stor_id` is part of the nonclustered indexes. There is no need to perform a bookmark lookup on the data page. By joining the two index result sets, SQL Server creates the same effect as having one covering index on `qty`, `ord_date`, and `stor_id` on the table. If you use the same numbers as in the "Index Intersection" section presented earlier, the cost of the index join would be as follows:

8	pages (1 root page + 1 intermediate page + the 6 leaf pages to find all the bookmarks for the 1,200 matching index rows on `qty`)
+ 4	pages (1 root page + 1 intermediate page + 2 leaf pages to find all the bookmarks for the 212 matching index rows on `ord_date`)
= 12	pages

Figure 35.13 shows an example of the execution plan for an index join. Notice that it does not include the bookmark lookup present in the index intersection execution plan (refer to Figure 35.8).

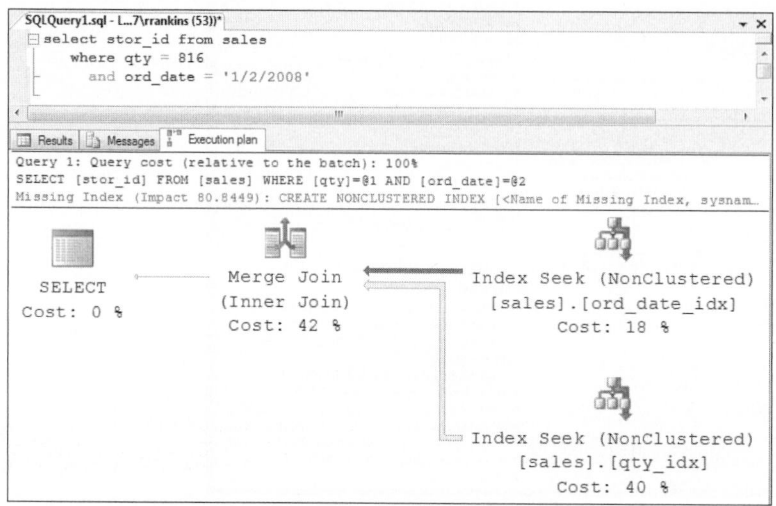

FIGURE 35.13 An execution plan for an index join.

Optimizing with Indexed Views

In SQL Server 2008, when you create a unique clustered index on a view, the result set for the view is materialized and stored in the database with the same structure as a table that has a clustered index. Changes made to the data in the underlying tables of the view are automatically reflected in the view the same way as changes to a table are reflected in its indexes. In the Developer and Enterprise Editions of SQL Server 2008, the Query Optimizer automatically considers using the index on the view to speed up access for queries run directly against the view. The Query Optimizer in the Developer and Enterprise Editions of SQL Server 2008 also looks at and considers using the indexed view for searches against the underlying base table, when appropriate.

NOTE

Although indexed views can be created in any edition of SQL Server 2008, they are considered for query optimization only in the Developer and Enterprise Editions of SQL Server 2008. In other editions of SQL Server 2008, indexed views are not used to optimize the query unless the view is explicitly referenced in the query and the `NOEXPAND` Query Optimizer hint is specified. For example, to force the Query Optimizer to consider using the `sales_Qty_Rollup` indexed view in the Standard Edition of SQL Server 2008, you execute the query as follows:

```
select * from sales_Qty_Rollup WITH (NOEXPAND)
    where stor_id between 'B914' and 'B999'
```

The NOEXPAND hint is allowed only in SELECT statements, and the indexed view must be referenced directly in the query. (Only the Developer and Enterprise Editions consider using an indexed view that is not directly referenced in the query.) As always, you should use Query Optimizer hints with care. When the NOEXPAND hint is included in the query, the Query Optimizer cannot consider other alternatives for optimizing the query.

Consider the following example, which creates an indexed view on the sales table, containing stor_id and sum(qty) grouped by stor_id:

```
set quoted_identifier on
go

if object_id('sales_Qty_Rollup') is not null
    drop view sales_Qty_Rollup
go
create view sales_qty_rollup
with schemabinding
as
   select stor_id, sum(qty) as total_qty, count_big(*) as id
      from dbo.sales
      group by stor_id
go

create unique clustered index idx1 on sales_Qty_Rollup (stor_id)
go
```

The creation of the clustered index on the view essentially creates a clustered table in the database with the three columns stor_id, total_qty, and id. As you would expect, the following query on the view itself uses a clustered index seek on the view to retrieve the result rows from the view instead of having to scan or search the sales table itself:

```
select * from sales_Qty_Rollup
   where stor_id between 'B914' and 'B999'
```

However, the following query on the sales table uses the indexed view sales_qty_rollup to retrieve the result set as well:

```
select stor_id,  sum(qty)
   from sales
   where stor_id between 'B914' and 'B999'
   group by stor_id
```

Essentially, the Query Optimizer recognizes the indexed view essentially as another index on the `sales` table that covers the query. The execution plan in Figure 35.14 shows the indexed view being searched in place of the table.

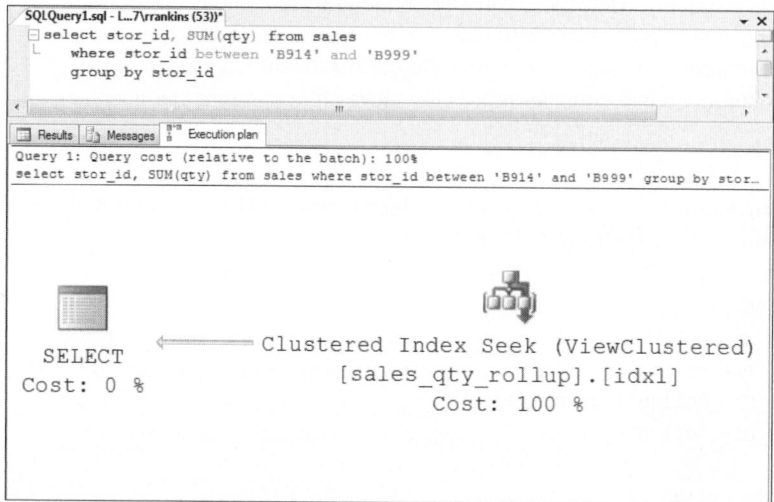

FIGURE 35.14 An execution plan showing an indexed view being searched to satisfy a query on a base table.

NOTE

In addition to the seven required `SET` options that need to be set appropriately when the indexed view is created, they must also be set the same way for a session to be able to use the indexed view in queries. The required `SET` option settings are as follows:

```
SET ARITHABORT ON
SET CONCAT_NULL_YIELDS_NULL ON
SET QUOTED_IDENTIFIER ON
SET ANSI_NULLS ON
SET ANSI_PADDING ON
SET ANSI_WARNINGS ON
SET NUMERIC_ROUNDABORT OFF
```

If these `SET` options are not set appropriately for the session running a query that could make use of an indexed view, the indexed view is not used, and the table is searched instead.

For more information on indexed views, see Chapters 27, "Creating and Managing Views," and 34, "Data Structures, Indexes, and Performance."

You might find rare situations when using the indexed view in the Enterprise, Datacenter, or Developer Editions of SQL Server 2008 leads to poor query performance, and you might want to avoid having the Query Optimizer use the indexed view. To force the Query Optimizer to ignore the indexed view(s) and optimize the query using the indexes on the underlying base tables, you specify the EXPAND VIEWS query option, as follows:

```
select * from sales_Qty_Rollup
   where stor_id between 'B914' and 'B999'
   OPTION (EXPAND VIEWS)
```

Optimizing with Filtered Indexes

SQL Server 2008 introduces the capability to define filtered indexes and statistics on a subset of rows rather than on the entire rowset in a table. This is done by specifying simple predicates in the index create statement to restrict the set of rows included in the index. Filtered statistics help solve a common problem in estimating the number of matching rows when the estimates become skewed due to a large number of duplicate values (or NULLs) in an index or due to data correlation between columns. Filtered indexes provide query optimization benefits when you frequently query specific subsets of your data rows.

If a filtered index exists on a table, the optimizer recognizes when a search predicate is compatible with the filtered index; it considers using the filtered index to optimize the query if the selectivity is good.

For example, the titles table in the bigpubs2008 database contains a large percentage of rows where ytd_sales is 0. A nonclustered index typically doesn't help for searches in which ytd_sales is 0 because the selectivity isn't adequate, and a table scan would be performed. An advantageous approach then is to create a filtered index on ytd_sales without including the values of 0 to reduce the size of the index and make it more efficient.

For example, first create an unfiltered index on ytd_sales on the titles table:

```
create index ytd_sales_unfiltered on titles (ytd_sales)
```

Then, execute the following two queries:

```
select * from titles where ytd_sales = 0
select * from titles where ytd_sales = 10
```

As you can see by the query plan displayed in Figure 35.15, a query where ytd_sales = 0 still uses a table scan instead of the index because the selectivity is poor, whereas it uses the index for ytd_sales = 10.

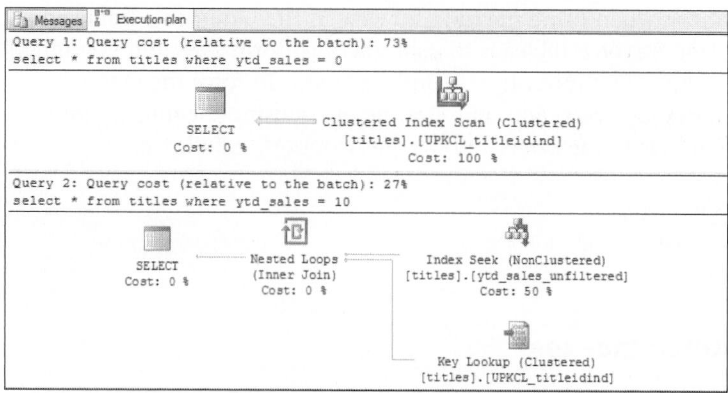

FIGURE 35.15 An execution plan showing index not being used due to poor selectivity.

Now, drop the unfiltered index and re-create a filtered index that excludes values of `0`:

```
drop index titles.ytd_sales_unfiltered
go
create index ytd_sales_filtered on titles (ytd_sales)
where ytd_sales <> 0
```

Re-run the queries and examine the query plan again. Figure 35.16 shows that the query where `ytd_sales = 0` still uses a table scan as before, but the query where `ytd_sales = 10` is able to use the filtered index.

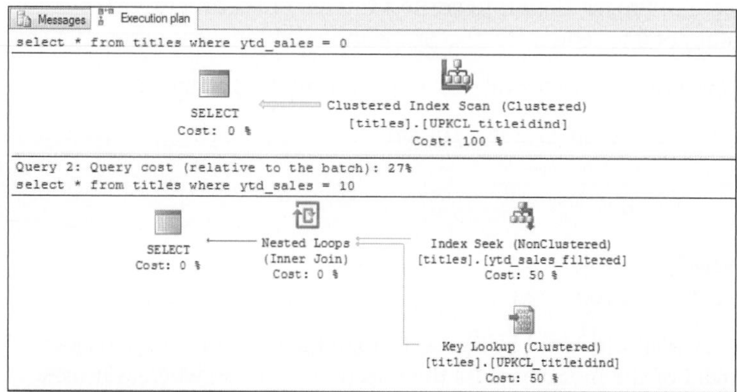

FIGURE 35.16 An execution plan showing the filtered index being used.

In this case, it may be beneficial to define the filtered index instead of a normal index on `ytd_sales` because the filtered index will require less space and be a more efficient index by excluding all the rows with ytd_sales values of `0`, especially if the majority of the queries against the table are searching for `ytd_sales` values that are nonzero.

NOTE

For more information on creating and using filtered indexes, see Chapter 34.

Join Selection

The job of the Query Optimizer is incredibly complex. The Query Optimizer can consider literally thousands of options when determining the optimal execution plan. The statistics are simply one of the tools that the Query Optimizer can use to help in the decision-making process.

In addition to examining the statistics to determine the most efficient access paths for SARGs and join clauses, the Query Optimizer must consider the optimum order in which to access the tables, the appropriate join algorithms to use, the appropriate sorting algorithms, and many other details too numerous to list here. The goal of the Query Optimizer during join selection is to determine the most efficient join strategy.

As mentioned at the beginning of this chapter, delving into the detailed specifics of the various join strategies and their costing algorithms is beyond the scope of a single chapter on optimization. In addition, some of these costing algorithms are proprietary and not publicly available. The goal of this section, then, is to present an overview of the most common query processing algorithms that the Query Optimizer uses to determine an efficient execution plan.

Join Processing Strategies

If you are familiar with SQL, you are probably very familiar with using joins between tables in creating SQL queries. A join occurs any time the SQL Server Query Optimizer has to compare two inputs to determine an output. The join can occur between one table and another table, between an index and a table, or between an index and another index (as described previously, in the section "Index Intersection").

The SQL Server Query Optimizer uses three primary types of join strategies when it must compare two inputs: nested loops joins, merge joins, and hash joins. The Query Optimizer must consider each one of these algorithms to determine the most appropriate and efficient algorithm for a given situation.

Each of the three supported join algorithms could be used for any join operation. The Query Optimizer examines all the possible alternatives, assigns costs to each, and chooses the least expensive join algorithm for a given situation. Merge and hash joins often greatly improve the query processing performance for very large data tables and data warehouses.

Nested Loops Joins

The nested loops join algorithm is by far the simplest of the three join algorithms. The nested loops join uses one input as the "outer" loop and the other input as the "inner" loop. As you might expect, SQL Server processes the outer input one row at a time. For each row in the outer input, the inner input is searched for matching rows.

Figure 35.17 illustrates a query that uses a nested loops join.

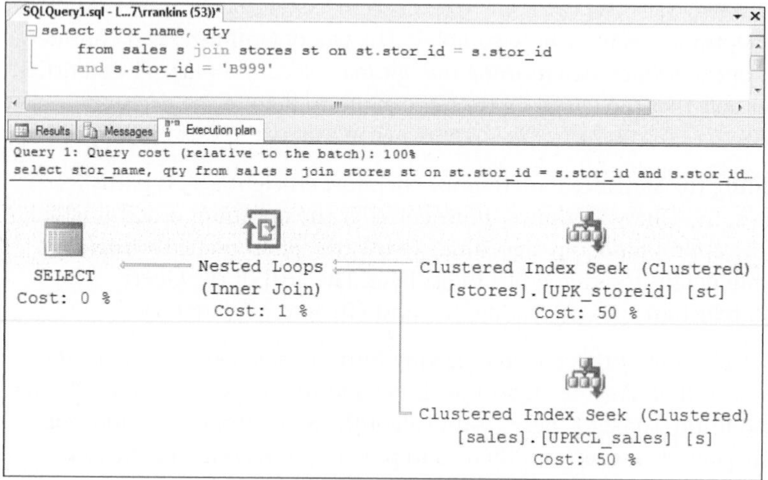

FIGURE 35.17 An execution plan for a nested loops join.

Note that in the graphical execution plan, the outer loop is represented as the top input table, and the inner loop is represented as the bottom input table. In most instances, the Query Optimizer chooses the input table with the fewest number of qualifying rows to be the outer loop to limit the number of iterative lookups against the inner table. However, the Query Optimizer may choose the input table with the greater number of qualifying rows as the outer table if the I/O cost of searching that table first and then performing the iterative loops on the other table is lower than the alternative.

The nested loop join is the easiest join strategy for which to estimate the I/O cost. The cost of the nested loop join is calculated as follows:

	Number of I/Os to read in outer input
+	Number of matching rows × Number of I/Os per lookup on inner input
=	Total logical I/O cost for query

The Query Optimizer evaluates the I/O costs for the various possible join orders as well as the various possible access paths and indexes available to determine the most efficient join order. The nested loops join is efficient for queries that typically affect only a small number of rows. As the number of rows in the outer loop increases, the effectiveness of the nested loops join strategy diminishes. The reason is the increased number of logical I/Os required as the number of qualifying rows increases.

Also, if there are no useful indexes on the join columns, the nested loop join is not an efficient join strategy because it requires a table scan lookup on the inner table for each row in the outer table. Lacking useful indexes for the join, the Query Optimizer often opts to perform a merge or hash join.

Merge Joins

The merge join algorithm is much more effective than the nested loops join for dealing with large data volumes or when the lack of limiting SARGs or useful indexes on SARGs leads to a table scan of one or both tables involved in the join. A merge join works by retrieving one row from each input and comparing them, matching on the join column(s). Figure 35.18 illustrates a query that uses a merge join.

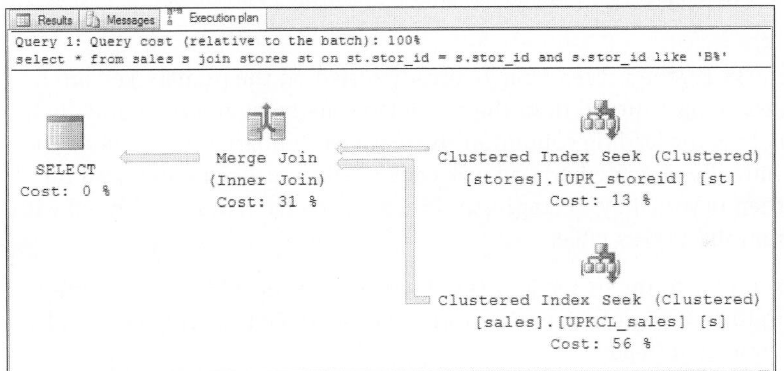

FIGURE 35.18 An execution plan for a merge join.

A merge join requires that both inputs be sorted on the merge columns—that is, the columns specified in the equality (`ON`) clauses of the join predicate. A merge join does not work if both inputs are not sorted. In the query shown in Figure 35.18, both tables have a clustered index on `stor_id`, so the merge column (`stor_id`) is already sorted for each table. If the merge columns are not already sorted, a separate sort operation may be required before the merge join operation. When the input is sorted, the merge join operation retrieves a row from each input and compares them, returning the rows if they are equal. If the inputs are not equal, the lower-value row is discarded, and another row is obtained from that input. This process repeats until all rows have been processed.

Usually, the Query Optimizer chooses a merge join strategy, as in this example, when the data volume is large and both columns are contained in an existing presorted index, such as a clustered primary key. If either of the inputs is not already sorted, the Query Optimizer has to perform an explicit sort before the join. Figure 35.19 shows an example of a sort being performed before the merge join is performed.

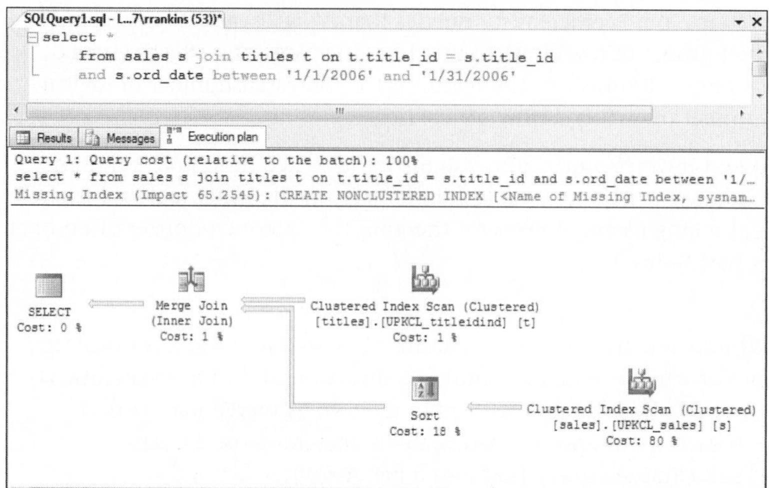

FIGURE 35.19 An execution plan for a merge join with a preliminary sort step.

In the query in Figure 35.19, the `titles` table is already sorted on the primary key on `title_id`, but the rows being returned from the `sales` table are being returned initially in `stor_id` order. (`stor_id` is the leading column in the clustered primary key on sales.) The resulting rows matching the search criteria on `ord_date` via the clustered index scan on the `sales` table are then re-sorted by `title_id`, and then the merge join is performed with the rows retrieved from the `titles` table.

If one or more of the inputs to the merge join is not sorted, and the additional sorting causes the merge join to be too expensive to perform, the Query Optimizer may consider using the hash join strategy instead.

Hash Joins

The final—and most complicated—join algorithm is the hash join. The hash join is an effective join strategy for dealing with large data volumes where the inputs might not be sorted and when no useful indexes exist on your tables for performing the join. Figure 35.20 illustrates a query that uses a hash join.

The basic hash join algorithm involves separating the two inputs into a build input and probe input. The Query Optimizer usually attempts to assign the smaller input as the build input. The hash join scans the build input and creates a hash table. Each row from the build input is inserted into the hash table based on a hash key value, which is computed. The probe input is then scanned, one row at a time. A hash key value is computed for each row in the probe, and the hash table is scanned for matches. The hash join is an effective join strategy when dealing with large data volumes and unsorted data inputs.

In a hash join, the keys that are common between the two tables are hashed into a hash bucket, using the same hash function. This bucket usually starts out in memory and then moves to disk, as needed. The type of hashing that occurs depends on the amount of

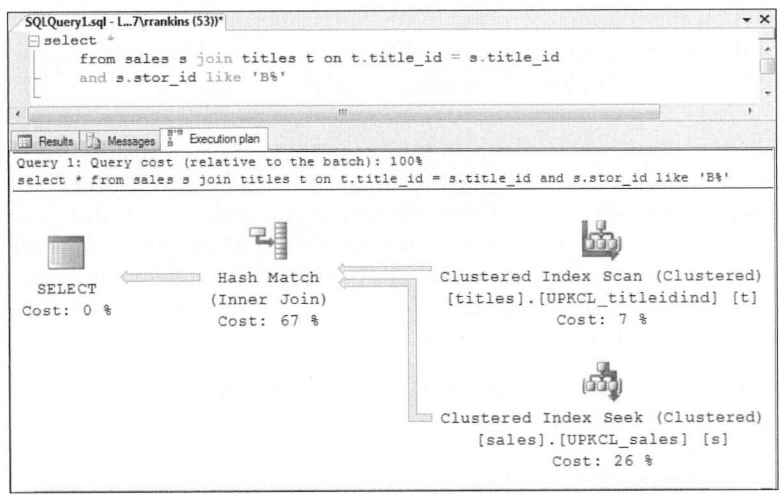

FIGURE 35.20 An execution plan for a hash join.

memory required. Hashing is commonly used for inner and outer joins, intersections, unions, and differences. The Query Optimizer often uses hashing for intermediate processing.

Pseudocode for a simple hash join might look like this:

```
create an empty hash table
for each row in the input table
    read the row
    hash the key value
    insert the hashed key into the hash bucket
for each row in the larger table
    read the row
    hash the key value
    if hashed key value is found in the hash bucket
        output hash key and both row identifiers
drop the hash table
```

Although hashing is useful when no useful indexes are on the tables for a join, the Query Optimizer still might not choose it as the join strategy if it has a high cost in terms of memory required. If the entire hash table doesn't fit in memory, SQL Server has to split both the build and probe inputs into partitions, each containing a different set of hash keys, and write those partitions out to disk. As each partition is needed, it is brought into memory. This increases the amount of I/O and general processing time for the query.

If you want to use the hashing strategy efficiently, it is best if the smaller input is used as the build input. If, during execution, SQL Server discovers that the build input is actually larger than the probe input, it might switch the roles of the build and probe input midstream. The Query Optimizer usually doesn't have a problem determining which input is smaller if the statistics on the columns involved in the query are current. Column-level statistics can also help the Query Optimizer determine the estimated number of rows matching a SARG, even if no actual index will be used.

Grace Hash Joins If the two inputs are too large to fit into memory for a normal hash join, SQL Server might use a modified method, called the *grace hash join*. This method partitions the smaller input table (also referred to as the *build input*) into a number of buckets. The total number of buckets is calculated by determining the bucket size that will fit in memory and dividing it into the number of rows in the table. The larger table (also referred to as the *probe input*) is then also partitioned into the same number of buckets. Each bucket from each input can then be read into memory and the matches made.

A *hybrid join* is a join method that uses elements of both a simple in-memory hash and grace hash.

NOTE

Hash and merge join strategies can be applied only when the join is an equijoin—that is, when the join condition compares columns from two inputs with the equality (=) operator. If the join is not based on an equality, (for example, using a `BETWEEN` clause), using nested loop joins is the only strategy that can be employed.

Determining the Optimal Join Order

In addition to determining the best join strategies, the Query Optimizer also evaluates and determines the optimal join order that would result in the most efficient query plan. In the query's execution plan, you might find that the order of the tables in the execution plan is a different order than specified in the query. Regardless of the join strategy used, the Query Optimizer needs to determine which table is the outer input and which is the inner input to the join strategy chosen. For example, consider the following query:

```
select a.au_lname, t.title, pubdate
   from authors a
   join titleauthor ta on a.au_id = ta.au_id
   join titles t on ta.title_id = t.title_id
```

In addition to the possible access paths and join strategies available, the server can consider the following pool of possible join orders:

```
authors → titleauthor → titles

titles → titleauthor → authors

titleauthor → titles → authors
```

```
titleauthor → authors → titles
authors → titles → titleauthor
titles → authors → titleauthor
```

For each of these join orders, the Query Optimizer considers the various access paths available for each table as well as the different join strategies available. For example, the Query Optimizer could consider the following possible join strategies:

- Perform a table scan on the `authors` table and for each row perform an index seek against the `auidind` index on `titleauthor` to find the matching rows by `au_id`. And for each matching row in `titleauthor`, perform an index seek against the primary key of the `titles` table to find the matching rows in titles by `title_id`.
- Perform a table scan on the titles table and for each row perform an index seek against the `titleidind` index on `titleauthor` to find the matching rows by `title_id`. And for each matching row in `titleauthor`, perform an index seek against the primary key of the `authors` table to find the matching rows in authors by `au_id`.
- Perform an index scan of the `titleidind` of the `titleauthor` table and use a hash join to match it with a clustered index scan of the `titles` table. And for each of the qualifying rows from this hash join, perform another hash join with an index scan of the `aunmind` index of the `authors` table.

35

NOTE

If you run this query yourself and examine the query plan, you'll likely see that the third alternative is the one chosen by the Query Optimizer. Index scans are performed on the `authors` and `titleauthor` tables because the nonclustered indexes on those tables cover the join query. That is, the nonclustered indexes contain all the columns necessary to satisfy the join conditions as well as the requested result columns.

These are just three of the possibilities. There are many more options for the Query Optimizer to consider as execution plans for processing this join. For example, for each of the three options, there are other indexes to consider, and there are other possible join orders and strategies to consider as well.

As you can see, there can be a large number of execution plan options for the Query Optimizer to consider for processing a join, and this example is a relatively simple three-table join. The number of options increases exponentially as the number of tables involved in the query increases. The "Execution Plan Selection" section, later in this chapter, describes how the Query Optimizer deals with the large number of possible execution plan options.

Subquery Processing

SQL Server optimizes subqueries differently, depending on how they are written. For example, SQL Server attempts to flatten some subqueries into joins when possible, to allow the Query Optimizer to select the optimal join order rather than be forced to process the query inside-out. The following sections examine the different types of subqueries and how SQL Server optimizes them.

IN, ANY, and EXISTS Subqueries

In SQL Server, any query that contains a subquery introduced with an `IN`, `= ANY`, or `EXISTS` predicate is usually flattened into an existence join unless the outer query also contains an `OR` clause or unless the subquery is correlated or contains one or more aggregates.

An existence join is optimized the same way as a regular join, with one exception: With an existence join, as soon as a matching row is found in the inner table, the value `TRUE` is returned, and SQL Server stops looking for further matches for that row in the outer table and moves on to the next row. A normal join would continue processing to find all matching rows. The following query provides an example of an existence join and a quantified predicate subquery that will be converted to an existence join:

```
select pub_name from publishers p
   where exists (select 1 from titles t
                 where type = 'business'
                 and t.pub_id = p.pub_id)

select pub_name from publishers
   where pub_id in (select pub_id from titles
                    where type = 'business')
```

Figure 35.21 shows an example of the execution plan for both of these queries. You can see that the query plans are the same, providing proof that the quantified predicate subquery is being flattened into an existence join.

Materialized Subqueries

If an outer query is comparing a column against the result of a subquery using any of the comparison operators (=, >, <, >=, <=, !=), and the subquery is not correlated, the results of the subquery are often resolved—that is, materialized—before comparison against the outer table column. For these types of queries, the Query Optimizer processes the query inside-out.

An example of this type of query is as follows:

```
select title from titles
   where ytd_sales = (select max(qty) from sales)
```

In this example, the subquery is resolved first to find the maximum `qty` value from the `sales` table to compare against `ytd_sales` in the outer query. Figure 35.22 shows an example of a query plan for this materialized subquery.

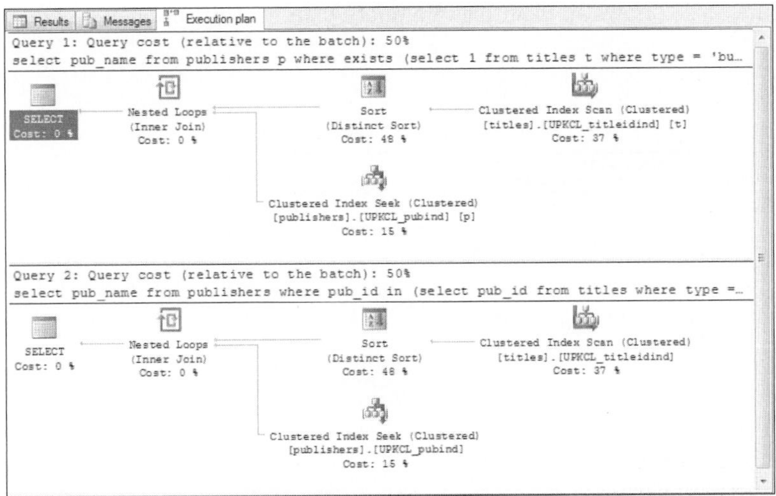

FIGURE 35.21 An execution plan for an existence join and a quantified predicate subquery flattened into an existence join.

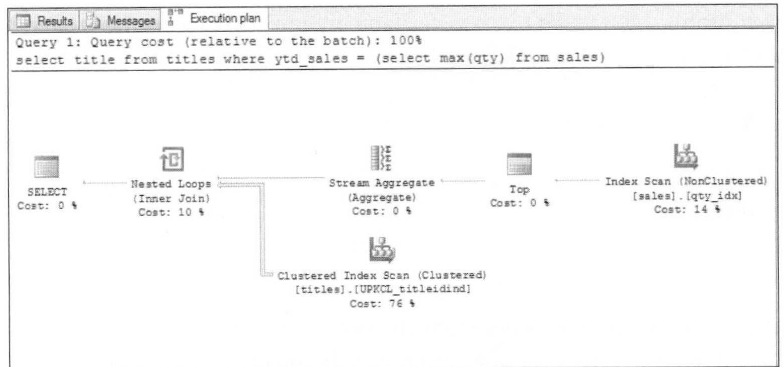

FIGURE 35.22 An execution plan for a materialized subquery.

The following query is an interesting case in which the subquery is not materialized first:

```
select title from titles
   where ytd_sales = (select max(ytd_sales) from titles)
```

In this example, with no index on the `ytd_sales` column, the Query Optimizer recognizes that a table scan is required on the `titles` table to find the maximum `ytd_sales` value. Rather than run the subquery first using a table scan and then use the value returned to perform another lookup against the `titles` table, it simply scans the `titles` table and returns and sorts the `ytd_sales` value in descending order. It then simply returns the rows with the top matching values because these rows are the ones where the `ytd_sales` value is the maximum. Figure 35.23 shows an example of a query plan for this subquery processing strategy.

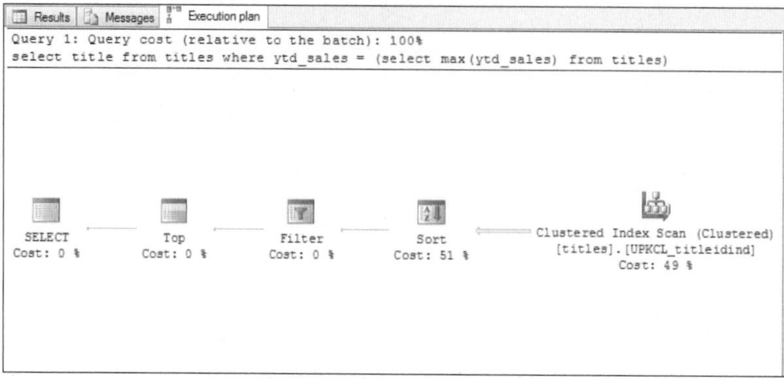

FIGURE 35.23 An execution plan for a subquery flattened into a table scan with sort.

Correlated Subqueries

A correlated subquery contains a reference to an outer table in a join clause in the subquery. Following is an example of a correlated subquery:

```
SELECT title_id, price
FROM titles
WHERE ytd_sales IN
    (SELECT qty
    FROM sales
    WHERE titles.title_id = sales.title_id)
```

Because correlated subqueries depend on values from the outer query for resolution, they cannot be processed independently. Instead, SQL Server usually processes correlated subqueries repeatedly, once for each qualifying outer row. Often, a correlated subquery looks like a nested loop join. A sample execution plan for the preceding correlated subquery example is shown in Figure 35.24. Notice that an inner join using a left semi join is performed. *Semi joins* are joins that return rows from one table based on the existence of related rows in the other table. A *left semi join* operation returns each row from the first (top or left) input when there is a matching row in the second (bottom or right) input. If the attributes are returned from the bottom (or right) table, it's referred to as a *right semi join*.

NOTE

The inverse of a semi join is an anti–semi join. An anti–semi join looks for rows in one table based on their nonexistence in the other, such as for a `NOT IN` or `NOT EXISTS` type subquery, or for some outer join queries.

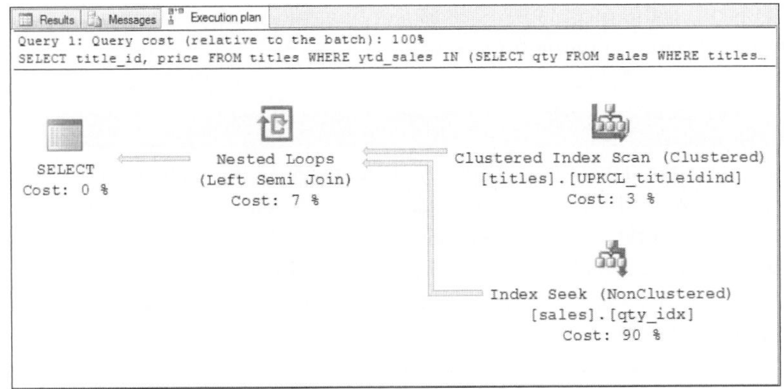

FIGURE 35.24 An execution plan for a correlated subquery.

However, if there is no useful index on the correlated columns to find the matching rows, the Query Optimizer may choose to perform a single search against each table separately and perform a hash join against the results.

Execution Plan Selection

At this point in the query optimization process, the Query Optimizer has examined the entire query and estimated the costs of all possible access paths for the SARGs and join clauses and also the various join orders and query-processing strategies. It now needs to choose which plan to pass on to SQL Server for execution.

For a single table query, choosing the best query plan typically involves choosing the access path and query processing strategy that results in the most efficient execution plan; usually, this is the plan that requires the fewest number of logical I/Os and typically requiring the least resources to process the query on that table. However, sometimes the Query Optimizer may choose a plan that returns rows faster to the user but with a greater, but reasonable, cost in resources (I/O plus CPU and memory). For example, processing a query in parallel (that is, using multiple CPUs simultaneously for the same query) typically requires more resources than processing it via a single CPU, but the query may complete much faster when processed in parallel. The Query Optimizer may choose to use such a parallel plan for execution if the load on the server is not adversely affected.

For a multitable query, choosing the best plan involves not only determining the cheapest access path and query processing strategy for each table individually but also determining the best access paths in conjunction with the optimal join strategy that results in the lowest estimated query cost, as discussed in the earlier section on join selection.

In addition, if any `UNION`, `ORDER BY`, `GROUP BY`, or `DISTINCT` clauses are present, the Query Optimizer chooses the most efficient method to process them.

For all its options, the overriding factor in selecting a plan is primarily the overall I/O cost. The Query Optimizer usually selects a query plan that results in the least amount of I/O processing because I/O is often the most expensive aspect of a query. After the plan is selected, it's passed to the Database Engine for execution.

NOTE

As you can see in examples throughout this chapter, you can examine the query plan chosen by the Query Optimizer with the graphical execution plan feature of SSMS. You can also display a text representation of the execution plan by enabling the `SHOWPLAN_TEXT`, `SHOWPLAN_ALL`, `SHOWPLAN_XML`, `STATISTICS PROFILE`, or `STATISTICS XML` option in a user session. How to interpret the output from these tools is covered in Chapter 36, "Query Analysis," along with a discussion of other tools available for examining the query plan selection process.

You also have the capability to influence or override the query plan selection process, using methods discussed later in this chapter, in the section "Managing the Optimizer."

The Query Optimizer can choose from many possible execution plans, especially when a large number of tables are involved in the query—and an even greater number of permutations of join strategies and index usage is possible. The number of permutations grows exponentially as the number of tables involved in the query grows. Some complex queries could potentially have millions of possible execution plans. In these cases, the Query Optimizer does not analyze all possible plan combinations. Instead, it tries to find an execution plan that has a cost reasonably close to the theoretical minimum.

Initially, SQL Server tries to determine whether only one viable plan for a query exists. This is called *trivial plan optimization*. For simple queries, this can save the Query Optimizer a lot of work. The idea behind trivial plan optimization is that cost-based optimization can be expensive to initialize and run. The Query Optimizer can try many possible variations in looking for the cheapest plan and the time required to find the optimal query plan could potentially be longer than the time required to execute the query itself. If the Query Optimizer can determine by investigating the query and the relevant metadata that there is only one viable plan for a query, it can avoid a lot of the work required to initialize and perform cost-based optimization.

An example of a trivial query plan is a single table `SELECT` statement with a SARG on a unique key or a `SELECT` on a table with no indexes or `GROUP BY` clause. Another example is an `INSERT` statement using a `VALUES` clause into a table that doesn't participate in indexed views: There is only one way to insert this record. For each of these examples, the query plans are fairly obvious plans that are typically very inexpensive, so the Query Optimizer generates the plan without trying to find something better. If the Query Optimizer tried to consider every possible plan, the optimization cost could actually exceed the query processing time, outweighing any benefit provided by well-optimized queries.

If a trivial plan is not available, the Query Optimizer next performs some query simplifications, usually syntactic transformations of the query itself, such as commutative properties and operations that can be rearranged. An example of simplification is evaluation of simple single-table SARG filters before processing the joins. While the filters are logically evaluated after the joins, evaluating the filters before the joins still produces the correct result and is more efficient because it removes unqualified rows before the join operation is performed, resulting in fewer iterations and, subsequently, fewer I/Os.

After any attempts at query simplification, the Query Optimizer begins a more thorough optimization process. To avoid just running through all the possibilities that would cause the optimization process to take a long time, it breaks up the optimization into three phases. After each phase, the Query Optimizer applies a set of rules to evaluate the cost of any resulting plan. If, according to these rules, the plan is cheap enough, it chooses and submits that plan for execution. If, according to the rules, no plan is cheap enough, the Query Optimizer continues on to the next phase, with its own set of (usually more complex) rules to apply. In the vast majority of cases, the Query Optimizer finds a viable execution plan in the preliminary phases.

The first phase of optimization, Phase 0, contains a limited set of rules and is applied to queries with at least four tables. As you've seen previously, join reordering alone generates many potential plan candidates, so the Query Optimizer uses a limited number of join orders in Phase 0 and considers using only the hash or nested-loop join strategies. If, at the end of this phase, the Query Optimizer finds a plan with an estimated cost below the threshold for Phase 0, the optimization ends. Phase 0 is also referred to as the *transaction processing phase* because the final query plans produced by Phase 0 are typically found in transaction processing applications.

The next phase is Phase 1, or quick plan optimization. This phase applies additional transformation rules and examines different possible join orders than were considered in Phase 0. If, at the end of Phase 1, the Query Optimizer finds a best plan with a cost less than the threshold for Phase 1, optimization ends and the best plan identified is returned.

Up to this point, the Query Optimizer has considered only nonparallel query plans. If more than one CPU is available to SQL Server and the cost of the least expensive plan produced by Phase 1 is greater than the Cost Threshold for Parallelism configuration setting, the Query Optimizer runs the Phase 1 optimization again, this time looking for the best parallel query plan. The costs of the nonparallel and parallel plans generated by Phase 1 are then compared and the Query Optimizer enters the last phase of optimization, Phase 2, for the cheaper of the two.

Phase 2 is also referred to as the full optimization phase. If the cost of the best nonparallel plan found so far is still below the parallelism threshold, or there is only a single CPU available, the full optimization phase continues using a brute-force method to find the best serial plan, checking additional combinations of indexes and processing strategies such as outer join reordering and automatic indexed view substitution for multitable views. In this phase, the Query Optimizer examines every possible execution plan and eventually chooses the cheapest one. The number of execution plans it considers during Phase 2 is restricted by a time limit. When the designated time limit for Phase 2 is reached, the Query Optimizer returns the cheapest plan found thus far.

Eventually, an execution plan is determined to be the most efficient. After this is determined, the execution plan is passed on to the SQL Server query processor to be executed.

Query Plan Caching

SQL Server 2008 has a pool of memory used to store both execution plans and data. The amount of memory allocated to execution plans or data changes dynamically, depending on the needs of the system. The portion of memory used to store execution plans is often referred to as the *plan cache*.

The first time a cacheable query is submitted to SQL Server, the query plan is compiled and put into the plan cache. Query plans are read-only re-entrant structures shared by multiple users. At most, there are two instances of a query plan at any time in the plan cache: a serial execution plan and parallel query execution plan. The same parallel execution plan is used for all parallel executions, regardless of the degree of parallelism.

When you execute subsequent SQL statements, the Database Engine first checks to see whether an existing execution plan for the same SQL statement already resides in the plan cache. If it finds one, SQL Server attempts to reuse the matching execution plan, thereby saving the overhead of having to recompile an execution plan for each ad hoc SQL statement issued. If no matching execution plan is found, SQL Server is forced to generate a new execution plan for the query.

The ability to reuse query plans for ad hoc queries in addition to caching query plans for stored procedures can help improve the performance for complex queries that are executed frequently because SQL Server can avoid having to compile a query plan every time it's executed if a matching query plan is found in memory first.

Query Plan Reuse

Query plan reuse for stored procedures is pretty straightforward. The whole idea behind stored procedures is to promote plan reuse. For stored procedures and triggers, plan reuse is simply based on the procedure or trigger name. The first time a stored procedure is executed, the query plan is generated based on the initial parameters. On subsequent executions, SQL Server checks the plan cache to see whether a query plan exists for a procedure with the same name, and if one is found, it simply substitutes the new parameter values into the existing query plan for execution.

Another method that promotes query plan reuse is using the `sp_executesql` stored procedure for executing dynamic SQL statements. When using `sp_executesql`, typically you specify a dynamic query with explicitly identified parameters for SARGs. Here's an example:

```
sp_executesql N'select t.title, pubdate from bigpubs2008.dbo.authors a
join bigpubs2008.dbo.titleauthor ta on a.au_id = ta.au_id
join bigpubs2008.dbo.titles t on ta.title_id = t.title_id
where a.au_lname = @name', N'@name varchar(30)', 'Smith'
```

When the same query is executed again via `sp_executesql`, SQL Server reuses the existing query plan (if it is still in the plan cache) and simply substitutes the different parameter values.

Although SQL Server can also match query plans for ad hoc SQL statements, there are some limitations as to when a plan can be reused. For SQL Server to match SQL statements to existing execution plans in the plan cache for ad hoc queries, all object references in the query must be qualified with at least the schema name, and fully qualified object names (database plus schema name) provide increased likelihood of plan reuse. In addition, plan caching for ad hoc queries requires an exact text match between the queries. The text match is both case sensitive and space sensitive. For example, the following two queries are logically identical, but because they are not textually identical, they would not share the same query plan:

```
select a.au_lname, t.title, pubdate
from authors a
join titleauthor ta on a.au_id = ta.au_id
join titles t on ta.title_id = t.title_id

select a.au_lname,
       t.title,
       pubdate
from authors a
join titleauthor ta on a.au_id = ta.au_id
join titles t on ta.title_id = t.title_id
```

Another factor that can prevent query plan reuse by matching queries is differences in certain SET options, database options, or configuration options in effect for the user session when the query is invoked. For example, a query might optimize differently for one session if the ANSI_NULLS option is turned on than it would if it were turned off. The following list of SET options must match for a query plan to be reused by a session:

- ANSI_PADDING
- FORCEPLAN
- CONCAT_NULL_YIELDS_NULL
- ANSI_WARNINGS
- ANSI_NULLS
- QUOTED_IDENTIFIER
- ANSI_NULL_DFLT_ON
- ANSI_NULL_DFLT_OFF

If any one of these setting values does not match the setting options for a cached plan, the session generates a new query plan. Likewise, if the session is using a different language or DATEFORMAT setting than that used by a cached plan, it needs to generate a new execution plan. As you can see, sometimes fairly subtle differences can prevent plan reuse.

Simple Query Parameterization

For certain simple queries executed without parameters, SQL Server 2008 automatically replaces constant literal values with parameters and compiles the query plan. This simple parameterization of the query plan increases the possibility of query plan matching for subsequent queries. If a subsequent query differs in only the values of the constants, it matches with the parameterized query plan and reuses the query plan.

Consider this query:

```
SELECT * FROM AdventureWorks.Production.Product WHERE ProductSubcategoryID = 1
```

The search value `1` at the end of the statement can be treated like a parameter. When the query plan is generated for this query, the Query Optimizer replaces the search value with a placeholder parameter, such as `@p1`. This process is called *simple parameterization*. Using the method of simple parameterization, SQL Server 2008 recognizes that following statement is identical to the first except for the search value of `9` and would generate essentially the same execution plan:

```
SELECT * FROM AdventureWorks.Production.Product WHERE ProductSubcategoryID = 9
```

This query will reuse the query plan generated by the first query.

NOTE

You can determine whether simple parameterization has been used for a query by examining the query plan information for the query. If the query plan information contains such placeholders as `@p1` and `@p2` in the search predicates when literal values were specified in the actual query, you know simple parameterization has been applied for the query. You can see an example of this in Figure 35.13 where parameters were substituted in the query plan for the search arguments against `qty` and `ord_date`.

Query Plan Aging

A query plan is saved in cache along with a cost factor that reflects the cost of actually creating the plan when compiling the query. For ad hoc query plans, SQL Server sets its cost to `0`, which indicates that the plan can be removed from the plan cache immediately if space is needed for other plans. For other query plans, such as for a stored procedure, the query plan cost is a measure of the amount of resources required to produce it. This cost is calculated in "number of ticks." The maximum plan cost is 31. The plan cost is determined as follows:

Every 2 I/Os required by the plan = 1 tick (with a maximum of 19 ticks)

Every 2 context switches in the plan = 1 tick (with a maximum of 8 ticks)

Every 16 pages (128KB) of memory required for the plan = 1 tick (with a maximum of 4 ticks)

All reusable query plans remain in cache until space is needed in the plan cache for a new plan. When space is needed, SQL Server removes the oldest unused execution plan from the plan cache that has the lowest plan cost.

As plans age in cache, the plan cost is not decremented until the size of the plan cache reaches 50% of the buffer pool size. When this occurs, the next access of the plan cache results in the plan cost for all query plans being decremented by 1. As plans reside in the plan cache over a period of time and are not reused, they eventually reach a plan cache cost of 0 and thus become eligible to be removed from cache the next time plan cache space is needed. However, when a query plan is reused, its plan cost is reset back to its initial value. This helps ensure that frequently accessed query plans remain in the plan cache.

Recompiling Query Plans

Certain changes in a database over time can cause existing execution plans to become either inefficient or invalid, based on the new state of the database. SQL Server detects the changes that invalidate an execution plan and marks the plan as not valid. A new plan is then automatically recompiled the next time the query that uses that query plan is invoked. Most query plan recompilations are required either for statement correctness or to obtain potentially faster query execution plans. The types of conditions that can invalidate a query plan include the following:

- Modifications made to the definition of a table or view referenced by the query using `ALTER TABLE` and `ALTER VIEW`
- Changes made to any indexes used by the execution plan
- Updates to the statistics used by the execution plan via either the `UPDATE STATISTICS` command or automatically
- Dropping of an index or indexed view used by the execution plan
- Execution of `sp_recompile` on a table referenced by the query plan
- Large numbers of changes to keys (generated by `INSERT` or `DELETE` statements from other users that modify a table referenced by the query)
- Adding or dropping a trigger on a table
- When the number of rows in the inserted or deleted tables grows significantly within a trigger defined on a table referenced in the query plan
- Execution of a stored procedure with the `WITH RECOMPILE` option specified

To avoid the unnecessary recompilation of statements that do not require it, SQL Server 2008 performs statement-level recompilation: only the statement inside the batch or stored procedure that requires recompilation is recompiled. Statement-level recompilation helps improve query performance because, in most cases, only a small number of statements within a batch or stored procedure cause recompilations and their associated penalties, in terms of CPU time and locks. These penalties are therefore avoided for the other statements in the batch that do not have to be recompiled.

Forcing Query Plan Recompiles

If you suspect that a query plan that is being reused is not appropriate for the current execution of a query, you can also manually force the query plan to be recompiled for the query. This capability can be especially useful for parameterized queries. Query parameterization provides a performance benefit by minimizing compilation overhead, but a parameterized query often provides less specific costing information to the Query Optimizer and can result in the creation of a more general plan, which can be less efficient than a more specific plan created for a specific set of literal values.

If the initial parameterized query plan generated for the query was not based on a representative set of parameters, or if you are invoking an instance of the query with a nonrepresentative set of search values, you might find it necessary to force the Query Optimizer to generate a new query plan. You can force query recompilation for a specific execution of a query by specifying the `RECOMPILE` query hint. For more information on specifying the `RECOMPILE` query hint, see the "Managing the Optimizer" section, later in this chapter.

Monitoring the Plan Cache

You can view and get information about the query plans currently in plan cache memory by using some of the DMVs available in SQL Server 2008. Following are some of the useful ones related to monitoring the plan cache:

- **`sys.dm_exec_cached_plans`**—Returns general information about the query execution plans currently in the plan cache.
- **`sys.dm_exec_query_stats`**—Returns aggregate performance statistics for cached query plans.
- **`sys.dm_exec_sql_text`**—Returns the text of the SQL statement for a specified plan handle.
- **`sys.dm_exec_cached_plan_dependent_objects`**—Returns one row for every dependent object of a compiled plan.
- **`sys.dm_exec_plan_attributes`**—Returns one row per attribute associated with the plan for a specified plan handle.

sys.dm_exec_cached_plans

The `sys.dm_exec_cached_plans` DMV provides information on all the execution plans currently in the plan cache. Because the cache can have a large number of plans, you usually want to limit the results returned from `sys.dm_exec_cached_plans` by using a filter on the `cacheobjtype` column and also using the `TOP` clause. For example, the query shown in Listing 35.1 returns the top 10 compiled plans currently in the plan cache, sorted in descending order by the number of times the plan has been reused (`usecounts`).

LISTING 35.1 Returning the Top 10 Compiled Plans, by Usage Count

```
select top 10 objtype, usecounts, size_in_bytes, plan_handle
   from sys.dm_exec_cached_plans
   where cacheobjtype = 'Compiled Plan'
   order by usecounts desc
go

objtype   usecounts size_in_bytes plan_handle
--------- --------- ------------- -------------------------------------------------
Prepared  127       65536         0x06000100962E9C11B820A20700000000000000000000000
Adhoc     110       49152         0x06000100804AD300B8E02D0C00000000000000000000000
Adhoc     40        16384         0x060001006CC40F18B860D80A00000000000000000000000
Adhoc     26        8192          0x0600040023900901B820A10600000000000000000000000
Adhoc     26        8192          0x060004003E77102CB8E0A30600000000000000000000000
Proc      17        8192          0x05000400F578A275B8405F0700000000000000000000000
Adhoc     17        8192          0x06000400EBC44D2AB880A00600000000000000000000000
Adhoc     15        8192          0x060001001AF2320BB8801A0800000000000000000000000
Proc      12        212992        0x05000400744F1F67B8604F0E00000000000000000000000
Proc      12        49152         0x050004006A934A11B8C0550E00000000000000000000000
```

The types of plans in the plan cache are listed under the `cacheobjtype` column and can be any of the following:

- **`Compiled Plan`**—The actual compiled plan generated that can be shared by sessions running the same procedure or query.
- **`Compiled Plan Stub`**—A small, compiled plan stub generated when a batch is compiled for the first time and the Optimize for Ad Hoc Workloads option is enabled. It helps to relieve memory pressure by not allowing the plan cache to become filled with compiled plans that are not reused.
- **`Executable Plan`**—The actual execution plan and the environment settings for the session that ran the compiled plan. Caching the environment settings for an execution plan makes subsequent executions more efficient. Each concurrent execution of the same compiled plan will have its own executable plan. All executable plans are associated with a compiled plan having the same `plan_handle`, but not all compiled plans have an associated executable plan.
- **`Parse Tree`**—The internal parsed form of a query generated before compilation and optimization.
- **`CLR Compiled Func`**—Execution plan for a CLR-based function.
- **`CLR Compiled Proc`**—Execution plan for a CLR-based procedure.
- **`Extended proc`**—The cached information for an extended stored procedure.

35

The type of object or query for which a plan is cached is stored in the objtype column. This column can contain one of the following values:

- **Proc**—The cached plan is for a stored procedure or inline function.
- **Prepared**—The cached plan is for queries submitted using sp_executesql or for queries using the prepare and execute method.
- **Adhoc**—The cached plan is for queries that don't fall into any other category.
- **ReplProc**—The cached plan is for replication agents.
- **Trigger**—The cached plan is for a trigger.
- **View**—The cached plan is for a view or a noninline function. You typically see a parse tree only for a view or noninline function, not a compiled plan. The view or function typically does not have its own separate plan because it is expanded as part of another query.
- **UsrTab** or **SysTab**—The cached plan is for a user or system table that has computed columns. This is typically associated with a parse tree.
- **Default**, **Check**, or **Rule**—The cached plan is simply a parse tree for these types of objects because they are expanded as part of another query in which they are applied.

To determine how often a plan is being reused, you can examine the value in the usecounts columns. The usecounts value is incremented each time the cached plan is looked up and reused.

sys.dm_exec_sql_text

Overall, the information returned by sys.dm_exec_cached_plans is not overly useful unless you know what queries or stored procedures these plans refer to. You can view the SQL text of these query plans by writing a query that joins sys.dm_exec_cached_plans with the sys.dm_exec_sql_text DMV. For example, you can use the query shown in Listing 35.2 to return the SQL text for the top 10 largest ad hoc query plans currently in the plan cache.

LISTING 35.2 Returning the Top 10 Largest Ad Hoc Query Plans

```
select top 10 objtype, usecounts, size_in_bytes,  plan_handle,
       -- the following removes newline and carriage return from the sql text
       replace(replace( text, char(13), ' '), char(10), ' ') as sqltext
   from sys.dm_exec_cached_plans as p
   cross apply sys.dm_exec_sql_text (p.plan_handle)
   where cacheobjtype = 'Compiled Plan'
     and objtype = 'Adhoc'
   order by size_in_bytes desc, usecounts desc
```

sys.dm_exec_query_stats

The plan cache also keeps track of useful statistics about each cached plan, such as the amount of CPU or the number of reads and writes performed by the query plan since it was placed into the plan cache. This information can be examined using the sys.dm_exec_query_stats DMV, which returns statistics for each statement in a stored procedure or a SQL batch. To provide statistics for the procedure or batch as a whole, you need to summarize the data. Listing 35.3 provides a sample query that returns the I/O, CPU, and elapsed time statistics for the 10 most recently executed stored procedures.

LISTING 35.3 Returning Query Plan Stats for the 10 Most Recently Executed Procedures

```
select TOP 10 usecounts, size_in_bytes,
   max(last_execution_time) as last_execution_time,
   sum(total_logical_reads) as total_logical_reads,
   sum(total_physical_reads) as total_physical_reads,
   sum(total_worker_time/1000) as total_CPU_time,
   sum(total_elapsed_time/1000) as total_elapsed_time,
   replace(substring (text,
                      patindex('%create procedure%', text),
                      datalength(text)),
           'create procedure', '') as procname
   from sys.dm_exec_query_stats s
   join sys.dm_exec_cached_plans p on s.plan_handle = p.plan_handle
   CROSS APPLY sys.dm_exec_sql_text(p.plan_handle) as st
   where p.objtype = 'Proc' and p.cacheobjtype = 'Compiled Plan'
   group by usecounts, size_in_bytes, text
   order by max(last_execution_time) desc
```

Table 35.1 describes some of the most useful columns returned by the sys.dm_exec_query_stats DMV.

TABLE 35.1 Description of Columns for **sys.dm_exec_query_stats**

Column Name	Description
statement_start_offset	The starting position of the query that the row describes within the text of its batch or stored procedure, indicated in bytes, beginning with 0.
statement_end_offset	The ending position of the query that the row describes within the text of its batch or stored proc. A value of -1 indicates the end of the batch.
plan_generation_num	The number of times the plan has been recompiled while it has remained in the cache.

TABLE 35.1 Description of Columns for **sys.dm_exec_query_stats**

Column Name	Description
plan_handle	A pointer to the plan. This value can be passed to the dm_exec_query_plan dynamic management function.
creation_time	The time the plan was compiled.
last_execution_time	The last time the plan was executed.
execution_count	The number of times the plan has been executed since it was last compiled.
total_worker_time	The total amount of CPU time, in microseconds, consumed by executions of this plan for the statement.
last_worker_time	The CPU time, in microseconds, consumed the last time the plan was executed.
min_worker_time	The minimum CPU time, in microseconds, this plan has ever consumed during a single execution.
max_worker_time	The maximum CPU time, in microseconds, this plan has ever consumed during a single execution.
total_physical_reads	The total number of physical reads performed by executions of this plan since it was compiled.
last_physical_reads	The number of physical reads performed the last time the plan was executed.
min_physical_reads	The minimum number of physical reads this plan has ever performed during a single execution.
max_physical_reads	The maximum number of physical reads this plan has ever performed during a single execution.
total_logical_writes	The total number of logical writes performed by executions of this plan since it was compiled.
last_logical_writes	The number of logical writes performed the last time the plan was executed.
min_logical_writes	The minimum number of logical writes this plan has ever performed during a single execution.
max_logical_writes	The maximum number of logical writes this plan has ever performed during a single execution.
total_logical_reads	The total number of logical reads performed by executions of this plan since it was compiled.
last_logical_reads	The number of logical reads performed the last time the plan was executed.

TABLE 35.1 Description of Columns for **sys.dm_exec_query_stats**

Column Name	Description
min_logical_reads	The minimum number of logical reads this plan has ever performed during a single execution.
max_logical_reads	The maximum number of logical reads this plan has ever performed during a single execution.
total_elapsed_time	The total elapsed time, in microseconds, for completed executions of this plan.
last_elapsed_time	The elapsed time, in microseconds, for the most recently completed execution of this plan.
min_elapsed_time	The minimum elapsed time, in microseconds, for any completed execution of this plan.
max_elapsed_time	The maximum elapsed time, in microseconds, for any completed execution of this plan.
query_hash	The binary hash value calculated on the query and used to identify queries with similar logic.
query_plan_hash	The binary hash value calculated on the query execution plan and used to identify similar query execution plans.

The query_hash and query_plan_hash values are new for SQL Server 2008. You can use these values to determine the aggregate resource usage for queries that differ only by literal values or with similar execution plans. You can use these values to write queries that you can use to help determine the aggregate resource usage for similar queries and similar query execution plans. For example, Listing 35.4 provides a query to find the query_hash and query_plan_hash values for queries that select from the titles table searching by ytd_sales. Looking at the results, you can see that even with different search arguments, each of the matching queries generates the same query hash value, but they have different query plan hash values for queries that use different query plans.

LISTING 35.4 Returning Query and Query Plan Hash Values for a Query

```
SELECT convert(varchar(41), substring(st.text, 1, 42)) AS 'Query Text',
        qs.query_hash AS 'Query Hash',
        qs.query_plan_hash as 'Query Plan Hash'
FROM sys.dm_exec_query_stats qs
CROSS APPLY sys.dm_exec_sql_text (qs.sql_handle) st
    WHERE st.text like 'SELECT * from titles where ytd_sales%'
go
```

```
Query Text                                  Query Hash         Query Plan Hash
-------------------------------------------------------------------------------
select * from titles where ytd_sales = 0  0x9AB21AC5889FE2D0 0x8D6DE6D258BABB2B
select * from titles where ytd_sales = 0  0x9AB21AC5889FE2D0 0x8D6DE6D258BABB2B
select * from titles where ytd_sales = 99 0x9AB21AC5889FE2D0 0xE889B5D23D917DFD
select * from titles where ytd_sales = 10 0x9AB21AC5889FE2D0 0xE889B5D23D917DFD
select * from titles where ytd_sales = 0  0x9AB21AC5889FE2D0 0x8D6DE6D258BABB2B
select * from titles where ytd_sales = 0  0x9AB21AC5889FE2D0 0xE889B5D23D917DFD
```

This query hash or query plan hash value can be used in a query to aggregate performance statistics for like queries. For example, the following query returns the average processing time and logical reads for the same queries that were returned in Listing 35.2:

```
SELECT
 SUM(total_worker_time) / SUM(execution_count)/1000. AS "Avg CPU Time(ms)",
 SUM(total_logical_reads) / SUM(execution_count) AS "Avg Reads"
FROM
sys.dm_exec_query_stats
where query_hash = 0x9AB21AC5889FE2D0
go

Avg CPU Time(ms)                        Avg Reads
--------------------------------------- --------------------
164.092000                              7
```

Listing 35.5 provides a sample query using the query hash value to return information about the top 25 queries ranked by average processing time.

LISTING 35.5 Returning Top 25 Queries Using Query Hash

```
SELECT TOP 25 query_stats.query_hash AS "Query Hash",
    SUM(query_stats.total_worker_time) / SUM(query_stats.execution_count) AS
 "Avg CPU Time",
    MIN(query_stats.statement_text) AS "Statement Text"
FROM
    (SELECT QS.*,
    SUBSTRING(ST.text, (QS.statement_start_offset/2) + 1,
    ((CASE statement_end_offset
        WHEN -1 THEN DATALENGTH(ST.text)
        ELSE QS.statement_end_offset END
            - QS.statement_start_offset)/2) + 1) AS statement_text
     FROM sys.dm_exec_query_stats AS QS
     CROSS APPLY sys.dm_exec_sql_text(QS.sql_handle) as ST) as query_stats
GROUP BY query_stats.query_hash
```

```
ORDER BY 2 DESC;
GO
```

sys.dm_exec_plan_attributes

If you want to get information about specific attributes of a specific query plan, you use sys.dm_exec_plan_attributes. This DMV takes a plan_handle as an input parameter (see Listing 35.1 for an example of a query that you can use to retrieve a query's plan handle) and returns one row for each attribute associated with the query plan. These attributes include information such as the ID of the database context the query plan was generated in, the ID of the user who generated the query plan, session SET options in effect at the time the plan was generated, and so on. Many of these attributes are used as part of the cache lookup key for the plan (indicated by the value 1 in the is_cache_key_column). Following is an example of the output for sys.dm_exec_plan_attributes:

```
select convert(varchar(30), attribute) as attribute,
       convert(varchar(12), value) as value,
       is_cache_key
FROM
sys.dm_exec_plan_attributes (0x06000400EBC44D2AB880A0060000000000000000000000000)
where is_cache_key = 1
go

attribute                      value        is_cache_key
--------------------------------------------------------
set_options                    187          1
objectid                       709739755    1
dbid                           4            1
dbid_execute                   0            1
user_id                        -2           1
language_id                    0            1
date_format                    1            1
date_first                     7            1
compat_level                   100          1
status                         0            1
required_cursor_options        0            1
acceptable_cursor_options      0            1
merge_action_type              0            1
is_replication_specific        0            1
optional_spid                  0            1
optional_clr_trigger_dbid      0            1
optional_clr_trigger_objid     0            1
```

35

Note the attributes flagged as cache keys for the plan. If one of these properties does not match the state of the current user session, the plan cannot be reused for that session, and a new plan must be compiled and stored in the plan cache. If you see multiple plans in cache for what appears to be the same query, you can determine the key differences between them by comparing the columns associated with the plan's cache keys to see where the differences lie.

TIP

If SQL Server has been running for a while, with a lot of activity, the number of plans in the plan cache can become quite large, resulting in a large number of rows being returned by the plan cache DMVs. To run your own tests to determine which query plans get cached and when specific query plans are reused, you should clear out the cache occasionally. You can use the `DBCC FREEPROCCACHE` command to clear all cached plans from memory. If you want to clear only the cached plans for objects or queries in a specific database, you execute the following command:

```
DBCC FLUSHPROCINDB (dbid)
```

Keep in mind that you should run these commands only in a test environment. Running these commands in production servers could impact the performance of the currently running applications.

Other Query Processing Strategies

In addition to the optimization strategies covered so far, SQL Server also has some additional strategies it can apply for special types of queries. These strategies are used to help further reduce the cost of executing various types of queries.

Predicate Transitivity

You might be familiar with the transitive property from algebra. The transitive property simply states that if A=B and B=C, then A=C. SQL Server supports the transitive property in its query predicates. Predicate transitivity enables SQL Server to infer a join equality from two given equalities. Consider the following example:

```
SELECT *
   FROM table1 t1
   join table2 t2 on t1.column1 = t2.column1
   join table3 t3 on t2.column1 = t3.column1
```

Using the principle of predicate transitivity, SQL Server is able to infer that `t1.column1` is equal to `t3.column1`. This capability provides the Query Optimizer with another join strategy to consider when optimizing this query. This might result in a much cheaper execution plan.

The transitive property can also be applied to SARGs used on join columns. Consider the following query:

```
select *
   from sales s
   join stores st on s.stor_id = st.stor_id
   and s.stor_id = 'B199'
```

Again, using transitive closure, it follows that `st.stor_id` is also equal to `'B199'`. SQL Server recognizes this and can compare the search value against the statistics on both tables to more accurately estimate the number of matching rows from each table.

Group by Optimization

One way SQL Server can process `GROUP BY` results is to retrieve the matching detailed data rows into a worktable and then sort the rows and calculate the aggregates on the groups formed. In SQL Server 2008, the Query Optimizer also may choose to use hashing to organize the data into groups and then compute the aggregates.

The hash aggregation strategy uses the same basic method for grouping and calculating aggregates as for a hash join. At the point where the probe input row is checked to determine whether it already exists in the hash bucket, the aggregate is computed if a hash match is found. The following pseudocode summarizes the hash aggregation strategy:

```
create a hash table
for each row in the input table
    read the row
    hash the key value
    search the hash table for matches
    if match found
        aggregate the value into the old record
    else
        insert the hashed key into the hash bucket
scan and output the hash table contents
drop the hash table
```

For some join queries that contain `GROUP BY` clauses, SQL Server might perform the grouping operation before processing the join. This could reduce the size of the input table to the join and lower the overall cost of executing the query.

NOTE

One important point to keep in mind is that regardless of the `GROUP BY` strategy employed, the rows are not guaranteed to be returned in sorted order by the grouping column(s) as they were in earlier releases. If the results must be returned in a specific sort order, you need to use the `ORDER BY` clause with `GROUP BY` to ensure ordered results. You might want to get into the habit of doing this regularly.

Queries with DISTINCT

When the `DISTINCT` clause is specified in a query, SQL Server can eliminate duplicate rows by the sorting the result set in a worktable to identify and remove the duplicates, similar to how a worktable is used for `GROUP BY` queries. In SQL Server 2008, the Query Optimizer can also employ a hashing strategy similar to that used for `GROUP BY` to return only the distinct rows before the final result set is determined.

In addition, if the Query Optimizer can determine at compile time that there will be no possibility of duplicate rows in the result set (for example, each row contains the table's primary key), the strategies for removing duplicate rows are skipped altogether.

Queries with UNION

When you specify `UNION` in a query, SQL Server merges the result sets, applying one of the merge or concatenation operators with sorting strategies to remove any duplicate rows. Figure 35.25 shows an example similar to the `OR` strategy where the rows are concatenated and then sorted to remove any duplicates.

If you specify `UNION ALL` in a query, SQL Server simply appends the result sets together. No intermediate sorting or merge step is needed to remove duplicates. Figure 35.26 shows the same query as in Figure 35.25, except that a `UNION ALL` is specified.

When you know that you do not need to worry about duplicate rows in a `UNION` result set, always specify `UNION ALL` to eliminate the extra overhead required for sorting.

When a `UNION` is used to merge large result sets together, SQL Server 2008 may opt to use a merge join or hash match operation to remove any duplicate rows. Figure 35.27 shows an example of a `UNION` query where the rows are concatenated, and then a hash match operation is used to remove any duplicates.

Parallel Query Processing

The query processor in SQL Server 2008 includes parallel query processing—an execution strategy that can improve the performance of complex queries on computers with more than one processor.

SQL Server inserts exchange operators into each parallel query to build and manage the query execution plan. The exchange operator is responsible for providing process management, data redistribution, and flow control. The exchange operators are displayed in the

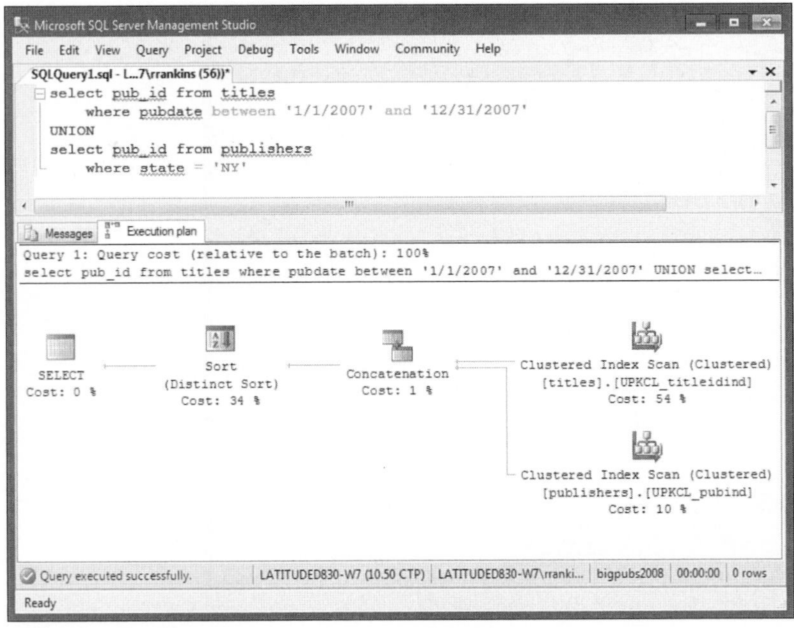

FIGURE 35.25 An execution plan for a **UNION** query.

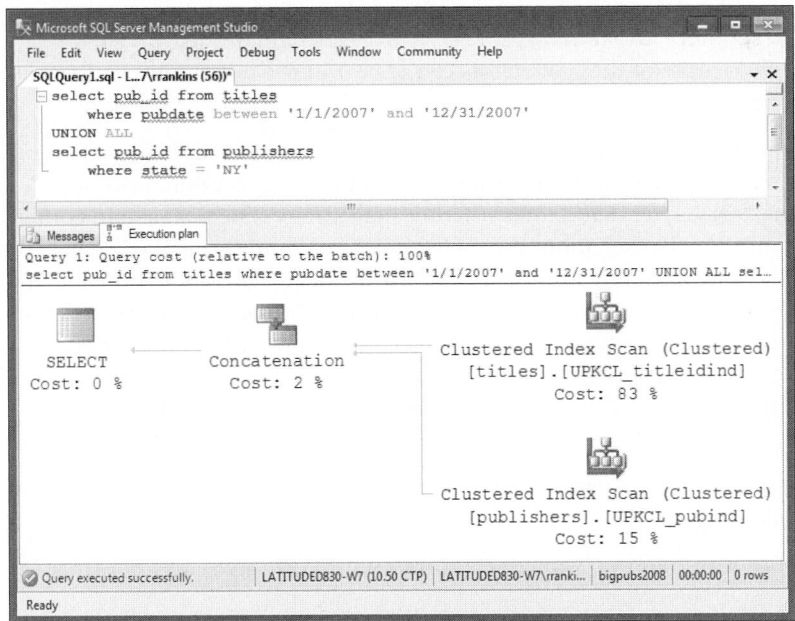

FIGURE 35.26 An execution plan for a **UNION ALL** query.

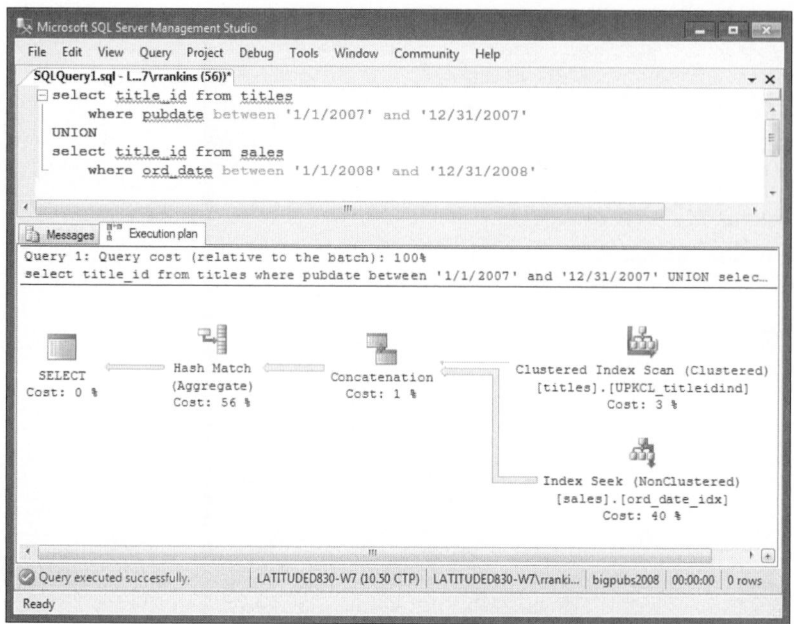

FIGURE 35.27 An execution plan for a **UNION** query, using a hash match to eliminate duplicate rows.

query plans as the `Distribute Streams`, `Repartition Streams`, and `Gather Streams` logical operators. One or more of these operators can appear in the execution plan output of a query plan for a parallel query.

Whereas a parallel query execution plan can use more than one thread, a serial execution plan, used by a nonparallel query, uses only a single thread for its execution. Prior to query execution time, SQL Server determines whether the current system state and configuration allow for parallel query execution. If parallel query execution is justified, SQL Server determines the optimal number of threads, called the degree of parallelism, and distributes the query workload execution across those threads. The parallel query uses the same number of threads until the query completes. SQL Server reexamines the optimal degree of parallelism each time a query execution plan is retrieved from the procedure cache. Individual instances of the same query could be assigned a different degree of parallelism.

SQL Server calculates the degree of parallelism for each instance of a parallel query execution by using the following criteria:

- How many processors does the computer running SQL Server have, and how many are allocated to SQL Server?

  If two or more processors are allocated to SQL Server, it can use parallel queries.

- What is the number of concurrent active users?

The degree of parallelism is inversely related to CPU usage. The Query Optimizer assigns a lower degree of parallelism if the CPUs are already busy.

- Is sufficient memory available for parallel query execution?

  Queries, like other processes, require resources to execute, particularly memory. Obviously, a parallel query demands more memory than a serial query. More importantly, as the degree of parallelism increases, so does the amount of memory required. The Query Optimizer carefully considers this in developing a query execution plan. The Query Optimizer could either adjust the degree of parallelism or use a serial plan to complete the query.

- What is the type of query being executed?

  Queries that use several CPU cycles justify using a parallel execution plan. Some examples are joins of large tables, substantial aggregations, and sorting of large result sets. The Query Optimizer determines whether to use a parallel or serial plan by checking the value of the cost threshold for parallelism.

- Are a sufficient number of rows processed in the given stream?

  If the Query Optimizer determines that the number of rows in a stream is too low, it does not execute a parallel plan. This prevents scenarios where the parallel execution costs exceed the benefits of executing a parallel plan.

Regardless of the answers to the previous questions, the Query Optimizer does not use a parallel execution plan for a query if any one of the following conditions is true:

- The serial execution cost of the query is not high enough to consider an alternative parallel execution plan.
- A serial execution plan exists that is estimated to be faster than any possible parallel execution plan for the particular query.
- The query contains scalar or relational operators that cannot be run in parallel.

Parallel Query Configuration Options

Two server configuration options—`maximum degree of parallelism` and `cost threshold for parallelism`—affect the consideration for a parallel query. Although doing so is not recommended, you can change the default settings for each. For single processor machines, these settings are ignored.

The `maximum degree of parallelism` option limits the number of threads to use in a parallel plan execution. The range of possible values is `0` to `32`. This value is configured to `0` by default, which allows the Query Optimizer to use up to the actual number of CPUs allocated to SQL Server. If you want to suppress parallel processing completely, set the value to `1`.

The `cost threshold for parallelism` option establishes a ceiling value the Query Optimizer uses to consider parallel query execution plans. If the calculated value to execute a serial plan is greater than the value set for the cost threshold for parallelism, a parallel plan is generated. This value is defined by the estimated time, in seconds, to execute the serial plan. The range of values for this setting is `0` to `32767`. The default value is `5`. If the maximum degree of parallelism is set to `1`, or if the computer has a single processor, the cost threshold for parallelism value is ignored.

You can modify the settings for the `maximum degree of parallelism` and the `cost threshold for parallelism` server configuration options either by using the `sp_configure` system stored procedure or through SSMS. To set the values for these options, use the `sp_configure` system stored procedure via SSMS or via SQLCMD, as follows:

```
USE master
go
exec sp_configure 'show advanced options', 1
GO
RECONFIGURE
GO
exec sp_configure 'max degree of parallelism', 2
exec sp_configure 'cost threshold for parallelism', 15
RECONFIGURE
GO
```

To set these configuration options via SSMS, right-click the SQL Server instance in the Object Explorer and then click Properties. In the Server Properties dialog, select the Advanced page. The parallelism options are near the bottom, as shown in Figure 35.28.

Identifying Parallel Queries

You can identify when a parallel execution plan is being chosen by displaying the graphical execution plan in SSMS. The graphical execution plan uses icons to represent the execution of specific statements and queries in SQL Server. The execution plan output for every parallel query has at least one of these three logical operators:

- **`Distribute Streams`**—Receives a single input stream of records and distributes multiple output streams. The contents and form of the record are unchanged. All records enter through the same single input stream and appear in one of the output streams, preserving the relative order.
- **`Gather Streams`**—Assembles multiple input streams of records and yields a single output stream. The relative order of the records, contents, and form is maintained.
- **`Repartition Streams`**—Accepts multiple input streams and produces multiple streams of records. The record contents and format are unchanged.

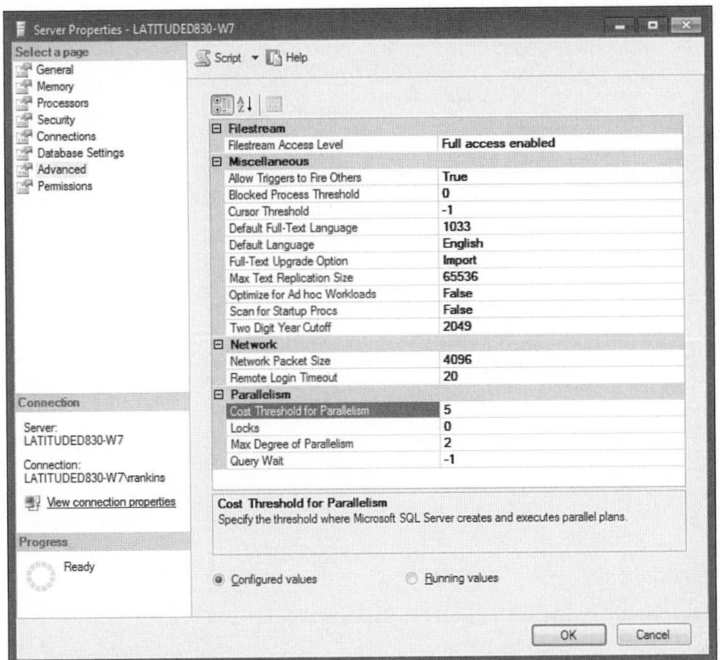

FIGURE 35.28 Setting SQL Server parallelism options.

Figure 35.29 shows a portion of a sample query plan that uses parallel query techniques—both repartition streams and gather streams.

Parallel Queries on Partitioned Objects

SQL Server 2008 provides improved query processing performance for partitioned objects when running parallel plans including changes in the way parallel and serial plans are represented, and enhancements to the partitioning information provided in both compile-time and runtime execution plans. SQL Server 2008 also automates and improves the thread partitioning strategy for parallel query execution plans on partitioned objects.

In addition to the performance improvements, query plan information has been improved as well in SQL Server 2008, now providing the following information related to partitioned objects:

- The partitions accessed by the query, available in runtime execution plans.
- An optional `Partitioned` attribute indicating that an operation, such as a `seek`, `scan`, `insert`, `update`, `merge`, or `delete`, is performed on a partitioned table.
- Summary information that provides a total count of the partitions accessed. This information is available only in runtime plans.

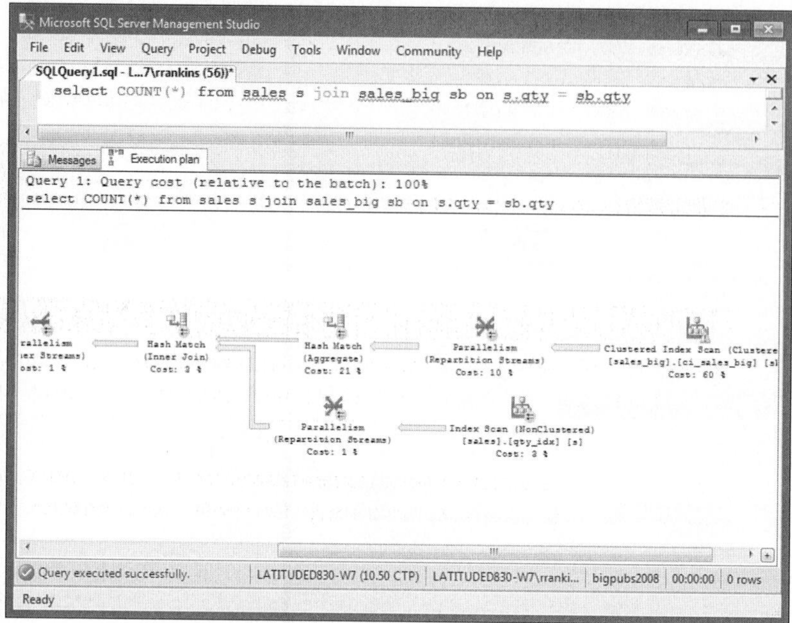

FIGURE 35.29 A graphical execution plan of a query using parallel query techniques.

Common Query Optimization Problems

So you've written a query and examined the query plan, and performance isn't what you expected. It might appear that SQL Server isn't choosing the appropriate query plan that you expect. Is something wrong with the query or with the Query Optimizer? Before delving into a detailed discussion about how to debug and analyze query plans (covered in detail in Chapter 36), the following sections look at some of the most common problems and SQL coding issues that can lead to poor query plan selection.

Out-of-Date or Insufficient Statistics

Admittedly, having out-of-date or unavailable statistics is not as big a problem as it was in SQL Server releases prior to 7.0. Back in those days, the first question asked when someone was complaining of poor performance was, "When did you last update statistics?" If the answer was "Huh?" we usually found the culprit.

With the Auto-Update Statistics and Auto-Create Statistics features in SQL Server 2008, this problem is not as prevalent as it used to be. If a query detects that statistics are out of date or missing, it causes them to be updated or created and then optimizes the query plan based on the new statistics.

NOTE

If statistics are missing or out of date, the first running query that detects this condition might run a bit more slowly as it updates or creates the statistics first, especially if the table is relatively large, and also if it has been configured for FULLSCAN when indexes are updated.

However, SQL Server 2008 provides the AUTO_UPDATE_STATISTICS_ASYNC database option. When this option is set to ON, queries do not wait for the statistics to be updated before compiling. Instead, the out-of-date statistics are put on a queue for updating by a worker thread in a background process, and the query and any other concurrent queries compile immediately, using the existing out-of-date statistics. Although there is no delay for updated statistics, the out-of-date statistics may cause the Query Optimizer to choose a less efficient query plan, but the response times are more predictable. Any queries invoked after the updated statistics are ready will use the updated statistics in generating a query plan. This may cause the recompilation of any cached plans that depend on the older statistics.

You should consider setting the AUTO_UPDATE_STATISTICS_ASYNC option to ON when any of your applications have experienced client request timeouts caused by queries waiting for updated statistics or when it is acceptable for your application to run queries with less efficient query plans due to outdated statistics so that you can maintain predictable query response times.

You could have insufficient statistics to properly optimize a query if the sample size used when the statistics were generated wasn't large enough. Depending on the nature of your data and size of the table, the statistics might not accurately reflect the actual data distribution and cardinality. If you suspect that this is the case, you can update statistics by specifying the FULLSCAN option or a larger sample size, so SQL Server examines more records to derive the statistics.

For more information on understanding and managing index statistics, see Chapter 34.

Poor Index Design

Poor index design is another reason—often a primary reason—why queries might not optimize as you expect them to. If no supporting indexes exist for a query, or if a query contains SARGs that cannot be optimized effectively to use the available indexes, SQL Server ends up performing either a table scan, an index scan, or another hash or merge join strategy that is less efficient. If this appears to be the problem, you need to reevaluate your indexing decisions or rewrite the query so it can take advantage of an available index. For more information on designing useful indexes, see Chapter 34.

Search Argument Problems

It's the curse of SQL that there are a number of ways to write a query and get the same result set. Some queries, however, might not be as efficient as others. A good understanding of the Query Optimizer can help you avoid writing search arguments that SQL Server can't optimize effectively. The following sections highlight some of the common "gotchas" encountered in SQL Server SARGs that can lead to poor or unexpected query performance.

Using Optimizable SARGs

As mentioned previously, in the section "Identifying Search Arguments," the Query Optimizer uses search arguments to help it narrow down the set of rows to evaluate. The search argument is in the form of a `WHERE` clause that equates a column to a constant. The SARGs that optimize most effectively are those that compare a column with a constant value that is not an expression or a variable, and with no operation performed against the column itself. The following is an example:

```
SELECT column1
   FROM table1
   WHERE column1 = 123
```

You should try to avoid using any negative logic in your SARGs (for example, `!=`, `<>`, `not in`) or performing operations on, or applying functions to, the columns in the SARG.

No SARGs

You need to watch out for queries in which the SARG might have been left out inadvertently, such as this:

```
select title_id from titles
```

A SQL query with no search argument (that is, no `WHERE` clause) always performs a table or clustered index scan unless a nonclustered index can be used to cover the query. (See Chapter 34 for a discussion of index covering.) If you don't want the query to affect the entire table, you need to be sure to specify a valid SARG that matches an index on the table to avoid table scans.

Unknown Values in WHERE Clauses

You need to watch out for expressions in which the search value in the SARG cannot be evaluated until runtime. In these expressions, often the search value is a local variable or subquery that can be materialized to a single value.

SQL Server treats these expressions as SARGs but can't use the statistics histogram to estimate the number of matching rows because it doesn't have a value to compare against the histogram values during query optimization. The values for the expressions aren't known until the query is actually executed. In this situation, the Query Optimizer uses the index density information. The Query Optimizer is generally able to better estimate the number of rows affected by a query when it can compare a known value against the statistics histogram than when it has to use the index density to estimate the average number of rows that match an unknown value. This is especially true if the data in a table isn't distributed evenly. When you can, you should try to avoid using constant expressions that can't be evaluated until runtime so that the statistics histogram can be used rather than the density value.

To avoid using constant expressions in `WHERE` clauses that can't be evaluated until runtime, you should consider putting the queries into stored procedures and passing in the constant expression as a parameter. Because the Query Optimizer evaluates the value of a parameter prior to optimization, SQL Server evaluates the expression prior to optimizing the stored procedure.

For best results when writing queries inside stored procedures, you should use stored procedure parameters rather than local variables in your SARGs whenever possible. This strategy allows the Query Optimizer to optimize the query by using the statistics histogram, comparing the parameter value against the statistics histogram to estimate the number of matching rows. If you use local variables as SARGs in stored procedures, the Query Optimizer is restricted to using index density, even if the local variable is assigned the value of a parameter.

Other types of constructs for which it is difficult for the Query Optimizer to accurately estimate the number of qualifying rows or the data distribution using the statistics histogram include aggregations in subqueries, scalar expressions, user-defined functions, and noninline table-valued functions.

Data Type Mismatches

Another common problem is data type mismatches. If you attempt to join tables on columns of different data types, the Query Optimizer might not be able to effectively use indexes to evaluate the join. This can result in a less efficient join strategy because SQL Server has to convert all values first before it can process the query. You should avoid this situation by maintaining data type consistency across the join key columns in your database.

Large Complex Queries

For complex queries with a large number of tables and join conditions, the number of possible execution plans can be enormous. The full optimization phase of the Query Optimizer has a time limit to restrict how long it spends analyzing all the possible query plans. There is no known general and effective shortcut to arrive at the optimal plan. To deal with such a large selection of plans, SQL Server 2008 implements a number of heuristics to deal with very large queries and attempt to come up with an efficient query plan within the time available. When it is not possible to analyze the entire set of plan alternatives and the heuristics are applied, it is not uncommon to encounter suboptimal query plans being chosen.

When is your query large enough to be a concern? Answering this question is difficult because the answer depends on the number of tables involved, the form of filter and join predicates, and the operations performed. If a query involves more than 12 tables, it is likely that the Query Optimizer is having to rely on heuristics and shortcuts to generate a query plan and may miss some optimal strategies.

In general, you get more optimal query plans if you can simplify your queries as much as possible.

Triggers

If you are using triggers on `INSERT`, `UPDATE`, or `DELETE`, it is possible that your triggers can cause performance problems. You might think that `INSERT`, `UPDATE`, or `DELETE` is performing poorly when actually it is the trigger that needs to be tuned. In addition, you might have triggers that fire other triggers. If you suspect that you are having performance problems with the triggers, you can monitor the SQL they are executing and the response time, as well as execution plans generated for statements within triggers using SQL Server Profiler. For more information on monitoring performance with SQL Server Profiler, see Chapter 6, "SQL Server Profiler." You can also see the query plans for statements executed in triggers by using SSMS if you enable the Include Actual Execution Plan option. For more information on using SSMS to view and analyze query plans, see Chapter 36.

Managing the Optimizer

Because the Query Optimizer might sometimes make poor decisions as to how to best process a query, you need to know how and when you may need to override the Query Optimizer and force SQL Server to process a query in a specific manner.

How often does SQL Server require manual intervention to execute a query optimally? Considering the overwhelming number of query types and circumstances in which those queries are run, SQL Server does a surprisingly effective job of query optimization in most instances. For all but the most grueling, complex query operations, experience has shown that SQL Server's Query Optimizer is quite clever—and very, very good at wringing the best performance out of any hardware platform. For this reason, you should treat the material covered in this chapter as a collection of techniques to be used only where other methods of getting optimal query performance have already failed.

Before indiscriminately applying the techniques discussed in this section, remember one very important point: use of these features can effectively hide serious fundamental design or coding flaws in your database, application, or queries. In fact, if you're tempted to use these features (with a few moderate exceptions), it should serve as an indicator that the problems might lie elsewhere in the application or queries.

If you are satisfied that no such flaws exist and that SQL Server is choosing the wrong plan to optimize your query, you can use the methods discussed in this section to override two of the three most important decisions the Query Optimizer makes:

- Choosing which index, if any, to resolve the query
- Choosing the join strategy to apply in a multitable query

The other decision made by the Query Optimizer is the locking strategy to apply. Using table hints to override locking strategies is discussed in Chapter 37, "Locking and Performance."

Throughout this and following sections, one point must remain clear in your mind: these options should be used only in *exception cases* to cope with specific optimization problems in specific queries in specific applications. There are therefore no standard or global rules to follow because the application of these features, by definition, means that normal SQL Server behavior isn't taking place.

The practical result of this idea is that you should test every option in *your* environment, with *your* data and *your* queries, and use the techniques and methods discussed in this chapter and the other performance-related chapters to optimize and fine-tune the performance of your queries. The fastest-performing query wins, so you shouldn't be afraid to experiment with different alternatives—but you shouldn't think that these statements and features are globally applicable or fit general categories of problems, either! There are, in fact, only three rules: *Test, test,* and *test*!

TIP

As a general rule, Query Optimizer and table hints should be used only as a last resort, when all other methods to get the Query Optimizer to generate a more efficient query plan have failed. Always try to find other ways to rewrite the queries to encourage the Query Optimizer to choose a better plan. This includes adding additional SARGs, substituting unknown values for known values in SARGS or trying to replace unknown values with known values, breaking up queries, converting subqueries to joins or joins to subqueries, and so on. Essentially, you should try other coding variations on the query itself to get the same result in a different way and try to see if one of the variations ends up using the more efficient query plan that you expect it to.

In reality, about the only time you should use these hints is when you're testing the performance of a query and want to see if the Query Optimizer is actually choosing the best execution plan. You can enable the various query analysis options, such as `STATISTICS PROFILE` and `STATISTICS IO`, and then see how the query plan and statistics change as you apply various hints to the query. You can examine the output to determine whether the I/O cost and/or runtime improves or gets worse if you force one index over another or if you force a specific join strategy or join order.

The problem with hard-coding table and Query Optimizer hints into application queries is that the hints prevent the Query Optimizer from modifying the query plan as the data in the tables changes over time. Also, if subsequent service packs or releases of SQL Server incorporate improved optimization algorithms or strategies, the queries with hard-coded hints will not be able to take advantage of them.

If you find that you must incorporate any of these hints to solve query performance problems, you should be sure to document which queries and stored procedures contain Query Optimizer and table hints. It's a good idea to periodically go back and test the queries to determine whether the hints are still appropriate. You might find that, over time, as the data values in the table change, the forced query plan generated because of the hints is no longer the most efficient query plan, and the Query Optimizer now generates a more efficient query plan on its own.

Optimizer Hints

You can specify three types of hints in a query to override the decisions made by the Query Optimizer:

- Table hints
- Join hints
- Query hints

The following sections examine and describe each type of table hint.

Forcing Index Selection with Table Hints

In addition to locking hints that can be specified for each table in a query, SQL Server 2008 allows you to provide table-level hints that enable you to specify the index SQL Server should use for accessing the table. The syntax for specifying an index hint is as follows:

```
SELECT column_list FROM tablename WITH (INDEX (indid | index_name [, ...]) )
```

This syntax allows you to specify multiple indexes. You can specify an index by name or by ID. It is recommended that you specify indexes by name as the IDs for nonclustered indexes can change if they are dropped and re-created in a different order than that in which they were created originally. You can specify an index ID of `0`, or the table name itself, to force a table scan.

When you specify multiple indexes in the hint list, all the indexes listed are used to retrieve the rows from the table, forcing an index intersection or index covering via an index join. If the collection of indexes listed does not cover the query, a regular row fetch is performed after all the indexed columns are retrieved.

To get a list of indexes on a table, you can use `sp_helpindex`. However, the stored procedure doesn't display the index ID. To get a list of all user-defined tables and the names of the indexes defined on them, you can execute a query against the `sys.indexes` catalog view similar to the one shown in Listing 35.6, which was run against the `bigpubs2008` database.

LISTING 35.6 Query Against **sys.indexes** Catalog View to Get Index Names and IDs

```
select 'Table name' = convert(char(20), object_name(object_id)),
       'Index name' = convert(char(30), name),
       'Index ID' = index_id,
       'Index Type' = convert(char(15), type_desc)
```

```
  from sys.indexes where object_id > 99 —only system tables have id less than 99
   and index_id between 1 and 254   /* do not include rows for text columns
                                    or tables without a clustered index*/
    /* do not include auto statistics */
   and is_hypothetical = 0
   and objectproperty(object_id, 'IsUserTable') = 1
order by 1, 3
go

Table name           Index name                     Index ID    Index Type
-------------------------------------------------------------------------------
authors              UPKCL_auidind                  1           CLUSTERED
authors              aunmind                        2           NONCLUSTERED
employee             employee_ind                   1           CLUSTERED
employee             PK_emp_id                      2           NONCLUSTERED
jobs                 PK__jobs__job_id__25319086     1           CLUSTERED
PARTS                PK__PARTS__09746778            1           CLUSTERED
PARTS                UQ__PARTS__0A688BB1            2           NONCLUSTERED
pub_info             UPKCL_pubinfo                  1           CLUSTERED
publishers           UPKCL_pubind                   1           CLUSTERED
roysched             titleidind                     2           NONCLUSTERED
sales                UPKCL_sales                    1           CLUSTERED
sales                titleidind                     2           NONCLUSTERED
sales                ord_date_idx                   7           NONCLUSTERED
sales                qty_idx                        8           NONCLUSTERED
sales_big            ci_sales_big                   1           CLUSTERED
sales_big            idx1                           2           NONCLUSTERED
sales_noclust        idx1                           2           NONCLUSTERED
sales_noclust        ord_date_idx                   3           NONCLUSTERED
sales_noclust        qty_idx                        4           NONCLUSTERED
stores               UPK_storeid                    1           CLUSTERED
stores               nc1_stores                     2           NONCLUSTERED
titleauthor          UPKCL_taind                    1           CLUSTERED
titleauthor          auidind                        2           NONCLUSTERED
titleauthor          titleidind                     3           NONCLUSTERED
titles               UPKCL_titleidind               1           CLUSTERED
titles               titleind                       2           NONCLUSTERED
titles               ytd_sales_filtered             11          NONCLUSTERED
```

SQL Server 2008 introduces the new FORCESEEK table hint, which provides an additional query optimization option. This hint specifies that the query optimizer use only an index seek operation as the access path to the data in the table or view referenced in the query rather than a index or table scan. If a query plan contains table or index scan operators, forcing an index seek operation may yield better query performance. This is especially true when inaccurate cardinality or cost estimations cause the optimizer to favor scan operations at plan compilation time.

Before using the FORCESEEK table hint, you should make sure that statistics on the table are current and accurate. Also, you should evaluate the query for items that can cause poor cardinality or cost estimates and remove these items if possible. For example, replace local variables with parameters or literals and limit the use of multistatement table-valued functions and table variables in the query.

Also, be aware that if you specify the FORCESEEK hint in addition to an index hint, the FORCESEEK hint can cause the optimizer to use an index other than one specified in the index hint.

Forcing Join Strategies with Join Hints

Join hints let you force the type of join that should be used between two tables. The join hints correspond with the three types of join strategies:

- LOOP
- MERGE
- HASH

You can specify join hints only when you use the ANSI-style join syntax—that is, when you actually use the keyword JOIN in the query. The hint is specified between the type of join and the keyword JOIN, which means you can't leave out the keyword INNER for an inner join. Thus, the syntax for the FROM clause when using join hints is as follows:

```
FROM table1 {INNER | OUTER} [LOOP | MERGE | HASH} JOIN table2
```

The following example forces SQL Server to use a hash join:

```
select st.stor_name, ord_date, qty
   from stores st INNER HASH JOIN sales s on st.stor_id = s.stor_id
   where st.stor_id between 'B100' and 'B599'
```

You can also specify a global join hint for all joins in a query by using a query processing hint.

Specifying Query Processing Hints

SQL Server 2008 enables you to specify additional query hints to control how your queries are optimized and processed. You specify query hints at the end of a query by using the OPTION keyword. There can be only one OPTION clause per query, but you can specify multiple hints in an OPTION clause, as shown in the following syntax:

```
OPTION (hint1 [, ...hintn])
```

Query hints are grouped into four categories: GROUP BY, UNION, join, and miscellaneous.

GROUP BY Hints GROUP BY hints specify how GROUP BY or COMPUTE operations should be performed. The following GROUP BY hints can be specified:

- **HASH GROUP**—This option forces the Query Optimizer to use a hashing function to perform the GROUP BY operation.
- **ORDER GROUP**—This option forces the Query Optimizer to use a sorting operation to perform the GROUP BY operation.

Only one GROUP BY hint can be specified at a time.

UNION Hints The UNION hints specify how UNION operations should be performed. The following UNION hints can be specified:

- **MERGE UNION**—This option forces the Query Optimizer to use a merge operation to perform the UNION operation.
- **HASH UNION**—This option forces the Query Optimizer to use a hash operation to perform the UNION operation.
- **CONCAT UNION**—This option forces the Query Optimizer to use the concatenation method to perform the UNION operation.

Only one UNION hint can be specified at a time, and it must come after the last query in the UNION. The following is an example of forcing concatenation for a UNION:

```
select stor_id from sales where stor_id like 'B19%'
UNION
select title_id from titles where title_id like 'C19%'
OPTION (CONCAT UNION)
```

Join Hints The join hint specified in the OPTION clause specifies that all join operations in the query are performed as the type of join specified in the hint. The join hints that can be specified in the query hints are the same as the table hints:

- LOOP JOIN
- MERGE JOIN
- HASH JOIN

If you also specify a join hint for a specific pair of tables, the table-level hints specified must be compatible with the query-level join hint.

Miscellaneous Hints The following miscellaneous hints can be used to override various query operations:

- **FORCE ORDER**—This option tells the Query Optimizer to join the tables in the order in which they are listed in the FROM clause and not to determine the optimal join order.

35

- **FAST *n***—This hint instructs SQL Server to optimize the query to return the first *n* rows as quickly as possible, even if the overall throughput is reduced. In other words, it improves response time at the expense of total query execution time. This option generally influences the Query Optimizer to retrieve data using a nonclustered index that matches the `ORDER BY` clause of a query instead of using a different access method that would require a sort operation first to return rows in the specified order. After *n* number of rows have been returned, the query continues execution normally to produce its full result set.
- **ROBUST PLAN**—This option forces the Query Optimizer to attempt a plan that works for the maximum potential row size, even if it means degrading performance. If you have very wide `VARCHAR` columns, some types of query plans might create intermediate tables, and if any of the internal operations need to store and process rows in these intermediate tables, some rows might exceed SQL Server's row size limit. If this happens, SQL Server generates an error during query execution. When the `ROBUST PLAN` hint is specified, the Query Optimizer does not consider any plans that might encounter this problem.
- **MAXDOP *number***—This hint overrides the server-level configuration setting for `max degree of parallelism` for the current query in which the hint is specified.
- **KEEP PLAN**—When this hint is specified, it forces the Query Optimizer to relax the estimated recompile threshold for a query. The estimated recompile threshold is the point at which a query is automatically recompiled when the estimated number of indexed column changes have been made to a table by updates, inserts, or deletes. Specifying `KEEP PLAN` ensures that the query is not recompiled as frequently when there are multiple updates to a table. This option is useful primarily for queries whose execution plan stays in memory, such as for stored procedures. You might want to specify this option for a stored procedure that does a lot of work with temporary tables, which can lead to frequent recompilations of the execution plan for the stored procedure.
- **KEEPFIXED PLAN**—This query hint tells the Query Optimizer not to recompile the query plan when there are changes in statistics or modifications to indexed columns used by the query via updates, deletes, or inserts. When this option is specified, the query is recompiled only if the schema of the underlying tables is changed or `sp_recompile` is executed against those tables.
- **EXPAND VIEWS**—This hint tells the Query Optimizer not to consider any indexed view as a substitute for any part of the query and to force the view to be expanded into its underlying query. This hint essentially prevents direct use of indexed views in the query plan.
- **MAXRECURSION *number***—This hint specifies the maximum number of recursions allowed for the common table expression query, where *`number`* is an integer between `0` and `32767`. When `0` is specified, no limit is applied. If this option is not specified, the default limit for the server is `100`. For more information on common table

expressions and recursive queries, see Chapter 43, "Transact-SQL Programming Guidelines, Tips, and Tricks."

- **`RECOMPILE`**—This hint forces SQL Server not to keep the execution plan generated for the query in the plan cache after it executes. This forces a new plan to be generated the next time the same or a similar query plan is executed. `RECOMPILE` is useful for queries with variable values that vary widely each time they are compiled and executed. This hint can be used for individual statements within a stored procedure in place of the global `WITH RECOMPILE` option when you want only a subset of queries inside the stored procedure to be recompiled rather than all of them.
- **`OPTIMIZE FOR ( @variable_name = literal_constant [ , ...n ] )`**—This hint instructs SQL Server to use a specified value to optimize the SARGs for a local variable that is otherwise unknown when the query is compiled and optimized. The value is used only during query optimization and not during query execution. `OPTIMIZE FOR` can help improve optimization by allowing the Query Optimizer to use the statistics histogram rather than index densities to estimate the rows that match the local variable, or can be used when you create plan guides.
- **`OPTIMIZE FOR UNKNOWN`**—This hint instructs the query optimizer to use statistical data instead of the initial values for local variables when the query is compiled and optimized, including parameters created with forced parameterization.
- **`TABLE HINT (object_name [ , table_hint [ [, ]...n ] ] )`**—New in SQL Server 2008, you can now specify table hints in the Query Hint `OPTION` clause. It is recommended that the `TABLE HINT` clause be used only in the context of a plan guide. For all other ad hoc queries, it is recommend that normal table hints be used.
- **`USE PLAN N'xml_plan'`**—This hint instructs SQL Server to use an existing query plan for a query as specified by the designated *`xml_plan`*. The `USE PLAN` query hint can be used for queries whose plans result in slow execution times but for which you know better plans exist.

NOTE

Optimizer hints are not always executed. For example, the Query Optimizer is likely to ignore a `HASH UNION` hint for a query using the `UNION ALL` statement. Because `UNION ALL` means to return all rows whether or not there are duplicates, you don't need to hash these values to determine uniqueness and remove duplicates, so the normal concatenation is likely to still take place.

Forced Parameterization

In SQL Server 2008, if a SQL statement is executed without parameters, the Query Optimizer parameterizes the statement internally to increase the possibility of matching it against an existing execution plan. This process is called *simple parameterization,* sometimes referred to as auto-parameterization. Simple parameterization is somewhat limited in that it can parameterize only a relatively small number of queries that match a small number of very simple and strictly defined query templates. For example, simple parameterization is not possible for queries that contain any of the following query elements:

- References to more than one table
- IN clauses or OR expressions
- UNION
- Any query hints
- DISTINCT
- TOP
- Subqueries
- GROUP BY
- Not equal (<> or !=) comparisons
- References to functions

SQL Server 2008 enables you to override the default simple parameterization behavior of SQL Server and provide parameterization for more complex queries by specifying that all SELECT, INSERT, UPDATE, and DELETE statements in a database be implicitly parameterized when they are compiled by the Query Optimizer. You enable this by setting the PARAMETERIZATION option to FORCED in the ALTER DATABASE statement:

```
ALTER DATABASE dbname SET PARAMETERIZATION {FORCED | SIMPLE}
```

Setting the PARAMETERIZATION option is an online operation that can be issued at any time and requires no database-level exclusive locks.

Forced parameterization may improve the performance of queries for certain databases by reducing the frequency of query compilations and recompilations. Essentially, forced parameterization provides the query plan reuse benefits of parameterized queries without requiring you to rewrite a single line of application code. The databases that may benefit from forced parameterization generally support OLTP-type applications that experience high volumes of concurrent queries, such as point-of-sale applications.

When the PARAMETERIZATION FORCED option is enabled, any literal value that appears in a SELECT, INSERT, UPDATE, or DELETE statement, submitted in any form, is converted to a parameter during query compilation. The exceptions are literals that appear in the following query constructs:

- INSERT...EXECUTE statements
- Statements inside the bodies of stored procedures, triggers, or user-defined functions. SQL Server already reuses query plans for these routines.
- Prepared statements that have already been parameterized by the client-side application.
- Statements inside a T-SQL cursor.

- Any statement run in a context where `ANSI_PADDING` or `ANSI_NULLS` is set to `OFF`.
- Statements that contain more than 2,097 literals eligible for parameterization.
- Statements that reference variables, such as `WHERE st.state = @state`.
- Statements that contain the `RECOMPILE` or `OPTIMIZE FOR` query hints.
- Statements that contain a `COMPUTE` clause.
- Statements that contain a `WHERE CURRENT OF` clause.

If an execution plan for a query is cached, you can determine whether the query is parameterized by referencing the `sql` column of the `sys.syscacheobjects` DMV. If a query is parameterized, the names and data types of parameters are listed in this column before the text of the submitted SQL (for example, `@1 tinyint`).

Guidelines for Using Forced Parameterization

Consider the following guidelines when determining whether to enable forced parameterization for a database:

- Forced parameterization, in effect, changes the literal constants in a query to parameters when the query is compiled, and thus, the Query Optimizer might choose suboptimal plans for queries. For example, the Query Optimizer may be less likely to match the query to an indexed view or an index on a computed column. It may also choose suboptimal plans for queries posed on partitioned tables and distributed partitioned views. Forced parameterization should not be used for environments that rely heavily on indexed views and indexes on computed columns.
- Enabling the `PARAMETERIZATION FORCED` option causes all query plans for the database to be flushed from the plan cache.
- Generally, the `PARAMETERIZATION FORCED` option should be used only by experienced database administrators after determining that doing this does not adversely affect performance.

If forced parameterization is enabled and you want to override this behavior and have simple parameterization used for a single query and any others that are syntactically equivalent but differ only in their parameter values, you can use plan guides and specify `PARAMETERIZATION SIMPLE` when creating the plan guides. Conversely, rather than enabling `PARAMETERIZATION FORCED` for an entire database, you can use plan guides and specify the `PARAMETERIZATION FORCED` query option only for a specific set of syntactically equivalent queries that you have determined would benefit from forced parameterization.

Using the USE PLAN Query Hint

The `USE PLAN` query hint in SQL Server 2008 can be used to encourage the Query Optimizer to use the specified XML query plan for processing the query. This option provides more control over influencing the execution of a query than is possible with the other available query hints, such as `FORCE ORDER`, `LOOP JOIN`, and `KEEP PLAN`. None of these options individually are powerful enough to influence the Query Optimizer to consistently choose a particular query plan, especially when the referenced table row counts, statistics, indexes, and other attributes of the environment change.

The `USE PLAN` query hint is specified in the `OPTION` clause, and you provide it with a query plan in XML format. Listing 35.7 provides an example of the `USE PLAN` hint being specified for a merge join for a simple query that consists of a join between two tables. (Note: For the sake of space, the full XML plan has been truncated.)

LISTING 35.7 Specifying the **USE PLAN** Query Option

```
select st.stor_name, s.ord_date
   from sales s join stores st on s.stor_id = st.stor_id
   WHERE st.state = 'NY'
OPTION (USE PLAN N'
<?xml version="1.0" encoding="utf-16"?>
<ShowPlanXML xmlns:xsi="http://www.w3.org/2001/XMLSchema-instance"
 xmlns:xsd="http://www.w3.org/2001/XMLSchema" Version="1.1"
 Build="10.50.1352.12" xmlns="http://schemas.microsoft.com/
 sqlserver/2004/07/showplan">
  <BatchSequence>
    <Batch>
      <Statements>
        <StmtSimple StatementCompId="1" StatementEstRows="10710.8"
 StatementId="1" StatementOptmLevel="FULL" StatementSubTreeCost="1.71032"
 StatementText="select st.stor_name, s.ord_date&#xD;&#xA;   from sales s join
 stores st on s.stor_id = st.stor_id&#xD;&#xA;   WHERE st.state =
 ''NY''&#xD;&#xA;" StatementType="SELECT" QueryHash="0x35DE42B697A8BAAF
 " QueryPlanHash="0x9F4AE50605763B05">
          <StatementSetOptions ANSI_NULLS="true" ANSI_PADDING="true"
 ANSI_WARNINGS="true" ARITHABORT="true" CONCAT_NULL_YIELDS_NULL="true"
 NUMERIC_ROUNDABORT="false" QUOTED_IDENTIFIER="true" />
          <QueryPlan DegreeOfParallelism="1" CachedPlanSize="16" CompileTime="6"
 CompileCPU="6" CompileMemory="232">
            <MissingIndexes>
              <MissingIndexGroup Impact="13.6636">
                <MissingIndex Database="[bigpubs2008]" Schema="[dbo]"
 Table="[stores]">
                  <ColumnGroup Usage="EQUALITY">
                    <Column Name="[state]" ColumnId="5" />
                  </ColumnGroup>
                  <ColumnGroup Usage="INCLUDE">
                    <Column Name="[stor_id]" ColumnId="1" />
                    <Column Name="[stor_name]" ColumnId="2" />
                  </ColumnGroup>
                </MissingIndex>
              </MissingIndexGroup>
```

```
          </MissingIndexes>
          <RelOp AvgRowSize="39" EstimateCPU="0.363144" EstimateIO="0"
EstimateRebinds="0" EstimateRewinds="0" EstimateRows="10710.8"
LogicalOp="Inner Join" NodeId="0" Parallel="false" PhysicalOp="Merge Join"
EstimatedTotalSubtreeCost="1.71032">
...
                  <Object Database="[bigpubs2008]" Schema="[dbo]" Table="[sales]"
Index="[UPKCL_sales]" Alias="[s]" IndexKind="Clustered" />
                 </IndexScan>
                </RelOp>
              </Merge>
            </RelOp>
          </QueryPlan>
        </StmtSimple>
      </Statements>
    </Batch>
  </BatchSequence>
</ShowPlanXML>
```


To obtain an XML-formatted query plan, which you can provide to the USE PLAN query hint, SQL Server 2008 provides the following methods:

- Using the SET SHOWPLAN_XML and SET STATISTICS XML session options
- Querying the plan column of the sys.dm_exec_query_plan dynamic management view for a cached query plan
- Using SQL Server Profiler and capturing either the Showplan XML, Showplan XML Statistics Profile, or Showplan XML For Query Compile event classes

NOTE

When the XML query plan contains a character string in single quotation marks ('), the quotation marks must be escaped by a second quotation mark before using the plan with the USE PLAN query hint. For example, a plan that contains WHERE A.varchar = 'This is a string' must be escaped by modifying the code to WHERE A.varchar = ''This is a string''; otherwise, it will generate a syntax error when submitted for execution.

You may choose to use the USE PLAN hint for queries where the execution plan chosen leads to slow execution times but for which you know a better plan exists. This scenario may commonly occur for queries that might have executed well in an earlier version of SQL Server but that perform poorly under an upgraded version. Another scenario could be a complex query that involves multiple tables where the compiled or recompiled query plan generated is occasionally not optimal, possibly as a result of out-of-date or missing statistics in any of the underlying tables or because of complex constructs in the query that cause the Query Optimizer to inaccurately estimate the size of the intermediate query results.

The `USE PLAN` query hint can be specified only for `SELECT` and `SELECT INTO` statements. Also, you can force only query plans that can be produced by the Query Optimizer's normal optimization strategy.

Because the `USE PLAN` option requires that the XML execution plan be hard-coded in the SQL statement itself, it is not a viable solution for deployed or third-party applications where it may not be possible or feasible to modify the queries directly. It's really useful only as a tool for troubleshooting poorly running queries. To force query plans to apply query hints to queries when you cannot or do not want to directly change the application or SQL code, you might consider using plan guides.

Using Plan Guides

At times, you might find it necessary to use query hints to improve the performance of queries for a particular query or a small set of queries. Although this may be easy to do when you have access to the application code, often the particular queries to be modified are embedded within a third-party application, and alteration of the queries themselves is virtually impossible. Also, if you start hard-coding query hints in your application code, changing them as necessary when data volumes change or when upgrading to a new version of SQL Server can be a difficult undertaking.

The plan guides feature in SQL Server 2008 provides an ideal solution for such scenarios by offering another mechanism for injecting query hints into the original query without having to modify the query itself. The plan guides mechanism uses an internal lookup system table, based on information in the `sys.plan_guides` catalog view, to map the original query to a substitute query or query template.

As described earlier in this chapter, when a SQL statement is submitted, it is first compared against the cached plans to check for a match. If a match exists, the cached query plan is used to execute the query. If no cached plan exists for the query, the Query Optimizer next looks for a match against the set of existing plan guides, if any, stored in the current database for a match. If an active plan guide that matches the SQL statement is found, the original matching statement is substituted with the one from the plan guide, the query plan is compiled and cached, and the query is executed using the plan generated from the plan guide.

Queries that can benefit from plan guides are generally those that are parameter based and those that are likely performing poorly because they use cached query plans whose parameter values do not represent a more representative scenario.

The plan guides feature essentially consists of two stored procedures to create, drop, enable, and disable plan guides and the `sys.plan_guides` metadata view that describes the stored plan guides. Plan guides are created and administered by using the two system stored procedures:

- `sp_create_plan_guide`

- sp_control_plan_guide

The syntax for these procedures is as follows:

```
sp_create_plan_guide [ @name = ] N'plan_guide_name'
    , [ @stmt = ] N'statement_text'
    , [ @type = ] N'{ OBJECT | SQL | TEMPLATE }'
    , [ @module_or_batch = ]
      {
                    N'[ schema_name. ] object_name'
        | N'batch_text'
        | NULL
      }
    , [ @params = ] { N'@parameter_name data_type [ ,...n ]' | NULL }
    , [ @hints = ] { N'OPTION ( query_hint [ ,...n ] )'
               | N'XML_execution plan'
                 | NULL }

sp_control_plan_guide [ @operation = ] N'<control_option>'
  [ , [ @name = ] N'plan_guide_name' ]

<control_option>::=
{
    DROP
  | DROP ALL
  | DISABLE
  | DISABLE ALL
  | ENABLE
  | ENABLE ALL
}
```

Note that in SQL Server 2008, the sp_create_plan_guide stored procedure enables you to pass an XML execution plan directly in the @hints parameter instead of embedding the output in a USE PLAN hint. This capability simplifies the process of applying a fixed query plan as a plan guide hint.

In addition, a new stored procedure, sp_create_plan_guide_from_handle, allows you to create one or more plan guides from a query plan in the plan cache. The syntax for sp_create_plan_guide_from_handle is as follows:

```
sp_create_plan_guide_from_handle [ @name = ] N'plan_guide_name'
    , [ @plan_handle = ] plan_handle
    , [ [ @statement_start_offset = ] { statement_start_offset | NULL } ]
```

Instead of specifying an actual XML execution plan, you pass the handle for a query plan currently in the plan cache to the @plan_handle parameter. As shown previously in this chapter, a plan_handle can be obtained from the sys.dm_exec_query_stats DMV. If the cached plan contains multiple queries in a SQL batch, you can specify the starting position of the statement within the batch via the `@statement_start_offset` parameter. The statement offset corresponds to the `statement_start_offset` column in the `sys.dm_exec_query_stats` dynamic management view. If no statement offset is specified, a plan guide is created for each statement in the batch using the query plan for the specified plan handle. The resulting plan guides are equivalent to plan guides that use the `USE PLAN` query hint to force the use of a specific plan.

Creating Plan Guides

Plan guides can be created to match queries executed in the following contexts:

- An `OBJECT` plan guide matches queries that execute in the context of T-SQL stored procedures, scalar functions, or multistatement table-valued functions.
- A `SQL` plan guide matches queries that execute in the context of ad hoc T-SQL statements and batches that are not part of a stored procedure or other compiled database object.
- A `TEMPLATE` plan guide matches ad hoc queries that parameterize to a specified form. These plan guides are used to override the current `SET PARAMETERIZATION` database option.

In the `sp_create_plan_guide` statement, you specify the query that you want optimized and provide the `OPTION` clause with the query hints necessary to optimize the query in the manner desired, or an XML execution plan for the query plan you want the query to use. When the query executes, SQL Server matches the query to the plan guide and applies the forced query plan to the query at runtime.

The plan guide can specify any of the following query hints individually or combined with others, when applicable:

- `{HASH | ORDER} GROUP`
- `{CONCAT | HASH | MERGE} UNION`
- `{LOOP | MERGE | HASH} JOIN`
- `FAST` *`n`*
- `FORCE ORDER`
- `MAXDOP` *`number_of_processors`*
- `OPTIMIZE FOR (` *`@variable_name = literal_constant ) [ ,...n ]`*
- `OPTIMIZE FOR UNKNOWN`
- `RECOMPILE`
- `ROBUST PLAN`
- `KEEP PLAN`
- `KEEPFIXED PLAN`

- EXPAND VIEWS
- MAXRECURSION *number*
- TABLE HINT (*object_name [, table_hint [[,]...n]]*)
- USE PLAN *<xmlplan>*
- PARAMETERIZATION { SIMPLE | FORCED }

The PARAMETERIZATION { SIMPLE | FORCED } query hint can be used only within a plan guide, and it specifies whether a query is parameterized as part of compiling a query plan. This option overrides the current setting of the PARAMETERIZATION option set at the database level.

Listing 35.8 provides a sample plan guide created for a simple SQL statement.

LISTING 35.8 Creating a Plan Guide for a Simple SQL Statement

```
sp_create_plan_guide @name = N'PlanGuide1',
@stmt = N'SELECT COUNT(*) AS Total
FROM dbo.sales s, dbo.titles t
WHERE s.title_id = t.title_id
and t.pubdate BETWEEN ''1/1/2004'' AND ''1/1/2006''
',
@type = N'SQL',
@module_or_batch = NULL,
@params = NULL,
@hints = N'OPTION (HASH JOIN)'
```

For plan guides of type 'SQL' or 'TEMPLATE' to match a query successfully, the values for *batch_text* and *@parameter_name data_type [,...n]* must be provided in exactly the same format as their counterparts submitted by the application. Specifically, they must match character for character, including comments and whitespaces.

TIP

When you are creating plan guides, be careful to specify the query in the @stmt parameter and any parameter names and values in the @params parameter exactly as they are received from the application. The best way to ensure this is to capture the batch or statement text from SQL Server Profiler. (See Chapter 6 for more information on using SQL Server Profiler to capture SQL queries.) Also, as with the XML query plans passed to the USE PLAN query hint, single-quoted literal values, such as '1/1/2000', need to be delimited with single quotation marks escaped by additional single quotation marks, as shown in Listing 35.6.

Managing Plan Guides

You use the sp_control_plan_guide stored procedure to enable, disable, or drop a plan guide. The following example drops the plan guide created in Listing 35.8:

```
sp_control_plan_guide N'DROP', N'PlanGuide1'
```

To execute sp_control_plan_guide on a plan guide of type OBJECT (for example, a plan guide created for a stored procedure), you must have at least ALTER permission on the object that is referenced by the plan guide. For all other plan guides, you must have at least ALTER DATABASE permission. Attempting to drop or alter a function or stored procedure that is referenced by a plan guide results in an error.

In SQL Server 2008, it is possible to define multiple plan guides for the same query. However, only one plan guide can be active at a time. You can use sp_control_plan_guide to enable and disable plan guides.

Validating Plan Guides

The new system function sys.fn_validate_plan_guide can be used to validate a plan guide. Plan guides can become invalid after changes such as dropping an index are made to the physical design of the database. By validating a plan guide, you can determine whether the plan guide can be used unmodified by the query optimizer. The sys.fn_validate_plan_guide function returns the first error message encountered when the plan guide is applied to its query. If the plan guide is valid, an empty rowset is returned.

The sys.plan_guides Catalog View

All plan guides are stored in the sys.plan_guides database system catalog view. You can get information about the plan guides defined in a database by running a query against the sys.plan_guides catalog view, as in the following example:

```
select name, is_disabled, scope_type_desc, scope_object_id,
       parameters, hints, query_text from sys.plan_guides
```

Table 35.2 describes the columns in the sys.plan_guides catalog view.

TABLE 35.2 **sys.plan_guides** Columns

Column Name	Description
plan_guide_id	Unique identifier of the plan guide.
Name	Name of the plan guide.
create_date	Date and time the plan guide was created.
modify_date	Date the plan guide was last modified.
is_disabled	1 = disabled and 0 = enabled.
query_text	Text of the query on which the plan guide is created.
scope_type	Scope of the plan guide: 1 = OBJECT, 2 = SQL, and 3 = TEMPLATE.
scope_type_desc	Description of scope of the plan guide: OBJECT, SQL, or TEMPLATE.

scope_object_id	If scope_type is OBJECT, the object_id of the object defining the scope of the plan guide; otherwise, NULL.
scope_batch	If scope_type is SQL, the text of the SQL batch. If NULL, either the batch type is not SQL or scope_type is SQL, and the value of query_text applies.
parameters	The string defining the list of parameters associated with the plan guide. If NULL, no parameter list is associated with the plan guide.
hints	The query OPTION hints associated with the plan guide.

Plan Guide Best Practices

Following are some of the recommended best practices for using the USE PLAN query hint and the plan guides feature:

- The USE PLAN query hint and plan guides should be used only when other standard query tuning options, such as tuning indexes and ensuring the table has current statistics, have been extensively tried and have failed to produce the necessary results. When a query plan is forced by using either the USE PLAN query hint or a plan guide, it prevents the Query Optimizer from adapting to changing data distributions, new indexes, or improved query execution algorithms in successive SQL Server releases or service packs.
- You need to be sure to have a full understanding of query optimization and of the implications and long-term ramifications of forcing query plans.
- You should try to force only a small fraction of the workload. If you find you are forcing more than a few dozen queries, you should check whether other issues with the configuration could be limiting performance, including insufficient system resources, incorrect database configuration settings, missing indexes, poorly written queries, and other factors.
- It is not advisable to attempt to code by hand or modify the XML execution plan that is specified in the USE PLAN query hint. You should capture and use a plan produced by SQL Server itself. The XML execution plan is a lengthy and complex listing, and improper changes could prevent it from identically matching one of the Query Optimizer–generated plans, which would result in the USE PLAN hint being ignored.
- The USE PLAN query hint should not be directly embedded into the application code because that would make the maintenance of the application across query plan and SQL Server version changes difficult to manage. Also, embedding USE PLAN directly into the query generally prevents the plan for the query from being cacheable. The USE PLAN hint is intended primarily for ad hoc performance tuning and test purposes, and for use with the plan guides feature.
- The plan guides created for an application should be well documented and regularly backed up because they constitute an integral part of the application's performance

tuning. You should also retain the scripts that you used to create plan guides and treat them as you would other source code for an application.

- After creating a plan guide, you should test to make sure that it is being applied to the intended queries.

Verifying That a Plan Guide Is Being Applied

When you have a plan guide defined, you might want to verify that the application query is making use of the plan guide. You can follow these steps to confirm whether a plan guide is being used:

1. After creating the plan guide, run SQL Server Profiler and configure it to capture the query text and XML execution plan for the application and the query in question and start the Profiler trace.
2. Run your application and cause it to invoke the query in question.
3. Stop the profiler trace and collect the query plan by right-clicking the Showplan XML Statistics Profile event that corresponds to the query and then selecting the Extract Event Data option.
4. Save the event data to a file.
5. Open the `Showplan.xml` file in any text file viewer or Internet Explorer to examine the XML code.
6. If the plan guide was used to generate the query plan, the XML execution plan output contains the `PlanGuideDB` and `PlanGuideName` tags, as shown in the following example:

```
<ShowPlanXML xmlns=
"http://schemas.microsoft.com/sqlserver/2004/07/showplan"
 Version="1.0" Build="9.00.1282.00">
  <BatchSequence>
    <Batch>
      <Statements>
        <StmtSimple PlanGuideDB="bigpubs2008"
 PlanGuideName="PlanGuide1">
...
        </StmtSimple>
      </Statements>
    </Batch>
  </BatchSequence>
   </ShowPlanXML>
```

As another option to help determine whether or not plan guides are being used, you can use two new event classes available in the SQL Server 2008 Profiler: Plan Guide Successful and Plan Guide Unsuccessful. These new event classes make it easier to verify whether plan guides are being used by the Query Optimizer. For example, if SQL Server cannot produce an execution plan for a query that contains a plan guide when the initial plan guide compilation is performed, the query is automatically compiled without using the plan guide, and the Plan Guide Unsuccessful event is raised. For more information on monitoring SQL Server using SQL Profiler, see Chapter 6.

NOTE

Note that the plan guide events are raised only during the initial compilation of a query that contains a plan guide when the query plan gets loaded into the plan cache. If you do not see either of these events, you may need to flush the plan cache using `DBCC FREEPROCCACHE`.

In addition, there are two new Performance Monitor counters: `Guided Plan Executions/sec` and `Misguided Plan Executions/sec`. These counters are available in the SQL Server, SQL Statistics Object. They report the number of plan executions in which the query plan has been successfully or unsuccessfully generated using a plan guide. For more information on monitoring SQL Server performance using Performance Monitor, see Chapter 39, "Monitoring SQL Server Performance."

Creating and Managing Plan Guides in SSMS

SQL Server 2008 enables you to create, delete, enable, disable, or script plan guides within SSMS. The plan guides options are available in the `Programmability` folder in Object Explorer. To create a new plan guide in SSMS, right-click on Plan Guides and select the New Plan Guide option. This brings up the dialog shown in Figure 35.30.

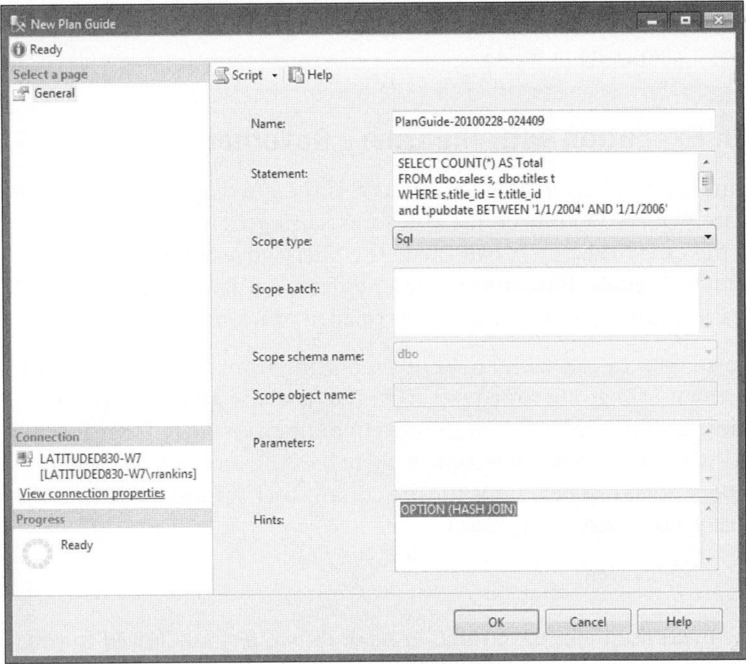

FIGURE 35.30 Creating a plan guide in SSMS.

To manage existing plan guides in SSMS, you can right-click on the plan guide name to bring up the context menu that allows you to enable, disable, delete, script, or view the properties of the plan guide, as shown in Figure 35.31.

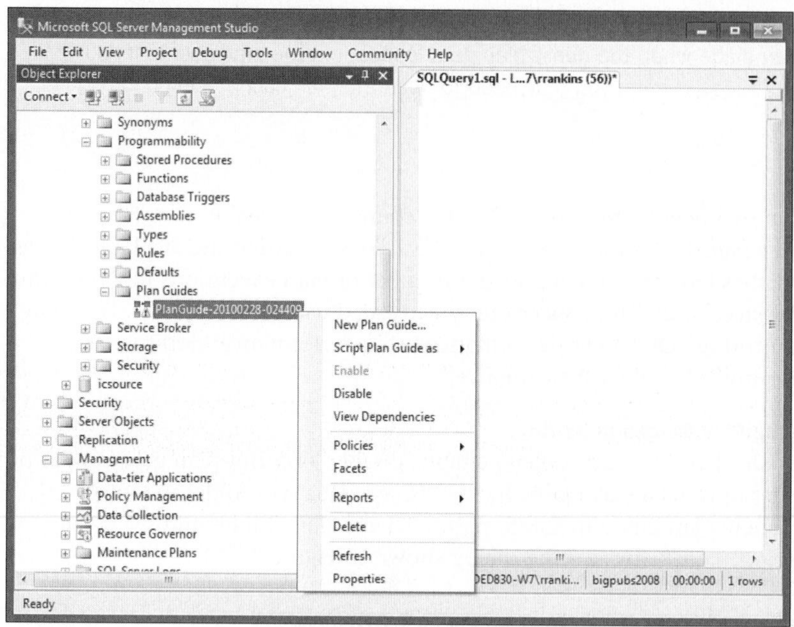

FIGURE 35.31 Managing a plan guide in SSMS.

Limiting Query Plan Execution with the Query Governor

Another tool for managing query plans in SQL Server 2008 is the query governor. Because SQL Server uses a cost-based Query Optimizer, the cost of executing a given query is always estimated before the query is actually executed. The query governor enables you to set a cost threshold to prevent certain long-running queries from being executed. This is not so much an optimization tuning tool as it is a performance problem prevention tool.

For example, if you have an application with an ad hoc reporting front end, you have no way of controlling what the user is going to request from the database and the type of query generated. The query governor allows you to prevent a runaway query from executing and using up valuable CPU and memory resources by processing a poorly formed query. You can set the query governor cost limit for the current user session by setting the session-level property `QUERY_GOVERNOR_COST_LIMIT`:

```
SET QUERY_GOVERNOR_COST_LIMIT value
```

The value specified is the maximum length of time, in seconds, a query is allowed to run. If the Query Optimizer estimates the query would take longer than the specified value, SQL Server does not execute it.

Although the option is specified in seconds, it is a relative value that corresponds to the estimated subtree cost, as calculated by the Query Optimizer. In other words, if you set the query governor cost limit to `100`, it prevents the execution of any queries whose estimated subtree cost is greater than 100 seconds. The estimated subtree cost time is based on the query cost algorithm in SQL Server and might not map exactly to how long the query actually takes to run on your own system. The actual runtime depends on a number of factors: CPU speed, I/O speed, network speed, the number of rows returned over the network, and so on. You need to correlate the Query Optimizer runtime estimate to how long the query actually takes to run on your system to set the query governor cost limit to a value related to actual query runtime.

The best way to figure out how to set the query governor is to run your queries with the `STATISTICS PROFILE` and `STATISTICS TIME` session settings enabled. (These settings are discussed in more detail in Chapter 36.) You then compare the values in the `TotalSubtree Cost` column for the first row of the `STATISTICS PROFILE` output with the `elapsed time` displayed by `STATISTICS TIME` for your query. If you do this for a number of your queries, you might be able to come up with an average correlation of the actual runtimes with the Query Optimizer's estimated query cost. For example, if the average cost estimate is 30 seconds and the actual runtimes are 15 seconds, you may need to double the setting for query governor cost limit to correspond to the actual execution time threshold; in other words, if you want the threshold to be 60 seconds for this example, you would want to set the query governor threshold to `120`.

To configure a query governor threshold for all user connections, you can also set it at the server level. In SSMS, right-click the server in the Object Browser and choose Properties from the menu. In the Server Properties dialog, select the Connections page. Enable the Use Query Governor to Prevent Long-Running Queries check box and specify the desired cost threshold (see Figure 35.32). The cost threshold is specified in the same units as specified for the `QUERY_GOVERNOR_COST_LIMIT` session setting.

Alternatively, you can configure the server-wide query governor setting by using `sp_configure`:

```
sp_configure query governor cost limit, 100
```

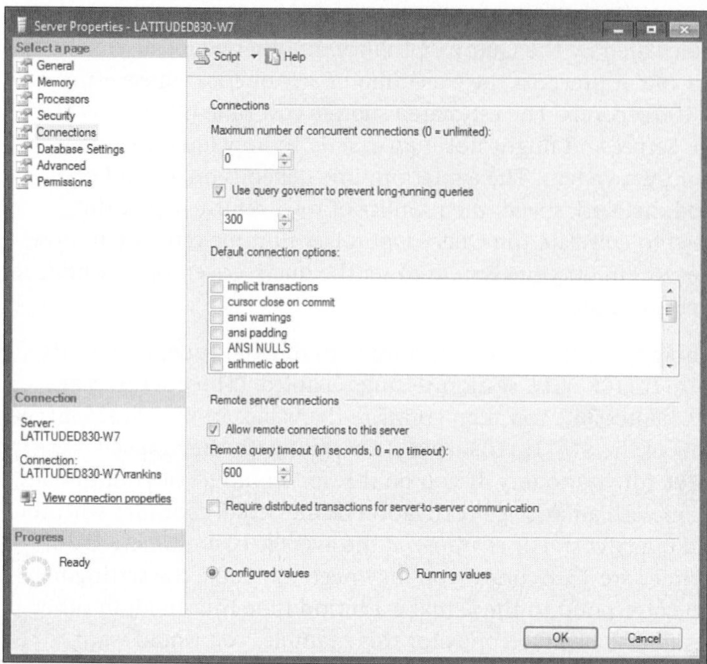

FIGURE 35.32 Configuring the query governor settings in the SQL Server Properties dialog.

Summary

The SQL Server Query Optimizer has improved over the years, taking advantage of new techniques and algorithms to improve its capability to find the most efficient execution plan. Understanding how queries are optimized and what information the Query Optimizer uses to generate and select an execution plan will help you write more efficient queries and choose better indexes. To help the Query Optimizer, you should at least try to write queries that can be optimized effectively by avoiding the common query optimization problems discussed in this chapter.

Most of the time, the Query Optimizer chooses the most efficient query plan. When it doesn't, the reason might be problems with the way the query itself is written, out-of-date or unavailable statistics, poor index design, or other common query performance problems, as discussed in this chapter. Still, on occasion, the Query Optimizer may make the wrong choice for an execution plan. When you suspect that the Query Optimizer is making the wrong decision, you can use SQL Server's table and Query Optimizer hints and the plan guide feature to override the Query Optimizer's decisions. However, before arbitrarily applying these hints, you should analyze the queries fully to try to determine why the Query Optimizer is choosing a particular plan. To aid you in this effort, SQL Server provides a number of tools to analyze the query plans generated and determine the source of the problem. These tools are described in Chapter 36.

CHAPTER 36

Query Analysis

IN THIS CHAPTER

- What's New in Query Analysis
- Query Analysis in SSMS
- SSMS Client Statistics
- Using the **SET SHOWPLAN** Options
- Using **sys.dm_exec_query_plan**
- Query Statistics
- Query Analysis with SQL Server Profiler

SQL Server's cost-based Query Optimizer typically does a good job of determining the best query plan for processing a query. At times, however, you might be a little bit skeptical about the plan the Query Optimizer generates or want to understand why it is choosing a specific plan. At the least, you will want to know the specifics about the query plans the Query Optimizer is generating, such as the following:

- Is the Query Optimizer using the indexes you have defined, or is it performing table or index scans?
- Are work tables being used to process the query?
- What join strategy is being applied?
- What join order is the Query Optimizer using?
- What statistics and cost estimates is the Query Optimizer using to make its decisions?
- How do the Query Optimizer's estimates compare to actual I/O costs and row counts?

Fortunately, SQL Server provides some tools to help you answer these questions. The primary tool is SQL Server Management Studio (SSMS). SSMS provides a number of features for monitoring the estimated or actual execution plan as well as viewing the actual runtime statistics for your queries. This chapter describes how to display the graphical execution plan as well as client statistics within SSMS.

Although SSMS is a powerful and useful tool for query analysis, SQL Server still provides some text-based query analysis utilities as well. These tools are also described in this chapter, along with tips on how to use them most effectively.

NOTE

The examples presented in this chapter use the `bigpubs2008` database because most examples require sufficient data to demonstrate many of the more interesting query plans. A copy of the `bigpubs2008` database is available on on the CD included with this book. Instructions on how to obtain and install the database are presented in the Introduction.

What's New in Query Analysis

There are not many significant changes or new features related to Query Analysis provided in SQL Server 2008. The tools and commands are mostly unchanged from what was introduced in SQL Server 2005. One new useful enhancement, however, is the Missing Index Hints feature available when displaying the Execution Plan of a query in SSMS.

Query Analysis in SSMS

The main tool for query analysis in SQL Server 2008 is the Query Editor available in SSMS. The SSMS Query Editor can produce a graphical execution plan that provides analysis information in an intuitive and easy-to-view manner. You can display the execution plan in one of two ways: the estimated execution plan or the actual execution plan.

You can display an estimated execution plan for the entire contents of the query window, or for any highlighted SQL code in the query window, by choosing Display Estimated Execution Plan from the Query menu. You can also invoke it by using the Ctrl+L keyboard shortcut. This feature is useful for displaying and analyzing execution plans for long-running queries or queries with large result sets without having to actually run the query and wait for the results to be returned.

You can also display the actual execution plans for queries as they are executed by selecting the Include Actual Execution Plan option from the Query menu or by using the Ctrl+M keyboard shortcut. This option is a toggle that remains on until you select it again to disable it. When this option is enabled, your query results are displayed, along with an Execution Plan tab in the Results panel. Click the Execution Plan tab to display the execution plan for the query or queries that are executed. This option is especially useful when you want to execute commands and compare the actual runtime and I/O statistics with the execution plan estimates. (These statistics can be displayed with the `SET STATISTICS` options described in the "Query Statistics" section, later in this chapter.)

The graphical execution plans display a series of nodes connected by lines. Each node is represented by an icon, which indicates the logical and physical operator executed for that node. The execution plan flows from right to left and top to bottom, eventually ending at a statement icon, which indicates the type of query that generated the execution plan.

This query might be a SELECT, INSERT, UPDATE, TABCREATE, and so on. The arrows between the icons indicate the movement of rows between operators. If the query window contains multiple statements, multiple query execution plans are displayed in the Execution Plan tab. For each query in the batch that is analyzed and displayed, the relative cost of the query is displayed as a percentage of the total cost of the batch.

To interpret and analyze the execution plan output, you start with the farthest icon on the right and read each ToolTip as you move left and down through the tree. Each icon in the query tree is called a *node*, and icons displayed under each other participate in the same level of the execution tree.

NOTE

The displayed width of each of the arrowhead lines in the graphical execution plan can indicate the relative cost, in estimated number of rows, and the row and data size of the data moving through the query. The smaller the width of the arrow, the smaller the estimated row count or row size. Moving the cursor over the line displays a ToolTip that indicates the estimated row count and row and data size.

Figure 36.1 shows a sample SSMS graphical execution plan window.

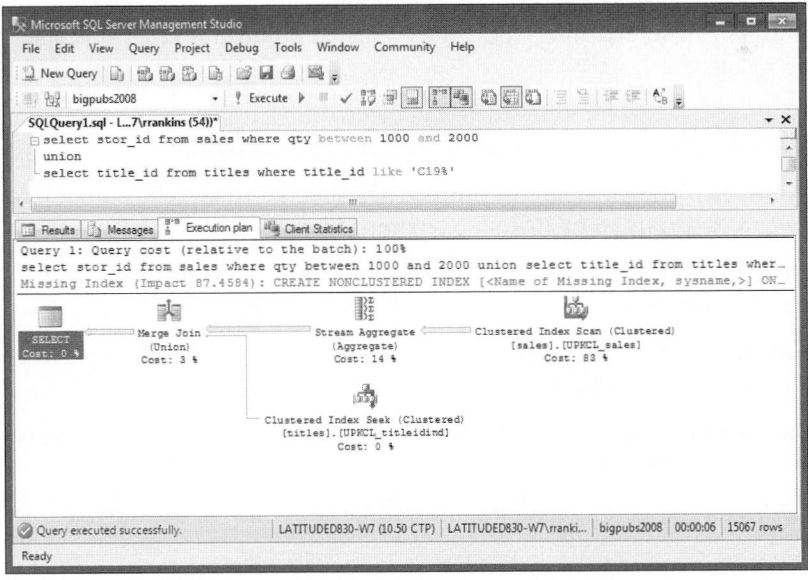

FIGURE 36.1 SSMS graphical execution plan.

The following sections describe the icons and information provided in the graphical execution plan.

Execution Plan ToolTips

When a graphical execution plan is presented in the Query Analyzer, you can get more information about each node in the execution plan by moving the mouse cursor over one of the icons. ToolTips for estimated execution plans are slightly different from the ToolTips displayed for an execution plan that is generated when a query is actually executed. The ToolTip displayed for an estimated execution plan provides the following information:

- **Physical Operation**—Lists the physical operation being performed for the node, such as a Clustered Index Scan, Index Seek, Aggregate, Hash or Nested Loop Join, and so on.
- **Logical Operation**—Lists the logical operation that corresponds with the physical operation, such as the logical operation of a union being physically performed as a merge join. The logical operator, if different from the physical operator, is listed in parentheses below the physical operator in the icon text in the graphical execution plan. Essentially, the logical operators describe the relational operation used to process a statement, while the physical operation describes how it is being performed.
- **Estimated I/O Cost**—Indicates the estimated relative I/O cost for the operation. Preferably, this value should be as low as possible.
- **Estimated CPU Cost**—Lists the estimated relative CPU cost for the operation.
- **Estimated Number of Executions**—Lists the estimated number of times this operation will be executed.
- **Estimated Operator Cost**—Indicates the estimated cost to execute the physical operation. For best performance, you want this value as low as possible.
- **Estimated Number of Rows**—Lists the estimated number of rows to be output by the operation and passed on to the parent operation.
- **Estimated Row Size**—Indicates the estimated average row size of the rows being passed through the operator.
- **Estimated Subtree Cost**—Lists the estimated cumulative total cost of this operation and all child operations preceding it in the same subtree.
- **Object**—Indicates which database object is being accessed by the operation being performed by the current node.
- **Predicate**—Indicates the search predicate specified for the object in the original query.
- **Seek Predicates**—Indicates the search predicate being used in the seek against the index when an index seek is being performed.
- **Output List**—Indicates which columns of data are being returned by the operation.

- **Ordered**—Indicates whether the rows are being retrieved via an index in sorted order.
- **Node ID**—Lists a unique identifier of the node within the execution plan.

Some operators may also include the Actual Rebinds and Actual Rewinds counts. When an operator is on the outer side of a loop join, Actual Rebinds equals 1 and Actual Rewinds equals 0. If an operator is on the inner side of a loop join, the sum of the number of rebinds and rewinds should equal the number of rows returned by the table on the outer side of the join. A rebind means that one or more of the correlated parameters of the join changed and the inner side must be reevaluated. A rewind means that none of the correlated parameters changed and the prior inner result set may be reused.

NOTE

Depending on the type of operator and other query characteristics, not all the preceding items are displayed in the ToolTip.

The ToolTips for an execution plan generated when the query is actually executed display the same information as the estimated execution plan, but the ToolTip also displays the actual number of rows returned by the operation and the actual number of executions. This information is useful in determining the effectiveness of the statistics on the column or index because it helps you compare how closely the estimated row count matches the actual row count. If a significant difference exists (significant being a relative term), you might need to update the statistics and possibly increase the sample size used when the statistics are updated to generate more accurate statistics.

Figure 36.2 displays a sample ToolTip. Notice the difference between the `Estimated Number of Rows` value (8325.01) and the `Actual Number of Rows` value (160). This indicates an obvious issue with missing or out-of-date statistics.

NOTE

To achieve the large difference between the actual row count and estimated row count shown in Figure 36.2, we disabled the `AUTO-CREATE STATISTICS` option for the database. If this option is not disabled, SQL Server automatically generates the missing statistics on the `ord_date` column before generating the execution plan. With the column statistics generated, it would likely come up with a better row estimate.

In this example, the ToolTip displays the information for a Table Scan physical operation. The Estimated I/O Cost and Estimated CPU Cost provide critical information about the relative performance of this query. You want these numbers to be as low as possible.

The Estimated Subtree Cost displays cumulated costs for this node and any previous nodes that feed into it. This number increases as you move from right to left in the execution plan diagram. For the next-to-last icon for a query execution path (the icon leading into the statement icon), the ToolTip displays the Total Estimated Subtree Cost for the entire query.

Table Scan

Scan rows from a table.

Physical Operation	Table Scan
Logical Operation	Table Scan
Actual Number of Rows	160
Estimated I/O Cost	1.14172
Estimated CPU Cost	0.185676
Estimated Number of Executions	1
Number of Executions	1
Estimated Operator Cost	1.3274 (100%)
Estimated Subtree Cost	1.3274
Estimated Number of Rows	8325.01
Estimated Row Size	48 B
Actual Rebinds	0
Actual Rewinds	0
Ordered	False
Node ID	0

Predicate
[bigpubs2008].[dbo].[new_sales].[ord_date] =CONVERT_IMPLICIT(datetime,[@1],0)
Object
[bigpubs2008].[dbo].[new_sales]
Output List
[bigpubs2008].[dbo].[new_sales].stor_id, [bigpubs2008].[dbo].[new_sales].ord_num, [bigpubs2008].[dbo].[new_sales].ord_date, [bigpubs2008].[dbo].[new_sales].qty, [bigpubs2008].[dbo].[new_sales].payterms, [bigpubs2008].[dbo].[new_sales].title_id
Warnings
Columns With No Statistics: [bigpubs2008].[dbo].[new_sales].ord_date

FIGURE 36.2 A ToolTip example.

NOTE

The total Estimated Subtree Cost displayed for the statement icon is the cost compared against the query governor cost limit setting, if enabled, to determine whether the query will be allowed to run. For more information on configuring and setting the query governor cost limit, see Chapter 35, "Understanding Query Optimization."

The Predicate section outlines the predicates and parameters the query uses. This information is useful in determining how the Query Optimizer is interpreting your search arguments (SARGs) and if they are being interpreted as SARGs that can be optimized effectively.

Putting all the ToolTip information together provides the key to understanding each operation and its potential cost. You can use this information to compare various incarnations of a query to determine whether changes to the query result in improved query plans and whether the estimated values are consistent with actual values.

NOTE

If the Query Optimizer has issued a warning about one of the execution plan operators, such as missing column statistics or missing join predicates, the icon is displayed with a yellow warning triangle (see Figure 36.3). These warnings indicate a condition that can cause the Query Optimizer to choose a less efficient query plan than otherwise expected. The ToolTip for the operation with the warning icon includes a Warnings item that indicates why the warning was generated.

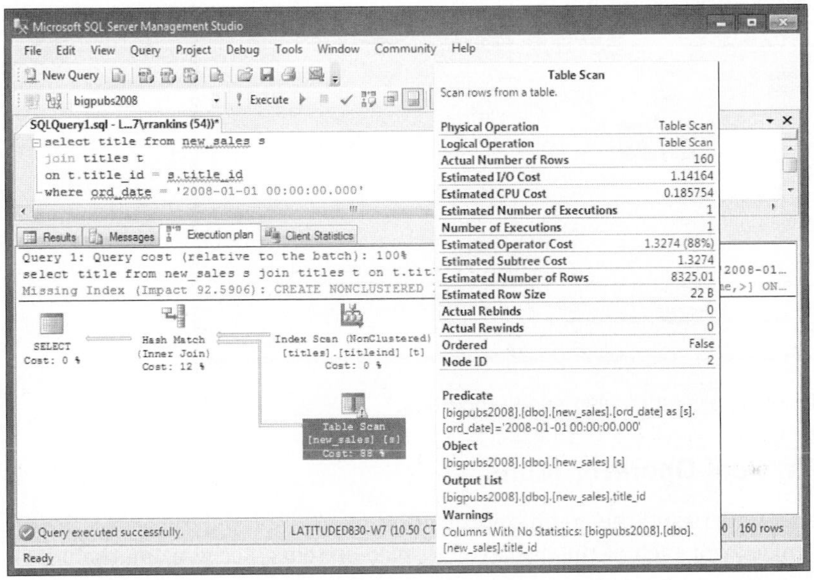

FIGURE 36.3 An example of an execution plan with warnings.

If you prefer to view the information about a node in an execution tree in more detail and with something more stable than a ToolTip, you can right-click the node and select Properties. This brings up the Properties window, as shown in Figure 36.4.

The Properties window provides all the same information available in the ToolTip and also provides some more detailed information, along with descriptions of the types of information provided.

NOTE

For more examples of graphical execution plans, see Chapter 35. The sections that discuss the different query strategies contain examples of the graphical showplans that correspond to the strategies. Many of these showplans provide various examples of the operator icons discussed in this section.

36

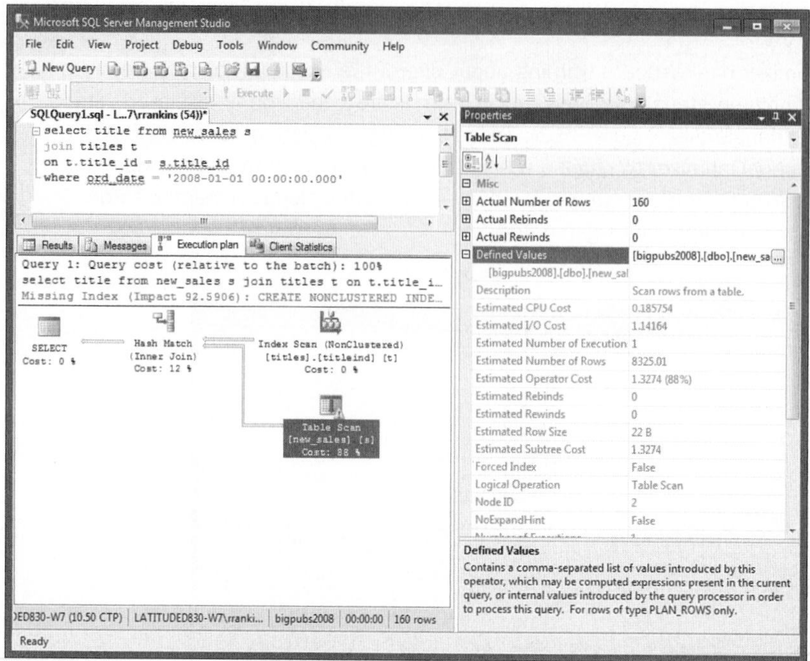

FIGURE 36.4 The query execution plan node properties.

Logical and Physical Operator Icons

If you want to better understand the graphical execution plans displayed in SSMS, it helps to be able to recognize what each of the displayed icons represents. Recognizing them is especially valuable when you need to quickly locate operations that appear out of place for the type of query being executed. The following sections cover the more common logical and physical operators displayed in the Query Analyzer execution plans.

Assert 

Assert is used to verify a condition, such as referential integrity (RI) or check constraint, or to ensure that a scalar subquery returns only a single row. It acts as sort of a roadblock, allowing a result stream to continue only if the check being performed is satisfied. The argument displayed in the Assert ToolTip spells out each check being performed.

For example, a deletion from the `titles` table in the `bigpubs2008` database has to be verified to ensure that it doesn't violate referential integrity with the `sales` and `titleauthors` table. The reference constraints need to check that the `title_id` being deleted does not exist in either the `sales` or `titleauthors` tables. If the result of the Assert returns a `NULL`, the stream continues through the query. Figure 36.5 shows the estimated execution plan and ToolTip of the Assert that appears for a delete on titles. The Predicate indicates that the reference constraint rejects any case in which the matching foreign key expression that returns from both child tables is `NOT NULL`. Notice that it returns a different value (`0` or 1), depending on the table on which the foreign key violation occurs so that the appropriate error message can be displayed.

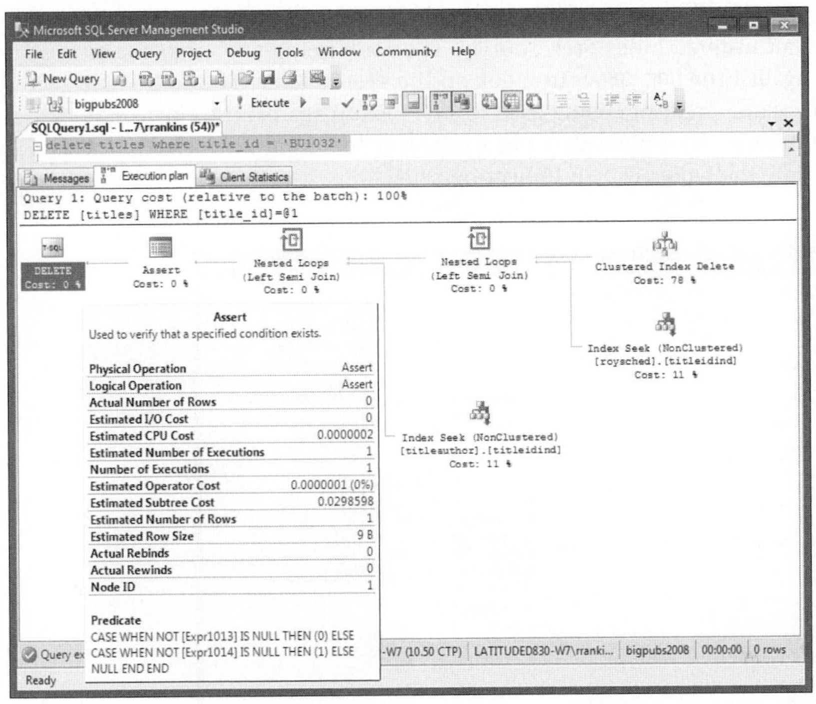

FIGURE 36.5 An Assert example.

Clustered Index Delete , Insert , and Update

The Clustered Index physical operators Delete, Insert, and Update indicate that one or more rows in the specified clustered index are being deleted, inserted, or updated. The index or indexes affected by the operation are specified in the Object item of the ToolTip. The Predicate indicates which rows are being deleted or which columns are being updated.

Nonclustered Index Delete , Insert , and Update

Similar to the Clustered Index physical operators Delete, Insert, and Update, the Nonclustered Index physical operators Delete, Insert, and Update indicate that one or more rows in the specified nonclustered index are being deleted, inserted, or updated.

Clustered Index Scan and Seek

A Clustered Index Seek is a logical and physical operator that indicates the Query Optimizer is using the clustered index to find the data rows via the index pointers. A Clustered Index Scan (also a logical and physical operator) indicates whether the Query

Optimizer is scanning all or a subset of the table or index rows. Note that a table scan against a table with a clustered index displays as a Clustered Index Scan; the Query Optimizer is performing a full scan against all data rows in the table, which are in clustered key order.

Figure 36.6 shows a Clustered Index Seek ToolTip. The ToolTip indicates that the seek is being performed against the `UPK_Storeid` index on the `stores` table. The Seek Predicates item indicates the search predicate being used for the lookup against the clustered index, and the Query Optimizer determines that the results will be output in clustered index order, as indicated by the Ordered item indicating `true`.

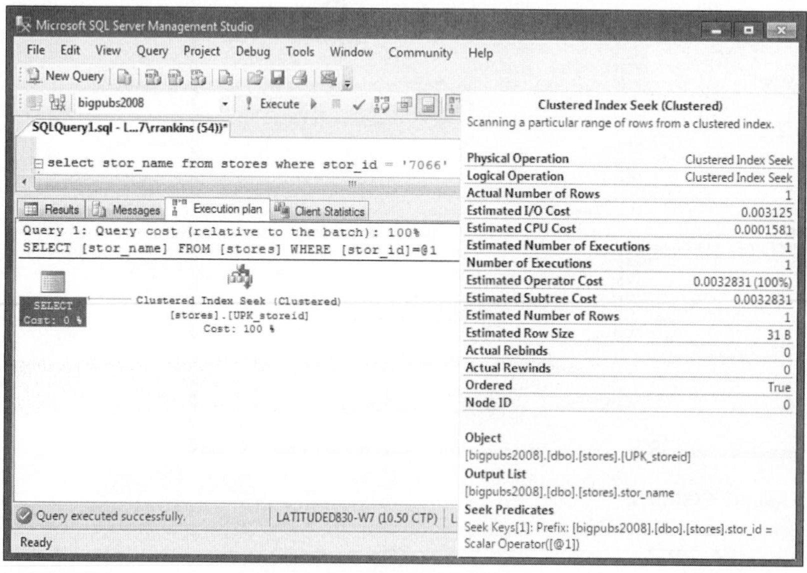

FIGURE 36.6 Clustered Index Seek ToolTip example.

Nonclustered Index Scan and Seek

A Nonclustered Index Seek is a logical and physical operator that indicates the Query Optimizer is using the nonclustered index to find the data rows via the index pointers. A Nonclustered Index Scan (also a logical and physical operator) indicates whether the Query Optimizer is scanning all or a subset of the nonclustered index rows. The Seek Predicates item in a Nonclustered Index Seek operator identifies the search predicate being used for the lookup against the nonclustered index. The Ordered item in the ToolTip indicates `true` if the rows will be returned in nonclustered index key order.

Collapse and Split

A Split physical and logical operator indicates that the Query Optimizer has decided to break the rows' input from the previous update optimization step into a separate delete and insert operation. The Estimated Number of Rows in the Split icon ToolTips is normally double the input row count, reflecting this two-step operation. If possible, the

Query Optimizer might choose later in the plan to collapse those rows, grouping by a key value. The collapse typically occurs if the query processor encounters adjacent rows that delete and insert the same key values.

Compute Scalar

The Query Optimizer uses the Compute Scalar operator to output a computed scalar value. This value might be returned in the result set or used as input to another operation in the query, such as a Filter operator. You might see this operator when data values that are feeding an input need to be converted to a different data type first.

Concatenation

The Concatenation operator indicates that the result sets from two or more input sources are being concatenated into a single output. You often see this when a `UNION ALL` is being used. You can force a concatenation union strategy by using the `OPTION` clause in the query and specifying a `CONCAT UNION`. Optimization of UNION queries, with examples of the execution plan outputs, is covered in Chapter 35.

Constant Scan

The Constant Scan operator introduces one or more constant rows into a query. A Compute Scalar operation sometimes is used to provide input to the Constant Scan operator. A Compute Scalar operator often follows a Constant Scan operator to add columns to any rows produced by the Constant Scan operator.

Deleted Scan and Inserted Scan

The Deleted Scan and Inserted Scan icons in the execution plan indicate that a trigger is being fired and that within that trigger, the Query Optimizer needs to scan either the deleted or inserted tables.

Filter

The Filter icon indicates that the input rows are being filtered according to the predicate indicated in the ToolTip. This operator is used primarily for intermediate operations that the Query Optimizer needs to perform.

Hash Match

Hash joins are covered in more detail in Chapter 35, but to understand the Hash Match physical operator, you must understand the basic concept of hash joins to some degree.

In a hash join, the keys common between the two tables are hashed into a hash bucket, using the same hash function. This bucket usually starts out in memory and then moves to disk as needed. The type of hashing that occurs depends on the amount of memory required. Hashing is commonly used for inner and outer joins, intersections, unions, and differences. The Query Optimizer often uses hashing for intermediate processing.

A hash join requires at least one equality clause in the predicate, which includes the clauses used to relate a primary key to a foreign key. Usually, the Query Optimizer selects a hash join when the input tables are unsorted or are different in size, when no appropriate indexes exist, or when specific ordering of the result is not required. Hash joins help provide better query performance for large databases, complex queries, and distributed tables.

A hash match operator uses the hash join strategy and might also include other criteria to be considered a match. The other criteria are indicated in the `Probe Residual` clause shown in the Hash Match ToolTip.

Nonclustered Index Spool, Row Count Spool, and Table Spool

An Index Spool, Row Count Spool, or Table Spool icon indicates that the rows are being stored in a hidden spool table in the `tempdb` database, which exists only for the duration of the query. Generally, this spool is created to support a nested iteration operation because the Query Optimizer might need to use the rows again. If the operator is rewound (for example, by a Nested Loops operator) but no rebinding is needed, the spooled data is used instead of rescanning the input data.

Often, you see a Spool icon under a Nested Loops icon in the execution plan. A Table Spool ToolTip does not show a predicate because no index is used. An Index Spool ToolTip shows a `SEEK` predicate. A temporary work table is created for an index spool, and then a temporary index is created on that table. These temporary work tables are local to the connection and live only as long as the query.

The Row Count Spool operator counts how many rows are present in the input and returns just the number of rows. This operator is used when checking for the existence of rows, rather than the actual data contained in the rows (for example, an existence subquery or an outer join when the actual data from the inner side is not needed).

Eager Spool or Lazy Spool

The Query Optimizer selects to use either an Eager or Lazy method of filling the spool, depending on the query. The Eager method means that the spool table is built all at once upon the first request for a row from the parent operator. The Lazy method builds the spool table as a row is requested by its parent operator.

Log Row Scan

The Log Row Scan icon indicates that the transaction log is being scanned.

Merge Join

The merge join is a strategy requiring that both the inputs be sorted on the common columns, defined by the predicate. The Merge Join operator may be preceded by an explicit sort operation in the query plan. A merge join performs one pass through each input table, matching the columns defined in the `WHERE` or `JOIN` clause as it steps through each input. A merge join looks similar to a simple nested loop but uses only a single pass of each table. Occasionally, you might see an additional sort operation prior to the merge join operation when the initial inputs are not sorted properly. Merge joins are often used to perform inner joins, left outer joins, left semi-joins, left anti-semi-joins, right outer joins, right semi-joins, right anti-semi-joins, and union logical operations.

Nested Loops

Nested loop joins are also known as nested iteration. Basically, in a nested iteration, every qualifying row in the outer table is compared to every qualifying row in the inner table. This is why you may at times see a Spool icon of some sort providing input to a Nested Loop icon. This allows the inner table rows to be reused (that is, rewound). When every row in each table is being compared, it is called a naïve nested loops join. If an index is used to find the qualifying rows, it is referred to as an index nested loops join. Nested loops can be used to perform inner joins, left outer joins, left semi-joins, and left anti-semi-joins.

The number of comparisons performed for a nested loop join is the calculation of the number of outer rows times the estimated number of matching inner rows for each lookup. This can become expensive. Generally, a nested loop join is considered to be most effective when both input tables are relatively small.

Parameter Table Scan 

The Parameter Table Scan icon indicates that a table is acting as a parameter in the current query. Typically, this icon is displayed when `INSERT` queries exist in a stored procedure.

Remote Delete, Remote Insert, Remote Query, Remote Scan,

and Remote Update

The Remote Delete, Remote Insert, Remote Query, Remote Scan, and Remote Update operators indicate that the operation is being performed against a remote object such as a linked table.

RID Lookup

The RID Lookup operator indicates that a bookmark lookup is being performed on a heap table using a row identifier (RID). The ToolTip indicates the bookmark label used to look up the row and the name of the table in which the row is being looked up. The RID Lookup operator is always accompanied by a Nested Loop Join operator.

Sequence

The Sequence operator executes each operation in its child node, moving from top to bottom in sequence, and returns only the end result from the bottom operator. You see this most often in the updates of multiple objects.

Sort 

The Sort operator indicates that the input is being sorted. The sort order is displayed in the ToolTip's Order By item.

Stream Aggregate

You most often see the Stream Aggregate operation when you are aggregating a single input, such as a `DISTINCT` clause or a `SUM`, `COUNT`, `MAX`, `MIN`, or `AVG` operator. The output of this operator may be referenced by later operators in the query, returned to the client, or both.

Because the Stream Aggregate operator requires input ordered by the columns within its groups, a Sort operator often precedes the Stream Aggregate operator unless the data is already sorted due to a prior Sort operator or due to an ordered index seek or scan.

Table Delete, Table Insert, Table Scan, and Table Update

You see the Table Delete, Table Insert, Table Scan, and Table Update operators when the indicated operation is being performed against that table as a whole. The presence of these operators does not always mean a problem exists, although a table scan can be an indicator that you might need some indexes to support the query. A table scan may be performed on small tables even if appropriate indexes exist, especially when the table is only a single page or two in size.

Table-valued Function

The Table-valued Function operator is displayed for queries with calls to table-valued functions. The Table-valued Function operator evaluates the table-valued function, and the resulting rows are stored in the `tempdb` database. When the parent operators request the rows, the Table-valued Function operator returns the rows from `tempdb`.

Top 

The Top operator indicates a limit that is set, either by number of rows or a percentage, on the number of results to be returned from the input. The ToolTip may also contain a list of the columns being checked for ties if the `WITH TIES` option has been specified.

Parallelism Operators

The Parallelism operators indicate that parallel query processing is being performed. The associated logical operator displayed is one of the Distribute Streams, Gather Streams, or Repartition Streams logical operators.

> **Distribute Streams** The Distribute Streams operator takes a single input stream of records and produces multiple output streams. Each record from the input stream appears in one of the output streams. Hashing is typically used to decide to which output stream a particular input record belongs.
>
> **Gather Streams** The Gather Streams operator consumes several input streams and produces a single output stream of records by combining the input streams. If the output is ordered, the ToolTip will contain an `Order By` item indicating the columns being ordered.
>
> **Repartition Streams** The Repartition Streams operator consumes multiple streams and produces multiple streams of records. Each record from an input stream is placed into one output stream. If the output is ordered, the ToolTip contains an `Order By` item indicating the columns being ordered.

NOTE

Parallel query processing strategies are covered in more detail in Chapter 35.

Analyzing Stored Procedures

When displaying the estimated execution plan for a stored procedure, you see multiple statement operators as inputs to the Stored Procedure operator, especially if you have any conditional branching in the stored procedure. One operator exists for each statement defined in the stored procedure. When conditional branching occurs in the stored procedure, SQL Server does not know at query optimization time which statements in the stored procedure will actually be executed, so it has to estimate a query plan for each individual statement. An example is shown in Figure 36.7.

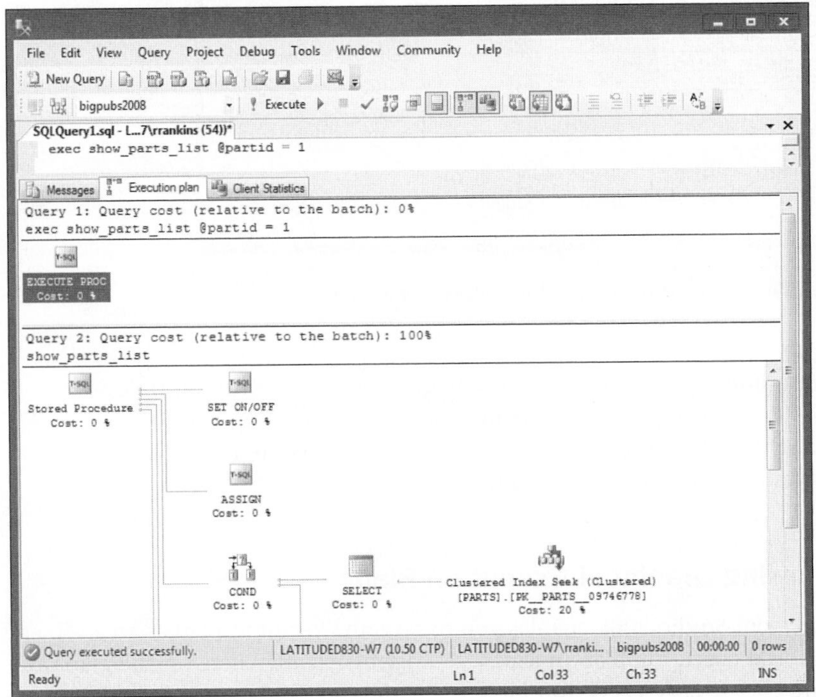

FIGURE 36.7 Estimated execution plan for a stored procedure.

When you execute the stored procedure with the Show Execution Plan option enabled, SSMS displays only the execution plans for the path or statements that are actually executed, as shown in Figure 36.8.

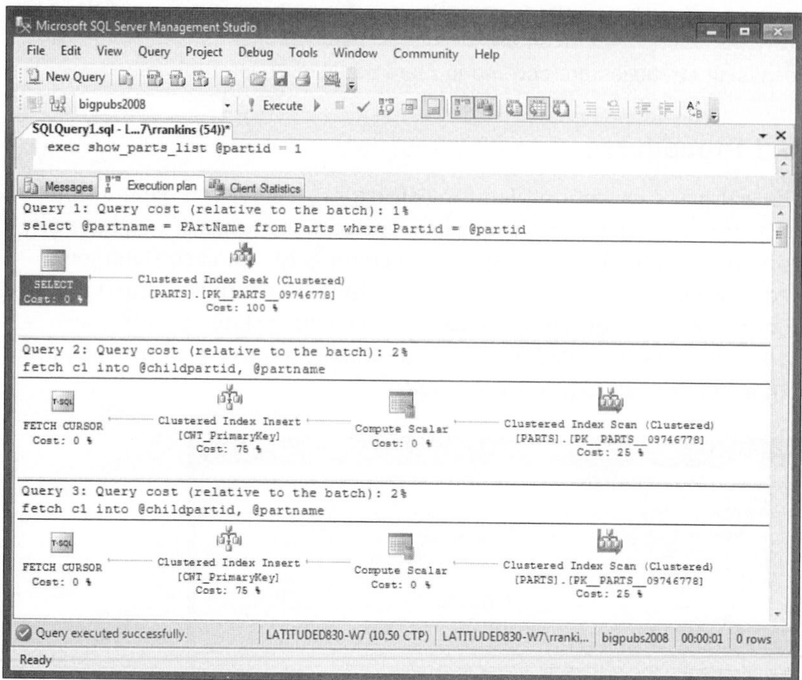

FIGURE 36.8 Actual execution plan used for a stored procedure.

In addition, because stored procedures can become quite complex, with multiple SQL statements, seeing the graphical execution plan in the SSMS Execution Plan window can be difficult. You might find it easier to break up the stored procedure into smaller batches or individual queries and analyze it a bit at a time.

Saving and Viewing Graphical Execution Plans

SQL Server Management Studio 2008 enables you to save an execution plan as an XML file. To save a graphical execution plan in SSMS, you right-click anywhere on the graphical execution plan and choose Save Execution Plan As to bring up the Save As dialog (alternatively, you can choose the Save Execution Plan As option from the File menu).

When you save the execution plan to a file, the graphical execution plan is saved as an XML, file with the `.sqlplan` file extension. To view a saved execution plan, click on the File menu; select Open and then File. In the Open File dialog, select Execution Plan files in the Files of Type drop-down to limit the files displayed to just Execution Plan Files (see Figure 36.9). After you identify the file you want to load, click the Open button, and SSMS opens a new window with the selected execution plan displayed. Just as when the execution plan was originally generated, you can mouse over the operators and display the detailed information contained in the ToolTips.

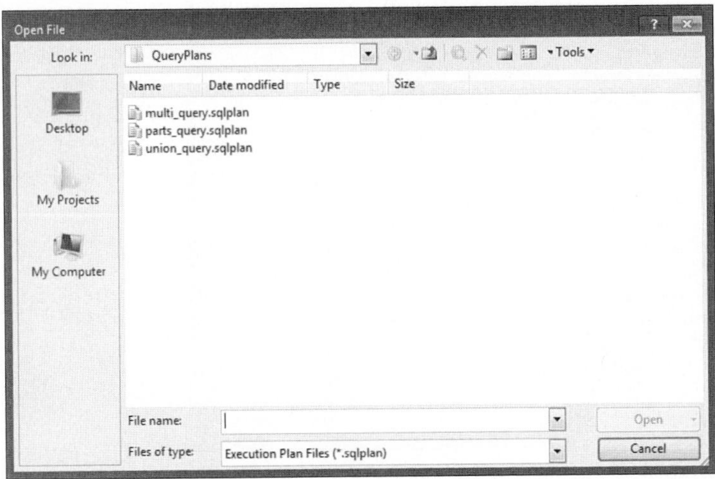

FIGURE 36.9 Loading an execution plan into SSMS.

Displaying Execution Plan XML

In addition to viewing the graphical execution plan in SSMS, you can also display the XML generated by the Query Optimizer that is used to create the graphical execution plan. Right-click on the execution plan and select the Show Execution Plan XML option (see Figure 36.10).

Selecting this option opens a new XML editor window with the `SHOWPLAN_XML` output generated by the query optimizer.

Missing Index Hints

One new feature in SQL Server Management Studio 2008 is Missing Index Hints when displaying the execution plan of a query. You can use the Missing Index Hints feature to help identify columns on which adding an index might help the query execute faster and more efficiently. Missing Index Hints is a lightweight, server-side, always-on feature using dynamic management objects and execution plans to provide information about missing indexes that could enhance query performance.

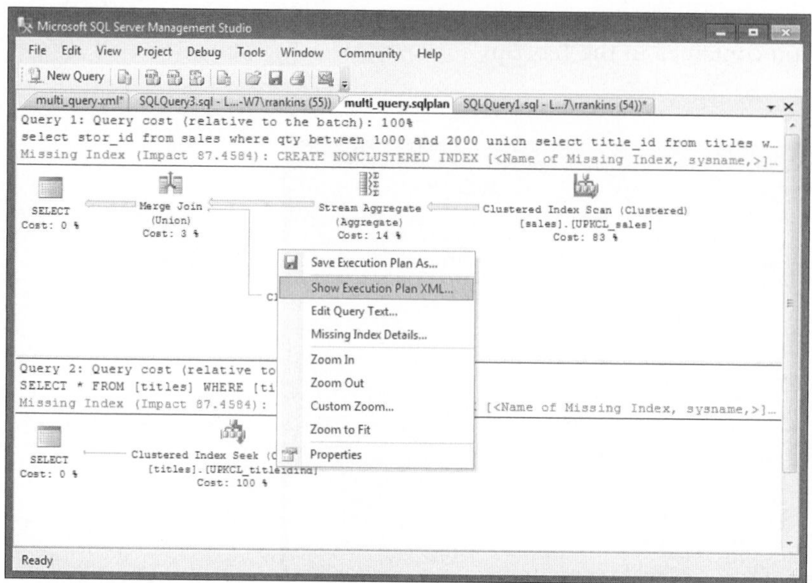

FIGURE 36.10 Generating execution plan XML in SSMS.

NOTE

The Missing Index Hints feature is separate from the Database Engine Tuning Advisor available in SQL Server 2008. The Database Engine Tuning Advisor is a more comprehensive tool that assesses the physical database design and recommends new physical design structures for performance improvement. In addition to index recommendations, it also considers whether indexed views or partitioning could be used to improve query performance.

When the query optimizer generates an execution plan, it analyzes what are the best available indexes for a the specified search and join conditions. If a useful index is not found, the query optimizer generates a suboptimal query plan but still stores information about the missing indexes. The Missing Index Hints feature enables you to view information about these indexes so you can decide whether they should be implemented.

If any missing indexes are identified by the Query Optimizer, the Execution Plan tab in SSMS displays information related to all the missing indexes. If you put the mouse pointer over the missing index text, it displays a ToolTip showing the T-SQL code required to create the suggested missing index as suggested, as shown in Figure 36.11.

In addition to displaying a ToolTip with the T-SQL code, you can also generate the SQL code to create the recommended index by right-clicking on the missing index text and then selecting the Missing Index Details option from the drop-down list (see Figure 36.12). SSMS generates the T-SQL code in a new query window. An example of the T-SQL code generated is shown in Listing 36.1.

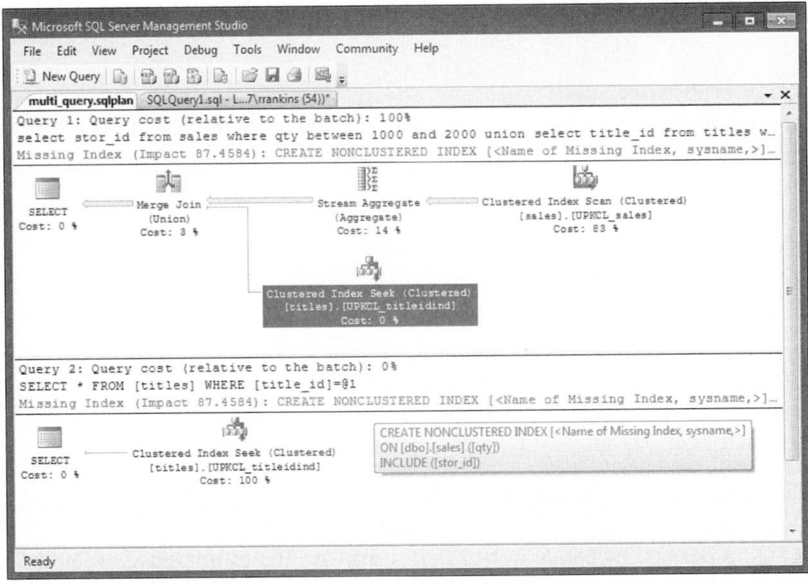

FIGURE 36.11 Displaying missing indexes in SSMS.

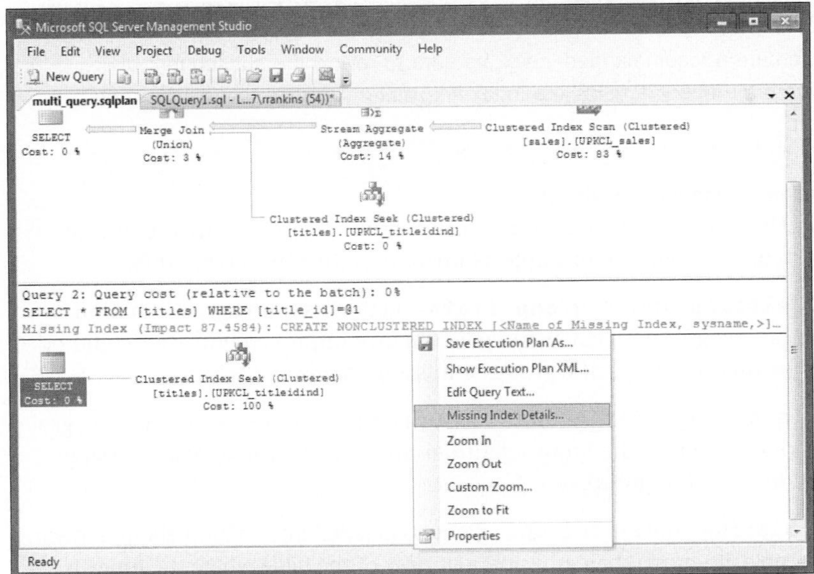

FIGURE 36.12 Generating T-SQL code to create a missing index.

LISTING 36.1 SQL Generated by SSMS Missing Index Hints Feature

```
/*
Missing Index Details from multi_query.sqlplan
The Query Processor estimates that implementing the following index could improve
 the query cost by 87.4584%.
*/

/*
USE [bigpubs2008]
GO
CREATE NONCLUSTERED INDEX [<Name of Missing Index, sysname,>]
ON [dbo].[sales] ([qty])
INCLUDE ([stor_id])
GO
*/
```

If you examine the SQL generated by SSMS, notice that it displays the estimated associated cost benefit expected by adding the recommended index. Also note that the script does not include an index name. You need to specify an index name based on your naming standards.

NOTE

If you decide to create a recommended index, be sure to review the subsequent query plan to determine if the query is using the index and that it provides the expected performance benefit.

Missing Index Dynamic Management Objects

The Missing Index Hints feature in SSMS draws information regarding missing indexes from a set of new dynamic management objects introduced in SQL Server 2008:

- **sys.dm_db_missing_index_group_stats**—Returns summary information about missing index groups, such as the performance improvements that could be gained by implementing a specific group of missing indexes.
- **sys.dm_db_missing_index_groups**—Returns information about a specific group of missing indexes, such as the group identifier and the identifiers of all missing indexes contained in that group.
- **sys.dm_db_missing_index_columns**—Returns detailed information about a missing index; for example, it returns the name and identifier of the table where the index is missing, and the columns and column types that should make up the missing index.
- **sys.dm_db_missing_index_details**—Returns information about the database table columns that are missing an index.

Although the missing indexes feature in SSMS is useful when analyzing individual queries, it's not convenient for analyzing missing indexes for a large set of SQL queries, like the set of queries executed by an application. This is where the dynamic management objects come in handy. After running a typical workload on SQL Server, you can retrieve information about missing indexes by querying the dynamic management functions directly. You can use the information returned by these dynamic management objects in scripts and use the information to generate CREATE INDEX statements to create the missing indexes. Listing 36.2 provides a sample query that displays the missing index information for a query on the sales table that was run between 10:30 and 10:40 p.m. on February 21, 2010.

LISTING 36.2 Querying the Missing Index Dynamic Management Objects

```
SELECT
     mig.index_group_handle as handle,
     convert(varchar(30), statement) AS table_name,
     convert(varchar(12), column_name) AS Column_name,
     convert(varchar(10), column_usage) as ColumnUsage,
     avg_user_impact as avg_impact
FROM sys.dm_db_missing_index_details AS mid
CROSS APPLY sys.dm_db_missing_index_columns (mid.index_handle)
INNER JOIN sys.dm_db_missing_index_groups AS mig
       ON mig.index_handle = mid.index_handle
inner join sys.dm_db_missing_index_group_stats AS migs
       ON migs.group_handle = mig.index_group_handle
where mid.object_id = object_id('sales')
and last_user_seek between '2010-02-21 22:30' and '2010-02-21 22:40'
ORDER BY mig.index_group_handle, mig.index_handle, column_id;
GO

handle      table_name                      Column_name  ColumnUsage avg_impact
----------- ------------------------------ ------------ ----------- ----------
2           [bigpubs2008].[dbo].[sales]    stor_id      INCLUDE     87.46
2           [bigpubs2008].[dbo].[sales]    qty          INEQUALITY  87.46
```

If you view the output of this query, you see that the optimizer is recommending an index on the qty column to support an inequality operator. It is also recommended that the stor_id column be specified as an included column in the index. This index is estimated to improve performance by 87.46%. When you use this information, the CREATE INDEX statement for the recommended index would be the following:

```
CREATE INDEX qty_idx on [bigpubs2008].[dbo].[sales] (qty) INCLUDE (stor_id)
```

Missing Index Hints Features Limitations

The Missing Index Hints feature provides some helpful information for identifying potentially missing indexes in your database, but it does have a few limitations:

- It is not intended to fine-tune the existing indexes, only to recommend additional indexes when no useful index is found that can be used to satisfy a search or join condition.
- It does not specify the order for columns to be specified in the index.
- For queries involving only inequality predicates, the cost information returned is less accurate than for equality operators.
- It only recommends adding included columns to indexes for some queries instead of creating composite indexes. You need to determine whether the included columns should be specified as additional index key columns instead.
- It returns only raw information about columns on which indexes might be missing.
- It may return different costs for the same missing index group for different executions.
- It does not suggest filtered indexes.
- The dynamic management objects can store information from a maximum of 500 missing indexes.
- It is unable to provide recommendations for clustered indexes, indexed views, or table partitioning. (Use the Database Engine Tuning Advisor instead for these recommendations.)
- After the SQL Server is restarted, all the information related to missing indexes is lost. To keep the information for later use, the DBA needs to back up all the data available within all the missing index dynamic management objects prior to restarting SQL Server.

NOTE

Although the Missing Index Hints feature is helpful for identifying indexes that may be useful for you to define, it's not a substitute for a well-thought-out index design. For more information on index design, see Chapter 34, "Data Structures, Indexes, and Performance."

SSMS Client Statistics

You can use SSMS to get some additional information related to the client-side performance of the query by toggling the Include Client Statistics option in the Query menu. When turned on, the Client Statistics tab is added to the Results panel. This tab displays useful performance statistics in a tabular format that is related to how much work the client had to do to submit the query and process the results, including statistics about the network packets and elapsed time of the query.

SSMS keeps track of the statistics for previous executions within a session so that you can compare the statistics between different query executions. It also keeps track of the overall average statistics across all executions. Figure 36.13 shows an example of the client statistics displayed after three separate query executions.

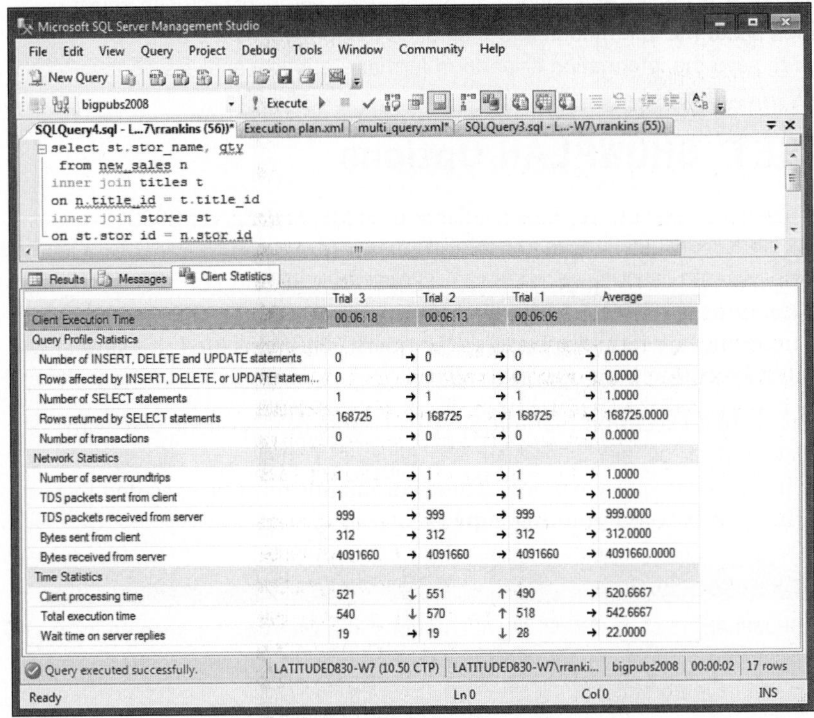

FIGURE 36.13 SSMS client statistics.

The first line in the Client Statistics tab displays the actual time the query was executed. The Time Statistics values are specified in number of milliseconds. Some of the most useful pieces of information include the number of rows returned by `SELECT` statements, total client processing time, total execution time, and number of bytes sent and received across the network.

The Average column contains the cumulative average since the Include Client Statistics option was enabled. Turning the option off and back on clears out all the historical statistics and resets the averages. Alternatively, you can also reset the client statistics by selecting the Reset Client Statistics option from the Query menu.

One of the most helpful features of the client statistics is the arrow indicators provided for the different executions, which makes it easy to identify which values increased, decreased, or stayed this same. This feature makes it easy to compare the runtime statistics between different queries or different executions of the same query.

36

TIP

Unlike the graphical execution plans, SSMS does not provide a way to save the client statistics. Fortunately, the statistics are displayed using a standard grid control. You can right-click the client statistics and choose Select All. Then you right-click and select Copy. You can then paste the information into a spreadsheet program such as Excel, which allows you to save the information or perform further statistical analysis on it.

Using the SET SHOWPLAN Options

In addition to the graphical execution plans available in SSMS, SQL Server 2008 provides three `SET SHOWPLAN` options to display the execution plan information in a text or XML format. These options are `SET SHOWPLAN_TEXT`, `SET SHOWPLAN_ALL`, and `SET SHOWPLAN_XML`. When one of these options is enabled, SQL Server returns the execution plan generated for the query, but no results are returned because the query is not executed. It's similar to the Display Estimated Execution Plan option in SSMS.

You can turn on the textual execution plan output in a couple of ways. One way is to issue the `SET SHOWPLAN_TEXT ON`, `SET SHOWPLAN_ALL ON`, or `SET SHOWPLAN_XML ON` command directly in the SSMS query window. These commands must be executed in a separate batch by themselves before running a query.

TIP

Before enabling `SHOWPLAN_TEXT` or `SHOWPLAN_ALL` options in a Query Editor session in SSMS, be sure to disable the Include Actual Execution Plan option; otherwise, the `SHOWPLAN` options will have no effect.

SHOWPLAN_TEXT

Typing the following command in an SSMS query window turns on the `SHOWPLAN_TEXT` option:

```
SET SHOWPLAN_TEXT ON
GO
```

Setting this option causes the textual showplan output to be displayed in the results panel but does not execute the query. You can also enable the `SHOWPLAN_TEXT` option by choosing the Query Options item from the Query menu. In the Query Options dialog, you click the Advanced item and check the `SET SHOWPLAN_TEXT` option.

The `SHOWPLAN_TEXT` option displays a textual representation of the execution plan. Listing 36.3 shows an example for a simple inner join query.

TIP

When you are displaying the `SHOWPLAN_TEXT` information in SSMS, it is usually easiest to view if you configure SSMS to return results to text rather than as a grid.

LISTING 36.3 An Example of **SHOWPLAN_TEXT** Output

```
set showplan_text on
go
select st.stor_name, ord_date, qty
from stores st join sales_noclust s on st.stor_id = s.stor_id
where st.stor_id between 'B100' and 'B199'
go
StmtText
-------------------------------------------------------------------------------
select st.stor_name, ord_date, qty
from stores st join sales_noclust s on st.stor_id = s.stor_id
where st.stor_id between 'B100' and 'B199'

(1 row(s) affected)

StmtText
-----------------------------------------------------------------------------
-----------------------------------------------------------------------------
-----------------------------------------------------------------------------
-------------------------
  |--Nested Loops(Inner Join, OUTER REFERENCES:([Bmk1002], [Expr1006]) WITH
 UNORDERED PREFETCH)
       |--Nested Loops(Inner Join, OUTER REFERENCES:([st].[stor_id]))
       |    |--Clustered Index
Seek(OBJECT:([bigpubs2008].[dbo].[stores].[UPK_storeid]
 AS [st]), SEEK:([st].[stor_id] >= 'B100' AND [st].[stor_id] <= 'B199')
 ORDERED FORWARD)
       |    |--Index Seek(OBJECT:([bigpubs2008].[dbo].[sales_noclust].[idx1] AS
 [s]), SEEK:([s].[stor_id]=[bigpubs2008].[dbo].[stores].[stor_id] as
 [st].[stor_id]),  WHERE:([bigpubs2008].[dbo].[sales_noclust].[stor_id] as
 [s].[stor_id]>='B100' AND [bigpubs
       |--RID Lookup(OBJECT:([bigpubs2008].[dbo].[sales_noclust] AS [s]),
 SEEK:([Bmk1002]=[Bmk1002]) LOOKUP ORDERED FORWARD)

(5 row(s) affected)
```

The output is read from right to left, similarly to the graphical execution plan. Each line represents a physical/logical operator. The text displayed matches the logical and physical operator names displayed in the graphical execution plan. If you can read the graphical query plan, you should have no trouble reading the SHOWPLAN_TEXT output.

In the example in Listing 36.3, SQL Server performs a clustered index seek on the stores table, using the UPK_storeid index, and a nonclustered index seek on sales_noclust, using index idx1. The inputs are combined using a nested loop join. Finally, a RID lookup is performed to retrieve the ord_date and qty information from the sales_noclust table.

When the SHOWPLAN_TEXT option is set to ON, execution plan information about all subsequent SQL Server 2008 statements is returned until the option is set to OFF. Also, all subsequent commands are optimized but not executed. To turn off the textual showplan output and allow execution of commands again, type the following command:

```
SET SHOWPLAN_TEXT OFF
GO
```

TIP

To switch from one SET SHOWPLAN option to another, remember that no commands are executed until the SET SHOWPLAN option is turned off. This includes setting the SET SHOWPLAN options. For example, to switch from SHOWPLAN_TEXT to either SHOWPLAN_ALL or SHOWPLAN_XML, you have to turn off SHOWPLAN_TEXT first with the SET SHOWPLAN_TEXT OFF command.

SHOWPLAN_ALL

The SHOWPLAN_ALL option displays the same textual execution plan information as the SHOWPLAN_TEXT option, and it also provides additional columns of output for each row of textual showplan output. These columns provide much of the same information available in the graphical execution ToolTips, and the column headings correspond to the ToolTip items listed in the "Execution Plan ToolTips" section, earlier in this chapter. Table 36.1 describes the information provided in the data columns returned by the SHOWPLAN_ALL option.

TABLE 36.1 Data Columns Returned by **SHOWPLAN_ALL**

Column Name	Description
StmtText	The text of the T-SQL statement and also each of the physical operators in the execution plan. (It may optionally also contain the logical operators.)
StmtId	The number of the statement in the current batch.
NodeId	The ID of the node in the current query.
Parent	The node ID of the parent operator for the current operator.
PhysicalOp	Physical operator description for the current node.
LogicalOp	Logical operator description for the current node.
Argument	Supplemental information about the operation being performed.
DefinedValues	A comma-separated list of values introduced by this operator. These may be either computed expressions present in the current query or internal values introduced by the query processor to be able to process this query.

TABLE 36.1 Data Columns Returned by **SHOWPLAN_ALL**

Column Name	Description
EstimateRows	Estimated number of rows of output produced by the operator.
EstimateIO	Estimated I/O cost for the operator.
EstimateCPU	Estimated CPU cost for the operator.
AvgRowSize	Estimated average row size (in bytes) of the row being passed through the operator.
TotalSubtreeCost	Estimated (cumulative) cost of this operation and all child operations.
OutputList	A comma-separated list of columns being projected by the current operation.
Warnings	A comma-separated list of warning messages relating to the current operation (for example, missing statistics).
Type	The type of node (either PLAN_ROW or the type of T-SQL statement).
Parallel	Whether the operator is running in parallel (1) or not (0).
EstimateExecutions	Estimated number of times this operator will be executed while running the current query.

TIP

When you are displaying the SHOWPLAN_ALL information in SSMS, it is usually easiest to view if you configure SSMS to return results to grid rather than as text.

SHOWPLAN_XML

When SET SHOWPLAN_XML is set to ON, SQL Server does not execute the query but returns execution information for each T-SQL batch as an XML document. The execution plan information for each T-SQL batch is contained in a single XML document. Each XML document contains the text of the statements in the batch, followed by the details of the execution steps and operators. The document includes the estimated costs, numbers of rows, indexes used, join order, and types of operators performed.

The SHOWPLAN_XML option generates the same XML output as the Show Estimated Execution Plan option in SSMS. In essence, you are looking at the same information, just without the pretty pictures. As a matter of fact, you can save the output from the SHOWPLAN_XML option to a file and open it back into SSMS as a SQL plan file. The recommended approach is to configure the query window to return results to a grid. If you return the results as text or to a file, the maximum output size for a character column in

SSMS is 8,192 bytes. If the XML document exceeds this length, it is truncated and does not load correctly. In the grid results, the maximum size of XML data is 2MB.

After you run the query and generate the grid results, you can right-click on the result row and choose the Save Results As option to specify the file to save the results to. If all goes well, you end up with a `.sqlplan` file that you can then load back into SSMS for further analysis at a later date.

NOTE

The document containing the XML schema for the `SET SHOWPLAN_XML` output is available in the same directory as the SQL Server installation, which by default is `C:\Program Files\Microsoft SQL Server\100\Tools\Binn\schemas\sqlserver\2004\07\showplan\showplanxml.xsd`.

Using `sys.dm_exec_query_plan`

Dynamic management views (DMVs) can return server state information that can be used to monitor and diagnose database engine issues and help tune performance. The `sys.dm_exec_query_plan` DMV returns the showplan information for a T-SQL batch whose query execution plan resides in the plan cache. This can be any SQL batch, not just the batch executed by the current user session. The `sys.dm_exec_query_plan` DMV also provides the capability to retrieve the execution plan for currently long-running processes to help diagnose why they may be running slowly.

The showplan information provided by `sys.dm_exec_query_plan` is returned in a column called `query_plan`, which is of the `xml` data type. This column provides the same information as `SET SHOWPLAN XML`. The syntax of `sys.dm_exec_query_plan` is

```
sys.dm_exec_query_plan ( plan_handle )
```

In SQL Server 2008, the query plans for various types of T-SQL batches are cached in an area of memory called the *plan cache*. Each cached query plan is identified by a unique identifier called a *plan handle*. To view the showplan for one of these batches, you need to provide the plan handle for the batch to the `sys.dm_exec_query_plan` DMV.

The tricky part about using `sys.dm_exec_query_plan` is determining the plan handle to use. First, you need to determine the SPID for the process with the long-running query. This is usually accomplished using `sp_who2` or via the SSMS Activity Monitor.

When you have the SPID, you can use the `sys.dm_exec_requests` DMV to obtain the plan handle (assume in this case that the SPID is 58):

```
select plan_handle from sys.dm_exec_requests where session_id = 58
go
```

```
plan_handle
---------------------------------------------------------------------------
0x06000A00E96E6D2CB8A1F505000000000000000000000000
```

When you have the plan handle, you can pass it on to the sys.dm_exec_query_plan DMV to return the query plan:

```
SELECT query_plan
FROM sys.dm_exec_query_plan (0x06000A00E96E6D2CB8A1F505000000000000000000000000)
```

Alternatively, to prevent having to copy and paste the plan handle from the sys.dm_exec_requests query into the query against sys.dm_exec_query_plan, you can use the CROSS APPLY clause, as in the following query:

```
SELECT query_plan FROM sys.dm_exec_requests cp
    CROSS APPLY sys.dm_exec_query_plan(cp.plan_handle)
    where cp.session_id = 58
```

If you return the results to grid, you can right-click the data in the query_plan column and save it to a file, which can then be loaded into SSMS to view the graphical execution plan, just like the output from the SET SHOWPLAN_XML option.

To return the query plan for all currently running T-SQL batches, you can run the following:

```
SELECT query_plan FROM sys.dm_exec_requests cp
    CROSS APPLY sys.dm_exec_query_plan(cp.plan_handle)
```


In addition to returning the query plans for the currently running T-SQL batches, SQL Server 2008 also provides the sys.dm_exec_query_stats and sys.dm_exec_cached_plans DMVs. The sys.dm_exec_cached_plans DMV can be used to return information about all query plans currently residing in the plan cache. For example, to retrieve a snapshot of all query plans residing in the plan cache, you use the CROSS APPLY operator to pass the plan handles from sys.dm_exec_cached_plans to sys.dm_exec_query_plan, as follows:

```
SELECT * FROM sys.dm_exec_cached_plans cp
   CROSS APPLY sys.dm_exec_query_plan(cp.plan_handle)
```

To retrieve a snapshot of all query plans that currently reside in the plan cache for which the server has gathered statistics, use the CROSS APPLY operator to pass the plan handles from sys.dm_exec_query_stats to sys.dm_exec_query_plan as follows:

```
SELECT * FROM sys.dm_exec_query_stats qs
   CROSS APPLY sys.dm_exec_query_plan(qs.plan_handle)
```

Because sys.dm_exec_query_plan provides the capability to view the query plan for any session, a user must be a member of the sysadmin fixed server role or have the VIEW SERVER STATE permission on the server to invoke it.

NOTE

The SET SHOWPLAN_ALL and SET SHOWPLAN_TEXT options are deprecated features and may be removed in a future version of SQL Server. It is recommended that you switch to using the SET SHOWPLAN_XML option instead.

Query Statistics

In addition to the new dynamic management objects, SQL Server 2008 still provides the SET STATISTICS IO and SET STATISTICS TIME options, which display the actual logical and physical page reads incurred by a query and the CPU and elapsed time, respectively. These two SET options return actual execution statistics, as opposed to the estimates returned by SSMS and the SHOWPLAN options discussed previously. These two tools can be invaluable for determining the actual cost of a query.

In addition to the IO and TIME statistics, SQL Server also provides the SET STATISTICS PROFILE and SET STATISTICS XML options. These options are provided to display execution plan information while still allowing the query to run.

STATISTICS IO

You can set the STATISTICS IO option for individual user sessions, and you can turn it on in an SSMS query window by typing the following:

```
SET STATISTICS IO ON
GO
```

You can also set this option for the query session in SSMS by choosing the Options item in the Query menu. In the Query Options dialog, click the Advanced item and check the SET STATISTICS IO check box, as shown in Figure 36.14.

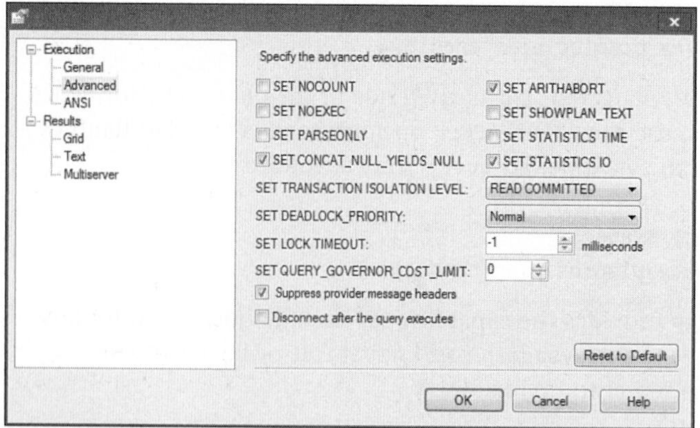

FIGURE 36.14 Enabling the **STATISTICS IO** option in SSMS.

The STATISTICS IO option displays the scan count (that is, the number of iterations), the logical reads (from cached data), the physical reads (from physical storage), and the read-ahead reads.

Listing 36.4 displays the STATISTICS IO output for the same query executed in Listing 36.3. (Note that the result set has been deleted to save space.)

LISTING 36.4 An Example of **STATISTICS IO** Output

```
set statistics io on
go
select st.stor_name, ord_date, qty
from stores st join sales_noclust s on st.stor_id = s.stor_id
where st.stor_id between 'B100' and 'B199'
go

-- output deleted

(1077 row(s) affected)
Table 'sales_noclust'. Scan count 100, logical reads 1383, physical reads 5,
 read-ahead reads 8, lob logical reads 0, lob physical reads 0,
 lob read-ahead reads 0.
Table 'stores'. Scan count 1, logical reads 3, physical reads 0,
 read-ahead reads 0, lob logical reads 0, lob physical reads 0,
 lob read-ahead reads 0.
```


Scan Count

The scan count value indicates the number of times the corresponding table was accessed during query execution. The outer table of a nested loop join typically has a scan count of 1. The scan count for the inner tables typically reflects the number of times the inner table is searched, which is usually the same as the number of qualifying rows in the outer table. The number of logical reads for the inner table is equal to the scan count multiplied by the number of pages per lookup for each scan. Note that the scan count for the inner table might sometimes be only 1 for a nested join if SQL Server copies the needed rows from the inner table into a work table in cache memory and reads from the work table for subsequent iterations (for example, if it uses the Table Spool operation). The scan count for hash joins and merge joins is typically 1 for both tables involved in the join, but the logical reads for these types of joins are usually substantially higher.

Logical Reads

The logical reads value indicates the total number of page accesses necessary to process the query. Every page is read from cache memory, even if it first has to be read from disk. Every physical read always has a corresponding logical read, so the number of physical reads will never exceed the number of logical reads. Because the same page might be accessed multiple times, the number of logical reads for a table could exceed the total number of pages in the table.

Physical Reads

The `physical reads` value indicates the actual number of pages read from disk. The value for physical reads can vary greatly and should decrease, or drop to zero, with subsequent executions of the query because the data will be loaded into the data cache by the first execution. The number of physical reads will also be lowered by pages brought into memory by the read-ahead mechanism.

Read-Ahead Reads

The `read-ahead reads` value indicates the number of pages read into cache memory using the read-ahead mechanism while the query was processed. Pages read by the read-ahead mechanism will not necessarily be used by the query. When a page read by the read-ahead mechanism is accessed by the query, it counts as a logical read, but not as a physical read.

The read-ahead mechanism can be thought of as an optimistic form of physical I/O, reading the pages into cache memory that it expects the query will need before the query needs them. When you are scanning a table or index, the table's index allocation map pages (IAMs) are looked at to determine which extents belong to the object. An extent consists of eight data pages. The eight pages in the extent are read with a single read, and the extents are read in the order that they are stored on disk. If the table is spread across multiple files, the read-ahead mechanism attempts parallel reads from up to eight files at a time instead of sequentially reading from the files.

LOB Reads

If the query retrieves text, ntext, image, or large value type (`varchar(max)`, `nvarchar(max)`, `varbinary(max)`) data, the `lob logical reads`, `lob physical reads`, and `lob read-ahead reads` values provide the logical, physical, and read-ahead read statistics for the large object (LOB) I/Os.

Analyzing `STATISTICS IO` Output

The output shown in Listing 36.4 indicates that the `sales_noclust` table was scanned 100 times, with 5 physical reads (that is, 5 physical I/Os were performed). The `stores` table was scanned once, with all reads coming from cache (physical reads = 0).

You can use the `STATISTICS IO` option to evaluate the effectiveness of the size of the data cache and to evaluate, over time, how long a table will stay in cache. The lack of physical reads is a good sign, indicating that memory is sufficient to keep the data in cache. If you keep seeing many physical reads when you are analyzing and testing your queries, you might want to consider adding more memory to the server to improve the cache hit ratio. You can estimate the cache hit ratio for a query by using the following formula:

```
Cache hit ratio = (Logical reads - Physical reads) / Logical reads
```

The number of physical reads appears lower than it actually is if pages are preloaded by read-ahead activity. Because read-ahead reads lower the physical read count, they give the indication of a good cache hit ratio, when in actuality, the data is still being physically read from disk. The system could still benefit from more memory so that the data remains in cache and the number of read-ahead reads is reduced. `STATISTICS IO` is generally more useful for evaluating individual query performance than for evaluating overall cache hit ratio. The pages that reside and remain in memory for subsequent executions are determined by the data pages being accessed by other queries executing at the same time and the number of data pages being accessed by the other queries. If no other activity is occurring, you are likely to see no physical reads for subsequent executions of the query if the amount of data being accessed fits in the available cache memory. Likewise, if the same data is being accessed by multiple queries, the data tends to stay in cache, and the number of physical reads for subsequent executions tends to be low. However, if other queries executing at the same time are accessing large volumes of data from different tables or ranges of values, the data needed for the query you are testing might end up being flushed from cache, and the physical I/Os will increase. Depending on the other ongoing SQL Server activity, the physical reads you see displayed by `STATISTICS IO` can be inconsistent.

When you are evaluating individual query performance, examining the logical reads value is usually more helpful because the information is consistent across all executions, regardless of other SQL Server activity. Generally speaking, the queries with the fewest logical reads are the fastest queries. If you want to monitor the overall cache hit ratio for all SQL Server activity to evaluate the SQL Server memory configuration, use the Performance Monitor, which is discussed in Chapter 39, "Monitoring SQL Server Performance."

STATISTICS TIME

You can set the `STATISTICS TIME` option for individual user sessions. In an SSMS query window, you type the following:

```
SET STATISTICS TIME ON
```

You can also set this option for the query session in SSMS by choosing the Options item in the Query menu. In the Query Options dialog, you click the Advanced item and check the `SET STATISTICS TIME` check box.

The `STATISTICS TIME` option displays the total CPU and elapsed time that it takes to actually execute a query. The `STATISTICS TIME` output for the query in Listing 36.3 returns the output shown in Listing 36.5. (Again, the data rows returned have been deleted to save space.)

LISTING 36.5 An Example of **STATISTICS TIME** Output

```
set statistics io on
set statistics time on
go

select st.stor_name, ord_date, qty
from stores st join sales_noclust s on st.stor_id = s.stor_id
```

```
where st.stor_id between 'B100' and 'B199'
go


SQL Server parse and compile time:
   CPU time = 0 ms, elapsed time = 0 ms.

--output deleted

(1077 row(s) affected)
Table 'sales_noclust'. Scan count 100, logical reads 1383, physical reads 0,
 read-ahead reads 0, lob logical reads 0, lob physical reads 0, lob read-ahead
 reads 0.
Table 'stores'. Scan count 1, logical reads 3, physical reads 0, read-ahead
 reads 0, lob logical reads 0, lob physical reads 0, lob read-ahead reads 0.

 SQL Server Execution Times:
   CPU time = 0 ms,  elapsed time = 187 ms.
```

Here, you can see that the total execution time, denoted by the elapsed time, was relatively low and not significantly higher than the CPU time. This is due to the lack of any physical reads and the fact that all activity is performed in memory.

NOTE

In some situations, you might notice that the parse and compile time for a query is displayed twice. This happens when the query plan is added to the plan cache for possible reuse. The first set of information output is the actual parse and compile before placing the plan in cache, and the second set of information output appears when SQL Server retrieves the plan from cache. Subsequent executions still show the same two sets of output, but the parse and compile time is 0 when the plan is reused because a query plan is not being compiled.

If elapsed time is much higher than CPU time, the query had to wait for something, either I/O or locks. If you want to see the effect of physical versus logical I/Os on the performance of a query, you need to flush the pages accessed by the query from memory. You can use the `DBCC DROPCLEANBUFFERS` command to clear all clean buffer pages out of memory. Listing 36.6 shows an example of clearing the pages from cache and rerunning the query with the `STATISTICS IO` and `STATISTICS TIME` options enabled.

TIP

To ensure that none of the table is left in cache, make sure all pages are marked as clean before running the DBCC DROPCLEANBUFFERS command. A buffer is dirty if it contains a data row modification that has either not been committed yet or has not been written out to disk yet. To clear the greatest number of buffer pages from cache memory, make sure all work is committed, checkpoint the database to force all modified pages to be written out to disk, and then execute the DBCC DROPCLEANBUFFERS command.

CAUTION

The DBCC DROPCLEANBUFFERS command should be executed in a test or development environment only. Flushing all data pages from cache memory in a production environment can have a significantly adverse impact on system performance.

LISTING 36.6 An Example of Clearing the Clean Pages from Cache to Generate Physical I/Os

```
USE bigpubs2008
go
CHECKPOINT
go
DBCC DROPCLEANBUFFERS
go

SET STATISTICS IO ON
SET STATISTICS TIME ON
go
select st.stor_name, ord_date, qty
from stores st join sales_noclust s on st.stor_id = s.stor_id
where st.stor_id between 'B100' and 'B199'
go

SQL Server parse and compile time:
   CPU time = 0 ms, elapsed time = 1 ms.

--output deleted

(1077 row(s) affected)
Table 'sales_noclust'. Scan count 100, logical reads 1383, physical reads 6,
 read-ahead reads 0, lob logical reads 0, lob physical reads 0, lob read-ahead
```

```
 reads 0.
Table 'stores'. Scan count 1, logical reads 3, physical reads 2, read-ahead
 reads 0, lob logical reads 0, lob physical reads 0, lob read-ahead reads 0.

 SQL Server Execution Times:
   CPU time = 0 ms,  elapsed time = 282 ms.
```

Notice that this time around, even though the reported CPU time was the same, the elapsed time was 282 milliseconds due to the physical I/Os that had to be performed during this execution.

You can use the `STATISTICS TIME` and `STATISTICS IO` options together in this way as a useful tool for benchmarking and comparing performance when modifying queries or indexes.

Using `datediff()` to Measure Runtime

Although the `STATISTICS TIME` option works fine for displaying the runtime of a single query, it is not as useful for displaying the total CPU time and elapsed time for a stored procedure. The `STATISTICS TIME` option generates time statistics for every command executed within the stored procedure. This makes it difficult to read the output and determine the total elapsed time for the entire stored procedure.

Another way to display runtime for a stored procedure is to capture the current system time right before it starts, capture the current system time as it completes, and display the difference between the two, specifying the appropriate-sized `datepart` parameter to the `datediff()` function, depending on how long your procedures typically run. For example, if a procedure takes minutes to complete, you probably want to display the difference in seconds or minutes, rather than milliseconds. If the time to complete is in seconds, you likely want to specify a `datepart` of seconds or milliseconds. Listing 36.7 displays an example of using this approach.

LISTING 36.7 Using **`datediff()`** to Determine Stored Procedure Runtime

```
set statistics time off
set statistics io off
go
declare @start datetime
select @start = getdate()
exec sp_help
select datediff(ms, @start, getdate()) as 'runtime(ms)'
go

-- output deleted
```

```
runtime(ms)
-----------
        3263
```

STATISTICS PROFILE

The SET STATISTICS PROFILE option is similar to the SET SHOWPLAN_ALL option but allows the query to actually execute. It returns the same execution plan information displayed with the SET SHOWPLAN_ALL statement, with the addition of two columns that display actual execution information. The Rows column displays the actual number of rows returned in the execution step, and the Executions column shows the actual number of executions for the step. The Rows column can be compared to the EstimatedRows column, and the Execution column can be compared to the EstimatedExecution column to determine the accuracy of the execution plan estimates.

You can set the STATISTICS PROFILE option for individual query sessions. In an SSMS query window, you type the following statement:

```
SET STATISTICS PROFILE ON
GO
```

36

NOTE

The SET STATISTICS PROFILE option has been deprecated and may be removed in a future version of SQL Server. It is recommended that you switch to using the SET STATISTICS XML option instead.

STATISTICS XML

Similar to the STATISTICS PROFILE option, the SET STATISTICS XML option allows a query to execute while also returning the execution plan information. The execution plan information returned is similar to the XML document displayed with the SET SHOWPLAN_XML statement.

To set the STATISTICS XML option for individual query sessions in SSMS or another query tool, you type the following statement:

```
SET STATISTICS XML ON
GO
```

NOTE

With all the fancy graphical tools available, why would you want to use the text-based analysis tools? Although the graphical tools are useful for analyzing individual queries one at a time, they can be a bit tedious if you have to perform analysis on a number of queries. As an alternative, you can put all the queries you want to analyze in a script file and set the appropriate options to get the query plan and statistics output you want to see. You can then run the script through a tool such as `sqlcmd` and route the output to a file. You can then quickly scan the file or use an editor's Find utility to look for the obvious potential performance issues, such as table scans or long-running queries. Next, you can copy the individual problem queries you identify from the output file into SSMS, where you can perform a more thorough analysis on them.

You could also set up a job to run this SQL script periodically to constantly capture and save performance statistics. This gives you a means to keep a history of the query performance and execution plans over time. This information can be used to compare performance differences as the data volumes and SQL Server activity levels change over time.

Another advantage of the textual query plan output over the graphical query plans is that for very complex queries, the graphical plan tends to get very big and spread out so much that it's difficult to read and follow. The textual output is somewhat more compact and easier to see all at once.

Query Analysis with SQL Server Profiler

SQL Server Profiler serves as another powerful tool available for query analysis. When you must monitor a broad range of queries and database activity and analyze the performance, it is difficult to analyze all those queries manually. For example, if you have a number of stored procedures to analyze, how would you know which ones to focus on as problem procedures? You would have to identify sample parameters for all of them and manually execute them individually to see which ones were running too slowly and then, after they were identified, do some query analysis on them.

With SQL Server Profiler, you can simply define a trace to capture performance-related statistics on the fly while the system is being used normally. This way, you can capture a representative sample of the type of activity your database will receive and capture statistics for the stored procedures as they are being executed with real data values. Also, to avoid having to look at everything, you can set a filter on the Duration column so that it displays only items with a runtime longer than the specified threshold.

The events you want to capture to analyze query performance are listed under the Performance events. They include Showplan All, Showplan Statistics Profile, Showplan Text, Showplan Text (Unencoded), Showplan XML, Showplan XML for Query Compile, and Showplan XML Statistics Profile. The data columns that you want to be sure to include when capturing the showplan events are TextData, CPU, StartTime, Duration, and Reads and Writes. Also, for the Showplan Statistics and Showplan All events, you must also select the BinaryData data column.

Capturing the showplan performance information with SQL Server Profiler provides you with all the same information you can capture with all the other individual tools discussed in this chapter. You can easily save the trace information to a file or table for replaying the sequence to test index or configuration changes, or simply for historical analysis. If you choose any of the Showplan XML options, you have the option of saving the XML Showplan events separately from the overall trace file. You can choose to save all XML Showplan events in a single file or separate file for each event (see Figure 36.15). You can then load the Showplan XML file into SSMS to view the graphical execution plans and perform your query analysis.

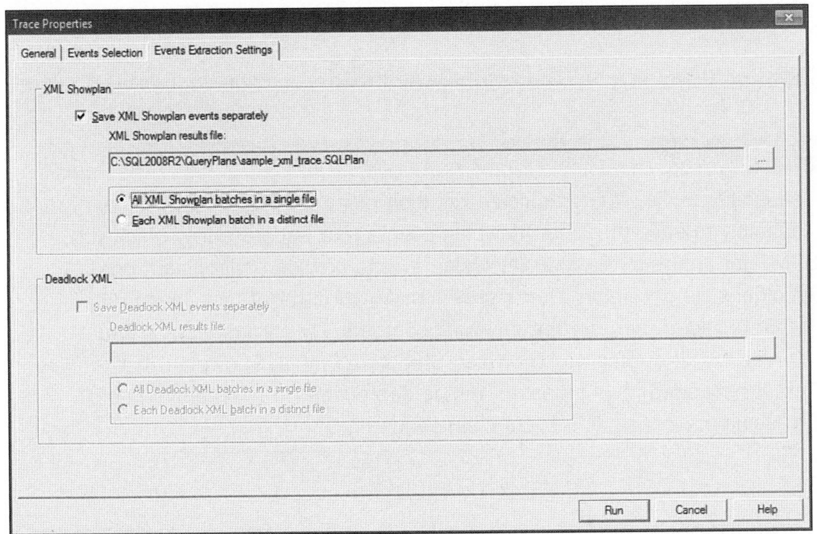

FIGURE 36.15 Saving XML Showplan events to a single file.

When you run a SQL Server Profiler trace with the Showplan XML event enabled, SQL Server Profiler displays the graphical execution plans captured in the bottom display panel of the Profiler window when you select a record with a Showplan XML EventClass. The graphical execution plans displayed in SQL Server Profiler are just like the ones displayed in SSMS, and they also include the same detailed information available via the ToolTips. Figure 36.16 shows an example of a graphical execution plan being displayed in SQL Server Profiler.

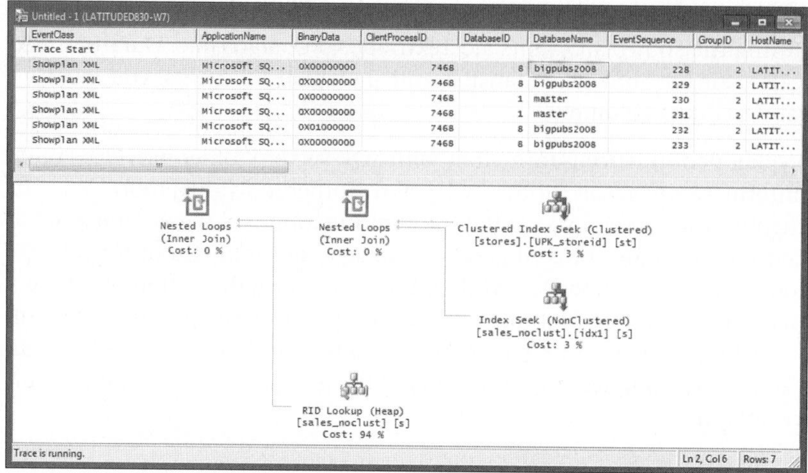

FIGURE 36.16 Displaying an XML Showplan event in SQL Server Profiler.

For more information on using SQL Server Profiler, see Chapter 6, "SQL Server Profiler."

NOTE

Because of the capability to view the graphical execution plans in SQL Server Profiler as well as the capability to save the XML Showplan events to a separate file, which you can bring into SSMS for analysis, the XML Showplan events provide a significant benefit over the other, older-style showplan events provided. As a matter of fact, these other showplan events are provided primarily for backward-compatibility purposes. In a future version of SQL Server, the Showplan All, Showplan Statistics Profile, Showplan Text, and Showplan Text (Unencoded) event classes will be deprecated. It is recommended that you switch to using the newer XML event classes instead.

Summary

Between the features of SSMS and the text-based query analysis tools, SQL Server 2008 provides a number of powerful utilities to help you analyze and understand how your queries are performing and also help you develop a better understanding of how queries in general are processed and optimized in SQL Server 2008. Such an understanding can help ensure that the queries you develop will be optimized more effectively by SQL Server.

The tools discussed in this chapter are useful for analyzing individual query performance. However, in a multiuser environment, query performance is often affected by more than just how a single query is optimized. One of those factors is locking contention. Chapter 37, "Locking and Performance," delves into locking in SQL Server, its impact on query and application performance, and ways to minimize locking performance issues in SQL Server systems.

CHAPTER 37

Locking and Performance

IN THIS CHAPTER

- What's New in Locking and Performance
- The Need for Locking
- Transaction Isolation Levels in SQL Server
- The Lock Manager
- Monitoring Lock Activity in SQL Server
- SQL Server Lock Types
- SQL Server Lock Granularity
- Lock Compatibility
- Locking Contention and Deadlocks
- Table Hints for Locking
- Optimistic Locking

This chapter examines locking and its impact on transactions and performance in SQL Server. It also reviews locking hints that you can specify in queries to override SQL Server's default locking behavior.

What's New in Locking and Performance

SQL Server 2008 doesn't provide any significant changes in locking behavior or features over what was provided in SQL Server 2005 (such as Snapshot Isolation and improved lock and deadlock monitoring). The main new feature in SQL Server 2008 is the capability to control lock escalation behavior at the table level. The new `LOCK_ESCALATION` table option allows you to enable or disable table-level lock escalation. This new feature can reduce contention and improve concurrency, especially for partitioned tables.

One other change for SQL Server 2008 is the deprecation of the Locks configuration setting. This option, while still visible and settable in `sp_configure`, is simply ignored by SQL Server 2008. Also deprecated in SQL Server 2008 is the `timestamp` data type. It has been replaced with the `rowversion` data type. For more information on using the `rowversion` data type, see the "Optimistic Locking" section in this chapter.

The Need for Locking

In any multiuser database, there must be a consistent set of rules for making changes to the data. For a true transaction-processing database, the database management system (DBMS) is responsible for resolving potential conflicts between two different processes that are attempting to change the same piece of information at the same time. Such a situation cannot occur because the consistency of a transaction cannot be guaranteed. For example, if two users were to change the same data at approximately the same time, whose change would be propagated? Theoretically, the results would be unpredictable because the answer is dependent on whose transaction completed last. Because most applications try to avoid "unpredictability" with data wherever possible (imagine a banking system returning "unpredictable" results, and you get the idea), some method must be available to guarantee sequential and consistent data changes.

Any relational database must support the ACID properties for transactions, as discussed in Chapter 31, "Transaction Management and the Transaction Log":

- Atomicity
- Consistency
- Isolation
- Durability

These ACID properties ensure that data changes in a database are correctly collected together and that the data is going to be left in a consistent state that corresponds with the actions being taken.

The main role of locking is to provide the isolation that transactions need. Isolation ensures that individual transactions don't interfere with one another, that a given transaction does not read or modify the data being modified by another transaction. In addition, the isolation that locking provides helps ensure consistency within transactions. Without locking, consistent transaction processing is impossible. Transactions are logical units of work that rely on a constant state of data, almost a "snapshot in time" of what they are modifying, to guarantee their successful completion.

Although locking provides isolation for transactions and helps ensure their integrity, it can also have a significant impact on the performance of the system. To keep your system performing well, you want to keep transactions as short, concise, and noninterfering as possible. This chapter explores the locking features of SQL Server that provide isolation for transactions. You'll come to understand the performance impact of the various levels and types of locks in SQL Server and how to define transactions to minimize locking performance problems.

Transaction Isolation Levels in SQL Server

Isolation levels determine the extent to which data being accessed or modified in one transaction is protected from changes to the data by other transactions. In theory, each transaction should be fully isolated from other transactions. However, in practice, for practical and performance reasons, this might not always be the case. In a concurrent environment in the absence of locking and isolation, the following four scenarios can happen:

- **Lost update**—In this scenario, no isolation is provided to a transaction from other transactions. Multiple transactions can read the same copy of data and modify it. The last transaction to modify the data set prevails, and the changes by all other transactions are lost.
- **Dirty reads**—In this scenario, one transaction can read data that is being modified by other transactions. The data read by the first transaction is inconsistent because the other transaction might choose to roll back the changes.
- **Nonrepeatable reads**—In this scenario, which is somewhat similar to zero isolation, a transaction reads the data twice, but before the second read occurs, another transaction modifies the data; therefore, the values read by the first read are different from those of the second read. Because the reads are not guaranteed to be repeatable each time, this scenario is called nonrepeatable reads.
- **Phantom reads**—This scenario is similar to nonrepeatable reads. However, instead of the actual rows that were read changing before the transaction is complete, additional rows are added to the table, resulting in a different set of rows being read the second time. Consider a scenario in which Transaction A reads rows with key values within the range of 1 through 5 and returns three rows with key values 1, 3, and 5. Before Transaction A reads the data again within the transaction, Transaction B adds two more rows with the key values 2 and 4 and commits the changes. Assuming that Transaction A and Transaction B both can run independently without blocking each other, when Transaction A runs the query a second time, it now gets five rows with key values 1, 2, 3, 4, and 5. This phenomenon is called *phantom reads* because in the second pass, you get records you did not expect to retrieve.

Ideally, a DBMS must provide levels of isolation to prevent these types of scenarios. Sometimes, for practical and performance reasons, databases relax some of the rules. The American National Standards Institute (ANSI) has defined four transaction isolation levels, each providing a different degree of isolation to cover the previous scenarios. ANSI SQL-92 defines the following four standards for transaction isolation:

- Read Uncommitted (Level 0)
- Read Committed (Level 1)
- Repeatable Read (Level 2)
- Serializable (Level 3)

SQL Server 2008 supports all the ANSI isolation levels; in addition, SQL Server 2008 also supports two additional transaction isolation levels that use row versioning. One is an alternative implementation of Read Committed isolation called Read Committed Snapshot, and the other is the Snapshot transaction isolation level.

You can set the default transaction isolation for a user session by using the `SET TRANSACTION ISOLATION LEVEL` T-SQL command, or for individual SQL statements, you can specify table-level isolation hints within the query. Using table-level hints is covered later in this chapter, in the section "Table Hints for Locking."

Read Uncommitted Isolation

If you set the Read Uncommitted mode for a session, no isolation is provided to the `SELECT` queries in that session. A transaction that is running with this isolation level is not immune to dirty reads, nonrepeatable reads, or phantom reads.

To set the Read Uncommitted mode for a session, you run the following statements from the client:

- **T-SQL**—Use `SET TRANSACTION ISOLATION LEVEL READ UNCOMMITTED`.
- **ODBC**—Use the function call `SQLSetConnectAttr` with `Attribute` set to `SQL_ATTR_TXN_ISOLATION` and `ValuePtr` set to `SQL_TXN_READ_UNCOMMITTED`.
- **OLE DB**—Use the function call `ITransactionLocal::StartTransaction` with the `isoLevel` set to `ISOLATIONLEVEL_READUNCOMMITTED`.
- **ADO**—Set the `IsolationLevel` property of the `Connection` object to `adXactReadUncommitted`.
- **ADO.NET**—For applications using the `System.Data.SqlClient` managed namespace, call the `SqlConnection.BeginTransaction` method and set the `IsolationLevel` option to `ReadUncommitted`.

You need to be careful when running queries at Read Uncommitted isolation; it is possible to read changes that have been made to data that are subsequently rolled back. In essence, the accuracy of the results cannot be guaranteed. You should use this mode only when you need to get information quickly from an online transaction processing (OLTP) database, without affecting or being affected by the ongoing updates and when the accuracy of the results is not critical.

Read Committed Isolation

The Read Committed mode is the default locking-isolation mode for SQL Server. With Read Committed as the transaction isolation level, read operations can read pages only for transactions that have already been committed. No "dirty reads" are allowed. Locks acquired by update transactions are held for the duration of the transaction. However, in this mode, read requests within the transaction release locks as soon as the query finishes reading the data. Although this improves concurrent access to the data for updates, it does not prevent nonrepeatable reads or phantom reads. For example, within a transaction, a process could read one set of rows early in the transaction and then, before reading the information again, another process could modify the result set, resulting in a different result set being read the second time.

Because Read Committed is the default isolation level for SQL Server, you do not need to do anything to set this mode. If you need to set the isolation level back to Read Committed mode for a session, you run the following statements from the client:

- **T-SQL**—Use `SET TRANSACTION ISOLATION LEVEL READ COMMITTED`.

- **ODBC**—Use the function call `SQLSetConnectAttr` with `Attribute` set to `SQL_ATTR_TXN_ISOLATION` and `ValuePtr` set to `SQL_TXN_READ_COMMITTED`.
- **OLE DB**—Use the function call `ITransactionLocal::StartTransaction` with `isoLevel` set to `ISOLATIONLEVEL_READCOMMITTED`.
- **ADO**—Set the `IsolationLevel` property of the `Connection` object to `adXactReadcommitted`.
- **ADO.NET**—For applications using the `System.Data.SqlClient` managed namespace, call the `SqlConnection.BeginTransaction` method and set the `IsolationLevel` option to `ReadCommitted`.

Read Committed Snapshot Isolation

When the `READ_COMMITTED_SNAPSHOT` database option is set to `ON`, sessions running with the Read Committed isolation mode use row versioning to provide statement-level read consistency. When this database option is enabled and a transaction runs at the Read Committed isolation level, all statements within the transaction see a snapshot of the data as it exists at the start of the statement.

When the `READ_COMMITTED_SNAPSHOT` option is enabled for a database, SQL Server maintains versions of each row that is modified. Whenever a transaction modifies a row, an image of the row before modification is copied into a page in the version store, which is a collection of data pages in `tempdb`. If multiple transactions modify a row, multiple versions of the row are linked in a version chain. Queries running with Read Committed Snapshot isolation retrieve the last version of each row that had been committed when the statement started, providing a statement-level snapshot of the data.

37

In the Read Committed Snapshot isolation mode, read operations do not acquire shared page or row locks on the data. Therefore, readers using row versioning do not block other processes modifying the same data, and, similarly, processes modifying the data do not block the readers. In addition, because the read operations do not acquire locks, locking overhead is reduced. However, processes modifying data still block other processes modifying data because two operations cannot modify the same data at the same time. Exclusive locks on modified data are still acquired and held until the end of the transaction.

While locking overhead is reduced for read operations when using Read Committed Snapshot isolation, it does introduce overhead to maintain the row versions in `tempdb`. In addition, `tempdb` must have sufficient space to hold the row versions in addition to the space required for normal `tempdb` operations.

You might want to consider enabling the `READ_COMMITTED_SNAPSHOT` database option when blocking that occurs between read and write operations affects performance to the point that the overhead of creating and managing row versions is offset by the concurrency benefits. You may also consider using Read Committed Snapshot isolation when an application requires absolute accuracy for long-running aggregations or queries where data values must be consistent to the point in time that the query starts.

NOTE

You can use Read Committed Snapshot isolation mode with most existing SQL Server applications without making any change to the application code itself if the applications are written to use the default Read Committed isolation level. The behavior of Read Committed, whether to use row versioning or not, is determined by the database option setting, and this can be enabled or disabled without requiring any changes to the application code.

Repeatable Read Isolation

In Repeatable Read mode, SQL Server provides the same level of isolation for updates as in Read Committed mode, but it also allows the data to be read many times within the same transaction and guarantees that the same values will be read each time. Repeatable Read isolation mode prevents other users from updating data that has been read within the transaction until the transaction in which it was read is committed or rolled back. This way, the reading transaction does not pick up changes to the rows it read previously within the transaction. However, this isolation mode does not prevent additional rows (that is, phantom reads) from appearing in the subsequent reads.

Although preventing nonrepeatable reads is desirable for certain transactions, it requires holding locks on the data that has been read until the transaction is completed. This reduces concurrent access for multiple update operations and causes performance degradation due to lock waits and locking contention between transactions. It can also potentially lead to deadlocks. (Deadlocking is discussed in more detail in the "Deadlocks" section, later in this chapter.)

To set Repeatable Read mode for a session, you run the following statements from the client:

- **T-SQL**—Use `SET TRANSACTION ISOLATION LEVEL REPEATABLE READ`.
- **ODBC**—Use the function call `SQLSetConnectAttr` with `Attribute` set to `SQL_ATTR_TXN_ISOLATION` and `ValuePtr` set to `SQL_TXN_REPEATABLEREAD`.
- **OLE DB**—Use the function call `ITransactionLocal::StartTransaction` with `isoLevel` set to `ISOLATIONLEVEL_REPEATABLEREAD`.
- **ADO**—Set the `IsolationLevel` property of the `Connection` object to `adXact REPEATABLEREAD`.
- **ADO.NET**—For applications using the `System.Data.SqlClient` managed namespace, call the `SqlConnection.BeginTransaction` method and set the `IsolationLevel` option to `RepeatableRead`.

Serializable Read Isolation

Serializable Read mode is similar to repeatable reads but adds to it the restriction that rows cannot be added to a result set that was read previously within a transaction. This prevents phantom reads. In other words, Serializable Read locks the existing data being read as well as rows that do not yet exist. It accomplishes this by locking the data being read. In addition, SQL Server puts locks on the range of values being read so that additional rows cannot be added to the range.

For example, say you run a query in a transaction that retrieves all records for the `Sales` table in the `bigpubs2008` database for a store with the `stor_id` of `7066`. To prevent additional sales records from being added to the `Sales` table for this store, SQL Server locks the range of values with `stor_id` of `7066`. It accomplishes this by using key-range locks, which are discussed in the "Serialization and Key-Range Locking" section, later in this chapter.

Although preventing phantom reads is desirable for certain transactions, Serializable Read mode, like Repeatable Read, reduces concurrent access for multiple update operations and can cause performance degradation due to lock waits and locking contention between transactions, and it can potentially lead to deadlocks.

To set Serializable Read mode for a session, you run the following statements from the client:

- **T-SQL**—Use `SET TRANSACTION ISOLATION LEVEL SERIALIZABLE`.
- **ODBC**—Use the function call `SQLSetConnectAttr` with `Attribute` set to `SQL_ATTR_TXN_ISOLATION` and `ValuePtr` set to `SQL_TXN_SERIALIZABLE`.
- **OLE DB**—Use the function call `ITransactionLocal::StartTransaction` with `isoLevel` set to `ISOLATIONLEVEL_SERIALIZABLE`.
- **ADO**—Set the `IsolationLevel` property of the `Connection` object to `adXact SERIALIZABLE`.
- **ADO.NET**—For applications using the `System.Data.SqlClient` managed namespace, call the `SqlConnection.BeginTransaction` method and set the `IsolationLevel` option to `Serializable`.

37

Snapshot Isolation

Snapshot Isolation is an additional isolation level available in SQL Server 2008. Similar to Read Committed Snapshot, Snapshot Isolation mode uses row versioning to take a point-in-time snapshot of the data. However, unlike Read Committed Snapshot isolation, which provides a statement-level snapshot of the data, Snapshot Isolation maintains a snapshot of the data for the duration of the entire transaction. A data snapshot is taken when the transaction starts and the snapshot remains consistent for the duration of the transaction.

Snapshot Isolation mode provides the benefit of repeatable reads without acquiring and holding shared locks on the data that is read. This can help minimize locking and blocking problems between read operations and update operations. Read operations do not have to wait for write operations and writes don't have to wait for reads.

To set the Snapshot Isolation mode for a session, you run the following statement:

```
SET TRANSACTION ISOLATION LEVEL SNAPSHOT
```

In addition, to be able to request the Snapshot Isolation mode in a session, you must enable the database option `ALLOW_SNAPSHOT_ISOLATION` with the `ALTER DATABASE` command:

```
ALTER DATABASE dbname SET ALLOW_SNAPSHOT_ISOLATION ON
```

When Snapshot Isolation mode is enabled, SQL Server assigns a transaction sequence number to each transaction that manipulates data using row versioning. When either the `READ_COMMITTED_SNAPSHOT` or `ALLOW_SNAPSHOT_ISOLATION` database option is set to `ON`, SQL Server stores a version of the previously committed image of the data row in `tempdb` whenever the row is modified by a transaction. Each of these versions is marked with the transaction sequence number of the transaction that made the change. The versions of the modified rows are linked together in a chain, with the most recent version of the row always stored in the current database and the versioned rows stored in `tempdb`.

When a transaction requests a read of data, it searches the version chain to locate the last committed version of the data row with a lower transaction sequence number than the current transaction. Row versions are kept in `tempdb` only long enough to satisfy the requirements of any transactions running under row versioning–based isolation levels. SQL Server keeps track of the sequence number of the oldest outstanding transaction and periodically deletes all row versions stamped with transaction sequence numbers lower than that.

You might consider using snapshot isolation in the following instances:

- When you want optimistic concurrency control
- When it is unlikely that your transaction would have to be rolled back because of an update conflict
- When an application generates reports based on long-running, multistatement queries that must have point-in-time consistency
- With systems that are incurring a high number of deadlocks because of read/write contention

There is a risk to using snapshot isolation, however. If two client applications both retrieve the same data and then both attempt to write changes to the data back to the database, the second application could potentially overwrite the first application's changes. This is called a *lost update error*. Fortunately, SQL Server 2008 resolves this problem by blocking the second transaction's writes. So, although snapshot isolation provides benefits for resolving conflicts between read and write operations, there can still be conflicts between multiple write operations. For systems with heavy read and insert activity and with little concurrent updating of the same resource, snapshot isolation can provide a solution for concurrency issues.

Another cost of snapshot isolation is that it can make heavy use of `tempdb`. For this reason, you should locate `tempdb` on its own high-performance drive system.

NOTE

Only one of the transaction isolation levels can be active at any given time for a user session. The isolation level you set within an application is active for the duration of the connection or until it is manually reset. To check the current transaction isolation level settings, you run the DBCC USEROPTIONS command and examine the value for isolation level, as in the following example:

```
DBCC USEROPTIONS
go

Set Option                         Value
---------------------------------- -------------
textsize                           2147483647
language                           us_english
dateformat                         mdy
datefirst                          7
lock_timeout                       -1
quoted_identifier                  SET
arithabort                         SET
ansi_null_dflt_on                  SET
ansi_warnings                      SET
ansi_padding                       SET
ansi_nulls                         SET
concat_null_yields_null            SET
isolation level                    snapshot
```

Be aware that `DBCC USEROPTIONS` reports an isolation level of Read Committed Snapshot when the database option `READ_COMMITTED_SNAPSHOT` is set to `ON` and the current transaction isolation level is set to Read Committed. The actual isolation level in effect for the user session is Read Committed.

The Lock Manager

The responsibility for ensuring lock conflict resolution between user processes falls on the SQL Server Lock Manager. SQL Server automatically assigns locks to processes to guarantee that the current user of a resource (for example, a data row or page, an index row or page, a table, an index, or a database) has a consistent view of that resource, from the beginning to the end of a particular operation. In other words, what you start with is what you work with throughout your transaction. Nobody can change what you are working on in midstate, thereby ensuring the consistency of your transaction.

The Lock Manager is responsible for deciding the appropriate lock type (for example, shared, exclusive, update) and the appropriate granularity of locks (for example, row, page, table), according to the type of operation being performed and the amount of data being affected. Based on the type of transaction, the SQL Server Lock Manager chooses different types of lock resources. For example, a `CREATE INDEX` statement might lock the entire table, whereas an `UPDATE` statement might lock only a specific row.

The Lock Manager also manages compatibility between lock types attempting to access the same resources, resolves deadlocks, and escalates locks to a higher level, if necessary.

The Lock Manager manages locks for both shared data and internal system resources. For shared data, the Lock Manager manages row locks, page locks, and table locks on tables, as well as data pages, text pages, and leaf-level index pages. Internally, the Lock Manager uses latches to manage locking on index rows and pages, controlling access to internal data structures and, in some cases, for retrieving individual rows of data. Latches provide better system performance because they are less resource intensive than locks. Latches also provide greater concurrency than locks. Latches are typically used for operations such as page splits, deletion of index rows, movement of rows in an index, and so on. The main difference between a lock and a latch is that a lock is held for the duration of the transaction, and a latch is held only for the duration of the operation for which it is required. Locks are used to ensure the logical consistency of data, whereas latches are used to ensure the physical consistency of the data and data structures.

The remainder of this chapter examines how the Lock Manager determines the type and level of lock to assign, based on the type of command being executed, number of rows affected, and lock isolation level in effect.

Monitoring Lock Activity in SQL Server

To monitor the performance of a system, you need to keep track of locking activity in SQL Server. The following are the most commonly used methods to do so:

- Querying the `sys.dm_tran_locks` dynamic management view directly
- Viewing locking activity with SQL Server Profiler
- Monitoring locks with Performance Monitor

As you read through the rest of this chapter, you might want to examine or monitor the locking activity for the examples presented. To assist you in that effort, the following sections describe the methods of examining lock activity in SQL Server 2008.

Querying the `sys.dm_tran_locks` View

The `sys.dm_tran_locks` dynamic management view returns information about all the locks currently granted or waiting to be granted in SQL Server. (The information is populated from the internal lock management structures in SQL Server 2008.) This view provides no historical information; rather, the data in this view corresponds to live Lock

Manager information. This data can change at any time for subsequent queries of the view as locks are acquired and released.

The information returned by the view can be divided into two main groups: resource information and lock request information. The resource information describes the resource on which the lock request is being made, and the request information provides details on the lock request itself. Table 37.1 describes the most useful data columns returned by the `sys.dm_tran_locks` view.

TABLE 37.1 Useful Columns Returned by the **`sys.dm_tran_locks`** View

Column Name	Description
`resource_type`	Indicates the type of resource the lock is being held or requested on.
`resource_subtype`	Indicates a subtype of the `resource_type`, if any.
`resource_database_id`	Indicates the database ID of the database where the resource resides.
`resource_description`	Provides information about the resource that is not available from other resource columns.
`resource_associated_entity_id`	Indicates the ID of the entity in a database that the resource is associated with.
`resource_lock_partition`	Indicates the ID of the associated partition for a resource that is partitioned.
`request_mode`	Indicates the lock mode of the request that has been granted or is being waited on.
`request_type`	Indicates the request type. (The only current value is `LOCK`.)
`request_status`	Indicates the current status of this request (`GRANT`, `CONVERT`, or `WAIT`).
`request_reference_count`	Returns an approximate number of times the same requestor has requested this resource.
`request_lifetime`	Specifies a code indicating when the lock on the resource is released.
`request_session_id`	Indicates the ID of the session that generated the corresponding request.
`request_exec_context_id`	Indicates the ID of the execution context of the process that generated the lock request.

TABLE 37.1 Useful Columns Returned by the **sys.dm_tran_locks** View

Column Name	Description
request_request_id	Indicates the batch ID of the process that generated the request.
request_owner_type	Indicates the type of entity that owns the request. Possible values include, but are not limited to, TRANSACTION, CURSOR, and SESSION.
request_owner_id	Specifies the ID of the specific owner of this request. This value is used for transactions for which this is the transaction ID.
request_owner_guid	Indicates the GUID of the specific owner of the lock request. This value is used only by a distributed transaction where the value corresponds to the MS DTC GUID for that transaction
request_owner_lockspace_id	Represents the lockspace ID of the requestor. The lockspace ID determines whether two requestors are compatible with each other and can be granted locks in modes that would otherwise conflict with one another.
lock_owner_address	Indicates the memory address of the internal data structure used to track the request.

Table 37.2 lists the possible lock request modes that can be displayed in the request_mode column of the sys.dm_tran_locks view.

TABLE 37.2 Lock Request Modes

Value	Lock Type	Description	Request Mode
1	N/A	No access provided to the requestor	NULL
2	Schema	Schema stability lock	Sch-S
3	Schema	Schema modification lock	Sch-M
4	Shared	Acquisition of a shared lock on the resource	S
5	Update	Acquisition of an update lock on the resource	U
6	Exclusive	Exclusive lock granted on the resource	X
7	Intent	Intent for a shared lock	IS
8	Intent	Intent for an update lock	IU
9	Intent	Intent for an exclusive lock	IX

TABLE 37.2 Lock Request Modes

Value	Lock Type	Description	Request Mode
10	Intent	Shared lock with intent for an update lock on subordinate resources	SIU
11	Intent	Shared lock with intent for an exclusive lock on subordinate resources	SIX
12	Intent	Update lock with an intent for an exclusive lock on subordinate resources	UIX
13	Bulk	BULK UPDATE lock used for bulk copy operations	BU
14	Key-Range	Shared lock on the range between keys and shared lock on the key at the end of the range; used for serializable range scan	Range_S_S
15	Key-Range	Shared lock on the range between keys, with an update lock on the key at the end of the range	Range_S_U
16	Key-Range	Exclusive lock used to prevent inserts into a range between keys	RangeIn-N
17	Key-Range	Key-range conversion lock created by overlap of RangeIn-N and shared (S) locks	RangeIn-S
18	Key-Range	Key-range conversion lock created by overlap of RangeIn-N and update (U) locks	RangeIn-U
19	Key-Range	Key-range conversion lock created by overlap of RangeIn-N and exclusive (X) locks	RangeIn-X
20	Key-Range	Key-range conversion lock created by overlap of RangeIn-N and RangeS_S locks	RangeX-S
21	Key-Range	Key-Range conversion lock created by overlap of RangeIn-N and RangeS_U locks	RangeX-U
22	Key-Range	Exclusive lock on range between keys, with an exclusive lock on the key at the end of the range	RangeX-X

Listing 37.1 provides an example of a query against the sys.dm_tran_locks view.

LISTING 37.1 An Example of a Query Against the **sys.dm_tran_locks** View

```
select str(request_session_id, 4,0) as spid,
       convert (varchar(12), db_name(resource_database_id)) As db_name,
       case when resource_database_id = db_id() and resource_type = 'OBJECT'
            then convert(char(20), object_name(resource_Associated_Entity_id))
            else convert(char(20), resource_Associated_Entity_id)
```

37

```
            end as object,
        convert(varchar(12), resource_type) as resrc_type,
        convert(varchar(12), request_type) as req_type,
        convert(char(1), request_mode) as mode,
        convert(varchar(8), request_status) as status
    from sys.dm_tran_locks
order by request_session_id, 3 desc
go

spid db_name      object          resrc_type req_type mode status
---- ---------- --------------- ----------- -------- ---- --------
 52 msdb         0               DATABASE   LOCK      S   GRANT
 55 bigpubs2008  titles          OBJECT     LOCK      I   GRANT
 55 bigpubs2008  sales_qty_rollup OBJECT    LOCK      X   GRANT
 55 bigpubs2008  sales           OBJECT     LOCK      X   GRANT
 55 bigpubs2008  679707671068672 PAGE       LOCK      I   GRANT
 55 bigpubs2008  679707671068672 KEY        LOCK      X   GRANT
 55 bigpubs2008  398232694358016 KEY        LOCK      X   GRANT
 55 bigpubs2008  398232694358016 PAGE       LOCK      I   GRANT
 55 bigpubs2008  0               DATABASE   LOCK      S   GRANT
 56 msdb         0               DATABASE   LOCK      S   GRANT
 58 bigpubs2008  sales           OBJECT     LOCK      I   WAIT
 58 bigpubs2008  0               DATABASE   LOCK      S   GRANT
```

Note that the query in Listing 37.1 contains a `CASE` expression for displaying the object name. If the resource type is `OBJECT` and the database ID of the locked resource is the same as the current database context, it returns the object name; otherwise, it returns the object ID because the `object_name()` function operates only in the current database context.

TIP

To save yourself the trouble of having to type in the query listed in Listing 37.1, or having to read it in from a file each time you want to run it, you might want to consider creating your own stored procedure or view that invokes this query.

NOTE

In SQL Server 2005, you could monitor lock activity via the Activity Monitor in SQL Server Management Studio (SSMS). If you're looking for this tool in SQL Server 2008, you won't find it. For some reason, this feature was removed from SSMS in SQL Server 2008. The only locking information provided by the SSMS Activity Monitor in SQL Server 2008 is the indication of lock blocking and wait time provided by the Process Monitor and the Lock Waits information provided by the Resource Waits Monitor. There is no GUI-based lock monitoring tool provided with SQL Server 2008 to display the specific locks being held by processes or the locks being held on objects as there was in SQL Server 2005.

Viewing Locking Activity with SQL Server Profiler

Another tool to help you monitor locking activity in SQL Server 2008 is SQL Server Profiler. SQL Server Profiler provides a number of lock events that you can capture in a trace. The trace information can be viewed in real-time or saved to a file or database table for further analysis at a later date. Saving the information to a table allows you to run different reports on the information to help in the analysis.

NOTE

This chapter provides only a brief overview of how to capture and view locking information using SQL Server Profiler. For more information on the features and capabilities of SQL Server Profiler and how to use it, see Chapter 6, "SQL Server Profiler."

SQL Profiler provides the following lock events that can be captured in a trace:

- **`Lock:Acquired`**—Indicates when a lock on a resource, such as a data page or row, has been acquired.
- **`Lock:Cancel`**—Indicates when the acquisition of a lock on a resource has been canceled (for example, as the result of a deadlock).
- **`Lock:Deadlock`**—Indicates when two or more concurrent processes have deadlocked with each other.
- **`Lock:Deadlock Chain`**—Provides the information for each of the events leading up to a deadlock. This information is similar to that provided by the 1204 trace flag, which is covered in the "Deadlocks" section, later in this chapter.
- **`Lock:Escalation`**—Indicates when a lower-level lock has been converted to a higher-level lock (for example, when page-level locks are escalated to table-level locks).
- **`Lock:Released`**—Indicates that a process has released a previously acquired lock on a resource.
- **`Lock:Timeout`**—Indicates that a lock request that is waiting on a resource has timed out due to another transaction holding a blocking lock.
- **`Lock:Timeout (timeout >0)`**—Is similar to `Lock:Timeout` but does not include any events where the lock timeout is 0 seconds.
- **`Deadlock Graph`**—Generates an XML description of a deadlock.

Figure 37.1 shows an example of choosing a set of locking events to monitor with SQL Server Profiler.

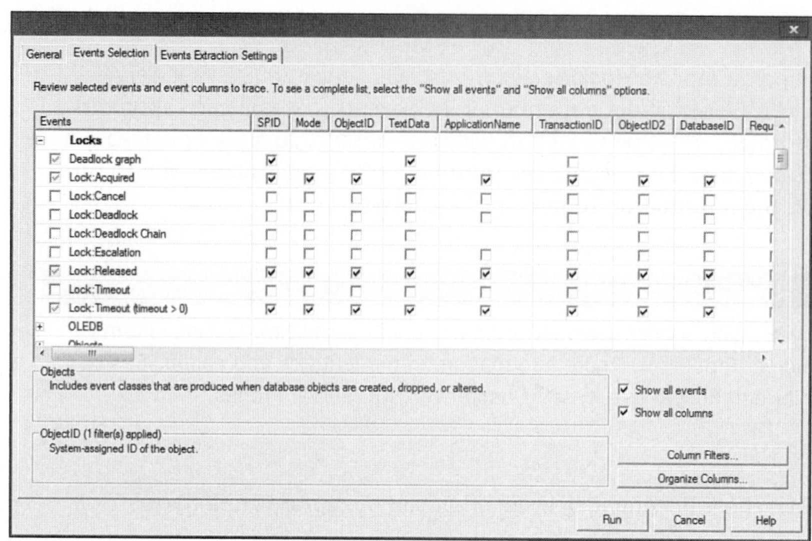

FIGURE 37.1 Choosing lock events in SQL Server Profiler.

SQL Server Profiler also provides a number of data values to display for the events being monitored. You might find the following data columns useful when monitoring locking activity:

- **spid**—The process ID of the process that generated the event.
- **EventClass**—The type of event being captured.
- **Mode**—For lock monitoring, the type of lock involved in the captured event.
- **ObjectID**—The ID of the object involved in the locking event—that is, the object that the lock is associated with.
- **DatabaseID**—The ID of the database involved in the locking event
- **TextData**—The query that generated the lock event.
- **LoginName**—The login name associated with the process.
- **ApplicationName**—The name of the application generating the lock event.

Keep in mind that many internal system processes also acquire locks in SQL Server. If you want to filter out those processes and focus on specific processes, users, or applications, you use the filters in SQL Server Profiler to include the information you want to trace or exclude the information you don't want to trace (see Figure 37.2).

After you set up your events, data columns, and filters, you can begin the trace. Figure 37.3 shows an example of the type of information captured.

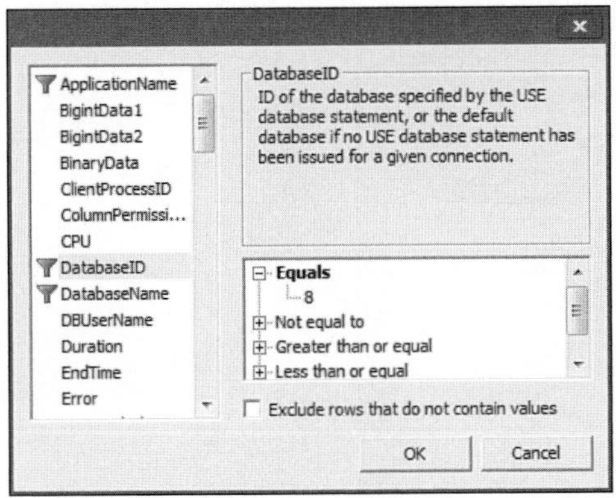

FIGURE 37.2 Filtering out unwanted information in SQL Server Profiler.

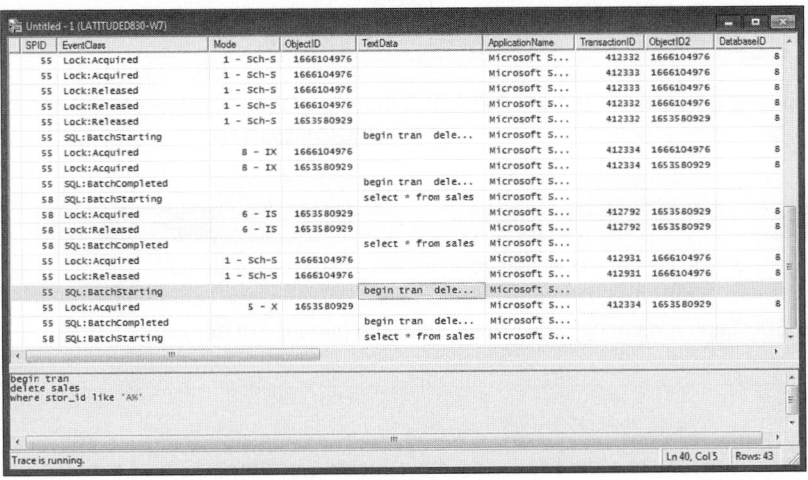

FIGURE 37.3 Lock information captured in a SQL Server Profiler trace.

Monitoring Locks with Performance Monitor

Another method of monitoring locking in SQL Server is through the Performance Monitor. The `sys.dm_tran_locks` view and SSMS Activity Monitor provide a snapshot of the actual locks currently in effect in SQL Server. If you want to monitor the locking activity as a whole on a continuous basis, you can use the Windows Performance Monitor and monitor the counters available for the `SQLServer:Locks` performance object (see Figure 37.4).

37

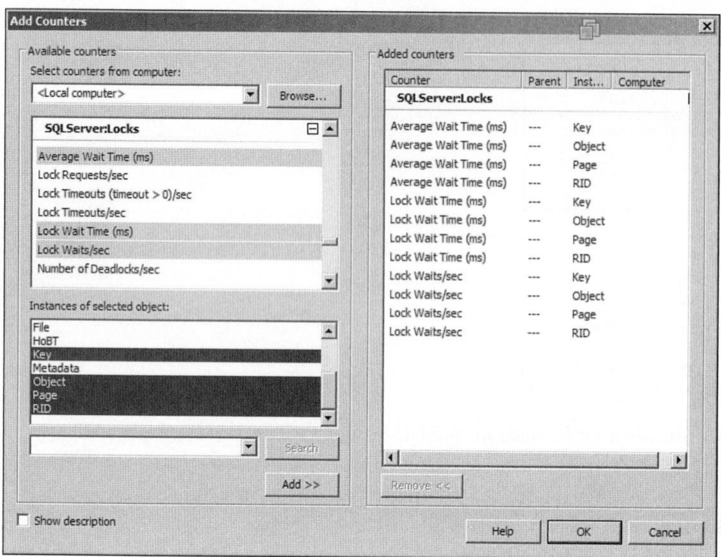

FIGURE 37.4 Choosing counters for the **SQLServer:Locks** performance object in Performance Monitor.

NOTE

If you are monitoring a SQL Server 2008 named instance rather than a default instance of SQL Server 2008, the SQL Server performance counters are listed under the name of the SQL Server instance rather than under the generic `SQLServer` performance counters.

You can use the `SQLServer:Locks` object to help detect locking bottlenecks and contention points in the system as well as to provide a summary of the overall locking activity in SQL Server. You can use the information that Performance Monitor provides to identify whether locking problems are the cause of any performance problems. You can then take appropriate corrective actions to improve concurrency and the overall performance of the system. The counters that belong to the `SQLServer:Locks` object are as follows:

- **Average Wait Time**—This counter represents the average wait time (in milliseconds) for each lock request. A high value is an indication of locking contention that could be affecting performance of concurrent processes.
- **Lock Requests/sec**—This counter represents the total number of new locks and lock conversion requests made per second. A high value for this counter is not necessarily a cause for alarm; it might simply indicate a system with a high number of concurrent users.
- **Lock Timeouts (timeout > 0)/sec**—This counter is similar to the LockTimeouts/sec counter but does not include `NOWAIT` lock requests that time out immediately.

- **Lock Timeouts/sec**—This counter represents the total number of lock timeouts per second that occur for lock requests on a resource that cannot be granted before the lock timeout interval is exceeded. By default, a blocked process waits indefinitely unless the application specifies a maximum timeout limit, using the `SET LOCK_TIMEOUT` command. A high value for this counter might indicate that the timeout limit is set to a low value in the application or that you are experiencing excessive locking contention.
- **Lock Wait Time**—This counter represents the cumulative wait time for each lock request. It is given in milliseconds. A high value here indicates that you might have long-running or inefficient transactions that are causing blocking and locking contention.
- **Lock Waits/sec**—This counter represents the total number of lock requests generated per second for which a process had to wait before a lock request on a resource was granted. A high value might indicate inefficient or long-running transactions or a poor database design that is causing a large number of transactions to block one another.
- **Number of Deadlocks/sec**—This number represents the total number of lock requests per second that resulted in deadlocks. Deadlocks and ways to avoid them are discussed in the "Deadlocks" section, later in this chapter.

For more information on using Windows Performance Monitor for monitoring SQL Server performance, see Chapter 39, "Monitoring SQL Server Performance."

SQL Server Lock Types

Locking is handled automatically in SQL Server. The Lock Manager chooses the type of lock, based on the type of transaction (such as `SELECT`, `INSERT`, `UPDATE`, or `DELETE`). Lock Manager uses the following types of locks:

- Shared locks
- Update locks
- Exclusive locks
- Intent locks
- Schema locks
- Bulk update locks

In addition to choosing the type of lock, the Lock Manager in SQL Server 2008 automatically adjusts the granularity of the locks (for example, row, page, table), based on the nature of the statement that is executed and the number of rows that are affected.

Shared Locks

By default, SQL Server uses shared locks for all read operations. A shared lock is, by definition, not exclusive. Theoretically, an unlimited number of shared locks can be held on a resource at any given time. In addition, shared locks are unique in that, by default, a process locks a resource only for the duration of the read on the resource (row, page, or table). For example, the query `SELECT * from authors` locks the first row in the `authors` table when the query starts. After the first row is read, the lock on that row is released, and a lock on the second row is acquired. After the second row is read, its lock is released, and a lock on the third row is acquired, and so on. In this fashion, a `SELECT` query allows other data rows that are not being read to be modified during the read operation. This increases concurrent access to the data.

Shared locks are compatible with other shared locks as well as with update locks. A shared lock does not prevent the acquisition of additional shared locks or an update lock by other processes on a given row or page. Multiple shared locks can be held at any given time, for a number of transactions or processes. These transactions do not affect the consistency of the data. However, shared locks do prevent the acquisition of exclusive locks. Any transaction attempting to modify data on a page or a row on which a shared lock is placed is blocked until all the shared locks are released.

NOTE

It is important to note that within a transaction running at the default isolation level of Read Committed, shared locks are not held for the duration of the transaction or even the duration of the statement that acquires the shared locks. Shared lock resources (row, page, table, and so on) are normally released as soon as the read operation on the resource is completed. SQL Server provides the `HOLDLOCK` clause for the `SELECT` statement, which you can use if you want to continue holding the shared lock for the duration of the transaction. `HOLDLOCK` is explained later in this chapter, in the section "Table Hints for Locking." Another way to hold shared locks for the duration of a transaction is to set the isolation level for the session or the query to Repeatable Read or Serializable Reads.

Update Locks

Update locks are used to lock rows or pages that a user process intends to modify. When a transaction tries to update a row, it must first read the row to ensure that it is modifying the appropriate record. If the transaction were to put a shared lock on the resource initially, it would eventually need to get an exclusive lock on the resource to modify the record and prevent any other transaction from modifying the same record. The problem is that this could lead to deadlocks in an environment in which multiple transactions are trying to modify data on the same resource at the same time. Figure 37.5 demonstrates how deadlocks can occur if lock conversion takes place from shared locks to exclusive locks. When both processes attempt to escalate the shared lock they both hold on a resource to an exclusive lock, it results in a deadlock situation.

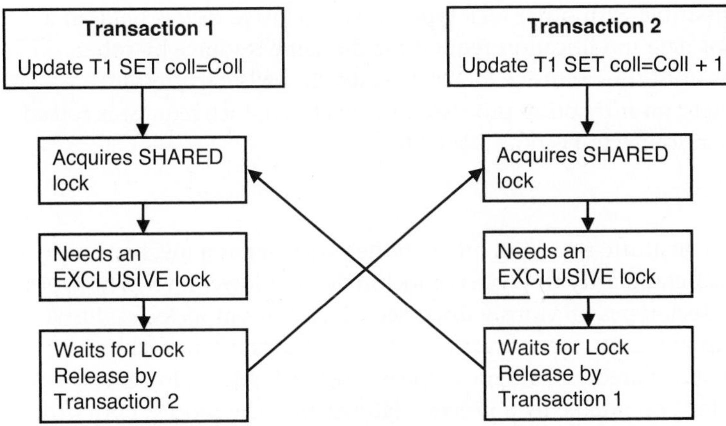

FIGURE 37.5 A deadlock scenario with shared and exclusive locks.

Update locks in SQL Server are provided to prevent this kind of deadlock scenario. Update locks are partially exclusive in that only one update lock can be acquired at a time on any resource. However, an update lock is compatible with shared locks, in that both can be acquired on the same resource simultaneously. In effect, an update lock signifies that a process wants to change a record, and it keeps out other processes that also want to change that record. However, an update lock allows other processes to acquire shared locks to read the data until the `UPDATE` or `DELETE` statement is finished locating the records to be affected. The process then attempts to escalate each update lock to an exclusive lock. At this time, the process waits until all currently held shared locks on the same records are released. After the shared locks are released, the update lock is escalated to an exclusive lock. The data change is then carried out, and the exclusive lock is held for the remainder of the transaction.

NOTE

Update locks are not used just for update operations. SQL Server uses update locks any time a search for data is required prior to performing the actual modification, such as with qualified updates and deletes (that is, when a `WHERE` clause is specified). Update locks are also used for insertions into a table with a clustered index because SQL Server must first search the data and clustered index to identify the correct position at which to insert the new row to maintain the sort order. After SQL Server has found the correct location and begins inserting the record, it escalates the update lock to an exclusive lock.

Exclusive Locks

As mentioned earlier, an exclusive lock is granted to a transaction when it is ready to perform data modifications. An exclusive lock on a resource makes sure no other transaction can interfere with the data locked by the transaction that is holding the exclusive lock. SQL Server releases the exclusive lock at the end of the transaction.

Exclusive locks are incompatible with other lock types. If an exclusive lock is held on a resource, any other read or data modification request for the same resource by other processes is forced to wait until the exclusive lock is released. Likewise, if a resource currently has read locks held on it by other processes, the exclusive lock request is forced to wait in a queue for the resource to become available.

Intent Locks

Intent locks do not really constitute a locking mode; rather, they act as a mechanism to indicate at a higher level of granularity the types of locks held at a lower level. The types of intent locks mirror the lock types previously discussed: shared intent locks, exclusive intent locks, and update intent locks. SQL Server Lock Manager uses intent locks as a mechanism to indicate that a shared, update, or exclusive lock is held at a lower level. For example, a shared intent lock on a table by a process signifies that the process currently holds a shared lock on a row or page within the table. The presence of the intent lock prevents other transactions from attempting to acquire a table-level lock that would be incompatible with the existing row or page locks.

Intent locks improve locking performance by allowing SQL Server to examine locks at the table level to determine the types of locks held on the table at the row or page level rather than searching through the multiple locks at the page or row level within the table. Intent locks also prevent two transactions that are both holding locks at a lower level on a resource from attempting to escalate those locks to a higher level while the other transaction still holds the intent lock. This prevents deadlocks during lock escalation.

You typically see three types of intent locks when monitoring locking activity: intent shared (`IS`) locks, intent exclusive (`IX`) locks, and shared with intent exclusive (`SIX`) locks. An `IS` lock indicates that the process currently holds, or has the intention of holding, shared locks on lower-level resources (row or page). An `IX` lock indicates that the process currently holds, or has the intention of holding, exclusive locks on lower-level resources. An `SIX` (pronounced as the letters *S-I-X*, not like the number six) lock occurs under special circumstances when a transaction is holding a shared lock on a resource, and later in the transaction, an `IX` lock is needed. At that point, the `IS` lock is converted to an `SIX` lock.

In the following example, the `SELECT` statement running at the serializable level acquires a shared table lock. It then needs an exclusive lock to update the row in the `sales_big` table:

```
SET TRANSACTION ISOLATION LEVEL serializable
go
BEGIN TRAN
 select sum(qty) FROM sales_big
UPDATE sales_big
    SET qty = 0
    WHERE sales_id = 1001
COMMIT TRAN
```

Because the transaction initially acquired a shared (S) table lock and then needed an exclusive row lock, which requires an intent exclusive (IX) lock on the table within the same transaction, the S lock is converted to an SIX lock.

NOTE

If only a few rows were in sales_big, SQL Server might acquire only individual row or key locks rather than a table-level lock. SQL Server would then have an intent shared (IS) lock on the table rather than a full shared (S) lock. In that instance, the UPDATE statement would then acquire a single exclusive lock to apply the update to a single row, and the X lock at the key level would result in the IS locks at the page and table levels being converted to an IX lock at the page and table level for the remainder of the transaction.

Schema Locks

SQL Server uses schema locks to maintain structural integrity of SQL Server tables. Unlike other types of locks that provide isolation for the data, schema locks provide isolation for the schema of database objects, such as tables, views, and indexes within a transaction. The Lock Manager uses two types of schema locks:

- **Schema stability locks**—When a transaction is referencing either an index or a data page, SQL Server places a schema stability lock on the object. This ensures that no other process can modify the schema of an object—such as dropping an index or dropping or altering a stored procedure or table—while other processes are still referencing the object.
- **Schema modification locks**—When a process needs to modify the structure of an object (for example, alter the table, recompile a stored procedure), the Lock Manager places a schema modification lock on the object. For the duration of this lock, no other transaction can reference the object until the changes are complete and committed.

Bulk Update Locks

A bulk update lock is a special type of lock used only when bulk copying data into a table using the bcp utility or the BULK INSERT command. This special lock is used for these operations only when either the TABLOCK hint is specified to bcp or the BULK INSERT command or when the table lock on bulk load table option has been set for the table. Bulk update locks allow multiple bulk copy processes to bulk copy data into the same table in parallel, while preventing other processes that are not bulk copying data from accessing the table. If there are any indexes on the table, or any other processes already holding locks on the table, a bulk update lock cannot be granted.

SQL Server Lock Granularity

Lock granularity is essentially the amount of data locked as part of a query or update to provide complete isolation and serialization for the transaction. The Lock Manager needs to balance the concurrent access to resources versus the overhead of maintaining a large number of lower-level locks. For example, the smaller the lock size, the greater the number of concurrent users who can access the same table at the same time but the greater the overhead in maintaining those locks. The greater the lock size, the less overhead required to manage the locks, but concurrency is also less. Figure 37.6 demonstrates the trade-offs between lock size and concurrency.

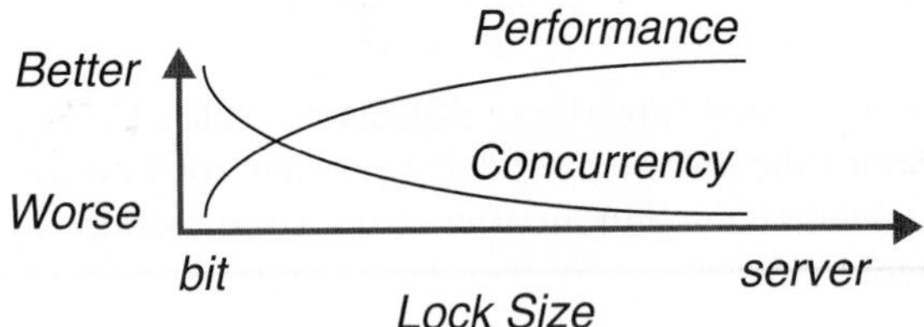

FIGURE 37.6 Trade-offs between performance and concurrency, depending on lock granularity.

Currently, SQL Server balances performance and concurrency by locking at the row level or higher. Based on a number of factors, such as key distribution, number of rows, row density, search arguments (SARGs), and so on, the Query Optimizer makes lock granularity decisions internally, and the programmer does not have to worry about such issues. SQL Server provides a number of T-SQL extensions that give you better control over query behavior from a locking standpoint. These Query Optimizer overrides are discussed in the "Table Hints for Locking" section, later in this chapter.

SQL Server provides the following locking levels:

- DATABASE—Whenever a SQL Server process is using a database other than `master`, the Lock Manager grants a database lock to the process. These are always shared locks, and they are used to keep track of when a database is in use to prevent another process from dropping the database, setting the database offline, or restoring the database. Note that because `master` and `tempdb` cannot be dropped or set offline, database locks are not required on those databases.
- FILE—A file lock is a lock acquired on a database file.
- EXTENT—Extent locks are used for locking extents, usually only during space allocation and deallocation. An extent consists of eight contiguous data or index pages. Extent locks can be shared extent or exclusive extent locks.
- ALLOCATION_UNIT—This type of lock is acquired on a database allocation unit.

- **TABLE**—With this type of lock, the entire table, inclusive of data and indexes, is locked. Examples of when table-level locks may be acquired include selecting all rows from a large table at the serializable level and performing unqualified updates or deletes on a table.
- **Heap or B-Tree (HOBT)**—This type of lock is acquired on a heap of data pages or on the B-Tree structure of an index.
- **PAGE**—With a page lock, the entire page, consisting of 8KB of data or index information, is locked. Page-level locks might be acquired when all rows on a page need to be read or when page-level maintenance needs to be performed, such as updating page pointers after a page split.
- **Row ID (RID)**—With an RID lock, a single row within a page is locked. RID locks are acquired whenever efficient and possible to do so in an effort to provide maximum concurrent access to the resource.
- **KEY**—SQL Server uses two types of key locks. The one that is used depends on the locking isolation level of the current session. For transactions that run in Read Committed or Repeatable Read isolation modes, SQL Server locks the actual index keys associated with the rows being accessed. (If a clustered index is on the table, the data rows are the leaf level of the index. You see key locks instead of row locks on those rows.) When in Serializable Read isolation mode, SQL Server prevents phantom rows by locking a range of key values so that no new rows can be inserted into the range. These are referred to as *key-range locks*. Key-range locks associated with a particular key value lock that key and the previous one in the index to indicate that all values between them are locked. Key-range locks are covered in more detail in the next section.
- **METADATA**—This type of lock is acquired on system catalog information
- **APPLICATION**—An application lock allows users to essentially define their own locks by specifying a name for the resource, a lock mode, an owner, and a timeout interval. Using application locks is discussed later in this chapter, in the section "Using Application Locks."

Serialization and Key-Range Locking

As mentioned in the previous section, SQL Server provides serialization (Isolation Level 3) through the `SET TRANSACTION ISOLATION SERIALIZABLE` command. One of the isolations provided by this isolation level is the prevention against phantom reads. Preventing phantom reads means that the recordset that a query obtains within a transaction must return the same result set when it is run multiple times within the same transaction. That is, while a transaction is active, another transaction should not be allowed to insert new rows that would appear in the recordset of a query that were not in the original recordset retrieved by the transaction. SQL Server provides this capability though key-range locking.

As described earlier in this chapter, key-range locking in SQL Server provides isolation for a transaction from data modifications made by other transactions. This means that a transaction should return the same recordset each time. The following sections show how key-range locking works with various lock modes. Key-range locking covers the scenarios of a range search that returns a result set as well as searches against nonexistent rows.

Key-Range Locking for a Range Search

In a scenario that involves key-range locking for a range search, SQL Server places locks on the index pages for the range of data covered in the WHERE clause of the query. (For a clustered index, the rows would be the actual data rows in the table.) Because the range is locked, no other transaction can insert new rows that fall within the range. In Figure 37.7, for example, transaction A has issued the following SELECT statement:

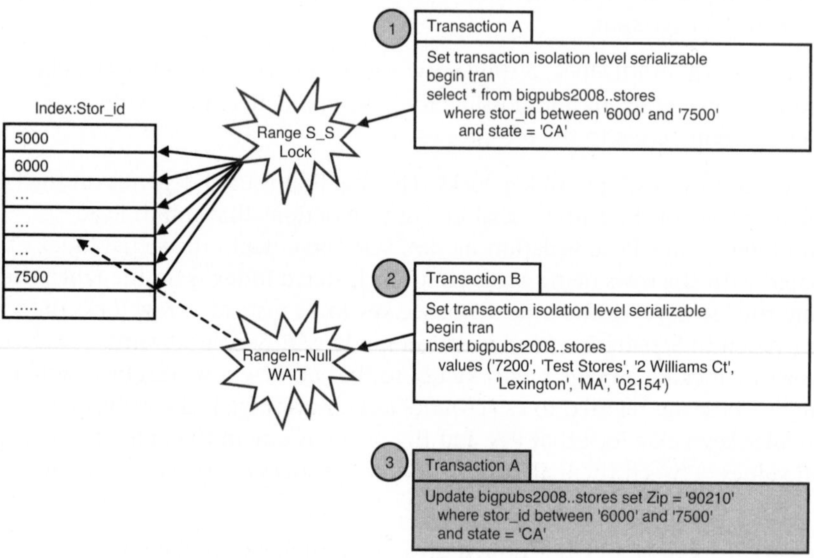

FIGURE 37.7 Key-range locking with a range search.

```
Set transaction isolation level serializable
begin tran
select * from bigpubs2008..stores
where stor_id between '6000' and '7500'
       and state = 'CA'
```

Transaction B is performing the following INSERT statement, attempting to insert a row that falls within the range being retrieved by transaction A (stor_id >= '6000' and stor_id <= '7500'):

```
begin tran
insert bigpubs2008..stores
values ('7200', 'Test Stores', '2 Williams Ct','Lexington', 'MA', '02154')
```

Listing 37.2 shows the locks acquired when using the sys.dm_tran_locks catalog view. (In this sample output, SPID 53 is executing the SELECT statement, and SPID 57 is attempting the INSERT.)

LISTING 37.2 Viewing Key-Range Locks Using the **sys.dm_tran_locks** View

```
select str(request_session_id, 4,0) as spid,
       convert (varchar(12), db_name(resource_database_id)) As db_name,
       case when resource_database_id = db_id() and resource_type = 'OBJECT'
            then convert(char(20), object_name(resource_Associated_Entity_id))
            else convert(char(20), resource_Associated_Entity_id)
            end as object,
       convert(varchar(12), resource_type) as resource_type,
       convert(varchar(10), request_mode) as mode,
       convert(varchar(8), request_status) as status
   from sys.dm_tran_locks
order by request_session_id, 3 desc
go

spid db_name      object          resource_type mode      status
---- ------------ --------------- ------------- --------- --------
  52 msdb         0               DATABASE      S         GRANT
  53 bigpubs2008  391941215944704 PAGE          IS        GRANT
  53 bigpubs2008  391941215944704 KEY           RangeS-S  GRANT
  53 bigpubs2008  391941215944704 KEY           RangeS-S  GRANT
  53 bigpubs2008  391941215944704 KEY           RangeS-S  GRANT
  53 bigpubs2008  391941215944704 KEY           RangeS-S  GRANT
  53 bigpubs2008  391941215944704 KEY           RangeS-S  GRANT
  53 bigpubs2008  1685581043      OBJECT        IS        GRANT
  53 bigpubs2008  0               DATABASE      S         GRANT
  57 bigpubs2008  673416192655360 PAGE          IX        GRANT
  57 bigpubs2008  673416192655360 KEY           X         GRANT
  57 bigpubs2008  391941215944704 PAGE          IX        GRANT
  57 bigpubs2008  391941215944704 PAGE          IX        GRANT
  57 bigpubs2008  391941215944704 KEY           RangeI-N  WAIT
  57 bigpubs2008  391941215944704 KEY           RangeI-N  GRANT
  57 bigpubs2008  391941215944704 KEY           X         GRANT
  57 bigpubs2008  391941215944704 PAGE          IX        GRANT
  57 bigpubs2008  1685581043      OBJECT        IX        GRANT
  57 bigpubs2008  0               DATABASE      S         GRANT
```

To provide key-range isolation, SQL Server places `RangeS-S` locks (that is, a shared lock on the key range and a shared lock on the key at the end of the range) on the index keys for the rows with the matching values. It also places intent share (`IS`) locks on the page(s) and the table that contain the rows. The insert process acquires intent exclusive (`IX`) locks on the destination page(s) and the table. In this case, the insert process is waiting for a `RangeIn-Null` lock on the key range until the `RangeS-S` locks in the key range are released. The `RangeIn-Null` lock is an exclusive lock on the range between keys, with no lock on the key. This lock is acquired because the insert process is attempting to insert a new store ID that has no associated key value.

Key-Range Locking When Searching Nonexistent Rows

In a scenario that involves key-range locking when searching nonexistent rows, if a transaction is trying to delete or retrieve a row that does not exist in the database, it still should not find any rows at a later stage in the same transaction with the same query. For example, in Figure 37.8, Transaction A is trying to fetch a nonexistent row with the key value `7200` using the following query:

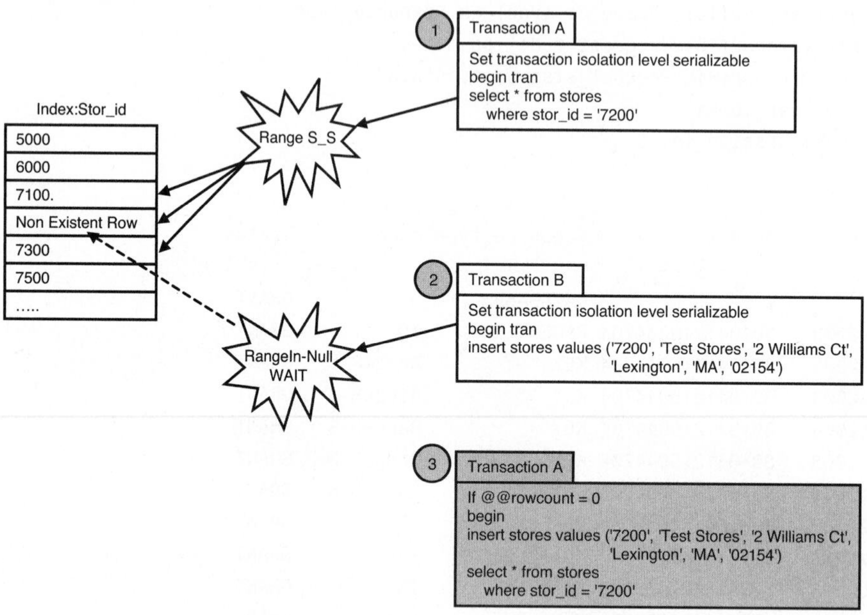

FIGURE 37.8 Key-range locking with a nonexistent data set.

```
SET TRANSACTION ISOLATION LEVEL serializable
go
BEGIN TRAN
 select * FROM bigpubs2008..stores
 where stor_id = '7200'
```

In another concurrent transaction, Transaction B is executing the following statement to insert a record with the same key value (`stor_id = 7200`):

```
begin tran
insert bigpubs2008..stores
values ('7200', 'Test Stores', '2 Williams Ct','Lexington', 'MA', '02154')
```

In this mode, SQL Server prevents Transaction B (SPID 57) from inserting a new row by using a `RangeS-S` lock for Transaction A (SPID 53). This lock is placed on the index key rows for the rows in the range between `MAX(stor_id) < 7200` (key value `7100` in Figure 37.8) and `MIN(stor_id) > 7200` (key value `7300` in Figure 37.8). Transaction B holds a `RangeIn-Null` lock and waits for the `RangeS-S` lock to be released.

Listing 37.3 provides an example of the query against the `sys.dm_tran_locks` catalog view for these two transactions.

LISTING 37.3 Viewing Key-Range Locks on Nonexistent Row

```
select str(request_session_id, 4,0) as spid,
       convert (varchar(12), db_name(resource_database_id)) As db_name,
       case when resource_database_id = db_id() and resource_type = 'OBJECT'
            then convert(char(20), object_name(resource_Associated_Entity_id))
            else convert(char(20), resource_Associated_Entity_id)
            end as object,
       convert(varchar(12), resource_type) as resource_type,
       convert(varchar(10), request_mode) as mode,
       convert(varchar(8), request_status) as status
   from sys.dm_tran_locks
order by request_session_id, 3 desc
go

spid db_name      object           resource_type mode       status
---- ------------ ---------------- ------------- ---------- --------
  53 bigpubs2008  391941215944704 PAGE          IS         GRANT
  53 bigpubs2008  391941215944704 KEY           RangeS-S   GRANT
  53 bigpubs2008  1685581043      OBJECT        IS         GRANT
  53 bigpubs2008  0               DATABASE      S          GRANT
  57 bigpubs2008  391941215944704 PAGE          IX         GRANT
  57 bigpubs2008  391941215944704 KEY           RangeI-N   WAIT
  57 bigpubs2008  1685581043      OBJECT        IX         GRANT
  57 bigpubs2008  0               DATABASE      S          GRANT
```

Using Application Locks

The SQL Server Lock Manager knows nothing about the object or the structure of the object it is locking. The Lock Manager simply checks whether two processes are trying to obtain incompatible locks on the same resource. If so, blocking occurs.

SQL Server allows you to extend the resources that can be locked beyond the ones automatically provided. You can define your own custom locking resources and let the Lock Manager control the access to those resources as it would for any resource in a database. This essentially allows you to choose to lock anything you want. These user-defined lock resources are called *application locks*. To define an application lock, you use the sp_getapplock stored procedure and specify a name for the resource you are locking, a mode, an optional lock owner, and an optional lock timeout interval. The syntax for sp_getapplock is as follows:

```
sp_getapplock [ @Resource = ] 'resource_name',
    [ @LockMode = ] 'lock_mode'
    [ , [ @LockOwner = ] { 'transaction'  | 'session' } ]
    [ , [ @LockTimeout = ] 'value' ]
    [ , [ @DbPrincipal = ] 'database_principal' ]
```

Two resources are considered to be the same resource and are subject to lock contention if they have the same name and the same lock owner in the same database. The resource name used in these procedures can be any identifier up to 255 characters long. The lock owner can be specified as either transaction or session. Multiple requests for locks on the same resource can be granted only if the locking modes of the requests are compatible. (See the "Lock Compatibility" section, later in this chapter, for a lock compatibility matrix.) The possible modes of the lock allowed are shared, update, exclusive, intent exclusive, and intent shared. The database principal is the user, role, or application role that has permissions to an object in a database. The default is public.

For what purpose can you use application locks, and how do you use them? Suppose you have a table that contains a queue of items to be processed by the system. You need a way to serialize the retrieval of the next item from the queue so that the multiple concurrent processes do not grab the same item at the same time. In the past, one way this could be accomplished was by forcing an exclusive lock on the table. (The use of table hints to override default locking behavior is covered in the "Table Hints for Locking" section, later in this chapter.) Only the first process to acquire the exclusive lock would be able to retrieve the next item from the queue. The other processes would have to wait until the exclusive lock was released. The problem with this approach is that the exclusive lock would also block other processes that might need to simply retrieve data from the table.

You can use application locks to avoid having to place an exclusive lock on the entire table. By using sp_getapplock, you can define and lock a custom lock resource for a transaction or session. Locks that are owned by the current transaction are released when the transaction commits or rolls back. Locks that are owned by the session are released when the session is closed. Locks can also be explicitly released at any time, with the sp_releaseapplock stored procedure. The syntax for sp_releaseapplock is as follows:

```
sp_releaseapplock [ @Resource = ] 'resource_name'
    [ , [ @LockOwner = ] { 'transaction' | 'session' }]
    [ , [ @DbPrincipal = ] 'database_principal' ]
```

NOTE

If a process calls sp_getapplock multiple times for the same lock resource, sp_releaseapplock must be called the same number of times to fully release the lock. In addition, if sp_getapplock is called multiple times on the same lock resource but specifies different lock modes each time, the resulting lock on the resource is a union of the different lock modes. Generally, the lock mode ends up being promoted to the more restrictive level of the existing lock mode and the newly requested mode. The resulting lock mode is held until the last lock release call is made to fully release the lock. For example, assume that a process initially called sp_getapplock requested a shared lock. If it subsequently called sp_getapplock again and requested an exclusive lock, an exclusive lock would be held on the resource until sp_releaseapplock was executed twice.

In the following example, you first request an exclusive lock on an application lock called 'QueueLock' by using sp_getapplock. You then invoke the procedure to get the next item in the queue. After the procedure returns, you call sp_releaseapplock to release the application lock called 'QueueLock' to let another session acquire the application lock:

```
exec sp_getapplock 'QueueLock', 'Exclusive', 'session'
exec get_next_item_from_queue
exec sp_releaseapplock 'QueueLock', 'session'
```

As long as all processes that need to retrieve items from the queue execute this same sequence of statements, no other process can execute the get_next_item_from_queue process until the application lock is released. The other processes block attempts to acquire the exclusive lock on the resource 'QueueLock'. For example, Listing 37.4 shows an example of a query against the sys.dm_tran_locks view, showing one process (SPID 53) holding an exclusive lock on QueueLock, while another process (SPID 57) is waiting for an exclusive lock on QueueLock. (The hash value generated internally for QueueLock is shown as 18fb067e in the Resource_Desc field.)

LISTING 37.4 Viewing Application Locks Using **sys.dm_tran_locks**

```
select str(request_session_id, 4,0) as spid,
       convert (varchar(12), db_name(resource_database_id)) As db_name,
       case when resource_database_id = db_id() and resource_type = 'OBJECT'
            then convert(char(6), object_name(resource_Associated_Entity_id))
            else convert(char(6), resource_Associated_Entity_id)
            end as object,
       convert(varchar(12), resource_type) as resource_type,
       convert(varchar(4), request_mode) as mode,
       convert(varchar(24), resource_description) as resource_desc,
```

```
      convert(varchar(6), request_status) as status
   from sys.dm_tran_locks
order by request_session_id, 3 desc
go

spid db_name       object resource_type mode resource_desc               status
---- ------------ ------ ------------- ---- -------------------------- ------
 52 msdb          0      DATABASE      S                               GRANT
 53 bigpubs2008   0      DATABASE      S                               GRANT
 53 bigpubs2008   0      APPLICATION   X    0:[QueueLock]:(18fb067e) GRANT
 57 bigpubs2008   0      APPLICATION   X    0:[QueueLock]:(18fb067e) WAIT
 57 bigpubs2008   0      DATABASE      S                               GRANT
```

CAUTION

This method of using application locks to control access to the queue works only if all processes that are attempting to retrieve the next item in the queue follow the same protocol. The `get_next_item_from_queue` procedure itself is not actually locked. If another process attempts to execute the `get_next_item_from_queue` process without attempting to acquire the application lock first, the Lock Manager in SQL Server does not prevent the session from executing the stored procedure.

Index Locking

As with locks on data pages, SQL Server manages locks on index pages internally. There is the opportunity for greater locking contention in index pages than in data pages. Contention at the root page of the index is the highest because the root is the starting point for all searches via the index. Contention usually decreases as you move down the various levels of the B-tree, but it is still higher than contention at the data page level due to the typically greater number of index rows per index page than data rows per data page.

If locking contention in the index becomes an issue, you can use `ALTER INDEX` to manage the locking behavior at the index level. The syntax of this command is as follows:

```
ALTER INDEX { index_name | ALL } ON object
{   ALLOW_ROW_LOCKS = { ON | OFF }
 | ALLOW_PAGE_LOCKS = { ON | OFF }
```

The default for both `ALLOW_ROW_LOCKS` and `ALLOW_PAGE_LOCKS` is `ON`. When both of these options are enabled, SQL Server automatically makes the decision whether to apply row or page locks on the indexes and can escalate locks from the row or page level to the table level. When `ALLOW_ROW_LOCKS` is set to `OFF`, row locks on indexes are not used. Only page- or table-level locks are applied. When `ALLOW_PAGE_LOCKS` is set to `OFF`, no page locks are used on indexes, and only row- or table-level locks are applied. When `ALLOW_ROW_LOCKS` and ALLOW_PAGE_LOCK are both set to OFF, only a table-level lock is applied when the index is accessed.

NOTE

When ALLOW_PAGE_LOCKS is set to OFF for an index, the index cannot be reorganized.

SQL Server usually makes good choices for the index locks, but based on the distribution of data and nature of the application, you might want to force a specific locking option on a selective basis. For example, if you are experiencing a high level of locking contention at the page level of an index, you might want to force SQL Server to use row-level locks by turning off page locks.

As another example, if you have a lookup table that is primarily read-only (for example, one that is only refreshed by a weekly or monthly batch process), it may be more efficient to turn off page and row locking so that all readers simply acquire shared table-level locks, thereby reducing locking overhead. When the weekly or monthly batch update runs, the update process acquires an exclusive table-level lock when refreshing the table.

To display the current locking option for a given index, you use the INDEXPROPERTY function:

```
select INDEXPROPERTY(object_ID , index_name,
                  { 'IsPageLockDisallowed' | 'IsRowLockDisallowed' } )
```

CAUTION

SQL Server generally makes the correct decision in choosing the appropriate locking granularity for a query. It is generally not recommended that you override the locking granularity choices that the Query Optimizer makes unless you have good reason to do so and have evaluated all options first. Setting the inappropriate locking level can adversely affect the concurrency for a table or index.

Row-Level Versus Page-Level Locking

For years, it was often debated whether row-level locking was better than page-level locking. That debate still goes on in some circles. Many people argue that if databases and applications are well designed and tuned, row-level locking is unnecessary. This is borne out somewhat by the number of large and high-volume applications that were developed when row-level locking wasn't even an option. (Prior to SQL Server version 7, the smallest unit of data that SQL Server could lock was the page.) However, at that time, the page size in SQL Server was only 2KB. With page sizes expanded to 8KB, a greater number of rows (four times as many) can be contained on a single page. Page-level locks on 8KB pages could lead to greater page-level contention because the likelihood of the data rows being requested by different processes residing on the same page is greater. Using row-level locking increases the concurrent access to the data.

On the other hand, row-level locking consumes more resources (memory and CPU) than page-level locks simply because there is a greater number of rows than pages in a table. If a process needed to access all rows on a page, it would be more efficient to lock the entire page than acquire a lock for each individual row. This would result in a reduction in the number of lock structures in memory that the Lock Manager would have to manage.

Which is better—greater concurrency or lower overhead? As shown earlier, in Figure 37.6, it's a trade-off. As lock size decreases, concurrency improves, but performance degrades due to the extra overhead. As the lock size increases, performance improves due to less overhead, but concurrency degrades. Depending on the application, the database design, and the data, either page-level or row-level locking can be shown to be better than the other in different circumstances.

SQL Server makes the determination automatically at runtime—based on the nature of the query, the size of the table, and the estimated number of rows affected—of whether to initially lock rows, pages, or the entire table. In general, SQL Server attempts to first lock at the row level more often than the page level, in an effort to provide the best concurrency. With the speed of today's CPUs and the large memory support, the overhead of managing row locks is not as expensive as in the past. However, as the query processes and the actual number of resources locked exceed certain thresholds, SQL Server might attempt to escalate locks from a lower level to a higher level, as appropriate.

At times, SQL Server might choose to do both row and page locking for the same query. For example, if a query returns multiple rows, and if enough contiguous keys in a nonclustered index page are selected to satisfy the query, SQL Server might place page locks on the index while using row locks on the data. This reduces the need for lock escalation.

Lock Escalation

When SQL Server detects that the locks acquired by a query are using too much memory and consuming too many system resources for the Lock Manager to manage the locks efficiently, it automatically attempts to escalate row, key, or page locks to table-level locks. For example, because a query on a table continues to acquire row locks and every row in the table will eventually be accessed, it makes sense for SQL Server to escalate the row locks to a table-level lock. After the table-level lock is acquired, the row-level locks are released. This helps reduce locking overhead and keeps the system from running out of available lock structures. Recall from earlier sections in this chapter that the potential need for lock escalation is reflected in the intent locks that are acquired on the table by the process locking at the row or page level. While the default behavior in SQL Server is to escalate to table-level locks, SQL Server 2008 introduces the capability to escalate row or page locks to a single partition via the `LOCK_ESCALATION` setting in `ALTER TABLE`. This new option allows you to specify whether escalation is always to the table or partition level. The `LOCK_ESCALATION` setting can also be used to prevent lock escalation entirely.

NOTE

SQL Server never escalates row locks to page locks, only to table or partition-level locks. Also, multiple partition-level locks are never escalated to a single table-level lock.

What are the lock escalation thresholds in SQL Server? Currently, SQL Server attempts lock escalation under the following conditions:

- Whenever a single T-SQL statement acquires at least 5,000 locks on a single reference of a table, table partition, or index (this value is subject to change in subsequent service packs). Note that lock escalation does not occur if the locks are spread across multiple objects in the same statement—for example, 4,000 locks on one index and 2,500 locks on another.
- When the amount of memory required by lock resources exceeds 40% of the available Database Engine memory pool

NOTE

Generally, if more memory is required for lock resources than is currently available in the Database Engine memory pool, the Database Engine allocates additional memory dynamically to satisfy the request for locks as long as more computer memory is available and the `max server memory` threshold has not been reached. However, if allocating additional memory would cause paging at the operating system level, more lock space is not allocated. If no more memory is available, or the amount of memory allocated to lock resources reaches 60% of the memory acquired by an instance of the Database Engine, further requests for locks generate an out-of-lock memory error.

If locks cannot be escalated because of lock conflicts, SQL Server reattempts lock escalation when every 1,250 additional locks are acquired. For example, if another process is also holding locks at the page or row level on the same table (indicated by the presence of that process's intent lock on the table), lock escalation cannot take place if the lock types are not compatible until the lower-level locks are released by the other processes. In this case, SQL Server continues acquiring locks at the row or page level until the table lock becomes available.

Controlling Lock Escalation

Escalating locks to the table or partition level can lead to locking contention or blocking for other transactions attempting to access a row or page in the same table. Under certain circumstances, you might want to disable lock escalation.

As mentioned previously, lock escalation can be enabled or disabled at the table level using the `ALTER TABLE` command:

```
ALTER TABLE tablename set (LOCK_ESCALATION ={ AUTO | TABLE | DISABLE } )
```

Setting the option to `AUTO` allows SQL Server to escalate to the table or partition level. Setting the option to `DISABLE` prevents escalation to the table or partition level.

SQL Server 2008 also supports disabling lock escalation for all tables in all databases within a SQL Server instance using either the 1211 or 1224 trace flags. Trace flag 1211 completely disables lock escalation, regardless of the memory required for lock resources. However, when the amount of memory required for lock resources exceeds 60% of the maximum available Database Engine memory, an out-of-lock memory error is generated. Alternatively, trace flag 1224 disables the built-in lock escalation based on the number of locks acquired, but lock escalation is still possible when the 40% of available Database Engine memory threshold is reached. However, as noted previously, if the locks cannot be escalated, SQL Server could still run out of available memory for locks.

NOTE

You should be extremely careful when considering disabling lock escalation via the trace flags. A poorly designed application could potentially exhaust the available SQL Server memory with excessive lock structures and seriously degrade SQL Server performance. It is usually preferable to control lock escalation at the object level via the `ALTER TABLE` command.

Lock Compatibility

If a process has already locked a resource, the granting of lock requests by other transactions on the same resource is governed by the lock compatibility matrix within SQL Server. Table 37.3 shows the lock compatibility matrix for the locks most commonly acquired by the SQL Server Lock Manager, indicating which lock types are compatible and which lock types are incompatible when requested on the same resource.

TABLE 37.3 SQL Server Lock Compatibility Matrix

Requested Lock Type	Existing Lock Type								
	IS	S	U	IX	SIX	X	Sch-S	SCH-M	BU
Intent shared	Yes	Yes	Yes	Yes	Yes	No	Yes	No	No
Shared	Yes	Yes	Yes	No	No	No	Yes	No	No
Update	Yes	Yes	No	No	No	No	Yes	No	No
Intent exclusive	Yes	No	No	Yes	No	No	Yes	No	No
Shared with intent exclusive	Yes	No	No	No	No	No	Yes	No	No
Exclusive	No	No	No	No	No	No	Yes	No	No
Schema stability	Yes	Yes	Yes	Yes	Yes	Yes	Yes	No	Yes
Schema modify	No	No	No	No	No	No	No	No	No
Bulk update	No	No	No	No	No	No	Yes	No	Yes

For example, if a transaction has acquired a shared lock on a resource, the possible lock types that can be acquired on the resource by other transactions are intent shared, shared, update, and schema stability locks. Intent exclusive, `SIX`, exclusive, schema modification, and bulk update locks are incompatible with a shared lock and cannot be acquired on the resource until the shared lock is released.

Locking Contention and Deadlocks

In the grand scheme of things, the most likely culprits of SQL Server application performance problems are typically poorly written queries, poor database and index design, and locking contention. Whereas the first two problems result in poor application performance, regardless of the number of users on the system, locking contention becomes more of a performance problem as the number of users increases. It is further compounded by increasingly complex or long-running transactions.

Locking contention occurs when a transaction requests a lock type on a resource that is incompatible with an existing lock type on the resource. By default, the process waits indefinitely for the lock resource to become available. Locking contention is noticed in the client application through the apparent lack of response from SQL Server.

Figure 37.9 demonstrates an example of locking contention. Process 1 has initiated a transaction and acquired an exclusive lock on page 1:325. Before Process 1 can acquire the lock that it needs on page 1:341 to complete its transaction, Process 2 acquires an exclusive lock on page 1:341. Until Process 2 commits or rolls back its transaction and releases the lock on Page 1:341, the lock continues to be held. Because this is not a deadlock scenario (which is covered in the "Deadlocks" section, later in this chapter), by default, SQL Server takes no action. Process 1 simply waits indefinitely.

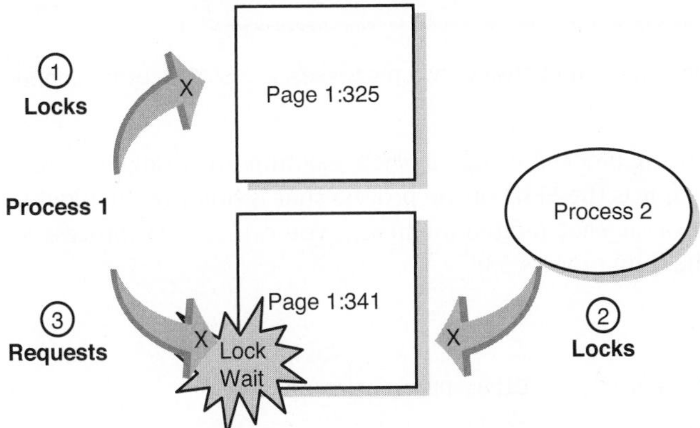

FIGURE 37.9 Locking contention between two processes.

37

Identifying Locking Contention

When a client application appears to freeze after submitting a query, this is often due to locking contention. To identify locking contention between processes, you can use the SSMS Activity Monitor, as discussed earlier in this chapter, in the "Monitoring Lock Activity in SQL Server" section; use the `sp_who2` stored procedure; or query the `sys.dm_tran_locks` system catalog view. Figure 37.10 shows an example of a blocking lock as viewed in the SSMS Activity Monitor.

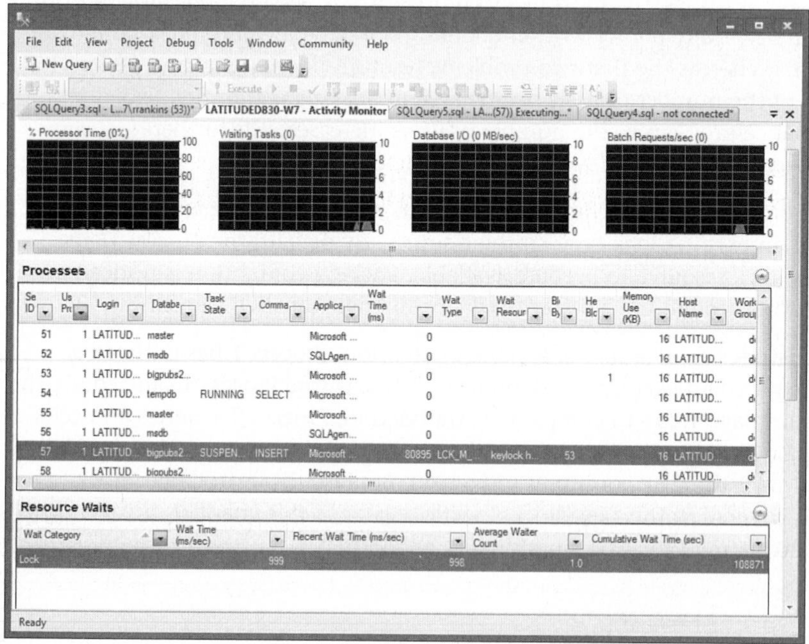

FIGURE 37.10 Examining locking contention between two processes in SSMS Activity Monitor.

To identify whether a process is being blocked using `sp_who2`, examine the `BlkBy` column. If any value besides '-' is displayed, it is the SPID of the process that is holding the blocking lock. In the following output of `sp_who2` (edited for space), you can see that process 57 is `SUSPENDED`, waiting on a lock held by process 53:

```
exec sp_who2
go
SPID  Status     Login     HostName          BlkBy DBName       Command
----- ---------- --------- ----------------- ----- ------------ ---------------
*** info for internal processes deleted ***
51    sleeping   rrankins  LATITUDED830-W7   .     master       AWAITING COMMAND
52    sleeping   SQLADMIN  LATITUDED830-W7   .     msdb         AWAITING COMMAND
53    sleeping   rrankins  LATITUDED830-W7   .     bigpubs2008  AWAITING COMMAND
54    sleeping   rrankins  LATITUDED830-W7   .     tempdb       AWAITING COMMAND
```

```
55    sleeping   rrankins  LATITUDED830-W7  .    master       AWAITING COMMAND
56    sleeping   SQLADMIN  LATITUDED830-W7  .    msdb         AWAITING COMMAND
57    SUSPENDED  rrankins  LATITUDED830-W7 53    bigpubs2008  INSERT
58    sleeping   rrankins  LATITUDED830-W7  .    bigpubs2008  AWAITING COMMAND
59    RUNNABLE   rrankins  LATITUDED830-W7  .    master       SELECT INTO
```

To determine what table, page, or rows are involved in blocking and at what level the blocking is occurring, you can query the `sys.dm_tran_locks` catalog view, as shown in Listing 37.5.

LISTING 37.5 Viewing Locking Contention by Using the **`sys.dm_tran_locks`** View

```
use bigpubs2008
go
select str(request_session_id, 4,0) as spid,
       convert (varchar(12), db_name(resource_database_id)) As db_name,
       case when resource_database_id = db_id() and resource_type = 'OBJECT'
            then convert(char(12), object_name(resource_Associated_Entity_id))
            else convert(char(16), resource_Associated_Entity_id)
            end as object,
       convert(varchar(12), resource_type) as resource_type,
       convert(varchar(8), request_mode) as mode,
       convert(varchar(14), resource_description) as resource_desc,
       convert(varchar(6), request_status) as status
   from sys.dm_tran_locks
order by request_session_id, 3 desc
go

spid db_name      object           resource_type mode     resource_desc status
---- ------------ ---------------- ------------ -------- -------------- ------
 52 msdb          0                DATABASE     S                       GRANT
 53 bigpubs2008  673416192655360   PAGE         IX       1:608          GRANT
 53 bigpubs2008  673416192655360   KEY          X        (928195c101b1) GRANT
 53 bigpubs2008  391941215944704   KEY          X        (59d1a826552c) GRANT
 53 bigpubs2008  391941215944704   PAGE         IX       1:280          GRANT
 53 bigpubs2008  stores            OBJECT       IX                      GRANT
 53 bigpubs2008  0                 DATABASE     S                       GRANT
 56 msdb         0                 DATABASE     S                       GRANT
 57 bigpubs2008  391941215944704   PAGE         IS       1:280          GRANT
 57 bigpubs2008  391941215944704   KEY          S        (59d1a826552c) WAIT
 57 bigpubs2008  stores            OBJECT       IS                      GRANT
 57 bigpubs2008  0                 DATABASE     S                       GRANT
```

From this output, you can see that Process 57 is waiting for a shared (`S`) lock on key `59d1a826552c` of page 1:280 of the `stores` table. Process 53 has an intent exclusive (`IX`) lock on that page because it has an exclusive (X) lock on a key on that page. (Both have the same resource_Associated_Entity_id of 59d1a826552c.)

As an alternative to sp_who and the sys.dm_tran_locks view, you can also get specific information on any blocked processes by querying the sys.dm_os_waiting_tasks system catalog view, as shown in Listing 37.6.

LISTING 37.6 Viewing Blocked Processes by Using the **sys.dm_os_waiting_tasks** View

```
select convert(char(4), session_id) as spid,
       convert(char(8), wait_duration_ms) as duration,
       convert(char(8), wait_type) as wait_type,
       convert(char(3), blocking_session_id) as blk,
       resource_description
from sys.dm_os_waiting_tasks
where blocking_session_id is not null
go

spid duration wait_type blk  resource_description
---- -------- --------- ---- --------------------------------------------------
-----------------------------------------
57   134118   LCK_M_S   53   keylock hobtid=391941215944704 dbid=8 id=lockfd43800
  mode=X associatedObjectId=391941215944704
```

Setting the Lock Timeout Interval

If you do not want a process to wait indefinitely for a lock to become available, SQL Server allows you to set a lock timeout interval by using the SET LOCK_TIMEOUT command. You specify the timeout interval in milliseconds. For example, if you want your processes to wait only 5 seconds (that is, 5,000 milliseconds) for a lock to become available, you execute the following command in the session:

```
SET LOCK_TIMEOUT 5000
```

If your process requests a lock resource that cannot be granted within 5 seconds, the statement is aborted, and you get the following error message:

```
Server: Msg 1222, Level 16, State 52, Line 1
Lock request time out period exceeded.
```

To examine the current LOCK_TIMEOUT setting, you can query the system function @@lock_timeout:

```
select @@lock_timeout
go

-----------
       5000
```

If you want processes to abort immediately if the lock cannot be granted (in other words, no waiting at all), you set the timeout interval to `0`. If you want to set the timeout interval back to infinity, execute the `SET_LOCK_TIMEOUT` command and specify a timeout interval of `-1`.

Minimizing Locking Contention

Although setting the lock timeout prevents a process from waiting indefinitely for a lock request to be granted, it doesn't address the cause of the locking contention. In an effort to maximize concurrency and application performance, you should minimize locking contention between processes as much as possible. Some general guidelines to follow to minimize locking contention include the following:

- Keep transactions as short and concise as possible. The shorter the period of time locks are held, the less chance for lock contention. Keep commands that are not essential to the unit of work being managed by the transaction (for example, assignment selects, retrieval of updated or inserted rows) outside the transaction.
- Keep statements that comprise a transaction in a single batch to eliminate unnecessary delays caused by network input/output (I/O) between the initial `BEGIN TRAN` statement and the subsequent `COMMIT TRAN` commands.
- Consider coding transactions entirely within stored procedures. Stored procedures typically run faster than commands executed from a batch. In addition, because they are server resident, stored procedures reduce the amount of network I/O that occurs during execution of the transaction, resulting in faster completion of the transaction.
- Commit updates in cursors frequently and as soon as possible. Cursor processing is much slower than set-oriented processing and causes locks to be held longer.

37

NOTE

Even though cursors might run more slowly than set-oriented processing, cursors can sometimes be used to minimize locking contention for updates and deletions of a large number of rows from a table, which might result in a table lock being acquired. The `UPDATE` or `DELETE` statement itself might complete faster; however, if it is running with an exclusive lock on the table, then no other process can access the table until it completes. By using a cursor to update a large number of rows one row at a time and committing the changes frequently, the cursor uses page- or row-level locks rather than a table-level lock. It might take longer for the cursor to complete the actual update or delete, but while the cursor is running, other processes are still able to access other rows or pages in the table that the cursor doesn't currently have locked.

- Use the lowest level of locking isolation required by each process. For example, if dirty reads are acceptable and accurate results are not imperative, consider using transaction Isolation Level 0. Use the Repeatable Read or Serializable Read isolation levels only if absolutely necessary.

- Never allow user interaction between a `BEGIN TRAN` statement and a `COMMIT TRAN` statement because doing so may cause locks to be held for an indefinite period of time. If a process needs to return rows for user interaction and then update one or more rows, consider using optimistic locking or Snapshot Isolation in your application. (Optimistic locking is covered in the "Optimistic Locking" section, later in this chapter.)
- Minimize "hot spots" in a table. Hot spots occur when the majority of the update activity on a table occurs within a small number of pages. For example, hot spots occur for concurrent insertions to the last page of a heap table or the last pages of a table with a clustered index on a sequential key. You can often eliminate hot spots by creating a clustered index in a table on a column or columns to order the rows in the table in such a way that insert and update activity is spread out more evenly across the pages in the table.

Deadlocks

A *deadlock* occurs when two processes are each waiting for a locked resource that the other process currently holds. Neither process can move forward until it receives the requested lock on the resource, and neither process can release the lock it is currently holding until it can receive the requested lock. Essentially, neither process can move forward until the other one completes, and neither one can complete until it can move forward.

Two primary types of deadlocks can occur in SQL Server:

- **Cycle deadlocks**—A cycle deadlock occurs when two processes acquire locks on different resources, and then each needs to acquire a lock on the resource that the other process has. Figure 37.11 demonstrates an example of a cycle deadlock.

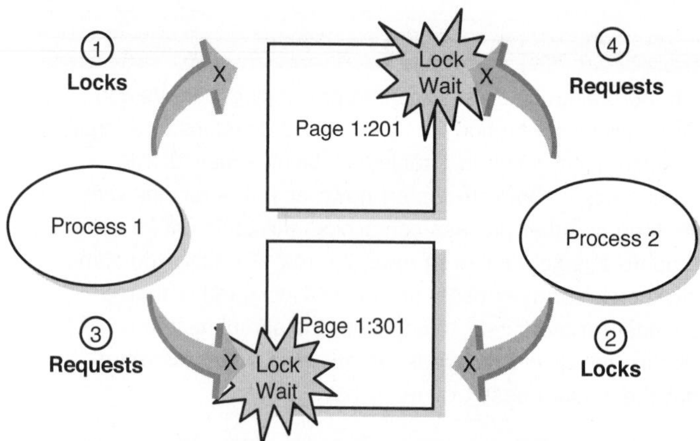

FIGURE 37.11 An example of a cycle deadlock.

In Figure 37.11, Process 1 acquires an exclusive lock on page 1:201 in a transaction. At the same time, Process 2 acquires an exclusive lock on page 1:301 in a transaction. Process 1 then attempts to acquire a lock on page 1:301 and begins waiting for the lock to become available. Simultaneously, Process 2 requests an exclusive lock on page 1:201, and a deadlock, or "deadly embrace," occurs.

- **Conversion deadlocks**—A conversion deadlock occurs when two or more processes each hold a shared lock on the same resource within a transaction and each wants to promote the shared lock to an exclusive lock, but neither can do so until the other releases the shared lock. An example of a conversion deadlock is shown in Figure 37.12.

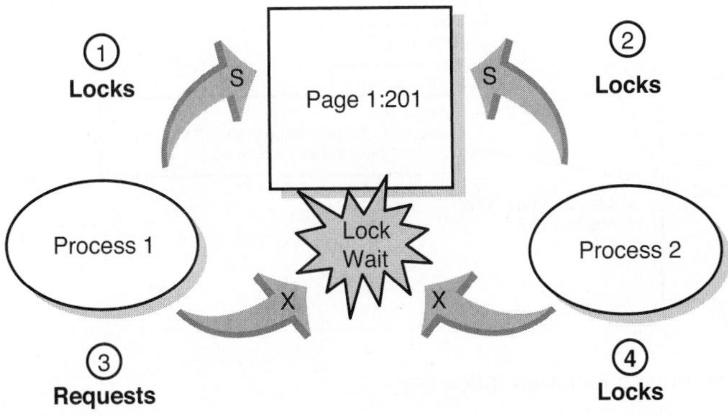

FIGURE 37.12 An example of a conversion deadlock.

It is often assumed that deadlocks happen at the data page or data row level. In fact, deadlocks often occur at the index page or index key level. Figure 37.13 depicts a scenario in which a deadlock occurs due to contention at the index key level.

SQL Server automatically detects when a deadlock situation occurs. A separate process in SQL Server, called `LOCK_MONITOR`, checks the system for deadlocks roughly every 5 seconds. In the first pass, this process detects all the processes that are waiting on a lock resource. The `LOCK_MONITOR` thread checks for deadlocks by examining the list of waiting lock requests to see if any circular lock requests exist between the processes holding locks and the processes waiting for locks. When the `LOCK_MONITOR` detects a deadlock, SQL Server aborts the transaction of one of the involved processes. How does SQL Server determine which process to abort? It attempts to choose as the deadlock victim the transaction that it estimates would be least expensive to roll back. If both processes involved in the deadlock have the same rollback cost and the same deadlock priority, the deadlock victim is chosen randomly.

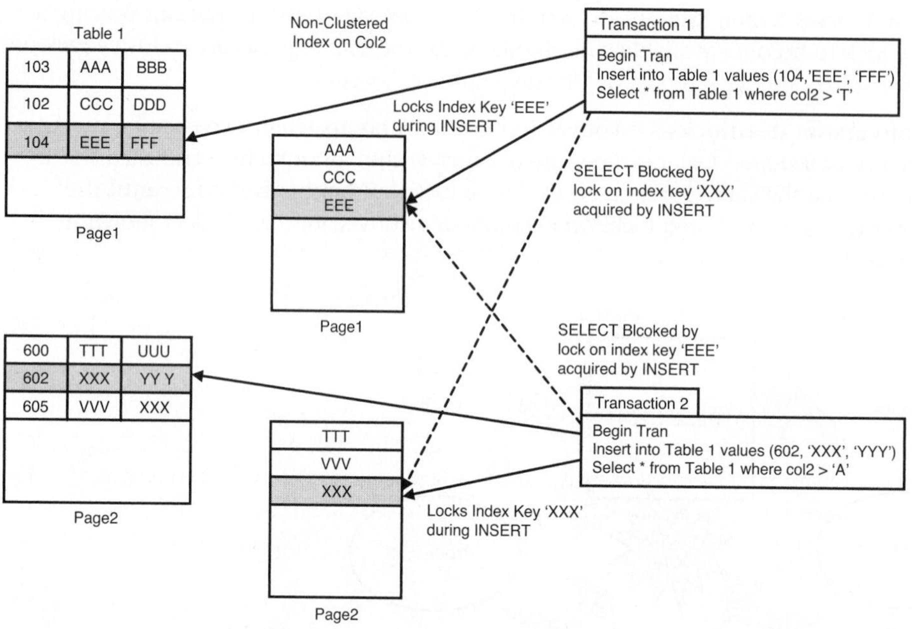

FIGURE 37.13 Deadlock scenario due to locks on index keys.

NOTE

As deadlocks occur, SQL Server begins reducing the deadlock detection interval and can potentially go as low as 100ms. In addition, the first few lock requests that cannot be satisfied after a deadlock is detected immediately trigger a deadlock search instead of waiting for the next deadlock detection interval. When deadlock frequency declines, the deadlock detection interval begins to increase back to 5 seconds.

You can influence which process will be the deadlock victim by using the >`SET DEADLOCK_PRIORITY` statement. `DEADLOCK_PRIORITY` can be set to `LOW`, `NORMAL`, or `HIGH`. Alternatively, `DEADLOCK_PRIORITY` can also be set to any integer value from `-10` to `10`. The default deadlock priority is `NORMAL`. When two sessions deadlock, and the deadlock priority has been set to something other than the default, the session with the lower priority is chosen as the deadlock victim. If you have lower-priority processes that you would prefer always be chosen as the deadlock victims, you might want to set the process's deadlock priority to `LOW`. Alternatively, for critical processes, you might want to set the deadlock priority to `HIGH` to specify processes that should always come out as the winners in a deadlock scenario.

Avoiding Deadlocks

Although SQL Server automatically detects and handles deadlocks, you should try to avoid deadlocks in your applications. When a process is chosen as a deadlock victim, it has to resubmit its work because it has been rolled back. Frequent deadlocks create performance problems if you have to keep repeating work.

You can follow a number of guidelines to minimize, if not completely eliminate, the number of deadlocks that occur in your application(s). Following the guidelines presented earlier to minimize locking contention and speed up your transactions also helps to eliminate deadlocks. The less time for which a transaction is holding locks, the less likely the transition will be around long enough for a conflicting lock request to be requested at the same time. In addition, you might want to follow this list of additional guidelines when designing applications:

- Be consistent about the order in which you access the data from tables to avoid cycle deadlocks.
- Minimize the use of `HOLDLOCK` or queries that are running using Repeatable Read or Serializable Read isolation levels. This helps avoid conversion deadlocks. If possible, perform `UPDATE` statements before `SELECT` statements so that your transaction acquires an update or exclusive lock first. This eliminates the possibility of a conversion deadlock. (Later, in the "Table Hints for Locking" section in this chapter, you see how to use table-locking hints to force `SELECT` statements to use update or exclusive locks as another strategy to avoid conversion deadlocks.)
- Choose the transaction isolation level judiciously. You might be able to reduce deadlocks by choosing lower isolation levels.

Handling and Examining Deadlocks

SQL Server returns error number 1205 to the client when it aborts a transaction as a result of deadlock. The following is an example of a 1205 error message:

```
Msg 1205, Level 13, State 51, Line 1
Transaction (Process ID 53) was deadlocked on lock resources with another process
 and has been chosen as the deadlock victim. Rerun the transaction.
```

Because a deadlock is not a logical error but merely a resource contention issue, the client can resubmit the entire transaction. To handle deadlocks in applications, be sure to trap for message 1205 in the error handler. When a 1205 error occurs, the application can simply resubmit the transaction automatically. It is considered bad form to allow end users of an application to see the deadlock error message returned from SQL Server.

Earlier in this chapter, you learned how to use `sp_who2` and the `sys.dm_tran_locks` and `sys.dm_os_waiting_tasks` system catalog views to monitor locking contention between processes. However, when a deadlock occurs, one transaction is rolled back, and one is allowed to continue. If you examine the output from `sp_who2` or the system catalog views after a deadlock occurs, the information likely will not be useful because the locks on the resources involved will have since been released.

Fortunately, SQL Server provides a couple of trace flags to monitor deadlocks within SQL Server. They are trace flag 1204 and trace flag 1222. When enabled, they print deadlock information to the SQL Server error log. Trace flag 1204 provides deadlock information generated by each process involved in the deadlock. Trace flag 1222 provides deadlock information by processes and by resources. Both trace flags can be enabled to capture a complete representation of a deadlock event.

You use the `DBCC TRACEON` command to turn on the trace flags and `DBCC TRACEOFF` to turn them off. The 1204 and 1222 trace flags are global trace flags. Global trace flags are set at the server level and are visible to every connection on the server. They cannot be set for a specific session only. They enable or disable a global trace flag, and the `-1` option must be specified as the second argument to the `DBCC TRACEON` and `DBCC TRACEOFF` commands. The following example shows how to globally enable the 1204 trace flag:

```
dbcc traceon(1204, -1)
```

If possible, it is best to set global trace flags whenever SQL Server is started up by adding the `-T` option with the appropriate trace flag value to the SQL Server startup parameters. For example, to have SQL Server turn on the 1204 trace flag automatically on startup, you use the SQL Server Configuration Manager. In the SQL Server Configuration Manager window, you click SQL Server 2005 Services; in the right pane, right-click the SQL Server service for the appropriate SQL Server instance name and then click Properties. On the Advanced tab, expand the Startup Parameters box and type a semicolon (;) and `-T1204` after the last startup parameter listed (see Figure 37.14); then click OK to save the changes. You then need to stop and restart SQL Server for the trace flag to take effect.

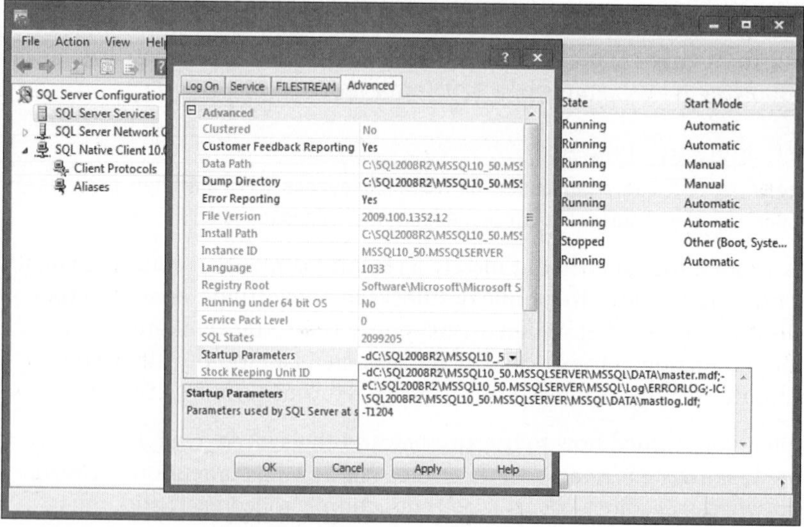

FIGURE 37.14 Setting the 1204 trace flag to be enabled on SQL Server startup.

CAUTION

The 1204 and 1222 trace flags may incur some additional processing overhead in SQL Server. They should be used only when you are debugging and tuning SQL Server performance, and they should not be left on indefinitely in a production environment. You should turn them off after you have diagnosed and fixed the problems.

The 1204 Trace Flag Trace flag 1204 prints useful information to the SQL Server error log when a deadlock is detected. The following output is from the error log for this trace flag:

```
2010-02-14 18:44:36.27 spid6s     Deadlock encountered .... Printing deadlock
 information
2010-02-14 18:44:36.27 spid6s     Wait-for graph
2010-02-14 18:44:36.27 spid6s
2010-02-14 18:44:36.27 spid6s     Node:1

2010-02-14 18:44:36.33 spid6s     KEY: 8:391941215944704 (59d1a826552c) CleanCnt:3
 Mode:S Flags: 0x1
2010-02-14 18:44:36.33 spid6s      Grant List 0:
2010-02-14 18:44:36.33 spid6s        Owner:0x0FE274C0 Mode: S       Flg:0x40
 Ref:0 Life:02000000 SPID:53 ECID:0XactLockInfo: 0x05626F00
2010-02-14 18:44:36.33 spid6s        SPID: 53 ECID: 0 Statement Type: DELETE
 Line #: 1
2010-02-14 18:44:36.33 spid6s        Input Buf: Language Event: delete
 bigpubs2008..stores
where stor_id = '7066'
2010-02-14 18:44:36.33 spid6s     Requested by:
2010-02-14 18:44:36.33 spid6s       ResType:LockOwner Stype:'OR'Xdes:0x06136280
 Mode: X SPID:57 BatchID:0 ECID:0 TaskProxy:(0x062DE354) Value:0xfe27580 Cost:(0/0)
2010-02-14 18:44:36.33 spid6s
2010-02-14 18:44:36.33 spid6s     Node:2

2010-02-14 18:44:36.33 spid6s     KEY: 8:391941215944704 (59d1a826552c)
 CleanCnt:3 Mode:S Flags: 0x1
2010-02-14 18:44:36.33 spid6s      Grant List 0:
2010-02-14 18:44:36.33 spid6s        Owner:0x0FE27480 Mode: S
Flg:0x40 Ref:0 Life:02000000 SPID:57 ECID:0 XactLockInfo: 0x061362A8
2010-02-14 18:44:36.33 spid6s        SPID: 57 ECID: 0 Statement Type: DELETE
 Line #: 1
2010-02-14 18:44:36.33 spid6s        Input Buf: Language Event: delete
 bigpubs2008..stores
where stor_id = '7066'
```

```
2010-02-14 18:44:36.33 spid6s     Requested by:
2010-02-14 18:44:36.33 spid6s       ResType:LockOwner Stype:'OR'Xdes:0x05626ED8
 Mode: X SPID:53 BatchID:0 ECID:0 TaskProxy:(0x06892354) Value:0xfe27240 Cost:(0/0)
2010-02-14 18:44:36.33 spid6s
2010-02-14 18:44:36.33 spid6s     Victim Resource Owner:
2010-02-14 18:44:36.33 spid6s      ResType:LockOwner Stype:'OR'Xdes:0x06136280

 Mode: X SPID:57 BatchID:0 ECID:0 TaskProxy:(0x062DE354) Value:0xfe27580 Cost:(0/0)
```

Although the 1204 output is somewhat cryptic, it is not too difficult to read if you know what to look for. If you look through the output, you can see where it lists the SPIDs of the processes involved in the deadlock (in this example, SPIDs 53 and 57) and indicates which process was chosen as the deadlock victim (`SPID:57`). The type of statement involved is indicated by `Statement Type`. In this example, both processes were attempting a `DELETE` statement. You can also examine the actual text of the query (`Input Buf`) that each process was executing at the time the deadlock occurred. The output also displays the locks granted to each process (`Grant List`), the lock types (`Mode:`) of the locks held, and the lock resources requested by the deadlock victim.

The 1222 Trace Flag Trace flag 1222 provides deadlock information, first by processes and then by resources. The information is returned in an XML-like format that does not conform to an XML schema definition. The output has three major sections:

- The first section declares the deadlock victim.
- The second section describes each process involved in the deadlock
- The third section describes the resources involved

The following example shows the 1222 trace flag output for the same deadlock scenario displayed by the 1204 trace flag output in the previous section:

```
2010-02-14 18:50:38.95 spid19s    deadlock-list
2010-02-14 18:50:38.95 spid19s     deadlock victim=process2e4be40
2010-02-14 18:50:38.95 spid19s      process-list
2010-02-14 18:50:38.95 spid19s       process id=process2e4be40 taskpriority=0
 logused=0 waitresource=KEY: 8:391941215944704 (59d1a826552c) waittime=4719
 ownerId=3060410 transactionname=user_transaction lasttranstarted=
 2010-02-14T18:50:19.863 XDES=0x5626ed8 lockMode=X schedulerid=1 kpid=
 8316 status=suspended spid=57 sbid=0 ecid=0 priority=0 trancount=2
 lastbatchstarted=2010-02-14T18:50:34.170 lastbatchcompleted=
 2010-02-14T18:50:19.867 lastattention=2010-02-14T18:40:55.483 clientapp=
 Microsoft SQL Server Management Studio - Query hostname=LATITUDED830-W7
 hostpid=940 loginname=LATITUDED830-W7\rrankins isolationlevel=serializable
 (4) xactid=3060410 currentdb=8 lockTimeout=4294967295 clientoption1=671090784
 clientoption2=390200
2010-02-14 18:50:38.95 spid19s        executionStack
2010-02-14 18:50:38.95 spid19s         frame procname=adhoc line=1 stmtstart=36
 sqlhandle=0x0200000091375f0a4f39d6bfb1addf384048ee0fa211d85f
```

```
2010-02-14 18:50:38.95 spid19s     DELETE [bigpubs2008]..[stores] WHERE
[stor_id]=@1
2010-02-14 18:50:38.95 spid19s          frame procname=adhoc line=1
sqlhandle=0x02000000748e4d288370bb86daf8048c94f6402aeacee742
2010-02-14 18:50:38.95 spid19s     delete bigpubs2008..stores
2010-02-14 18:50:38.95 spid19s     where stor_id = '7066'
2010-02-14 18:50:38.95 spid19s         inputbuf
2010-02-14 18:50:38.95 spid19s     delete bigpubs2008..stores
2010-02-14 18:50:38.95 spid19s     where stor_id = '7066'
2010-02-14 18:50:38.95 spid19s        process id=process2e4b390 taskpriority=0
logused=0 waitresource=KEY: 8:391941215944704 (59d1a826552c) waittime=9472
ownerId=3060605 transactionname=user_transaction lasttranstarted=
2010-02-14T18:50:24.447 XDES=0x6136280 lockMode=X schedulerid=1 kpid=7384
status=suspended spid=53 sbid=0 ecid=0 priority=0 trancount=2
lastbatchstarted=2010-02-14T18:50:29.413 lastbatchcompleted=
2010-02-14T18:50:24.447 clientapp=Microsoft SQL Server Management Studio -
Query hostname=LATITUDED830-W7 hostpid=940 loginname=LATITUDED830-W7\rrankins
isolationlevel=serializable (4) xactid=3060605 currentdb=8 lockTimeout=4294967295
clientoption1=671090784 clientoption2=390200
2010-02-14 18:50:38.95 spid19s         executionStack
2010-02-14 18:50:38.95 spid19s          frame procname=adhoc line=1 stmtstart=36
sqlhandle=0x0200000091375f0a4f39d6bfb1addf384048ee0fa211d85f
2010-02-14 18:50:38.95 spid19s     DELETE [bigpubs2008]..[stores] WHERE
[stor_id]=@1
2010-02-14 18:50:38.95 spid19s          frame procname=adhoc line=1
sqlhandle=0x02000000748e4d288370bb86daf8048c94f6402aeacee742
2010-02-14 18:50:38.95 spid19s     delete bigpubs2008..stores
2010-02-14 18:50:38.95 spid19s     where stor_id = '7066'
2010-02-14 18:50:38.95 spid19s        inputbuf
2010-02-14 18:50:38.95 spid19s     delete bigpubs2008..stores
2010-02-14 18:50:38.95 spid19s     where stor_id = '7066'
2010-02-14 18:50:38.95 spid19s       resource-list
2010-02-14 18:50:38.95 spid19s        keylock hobtid=391941215944704 dbid=8
objectname=bigpubs2008.dbo.stores indexname=UPK_storeid id=lockfd432c0 mode=S
associatedObjectId=391941215944704
2010-02-14 18:50:38.95 spid19s         owner-list
2010-02-14 18:50:38.95 spid19s          owner id=process2e4b390 mode=S
2010-02-14 18:50:38.95 spid19s         waiter-list
2010-02-14 18:50:38.95 spid19s          waiter id=process2e4be40 mode=X
requestType=convert
2010-02-14 18:50:38.95 spid19s        keylock hobtid=391941215944704 dbid=8
objectname=bigpubs2008.dbo.stores indexname=UPK_storeid id=lockfd432c0 mode=S
associatedObjectId=391941215944704
2010-02-14 18:50:38.95 spid19s         owner-list
2010-02-14 18:50:38.95 spid19s          owner id=process2e4be40 mode=S
2010-02-14 18:50:38.95 spid19s         waiter-list
```

37

```
2010-02-14 18:50:38.95 spid19s          waiter id=process2e4b390 mode=X
 requestType=convert
```

Monitoring Deadlocks with SQL Server Profiler

If you still find the 1204 and 1222 trace flag output too difficult to interpret, you'll be pleased to know that SQL Server Profiler provides a much more user-friendly way of capturing and examining deadlock information. As discussed in the "Monitoring Lock Activity in SQL Server" section, earlier in this chapter, SQL Profiler provides three deadlock events that can be monitored:

- `Lock:Deadlock`
- `Lock:Deadlock Chain`
- `Deadlock Graph`

The `Lock:Deadlock` and `Lock:Deadlock Chain` events aren't really very useful in SQL Server 2008. The `Lock:Deadlock` event generates a simple trace record that indicates when a deadlock occurs between two processes. The SPID column indicates what process was chosen as the deadlock victim. The `Lock:Deadlock Chain` event generates a trace record for each process involved in the deadlock. Unfortunately, neither of these trace events provides any detailed information, such as the queries involved in the deadlock. (You would need to also trace the T-SQL commands executed to capture this information, but you would then be capturing all SQL statements, not just those involved in the deadlock.)

Fortunately, SQL Server Profiler provides the new `Deadlock Graph` event. When this event is enabled, SQL Server Profiler populates the `TextData` data column in the trace with XML data about the process and objects involved in the deadlock. This XML data can then be used to display a Deadlock Graph in SQL Server Profiler itself, or the XML can be extracted to a file, which can be read in and viewed in SSMS. Figure 37.15 shows an example of a Deadlock Graph being displayed in SQL Server Profiler.

The Deadlock Graph displays the processes, resources, and relationships between the processes and resources. The following components make up a Deadlock Graph:

- **Process node**—An oval containing information about each thread that performs a task involved in the deadlock (for example, `INSERT`, `UPDATE`, or `DELETE`).
- **Resource node**—A rectangle containing information about each database object being referenced (for example, a table, an index, a page, a row, or a key).
- **Edge**—A line representing a relationship between a process and resource. A request edge occurs when a process waits for a resource. An owner edge occurs when a resource waits for a process. The lock mode is included in the edge description.

Figure 37.15 displays the deadlock information for the processes involved in the deadlocks displayed by the 1204 and 1222 trace flag output listed in the previous sections. You can see that it displays the resource(s) involved in the deadlock in the Resource node (`Key Lock`), the lock type held on the resource by each process (`Owner Mode: S`), the lock type being requested by each process (`Request Mode: X`), and general information about each

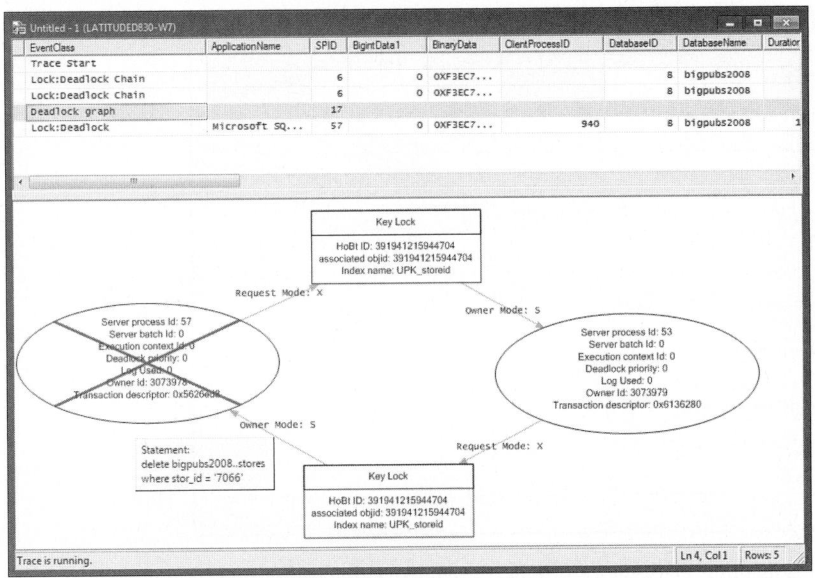

FIGURE 37.15 Displaying a Deadlock Graph in SQL Server Profiler.

process (for example, SPID, deadlock priority) displayed in each process node. The process node of the process chosen as the deadlock victim has an X through it. If you place the mouse pointer over a process node, a ToolTip displays the SQL statement for that process involved in the deadlock. If the graph appears too large or too small for the profiler window, you can right-click anywhere within the graph to bring up a context menu that allows you to increase or decrease the size of the graph.

To save a Deadlock Graph to a file for further analysis at a later date, you can right-click the Deadlock Graph event in the top panel and choose the Extract Event Data option. To save all Deadlock Graph events contained in a SQL Server trace to one or more files, you select File, Export, Extract SQL Server Events and then choose the Extract Deadlock Events option. In the dialog that appears, you have the option to save all Deadlock Graphs contained in the trace to a single file or to save each to a separate file.

SQL Server Profiler can also save all Deadlock Graphs to a file automatically. When you are configuring a trace with the `Deadlock Graph` event selected, you go to the Events Extraction Settings tab and click Save Deadlock XML Events Separately. Then you specify the file where you want the deadlock events to be saved. You can select to save all Deadlock Graph events in a single XML file or to create a new XML file for each Deadlock Graph. If you choose to create a new XML file for each Deadlock Graph, SQL Server Profiler automatically appends a sequential number to the filename. Figure 37.16 shows an example of the Events Extraction Settings tab to have a Profiler trace automatically generate a separate file for each deadlock trace.

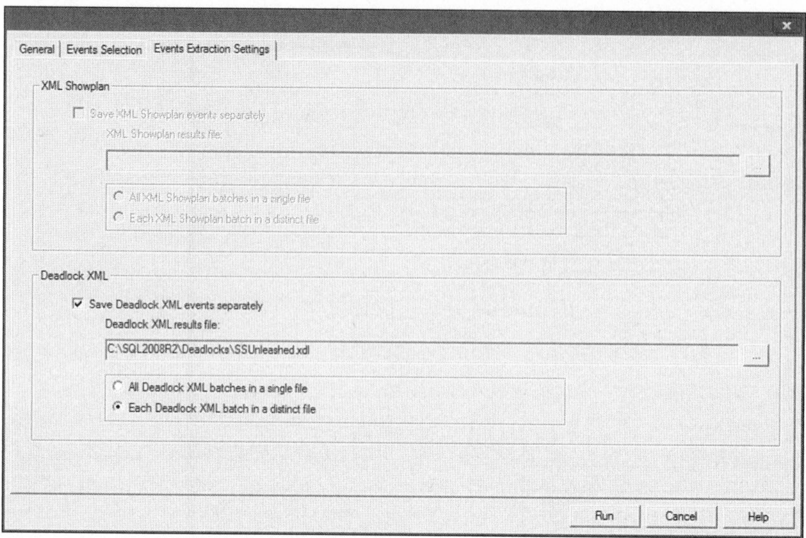

FIGURE 37.16 Configuring SQL Server Profiler to export Deadlock Graphs to individual files.

You can use SSMS to open and analyze any SQL Server Profiler Deadlock Graphs that you have saved to a file. To do so, in SSMS you choose File, Open and then click File. In the Open File dialog box, you select the `.xdl` file type as the type of file. You now have a filtered list of only deadlock files (see Figure 37.17). After you select the file or files, you are able to view them in SSMS.

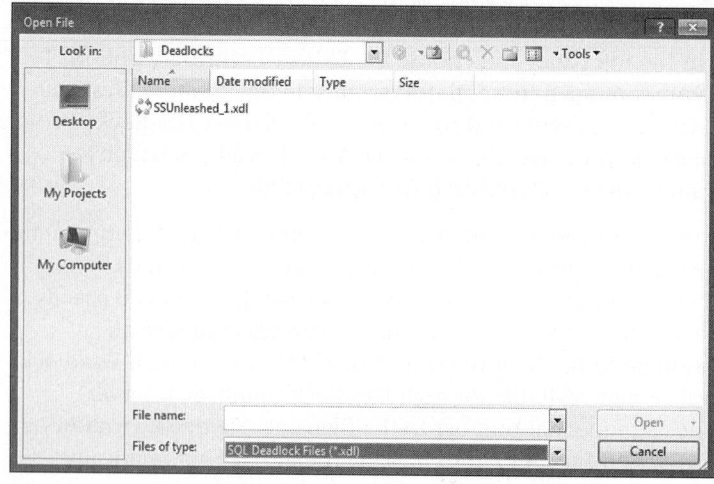

FIGURE 37.17 Opening a Deadlock Graph file in SSMS.

Table Hints for Locking

As mentioned previously in this chapter, in the "Transaction Isolation Levels in SQL Server" section, you can set an isolation level for your connection by using the `SET TRANSACTION ISOLATION LEVEL` command. This command sets a global isolation level for an entire session, which is useful if you want to provide a consistent isolation level for an application. However, sometimes you might want to specify different isolation levels for specific queries or for different tables within a single query. SQL Server allows you to do this by supporting table hints in the `SELECT`, `MERGE`, `UPDATE`, `INSERT`, and `DELETE` statements. In this way, you can override the isolation level currently set at the session level.

In this chapter, you have seen that locking is dynamic and automatic in SQL Server. Based on certain factors (for example, SARGs, key distribution, data volume), the Query Optimizer chooses the granularity of the lock (that is, row, page, or table level) on a resource. Although it is usually best to leave such decisions to the Query Optimizer, you might encounter certain situations in which you want to force a different lock granularity on a resource than what the optimizer has chosen. SQL Server provides additional table hints that you can use in the query to force lock granularity for various tables participating in a join.

SQL Server also automatically determines the lock type (`SHARED`, `UPDATE`, `EXCLUSIVE`) to use on a resource, depending on the type of command being executed on the resource. For example, a `SELECT` statement uses a shared lock. SQL Server also provides additional table hints to override the default lock type.

The table hints to override the lock isolation, granularity, or lock type for a table can be provided using the `WITH` operator of the `SELECT`, `UPDATE`, `INSERT`, and `DELETE` statements.

The following sections discuss the various locking hints that can be passed to an optimizer to manage isolation levels and the lock granularity of a query.

37

NOTE

Although many of the table-locking hints can be combined, you cannot combine more than one isolation level or lock granularity hint at a time on a single table. Also, the `NOLOCK`, `READUNCOMMITTED`, and `READPAST` hints described in the following sections cannot be used on tables that are the target of `INSERT`, `UPDATE`, `MERGE`, or `DELETE` queries.

Transaction Isolation–Level Hints

SQL Server provides a number of hints that you can use in a query to override the default transaction isolation level:

- **HOLDLOCK**—`HOLDLOCK` maintains shared locks for the duration of the entire statement or for the entire transaction, if the statement is in a transaction. This option is equivalent to the Serializable Read isolation level. The following hypothetical example demonstrates the usage of the HOLDLOCK statement within a transaction:

```
declare @seqno int
begin transaction
-- get a UNIQUE sequence number from sequence table
SELECT @seqno = isnull(seq#,0) + 1
from sequence WITH (HOLDLOCK)

-- in the absence of HOLDLOCK, shared lock will be released
-- and if some other concurrent transaction ran the same
-- command, both of them could get the same sequence number

UPDATE sequence
set   seq# = @seqno

--now go do something else with this unique sequence number
commit tran
```

NOTE

As discussed earlier in this chapter, in the "Deadlocks" section, using HOLDLOCK in this manner leads to potential deadlocks between processes executing the transaction at the same time. For this reason, the HOLDLOCK hint, as well as the REPEATABLEREAD and SERIALIZABLE hints, should be used sparingly, if at all. In this example, it might be better for the SELECT statement to use an update or an exclusive lock on the sequence table, using the hints discussed later in this chapter, in the section "Lock Type Hints." Another option would be to use an application lock, as discussed previously in this chapter, in the section "Using Application Locks."

- **NOLOCK**—You can use this option to specify that no shared lock be placed on the resource. This option is similar to running a query at Isolation Level 0 (Read Uncommitted), which allows the query to ignore exclusive locks and read uncommitted changes. The NOLOCK option is a useful feature in reporting environments, where the accuracy of the results is not critical.
- **READUNCOMMITTED**—This is the same as specifying the Read Uncommitted mode when using the SET TRANSACTION ISOLATION LEVEL command, and it is the same as the NOLOCK table hint.
- **READCOMMITTED**—This is the same as specifying the Read Committed mode when you use the SET TRANSACTION ISOLATION LEVEL command. The query waits for exclusive locks to be released before reading the data. This is the default locking isolation mode for SQL Server. If the database option READ_COMMITTED_SNAPSHOT is ON, SQL Server does not acquire shared locks on the data and uses row versioning.

- **READCOMMITTEDLOCK**—This option specifies that read operations acquire shared locks as data is read and release those locks when the read operation is completed, regardless of the setting of the READ_COMMITTED_SNAPSHOT database option.
- **REPEATABLEREAD**—This is the same as specifying Repeatable Read mode with the SET TRANSACTION ISOLATION LEVEL command. It prevents nonrepeatable reads within a transaction and behaves similarly to the HOLDLOCK hint.
- **SERIALIZABLE**—This is the same as specifying Serializable Read mode with the SET TRANSACTION ISOLATION LEVEL command. It prevents phantom reads within a transaction and behaves similarly to using the HOLDLOCK hint.
- **READPAST**—This hint specifies that the query skip over the rows or pages locked by other transactions, returning only the data that can be read. Read operations specifying READPAST are not blocked. When specified in an UPDATE or DELETE statement, READPAST is applied only when reading data to identify which records to update. READPAST can be specified only in transactions operating at the Read Committed or Repeatable Read isolation levels. This lock hint is useful when reading information from a SQL Server table used as a work queue. A query using READPAST skips past queue entries locked by other transactions to the next available queue entry, without having to wait for the other transactions to release their locks.

Lock Granularity Hints

You can use to override lock granularity:

- **ROWLOCK**—You can use this option to force the Lock Manager to place a row-level lock on a resource instead of a page-level or a table-level lock. You can use this option in conjunction with the XLOCK lock type hint to force exclusive row locks.
- **PAGLOCK**—You can use this option to force a page-level lock on a resource instead of a row-level or table-level lock. You can use this option in conjunction with the XLOCK lock type hint to force exclusive page locks.
- **TABLOCK**—You can use this option to force a table-level lock instead of a row-level or page-level lock. You can use this option in conjunction with the HOLDLOCK table hint to hold the table lock until the end of the transaction.
- **TABLOCKX**—You can use this option to force a table-level exclusive lock instead of a row-level or page-level lock. No shared or update locks are granted to other transactions as long as this option is in effect. If you are planning maintenance on a SQL Server table and you don't want interference from other transactions, using this option is one of the ways to essentially put a table into a single-user mode.

Lock Type Hints

You can use the following optimizer hints to override the lock type that SQL Server uses:

- **UPDLOCK**—This option is similar to HOLDLOCK except that whereas HOLDLOCK uses a shared lock on the resource, UPDLOCK places an update lock on the resource for the duration of the transaction. This allows other processes to read the information, but not acquire update or exclusive locks on the resource. This option provides read repeatability within the transaction while preventing deadlocks that can result when using HOLDLOCK.

- **XLOCK**—This option places an exclusive lock on the resource for the duration of the transaction. This prevents other processes from acquiring locks on the resource.

Optimistic Locking

With many applications, clients need to fetch the data to browse through it, make modifications to one or more rows, and then post the changes back to the database in SQL Server. These human-speed operations are slow in comparison to machine-speed operations, and the time lag between the fetch and post might be significant. (Consider a user who goes to lunch after retrieving the data.)

For these applications, you would not want to use normal locking schemes such as SERIALIZABLE or HOLDLOCK to lock the data so it can't be changed from the time the user retrieves it to the time he or she applies any updates. This would violate one of the key rules for minimizing locking contention and deadlocks that you should not allow user interaction within transactions. You would also lose all control over the duration of the transaction. In a multiuser OLTP environment, the indefinite holding of the shared locks could significantly affect concurrency and overall application performance due to blocking on locks and locking contention.

On the other hand, if the locks are not held on the rows being read, another process could update a row between the time it was initially read and when the update is posted. When the first process applies the update, it would overwrite the changes made by the other process, resulting in a lost update.

So how do you implement such an application? How do you allow users to retrieve information without holding locks on the data and still ensure that lost updates do not occur?

Optimistic locking is a technique used in situations in which reading and modifying data processes are widely separated in time. Optimistic locking helps a client avoid overwriting another client's changes to a row without holding locks in the database.

One approach for implementing optimistic locking is to use the `rowversion` data type. Another approach is to take advantage of the optimistic concurrency features of snapshot isolation.

Optimistic Locking Using the `rowversion` Data Type

SQL Server 2008 provides a special data type called `rowversion` that can be used for optimistic locking purposes within applications. The purpose of the `rowversion` data type is to serve as a version number in optimistic locking schemes. SQL Server automatically generates the value for a `rowversion` column whenever a row that contains a column of this type is inserted or updated. The `rowversion` data type is an 8-byte binary data type, and other than guaranteeing that the value is unique and monotonically increasing, the value is not meaningful; you cannot look at the individual bytes and make any sense of them.

NOTE

In previous versions of SQL Server, the `rowversion` data type was also referred to as the `timestamp` data type. While this data type synonym still exists in SQL Server 2008, it has been deprecated and the `rowversion` data type name should be used instead to ensure future compatibility.

In an application that uses optimistic locking, the client reads one or more records from the table, being sure to retrieve the primary key and current value of the `rowversion` column for each row, along with any other desired data columns. Because the query is not run within a transaction, any locks acquired for the `SELECT` are released after the data has been read. At some later time, when the client wants to update a row, it must ensure that no other client has changed the same row in the intervening time. The `UPDATE` statement must include a `WHERE` clause that compares the `rowversion` value retrieved with the original query, with the current `rowversion` value for the record in the database. If the `rowversion` values match—that is, if the value that was read is the same as the value currently in the database—no changes to that row have occurred since it was originally retrieved. Therefore, the change attempted by the application can proceed. If the `rowversion` value in the client application *does not* match the value in the database, that particular row has been changed since the original retrieval of the record. As a result, the state of the row that the application is attempting to modify is not the same as the row that currently exists in the database. As a result, the transaction should not be allowed to take place, to avoid the lost update problem.

To ensure that the client application does not overwrite the changes made by another process, the client needs to prepare the T-SQL `UPDATE` statement in a special way, using the `rowversion` column as a versioning marker. The following pseudocode represents the general structure of such an update:

```
UPDATE theTable
  SET theChangedColumns = theirNewValues
  WHERE primaryKeyColumns = theirOldValues
    AND rowversion = itsOldValue
```

Because the `WHERE` clause includes the primary key, the `UPDATE` can apply only to exactly one row or to no rows; it cannot apply to more than one row because the primary key is unique. The second part of the `WHERE` clause provides the optimistic "locking." If another client has updated the row, the `rowversion` no longer has its old value (remember that the server changes the `rowversion` value automatically with each update), and the `WHERE` clause does not match any rows. The client needs to check whether any rows were updated. If the number of rows affected by the update statement is zero, the row has been modified since it was originally retrieved. The application can then choose to reread the data or do whatever recovery it deems appropriate. This approach has one problem: how does the application know whether it didn't match the row because the `rowversion` was changed, because the primary key had changed, or because the row had been deleted altogether?

In SQL Server 2000, there was an undocumented `tsequal()` function (which was documented in prior releases) that could be used in a `WHERE` clause to compare the `rowversion` value retrieved by the client application with the `rowversion` value in the database. If the `rowversion` values matched, the update would proceed. If not, the update would fail, with error message 532, to indicate that the row had been modified. Unfortunately, this function is no longer provided in SQL Server 2005 and later releases. Any attempt to use it now results in a syntax error. As an alternative, you can programmatically check whether the update modified any rows, and if not, you can check whether the row still exists and return the appropriate message. Listing 37.7 provides an example of a stored procedure that implements this strategy.

LISTING 37.7 An Example of a Procedure for Optimistic Locking

```
create proc optimistic_update
      @id int, -- provide the primary key for the record
      @data_field_1 varchar(10), -- provide the data value to be updated
      @rowversion rowversion -- pass in the rowversion value retrieved with
                             -- the initial data retrieval
as
-- Attempt to modify the record
update data_table
  set data_field_1 = @data_field_1
  where id = @id
    and versioncol = @rowversion
-- Check to see if no rows updated
IF @@ROWCOUNT=0
BEGIN
  if exists (SELECT * FROM data_table WHERE id=@id)
  -- The row exists but the rowversions don't match
  begin
     raiserror ('The row with id "%d" has been updated since it was read',
                10, 1, @id)
     return -101
  end
  else -- the row has been deleted
  begin
     raiserror ('The row with id "%d" has been deleted since it was read',
                 10, 2, @id)
     return -102
  end
end
```

```
ELSE
  PRINT 'Data Updated'
return 0
```

Using this approach, if the update doesn't modify any rows, the application receives an error message and knows for sure that the reason the update didn't take place is that either the `rowversion` value didn't match or the row was deleted. If the row is found and the `rowversion` values match, the update proceeds normally.

Optimistic Locking with Snapshot Isolation

SQL Server 2008's Snapshot Isolation mode provides another mechanism for implementing optimistic locking through its automatic row versioning. If a process reads data within a transaction when Snapshot Isolation mode is enabled, no locks are acquired or held on the current version of the data row. The process reads the version of the data at the time of the query. Because no locks are held, it doesn't lead to blocking, and another process can modify the data after it has been read. If another process does modify a data row read by the first process, a new version of the row is generated. If the original process then attempts to update that data row, SQL Server automatically prevents the lost update problem by checking the row version. In this case, because the row version is different, SQL Server prevents the original process from modifying the data row. When it attempts to modify the data row, the following error message appears:

```
Msg 3960, Level 16, State 4, Line 2
Snapshot isolation transaction aborted due to update conflict. You cannot use
 snapshot isolation to access table 'dbo.data_table' directly or indirectly in
 database 'bigpubs2008' to update, delete, or insert the row that has been modified
 or deleted by another transaction. Retry the transaction or change the isolation
 level for the update/delete statement.
```

To see how this works, you can create the following table:

```
use bigpubs2008
go
--The first statement is used to disable any previously created
--DDL triggers in the database which would prevent creating a new table.
DISABLE TRIGGER ALL ON DATABASE
go
create table data_table
   (id int identity,
    data_field_1 varchar(10),
    timestamp timestamp)
go
insert data_table (data_field_1) values ('foo')
go
```

Next, you need to ensure that `bigpubs2008` is configured to allow snapshot isolation:

```
ALTER DATABASE bigpubs2008 SET ALLOW_SNAPSHOT_ISOLATION ON
```

In one user session, you execute the following SQL statements:

```
SET TRANSACTION ISOLATION LEVEL SNAPSHOT
go
begin tran
select * from data_table
go

id          data_field_1 timestamp
----------- ------------ ------------------
1           foo          0x0000000000000BC4
```

Now, in another user session, you execute the following UPDATE statement:

```
update data_table set data_field_1 = 'bar'
  where id = 1
```

Then you go back to the original session and attempt the following update:

```
update data_table set data_field_1 = 'fubar'
  where id = 1
go

Msg 3960, Level 16, State 4, Line 2
Snapshot isolation transaction aborted due to update conflict. You cannot use
 snapshot isolation to access table 'dbo.data_table' directly or indirectly in
 database 'bigpubs2008' to update, delete, or insert the row that has been modified
 or deleted by another transaction. Retry the transaction or change the isolation
 level for the update/delete statement.
```

Note that for the first process to hold on to the row version, the SELECT and UPDATE statements must be run in the same transaction. When the transaction is committed or rolled back, the row version acquired by the SELECT statement is released. However, because the SELECT statement run at the Snapshot Isolation level does not hold any locks, there are no locks being acquired or held by that SELECT statement within the transaction, so it avoids the problems that would normally be encountered by using HOLDLOCK or the Serializable Read isolation level. Because no locks were held on the data row, the other process was allowed to update the row after it was retrieved, generating a new version of the row. The automatic row versioning provided by SQL Server's Snapshot Isolation mode prevented the first process from overwriting the update performed by the second process, thereby preventing a lost update.

CAUTION

Locking contention is prevented in the preceding example only because the transaction performed only a `SELECT` before attempting the `UPDATE`. A `SELECT` run with Snapshot Isolation mode enabled reads the current version of the row and does not acquire or hold locks on the actual data row. However, if the process were to perform any other modification on the data row, the update or exclusive locks acquired would be held until the end of the transaction, which could lead to locking contention, especially if user interaction is allowed within the transaction after the update or exclusive locks are acquired.

Also, be aware of the overhead generated in `tempdb` when Snapshot Isolation mode is enabled for a database, as described in the section "Transaction Isolation Levels in SQL Server," earlier in this chapter.

Because of the overhead incurred by snapshot isolation and the cost of having to roll back update conflicts, you should consider using Snapshot Isolation mode only to provide optimistic locking for systems where there is little concurrent updating of the same resource so that it is unlikely that your transactions have to be rolled back because of an update conflict.

Summary

Locking is critical in a multiuser environment for providing transaction isolation. SQL Server supports all ANSI-defined transaction isolation levels, including the Snapshot Isolation level for applications that can benefit from optimistic concurrency. The Lock Manager in SQL Server automatically locks data at the row level or higher, as necessary, to provide the appropriate isolation while balancing the locking overhead with concurrent access to the data. It is important to understand how locking works and what its effect is on application performance to develop efficient queries and applications.

SQL Server provides a number of tools for monitoring and identifying locking problems and behavior. In addition, SQL Server provides a number of table-locking hints that give the developer better control over the default lock types and granularity used for certain queries.

Although following the guidelines to minimize locking contention in applications is important, another factor that affects locking behavior and query performance is the actual database design. Chapter 38, "Database Design and Performance," discusses database design and its effect on database performance and provides guidelines to help ensure that transactions and T-SQL code run efficiently.

CHAPTER 38

Database Design and Performance

IN THIS CHAPTER

- What's New in Database Design and Performance
- Basic Tenets of Designing for Performance
- Logical Database Design Issues
- Denormalizing a Database
- Database Filegroups and Performance
- RAID Technology
- SQL Server and SAN Technology

Various factors contribute to the optimal performance of a database application. Some of these factors include logical database design (rules of normalization), physical database design (denormalization, indexes, data placement), choice of hardware (SMP servers/multiprocessor servers), network bandwidth (LAN versus WAN), client and server configuration (memory, CPU), data access techniques (ODBC, ADO, OLEDB), and application architecture (two-tier versus n-tier). This chapter helps you understand some of the key database design issues to ensure that you have a reliable high-performance application.

NOTE

Index design is often considered part of physical database design. Because index design guidelines and the impact of indexes on query and update performance are covered in detail in Chapter 34, "Data Structures, Indexes and Performance," this chapter does not discuss index design. It focuses instead on other aspects of database design and performance.

What's New in Database Design and Performance

Many of the database design and performance considerations that applied to previous versions of SQL Server still apply to SQL Server 2008. These principles are basic in nature and are not affected by the version of the database management system. This chapter focuses on those relatively unchanged principles.

There are, however, some new features in SQL Server 2008 that will augment these basic principles. Filtered indexes, new query and table hints, plus other table-oriented features are just a few things you should consider when designing your database for performance. These features are discussed in detail in Chapter 24, "Creating and Managing Tables," Chapter 34, "Data Structures, Indexes, and Performance," and other chapters in Part V, "SQL Server Performance and Optimization."

Basic Tenets of Designing for Performance

Designing for performance requires making trade-offs. For example, to get the best write performance out of a database, you must sacrifice read performance. Before you tackle database design issues for an application, it is critical to understand your goals. Do you want faster read performance? Faster write performance? A more understandable design?

Following are some basic truths about physical database design for SQL Server 2008 and the performance implications of each:

- It's important to keep table row sizes as small as possible. Doing so is not about saving disk space. Having smaller rows means more rows fit on a single 8KB page, which means fewer physical disk reads are required to read a given number of rows.
- You should use indexes to speed up read access. However, the more indexes a table has, the longer it takes to insert, update, and delete rows from the table.
- Using triggers to perform any kind of work during an insert, an update, or a delete exacts a performance toll and decreases concurrency by lengthening transaction duration.
- Implementing declarative referential integrity (via primary and foreign keys) helps maintain data integrity, but enforcing foreign key constraints requires extra lookups on the primary key table to ensure existence.
- Using `ON DELETE CASCADE` referential integrity constraints helps maintain data integrity but requires extra work on the server's part.

Keeping tables as narrow as possible—that is, ensuring that the row size is as small as possible—is one of the most important things you can do to ensure that a database performs well. To keep your tables narrow, you should choose column data types with size in mind. You shouldn't use the `bigint` data type if the `int` will do. If you have zero-to-one relationships in tables, you should consider vertically partitioning the tables. (See the "Vertical Data Partitioning" section, later in this chapter, for details on this scenario.)

Cascading deletes (and updates) cause extra lookups to be done whenever a delete runs against the parent table. In many cases, the optimizer uses worktables to resolve delete and update queries. Enforcing these constraints manually, from within stored procedures, for example, can give better performance. This is not a wholehearted endorsement against referential integrity constraints. In most cases, the extra performance hit is worth the saved aggravation of coding everything by hand. However, you should be aware of the cost of this convenience.

Logical Database Design Issues

A good database design is fundamental to the success of any application. Logical database design for relational databases follows rules of normalization. As a result of normalization, you create a data model that is usually, but not necessarily, translated into a physical data model. A logical database design does not depend on the relational database you intend to use. The same data model can be applied to Oracle, Sybase, SQL Server, or any other relational database. On the other hand, a physical data model makes extensive use of the features of the underlying database engine to yield optimal performance for the application. Physical models are much less portable than logical models.

TIP

If portability is a big concern to you, consider using a third-party data modeling tool, such as ERwin or ERStudio. These tools have features that make it easier to migrate your logical data models to physical data models on different database platforms. Of course, using these tools just gets you started; to get the best performance out of your design, you need to tweak the physical design for the platform you have chosen.

Normalization Conditions

Any database designer must address two fundamental issues:

- Designing the database in a simple, understandable way that is maintainable and makes sense to its developers and users
- Designing the database such that data is fetched and saved with the fastest response time, resulting in high performance

Normalization is a technique used on relational databases to organize data across many tables so that related data is kept together based on certain guidelines. Normalization results in controlled redundancy of data; therefore, it provides a good balance between disk space usage and performance. Normalization helps people understand the relationships between data and enforces rules to ensure that the data is meaningful.

TIP

Normalization rules exist, among other reasons, to make it easier for people to understand the relationships between data. But a perfectly normalized database sometimes doesn't perform well under certain circumstances, and it may be difficult to understand. There are good reasons to deviate from a perfectly normalized database.

Normalization Forms

Five normalization forms exist, represented by the symbol 1NF for first normal form, 2NF for second normal form, and so on. If you follow the rules for the first rule of normalization, your database can be described as "in first normal form."

Each rule of normalization depends on the previous rule for successful implementation, so to be in second normal form (2NF), your database must also follow the rules for first normal form.

A typical relational database used in a business environment falls somewhere between second and third normal forms. It is rare to progress past the third normal form because fourth and fifth normal forms are more academic than practical in real-world environments.

Following is a brief description of the first three rules of normalization.

First Normal Form

The first rule of normalization requires removing repeating data values and specifies that no two rows in a table can be identical. This means that each table must have a logical primary key that uniquely identifies a row in the table.

Consider a table that has four columns—`PublisherName`, `Title1`, `Title2`, and `Title3`—for storing up to three titles for each publisher. This table is not in first normal form due to the repeating `Title` columns. The main problem with this design is that it limits the number of titles associated with a publisher to three.

Removing the repeating columns so there is just a `PublisherName` column and a single `Title` column puts the table in first normal form. A separate data row is stored in the table for each title published by each publisher. The combination of `PublisherName` and `Title` becomes the primary key that uniquely identifies each row and prevents duplicates.

Second Normal Form

A table is considered to be in second normal form if it conforms to the first normal form and all nonkey attributes of the table are fully dependent on the entire primary key. If the primary key consists of multiple columns, nonkey columns should depend on the entire key and not just on a part of the key. A table with a single column as the primary key is automatically in second normal form if it satisfies first normal form as well.

Assume that you need to add the publisher address to the database. Adding it to the table with the `PublisherName` and `Title` column would violate second normal form. The primary key consists of both `PublisherName` and `Title`, but the `PublisherAddress` attribute is an attribute of the publisher only. It does not depend on the entire primary key.

To put the database in second normal form requires adding an additional table for storing publisher information. One table consists of the `PublisherName` column and `PublisherAddress`. The second table contains the `PublisherName` and `Title` columns. To retrieve the `PublisherName`, `Title`, and `PublisherAddress` information in a single result would require a join between the two tables on the `PublisherName` column.

Third Normal Form

A table is considered to be in third normal form if it already conforms to the first two normal forms and if none of the nonkey columns are dependent on any other nonkey columns. All such attributes should be removed from the table.

Let's look at an example that comes up often during database architecture. Suppose that an employee table has four columns: `EmployeeID` (the primary key), `salary`, `bonus`, and `total_salary`, where `total_salary = salary + bonus`. Existence of the `total_salary` column in the table violates the third normal form because a nonkey column (`total_salary`) is dependent on two other nonkey columns (`salary` and `bonus`). Therefore, for the table to conform to the third rule of normalization, you must remove the `total_salary` column from the employee table.

Benefits of Normalization

Following are the major advantages of normalization:

- Because information is logically kept together, normalization provides improved overall understanding of the system.
- Because of controlled redundancy of data, normalization can result in fast table scans and searches (because less physical data has to be processed).
- Because tables are smaller with normalization, index creation and data sorts are much faster.
- With less redundant data, it is easier to maintain referential integrity for the system.
- Normalization results in narrower tables. Because you can store more rows per page, more rows can be read and cached for each I/O performed on the table. This results in better I/O performance.

Drawbacks of Normalization

One result of normalization is that data is stored in multiple tables. To retrieve or modify information, you usually have to establish joins across multiple tables. Joins are expensive from an I/O standpoint. Multitable joins can have an adverse impact on the performance of the system. The following sections discuss some of the denormalization techniques you can use to improve the performance of a system.

TIP

An adage for normalization is "Normalize 'til it hurts; denormalize 'til it works." To put this maxim into use, try to put your database in third normal form initially. Then, when you're ready to implement the physical structure, drop back from third normal form, where excessive table joins are hurting performance. A common mistake is that developers make too many assumptions and over-denormalize the database design before even a single line of code has been written to even begin to assess the database performance.

Denormalizing a Database

After a database has been normalized to the third form, database designers intentionally backtrack from normalization to improve the performance of the system. This technique of rolling back from normalization is called *denormalization*. Denormalization allows you to keep redundant data in the system, reducing the number of tables in the schema and reducing the number of joins to retrieve data.

TIP

Duplicate data is more helpful when the data does not change very much, such as in data warehouses. If the data changes often, keeping all "copies" of the data in sync can create significant performance overhead, including long transactions and excessive write operations.

Denormalization Guidelines

When should you denormalize a database? Consider the following points:

- Be sure you have a good overall understanding of the logical design of the system. This knowledge helps in determining how other parts of the application are going to be affected when you change one part of the system.
- Don't attempt to denormalize the entire database at once. Instead, focus on the specific areas and queries that are accessed most frequently and are suffering from performance problems.
- Understand the types of transactions and the volume of data associated with specific areas of the application that are having performance problems. You can resolve many such issues by tuning the queries without denormalizing the tables.
- Determine whether you need virtual (computed) columns. Virtual columns can be computed from other columns of the table. Although this violates third normal form, computed columns can provide a decent compromise because they do not actually store another exact copy of the data in the same table.
- Understand data integrity issues. With more redundant data in the system, maintaining data integrity is more difficult, and data modifications are slower.

- Understand storage techniques for the data. You may be able to improve performance without denormalization by using RAID, SQL Server filegroups, and table partitioning.
- Determine the frequency with which data changes. If data is changing too often, the cost of maintaining data and referential integrity might outweigh the benefits provided by redundant data.
- Use the performance tools that come with SQL Server (such as SQL Server Profiler) to assess performance. These tools can help isolate performance issues and give you possible targets for denormalization.

TIP

If you are experiencing severe performance problems, denormalization should *not* be the first step you take to rectify the problem. You need to identify specific issues that are causing performance problems. Usually, you discover factors such as poorly written queries, poor index design, inefficient application code, or poorly configured hardware. You should try to fix these types of issues *before* taking steps to denormalize database tables.

Essential Denormalization Techniques

You can use various methods to denormalize a database table and achieve desired performance goals. Some of the useful techniques used for denormalization include the following:

- Keeping redundant data and summary data
- Using virtual columns
- Performing horizontal data partitioning
- Performing vertical data partitioning

Redundant Data

From an I/O standpoint, joins in a relational database are inherently expensive. To avoid common joins, you can add redundancy to a table by keeping exact copies of the data in multiple tables. The following example demonstrates this point. This example shows a three-table join to get the title of a book and the primary author's name:

```
select c.title,
       a.au_lname,
       a.au_fname
   from   authors a join titleauthor b on a.au_id = b.au_id
   join titles c on b.title_id = c.title_id
   where  b.au_ord = 1
   order by c.title
```

You could improve the performance of this query by adding the columns for the first and last names of the primary author to the `titles` table and storing the information in the titles table directly. This would eliminate the joins altogether. Here is what the revised query would look like if this denormalization technique were implemented:

```
select title,
       au_lname,
       au_fname
   from  titles
   order by title
```

As you can see, the au_lname and au_fname columns are now redundantly stored in two places: the titles table and authors table. It is obvious that with more redundant data in the system, maintaining referential integrity and data integrity is more difficult. For example, if the author's last name changed in the authors table, to preserve data integrity, you would also have to change the corresponding au_lname column value in the titles table to reflect the correct value. You could use SQL Server triggers to maintain data integrity, but you should recognize that update performance could suffer dramatically. For this reason, it is best if redundant data is limited to data columns whose values are relatively static and are not modified often.

Computed Columns

A number of queries calculate aggregate values derived from one or more columns of a table. Such computations can be CPU intensive and can have an adverse impact on performance if they are performed frequently. One of the techniques to handle such situations is to create an additional column that stores the computed value. Such columns are called *virtual columns*, or *computed columns*. Since SQL Server 7.0, computed columns have been natively supported. You can specify such columns in create table or alter table commands. The following example demonstrates the use of computed columns:

```
create table emp (
        empid int not null primary key,
        salary money not null,
        bonus money not null default 0,
        total_salary as ( salary+bonus )
        )
go
insert emp (empid, salary, bonus) values (100, $150000.00, $15000)
go
select * from emp
go
empid       salary          bonus                 total_salary
----------- --------------- --------------------- ---------------
100         150000.0000     15000.0000            165000.0000
```

By default, virtual columns are not physically stored in SQL Server tables. SQL Server internally maintains a column property named iscomputed that can be viewed from the sys.columns system view. It uses this column to determine whether a column is computed. The value of the virtual column is calculated at the time the query is run. All columns referenced in the computed column expression must come from the table on which the computed column is created. You can, however, reference a column from another table by using a function as part of the computed column's expression. The function can contain a reference to another table, and the computed column calls this function.

Since SQL Server 2000, computed columns have been able to participate in joins to other tables, and they can be indexed. Creating an index that contains a computed column creates a physical copy of the computed column in the index tree. Whenever a base column participating in the computed column changes, the index must also be updated, which adds overhead and may possibly slow down update performance.

In SQL Server 2008, you also have the option of defining a computed column so that its value is physically stored. You accomplish this with the `ADD PERSISTED` option, as shown in the following example:

```
--Alter the computed SetRate column to be PERSISTED
ALTER TABLE Sales.CurrencyRate
 alter column SetRate ADD PERSISTED
```

SQL Server automatically updates the persisted column values whenever one of the columns that the computed column references is changed. Indexes can be created on these columns, and they can be used just like nonpersisted columns. One advantage of using a computed column that is persisted is that it has fewer restrictions than a nonpersisted column. In particular, a persisted column can contain an imprecise expression, which is not possible with a nonpersisted column. Any float or real expressions are considered imprecise. To ensure that you have a precise column you can use the `COLUMNPROPERTY` function and review the `IsPrecise` property to determine whether the computed column expression is precise.

Summary Data

Summary data is most helpful in a decision support environment, to satisfy reporting requirements and calculate sums, row counts, or other summary information and store it in a separate table. You can create summary data in a number of ways:

- **Real-time**—Every time your base data is modified, you can recalculate the summary data, using the base data as a source. This is typically done using stored procedures or triggers.
- **Real-time incremental**—Every time your base data is modified, you can recalculate the summary data, using the old summary value and the new data. This approach is more complex than the real-time option, but it could save time if the increments are relatively small compared to the entire dataset. This, too, is typically done using stored procedures or triggers.
- **Delayed**—You can use a scheduled job or custom service application to recalculate summary data on a regular basis. This is the recommended method to use in an OLTP system to keep update performance optimal.

Horizontal Data Partitioning

As tables grow larger, data access time also tends to increase. For queries that need to perform table scans, the query time is proportional to the number of rows in the table. Even when you have proper indexes on such tables, access time slows as the depth of the index trees increases. The solution is splitting the table into multiple tables such that each table has the same table structure as the original one but stores a different set of data. Figure 38.1 shows a billing table with 90 million records. You can split this table into 12 monthly tables (all with the identical table structure) to store billing records for each month.

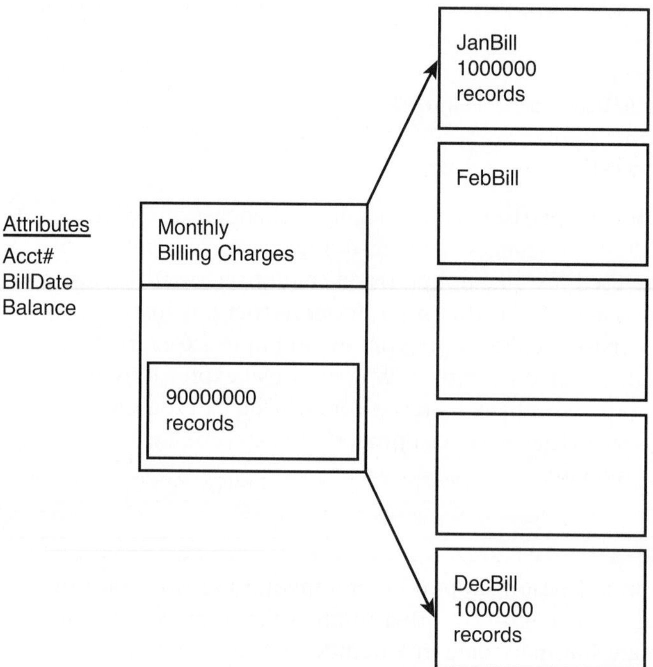

FIGURE 38.1 Horizontal partitioning of data.

You should carefully weigh the options when performing horizontal splitting. Although a query that needs data from only a single month gets much faster, other queries that need a full year's worth of data become more complex. Also, queries that are self-referencing do not benefit much from horizontal partitioning. For example, the business logic might dictate that each time you add a new billing record to the billing table, you need to check any outstanding account balance for previous billing dates. In such cases, before you do an insert in the current monthly billing table, you must check the data for all the other months to find any outstanding balance.

TIP

Horizontal splitting of data is useful where a subset of data might see more activity than the rest of the data. For example, say that in a healthcare provider setting, 98% of the patients are inpatients, and only 2% are outpatients. In spite of the small percentage involved, the system for outpatient records sees a lot of activity. In this scenario, it makes sense to split the patient table into two tables—one for the inpatients and one for the outpatients.

When splitting tables horizontally, you must perform some analysis to determine the optimal way to split the table. You need to find a logical dimension along which to split the data. The best choice takes into account the way your users use your data. In the example that involves splitting the data among 12 tables, date was mentioned as the optimal split candidate. However, if the users often did ad hoc queries against the billing table for a full year's worth of data, they would be unhappy with the choice to split that data among 12 different tables. Perhaps splitting based on a customer type or another attribute would be more useful.

NOTE

You can use partitioned views to hide the horizontal splitting of tables. The benefit of using partitioned views is that multiple horizontally split tables appear to the end users and applications as a single large table. When this is properly defined, the optimizer automatically determines which tables in the partitioned view need to be accessed, and it avoids searching all tables in the view. The query runs as quickly as if it were run only against the necessary tables directly. For more information on defining and using partitioned views, see Chapter 27, "Creating and Managing Views."

In SQL Server 2008, you also have the option of physically splitting the rows in a single table over more than one partition. This feature, called *partitioned tables*, utilizes a partitioning function that splits the data horizontally and a partitioning scheme that assigns the horizontally partitioned data to different filegroups. When a table is created, it references the partitioned schema, which causes the rows of data to be physically stored on different filegroups. No additional tables are needed, and the table is still referenced with the original table name. The horizontal partitioning happens at the physical storage level and is transparent to the user.

Vertical Data Partitioning

As you know, a database in SQL Server consists of 8KB pages, and a row cannot span multiple pages. Therefore, the total number of rows on a page depends on the width of the table. This means the wider the table, the smaller the number of rows per page. You can achieve significant performance gains by increasing the number of rows per page, which in turn reduces the number of I/Os on the table. Vertical splitting is a method of reducing the width of a table by splitting the columns of the table into multiple tables. Usually, all frequently used columns are kept in one table, and others are kept in the other table. This way, more records can be accommodated per page, fewer I/Os are generated, and more data can be cached into SQL Server memory. Figure 38.2 illustrates a vertically partitioned table. The frequently accessed columns of the `authors` table are stored in the `author_primary` table, whereas less frequently used columns are stored in the `author_secondary` table.

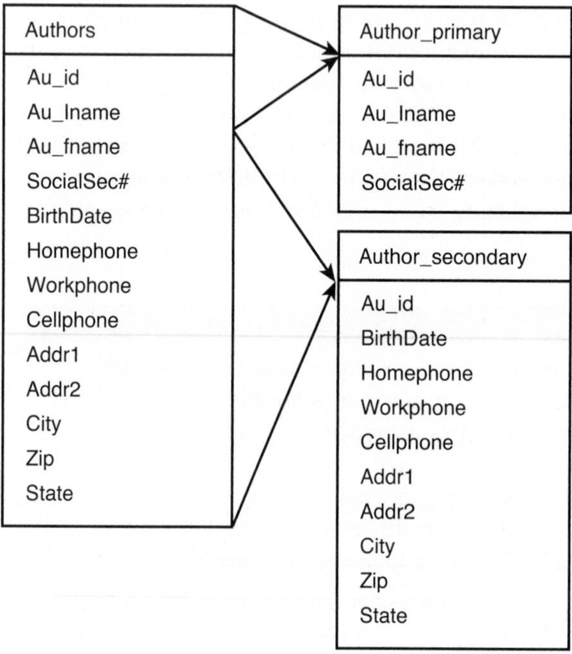

FIGURE 38.2 Vertical partitioning of data.

TIP

Make the decision to split data very carefully, especially when the system is already in production. Changing the data structure might have a system-wide impact on a large number of queries that reference the old definition of the object. In such cases, to minimize risks, you might want to use SQL Server views to hide the vertical partitioning of data. Also, if you find that users and developers are frequently joining between the vertically split tables because they need to pull data together from the two tables, you might want to reconsider the split point or the splitting of the table itself. Doing frequent joins between split tables with smaller rows requires more I/Os to retrieve the same data than if the data resided in a single table with wider rows.

Performance Implications of Zero-to-One Relationships

Suppose that one of the development managers in your company, Bob, approaches you to discuss some database schema changes. He is one of several managers whose groups all use the central `User` table in your database. Bob's application makes use of about 5% of the users in the `User` table. Bob has a requirement to track five yes/no/undecided flags associated with those users. He would like you to add five one-character columns to the `User` table to track this information. What do you tell Bob?

Bob has a classic zero-to-one problem. He has some data he needs to track, but it applies to only a small subset of the data in the table. You can approach this problem in one of three ways:

- **Option 1: Add the columns to the `User`** table—In this case, 95% of your users will have `NULL` values in those columns, and the table will become wider for everybody.
- **Option 2: Create a new table with a vertical partition of the `User`** table—The new table will contain the `User` primary key and Bob's five flags. In this case, 95% of your users will still have `NULL` data in the new table, but the `User` table is protected against these effects. Because other groups don't need to use the new partition table, this is a nice compromise.
- **Option 3: Create a new vertically partitioned table as in Option 2 but populate it only with rows that have at least one non-`NULL`** value for the columns in the new partition—This option is great for database performance, and searches in the new table will be wonderfully fast. The only drawback to this approach is that Bob's developers will have to add additional logic to their applications to determine whether a row exists during updates. Bob's folks will need to use an outer join to the table to cover the possibility that a row doesn't exist.

Depending on the goals of the project, any one of these options can be appropriate. Option 1 is simple and is the easiest to code for and understand. Option 2 is a good compromise between performance and simplicity. Option 3 gives the best performance in certain circumstances but impacts performance in certain other situations and definitely requires more coding work to be done.

Database Filegroups and Performance

Filegroups allow you to decide where on disk a particular object should be placed. You can do this by defining a filegroup within a database, extending the database onto a different drive or set of drives, and then placing a database object on the new filegroup.

Every database, by default, has a primary filegroup that contains the primary data file. There can be only one primary filegroup. This primary filegroup contains all the pages assigned to system tables. It also contains any additional database files created without specifying filegroup. Initially, the primary filegroup is also the default file group. There can be only one default filegroup, and indexes and tables that are created without specifying a filegroup are placed in the default filegroup. You can change the default filegroup to another filegroup after it has been created for a database.

In addition to the primary filegroup, you can add one or more additional filegroups to the database that are named user-defined filegroups. Each of those filegroups can contain one or more files. The main purpose of using filegroups is to provide more control over the placement of files and data on the server. When you create a table or an index, you can map it to a specific filegroup, thus controlling the placement of data. A typical SQL Server database installation generally uses a single RAID array to spread I/O across disks and create all files in the primary filegroup; more advanced installations or installations with very large databases spread across multiple array sets can benefit from the finer level of control of file and data placement afforded by additional filegroups.

For example, for a simple database such as `AdventureWorks2008`, you can create just one primary file that contains all data and objects and a log file that contains the transaction log information. For a larger and more complex database, such as a securities trading system, where large data volumes and strict performance criteria are the norm, you might create the database with one primary file and four secondary files. You can then set up filegroups so you can place the data and objects within the database across all five files. If you have a table that itself needs to be spread across multiple disk arrays for performance reasons, you can place multiple files in a filegroup, each of which resides on a different disk, and create the table on that filegroup. For example, you can create three files (`Data1.ndf`, `Data2.ndf`, and `Data3.ndf`) on three disk arrays and then assign them to the filegroup called `spread_group`. Your table can then be created specifically on the `spread_group` filegroup. Queries for data from the table are then spread across the three disk arrays, thereby improving I/O performance.

Filegroups are most often used in high-performance environments to isolate key tables or indexes on their own set of disks, which are in turn typically part of a high-performance RAID array. Assuming that you start with a database that has just a `PRIMARY` filegroup (the default), the following example shows how you would add an index filegroup on a new drive and move some nonclustered indexes to it:

```
-- add the filegroup
alter database Grocer
      add filegroup FG_INDEX

-- Create a new database file and add it to the FG_INDEX filegroup
alter database Grocer
add file(
    NAME = Grocer_Index,
       FILENAME = 'g:\Grocer_Index.ndf',
       SIZE = 2048MB,
       MAXSIZE = 8192MB,
```

```
    FILEGROWTH = 10%
) to filegroup FG_INDEX

create nonclustered index xOrderDetail_ScanDT
   on OrderDetail(ScanDT)
   on FG_INDEX
```

Moving the indexes to a separate RAID array minimizes I/O contention by spreading out the I/O generated by updates to the data that affect data rows and require changes to index rows as well.

NOTE

Because the leaf level of a clustered index is the data page, if you create a clustered index on a filegroup, the entire table moves from the existing filegroup to the new filegroup. If you want to put indexes on a separate filegroup, you should reserve that space for nonclustered indexes only.

Having your indexes on a separate filegroup gives you the following advantages:

- Index scans and index page reads come from a separate disk, so they need not compete with other database processes for disk time.
- Inserts, updates, and deletes on the table are spread across two separate disk arrays. The clustered index, including all the table data, is on a separate array from the nonclustered indexes.
- You can target your budget dollars more precisely because the faster disks improve system performance more if they are given to the index filegroup rather than the database as a whole.

The next section gives specific recommendations on how to architect a hardware solution based on using separate filegroups for data and indexes.

RAID Technology

Redundant array of inexpensive disks (RAID) is used to configure a disk subsystem to provide better performance and fault tolerance for an application. The basic idea behind using RAID is that you spread data across multiple disk drives so that I/Os are spread across these drives. RAID has special significance for database-related applications, where you want to spread random I/Os (data changes) and sequential I/Os (for the transaction log) across different disk subsystems to minimize disk head movement and maximize I/O performance.

The four significant levels of RAID implementation that are of most interest in database implementations are as follows:

- RAID 0 is data striping with no redundancy or fault tolerance.
- RAID 1 is mirroring, where every disk in the array has a mirror (copy).
- RAID 5 is striping with parity, where parity information for data on one disk is spread across the other disks in the array. The contents of a single disk can be re-created from the parity information stored on the other disks in the array.
- RAID 10, or 1+0, is a combination of RAID 1 and RAID 0. Data is striped across all drives in the array, and each disk has a mirrored duplicate, offering the fault tolerance of RAID 1 with the performance advantages of RAID 0.

RAID Level 0

RAID Level 0 provides the best I/O performance among all other RAID levels. A file has sequential segments striped across each drive in the array. Data is written in a round-robin fashion to ensure that data is evenly balanced across all drives in the array. However, if a media failure occurs, no fault tolerance is provided, and all data stored in the array is lost. RAID 0 should not be used for a production database where data loss or loss of system availability is not acceptable. RAID 0 is occasionally used for `tempdb` to provide the best possible read and (especially) write performance. RAID 0 is helpful for random read requirements, such as those that occur on `tempdb` and in data segments.

TIP

Although the data stored in `tempdb` is temporary and noncritical data, failure of a RAID 0 stripeset containing `tempdb` results in loss of system availability because SQL Server requires a functioning `tempdb` to carry out many of its activities. If loss of system availability is not an option, you should not put `tempdb` on a RAID 0 array. You should use one of the RAID technologies that provides redundancy.

If momentary loss of system availability is acceptable in exchange for the improved I/O and reduced cost of RAID 0, recovery of `tempdb` is relatively simple. The `tempdb` database is re-created each time the SQL Server instance is restarted. If the disk that contained your `tempdb` was lost, you could replace the failed disk, restart SQL Server, and the files would automatically be re-created. This scenario is complicated if the failed disk with the `tempdb` file also contains your `master` database or other system databases. See Chapter 14, "Database Backup and Restore," for a more detailed discussion of restoring system databases.

RAID 0 is the least expensive of the RAID configurations because 100% of the disks in the array are available for data, and none are used to provide fault tolerance. Performance is also the best of the RAID configurations because there is no overhead required to maintain redundant data.

Figure 38.3 depicts a RAID 0 disk array configuration.

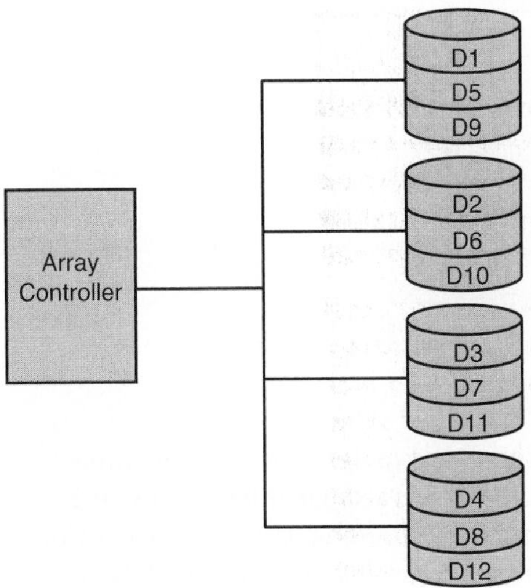

FIGURE 38.3 RAID Level 0.

RAID Level 1

With RAID 1, known as disk mirroring, every write to the primary disk is written to the mirror set. Either member of the set can satisfy a read request. RAID 1 devices provide excellent fault tolerance because in the event of a media failure, either on the primary disk or mirrored disk, the system can still continue to run. Writes are much faster than with RAID 5 arrays because no parity information needs to be calculated first. The data is simply written twice.

RAID 1 arrays are best for transaction logs and index filegroups. RAID 1 provides the best fault tolerance and best write performance, which is critical to log and index performance. Because log writes are sequential write operations and not random access operations, they are best supported by a RAID 1 configuration.

RAID 1 arrays are the most expensive RAID configurations because only 50% of total disk space is available for actual storage. The rest is used to provide fault tolerance.

Figure 38.4 shows a RAID 1 configuration.

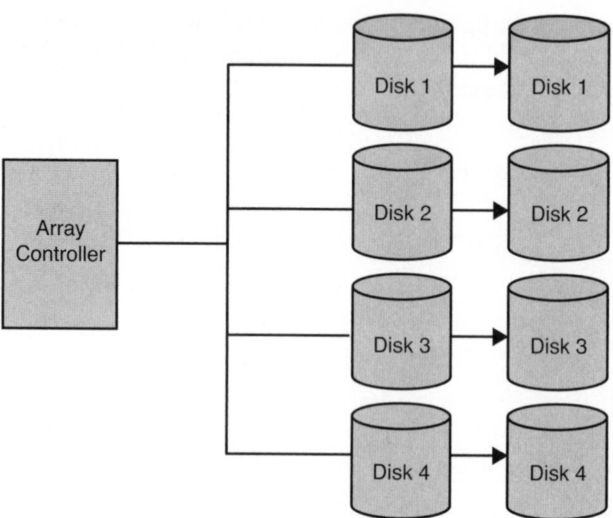

FIGURE 38.4 RAID Level 1.

Because RAID 1 requires that the same data be written to two drives at the same time, write performance is slightly less than when writing data to a single drive because the write is not considered complete until both writes have been done. Using a disk controller with a battery-backed write cache can mitigate this write penalty because the write is considered complete when it occurs to the battery-backed cache. The actual writes to the disks occur in the background.

RAID 1 read performance is often better than that of a single disk drive because most controllers now support split seeks. Split seeks allow each disk in the mirror set to be read independently of each other, thereby supporting concurrent reads.

RAID Level 10

RAID 10, or RAID 1+0, is a combination of mirroring and striping. It is implemented as a stripe of mirrored drives. The drives are mirrored first, and then a stripe is created across the mirrors to improve performance. This should not be confused with RAID 0+1, which is different and is implemented by first striping the disks and then mirroring.

Many businesses with high-volume OLTP applications opt for RAID 10 configurations. The shrinking cost of disk drives and the heavy database demands of today's business applications are making this a much more viable option. If you find that your transaction log or index segment is pegging your RAID 1 array at 100% usage, you can implement a RAID 10 array to get better performance. This type of RAID carries with it all the fault tolerance (and cost!) of a RAID 1 array, with all the performance benefits of RAID 0 striping.

RAID Level 5

RAID 5 is most commonly known as striping with parity. In this configuration, data is striped across multiple disks in large blocks. At the same time, parity bits are written across all the disks for a given block. Information is always stored in such a way that any one disk can be lost without any information in the array being lost. In the event of a disk failure, the system can still continue to run (at a reduced performance level) without downtime by using the parity information to reconstruct the data lost on the missing drive.

Some arrays provide "hot-standby" disks. The RAID controller uses the standby disk to rebuild a failed drive automatically, using the parity information stored on all the other drives in the array. During the rebuild process, performance is markedly worse.

The fault tolerance of RAID 5 is usually sufficient, but if more than one drive in the array fails, you lose the entire array. It is recommended that a spare drive be kept on hand in the event of a drive failure, so the failed drive can be replaced quickly before any other drives fail.

NOTE

Many of the RAID solutions available today support "hot-spare" drives. A hot-spare drive is connected to the array but doesn't store any data. When the RAID system detects a drive failure, the contents of the failed drive are re-created on the hot-spare drive, and it is automatically swapped into the array in place of the failed drive. The failed drive can then be manually removed from the array and replaced with a working drive, which becomes the new hot spare.

RAID 5 provides excellent read performance but expensive write performance. A write operation on a RAID 5 array requires two writes: one to the data drive and one to the parity drive. After the writes are complete, the controller reads the data to ensure that the information matches (that is, that no hardware failure has occurred). A single write operation causes four I/Os on a RAID 5 array. For this reason, putting log files or `tempdb` on a RAID 5 array is not recommended. Index filegroups, which suffer worse than data filegroups from bad write performance, are also poor candidates for RAID 5 arrays. Data filegroups where more than 10% of the I/Os are writes are also not good candidates for RAID 5 arrays.

Note that if write performance is not an issue in your environment—for example, in a DSS/data warehousing environment—you should, by all means, use RAID 5 for your data and index segments.

In any environment, you should avoid putting `tempdb` on a RAID 5 array. `tempdb` typically receives heavy write activity, and it performs better on a RAID 1 or RAID 0 array.

RAID 5 is a relatively economical means of providing fault tolerance. No matter how many drives are in the array, only the space equivalent to a single drive is used to support fault tolerance. This method becomes more economical with more drives in the array. You must have at least three drives in a RAID 5 array. Three drives would require that 33% of available disk space be used for fault tolerance, four would require 25%, five would require 20%, and so on.

Figure 38.5 shows a RAID 5 configuration.

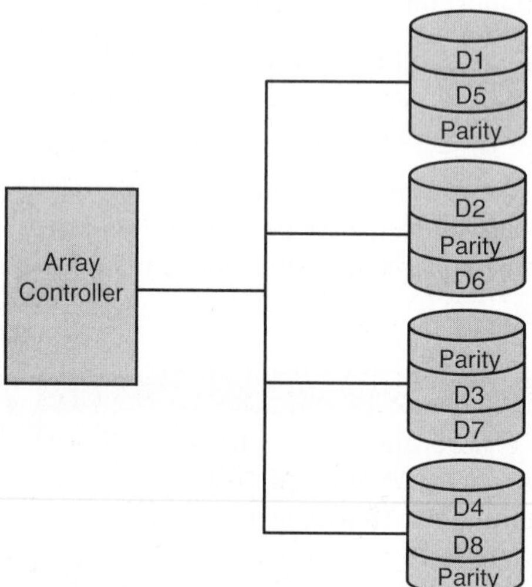

FIGURE 38.5 RAID Level 5.

NOTE

Although the recommendations for using the various RAID levels presented here can help ensure that your database performance will be optimal, reality often dictates that your optimum disk configuration might not be available. You may be given a server with a single RAID 5 array and told to make it work. Although RAID 5 is not optimal for `tempdb` or transaction logs, the write performance can be mitigated by using a controller with a battery-backed write cache.

If possible, you should also try to stripe database activity across multiple RAID 5 arrays rather than a single large RAID 5 array to avoid overdriving the disks in the array.

SQL Server and SAN Technology

With to the increased use of storage area networks (SANs) in SQL Server environments, it is important to understand the design and performance implications of implementing SQL Server databases on SANs. SANs are becoming increasingly more common in SQL Server environments these days for a number of reasons:

- Increasing database sizes
- The increasing prevalence of clustered environments
- The performance advantages and storage efficiencies and flexibilities of SANs
- The increasing needs of recoverability and disaster recovery
- Simplified disk administration

In large enterprises, a SAN can be used to connect multiple servers to a centralized pool of disk storage. Compared to managing hundreds of servers, each with its own separate disk arrays, SANs help simplify disk administration by treating all the company's storage as a single resource. Disk allocation, maintenance, and routine backups are easier to manage, schedule, and control. In some SANs, the disks themselves can copy data to other disks for backup without any processing overhead at the host computers.

What Is a SAN?

A SAN contains multiple high-performance hard drives coupled with high-performance caching controllers. The hard drives are often configured into various RAID configurations. These drive configurations are virtualized so that the consumer does not know which hard drives a SQL Server or other device connected to the SAN will access. Essentially, the SAN presents blocks of storage to servers that can consist of a single hard drive, multiple hard drives, or portions of hard drives in a logical unit called a Logical Unit Number (LUN). Connection to a SAN is typically through fiber channel, a high-speed optical network.

SANS can provide advantages over locally attached storage. Most SANs provide features that allow you to clone, snapshot, or rapidly move data (replicate) from one location to another, much faster than file copies or data transfers over your network. This increases the usefulness of SANs for disaster recovery. SANs also provide a shared disk resource for building server clusters, even allowing a cluster or server to boot off a SAN.

Another reason for the increased use of SANs is that they offer increased utilization of storage. With locally attached storage, large amounts of disk space can end up being wasted. With a SAN, you can expand or contract the amount of disk space allocated to a server or cluster as needed.

Due to their cost and complexity, however, SANs are not for everybody. They only really make sense in large enterprises. They are not a good choice for small environments with relatively small databases, for companies with limited budgets (SANs are expensive), or for companies that require disaster recovery on only one or a few SQL Servers.

SAN Considerations for SQL Server

Before you rush out and purchase a SAN or two for your SQL Server environments, there are some considerations to keep in mind when using SANs with SQL Server.

Cache Performance

One of the reasons SANs can offer superior performance to locally attached storage is they typically are configured with a significant amount of cache space. This is normally a good thing. However, because the SAN provides storage services to multiple servers, the available cache space is shared as well. If there is significant activity against the SAN, there can be extensive cache turnover. This means that the large cache space may not always be available to SQL Server, so some of the performance gains provided by the large cache are not realized.

NOTE

Cache turnover in a SAN can lead to widely varying physical I/O response times. When SQL Server performs I/O against the SAN, it's considered a physical I/O whether or not the data resides in the SAN cache. When the physical I/O performance for SQL Server is measured, the performance can be orders of magnitude faster when the data is residing in the SAN cache than when the data has to be physically read from the disks in the SAN. It is important that you perform benchmarking with your SAN vendor to ensure that your SAN cache will be adequate to provide optimal database performance.

Avoid Disk Drive Contention

SAN storage is divided into LUNs. Servers attached to the SAN recognize one or more of these units as a disk partition or drive. However, these LUNs may share the same disk drives. For example, consider six 100GB drives in the SAN. Theoretically, this could be divided into two LUNs of 300GB each. Although each LUN may be allocated to different SQL Servers, some of the drives shared between the two LUNs could experience twice the I/O from both servers than if the drives were dedicated to a single server. To avoid this situation, most SANs support *zoning*, which allows the SAN administrator to dedicate entire disks in the SAN to your LUN to isolate the I/O on the drives in the LUN to your SQL Server.

In addition, you should try to ensure that your database log files are on a LUN consisting of dedicated drives separate from the LUN (or LUNs) used for your SQL Server data files. Log files typically are written sequentially, unlike data files where data access tends to consist more of random reads and writes. Sharing a LUN between data files and log files generally does not provide optimal IO performance. Unfortunately, your SAN administrator may not permit you to dedicate a separate disk or set of disks to your log files. An alternative may be to place your log files on a local RAID 1 or RAID 10 array. However, you might want to benchmark to determine which solution provides better performance because the caching capabilities of the SAN may offset the potential drive contention in the SAN.

Additional SAN Performance Considerations

Some SAN administrators may attempt to convince you to use RAID 5 for all data and log files. Before following their advice, you should benchmark the system using a representative load to ensure that RAID 5 will offer the best performance for your log files, `tempdb`, and any write-intensive filegroups.

You should also ensure that the hardware your SQL Server system uses to connect to the SAN provides optimal performance. Make sure that you have the correct and most up-to-date drivers for your SAN components. If you can, consider using multiple high-speed host bus adapters (HBAs) to connect your servers to your SAN to avoid the I/O contention that can occur with a single HBA. If you do use multiple HBAs, try to ensure they are on different buses to prevent bus saturation and that the HBAs are plugged into the PCI slots offering the highest speed.

SANs are complex, and delivering optimal performance for a SQL Server solution using a SAN is challenging. Benchmark your SQL Server to determine if bottlenecks exist with your SAN. Be willing to work with your SAN administrator or vendor to fine-tune your SAN configuration and carefully consider and benchmark any recommendations they may make to ensure optimal performance.

Summary

A good database design is the best place to start to ensure that your database application runs smoothly. This chapter outlined some of the fundamental aspects a database design that you should consider. If you have the luxury of designing the database system from the ground up, be sure to use what you learned in this chapter in the early stages of developing your database system. If you inherit a database with an inadequate design, the design principles described in this chapter still apply, but they may be a bit harder to implement.

The next chapter, "Monitoring SQL Server Performance," delves into the tools and techniques you can use to evaluate the performance of your SQL Server instance. Monitoring is tightly linked to database design and is essential in achieving optimal database performance.

CHAPTER 39

Monitoring SQL Server Performance

IN THIS CHAPTER

- What's New in Monitoring SQL Server Performance
- Performance Monitoring Tools
- A Performance Monitoring Approach

No SQL Server implementation is perfect out of the box. As you build and add SQL Server–based applications to your server, you should take an active approach to monitoring performance. You also need to keep reevaluating as more and more load is placed on your servers and data volumes grow. This chapter focuses on SQL Server monitoring and leaves monitoring of the other types of servers (including application servers, backup servers, domain controllers, file and print servers, mail/messaging servers, and web servers) for the specialists in those areas.

You can monitor many things on your SQL Server platform, ranging from physical and logical I/O to the network packets passing between the server and your client applications. To make this monitoring task a little cleaner, this chapter classifies the key monitoring elements into network, processors, memory/cache, and disk systems. Figure 39.1 shows how these key elements interrelate with SQL Server 2008 and Windows. The aspect of utilization—whether CPU utilization, memory utilization, or something else—is at the center of most of the discussions in this chapter. The important concept to remember is how to monitor or measure utilization and how to make changes to improve this utilization because you are still not in a perfect world of infinite CPU power, infinite disk space, infinite network load capability, and infinite memory.

It is essential that you know which tools you can use to get this valuable information. These tools include SQL Server Management Studio (SSMS) Activity Monitor, Data Collector, Extended Events, Windows Performance Monitor and its various counters, a few SQL Server DBCC options, SQL Server Profiler, and a variety of SQL Server dynamic management views (DMVs). Although many other third-party products are available for performance monitoring, some of which do a fantastic job of gathering and aggregating performance data from a number of sources, there is just not enough space in this chapter to cover all the various third-party tools and their features. Instead, this chapter focuses on the performance monitoring tools provided out of the box with SQL Server 2008.

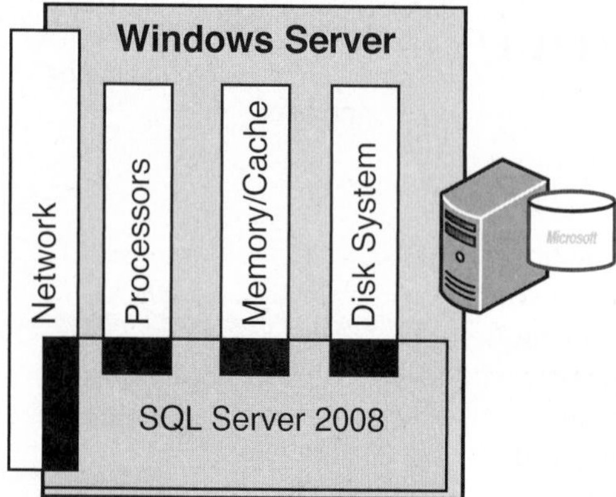

FIGURE 39.1 Key elements of SQL Server 2008 performance monitoring: network, processors, memory/cache, and disks.

What's New in Monitoring SQL Server Performance

Performance tuning and troubleshooting are time-consuming tasks for the administrator. To help provide insights quickly into performance issues, SQL Server 2008 provides a number of new and enhanced features for monitoring SQL Server performance.

In SQL Server 2005, the Activity Monitor in SSMS showed only the current running processes and the locks currently being held in the system. In SQL Server 2008, the Activity Monitor has been enhanced and now provides a graphical overview of SQL Server activity, as well as information on active user tasks, resource waits, data file I/O, and the recent most expensive queries. Unfortunately, the new information and fancier interface come with the loss of the useful lock monitor that was available in SQL Server 2005 Activity Monitor.

SQL Server 2008 also introduced a new performance monitoring tool called the Data Collector. The Data Collector gathers performance data from multiple sources and stores the data in the management data warehouse (MDW). The MDW is simply a database setup within a SQL Server instance where the data is collected for subsequent viewing and reporting.

SQL Server Extended Events is a general event-handling system for the server. The Extended Events infrastructure is a lightweight mechanism that supports capturing, filtering, and acting on events generated by the server process. Extended Events is designed to be a foundation that users can configure to monitor and capture different types of data, including performance data. It's a flexible and powerful way to provide a low granular level of information about the server system. Events can be used to diagnose runtime problems by adding contextual data, such as Transact-SQL (T-SQL) call stacks or query plan handles, to any event. Events can be captured into several different output types, including Event Tracing for Windows (ETW), which enables you to correlate events with operating system and application events and performance counters.

SQL Server 2008 also introduces a number of new dynamic management views to simplify retrieval of information that can be helpful with memory troubleshooting. These new DMVs are described in more detail later in this chapter.

Performance Monitoring Tools

In prior versions of SQL Server, the tools available for monitoring SQL Server performance were somewhat limited. Yes, you had the Windows Performance Monitor, Activity Monitor, SQL Server Profiler, and SQL Trace, but performing in-depth performance monitoring usually required the purchase of third-party tools to collect, monitor, and view performance information in a useful way.

SQL Server 2008 provide a number of tools you can use to collect, analyze, monitor, and report performance-related data. The usual old-timers such as SQL Server Profiler and Database Engine Tuning Advisor still exist and are available to you, but SQL Server 2008 also includes a new Activity Monitor, the Data Collector and management data warehouse, SQL Utility, and SQL Server Extended Events.

NOTE

For a discussion on using SQL Server Profiler for monitoring and analyzing performance, see Chapter 6, "SQL Server Profiler." For more information on the Database Engine Tuning Advisor, see Chapter 55, "Configuring, Tuning, and Optimizing SQL Server Options." In addition, the Activity Monitor is already covered in detail in Chapter 4, "SQL Server Management Studio," so detailed information on Activity Monitor is not provided in this chapter.

The Data Collector and the MDW

As mentioned previously, SQL Server 2008 introduces a new performance monitoring tool called the Data Collector. The Data Collector is designed to collect performance-related data from multiple sources from one or more SQL Servers, store it in a central data warehouse, and present the data through reports in SQL Server Management Studio. The main purpose of the Data Collector is to provide an easy way to automate the collection of critical performance data. The Data Collector gathers information from Windows performance counters, snapshots of data grabbed from dynamic management views, and details on disk utilization.

Data collection can be configured to run continuously or on a user-defined schedule. You can adjust the scope of data collection to suit the needs of your test and production environments. The Data Collector provides a single central point for data collection across your database servers and applications and, unlike SQL Trace, is not limited to collecting performance data only.

The Data Collector feature consists of the following components:

- **Data collection sets**—These are the definitions and scheduled jobs for collecting performance data. They are stored in the `msdb` system database.
- **The Data Collector runtime component**—This standalone process, called `Dcexec.exe`, is responsible for loading and executing the SSIS packages that are part of a collection set.
- **SQL Server Integration Services (SSIS) packages**—These packages are used to collect and upload the data.
- **The management data warehouse database**—This is a relational database where the collected data is stored. It also contains the views and stored procedures needed for collection management.
- **MDW Reports**—These reports are built in to SSMS for viewing the collected performance data.

Figure 39.2 provides an overview of the Data Collector architecture and how the various components interact.

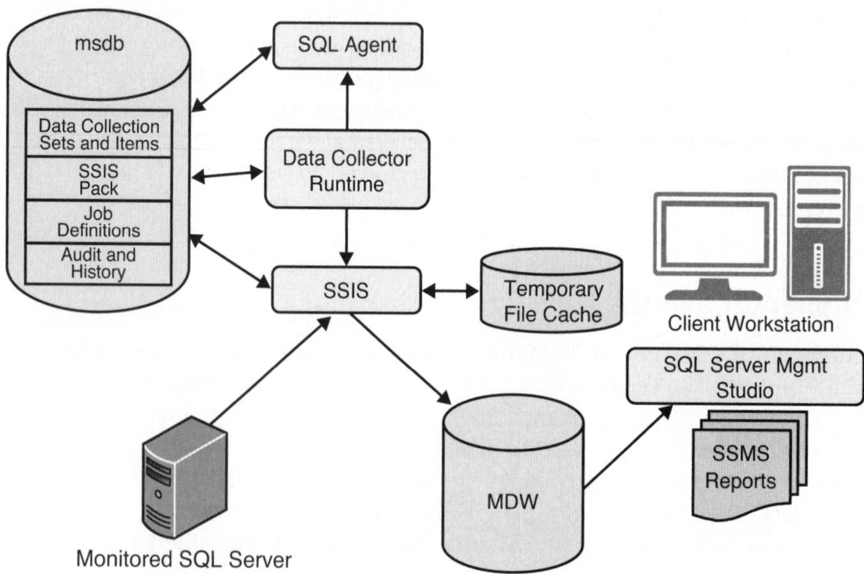

FIGURE 39.2 Data Collector architecture.

NOTE

The Data Collector is not a zero-impact monitoring solution. It incurs approximately a 2% to 5% performance hit on the servers where it's collecting data. This performance hit is mainly on the CPU.

Data Collection Sets

A *data collection set* is group of collection items. A *collection set* is the unit of data collection that a user can interact with through the user interface. Data collection sets are defined and deployed on a SQL Server 2008 instance and can be run independently of each other. Each collection set is run by a SQL Server Agent job or jobs, and data is uploaded to the management data warehouse on a predefined schedule.

Out of the box, SQL Server 2008 provides the following built-in system data collection sets and reports:

- **Disk Usage**—Collects local disk usage information for all the databases of the SQL Server instance. This information can help you determine current space utilization and future disk space requirements for disk capacity planning.
- **Server Activity**—Collects SQL Server instance-level resource usage information like CPU, memory, and I/O. This information can help you monitor short-term to long-term resource usage trends and identify potential resource bottlenecks on the system. It can also be used for resource capacity planning.
- **Query Statistics**—Collects individual statement-level query statistics, including query text and query plans. This information can help you identify the top resource-consuming queries that may need performance tuning.

The definition of the system collection sets cannot be modified. However, you can define your own collection sets or define your own custom reports for this data.

Data Collector Runtime Component

The Data Collector runtime component is invoked by a standalone process called `Dcexec.exe`. This component manages data collection based on the definitions provided in a collection set. The Data Collector runtime component is responsible for loading and executing the SSIS packages that are part of a collection set.

A collection set can be run in one of the following collection and upload modes:

- **Noncached mode**—Data collection and upload are executed on the same schedule. The packages collect data as scheduled and then immediately upload data.
- **Cached mode**—Data collection and upload are performed on different schedules. The collection package continues to collect and cache data until stopped. Data is uploaded from the local cache according to the schedule specified by the user.

NOTE

The Data Collector runtime component can perform only data collection or data upload. It cannot run these tasks concurrently.

SSIS Packages

The Data Collector is implemented as SSIS packages that are invoked by the Data Collector runtime component. These packages can be configured to run manually, continuously, or scheduled as SQL Server Agent jobs to periodically collect and upload data to the management data warehouse.

The two most important tasks for the SSIS packages are data collection and data upload. These tasks are carried out by separate packages. A collection package gathers data from a data provider and keeps it in temporary storage. An upload package reads the data in temporary storage, processes the data as required (for example, removing unnecessary data points, normalizing the data, and data aggregation) and then uploads the data to the management data warehouse. The upload is done as a bulk insert to minimize the impact on server performance.The separation of data collection and data upload into separate packages provides more flexibility and efficiency. This design supports scenarios in which snapshots of the data are captured at frequent intervals (for example, every 15 seconds), but the collected data needs to be uploaded only every hour. Data collection and upload frequency should be determined by the monitoring requirements of a particular SQL Server installation.

The Management Data Warehouse

The management data warehouse is a relational database where the Data Collector stores its data. A single MDW database can serve as the central repository for data collectors running on one or more target SQL Server instances. A data collector is configured on each target server, and it collects and uploads data to the MDW database, which may be on a remote server. Between the time the data is captured and the time it is uploaded, the Data Collector may write temporary data into cache files on the target server.

NOTE

You can install the MDW on the same instance of SQL Server that is running the Data Collector. However, if server resources or performance are an issue on the server that is being monitored, you might want to install the management data warehouse on a different computer to avoid additional CPU and I/O contention.

The MDW can become quite large, growing at approximately 250–500MB per day. This is roughly around 2GB of database storage per server each week. You need to decide how long you want to retain the data based on on your performance monitoring needs and your storage availability. For the most part, you can probably stick with the default retention settings, which are 14 days for Query Statistics and Server Activity History data collections and two years for Disk Usage Summary collections.

The required schemas and the objects to support the predefined system collection sets are created when you run the wizard to create the MDW. Two schemas are created: `core` and `snapshots`. The `core` schema describes the tables, stored procedures, and views used to organize and identify collected data. These tables are shared among all the data tables created for individual collector types. The `snapshots` schema describes the objects needed to store and maintain the data collected by the collector types that are provided.

A third schema, `custom_snapshots`, is created if you create your own user-defined collection sets that include collection items that use the Generic T-SQL Query collector type.

CAUTION

You should not directly modify any data stored in the management data warehouse. Changing the data that you have collected invalidates the legitimacy of the collected data. Also, instead of directly accessing the MDW tables, you should always use the documented stored procedures and functions provided with the Data Collector to access instance and application data.

MDW Reports

The MDW reports included in SSMS present the information gathered by the Data Collector in the following areas:

- Query performance statistics and use of indexes
- Server activity information, including waiting processes, memory usage, CPU/scheduler usage, and disk I/O
- Disk usage information

Each of the reports present a summary of the data at a high level, with the capability to drill down into the details. Sometimes the reports can provide information to help direct you to a solution for a performance problem. For example, if the query performance statistics report shows an extremely slow-running query, you can drill down through the report to expose more details on the query, right down to the query plan. The query plan could indicate that there is a missing index on that table, and creating that index could make a major difference in the query performance.

Installing and Configuring the Data Collector

Before you can use the Data Collector, you must complete the following tasks:

- Create logins and map them to Data Collector roles.
- Configure the management data warehouse.

NOTE

The management data warehouse can be installed only on a server running SQL Server 2008 or SQL Server 2008 R2.

The Data Collector has specific roles for data collection and management data warehouse tasks. The logins and roles required for data collection need to be created on the server that performs the data collection. Logins and roles for the MDW need to be created in the server that hosts the MDW. These logins and the MDW are created using the Configure Management Data Warehouse Wizard, which performs the following tasks:

- Creates the management data warehouse
- Installs the predefined System Data collection sets
- Maps logins to management data warehouse roles
- Enables data collection
- Starts the System Data collection sets

To invoke the Configure Management Data Warehouse Wizard, perform the following tasks on the SQL Server instance where you want to host the MDW:

1. Ensure that SQL Server Agent is running (for information on starting SQL Server Agent, see Chapter 16, "SQL Server Scheduling and Notification").
2. In Object Explorer in SSMS, expand the server instance that will host the MDW and expand the `Management` node for that server.
3. Right-click Data Collection and then click Configure Management Data Warehouse. This starts the Configure Management Data Warehouse Wizard.
4. Click on Next to display the Select Configuration Task window, as shown in Figure 39.3.

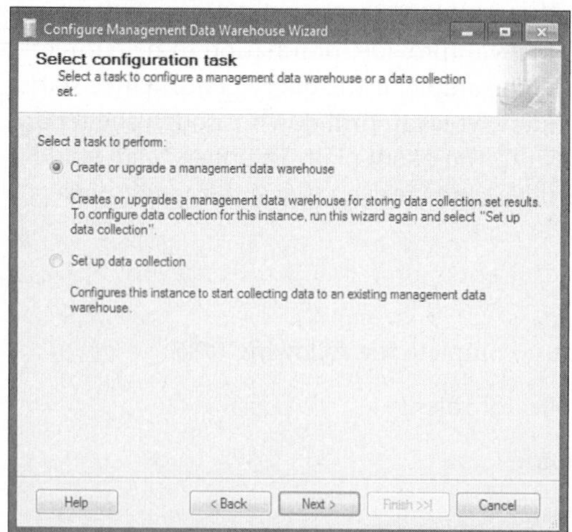

FIGURE 39.3 The Configure Management Data Warehouse Wizard's Select Configuration Task window.

TIP

If you've already created a repository database for the SQL Server Utility (see the "SQL Server Utility" section later in this chapter), you must use this same database as the MDW for the Data Collector. You can skip the process of creating the MDW and jump right to the configuration of the Data Collector. On the Configure Management Data Warehouse Storage screen (look ahead to Figure 39.6), you specify the name of the server that was set up as the utility control point (UCP) and specify the name of the utility data warehouse database that was set up to collect the SQL Server Utility performance statistics.

In the Select Configuration Task window, make sure the radio button for Create or Upgrade a Management Data Warehouse is selected and click Next. Specify the name of the server instance that will host the MDW and click on New to create the MDW database. This brings up the standard New Database dialog. Enter the name you want to use for the MDW database and specify the location of the database files if you want the database created in different drive or directory than the default data file directory.

TIP

If you are creating the MDW on a server that you will also be monitoring with the Data Collector, it's a good idea to put the MDW on drives separate from where your production databases reside to avoid the potential for any I/O contention between the MDW and your production databases.

Also, because of the anticipated growth of the MDW, you might want to change the default autogrow size of the MDW from 50MB to possibly 250 or 500MB and set the initial size to at least 500MB or 1GB.

Before saving your settings and creating the MDW database, display the Options page and make sure that the database is configured for Simple recovery mode. For the current release of the Data Collector, the management data warehouse should be created using the Simple recovery model, to minimize logging.

When you are satisfied with the database configuration, click on OK to create the MDW database. After the database is created and you are brought back to the Configure Management Data Warehouse Storage screen (see Figure 39.4), click Next to continue to the Map Logins and Users screen. On this screen, assign the appropriate MDW roles to your SQL Server users (see Figure 39.5). Any users who need to view the Data Collector reports need the `mdw_reader` role.

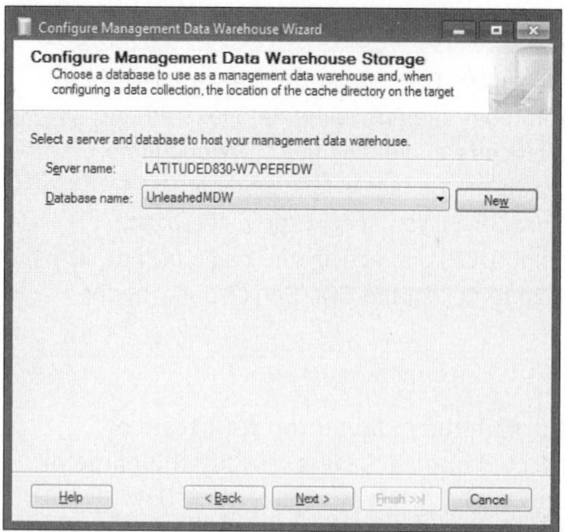

FIGURE 39.4 The Configure Management Data Warehouse Storage screen.

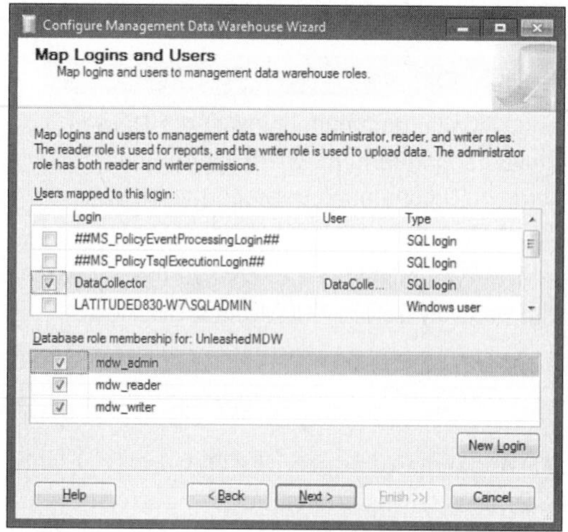

FIGURE 39.5 The Map Logins and Users screen.

By default, no user is a member of the MDW database roles. User membership in these roles must be granted explicitly. Members of the `mdw_admin` role have Read, Write, Update, and Delete access to the management data warehouse. Members of this role can change the management data warehouse schema when required (for example, adding a new table when a new collection type is installed) and run maintenance jobs on the management data warehouse, such as archive or cleanup. Members of the `mdw_writer` role can upload and write data to the management data warehouse; any Data Collector that stores data in the management data warehouse has to be a member of this role. Members of the `mdw_reader` role have Read access to the management data warehouse primarily for the purpose of supporting troubleshooting by providing access to historical data.

It is recommended that you create a new login for data collection and map it as shown in Figure 39.5.

After you map the users, click on Next to bring up the Complete the Wizard screen, which provides a summary of the tasks to be performed. If everything looks okay, click Finish to perform the configuration of the MDW, which includes running the installation script to install the required schema objects in the MDW.

After you have created the MDW and made it available, the next step is to begin data collection for one or more of your SQL Server 2008 instances. Right-click on the `Data Collection` node in Object Explorer and select the Configure Management Data Warehouse option again. On the Select Configuration Task screen (refer to Figure 39.3), select the Set Up Data Collection radio button and click Next. On the Configure Management Data Warehouse Storage screen (see Figure 39.6), specify the name of the server that hosts the MDW and the name of the MDW database created previously. When specifying the server, you can also specify which directory you want the Data Collector to use for its local file cache (again, if possible, this should be on a different drive than where your database data files reside to minimize I/O contention). If you leave the value blank, it uses the default SQL Agent `TEMP` directory.

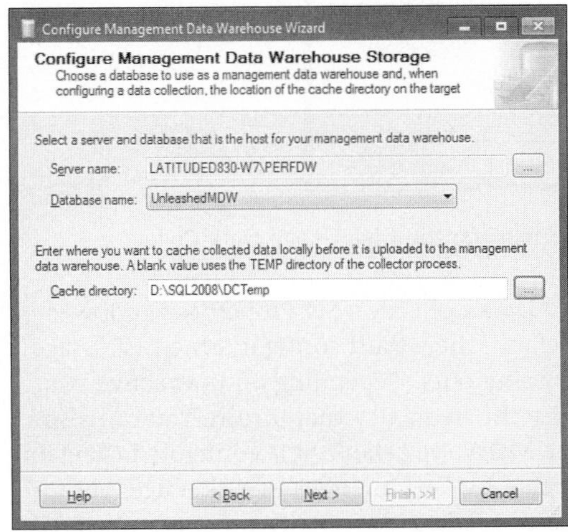

FIGURE 39.6 The Configure Management Data Warehouse Storage screen when configuring data collection.

When you finish making your selections, click Next to bring up the Complete the Wizard screen, which provides a summary of the tasks to be performed. If everything looks okay, click Finish to have the wizard perform the configuration of the system collection sets and enable data collection.

The System Data Collectors

When the Configure Management Data Warehouse Wizard is finished, you should see three additional nodes under the `Data Collector` node: `Disk Usage`, `Query Statistics`, and `Server Activity`. You can double-click each node, or right-click and select Properties, to open the Properties window. The Properties window for the Disk Usage Data Collector is shown in Figure 39.7.

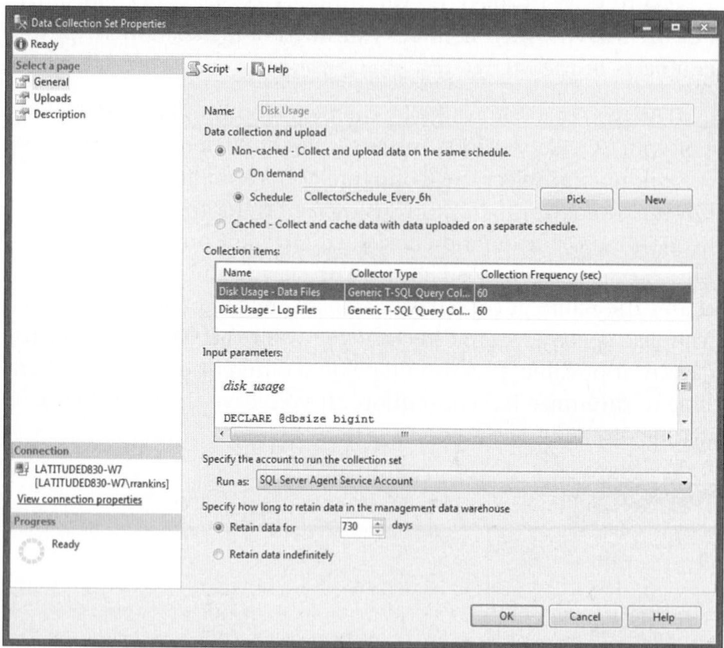

FIGURE 39.7 Data Collection Set Properties window for the Disk Usage Data Collector.

The main item you may want to change in the Data Collection Set Properties window is the data collection and upload schedule. By default, the wizard configures the Disk Usage Collection set to run in noncached mode every six hours. Depending on how active your server is, you might want to increase or decrease the frequency that it runs. You can also configure how long it should retain data in the MDW. By default, it is configured to retain data for two years (730 days). This is probably fine for keeping track of disk usage, but for more active Data Collector Sets, you might want to reduce the retention period to reduce the size of the MDW. For example, the default retention period for the Query Statistics and Server Activity Data Collectors is 14 days.

Both the Query Statistics and Server Activity Data Collectors are configured to cache data and upload to the MDW on a separate schedule. If you look in the General page of the Data Collection Set Properties window for these Data Collectors, you see that the schedule Query Statistics Data Collector is to gather information every 10 seconds, and the Server Activity collector gathers information every 60 seconds. To view the upload schedule, click on the Uploads page (see Figure 39.8). Both Data Collectors, by default, are configured to upload the cached data to the MDW every 15 minutes. To change the upload schedule, you can either pick from an existing schedule or create a new one (Figure 39.8 shows the Pick Schedule list). The Upload Properties page also displays the last time the cached data was uploaded to the MDW.

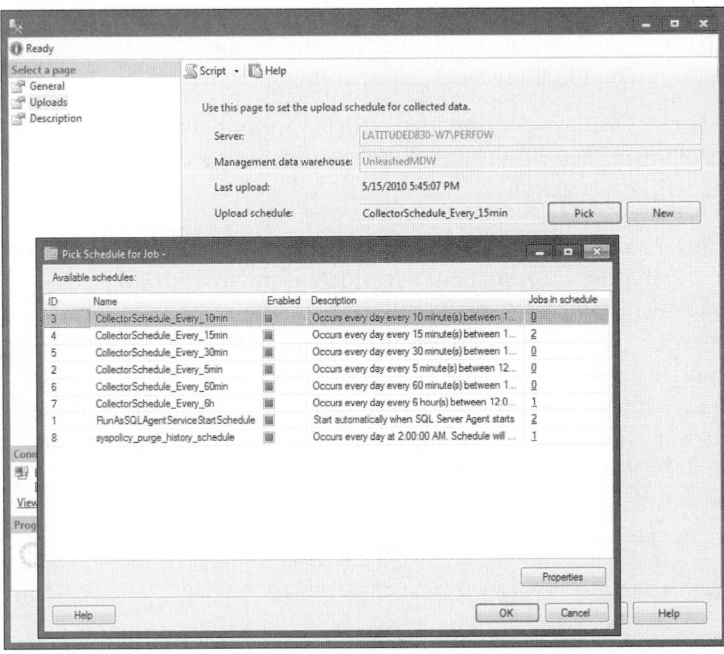

FIGURE 39.8 Data Collection Set upload schedule.

In very active servers, the Data Collector can generate a lot of data, and its storage tables can fill up with millions of rows within hours. You might want to modify the collector job schedules and decrease the frequency of data collections depending on the use of each server and your monitoring requirements.

NOTE

Data collection for the built-in system collection sets begins automatically after the Configure Management Data Warehouse completes. Depending on how active your servers are, it likely will take awhile for some meaningful data to accumulate. You might want to wait an hour or so before looking at the reports.

Data Collector Reports

After you set up data collection, SQL Server Management Studio provides three new reports for viewing data accumulated by the Data Collector: Server Activity History, Disk

Usage Summary and Query Statistics History. You can view these reports by right-clicking on the `Data Collection` node and selecting Reports, and then select Management Data Warehouse. From there, you can choose one of the three built-in reports:

- **Disk Usage Summary**—Displays data and log file sizes (starting size and current size) and average daily growth
- **Query Statistics History**—Displays query execution statistics including the top 10 queries by CPU, Duration, Total I/O, Physical Reads, and Logical Writes
- **Server Activity History**—Displays performance statistics in four general areas: CPU %, Disk I/O Usage, Memory Usage, and Network Usage, plus SQL Server Wait statistics by wait type and SQL Server activity

Figure 39.9 displays an example of the Disk Usage Summary Report. All the data collection reports provide drill-down capabilities on just about every data element and widget displayed in the main report. For example, in the Disk Usage Summary report, you can click on the database name to display a more detailed breakdown of the disk usage for that specific database. Figure 39.10 shows the Disk Usage details for the `AdventureWorks2008R2` database. If you click on the Trend graph or the current database or log size, it displays a more detailed graph showing the growth trends for the database over time since the data collection session started.

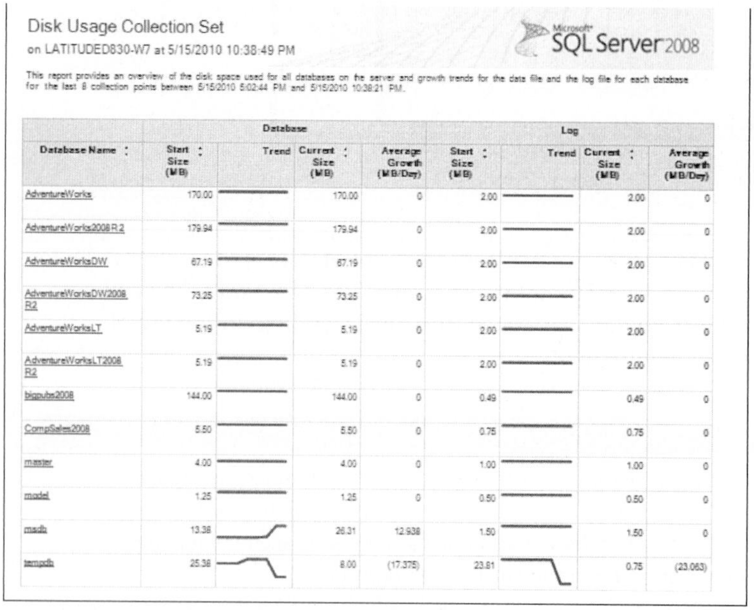

Disk Usage Collection Set

on LATITUDED830-W7 at 5/15/2010 10:38:49 PM

Microsoft SQL Server 2008

This report provides an overview of the disk space used for all databases on the server and growth trends for the data file and the log file for each database for the last 8 collection points between 5/15/2010 5:02:44 PM and 5/15/2010 10:38:21 PM.

	Database				Log			
Database Name	Start Size (MB)	Trend	Current Size (MB)	Average Growth (MB/Day)	Start Size (MB)	Trend	Current Size (MB)	Average Growth (MB/Day)
AdventureWorks	170.00		170.00	0	2.00		2.00	0
AdventureWorks2008R2	179.94		179.94	0	2.00		2.00	0
AdventureWorksDW	67.19		67.19	0	2.00		2.00	0
AdventureWorksDW2008R2	73.25		73.25	0	2.00		2.00	0
AdventureWorksLT	5.19		5.19	0	2.00		2.00	0
AdventureWorksLT2008R2	5.19		5.19	0	2.00		2.00	0
bigpubs2008	144.00		144.00	0	0.49		0.49	0
CompSales2008	5.50		5.50	0	0.75		0.75	0
master	4.00		4.00	0	1.00		1.00	0
model	1.25		1.25	0	0.50		0.50	0
msdb	13.38		26.31	12.938	1.50		1.50	0
tempdb	25.38		8.00	(17.375)	23.81		0.75	(23.063)

FIGURE 39.9 Disk Usage Summary report.

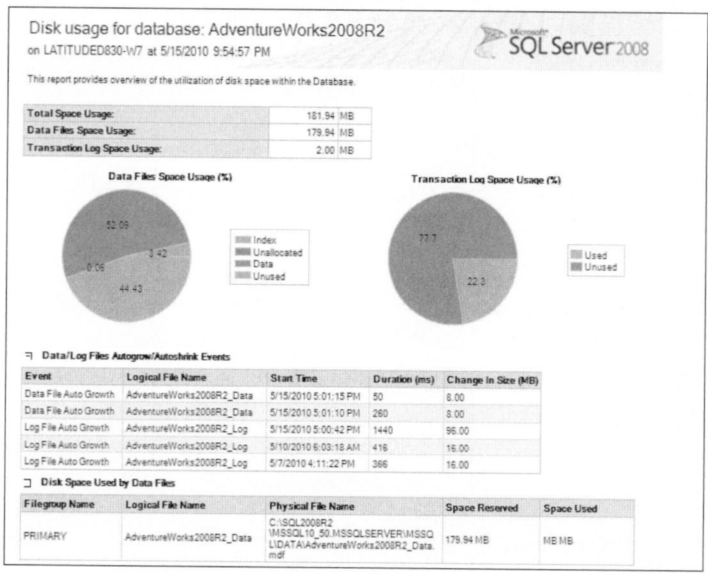

Disk usage for database: AdventureWorks2008R2

on LATITUDED830-W7 at 5/15/2010 9:54:57 PM

Microsoft SQL Server 2008

This report provides overview of the utilization of disk space within the Database.

Total Space Usage:	181.94	MB
Data Files Space Usage:	179.94	MB
Transaction Log Space Usage:	2.00	MB

Data/Log Files Autogrow/Autoshrink Events

Event	Logical File Name	Start Time	Duration (ms)	Change In Size (MB)
Data File Auto Growth	AdventureWorks2008R2_Data	5/15/2010 5:01:15 PM	50	8.00
Data File Auto Growth	AdventureWorks2008R2_Data	5/15/2010 5:01:10 PM	260	8.00
Log File Auto Growth	AdventureWorks2008R2_Log	5/15/2010 5:00:42 PM	1440	96.00
Log File Auto Growth	AdventureWorks2008R2_Log	5/10/2010 6:03:18 AM	416	16.00
Log File Auto Growth	AdventureWorks2008R2_Log	5/7/2010 4:11:22 PM	366	16.00

Disk Space Used by Data Files

Filegroup Name	Logical File Name	Physical File Name	Space Reserved	Space Used
PRIMARY	AdventureWorks2008R2_Data	C:\SQL2008R2 \MSSQL10_50.MSSQLSERVER\MSSQL\DATA\AdventureWorks2008R2_Data.mdf	179.94 MB	MB MB

FIGURE 39.10 Disk Usage report for **AdventureWorks2008R2** database.

If you want to run reports for any of the monitored servers without having navigate to the `Data Collection` node for each server instance, you can open the server instance that hosts the MDW. Browse to the MDW database in the SSMS Object Browser and right-click on that database. Then select Reports and select the the Management Data Warehouse Overview report (see Figure 39.11).

Management Data Warehouse Overview: UnleashedMDW

on LATITUDED830-W7\PERFDW at 5/15/2010 10:41:38 PM

Microsoft SQL Server 2008

This report provides an overview of the data collector instances that record their data in this management data warehouse. Click on the last snapshot upload time hyperlink to display the report for the associated system collection set.

	Last Snapshot Upload Times for System Collection Sets		
Instance Name	Server Activity	Query Statistics	Disk Usage
LATITUDED830-W7	5/15/2010 10:38:13 PM	5/15/2010 10:38:13 PM	5/15/2010 10:38:13 PM
LATITUDED830-W7\PERFDW	5/15/2010 10:35:50 PM	5/15/2010 10:35:50 PM	5/15/2010 10:35:50 PM

FIGURE 39.11 Management Data Warehouse Overview report.

The Management Data Warehouse Overview report lists which servers the data collection is running on and shows the most recent times data was uploaded for each of the collection sets. You can click on the hyperlinks below each of the listed collection sets to bring up that corresponding report for that server. For example, if you click on the link below Server Activity for the LATITUDED830-W7 server, it displays the Server Activity History report, as shown in Figure 39.12.

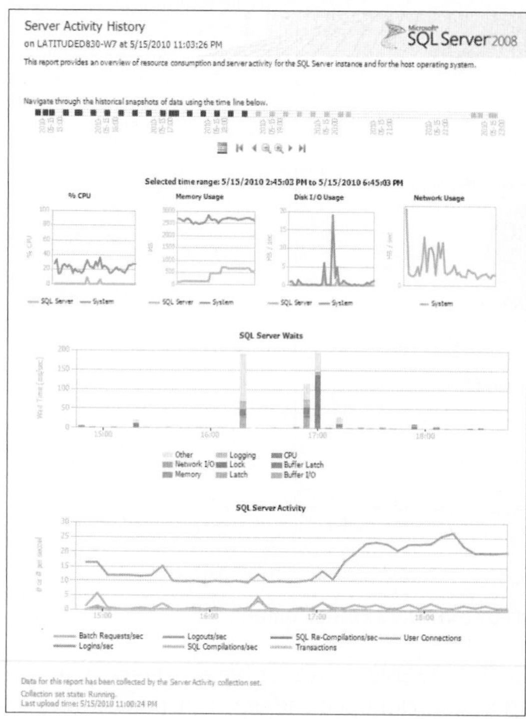

FIGURE 39.12 The Server Activity History report.

Like the Disk Usage report, most of the data elements in the Server Activity History report are hyperlinks that let you drill down into more detail. For example, you can click in the line in the Disk I/O Usage graph to bring up additional detail by disk of the Disk Response Time, Average Disk Queue Length, Disk Transfer Rate, as well as the average, minimum, and maximum I/O reads and writes for the processes running during the data collection session.

If you want to narrow down the report to a specific time frame, you can click on a point in the timeline shown on the report to set the end time of the data displayed. You can click on the magnifying glass to increase or decrease the size of the interval displayed and click the arrow buttons to move to the next or previous interval. For finer control over the time period displayed, click on the calendar icon to bring up the dialog shown in Figure 39.13. Here, you can set the specific start time and choose an interval (15 minutes or 1, 4, 12, or 24 hours) to display from that start time.

The Data Collector reports contain a lot of data, especially if you drill down into the details. There are more details than we have space to get into in this chapter. You should plan to spend some time examining each of these reports by drilling down into the various details and selecting different time frames and so on to get familiar with what they have to offer. For example, you can drill from the Query Statistics History report to the individual query details, including the graphical execution plan.

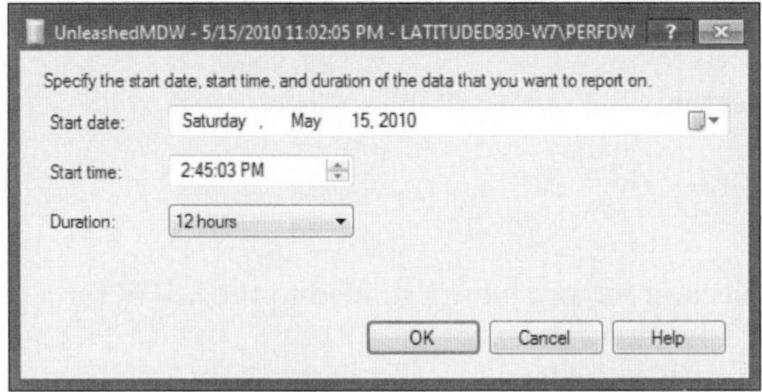

FIGURE 39.13 Defining the time frame to display in a data collection report.

Managing the Data Collector

To stop collecting performance data for a SQL Server instance, right-click on `Data Collection` in the `Management` node and click Disable Data Collection. If you want to stop a specific data collection set, expand the `Data Collection` node and then expand the `System Data Collection Sets` folder. Right-click on the data collection set you want to stop and select Stop Data Collection Set.

You can also force a collection set to gather data and upload statistics manually by right-clicking on the data collection set and selecting Collect and Upload Now.

To check on the status and history of the Data Collectors, you can right click on the `Data Collection` node and select View Logs. This launches the log viewer that displays the activity that has occurred for each of the data collection sets, such as which collection sets are active and the collection and upload history of each of the collection sets.

Managing the Data Collector in T-SQL

Much of the Data Collector can be managed effectively within SSMS. However, if you have to perform a number of tasks repeatedly, using the wizards and SSMS dialogs can sometimes become tedious. Fortunately, the Data Collector provides an extensive collection of stored procedures that you can use to perform any data collection task. In addition, you can use functions and views to retrieve configuration data from the `msdb` and management data warehouse databases, execution log data, as well as the performance data stored in the management data warehouse.

39

TIP

As with most tools in SSMS, when using the GUI, you can click the Script buttion to generate a script for the actions being performed. This is a great way to become more familiar with the T-SQL commands and procedures for managing the Data Collector.

For example, to enable or disable the Data Collector in a SQL Server instance, you can use the `sp_syscollector_enable_collector` and `sp_syscollector_disable_collector` stored procedures:

```
USE msdb;
GO
EXEC dbo.sp_syscollector_disable_collector;
GO
EXEC dbo.sp_syscollector_enable_collector;
GO
```

To force the running of a noncached collection set and have it upload to the MDW for collection sets configured in noncached collection mode, use the `sp_syscollector_run_collection_set` system procedure:

```
sp_syscollector_run_collection_set
          [[ @collection_set_id = ] collection_set_id]
          , [[ @name = ] 'name' ]
```

You can pass either the collection set ID or the collection name. When you are passing one, the other parameter can be `NULL`:

```
USE msdb;
GO
EXEC sp_syscollector_run_collection_set @name = 'Disk Usage'
go
```

To force a manual update of a cached mode Data Collector, you can use the `sp_syscollector_upload_collection_set` procedure:

```
USE msdb;
GO
EXEC sp_syscollector_upload_collection_set @name = 'Server Activity'
go
```

To stop or start a specific collector set, you can use the `sp_syscollector_start_collection_set` and `sp_syscollector_stop_collection` set stored procedures:

```
USE msdb;
GO
EXEC dbo.sp_syscollector_stop_collection_set @name = 'Disk Usage'
GO
EXEC dbo.sp_syscollector_start_collection_set @name = 'Disk Usage'
GO
```

To modify a collection set, you can use the `sp_syscollector_update_collection_set` procedure. The syntax is as follows:

```
sp_syscollector_update_collection_set
    [ [ @collection_set_id = ] collection_set_id ]
        , [ [ @name = ] 'name' ]
        , [ [ @new_name = ] 'new_name' ]
```

```
, [ [ @target = ] 'target' ]
, [ [ @collection_mode = ] collection_mode ]
, [ [ @days_until_expiration = ] days_until_expiration ]
, [ [ @proxy_id = ] proxy_id ]
, [ [ @proxy_name = ] 'proxy_name' ]
, [ [ @schedule_uid = ] 'schedule_uid' ]
, [ [ @schedule_name = ] 'schedule_name' ]
, [ [ @logging_level = ] logging_level ]
, [ [ @description = ] 'description' ]
```

If the collection set is running, the only options you can modify are the *schedule_uid* and *description*. You need to stop the collection set with sp_syscollector_stop_collection_set first to change other options like the *collection-mode* or *days_until_expiration*. For example, the following code changes the number of days to retain collection set data to seven days for the Server Activity collection set:

```
USE msdb;
GO
EXEC dbo.sp_syscollector_stop_collection_set @name = 'Disk Usage'
GO
EXEC dbo.sp_syscollector_update_collection_set
@name = N'Server Activity',
@days_until_expiration = 7;
GO
EXEC dbo.sp_syscollector_start_collection_set @name = 'Disk Usage'
GO
```

To view information about the configured collection sets, you can run a query on the syscollector_collection_sets table similar to the following:

```
select collection_set_id as ID,
       cast (scs.name as varchar(20)) as name,
       is_running as 'running',
       case collection_mode when 0 then 'cached'
            else 'noncached' end as coll_mode,
       days_until_expiration as retntn,
       cast (s.name as varchar(30)) as schedule
 from syscollector_collection_sets scs
        inner join
      sysschedules s
        on scs.schedule_uid = s.schedule_uid
go

ID name                 running coll_mode retntn schedule
-- -------------------- ------- --------- ------ ------------------------------
2  Server Activity      1       cached    7      CollectorSchedule_Every_15min
3  Query Statistics     1       cached    14     CollectorSchedule_Every_15min
```

39

```
4  Utility Information  1       noncached 1      CollectorSchedule_Every_30min
1  Disk Usage           1       noncached 730    CollectorSchedule_Every_6h
```

There are other informational views you can use to view the data collection configuration:

```
-- To display the location of the temporary cache and the MDW
select * From syscollector_config_store
go
parameter_name     parameter_value
------------------ ----------------------
CacheDirectory     D:\SQL2008\DCTemp
CacheWindow        1
CollectorEnabled   1
MDWDatabase        UnleashedMDW
MDWInstance        LATITUDED830-W7\PERFDW

-- To display the data collection capture and upload
--  information from the execution log
select * From syscollector_config_store
go
select csc.name as collection_set, start_time
 From syscollector_execution_log sel
        inner join
      syscollector_collection_sets csc
        on sel.collection_set_id = csc.collection_set_id
order by csc.name, start_time
go
```

You can also use the stored procedures, functions, and views that are provided to create your own end-to-end data collection scenarios.

Creating a Customized Data Collection Set

Although you cannot change or delete the built-in system Data Collectors, you can define your own custom data collection sets. However, currently, you can define them only in T-SQL. There are four different collector types that you can use to build a collector set:

- **T-SQL query**—Executes a user-provided T-SQL statement as an input parameter, saves the output from the query, and then uploads the output to the management data warehouse.
- **SQL Trace**—Uses SQL Trace to monitor the SQL Server Relational Engine, with trace data coming from the system default trace or from one or more custom traces.
- **Performance counters**—Collects specific performance counter information from Windows Performance Monitor on the computer running SQL Server 2008.
- **Query activity**—Collects query statistics and query activity information along with the query plan and query text for queries that meet predefined criteria. Essentially, this collector type collects the same information as the Query Statistics collection

set, so it is recommended that you simply use the predefined Query Statistics collection set.

One of the reasons you might create a customized data collection set is that the default system Data Collector for Query Statistics does not store all the statements. It captures only the worst-performing queries based on the algorithms specified in the collection set. You might want to collect more queries than the top three worst performing ones. However, if you create your own data collection for query statistics, you should probably disable the default system collector to reduce data collection overhead.

This chapter shows how to create a custom collection set to monitor a few Performance Monitor counters.

TIP

To see an example of a collection set based on performance counters, DMVs, and T-SQL queries, you can look at the definition of the default Server Activity collection set. You can easily see this definition by right-clicking on Server Activity in the System `Data Collection Sets` folder in SSMS and selecting Script Data Collection.

There is also GUI support for creating a collection set based on a SQL Server Profiler trace. After you define a trace in SQL Server Profiler with the events you want to capture, select Export from the File menu; then choose Script Trace Definition and select For SQL Trace Collection Set. Doing so generates a T-SQL script that you can use to create a custom Data Collector Set based on a SQL Server Profiler Trace definition.

Assuming you've already set up your MDW, you can begin by creating the data collection set and adding the collection items you want it to contain. To create the data collection set, use the `sp_syscollector_create_collection_set` procedure. Next, you need to create the `collection_items` to indicate what information you want the collection set to collect. If you are creating collection items for Performance Monitor counters, The Performance Counter collector type takes three input parameters:

- **Objects**—The SQL Server objects running in an instance of SQL Server
- **Counters**—The counters associated with a SQL Server object
- **Instances**—The instances of the specified object

Some input parameters support wildcard characters, which enable you to include multiple counters in a single statement. However, you can use wild cards only at the Counters and Instances levels and, even then, only at the beginning of the string (for example, `'* Processor'`) or at the end of the string (for example, `'Memory *'`).

An example of the creation of custom collection set for capturing information for the `Logical Disk` and `Process` Performance Monitor counters is shown in Listing 39.1.

LISTING 39.1 Creating a Custom Collection Set

```
Use msdb
go

Declare @collection_set_id_1 int
Declare @collection_set_uid_2 uniqueidentifier
EXEC [dbo].[sp_syscollector_create_collection_set]
     @name=N'Disk I/O Perf and SQL CPU',
     @collection_mode=1, — non-cached
     @description=
  N'Collects logical disk performance counters and SQL Process CPU',
     @target=N'',
     @logging_level=0,
     @days_until_expiration=7,
     @proxy_name=N'',
     @schedule_name=N'CollectorSchedule_Every_5min',
     @collection_set_id=@collection_set_id_1 OUTPUT,
     @collection_set_uid=@collection_set_uid_2 OUTPUT
Select collection_set_id_1=@collection_set_id_1,
       collection_set_uid_2=@collection_set_uid_2

/********************************************
** Now, create the desired collection items
********************************************/

Declare @collector_type_uid_3 uniqueidentifier
Select @collector_type_uid_3 = collector_type_uid
   From [dbo].[syscollector_collector_types]
   Where name = N'Performance Counters Collector Type';
Declare @collection_item_id_4 int
EXEC [dbo].[sp_syscollector_create_collection_item]
@name=N'Logical Disk Collection and SQL Server CPU',
@parameters=N'<ns:PerformanceCountersCollector xmlns:ns="DataCollectorType">
     <PerformanceCounters Objects="LogicalDisk"
          Counters="Avg. Disk Bytes/Read"
          Instances="*" />
     <PerformanceCounters Objects="LogicalDisk"
          Counters="Avg. Disk Bytes/Write"
          Instances="*" />
     <PerformanceCounters Objects="LogicalDisk"
          Counters="Avg. Disk sec/Read"
          Instances="*" />
     <PerformanceCounters Objects="LogicalDisk"
```

```
        Counters="Avg. Disk sec/Write"
        Instances="*" />
    <PerformanceCounters Objects="LogicalDisk"
        Counters="Disk Read Bytes/sec"
        Instances="*" />
    <PerformanceCounters Objects="LogicalDisk"
        Counters="Disk Write Bytes/sec"
        Instances="*" />
    <PerformanceCounters Objects="Process"
        Counters="% Privileged Time"
        Instances="sqlservr" />
    <PerformanceCounters Objects="Process"
        Counters="% Processor Time"
        Instances="sqlservr" />
</ns:PerformanceCountersCollector>',
@collection_item_id=@collection_item_id_4 OUTPUT,
@frequency=5,
@collection_set_id=@collection_set_id_1,
@collector_type_uid=@collector_type_uid_3
Select @collection_item_id_4
Go
```

After you create the collection set, you can start this data collection, either through SSMS (your user-defined collection sets will be listed directly within the `Data Collection` node) or with the following stored procedure call:

```
Declare @collection_set_id int
select @collection_set_id = collection_set_id
from syscollector_collection_sets
where name = 'Disk I/O Perf and SQL CPU'

EXEC sp_syscollector_start_collection_set
        @collection_set_id = @collection_set_id
go
```

Because there aren't any custom reports available for displaying the results of the custom collection set just defined, you need to run a query in the MDW database to view the collected Performance Monitor counter values. A sample query (which could serve as the basis for a customer report) is provided in Listing 39.2.

LISTING 39.2 Querying the MDW for Custom Data Collection Values

```
Use UnleashedMDW
Go
select spci.path as 'Counter Path', spci.object_name as 'Object Name',
spci.counter_name as 'counter Name', spci.instance_name,
spcv.formatted_value as 'Formatted Value',
spcv.collection_time as 'Collection Time',
sii.instance_name as 'SQL Server Instance'
from snapshots.performance_counter_values spcv
        inner join
    snapshots.performance_counter_instances spci
        on spcv.performance_counter_instance_id = spci.performance_counter_id
        inner join
   core.snapshots_internal si
        on si.snapshot_id = spcv.snapshot_id
        inner join
    core.source_info_internal sii
        on sii.source_id = si.source_id
where
    sii.collection_set_uid = '5D9849BE-1526-4159-99EB-6B0E690C31EA'
order by spcv.collection_time desc
```

It is possible to create your own custom reports using SQL Server Reporting Services that query the information for your custom collection sets in the MDW database. For more information on creating custom reports, see Chapter 53, "SQL Server 2008 Reporting Services."

Data Collector Limitations and Recommendations

Although the Data Collector is a great start to a built-in performance monitoring tool, it does have some limitations still, which are not wholly unexpected in a product that's still early in its release cycle. One key limitation is the limited number of built-in data providers and the reports available. It is hoped that future versions will make it easier to extend the Data Collector to add additional collection sets and reports.

If you are defining your own custom Data Collectors, consider these recommendations:

- Combine multiple performance counter or query collection items into a single collection item wherever possible.
- Combine collection items into a single collection set whenever possible unless you need separate data retention periods or different collection schedules for the collection items.
- If you collect data frequently, it is more efficient to run the collection set in cached collection mode than starting and stopping a new process every time new data must be collected. In cached collection mode, the collection process runs continuously. As a general rule, if you will be capturing data every five minutes or less, consider using a collection set that runs in cached collection mode.

- If you are collecting data less frequently than every five minutes, using noncached mode is more efficient than leaving a generally idle process running all the time.
- Although the collection frequency for cached collection sets can be set to run as frequently as every five seconds, be aware that more frequent collection has correspondingly high overhead. Always choose the lowest collection frequency that will meet your needs.

Currently, removing data collection after it has been configured is not supported. You can disable data collections but cannot remove them or the SSIS packages and jobs associated with them after they have been defined. Attempting to manually remove data collection may lead to errors if you try to re-implement data collection in the future. In addition, you should not drop or change the name of the MDW database because all the jobs are based on the original database name.

Another key limitation in the Data Collector is the lack of built-in alerting in the event that certain performance thresholds are crossed while monitoring the system. In contrast, the SQL Server Utility, which performs more limited monitoring and data capture than the Data Collector, does provide a threshold and alerting mechanism.

SQL Server Utility

SQL Server 2008 R2 introduces a new multiserver management tool named the SQL Server Utility. This new tool takes performance monitoring in SQL Server to the next level by providing the capability to monitor specific performance metrics for one or more SQL Server instances in a single view from a single SQL Server instance. The performance information is captured in a database, and you can view this information in one convenient place from within the SSMS environment.

Some basic setup is required to start using the SQL Utility. You accomplish this basic setup by using the new Utility Explorer available in SSMS. You click View on the SSMS menu bar and then select Utility Explorer. This Utility Explorer has a tree-like structure similar to the Object Explorer, and it integrates into the SSMS environment in much the same way.

NOTE

The option to view the Utility Explorer is not available if you are running a version of SQL Server prior to SQL Server 2008 R2.

The first page displayed when you launch the Utility Explorer is shown in Figure 39.14. This screen outlines all the utility configuration steps and is a handy launch point into wizards that guide you through the setup process. You can also click on the Video link next to each step to obtain further help on configuring that step.

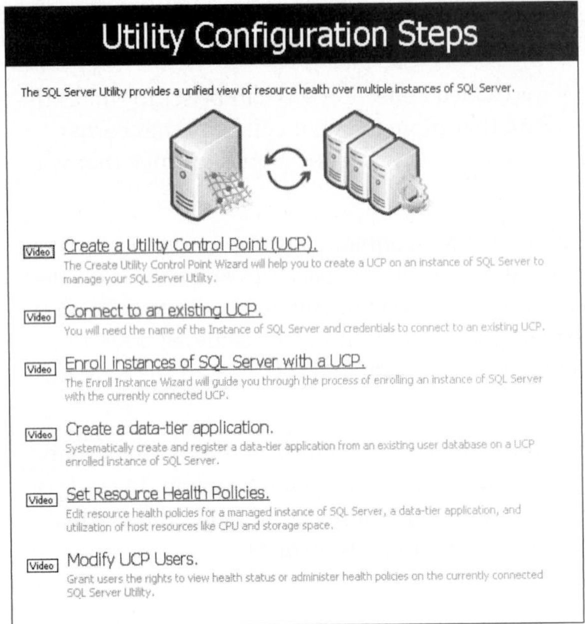

FIGURE 39.14 Utility Configuration Steps.

These steps and the details related to configuring the Utility Explorer are covered in more depth in Chapter 4. This chapter focuses on the performance monitoring capabilities of the SQL Server Utility and the specific metrics available for collection. To enable these capabilities, you only need to do the following:

1. Create a utility control point.
2. Connect to an existing UCP.
3. Enroll instances of SQL Server into the UCP.

The UCP is a central repository for storing configuration information and performance data for all the instances that have been enrolled in the SQL Server Utility. Each SQL Server Utility has only one UCP that you define by clicking on the first link listed in the Utility Configurations Steps. A wizard guides you through the creation.

NOTE

The SQL Server Utility collection set can work side by side with non–SQL Server Utility collection sets, such as those set up for data collection in the MDW. In other words, a managed instance of SQL Server can be monitored by other collection sets while it is a member of a SQL Server Utility. However, you must disable data collection while the instance of SQL Server is being enrolled into the SQL Server Utility.

In addition, after the instance is enrolled with the UCP, when you restart the non–SQL Server Utility collection sets, all collection sets on the managed instance upload their data to the utility management data warehouse (UMDW), `sysutility_mdw`.

After you create the UCP, a new tab named Utility Explorer Content is displayed within the Utility Explorer (see Figure 39.15). This Utility Explorer window is also called the SQL Server Utility *dashboard*. This dashboard is the main window for viewing performance metrics captured by the SQL Server Utility. The information displayed on this screen immediately after creating the UCP is the performance information for the UCP itself. Each UCP is automatically a managed instance and thus has performance data collected for it.

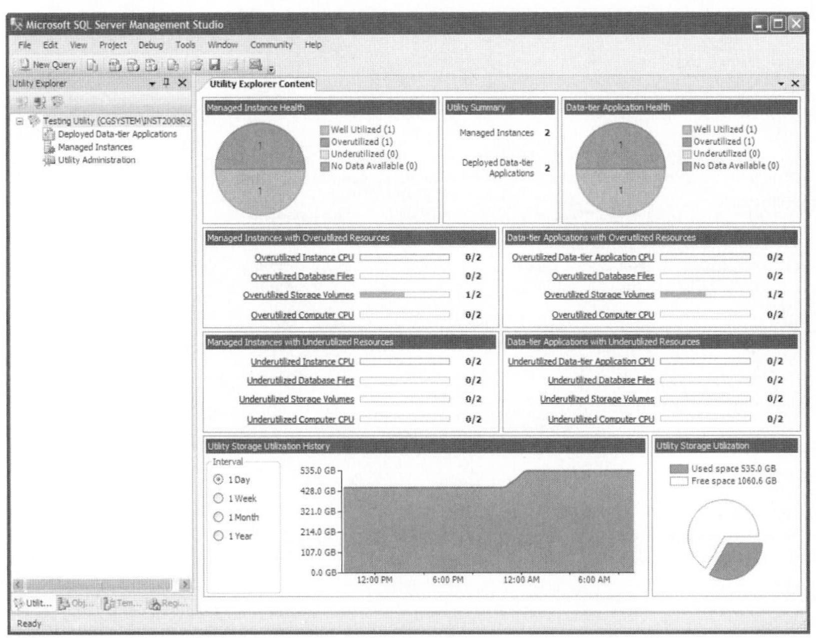

FIGURE 39.15 SQL Server Utility dashboard.

The following four performance utilization metrics are captured by the SQL Server Utility and displayed on the Utility Explorer Content screen:

- CPU utilized by the SQL Server instance
- Database file utilization
- Storage volume utilization

- CPU utilized by the computer running the instance

This performance data is broken down based on utilization thresholds and displayed in the dashboard window based on whether the specific metric is overutilized, underutilized, or well utilized. This breakdown is created for each managed instance as well as data-tier applications, a discussion of which is beyond the scope of this chapter.

The key to making this performance information valuable for you is defining the thresholds for each one of these metrics. Overutilization or underutilization, to some degree, is a matter of personal preference. A CPU that is at 70% utilization may be considered overutilized for some but not for others. The thresholds for these metrics can be defined using the `Utility Administration` node in the Utility Explorer. Figure 39.16 shows the policy screen where the global policies for the managed instances can be defined. These policies are essentially the thresholds for each of the four performance categories displayed in the SQL Server Utility dashboard.

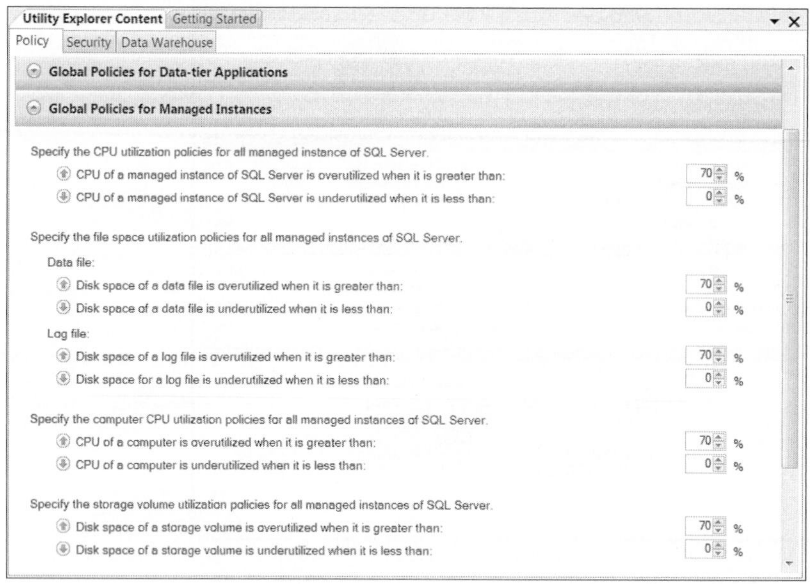

FIGURE 39.16 Global policies for managed instances.

The real power of the SQL Server Utility lies in its capability to collect the kind of performance data that we have been talking about for other SQL Server instances. This multi-server management capability is easy to implement and simply requires that you enroll the other SQL Server instances with a UCP. As mentioned earlier, you can do this by using the third link on the Utility Configuration Steps page. You can also right-click on the `Managed Instances` node in the Utility Explorer and select Enroll Instance. The Enroll Instance Wizard guides you through the enrollment steps. Upon completion of the wizard, the new instance appears in the Utility Explorer Content tab, as shown in Figure 39.17.

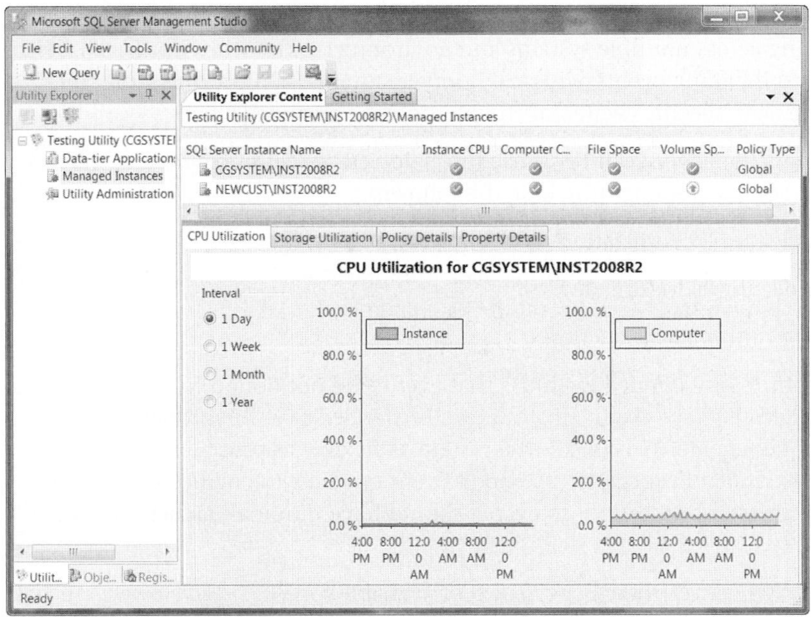

FIGURE 39.17 Managed instances.

The performance data collected by the SQL Server Utility is stored in the utility management data warehouse. The UMDW is a database named `sysutility_mdw` that is automatically created on the UCP instance when the UCP is created. It can be viewed in the list of databases in Object Explorer. By default, each managed instance enrolled in the UCP sends configuration and performance data to the UCP database every 15 minutes. The frequency of data collections provides for a comprehensive set of historical information. This data can be viewed in the Utility Explorer across different intervals, including daily, weekly, monthly, and yearly views. These views provide a sound foundation for identifying problems or identifying trends that can lead to problems in the enrolled SQL Server instances.

CAUTION

The frequency of collection of data in the UMDW database can also lead to a large database. Make sure that you monitor the size of the `sysutility_mdw` database over time. You can manage the data retention period through the SQL Server Utility Explorer. Click on Utility Administration and then select the Data Warehouse tab. You can drag the slider to change the retention period from the default value of one year to one, three, or six months if the UMDW database is becoming too large.

SQL Server Extended Events

SQL Server Extended Events (SSEE) are truly the future event-oriented framework that all SQL Server–based systems and applications will be using going forward. Extended Events are highly flexible to define, are able to capture almost any action or event within your reach, are lightweight in their implementation, and are flexible enough to create simple or complex monitoring across multiple systems and environments. In other words, SSEE is a unified approach to handling events across SQL Server systems, while at the same time enabling users to isolate specific events for troubleshooting purposes.

The Extended Events framework can be utilized to help SQL Server implementations in many ways. Some approaches might include the following:

- Isolating excessive CPU utilization
- Looking for deadlocks/locking
- Locating long-running SQL queries

One of the key features of Extended Events is that events are not bound to a general set of output columns like SQL Trace events. Instead, each Extended Event publishes its data using its own unique schema. This makes the system as flexible as possible for what can be returned from Extended Events. The Extended Event system was engineered from the ground up with performance in mind, so events should have minimal impact on system performance.

SSEE currently is T-SQL based (there is no GUI tool available for SSEE yet). However, it has several predefined SQL Server catalog and dynamic management views and also is integrated with the Event Tracing for Windows (ETW) tools. Figure 39.18 shows the overall makeup of the new SSEE framework.

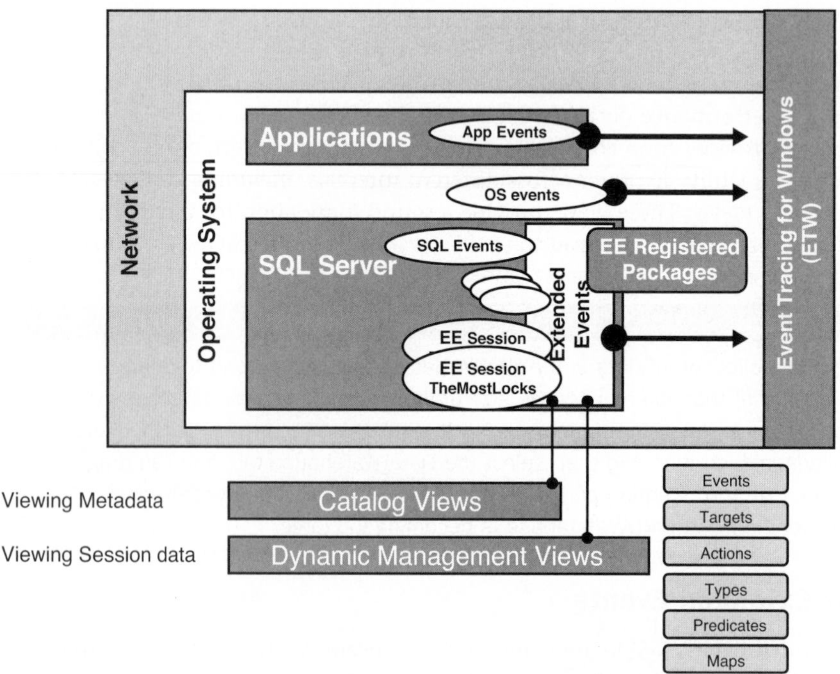

FIGURE 39.18 SQL Server Extended Event framework.

There is basically an Extended Event engine that runs within SQL Server and drives the event gathering for active sessions. This capability essentially provides a standard and powerful way to dynamically monitor active processes, while at the same time having minimal effect on those processes.

Looking a little closer at Figure 39.18, you can see the concept of Extended Events packages (a package), which contain one or more Extended Events objects. The Extended Events engine allows any event to be bound to any target. In other words, events can push their results to any location for consumption (like the ETW) or can be exposed via Views in SMSS, and so on.

Predicates are used to filter what events (that are firing) get pushed to the target (consumer). This capability greatly adds to the flexibility of the Extended Events infrastructure.

The next sections examine the main elements of Extended Events.

Packages

A *package* is a container for SQL Server Extended Events objects. It is the basic unit within which all other Extended Event objects ship. Four kinds of Extended Events packages are included in SQL Server 2008:

- **`package0`—Extended Events system objects. This is the default package.**
- **`sqlserver`—SQL Server–related objects.**
- **`sqlos`—SQL Server Operating System (SQLOS)–related objects.**
- **`SecAudit`—Security Audit events.**

You can see these four packages by running the following query:

```
select * from sys.dm_xe_packages
```

Packages can interact with one another to avoid having to provide the same code in multiple contexts. In other words, if one package exposes an action that can be bound to an event, any number of other events in other packages can also use it. For example, the `package0` package that ships with SQL Server 2008 contains objects designed to be used by all the other packages.

A package can contain any or all of the following objects:

- Events
- Targets
- Actions
- Types
- Predicates
- Maps

Events

Events are monitoring points of interest in the execution path of a program, such as SQL Server. An event firing indicates that the point of interest was reached and provides state information from the time the event was fired. Events can be used solely for tracing purposes or for triggering actions. These actions can either be synchronous or asynchronous. There can be one or more events in an event session package.

To see a list of the events provided with SQL Server, you can run the following query:

```
select * from sys.dm_xe_objects where object_type = 'event'
```

As stated previously, events have a schema that defines their contents. This schema is composed of event columns with well-defined types. You can view the event schema by querying `sys.dm_xe_object_columns`, as in the following example:

```
select name, column_id, type_name, column_type
from sys.dm_xe_object_columns
where object_name = 'page_split'
go

name     column_id    type_name     column_type
------- ----------- ------------ -----------
ID       0            uint16        readonly
UUID     1            guid_ptr      readonly
VERSION  2            uint8         readonly
CHANNEL  3            etw_channel   readonly
KEYWORD  4            keyword_map   readonly
file_id  0            uint16        data
page_id  1            uint32        data
```

Columns marked with `column_type` data are the values that will be filled in at runtime. The read-only columns provide metadata about the event. Notice that one of the columns in the output is the channel for the event; this indicates the category of the event. The available event channels in SQL Server 2008 are as follows:

- **Admin**—Admin events are primarily targeted to the end users, administrators, and support. They include events such as error reports and deprecation announcements.
- **Operational**—Operational events are used for analyzing and diagnosing a problem or occurrence. They can be used to trigger tools or tasks based on the problem or occurrence. An example of an operational event is one in which a database is attached or detached.
- **Analytic**—Analytic events are those that fire on a regular basis, often in high volume. They describe program operation such as lock acquisition and SQL Server statement execution. They are typically aggregated to support performance analysis.
- **Debug**—Debug events are used solely by DBAs and support engineers to help diagnose and solve engine-related problems.

Targets

Targets are event session consumers and indicate where output is located, such as a file, ring buffer, or a bucket with aggregation. Targets can process events synchronously or asynchronously. Extended Events provides several predefined targets you can use as appropriate for directing event output. An example of one of our favorites is provided later in this chapter.

You can find a list of available targets in SQL Server 2008 by running the following query:

```
select * from sys.dm_xe_objects where object_type ='target'
```

Predicates

Predicates are a set of logical evaluation rules for events when they are processed that serve to filter events. They help reduce the volume of captured data and tailor down the output for analysis. In effect, they enable the Extended Events user to selectively capture event data based on specific criteria.

There are two different types of predicates in SQL Server 2008: `pred_compare` and `pred_source`. The `pred_compare` predicates are comparison functions, such as >=.

To view a list of the `pred_compare` predicates available in SQL Server 2008, you can run the following query:

```
select * from sys.dm_xe_objects where object_type = 'pred_compare'
```

If you run this query, you'll notice that there are a number of similar `pred_compare` predicates with the same comparison function but for different data types (for example, `greater_than_int64` and `greater_than_float64`).

The `pred_source` predicates are extended attributes that can be used within predicates to filter on attributes not carried by the event's own schema (such as `transaction_id` or `database_id`). The available `pred_source` predicates can be listed by using the following query:

```
select * from sys.dm_xe_objects where object_type = 'pred_source'
```


Actions

Actions are programmatic responses or series of responses to an event. Actions are bound to an event, and each event may have a unique set of actions. Actions are performed synchronously in association with bound events. They can be used to accomplish certain tasks or simply provide more information relevant to the events.

There are many types of actions, and they have a wide range of capabilities:

- Receive a stack dump and inspect data.
- Store state information in a variable.
- Bring event data from multiple places together.

- Append new data to existing event data.

To view a list of the actions available in SQL Server 2008, you can run the following query:

```
select * from sys.dm_xe_objects where object_type = 'action'
```

Types and Maps

Two kinds of data types can be defined in an event: scalar types and maps. *Scalar types* are single values, like integers. *Maps* are tables that map internal object values to static, predefined, user-friendly descriptions. They help you see what the internal values stand for (making them human consumable) but allow the event to more efficiently store the integer map value rather than the actual text.

Like all the other elements discussed thus far, types and maps can also be viewed by querying the `sys.dm_xe_objects` catalog view:

```
select * from sys.dm_xe_objects
where object_type in ('type', 'map')
```

Although types are relatively self-explanatory, maps require a lookup to expose the associated human-readable text when appropriate. The map values are stored in the DMV called `sys.dm_xe_map_values`. To list the `map_keys` and `map_values` for lock types, for example, you can run the following query:

```
select * from sys.dm_xe_map_values where name = 'lock_mode'
```

Extended Events Catalog Views and DMVs

To get metadata information about what events, actions, fields, and targets have been defined, you can use the catalog views supplied with SQL Server.

> **NOTE**
>
> Examples of the queries presented in this section are provided in the file named `Extended Events Views.sql` on the CD for this book.

For catalog views, the following short list shows the `SELECT` statements and their purposes (that use the predefined SSEE catalog views).

To see event sessions, you use the following:

```
SELECT * FROM sys.server_event_sessions;
```

To see actions on each event (of an event session), run this:

```
SELECT * FROM sys.server_event_session_actions;
```

To see events in an event session, run the following:

```
SELECT * FROM sys.server_event_session_events;
```

To see columns of events and targets, use this statement:

```
SELECT * FROM sys.server_event_session_fields;
```

And, to see event targets for an event session, you use the following:

```
SELECT * FROM sys.server_event_session_targets;
```

You use the dynamic management views to obtain session metadata and session data itself (as it is being gathered during execution). The metadata is obtained from the catalog views, and the session data is created when you start and run an event session.

To see session dispatcher pools, you use the following statement:

```
SELECT * FROM sys.dm_os_dispatcher_pools;
```

To see event package objects, use this:

```
SELECT * FROM sys.dm_xe_objects;
```

To see the schema for all objects, run this statement:

```
SELECT * FROM sys.dm_xe_object_columns;
```

To see the registered packages in the Extended Events engine, use this:

```
SELECT * FROM sys.dm_xe_packages;
```

To see the active Extended Events sessions, run the following:

```
SELECT * FROM sys.dm_xe_sessions;
```

To see session targets, run this statement:

```
SELECT * FROM sys.dm_xe_session_targets;
```

To see session events, use this:

```
SELECT * FROM sys.dm_xe_session_events;
```


To see event session actions, use this:

```
SELECT * FROM sys.dm_xe_session_event_actions;
```

To see the mapping of internal keys to readable text, use the following:

```
SELECT * FROM sys.dm_xe_map_values;
```

Specific variations might be as follows:

```
SELECT map_value Keyword from sys.dm_xe_map_values
where name = 'keyword_map';
```

```
SELECT map_key, map_value from sys.dm_xe_map_values
where name = 'lock_mode';
```

And finally, to see the configuration values for objects bound to a session, you use the following:

```
SELECT * FROM sys.dm_xe_session_object_columns;
```

Creating an Extended Events Session

Microsoft uses the same common paradigm (CREATE, ALTER, DROP) for most of its newer capabilities, such as Create Audit.. (for SQL Auditing), Create Endpoint.. (for database mirroring), and many others. SSEE follows the same path in that you basically create an Extended Events session, alter it to start the monitoring session, alter it again to stop the monitoring, and then leverage the catalog and dynamic management views before, during, and after the session monitoring to view the event information.

Creating events (event sessions) is fairly easy to do using the CREATE, ALTER and DROP EVENT statements. These Data Definition Language (DDL) statements completely control the creation and activation of Extended Events. All the SSEE objects are created in the msdb database. Only those users with CONTROL SERVER permissions can create, alter, or drop SSEE objects. To use the catalog and dynamic management views, you need at least VIEW SERVER STATE permission.

In this section, you quickly set up and define a new Extended Events session object that includes operating system IO requests and SQL Server lock-acquired counts. The purpose is to isolate the database objects (tables) that are being hit hardest with locks to better understand the behavior of the database design.

Included on the CD for this book is a SQL script file named TheMostLocks.sql. Locate this SQL script now; then start SSMS and open a new query connection with the CREATE EVENT SESSION script in it. Figure 39.19 shows a current connection to SQL Server with TheMostLocks.sql file open and the event session named TheMostLocks ready to be created.

As you examine the CREATE EVENT SESSION T-SQL code, notice that two events are being created with the ADD EVENT statements. One will gather async IO requests, and the other will retrieve SQL Server–acquired locks on an object's information. Also, notice the TARGET statement, which uses a predefined target location that allows you to retrieve the results within SQL Server during execution and that filters on showing only the lock's acquired information.

The CREATE EVENT SESSION T-SQL code is as follows:

```
IF EXISTS(SELECT * FROM sys.server_event_sessions WHERE name='TheMostLocks')
DROP EVENT session TheMostLocks ON SERVER;

CREATE EVENT SESSION TheMostLocks
ON SERVER
```

```
        ADD EVENT sqlos.async_io_requested,
        ADD EVENT sqlserver.lock_acquired
        ADD TARGET package0.synchronous_bucketizer (
        SET filtering_event_name='sqlserver.lock_acquired',
source_type=0, source='resource_0')
        WITH (MAX_MEMORY=4MB, MAX_EVENT_SIZE=4MB);
```

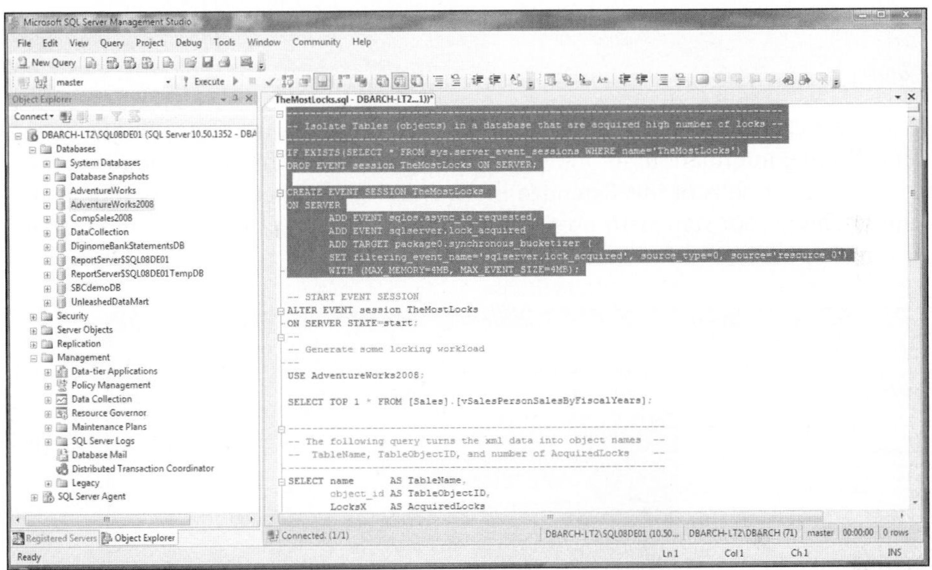

FIGURE 39.19 SSMS creating an event session named **TheMostLocks**.

Alternatively, you can direct the TARGET output to a file by using the following TARGET statement, for example:

```
ADD TARGET package0.etw_classic_sync_target
 (SET default_etw_session_logfile_path  = N'C:\TEMP\EESessionFile.etl' )
```

You could then use the resulting file with the ETW to assemble this and other events from other portions of your environment.

After the event session is created, you are able to start it by using the ALTER EVENT SESSION command, generate some activity on your server that will be captured by the event session, view the dynamic results during the execution of the activity, and then stop the event session.

Go ahead and create the event session as it is listed now. Simply highlight the CREATE EVENT SESSION T-SQL statements shown previously and execute this code from SSMS. When it is complete, you are ready to start the event session by using the following command:

```
-- START EVENT SESSION
ALTER EVENT SESSION TheMostLocks ON SERVER STATE=start;
```

Using the AdventureWorks2008 database, you can generate some simple activity that is known to acquire share locks on tables. Use the following T-SQL that references the [Sales].[vSalesPersonSalesByFiscalYears] view:

```
--
-- Generate some lock acquiring workload
--
USE AdventureWorks2008;

SELECT TOP 1 * FROM [Sales].[vSalesPersonSalesByFiscalYears];
```

As soon as the preceding SELECT statement is generated, the Extended Event begins doing its job of collecting information. As you can see in Figure 39.20, this fairly complex join statement grabs the results of this Extended Event and displays them in a very nice readable fashion. This SELECT statement uses the dynamic management views previously identified in this chapter during the Extended Events active session.

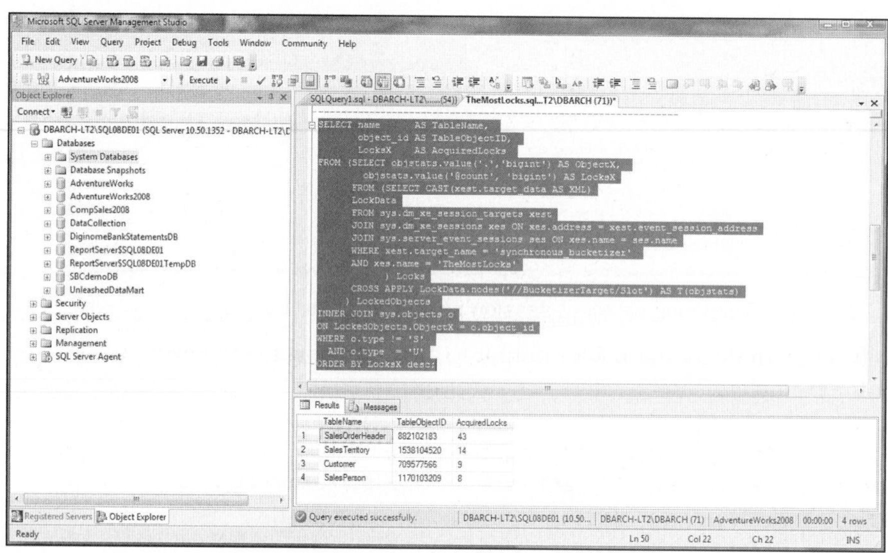

FIGURE 39.20 Displaying the results of acquired locks from the Extended Events session.

As you can see, this session isolates the table objects that have the most acquired locks on them during execution. This capability is very powerful.

The T-SQL code is as follows:

```
-------------------------------------------------------------------
-- The following query turns the xml data that is accumulating   --
-- from the Extended Event Session and displays it more clearly  --
--  TableName, TableObjectID, and number of AcquiredLocks        --
-------------------------------------------------------------------
SELECT name      AS TableName,
```

```
        object_id AS TableObjectID,
        LocksX    AS AcquiredLocks
FROM (SELECT objstats.value('.','bigint') AS ObjectX,
         objstats.value('@count', 'bigint') AS LocksX
      FROM (SELECT CAST(xest.target_data AS XML)
      LockData
      FROM sys.dm_xe_session_targets xest
      JOIN sys.dm_xe_sessions xes ON xes.address = xest.event_session_address
      JOIN sys.server_event_sessions ses ON xes.name = ses.name
      WHERE xest.target_name = 'synchronous_bucketizer'
      AND xes.name = 'TheMostLocks'
            ) Locks
      CROSS APPLY LockData.nodes('//BucketizerTarget/Slot') AS T(objstats)
     ) LockedObjects
INNER JOIN sys.objects o
ON LockedObjects.ObjectX = o.object_id
WHERE o.type != 'S'
  AND o.type  = 'U'
ORDER BY LocksX desc;
```

To turn off the Extended Events session, you simply issue another `ALTER EVENT SESSION` command with the `STATE` equal to `stop`, as shown here:

```
-- STOP EVENT SESSION
ALTER EVENT SESSION TheMostLocks
ON SERVER STATE=stop ;
```

Various Extended Events can be defined for monitoring purposes within the SQL Server environment, your application environment, and at the operating system level. You will likely build up a complete library of Extended Events that represent what you are most interested in monitoring about your environment. They will then become valuable tools for years to come. We also expect forums and Microsoft to create many templates of Extended Events to aid you in creating this extensive library of monitoring capability.

Windows Performance Monitor

Windows Performance Monitor is a graphical tool that provides a visual display of built-in Windows performance counters, either in real-time or as a way to review historical data. It is supplied as part of the installation of any Windows server or workstation (in Windows Server 2008 it is called *Reliability and Performance Monitor*). Hundreds of performance counters are available. These counters can be monitored on the local machine or remotely over the network, and they can be set up to monitor any object and counter on multiple systems at once from one session. A small subset of performance information is also available via the Windows Task Manager Performance tab. However, all this information and more is available using the Performance Monitor facility.

NOTE

This chapter covers the version of Performance Monitor available in Windows Server 2008, Windows Server 2008 R2, Windows Vista, and Windows 7. If you are running on Windows XP, Windows Server 2003, or earlier versions of Windows, the interface and functionality of Performance Monitor are a bit more limited than the version presented here. However, many of the concepts of using Performance Monitor and performance counters are still similar.

Performance Monitor features multiple graph views that enable you to visually review performance log data. You can add performance counters to Performance Monitor individually or by creating custom Data Collector Sets. The recent version of Windows Performance Monitor combines the functionality of previous standalone tools including Performance Logs and Alerts (PLA), Server Performance Advisor (SPA), and System Monitor.

You can use Windows Performance Monitor to examine how programs you run affect your computer's performance, both in real-time and by collecting log data for later analysis. When you install SQL Server, additional performance counters are installed that you can use to monitor SQL Server performance elements such as cache utilization, locking, wait states, and I/O performance. Performance Monitor can be launched from many different points. From SQL Profiler, choose the Tools menu option and choose the Performance Monitor item. Figure 39.21 shows this menu option from SQL Profiler. You can also launch it from the `Administrative Tools` folder in the Windows Start menu.

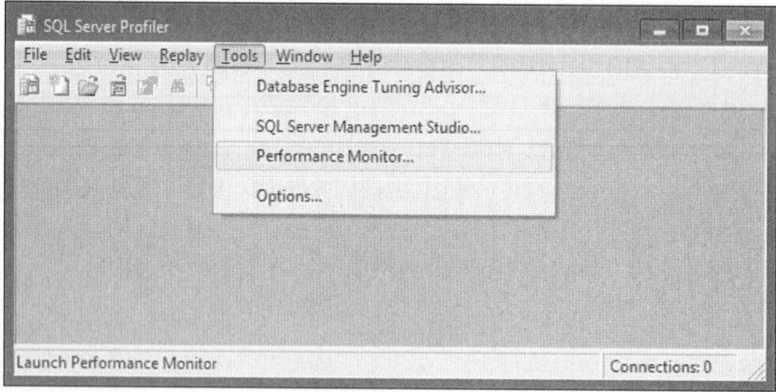

FIGURE 39.21 Launching Performance Monitor from SQL Profiler.

Performance Monitor Views

When you first launch Performance Monitor, you are presented with the welcome screen (in Windows 2008, the welcome screen is the Resource Overview). Click on Performance Monitor in the `Monitoring Tools` folder to bring up the Performance Monitor main display. In the Performance Monitor main display, you can view the performance information in one of three different modes:

- **Graphic chart**—This view, the default, shows the selected counters as colored lines over a timeline with the y-axis representing the value and the x-axis representing time. You can also add gridlines (horizontal and vertical). This view lets you view performance trends over time.

- **Histogram chart**—This view shows the selected counters as colored horizontal bars (as in a histogram). These histogram bars change dynamically to reflect the data sampling values. With this view, you see a current snapshot of the performance counters rather than the trend of activity over time.
- **Report display**—In this mode, you see the current values for counters collected under their parent object in a textual display format. Like the histogram view, this view does not show you the activity trends, just the current sampling value, but it is great for showing what counters you are collecting data with.

Figure 39.22 shows the basic graphic chart view interface for Performance Monitor displaying several useful system counters that are explained later in this chapter. These counters are added to Performance Monitor through the creation of Performance Monitor Data Collector Sets.

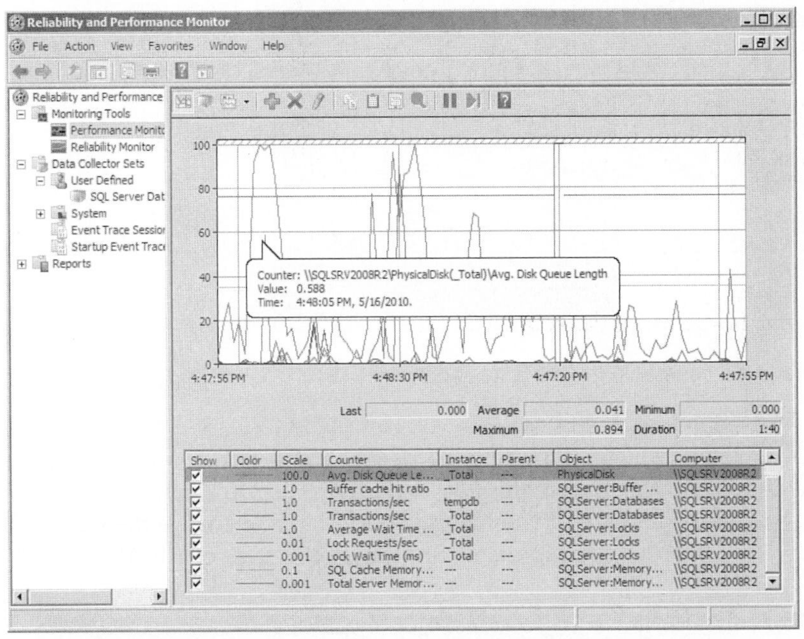

FIGURE 39.22 Performance Monitor chart view, with various counters.

When you open the Performance Monitor view, depending on the OS version you are running, you see up to three default performance counters: Memory: Pages/sec, PhysicalDisk:Avg.Disk Queue Length, and Processor:% Processor Time. These counters provide a good start, but you really want to see many other counters that reflect the complete picture of how your server is behaving. This chapter explains the recommended ones to use for SQL Server in the "SQL Server Performance Counters" section.

You add a counter by clicking the large plus sign toolbar button near the top. The Add Counters dialog that appears (see Figure 39.23) allows you to select the computer to monitor (this can be a remote server), a performance object, any specific counters, and an instance of the counter, if applicable. You can select the Show Description check box to get a simple explanation of the currently selected counter. When you are done making your selections of counters to add, click OK to return to the Performance Monitor screen.

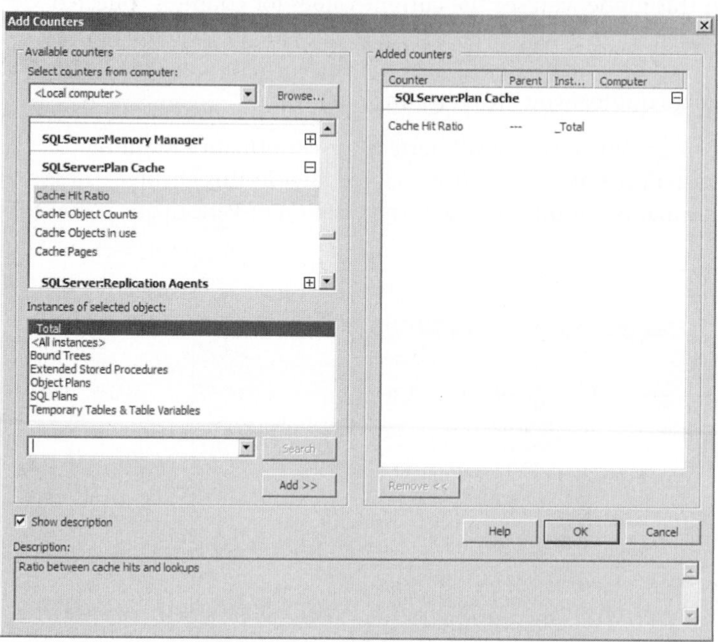

FIGURE 39.23 Adding a counter in Performance Monitor.

You can customize the look of the lines in the chart view by right-clicking and selecting Properties. On the Data tab of the System Monitor Properties dialog, you can specify the color, width, and style of line for each of your counters. You can also change the scale of a counter's value as well so that the line appears within the graph's scale of 1 to 100.

TIP

To quickly rescale all the counters, select all the counters in the bottom panel of the Chart view window, right-click, and select Scale Selected Counters. Performance Monitor automatically selects a scale for each counter such that all lines appear within the display.

To remove a counter, you simply highlight the line in the bottom area of the Chart view window and press the Delete key or click on the X button in the toolbar. If you just want to temporarily hide a counter to make the display a little less busy, you can right-click a counter in the bottom area of the Chart view and select Hide Selected Counters.

The Chart view also provides a way to make a specific counter or set of counters stand out in the display by making the line or lines black and bold. This capability can help you focus on the trend of a specific counter. To turn on highlighting, select one or more counters in the bottom area of the Chart view and click on the Highlight button on the toolbar (the one that looks like highlighter pen just to the right of the big red X).

Adding counters like this in an ad hoc manner is fine for a quick monitoring session. However, after you close the Performance Monitor tool, you lose the counters you have selected, so they are not available the next time you open Performance Monitor. Typically, you need to set up those counters you want to reuse or to have running continuously or on a schedule that captures the performance counters to a log file. To do this, you create one or more Data Collector Sets.

Creating Data Collector Sets in Performance Monitor

A *Data Collector Set* is the building block of performance monitoring and reporting in Windows Performance Monitor. It organizes multiple data collection points into a single component that can be used for review or to log performance counters. A Data Collector Set can be created and then recorded individually, grouped with other Data Collector Sets and incorporated into logs, viewed in Performance Monitor, or configured to generate alerts when thresholds are reached. You can set up schedules on your Data Collector Sets to have them run the data collection at specific times.

Data collector sets can contain the following types of Data Collectors:

- Performance counters
- Event trace data
- System configuration information (Registry key values)

Performance counters are measurements of system state or activity. They can be included in the operating system or can be part of individual applications. When you install SQL Server, a number of SQL Server–specific performance counters are installed (a number of the more useful ones are described later in this chapter). Windows Performance Monitor requests the current value of performance counters at specified time intervals.

Event trace data is collected from trace providers, which are components of the operating system or of individual applications that report actions or events. Output from multiple trace providers can be combined into a trace session.

Configuration information is collected from key values in the Windows Registry. Windows Performance Monitor can record the value of a Registry key at a specified time or interval as part of a log file.

The easiest way to created a Data Collector Set is to create a custom view of counters in Performance Monitor (similar to what was shown in the previous section). When you are satisfied with the counters and settings you have configured, right-click on the `Performance Monitor` node in the `Monitoring Tools` folder, select New, and then select

Data Collector Set. This starts the Create Data Collector Set Wizard, which walks you through the following steps:

1. The wizard prompts for a name for the Data Collector Set. Enter a name and click Next.
2. Specify the root directory where the Performance Monitor log files will be written and click Next.
3. Specify if you want the Data Collector to run under a different user ID and if you want to start the Data Collector immediately or to just save the Data Collector Set. Click Finish to return to Performance Monitor.

The newly created Data Collector Set is listed under the `User Defined` folder in the `Data Collector Sets` node in Performance Monitor.

You can also create a Data Collector Set manually or from a template by right-clicking on the `User Defined` folder in the `Data Collector Sets` node and selecting New, Data Collector Set. This launches a modified version of the Create New Data Collector Set Wizard, as shown in Figure 39.24.

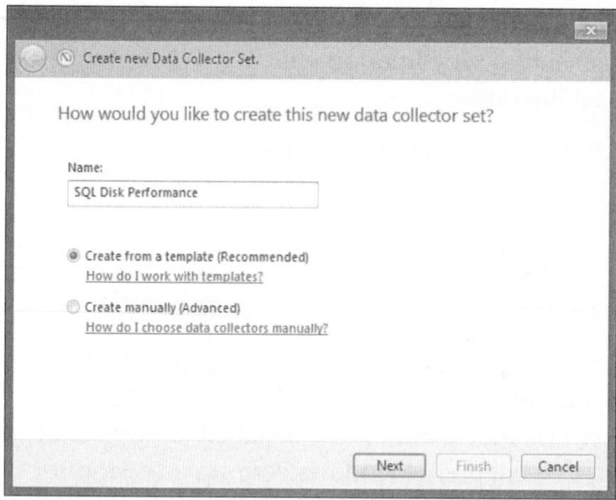

FIGURE 39.24 The Create New Data Collector Set Wizard.

You first specify a name for the collector set and then choose whether to create it from a template or manually. Then you click Next.

If you choose to create from a template, the next screen displays the built-in templates provided with Windows; these standard templates focus on general system performance or diagnostics. You can also choose to import your own templates by clicking on the Browse button.

NOTE

Creating your own Data Collector Set templates in Performance Monitor is relatively easy. If you have a Data Collector Set that you've set up with the performance counters and settings that you would like to reuse, simply right-click the Data Collector Set you want to export and click Save Template. Select a directory in which to store the collector set as an XML file and click Save. You can now copy this template for use on other computers.

After selecting the template, navigate to the next screen to specify the root directory for the log files. On the final screen, you have the option again to start the collector immediately, save it, or open the properties for the Data Collector Set so you can make further modifications to it, such as specifying a schedule or how it should handle.

If you choose to create a new Data Collector Set manually instead of using a template, you are presented with the screen shown in Figure 39.25. You have the option to create a Data Collector Set that generates data logs or to create a Performance Counter Alert. If you are creating data logs, you can specify what sort of information you want to include in the collector set (in this example, we're logging performance counters only).

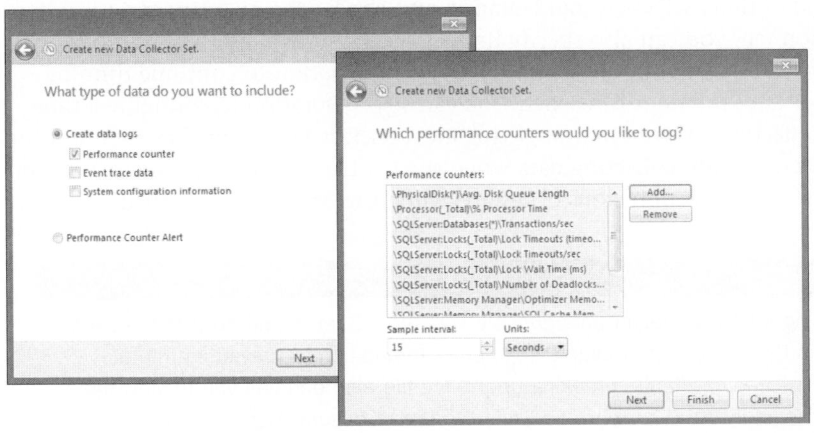

FIGURE 39.25 Creating a new Data Collector Set manually to capture performance counters.

Depending on the Data Collector types you select, you are presented with dialogs to add Data Collectors to your Data Collector Set. In this example, you are presented with the dialog to add performance counters, as shown in Figure 39.25.

After defining the counters, and so on, you are presented with the familiar options to specify the root directory and whether to save, run, or edit the properties of the Data Collector Set.

After you create a Data Collector Set, you can add additional Data Collectors to it as desired. They can be additional performance counter event traces, configuration Data Collectors, or performance counter alerts.

Running a Data Collector Set in Performance Monitor

The easiest way to run a Data Collector Set is to right-click on it and choose Start. When you are done capturing, right-click again and choose Stop. However, this is probably not the most effective way to execute your Data Collector Sets. A more effective approach is to set up a schedule for data collection.

During Data Collector Set creation, you can configure the schedule by selecting Open Properties for this Data Collector Set at the end of the Create New Data Collector Set Wizard. After a Data Collector Set is created, you can access the schedule options by right-clicking the Data Collector Set name in the Microsoft Management Console (MMC) navigation pane and selecting Properties. When the Properties dialog is displayed, click the Schedule tab to specify the schedule when you want the Data Collector to run. You can specify the start date, time, or day for data collection. If you do not want to collect new data after a certain date, select Expiration Date and choose a date from the calendar. You can create multiple schedules for a single Data Collector Set.

The Data Collector runs continuously unless you specify a Stop condition for a Data Collector Set. The Stop condition can be set in the Stop Condition tab. To stop collecting data after a period of time, select Overall Duration and choose the quantity and units. On the Stop Condition tab, you can also specify limits to segment data collection into separate logs. Select the Restart the Data Collector Set at Limits option to continue running the Data Collector after the limit is reached. You can select Duration to configure a time period for data collection to write to a single log file, or select Maximum Size to restart the Data Collector Set or to stop collecting data when the log file reaches a specific size. If you select both limits, data collection stops or restarts when the first limit is reached.

TIP

If you are running a Data Collector continuously, you should set a limit so that the Data Collector breaks the log file into multiple segments. In addition to preventing the file from becoming exceedingly large, breaking up the log file also enables you to view the log file segments prior to the current one while the Data Collector Set is running. Unfortunately, you cannot directly open the currently active log file for a Data Collector Set to view the live data collection. However, if you have a previous report available, you can open the report in the Performance Monitor window. When this report is open, click the View Current Activity button (or press Ctrl+T) and you can view the current activity in real-time as it's being captured.

Viewing Data Collector Set Results in Performance Monitor

To view a Data Collector Set report in Windows Performance Monitor, expand Reports and click User Defined or System. Then expand the Data Collector Set that you want to view as a report. Simply click the report that you want to view from the list of available reports. The report opens in the console pane.

If you want to open one or more log files in Performance Monitor (perhaps you have a set of log files copied from another server), in the Windows Performance Monitor navigation pane, expand Monitoring Tools and click Performance Monitor. In the console pane toolbar, click the Add Log Data button (or press Ctrl+L). The Performance Monitor Properties page opens with the Source tab active (see Figure 39.26). In the Data Source section, follow these steps:

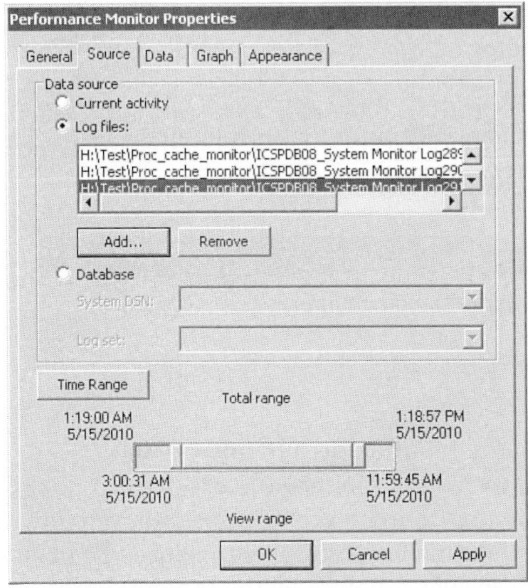

FIGURE 39.26 Importing log files into Performance Monitor.

1. Select Log Files and click Add.
2. Browse to the log file you want to view and click Open.
3. To add multiple log files to the Performance Monitor view, click Add again.
4. Click Time Range to see times included in the log or logs you selected.
5. When you are finished selecting log files, click OK.
6. Right-click in the Performance Monitor display and click Add Counters to select the counters you want to display in Performance Monitor. Only the counters included in the log file or files you selected in step 4 are made available.

For a single log file, you can move the beginning and ending time sliders to view only a portion of the log file in Performance Monitor.

For multiple log files, you can move the beginning and ending time sliders to choose the time period (from all the selected log files) to view in Performance Monitor. If a log has data from the time period you select, it is available in the display.

Why Use Performance Monitor?

You might be asking, "With all the new performance monitoring tools provided with SQL Server, is there a need to continue to use Performance Monitor?"

Even though many of the performance counters and relevant information are now available in the SQL Server Data Collector, as mentioned previously, the Data Collector does incur some overhead on SQL Server. Performance Monitor, on the other hand, incurs significantly less impact on SQL Server performance.

In addition, the SQL Server Data Collector currently doesn't have a built-in alerting capability. As mentioned previously, you can set up performance counter alerts in Performance Monitor. In addition, Performance Monitor enables you to monitor more than what is provided with SQL Server Data Collector, including all aspects of the operating system as well as other applications.

One other feature that's very useful with Performance Monitor logs is the capability to import performance counter logs into SQL Server Profiler.

NOTE

For more information on importing and viewing performance counter logs in SQL Server Profiler, see Chapter 6.

SQL Server Performance Counters

For each SQL Server instance installed, Performance Monitor has a number of SQL Server–specific performance objects added to it, each with a number of associated counters. Each SQL Server instance has its own set of monitoring objects because you certainly wouldn't want to mix monitoring values across multiple instances. Performance counters for named instances use the naming convention `MSSQL$` followed by the instance name (for example, `MSSQL$SQL2008DEV:General Statistics`). Performance counters for the default instance of SQL Server use the naming convention of SQLSERVER followed by the counter name (for example, `SQLServer:General Statistics`).

Table 39.1 provides a list of the SQL Server performance counters available for SQL Server 2008

TABLE 39.1 SQL Server Performance Objects

Performance Object	Description
`SQLServer:Access Methods`	Information on searches and allocations of SQL Server database objects (for example, the number of index searches or number of pages allocated to indexes and data).
`SQLServer:Backup Device`	Information about backup devices, such as the throughput of the backup device.
`SQLServer:Buffer Manager`	Information about the memory buffers used by SQL Server.
`SQLServer:Buffer Partition`	Information about buffer free page accesses.

TABLE 39.1 SQL Server Performance Objects

Performance Object	Description
SQLServer:CLR	Information about common language runtime (CLR)
SQLServer:Cursor Manager by Type SQLServer:Cursor Manager Total	Information about cursors.
SQLServer:Database Mirroring	Information about database mirroring.
SQLServer:Databases	Database-specific information such as the amount of free log space available or the number of active transactions in the database.
SQL Server:Deprecated Features	Information on the number of times deprecated features are used.
SQLServer:Exec Statistics	Execution statistics information.
SQLServer:General Statistics	General server-wide activity, such as the number of logins per second.
SQLServer:Latches	Information about the latches on internal resources, such as database pages.
SQLServer:Locks	Information about the individual lock requests made by SQL Server, such as lock timeouts and deadlocks.
SQLServer:Memory Manager	Information about SQL Server memory usage, such as the total number of lock structures currently allocated.
SQLServer:Plan Cache	Information about the SQL Server cache used to store objects such as stored procedures, triggers, and query plans.
SQLServer: Resource Pool Stats	Information about Resource Governor resource pool statistics.
SQLServer:SQL Errors	Information about SQL Server errors.
SQLServer:SQL Statistics	Query statistics, such as the number of batches of T-SQL statements received by SQL Server.
SQLServer:Transactions	Transaction statistics, such as the overall number of transactions and the number of snapshot transactions.
SQLServer:User Settable	Custom counters that can be a custom stored procedure or any T-SQL statement that returns a value to be monitored.

TABLE 39.1 SQL Server Performance Objects

Performance Object	Description
SQLServer: Wait Statistics	Information about waits.
SQLAgent:Alerts	Information about SQL Server Agent alerts.
SQLAgent:Jobs	Information about SQL Server Agent jobs.
SQLAgent:JobSteps	Information about SQL Server Agent job steps.
SQLAgent:Statistics	General information about SQL Server Agent.
SQLServer:Replication Agents SQLServer:Replication Snapshot SQLServer:Replication Logreader SQLServer:Replication Dist. SQLServer:Replication Merge	Information about replication agent activity.

User-Defined Counters

You can extend the range of information that Performance Monitor displays by creating up to 10 of your own counters. These user-defined counters appear under the SQLServer:User Settable:Query object, which contains the 10 counters as instances, starting with User Counter 1. You define your own counters by calling stored procedures with the names sp_user_counter1 through sp_user_counter10, which are located in the master database.

These counters work differently than they did under previous versions of SQL Server and require you to call the stored procedures to update the information they return to Performance Monitor. To make any real use of these stored procedures, you now need to call them within a loop or as part of a job that is scheduled on some recurring basis.

Using these counters allows you to monitor any information you want, whether it is system, database, or even object specific. The only restriction is that the stored procedure can take only a single integer value argument.

The following sample user-defined counter procedure sets the counter value to the average connection time for all user connections. Processes that have a session_id less than 50 are internal system processes (checkpoint, Lazy Writer, and so on):

```
DECLARE @value INT


SELECT @value = AVG( DATEDIFF( mi, login_time, GETDATE()))
FROM sys.dm_exec_sessions
WHERE session_id > 50

EXEC sp_user_counter1 @value
```

You could further extend this information by creating additional user procedures for returning the minimum and maximum times connected, as well as database usage. Your only limitation is that you can monitor only a maximum of 10 pieces of information at one time.

Accessing Performance Counters via T-SQL

Most of the SQL Server–oriented performance counter values can also be seen at any point in time via the system catalog view named `sys.sysperfinfo`:

```
SELECT * from sys.sysperfinfo
```

This view shows the performance object name, counter name, and current counter value as of the time the system view is executed.

You should keep in mind that many of the performance counters are accumulation counters, and you have to run them at intervals and determine the difference (change) from one interval to the next. Others are current values of aspects such as transaction rates, memory usage, and hit ratios.

A Performance Monitoring Approach

If you take a closer look at the performance monitoring areas depicted in Figure 39.1, you can see that SQL Server spans them all. SQL Server must process requests submitted to it via the network, service those requests with one or more processors, and rely on accessing a request's data from both memory/cache and the disk system. If you maximize utilization on these resources from the point of view of SQL Server and the operating system, you end up with a well-tuned database server. However, an optimally tuned system doesn't guarantee good performance. It's still important to have a good database design and to implement optimal index strategies. The whole picture is important to tuning your SQL Server implementation, but the database, table designs, indexing strategy, and SQL statement tuning are described in much more detail in other chapters. This section focuses on the SQL Server instance as it sits on the OS and the hardware, along with the major monitoring capabilities available to you.

One area of interest is the amount of network traffic handled by SQL Server and the size of these network requests. Another area of interest is the capability of the available processors to service the load presented to them by SQL Server without exceeding the CPU capacity of the system. This section also looks at SQL Server memory utilization of the available system memory and how effectively SQL Server is utilizing the disk system.

In general, you want to start from the bottom, with the network, and work your way up into the SQL Server–specific elements. This allows you to quickly isolate certain issues that are paramount in performance tuning. In each of these areas, this section provides a list of minimum detail performance handles or counters that can be examined. This approach can be summarized into the following steps:

1. Understand and monitor network request characteristics as they relate to SQL Server and the machine on which SQL Server has been installed. This means a

complete profile of what is coming into and being sent back out over the network from SQL Server.

2. Understand processor utilization. Processing power might be the biggest issue affecting performance. You need to get a handle on this aspect of performance early.
3. Understand and monitor memory and cache utilization. This is the next step, monitoring the overall memory usage from the operating system level point of view and monitoring the memory that SQL Server is using for data buffers, plan cache, and so on.
4. Understand and monitor disk system utilization. You are often rewarded for implementing a simple (and less expensive) disk configuration or data storage approach. However, a simple configuration may not provide the best performance for your system. And you often don't know you have a problem unless you look for it. Techniques that are often used to alleviate disk performance issues include disk striping, isolation of logs from data, and so on.

You need to repeat steps 1 through 4 on a regular basis. Your continued success (and, it is hoped, salary increases) will reflect your diligence here. For each step, certain tools and facilities are available for you to use that gather the information needed to identify and monitor performance issues. Let's look now at how to use these tools to monitor and analyze the network, processor, memory, and disk utilization and performance.

Monitoring the Network Interface

One area of possible congestion is the network card or network interface; it does not matter how fast the server's work is if it has to queue up to go out through a small pipe. Remember that any activity on the server machine might be consuming some of the bandwidth of the network interface card. With the increasing implementations of gigabit networks and the increases in network bandwidth over wide area networks (WANs), network throughput is not as much of a bottleneck as it used to be. That's not to say network performance issues do not arise. For example, a bad or misconfigured router can cause all sorts of network performance issues, especially if your users and your SQL Server are on different sides of the router. If you are not detecting query performance issues in SQL Server but users are still complaining about slow query performance, the network is a likely culprit.

You can monitor network activity via Performance Monitor. Table 39.2 shows the typical network performance object and counters you can use to monitor network interface activity.

TABLE 39.2 Network Interface Performance Objects and Counters

Performance Monitor Object	Description
`Network Interface: Bytes Received`	The rate at which bytes are received on the interface.
`Network Interface: Bytes Sent`	The rate at which bytes are sent on the interface.

TABLE 39.2 Network Interface Performance Objects and Counters

Performance Monitor Object	Description
`Network Interface: Bytes Total`	The rate at which all bytes are sent and received on the interface.
`Network Interface: Current Bandwidth`	The bits per second (bps) of the interface card.
`Network Interface: Output Queue Length`	The length of the output packet queue (in packets). If this is longer than two, delays are occurring, and a bottleneck exists.
`Network Interface: Packets Received`	The rate at which packets are received on the network interface.
`Network Interface: Packets Sent`	The rate at which packets are sent on the network interface.
`Network Interface: Packets`	The rate at which packets are sent and received on the network interface.
`Server: Bytes Received`	The number of bytes the server has received from the network. This is the big-picture indicator of how busy the server is.
`Server: Bytes Transmitted`	The number of bytes the server has sent/transmitted to the network. Again, this is a good overall picture of how busy the server is.

In general, if the SQL Server packet sends or receives are grossly lower than the overall server's packet sends and receives, other activity on the server is occurring that is potentially bogging down this server or not allowing SQL Server to be used optimally. The rule of thumb here is to isolate all other functionality to other servers if you can and let SQL Server be the main application on a machine.

The `sp_monitor` system stored procedure, as well as several SQL Server system variables, can be used to see how many requests are queuing up, waiting to make use of the network interface. The following `SELECT` statement retrieves a current picture of what is being handled by SQL Server from a network packet's point of view:

```
SELECT  @@connections as Connections,
        @@pack_received as Packets_Received,
        @@pack_sent as Packets_Sent,
        getdate() as 'As of datetime'
go
Connections Packets_Received Packets_Sent As of datetime
----------- ---------------- ------------ -----------------------
39407       395569           487258       2010-05-16 22:34:19.650
```

39

The sp_monitor system stored procedure provides packets sent and received as a running total and since the last time it was run (difference in seconds). Here's an example of what would result (the network- and packets-related results):

```
EXEC sp_monitor
GO
last_run                current_run             seconds
----------------------- ----------------------- -----------
2010-04-02 17:34:58.817 2010-05-16 22:35:08.940 3819610

cpu_busy     io_busy    idle
------------ ---------- -----------------
318(318)-0%  62(62)-0%  182952(182928)-4%

packets_received packets_sent   packet_errors
---------------- -------------- --------------
395781(395753)   487483(487455) 1(1)

total_read   total_write   total_errors connections
------------ ------------- ------------ ------------
8084(8084)   69921(69921)  0(0)         39432(39418)
```

The values within the parentheses are the amounts since the last time sp_monitor was run, and the seconds column shows how long that period was. You can actually see the rate at which traffic is coming into and out of SQL Server.

Monitoring the Processors

The main processors of a server do the majority of the hard work, executing the operating system code and all applications. This is the next logical place to start looking at the performance of a system. With SQL Server 2008, you can identify the number of CPUs you want to utilize on your physical machine. If your physical machine has 32 CPUs, you might not necessarily want to make all 32 CPUs available to SQL Server. In fact, in some cases, this would be a detriment; some CPU processing should be reserved for the OS and the network management on heavily loaded servers (5% of the CPUs). SQL Server allows you to identify how many CPUs it can use from what is available on the physical machine. In Figure 39.27, you can see the number of CPUs available to SQL Server on a typical server from the SSMS Server Properties page. In this example, all CPUs are being made available to SQL Server.

In a 32-CPU server example and using the 5% number just mentioned, you should let SQL Server use 30 of the CPUs and reserve 2 CPUs for dedicated network- and OS-related activity ($0.05 \times 32 = 1.6$, rounded up to 2 CPUs). This also allows SQL Server to utilize SQL parallelism effectively.

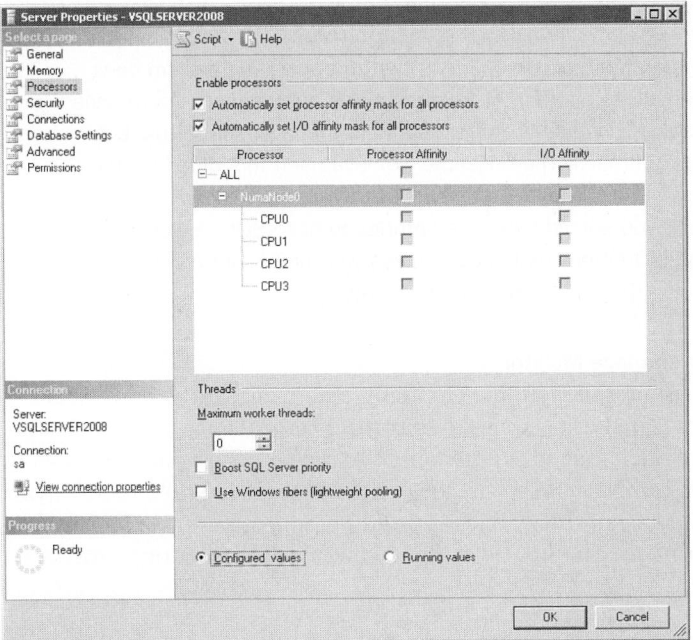

FIGURE 39.27 Processor (CPU) properties of a SQL Server instance.

Keep in mind that from a multitasking point of view, Windows servers often move process threads among different processors. This process thread movement activity can reduce Microsoft SQL Server performance under heavy system loads because each processor cache is repeatedly reloaded with data. It is possible to assign processors to specific threads, which can improve performance under these types of conditions by eliminating processor reloads. This association between a thread and processor is called *processor affinity*. SQL Server 2008 supports processor affinity by means of two affinity mask options: affinity mask (also known as CPU affinity mask) and affinity I/O mask. If you do nothing, SQL Server is allowed to use each CPU for all its processing, with no affinity whatsoever. The operating system distributes threads from instances of SQL Server evenly among these CPUs.

The affinity I/O mask option binds SQL Server disk I/O to a specified subset of CPUs. In high-end SQL Server online transaction processing (OLTP) environments, this extension can enhance the performance of SQL Server threads issuing a high number of I/Os. This enhancement does not support hardware affinity for individual disks or disk controllers, though. Perhaps this will be a future enhancement to SQL Server.

NOTE

A side effect of specifying the affinity mask option is that the operating system does *not* move threads from one CPU to another. Most systems obtain optimal performance by letting the operating system schedule the threads among the available CPUs, but there are exceptions to this approach. The only time we have used this affinity setting was to isolate CPUs to specific SQL Server instances on the same box that had numerous CPUs to utilize. Typically, you should leave the settings to have SQL Server automatically set processor and I/O affinity as needed unless your processor monitoring indicates manually configuring the affinity may be necessary.

Monitoring Processors in Performance Monitor

From a Performance Monitor point of view, the emphasis is on seeing if the processors that are allocated to the server are busy enough to maximize performance but not so saturated as to create a bottleneck. The rule of thumb here is to see whether your processors are working at between 20% and 50%. If this usage is consistently above 80% to 95%, you should consider splitting off some of the workload or adding processors. Table 39.3 indicates some of the key Performance Monitor objects and counters for measuring processor utilization.

TABLE 39.3 Processor-Related Performance Objects and Counters

Performance Monitor Object	Description
`Processor: % Processor Time`	The rate at which bytes are received on the interface.
`System: Processor Queue Length`	The number of threads in the processor queue. A sustained processor queue of greater than two threads indicates a processor bottleneck.
`System: Threads`	The number of threads executing on the machine. A thread is the basic executable entity that can execute instructions in a processor.
`System: Context Switches`	The rate at which the processor and SQL Server has to change from executing on one thread to executing on another. This costs CPU resources.
`Processor: % Interrupt Time`	The percentage of time that the processor spends receiving and servicing hardware interrupts.
`Processor: Interrupts/sec`	The average number of hardware interrupts the processor is receiving and servicing.

The counters `System: % Total Processor Time`, `System: Processor Queue Length`, and `Processor: % Processor Time` are the most critical to watch. If the percentages are consistently high (above that 80% to 95% level), you need to identify which specific processes and threads are consuming so many CPU cycles. The ideal Windows setup is to run SQL Server on a standalone member server to the Windows domain. You should not install SQL Server on a primary domain controller (PDC) or backup domain controller (BDC) because the PDC and BDC run additional services that consume memory, CPU, and network resources.

Before you upgrade to the latest processor just because the `% Processor Time` counter is constantly high, you might want to check the load placed on the CPU by your other devices. By checking `Processor: % Interrupt Time` and `Processor: Interrupts/Sec`, you can tell whether the CPU is interrupted more than normal by devices such as disk controllers.

The `% Interrupt Time` value should be as close to `0` as possible; controller cards should handle any processing requirements.

The `System: Context Switches` counter can reveal when excessive context switching occurs, which usually directly affects overall performance. In addition, the `System: Threads` counter can give a good picture of the excessive demand on the CPU of having to service huge numbers of threads. In general, you should look at these counters only if processor queuing is happening.

By upgrading inefficient controllers to bus-mastering controllers, you can take some of the load from the CPU and put it back on the adapter. You should also keep the controller patched with the latest drivers from the hardware vendor.

Monitoring Processor Performance in SSMS

The Activity Monitor in SSMS provides some basic information on processor performance, such as the `% Processor Time` that SQL Server is consuming and a list of the current user connections into SQL Server.

If you've enabled the SQL Server Utility for your SQL Server instance, you can get a high-level view of CPU utilization on the CPU Utilization page of the Utility Explorer (see Figure 39.28). This view displays CPU utilization for the SQL Server instance and the overall CPU utilization for the server.

If you are collecting performance data into the MDW using the Data Collector for a SQL Server instance, you can view more detailed CPU utilization and CPU wait information in the Server Activity History report (refer to Figure 39.12). If you see high CPU utilization, you can click on the CPU Usage graph to drill down and examine the details of the top 10 processes consuming CPU resources.

If there is an indication of excessive CPU waits, you can click on the SQL Server Waits graph to drill down into the details regarding the queries experiencing high CPU waits.

Dynamic Management Views or System Views for Monitoring Processor Items

Within SQL Server, you can execute a simple `SELECT` statement that yields the SQL Server processes and their corresponding threads:

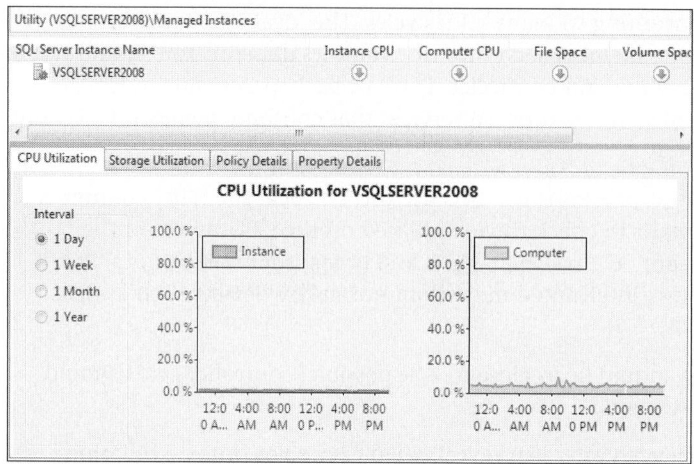

FIGURE 39.28 Viewing CPU utilization in the Utility Explorer.

```
SELECT top 10 spid, lastwaittype, dbid, uid, cpu, physical_io, memusage,status,
       loginame, program_name
from sys.sysprocesses
ORDER BY cpu desc
```

This statement lists the top 10 CPU resource hogs active in SQL Server. After you identify which processes are causing a burden on the CPU, you can check whether they can be either turned off or moved to a different server. If they cannot be turned off or moved, you might want to consider upgrading the processor. The same information is available via the new DMV:

```
SELECT top 10 session_id, command, database_id, user_id,
 cpu_time, reads,        writes, logical_reads
from sys.dm_exec_requests
order by cpu_time desc
```

Taking a peek at the SQL Server schedulers (using the `sys.dm_os_schedulers` DMV) also shows whether the number of runnable tasks is getting bogged down. If the `runnable_tasks_count` values are nonzero, there aren't enough CPU time slices available to run the current SQL Server workload. The following example shows how you query the `dm_os_schedulers` view for this information:

```
SELECT scheduler_id, current_tasks_count, runnable_tasks_count
FROM Sys.dm_os_schedulers
```

And finally, to get an idea of the top CPU hogs in SQL Server cached SQL and stored procedures, you can query the `sys.dm_exec_query_stats` DMV and aggregate on `total_worker_time` to get the total CPU consumption, as follows:

```
SELECT top 50 sum(total_worker_time) as Total_CPU,
              sum(execution_count) as Total_Count,
              count(*) as Total_Statements,
              plan_handle
FROM   sys.dm_exec_query_stats
GROUP BY plan_handle
Order by 1 desc
GO
```

To actually see the SQL code that is behind the `plan_handle`, you can execute the `dm_exec_sql_text` function to get your "hog" list:

```
SELECT total_worker_time, b.text
FROM sys.dm_exec_query_stats A
CROSS APPLY sys.dm_exec_sql_text (A.plan_handle) AS B
order by 1 desc
```

Monitoring Memory

Memory, like a processor, is divided into segments for each process running on the server. If there is a demand for more memory than is available, the operating system has to use virtual memory to supplement the physical memory. Virtual memory is storage allocated on the hard disk; it is named `PAGEFILE.SYS` under Windows.

It is important to remember that when the operating system or SQL Server isn't able to use memory to find something and has to use virtual memory stored on the disk, performance degrades. You need to work on minimizing this situation, known as *swapping* or *page faulting*.

Monitoring Memory with Performance Monitor

Table 39.4 reflects the main performance objects and counters that are best utilized to monitor memory for SQL Server.

TABLE 39.4 Memory-Related Performance Objects and Counters

Performance Monitor Object	Description
`Process: Working Set|sqlservr`	The set of memory pages touched recently by the threads in the process (SQL Server, in this case).
`SQLSERVER:Buffer Manager: Buffer cache hit ratio`	The percentage of pages that were found in the buffer pool without having to incur a read from disk.
`SQLSERVER:Buffer Manager: Total Pages`	The total number of pages in the buffer pool, including database pages, free pages, and stolen pages.
`SQLSERVER:Memory Manager: Total Server Memory(KB)`	The total amount of dynamic memory the server is currently consuming.
`SQLSERVER:Memory Manager: SQL Cache Memory(KB)`	The total amount of dynamic memory the SQL Server cache is currently consuming.

TABLE 39.4 Memory-Related Performance Objects and Counters

Performance Monitor Object	Description
`SQLSERVER:Plan Cache: Cache hit ratio`	The ratio between lookups and cache hits for query plans in the plan cache.
`SQLSERVER:Buffer Manager: Total Pages`	The total number of pages in the plan cache.
`Memory: Pages/sec`	The number of pages read from or written to disk to resolve hard page faults. This value usually gives a direct indication of memory issues.
`Memory: Pages Read/sec`	The number of times the disk was read to resolve hard page faults.
`Memory: Page Faults/sec`	The overall rate at which faulted pages are handled by the processor.
`Process: Page Faults/sec|sqlservr`	The rate of page faults occurring in the threads associated with a process (SQL Server, in this case).

To observe the level of the page faulting, you can look at the `Memory: Page Faults/sec` and `Process: Page Faults` (for a SQL Server instance) counters. Next in line are the `MSSQL Buffer Manager: Buffer Cache hit ratio` and `MSSQL Buffer Manager: Total Pages` counters. They directly indicate how well SQL Server is finding data in its controlled memory (cache). You want to achieve a near 90% or higher ratio here.

If the `Memory: Pages/sec` counter is greater than `0` or the `Memory: Page Reads/sec counter` is greater than `5`, the operating system is being forced to use the disk to resolve memory references. These are called *hard faults*. The `Memory: Pages/sec` counter is one of the best indicators of the amount of paging that Windows is doing and the adequacy of SQL Server's current memory configuration.

Because the memory used by SQL Server 2008 dynamically grows and shrinks, you might want to track the exact usage by using either `Process: Working Set: SQLServer` or `MSSQL: Memory Manager: Total Server Memory (KB)` counters. These counters indicate the current size of the memory used by the SQL Server process. If these numbers are consistently high, compared to the amount of physical memory in the machine, you are probably ready to install more memory on the server. If you see a performance degradation because SQL Server must continually grow and shrink its memory, you should either remove some of the other services or processes running or configure SQL Server to use a fixed memory allocation.

Monitoring Memory in SSMS

If you are collecting performance data into the MDW using the Data Collector for a SQL Server instance, you can view more detailed memory usage and memory wait information in the Server Activity History report (refer to Figure 39.12). You can click on the Memory Usage graph to drill down and examine the details of the total memory usage in SQL

Server and the cache and page ratios. It also displays a list of all processes in the server and the total working set size. You can use this information to see if other running processes may be using memory that should be left available for SQL Server.

DMVs or System Views for Monitoring Memory

The DMVs associated with memory are numerous. The ones you'll most likely utilize are memory clerks, memory pools, and cache counters.

You can find memory allocations by type by using the `sys.dm_os_memory_clerks` DMV view:

```
SELECT type, sum(multi_pages_kb) from sys.dm_os_memory_clerks
WHERE multi_pages_kb <> 0
GROUP BY type
order by 2 desc
```

To see how the cache is being used, you can query `sys.dm_os_memory_cache_counters`:

```
SELECT substring(name,1,25) AS Name, single_pages_kb,
       single_pages_in_use_kb
FROM sys.dm_os_memory_cache_counters
order by single_pages_kb desc
```

Finally, when you want to see the total pages allocated to the different objects in memory, you use the `sys.dm_os_memory_objects` DMV:

```
SELECT substring(type,1,25) as Type,
       sum(pages_allocated_count) as Total_Memory_Allocated
FROM sys.dm_os_memory_objects
group by type
order by 2 desc
```

Several new DMVs were introduced in SQL Server 2008 to simplify retrieval of information that can be helpful with memory troubleshooting. In some cases, the newly introduced DMVs provide information that was previously available only in `DBCC MEMORYSTATUS` output. Table 39.5 provides a summary of the new DMVs available for memory troubleshooting.

TABLE 39.5 New Memory-Related DMVs in SQL Server 2008

DMV	Description
`sys.dm_os_memory_brokers`	Provides information about memory allocations using the internal SQL Server memory manager. The information provided can be useful in determining very large memory consumers.

TABLE 39.5 New Memory-Related DMVs in SQL Server 2008

DMV	Description
sys.dm_os_memory_nodes and sys.dm_os_memory_node_access_stats	Provide information about physical nonuniform memory access (NUMA) memory nodes and node access statistics grouped by the type of the page. (sys.dm_os_memory_node_access_stats is populated only if dynamic trace flag 842 is enabled due to its performance impact.)
sys.dm_os_nodes	Provides information about CPU node configuration for SQL Server. This DMV also reflects software NUMA (soft-NUMA) configuration.
sys.dm_os_process_memory	Provides overview information about SQL Server memory usage, including the total physical memory in use and the memory utilization percentage
sys.dm_os_sys_memory	Provides overview information about the system memory usage including total physical memory on the system and the available physical memory.
sys.dm_resource_governor_configuration, sys.dm_resource_governor_resource_pools, and sys.dm_resource_governor_workload_groups	Provide information about the state of the Resource Governor feature of SQL Server 2008. Some of the configuration parameters of Resource Governor affect how SQL Server allocates memory; you should check these parameters during memory troubleshooting. For more information on using Resource Governor and its impact on memory allocation, see Chapter 40, "Managing Workloads with the Resource Governor."

Monitoring the Disk System

SQL Server performance depends heavily on the I/O subsystem. SQL Server is constantly reading pages from and writing pages to disk via the data cache. It is also constantly writing to disk via the transaction log. Focusing on the database data files, transaction log files, and especially tempdb can yield great performance for your SQL Server platform. Table 39.6 lists the essential performance objects and counters related to monitoring the disk system.

TABLE 39.6 Disk Usage-Related Performance Objects and Counters

Performance Monitor Object	Description
`Physical Disk: Current Disk Queue Length`	The number of outstanding requests (read/write) for a disk.
`Physical Disk: Avg. Disk Queue Length`	The average number of both read and write requests queued for disks.
`Physical Disk: Disk Read Bytes`	The rate at which bytes are transferred from the disk during read operations.
`Physical Disk: Disk Write Bytes`	The rate at which bytes are transferred to the disk during write operations.
`Physical Disk: % Disk Time`	The percentage of elapsed time that the selected disk drive is busy servicing read or write requests.
`Logical Disk: Current Disk Queue Length`	The number of outstanding requests (read/write) for a disk.
`Logical Disk: Avg. Disk Queue Length`	The average number of both read and write requests queued for disks.
`Logical Disk: Disk Read Bytes`	The rate at which bytes are transferred from the disk during read operations.
`Logical Disk: Disk Write Bytes`	The rate at which bytes are transferred to the disk during write operations.
`Logical Disk: % Disk Time`	The percentage of elapsed time that the selected disk drive is busy servicing read or write requests.

Slow disk I/O causes a reduction in the transaction throughput. To identify which disks are receiving all the attention, you should monitor both the `Physical Disk` and `Logical Disk` performance objects. You have many more opportunities to tune at the disk level than with other components, such as processors. This has long been the area where database administrators and system administrators have been able to get better performance. You can start by looking at the behavior of the `Physical Disk: Current Disk Queue Length` and `Physical Disk: Avg. Disk Queue Length` counters for all disks or for each particular disk. This way, you can identify where most of the activity is, from a disk-usage point of view.

As you monitor each individual disk, you might see that some drives are not as busy as others. You can relocate heavily used resources to minimize these long queue lengths that you have uncovered and spread out the disk activity. Common techniques for this are to relocate indexes away from tables, isolate read-only tables away from volatile tables, and so on. You need to take special care with `tempdb`. The best practice is to isolate it away from all other disk I/O processing.

The Physical Disk: % Disk Time counter for each physical disk drive shows the percentage of time that the disk is active; a continuously high value could indicate an underperforming disk subsystem.

Of course, the monitoring up to this point shows only half the picture if drives are partitioned into multiple logical drives. To see the work on each logical drive, you need to examine the logical disk counters; in fact, you can monitor read and write activity separately with Logical Disk: Disk Write Bytes/sec and Logical Disk: Disk Read Bytes/sec. You should be looking for average times below 20ms. If the averages are over 50ms, the disk subsystem is in serious need of replacement, reconfiguration, or redistribution.

If you use RAID, you need to know how many physical drives are in each RAID array to figure out the monitored values of disk queuing for any one disk. In general, you just divide the disk queue value by the number of physical drives in the disk array. This calculation gives you a fairly accurate number for each physical disk's queue length.

Monitoring SQL Server's Disk Activity

In the preceding section, we looked at monitoring overall disk activity. In this section, we examine what SQL Server's contribution is to all this disk activity. Disk activity can be categorized into reads and writes. SQL Server carries out writes to the disk for the following processes:

- Logging records
- Writing dirty cache pages at the end of a transaction
- Freeing space in the page cache

Logging is a constant occurrence in any database that allows modifications, and SQL Server attempts to optimize this process by batching a number of writes together. To see how much work is done on behalf of the database logs, you can examine the SQLServer:Databases:Log Bytes Flushed and SQLServer:Databases:Log Flushes/sec counters. The first tells you the quantity of the work, and the second tells you the frequency.

The third kind of write occurs to make space within the page cache. This is carried out by the Lazy Writer process, which you can track with the counter SQLServer:Buffer Manager:Lazy Writes.

You also can easily monitor the amount of reading SQL Server is doing by using the counter SQLServer:Buffer Manager:Page Reads.

Monitoring Disk Performance in SSMS

If you are collecting performance data into the MDW using the Data Collector for a SQL Server instance, you can view more detailed disk performance in the Server Activity History report (refer to Figure 39.12). You can click on the Disk Usage graph to drill down and examine the details on Disk Response Time, Average Disk Queue Length, and Disk

Transfer Rate. In addition, the System Disk Usage detail report also lists the top 20 processes with the highest I/O writes or highest I/O reads per second. This information can help you determine which processes besides SQL Server are performing a large number of disk reads and/or writes that could be affecting the I/O performance of SQL Server.

DMVs or System Views for Monitoring Disk System Items

There are several I/O-related DMVs and functions. They cover backup tape I/O, pending I/O requests, I/O on cluster shared drives, and virtual file I/O statistics.

The best of these is the `sys.dm_io_virtual_file_stats` function, which allows you to see the file activity within a database allocation. You supply the database ID as the first parameter, along with the file ID of the database file as the second parameter. This yields an accumulating set of statistics that can be used to isolate and characterize heavy I/O:

```
SELECT cast(db_name(database_id) as varchar(12)) as dbname,
       file_id,
       num_of_reads as numreads,
       num_of_bytes_read as bytesread,
       num_of_bytes_written as byteswritten,
       size_on_disk_bytes as size
FROM sys.dm_io_virtual_file_stats (5,1)
GO
dbname       file_id numreads bytesread byteswritten size
------------ ------- -------- --------- ------------ ----------
UnleashedMDW 1       7022     411140096 759291904    1048576000
```

In addition, the OS wait stats for I/O latch waits are great for identifying when reading or writing of a page is not available from the data cache. These latch waits account for the physical I/O waits when a page is accessed for reading or writing. When the page is not found in the cache, an asynchronous I/O gets posted. If there is any delay in the I/O, the `PAGEIOLATCH_EX` or `PAGEIOLATCH_SH` latch waits are affected. An increased number of latch waits indicates that an I/O bottleneck exists. The following query reveals this latch wait information:

```
SELECT substring(wait_type,1,15) AS Latch_Waits, waiting_tasks_count, wait_time_ms
FROM sys.dm_os_wait_stats
WHERE wait_type like 'PAGEIOLATCH%'
ORDER BY wait_type
GO
Latch_Waits     waiting_tasks_count  wait_time_ms
--------------- -------------------- --------------------
PAGEIOLATCH_DT  0                    0
PAGEIOLATCH_EX  2871                 61356
PAGEIOLATCH_KP  0                    0
PAGEIOLATCH_NL  0                    0
PAGEIOLATCH_SH  7305                 98120
PAGEIOLATCH_UP  1372                 7318
```

Monitoring Other SQL Server Performance Items

In addition to the main system items that affect performance which have been covered already, there are other items in SQL Server that affect system performance that you should include in your performance monitoring approach.

Monitoring Locks

One of the often-overlooked areas of performance degradation is locking. You need to ensure that the correct types of locks are issued and that the worst kind of lock, a blocking lock, is kept to a minimum. A *blocking lock*, as its name implies, prevents other users from continuing their own work. An easy way to identify the level of blocking locks is to use the counter `SQLServer:Memory Manager:Lock Blocks`. If this counter frequently indicates a value greater than `0`, you need to examine the queries being executed or even revisit the database design.

For a more detailed discussion on monitoring locking in SQL Server and minimizing locking contention, see Chapter 37, "Locking and Performance."

Monitoring Users

Even though you cannot always trace performance problems directly to the number of users connected, it is a good idea to occasionally monitor how this number fluctuates. It is fairly easy to trace one particular user who is causing a massive performance problem.

The leverage point here is to see the current number of user connections with the `SQLServer:General Statistics:User Connections` counter in conjunction with other objects and counters. It is easy to say that the disk subsystem is a bottleneck, but how many users is SQL Server supporting at the time?

Summary

Attacking SQL Server performance is not a simple task because so many variables are involved. Tuning queries and proper database design are a huge part of this, but dealing with SQL Server as an engine that consumes resources and the physical machine is equally important. This is why it is so critical to take an orderly, methodical approach when undertaking this task. As pointed out in this chapter, you need to basically peel apart the box on which SQL Server has been installed, one component at a time (network, CPU, memory, and disk). This way, you can explore the individual layer or component in a clear and concise manner. Within a short amount of time, you will be able to identify the biggest performance offenders and resolve them.

The next chapter, "Managing Workloads with Resource Governor," discusses the new feature in SQL Server 2008 that lets you control the allocation of resources to SQL Server sessions. This feature can help avoid situations in which a runaway query consumes excessive resources in SQL Server.

CHAPTER 40

Managing Workloads with the Resource Governor

IN THIS CHAPTER

- Overview of Resource Governor
- Resource Governor Components
- Configuring Resource Governor
- Monitoring Resource Usage
- Modifying Your Resource Governor Configuration

If you have ever had a user kick off a runaway report that brought the system to its knees, effectively halting your production online transaction processing (OLTP) activity, you might have wished for a mechanism in SQL Server that would limit the amount of hardware resources allocated to ad hoc reporting requests so that normal production activity was not affected. Such a mechanism could prevent certain processes from consuming too many of the available SQL Server resources, ensuring that your more critical, higher-priority processes would consistently have access to the resources they need.

Fortunately, SQL Server 2008 now provides such a mechanism: Resource Governor. Resource Governor allows you to classify different types of sessions on your server, which in turn allows you to control how server resources are assigned to a given activity. In SQL Server 2005 and earlier, queries fought among themselves to decide which one would grab the necessary resources first, and it was hard to predict who would win out. By using Resource Governor, you are able to instruct SQL Server to limit the resources a particular session can access. This capability can help ensure that your OLTP processes continue to provide predictable performance that isn't adversely affected by unpredictable activity. For example, with Resource Governor, you can specify that no more than 20% of CPU and/or memory resources should be allocated to running reports. When this feature is enabled, no matter how many reports are run, they can never exceed their designated resource allocation. Of course, this reduces the performance of the reports, but at least your production OLTP performance isn't as negatively affected by runaway reports anymore.

NOTE

Resource Governor is available only in the Enterprise, Datacenter, and Developer Editions of SQL Server 2008 and SQL Server 2008 R2.

Overview of Resource Governor

Resource Governor works by controlling the allocation of resources according to workloads. When a connection request is submitted to the Database Engine, the request is classified based on a classification function. The classification function is a scalar function that you define via T-SQL. The classification function evaluates information about the connection (for example, login ID, application name, hostname, server role) to determine how it should be classified. After the connection request is classified, it is routed to a workload group defined for that classification (or if the connection cannot be classified, it is routed to the default workload group). Each workload group is associated with a resource pool. A resource pool represents the physical resources of SQL Server (currently in SQL Server 2008, the only physical resources available for configuration are CPU and memory) and specifies the maximum amount of CPU and/or memory resources that are to be allocated to a specific type of workload. When a connection is classified and put into the correct workload group, the connection is allocated the CPU and memory resources assigned to it, and then the query is passed on to the query optimizer for execution. This process is illustrated in Figure 40.1.

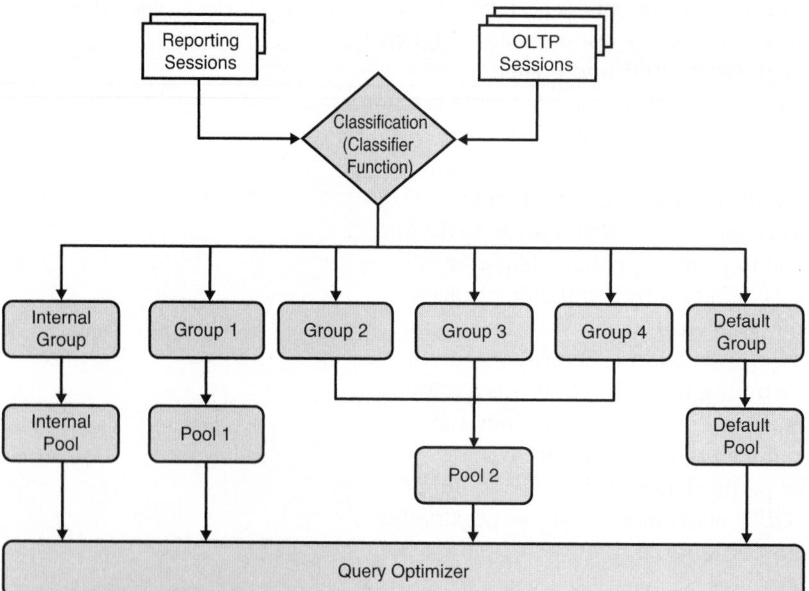

FIGURE 40.1 Overview of the Resource Governor.

Resource Governor is designed to address the following types of resource issues, which are commonly found in a database environment:

- **Runaway queries**—These resource-intensive queries can take up most or all of the server resources.
- **Unpredictable workload execution**—This situation occurs when you have concurrent applications on the same server that are not isolated from each other, and the resulting resource contention causes unpredictable performance.
- **Workload prioritization**—You might want to ensure that a critical workload is given priority to the system resources so it can process faster than other workloads or is guaranteed to complete if there is resource contention.

In addition to enabling you to classify incoming connections and route their workloads to a specific group, Resource Governor also enables you to do the following:

- Monitor resource usage for each workload in a group
- Pool resources and set pool-specific limits on CPU usage and memory allocation, which can prevent or minimize the probability of runaway queries
- Associate grouped workloads with a specific pool of resources
- Identify and set priorities for workloads

The current release of Resource Governor has the following limitations:

- Resource allocation is only for CPU and memory usage. There is no support for managing network and disk I/O resource utilization.
- Resource Governor manages only resource consumption of the Database Engine. You cannot use Resource Governor to manage workloads within SSAS, SSIS, or SSRS.

In the following sections, you learn how to set up and configure Resource Governor for use, how Resource Governor works under the hood, and how you can use Resource Governor to better prioritize and manage a SQL Server's workload.

Resource Governor Components

Resource Governor consists of three main components: classification, workload groups, and resource pools. Understanding these three components and how they interact is important to understanding and using Resource Governor.

Classification

Classification is the process of evaluating incoming user connections and assigning them to a workload group. Classification is performed by logic contained in a user-defined function. The function returns the workload group name, which Resource Governor uses to route the sessions into the appropriate workload groups.

When Resource Governor is configured, the login process for a session consists of the following steps:

1. Login authentication
2. LOGON trigger execution
3. Classification

Workload Groups

Workload groups are the containers for similar connections, which are grouped together as similar according to the classification criteria applied to each connection. A workload group also provides the mechanism for aggregate monitoring of resource consumption.

Resource Governor has two predefined workload groups: the internal group and default group. The internal workload group is used solely by internal Database Engine processes. You cannot change the classification criteria for the internal group, and you also cannot classify any user requests for assignment to the internal group. You can, however, monitor the internal group.

Connection requests are automatically classified into the default group when the following conditions exist:

- There are no criteria to classify a request.
- There is an attempt to classify the request into a nonexistent group.
- There is a general classification failure.

Resource governor supports a total of 20 workload groups. Because two of them are reserved for the internal and default workload groups, a total of 18 user-defined workload groups can be defined.

Resource Pools

A *resource pool*, or *pool*, represents the allocation of physical resources of the SQL Server. A resource pool has two parts:

- The first part specifies the minimum resource reservation. This part of the resource pool does not overlap with other pools.
- The other part specifies the maximum possible resource reservation for the pool. The resource allocation is shared with other pools.

In SQL Server 2008 and SQL Server 2008 R2, the pool resources are set by specifying a `MIN` or `MAX` allocation for CPU and a `MIN` or `MAX` allocation for memory. The `MIN` setting specifies the minimum guaranteed resource availability of the pool. The `MAX` setting sets the maximum size of the pool for each of the resources.

Because there cannot be any overlap in the minimum resource reservation, the sum of the `MIN` values across all pools cannot exceed 100% of the total server resources. The ensures that each pool is guaranteed the specified resource allocation.

The MAX value can be set anywhere in the range between the MIN value and 100% inclusive. The MAX setting represents the maximum amount of resources a session can consume, as long as the resources are available and not in use by another pool that is configured with a nonzero MIN value. When a pool has a nonzero MIN percentage defined, the effective MAX value of other pools is readjusted down, as necessary, to the existing MAX value minus the sum total of the MIN values of other pools.

For example, consider you have two user-defined pools. One pool, Pool1, is defined with a MIN setting of 20% and a MAX setting of 100%. The other pool, Pool2, is defined with a MIN setting of 50% and a MAX setting of 70%. The resulting effective MAX setting for Pool1 is 50% (100% minus the MIN 50% of Pool2). The effective MAX setting of Pool2, however, remains at 70% rather than 80% because 70% is the configured MAX value of Pool2.

The shared part of the pool (the amount between the MIN and effective MAX values) is used to determine the amount of resources that can be consumed by the pool if the resources are available and not being consumed by another pool. When resources are consumed by a pool, they are assigned to the specified pool and are not shared until processing completes in that pool.

To illustrate this further, consider a scenario in which there are three user-defined resource pools:

- PoolA is defined with a MIN % of 10 and MAX % of 100.
- PoolB is defined with a MIN % of 35 and a MAX % of 90.
- PoolC is defined with a MIN % of 30 and a MAX % of 80.

The effective MAX of PoolA would be calculated as follows:

MAX % of PoolA	100
minus MIN % of PoolB	35
minus MIN % of PoolC	30
equals EFF MAX of PoolA	35

The total Shared % of resources of PoolA would then be calculated as follows:

Effective MAX % of PoolA	35
minus MIN % of PoolA	10
equals Shared % of PoolA	25

Table 40.1 illustrates the calculated effective MAX and Shared % values for all pools in this configuration.

TABLE 40-1 Effective **MAX** and **Shared** % Values for Multiple Pools

ResourcePool	MIN %	MAX %	**Effective** MAX %	Shared %
Internal	0	100	100	100
Default	0	100	25	25
PoolA	10	100	35	25
PoolB	35	90	50	15
PoolC	30	80	35	5

To coincide with the predefined workload groups, Resource Governor also has two predefined resource pools: the internal pool and default pool.

The internal pool represents the resources consumed by the internal processes of the Database Engine. This pool always contains only the internal group, and the pool is not alterable in any way. The Internal Pool has a fixed `MIN %` of 0 and a `MAX %` of 100, and resource consumption by the internal pool is not restricted or reduced by any settings in other pools. In other words, the effective `MAX` of the Internal Pool is always 100%. Any workloads in the internal pool are considered critical for server function, and Resource Governor allows the internal pool to consume 100% of available resources if necessary, even if it means the violation of the resource requirements of the other pools.

The default pool is the first predefined user pool. Prior to any configuration, the default pool contains only the default group. The default pool cannot be created or dropped, but it can be altered. The default pool can contain user-defined groups in addition to the default group.

Now that you have an understanding of the Resource Governor components, let's put them into use by enabling and setting up some resource groups.

Configuring Resource Governor

To begin using Resource Governor for managing the resources of your workloads, follow these steps:

1. Enable Resource Governor.
2. Create your user-defined resource pools.
3. Define your workload groups and assign them to pools.
4. Create the classifier function.
5. Register the classifier function with the Resource Governor.

NOTE

Resource Governor can be set up and managed using either SQL Server Management Studio (SSMS) or via T-SQL commands. In the following sections, we first show you how to perform the tasks in SSMS and how the same actions can be implemented using T-SQL.

Enabling Resource Governor

Before you can begin creating your resource pools, you need to enable the Resource Governor first. To enable Resource Governor in SSMS, in Object Explorer, expand the `Management` node, right-click on the `Resource Governor` node, and select Enable (see Figure 40.2).

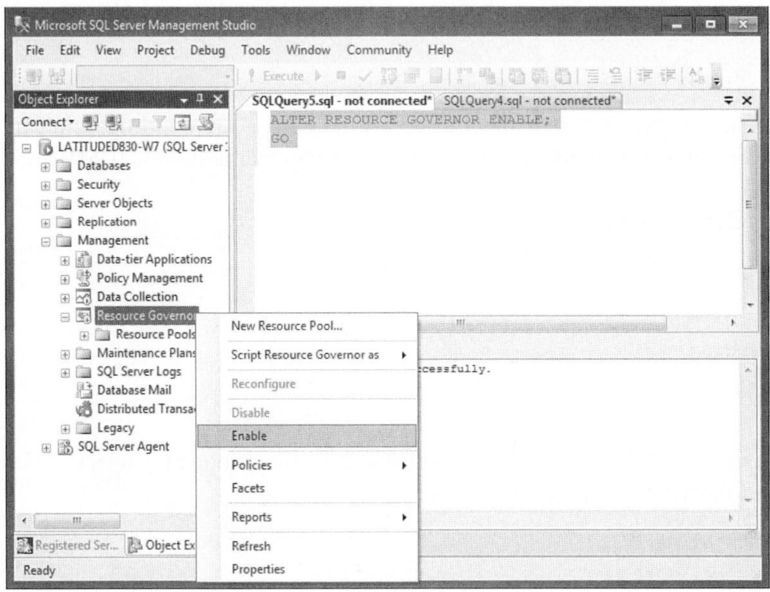

FIGURE 40.2 Enabling Resource Governor in SSMS.

Alternatively, you can also enable Resource Governor by using the `ALTER RESOURCE GOVERNOR` command in T-SQL:

```
ALTER RESOURCE GOVERNOR RECONFIGURE
```

When Resource Governor is not enabled, the `RECONFIGURE` option enables Resource Governor. Enabling Resource Governor has the following results:

- The classifier function, if defined, is executed for new connections so that their workload can be assigned to workload groups.
- The resource limits specified in the Resource Governor configuration are honored and enforced.
- Any connections that existed before Resource Governor was enabled are now affected by any configuration changes made when Resource Governor was disabled.

When Resource Governor is already enabled, the `RECONFIGURE` option must be executed to apply any configuration changes made using the `CREATE|ALTER|DROP WORKLOAD GROUP` or `CREATE|ALTER|DROP RESOURCE POOL` statements.

To determine whether Resource Governor is currently enabled, you can run a `SELECT` statement against the `sys.resource_governor_configuration` system catalog table to view the `is_enabled` column:

```
select is_enabled from sys.resource_governor_configuration
go

is_enabled
----------
1
```

To determine whether any `RESOURCE GOVERNOR` configuration changes are pending, you can use the `sys.dm_resource_governor_configuration` dynamic management view (DMV):

```
select is_reconfiguration_pending
    from sys.dm_resource_governor_configuration
go

is_reconfiguration_pending
----------------------------
0
```

To disable Resource Governor, right-click on the `Resource Governor` node and select Disable or execute the following command in T-SQL:

```
ALTER RESOURCE GOVERNOR DISABLE
```

Defining Resource Pools

When setting up a Resource Pool, you have to specify a name for the pool and set its properties. The properties available for a resource pool are

- **`Name`**—The name used to refer to the resource pool
- **`Minimum CPU %`**—The guaranteed average CPU bandwidth for all requests to the resource pool *when there is CPU contention*
- **`Maximum CPU %`**—The maximum average CPU bandwidth for all requests to the resource pool *when there is CPU contention*
- **`Min Memory %`**—The guaranteed minimum amount of memory reserved for the resource pool that *cannot be shared with other resource pools*
- **`Max Memory %`**—The total server memory that can be used by requests to the resource pool

Creating a Resource Pool in SSMS

The following steps walk you through using SSMS to create a resource pool named `ReportPool` that you'll configure for handling report query workloads:

1. In Object Explorer, expand the `Management` node for a SQL Server Instance and expand the `Resource Governor` node.
2. Right-click on Resource Pools and select New Resource Pool to open the Resource Governor Properties page (see Figure 40.3).

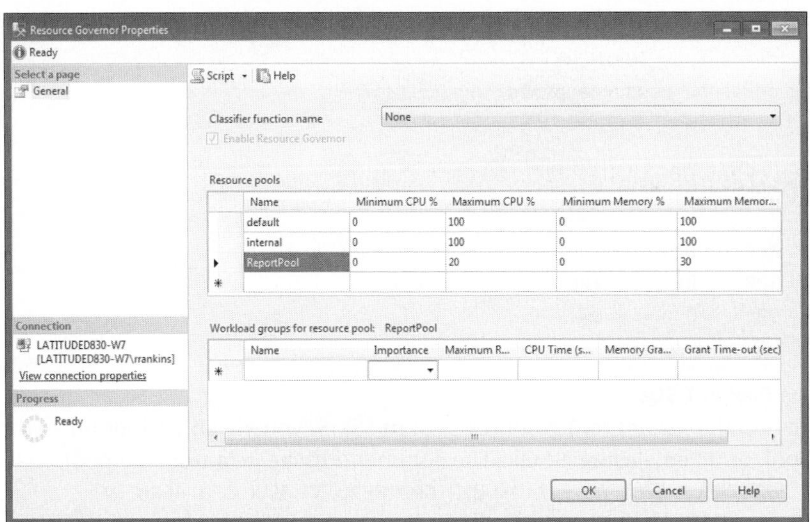

FIGURE 40.3 Creating a resource pool in SSMS.

3. In the Resource Pools grid, click the first column in the empty row. This row is labeled with an asterisk (*).

NOTE

If the Resource Pools grid does not have a row labeled with an asterisk, Resource Governor has not been enabled yet. You can enable Resource Governor without leaving the Resource Governor Properties page by putting a check mark in the Enable Resource Governor check box.

4. Double-click the empty cell in the `Name` column. Type in the name that you want to use for the resource pool. For this example, use the name `ReportPool`.
5. Set the CPU and Memory resource values. In this example, leave the `Min CPU %` and `Min Memory %` values at 0 and configure the `Max CPU %` and `Max Memory %` values at 20 and 30, respectively.
6. To create the pool and exit the dialog, click OK.

To verify that the new pool was created, you expand the `Resource Pools` folder under the `Resource Governor` node and look for a node named `ReportPool`. Alternatively, you can run a query against the `sys.resource_governor_resource_pools` dynamic management view, similar to the following, which also displays the resource pool configuration:

```
select name,
       min_cpu_percent as MinCPU,
       max_cpu_percent as MaxCPU,
       min_memory_percent as 'MinMEM%' ,
       max_memory_percent as 'MaxMEM%'
from sys.resource_governor_resource_pools
go

name       MinCPU MaxCPU MinMEM% MaxMEM%
---------- ------ ------ ------- -------
internal   0      100    0       100
default    0      100    0       100
ReportPool 0      20     0       30
```

Creating a Resource Pool in T-SQL

Now that you've set up the `ReportPool` resource pool in SSMS, you are able to set up a second resource pool, `OLTPPool`, using T-SQL. The command to create a resource pool, `CREATE RESOURCE POOL`, takes four arguments: `MIN_CPU_PERCENT`, `MAX_CPU_PERCENT`, `MIN_MEMORY_PERCENT`, and `MAX_MEMORY_PERCENT`. After creating the resource pool, you need to run `ALTER RESOURCE GOVERNOR RECONFIGURE` to apply the new resource pool:

```
CREATE RESOURCE POOL OLTPPool
   WITH
         (min_cpu_percent=80,
          max_cpu_percent=100,
          min_memory_percent=75,
          max_memory_percent=100)
GO
ALTER RESOURCE GOVERNOR RECONFIGURE;
GO
```

Now that you've defined the resource pools needed, the next step is to define your workload groups and associate them with a resource pool.

Defining Workload Groups

After you define your resource pools, the next step is to create the workload groups and associate them with the appropriate resource pools. Multiple workgroups can be assigned to that same pool, but a workgroup cannot be assigned to multiple resource pools.

Creating Workload Groups in SSMS

To create a workload group in SSMS, perform the following steps:.

1. In Object Explorer, expand the `Management` node, right-click `the Resource Governor node`, and then click Properties to bring up the Resource Governor Properties page.
2. In the Resource Pools grid, click the row for the resource pool you want to create a `workload group` for (in this example, the `ReportPool` resource pool). This creates a new empty row in the Workload Groups for Resource Pool grid for that pool.
3. Double-click the empty cell in the `Name` column for the empty workload group row and type in the name you want to use for the workload group (for this example, `ReportWG1`) and any other properties you want to specify (see Figure 40.4)

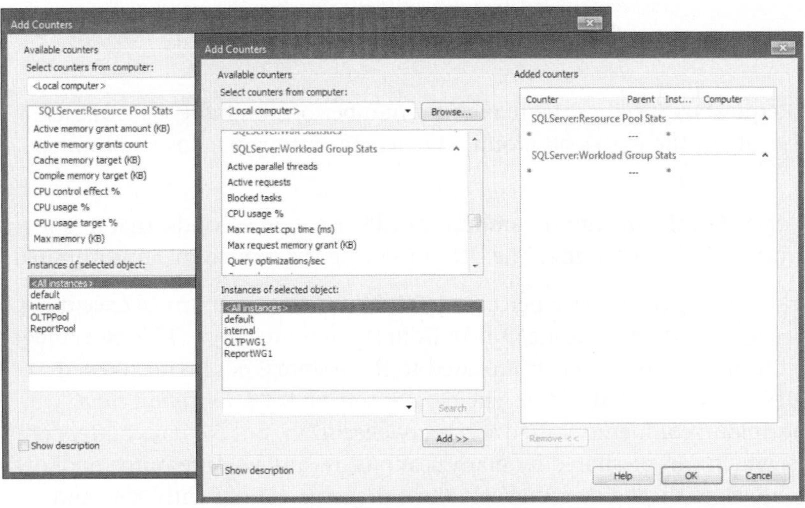

FIGURE 40.4 Creating a Workload Group in SSMS.

4. Click OK to exit the Properties page and create the workload group.

The additional, optional properties available for workload groups let you set a finer level of control over the execution of queries within a workload group. The options available are

- **Importance**—Specifies the relative importance (`LOW`, `MEDIUM`, or `HIGH`) of the workload group within the resource pool. If you define multiple workload groups in a resource pool, this setting determines whether requests within one workload group run at a higher or lower priority than other workload groups within the same resource pool. MEDIUM is the default setting. Currently, the weighting factors for each setting is LOW=1, MEDIUM=3, and HIGH=9. This means that the scheduler will attempt to execute sessions in workgroups with importance of HIGH three times more often than workgroups with MEDIUM importance, and nine times more often workgroups with LOW importance.

NOTE

Try to avoid having too many sessions in groups with high importance or assigning high importance to too many groups because the sessions will likely end up getting only equal time on the scheduler as your medium and low priority sessions.

- **Maximum Requests**—Specifies the maximum number of simultaneous requests allowed to execute in the workload group. The default setting, 0, allows unlimited requests.
- **CPU Time**—Specifies the maximum amount of CPU time, in seconds, that a request within the workload group can use. The default setting is 0, which means unlimited.
- **Memory Grant %**—Specifies, as a percentage, the maximum amount of execution grant memory that a single request can take from the resource pool. This percentage is relative to the amount of memory allocated to the resource pool. The allowed range of values is from 0 through 100. The default setting is 25. *Execution grant memory* is the amount of memory used for query execution, not for data buffers or cached plans, which can be shared by many sessions, regardless of resource pool or workload group. Note that setting this value to 0 prevents queries with SORT and HASH JOIN operations in user-defined workload groups from running. It is also not recommended that this value be set greater than 70 because the server may be unable to set aside enough free memory if other concurrent queries are running.
- **Grant Time-out**—Specifies the maximum time, in seconds, that a query waits for a resource to become available. If the resource does not become available, the process may fail with a time-out error. Note that a query does not always fail when the grant time-out is reached. A query fails only if there are too many concurrent queries running. Otherwise, the query may run with reduced resources, resulting in reduced query performance. The default setting is 0, which means the server calculates the time-out using an internal calculation based on query cost to determine the maximum time.
- **Degree of Parallelism**—Specifies the maximum degree of parallelism (DOP) for parallel queries. This values takes precedence over the global max degree of parallelism configuration setting, as well as any query hints. The allowed range of values is from 0 through 64. The default setting is 0, which means that processes use the global setting. Be aware that MAX_DOP specifies an upper limit only. The actual degree

of parallelism is determined by the server based on the actual number of schedulers and available number of parallel threads, which may be less than the specified MAX_DOP. To better understand how the MAX_DOP setting is handled, consider the following:

- MAX_DOP as a query hint is considered only if it does not exceed the workload group MAX_DOP setting.
- MAX_DOP as a query hint always overrides the max degree of parallelism server configuration option.
- Workload group MAX_DOP always overrides the max degree of parallelism server configuration option
- If a query is marked as serial at compile time, it cannot be changed back to parallel at runtime regardless of the workload group or server configuration setting.
- When the degree of parallelism is decided, it can be lowered only when memory pressure occurs. Workload group reconfiguration is not seen for tasks already waiting in the grant memory queue.

To verify that the new workload group was created, in SSMS Object Explorer, expand the Resource Governor node, expand the Resource Pools folder, expand the ReportPool node, and finally, expand the Workload Groups folder. You should then see a folder named ReportWG1.

Creating Workload Groups in T-SQL

Now that you've set up the ReportWG1 workload group in SSMS, you are able to set up a second workload group, OLTPWG1, using T-SQL. The command to create a resource pool, CREATE RESOURCE POOL, takes five optional arguments: REQUEST_MAX_MEMORY_GRANT_PERCENT, REQUEST_MAX_CPU_TIME_SEC, GROUP_MAX_REQUESTS, REQUEST_MEMORY_GRANT_TIMEOUT_SEC, and MAX_DOP, which were described in the preceding section.

```
CREATE WORKLOAD GROUP OLTPWG1
    WITH ( IMPORTANCE  = HIGH )
    USING OLTPPool
ALTER RESOURCE GOVERNOR RECONFIGURE
GO
```

To view the workload groups in T-SQL, you can run a query against the sys.resource_governor_workload_groups system catalog view, similar to the following, which also displays the workload group settings:

```
select wg.name,
       p.name as 'pool',
       group_max_requests as max_req,
       request_max_cpu_time_sec as max_cpu,
       request_max_memory_grant_percent as max_mem,
```

```
        request_memory_grant_timeout_sec as grant_timeout,
        max_dop
 from sys.resource_governor_workload_groups wg
         inner join
       sys.resource_governor_resource_pools p
         on wg.pool_id = p.pool_id
go

name      pool       max_req max_cpu max_mem grant_timeout max_dop
--------- ---------- ------- ------- ------- ------------- -------
internal  internal   0       0       25      0             0
default   default    0       0       25      0             0
ReportWG1 ReportPool 0       0       25      0             0
OLTPWG1   OLTPPool   0       0       25      0             0
```

Creating a Classification Function

After you define your resource pools and workload groups, you need to create a classification function that contains the logic to evaluate the connections and assign them to the appropriate workload group. The classification function applies to each new session connection to SQL Server. Each session stays in the assigned workload group until it terminates, unless is it reassigned explicitly to a different group. There can be only one classification function active at any given time. If no classifier function is defined or active, all connections are assigned to the default workload group.

The classification function is a scalar function created with the `CREATE FUNCTION` statement, which must return a workgroup name as value of type `SYSNAME` (`SYSNAME` is a data type alias for `nvarchar(128)`). If the user-defined function returns `NULL`, `'default'`, or the name of nonexistent group, the session is assigned to the default workload group. The session is also assigned to the default context if the function fails for any reason.

The logic of the classification function is typically based on connection properties and often determines the `workload_group` the connection should be assigned to based on values returned by system functions such as `SUSER_NAME()`, `SUSER_SNAME()`, `IS_SRVROLEMEMBER()`, `IS_MEMBER()`, `HOST_NAME()`, or `APP_NAME()`.In addition to these functions, you can use other available property functions when making classification decisions. The `LOGINPROPERTY()` function now includes two properties (`DefaultDatabase` and `DefaultLanguage`) that can be used in classification functions. In addition, the `CONNECTIONPROPERTY()` function provides access to the network transport and protocol being used for the connection, as well as details of the authentication scheme, the local IP address and TCP port, and the client's IP address. For example, you could assign a connection to a workload group based on which subnet a connection is coming in from.

TIP

If you decide to use either HOST_NAME() or APP_NAME() in your classifier function, be aware that it's possible for the values returned by these functions to be altered by users. In general, however, the APP_NAME() function tends to work very well for classifying connections.

TIP

A client session may time out if the classification function does not complete within the specified time-out for the login. Login time-out is a client property, and as such, the server is unaware of a time-out. A long-running classifier function can leave the server with orphaned connections for long periods. It is important that you create efficient classifier functions that finish execution before a connection time-out.

If you are using the Resource Governor, it is recommended that you enable the dedicated administrator connection (DAC) on the server. The DAC is not subject to Resource Governor classification and can be used to monitor and troubleshoot a classification function.

For simplicity, the example presented in this chapter uses the SUSER_NAME() function. Listing 40.1 first creates a couple of SQL Server logins (report_user and oltp_user), which will be used within the classification function to identify which workload group session connections should be assigned to. After adding the logins as users in the AdventureWorks2008R2 database, it then creates the classification function in the master database.

LISTING 40.1 Classification Function Example

```
use master;
create login report_user with password='Rep0rter1'
create login oltp_user with password='01tPus3r1'
go

use AdventureWorks2008R2;
create user report_user
create user oltp_user
EXEC sp_addrolemember N'db_datawriter', N'report_user'
EXEC sp_addrolemember N'db_datareader', N'report_user'
EXEC sp_addrolemember N'db_datawriter', N'oltp_user'
EXEC sp_addrolemember N'db_datareader', N'oltp_user'
go
```

```
use master
go
CREATE FUNCTION dbo.WorkgroupClassifier ()
  RETURNS SYSNAME WITH SCHEMABINDING
AS
BEGIN
  DECLARE @WorkloadGroup SYSNAME = N'Unidentified';
  SET @WorkloadGroup = CASE suser_name()
    WHEN N'report_user' THEN
      N'ReportWG1'
    WHEN N'oltp_user' THEN
      N'OLTPWG1'
    ELSE N'Unidentified'
  END;
  RETURN @WorkloadGroup;
END;
Go
GRANT EXECUTE on dbo.WorkgroupClassifier to public
go
```

Before you put the classification function into use, it's a good idea to test it. A poorly written classification function could cause your system to become unresponsive. For example, you can test the `WorkgroupClassifier()` function in SSMS by executing the following commands under different login IDs:

```
-- Executed logged in as report_user
select dbo.WorkgroupClassifier()
go
---------
ReportWG1
-- Executed logged in as report_user
select dbo.WorkgroupClassifier()
go
---------
OLTPWG1
-- Executed Logged in as another user
select dbo.WorkgroupClassifier()
go
------------------------
Unidentified
```

After you verify the classification function works as expected, you can then configure it as the classification function using the `ALTER RESOURCE GOVERNOR` command:

```
ALTER RESOURCE GOVERNOR
  WITH (CLASSIFIER_FUNCTION = dbo.WorkgroupClassifier);
ALTER RESOURCE GOVERNOR RECONFIGURE;
```

After you create the function and apply the configuration changes, the Resource Governor classifier will use the workload group name returned by the function to send new requests to the appropriate workload group.

NOTE

You can also set the classification function for Resource Governor on the Resource Governor Properties page, as shown in Figure 40.4. Click the Classifier Function Name drop-down list and choose from the list of available functions presented. Click OK to save the changes and reconfigure Resource Governor.

You can verify which classification function Resource Governor is currently using by running the following query against the `sys.resource_governor_configuration` system catalog view:

```
select object_name(classifier_function_id) AS 'Classifier UDF name',
    is_enabled
from sys.resource_governor_configuration
go

Classifier UDF name  is_enabled
-------------------- ----------
WorkgroupClassifier  1
```

At this point, your Resource Governor configuration is complete. You then should monitor the system to make sure it's working as it should.

TIP

To help make setting up and configuring Resource Governor easy and make sure you get all the pieces together in the right sequence, you can configure Resource Governor by using a template provided in SQL Server Management Studio. From the View menu in SSMS, select Template Explorer to display the Template Explorer. In the Template Explorer, expand Resource Governor and then double-click Configure Resource Governor. Provide the connection information, and the template `Configure Resource Governor.sql` opens in a query editor window. This template contains template code to create and configure a resource pool, workload group, and classifier function.

Monitoring Resource Usage

SQL Server provides three dynamic management views you can use to view and monitor your Resource Governor configuration:

- **`sys.dm_resource_governor_workload_groups`**—Returns workload group statistics along with the current in-memory configuration of the workload groups.

- **sys.dm_resource_governor_resource_pools**—Returns information about current state of your resource pools and resource pool statistics.
- **sys.dm_resource_governor_configuration**—Returns the in-memory configuration state of the Resource Governor. Output is the same as the `sys.resource_governor_configuration` system catalog view.

For example, the following query against the `sys.dm_resource_governor_resource_pools` DMV returns the configuration settings for each of the pools along with the actual memory allocated:

```
select name,
       min_cpu_percent as MinCPU,
       max_cpu_percent as MaxCPU,
       min_memory_percent as 'MinMEM%' ,
       max_memory_percent as 'MaxMEM%',
       max_memory_kb as 'MaxMemKB',
       used_memory_kb as 'UsedMemKB',
       target_memory_kb as 'TgtMemKB'
 from sys.dm_resource_governor_resource_pools
GO

name       MinCPU MaxCPU MinMEM% MaxMEM% MaxMemKB UsedMemKB TgtMemKB
---------- ------ ------ ------- ------- -------- --------- --------
internal   0      100    0       100     1556232  8296      1556232
default    0      100    0       100     389064   8336      389064
ReportPool 0      20     0       30      389064   280       389064
OLTPPool   80     100    75      100     1556232  40        1556232
```

The following example displays statistics on the requests received within the defined workgroups:

```
select
    cast(g.name as nvarchar(10)) as wg_name,
    cast(p.name as nvarchar(10)) as pool_name,
    total_request_count as totreqcnt,
    active_request_count as actreqcnt,
    g.total_cpu_usage_ms as tot_cpu_use,
    total_cpu_limit_violation_count as tot_clvc,
    g.request_max_cpu_time_sec as req_mcts,
    g.total_reduced_memgrant_count as tot_rmc
 from sys.dm_resource_governor_workload_groups g
    inner join
    sys.dm_resource_governor_resource_pools p
    on p.pool_id = g.pool_id
go
```

```
wg_name   pool_name  totreqcnt actreqcnt tot_cpu_use tot_clvc req_mcts tot_rmc
--------- ---------- --------- --------- ----------- -------- -------- -------
internal  internal   0         0         37314       0        0        0
default   default    784       2         97938       0        0        0
ReportWG1 ReportPool 170       1         476016      0        0        0
OLTPWG1   OLTPPool   161       0         1834        0        0        0
```

Six other DMVs in SQL Server 2008 contain information related to Resource Governor:

- **sys.dm_exec_query_memory_grants**—Returns information about the queries that have acquired a memory grant or that still require a memory grant to execute. Resource Governor–related columns in this table are the `group_id`, `pool_id`, `is_small`, and `ideal_memory_kb` columns.
- **sys.dm_exec_query_resource_semaphores**—Returns information about the current `query_resource` semaphore status, providing general query-execution memory status information. The `pool_id` column provides a link to Resource Governor information.
- **sys.dm_exec_session**—Returns one row per session on SQL Server. The `group_id` column relates the information to Resource Governor workload groups.
- **sys.dm_exec_requests**—Returns information about each request currently executing within SQL Server. The `group_id` column relates the information to Resource Governor workload groups.
- **sys.dm_exec_cached_plans**—Returns a row for each query plan cached by SQL Server in the plan cache. The `pool_id` column relates the information to Resource Governor resource pools.
- **sys.dm_os_memory_brokers**—Returns information about internal allocations within SQL Server that use the Memory Manager. This information includes the following columns for the Resource Governor: `pool_id`, `allocations_db_per_sec`, `predicted_allocations_kb`, and `overall_limit_kb`.

The following query joins between `sys.dm_exec_session` and `sys.dm_resource_governor_workload_groups` to display which sessions are in which workload group:

```
SELECT
    CAST(g.name as nvarchar(10)) as poolname,
    s.session_id as 'session',
    s.login_time,
    CAST(s.host_name as nvarchar(15)) as host_name,
    CAST(s.program_name AS nvarchar(20)) as program_name
          FROM sys.dm_exec_sessions s
     INNER JOIN sys.dm_resource_governor_workload_groups g
          ON g.group_id = s.group_id
where g.name in ('default', 'ReportWG1', 'OLTPWG1')
```

40

```
go
poolname   session login_time              host_name         program_name
---------- ------- ----------------------- ---------------- --------------------
default    51      2010-05-02 14:31:18.530 LATITUDED830-W7 Microsoft SQL Server
default    52      2010-05-02 14:31:21.990 LATITUDED830-W7 SQLAgent - Generic R
default    53      2010-05-02 14:31:23.533 LATITUDED830-W7 SQLAgent - TSQL JobS
default    55      2010-05-02 14:47:27.250 LATITUDED830-W7 Microsoft SQL Server
ReportWG1  60      2010-05-02 19:06:21.100 LATITUDED830-W7 Microsoft SQL Server
OLTPWG1    54      2010-05-02 21:03:03.020 LATITUDED830-W7 Microsoft SQL Server
```

You can also monitor CPU and memory resources allocated by the Resource Governor through the Windows Performance Monitor via a couple of new performance counters:

- `SQLServer: Resource Pool Stats`
- `SQLServer: Workload Stats`

An instance of the `SQLServer: Resource Pool Stats` counter is available for each of the configured resource pools. Likewise, an instance of the `SQLServer: Workload Stats` counter is available for each of the configured workload groups (see Figure 40.5). These performance counters return the same information as that returned by the `sys.dm_resource_governor_workload_groups` and `sys.dm_resource_governor_resource_pools` DMVs but enable you to monitor these statistics over time.

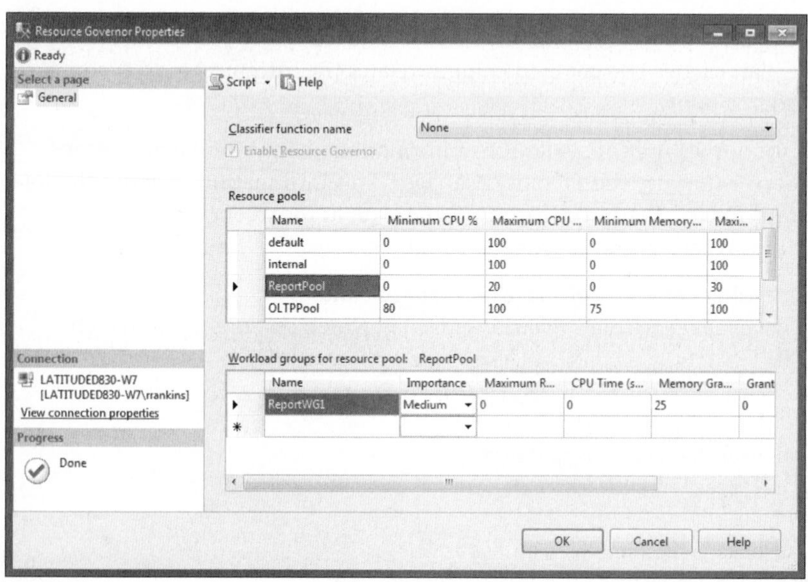

FIGURE 40.5 Monitoring resource pool and workload group statistics in Performance Monitor.

Modifying Your Resource Governor Configuration

You can modify settings for resource pools or workload groups in SQL Server Management Studio via the Resource Governor Properties page, as shown previously in Figure 40.4. You simply make the changes desired (for example, a Resource Pool Maximum CPU% or Workload Group Importance) and click OK to save the changes.

Alternatively, you can modify the resource pool using the `ALTER RESOURCE POOL` command. With this command, you can modify the minimum and maximum CPU and memory percentages for a resource pool. The syntax is as follows:

```
ALTER RESOURCE POOL { pool_name | "default" }
[WITH
          ( [ MIN_CPU_PERCENT = value ]
     [ [ , ] MAX_CPU_PERCENT = value ]
     [ [ , ] MIN_MEMORY_PERCENT = value ]
     [ [ , ] MAX_MEMORY_PERCENT = value ] )
]
```

You can modify workload group settings using the `ALTER WORKLOAD GROUP` command. You can change the workload group settings as well as move the workload group to another resource pool. The syntax is as follows:

```
ALTER WORKLOAD GROUP { group_name | "default" }
[ WITH
    ([ IMPORTANCE = { LOW | MEDIUM | HIGH } ]
           [ [ , ] REQUEST_MAX_MEMORY_GRANT_PERCENT = value ]
           [ [ , ] REQUEST_MAX_CPU_TIME_SEC = value ]
           [ [ , ] REQUEST_MEMORY_GRANT_TIMEOUT_SEC = value ]
           [ [ , ] MAX_DOP = value ]
           [ [ , ] GROUP_MAX_REQUESTS = value ] )
 ]
[ USING { pool_name | "default" } ]
```

NOTE

After executing your `ALTER WORKLOAD GROUP` or `ALTER RESOURCE POOL` commands, you need to run the `ALTER RESOURCE GOVERNOR RECONFIGURE` command to apply the changes.

40

The following example moves the `ReportWG1` workload group from the `ReportPool` resource pool to the default resource pool:

```
ALTER WORKLOAD GROUP ReportWG1
USING [default];
GO
```

```
ALTER RESOURCE GOVERNOR RECONFIGURE
GO
```

You can also move a workload group to another resource pool in SSMS using the Resource Governor Properties page. Click the Resource Pool name in the Resource Pools grid; then right-click on Workload Group in the Workload Groups grid and select Move To (see Figure 40.6). This brings up the Move Workload Group dialog, which lists the available resource pools the workload group can be moved to. Select the desired resource pool and click OK.

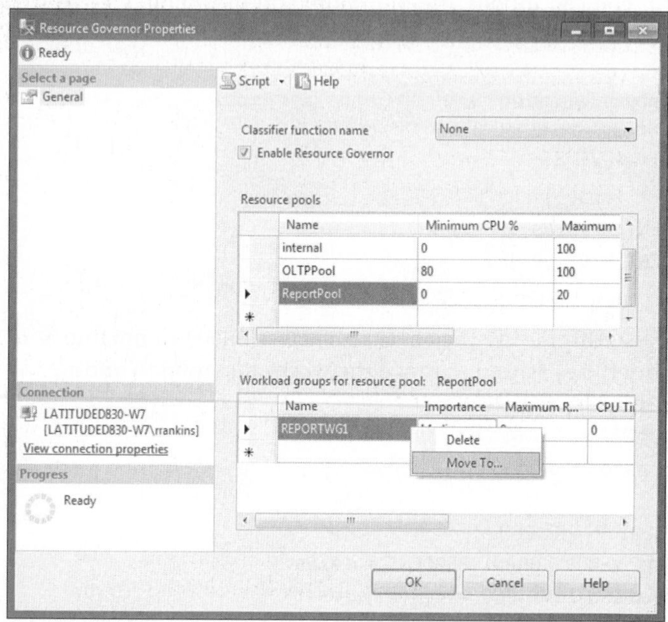

FIGURE 40.6 Moving a workload group in SSMS.

Why move a workload group to a different resource pool? You might decide that a workload group should be in a resource pool that has different configuration settings, or you might want to move workload groups out of a resource pool so that you can drop the resource pool.

Deleting Workload Groups

You can delete a workload group or resource pool by using SQL Server Management Studio or T-SQL. To drop a workload group in SSMS, follow these steps:

1. Expand the `Management` node in Object Explorer and expand the `Resource Governor` node to display the `Resource Pools` folder.
2. Expand the node of the resource pool where the workload group is defined to display the `Workload Groups` folder.

3. Expand the `Workload Groups` folder to list the workload groups.
4. Right-click the workload group you want to drop and select Delete.
5. In the Delete Object window, the Workload Group is listed in the Object to Be Deleted list. Click OK to confirm the deletion.

To drop a workload group using T-SQL, use the `DROP WORKLOAD GROUP` command:

```
DROP WORKLOAD GROUP OLTPWG1
ALTER RESOURCE GOVERNOR RECONFIGURE
go
```

You cannot drop a workload group if there are any active sessions assigned to it. If a workload group contains active sessions, deleting the workload group or moving it to a different resource pool will fail when the `ALTER RESOURCE GOVERNOR RECONFIGURE` statement is called to apply the change. The following options provide a way to work around this problem:

- Wait until all the sessions from the affected group have disconnected and then rerun the `ALTER RESOURCE GOVERNOR RECONFIGURE` statement.
- Explicitly stop sessions in the affected group by using the KILL command and then rerun the `ALTER RESOURCE GOVERNOR RECONFIGURE` statement.
- Restart SQL Server. When the restart process is complete, the deleted group will not be created, and a moved group will automatically use the new resource pool assignment.

NOTE

If an attempt to reconfigure Resource Governor fails after dropping a workload group because of active sessions and you change your mind about dropping the workload group, you can restore it by rerunning the `CREATE WORKLOAD GROUP` command for that workgroup. After re-creating the workload group, run the `ALTER RESOURCE GROUP RECONFIGURE` command again, and the workload group is restored.

Deleting Resource Pools

To drop a resource pool in SSMS, follow these steps:

1. Expand the `Management` node in Object Explorer and expand the `Resource Governor` node to display the `Resource Pools` folder.
2. Expand the `Resource Pools` folder to list the resource pools defined.
3. Right-click the resource pool you want to drop and select Delete.
4. In the Delete Object window, the resource pool is listed in the Object to Be Deleted list. Click OK to confirm the deletion.

To drop a workload group using T-SQL, use the `DROP RESOURCE POOL` command:

```
DROP RESOURCE POOL OLTPPOOL
ALTER RESOURCE GOVERNOR RECONFIGURE
go
```

You cannot drop a resource pool if any workload groups are still assigned to the resource pool. You need to drop the workload group or move it to another resource pool first.

Modifying a Classification Function

If you need to make a change to the classification function, it's important to note that the function cannot be dropped or altered while it is marked as the classification function for the Resource Governor. Before you can modify or drop the classification function, you first need to disable Resource Governor. Alternatively, you can replace the classification function with another by running the `ALTER RESOURCE GOVERNOR` command and passing it a different `CLASSIFIER_FUNCTION` name. You can also simply disable the current classifier function by executing the following command:

```
ALTER RESOURCE GOVERNOR
  WITH (CLASSIFIER_FUNCTION = NULL);
ALTER RESOURCE GOVERNOR RECONFIGURE;
```

The sample classification function shown in Listing 40.1 uses a simple case expression to determine the workload group based on only two login IDs. If you have a more complex set of rules to apply or want to be able to make changes more dynamically than having to replace the classification function each time you need to make a change, you can define your classifier function to look up the workload group names from a database table, rather than hard-coding the workload group names and matching criteria into the function. Performance should not be greatly affected when accessing the table to look up the workload group. The reason is that the table likely won't be very large and should remain cached in the buffer pool because it's being accessed repeatedly every time a connection is made to SQL Server.

Summary

Resource Governor offers many potential benefits, primarily the capability to prioritize SQL Server resources for critical applications and users and preventing "runaway" or unexpected queries from adversely impacting SQL Server performance significantly. It fits in with Microsoft's goal of providing predictable performance for your SQL Server applications.

Resource Governor also offers some potential pitfalls, however. For example, a misconfigured Resource Governor can not only hurt a server's overall performance, but can potentially lock up your server, requiring you to use the dedicated administrator connection to attach to the locked-up SQL Server to troubleshoot and fix the problem. Therefore, it is recommended that you implement Resource Governor only if you are an experienced DBA and have a good understanding of, and familiarity with, the workloads executed against your SQL Server databases. Even then, it's imperative that you test your configuration on a test server before rolling it out into production.

Also, after implementing a Resource Governor configuration, you should monitor your SQL Server performance to make sure the configuration has the desired effect. The next chapter, "A Performance and Tuning Methodology," provides guidelines for monitoring and tuning the performance of your SQL Server environment.

CHAPTER 41

A Performance and Tuning Methodology

IN THIS CHAPTER

- ▶ The Full Architectural Landscape
- ▶ Primary Performance and Tuning Handles
- ▶ A Performance and Tuning Methodology
- ▶ Performance and Tuning Design Guidelines
- ▶ Tools of the Performance and Tuning Trade

Yes, you can tune your SQL Server implementation to perform optimally for you. However, random jabs at bleeding arteries may stop immediate bleeding, but the patient will die before too long. Forgive the graphic analogy, but all too often, performance and tuning is crudely attempted with extremely serious oversights and very often extremely poor results. Usually, you can avoid this outcome if you follow basic, orderly steps when tuning your SQL Server platform and understand the complete SQL Server ecosystem. This chapter describes a repeatable performance and tuning methodology that has been refined over the past decade during hundreds of performance and tuning consulting engagements on SQL Server implementations running at some of the largest companies on the planet.

Good performance really starts when you design it into your implementation from the beginning. Even the best-designed applications require fine-tuning over time. Unfortunately, dealing with performance is very often put off or not considered at all until it becomes a problem in production!

As a part of introducing a formal performance and tuning approach, we describe the overall architectural landscape of most applications and how SQL Server sits within this environment. You should keep in mind that addressing performance and tuning of your SQL Server implementation is a layered exercise and all layers must be considered; all layers factor into your results. We also discuss an assortment of design considerations (guidelines) that you should incorporate into your designs from the beginning. And lastly, we outline several tools of the trade when focusing on performance and tuning. Some are out-of-the-box from Microsoft;

others are from third-party providers that allow you to visualize and rapidly isolate your performance issues as they are happening. A number of other chapters in this book are dedicated to the actual performance tuning of a SQL Server instance, SQL tables, and SQL statements. This chapter provides you with a framework and ordered process to attack a SQL Server–based environment from top to bottom that will yield thorough and complete results. No more just stopping the bleeding artery. We want to cure the patient!

The Full Architectural Landscape

As mentioned previously, understanding all layers of your implementation is critical to performance and tuning of your SQL Server application. Even the smallest aspect, such as locking, could be at the heart of your poor performing system. You just don't truly know until you have evaluated all layers and all interactions that come into play in your SQL Server application. Figure 41.1 provides an overall perspective of all the layers of the architecture that you need to better understand and potentially tune.

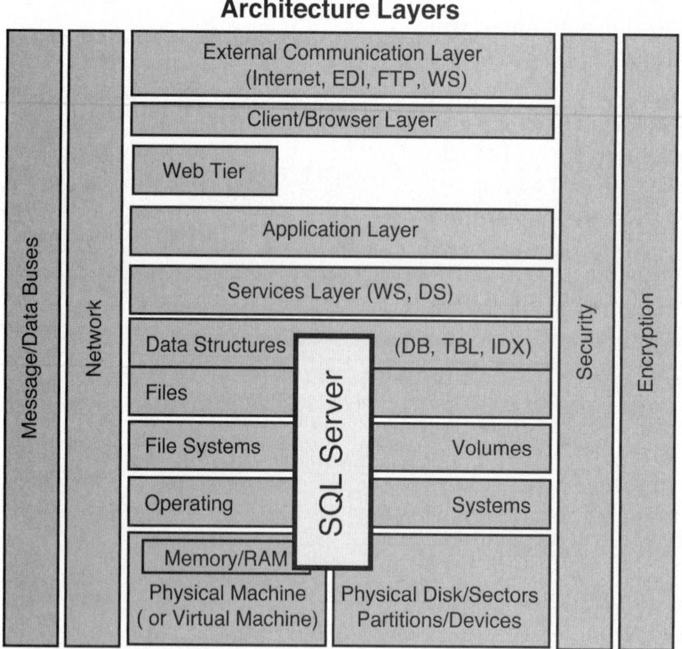

FIGURE 41.1 The overall architectural landscape of a SQL Server implementation.

As you can see in Figure 41.1, your SQL Server environment sits at the heart of many different layers. They include the hardware (either physical or virtual footprint), memory, physical disks/devices, operating system, file systems, and database, to name a few. Quite often, a combined effort is needed between the infrastructure, application, database, and network teams to deliver the final, well-tuned SQL Server environment. If you can understand that you have not just a database problem or just an application design problem, you will likely be more successful at delivering "optimal" results when tuning your environment. You can treat Figure41.1 as a checklist that you make sure you cover when doing performance and tuning. Then, when you make a change in one layer, you can make sure you test the full impact throughout all the other layers. Often, when you solve one issue in one layer, other issues bubble up to the surface of another layer.

Primary Performance and Tuning Handles

Now, let's peel the onion a little more into the core architecture of SQL Server itself. Figure 41.2 shows the primary components within a SQL Server instance. The major issues to worry about at the instance level are the caches that comprise the memory pool and the number of CPUs available for processing to SQL Server itself (shown as white boxes, not dark ones). Of course, the disk I/O subsystem and files have to be carefully evaluated and used effectively as well. All other darker boxed items such as the SQL Server kernel are not within your control.

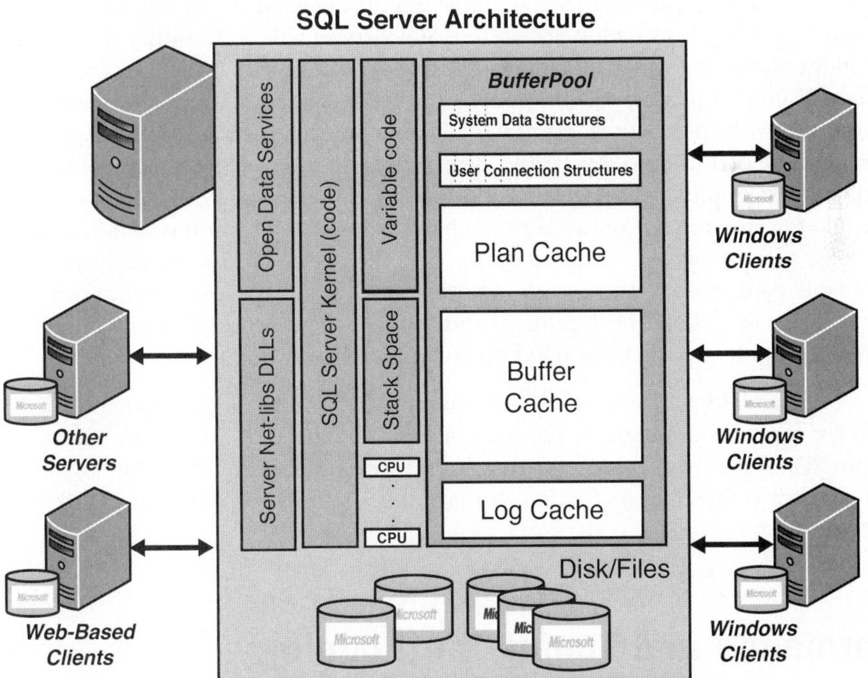

FIGURE 41.2 SQL Server instance architecture (memory, CPU, I/O).

The rule of thumb here is to treat these instance-level resources as "scarce" resources and monitor the CPU and disk I/O for their saturation levels (never exceeding 80%) and memory for its hit ratio and capability to service the desired amount of concurrent work at or better than the service-level requirements of your end users (even during peak usage times).

Figure 41.3 shows a more readily recognizable combination of "handles" that are the major areas a human can adjust to achieve optimal performance.

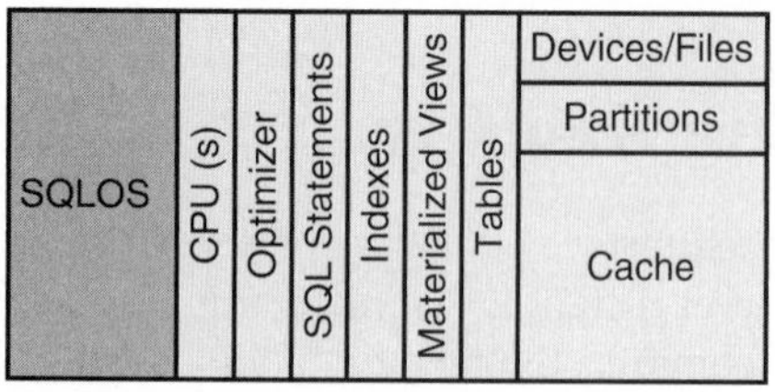

FIGURE 41.3 SQL Server handles available for performance tuning.

We've already mentioned CPU, cache/memory, and disk I/O; these and all the other handles listed in Figure 41.3 work together and must be considered together when doing performance and tuning. A change in a SQL statement affects what the optimizer (which makes decisions regarding how data is accessed in SQL Server) will do to satisfy the query. The correct index allows the query to get data the most effective way. The correct table design drastically affects updates, deletes, inserts, and reads. The number of CPUs available to SQL Server can invoke parallelism. What work is done in `tempdb` (and where `tempdb` is located) can improve performance by 1000%. The index and table level fill factor (free space), number of page splits, and page allocations being done within your databases can hurt you by 1000%. Hints to the optimizer can change the way execution is handled. And other issues such as materialized views, partitions, and file placement (at the disk subsystem level) directly contribute to the overall performance of every SQL execution. Even something as simple as locking (or deadlocks) and the consistent order of update operations within transactions can make or break an entire SQL Server implementation.

We explain a bit more of what to look for with the primary handles in the guideline section later. For most development or production support teams, tackling performance and tuning for SQL Server can truly be overwhelming. The next section describes an orderly performance and tuning methodology that most should be able to follow and use to yield great results.

A Performance and Tuning Methodology

A *methodology* is a process or procedure, for example, designed for repeatability that has been proven to work for a certain paradigm. In our case, it is a repeatable and thorough SQL Server–focused performance and tuning process. We generalized this focused process into a repeatable methodology and identified two possible paths that can be taken through it: one for a *new* SQL Server implementation that will have performance and tuning designed into it from the start and another for performance and tuning of an *existing* SQL Server implementation (one that needs to be scaled out or rescued—or in other words, "optimized").

Figure 41.4 illustrates this overall performance and tuning methodology within a traditional waterfall development methodology context. But, as you will see, it is very iterative in nature and can be followed within any organization's formal development methodology.

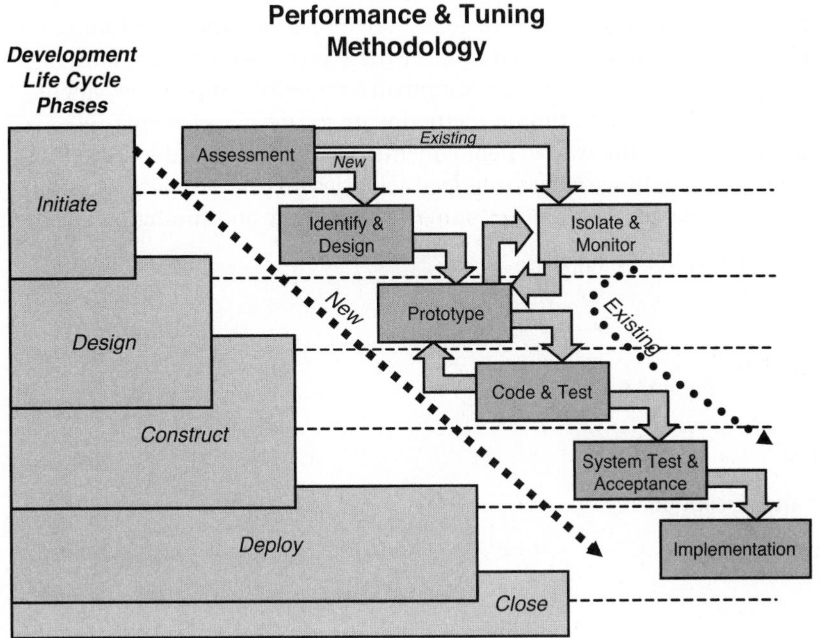

FIGURE 41.4 Generalized performance and tuning methodology for SQL Server.

Notice the two distinct paths labeled "New" and "Existing" indicated by the dashed arrowed lines. As mentioned earlier, one path is for new implementations, and the other is for existing implementations. The following sections describe each of these distinct paths through the methodology.

Designing In Performance and Tuning from the Start

If you are just starting to design and develop a new SQL Server–based implementation, it would be great to factor in all possible performance and tuning considerations from the beginning. In real life, this is rarely done primarily because much is unknown from a data access, number of users, and table design point of view. However, you are not precluded from designing in certain common performance and tuning considerations, nor are you precluded from incorporating a performance and tuning "prototyping" step in your methodology so that you have known and predictable results of what you are building "as you go" and not "at the end." As you have no doubt experienced (or heard many times), changing something after it is built is more expensive than if you had considered it much earlier in the development process. In fact, such changes are likely at least 10 or more times more expensive from both a monetary point of view and from a time point of view.

As you can see in Figure 41.4, each path begins with an assessment step. For new development, this step covers the traditional "initiation" type of activities, such as project sizing, scheduling, scope refinement, and resourcing. As you identify project sizing, scheduling, and resourcing, you should add in 5% to each subsequent phase of your traditional development life cycle for performance and tuning activities. We outline these activities shortly. In general, they include capturing performance goals, having performance and tuning design reviews, building prototypes optimized to meet these performance goals, and setting final checkpoints that demonstrate full compliance of performance achievement under full loads. Our performance and tuning methodology for new implementations focuses on six major steps along the way to deployments. We don't list all the tasks or activities around your programming or user interface activities. Instead, we just focus on the SQL Server–oriented items that pertain to optimal performance and tuning.

The six development methodology steps are

- Assessment
- Identify and Design
- Prototype
- Code and Test
- System Test and Acceptance
- Implementation

Assessment

During this project initiation phase, a complete picture of the effort is usually identified and assessed at a high level. This includes

- **Project sizing**—Determines if this is a small, medium, or larger project.
- **Project scope clarifications**—Describe the intent and application scope to be created.
- **Deliverables identified**—Identifies deliverables for all subsequent phases of the project. This should also include new tasks for performance and tuning activities.
- **Schedules/milestones**—Reflect what is needed to build this application, when it must be delivered, and everything along the way.
- **Resources identified and committed to project**—Includes some specialized resources that enable your performance and tuning tasks and reviews.

All organizations have their own version of this step/phase, but you should note that you need to plan in time for performance and tuning from the beginning. We suggest at least adding 5% to the number of hours to performance and tuning tasks for each subsequent step in the development life cycle. That 5% will save you enormous heartache and grief later and will ensure the success of your implementation.

Identify and Design

The identification and design step is centered around the clear identification of what must be built, what service-level agreements are needed, and what performance goals must be met. The performance and tuning-oriented tasks are as follows:

- **Identify the primary service-level agreements (SLAs)/performance goals**—This task is critical and must be stated clearly and realistically. Sub-second response rates are likely not realistic for every element of an application. You will be measured against these goals.
- **Estimate work load/use profiles**—These profiles are the general volumes of major activity this application must support, such as 68% online activity, 32% reporting activity, and availability such as 24×7×365. These profiles should also include any known growth estimates for different increments of time such as 6-month growth numbers, 12-month growth numbers, so on.
- **Generalize to major access patterns**—This task quantifies the major data access patterns that must be supported by the application. Knowing these patters is essential in order to design in performance from the start. Examples of data access patterns are a shopping cart access pattern and an ATM access pattern. They would be vastly different in their table, indexing, and transactional designs.
- **Design for all layers of the architecture**—Based on the performance goals, workloads, and major data access patterns, your initial designs should not only cover the SQL Server objects (such as table designs, index designs, and so on), but must also reach out to each other's architectural layer previously identified. Now is the time to design on the correct partitioning scheme, correct transactional model, correct file placement approach, correct disk subsystem to use, correct servers needed, and memory management needs of your application. You should include a task in your project plan for a complete performance and design review.

Prototype

We added a formal prototyping step into this methodology to stress how important it is to fully evaluate and understand the performance expectations of the application you are building. This very iterative process can help greatly in refining the designs being considered. Go ahead and build a prototyping environment where you can thoroughly try out what you have designed in the preceding "Identify and Design" step. Your prototype should illustrate (and implement) the major data access patterns you must support, show how they are achieving planned performance goals, and indicate whose results must be signed off on to pass to the next development phase step. You may have to iterate back through this and the preceding step several times to narrow in on a more optimal design solution. Use this time now to ensure success later.

- **In a prototype environment, prototype possible solutions**—This is for a generalized design and does not have to include every column of data or functionality of the application. There may be one or more possible solutions that you must prototype. The prototype is at the generic "pattern" level. Often we use tables that have artificial columns as placeholders of known unusual data types along with the minimal known columns needed to implement a data access pattern and table design.

- **Dissect trouble areas**—During the prototyping, you will have issues around your design and the performance results you are getting. Now is the right time to solve these types of issues. Not later.
- **Ramp up for load/stress testing**—Your prototypes should include some level of volume or peak stress testing results so you can have a good understanding of what to expect at peak times. In addition, it is beneficial to prototype and test with data volumes that are representative of your expected production data volumes. This helps to identify ahead of time any performance issues that may arise when querying and processing larger data volumes.

NOTE

Very large volumes of data may require modifications to the database design to provide good performance. The earlier this need is determined in the design/testing process, the less expensive it will be to implement these changes in the system while code is still being developed rather than having to make changes after the system has been put into production.

- **Iterate back to the "Identify and Design" step (as needed)**—Design and redesign as much as is needed. Prototyping helps you narrow in on an optimized solution quickly. In general, shoot for a 90% solution (one that meets performance within 10% of stated goals).

You should also have the right tools available to you during this prototyping step. This includes monitoring tools, performance and tuning tools, and other instrumentation needed to better understand and resolve any early issues that surface. Later in this chapter, we outline several tools of the trade for performance and tuning in a SQL Server platform and performance and tuning guidelines that you can follow.

Code and Test

In the "Code and Test" stage, you fully code all elements of your application. This includes all table designs, index designs, application coding, and complete testing prior to the system test and user acceptance.

- **Perform full coding and unit/load testing**—At this point, perform complete coding of your application and database. Each unit test must also include a step to determine how it is meeting performance goals/SLAs. Most programmers are not accustomed to this checkpoint. The code does not go forward unless the goals/SLAs are fully met. No exceptions. Again, whenever possible, testing should be done with data volumes and values that are representative of the expected production data after the system has been running for an extended period of time. Doing so is very important to help avoid future performance issues when the system is in production, because as data volumes grow, queries may optimize differently. Queries that run quickly with small data volumes may optimize differently and run slowly with larger data volumes. However, if you can optimize the database design and queries to provide good performance when you have large data volumes, performance should be just as good or even better with smaller data volumes as well.

- **Perform regression testing if desired**—Utilize full regression testing if you desire. This step usually requires complex testing harnesses and dedicated quality assurance resources.
- **Iterate back to the "Prototype" step (as needed)**—Don't be afraid to iterate back into the prototyping mode to flesh out a serious issue. You need to solve issues now, not later in production or in acceptance testing.
- **Assess if service levels have been met**—Create a formal checkpoint that must be passed around the service levels and performance goals being met. You cannot proceed to the next step unless they are met!

System Test and Acceptance

The "System Test and Acceptance" stage is the full-blown integrated system test in a production-like environment. You do final user acceptance and full system-level stress tests here. All your performance goals must be fully met! Again, you need to have a formal checkpoint identified here that requires signoff of the SLAs/performance goals and fully document the results for the system stress tests.

In the full system/stress test/user acceptance, your fully loaded application and database are thoroughly tested by your users, and a full stress test is done to reflect peak system usage. The users should not sign off on this step unless the performance goals are met, and the application's functional test is successful.

If possible, this stage should reflect what the complete production hardware and software stack will look like. By now, you should also be able to set expectations for both current and future scalability of this application.

Implementation

By design, the implementation should be merely a formality. Certainly, all performance concerns should have been met, documented, and verified even under peak processing scenarios. It is also recommended that any production implementation include a certain amount of performance and tuning instrumentation and monitoring. This should be a standard part of any production implementation environment now.

- **Production build/implementation**—You should perform a complete buildout of your application in production.
- **Production performance and monitoring**—You need to have complete performance and tuning instrumentation and monitoring in place and tied to your system monitoring services (SMS) environment. There is usually a proactive monitoring following a new implementation for an extended amount of time. Don't just implement and walk away. There is likely something that must be adjusted.

- **Final documentation/results**—In this step, you create a set of documents that reflect what you built and also the current performance levels being achieved. These documents will be valuable later as the application changes and workloads increase.

Figure 41.5 shows a holistic picture of the different layers that you have been building on and how these different layers depend on each other and are built on each other. Make sure you have checked off and considered each of them in your pursuit of optimizing your SQL Server–based implementation.

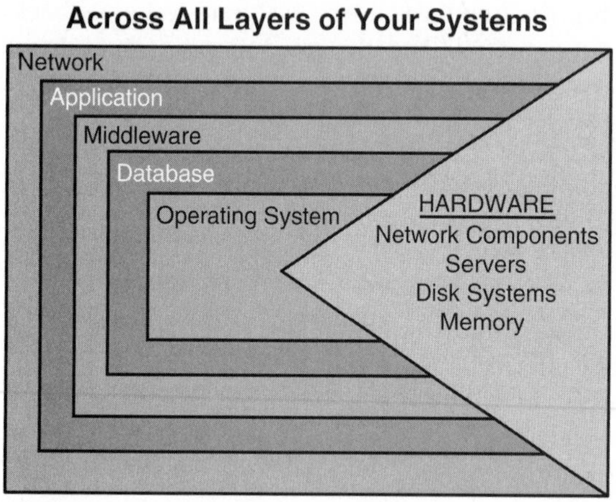

FIGURE 41.5 The many interrelated layers of your system.

Starting at the hardware footprint, to the operating systems that sit on top of the hardware, to the database and middleware implemented on top of the OS, to the application itself (however many application tiers), and the network supporting the communication to the users—all have a part in delivering an optimal implementation.

The next section describes our formal performance and tuning methodology applied to an existing implementation.

Performance and Tuning for an Existing Implementation

Many of you may have just skipped down to this section because you have already built something and are trying to get to some serious performance and tuning for your existing implementation. Regardless of your situation, the essence of this section is describing the methodology for isolation, identification, and migration to get your existing implementation to a well-performing and tuned implementation. We use *isolation* in the sense that you must isolate the major performance issues quickly, *identification* in the sense of locating the exact issues to focus on, and *migration* in the sense of having to get from the current issues to a new issue-free implementation. This last part is often incredibly hard to do—like changing tires on a car while it is still moving. With this in mind, a different path through the performance and tuning methodology is needed—one that starts with an assessment, but an assessment of what issues or shortcomings exist, and then a separate branch (path) that includes isolation, monitoring, and identification of the issues rapidly. This is then followed by rapid prototyping and further isolation and monitoring and eventual full system testing and rolling out the changes into your production implementation.

One big advantage of doing performance and tuning on an existing implementation is that you have live transactional information, live data, and other production execution history to work from. From all of these, you should be able to piece together a good execution profile, all the major data access patterns, and other major characteristics critical to tuning what you have. You also are able to include new information or scalability needs as well.

Another initial decision you need to make is whether you want only transparent changes (ones that have no application changes whatsoever, such as index changes, server instance changes, file placement changes, some stored procedure changes, and so on) or if you can tolerate making nontransparent changes (ones that force you to also make schema, structure, and SQL statement changes, and even application changes). Of course, your decision depends on how much trouble you are in.

Now, let's look back at Figure 41.4 and focus on the far right-most path through this methodology. We start by recasting the traditional "initiation" type of activities such as project sizing, scheduling, scope refinement, and resourcing to focus on just the performance and tuning tasks at hand. Again, we don't list all the tasks or activities around your programming or user interface activities; we just focus on the SQL Server–oriented items that pertain to optimal performance and tuning.

Performance and tuning methodology steps for an existing implementation are as follows:

- Assessment
- Isolation and Monitor
- Prototype
- Code and Test
- System Test and Acceptance
- Implementation

Assessment

For this first step, assessment, a complete picture of the performance issues or expectations must be outlined. This includes

- **Project sizing**—Determines if the performance and tuning effort you are about to engage in will be a small, medium, or large project. Although it is not a full-blown development project, it could certainly be bigger than you realize.
- **Project scope clarifications**—Identify mostly whether you can tolerate only transparent changes versus nontransparent changes to resolve your performance issues.

- **Deliverables identified**—Focuses mostly on performance and tuning activities but may be expanded to application activities if the changes needed must extend into the application itself.
- **Schedules/milestones**—Reflect what is needed to monitor, isolate, identify, and roll out the changes needed.
- **Resources identified and committed to project**—Identifies resources centered around your best performance and tuning folks. Don't scrimp here. Even if you have to hire some experts to help with this effort, this is money well invested.

Isolate and Monitor

Now comes the specialized path down the performance and tuning methodology for existing implementations. It is time to monitor, isolate, and identify exactly where your problems are. In addition, you must not lose sight of the complete stack and all the layers that will potentially be a part of your performance issues.

You also need to revisit (or define for the first time) what service-level agreements are needed and what performance goals must be met. The performance and tuning-oriented tasks are as follows:

- **Identify the primary service-level agreements (SLAs)/performance goals**—If you haven't performed this task yet, the time is now. If you did it previously, it is time to revisit what these SLAs should be realistically. Again, subsecond response rates are likely not realistic for every element of an application. You should also add new or emerging scalability and growth needs to your goals now. This may have some very significant impact to new design decisions or performance and tuning approaches that would be different if all you needed to do was tune for an existing, unchanging workload.
- **Set up your execution capture and monitoring capabilities**—You should perform this task at each of the layers in your architecture if you can. Remember, many performance issues often are spread across multiple areas. Our preference is to get peak production monitoring. This includes basic monitoring using Perfmon counters, SQL Server Profiler tracing, and even third-party monitoring tools that can help you see major issues graphically as they are happening. We talk about tools of the trade later in the chapter.
- **Isolate hottest issues**—We like to use the 90/10 rule such that 10% of your execution transactions or implementation configurations are likely causing 90% of your problems. If you solve that 10%, you have a well-performing platform. These issues must be isolated layer by layer (network, hardware, OS, application server/application, SQL Server instance, database, SQL statements, and so on).
- **Create workloads/use profiles**—Utilizing the tracing/capture tools, you need to capture and organize where the problem issues are located at each layer. For SQL statements, this means capturing and ordering the worst-performing SQL into the top 100 worst by I/O and CPU consumption usually. You also need to identify concurrency issues (locking/deadlocks), disk/file utilization queues, cache utilization,

and many other handles. It is from these issues that you must create repeatable execution patterns so that you can tune to support them. You must also execute all activities such as batch processes and so on that might not normally come into play until scheduled events have occurred. For new growth or scalability increases, add the appropriate workloads, use profiles, and SQL statements into the mix.

- **Identify issues and possible solutions for all layers of the architecture**—Based on the performance goals, workloads, and major data access patterns, you need to come up with a series of performance changes prioritized by the biggest impact. These changes may include SQL Server objects changes (such as table changes, new or different indexes, and so on) but could also reach out to other architectural layers previously identified. These changes can also affect adding or changing a partitioning scheme, fixing a transactional model, correcting the file placements, changing the disk subsystem or server configurations, and adjusting the memory requirements of your application. Before you make any changes, you should have a comprehensive performance review that outlines all issues identified and proposes solutions to each.

Prototype

You now enter an iterative cycle between isolate, monitor, prototype, isolate, monitor, and prototype. This cycle may repeat for any number of iterations as you deem necessary. You should set your overall goals to achieve at least 95% of your performance goals. It isn't too hard to get to that point. However, it is hard to squeeze out that last 5%, though. Often, getting those last few yards isn't really going to buy you that much more relief.

When you want to get good performance and tuning results, it's always best to utilize a prototyping environment that is very much like your production environment (or at least as close to the same as possible in all aspects—memory, CPU, disk subsystems, data volumes, and so on). Optimizer decisions and I/O times, for example, vary greatly from one configuration to another. If your prototyping system is completely different from your production system or configuration, you will likely be able to achieve only 80% of your performance goals and SLAs. Often, we are able to use a company's QA/User Acceptance Testing environment, which is a mirror image of the production system, including a very current and complete production database backup image being used for the system testing. You need to negotiate time with this type of environment. Some prototyping can be accomplished on smaller environments (such as testing new partitioning schemes, new SQL query statements, and so on). But you need to run this all on a full-blown production-like environment before it is all said and done.

Again, your prototype should illustrate (and implement) the major data access patterns you must support, show how they are achieving planned performance goals, and indicate whose results must be signed off on to pass to the next development phase step. You may have to iterate back through this and the preceding step several times to narrow in on a more optimal design solution. You need to have full execution monitoring and tracing set up in this prototyping environment.

- **Create a complete prototype environment**—Remember that you have to test existing and new solutions, not just one or the other. A change in something new may adversely affect something that was fine before, but becomes slow performing with the new solution. There may be one or more possible solutions that you must prototype to get the best results. You will be using "live" patterns based on production queries for the most part now. Any new functionality or solutions will be added to this mix.

- **Ramp up for load/stress testing**—Your prototypes should include some full level of volume or peak stress testing results so you can have a good understanding of what to expect at peak times and the potential impact of performance changes to one aspect of the system on another, such as increased locking contention.
- **Iterate back to the "Isolate and Monitor" step (as needed)**—Change, enhance, and try out new solutions in this iterative circle. Using a prototyping approach allows you to narrow down to what works best rather quickly.

Remember that you should have the right tools available to you during this prototyping step. They include monitoring tools, performance and tuning tools, and other instrumentation needed to better understand and resolve any early issues that surface. Again, later in this chapter we outline several tools of the trade for performance and tuning in a SQL Server platform and performance and tuning guidelines that you can follow.

Code and Test

The "Code and Test" step takes on a more formal process after the prototyping of all possible performance and tuning enhancements has been completed. In this step, you fully code all elements of your application with any changes that have resulted from the prototyping effort. This includes all table designs, index designs, and application coding prior to the final system test and user acceptance. Remember, if you are doing only the transparent changes, this part should be fairly easy; but if your changes are nontransparent, this will be a full-blown code and test phase of your entire application.

- **Perform full coding and unit/load testing**—Perform complete coding of the application and database. Each unit test must also include a step determining how they are meeting performance goals/SLAs. Most programmers are not accustomed to this checkpoint. The code does not go forward unless the goals/SLAs are fully met. No exceptions.
- **Perform regression testing if desired**—Utilize full regression testing if you desire. This step usually requires complex testing harnesses and dedicated quality assurance resources.
- **Iterate back to the "Prototype" step (as needed)**—Don't be afraid to iterate back into the prototyping mode to flesh out a serious issue. You need to solve issues now, not later in production or in acceptance testing.
- **Assess if service levels have been met**—Create a formal checkpoint that must be passed around the service levels and performance goals being met. You cannot proceed to the next step unless these goals are met!

System Test and Acceptance

The next step is the full-blown integrated system test in a production-like environment. You do final user acceptance and full system-level stress tests here. All your performance goals must be fully met! Again, you need to have a formal checkpoint identified here that requires signoff of the SLAs/performance goals and fully document the results for the system stress tests.

In the full system/stress test/user acceptance, your fully loaded application is thoroughly tested by your users, and a full stress test is done to reflect peak system usage. The users should not sign off on this step unless the performance goals are met, and the application's functional test is successful.

If possible, this stage should reflect what the complete production hardware and software stack will look like. By now, you should also be able to set expectations for both current and future scalability of this application.

Implementation

The biggest issues now are migrating your new changes into the existing production implementation. This may include complex data structure changes and data migrations from old structures to new structures, or may simply involve dropping and re-creating indexes. You should plan all steps of your changes to the nth degree and test the upgrades on your QA platform a few times. You may have to schedule downtime for extensive nontransparent changes. You should make full backups at all layers prior to your live upgrade in production. Be sure to have a set of performance benchmark operations ready to run in production to verify the results you intended.

- **Production build/implementation**—You should perform a complete buildout of your application in production and full migration upgrade scripts/data conversions.
- **Production performance and monitoring**—You need to have complete performance and tuning instrumentation and monitoring in place and running. Run a series of performance testing scripts/queries as a part of your production upgrade process. Don't just implement and walk away. There is likely something that must be adjusted even at this late stage.
- **Final documentation/results**—In this step, you create a set of documents that reflect what you built and also the current performance levels being achieved.

In theory, you should now be in an optimized execution implementation. You should be prepared to monitor, monitor, and monitor some more. We traditionally keep a close monitoring eye for about five days of execution and then switch back to a normal amount of proactive monitoring after that.

The following sections highlight some common design techniques, approaches, and guidelines you should consider or utilize as you tune your SQL Server implementation.

Performance and Tuning Design Guidelines

We outline some of the major performance and tuning design guidelines here. There are, of course, many more, but if you a least consider and apply the ones outline here, you should end up with a decently performing SQL Server implementation. As we have described previously, performance and tuning should first be "designed in" to your SQL Server implementation. Many of the guidelines discussed here can be adopted easily in this way. However, when you put off the performance and tuning until later, you have fewer options to apply and less performance improvement when you do make changes. Remember, addressing performance and tuning is like peeling an onion. And, for this reason, we present our guidelines in that way—layer by layer. This approach helps provide you with a great reference point for each layer and a list you can check off as you develop your SQL Server–based implementation. Just ask yourself whether you have considered the specific layer guidelines when you are dealing with that layer. Also, several chapters take you through the full breadth and depth of options and techniques introduced in many of these guidelines. We point you to those chapters as we outline the guidelines.

Hardware and Operating System Guidelines

Let's start with the salient hardware and operation system guidelines that you should be considering:

Hardware/Physical Server:

- **Server sizing/CPUs**—Physical (or virtual) servers that will host a SQL Server instance should be roughly sized to handle the maximum processing load plus 35% more CPUs (and you should always round up). As an example, for a workload that you anticipate may be fully handled by a four-CPU server configuration, we recommend automatically increasing the number of CPUs to six. We also *always* leave at least one CPU for the operating system. So, if six CPUs are on the server, you should allocate only five to SQL Server to use. You can find details on configuring CPUs in Chapter 55, "Configuring, Tuning, and Optimizing SQL Server Options," and details on monitoring CPU utilization in Chapter 39, "Monitoring SQL Server Performance."
- **Memory**—The amount of memory you might need is often directly related to the amount of data you need to be in the cache to achieve 100% or near 100% cache hit ratios. This, of course, yields higher overall performance. We don't believe there is too much memory for SQL Server, but we do recognize that some memory must be left to the operating system to handle OS-level processing, connections, and so on. So, in general, you should make 90% of memory available to SQL Server and 10% to the OS. You can find details on configuring memory in Chapter 49 and details on monitoring memory utilization in Chapter 39.
- **Disk/SAN/NAS/RAID**—Your disk subsystem can be a major contributor to performance degradation if not handled properly. We recognize that there are many different options available here. We generally try to have some separate devices on

different I/O channels so that disk I/O isolation techniques can be used. This means that you isolate heavy I/O away from other heavy I/O activity; otherwise, disk head contention causes massive slowdowns in physical I/O. When you use SAN/NAS storage, much of the storage is just logical drives that are heavily cached. This type of situation limits the opportunity to spread out heavy I/O, but the caching layers often alleviate that problem. In general, RAID 10 is great for high update activity, and RAID 5 is great for mostly read-only activity. You can find more information on RAID and storage options in Chapter 38, "Database Design and Performance."

Operating System:

- **Page file location**—When physical memory is exceeded, paging occurs to the page file. You need to make sure that the page file is not located on one of your database disk locations; otherwise, performance of the whole server degrades rapidly.
- **Processes' priority**—You should never lower the SQL Server processes in priority or to the background. You should always have them set as high as possible.
- **Memory**—As mentioned earlier, you should make sure that at least 10% of memory is available to the OS for all its housekeeping, connection handling, process threads, and so on.
- **OS version**—You should make sure you are using the most recent version of the operating systems as you can and have updated with the latest patches or service packs. Also, often you must remove other software on your server, such as specialized virus protection. We have lost track of the number of SQL Server implementations we have found that had some third-party virus software installed (and enabled) on it, and all files and communication to the server were interrupted by the virus scans. Rely on Microsoft Windows and your firewalls for this protection rather than a third-party virus solution that gets in the way of SQL Server. If your organization requires some type of virus protection on the server, at least disable scanning of the database device files.

Network:

- **Packet sizes/traffic**—With broader bands and faster network adapters (typically at least 1GB now), we recommend you utilize the larger packet sizes to accommodate your heavier-traffic SQL Server instances. Packets of 8KB and larger are easily handled now. Information on configuring the SQL Server packet size is available in Chapter 49.
- **Routers/switches/balancers**—Depending on if you are using SQL clustering or have multitiered application servers, you likely should utilize some type of load balancing at the network level to spread out connections from the network and avoid bottlenecks.

SQL Server Instance Guidelines

Next comes the SQL Server instance itself and the critical items that must be considered:

- **SQL Server configuration**—We do not list many of the SQL Server instance options here, but many of the default options are more than sufficient to deal with most SQL Server implementations. See Chapter 49 for information on all the available options.
- **SQL Server device allocations**—Devices should be treated with care and not overallocated. SQL databases utilize files and devices as their underlying allocation from the operating system. You do not want dozens and dozens of smaller files or devices for each database. Having all these files or devices becomes harder to administer, move, and manipulate. We often come into a SQL Server implementation and simplify the device allocations before we do any other work on the database. At a minimum, you should create data devices and log devices so that you can easily isolate (separate) them.
- **`tempdb`** database—Perhaps the most misunderstood SQL Server shared resource is `tempdb`. General guidelines for `tempdb` is to minimize explicit usage (overusage) of it by limiting temp table creation, sorts, queries using DISTINCT clause, so on. You are creating a hot spot in your SQL Server instance that is mostly *not* in your control. You might find it hard to believe, but indexing, table design, and even not executing certain SQL statements can have a huge impact on what gets done in `tempdb` and have a huge effect on performance. And, of course, you need to isolate `tempdb` away from all other databases. For additional information on placing and monitoring `tempdb`, see Chapters 38 and 39.
- **`master`** database—There is one simple guideline here: *protect the `master` database at all costs*. This means frequent backups and isolation of *`master`* away from all other databases.
- **`model`** database—It seems harmless enough, but all databases in SQL Server utilize the `model` database as their base allocation template. We recommend you tailor this for your particular environment.
- **Memory**—The best way to utilize and allocate memory to SQL Server depends on a number of factors. One is how many other SQL Server instances are running on the same physical server. Another is what type of SQL Server–based application it is: heavy update versus heavy reads. And yet another is how much of your application has been written with stored procedures, triggers, and so on. In general, you want to give as much of the OS memory to SQL Server as you can. But this amount should never exceed 90% of the available memory at the OS level. You don't want SQL Server or the OS to start thrashing via the page file or competing against each other for memory. Also, when more than one SQL Server instance is on the same physical server, you need to divide the memory correctly for each. Don't pit them against

each other. More information on configuring and monitoring SQL Server memory is available in Chapters 39 and 49.

Database-Level Guidelines

- **Database allocations**—We like to use an approach of putting database files for heavily used databases on the same drives as lightly used databases when more than one database is being managed by a single SQL Server instance. In other words, pair big with small, not big with big. This approach is termed *reciprocal database pairing*.

  You should also not have too many databases on a single SQL Server instance. If the server fails, so do all the applications that were using the databases managed by this one SQL Server instance. It's all about risk mitigation. Remember the adage "never put all your eggs in one basket."

  Databases have two primary file allocations: one for their data portion and the other for their transaction log portion. You should always isolate these file allocations from each other onto separate disk subsystems with separate I/O channels if possible. The transaction log is a hot spot for highly volatile applications (that have frequent update activity). Isolate, isolate, and isolate some more. There is also a notion of something called *reciprocal database device location*. More information is available on this issue in Chapters 38 and 39.

  You need to size your database files appropriately large enough to avoid database file fragmentation. Heavily fragmented database files can lead to excessive file I/O within the operating system and poor I/O performance. For example, if you know your database is going to grow to 500GB, size your database files at 500GB from the start so that the operating system can allocate a contiguous 500GB file. In addition, be sure to disable the Auto-Shrink database option. Allowing your database files to continuously grow and shrink also leads to excessive file fragmentation as file space is allocated and deallocated in small chunks.

- **Database backup/recovery/administration**—You should create a database backup and recovery schedule that matches the database update volatility and recovery point objective. All too often a set schedule is used when, in fact, it is not the schedule that drives how often you do backups or how fast you must recover from failure.

Table Design Guidelines

- **Table designs**—Given the massively increased CPU, memory, and disk I/O speeds that now exist, you should use a general guideline to create as "normalized" a table design as is humanly possible. No longer is it necessary to massively denormalize for performance. Most normalized table designs are easily supported by SQL Server. Normalized table designs ensure that data has high integrity and low overall redundant data maintenance. See Dr. E. F. Codd's original work on relational database design (*The Relational Model for Database Management: Version 2,* Addison Wesley,

1990). Denormalize for performance as a last resort! For more information on normalization and denormalization techniques, see Chapter 38.

NOTE

Too often, we have seen attempts by developers and database designers to guess at the performance problems they expect to encounter denormalizing the database design before any real performance testing has even been done, This, more often than not, results in an unnecessarily, and sometimes excessively, denormalized database design. Overly denormalized databases require creating additional code to maintain the denormalized data, and this often ends up creating more performance problems than it attempts to solve, not to mention the greater potential for data integrity issues when data is heavily denormalized. It is always best to start with as normalized a database as possible, and begin testing early in the development process with real data volumes to identify potential areas where denormalization may be necessary for performance reasons. Then, and only when absolutely necessary, you can begin to look at areas in your table design where denormalization may provide a performance benefit.

- **Data types**—You must be consistent! In other words, you need to take the time to make sure you have the same data type definitions for columns that will be joined and/or come from the same data domain—`Int` to `Int`, and so on. Often the use of user-defined data types goes a long way to standardize the underlying data types across tables and databases. This is a very strong method of ensuring consistency.
- **Defaults**—Defaults can help greatly in providing valid data values in columns that are common or that have been specified as mandatory (not `NULL`). Defaults are tied to the column and are consistently applied, regardless of the application that touches the table.
- **Check constraints**—Check constraints can also be useful if you need to have checks of data values as part of your table definition. Again, it is a consistency capability at the column level that guarantees that only correct data ends up in the column. Let us add a word of warning, though: you have to be aware of the insert and update errors that can occur in your application from invalid data values that don't meet the check constraints.
- **Triggers**—Often triggers are used to maintain denormalized data, custom audit logs, and referential integrity. Triggers are often used when you want certain behavior to occur when updates, inserts, and deletes occur, regardless of where they are initiated from. Triggers can result in cascading changes to related (dependent) tables or failures to perform modifications because of restrictions. Keep in mind that triggers add overhead to even the simplest of data modification operations in your database and are a classic item to look at for performance issues. You should implement triggers sparingly and implement only triggers that are "appropriate" for the level of integrity or activity required by your applications, and no more than is necessary. Also, you need to be careful to keep the code within your triggers as efficient as

possible so the impact on your data modifications is kept to a minimum. For more information on coding and using triggers, see Chapter 30, "Creating and Managing Triggers."

- **Primary keys/foreign keys**—For OLTP and normalized table designs, you need to utilize explicit primary key and foreign key constraints where possible. For many read-only tables, you may not even have to specify a primary key or foreign key at all. In fact, you will often be penalized with poorer load times or bulk updates to tables that are used mostly as lookup tables. SQL Server must invoke and enforce integrity constraints if they are defined. If you don't absolutely need them (such as with read-only tables), don't specify them.

- **Table allocations**—When creating tables, you should consider using the fill factor (free space) options (when you have a clustered index) to correspond to the volatility of the updates, inserts, and deletes that will be occurring in the table. Fill factor leaves free space in the index and data pages, allowing room for subsequent inserts without incurring a page split. You should avoid page splits as much as possible because they increase the I/O cost of insert and update operations. For more information on fill factor and page splits, see Chapter 34, "Data Structures, Indexes, and Performance."

- **Table partitioning**—It can be extremely powerful to segregate a table's data into physical partitions that are naturally accessed via some natural subsetting such as date or key range. Queries that can take advantage of partitions can help reduce I/O by searching only the appropriate partitions rather than the entire table. For more information on table partitioning, see Chapters 24, "Creating and Managing Tables," and 34.

- **Purge/archive strategy**—You should anticipate the growth of your tables and determine whether a purge/archive strategy will be needed. If you need to archive or purge data from large tables that are expected to continue to grow, it is best to plan for archiving and purging from the beginning. Many times, your archive/purge method may require modifications to your table design to support an efficient archive/purge method. In addition, if you are archiving data to improve performance of your OLTP applications, but the historical data needs to be maintained for reporting purposes, this also often requires incorporating the historical data into your database and application design. It is much easier to build in an archive/purge method to your database and application from the start than have to retrofit something back into an existing system. Performance of the archive/purge process often is better when it's planned from the beginning as well.

Indexing Guidelines

In general, you need to be sure not to overindex your tables, especially for tables that require good performance for data modifications! Common mistakes include creating redundant indexes on primary keys that already have primary key constraints defined or creating multiple indexes with the same set of leading columns. You should understand when an index is required based on need, not just the desire to have an index. Also, you should make sure that the indexes you define have sufficient cardinality to be useful for your queries. In most performance and tuning engagements that we do, we spend a good portion of our time removing indexes or redefining them correctly to better support the queries being executed against the tables. For more information on defining useful indexes and how queries are optimized, see Chapters 34, and 35, "Understanding Query Optimization."

Following are some indexing guidelines:

- Have an indexing strategy that matches the database/table usages; this is paramount. Do not index OLTP tables with a DSS indexing strategy and vice versa.
- For composite indexes, try to keep the more selective columns leftmost in the index.
- Be sure to index columns used in joins. Joins are processed inefficiently if no index on the column(s) is specified in a join.
- Tailor your indexes for your most critical queries and transactions. You cannot index for every possible query that might be run against your tables. However, your applications will perform better if you can identify your critical and most frequently executed queries and design indexes to support them.
- Avoid indexes on columns that have poor selectivity. The Query Optimizer is not likely to use the indexes, so they would simply take up space and add unnecessary overhead during inserts, updates, and deletes.
- Use clustered indexes when you need to keep your data rows physically sorted in a specific column order. If your data is growing sequentially or is primarily accessed in a particular order (such as range retrievals by date), the clustered index allows you to achieve this more efficiently.
- Use nonclustered indexes to provide quicker direct access to data rows than a table scan when searching for data values not defined in your clustered index. Create nonclustered indexes wisely. You can often add a few other data columns in the nonclustered index (to the end of the index definition) to help satisfy SQL queries completely in the index (and not have to read the data page and incur some extra I/O). This is termed "covering your query." All query columns can be satisfied from the index structure.
- Consider specifying a clustered index fill factor (free space) value to minimize page splits for volatile tables. Keep in mind, however, that the fill factor is lost over time as rows are added to the table and pages fill up. You might need to implement a database maintenance job that runs periodically to rebuild your indexes and reapply the fill factor to the data and index pages.
- Be extremely aware of the table/index statistics that the optimizer has available to it. When your table has changed by more than 20% from updates, inserts, or deletes, the data distribution can be affected quite a bit, and the optimizer decisions can change greatly. You'll often want to ensure that the Auto-Update Statistics option is enabled for your databases to help ensure that index statistics are kept up-to-date as your data changes.

View Design Guidelines

In general, you can have as many views as you want. Views are *not* tables and do not take up any storage space (unless you create an index on the view). They are merely an abstraction for convenience. Except for indexed views, views do not store any data; the results of a view are materialized at the time the query is run against the view and the data is retrieved from the underlying tables. Views can be used to hide complex queries, can be used to control data access, and can be used in the same place as a table in the `FROM` statement of any SQL statement.

Following are some view design guidelines:

- Use views to hide tables that change their structure often. By using views to provide a stable data access view to your application, you can greatly reduce programming changes.
- Utilize views to control security and control access to table data at the data value level.
- Be careful of overusing views containing complex multitable queries, especially code that joins such views together. When the query is materialized, what may appear as a simple join between two or three views can result in an expensive join between numerous tables, sometimes including joins to a single table multiple times.
- Use indexed views to dramatically improve performance for data accesses done via views. Essentially, SQL Server creates an indexed lookup via the view to the underlying table's data. There is storage and overhead associated with these views, so be careful when you utilize this performance feature. Although indexed views can help improve the performance of `SELECT` statements, they add overhead to `INSERT`, `UPDATE`, and `DELETE` statements because the rows in the indexed view need to be maintained as data rows are modified, similar to the maintenance overhead of indexes.

For more information on creating and using views, see Chapter 27, "Creating and Managing Views."

Transact-SQL Guidelines

Overall, how you write your Transact-SQL (T-SQL) code can have one of the greatest impacts on your SQL Server performance. Regardless of how well you've optimized your server configuration and database design, poorly written and inefficient SQL code still results in poor performance. The following sections list some general guidelines to help you write efficient, faster-performing code.

General T-SQL Coding Guidelines

- Use `IF EXISTS` instead of `SELECT COUNT(*)` when checking only for the existence of any matching data values. `IF EXISTS` stops the processing of the `SELECT` query as soon as the first matching row is found, whereas `SELECT COUNT(*)` continues searching until all matches are found, wasting I/O and CPU cycles.

- Using Exists/Not Exists in a sub-query is preferable to IN/ NOT IN for sets that are queried. As the potential target size of the set used in the IN gets larger, the performance benefit increases.
- Avoid unnecessary `ORDER BY` or `DISTINCT` clauses. Unless the Query Optimizer determines that the rows will be returned in sorted order or all rows are unique, these operations require a worktable for processing the results, which incurs extra overhead and I/O. Avoid these operations if it is not imperative for the rows to be returned in a specific order or if it's not necessary to eliminate duplicate rows.
- Use `UNION ALL` instead of `UNION` if you do not need to eliminate duplicate result rows from the result sets being combined with the `UNION` operator. The `UNION` statement has to combine the result sets into a worktable to remove any duplicate rows from the result set. `UNION ALL` simply concatenates the result sets together, without the overhead of putting them into a worktable to remove duplicate rows.
- Use table variables instead of temporary tables whenever possible or feasible. Table variables are memory resident and do not incur the I/O overhead and system table and I/O contention that can occur in `tempdb` with normal temporary tables.
- If you need to use temporary tables, keep them as small as possible so they are created and populated more quickly and use less memory and incur less I/O. Select only the required columns rather than using `SELECT *`, and retrieve only the rows from the base table that you actually need to reference. The smaller the temporary table, the faster it is to create and access the table.
- If a temporary table is of sufficient size and will be accessed multiple times, it is often cost effective to create an index on it on the column(s) that will be referenced in the search arguments (SARGs) of queries against the temporary table. Do this only if the time it takes to create the index plus the time the queries take to run using the index is less than the sum total of the time it takes the queries against the temporary table to run without the index.
- Avoid unnecessary function executions. If you call a SQL Server function (for example, `getdate()`) repeatedly within T-SQL code, consider using a local variable to hold the value returned by the function and use the local variable repeatedly throughout your SQL statements rather than repeatedly executing the SQL Server function. This saves CPU cycles within your T-SQL code.
- Try to use set-oriented operations instead of cursor operations whenever possible and feasible. SQL Server is optimized for set-oriented operations, so they are almost always faster than cursor operations performing the same task. However, one potential exception to this rule is if performing a large set-oriented operation lead to locking concurrency issues. Even though a single update runs faster than a cursor, while it is running, the single update might end up locking the entire table, or large portions of the table, for an extended period of time. This would prevent other users from accessing the table during the update. If concurrent access to the table is more important than the time it takes for the update itself to complete, you might want to consider using a cursor.

- Consider using the `MERGE` statement introduced in SQL Server 2008 when you need to perform multiple updates against a table (`UPDATE`, `INSERT`, or `DELETE`) because it enables you to perform these operations in a single pass of the table rather than perform a separate pass for each operation.

- Consider using the `OUTPUT` clause to return results from `INSERT`, `UPDATE`, or `DELETE` statements rather than having to perform a separate lookup against the table.

- Use search arguments that can be effectively optimized by the Query Optimizer. Try to avoid using any negative logic in your SARGs (for example, `!=`, `<>`, `not in`) or performing operations on, or applying functions to, the columns in the SARG. Avoid using expressions in your SARGs where the search value cannot be evaluated until runtime (such as local variables, functions, and aggregations in subqueries) because the optimizer cannot accurately determine the number of matching rows because it doesn't have a value to compare against the histogram values during query optimization. Consider putting the queries into stored procedures and passing in the value of the expression as a parameter. The Query Optimizer evaluates the value of a parameter prior to optimization. SQL Server evaluates the expression prior to optimizing the stored procedure.

- Avoid data type mismatches on join columns.

- Avoid writing large complex queries whenever possible. Complex queries with a large number of tables and join conditions can take a long time to optimize. It may not be possible for the Query Optimizer to analyze the entire set of plan alternatives, and it is possible that a suboptimal query plans could be chosen. Typically, if a query involves more than 12 tables, it is likely that the Query Optimizer will have to rely on heuristics and shortcuts to generate a query plan and may miss some optimal strategies.

For more tips and information on coding effective and efficient queries, see Chapters 43, "Transact-SQL Programming Guidelines, Tips, and Tricks," and 35.

Stored Procedure Guidelines

- Use stored procedures for SQL execution from your applications. Stored procedure execution can be more efficient that ad hoc SQL due to reduced network traffic and query plan caching for stored procedures.

- Use stored procedures to make your database sort of a "black box" as far as the as your application code is concerned. If all database access is managed through stored procedures, the applications are shielded from possible changes to the underlying database structures. You can simply modify the existing stored procedures to reflect the changes to the database structures without requiring any changes to the front-end application code.

- Ensure that your parameter data types match the column data types they are being compared against to avoid data type mismatches and poor query optimization.

- Avoid transaction nesting issues in your stored procedures by developing a consistent error-handling strategy for failed transactions or other errors that occur in transactions within your stored procedures. Implement that strategy consistently across all procedures and applications. Within stored procedures that might be nested, you need to check whether the procedure is already being called from within a transaction before issuing another `BEGIN TRAN` statement. If a transaction is already active, you can issue a `SAVE TRAN` statement so that the procedure can roll back only the work that it has performed and allow the calling procedure that initiated the transaction to determine whether to continue or abort the overall transaction.
- Break up large, complex stored procedures into smaller, more manageable stored procedures. Try to create very modular pieces of code that are easily reused and/or nested.

For more information on using and optimizing stored procedures, see Chapter 28, "Creating and Managing Stored Procedures."

Coding Efficient Transactions and Minimizing Locking Contention

Poorly written or inefficient transactions can have a detrimental effect on concurrency of access to data and overall application performance. To reduce locking contention for resources, you should keep transactions as short and efficient as possible. During development, you might not even notice that a problem exists; the problem might become noticeable only after the system load is increased and multiple users are executing transactions simultaneously.

Following are some guidelines to consider when coding transactions to minimize locking contention and improve application performance:

- Do not return result sets within a transaction. Doing so prolongs the transaction unnecessarily. Perform all data retrieval and analysis outside the transaction.
- *Never* prompt for user input during a transaction. If you do, you lose all control over the duration of the transaction. (Even the best programmers miss this one on occasion.) On the failure of a transaction, be sure to issue the rollback before putting up a message box telling the user that a problem occurred.
- Use optimistic locking or snapshot isolation. If user input is unavoidable between data retrieval and modification and you need to handle the possibility of another user modifying the data values read, leverage the necessary locking strategy (or isolation) to guarantee that no other user corrupts this data. Simple things like re-read and compare, as opposed to holding the resource.
- Keep statements that comprise a transaction in a single batch to eliminate unnecessary delays caused by network input/output between the initial `BEGIN TRAN` statement and the subsequent `COMMIT TRAN` commands. Additionally, keeping the `BEGIN TRAN` and `COMMIT/ROLLBACK` statements within the same batch helps avoid the possibility of leaving transactions open should the `COMMIT/ROLLBACK` statement not be issued in a subsequent batch.

- Consider coding transactions entirely within stored procedures. Stored procedures typically run faster than commands executed from a batch. In addition, because they are server resident, stored procedures reduce the amount of network I/O that occurs during execution of the transaction, resulting in faster completion of the transaction.
- Keep transactions as short and concise as possible. The shorter the period of time locks are held, the less chance for lock contention. Keep commands that are not essential to the unit of work being managed by the transaction (for example, assignment selects, retrieval of updated or inserted rows) outside the transaction.
- Use the lowest level of locking isolation required by each process. For example, if dirty reads are acceptable and accurate results are not imperative, consider using transaction Isolation Level 0. Use the Repeatable Read or Serializable Read isolation levels only if absolutely necessary.

For more information on managing transactions and minimizing locking contention, see Chapters 37, "Locking and Performance," and 31, "Transaction Management and the Transaction Log."

Application Design Guidelines

- **Locking/deadlock considerations**—These considerations are often the most misunderstood part of SQL Server implementations. Start by standardizing on update, insert, and delete order for all applications that modify data. You do not want to design in locking or deadlocking issues because of inconsistent resource locking orders that result in a "deadly embrace." For a more in-depth discussion on locking and deadlocking and recommendations for avoiding locking performance issues, see Chapter 37.
- **Stateless application design**—To scale out, your application needs to take advantage of load-balancing tiers, application server clustering, and other scaleout options. If you don't force the application or database to carry state, you will have much more success in your scaleout plans.
- **Remote Procedure Calls/linked servers**—Often data can be accessed via linked server connections rather than by redundantly copying or replicating data into a database. You can take advantage of this capability with SQL Server to reduce the redundant storage of data and eliminate synchronization issues between redundant data stores. Because Remote Procedure Calls are being deprecated in SQL Server, you should stay away from them.
- **Transactional integrity**—There is no excuse for sacrificing transactional integrity for performance. The extra overhead (and possible performance impact) comes with holding resources (and locks) until the transaction commit point to ensure data integrity. However, if you keep the logical unit of work (the business transaction) as small as possible, you can usually minimize the impact. In other words, you should keep your transaction sizes small and tight.

Distributed Data Guidelines

- **Distribute for disaster recovery**—Those organizations that have a disaster recovery requirement that they would like to fulfill with distributed data can use several options. One is traditional bit-level stretch clustering (using third-party products such as from Symantec) to your disaster recovery site. Another is simple log shipping to a secondary data center at some interval. Keep in mind, though, that log shipping will be deprecated at some point. Other options include database mirroring (asynchronous mode), periodic full database backups that are sent to another site and restored to a standby server, and a few variations of data replication.
- **Distribute to satisfy partitioned data accesses**—If you have very discrete and separate data access by some natural key such as geography or product types, it is often easy to have a huge performance increase by distributing or partitioning your tables to serve these accesses. Data replication options such as peer-to-peer and multiple publishers fit this well when you also need to isolate the data to separate servers and even on separate continents. Chapter 19, "Replication," describes all replication variations.
- **Distribute for performance**—Taking the isolation approach a bit further, you can devise a variety of SQL Server configurations that greatly isolate entire classes of data access, such as reporting access isolated away from online transactional processing, and so on. Classic SQL Server–based methods for this now include the use of database mirroring and snapshots on the mirror, a few of the data replication options, and others. Check in both Chapters 20, "Database Mirroring," and 32, "Database Snapshots," for details.

High-Availability Guidelines

- **Understand your high-availability (HA) needs first**—More important than applying a single technical solution to achieve high availability is to actually decide what you really need. You should evaluate exactly what your HA requirements might be with a formal assessment and a cost to the company if you do not have HA for your application. See Chapter 18, "SQL Server High Availability," for a complete depiction of your needs and options.
- **Know your options for different levels of HA achievement**—With SQL Server, there are several ways to achieve nearly the same level of high availability, including SQL clustering, data replication, database mirroring, log shipping, so on. But deciding on the right one often depends on many other variables. Again, refer to Chapter 18 for details or pick up *Microsoft SQL Server High Availability* by Sams Publishing as soon as you can to see how to do a complete HA assessment and technology deployment. This book covers it all!
- **Be aware of sacrifices for HA at the expense of performance**—High availability often comes at the expense of performance. As an example, if you use database mir-

roring in its high availability/automatic failover configuration, you actually end up with slower transaction processing. This can hurt if your SLAs are for subsecond transactions. Be extremely careful here. Apply the HA solution that matches your entire application's service-level agreements.

We have listed many guidelines for you to consider. Our hope is that you run through them for every SQL Server–based system you build. Use them as a checklist so that you catch the big design issues early and that you are designing in performance from the start.

Tools of the Performance and Tuning Trade

If you are going off to war (Performance and Tuning war), you should not come empty handed. Bring all your heaviest artillery. In other words, make sure you have plenty of performance and tuning tools to help you diagnose and resolve your issues (to fight your war). One tool we are providing you is this formal performance and tuning methodology outlined in this chapter. But methodologies are only part of the process. There are tools you can use out of the box from Microsoft as well as plenty of third-party tools that will help you shed much light on any issues you may be having. In the following sections, we outline a few of both so you can see various methods of getting to the heart of your performance and tuning problems. Some tools are highly graphic and easy to use; others are more text-based and require much more effort and organizing. But you need to come prepared to fight the war. Do not wait until you have a performance problem in your production environment to learn how to use one of these tools or to have bought a performance and tuning tool. Get what you need upfront.

Microsoft Out-of-the-Box

Microsoft continues to offer some built-in capabilities around performance and tuning with tools such as SQL Server Profiler, Data Collection Services, Performance Monitor counters that monitor many of the execution aspects of SQL Server, and plenty of SQL options at the server level to ensure optimal execution. We mention a few here, but other chapters in this book describe these offerings in greater detail:

- **SQL Server Profiler**—This rock-solid Microsoft-bundled offering is slowly getting better and better. As you can see in Figure 41.6, the SQL statements across a SQL Server instance are captured along with the execution statistics and other performance handles. You can save your traces and even import them into SQL Server tables for analysis by sorting the raw SQL code into the Top 10 (or 100) worst-performing queries. We include SQL statements on the CD of this book to help you manipulate the raw queries and organize them into a usable order (such as the top 100 worst queries).

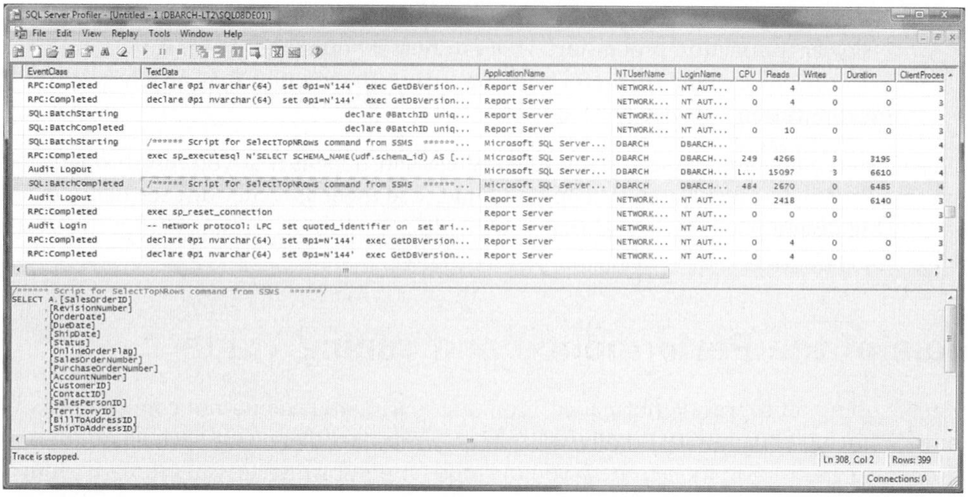

FIGURE 41.6 SQL Server Profiler tracing SQL statements.

- **Other Microsoft tools**—As mentioned previously, you can also use other tools such as Perfmon counters to isolate locking, deadlocking, memory utilization, CPU utilization, cache hit ratios, physical and logical disk I/Os, disk queue lengths, and a host of others. This includes counters for database mirroring execution, data replication execution, and many others. Even DBCC is still a viable tool for helping track down pesky things like excessive page splits that play havoc on performance. Chapters 39 and 49 take you deep into these out-of-the-box capabilities for SQL Server.

Third-Party Performance and Tuning Tools

There are a number of performance monitoring and tuning tools available for third-party vendors. Here, we list a few that we have some personal experience with:

- **Precise 8.5**—For database and other tier monitoring in one package, Precise TPM (formerly Precise i3 from Symantec but spun out a few years ago) is one of the best out there. It's a bit pricey, but for larger organizations that have vast implementations, investing in this type of holistic toolset can pay dividends. See www.precise.com for a current release of database and J2EE monitoring capabilities.

- **SQL Shot**—This tool uses a different approach from Microsoft. In particular, SQL Shot bubbles up all SQL Server–based execution information into a cockpit of visuals (or graphics). Figure 41.7 shows how easy it is to see trouble spots in your SQL Server–based system by using SQL Shot's main GUI. See www.dbarchitechs.com for a current release of the SQL Server 2008 R2 version.

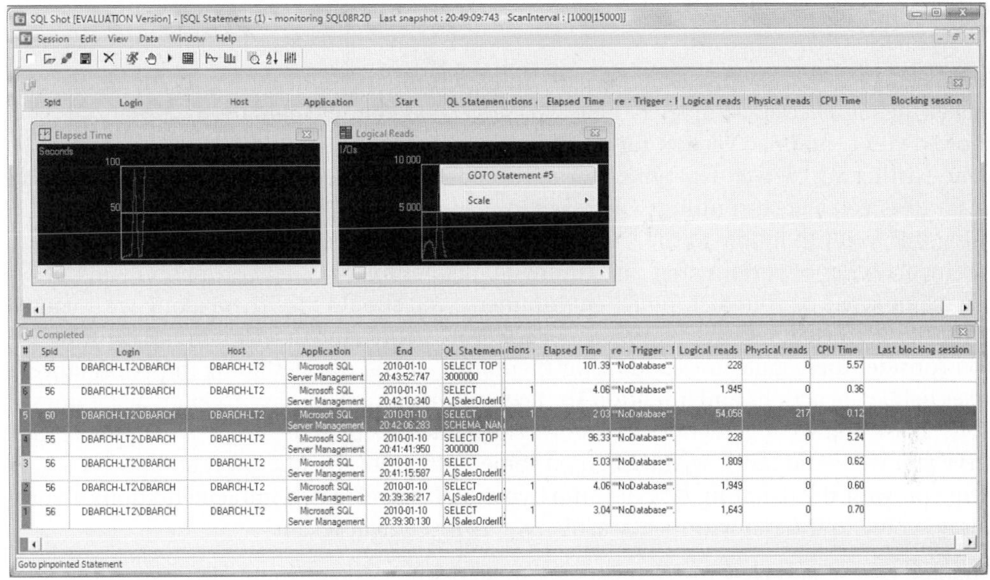

FIGURE 41.7 Graphic depiction of SQL Server performance issues using SQL Shot.

- **Proactive DBA SQL Capture**—This tool provides no-impact database monitoring of end-user response times and SQL activity. SQL Capture works by "sniffing" network SQL conversations between clients and SQL Server, gathering a wide variety of metrics on the SQL executed by clients. Capturing can occur right on the target server for convenient, low-impact monitoring or on a separate machine for true, no-impact capturing of database activity. You can log all or only selected SQL details to a repository database of your choice and/or to operating system flat files for later viewing and analysis. See www.proactivedba.com for more detailed information on the current release.
- **Idera SQL Diagnostic Monitor SQL**—This performance monitoring and diagnostics solution can proactively alert administrators to health, performance, or availability problems within their SQL Server environment, all from a central console. In addition to real-time monitoring and analysis, current versions also provide the History Browser, which allows you to diagnose historical SQL Server performance problems by selecting a historical point-in-time to view. See www.idera.com for information on the current release.

Again, come to the war with all your weapons. This is critical work, and you need to make great performance and tuning decisions, be able to isolate issues quickly, and uncover even the most complex problems.

Summary

In this chapter, you saw the difference a formal performance and tuning methodology can make when applied to completely new SQL Server–based implementations. We also showed you a modified version for attacking performance issues you might have with your existing SQL Server deployment. You should use the one that fits your needs best and guarantees you a great-running SQL Server implementation. But you need to use something that you can follow to the letter so that nothing falls between the cracks. We also outlined a series of performance and tuning guidelines for you that correspond with all the major layers of your SQL Server environment. You should take these along with you to every design review, code walkthrough, or solution architecture checkpoint. Make sure you consider these guidelines and factor them into all you do. Designing in performance takes deliberate actions and attention to the bigger picture. You have to know what questions to ask and what guidelines to follow. The guidelines presented in this chapter should serve you well. And lastly, we highlighted some of the tools by Microsoft and others to help you with the daunting task of tuning your SQL Server–based implementation. If you always come to the war with heavy artillery, you'll get great results!

Chapter 42, "What's New for Transact-SQL in SQL Server 2008," highlights new features and changes to some existing ones to help you stay current with the ever-expanding Transact-SQL offering.

Index

Symbols

` (backtick), 492

[ ] (brackets), 495

+= compound operator, CD:1569

-= compound operator, CD:1569

*= compound operator, CD:1569

/= compound operator, CD:1569

%= compound operator, CD:1569

^= compound operator, CD:1569

|= compound operator, CD:1569

&= compound operator, CD:1569

$( ) designators, 108

$ (dollar sign), 492

| (pipe character), 483

+ (plus sign), 493

(pound sign), 491, 879

$_ special variable, 493

1204 trace flags (error logs), 1386-1388

1222 trace flags (error logs), 1388-1390

A

access

- clients. *See* client data access technologies
- Database Engine data access, 11-12
- identity access management, 364, 366
- of performance counters via T-SQL, 1477

access check cache bucket count configuration option, CD:2284

access check cache quota configuration option, CD:2285

access path costs, estimating, 1221-1222

clustered indexes, 1222-1223

nonclustered indexes, 1223-1227

table scans, 1227-1228

Account Provisioning page (SQL Server Installation Center), 205-206

accounts

for Database Mail, creating, 429-432

SQL Server Agent proxy accounts, 455-456

startup accounts for SQL Server Agent, 452-453

ACID properties, 996

@action parameter, CD:2013

actions (SSEE), 1459

active multisite DR pattern, CD:2334

active/active configuration

DR sites pattern, CD:2333-CD:2334

SQL Server Clustering, 657

active/passive configuration

DR sites pattern, CD:2332-CD:2333

SQL Server Clustering, 657

ActiveX Data Object Multidimensional (ADO MD), CD:2032, CD:2077

Activity Monitor, 75-77, 1483

ad hoc distributed queries configuration option, CD:2285

adapters (SSIS), Attunity CDC Suite, CD:2147

Add-Content cmdlet, 491

ADD COLUMN clause, 767

ADD parameter (ALTER FULLTEXT INDEX), CD:2011-CD:2012

AddHours method, 502

adding

CLR functions to databases, 944-945

CLR stored procedures to databases, CD:1780-CD:1781

columns (T-SQL), 767-768

counters, 1469

data sources to OLAP databases, CD:2044-CD:2046

extended stored procedures to SQL Server, CD:1782-CD:1783

linked servers, CD:2253-CD:2260

AddMilliseconds method, 502

AddMinutes method, 502

AddMonths method, 503

AddSeconds method, 503

AddYears method, 503

administration tools (SSMS), 71

Activity Monitor, 75-77

Log File Viewer, 77, 79

Object Explorer. *See* Object Explorer

registered servers, 71-72

SQL Server Utility, 79-83, 85

ADO MD (ActiveX Data Object Multidimensional), CD:2032, CD:2077

ADO.NET, CD:1788-CD1793, CD:1804, CD:1810

ADO.NET Data Services (ADODS), CD:1787, CD:1803-CD:1805

building data services, CD:1806-CD:1811

CRUD operations, CD:1811-CD:1816

Advanced Encryption Standard (AES), 338

Advanced menu (SQL Server Installation Center), 211

Advanced page (SQL Server Agent), 451

Advanced Windowing Extensions (AWE), CD:2289-CD:2291

adXactReadcommitted function, 1345

AES (Advanced Encryption Standard), 338

affinity I/O mask configuration option, CD:2286-CD:2287

affinity mask configuration option, CD:2287-CD:2288

AFTER triggers
- combining with INSTEAD OF triggers, 971-972
- example, 954-955
- executing, 955
- explained, 953-954
- special considerations, 956-957
- trigger firing order, 956
- versus INSTEAD OF triggers, 970

agent history clean up: distribution, 571

Agent XP configuration option, CD:2289

agents. *See* replication agents

aggregates. *See* UDAs (user-defined aggregates)

aggregating data within cubes in OLAP database creation, CD:2066-CD:2071

Aggregation Design Wizard, CD:2070

aging query plans, 1256-1257

alert mail notifications (SQL Server Agent Mail), 443-444

alert responses, 472, 474

Alert System page (SQL Server Agent), 451

alerts
- creating with SQL Server Agent Mail, 443-444
- defined, 449
- scripting, 474-475
- SQL Server Agent, 469
  - alert properties, 469-472
  - alert responses, 472, 474

algorithms, 338

alias data types, 753

aliases, 277, 484

allocating space
- extents, 1113-1114
- GAM pages, 1114

AllocUnit locking level (SQL Server), 1364

ALLOW_PAGE_LOCK, 1373

ALLOW_PAGE_LOCKS, 799, 1372-1373

ALLOW_ROW_LOCKS, 799, 1372

ALLOW_SNAPSHOT_ISOLATION, 1348

ALTER, 312

ALTER ASSEMBLY, CD:1828

ALTER COLUMN, 766-767

ALTER DATABASE, 632, 644, 714, 722, 726, 736, 1099

ALTER FULLTEXT INDEX, CD:2010
- ADD parameter, CD:2011-CD:2012
- DISABLE parameter, CD:2010-CD:2011
- DROP parameter, CD:2012
- ENABLE parameter, CD:2010-CD:2011
- SET CHANGE_TRACKING parameter, CD:2011
- START parameter, CD:2012-CD:2013
- STOP parameter, CD:2012-CD:2013

ALTER FUNCTION, 939

ALTER INDEX, 803, 1175-1176, 1178, 1372

ALTER INDEX REBUILD, 805

ALTER INDEX REORGANIZE, 1077

ALTER PARTITION SCHEME, 783

ALTER PROCEDURE, 891-892

ALTER RESOURCE GOVERNOR, 1499

ALTER RESOURCE GOVERNOR RECONFIGURE, 1515

ALTER RESOURCE POOL, 1513

ALTER ROLE, 322

ALTER SERVER AUDIT, 372, 374

ALTER TABLE
- ADD COLUMN clause, 767
- ALTER COLUMN clause, 766-767
- creating constraints, 764, 823
- DROP COLUMN clause, 768

ALTER USER, 320

ALTER VIEW, 852

ALTER WORKLOAD GROUP, 1513

altering views with T-SQL, 852

American National Standards Institute (ANSI), 301

analysis phase (transaction recovery process), 1029

Analysis Services. *See* SSAS (SQL Server Analysis Services)

Analysis Services Migration Wizard, 253

Analysis Wizard, 230-235

analyzing

slow stored procedures or queries with SQL Server Profiler, 157-158

STATISTICS IO, 1332-1333

stored procedures with Query Analyzer, 1315-1316

traces (SQL Server Profiler) with Database Engine Tuning Advisor, 138

anonymous subscriptions, 563

ANSI (American National Standards Institute), 301

ANY, 1248

application data values, CD:2337

Application locking level (SQL Server), 1365

application locks, granularity, 1369-1372

application progress, monitoring (SQL Server Profiler), 162-164

application roles, 309

ApplicationName data column (SQL Profiler), 1356

applications

DAC (data-tier application), 82-83

OLTP (online transaction processing) applications, 53

OLTP ERP, 53-56

OLTP shopping cart, 56-57

troubleshooting with ssbiagnose.exe, CD:1993-CD:1994

tuning guidelines, 1545

APPLY operator, CD:1722

CROSS APPLY, CD:1722-CD1723

OUTER APPLY, CD:1723-CD:1724

APP_NAME( ) function, 1507

architectural layers in tuning, 1520-1521

architecture

delivery architecture, subscriptions, CD:2237

SQL Server instance architecture, CD:2274-CD:2275

SQL Server Profiler, 122-123

SSIS (SQL Server Integration Services), CD:2105-CD:2110

SSRS (SQL Server Reporting Services), CD:2179-CD:2181

archiving, tuning guidelines, 1539

arguments, passing, 494

arithmetic operators, 496

arrays

explained, 495-496

short data cluster array, 1119

articles, filtering, 550-554

AS DEFAULT (CREATE FULLTEXT CATALOG), CD:2004

AS HTTP, CD:1934-CD:1937

ASC (CREATE INDEX), 796

assemblies, creating (managed stored procedures), CD:1833-CD:1834

Assert icon (Query Analyzer), 1308-1309

assessment stage (tuning methodology), 1524, 1529-1530

association rules (data mining algorithms), CD:2084

asymmetric key encryption, 338

asynchronous operations, 622

asynchronous statistics updating (indexes), 1163

Atom Publishing Protocol (AtomPub), CD:1803

Attach Databases dialog, 738

attaching databases, 737-739

attachments (email), sending

CSV files, 440-441

XML attachments, 439-440

ATTACH_REBUILD_LOG, 739

attributes, managed stored procedures, CD:1830-CD:1832
Attunity CDC Suite, CD:2147
audit methods, 40
auditing
  with SQL Server Audit, 368-372
  with T-SQL, 372-374
authentication, 294
  authentication modes, setting, 295
  mixed authentication mode, 294
  Windows Authentication mode, 294
AUTHORIZATION, CD:1933, CD:1966, CD:1987, CD:2005
authorization for web services, CD:1933
Auto Close, 723
AUTO_CREATE_STATISTICS, 1216
AUTO mode (XML), CD:1873-CD:1877
auto-parameterization, 1285
Auto Shrink, 723
AUTO_UPDATE_STATISTICS, 162, 723-725, 1216
AUTO_UPDATE_STATISTICS_ASYNC, 1275
AutoCommit transactions, 997-998
automated installs, 217
automatic checkpoints (logs), 1027-1028
automatic failover, 623
automatic query plan recompilation (stored procedures), performance, CD:1767
automatically updating index statistics, 1161-1163
AUTOSHRINK, 731
availability, enterprise computing, 655
Average Wait Time counter (SQLServer Locks object), 1358
AveragePricebyType( ) function, 924
AveragePricebyType2( ) function, 924
AvgBookPrice( ) function, 922
avoiding transaction nesting, CD:1736
awe enabled configuration option, CD:2289-CD:2291

B

B-tree indexes, 1132-1133
backtick (`), 492
Backup and Restore Events report, 413
BACKUP CERTIFICATE, 278, CD:1986
backup compression, 40
backup compression default configuration option, CD:2291
BACKUP DATABASE, 390, 392-393
backup devices, 385. *See also* backups
  creating, 387-388
  disk devices, 386
  media sets and families, 387
  network shares, 386-387
  tape devices, 386
BACKUP LOG, 391, 394-395
backupfile, 412
backupfilegroup, 412
backupmediafamily, 412
backupmediaset, 412
backups. *See also* backup devices
  Backup and Restore Events report, 413
  compressed backups, 402-403
  considerations for very large databases, 425
  copy backups, 402
  copy-only backups, 382
  creating
    with SSMS, 388-390
    with T-SQL, 390-391, 393
  databases, 516-518
  developing backup plans, 378-379
  differential backups, 380, 397-398
  differential partial backups, 381
  file/filegroup backups, 381, 400-401
  frequency of, 423-424
  full database backups, 380, 396-397

HA (high availability), 527
Maintenance Plan Wizard, 1072, 1074-1075
maintenance plans, 426
mirrored backups, 401-402
new features, 377-378
partial backups, 381, 398-400
recovery models. *See* recovery, recovery models
replication monitoring, 612-613
restoring to new locations, 736
snapshot backups, 425
standby servers, 424-425
system database backups, 403
system tables, 412-413
tail of transaction logs, 418
TDE certificates and keys, 353-355
transaction log backups, 382
transaction logs, 393
creating with SSMS, 394
creating with T-SQL, 394-395
tuning guidelines, 1537

backupset, 412

balancers, tuning guidelines, 1535

base tables, 854-858

baselines, providing with database snapshots, 1054

BASIC authentication, CD:1934

.BAT files, 104

batches
bulk-copy operations (SSIS), CD:2164
transactions, 1007-1009

BATCHES option (WEBMETHOD) 1940

BCM (bulk changed map) pages, 1116

bcp (Bulk Copy Program) utility, CD:2099
hints, supplying to, CD:2165-CD:2166
SSIS (SQL Server Integration Services), CD:2147-CD:2153
file, CD:2153
format, CD:2153-CD:2163
views, CD:2163
syntax, 115-116

BEGIN CONVERSATION DIALOG, CD:1974-CD:1976

BEGIN DISTRIBUTED TRANSACTION, CD:1764

BEGIN TRANSACTION, 998, 1001, 1006, 1016, 1019, CD:1764

best practices
checking best practices compliance, 706
MERGE statement, CD:1558-CD:1559
Policy-Based Management, 706-707
T-SQL. *See* T-SQL, coding recommendations

bidirectional traffic, 288

BIDS
developing reports with, CD:2196-CD:2199
overview, CD:2190

bigint data type, 748

binary columns, RAW XML mode, CD:1871

binary data type, 748

bipubs2005 database, installing, 7

bit data type, 748

BLOBs, full-text indexing of, CD:2006-CD:2007. *See also* unstructured data in FILESTREAM storage

blocked process threshold configuration option, CD:2291

BLOCKSIZE (BACKUP DATABASE), 392

bottlenecks, identifying with SQL Server Profiler, 160-162

bound connections (transactions), 1039-1040

bound defaults, 833

brackets ([ ]), 495

breadth-first indexing, CD:1581

Browser role, CD:2234

browsing data within cubes in OLAP database creation, CD:2071-CD:2075

built-in methods, CD:1899-CD:1918

built-in roles, securing reports, CD:2234-CD:2235

BUILTIN\Administrators, 297

bulk changed map (BCM) pages, 1116

Bulk Copy Program. See bcp (Bulk Copy Program) utility

BULK INSERT statement, 115

bulk update locks, 1363

bulk-copy operations (SSIS), CD:2163-CD2166

bulkadmin, 303

C

C# client application examples

- calling web methods–bound stored procedures that return XML, CD:1951-CD:1953
- running a web method bound to a stored procedure, CD:1942-CD:1947
- running ad hoc T-SQL batches from SQL Server web services, CD:1947-CD1951

C2 audit mode, CD:2291-CD:2292

cache refresh plans (CRPs), CD:2239

cached reports

- CRPs (cache refresh plans), CD:2239
- report execution options, CD:2237-CD:2238

caching

- procedure caches, stored procedures, CD:1766
- query plan caching. *See* query plan, caching
- SANs (storage area networks), 1424

calculated members (calculations), OLAP database creation, CD:2078-CD:2079

calculating dates. *See* date calculations

CALLED ON NULL INPUT (CREATE FUNCTION), 928-929

CALLER (EXECUTE AS), 883

calling stored procedures from transactions, CD:1735-CD:1738

capture instances, CD:1620

CAS (Code Access Security) permission sets, CD:1827

CASCADE, 819

cascading deletes, 963-965, 1404

cascading FOREIGN KEY constraints, 967

cascading referential integrity, 818-820

cascading updates, 965-966

catalog views, 175-177

- system stored procedures and, CD:1954-CD:1955
- viewing DDL triggers, 987

catalogs, full-text, CD:2002

CATCH block, CD:1738-CD:1739

categories (policies)

- creating, 701
- explained, 693

CDC (Change Data Capture), CD:1614-CD:1626

- Change Tracking versus, CD:1627
- DDL changes to source tables, CD:1626
- enabling for databases, CD:1617
- enabling for tables, CD:1617-CD:1619
- explained, 41
- tables for, CD:1615-CD:1617
  - querying, CD:1619-CD:1626

cdc.captured_columns metadata table, CD:1616

cdc.change_tables metadata table, CD:1616

cdc.ddl_history metadata table, CD:1616

cdc.index_columns metadata table, CD:1616

cdc.lsn_time_mapping metadata table, CD:1616

Central Management Servers

- creating, 695-696
- explained, 695
- importing and evaluating policies to, 696-697
- registering SQL Server instances in, 696

central publisher replication model, 555-556

central publisher with remote distributor replication model, 557

central subscriber replication model, 559

certificates, 338

- backing up TDE certificates, 353-355
- conversation encryption, CD:1985-CD:1992
- encrypting columns with, 346-349
- root-level certificates, 278

Change Data Capture (CDC), CD:1614-CD:1626

- Change Tracking versus, CD:1627
- DDL changes to source tables, CD:1626
- enabling for databases, CD:1617
- enabling for tables, CD:1617-CD:1619
- explained, 41
- tables for, CD:1615-CD:1617
  - querying, CD:1619-CD:1626

Change Tracking, CD:1627-CD:1635

- explained, 41
- identifying changed columns, CD:1633-CD:1634
- identifying tracked changes, CD:1630-CD:1633
- implementing, CD:1628-CD:1630
- performance overhead of, CD:1634-CD:1635

changed columns, identifying, CD:1633-CD:1634

char data type, 748

CHARACTER SET, CD:1941

CHARACTER_SET (WEBMETHOD) 1941

Chart control, CD:2175, CD:2203

CHECK constraint, 764, 820-821

- tuning guidelines, 1538

checkpoints, 717

- logs, 1024-1028

CHECKSUM (BACKUP DATABASE), 392

CHECKSUM (RESTORE DATABASE), 405

CHECK_CONSTRAINTS hint, CD:2166

Children's Online Privacy Protection Act, 367

Choose a Chart Type window (Report Builder) 2219

CI record, 1122

classification functions

- creating, 1506-1509
- defined, 1495-1496
- modifying, 1516

CLEAR PORT, CD:1935

client access provisioning, 268-270

client applications, redistributing SNAC, 274

client data access technologies, 279

- drivers, 281
- JDBC, 287
- MDAC, 285-286
- .NET Framework, 283-284
- providers, 280
- SNAC, 281
- SNAC (ADO), 283
- SNAC (ODBC), 282-283
- SNAC (OLE DB), 282
- SQLCLR context connections, 284-285

client tools (client installation), 271-272

clients

- configuring, 274
  - connection encryption, 278-279
  - for database mirroring, 647-648
  - new features, 263-264
  - SSCM, 275-277
- defined, 265
- installing
  - client tools, 271-272
  - installation requirements, 271
  - new features, 263-264
  - SNAC, 272-274

CLOSE SYMMETRIC KEY, 348

CLR (common language runtime), 754, CD:1825
functions, 944-947
stored procedures, CD:1779
adding to databases, CD:1780-CD:1781
versus CLR stored procedures, CD:1781
triggers, 988-991
user-defined data types, 754
clr enabled configuration option, CD:2292
Cluster Administrator, viewing properties, 679
CLUSTERED (CREATE INDEX), 796
Clustered Index Delete icon (Query Analyzer), 1309
clustered index fill factors, tuning guidelines, 1540
Clustered Index Scan icon (Query Analyzer), 1309
clustered indexes, 792-793, 1112, 1133-1134
costs, 1222-1223
designing, 1185-1186
indexed views, 1192-1193
nonunique, 1135-1136
row structure, 1134-1135
tuning guidelines, 1540
clustered tables, 1130-1131
clusters, 658
building solutions with HA (high availability) options, 531-534
data mining algorithms, CD:2084
server clusters, 658
cmdlets
Add-Content, 491
Convert-UrnToPath, 509
Decode-SqlName, 509
defined, 483
Encode-SqlName, 509
Export-Csv, 501
filtering cmdlets, 499-500
ForEach-Object, 499
Format-List, 500
Format-Table, 500
formatting cmdlets, 500-501
Get-Alias, 490
Get-ChildItem, 490
Get-Command, 488
Get-Content, 490, 514
Get-Help, 488-489
Get-Item, 520
Get-Member, 489-490
Get-Process, 513
Get-Service, 513
Group-Object, 490
Import-Csv, 501
Invoke-PolicyEvaluation, 508, 521
Invoke-SqlCmd, 508, 520-521
Measure-Command, 490
New-Object, 490
Read-Host, 490
Select-Object, 490
Select-String, 515
Set-Content, 491
Set-ExecutionPolicy, 487
Sort-Object, 490
Start-Service, 513
Start-Transcript, 491
Where-Object, 499
Write-Host, 490
Codd, E. F., 1537
Code Access Security (CAS) permission sets, CD:1827
Codezone Community, 68
coding and testing stage (tuning methodology), 1526-1527, 1532
coding recommendations for T-SQL. ***See* T-SQL, coding recommendations**
coding transactions, 1022-1023

Collapse icon (Query Analyzer), 1310

collation, 720

Collation property, 726

column lists (T-SQL), CD:1638-CD:1640

COLUMN NAME (CREATE FULLTEXT INDEX), CD:2005-CD:2006

column operator values (sp trace setfilter), 151

column sets, 36, CD:1600-CD:1601

column-level encryption

with certificates, 346-349

explained, 343

with passphrases, 344-346

TDE (transparent data encryption)

backing up TDE certificates and keys, 353-355

compared to column-level encryption, 356-357

explained, 350-351

implementing, 351-352

limitations, 355-356

managing in SSMS, 352-353

ColumnCount parameter (SqlTriggerContext), CD:1856

COLUMNPROPERTY function, CD:2015

columns

adding in T-SQL, 767-768

checking for updates, 959-961

column sets, 36, 759-761

computed columns

denormalization, 1410-1411

indexes, 1193-1195

data types. *See* data types

FILESTREAM storage, 759

indexes

included columns, 1190-1191

joins, 1184

joining, 521-522

naming, 747

new xml data type, CD:1892-CD:1894

overview, 747

properties, 755

changing with T-SQL, 766-767

computed columns, 758

IDENTITY, 755-757

NULL and NOT NULL, 755

ROWGUIDCOL, 757

renumbering, CD:2162-CD:2163

sparse columns, 36, 759-761, 1107-1108, CD:1600-CD:1605

statistics, generating, 1161-1167, 1169

xml columns

full-text indexing, CD:1924-CD:1925

indexing, CD:1918-CD:1924

command lines, DTA (Database Engine Tuning Advisor), CD:2321-CD:2326

command sourcing phase (dtexec) 2136

command-line utilities

bcp. *See* bcp (Bulk Copy Program) utility

dta, 109-112

installation locations, 104

isql, 105

new features, 104-105

osql, 105

sac, 105

sqlcmd

executing, 106-108

scripting variables with, 108-109

syntax, 105-106

sqldiag, 116-117

sqlps, 105

sqlservr, 118

ssbdiagnose, 47

SSIS (SQL Server Integration Services), CD:2112

tablediff, 112-115

comments

adding to scripts, 491

in T-SQL code, CD:1652-CD:1653

COMMIT, 999

COMMIT TRAN, 999

common criteria compliance enabled configuration option, CD:2292

Common Language Runtime (CLR), 754, CD:1825

common table expressions. *See* **CTE (common table expressions)**

Compact 3.5 Edition (SQL Server)

features, 29

licensing, 32

comparing

contents of two tables, 112-115

dates, CD:1666-CD:1669

comparison operators, 496

ComparisonStyle property, 726

compatibility levels, 242

compatibility locks, 1376-1377

compatibility views, 172-175

compiling

DML statements, 1212-1213

queries. *See* queries

query plans, 1257-1258

Complete page (SQL Server Installation Center), 210-211

complex expressions, CD:2200-CD:2202

complex queries, tuning guidelines, 1543

compliance

checking best practices compliance, 706

SQL Server and, 366-367

composite indexes

designing, 1184

tuning guidelines, 1540

compound operators, 37, CD:1568-CD:1569

compressed backups, 402-403

compression

CI record, 1122

explained, 1117

managing with SSMS, 1126-1127

page-level compression, 1119-1121

evaluating, 1123-1126

implementing, 1122-1123

row-level compression, 1117-1119

COMPRESSION, 392, CD:1937

CompSales database, installing, 7

CompSales International (OLAP requirements example), CD:2040-CD:2041, CD:2081-CD:2082, CD:2095-CD:2096

cube, CD:2042, CD:2082

data, CD:2084-CD:2091

KPIs, CD:2082

OLAP, CD:2044

SQL, CD:2042-CD:2043

Compute Scalar icon (Query Analyzer), 1311

computed columns, 758

denormalization, 1410-1411

indexes, 1193-1195

SARG on, 1220-1221

CONCAT UNION, 1283

Concatenation icon (Query Analyzer), 1311

condition expressions, 830

conditional statements, 496-497

conditions

creating based on facets, 697-698

defined, 693

configuration data, CD:2337

configuration files, upgrading with, 250-251

configuration options (SQL Server 2008), CD:2275

access check cache bucket count, CD:2284

access check cache quota, CD:2285

ad hoc distributed queries, CD:2285

affinity I/O mask, CD:2286-CD:2287

affinity mask, CD:2287-CD:2288
Agent XP, CD:2289
awe enabled, CD:2289-CD:2291
backup compression default, CD:2291
blocked process threshold, CD:2291
c2 audit mode, CD:2291-CD:2292
clr enabled, CD:2292
common criteria compliance enabled, CD:2292
cost threshold for parallelism, CD:2293
cross db ownership chaining, CD:2293
cursor threshold, CD:2294
default full-text language, CD:2294-CD:2296
default language, CD:2296-CD:2298
EKM provider enabled, CD:2298
filestream_access_level, CD:2299
fill factor, CD:2299-CD:2300
fixing incorrect option settings, CD:2283
in-doubt xact resolution, CD:2300
index create memory, CD:2300
lightweight pooling, CD:2301
locks, CD:2301-CD:2302
max degree of parallelism, CD:2302
max server memory, CD:2302-CD:2303
max text repl size, CD:2304
max worker threads, CD:2305
min memory per query, CD:2306
min server memory, CD:2302-CD:2303
miscellaneous options, CD:2316
nested triggers, CD:2306
network packet size, CD:2306-CD:2307
new features, CD:2274
obsolete configuration options, CD:2283-CD:2284
optimize for ad hoc workloads, CD:2307-CD:2308
overview, CD:2275-CD:2283
parallelism, CD:2293
PH_timeout, CD:2308
priority boost, CD:2308-CD:2309
query governor cost limit, CD:2309-CD:2310
query wait, CD:2310
recovery interval, CD:2310-CD:2311
remote admin connections, CD:2311
remote login timeout, CD:2311
remote proc trans, CD:2312
remote query timeout, CD:2312-CD:2313
scan for startup procs, CD:2313
self-configuring options, CD:2276
setting with SSMS, CD:2283
show advanced options, CD:2313
user connections, CD:2313-CD:2314
user options, CD:2315-CD:2316
XP-related configuration options, CD:2316

configuration phase (dtexec) 2137

ConfigurationFile.ini file, 212-216

configuring. ***See also*** **configuration options (SQL Server 2008)**

clients, 274
  connection encryption, 278-279
  new features, 263-264
  SSCM, 275-277
Data Collector, 1433-1437
Database Mail
  mail profiles and accounts, 429-432
  overview, 428-429
  systemwide mail settings, 433
  testing setup, 433-434
database mirroring
  client setup and configuration, 647-648
  with Database Mirroring Wizard, 633-639
event forwarding, 477-478
linked servers, CD:2261-CD:2263

parallel queries, 1271-1272
query governors, 1299
remote servers, CD:2246-CD:2251
Resource Governor
creating resource pools, 1500-1502
enabling Resource Governor, 1499-1500
modifying configuration, 1513-1516
SQL Server Agent, 450
email notification, 454
properties, 450-452
proxy accounts, 455-456
startup account, 452-453
SQL Server database disks, 666-667
SSIS (SQL Server Integration Services), CD:2108
SSRS (SQL Server Reporting Services)
databases, CD:2187-CD:2188
email and, CD:2189
encryption, CD:2189-CD:2190
overview, CD:2186
Report, CD:2189
scale-out, CD:2190
Web, CD:2186-CD:2187
Windows, CD:2186

-confirm parameters, 503

connection encryption, configuring clients, 278-279

Connection page (SQL Server Agent), 451

Connection Test Program for SQL Server Cluster, 681-684

CONNECTIONPROPERTY( ) function, 1506

connections, bound, 1039-1040

connectivity
firewalls, 288
testing, 288-289
troubleshooting, 287

consistency (transactions), 572

Constant Scan icon (Query Analyzer), 1311

constraints, 813
CHECK, 820-821
creating, 821
with ALTER TABLE, 764
with CREATE TABLE, 764
with SSMS, 823-826
with T-SQL, 822-823
defining table constraints, 763-765
disabling, 829-830
dropping, 829
FOREIGN KEY, 816-818
cascading referential integrity, 818-820
gathering constraint information, 827-829
PRIMARY KEY, 813-814
UNIQUE, 815-816

construction phase (OLAP design methodologies), CD:2039

constructors, row, CD:1569-CD:1572

constructs (SQL Server Service Broker), CD:1965
creating queues for, CD:1970-CD:1972
defining messages and, CD:1965-CD:1969
defining services to, CD:1973
planning conversations, CD:1974-CD:1976
prioritizing, CD:1984
setting up contracts, CD:1970

containers (SSIS), CD:2106

CONTAINS, CD:2020
generation, CD:2021-CD:2022
LANGUAGE, CD:2022
proximity, CD:2022
search phrase, CD:2020-CD:2021
weighted, CD:2022

CONTAINSTABLE, CD:2020, CD:2023
generation, CD:2021-CD:2022
LANGUAGE, CD:2022
proximity, CD:2022
search phrase, CD:2020-CD:2021
weighted, CD:2022

Content Manager role, CD:2234

contention, locking, 1377-1380

identifying, 1378, 1380

minimizing, 1381-1382

context connection string (managed stored procedures), CD:1832

context connections, 284-285

CONTEXT INFO, CD:1671-CD:1673

context switching, 331-333

CONTINUE AFTER ERROR option

BACKUP DATABASE, 392

RESTORE DATABASE, 405

contracts, setting up for communication (SQL Server Service), CD:1970

CONTROL, 312, CD:1956

control of flow, 464, CD:2106

conversation encryption (SQL Server Service), CD:1985-CD:1992

conversation initiators, creating, CD:1976-CD:1979

conversation targets, creating, CD:1980-CD:1984

conversations, CD:1974

building routes to map conversations between, CD:1992

conversation initiator, creating, CD:1976-CD:1979

conversation targets, creating, CD:1980-CD:1984

remote service bindings, creating, CD:1992

planning between services (SQL Server Service), CD:1974-CD:1976

prioritizing (SQL Server Service Broker), CD:1984

conversion deadlocks, 1383

Convert-UrnToPath cmdlet, 509

converting dates, CD:1575-CD:1576, CD:1666-CD:1669

Copy Database Wizard, 238-241

COPY ONLY (BACKUP DATABASE), 393

copy-on-write technology, 620-621, 1048, 1050

copy-only backups, 382, 402

copying packages (dtutil utility), CD:2141-CD:2144

correlated subqueries, 1250-1251

cost (parallelism), CD:2293

cost threshold for parallelism configuration option, CD:2293

costs of SQL Server 2008, 31

counters

adding, 1469

performance counters, accessing via T-SQL, 1477

removing, 1468

user-defined counters, 1476-1477

covering indexes, 795, 1188-1190

CPU Utilization page, 1483

CPUs, tuning guidelines for, 1534

CREATE, creating stored procedures, 871-872

CREATE ASSEMBLY, 944-945, CD:1780, CD:1828

CREATE CERTIFICATE, 278, 346, CD:1985

CREATE DATABASE, 14, 713, 721-722, 1099

CREATE DEFAULT, 833

CREATE ENDPOINT, 627-629, CD:1931-CD:1933

CREATE FULLTEXT CATALOG, CD:2003-CD:2005

CREATE FULLTEXT INDEX, CD:2005

BLOBs and XML, CD:2006-CD:2007

COLUMN NAME, CD:2005-CD:2006

KEY INDEX, CD:2008

LANGUAGE, CD:2007-CD:2008

ON FULLTEXT CATALOG, CD:2008

POPULATION TYPE, CD:2008-CD:2010

TYPE COLUMN, CD:2006

CREATE FUNCTION, 925-926, 935, 945

CREATE INDEX, 796

arguments, 796-797

relational index options, 798-799

CREATE INDEX WITH DROP EXISTING, 805

CREATE LOGIN, CD:2250

CREATE MASTER KEY ENCRYPTION, 355

Create New Data Collector Set Wizard, 1470

CREATE PARTITION FUNCTION, 776-777, 782

CREATE PARTITION SCHEME, 782

CREATE PROCEDURE, 877-879, CD:1780

CREATE RESOURCE POOL, 1502

CREATE STATISTICS, 1167, 1169, 1216

CREATE TABLE, 745-747, 764, 822

CREATE TYPE, 753, 901

CREATE USER, 320

Create Utility Control Point Wizard, 82

CREATE WORKLOAD GROUP, 1505

credentials, 455

CROSS APPLY operator, CD:1722-CD:1723

cross db ownership chaining configuration option, CD:2293

crosstabs, CD:1718

CRPs (cache refresh plans), CD:2239

CRUD operations (ADO.NET Data Services), CD:1811-CD:1816

***Cryptography in the Database* (Kenan), 367**

CSV files

handling in PowerShell, 501-502

sending as attachments with Database Mail, 440-441

CTE (common table expressions), CD:1698-CD:1700

recursive, CD:1707-CD:1708

recursive queries, CD:1700

expanding, CD:1701-CD:1707

CUBE operator, CD:1561-CD:1562

cube perspectives, CD:2082

cubes

OLAP cube creation, CD:2042

OLAP database creation

aggregating with data, CD:2066-CD:2071

browsing data, CD:2071-CD:2075

building and deploying, CD:2064-CD:2065

creating, CD:2060-CD:2064

populating with data, CD:2065-CD:2066

SSAS, CD:2032-CD:2036

cumulative updates, installing, 218, 220, 222

CURSOR variables, CD:1748-CD:1753

cursor operations, tuning guidelines, 1542

CURSOR STATUS, CD:1750

cursor threshold configuration option, CD:2294

cursors

in multitier environments, CD:1659

performance, CD:1656-CD:1659

stored procedures, CD:1743-CD:1753

custom function templates, creating, 933-936

custom managed database objects

developing, CD:1825-CD:1864

managed triggers, CD:1856-CD:1861

permissions, CD:1827-CD:1829

related system catalogs, CD:1863-CD:1864

stored procedures, CD:1829-CD:1835

assembly creation, CD:1833-CD:1834

attributes, CD:1830-CD:1832

debugging, CD:1834-CD:1835

implementation contract, CD:1830-CD:1832

Microsoft.SqlServer.Server objects, CD:1832-CD:1833

transactions, CD:1861-CD:1863

UDAs (user-defined aggregates), CD:1853-CD:1856

UDFs (user-defined functions)

scalar UDFs, CD:1835-CD:1839

TVFs (table-valued UDFs), CD:1839-CD:1844

UDTs (user-defined types), CD:1844-CD:1852

Visual Studio, CD:2008 1829

custom stored procedure templates, creating, 875-879

customized data collection sets, 1446-1450

customizing format files (bcp utility), CD:2153-CD:2154

cycle deadlocks, 1382

D

DAC (data-tier application), 82-83

data

application data values, CD:2337

configuration data, CD:2337

controlling access with views, 842-844

delivering to users in OLAP database creation, CD:2076

metadata, CD:2337

data abstraction (views), 841-842

data access

client technologies, 279

drivers, 281

JDBC, 287

MDAC, 285-286

.NET Framework data provider for SQL Server, 283-284

providers, 280

SNAC, 281

SNAC (ADO), 283

SNAC (ODBC), 282-283

SNAC (OLE DB), 282

SQLCLR context connections, 284-285

Database Engine, 11-12

data bars, CD:2174, CD:2203

data characteristics (data replication), 578-579

Data Collection services, CD:2326-CD:2327

Data Collector, 1429-1430

customized data collection sets, 1446-1450

data collection sets, 1431

installing and configuring, 1433-1437

limitations and recommendations, 1450-1451

managing, 1443-1446

MDW, 1432-1433

reports, 1439-1442

runtime component, 1431

SSIS packages, 1432

system data collectors, 1437-1439

Data Collector Set (Windows Performance Monitor), 1469-1473

data columns

FILESTREAM storage for, CD:1597-CD:1599

SQL Profiler, 1356

traces (SQL Server Profiler), 127-128, 130

data compression

CI record, 1122

defined, 37

explained, 1117

managing with SSMS, 1126-1127

page-level compression, 1119-1121

evaluating, 1123-1126

implementing, 1122-1123

row-level compression, 1117-1119

Data Compression Wizard, 1127

Data Definition Language (DDL), CD:1892

Data Directories page (SQL Server Installation Center), 206-207

data distribution, 573-574

data encryption. *See* encryption

data files, 710

data flow (SSIS), CD:2107

data flow task (SSIS), CD:2107

data insertion with row constructors, CD:1569-CD:1572

data integrity
checking with Maintenance Plan Wizard, 1075-1076
constraints, 813
CHECK, 820-821
creating, 821
creating with SSMS, 823-826
creating with T-SQL, 822-823
disabling, 829-830
dropping, 829
FOREIGN KEY, 816-820
gathering constraint information, 827-829
PRIMARY KEY, 813-814
UNIQUE, 815-816
Database Engine, 12
declarative data integrity, 812
domain integrity, 812
enforcing, 812-813
entity integrity, 812
new features, 811
procedural data integrity, 813
referential integrity, 812
rules, 830-831
Data Junction, CD:2099
data manipulation
deleting rows, 1144
simplifying with views, 839-840
updating rows, 1145-1146
Data Manipulation Language. *See* DML
data mining, CD:2084-CD:2091
OLAP performance, CD:2093-CD:2094
SSIS, CD:2093
Data Mining Wizard, CD:2085-CD:2087
data modification
inserting data, 1141-1143
views and, 853-854
data pages
data rows
overview, 1104-1105
sparse columns, 1107-1108
sql_variant data type, 1107
structure of, 1105-1107
defined, 1103
page header, 1103-1104
row offset table, 1108-1109
data partitioning
HA (high availability), 539
horizontal data partitioning, 1412-1413
vertical data partitioning, 1413-1414
data region templates, CD:2173, CD:2199
data replication, 547-549, CD:2338-CD:2340
articles, filtering, 550-551, 553-554
building solutions with HA (high availability) options, 534-535
central publisher replication model, 555-556
central publisher with remote distributor replication model, 557
central subscriber replication model, 559
database mirroring and, 614
distribution server, 550
log shipping, 614
merge replication, 575-576
methods of data distribution, 573-574
monitoring, 603
backup and recovery, 612-613
in heterogeneous environments, 611-612
peer-to-peer replication, 609-610
Performance Monitor, 610-611
within SQL Server Management Studio, 606-607
SQL statements, 603-606
troubleshooting replication failures, 608

multiple publishers or multiple subscribers replication model, 559-560

new features, 546-547

peer-to-peer replication model, 561-562, 609-610

performance, 613-614

planning for, 572-573

publication server, 549-550

publications, 550

publisher subscriber replication model, 558

replication agents. *See* replication agents

scripting replication, 600, 602

setting up, 579-580

creating distributors and enabling publishing, 581-584

creating publications, 584-592

creating subscriptions, 594-600

horizontal and vertical filtering, 592, 594

snapshot replication, 574

subscription server, 550

subscriptions. *See* subscriptions

transactional replication, 574-575

updating subscribers replication model, 560-561

user requirements, 577-579

data rows (database pages)

overview, 1104-1105

sparse columns, 1107-1108

sql_variant data type, 1107

structure of, 1105-1107

Data Source View Wizard, CD:2048

data source views, creating, CD:2046-CD:2050

data sources

adding to OLAP databases, CD:2044-CD:2046

report data source, CD:2175

shared data sources, CD:2193

data storage, 710-711

FILESTREAM storage, CD:1592-CD:1593

for data columns, CD:1597-CD:1599

database setup, CD:1596

enabling, CD:1593-CD:1596

data structures, 1092-1093. *See also* specific data structures (i.e. indexes, tables)

data transformation requirement (SSIS), CD:2113-CD:2116

Data Transformation Services. *See* DTS (Data Transformation Services)

data types

CLR user-defined data types, 754

date and time, 751, CD:1572-CD:1575

file data types, CD:2153

hierarchyid, 751, CD:1580-CD:1590, CD:1592

creating hierarchies, CD:1580-CD:1581

modifying hierarchies, CD:1587-CD:1590, CD:1592

populating hierarchies, CD:1581-CD:1583

querying hierarchies, CD:1583-CD:1587

large row support, 753

large-value data types, 752

new features, 37

new xml data type, CD:1890-CD:1891

built-in methods, CD:1899-CD:1918

columns, CD:1892-CD:1894

schema collections, CD:1894-CD:1899

overview, 750

search argument problems, 1277

spatial data types, 751-752, CD:1605-CD:1614

table of, 748-750

tuning guidelines, 1538

user-defined data types, 753-754

xml, 751

data-centric approach to disaster recovery, CD:2337-CD:2338

data-driven subscriptions, CD:2236-CD:2237

data-tier application (DAC), 82-83

DataAccess parameter

scalar UDFs, CD:1836

SqlMethod, CD:1849

database administration, new features, 40-41

database allocations, tuning guidelines, 1537

Database Audit Specification, 369

database backups. ***See*** **backups**

database compatibility levels, 242

database design

denormalization

computed columns, 1410-1411

defined, 1408

guidelines, 1408-1409

horizontal data partitioning, 1412-1413

redundant data, 1409-1410

summary data, 1411

vertical data partitioning, 1413-1414

zero-to-one relationships, 1415

designing for performance, 1404-1405

filegroups and performance, 1415-1417

new features, 1403-1404

normalization

benefits of, 1407

first normal form, 1406

limitations of, 1407-1408

normalization conditions, 1405

second normal form, 1406-1407

third normal form, 1407

RAID (redundant array of inexpensive disks), 1417

RAID Level 0, 1418-1419

RAID Level 1, 1419-1420

RAID Level 5, 1421-1422

RAID Level 10, 1420

SANs (storage area networks)

cache, 1424

disk drive contention, 1424

explained, 1422-1423

performance, 1424-1425

Database Diagram Editor

creating constraints, 825

creating tables, 743-744

database diagrams, modifying tables, 772-773

database encryption key (DEK), 350

Database Engine

access to data, 11-12

data integrity, 12

explained, 10

storage, 10

upgrading, 243, 245-246

Database Engine Configuration page (SQL Server Installation Center), 205, 207-208

Database Engine Tuning Advisor. ***See*** **DTA**

database files, 711

file management, 1096-1097

filegroups, 713-715

log files, 1096

master database files, 719

primary data files, 712, 1095

properties, 1093

secondary data files, 712, 1095

transaction log files, 716-717

Database locking level (SQL Server), 1364

Database Mail, 427, 454

configuration

mail profiles and accounts, 429-432

overview, 428-429

systemwide mail settings, 433

testing, 433-434

deleting mail objects with T-SQL, 432-433

email attachments, 439-441

mail configuration objects, viewing, 445-446
mail message data, viewing, 446-447
new features, 427
receiving email, 441
security profiles, 431
sending email, 435-441
Service Broker (SSB), 434-435
updating with T-SQL, 432-433

Database Mail Configuration Wizard, 428-432

database maintenance
executing maintenance plans, 1088
Maintenance Plan Wizard
backing up databases, 1072, 1074-1075
checking database integrity, 1075-1076
maintaining indexes and statistics, 1077-1080
overview, 1070-1072
scheduling maintenance plans, 1080-1083
shrinking databases, 1076-1077
manual maintenance, 1084-1088
new features, 1070
policies, 1090
without a plan, 1089

database management system (DBMS). *See* DBMS

database master keys, 340-341

database mirroring, 46, CD:2341-CD:2342
asynchronous operations, 622
automatic failover, 623
building solutions with HA (high availability) options, 537-538
client setup and configuration, 647-648
combining with replication, 651-652
configuring with Database Mirroring Wizard, 633-639
copy-on-write technology, 620-621
creating databases on mirror server, 630-631
data replication and, 614
endpoints
creating, 627-628
dropping, 632
identifying, 632-633
explained, 17, 618-620
forced service, 623
manual failover, 623
mirror database server, 619, 622
monitoring, 639-642
new features, 617-618
operating modes, 622-623
permissions, 629-630
preparing for, 624-627
principal database server, 619, 622
removing mirroring, 643-645
reporting via database snapshots from mirror, 652-653
requirements, 624
role switching, 623
roles, 622
SQL Server 2005 versus SQL Server 2008, 649-650
synchronous operations, 622
testing failover from principal to mirror, 645-646
when to use, 621
witness database server, 620, 622

Database Mirroring Monitor, 639-642

Database Mirroring Wizard, 633-639

database mirrors
providing reporting databases from, 1055-1056
reciprocal principal/mirror reporting configuration, 1065-1066
setting up database snapshots against, 1064-1065

DATABASE option (WEBMETHOD) 1941

Database Properties dialog, 723

Database Read-Only, 724

database roles, managing, 321-322

database snapshots, 1043

copy-on-write technology, 1048, 1050

creating, 1057-1061

database snapsphot sparse files, 1048

dropping, 1062

explained, 1044-1048

limitations and restrictions, 1048, 1050

new features, 1044

number of database snapshots per source database, 1067

reciprocal principal/mirror reporting configuration, 1065-1066

reverting to, 1048, 1052-1053, 1062

source databases, 1063-1064

security, 1067

setting up against database mirrors, 1064-1065

snapshot databases, 1048

source databases, 1048

sparse file size management, 1067

testing with QA, 1064

when to use, 1051

providing baseline, 1054

providing point-in-time reporting databases, 1054-1055

providing reporting databases from a database mirror, 1055-1056

reverting to snapshots for recovery purposes, 1052-1053

safeguarding databases prior to making mass changes, 1053

database snapsphot sparse files, 1048

DATABASEPROPERTYEX, 726-729

databases

ALTER DATABASE, 736

attaching, 737-739

backing up. *See* backups

baselines, providing with database snapshots, 1054

bigpubs2005. *See* bigpubs2005 database

checking database usage, 519

checking integrity, 1075-1076

CLR functions, adding to, 944-945

CLR stored procedures, adding to, CD:1780-CD:1781

columns, joining, 521-522

CompSales database, installing, 7

configuring for SSRS (SQL Server Reporting Services), CD:2187-CD:2188

creating, 717-718

with SSMS, 718-721

with T-SQL, 721-722

data structure, 710-711

database mirroring. *See* database mirroring

database options

Auto Close, 723

Auto Create Statistics, 723

Auto Shrink, 723

Database Read-Only, 724

explained, 722-725

Page Verify, 724

Restrict Access, 724

retrieving option information, 726-729

setting with T-SQL, 725

defined, 709

detaching, 737-739, CD:2350

enabling CDC for, CD:1617

expanding, 730-731

filegroups. *See* filegroups

maintenance. *See* database maintenance

managing file growth, 729-730

migrating

compatibility levels, 242

Copy Database Wizard, 238-241

explained, 238

moving, 736
new features, 710
OLAP database creation, CD:2044
adding data sources, CD:2044-CD:2046
ADO MD, CD:2077
aggregating data within, CD:2066-CD:2071
browsing data in the cube, CD:2071-CD:2075
building and deploying the cube, CD:2064-CD:2065
calculated members, CD:2078-CD:2079
creating data source views, CD:2046-CD:2050
creating the cube, CD:2060-CD:2064
defining dimensions and hierarchies, CD:2050-CD:2060
delivering data to users, CD:2076
multidimensional expressions, CD:2076-CD:2077
populating cubes with data, CD:2065-CD:2066
query analysis and, CD:2079-CD:2081
pages. *See* pages (databases)
relational databases
generating, CD:2081
limitations of, CD:2082
ReportServer, CD:2180
ReportServerTempDB, CD:2180
restoring. *See* restores
rows. *See* rows
safeguarding prior to making mass changes, 1053
setting up for FILESTREAM storage, CD:1596
shrinking, 731
DBCC SHRINKDATABASE, 731-732
DBCC SHRINKFILE, 732-733
log files, 734
in Maintenance Plan Wizard, 1076-1077
with SSMS, 734-735
snapshots. *See* database snapshots
system databases, 709
associated database files, 167
distribution database, 168
explained, 166-167
maintaining, 169-170
master database, 167
model database, 168
msdb database, 168
resource database, 168
tempdb database, 169
tables. *See* tables
tuning guidelines, 1537
user databases, 709

Datacenter Edition (SQL Server 2008), 42-43

DATAllegro v3, CD:2094

datasets, CD:2193-CD:2194
shared datasets, CD:2175, CD:2194-CD:2195

DATA_COMPRESSION argument (CREATE INDEX), 799

date calculations
PowerShell, 502-503
T-SQL, CD:1663-CD:1666
converting dates for comparison, CD:1666-CD:1669
first day of month, CD:1664
first day of quarter, CD:1665
first day of year, CD:1664
midnight for the current day, CD:1665
Monday of the current week, CD:1665

DATE data type, 37, 748, 751, CD:1572

date data types, 751, CD:1572-CD:1576

DATEADD function, CD:1663

DATEDIFF function, CD:1663

datediff( ) function, 1336-1337

datetime data type, 748, 751, CD:1572

DATETIME2 data type, 37, 748, 751, CD:1573

DATETIMEOFFSET data type, 37, 748, 751, CD:1573

db backupoperator, 305

db datareader, 305, 307

db datawriter, 305, 307

db ddladmin, 305

db denydatareader, 305

db denydatawriter, 305

db owner, 305

db securityadmin, 305

DBCC, 1548

DBCC DROPCLEANBUFFERS, 1335

DBCC FREEPROCCACHE, 1266

DBCC OPENTRAN, 1038

DBCC SHOW_STATISTICS, 1153-1157, 1219

DBCC SHRINKDATABASE, 731-732

DBCC SHRINKFILE, 732-733

dbcreator, 303

DBMS (database management system), 1342

dbo users, 299

DB_accessadmin, 305

DCM (differential changed map) pages, 1116

DDL (Data Definition Language), CD:1892

- changes to CDC source tables, CD:1626
- statements, 983
- triggers, 976
  - creating, 983-986
  - managing, 986-987
  - table of, 983

de-duping data with ranking functions, CD:1684-CD:1687

Deadlock Graph event (SQL Profiler), 1355

deadlocks, 1382-1384

- 1204 trace flags, setting, 1386-1388
- 1222 trace flags, setting, 1388-1390
- avoiding, 1384-1385
- conversion deadlocks, 1383
- cycle deadlocks, 1382
- examining, 1385-1386
- handling, 1385-1387
- monitoring, 1390-1392
- SQL Server Profiler, 158-159
- tuning guidelines, 1545

DEADLOCK_PRIORITY, 1384

debugger (T-SQL), 41

debugging

- managed code, CD:1834-CD:1835
- stored procedures, 905-908
- T-SQL, 100-101

decimal data type, 748

Decision Support Systems (DSS), 666

decision trees (data mining algorithms), CD:2085

declarative data integrity, implementing, 812

declarative defaults, 831-833

declarative referential integrity (DRI), 951

DECLARE (variable assignment), CD:1568

Decode-SqlName cmdlet, 509

DecryptByAsymKey( ) function, 343

DecryptByCert( ) function, 343

DecryptByKey( ) function, 343, 348

DecryptByPassphrase( ) function, 343

dedicated administrator connections, HA (high availability), 540

DEFAULT, 764, 832-835

default full-text language configuration option, CD:2294-CD:2296

default language configuration option, CD:2296-CD:2298

default values, setting for stored procedure input parameters, 895-898

defaults, 831

- application of, 833-835

bound defaults, 833

declarative defaults, 831-833

restrictions on, 835

tuning guidelines, 1538

deferred name resolution (stored procedures), 885-888

defining user-defined table types, CD:1577

DEK (database encryption key), 350

Deleted Scan icon (Query Analyzer), 1311

deleted tables (DML triggers), 957-959

deleting

database snapshots, 1062

logins (SSMS), 317

mail objects from Database Mail with T-SQL, 432-433

packages (dtutil utility), CD:2141-CD:2144

resource pools, 1515-1516

rows, 1144

LINQ to SQL, CD:1801

delivery architecture (subscriptions), CD:2237

denormalization

computed columns, 1410-1411

defined, 1408

guidelines, 1408-1409

horizontal data partitioning, 1412-1413

redundant data, 1409-1410

summary data, 1411

tuning guidelines, 1537-1538

vertical data partitioning, 1413-1414

zero-to-one relationships, 1415

DENSE RANK function, CD:1711-CD:1712

densities of indexes, 1158-1159

DENY, 311, 330

deploying

cubes in OLAP database creation, CD:2064-CD:2065

reports, CD:2207-CD:2209

deprecated features, 49

DESC (CREATE INDEX), 796

DESCRIPTION (BACKUP DATABASE), 392

design. *See also* guidelines

databases. *See* database design

example systems (SQL Server Service Broker), CD:1964-CD:1965

indexes, 1184, 1403

clustered indexes, 1185-1186

composite indexes, 1184

covering, 1188-1190

included columns, 1190-1191

multiple indexes, 1191-1192

nonclustered indexes, 1186-1188

wide indexes, 1191-1192

for performance, 1523-1528

assessment stage, 1524

coding and testing stage, 1526-1527

identification and design stage, 1525

implementation stage, 1527-1528

prototyping stage, 1525-1526

system testing and acceptance stage, 1527

report design, CD:2202

enhancements in, CD:2172-CD:2175

tables, tuning guidelines, 1537-1538

Design a Query window (Report Builder), CD:2218-CD:2219

design methodologies for OLAP, CD:2038

construction phase, CD:2039

design phase, CD:2039

implementation phase, CD:2040

maintenance phase, CD:2040

requirements phase, CD:2039

design phase (OLAP design methodologies), CD:2039

Designer IDE (SSIS), CD:2110-CD:2112, CD:2126-CD:2135

detaching databases, 737-739, CD:2350

deterministic function, 1194

Developer Edition (SQL Server 2008)

features, 27

licensing, 32

developing

custom managed database objects, CD:1825-CD:1864

managed triggers, CD:1856-CD:1861

permissions, CD:1827-CD:1829

related system catalogs, CD:1863-CD:1864

stored procedures, CD:1829-CD:1835

transactions, CD:1861-CD:1863

UDAs (user-defined aggregates), CD:1853-CD:1856

UDFs (user-defined functions), CD:1835-CD:1844

UDTs (user-defined types), CD:1844-CD:1852

Visual Studio 2008, CD:1829

reports

with BIDS, CD:2196-CD:2199

Chart control, CD:2203

controls summary, CD:2202-CD:2204

data bars, CD:2203

data planning and preparation, CD:2193

datasets, CD:2193-CD:2194

deployment, CD:2207-CD:2209

design, CD:2202

expressions, CD:2200-CD:2202

gauges, CD:2203

Image control, CD:2203

indicators, CD:2203-CD:2207

interactivity, CD:2211-CD:2213

Line control, CD:2203

List control, CD:2203

Map control, CD:2203

Matrix control, CD:2202

overview of development process, CD:2192

Rectangle control, CD:2203

Report Builder. *See* Report Builder

Report Manager, CD:2209-CD:2210

shared data sources, CD:2193

shared datasets, CD:2194-CD:2195

Sparklines, CD:2203-CD:2207

Subreport control, CD:2204

Table control, CD:2202

tables and hierarchies in, CD:2210-CD:2211

Tablix, CD:2199-CD:2202

Text Box control, CD:2204

development life cycle (security), 361-362

development tools (SSMS), Query Editor

disconnected editing, 88

editing sqlmd scripts, 88-89

IntelliSense, 87

overview, 85-87

performance, 91-92

Query Designer, 92-93

query types, 87-88

regular expressions and wildcards, 89-91

device allocations, tuning guidelines, 1536

device CALs, 31

diagnostics

full-text indexes, CD:2014

COLUMNPROPERTY function, CD:2015

example, CD:2016-CD:2017

FULLTEXTCATALOGPROPERTY, CD:2015-CD:2016

OBJECTPROPERTY function, CD:2014-CD:2015

sqldiag, 116-117

ssbdiagnose, 47

dialog handles, CD:1974

DialogTimer, CD:1969

differential backups, 380, 397-398

differential changed map (DCM) pages, 1116

DIFFERENTIAL option (BACKUP DATABASE), 392

differential partial backups, 381

DIGEST authentication, CD:1934

digital certificates, 338

compared to TDE (transparent data encryption), 356-357

encrypting columns with, 346-349

Dimension Wizard, CD:2051-CD:2052

dimensions, defining in OLAP database creation, CD:2050, CD:2054-CD:2060

direct recursion, 993

dirty pages, 717

dirty reads (transaction isolation levels), 1343

Dirty Writer process (logs), 1024-1028

DISABLE (ALTER FULLTEXT INDEX), CD:2010-CD:2011

DISABLE BROKER, CD:1961

disabling

constraints, 829-830

indexes, 1182

disaster recovery

data-centric approach, CD:2337-CD:2338

focus of, CD:2342-CD:2347

Level 0, CD:2331

Level 1, CD:2331

Level 2, CD:2331

Level 3, CD:2331

Level 4, CD:2331

new features, CD:2330

options for, CD:2338

data replication, CD:2338-CD:2340

database mirroring and snapshots, CD:2341-CD:2342

log shipping, CD:2339-CD:2341

overview, CD:2329-CD:2331

patterns, CD:2332

active multisite DR pattern, CD:2334

active/active DR sites pattern, CD:2333-CD:2334

active/passive DR sites pattern, CD:2332-CD:2333

choosing, CD:2334-CD:2335

planning and executing, CD:2349-CD:2350

process, CD:2342

sqldiag.exe, CD:2347-CD:2349

recovery objectives, CD:2336-CD:2337

reverting to database snapshots, 1052-1053, 1062-1064

third-party alternatives, CD:2350-CD:2351

tuning guidelines, 1546

disconnected editing, 88

discovery, CD:1929

disk activity, monitoring, 1490

disk devices, 386

disk drive contention, 1424

disk performance, monitoring in SSMS, 1490

Disk Queue Length counter, 713

disk space requirements for SQL Server 2008, 187

Disk Space Requirements page (SQL Server Installation Center), 203

disk subsystem, tuning guidelines for, 1534

disk systems, monitoring, 1488-1490

diskadmin, 303

displaying execution plan XML, 1317

DISTINCT, CD:1654

query processing, 1268

tuning guidelines, 1542

distribute streams, 1272

Query Analyzer, 1314

distributed data, tuning guidelines, 1546

distributed messaging, CD:1960

distributed partitioned views, 859-860, 975

distributed queries (linked servers), CD:2252

Distributed Transaction Coordinator (DTC), 572, 657

distributed transactions, 573

linked servers, CD:2252-CD:2253

managing, 1040

distribution agent, 569-570

distribution clean up: distribution, 571

distribution database, 168, 564-565

distribution server (data replication), 550

distributors, creating for data replication, 581-584

dm exe sql text, CD:1766

dm exec cached plans, CD:1766

dm exec plan attributes, CD:1766

DML (Data Manipulation Language)

Insert over DML, CD:1559-CD:1561

statements, compiling, 1212-1213

triggers

AFTER triggers. *See* AFTER triggers

cascading deletes, 963-965

cascading updates, 965-966

creating, 951-953

explained, 950-951

inserted and deleted tables, 957-961

INSTEAD OF triggers. *See* INSTEAD OF triggers

referential integrity, 961-963

DMVs (dynamic management views), 45-46, 179-181, CD:1994

disk system items, monitoring, 1491

memory items, monitoring, 1487

processor items, monitoring, 1483

SEE (SQL Server Extended Events), 1460-1462

sys.dm exec query plan, 1328-1329

sys.dm_exec_cached_plans, 1511

sys.dm_exec_query_memory_grants, 1511

sys.dm_exec_query_resource_semaphores, 1511

sys.dm_exec_requests, 1511

sys.dm_exec_session, 1511

sys.dm_os_memory_brokers, 1511

sys.dm_resource_governor_configuration, 1510

sys.dm_resource_governor_resource_pools, 1510

sys.dm_resource_governor_workload_groups, 1509

dm_db_index_physical_stats, 1171-1174

Document Type Definition (DTD), CD:1866

documents, XML, CD:1866

dollar sign ($), 492

domain integrity, 812. *See also* **data integrity**

DPVs (distributed partitioned views), 859-860, 975

DR. *See* **disaster recovery**

DRI (declarative referential integrity), 951

drivers, 281

DROP (ALTER FULLTEXT INDEX) 2012

DROP COLUMN, 768

DROP DATABASE, 1062

DROP ENDPOINT, 632, 644

DROP INDEX, 807

DROP RESOURCE POOL, 1516

DROP ROLE, 322

DROP TABLE, 773

DROP USER, 320

DROP VIEW, 853

DROP WORKLOAD GROUP, 1515

dropping

constraints, 829

database snapshots, 1062

endpoints, 632

indexes, 807

tables, 773-774

views with T-SQL, 853

DROP_EXISTING argument (CREATE INDEX), 798

DSS (Decision Support Systems), 57, 666

hybrid SQL Server reporting configuration, 59, 61

multidimensional OLAP cube, 58-59

star schema data warehouse for global computer sales, 57-58

DTA (Database Engine Tuning Advisor), 109-112, 138, 1149, 1201-1204, CD:2274

command line, CD:2321-CD:2326

GUI, CD:2317-CD:2320

overview, CD:2317

DTC (Distributed Transaction Coordinator), 572, 657

DTD (Document Type Definition), CD:1866

dtexec utility, CD:2135-CD:2137

packages, running, CD:2137, CD:2141

phases, CD:2136

DTS (Data Transformation Services), 228, 259-261

DTS Package Migration Wizard, 259-261

DTS Parameters, 233-234

dtsrun utility, CD:2135

dtutil utility, CD:2141-CD:2145

duplicate data, de-duping with ranking functions, CD:1684-CD:1687

dynamic management objects, Missing Index Hints, 1320-1321

dynamic management views. *See* DMVs

dynamic SQL

SQL injection attacks, avoiding, CD:1643-CD:1652

stored procedures, CD:1774-CD:1779

E

Eager Spool (Query Analyzer), 1312

editing sqlmd scripts, 88-89

editions of SQL Server

Compact 3.5 Edition, 29, 32

comparison of, 25

Developer Edition, 27, 32

Enterprise Edition, 24-26

Express Edition, 28-29, 32

R2 Datacenter Edition, 29, 42-43

R2 Parallel Data Warehouse Edition, 30, 43

Standard Edition, 23-26

Web Edition, 27-28, 32

Workgroup Edition, 27

EKM (Extensible Key Management), 40, 341-342

EKM provider enabled configuration option, CD:2298

element-centric XML shape, CD:1868

email

configuring in SSRS (SQL Server Reporting Services) 2189

notification, configuring in SQL Server Agent, 454

receiving with Database Mail, 441

sending with Database Mail, 435-441

SQL Server Agent Mail. *See* SQL Server Agent Mail

EMC Corporation, CD:2351

ENABLE (ALTER FULLTEXT INDEX), CD:2010-CD:2011

ENABLE BROKER, 405, CD:1961

enabling

CDC

for databases, CD:1617

for tables, CD:1617-CD:1619

Change Tracking, CD:1628-CD:1630

FILESTREAM storage, CD:1593-CD:1596

Report Builder, CD:2233-CD:2234

Resource Governor, 1499-1500

SQL Server Agent Mail, 442

Encode-SqlName cmdlet, 509

EncryptByAsymKey( ) function, 343

EncryptByCert( ) function, 343

EncryptByKey( ) function, 343, 347

EncryptByPassphrase( ) function, 343

ENCRYPTION, 847-848

encryption

algorithms, 338

asymmetric key encryption, 338

column-level encryption

with certificates, 346-349

compared to TDE (transparent data encryption), 356-357

explained, 343

with passphrases, 344-346

configuring in SSRS, CD:2189-CD:2190

connection encryption, configuring clients, 278-279

key management, 339, 341

database master keys, 340-341

EKM (Extensible Key Management), 341-342

service master keys, 340

new features, 336

overview, 335, 338-339

private keys, 338

public keys, 338

symmetric key encryption, 338

TDE (transparent data encryption)

backing up TDE certificates and keys, 353-355

compared to column-level encryption, 356-357

explained, 350-351

implementing, 351-352

limitations, 355-356

managing in SSMS, 352-353

when to use, 339

END CONVERSATION, CD:1979

EndDialog, CD:1969

__$end_lsn column (CDC table), CD:1615

endpoints, CD:1931

catalog views and system stored procedures, CD:1954-CD:1955

controlling access permissions, CD:1955-CD:1956

creating, 627-628

creating for web services, CD:1931-CD:1933

defined, 267

dropping, 632

FOR SOAP, CD:1955

identifying, 632-633

server endpoint layers, 267-268

TDS endpoints, 267

enforcement layers (security), 362-364

enforcing

data integrity, 812-813

referential integrity with DML triggers, 961-963

enhancements in SQL Server 2008, 45

enterprise computing, 655

Enterprise Edition (SQL Server 2008), 24-26

entitization, CD:1941

entity integrity, 812

envelopes (SOAP) 1930

EOIO (exactly-once-in-order) messaging, CD:1974

@@ERROR, CD:1683-CD:1684, CD:1738

ERROR BROKER CONVERSATIONS, CD:1961

Error, CD:1969

error handling

with @@ERROR and @@ROWCOUNT, CD:1683-CD:1684

TRY...CATCH construct, CD:1724-CD:1727

ERROR LINE, CD:1725, CD:1739

error list window (SSMS), 42

error logs, SQL Server Agent, 456-457

ERROR MESSAGE, CD:1725, CD:1739
ERROR NUMBER, CD:1725, CD:1739
ERROR PROCEDURE, CD:1725, CD:1739
ERROR SEVERITY, CD:1725, CD:1739
ERROR STATE, CD:1725, CD:1739
errors, stored procedures from, CD:1738-CD:1741
ERROR_BROKER_CONVERSATIONS (RESTORE DATABASE), 406
escalation locks, 1374-1376
escape characters, 492
Estimated Subtree Cost, 1305
ETL (extraction, transformation, and loading), CD:2099
ETW (Event Tracing for Windows), 1429
evaluating
  indexes, 1150-1153
  page compression, 1123-1126
  policies, 702-703
  recovery models, 705
event forwarding, 477-478
event handlers (SSIS), CD:2107
Event parameter (SqlTrigger), CD:1856
Event Tracing for Windows (ETW), 1429
EventClass data column (SQL Profiler), 1356
EVENTDATA, 985
EventData parameter (SqlTriggerContext), CD:1857
events
  SSEE (SQL Server Extended Events), 1458
  trace events and categories, 141-147
  traces (SQL Server Profiler), 125-127
exactly-once-in-order (EOIO) messaging, CD:1974
EXCEPT IP, CD:1936
exclusive locks, 1361
EXEC, 880-881, 923
exec sp spaceused, CD:2344
exec sp_configure, CD:2344
exec sp_helpdb dbnamexyz, CD:2344
exec sp_helplinkedsrvlogin, CD:2344
exec sp_helplogins, CD:2343
exec sp_helpserver, CD:2343
exec sp_linkedservers, CD:2344
exec sp_server_info, CD:2344
EXECUTE AS, 332-333, 883-885, 929
Execute Report Definitions, CD:2233
executing
  AFTER triggers, 955
  disaster recovery, CD:2349-CD:2350
  INSTEAD OF triggers, 968-970
  maintenance plans, 1088
  sqlcmd, 106-108
  stored procedures
    execution context and EXECUTE AS, 883-885
    via linked servers, CD:2268
    in SSMS, 881-882
    syntax, 880-881
  traces (SQL Server Profiler), 132
execution accounts, configuring in SSRS (SQL Server, CD:2189
execution context, 331-333, CD:1766
execution log (SSRS), CD:2240
execution modes, 694-695
execution options (reports), CD:2237
  cached reports, CD:2237-CD:2238
  CRPs (cache refresh plans) 2239
  execution snapshots, CD:2238
  history snapshots, CD:2238
  live reports and sessions, CD:2237
  user-specific data limitations, CD:2239
execution plan selection (Query Optimizer), 1251-1253
execution plans
  graphical execution plans, saving and viewing, 1317
  XML, displaying, 1317

execution policy (PowerShell), 487
execution snapshots, CD:2238
existing implementations, tuning methodology for, 1528-1533
assessment stage, 1529-1530
coding and testing stage, 1532
implementation stage, 1533
isolation and monitoring stage, 1530-1531
prototyping stage, 1531-1532
system test and acceptance stage, 1533
EXISTS, 1248
exists( ) new xml data type method, CD:1900, CD:1908-CD:1909
EXPAND VIEWS, 1284
expanding
databases, 730-731
hierarchies with recursive CTEs, CD:1701-CD:1707
expansion, CD:2021
indexed views, 866-867
expired subscription clean up, 571
EXPIREDATE (BACKUP DATABASE), 392
explicit context switching, 332
EXPLICIT mode (XML), CD:1877-CD:1881
explicit transactions, 997
explicit user-defined transactions
compared to implicit transactions, 1006
processing, 998-1000
nested transactions, 1001-1003
savepoints, 1000-1001
Export-Csv cmdlet, 501
exporting
with bcp utility, CD:2151-CD:2153
current state as policy, 700-701
policies, 703-704
traces (SQL Server Profiler), 132
exposure endpoints, 360
Express Edition (SQL Server 2008)
features, 28-29
licensing, 32
Expression Builder (SSIS), CD:2112, CD:2115
expressions
complex expressions, CD:2200-CD:2202
enhancements to, CD:2179
multidimensional expressions in OLAP database, CD:2076-CD:2077
simple expressions, CD:2178
Extended Events, 40
extended events catalog views (SSEE), 1460-1462
extended events sessions (SSEE), 1462-1465
Extended MAPI (Extended Messaging Application Programming Interface), 427
extended stored procedures, CD:1782
adding to SQL Server, CD:1782-CD:1783
obtaining information on, CD:1783
provided with SQL Server, CD:1783-CD:1784
xp cmdshell, CD:1784-CD:1786
Extensible Key Management (EKM), 40, 341-342
extensions, 712
Extent locking level (SQL Server), 1364
extents, 710
allocating space, 1113-1114
defined, 10
EXTERNAL ACCESS permission, 945, CD:1780
external activation, CD:1964
external fragmentation (indexes), 1169
ExternalMailQueue, 434
extraction, transformation, and loading (ETL), CD:2099

F

facets

creating conditions based on, 697-698

explained, 689, 692

table of, 690-692

failover, 623

combining with scale-out options, 538

testing from principal to mirror, 645-646

FAST n hints, 1284

Feature Selection page (SQL Server Installation Center), 200-201

fields, format files

lengths, CD:2157-CD:2158

terminators, CD:2158-CD:2162

file backups, 381, 400-401

file data types (bcp utility), CD:2153

file growth, managing for databases, 729-730

File locking level (SQL Server), 1364

FILE option (RESTORE DATABASE), 406

filegroup backups, 381, 400-401

filegroups, 713-715

controlling table placement with, 1098

FILESTREAM filegroups, 1100-1101

overview, 1097-1100

performance and, 1415-1417

FILEGROWTH, 722

files, 1095

.BAT files, 104

configuration files, upgrading with, 250-251

ConfigurationFile.ini, 212-216

CSV files

handling in PowerShell, 501-502

sending as attachments with Database Mail, 440-441

data files, 710

database files, 711-712

file management, 1096-1097

format files, bcp utility, CD:2153-CD:2163

log files, 1096

mssqlsystemresource.mdf, 169

primary data files, 712, 1095

properties, 1093

saving trace output to, 133

secondary data files, 712, 1095

transaction log files, 710, 716-717

FILESTREAM filegroups, 1100-1101

FILESTREAM storage, 207-208, 759, CD:1592-CD:1593

for data columns, CD:1597-CD:1599

database setup, CD:1596

defined, 36

enabling, CD:1593-CD:1596

filestream_access_level configuration option, CD:2299

fill factor configuration option, CD:2299-CD:2300

fill factors

indexes, setting, 1179-1181

tuning guidelines, 1540

FILLFACTOR argument (CREATE INDEX), 798

FillRowMethodName parameter (TVFs), CD:1839

Filter icon, 1311

filtered indexes, 38

advantages, 1195-1196

creating, 1196-1198

optimizing with, 1239-1241

statistics, 1198-1199

filtered statistics, 38

filtering

articles, 550-551, 553-554

horizontal filtering, 592, 594

MDS-based filtering, CD:2095-CD:2096

vertical filtering, 592, 594

filtering cmdlets, 499-500

filters, traces (SQL Server Profiler), 130-132

finding foreign key references, 774

FIRE TRIGGERS, 956

firewalls, connectivity, 288

FIRE_TRIGGER hint, CD:2166

firing order (AFTER triggers), 956

first day of month, calculating, CD:1664

first day of quarter, calculating, CD:1665

first day of year, calculating, CD:1664

first normal form, 1406

fixed-database roles, 304-306

fixed-server roles, 303-304

flat-earth data, CD:1605

float data type, 748

flow control, 465

fn trace geteventinfo, 153

fn trace getfilterinfo, 153

fn trace getinfo, 153

focus of disaster recovery, CD:2342-CD:2347

focusing on specific data with views, 840-841

FOR ATTACH option (CREATE DATABASE), 737-738

for clause (query( ) new xml data type method), CD:1902-CD:1903

FOR SOAP, CD:1938-CD:1942, CD:1955

FOR XML modes, CD:1866, CD:1687

- AUTO mode, CD:1873-CD:1877
- EXPLICIT mode, CD:1877-CD:1881
- new xml data type, CD:1884-CD:1887
- PATH mode, CD:1881-CD:1884
- RAW mode, CD:1867-CD:1871

FORCE ORDER hints, 1283

forced parameterization, managing Query Optimizer, 1285-1287

forced service, 623

FORCESEEK, 38, 1281-1282

forcing query plan recompiles, 1258, CD:1770-CD:1773

ForEach-Object cmdlet, 499

FOREIGN KEY constraint, 764, 816-818, 963

- cascading referential integrity, 818-820, 967

foreign key references, finding, 774

foreign keys, tuning guidelines, 1539

format files

- bcp utility, CD:2153-CD:2163
  - creating, CD:2154-CD:2155
  - customizing, CD:2153-CD:2154
- fields
  - lengths, CD:2157-CD:2158
  - terminators, CD:2158-CD:2162
- prefixes, lengths, CD:2157
- storage types, CD:2155-CD:2156

FORMAT option

- BACKUP DATABASE, 392
- WEBMETHOD, 1939

Format parameter

- SqlUserDefinedAggregate, CD:1853
- SqlUserDefinedType, CD:1845

Format-List cmdlet, 500

Format-Table cmdlet, 500

formatting cmdlets, 500-501

forward pointers, 1146

fragmentation of indexes, 1169-1170

fragments (XML), CD:1866

FREETEXT, CD:2020-CD:2024

FREETEXTTABLE, CD:2020-CD:2024

frequency of backups, 423-424

FT Daemon Host, CD:1999

FTS (Full-Text Search) 1997

- CONTAINS, CD:2020
  - generation, CD:2021-CD:2022
  - LANGUAGE, CD:2022
  - proximity, CD:2022
  - search phrase, CD:2020-CD:2021
  - weighted, CD:2022

CONTAINSTABLE, CD:2020, CD:2023
generation, CD:2021-CD:2022
LANGUAGE, CD:2022
proximity, CD:2022
search phrase, CD:2020-CD:2021
weighted, CD:2022
explained, 17-18
FREETEXT, CD:2020-CD:2024
FREETEXTTABLE, CD:2020-CD:2024
full-text catalogs, CD:2002
full-text indexes. *See* full-text indexes
indexing, CD:1999-CDL2001
maintenance, CD:2024-CD:2025
new features, CD:1998
overview, CD:1997
performance, CD:2025-CD:2026
searching, CD:2001-CD:2002
stop lists, CD:2024
troubleshooting, CD:2026-CD:2028
full database backups, 380, 396-397
full outer joins, CD:1680-CD:1682
full recovery model, 383
full-text catalogs, CD:2002
full-text indexes, CD:2003
creating with T-SQL, CD:2003
ALTER FULLTEXT INDEX, CD:2010-CD:2013
CREATE FULLTEXT, CD:2003-CD:2005
CREATE FULLTEXT INDEX, CD:2005-CD:2010
managing MSFTESQL, CD:2013-CD:2014
diagnostics, CD:2014
COLUMNPROPERTY, CD:2015
example, CD:2016-CDL2017
FULLTEXTCATALOGPROPERTY, CD:2015-CD:2016
OBJECTPROPERTY, CD:2014-CD:2015
Full-Text Indexing Wizard, CD:2017-CD:2019
xml columns, CD:1924-CD:1925
Full-Text Indexing Wizard, CD:2017-CD:2019
Full-Text Search. *See* FTS
FULLTEXTCATALOGPROPERTY, CD:2015-CD:2016
Function Properties dialog (SSMS), 941
functions, 497-498. *See also* UDFs (user-defined functions); *names of specific functions*
avoiding unnecessary executions, CD:1656
classification functions
creating, 1506-1509
defined, 1495-1496
modifying, 1516
CLR functions, 944-945
deciding between T-SQL and CLR functions, 946-947
object definition, 891
partition functions, creating, 776-778
rewriting stored procedures as, 942-943
tuning guidelines, 1542

G

GAM (global allocation map), 711, 1114-1115
gather streams, 1272
Query Analyzer, 1314
gauge panels, CD:2173
gauges, CD:2173, CD:2203
generating
column statistics, 1161-1167, 1169
index statistics, 1161-1167, 1169
page numbers with NTILE, CD:1717
relational databases, CD:2081-CD:2082
T-SQL statements, CD:1682-CD:1683
generation, CD:2021-CD:2022
generics, CD:1796
geography data type, 37, 748, 751, CD:1605, CD:1609-CD:1611

Geography Markup Language (GML), CD:1606

geometry data type, 37, 748, CD:1605, CD:1607-CD:1609. *See also* spatial data types

GEOMETRYCOLLECTION, CD:1606

GET CONVERSATION DIALOG, CD:1980, CD:1983

Get-Alias cmdlet, 490

Get-ChildItem cmdlet, 490

Get-Command cmdlet, 488

Get-Content cmdlet, 490, 514

Get-Help cmdlet, 488-489

Get-Item cmdlet, 520

Get-Member cmdlet, 489-490

Get-Process cmdlet, 513

Get-Service cmdlet, 513

getdate( ) function, 918

getonlydate( ) function, 919, 930

ghost records, 1144

GLBA (Gramm-Leach-Bliley Act), 367

global allocation map (GAM), 711, 1114-1115

global variables, simulating with CONTEXT INFO setting, CD:1671-CD:1673

GML (Geography Markup Language), CD:1606

Gramm-Leach-Bliley Act (GLBA), 367

GRANT, 311, 330, 629

granting permissions, 629-630

granularity locks, 1364-1376

- application locks, 1369-1372
- index locks, 1372-1373
- key-range locking, 1365-1369
- serialization locking, 1365-1369

graphic charts, 1467

graphical execution plans, saving and viewing, 1317

GROUP BY, 1283, CD:1561

- CUBE operator, CD:1561-CD:1562
- GROUPING SETS operator, CD:1562-CD:1565
- grouping_id( ) function, CD:1565-CD:1568
- query processing, 1267
- ROLLUP operator, CD:1561-CD:1562

Group-Object cmdlet, 490

GROUPING, sorting results, CD:1669-CD:1671

GROUPING SETS, 38, CD:1562-CD:1565

grouping_id( ) function, CD:1565-CD:1568

groups, workload

- creating, 1503-1505
- deleting, 1514-1515
- explained, 1496
- viewing, 1505-1506

guest users, 299-300

GUI for DTA (Database Engine Tuning Advisor), CD:2317-CD:2320

guidelines

- MERGE statement, CD:1558-CD:1559
- for tuning, 1534
  - applications, 1545
  - database-level guidelines, 1537
  - distributed data, 1546
  - hardware and operating system, 1534-1535
  - high availability, 1546-1547
  - indexing, 1539-1540
  - SQL Server instance, 1536-1537
  - table-level guidelines, 1537-1539
  - Transact-SQL, 1541-1545
  - views, 1541

H

HA (high-availability), 523

- backups, 527
- building solutions, 530
  - combining failover with scale-out options, 538

data replication, 534-535
database mirroring, 537-538
log shipping, 535-537
MSCS, 530-531
SQL Clustering, 531-534
data partitioning, 539
data replication and database mirroring, 614
database snapshots, 539
dedicated administrator connections, 540
defined, 525-526
fast recovery, 538
hardware, 527
Microsoft Virtual Server 2005, 541-542
new features, 524-525
online indexing, 538
online restore, 538
operating systems, 527
overview, 523
quality assurance, 528
server instance isolation, 528, 530
snapshot isolation levels, 540
standards/procedures, 528
training, 528
tuning guidelines, 1546-1547
vendor agreements, 528

handles for tuning, 1521-1522

hardware
HA (high availability), 527
requirements for SQL Server 2008, 186-187
tuning guidelines, 1534-1535

HASH GROUP, 1283

hash joins, 1244-1246

Hash Match icon (Query Analyzer), 1311

HASH UNION, 1283

headers, page, 1103-1104

Health Insurance Portability and Accountability Act (HIPAA), 366

heap, deleting rows, 1144

Heap or B-Tree (HOBT) locking level (SQL Server), 1365

heap tables, 1129-1130

heartbeat, 659

help features
PowerShell, 487-490
SSMS, 68-70

heterogeneous environments, replication monitoring, 611-612

hierarchies
creating, CD:1580-CD:1581
defining in OLAP database creation, CD:2050, CD:2054-CD:2060
expanding with recursive CTEs, CD:1701-CD:1707
modifying, CD:1587-CD:1590, CD:1592
populating, CD:1581-CD:1583
querying, CD:1583-CD:1587
in reports, CD:2210-CD:2211

Hierarchyid data type, 37, 748, 751, CD:1580-CD:1590, CD:1592
creating hierarchies, CD:1580-CD:1581
modifying hierarchies, CD:1587-CD:1590, CD:1592
populating hierarchies, CD:1581-CD:1583
querying hierarchies, CD:1583-CD:1587

high-availability. *See* HA (high availability)

hints
bulk-copy operations, CD:2165-CD:2166
Query Optimizer, 1280
EXPAND VIEWS, 1284
FAST n, 1284
FORCE ORDER, 1283
GROUP BY, 1283
join, 1282-1283
KEEP PLAN, 1284

KEEPFIXED PLAN, 1284
MAXDOP number, 1284
MAXRECURSION number, 1284
OPTIMIZE FOR UNKNOWN, 1285
OPTIMIZER FOR, 1285
processing hints, 1282, 1285
RECOMPILE, 1285
ROBUST PLAN, 1284
TABLE HINT, 1285
table hints, 1280-1282
UNION, 1283
USE PLAN, 1287-1290
USE PLAN N, 1285
table hints for locking
lock granularity hints, 1395
lock type hints, 1395-1396
transaction isolation–level hints, 1393-1395
HIPAA (Health Insurance Portability and Accountability Act), 366
histogram charts, 1155-1158, 1467
History page (SQL Server Agent), 452
history snapshots, CD:2238
HOLAP (hybrid OLAP), CD:2037
HOLDLOCK, 1021, 1393, CD:1661
HOME\Administrator, 297
horizontal data partitioning, 1412-1413
horizontal filtering, data replication, 592, 594
Hosting API, CD:1825
HOST_NAME( ) function, 1507
hot-add CPU, 39
hybrid joins, 1246
hybrid OLAP (HOLAP), CD:2037
hybrid SQL Server reporting configuration, 59, 61

I

IAM (index allocation map), 710, 1115-1116
IDDL statements, 976-982
IDDL triggers, table of, 976-982
identification and design stage (tuning methodology), 1525
identifying
ad hoc queries (SQL Server Profiler), 159-160
endpoints, 632-633
JOIN clauses, 1215-1216
missing indexes, 1201
with Database Engine Tuning Advisor, 1201-1204
missing index dynamic management objects, 1202-1204
objects referenced in stored procedures, 887-888
OR clauses, 1214-1215
parallel queries, 1272-1273
performance bottlenecks, 160-162
search arguments, 1214
unused indexes, 1205-1207
IDENTITY, 755-757
identity access management, 364, 366
identity columns, 755-757
Idera SQL Diagnostic Monitor SQL, 1549
IDEs (integrated development environments), CD:1928
IF EXISTS, 1541, CD:1654
IFilters, CD:1999
IGNORE_DUP_KEY (CREATE INDEX), 798
Image control, CD:2203
image data type, 748
immediate transactional consistency, 572
immediate updating, 17
IMPERSONATE, 312, 332

implementation contract (managed stored procedures), CD:1830-CD:1832

implementation phase

OLAP design methodologies, CD:2040

tuning methodology, 1527-1528, 1533

implementations of SQL Server, 51-53

DSS (decision support systems) application examples, 57

hybrid SQL Server reporting configuration, 59, 61

multidimensional OLAP cube, 58-59

OLTP (online transaction processing) application examples, 53

OLTP ERP, 53-56

OLTP shopping cart, 56-57

implementing

declarative data integrity, 812

procedural data integrity, 813

implicit context switching, 333

implicit transactions, 997

compared to explicit transactions, 1006

processing, 1003-1006

Import and Export Wizard (SSIS), CD:2110-CD:2111

Import-Csv cmdlet, 501

importing

with bcp utility, CD:2151-CD:2153

policies, 696-697, 703-704

traces (SQL Server Profiler), 135-136

IN, 1248

in-doubt xact resolution configuration option, CD:2300

in-place updates, 1145

INCLUDE (CREATE INDEX), 796

included columns (indexes), 1190-1191

index allocation map (IAM), 710, 1115-1116

index create memory configuration option, CD:2300

INDEX CREATE, 986

index locks, granularity, 1372-1373

index pages, 1112-1113

extents, 1113-1114

nonleaf indexes, 1112

space allocation structures, 1113

index selection, evaluating SARG and join selectivity, 1218

indexed views, 844, 860, 1192-1193

creating, 861-863

expansion, 866-867

optimizing with, 1236-1237, 1239

performance and, 863-866

indexes

B-tree indexes, 1132-1133

choosing, 1199-1201

clustered indexes, 792-793, 1133-1134

costs, 1222-1223

designing, 1185-1186

indexed views, 1192-1193

nonunique, 1135-1136

row structure, 1134-1135

columns

computed columns, 1193-1195

included columns, 1190-1191

joins, 1184

composite indexes, design, 1184

covering, 795, 1188-1190

creating

with SSMS, 800-801, 803

with T-SQL, 795-800

deleting rows, 1144

densities, 1158-1159

design, 1184, 1275, 1403

disabling, 1182

dropping, 807

evaluating, 1150-1153

fill factor

reapplying, 1181
setting, 1179-1181
filtered indexes, 38
advantages, 1195-1196
creating, 1196-1198
optimizing with, 1239-1241
statistics, 1198-1199
fragmentation, 1169-1170
in FTS (Full-Text Search), CD:1999-CD:2001
full-text indexes. *See* full-text indexes
index intersection, 1229-1231
index union strategy, 1232-1234
intermediate nodes, 792
joins, 1234, 1236
maintenance, 1169-1179
ALTER INDEX, 1175-1176, 1178
disabling indexes, 1182
dm_db_index_physical_stats, 1171-1175
fill factor, 1179-1181
with Maintenance Plan Wizard, 1077-1080
SSMS, 1183
managing, 803
with SSMS, 806-807
with T-SQL, 803-806
missing indexes, identifying, 1201
with Database Engine Tuning Advisor, 1201-1204
missing index dynamic management objects, 1202-1204
multiple indexes, 1191-1192, 1228
index intersection, 1229-1231
index joins, 1234, 1236
index union strategy, 1232-1234
new features, 791-792, 1092
nonclustered, 793-795, 1136-1138
costs, 1223-1227
designing, 1186-1188
leaf rows, 1138-1139
nonleaf rows, 1139-1140
rebuilding, 1179
online indexing operations, 538, 807-808
overview, 1132
poor selectivity, 1159, 1184
query indexes, 1199-1201
querying, 1146-1149
selecting, 1149-1150, 1216
estimating access path costs, 1221-1228
evaluating SARG and join selectivity, 1216-1221
multiple indexes, 1228-1234, 1236
statistics, 1153, 1155
generating, 1161-1167, 1169
histograms, 1155-1158
rows, estimating, 1159-1160
string summary statistics, 1169
tables, over-definition, 1148
tuning guidelines, 1539-1540
unused indexes, identifying, 1205-1207
update performance indexes, 1199-1201
on views, 809-810
wide indexes, 1191-1192
xml columns, CD:1918-CD:1925
indicators, CD:2173, CD:2203-CD:2207
indirect recursion, 993
inequality operators, SARG and, 1218
Informatica, CD:2099
Information Practices Act of 2005, 367
INFORMATION SCHEMA, 936-937
information schema views, 177-178
INFORMATION_SCHEMA users, 300
Infoset (XML), CD:1920-CD:1921
INIT (BACKUP DATABASE), 392
INITIATOR, CD:1970

inline table-valued functions, 923-926

input parameters for stored procedures

explained, 893-894

passing object names as, 898-899

setting default values for, 895-898

table-valued parameters, 901-902

wildcards in, 899-900

INSERT, 311

Insert over DML, CD:1559-CD:1561

Insert Scan icon (Query Analyzer), 1311

inserted tables (DML triggers), 957-959

inserting

data, 1141-1142

trace data, 136-137

Installation Configuration page (SQL Server Installation Center), 201, 203

Installation Configuration Rules page (SQL Server Installation Center), 209

installation paths, 202

Installation Rules page (SQL Server Installation Center), 201-202

installing

bigpubs2005 database, 7

clients

client tools, 271-272

installation requirements, 271

new features, 263-264

SNAC, 272-274

CompSales database, 7

Data Collector, 1433-1437

installation enhancements, 49

PowerShell, 485

Report Builder, CD:2213-CD:2214

SQL Server 2008, 236. *See also* side-by-side migration; SQL Server Installation Center

automated installs, 217

with ConfigurationFile.ini file, 212-216

cumulative updates, 218, 220, 222

disk space requirements, 187

hardware requirements, 186-187

installation paths, 202

manual installs, 217

network protocols, 191

new features, 185-186

running multiple simultaneous editions, 191

Service Packs, 218, 220, 222

Slipstream installations, 222-224

software requirements, 188-191

SQL Server Clustering, 665-666

configuring SQL Server database disks, 666-667

Connection Test Program, 681-684

failure of nodes, 679, 681

MSCS, installing, 668

network interfaces, installing, 668

SQL Server, installing, 668-679

SSRS (SQL Server Reporting Services), CD:2182-CD:2185

UA (SQL Server Upgrade Advisor), 229

instances

SQL Browser, 270-271

XML, CD:1866

INSTEAD OF triggers

combining with AFTER triggers, 971-972

example, 968

executing, 968-970

explained, 967

restrictions, 975

versus AFTER triggers, 970

views, 972-975

int data type, 748

INTEGRATED, CD:1934

integrated development environments (IDEs) 1928

Integration Services (IS_. *See* SSIS (SQL Server Integration Services)

IntelliSense, 87

intent locks, 1362-1363

interactivity

of PowerShell, 486

in reports, CD:2211-CD:2213

interdependencies in tuning, 1521-1522

intergrating SSMS with source control, 95-97

intermediate nodes, 792

intermediate processing products, CD:2180

internal activation, CD:1964

internal fragmentation, 1169-1170

InternalMailQueue, 434

interoperability in enterprise computing, 655

Invoke-PolicyEvaluation cmdlet, 508, 521

Invoke-SqlCmd cmdlet, 508, 520-521

InvokeIfReceiverIsNull parameter (SqlMethod), CD:1850

IS (Integration Services). See SSIS (SQL Server Integration Services)

IsAnsiNullDefault property, 727

IsAnsiNullsEnabled property, 727

IsAnsiPaddingEnabled property, 727

IsAnsiWarningsEnabled property, 727

IsArithmeticAbortEnabled property, 727

IsAutoClose property, 727

IsAutoCreateStatistics property, 727

IsAutoShrink property, 727

IsAutoUpdateStatistics property, 727

IsByteOrdered parameter (SqlUserDefinedType), CD:1845

IsCloseCursorsOnCommitEnabled property, 727

IsDeterministic parameter, 938

IsDeterministic parameter (scalar UDFs), CD:1836

IsDeterministic parameter (SqlMethod), CD:1849

IsFixedLength parameter (SqlUserDefinedType), CD:1845

IsFulltextEnabled property, 727

IsInlineFunction parameter, 938

IsInStandBy property, 727

IsInvariantToDuplicates parameter (SqlUserDefinedAggregate), CD:1853

IsInvariantToNulls parameter (SqlUserDefinedAggregate), CD:1853

IsInvariantToOrder parameter (SqlUserDefinedAggregate), CD:1853

IsLocalCursorsDefault property, 727

IsMergePublished property, 727

IsMutator parameter (SqlMethod), CD:1849

IsNullConcat property, 727

IsNullIfEmpty parameter (SqlUserDefinedAggregate), CD:1854

IsNumericRoundAbortEnabled property, 727

isolation and monitoring stage (tuning methodology), 1530-1531

isolation levels (transactions), 1342-1344

dirty reads, 1343

lost updates, 1343

nonrepeatable reads, 1343

phantom reads, 1343

read committed isolation, 1344-1345

read committed snapshot isolation, 1345-1346

read uncommitted isolation, 1344

repeatable read isolation, 1346

serializable read isolation, 1346-1347

snapshot isolation, 1347-1349

IsParameterizationForced property, 727

IsPrecise parameter (scalar UDFs), CD:1837

IsPublished property, 728

isql, 105

IsQuotedIdentifiersEnabled property, 728

IsRecursiveTriggersEnabled property, 728

IsScalarFunction parameter, 938

IsSchemaBound parameter, 938
IsSubscribed property, 728
IsSyncWithBackup property, 728
IsTableFunction parameter, 938
IsTornPageDetectionEnabled property, 728
IsUpdatedColumn parameter (SqlTriggerContext), CD:1856
ITransactionLocal::StartTransaction function, 1345

J

JavaScript Object Notation (JSON), CD:1803, CD:1811
JDBC (Java Database Connectivity), 281, 287
job history, viewing, 468-469
job mail notifications (SQL Server Agent Mail), 442-443
job notifications, 467-468
job schedules, 465-467
job steps, 462-465
Job System page (SQL Server Agent), 451
jobs
- creating with SQL Server Agent Mail, 443
- defined, 449
- managing in SQL Server Agent, 461
  - job history, 468-469
  - job notifications, 467-468
  - job properties, 461-462
  - job schedules, 465-467
  - job steps, 462-465
- multiserver job management, 476-477
- scripting, 474-475

JOIN clauses, identifying for query analysis, 1215-1216
join hints, 1282-1283
join selectivity, evaluating, 1216-1221
joining
- columns, 521-522, 1184
- strings, 493
- variables, 493

joins, 1241
- determining optimal join order, 1246-1247
- hash joins, 1244-1246
- hybrid joins, 1246
- index joins, 1234, 1236
- merge joins, 1243-1244
- nested loops joins, 1242-1243
- outer joins, CD:1673-CD:1674
  - full outer joins, CD:1680-CD:1682
  - nested outer joins, CD:1679-CD:1680
  - WHERE clause versus, CD:1675-CD:1679
- processing strategies, 1241-1242
  - hash joins, 1244-1246
  - merge joins, 1243-1244
  - nested loops joins, 1242-1243
- semi joins, 1250
- subquery processing, 1248
  - correlated subqueries, 1250-1251
  - IN, ANY, and EXISTS subqueries, 1248
  - materialized subqueries, 1248-1250
- tuning guidelines, 1540
- for WHEN clauses (MERGE statement), CD:1554

JSON (JavaScript Object Notation), CD:1803, CD:1811

K

KEEP PLAN, 1284
KEEP REPLICATION, 406, 410
KEEPFIXED PLAN, 1284
KERBEROS, CD:1934

KEY INDEX (CREATE FULLTEXT INDEX) 2008

Key locking level (SQL Server), 1365

key management, 339, 341

database master keys, 340-341

EKM (Extensible Key Management), 341-342

service master keys, 340

key performance indicators (KPIs), CD:2082, CD:2173

key-range locking

granularity, 1365-1369

nonexistent row searches, 1368-1369

range searches, 1366-1367

keywords. ***See names of specific keywords***

KEY_GUID( ) function, 347

KILOBYTES_PER_BATCH, CD:2166

KPIs (key performance indicators), CD:2082, CD:2173

L

LANGUAGE (CREATE FULLTEXT INDEX), CD:2007-CD:2008

large object (LOB), 713

data pages, 1110-1112

reads, 1332

large row support data types, 753

large-value data types, 752

latent transactional consistency, 572

Lazy Spool (Query Analyzer), 1312

LCID property, 728

leaf rows, nonclustered indexes, 1138-1139

left semi joins, 1250

legislation, 366-367

Level 0 disaster recovery, CD:2331

Level 1 disaster recovery, CD:2331

Level 2 disaster recovery, CD:2331

Level 3 disaster recovery, CD:2331

Level 4 disaster recovery, CD:2331

License Terms page (SQL Server Installation Center), 197, 199

licensing models

choosing, 32

Compact Edition 3.5 Edition, 32

Developer Edition, 32

estimated retail pricing, 31

explained, 30-31

Express Edition, 32

mixing, 33

multi-instancing, 34

passive server/failover licensing, 33

virtual server licensing, 33-34

Web Edition, 32

life cycle, security, 361-362

lightweight pooling configuration option, CD:2301

LIKE, SARG and, 1219-1220

limitations

of relational databases, CD:2082

of web services, CD:1956-CD:1957

Line control, CD:2203

linear regression, data mining algorithms, CD:2085

LINESTRING instance type, CD:1606

linked servers

adding, CD:2253-CD:2260

configuring with sp serveroption, CD:2261-CD:2263

distributed queries, CD:2252

distributed transactions, CD:2252-CD:2253

executing stored procedures, CD:2268

mapping local logins to logins, CD:2263-CD:2267

obtaining general information about, CD:2267-CD:2268

overview, CD:2251-CD:2252

setting up through SQL Server Management, CD:2269-CD:2271
tuning guidelines, 1545
unregistering, CD:2261
viewing, CD:2260-CD:2261
LINQ to SQL, CD:1793-CD:1798
deleting rows, CD:1801
generics, CD:1796
Linqpad, CD:1798-CD:1801
updating rows, CD:1802
Linqpad, CD:1798-CD:1801
List control (SSMS) 2203
LISTENER IP, CD:1934
LISTENER PORT, CD:1934
live reports, report execution options, CD:2237
load testing in tuning methodology, 1526, 1532
LOB (large object), 713
data pages, 1110-1112
reads, 1332
local mode (Report Viewer) 2181
Local Security Policy editor, 453
Lock:Acquired event (SQL Profiler), 1355
Lock:Cancel event (SQL Profiler), 1355
Lock:Deadlock Chain event (SQL Profiler), 1355
Lock:Deadlock event (SQL Profiler), 1355
Lock:Escalation event (SQL Profiler), 1355
Lock:Released event (SQL Profiler), 1355
Lock:Timeout event (SQL Profiler), 1355
lock activity, monitoring, 1350
lock request modes, 1352-1353
Performance Monitor, 1357-1359
SQL Server Profiler, 1355-1357
sys.dm_tran_locks view, 1350, 1352-1354
LOCK ESCALATION, 39
lock events (SQL Profiler), 1355
lock granularity hints, 1395
Lock Manager, 1349-1350, 1359
bulk update locks, 1363
exclusive locks, 1361
granularity of locks, 1364-1376
intent locks, 1362-1363
schema locks, 1363
shared locks, 1360
update locks, 1360-1361
Lock Requests/sec counter (SQLServer:Locks object), 1358
Lock Timeouts/sec counter (SQLServer:Locks object), 1358-1359
lock type hints, 1395-1396
Lock Wait Time counter (SQLServer:Locks object), 1359
Lock Waits/sec counter (SQLServer:Locks object), 1359
locks, 1359
bulk update locks, 1363
compatibility, 1376-1377
contention, 1377-1380
identifying, 1378, 1380
minimizing, 1381-1382
tuning guidelines, 1544-1545
deadlocks, 1382-1384
1204 trace flags, 1386-1388
1222 trace flags, 1388-1390
avoiding, 1384-1385
conversion deadlocks, 1383
cycle deadlocks, 1382
examining, 1385-1386
handling, 1385-1387
monitoring, 1390-1392
escalation, 1374-1376
exclusive locks, 1361
granularity, 1364-1376
application locks, 1369-1372
index locks, 1372-1373
key-range locking, 1365-1369
serialization locking, 1365-1369

importance of, 1342
intent locks, 1362-1363
Lock Manager, 1349-1350
monitoring lock activity, 1350, 1358
lock request modes, 1352-1353
with Performance Monitor, 1357-1359
with SQL Server Profiler, 1355-1357
sys.dm_tran_locks view, 1350, 1352-1354
new features, 1341
optimistic locking, 1396
with rowversion data type, 1396-1399
with snapshot isolation, 1399-1401
page-level locking, 1373-1374
row-level locking, 1373-1374
schema locks, 1363
shared locks, 1360
SQL Server levels, 1364
SQL Server performance counters, 1492
table hints, 1393-1395
lock granularity hints, 1395
lock type hints, 1395-1396
transaction isolation–level hints, 1393-1395
timeout intervals, setting, 1380-1381
transaction isolation levels, 1342-1344
dirty reads, 1343
lost updates, 1343
nonrepeatable reads, 1343
phantom reads, 1343
read committed isolation, 1344-1345
read committed snapshot isolation, 1345-1346
read uncommitted isolation, 1344
repeatable read isolation, 1346
serializable read isolation, 1346-1347
snapshot isolation, 1347-1349
on transactions, 1021-1022
tuning guidelines, 1545
update locks, 1360-1361
locks configuration option, CD:2301-CD:2302
lock_owner_address column, 1352
Log File Viewer, 77, 79, 372-373, 468
log files, 1096
shrinking, 734, 1035-1037
viewing, 77, 79, 372-373, 468
log reader agent, 569
Log Row Scan (Query Analyzer), 1312
log sequence numbers (LSNs), 996
log shipping, CD:2339-CD:2341
building solutions with HA (high availability) options, 535-537
data replication, 614
logged bulk-copy operations, CD:2163-CD:2166
logging
SSIS, CD:2109
transaction logging, 1023-1037
logical and physical operator icons (Query Analyzer), 1308
Assert, 1308-1309
Clustered Index Delete, 1309
Clustered Index Scan, 1309
Collapse, 1310
Compuate Scalar, 1311
Concatenation, 1311
Constant Scan, 1311
Deleted Scan, 1311
Distribute Streams, 1314
Eager Spool, 1312
Gather Streams, 1314
Hash Match, 1311
Insert Scan, 1311
Lazy Spool, 1312
Log Row Scan, 1312

Merge Join, 1312
Nested Loops, 1313
Nonclustered Index Delete, 1309
Nonclustered Index Scan, 1310
Nonclustered Index Spool, 1312
Parallelism, 1314
Parameter Table Scan, 1313
Remote Delete, 1313
Remote Insert, 1313
Remote Query, 1313
Remote Scan, 1313
Remote Update, 1313
RID Lookup, 1313
Row Count Spool, 1312
Sequence, 1313
Sort, 1313
Stream Aggregate, 1314
Table Delete, 1314
Table Insert, 1314
Table Scan, 1314
Table Spool, 1312
Table Update, 1314
Table-valued Function, 1314
Top, 1314

logical database design. ***See*** **database design**

logical reads, 1331

LoginName data column (SQL Profiler), 1356

LOGINPROPERTY( ) function, 1506

logins, 296-297
managing, 313
with SSMS, 313-317
with T-SQL, 317-318
users, 298

LOGIN_TYPE (WEBMETHOD) 1940

logistic regression, data mining algorithms, CD:2085

logmarkhistory, 412

logs
checkpoints, 1024-1028
SQL Server Agent error log, 456-457
SSMS logs
execution log, CD:2240
server trace log, CD:2239-CD:2240
windows event log, CD:2240
transaction log files. *See* transaction logs
write-ahead logs, 717

long-running transactions, managing, 1037-1039

Lookup function, CD:2179

LookupSet function, CD:2179

looping statements, 498-499
nested loops joins, 1242-1243

loosely coupled, CD:1960

lost updates, transaction isolation levels, 1343

LSNs (log sequence numbers), 996

M

mail configuration objects, viewing, 445-446

mail message data, viewing, 446-447

mail profiles
creating in Database Mail, 429-432
defined, 429

maintenance
database. *See* database maintenance
FTS (Full-Text Search), CD:2024-CD:2025
indexes, 1169-1179
ALTER INDEX, 1175-1178
disabling, 1182
dm_db_index_physical_stats, 1171-1175
fill factor, 1179-1181
Maintenance Plan Wizard, 1077-1080
SSMS, 1183
system databases, 169-170

Maintenance menu (SQL Server Installation Center), 211

maintenance phase (OLAP design methodologies), CD:2040

Maintenance Plan Wizard

- backing up databases, 1072, 1074-1075
- checking database integrity, 1075-1076
- maintaining indexes and statistics, 1077-1080
- overview, 1070-1072
- scheduling maintenance plans, 1080-1083
- shrinking databases, 1076-1077

maintenance plans, 426

- executing, 1088
- managing manually, 1084-1088
- scheduling with Maintenance Plan Wizard, 1080-1083

majority node sets, 660

managed database objects. ***See*** **custom managed database objects**

managed stored procedures, CD:1829-CD:1835

managed triggers, developing, CD:1856-CD:1861

management data warehouse. ***See*** **MDW**

Management Studio, 504

managing

- alerts (SQL Server Agent), 469
  - properties, 469-472
  - responses, 472, 474
- constraints
  - disabling, 829-830
  - dropping, 829
  - gathering constraint information, 827-829
- Data Collector, 1443-1446
- database roles, 321-322
- databases
  - ALTER DATABASE, 736
  - expanding, 730-731
  - file growth, 729-730
  - shrinking, 731-735
- DDL triggers, 986-987
- indexes, 803
  - with SSMS, 806-807
  - with T-SQL, 803-806
- jobs (SQL Server Agent), 461
  - job history, 468-469
  - job notifications, 467-468
  - job properties, 461-462
  - job schedules, 465-467
  - job steps, 462-465
- logins, 313
  - with SSMS, 313-317
  - with T-SQL, 317-318
- maintenance plans manually, 1084-1088
- MSFTESQL, CD:2013-CD:2014
- operators (SQL Server Agent), 458-460
- permissions, 322
  - with SSMS, 323-329
  - with T-SQL, 330-331
  - for user-defined functions, 941-942
- plan guides, 1293-1294
- projects in SSMS, 93-95
- Query Optimizer, 1278-1280
  - forced parameterization, 1285-1287
  - join hints, 1282
  - plan guides, 1290-1298
  - processing hints, 1282, 1285
  - query governor, 1298-1299
  - table hints, 1280-1282
  - USE PLAN, 1287-1290
- remote servers, CD:2244-CD:2246
- users, 318
  - with SSMS, 318, 320
  - with T-SQL, 320-321
- views, 852-853

manual checkpoints (logs), 1028
manual failover, 623
manual installs, 217
manual synchronization, 567
manually updating index statistics, 1164
Map control, CD:2174, CD:2203
map reports, CD:2222-CD:2226
mapping local logins to logins on linked servers, CD:2263-CD:2267
maps, 1460
markups (XML documents), CD:1866
Martin, John, 650
masks
  affinity I/O masks, CD:2286-CD:2287
  affinity masks, CD:2287-CD:2288
Master Data Services, CD:2095
master database, 167, 421, 1536
master database files, 719
master merges, CD:2001
Master Server Wizard, 476
master servers, 476-477
materialized subqueries, 1248-1250
Matrix control (SSMS) 2202
MAX data, storing, 1112
max degree of parallelism configuration option, CD:2302
max server memory configuration option, CD:2302-CD:2303
max specifier, CD:1688-CD:1689
max text repl size configuration option, CD:2304
MAX values (resource pools), 1496-1498
max worker threads configuration option, CD:2305
MaxByteSize parameter
  SqlUserDefinedAggregate, CD:1854
  SqlUserDefinedType, CD:1845
MAXDOP, 799, 1284
MAXRECURSION, 1284, CD:1707-CD:1708
MAX_SOAP_HEADERS_SIZE (WEBMETHOD) 1942
MDAC (Microsoft Data Access Components), 285-286, CD:1929
.mdf extension, 712
MDW (management data warehouse), 1428
  custom data collection values, querying, 1450
  Data Collector, 1432-1433
MDX-based filtering, CD:2095-CD:2096
Measure-Command cmdlet, 490
measuring runtime, 1336-1337
media families, 387
media sets, 387
MEDIADESCRIPTION (BACKUP DATABASE), 392
MEDIANAME option
  BACKUP DATABASE, 393
  RESTORE DATABASE, 406
MEDIAPASSWORD option
  BACKUP DATABASE, 393
  RESTORE DATABASE, 406
member tables, 854-858
memory
  monitoring, 1485-1487
  tuning guidelines, 1534-1536
MERGE, 38, CD:1552-CD:1559, CD:1656
  tuning guidelines, 1543
  VALUES clause, CD:1571
merge agent, 570-571
Merge Join (Query Analyzer), 1312
merge joins, 1243-1244
merge replication, 16-17, 574-576
MERGE UNION, 1283
message storage (SQL Server Service Broker), CD:1970-CD:1972
message types, choosing for SQL Server Service Broker, CD:1965-CD:1969

messages, defining in SQL Server Service Broker, CD:1965-CD:1969

metadata, CD:2337

Metadata locking level (SQL Server), 1365

metadata tables (CDC), CD:1616

methodology for tuning, 1522-1523

- for existing implementations, 1528-1533
- for new implementations, 1523-1528

Microsoft Cluster Services. *See* **MSCS**

Microsoft Data Access Components (MDAC) 1929

Microsoft Full-Text Engine for SQL Server (MSFTESQL), 17

- managing, CD:2013-CD:2014

Microsoft Message Queuing (MSMQ), CD:1960

Microsoft ODBC driver for SQL Server, 281

Microsoft OLE DB provider for ODBC, 280

Microsoft OLE DB provider for SQL Server, 280

***Microsoft SQL Server High Availability*, 526**

Microsoft Sync Framework (MSF), CD:1816-CD:1817

- building OCA, CD:1818-CD:1823
- sync services for ADO.NET, CD:1817-CD:1818

Microsoft Tape Format (MTF), 386

Microsoft Virtual Server 2005, 541-542

Microsoft.SqlServer.Server objects, CD:1832-CD:1833

midnight for the current day, calculating, CD:1665

migration

- Analysis Services, 253-254
- Reporting Services, 255
  - in-place upgrades, 255-257
  - migrating to Reporting Services 2008, 257-258
- side-by-side migration. *See* side-by-side migration
- web services, CD:1928

min memory per query configuration option, CD:2306

min server memory configuration option, CD:2302-CD:2303

MIN values (resource pools), 1496-1498

mirror database server, 619, 622

mirrored backups, 401-402

mirroring. *See* **database mirroring**

missing index dynamic management objects, 1202-1204

Missing Index Hints, 1317-1318, 1320

- dynamic management objects, 1320-1321
- limitations of, 1321-1322

missing indexes, identifying, 1201

- with Database Engine Tuning Advisor, 1201-1204
- missing index dynamic management objects, 1202-1204

mixed authentication mode, 294

mixed extent, 710

Mode data column (SQL Profiler), 1356

model database, 168, 1536

models, setting permissions, CD:2233

modify( ) new xml data type method, CD:1900, CD:1913-CD:1918

modifying

- classification functions, 1516
- data through partitioned views, 858-859
- hierarchies, CD:1587-CD:1590, CD:1592
- logins (SSMS), 316
- Resource Governor configuration, 1513-1516
- stored procedures
  - with ALTER PROCEDURE, 891-892
  - with SSMS, 892-893
- tables, 765-766
  - with database diagrams, 772-773
  - with Object Explorer and Table Designer, 769-772
  - with T-SQL, 766-768
- user-defined functions, 939-940

MOLAP (Multidimensional OLAP), 58-59, CD:2037

Monday of the current week, calculating, CD:1665

money data type, 749

monitoring

- application progress with SQL Server Profiler, 162-164
- auto-update statistics with SQL Server Profiler, 162
- data replication, 603
  - backup and recovery, 612-613
  - in heterogeneous environments, 611-612
  - peer-to-peer replication, 609-610
  - Performance Monitor, 610-611
  - SQL statements, 603-606
  - troubleshooting replication failures, 608
  - within SQL Server Management Studio, 606-607
- database mirroring, 639-642
- deadlocks, 1390-1392
- disk performance (SSMS), 1490
- disk systems, 1488-1490
- lock activity, 1350
  - lock request modes, 1352-1353
  - Performance Monitor, 1357-1359
  - SQL Server Profiler, 1355-1357
  - sys.dm_tran_locks view, 1350, 1352-1354
- memory, 1485-1487
- network interfaces, 1478-1480
- plan cache, 1258
  - sys.dm exec sql text, 1260
  - sys.dm_exec_cached_plans, 1258-1260
  - sys.dm_exec_plan_attributes, 1265-1266
  - sys.dm_exec_query_stats, 1261-1265
  - sys.dm_exec_sql_text, 1260
- processors, 1480-1485
- resource usage, 1509-1512
- running traces, 153-154
- SQL Server disk activity, 1490
- SQL Server performance, 1427
- store procedure recompilation, CD:1767-CD:1773

monitoring and isolation stage (tuning methodology), 1530-1531

MOVE (RESTORE DATABASE), 406

moving

- databases, 736
- hierarchy nodes, CD:1589
- packages (dtutil utility), CD:2141-CD:2144

MSCS (Microsoft Cluster Services)

- building solutions with HA (high availability) options, 530-531
- extending with NLB, 662
- installing, 668
- SQL Server Clustering, 657-665

MSDASQL, 280

msdb database, 168

MSDN Online, 68

MSF (Microsoft Sync Framework), CD:1816-CD:1817

- building OCA, CD:1818-CD:1823
- sync services for ADO.NET, CD:1817-CD:1818

MSFTESQL (Microsoft Full-Text Engine for SQL Server), 17

- managing, CD:2013-CD:2014

MSMQ (Microsoft Message Queuing) 1960

mssqlsystemresource.mdf file, 169

MTF (Microsoft Tape Format), 386

multi-instancing, 34

multidimensional expressions in OLAP database creation, CD:2076-CD:2077

Multidimensional OLAP (MOLAP), 58-59, CD:2037

MULTILINESTRING, CD:1606

MultiLookup function, CD:2179

multiple indexes, 1228

index intersection, 1229-1231

index joins, 1234, 1236

index union strategy, 1232-1234

wide indexes, compared, 1191-1192

multiple job steps, defining, 464

multiple publishers or multiple subscribers replication model, 559-560

multiple simultaneous editions, running, 191

MULTIPOINT, CD:1606

MULTIPOLYGON, CD:1606

multiserver job management, 476-477

multiserver jobs, creating, 477

multiserver queries, 42, 101-102

multistatement table-valued functions, 924-926

multistatement transactions, triggers, 1017-1019

multitier environments, cursors in, CD:1659

My Reports role, CD:2235

N

NAME option

BACKUP DATABASE, 393

WEBMETHOD, 1939

Name parameter

scalar UDFs, CD:1837

SqlMethod, CD:1849

SqlTrigger, CD:1856

SqlUserDefinedAggregate, CD:1854

SqlUserDefinedType, CD:1845

name resolution, 885-888

names

columns, 747

naming conventions, ensuring, 706

object names

passing as parameters, 898-899

qualifying with schema names, CD:1640-CD:1643

qualifying names, CD:1941

NAMESPACE, CD:1937

namespaces, CD:1788

navigational property, CD:1810

nchar data type, 749

.ndf extension, 712

nested loops

joins, 1242-1243

Query Analyzer, 1313

nested outer joins, CD:1679-CD:1680

nested stored procedures, CD:1753-CD:1755

recursion, CD:1755-CD:1758

tuning guidelines, 1544

nested transactions, 1001-1003, 1015-1017

nested triggers, 991-992, CD:2306

.NET classes, CD:1812

.NET Framework

ADO.NET, CD:1788-CD:1793, CD:1804, CD:1810

custom managed database objects

developing, CD:1825-CD:1864

managed triggers, CD:1856-CD:1861

permissions, CD:1827-CD:1829

related system catalogs, CD:1863-CD:1864

stored procedures, CD:1829-CD:1835

transactions, CD:1861-CD:1863

UDAs (user-defined aggregates), CD:1853-CD:1856

UDFs (user-defined functions), CD:1835-CD:1844

UDTs (user-defined types), CD:1844-CD:1852

Visual Studio 2008, CD: 1829

Code Access Security (CAS) permission sets, CD:1827
data provider for SQL Server, 280, 283-284
namespaces, CD:1788
NET SEND, 459
NET START, 118
NET STOP, 118
net-libraries, 280
network interfaces
installing, 668
monitoring, 1478-1480
Network Load Balancing (NLB), extending MSCS with, 662
network packet size configuration option, CD:2306-CD:2307
network protocols. *See* protocols
network shares, 386-387
network tuning, 1535
neural networks, CD:2085
New Alert dialog, 470
NEW BROKER, 406, CD:1961
new implementations, tuning methodology for, 1523-1528
assessment stage, 1524
coding and testing stage, 1526-1527
identification and design stage, 1525
implementation stage, 1527-1528
prototyping stage, 1525-1526
system testing and acceptance stage, 1527
New Job Step dialog, 462
new xml data type, CD:1890-CD:1891
built-in methods, CD:1899-CD:1918
exists() method, CD:1900, CD:1908-CD:1909
modify() method, CD:1900, CD:1913-CD:1918
nodes() method, CD:1900, CD:1911-CD:1912
query() method, CD:1900-CD:1908
value() method, CD:1900, CD:1910
columns, CD:1892-CD:1894
FOR XML modes, CD:1884-CD:1887
schema collections, CD:1894-CD:1899
New-Object cmdlet, 490
NEXT USED, 783
NLB (Network Load Balancing), extending MSCS with, 662
NO ACTION, 818
NO CHECKSUM option
BACKUP DATABASE, 392
RESTORE DATABASE, 405
NO COMPRESSION option (BACKUP DATABASE), 392
NO RECOVERY option (RESTORE), 630
NO TRUNCATE option (BACKUP LOG), 395
nodes, 1303
failure of, 679-681
in hierarchies, CD:1589
XML documents, CD:1866
nodes(), CD:1900, CD:1911-CD:1912
NOEXPAND, 1236
NOLOCK, 1394
NON-CLUSTERED argument (CREATE INDEX), 796
non-logged bulk-copy operations (SSIS), CD:2163-CD:2166
non-Transact-SQL (non-T-SQL), 455
Nonclustered Index Delete icon (Query Analyzer), 1309
Nonclustered Index Scan icon (Query Analyzer), 1310
Nonclustered Index Spool (Query Analyzer), 1312
nonclustered indexes, 793-795, 1112, 1136-1138
costs, 1223-1227
designing, 1186-1188

leaf rows, 1138-1139
nonleaf rows, 1139-1140
rebuilding, 1179
tuning guidelines, 1540

nonexistent rows, searching, 1368-1369

nonleaf pages, 1112

nonleaf rows, 1139-1140

nonrepeatable reads, 1343

nonunique clustered indexes, 1135-1136

NORECOVERY option, 393-395, 406-408

normalization. *See also* **denormalization**
benefits of, 1407
conditions, 1405
first normal form, 1406
limitations of, 1407-1408
second normal form, 1406-1407
third normal form, 1407
tuning guidelines, 1537-1538

NOSKIP option (BACKUP DATABASE), 392

not-in-place updates, 1145-1146

NOT NULL, 755

notifications
job notifications, 467-468
managing operators, 460

NOTRUNCATE option (DBCC SHRINKDATABASE), 732

NOUNLOAD option
BACKUP DATABASE, 393
RESTORE DATABASE, 407

ntext data type, 749

NTILE function, CD:1717-CD:1714

NULL, 755, CD:1600-CD:1605

Number of Deadlocks/sec counter, 1359

numeric data type, 749

nvarchar data type, 749, 752

O

object definition function, 891

Object Explorer, 68, 73-75
creating databases, 718-721
creating tables, 742-743
data types, 750
dropping tables, 773-774
modifying tables, 769-772

object-based functionality (PowerShell), 484

ObjectID data column (SQL Profiler), 1356

objectives of disaster recovery, CD:2336-CD:2337

OBJECTPROPERTY function, 938, CD:2014-CD:2015

object_definition() function, 891

object_id() function, 891

obsolete configuration options, CD:2283-CD:2284

OCA (Occasionally Connected Application), CD:1816-CD:1823

ODBC (Open Database Connectivity), 281, CD:1929

OGC (Open Geospatial Consortium, Inc.), CD:1606

OLAP (online analytical processing), 228, CD:2029
design methodologies
construction phase, CD:2039
design phase, CD:2039
implementation phase, CD:2040
maintenance phase, CD:2040
requirements phase, CD:2039
design methodologies, CD:2038
HOLAP, CD:2037
MOLAP, CD:2037
performance, CD:2093-CD:2094
preparing for database creation, CD:2038
requirements example (CompSales),

CD:2040-CD:2041, CD:2081-CD:2082
cube, CD:2042, CD:2082
data, CD:2084-CD:2091
KPIs, CD:2082
OLAP, CD:2044
security, CD:2095-CD:2096
SQL, CD:2042-CD:2043
ROLAP, CD:2037
SSAS and, CD:2030-CD:2032
versus OLTP, CD:2036-CD:2037
OLE DB, CD:2251
OLTP (online transaction processing), 53, 666, CD:2030
OLTP ERP, 53-56
OLTP shopping cart, 56-57
versus OLAP, CD:2036-CD:2037
On Change Log Only execution mode, 695
On Change Prevent execution mode, 694
ON clause (MERGE statement), CD:1552
ON DELETE CASCADE, 963, 1404
On Demand execution mode, 694
on failure workflows, CD:2106
ON FULLTEXT CATALOG parameter (CREATE FULLTEXT INDEX) 2008
On Schedule execution mode, 694
on success workflows, CD:2106
ON UPDATE CASCADE, 963
online analytical processing. *See* OLAP (online analytical processing)
ONLINE argument (CREATE INDEX), 798
online indexing
HA (high availability), 538
operations, 807-808
online restores, 421, 538
online transaction processing. *See* OLTP (online transaction processing)
OnNullCall parameter (SqlMethod), CD:1849
Open Database Connectivity (ODBC), 281, CD:1929
Open Geospatial Consortium, Inc. (OGC), CD:1606
OPENXML, CD:1887-CD:1890
operating modes for database mirroring, 622-623
operating systems
HA (high availability), 527
tuning guidelines, 1534-1535
__$operation column (CDC table), CD:1616
operations (SSIS), CD:2163-CD:2164
batches, CD:2164
hints, CD:2165-CD:2166
parallel, CD:2164-CD:2165
operators, 496
compound operators, 37, CD:1568-CD:1569
creating with SQL Server Agent Mail, 442
defined, 449
inequality operators, SARG and, 1218
managing in SQL Server Agent, 458-460
optimal join order, determining, 1246-1247
optimistic locking
with rowversion data type, 1396-1399
with snapshot isolation, 1399-1401
optimizing performance. *See* performance
optimize for ad hoc workloads configuration option, CD:2307-CD:2308
OPTIMIZE FOR UNKNOWN hints, 1285
OPTIMIZER FOR hints, 1285
@@options function, 1006
OR clauses, identifying for query analysis, 1214-1215
ORDER BY, CD:1654
query() method, CD:1905-CD:1906
tuning guidelines, 1542
ORDER GROUP, 1283
ORDER hint, CD:2166
order of joins, determining, 1246-1247

OS-related tasks (PowerShell), 512-514

osql, 105

OUTER APPLY operator, CD:1723-CD:1724

outer joins, CD:1673-CD:1674

full outer joins, CD:1680-CD:1682

nested outer joins, CD:1679-CD:1680

WHERE clause versus, CD:1675-CD:1679

OUTPUT clause, 902-903, CD:1693-CD:1697

Insert over DML, CD:1559-CD:1561

MERGE statement, CD:1553

tuning guidelines, 1543

output parameters for stored procedures, 902-903, CD:1777-CD:1779

OverallPageNumber variable, CD:2179

OverallTotalPages variable, CD:2179

OWNER option (EXECUTE AS), 884

P

Package Execution Utility, CD:2135-CD:2136

dtexec utility, CD:2135-CD:2137

dtsrun utility, CD:2135

dtutil utility, CD:2141-CD:2145

packages, running, CD:2137-CD:2141

package loading phase (dtexec), CD:2137

Package Migration Wizard, 260

packages

running, CD:2137-CD:2141

SSEE (SQL Server Extended Events), 1457

SSIS, CD:2106, CD:2109

packet sizes, tuning guidelines for, 1535

PAD_INDEX option, 798, 1181

page compression

evaluating, 1123-1126

implementing, 1122-1123

page files, tuning guidelines, 1535

page free space (PFS), 711, 1115

page headers, 1103-1104

page-level compression, 1119-1121

page-level locking, 1373-1374

Page locking level (SQL Server), 1365

page splits, 1141-1143

Page Verify, 724

PageName variable, CD:2179

pages (database)

BCM (bulk changed map) pages, 1116

data pages

data rows, 1104-1108

defined, 1103

page header, 1103-1104

row offset table, 1108-1109

DCM (differential changed map) pages, 1116

defined, 10

dirty pages, 717

GAM (global allocation map) pages, 1114-1115

IAM (index allocation map), 1115-1116

index pages, 1112-1113

extents, 1113-1114

space allocation structures, 1113

LOB data pages, 1110-1112

overview, 1101

PFS (page free space), 1115

row-overflow pages, 1109-1110

SGAM (shared global allocation map) pages, 1114

space allocation, 1113-1114

table of page types, 1102

paging results, CD:1714-CD:1717

PAGLOCK optimizer hint, 1395

Parallel Data Warehouse (SQL Server 2008), 43

parallel loading, CD:2164-CD:2165

parallel query processing, 1268-1271
configuration options, 1271-1272
identifying, 1272-1273
parallel queries on partitioned objects, 1273
parallelism, 1314, CD:2293
param construct, 494
Parameter Table Scan, 1313
PARAMETERIZATION FORCED, 1286-1287
parameterization of queries, 1256
PARAMETERIZATION SIMPLE, 1287
partial backups, 381, 398-400
PARTIAL option (RESTORE DATABASE), 406
partitions, 774
horizontal data partitioning, 1412-1413
partition functions, 776-778
partitioned objects, parallel queries on, 1273
partitioned tables, 774-775
adding partitions, 782-783
creating, 779-781
creating partition functions, 776-778
creating partition schemes, 778-779
dropping partitions, 784-785
switching partitions, 785-789
viewing information, 781
partitioned views, 844
base tables, 854-858
distributed partitioned views, 859-860
modifying data through, 858-859
by ROW NUMBER function, CD:1710-CD:1711
schemes, 778-779
tuning guidelines, 1539, 1546
vertical data partitioning, 1413-1414
passing
arguments, 494
object names as parameters, 898-899
passive server/failover licensing, 33
passphrases, encrypting columns with, 344-346
PASSWORD option
BACKUP DATABASE, 392
RESTORE DATABASE, 406
PATH, CD:1881-CD:1884, CD:1922, CD:1935
patterns of disaster recovery
active multisite DR patterns, CD:2334
active/active DR site patterns, CD:2333-CD:2334
active/passive DR site patterns, CD:2332-CD:2333
choosing, CD:2334-CD:2335
PCI (Payment Card Industry) data security standard, 367
peer-to-peer replication, 561-562, 609-610
Perfmon, 1548
performance. ***See also*** **performance-monitoring tools**
Change Tracking, CD:1634-CD:1635
configuration options
access check cache bucket count, CD:2284
access check cache quota, CD:2285
ad hoc distributed queries, CD:2285
affinity I/O mask, CD:2286-CD:2287
affinity mask, CD:2287-CD:2288
Agent XP, CD:2289
awe enabled, CD:2289-CD:2291
backup compression default, CD:2291
blocked process threshold, CD:2291
c2 audit mode, CD:2291-CD:2292
clr enabled, CD:2292
common criteria compliance enabled, CD:2292
cost threshold for parallelism, CD:2293
cross db ownership chaining, CD:2293
cursor threshold, CD:2294
default full-text language, CD:2294-CD:2296

default language, CD:2296-CD:2298
EKM provider enabled, CD:2298
filestream_access_level, CD:2299
fill factor, CD:2299-CD:2300
in-doubt xact resolution, CD:2300
index create memory, CD:2300
lightweight pooling, CD:2301
locks, CD:2301-CD:2302
max degree of parallelism, CD:2302
max server memory, CD:2302-CD:2303
max text repl size, CD:2304
max worker threads, CD:2305
min memory per query, CD:2306
min server memory, CD:2302-CD:2303
miscellaneous options, CD:2316
nested triggers, CD:2306
network packet size, CD:2306-CD:2307
optimize for ad hoc workloads, CD:2307-CD:2308
parallelism, CD:2293
PH_timeout, CD:2308
priority boost, CD:2308-CD:2309
query governor cost limit, CD:2309-CD:2310
query wait, CD:2310
recovery interval, CD:2310-CD:2311
remote admin connections, CD:2311
remote login timeout, CD:2311
remote proc trans, CD:2312
remote query timeout, CD:2312-CD:2313
scan for startup procs, CD:2313
show advanced options, CD:2313
user connections, CD:2313-CD:2314
user options, CD:2315-CD:2316
XP-related configuration options, CD:2316

counters
  SSRS (SQL Server Reporting Services) 2240
  Windows Performance Monitor, 1474-1476
data replication, 613-614
designing for database performance, 1404-1405
filegroups and, 1415-1417
FTS (Full-Text Search), CD:2025-CD:2026
indexed views and, 863-866
monitoring SQL Server performance, 1427
new features, 38-39
OLAP database creation, CD:2079-CD:2081
performance monitoring approach, 1477
processors, monitoring in SSMS, 1483
Query Editor, 91-92
SANs (storage area networks), 1424-1425
SQL Server performance, 1428-1429, 1490-1492
stored procedures, CD:1764-CD:1765
  automatic query plan recompilation, CD:1767
  query plan caching, CD:1765
  shared query plans, CD:1766
  SQL Server procedure cache, CD:1766
T-SQL
  avoiding unnecessary function executions, CD:1656
  cursors, CD:1656-CD:1659
  DISTINCT, CD:1654
  IF EXISTS, CD:1654
  ORDER BY, CD:1654
  temporary tables versus table variables, CD:1654-CD:1656
  UNION versus UNION ALL, CD:1654
  UPDATE, CD:1659-CD:1663
tuning
  architectural layers, 1520-1521

guidelines, 1534-1545
methodology, 1522-1533
primary handles for, 1521-1522
system interdependencies in, 1521-1522
tools for, 1547-1549
third-party tools, 1548-1549
Windows performance, 1478-1487, 1489-1490

performance-monitoring tools
Data Collector, 1429-1432
customized data, 1446-1450
installing and, 1433-1437
limitations and, 1450-1451
managing, 1443
managing in T, 1443-1446
MDW, 1432-1433
MDW reports, 1433
reports, 1439-1442
system data, 1437-1439
SQL Server Extended Events, 1455-1465
SQL Server Utility, 1451-1455
Windows Performance, 1466-1477
Windows Performance Monitor, 1465-1466
Data Collector Sets, 1467
lock activity monitoring, 1357-1359
memory monitoring, 1485-1486
replication monitoring, 610-611

permissions, 292, 311-312
access permissions, CD:1955-CD:1956
Execute Report Definitions, CD:2233
granting, 629-630
managed database objects, CD:1827-CD:1829
managing with SSMS, 322-323
at database level, 326-328
at object level, 328-329
at server level, 323-325
managing with T-SQL, 330-331
roles, 302
securing reports, CD:2234-CD:2235
setting on models, CD:2233
system permissions, CD:2235
for user-defined functions, 941-942

Personal Identifiable Information (PII), 366-367

perspectives. *See* cube perspectives

PFS (page free space), 711, 1115

PH_timeout configuration option, CD:2308

phantom reads, 1343

physical reads, 1332

PhysicalDisk object, 713

PII (Personal Identifiable Information), 366-367

pipe character (|), 483

pipelines, 483

pipes, 270-271

PIVOT clause, CD:1718-CD:1721

plan cache, 1254, 1260

plan guides, 39
best practices, 1295-1296
creating, 1292-1293, 1297-1298
managing, 1293-1294
overview, 1290-1292
sys.plan_guides catalog view, 1294-1295
validating, 1294
verifying application of, 1296-1297

planning
disaster recovery, CD:2349-CD:2350
for backups and restoration, 378-379
for data replication, 572-573
maintenance plans, 426

plus sign (+), 493

point in time, restoring to, 419-420

POINT instance type, CD:1605

point-in-time reporting databases, providing with database snapshots, 1054-1055

point of failure, restoring to, 417-419

pointers, 1146

policies

categories, 693, 701

creating, 699-700

database maintenance policies, 1090

defined, 693

evaluating, 702-703

exporting, 703-704

exporting current state as, 700-701

importing, 696-697, 703-704

Policy-Based Management, 450

advantages of, 687-688

best practices, 706-707

categories, 693, 701

Central Management Servers

creating, 695-696

explained, 695

importing and evaluating policies to, 696-697

registering SQL Server instances in, 696

conditions

creating based on facets, 697-698

defined, 693

execution modes

On Change Log Only, 695

On Change Prevent, 694

On Demand, 694

On Schedule, 694

explained, 40

facets

creating conditions based on, 697-698

explained, 689, 692

table of, 690-692

goals of, 688-689

online resources, 689

policies

categories, 693, 701

creating, 699-700

database maintenance policies, 1090

defined, 693

evaluating, 702-703

exporting, 703-704

exporting current state as, 700-701

importing, 696-697, 703-704

real-world examples

checking best practices compliance, 706

ensuring object naming conventions, 706

evaluating recovery models, 705

implementing Surface Area Configuration checks, 705

performing server health checks, 705

sample templates, 704-705

targets, 693

POLYGON instance type, CD:1606

pools

creating

in SSMS, 1500-1502

in T-SQL, 1502

deleting, 1515-1516

explained, 1496

MIN/MAX values, 1496-1498

populating

cubes with data in OLAP database creation, CD:2065-CD:2066

hierarchies, CD:1581-CD:1583

population, CD:2008

POPULATION TYPE parameter (CREATE FULLTEXT INDEX), CD:2008-CD:2010

ports, 270-271, CD:1935

pound sign (#), 491, 879

PowerPivot, 43-44

PowerShell

adding PowerShell support, 504

aliases, 484

arguments, passing, 494

arrays, 495-496
cmdlets
- Add-Content, 491
- Convert-UrnToPath, 509
- Decode-SqlName, 509
- defined, 483
- Encode-SqlName, 509
- Export-Csv, 501
- filtering cmdlets, 499-500
- ForEach-Object, 499
- Format-List, 500
- Format-Table, 500
- formatting cmdlets, 500-501
- Get-Alias, 490
- Get-ChildItem, 490
- Get-Command, 488
- Get-Content, 490, 514
- Get-Help, 488-489
- Get-Item, 520
- Get-Member, 489-490
- Get-Process, 513
- Get-Service, 513
- Group-Object, 490
- Import-Csv, 501
- Invoke-PolicyEvaluation, 508, 521
- Invoke-SqlCmd, 508, 520-521
- Measure-Command, 490
- New-Object, 490
- Read-Host, 490
- Select-Object, 490
- Select-String, 515
- Set-Content, 491
- Set-ExecutionPolicy, 487
- Sort-Object, 490
- Start-Service, 513
- Start-Transcript, 491
- Where-Object, 499
- Write-Host, 490

conditional statements, 496-497
console, 485-486
CSV files, handling, 501-502
databases
- backing up, 516-518
- checking database usage, 519
- creating database tables, 515-516
- getting table properties, 520
- joining columns, 521-522

date/time calculations, 502-503
escape characters, 492
execution policy, 487
functions, 497-498
general tasks, 509-510
help features
- Get-Command cmdlet, 488
- Get-Help cmdlet, 488-489
- Get-Member cmdlet, 489-490
- overview, 487

installing, 485
integrated support for, 42
interactivity, 486
looping statements, 498-499
new features, 481-482
object-based functionality, 484
online resources, 483
operators, 496
overview, 482-483
param construct, 494
pipeline, 483
profiles, 487
providers, 484
retrieving entries, 522
scripts
- comments, 491
- creating, 491
- defined, 483
- OS-related tasks, 512-514

scheduling, 510-512
SQL Server–specific tasks, 514-515
security, 486
server settings, checking, 518
SMO (SQL Server Management Objects), 484
snap-ins, 484
SQL Server PowerShell
accessing, 505
cmdlets, 508-509
defined, 505
overview, 506-507
SQL providers, 507, 515
SQL Server Agent support, 509
strings, joining, 493
support for, 450
variables
$_ special variable, 493
explained, 491-492
joining, 493
versions, 483
-whatif/-confirm parameters, 503
WMI (Windows Management Instrumentation), 484-485

Precise 8.5, 1548

predicates, 1306
SSEE (SQL Server Extended Events), 1459
transitivity, 1266-1267

primary data files, 712, 1095

primary filegroups, 713

primary handles for tuning, 1521-1522

PRIMARY KEY constraint, 764, 813-814

primary keys, 1539

principals, 292, 295, 619, 622
logins, 296-297
roles, 302
application roles, 309
fixed-database roles, 304-306
fixed-server roles, 303-304
public roles, 306-307
user-defined roles, 307-309
user/schema separation, 301-302
users
dbo users, 299
explained, 298-299
guest users, 299-300
INFORMATION_SCHEMA users, 300
sys users, 300

PRINT, CD:1983

priorities
prioritizing conversations, CD:1984
tuning guidelines, 1535

priority boost configuration option, CD:2308-CD:2309

private keys, 338

Proactive DBA SQL Capture, 1549

procedural data integrity, 813

procedure caches, CD:1766

procedures. ***See specific procedures***

Proceedings of the, 31st International Conference on Very Large Data Bases, **CD:1920**

processadmin, 303

processes
deadlocks, 1382-1384
1204 trace flags, 1386-1388
1222 trace flags, 1388-1390
avoiding, 1384-1385
conversion deadlocks, 1383
cycle deadlocks, 1382
examining, 1385-1386
handling, 1385-1387
monitoring, 1390-1392
locking contention, 1377-1380
identifying, 1378-1380
minimizing, 1381-1382
priority, 1535

processing
- processing hints, 1282, 1285
- processing instructions (XML), CD:1866
- reports, CD:2176
- snapshot agents, 567-568
- transactions, 997

processor affinity, 1481, CD:2286

processors, monitoring, 1480-1485

Product Key entry page (SQL Server Installation Center), 197-198

Profiler, 132-135, 1338-1340, 1547
- analyzing slow stored procedures or queries, 157-158
- application progress, monitoring, 162-164
- architecture, 122-123
- auto-update statistics, monitoring, 162
- deadlocks, 158-159, 1390-1392
- explained, 15
- indexes, selecting, 1149
- lock activity, monitoring, 1355-1357
- new features, 121
- performance bottlenecks, identifying, 160-162
- queries, identifying ad hoc queries, 159-160
- replaying trace data, 138-140
- traces
  - analyzing trace output with Database Engine Tuning Advisor, 138
  - creating, 123-125
  - data columns, 127-128, 130
  - defining server-side traces, 140-141, 148-152
  - events, 125-127
  - executing, 132
  - exporting, 132
  - filters, 130-132
  - importing, 135
  - importing into tables, 135-136
  - saving, 132
  - saving Profiler GUI output, 134-135
  - saving to files, 133
  - saving to tables, 134
  - stopping server-side traces, 155-156
  - trace events and categories, 141-147
- traces, monitoring, 153-154
- user configurable events, 163

profiles
- creating in Database Mail, 429-432
- PowerShell, 487

projects, managing in SSMS, 93-95

properties. ***See specific properties***

PROPERTY secondary index (XML) 1923

protocols
- ensuring appropriate network protocols are configured on server, 264-267
- support for, 191

prototyping stage (tuning methodology), 1525-1526, 1531-1532

providers, 280
- defined, 484
- SQL providers, 507, 515

provisioning, 268-270

proximity, CD:2022

proxy accounts, 455-456

public keys, 338

public roles, 306-307

publication server, 549-550

publications, 550
- creating, 584-592
- data replication, 550

Publisher role, CD:2234

publisher subscriber replication model, 558

publishing, 581-584

pull subscriptions, 563

Q

QA (quality assurance)
HA (high availability), 528
testing database snapshots, 1064
QNames, CD:1941
qualifying names, CD:1941
quality assurance (QA)
HA (high availability), 528
testing database snapshots, 1064
queries
ad hoc queries, 159-160, CD:2285
analyzing, 157-158, 1213
identifying JOIN clauses, 1215-1216
identifying OR clauses, 1214-1215
identifying search arguments, 1214
OLAP database creation, CD:2079-CD:2081
Query Analyzer. *See* Query Analyzer
SQL Server Profiler, 1338-1340
compiling. *See* query compilation
DISTINCT, 1268
distributed queries, CD:2252
execution plan, 1211
GROUP BY, 1267
multiserver queries, 42, 101-102
optimizing. *See* Query Optimizer
parallel query processing, 1268-1271
configuration options, 1271-1272
identifying, 1272-1273
parallel queries on partitioned objects, 1273
parameterization, 1256
partitioned tables, 775
predicate transitivity, 1266-1267
query governor, 1298-1299
query plan caching. *See* query plan caching
recursive queries, CD:1700-CD:1708
statistics, 1330
datediff(), 1336-1337
STATISTICS IO, 1330-1333
STATISTICS PROFILE, 1337
STATISTICS TIME, 1333-1336
STATISTICS XML, 1337-1338
subquery processing, 1248
correlated subqueries, 1250-1251
IN, ANY, and EXISTS subqueries, 1248
materialized subqueries, 1248-1250
troubleshooting
index design, 1275
large complex queries, 1277-1278
search arguments, 1276-1277
statistics, 1274-1275
triggers, 1278
tuning guidelines, 1543
types, 87-88
UNION, 1268
Query Analyzer, 1302-1303
execution plan ToolTips, 1304-1307
graphical execution plans, saving and viewing, 1317
logical and physical operator icons
Assert, 1308-1309
Clustered Index Delete, 1309
Clustered Index Scan, 1309
Collapse, 1310
Compute Scalar, 1311
Concatenation, 1311
Constant Scan, 1311
Deleted Scan, 1311
Distribute Streams, 1314
Eager Spool, 1312
Gather Streams, 1314
Hash Match, 1311
Insert Scan, 1311

Lazy Spool, 1312
Log Row Scan, 1312
Merge Join, 1312
Nested Loops, 1313
Nonclustered Index Delete, 1309
Nonclustered Index Scan, 1310
Nonclustered Index Spool, 1312
Parallelism, 1314
Parameter Table Scan, 1313
Remote Delete, 1313
Remote Insert, 1313
Remote Query, 1313
Remote Scan, 1313
Remote Update, 1313
RID Lookup, 1313
Row Count Spool, 1312
Sequence, 1313
Sort, 1313
Stream Aggregate, 1314
Table Delete, 1314
Table Insert, 1314
Table Scan, 1314
Table Spool, 1312
Table Update, 1314
Table-valued Function, 1314
Top, 1314
SSMS, 1302
stored procedures, analyzing, 1315-1316

Query Builder, CD:2112-CD:2114

query compilation
DML statements, 1212-1213
execution plan selection, 1251-1253
join selection
determining optimal join order, 1246-1247
join processing strategies, 1241-1246
subquery processing, 1248-1251
optimization steps, 1218
overview, 1213
query analysis, 1213
identifying JOIN clauses, 1215-1216
identifying OR clauses, 1214-1215
identifying search arguments, 1214
row estimation and index selection
estimating access path costs, 1221-1228
evaluating SARG and join selectivity, 1216-1221
multiple indexes, 1228-1236
optimizing with filtered indexes, 1239-1241
optimizing with indexed views, 1236-1239

Query Designer, 92-93

Query Editor
disconnected editing, 88
editing sqlmd scripts, 88-89
IntelliSense, 87
overview, 85-87
performance, 91-92
Query Designer, 92-93
query types, 87-88
regular expressions and wildcards, 89-91

QUERY_GOVERNOR_COST_LIMIT, 1298-1299, CD:2309-CD:2310

Query Optimizer, 1301
execution plan selection, 1251-1253
indexes, evaluating, 1150-1153
join selection
determining optimal join order, 1246-1247
join processing strategies, 1241-1246
subquery processing, 1248-1251
managing, 1278-1280
forced parameterization, 1285-1287
join hints, 1282

processing hints, 1282, 1285
query governor, 1298-1299
table hints, 1280-1282
USE PLAN, 1287-1290
multiple indexes, 1228
index intersection, 1229-1231
index joins, 1234-1236
index union strategy, 1232-1234
new features, 1210-1211
optimization steps, 1218
overview, 1209-1213
plan guides
best practices, 1295-1296
creating, 1292-1293, 1297-1298
managing, 1293-1294
overview, 1290-1292
sys.plan_guides catalog view, 1294-1295
validating, 1294
verifying application of, 1296-1297
query analysis, 1213
identifying JOIN clauses, 1215-1216
identifying OR clauses, 1214-1215
identifying search arguments, 1214
row estimation and index selection
estimating access path costs, 1221-1228
evaluating SARG and join selectivity, 1216-1221
multiple indexes, 1228-1236
optimizing with filtered indexes, 1239-1241
optimizing with indexed views, 1236-1239
table scans, 1132

query plan caching
monitoring plan cache
sys.dm_exec_cached_plans, 1258-1260
sys.dm_exec_plan_attributes, 1265-1266
sys.dm_exec_query_stats, 1261-1265
sys.dm_exec_sql_text, 1260
query plan aging, 1256-1257
query plan reuse, 1254-1256
recompiling query plans, 1257-1258
stored procedures, CD:1765

query plans
automatic query plan recompilation, CD:1767
caching
monitoring plan cache, 1258-1266
query plan aging, 1256-1257
query plan reuse, 1254-1256
recompiling query plans, 1257-1258
stored procedures, CD:1765
forcing recompilation, CD:1770-CD:1773
hash values, 39

query trees, 1212

query wait configuration option, CD:2310

query() method, CD:1900-CD:1908
for clause, CD:1902-CD:1903
order by clause, CD:1905-CD:1906
return clause, CD:1907-CD:1908
where clause, CD:1905

Questions option (SSMS), 68

queues
creating for message storage, CD:1970-CD:1972
queue monitor, CD:1995
transmission queues, CD:1974

quorum drives, 660

quorums, 660

R

R2 Datacenter Edition (SQL Server 2008), 29

R2 Parallel Data Warehouse Edition (SQL Server 2008), 30

RAID (redundant array of inexpensive disks), 1417-1418

RAID Level 0, 1418-1419

RAID Level 1, 1419-1420

RAID Level 5, 1421-1422

RAID Level 10, 1420

tuning guidelines for, 1535

RANGE LEFT partitions, 778

RANGE RIGHT partitions, 777-778

range searching, 1366-1367

RANK function, CD:1711-CD:1712

ranking functions

de-duping data with, CD:1684-CD:1687

DENSE RANK, CD:1711-CD:1712

NTILE, CD:1712-CD:1714, CD:1717

RANK, CD:1711-CD:1712

ROW NUMBER

paging results, CD:1714-CD:1717

partitioning by, CD:1710-CD:1711

ROW NUMBER, CD:1708-CD:1710

RAW mode, CD:1867-CD:1871

RCE (Report Customization Extension) 2179

RDL (Report Definition Language), 257, CD:2175

read-ahead reads, 1332

read committed isolation, 1344-1345

READ COMMITTED option (SET TRANSACTION ISOLATION LEVEL statement), 1021

READ_COMMITTED_SNAPSHOT, 1022, 1345-1346

Read-Host cmdlet, 490

read uncommitted isolation, 1344

READ UNCOMMITTED option (SET TRANSACTION ISOLATION LEVEL statement), 1021

READCOMMITTED transaction isolation level, 1394

READCOMMITTEDLOCK transaction isolation level, 1395

READPAST transaction isolation level, 1395

READUNCOMMITTED transaction isolation level, 1394

Ready to Install page (SQL Server Installation Center), 210

real data type, 749

REBUILD, 804

Rebuild Index task, 1078

rebuilding nonclustered indexes, 1179

RECEIVE, CD:1980, CD:1984

receiving email with Database Mail, 441

reciprocal database device location, 1537

reciprocal database pairing, 1537

reciprocal principal/mirror reporting configuration, 1065-1066

reclaiming space, 1144

RECOMPILE hints, 1285

recompiling query plans, 1257-1258

RECONFIGURE option (ALTER RESOURCE GOVERNOR), 1499

records, CI, 1122

recovery. *See also* **disaster recovery**

full database recovery, 418

HA (high availability), 538

recovery models, 382-383

bulk-logged recovery, 384-385

evaluating, 705

full recovery, 383

simple recovery, 385

recovery point objective (RPO) 2336

recovery time objective (RTO) 2337

replication monitoring, 612-613

transactions, 1023-1024, 1028-1030

analysis phase, 1029

checkpoint process, 1024-1028

redo (roll-forward) phase, 1029
undo (rollback) phase, 1029
recovery interval configuration option, CD:2310-CD:2311
Recovery Model setting, 720
RECOVERY option (RESTORE DATABASE), 406
recovery point objective (RPO) 2336
Recovery property, 728
recovery time objective (RTO) 2337
Rectangle control, CD:2203
recursion, 993
stored procedures, CD:1755-CD:1758
queries, CD:1700
expanding hierarchies, CD:1701-CD:1707
MAXRECURSION option, CD:1707-CD:1708
triggers, 992-993
redo (roll-forward) phase (transaction recovery process), 1029
redundant array of inexpensive disks. *See* RAID
redundant data, denormalization, 1409-1410
referential integrity, 812
cascading, 818-820
DML triggers, 961-963
registered servers (SSMS), 71-72
registering SQL Server instances in Central Management Servers, 696
regression testing, 1527, 1532
regular expressions, 89-91
reinitialize subscriptions having data validation failures, 571
RELATED CONVERSATION keyword, CD:1976
related system catalogs, CD:1863-CD:1864
relational data (XML)
FOR XML modes, CD:1866-CD:1887
OPENXML, CD:1887-CD:1890
relational databases, generating, CD:2081-CD:2082
relational index options, 798-799
Relational OLAP (ROLAP), CD:2037
relationships, zero-to-one, 1415
reliability of enterprise computing, 655
remote admin connections configuration option, CD:2311
Remote Delete (Query Analyzer), 1313
Remote Insert (Query Analyzer), 1313
remote login timeout configuration option, CD:2311
remote mode (Report Viewer) 2181
remote proc trans configuration option, CD:2312
remote procedure calls (RPC), 1545, CD:2243
Remote Query (Query Analyzer), 1313
remote query timeout, CD:2312-CD:2313
Remote Scan (Query Analyzer), 1313
remote servers, CD:2243
configuring, CD:2246-CD:2251
managing, CD:2244-CD:2246
new features, CD:2244
remote service bindings, CD:1992
remote stored procedures, CD:1764
Remote Update (Query Analyzer), 1313
removing
counters, 1468
database mirroring, 643-645
mappings for linked servers, CD:2265
snapshots from cache reports, CD:2238
RenderFormat.Name variable, CD:2179
rendering reports, CD:2176
renumbering columns, CD:2162-CD:2163
REORGANIZE, 804
Reorganize Index task, 1078
repartition streams, 1272, 1314
repeatable read isolation, 1346
REPEATABLE READ option (SET TRANSACTION ISOLATION LEVEL statement), 1021

REPEATABLEREAD transaction isolation level, 1395

REPLACE option (RESTORE DATABASE), 407

replaying trace data, 138-140

replication, 547-549, CD:2338-CD:2340

- articles, 550-554
- building solutions with HA (high availability) options, 534-535
- central publisher replication model, 555-556
- central publisher with remote distributor replication model, 557
- central subscriber replication model, 559
- combining with database mirroring, 614, 651-652
- distribution server, 550
- enhancements, 46-47
- explained, 15
- immediate updating, 17
- log shipping, 614
- merge replication, 16-17, 575-576
- methods of data distribution, 573-574
- monitoring
  - backup and recovery, 612-613
  - in heterogeneous environments, 611-612
  - peer-to-peer replication, 609-610
  - Performance Monitor, 610-611
  - SQL statements, 603-606
  - troubleshooting replication failures, 608
  - within SQL Server Management Studio, 606-607
- multiple publishers or multiple subscribers replication model, 559-560
- new features, 546-547
- peer-to-peer replication, 561-562, 609-610
- performance, 613-614
- planning for, 572-573
- publication server, 549-550
- publications, 550
- publisher subscriber replication model, 558
- replication agents. *See* replication agents
- scripting replication, 600-602
- setting up, 579-580
  - creating distributors and enabling publishing, 581-584
  - creating publications, 584-592
  - creating subscriptions, 594-600
  - horizontal and vertical filtering, 592-594
- snapshot replication, 16, 574
- subscription server, 550
- subscriptions. *See* subscriptions
- transactional replication, 16, 574-575
- updating subscribers replication model, 560-561
- user requirements, 577-579

replication agents, 565-566

- agent history cleanup: distribution, 571
- checkup, 572
- distribution agent, 569-570
- distribution cleanup: distribution, 571
- expired subscription cleanup, 571
- log reader agent, 569
- merge agent, 570-571
- reinitialize subscriptions having data validation failures, 571
- replication agents checkup, 572
- snapshot agent
  - processing, 567-568
  - synchronization, 566-567

Replication Monitor, 46

Report Builder

- Choose a Chart Type window, CD:2219
- Design a Query window, CD:2218-CD:2219
- enabling, CD:2233-CD:2234
- installing, CD:2213-CD:2214
- map reports, CD:2222-CD:2226

overview, CD:2176, CD:2190-CD:2191
RB3 ribbon bar features, CD:2215-CD:2217
RB3 versions, CD:2213
report models, CD:2226
report models, CD:2227-CD:2231
report parts, CD:2220-CD:2222
security, CD:2233

Report Customization Extension (RCE), CD:2179

Report Definition Language (RDL), 257, CD:2175

Report Designer
Chart control, CD:2175
data bar, CD:2174
enhancements, CD:2172-CD:2175
gauge panels, CD:2173
gauges, CD:2173
indicator, CD:2173
Map control, CD:2174
Sparklines, CD:2174
Tablix, CD:2173

Report Manager, CD:2177, CD:2189, CD:2209-CD:2210

Report Server Service, CD:2178

Report Viewer, 234-235, CD:2181

ReportExecution2005.asmx, CD:2180

Reporting Services. *See* SSRS (SQL Server Reporting Services)

reports
Backup and Restore Events report, 413
cached reports, CD:2237-CD:2238
Chart control, CD:2203
controls summary, CD:2202-CD:2204
data bars, CD:2203
Data Collector, 1439-1442
data planning and preparation, CD:2193
via database snapshots from mirror, 652-653
datasets, CD:2193-CD:2194
deploying, CD:2207-CD:2209
designing, CD:2172-CD:2175, CD:2202
Choose a Chart Type window, CD:2219
Design a Query window, CD:2218-CD:2219
enabling Report Builder, CD:2233-CD:2234
installing RB3, CD:2213-CD:2214
map reports, CD:2222-CD:2226
RB3 ribbon bar features, CD:2215-CD:2217
RB3 versions, CD:2213
report models, CD:2226-CD:2231
report parts, CD:2220-CD:2222
security, CD:2233
developing, CD:2192, CD:2196-CD:2199
Execute Report Definitions, CD:2233
execution options, CD:2237
cached reports, CD:2237-CD:2238
CRPs (cache refresh plans) 2239
execution snapshots, CD:2238
history snapshots, CD:2238
live reports and sessions, CD:2237
user-specific data limitations, CD:2239
expressions, CD:2200-CD:2202
gauges, CD:2203
Image control, CD:2203
indicators, CD:2203-CD:2207
interactivity, CD:2211-CD:2213
Line control, CD:2203-CD:2203
Map control, CD:2203
map reports, CD:2222-CD:2226
Matrix control, CD:2202
overview, CD:2191-CD:2192
processing and rendering, CD:2176
RCE (Report Customization Extension) 2179
Rectangle control, CD:2203
report data source, CD:2175

report displays, 1467
report models, CD:2226-CD:2231
report parts, CD:2175
securing
built-in roles and permissions, CD:2234-CD:2235
system roles and system permissions, CD:2235
securing, CD:2234
Server Activity History report, 1441
shared data sources, CD:2193
shared datasets, CD:2194-CD:2195
Sparklines, CD:2203-CD:2207
Subreport control, CD:2204
subscriptions, CD:2235-CD:2236
data-driven subscriptions, CD:2236-CD:2237
delivery architecture, CD:2237
Table control, CD:2202
tables and hierarchies in, CD:2210-CD:2211
Tablix, CD:2199-CD:2202
Text Box control, CD:2204
ReportServer database, CD:2180
ReportServerTempDB database, CD:2180
ReportService2005.asmx, CD:2180
ReportService2006.asmx, CD:2180
ReportService2010.asmx, CD:2180
request_exec_context_id column, 1351
request_lifetime column, 1351
request_mode column, 1351
request_owner_guid column, 1352
request_owner_id column, 1352
request_owner_lockspace_id column, 1352
request_owner_type column, 1352
request_reference_count column, 1351
request_request_id column, 1352
request_session_id column, 1351
request_status column, 1351
request_type column, 1351
requirements phase (OLAP design methodologies), CD:2039
resource_associated_entity_id column, 1351
resource_database_id column, 1351
resource_description column, 1351
resource database, 168
Resource Governor
classification functions
creating, 1506-1509
defined, 1495-1496
modifying, 1516
enabling, 1499-1500
explained, 41
modifying configuration of, 1513-1516
monitoring resource usage, 1509-1512
overview, 1493-1495
resource pools
creating, 1500-1502
deleting, 1515-1516
explained, 1496
MIN/MAX values, 1496-1498
workload groups
creating, 1503-1505
deleting, 1514-1515
explained, 1496
viewing, 1505-1506
resource_lock_partition column, 1351
resource pools
creating, 1500-1502
deleting, 1515-1516
explained, 1496
MIN/MAX values, 1496-1498
resource_subtype column, 1351
resource_type column, 1351
resource usage, monitoring, 1509-1512

RESTART option
- BACKUP DATABASE, 393
- RESTORE DATABASE, 407

restoorefilegroup, 412

RESTORE, 404, 630

RESTORE DATABASE, 404-407

Restore dialog, 66

RESTORE FILELISTONLY, 411

RESTORE HEADERONLY, 411

RESTORE VERIFYONLY, 411-412

restorefile, 412

restorehistory, 412

restores
- Backup and Restore Events report, 413
- developing restore plans, 378-379
- overview, 403
- restore information, retrieving
  - RESTORE FILELISTONLY, 411
  - RESTORE HEADERONLY, 411
  - RESTORE VERIFYONLY, 411-412
- restoring database backups to new locations, 736
- scenarios, 414
  - online restorations, 421
  - restoring snapshots, 416
  - restoring system databases, 421-423
  - restoring to a different database, 414-415
  - restoring to point in time, 419-420
  - restoring to point of failure, 417-419
  - restoring transaction logs, 416, 419
- with SSMS, 409-410
- system tables, 412-413
- with T-SQL
  - database restores, 404-407
  - transaction log restores, 407-408

Restrict Access, 724

RESTRICT IP, CD:1936

RESTRICTED_USER option (RESTORE DATABASE), 407

restrictions
- INSTEAD OF triggers, 975
- on defaults, 835

RETAINDAYS option (BACKUP DATABASE), 392

retrieving
- database option information, 726-729
- entries, 522

Retry Attempts, 464

Retry Interval, 464

Retry options, 464

return clause (query() method), CD:1907-CD:1908

returning procedure status, 904-905

RETURNS NULL ON NULL INPUT option (CREATE FUNCTION), 928

reusing query plans, 1254-1256

reverting to database snapshots, 1048, 1052-1053, 1062-1064

REVOKE, 311, 330

REWIND option
- BACKUP DATABASE, 393
- RESTORE DATABASE, 407

rewriting stored procedures as functions, 942-943

RIAs (Rich Internet Applications), CD:1787

RID Lookup, 1313

Riedberger, Jason, 650

right semi joins, 1250

risk management, 360-361

ROBUST PLAN hints, 1284

ROLAP (Relational OLAP), CD:2037

roles, 302
- application roles, 309
- assignments, CD:2234
- for database mirroring, 622

database roles
managing with SSMS, 321-322
managing with T-SQL, 322
fixed-database roles, 304-306
fixed-server roles, 303-304
OLAP, CD:2095-CD:2096
public roles, 306-307
switching, 623
user-defined roles, 307-309

ROLLBACK, 999, CD:1984

ROLLBACK TRAN, 999, 1016-1017

rollback transaction statement, CD:1736

ROLLUP operator, CD:1561-CD:1562

root-level certificate, 278

round-earth data, CD:1605

routers, 1535

row constructors, 38, CD:1569-CD:1572

Row Count Spool, 1312

Row ID (RID) locking level, 1365

row-level compression, 1117-1119

row-level locking, 1373-1374

ROW NUMBER function, CD:1708-CD:1710
paging results, CD:1714-CD:1717
partitioning by, CD:1710-CD:1711

row offset table, 1108-1109

ROW OVERFLOW DATA, 753

row-overflow pages, 1109-1110

@@ROWCOUNT, CD:1683-CD:1684

ROWGUIDCOL, 757

ROWLOCK optimizer hint, 1395

rows
in database pages
overview, 1104-1105
sparse columns, 1107-1108
sql_variant data type, 1107
structure of, 1105-1107
deleting
from heap, 1144
from index, 1144
reclaiming space, 1144
with LINQ to SQL, CD:1801
indexes, 1134-1135
leaf rows, 1138-1139
nonleaf rows, 1139-1140
row constructors, 38, CD:1569-CD:1572
row estimation
estimating access path costs, 1221-1228
evaluating SARG and join selectivity, 1216-1221
multiple indexes, 1228-1236
updating
forward pointers, 1146
index statistics, 1159-1160
in-place updates, 1145
not-in-place updates, 1145-1146
with LINQ to SQL, CD:1802

ROWS_PER_BATCH hint, CD:2165-CD:2166

rowversion data type, 749, 1396-1399

ROW_OVERFLOW_DATA, 1109

RPC (remote procedure calls), 1545, CD:2243

RPO (recovery point objective) 2336

RS.exe, CD:2180

RSCM, SSRS configuration
databases, CD:2187-CD:2188
email and execution accounts, CD:2189
encryption, CD:2189-CD:2190
overview, CD:2186
Report Manager, CD:2189
scale-out architecture configuration, CD:2190
Web Service, CD:2186-CD:2187
Windows Service, CD:2186

RSConfig.exe, CD:2180

RSKeyMgmt.exe, CD:2180, CD:2190

RTO (recovery time objective) 2337

running traces, monitoring, 153-154

runtime, measuring with datediff(), 1336-1337

runtime component (Data Collector), 1431

S

SAC (Surface Area Configuration) tool, 105, 705

safeguarding databases prior to making mass changes, 1053

SAFETY option, 622

SANs (storage area networks), 661, 711

- cache, 1424
- disk drive contention, 1424
- explained, 1422-1423
- performance, 1424-1425
- tuning guidelines for, 1535

Sarbanes-Oxley Act (SOX), 367

SARG

- computed columns, 1220-1221
- evaluating, 1216-1221
- inequality operators, 1218
- LIKE clauses, 1219-1220
- search argument problems, 1276

SAVE TRAN, 1000

savepoints, 1000-1001, 1019-1020

saving

- graphical execution plans, 1317
- traces (SQL Server Profiler), 132
  - to files, 133
  - Profiler GUI output, 134-135
  - to tables, 134

scalability, 655

scalar functions, 921-925, CD:1835-CD:1839

scalar types, 1460

scale-out architecture configuration (SSRS) 2190

scaling out, 662

scan for startup procs configuration option, CD:2313

scans

- scan count, 1331
- table scans, 1227-1228

SCC (System Configuration Checker), 186

scheduling

- maintenance plans, 1080-1083
- scripts, 510-512

schema collections, CD:1894-CD:1899

schema locks, 1363

schema names, qualifying object names with, CD:1640-CD:1643

SCHEMA option (WEBMETHOD), CD:1939-CD:1941

SCHEMABINDING, 809-810, 848, 927-928

scripts

- alerts, 474-475
- comments, 491
- creating, 491
- defined, 483
- jobs, 474-475
- replication, 600-602
- scheduling, 510-512
- sqlmd scripts, 88-89
- variables, 108-109

searches

- arguments
  - identifying for query analysis, 1214
  - troubleshooting, 1276-1277
  - tuning guidelines, 1543
- full-text. *See* Full-Text Search

second normal form, 1406-1407

secondary data files, 712, 1095

secondary GAM (SGAM), 711

securables, 292, 310

Secure Sockets Layer. ***See*** **SSL (Secure Sockets Layer)**

security

across the life cycle, 361-362

auditing

with SQL Server Audit, 368-372

with T-SQL, 372-374

authentication, 294-295

compliance, 366-367

data security, 336-337

database snapshots, 1067

EKM (Extensible Key Management), 40

encryption. *See* encryption

enforcement layers and components, 362-364

execution context, 331

explicit context switching, 332

implicit context switching, 333

exposure endpoints, 360

identity access management, 364, 366

logins. *See* logins

new features, 39-40, 291-292

OLAP, CD:2095-CD:2096

overview, 292-294, 359-360

permissions. *See* permissions

PII (Personal Identifiable Information), 366-367

PowerShell, 486

Report Builder, CD:2233

reports

built-in roles and permissions, CD:2234-CD:2235

system roles and system permissions, CD:2235

risk management, 360-361

roles, 302, CD:2234

application roles, 309

database roles, 321-322

fixed-database roles, 304-306

fixed-server roles, 303-304

public roles, 306-307

user-defined roles, 307-309

securables, 310

SQL injection, 374-376

SQL Server Agent, 458

SQL Server Service Broker, CD:1985-CD:1992

TDE (transparent data encryption), 39

users

dbo users, 299

explained, 298-299

guest users, 299-300

INFORMATION_SCHEMA users, 300

logins, 298

sys users, 300

user/schema separation, 301-302

securityadmin, 303

SELECT statement, 300

select @@SERVERNAME, CD:2343

select @@SERVICENAME, CD:2343

select @@VERSION, CD:2343

SELECT COUNT(*), CD:1654

Select-Object cmdlet, 490

Select-String cmdlet, 515

self-configuring options, CD:2276

SELF option (EXECUTE AS), 884

self-signed certificates, CD:1985

semi joins, 1250

SEND, CD:1979

SEND ON CONVERSATION, CD:1980

sending email with Database Mail, 435-441

__$seqval column (CDC table), CD:1615

Sequence (Query Analyzer), 1313

sequence clustering, CD:2085

sequence trees, 1212

SERIALIZABLE option (SET TRANSACTION ISOLATION LEVEL statement), 1022

serializable read isolation, 1346-1347

SERIALIZABLE transaction isolation level, 1395

serialization locking, 1365-1369

Server Activity History report, 1441

Server Audit object, 369

Server Audit Specification object, 369

Server Configuration page (SQL Server Installation Center), 203-205

server endpoint layer, 267-270

SERVER ROLE, 297

server trace log (SSRS), CD:2239-CD:2240

server-side traces

- creating and starting, 151
- defining, 140-141, 148-152
- stopping, 155-156

serveradmin, 303

servers

- aliases, 277
- clusters, 658
- health checks, 705
- linked. *See* linked servers
- master servers, 476-477
- multiserver jobs, 477
- registered servers (SSMS), 71-72
- remote. *See* remote servers
- server instance isolation, 528-530
- settings, checking, 518
- sizing, 1534
- standby servers, 424-425
- target servers, 476-477

Service Broker, 434-435

- basics of, CD:1960-CD:1963
- constructs
  - creating queues for, CD:1970-CD:1972
  - defining messages and, CD:1965-CD:1969
  - defining services to, CD:1973
  - planning conversations, CD:1974-CD:1976
  - prioritizing, CD:1984
  - setting up contracts, CD:1970
- constructs, CD:1965
- designing example systems, CD:1964-CD:1965
- distributed messaging, CD:1960
- enhancements, 47-48
- explained, 22-23
- routing and security, CD:1985-CD:1992
- system catalogs, CD:1994-CD:1995

service master keys, 340

Service Packs, installing, 218-222

service program, CD:1964

services. *See specific services*

session snapshots, CD:2237-CD:2238

SESSION_TIMEOUT option (WEBMETHOD), CD:1941

SESSIONS option (WEBMETHOD), CD:1941

set-based processing language, SQL as, CD:1656

SET CHANGE_TRACKING parameter (ALTER FULLTEXT INDEX), CD:2011

Set-Content cmdlet, 491

SET DEFAULT, 819

Set-ExecutionPolicy cmdlet, 487

SET LOCK_TIMEOUT, 1380

set nocount on, CD:1765

SET NULL, 819

SET PARTNER, 632

SET REMOTE PROC TRANSACTIONS, CD:1764

SET ROWCOUNT, CD:1692

SET SHOWPLAN

- SHOWPLAN_ALL, 1326-1327
- SHOWPLAN_TEXT, 1324-1326
- SHOWPLAN_XML, 1327-1328
- SHOWPLAN XML ON, 92

SET TRANSACTION ISOLATION LEVEL, 1021-1022, 1393

SET TRANSACTION ISOLATION LEVEL READ COMMITTED, 1344

SET TRANSACTION ISOLATION SERIALIZABLE, 1365

SET USER, 332

SET WITNESS, 632

set-oriented operations, 1542

setting. *See* configuring

Setup Role page (SQL Server Installation Center), 200

Setup Support Files installation screen (SQL Server Installation Center), 197

Setup Support Rules for Setup Support Files detail (SQL Server Installation Center), 196

Setup Support Rules for SQL Server installation detail (SQL Server Installation Center), 197-198

setupadmin, 303

SGAM (secondary GAM), 711

SGAM (shared global allocation map) pages, 1114

SGML (Standard Generalized Markup Language), CD:1866

shapefiles, CD:2174

shared data sources, CD:2193

shared datasets, CD:2175, CD:2194-CD:2195

shared disk arrays, 660

shared global allocation map (SGAM) pages, 1114

shared locks, 1360

shared nothing disk arrays, 660

shared query plans, CD:1766

SharePoint, integration with SSRS (SQL Server Reporting Services), CD:2177

shopping cart example (OLTP), 56-57

short data cluster array, 1119

show advanced options configuration option, CD:2313

SHOWPLAN_ALL, 1326-1327

SHOWPLAN_TEXT, 1324-1326

SHOWPLAN_XML, 1327-1328

Shrink Database dialog, 734

shrinking

- databases, 731
  - DBCC SHRINKDATABASE, 731-732
  - DBCC SHRINKFILE, 732-733
  - Maintenance Plan Wizard, 1076-1077
  - shrinking log files, 734
  - with SSMS, 734-735
- log files, 734

side-by-side migration (installing SQL Server 2008), 236-237

- avoiding an unintentional in-place upgrade during setup, 237
- migrating Analysis Services, 253-254
- migrating databases
  - Copy Database Wizard, 238-241
  - database compatibility levels, 242
  - explained, 238
- migrating Reporting Services
  - in-place upgrades, 255-257
  - migrating to Reporting Services 2008, 257-258

simple expressions, CD:2178

Simple Mail Transfer Protocol. *See* SMTP (Simple Mail Transfer Protocol)

Simple Object Access Protocol. *See* SOAP (Simple Object Access Protocol)

simple recovery model, 385

site autonomy, 573

SITE, CD:1937

slipstream installations, 49, 222-224

slipstreaming upgrades, 251-252

smalldatetime data type, 749, CD:1572

smallint data type, 749

smallmoney data type, 749

SMO (SQL Server Management Objects), 484

SMTP (Simple Mail Transfer Protocol), 427

creating accounts in Database Mail, 430

failover priority, 431

SNAC

client data access technologies, 281

ADO, 283

ODBC, 282-283

OLE DB, 282

installing for clients, 272-274

redistributing with custom client applications, 274

snap-ins, 484

SNAPSHOT option (SET TRANSACTION ISOLATION LEVEL statement), 1022

snapshots, CD:2341-CD:2342

backups, 425

databases, 1048

execution snapshots, CD:2238

history snapshots, CD:2238

isolation, 1347-1349

HA (high availability), 539-540

optimistic locking with, 1399-1401

replication, 16, 574

reporting via database snapshots from mirror, 652-653

restoring, 416

snapshot agent

processing, 567-568

synchronization, 566-567

SOAP (Simple Object Access Protocol), CD:1928-CD:1931

software requirements for SQL Server, 188-191

software scaling, 662

Solution Explorer, 95

Sort (Query Analyzer), 1313

SORT_IN_TEMPDB argument (CREATE INDEX), 798

Sort-Object cmdlet, 490

sorting results with GROUPING function, CD:1669-CD:1671

source code control

integrating with SSMS, 95-97

stored procedures, CD:1741-CD:1742

source databases, 1048

number of database snapshots per, 1067

reverting from database snapshots, 1063-1064

source tables for CDC, CD:1626

SOX (Sarbanes-Oxley Act), 367

sp addextendedproc, CD:1782

sp addlinkedserver, CD:2253-CD:2260

sp addlinkedsrvlogin, CD:2263-CD:2265

sp catalogs, CD:2267

sp cdc enable Table stored procedure, CD:1617-CD:1618

sp columns ex, CD:2267

sp configure, 182, 910, CD:2277-CD:2278

SP Counts, 124

sp createstats, 182

sp dboption, 725-726

sp delete jobsteplog, 464

sp dropserver, CD:2261

sp executesql, 880, CD:1776-CD:1779

sp foreignkeys, CD:2267

sp help, 182, 910

sp helpdb, 910

sp helpfile, 176

sp helptext, 936

sp help constraint, 827

sp helparticle, 603

sp helpconstraint, 774

sp helpdb, 182, 729

SP HELPDINDEX, 807

sp helpdistributor, 603

sp helpextendedproc, CD:1783

sp helpfile, 183

sp helplinkedsrvlogin, CD:2266-CD:2267
sp helppublication, 603
sp helpsubscriberinfo, 603
sp helpsubscription, 603
sp helptext, 889
sp indexes, CD:2267
sp linkedservers, CD:2260-CD:2261, CD:2267
sp lock, 183
sp monitor, 1479
sp primarykeys, CD:2267
sp processmail, 441
sp procoption, 153
sp recompile, CD:1773
sp refreshview, 845
sp send dbmail, 435-438
sp serveroption, CD:2261-CD:2263
sp setapprole, 309
sp settriggerorder, 956
sp spaceused, 183, 759
sp tables ex, CD:2267
sp trace create, 141
sp trace setevent, 141
sp trace setfilter, 141, 151
sp trace setstatus, 141, 155
sp who, 183, 910
sp who2, 910
space allocation, database pages
  extents, 1113-1114
  GAM pages, 1114
Sparklines, CD:2174, CD:2203-CD:2207
sparse columns, 36, 759-761, 1107-1108, CD:1600-CD:1605
sparse file size management, 1067
spatial data types, 37, 751-752, CD:1605-CD:1614
spid data column (SQL Profiler), 1356
SPLIT RANGE, 782
SQL Browser
  instances, 270-271
  overview, 270
  pipes, 270-271
  ports, 270-271
SQL Capture, 1549
SQL Clustering, 531-534
SQL injection, 374-376, CD:1643-CD:1652
SQL_LOGIN, 296
SQL Mail, 427, 454
SQL Native Client ODBC driver, 281
SQL Native Client OLE DB provider, 280
SQL Profiler
  data columns, 1356
  lock events, 1355
  templates, 124
SQL Server 6.5, upgrading from, 252
SQL Server 7, upgrading from, 252
SQL Server 2008 Developer Edition, 27, 32
SQL Server 2008 Enterprise Edition, 24-26
SQL Server 2008 Express Edition, 28-29, 32
SQL Server 2008 R2 Datacenter Edition, 29, 42-43
SQL Server 2008 R2 Parallel Data Warehouse, 43
SQL Server 2008 R2 Parallel Data Warehouse Edition, 30
SQL Server 2008 Standard Edition, 23-26
SQL Server 2008 Web Edition, 27-28, 32
SQL Server 2008 Workgroup Edition, 27
SQL Server Agent, 509
  alerts
    defined, 449
    properties, 469-472
    responses, 472-474
  capabilities, 449

configuring
email notification, 454
properties, 450-452
proxy accounts, 455-456
startup account, 452-453
error logs, 456-457
explained, 14-15
jobs. *See* jobs
operators, 449, 458-460
proxy accounts, 455-456
security, 458
SQL Server Agent Mail, 441
alert mail notifications, 443
creating alerts, 443-444
testing, 444
job mail notifications
creating jobs, 443
creating operators, 442
enabling, 442
testing, 443
SQL Server Analysis Services. *See* SSAS (SQL Server Analysis Services)
SQL Server Audit, 40, 368-372
SQL Server BIDS, CD:2042-CD:2043
SQL Server Clustering
active/active configuration, 657
active/passive configuration, 657
installing, 665-666
configuring SQL Server database disks, 666-667
Connection Test Program, 681-684
failure of nodes, 679-681
MSCS, 668
network interfaces, 668
SQL Server, 668-679
MSCS, 657-665
new features, 656
problems with, 684-685
SQL Server Compact 3.5 Edition, 29, 32
SQL Server Configuration Manager, 14, 452
SQL Server Extended Events. *See* SSEE (SQL Server Extended Events)
SQL Server Installation Center
Account Provisioning page, 205-206
Advanced menu, 211
Complete page, 210-211
Data Directories page, 206-207
Database Engine Configuration page, 205-208
Disk Space Requirements page, 203
Feature Selection page, 200-201
Installation Configuration page, 201-203
Installation Configuration Rules page, 209
Installation Rules page, 201-202
launching, 192-193
License Terms page, 197-199
Maintenance menu, 211
Product Key entry page, 197-198
Ready to Install page, 210
Server Configuration page, 203-205
Setup Role page, 200
Setup Support Files installation screen, 197
Setup Support Rules for Setup Support Files detail, 196
Setup Support Rules for SQL Server installation detail, 197-198
SQL Server Installation menu, 194-195
System Configuration Checker HTML report, 194-195
System Configuration Checker window, 194
Tools menu, 211
SQL Server Installation menu (SQL Server Installation Center), 194-195
SQL Server instance architecture, CD:2274-CD:2275
SQL Server Integration Services. *See* SSIS (SQL Server Integration Services)

SQL Server Lock Manager, 1349-1350

SQL Server Management Studio

linked server configuration, CD:2269-CD:2271

replication monitoring, 606-607

SQL Server Management Studio. *See* SSMS (SQL Server Management Studio)

SQL Server Performance objects, 1474-1476

SQL Server PowerShell. *See also* PowerShell

accessing, 505

cmdlets, 508-509

defined, 505

overview, 506-507

SQL providers, 507, 515

SQL Server Agent support, 509

SQL Server Profiler. *See* Profiler

SQL Server Reporting Services. *See* SSRS (SQL Server Reporting Services)

SQL Server sample implementations, 51-53

DSS (decision support systems) application examples, 57

hybrid SQL Server reporting configuration, 59-61

multidimensional OLAP cube, 58-59

OLTP (online transaction process) application examples

OLTP ERP, 53-56

OLTP shopping cart, 56-57

SQL Server Service Broker. *See* Service Broker

SQL Server Utility, 43, 79-85, 1451-1455

SQL Shot, 1548

SQL statements. *See specific statements*

sql_variant data type, 749, 1107

SQLAgentOperatorRole, 458

SQLAgentReaderRole, 458

SQLAgentUserRole, 458

SQLCLR

context connections, 284-285

enhancements, 46

SQLCMD, 504

executing, 106-108

scripting variables with, 108-109

syntax, 105-106

SqlConnection.BeginTransaction, 1345

SqlContext object, CD:1832

SqlContext.Pipe object, CD:1832

SqlDataRecord object, CD:1833

sqldiag, 116-117, CD:2347-CD:2349

sqlmd scripts, editing, 88-89

SqlMetaData object, CD:1833

SqlMethod, CD:1849-CD:1850

SQLOLEDB, 280

sqlps, 105, 481

sqlservr, 118

SQLSetConnectAttr(), 1345

SQLSortOrder property, 728

SqlTrigger attribute, CD:1856

SqlTriggerContext attribute, CD:1856

SqlUserDefinedAggregate attribute, CD:1853

SqlUserDefinedType, CD:1845

SSADO (Sync Services for ADO.NET), CD:1817

SSAS (SQL Server Analysis Services)

cube perspectives. *See* cube perspectives

enhancements, 48

migrating, 253-254

new features, CD:2029

OLAP. *See* OLAP (online analytical processing)

wizards, CD:2032

explained, 19-20

SSB. *See* Service Broker

ssbdiagnose.exe, 47, CD:1993-CD:1994

SSCM

configuring clients, 275-277

testing connectivity, 288

SSEE (SQL Server Extended Events), 1455-1457

actions, 1459
events, 1458
extended events and, 1460-1462
extended events sessions, 1462-1465
packages, 1457
predicates, 1459
targets, 1459
types and maps, 1460

SSIS (SQL Server Integration Services), 572, CD:2100-CD:2105, CD:2113
architecture, CD:2105-CD:2110
Attunity CDC Suite, CD:2147
bcp utility, CD:2147-CD:2150
exporting/importing data, CD:2151-CD:2153
file data types, CD:2153
format files, CD:2153-CD:2163
views, CD:2163
bulk-copy operations, CD:2163-CD:2164
batches, CD:2164
hints, CD:2165-CD:2166
parallel loading, CD:2164-CD:2165
configurations, CD:2108
containers, CD:2106
control flow, CD:2106
data flow, CD:2107
data flow task, CD:2107
data mining, CD:2093
data transformation requirement, CD:2113-CD:2116
Designer, CD:2110-CD:2112, CD:2126-CD:2135
enhancements, 47
event handlers, CD:2107
explained, 18-19
logging, CD:2109
new features, CD:2100
Package Execution utility
dtexec utility, CD:2135-CD:2137
dtsrun utility, CD:2135
dtutil utility, CD:2141-CD:2145
running packages, CD:2137-CD:2141
Package Execution utility, CD:2135-CD:2136
Package Upgrade Wizard, 258
packages, 1432, CD:2106-CD:2109
SSIS Wizard, CD:2115-CD:2126
tasks, CD:2106
tools, CD:2110-CD:2111
command-prompt utilities, CD:2112
Expression Builder, CD:2112-CD:2115
Import and Export Wizard, CD:2110-CD:2111
integration services, CD:2113
Query Builder, CD:2112-CD:2114
SSIS Designer, CD:2110-CD:2112, CD:2126-CD:2135
transformations, CD:2107
upgrading SSIS packages, 258-259
variables, CD:2109
Visual Studio Integration Services Connection Project, CD:2145
workflows, CD:2106
XML configuration file, CD:2108

SSL (Secure Sockets Layer) 1934

SSL PORT, CD:1935

SSMS (SQL Server Management Studio), 12, 800, 1301
Activity Monitor, 75-77, 1483
backups, creating, 388-390
BIDS
developing reports with, CD:2196-CD:2199
overview, CD:2190
client statistics, 1322-1323
configuration options, CD:2283

constraints, creating, 823-826
controls summary, CD:2202-CD:2204
creating user-defined functions, 930-933
data bars, CD:2203
data compression, managing, 1126-1127
Database Diagram Editor, 743-744
databases
- creating, 718-721
- database roles, 321-322
- restores, 409-410
- shrinking, 734-735

disk performance, monitoring, 1490
enhanced features, 45
explained, 12-14
expressions, CD:2200-CD:2202
gauges, CD:2203
Image control, CD:2203
indexes
- creating, 800-803
- managing, 806-807, 1183

indicators, CD:2203-CD:2207
integrated help, 68-70
integrating with source control, 95-97
Line control, CD:2203
Log File Viewer, 77-79
logins
- deleting, 317
- managing, 313-317
- modifying, 316

Map control, CD:2203
memory, monitoring, 1486
Missing Index Hints, 1320
multiserver queries, 101-102
new features, 41-42, 63-64
Object Explorer, 73-75
- creating tables, 742-743
- data types, 750
- dropping tables, 773-774
- modifying tables with Table Designer, 769-772

permissions, managing
- at database level, 326-328
- at object level, 328-329
- at server level, 323-325

plan guides, creating and managing, 1297-1298
project management, 93-95
Query Analyzer, 1302-1307
Query Editor
- disconnected editing, 88
- editing sqlmd scripts, 88-89
- IntelliSense, 87
- overview, 85-87
- performance, 91-92
- Query Designer, 92-93
- query types, 87-88
- regular expressions and wildcards, 89-91

Rectangle control, CD:2203
registered servers, 71-72
reports. *See* reports
resource pools
- creating, 1500-1502
- deleting, 1515

security
- built-in roles and permissions, CD:2234-CD:2235
- role assignments, CD:2234
- security roles, CD:2234
- system roles and permissions, CD:2235

Shrink File dialog, 1036
Sparklines, CD:2203-CD:2207
spatial data support in, CD:1611-CD:1614
SQL Server Utility, 79-85

stored procedures. *See* stored procedures
Subreport control, CD:2204
subscriptions, CD:2235-CD:2236
data-driven subscriptions, CD:2236-CD:2237
delivery architecture, CD:2237
T-SQL debugging, 100-101
Tablix, CD:2199-CD:2202
TDE (transparent data encryption) in, 352-353
Template Explorer, 97-99, 874
templates, 97-100
Text Box control, CD:2204
transaction logs, 394
user-defined functions
modifying, 939-940
viewing, 939-940
users, managing, 318-320
views, 853
window management, 65-67
workload groups
creating, 1503-1505
deleting, 1514-1515

SSRS (SQL Server Reporting Services)
architecture, CD:2179-CD:2181
configuring
databases, CD:2187-CD:2188
email and execution accounts, CD:2189
encryption, CD:2189CD:2190
overview, CD:2186
Report Manager, CD:2189
scale-out architecture configuration, CD:2190
Web Service, CD:2186-CD:2187
Windows Service, CD:2186
discontinued features, CD:2170-CD:2172
encryption, CD:2189-CD:2190
explained, 20-22
expressions
enhancements to, CD:2179
simple expressions, CD:2178
installing
file locations, CD:2184-CD:2185
installation sequence, CD:2182-CD:2184
new features, 44-45
overview, CD:2169
performance and monitoring tools
execution log, CD:2240
performance counters, CD:2240
server trace log, CD:2239-CD:2240
windows event log, CD:2240
performance and monitoring tools, CD:2239
RCE (Report Customization Extension), CD:2179
RDL (Report Definition Language), CD:2175
Report Builder, CD:2176, CD:2226
report data source, CD:2175
report design enhancements, CD:2172-CD:2175
Report Designer
Chart control, CD:2175
data bar, CD:2174
gauge panels, CD:2173
gauges, CD:2173
indicator, CD:2173
Map control, CD:2174
Sparklines, CD:2174
Tablix, CD:2173
Report Manager, CD:2177, CD:2189
report parts, CD:2175
report processing and rendering, CD:2176
Report Server Service, CD:2178
shared datasets, CD:2175
SharePoint integration, CD:2177
upgrading

in-place upgrades, 255-257

migrating to Reporting Services 2008, 257-258

Standard Edition (SQL Server 2008), 23-26

Standard Generalized Markup Language (SGML), CD:1866

standard views, 844

STANDBY, 395, 406-408

standby servers, 424-425

star schema data warehouse for global computer sales, 57-58

START parameter (ALTER FULLTEXT INDEX), CD:2012-CD:2013

Start-Service cmdlet, 513

Start-Transcript cmdlet, 491

__$start_lsn column (CDC table), CD:1615

startup accounts for SQL Server Agent, 452-453

startup procedures, 911-915

stateless application design, 1545

statements. *See* specific statements

statistics

columns, generating, 1161-1169

filtered statistics, 1198-1199

indexes, 1153-1155

generating, 1161-1169

histograms, 1155-1158

maintaining with Maintenance Plan Wizard, 1077-1080

problems with query optimization, 1274-1275

query statistics

datediff(), 1336-1337

STATISTIC IO, 1332-1333

STATISTICS IO, 1330-1332

STATISTICS PROFILE, 1337

STATISTICS TIME, 1333-1336

STATISTICS XML, 1337-1338

tuning guidelines, 1540

STATISTICS IO, 1330-1331

analyzing output, 1332-1333

LOB reads, 1332

logical reads, 1331

physical reads, 1332

read-ahead reads, 1332

scan count, 1331

STATISTICS_NO_RECOMPUTE argument (CREATE INDEX), 798

STATISTICS PROFILE, 1299, 1337

STATISTICS TIME, 1299, 1333-1336

STATISTICS XML, 1337-1338

STATS option

BACKUP DATABASE, 393

RESTORE DATABASE, 407

status of procedures, returning, 904-905

Status property, 728

SteelEye LifeKeeper, CD:2350

stop lists, CD:2024

STOP ON ERROR option

BACKUP DATABASE, 392

RESTORE DATABASE, 405

STOP parameter (ALTER FULLTEXT INDEX), CD:2012-CD:2013

STOPAT option (RESTORE DATABASE), 407

STOPATMARK option (RESTORE DATABASE), 407

STOPBEFOREMARK option (RESTORE DATABASE), 407

stopping server-side traces, 155-156

storage, 710-711

for data columns, CD:1597-CD:1599

Database Engine, 10

FILESTREAM storage, 207-208, 759, CD:1592-CD:1593

database setup, CD:1596

enabling, CD:1593-CD:1596

format files, CD:2155-CD:2156

new features, 36-37

stored procedures. ***See also specific procedures***

advantages of, 870-871

analyzing

with Query Analyzer, 1315-1316

with SQL Server Profiler, 157-158

calling from transactions, CD:1735-CD:1738

CLR stored procedures, CD:1779

adding to databases, CD:1780-CD:1781

versus T-SQL stored procedures, CD:1781

creating

custom stored procedure templates, 875-879

example, 872

in SSMS, 872-874

syntax, 871

for web services, CD:1931

cursors, CD:1743-CD:1753

debugging, 905-908

deferred name resolution, 885-888

defined, 869

dynamic SQL, CD:1774-CD:1779

errors, CD:1738-CD:1741

executing

execution context and EXECUTE AS, 883-885

via linked servers, CD:2268

in SSMS, 881-882

syntax, 880-881

extended stored procedures

adding to SQL Server, CD:1782-CD:1783

obtaining information on, CD:1783

provided with SQL Server, CD:1783-CD:1784

xp cmdshell, CD:1784-CD:1786

for managing logins, 317

identifying objects references in, 887-888

input parameters

explained, 893-894

passing object names as, 898-899

setting default values for, 895-898

table-valued parameters, 901-902

wildcards in, 899-900

managed database objects, CD:1829-CD:1835

modifying

with ALTER PROCEDURE, 891-892

with SSMS, 892-893

monitoring recompilation, CD:1767-CD:1773

nested stored procedures, CD:1753-CD:1758

new features, 869-870

output parameters, 902-903

performance, CD:1764-CD:1765

automatic query plan recompilation, CD:1767

query plan caching, CD:1765

shared query plans, CD:1766

SQL Server procedure cache, CD:1766

remote stored procedures, CD:1764

returning procedure status, 904-905

rewriting as functions, 942-943

running web methods bound to stored, CD:1942-CD:1947

system stored procedures, 181-183

categories of, 909-910

explained, 908-909

table of, 910

T-SQL

calling from transactions, CD:1735-CD:1738

coding guidelines, CD:1733-CD:1735

errors, CD:1738-CD:1741

source code control, CD:1741-CD:1742

table-valued parameters, CD:1576-CD:1580

temporary stored procedures, 879-880
temporary tables, CD:1759-CD:1760
performance tips, CD:1760-CD:1762
table data type, CD:1762-CD:1763
transactions, 1009-1014
tuning guidelines, 1543-1544
viewing, 889-891
Stream Aggregate (Query Analyzer), 1314
streams, 1272
strings
joining, 493
summary statistics, 1169
structures. *See* data structures
stub, CD:1929
subquery processing
correlated subqueries, 1250-1251
IN, ANY, and EXISTS subqueries, 1248
materialized subqueries, 1248-1250
Subreport control, CD:2204
subscriptions, 562-563
anonymous subscriptions, 563
creating for data replication, 594-600
distribution database, 564-565
reports
data-driven subscriptions, CD:2236-CD:2237
delivery architecture, CD:2237
reports, CD:2235-CD:2236
subscription servers, 550
subtrees in hierarchies, reparenting, CD:1590
summary data, denormalization, 1411
Surface Area Configuration (SAC) tool, 105, 705
Surface Area Configuration checks, 705
SUSER_NAME() function, 1507
suspect pages, 412
SWITCH, 789
switches, 1535
switching table partitions, 785-789
SWITCHOFFSET(), 38, CD:1573
Symantec, CD:2350
symmetric key encryption, 338
Sync Services for ADO.NET (SSADO), CD:1817
synchronization, CD:1630. *See also* Change Tracking
manual synchronization, 567
snapshot agents, 566-567
synchronous operations, 622
sys users, 300
sys.conversation groups, CD:1994
sys.databases catalog view, 729
sys.dm broker activated tasks, CD:1995
sys.dm broker connections, CD:1995
sys.dm broker forwarded messages, CD:1995
sys.dm broker queue monitors, CD:1995
sys.dm broker transmission status, CD:1995
sys.dm_db_index_physical_stats, 1174
sys.dm_exec_cached_plans, 1258-1260, 1511
sys.dm_exec_cached_plan_dependent _objects, 1258
sys.dm_exec_plan_attributes, 1258, 1265-1266
sys.dm_exec_query_memory_grants, 1511
sys.dm_exec_query_plan, 1328-1329
sys.dm_exec_query_resource_semaphores, 1511
sys.dm_exec_query_stats, 1258, 1261-1265
sys.dm_exec_requests, 1511
sys.dm_exec_session, 1511
sys.dm_exec_sql_text, 1258-1260
sys.dm_os_memory_brokers, 45, 1511
sys.dm_os_memory_nodes, 45
sys.dm_os_nodes, 46
sys.dm_os_process_memory, 46
sys.dm_os_sys_memory, 46
sys.dm_resource_governor_configuration, 1510
sys.dm_resource_governor_resource_pools, 1510

sys.dm_resource_governor_workload_groups, 1509

sys.dm_tran_locks, 1350-1354

sys.endpoint webmethods, CD:1954

sys.endpoints, CD:1954

sys.filegroups system catalog view, 1099

sys.indexes, 1280-1282

sys.master files, 712

sys.plan_guides catalog view, 1294-1295

sys.service contract message usages, CD:1995

sys.service contracts, CD:1995

sys.service message types, CD:1995

sys.service queues, CD:1994

sys.services, CD:1994

sysadmin, 303

SYSDATETIME(), 38, CD:1573

SYSDATETIMEOFFSET(), 38, CD:1573

sysfiles table, 1093-1094

sysjobstepslogs table, 464

sysmail configuration, 445-446

sysmail configure sp, 433

sysmail delete account sp, 432

sysmail delete log sp, 433, 447

sysmail delete principalprofile sp, 432

sysmail delete profile sp, 432

sysmail delete profileaccount sp, 432

sysmail faileditems, 447

sysmail help queue sp, 447

sysmail help status sp, 435, 447

sysmail principalprofile, 445

sysmail profile, 445

sysmail profileaccount, 446

sysmail server, 445

sysmail servertype, 445

sysmail start sp, 435

sysmail stop sp, 435

sysmail unsentitems, 447

sysmail update account sp, 432

sysmail update principalprofile sp, 432

sysmail update profile sp, 432

sysmail update profileaccount sp, 432

sysmessages, 470-471

sysopentapes, 412

system administrators

- new system administration features, 165
- responsibilities of, 166

system catalogs, CD:1994-CD:1995

System Configuration Checker HTML report, 194-195

System Configuration Checker window, 194

System Configuration Checker. *See* SCC (System Configuration Checker)

system databases, 709

- associated database files, 167
- backups, 403
- distribution database, 168
- explained, 166-167
- maintaining, 169-170
- master database, 167
- model database, 168
- msdb database, 168
- resource database, 168
- restoring, 421-423
- tempdb database, 169

system interdependencies, 1521-1522

system stored procedures, 181-183, 910

- catalog views and, CD:1954-CD:1955
- categories of, 909-910
- explained, 908-909
- table of, 910

system tables, 170-171, 412-413

system test and acceptance stage (tuning methodology), 1527, 1533

system views

catalog views, 175-177

compatibility views, 172-175

DMVs (dynamic management views), 179-181

explained, 171-172

information schema views, 177-178

monitoring disk system items, 1491

monitoring memory items, 1487

monitoring processor items, 1483

System.Data namespace (.NET Framework), CD:1788

System.Data.SqlClient namespace (.NET Framework), CD:1788

System.Xml namespace (.NET Framework), CD:1788

SystemDataAccess parameter, CD:1836, CD:1849

SYSUTCDATETIME() function, 38, CD:1573

T

T-SQL

auditing with, 372-374

backups, 390-393

CDC (Change Data Capture), CD:1614-CD:1626

Change Tracking versus, CD:1627

DDL changes to source, CD:1626

enabling for databases, CD:1617

enabling for tables, CD:1617-CD:1619

querying CDC tables, CD:1619-CD:1626

tables for, CD:1615-CD:1617

Change Tracking, CD:1627-CD:1635

identifying changed columns, CD:1633-CD:1634

identifying tracked changes, CD:1630-CD:1633

implementing, CD:1628-CD:1630

performance overhead of, CD:1634-CD:1635

coding recommendations

avoiding SQL injection attacks, CD:1643-CD:1652

commenting, CD:1652-CD:1653

explicit column lists, CD:1638-CD:1640

qualifying object names with, CD:1640-CD:1643

compound operators, CD:1568-CD:1569

constraints, 822-823

CONTEXT INFO setting, CD:1671-CD:1673

Data Collector, managing, 1443-1446

databases

creating, 721-722

managing database roles, 322

options, 725

restores, 404-407

date and time data types, CD:1572-CD:1576

date calculations, CD:1663-CD:1666

de-duping data with ranking functions, CD:1684-CD:1687

debugging, 41, 100-101, 905-908

error handling, CD:1724-CD:1727

execution engine, 242

FILESTREAM storage, CD:1592-CD:1593

for data columns, CD:1597-CD:1599

database setup, CD:1596

enabling, CD:1593-CD:1596

full-text indexes, creating

ALTER FULLTEXT INDEX, CD:2010-CD:2013

CREATE FULLTEXT CATALOG, CD:2003-CD:2005

CREATE FULLTEXT INDEX, CD:2005-CD:2010

managing MSFTESQL, CD:2013-CD:2014

generating statements, CD:1682-CD:1683
GROUPING function, CD:1669-CD:1671
Hierarchyid data type, CD:1580-CD:1592
- creating hierarchies, CD:1580-CD:1581
- modifying hierarchies, CD:1587-CD:1592
- populating hierarchies, CD:1581-CD:1583
- querying hierarchies, CD:1583-CD:1587

indexes
- creating, 795-800
- managing, 803-806

Insert over DML, CD:1559-CD:1561
logins, managing, 317-318
mail objects, deleting, 432-433
modifying tables
- adding and dropping columns, 767-768
- changing column properties, 766-767

new features, 37-38
outer joins, CD:1673-CD:1674
- full outer joins, CD:1680-CD:1682
- nested outer joins, CD:1679-CD:1680
- WHERE clause versus, CD:1675-CD:1679

performance
- avoiding unnecessary function executions, CD:1656
- counters, 1477
- cursors, CD:1656-CD:1659
- DISTINCT, CD:1654
- IF EXISTS, CD:1654
- ORDER BY, CD:1654
- temporary tables versus table variables, CD:1654-CD:1656
- UNION versus UNION ALL, CD:1654
- UPDATE, CD:1659-CD:1663

permissions, managing, 330-331
resource pools
- creating, 1502
- deleting, 1516

row constructors, CD:1569-CD:1572
running ad hoc T-SQL batches from web services, CD:1947-CD:1951
sparse columns, CD:1600-CD:1605
spatial data types, CD:1605-CD:1614
statements. *See specific statements*
stored procedures. *See stored procedures*
T-SQL functions versus CLR functions, 946-947
table-valued parameters, CD:1576-CD:1580
tables, creating, 744-747
transaction logs
- creating, 394-395
- restores, 407-408

tuning guidelines, 1541-1545
updating Database Mail, 432-433
user-defined functions
- creating, 925-930
- modifying, 939
- viewing, 936-939

users, managing, 320-321
views
- altering, 852
- creating, 845-849
- dropping views, 853

workload groups
- creating, 1505
- deleting, 1514-1515
- viewing, 1505-1506

xml data type, CD:1687-CD:1688

Table control (SSMS) 2202

Table Delete (Query Analyzer), 1314

Table Designer, 769-772

table expressions. ***See*** **CTE (common table expressions)**

table hints, 1285
- locking, 1393-1395
  - lock granularity hints, 1395

lock type hints, 1395-1396

transaction isolation–level hints, 1393-1395

Query Optimizer, 1280-1282

Table Insert (Query Analyzer), 1314

Table locking level (SQL Server), 1365

Table Scan (Query Analyzer), 1314

table scans, 1132, 1227-1228

Table Spool (Query Analyzer), 1312

Table Update (Query Analyzer), 1314

table-valued functions, 1314

inline table-valued functions, 923-924

multistatement table-valued functions, 924-925

table-valued parameters, 38, 901-902, CD:1576-CD:1580

TableDefinition parameter (TVFs), CD:1839

tablediff, 112-115

tables

base tables, 854-858

CDC tables, CD:1615-CD:1626

clustered tables, 1130-1131

columns. *See* columns

comparing with tablediff, 112-115

constraints, 763-765

creating, 515-516

with Database Diagram Editor, 743-744

with Object Explorer, 742-743

with sparse columns, CD:1601

with T-SQL, 744-747

CTE (common table expressions), CD:1698-CD:1708

dropping, 773-774

enabling CDC for, CD:1617-CD:1619

explained, 1127-1129

fragmentation, 1169

getting table properties, 520

heap tables, 1129-1130

importing trace files into, 135-136

indexes. *See* indexes

inserting trace data into trace tables, 136-137

location, defining, 761-763

modifying, 765-766

with database diagrams, 772-773

with Object Explorer and Table Designer, 769-772

with T-SQL, 766-768

new features, 741-742

partitions. *See* partitions

in reports, CD:2210-CD:2211

row offset table, 1108-1109

saving trace output to, 134

synchronizing, CD:1552-CD:1559

sysfiles, 1093-1094

sysjobstepslogs, 464

system tables, 170-171, 412-413

temporary tables. *See* temporary tables

tuning guidelines, 1537-1539

user-defined table types, CD:1577

variables

temporary tables and common table, CD:1654-CD:1656

tuning guidelines, 1542

TABLESAMPLE clause, CD:1727-CD:1730

Tablix, CD:2173, CD:2199-CD:2202

TABLOCK optimizer hint, 1395, CD:2166

TABLOCKX optimizer hint, 1395

Tabular Data Stream (TDS), 267, CD:1929

tape devices, 386

TARGET, CD:1970

Target parameter (SqlTrigger), CD:1856

Target Server Wizard, 477

target servers, 476-477

TARGET SIZE, 733

targets, 693, 1459

tasks (SSIS), CD:2106

TDE (transparent data encryption), 39

- backing up TDE certificates and keys, 353-355
- compared to column-level encryption, 356-357
- explained, 350-351
- implementing, 351-352
- limitations, 355-356
- managing in SSMS, 352-353

TDS (Tabular Data Stream), 267, CD:1929

tempdb database, 169, 1536, CD:1760-CD:1762

Template Explorer, 97-99, 874, 953

templates

- custom function templates, 933-936
- custom stored procedure templates, 875-879
- data region templates, CD:2173, CD:2199
- Policy-Based Management sample templates, 704-705
- SQL Profiler templates, 124
- SSMS templates, 97-100

temporary stored procedures, 879-880

temporary tables

- creating, 789-790
- stored procedures
  - performance tips, CD:1760-CD:1762
  - table data types, CD:1762-CD:1763
- stored procedures, CD:1759-CD:1760
- table-valued parameters versus, CD:1580
- table variables and common table, CD:1654-CD:1656
- tuning guidelines, 1542

terminators, CD:2158-CD:2162

testing

- alerts, 444
- connectivity, 288-289
- Database Mail setup, 433-434
- failover from principal to mirror, 645-646
- job-completion notification, 443
- testing and coding stage (tuning), 1526-1527, 1532

Text Box control, CD:2204

text data type, 749

TextData data column (SQL Profiler), 1356

third normal form, 1407

third-party disaster recovery alternatives, CD:2350-CD:2351

three-permission sets, CD:1827-CD:1829

time

- PowerShell date/time calculations, 502-503
- time data types, 37, 749, 751, CD:1572-CD:1575-CD:1576
- time series, CD:2085

time slices, 659

timeout intervals, 1380-1381

timestamp data type, 749

tinyint data type, 750

TODATETIMEOFFSET(), 38, CD:1573

tokens, 606

tools. *See specific tools*

Tools menu (SQL Server Installation Center), 211

ToolTips, 1304-1307

Top (Query Analyzer), 1314

TOP clause, CD:1689-CD:1693

topological sorting, CD:1581

Trace Name, 125

traces

- 1204 trace flags, 1386-1388
- 1222 trace flags, 1388-1390
- analyzing output with Database Engine Tuning Advisor, 138
- creating with SQL Server Profiler, 123-125
- data columns, 127-130
- events, 125-127

- executing, 132
- exporting, 132
- filters, 130-132
- importing, 135-136
- inserting trace data into trace tables, 136-137
- monitoring running traces, 153-154
- replaying trace data, 138-140
- saving, 132
  - Profiler GUI output, 134-135
  - to files, 133
  - to tables, 134
- server-side traces
  - defining, 140-141, 148-152
  - stopping, 155-156
- trace events and categories, 141-147

tracked changes, identifying, CD:1630-CD:1633

traffic, tuning guidelines, 1535

@@trancount function, 1001, 1003, CD:1735

Transact-SQL. *See* T-SQL

transaction isolation–level hints, 1393-1395

transaction logs, 393, 710, 716-717

- backups, 382, 418
- creating with SSMS, 394
- creating with T-SQL, 394-395
- data rows, 1104
- full database backups, 396-397
- restoring, 416, 419
- restoring with T-SQL, 407-408

Transaction.Current object, CD:1861

transactional replication, 16, 573-575

transactions

- ACID properties, 996
- batches, 1007-1009
- bound connections, 1039-1040
- calling stored procedures from, CD:1735-CD:1738
- coding, 1022-1023
- defined, 52, 995
- distributed transactions
  - linked servers, CD:2252-CD:2253
  - managing, 1040
- explicit transactions, 997
- implicit transactions, 997
- isolation levels, 1342-1344
  - dirty reads, 1343
  - lost updates, 1343
  - nonrepeatable reads, 1343
  - phantom reads, 1343
  - read committed isolation, 1344-1345
  - read committed snapshot isolation, 1345-1346
  - read uncommitted isolation, 1344
  - repeatable read isolation, 1346
  - serializable read isolation, 1346-1347
  - snapshot isolation, 1347-1349
- locks, 1021-1022
- long-running transactions, 1037-1039
- managed database objects, developing, CD:1861-CD:1863
- nested transactions, CD:1736
- processing, 997, 1253
  - AutoCommit, 997-998
  - explicit user-defined transactions, 998-1003, 1006
  - implicit transactions, 1003-1006
- stored procedures, 1009-1014
- transaction logging, 1023-1037
- transaction management
  - AutoCommit, 997-998
  - batches, 1007-1009
  - bound connections, 1039-1040
  - coding, 1022-1023
  - distributed transactions, 1040
  - explicit user-defined transactions, 998-1006

implicit transactions, 1003-1006
locks, 1021-1022
long-running transactions, 1037-1039
new features, 995
overview, 996-997
recovery process, 1023-1030
stored procedures, 1009-1014
transaction logging, 1023-1037
transaction processing, 997
triggers, 1014-1015
multistatement transactions, 1017-1019
savepoints, 1019-1020
transaction nesting, 1015-1017
tuning guidelines, 1544-1545

TransactionScope object, CD:1862

transformations (SSIS), CD:2107

transmission queues, CD:1974

transparent data encryption. ***See* TDE (transparent data encryption)**

tree relationships, expanding with recursive procedures, CD:1756

TriggerAction parameter (SqlTriggerContext), CD:1856

triggers
AFTER triggers
combining with INSTEAD OF triggers, 971-972
example, 954-955
executing, 955
explained, 953-954
special considerations, 956-957
trigger firing order, 956
versus INSTEAD OF triggers, 970
CLR triggers, 988-991
DDL triggers. *See* DDL, triggers
DML triggers
AFTER triggers, 953-957
cascading deletes, 963-965
cascading updates, 965-966
creating, 951-953
explained, 950-951
inserted and deleted tables, 957-961
referential integrity, 961-963
INSTEAD OF
combining with AFTER triggers, 971-972
example, 968
executing, 968-970
explained, 967
restrictions, 975
versus AFTER triggers, 970
views, 972-975
managed triggers, CD:1856-CD:1861
nested triggers, 991-992, CD:2306
new features, 950
recursive triggers, 992-993
troubleshooting, 1278
tuning guidelines, 1538

trivial plan optimization, 1252

troubleshooting
applications with ssbdiagnose.exe, CD:1993-CD:1994
connectivity issues, 287
FTS (Full-Text Search), CD:2026-CD:2028
incorrect configuration options, CD:2283
query optimization
index design, 1275
large complex queries, 1277-1278
search arguments, 1276-1277
statistics, 1274-1275
triggers, 1278
replication failures, 608

TRUNCATE, 333

TRUNCATE TABLE, 956

TRUNCATEONLY option (DBCC SHRINKDATABASE), 732

TRY, CD:1738

TRY...CATCH, CD:1724-CD:1727, CD:1738

TSQL, 124

TSQL Default TCP, 269

TSQL Duration, 124

TSQL Grouped, 124

TSQL Locks, 124

TSQL Replay, 124

TSQL SPs, 124

tuning. *See also* performance

architectural layers, 1520-1521

guidelines, 1534

for applications, 1545

database-level guidelines, 1537

for distributed data, 1546

for hardware and operating system, 1534-1535

for high availability, 1546-1547

for indexing, 1539-1540

for SQL Server instance, 1536-1537

for Transact-SQL, 1541-1545

for views, 1541

table-level guidelines, 1537-1539

methodology, 1522-1523

for existing implementations, 1528-1533

for new implementations, 1523-1528

primary handles for, 1521-1522

system interdependencies in, 1521-1522

tools for, 1547-1549

Microsoft tools, 1547-1548

third-party tools, 1548-1549

TVFs (table-valued UDFs), CD:1839-CD:1844

two-phase commit, 572

two-way synchronization applications, CD:1627

TYPE COLUMN parameter (CREATE FULLTEXT INDEX) 2006

types. *See specific types*

U

UA (SQL Server Upgrade Advisor), 228-229

Analysis Wizard, 230-235

installing, 229

Report Viewer, 235

system requirements, 229-230

UDAs (user-defined aggregates), CD:1853-CD:1856

UDFs (user-defined functions)

managed database, CD:1835-CD:1844

scalar UDFs, CD:1835-CD:1839

TVFs (table-valued UDFs), CD:1839-CD:1844

UDTs (user-defined types), 754, CD:1844-CD:1852

UMDW database, 1455

UNC (Universal Naming Convention), 386

unconditional workflows, CD:2106

undo phase (transaction recovery process), 1029

uniform extent, 711

UNION

query processing, 1268

tuning guidelines, 1542

versus UNION ALL, CD:1654

UNION ALL, 854

tuning guidelines, 1542

versus UNION, CD:1654

UNION hints, 1283

UNIQUE keyword, 764, 796, 815-816

uniqueidentifier data type, 750

unit testing, 1526, 1532

Universal Naming Convention. *See* UNC (Universal Naming Convention)

UNLOAD option

BACKUP DATABASE, 393

RESTORE DATABASE) 407

UNPIVOT clause, CD:1718-CD:1721

unregistering linked servers, CD:2261

UNSAFE, 945, CD:1780

unstructured data in FILESTREAM storage, CD:1592-CD:1593

- database setup, CD:1596
- enabling, CD:1593-CD:1596
- for data columns, CD:1597-CD:1599

unused indexes, identifying, 1205-1207

update locks, 1360-1361

update performance indexes, 1199-1201

UPDATE, 959-961, CD:1659-CD:1663

__$update_mask column (CDC table), CD:1616

UPDATE STATISTICS, 1161-1164, 1216

Updateability property, 728

updating

- checking for column updates, 959-961
- column statistics, 1161-1169
- Database Mail with T-SQL, 432-433
- index statistics, 1161-1169
- rows
  - forward pointers, 1146
  - in-place updates, 1145
  - with LINQ to SQL, CD:1802
  - not-in-place updates, 1145-1146
- subscribers replication model, 560-561

UPDLOCK optimizer hint, 1395

Upgrade Advisor. *See* UA (SQL Server Upgrade Advisor)

upgrading

- Analysis Services, 253-254
- with configuration files, 250-251
- DTS, 259-261
- from SQL Server 7 or SQL Server 6.5, 252
- new features, 227-228
- Reporting Services
  - in-place upgrades, 255-257
  - migrating to Reporting Services 2008, 257-258
- side-by-side migration. *See* side-by-side migration
- slipstreaming upgrades, 251-252
- SSIS packages, 258-259
- Upgrade Advisor. See UA (SQL Server Upgrade Advisor), 228
- upgrading in-place
  - SQL Server 2008 upgrade matrix, 246-250
  - upgrading database engine, 243-246
- upgrade options, CD:1998-CD:1999

Usage-Based Optimization Wizard, CD:2080

USE PLAN, 1287-1290

USE PLAN *N* hints, 1285

user CALs, 31

user configurable events, 163

user connections configuration option, CD:2313-CD:2314

user databases, 709

user-defined counters, 1476-1477

user-defined data types, 753-754

user-defined functions. *See* UDFs (user-defined functions)

user-defined roles, 307-309

user-defined types (UDTs), 754, CD:1577

user options configuration option, CD:2315-CD:2316

UserAccess property, 728

users

- dbo users, 299
- delivering data to, CD:2076
- explained, 298-299
- guest users, 299-300
- INFORMATION_SCHEMA users, 300
- logins, 298
- managing
  - with SSMS, 318-320
  - with T-SQL, 320-321

- SQL Server performance counters, 1492
- sys users, 300
- user/schema separation, 301-302
- user-specific data limitations, CD:2239

USING clause (MERGE statement), CD:1552

utilities. ***See specific utilities***

V

valid documents (XML), CD:1866

validating plan guides, 1294

validation and execution phase (dtexec) 2137

ValidationMethodName parameter (SqlUserDefinedType), CD:1845

VALUE secondary index (XML) 1922

value() method, CD:1900, CD:1910, CD:1923

VALUES clause
- in MERGE statement, CD:1571
- in views, CD:1570

varbinary data type, 750-752, CD:1688-CD:1689

varchar data type, 750-752, CD:1688-CD:1689

variables
- $_ special variable, 493
- assignment
  - in DECLARE statement, CD:1568
  - in UPDATE statement, CD:1659-CD:1663
- CURSOR, CD:1748-CD:1753
- explained, 491-492
- joining, 493
- scripting with sqlcmd, 108-109
- SSIS, CD:2109

verifying
- application of plan guides, 1296-1297
- packages, CD:2141-CD:2144

VeriSign, 278

Veritas Storage Replicator, CD:2350

Veritas Volume Replicator, CD:2350

version numbers in Change Tracking, CD:1633

Version property, 728

vertical data partitioning, 1413-1414

vertical filtering, 592-594

VHD (Virtual Hard Disk), 542

VIEW DEFINITION, 312

View Designer, 849-851

VIEW METADATA, 849

viewing
- Data Collector Sets in Performance Monitor, 1472-1473
- DDL triggers with catalog views, 987
- graphical execution plans, 1317
- job history, 468-469
- last generated report, 234
- linked servers, CD:2260-CD:2261
- lock activity
  - Performance Monitor, 1357-1359
  - SQL Server Profiler, 1355-1357
- mail configuration objects, 445-446
- mail message data, 446-447
- partitioned table information, 781
- SQL Server Agent error log, 456-457
- stored procedures, 889-891
- user-defined functions
  - with SSMS, 939-940
  - with T-SQL, 936-939
- workload groups, 1505-1506

views. ***See also specific views***
- altering with T-SQL, 852
- bcp utility, CD:2163
- catalog views, CD:1954-CD:1955
- controlling access to data, 842-844
- creating with T-SQL, 845-847
  - ENCRYPTION, 847-848
  - SCHEMABINDING, 848

VIEW METADATA, 849
WITH CHECK OPTION, 849
creating with View Designer, 849-851
data abstraction, 841-842
data modifications and, 853-854
defined, 837-838
distributed partitioned view, 975
dropping, 853
dynamic management views, 45-46
focusing on specific data, 840-841
indexed views, 809-810, 844, 860, 1192-1193
creating, 861-863
expansion, 866-867
performance and, 863-866
INSTEAD OF triggers, 972-975
managing, 852-853
new features, 837
partitioned views, 844
base tables, 854-858
distributed partitioned views, 859-860
modifying data through, 858-859
restrictions, 844-845
simplifying data manipulation, 839-840
standard views, 844
system views. *See* system views
tuning guidelines, 1541
VALUES clause in, CD:1570
Windows Performance Monitor, 1466-1469

Virtual Hard Disk (VHD), 542

Virtual Machine Monitor (VMM), 542

Virtual Server, 541-542

virtual server licensing, 33-34

virtualization, 33

Visual Studio, CD:1829, CD:2008

Visual Studio Integration Services Connection Project, CD:2145

Visual Studio Tools for Applications (VSTA), 47

VMM (Virtual Machine Monitor), 542

VSTA (Visual Studio Tools for Applications), 47

W

W3C (World Wide Web) 1928

Web Edition (SQL Server 2008), 27-28, 32

web services
catalog views and system stored procedures, CD:1954-CD:1955
configuring, CD:2186-CD:2187
controlling access permissions, CD:1955-CD:1956
creating, CD:1930-CD:1934
AS HTTP keyword group, CD:1934-CD:1937
authorization, CD:1933
endpoints, CD:1931-CD:1933
FOR SOAP keyword group, CD:1938-CD:1942
stored procedures, CD:1931
examples
calling web methods–bound stored, CD:1951-CD:1953
running ad hoc T-SQL batches from web, CD:1947-CD:1951
running web methods bound to stored, CD:1942-CD:1947
history and overview, CD:1928-CD:1929
limitations, CD:1956-CD:1957
migration path, CD:1928
new features, CD:1927-CD:1928
patterns, CD:1929-CD:1930

Web Services Description Language (WSDL) 1928

Web Sites Properties dialog, CD:1938

WEBMETHOD, CD:1938-CD:1940

weightedsearches, CD:2022

well formed documents (XML), CD:1866

Well-Known Binary (WKB), CD:1606

Well-Known Text (WKT), CD:1606

-whatif parameters, 503

WHEN MATCHED clause (MERGE statement), CD:1552

WHEN NOT MATCHED BY SOURCE clause (MERGE statement),, CD:1553

WHEN NOT MATCHED BY TARGET clause (MERGE statement),, CD:1552

WHERE argument, 797

- outer joins versus, CD:1675-CD:1679
- query() method, CD:1905
- search argument problems, 1276-1277

Where-Object cmdlet, 499

wide indexes, 1191-1192

wildcards

- in Query Editor, 89-91
- in stored procedure input parameters, 899-900

window management (SSMS), 65-67

Windows Authentication mode, 294, 313

windows event log, CD:2240

Windows Firewall, 288

WINDOWS GROUP, 296

Windows Installer 3.1, 271

WINDOWS LOGIN, 297

Windows Management Instrumentation (WMI), 484-485, CD:2181

Windows Performance Monitor, 1465-1466

- accessing performance counters, 1477
- Data Collector Sets, 1469-1472
  - running, 1472
  - viewing, 1472-1473
- performance counters, 1474-1476
  - monitoring disk systems, 1489-1490
  - monitoring memory, 1486-1487
  - monitoring network interfaces, 1478-1480
  - monitoring processors, 1480-1485
- reasons for using, 1473-1474
- replication monitoring, 610-611
- user-defined counters, 1476-1477
- views, 1466-1469

Windows PowerShell. *See* PowerShell

Windows Service, CD:2186

Windows Service Control Manager, 452

WITH, CD:1698, CD:1975

WITH ACCENT_SENSITIVITY, CD:2004

WITH CHECK OPTION, 849

WITH CLEANUP, CD:1979

WITH MARK, 999

WITH RECOMPILE, CD:1771

witness database server, 620, 622

wizards. *See specific wizards*

WKB (Well-Known Binary), CD:1606

WKT (Well-Known Text), CD:1606

WMI (Windows Management Instrumentation), 484-485, CD:2181

word breakers, CD:2000-CD:2001

workflows (SSIS), CD:2106

Workgroup Edition (SQL Server 2008), 27

WorkgroupClassifier() function, 1508

workload groups

- creating
  - in SSMS, 1503-1505
  - in T-SQL, 1505
- deleting, 1514-1515
- explained, 1496
- viewing, 1505-1506

World Wide Web Consortium (W3C) 1928

write-ahead logs, 717

Write-Host cmdlet, 490

WRITETEXT, 956

WSDL (Web Services Description Language), CD:1928, CD:1941

WSDL option (WEBMETHOD) 1940

X

XLOCK hint, 1396, CD:1661

XML, CD:1866

- attribute-centric XML shape, CD:1867
- calling web methods–bound stored procedure that returns, CD:1951-CD:1953
- displaying execution plans, 1317
- documents
  - fragments, CD:1866
  - instances, CD:1866
  - markups, CD:1866
  - processing instructions, CD:1866
  - valid documents, CD:1866
  - well formed documents, CD:1866
- documents, CD:1866
- element-centric XML shape, CD:1868
- FOR XML modes, CD:1866
  - AUTO mode, CD:1873-CD:1877
  - EXPLICIT mode, CD:1877-CD:1881
  - newxml data type, CD:1884-CD:1887
  - PATH mode, CD:1881-CD:1884
  - RAW mode, CD:1867-CD:1871
- Infoset, CD:1920-CD:1921
- new features, CD:1865
- new xml data type, CD:1890-CD:1891
  - built-in methods, CD:1899-CD:1918
  - columns, CD:1892-CD:1894
  - schema collections, CD:1894-CD:1899
- nodes, CD:1866
- OPENXML, CD:1887-CD:1890
- sending as attachments with Database Mail, 439-440
- xml columns, CD:1918-CD:1925
- XMLDML (XML Data Modification Language), CD:1913
- XSD (XML Schema Definition), CD:1866

XML configuration file, CD:2108

xml data type, 750-751, CD:1687-CD:1688

XML Schema Definition (XSD), CD:1866

XMLDATA keyword, CD:1871

XMLDML (XML Data Modification Language), CD:1913

xp cmdshell, CD:1784-CD:1786

XP-related configuration options, CD:2316

XSD (XML Schema Definition), CD:1866

Y-Z

Yuhanna, Noel, 1

zero-to-one relationships, 1415

zoning, 1424

informIT.com THE TRUSTED TECHNOLOGY LEARNING SOURCE

PEARSON

Addison-Wesley | Cisco Press | EXAM/CRAM | IBM Press | QUE | PRENTICE HALL | SAMS | Safari Books Online